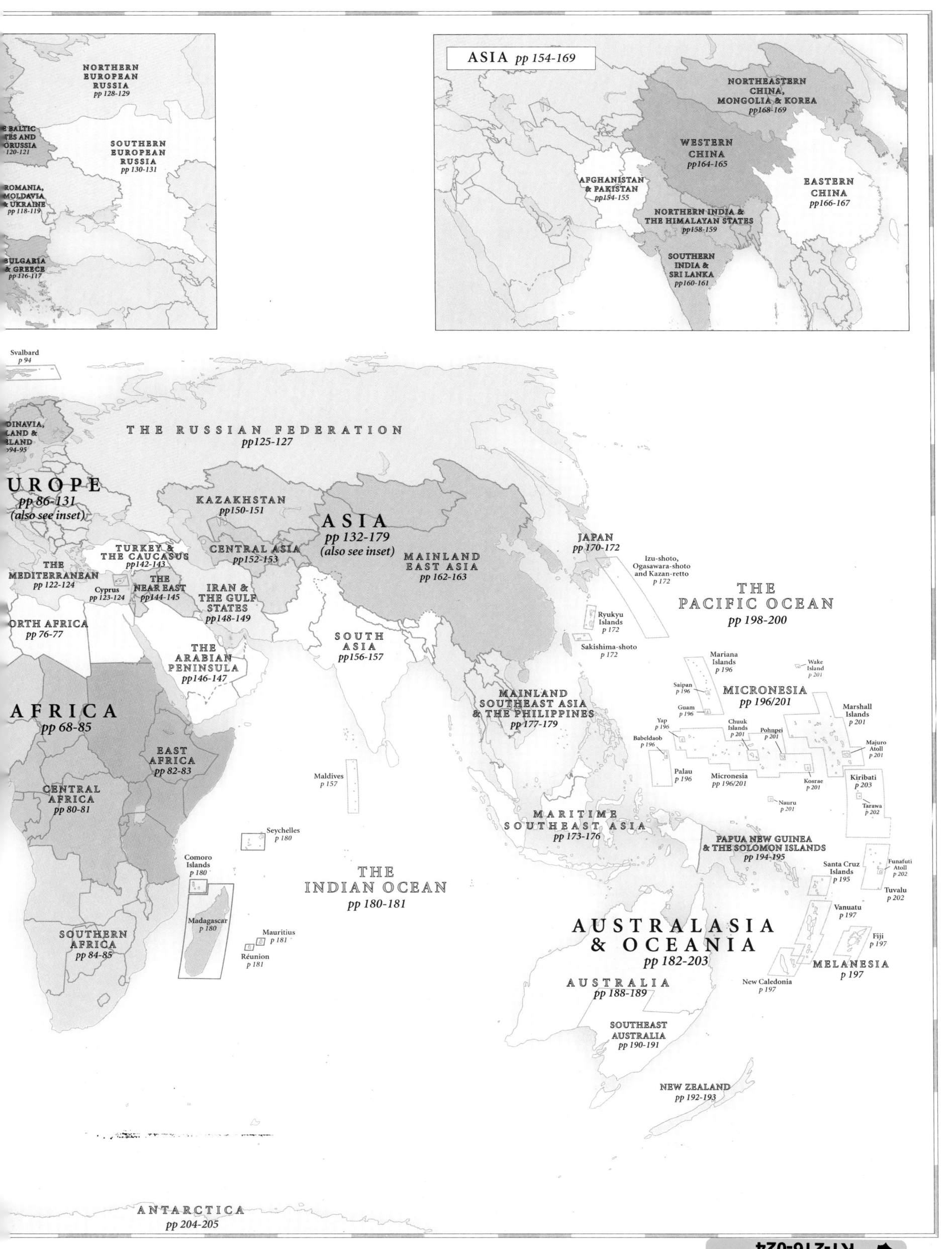

DORLING KINDERSLEY

WORLD ATLAS

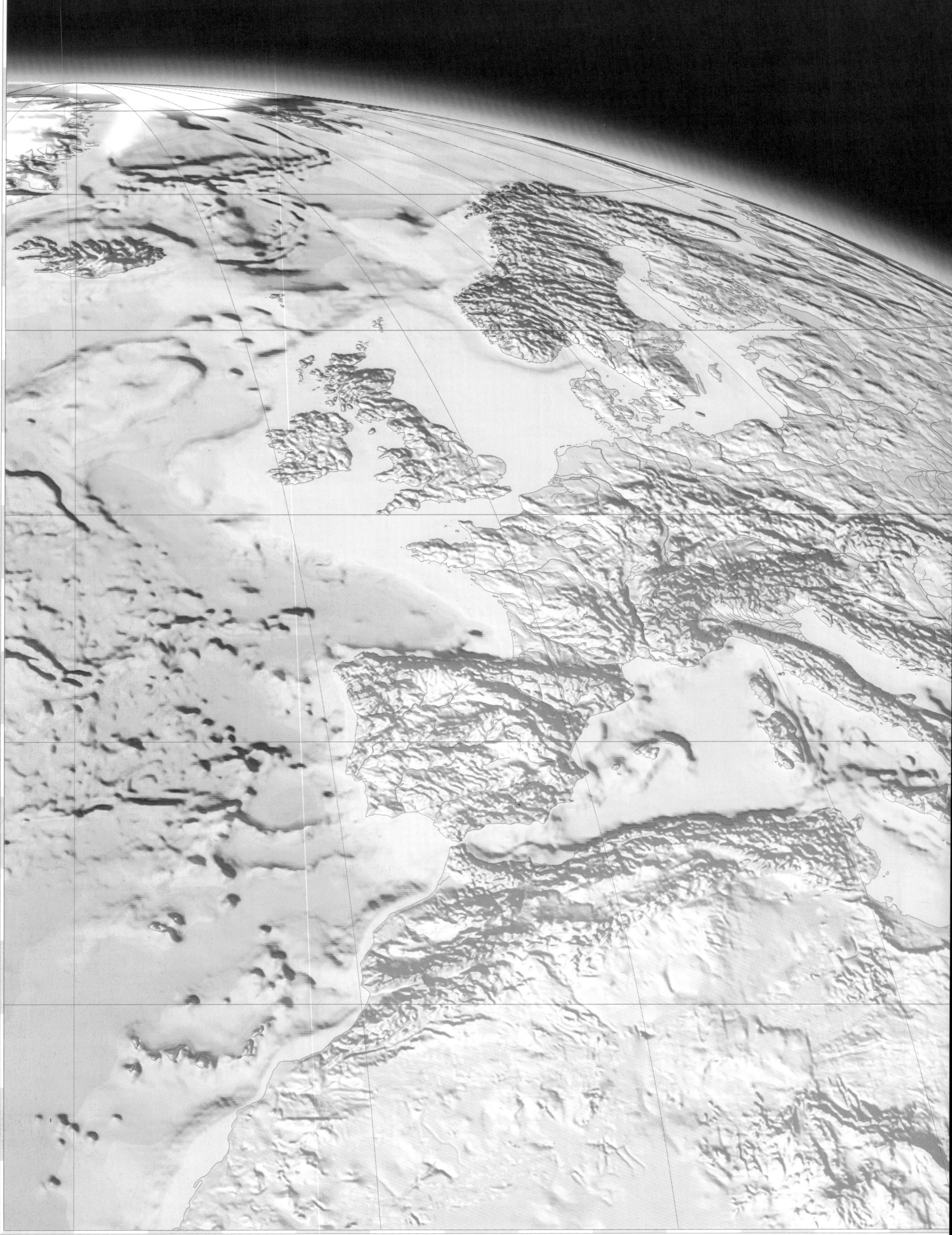

DORLING KINDERSLEY

WORLD ATLAS

London • New York • Sydney • Moscow

A DORLING KINDERSLEY BOOK

GENERAL GEOGRAPHICAL CONSULTANTS

PHYSICAL GEOGRAPHY • Denys Brunsden, Emeritus Professor, Department of Geography, King's College, London

HUMAN GEOGRAPHY • Professor J Malcolm Wagstaff, Department of Geography, University of Southampton

PLACE NAMES • Caroline Burgess, Permanent Committee on Geographical Names, London

BOUNDARIES • International Boundaries Research Unit, Mountjoy Research Centre, University of Durham

DIGITAL MAPPING CONSULTANTS

DK Cartopia developed by George Galfalvi and XMap Ltd, London

Professor Jan-Peter Muller, Department of Photogrammetry and Surveying, University College, London

Cover globes, planets and information on the Solar System provided by Philip Eales and Kevin Tildsley, Planetary Visions Ltd, London

REGIONAL CONSULTANTS

NORTH AMERICA • Dr David Green, Department of Geography, King's College, London
Jim Walsh, Head of Reference, Wessell Library, Tufts University, Medford, Massachussetts

SOUTH AMERICA • Dr David Preston, School of Geography, University of Leeds

EUROPE • Dr Edward M Yates, formerly of the Department of Geography, King's College, London

AFRICA • Dr Philip Amis, Development Administration Group, University of Birmingham
Dr Ieuan Ll Griffiths, Department of Geography, University of Sussex
Dr Tony Binns, Department of Geography, University of Sussex

CENTRAL ASIA • Dr David Turnock, Department of Geography, University of Leicester

SOUTH AND EAST ASIA • Dr Jonathan Rigg, Department of Geography, University of Durham

AUSTRALASIA AND OCEANIA • Dr Robert Allison, Department of Geography, University of Durham

ACKNOWLEDGEMENTS

Digital terrain data created by Eros Data Center, Sioux Falls, South Dakota, USA. Processed by GVS Images Inc, California, USA and Planetary Visions Ltd, London, UK
• CIRCA Research and Reference Information, Cambridge, UK • Digitization by Robertson Research International, Swanley, UK • Peter Clark
British Isles maps generated from a dataset supplied by Map Marketing Ltd/European Map Graphics Ltd in combination with DK Cartopia copyright data

DORLING KINDERSLEY CARTOGRAPHY

EDITOR-IN-CHIEF
Andrew Heritage

MANAGING CARTOGRAPHER   SENIOR CARTOGRAPHIC EDITOR
David Roberts   Roger Bullen

CARTOGRAPHERS
Pamela Alford • James Anderson • Sarah Baker-Ede • Caroline Bowie • Dale Buckton • Tony Chambers • Jan Clark • Bob Croser • Martin Darlison • Claire Ellam
Sally Gable • Jeremy Hepworth • Geraldine Horner • Chris Jackson • Christine Johnston • Julia Lunn • Michael Martin • James Mills-Hicks • Simon Mumford • John Plumer
John Scott • Ann Stephenson • Julie Turner • Jane Voss • Scott Wallace • Iorwerth Watkins • Bryony Webb • Alan Whitaker • Peter Winfield

DIGITAL MAPS CREATED IN DK CARTOPIA BY   PLACENAMES DATABASE TEAM
Tom Coulson • Thomas Robertshaw   Natalie Clarkson • Ruth Duxbury • Caroline Falce • John Featherstone • Dan Gardiner
Philip Rowles • Rob Stokes   Ciárán Hynes • Margaret Hynes • Helen Rudkin • Margaret Stevenson • Annie Wilson

DATABASE MANAGER
Simon Lewis

MANAGING EDITOR   SENIOR MANAGING ART EDITOR
Lisa Thomas   Philip Lord

EDITORS   DESIGNERS
Thomas Heath • Wim Jenkins • Jane Oliver   Scott David • Carol Ann Davis • David Douglas
Siobhán Ryan • Elizabeth Wyse   Rhonda Fisher • Karen Gregory • Nicola Liddiard • Paul Williams

EDITORIAL RESEARCH   ILLUSTRATIONS
Helen Dangerfield • Andrew Rebeiro-Hargrave   Ciárán Hughes • Advanced Illustration, Congleton, UK

ADDITIONAL EDITORIAL ASSISTANCE   PICTURE RESEARCH
Debra Clapson • Robert Damon • Ailsa Heritage • Constance Novis • Jayne Parsons • Chris Whitwell   Melissa Albany • James Clarke • Anna Lord • Christine Rista • Sarah Moule

EDITORIAL DIRECTION • Louise Cavanagh   ART DIRECTION • Chez Picthall

PRODUCTION
David Proffit • Hilary Stephens

First published in Great Britain in 1997 by Dorling Kindersley Limited, 9 Henrietta Street, London WC2E 8PS. Reprinted with revisions 1998.

Visit us on the World Wide Web at http://www.dk.com

A CIP catalogue record for this book is available from the British Library / ISBN: 0-7515-0341-0

Reproduction by Colourscan, Singapore, and The Printed Word, London. Printed and bound by Mondadori, Italy

INTRODUCTION

For many, the outstanding legacy of the twentieth century has been the way in which the Earth has shrunk. As we approach the end of this most dramatic of centuries, and the end of the second millennium, there is a greater need than ever for a clear vision of the World in which we live. The human population has increased fourfold since 1900. The last scraps of *terra incognita* – the polar regions and ocean depths – have been penetrated and mapped. New regions have been colonized, and previously hostile realms claimed for habitation. The advent of aviation technology and mass tourism has allowed many of us to travel further, faster and more frequently than ever before. In doing so we are given a bird's-eye view of the Earth's surface denied to our forebears.

At the same time, the amount of information about our World has grown enormously. Telecommunications can span the greatest distances in fractions of a second: our multi-media environment hurls uninterrupted streams of data at us, on the printed page, through the airwaves and across our television and computer screens; events from all corners of the globe reach us instantaneously, and are witnessed as they unfold. Our sense of stability and certainty has been eroded; instead, we are aware that the World is in a constant state of flux and change. Natural disasters, man-made cataclysms and conflicts between nations remind us daily of the enormity and fragility of our domain.

Our current 'global' culture has made the need greater than ever before for everyone to possess an atlas. The *DK World Atlas* has been conceived to meet this need. At its core, like all atlases, it seeks to define where places are, to describe their main characteristics, and to locate them in relation to other places. Every attempt has been made to make the information on the maps as clear and accessible as possible. In addition, each page of the Atlas provides a wealth of further information, bringing the maps to life. Using photographs, diagrams, 'at-a-glance' maps, introductory texts and captions, the Atlas builds up a detailed portait of those features – cultural, political, economic and geomorphological – which make each region unique, and which are also the main agents of change.

A map only provides a snapshot of the World at a given time. Drawing on the resources of a wide range of sciences and using the latest technology, the *DK World Atlas* is intended to equip the reader with the information needed to understand why the World today is the shape it is, and to recognize the processes of change which will determine its evolution in the next century.

PETER KINDERSLEY

CONTENTS

EUROPE

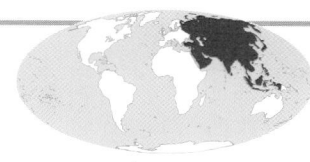

ASIA

AUSTRALASIA AND OCEANIA

INDEX–GAZETTEER

KEY TO REGIONAL MAPS

PHYSICAL FEATURES

elevation

- 6000m / 19,686ft
- 4000m / 13,124ft
- 3000m / 9843ft
- 2000m / 6562ft
- 1000m / 3281ft
- 500m / 1640ft
- 250m / 820ft
- 100m / 328ft
- sea level
- below sea level

- ▲ elevation above sea level (mountain height)
- ▲ volcano
- ✕ pass
- ▼ elevation below sea level (depression depth)

- sand desert
- lava flow
- coastline
- reef
- atoll

sea depth

- sea level
- -250m / -820ft
- -500m / -1640ft
- -1000m / -3281ft
- -2000m / -6562ft
- -3000m / -9843ft

- ▲ seamount / guyot symbol
- ▼ undersea spot depth

DRAINAGE FEATURES

- main river
- secondary river
- tertiary river
- minor river
- main seasonal river
- secondary seasonal river
- canal
- waterfall
- rapids
- dam
- perennial lake
- seasonal lake
- perennial salt lake
- seasonal salt lake
- reservoir
- salt flat / salt pan
- marsh / salt marsh
- mangrove
- wadi
- spring / well / waterhole / oasis

ICE FEATURES

- ice cap / sheet
- ice shelf
- glacier
- summer pack ice limit
- winter pack ice limit

COMMUNICATIONS

- motorway / highway
- motorway / highway (under construction)
- major road
- minor road
- tunnel (road)
- main line
- minor line
- tunnel (rail)
- ✈ international airport

BORDERS

- full international border
- undefined international border
- disputed *de facto* border
- disputed territorial claim border
- indication of country extent (Pacific only)
- indication of dependent territory extent (Pacific only)
- demarcation / cease fire line
- autonomous / federal region border
- 2nd order internal administrative border
- 3rd order internal administrative border

SETTLEMENTS

- built up area

settlement population symbols

- ▣ more than 5 million
- ◙ 1 million to 5 million
- ◉ 500,000 to 1 million
- ◎ 100,000 to 500,000
- ⊚ 50,000 to 100,000
- ○ 10,000 to 50,000
- ○ fewer than 10,000

- ▣ ■ ● country/dependent territory capital city
- ▣ ■ ● autonomous / federal region / 2nd order internal administrative centre
- ▣ ■ ● 3rd order internal administrative centre

MISCELLANEOUS FEATURES

- ⁝⁝⁝⁝⁝ ancient wall
- ◇ site of interest
- ⚬ scientific station

GRATICULE FEATURES

- lines of latitude and longitude / Equator
- Tropics / Polar circles
- degrees of longitude / latitude

TYPOGRAPHIC KEY

PHYSICAL FEATURES

landscape features	*Namib Desert*
	Massif Central
	ANDES
headland	*Nordkapp*
elevation / volcano / pass	Mount Meru 4556 m
drainage features	*Lake Rudolf*
rivers / canals spring / well / waterhole / oasis / waterfall / rapids / dam	*Mekong*
ice features	*Vatnajökull*
sea features	*Golfe de Lion*
	Andaman Sea
	INDIAN OCEAN
undersea features	*Barracuda Fracture Zone*

REGIONS

country	**ARMENIA**
dependent territory with parent state	**NIUE (to NZ)**
region outside feature area	ANGOLA
autonomous / federal region	MINAS GERAIS
2nd order internal administrative region	MINSKAYA VOBLASTS'
3rd order internal administrative region	Vaucluse
cultural region	New England

SETTLEMENTS

capital city	**BEIJING**
dependent territory capital city	FORT-DE-FRANCE
other settlements	**Chicago**
	Adana
	Tizi Ozou
	Yonezawa
	Farnham

MISCELLANEOUS

sites of interest / miscellaneous	*Valley of the Kings*
Tropics / Polar circles	*Antarctic Circle*

HOW TO USE THIS ATLAS

THE ATLAS IS ORGANIZED BY CONTINENT, moving eastwards from the International Date Line. The opening section describes the world's structure, systems and its main features. The Atlas of the World which follows, is a continent-by-continent guide to today's world, starting with a comprehensive insight into the physical, political and economic structure of each continent, followed by integrated mapping and descriptions of each region or country.

THE WORLD

THE INTRODUCTORY SECTION of the Atlas deals with every aspect of the planet, from physical structure to human geography, providing an overall picture of the world we live in. Complex topics such as the landscape of the Earth, climate, oceans, population and economic patterns are clearly explained with the aid of maps and diagrams drawn from the latest information.

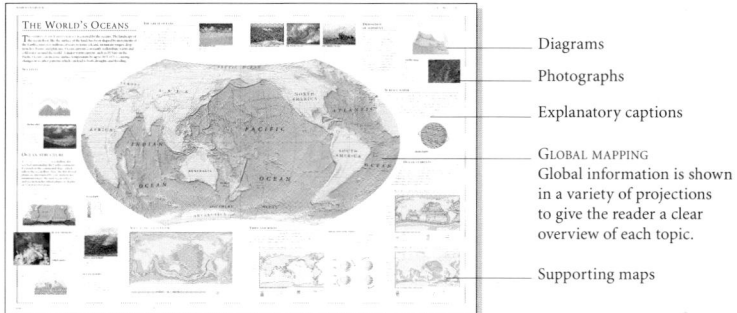

- Diagrams
- Photographs
- Explanatory captions
- GLOBAL MAPPING Global information is shown in a variety of projections to give the reader a clear overview of each topic.
- Supporting maps

THE POLITICAL CONTINENT

THE POLITICAL PORTRAIT of the continent is a vital reference point for every continental section, showing the position of countries relative to one another, and the relationship between human settlement and geographic location. The complex mosaic of languages spoken in each continent is mapped, as is the effect of communications networks on the pattern of settlement.

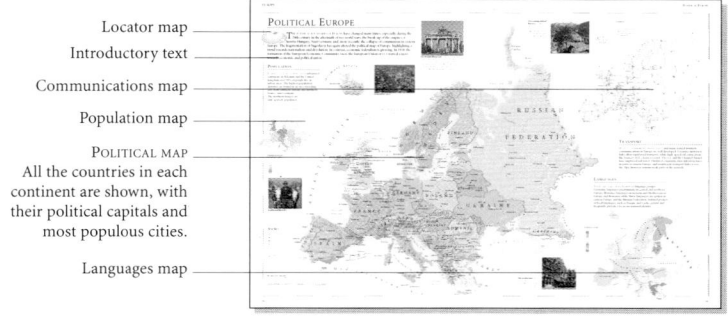

- Locator map
- Introductory text
- Communications map
- Population map
- POLITICAL MAP All the countries in each continent are shown, with their political capitals and most populous cities.
- Languages map

CONTINENTAL RESOURCES

THE EARTH'S RICH NATURAL RESOURCES, including oil, gas, minerals and fertile land, have played a key role in the development of society. These pages show the location of minerals and agricultural resources on each continent, and how they have been instrumental in dictating industrial growth and the varieties of economic activity across the continent.

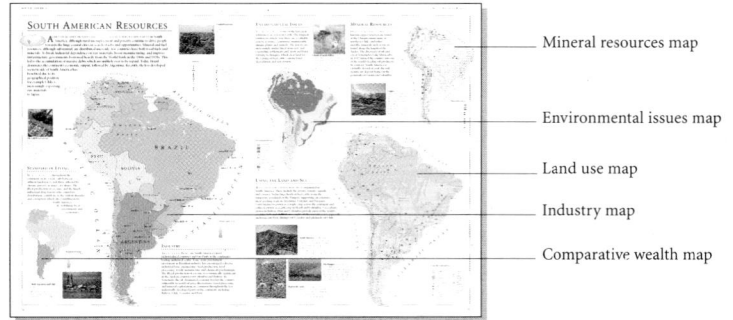

- Mineral resources map
- Environmental issues map
- Land use map
- Industry map
- Comparative wealth map

THE PHYSICAL CONTINENT

THE ASTONISHING VARIETY of landforms, and the dramatic forces that created and continue to shape the landscape, are explained in the continental physical spread. Cross-sections, illustrations and terrain maps highlight the different parts of the continent, showing how nature's forces have produced the landscapes we see today.

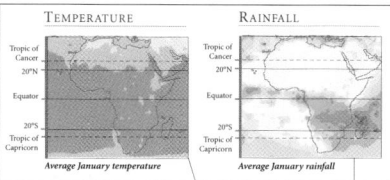

CLIMATE CHARTS
Rainfall and temperature charts clearly show the continental patterns of rainfall and temperature.

CLIMATE MAP
Climatic regions vary across each continent. The map displays the differing climatic regions, as well as daily hours of sunshine at selected weather stations.

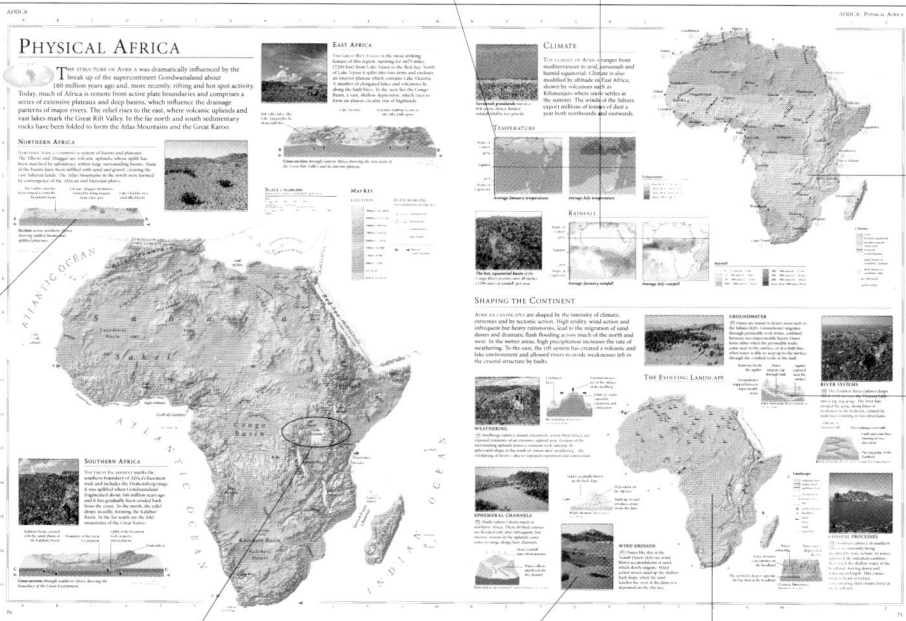

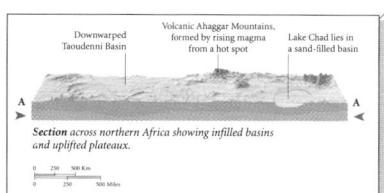

CROSS-SECTIONS
Detailed cross-sections through selected parts of the continent show the underlying geomorphic structure.

LANDFORM DIAGRAMS
The complex formation of many typical landforms is summarized in these easy-to-understand illustrations.

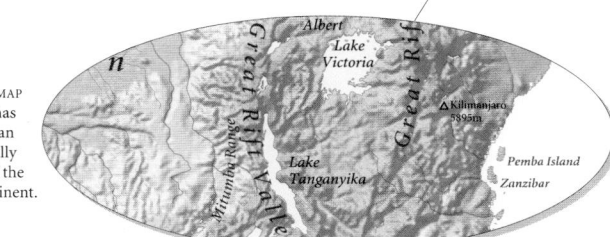

MAIN PHYSICAL MAP
Detailed satellite data has been used to create an accurate and visually striking picture of the surface of the continent.

PHOTOGRAPHS
A wide range of beautiful photographs bring the world's regions to life.

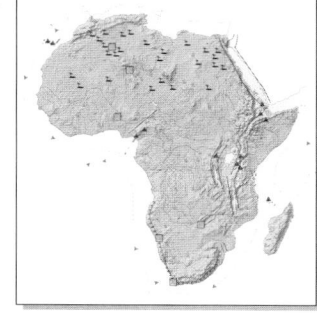

LANDSCAPE EVOLUTION MAP
The physical shape of each continent is affected by a variety of forces which continually sculpt and modify the landscape. This map shows the major processes which affect different parts of the continent.

REGIONAL MAPPING

THE MAIN BODY of the Atlas is a unique regional map set, with detailed information on the terrain, the human geography of the region and its infrastructure. Around the edge of the map, additional 'at-a-glance' maps, give an instant picture of regional industry, land use and agriculture. The detailed terrain map (shown in perspective), focuses on the main physical features of the region, and is enhanced by annotated illustrations, and photographs of the physical structure.

REGIONAL LOCATOR
This small map shows the location of each country in relation to its continent.

THE TRANSPORT NETWORK

340,090 miles (544,144 km)	4813 miles 7700 km
12,872 miles (20,592 km)	2108 miles (3389 km)

New York's commercial success is tied historically to its transport connections. The Erie Canal, completed in 1825, opened up the Great Lakes and the interior to New York's markets and carried a stream of immigrants into the Midwest.

TRANSPORT NETWORK
The differing extent of the transport network for each region is shown here, along with key facts about the transport system.

KEY TO MAIN MAP
A key to the population symbols and land heights accompanies the main map.

WORLD LOCATOR
This locates the continent in which the region is found on a small world map.

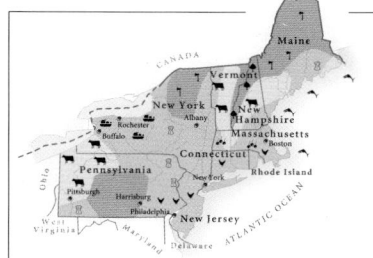

LAND USE MAP
This shows the different types of land use which characterize the region, as well as indicating the principal agricultural activities.

GRID REFERENCE
The framing grid provides a location reference for each place listed in the Index.

MAP KEYS
Each supporting map has its own key.

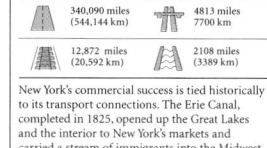

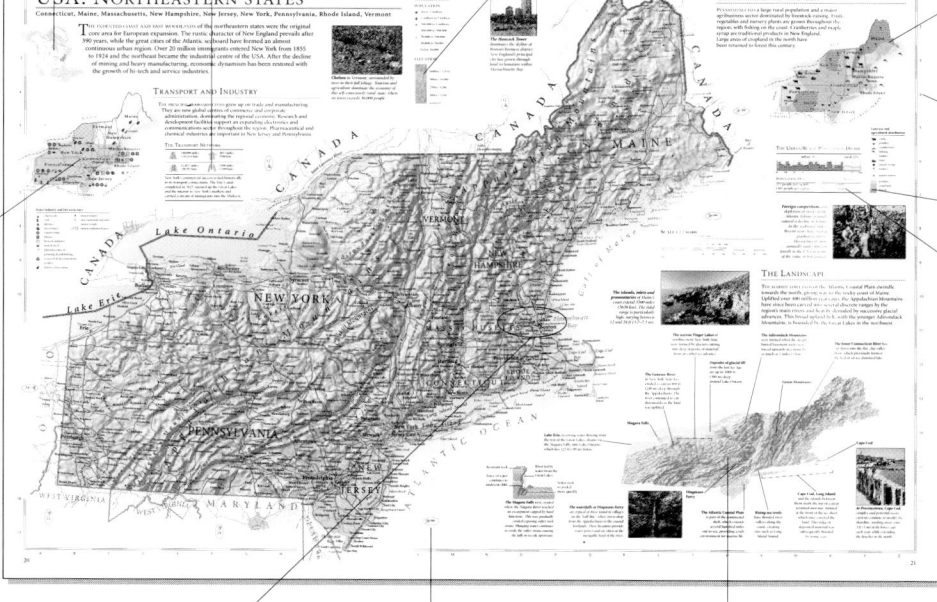

THE URBAN/RURAL POPULATION DIVIDE

urban 78%   rural 22%

0 10 20 30 40 50 60 70 80 90 100

POPULATION DENSITY	TOTAL LAND AREA
277 people per sq mile (107 people per sq km)	161,096 sq miles (417,222 sq km)

URBAN/RURAL POPULATION DIVIDE
The proportion of people in the region who live in urban and rural areas, as well as the overall population density and land area are clearly shown in these simple graphics.

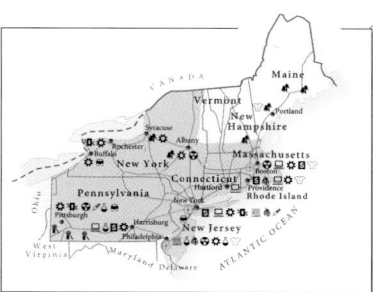

TRANSPORT AND INDUSTRY MAP
The main industrial areas are mapped, and the most important industrial and economic activities of the region are shown.

CONTINUATION SYMBOLS
These symbols indicate where adjacent maps can be found.

MAIN REGIONAL MAP
A wealth of information is displayed on the main map, building up a rich portrait of the interaction between the physical landscape and the human and political geography of each region. The key to the regional maps can be found on page viii.

LANDSCAPE MAP
The computer-generated terrain model accurately portrays an oblique view of the landscape. Annotations highlight the most important geographic features of the region.

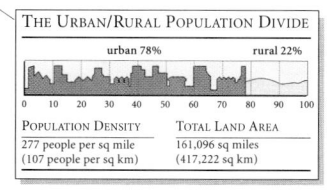

JUPITER

- **Diameter:** 88,846 miles (142,984 km)
- **Mass:** 1,900,000 million million million tons
- **Temperature:** -153°C (extremes not available)
- **Distance from Sun:** 483 million miles (778 million km)
- **Length of day:** 9.84 hours
- **Length of year:** 11.86 years
- **Surface gravity:** 1 kg = 2.53 kg

MARS

- **Diameter:** 4217 miles (6786 km)
- **Mass:** 642 million million million tons
- **Temperature:** -137 to 37°C
- **Distance from Sun:** 142 million miles (228 million km)
- **Length of day:** 24.623 hours
- **Length of year:** 1.88 years
- **Surface gravity:** 1 kg = 0.38 kg

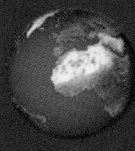

EARTH

- **Diameter:** 7926 miles (12,756 km)
- **Mass:** 5976 million million million tons
- **Temperature:** -70 to 55°C
- **Distance from Sun:** 93 million miles (150 million km)
- **Length of day:** 23.92 hours
- **Length of year:** 365.25 days
- **Surface gravity:** 1 kg = 1 kg

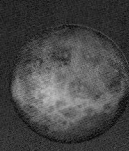

VENUS

- **Diameter:** 7520 miles (12,102 km)
- **Mass:** 4870 million million million tons
- **Temperature:** 457°C (extremes not available)
- **Distance from Sun:** 67 million miles (108 million km)
- **Length of day:** 243.01 days
- **Length of year:** 224.7 days
- **Surface gravity:** 1 kg = 0.88 kg

MERCURY

- **Diameter:** 3031 miles (4878 km)
- **Mass:** 330 million million million tons
- **Temperature:** -173 to 427°C
- **Distance from Sun:** 36 million miles (58 million km)
- **Length of day:** 58.65 days
- **Length of year:** 87.97 days
- **Surface gravity:** 1 kg = 0.38 kg

THE SOLAR SYSTEM

NINE MAJOR PLANETS, their satellites, and countless minor planets (asteroids) orbit the Sun to form the Solar System. The Sun, our nearest star, creates energy from nuclear reactions deep within its interior, providing all the light and heat which make life on Earth possible. The Earth is unique in the solar system in that it supports life: its size, gravitational pull and distance from the Sun have all created the optimum conditions for the evolution of life. The planetary images seen here are composites derived from actual spacecraft images (not shown to scale).

THE SUN

- **Diameter:** 864,948 miles (1,392,000 km)
- **Mass:** 1990 million million million million tons

THE SUN was formed when a swirling cloud of dust and gas contracted, pulling matter into its centre. When the temperature at the centre rose to 1,000,000°C, nuclear fusion – the fusing of hydrogen into helium, creating energy – occurred, releasing a constant stream of heat and light.

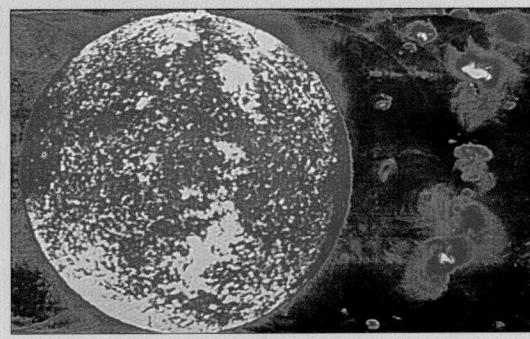

Solar flares are sudden bursts of energy from the Sun's surface. They can be 125,000 miles (200,000 km) long.

THE FORMATION OF THE SOLAR SYSTEM

The cloud of dust and gas thrown out by the Sun during its formation cooled to form the Solar System. The smaller planets nearest the Sun are formed of minerals and metals. The outer planets were formed at lower temperatures, and consist of swirling clouds of gases.

THE MILANKOVITCH CYCLE

The amount of radiation from the Sun which reaches the Earth is affected by variations in the Earth's orbit and the tilt of the Earth's axis, as well as by 'wobbles' in the axis. These variations cause three separate cycles, corresponding with the durations of recent ice ages.

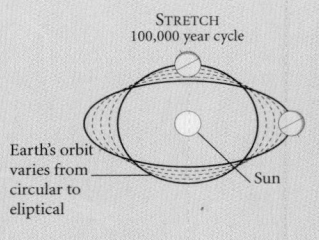

STRETCH
100,000 year cycle

Earth's orbit varies from circular to elliptical

Sun

TILT
41,000 year cycle

Sun

Angle of tilt varies by 2.4°

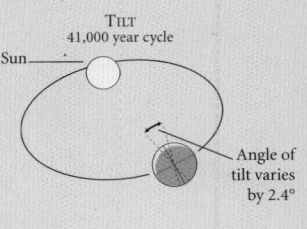

WOBBLE
21,000 year cycle

The Earth wobbles like a spinning top as it rotates

Sun

SATURN

- **Diameter:** 74,974 miles (120,660 km)
- **Mass:** 570,000 million million million tons
- **Temperature:** -185°C (extremes not available)
- **Distance from Sun:** 887 million miles (1427 million km)
- **Length of day:** 10.23 hours
- **Length of year:** 29.46 years
- **Surface gravity:** 1 kg = 1.07 kg

URANUS

- **Diameter:** 31,763 miles (51,118 km)
- **Mass:** 86,800 million million million tons
- **Temperature:** -214°C (extremes not available)
- **Distance from Sun:** 1783 million miles (2870 million km)
- **Length of day:** 17.9 hours
- **Length of year:** 84.01 years
- **Surface gravity:** 1 kg = 0.92 kg

NEPTUNE

- **Diameter:** 30,775 miles (49,528 km)
- **Mass:** 102,000 million million million tons
- **Temperature:** -225°C (extremes not available)
- **Distance from Sun:** 2794 million miles (4497 million km)
- **Length of day:** 19.2 hours
- **Length of year:** 164.79 years
- **Surface gravity:** 1 kg = 1.18 kg

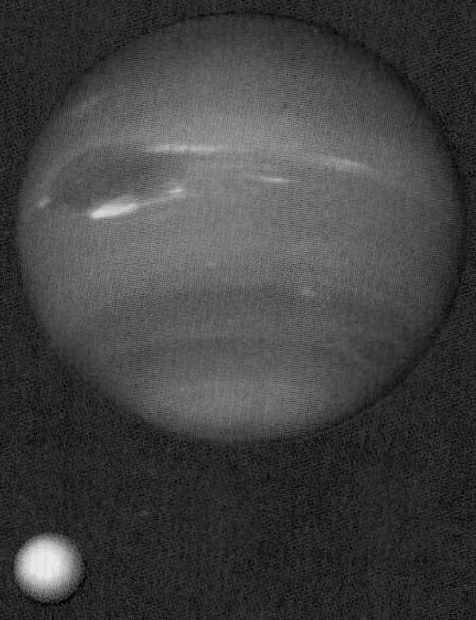

SPACE DEBRIS

MILLIONS OF OBJECTS, remnants of planetary formation, circle the Sun in a zone lying between Mars and Jupiter: the asteroid belt. Fragments of asteroids break off to form meteoroids, which can reach the Earth's surface. Comets, composed of ice and dust, originated outside our solar system. Their elliptical orbit brings them close to the Sun and into the inner solar system.

Meteor Crater in Arizona is 4200 ft (1300 m) wide and 660 ft (200 m) deep. It was formed over 10,000 years ago.

METEOROIDS

Meteoroids are fragments of asteroids which hurtle through space at great velocity. Although millions of meteoroids enter the Earth's atmosphere, the vast majority burn up on entry, and fall to the Earth as a meteor or shooting star. Large meteoroids travelling at speeds of 155,000 mph (250,000 kmph) can sometimes withstand the atmosphere and hit the Earth's surface with tremendous force, creating large craters on impact.

POSSIBLE AND ACTUAL METEORITE CRATERS

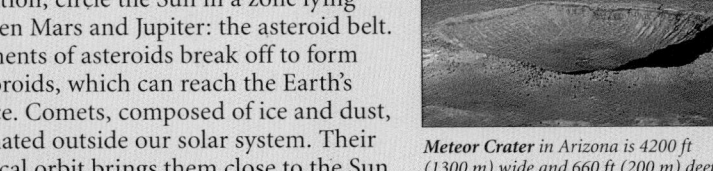

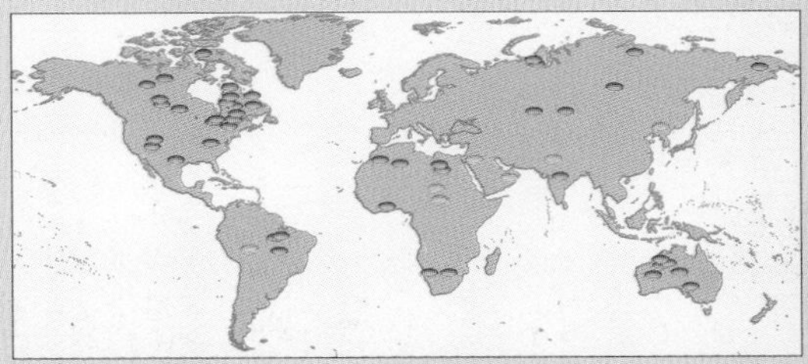

Map key

◯ Possible impact craters ◯ Meteorite impact craters

THE EARTH'S ATMOSPHERE

DURING THE EARLY STAGES of the Earth's formation, ash, lava, carbon dioxide and water vapour were discharged onto the surface of the planet by constant volcanic eruptions. The water formed the oceans, while carbon dioxide entered the atmosphere or was dissolved in the oceans. Clouds, formed of water droplets, reflected some of the Sun's radiation back into space. The Earth's temperature stabilized and early life forms began to emerge, converting carbon dioxide into life-giving oxygen.

It is thought that the gases that make up the Earth's atmosphere originated deep within the interior, and were released many millions of years ago during intense volcanic actvity, similar to this eruption at Mount St. Helens.

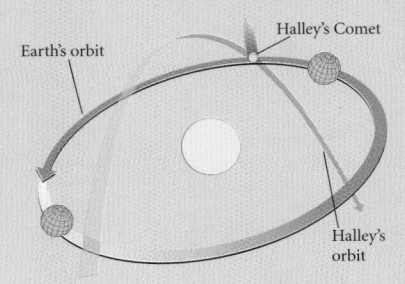

The orbit of Halley's Comet brings it close to the Earth every 76 years. It last visited in 1986.

Halley's Comet

Earth's orbit

Halley's orbit

ORBIT OF HALLEY'S COMET AROUND THE SUN

PLUTO

- **Diameter:** 1429 miles (2300 km)
- **Mass:** 13 million million million tons
- **Temperature:** -236°C (extremes not available)
- **Distance from Sun:** 3666 million miles (5900 million km)
- **Length of day:** 6.39 hours
- **Length of year:** 248.54 years
- **Surface gravity:** 1 kg = 0.30 kg

ORDER AND RELATIVE DISTANCE FROM THE SUN OF PLANETS

SUN MERCURY VENUS EARTH MARS JUPITER SATURN URANUS NEPTUNE PLUTO

0   500   1000   1500   2000   2500   3000   3500   4000   4500   5000   5500   6000 mill. km

0   500   1000   1500   2000   2500   3000   3500   4000 mill. miles

THE PHYSICAL WORLD

THE EARTH'S SURFACE is constantly being transformed: it is uplifted, folded and faulted by tectonic forces; weathered and eroded by wind, water and ice. Sometimes change is dramatic, the spectacular results of earthquakes or floods. More often it is a slow process lasting millions of years. A physical map of the world represents a snapshot of the ever-evolving architecture of the Earth. This terrain map shows the whole surface of the Earth, both above and below the sea.

THE WORLD IN SECTION

These cross-sections around the Earth, one in the northern hemisphere; one straddling the Equator, reveal the limited areas of land above sea level in comparison with the extent of the sea floor. The greater erosive effects of weathering by wind and water limit the upward elevation of land above sea level, while the deep oceans retain their dramatic mountain and trench profiles.

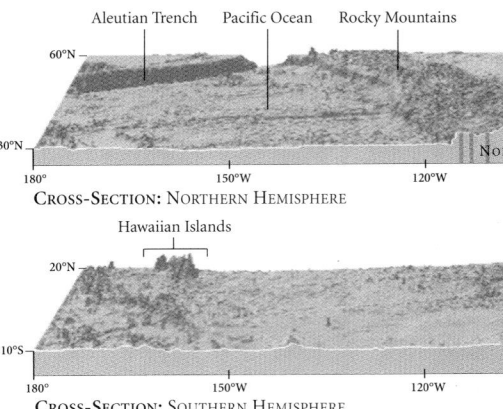

Aleutian Trench   Pacific Ocean   Rocky Mountains

CROSS-SECTION: NORTHERN HEMISPHERE

Hawaiian Islands

CROSS-SECTION: SOUTHERN HEMISPHERE

MAP KEY

GEOGRAPHICAL REGIONS

- ice
- tundra
- needleleaf forest
- broadleaf forest
- cultivated land
- hot desert
- cold desert
- tropical grassland
- tropical rainforest
- mountain
- submarine regions

SCALE 1:66,000,000
(projection: Wagner VII)

Km
0   250   500   1,000   1,500   2,000

Miles
0   250   500   1,000   1,500   2,000

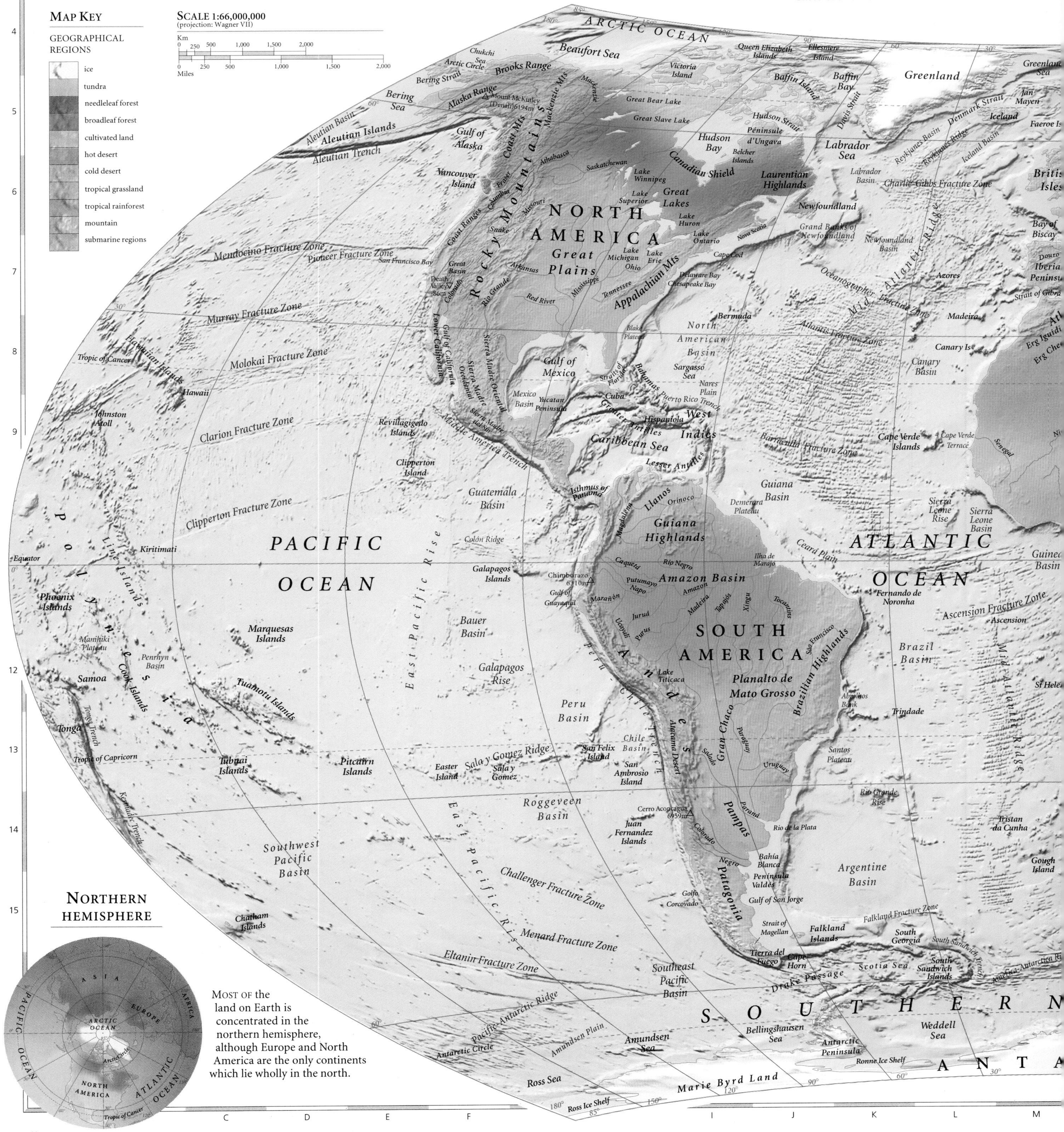

NORTHERN HEMISPHERE

MOST OF the land on Earth is concentrated in the northern hemisphere, although Europe and North America are the only continents which lie wholly in the north.

Map labels

ARCTIC OCEAN
Beaufort Sea
Chukchi Sea
Arctic Circle
Bering Strait
Brooks Range
Bering Sea
Alaska Range
Mount McKinley (Denali) 6194m
Coast Mts
Mackenzie Mts
Mackenzie
Victoria Island
Queen Elizabeth Islands
Ellesmere Island
Greenland
Greenland Sea
Jan Mayen
Iceland
Faeroe Is
Baffin Island
Baffin Bay
Davis Strait
Denmark Strait
Reykjanes Basin
Reykjanes Ridge
Iceland Basin
Great Bear Lake
Hudson Strait
Péninsule d'Ungava
British Isles
Aleutian Basin
Aleutian Islands
Aleutian Trench
Gulf of Alaska
Vancouver Island
Fraser
Columbia
Snake
Rocky Mountains
Great Slave Lake
Saskatchewan
Athabasca
Lake Winnipeg
Canadian Shield
Great Bear Lake
Hudson Bay
Belcher Islands
Laurentian Highlands
Labrador Sea
Newfoundland
Labrador Basin
Grand Banks of Newfoundland
Newfoundland Basin
Charlie-Gibbs Fracture Zone
Bay of Biscay
NORTH AMERICA
Great Plains
Coast Ranges
Missouri
Great Basin
Death Valley
Colorado
Rio Grande
Arkansas
Red River
Tennessee
Mississippi
Lake Superior
Lake Michigan
Lake Huron
Lake Erie
Lake Ontario
Great Lakes
Ohio
Appalachian Mts
Delaware Bay
Chesapeake Bay
Cape Cod
Nova Scotia
Oceanographer Fracture Zone
Mid-Atlantic Ridge
Iberian Peninsula
Strait of Gibraltar
Madeira
Azores
Atl
Mendocino Fracture Zone
Pioneer Fracture Zone
San Francisco Bay
Murray Fracture Zone
Molokai Fracture Zone
Tropic of Cancer
Hawaiian Islands
Hawaii
Johnston Atoll
Sierra Madre Occidental
Sierra Madre Oriental
Gulf of California
Lower California
Mexico Basin
Yucatan Peninsula
Sierra Madre
Blake Plateau
Bermuda
North American Basin
Atlantis Fracture Zone
Canary Is
Canary Basin
Erg Iguidi
Erg Chech
Strait of Florida
Bahamas
Gulf of Mexico
Cuba
Greater Antilles
Hispaniola
Puerto Rico Trench
Nares Plain
Sargasso Sea
West Indies
Clarion Fracture Zone
Revillagigedo Islands
Clipperton Island
Clipperton Fracture Zone
Middle America Trench
Guatemala Basin
Isthmus of Panama
Caribbean Sea
Lesser Antilles
Barracuda Fracture Zone
Cape Verde Islands
Cape Verde Terrace
Ni
Senegal
PACIFIC OCEAN
Galapagos Islands
Galapagos Rise
East Pacific Rise
Colón Ridge
Guiana Basin
Llanos
Orinoco
Demerara Plateau
Ceará Plain
Sierra Leone Rise
Sierra Leone Basin
Kiritimati
Line Islands
Equator
Phoenix Islands
Polynesia
Marquesas Islands
Bauer Basin
Chimborazo 6310m
Gulf of Guayaquil
Marañón
Napo
Putumayo
Caquetá
Rio Negro
Guiana Highlands
Amazon Basin
Amazon
Ilha de Marajó
Tocantins
Xingu
Tapajós
Madeira
Juruá
Jurua
Ucayali
ATLANTIC OCEAN
Guinea Basin
Fernando de Noronha
Ascension
Ascension Fracture Zone
SOUTH AMERICA
Manihiki Plateau
Penrhyn Basin
Samoa
Cook Islands
Tonga
Tonga Trench
Tropic of Capricorn
Kermadec Trench
Tubuai Islands
Pitcairn Islands
Easter Island
Sala y Gomez Ridge
Sala y Gomez
San Felix Island
San Ambrosio Island
Chile Basin
Andes
Peru Basin
Peru-Chile Trench
Lake Titicaca
Planalto de Mato Grosso
Brazilian Highlands
São Francisco
Paraguay
Brazil Basin
Abrolhos Bank
Trindade
St Helena
Santos Plateau
Roggeveen Basin
Cerro Aconcagua 6959m
Juan Fernandez Islands
Gran Chaco
Paraná
Uruguay
Colorado
Pampas
Río de la Plata
Rio Grande Rise
Chatham Islands
Southwest Pacific Basin
Challenger Fracture Zone
Menard Fracture Zone
Eltanin Fracture Zone
Pacific-Antarctic Ridge
Antarctic Circle
Negro
Bahía Blanca
Peninsula Valdés
Gulf of San Jorge
Golfo Corcovado
Patagonia
Argentine Basin
Gough Island
Tristan da Cunha
Strait of Magellan
Falkland Islands
Falkland Fracture Zone
South Georgia
South Sandwich Islands
Tierra del Fuego
Cape Horn
Scotia Sea
Drake Passage
Southeast Pacific Basin
Amundsen Plain
Amundsen Sea
Bellingshausen Sea
Antarctic Peninsula
Weddell Sea
SOUTHERN
ANTA
Ross Sea
Ross Ice Shelf
Marie Byrd Land
Ronne Ice Shelf
South Atlantic Ridge

ASIA
EUROPE
AFRICA
ARCTIC OCEAN
PACIFIC OCEAN
ATLANTIC OCEAN
NORTH AMERICA
Arctic Circle
Tropic of Cancer

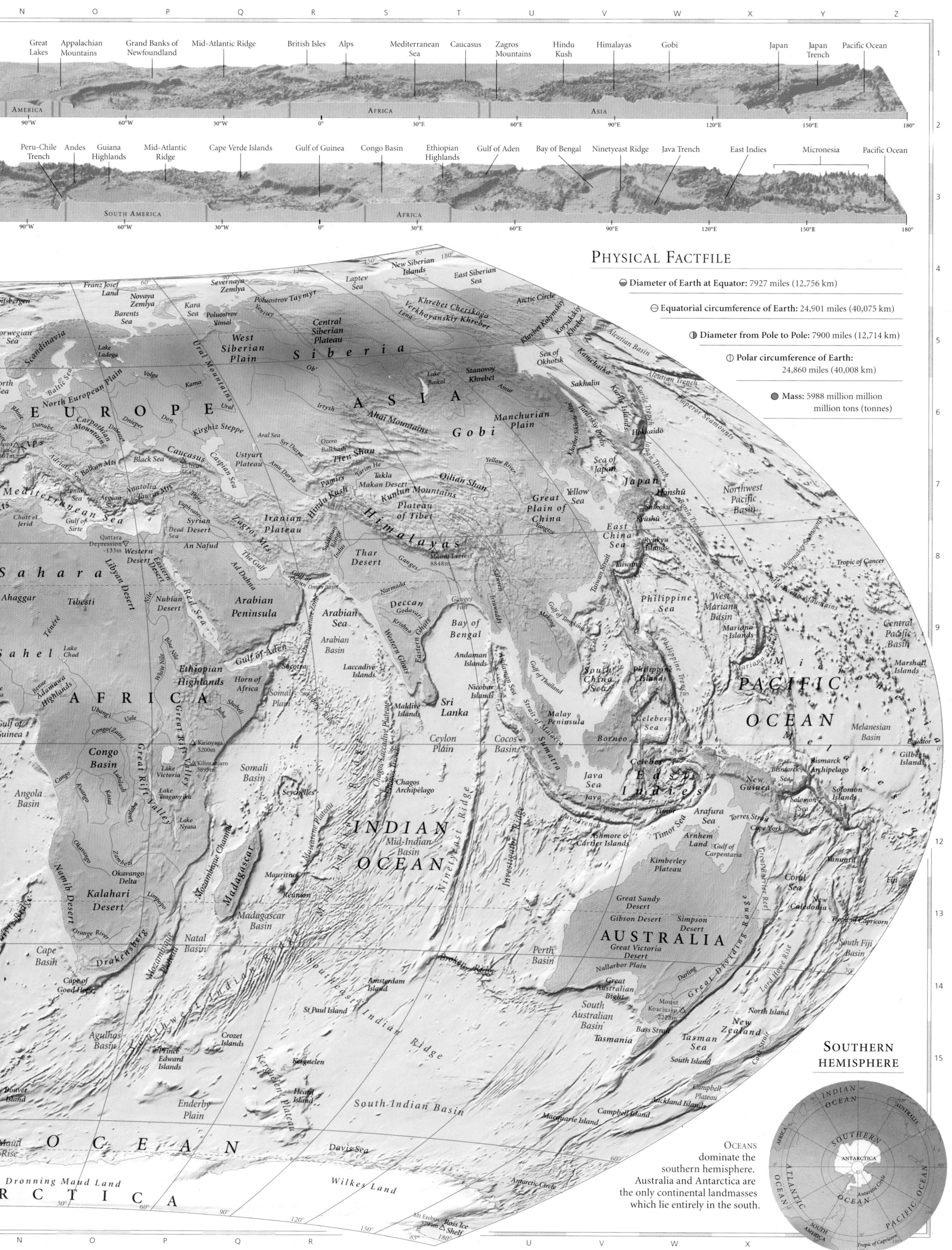

PHYSICAL FACTFILE

- **Diameter of Earth at Equator:** 7927 miles (12,756 km)
- **Equatorial circumference of Earth:** 24,901 miles (40,075 km)
- **Diameter from Pole to Pole:** 7900 miles (12,714 km)
- **Polar circumference of Earth:** 24,860 miles (40,008 km)
- **Mass:** 5988 million million million tons (tonnes)

SOUTHERN HEMISPHERE

OCEANS dominate the southern hemisphere. Australia and Antarctica are the only continental landmasses which lie entirely in the south.

STRUCTURE OF THE EARTH

THE EARTH AS IT IS TODAY is just the latest phase in a constant process of evolution which has occurred over the past 4.5 billion years. The Earth's continents are neither fixed nor stable; over the course of the Earth's history, propelled by currents rising from the intense heat at its centre, the great plates on which they lie have moved, collided, joined together, and separated. These processes continue to mould and transform the surface of the Earth, causing earthquakes and volcanic eruptions and creating oceans, mountain ranges, deep ocean trenches and island chains.

INSIDE THE EARTH

THE EARTH'S HOT INNER CORE is made up of solid iron, while the outer core is composed of liquid iron and nickel. The mantle nearest the core is viscous, whereas the rocky upper mantle is fairly rigid. The crust is the rocky outer shell of the Earth. Together, the upper mantle and the crust form the lithosphere.

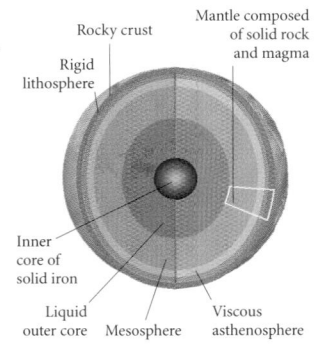

Rocky crust
Mantle composed of solid rock and magma
Rigid lithosphere
Inner core of solid iron
Liquid outer core
Mesosphere
Viscous asthenosphere

THE DYNAMIC EARTH

THE EARTH'S CRUST is made up of eight major (and several minor) rigid continental and oceanic tectonic plates, which fit closely together. The positions of the plates are not static. They are constantly moving relative to one another. The type of movement between plates affects the way in which they alter the structure of the Earth. The oldest parts of the plates, known as shields, are the most stable parts of the Earth and little tectonic activity occurs here.

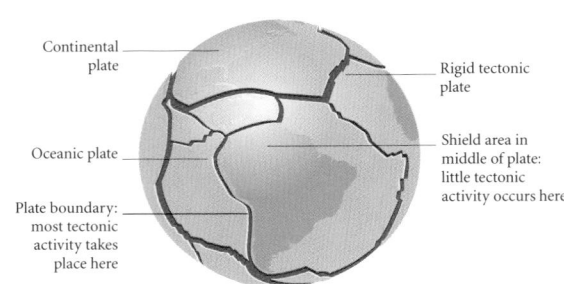

Continental plate
Oceanic plate
Plate boundary: most tectonic activity takes place here
Rigid tectonic plate
Shield area in middle of plate: little tectonic activity occurs here

CONVECTION CURRENTS

DEEP WITHIN THE EARTH, at its inner core, temperatures may exceed 8100°F (4000°C). This heat warms rocks in the mesosphere which rise through the partially molten mantle, displacing cooler rocks just below the solid crust, which sink, and are warmed again by the heat of the mantle. This process is continually repeated, creating convection currents which form the moving force beneath the Earth's crust.

Inner core
Outer core
Subduction zone
Ocean crust
Movement of plate
Mid-ocean ridge
Lithosphere
Asthenosphere
Mesosphere
Continental crust

PLATE BOUNDARIES

THE BOUNDARIES BETWEEN THE PLATES are the areas where most tectonic activity takes place. Three types of movement occur at plate boundaries: the plates can either move towards each other, move apart, or slide past each other. The effect this has on the Earth's structure depends on whether the margin is between two continental plates, two oceanic plates or an oceanic and continental plate.

Tectonic Activity

- – – – – uncertain plate boundary
- ▲ volcanic zone
- ● earthquake zone
- ● hot spot
- ⋎⋎⋎⋎⋎ rift valley

MID-OCEAN RIDGES

Mid-ocean ridges are formed when two adjacent oceanic plates pull apart, allowing magma to force its way up to the surface, which then cools to form solid rock. Vast amounts of volcanic material are discharged at these mid-ocean ridges which can reach heights of 10,000 ft (3000 m).

The Mid-Atlantic Ridge rises above sea level in Iceland, producing geysers and volcanoes.

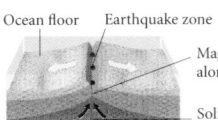

Ocean floor
Earthquake zone
Magma pushed upwards along centre of ridge
Solid mantle

FORMATION OF A MID-OCEAN RIDGE

OCEAN PLATES MEETING

▲▲ Oceanic crust is denser and thinner than continental crust; on average it is 3 miles (5 km) thick, while continental crust averages 18–24 miles (30–40 km). When oceanic plates of similar density meet, the crust is contorted as one plate overrides the other, forming deep sea trenches and volcanic island arcs above sea level.

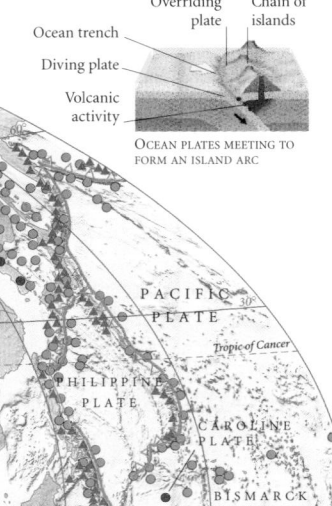

Overriding plate
Chain of islands
Ocean trench
Diving plate
Volcanic activity

OCEAN PLATES MEETING TO FORM AN ISLAND ARC

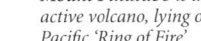

Mount Pinatubo is an active volcano, lying on the Pacific 'Ring of Fire'.

DIVING PLATES

▲▲ When an oceanic and a continental plate meet, the denser oceanic plate is driven underneath the continental plate, which is crumpled by the collision to form mountain ranges. As the ocean plate plunges downward, it heats up, and molten rock (magma) is forced up to the surface.

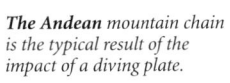

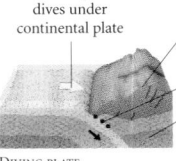

The Andean mountain chain is the typical result of the impact of a diving plate.

Oceanic plate dives under continental plate
Mountains thrust up by collision
Earthquake zone
Continental plate

DIVING PLATE

SLIDING PLATES

When two plates slide past each other, friction is caused along the fault line which divides them. The plates do not move smoothly, and the uneven movement causes earthquakes.

The deep fracture caused by the sliding plates of the San Andreas Fault can be clearly seen in parts of California.

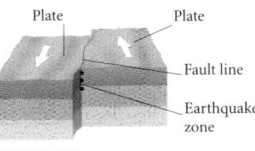

Plate
Plate
Fault line
Earthquake zone

SLIDING PLATES

COLLIDING PLATES

▲▲ When two continental plates collide, great mountain chains are thrust upwards as the crust buckles and folds under the force of the impact.

The Alps were formed when the African Plate collided with the Eurasian Plate, about 65 million years ago.

Plate buckles as it collides
Mountains thrust upwards
Earthquake zone
Crust thickens in response to the impact

CONTINENTAL PLATES COLLIDING TO FORM A MOUNTAIN RANGE

Map labels

JUAN DE FUCA PLATE
NORTH AMERICAN PLATE
EURASIAN PLATE
ANATOLIAN PLATE
IRANIAN PLATE
ARABIAN PLATE
PACIFIC PLATE
PHILIPPINE PLATE
CAROLINE PLATE
BISMARCK PLATE
CARIBBEAN PLATE
COCOS PLATE
PACIFIC PLATE
AFRICAN PLATE
SOUTH AMERICAN PLATE
NAZCA PLATE
INDO AUSTRALIAN PLATE
SOLOMON PLATE
FIJI PLATE
SCOTIA PLATE
ANTARCTIC PLATE

Arctic Circle
Tropic of Cancer
Equator
Tropic of Capricorn
Antarctic Circle

CONTINENTAL DRIFT

ALTHOUGH THE PLATES which make up the Earth's crust move only a few centimetres in a year, over the millions of years of the Earth's history, its continents have moved many thousands of kilometres, to create new continents, oceans and mountain chains.

4: TRIASSIC PERIOD

245–208 million years ago. All three major continents have joined to form the supercontinent of Pangea.

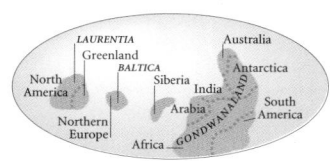

1: CAMBRIAN PERIOD

570–510 million years ago. Most continents are in tropical latitudes. The supercontinent of Gondwanaland reaches the South Pole.

5: JURASSIC PERIOD

208–145 million years ago. The supercontinent of Pangea begins to break up, causing an overall rise in sea levels.

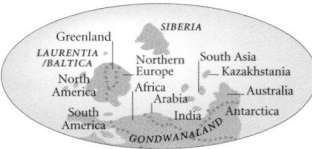

2: DEVONIAN PERIOD

408–362 million years ago. The continents of Gondwanaland and Laurentia are drifting northwards.

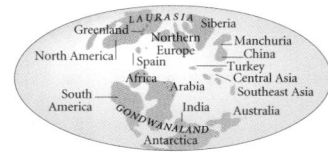

6: CRETACEOUS PERIOD

145–65 million years ago. Warm shallow seas cover much of the land: sea levels are about 80 ft (25 m) above present levels.

3: CARBONIFEROUS PERIOD

362–290 million years ago. The Earth is dominated by three continents; Laurentia, Angaraland and Gondwanaland.

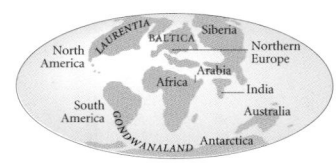

7: TERTIARY PERIOD

65–2 million years ago. Although the world's geography is becoming more recognizable, major events such as the creation of the Himalayan mountain chain, are still to occur during this period.

CONTINENTAL SHIELDS

THE CENTRES OF THE EARTH'S CONTINENTS, known as shields, were established between 2500 and 500 million years ago; some contain rocks over two billion years old. They were formed by a series of turbulent events: plate movements, earthquakes and volcanic eruptions. Since the Pre-Cambrian period, over 570 million years ago, they have experienced little tectonic activity, and today, these flat, low-lying slabs of solidified molten rock form the stable centres of the continents. They are bounded or covered by successive belts of younger sedimentary rock.

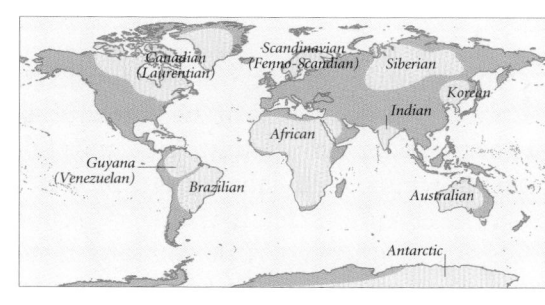

CREATION OF THE HIMALAYAS

BETWEEN 10 AND 20 MILLION YEARS AGO, the Indian subcontinent, part of the ancient continent of Gondwanaland, collided with the continent of Asia. The Indo-Australian Plate continued to move northwards, displacing continental crust and uplifting the Himalayas, the world's highest mountain chain.

MOVEMENTS OF INDIA

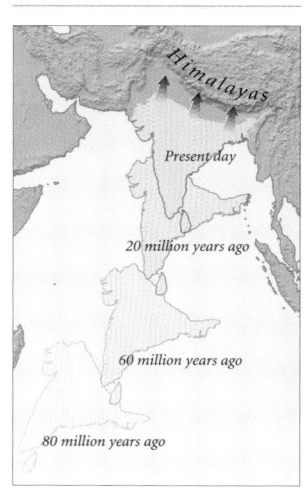

Present day

20 million years ago

60 million years ago

80 million years ago

Force of collision pushes up mountains

CROSS-SECTION THROUGH THE HIMALAYAS

The Himalayas were uplifted when the Indian subcontinent collided with Asia.

THE HAWAIIAN ISLAND CHAIN

A HOT SPOT lying deep beneath the Pacific Ocean pushes a plume of magma from the Earth's mantle up through the Pacific Plate to form volcanic islands. While the hot spot remains stationary, the plate on which the islands sit is moving slowly. A long chain of islands has been created as the plate passes over the hot spot.

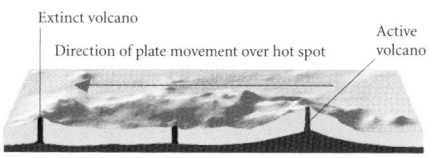

Extinct volcano

Direction of plate movement over hot spot

Active volcano

CROSS-SECTION THROUGH THE HAWAIIAN ISLANDS

EVOLUTION OF THE HAWAIIAN ISLANDS

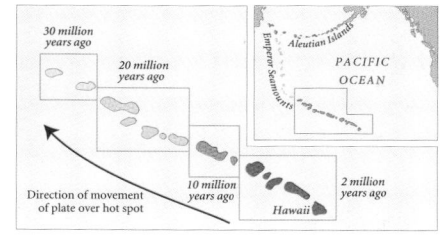

30 million years ago

20 million years ago

10 million years ago

2 million years ago

PACIFIC OCEAN

Direction of movement of plate over hot spot

Hawaii

THE EARTH'S GEOLOGY

THE EARTH'S ROCKS are created in a continual cycle. Exposed rocks are weathered and eroded by wind, water and chemicals and deposited as sediments. If they pass into the Earth's crust they will be transformed by high temperatures and pressures into metamorphic rocks or they will melt and solidify as igneous rocks.

GNEISS

1 Gneiss is a metamorphic rock made at great depth during the formation of mountain chains, when intense heat and pressure transform sedimentary or igneous rocks.

Gneiss formations in Norway's Jotunheimen Mountains.

Basalt columns at Giant's Causeway, Northern Ireland, UK.

BASALT

2 Basalt is an igneous rock, formed when small quantities of magma lying close to the Earth's surface cool rapidly.

LIMESTONE

3 Limestone is a sedimentary rock, which is formed mainly from the calcite skeletons of marine animals which have been compressed into rock.

Limestone hills, Guilin, China.

SANDSTONE

8 Sandstones are sedimentary rocks formed mainly in deserts, beaches and deltas. Desert sandstones are formed of grains of quartz which have been well rounded by wind erosion.

Rock stacks of desert sandstone, at Bryce Canyon National Park, Utah, USA.

Extrusive igneous rocks are formed during volcanic eruptions, as here in Hawaii.

ANDESITE

7 Andesite is an extrusive igneous rock formed from magma which has solidified on the Earth's crust after a volcanic eruption.

THE WORLD'S MAJOR GEOLOGICAL REGIONS

Geological Regions

- continental shield
- sedimentary cover
- coral formation
- igneous rock types

Mountain Ranges

- Alpine (new)
- Hercynian (old)
- Caledonian (ancient)

CORAL

4 Coral reefs are formed from the skeletons of millions of individual corals.

Great Barrier Reef, Australia.

SCHIST

6 Schist is a metamorphic rock formed during mountain building, when temperature and pressure are comparatively high. Both mudstones and shales reform into schist under these conditions.

Schist formations in the Atlas Mountains, northwestern Africa.

GRANITE

5 Granite is an intrusive igneous rock formed from magma which has solidified deep within the Earth's crust. The magma cools slowly, producing a coarse-grained rock.

Namibia's Namaqualand Plateau is formed of granite.

SHAPING THE LANDSCAPE

THE BASIC MATERIAL OF THE EARTH'S SURFACE is solid rock: valleys, deserts, soil and sand are all evidence of the powerful agents of weathering, erosion and deposition which constantly shape and transform the Earth's landscapes. Water, either flowing continually in rivers or seas, or frozen and compacted into solid sheets of ice, has the most clearly visible impact on the Earth's surface. But wind can transport fragments of rock over huge distances and strip away protective layers of vegetation, exposing rock surfaces to the impact of extreme heat and cold.

WATER

LESS THAN 2% of the world's water is on the land, but it is the most powerful agent of landscape change. Water, as rainfall, groundwater and rivers, can transform landscapes through both erosion and deposition. Eroded material carried by rivers forms the world's most fertile soils.

Waterfalls such as the Iguaçu Falls on the border between Argentina and southern Brazil, erode the underlying rock, causing the falls to retreat.

COASTAL WATER

THE WORLD'S COASTLINES are constantly changing; every day, tides deposit, sift and sort sand and gravel on the shoreline. Over longer periods, powerful wave action erodes cliffs and headlands and carves out bays.

A low, wide sandy beach on South Africa's Cape Peninsula is continually re-shaped by the action of the Atlantic waves.

The sheer chalk cliffs at Seven Sisters in southern England are constantly under attack from waves.

GROUNDWATER

IN REGIONS where there are porous rocks such as chalk, water is stored underground in large quantities; these reservoirs of water are known as aquifers. Rain percolates through topsoil into the underlying bedrock, creating an underground store of water. The limit of the saturated zone is called the water table.

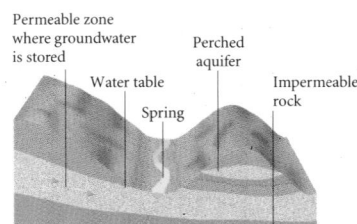

Permeable zone where groundwater is stored
Water table
Perched aquifer
Spring
Impermeable rock

STORAGE OF GROUNDWATER IN AN AQUIFER

World river systems:
Sediment deposited annually per drainage basin

tons per sq mile per year
9120   2400
6080   1600
1520   400
760   200 and less
tonnes per sq km per year

World river systems

drainage basin

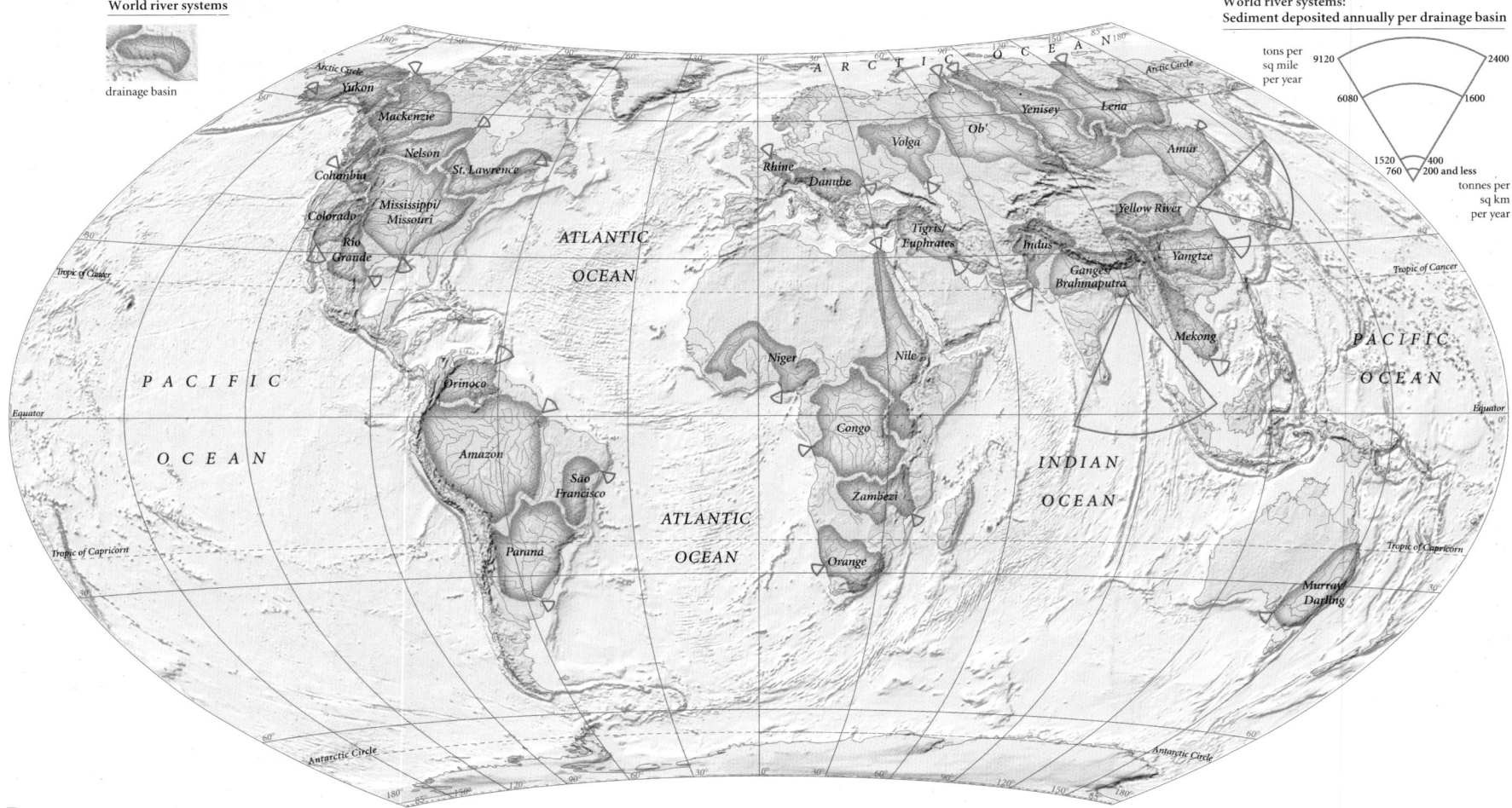

ARCTIC OCEAN

Yukon
Mackenzie
Nelson
Columbia
St. Lawrence
Colorado
Mississippi Missouri
Rio Grande

ATLANTIC OCEAN

Yenisey   Lena
Volga   Ob'
Rhine   Amur
Danube
Tigris/Euphrates   Yellow River
Indus
Ganges/Brahmaputra   Yangtze
Mekong

PACIFIC OCEAN

Orinoco
Amazon
São Francisco
Paraná

Niger   Nile
Congo
Zambezi
Orange

INDIAN OCEAN

Murray/Darling

PACIFIC OCEAN

Tropic of Cancer
Equator
Tropic of Capricorn
Arctic Circle
Antarctic Circle

RIVERS

RIVERS ERODE THE LAND by grinding and dissolving rocks and stones. Most erosion occurs in the river's upper course as it flows through highland areas. Rock fragments are moved along the river bed by fast-flowing water and deposited in areas where the river slows down, such as flat plains, or where the river enters seas or lakes.

RIVER VALLEYS

Over long periods of time rivers erode uplands to form characteristic V-shaped valleys with smooth sides.

Resistant rock
River
Chemical erosion cuts valley in softer rock

RIVER VALLEY EROSION

DELTAS

When a river deposits its load of silt and sediment (alluvium) on entering the sea, it may form a delta. As this material accumulates, it chokes the mouth of the river, forcing it to create new channels to reach the sea.

The Nile forms a broad delta as it flows into the Mediterranean.

DRAINAGE BASINS

The drainage basin is the area of land drained by a major trunk river and its smaller branch rivers or tributaries. Drainage basins are separated from one another by natural boundaries known as watersheds.

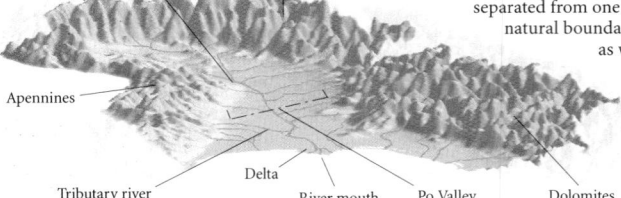

Watershed
Major trunk river
Alps
Apennines
Tributary river
Delta
River mouth
Po Valley
Dolomites

The drainage basin of the Po River, northern Italy.

MEANDERS

In their lower courses, rivers flow slowly. As they flow across the lowlands, they form looping bends called meanders.

The Mississippi River forms meanders as it flows across the southern USA.

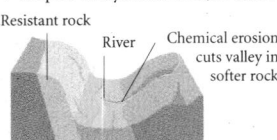

The meanders of Utah's San Juan River have become deeply incised.

DEPOSITION

When rivers have deposited large quantities of fertile alluvium, they are forced to find new channels through the alluvium deposits, creating braided river systems.

Mud is deposited by China's Yellow River in its lower course.

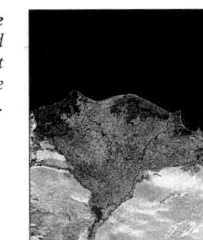

A huge landslide in the Swiss Alps has left massive piles of rocks and pebbles called scree.

LANDSLIDES

Heavy rain and associated flooding on slopes can loosen underlying rocks, which crumble, causing the top layers of rock and soil to slip.

GULLIES

In areas where soil is thin, rainwater is not effectively absorbed, and may flow overland. The water courses downhill in channels, or gullies, and may lead to rapid erosion of soil.

A deep gully in the French Alps caused by the scouring of upper layers of turf.

ICE

DURING ITS LONG HISTORY, the Earth has experienced a number of glacial episodes when temperatures were considerably lower than today. During the last Ice Age, 18,000 years ago, ice covered an area three times larger than it does today. Over these periods, the ice has left a remarkable legacy of transformed landscapes.

GLACIERS

GLACIERS ARE FORMED by the compaction of snow into 'rivers' of ice. As they move over the landscape, glaciers pick up and carry a load of rocks and boulders which erode the landscape they pass over, and are eventually deposited at the end of the glacier.

A massive glacier advancing down a valley in southern Argentina.

POST-GLACIAL FEATURES

WHEN A GLACIAL EPISODE ENDS, the retreating ice leaves many features. These include depositional ridges called moraines, which may be eroded into low hills known as drumlins; sinuous ridges called eskers; kames which are rounded hummocks; depressions known as kettle holes; and finely-ground loess deposits.

GLACIAL VALLEYS

GLACIERS CAN ERODE much more powerfully than rivers. They form steep-sided, flat-bottomed valleys with a typical U-shaped profile. Valleys created by tributary glaciers, whose floors have not been eroded to the same depth as the main glacial valley floor, are called hanging valleys.

The U-shaped profile and piles of morainic debris are characteristic of a valley once filled by a glacier.

A series of hanging valleys high up in the Chilean Andes.

The profile of the Matterhorn has been formed by three cirques lying 'back-to-back'.

CIRQUES

Cirques are basin-shaped hollows which mark the head of a glaciated valley. Where neighbouring cirques meet, they are divided by sharp rock ridges called arêtes. It is these arêtes which give the Matterhorn its characteristic profile.

FJORDS

Fjords are ancient glacial valleys flooded by the sea following the end of a period of glaciation. Beneath the water, the valley floor can be 4000 ft (1300 m) deep.

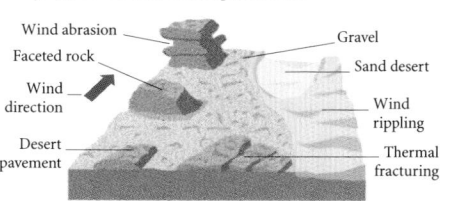

A fjord fills a former glacial valley in southern New Zealand.

PAST AND PRESENT WORLD ICE-COVER AND GLACIAL FEATURES

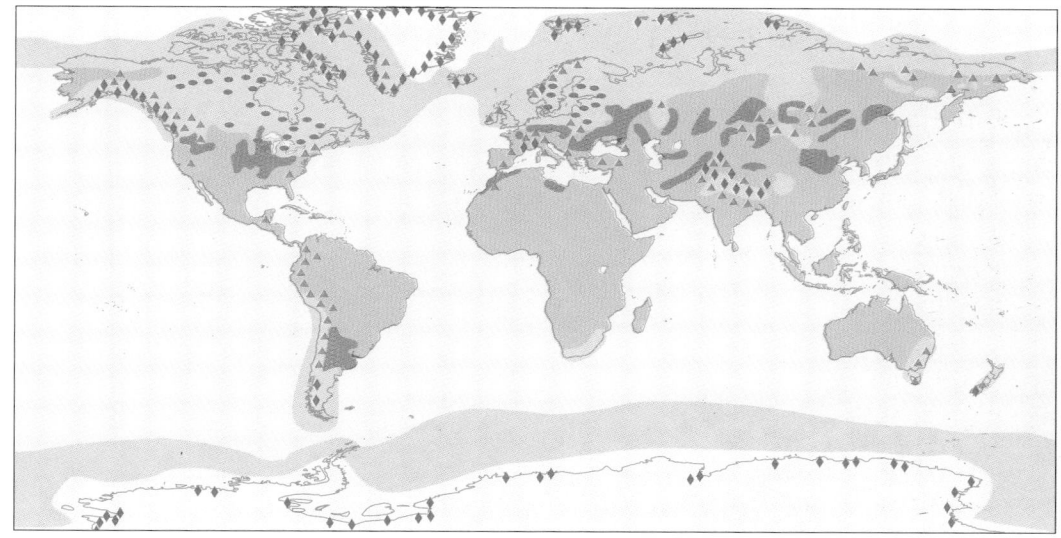

POST-GLACIAL LANDSCAPE FEATURES

- Kame terrace
- Kettle hole
- Esker
- Braided river
- Windblown loess
- Retreating glacier
- Drumlin
- Terminal moraine
- Glacial till
- Bedrock

Past and present world ice cover and glacial features

- extent of last Ice Age
- loess deposits
- post-glacial feature
- glacial feature
- present day ice cover
- glacial field

ICE SHATTERING

Water drips into fissures in rocks and freezes, expanding as it does so. The pressure weakens the rock, causing it to crack, and eventually to shatter into polygonal patterns.

Irregular polygons show through the sedge-grass tundra in the Yukon, Canada.

PERIGLACIATION

Periglacial areas occur near to the edge of ice sheets. A layer of frozen ground lying just beneath the surface of the land is known as permafrost. When the surface melts in the summer, the water is unable to drain into the frozen ground, and so 'creeps' downhill, a process known as solifluction

WIND

STRONG WINDS can transport rock fragments great distances, especially where there is little vegetation to protect the rock. In desert areas, wind picks up loose, unprotected sand particles, carrying them over great distances. This powerfully abrasive debris is blasted at the surface by the wind, 'weathering' the landscape into dramatic shapes.

DEPOSITION

THE ROCKY, STONY FLOORS of the world's deserts are swept and scoured by strong winds. The smaller, finer particles of sand are shaped into surface ripples, dunes, or sand mountains, which rise to a height of 650 ft (200 m). Dunes usually form single lines, running perpendicular to the direction of the prevailing wind. These long, straight ridges can extend for over 100 miles (160 km).

DUNES

Dunes are shaped by wind direction and sand supply. Where sand supply is limited, crescent-shaped barchan dunes are formed.

PREVAILING WINDS AND DUST TRAJECTORIES

Prevailing winds
- northeast trade
- southeast trade
- westerly
- westerly
- polar easterly
- polar easterly

Dust trajectories
- trajectory of aeolian dust

Barchan dunes in the Arabian Desert.

Complex dune system in the Sahara.

TYPES OF DUNE

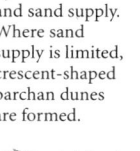
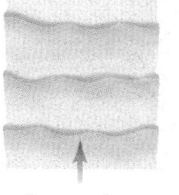
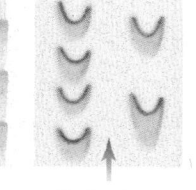
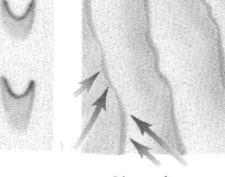

- wind direction
- Transverse dune
- Barchan dune
- Linear dune
- Star dune

TEMPERATURE

HOT AND COLD DESERTS

- Arctic Circle
- Tropic of Cancer
- Equator
- Tropic of Capricorn
- Antarctic Circle

Main desert types
- hot arid
- semi-arid
- cold polar

MOST OF THE WORLD'S deserts are in the tropics. The cold deserts which occur elsewhere are arid because they are a long way from the rain-giving sea. Rock in deserts is exposed because of lack of vegetation and is susceptible to changes in temperature; extremes of heat and cold can cause both cracks and fissures to appear in the rock.

HEAT

FIERCE SUN can heat the surface of rock, causing it to expand more rapidly than the cooler, underlying layers. This creates tensions which force the rock to crack or break up. In arid regions, the evaporation of water from rock surfaces dissolves certain minerals within the water, causing salt crystals to form in small openings in the rock. The hard crystals force the openings to widen into cracks and fissures.

The cracked and parched floor of Death Valley, California. This is one of the hottest deserts on Earth.

DESERT ABRASION

Abrasion creates a wide range of desert landforms from faceted pebbles and wind ripples in the sand, to large-scale features such as yardangs (low, streamlined ridges), and scoured desert pavements.

- Wind abrasion
- Faceted rock
- Wind direction
- Desert pavement
- Gravel
- Sand desert
- Wind rippling
- Thermal fracturing

FEATURES OF A DESERT SURFACE

This dry valley at Ellesmere Island in the Canadian Arctic is an example of a cold desert. The cracked floor and scoured slopes are features also found in hot deserts.

THE WORLD'S OCEANS

TWO-THIRDS OF THE EARTH'S SURFACE is covered by the oceans. The landscape of the ocean floor, like the surface of the land, has been shaped by movements of the Earth's crust over millions of years to form volcanic mountain ranges, deep trenches, basins and plateaux. Ocean currents constantly redistribute warm and cold water around the world. A major warm current, such as El Niño in the Pacific Ocean, can increase surface temperature by up to 46°F (8°C), causing changes in weather patterns which can lead to both droughts and flooding.

SEA LEVEL

IF THE INFLUENCE of tides, winds, currents and variations in gravity were ignored, the surface of the Earth's oceans would closely follow the topography of the ocean floor, with an underwater ridge 3000 ft (915 m) high producing a rise of up to 3 ft (1 m) in the level of the surface water.

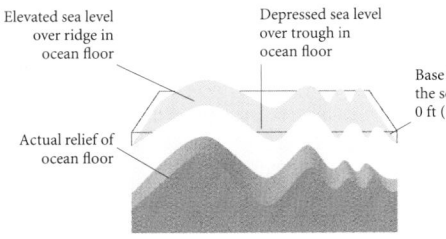

Elevated sea level over ridge in ocean floor

Depressed sea level over trough in ocean floor

Base level of the sea surface at 0 ft (0 m)

Actual relief of ocean floor

HOW SURFACE WATERS REFLECT THE RELIEF OF THE OCEAN FLOOR

The low relief of many small Pacific islands such as these atolls at Huahine in French Polynesia makes them vulnerable to changes in sea level.

OCEAN STRUCTURE

THE CONTINENTAL SHELF is a shallow, flat sea-bed surrounding the Earth's continents. It extends to the continental slope, which falls to the ocean floor. Here, the flat abyssal plains are interrupted by vast, underwater mountain ranges, the mid-ocean ridges, and ocean trenches which plunge to depths of 35,828 ft (10,920 m).

Flat-topped guyot   Trench   Abyssal plain   Volcanic island
Seamount   Oceanic ridge   Continental shelf

TYPICAL SEA-FLOOR FEATURES

THE GREAT OCEANS

THERE ARE FIVE OCEANS on Earth: the Pacific, Atlantic, Indian and Southern oceans, and the much smaller Arctic Ocean. These five ocean basins are relatively young, having evolved within the last 80 million years. One of the most recent plate collisions, between the Eurasian and African plates, created the present-day arrangement of continents and oceans.

The Indian Ocean accounts for approximately 20% of the total area of the world's oceans.

Ocean depth

	Sea level
	200m / 656ft
	1000m / 3281ft
	2000m / 6562ft
	3000m / 9843ft
	4000m / 13,124ft
	5000m / 16,400ft
	6000m / 19,686ft

BLACK SMOKERS

These vents in the ocean floor disgorge hot, sulphur-rich water from deep in the Earth's crust. Despite the great depths, a variety of lifeforms have adapted to the chemical-rich environment which surrounds black smokers.

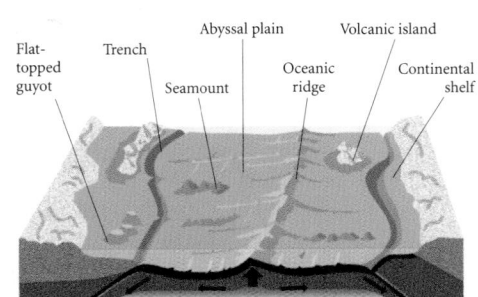

A black smoker in the Atlantic Ocean.

Surtsey, near Iceland, is a volcanic island lying directly over the Mid-Atlantic Ridge. It was formed in the 1960s following intense volcanic activity nearby.

Chimney   Plume of hot mineral laden water   Water heated by hot basalt
Water percolates into the sea floor   Ocean floor

FORMATION OF BLACK SMOKERS

OCEAN FLOORS

Mid-ocean ridges are formed by lava which erupts beneath the sea and cools to form solid rock. This process mirrors the creation of volcanoes from cooled lava on the land. The ages of sea floor rocks increase in parallel bands outwards from central ocean ridges.

AGES OF THE OCEAN FLOOR

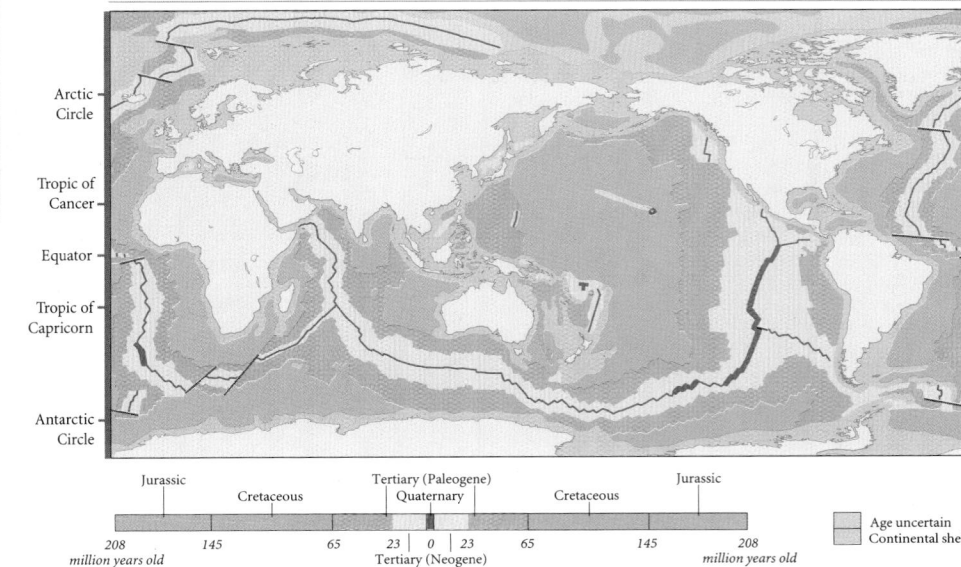

Arctic Circle
Tropic of Cancer
Equator
Tropic of Capricorn
Antarctic Circle

Jurassic   Cretaceous   Tertiary (Paleogene)   Quaternary   Cretaceous   Jurassic

208 million years old   145   65   23 | 0 | 23   65   145   208 million years old

Tertiary (Neogene)

Age uncertain
Continental shelf

Map labels: ARCTIC, Arctic Circle, Barents Sea, Kara Sea, Laptev Sea, East Siberian Sea, North Sea, Baltic Sea, Sea of Okhotsk, EUROPE, ASIA, Black Sea, Mediterranean Sea, Caspian Sea, Sea of Japan, Kurile Trench, Northwest Pacific Basin, Tropic of Cancer, Red Sea, The Gulf, Arabian Sea, Yellow Sea, East China Sea, Bay of Bengal, Gulf of Thailand, South China Sea, Philippine Sea, Mariana Trench, Mid-Pacific Mountains, AFRICA, Gulf of Guinea, Equator, Somali Basin, INDIAN, Sunda Shelf, Celebes Sea, Bismarck Sea, Melanesian Basin, Angola Basin, Mid-Indian Basin, Arafura Sea, Timor Sea, Solomon Sea, Coral Sea, Great Barrier Reef, Mozambique Channel, Madagascar Basin, AUSTRALIA, Perth Basin, South Fiji Basin, Tropic of Capricorn, Mascarene Plateau, Ninety East Ridge, Cape Basin, Madagascar Basin, OCEAN, South Australian Basin, Bass Strait, Tasman Sea, Agulhas Basin, Kerguelen Plateau, Southeast Indian Ridge, Campbell Plateau, South Indian Basin, SOUTHERN, Enderby Plain, Antarctic Circle, ANTARCTICA

Currents in the Southern Ocean are driven by some of the world's fiercest winds, including the Roaring Forties, Furious Fifties and Shrieking Sixties.

The Pacific Ocean is the world's largest and deepest ocean, covering over one-third of the surface of the Earth.

The Atlantic Ocean was formed when the landmasses of the eastern and western hemispheres began to drift apart 180 million years ago.

DEPOSITION OF SEDIMENT

STORMS, EARTHQUAKES, and volcanic activity trigger underwater currents known as turbidity currents which scour sand and gravel from the continental shelf, creating underwater canyons. These strong currents pick up material deposited at river mouths and deltas, and carry it across the continental shelf and through the underwater canyons, where it is eventually laid down on the ocean floor in the form of fans.

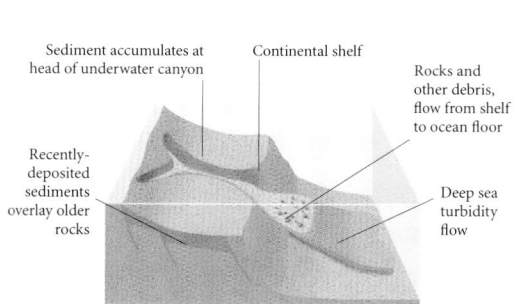

HOW SEDIMENT IS DEPOSITED ON THE OCEAN FLOOR

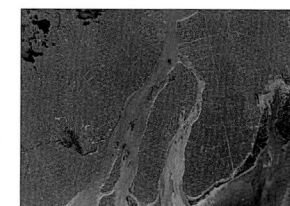

Satellite image of the Yangtze (Chang Jiang) Delta, in which the land appears red. The river deposits immense quantities of silt into the East China Sea, much of which will eventually reach the deep ocean floor.

SURFACE WATER

OCEAN CURRENTS move warm water away from the Equator towards the poles, while cold water is, in turn, moved towards the Equator. This is the main way in which the Earth distributes surface heat and is a major climatic control. Approximately 4000 million years ago, the Earth was dominated by oceans and there was no land to interrupt the flow of the currents, which would have flowed as straight lines, simply influenced by the Earth's rotation.

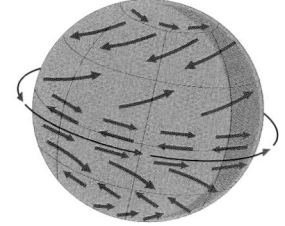

Idealized globe showing the movement of water around a landless Earth.

OCEAN CURRENTS

SURFACE CURRENTS are driven by the prevailing winds and by the spinning motion of the Earth, which drives the currents into circulating whirlpools, or gyres. Deep sea currents, over 330 ft (100 m) below the surface, are driven by differences in water temperature and salinity, which have an impact on the density of deep water and on its movement.

SURFACE TEMPERATURE AND CURRENTS

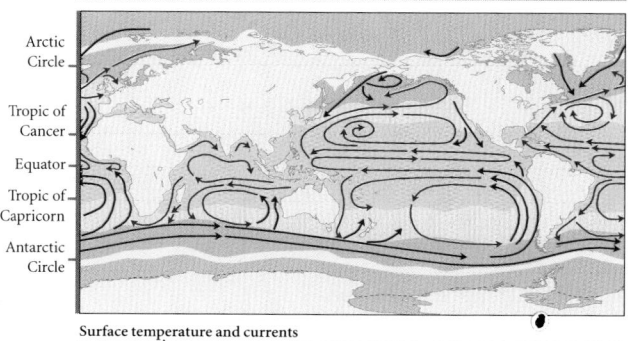

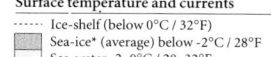

Surface temperature and currents

---- Ice-shelf (below 0°C / 32°F)	0–10°C / 32–50°F	→ warm current
Sea-ice* (average) below -2°C / 28°F	10–20°C / 50–68°F	→ cold current
Sea-water -2–0°C / 28-32°F	20–30°C / 68–86°F	
* Sea-water freezes at -1.9°C / 28.4°F		

DEEP SEA TEMPERATURE AND CURRENTS

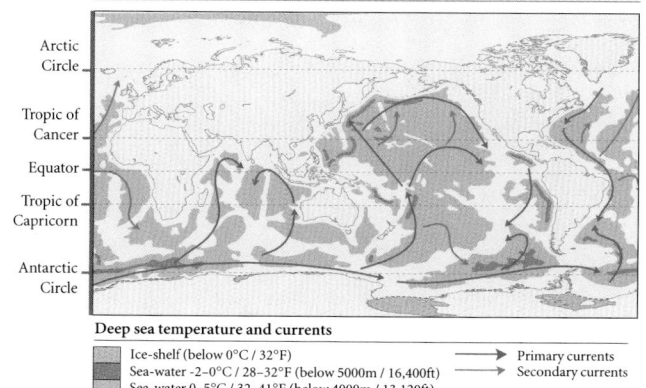

Deep sea temperature and currents

Ice-shelf (below 0°C / 32°F)		→ Primary currents
Sea-water -2–0°C / 28-32°F (below 5000m / 16,400ft)		→ Secondary currents
Sea-water 0–5°C / 32-41°F (below 4000m / 13,120ft)		

TIDES AND WAVES

TIDES ARE CREATED by the pull of the Sun and Moon's gravity on the surface of the oceans. The levels of high and low tides are influenced by the position of the Moon in relation to the Earth and Sun. Waves are formed by wind blowing over the surface of the water.

HIGH AND LOW TIDES

The highest tides occur when the Earth, the Moon and the Sun are aligned *(below left)*.
The lowest tides are experienced when the Sun and Moon align at right angles to one another *(below right)*.

TIDAL RANGE AND WAVE ENVIRONMENTS

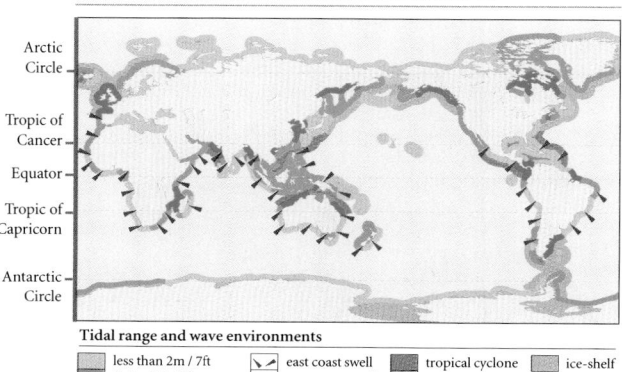

Tidal range and wave environments

less than 2m / 7ft	east coast swell	tropical cyclone
2–4m / 7–13ft	west coast swell	storm wave
greater than 4m / 13ft		ice-shelf

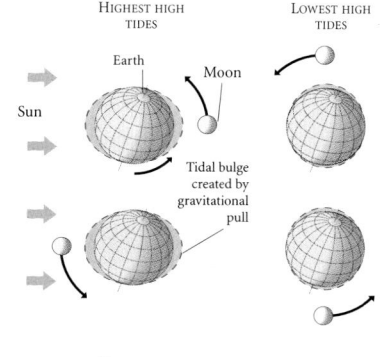

HIGHEST HIGH TIDES

LOWEST HIGH TIDES

Earth
Moon
Sun
Tidal bulge created by gravitational pull

HIGHEST HIGH TIDES

LOWEST HIGH TIDES

THE GLOBAL CLIMATE

THE EARTH'S CLIMATIC TYPES CONSIST of stable patterns of weather conditions averaged out over a long period of time. Different climates are categorized according to particular combinations of temperature and humidity. By contrast, weather consists of short-term fluctuations in wind, temperature and humidity conditions. Different climates are determined by latitude, altitude, the prevailing wind and circulation of ocean currents. Longer-term changes in climate, such as global warming or the onset of ice ages, are punctuated by shorter-term events which comprise the day-to-day weather of a region, such as frontal depressions, hurricanes and blizzards.

THE ATMOSPHERE, WIND AND WEATHER

THE EARTH'S ATMOSPHERE has been compared to a giant ocean of air which surrounds the planet. Its circulation patterns are similar to the currents in the oceans and are influenced by three factors; the Earth's orbit around the Sun and rotation about its axis, and variations in the amount of heat radiation received from the Sun. If both heat and moisture were not redistributed between the Equator and the poles, large areas of the Earth would be uninhabitable.

Heavy fogs, as here in southern England, form as moisture-laden air passes over cold ground.

TEMPERATURE

THE WORLD CAN BE DIVIDED into three major climatic zones, stretching like large belts across the latitudes: the tropics which are warm; the cold polar regions and the temperate zones which lie between them. Temperatures across the Earth range from above 30°C (86°F) in the deserts to as low as -55°C (-70°F) at the poles. Temperature is also controlled by altitude; because air becomes cooler and less dense the higher it gets, mountainous regions are typically colder than those areas which are at, or close to, sea level.

AVERAGE JANUARY TEMPERATURES

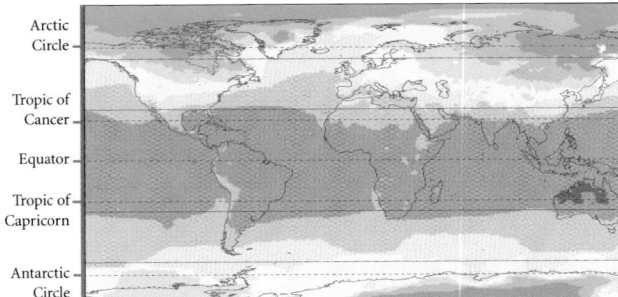

AVERAGE JULY TEMPERATURES

below - 30°C (-22°F)	-10 to 0°C (14 to 32°F)
-30 to - 20°C (-22 to -4°F)	0 to 10°C (32 to 50°F)
-20 to - 10°C (-4 to 14°F)	10 to 20°C (50 to 68°F)
	20 to 30°C (68 to 86°F)
	above 30°C (86°F)

GLOBAL AIR CIRCULATION

AIR DOES NOT SIMPLY FLOW FROM THE EQUATOR TO THE POLES, it circulates in giant cells known as Hadley and Ferrel cells. As air warms it expands, becoming less dense and rising; this creates areas of low pressure. As the air rises it cools and condenses, causing heavy rainfall over the tropics and slight snowfall over the poles. This cool air then sinks, forming high pressure belts. At surface level in the tropics these sinking currents are deflected polewards as the westerlies and towards the Equator as the trade winds. At the poles they become the polar easterlies.

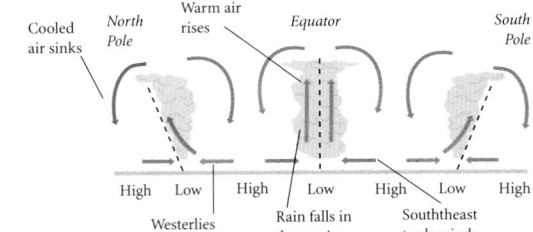

The Antarctic pack-ice expands its area by almost seven times during the winter as temperatures drop and surrounding seas freeze.

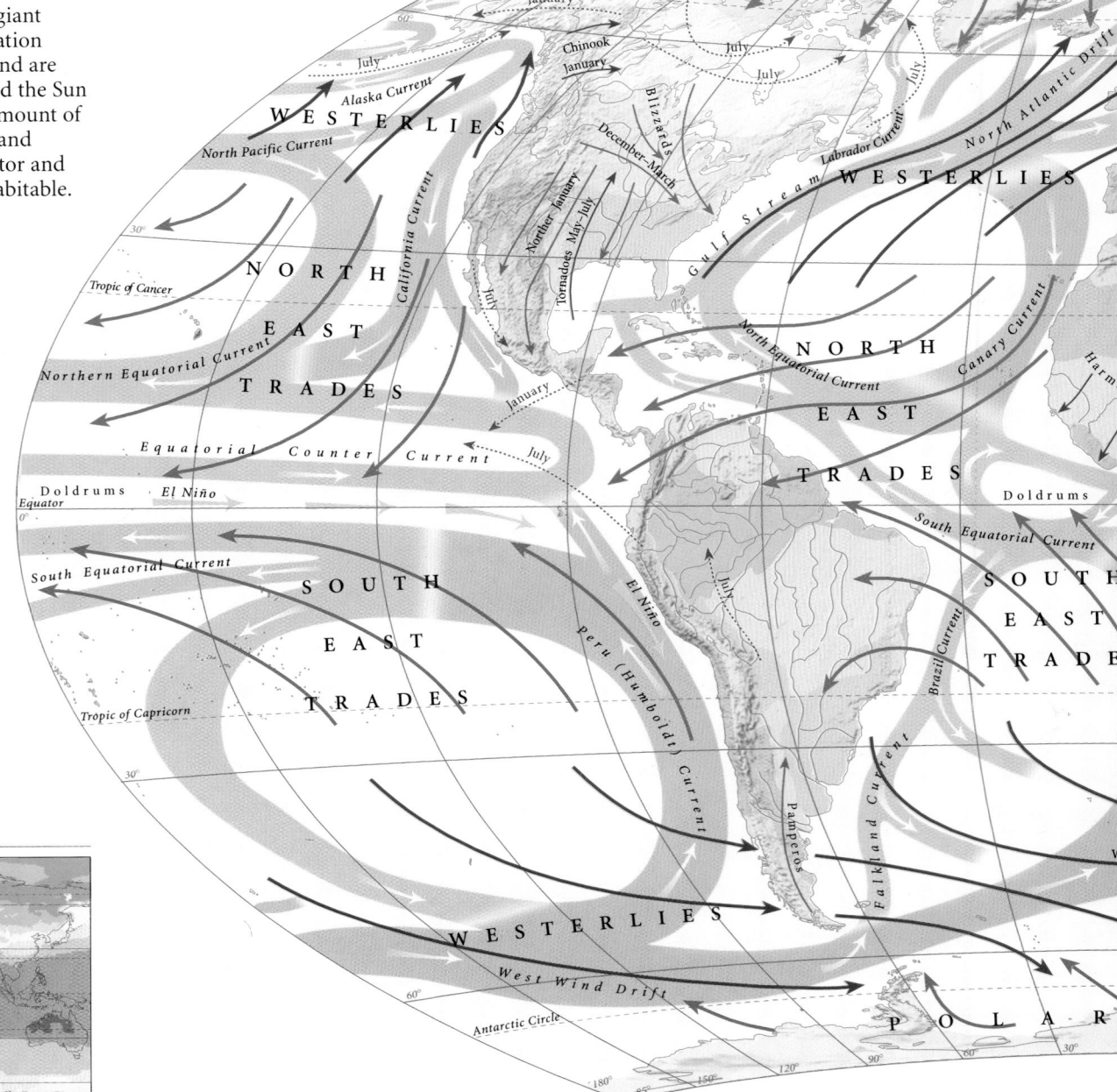

CLIMATIC CHANGE

THE EARTH IS CURRENTLY IN A WARM PHASE between ice ages. Warmer temperatures result in higher sea levels as more of the polar ice caps melt. Most of the world's population lives near coasts, so any changes which might cause sea levels to rise, could have a potentially disastrous impact.

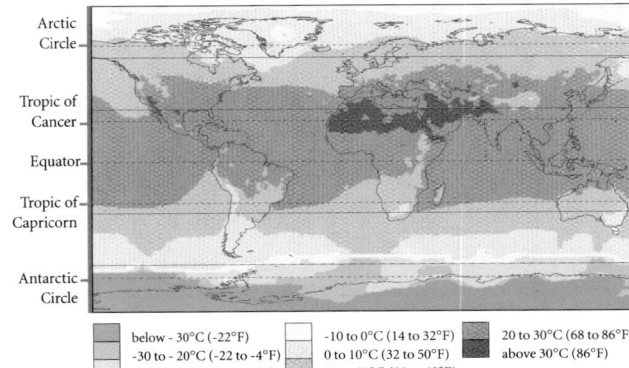

This ice fair, painted by Pieter Brueghel the Younger in the 17th century, shows the Little Ice Age which peaked around 300 years ago.

THE GREENHOUSE EFFECT

Gases such as carbon dioxide are known as 'greenhouse gases' because they allow shortwave solar radiation to enter the Earth's atmosphere, but help to stop longwave radiation from escaping. This traps heat, raising the Earth's temperature. An excess of these gases, such as that which results from the burning of fossil fuels, helps trap more heat and can lead to global warming.

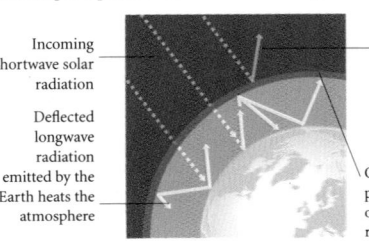

Incoming shortwave solar radiation

Deflected shortwave solar radiation

Deflected longwave radiation emitted by the Earth heats the atmosphere

Greenhouse gases prevent the escape of longwave radiation

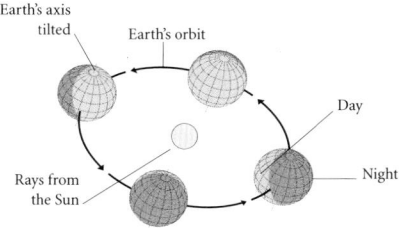

The islands of the Caribbean, Mexico's Gulf coast and the southeastern USA are often hit by hurricanes formed far out in the Atlantic.

OCEANIC WATER CIRCULATION

IN GENERAL, OCEAN CURRENTS parallel the movement of winds across the Earth's surface. Incoming solar energy is greatest at the Equator and least at the poles. So, water in the oceans heats up most at the Equator and flows polewards, cooling as it moves north or south towards the Arctic or Antarctic. The flow is eventually reversed and cold water currents move back towards the Equator. These ocean currents act as a vast system for moving heat from the Equator towards the poles and are a major influence on the distribution of the Earth's climates.

In marginal climatic zones years of drought can completely dry out the land and transform grassland to desert.

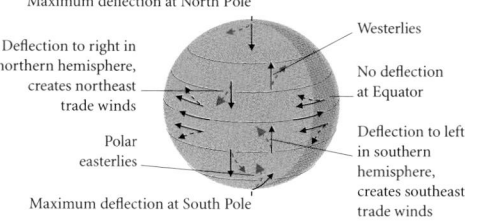

The wide range of environments found in the Andes is strongly related to their altitude, which modifies climatic influences. While the peaks are snow-capped, many protected interior valleys are semi-tropical.

TILT AND ROTATION

The tilt and rotation of the Earth during its annual orbit largely control the distribution of heat and moisture across its surface, which correspondingly controls its large-scale weather patterns. As the Earth annually rotates around the Sun, half its surface is receiving maximum radiation, creating summer and winter seasons. The angle of the Earth means that on average the tropics receive two and a half times as much heat from the Sun each day as the poles.

Earth's axis tilted
Earth's orbit
Day
Rays from the Sun
Night

THE CORIOLIS EFFECT

The rotation of the Earth influences atmospheric circulation by deflecting winds and ocean currents. Winds blowing in the northern hemisphere are deflected to the right and those in the southern hemisphere are deflected to the left, creating large-scale patterns of wind circulation, such as the northeast and southeast trade winds and the westerlies. This effect is greatest at the poles and least at the Equator.

Maximum deflection at North Pole
Westerlies
Deflection to right in northern hemisphere, creates northeast trade winds
No deflection at Equator
Polar easterlies
Deflection to left in southern hemisphere, creates southeast trade winds
Maximum deflection at South Pole

MAP KEY

Climate zones
- ice cap
- tundra
- subarctic
- cool continental
- warm humid
- mediterranean
- semi-arid
- arid
- tropical
- humid equatorial

Ocean currents
- warm
- cold

Prevailing winds
- → warm
- → cold

Local winds
- → warm
- → cold
- seasonal*
- * (seasonal winds which can either be warm or cold)

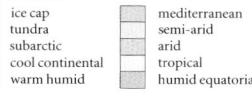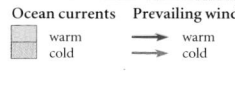

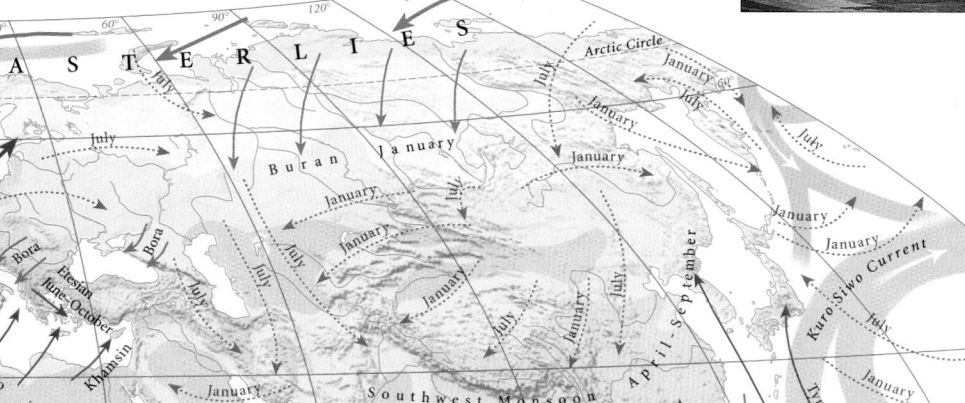

PRECIPITATION

WHEN WARM AIR EXPANDS, it rises and cools, and the water vapour it carries condenses to form clouds. Heavy, regular rainfall is characteristic of the equatorial region, while the poles are cold and receive only slight snowfall. Tropical regions have marked dry and rainy seasons, while in the temperate regions rainfall is relatively unpredictable.

Monsoon rains, which affect southern Asia from May to September, are caused by sea winds blowing across the warm land.

Heavy tropical rainstorms occur frequently in Papua New Guinea, often causing soil erosion and landslides in cultivated areas.

AVERAGE JANUARY RAINFALL

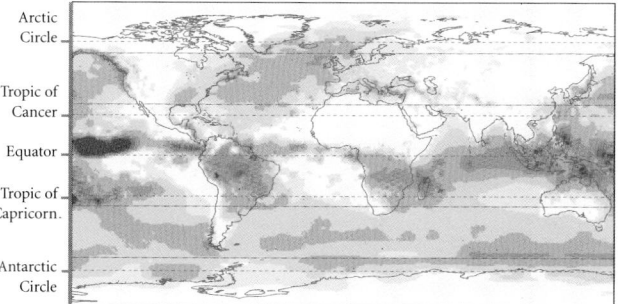

Arctic Circle
Tropic of Cancer
Equator
Tropic of Capricorn
Antarctic Circle

AVERAGE JULY RAINFALL

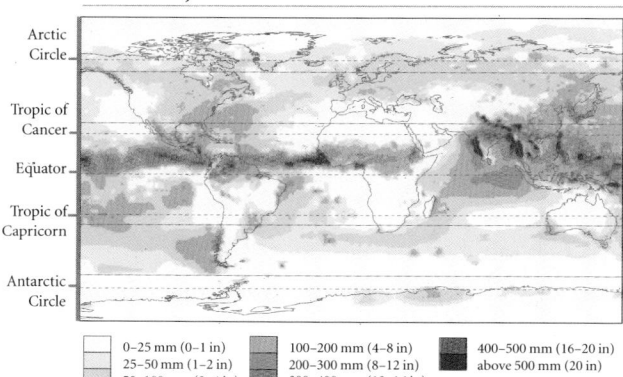

Arctic Circle
Tropic of Cancer
Equator
Tropic of Capricorn
Antarctic Circle

- 0–25 mm (0–1 in)
- 25–50 mm (1–2 in)
- 50–100 mm (2–4 in)
- 100–200 mm (4–8 in)
- 200–300 mm (8–12 in)
- 300–400 mm (12–16 in)
- 400–500 mm (16–20 in)
- above 500 mm (20 in)

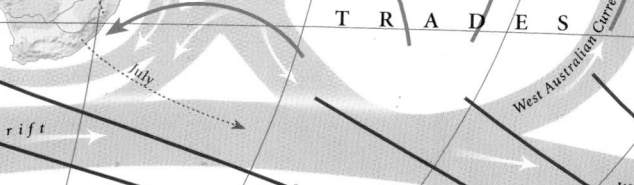

The intensity of some blizzards in Canada and the northern USA can give rise to snowdrifts as high as 10 ft (3 m).

The Atacama Desert in Chile is one of the driest places on Earth, with an average rainfall of less than 2 inches (50 mm) per year.

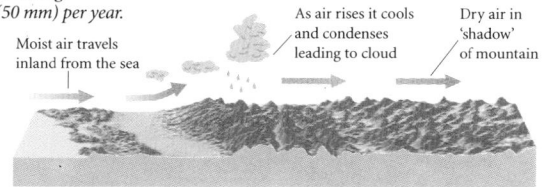

Violent thunderstorms occur along advancing cold fronts, when cold, dry air masses meet warm, moist air, which rises rapidly, its moisture condensing into thunderclouds. Rain and hail become electrically charged, causing lightning.

THE RAINSHADOW EFFECT

When moist air is forced to rise by mountains, it cools and the water vapour falls as precipitation, either as rain or snow. Only the dry, cold air continues over the mountains, leaving inland areas with little or no rain. This is called the rainshadow effect and is one reason for the existence of the Mojave Desert in California, which lies east of the Coast Ranges.

Moist air travels inland from the sea
As air rises it cools and condenses leading to cloud
Dry air in 'shadow' of mountain

THE RAINSHADOW EFFECT

LIFE ON EARTH

A UNIQUE COMBINATION of an oxygen-rich atmosphere and plentiful water is the key to life on Earth. Apart from the polar ice caps, there are few areas which have not been colonized by animals or plants over the course of the Earth's history. Plants process sunlight to provide them with their energy, and ultimately all the Earth's animals rely on plants for survival. Because of this reliance, plants are known as primary producers, and the availability of nutrients and temperature of an area is defined as its primary productivity, which affects the quantity and type of animals which are able to live there. This index is affected by climatic factors – cold and aridity restrict the quantity of life, whereas warmth and regular rainfall allow a greater diversity of species.

BIOGEOGRAPHICAL REGIONS

THE EARTH CAN BE DIVIDED into a series of biogeographical regions, or biomes, ecological communities where certain species of plant and animal co-exist within particular climatic conditions. Within these broad classifications, other factors including soil richness, altitude and human activities such as urbanization, intensive agriculture and deforestation, affect the local distribution of living species within each biome.

POLAR REGIONS

A layer of permanent ice at the Earth's poles covers both seas and land. Very little plant and animal life can exist in these harsh regions.

TUNDRA

A desolate region, with long, dark freezing winters and short, cold summers. With virtually no soil and large areas of permanently frozen ground known as permafrost, the tundra is largely treeless, though it is briefly clothed by small flowering plants in the summer months.

NEEDLELEAF FORESTS

With milder summers than the tundra and less wind, these areas are able to support large forests of coniferous trees.

BROADLEAF FORESTS

Much of the northern hemisphere was once covered by deciduous forests, which occurred in areas with marked seasonal variations. Most deciduous forests have been cleared for human settlement.

TEMPERATE RAINFORESTS

In warmer wetter areas, such as southern China, temperate deciduous forests are replaced by evergreen forest.

DESERTS

Deserts are areas with negligible rainfall. Most hot deserts lie within the tropics; cold deserts are dry because of their distance from the moisture-providing sea.

MEDITERRANEAN

Hot, dry summers and short winters typify these areas, which were once covered by evergreen shrubs and woodland, but have now been cleared by humans for agriculture.

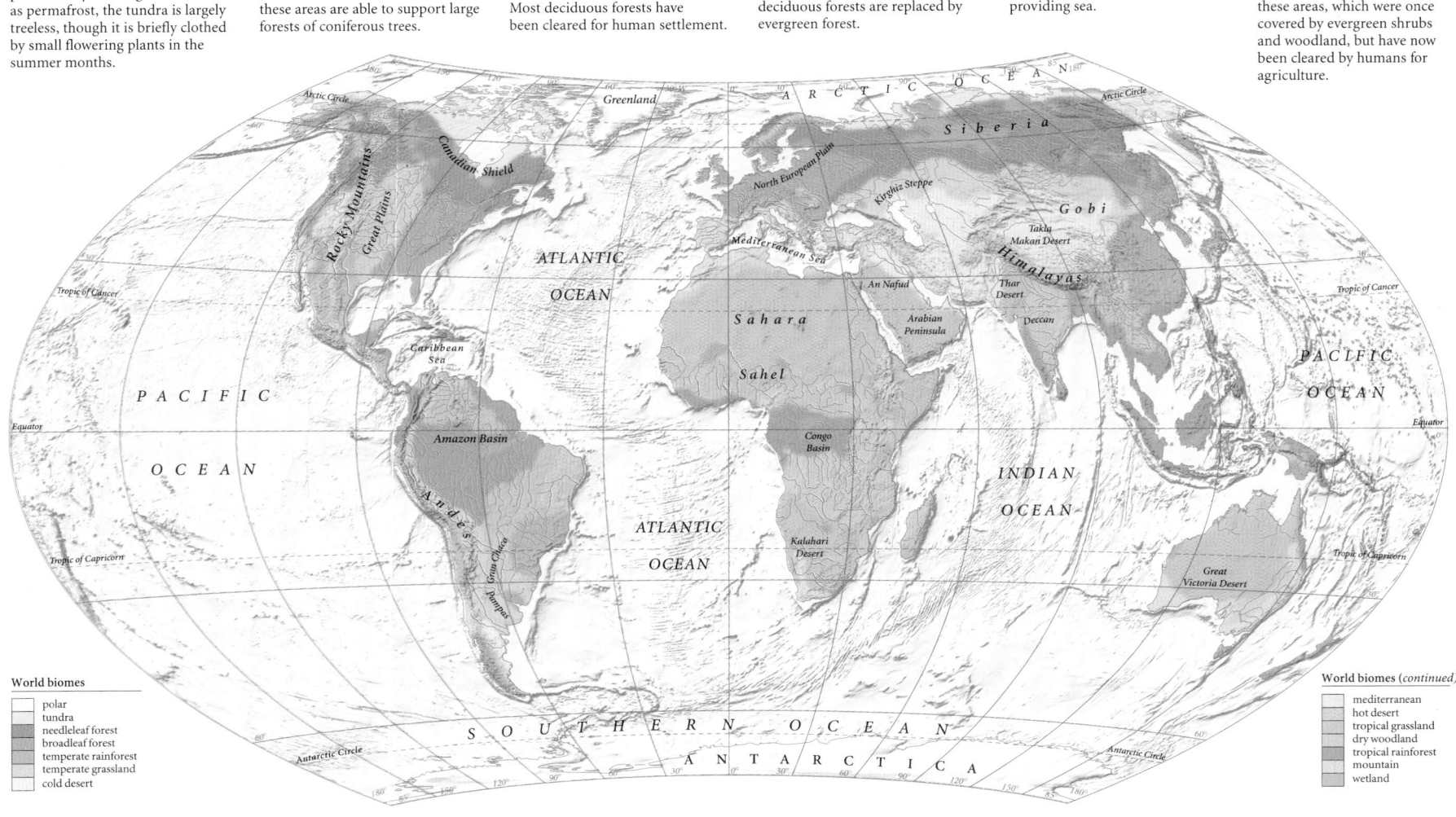

World biomes
- polar
- tundra
- needleleaf forest
- broadleaf forest
- temperate rainforest
- temperate grassland
- cold desert

World biomes (continued)
- mediterranean
- hot desert
- tropical grassland
- dry woodland
- tropical rainforest
- mountain
- wetland

TROPICAL AND TEMPERATE GRASSLANDS

The major grassland areas are found in the centres of the larger continental landmasses. In Africa's tropical savannah regions, seasonal rainfall alternates with drought. Temperate grasslands, also known as *steppes* and *prairies* are found in the northern hemisphere, and in South America, where they are known as the *pampas*.

DRY WOODLANDS

Trees and shrubs, adapted to dry conditions, grow widely spaced from one another, interspersed by savannah grasslands.

TROPICAL RAINFORESTS

Characterized by year-round warmth and high rainfall, tropical rainforests contain the highest diversity of plant and animal species on Earth.

MOUNTAINS

Though the lower slopes of mountains may be thickly forested, only ground-hugging shrubs and other vegetation will grow above the tree line which varies according to both altitude and latitude.

WETLANDS

Rarely lying above sea level, wetlands are marshes, swamps and tidal flats. Some, with their moist, fertile soils, are rich feeding grounds for fish and breeding grounds for birds. Others have little soil structure and are too acidic to support much plant and animal life.

BIODIVERSITY

THE NUMBER OF PLANT AND ANIMAL SPECIES, and the range of genetic diversity within the populations of each species, make up the Earth's biodiversity. The plants and animals which are endemic to a region – that is, those which are found nowhere else in the world – are also important in determining levels of biodiversity. Human settlement and intervention have encroached on many areas of the world once rich in endemic plant and animal species. Increasing international efforts are being made to monitor and conserve the biodiversity of the Earth's remaining wild places.

ANIMAL ADAPTATION

THE DEGREE OF AN ANIMAL'S ADAPTABILITY to different climates and conditions is extremely important in ensuring its success as a species. Many animals, particularly the largest mammals, are becoming restricted to ever-smaller regions as human development and modern agricultural practices reduce their natural habitats. In contrast, humans have been responsible – both deliberately and accidentally – for the spread of some of the world's most successful species. Many of these introduced species are now more numerous than the indigenous animal populations.

POLAR ANIMALS

The frozen wastes of the polar regions are able to support only a small range of species which derive their nutritional requirements from the sea. Animals such as the walrus *(left)* have developed insulating fat, stocky limbs and double-layered coats to enable them to survive in the freezing conditions.

DIVERSITY OF ANIMAL SPECIES

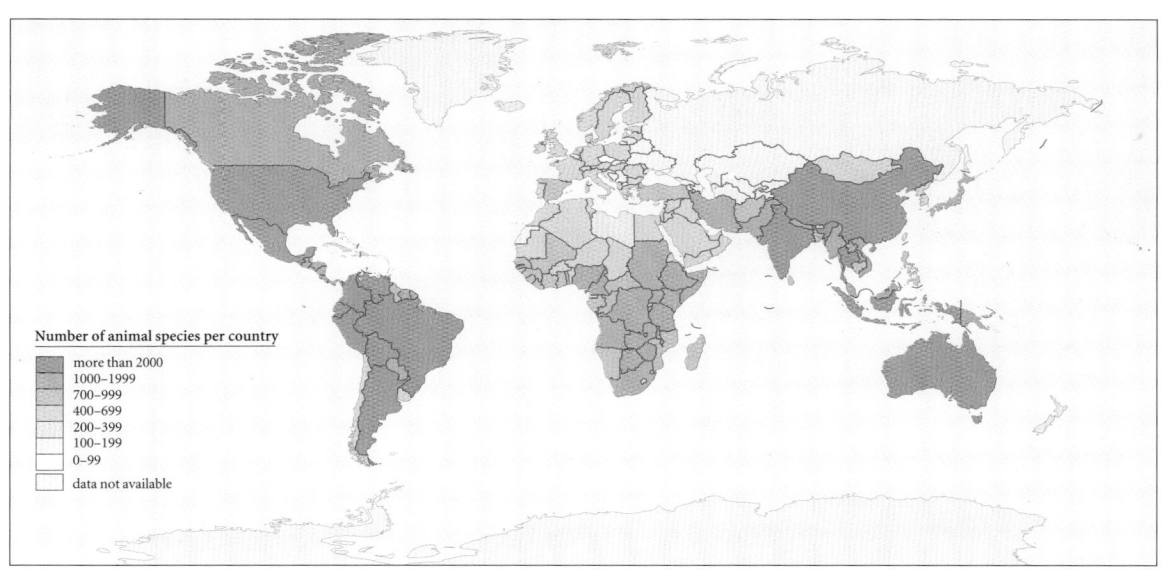

Number of animal species per country
- more than 2000
- 1000–1999
- 700–999
- 400–699
- 200–399
- 100–199
- 0–99
- data not available

DESERT ANIMALS

Many animals which live in the extreme heat and aridity of the deserts are able to survive for days and even months with very little food or water. Their bodies are adapted to lose heat quickly and to store fat and water. The Gila monster *(above)* stores fat in its tail.

AMAZON RAINFOREST

The vast Amazon Basin is home to the world's greatest variety of animal species. Animals are adapted to live at many different levels from the treetops to the tangled undergrowth which lies beneath the canopy. The sloth *(below)* hangs upside down in the branches. Its fur grows from its stomach to its back to enable water to run off quickly.

MARINE BIODIVERSITY

The oceans support a huge variety of different species, from the world's largest mammals like whales and dolphins down to the tiniest plankton. The greatest diversities occur in the warmer seas of continental shelves, where plants are easily able to photosynthesize, and around coral reefs, where complex ecosystems are found. On the ocean floor, nematodes can exist at a depth of more than 10,000 ft (3000 m) below sea level.

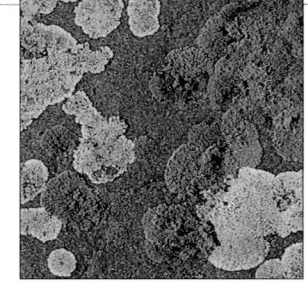

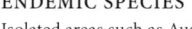

HIGH ALTITUDES

Few animals exist in the rarefied atmosphere of the highest mountains. However, birds of prey such as eagles and vultures *(above)*, with their superb eyesight can soar as high as 23,000 ft (7000 m) to scan for prey below.

URBAN ANIMALS

The growth of cities has reduced the amount of habitat available to many species. A number of animals are now moving closer into urban areas to scavenge from the detritus of the modern city *(left)*. Rodents, particularly rats and mice, have existed in cities for thousands of years, and many insects, especially moths, quickly develop new colouring to provide them with camouflage.

ENDEMIC SPECIES

Isolated areas such as Australia and the island of Madagascar, have the greatest range of endemic species. In Australia, these include marsupials such as the kangaroo *(below)*, which carry their young in pouches on their bodies. Destruction of habitat, pollution, hunting, and predators introduced by humans, are threatening this unique biodiversity.

PLANT ADAPTATION

ENVIRONMENTAL CONDITIONS, particularly climate, soil type and the extent of competition with other organisms, influence the development of plants into a number of distinctive forms. Similar conditions in quite different parts of the world create similar adaptations in the plants, which may then be modified by other, local, factors specific to the region.

COLD CONDITIONS

In areas where temperatures rarely rise above freezing, plants such as lichens *(left)* and mosses grow densely, close to the ground.

RAINFORESTS

Most of the world's largest and oldest plants are found in rainforests; warmth and heavy rainfall provide ideal conditions for vast plants like the world's largest flower, the rafflesia *(left)*.

HOT, DRY CONDITIONS

Arid conditions lead to the development of plants whose surface area has been reduced to a minimum to reduce water loss. In cacti *(above)*, which can survive without water for months, leaves are minimal or not present at all.

ANCIENT PLANTS

Some of the world's most primitive plants still exist today, including algae, cyclads and many ferns *(above)*, reflecting the success with which they have adapted to changing conditions.

DIVERSITY OF PLANT SPECIES

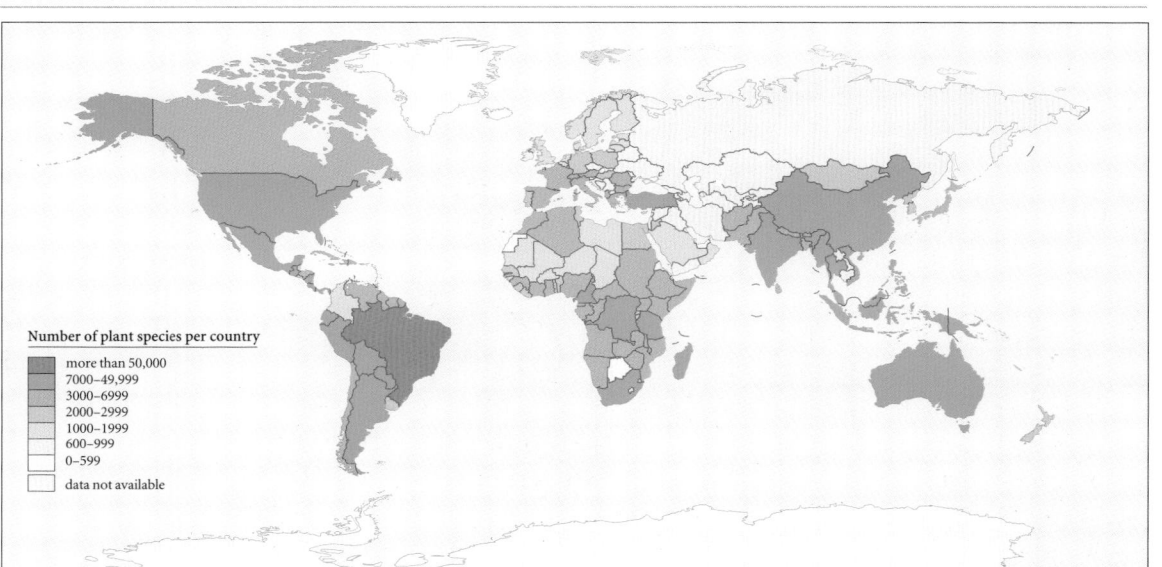

Number of plant species per country
- more than 50,000
- 7000–49,999
- 3000–6999
- 2000–2999
- 1000–1999
- 600–999
- 0–599
- data not available

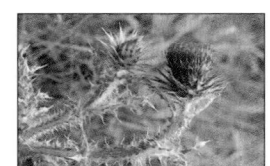

RESISTING PREDATORS

A great variety of plants have developed devices including spines *(above)*, poisons, stinging hairs and an unpleasant taste or smell to deter animal predators.

WEEDS

Weeds such as bindweed *(above)* are fast-growing, easily dispersed, and tolerant of a number of different environments, enabling them to quickly colonize suitable habitats. They are among the most adaptable of all plants.

POPULATION AND SETTLEMENT

THE EARTH'S POPULATION IS PROJECTED to rise from its current level of about 5.7 billion to reach some 10 billion by 2025. The global distribution of this rapidly growing population is very uneven, and is dictated by climate, terrain and natural and economic resources. The great majority of the Earth's people live in coastal zones, and along river valleys. Deserts cover over 20% of the Earth's surface, but support less than 5% of the world's population. By the year 2000 it is estimated that over half the Earth's population will live in cities – most of them in Asia – as a result of mass migration from rural areas in search of jobs. Many of these people will live in the so-called 'megacities', some with populations as great as 40 million.

PATTERNS OF SETTLEMENT

THE PAST 200 YEARS have seen the most radical shift in world population patterns in recorded history.

NOMADIC LIFE

ALL THE WORLD'S PEOPLES were hunter-gatherers 10,000 years ago. Today nomads, who live by following available food resources, account for less than 0.0001% of the world's population. They are mainly pastoral herders, moving their livestock from place to place in search of grazing land.

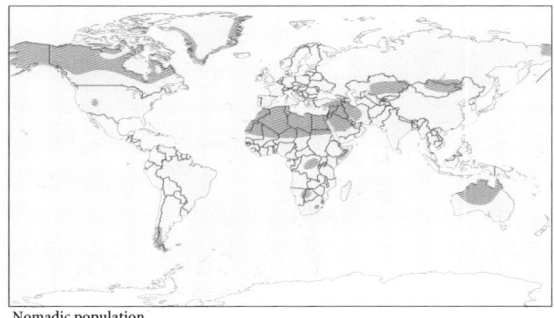

Nomadic population

Nomadic population area

THE GROWTH OF CITIES

IN 1900 there were only 13 cities in the world with populations of more than a million, mostly in the northern hemisphere. Today, as more and more people in the developing world migrate to towns and cities, there are 23 cities whose population exceeds 5 million, and over 284 million-cities.

MILLION-CITIES IN 1900

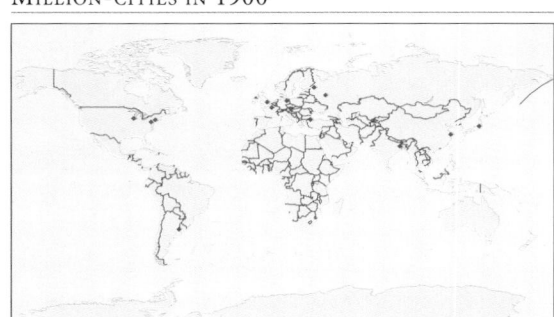

Million-cities in 1900

• Cities over 1 million population

MILLION-CITIES IN 1995

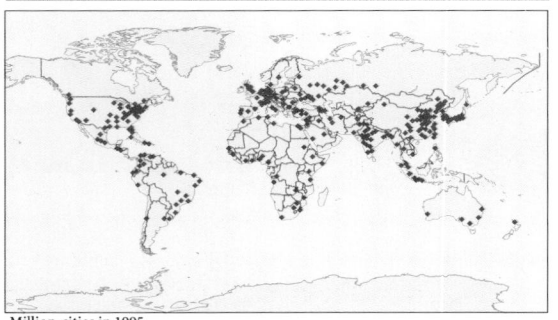

Million-cities in 1995

• Cities over 1 million population

NORTH AMERICA

THE EASTERN AND WESTERN SEABOARDS of the USA, with huge expanses of interconnected cities, towns and suburbs, are vast, densely-populated megalopolises. Central America and the Caribbean also have high population densities. Yet, away from the coasts and in the wildernesses of northern Canada the land is very sparsely settled.

Vancouver on Canada's west coast, grew up as a port city. In recent years it has attracted many Asian immigrants, particularly from the Pacific Rim.

North America's central plains, the continent's agricultural heartland, are thinly populated and highly productive.

EUROPE

WITH ITS TEMPERATE CLIMATE, and rich mineral and natural resources, Europe is generally very densely settled. The continent acts as a magnet for economic migrants from the developing world, and immigration is now widely restricted. Birth rates in Europe are generally low, and in some countries, such as Germany, the populations have stabilized at zero growth, with a fast-growing elderly population.

Many European cities, like Siena, once reflected the 'ideal' size for human settlements. Modern technological advances have enabled them to grow far beyond the original walls.

Within the densely-populated Netherlands the reclamation of coastal wetlands is vital to provide much-needed land for agriculture and settlement.

Population density
(inhabitants per sq km)

More than 200
101–200
51–100
21–50
11–20
6–10
1–5
Less than 1

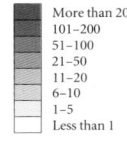

NORTH AMERICA

Population 9%   World land area 17%

EUROPE

Population 14%   World land area 7.1%

AFRICA

Population 12%   World land area 20.2%

SOUTH AMERICA

Population 5.5%   World land area 11.8%

SOUTH AMERICA

MOST SETTLEMENT IN SOUTH AMERICA is clustered in a narrow belt in coastal zones and in the northern Andes. During the 20th century, cities such as São Paulo and Buenos Aires have grown enormously, acting as powerful economic magnets to the rural population. Shanty towns have grown up on the outskirts of many major cities to house these immigrants, often lacking basic amenities.

Many people in western South America live at high altitudes in the Andes, both in cities and in villages such as this one in Bolivia.

Venezuela is the most highly urbanized country in South America, with more than 90% of the population living in cities such as Caracas.

AFRICA

THE ARID CLIMATE of much of Africa means that settlement of the continent is sparse, focusing in coastal areas and fertile regions such as the Nile Valley. Africa still has a high proportion of nomadic agriculturalists, although many are now becoming settled, and the population is predominantly rural.

Cities such as Nairobi (above), Cairo and Johannesburg have grown rapidly in recent years, although only Cairo has a significant population on a global scale.

Traditional lifestyles and homes persist across much of Africa, which has a higher proportion of rural or village-based population than any other continent.

ASIA

MOST ASIAN SETTLEMENT originally centred around the great river valleys such as the Indus, the Ganges and the Yangtze. Today, almost 60% of the world's population lives in Asia, many in burgeoning cities – particularly in the economically-buoyant Pacific Rim countries. Even rural population densities are high in many countries; practices such as terracing in Southeast Asia making the most of the available land.

Many of China's cities are now vast urban areas with populations of more than 5 million people.

This stilt village in Bangladesh is built to resist the regular flooding. Pressure on land, even in rural areas, forces many people to live in marginal areas.

POPULATION STRUCTURES

POPULATION PYRAMIDS are an effective means of showing the age structures of different countries, and highlighting changing trends in population growth and decline. The typical pyramid for a country with a growing, youthful population, is broad-based *(left)*, reflecting a high birth rate and a far larger number of young rather than elderly people. In contrast, countries with populations whose numbers are stabilizing have a more balanced distribution of people in each age band, and may even have lower numbers of people in the youngest age ranges, indicating both a high life expectancy, and that the population is now barely replacing itself *(right)*. The Russian Federation *(centre)* still bears the scars of the Second World War, reflected in the dramatically lower numbers of men than women in the 60–80+ age range.

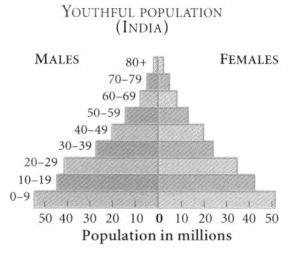

YOUTHFUL POPULATION (INDIA)

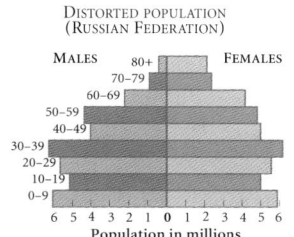

DISTORTED POPULATION (RUSSIAN FEDERATION)

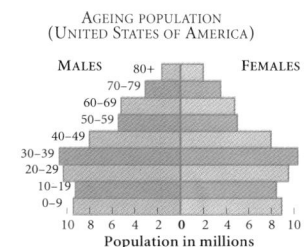

AGEING POPULATION (UNITED STATES OF AMERICA)

POPULATION GROWTH

IMPROVEMENTS IN FOOD SUPPLY and advances in medicine have both played a major role in the remarkable growth in global population, which has increased five-fold over the last 150 years. Food supplies have risen with the mechanization of agriculture and improvements in crop yields. Better nutrition, together with higher standards of public health and sanitation, have led to increased longevity and higher birth rates.

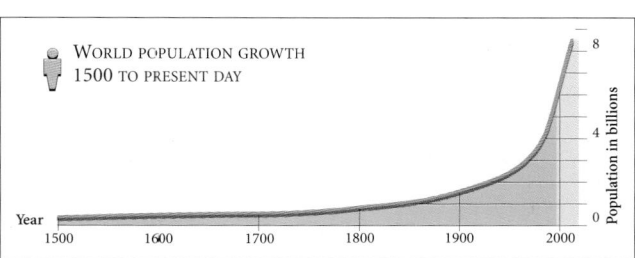

WORLD POPULATION GROWTH 1500 TO PRESENT DAY

WORLD NUTRITION

TWO-THIRDS OF THE WORLD's food supply is consumed by the industrialized nations, many of which have a daily calorific intake far higher than is necessary for their populations to maintain a healthy body weight. In contrast, in the developing world, about 800 million people do not have enough food to meet their basic nutritional needs.

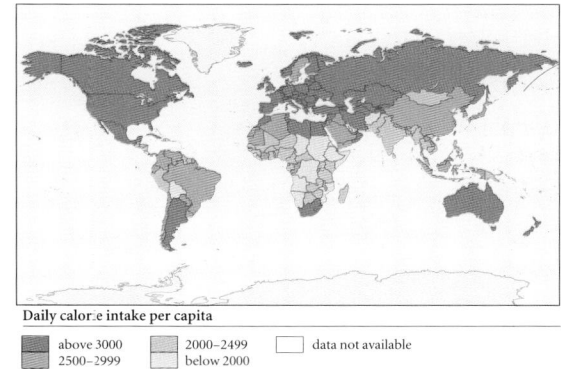

Daily calorie intake per capita

above 3000 / 2500–2999 / 2000–2499 / below 2000 / data not available

WORLD LIFE EXPECTANCY

IMPROVED PUBLIC HEALTH and living standards have greatly increased life expectancy in the developed world, where people can now expect to live twice as long as they did 100 years ago. In many of the world's poorest nations, inadequate nutrition and disease, means that the average life expectancy still does not exceed 45 years.

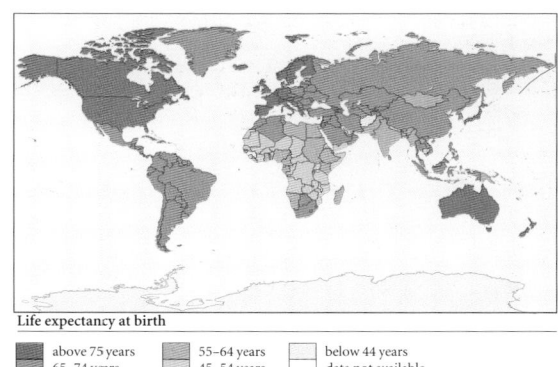

Life expectancy at birth

above 75 years / 65–74 years / 55–64 years / 45–54 years / below 44 years / data not available

WORLD INFANT MORTALITY

IN PARTS OF THE DEVELOPING WORLD infant mortality rates are still high; access to medical services such as immunization, adequate nutrition and the promotion of breast-feeding have been important in combating infant mortality.

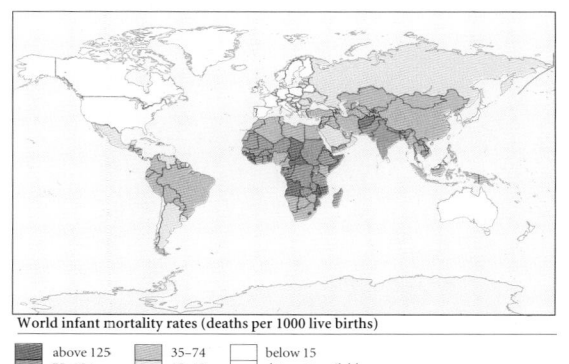

World infant mortality rates (deaths per 1000 live births)

above 125 / 75–124 / 35–74 / 15–43 / below 15 / data not available

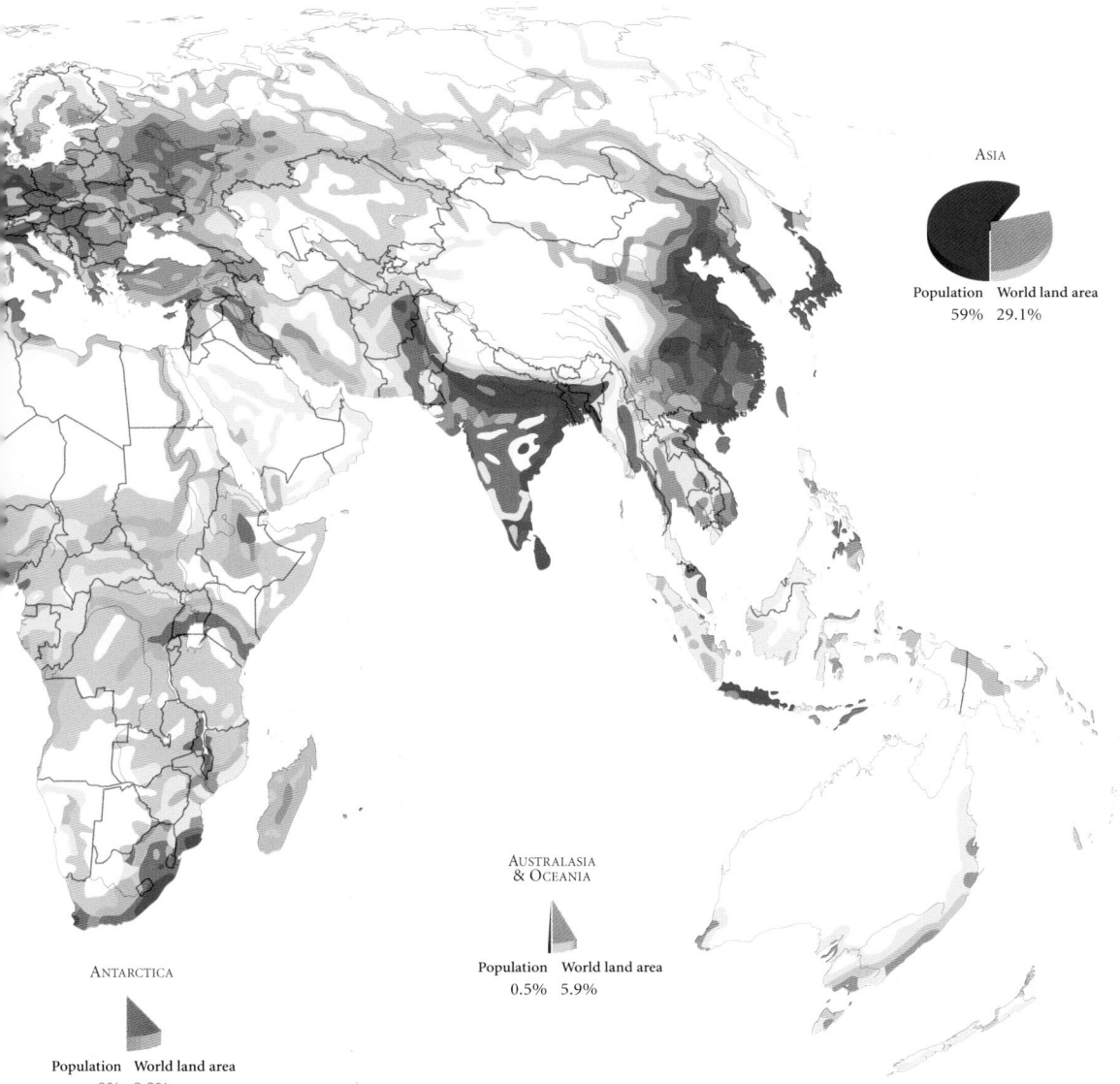

ASIA

Population 59% / World land area 29.1%

AUSTRALASIA & OCEANIA

Population 0.5% / World land area 5.9%

ANTARCTICA

Population 0% / World land area 8.9%

AUSTRALASIA & OCEANIA

THIS IS THE WORLD's most sparsely settled region. The peoples of Australia and New Zealand live mainly in the coastal cities, with only scattered settlements in the arid interior. The Pacific islands can only support limited populations because of their remoteness and lack of resources.

Brisbane, on Australia's Gold Coast is the most rapidly expanding city in the country. The great majority of Australia's population lives in cities near the coasts.

The remote highlands of Papua New Guinea are home to a wide variety of peoples, many of whom still subsist by traditional hunting and gathering.

AVERAGE WORLD BIRTH RATES

BIRTH RATES ARE MUCH HIGHER in Africa, Asia and South America than in Europe and North America. Increased affluence and easy access to contraception are both factors which can lead to a significant decline in a country's birth rate.

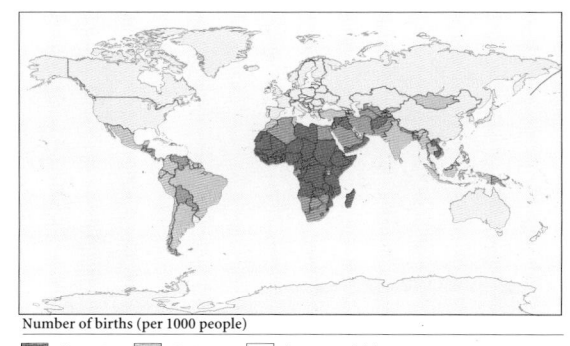

Number of births (per 1000 people)

above 40 / 30–39 / 20–29 / below 20 / data not available

THE ECONOMIC SYSTEM

THE WEALTHY COUNTRIES OF THE DEVELOPED WORLD, with their aggressive, market-led economies and their access to productive new technologies and international markets, dominate the world economic system. At the other extreme, many of the countries of the developing world are locked in a cycle of national debt, rising populations and unemployment. The state-managed economies of the former communist bloc began to be dismantled during the 1990s, and China is emerging as a major economic power following decades of isolation.

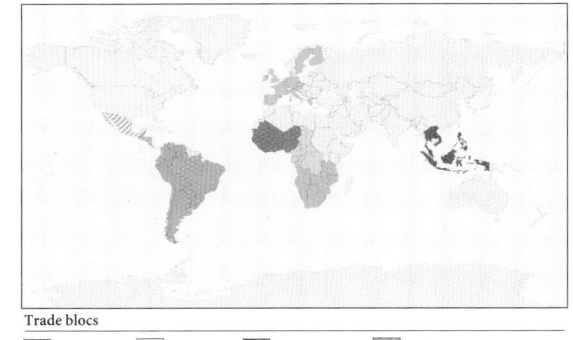

Trade blocs

	EU		NAFTA		ASEAN		LAIA
	CACM		SADC		ECOWAS		CEEAC

TRADE BLOCS

INTERNATIONAL TRADE BLOCS are formed when groups of countries, often already enjoying close military and political ties, join together to offer mutually preferential terms of trade for both imports and exports. Increasingly, global trade is dominated by three main blocs: the EU, NAFTA, and ASEAN. They are supplanting older trade blocs such as the Commonwealth, a legacy of colonialism.

INTERNATIONAL TRADE FLOWS

WORLD TRADE acts as a stimulus to national economies, encouraging growth. Over the last three decades, as heavy industries have declined, services – banking, insurance, tourism, airlines and shipping – have taken an increasingly large share of world trade. Manufactured articles now account for nearly two-thirds of world trade; raw materials and food make up less than a quarter of the total.

SHIPPING
Ships carry 80% of international cargo, and extensive container ports, where cargo is stored, are vital links in the international transport network.

MULTINATIONALS
Multinational companies are increasingly penetrating inaccessible markets. The reach of many American commodities is now global.

PRIMARY PRODUCTS
Many countries, particularly in the Caribbean and Africa, are still reliant on primary products such as rubber and coffee, which makes them vulnerable to fluctuating prices.

SERVICE INDUSTRIES
Service industries such as banking, tourism and insurance have been the fastest-growing industrial sector in the last half of the 20th century. Lloyds of London is the centre of the world insurance market.

Countries reliant on a single export
- bananas
- coffee
- oil/petroleum
- copper

Balance of trade (millions US$)
over 30,000	
10,000–29,000	
1000–9999	Surplus
0–999	
0–999	
1000–9999	
10,000–29,999	Deficit
below 30,000	
data unavailable	

Direct investment
- from USA
- from Europe
- from Japan

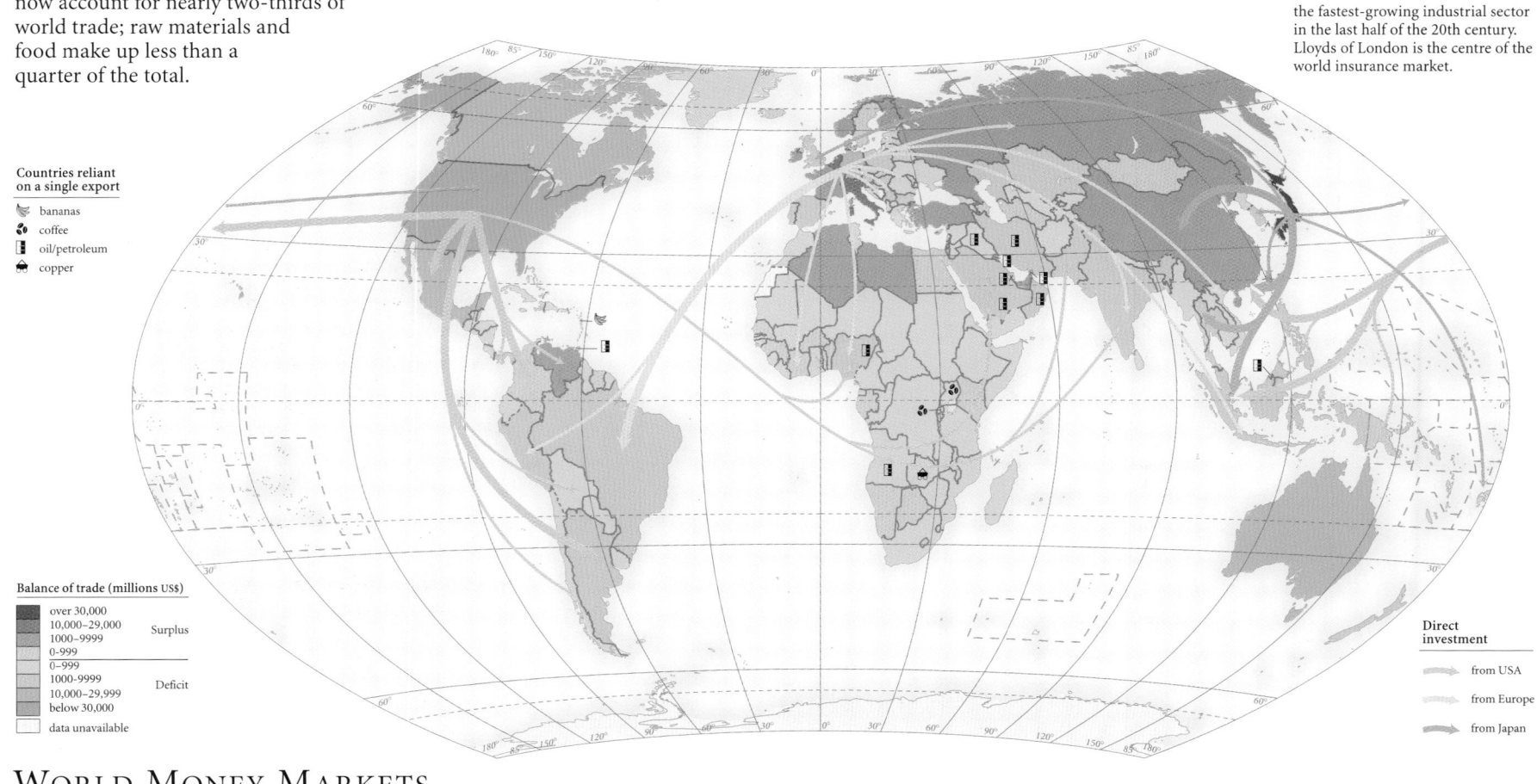

WORLD MONEY MARKETS

THE FINANCIAL WORLD has traditionally been dominated by three major centres – Tokyo, New York and London, which house the headquarters of stock exchanges, multinational corporations and international banks. Their geographic location means that, at any one time in a 24-hour day, one major market is open for trading in shares, currencies and commodities. Since the late 1980s, technological advances have enabled transactions between financial centres to occur at ever-greater speed, and new markets have sprung up throughout the world.

NEW STOCK MARKETS

NEW STOCK MARKETS are now opening in many parts of the world, where economies have recently emerged from state controls. In Moscow and Beijing, and several countries in eastern Europe, newly-opened stock exchanges reflect the transition to market-driven economies.

THE DEVELOPING WORLD

INTERNATIONAL TRADE in capital and currency is dominated by the rich nations of the northern hemisphere. In parts of Africa and Asia, where exports of any sort are extremely limited, home-produced commodities are simply sold in local markets.

MAJOR MONEY MARKETS

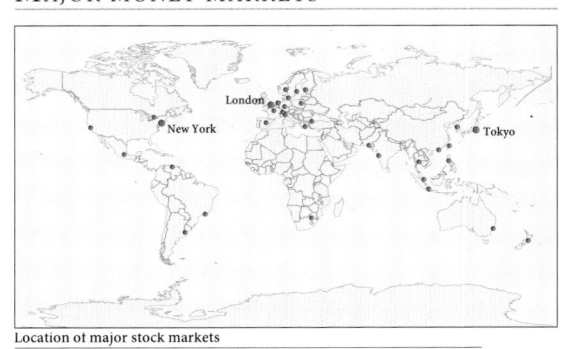

Location of major stock markets
- Major stock markets

The Tokyo Stock Market *crashed in 1990, leading to a slow-down in the growth of the world's most powerful economy, and a refocusing on economic policy away from export-led growth and towards the domestic market.*

Dealers at the Calcutta Stock Market. *The Indian economy has been opened up to foreign investment and many multinationals now have bases there.*

Markets have thrived *in communist Vietnam since the introduction of a liberal economic policy.*

WORLD WEALTH DISPARITY

A GLOBAL ASSESSMENT of Gross Domestic Product (GDP) by nation reveals great disparities. The developed world, with only a quarter of the world's population, has 80% of the world's manufacturing income. Civil war, conflict and political instability further undermine the economic self-sufficiency of many of the world's poorest nations.

Cities such as Detroit have been badly hit by the decline in heavy industry.

URBAN DECAY

ALTHOUGH THE USA still dominates the global economy, it faces deficits in both the federal budget and the balance of trade. Vast discrepancies in personal wealth, high levels of unemployment, and the dismantling of welfare provisions throughout the 1980s have led to severe deprivation in several of the inner cities of North America's industrial heartland.

BOOMING CITIES

SINCE THE 1980s the Chinese government has set up special industrial zones, such as Shanghai, where foreign investment is encouraged through tax incentives. Migrants from rural China pour into these regions in search of work, creating 'boomtown' economies.

Foreign investment has encouraged new infrastructure development in cities like Shanghai.

URBAN SPRAWL

CITIES ARE EXPANDING all over the developing world, attracting economic migrants in search of work and opportunities. In cities such as Rio de Janeiro, housing has not kept pace with the population explosion, and squalid shanty towns *(favelas)* rub shoulders with middle-class housing.

The favelas of Rio de Janeiro sprawl over the hills surrounding the city.

COMPARATIVE WORLD WEALTH

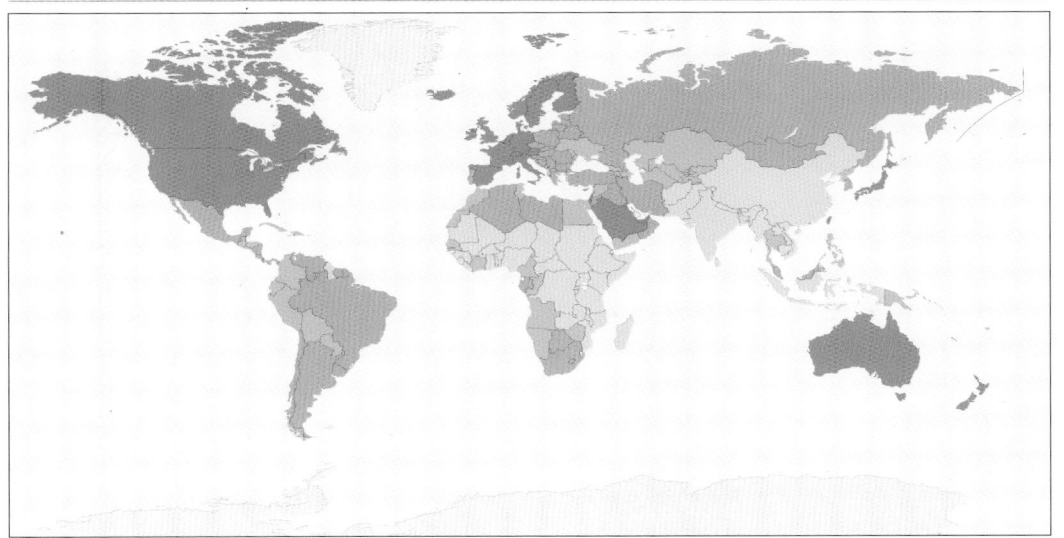

World economies
- high income
- upper-middle income
- lower-middle income
- low income
- data unavailable

ECONOMIC 'TIGERS'

THE ECONOMIC 'TIGERS' of the Pacific Rim – Taiwan, Singapore, and South Korea – have grown faster than Europe and the USA over the last decade. Their export- and service-led economies have benefited from stable government, low labour costs, and foreign investment.

Hong Kong, with its fine natural harbour, is one of the most important ports in Asia.

AGRICULTURAL ECONOMIES

IN PARTS OF THE DEVELOPING WORLD, people survive by subsistence farming – only growing enough food for themselves and their families. With no surplus product, they are unable to exchange goods for currency, the only means of escaping the poverty trap. In other countries, farmers have been encouraged to concentrate on growing a single crop for the export market. This reliance on cash crops leaves farmers vulnerable to crop failure and to changes in the market price of the crop.

The Ugandan uplands are fertile, but poor infrastructure hampers the export of cash crops.

A shopping arcade in Paris displays a great profusion of luxury goods.

THE AFFLUENT WEST

THE CAPITAL CITIES of many countries in the developed world are showcases for consumer goods, reflecting the increasing importance of the service sector, and particularly the retail sector, in the world economy. The idea of shopping as a leisure activity is unique to the western world. Luxury goods and services attract visitors, who in turn generate tourist revenue.

TOURISM

IN 1990, THERE WERE 425 million tourists worldwide. Tourism is now the world's biggest single industry, employing 127 million people, though frequently in low-paid unskilled jobs. While tourists are increasingly exploring inaccessible and less-developed regions of the world, the benefits of the industry are not always felt at a local level. There are also worries about the environmental impact of tourism, as the world's last wildernesses increasingly become tourist attractions.

Botswana's Okavango Delta is an area rich in wildlife. Tourists make safaris to the region, but the impact of tourism is controlled.

MONEY FLOWS

FOREIGN INVESTMENT in the developing world during the 1970s led to a global financial crisis in the 1980s, when many countries were unable to meet their debt repayments. The International Monetary Fund (IMF) was forced to reschedule the debts and, in some cases, write them off completely. Within the developing world, austerity programmes have been initiated to cope with the debt, leading in turn to high unemployment and galloping inflation. In many parts of Africa, stricken economies are now dependent on international aid.

In rural Southeast Asia, babies are given medical checks by UNICEF as part of a global aid programme sponsored by the UN.

TOURIST ARRIVALS

Tourist arrivals
- over 20 million
- 10–20 million
- 5–10 million
- 2.5–5 million
- 1–2.5 million
- 700,000–999,000
- under 700,000
- data unavailable

INTERNATIONAL DEBT: DONORS AND RECEIVERS

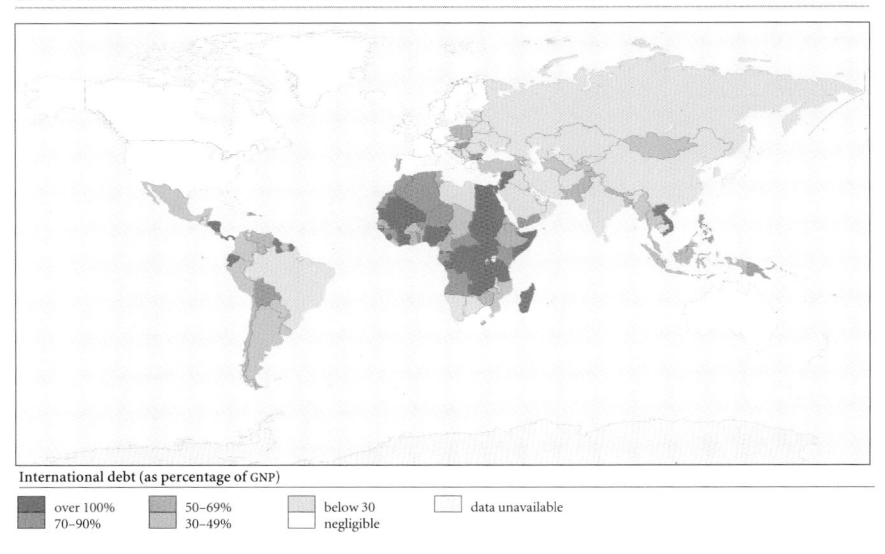

International debt (as percentage of GNP)
- over 100%
- 70–90%
- 50–69%
- 30–49%
- below 30
- negligible
- data unavailable

THE POLITICAL WORLD

THERE ARE 192 INDEPENDENT COUNTRIES in the world today. With the exception of Antarctica, where territorial claims have been deferred by international treaty, every land area of the Earth's surface either belongs to, or is claimed by, one country or another. The largest country in the world is the Russian Federation, the smallest is Vatican City. Some 60 overseas dependent territories remain, administered variously by France, Australia, Denmark, New Zealand, Norway, Portugal, the UK, the USA and the Netherlands.

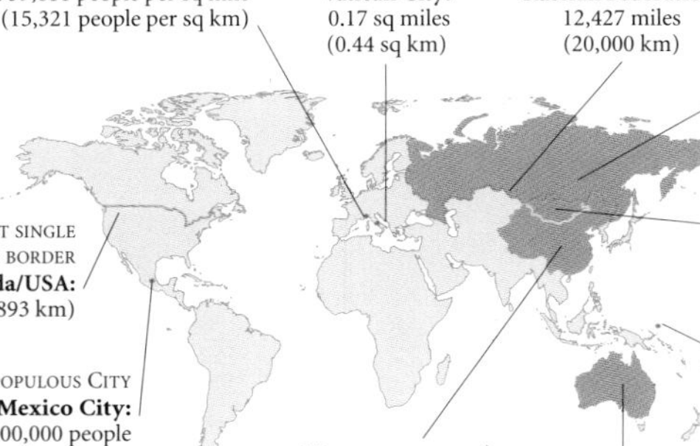

INTERNATIONAL BORDERS

THE MAP SHOWS three main types of boundary between states. Full borders represent internationally agreed and recognized territorial boundaries. Undefined borders exist where no fixed boundary between states has been demarcated; the boundaries indicated in this way show approximate areas of sovereignty. A disputed border is indicated where a *de facto* territorial boundary exists, which is not agreed or is subject to arbitration.

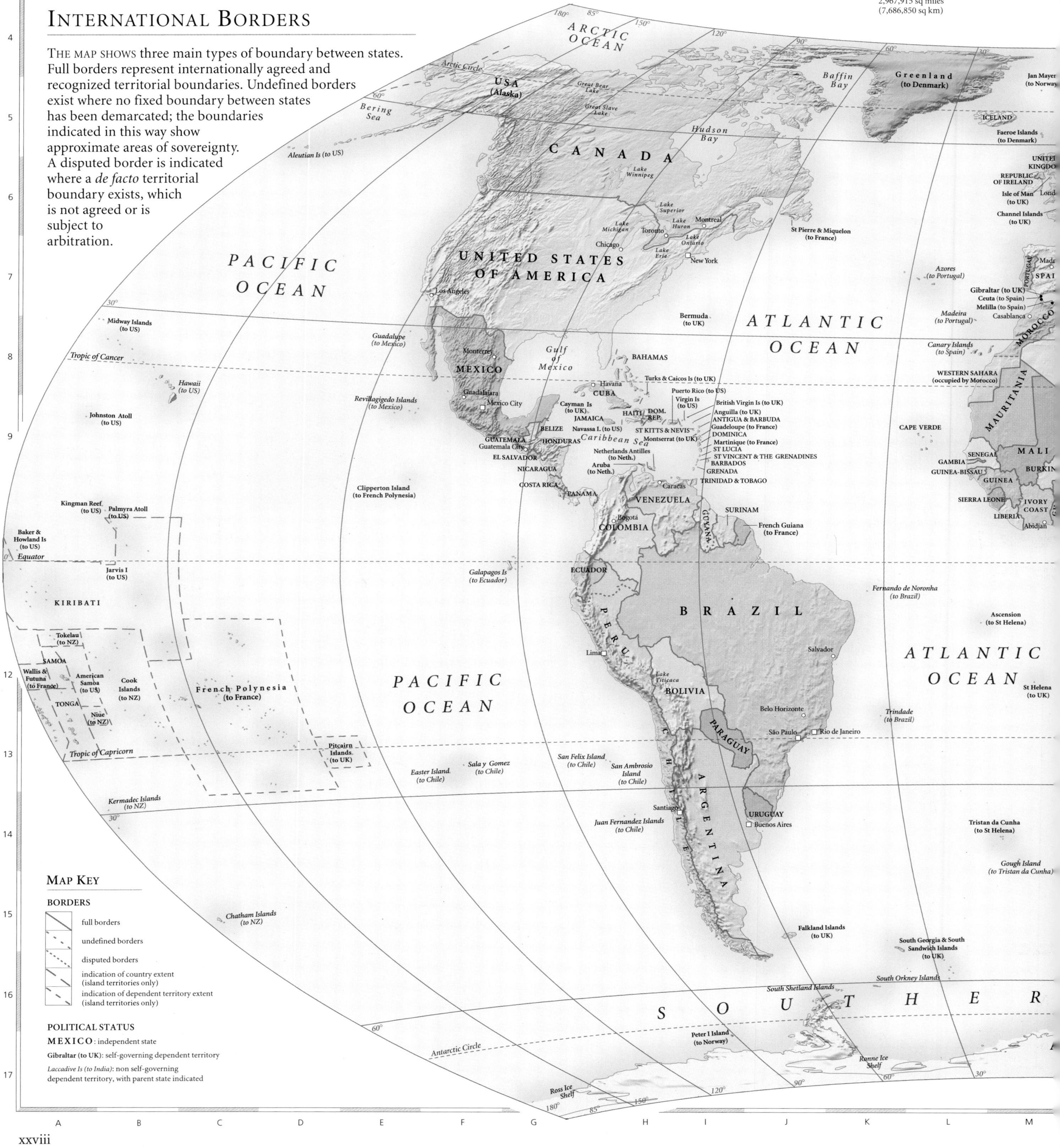

MOST DENSELY POPULATED COUNTRY
Monaco: 39,681 people per sq mile (15,321 people per sq km)

SMALLEST COUNTRY
Vatican City: 0.17 sq miles (0.44 sq km)

LONGEST LAND BORDERS
Russian Federation: 12,427 miles (20,000 km)

LARGEST COUNTRY
Russian Federation: 6,592,863 sq miles (17,075,400 sq km)

LONGEST SINGLE LAND BORDER
Canada/USA: 5526 miles (8893 km)

LEAST DENSELY POPULATED COUNTRY
Mongolia: 3.6 people per sq mile (1.5 people per sq km)

MOST POPULOUS CITY
Mexico City: 21,000,000 people

SMALLEST ISLAND COUNTRY
Nauru: 8.2 sq miles (21 sq km)

MOST POPULOUS COUNTRY
China: 1,118,000,000 people (estimated)

LARGEST ISLAND COUNTRY
Australia: 2,967,915 sq miles (7,686,850 sq km)

MAP KEY

BORDERS

- full borders
- undefined borders
- disputed borders
- indication of country extent (island territories only)
- indication of dependent territory extent (island territories only)

POLITICAL STATUS

MEXICO: independent state

Gibraltar (to UK): self-governing dependent territory

Laccadive Is (to India): non self-governing dependent territory, with parent state indicated

ARCTIC OCEAN
Arctic Circle
USA (Alaska)
Bering Sea
Aleutian Is (to US)
Great Bear Lake
Great Slave Lake
CANADA
Hudson Bay
Baffin Bay
Greenland (to Denmark)
Jan Mayen (to Norway)
ICELAND
Faeroe Islands (to Denmark)
UNITED KINGDOM
REPUBLIC OF IRELAND
Isle of Man (to UK)
Channel Islands (to UK)
Lake Winnipeg
Lake Superior
Lake Michigan
Lake Huron
Lake Ontario
Lake Erie
Montreal
Toronto
Chicago
New York
UNITED STATES OF AMERICA
St Pierre & Miquelon (to France)
PACIFIC OCEAN
Los Angeles
Bermuda (to UK)
ATLANTIC OCEAN
Azores (to Portugal)
Madeira (to Portugal)
Gibraltar (to UK)
Ceuta (to Spain)
Melilla (to Spain)
Casablanca
MOROCCO
SPAIN
Midway Islands (to US)
Tropic of Cancer
Guadalupe (to Mexico)
Monterrey
Gulf of Mexico
BAHAMAS
Canary Islands (to Spain)
WESTERN SAHARA (occupied by Morocco)
MAURITANIA
Hawaii (to US)
MEXICO
Havana
CUBA
Turks & Caicos Is (to UK)
Johnston Atoll (to US)
Revillagigedo Islands (to Mexico)
Guadalajara
Mexico City
Cayman Is (to UK)
HAITI
DOM. REP.
Puerto Rico (to US)
Virgin Is (to US)
British Virgin Is (to UK)
Anguilla (to UK)
ANTIGUA & BARBUDA
Guadeloupe (to France)
DOMINICA
Martinique (to France)
ST LUCIA
ST VINCENT & THE GRENADINES
BARBADOS
GRENADA
TRINIDAD & TOBAGO
JAMAICA
Navassa I. (to US)
BELIZE
ST KITTS & NEVIS
Montserrat (to UK)
GUATEMALA
Guatemala City
HONDURAS
EL SALVADOR
Netherlands Antilles (to Neth.)
Aruba (to Neth.)
NICARAGUA
COSTA RICA
PANAMA
Caracas
VENEZUELA
CAPE VERDE
GAMBIA
SENEGAL
GUINEA-BISSAU
GUINEA
MALI
BURKINA
SIERRA LEONE
IVORY COAST
LIBERIA
Abidjan
Kingman Reef (to US)
Palmyra Atoll (to US)
Baker & Howland Is (to US)
Equator
Jarvis I (to US)
KIRIBATI
Galapagos Is (to Ecuador)
ECUADOR
COLOMBIA
Bogotá
SURINAM
GUYANA
French Guiana (to France)
Fernando de Noronha (to Brazil)
Ascension (to St Helena)
PERU
Lima
BRAZIL
Salvador
ATLANTIC OCEAN
Tokelau (to NZ)
SAMOA
Wallis & Futuna (to France)
American Samoa (to US)
Cook Islands (to NZ)
French Polynesia (to France)
TONGA
Niue (to NZ)
PACIFIC OCEAN
BOLIVIA
Lake Titicaca
Belo Horizonte
São Paulo
Rio de Janeiro
Trindade (to Brazil)
St Helena (to UK)
Pitcairn Islands (to UK)
Tropic of Capricorn
Easter Island (to Chile)
Sala y Gomez (to Chile)
San Felix Island (to Chile)
San Ambrosio Island (to Chile)
PARAGUAY
CHILE
ARGENTINA
Kermadec Islands (to NZ)
Juan Fernandez Islands (to Chile)
Santiago
URUGUAY
Buenos Aires
Tristan da Cunha (to St Helena)
Gough Island (to Tristan da Cunha)
Chatham Islands (to NZ)
Falkland Islands (to UK)
South Georgia & South Sandwich Islands (to UK)
South Orkney Islands
South Shetland Islands
SOUTHERN
Peter I Island (to Norway)
Antarctic Circle
Ronne Ice Shelf
Ross Ice Shelf
Clipperton Island (to French Polynesia)

THE WORLD IN 1914

THE EARLY YEARS of the 20th century saw the mainly European colonial empires reaching their greatest extents by 1914. Two world wars inaugurated their disintegration, but even in 1950 there were only 82 independent countries. Since then, over 100 have gained their independence, culminating in the break-up of the Soviet Union after 1990.

PERCENTAGE OF EARTH'S LAND SURFACE CONTROLLED BY COLONIAL EMPIRES IN 1914

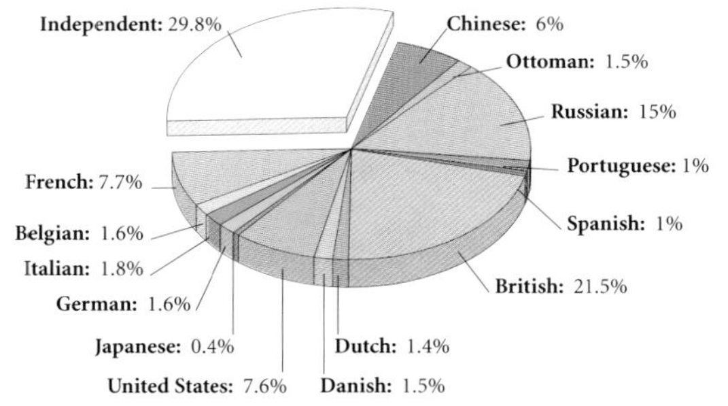

- Independent: 29.8%
- Chinese: 6%
- Ottoman: 1.5%
- Russian: 15%
- Portuguese: 1%
- Spanish: 1%
- British: 21.5%
- Danish: 1.5%
- Dutch: 1.4%
- United States: 7.6%
- Japanese: 0.4%
- German: 1.6%
- Italian: 1.8%
- Belgian: 1.6%
- French: 7.7%

COLONIAL EMPIRES IN 1914

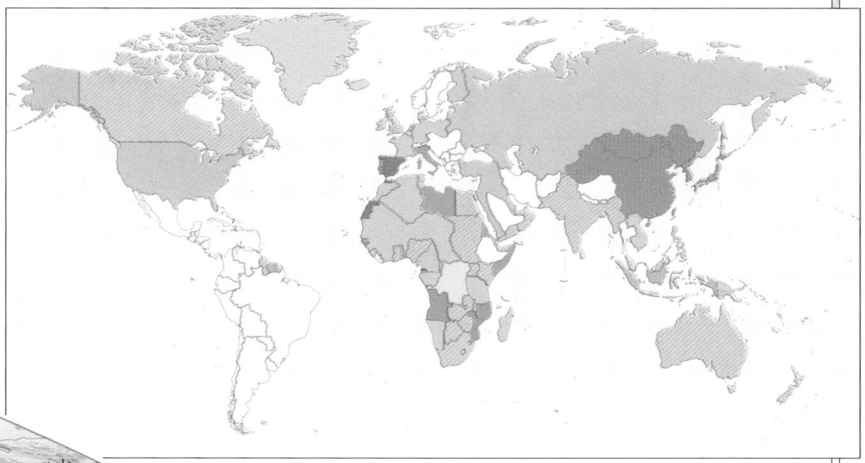

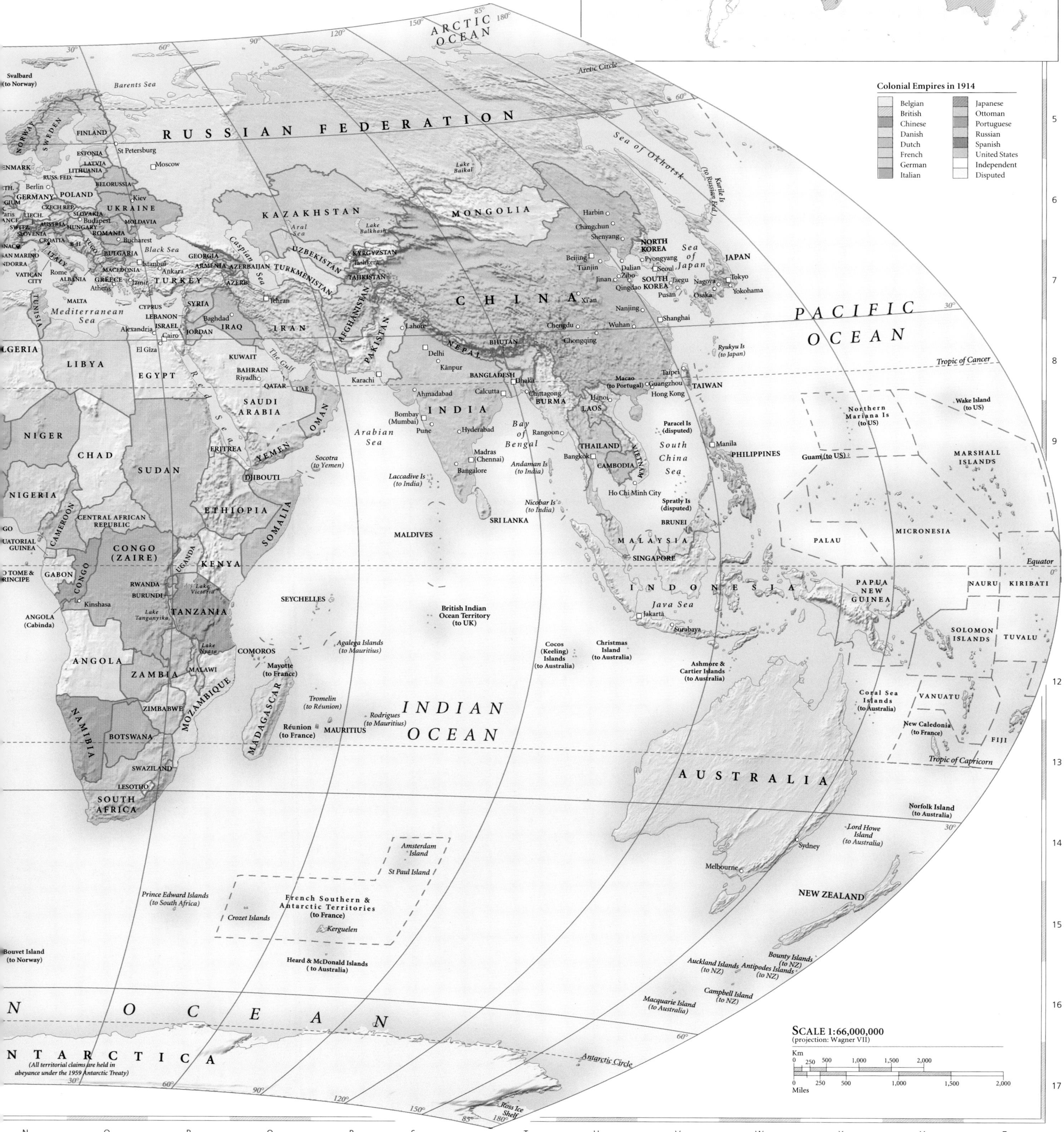

Colonial Empires in 1914

- Belgian
- British
- Chinese
- Danish
- Dutch
- French
- German
- Italian
- Japanese
- Ottoman
- Portuguese
- Russian
- Spanish
- United States
- Independent
- Disputed

SCALE 1:66,000,000
(projection: Wagner VII)

Km
0 250 500 1,000 1,500 2,000

Miles
0 250 500 1,000 1,500 2,000

xxix

STATES AND BOUNDARIES

THERE ARE OVER 190 SOVEREIGN STATES in the world today; in 1950 there were only 82. Over the last half-century national self-determination has been a driving force for many states with a history of colonialism and oppression. As more borders are added to the world map, the number of international border disputes increases.

In many cases, where the impetus towards independence has been religious or ethnic, disputes with minority groups have also caused violent internal conflict. While many newly-formed states have moved peacefully towards independence, successfully establishing government by multi-party democracy, dictatorship by military regime or individual despot is often the result of the internal power-struggles which characterize the early stages in the lives of new nations.

THE NATURE OF POLITICS

Democracy is a broad term: it can range from the ideal of multiparty elections and fair representation to, in countries such as Singapore and Indonesia, a thin disguise for single-party rule. In despotic regimes, on the other hand, a single, often personal authority has total power; institutions such as parliament and the military are mere instruments of the dictator.

The stars and stripes of the US flag are a potent symbol of the country's status as a federal democracy.

Types of government

- Multiparty democracy for more than 10 yrs
- Multiparty/transitional democracy within last 10 yrs
- Single-party government
- Military regime
- Theocracy
- Absolute monarchy
- Current civil unrest

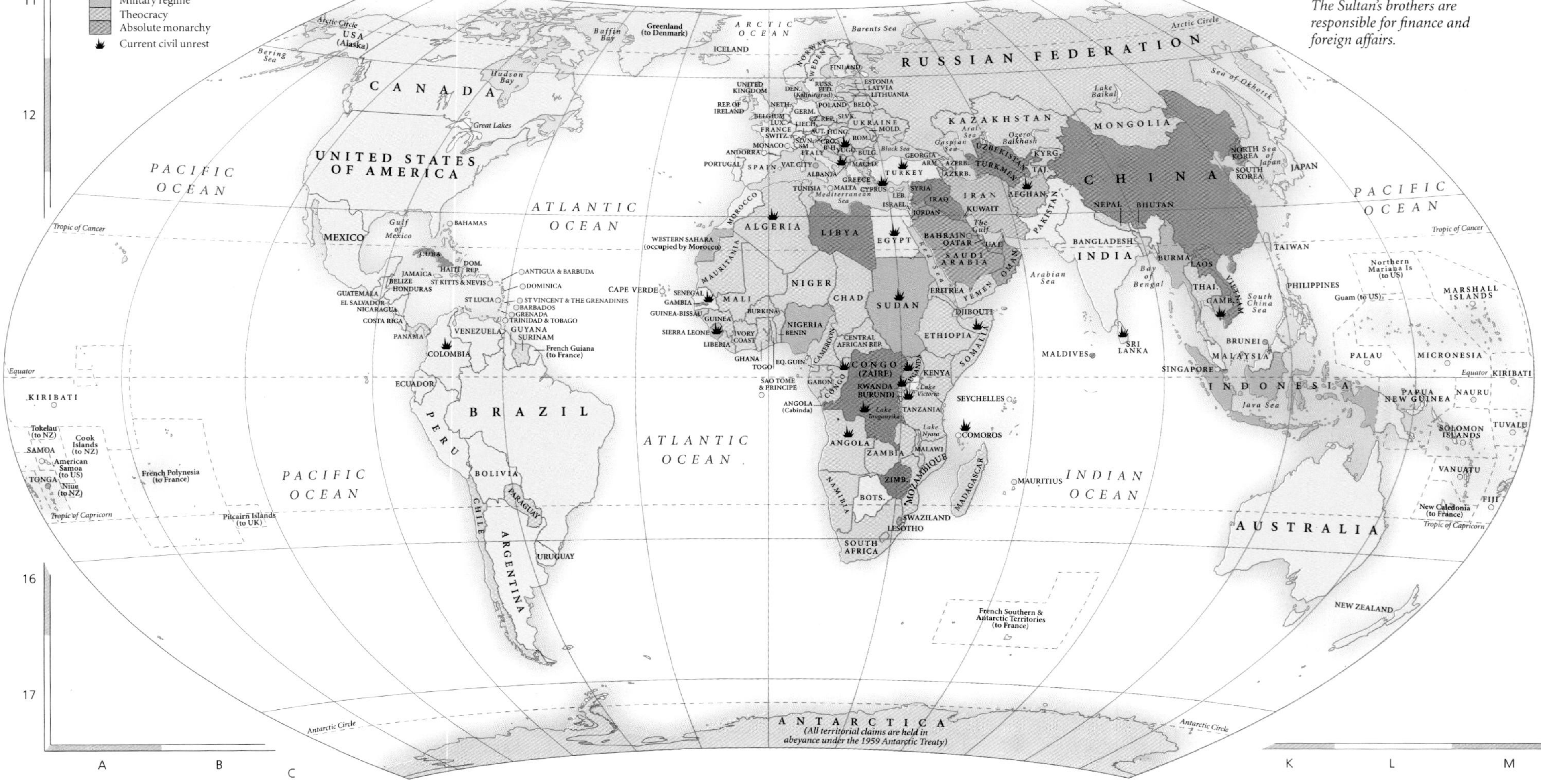

THE CHANGING WORLD MAP

DECOLONIZATION

In 1950, large areas of the world remained under the control of a handful of European countries (*page xxviii*). The process of decolonization had begun in Asia, where, following the Second World War, much of south and southeast Asia sought and achieved self-determination. In the 1960s, a host of African states achieved independence, so that by 1965, most of the larger tracts of the European overseas empires had been substantially eroded. The final major stage in decolonization came with the break-up of the Soviet Union and the Eastern bloc after 1990. The process continues today as the last toeholds of European colonialism, often tiny island nations, press increasingly for independence.

Icons of communism, including statues of former leaders such as Lenin and Stalin, were destroyed when the Soviet bloc was dismantled in 1989, creating several new nations.

Iran is one of the world's true theocracies; Islam has an impact on every aspect of political life.

Saddam Hussein overthrew his predecessor in 1979. Since then he has promoted an extreme personality cult, with autocratic control over 19.3 million Iraqis.

NEW NATIONS 1945–1965

NEW NATIONS 1965–1996

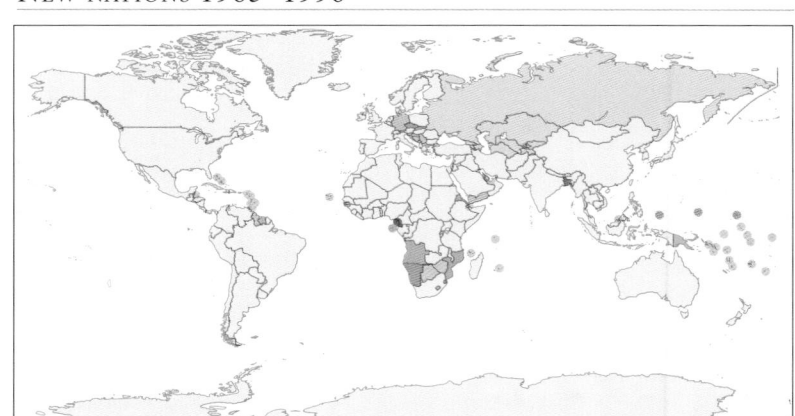

Administration at the time of independence

Australia	Netherlands
Aust/NZ/UK	New Zealand
Belgium	Pakistan
China	Portugal
Czechoslovakia	South Africa
Egypt/UK	Spain
Ethiopia	UK
France	Unified country
France/UK	USA
Italy	USSR
Japan	Yugoslavia
Malaysia	

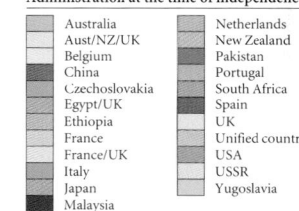

North Korea is an independent communist republic. Power is concentrated in the hands of Kim Jong Il.

South Africa became a democracy in 1994, when elections ended over a century of white minority rule.

In Brunei the Sultan has ruled by decree since 1962; power is closely tied to the royal family. The Sultan's brothers are responsible for finance and foreign affairs.

LINES ON THE MAP

THE DETERMINATION OF INTERNATIONAL BOUNDARIES can use a variety of criteria. Many of the borders between older states follow physical boundaries; some mirror religious and ethnic differences; others are the legacy of complex histories of conflict and colonialism, while others have been imposed by international agreements or arbitration.

POST-COLONIAL BORDERS

WHEN THE EUROPEAN COLONIAL EMPIRES IN AFRICA were dismantled during the second half of the 20th century, the outlines of the new African states mirrored colonial boundaries. These boundaries had been drawn up by colonial administrators, often based on inadequate geographical knowledge. Such arbitrary boundaries were imposed on people of different languages, racial groups, religions and customs. This confused legacy often led to civil and international war.

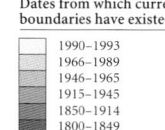

Dates from which current boundaries have existed
1990–1993
1966–1989
1946–1965
1915–1945
1850–1914
1800–1849
Pre-1800

The conflict that has plagued many African countries since independence has caused millions of people to become refugees.

PHYSICAL BORDERS

MANY OF THE WORLD'S COUNTRIES are divided by physical borders: lakes, rivers, mountains. The demarcation of such boundaries can, however, lead to disputes. Control of waterways, water supplies and fisheries are frequent causes of international friction.

ENCLAVES

THE SHIFTING POLITICAL MAP over the course of history has frequently led to anomalous situations. Parts of national territories may become isolated by territorial agreement, forming an enclave. The West German part of the city of Berlin, which until 1989 lay several hundred kilometres within East German territory, was a famous example.

ANTARCTICA

WHEN ANTARCTIC EXPLORATION began a century ago, seven nations, Australia, Argentina, Britain, Chile, France, New Zealand and Norway, laid claim to the new territory. In 1961 the Antarctic Treaty, signed by 39 nations, agreed to hold all territorial claims in abeyance.

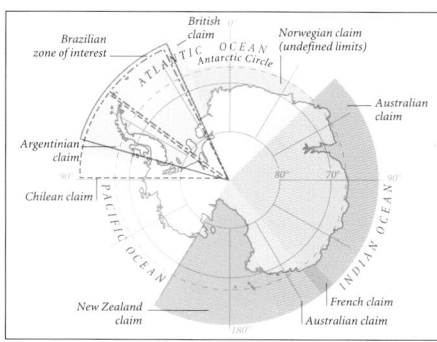

WORLD BOUNDARIES

Since the independence of Lithuania and Belorussia, the peoples of the Russian enclave of Kaliningrad have become physically isolated.

GEOMETRIC BORDERS

STRAIGHT LINES and lines of longitude and latitude have occasionally been used to determine international boundaries; and indeed the world's longest international boundary, between Canada and the USA follows the 49th Parallel for over one-third of its course. Many Canadian, American and Australian internal administrative boundaries are similarly determined using a geometric solution.

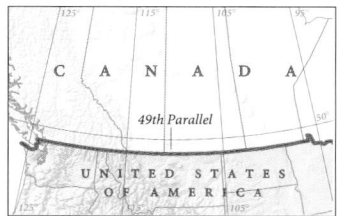

Different farming techniques in Canada and the USA clearly mark the course of the international boundary in this satellite map.

LAKE BORDERS
Countries which lie next to lakes usually fix their borders in the middle of the lake. Unusually the Lake Nyasa border between Malawi and Tanzania runs along Tanzania's shore.

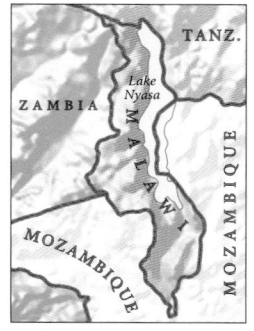

Complicated agreements between colonial powers led to the awkward division of Lake Nyasa.

RIVER BORDERS
Rivers alone account for one-sixth of the world's borders. Many great rivers form boundaries between a number of countries. Changes in a river's course and interruptions of its natural flow can lead to disputes, particularly in areas where water is scarce. The centre of the river's course is the nominal boundary line.

The Danube forms all or part of the border between nine European nations.

MOUNTAIN BORDERS
Mountain ranges form natural barriers and are the basis for many major borders, particularly in Europe and Asia. The watershed is the conventional boundary demarcation line, but its accurate determination is often problematic.

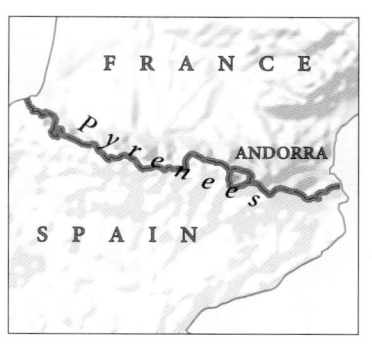

The Pyrenees form a natural mountain border between France and Spain.

SHIFTING BOUNDARIES – POLAND

BORDERS BETWEEN COUNTRIES can change dramatically over time. The nations of eastern Europe have been particularly affected by changing boundaries. Poland is an example of a country whose boundaries have changed so significantly that it has literally moved around Europe. At the start of the 16th century, Poland was the largest nation in Europe. Between 1772 and 1795, it was absorbed into Prussia, Austria and Russia, and it effectively ceased to exist. After the First World War, Poland became an independent country once more, but its borders changed again after the Second World War following invasions by both Soviet Russia and Nazi Germany.

In 1634, Poland was the largest nation in Europe, its eastern boundary reaching towards Moscow.

From 1772–1795, Poland was gradually partitioned between Austria, Russia and Prussia. Its eastern boundary receded by over 100 miles (160 km).

Following the First World War, Poland was reinstated as an independent state, but it was less than half the size it had been in 1634.

After the Second World War the Baltic Sea border was extended westwards, but much of the eastern territory was annexed by Russia.

INTERNATIONAL DISPUTES

THERE ARE MORE THAN 60 DISPUTED BORDERS or territories in the world today. Although many of these disputes can be settled by peaceful negotiation, some areas have become a focus for international conflict. Ethnic tensions have been a major source of territorial disagreement throughout history, as has the ownership of, and access to, valuable natural resources. The turmoil of the post-colonial era in many parts of Africa is partly a result of the 19th century 'carve-up' of the continent, which created potential for conflict by drawing often arbitrary lines through linguistic and cultural areas.

JAMMU AND KASHMIR

DISPUTES OVER JAMMU AND KASHMIR have caused three serious wars between India and Pakistan since 1947. Pakistan wishes to annex the largely Muslim territory, while India refuses to cede any territory or to hold a referendum, and also lays claim to the entire territory. Most international maps show the 'line of control' agreed in 1972 as the *de facto* border. In addition, both Pakistan and India have territorial disputes with neighbouring China. The situation is further complicated by a Kashmiri independence movement, active since the late 1980s.

Indian army troops maintain their positions in the mountainous terrain of northern Kashmir.

NORTH AND SOUTH KOREA

SINCE 1953, the *de facto* border between North and South Korea has been a ceasefire line which straddles the 38th Parallel and is designated as a demilitarized zone. Both countries have heavy fortifications and troop concentrations behind this zone.

Heavy fortifications on the border between North and South Korea.

CYPRUS

CYPRUS WAS PARTITIONED in 1974, following an invasion by Turkish troops. The south is now the Greek Cypriot Republic of Cyprus, while the self-proclaimed Turkish Republic of Northern Cyprus is recognized only by Turkey.

The so-called 'green line' divides Cyprus into Greek and Turkish sectors.

TURKISH REPUBLIC OF NORTHERN CYPRUS

Mediterranean Sea — Kyrenia Mountains — Karpasia
NICOSIA
CYPRUS — Troodos — Lárnaca
UK Sovereign Base Area
Lemesós (Limassol) — Mediterranean Sea
UK Sovereign Base Area

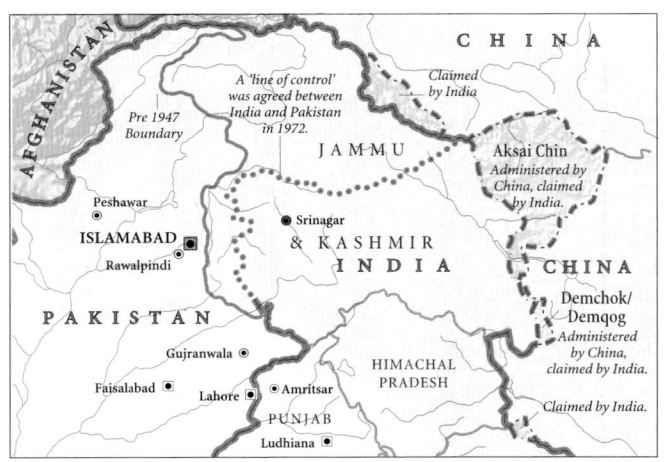

AFGHANISTAN — CHINA
A 'line of control' was agreed between India and Pakistan in 1972.
Claimed by India
Pre 1947 Boundary
JAMMU
Peshawar
Aksai Chin — Administered by China, claimed by India.
Srinagar
ISLAMABAD
Rawalpindi — & KASHMIR — INDIA — CHINA
PAKISTAN
Demchok/ Demqog — Administered by China, claimed by India.
Gujranwala
Faisalabad — Lahore — Amritsar — HIMACHAL PRADESH
Claimed by India.
Ludhiana — PUNJAB

Disputed territories and borders

- Countries involved in active territorial or border disputes
- Disputed borders
- Undefined borders
- Disputed territories

[World map with labels: ICELAND, Rockall, NORWAY, RUSSIAN FEDERATION, Northern Ireland, UNITED KINGDOM, DEN., LAT., EST., LITH., REP. OF IRELAND, RUS. FED., UKRAINE, MOLD., KAZAKHSTAN, Kurile Islands, MAC., CRO., B-H., YUGO., ROM., Serpent's Island, ALBANIA, GEORG., ARM., AZERB., Liancourt Rocks, GREECE, TURKEY, Alexandretta, TURKMEN., NORTH KOREA, JAPAN, Gibraltar, SPAIN, CYPRUS, LEB., SYRIA, Hatay, IRAN, CHINA, SOUTH KOREA, Ceuta, Melilla, ISRAEL, Golan Heights, IRAQ, Matsu, Senkaku Islands, MOROCCO, JORDAN, Askai Chin, Quemoy, TAIWAN, WESTERN SAHARA, EGYPT, BAHRAIN, QATAR, UAE, PAKISTAN, Jammu and Kashmir, Paracel Islands, PHILIPPINES, CUBA, Guantanamo Bay, SAUDI ARABIA, YEMEN, INDIA, BELIZE, GUATEMALA, EL SALVADOR, NICARAGUA, NIGERIA, ERITREA, Hanish Islands, THAI., VIETNAM, Spratly Islands, Sipidan and Ligitan, VENEZUELA, GUYANA, SURINAM, French Guiana, SUDAN, ETHIOPIA, SOMALIA, CAMB., MALAYSIA, COLOMBIA, GHANA, TOGO, CAMEROON, KENYA, SINGAPORE, INDONESIA, ECUADOR, British Indian Ocean Territory, East Timor, PERU, BRAZIL, COMOROS, BOLIVIA, MADAGASCAR, MAURITIUS, NAMIBIA, BOTSWANA, New Caledonia, ARGENTINA, URUGUAY, CHILE, SOUTH AFRICA, Falkland Islands]

THE FALKLAND ISLANDS

THE BRITISH DEPENDENT TERRITORY of the Falkland Islands was invaded by Argentina in 1982, sparking a full-scale war with the UK. In 1995, the UK and Argentina reached an agreement on the exploitation of oil reserves around the islands.

British warships in Falkland Sound during the 1982 war with Argentina.

[Korea inset map: CHINA, NORTH KOREA, PYONGYANG, Sea of Japan, SEOUL, SOUTH KOREA, Yellow Sea]

ISRAEL

ISRAEL WAS CREATED IN 1947 following the UN Resolution (147) on Palestine. Until 1979 Israel had no borders, only ceasefire lines from a series of wars in 1948, 1967 and 1973. Treaties with Egypt in 1979 and Jordan in 1994 led to these borders being defined and agreed. Negotiations over Israeli settlements in disputed territories such as the West Bank, and the issue of self-government for the Palestinians, continue.

[Israel inset map: ISRAEL, Jenin, Qabatiya, Tulkarm, Nablus, Qalqiliya, WEST BANK, Mas-ha, Jiftlik Post, Kefar Tappuah, Auja et Tahta, Nahal Elisha, Nu'eima, Ramallah, Jericho, JERUSALEM, JORDAN, Bethlehem, Hebron (Israel retains 15% control), Dead Sea]

- Israeli settlement
- Major settlement
- Palestinian settlement
- Area under Palestinian control

[Golan Heights inset map: LEBANON, Mediterranean Sea, GOLAN HEIGHTS, SYRIA, GAZA STRIP, WEST BANK, ISRAEL, JORDAN, EGYPT]

Barbed-wire fences surround a settlement in the Golan Heights.

YUGOSLAVIA

FOLLOWING THE DISINTEGRATION in 1990 of the communist state of Yugoslavia, the breakaway states of Croatia and Bosnia-Herzegovina came into conflict with the 'parent' state (consisting of Serbia and Montenegro). Warfare focused on ethnic and territorial ambitions in Bosnia. The tenuous Dayton Accord of 1995 sought to recognize the post-1990 borders, whilst providing for ethnic partition and required international peace-keeping troops to maintain the terms of the peace.

[Yugoslavia inset map: CROATIA, Bihać, Sava, Brčko, SERBIA, Banja Luka, Tuzla, Jajce, Srebrenica, BOSNIA-HERZEGOVINA, Gornji Vakuf, SARAJEVO, Goražde, Split, YUGOSLAVIA, Adriatic Sea, Mostar, Dubrovnik, MONTENEGRO]
- Invaded by Serbia
- Muslim/Croat federation

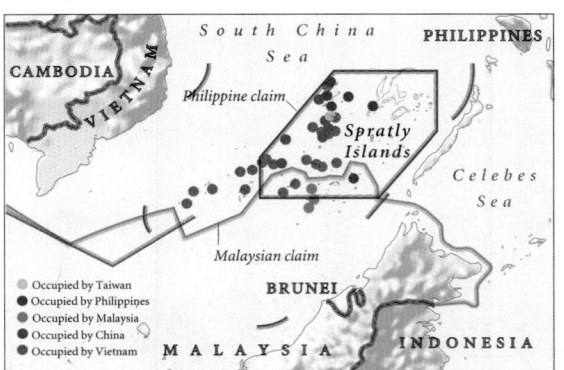

Most claimant states have small military garrisons on the Spratly Islands.

THE SPRATLY ISLANDS

THE SITE OF POTENTIAL OIL and natural gas reserves, the Spratly Islands in the South China Sea have been claimed by China, Vietnam, Taiwan, Malaysia and the Philippines since the Japanese gave up a wartime claim in 1951.

[Spratly Islands inset map: CAMBODIA, VIETNAM, South China Sea, PHILIPPINES, Philippine claim, Spratly Islands, Celebes Sea, Malaysian claim, BRUNEI, MALAYSIA, INDONESIA]
- Occupied by Taiwan
- Occupied by Philippines
- Occupied by Malaysia
- Occupied by China
- Occupied by Vietnam

THE
BRITISH
ISLES

POLITICAL BRITISH ISLES

THE UNITED KINGDOM'S SYSTEM OF GOVERNMENT has evolved over a long period, uninterrupted by any successful foreign invasion since 1066. Democracy takes the form of a constitutional monarchy, in which the monarch is a passive figurehead. The identity of the UK is being challenged by the prospect of a federal Europe, by Scottish and Welsh demands for devolution, and by the volatile condition of Northern Ireland, where Republicans face a majority who wish to remain under British government. The Republic of Ireland grew out of the Irish Free State, established in 1921, and has become an independent democracy with membership of the UN and the EU. The Anglo-Irish Accord of 1985 established a permanent cabinet-level channel for dialogue between Britain and Ireland.

4 THE NORTHWEST

1 CENTRAL SCOTLAND

2 THE NORTHEAST

3 TEESSIDE

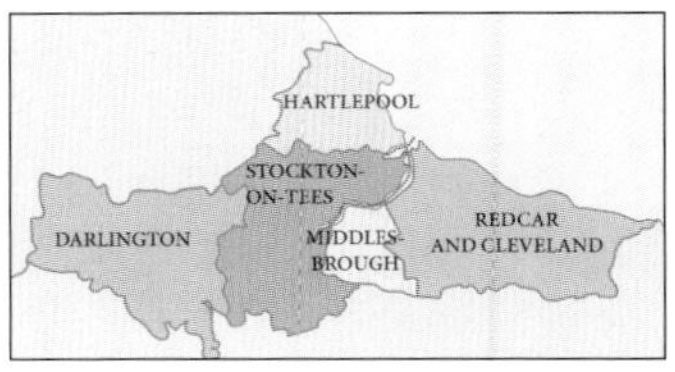

UK ADMINISTRATIVE REGIONS
The UK has radically reformed its administrative structure since the mid-1990s. A single-tier system of unitary authorities for local government has been introduced for Scotland and Wales and the most densely-populated parts of England. The traditional two-tier system of counties subdivided into districts remains in the more rural parts of England. Northern Ireland has had a system of unitary authorities since 1972, although the county names are still commonly used.

SCALE 1:4,200,000
(projection: Lambert Conformal Conic)

Km
0 5 10 20 30 40 50 60 70 80

Miles
0 5 10 20 30 40 50 60 70 80

REPUBLIC OF IRELAND ADMINISTRATIVE REGIONS
The Republic of Ireland has been divided into 26 counties since independence in 1921. When the six counties of Northern Ireland were included, the island could be divided into the four historic provinces of Ulster, Connaught, Leinster and Munster (see map of Ireland on page xliv), although these have little or no administrative function today.

5 SOUTH WALES

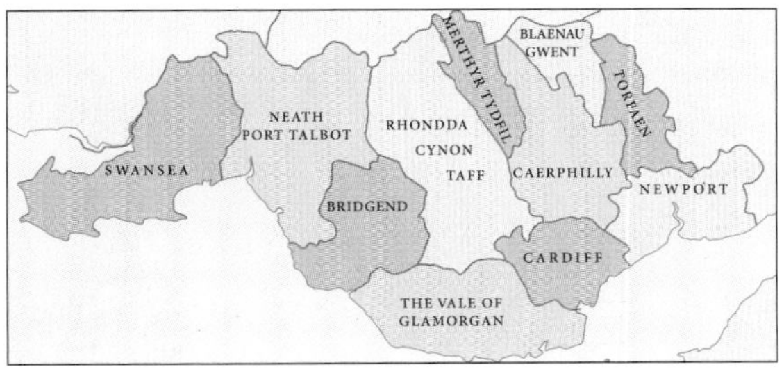

6 THE WEST MIDLANDS

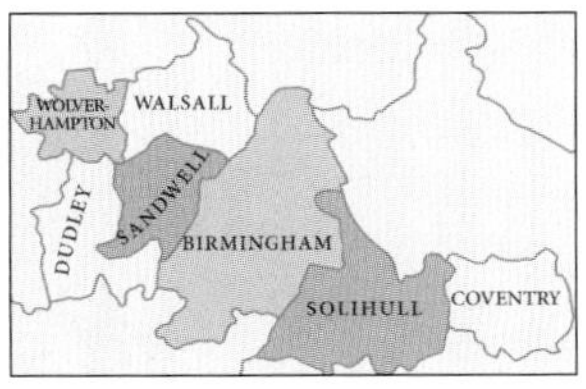

GUERNSEY (British Crown dependency)

JERSEY (British Crown dependency)

GREATER LONDON ADMINISTRATIVE REGIONS
London is divided into 32 boroughs (plus the Corporation of the City of London), which effectively have the same status as other unitary authorities in the UK. There has not been a citywide administrative body since the abolition of the Greater London Council (GLC) in 1986.

7 GREATER LONDON

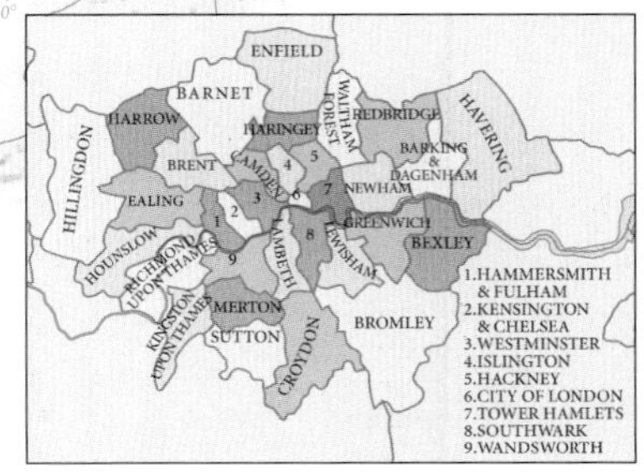

1. HAMMERSMITH & FULHAM
2. KENSINGTON & CHELSEA
3. WESTMINSTER
4. ISLINGTON
5. HACKNEY
6. CITY OF LONDON
7. TOWER HAMLETS
8. SOUTHWARK
9. WANDSWORTH

WALES

THE ANCIENT CAMBRIAN MOUNTAINS form the backbone of this green, mountainous country, which has been a stronghold of Celtic culture for about 3000 years. Wales has been incorporated with England since 1535 but retains a strong national identity. Over one-fifth of the people speak Welsh, a Celtic language with a rich poetic tradition. About 60% of the country's 2.8 million population live in the south or extreme northeast. The old coal-based industries that transformed these areas last century have since given way to a service-led economy.

TRANSPORT AND INDUSTRY

THE MINING INDUSTRIES, particularly slate and coal, have declined greatly this century. Factories in South Wales are served by deepwater ports such as Milford Haven, which has a large oil refinery and steel works. Electronics and light manufacturing industries, supported by government incentives, have grown rapidly in the south and also in central rural areas.

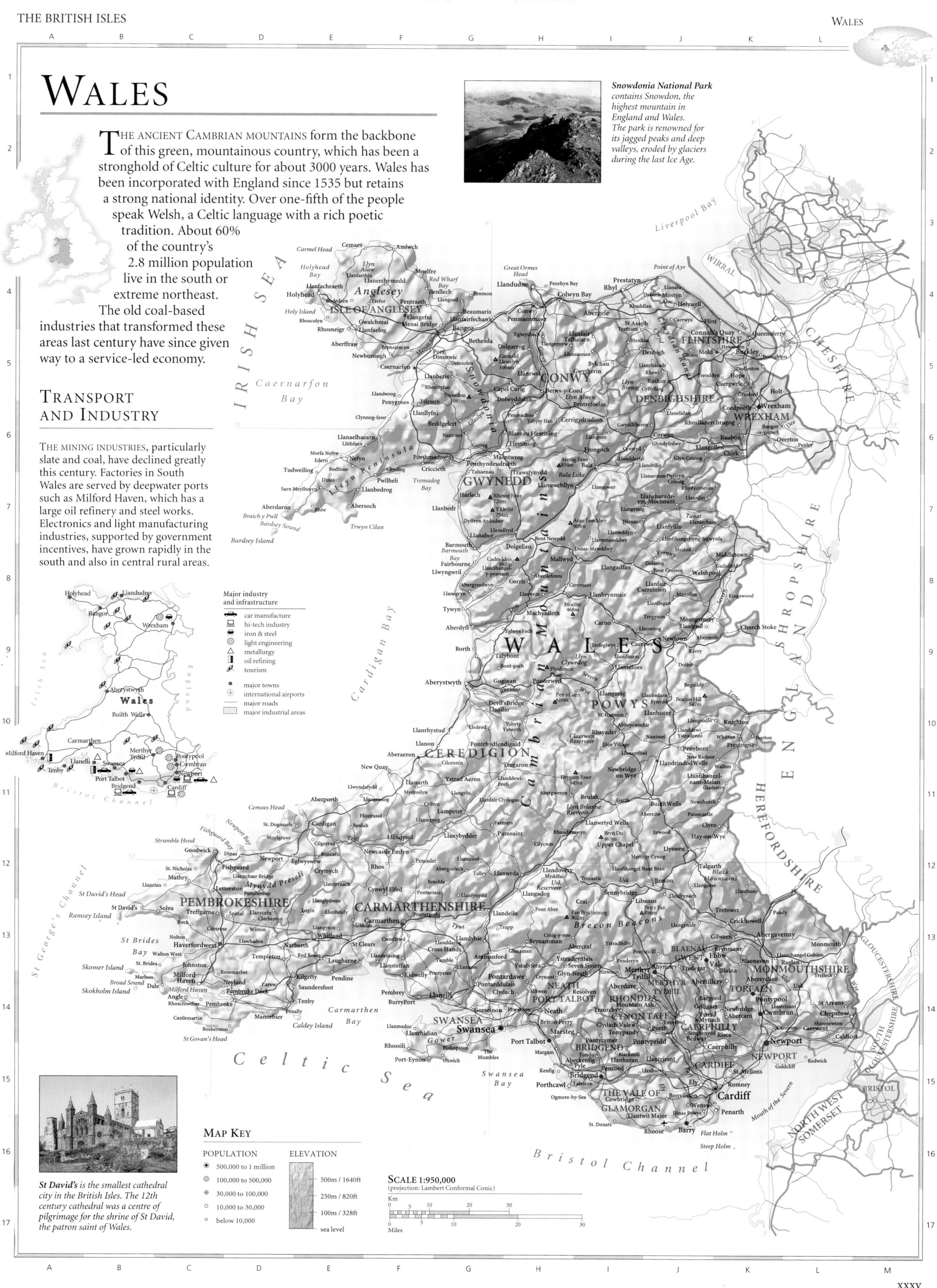

Snowdonia National Park contains Snowdon, the highest mountain in England and Wales. The park is renowned for its jagged peaks and deep valleys, eroded by glaciers during the last Ice Age.

Major industry and infrastructure
- car manufacture
- hi-tech industry
- iron & steel
- light engineering
- metallurgy
- oil refining
- tourism
- major towns
- international airports
- major roads
- major industrial areas

St David's is the smallest cathedral city in the British Isles. The 12th century cathedral was a centre of pilgrimage for the shrine of St David, the patron saint of Wales.

MAP KEY

POPULATION
- 500,000 to 1 million
- 100,000 to 500,000
- 30,000 to 100,000
- 10,000 to 30,000
- below 10,000

ELEVATION
- 500m / 1640ft
- 250m / 820ft
- 100m / 328ft
- sea level

SCALE 1:950,000
(projection: Lambert Conformal Conic)

SOUTHERN ENGLAND

SOUTHERN ENGLAND is the most affluent part of the British Isles, benefiting from close proximity to Europe, fertile agricultural land, and the capital, London, as a focus of wealth, political power and population. The physical landscape varies dramatically from the bleak uplands of the southwestern Cornish peninsula through the rolling Cotswold Hills to the flat, often marshy, expanses of Essex.

The southeast of England is the most densely populated region of the UK, and the growth of industries such as communications and financial services since the 1980s, has put considerable strain on transport and housing provision, with the building of new infrastructure becoming an issue of political controversy in the 1990s.

The city of Bath is built on the site of the Roman spa, Aquae Sulis. It is one of the most architecturally distinguished of British cities, noted for its elegant Georgian crescents built from the distinctive honey-coloured local stone.

MAP KEY

POPULATION

- ■ above 5 million
- ■ 1 million to 5 million
- ◉ 500,000 to 1 million
- ◎ 100,000 to 500,000
- ⊕ 30,000 to 100,000
- ○ 10,000 to 30,000
- ∘ below 10,000

ELEVATION

500m / 1640ft
250m / 820ft
100m / 328ft
sea level

Clifton Suspension Bridge, which spans the Avon Gorge, was designed by the great Victorian engineer, Isambard Kingdom Brunel and completed in 1864. It served as an important transport link for Bristol's then growing import and export trade in meat, tobacco and fruit.

LONDON

SCALE 1:230,000

The cliffs of north Devon bear the full force of the Atlantic Ocean. The entire British land mass is gradually tilting, with uplift continuing on the west coast, while the east faces the increasing threat of flooding by the sea.

Isles of Scilly

(same scale as main map)

TRANSPORT AND INDUSTRY

THROUGHOUT THE SOUTHEAST, service industries are growing, most notably in the areas of tourism, business support and retailing. At the heart of the capital, the City of London is one of the world's leading financial centres. In contrast to the flourishing service sector, engineering industries such as aerospace and car manufacture have faced long-term decline. Lightweight manufacturing industries such as pharmaceuticals and electronics are expanding around cities and along major transport corridors such as the M4. The southwest remains far less industrialized.

The luxury homes and offices at Canary Wharf are part of the Docklands development project, an attempt to revitalize east London following the decline of the dockyards and provide space for the expansion of the City of London.

Major industry and infrastructure

✈ aerospace	🏭 food processing	■ capital cities
🚗 car manufacture	hi-tech industry	● major towns
chemicals	⚙ light engineering	✈ international airports
⚙ engineering	printing & publishing	— major roads
S finance	tourism	major industrial areas

Leeds Castle, near Maidstone, is one of a number of important castles in the southeast. First started in the 12th century, the castle has been inhabited continuously, and has been extended and rebuilt countless times.

CHANNEL ISLANDS (to UK)

(same scale as main map)

SCALE 1:1,000,000
(projection: Lambert Conformal Conic)

Km
0   5   10   20   30

Miles
0   5   10   20   30

CENTRAL ENGLAND

THE INDUSTRIAL REGIONS around Birmingham, Coventry and the Potteries of Stoke-on-Trent, the dramatic hills of the Derbyshire's Peak District, and the windy fenlands of Lincolnshire and Norfolk, all illustrate the great diversity of England's central counties. Many of the most important developments of the Industrial Revolution occurred in this area, including the construction of the canal system. The traditional industrial heartland remains the most populous part of this region with far lower densities in East Anglia, although counties such as Cambridgeshire have recently seen large influxes of people from the crowded southeast.

TRANSPORT AND INDUSTRY

THE MASS PRODUCTION of iron and steel, ceramics and textiles was important in this region from the end of the 18th century onwards. This great industrial base provided an ideal location for automotive manufacturing throughout much of the 20th century, particularly around Coventry and Birmingham. In recent years, the growth of hi-tech and service industries, particularly in and around Cambridge, has attracted new investment, while agriculture remains important in both Hereford and the East Anglian counties.

Major industry and infrastructure

- ✈ aerospace
- 🍺 brewing
- 🚗 car manufacture
- ceramics
- chemicals
- ⚙ engineering
- 🐟 fish processing
- 🍲 food processing
- hi-tech industry
- △ metallurgy
- pharmaceuticals
- printing & publishing
- textiles
- • major towns
- ✈ international airports
- major roads
- major industrial areas

THE WEST MIDLANDS

SCALE 1:560,000

One of the most important developments of the Industrial Revolution took place at Ironbridge. In 1709, Abraham Darby I discovered how to smelt iron ore using local coke, rather than charcoal, of which there was a shortage. This paved the way for the mass production of iron, used for bridges, ships and buildings.

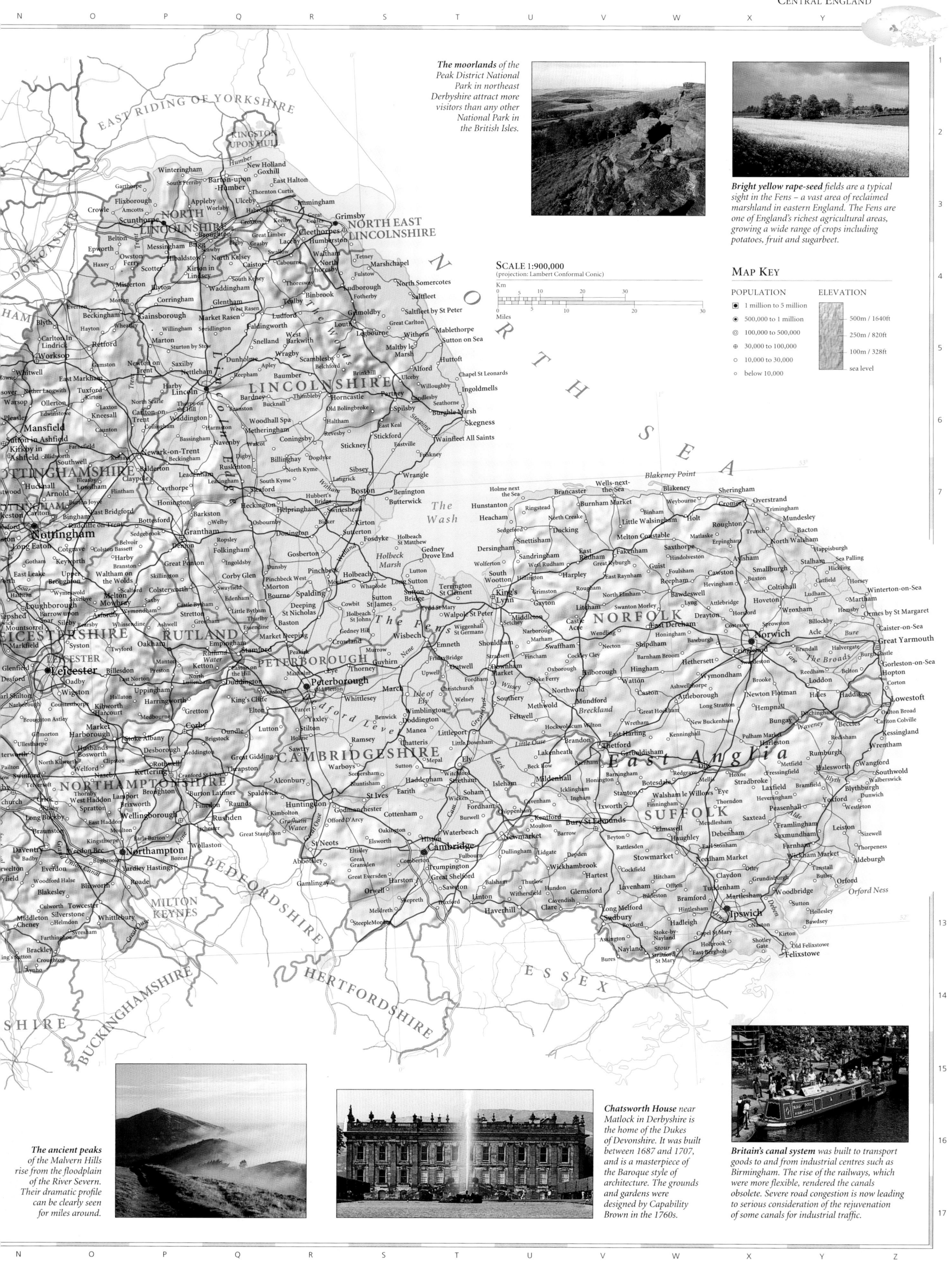

The moorlands of the Peak District National Park in northeast Derbyshire attract more visitors than any other National Park in the British Isles.

Bright yellow rape-seed fields are a typical sight in the Fens – a vast area of reclaimed marshland in eastern England. The Fens are one of England's richest agricultural areas, growing a wide range of crops including potatoes, fruit and sugarbeet.

SCALE 1:900,000
(projection: Lambert Conformal Conic)

Km
0   10   20   30

Miles
0   10   20   30

MAP KEY

POPULATION

- 1 million to 5 million
- 500,000 to 1 million
- 100,000 to 500,000
- 30,000 to 100,000
- 10,000 to 30,000
- below 10,000

ELEVATION

500m / 1640ft
250m / 820ft
100m / 328ft
sea level

The ancient peaks of the Malvern Hills rise from the floodplain of the River Severn. Their dramatic profile can be clearly seen for miles around.

Chatsworth House near Matlock in Derbyshire is the home of the Dukes of Devonshire. It was built between 1687 and 1707, and is a masterpiece of the Baroque style of architecture. The grounds and gardens were designed by Capability Brown in the 1760s.

Britain's canal system was built to transport goods to and from industrial centres such as Birmingham. The rise of the railways, which were more flexible, rendered the canals obsolete. Severe road congestion is now leading to serious consideration of the rejuvenation of some canals for industrial traffic.

NORTHERN ENGLAND

THE DRAMATIC PENNINE RANGE provides a central upland spine for northern England's fine and varied landscape, flanked to the west by the famous Lake District. The modern world's first industrial cities, including Manchester, Sheffield and Bradford, rose to greatness across this region from the mid 18th century, fuelled by local coal fields, with each specializing in particular trades including textiles, metal products and shipbuilding. The decline of manufacturing – particularly in the heavy industries – in the 20th century hit northern England hard, leading to prolonged economic depression. However, following major economic restructuring in the late 1980s, the north has been highly successful in attracting foreign investment. The great industrial cities such as Manchester, Liverpool, Leeds and Newcastle have maintained their position at the centre of northern England's cultural and economic life.

Blackpool's famous tower, built in 1895, stands as a testament to the rise of the tourist industry in late 19th century Britain, as workers from the nearby Lancashire cotton mills and Yorkshire woollen mills flocked to the town on their annual holidays. Blackpool remains a popular tourist resort today.

TRANSPORT AND INDUSTRY

ONCE THE CENTRE of heavy manufacturing, service industries now dominate the northern economy, following a difficult period of transition. Massive inward investment by multinational companies has helped northern England retain a majority share of current manufacturing activity in the UK. New light engineering and car production plants have developed in and around the region's cities, alongside more traditional industries such as iron and steel, textiles.

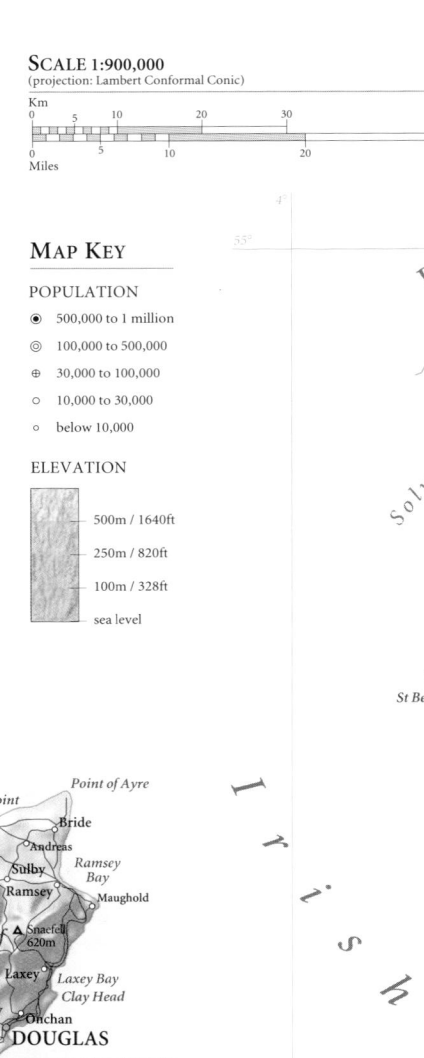

The Laxey Wheel on the Isle of Man – 72 ft (22 m) high is the largest steam-powered waterwheel in the world. During the 19th century it was used to pump water from the nearby iron ore mines. The 'Three Legs of Man' on the front of the wheel is an ancient symbol, first thought to have been used by the Vikings.

SCALE 1:900,000
(projection: Lambert Conformal Conic)

MAP KEY

POPULATION

⊙ 500,000 to 1 million
◉ 100,000 to 500,000
⊕ 30,000 to 100,000
○ 10,000 to 30,000
• below 10,000

ELEVATION

500m / 1640ft
250m / 820ft
100m / 328ft
sea level

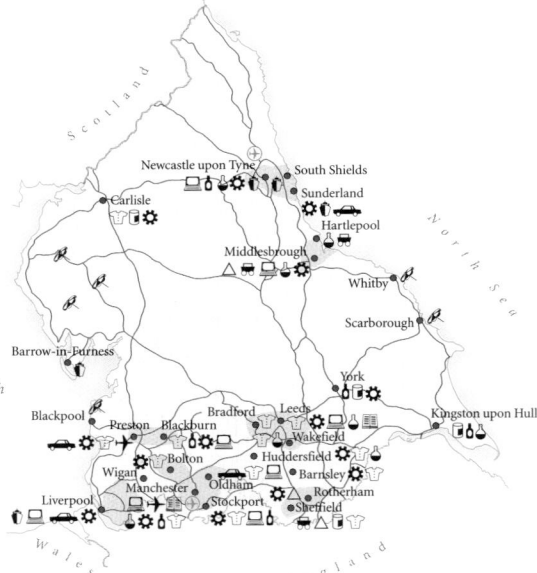

Major industry and infrastructure

✈ aerospace	△ iron & steel	• major towns
brewing	△ metallurgy	⊕ international airports
car manufacture	printing & publishing	major roads
chemicals	⚓ shipbuilding	major industrial areas
engineering	textiles	
food processing	tourism	
hi-tech industry		

ISLE OF MAN
(to UK)

THE NORTHWEST

SCALE 1:560,000

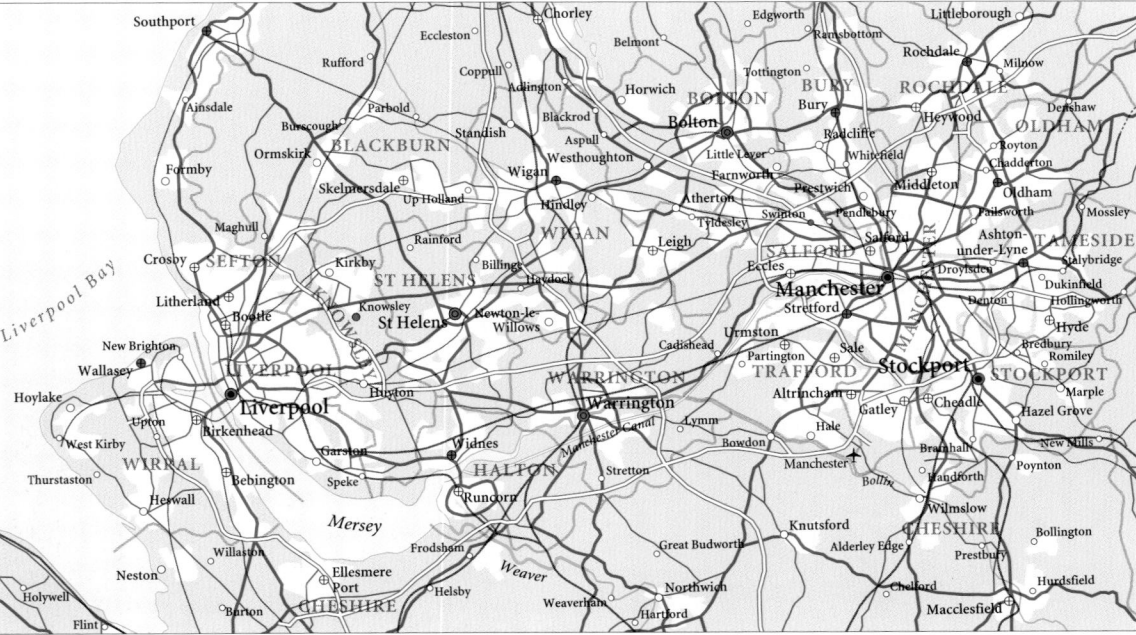

The spectacular gothic-revival architecture of Manchester Town Hall recalls the great wealth and civic pride of the city at the height of the Industrial Revolution.

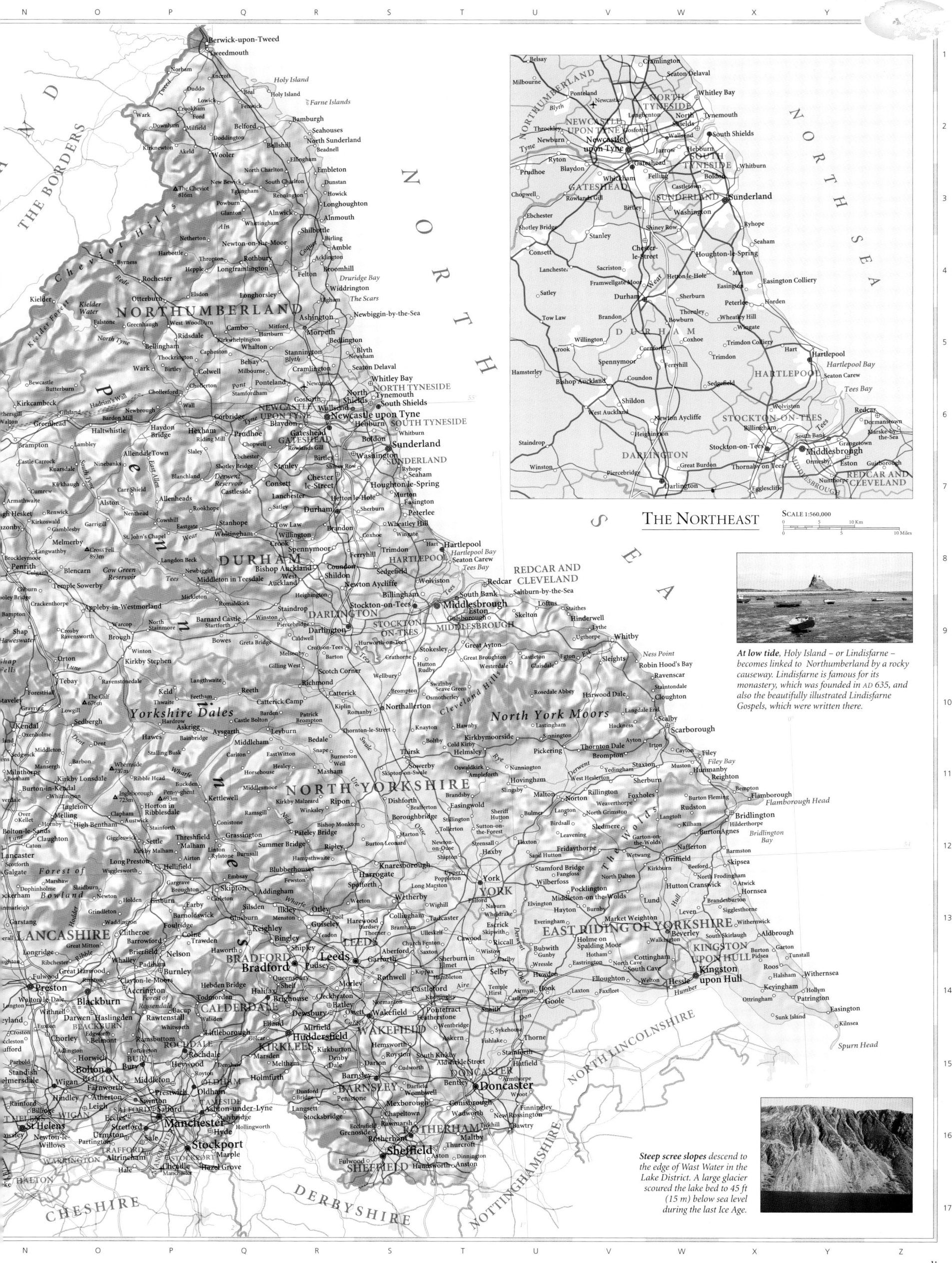

THE NORTHEAST

SCALE 1:560,000

At low tide, Holy Island – or Lindisfarne – becomes linked to Northumberland by a rocky causeway. Lindisfarne is famous for its monastery, which was founded in AD 635, and also the beautifully illustrated Lindisfarne Gospels, which were written there.

Steep scree slopes descend to the edge of Wast Water in the Lake District. A large glacier scoured the lake bed to 45 ft (15 m) below sea level during the last Ice Age.

SCOTLAND

THIS RUGGED NORTHERN REGION of Britain was an independent state until the Act of Union with England in 1707. Almost three quarters of the people live in the heavily industrialized central lowlands, which lie between the high moors of the southern uplands and the rugged highlands and islands of the north. English is the main language, with Gaelic also spoken, especially in highland areas. Development of the North Sea oilfields since the 1970s has given Scotland a critical role in the British energy industry, lending potency to the 'Home Rule' campaign for a Scottish parliament.

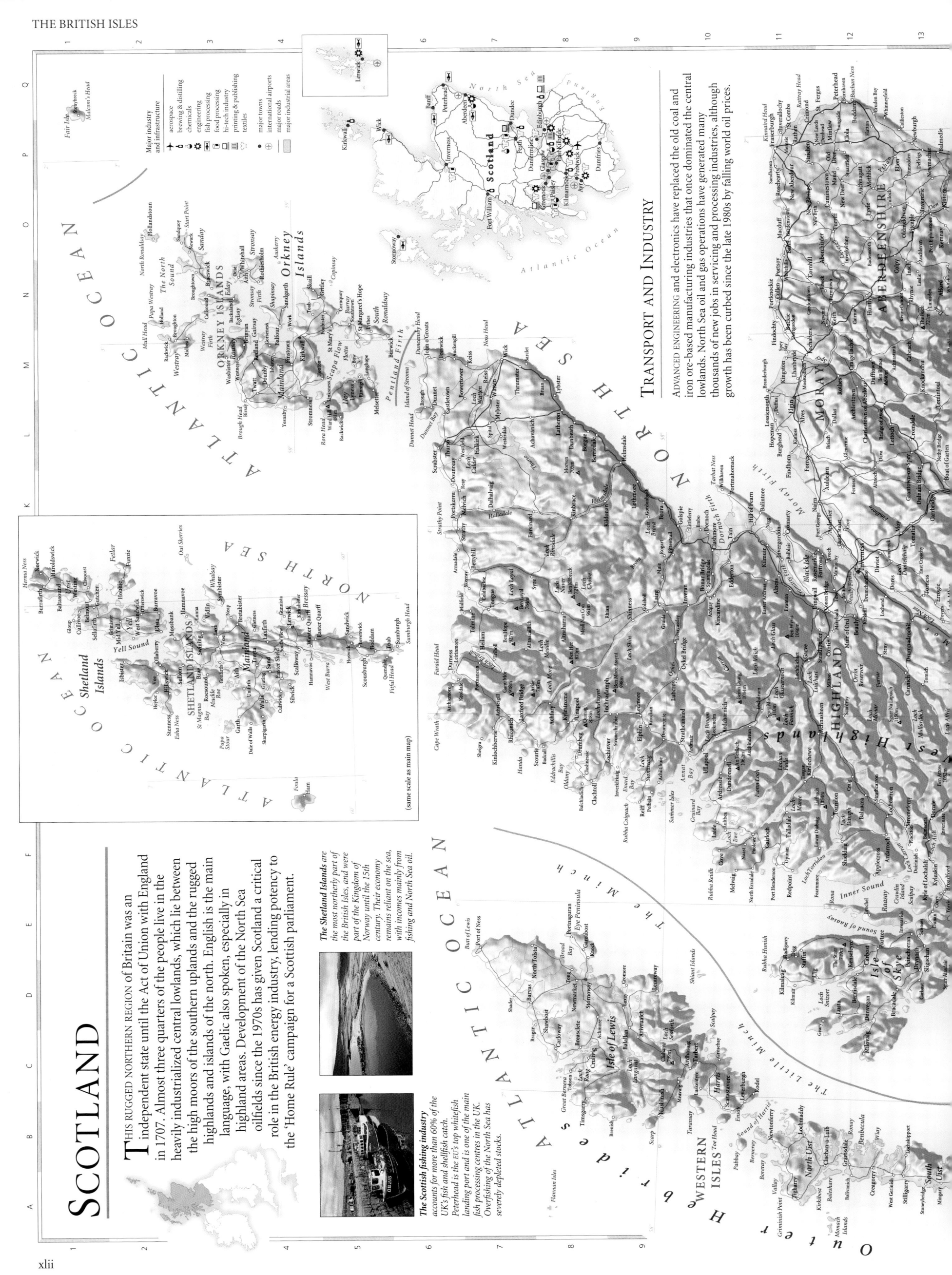

The Scottish fishing industry accounts for more than 60% of the UK's fish and shellfish catch. Peterhead is the EU's top whitefish landing port and is one of the main fish processing centres in the UK. Overfishing of the North Sea has severely depleted stocks.

The Shetland Islands are the most northerly part of the British Isles, and were part of the Kingdom of Norway until the 15th century. Their economy remains reliant on the sea, with incomes mainly from fishing and North Sea oil.

TRANSPORT AND INDUSTRY

ADVANCED ENGINEERING and electronics have replaced the old coal and iron ore-based manufacturing industries that once dominated the central lowlands. North Sea oil and gas operations have generated many thousands of new jobs in servicing and processing industries, although growth has been curbed since the late 1980s by falling world oil prices.

Major industry and infrastructure
aerospace
brewing & distilling
chemicals
engineering
food processing
hi-tech industry
printing & publishing
textiles
major towns
international airports
major roads
major industrial areas

MAP KEY

POPULATION
- ☐ 1 million to 5 million
- ⊙ 500,000 to 1 million
- ◉ 100,000 to 500,000
- ⊕ 30,000 to 100,000
- ○ 10,000 to 30,000
- ∘ below 10,000

ELEVATION
- 1000m / 3281ft
- 500m / 1640ft
- 250m / 820ft
- 100m / 328ft
- sea level

Edinburgh is Scotland's capital city. The city is host annually to the world-renowned Edinburgh Festival, a celebration of the performing arts.

Glasgow, an ancient river port on the banks of the Clyde, grew rapidly during the Industrial Revolution to become Scotland's leading industrial city.

The Scottish Highlands contain the highest and oldest mountains in the British Isles. Glacial lakes and sharp-edged arêtes recall the Ice Age which shaped this region 18,000 years ago.

SCALE 1:1,125,000
(projection: Lambert Conformal Conic)

IRELAND

THE UNSPOILT SCENERY and folk culture of Ireland reflect its remote position on the western fringe of Europe, and contrast with the so-called 'troubles' which have long hindered its development. The Republic of Ireland emerged from British rule as a free state in 1921 and is separated from Northern Ireland by the UK's only land border. Coastal hill ranges encircle a central undulating plain, strewn with many lakes and bogs. The Republic has benefited from EC grants since the 1980s, which have contributed to the growth of industry and infrastructure.

MAP KEY

POPULATION

◎ 100,000 to 500,000
⊕ 30,000 to 100,000
⊙ 10,000 to 30,000
○ below 10,000

ELEVATION

1000m / 3281ft
500m / 1640ft
250m / 820ft
100m / 328ft
sea level

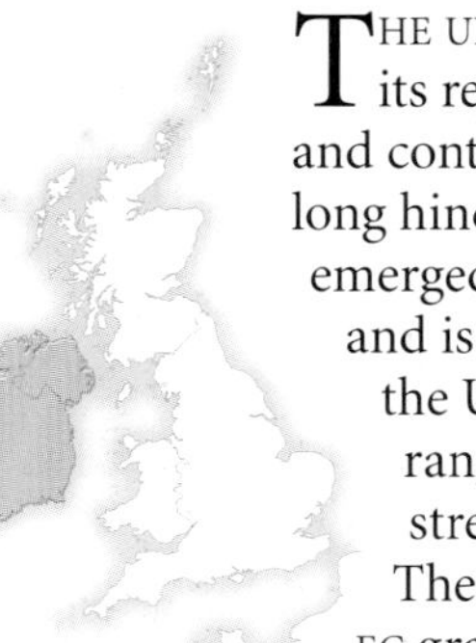

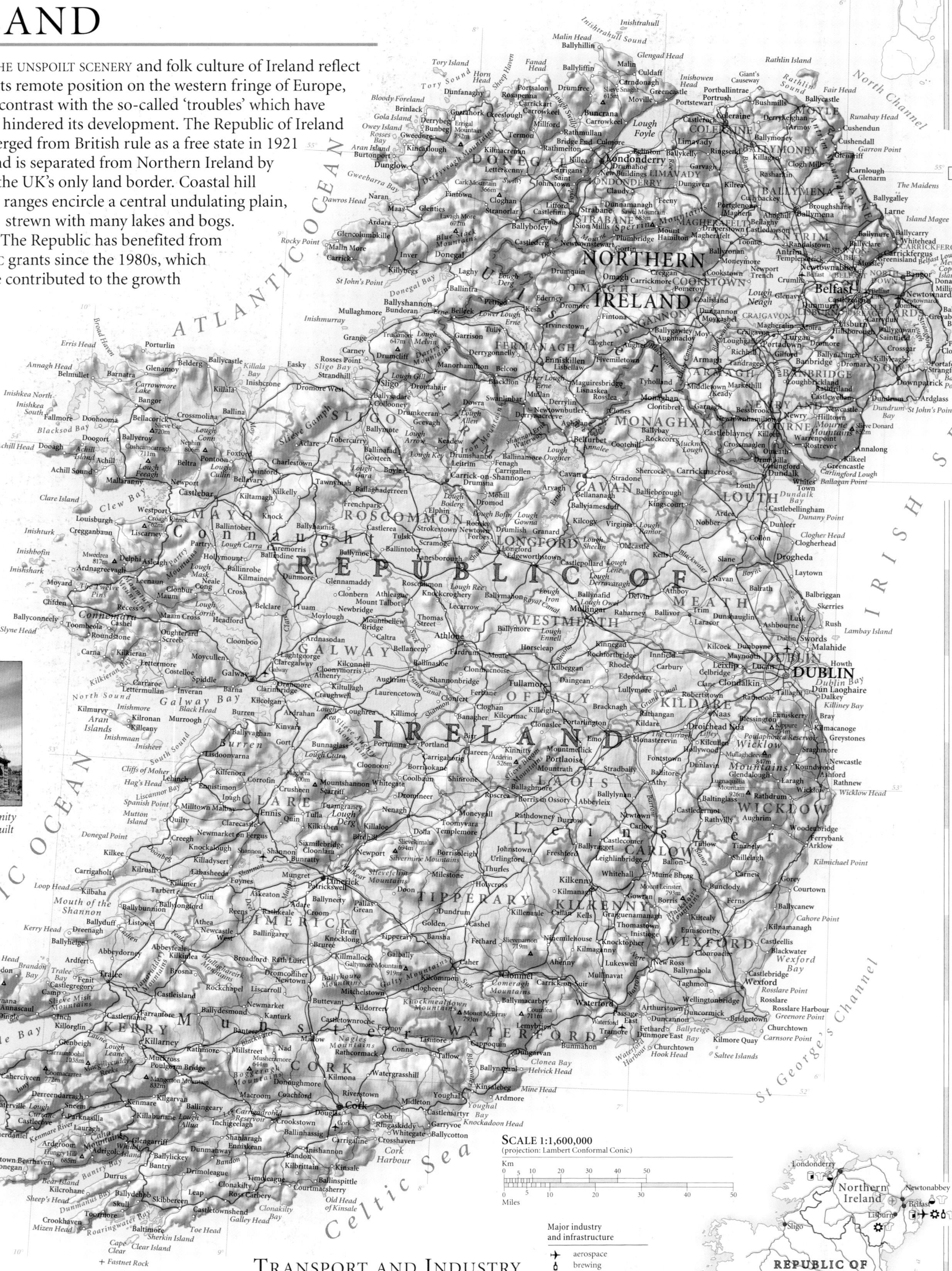

The Campanile in Trinity College, Dublin, was built by Sir Charles Lanyon, architect of Queen's College, Belfast. It is 98 ft (30 m) high.

The Burren is a massive limestone plateau in the northwest of County Clare. A wide range of Mediterranean and Alpine plants flourish in the pastures, near shallow lakes and in the cracks in the limestone pavement.

SCALE 1:1,600,000
(projection: Lambert Conformal Conic)

Km
0 5 10   20   30   40   50
Miles
0 5 10   20   30   40   50

TRANSPORT AND INDUSTRY

NORTHERN IRELAND'S industries are concentrated in Belfast, once a great textiles and shipbuilding centre which has faced chronic recession since the 1970s. Industrialization in the Republic of Ireland began properly in the 1950s. A broad range of goods are now produced for export near Dublin, and in many other larger towns.

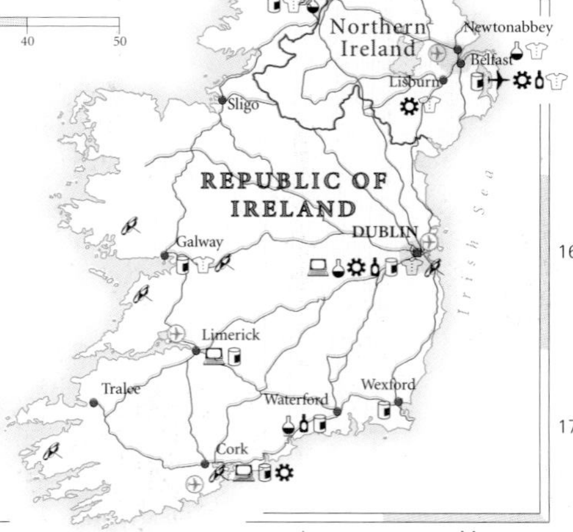

Major industry and infrastructure

↟ aerospace
⌂ brewing
△ chemicals
⚙ engineering
▣ food processing
⊡ hi-tech industry
⊽ textiles
⚑ tourism

● capital cities
• major towns
⊕ international airports
— major roads
▦ major industrial areas

ATLAS
OF THE
WORLD

THE MAPS IN THIS ATLAS ARE ARRANGED CONTINENT BY CONTINENT, STARTING FROM THE INTERNATIONAL DATE LINE, AND MOVING EASTWARDS. THE MAPS PROVIDE A UNIQUE VIEW OF TODAY'S WORLD, COMBINING TRADITIONAL CARTOGRAPHIC TECHNIQUES WITH THE LATEST REMOTE-SENSED AND DIGITAL TECHNOLOGY.

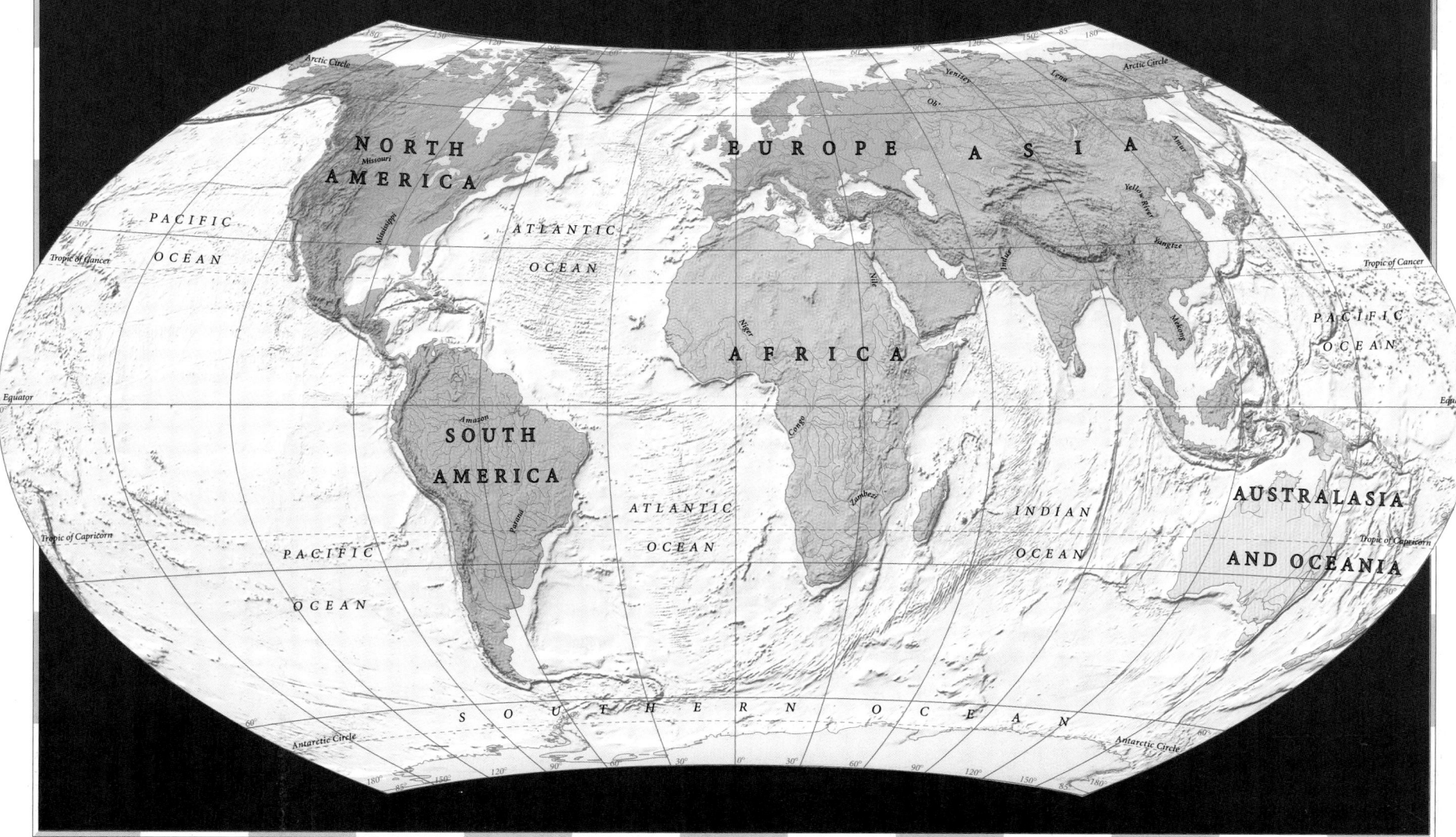

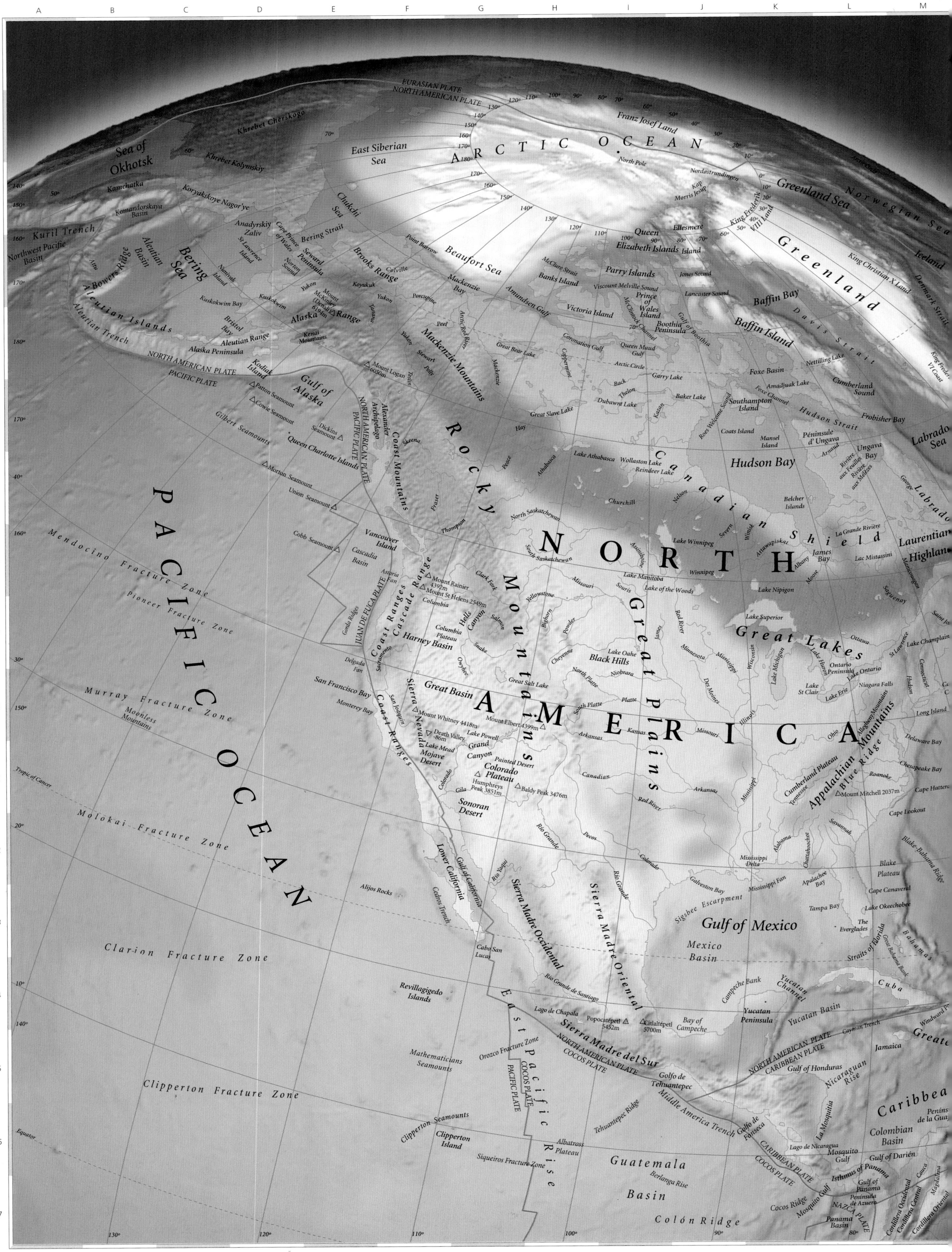

Column markers (top and bottom): A B C D E F G H I J K L M

Row markers (left and right): 1 2 3 4 5 6 7 8 9 10 11 12 13 14 15 16 17

EURASIAN PLATE
NORTH AMERICAN PLATE

Sea of Okhotsk
Khrebet Cherskogo
Khrebet Kolymskiy
East Siberian Sea
ARCTIC OCEAN
Franz Josef Land
North Pole
Nordaustlandet
Greenland Sea
Norwegian Sea

Kamchatka
Koryakskoye Nagor'ye
Chukchi Sea
Kap Morris Jesup
King Frederik VIII Land
Iceland
Denmark Strait

Komandorskaya Basin
Anadyrskiy Zaliv
Cape Prince of Wales
Seward Peninsula
Point Barrow
Beaufort Sea
Queen Elizabeth Islands
Ellesmere Island
King Christian X Land
King Frederik VI Land

Kuril Trench
Northwest Pacific Basin
Bowers Ridge
Aleutian Basin
Bering Sea
St Lawrence Island
Norton Sound
Colville
Brooks Range
McClure Strait
Parry Islands
Banks Island
Viscount Melville Sound
Jones Sound
Lancaster Sound
Greenland
Baffin Bay
Baffin Island
Davis Strait

Aleutian Ridge
Aleutian Islands
Anu
Nunivak Island
Bristol
Kuskokwim Bay
Kuskokwim
Yukon
Mount (McKinley) Denali
Alaska Range
Kenai Mountains
Yukon
Mackenzie Bay
Mackenzie
Amundsen Gulf
Victoria Island
Prince of Wales Island
Boothia Peninsula
Gulf of Boothia
Coronation Gulf
Queen Maud Gulf
Foxe Basin
Nettilling Lake
Cumberland Sound
Frobisher Bay
Labrador Sea

Aleutian Trench
Alaska Peninsula
Kodiak Island
Gulf of Alaska
Mount Logan 6050m
Mackenzie Mountains
Peel
Arctic Red River
Great Bear Lake
Coppermine
Arctic Circle
Garry Lake
Back
Baker Lake
Thelon
Dubawnt Lake
Southampton Island
Roes Welcome Sound
Coats Island
Mansel Island
Hudson Strait
Péninsule d'Ungava
Rivière aux Feuilles
Rivière aux Mélèzes
Ungava Bay

NORTH AMERICAN PLATE
PACIFIC PLATE
Patton Seamount
Cowie Seamount
Dickins Seamount
Queen Charlotte Islands
Alexander Archipelago
Coast Mountains
Skeena
Rocky Mountains
Hay
Peace
Lake Athabasca
Wollaston Lake
Reindeer Lake
Hudson Bay
Belcher Islands
George
Labrador

Gilbert Seamounts
Morton Seamount
Union Seamount
Cobb Seamount
Vancouver Island
Cascadia Basin
Fraser
Thompson
North Saskatchewan
Churchill
Nelson
Lake Winnipeg
Severn
Winisk
Attawapiskat
Lac Mistassini
James Bay
La Grande Rivière
Rupert
Laurentian Highlands

PACIFIC OCEAN
Mendocino Fracture Zone
Pioneer Fracture Zone
JUAN DE FUCA PLATE
NORTH AMERICAN PLATE
PACIFIC PLATE
Gorda Ridge
Astoria Fan
Cascade Range
Mount Rainier 4392m
Mount St Helens 2549m
Columbia
Columbia Plateau
Coast Ranges
Harney Basin
Snake
Clark Fork
Salmon
Yellowstone
Missouri
Souris
Red River
Lake Manitoba
Lake of the Woods
Lake Winnipeg
NORTH
Lake Nipigon
Lake Superior
Ottawa
St Lawrence
Lake Champlain

Delgada Fan
San Francisco Bay
Monterey Bay
Sacramento
San Joaquin
Coast Ranges
Sierra Nevada
Great Basin
Owyhee
Bighorn
Powder
North Platte
Cheyenne
Black Hills
Lake Oahe
Missouri
Niobrara
AMERICA
Great Plains
Minnesota
Wisconsin
Des Moines
Lake Michigan
Lake Huron
Georgian Bay
Lake St Clair
Lake Erie
Lake Ontario
Niagara Falls
Great Lakes
Hudson
Long Island

Murray Fracture Zone
Moonless Mountains
Mount Whitney 4418m
Lake Powell
Grand Canyon
Mount Elbert 4399m
Lake Mead
Death Valley -86m
Colorado Plateau
Humphreys Peak 3851m
Baldy Peak 3476m
Great Salt Lake
South Platte
Platte
Kansas
Arkansas
Missouri
Illinois
Ohio
Allegheny Mountains
Appalachian Mountains
Blue Ridge
Mount Mitchell 2037m
Delaware Bay
Chesapeake Bay
Cape Hatteras
Roanoke
Cumberland Plateau
Tennessee

Tropic of Cancer
Mojave Desert
Colorado
Gila
Sonoran Desert
Canadian
Red River
Arkansas
Mississippi
Alabama
Chattahoochee
Savannah
Cape Lookout

Molokai Fracture Zone
Lower California
Río Yaqui
Río Grande
Pecos
Colorado
Río Grande
Mississippi Delta
Galveston Bay
Mississippi Fan
Apalachee Bay
Blake Plateau
Cape Canaveral

Alijos Rocks
Gulf of California
Cedros Trench
Sierra Madre Occidental
Sigsbee Escarpment
Gulf of Mexico
Mexico Basin
Tampa Bay
Lake Okeechobee
The Everglades
Blake-Bahama Ridge
Straits of Florida
Bahamas

Clarion Fracture Zone
Cabo San Lucas
Sierra Madre Oriental
Río Grande de Santiago
Compeche Bank
Yucatan Channel
Cuba
Great Bahama Bank

Revillagigedo Islands
East Pacific Rise
Lago de Chapala
Popocatépetl 5452m
Citlaltépetl 5700m
Bay of Campeche
Yucatan Peninsula
Yucatan Basin
Windward Passage
Greater

Mathematicians Seamounts
Orozco Fracture Zone
COCOS PLATE
PACIFIC PLATE
Sierra Madre del Sur
NORTH AMERICAN PLATE
CARIBBEAN PLATE
Gulf of Honduras
Nicaraguan Rise
Jamaica
Cayman Trench
Caribbea
Peninsula de la Gua

Clipperton Fracture Zone
Clipperton Seamounts
Clipperton Island
Albatross Plateau
Tehuantepec Ridge
Middle America Trench
Golfo de Tehuantepec
Golfo de Fonseca
COCOS PLATE
CARIBBEAN PLATE
La Mosquitia
Lago de Nicaragua
Mosquito Gulf
Colombian Basin
Gulf of Darién

Equator
Siqueiros Fracture Zone
Guatemala Basin
Berlanga Rise
Cocos Ridge
Colón Ridge
Gulf of Panama
Isthmus of Panama
Peninsula de Azuero
Panama Basin
NAZCA PLATE
Cordillera Occidental
Cordillera Central
Magdalena

NORTH AMERICA

NORTH AMERICA IS THE WORLD'S THIRD LARGEST CONTINENT WITH A
TOTAL AREA OF 9,358,340 SQ MILES (24,238,000 SQ KM) INCLUDING
GREENLAND AND THE CARIBBEAN ISLANDS. IT LIES WHOLLY
WITHIN THE NORTHERN HEMISPHERE.

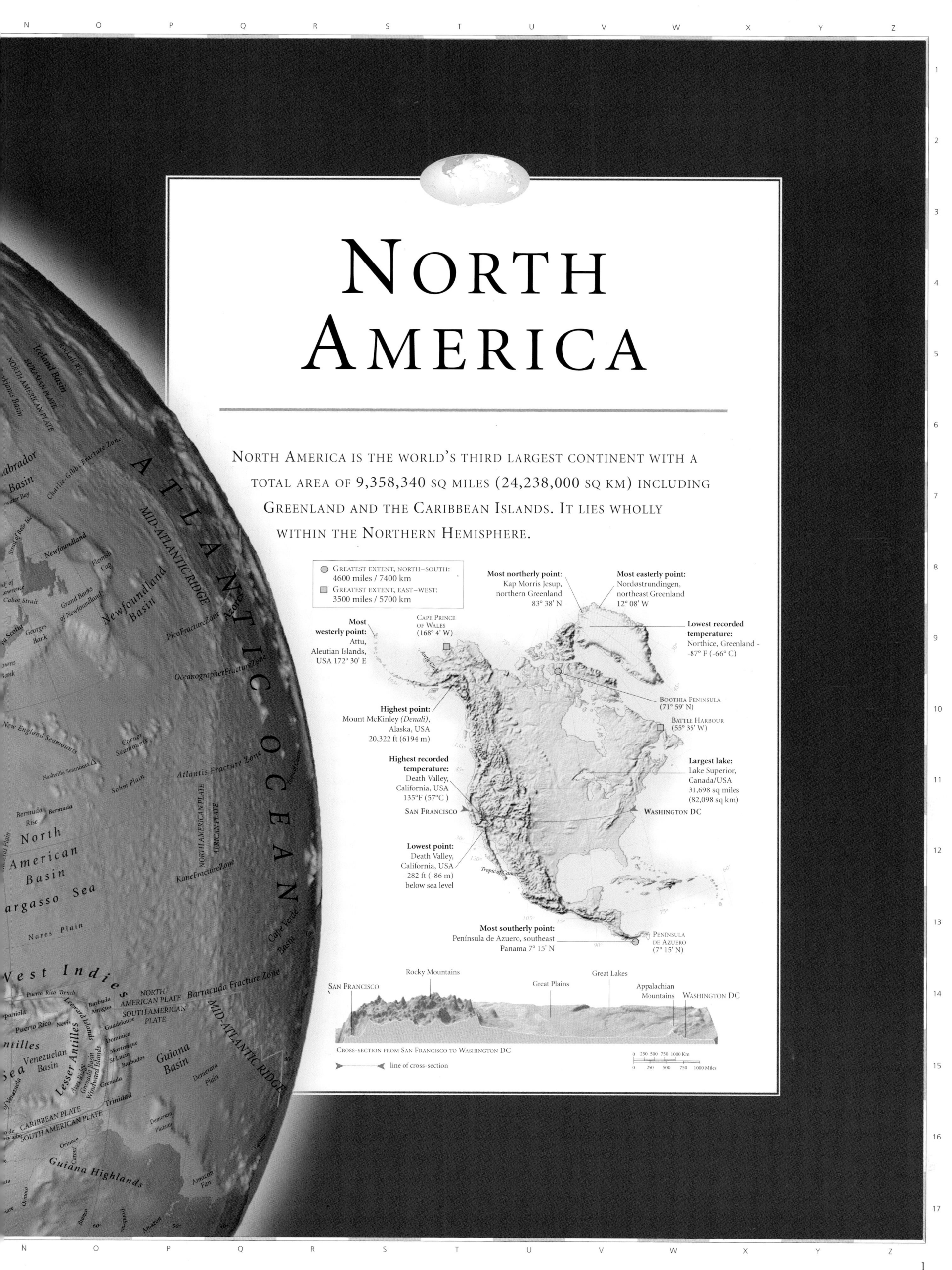

- GREATEST EXTENT, NORTH–SOUTH: 4600 miles / 7400 km
- GREATEST EXTENT, EAST–WEST: 3500 miles / 5700 km

Most northerly point:
Kap Morris Jesup,
northern Greenland
83° 38' N

Most easterly point:
Nordøstrundingen,
northeast Greenland
12° 08' W

CAPE PRINCE
OF WALES
(168° 4' W)

**Lowest recorded
temperature:**
Northice, Greenland -
-87° F (-66° C)

**Most
westerly point:**
Attu,
Aleutian Islands,
USA 172° 30' E

BOOTHIA PENINSULA
(71° 59' N)

BATTLE HARBOUR
(55° 35' W)

Highest point:
Mount McKinley (Denali),
Alaska, USA
20,322 ft (6194 m)

**Highest recorded
temperature:**
Death Valley,
California, USA
135°F (57°C)

Largest lake:
Lake Superior,
Canada/USA
31,698 sq miles
(82,098 sq km)

SAN FRANCISCO

WASHINGTON DC

Lowest point:
Death Valley,
California, USA
-282 ft (-86 m)
below sea level

Most southerly point:
Península de Azuero, southeast
Panama 7° 15' N

PENÍNSULA
DE AZUERO
(7° 15' N)

SAN FRANCISCO — Rocky Mountains — Great Plains — Great Lakes — Appalachian Mountains — WASHINGTON DC

CROSS-SECTION FROM SAN FRANCISCO TO WASHINGTON DC

line of cross-section

0 250 500 750 1000 Km
0 250 500 750 1000 Miles

ATLANTIC OCEAN
MID-ATLANTIC RIDGE
Iceland Basin
EURASIAN PLATE
NORTH AMERICAN PLATE
Reykjanes Basin
Labrador Basin
Charlie-Gibbs Fracture Zone
Newfoundland
Flemish Cap
Newfoundland Basin
Grand Banks of Newfoundland
Cabot Strait
Georges Bank
Pico Fracture Zone
Oceanographer Fracture Zone
New England Seamounts
Corner Seamounts
Nashville Seamount
Atlantis Fracture Zone
Sohm Plain
Bermuda Rise
NORTH AMERICAN PLATE
AFRICAN PLATE
Kane Fracture Zone
North American Basin
Sargasso Sea
Nares Plain
Cape Verde Basin
West Indies
Puerto Rico Trench
Barracuda Fracture Zone
NORTH AMERICAN PLATE
SOUTH AMERICAN PLATE
Puerto Rico
Nevis
Leeward Islands
Barbuda
Antigua
Guadeloupe
Dominica
Martinique
St Lucia
Barbados
Windward Islands
Grenada
Antilles
Lesser Antilles
Venezuelan Basin
Guiana Basin
Trinidad
MID-ATLANTIC RIDGE
CARIBBEAN PLATE
SOUTH AMERICAN PLATE
Orinoco
Guiana Highlands
Amazon Fan

PHYSICAL NORTH AMERICA

THE NORTH AMERICAN CONTINENT can be divided into a number of major structural areas: the Western Cordillera, the Canadian Shield, the Great Plains and Central Lowlands, and the Appalachians. Other smaller regions include the Gulf Atlantic Coastal Plain which borders the southern coast of North America from the southern Appalachians to the Great Plains. This area includes the expanding Mississippi Delta. A chain of volcanic islands, running in an arc around the margin of the Caribbean Plate, lie to the east of the Gulf of Mexico.

THE CANADIAN SHIELD

SPANNING NORTHERN CANADA and Greenland, this geologically stable plain forms the heart of the continent, containing rocks over two billion years old. A long history of weathering and repeated glaciation has scoured the region, leaving flat plains, gentle hummocks, numerous small basins and lakes, and the bays and islands of the Arctic.

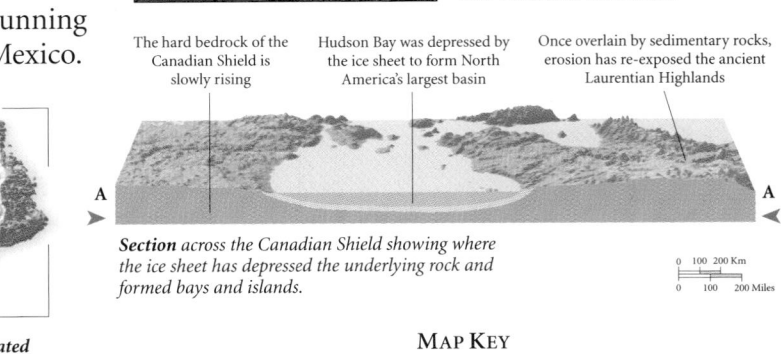

The hard bedrock of the Canadian Shield is slowly rising

Hudson Bay was depressed by the ice sheet to form North America's largest basin

Once overlain by sedimentary rocks, erosion has re-exposed the ancient Laurentian Highlands

A A

Section across the Canadian Shield showing where the ice sheet has depressed the underlying rock and formed bays and islands.

0 100 200 Km
0 100 200 Miles

THE WESTERN CORDILLERA

ABOUT 80 MILLION YEARS ago the Pacific and North American plates collided, uplifting the Western Cordillera. This consists of the Aleutian, Coast, Cascade and Sierra Nevada mountains, and the inland Rocky Mountains. These run parallel from the Arctic to Mexico.

The weight of the ice sheet, 1.8 miles (3 km) thick, has depressed the land to 0.6 miles (1 km) below sea level

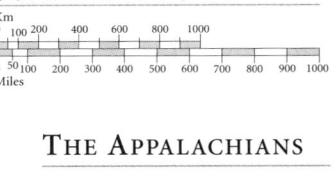

Strata have been thrust eastward along fault lines

The Rocky Mountain Trench is the longest linear fault on the continent

This computer-generated view shows the ice-covered island of Greenland without its ice cap.

B B

Volcanic rock *Cross-section* through the Western Cordillera showing direction of mountain building.

0 50 100 Km
0 50 100 Miles

MAP KEY

ELEVATION

3500m / 11,484ft
3000m / 9843ft
2500m / 8203ft
2000m / 6562ft
1500m / 4922ft
1000m / 3281ft
500m / 1640ft
250m / 820ft
100m / 328ft
sea level

PLATE MARGINS
(for explanation see page xiv)

constructive
△   △   destructive
conservative
.... uncertain

physiographic regions

line of cross-section

SCALE 1:38,000,000
(projection: Lambert Azimuthal Equal Area)

Km
0 100 200 400 600 800 1000
0 50 100 200 300 400 500 600 700 800 900 1000
Miles

THE GREAT PLAINS & CENTRAL LOWLANDS

DEPOSITS LEFT by retreating glaciers and rivers have made this vast flat area very fertile. In the north this is the result of glaciation, with deposits up to one mile (1.7 km) thick, covering the basement rock. To the south and west, the massive Missouri/Mississippi river system has for centuries deposited silt across the plains, creating broad, flat flood plains and deltas.

Sedimentary layers overlay domed basement rock

Upland rivers drain south towards the Mississippi Basin

Confluence of the Missouri and Mississippi rivers

D D

Section across the Great Plains and Central Lowlands showing river systems and structure.

0 200 400 Km
0 200 400 Miles

THE APPALACHIANS

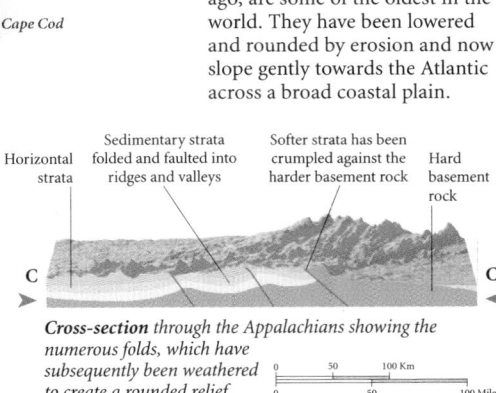

THE APPALACHIAN MOUNTAINS, uplifted about 400 million years ago, are some of the oldest in the world. They have been lowered and rounded by erosion and now slope gently towards the Atlantic across a broad coastal plain.

Horizontal strata

Sedimentary strata folded and faulted into ridges and valleys

Softer strata has been crumpled against the harder basement rock

Hard basement rock

C C

Cross-section through the Appalachians showing the numerous folds, which have subsequently been weathered to create a rounded relief.

0 50 100 Km
0 50 100 Miles

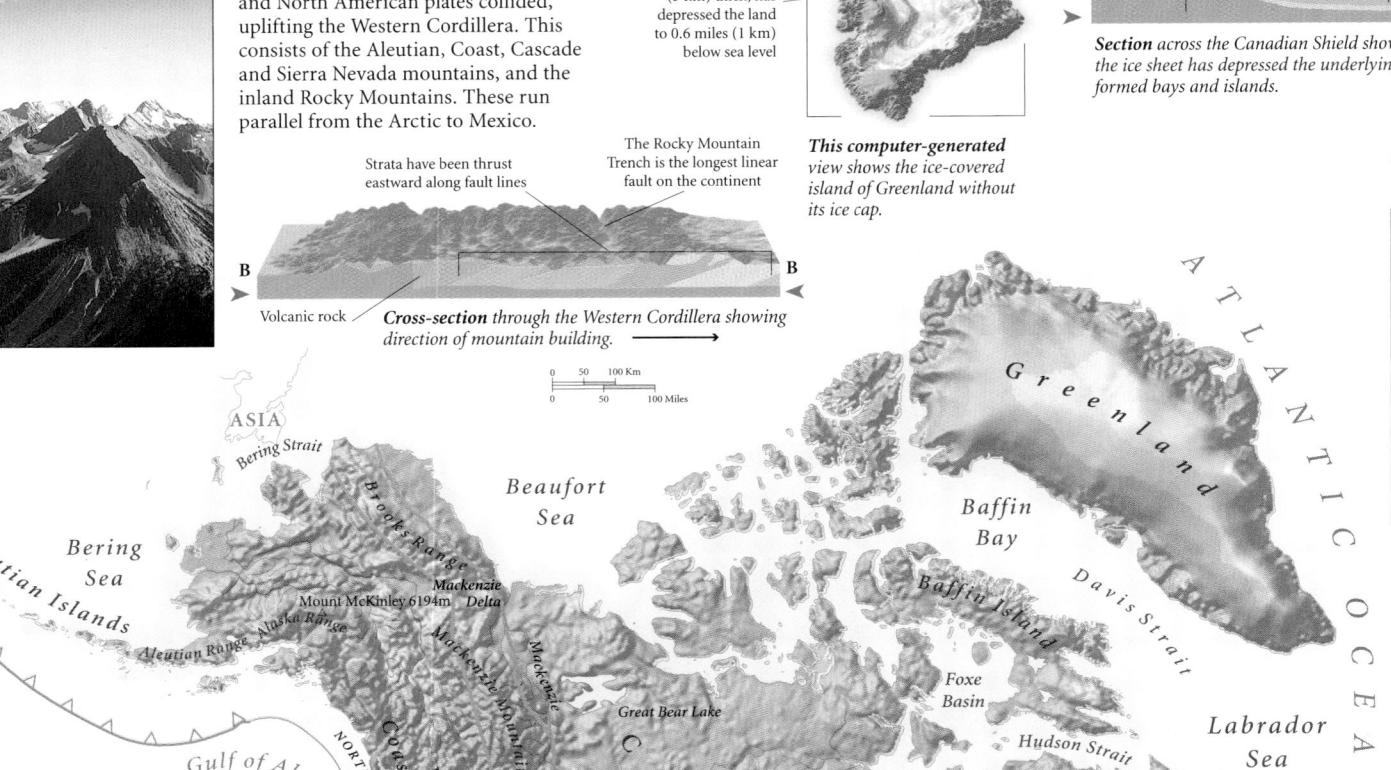

Map labels:

ASIA
Bering Strait
Aleutian Islands
Bering Sea
Gulf of Alaska
Beaufort Sea
Brooks Range
Mount McKinley 6194m
Mackenzie Delta
Aleutian Range Alaska Range
Mackenzie Mountains
Mackenzie
NORTH AMERICAN PLATE
PACIFIC PLATE
Coast Mountains
WESTERN
ROCKY MOUNTAINS
CORDILLERA
Great Bear Lake
Great Slave Lake
Lake Athabasca
Reindeer Lake
CANADIAN
CENTRAL LOWLANDS
GREAT PLAINS
SHIELD
Lake Winnipeg
Lake Manitoba
Hudson Bay
Foxe Basin
Hudson Strait
Baffin Island
Baffin Bay
Davis Strait
Greenland
ATLANTIC OCEAN
Labrador Sea
Labrador
Laurentian Highlands
Newfoundland
Lake Superior
Lake Huron
Lake Michigan
Great Lakes
Lake Ontario
Lake Erie
St Lawrence
Nova Scotia
Cape Cod
APPALACHIAN MOUNTAINS
APPALACHIANS
Mount Rainier 4392m
Mount St Helens 2549m
Cascade Range
Sierra Nevada
San Joaquin Valley
Great Basin
Great Salt Lake
San Andreas Fault
Coast Ranges
Death Valley 86m Mojave Desert
Grand Canyon
Colorado Plateau
Colorado
Sonoran Desert
Missouri
Arkansas
Ohio
Mississippi
GULF ATLANTIC COASTAL PLAIN
Rio Grande
Sierra Madre Occidental
Gulf of California
PACIFIC OCEAN
Lower California
Mississippi Delta
Gulf of Mexico
Citlaltépetl 5700m
Sierra Madre Oriental
Yucatán Peninsula
West Indies
NORTH AMERICAN PLATE
CARIBBEAN PLATE
Greater Antilles
Lesser Antilles
Caribbean Sea
Sierra Madre del Sur
COCOS PLATE
CARIBBEAN PLATE
Lago de Nicaragua
Isthmus of Panama
CARIBBEAN PLATE
SOUTH AMERICAN PLATE
SOUTH AMERICA

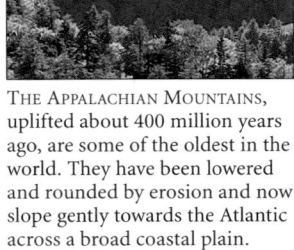
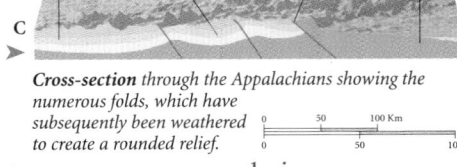

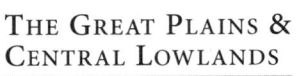

CLIMATE

NORTH AMERICA'S climate includes extremes ranging from freezing Arctic conditions in Alaska and Greenland, to desert in the southwest, and tropical conditions in southeastern Florida, the Caribbean and Central America. Central and southern regions are prone to severe storms including tornadoes and hurricanes.

'Tornado alley' in the Mississippi Valley suffers frequent tornadoes.

Climate
- ice cap
- tundra
- subarctic
- cool continental
- warm humid
- semi-arid
- arid
- humid equatorial
- tropical

- daily hours of sunshine, January
- daily hours of sunshine, July
- direction of hurricanes
- tornado zones

TEMPERATURE

Arctic Circle
60° N
40° N
Tropic of Cancer
20° N

Average January temperature

Average July temperature

Temperature
- below -30°C (-22°F)
- -30 to -20°C (-22 to -4°F)
- -20 to -10°C (-4 to 14°F)
- -10 to 0°C (14 to 32°F)
- 0 to 10°C (32 to 50°F)
- 10 to 20°C (50 to 68°F)
- 20 to 30°C (68 to 86°F)
- above 30°C (86 °F)

RAINFALL

Arctic Circle
60° N
40° N
Tropic of Cancer
20° N

Average January rainfall

Average July rainfall

Rainfall
- 0–25 mm (0–1 in)
- 25–50 mm (1–2 in)
- 50–100 mm (2–4 in)
- 100–200 mm (4–8 in)
- 200–300 mm (8–12 in)
- 300–400 mm (12–16 in)
- 400–500 mm (16–20 in)
- more than 500 mm (20 in)

Much of the southwest is semi-desert; receiving less than 12 inches (300 mm) of rainfall a year.

The lush, green mountains of the Lesser Antilles receive annual rainfalls of up to 360 inches (9000 mm).

(Map labels: Nome, Eismitte, Fairbanks, Resolute, Aklavik, Coppermine, Frobisher Bay, Haines Junction, Juneau, Happy Valley - Goose Bay, Torbay, Fort Vermillon, Churchill, Fort St John, Vancouver, Winnipeg, Montréal, Medicine Hat, Toronto, Boise, Sioux City, New York, Salt Lake City, Denver, San Francisco, Cape Hatteras, Las Vegas, Atlanta, Phoenix, Los Angeles, Little Rock, Houston, Miami, Guaymas, New Orleans, Nassau, Chihuahua, Santo Domingo, Fort-de-France, Mérida, Kingston, Acapulco, San Salvador, San José, Arctic Circle, Tropic of Cancer)

SHAPING THE CONTINENT

GLACIAL PROCESSES affect much of northern Canada, Greenland and the Western Cordillera. Along the western coast of North America, Central America and the Caribbean, underlying plates moving together lead to earthquakes and volcanic eruptions. The vast river systems, fed by mountain streams, constantly erode and deposit material along their paths.

VOLCANIC ACTIVITY

[1] Mount St Helens volcano *(right)* in the Cascade Range erupted violently in May 1980, killing 57 people and levelling large areas of forest. The lateral blast filled a valley for 15 miles (25 km) with debris.

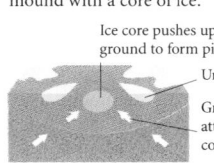

Molten rock at volcano's core
Vertical eruption
Lateral explosion increases extent of damage
Landslide fills valley

VOLCANIC ACTIVITY: ERUPTION OF MOUNT ST HELENS

PERIGLACIATION

[2] The ground in the far north is nearly always frozen: the surface thaws only in summer. This freeze-thaw process produces features such as pingos *(left)*; formed by the freezing of groundwater. With each successive winter ice accumulates producing a mound with a core of ice.

Ice core pushes up ground to form pingo
Unfrozen lake
Groundwater attracted to ice core

PERIGLACIATION: FORMATION OF A PINGO IN THE MACKENZIE DELTA

THE EVOLVING LANDSCAPE

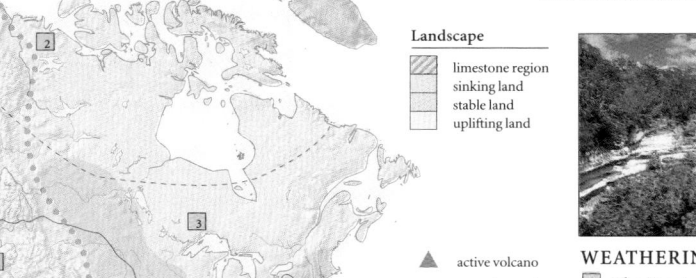

Landscape
- limestone region
- sinking land
- stable land
- uplifting land

- active volcano
- area of tectonic activity
- limit of permafrost
- maximum limit of glaciation
- ocean current

POST-GLACIAL LAKES

[3] A chain of lakes from Great Bear Lake to the Great Lakes *(above)* was created as the ice retreated northwards. Glaciers scoured hollows in the softer lowland rock. Glacial deposits at the lip of the hollows, and ridges of harder rock, trapped water to form lakes.

Retreating glacier
Ice-scoured hollow filled with glacial meltwater to form a lake
Harder rock creates a barrier between lakes
Softer lowland rock

POST-GLACIAL LAKES: FORMATION OF THE GREAT LAKES

SEISMIC ACTIVITY

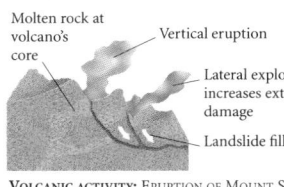

[5] The San Andreas Fault *(above)* places much of the North America's west coast under constant threat from earthquakes. It is caused by the Pacific Plate grinding past the North American Plate at a faster rate, though in the same direction.

Pacific Plate
San Andreas Fault
Fault is caused by faster movement of Pacific Plate
North American Plate

SEISMIC ACTIVITY: ACTION OF THE SAN ANDREAS FAULT

RIVER EROSION

[6] The Grand Canyon *(above)* in the Colorado Plateau was created by the downward erosion of the Colorado River, combined with the gradual uplift of the plateau, over the past 30 million years. The contours of the canyon formed as the softer rock layers eroded into gentle slopes, and the hard rock layers into cliffs. The depth varies from 3855–6560 ft (1175–2000 m).

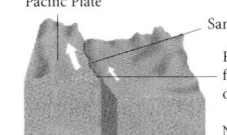

Soft rock is easily eroded into gentle slopes
Hard rock resists erosion
Colorado River cuts down through rock

RIVER EROSION: FORMATION OF THE GRAND CANYON

WEATHERING

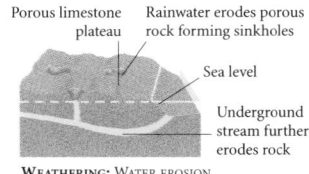

[4] The Yucatan Peninsula is a vast, flat limestone plateau in southern Mexico. Weathering action from both rainwater and underground streams has enlarged fractures in the rock to form caves and hollows, called sinkholes *(above)*.

Porous limestone plateau
Rainwater erodes porous rock forming sinkholes
Sea level
Underground stream further erodes rock

WEATHERING: WATER EROSION ON THE YUCATAN PENINSULA

POLITICAL NORTH AMERICA

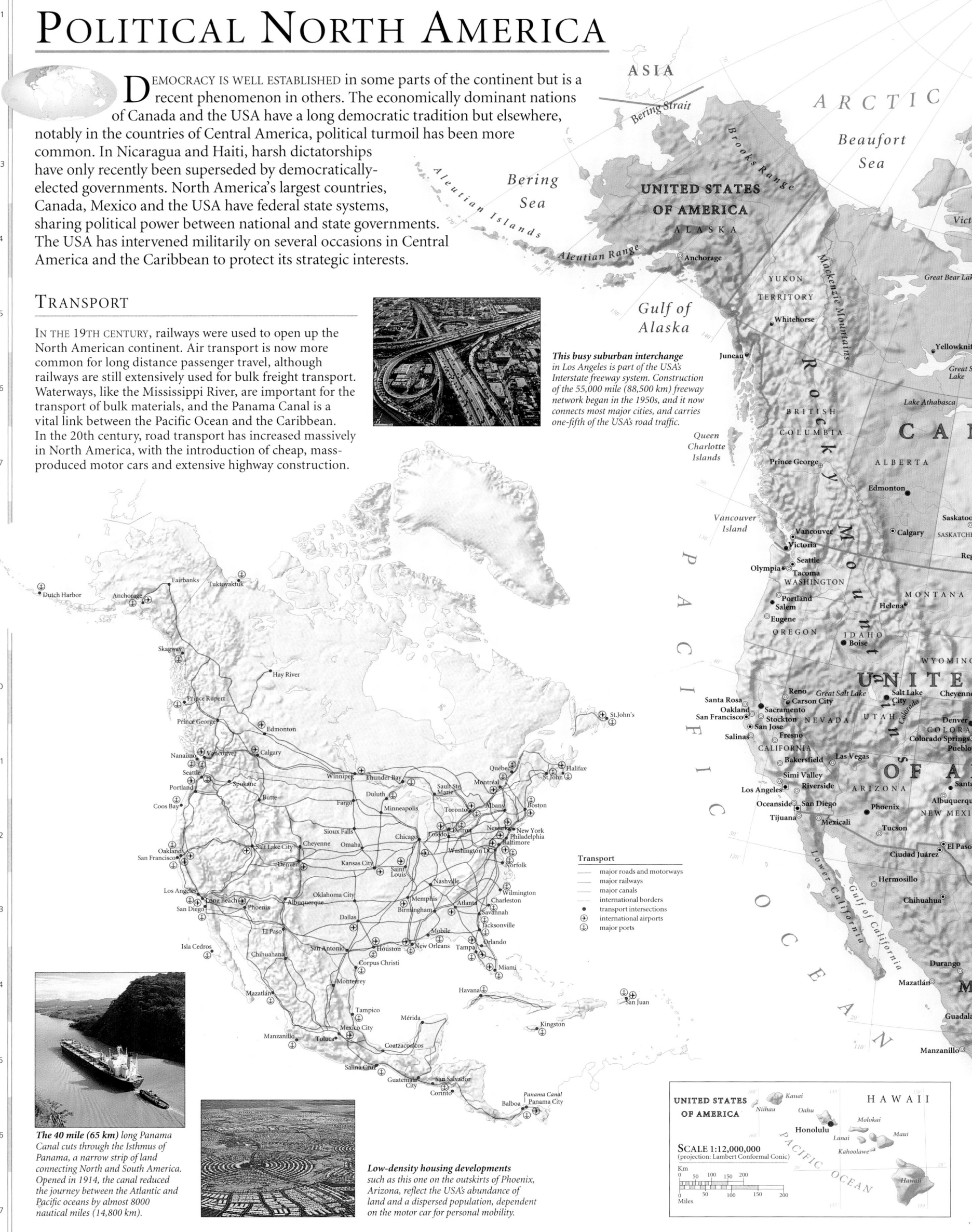

DEMOCRACY IS WELL ESTABLISHED in some parts of the continent but is a recent phenomenon in others. The economically dominant nations of Canada and the USA have a long democratic tradition but elsewhere, notably in the countries of Central America, political turmoil has been more common. In Nicaragua and Haiti, harsh dictatorships have only recently been superseded by democratically-elected governments. North America's largest countries, Canada, Mexico and the USA have federal state systems, sharing political power between national and state governments. The USA has intervened militarily on several occasions in Central America and the Caribbean to protect its strategic interests.

TRANSPORT

IN THE 19TH CENTURY, railways were used to open up the North American continent. Air transport is now more common for long distance passenger travel, although railways are still extensively used for bulk freight transport. Waterways, like the Mississippi River, are important for the transport of bulk materials, and the Panama Canal is a vital link between the Pacific Ocean and the Caribbean. In the 20th century, road transport has increased massively in North America, with the introduction of cheap, mass-produced motor cars and extensive highway construction.

This busy suburban interchange in Los Angeles is part of the USA's Interstate freeway system. Construction of the 55,000 mile (88,500 km) freeway network began in the 1950s, and it now connects most major cities, and carries one-fifth of the USA's road traffic.

The 40 mile (65 km) long Panama Canal cuts through the Isthmus of Panama, a narrow strip of land connecting North and South America. Opened in 1914, the canal reduced the journey between the Atlantic and Pacific oceans by almost 8000 nautical miles (14,800 km).

Low-density housing developments such as this one on the outskirts of Phoenix, Arizona, reflect the USA's abundance of land and a dispersed population, dependent on the motor car for personal mobility.

Transport
— major roads and motorways
— major railways
— major canals
---- international borders
• transport intersections
⊕ international airports
⊕ major ports

UNITED STATES OF AMERICA
SCALE 1:12,000,000
(projection: Lambert Conformal Conic)

HAWAII

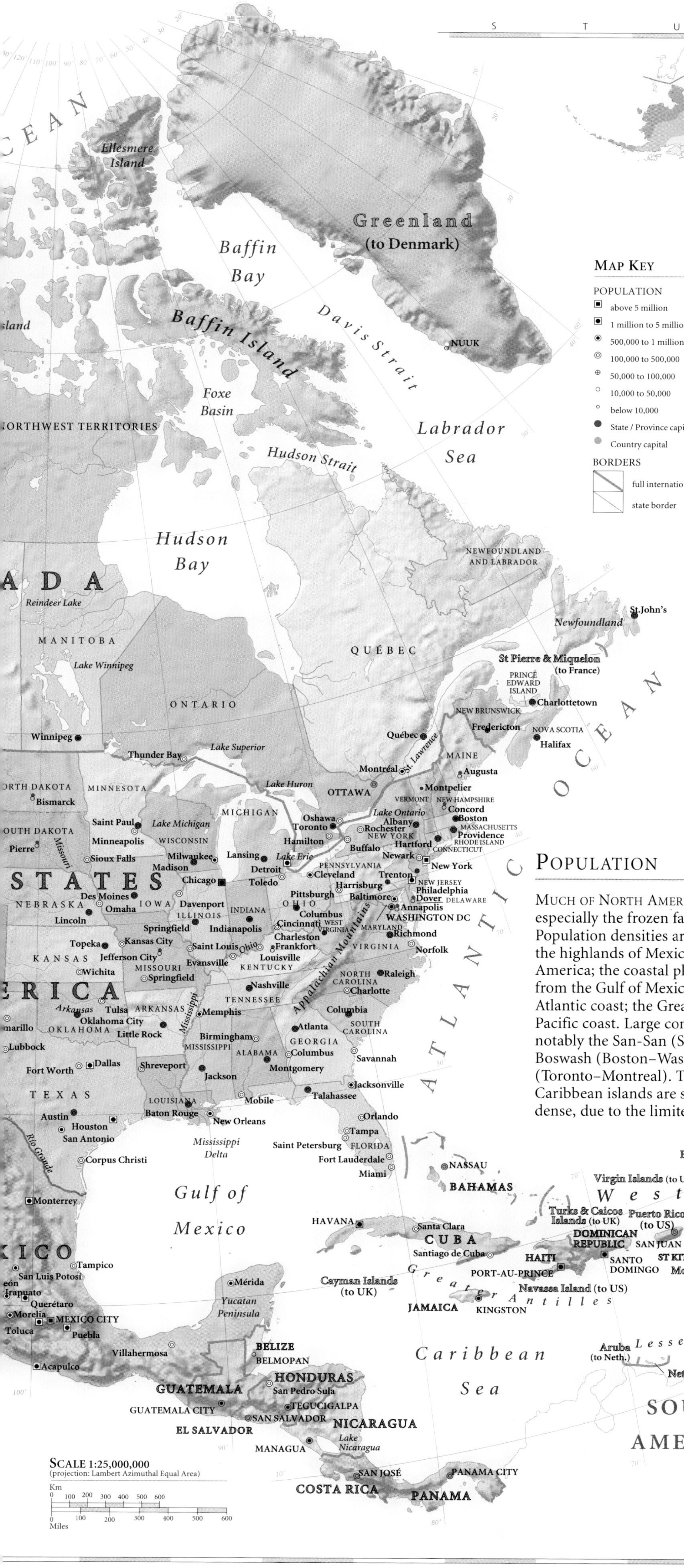
Map Key
POPULATION
above 5 million
1 million to 5 million
500,000 to 1 million
100,000 to 500,000
50,000 to 100,000
10,000 to 50,000
below 10,000
State / Province capital
Country capital
BORDERS
full international border
state border
Greenland
(to Denmark)
Ellesmere Island
Baffin Bay
Baffin Island
Davis Strait
NUUK
Foxe Basin
Labrador Sea
Hudson Strait
Hudson Bay
NORTHWEST TERRITORIES
NEWFOUNDLAND AND LABRADOR
Newfoundland
St John's
QUÉBEC
MANITOBA
Lake Winnipeg
Reindeer Lake
ONTARIO
Winnipeg
Thunder Bay
Lake Superior
St Pierre & Miquelon (to France)
PRINCE EDWARD ISLAND
Charlottetown
NEW BRUNSWICK
Fredericton
NOVA SCOTIA
Halifax
Québec
St. Lawrence
Montréal
OTTAWA
MAINE
Augusta
Montpelier
VERMONT
NEW HAMPSHIRE
Concord
Boston
MASSACHUSETTS
Providence
RHODE ISLAND
CONNECTICUT
Hartford
Lake Ontario
Albany
Rochester
NEW YORK
Buffalo
Oshawa
Toronto
Hamilton
Lake Huron
MICHIGAN
Lake Michigan
Lansing
Detroit
Lake Erie
Toledo
Cleveland
PENNSYLVANIA
Harrisburg
Pittsburgh
Newark
New York
Trenton
NEW JERSEY
Philadelphia
Dover
DELAWARE
Baltimore
Annapolis
WASHINGTON DC
MARYLAND
WEST VIRGINIA
Richmond
VIRGINIA
Norfolk
ATLANTIC OCEAN
NORTH DAKOTA
Bismarck
MINNESOTA
Saint Paul
Minneapolis
SOUTH DAKOTA
Pierre
Sioux Falls
WISCONSIN
Milwaukee
Madison
Chicago
Missouri
STATES
NEBRASKA
Des Moines
Omaha
Lincoln
IOWA
Davenport
ILLINOIS
INDIANA
OHIO
Columbus
Springfield
Indianapolis
Cincinnati
Charleston
Frankfort
Topeka
Kansas City
KANSAS
Jefferson City
Saint Louis
Ohio
Louisville
KENTUCKY
Evansville
MISSOURI
Wichita
Springfield
NORTH CAROLINA
Raleigh
Charlotte
Appalachian Mountains
Nashville
TENNESSEE
ERICA
Arkansas
Tulsa
ARKANSAS
Memphis
Mississippi
Oklahoma City
OKLAHOMA
Little Rock
Amarillo
Lubbock
Columbia
SOUTH CAROLINA
Atlanta
Birmingham
MISSISSIPPI
GEORGIA
ALABAMA
Columbus
Savannah
Montgomery
Dallas
Fort Worth
Shreveport
Jackson
TEXAS
Jacksonville
LOUISIANA
Baton Rouge
Mobile
Talahassee
Austin
Houston
San Antonio
New Orleans
Orlando
Tampa
Saint Petersburg
FLORIDA
Fort Lauderdale
Miami
Mississippi Delta
Rio Grande
Corpus Christi
NASSAU
BAHAMAS
Gulf of Mexico
Monterrey
HAVANA
Santa Clara
CUBA
Santiago de Cuba
British Virgin Islands (to UK)
Virgin Islands (to US)
Anguilla (to UK)
West Indies
Turks & Caicos Islands (to UK)
Puerto Rico (to US)
ANTIGUA & BARBUDA
DOMINICAN REPUBLIC
SAN JUAN
Guadeloupe (to France)
HAITI
SANTO DOMINGO
ST KITTS & NEVIS
DOMINICA
PORT-AU-PRINCE
Montserrat (to UK)
Martinique (to France)
ST LUCIA
BARBADOS
Cayman Islands (to UK)
Greater Antilles
Navassa Island (to US)
ST VINCENT & THE GRENADINES
GRENADA
JAMAICA
KINGSTON
Lesser Antilles
TRINIDAD & TOBAGO
PORT-OF-SPAIN
Aruba (to Neth.)
Netherlands Antilles (to Neth.)
XICO
Tampico
San Luis Potosí
León
Irapuato
Querétaro
Morelia
MEXICO CITY
Toluca
Puebla
Mérida
Yucatan Peninsula
Villahermosa
Acapulco
BELIZE
BELMOPAN
HONDURAS
San Pedro Sula
GUATEMALA
GUATEMALA CITY
TEGUCIGALPA
SAN SALVADOR
EL SALVADOR
NICARAGUA
Lake Nicaragua
MANAGUA
SAN JOSÉ
COSTA RICA
PANAMA CITY
PANAMA
Caribbean Sea
SOUTH AMERICA
SCALE 1:25,000,000
(projection: Lambert Azimuthal Equal Area)
Km
0 100 200 300 400 500 600
0 100 200 300 400 500 600
Miles

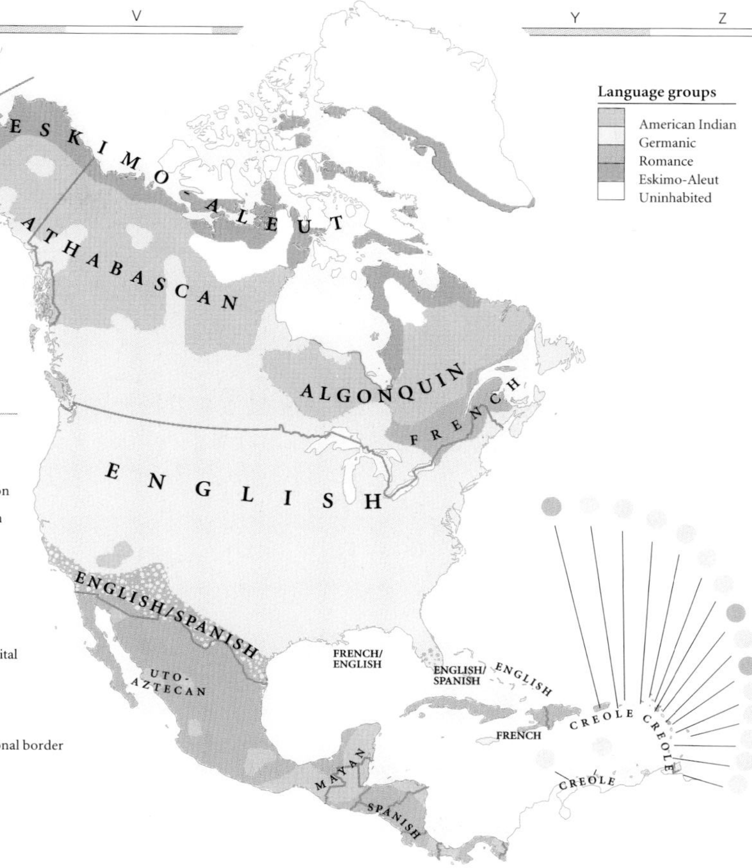
Language groups
American Indian
Germanic
Romance
Eskimo-Aleut
Uninhabited
ESKIMO-ALEUT
ATHABASCAN
ALGONQUIN
FRENCH
ENGLISH
ENGLISH/SPANISH
UTO-AZTECAN
FRENCH/ENGLISH
ENGLISH/SPANISH
ENGLISH
FRENCH
CREOLE
CREOLE
CREOLE
MAYAN
SPANISH

Land in northern Canada is being set aside for Inuit reserves, allowing the Inuit and other Native American groups to maintain their traditional practices and culture.

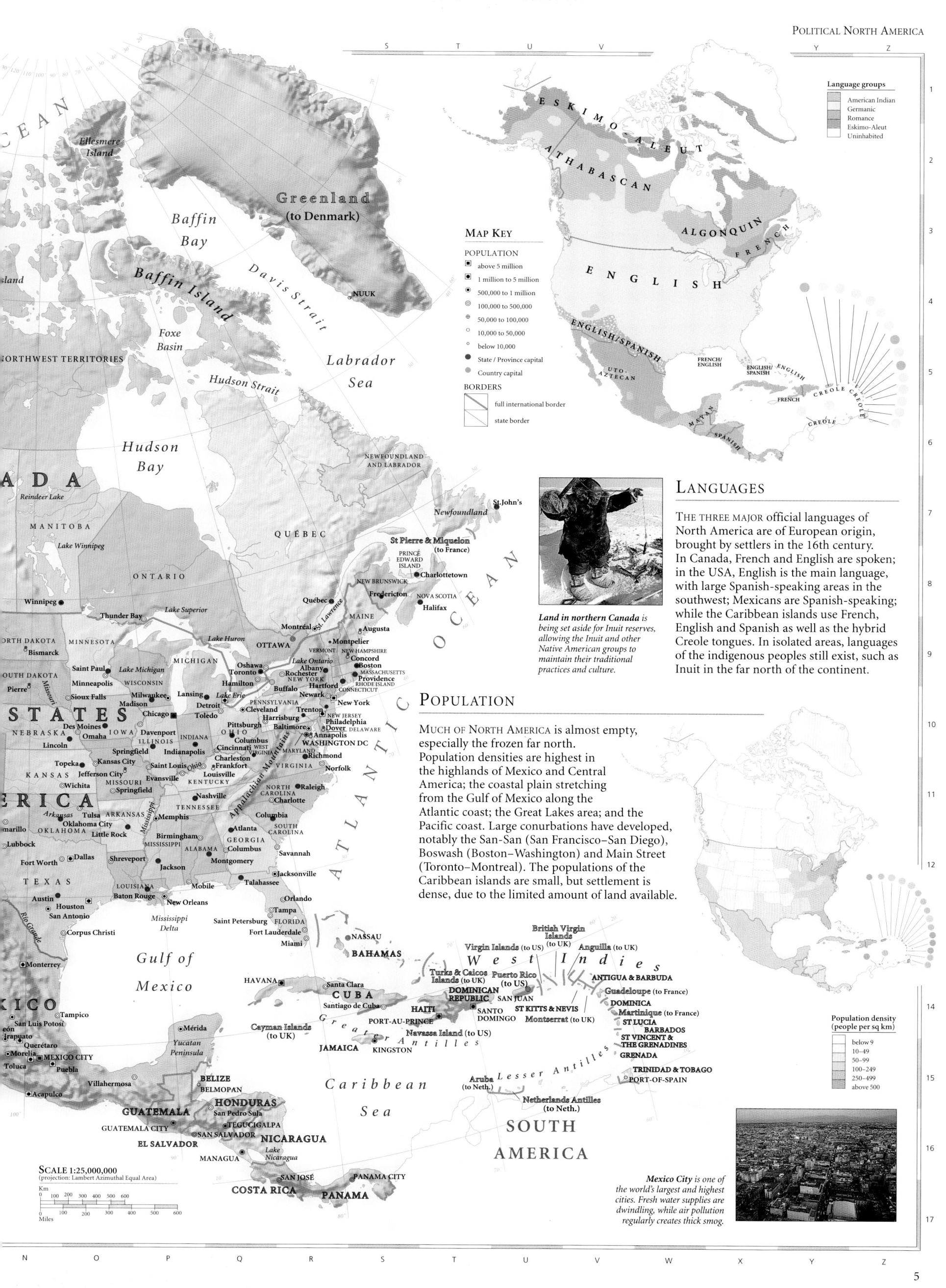

Languages

The three major official languages of North America are of European origin, brought by settlers in the 16th century. In Canada, French and English are spoken; in the USA, English is the main language, with large Spanish-speaking areas in the southwest; Mexicans are Spanish-speaking; while the Caribbean islands use French, English and Spanish as well as the hybrid Creole tongues. In isolated areas, languages of the indigenous peoples still exist, such as Inuit in the far north of the continent.

Population

Much of North America is almost empty, especially the frozen far north. Population densities are highest in the highlands of Mexico and Central America; the coastal plain stretching from the Gulf of Mexico along the Atlantic coast; the Great Lakes area; and the Pacific coast. Large conurbations have developed, notably the San-San (San Francisco–San Diego), Boswash (Boston–Washington) and Main Street (Toronto–Montreal). The populations of the Caribbean islands are small, but settlement is dense, due to the limited amount of land available.

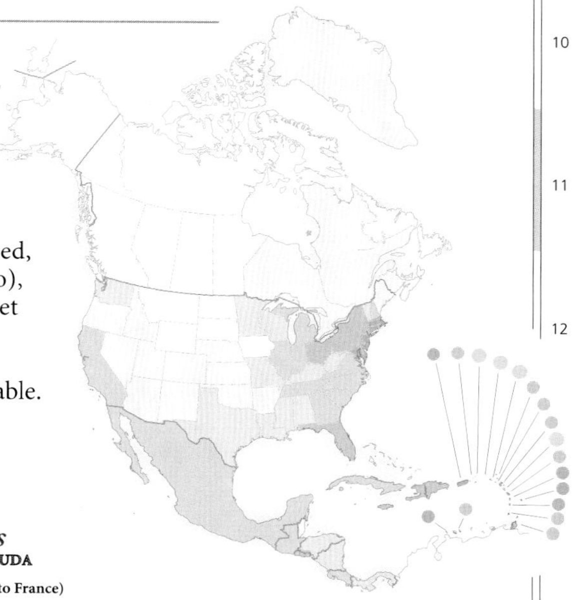
Population density (people per sq km)
below 9
10–49
50–99
100–249
250–499
above 500

Mexico City is one of the world's largest and highest cities. Fresh water supplies are dwindling, while air pollution regularly creates thick smog.

NORTH AMERICAN RESOURCES

THE TWO NORTHERN COUNTRIES of Canada and the USA are richly endowed with natural resources which have helped to fuel economic development. The USA is the world's largest economy, although today it is facing stiff competition from the Far East. Mexico has relied on oil revenues but there are hopes that the North American Free Trade Agreement (NAFTA), will encourage trade growth with Canada and the USA. The poorer countries of Central America and the Caribbean depend largely on cash crops and tourism.

INDUSTRY

THE MODERN, INDUSTRIALIZED economies of the USA and Canada contrast sharply with those of Mexico, Central America and the Caribbean. Manufacturing is especially important in the USA; vehicle production is concentrated around the Great Lakes, while electronic and hi-tech industries are increasingly found in the western and southern states. Mexico depends on oil exports and assembly work, taking advantage of cheap labour. Many Central American and Caribbean countries rely heavily on agricultural exports.

South of San Francisco, 'Silicon Valley' is both a national and international centre for hi-tech industries, electronic industries and research institutions.

Multinational companies rely on cheap labour and tax benefits to assemble vehicles in Mexican factories.

STANDARD OF LIVING

THE USA AND CANADA have one of the highest overall standards of living in the world. However, many people still live in poverty, especially in inner city ghettos and some rural areas. Central America and the Caribbean are markedly poorer than their wealthier northern neighbours. Haiti is the poorest country in the western hemisphere.

After its purchase from Russia in 1867, Alaska's frozen lands were largely ignored by the USA. Oil reserves similar in magnitude to those in eastern Texas were discovered in Prudhoe Bay, Alaska in 1968. Freezing temperatures and a fragile environment hamper oil extraction.

Standard of Living
(UN Human Development Index)

high

low

Fish such as cod, flounder and plaice are caught in the Grand Banks, off the Newfoundland coast, and processed in many North Atlantic coastal settlements.

The twin towers of the World Trade Center dominate the Manhattan skyline. New York is one of the world's leading trade and finance centres.

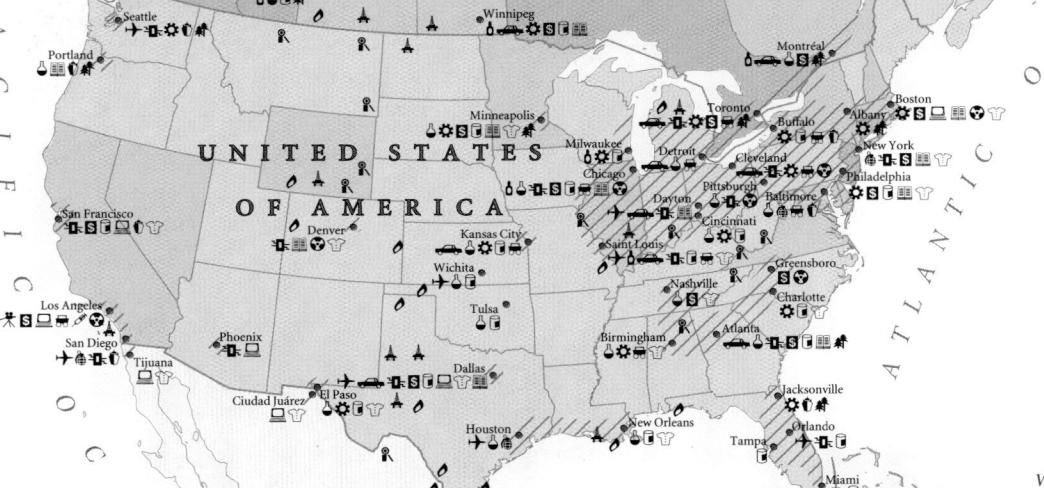

Industry

✈ aerospace	🏭 printing & publishing
🍺 brewing	⚙ research & development
🚗 car/vehicle manufacture	⚓ shipbuilding
🧪 chemicals	sugar processing
🛡 defence	⊺ textiles
📺 electronics	timber processing
⚙ engineering	tobacco processing
film industry	
finance	coal
food processing	oil
hi-tech industry	gas
iron & steel	industrial cities
pharmaceuticals	major industrial areas

GNP per capita (US$)

- 0–1999
- 2000–4999
- 5000–9999
- 10,000–19,999
- 20,000–24,999
- 25,000+

Map labels: RUSS. FED., Bering Strait, ARCTIC OCEAN, Beaufort Sea, Prudhoe Bay, Greenland (to Denmark), Baffin Bay, Bering Sea, USA, Gulf of Alaska, Labrador Sea, Hudson Strait, Hudson Bay, CANADA, Vancouver, Calgary, Seattle, Winnipeg, Montréal, Portland, Boston, Minneapolis, Toronto, Buffalo, Albany, Milwaukee, Detroit, Cleveland, New York, UNITED STATES, Chicago, Pittsburgh, Philadelphia, OF AMERICA, Dayton, Baltimore, San Francisco, Denver, Cincinnati, St Louis, Kansas City, Greensboro, Wichita, Nashville, Charlotte, Los Angeles, Tulsa, Atlanta, San Diego, Phoenix, Birmingham, Tijuana, Dallas, Ciudad Juárez, El Paso, Jacksonville, Houston, New Orleans, Orlando, Tampa, PACIFIC OCEAN, Monterrey, Gulf of Mexico, Miami, BAHAMAS, Havana, CUBA, West Indies, Turks & Caicos Islands (to UK), British Virgin Islands (to UK), Virgin Islands (to US), Anguilla (to UK), ST KITTS & NEVIS, ANTIGUA & BARBUDA, Montserrat (to UK), Guadeloupe (to France), Puerto Rico (to US), San Juan, Cayman Islands (to UK), JAMAICA, HAITI, DOMINICAN REPUBLIC, Port-au-Prince, Santo Domingo, DOMINICA, Martinique (to France), ST LUCIA, BARBADOS, ST VINCENT & THE GRENADINES, GRENADA, TRINIDAD & TOBAGO, Port-of-Spain, Greater Antilles, Lesser Antilles, Navassa Island (to US), Aruba (to Neth.), Netherlands Antilles (to Neth.), Caribbean Sea, MEXICO, Guadalajara, Mexico City, BELIZE, GUATEMALA, Guatemala City, HONDURAS, Tegucigalpa, EL SALVADOR, San Salvador, NICARAGUA, Managua, COSTA RICA, San José, PANAMA, Panama City, COLOMBIA, VENEZUELA, ATLANTIC OCEAN

ENVIRONMENTAL ISSUES

MANY FRAGILE ENVIRONMENTS ARE UNDER THREAT throughout the region. In Haiti, all the primary rainforest has been destroyed, while air pollution from factories and cars in Mexico City is amongst the worst in the world. Elsewhere, industry and mining pose threats, particularly in the delicate arctic environment of Alaska where oil spills have polluted coastlines and decimated fish stocks.

Environmental Issues

- national parks
- acid rain
- tropical forest
- forest destroyed
- desert
- desertification
- polluted rivers
- radioactive contamination
- marine pollution
- heavy marine pollution
- poor urban air quality

Wild bison graze in Yellowstone National Park, the world's first national park. Designated in 1870, geothermal springs and boiling mud are among its natural spectacles, making it a major tourist attraction.

MINERAL RESOURCES

FOSSIL FUELS ARE EXPLOITED in considerable quantities throughout the continent. Coal mining in the Appalachians is declining but vast open pits exist further west in Wyoming. Oil and natural gas are found in Alaska, Texas, the Gulf of Mexico, and the Canadian West. Canada has large quantities of nickel, while Jamaica has considerable deposits of bauxite, and Mexico has large reserves of silver.

Mineral Resources

- oil field
- gas field
- coal field
- bauxite
- copper
- gold
- iron
- lead
- nickel
- phosphates
- silver
- uranium

In addition to fossil fuels, North America is also rich in exploitable metallic ores. This vast, mile-deep (1.6 km) pit is a copper mine in New Mexico.

In agriculturally marginal areas where the soil is either too poor, or the climate too dry for crops, cattle ranching proliferates – especially in Mexico and the western reaches of the Great Plains.

USING THE LAND AND SEA

ABUNDANT LAND AND FERTILE SOILS stretch from the Canadian prairies to Texas creating North America's agricultural heartland. Cereals and cattle ranching form the basis of the farming economy, with corn and soya beans also important. Fruit and vegetables are grown in California using irrigation, while Florida is a leading producer of citrus fruits. Caribbean and Central American countries depend on cash crops such as bananas, coffee and sugar cane, often grown on large plantations. This reliance on a single crop can leave these countries vulnerable to fluctuating world crop prices.

Sugar cane is Cuba's main agricultural crop, and is grown and processed throughout the Caribbean. Fermented sugar is used to make rum.

The Great Plains support large-scale arable farming throughout central North America. Corn is grown in a belt south and west of the Great Lakes, while further west where the climate is drier, wheat is grown.

Using the Land and Sea

- cropland
- forest
- ice cap
- mountain region
- pasture
- tundra
- wetland
- desert
- major conurbations
- cattle
- goats
- pigs
- poultry
- reindeer
- sheep
- bananas
- citrus fruits
- coffee
- corn (maize)
- cotton
- fishing
- fruit
- maple syrup
- peanuts
- rice
- shellfish
- soya beans
- sugar cane
- timber
- tobacco
- vineyards
- wheat

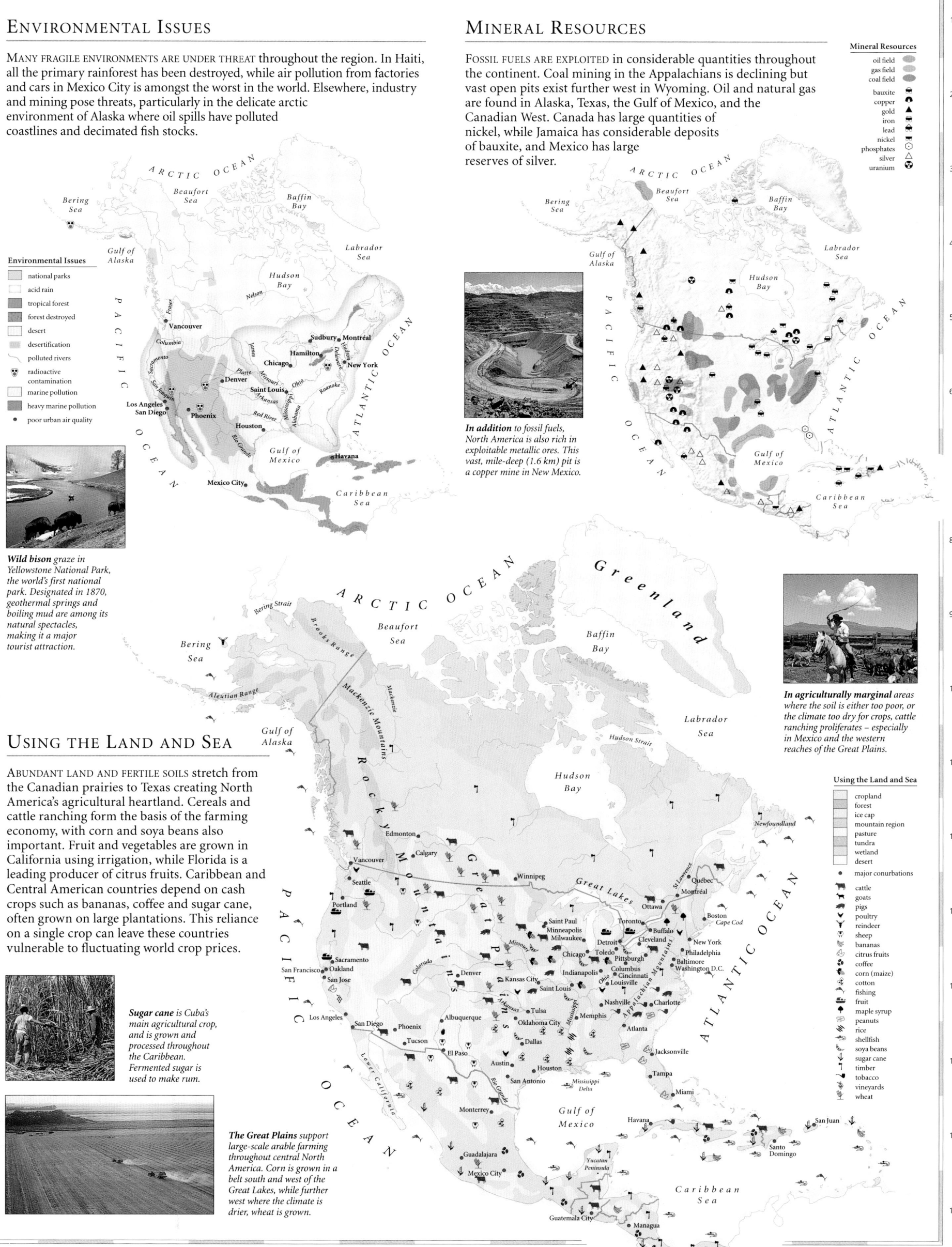

CANADA: WESTERN PROVINCES

Alberta, British Columbia, Manitoba, Saskatchewan, Yukon Territory

THE MOUNTAINS OF THE WEST COAST, incorporating British Columbia and the Yukon Territory, descend into the vast, flat prairies of Alberta, Saskatchewan and Manitoba. The empty lands and fertile soils of the prairie provinces attracted migrants, and the descendants of early European immigrants still make up a large proportion of the population. The mechanization of agriculture has reduced the need for labour, and rural population densities remain low. The majority of the people live within 100 miles (160 km) of the southern Canada–USA border, and in British Columbia, one of the leading Canadian provinces in terms of economic wealth. The Yukon Territory, in the far north, remains a relatively unspoilt wilderness, containing large, untapped mineral reserves. This province has a significant population of Native Americans, many of whom maintain a traditional lifestyle.

USING THE LAND AND SEA

WHEAT FARMING IS THE ECONOMIC MAINSTAY of Alberta, Manitoba and Saskatchewan, which contain 82% of farmland in Canada. Cattle are also raised on the prairies. Forestry and fishing are the most prominent resource-based industries in British Columbia. Despite the mountainous terrain, fruit and specialized grains can be grown in the Okanagan and Fraser valleys.

Land use and agricultural distribution

- cattle
- cereals
- fishing
- fruit
- timber
- major towns

pasture
cropland
forest
wetland
barren
tundra

THE URBAN/RURAL POPULATION DIVIDE

77% urban   23% rural

0 10 20 30 40 50 60 70 80 90 100

POPULATION DENSITY	TOTAL LAND AREA
6 people per sq mile (2 people per sq km)	1,224,449 sq miles (3,172,150 sq km)

Large, highly-mechanized and often very specialized farms, requiring huge investment but little labour, characterize modern farming in the prairies.

TRANSPORT AND INDUSTRY

THE WESTERN PROVINCES contain a wealth of mineral resources. Alberta holds the bulk of Canada's fossil fuels; the other provinces contain reserves of metallic ores, such as zinc, lead and silver. Isolation from markets has slowed the development of manufacturing, restricting it to the large cities like Vancouver, Winnipeg and Calgary. Hydro-electric power is widely exploited, although there is increasing concern about potential ecological damage.

THE TRANSPORT NETWORK

82,438 miles (135,145 km)

6459 miles (10,401 km)

10,811 miles (17,410 km)

None

The transport network of the western provinces is dominated by east–west routes that weave through mountain passes and spread across the plains. Access to some northern areas is restricted to air travel.

Major industry and infrastructure

- aerospace
- chemicals
- coal
- engineering
- food processing
- hydro-electric power
- mining
- oil & gas
- timber processing
- major towns
- international airports
- major roads
- major industrial areas

The Fraser River valley is a major area of settlement in British Columbia. Railways cross the Rocky Mountains via this valley.

Established in 1907, Jasper National Park lies in the heart of the Rocky Mountains. It is noted for its spectacular alpine scenery and contains part of the large Columbia Icefield.

Much of the Yukon Territory is uninhabited tundra. Industry is based on the extraction of mineral resources, and to a lesser extent, on the scattered forests of the south.

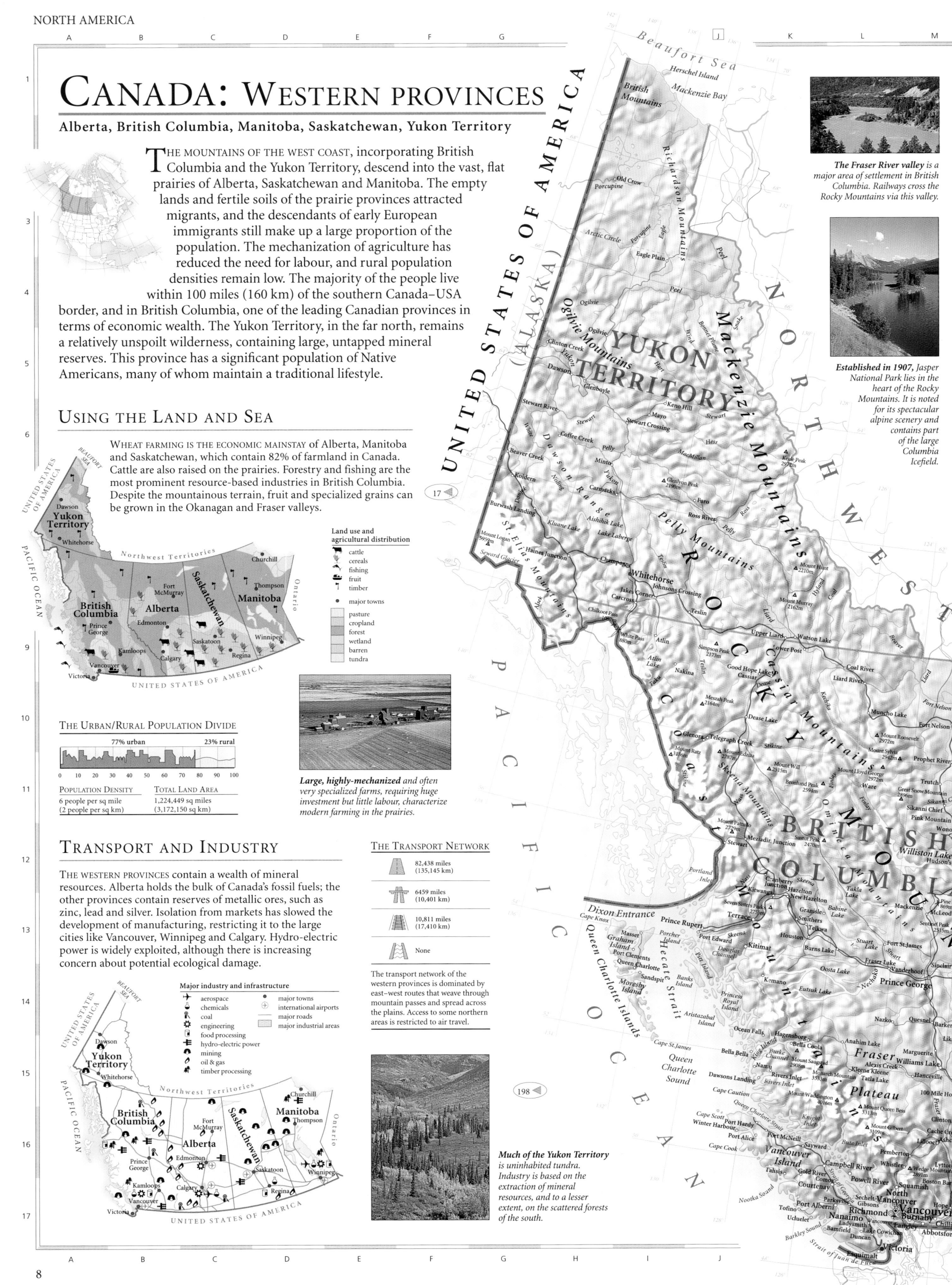

N O P Q R S T U V W X Y

THE LANDSCAPE

THE MASSIVE ROCKY MOUNTAINS form a continental divide between rivers flowing eastward and westward. East of the mountains, stretching from the Arctic Circle south into the USA, lie the interior plains. Covered with glacial deposits from the last Ice Age, these are interspersed with hilly regions and long, steep escarpments.

MAP KEY

POPULATION

◉ 500,000 to 1 million
◎ 100,000 to 500,000
⊕ 50,000 to 100,000
○ 10,000 to 50,000
○ below 10,000

ELEVATION

6000m / 19,686ft
4000m / 13,124ft
3000m / 9843ft
2000m / 6562ft
1000m / 3281ft
500m / 1640ft
250m / 820ft
100m / 328ft
sea level

SCALE 1:7,500,000
(projection: Lambert Conformal Conic)

Km
0 25 50 100 150 200 250

Miles
0 25 50 100 150 200 250

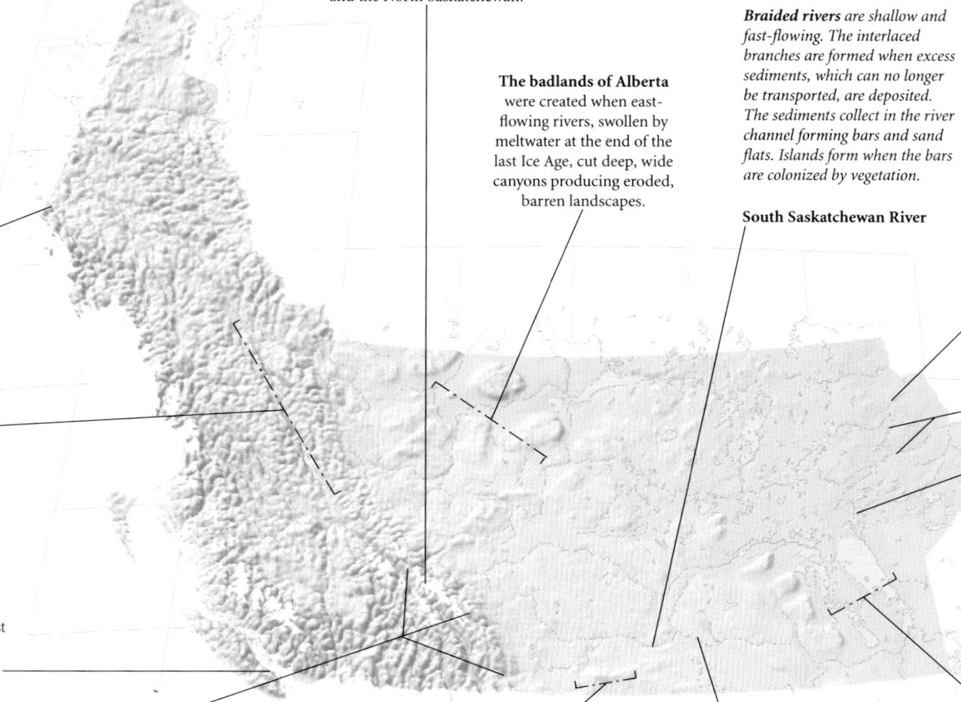

Mount Logan rises 19,551 ft (5959 m). It is the highest peak in Canada.

The Rocky Mountain Trench is the longest linear fault in the world. It has formed a straight, flat-bottomed valley between 2–9 miles (4–15 km) wide, and up to 3280 ft (1000 m) deep.

Hundreds of islands dot the fjord-indented coast of British Columbia; the largest is Vancouver Island.

Three major passes cut through the Rocky Mountains: Yellowhead, Kicking Horse and Crowsnest. They are all used as transport routes through the mountains.

The Cypress Hills rise to 4806 ft (1465 m) above the surrounding plain. Having escaped the last glaciation they contain unique plant and animal life. The silvery lupine, bunchberry and lodgepole pine all grow in the cool, moist climate of the hills.

The Columbia Icefield in the Rocky Mountains is the source of two major rivers, the Athabasca and the North Saskatchewan.

The badlands of Alberta were created when east-flowing rivers, swollen by meltwater at the end of the last Ice Age, cut deep, wide canyons producing eroded, barren landscapes.

South Saskatchewan River

Vegetated island
River flow is diverted by deposited sediments

Bar
Sand flat

Braided rivers are shallow and fast-flowing. The interlaced branches are formed when excess sediments, which can no longer be transported, are deposited. The sediments collect in the river channel forming bars and sand flats. Islands form when the bars are colonized by vegetation.

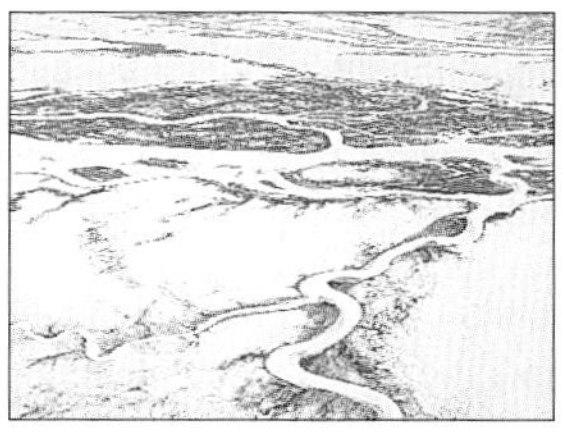

Across the tundra of northern Manitoba, widespread permafrost inhibits water from permeating the soil. This causes rivers like the Churchill to flow in many channels, which can be frozen for up to six months during the winter.

The Nelson and Churchill rivers drain northward across the Canadian Shield to Hudson Bay. The shield covers three-fifths of Saskatchewan.

Setting Lake

Ancient granite outcrops, part of the Canadian Shield, rise above the surface of Setting Lake, which was initially formed by meltwater from the last Ice Age.

The Alberta and Saskatchewan plains bear strong testament to past glaciations. The Assiniboine, Saskatchewan and Qu'Appelle rivers occupy flat-bottomed, steep-sided valleys eroded during the last Ice Age by glacial meltwater.

The lowlands of Manitoba are a basin that once held the vast post-glacial Lake Agassiz, remnants of which include Lake Winnipeg, Lake Winnipegosis and Lake Manitoba.

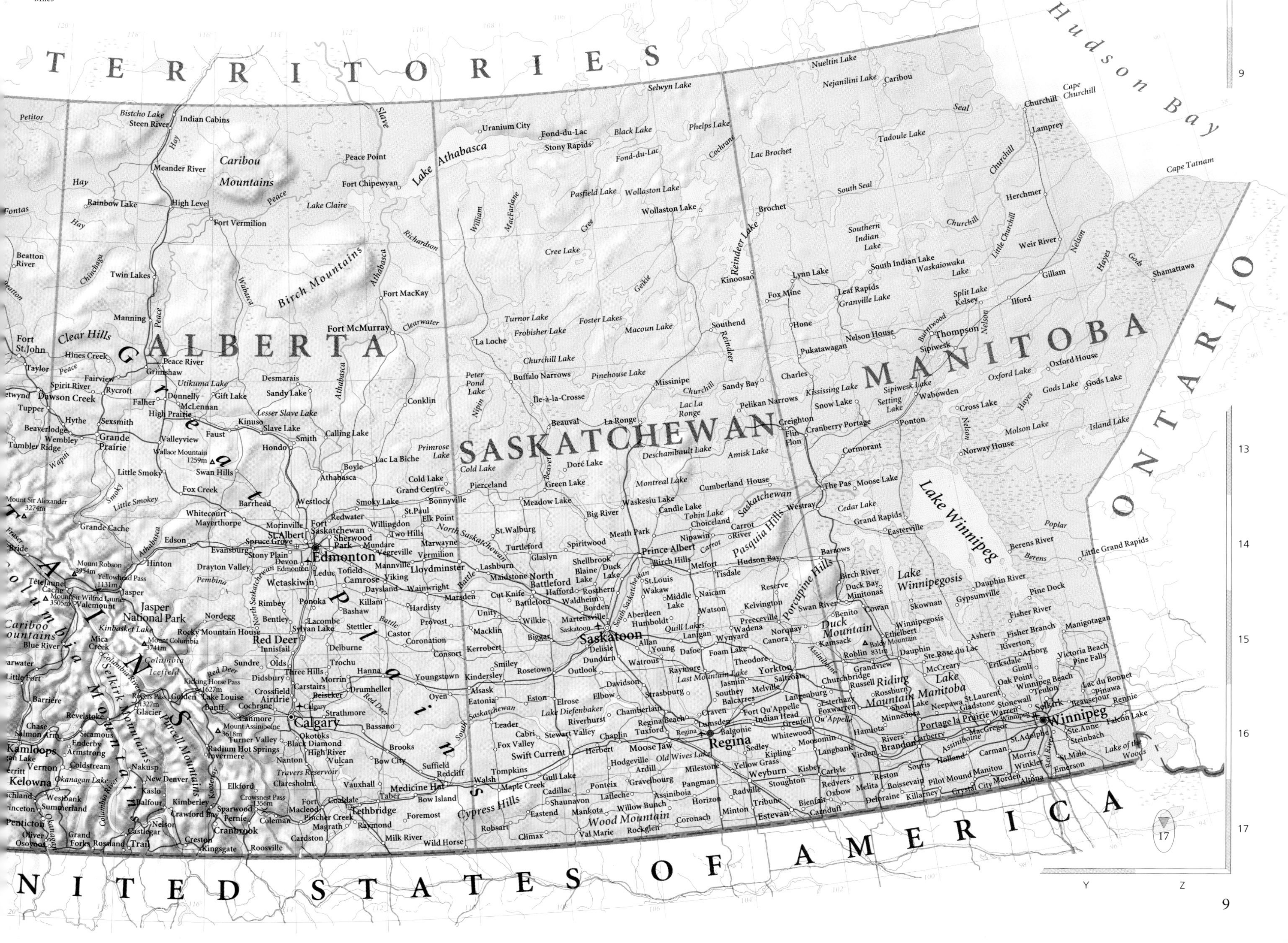

TERRITORIES

ALBERTA

SASKATCHEWAN

MANITOBA

ONTARIO

Hudson Bay

UNITED STATES OF AMERICA

17

9

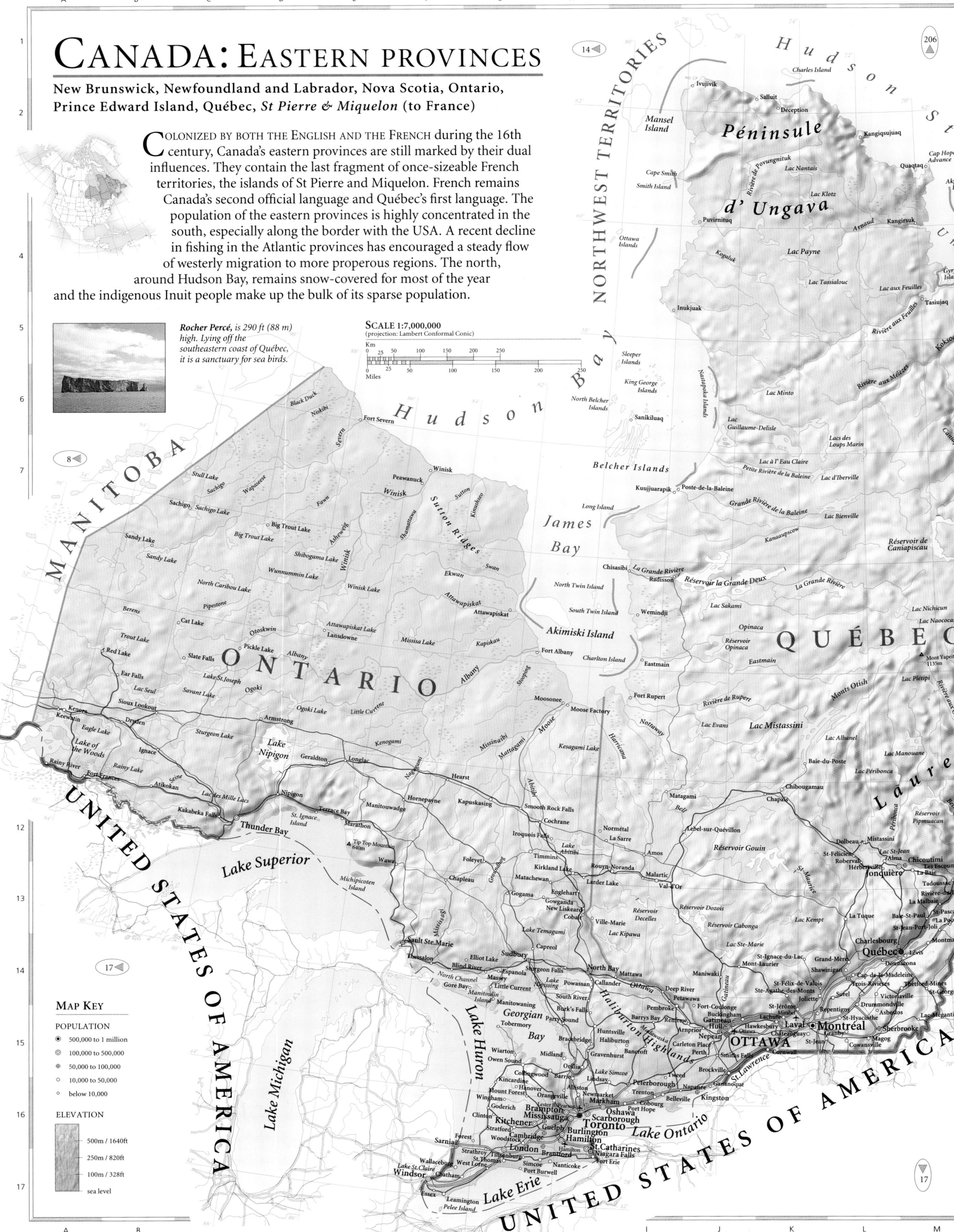

CANADA: EASTERN PROVINCES

New Brunswick, Newfoundland and Labrador, Nova Scotia, Ontario, Prince Edward Island, Québec, *St Pierre & Miquelon* (to France)

COLONIZED BY BOTH THE ENGLISH AND THE FRENCH during the 16th century, Canada's eastern provinces are still marked by their dual influences. They contain the last fragment of once-sizeable French territories, the islands of St Pierre and Miquelon. French remains Canada's second official language and Québec's first language. The population of the eastern provinces is highly concentrated in the south, especially along the border with the USA. A recent decline in fishing in the Atlantic provinces has encouraged a steady flow of westerly migration to more properous regions. The north, around Hudson Bay, remains snow-covered for most of the year and the indigenous Inuit people make up the bulk of its sparse population.

Rocher Percé, is 290 ft (88 m) high. Lying off the southeastern coast of Québec, it is a sanctuary for sea birds.

SCALE 1:7,000,000
(projection: Lambert Conformal Conic)

Km
0 25 50   100   150   200   250

Miles
0 25 50   100   150   200   250

MAP KEY

POPULATION

- 500,000 to 1 million
- 100,000 to 500,000
- 50,000 to 100,000
- 10,000 to 50,000
- below 10,000

ELEVATION

500m / 1640ft
250m / 820ft
100m / 328ft
sea level

THE LANDSCAPE

MUCH OF EASTERN CANADA is part of the Canadian Shield. Glaciers have scoured the land leaving deposits that have dammed and diverted streams, to create a rocky landscape strewn with lakes and swamps. Much of the ground is subject to permafrost, which further impedes drainage. The uplands in the far east are the most northerly extension of the Appalachian mountain chain.

The Péninsule d'Ungava is littered with erratics – isolated rocks which were carried by glaciers and deposited away from their place of origin when the glacier melted.

Labrador's indented coast is a product of past glaciations, which caused sea level change, and wave erosion. There are countless offshore islands, fjords and exposed headlands.

Lake Superior is the world's largest expanse of fresh water, covering 32,150 sq miles (83,270 sq km). It is crossed by the Canada–USA border.

The eroded highlands of New Brunswick, Nova Scotia and Newfoundland are part of the Appalachian mountain chain, formed over 400 million years ago.

Laurentides Park

Bay of Fundy

Tidal waters are channelled down the bay

Steep cliffs bound the bay

The bay is 94 miles (151 km) long

The forested Laurentides Park incorporates part of the Laurentian Highlands. Within its boundaries are over 1600 lakes.

At the Bay of Fundy, incoming waves are funnelled down the long, narrow, steep-sided bay. These topographical features cause fast-flowing tides which can rise 70 ft (21 m).

The tides at the Bay of Fundy are among the highest in the world. At low tide the tree-topped rocks have been likened to flowerpots.

TRANSPORT AND INDUSTRY

BOTH QUÉBEC AND ONTARIO have a diversified manufacturing sector located in the south. Across the rest of the region, industry is largely based around local resources, which accounts for the large number of fish and timber processing plants and mines. Many of the fast-flowing rivers are also gradually being harnessed for hydro-electric power.

Major industry and infrastructure

- ✈ aerospace
- 🚗 vehicle manufacture
- chemicals
- 🐟 fish processing
- food processing
- hi-tech industry
- hydro-electric power
- mining
- 🌲 timber processing
- ■ capital cities
- ● major towns
- ✈ international airports
- — major roads
- major industrial areas

Fish processing is a major industry in the Atlantic provinces. Fogo Island, off Newfoundland, has barely a thousand inhabitants but it is able to sustain a number of cod canneries.

THE TRANSPORT NETWORK

84,522 miles (136,325 km)	
1858 miles (2998 km)	
12,774 miles (20,602 km)	
376 miles (606 km)	

The majority of Canada's large ports lie in the east. Since the 1960s the region's rail network has been steadily reduced; Newfoundland recently lost its last remaining line, the Long-Cross Island line.

USING THE LAND AND SEA

WITH THIN SOILS restricting farming to the south, the forests which grow in vast unbroken tracts across eastern Canada provide an important source of revenue. Coastal communities rely heavily on the rich fishing grounds of the Atlantic Ocean, although foreign competition and overfishing have resulted in strict policies to conserve stocks.

THE URBAN/RURAL POPULATION DIVIDE

77% urban   23% rural

POPULATION DENSITY	TOTAL LAND AREA
17 people per sq mile (7 people per sq km)	1,061,600 sq miles (2,750,260 sq km)

Land use and agricultural distribution

- 🐄 cattle
- cereals
- 🐟 fishing
- 🍎 fruit
- 🌲 timber
- ■ capital cities
- ● major towns
- pasture
- cropland
- forest
- tundra

Prince Edward Island is the only Atlantic province with notable agricultural land. The island is Canada's leading producer of potatoes.

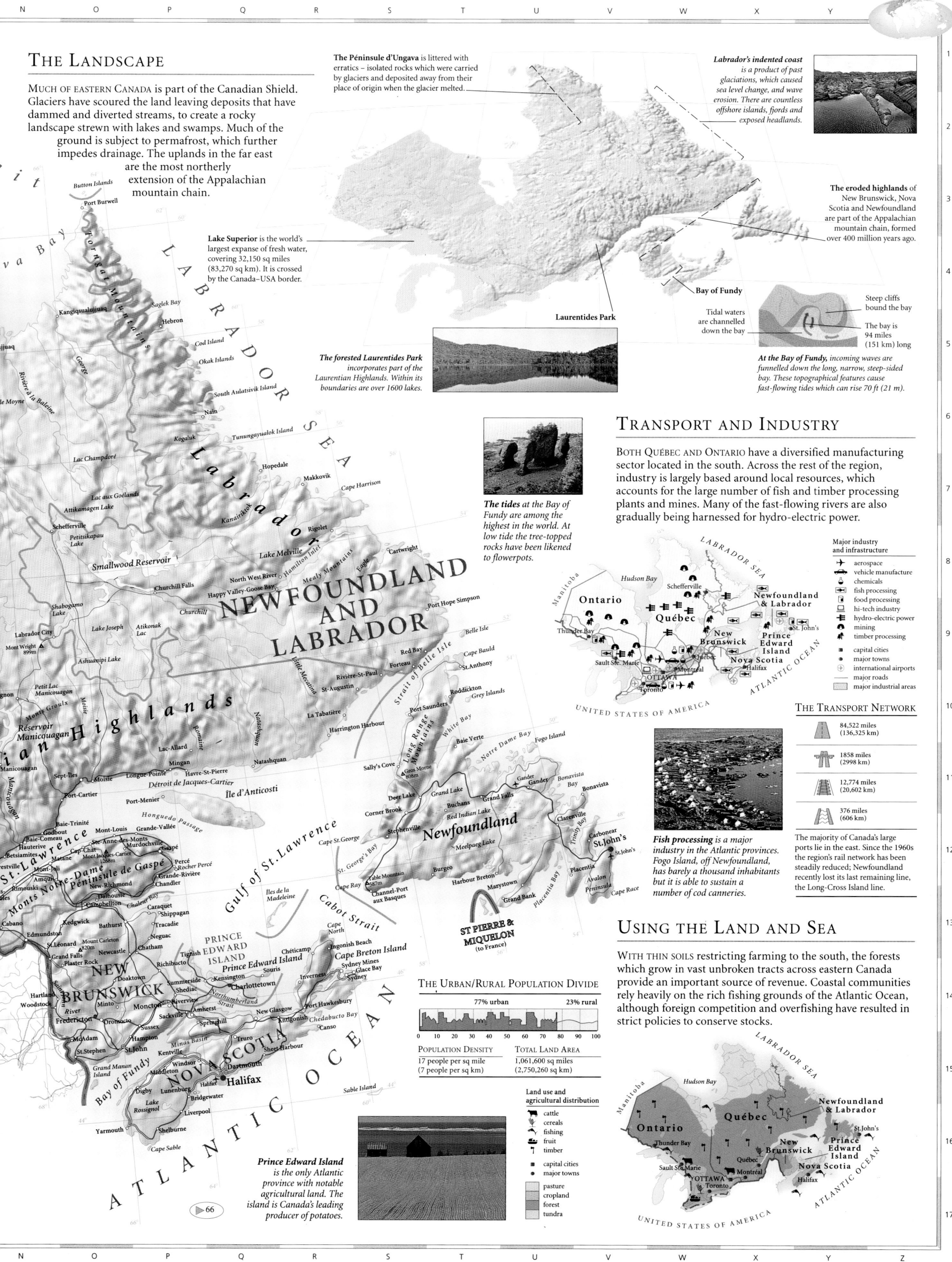

▶ 66

SOUTHEASTERN CANADA

Southern Ontario, Southern Quebec

THE SOUTHERN PARTS of Québec and Ontario form the economic heart of Canada. The two provinces are divided by their language and culture; in Québec, French is the main language, whereas English is spoken in Ontario. Separatist sentiment in Québec has led to a provincial referendum on the question of a sovereignty association with Canada. The region contains Canada's capital, Ottawa and its two largest cities: Toronto, the centre of commerce and Montréal, the cultural and administrative heart of French Canada.

Niagara Falls lies on the border between Canada and the USA. It comprises a system of two falls: American Falls, in New York, is separated from Horseshoe Falls, in Ontario, by Goat Island. Horseshoe Falls, seen here, plunges 160 ft (48 m) and is 2500 ft (762 m) wide.

The port at Montréal is situated on the St. Lawrence Seaway. A network of 16 locks allows sea-going vessels access to routes once plied by fur-trappers and early settlers.

TRANSPORT AND INDUSTRY

THE CITIES OF SOUTHERN QUÉBEC AND ONTARIO, and their hinterlands, form the heart of Canadian manufacturing industry. Toronto is Canada's leading financial centre, and Ontario's motor and aerospace industries have developed around the city. A major centre for nickel mining lies to the north of Toronto. Most of Québec's industry is located in Montréal, the oldest port in North America. Chemicals, paper manufacture and the construction of transport equipment are leading industrial activities.

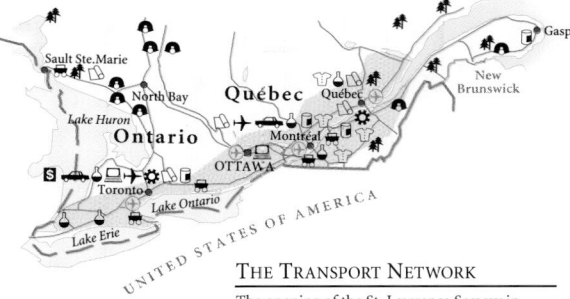

Major industry and infrastructure

car manufacture	textiles
chemicals	paper industry
engineering	timber processing
finance	capital cities
food processing	major towns
hi-tech industry	international airports
mining	major roads
iron & steel	major industrial areas

THE TRANSPORT NETWORK

The opening of the St. Lawrence Seaway in 1959 finally allowed ocean-going ships (up to 24,000 tons (tonnes)) access to the interior of Canada, creating a vital trading route.

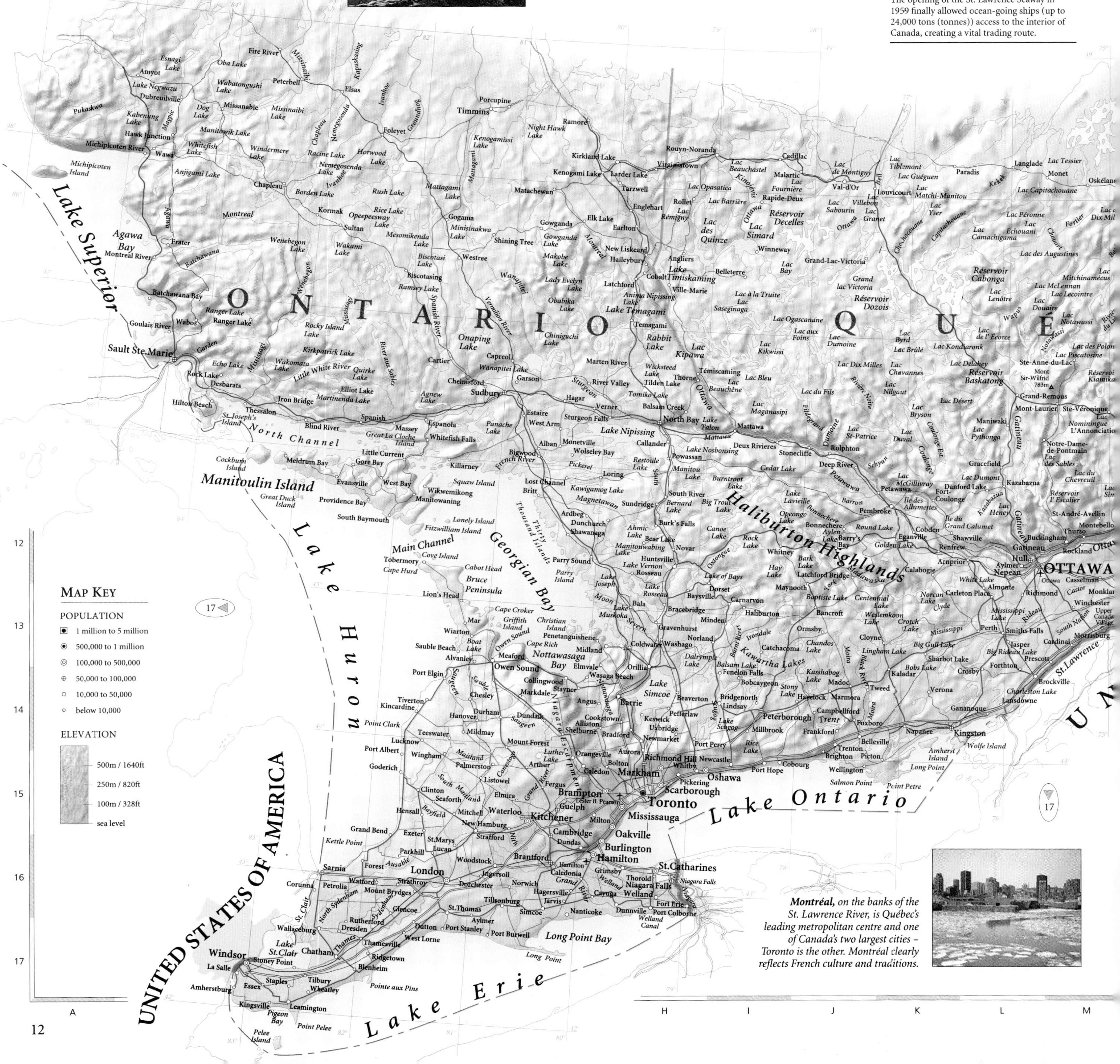

MAP KEY

POPULATION

- 1 million to 5 million
- 500,000 to 1 million
- 100,000 to 500,000
- 50,000 to 100,000
- 10,000 to 50,000
- below 10,000

ELEVATION

- 500m / 1640ft
- 250m / 820ft
- 100m / 328ft
- sea level

Montréal, on the banks of the St. Lawrence River, is Québec's leading metropolitan centre and one of Canada's two largest cities – Toronto is the other. Montréal clearly reflects French culture and traditions.

USING THE LAND AND SEA

THE PRODUCTIVE NIAGARA 'FRUIT BELT' on the shores of Lake Erie and Lake Ontario is a major farming region, although available farmland is being challenged by urban expansion. Québec is Canada's leading producer of maple syrup and dairy products. In the north, farmland gives way to extensive areas of forest, partly used for commercial logging. Fishing occurs in Atlantic waters and in the Great Lakes.

THE URBAN/RURAL POPULATION DIVIDE

urban 87%   rural 13%

0 10 20 30 40 50 60 70 80 90 100

POPULATION DENSITY	TOTAL LAND AREA
64 people per sq mile	214,230 sq miles
(25 people per sq km)	(555,000 sq km)

Land use and agricultural distribution

- cattle
- fish
- cereals
- fruit
- maple syrup
- timber
- tobacco
- capital cities
- major towns
- pasture
- cropland
- forest

Pumpkins are just one of the crops grown in the Niagara 'fruit belt'. The mild climate, moderated by the lakes, allows the cultivation of a wide range of fruit and vegetables, including cherries, apples, peaches, grapes and asparagus. Fruit and vegetable growing is confined to southern Canada, due to the colder climate and short growing season of the northern regions.

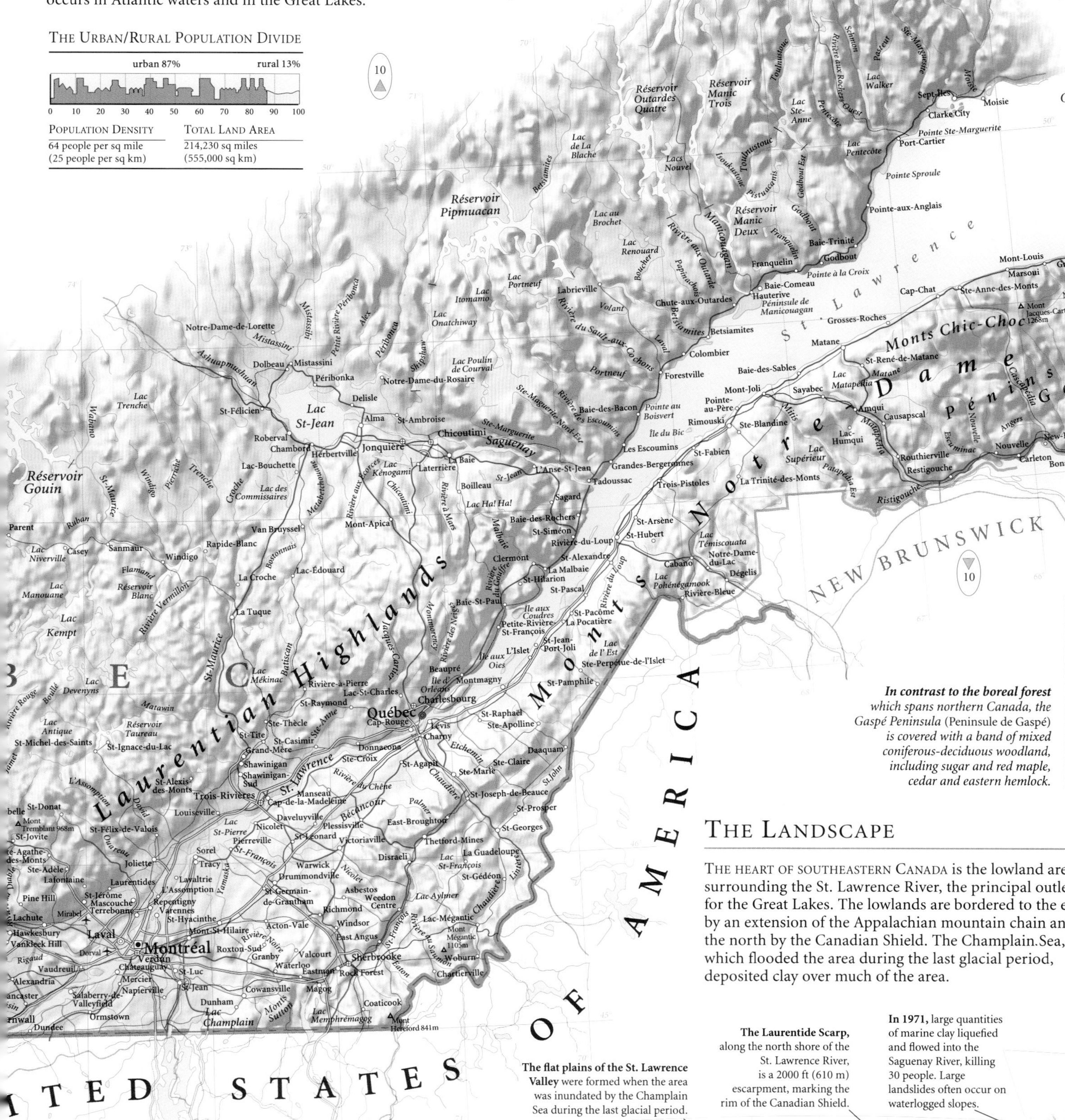

In contrast to the boreal forest which spans northern Canada, the Gaspé Peninsula (Péninsule de Gaspé) is covered with a band of mixed coniferous-deciduous woodland, including sugar and red maple, cedar and eastern hemlock.

THE LANDSCAPE

THE HEART OF SOUTHEASTERN CANADA is the lowland area surrounding the St. Lawrence River, the principal outlet for the Great Lakes. The lowlands are bordered to the east by an extension of the Appalachian mountain chain and to the north by the Canadian Shield. The Champlain.Sea, which flooded the area during the last glacial period, deposited clay over much of the area.

The wooded Gaspé Peninsula (Péninsule de Gaspé) includes the Notre Dame and Shickshock mountains (Monts Chic-Choc). These are a northerly outcrop of the Appalachian mountain chain.

The flat plains of the St. Lawrence Valley were formed when the area was inundated by the Champlain Sea during the last glacial period.

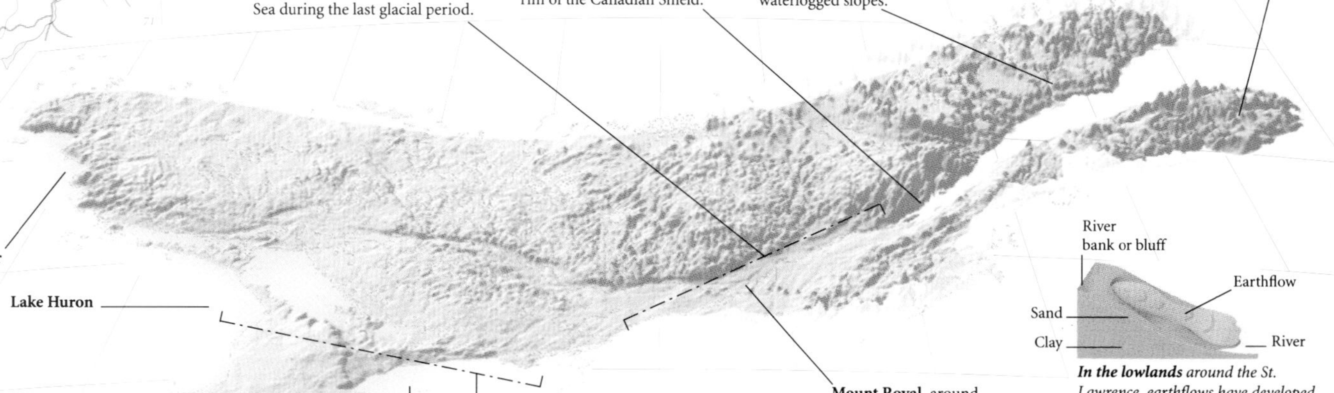

The Laurentide Scarp, along the north shore of the St. Lawrence River, is a 2000 ft (610 m) escarpment, marking the rim of the Canadian Shield.

In 1971, large quantities of marine clay liquefied and flowed into the Saguenay River, killing 30 people. Large landslides often occur on waterlogged slopes.

Mount Royal, around which the city of Montréal has developed, is the result of an igneous intrusion which occurred between 135 and 65 million years ago.

Point Pelee is a world-famous site for bird migration. Over 250 species of bird have been sighted on the sandspit which forms the southern tip of the Canadian mainland.

The Great Lakes moderate the climate of the area surrounding the St. Lawrence River. Their water, which cools more slowly than the land, acts as a reservoir for warmth, extending the growing season into the early autumn.

In the lowlands around the St. Lawrence, earthflows have developed along gentle river banks where sand overlies clay, making the surface layers very unstable. When the slope's natural equilibrium is disturbed, an earthflow can occur.

Lake Superior
Lake Huron
Lake Erie
Lake Ontario

River bank or bluff
Earthflow
Sand
Clay
River

SCALE 1:3,000,000
(projection: Lambert Conformal Conic)

Km
0 5 10 20 30 40 50 60 70 80
Miles
0 5 10 20 30 40 50 60 70 80

A   Aa   B   Bb   C   Cc   D   Dd   E   Ee   F   Ff   G

CANADA

ANADA IS THE SECOND LARGEST COUNTRY in the world, and with only about one-tenth of its land area inhabited, it is one of the most sparsely populated. Canada became a confederation in 1867, though Newfoundland did not join until 1949. As a founding member of the UN and of the Commonwealth, Canada has played an important role in international affairs. A constitutional crisis, focusing on the French-speaking Québécois, and Inuit and Native American land rights, have dominated politics in the 1990s. In 1999, part of the Northwest Territories, Nunavut, will become a self-governing homeland for the Inuit.

The Selwyn Mountains
in northwestern Canada form part of the Rocky Mountains. The highest point, Keele Peak, rises to 9750 ft (2972 m).

TRANSPORT AND INDUSTRY

ABUNDANT ENERGY in the form of coal, oil, natural gas and hydro-electric power underpins Canadian industry. Over 75% of manufacturing is concentrated in the Great Lakes–St. Lawrence region, including prospering aerospace, transport and hi-tech industries. Across Canada as a whole, manufacturing has developed around a diversified, high-quality resource base and a wide range of metallic and non-metallic minerals.

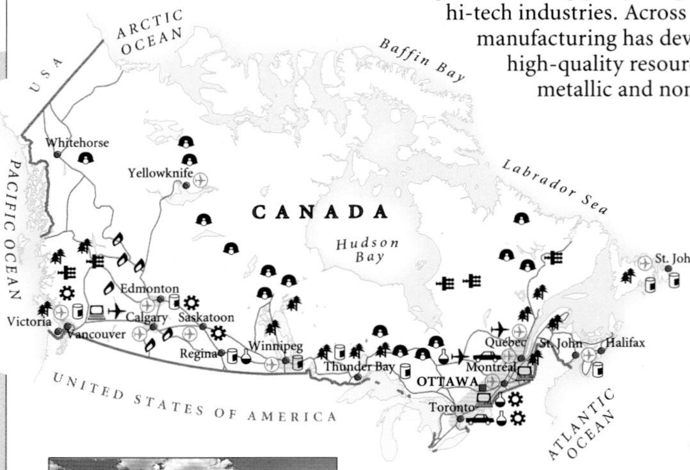

Major industry and infrastructure

✈ aerospace	■	capital cities
🚗 car manufacture	•	major towns
⚙ chemicals	✈	international airports
🏭 engineering		major roads
🖥 food processing		major industrial areas
💻 hi-tech industry		
⚡ hydroelectric power		
🛢 oil & gas		
⛏ mining		
🌲 timber processing		

Canada has one of the world's highest rates of energy consumption per person. It is endowed with vast hydro-electric potential from which more than 60% of its electricity requirements are generated.

THE TRANSPORT NETWORK

🛣 549,460 miles (884,272 km)		🛤 4860 miles (7819 km)	
🚆 120,546 miles (194,000 km)		⛴ 1864 miles (3000 km)	

In recent years the road network has been expanded, especially links to remote areas. Meanwhile, for long-distance travel, air transport now supersedes the declining rail network, which focuses mainly on east–west routes.

THE LANDSCAPE

GLACIERS ON ISLANDS IN THE ARCTIC OCEAN are the last remnants of the ice sheet that once covered and shaped Canada. Hudson Bay is the centre of the Canadian Shield, a huge, eroded plateau marked at its southern extremity by a string of lakes running southeastwards from Great Bear Lake to the Great Lakes. In contrast to the rolling relief of the Shield and the central lowland region, the Rocky Mountains rise to peaks of over 13,000 ft (4000 m), stretching 500 miles (800 km) along the west coast.

Along the northeastern coast of Baffin Island the mountains rise to 8000 ft (2440 m). Glaciers move down through the valleys to the sea, eroding wide U-shaped valleys.

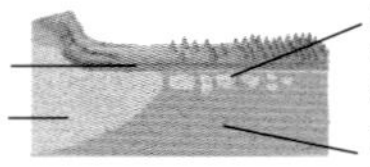

Top layer thaws in the summer

Permanently frozen ground

Marginal areas of permafrost thaw in summer

Unfrozen ground where temperature is more moderate

Permanently frozen ground known as permafrost is common in Canada's northern tundra. It thickens further north, becoming hundreds of metres deep in parts of the Arctic.

The Mackenzie River, flowing north over the permafrost, forms a wide river channel with many tributaries. Together with the Peel River it has created a long, narrow delta at its mouth. The entire river freezes during the winter.

Great Bear Lake

Exposure to three phases of mountain-building and subsequent erosion over millions of years has moulded the ancient Canadian Shield into a series of basins and ridges.

The Rocky Mountains were formed some 80 million years ago, when the Pacific Plate was driven under the North American Plate, forcing up the land.

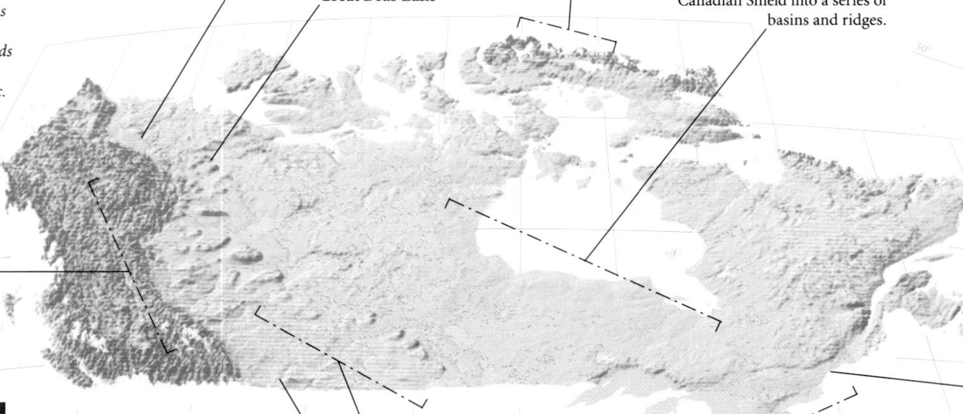

Isolated pillars, known as hoodoos near Red Deer River in the badlands of Alberta are a product of wind and water erosion, especially flash floods. The badlands lie in the rain shadow of the Rocky Mountains, which creates a semi-arid climate.

Fertile prairies stretch from the southern rim of the Canadian Shield, south into the USA.

The Great Lakes lie on the Canada–USA border. The basins they now occupy were fashioned by repeated ice advance. Once, Lakes Superior, Huron and Michigan formed one large lake, Lake Nipissing.

The St. Lawrence River is 2350 miles (3782 km) long. It flows from the western shore of Lake Superior through the Great Lakes and on to the Atlantic Ocean. From December to April, the St. Lawrence Seaway freezes between Lake Ontario and Montréal.

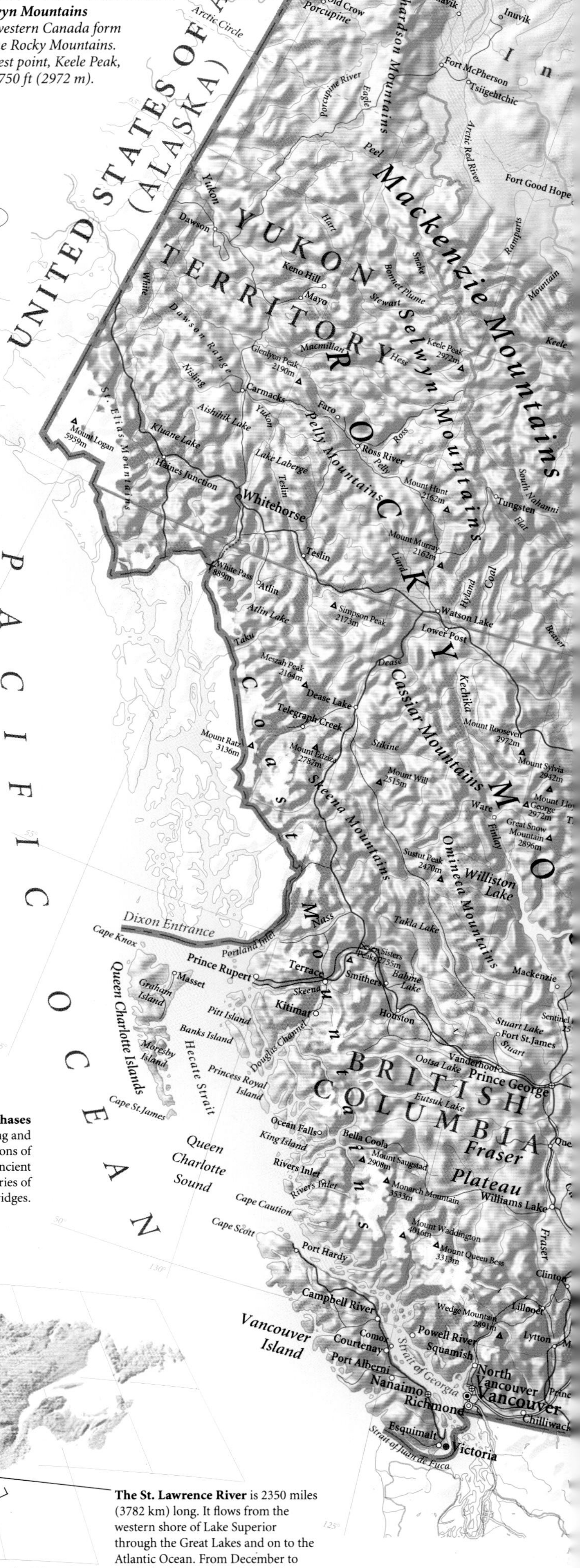

A   Aa   B   Bb   C   Cc   D   Dd   E   Ee   F

THE UNITED STATES OF AMERICA

CONTERMINOUS USA (FOR ALASKA AND HAWAII SEE PAGES 40-41)

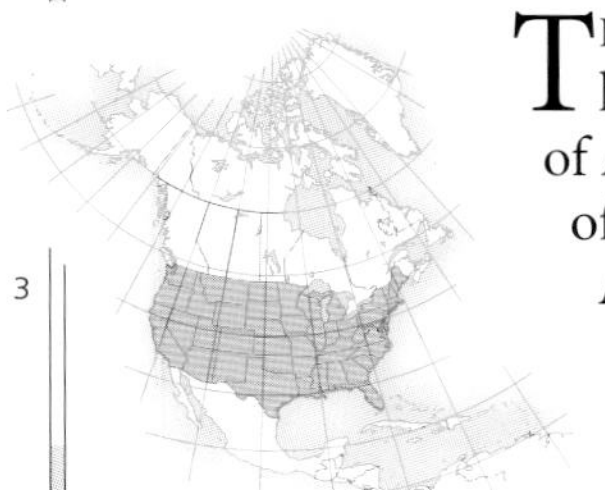

THE USA'S PROGRESSION FROM FRONTIER TERRITORY to economic and political superpower has taken less than 200 years. The 48 conterminous states, along with the outlying states of Alaska and Hawaii, are part of a federal union, held together by the guiding principles of the US Constitution, which enshrines the ideals of democracy and liberty for all. Abundant fertile land and a rich resource-base fuelled and sustained the USA's economic development. With the spread of agriculture and the growth of trade and industry came the need for a larger workforce, which was supplied by millions of immigrants, many seeking an escape from poverty and political or religious persecution. Immigration continues today, particularly from Central America and Asia.

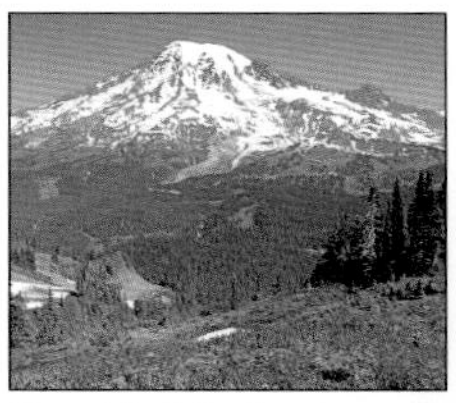

Mount Rainier is a dormant volcano in the Cascade Range, Washington. This 14,090 ft (4392 m) peak is flanked by the most extensive glacier outside Alaska.

TRANSPORT AND INDUSTRY

THE USA HAS BEEN THE INDUSTRIAL POWERHOUSE of the world since the Second World War, pioneering mass-production and the consumer lifestyle. Initially, heavy engineering and manufacturing in the northeast led the economy. Today, heavy industry has declined and the USA's economy is driven by service and financial industries, with the most important being defence, hi-tech and electronics.

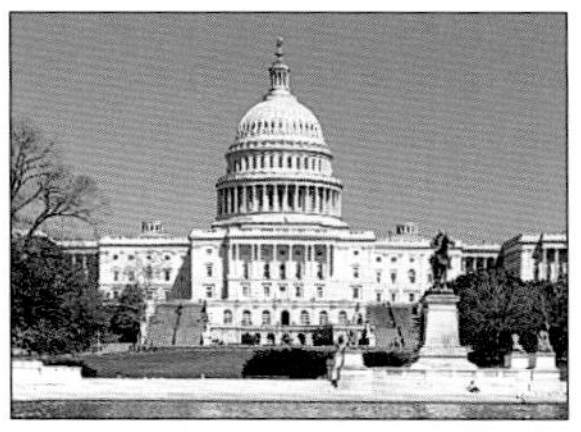

Washington dc was established as the site for the nation's capital in 1790. It is home to the seat of national government, on Capitol Hill, as well as the President's official residence, the White House.

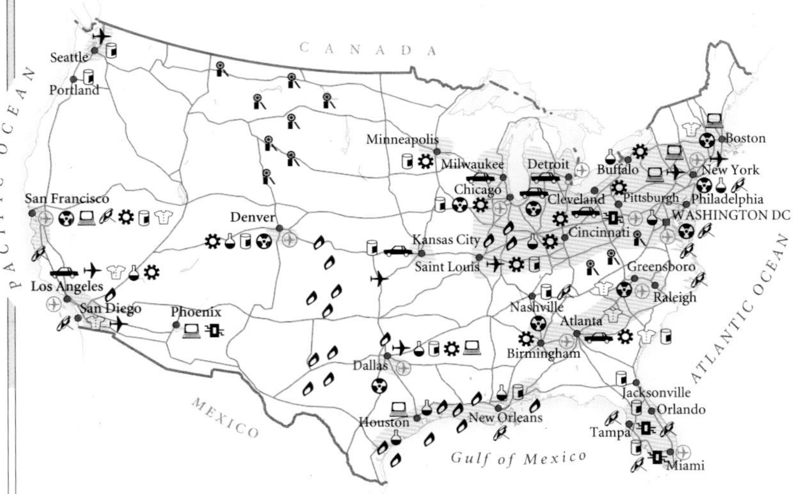

Major industry and infrastructure

✈	aerospace	⚙	research & development
🚗	car manufacture		textiles
	chemicals		tourism
	coal		
	electronics	■	capital cities
⚙	engineering	■	major towns
	food processing	✈	international airports
	hi-tech industry		major roads
♦	oil & gas		major industrial areas

THE TRANSPORT NETWORK

3,955,393 miles (6,365,590 km)		52,419 miles (84,361 km)	
148,308 miles (238,628 km)		25,482 miles (41,009 km)	

Transport in the USA is dominated by the car which, with the extensive Interstate Highway system, allows great personal mobility. Today, internal air flights between major cities provide the most rapid cross-country travel.

THE LANDSCAPE

THE HIGH, RUGGED MOUNTAIN RANGES of the west are about 80 million years old, geologically young compared to the old, eroded, Appalachian mountain chain, which dates from when North America and Europe were joined together as part of the supercontinent Pangaea, 400 million years ago. In contrast, the Great Plains and Mississippi Basin have a low relief and fertile soils.

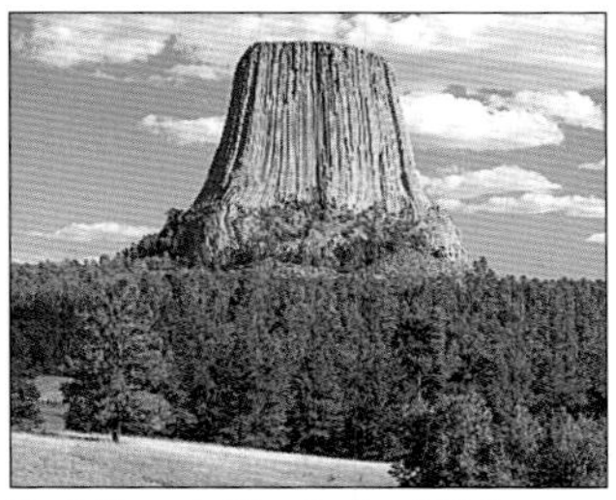

Devils Tower, in Wyoming is a 1280 ft (390 m) intrusion of basalt rock, which cooled to form octagonal pillars. In 1906 it became the first US National Monument.

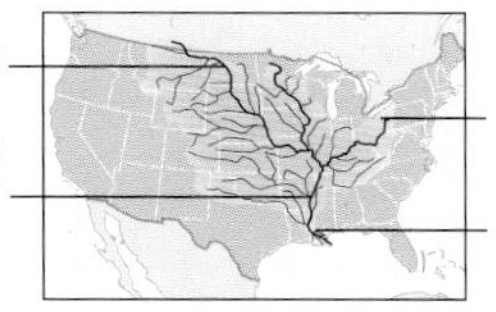

Missouri River
Mississippi River
Ohio River
Mississippi Delta

The massive drainage basin of the Mississippi covers 1,250,000 sq miles (3,200,000 sq km). It includes all areas drained by the Mississippi and its chief tributaries, the Missouri and Ohio rivers, and drains the entire region from the Appalachians to the Rockies.

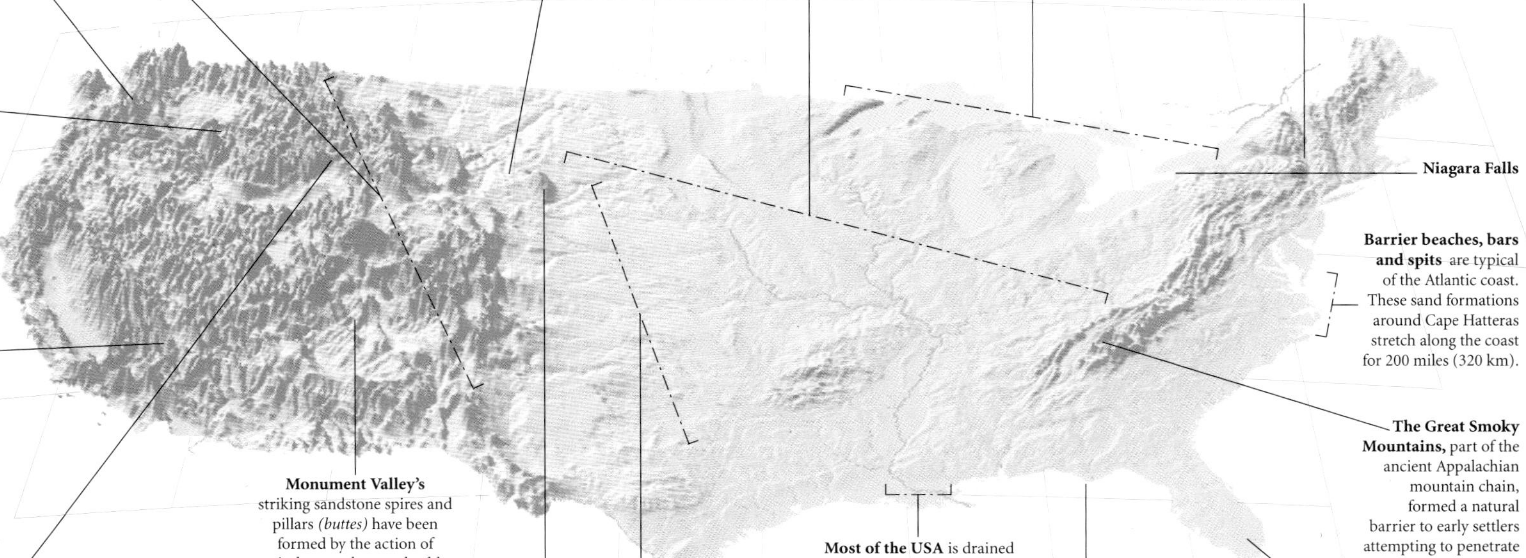

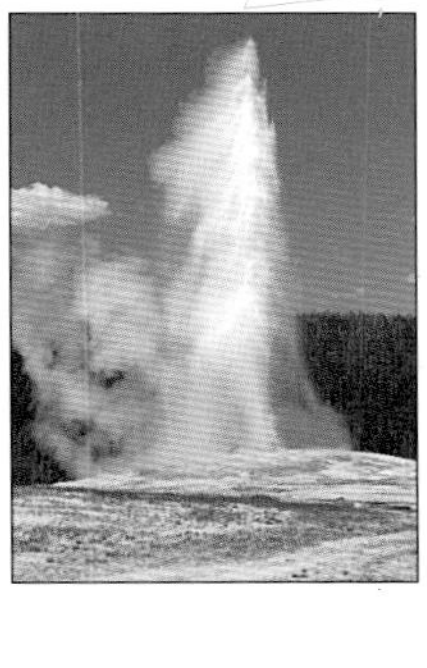

Mount Rainier

Hell's Canyon running through part of Idaho and Oregon, is North America's deepest gorge. It was formed by the down-cutting of the Snake River through the thick basalt rocks of the Columbia–Snake Plateau.

Death Valley, California, 282 ft (86 m) below sea level, is the lowest point in the western hemisphere, and one of the hottest places on Earth. Temperatures of 190° F (88° C) have been recorded here.

The Rocky Mountains form the backbone of the USA, running from Alaska to New Mexico. They contain the USA's highest mountains and many active volcanoes.

The Hudson-Mohawk Gap, lying at the point where the two rivers join, allows passage from the Atlantic Ocean to the continental interior.

The Great Lakes

Niagara Falls

Barrier beaches, bars and spits are typical of the Atlantic coast. These sand formations around Cape Hatteras stretch along the coast for 200 miles (320 km).

The Great Smoky Mountains, part of the ancient Appalachian mountain chain, formed a natural barrier to early settlers attempting to penetrate the country's interior.

Monument Valley's striking sandstone spires and pillars *(buttes)* have been formed by the action of wind, water, heat and cold.

Volcanically heated water erupts every 40-80 minutes from Old Faithful geyser in Yellowstone National Park, Wyoming. The 170 ft (50 m) column of water and steam persists for 4 minutes.

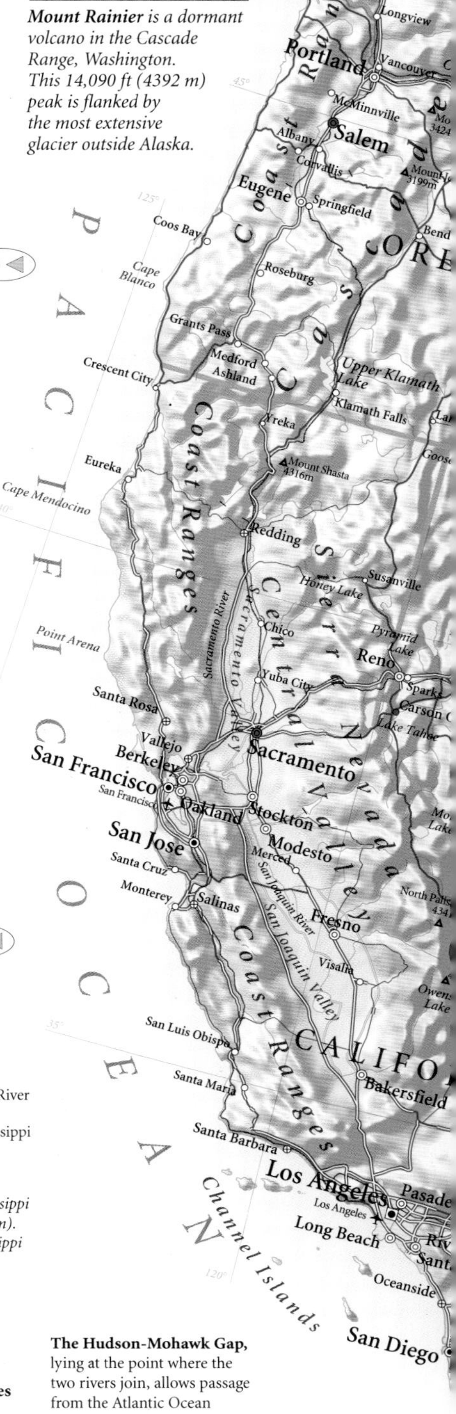

The deep gullies of South Dakota's badlands are created by periodic, torrential rainfall, which erodes the soft soils and rocks. Their form has been greatly affected by changes in land use.

Great Plains

Most of the USA is drained by the great Mississippi River system. At its mouth, where levées are breached, floodwaters are carried to the swamps through a series of channels. This region is known as the bayou.

The USA's Gulf Coast is seriously affected by hurricane erosion which reshapes its beaches and sandbanks.

The Everglades are a vast area of saw-grass swamp covering 4000 sq miles (10,300 sq km) of southern Florida.

USING THE LAND AND SEA

THE MAJORITY OF CANADA's agricultural land is found in the prairies, which cover 140 million acres (57 million ha) and support wheat and grain-fed cattle. More specialized crops, such as fruit and vegetables, are grown in pockets of agricultural land in the east and west. Of Canada's many islands, only Prince Edward Island has notable farmland. Further north, boreal forests, exploited for timber, run in an almost unbroken arc, giving way to uncultivable tundra and ice sheets in the far north.

Land use and agricultural distribution

- cattle
- cereals
- fishing
- fruit
- timber
- ■ capital cities
- ● major towns

pasture
cropland
forest
wetland
mountain region
barren
tundra

THE URBAN/RURAL POPULATION DIVIDE

urban 78%   rural 22%

0 10 20 30 40 50 60 70 80 90 100

POPULATION DENSITY	TOTAL LAND AREA
8 people per sq mile (3 people per sq km)	3,559,294 sq miles (9,220,970 sq km)

The climate and topography of the prairies makes them ideally suited to farming. Long summer days, moderate temperatures, limited rainfall and flat plains provide excellent conditions for wheat farming.

Ottawa was selected by Queen Victoria as the Canadian capital in 1858. Prior to this date it was a notorious work camp centred around the lumber industry. Today, the city is known as 'Silicon Valley North', due to its concentration of hi-tech industries.

MAP KEY

POPULATION
- ◉ 500,000 to 1 million
- ◎ 100,000 to 500,000
- ⊕ 50,000 to 100,000
- ○ 10,000 to 50,000
- ∘ below 10,000

ELEVATION
- 6000m / 19,686ft
- 4000m / 13,124ft
- 3000m / 9843ft
- 2000m / 6562ft
- 1000m / 3281ft
- 500m / 1640ft
- 250m / 820ft
- 100m / 328ft
- sea level

The Great Lakes are drained by the St. Lawrence River which flows down through a wide tectonic depression. It forms a broad estuary for much of its course, the width varying from 1.2 miles (1.9 km) in the upper reaches to 90 miles (145 km) at its mouth.

SCALE 1:9,250,000
projection: Lambert Azimuthal Equal Area

Km
25 50   100   150   200   250   300   350
Miles
       50   100   150   200   250   300   350

Sea

Banks
Island

Cape Kellett
Sachs Harbour
Cape Wollaston
Prince Albert
Peninsula

Cape Parry
Cape Lambton
Cape Lyon
Cape Bathurst
Franklin
Bay
Paulatuk
Holman

Amundsen Gulf

Prince Albert Sound

Dolphin & Union Strait

Wollaston
Peninsula

Victoria
Island

Viscount Melville Sound

Passage Point
Peel Point

Stefansson
Island

206

Prince of Wales
Island

Peel
Sound

Somerset
Island

Brodeur
Peninsula

Borden
Peninsula

Admiralty Inlet

Baffin

Baffin Bay

Cape
Henry Kater

Hadley Bay
McClintock Channel
Franklin Strait
Gulf of Boothia
Boothia
Peninsula
Prince Regent Inlet

Zeta Lake
Gateshead Island
Cape Englefield

Cape Chapman

Igloolik
Jens Munk
Island
Rowley
Island
Baird
Peninsula

Air Force
Island

Nettilling
Lake

Prince Charles
Island

Hall Beach

Melville
Peninsula

Wales
Island

Taloyoak

Pelly Bay

Simpson
Peninsula

Committee
Bay

Hantzsch

Koukdjuak

Foxe
Basin

Cape Dorchester
Foxe Peninsula
Cape Dorset
Salisbury
Island

Bluenose Lake
Rae

Cape Krusenstern
Coronation Gulf
Coppermine

Kent Peninsula
Bathurst Inlet

Jenny Lind Island
Queen Maud Gulf
Bowes
Point
Ellice

Cambridge Bay

King William
Island
Gjoa Haven
Adelaide
Peninsula
Chantrey Inlet

Rae Strait

Kitikmeot

Hayes
Repulse Bay
Vansittart Island
Foxe Channel

Nottingham
Island

Ivujivik

Coppermin

Hood
Burnside

Back

Wager Bay

Southampton
Island
Roes Welcome Sound
Coral Harbour

Cape Kendall
Cape Low

Evans Strait

Mansel Island

NORTH WEST TERRITORIES

C A N

Great Bear Lake
Echo Bay
Takijuq
Lake

Garry Lake

Back

Aberdeen Lake
Baker Lake
Baker Lake
Chesterfield Inlet
Chesterfield Inlet

Rankin Inlet

Coats
Island

Cape Dorchester

man Wells
Fort Norman

Hottah Lake

Déline

Aylmer
Lake
Clinton-Colden Lake

Thelon

Keewatin

Dubawnt Lake

Yathkyed
Lake

Whale Cove

Wrigley

Lac La Martre

Snare
Yellowknife

Hanbury

Lac La Martre
Rae-Edzo
Reliance

Fort Smith

Dubawnt

Kazan

Eskimo Point
Arviat

Willowlake
Horn

Yellowknife
Łutselk'e
Snowdrift
Nonacho Lake

Tha-Anne

Hudson

Fort Simpson

Fort Providence
Great Slave Lake
Fort Resolution

Tazin

Thlewiaza

Bay

Trout
Hay River
Pine Point

Thoa
Wholdaia Lake
Kasba Lake
Nueltin Lake

Nejanilini Lake

Fort Liard
Petitot

Fort Smith
Slave

Uranium City
Selwyn Lake
Phelps Lake

Seal

Cape Churchill

Bistcho Lake
Steen River

Fort Chipewyan
Lake Athabasca
Black Lake
Lac Brochet

Tadoule Lake

Churchill
Churchill

Fort
Fort Nelson
Fontas

High Level
Fort Vermilion
Lake Claire

William
MacFarlane
Pasfield Lake
Wollaston Lake
Wollaston Lake

South Seal

Southern Indian Lake

Cape Tatnam

Caribou
Mountains
Peace

Birch
Mountains

Cree Lake
Cree

Geikie

Reindeer Lake

Split Lake
Gods
Nelson

Fort Severn

Chinchaga

Manning
Wabasca

A L B E R T A

SASKATCHEWAN

Clearwater
Turnor Lake
Lynn Lake

Leaf Rapids

Granville Lake

Waskaiowaka Lake

Gillam

Winisk

Beatton
Fort
St.John
Grimshaw
Fairview
Peace River

Athabasca
Fort McMurray
La Loche

Foster Lakes
Macoun Lake

Thompson
Burntwood

Sipiwesk
Lake

Oxford Lake
Gods Lake

Big Trout Lake

Dawson Creek
Grande Prairie
Wapiti

Valleyview
Slave Lake
Utikuma Lake
Lesser Slave Lake

Churchill Lake
Peter Pond
Lake
Buffalo Narrows
Missinipe
Churchill

Kississing Lake
Wabowden

Melson
Lake

Island Lake

Sachigo Lake

Winisk Lake

Chetwynd

Wallace Mountain
1259m
Swan Hills

Primrose Lake

La Ronge
Lac La Ronge

Creighton
Deschambault
Lake
Flin Flon

The Pas

Sandy Lake
Sandy Lake
North Caribou Lake

Attawapiskat Lake

Grande Cache
Mount Robson
3954m

Whitecourt

Cold Lake
Cold Lake
Grand Centre

Meadow Lake

Amisk Lake
Montreal Lake

Tobin Lake

Saskatchewan

Cedar Lake
Grand Rapids

M A N I T O B A

Lake Winnipeg

Poplar

O N T A R I O

Red Lake

Trout Lake

Pipestone

Hinton
Edson
Drayton Valley
Pembina

St.Albert
Fort Saskatchewan
Edmonton
Spruce Grove
Stony Plain
Devon
Leduc
Camrose

Morinville
Vegreville
Vermilion
St.Walburg
Lloydminster

North Saskatchewan
Prince Albert
Nipawin
Porcupine Hills
Hudson Bay

Swan River

Duck
Mountain
Baldy Mountain
831m

Porcupine Hills
Gypsumville

Trout Lake
Lac
St.Joseph

Armstrong

Mount
Sir Wilfrid Laurier 3505m
Mount
954m

Wetaskiwin
Ponoka

Wainwright
Battleford
North Battleford
Melfort
Tisdale

Riding
Mountain
Dauphin

Eriksdale

Red Lake

Lac Seul

Sioux Lookout
Lake
Nipigon

Kinbasket Lake

Rocky
Mountain
House
Sylvan Lake
Red Deer
Lacombe
Stettler
Innisfail

Unity
Martensville
Saskatoon
Humboldt
Lanigan
Watrous
Quill Lakes
Wynyard
Canora
Yorkton
Kamsack

Neepawa
Minnedosa
Gladstone

Dauphin
Lake Manitoba

Gimli
Stonewall

Ear Falls

Dryden

Eagle Lake

Kenora

Mount Columbia
3747m

Golden

Red Deer
Didsbury
1627m
Olds

Biggar

Rosetown
Outlook

Lumsden

Portage la Prairie
Winnipeg
Selkirk
Beausejour
Pinawa

Lac des Mille Lacs

Salmon Arm
Kamloops

Canmore
Mount Assiniboine
3618m
Banff
Invermere
Kimberley

Kicking Horse Pass
1627m
Airdrie
Calgary
Okotoks
Strathmore

Drumheller
Oyen

Kindersley
Lake Diefenbaker
Fort Qu'Appelle
Indian Head
Qu'Appelle
Regina

Brandon
Assiniboine
Carman

Steinbach

Winkler
Morden
Altona

Rainy Lake
Fort Frances

Atikokan

Thunder Bay

Lake

Kelowna
Penticton
Nelson
Castlegar
Cranbrook

High River
Claresholm
Fort Macleod
Lethbridge
Pincher Creek
Coaldale
Cardston
Raymond
Milk River

Travers
Reservoir
Medicine Hat
Redcliff
Taber
Maple Creek

Cypress Hills

Swift Current
Moose Jaw
Old Wives Lake

Val Marie
Wood Mountain

Assiniboia

Weyburn
Carlyle
Estevan
Rockglen

Virden
Melita

Killarney

Moosomin

Souris

U N I T E D   S T A T E S   O F   A M E R I C A

17

g   H   Hh   I   Ii   J   Jj   K   Kk   L   Ll   M   Mm

The Sonoran Desert in southwestern Arizona stretches into Mexico and merges to the northwest with California's Mojave Desert. Much of the southwest is very arid, especially the 'rain-starved' areas between the Coast Ranges and the Rocky Mountains.

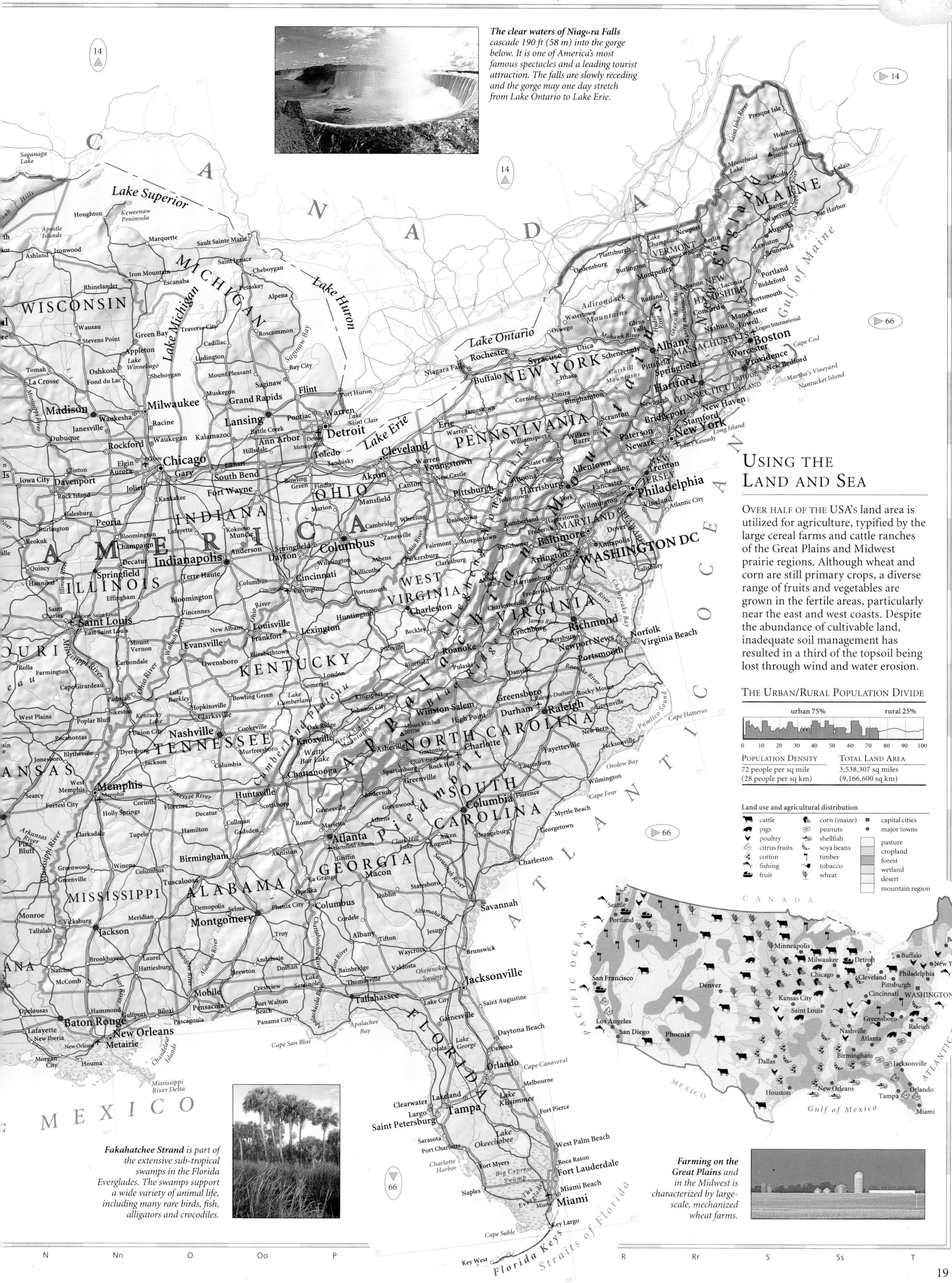

The clear waters of Niagara Falls cascade 190 ft (58 m) into the gorge below. It is one of America's most famous spectacles and a leading tourist attraction. The falls are slowly receding and the gorge may one day stretch from Lake Ontario to Lake Erie.

USING THE LAND AND SEA

OVER HALF OF THE USA's land area is utilized for agriculture, typified by the large cereal farms and cattle ranches of the Great Plains and Midwest prairie regions. Although wheat and corn are still primary crops, a diverse range of fruits and vegetables are grown in the fertile areas, particularly near the east and west coasts. Despite the abundance of cultivable land, inadequate soil management has resulted in a third of the topsoil being lost through wind and water erosion.

THE URBAN/RURAL POPULATION DIVIDE

urban 75%   rural 25%

POPULATION DENSITY	TOTAL LAND AREA	
72 people per sq mile (28 people per sq km)	3,538,307 sq miles (9,166,600 sq km)	

Land use and agricultural distribution

- cattle
- pigs
- poultry
- citrus fruits
- cotton
- fishing
- fruit
- corn (maize)
- peanuts
- shellfish
- soya beans
- timber
- tobacco
- wheat
- capital cities
- major towns

pasture
cropland
forest
wetland
desert
mountain region

Fakahatchee Strand is part of the extensive sub-tropical swamps in the Florida Everglades. The swamps support a wide variety of animal life, including many rare birds, fish, alligators and crocodiles.

Farming on the Great Plains and in the Midwest is characterized by large-scale, mechanized wheat farms.

USA: NORTHEASTERN STATES

Connecticut, Maine, Massachusetts, New Hampshire, New Jersey, New York, Pennsylvania, Rhode Island, Vermont

THE INDENTED COAST AND VAST WOODLANDS of the northeastern states were the original core area for European expansion. The rustic character of New England prevails after 390 years, while the great cities of the Atlantic seaboard have formed an almost continuous urban region. Over 20 million immigrants entered New York from 1855 to 1924 and the northeast became the industrial centre of the USA. After the decline of mining and heavy manufacturing, economic dynamism has been restored with the growth of hi-tech and service industries.

Chelsea in Vermont, surrounded by trees in their fall foliage. Tourism and agriculture dominate the economy of this self-consciously rural state, where no town exceeds 30,000 people.

MAP KEY

POPULATION

- above 5 million
- 1 million to 5 million
- 500,000 to 1 million
- 100,000 to 500,000
- 50,000 to 100,000
- 10,000 to 50,000
- below 10,000

ELEVATION

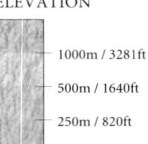

- 1000m / 3281ft
- 500m / 1640ft
- 250m / 820ft
- 100m / 328ft
- sea level

TRANSPORT AND INDUSTRY

THE PRINCIPAL SEABOARD CITIES grew up on trade and manufacturing. They are now global centres of commerce and corporate administration, dominating the regional economy. Research and development facilities support an expanding electronics and communications sector throughout the region. Pharmaceutical and chemical industries are important in New Jersey and Pennsylvania.

THE TRANSPORT NETWORK

340,090 miles (544,144 km)	4813 miles 7700 km
12,872 miles (20,592 km)	2108 miles (3389 km)

New York's commercial success is tied historically to its transport connections. The Erie Canal, completed in 1825, opened up the Great Lakes and the interior to New York's markets and carried a stream of immigrants into the Midwest.

Major industry and infrastructure

- chemicals
- coal
- defence
- electronics
- engineering
- finance
- hi-tech industry
- iron & steel
- pharmaceuticals
- printing & publishing
- research & development
- textiles
- timber processing
- major towns
- international airports
- major roads
- major industrial area

(Inset map labels: CANADA, Maine, Vermont, New Hampshire, Syracuse, Portland, Rochester, Albany, Buffalo, New York, Massachusetts, Boston, Connecticut, Hartford, Providence, Rhode Island, Pennsylvania, New York, New Jersey, Pittsburgh, Harrisburg, Philadelphia, Ohio, West Virginia, Maryland, Delaware, ATLANTIC OCEAN)

(Main map place names include:)

CANADA

Lake Ontario — Lake Erie

NEW YORK — Buffalo, Rochester, Syracuse, Utica, Albany, Schenectady, Troy, Niagara Falls, Lockport, Batavia, Elmira, Binghamton, Ithaca, Watertown, Oswego, Fulton, Oneida Lake, Finger Lakes, Cayuga Lake, Seneca Lake, Adirondack Mountains, Lake Champlain, Lake Placid, Catskill Mountains, Hudson River, Mohawk River

VERMONT — Burlington, Montpelier, Rutland, Bennington

MASSACHUSETTS — Springfield, Pittsfield

CONNECTICUT — Hartford, Waterbury, New Haven, Bridgeport, Stamford, Danbury

NEW YORK (city) — Yonkers, White Plains, New Rochelle, Long Island, Jersey City, Newark

PENNSYLVANIA — Pittsburgh, Scranton, Wilkes Barre, Williamsport, Allentown, Bethlehem, Reading, Harrisburg, Lancaster, York, Erie, Altoona, Johnstown, Philadelphia, Appalachian Mountains, Allegheny Plateau, Allegheny Mountains, Blue Mountain, Laurel Hill

NEW JERSEY — Trenton, Camden, Atlantic City, New Brunswick, Princeton

OHIO — WEST VIRGINIA — MARYLAND — DELAWARE

ATLANTIC OCEAN

The Hancock Tower dominates the skyline of Boston's business district. New England's principal city has grown through land reclamation within Massachusetts Bay.

USING THE LAND AND SEA

PENNSYLVANIA HAS a large rural population and a major agribusiness sector dominated by livestock-raising. Fruit, vegetables and nursery plants are grown throughout the region, with fishing on the coast. Cranberries and maple syrup are traditional products in New England. Large areas of cropland in the north have been returned to forest this century.

CANADA
Maine
Vermont
New York
Albany
New Hampshire
Rochester
Massachusetts
Buffalo
Boston
Connecticut
Ohio
Pennsylvania
New York
Rhode Island
Pittsburgh
Harrisburg
West Virginia
Philadelphia
New Jersey
Maryland
Delaware
ATLANTIC OCEAN

Land use and agricultural distribution

- cattle
- poultry
- cranberries
- fishing
- fodder
- fruit
- maple syrup
- timber
- major towns

pasture
cropland
forest

THE URBAN/RURAL POPULATION DIVIDE

urban 78%   rural 22%

0 10 20 30 40 50 60 70 80 90 100

POPULATION DENSITY	TOTAL LAND AREA
277 people per sq mile (107 people per sq km)	161,096 sq miles (417,222 sq km)

Foreign competition and depletion of stocks in the Atlantic fishing grounds caused a decline in fishing in the seaboard states. Recent years have seen a gradual recovery; Massachusetts now annually ranks third or fourth in the USA in terms of the value of fish landed.

THE LANDSCAPE

THE MARSHY LOWLANDS of the Atlantic Coastal Plain dwindle towards the north, giving way to the rocky coast of Maine. Uplifted over 400 million years ago, the Appalachian Mountains have since been carved into several discrete ranges by the region's main rivers and heavily denuded by successive glacial advances. This broad upland belt, with the younger Adirondack Mountains, is bounded by the Great Lakes in the northwest.

The islands, inlets and promontories of Maine's coast extend 3500 miles (5630 km). The tidal range is particularly high, varying between 12 and 24 ft (3.7–7.3 m).

The narrow Finger Lakes of northwestern New York State were formed by glaciers cutting into deep deposits of material from an earlier ice advance.

The Adirondack Mountains were formed when the deeply buried basement rocks were forced upwards in a dome by as much as 2 miles (3 km).

The lower Connecticut River has cut down into the flat, clay valley floor, which previously formed the bed of an ice-dammed lake.

Deposits of glacial till from the last Ice Age are up to 1000 ft (300 m) deep around Lake Ontario.

The Genesee River in New York State has eroded a canyon 800 ft (240 m) deep through the Appalachians. The river continued to cut downwards as the land was uplifted.

Green Mountains

Niagara Falls

Cape Cod

Lake Erie, receiving water flowing from the rest of the Great Lakes, drains via the Niagara Falls, into Lake Ontario, which lies 325 ft (99 m) below.

Resistant rock
River fed by water from the Great Lakes
Force of water continues to undercut cliffs
Softer rock is eroded more quickly

The Niagara Falls were created where the Niagara River reached an escarpment capped by hard limestone. This was gradually eroded exposing softer rock strata. Plunging water continues to erode the softer strata causing the falls to recede upstream.

The waterfalls at Dingmans Ferry are typical of those found in villages on the 'Fall-line', where rivers drop from the Appalachians to the coastal lowlands. These locations provide water power and are often at the navigable head of the river.

Dingmans Ferry

The Atlantic Coastal Plain is part of the continental shelf, which extends several hundred miles out to sea, providing a rich environment for marine life.

Rising sea levels have flooded river valleys along the coast, creating rias such as Long Island Sound.

Cape Cod, Long Island and the islands between them mark the top of a great terminal moraine, formed at the front of the ice sheet which once covered the land. This ridge of deposited material was subsequently flooded by rising seas.

Cape Cod

At Provincetown, Cape Cod, complex and powerful ocean currents continue to modify the shoreline, washing away some 3 ft (1 m) of the lower cape each year, while extending the beaches in the north.

SCALE 1:2,750,000
(projection: Lambert Conformal Conic)

Km
0 10 20 30 40 50 60 70 80 90 100

0 5 10 20 30 40 50 60 70 80 90 100
Miles

▷ 10
▷ 66

CANADA
Madawaska
Saint John River
Fort Kent
Long Lake
Beau Lake
Dickey
Van Buren
Eagle Lake
Limestone
Saint John River
Allagash River
Fish River Lake
Washburn
Caribou
Presque Isle
Fort Fairfield
Squa Pan Mountain 451m
Machias River
Ashland
Mars Hill
Aroostook River
Saddleback Mountain 517m
Churchill Lake
Eagle Lake
Chamberlain Lake
Mount Chase 744m
Houlton
Island Falls
Seboomook Lake
Chesuncook Lake
Mount Katahdin 1605m
Mattawamkeag
Sherman Mills
Danforth
Chiputneticook Lakes
Moosehead Lake
Millinocket Lake
Millinocket
Penobscot River
Boundary Bald Mountain 1109m
Vanceboro
Jackman
Big Squaw Mountain 978m
White Cap Mountain 1111m
Greenville
Lincoln
Saint Croix River
Woodland
Calais
Moose River
Coburn Mountain 1133m
Brownville Junction
Sebec Lake
Milo
Mattawamkeag
West Grand Lake
Bay of Fundy
MAINE
Flagstaff Lake
Bigelow Mountain 1265m
Guildford
Big Lake
Trumbledown Mountain 1080m
Bingham
Lake Memphremagog
Aziscohos Lake
Stratton
Sebasticook Lake
Old Town
Milford
Eastport
Lubec
Gore Mountain 1015m
Colebrook
Rangeley
Saddleback Mountain 1255m
Madison
Bangor
Brewer
Lead Mountain 466m
Gardner Lake
Machias
Grand Manan Channel
Newport
Island Pond
Blue Mountain 988m
Mooselookmeguntic Lake
Farmington
Skowhegan
Pittsfield
Hampden
Graham Lake
Cross Island
Barton
Old Speck Mountain 1274m
Rumford
Wilton
Oakland
Winslow
China Lake
Searsport
Buckstown
Ellsworth
Milbridge
Jonesport
Great Wass Island
Guildhall
Lancaster
Berlin
Bethel
Norway
South Paris
Augusta
Belfast
Blue Hill
Bar Harbor
Mount Desert Island
Lyndonville
Gardiner
Lewiston
Auburn
Camden
Rockland
Thomaston
Deer Isle
Swans Island
Petit Manan Point
Moore Reservoir
Mount Washington 1917m
Littleton
Mount Lafayette 1600m
Bridgton
Lisbon Falls
Bath
Brunswick
Wiscasset
Waldoboro
Vinalhaven Island
Isle au Haut
Lisbon
Woodsville
North Conway
Conway
Pinkham Mountain 612m
Sebago Lake
North Windham
Boothbay Harbor
Matinicus Island
Seal Island
Ragged Island
Plymouth
Squam Lake
Mount Cardigan 951m
Meredith
Lake Winnipesaukee
Wolfeboro
Gorham
Portland
South Portland
Cape Elizabeth
Casco Bay
Gulf of Maine
Lebanon
Bristol
Laconia
Alfred
Saco
Biddeford
NEW HAMPSHIRE
Northfield
Farmington
Sanford
Kennebunk
Claremont
Sunapee Lake
Concord
Rochester
Somersworth
York Harbor
Henniker
Dover
Kittery
Hillsboro
Goffstown
Newmarket
Portsmouth
Keene
Manchester
Exeter
Hampton
Jaffrey
Peterborough
Amesbury
Newburyport
Winchester
Milford
Nashua
Haverhill
Methuen
Plum Island
Athol
Winchendon
Fitchburg
Lowell
Lawrence
Danvers
Gloucester
Quabbin Reservoir
Leominster
Woburn
Salem
Cape Ann
Beverly
Clinton
Medford
Lynn
Barre
Hudson
Cambridge
Malden
Massachusetts Bay
MASSACHUSETTS
Worcester
Framingham
Newton
Boston
Quincy
Logan International
Palmer
Auburn
Dedham
Weymouth
Whitinsville
Stoughton
Randolph
Marshfield
Race Point
Provincetown
Stafford Springs
Southbridge
Milford
Mansfield
Bridgewater
Brockton
Kingston
Plymouth
Putnam
Greenville
Attleboro
Taunton
Cape Cod Bay
Orleans
Danielson
Pawtucket
East Providence
Somerset
Fall River
Cape Cod
Barnstable
Nauset Beach
Moosup
Cranston
Warwick
Fairhaven
Hyannis
South Yarmouth
Jewett City
Colchester
RHODE ISLAND
New Bedford
East Falmouth
Monomoy Island
Norwich
Tiverton
Falmouth
Great Point
New London
Westerly
Rhode Island
Newport
Oak Bluffs
Nantucket Sound
Niantic
Groton
Rhode Island Sound
Block Island Sound
Edgartown
Martha's Vineyard
Nantucket
Nantucket Island
Fishers Island
Gardiners Island
Block Island
Southold
Montauk Point
Sag Harbor
Montauk
Southampton
OCEAN

USA: MID-EASTERN STATES

Delaware, District of Columbia, Kentucky, Maryland, North Carolina, South Carolina, Tennessee, Virginia, West Virginia

KEY EVENTS IN THE HISTORY OF THE USA took place in this diverse region, which became the front line in the Civil War of 1861–65 between North and South. Strong regional contrasts exist between the fertile coastal plains, the isolated upcountry of the Appalachian Mountains and the cotton-growing areas of the Mississippi lowlands to the west. Whilst coal mining, a traditional industry in the Appalachians, has declined in recent years leaving much rural poverty, service industries elsewhere have increased, especially in the US federal capital, Washington DC.

MAP KEY

POPULATION

- 500,000 to 1 million
- 100,000 to 500,000
- 50,000 to 100,000
- 10,000 to 50,000
- below 10,000

ELEVATION

- 6000m / 19,686ft
- 4000m / 13,124ft
- 3000m / 9843ft
- 2000m / 6562ft
- 1000m / 3281ft
- 500m / 1640ft
- 250m / 820ft
- 100m / 328ft
- sea level

SCALE 1:3,000,000
(projection: Lambert Conformal Conic)

The Bluegrass region of Kentucky centres on the town of Lexington. This exceptionally fertile rolling plain is well known for its thoroughbred horse-breeding ranches.

TRANSPORT AND INDUSTRY

IN THE URBANIZED NORTHEAST, manufacturing remains important, alongside a burgeoning service sector. North Carolina is a major centre for industrial research and development. Traditional industries include Tennessee whiskey, and textiles in South Carolina. The decline of open-cast coal mining in the Appalachians has been hastened by environmental controls, although adventure-tourism is a flourishing new industry.

Major industry and infrastructure

- adventure-tourism
- car manufacture
- coal
- electronics
- engineering
- finance
- food processing
- hi-tech industry
- mining
- research & development
- textiles
- capital cities
- major towns
- international airports
- major roads
- major industrial areas

THE TRANSPORT NETWORK

452,218 miles (723,548 km)	5737 miles (8267 km)
18,336 miles (29,503 km)	4404 miles (7081 km)

Tennessee's rivers are part of an important inland bulk-transport network. Memphis is connected with New Orleans in the south, and with cities as distant as Minneapolis, Sioux City, Chicago and Pittsburgh, via the Mississippi and its tributaries.

THE LANDSCAPE

THE EASTERN TRIBUTARIES OF THE MISSISSIPPI drain the interior lowlands. The Cumberland Plateau and the parallel ranges of the Appalachians have been successively uplifted and eroded over time, with the eastern side reduced to a series of foothills known as the Piedmont. The broad coastal plain gradually falls away into salt marshes, lagoons and offshore bars, broken by flooded estuaries along the shores of the Atlantic.

The Mammoth Cave is part of an extensive cave system in the limestone region of southwestern Kentucky. It stretches for over 300 miles (485 km) on five different levels and contains three rivers and three lakes.

The Mississippi River and its tributary the Ohio River form the western border of the region.

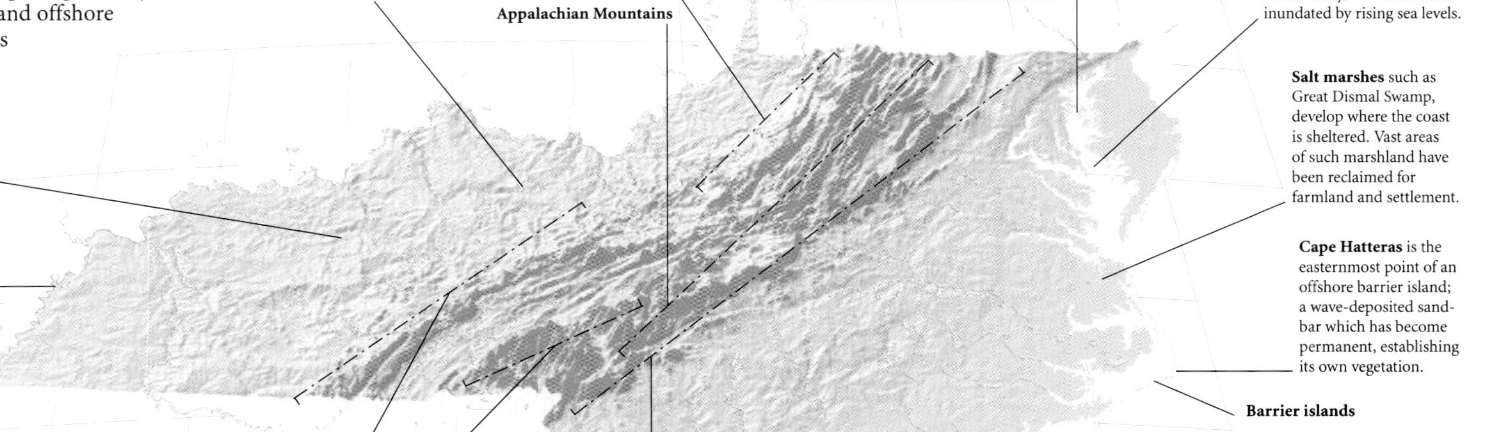

Natural Bridge in eastern Kentucky is an arch 78 ft (26 m) long and 65 ft (20 m) high. It has been shaped from resistant sandstone by gradual weathering processes, which removed the softer rock lying underneath.

The Allegheny Mountains form the northwestern edge of the Appalachian mountain chain. Continuous folding has formed rich seams of bituminous coal.

Appalachian Mountains

Farmland on the eastern shores of Chesapeake Bay is sustained by artificial drainage. The area also provides refuge for a variety of waterfowl.

The many inlets of Chesapeake Bay are the flooded tributaries of the main river valley, which have been inundated by rising sea levels.

Salt marshes such as Great Dismal Swamp, develop where the coast is sheltered. Vast areas of such marshland have been reclaimed for farmland and settlement.

Cape Hatteras is the easternmost point of an offshore barrier island; a wave-deposited sand-bar which has become permanent, establishing its own vegetation.

Barrier islands

Tidal inlet
Barrier island

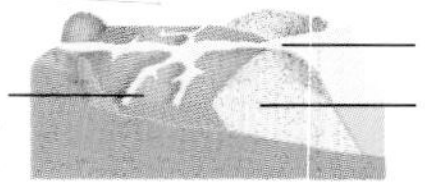

These intertidal mudflats become submerged at high tide

Barrier islands are common along the coasts of North and South Carolina. As sea levels rise, wave action builds up ridges of sand and pebbles parallel to the coast, separated by lagoons or intertidal mudflats, which are flooded at high tide.

The Cumberland Plateau is the most southwesterly part of the Appalachians. Big Black Mountain at 4180 ft (1274 m) is the highest point in the range.

The Great Smoky Mountains form the western escarpment of the Appalachians. The region is heavily forested, with over 130 species of tree.

The Blue Ridge Mountains are a steep ridge, culminating in Mount Mitchell, the highest point in the Appalachians, at 6684 ft (2037 m).

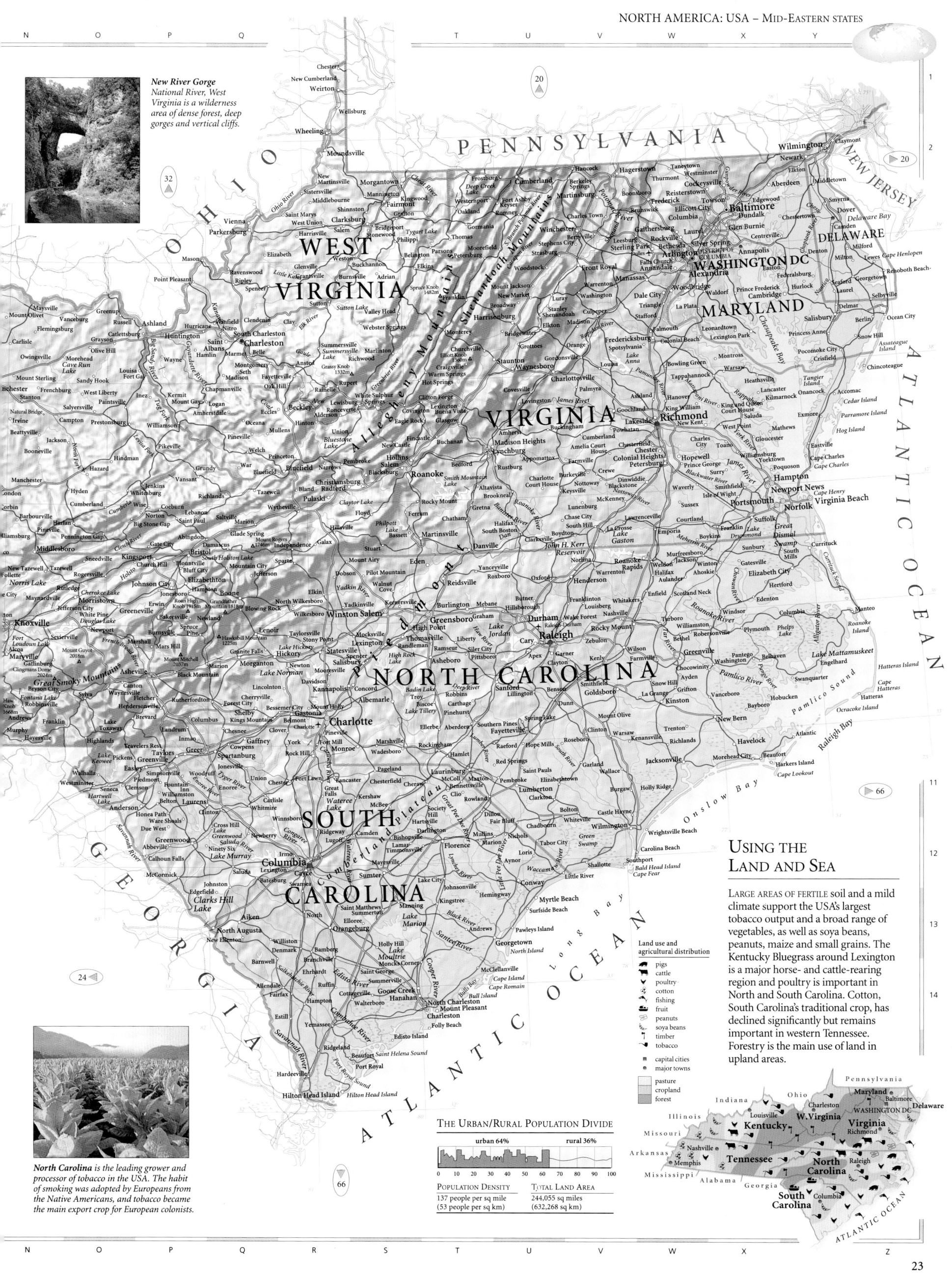

New River Gorge National River, West Virginia is a wilderness area of dense forest, deep gorges and vertical cliffs.

North Carolina is the leading grower and processor of tobacco in the USA. The habit of smoking was adopted by Europeans from the Native Americans, and tobacco became the main export crop for European colonists.

USING THE LAND AND SEA

LARGE AREAS OF FERTILE soil and a mild climate support the USA's largest tobacco output and a broad range of vegetables, as well as soya beans, peanuts, maize and small grains. The Kentucky Bluegrass around Lexington is a major horse- and cattle-rearing region and poultry is important in North and South Carolina. Cotton, South Carolina's traditional crop, has declined significantly but remains important in western Tennessee. Forestry is the main use of land in upland areas.

Land use and agricultural distribution

- pigs
- cattle
- poultry
- cotton
- fishing
- fruit
- peanuts
- soya beans
- timber
- tobacco

- capital cities
- major towns

- pasture
- cropland
- forest

THE URBAN/RURAL POPULATION DIVIDE

urban 64%   rural 36%

POPULATION DENSITY
137 people per sq mile
(53 people per sq km)

TOTAL LAND AREA
244,055 sq miles
(632,268 sq km)

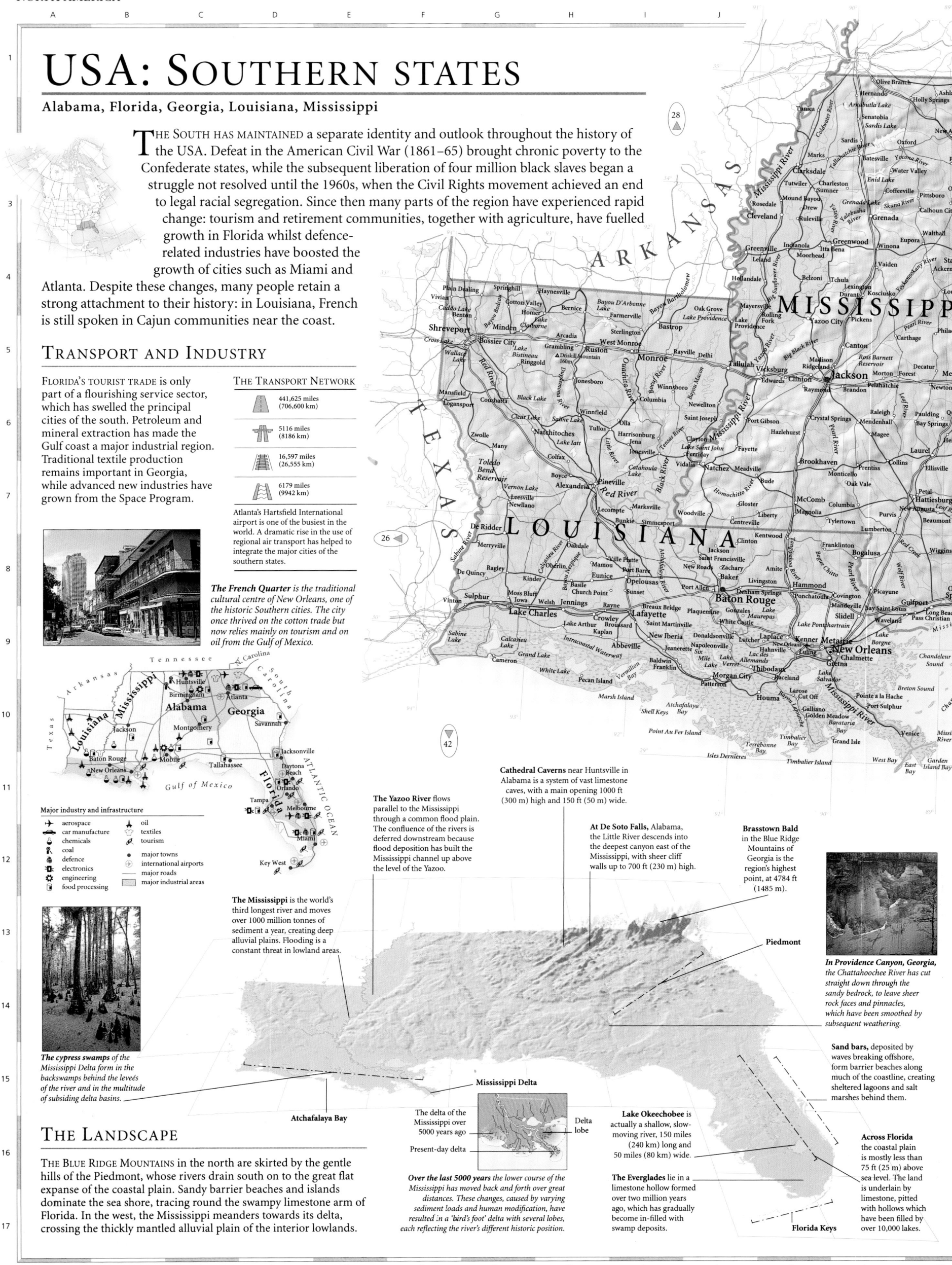

USA: SOUTHERN STATES

Alabama, Florida, Georgia, Louisiana, Mississippi

THE SOUTH HAS MAINTAINED a separate identity and outlook throughout the history of the USA. Defeat in the American Civil War (1861–65) brought chronic poverty to the Confederate states, while the subsequent liberation of four million black slaves began a struggle not resolved until the 1960s, when the Civil Rights movement achieved an end to legal racial segregation. Since then many parts of the region have experienced rapid change: tourism and retirement communities, together with agriculture, have fuelled growth in Florida whilst defence-related industries have boosted the growth of cities such as Miami and Atlanta. Despite these changes, many people retain a strong attachment to their history: in Louisiana, French is still spoken in Cajun communities near the coast.

TRANSPORT AND INDUSTRY

FLORIDA'S TOURIST TRADE is only part of a flourishing service sector, which has swelled the principal cities of the south. Petroleum and mineral extraction has made the Gulf coast a major industrial region. Traditional textile production remains important in Georgia, while advanced new industries have grown from the Space Program.

THE TRANSPORT NETWORK

441,625 miles (706,600 km)	
5116 miles (8186 km)	
16,597 miles (26,555 km)	
6179 miles (9942 km)	

Atlanta's Hartsfield International airport is one of the busiest in the world. A dramatic rise in the use of regional air transport has helped to integrate the major cities of the southern states.

The French Quarter is the traditional cultural centre of New Orleans, one of the historic Southern cities. The city once thrived on the cotton trade but now relies mainly on tourism and on oil from the Gulf of Mexico.

Major industry and infrastructure

- ✈ aerospace
- 🚗 car manufacture
- chemicals
- coal
- defence
- electronics
- engineering
- food processing
- oil
- textiles
- tourism
- major towns
- international airports
- major roads
- major industrial areas

THE LANDSCAPE

THE BLUE RIDGE MOUNTAINS in the north are skirted by the gentle hills of the Piedmont, whose rivers drain south on to the great flat expanse of the coastal plain. Sandy barrier beaches and islands dominate the sea shore, tracing round the swampy limestone arm of Florida. In the west, the Mississippi meanders towards its delta, crossing the thickly mantled alluvial plain of the interior lowlands.

The cypress swamps of the Mississippi Delta form in the backswamps behind the levées of the river and in the multitude of subsiding delta basins.

The Yazoo River flows parallel to the Mississippi through a common flood plain. The confluence of the rivers is deferred downstream because flood deposition has built the Mississippi channel up above the level of the Yazoo.

The Mississippi is the world's third longest river and moves over 1000 million tonnes of sediment a year, creating deep alluvial plains. Flooding is a constant threat in lowland areas.

Cathedral Caverns near Huntsville in Alabama is a system of vast limestone caves, with a main opening 1000 ft (300 m) high and 150 ft (50 m) wide.

At De Soto Falls, Alabama, the Little River descends into the deepest canyon east of the Mississippi, with sheer cliff walls up to 700 ft (230 m) high.

Brasstown Bald in the Blue Ridge Mountains of Georgia is the region's highest point, at 4784 ft (1485 m).

In Providence Canyon, Georgia, the Chattahoochee River has cut straight down through the sandy bedrock, to leave sheer rock faces and pinnacles, which have been smoothed by subsequent weathering.

Sand bars, deposited by waves breaking offshore, form barrier beaches along much of the coastline, creating sheltered lagoons and salt marshes behind them.

Piedmont

Atchafalaya Bay

Mississippi Delta

The delta of the Mississippi over 5000 years ago

Present-day delta

Delta lobe

Over the last 5000 years the lower course of the Mississippi has moved back and forth over great distances. These changes, caused by varying sediment loads and human modification, have resulted in a 'bird's foot' delta with several lobes, each reflecting the river's different historic position.

Lake Okeechobee is actually a shallow, slow-moving river, 150 miles (240 km) long and 50 miles (80 km) wide.

The Everglades lie in a limestone hollow formed over two million years ago, which has gradually become in-filled with swamp deposits.

Across Florida the coastal plain is mostly less than 75 ft (25 m) above sea level. The land is underlain by limestone, pitted with hollows which have been filled by over 10,000 lakes.

Florida Keys

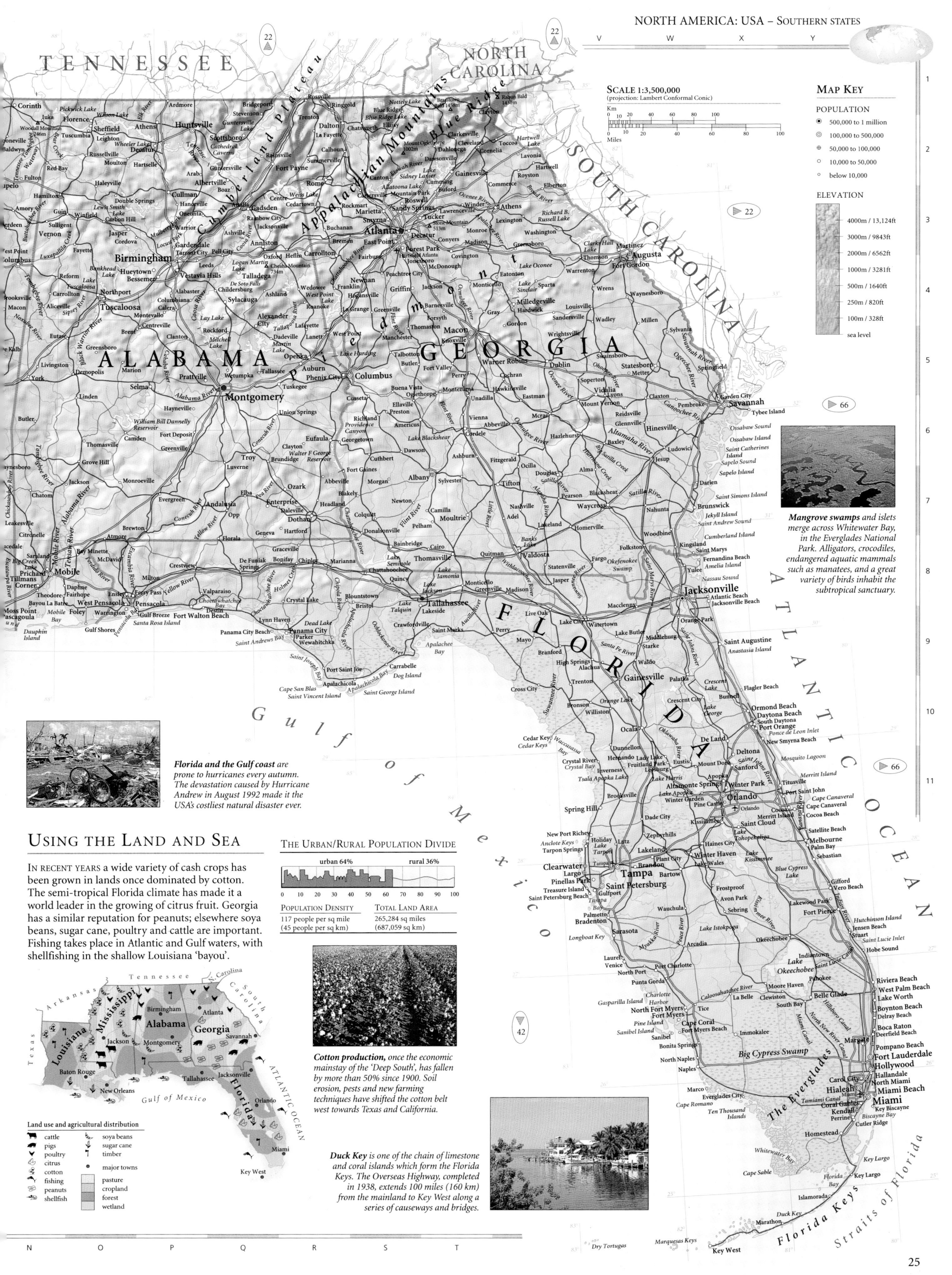

SCALE 1:3,500,000
(projection: Lambert Conformal Conic)

MAP KEY

POPULATION

- 500,000 to 1 million
- 100,000 to 500,000
- 50,000 to 100,000
- 10,000 to 50,000
- below 10,000

ELEVATION

- 4000m / 13,124ft
- 3000m / 9843ft
- 2000m / 6562ft
- 1000m / 3281ft
- 500m / 1640ft
- 250m / 820ft
- 100m / 328ft
- sea level

Mangrove swamps and islets merge across Whitewater Bay, in the Everglades National Park. Alligators, crocodiles, endangered aquatic mammals such as manatees, and a great variety of birds inhabit the subtropical sanctuary.

Florida and the Gulf coast are prone to hurricanes every autumn. The devastation caused by Hurricane Andrew in August 1992 made it the USA's costliest natural disaster ever.

USING THE LAND AND SEA

IN RECENT YEARS a wide variety of cash crops has been grown in lands once dominated by cotton. The semi-tropical Florida climate has made it a world leader in the growing of citrus fruit. Georgia has a similar reputation for peanuts; elsewhere soya beans, sugar cane, poultry and cattle are important. Fishing takes place in Atlantic and Gulf waters, with shellfishing in the shallow Louisiana 'bayou'.

THE URBAN/RURAL POPULATION DIVIDE

urban 64%   rural 36%

POPULATION DENSITY
117 people per sq mile
(45 people per sq km)

TOTAL LAND AREA
265,284 sq miles
(687,059 sq km)

Cotton production, once the economic mainstay of the 'Deep South', has fallen by more than 50% since 1900. Soil erosion, pests and new farming techniques have shifted the cotton belt west towards Texas and California.

Land use and agricultural distribution
- cattle
- pigs
- poultry
- citrus
- cotton
- fishing
- peanuts
- shellfish
- soya beans
- sugar cane
- timber
- major towns
- pasture
- cropland
- forest
- wetland

Duck Key is one of the chain of limestone and coral islands which form the Florida Keys. The Overseas Highway, completed in 1938, extends 100 miles (160 km) from the mainland to Key West along a series of causeways and bridges.

USA: Texas

First explored by Spaniards moving north from Mexico in search of gold, Texas was controlled by Spain and then Mexico, before becoming an independent republic in 1836, and joining the Union of States in 1845. During the 19th century, many of the migrants who came to Texas raised cattle on the abundant land; in the 20th century, they were joined by prospectors attracted by the promise of oil riches. Today, although natural resources, especially oil, still form the basis of its wealth, the diversified Texan economy includes thriving hi-tech and finance industries. The major urban centres, home to 80% of the population, lie in the south and east, and include Houston, the 'oil-city', and Dallas–Fort Worth. Hispanic influences remain strong, especially in the south and west.

Dallas was founded in 1841 as a prairie trading post and its development was stimulated by the arrival of railroads. Cotton and then oil funded the town's early growth. Today, the modern, high-rise skyline of Dallas reflects the city's position as a leading centre of banking, insurance and the petroleum industry in the southwest.

Using the Land

Cotton production and livestock-raising, particularly cattle, dominate farming, although crop failures and the demands of local markets have led to some diversification. Following the introduction of modern farming techniques, cotton production spread out from the east to the plains of western Texas. Cattle ranches are widespread, while sheep and goats are raised on the dry Edwards Plateau.

Land use and agricultural distribution
- cattle
- goats
- sheep
- cereals
- cotton
- major towns
- pasture
- cropland
- forest
- barren

THE URBAN/RURAL POPULATION DIVIDE

urban 80%   rural 20%

0 10 20 30 40 50 60 70 80 90 100

POPULATION DENSITY
66 people per sq mile
(26 people per sq km)

TOTAL LAND AREA
267,338 sq miles
(692,402 sq km)

38

The huge cattle ranches of Texas developed during the 19th century when land was plentiful and could be acquired cheaply. Today, more cattle and sheep are raised in Texas than in any other state.

The Landscape

Texas is made up of a series of massive steps descending from the mountains and high plains of the west and northwest to the coastal lowlands in the southeast. Many of the state's borders are delineated by water. The Rio Grande flows from the Rocky Mountains to the Gulf of Mexico, marking the border with Mexico.

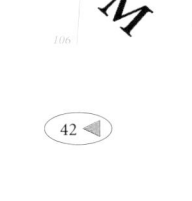

Cap Rock Escarpment *juts out from the plains, running 200 miles (320 km) from north to south. Its height varies from 300 ft (90 m) rising to sheer cliffs up to 1000 ft (300 m).*

42

The Llano Estacado or Staked Plain in northern Texas is known for its harsh environment. In the north, freezing winds carrying ice and snow sweep down from the Rocky Mountains, and to the south, sandstorms frequently blow up, scouring anything in their paths. Flash floods, in the wide, flat river beds that remain dry for most of the year, are another hazard.

The Guadalupe Mountains lie in the southern Rocky Mountains. They incorporate Guadalupe Peak, the highest in Texas, rising 8749 ft (2667 m).

The Red River flows for 1300 miles (2090 km), marking most of the northern border of Texas. A dam and reservoir along its course provide vital irrigation and hydro-electric power to the surrounding area.

The Rio Grande flows from the Rocky Mountains through semi-arid land, supporting sparse vegetation. The river actually shrinks along its course, losing more water through evaporation and seepage than it gains from its tributaries and rainfall.

Big Bend National Park

Sabine River

Extensive forests of pine and cypress grow in the eastern corner of the coastal lowlands where the average rainfall is 45 inches (1145 mm) a year. This is higher than the rest of the state and over twice the average in the west.

In the coastal lowlands of southeastern Texas the Earth's crust is warping, causing the land to subside and allowing the sea to invade. Around Galveston, the rate of downward tilting is 6 inches (15 cm) per year. Erosion of the coast is also exacerbated by hurricanes.

Edwards Plateau is a limestone outcrop. It is part of the Great Plains, bounded to the southeast by the Balcones Escarpment, which marks the southerly limit of the plains.

Flowing through 1500 ft (450 m) high gorges, *the shallow, muddy Rio Grande makes a 90° bend, which marks the southern border of Big Bend National Park, giving it its name. The area is a mixture of forested mountains, deserts and canyons.*

Padre Island

Laguna Madre in southern Texas has been almost completely cut off from the sea by Padre Island. This sand bank was created by wave action, carrying and depositing material along the coast. The process is known as longshore drift.

Oil deposits

Oil trapped by fault

Oil deposits migrate through reservoir rocks such as shale

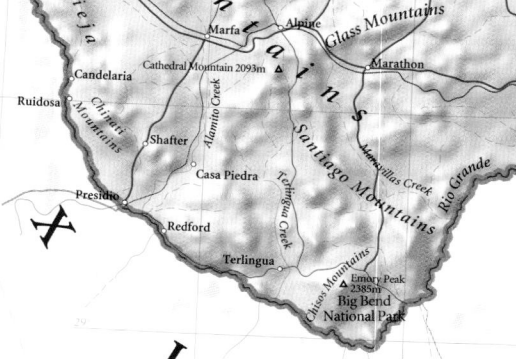

Oil accumulates beneath impermeable cap rock

Impermeable rock strata

Salt dome

Oil deposits *are found beneath much of Texas. They collect as oil migrates upwards through porous layers of rock until it is trapped, either by a cap of rock above a salt dome, or by a fault line which exposes impermeable rock through which the oil cannot rise.*

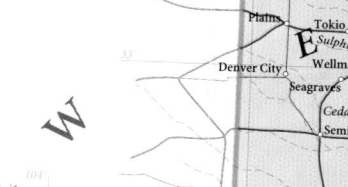

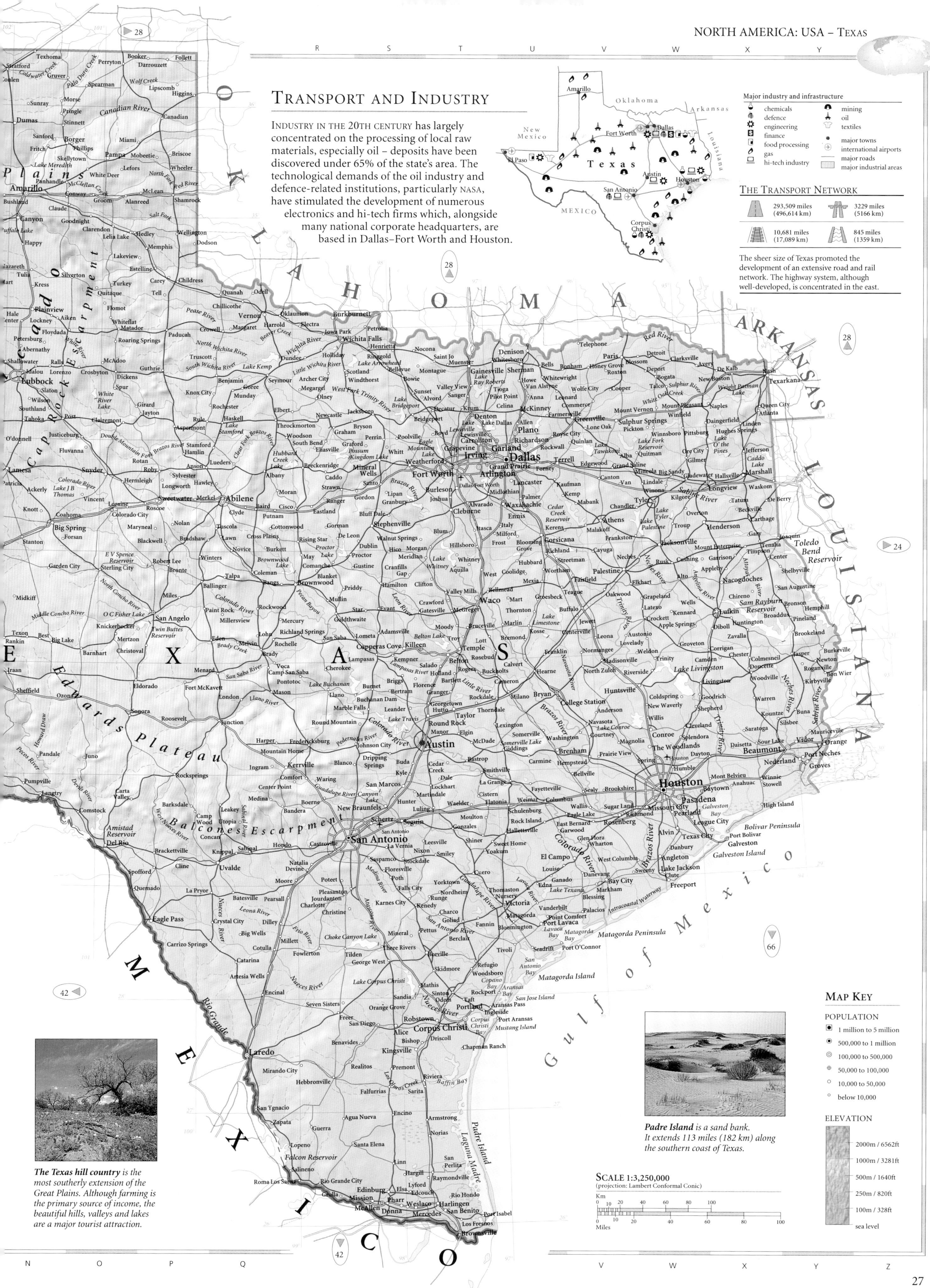

TRANSPORT AND INDUSTRY

INDUSTRY IN THE 20TH CENTURY has largely concentrated on the processing of local raw materials, especially oil – deposits have been discovered under 65% of the state's area. The technological demands of the oil industry and defence-related institutions, particularly NASA, have stimulated the development of numerous electronics and hi-tech firms which, alongside many national corporate headquarters, are based in Dallas–Fort Worth and Houston.

Major industry and infrastructure

chemicals	mining
defence	oil
engineering	textiles
finance	major towns
food processing	international airports
gas	major roads
hi-tech industry	major industrial areas

THE TRANSPORT NETWORK

293,509 miles (496,614 km)	3229 miles (5166 km)
10,681 miles (17,089 km)	845 miles (1359 km)

The sheer size of Texas promoted the development of an extensive road and rail network. The highway system, although well-developed, is concentrated in the east.

The Texas hill country is the most southerly extension of the Great Plains. Although farming is the primary source of income, the beautiful hills, valleys and lakes are a major tourist attraction.

Padre Island is a sand bank. It extends 113 miles (182 km) along the southern coast of Texas.

MAP KEY

POPULATION

- 1 million to 5 million
- 500,000 to 1 million
- 100,000 to 500,000
- 50,000 to 100,000
- 10,000 to 50,000
- below 10,000

ELEVATION

2000m / 6562ft
1000m / 3281ft
500m / 1640ft
250m / 820ft
100m / 328ft
sea level

SCALE 1:3,250,000
(projection: Lambert Conformal Conic)

Km
0 10 20 40 60 80 100

Miles
0 10 20 40 60 80 100

27

USA: SOUTH MIDWESTERN STATES

Arkansas, Kansas, Missouri, Oklahoma

THE EXPANSION OF THE USA focused on this region in the mid-19th century. Settlers spread from the confluence of the Missouri and Mississippi rivers up onto the Great Plains. This treeless expanse, which early explorers had called the 'Great American Desert', was turned into one of the world's richest agricultural regions; but periodic droughts, coupled with over-intensive farming, led to the 'Dustbowl' soil erosion crisis of the 1930s, the abandonment of many farms, and a mass exodus to the west coast. The land has since recovered, although the mechanization of agriculture has led to a decline in the rural population. In recent years, suburban residential development has spread rapidly across the wooded Ozark Plateau in the east of the region.

TRANSPORT AND INDUSTRY

THE PROCESSING OF AGRICULTURAL PRODUCTS, such as brewing and meat packing, has been traditionally important in these states. In Kansas and Oklahoma, diversified manufacturing now supplements income from fossil fuels; Wichita has become a world centre for aeronautical engineering, an industry which also employs many people in neighbouring Missouri.

Major industry and infrastructure

- ✈ aerospace
- ⚙ engineering
- $ finance
- 🗎 food processing
- ◊ gas
- ⛏ mining
- • oil
- 🚚 vehicle manufacture
- ■ major towns
- ✈ international airports
- — major roads
- major industrial areas

Agricultural produce *from the plains is moved by barges along the Mississippi. The river now carries a far greater tonnage of freight than any other waterway system in the USA.*

THE TRANSPORT NETWORK

380,307 miles (608,491 km)	4068 miles (6508 km)
16,185 miles (25,896 km)	1994 miles (3208 km)

The Arkansas River and its tributaries allow access to over half of the USA's navigable inland waterways. A system of locks and dams along the river provides Tulsa in Oklahoma with a navigable water route to the Gulf of Mexico.

MAP KEY

POPULATION
- ◉ 100,000 to 500,000
- ⊕ 50,000 to 100,000
- ○ 10,000 to 50,000
- • below 10,000

ELEVATION
- 1000m / 3281ft
- 500m / 1640ft
- 250m / 820ft
- 100m / 328ft
- sea level

THE LANDSCAPE

MOST OF THE REGION consists of high, treeless plains, which gradually descend east from the Rocky Mountains. Drainage follows this slope, with rivers flowing towards the alluvial lowlands of the Mississippi in the southeast. Between the plains and the lowlands lie various ranges of wooded hills, including the deeply incised Ozark Plateau.

Collapsed limestone caverns led to the formation of Big Basin in Kansas; a depression 100 ft (33 m) deep and 1 mile (1.6 km) wide.

The Great Salt Plains of northern Oklahoma cover 45 sq miles (116 sq km). The arid, white flats were left by the gradual evaporation of an ancient salt lake.

Underground water reserves
- Extent of the aquifer
- Kansas
- Oklahoma

The Ogallala Aquifer, *beneath the Great Plains, is the largest known source of underground water in the world. There is concern about the rapid depletion of this finite water supply by irrigation schemes.*

Flint Hills is the region's easternmost major escarpment. Steep, grassy uplands are interspersed with rocky, wooded ravines and outcrops of limestone and chert.

Missouri River

The Mississippi, *North America's longest river, is joined by the Missouri, its main tributary, on a flood plain which spreads south to the Gulf of Mexico.*

Red River

Devil's Den is a dry badland area. The rugged landscape, strewn with large boulders, is the eroded remnant of a spur extending from the Arbuckle Mountains to the west.

Ouachita Mountains

The Ozark Plateau is a wooded, hilly region of rivers and narrow, winding lakes. The Lake of the Ozarks was created by the damming of the Osage River in 1930.

Lake Ouachita, *in Arkansas is one of a number of irregularly-shaped lakes found among the ridges of the Ouachita Mountains.*

Crowleys Ridge is a long, sandy ridge, rising from the Mississippi flood plain. It was formed over thousands of years by the deposition of sand blown eastwards from the Great Plains.

Mississippi River

SCALE 1:3,000,000
(projection: Lambert Conformal Conic)

Km
0 5 10 20 30 40 50 60 70
Miles
0 5 10 20 30 40 50 60 70

The landscape of northeast Kansas is *interlaced by rivers which have cut broad wooded valleys through the gentle hills. All the rivers in Kansas form part of the massive Missouri/Mississippi drainage basin.*

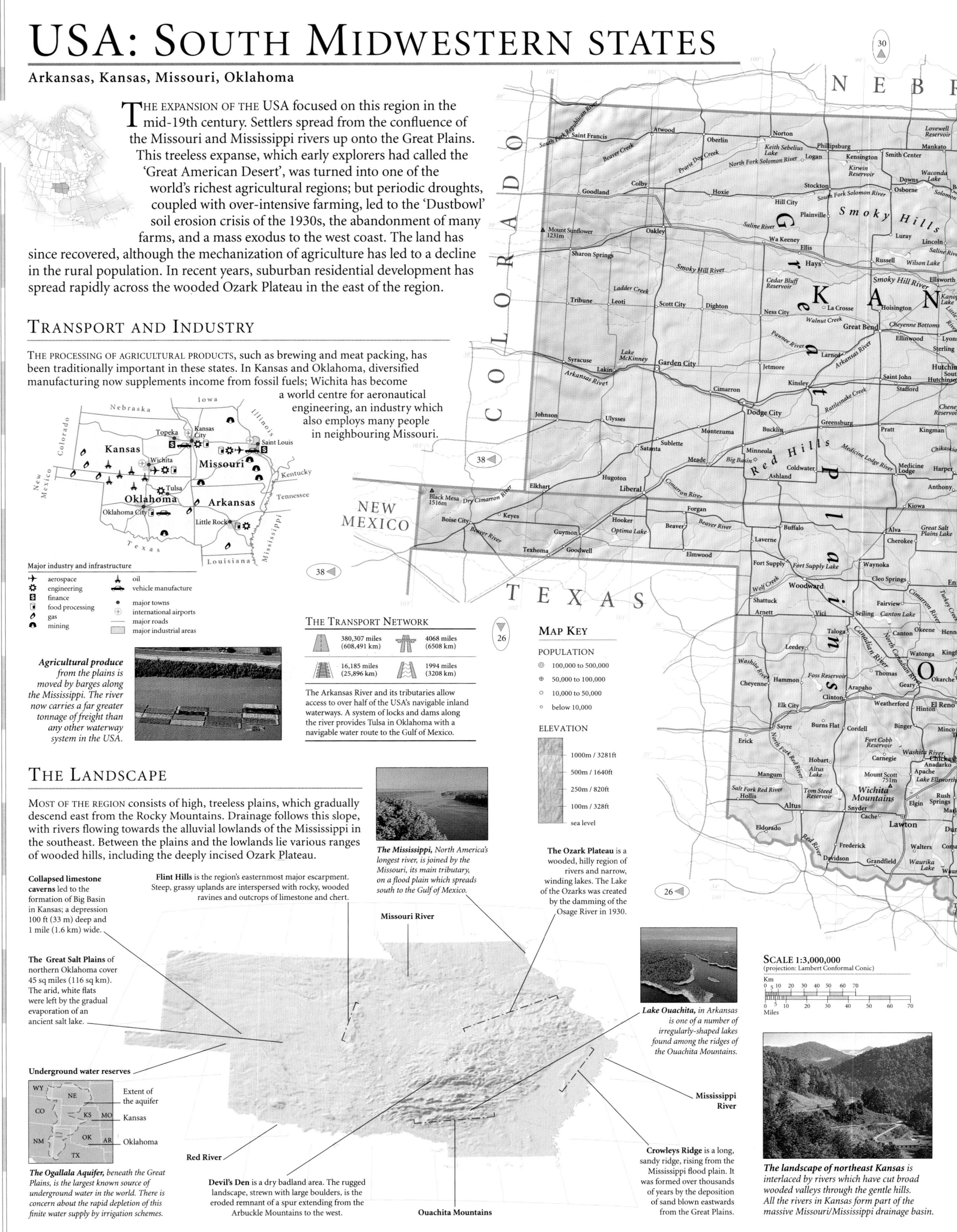

Gateway Arch, in Saint Louis, Missouri, is 634 ft (192 m) high. The huge steel arch symbolizes the city's historic role as the 'Gateway to the West'.

USING THE LAND

THE PROBLEMS of a harsh continental climate, with severe winters and hot, dry summers, are partially offset by the rich soils of the plains. Kansas is a major cereal producer, ranking first in the USA for the production of wheat and sorghum. Rainfall increases towards the east, favouring the cultivation of soya beans, cotton and rice, with corn concentrated in Missouri. Huge herds of cattle are raised in Oklahoma, Kansas and Missouri.

A combine harvester works the land on the Great Plains. A hundred years ago this region, also known as the prairies – the French word for pasture – was covered with tall, wild grasses.

THE URBAN/RURAL POPULATION DIVIDE

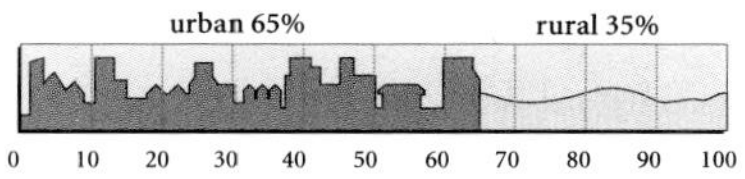

urban 65%   rural 35%

0 10 20 30 40 50 60 70 80 90 100

POPULATION DENSITY
48 people per sq mile
(19 people per sq km)

TOTAL LAND AREA
274,900 sq miles
(712,177 sq km)

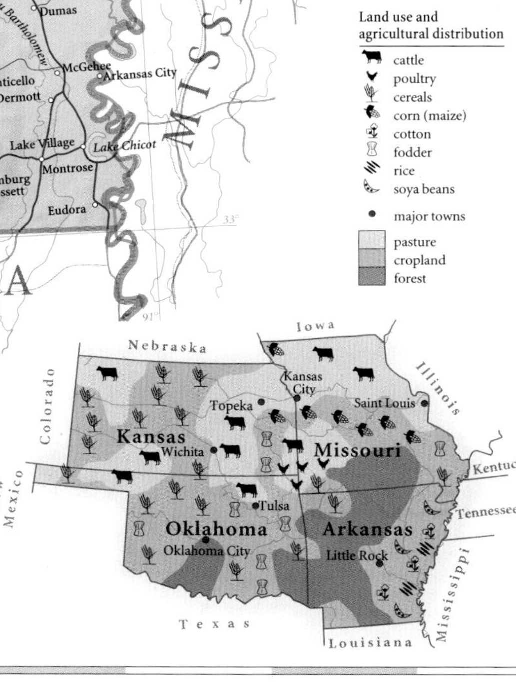

Land use and agricultural distribution
- cattle
- poultry
- cereals
- corn (maize)
- cotton
- fodder
- rice
- soya beans
- major towns
- pasture
- cropland
- forest

IOWA
ILLINOIS
MISSOURI
KANSAS
OKLAHOMA
ARKANSAS
TEXAS
LOUISIANA
TENNESSEE
KENTUCKY

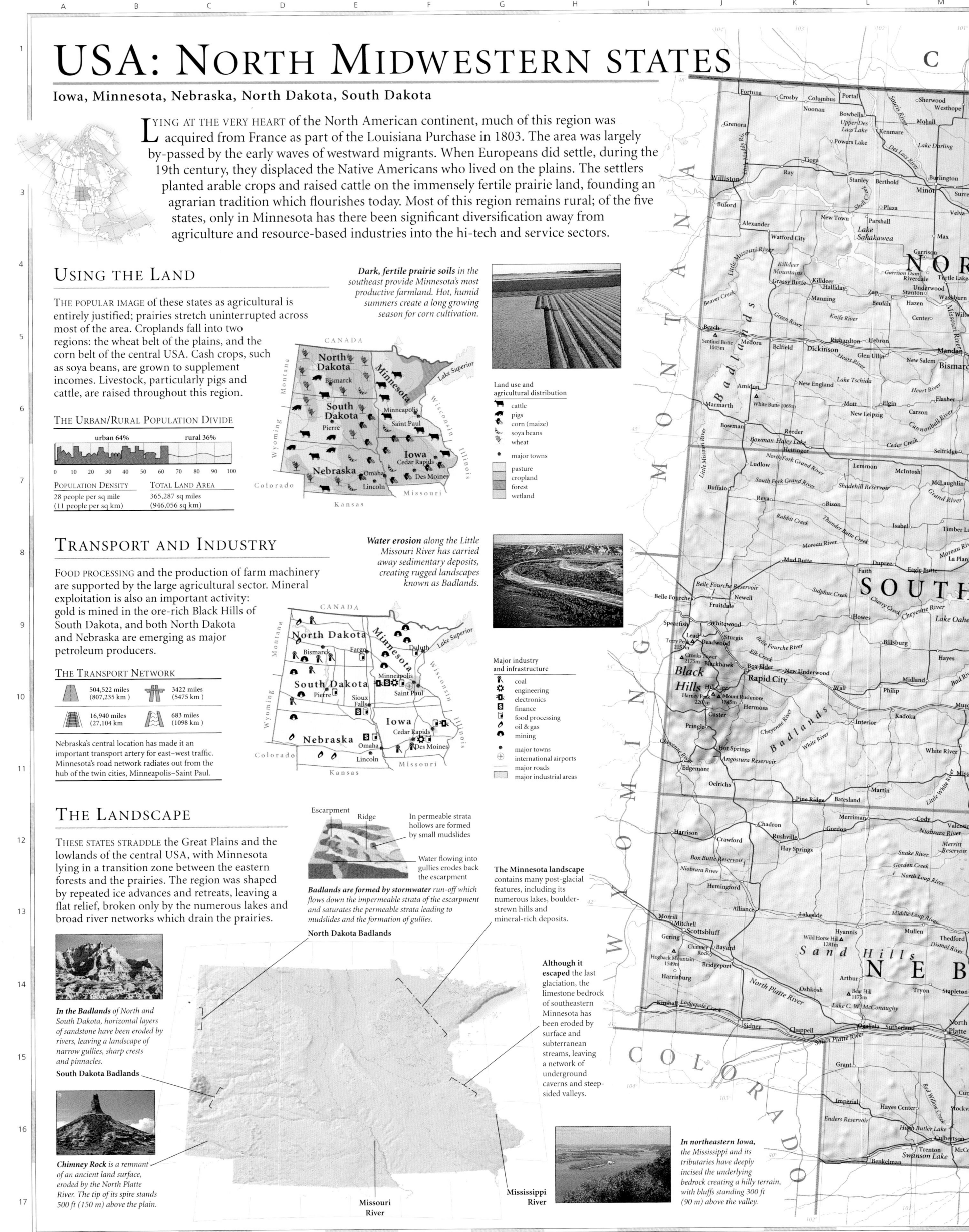

USA: NORTH MIDWESTERN STATES

Iowa, Minnesota, Nebraska, North Dakota, South Dakota

LYING AT THE VERY HEART of the North American continent, much of this region was acquired from France as part of the Louisiana Purchase in 1803. The area was largely by-passed by the early waves of westward migrants. When Europeans did settle, during the 19th century, they displaced the Native Americans who lived on the plains. The settlers planted arable crops and raised cattle on the immensely fertile prairie land, founding an agrarian tradition which flourishes today. Most of this region remains rural; of the five states, only in Minnesota has there been significant diversification away from agriculture and resource-based industries into the hi-tech and service sectors.

USING THE LAND

THE POPULAR IMAGE of these states as agricultural is entirely justified; prairies stretch uninterrupted across most of the area. Croplands fall into two regions: the wheat belt of the plains, and the corn belt of the central USA. Cash crops, such as soya beans, are grown to supplement incomes. Livestock, particularly pigs and cattle, are raised throughout this region.

Dark, fertile prairie soils in the southeast provide Minnesota's most productive farmland. Hot, humid summers create a long growing season for corn cultivation.

Land use and agricultural distribution
- cattle
- pigs
- corn (maize)
- soya beans
- wheat
- major towns
- pasture
- cropland
- forest
- wetland

THE URBAN/RURAL POPULATION DIVIDE

urban 64%   rural 36%

0 10 20 30 40 50 60 70 80 90 100

POPULATION DENSITY	TOTAL LAND AREA
28 people per sq mile (11 people per sq km)	365,287 sq miles (946,056 sq km)

TRANSPORT AND INDUSTRY

FOOD PROCESSING and the production of farm machinery are supported by the large agricultural sector. Mineral exploitation is also an important activity: gold is mined in the ore-rich Black Hills of South Dakota, and both North Dakota and Nebraska are emerging as major petroleum producers.

Water erosion along the Little Missouri River has carried away sedimentary deposits, creating rugged landscapes known as Badlands.

Major industry and infrastructure
- coal
- engineering
- electronics
- finance
- food processing
- oil & gas
- mining
- major towns
- international airports
- major roads
- major industrial areas

THE TRANSPORT NETWORK

504,522 miles (807,235 km)	3422 miles (5475 km)
16,940 miles (27,104 km)	683 miles (1098 km)

Nebraska's central location has made it an important transport artery for east–west traffic. Minnesota's road network radiates out from the hub of the twin cities, Minneapolis–Saint Paul.

THE LANDSCAPE

THESE STATES STRADDLE the Great Plains and the lowlands of the central USA, with Minnesota lying in a transition zone between the eastern forests and the prairies. The region was shaped by repeated ice advances and retreats, leaving a flat relief, broken only by the numerous lakes and broad river networks which drain the prairies.

Escarpment   Ridge   In permeable strata hollows are formed by small mudslides

Water flowing into gullies erodes back the escarpment

Badlands are formed by stormwater run-off which flows down the impermeable strata of the escarpment and saturates the permeable strata leading to mudslides and the formation of gullies.

North Dakota Badlands

The Minnesota landscape contains many post-glacial features, including its numerous lakes, boulder-strewn hills and mineral-rich deposits.

In the Badlands of North and South Dakota, horizontal layers of sandstone have been eroded by rivers, leaving a landscape of narrow gullies, sharp crests and pinnacles.

South Dakota Badlands

Chimney Rock is a remnant of an ancient land surface, eroded by the North Platte River. The tip of its spire stands 500 ft (150 m) above the plain.

Although it escaped the last glaciation, the limestone bedrock of southeastern Minnesota has been eroded by surface and subterranean streams, leaving a network of underground caverns and steep-sided valleys.

In northeastern Iowa, the Mississippi and its tributaries have deeply incised the underlying bedrock creating a hilly terrain, with bluffs standing 300 ft (90 m) above the valley.

Missouri River

Mississippi River

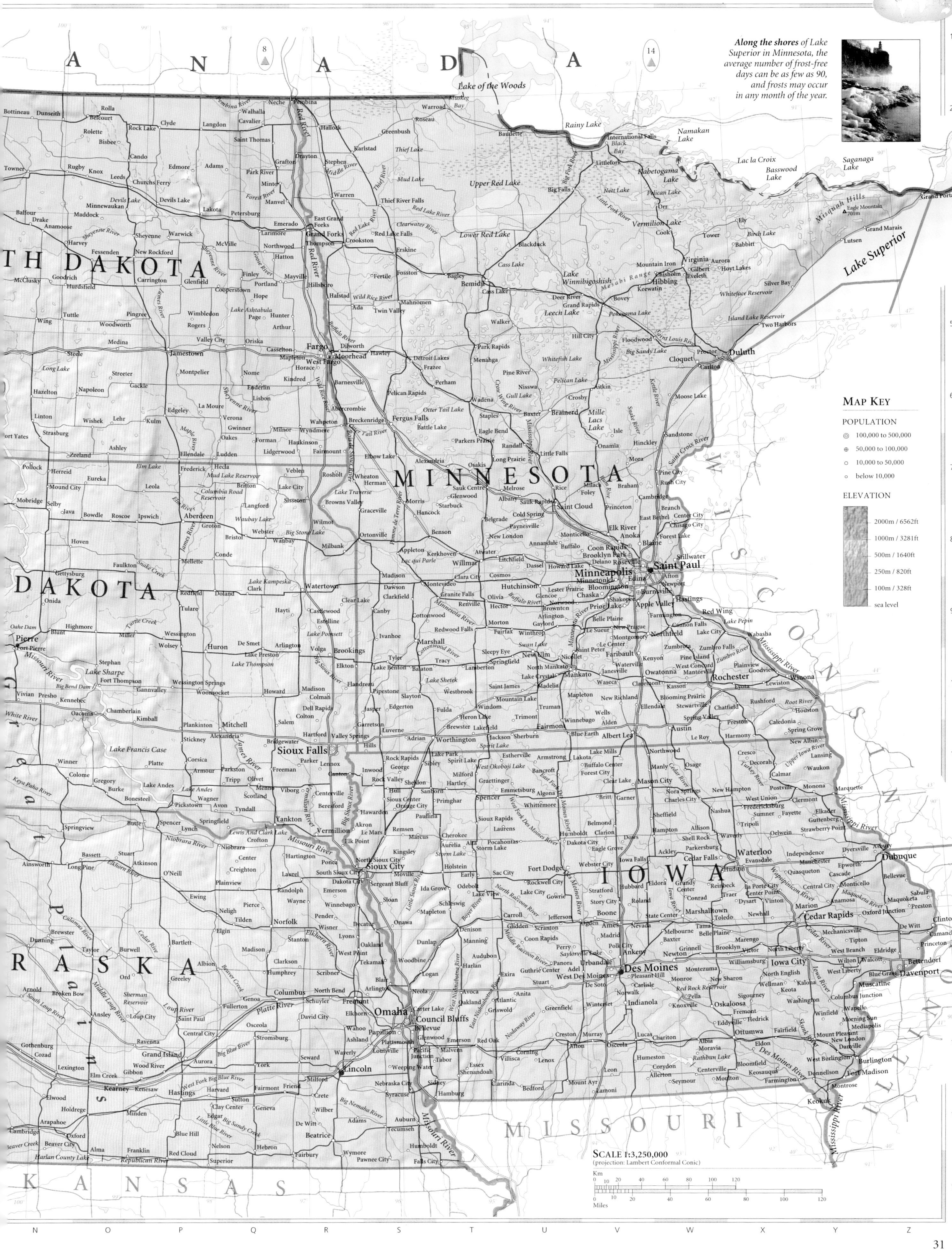

Along the shores of Lake Superior in Minnesota, the average number of frost-free days can be as few as 90, and frosts may occur in any month of the year.

MAP KEY

POPULATION

◉ 100,000 to 500,000
⊕ 50,000 to 100,000
○ 10,000 to 50,000
∘ below 10,000

ELEVATION

2000m / 6562ft
1000m / 3281ft
500m / 1640ft
250m / 820ft
100m / 328ft
sea level

SCALE 1:3,250,000
(projection: Lambert Conformal Conic)

Km
0 10 20   40   60   100   120

Miles
0   10   20   40   60   100   120

CANADA

NORTH DAKOTA

SOUTH DAKOTA

NEBRASKA

MINNESOTA

WISCONSIN

IOWA

ILLINOIS

MISSOURI

KANSAS

Lake Superior

USA: GREAT LAKES STATES

Illinois, Indiana, Michigan, Ohio, Wisconsin

THE STATES BORDERING THE GREAT LAKES developed rapidly in the second half of the 19th century as a result of improvements in communications: rail to the west and waterways to the south and east. Fertile land and good links with growing eastern seaboard cities encouraged the development of agriculture and food processing. Migrants from Europe and other parts of the USA flooded into the region and for much of this century the region's economy boomed. However, in recent years heavy industry has declined, earning the region the unwanted label the 'Rustbelt'.

TRANSPORT AND INDUSTRY

THE GREAT LAKES REGION IS THE CENTRE of the USA's car industry. Since the early part of this century, its prosperity has been closely linked to the fortunes of automobile manufacturing. Iron and steel production has expanded to meet demand from this industry. In the 1970s, nationwide recession, cheaper foreign competition in the automobile sector, pollution in and around the Great Lakes and the collapse of the meat-packing industry, centred on Chicago, forced these states to diversify their industrial base. New industries have emerged, notably electronics, service and finance industries.

THE TRANSPORT NETWORK

540,682 miles (865,091 km)	6550 miles (10,480 km)
24,928 miles (39,884 km)	2330 miles (3748 km)

Few areas of the USA have a comparable transport system. Chicago is a principal transport terminus with a dense network of roads, railways and Interstate freeways radiating from the city.

Ever since Ransom Olds and Henry Ford started mass-producing automobiles in Detroit early this century, the city's name has become synonymous with the American automotive industry.

Major industry and infrastructure

- car manufacture
- coal
- electronics
- engineering
- finance
- food processing
- iron & steel
- oil
- research & development
- textiles
- major towns
- international airports
- major roads
- major industrial areas

THE LANDSCAPE

MUCH OF THIS REGION shows the impact of glaciation which lasted until about 10,000 years ago, and extended as far south as Illinois and Ohio. Although the relief of the region slopes towards the Great Lakes, because the ice sheets blocked northerly drainage, most of the rivers today flow southwards, forming part of the massive Mississippi/Missouri drainage basin.

Lake Michigan

The dunes near Sleeping Bear Point rise 400 ft (120 m) from the banks of Lake Michigan. They are constantly being resculpted by wind action.

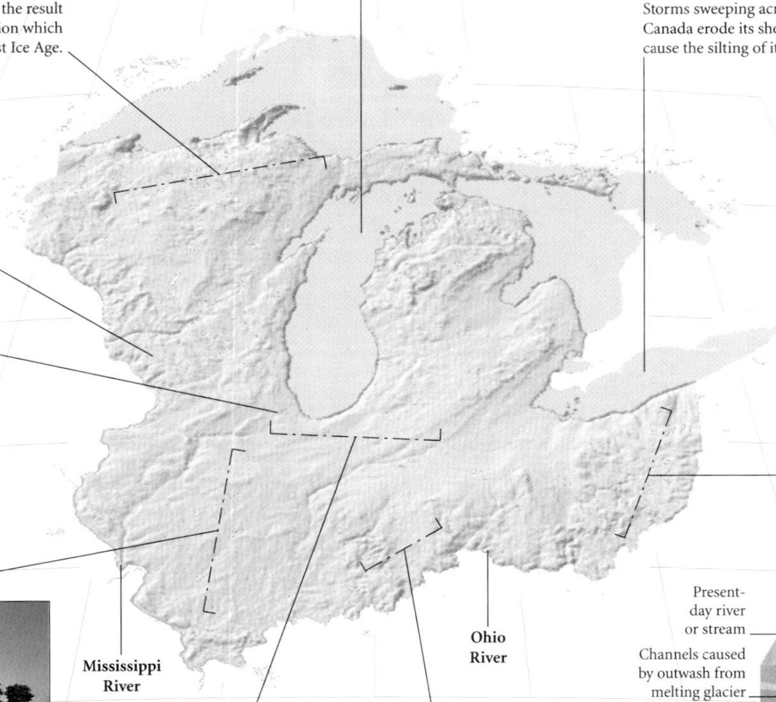

Lake Erie is the shallowest of the five Great Lakes. Its average depth is about 62 ft (19 m). Storms sweeping across from Canada erode its shores and cause the silting of its harbours.

The many lakes and marshes of Wisconsin and Michigan are the result of glacial erosion and deposition which occurred during the last Ice Age.

Southwestern Wisconsin is known as a 'driftless' area. Unlike most of the region, low hills protected it from erosion by the advancing ice sheet.

Most of the water used in northern Illinois is pumped from underground reservoirs. Due to increased demand, many areas now face a water shortage. Around Joliet, the water table has been lowered by more than 700 ft (210 m) over the last century.

The Appalachian Plateau stretches eastward from Ohio. It is dissected by streams flowing west into the Mississippi and Ohio rivers.

Illinois plains

The plains of Illinois are characteristic of drift landscapes, scoured and flattened by glacial erosion and covered with fertile glacial deposits.

Mississippi River

Relict landforms from the last glaciation, such as shallow basins and ridges, cover all but the south of this region. Ridges, known as moraines, up to 300 ft (100 m) high, lie to the south of Lake Michigan.

Ohio River

Unlike the level prairie to the north, southern Indiana is relatively rugged. Limestone in the hills has been dissolved by water, producing features such as sinkholes and underground caves.

Present-day river or stream

Channels caused by outwash from melting glacier

Glacial till

Most recent till deposits

Older till sheet

Bedrock

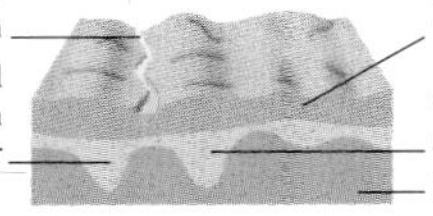

As a result of successive glacial depositions, the total depth of till along the former southern margin of the Laurentide ice sheet can exceed 1300 ft (400 m).

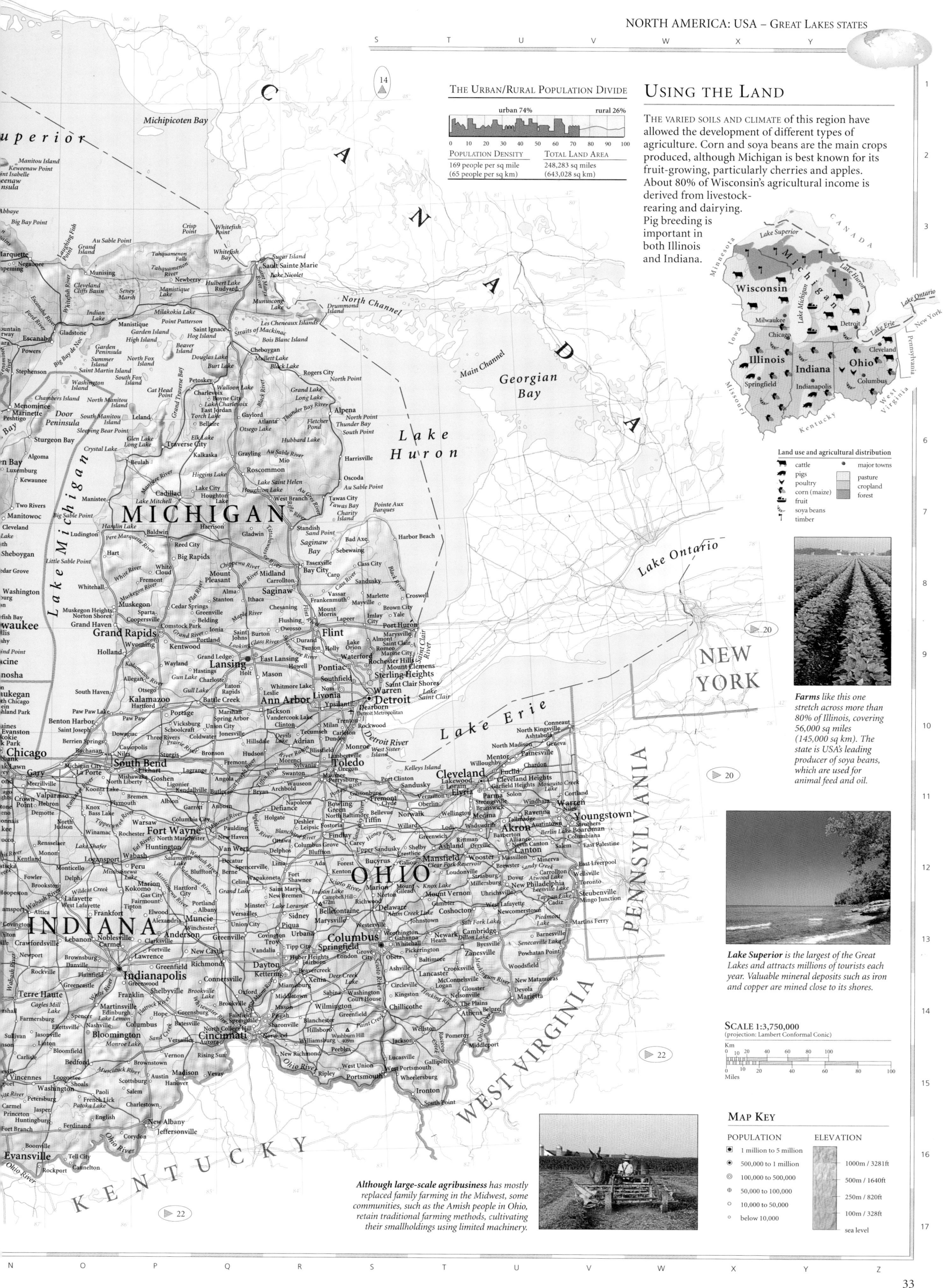

THE URBAN/RURAL POPULATION DIVIDE

urban 74%   rural 26%

POPULATION DENSITY	TOTAL LAND AREA
169 people per sq mile (65 people per sq km)	248,283 sq miles (643,028 sq km)

USING THE LAND

THE VARIED SOILS AND CLIMATE of this region have allowed the development of different types of agriculture. Corn and soya beans are the main crops produced, although Michigan is best known for its fruit-growing, particularly cherries and apples. About 80% of Wisconsin's agricultural income is derived from livestock-rearing and dairying. Pig breeding is important in both Illinois and Indiana.

Land use and agricultural distribution

- cattle
- pigs
- poultry
- corn (maize)
- fruit
- soya beans
- timber
- major towns
- pasture
- cropland
- forest

Farms like this one stretch across more than 80% of Illinois, covering 56,000 sq miles (145,000 sq km). The state is USA's leading producer of soya beans, which are used for animal feed and oil.

Lake Superior is the largest of the Great Lakes and attracts millions of tourists each year. Valuable mineral deposits such as iron and copper are mined close to its shores.

SCALE 1:3,750,000
(projection: Lambert Conformal Conic)

Km
0 10 20 40 60 80 100

Miles
0 10 20 40 60 80 100

MAP KEY

POPULATION
- 1 million to 5 million
- 500,000 to 1 million
- 100,000 to 500,000
- 50,000 to 100,000
- 10,000 to 50,000
- below 10,000

ELEVATION
- 1000m / 3281ft
- 500m / 1640ft
- 250m / 820ft
- 100m / 328ft
- sea level

Although large-scale agribusiness has mostly replaced family farming in the Midwest, some communities, such as the Amish people in Ohio, retain traditional farming methods, cultivating their smallholdings using limited machinery.

USA: NORTH MOUNTAIN STATES

Idaho, Montana, Oregon, Washington, Wyoming

THE REMOTENESS OF THE NORTHWESTERN STATES, coupled with the rugged landscape, ensured that this was one of the last areas settled by Europeans in the 19th century. Fur-trappers and gold-prospectors followed the Snake River westwards as it wound its way through the Rocky Mountains. The states of the northwest have pioneered many conservationist policies, with the USA's first national park opened at Yellowstone in 1872. More recently, the Cascades and Rocky Mountains have become havens for adventure tourism. The mountains still serve to isolate the western seaboard from the rest of the continent. This isolation has encouraged west coast cities to expand their trade links with countries of the Pacific Rim.

The Snake River has cut down into the basalt of the Columbia Basin to form Hells Canyon, the deepest in the USA, with cliffs up to 7900 ft (2408 m) high.

MAP KEY

POPULATION
- 500,000 to 1 million
- 100,000 to 500,000
- 50,000 to 100,000
- 10,000 to 50,000
- below 10,000

ELEVATION
- 4000m / 13,124ft
- 3000m / 9843ft
- 2000m / 6562ft
- 1000m / 3281ft
- 500m / 1640ft
- 250m / 820ft
- 100m / 328ft
- sea level

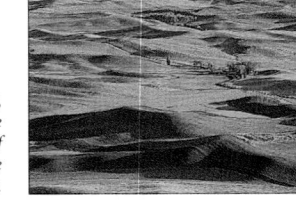

Fine-textured, volcanic soils in the hilly Palouse region of eastern Washington are susceptible to erosion.

USING THE LAND

WHEAT FARMING IN THE EAST gives way to cattle ranching as rainfall decreases. Irrigated farming in the Snake River valley produces large yields of potatoes and other vegetables. Dairying and fruit-growing take place in the wet western lowlands between the mountain ranges.

THE URBAN/RURAL POPULATION DIVIDE

urban 70%   rural 30%

POPULATION DENSITY
20 people per sq mile
(8 people per sq km)

TOTAL LAND AREA
493,782 sq miles
(1,278,846 sq km)

SCALE 1:3,750,000
(projection: Lambert Conformal Conic)

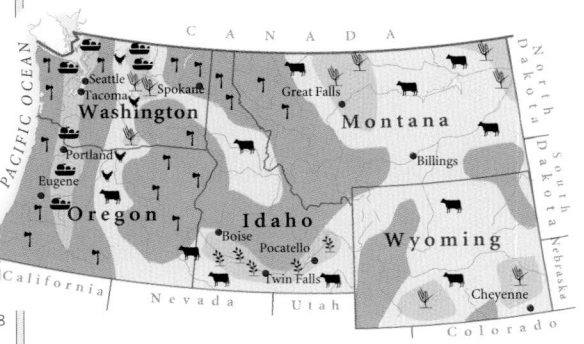

Land use and agricultural distribution
- cattle
- poultry
- cereals
- fruit
- potatoes
- timber
- major towns
- pasture
- cropland
- forest

198 ◄

TRANSPORT AND INDUSTRY

MINERALS AND TIMBER are extremely important in this region. Uranium, precious metals, copper and coal are all mined, the latter in vast open-cast pits in Wyoming; oil and natural gas are extracted further north. Manufacturing, notably related to the aerospace and electronics industries, is important in western cities.

THE TRANSPORT NETWORK

- 347,857 miles (556,571 km)
- 4200 miles (6720 km)
- 12,354 miles (19,766 km)
- 1108 miles (1782 km)

Major industry and infrastructure
- adventure tourism
- aerospace
- coal
- chemicals
- electronics
- food processing
- mining
- oil & gas
- timber processing
- major towns
- international airports
- major roads
- major industrial areas

The Union Pacific Railroad has been in service across Wyoming since 1867. The route through the Rocky Mountains is now shared with the Interstate 80, a major east–west highway.

Seattle lies in one of Puget Sound's many inlets. The city receives oil and other resources from Alaska, and benefits from expanding trade across the Pacific.

Crater Lake, Oregon, is 6 miles (10 km) wide and 1800 ft (600 m) deep. It marks the site of a volcanic cone, which collapsed after an eruption within the last 7000 years.

THE LANDSCAPE

THE ROCKY MOUNTAINS are flanked by lower parallel ranges, which spread onto the Great Plains in the east and surmount the broad lava plateau which extends westwards. The Cascade Range divides the Columbia Basin from the coastlands, where the low areas skirting Puget Sound are broken by the steep, volcanic Olympic Mountains and the wooded hills of the Coast Ranges.

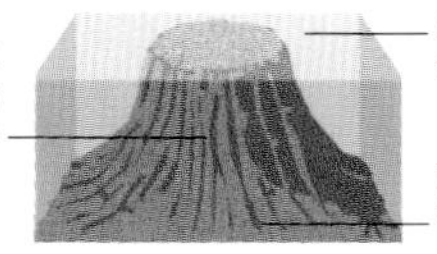

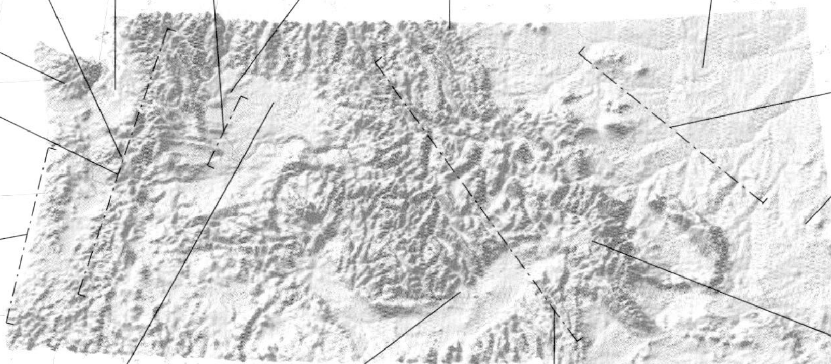

Glacial valleys on the seaward side of the Olympic Mountains receive about 142 inches (3600 mm) of rain per year, supporting the only true rainforest of the northern hemisphere.

Mount St Helens erupted in 1980, killing 57 people and devastating a huge area.

Puget Sound

Columbia Basin

Grand Coulee and the lesser *coulées* (ravines) were cut by cataclysmic floods, from the release of an ice-dammed lake, at the end of the last Ice Age.

The Continental Divide, or watershed, crosses the Lewis Range. From here, rivers flow west to Hudson Bay, south to the Gulf of Mexico and east to the Pacific Ocean.

Piney Buttes are the remnants of an older, higher land surface gradually weathered and eroded into isolated outcrops with flat tops and steep sides.

The Cascades are glacially scoured volcanic mountains, the highest of which is Mount Rainier, a dormant volcano at 14,409 ft (4392 m).

Great Plains

Devil's Tower

Coast Ranges

Molten rock cools, forming parallel columns

Surrounding strata eroded away

Molten rock wells up from the Earth's core

Devil's Tower in Wyoming is an igneous intrusion, formed below the Earth's surface. Molten rock intruded through cracks in the overlying strata and cooled. Over time, the softer rock layers have been eroded away, leaving only the tower standing.

The plateaux of the Columbia and Snake rivers represent one of the world's largest accumulations of lava. Over 5 million years ago, successive flows of molten basalt buried the existing land surface by up to 450 ft (150 m).

The contorted rock shapes at 'Craters of the Moon' National Monument in Idaho were left 2000 years ago by the sporadic upwelling of viscous lava from fissures in the basalt plateau.

Rocky Mountains

Water from the hot springs in Yellowstone National Park deposits minerals as it cools in rock pools. Long periods of deposition have created these rock terraces.

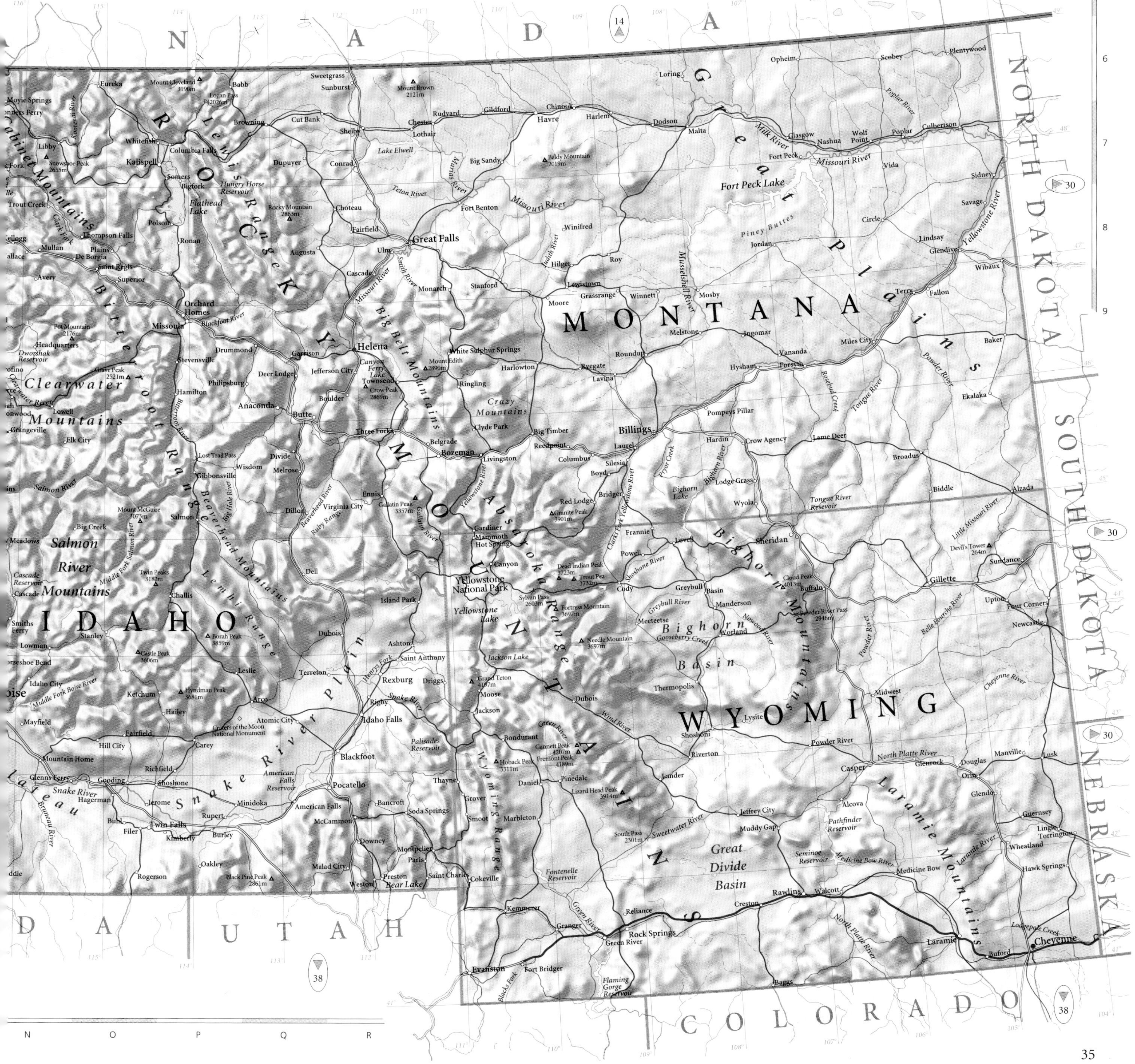

USA: CALIFORNIA & NEVADA

THE 'GOLD RUSH' OF 1849 attracted the first major wave of European settlers to the USA's west coast. The pleasant climate, beautiful scenery and dynamic economy continue to attract immigrants – despite the ever-present danger of earthquakes – and California has become the USA's most populous state. The overwhelmingly urban population is concentrated in the vast conurbations of Los Angeles, San Francisco and San Diego; new immigrants include people from South Korea, the Philippines, Vietnam and Mexico. Nevada's arid lands were initially exploited for minerals; in recent years, revenue from mining has been superseded by income from the tourist and gambling centres of Las Vegas and Reno.

MAP KEY

POPULATION

- ◼ 1 million to 5 million
- ◉ 500,000 to 1 million
- ◎ 100,000 to 500,000
- ⊕ 50,000 to 100,000
- ○ 10,000 to 50,000
- · below 10,000

ELEVATION

- 4000m / 13,124ft
- 3000m / 9843ft
- 2000m / 6562ft
- 1000m / 3281ft
- 500m / 1640ft
- 250m / 820ft
- 100m / 328ft
- sea level

SCALE 1:3,000,000
(projection: Lambert Conformal Conic)

Km 0 5 10 20 30 40 50 60 70 80
Miles 0 5 10 20 30 40 50 60 70 80

TRANSPORT AND INDUSTRY

NEVADA'S RICH MINERAL RESERVES ushered in a period of mining wealth which has now been replaced by revenue generated from gambling. California supports a broad set of activities including defence-related industries and research and development facilities. 'Silicon Valley', near San Francisco, is a world leading centre for micro-electronics, while tourism and the Los Angeles film industry also generate large incomes.

Gambling was legalized in Nevada in 1931; Las Vegas has since become the centre of this multi-million dollar industry.

Major industry and infrastructure

- ✈ aerospace
- 🚗 car manufacture
- defence
- 🎬 film industry
- $ finance
- 🍴 food processing
- gambling
- 💻 hi-tech industry
- ⛏ mining
- pharmaceuticals
- research & development
- ⊤ textiles
- tourism
- · major towns
- ⊕ international airports
- major roads
- major industrial areas

THE TRANSPORT NETWORK

🛣	211,459 miles (338,334 km)
	2944 miles (4710 km)
🛤	7872 miles (12,595 km)
	190 miles (306 km)

In California, the motor vehicle is a vital part of daily life, and an extensive freeway system runs throughout the state, which has a greater *per capita* car ownership than anywhere else in the world.

THE LANDSCAPE

THE BROAD CENTRAL VALLEY divides California's coastal mountains from the Sierra Nevada. The San Andreas Fault, running beneath much of the state, is the site of frequent earth tremors and sometimes more serious earthquakes. East of the Sierra Nevada, the landscape is characterized by the basin and range topography with stony deserts and many salt lakes.

Rising molten rock causes stretching of the Earth's crust

Extensive cracking (faulting) uplifted a series of ridges

As ridges are eroded they fill intervening valleys with sediments

Molten rock (magma) welling up to form a dome in the Earth's interior, causes the brittle surface rocks to stretch and crack. Some areas were uplifted to form mountains (ranges), while others sunk to form flat valleys (basins).

The General Sherman sequoia tree in Sequoia National Park is 3000 years old and at 275 ft (84 m) is one of the largest living things on earth.

Most of California's agriculture is confined to the fertile and extensively irrigated Central Valley, running between the Coast Ranges and the Sierra Nevada. It incorporates the San Joaquin and Sacramento valleys

The dramatic granitic rock formations of Half Dome and El Capitan, and the verdant coniferous forests, attract millions of visitors annually to Yosemite National Park in the Sierra Nevada.

The Great Basin dominates most of Nevada's topography containing large open basins, punctuated by eroded features such as *buttes* and *mesas*. River flow tends to be seasonal, dependent upon spring showers and winter snow melt.

Sierra Nevada

Wheeler Peak is home to some of the world's oldest trees, bristlecone pines, which live for up to 5000 years.

When the Hoover Dam across the Colorado River was completed in 1936, it created Lake Mead, one of the largest artificial lakes in the world, extending for 115 miles (285 km) upstream.

The San Andreas Fault is a transverse fault which extends for 650 miles (1050 km) through California. Major earthquakes occur when the land either side of the fault moves at different rates. San Francisco was devastated by an earthquake in 1906.

Death Valley

Named by migrating settlers in 1849, Death Valley is the driest, hottest place in North America, as well as being the lowest point on land in the western hemisphere, at 282 ft (86 m) below sea level.

The sparsely populated Mojave Desert receives less than 8 inches (200 mm) of rainfall a year. It is used extensively for weapons-testing and military purposes.

The Salton Sea was created accidentally between 1905 and 1907 when an irrigation channel from the Colorado River broke out of its banks and formed this salty 300 sq mile (777 sq km), land-locked lake.

Amargosa Desert

The Sierra Nevada create a 'rainshadow', preventing rain from reaching much of Nevada. Pacific air masses, passing over the mountains, are stripped of their moisture.

USING THE LAND

CALIFORNIA is the USA's leading agricultural producer, although low rainfall makes irrigation essential. The long growing season and abundant sunshine allow many crops to be grown in the fertile Central Valley including grapes, citrus fruits, vegetables and cotton. Almost 17 million acres (6.8 million hectares) of California's forests are used commercially. Nevada's arid climate and poor soil are largely unsuitable for agriculture; 85% of its land is state owned and large areas are used for underground testing of nuclear weapons.

Land use and agricultural distribution

- 🐄 cattle
- citrus fruits
- fruit
- irrigation
- timber
- vineyards
- · major towns
- pasture
- cropland
- forest
- desert

Without considerable irrigation, this fertile valley at Palm Springs would still be part of the Sonoran Desert. California's farmers account for about 80% of the state's total water usage.

THE URBAN/RURAL POPULATION DIVIDE

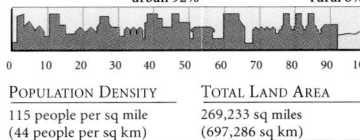

urban 92%   rural 8%

0 10 20 30 40 50 60 70 80 90 100

POPULATION DENSITY
115 people per sq mile
(44 people per sq km)

TOTAL LAND AREA
269,233 sq miles
(697,286 sq km)

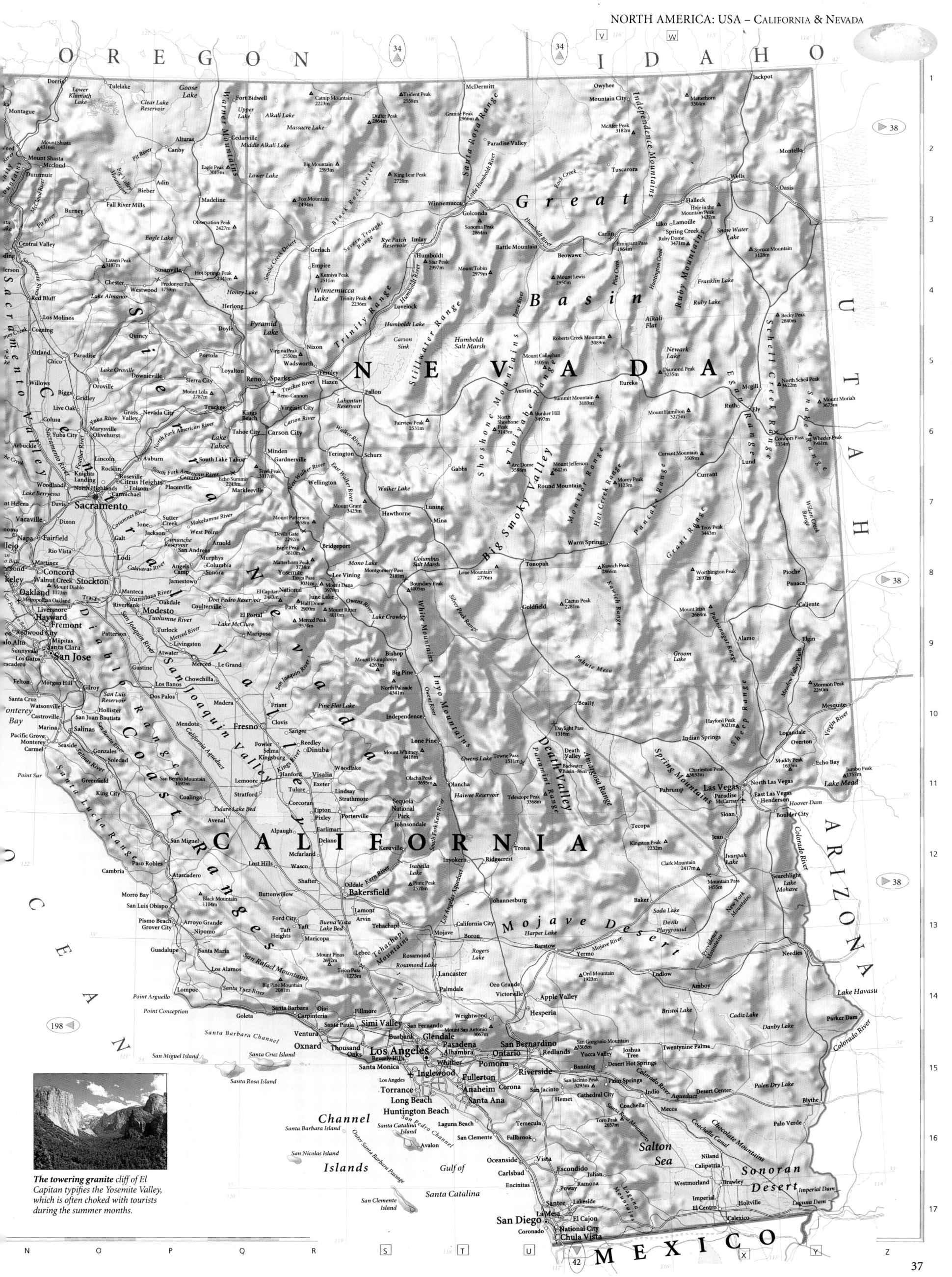

The towering granite cliff of El Capitan typifies the Yosemite Valley, which is often choked with tourists during the summer months.

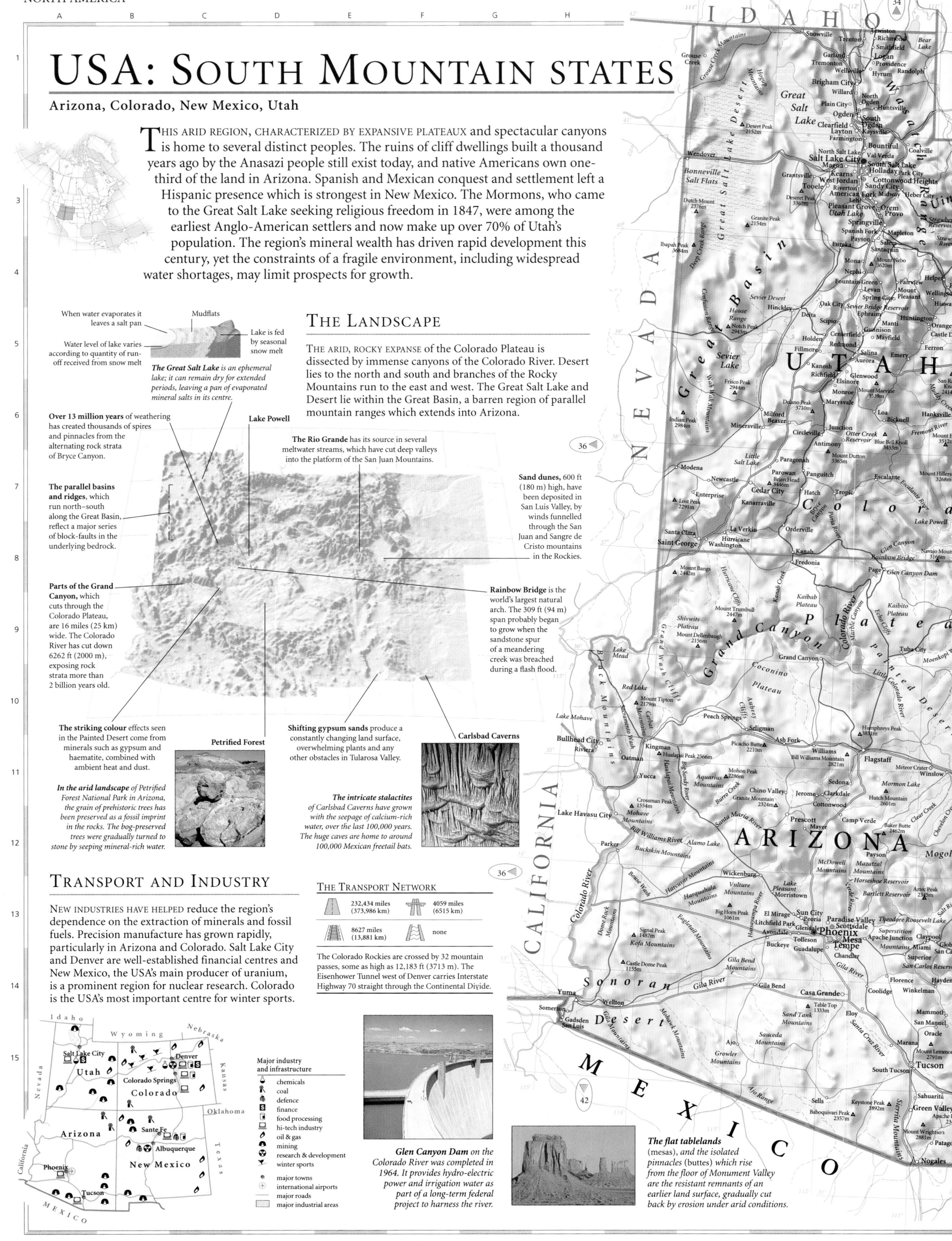

USA: South Mountain states

Arizona, Colorado, New Mexico, Utah

This arid region, characterized by expansive plateaux and spectacular canyons is home to several distinct peoples. The ruins of cliff dwellings built a thousand years ago by the Anasazi people still exist today, and native Americans own one-third of the land in Arizona. Spanish and Mexican conquest and settlement left a Hispanic presence which is strongest in New Mexico. The Mormons, who came to the Great Salt Lake seeking religious freedom in 1847, were among the earliest Anglo-American settlers and now make up over 70% of Utah's population. The region's mineral wealth has driven rapid development this century, yet the constraints of a fragile environment, including widespread water shortages, may limit prospects for growth.

When water evaporates it leaves a salt pan

Mudflats

Lake is fed by seasonal snow melt

Water level of lake varies according to quantity of run-off received from snow melt

The Great Salt Lake is an ephemeral lake; it can remain dry for extended periods, leaving a pan of evaporated mineral salts in its centre.

The Landscape

The arid, rocky expanse of the Colorado Plateau is dissected by immense canyons of the Colorado River. Desert lies to the north and south and branches of the Rocky Mountains run to the east and west. The Great Salt Lake and Desert lie within the Great Basin, a barren region of parallel mountain ranges which extends into Arizona.

Over 13 million years of weathering has created thousands of spires and pinnacles from the alternating rock strata of Bryce Canyon.

Lake Powell

The parallel basins and ridges, which run north–south along the Great Basin, reflect a major series of block-faults in the underlying bedrock.

The Rio Grande has its source in several meltwater streams, which have cut deep valleys into the platform of the San Juan Mountains.

Sand dunes, 600 ft (180 m) high, have been deposited in San Luis Valley, by winds funnelled through the San Juan and Sangre de Cristo mountains in the Rockies.

Parts of the Grand Canyon, which cuts through the Colorado Plateau, are 16 miles (25 km) wide. The Colorado River has cut down 6262 ft (2000 m), exposing rock strata more than 2 billion years old.

Rainbow Bridge is the world's largest natural arch. The 309 ft (94 m) span probably began to grow when the sandstone spur of a meandering creek was breached during a flash flood.

The striking colour effects seen in the Painted Desert come from minerals such as gypsum and haematite, combined with ambient heat and dust.

Petrified Forest

Shifting gypsum sands produce a constantly changing land surface, overwhelming plants and any other obstacles in Tularosa Valley.

Carlsbad Caverns

In the arid landscape of Petrified Forest National Park in Arizona, the grain of prehistoric trees has been preserved as a fossil imprint in the rocks. The bog-preserved trees were gradually turned to stone by seeping mineral-rich water.

The intricate stalactites of Carlsbad Caverns have grown with the seepage of calcium-rich water, over the last 100,000 years. The huge caves are home to around 100,000 Mexican freetail bats.

Transport and Industry

New industries have helped reduce the region's dependence on the extraction of minerals and fossil fuels. Precision manufacture has grown rapidly, particularly in Arizona and Colorado. Salt Lake City and Denver are well-established financial centres and New Mexico, the USA's main producer of uranium, is a prominent region for nuclear research. Colorado is the USA's most important centre for winter sports.

The Transport Network

🛣	232,434 miles (373,986 km)	🛤	4059 miles (6515 km)
🚆	8627 miles (13,881 km)	⚓	none

The Colorado Rockies are crossed by 32 mountain passes, some as high as 12,183 ft (3713 m). The Eisenhower Tunnel west of Denver carries Interstate Highway 70 straight through the Continental Divide.

Major industry and infrastructure

- chemicals
- coal
- defence
- finance
- food processing
- hi-tech industry
- oil & gas
- mining
- research & development
- winter sports
- major towns
- international airports
- major roads
- major industrial areas

Glen Canyon Dam on the Colorado River was completed in 1964. It provides hydro-electric power and irrigation water as part of a long-term federal project to harness the river.

The flat tablelands (mesas), and the isolated pinnacles (buttes) which rise from the floor of Monument Valley are the resistant remnants of an earlier land surface, gradually cut back by erosion under arid conditions.

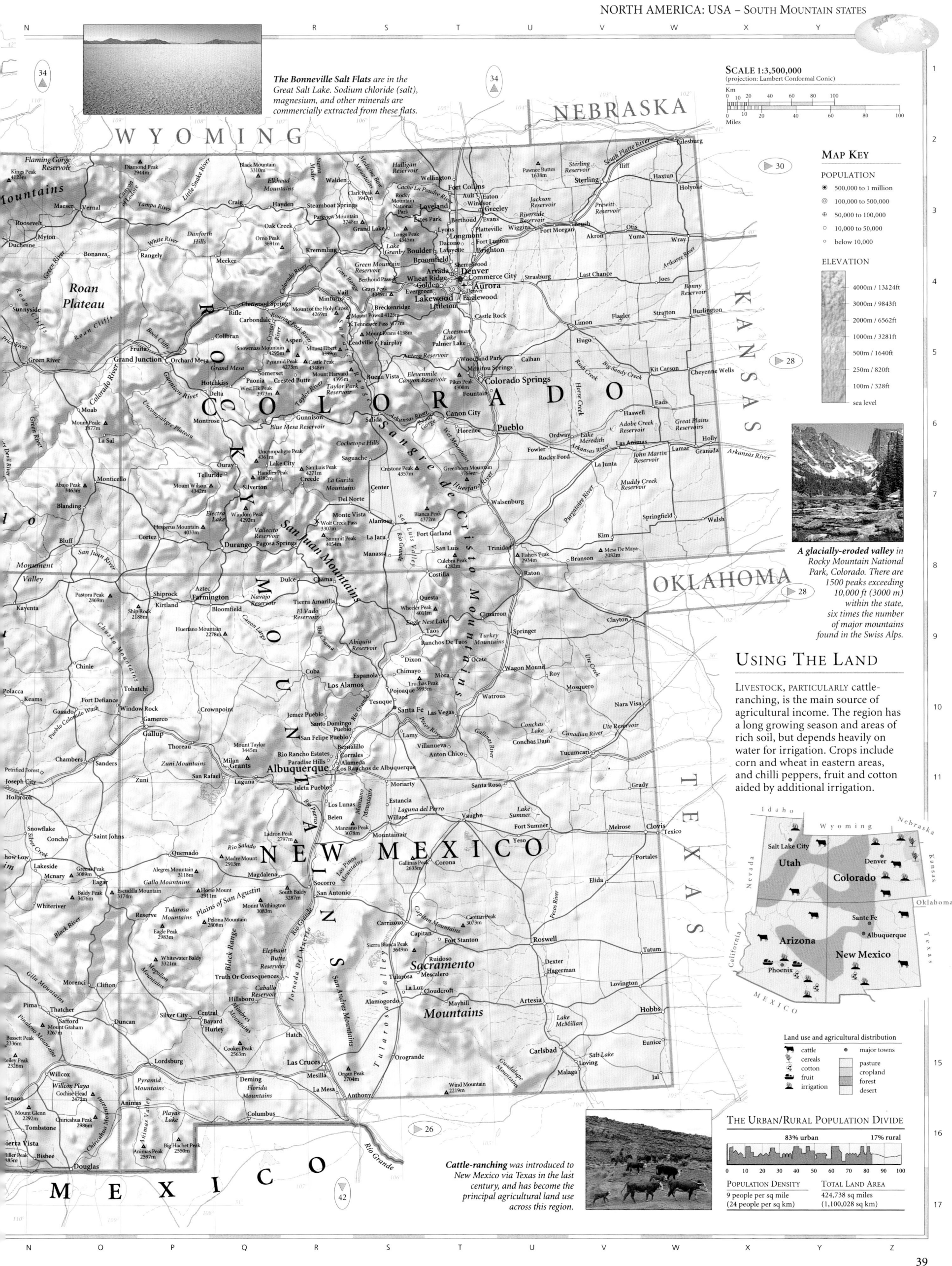

The Bonneville Salt Flats are in the Great Salt Lake. Sodium chloride (salt), magnesium, and other minerals are commercially extracted from these flats.

SCALE 1:3,500,000
(projection: Lambert Conformal Conic)

Km
0   20   40   60   80   100

Miles
0   20   40   60   80   100

MAP KEY

POPULATION

- ⊙ 500,000 to 1 million
- ⊚ 100,000 to 500,000
- ⊕ 50,000 to 100,000
- ⊙ 10,000 to 50,000
- ○ below 10,000

ELEVATION

- 4000m / 13124ft
- 3000m / 9843ft
- 2000m / 6562ft
- 1000m / 3281ft
- 500m / 1640ft
- 250m / 820ft
- 100m / 328ft
- sea level

A glacially-eroded valley in Rocky Mountain National Park, Colorado. There are 1500 peaks exceeding 10,000 ft (3000 m) within the state, six times the number of major mountains found in the Swiss Alps.

USING THE LAND

LIVESTOCK, PARTICULARLY cattle-ranching, is the main source of agricultural income. The region has a long growing season and areas of rich soil, but depends heavily on water for irrigation. Crops include corn and wheat in eastern areas, and chilli peppers, fruit and cotton aided by additional irrigation.

Land use and agricultural distribution

- cattle
- cereals
- cotton
- fruit
- irrigation
- major towns
- pasture
- cropland
- forest
- desert

Cattle-ranching was introduced to New Mexico via Texas in the last century, and has become the principal agricultural land use across this region.

THE URBAN/RURAL POPULATION DIVIDE

83% urban   17% rural

0   10   20   30   40   50   60   70   80   90   100

POPULATION DENSITY	TOTAL LAND AREA
9 people per sq mile	424,738 sq miles
(24 people per sq km)	(1,100,028 sq km)

A B C D E F G H I J K L M

USA: HAWAII

THE 122 ISLANDS of the Hawaiian archipelago – which are part of Polynesia – are the peaks of the world's largest volcanoes. They rise approximately 6 miles (9.7 km) from the floor of the Pacific Ocean. The largest, the island of Hawaii, remains highly active. Hawaii became the USA's 50th state in 1959. A tradition of receiving immigrant workers is reflected in the islands' ethnic diversity, with peoples drawn from around the rim of the Pacific. Only 2% of the current population are native Polynesians.

The island of Molokai is formed from volcanic rock. Mature sand dunes cover the rocks in coastal areas.

TRANSPORT AND INDUSTRY

TOURISM DOMINATES the economy, with over half of the population employed in services. The naval base at Pearl Harbor is also a major source of employment. Industry is concentrated on the island of Oahu and relies mostly on imported materials, while agricultural produce is processed locally.

Major industry and infrastructure

- food processing
- military base
- textiles
- tourism
- major towns
- international airports
- major roads
- major industrial areas

THE TRANSPORT NETWORK

4102 miles (6600 km)	43 miles (69 km)
none	none

Hawaii relies on ocean-surface transportation. Honolulu is the main focus of this network, bringing foreign trade and the markets of mainland USA to Hawaii's outer islands.

Haleakala's extinct volcanic crater is the world's largest. The giant caldera, containing many secondary cones, is 2000 ft (600 m) deep and 20 miles (32 km) in circumference.

USING THE LAND AND SEA

THE VOLCANIC SOILS are extremely fertile and the climate hot and humid on the lower slopes, supporting large commercial plantations growing sugar cane, bananas, pineapples and other tropical fruit, as well as nursery plants and flowers. Some land is given to pasture, particularly for beef and dairy cattle.

Land use and agricultural distribution

- cattle
- fishing
- fruit
- sugar cane
- major towns
- pasture
- cropland
- forest
- mountain region

The island of Kauai is one of the wettest places in the world, receiving some 450 inches (11,500 mm) of rain a year.

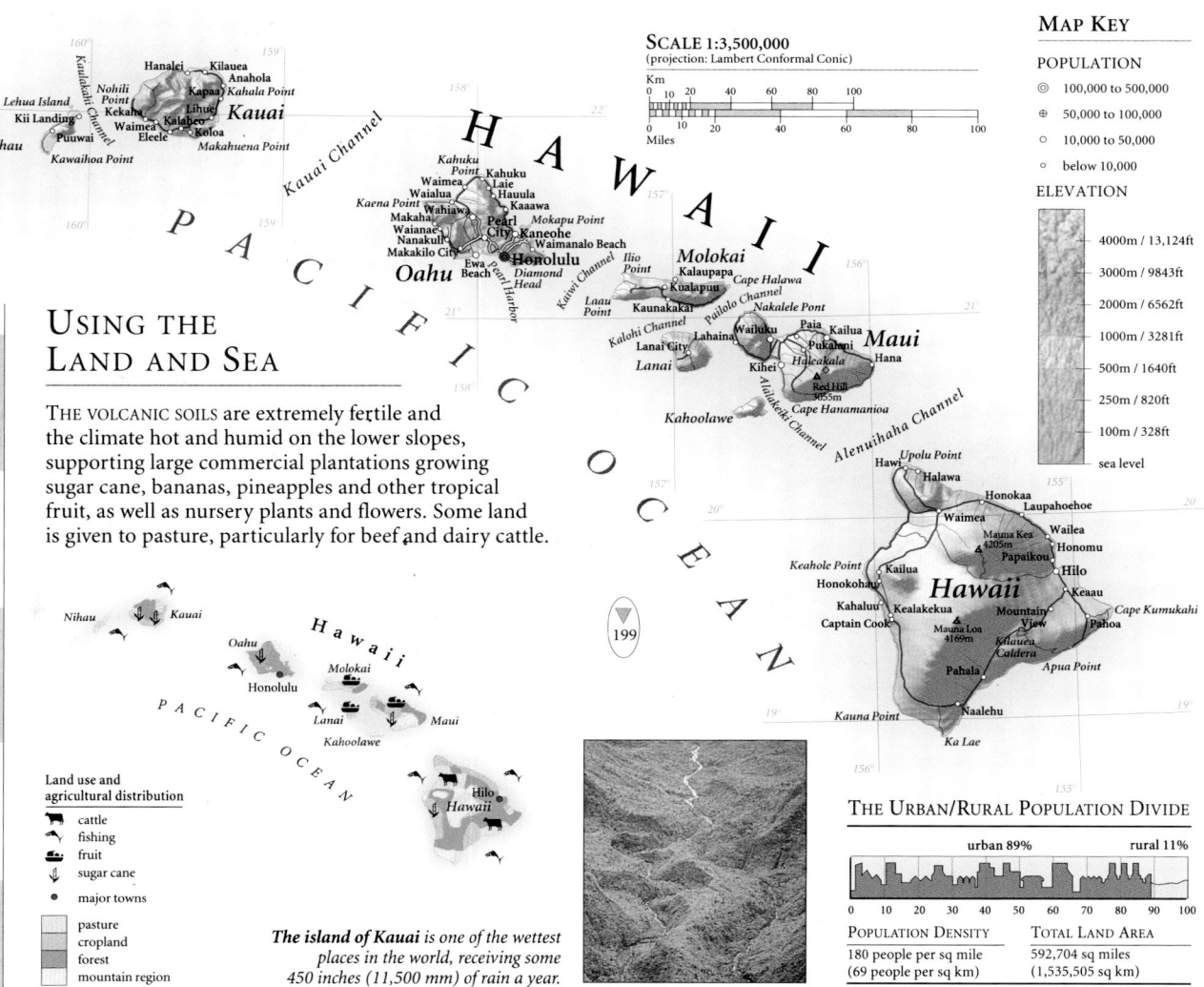

SCALE 1:3,500,000
(projection: Lambert Conformal Conic)

MAP KEY

POPULATION

- 100,000 to 500,000
- 50,000 to 100,000
- 10,000 to 50,000
- below 10,000

ELEVATION

- 4000m / 13,124ft
- 3000m / 9843ft
- 2000m / 6562ft
- 1000m / 3281ft
- 500m / 1640ft
- 250m / 820ft
- 100m / 328ft
- sea level

THE URBAN/RURAL POPULATION DIVIDE

urban 89%   rural 11%

0 10 20 30 40 50 60 70 80 90 100

POPULATION DENSITY	TOTAL LAND AREA
180 people per sq mile (69 people per sq km)	592,704 sq miles (1,535,505 sq km)

USING THE LAND AND SEA

THE ICE-FREE COASTLINE of Alaska provides access to salmon fisheries and more than 5.5 million acres (2.2 million ha) of forest. Most of Alaska is uncultivable, and around 90% of food is imported. Barley, hay and hothouse products are grown around Anchorage, where dairy farming is also concentrated.

THE URBAN/RURAL POPULATION DIVIDE

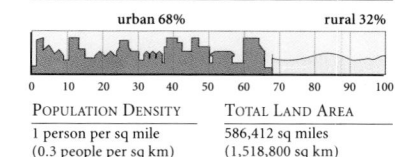

urban 68%   rural 32%

0 10 20 30 40 50 60 70 80 90 100

POPULATION DENSITY	TOTAL LAND AREA
1 person per sq mile (0.3 people per sq km)	586,412 sq miles (1,518,800 sq km)

A raft of timber from the Tongass Forest is hauled by a tug, bound for the pulp mills of the Alaskan coast between Juneau and Ketchikan.

CHUKCHI SEA

RUSSIAN FEDERATION

Bering Strait

BERING SEA

Saint Lawrence Island

Pribilof Islands

Kuskokwim Bay

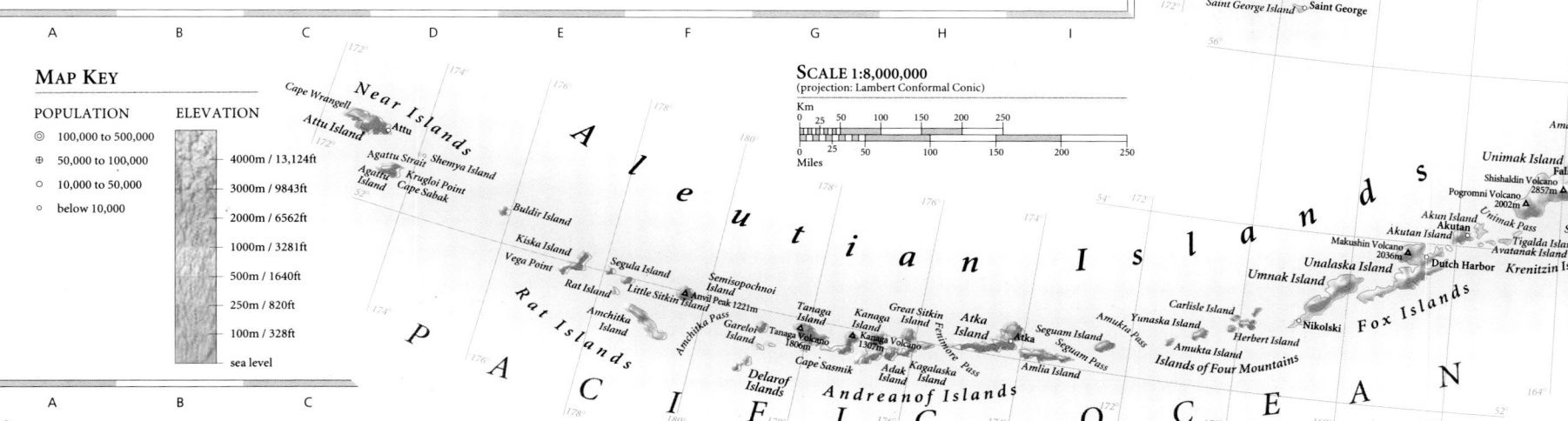

MAP KEY

POPULATION

- 100,000 to 500,000
- 50,000 to 100,000
- 10,000 to 50,000
- below 10,000

ELEVATION

- 4000m / 13,124ft
- 3000m / 9843ft
- 2000m / 6562ft
- 1000m / 3281ft
- 500m / 1640ft
- 250m / 820ft
- 100m / 328ft
- sea level

SCALE 1:8,000,000
(projection: Lambert Conformal Conic)

Aleutian Islands

Near Islands
Rat Islands
Andreanof Islands
Fox Islands

PACIFIC OCEAN

USA: ALASKA

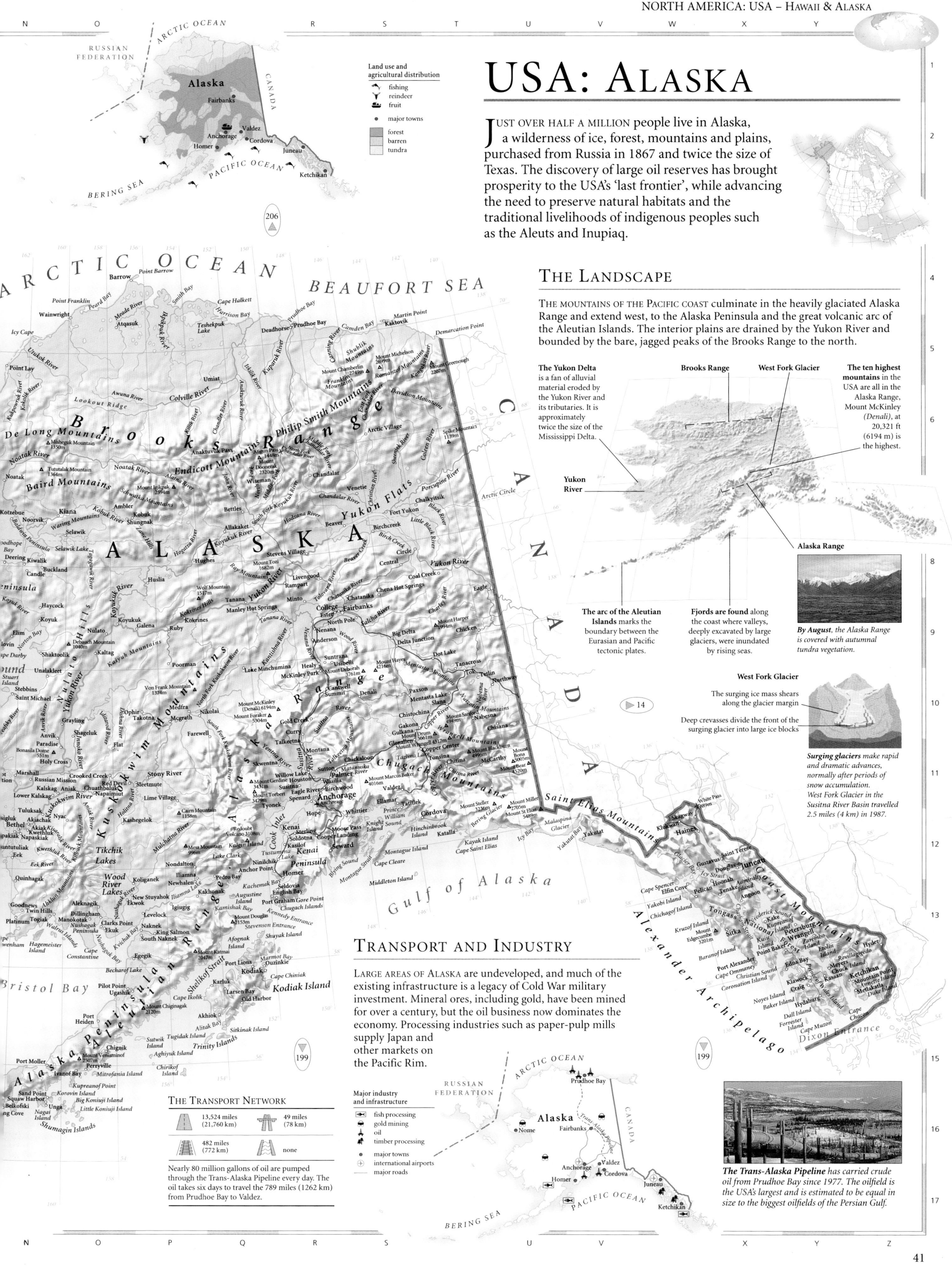

JUST OVER HALF A MILLION people live in Alaska, a wilderness of ice, forest, mountains and plains, purchased from Russia in 1867 and twice the size of Texas. The discovery of large oil reserves has brought prosperity to the USA's 'last frontier', while advancing the need to preserve natural habitats and the traditional livelihoods of indigenous peoples such as the Aleuts and Inupiaq.

THE LANDSCAPE

THE MOUNTAINS OF THE PACIFIC COAST culminate in the heavily glaciated Alaska Range and extend west, to the Alaska Peninsula and the great volcanic arc of the Aleutian Islands. The interior plains are drained by the Yukon River and bounded by the bare, jagged peaks of the Brooks Range to the north.

The Yukon Delta is a fan of alluvial material eroded by the Yukon River and its tributaries. It is approximately twice the size of the Mississippi Delta.

The ten highest mountains in the USA are all in the Alaska Range, Mount McKinley (Denali), at 20,321 ft (6194 m) is the highest.

By August, the Alaska Range is covered with autumnal tundra vegetation.

The arc of the Aleutian Islands marks the boundary between the Eurasian and Pacific tectonic plates.

Fjords are found along the coast where valleys, deeply excavated by large glaciers, were inundated by rising seas.

West Fork Glacier

The surging ice mass shears along the glacier margin

Deep crevasses divide the front of the surging glacier into large ice blocks

Surging glaciers make rapid and dramatic advances, normally after periods of snow accumulation. West Fork Glacier in the Susitna River Basin travelled 2.5 miles (4 km) in 1987.

TRANSPORT AND INDUSTRY

LARGE AREAS OF ALASKA are undeveloped, and much of the existing infrastructure is a legacy of Cold War military investment. Mineral ores, including gold, have been mined for over a century, but the oil business now dominates the economy. Processing industries such as paper-pulp mills supply Japan and other markets on the Pacific Rim.

THE TRANSPORT NETWORK

13,524 miles (21,760 km)		49 miles (78 km)	
482 miles (772 km)		none	

Nearly 80 million gallons of oil are pumped through the Trans-Alaska Pipeline every day. The oil takes six days to travel the 789 miles (1262 km) from Prudhoe Bay to Valdez.

The Trans-Alaska Pipeline has carried crude oil from Prudhoe Bay since 1977. The oilfield is the USA's largest and is estimated to be equal in size to the biggest oilfields of the Persian Gulf.

Land use and agricultural distribution
- fishing
- reindeer
- fruit
- major towns
- forest
- barren
- tundra

Major industry and infrastructure
- fish processing
- gold mining
- oil
- timber processing
- major towns
- international airports
- major roads

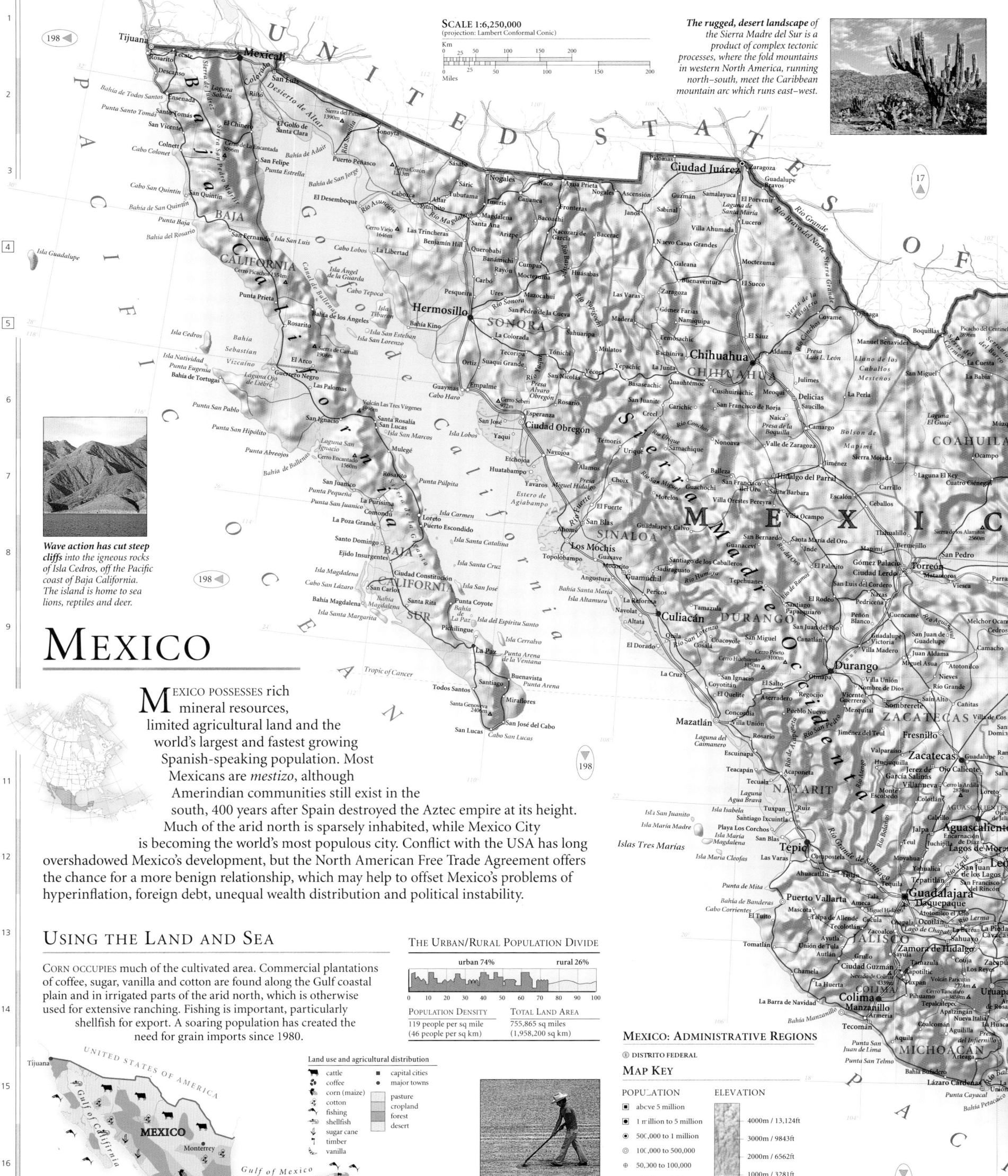

SCALE 1:6,250,000
(projection: Lambert Conformal Conic)

The rugged, desert landscape of the Sierra Madre del Sur is a product of complex tectonic processes, where the fold mountains in western North America, running north–south, meet the Caribbean mountain arc which runs east–west.

Wave action has cut steep cliffs into the igneous rocks of Isla Cedros, off the Pacific coast of Baja California. The island is home to sea lions, reptiles and deer.

MEXICO

M EXICO POSSESSES rich mineral resources, limited agricultural land and the world's largest and fastest growing Spanish-speaking population. Most Mexicans are *mestizo*, although Amerindian communities still exist in the south, 400 years after Spain destroyed the Aztec empire at its height. Much of the arid north is sparsely inhabited, while Mexico City is becoming the world's most populous city. Conflict with the USA has long overshadowed Mexico's development, but the North American Free Trade Agreement offers the chance for a more benign relationship, which may help to offset Mexico's problems of hyperinflation, foreign debt, unequal wealth distribution and political instability.

USING THE LAND AND SEA

CORN OCCUPIES much of the cultivated area. Commercial plantations of coffee, sugar, vanilla and cotton are found along the Gulf coastal plain and in irrigated parts of the arid north, which is otherwise used for extensive ranching. Fishing is important, particularly shellfish for export. A soaring population has created the need for grain imports since 1980.

THE URBAN/RURAL POPULATION DIVIDE

urban 74%	rural 26%

0 10 20 30 40 50 60 70 80 90 100

POPULATION DENSITY	TOTAL LAND AREA
119 people per sq mile	755,865 sq miles
(46 people per sq km)	(1,958,200 sq km)

Land use and agricultural distribution

- cattle
- coffee
- corn (maize)
- cotton
- fishing
- shellfish
- sugar cane
- timber
- vanilla

- capital cities
- major towns
- pasture
- cropland
- forest
- desert

Coffee beans spread out to dry in the sun. Coffee, grown mainly on the Gulf coastal plain, is Mexico's most valuable export crop.

MEXICO: ADMINISTRATIVE REGIONS

① DISTRITO FEDERAL

MAP KEY

POPULATION	ELEVATION
▪ above 5 million	4000m / 13,124ft
▪ 1 million to 5 million	3000m / 9843ft
◎ 500,000 to 1 million	2000m / 6562ft
◉ 100,000 to 500,000	1000m / 3281ft
⊕ 50,000 to 100,000	500m / 1640ft
⊙ 10,000 to 50,000	250m / 820ft
○ below 10,000	100m / 328ft
	sea level

THE LANDSCAPE

THE GREAT CENTRAL PLATEAU rises gently southwards from the Rio Grande, isolated from the coastal plains by the Sierra Madre Oriental and Occidental. The two ranges converge from east and west respectively, culminating in high volcanic peaks around Mexico City. Further ranges of the Sierra Madre rise to the south of the Balsas Basin, skirted by the low-lying Isthmus of Tehuantepec (*Istmo de Tehuantepec*) and Yucatan Peninsula.

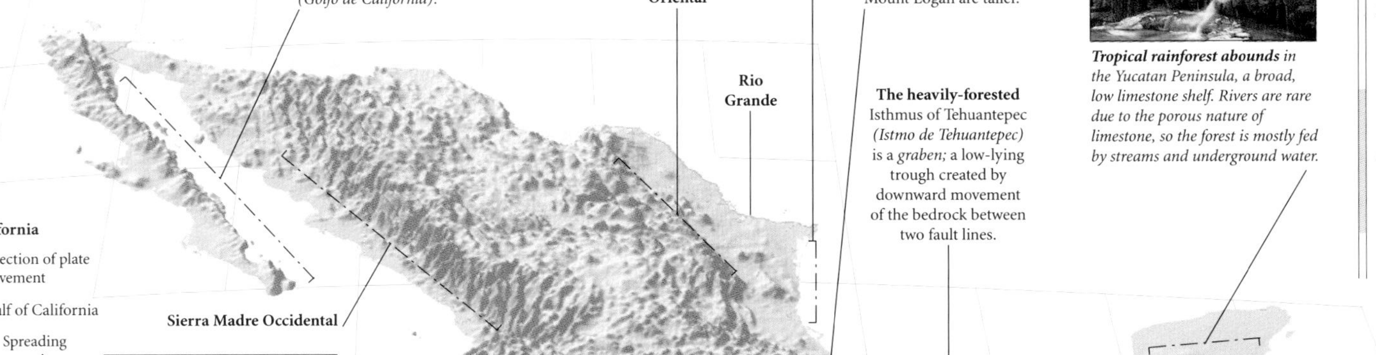

The long, narrow, extremely arid peninsula of Baja (lower) California is an elongated granite block, separated from the mainland by the flooded rift valley of the Gulf of California (*Golfo de California*).

Wave action has constructed sand bars which shelter lagoons along the shore of the Gulf coastal plain.

The dormant cone of Volcán Pico de Orizaba is, at 18,700 ft (5700 m), the highest peak in Mexico. In North America, only Mount McKinley and Mount Logan are taller.

Tropical rainforest abounds in the Yucatan Peninsula, a broad, low limestone shelf. Rivers are rare due to the porous nature of limestone, so the forest is mostly fed by streams and underground water.

Sierra Madre Oriental

Rio Grande

The heavily-forested Isthmus of Tehuantepec (*Istmo de Tehuantepec*) is a *graben*; a low-lying trough created by downward movement of the bedrock between two fault lines.

Sierra Madre Occidental

Formation of the Gulf of California

Baja California — Transform fault — Edge of continental crust — Direction of plate movement — Gulf of California — Spreading oceanic ridge

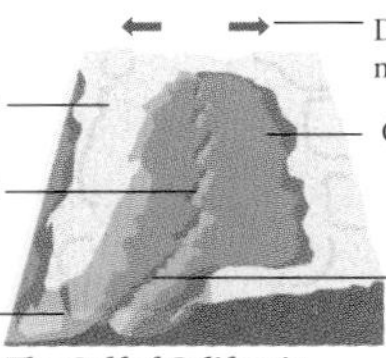

The Gulf of California (Golfo de California) began to open out about 4 million years ago as a result of rifting and plate displacement along transform faults.

Popocatépetl is a dormant volcano, part of the Pacific 'Rim of Fire'. The crater is over half a mile (1 km) wide.

Río Balsas

Popocatépetl

The unstable, earthquake-prone, upland basin around Mexico City was once a region of shallow lakes. Flood control measures and domestic consumption over the last four centuries have caused the virtual disappearance of this surface water.

The highlands of Chiapas are a series of *horsts*, blocks of land thrust upwards between two fault lines. Volcanic cones have developed where lava has flowed out from the faults.

TRANSPORT AND INDUSTRY

OIL AND GAS ON THE GULF COAST are Mexico's main sources of export income. Metal mining has declined but the country remains a leading global producer of silver. Manufacturing is heavily concentrated around the Mexico City metropolitan area, while the duty-free movement of goods in the USA border region, under the *Maquiladora* (twin plant) scheme, has created new hi-tech and service growth centres.

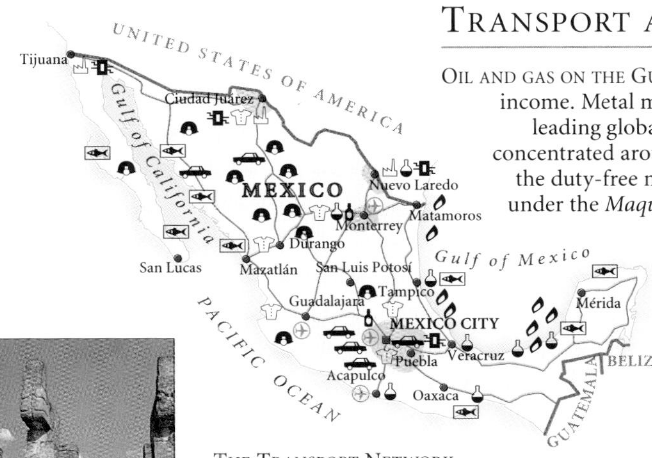

Major industry and infrastructure: brewing, car manufacture, chemicals, electronics, fish processing, maquiladoras, mining, oil & gas, textiles, capital cities, major towns, international airports, major roads, major industrial areas

THE TRANSPORT NETWORK

151,951 miles (373,986 km)
1935 miles (3116 km)
12,684 miles (20,425 km)
1801 miles (2900 km)

Fast, modern highways or *autopistas* now link Mexico City with Toluca, Puebla and other satellite cities, yet distant centres like Chihuahua are still served by narrow roads and an outdated rail network.

A stone figure reclines by the Temple of Warriors, within the Mayan city of Chichén-Itzá. The Maya civilization flourished across the Yucatan Peninsula between 200 and 900 AD.

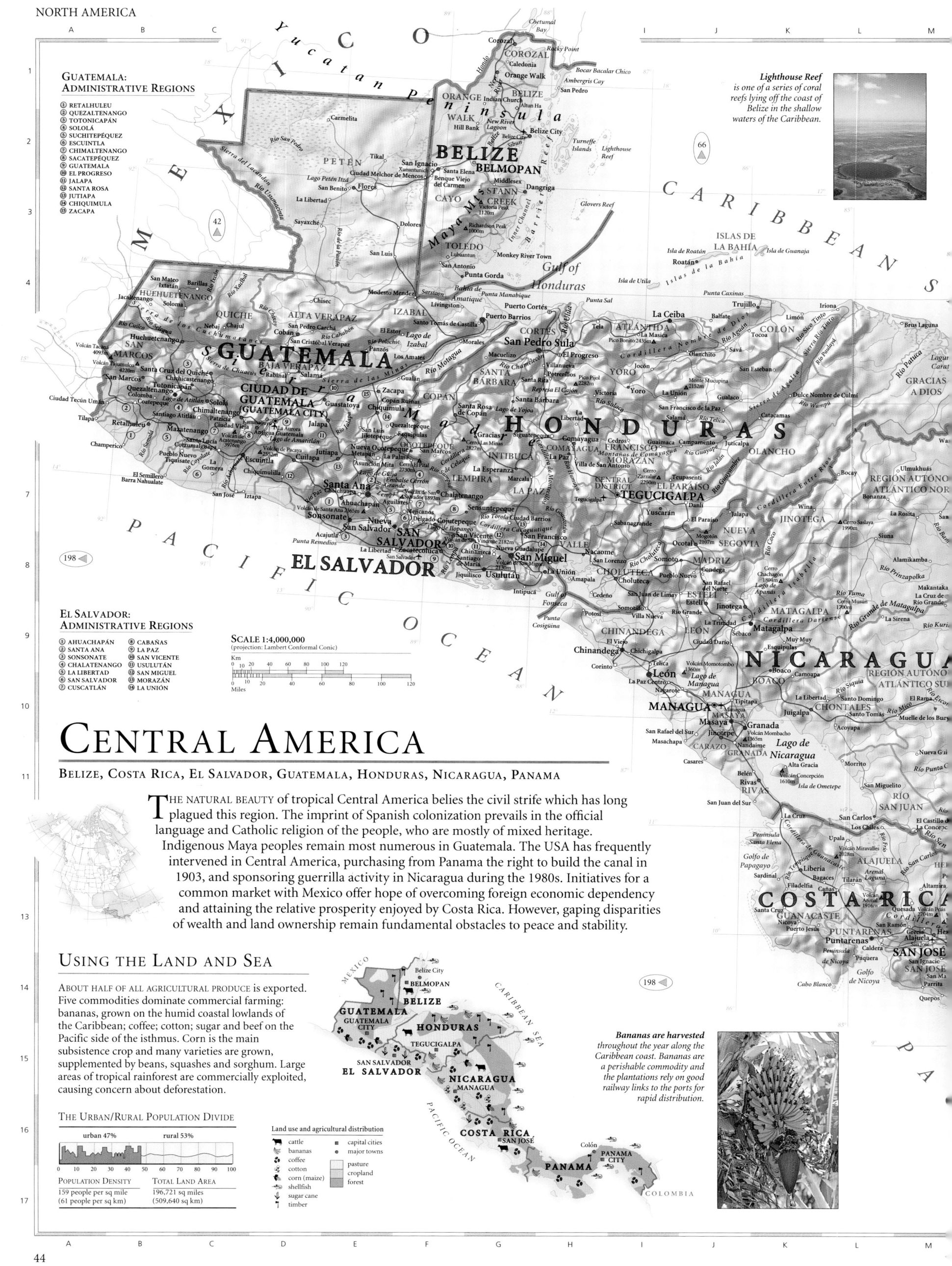

GUATEMALA:
ADMINISTRATIVE REGIONS
① RETALHULEU
② QUEZALTENANGO
③ TOTONICAPÁN
④ SOLOLÁ
⑤ SUCHITEPÉQUEZ
⑥ ESCUINTLA
⑦ CHIMALTENANGO
⑧ SACATEPÉQUEZ
⑨ GUATEMALA
⑩ EL PROGRESO
⑪ JALAPA
⑫ SANTA ROSA
⑬ JUTIAPA
⑭ CHIQUIMULA
⑮ ZACAPA

Lighthouse Reef
is one of a series of coral
reefs lying off the coast of
Belize in the shallow
waters of the Caribbean.

EL SALVADOR:
ADMINISTRATIVE REGIONS
① AHUACHAPÁN   ⑧ CABAÑAS
② SANTA ANA   ⑨ LA PAZ
③ SONSONATE   ⑩ SAN VICENTE
④ CHALATENANGO   ⑪ USULUTÁN
⑤ LA LIBERTAD   ⑫ SAN MIGUEL
⑥ SAN SALVADOR   ⑬ MORAZÁN
⑦ CUSCATLÁN   ⑭ LA UNIÓN

SCALE 1:4,000,000
(projection: Lambert Conformal Conic)

CENTRAL AMERICA

BELIZE, COSTA RICA, EL SALVADOR, GUATEMALA, HONDURAS, NICARAGUA, PANAMA

THE NATURAL BEAUTY of tropical Central America belies the civil strife which has long plagued this region. The imprint of Spanish colonization prevails in the official language and Catholic religion of the people, who are mostly of mixed heritage. Indigenous Maya peoples remain most numerous in Guatemala. The USA has frequently intervened in Central America, purchasing from Panama the right to build the canal in 1903, and sponsoring guerrilla activity in Nicaragua during the 1980s. Initiatives for a common market with Mexico offer hope of overcoming foreign economic dependency and attaining the relative prosperity enjoyed by Costa Rica. However, gaping disparities of wealth and land ownership remain fundamental obstacles to peace and stability.

USING THE LAND AND SEA

ABOUT HALF OF ALL AGRICULTURAL PRODUCE is exported. Five commodities dominate commercial farming: bananas, grown on the humid coastal lowlands of the Caribbean; coffee; cotton; sugar and beef on the Pacific side of the isthmus. Corn is the main subsistence crop and many varieties are grown, supplemented by beans, squashes and sorghum. Large areas of tropical rainforest are commercially exploited, causing concern about deforestation.

THE URBAN/RURAL POPULATION DIVIDE

urban 47%	rural 53%

POPULATION DENSITY   TOTAL LAND AREA
159 people per sq mile   196,721 sq miles
(61 people per sq km)   (509,640 sq km)

Land use and agricultural distribution
- cattle
- bananas
- coffee
- cotton
- corn (maize)
- shellfish
- sugar cane
- timber
- capital cities
- major towns
- pasture
- cropland
- forest

Bananas are harvested
throughout the year along the
Caribbean coast. Bananas are
a perishable commodity and
the plantations rely on good
railway links to the ports for
rapid distribution.

N O P Q R S T U V W X Y

Over 40 active volcanoes line the Pacific coast north of Panama, including Volcán Tajumulco which, at 13,846 ft (4220 m), is the highest point in Central America.

The high plateau of the Sierra de los Cuchumatanes is a *horst*, an upthrusted block of land. The limestone rock is deeply incised with canyons along the plateau edge.

Lake Petén Itzá is typical of the swampy depressions or *bajos* of the Petén region, formed by intense weathering of limestone in the hot and humid climate.

Low, white limestone cliffs, mangrove swamps and coral reefs characterize the coast of Belize, which is part of the Yucatan Peninsula.

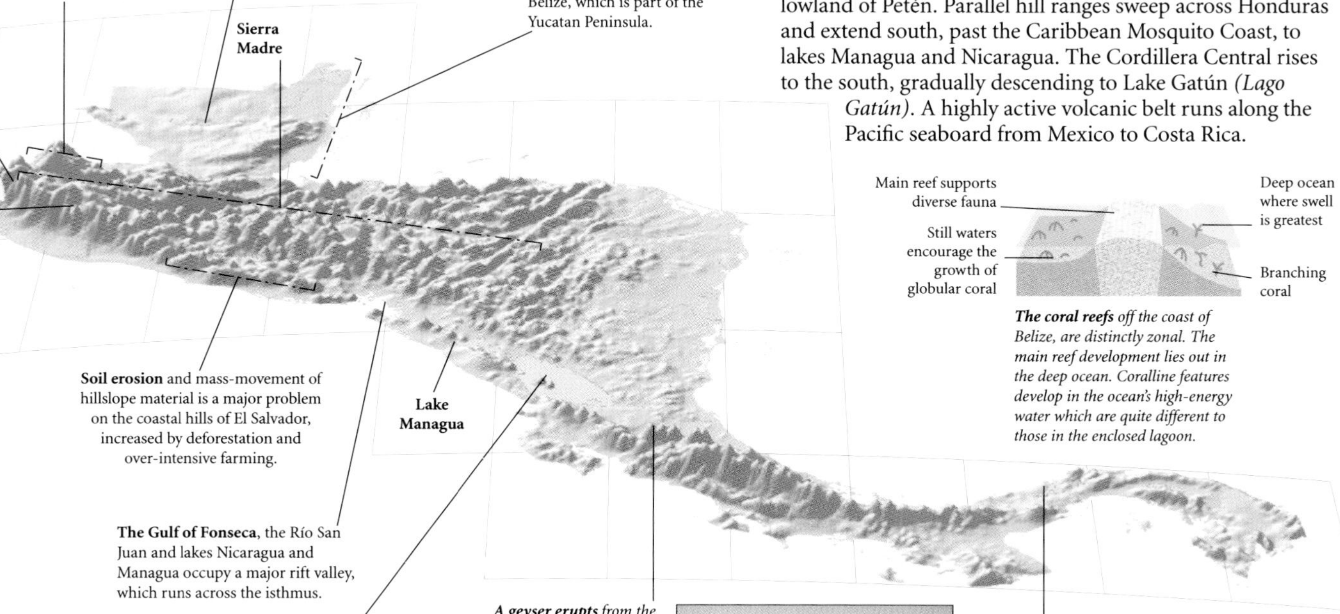

Sierra Madre

THE LANDSCAPE

THE SIERRA MADRE RANGE spreads west from Mexico, between the narrow Pacific coastal plain and the limestone lowland of Petén. Parallel hill ranges sweep across Honduras and extend south, past the Caribbean Mosquito Coast, to lakes Managua and Nicaragua. The Cordillera Central rises to the south, gradually descending to Lake Gatún (*Lago Gatún*). A highly active volcanic belt runs along the Pacific seaboard from Mexico to Costa Rica.

The 990 ft (300 m) deep crater occupied by Lake Atitlán (Lago de Atitlán) was created after a volcanic explosion caused the original cone to collapse in on itself. On its shores lie other volcanic cones.

Main reef supports diverse fauna

Still waters encourage the growth of globular coral

Deep ocean where swell is greatest

Branching coral

The coral reefs off the coast of Belize, are distinctly zonal. The main reef development lies out in the deep ocean. Coralline features develop in the ocean's high-energy water which are quite different to those in the enclosed lagoon.

Soil erosion and mass-movement of hillslope material is a major problem on the coastal hills of El Salvador, increased by deforestation and over-intensive farming.

Lake Managua

The Gulf of Fonseca, the Río San Juan and lakes Nicaragua and Managua occupy a major rift valley, which runs across the isthmus.

A geyser erupts from the central cone of Volcán Poás, an active volcano in the Cordillera Central of Costa Rica, which frequently produces spectacular lava flows.

Over half of the route of the Panama Canal runs through Lake Gatún (*Lago Gatún*), the highest stretch of the journey. The freshwater lake also acts as a holding reservoir for the canal, providing water to operate the locks.

Lake Nicaragua (*Lago de Nicaragua*) contains around 400 islands, some of which are active volcanoes. Unique freshwater species of shark and swordfish have evolved over the long period since the lake was cut off from the Pacific by a belt of volcanic cones.

An ox-drawn plough tills fields of tobacco in the Copán region of Honduras. Only about 25% of the land is cultivated, in this sparsely-populated country.

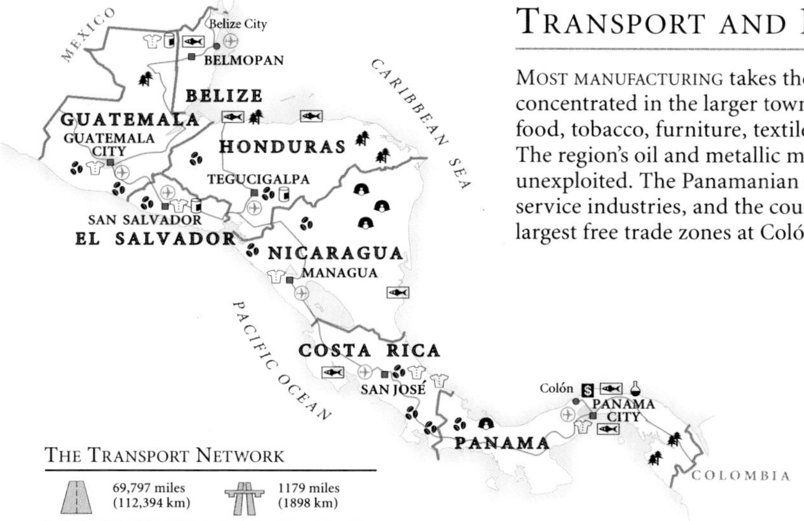

TRANSPORT AND INDUSTRY

MOST MANUFACTURING takes the form of cottage industries concentrated in the larger towns, and the production of food, tobacco, furniture, textiles, clothing and footwear. The region's oil and metallic mineral potential is largely unexploited. The Panamanian economy is dominated by service industries, and the country has one of the world's largest free trade zones at Colón.

MEXICO
Belize City
BELMOPAN
BELIZE
GUATEMALA
GUATEMALA CITY
HONDURAS
TEGUCIGALPA
CARIBBEAN SEA
SAN SALVADOR
EL SALVADOR
NICARAGUA
MANAGUA
PACIFIC OCEAN
COSTA RICA
SAN JOSÉ
Colón
PANAMA CITY
PANAMA
COLOMBIA

Major industry and infrastructure
- chemicals
- coffee processing
- fish processing
- finance
- food processing
- mining
- textiles
- timber processing
- capital cities
- major towns
- international airports
- major roads
- major industrial areas

MAP KEY

POPULATION
- 500,000 to 1 million
- 100,000 to 500,000
- 50,000 to 100,000
- 10,000 to 50,000
- below 10,000

ELEVATION
- 4000m / 13,124ft
- 3000m / 9843ft
- 2000m / 6562ft
- 1000m / 3281ft
- 500m / 1640ft
- 250m / 820ft
- 100m / 328ft
- sea level

166

THE TRANSPORT NETWORK

69,797 miles (112,394 km)		1179 miles (1898 km)	
2607 miles (4198 km)		3869 miles (6230 km)	

The completion of a major oil pipeline across Panama in 1982 has reduced crude oil shipments via the Panama Canal, further contributing to a long-term decline in canal traffic.

Panama's rainforests are home to many mammals which originated in North America, including jaguars, tapirs and deer, as well as sloths, anteaters and armadillos, which long ago migrated from South America.

Puerto Lempira
Arrecifes de la Media Luna
Coco
Cabo de Gracias a Dios
Laguna Bismuna
Boom
Arrecife Edinburgh
Dákura
Cayo Muerto
Cayos Miskitos
Cayos Londres
Tuapi
Puerto Cabezas
Wounta
Prinzapolka
Cayos Guerrero
Barra de Río Grande
Kara
Cayos King
Laguna de Perlas
Cayos de Perlas
Punta de Perlas
Punta Mosquito
Islas del Maíz
Bahía de Bluefields
El Bluff
Bluefields
Monkey Point
Punta Gorda
San Juan del Norte
Barra del Colorado
LIMÓN
Goápiles
Siquirres
Matina
Limón
Turrialba
Punta Mona
Bribri
CARIBBEAN SEA
Cerro La Muerte 3491m
Río Telire
Guabito
Cerro Chirripó
Guápiles
Cerro Kamuk 3554m
Bocas del Toro
Changuinola
San Isidro
Río Teribe
Almirante
Archipiélago de Bocas del Toro
Buenos Aires
Península Valiente
Cortés
BOCAS
Laguna de Chiriquí
PUNTARENAS
DEL
Chiriquí Grande
Río Grande de Térraba
Palmar Sur
TORO
Santa Catalina
San Vito
Volcán Barú 3475m
Golfo de los Mosquitos
Península de Osa
Boquete
Cerro Chorcha 2238m
Volcán
Cordillera Central
Golfito
La Concepción
CHIRIQUÍ
David
Cerro Santiago 2121m
Puerto Armuelles
Horconcitos
Alanje
Pedregal
Las Palmas
Isla Sevilla
Remedios
Punta Burica
Golfo de Chiriquí
Isla Parida
VERAGUAS
Soná
Santiago
Río de Jesús
HERRERA
Guarumal
Macaracas
Ponuga
Isla Cébaco
Península de Azuero
LOS SANTOS
Isla de Coiba
Cerro Hoya 1560m
Tonosí

Santa Isabel
Portobelo
El Porvenir
Colón
Lago Alajuela
Cristóbal
SAN BLAS
Archipiélago de San Blas
Nuevo Chagres
Lago Gatún
Cordillera de San Blas
Ailigandí
Miguel de la Borda
Istmo de Panamá
Coclé del Norte
Arenosa Canal
Chepo
Lago Bayano
Punta Mosquito
La Chorrera
Balboa
Cerro Chucanti 1439m
Puerto Obaldía
Capira
San Miguelito
PANAMÁ (PANAMA CITY)
Bahía de Panamá
Chimán
El Valle
Punta Chame
Cerro Azul 1173m
Archipiélago de las Perlas
COCLÉ
Blanca 1314m
Río Hato
Isla del Rey
El Real
Cerro Pirre 1200m
Penonomé
San Carlos
Isla San José
San Miguel
Golfo de San Miguel
La Palma
Punta Brava
Cerro Tacarcuna 1875m
Aguadulce
Punta Garachiné
Yaviza
Calobre
Río Santa María
Garachiné
DARIÉN
San Francisco
Bahía de Parita
Río Tuira
Cañazas
Parita
Monagrillo
Chitré
Los Santos
Ocú
Las Tablas
Montijo
COLOMBIA
Pedasí
Punta Mala

PANAMA

Golfo de Panamá

PACIFIC OCEAN

128

56

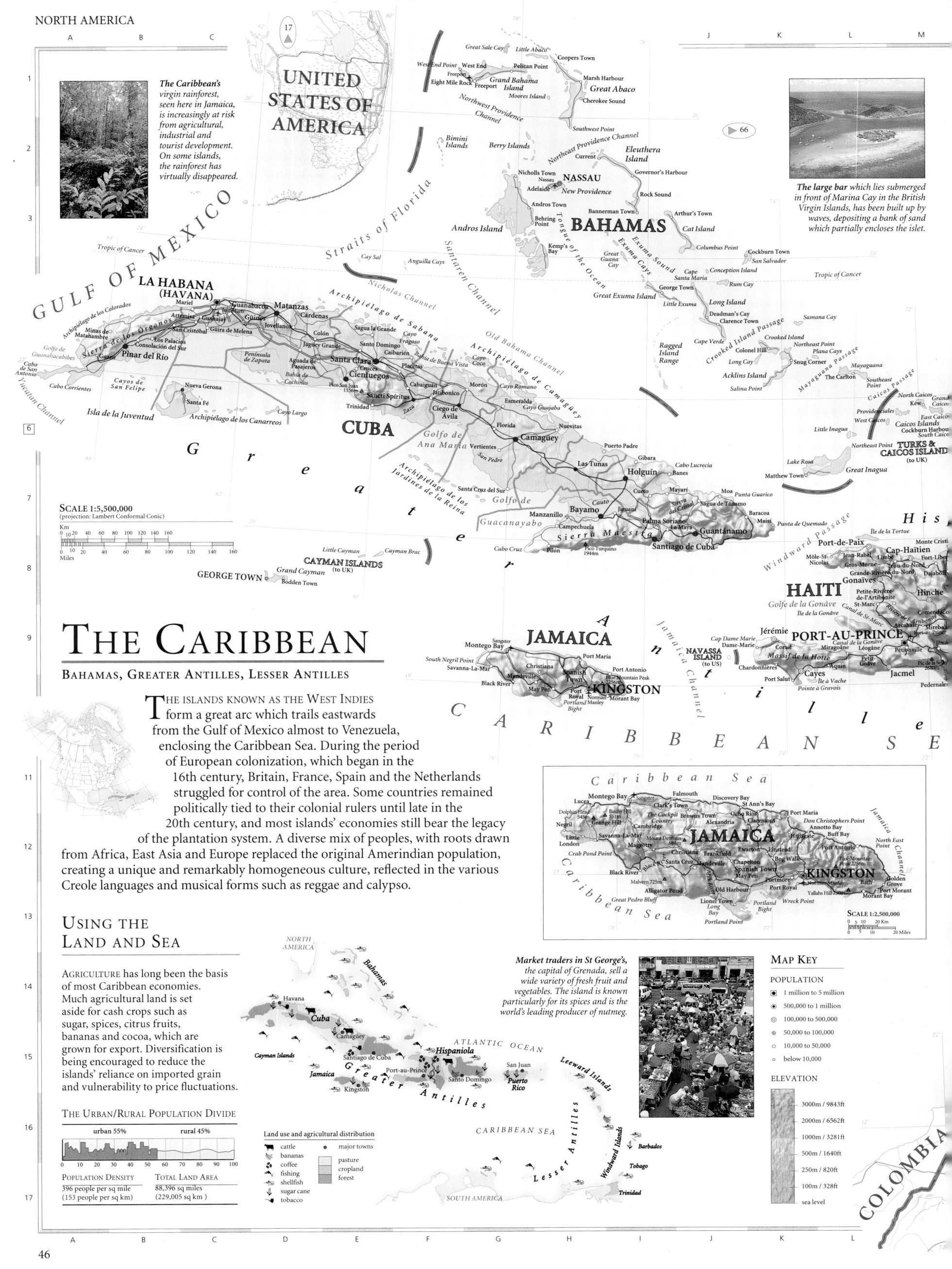

The Caribbean's virgin rainforest, seen here in Jamaica, is increasingly at risk from agricultural, industrial and tourist development. On some islands, the rainforest has virtually disappeared.

The large bar which lies submerged in front of Marina Cay in the British Virgin Islands, has been built up by waves, depositing a bank of sand which partially encloses the islet.

THE CARIBBEAN

BAHAMAS, GREATER ANTILLES, LESSER ANTILLES

THE ISLANDS KNOWN AS THE WEST INDIES form a great arc which trails eastwards from the Gulf of Mexico almost to Venezuela, enclosing the Caribbean Sea. During the period of European colonization, which began in the 16th century, Britain, France, Spain and the Netherlands struggled for control of the area. Some countries remained politically tied to their colonial rulers until late in the 20th century, and most islands' economies still bear the legacy of the plantation system. A diverse mix of peoples, with roots drawn from Africa, East Asia and Europe replaced the original Amerindian population, creating a unique and remarkably homogeneous culture, reflected in the various Creole languages and musical forms such as reggae and calypso.

USING THE LAND AND SEA

AGRICULTURE has long been the basis of most Caribbean economies. Much agricultural land is set aside for cash crops such as sugar, spices, citrus fruits, bananas and cocoa, which are grown for export. Diversification is being encouraged to reduce the islands' reliance on imported grain and vulnerability to price fluctuations.

THE URBAN/RURAL POPULATION DIVIDE

urban 55%   rural 45%

POPULATION DENSITY   TOTAL LAND AREA
396 people per sq mile   88,396 sq miles
(153 people per sq km)   (229,005 sq km)

Land use and agricultural distribution
- cattle
- bananas
- coffee
- fishing
- shellfish
- sugar cane
- tobacco
- major towns
- pasture
- cropland
- forest

Market traders in St George's, the capital of Grenada, sell a wide variety of fresh fruit and vegetables. The island is known particularly for its spices and is the world's leading producer of nutmeg.

MAP KEY

POPULATION
- 1 million to 5 million
- 500,000 to 1 million
- 100,000 to 500,000
- 50,000 to 100,000
- 10,000 to 50,000
- below 10,000

ELEVATION
- 3000m / 9843ft
- 2000m / 6562ft
- 1000m / 3281ft
- 500m / 1640ft
- 250m / 820ft
- 100m / 328ft
- sea level

SCALE 1:5,500,000
(projection: Lambert Conformal Conic)

SCALE 1:2,500,000

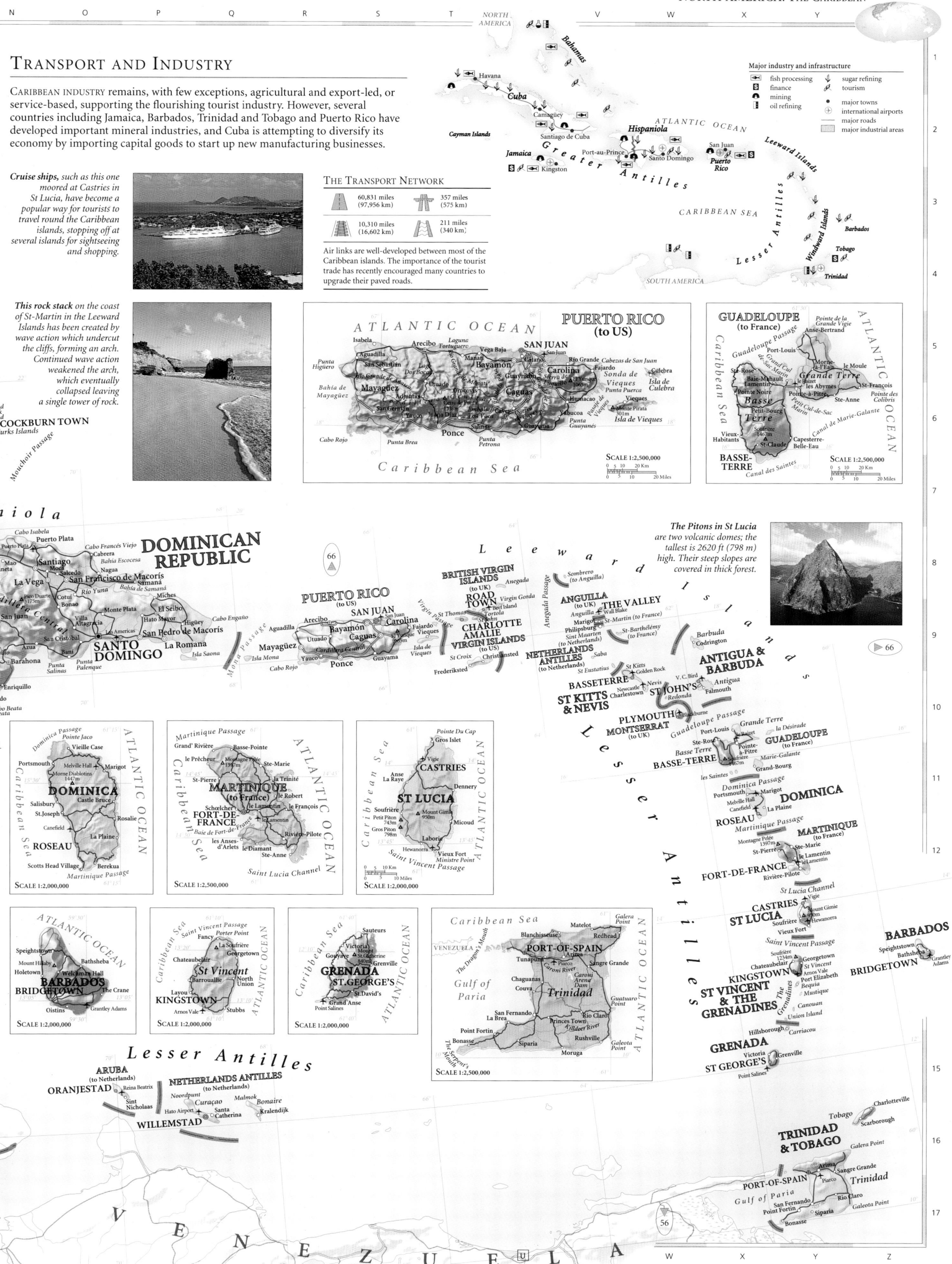

TRANSPORT AND INDUSTRY

CARIBBEAN INDUSTRY remains, with few exceptions, agricultural and export-led, or service-based, supporting the flourishing tourist industry. However, several countries including Jamaica, Barbados, Trinidad and Tobago and Puerto Rico have developed important mineral industries, and Cuba is attempting to diversify its economy by importing capital goods to start up new manufacturing businesses.

Cruise ships, such as this one moored at Castries in St Lucia, have become a popular way for tourists to travel round the Caribbean islands, stopping off at several islands for sightseeing and shopping.

This rock stack on the coast of St-Martin in the Leeward Islands has been created by wave action which undercut the cliffs, forming an arch. Continued wave action weakened the arch, which eventually collapsed leaving a single tower of rock.

THE TRANSPORT NETWORK

60,831 miles (97,956 km)		357 miles (575 km)	
10,310 miles (16,602 km)		211 miles (340 km)	

Air links are well-developed between most of the Caribbean islands. The importance of the tourist trade has recently encouraged many countries to upgrade their paved roads.

Major industry and infrastructure

- fish processing
- finance
- mining
- oil refining
- sugar refining
- tourism
- major towns
- international airports
- major roads
- major industrial areas

The Pitons in St Lucia are two volcanic domes; the tallest is 2620 ft (798 m) high. Their steep slopes are covered in thick forest.

PUERTO RICO (to US) — SCALE 1:2,500,000

GUADELOUPE (to France) — SCALE 1:2,500,000

DOMINICA — SCALE 1:2,000,000

MARTINIQUE (to France) — SCALE 1:2,500,000

ST LUCIA — SCALE 1:2,000,000

BARBADOS — SCALE 1:2,000,000

ST VINCENT — SCALE 1:2,000,000

GRENADA — SCALE 1:2,000,000

Trinidad — SCALE 1:2,500,000

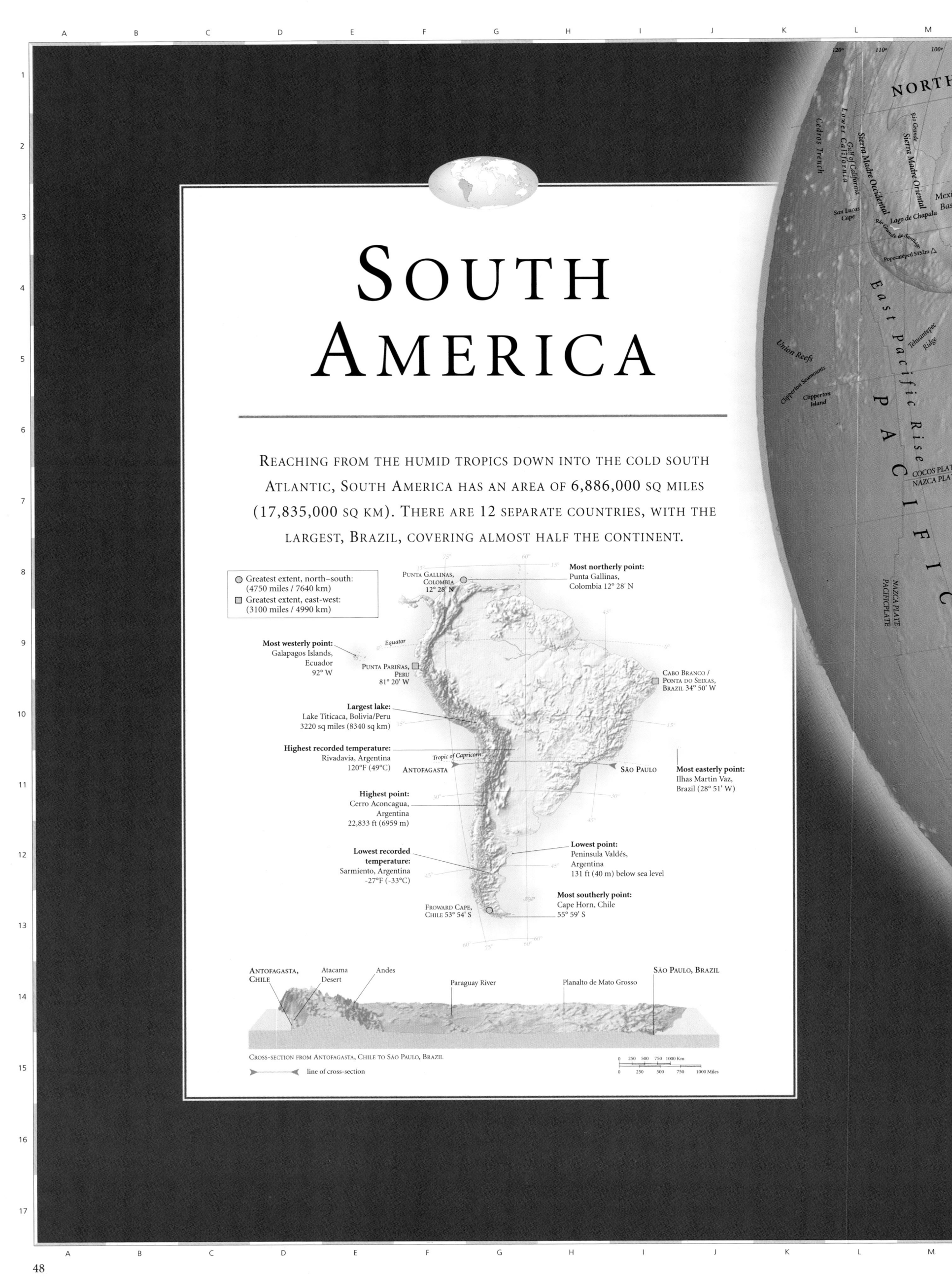

SOUTH AMERICA

REACHING FROM THE HUMID TROPICS DOWN INTO THE COLD SOUTH ATLANTIC, SOUTH AMERICA HAS AN AREA OF 6,886,000 SQ MILES (17,835,000 SQ KM). THERE ARE 12 SEPARATE COUNTRIES, WITH THE LARGEST, BRAZIL, COVERING ALMOST HALF THE CONTINENT.

○ Greatest extent, north–south:
(4750 miles / 7640 km)
□ Greatest extent, east-west:
(3100 miles / 4990 km)

Most northerly point:
Punta Gallinas,
Colombia 12° 28' N

Punta Gallinas,
Colombia
12° 28' N

Most westerly point:
Galapagos Islands,
Ecuador
92° W

Punta Pariñas,
Peru
81° 20' W

Cabo Branco /
Ponta do Seixas,
Brazil 34° 50' W

Largest lake:
Lake Titicaca, Bolivia/Peru
3220 sq miles (8340 sq km)

Highest recorded temperature:
Rivadavia, Argentina
120°F (49°C)

ANTOFAGASTA

SÃO PAULO

Most easterly point:
Ilhas Martin Vaz,
Brazil (28° 51' W)

Highest point:
Cerro Aconcagua,
Argentina
22,833 ft (6959 m)

Lowest recorded
temperature:
Sarmiento, Argentina
-27°F (-33°C)

Lowest point:
Peninsula Valdés,
Argentina
131 ft (40 m) below sea level

Most southerly point:
Cape Horn, Chile
55° 59' S

FROWARD CAPE,
CHILE 53° 54' S

ANTOFAGASTA,
CHILE

Atacama
Desert

Andes

Paraguay River

Planalto de Mato Grosso

SÃO PAULO, BRAZIL

CROSS-SECTION FROM ANTOFAGASTA, CHILE TO SÃO PAULO, BRAZIL

line of cross-section

0 250 500 750 1000 Km
0 250 500 750 1000 Miles

AMERICA

Mississippi Fan
Sigsbee Escarpment
Apalachee Bay
Cape Canaveral
Lake Okeechobee
Hatteras plain
Sargasso Sea
Nares Plain
Gulf of Mexico
Straits of Florida
Bahamas
Great Bahama Bank
Yucatan Peninsula
Yucatan Basin
Cuba
Puerto Rico Trench
West Indies
Tropic of Cancer

Greater Antilles
Cayman Trench
Jamaica
Gulf of Honduras
Hispaniola
Windward Passage
Puerto Rico
Nevis
Leeward Islands
Barbuda
Antigua
Guadeloupe
Dominica
Martinique
Saint Lucia
Barbados
NORTH AMERICAN PLATE
SOUTH AMERICAN PLATE

Sierra Madre del Sur
Gulf of Fonseca
Mosquito Coast
Nicaraguan Rise
Caribbean Sea
Punta Gallinas
Aruba
Bonaire
Curaçao
Isla de Margarita
Windward Islands
Grenada
Trinidad
Tobago
Lesser Antilles
AFRICAN PLATE

Middle America Trench
Lake Nicaragua
Mosquito Gulf
Isthmus of Panama
Gulf of Darien
Peninsula de la Guajira
Serrania de Perijá
Lake Maracaibo
Cordillera de la Costa
Orinoco
Caroni
Demerara Plain
MID-ATLANTIC RIDGE
Doldrums Fracture Zone

Guatemala Basin
Peninsula de Azuero
Gulf of Panama
Colombian Basin
Meta
Apure
Arauca
Llanos
Esequibo
Cuyuni
Manari
Oyapock
Guiana Basin
Four North Fracture Zone
Saint Paul Fracture Zone

Colón Ridge
Panama Basin
Cordillera Occidental
Magdalena
Cordillera Central
Cordillera Oriental
CARIBBEAN PLATE
SOUTH AMERICAN PLATE
Vichada
Guaviare
Guiana Highlands
Uraricoera
Serra Parima
Branco
Uatumã
Tumuc-Humac Mountains
Araguari
Ceará Plain
Equator

Galapagos Islands
Guainia
Caquetá
Putumayo
Uaupés
Napo
Içá
Rio Negro
Jutaí
Jurupari
Purus
Represa Balbina
Amazon Basin
Amazon
Para de Oeste
Jari
Paru
Amazon
Xingu
Ilha de Marajó
Amazon Fan
Baía de Marajó
Represa de Tucuruí
Tocantins
Baía de São Marcos
Atol das Rocas
Fernando de Noronha
Cabo de São Roque

Cordillera Real
Chimborazo 6310m
Gulf of Guayaquil
Marañón
Ucayali
Jutaí
Jurua
Tapauá
Purus
Madeira
SOUTH AMERICA
Tapajós
Serra do Cachimbo
Teles Pires
Arinos
Juruena
São Manuel
Serra Grande
Mearim
Itapicuru
Parnaiba
Planalto da Borborema
Cabo Branco
Pernambuco Plain
Represa de Itaparica

Punta Pariñas
Cordillera Oriental
Cochabamba
Madre de Dios
Beni
Mamoré
Guaporé
Chapada dos Parecis
AMERICA
Tocantins
Araguaia
Serra Formosa
Serra do Roncador
Manso
São Francisco
Chapada das Mangabeiras
Serra Geral de Goiás
Represa de Sobradinho
Chapada Diamantina
Brazilian Highlands
Serra da Espinhaço
Paraguaçu
Baía de Todos os Santos
Brazil Basin

Cordillera Occidental
Apurimac
Lake Titicaca
Yungas
Rapulo
Rio Grande
Planalto de Mato Grosso
Paraguay
Taquari
Pantanal
São Francisco
Paranaíba
Trindade Spur
Abrolhos Bank
Doce

Peru Basin
Mendaña Fracture Zone
Altiplano
Lago Poopó
ANDES
Pilcomayo
Aporé
Rio Grande
Serra do Paranapiacaba
Serra da Mantiqueira
Ilha de São Sebastião
Santos Plateau
Tropic of Capricorn

Nazca Ridge
Chile Basin
Peru-Chile Trench
Atacama Desert
Gran Chaco
Salinas Grandes
Salado
Bermejo
Mesopotamia
Uruguay
Serra Geral
Serra do Mar
Ilha de São Francisco
Rio Grande Rise

Easter Island
Sala y Gomez Fracture Zone
Islas de los Desventurados
Sierras de Córdoba
Laguna Mar Chiquita
Dulce
Pampas
Paraná
Embalse de Río Negro
Río Negro
Cuchilla Grande
Mirim Lagoon
Lagoa dos Patos

East Pacific Rise
Roggeveen Basin
Juan Fernandez Islands
Cerro Aconcagua 6959m
Colorado
Rio Negro
Bahía Blanca
Golfo San Matías
Río de la Plata
Argentine Basin

NAZCA PLATE
ANTARCTIC PLATE
Neuquén
Limay
Chubut
Patagonia
Gulf of San Jorge
Argentine Plain
Falkland Escarpment

ANTARCTIC PLATE
PACIFIC PLATE
Lago Buenos Aires
Golfo Corcovado
Deseado
Chico
Bahía Grande
Falkland Plateau
Falkland Islands
Maurice Ewing Bank
South Georgia
South Sandwich Trench
South Georgia Ridge
South Sandwich Islands

Archipiélago de los Chonos
Strait of Magellan
Tierra del Fuego
Scotia Ridge
SOUTH AMERICAN PLATE
SCOTIA PLATE
Scotia Sea
SCOTIA PLATE
ANTARCTIC PLATE
Antarctic Circle

Froward Cape
Cape Horn
South Shetland Trough
South Shetland Islands
South Orkney Islands

Weddell Sea
ANTARCTICA

ATLANTIC OCEAN

OCEAN

Gambia Plain
Cape Verde Basin
Cape Verde Islands

PACIFIC OCEAN

PHYSICAL SOUTH AMERICA

THREE MAJOR PHYSIOGRAPHIC REGIONS characterize South America. The oldest, the ancient Brazilian Shield and the smaller Guyana and Patagonian shields, form the stable core of the continent. Stretching along the entire west coast are the younger Andean fold mountains with many summits rising to 20,000 ft (6100 m). These two diverse regions are separated by a number of sedimentary basins carrying South America's large river systems to the sea. These include the massive Amazon Basin and the basin of the Gran Chaco.

THE AMAZON BASIN AND GUYANA SHIELD

THE RIVER AMAZON occupies a large depression in the Earth's crust, formed by the uplift of the Andes. It is covered by thick volcanic deposits and layers of alluvium – these have been laid down by the Amazon's many tributaries. To the north is the smaller Guyana Shield.

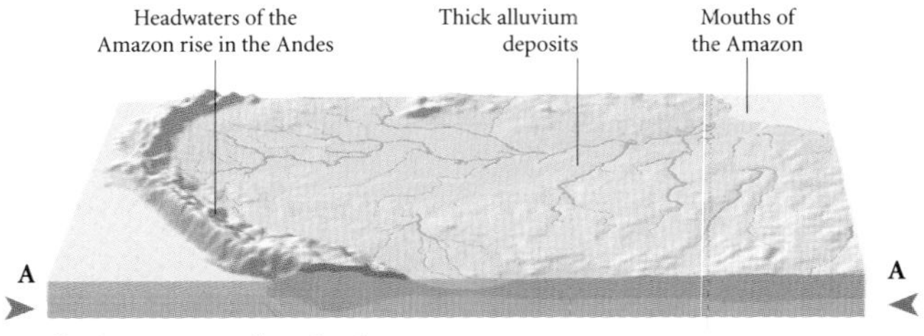

Headwaters of the Amazon rise in the Andes

Thick alluvium deposits

Mouths of the Amazon

Section across northern South America showing Amazon Basin and its drainage pattern.

0   500   1000 Km
0   500   1000 Miles

SCALE 1:27,500,000
(projection: Lambert Azimuthal Equal Area)

Km
0 100 200   400   600   800
Miles
0 100 200   400   600   800

THE ANDEAN UPLANDS

THE ANDEAN UPLANDS run along the west coast of South America. They are being uplifted as the Nazca Plate is subducted beneath the South American Plate. They contain some of the world's largest volcanoes, such as Cotopaxi, and Lake Titicaca which occupies a dormant site. The far south has many large ice-sheets and a fragmented coastline.

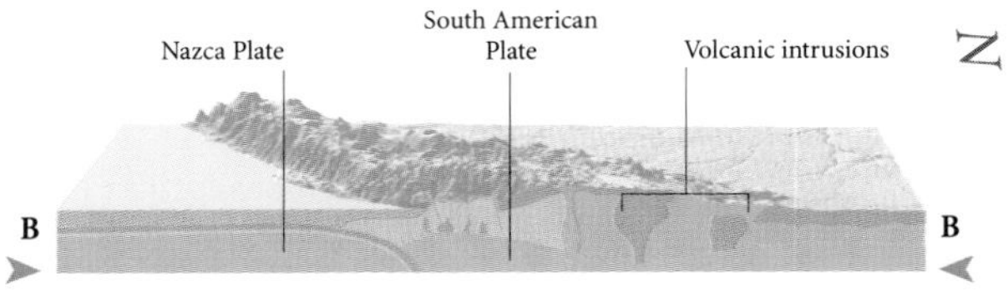

Nazca Plate

South American Plate

Volcanic intrusions

Cross-section through the Andes showing the subduction of the Nazca Plate beneath the South American Plate.

0   200   400 Km
0   200   400 Miles

MAP KEY

ELEVATION

6000m / 19,686ft
4000m / 13,124ft
3000m / 9843ft
2000m / 6562ft
1500m / 4922ft
1000m / 3281ft
500m / 1640ft
250m / 820ft
100m / 328ft
sea level

PLATE MARGINS
(for explanation see page xiv)

———— constructive
△ △ destructive
———— conservative
············ uncertain

———— physiographic regions
▶——— line of cross-section

THE BRAZILIAN SHIELD AND GRAN CHACO

THE IMMENSE BRAZILIAN SHIELD underlies more than one-third of South America. It is pitted with numerous volcanic intrusions, and a large basaltic plateau exists between the Paraná River and the Atlantic Ocean. The flat Gran Chaco lies to the west of the shield, covered by sedimentary deposits eroded from the Andes, and transported by South America's mighty rivers.

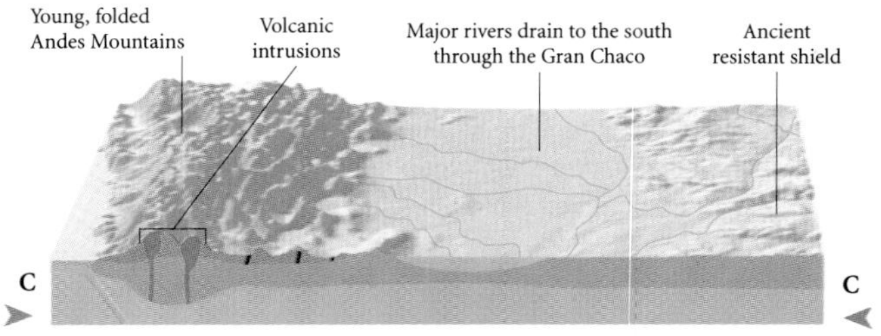

Young, folded Andes Mountains

Volcanic intrusions

Major rivers drain to the south through the Gran Chaco

Ancient resistant shield

Section across central South America showing the flat basin of the Gran Chaco and the ancient Brazilian Shield.

0   200   400 Km
0   200   400 Miles

Map labels

Punta Gallinas
Gulf of Venezuela
Lake Maracaibo
Gulf of Darien
Gulf of Panama
COCOS PLATE
NAZCA PLATE
Llanos
Orinoco
Cauca
Cordillera Occidental
Cordillera Central
Cordillera Oriental
Magdalena
GUYANA SHIELD
Guiana Highlands
Pakaraima Mountains
Tumuc-Humac Mountains
Río Negro
Branco
Japurá
Represa Balbina
Amazon
Ilha de Marajó
Cabo de São Roque
Planalto de Borborema
Cordillera Real
Cotopaxi 5897m
Chimborazo 6310m
Gulf of Guayaquil
Putumayo
Amazon
Amazon Basin
Marañón
Purus
Madeira
Tapajós
Xingu
Tocantins
Serra dos Carajás
Araguaia
Tocantins
BRAZILIAN SHIELD
Represa de Sobradinho
Serra do Cachimbo
Punta Negra
NAZCA PLATE
SOUTH AMERICAN PLATE
Nevado Huascarán 6768m
Ucayali
Madre de Dios
Guaporé
Chapada dos Parecis
Serra Formosa
Serra do Roncador
Serra Dourada
São Francisco
Serra do Espinhaço
Planalto de Mato Grosso
Brazilian Highlands
PACIFIC OCEAN
Lake Titicaca
Lago Poopó
Pantanal
Serra de Maracaju
Serra do Caiapó
Serra Geral
Serra da Mantiqueira
Altiplano
Atacama Desert
Gran Chaco
Pilcomayo
Paraná
Paraguay
Serra do Mar
Nevado Ojos del Salado 6880m
Cerro Aconcagua 6959m
Paraná
Mesopotamia
Uruguay
Lagoa dos Patos
Mirim Lagoon
Río de la Plata
NAZCA PLATE
SOUTH AMERICAN PLATE
Pampas
Salado
Colorado
Río Negro
ATLANTIC OCEAN
PATAGONIAN SHIELD
Isla de Chiloé
Península Valdés
Chico
Lago Colhué Huapí
Gulf of San Jorge
Deseado
Golfo de Penas
Patagonia
Andes
Bahía Grande
Falkland Islands
Strait of Magellan
ANTARCTIC PLATE
Tierra del Fuego
SOUTH AMERICAN PLATE
SCOTIA PLATE
Cape Horn
ATLANTIC OCEAN

A A Section across northern South America
B B Cross-section through the Andes
C C Section across central South America

CLIMATE

THE CLIMATE OF SOUTH AMERICA is influenced by three principal factors: the seasonal shift of high pressure air masses over the tropics, cold ocean currents along the western coast, affecting temperature and precipitation, and the mountain barrier produced by by the Andes, which creates a rain shadow over much of the south.

Climate
- tundra
- cool continental
- warm humid
- semi-arid
- arid
- humid equatorial
- tropical
- daily hours of sunshine, January
- daily hours of sunshine, July
- → cold wind

Mild winters and cool summers typify the extensive Pampas grasslands of Argentina.

Chile's hyper-arid Atacama Desert is renowned as one of the driest places on Earth.

TEMPERATURE

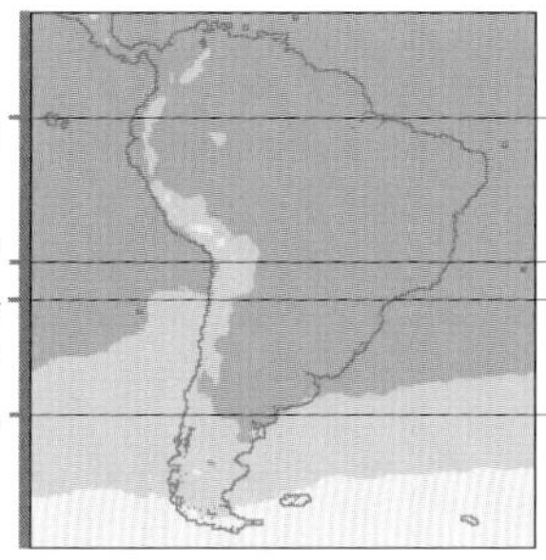

Average January temperature

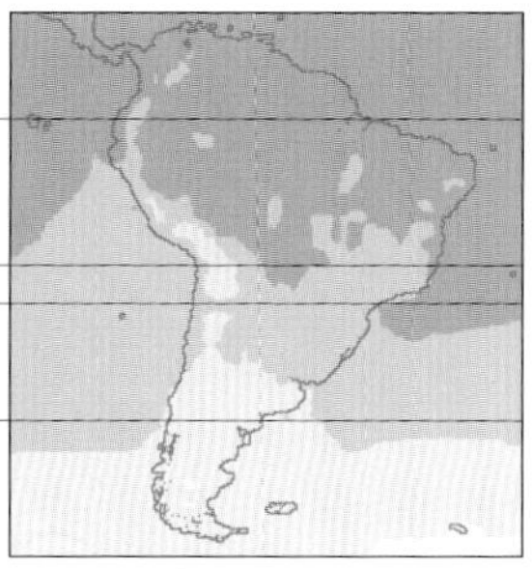

Average July temperature

Temperature
- below -30°C (-22°F)
- -30 to -20°C (-22 to -4°F)
- -20 to -10°C (-4 to 14°F)
- -10 to 0°C (14 to 32°F)
- 0 to 10°C (32 to 50°F)
- 10 to 20°C (50°F)
- 20 to 30°C (68 to 86°F)
- above 30°C (86°F)

RAINFALL

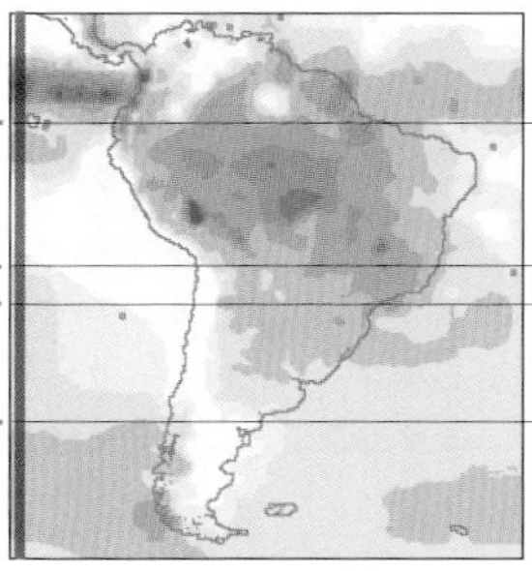

Average January rainfall

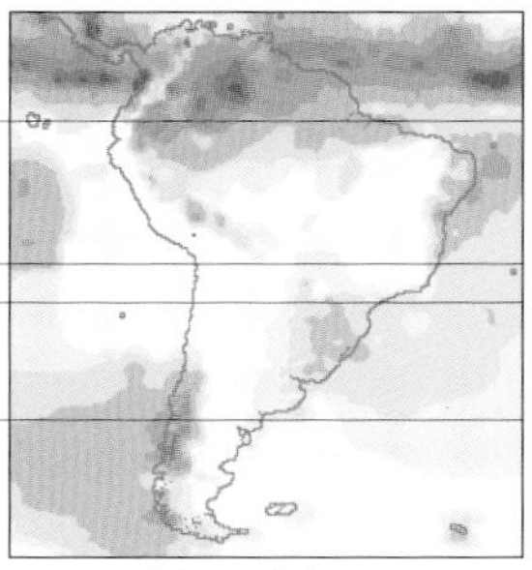

Average July rainfall

Rainfall
- 0–25 mm (0–1 in)
- 25–50 mm (1–2 in)
- 50–100 mm (2–4 in)
- 100–200 mm (4–8 in)
- 200–300 mm (8–12 in)
- 300–400 mm (12–16 in)
- 400–500 mm (16–20 in)
- more than 500 mm (20 in)

Tropical conditions are found across over half of South America. When both rainfall and temperatures are high, hot humid rainforests prevail.

SHAPING THE CONTINENT

SOUTH AMERICA'S ACTIVE TECTONIC BELT has been extensively folded over millions of years; landslides are still frequent in the mountains. The large river systems that erode the mountains flow across resistant shield areas, depositing sediment. Present-day glaciation affects the distinctive landscape of the far south.

MASS MOVEMENT

6 Debris slides are common in the highlands of South America (left). They occur where soil on a slope is saturated by rainwater and therefore less stable. The actual slides are often triggered by earthquakes.

- Scarp face left after soil has moved to the base of the slope
- Failure plane
- Toe of debris slide

MASS MOVEMENT: A SECTION OF A DEBRIS SLIDE

CHEMICAL WEATHERING

1 Table mountains (left) are the eroded remnants of an ancient upland. As water percolates along cracks in these high, flat-topped mountains it forms intricate cave systems. Chemical weathering also isolates large blocks which then collapse, accumulating as rockfalls at the foot of scarp slopes.

- Smooth summit dissected by deep gorges
- Rainfall
- Run-off surges down caverns as waterfalls

CHEMICAL WEATHERING: EROSION OF THE GUYANA SHIELD

THE EVOLVING LANDSCAPE

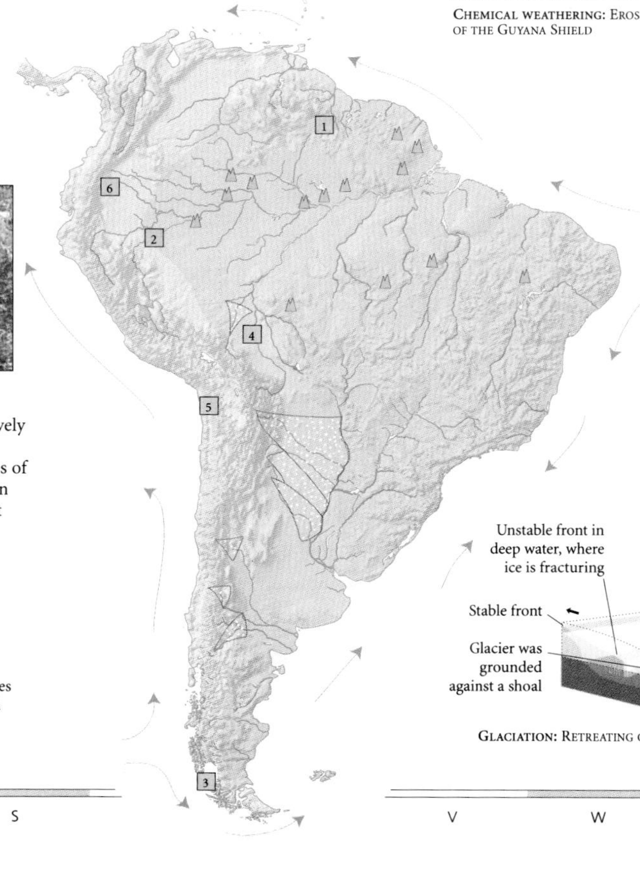

RIVER SYSTEMS

2 Along the Amazon (above) there is a great variation in rates of erosion. As the headwaters of the Amazon flow down from the Andes, they erode and transport vast quantities of sediment, and are known as whitewaters. Across the shield areas erosion rates are very low. These rivers, carrying rotting vegetation, are called blackwaters.

- Whitewater river
- Blackwater river
- Little erosion in shield areas
- Confluence of whitewater with blackwater

RIVER SYSTEMS: SUSPENDED SEDIMENTS IN THE AMAZON

Landscape
- uplifting land
- stable land
- sinking land
- glacier
- ocean current
- aluvial fan
- inselberg
- river

FOLDING

5 Folding occurs beneath the surface under high temperatures and pressures. Rocks become sufficiently malleable to flow and not fracture as tectonic plates collide. In the Valley of the Moon in Chile (above), anticlines (or upfolds) and synclines (or troughs) have been exploited by erosion.

- Fold axis
- Anticline
- Syncline
- Fold axis

FOLDING: SYNCLINES AND ANTICLINES

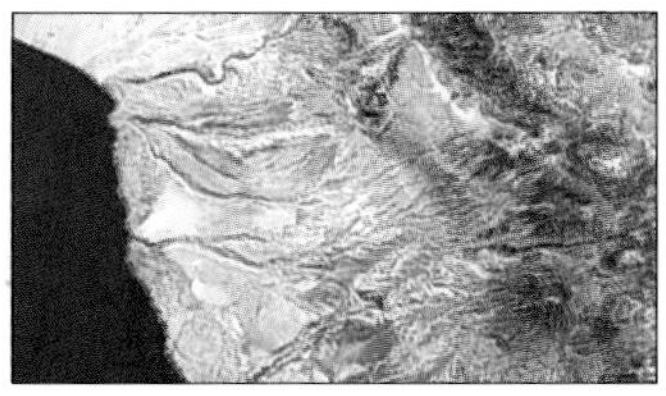

DEPOSITION

4 Large alluvial fans are found extensively across South America (above). Confined mountain rivers, carrying large quantities of eroded material, emerge from a mountain gorge onto the plains, where they deposit their load in huge fans.

- Mountain front
- Subsequent fan
- Confined stream in the mountains
- Fan forms as stream emerges onto the plain

DEPOSITION: FORMATION OF AN ALLUVIAL FAN

- Unstable front in deep water, where ice is fracturing
- Original extent of glacier
- Icebergs
- Stable front
- Glacier was grounded against a shoal

GLACIATION: RETREATING GLACIER IN PATAGONIA

GLACIATION

3 As fjord glaciers in Patagonia (above) retreat, they become grounded on shoals. In deeper water the base of the glacier becomes unstable, and icebergs break off (calve) until the glacier snout grounds once more.

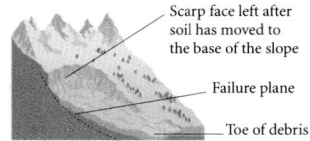

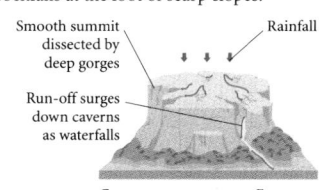
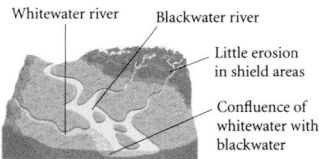

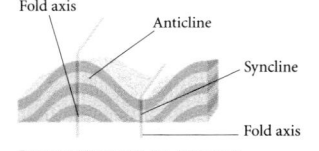
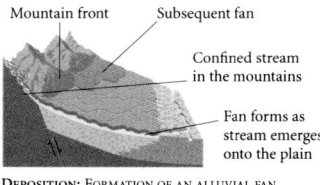
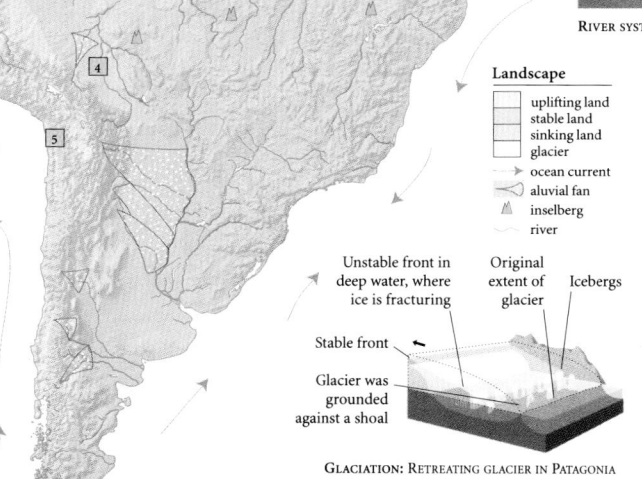

POLITICAL SOUTH AMERICA

MODERN SOUTH AMERICA'S POLITICAL BOUNDARIES have their origins in the territorial endeavours of explorers during the 16th century, who claimed almost the entire continent for Portugal and Spain. The Portuguese land in the east later evolved into the federal states of Brazil, while the Spanish vice-royalties eventually emerged as separate independent nation-states in the early 19th century. South America's growing population has become increasingly urbanized, with the expansion of coastal cities into large conurbations like Rio de Janeiro and Buenos Aires. In Brazil, Argentina, Chile and Uruguay, a succession of military dictatorships has given way to fragile, but strengthening, democracies.

Europe retains a small foothold in South America. Kourou in French Guiana is the site chosen by the European Space Agency to launch the Ariane rocket. As a result of its status as a French overseas department, French Guiana is actually part of the European Union.

SCALE 1:21,500,000
(projection: Lambert Azimuthal Equal Area)

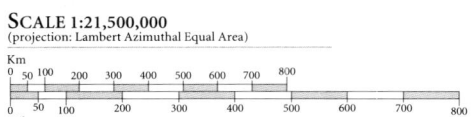

TRANSPORT

MOST MAJOR ROAD AND RAIL ROUTES are confined to the coastal regions by the forbidding natural barriers of the Andes Mountains and the Amazon Basin. Few major cross-continental routes exist, although Buenos Aires serves as a transport centre for the main rail links to La Paz and Valparaíso, while the construction of the Trans-Amazon and Pan-American Highways have made direct road travel possible from Recife to Lima and from Puerto Montt up the coast into central America. A new waterway project is proposed to transform the River Paraguay into a major shipping route, although it involves considerable wetland destruction.

South America's most extensive rail network is centred on the Argentinian capital, Buenos Aires. The construction of new rail lines from this important port, allowed the colonization of the Pampas lands for agriculture.

LANGUAGES

PRIOR TO EUROPEAN EXPLORATION in the 16th century, a diverse range of indigenous languages were spoken across the continent. With the arrival of Iberian settlers, Spanish became the dominant language, with Portuguese spoken in Brazil, and Native American languages such as Quechua and Guaraní, becoming concentrated in the continental interior. Today this pattern persists, although successive European colonization has led to Dutch being spoken in Surinam, English in Guyana, and French in French Guiana, while in large urban areas, Japanese and Chinese are increasingly common.

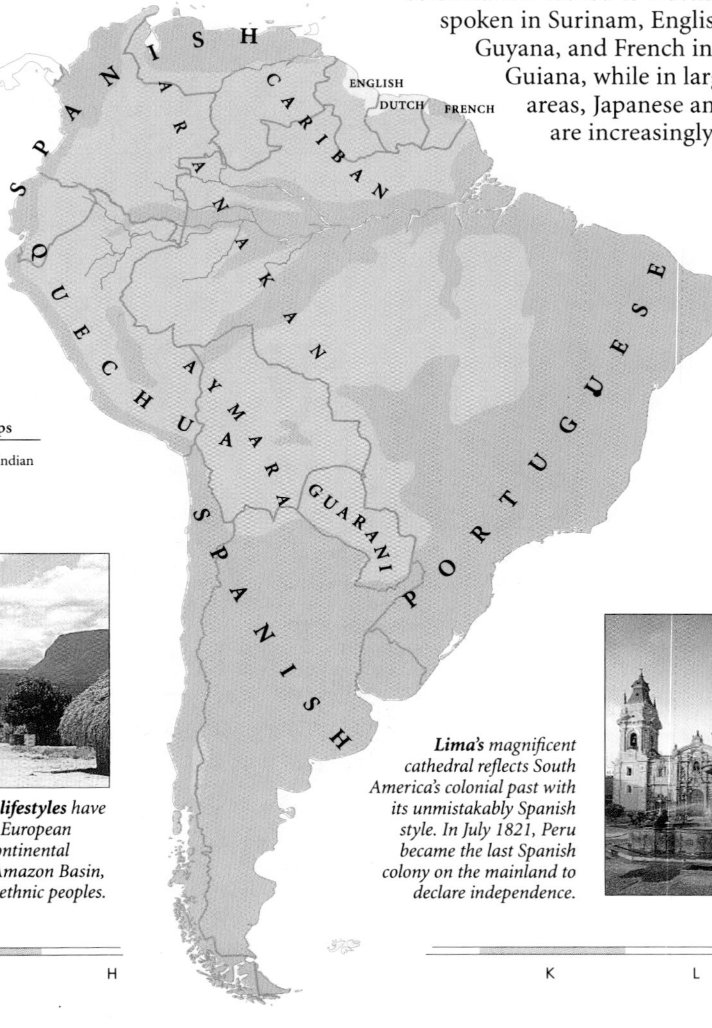

Transport

— major roads and motorways
— major railways
— international borders
• transport intersections
⊕ international airports
⊥ major ports

Language groups

American Indian
Germanic
Romance

Chile's main port, Valparaíso, is a vital national shipping centre, in addition to playing a key role in the growing trade with Pacific nations. The country's awkward, elongated shape means that sea transport is frequently used for internal travel and communications in Chile.

Indigenous South American lifestyles have not been totally submerged by European cultures and languages. The continental interior, and particularly the Amazon Basin, is still home to many different ethnic peoples.

Lima's magnificent cathedral reflects South America's colonial past with its unmistakably Spanish style. In July 1821, Peru became the last Spanish colony on the mainland to declare independence.

Caribbean Sea

Q R S T

NORTH AMERICA

Santa Marta
Barranquilla
Cartagena
Gulf of Darien
Maracaibo
Valledupar
Cabimas
Lake Maracaibo
Valencia
Barquisimeto
Maracay
CARACAS
Cumaná
TRINIDAD & TOBAGO

V W X Y Z

Gulf of Venezuela

Montería
Cúcuta
San Cristóbal
Barinas
Orinoco
VENEZUELA
Ciudad Guayana
Venezuelan territorial claim

Medellín
Manizales
Pereira
Armenia
Ibagué
Cali
BOGOTÁ
Bucaramanga
Magdalena
Cauca
Llanos
Rio Negro
Boa Vista
RORAIMA
Guiana Highlands
Linden
GEORGETOWN
GUYANA
SURINAM
PARAMARIBO
CAYENNE
French Guiana (to France)
Surinamese territorial claims

In April 1960, Brazil's government began the move from Rio de Janeiro to Brasília, a futuristic new city built in the sparsely populated interior. Brasília is now the federal capital of Brazil.

COLOMBIA
Pasto

Esmeraldas
Equator
QUITO
ECUADOR
Ambato
Riobamba
Babahoyo
Cuenca
Portoviejo
Guayaquil
Machala
Ecuadorean territorial claim
Piura
Chiclayo
Trujillo

Branco
Japurá
Marañón
Putumayo
Amazon
Amazon
Juruá
Purus
AMAZONAS
Amazon Basin
Madeira
Manaus
Tapajós
Santarém
Xingu
PARÁ
Tocantins
Araguaia
Belém
AMAPÁ
Macapá
Equator
São Luís
MARANHÃO
Teresina
CEARÁ
Fortaleza

Iquitos
Ucayali
PERU
Madre de Dios
ACRE
Rio Branco
Porto Velho
RONDÔNIA
PIAUÍ
Palmas do Tocantins
TOCANTINS
Juazeiro
Represa de Sobradinho
RIO GRANDE DO NORTE
Natal
PARAÍBA
João Pessoa
Jaboatão
PERNAMBUCO
Recife
ALAGOAS
Maceió
SERGIPE
Aracaju

Callao
LIMA
Huancayo
Cusco
BRAZIL
MATO GROSSO
Planalto de Mato Grosso
Cuiabá
BRASÍLIA
DISTRITO FEDERAL
Goiânia
GOIÁS
São Francisco
MINAS GERAIS
Brazilian Highlands
BAHIA
Salvador

Arequipa
Lake Titicaca
LA PAZ
BOLIVIA
Cochabamba
Oruro
Santa Cruz
SUCRE
Lago Poopó
Tacna
Arica
Iquique
Pilcomayo
Campo Grande
MATO GROSSO DO SUL
Ribeirão Preto
SÃO PAULO
Belo Horizonte
Vitória
ESPÍRITO SANTO
Juiz de Fora

Tocopilla
Atacama Desert
PARAGUAY
Gran Chaco
Paraná
Pilcomayo
Londrina
Campinas
Nova Iguaçu
Duque de Caxias
RIO DE JANEIRO
Niterói
Rio de Janeiro
Antofagasta
Tropic of Capricorn
San Salvador de Jujuy
ASUNCIÓN
Ciudad del Este
PARANÁ
São Paulo
Osasco
Sorocaba
Santo André
Santos
Tropic of Capricorn

Rapid urbanization has been a feature of most South American countries in the latter half of the 20th century. In many cases, this unchecked growth has led to the development of sprawling slums, lacking adequate water and sewerage facilities.

Salta
Formosa
Villarrica
Curitiba
San Miguel de Tucumán
SANTA CATARINA
Resistencia
Corrientes
Posadas
Florianópolis
Santiago del Estero
Paraguay
La Rioja
RIO GRANDE DO SUL
Santa Maria
Porto Alegre

La Serena
Coquimbo
CHILE
San Juan
Córdoba
ARGENTINA
Santa Fe
Paraná
Uruguay
Tacuarembó
Melo
URUGUAY
Viña del Mar
Valparaíso
SANTIAGO
Mendoza
San Luis
Rosario
Pampas
BUENOS AIRES
La Plata
MONTEVIDEO
Río de la Plata

Linares
Santa Rosa
Bahía Blanca
Mar del Plata
Concepción
Salado
Colorado
Lota
Neuquén
Temuco
Río Negro
Valdivia
Puerto Montt

MAP KEY

POPULATION
■ above 5 million
▣ 1 million to 5 million
◉ 500,000 to 1 million
◎ 100,000 to 500,000
⊕ 50,000 to 100,000
○ 10,000 to 50,000
· below 10,000
● Country capital
• State capital

BORDERS
▨ full international border
▨ disputed de facto border
▨ disputed territorial claim border
▨ state border

Lago Colhué Huapí
Rawson
PATAGONIA
Lago Buenos Aires
Gulf of San Jorge
Golfo de Penas
Deseado
Bahía Grande
Falkland Islands (to UK)
STANLEY
Río Gallegos
Strait of Magellan
Punta Arenas
Ushuaia
Beagle Channel
Cape Horn

Perched high in the Andes like many of the cities in western South America, La Paz, Bolivia is the world's highest capital city at over 11,500 ft (3500 m).

POPULATION

ALMOST HALF OF SOUTH AMERICA'S population lives in Brazil but, due to the large uninhabited expanses of the Amazon Basin, its overall population density is much lower than in other countries. During the 20th century the most important population trend has been the movement from rural to urban areas, giving rise to great population concentrations in large cities like São Paulo, Rio de Janeiro, Caracas, Lima, Bogotá and Buenos Aires.

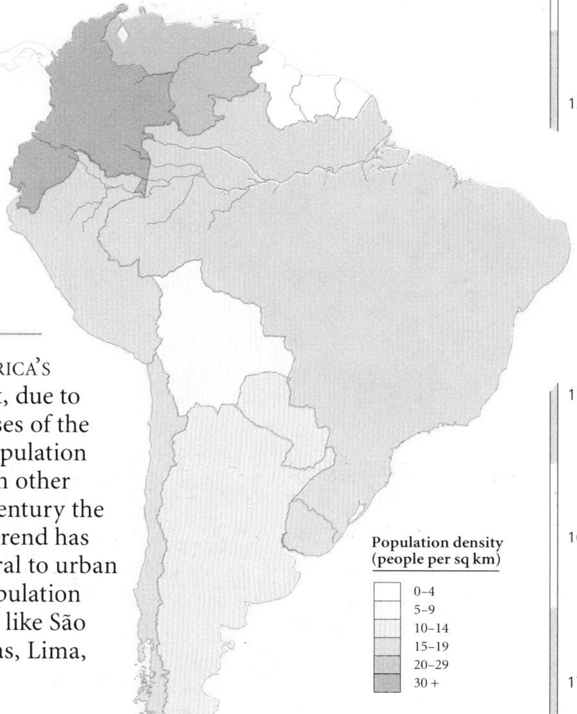

Population density (people per sq km)
0–4
5–9
10–14
15–19
20–29
30 +

PACIFIC OCEAN

ATLANTIC OCEAN

SOUTH AMERICAN RESOURCES

AGRICULTURE STILL PROVIDES THE LARGEST SINGLE FORM OF EMPLOYMENT in South America, although rural unemployment and poverty continue to drive people towards the huge coastal cities in search of jobs and opportunities. Mineral and fuel resources, although substantial, are distributed unevenly; few countries have both fossil fuels and minerals. To break industrial dependence on raw materials, boost manufacturing, and improve infrastructure, governments borrowed heavily from the World Bank in the 1960s and 1970s. This led to the accumulation of massive debts which are unlikely ever to be repaid. Today, Brazil dominates the continent's economic output, followed by Argentina. Recently, the less-developed western side of South America has benefited due to its geographical position; for example Chile is increasingly exporting raw materials to Japan.

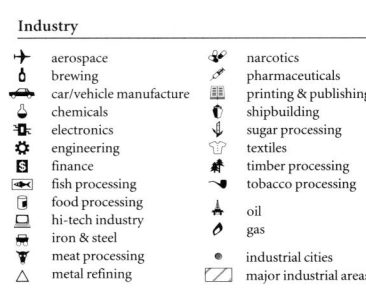

Ciudad Guayana is a planned industrial complex in eastern Venezuela, built as an iron and steel centre to exploit the nearby iron ore reserves.

The cold Peru Current flows north from the Antarctic along the Pacific coast of Peru, providing rich nutrients for one of the world's largest fishing grounds. However, over-exploitation has severely reduced Peru's anchovy catch.

STANDARD OF LIVING

WEALTH DISPARITIES throughout the continent create a wide gulf between affluent landowners and those afflicted by chronic poverty in inner-city slums. The illicit production of cocaine, and the hugely influential drug barons who control its distribution, contribute to the violent disorder and corruption which affect northwestern South America, de-stabilizing local governments and economies.

Standard of Living
(UN Human Development Index)

- low
- high

Both Argentina and Chile are now exploring the southernmost tip of the continent in search of oil. Here in Punta Arenas, a drilling rig is being prepared for exploratory drilling in the Strait of Magellen.

INDUSTRY

Industry

aerospace	narcotics
brewing	pharmaceuticals
car/vehicle manufacture	printing & publishing
chemicals	shipbuilding
electronics	sugar processing
engineering	textiles
finance	timber processing
fish processing	tobacco processing
food processing	oil
hi-tech industry	gas
iron & steel	industrial cities
meat processing	major industrial areas
metal refining	

ARGENTINA AND BRAZIL are South America's most industrialized countries and São Paulo is the continent's leading industrial centre. Long-term government investment in Brazilian industry has encouraged a diverse industrial base; engineering, steel production, food processing, textile manufacture and chemicals predominate. The illegal production of cocaine is economically significant in the Andean countries of Colombia and Bolivia. In Venezuela, the oil-dominated economy has left the country vulnerable to world oil price fluctuations. Food processing and mineral exploitation are common throughout the less industrially developed parts of the continent, including Bolivia, Chile, Ecuador and Peru.

GNP per capita (US$)

- 0–499
- 500–999
- 1000–1499
- 1500–2999
- 3000–5999
- 6000+

Caribbean Sea
PANAMA
Gulf of Panama
Barranquilla
Cartagena
Maracaibo
Barquisimeto
Caracas
Valencia
VENEZUELA
Ciudad Guayana
Georgetown
GUYANA
Paramaribo
SURINAM
French Guiana (to France)
Medellín
Bogotá
Cali
COLOMBIA
Quito
ECUADOR
Guayaquil
Iquitos
Belém
Manaus
Amazon Basin
BRAZIL
Fortaleza
Natal
Chiclayo
Chimbote
Recife
Lima
PERU
Maceió
Cusco
Salvador
Arequipa
BOLIVIA
La Paz
Santa Cruz
Sucre
Brasília
Iquique
Belo Horizonte
Chuquicamata
PARAGUAY
São Paulo
Rio de Janeiro
Antofagasta
Asunción
Ciudad del Este
Curitiba
San Miguel de Tucumán
Corrientes
Porto Alegre
Córdoba
Santa Fe
Rosario
URUGUAY
Rio Grande
Valparaíso
Mendoza
Buenos Aires
Montevideo
Santiago
Talca
Concepción
ARGENTINA
Bahía Blanca
Neuquén
Valdivia
Comodoro Rivadavia
Gulf of San Jorge
Falkland Islands (to UK)
Bahía Grande
Punta Arenas
Strait of Magellan
Cape Horn

ATLANTIC OCEAN
PACIFIC OCEAN
CHILE

ENVIRONMENTAL ISSUES

THE AMAZON BASIN is one of the last great wilderness areas left on Earth. The tropical rainforests which grow there are a valuable genetic resource, containing innumerable unique plants and animals. The forests are increasingly under threat from new and expanding settlements and 'slash and burn' farming techniques, which clear land for the raising of beef cattle, causing land degradation and soil erosion.

Clouds of smoke billow from the burning Amazon rainforest. Over 25,000 sq miles (60,000 sq km) of virgin rainforest are being cleared annually, destroying an ancient, irreplaceable, natural resource and biodiverse habitat.

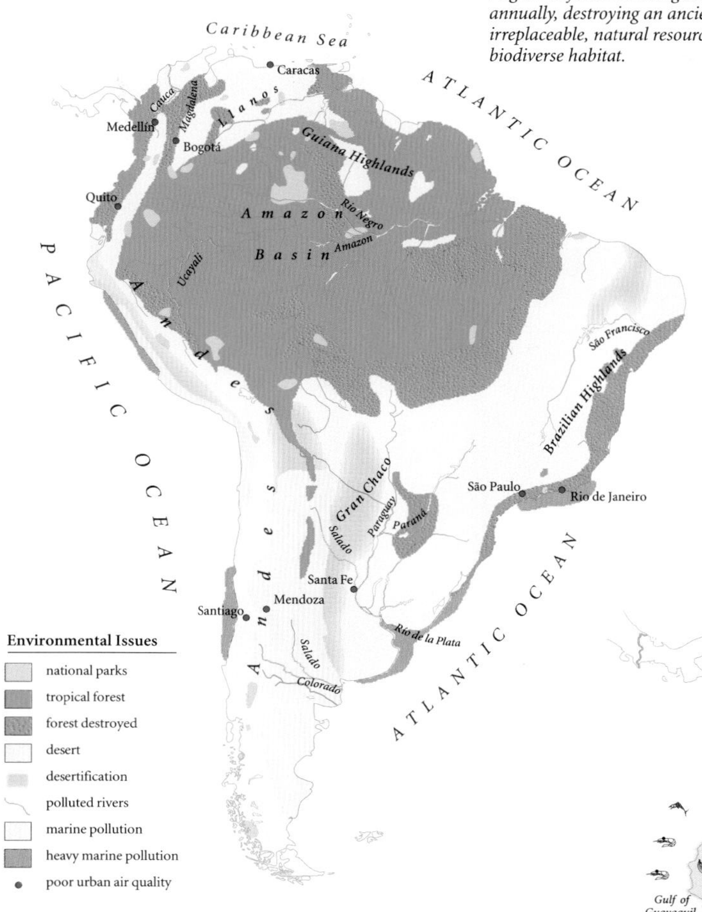

Environmental Issues

	national parks
	tropical forest
	forest destroyed
	desert
	desertification
	polluted rivers
	marine pollution
	heavy marine pollution
•	poor urban air quality

USING THE LAND AND SEA

MANY FOODS NOW COMMON WORLDWIDE originated in South America. These include the potato, tomato, squash, and cassava. Today, large herds of beef cattle roam the temperate grasslands of the Pampas, supporting an extensive meat-packing trade in Argentina, Uruguay and Paraguay. Corn (maize) is grown as a staple crop across the continent and coffee is grown as a cash crop in Brazil and Colombia. Coca plants grown in Bolivia, Peru and Colombia provide most of the world's cocaine. Fish and shellfish are caught off the western coast, especially anchovies off Peru, shrimps off Ecuador and pilchards off Chile.

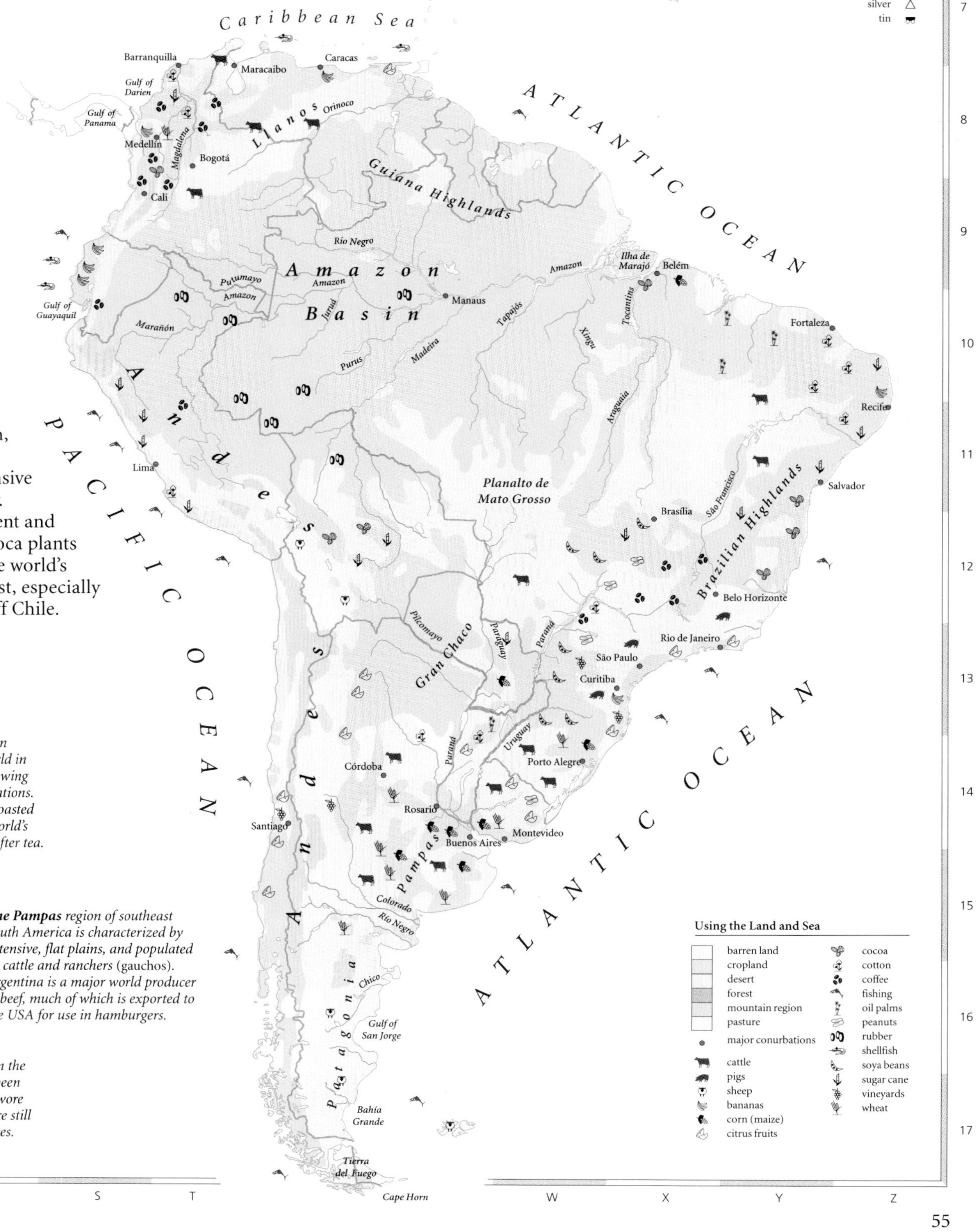

South America, and Brazil in particular, now leads the world in coffee production, mainly growing Coffea Arabica in large plantations. Coffee beans are harvested, roasted and brewed to produce the world's second most popular drink, after tea.

The Pampas region of southeast South America is characterized by extensive, flat plains, and populated by cattle and ranchers (gauchos). Argentina is a major world producer of beef, much of which is exported to the USA for use in hamburgers.

High in the Andes, hardy alpacas graze on the barren land. Alpacas are thought to have been domesticated by the Incas, whose nobility wore robes made from their wool. Today, they are still reared and prized for their soft, warm fleeces.

MINERAL RESOURCES

OVER A QUARTER OF THE WORLD'S known copper reserves are found at the Chuquicamata mine in northern Chile, and other metallic minerals such as tin are found along the length of the Andes. The discovery of oil and gas at Venezuela's Lake Maracaibo in 1917 turned the country into one of the world's leading oil producers. In contrast, South America is virtually devoid of coal, the only significant deposit being on the peninsula of Guajira in Colombia.

Copper is Chile's largest export, most of which is mined at Chuquicamata. Along the length of the Andes, metallic minerals like copper and tin are found in abundance, formed by the excessive pressures and heat involved in mountain-building.

Mineral Resources

	oil field
	gas field
	coal field
	bauxite
	copper
	diamonds
	gold
	iron
	lead
	silver
	tin

Using the Land and Sea

	barren land		cocoa
	cropland		cotton
	desert		coffee
	forest		fishing
	mountain region		oil palms
	pasture		peanuts
•	major conurbations		rubber
	cattle		shellfish
	pigs		soya beans
	sheep		sugar cane
	bananas		vineyards
	corn (maize)		wheat
	citrus fruits		

NORTHERN SOUTH AMERICA

COLOMBIA, GUYANA, SURINAM, VENEZUELA, *French Guiana* (to France)

FRINGED BY THE PACIFIC AND ATLANTIC OCEANS and the Caribbean Sea, South America's northern region has a rich range of natural resources, some exploited for centuries by colonial powers including the Spanish, French, Dutch and British, others still to be fully explored. The prospects for further economic development in Colombia, Guyana and Surinam are blighted by drug-related violence and political instability. Venezuela, despite huge incomes from its oil reserves, remains less developed in other industrial sectors.

French Guiana is an overseas *département* of France, now seeking greater autonomy. Most of the major population centres, such as Bogotá, have grown up in the temperate conditions of the high Andes or, like Caracas, at strategic points along the Caribbean coast.

Flowers grown in Colombia are exported all over the world, and include fine carnations and roses. Here, workers are cutting roses which have been grown in plastic greenhouses.

MAP KEY

POPULATION

- 1 million to 5 million
- 500,000 to 1 million
- 100,000 to 500,000
- 50,000 to 100,000
- 10,000 to 50,000
- below 10,000

ELEVATION

- 4000m / 13,124ft
- 3000m / 9843ft
- 2000m / 6562ft
- 1000m / 3281ft
- 500m / 1640ft
- 250m / 820ft
- 100m / 328ft
- sea level

Large open squares like the Plaza Bolivia in Bogotá are characteristic of many cities founded by the Spanish.

Scattered farms and villages have grown up on the gentle slopes of this Colombian river valley, utilizing the fertile soils for farming.

SCALE 1:6,500,000
(projection: Lambert Azimuthal Equal Area)

Km
0   25   50   100   150   200
Miles
0   25   50   100   150   200

The Orinoco River flows from its source in the southern Guiana Highlands to form a broad delta on Venezuela's Atlantic coast. One of its distributary channels opens into a wide bay called the Serpent's Mouth.

TRANSPORT AND INDUSTRY

MANY MINERAL RESOURCES are mined in Colombia, including fuels, gold and precious and semi-precious stones. Revenues from coffee and exports of illegal narcotics are crucial to the economy. Venezuela's major economic activity is the oil industry around Lake Maracaibo *(Lago de Maracaibo)*. Sugar and bauxite are exported from Guyana and Surinam.

THE TRANSPORT NETWORK

	153,755 miles (247,593km)
	925 miles (1490 km)
	2541 miles (4092 km)
	18,233 miles (29,360 km)

Rivers are an important means of transport in Colombia; many are extensively navigable. The Pan-American Highway runs through Colombia. In Venezuela, much infrastructure investment is linked to the oil industry.

▶ 66

Major industry and infrastructure

- chemicals
- finance
- food processing
- iron & steel
- narcotics
- mining
- oil
- oil refining
- pharmaceuticals
- textiles
- timber processing
- capital cities
- major towns
- international airports
- major roads
- major industrial areas

Vast oil reserves around Lake Maracaibo (Lago de Maracaibo) form the focus of Venezuelan industry. Incomes from oil are used to invest in other industries and in the development of infrastructure.

USING THE LAND

THE ANDEAN BASINS support cereals and potatoes. Livestock graze at higher altitudes and on the drier tropical grasslands known as the *llanos*; hardy goats are reared in scrubland areas. Grown at higher elevations, coffee is an important cash crop, as is cotton, sugar cane, bananas, citrus fruits, cocoa and rice, farmed on the Caribbean lowlands. Coca is the most widely-grown narcotic plant, with heroin poppies grown in Colombia and marijuana in lowland areas throughout the region.

Land use and agricultural distribution

- cattle
- goats
- bananas
- cereals
- coffee
- cotton
- sugar cane
- capital cities
- major towns
- pasture
- cropland
- forest
- wetlands
- mountain region

THE URBAN/RURAL POPULATION DIVIDE

urban 78%   rural 22%

0 10 20 30 40 50 60 70 80 90 100

POPULATION DENSITY
50 people per sq mile
(19 people per sq km)

TOTAL LAND AREA
1,111,317 sq miles
(2,879,060 sq km)

THE LANDSCAPE

AT ITS NORTHERNMOST REACHES, in western Colombia and Venezuela, the great Andean mountain chain splits into three distinct ranges: the Cordillera Oriental, Cordillera Central and Cordillera Occidental, intercut by a complex series of lesser ranges and basins. The relief becomes lower toward the coast and the interior plains of the northern Amazon Basin, rising again into the tropical hills of the Guiana Highlands.

The Sierra Nevada de Santa Marta is a granite massif which rises sharply from the Caribbean lowlands to snow-covered peaks, the tallest of which is 18,947 ft (5775 m) high.

Lake Maracaibo *(Lago de Maracaibo)* is not a true lake but a shallow inlet of the Caribbean Sea. It is the main source of Venezuela's oil.

The drainage basin of the Magdalena River and the Cauca, its main tributary, covers over 20% of Colombia's total surface area.

Cordillera Occidental

Cordillera Central

Cordillera Oriental

Colombia's eastern lowlands are known locally as *llanos*, meaning grasslands.

In the Guiana Highlands, Venezuela's most remote region, the ancient crystalline rocks contain deposits of iron ore, gold and diamonds.

Angel Falls *(Salto Ángel)*, at 3212 ft (979 m), is the world's highest waterfall.

Igneous intrusions into the crystalline plateau which forms most of central Guyana have led to the formation of the many rapids which characterize Guyana's rivers.

Potaru River

The Potaru River descends 741 ft (226 m) over a sandstone ledge at the Kaieteur Falls in Guyana.

Guyana Shield
- Alluvial plains
- Inselbergs
- Table mountains

The Guyana Shield is one of the oldest land surfaces in the world – probably formed more than 4 billion years ago. Chemical weathering over millions of years has created flat-topped table mountains and large numbers of inselbergs.

Over 80% of Surinam is covered by tropical rainforest.

Most of the land in French Guiana is low-lying; here, the rocks of the Guiana Highlands have been eroded by rivers flowing towards the sea.

▼ 60

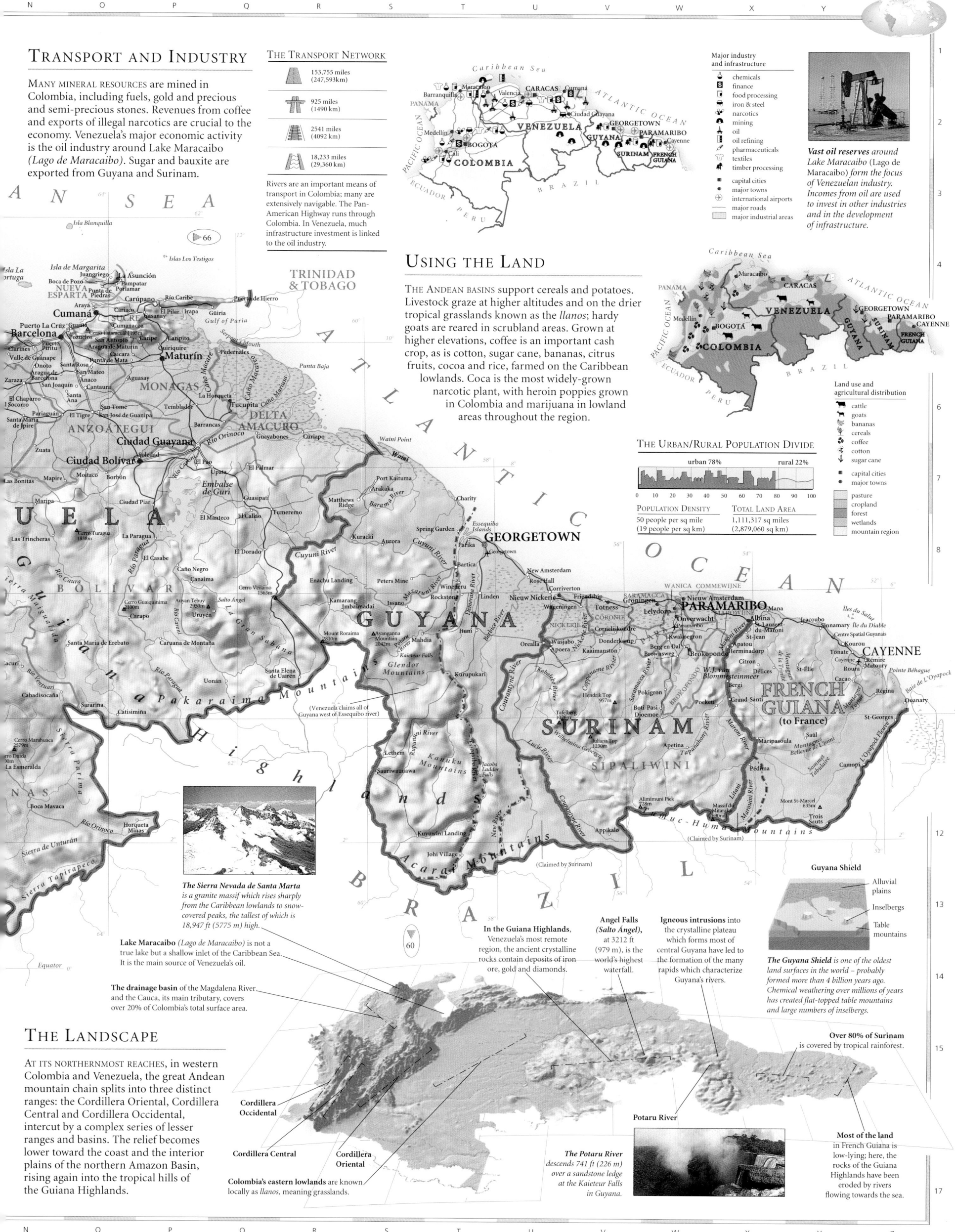

WESTERN SOUTH AMERICA

BOLIVIA, ECUADOR, PERU

THE THREE STATES OF WESTERN SOUTH AMERICA share a similar geography and recent history. Dominated by the Inca empire until Spanish conquest in the 16th century, they achieved independence from Spain in the early 19th century. The precipitous terrain of the Andes presents severe difficulties for overland transport and continues to be a barrier to national unity and stability. Although Ecuador is now a relatively stable democracy, the military is highly influential in Peru and Bolivia, while the drug trade and associated corruption discourages external aid and economic progress. Wealth and power are still largely concentrated in the hands of a small elite of families, who attained their position during the Spanish colonial period. Land rights and political recognition for the indigenous peoples are becoming increasingly important issues, particularly in Ecuador.

THE LANDSCAPE

BOLIVIA, PERU AND ECUADOR each possess a high Andean mountain region and an eastern region consisting of tropical lowlands and the Andean slope leading down to them. Towards the south of the region, the mountains widen to form the high plateau of the Altiplano. Peru and Ecuador also have fertile, lowland coastal plains. A wide variety of environments include *selva* (tropical rainforest), *montaña* (mountain forest) and grassland.

Ecuador's capital city, Quito, lies high in the Andes, nestling between snow-capped peaks. At 9350 ft (2850 m), Quito is the second highest capital in the world – La Paz in Bolivia is the highest.

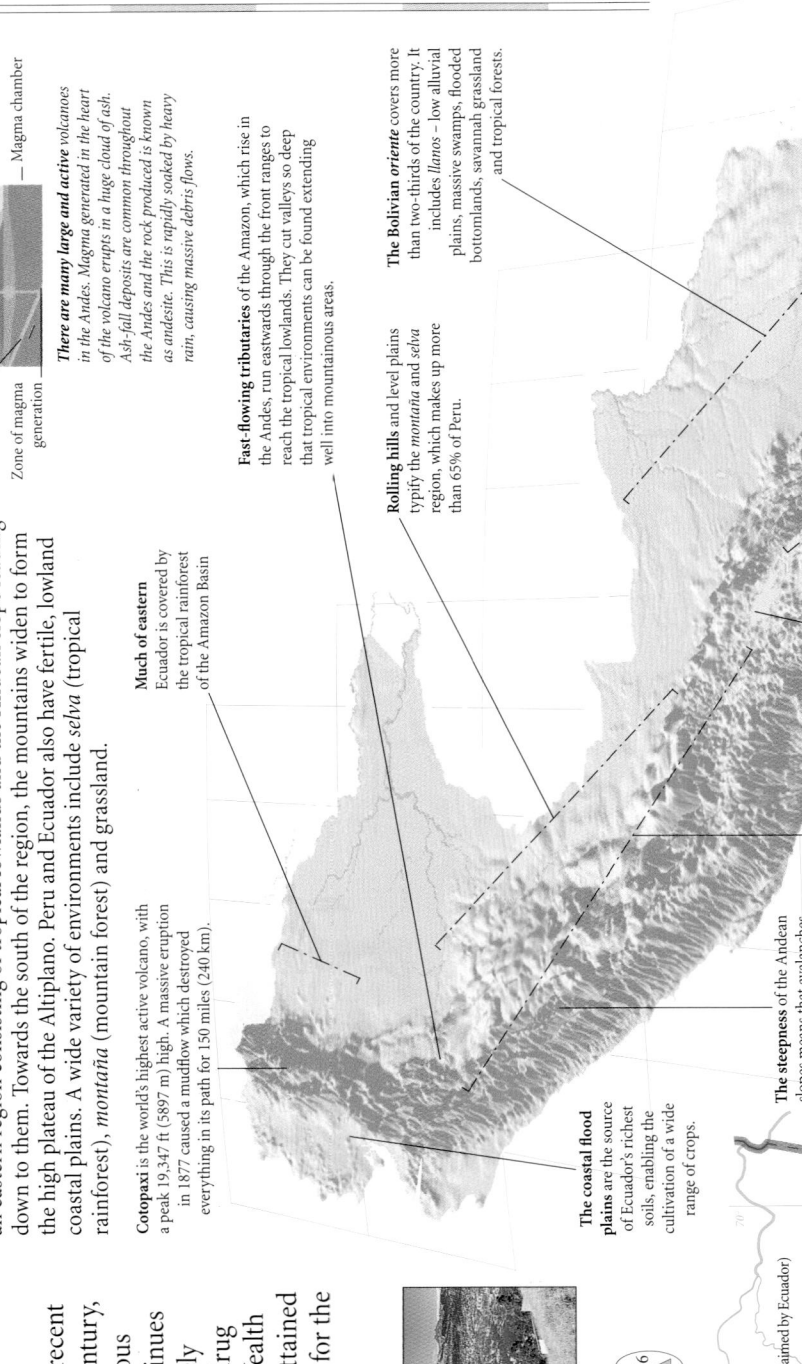

There are many large and active volcanoes in the Andes. Magma generated in the heart of the volcano erupts in a huge cloud of ash. Ash-fall deposits are common throughout the Andes and the rock produced is known as andesite. This is rapidly soaked by heavy rain, causing massive debris flows.

- Falling ash
- Lava flows
- Magma chamber
- Eruption column
- Subduction zone
- Zone of magma generation

Cotopaxi is the world's highest active volcano, with a peak 19,347 ft (5897 m) high. A massive eruption in 1877 caused a mudflow which destroyed everything in its path for 150 miles (240 km).

Fast-flowing tributaries of the Amazon, which rise in the Andes, run eastwards through the front ranges to reach the tropical lowlands. They cut valleys so deep that tropical environments can be found well into mountainous areas.

Much of eastern Ecuador is covered by the tropical rainforest of the Amazon Basin.

Rolling hills and level plains typify the *montaña* and *selva* region, which makes up more than 65% of Peru.

The Bolivian oriente covers more than two-thirds of the country. It includes *llanos* – low alluvial plains, massive swamps, flooded bottomlands, savannah grassland and tropical forests.

The coastal flood plains are the source of Ecuador's richest soils, enabling the cultivation of a wide range of crops.

The steepness of the Andean slopes means that avalanches and debris flows are an ever-present danger. A landslide starting from Nevado Huascarán in Peru in 1970 killed 20,000 people in 2.5 minutes when it engulfed an inhabited valley.

The Peruvian Andes are relatively young mountains which are continually being uplifted, making the area very unstable, with frequent earthquakes. The transport difficulties that they present continue to form a barrier to national unity.

The Altiplano is a flat, high plateau lying between the Cordillera Oriental and the Cordillera Occidental at a height of up to 12,500 ft (3800 m). At its margins lie many spurs and alluvial fans.

Bolivian Andes

Nevado de Illampu and *Nevado de Ancohuma*, at 21,275 ft (6485 m) and 21,490 ft (6550 m) respectively, form Illampu, the highest mountain in the Bolivian Andes.

Lake Titicaca

Lake Titicaca, which forms part of the border between Peru and Bolivia, is the largest lake in South America and the highest significant body of water in the world at an altitude of 12,507 ft (3812 m).

SCALE 1:7,750,000
(projection: Lambert Azimuthal Equal Area)

MAP KEY

POPULATION
- ■ above 5 million
- ● 1 million to 5 million
- ◎ 500,000 to 1 million
- ⊕ 100,000 to 500,000
- ○ 50,000 to 100,000
- ○ 10,000 to 50,000
- ○ below 10,000

ELEVATION
- 6000m / 19,686ft
- 4000m / 13,124ft
- 3000m / 9843ft
- 2000m / 6562ft
- 1000m / 3281ft
- 500m / 1640ft
- 250m / 820ft
- 100m / 328ft
- sea level

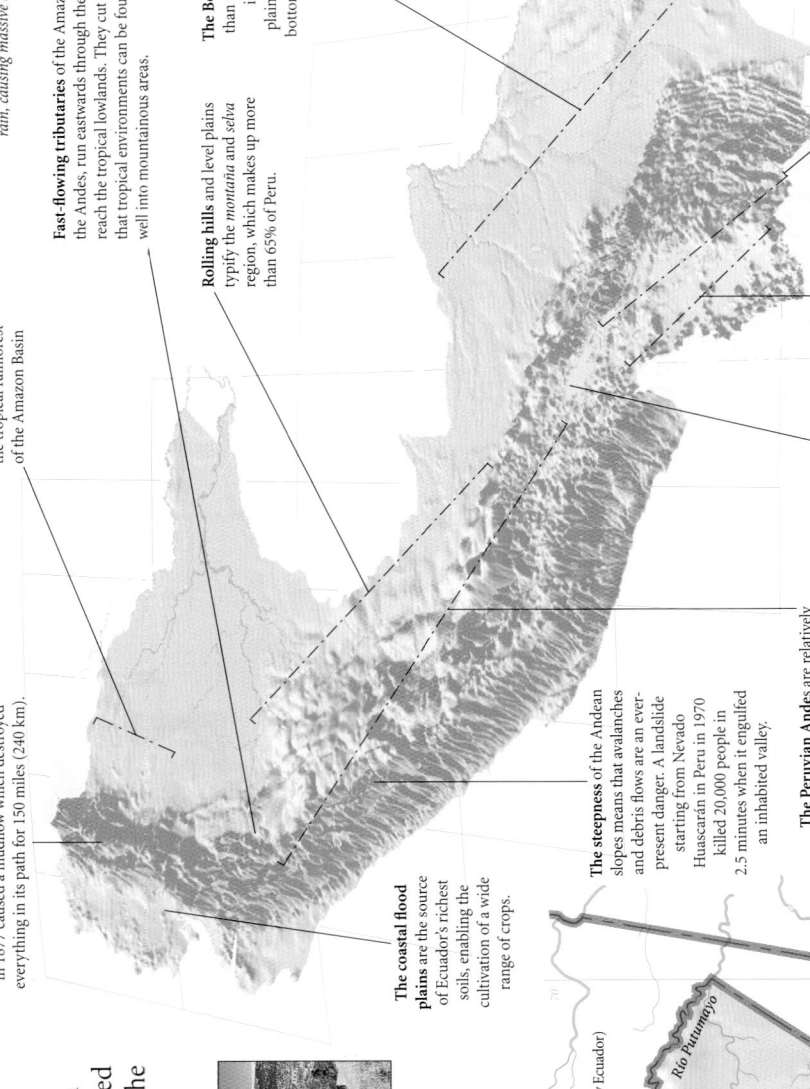

ECUADOREAN ADMINISTRATIVE REGIONS

1. CARCHI
2. TUNGURAHUA
3. BOLIVAR
4. CHIMBORAZO
5. ZAMORA CHINCHIPE

Llamas, with alpacas and vicuñas, are indigenous to South America. They thrive in Andean conditions and their wool is both exported and used in the manufacture of local textiles.

BOLIVIA'S TWO CAPITALS

LA PAZ – legislative and administrative capital
SUCRE – legal capital

THE URBAN/RURAL POPULATION DIVIDE

urban 64%   rural 36%

TOTAL LAND AREA
1,019,515 sq miles
(2,641,230 sq km)

POPULATION DENSITY
41 people per sq mile
(16 people per sq km)

Clearance of the forest in coca-growing regions is encouraged by the Bolivian government. The inaccessible terrain makes policing the growers very difficult. Coca is a popular crop because it is simple to grow and to transport, and is very profitable when illegally processed as cocaine.

USING THE LAND AND SEA

THE COASTAL REGIONS support a variety of cash crops including rice, sugar cane, bananas, coffee and cocoa, watered by rainfall or by irrigation schemes. The grasslands of the high *sierra* are used mainly for grazing a wide range of livestock; cattle and sheep are reared, along with pigs, and the indigenous llama and alpaca. Subsistence crops, especially potatoes and cereals, are grown lower down the mountain flanks. Despite government incentives to grow alternative crops, coca, used for cocaine, is the Bolivian and Peruvian *oriente's* most profitable commercial crop.

Land use and agricultural distribution

capital cities
major towns

cattle
sheep
bananas
cereals
cocoa
coffee
fishing
rubber
sugar cane

pasture
cropland
forest
mountain region
desert
wetlands

The ancient city of Machupicchu, in the Peruvian Andes was built prior to the Inca period. Its impressive ruins reflect a culture which had developed a high degree of sophistication.

The Galapagos Islands are mainly composed of lava, with very little vegetation near to the coasts, although the wetter inland slopes are mantled with forest.

A colony of marine iguanas basks on the rocks of Isla Fernandina in the Galapagos Islands. Charles Darwin's theory of evolution was inspired by the differences he found between the animal species on neighbouring islands in the Galapagos.

Galapagos Islands
(Archipiélago de Colón)

GALAPAGOS
(to Ecuador)

(same scale as main map)

TRANSPORT AND INDUSTRY

THE MOUNTAIN REGIONS are rich in minerals including lead, copper, silver, gold, zinc and tungsten, though high production and transport costs have meant that they are expensive to extract and vulnerable to price collapses. Foreign debt remains a major burden, hampering industrial development. Manufacturing tends to be small-scale and concentrates on products for local needs, including textiles, food processing and pharmaceuticals. Narcotics are an important, though illegal, export.

Major industry and infrastructure

car manufacture
chemicals
engineering
fish processing
food processing
iron & steel
mining
narcotics
oil
pharmaceuticals
shipbuilding

capital cities
major towns
international airports
major roads
major industrial areas

At Potosí in Bolivia, silver has been mined for over 400 years.

THE TRANSPORT NETWORK

96,070 miles (154,702km)
4417 miles (7112km)
14,966 miles (24,100km)
none

By the year 2000, a trans-continental highway should link Ilo, on Peru's Pacific coast, to Porto Esperança in Brazil, via Puerto Suárez in Bolivia. Establishing port facilities on the Pacific coast is crucial to landlocked Bolivia's further development.

BRAZIL

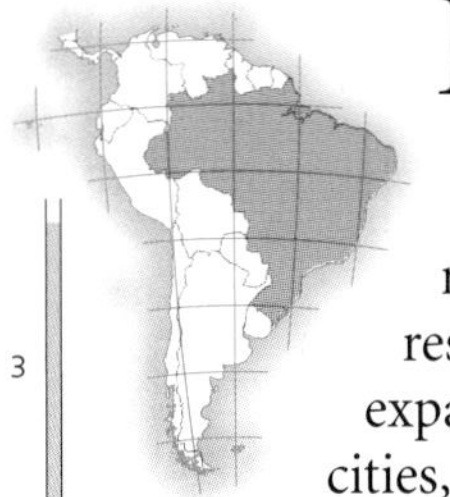

B RAZIL IS THE LARGEST COUNTRY in South America, with a population of
nearly 160 million – greater than the combined total for the whole of the
rest of the continent. The 26 states which make up the federal republic of
Brazil are administered from the purpose-built capital, Brasília. Tropical
rainforest, covering more than one-third of the country, contains rich natural
resources, but great tracts are sacrificed to agriculture, industry and urban
expansion on a daily basis. Most of Brazil's multi-ethnic population now live in
cities, some of which are vast areas of urban sprawl; São Paulo is one of the world's
biggest conurbations, with more than 17 million inhabitants. Although prosperity
is a reality for some, many people still live in great poverty, and mounting foreign debts
continue to damage Brazil's prospects of economic advancement.

USING THE LAND

BRAZIL HAS IMMENSE NATURAL RESOURCES, including minerals and
hardwoods, many of which are found in the fragile rainforest.
Brazil is the world's leading coffee grower and a major producer
of livestock, sugar and orange juice concentrate. Soya beans for
animal feed, particularly for poultry feed, have become the
country's most significant crop.

THE LANDSCAPE

THE AMAZON BASIN, containing the largest area of
tropical rainforest on Earth, covers nearly half of Brazil.
It is bordered by two shield areas: in the south by the
Brazilian Highlands, and in the north by the Guiana
Highlands. The east coast is dominated by a great
escarpment which runs for 1600 miles (2565 km).

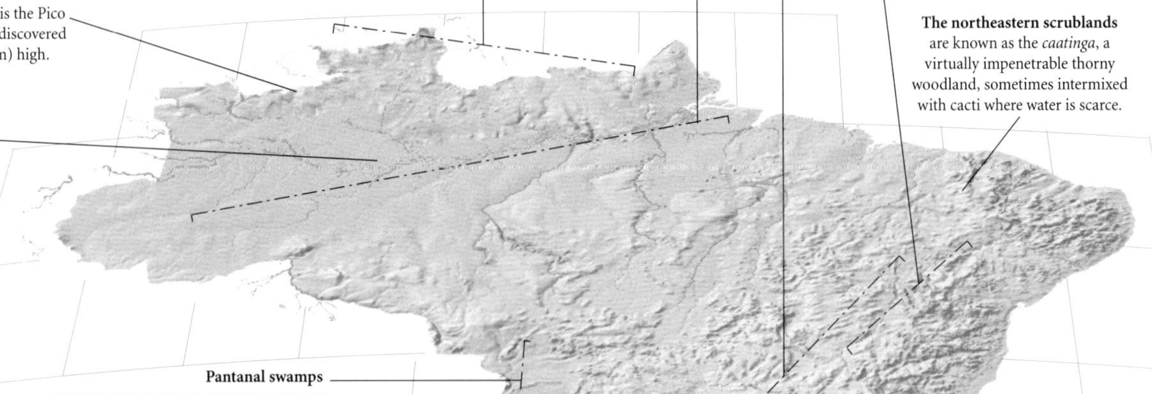

THE URBAN/RURAL POPULATION DIVIDE

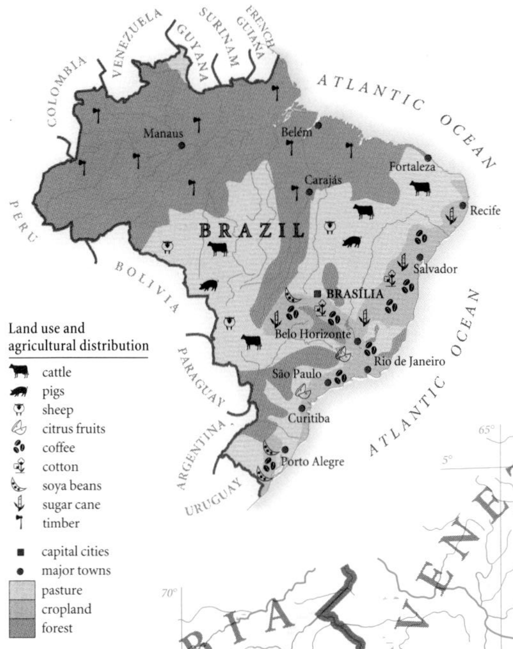

*The fecundity of parts of
Brazil's rainforest results
from exceptionally high
levels of rainfall and the
quantities of silt deposited
by the Amazon river system.*

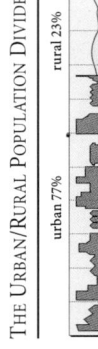
Pantanal swamps

*The Pantanal region in the
south of Brazil is an extension
of the Gran Chaco plain. The
swamps and marshes of this area
are renowned for their beauty,
and abundant and unique
wildlife, including wildfowl and
these caimans, a type of crocodile.*

*The Iguaçu River surges over the
spectacular Iguaçu Falls (Saltos do
Iguaçu) towards the Paraná River.
Falls like these are increasingly under
pressure from large-scale hydro-electric
projects such as that at Itaipú.*

The ancient Brazilian Highlands have a
varied topography. Their plateaux, hills and deep
valleys are bordered by highly-eroded mountains
containing important mineral deposits. They are
drained by three great river systems, the Amazon,
the Paraguay–Paraná and the São Francisco.

The São Francisco Basin has a climate unique
in Brazil. Known as the drought polygon, it
has almost no rain during the dry season,
leading to regular disastrous droughts.

The northeastern scrublands
are known as the caatinga, a
virtually impenetrable thorny
woodland, sometimes intermixed
with cacti where water is scarce.

The famous Sugar Loaf
Mountain (Pão de Açúcar)
which overlooks Rio de
Janeiro is a fine example of
a volcanic plug – a domed
core of solidified lava left
after the slopes of the original
volcano have eroded away.

Deep natural harbours such as
Baía de Guanabara were created
where the steep slopes of the
Serra da Mantiqueira plunge
directly into the ocean.

The Amazon Basin is the largest river basin
in the world. The Amazon River and over
a thousand tributaries drain an area of
2,375,000 sq miles (6,150,000 sq km)
and carry one-fifth of the world's
fresh water out to sea.

Guiana Highlands

Brazil's highest mountain is the Pico
da Neblina which was only discovered
in 1962. It is 9888 ft (3014 m) high.

The flood plains which
border the Amazon River
are made up of a variety
of different features
including shallow lakes
and swamps, mangrove
forests in the tidal
delta area and fertile
levées on river banks
and point bars.

Hillslope gullying

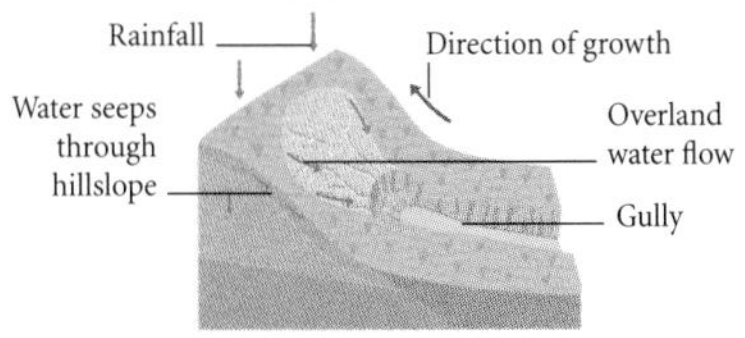

*Large-scale gullies
are common in Brazil,
particularly on hillslopes from
which vegetation has been
removed. Gullies grow
headwards (up the slope),
aided by a combination
of erosion through water
seepage and rainwater runoff.*

Direction of growth
Overland
water flow
Gully
Rainfall
Water seeps
through
hillslope

MAP KEY

POPULATION
▪ above 5 million
■ 1 million to 5 million
◉ 500,000 to 1 million
⊚ 100,000 to 500,000
⊕ 50,000 to 100,000
○ 10,000 to 50,000
∘ below 10,000

ELEVATION
3000m / 9843ft
2000m / 6562ft
1000m / 3281ft
500m / 1640ft
250m / 820ft
100m / 328ft
sea level

Land use and
agricultural distribution
cattle
pigs
sheep
citrus fruits
coffee
cotton
soya beans
sugar cane
timber
capital cities
major towns
pasture
cropland
forest

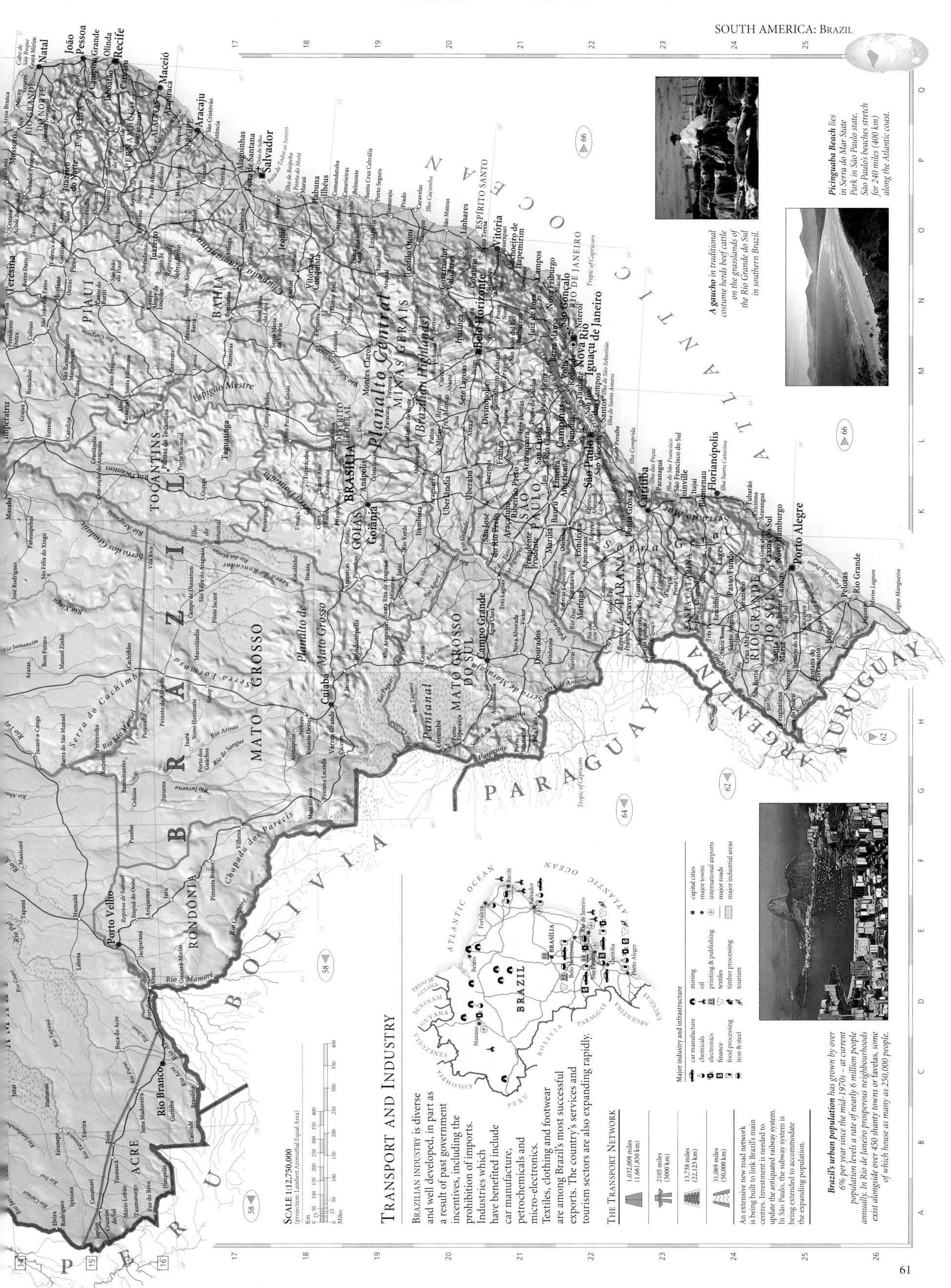

Picinguaba Beach lies in Serra do Mar State Park in São Paulo state. São Paulo's beaches stretch for 240 miles (400 km) along the Atlantic coast.

A gaucho in traditional costume herds beef cattle on the grasslands of the Rio Grande do Sul in southern Brazil.

Transport and Industry

BRAZILIAN INDUSTRY is diverse and well developed, in part as a result of past government incentives, including the prohibition of imports. Industries which have benefited include car manufacture, petrochemicals and micro-electronics. Textiles, clothing and footwear are among Brazil's most successful exports. The country's services and tourism sectors are also expanding rapidly.

THE TRANSPORT NETWORK

1,032,008 miles (1,661,850 km)	
2105 miles (3389 km)	
13,738 miles (22,123 km)	
31,069 miles (50,000 km)	

An extensive new road network is being built to link Brazil's main centres. Investment is needed to update the antiquated railway system. In São Paulo, the subway system is being extended to accommodate the expanding population.

SCALE 1:12,750,000
(projection: Lambert Azimuthal Equal Area)

Km
0 25 50 100 150 200 250 300 350 400

Miles
0 25 50 100 150 200 250 300

Brazil's urban population has grown by over 6% per year since the mid-1970s – at current population levels a rate of nearly 6 million people annually. In Rio de Janeiro prosperous neighbourhoods exist alongside over 450 shanty towns or favelas, some of which house as many as 250,000 people.

Major industry and infrastructure

car manufacture
chemicals
electronics
finance
food processing
iron & steel
mining
oil
printing & publishing
textiles
timber processing
tourism

capital cities
major towns
international airports
major roads
major industrial areas

EASTERN SOUTH AMERICA

URUGUAY, NORTHEAST ARGENTINA, SOUTHEAST BRAZIL

T HE VAST CONURBATIONS OF RIO DE JANEIRO, São Paulo and Buenos Aires form the core of South America's highly-urbanized eastern region. São Paulo state, with almost 34 million inhabitants, is among the world's 20 most powerful economies, and São Paulo is the fastest growing city on the continent. Rio de Janeiro and Buenos Aires, transformed in the last hundred years from port cities to great metropolitan areas each with more than 10 million inhabitants, typify the unstructured growth and wealth disparities of South America's great cities. In Uruguay, over half of the population lives in the capital, Montevideo, which faces Buenos Aires across the River Plate (Rio de la Plata). Immigration from the countryside has created severe pressure on the urban infrastructure, particularly on available housing, leading to a profusion of crowded shanty settlements (favelas or barrios).

USING THE LAND

MOST OF URUGUAY and the Pampas of northern Argentina are devoted to the rearing of livestock, especially cattle and sheep, which are central to both countries' economies. Soya beans, first produced in Brazil's Rio Grande do Sul, are now more widely grown for large-scale export, as are cereals, sugar cane and grapes. Subsistence crops, including potatoes, corn and sugar beet, are grown on the remaining arable land.

Land use and agricultural distribution
- cattle
- sheep
- cereals
- coffee
- fruit
- soya beans
- sugar cane
- capital cities
- major towns

- pasture
- cropland
- forest
- wetlands
- barren land

The rolling grasslands of Uruguay are ideally suited to the rearing of cattle, which are concentrated in great herds throughout the region.

TRANSPORT AND INDUSTRY

SOUTHEAST BRAZIL IS HOME TO MUCH of the important motor and capital goods industry, largely based around São Paulo; iron and steel production is also concentrated in this region. Uruguay's economy continues to be based mainly on the export of livestock products including meat and leather goods. Buenos Aires is Argentina's chief port, and the region has a varied and sophisticated economic base including service-based industries such as finance and publishing, as well as primary processing.

Major industry and infrastructure
- car manufacture
- chemicals
- engineering
- finance
- food processing
- iron & steel
- meat processing
- printing & publishing
- shipbuilding
- textiles
- timber processing
- capital cities
- major towns
- major roads
- international airports
- major industrial areas

THE TRANSPORT NETWORK
Throughout the region, road networks need to be expanded to cope with urban development. Plans are underway to build a road tunnel under the River Plate (Rio de la Plata) to link Montevideo and Buenos Aires.

MAP KEY

POPULATION
- above 5 million
- 1 million to 5 million
- 500,000 to 1 million
- 100,000 to 500,000
- 50,000 to 100,000
- 10,000 to 50,000
- below 10,000

ELEVATION
- 2000m / 6562ft
- 1000m / 3281ft
- 500m / 1640ft
- 250m / 820ft
- 100m / 328ft
- sea level

SCALE 1: 6,250,000
(projection: Lambert Azimuthal Equal Area)

Soya beans are harvested, pressed, and processed into soya cake, which is used as animal feed. The cake is fed mainly to chickens on large-scale factory farms, and the growth in soya production has been an important factor in the expansion of the Brazilian poultry trade.

The Itaipú dam on the Paraná River is one of the largest hydro-electric projects in the world, jointly financed by Brazil and Paraguay.

Rio de Janeiro's annual carnival, Mardi Gras, which ushers in the start of Lent, is an extravagant five-day parade through the city, characterized by fantastically decorated floats, exuberant dancing and samba music.

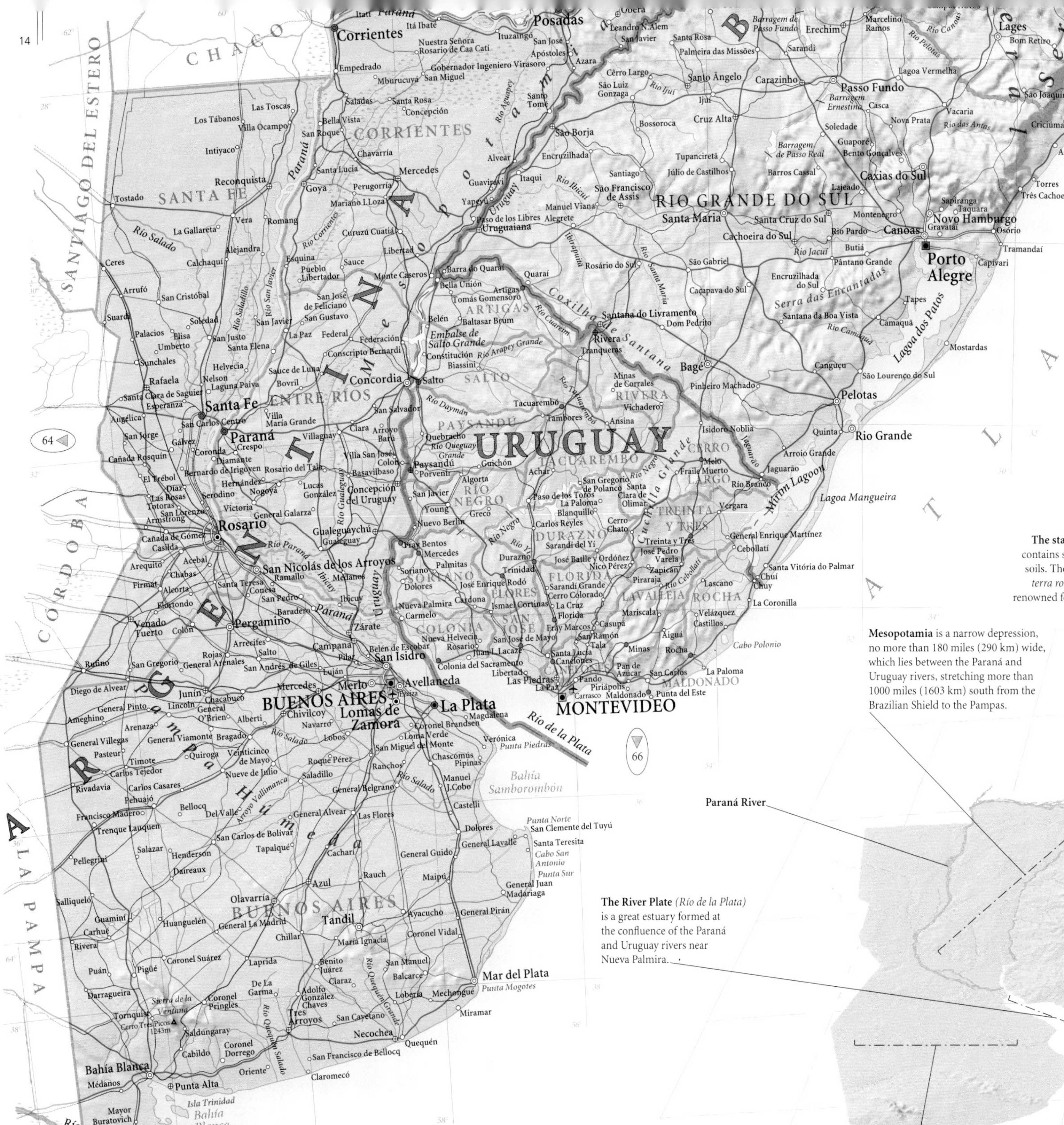

THE LANDSCAPE

THE SOUTHERN REACHES of the Brazilian Highlands follow the Atlantic coast to form low, rolling hills in the northeast of Uruguay. Much of South America's mid-eastern region and all of Uruguay has a gentle relief with land rarely rising above 300 ft (100 m). Argentina's northeast comprises two main regions: a long, narrow lowland known as Mesopotamia; and part of the Pampas grasslands.

In 1900, Buenos Aires was a modest port city with a population of less than 1 million. Today, more than 12 million people live in the city and its environs.

Tall lines of palm trees edge the savannah landscape of Mesopotamia in northeastern Argentina.

Tracing the edge of São Paulo state, the Paraná River drains the Brazilian Highlands, finally reaching the sea at the River Plate (Río de la Plata). Along with the Paraguay River, it is at the centre of a controversial scheme to turn the largely unnavigable route into a great shipping canal.

In winter, polar air masses and the cyclonic storms associated with them, can bring heavy rain, frosts and even snow, as far north as São Paulo.

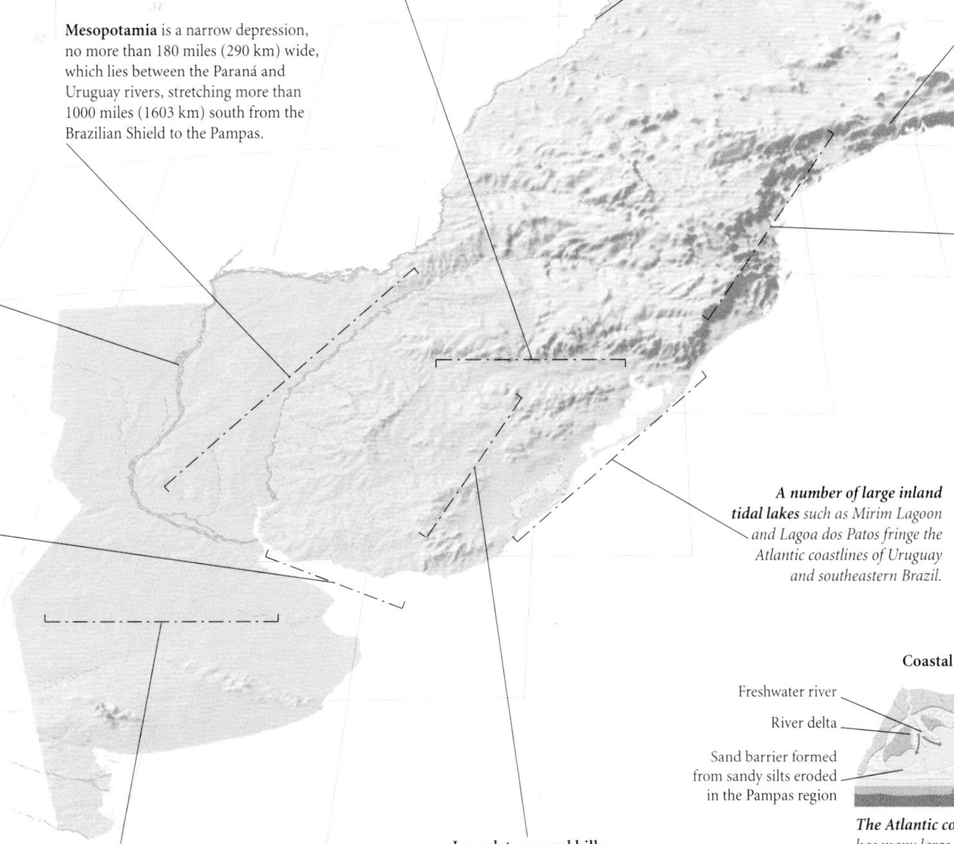

The Serra do Mar runs along the Atlantic coast towards Porto Alegre. South of this, the land slopes away to become lower and more level in Uruguay.

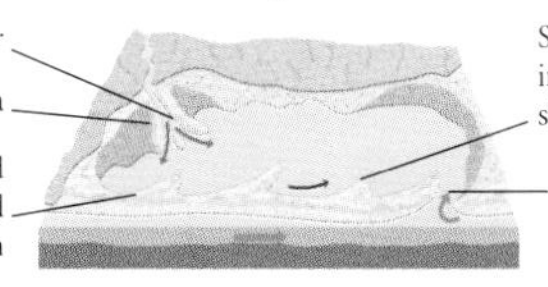

The Atlantic coast of Uruguay and southern Brazil has many large lagoons. Long-term lagoons are formed when sea levels change: 6000 years ago, the sea level near Buenos Aires was 6.5 ft (2 m) higher than it is today. More temporary lagoons are enclosed by spits and sand bars, created by the drifting of sand and sediment in parallel with the shoreline.

Coastal lagoons

Sand bar builds in parallel to the shoreline

Saltwater

Freshwater river

River delta

Sand barrier formed from sandy silts eroded in the Pampas region

A number of large inland tidal lakes such as Mirim Lagoon and Lagoa dos Patos fringe the Atlantic coastlines of Uruguay and southeastern Brazil.

The state of Rio Grande do Sul contains some of Brazil's most fertile soils. The weathered rocks produce terra rossa, a reddish-purple soil renowned for the rich coffee it produces.

Mesopotamia is a narrow depression, no more than 180 miles (290 km) wide, which lies between the Paraná and Uruguay rivers, stretching more than 1000 miles (1603 km) south from the Brazilian Shield to the Pampas.

Low plateaux and hills, like the Cuchilla Grande, dominate the landscape of Uruguay, which lies in a transitional zone between the humid Pampas of Argentina and the hilly uplands of Brazil.

The Argentinian Pampas lie to the south of the River Plate (Río de la Plata), meeting southern Mesopotamia in the north and the Atlantic Ocean to the east. They are covered by deposits of silt, alluvium and volcanic ash.

Paraná River

Montevideo became the capital of Uruguay following independence in 1828. The focus for Uruguayan industry and trade, it is also a popular destination for tourists from other South American countries.

The River Plate (Río de la Plata) is a great estuary formed at the confluence of the Paraná and Uruguay rivers near Nueva Palmira.

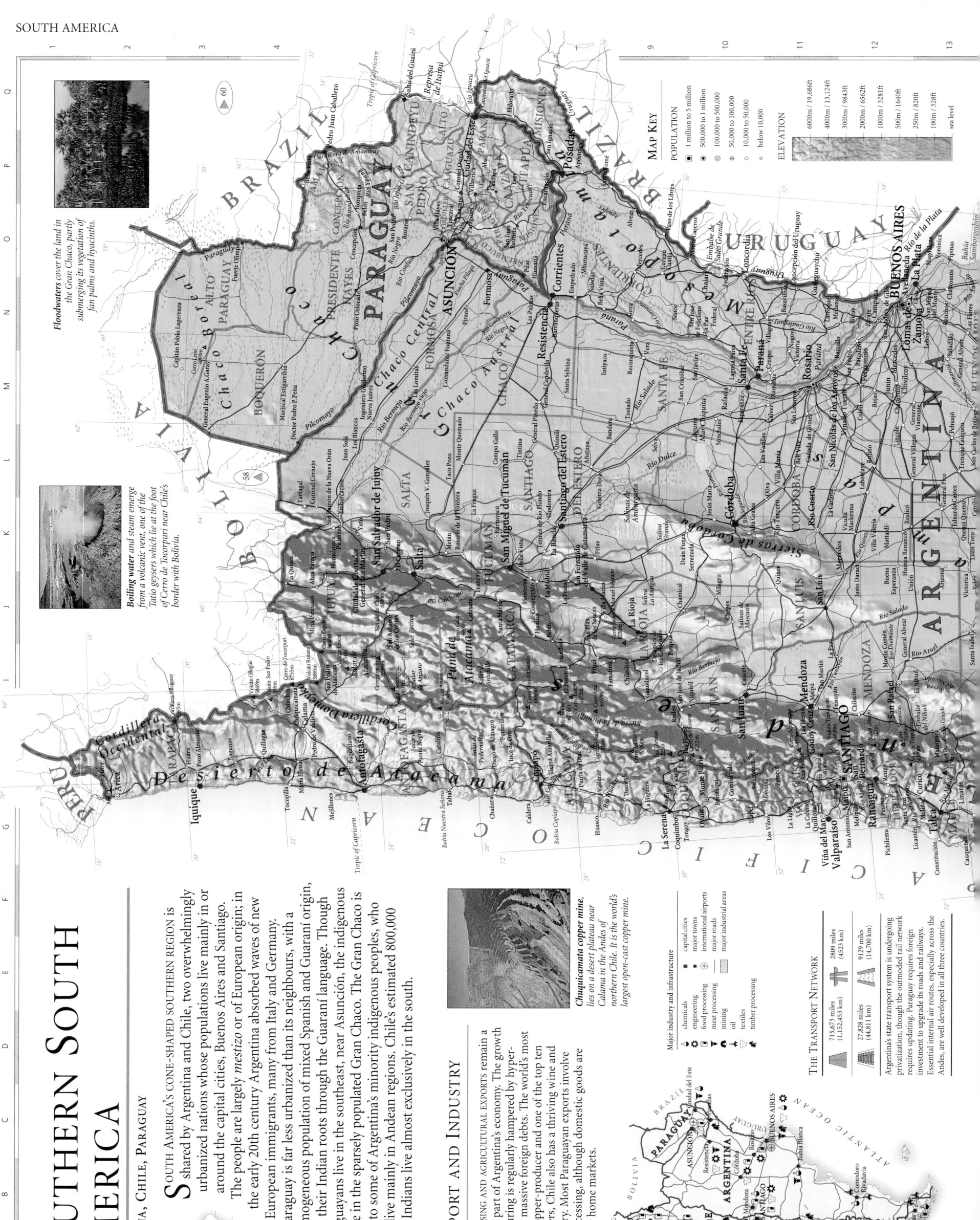

Floodwaters cover the land in the Gran Chaco, partly submerging its vegetation of fan palms and hyacinths.

Boiling water and steam emerge from a volcanic vent, one of the Tatio geysers which lie at the foot of Cerro de Tocorpuri near Chile's border with Bolivia.

SOUTHERN SOUTH AMERICA

ARGENTINA, CHILE, PARAGUAY

SOUTH AMERICA'S CONE-SHAPED SOUTHERN REGION is shared by Argentina and Chile, two overwhelmingly urbanized nations whose populations live mainly in or around the capital cities, Buenos Aires and Santiago. The people are largely *mestizo* or of European origin; in the early 20th century Argentina absorbed waves of new European immigrants, many from Italy and Germany. Paraguay is far less urbanized than its neighbours, with a homogeneous population of mixed Spanish and Guaraní origin, who retain their Indian roots through the Guaraní language. Though most Paraguayans live in the southeast, near Asunción, the indigenous Indians live in the sparsely populated Gran Chaco. The Gran Chaco is also home to some of Argentina's minority indigenous peoples, who otherwise live mainly in Andean regions. Chile's estimated 800,000 Mapuche Indians live almost exclusively in the south.

TRANSPORT AND INDUSTRY

FOOD PROCESSING AND AGRICULTURAL EXPORTS remain a fundamental part of Argentina's economy. The growth of manufacturing is regularly hampered by hyper-inflation and massive foreign debts. The world's most important copper-producer and one of the top ten gold producers, Chile also has a thriving wine and grape industry. Most Paraguayan exports involve primary processing, although domestic goods are produced for home markets.

Chuquicamata copper mine, lies on a desert plateau near Calama in the Andes of northern Chile. It is the world's largest open-cast copper mine.

Argentina's state transport system is undergoing privatization, though the outmoded rail network requires updating. Paraguay requires foreign investment to upgrade its roads and railways. Essential internal air routes, especially across the Andes, are well developed in all three countries.

MAP KEY

POPULATION
- 1 million to 5 million
- 500,000 to 1 million
- 100,000 to 500,000
- 50,000 to 100,000
- 10,000 to 50,000
- below 10,000

ELEVATION

6000m / 19,686ft	
4000m / 13,124ft	
3000m / 9843ft	
2000m / 6562ft	
1000m / 3281ft	
500m / 1640ft	
250m / 820ft	
100m / 328ft	
sea level	

THE TRANSPORT NETWORK

715,673 miles (1,152,453 km)	2809 miles (4523 km)
27,828 miles (44,811 km)	9129 miles (14,700 km)

Major industry and infrastructure
- chemicals
- engineering
- food processing
- meat processing
- mining
- oil
- textiles
- timber processing
- capital cities
- major towns
- international airports
- major roads
- major industrial areas

PACIFIC OCEAN

ATLANTIC OCEAN

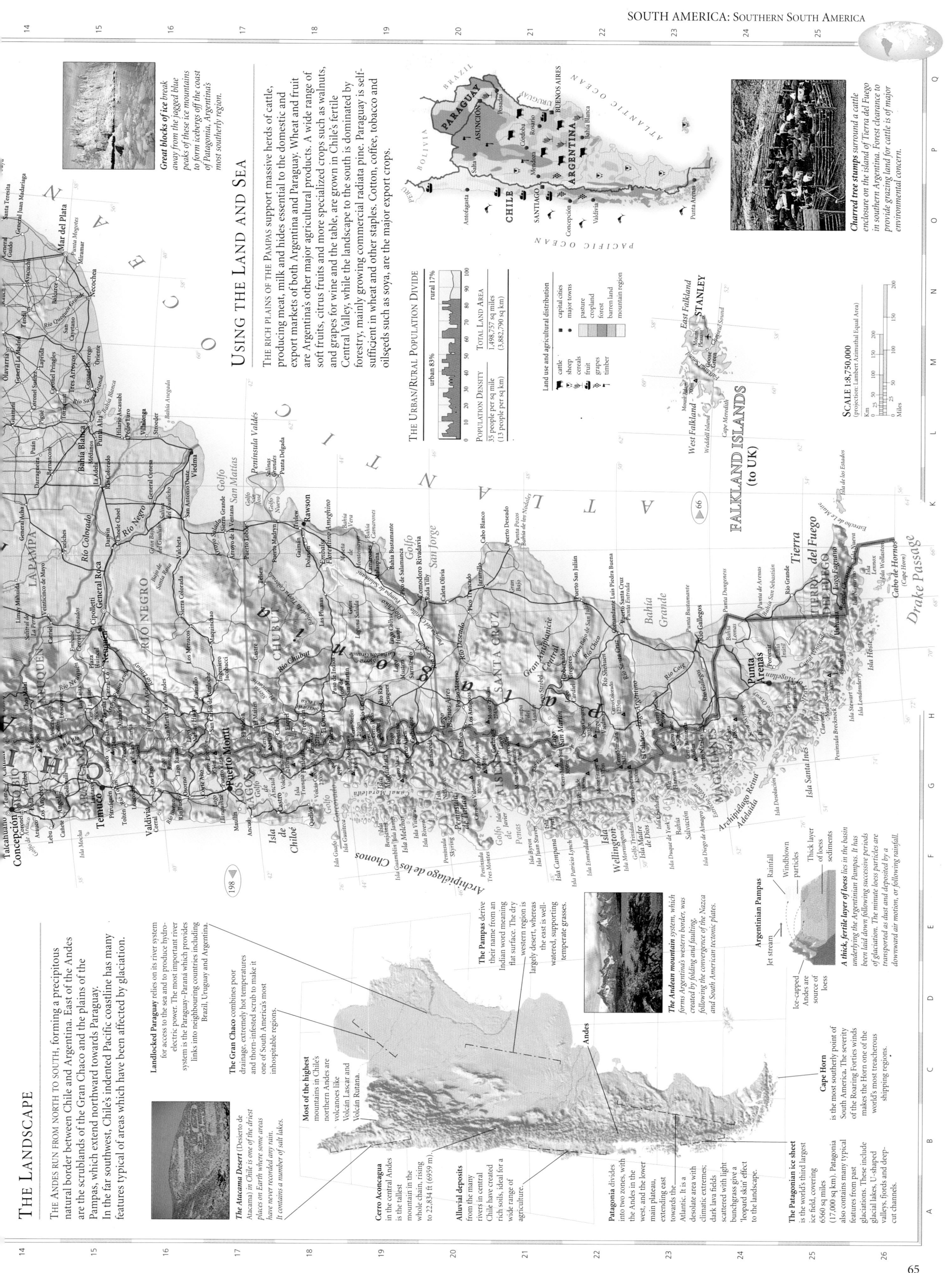

THE LANDSCAPE

THE ANDES RUN FROM NORTH TO SOUTH, forming a precipitous natural border between Chile and Argentina. East of the Andes are the scrublands of the Gran Chaco and the plains of the Pampas, which extend northward towards Paraguay. In the far southwest, Chile's indented Pacific coastline has many features typical of areas which have been affected by glaciation.

The Atacama Desert (Desierto de Atacama) in Chile is one of the driest places on Earth where some areas have never recorded any rain. It contains a number of salt lakes.

Most of the highest mountains in Chile's northern Andes are volcanoes like Volcán Lascar and Volcán Rutana.

Cerro Aconcagua in the central Andes is the tallest mountain in the whole chain, rising to 22,834 ft (6959 m).

Alluvial deposits from the many rivers in central Chile have created rich soils, ideal for a wide range of agriculture.

The Patagonian ice sheet is the world's third largest ice field, covering 6560 sq miles (17,000 sq km). Patagonia also contains many typical features from past glaciations. These include glacial lakes, U-shaped valleys, fjords and deep-cut channels.

Patagonia divides into two zones, with the Andes in the west, and the lower main plateau, extending east towards the Atlantic. It is a desolate area with climatic extremes; dark lava fields scattered with light bunchgrass give a 'leopard skin effect' to the landscape.

Cape Horn is the most southerly point of South America. The severity of the Roaring Forties winds makes the Horn one of the world's most treacherous shipping regions.

The Gran Chaco combines poor drainage, extremely hot temperatures and thorn-infested scrub to make it one of South America's most inhospitable regions.

Landlocked Paraguay relies on its river system for access to the sea and to produce hydro-electric power. The most important river system is the Paraguay–Paraná which provides links into neighbouring countries including Brazil, Uruguay and Argentina.

The Pampas derive their name from an Indian word meaning flat surface. The dry western region is largely desert, whereas the east is well-watered, supporting temperate grasses.

Argentinian Pampas

Ice-capped Andes are source of loess

Jet stream

Rainfall

Windblown particles

Thick layer of loess sediments

Andes

A thick, fertile layer of loess lies in the basin underlying the Argentinian Pampas. It has been laid down following successive periods of glaciation. The minute loess particles are transported as dust and deposited by a downward air motion, or following rainfall.

The Andean mountain system, which forms Argentina's western border, was created by folding and faulting following the convergence of the Nazca and South American tectonic plates.

Great blocks of ice break away from the jagged blue peaks of these ice mountains to form icebergs off the coast of Patagonia, Argentina's most southerly region.

USING THE LAND AND SEA

THE RICH PLAINS OF THE PAMPAS support massive herds of cattle, producing meat, milk and hides essential to the domestic and export markets of both Argentina and Paraguay. Wheat and fruit are Argentina's other major agricultural products. A wide range of soft fruits, citrus fruits and more specialized crops such as walnuts, and grapes for wine and the table, are grown in Chile's fertile Central Valley, while the landscape to the south is dominated by forestry, mainly growing commercial radiata pine. Paraguay is self-sufficient in wheat and other staples. Cotton, coffee, tobacco and oilseeds such as soya, are the major export crops.

Charred tree stumps surround a cattle enclosure on the island of Tierra del Fuego in southern Argentina. Forest clearance to provide grazing land for cattle is of major environmental concern.

THE URBAN/RURAL POPULATION DIVIDE

urban 83% rural 17%

POPULATION DENSITY
35 people per sq mile
(13 people per sq km)

TOTAL LAND AREA
1,498,757 sq miles
(3,882,790 sq km)

Land use and agricultural distribution

- cattle
- sheep
- cereals
- fruit
- grapes
- timber

- capital cities
- major towns

- pasture
- cropland
- forest
- barren land
- mountain region

SCALE 1:8,750,000
(projection: Lambert Azimuthal Equal Area)

FALKLAND ISLANDS
(to UK)

STANLEY

East Falkland

West Falkland

The Atlantic Ocean

THE ATLANTIC IS THE YOUNGEST OF THE WORLD'S OCEANS, formed about 180 million years ago when the landmasses of the eastern and western hemispheres separated. Its underwater topography is dominated by the Mid-Atlantic Ridge, a huge mountain system running north to south along the centre of the ocean. Although most of the ridge's peaks lie below the sea, some emerge as volcanic islands, like Iceland and the Azores. The Atlantic contains a wealth of resources, including substantial oil and gas reserves and rich fishing grounds. Until the 1950s, the north Atlantic was the world's busiest shipping route; cheaper air transport and alternative routes have shifted patterns of world trade.

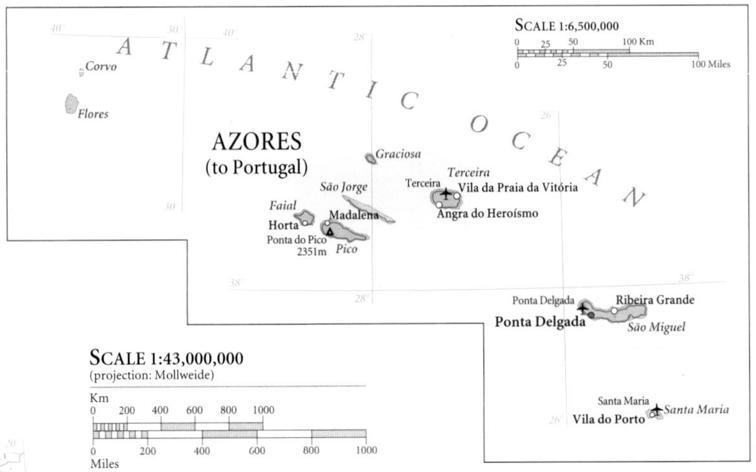

RESOURCES

DEVELOPMENT OF THE OIL AND GAS RESERVES in the Atlantic began in the 1940s around the Gulf of Mexico. Since then other areas have been exploited, including the North Sea, the west coast of Africa and the area east of Newfoundland and Nova Scotia. There is also extensive mining of sand, gravel and shell deposits by the USA and UK. For centuries, the north Atlantic's fishing grounds have been utilized more heavily than other oceans, leading to a serious decline in many fish stocks.

Resources (including wildlife)
- fish
- whales
- aggregates
- oil & gas
- major towns
- major ports

Surtsey near Iceland, lies on the Mid-Atlantic Ridge. The island was formed in 1963 following a volcanic eruption caused by sea-floor spreading.

Fishing in the seas around northwestern Europe dates back over 1500 years. The high nutrient content of the seas makes them ideal breeding grounds for many species of fish.

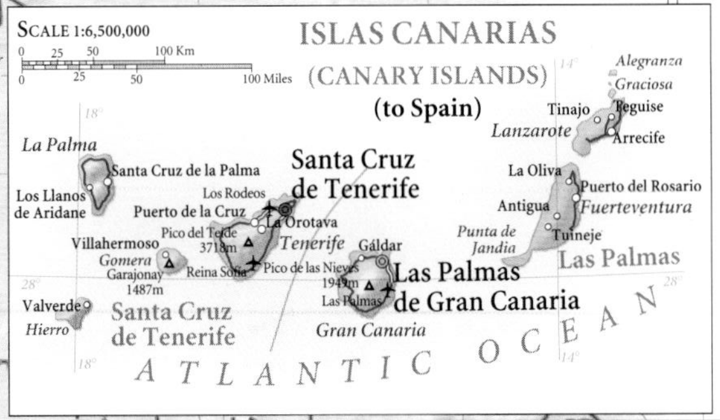

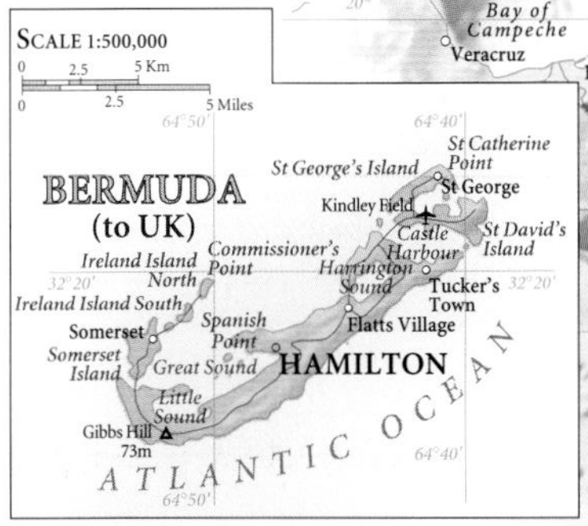

On 5 January 1993, the oil tanker Braer ran aground in the Shetland Islands, spilling 83,660 tons (85,000 tonnes) of light crude oil into the ocean, devastating the local marine ecosystem.

AZORES (to Portugal)

SCALE 1:6,500,000

Corvo, Flores, Graciosa, São Jorge, Terceira, Vila da Praia da Vitória, Angra do Heroísmo, Faial, Horta, Pico, Ponta do Pico 2351m, Madalena, São Miguel, Santa Maria, Vila do Porto, Ponta Delgada, Ribeira Grande

MADEIRA (to Portugal)

SCALE 1:2,500,000

Ponta do Pargo, Porto Santo, Ilhéu de Baixo, Camacha, São Vicente, Porto do Moniz, Faial, Machico, Ribeira Brava, Calheta, Câmara de Lobos, Funchal, Santa Cruz, Ilhas Desertas, Ilhéu Chão, Deserta Grande, Bugio

ISLAS CANARIAS (CANARY ISLANDS) (to Spain)

SCALE 1:6,500,000

Alegranza, Graciosa, Puerto del Rosario, Arrecife, Lanzarote, Tinajo, Teguise, Las Palmas, Fuerteventura, La Oliva, Antigua, Gran Canaria, Las Palmas de Gran Canaria, Santa Cruz de Tenerife, Orotava, Puerto de la Cruz, La Laguna, Tenerife, Pico de las Nieves 1949m, Galdar, Gáldar, La Palma, Santa Cruz de la Palma, Los Llanos de Aridane, Pico de la Cruz, San Sebastián de la Gomera, Gomera, Valverde, Hierro, Villahermoso, Pico de Teide 3718m

BERMUDA (to UK)

SCALE 1:500,000

St George's Island, St George, St David's Island, Bailey's Bay, Hamilton, Harrington Sound, Tucker's Town, Flatts Village, Somerset, Spanish Point, Great Sound, Ireland Island North, Ireland Island South, Spittal Pond, Gibbs Hill 76m

SCALE 1:43,000,000 (projection: Mollweide)

NORTH AMERICA: Baffin Bay, Baffin Basin, Baffin Island, Davis Strait, Foxe Channel, Foxe Basin, Hudson Strait, Ungava Bay, Labrador Sea, Labrador Basin, Hamilton Bank, Saglek Bank, Cumberland Sound, Arctic Circle, CANADA, Newfoundland, Grand Banks of Newfoundland, Flemish Cap, Orphan Knoll, Gulf of St Lawrence, St Lawrence, Nova Scotia, Halifax, Georges Bank, Boston, New York, Montreal, UNITED STATES OF AMERICA, Baltimore, Savannah, Jacksonville, Mobile, New Orleans, Gulf of Mexico, Tampico, Veracruz, MEXICO, Bay of Campeche, Yucatan, Yucatan Channel, Campeche Bank, BELIZE, Belize City, GUATEMALA, HONDURAS, Puerto Cortés, NICARAGUA, Bluefields, COSTA RICA, Limón, Puerto Limón, PANAMA, Cristóbal, Colón

Caribbean: BAHAMAS, Great Bahama Bank, Little Bahama Bank, Blake Plateau, Blake Bahama Ridge, CUBA, JAMAICA, HAITI, DOMINICAN REPUBLIC, Turks & Caicos Islands (to UK), PUERTO RICO (to USA), Puerto Rico Trench, Windward Passage, Caribbean Sea, Colombian Basin, Venezuelan Basin, Leeward Islands, BARBADOS, TRINIDAD & TOBAGO, Barbuda Ridge, Aves Ridge

SOUTH AMERICA: COLOMBIA, Gulf of Darien, Barranquilla, Cartagena, Maracaibo, Gulf of Maracaibo, VENEZUELA, La Guaira, Caracas, GUYANA, Georgetown, Demerara Plateau, Demerara Plain, Paramaribo, SURINAM, Ceará Plain, Orinoco, Magdalena, Amazon

ATLANTIC (ocean floor features): Mid-Atlantic Ridge, Reykjanes Ridge, Charlie-Gibbs Fracture Zone, Northwest Atlantic Mid-Ocean Canyon, Newfoundland Basin, Newfoundland Ridge, Newfoundland Seamounts, Sohm Plain, Nashville Seamount, Nares Plain, Hatteras Plain, Bermuda Rise, Bermuda (to UK), Bermuda Fracture Zone, Sargasso Sea, Atlantis Fracture Zone, Kane Fracture Zone, Oceanographer Fracture Zone, Barracuda Fracture Zone, Vema Fracture Zone, Doldrums Fracture Zone, Four North Fracture Zone, East Azores Fracture Zone, Corner Seamounts, Muir Seamounts, Milne Seamounts

EUROPE: ICELAND, Reykjavik, Surtsey, Iceland Basin, Reykjanes Basin, Irminger Basin, Denmark Strait, Greenland (to Denmark), Nuuk, Eirik Ridge, Faeroe Islands (to Denmark), Faeroe-Iceland Ridge, Shetland Islands, Orkney Islands, North Sea, British Isles, UNITED KINGDOM, Southampton, Milford Haven, Belfast, REPUBLIC OF IRELAND, Cork, Celtic Sea, Celtic Shelf, English Channel, St George's Channel, Rockall, Rockall Bank, Rockall Trough, Hatton Bank, Porcupine Bank, Porcupine Plain, Goban Spur, Biscay Plain, Bay of Biscay, FRANCE, Nantes, Bordeaux, Loire, Gironde, Bilbao, Gijón, SPAIN, Lisbon, PORTUGAL, Tagus Plain, Tagus, Guadiana, Gulf of Cadiz, Strait of Gibraltar, Gibraltar, Rotterdam

AFRICA: MOROCCO, Casablanca, Safi, Western Sahara (occupied by Morocco), ALGERIA, MAURITANIA, Nouakchott, Nouâdhibou, SENEGAL, Dakar, THE GAMBIA, Banjul, GUINEA-BISSAU, GUINEA, SIERRA LEONE, Freetown, LIBERIA, Monrovia, IVORY COAST, Abidjan, GHANA, TOGO, BENIN, NIGERIA, Lagos, Porto-Novo, CAMEROON, Douala, Malabo, Accra, Sekondi-Takoradi, Niger, Senegal, Gambia, Cape Verde Terrace, CAPE VERDE, Cape Verde Plain, Cape Verde Basin, Gambia Plain, Canary Islands (to Spain), Canary Islands Plain, Madeira (to Portugal), Madeira Plain, Great Meteor Tablemount, Cruiser Tablemount, Tropic Seamount, Saharan Seamounts

Inset globe: Reykjavik, Rotterdam, EUROPE, Gibraltar, NORTH AMERICA, New York, New Orleans, Sargasso Sea, Caribbean Sea, AFRICA, Lagos, Cape Town, ATLANTIC OCEAN, Rio de Janeiro, SOUTH AMERICA, Buenos Aires, Scotia Sea, Weddell Sea, ANTARCTICA, Cristóbal

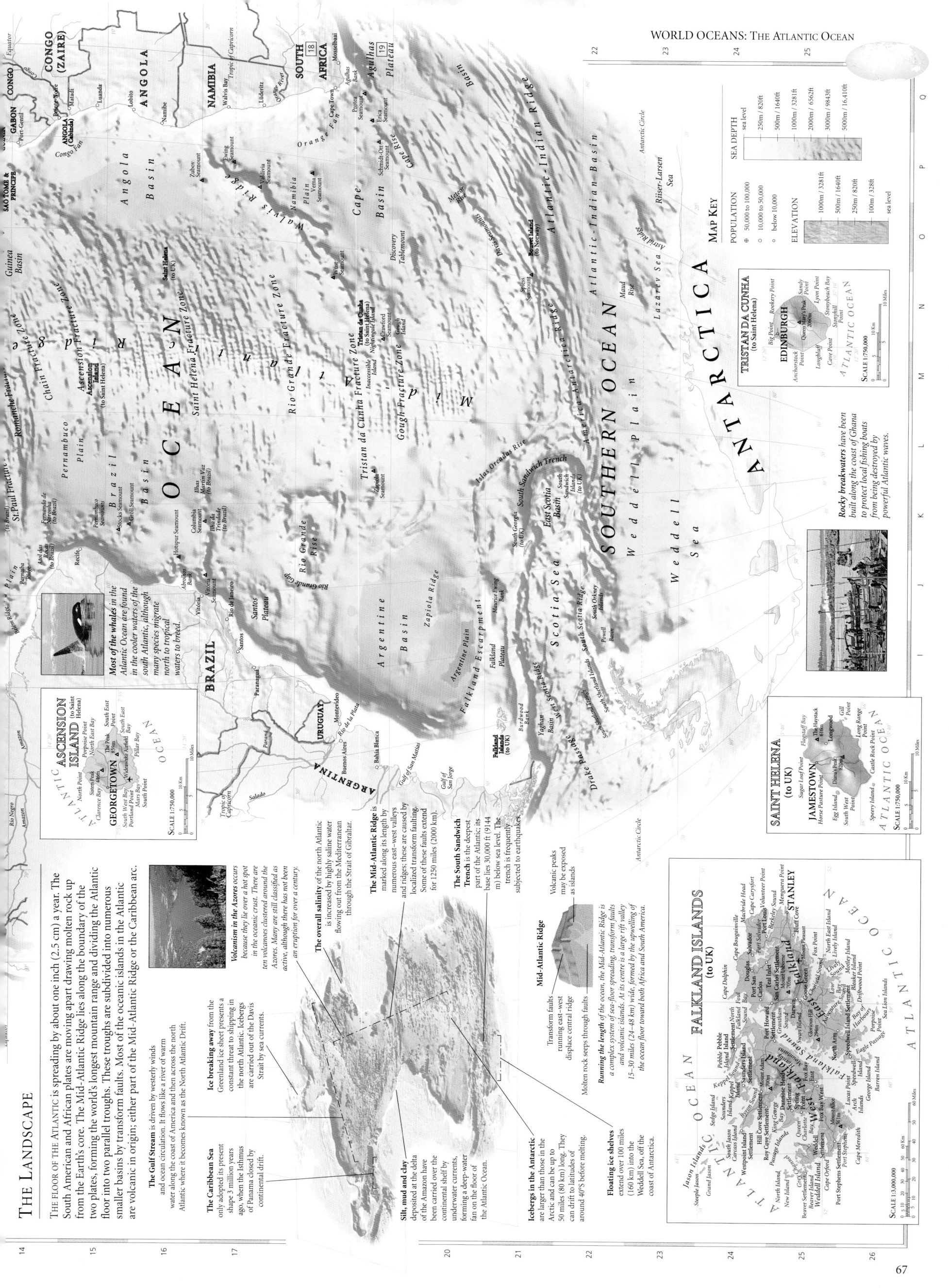

THE LANDSCAPE

THE FLOOR OF THE ATLANTIC is spreading by about one inch (2.5 cm) a year. The South American and African plates are moving apart drawing molten rock up from the Earth's core. The Mid-Atlantic Ridge lies along the boundary of the two plates, forming the world's longest mountain range and dividing the Atlantic floor into two parallel troughs. These troughs are subdivided into numerous smaller basins by transform faults. Most of the oceanic islands in the Atlantic are volcanic in origin; either part of the Mid-Atlantic Ridge or the Caribbean arc.

Most of the whales in the Atlantic Ocean are found in the cooler waters of the south Atlantic, although many species migrate north to tropical waters to breed.

The Gulf Stream is driven by westerly winds and ocean circulation. It flows like a river of warm water along the coast of America and then across the north Atlantic where it becomes known as the North Atlantic Drift.

Ice breaking away from the Greenland ice sheet presents a constant threat to shipping in the north Atlantic. Icebergs are carried out of the Davis Strait by sea currents.

The Caribbean Sea only adopted its present shape 3 million years ago, when the Isthmus of Panama closed by continental drift.

Silt, mud and clay deposited at the delta of the Amazon have been carried over the continental shelf by underwater currents, forming a deep-water fan on the floor of the Atlantic Ocean.

Icebergs in the Antarctic are larger than those in the Arctic and can be up to 50 miles (80 km) long. They can drift to latitudes of around 40°S before melting.

Floating ice shelves extend over 100 miles (160 km) into the Weddell Sea, off the coast of Antarctica.

Volcanism in the Azores occurs because they lie over a hot spot in the oceanic crust. There are ten volcanoes clustered around the Azores. Many are still classified as active, although there has not been an eruption for over a century.

The overall salinity of the north Atlantic is increased by highly saline water flowing out from the Mediterranean through the Strait of Gibraltar.

The Mid-Atlantic Ridge is marked along its length by numerous east–west valleys and ridges; these are caused by localized transform faulting. Some of these faults extend for 1250 miles (2000 km).

The South Sandwich Trench is the deepest part of the Atlantic; its base lies 30,000 ft (9144 m) below sea level. The trench is frequently subjected to earthquakes.

Volcanic peaks may be exposed as islands.

Mid-Atlantic Ridge

Transform faults running east-west displace central ridge

Molten rock seeps through faults

Running the length of the ocean, the Mid-Atlantic Ridge is a complex system of sea-floor spreading, transform faults and volcanic islands. At its centre is a large rift valley 15–30 miles (24–48 km) wide, formed by the upwelling of the ocean floor toward both Africa and South America.

Rocky breakwaters have been built along the coast of Ghana to protect local fishing boats from being destroyed by powerful Atlantic waves.

ASCENSION ISLAND (to Saint Helena)
GEORGETOWN
SCALE 1:750,000

TRISTAN DA CUNHA (to Saint Helena)
EDINBURGH
SCALE 1:750,000

SAINT HELENA (to UK)
JAMESTOWN
SCALE 1:750,000

FALKLAND ISLANDS (to UK)
STANLEY
SCALE 1:3,000,000

MAP KEY

SEA DEPTH
sea level
250m / 820ft
500m / 1640ft
1000m / 3281ft
2000m / 6562ft
3000m / 9843ft
5000m / 16,410ft

POPULATION
⊕ 50,000 to 100,000
○ 10,000 to 50,000
○ below 10,000

ELEVATION
1000m / 3281ft
500m / 1640ft
250m / 820ft
100m / 328ft
sea level

67

AFRICA

THE WORLD'S SECOND LARGEST CONTINENT, AFRICA COVERS AN
AREA OF 11,712,434 SQ MILES (30,335,000 SQ KM). IT HAS
53 SEPARATE COUNTRIES, INCLUDING MADAGASCAR IN THE
INDIAN OCEAN – THE HIGHEST NUMBER OF ANY CONTINENT.

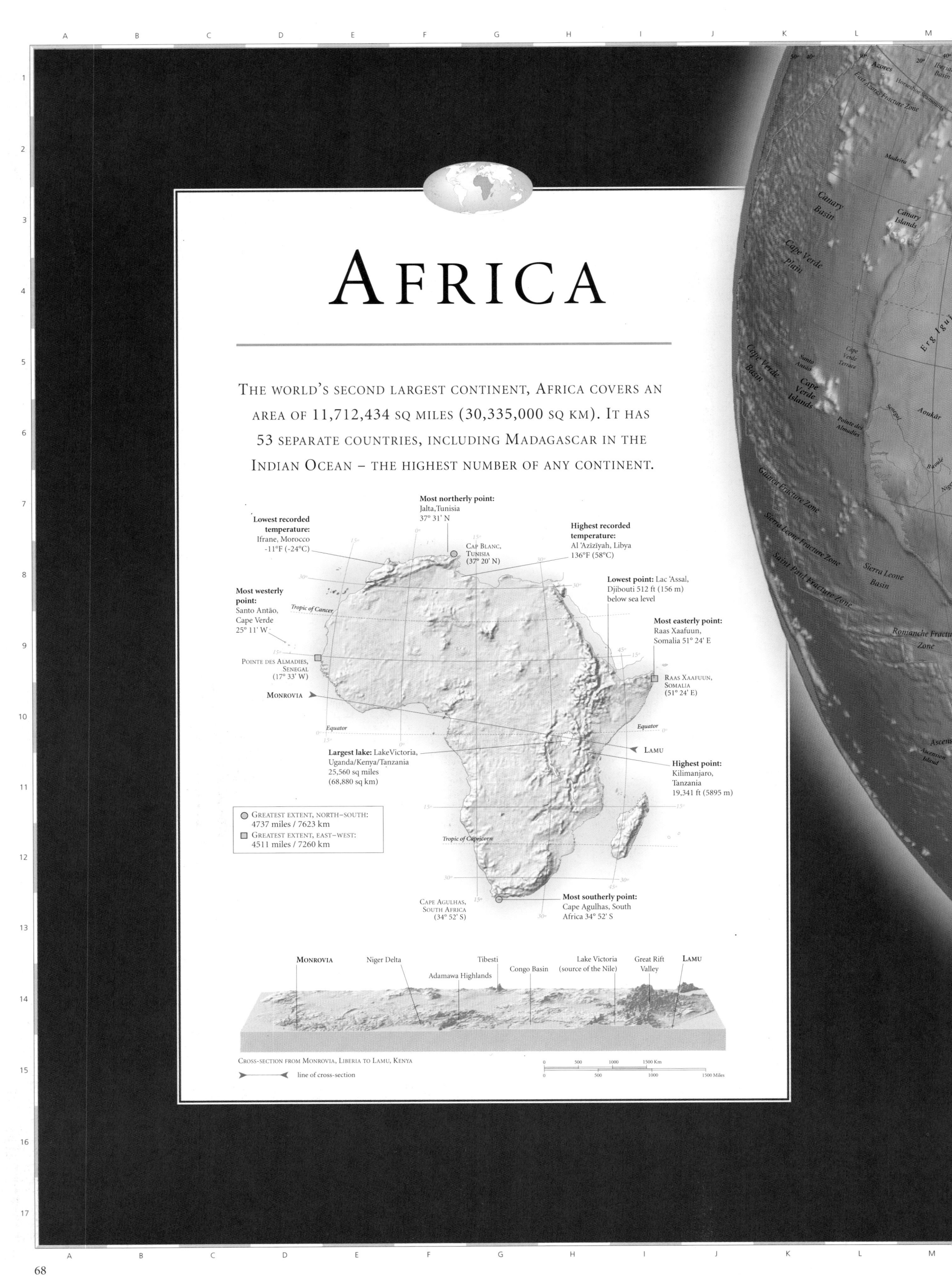

Most northerly point:
Jalta, Tunisia
37° 31' N

**Lowest recorded
temperature:**
Ifrane, Morocco
-11°F (-24°C)

**Highest recorded
temperature:**
Al 'Azīzīyah, Libya
136°F (58°C)

CAP BLANC,
TUNISIA
(37° 20' N)

Lowest point: Lac 'Assal,
Djibouti 512 ft (156 m)
below sea level

**Most westerly
point:**
Santo Antão,
Cape Verde
25° 11' W

Most easterly point:
Raas Xaafuun,
Somalia 51° 24' E

Tropic of Cancer

POINTE DES ALMADIES,
SENEGAL
(17° 33' W)

RAAS XAAFUUN,
SOMALIA
(51° 24' E)

MONROVIA

Equator

Equator

LAMU

Largest lake: LakeVictoria,
Uganda/Kenya/Tanzania
25,560 sq miles
(68,880 sq km)

Highest point:
Kilimanjaro,
Tanzania
19,341 ft (5895 m)

○ GREATEST EXTENT, NORTH–SOUTH:
4737 miles / 7623 km

□ GREATEST EXTENT, EAST–WEST:
4511 miles / 7260 km

Tropic of Capricorn

CAPE AGULHAS,
SOUTH AFRICA
(34° 52' S)

Most southerly point:
Cape Agulhas, South
Africa 34° 52' S

MONROVIA | Niger Delta | Tibesti | Congo Basin | Lake Victoria (source of the Nile) | Great Rift Valley | LAMU

Adamawa Highlands

CROSS-SECTION FROM MONROVIA, LIBERIA TO LAMU, KENYA

➤——◀—— line of cross-section

| 0 | 500 | 1000 | 1500 Km |
| 0 | 500 | 1000 | 1500 Miles |

PHYSICAL AFRICA

THE STRUCTURE OF AFRICA was dramatically influenced by the break up of the supercontinent Gondwanaland about 160 million years ago and, more recently, rifting and hot spot activity. Today, much of Africa is remote from active plate boundaries and comprises a series of extensive plateaux and deep basins, which influence the drainage patterns of major rivers. The relief rises to the east, where volcanic uplands and vast lakes mark the Great Rift Valley. In the far north and south sedimentary rocks have been folded to form the Atlas Mountains and the Great Karoo.

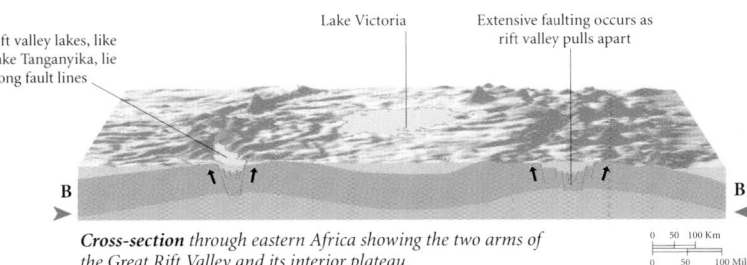

EAST AFRICA

THE GREAT RIFT VALLEY is the most striking feature of this region, running for 4475 miles (7200 km) from Lake Nyasa to the Red Sea. North of Lake Nyasa it splits into two arms and encloses an interior plateau which contains Lake Victoria. A number of elongated lakes and volcanoes lie along the fault lines. To the west lies the Congo Basin, a vast, shallow depression, which rises to form an almost circular rim of highlands.

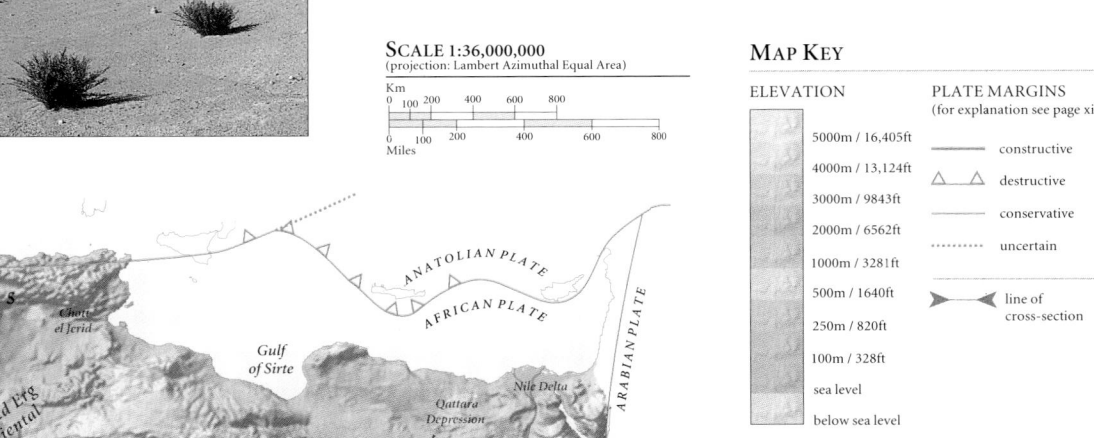

Rift valley lakes, like Lake Tanganyika, lie along fault lines

Lake Victoria

Extensive faulting occurs as rift valley pulls apart

Cross-section *through eastern Africa showing the two arms of the Great Rift Valley and its interior plateau.*

0 50 100 Km
0 50 100 Miles

NORTHERN AFRICA

NORTHERN AFRICA COMPRISES a system of basins and plateaux. The Tibesti and Ahaggar are volcanic uplands, whose uplift has been matched by subsidence within large surrounding basins. Many of the basins have been infilled with sand and gravel, creating the vast Saharan lands. The Atlas Mountains in the north were formed by convergence of the African and Eurasian plates.

The Earth's crust has been warped to form the Taoudenni Basin

Volcanic Ahaggar Mountains, formed by rising magma from a hot spot

Lake Chad lies in a sand-filled basin

Section *across northern Africa showing infilled basins and uplifted plateaux.*

0 250 500 Km
0 250 500 Miles

SCALE 1:36,000,000
(projection: Lambert Azimuthal Equal Area)

Km
0 100 200 400 600 800
0 100 200 400 600 800
Miles

MAP KEY

ELEVATION

5000m / 16,405ft
4000m / 13,124ft
3000m / 9843ft
2000m / 6562ft
1000m / 3281ft
500m / 1640ft
250m / 820ft
100m / 328ft
sea level
below sea level

PLATE MARGINS
(for explanation see page xiv)

—————— constructive
△△△△ destructive
————— conservative
············ uncertain
►———◄ line of cross-section

SOUTHERN AFRICA

THE GREAT ESCARPMENT marks the southern boundary of Africa's basement rock and includes the Drakensberg range. It was uplifted when Gondwanaland fragmented about 160 million years ago and it has gradually been eroded back from the coast. To the north, the relief drops steadily, forming the Kalahari Basin. In the far south are the fold mountains of the Great Karoo.

Kalahari Basin, covered with the sandy plains of the Kalahari Desert

Boundary of the Great Escarpment

Uplift of the basement rock created a raised plateau

Drakensberg

Cross-section *through southern Africa showing the boundary of the Great Escarpment.*

0 100 200 Km
0 100 200 Miles

Map labels

EURASIAN PLATE
AFRICAN PLATE
ANATOLIAN PLATE
AFRICAN PLATE
ARABIAN PLATE

ATLANTIC OCEAN

Atlas Mountains
Chott el Jerid
Gulf of Sirte
Qattara Depression
Nile Delta
Western Desert
Libyan Desert
Great Sand Sea
Lake Nasser
Nubian Desert
Red Sea
ARABIAN PLATE
AFRICAN PLATE
ASIA

Erg Iguidi
Grand Erg Occidental
Grand Erg Oriental
Erg Chech
Ahaggar
Tibesti
Nile

S a h a r a

Cape Verde Islands
Senegal
Taoudenni Basin
Niger
Massif de l'Aïr
Ténéré
Blue Nile
White Nile
Lake Tana
Gulf of Aden

Niger
Sahel
Lake Volta
White Volta
Niger
Benue
Grain Coast
Ivory Coast
Gold Coast
Slave Coast
Bight of Benin
Niger Delta
Adamawa Highlands
△ Cameroon Mountain 4070m
Gulf of Guinea
São Tomé
Chari
Massif des Bongo
Sudd
Ethiopian Highlands
Shebeli
Horn of Africa
Lake Rudolf
Juba

A T L A N T I C   O C E A N

Congo (Zaïre)
Congo Basin
Congo
Congo (Zaïre)
Lake Albert
Lake Victoria
Great Rift Valley
△ Kilimanjaro 5895m
Lake Tanganyika
Pemba Island
Zanzibar
Seychelles

Bié Plateau
Lake Nyasa
Comoro Islands
Zambezi
Zambezi
Madagascar
Mozambique Channel
Mauritius
Réunion

Namib Desert
Okavango Delta
Kalahari Basin
Kalahari Desert
Limpopo
Orange River
Great Karoo
Drakensberg
Cape of Good Hope

I N D I A N   O C E A N

CLIMATE

THE CLIMATES OF AFRICA range from mediterranean to arid, dry savannah and humid equatorial. In East Africa, where snow settles at the summit of volcanoes such as Kilimanjaro, climate is also modified by altitude. The winds of the Sahara export millions of tonnes of dust a year both northwards and eastwards.

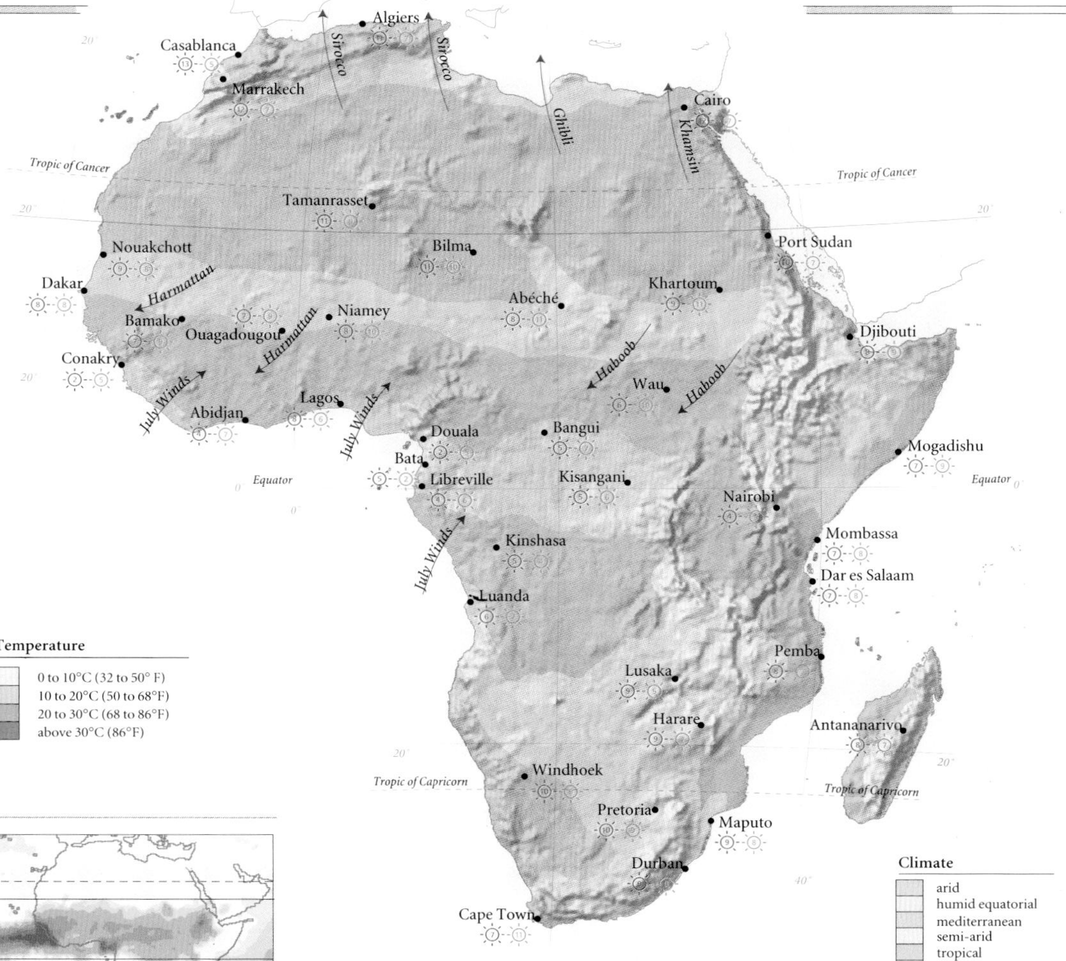

Savannah grasslands run in a belt across Africa; limited rainfall inhibits tree growth.

TEMPERATURE

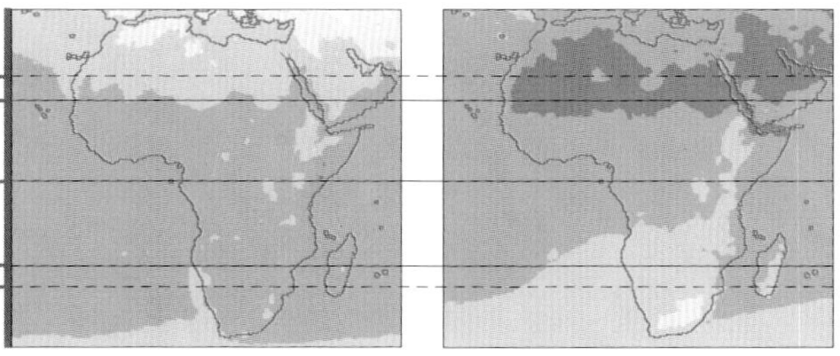

Average January temperature

Average July temperature

Temperature
- 0 to 10°C (32 to 50° F)
- 10 to 20°C (50 to 68°F)
- 20 to 30°C (68 to 86°F)
- above 30°C (86°F)

RAINFALL

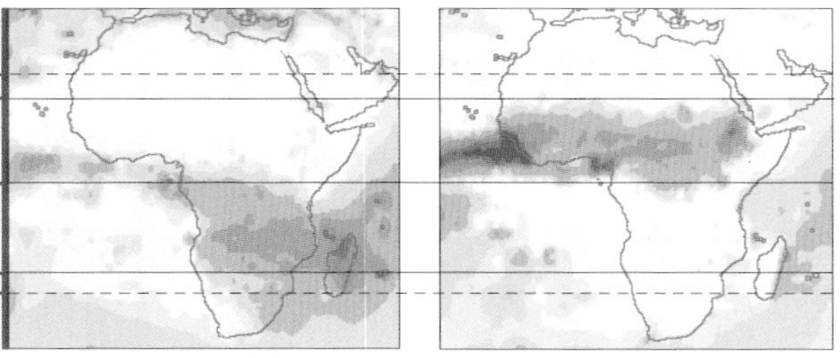

Average January rainfall

Average July rainfall

Rainfall
- 0–25 mm (0–1 in)
- 25–50 mm (1–2 in)
- 50–100 mm (2–4 in)
- 100–200 mm (4–8 in)
- 200–300 mm (8–12 in)
- 300–400 mm (12–16 in)
- 400–500 mm (16–20 in)
- more than 500 mm (20 in)

The hot, equatorial basin of the Congo River receives over 48 inches (1200 mm) of rainfall per year.

Climate
- arid
- humid equatorial
- mediterranean
- semi-arid
- tropical
- warm humid
- daily hours of sunshine, January
- daily hours of sunshine, July
- cold wind
- hot wind

SHAPING THE CONTINENT

AFRICAN LANDSCAPES are shaped by the intensity of climatic extremes and by tectonic action. High aridity, wind action and infrequent but heavy rainstorms, lead to the migration of sand dunes and dramatic flash flooding across much of the north and west. In the wetter areas, high precipitation increases the rate of weathering. To the east, the rift system has created a volcanic and lake environment and allowed rivers to erode weaknesses left in the crustal structure by faults.

GROUNDWATER

[1] Oases are found in desert areas such as the Sahara (*left*). Groundwater migrates through permeable rock strata, confined between two impermeable layers. Oases form either when the permeable rocks come near to the surface, or at a fault line, when water is able to seep up to the surface through the crushed rocks at the fault.

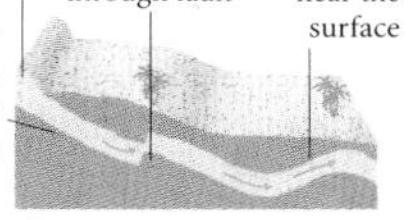

Rainwater feeds the aquifer
Water migrates up through fault
Aquifer exposed near the surface
Groundwater trapped between impermeable strata

GROUNDWATER: REPLENISHMENT OF AN OASIS

RIVER SYSTEMS

[2] The Zambezi River (*above*) drops 360 ft (110 m) over the Victoria Falls into a zig-zag gorge. The river has eroded the gorge along lines of weakness in the bedrock, created by fault lines running in two directions.

Old site of Victoria Falls
River plunges over falls
Fault and joint lines running in two directions
Zig-zag gorge of the Zambezi

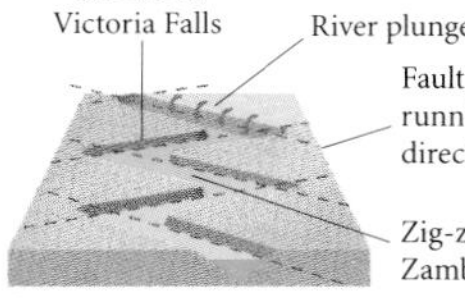

RIVER SYSTEMS: RETREATING OF THE VICTORIA FALLS

THE EVOLVING LANDSCAPE

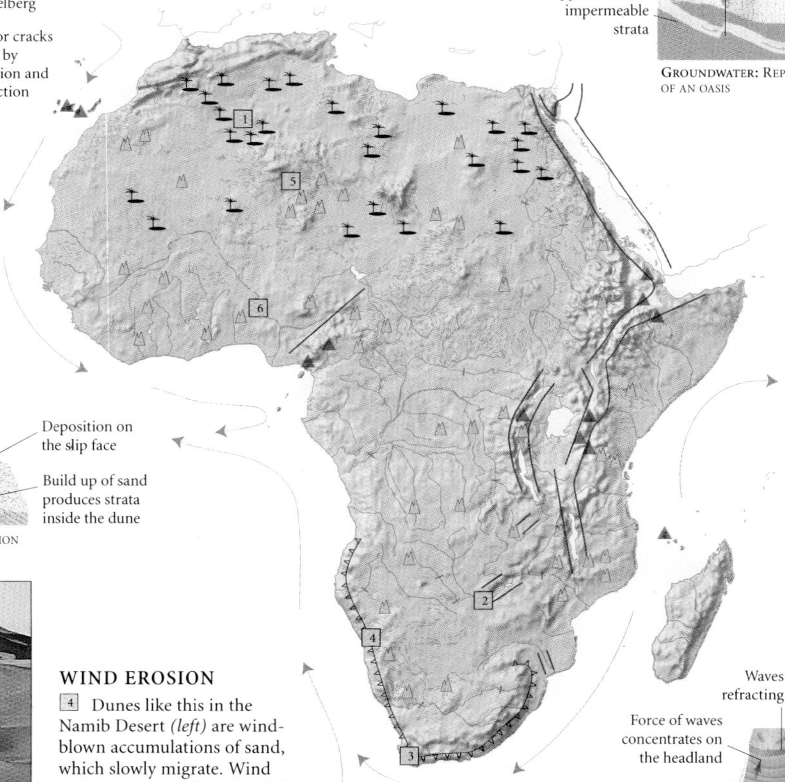

WEATHERING

Exfoliated layers
External stresses act on the surface of the inselberg
Joints or cracks caused by expansion and contraction

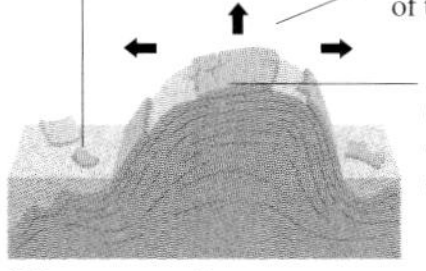

WEATHERING: FORMATION OF AN INSELBERG

[6] Inselbergs (*above*), found extensively across West Africa, are exposed remnants of an extensive upland area. Erosion of the surrounding uplands leaves a resistant rock outcrop. Its spheroidal shape is the result of 'onion-skin' weathering – the exfoliating layers – due to repeated expansion and contraction.

EPHEMERAL CHANNELS

[5] Wadis (*above*) drain much of northern Africa. These drybed courses are flooded only after infrequent, but intense, storms in the uplands cause water to surge along their channels.

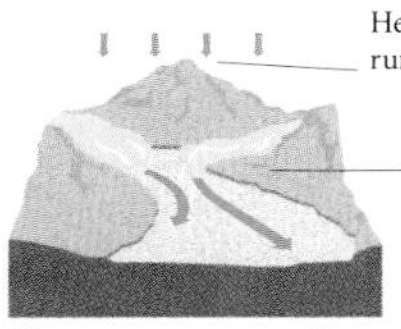

Heavy rainfall runs off mountains
Water collects and floods the dry channel

EPHEMERAL CHANNELS: FLASH FLOODING OF A WADI

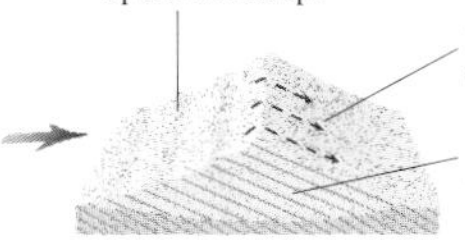

Sand is gradually blown up the back slope
Deposition on the slip face
Build up of sand produces strata inside the dune

WIND EROSION: MIGRATION OF A DUNE

WIND EROSION

[4] Dunes like this in the Namib Desert (*left*) are wind-blown accumulations of sand, which slowly migrate. Wind action moves sand up the shallow back slope; when the sand reaches the crest of the dune it is deposited on the slip face.

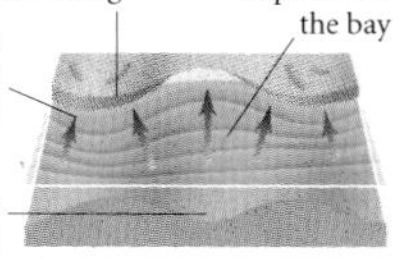

Landscape
- sinking land
- stable land
- uplifting land
- escarpment
- ocean current
- rift
- active volcano
- inselberg
- oasis
- river
- wadi
- waterfall

Waves refracting
Wave energy dispersed in the bay
Force of waves concentrates on the headland
The sea bed is deeper opposite the bay than at the headland

COASTAL PROCESSES: EROSION OF A BAY

COASTAL PROCESSES

[3] Houtbaai (*above*), in southern Africa, is constantly being modified by wave action. As waves approach the indented coastline, they reach the shallow water of the headland, slowing down and reducing in length. This causes them to bend or refract, concentrating their erosive force at the headlands.

POLITICAL AFRICA

THE POLITICAL MAP OF MODERN AFRICA only emerged following the end of the Second World War. Over the next half-century, all of the countries formerly controlled by European powers gained independence from their colonial rulers – only Liberia and Ethiopia were never colonized. The post-colonial era has not been an easy period for many countries, but there have been moves towards multi-party democracy in much of West Africa, and in Zambia, Tanzania and Kenya. In South Africa, democratic elections replaced the internationally-condemned apartheid system only in 1994. Other countries have still to find political stability; corruption in government and ethnic tensions are serious problems. National infrastructures, based on the colonial transport systems built to exploit Africa's resources, are often inappropriate for independent economic development.

LANGUAGES

THREE MAJOR WORLD LANGUAGES act as *lingua francas* across the African continent: Arabic in North Africa; English in southern and eastern Africa and Nigeria; and French in Central and West Africa, and in Madagascar. A huge number of African languages are spoken as well – over 2000 have been recorded, with more than 400 in Nigeria alone – reflecting the continuing importance of traditional cultures and values. In the north of the continent, the extensive use of Arabic reflects Middle Eastern influences while Bantu is widely-spoken across much of southern Africa.

Language groups

- Afro-Asiatic (Hamito-Semitic)
- Niger-Congo
- Sudanic
- Saharan
- Khoisan
- Indo-European
- Austronesian

OFFICIAL AFRICAN LANGUAGES

Official languages
- French
- English
- Arabic
- Portuguese
- Swahili
- Ahmaric
- Spanish
- French/English
- French/Arabic
- English/Swahili

Islamic influences are evident throughout North Africa. The Great Mosque at Kairouan, Tunisia, is Africa's holiest Islamic place.

In northeastern Nigeria, people speak Kanuri – a dialect of the Saharan language group.

TRANSPORT

AFRICAN RAILWAYS WERE BUILT to aid the exploitation of natural resources, and most offer passage only from the interior to the coastal cities, leaving large parts of the continent untouched – five land-locked countries have no railways at all. The Congo (Zaire), Nile and Niger river networks offer limited access to land within the continental interior, but have a number of waterfalls and cataracts which prevent navigation from the sea. Many roads were developed in the 1960s and 1970s, but economic difficulties are making the maintenance and expansion of the networks difficult.

South Africa has the largest concentration of railways in Africa. Over 20,000 miles (32,000 km) of routes have been built since 1870.

The Congo (Zaire) River, though not suitable for river transport along its entire length, forms a vital link for people and goods in its navigable inland reaches.

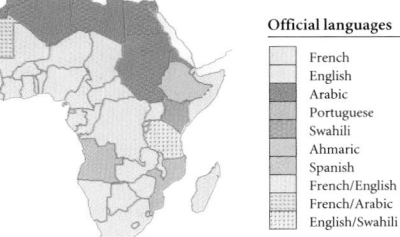

Traditional means of transport, such as the camel, are still widely used across the less accessible parts of Africa.

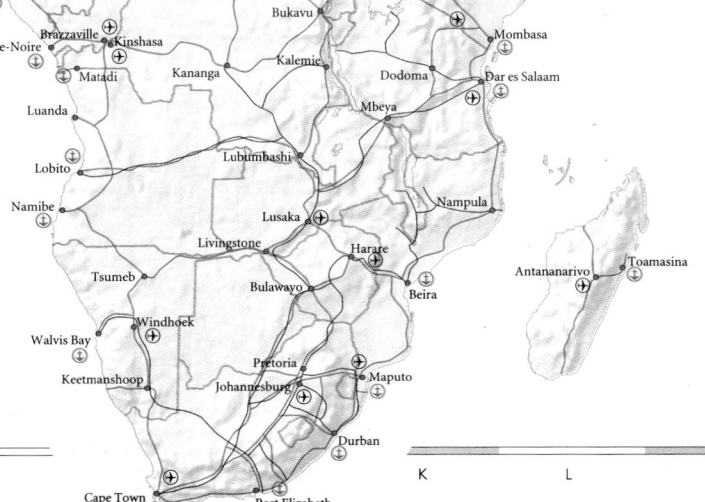

Transport
- major roads and motorways
- major railways
- major canal
- international borders
- transport intersections
- international airports
- major ports

PORTUGAL

Madeira (to Portugal)

Casablanca
Safi
Marrakech
MOROCCO
Agadir

Canary Islands (to Spain)

LAÂYOUNE
Western Sahara (Occupied by Morocco)

Tropic of Cancer

S
MAURITANIA
NOUAKCHOTT

CAPE VERDE

PRAIA

Senegal

SENEGAL
DAKAR   Kaolack
GAMBIA BANJUL
GUINEA-BISSAU BISSAU

Niger
BAMAKO

GUINEA

CONAKRY   Koidu
FREETOWN
SIERRA LEONE   YAMOUSSOUKRO
MONROVIA
LIBERIA

IVO
COA

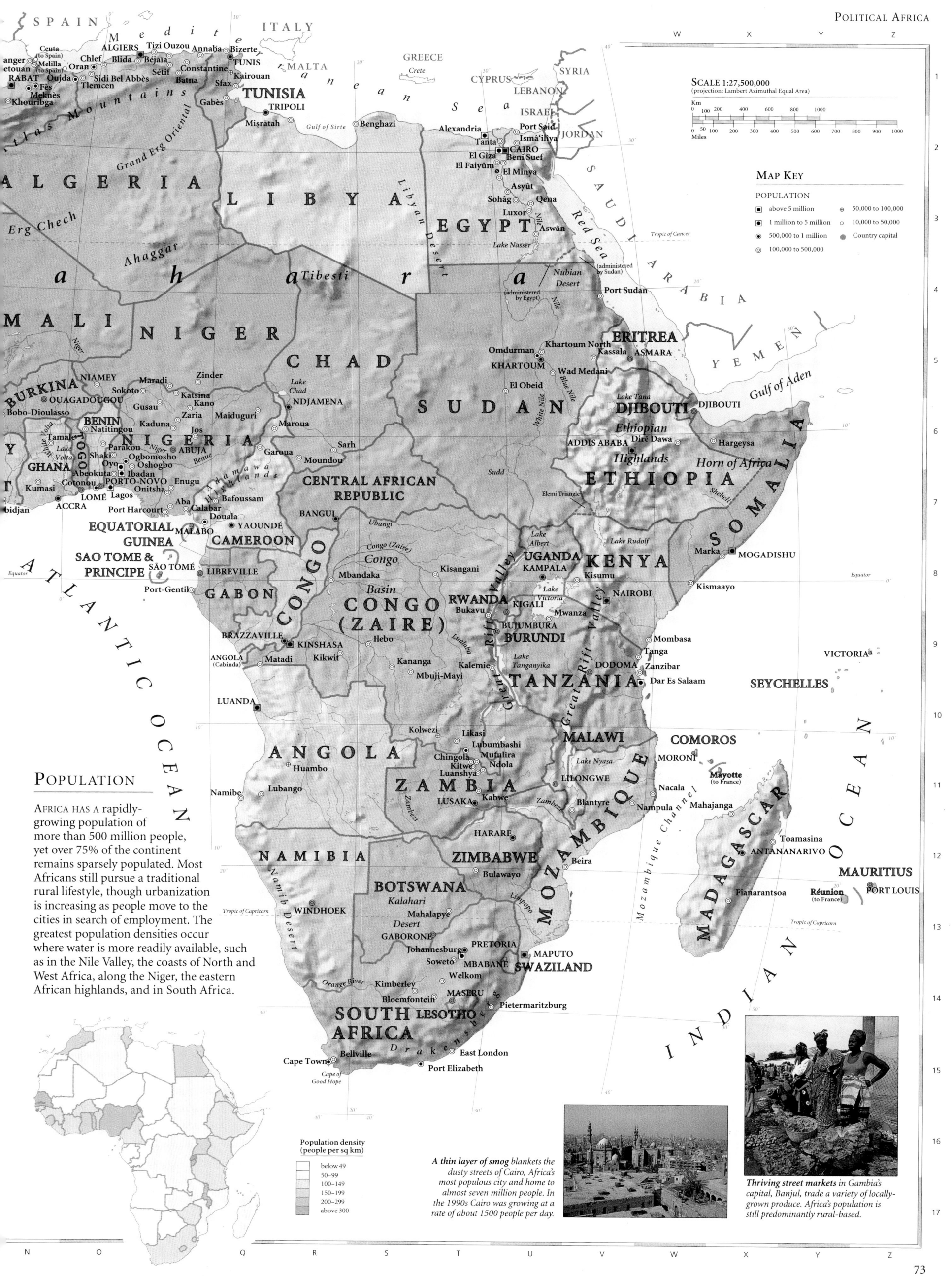

POLITICAL AFRICA

POPULATION

AFRICA HAS A rapidly-growing population of more than 500 million people, yet over 75% of the continent remains sparsely populated. Most Africans still pursue a traditional rural lifestyle, though urbanization is increasing as people move to the cities in search of employment. The greatest population densities occur where water is more readily available, such as in the Nile Valley, the coasts of North and West Africa, along the Niger, the eastern African highlands, and in South Africa.

Population density (people per sq km)
below 49
50–99
100–149
150–199
200–299
above 300

A thin layer of smog blankets the dusty streets of Cairo, Africa's most populous city and home to almost seven million people. In the 1990s Cairo was growing at a rate of about 1500 people per day.

Thriving street markets in Gambia's capital, Banjul, trade a variety of locally-grown produce. Africa's population is still predominantly rural-based.

73

AFRICAN RESOURCES

THE ECONOMIES OF MOST AFRICAN COUNTRIES are dominated by subsistence and cash crop agriculture, with limited industrialization. Manufacturing industry is largely confined to South Africa. Many countries depend on a single resource, such as copper or gold, or a cash crop, such as coffee, for export income, which can leave them vulnerable to fluctuations in world commodity prices. In order to diversify their economies and develop a wider industrial base, investment from overseas is being actively sought by many African governments.

INDUSTRY

MANY AFRICAN INDUSTRIES concentrate on the extraction and processing of raw materials. These include the oil industry, food processing, mining and textile production. South Africa accounts for over half of the continent's industrial output with much of the remainder coming from the countries along the northern coast. Over 60% of Africa's workforce is employed in agriculture.

The unspoilt natural splendour of wildlife reserves, like the Serengeti National Park in Tanzania, attract tourists to Africa from around the globe. The tourist industry in Kenya and Tanzania is particularly well developed, where it accounts for almost 10% of GNP.

STANDARD OF LIVING

SINCE THE 1960s most countries in Africa have seen significant improvements in life expectancy, healthcare and education. However, 18 of the 20 most deprived countries in the world are African, and the continent as a whole lies well behind the rest of the world in terms of meeting many basic human needs.

Standard of Living
(UN Human Development Index)

high

low

GNP per capita (US$)

0–199
200–399
400–599
600–899
900–1999
2000+

Industry

- brewing
- car/vehicle manufacture
- cement
- chemicals
- coffee processing
- electronics
- engineering
- finance
- fish processing
- food processing
- iron & steel

- mining
- palm oil processing
- peanut processing
- pharmaceuticals
- rice milling
- shipbuilding
- sugar processing
- tea processing
- textiles
- timber processing
- tobacco processing

- coal
- oil
- gas

- industrial cities
- major industrial areas

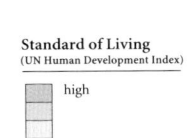

The discovery of oil in the swampy Niger Delta during the 1960s made Nigeria one of Africa's richer nations. As world oil prices fell in the 1980s, the Nigerian economy faltered.

Exotic rugs and brightly-coloured textiles are sold in a street market along the banks of the River Nile in Luxor, Egypt.

The Rössing uranium mines in Namibia are the largest in the world. Africa and the USA produce over half the world's uranium ore, used to fuel nuclear power plants. Elsewhere, South Africa and Niger also mine uranium on a large scale.

PORTUGAL   SPAIN   *Mediterranean Sea*   ITALY

CYPRUS   SYRIA   LEBANON   ISRAEL

Algiers   Annaba   Tunis
Oran
Casablanca   Rabat   Tripoli   TUNISIA
Safi   Benghazi   Alexandria   Port Said
MOROCCO   Cairo

Western Sahara (occupied by Morocco)

ALGERIA   LIBYA   EGYPT

Aswān   SAUDI ARABIA

Red Sea

MAURITANIA   Port Sudan   YEMEN

CAPE VERDE
MALI   NIGER   Khartoum   ERITREA   Asmara   Gulf of Aden

Dakar   SENEGAL   CHAD   SUDAN   DJIBOUTI
Banjul
GAMBIA   Bamako   BURKINA   Katsina   Kano
GUINEA-BISSAU   Kaduna   Addis Ababa
Conakry   GUINEA   BENIN   NIGERIA   ETHIOPIA
Freetown   IVORY   GHANA   TOGO   Ibadan   CENTRAL AFRICAN
SIERRA LEONE   COAST   Kumasi   Lagos   REPUBLIC   SOMALIA
Monrovia   LIBERIA   Accra   Bangui
Abidjan   Sekondi-Takoradi   Port Harcourt   CAMEROON   UGANDA   KENYA   Mogadishu
Douala   Kisangani   Kampala
EQUATORIAL GUINEA   Libreville   CONGO   RWANDA   Nairobi
SAO TOME & PRINCIPE   GABON   CONGO (ZAIRE)   Bukavu   BURUNDI   Mombasa
Gulf of Guinea   Port-Gentil   Brazzaville   Kananga   Dodoma   Zanzibar   Dar es Salaam
Pointe-Noire   Kinshasa   TANZANIA   SEYCHELLES
Luanda   Lubumbashi   MALAWI   COMOROS
Lobito   ANGOLA   Ndola   Blantyre   Mayotte (to France)
ZAMBIA   Lusaka   Antananarivo
Harare   Beira   MADAGASCAR   MAURITIUS
NAMIBIA   ZIMBABWE   Kwekwe   MOZAMBIQUE   Réunion (to France)
Walvis Bay   Bulawayo   Mozambique Channel
Windhoek   BOTSWANA   Maputo
Pretoria   SWAZILAND
Johannesburg   INDIAN OCEAN
Kimberley   LESOTHO   Durban
SOUTH AFRICA   East London
Cape Town   Port Elizabeth

ATLANTIC OCEAN

ENVIRONMENTAL ISSUES

ONE OF AFRICA'S most serious environmental problems occurs in marginal areas such as the Sahel where scrub and forest clearance, often for cooking fuel, combined with overgrazing, are causing desertification. Game reserves in southern and eastern Africa have helped to preserve many endangered animals, although the needs of growing populations have led to conflict over land use, and poaching is a serious problem.

Environmental Issues

- national parks
- tropical forest
- forest destroyed
- desert
- desertification
- polluted rivers
- radioactive contamination
- marine pollution
- heavy marine pollution
- poor urban air quality

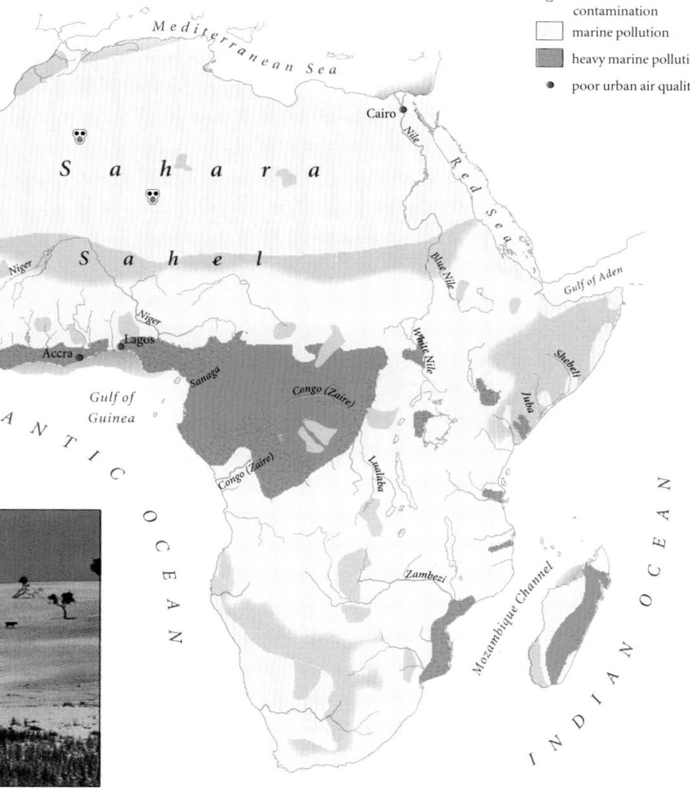

The Sahel's delicate natural equilibrium is easily destroyed by the clearing of vegetation, drought and overgrazing. This causes the Sahara to advance south, engulfing the savannah grasslands.

MINERAL RESOURCES

AFRICA'S ANCIENT PLATEAUX contain some of the world's most substantial reserves of precious stones and metals. Over 40% of the world's gold is mined in South Africa; Zambia has great copper deposits; and diamonds are mined in Botswana, Congo (Zaire) and South Africa. Oil has brought great economic benefits to Algeria, Libya and Nigeria.

Mineral Resources

- oil field
- gas field
- coal field
- bauxite
- copper
- diamonds
- gold
- iron
- phosphates
- tin
- uranium

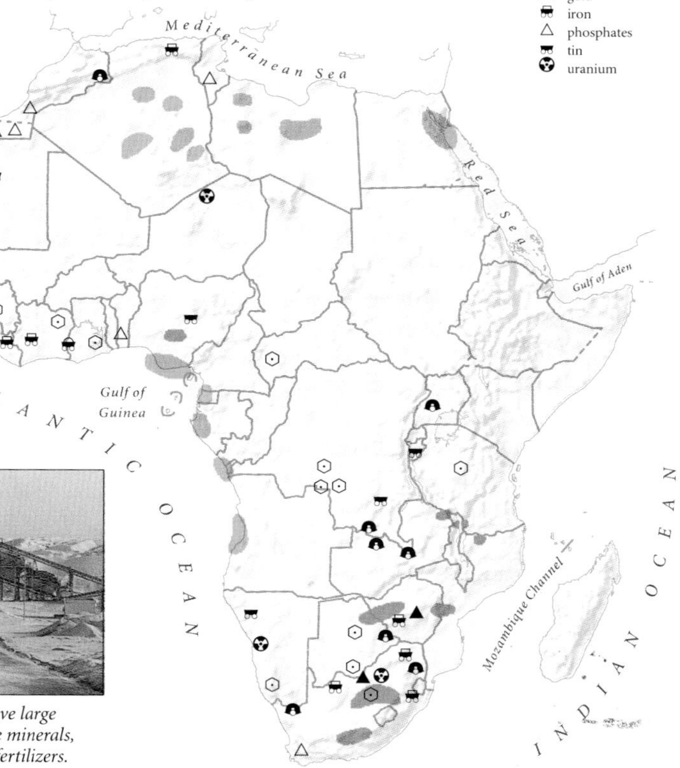

North and West Africa have large deposits of white phosphate minerals, which are used in making fertilizers. Morocco, Senegal, and Tunisia are the continent's leading producers.

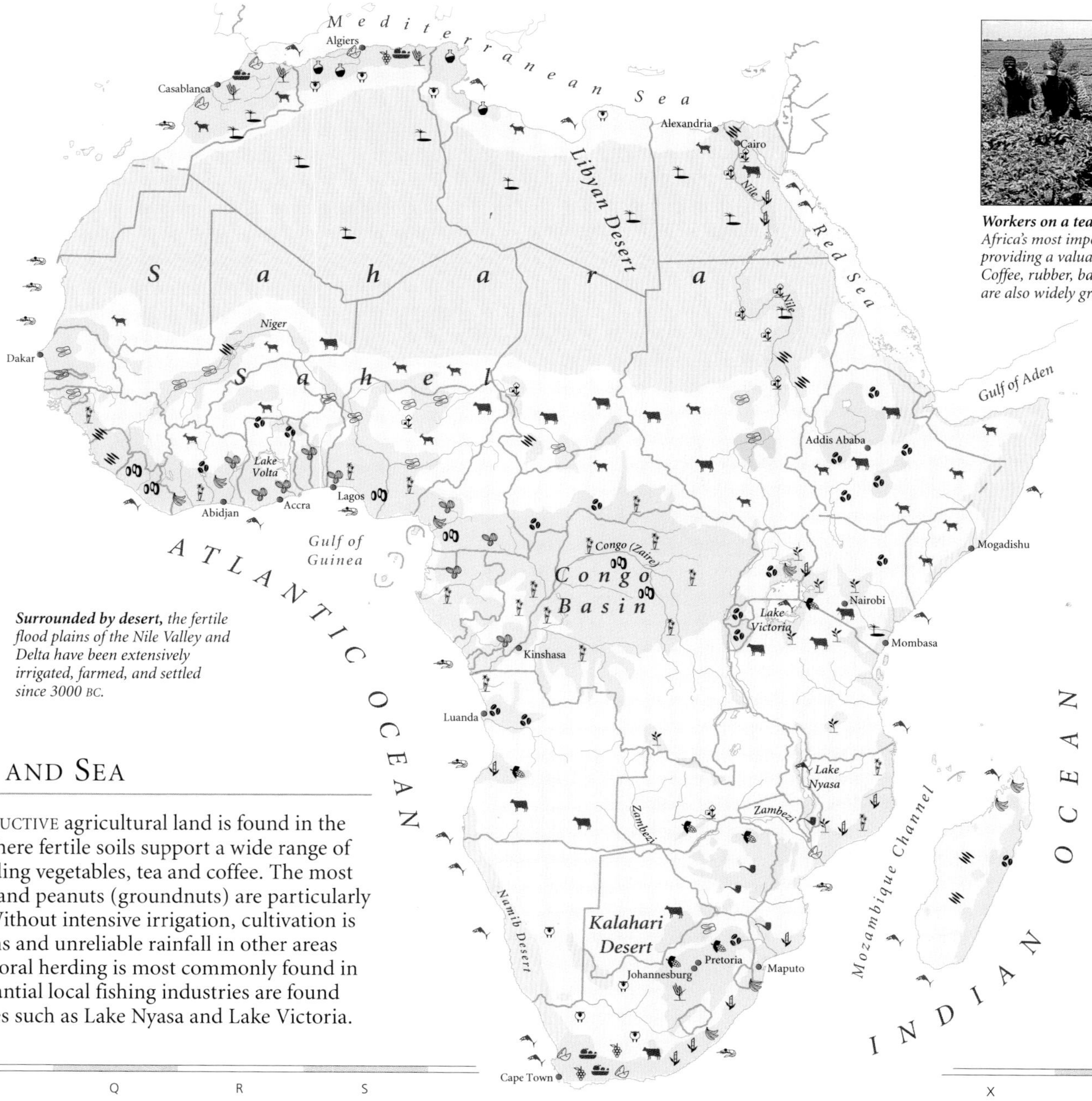

Workers on a tea plantation gather one of Africa's most important cash crops, providing a valuable source of income. Coffee, rubber, bananas, cotton and cocoa are also widely grown as cash crops.

Surrounded by desert, the fertile flood plains of the Nile Valley and Delta have been extensively irrigated, farmed, and settled since 3000 BC.

USING THE LAND AND SEA

SOME OF AFRICA'S MOST PRODUCTIVE agricultural land is found in the eastern volcanic uplands, where fertile soils support a wide range of valuable export crops including vegetables, tea and coffee. The most widely-grown grain is corn and peanuts (groundnuts) are particularly important in West Africa. Without intensive irrigation, cultivation is not possible in desert regions and unreliable rainfall in other areas limits crop production. Pastoral herding is most commonly found in these marginal lands. Substantial local fishing industries are found along coasts and in vast lakes such as Lake Nyasa and Lake Victoria.

Using the Land and Sea

- cropland
- desert
- forest
- pasture
- wetland
- major conurbations
- cattle
- goats
- sheep
- bananas
- corn (maize)
- citrus fruits
- cocoa
- cotton
- coffee
- dates
- fishing
- fruit
- oil palms
- olives
- peanuts
- rice
- rubber
- shellfish
- sugar cane
- tea
- tobacco
- vineyards

NORTH AFRICA

ALGERIA, EGYPT, LIBYA, MOROCCO, TUNISIA, WESTERN SAHARA

FRINGED BY THE MEDITERRANEAN along the northern coast and by the arid Sahara in the south, North Africa reflects the influence of many invaders, both European and, most importantly, Arab, giving the region an almost universal Islamic flavour and a common Arabic language. The countries lying to the west of Egypt are often referred to as the Maghreb, an Arabic term for 'west'. Today, Morocco and Tunisia exploit their culture and landscape for tourism, while rich oil and gas deposits aid development in Libya and Algeria, despite political turmoil. Egypt, with its fertile, Nile-watered agricultural land and varied industrial base, is the most populous nation.

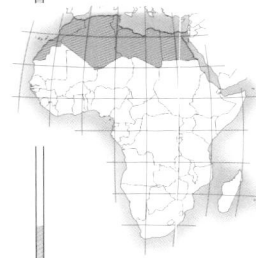

THE LANDSCAPE

THE ATLAS MOUNTAINS, which extend across much of Morocco, northern Algeria and Tunisia, are part of the fold mountain system which also runs through much of southern Europe. They recede to the south and east, becoming a steppe landscape before meeting the Sahara desert which covers more than 90% of the region. The sediments of the Sahara overlie an ancient plateau of crystalline rock, some of which is more than four billion years old.

These rock piles in Algeria's Ahaggar Mountains are the result of weathering caused by extremes of temperature. Great cracks or joints appear in the rocks, which are then worn and smoothed by the wind.

MAP KEY

POPULATION
- ■ above 5 million
- ■ 1 million to 5 million
- ◉ 500,000 to 1 million
- ◎ 100,000 to 500,000
- ⊕ 50,000 to 100,000
- ⊙ 10,000 to 50,000
- ○ below 10,000

ELEVATION
- 4000m / 13,124ft
- 3000m / 9843ft
- 2000m / 6562ft
- 1000m / 3281ft
- 500m / 1640ft
- 250m / 820ft
- 100m / 328ft
- sea level

SCALE 1:11,000,000
(projection: Lambert Azimuthal Equal Area)

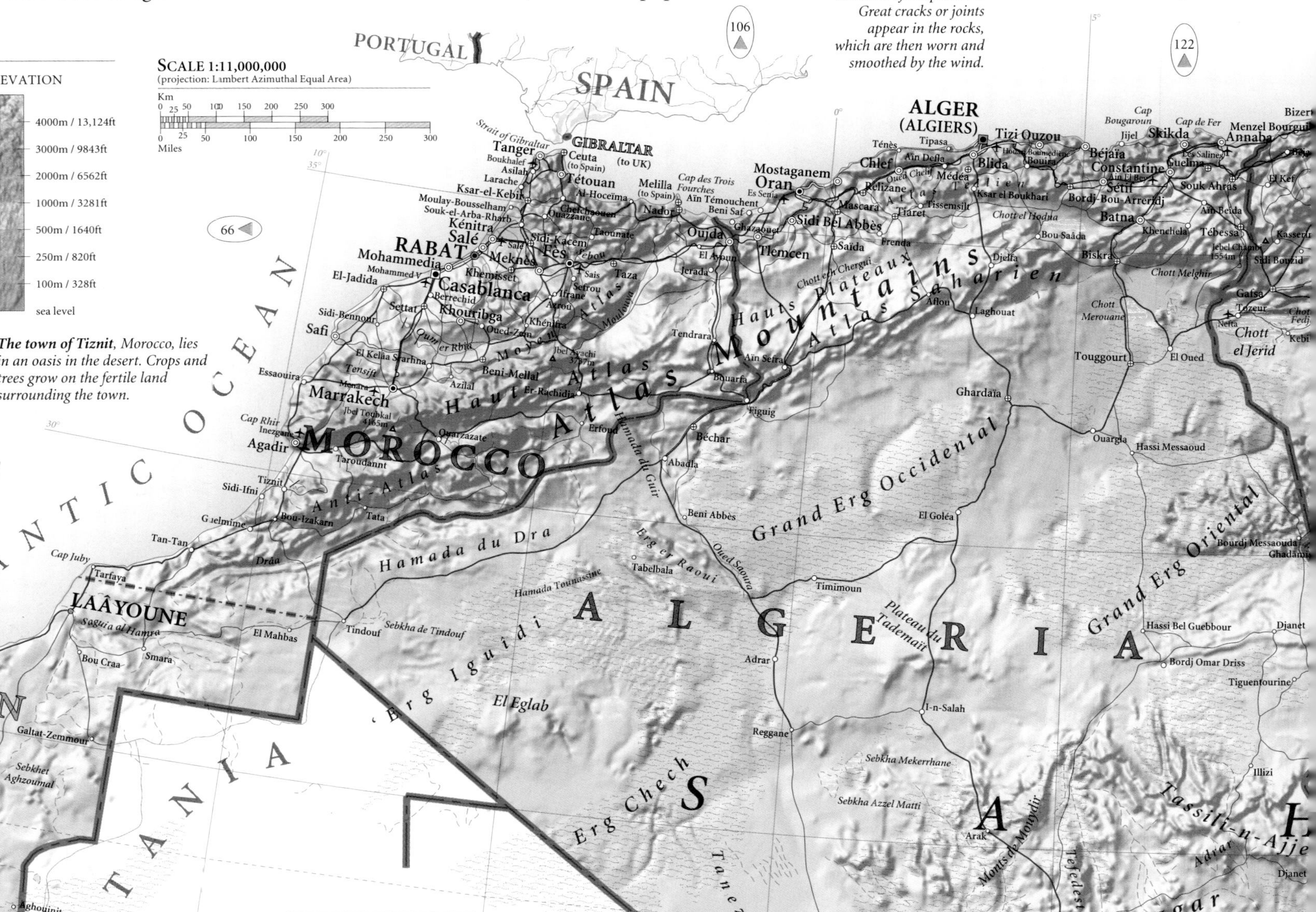

The town of Tiznit, Morocco, lies in an oasis in the desert. Crops and trees grow on the fertile land surrounding the town.

The Grand Erg Occidental is one of Algeria's great Saharan sand seas. Wind force and direction determines the nature of landforms such as the linear or seif dunes in the foreground.

USING THE LAND AND SEA

SHELTERED VALLEYS IN THE ATLAS MOUNTAINS, the Nile Valley and Delta, and the Mediterranean coast are the main sources of good farming land. A wide variety of valuable crops including cereals, rice and cotton, and woods such as cedar and cork, are grown. Typical Mediterranean crops such as olives, figs, dates and citrus fruits also thrive in these areas. The Nile Valley is particularly fertile, and most of Egypt's population lives close to the river. Elsewhere, irrigation is essential to improve crop yields on the desert margins.

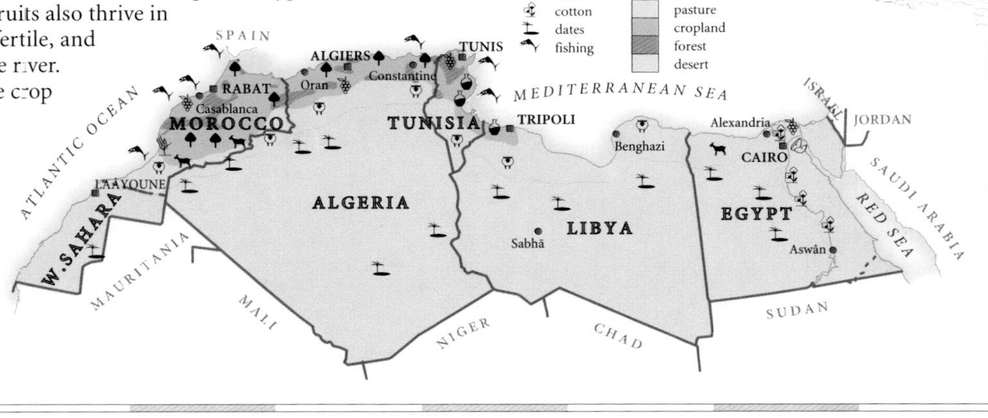

Land use and agricultural distribution
- goats
- sheep
- cereals
- citrus fruits
- cork
- cotton
- dates
- fishing
- olives
- vineyards
- ■ capital cities
- ■ major towns
- pasture
- cropland
- forest
- desert

THE URBAN/RURAL POPULATION DIVIDE

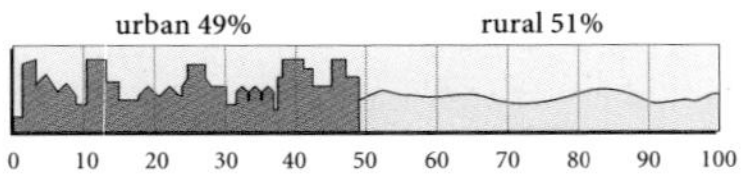

urban 49%   rural 51%

0 10 20 30 40 50 60 70 80 90 100

POPULATION DENSITY	TOTAL LAND AREA
56 people per sq mile (22 people per sq km)	2,215,020 sq miles (5,738,394 sq km)

Many North African nomads, such as the Bedouin, maintain a traditional pastoral lifestyle on the desert fringes, moving their herds of sheep, goats and camels from place to place – crossing country borders in order to find sufficient grazing land.

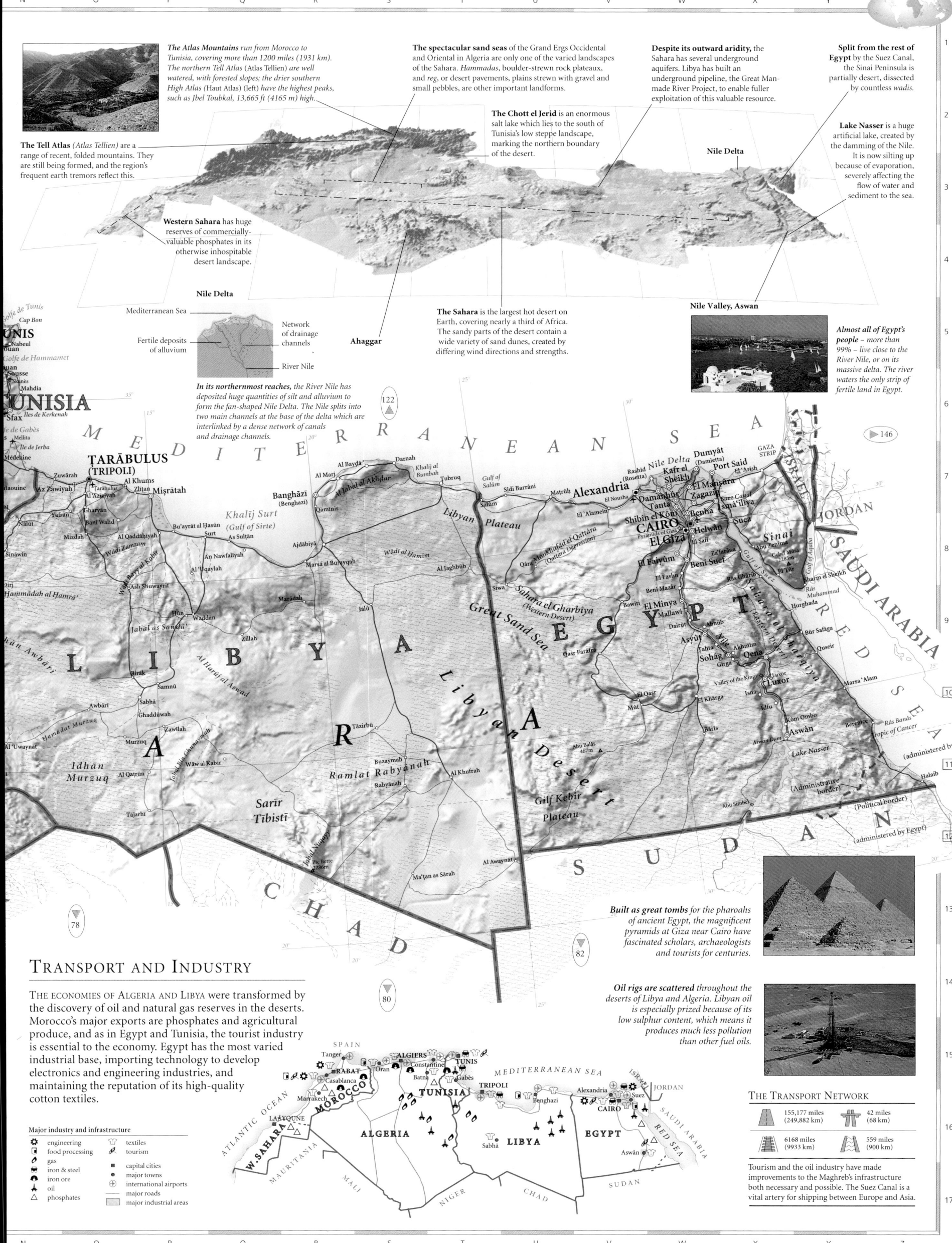

N O P Q R S T U V W X Y

The Atlas Mountains *run from Morocco to Tunisia, covering more than 1200 miles (1931 km). The northern Tell Atlas (Atlas Tellien) are well watered, with forested slopes; the drier southern High Atlas (Haut Atlas) (left) have the highest peaks, such as Jbel Toubkal, 13,665 ft (4165 m) high.*

The spectacular sand seas of the Grand Ergs Occidental and Oriental in Algeria are only one of the varied landscapes of the Sahara. *Hammadas*, boulder-strewn rock plateaux, and *reg*, or desert pavements, plains strewn with gravel and small pebbles, are other important landforms.

Despite its outward aridity, the Sahara has several underground aquifers. Libya has built an underground pipeline, the Great Man-made River Project, to enable fuller exploitation of this valuable resource.

Split from the rest of Egypt by the Suez Canal, the Sinai Peninsula is partially desert, dissected by countless *wadis*.

The Tell Atlas (*Atlas Tellien*) are a range of recent, folded mountains. They are still being formed, and the region's frequent earth tremors reflect this.

The Chott el Jerid is an enormous salt lake which lies to the south of Tunisia's low steppe landscape, marking the northern boundary of the desert.

Lake Nasser is a huge artificial lake, created by the damming of the Nile. It is now silting up because of evaporation, severely affecting the flow of water and sediment to the sea.

Nile Delta

Western Sahara has huge reserves of commercially-valuable phosphates in its otherwise inhospitable desert landscape.

Nile Delta

Mediterranean Sea

Fertile deposits of alluvium

Network of drainage channels

River Nile

Ahaggar

The Sahara is the largest hot desert on Earth, covering nearly a third of Africa. The sandy parts of the desert contain a wide variety of sand dunes, created by differing wind directions and strengths.

Nile Valley, Aswan

Almost all of Egypt's people – more than 99% – live close to the River Nile, or on its massive delta. The river waters the only strip of fertile land in Egypt.

In its northernmost reaches, the River Nile has deposited huge quantities of silt and alluvium to form the fan-shaped Nile Delta. The Nile splits into two main channels at the base of the delta which are interlinked by a dense network of canals and drainage channels.

Built as great tombs for the pharoahs of ancient Egypt, the magnificent pyramids at Giza near Cairo have fascinated scholars, archaeologists and tourists for centuries.

Oil rigs are scattered throughout the deserts of Libya and Algeria. Libyan oil is especially prized because of its low sulphur content, which means it produces much less pollution than other fuel oils.

TRANSPORT AND INDUSTRY

THE ECONOMIES OF ALGERIA AND LIBYA were transformed by the discovery of oil and natural gas reserves in the deserts. Morocco's major exports are phosphates and agricultural produce, and as in Egypt and Tunisia, the tourist industry is essential to the economy. Egypt has the most varied industrial base, importing technology to develop electronics and engineering industries, and maintaining the reputation of its high-quality cotton textiles.

Major industry and infrastructure

- ⚙ engineering
- 🏭 food processing
- ◔ gas
- iron & steel
- iron ore
- oil
- △ phosphates
- ⚲ textiles
- 🏖 tourism
- ■ capital cities
- ■ major towns
- ⊕ international airports
- major roads
- major industrial areas

THE TRANSPORT NETWORK

155,177 miles (249,882 km)	42 miles (68 km)
6168 miles (9933 km)	559 miles (900 km)

Tourism and the oil industry have made improvements to the Maghreb's infrastructure both necessary and possible. The Suez Canal is a vital artery for shipping between Europe and Asia.

WEST AFRICA

BENIN, BURKINA, CAPE VERDE, GAMBIA, GHANA, GUINEA, GUINEA-BISSAU, IVORY COAST, LIBERIA, MALI, MAURITANIA, NIGER, NIGERIA, SENEGAL, SIERRA LEONE, TOGO

WEST AFRICA IS AN IMMENSELY DIVERSE REGION, encompassing the desert landscapes and mainly Muslim populations of the southern Saharan countries, and the tropical rainforests of the more humid south, with a great variety of local languages and cultures. The rich natural resources and accessibility of the area were quickly exploited by Europeans; most of the Africans taken by slave traders came from this region, causing serious depopulation. The very different influences of West Africa's leading colonial powers, Britain and France, remain today, reflected in the languages and institutions of the countries they once governed.

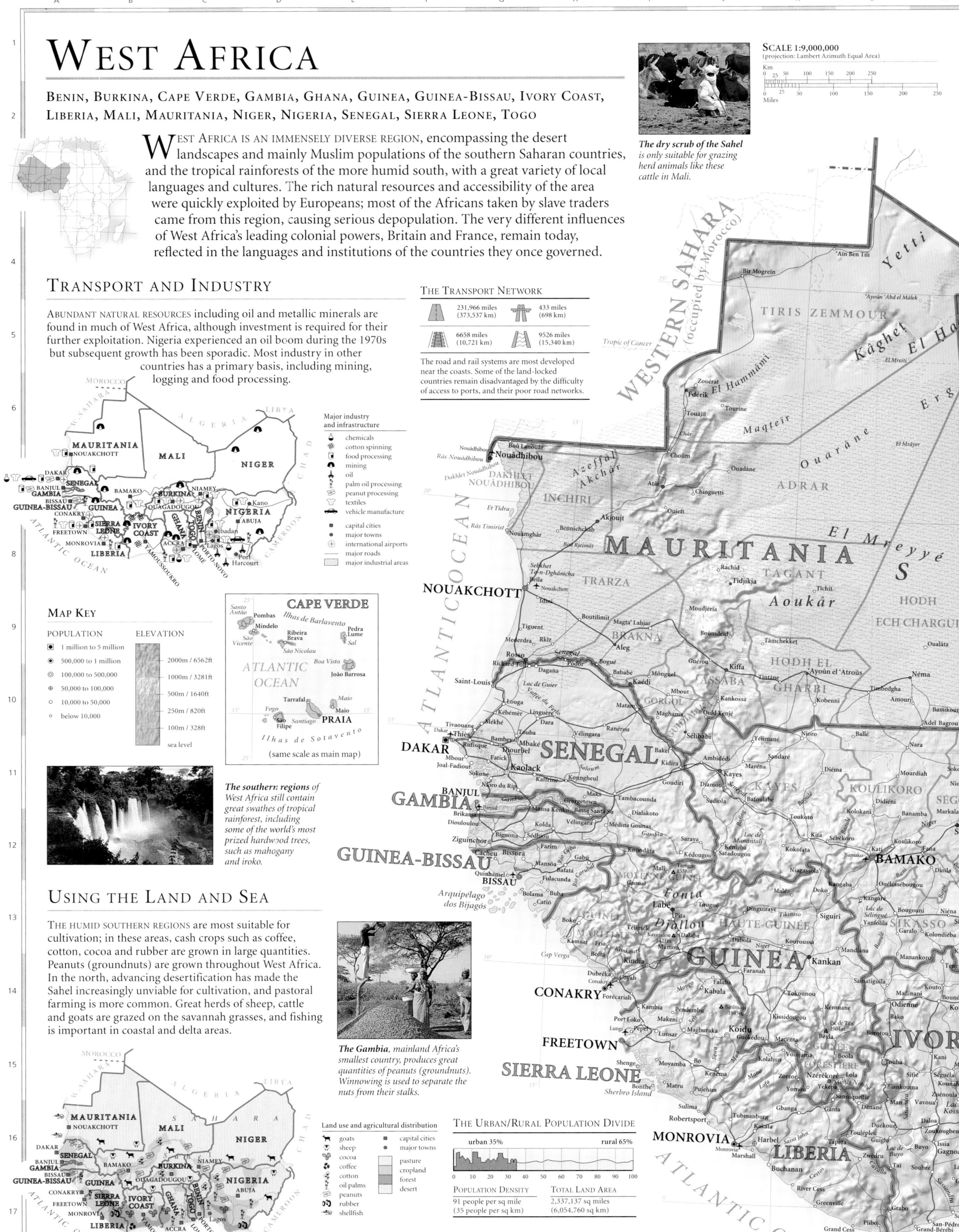

The dry scrub of the Sahel is only suitable for grazing herd animals like these cattle in Mali.

TRANSPORT AND INDUSTRY

ABUNDANT NATURAL RESOURCES including oil and metallic minerals are found in much of West Africa, although investment is required for their further exploitation. Nigeria experienced an oil boom during the 1970s but subsequent growth has been sporadic. Most industry in other countries has a primary basis, including mining, logging and food processing.

THE TRANSPORT NETWORK

231,966 miles (373,537 km)	433 miles (698 km)
6658 miles (10,721 km)	9526 miles (15,340 km)

The road and rail systems are most developed near the coasts. Some of the land-locked countries remain disadvantaged by the difficulty of access to ports, and their poor road networks.

Major industry and infrastructure

- chemicals
- cotton spinning
- food processing
- mining
- oil
- palm oil processing
- peanut processing
- textiles
- vehicle manufacture
- ■ capital cities
- □ major towns
- ✈ international airports
- — major roads
- ▨ major industrial areas

CAPE VERDE

Santo Antão, Pombas, Mindelo, São Vicente, Ribeira Brava, São Nicolau, Pedra Lume, Sal, Boa Vista, João Barrosa, ATLANTIC OCEAN, Tarrafal, Fogo, São Filipe, Santiago, Maio, Maio, **PRAIA**, Ilhas de Sotavento

Ilhas de Barlavento

(same scale as main map)

MAP KEY

POPULATION
- ▣ 1 million to 5 million
- ◉ 500,000 to 1 million
- ◎ 100,000 to 500,000
- ⊕ 50,000 to 100,000
- ⊙ 10,000 to 50,000
- • below 10,000

ELEVATION
- 2000m / 6562ft
- 1000m / 3281ft
- 500m / 1640ft
- 250m / 820ft
- 100m / 328ft
- sea level

The southern regions of West Africa still contain great swathes of tropical rainforest, including some of the world's most prized hardwood trees, such as mahogany and iroko.

USING THE LAND AND SEA

THE HUMID SOUTHERN REGIONS are most suitable for cultivation; in these areas, cash crops such as coffee, cotton, cocoa and rubber are grown in large quantities. Peanuts (groundnuts) are grown throughout West Africa. In the north, advancing desertification has made the Sahel increasingly unviable for cultivation, and pastoral farming is more common. Great herds of sheep, cattle and goats are grazed on the savannah grasses, and fishing is important in coastal and delta areas.

The Gambia, mainland Africa's smallest country, produces great quantities of peanuts (groundnuts). Winnowing is used to separate the nuts from their stalks.

Land use and agricultural distribution
- goats
- sheep
- cocoa
- coffee
- cotton
- oil palms
- peanuts
- rubber
- shellfish
- ■ capital cities
- • major towns
- pasture
- cropland
- forest
- desert

THE URBAN/RURAL POPULATION DIVIDE

urban 35% rural 65%

0 10 20 30 40 50 60 70 80 90 100

POPULATION DENSITY
91 people per sq mile (35 people per sq km)

TOTAL LAND AREA
2,337,137 sq miles (6,054,760 sq km)

SCALE 1:9,000,000
(projection: Lambert Azimuth Equal Area)

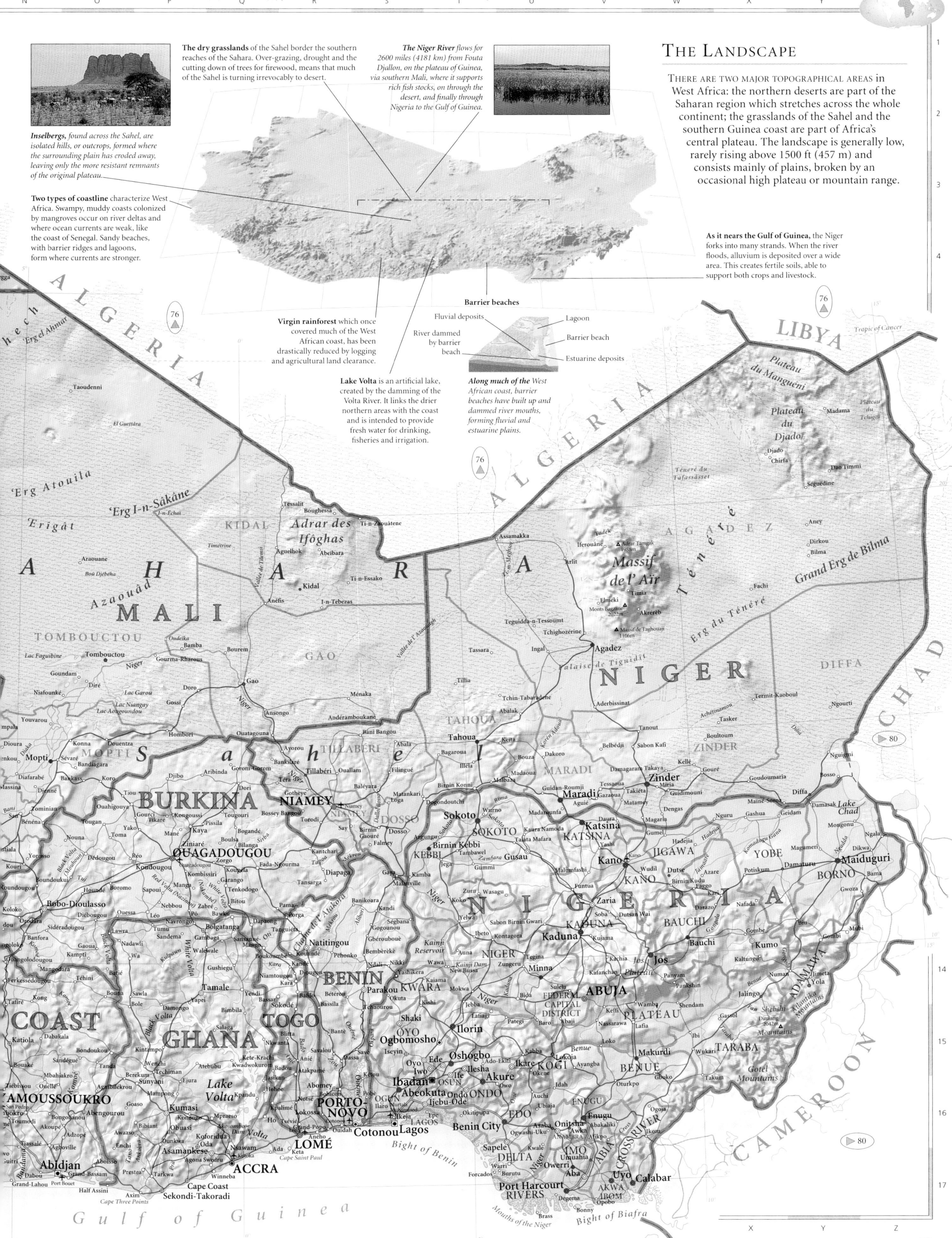

The dry grasslands of the Sahel border the southern reaches of the Sahara. Over-grazing, drought and the cutting down of trees for firewood, means that much of the Sahel is turning irrevocably to desert.

The Niger River flows for 2600 miles (4181 km) from Fouta Djallon, on the plateau of Guinea, via southern Mali, where it supports rich fish stocks, on through the desert, and finally through Nigeria to the Gulf of Guinea.

Inselbergs, *found across the Sahel, are isolated hills, or outcrops, formed where the surrounding plain has eroded away, leaving only the more resistant remnants of the original plateau.*

Two types of coastline characterize West Africa. Swampy, muddy coasts colonized by mangroves occur on river deltas and where ocean currents are weak, like the coast of Senegal. Sandy beaches, with barrier ridges and lagoons, form where currents are stronger.

THE LANDSCAPE

THERE ARE TWO MAJOR TOPOGRAPHICAL AREAS in West Africa: the northern deserts are part of the Saharan region which stretches across the whole continent; the grasslands of the Sahel and the southern Guinea coast are part of Africa's central plateau. The landscape is generally low, rarely rising above 1500 ft (457 m) and consists mainly of plains, broken by an occasional high plateau or mountain range.

As it nears the Gulf of Guinea, the Niger forks into many strands. When the river floods, alluvium is deposited over a wide area. This creates fertile soils, able to support both crops and livestock.

Virgin rainforest which once covered much of the West African coast, has been drastically reduced by logging and agricultural land clearance.

Barrier beaches

Fluvial deposits — Lagoon
River dammed by barrier beach — Barrier beach
— Estuarine deposits

Lake Volta is an artificial lake, created by the damming of the Volta River. It links the drier northern areas with the coast and is intended to provide fresh water for drinking, fisheries and irrigation.

Along much of the West African coast, barrier beaches have built up and dammed river mouths, forming fluvial and estuarine plains.

CENTRAL AFRICA

CAMEROON, CENTRAL AFRICAN REPUBLIC, CHAD, CONGO, CONGO (ZAIRE), EQUATORIAL GUINEA, GABON, SAO TOME & PRINCIPE

THE GREAT RAINFOREST BASIN of the Congo River embraces most of remote Central Africa. The interior was largely unknown to Europeans until late in the 19th century, when its tribal kingdoms were split – principally between France and Belgium – with Sao Tome and Principe the lone Portuguese territory, and Equatorial Guinea controlled by Spain. Open democracy and regional economic integration are important goals for these nations – several of which have only recently emerged from restrictive regimes – and investment is needed to improve transport infrastructures. Many of the small, but fast-growing and increasingly urban population, speak French, the regional *lingua franca*, along with several hundred Pygmy, Bantu and Sudanic dialects.

TRANSPORT AND INDUSTRY

LARGE RESERVES OF VALUABLE MINERALS are found in Central Africa: copper, cobalt, zinc and tin are mined in Congo (Zaire) and Cameroon; diamonds in the Central African Republic, and manganese in Gabon. Congo, Cameroon, Gabon, and Congo (Zaire) have oil deposits and oil has also been recently discovered in Chad. Goods such as palm oil and rubber are processed for export.

THE TRANSPORT NETWORK

✈	181,633 miles (292,485 km)	
⛴	342 miles (550 km)	
🚂	4774 miles (7688 km)	
	15,261 miles (24,475 km)	

The Trans-Gabon railway, which began operating in 1987, has opened up new sources of timber and manganese. Elsewhere, much investment is needed to update and improve road, rail and water transport.

THE LANDSCAPE

LAKE CHAD LIES in a desert basin bounded by the volcanic Tibesti Mountains in the north, plateaux in the east and, in the south, the broad watershed of the Congo Basin. The vast circular depression of the Congo is isolated from the coastal plain by the granite Massif du Chaillu. To the northwest, the volcanoes and fold mountains of the Cameroon Ridge (*Dorsale Camerounaise*) extend as islands into the Gulf of Guinea. The high fold mountains, fringing the east of the Congo Basin fall steeply, to the lakes of the Great Rift Valley.

A plug of resistant lava, at the southwestern end of the Cameroon Ridge (Dorsale Camerounaise), is all that remains of an eroded volcano.

The volcanic massif of Cameroon Mountain occupies an area which remains volcanically active.

Gulf of Guinea

Massif du Chaillu

Lake Chad is the remnant of an inland sea, which once occupied much of the surrounding basin. A series of droughts since the 1970s has reduced the area of this shallow freshwater lake to about 1000 sq miles (2599 sq km).

The Tibesti Mountains are the highest in the Sahara. They were pushed up by the movement of the African Plate over a hot spot, which first formed the northern Ahaggar Mountains and is now thought to lie under the Great Rift Valley.

The Congo River is second only to the Amazon in the volume of water it carries, and in the size of its drainage basin.

Lake Tanganyika, the world's second deepest lake, is the largest of a series of linear 'ribbon' lakes occupying a trench within the Great Rift Valley.

Rich mineral deposits in the 'Copper Belt' of Congo (Zaire) were formed under intense heat and pressure when the ancient African Shield was uplifted to form the region's mountains.

The lake-like expansion of the Congo River at Stanley Pool is the lowest point of the interior basin, although the river still descends more than 1000 ft (300 m) to reach the sea.

Virgin tropical rainforest covers the Ruwenzori range on the borders of Congo (Zaire) and Uganda.

The Congo River flows sluggishly through the rainforest of the interior basin. Towards the coast, the river drops steeply in a series of waterfalls and cataracts. At this point, the erosional power of the river becomes so great that it has formed a deep submarine canyon offshore.

Waterfalls and cataracts

Submarine canyon

Broad, shallow basin

The vast sand flats surrounding Lake Chad were once covered by water. Changing climatic patterns caused the lake to shrink, and desert now covers much of its previous area.

MAP KEY

POPULATION
- ◉ 1 million to 5 million
- ◎ 500,000 to 1 million
- ⊗ 100,000 to 500,000
- ⊕ 50,000 to 100,000
- ○ 10,000 to 50,000
- ◦ below 10,000

ELEVATION
- 4000m / 13,124ft
- 3000m / 9843ft
- 2000m / 6562ft
- 1000m / 3281ft
- 500m / 1640ft
- 250m / 820ft
- 100m / 328ft
- sea level

SCALE 1:9,500,000
(projection: Lambert Azimuthal Equal Area)

The ancient rocks of Congo (Zaire) hold immense and varied mineral reserves. This open pit copper mine is at Kolwezi in the far south.

Major industry and infrastructure
- brewing
- chemicals
- cobalt
- copper
- diamonds
- food processing
- manganese
- oil
- palm oil processing
- textiles
- tin
- capital cities
- major towns
- international airports
- major roads
- major industrial areas

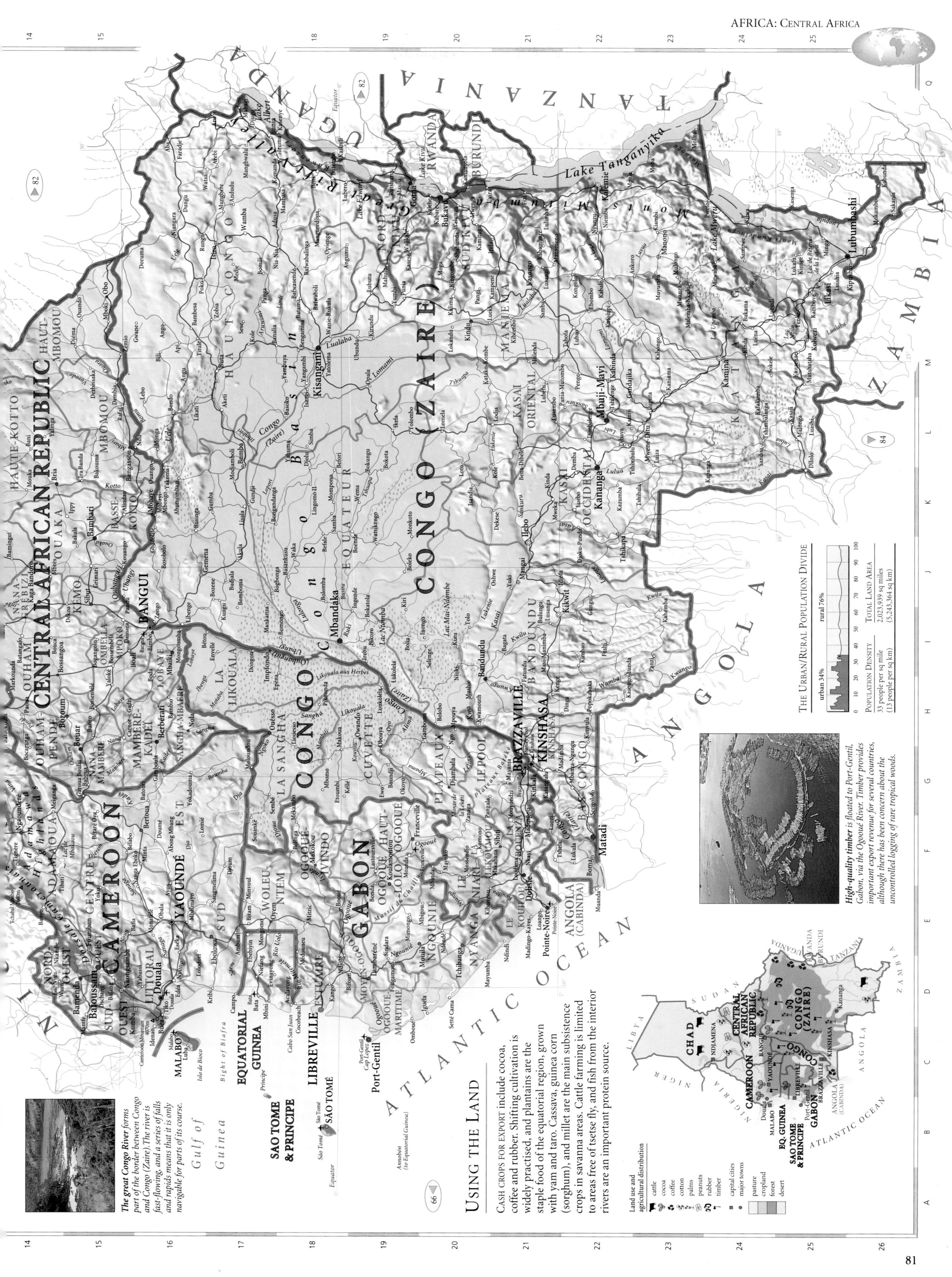

The great Congo River forms part of the border between Congo and Congo (Zaire). The river is fast-flowing, and a series of falls and rapids means that it is only navigable for parts of its course.

USING THE LAND

CASH CROPS FOR EXPORT include cocoa, coffee and rubber. Shifting cultivation is widely practised, and plantains are the staple food of the equatorial region, grown with yam and taro. Cassava, guinea corn (sorghum), and millet are the main subsistence crops in savanna areas. Cattle farming is limited to areas free of tsetse fly, and fish from the interior rivers are an important protein source.

High-quality timber is floated to Port-Gentil, Gabon, via the Ogooué River. Timber provides important export revenue for several countries, although there has been concern about the uncontrolled logging of rare tropical woods.

THE URBAN/RURAL POPULATION DIVIDE

urban 34%   rural 76%

POPULATION DENSITY	TOTAL LAND AREA
33 people per sq mile	2,023,939 sq miles
(13 people per sq km)	(5,243,363 sq km)

Land use and agricultural distribution

cattle, cocoa, coffee, cotton, palms, peanuts, rubber, timber

capital cities
major towns

pasture, cropland, forest, desert

EAST AFRICA

BURUNDI, DJIBOUTI, ERITREA, ETHIOPIA, KENYA, RWANDA, SOMALIA, SUDAN, TANZANIA, UGANDA

THE COUNTRIES OF EAST AFRICA divide into two distinct cultural regions. Sudan and the 'Horn' nations have been influenced by the Middle East; Ethiopia was the home of one of the earliest Christian civilizations, and Sudan reflects both Muslim and Christian influences, while the southern countries share a closer cultural affinity with other sub-Saharan nations. Some of Africa's most densely-populated countries lie in this region, and the needs of a growing population have put pressure on marginal lands and fragile environments. Although most East African economies remain strongly agricultural, Kenya has developed a varied industrial base.

THE LANDSCAPE

EAST AFRICA'S MOST SIGNIFICANT landscape feature is the Great Rift Valley, which formed during the most recent phase of continental movement when the rigid basement rocks cracked and buckled. Great blocks of land were raised and lowered, creating huge flat-bottomed valleys and steep escarpments, sometimes covered by volcanic extrusions in highland areas.

Central block slopes towards main fault

Ephemeral lake forms at far edge of slope

Boundary fault

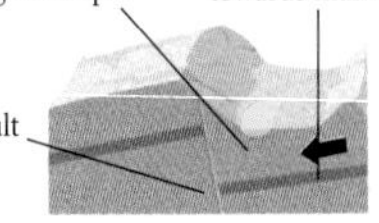

The eastern arm of the Great Rift Valley is gradually being pulled apart; however the forces on one side are greater than the other causing the land to slope. This affects regional drainage which migrates down the slope.

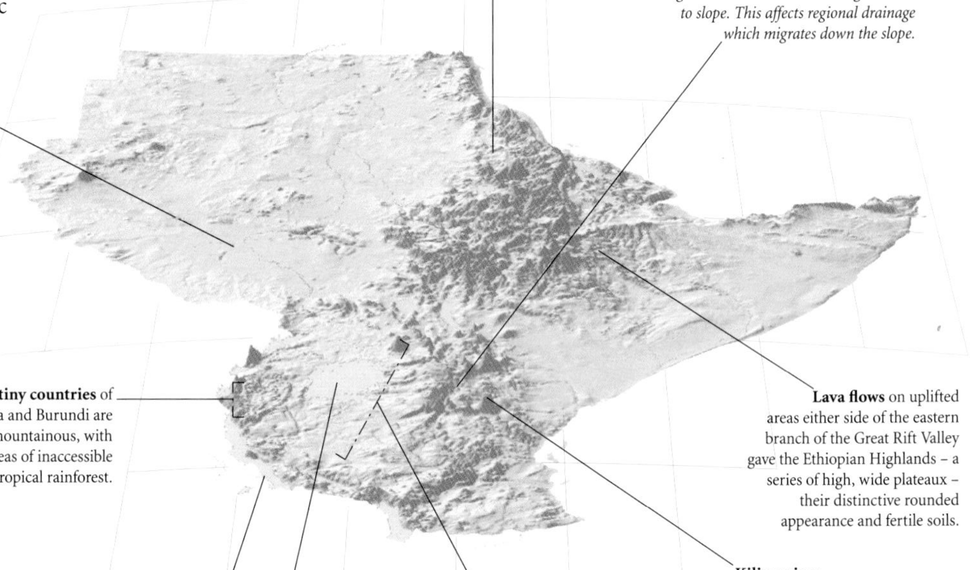

This dome at Gonder, in Ethiopia, is a volcanic intrusion, formed when molten rock pushed up the surface of the Earth and then solidified, leaving an outcrop of igneous rock.

Lava flows on uplifted areas either side of the eastern branch of the Great Rift Valley gave the Ethiopian Highlands – a series of high, wide plateaux – their distinctive rounded appearance and fertile soils.

Kilimanjaro

An extinct volcano, Kilimanjaro is Africa's highest mountain, rising 19,340 ft (5895 m). It is one of the few places in Africa where snow settles, allowing glacier ice to form.

A vast plateau lies between the eastern and western rift valleys in Kenya, Uganda and western Tanzania. It has been levelled by long periods of erosion to form a peneplain, but is dotted with insebergs – outcrops of more resistant rocks.

The Kassala region in eastern Sudan is watered by the Atbara River, an important tributary of the Nile. Most of the population is engaged in agriculture, growing cotton and cereals.

Lake Victoria occupies a vast basin between the two arms of the Great Rift Valley. It is the world's second largest lake in terms of surface area, extending 26,828 sq miles (69,484 sq km). The lake contains numerous islands and coral reefs.

Lake Tanganyika lies 8202 ft (2500 m) above sea level. It has a depth of nearly 16,400 ft (5000 m). The lake traces the valley floor for some 400 miles (644 km) of the western arm of the Great Rift Valley.

The tiny countries of Rwanda and Burundi are mainly mountainous, with large areas of inaccessible tropical rainforest.

Much of northern Sudan is covered by desert. However, in the tropical wetlands of the southern Sudd region, annual rainfall can sometimes exceed 40 inches (1000 mm).

MAP KEY

POPULATION
- ◉ 1 million to 5 million
- ● 500,000 to 1 million
- ◎ 100,000 to 500,000
- ⊕ 50,000 to 100,000
- ○ 10,000 to 50,000
- ○ below 10,000

ELEVATION
- 4000m / 13,124ft
- 3000m / 9843ft
- 2000m / 6562ft
- 1000m / 3281ft
- 500m / 1640ft
- 250m / 820ft
- 100m / 328ft
- sea level

SCALE 1:9,500,000
(projection: Lambert Azimuthal Equal Area)

USING THE LAND

THE LAKE VICTORIA BASIN and rich volcanic soils of the Kenyan, Tanzanian and Ugandan uplands support subsistence crops and cash crops, such as coffee, tea, cotton, sugar cane and a variety of high-quality vegetables. Where rainfall is too variable for cultivation, pastoralism predominates. In the most arid regions camels are common; elsewhere large herds of cattle, sheep and goats are raised. Tsetse fly infestation limits human settlement and agriculture in much of this region.

Land use and agricultural distribution
- cattle
- goats
- sheep
- coffee
- cotton
- sugar cane
- sisal
- tea
- timber
- capital cities
- major towns
- pasture
- cropland
- forest
- wetland
- desert

THE URBAN/RURAL POPULATION DIVIDE
- urban 19%
- rural 81%

POPULATION DENSITY
75 people per sq mile
(29 people per sq km)

TOTAL LAND AREA
2,413,758 sq miles
(6,253,259 sq km)

This flat valley floor in Burundi is criss-crossed by irrigation channels which provide a constant source of water for the coffee grown here.

TRANSPORT AND INDUSTRY

MOST EXPORTS FROM THIS REGION consist of raw materials which have undergone primary processing. These include cotton, sugar, tea, sisal and coffee. Fast-flowing rivers in the highlands generate hydro-electric power, which has great future potential. The appeal of Kenya's wildlife and beaches has made tourism a crucial part of the economy.

The great Ngorongoro Crater in Tanzania is an immense relic of past volcanic activity. Other examples are found throughout Kenya and Tanzania.

Major industry and infrastructure
- chemicals
- cement
- coffee processing
- frankincense
- hydro-electric power
- sisal processing
- sugar refining
- tea processing
- textiles
- wildlife reserves
- capital cities
- major towns
- international airports
- major roads
- major industrial areas

THE TRANSPORT NETWORK

- 149,852 miles (241,308 km)
- 8619 miles (13,879 km)
- 62 miles (100 km)
- 2837 miles (4568 km)

The land-locked nations suffer economically from their restricted access to the coast and from underdeveloped infrastructures. Kenya and Tanzania are investing in new transport links.

The magnificent National Parks of Kenya and Tanzania provide essential refuges for many of Africa's rarest animals. Tourism brings in much-needed cash to sustain these important conservation projects.

SOUTHERN AFRICA

ANGOLA, BOTSWANA, LESOTHO, MALAWI, MOZAMBIQUE, NAMIBIA, SOUTH AFRICA, SWAZILAND, ZAMBIA, ZIMBABWE

AFRICA'S VAST SOUTHERN PLATEAU has been a contested homeland for many centuries. The European incursion began with the slave trade and quickened last century, when the discovery of enormous mineral wealth secured South Africa's regional economic dominance. The struggle against white minority rule led to strife in Namibia, Zimbabwe, and the former Portuguese territories of Angola and Mozambique. South Africa's notorious apartheid laws, which denied basic human rights to more than 75% of the people, led to the state being internationally ostracized until 1994, when the first fully democratic elections inaugurated a new era of racial justice.

TRANSPORT AND INDUSTRY

SOUTH AFRICA, the world's largest exporter of gold, has a varied economy which generates about 75% of the region's income and draws migrant labour from neighbouring states. Angola exports petroleum; Botswana and Namibia rely on diamond mining; and Zambia is seeking to diversify its economy to compensate for declining copper reserves.

Almost all new mining ventures in Zimbabwe are now subject to government control. This mine at Bindura produces nickel, one of the country's top three minerals in terms of economic value.

Major industry and infrastructure

car manufacture	gold	capital cities
coal	oil	major towns
copper	textiles	international airports
diamonds	uranium	major roads
food processing	wildlife reserves	major industrial areas

THE LANDSCAPE

MOST OF SOUTHERN AFRICA rests on a concave plateau comprising the Kalahari basin and a mountainous fringe, skirted by a coastal plain which widens out in Mozambique. The plateau extends north, towards the Planalto de Bié in Angola, the Congo Basin and the lake-filled troughs of the Great Rift Valley. The eastern region is drained by the Zambezi and Limpopo rivers, and the Orange is the major western river.

Thousands of years of evaporating water have produced the Etosha Pan, one of the largest salt flats in the world. Lake and river sediments in the area indicate that the region was once less arid.

Finger Rock, near Khorixas, Namibia is a remnant of a former land surface, which has been denuded by erosion over the last 5 million years. These occasional stacks of partially weathered rocks interrupt the plains of the dry southern interior.

THE TRANSPORT NETWORK

196,477 miles (316,388 km)	1267 miles (2040 km)
24,137 miles (38,868 km)	5090 miles (8196 km)

Southern Africa's Cape-gauge rail network is by far the largest in the continent. About two-thirds of the 20,000 mile (32,000 km) system lies within South Africa. Lines such as the Harare–Bulawayo route have become corridors for industrial growth.

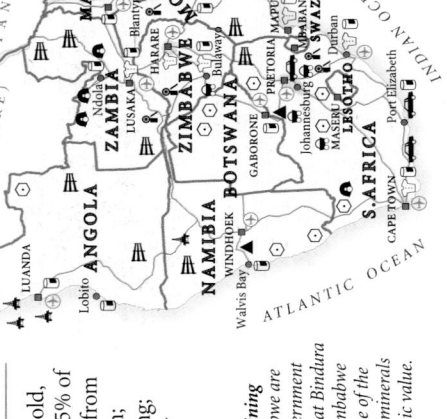

Following a series of droughts, this baobab tree in Zimbabwe now stands alone in a field once filled by sugar cane. The thick trunk and small leaves of the baobab help it to conserve water, enabling it to survive even in drought conditions.

At Victoria Falls, the Zambezi River has cut a spectacular gorge taking advantage of large joints in the basalt, which were first formed as the lava cooled and contracted.

Lake Nyasa occupies one of the deep troughs of the Great Rift Valley, where the land has been displaced downwards by as much as 3000 ft (920 m).

The fast-flowing Zambezi River cuts a deep, wide channel as it flows along the Zimbabwe/Zambia border.

The Okavango/Cubango River flows from the Planalto de Bié to the swamplands of the Okavango Delta, one of the world's largest inland deltas, where it divides into countless distributary channels, feeding out into the desert.

Great Rift Valley

Bushveld intrusion

Limpopo River

Volcanic lava, over 250 million years old, caps the peaks of the Drakensberg range, which lie on the mountainous rim of southern Africa's interior plateau.

Broad, flat-topped mountains characterize the Great Karoo, which have been cut from level rock strata under extremely arid conditions.

The mountains of the Little Karoo are composed of sedimentary rocks which have been substantially folded and faulted.

The Orange River, one of the longest in Africa, rises in Lesotho and is the only major river in the south which flows westward, rather than to the east coast.

The Kalahari Desert is the largest continuous sand surface in the world. Iron oxide gives a distinctive red colour to the windblown sand, which, in eastern areas, covers the bedrock by over 200 ft (60 m).

Planalto de Bié

Namib Desert

Khorixas, Namibia

MAP KEY

POPULATION

■ 1 million to 5 million
● 500,000 to 1 million
◉ 100,000 to 500,000
⊕ 50,000 to 100,000
○ 10,000 to 50,000
∘ below 10,000

ELEVATION

3000m / 9843ft
2000m / 6562ft
1000m / 3281ft
500m / 1640ft
250m / 820ft
100m / 328ft
sea level

Bushveld intrusion

The Bushveld intrusion lies on South Africa's high 'veld'. Molten magma intruded into the Earth's crust creating a saucer-shaped feature, more than 180 miles (300 km) across, containing regular layers of precious minerals, overlain by a dome of granite.

Granite
Chromite
Gabbro and peridotite
Magnetite
Platinum minerals

SCALE 1:9,500,000
(projection: Lambert Azimuthal Equal Area)

SOUTH AFRICA'S THREE CAPITALS

PRETORIA – administrative capital
CAPE TOWN – legislative capital
BLOEMFONTEIN – judicial capital

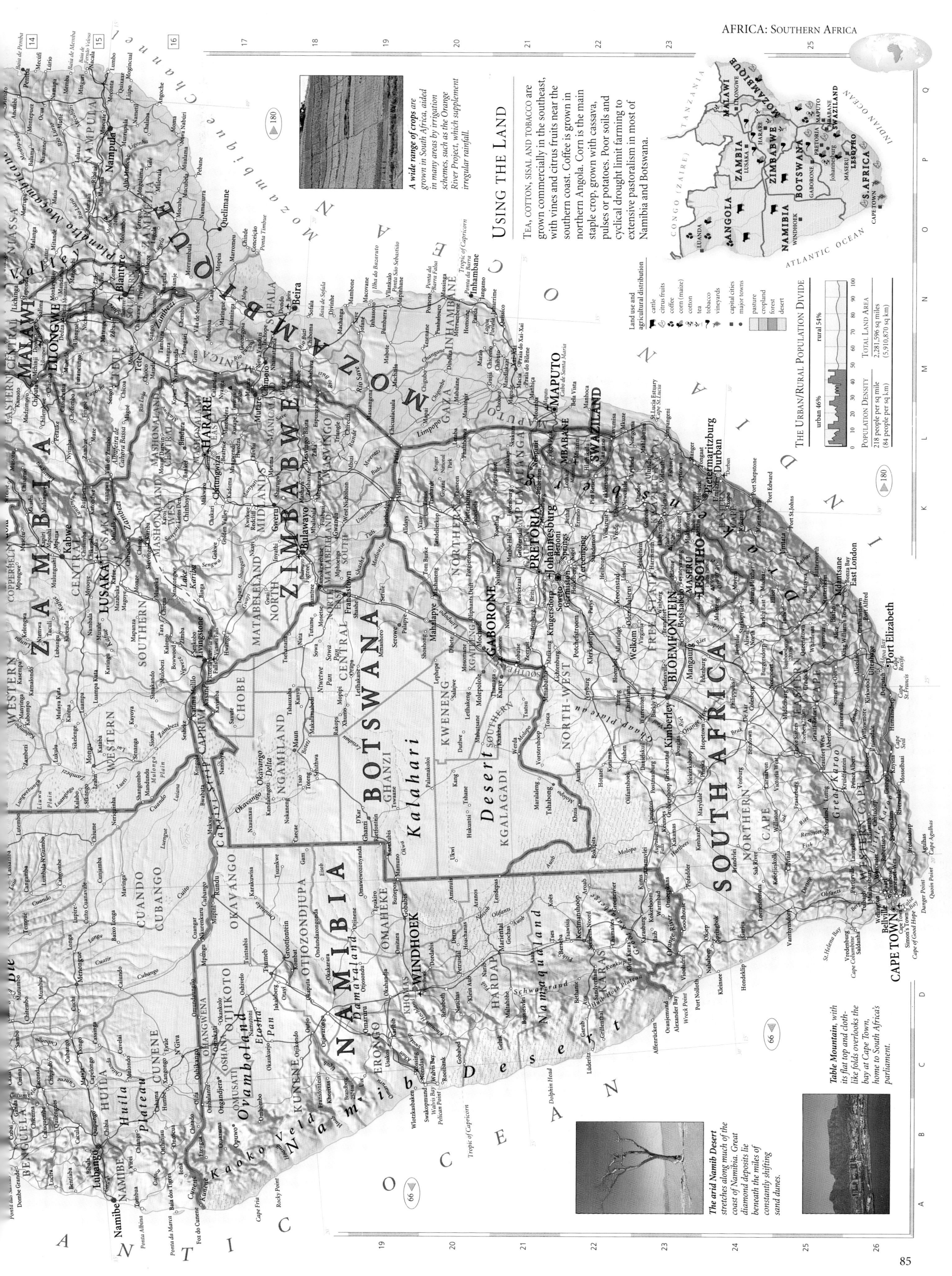

A wide range of crops are grown in South Africa, aided in many areas by irrigation schemes, such as the Orange River Project, which supplement irregular rainfall.

USING THE LAND

TEA, COTTON, SISAL AND TOBACCO are grown commercially in the southeast, with vines and citrus fruits near the southern coast. Coffee is grown in northern Angola. Corn is the main staple crop, grown with cassava, pulses or potatoes. Poor soils and cyclical drought limit farming to extensive pastoralism in most of Namibia and Botswana.

Land use and agricultural distribution

- cattle
- citrus fruits
- coffee
- corn (maize)
- cotton
- tea
- tobacco
- vineyards
- capital cities
- major towns

- pasture
- cropland
- forest
- desert

THE URBAN/RURAL POPULATION DIVIDE

urban 46%   rural 54%

POPULATION DENSITY	TOTAL LAND AREA
218 people per sq mile	2,281,596 sq miles
(84 people per sq km)	(5,910,870 sq km)

The arid Namib Desert stretches along much of the coast of Namibia. Great diamond deposits lie beneath the miles of constantly shifting sand dunes.

Table Mountain, with its flat and cloth-like folds overlooks the bay at Cape Town, home to South Africa's parliament.

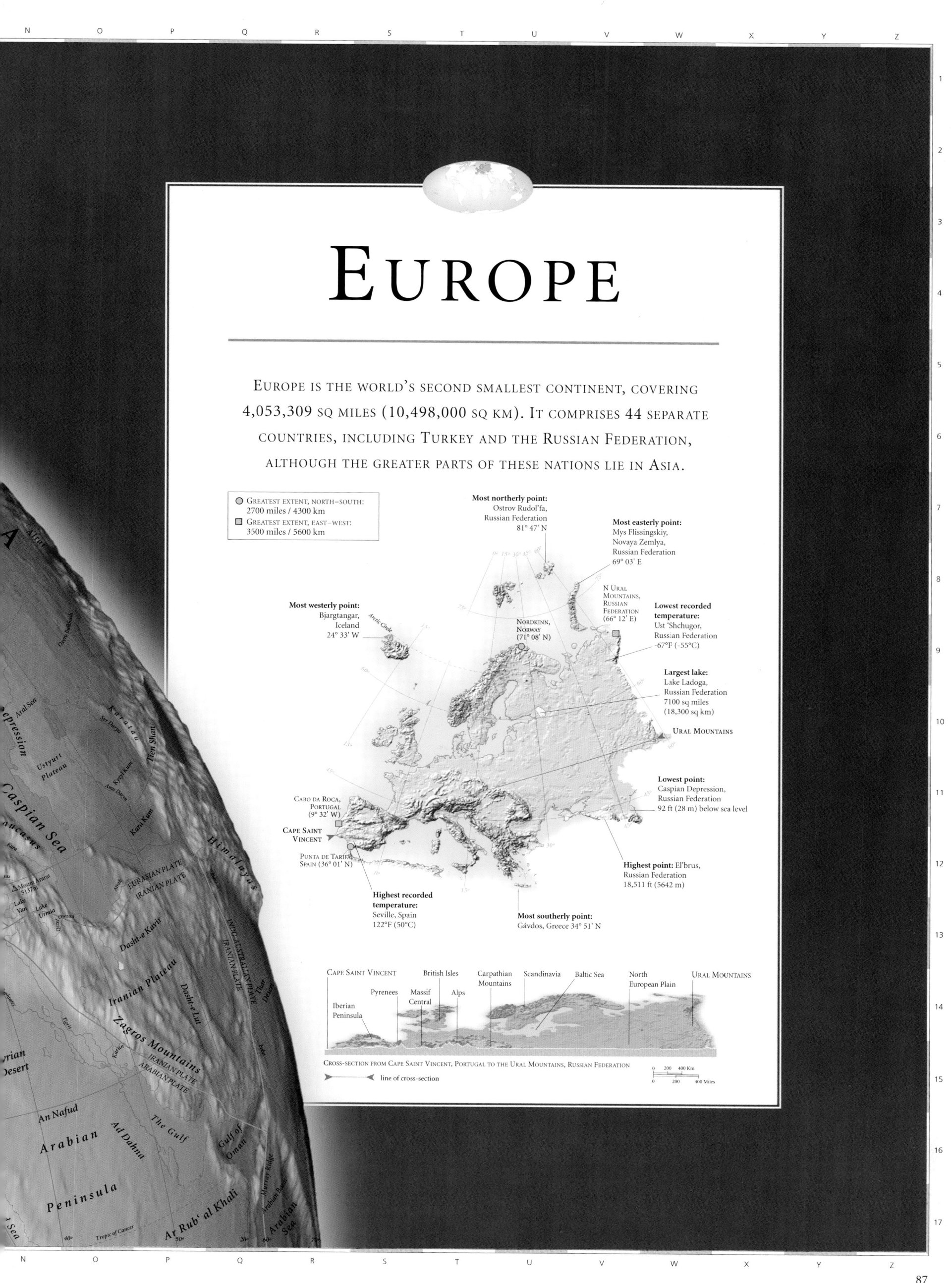

EUROPE

EUROPE IS THE WORLD'S SECOND SMALLEST CONTINENT, COVERING
4,053,309 SQ MILES (10,498,000 SQ KM). IT COMPRISES 44 SEPARATE
COUNTRIES, INCLUDING TURKEY AND THE RUSSIAN FEDERATION,
ALTHOUGH THE GREATER PARTS OF THESE NATIONS LIE IN ASIA.

● GREATEST EXTENT, NORTH–SOUTH:
2700 miles / 4300 km
■ GREATEST EXTENT, EAST–WEST:
3500 miles / 5600 km

Most northerly point:
Ostrov Rudol'fa,
Russian Federation
81° 47' N

Most easterly point:
Mys Flissingskiy,
Novaya Zemlya,
Russian Federation
69° 03' E

Most westerly point:
Bjargtangar,
Iceland
24° 33' W

N URAL
MOUNTAINS,
RUSSIAN
FEDERATION
(66° 12' E)

NORDKINN,
NORWAY
(71° 08' N)

Lowest recorded
temperature:
Ust 'Shchugor,
Russian Federation
-67°F (-55°C)

Largest lake:
Lake Ladoga,
Russian Federation
7100 sq miles
(18,300 sq km)

URAL MOUNTAINS

Lowest point:
Caspian Depression,
Russian Federation
92 ft (28 m) below sea level

CABO DA ROCA,
PORTUGAL
(9° 32' W)

CAPE SAINT
VINCENT

PUNTA DE TARIFA,
SPAIN (36° 01' N)

Highest point: El'brus,
Russian Federation
18,511 ft (5642 m)

Highest recorded
temperature:
Seville, Spain
122°F (50°C)

Most southerly point:
Gávdos, Greece 34° 51' N

CAPE SAINT VINCENT
Iberian
Peninsula
Pyrenees
Massif
Central
British Isles
Alps
Carpathian
Mountains
Scandinavia
Baltic Sea
North
European Plain
URAL MOUNTAINS

CROSS-SECTION FROM CAPE SAINT VINCENT, PORTUGAL TO THE URAL MOUNTAINS, RUSSIAN FEDERATION

0   200   400 Km
0   200   400 Miles

➤━━━ line of cross-section

PHYSICAL EUROPE

THE PHYSICAL DIVERSITY of Europe belies its relatively small size. To the northwest and south it is enclosed by mountains. The older, rounded Atlantic Highlands of Scandinavia and the British Isles lie to the north and the younger, rugged peaks of the Alpine Uplands to the south. In between lies the North European Plain, stretching 2485 miles (4000 km) from The Fens in England to the Ural Mountains in Russia. South of the plain lies a series of gently folded sedimentary rocks separated by ancient plateaux, known as massifs.

THE NORTH EUROPEAN PLAIN

RISING LESS THAN 1000 ft (300 m) above sea level, the North European Plain strongly reflects past glaciation. Ridges of both coarse moraine and finer, wind-blown deposits have accumulated over much of the region. The ice sheet also diverted a number of river channels from their original courses.

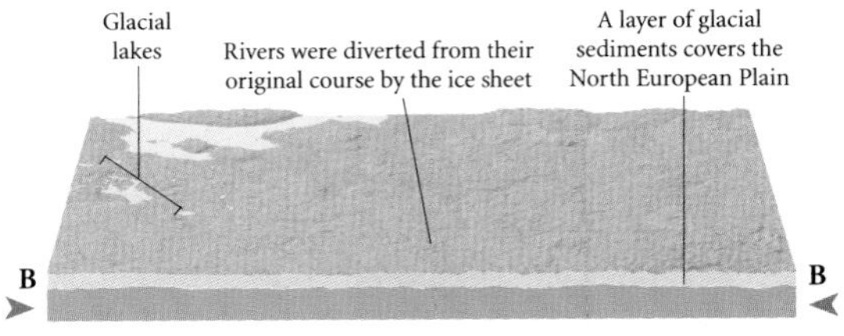

Glacial lakes

Rivers were diverted from their original course by the ice sheet

A layer of glacial sediments covers the North European Plain

B — B

Section across the North European Plain showing its low relief and drainage.

0 100 200 Km
0 100 200 Miles

THE ATLANTIC HIGHLANDS

THE ATLANTIC HIGHLANDS were formed by compression against the Scandinavian Shield during the Caledonian mountain-building period over 500 million years ago. The highlands were once part of a continuous mountain chain, now divided by the North Sea and a submerged rift valley.

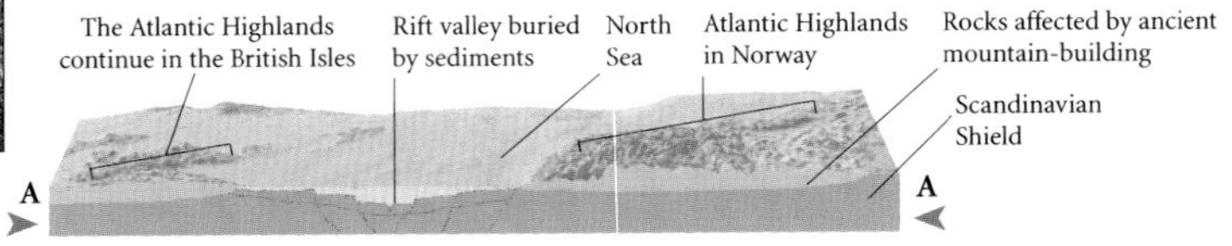

The Atlantic Highlands continue in the British Isles

Rift valley buried by sediments

North Sea

Atlantic Highlands in Norway

Rocks affected by ancient mountain-building

Scandinavian Shield

A — A

Cross-section through northeastern Europe showing the continuous mountain chain and rift valley system.

0 100 200 Km
0 100 200 Miles

SCALE 1:23,000,000
(projection: Lambert Azimuthal Equal Area)

Km
0 100 200 400 600
0 50 100 200 300 400 500 600
Miles

MAP KEY

ELEVATION

4000m / 13,124ft
3000m / 9843ft
2000m / 6562ft
1000m / 3281ft
500m / 1640ft
250m / 820ft
100m / 328ft
sea level

PLATE MARGINS
(for explanation see page xiv)

—— constructive
△△ destructive
—— conservative
······ uncertain
—— physiographic regions
>—< line of cross-section

Map labels

Iceland
NORTH AMERICAN PLATE
EURASIAN PLATE
Novaya Zemlya
Kara Sea
Barents Sea
Ostrov Kolguyev
Kola Peninsula
White Sea
Ural Mountains
Norwegian Sea
ATLANTIC HIGHLANDS
Kölen
Northern Dvina
Faeroe Islands
Shetland Islands
Outer Hebrides
SCANDINAVIAN SHIELD
Gulf of Bothnia
Lake Onega
Lake Ladoga
British Isles
Ireland
Shannon
North Sea
Vänern
Vättern
Gulf of Riga
Baltic Sea
Western Dvina
Central Russian Upland
Volga Upland
Britain
The Fens
Thames
Jylland
NORTH EUROPEAN PLAIN
Elbe
Oder
Vistula
Dnieper
Volga
English Channel
Rhine
Harz
Caspian Sea
PLATEAUX AND LOWLANDS
Ardennes
Danube
Carpathian Mountains
Don
Dniester
Sea of Azov
Seine
Loire
PLATEAUX AND LOWLANDS
ALPS
Mt Blanc 4807m
Po
Rhône
Great Hungarian Plain
Danube
Crimea
Caucasus Elbrus 5642m
Bay of Biscay
Massif Central
Garonne
Pyrenees
APENNINES
Adriatic Sea
DINARIC ALPS
Balkan Mountains
Black Sea
Duero
Iberian Peninsula
Ebro
Corsica
Tyrrhenian Sea
Vesuvius 1171m
ASIA
Guadalquivir
EURASIAN PLATE
AFRICAN PLATE
Balearic Islands
Sardinia
Sicily
Etna 3263m
Malta
EURASIAN PLATE
ANATOLIAN PLATE
AFRICAN PLATE
Peloponnese
Aegean Sea
Ionian Sea
Crete
ATLANTIC OCEAN
Mediterranean Sea

THE PLATEAUX AND LOWLANDS

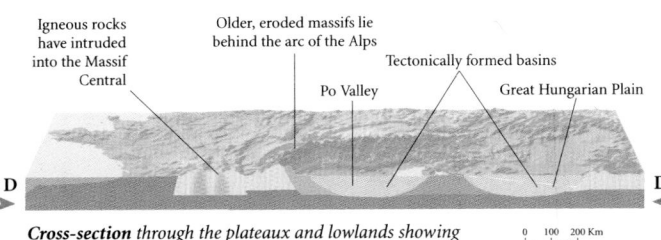

THE UPLIFTED PLATEAUX or massifs of southern central Europe are the result of long-term erosion, later followed by uplift. They are the source areas of many of the rivers which drain Europe's lowlands. In some of the higher reaches, fractures have enabled igneous rocks from deep in the Earth to reach the surface.

THE ALPINE UPLANDS

THE COLLISION OF the African and European continents, which began about 65 million years ago, folded and then uplifted a series of mountain ranges running across southern Europe and into Asia. Two major lines of folding can be traced: one includes the Pyrenees, the Alps and the Carpathian Mountains; the other incorporates the Apennines and the Dinaric Alps.

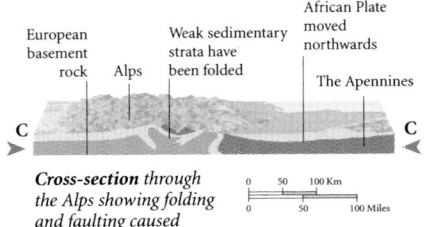

European basement rock

Alps

Weak sedimentary strata have been folded

African Plate moved northwards

The Apennines

C — C

Cross-section through the Alps showing folding and faulting caused by plate tectonics.

0 50 100 Km
0 50 100 Miles

Igneous rocks have intruded into the Massif Central

Older, eroded massifs lie behind the arc of the Alps

Tectonically formed basins

Po Valley

Great Hungarian Plain

D — D

Cross-section through the plateaux and lowlands showing the lower elevation of the ancient massifs.

0 100 200 Km
0 100 200 Miles

N O P Q R S T U V W X Z

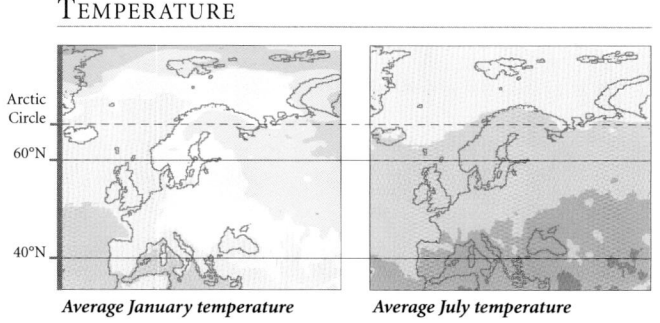

Frost grips northern and eastern Europe during the long cold winters. Lakes and rivers frequently freeze.

CLIMATE

EUROPE EXPERIENCES few extremes in either rainfall or temperature, with the exception of the far north and south. Along the west coast, the warm currents of the North Atlantic Drift moderate temperatures. Although east–west air movement is relatively unimpeded by relief, the Alpine Uplands halt the progress of north–south air masses, protecting most of the Mediterranean from cold, north winds.

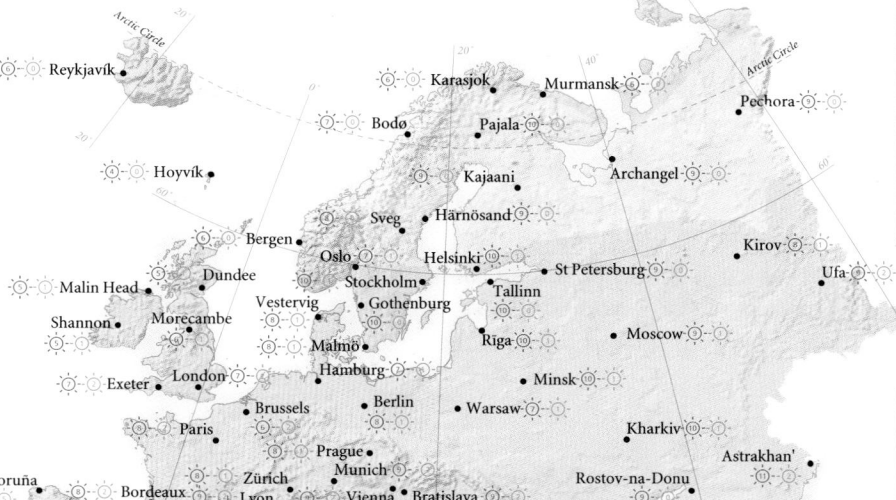

TEMPERATURE

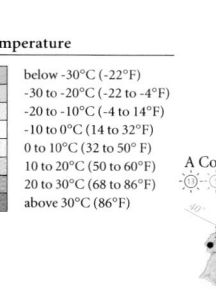

Temperature

	below -30°C (-22°F)
	-30 to -20°C (-22 to -4°F)
	-20 to -10°C (-4 to 14°F)
	-10 to 0°C (14 to 32°F)
	0 to 10°C (32 to 50°F)
	10 to 20°C (50 to 60°F)
	20 to 30°C (68 to 86°F)
	above 30°C (86°F)

Average January temperature *Average July temperature*

RAINFALL

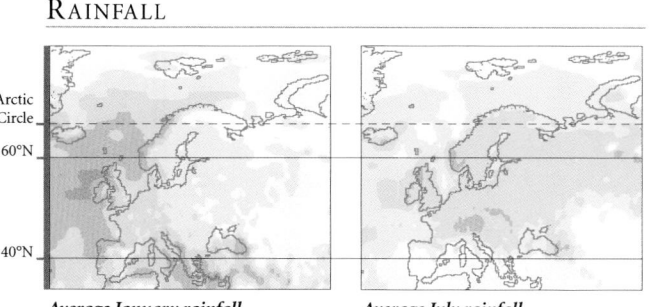

Rainfall

	0–25 mm (0–1 in)
	25–50 mm (1–2 in)
	50–100 mm (2–4 in)
	100–200 mm (4–8 in)
	200–300 mm (8–12 in)
	300–400 mm (12–16 in)
	400–500 mm (16–20 in)
	more than 500 mm (20 in)

Average January rainfall *Average July rainfall*

Climate

	tundra
	subarctic
	cool continental
	warm humid
	mediterranean
	semi-arid
☼	daily hours of sunshine, January
☀	daily hours of sunshine, July
→	cold wind
→	hot wind

Mild temperatures and frequent rainfall contribute to the fertile farming land found over much of northwestern Europe.

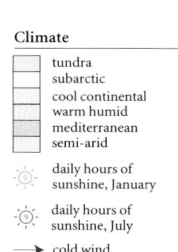

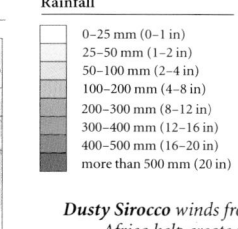

Dusty Sirocco winds from Africa help create the semi-arid scrubland common across the Mediterranean coastlands of southern Europe.

SHAPING THE CONTINENT

SUCCESSIVE ICE AGES have left many relict landforms across Europe. Present glaciers continue to carve peaks and valleys in the northern Atlantic Highlands and Alpine Uplands. Tectonic activity, both past and present, has shaped southern Europe and Iceland. Active volcanoes and earthquakes still occur in Italy and Greece. Europe's extensive coastline, particularly in the northwest, is constantly modified by wave action and fluvial deposits.

GLACIATION

[1] Valley glaciers, such as this one *(left)* in Iceland, form in hollows at the top of valleys and flow downwards, drawn by gravity. Their growth is dynamic; new snowfall constantly accumulates at the head of the glacier, while the snout melts, depositing material eroded and carried by the glacier.

Snow accumulates at the head of glacier
Glacier movement erodes valley
Glacier snout melts depositing eroded debris

GLACIATION: DEVELOPMENT OF A GLACIER

COASTAL PROCESSES

[5] Spits are narrow bands of sand or shingle, formed by longshore drift; a process whereby waves carry material along the beach. They usually form where the coastline changes direction, and their growth is then halted by an opposing river current, as at Spurn Head, in the British Isles *(left)*. Coastal features such as these are constantly being created and destroyed.

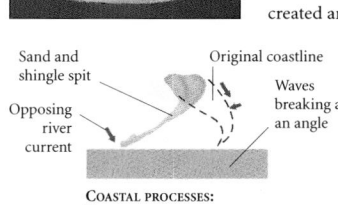

Sand and shingle spit
Original coastline
Opposing river current
Waves breaking at an angle

COASTAL PROCESSES: FORMATION OF A SPIT

Landscape

	uplifting land
	stable land
	sinking land
	limestone region
	glacier
▲	active volcano
→	ocean current
⋯	area of tectonic activity
—	maximum limit of glaciation

THE EVOLVING LANDSCAPE

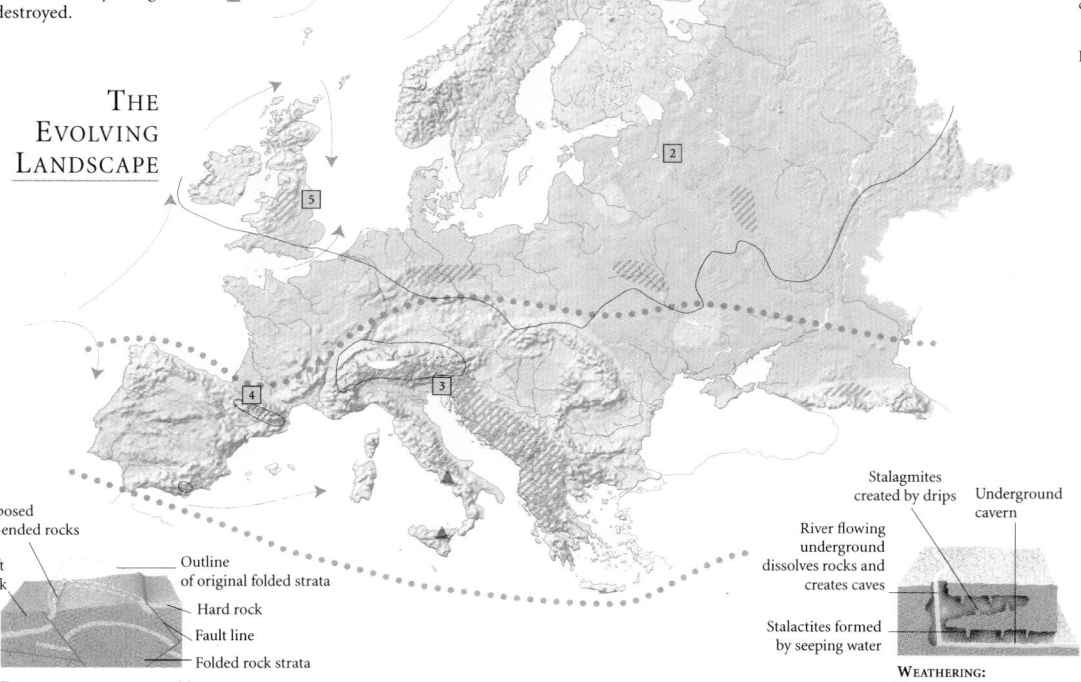

RIVER SYSTEMS

[2] Rivers are continuously transporting eroded material towards the sea. Slow-moving, low-gradient rivers, like this one in western Russia *(above)*, deposit their alluvium load, infilling valleys creating a flood plain. Subsequent climatic and tectonic fluctuations may erode the flood plain to form terraces.

Terrace created by erosion
Flood plain
Deposited alluvium
River channel

RIVER SYSTEMS: FORMATION OF A FLOOD PLAIN AND TERRACES

WEATHERING

[3] As surface water filters through permeable limestone, the rock dissolves to form underground caves, like Postojna in the Karst region of Slovenia *(above)*. Stalactites grow downwards as lime-enriched water seeps from roof fractures; stalagmites grow upwards where drips splash down.

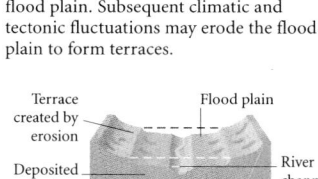

EROSION AND WEATHERING

[4] Much of Europe was once subjected to folding and faulting, exposing hard and soft rock layers. Subsequent erosion and weathering has worn away the softer strata, leaving up-ended layers of hard rock as in the French Pyrenees *(above)*.

Exposed up-ended rocks
Soft rock
Outline of original folded strata
Hard rock
Fault line
Folded rock strata

EROSION AND WEATHERING: MODIFICATION OF A FOLD

Stalagmites created by drips
Underground cavern
River flowing underground dissolves rocks and creates caves
Stalactites formed by seeping water

WEATHERING: FORMATION OF A CAVE

N O P Q R S T U V W X Y Z

POLITICAL EUROPE

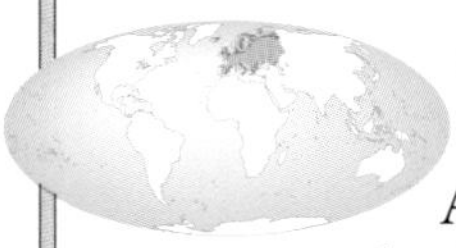

THE POLITICAL BOUNDARIES OF EUROPE have changed many times, especially during the 20th century in the aftermath of two world wars, the break-up of the empires of Austria-Hungary, Nazi Germany and, more recently, the collapse of communism in eastern Europe. The fragmentation of Yugoslavia has again altered the political map of Europe, highlighting a trend towards nationalism and devolution. In contrast, economic federalism is growing. In 1958, the formation of the European Economic Community (now the European Union or EU) started a move towards economic and political union.

The Brandenburg Gate in Berlin is a potent symbol of German reunification. From 1961, the road beneath it ended in a wall, built to stop the flow of refugees to the West. It was opened again in 1989 when the wall was destroyed and East and West Germany were reunited.

POPULATION

EUROPE IS A DENSELY POPULATED, urbanized continent; in Belgium and the United Kingdom over 90% of people live in urban areas. The highest population densities are found in an area stretching east from southern Britain and northern France, into Germany. The northern fringes are only sparsely populated.

Demand for space in densely populated European cities like London has led to the development of high-rise offices and urban sprawl.

Population density (people per sq km)
- below 49
- 50–99
- 100–149
- 150–199
- 200–299
- above 300

Traditional lifestyles still persist in many remote and rural parts of Europe, especially in the south, east, and in the far north.

MAP KEY

POPULATION
- ■ above 5 million
- ■ 1 million to 5 million
- ◉ 500,000 to 1 million
- ◎ 100,000 to 500,000
- ⊕ 50,000 to 100,000
- ○ 10,000 to 50,000
- ● Country capital

SCALE 1:15,500,000
(projection: Lambert Azimuthal Equal Area)

Km
0 50 100 200 300 400 500 600 700 800 900 1000
Miles
0 50 100 200 300 400 500 600 700

Map place names: Denmark Strait, REYKJAVÍK, ICELAND, Arctic Circle, Faeroe Islands (to Denmark), Norwegian Sea, Shetland Islands, Outer Hebrides, Orkney Islands, Bergen, Stavanger, Kristiansand, NORWAY, Trondheim, SWEDEN, Gulf of Bothnia, FINLAND, Lake Ladoga, Murmansk, Tampere, Turku, HELSINKI, Åland, OSLO, Uppsala, Örebro, STOCKHOLM, TALLINN, ESTONIA, St Petersburg, Vänern, Vättern, Gotland, Baltic Sea, RIGA, LATVIA, Western Dvina, Gothenburg, Jönköping, Ventspils, Liepāja, LITHUANIA, Vitsyebsk, SCOTLAND, Aberdeen, Dundee, Glasgow, NORTHERN IRELAND, Edinburgh, North Sea, Ålborg, DENMARK, Helsingborg, COPENHAGEN, Odense, Malmö, RUSS. FED. (Kaliningrad), Kaliningrad, Gdańsk, Kaunas, VILNIUS, MINSK, Babruysk, BELORUSSIA, Homyel, REPUBLIC OF IRELAND, Belfast, Isle of Man (to UK), DUBLIN, UNITED KINGDOM, Liverpool, Leeds, Manchester, Sheffield, WALES, Birmingham, Cardiff, ENGLAND, Newcastle upon Tyne, Groningen, Hamburg, Bremen, Elbe, Bydgoszcz, Poznań, Oder, Vistula, WARSAW, Brest, Łódź, POLAND, Wrocław, Kraków, L'viv, UKRAINE, KIEV, LONDON, Southampton, Thames, AMSTERDAM, THE HAGUE, NETH., Rotterdam, Nijmegen, Hannover, BERLIN, Leipzig, Dresden, PRAGUE, CZECH REPUBLIC, Chernivtsi, Dniester, MOLDAVIA, CHIŞINĂU, Channel Islands (to UK), English Channel, le Havre, Antwerp, BELGIUM, BRUSSELS, Liège, Düsseldorf, Bonn, GERMANY, Rhine, Frankfurt am Main, Nuremberg, Stuttgart, Strasbourg, LUXEMBOURG, Seine, PARIS, Orléans, Munich, Salzburg, VIENNA, BRATISLAVA, SLOVAKIA, Győr, Miskolc, Cluj-Napoca, ROMANIA, Braşov, Rennes, St-Nazaire, Nantes, Loire, FRANCE, Limoges, Lyon, Zürich, BERN, SWITZERLAND, Innsbruck, AUSTRIA, Alps, LIECHTENSTEIN, BUDAPEST, HUNGARY, BUCHAREST, Constanţa, Bordeaux, Toulouse, Marseille, Nice, Milan, Turin, Verona, Po, Venice, Trieste, LJUBLJANA, SLOVENIA, ZAGREB, CROATIA, BELGRADE, SERBIA, Danube, Ruse, A Coruña, Porto, Douro, Valladolid, Ebro, Zaragoza, ANDORRA LA VELLA, ANDORRA, Genoa, Bologna, Florence, SAN MARINO, MONACO, Corsica, Pisa, VATICAN CITY, ROME, Adriatic Sea, BOS. & HERZ., SARAJEVO, Mostar, YUGOSLAVIA, MONTENEGRO, SOFIA, BULGARIA, Varna, Burgas, Pyrenees, Rhône, PORTUGAL, LISBON, Setúbal, Tagus, MADRID, SPAIN, Barcelona, Valencia, Seville, Córdoba, Eivissa, Mallorca, Menorca, Palma, Murcia, Balearic Islands, Sardinia, ITALY, Tyrrhenian Sea, Naples, Bari, TIRANA, ALBANIA, SKOPJE, MACEDONIA, Larisa, Istanbul, TURKEY, Gibraltar (to UK), Cádiz, Málaga, Ceuta (to Spain), Melilla (to Spain), Mediterranean Sea, Palermo, Sicily, Catania, Messina, Cosenza, Cagliari, GREECE, Aegean Sea, Salonica, MALTA, VALLETTA, Ionian Sea, ATHENS, Piraeus, Irákleio, Crete, ATLANTIC OCEAN, Bay of Biscay

N O P Q R S T U V W X Y Z

Overcoming natural barriers, the Brenner Autobahn, one of the main routes across the Alps, links Innsbruck in Austria with Verona in Italy.

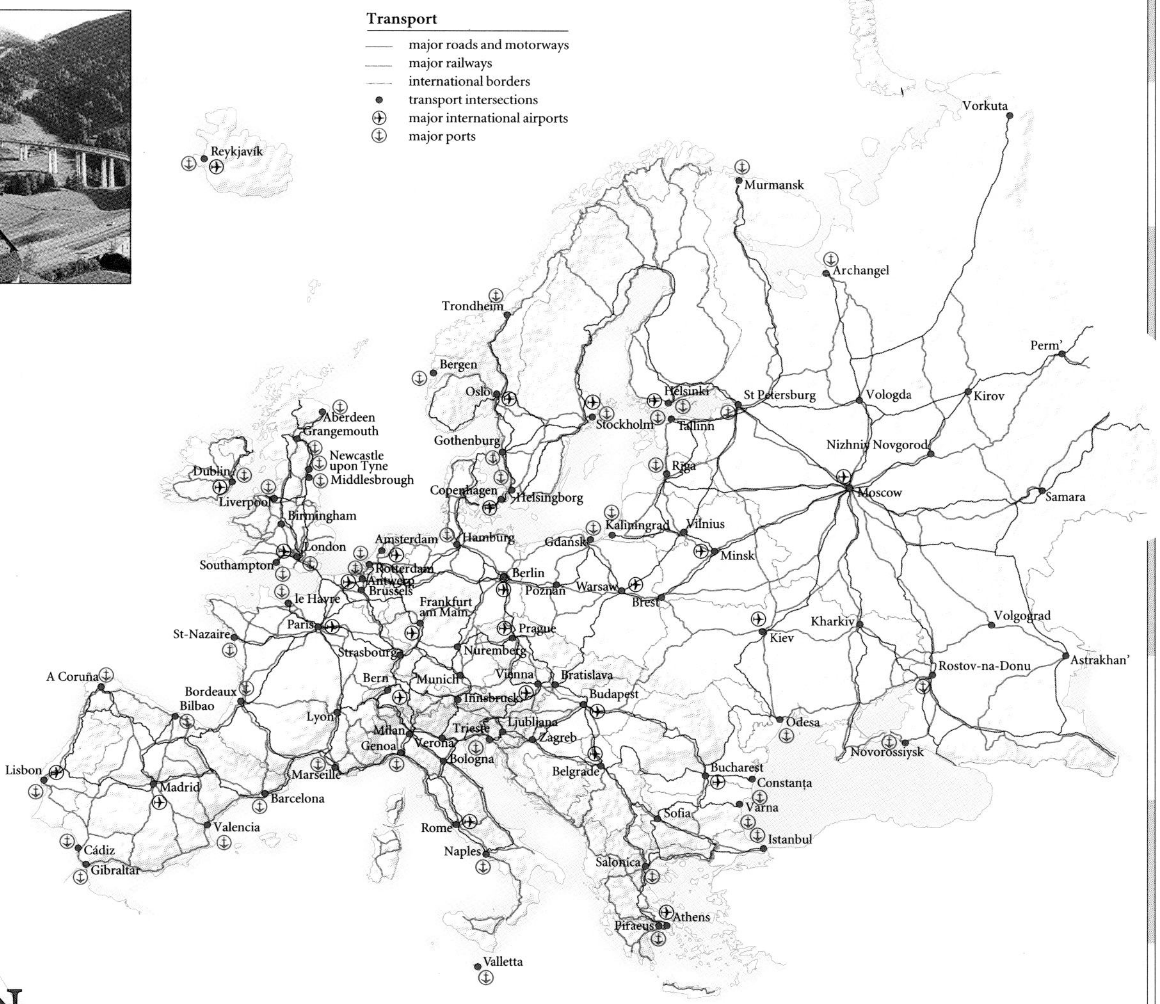

Transport
- major roads and motorways
- major railways
- international borders
- ● transport intersections
- ⊕ major international airports
- ⊕ major ports

Reykjavík

Vorkuta

Murmansk

Archangel

Novaya Zemlya

Kara Sea

Perm'

Trondheim

Bergen

Oslo
Helsinki
St Petersburg
Vologda
Kirov

Aberdeen
Grangemouth
Gothenburg
Stockholm
Tallinn
Nizhniy Novgorod

Dublin
Liverpool
Newcastle upon Tyne
Middlesbrough
Copenhagen
Helsingborg
Riga
Moscow
Samara

Southampton
London
Birmingham
Amsterdam
Hamburg
Kaliningrad
Vilnius
Minsk

Le Havre
Rotterdam
Antwerp
Brussels
Berlin
Gdansk
Poznan
Warsaw
Brest
Volgograd

St-Nazaire
Paris
Frankfurt am Main
Prague
Kiev
Kharkiv
Astrakhan'

A Coruña
Bordeaux
Bilbao
Strasbourg
Nuremberg
Bern
Munich
Vienna
Bratislava
Budapest
Odesa
Rostov-na-Donu

Lyon
Innsbruck
Ljubljana
Zagreb
Bucharest
Novorossiysk

Lisbon
Genoa
Verona
Trieste
Belgrade
Constanța
Varna

Madrid
Marseille
Bologna
Sofia
Istanbul

Barcelona
Rome
Salonica

Cádiz
Valencia
Naples
Piraeus
Athens

Gibraltar

Valletta

White Sea

Arkhangel'sk

Lake Onega

Barents Sea

RUSSIAN FEDERATION

Ural Mountains

Vorkuta

Perm'

Kirov

Vologda

Ufa

Yaroslavl'

Kazan'

Nizhniy Novgorod

MOSCOW

Ul'yanovsk

Tol'yatti
Samara

Orenburg

Tula

KAZAKHSTAN

Saratov

Voronezh

Kharkiv

Volgograd

AINE

Dnipropetrovs'k

Donets'k

Rostov-na-Donu

Astrakhan'

Volga

Odesa

Sea of Azov

Stavropol'

Novorossiysk

Grozny

Simferopol'

Caucasus

Caspian Sea

GEORGIA

AZERBAIJAN

Black Sea

EY

The architecture of the Grand Place lies at the heart of Brussels – home city to one of the EU headquarters.

Transport

DESPITE ITS FRAGMENTED GEOGRAPHY and many natural frontiers, communications in Europe are well developed. Extensive motorway links allow rapid road transport, while high-speed rail connections like France's TGV (*Train à Grande Vitesse*), and the Channel Tunnel have improved rail travel. Outdated communication infrastructures in parts of eastern Europe, and insufficient transport links across the Alps, however, remain weak parts of the network.

Languages

THERE ARE THREE MAIN EUROPEAN language groups: Germanic languages predominate in central and northern Europe; Romance languages in western and Mediterranean Europe and Romania; while Slavic languages are spoken in eastern Europe and the Russian Federation. Isolated pockets of local languages, such as Basque and Gaelic, persist and frequently provide a focus for national identity.

Language groups
- Turkic
- Albanian
- Finnic/Ugric
- Germanic
- Slavic
- Romance
- Basque
- Baltic
- Celtic
- Greek

ICELANDIC

FAEROESE

NORWEGIAN
SWEDISH
FINNISH
LAPPISH (SAMI)
SWEDISH
RUSSIA

GAELIC
ENGLISH
ESTONIAN
LATVIAN
LITHUANIAN
RUSSIAN

IRISH
ENGLISH
DANISH
BELORUSSIAN

WELSH
FRISIAN
DUTCH
GERMAN
POLISH
UKRAINIAN

BRETON
FRENCH
GERMAN
CZECH
SLOVAK

GALICIAN
FRENCH
ITALIAN
SLOVENE
HUNGARIAN
ROMANIAN

PORTUGUESE
SPANISH
BASQUE
CATALAN
SERBO-CROAT
BULGARIAN
MACEDONIAN
TURKISH

FRENCH
CATALAN
ITALIAN
ALBANIAN
GREEK

ITALIAN

MALTESE

EUROPEAN RESOURCES

Europe's large tracts of fertile, accessible land, combined with its generally temperate climate, have allowed a greater percentage of land to be used for agricultural purposes than in any other continent. Extensive coal and iron ore deposits were used to create steel and manufacturing industries during the 19th and 20th centuries. Today, although natural resources have been widely exploited, and heavy industry is of declining importance, the growth of hi-tech and service industries has enabled Europe to maintain its wealth.

INDUSTRY

EUROPE'S WEALTH WAS GENERATED by the rise of industry and colonial exploitation during the 19th century. The mining of abundant natural resources made Europe the industrial centre of the world. Adaptation has been essential in the changing world economy, and a move to service-based industries has been widespread except in eastern Europe, where heavy industry still dominates.

Countries like Hungary are still struggling to modernize inefficient factories left over from extensive, centrally-planned industrialization during the communist era.

Other power sources are becoming more attractive as fossil fuels run out; 16% of Europe's electricity is now provided by hydro-electric power.

Frankfurt am Main is an example of a modern service-based city. The skyline is dominated by headquarters from the worlds of banking and commerce.

STANDARD OF LIVING

LIVING STANDARDS IN WESTERN EUROPE are among the highest in the world, although there is a growing sector of homeless, jobless people. Eastern Europeans have lower overall standards of living – a legacy of stagnated economies.

Standard of Living
(UN Human Development Index)

low

high

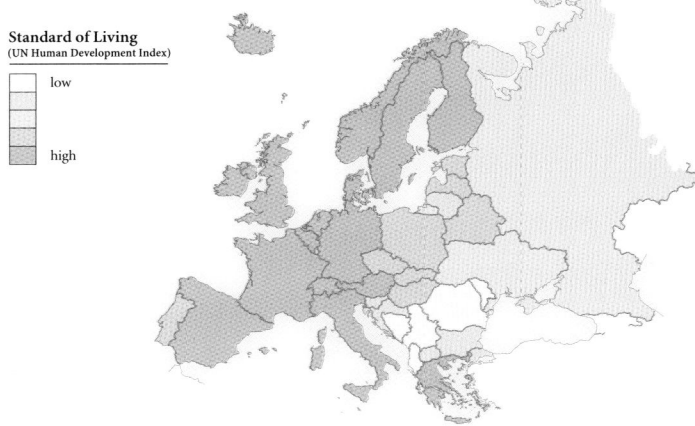

Skiing brings millions of tourists to the slopes each year, which means that even unproductive, marginal land is used to create wealth in the French, Swiss, Italian and Austrian Alps.

GNP per capita (US$)

below 1999
2000–4999
5000–9999
10,000–19,999
20,000–24,999
above 25,000

Industry

- aerospace
- brewing
- car/vehicle manufacture
- chemicals
- defence
- electronics
- finance
- food processing
- hi-tech industry
- iron & steel
- pharmaceuticals
- printing & publishing
- shipbuilding
- textiles
- timber processing
- wine
- coal
- oil
- gas
- industrial cities
- major industrial areas

ATLANTIC OCEAN

Norwegian Sea

Faeroe Islands (to Denmark)

Reykjavík · ICELAND

Barents Sea

Ostrov Kolguyev

Novaya Zemlya

Murmansk

Archangel

Trondheim

Bergen

Oslo

NORWAY

SWEDEN

Stockholm

Gothenburg

Gulf of Bothnia

FINLAND

Turku · Helsinki

St Petersburg

RUSSIAN FEDERATION

Perm'

Cherepovets

Yaroslavl

Kazán

Ufa

Ivanovo

Nizhniy Novgorod

Moscow

Tol'yatti

Samara

Ryazan'

Saratov

Tula

Volgograd

Glasgow

Belfast

REPUBLIC OF IRELAND

Dublin

Isle of Man (to UK)

Liverpool

Manchester

UNITED KINGDOM

Newcastle upon Tyne

North Sea

DENMARK

Copenhagen

Malmö

Baltic Sea

Tallinn

ESTONIA

Riga

LATVIA

LITHUANIA

Vilnius

RUSS. FED. (Kaliningrad)

Minsk

BELORUSSIA

Voronezh

Kursk

Kiev

Kharkiv

UKRAINE

Dnipropetrovs'k

Kryvyy Rih

Donets'k

Rostov-na-Donu

Cardiff

Birmingham

London

Channel Islands (to UK)

Amsterdam

Rotterdam

NETH.

Antwerp

BELG.

Brussels

Liège

Cologne

Hamburg

Berlin

Poznań

Łódź

Warsaw

POLAND

GERMANY

Leipzig

Dresden

Katowice

Kraków

CZECH REP.

Prague

SLOVAKIA

Bratislava

Lille

Rouen

Paris

Metz

Strasbourg

Frankfurt am Main

LUX.

Nantes

FRANCE

Bay of Biscay

Bordeaux

Lyon

Toulouse

Zürich

SWITZ.

LIECH.

Munich

Linz

Vienna

AUSTRIA

Budapest

HUNGARY

SLVN.

Zagreb

CROATIA

Turin

Milan

Venice

Genoa

Bologna

ITALY

MONACO

SAN MARINO

Corsica

VATICAN CITY

Rome

Sardinia

Naples

Taranto

Palermo

Sicily

Tyrrhenian Sea

A Coruña

Porto

PORTUGAL

Lisbon

SPAIN

Madrid

Bilbao

ANDORRA

Barcelona

Marseille

Seville

Gibraltar (to UK)

Ceuta (to Spain)

Melilla (to Spain)

MOROCCO

Mediterranean Sea

Balearic Islands

MOLDOVA

ROMANIA

Ploești

Bucharest

Constanța

Belgrade

YUGOSLAVIA

BOSNIA & HERZ.

Sofia

BULGARIA

Varna

Black Sea

Odesa

Caspian Sea

GEORGIA

AZERBAIJAN

KAZAKHSTAN

ALBANIA

MACED.

Salonica

GREECE

Piraeus

Athens

Istanbul

TURKEY

Aegean Sea

Ionian Sea

MALTA

Crete

Adriatic Sea

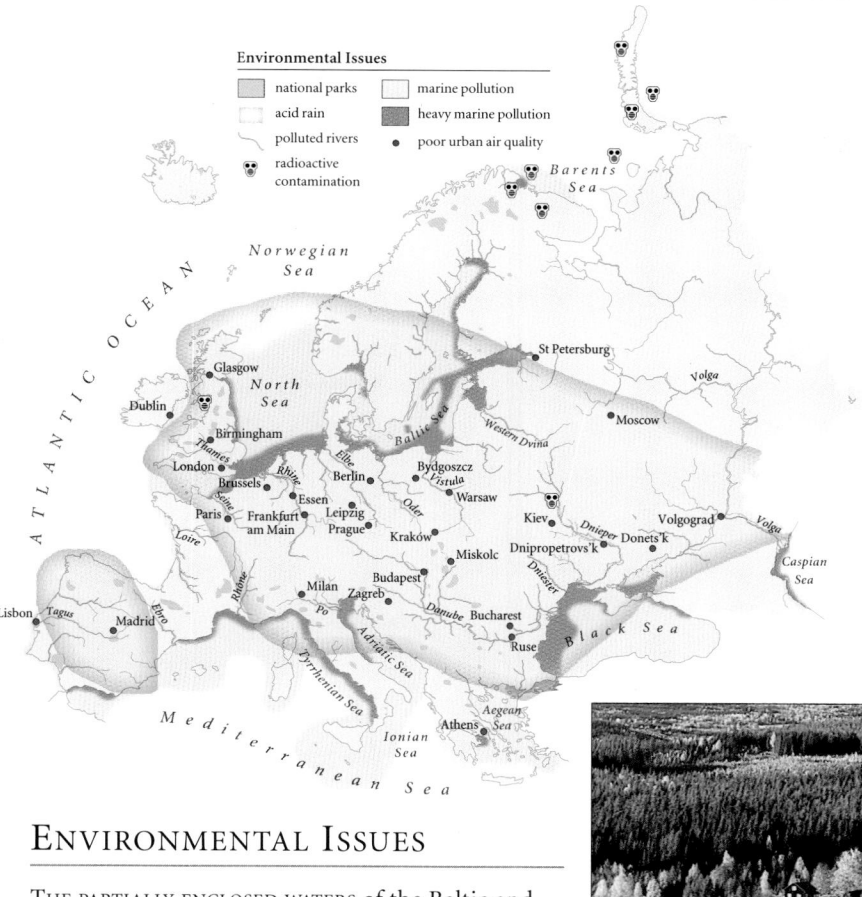

Environmental Issues

national parks
acid rain
polluted rivers
radioactive contamination
marine pollution
heavy marine pollution
• poor urban air quality

MINERAL RESOURCES

FOSSIL FUELS ARE EUROPE'S main mineral resource, although fuel demand far outstrips production. Sizeable coal reserves remain in the Donbass in Ukraine, Germany's Ruhr Valley, Poland, and in the British Isles. Oil and gas reserves are found mainly in the North Sea, and in the Volga Basin.

The valuable oil and gas reserves in the North Sea were first discovered in the early 1960s, and are exploited by the UK, Denmark, Germany and Norway.

Mineral Resources

oil field
gas field
coal field

bauxite
iron
lead
mercury △
potassium ▲
uranium
zinc

ENVIRONMENTAL ISSUES

THE PARTIALLY ENCLOSED WATERS of the Baltic and Mediterranean seas have become heavily polluted, while the Barents Sea is contaminated with spent nuclear fuel from Russia's navy. Acid rain, caused by emissions from factories and power stations, is actively destroying northern forests. As a result, pressure is growing to safeguard Europe's natural environment and prevent further deterioration.

Coniferous forest covers vast swathes of northern Scandinavia and the Russian Federation. Pollutants from other parts of Europe mixing with rainfall are causing defoliation and serious damage to many forests.

The Camargue in the Rhône Delta, southern France, is a protected wetland area, famous for its native population of white horses, and unique bird and plant life.

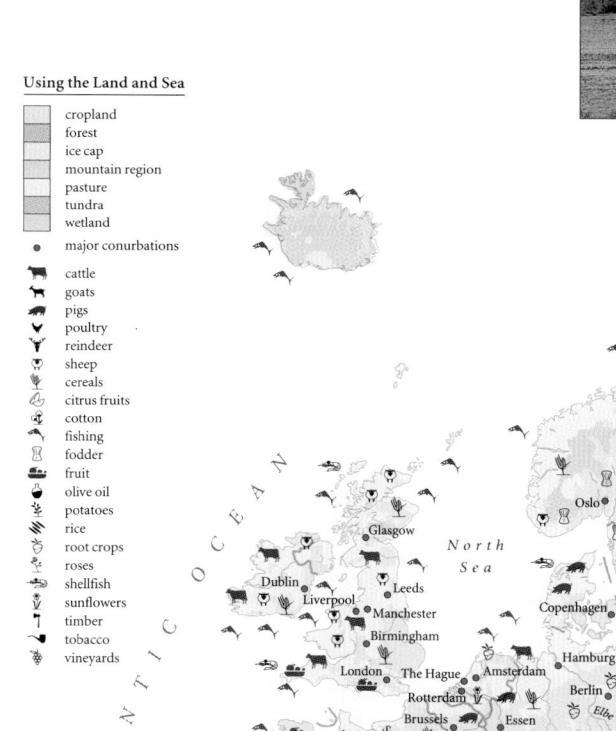

USING THE LAND AND SEA

EUROPE'S SWELLING URBAN POPULATION and the outward expansion of many cities has created acute competition for land. Despite this, European resourcefulness has maximized land potential, and over half of Europe's land is still used for a wide variety of agricultural purposes. Land in northern Europe is used for cattle-rearing, pasture, and arable crops. Towards the Mediterranean, the mild climate allows the growing of grapes for wine; olives, sunflowers, tobacco and citrus fruits. EU subsidies, however, have resulted in massive overproduction and a land 'set-aside' policy has been introduced.

Bulgarian roses are one of the many diverse crops grown in Europe. Rose oil, extracted from the petals, is used in perfume making.

Using the Land and Sea

cropland
forest
ice cap
mountain region
pasture
tundra
wetland
• major conurbations

cattle
goats
pigs
poultry
reindeer
sheep
cereals
citrus fruits
cotton
fishing
fodder
fruit
olive oil
potatoes
rice
root crops
roses
shellfish
sunflowers
timber
tobacco
vineyards

Lowland pastures are used for dairy farming. Good transport links and refrigeration allow fresh milk to be distributed throughout Europe.

SCANDINAVIA, FINLAND & ICELAND

DENMARK, NORWAY, SWEDEN, FINLAND, ICELAND

JUTTING INTO THE ARCTIC CIRCLE, this northern swathe of Europe has some of the continent's harshest environments, but benefits from great reserves of oil, gas and natural evergreen forests. While most early settlers came from the south, migrants to Finland came from the east, giving it a distinct language and culture. Since the late 19th century, the Scandinavian states have developed strong egalitarian traditions. Today, their welfare benefits systems are among the most extensive in the world, and standards of living are high. The Lapps, or Sami, maintain their traditional lifestyle in the northern regions of Norway, Sweden and Finland.

THE LANDSCAPE

GLACIERS UP TO 10,000 ft (3000 m) deep covered most of Scandinavia and Finland during the last Ice Age. The effects of glaciation mark the entire landscape, from the mountains to the lowlands, across the tundra landscape of Lapland, and the lake districts of Sweden and Finland.

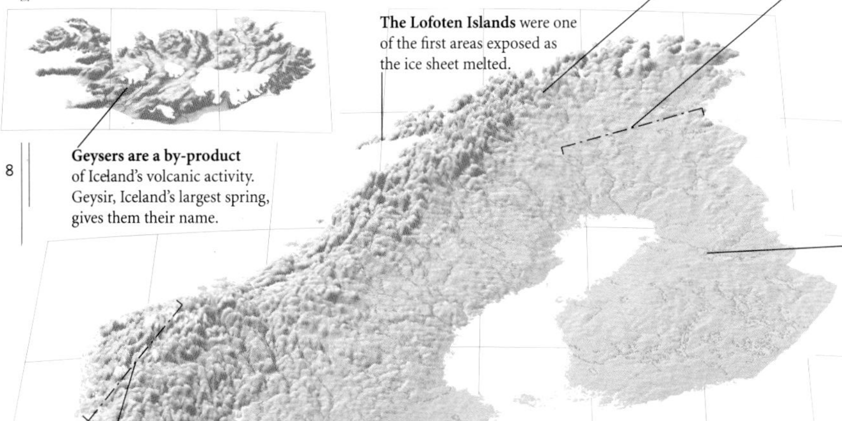

Geysers are a by-product of Iceland's volcanic activity. Geysir, Iceland's largest spring, gives them their name.

The Lofoten Islands were one of the first areas exposed as the ice sheet melted.

Halti Mountain is Finland's highest point, at 4356 ft (1328 m).

Lapland, north of the Arctic Circle, is an area of undulating fells and plains known as tundra. The subsoil is permanently frozen and therefore impermeable. There are many peat bogs. Pools reappear in the summer when the surface thaws.

Finland's landscape was fashioned by ice action. Glaciers gouged out its distinctive shallow lake basins, such as Oulujärvi, and left debris called moraines in their wake.

Oulujärvi

Area of maximum yearly uplift 0.3 in/yr (9 mm/yr)

Slower rates of uplift 0.1 in/yr (3 mm/yr)

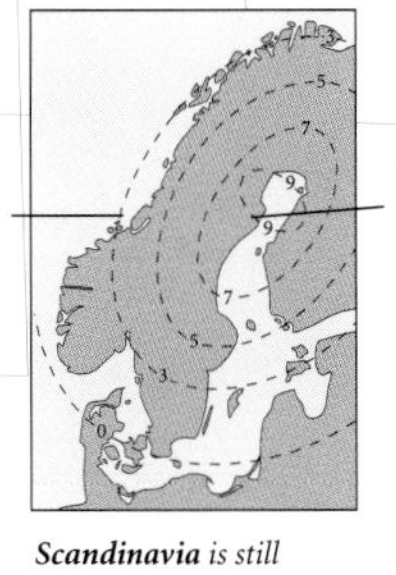

Scandinavia is still recovering from the last Ice Age, when ice depressed the land by 2000 ft (600 m). This gradual uplift is known as isostatic rebound.

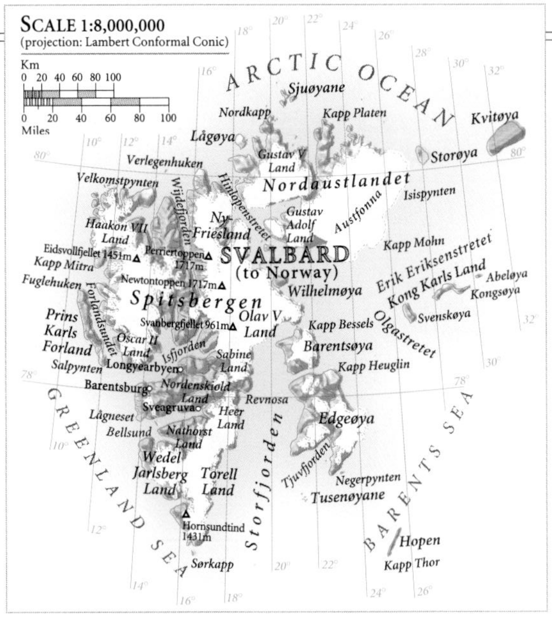

Sjælland coast

On the coast of Sjælland, the cliffs have been eroded by the sea, exposing layers of chalk and limestone.

The fjords on the western coast of Norway were once gentle river valleys. Their deep floors and steep sides were carved out by glaciers during the last Ice Age, and they were later flooded by the sea.

Fjords

USING THE LAND AND SEA

THE COLD CLIMATE, short growing season, poorly developed soil, steep slopes, and exposure to high winds across northern regions means that most agriculture is concentrated, with the population, in the south. Most of Finland and much of Norway and Sweden are covered by dense forests of pine, spruce and birch, which supply the timber industries.

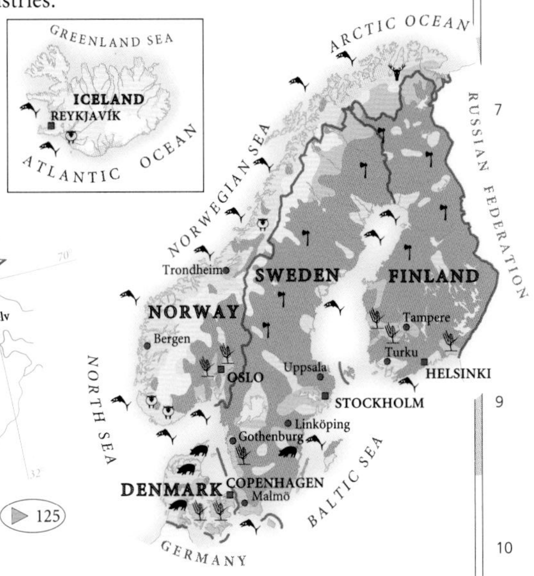

Land use and agricultural distribution

- fishing
- pigs
- sheep
- timber
- capital cities
- major towns
- pasture
- cropland
- forest
- mountain region
- tundra

THE URBAN/RURAL POPULATION DIVIDE

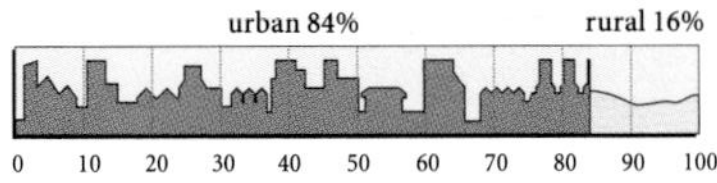

urban 84% — rural 16%

POPULATION DENSITY	TOTAL LAND AREA
269 people per sq mile (104 people per sq km)	329,380 sq miles (853,090 sq km)

SCALE 1:8,000,000
(projection: Lambert Conformal Conic)

SCALE 1:5,000,000
(projection: Lambert Conformal Conic)

(same scale as main map)

Svalbard map labels

ARCTIC OCEAN

Kvitøya
Storøya
Siøvane
Kapp Platen
Isøpynten
Nordaustlandet
Kapp Mitra
Gustav Adolf Land
Abeløya
Kongsøya
Svenskøya
Erik Eriksenstretet
Karls Land
BARENTS SEA
Nordkapp
Lågøya
Storfjorden
SVALBARD
(to Norway)
Spitsbergen
Hopen
Kapp Thor
Prins Karls Forland

ATLANTIC OCEAN

GREENLAND SEA
Denmark Strait
ICELAND
REYKJAVIK
VESTURLAND
NORDURLAND VESTRA
NORDURLAND EYSTRA
AUSTURLAND
SUDURLAND
Arctic Circle

RUSSIAN FEDERATION

ARCTIC OCEAN
FINLAND
HELSINKI
Tampere
Turku
SWEDEN
STOCKHOLM
Linköping
Uppsala
NORWAY
OSLO
Göteborg
Trondheim
Bergen
DENMARK COPENHAGEN
Malmö
GERMANY
NORTH SEA
BALTIC SEA
NORWEGIAN SEA

GREENLAND SEA
ICELAND
REYKJAVIK
ATLANTIC OCEAN

▲125

BARENTS SEA
ARCTIC OCEAN
RUSSIAN FED
Nordkapp (North Cape)
FINNMARK
Tromsø
TROMS
NORDLAND
Lofoten Vesterålen
LAPPI
Oulujärvi
LAPLAND
NORRBOTTEN

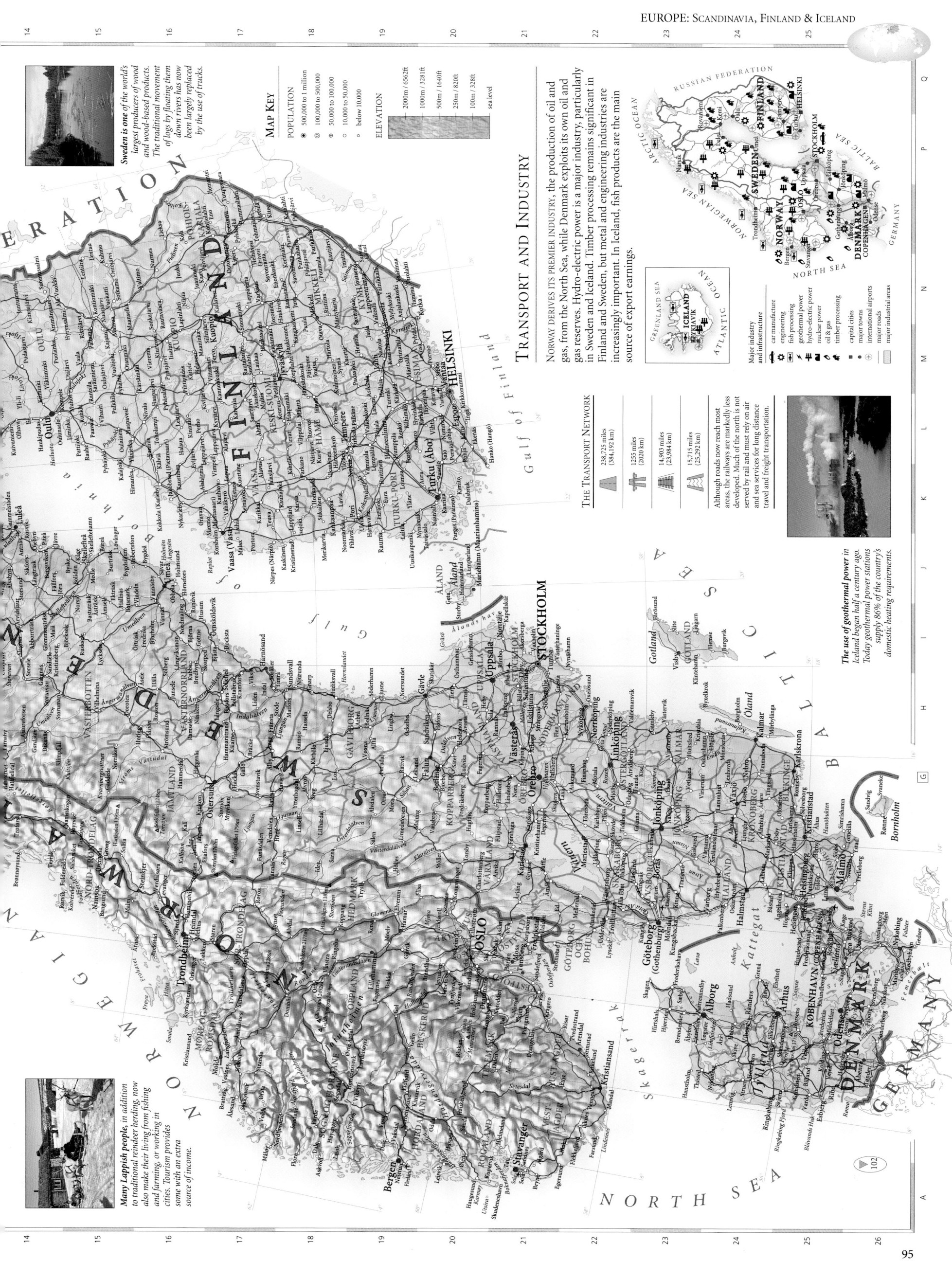

Sweden is one of the world's largest producers of wood and wood-based products. The traditional movement of logs by floating them down rivers has now been largely replaced by the use of trucks.

MAP KEY

POPULATION
- ◉ 500,000 to 1 million
- ◎ 100,000 to 500,000
- ⊕ 50,000 to 100,000
- ○ 10,000 to 50,000
- ∘ below 10,000

ELEVATION
- 2000m / 6562ft
- 1000m / 3281ft
- 500m / 1640ft
- 250m / 820ft
- 100m / 328ft
- sea level

TRANSPORT AND INDUSTRY

Norway derives its premier industry, the production of oil and gas, from the North Sea, while Denmark exploits its own oil and gas reserves. Hydro-electric power is a major industry, particularly in Sweden and Iceland. Timber processing remains significant in Finland and Sweden, but metal and engineering industries are increasingly important. In Iceland, fish products are the main source of export earnings.

THE TRANSPORT NETWORK

- 238,725 miles (384,192 km)
- 1255 miles (2020 km)
- 14,903 miles (23,984 km)
- 15,715 miles (25,292 km)

Although roads now reach most areas, the railways are markedly less developed. Much of the north is not served by rail and must rely on air and sea services for long distance travel and freight transportation.

Major industry and infrastructure
- car manufacture
- engineering
- fish processing
- geothermal power
- hydro-electric power
- nuclear power
- oil & gas
- timber processing
- capital cities
- major cities
- major towns
- international airports
- major roads
- major industrial areas

The use of geothermal power in Iceland began half a century ago. Today geothermal power stations supply 86% of the country's domestic heating requirements.

Many Lappish people, in addition to traditional reindeer herding, now also make their living from fishing and farming, or working in cities. Tourism provides some with an extra source of income.

SOUTHERN SCANDINAVIA

SOUTHERN NORWAY, SOUTHERN SWEDEN, DENMARK

SCANDINAVIA'S ECONOMIC AND POLITICAL HUB is the more habitable and accessible southern region. Many of the area's major cities are on the southern coasts, including Oslo and Stockholm, the capitals of Norway and Sweden. In Denmark, most of the population and the capital, Copenhagen, are located on its many islands. A cultural unity links the three Scandinavian countries. Their main languages, Danish, Swedish and Norwegian, are mutually intelligible, and they all retain their monarchies, although the parliaments have legislative control.

USING THE LAND

AGRICULTURE IN SOUTHERN SCANDINAVIA is highly mechanized although farms are small. Denmark is the most intensively farmed country and its western pastureland is used mainly for pig farming. Cereal crops including wheat, barley and oats, predominate in eastern Denmark and in the far south of Sweden. Southern Norway and Sweden have large tracts of forest which are exploited for logging.

THE URBAN/RURAL POPULATION DIVIDE

urban 87%   rural 13%

TOTAL LAND AREA
173,487 sq miles
(456,564 sq km)

POPULATION DENSITY
152 people per sq mile
(61 people per sq km)

Land use and agricultural distribution

capital cities
major towns

pasture
cropland
forest
mountain region

cattle
pigs
sheep
cereals
fodder
root crops
timber

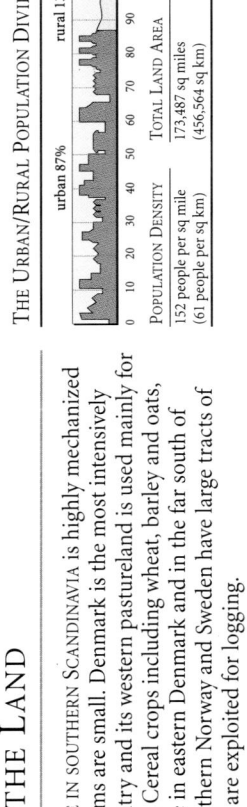

In Norway winters are longer and colder inland than in coastal areas, where the warm current of the North Atlantic Drift moderates the climate.

THE LANDSCAPE

SOUTHERN SCANDINAVIA, with the exception of Norway, has a flatter terrain than the rest of the region. Denmark and southern Sweden are both extensions of the North European Plain. In this area, because of glacial deposition rather than erosion, the soils are deeper and more fertile.

Acid rain, caused by industrial pollution carried north from elsewhere in Europe, harms plant and animal life in Scandinavian forests and lakes. The region's surface rocks lack lime to neutralize the acid, so making the problem more serious.

In the past, glaciers such as this one in Olden, Norway, were much larger. Today, many are retreating to yield the spectacular glacial scenery.

Limestone pillars eroded by the sea dot the coast of Gotland and surrounding islands.

Distinctive low ridges, called eskers, are found across southern Sweden. They are formed from sand and gravel deposits left by retreating glaciers.

The lakes of southern Sweden remain from a period when the land was completely flooded. As the ice melted, the land rose, leaving lakes in shallow, ice-scoured depressions. Sweden has over 90,000 lakes.

The peak of Glittertind in the Jotunheimen Mountains is 8044 ft (2452 m) high.

Vänern in Sweden is the largest lake in Scandinavia. It covers an area of 2080 sq miles (5390 sq km).

Denmark's flat and fertile soils are formed on glacial deposits between 100–160 ft (30–50 m) deep.

Olden

Sognefjorden

When the ice retreated the valley was flooded by the sea

Old valley floor

Erosion by glaciers deepened existing river valleys

Sea level

Sognefjorden is the deepest of Norway's many fjords. It drops to 4291 ft (1308 m) below sea level.

MAP KEY

POPULATION
- ● 500,000 to 1 million
- ◉ 100,000 to 500,000
- ⊕ 50,000 to 100,000
- ○ 10,000 to 50,000
- ∘ below 10,000

ELEVATION
- 2000m / 6562ft
- 1000m / 3281ft
- 500m / 1640ft
- 250m / 820ft
- 100m / 328ft
- sea level

SCALE 1:2,900,000
(projection: Lambert Conformal Conic)

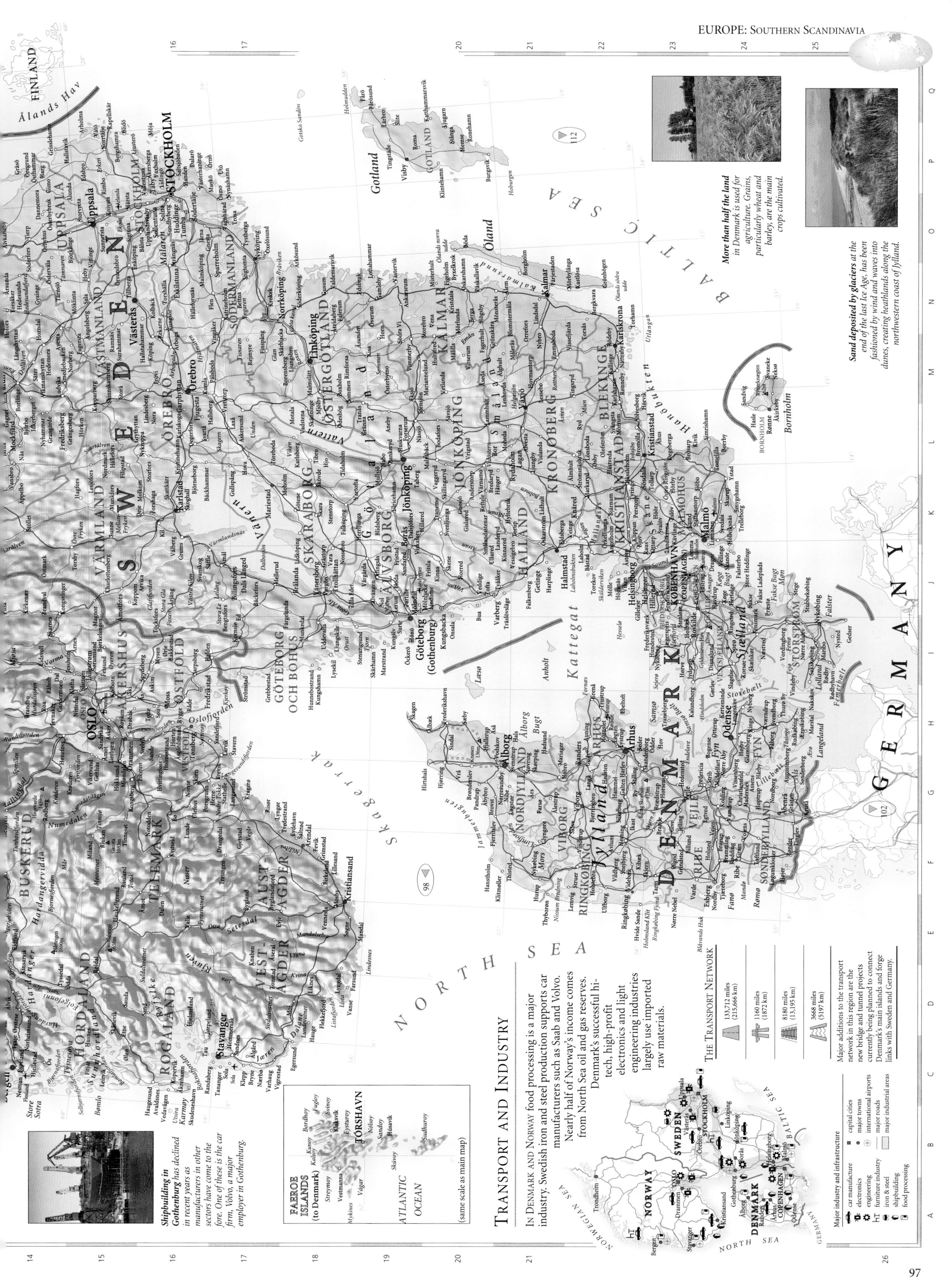

More than half the land in Denmark is used for agriculture. Grains, particularly wheat and barley, are the main crops cultivated.

Sand deposited by glaciers at the end of the last Ice Age, has been fashioned by wind and waves into dunes, creating heathlands along the northwestern coast of Jylland.

Shipbuilding in Gothenburg has declined in recent years as manufacturers in other sectors have come to the fore. One of these is the car firm, Volvo, a major employer in Gothenburg.

TRANSPORT AND INDUSTRY

In Denmark and Norway food processing is a major industry. Swedish iron and steel production supports car manufacturers such as Saab and Volvo. Nearly half of Norway's income comes from North Sea oil and gas reserves. Denmark's successful hi-tech, high-profit electronics and light engineering industries largely use imported raw materials.

THE TRANSPORT NETWORK

- 133,712 miles (215,666 km)
- 1160 miles (1872 km)
- 8180 miles (13,195 km)
- 3668 miles (5197 km)

Major additions to the transport network in this region are the new bridge and tunnel projects currently being planned to connect Denmark's main islands and forge links with Sweden and Germany.

FAEROE ISLANDS (to Denmark)

TORSHAVN

ATLANTIC OCEAN

(same scale as main map)

Major industry and infrastructure

- car manufacture
- electronics
- engineering
- furniture industry
- iron & steel
- shipbuilding
- food processing
- capital cities
- major towns
- international airports
- major roads
- major industrial areas

97

THE BRITISH ISLES

UNITED KINGDOM, REPUBLIC OF IRELAND

THE BRITISH ISLES have for centuries played a central role in European and world history. England, Wales, Scotland and Northern Ireland together form the United Kingdom (UK), while the southern portion of Ireland is an independent country, self-governing since 1921. Although England has tended to be the politically and economically dominant partner in the UK, the Scots, Welsh and Irish maintain independent cultures, distinct national identities and languages. Southeastern England is the most densely populated part of this crowded region, with over nine million people living in and around the London area.

TRANSPORT AND INDUSTRY

THE BRITISH ISLES' INDUSTRIAL BASE was founded primarily on coal, iron and textiles, based largely in the north. Today, the most productive sectors include hi-tech industries clustered mainly in southeastern England, chemicals, finance and the service sector, particularly tourism.

Major industry and infrastructure

- ⚙ car manufacture
- chemicals
- engineering
- hi-tech industry
- iron & steel
- tourism

- capital cities
- • major towns
- ✈ international airports
- — major roads
- ▢ major industrial areas

The UK's congested roads have become a major focus of environmental concern in recent years. No longer an island, the UK was finally linked to continental Europe by the Channel Tunnel in 1994.

THE TRANSPORT NETWORK

- 278,898 miles (448,844 km)
- 1927 miles (3101 km)
- 11,514 miles (18,530 km)
- 2255 miles (3629 km)

Clew Bay in western Ireland, is characteristic of the heavily indented west coast, where deep wide-mouthed bays separate the mountains of Mayo, Donegal and Kerry as they thrust out into the Atlantic Ocean.

The valley of Glen Coe in the Scottish Highlands is a U-shaped valley, typical of the north and west of the British Isles, where glaciers shaped much of the landscape.

THE LANDSCAPE

RUGGED UPLANDS dominate the landscape of Scotland, Wales and northern England. All the peaks in the British Isles over 4000 ft (1219 m) lie in highland Scotland. Lowland England rises into several ranges of rolling hills, including the older Mendips, and the Cotswolds and the Chilterns, which were formed at the same time as the Alps in southern Europe.

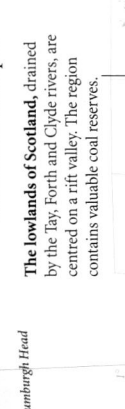

The Pennines, sometimes called 'the backbone of England', are formed of limestones and grits.

Ullswater in the Lake District fills a deep valley formed by glacial erosion.

The Fens are a low-lying area reclaimed from the sea.

Chiltern Hills

The Cotswold Hills are characterized by a series of limestone ridges overlooking clay vales.

Durdle Door

Coastal erosion around the British Isles forms striking features such as this limestone arch, Durdle Door in Dorset.

The lowlands of Scotland, drained by the Tay, Forth and Clyde rivers, are centred on a rift valley. The region contains valuable coal reserves.

Ben Nevis at 4409 ft (1343 m) is the highest peak in the UK.

Lake District

Mendip Hills

Dartmoor, studded with tors, is an exposed part of a vast granite dome, formed when molten rock intruded into the Earth's crust.

Snowdon is the highest mountain in England and Wales reaching 3556 ft (1085 m).

Black Ven, Lyme Regis

Much of the south coast is subject to landslides. Following rain, porous sandstones feed water into the underlying less permeable clays which then crumble and slide into the sea.

- Cracks
- Sandstone
- Clay
- Limestone
- Water
- Mudslide
- Sea

Over 600 islands, mostly uninhabited, lie west and north of the Scottish mainland.

Thousands of hexagonal basalt columns form Giant's Causeway on the north coast of Antrim. These were created by volcanic activity.

The British Isles have no large-scale river systems. The Shannon is the longest, at 230 miles (370 km).

Peat bogs dot the poorly-drained Irish lowlands.

MAP KEY

POPULATION
- ▪ above 5 million
- ▪ 1 million to 5 million
- ◉ 500,000 to 1 million
- ⊕ 100,000 to 500,000
- ⊕ 50,000 to 100,000
- ○ 10,000 to 50,000
- ○ below 10,000

ELEVATION
- 1000m / 3281ft
- 500m / 1640ft
- 250m / 820ft
- 100m / 328ft
- sea level

Map labels

Shetland Islands

Orkney Islands

SCOTLAND

Aberdeen

Dundee

Edinburgh

Glasgow

ATLANTIC OCEAN

NORTH SEA

English Channel

UNITED KINGDOM

LONDON

REPUBLIC OF IRELAND

DUBLIN

Belfast

Cardiff

Bristol

Liverpool

Manchester

Leeds

Birmingham

Nottingham

Oxford

Sheffield

Newcastle upon Tyne

Norwich

Cork

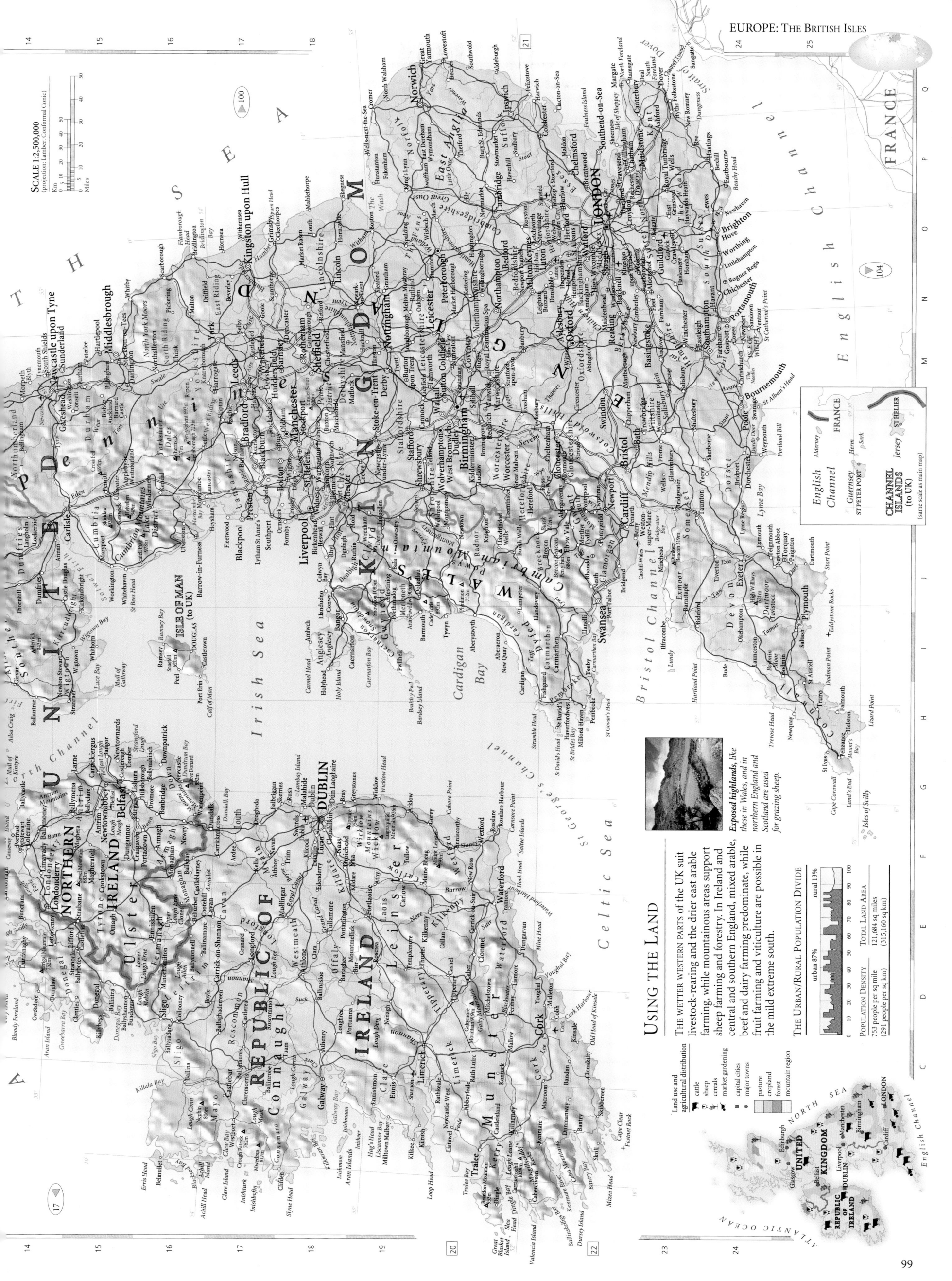

SCALE 1:2 500 000
(projection: Lambert Conformal Conic)

Exposed highlands, like these in Wales, and in northern England and Scotland are used for grazing sheep.

USING THE LAND

THE WETTER WESTERN PARTS of the UK suit livestock-rearing and the drier east arable farming, while mountainous areas support sheep farming and forestry. In Ireland and central and southern England, mixed arable, beef and dairy farming predominate, while fruit farming and viticulture are possible in the mild extreme south.

THE URBAN/RURAL POPULATION DIVIDE

urban 87%   rural 13%

POPULATION DENSITY	TOTAL LAND AREA
753 people per sq mile	121,684 sq miles
(291 people per sq km)	(315,160 sq km)

Land use and agricultural distribution
- cattle
- sheep
- cereals
- market gardening
- capital cities
- major towns
- pasture
- cropland
- forest
- mountain region

CHANNEL ISLANDS (to UK)
(same scale as main map)

English Channel
Alderney
Guernsey
ST PETER PORT
Herm
Sark
Jersey ST HELIER
FRANCE

THE LOW COUNTRIES

BELGIUM, LUXEMBOURG, NETHERLANDS

ONE OF NORTHWESTERN EUROPE'S strategic crossroads, the Low Countries are united by a common history in which they have often been a battleground in European wars. For over a thousand years they were ruled by foreign powers. Even after they achieved independence, the three countries maintained close links, later forming the world's first totally free labour and goods market, the Benelux Economic Union, which became the core of the European Community (now the European Union or EU). These states have remained at the forefront of wider European co-operation; Brussels, The Hague and Luxembourg are hosts to major institutions of the EU.

THE LANDSCAPE

THE MAIN GEOGRAPHICAL REGIONS of the Netherlands are the northern glacial heathlands, the low-lying lands of the Rhine and Maas/Meuse, the reclaimed polders, and the dune coast and islands. Belgium includes part of the Ardennes, together with the coalfields on its northern flanks, and the fertile Flanders Plain.

The loess soils of the Flanders Plain in western Belgium provide excellent conditions for arable farming.

Uplifted and folded 220 million years ago, the Ardennes have since been reduced to relatively level plateaux, then sharply incised by rivers such as the Maas/Meuse.

Since the Middle Ages the people of the Netherlands have used ditches and drainage dykes to reclaim land from the sea. These reclaimed areas are known as polders.

Extensive sand dune systems along the coast have prevented flooding of the land. Behind the dunes, marshy land is drained to form polders, usable land suitable for agriculture.

Sand dunes

Sea
Dune system
Polder
Drainage ditch

Schoorl

Heathlands, like these at Schoorl, are found along the coast of the Netherlands. Much of the coast was breached by the sea in the 5th century, creating its distinctive inlets and islands.

One-third of the Netherlands lies below sea level and flooding is a constant threat. Barrages have been built across the mouths of many rivers to contain floodwaters.

The parallel valleys of the Maas/Meuse and Rhine rivers were created when the Rhine was deflected from its previous course by the ice sheet which formed during the last Ice Age.

Silts and sands eroded by the Rhine throughout its course are deposited to form a delta on the west coast of the Netherlands.

Hautes Fagnes is the highest part of Belgium. The bogs and streams in this upland region result from high rainfall and low temperatures.

Ardennes

TRANSPORT AND INDUSTRY

IN THE WESTERN NETHERLANDS, a massive, sprawling industrialized zone encompasses many new hi-tech and service industries. Belgium's central region has emerged as the country's light manufacturing and services centre. Luxembourg city is home to more than 160 banks and the European headquarters of many international companies.

THE TRANSPORT NETWORK

✈	155,154 miles (249,697 km)	✈	1065 miles (1714 km)
🛤	4280 miles (6888 km)	🛤	4369 miles (7031 km)

The Low Countries hold a key position on the North Sea, containing Europe's two largest ports, Rotterdam and Antwerp, which are connected to a comprehensive system of inland waterways.

Major industry and infrastructure
- ✈ aerospace
- 💲 finance
- ⚙ engineering
- 💻 hi-tech industry
- 💉 pharmaceuticals
- ✂ textiles
- ● capital cities
- ● major cities
- ● major towns
- ✈ international airports
- major roads
- major industrial areas

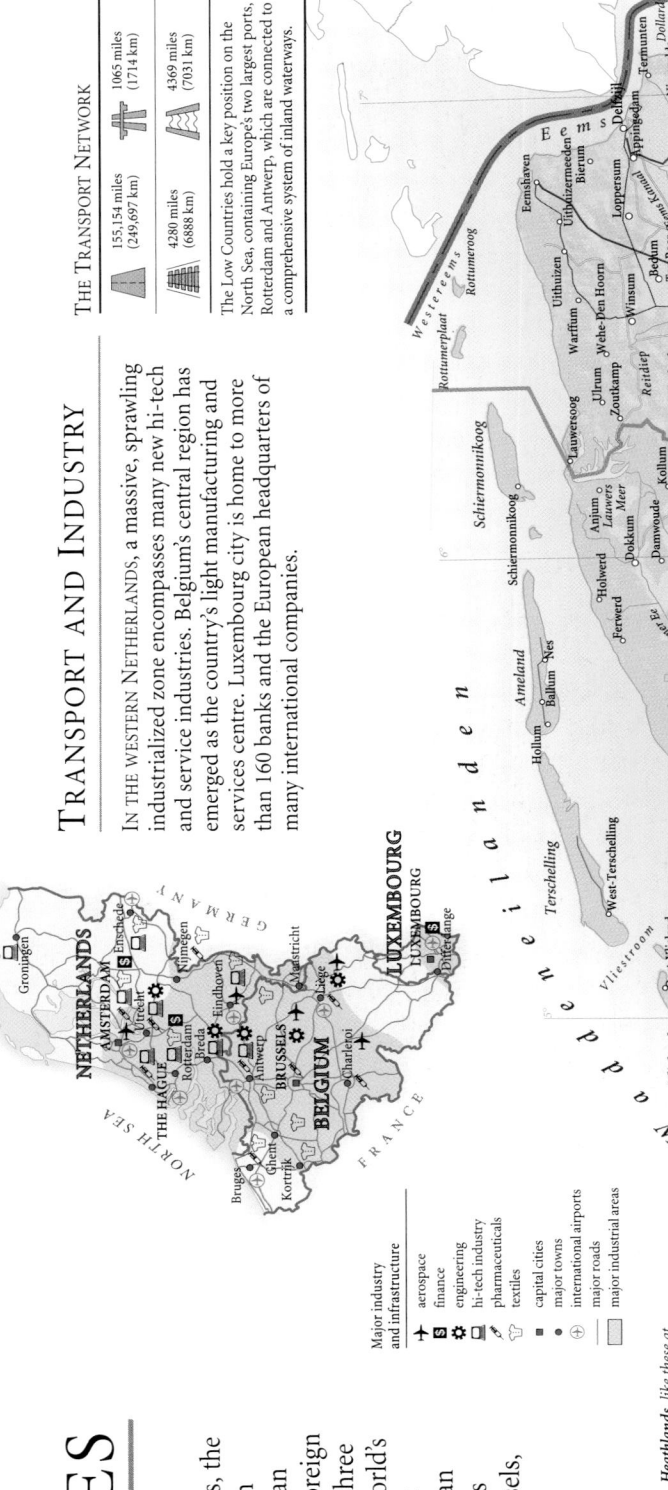

▲102

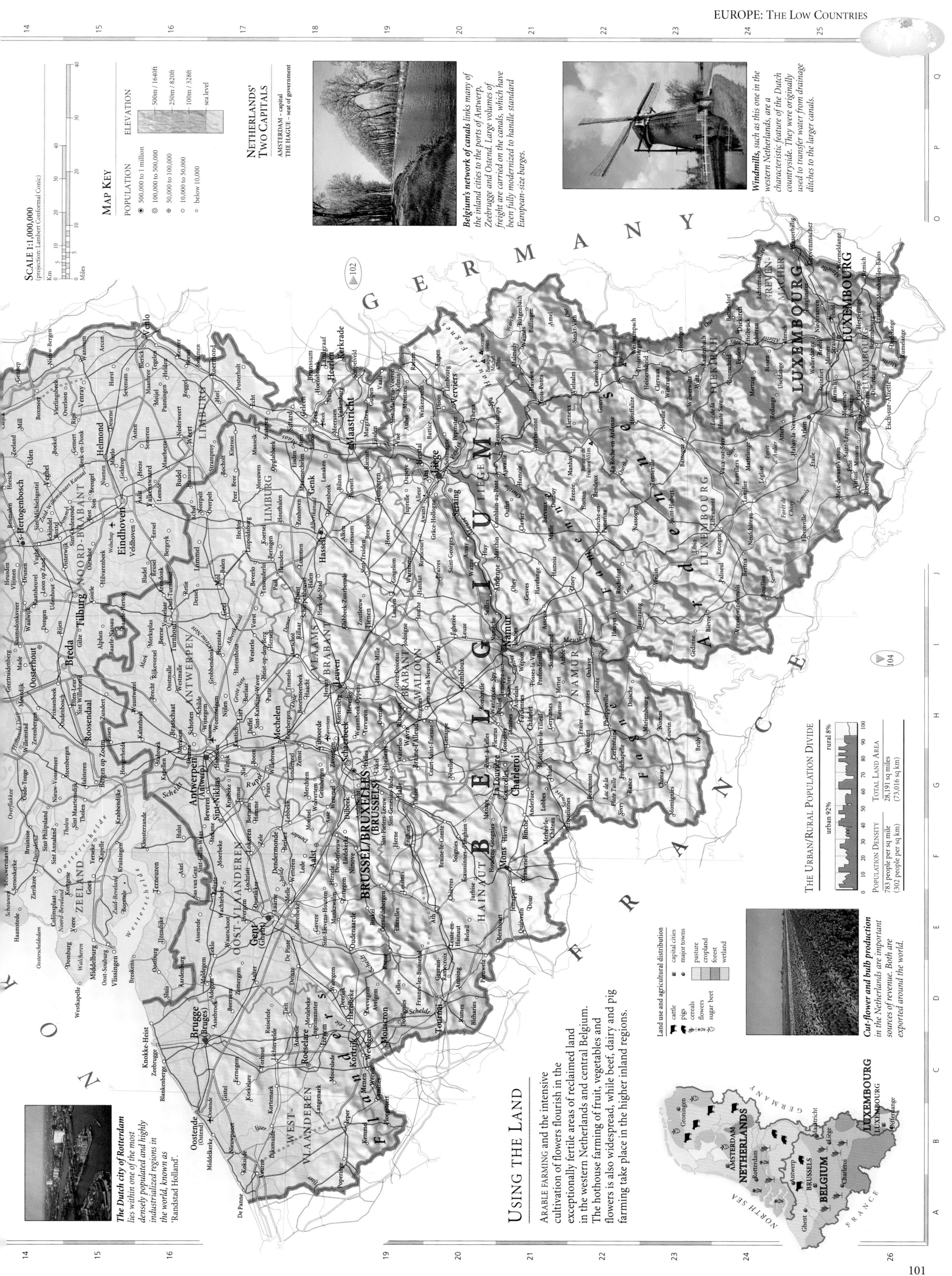

SCALE 1:1,000,000
(projection: Lambert Conformal Conic)

MAP KEY

ELEVATION

500m / 1640ft
250m / 820ft
100m / 328ft
sea level

POPULATION

● 500,000 to 1 million
◉ 100,000 to 500,000
⊕ 50,000 to 100,000
○ 10,000 to 50,000
○ below 10,000

NETHERLANDS'
TWO CAPITALS

AMSTERDAM – capital
THE HAGUE – seat of government

Belgium's network of canals links many of the inland cities to the ports of Antwerp, Zeebrugge and Ostend. Large volumes of freight are carried on the canals, which have been fully modernized to handle standard European-size barges.

Windmills, such as this one in the western Netherlands, are a characteristic feature of the Dutch countryside. They were originally used to transfer water from drainage ditches to the larger canals.

The Dutch city of Rotterdam lies within one of the most densely populated and highly industrialized regions in the world, known as 'Randstad Holland'.

USING THE LAND

ARABLE FARMING and the intensive cultivation of flowers flourish in the exceptionally fertile areas of reclaimed land in the western Netherlands and central Belgium. The hothouse farming of fruit, vegetables and flowers is also widespread, while beef, dairy and pig farming take place in the higher inland regions.

Land use and agricultural distribution

■ capital cities
• major towns
pasture
cropland
forest
wetland

🐄 cattle
🐷 pigs
cereals
flowers
sugar beet

Cut-flower and bulb production in the Netherlands are important sources of revenue. Both are exported around the world.

THE URBAN/RURAL POPULATION DIVIDE

urban 92%   rural 8%

POPULATION DENSITY	TOTAL LAND AREA
783 people per sq mile	28,191 sq miles
(302 people per sq km)	(73,016 sq km)

GERMANY

DESPITE THE DEVASTATION of its industry and infrastructure during the Second World War and its separation from eastern Germany during the Cold War, West Germany made a rapid recovery in the following generation to become Europe's most formidable economic power. When the Berlin Wall was dismantled in 1989, the two halves of Germany were politically united for the first time in 40 years. Complete social and economic unity remain a longer term goal, as East German industry and society adapt to a free market. Germany has been a key player in the creation of the European Union (EU) and in moves toward a single European currency.

USING THE LAND

GERMANY has a large, efficient agricultural sector, and produces more than three-quarters of its own food. The major crops grown are cereals and sugar beet on the more fertile soils, and root crops, rye, oats and fodder on the poorer soils of the northern plains and central uplands. Southern Germany is also a principal producer of high quality wines. Vineyards cover the slopes surrounding the Rhine and its tributaries.

Land use and agricultural distribution

- cattle
- pigs
- cereals
- sugar beet
- vineyards
- capital cities
- major towns
- pasture
- cropland
- forest

THE URBAN/RURAL POPULATION DIVIDE

urban 86%   rural 14%

POPULATION DENSITY	TOTAL LAND AREA
593 people per sq mile (229 people per sq km)	137,804 sq miles (356,910 sq km)

The Moselle River flows through the Rhine State Uplands (Rheinisches Schiefergebirge). During a period of uplift, pre-existing river meanders were deeply incised, to form its present dramatic contours.

THE LANDSCAPE

THE PLAINS OF NORTHERN GERMANY, the volcanic plateaux and mountains of the central uplands, and the Bavarian Alps are the three principal geographic regions in Germany. North to south the land rises steadily from barely 300 ft (90 m) in the plains to 6500 ft (2000 m) in the Bavarian Alps, which are a small but distinct region in the far south.

The heathlands of northern Germany are covered by glacial deposits of sandy outwash soil which makes them largely infertile. They support only sheep and solitary trees.

Lüneburg Heath *(Lüneburger Heide)*

Much of the landscape of northern Germany has been shaped by glaciation. During the last Ice Age, the ice sheet advanced as far the northern slopes of the central uplands.

Fault lines

Rhine

Downfaulted block

Part of the floor of the Rhine Rift Valley was let down between two parallel faults in the Earth's crust.

Rhine Rift Valley

Müritz Lake covers 45 sq miles (117 sq km), but is only 108 ft (33 m) deep. It lies in a shallow valley formed by glacial meltwater flowing out from a retreating ice sheet. These valleys are known as Urstromtäler.

The Harz Mountains were formed 300 million years ago. They are block-faulted mountains, formed when a section of the Earth's crust was thrust up between two faults.

The Elbe flows in wide meanders across the North German Plain to the North Sea. At its mouth it is 10 miles (16 km) wide.

Elbe River

The Danube rises in the Black Forest (*Schwarzwald*) and flows east, across a wide valley, on its course to the Black Sea.

Zugspitze, the highest peak in Germany at 9719 ft (2962 m), was formed during the Alpine mountain-building period, 30 million years ago.

The Rhine is Germany's principal waterway and one of Europe's longest rivers, flowing 820 miles (1320 km).

SCALE 1:2,250,000
(projection: Lambert Conformal Conic)

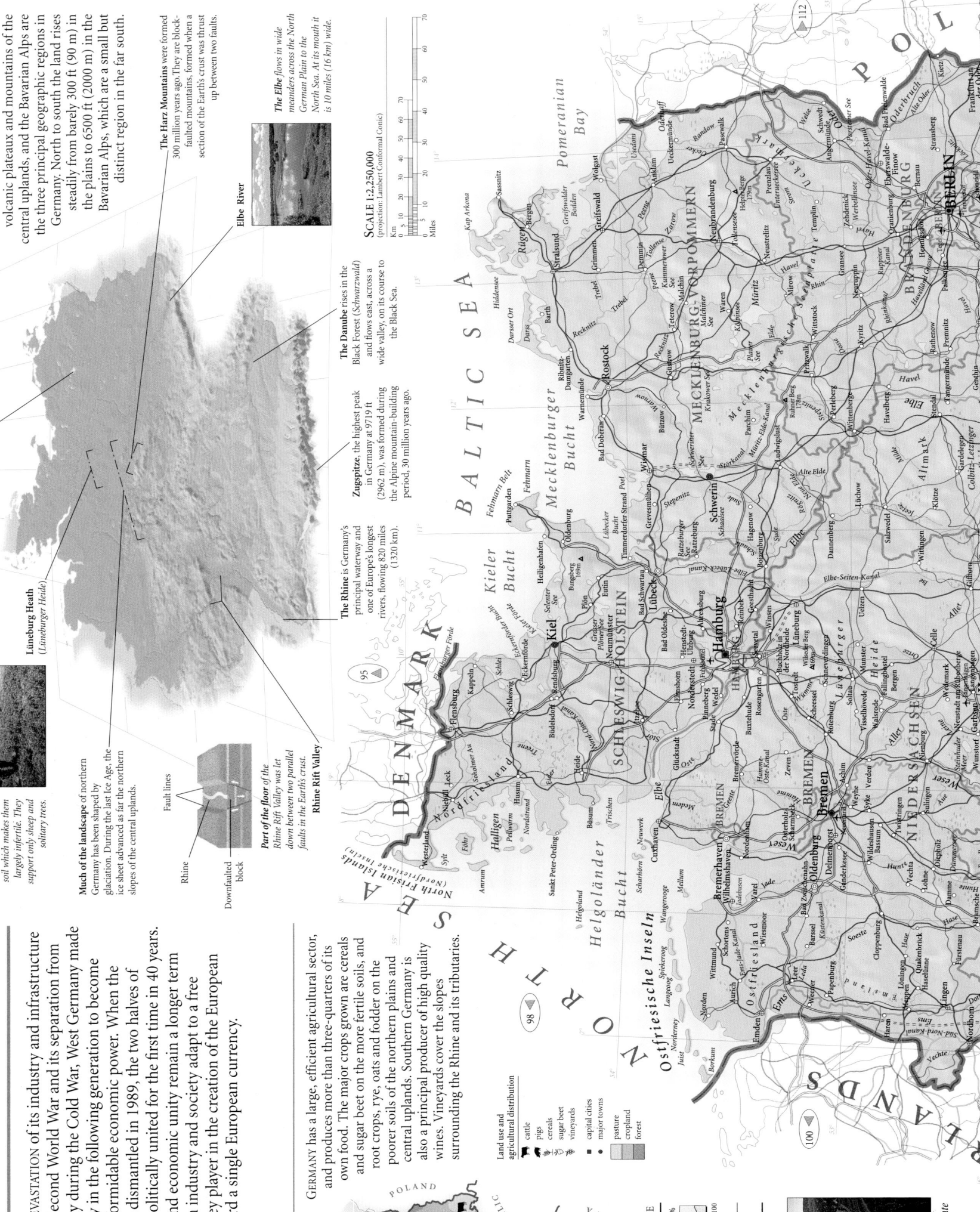

POLAND

BALTIC SEA

Pomeranian Bay

NORTH SEA

DENMARK

NETHERLANDS

MECKLENBURG-VORPOMMERN

BRANDENBURG

BERLIN

Potsdam

SCHLESWIG-HOLSTEIN

Kiel

Hamburg

NIEDERSACHSEN

BREMEN

Bremen

Hannover

Oldenburg

Nordfriesische Inseln

Ostfriesische Inseln

North Frisian Islands (*Nordfriesische Inseln*)

Helgoländer Bucht

Kieler Bucht

Mecklenburger Bucht

Rostock

Schwerin

Lübeck

Rügen

Stralsund

Greifswald

The Bavarian Alps straddle the country's southern border at an average height of 6500 ft (2000 m).

In the Black Forest (Schwarzwald), in southwestern Germany, woodland cloaks sandstone and granite hills, which contain rich mineral springs.

TRANSPORT AND INDUSTRY

TODAY, THE MAIN INDUSTRIES which contribute to Germany's economic power are industrial machine building, electronics, chemicals and car manufacture, including the famous Mercedes and BMW firms. While the introduction of a free market in the east has forced the closure of many less efficient companies there, west German manufacturers have moved in to set up new plants and businesses.

Germany has a complex network of inland waterways. The Rhine and Danube are at the centre of a vast canal system which links central and eastern Europe to the north.

THE TRANSPORT NETWORK

386,056 miles (621,297 km)

3406 miles (5482 km)

26,098 miles (42,000 km)

4598 miles (7100 km)

Major industry and infrastructure

- car manufacture
- chemicals
- hi-tech industry
- iron & steel
- mining
- precision engineering
- research & development
- shipbuilding
- capital cities
- major towns
- international airports
- major roads
- major industrial areas

MAP KEY

POPULATION

- more than 1 million to 5 million
- 500,000 to 1 million
- 100,000 to 500,000
- 50,000 to 100,000
- 10,000 to 50,000
- below 10,000

ELEVATION

- 2000m / 6562ft
- 1000m / 3281ft
- 500m / 1640ft
- 250m / 820ft
- 100m / 328ft
- sea level

103

FRANCE

FRANCE, MONACO

A MAJOR CENTRE OF CULTURE AND FASHION, and a leading producer of both industrial and agricultural goods, France is a key player in the push towards European unity. The founder of modern Republican government in the 18th century, France has been closely involved in European events for many centuries. The Paris Basin is the most highly populated area; Île de France is home to over nine million people. Large parts of rural France remain thinly populated, particularly the mountainous Massif Central, Pyrennees and southern Alps.

The chalk cliffs of Normandy (Normandie) *and southeastern England form part of a single geological region, now divided in two by the English Channel.*

THE LANDSCAPE

FRANCE'S LANDSCAPE was fashioned by two phases of mountain-building. The northwestern peninsula, the Massif Central and the Vosges date from 220 million years ago. The complex folds of the Alps and Pyrenees, the gently-folded Jura, and the low-lying sedimentary areas of the Paris, Garonne and Rhône basins started to form 65 million years ago.

The coast of Brittany (Bretagne) is highly indented where deep valleys in the northwestern peninsula were drowned by the sea.

The Normandy (Normandie) coastline is characterized by high chalk cliffs.

The coastline of France is 2141 miles (3427 km) long.

The Paris Basin consists of a layered sequence of sedimentary rocks. Fertile soils over much of the area make good agricultural land.

The gently rounded summits of the Vosges are over 200 million years old.

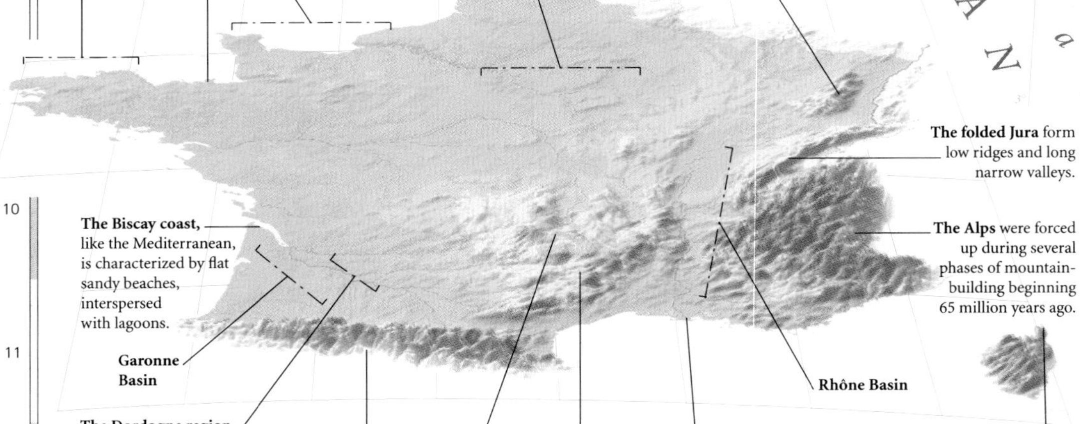

The folded Jura form low ridges and long narrow valleys.

The Alps were forced up during several phases of mountain-building beginning 65 million years ago.

The Biscay coast, like the Mediterranean, is characterized by flat sandy beaches, interspersed with lagoons.

Garonne Basin

The Dordogne region contains spectacular examples of limestone scenery including caves and gorges.

The Pyrenees form a natural border between France and Spain.

The ancient Massif Central, disturbed by the formation of the Alps, was subject to volcanism that only ceased during the last 10,000 years.

Rhône Delta

Rhône

The marshes of the Camargue

Delta plain

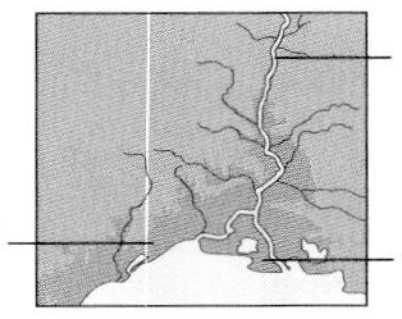

Deposition in the Rhône Delta is wave-dominated. Sea currents carry river sediments extending the delta plain westwards.

Rhône Basin

Corsica's northeastern peninsula has dramatic cliffs of folded limestone.

The volcanic landscape of the Auvergne where the cones of its extinct volcanoes have worn away to leave 'plugs' of lava.

TRANSPORT AND INDUSTRY

TODAY THE MAIN FRENCH GROWTH INDUSTRIES are hi-tech, including micro-electronics, telecommunications and aerospace. Other important sectors are the nuclear industry, only rivalled in scale by that of the USA, car manufacture, dominated by the giants Renault and Peugeot and a highly diversified tourist industry.

Major industry and infrastructure
- ✈ aerospace industry
- 🚗 car manufacture
- ⚙ chemicals
- ⚙ engineering
- 💻 hi-tech industry
- nuclear power
- 🏖 tourism
- ■ capital cities
- major towns
- ✈ international airports
- — major roads
- major industrial areas

THE TRANSPORT NETWORK

516,359 miles (831,000 km)	4142 miles (6680 km)
21,170 miles (34,070 km)	5270 miles (8500 km)

The French TGV (*Train à Grande Vitesse*) leads the world in high-speed train technology, and provides a service which is faster, door-to-door, than air travel.

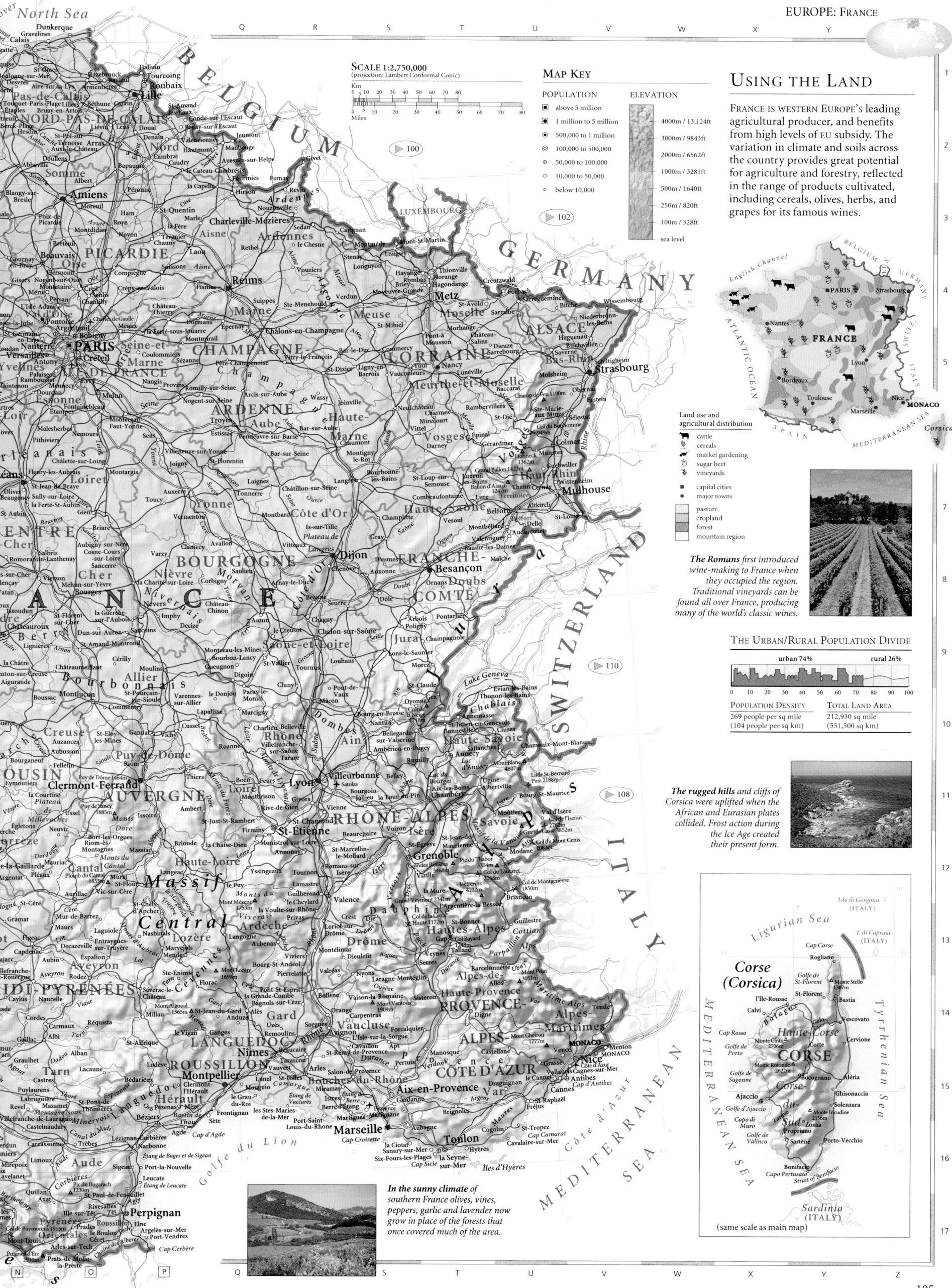

USING THE LAND

FRANCE IS WESTERN EUROPE'S leading agricultural producer, and benefits from high levels of EU subsidy. The variation in climate and soils across the country provides great potential for agriculture and forestry, reflected in the range of products cultivated, including cereals, olives, herbs, and grapes for its famous wines.

Land use and agricultural distribution
- cattle
- cereals
- market gardening
- sugar beet
- vineyards
- capital cities
- major towns
- pasture
- cropland
- forest
- mountain region

The Romans first introduced wine-making to France when they occupied the region. Traditional vineyards can be found all over France, producing many of the world's classic wines.

THE URBAN/RURAL POPULATION DIVIDE

urban 74%   rural 26%

POPULATION DENSITY	TOTAL LAND AREA
269 people per sq mile (104 people per sq km)	212,930 sq mile (551,500 sq km)

The rugged hills and cliffs of Corsica were uplifted when the African and Eurasian plates collided. Frost action during the Ice Age created their present form.

In the sunny climate of southern France olives, vines, peppers, garlic and lavender now grow in place of the forests that once covered much of the area.

SCALE 1:2,750,000
(projection: Lambert Conformal Conic)

MAP KEY

POPULATION
- above 5 million
- 1 million to 5 million
- 500,000 to 1 million
- 100,000 to 500,000
- 50,000 to 100,000
- 10,000 to 50,000
- below 10,000

ELEVATION
- 4000m / 13,124ft
- 3000m / 9843ft
- 2000m / 6562ft
- 1000m / 3281ft
- 500m / 1640ft
- 250m / 820ft
- 100m / 328ft
- sea level

Corse (Corsica)

(same scale as main map)

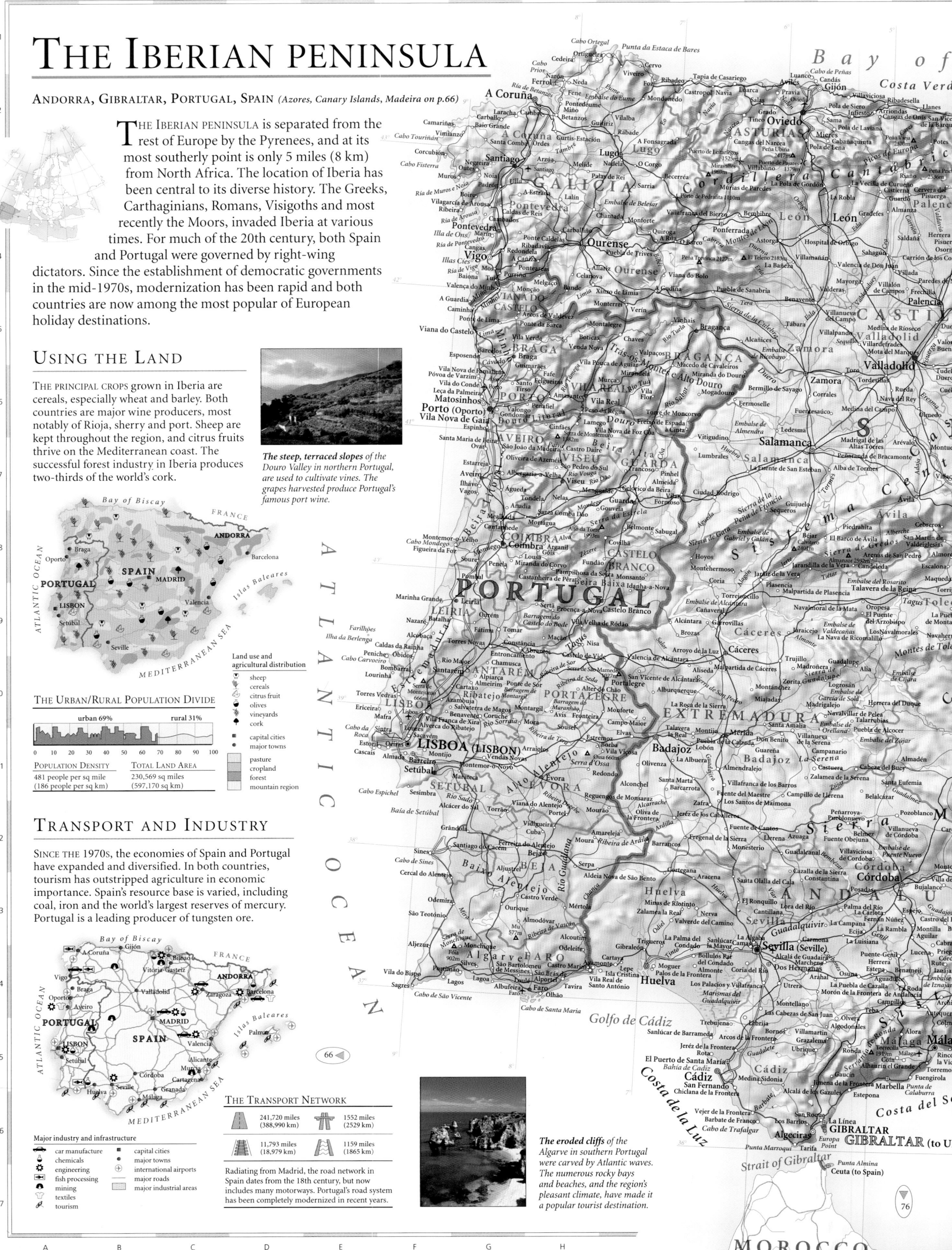

THE IBERIAN PENINSULA

ANDORRA, GIBRALTAR, PORTUGAL, SPAIN *(Azores, Canary Islands, Madeira on p.66)*

THE IBERIAN PENINSULA is separated from the rest of Europe by the Pyrenees, and at its most southerly point is only 5 miles (8 km) from North Africa. The location of Iberia has been central to its diverse history. The Greeks, Carthaginians, Romans, Visigoths and most recently the Moors, invaded Iberia at various times. For much of the 20th century, both Spain and Portugal were governed by right-wing dictators. Since the establishment of democratic governments in the mid-1970s, modernization has been rapid and both countries are now among the most popular of European holiday destinations.

USING THE LAND

THE PRINCIPAL CROPS grown in Iberia are cereals, especially wheat and barley. Both countries are major wine producers, most notably of Rioja, sherry and port. Sheep are kept throughout the region, and citrus fruits thrive on the Mediterranean coast. The successful forest industry in Iberia produces two-thirds of the world's cork.

The steep, terraced slopes of the Douro Valley in northern Portugal, are used to cultivate vines. The grapes harvested produce Portugal's famous port wine.

THE URBAN/RURAL POPULATION DIVIDE

urban 69%   rural 31%

0 10 20 30 40 50 60 70 80 90 100

POPULATION DENSITY	TOTAL LAND AREA
481 people per sq mile (186 people per sq km)	230,569 sq miles (597,170 sq km)

Land use and agricultural distribution
- sheep
- cereals
- citrus fruit
- olives
- vineyards
- cork
- capital cities
- major towns

pasture
cropland
forest
mountain region

TRANSPORT AND INDUSTRY

SINCE THE 1970S, the economies of Spain and Portugal have expanded and diversified. In both countries, tourism has outstripped agriculture in economic importance. Spain's resource base is varied, including coal, iron and the world's largest reserves of mercury. Portugal is a leading producer of tungsten ore.

THE TRANSPORT NETWORK

241,720 miles (388,990 km)	1552 miles (2529 km)
11,793 miles (18,979 km)	1159 miles (1865 km)

Radiating from Madrid, the road network in Spain dates from the 18th century, but now includes many motorways. Portugal's road system has been completely modernized in recent years.

Major industry and infrastructure
- car manufacture
- chemicals
- engineering
- fish processing
- mining
- textiles
- tourism
- capital cities
- major towns
- international airports
- major roads
- major industrial areas

The eroded cliffs of the Algarve in southern Portugal were carved by Atlantic waves. The numerous rocky bays and beaches, and the region's pleasant climate, have made it a popular tourist destination.

The climate in northwestern Spain is milder in both summer and winter than in the rest of the country, creating a verdant environment, more commonly associated with northwestern Europe.

MAP KEY

POPULATION
- 1 million to 5 million
- 500,000 to 1 million
- 100,000 to 500,000
- 50,000 to 100,000
- 10,000 to 50,000
- below 10,000

ELEVATION
- 3000m / 9843ft
- 2000m / 6562ft
- 1000m / 3281ft
- 500m / 1640ft
- 250m / 820ft
- 100m / 328ft
- sea level

SCALE 1:2,750,000
(projection: Lambert Conformal Conic)

THE LANDSCAPE

A VAST PLATEAU, the Meseta dominates the centre of the peninsula, enclosed by the Cordillera Cantábrica to the north and the Sierra Morena to the south. It is drained by three major rivers, the Douro/Duero, the Tagus, and the Guadalquivir. The peninsula experiences great variations in climate and rainfall, both regionally and locally.

The Pyrenees form Iberia's northeastern boundary, running for 270 miles (440 km), dividing the peninsula from the rest of Europe.

The Ebro River has formed the peninsula's largest delta. Recently, sediment flows have been seriously disturbed by nearby reservoirs.

On the northeastern coast sea level changes are evident from wave-cut beaches which rise up to 200 ft (60 m) above the present sea level.

Cordillera Cantábrica

Douro/Duero River

The Meseta plateau averages 1970 ft (600 m) in height and is now largely dry and treeless.

Tagus River

Mountain front

Pediment

Weathered material

Pediments are characteristic of semi-arid lands across Iberia. A pediment is a flat, low-lying, eroded platform, cut into the bedrock. Weathered material is transported by streams and deposited in broad fan shapes on the pediment.

The Guadalquivir River brings vital irrigation water to the plains, and like many of Iberia's rivers, is prone to flooding.

Sierra Morena

The Sierra Nevada in southern Spain contain Iberia's highest peak, Mulhacén, which rises 11,418 ft (3481 m).

In the Sierra de los Filabres deforestation and overgrazing, which cause soil erosion, have created semi-desert badlands.

The Balearic Islands (Islas Baleares) are characterized by jagged limestones and plains.

THE ITALIAN PENINSULA

ITALY, SAN MARINO, VATICAN CITY

THE LANDSCAPE

THE MAINLY MOUNTAINOUS and hilly Italian peninsula took its present form following a collision between the African and Eurasian tectonic plates. The Alps in the northwest rise to a high point of 15,772 ft (4807 m) at Mont Blanc (*Monte Bianco*) on the French border, while the Apennines (*Appennino*) form a rugged backbone, running along the entire length of the country.

THE ITALIAN PENINSULA is a land of great contrasts. Until unification in 1860, Italy was a collection of independent city states, whose competitiveness during the Renaissance resulted in the architectural and artistic magnificence of cities such as Rome, Florence and Venice. The majority of Italy's population and economic activity is concentrated in the north, centred on the sophisticated industrial city of Milan. Southern Italy, the *Mezzogiorno*, has a harsh and difficult terrain, and remains far less developed than the north. Attempts to attract industry and investment in the south are frequently deterred by the entrenched network of organized crime and corruption.

Mont Blanc (*Monte Bianco*)

Costa Smeralda

The island of Sardinia is an ancient land mass; an uplifted section of very old igneous rocks. Its rugged mountainous regions provide pasture for sheep and goats, while its valleys support some agriculture.

The Po Valley once formed part of the Adriatic Sea. Sediments of gravel, sand and clay washed down from the Alps gradually filling the bay and forming a broad, cultivable plain.

The Apennines (*Appennino*) are the source of most of Italy's rivers. They run 823 miles (1324 km) down the length of the peninsula.

Sardinia is the second largest island in the Mediterranean Sea. The highest point is Punta La Marmora at 6017 ft (1834 m).

The Dolomites (Alpi Dolomitiche) are formed of thick limestones, overlying weaker marine strata. They have distinctive serrated peaks and many massive landslides occur.

The distinctive square shape of the Gulf of Taranto (*Golfo di Taranto*) was defined by numerous block faults. Earthquakes are common in this region.

Vesuvius (*Vesuvio*)

The Pontine Marshes (*Agro Pontino*) are bounded by low sand hills which prevent natural drainage.

The Strait of Messina (*Stretto di Messina*) is between 2 and 12 miles (3–19 km) wide, and is a rich fishing ground.

The southwestern tip of Sicily lies 95 miles (152 km) from the north African mainland and is part of the same geological region.

Sicily is the largest island in the Mediterranean at 9926 sq miles (25,708 sq km).

Present-day crater has developed within the old crater of Monte Somma

Old crater

Monte Somma

Old crater

Vesuvius (*Vesuvio*)

There have been four volcanoes on the site of Vesuvius since volcanic activity began here more than 10,000 years ago.

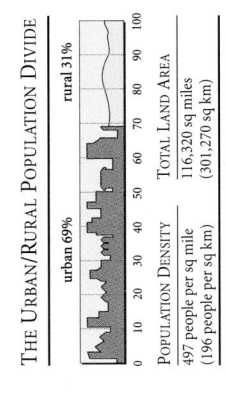

USING THE LAND

ITALY PRODUCES 95% of its own food. The best farming land is in the Po Valley in northern Italy, where soft wheat and rice are grown. Irrigation is essential to agriculture in much of the south. Italy is a major producer and exporter of citrus fruits, olives, tomatoes and wine.

THE URBAN/RURAL POPULATION DIVIDE

urban 69%   rural 31%

POPULATION DENSITY
497 people per sq mile
(196 people per sq km)

TOTAL LAND AREA
116,320 sq miles
(301,270 sq km)

Land use and agricultural distribution

- capital cities
- major towns
- pasture
- cropland
- forest
- mountain region

- cattle
- cereals
- citrus fruits
- olive oil
- rice
- vineyards

SCALE 1:2,500,000
(projection: Lambert Conformal Conic)

108

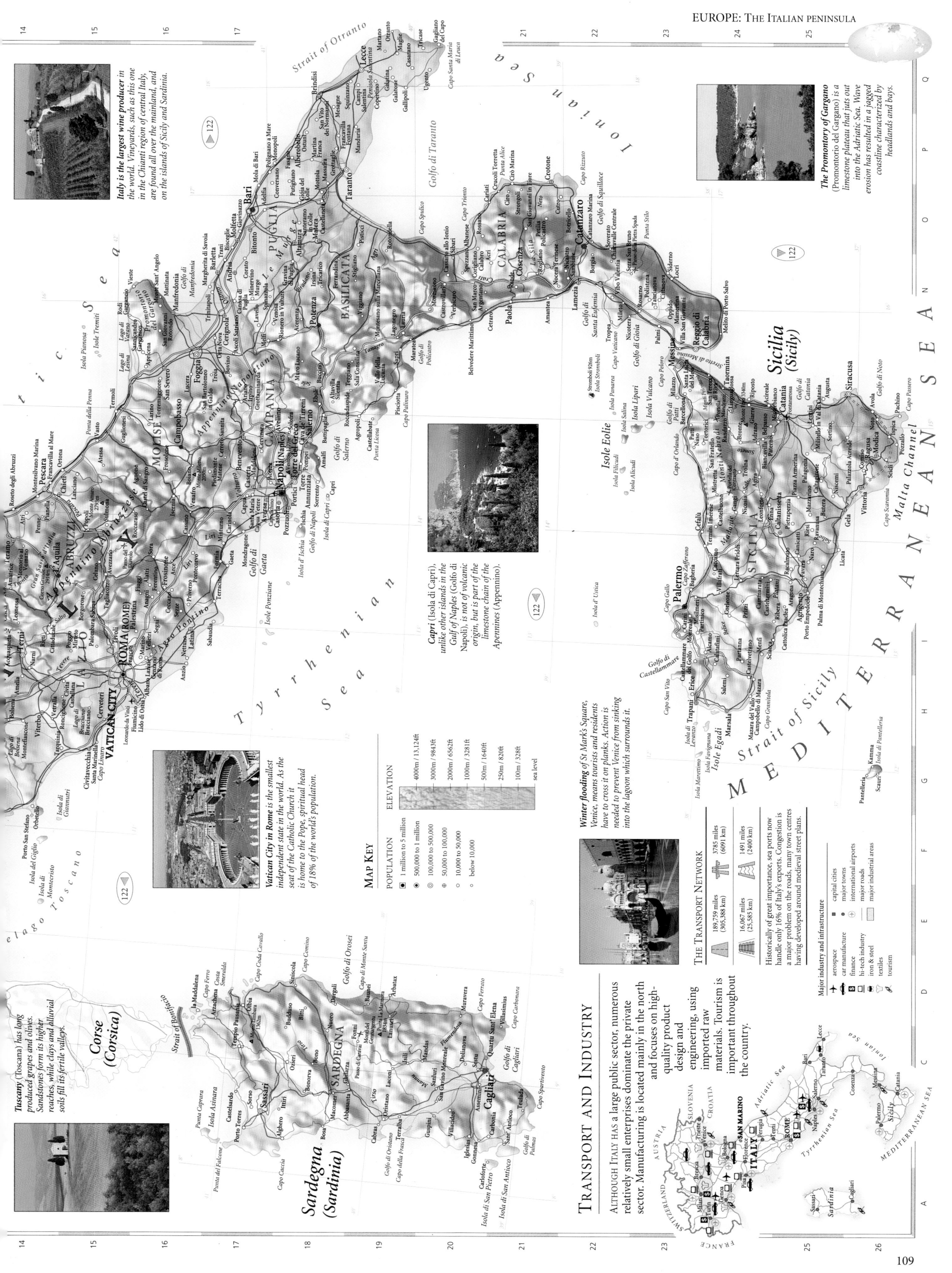

Italy is the largest wine producer in the world. Vineyards, such as this one in the Chianti region of central Italy, are found all over the mainland, and on the islands of Sicily and Sardinia.

The Promontory of Gargano (Promontorio del Gargano) is a limestone plateau that juts out into the Adriatic Sea. Wave erosion has resulted in a jagged coastline characterized by headlands and bays.

Vatican City in Rome is the smallest independent state in the world. As the seat of the Catholic Church it is home to the Pope, spiritual head of 18% of the world's population.

Capri (Isola di Capri), unlike other islands in the Gulf of Naples (Golfo di Napoli), is not of volcanic origin, but is part of the limestone chain of the Apennines (Appennino).

Winter flooding of St Mark's Square, Venice, means tourists and residents have to cross it on planks. Action is needed to prevent Venice from sinking into the lagoon which surrounds it.

Tuscany (Toscana) has long produced grapes and olives. Sandstones form its higher reaches, while clays and alluvial soils fill its fertile valleys.

MAP KEY

POPULATION
- 1 million to 5 million
- 500,000 to 1 million
- 100,000 to 500,000
- 50,000 to 100,000
- 10,000 to 50,000
- below 10,000

ELEVATION
- 4000m / 13,124ft
- 3000m / 9843ft
- 2000m / 6562ft
- 1000m / 3281ft
- 500m / 1640ft
- 250m / 820ft
- 100m / 328ft
- sea level

TRANSPORT AND INDUSTRY

ALTHOUGH ITALY HAS a large public sector, numerous relatively small enterprises dominate the private sector. Manufacturing is located mainly in the north and focuses on high-quality product design and engineering, using imported raw materials. Tourism is important throughout the country.

THE TRANSPORT NETWORK

189,759 miles (305,388 km)	3785 miles (6091 km)
16,067 miles (25,585 km)	1491 miles (2400 km)

Historically of great importance, sea ports now handle only 16% of Italy's exports. Congestion is a major problem on the roads, many town centres having developed around medieval street plans.

Major industry and infrastructure
- aerospace
- car manufacture
- finance
- hi-tech industry
- iron & steel
- textiles
- tourism
- capital cities
- major towns
- international airports
- major roads
- major industrial areas

THE ALPINE STATES

AUSTRIA, LIECHTENSTEIN, SLOVENIA, SWITZERLAND

THE ALPINE COUNTRIES of Austria, Switzerland, Liechtenstein and Slovenia form a narrow strip across western Europe's geographical core, lying on the main north–south trading routes across the Alps. Switzerland, politically neutral since 1815, is an important international meeting place and houses one of the headquarters of the United Nations, although not itself a member. Austria, once at the heart of the great Habsburg Empire has been a fully independent nation since 1955, and maintains a deserved reputation as an international centre of culture. Slovenia declared independence from the former Yugoslavia in 1991 and despite initial economic hardship, is now starting to achieve the prosperity enjoyed by its Alpine neighbours.

USING THE LAND

THE ALPINE REGION's mountainous terrain discourages cultivation over much of the land area. The primary agricultural activity is the raising of dairy and beef cattle on the pasture land of the lower mountain slopes. Austria is self-supporting in grains, and crops such as wheat, barley and grapes are grown on the east Austrian lowlands. Woodlands are more prevalent in the eastern Alps; both Austria and Slovenia have large tracts of forest.

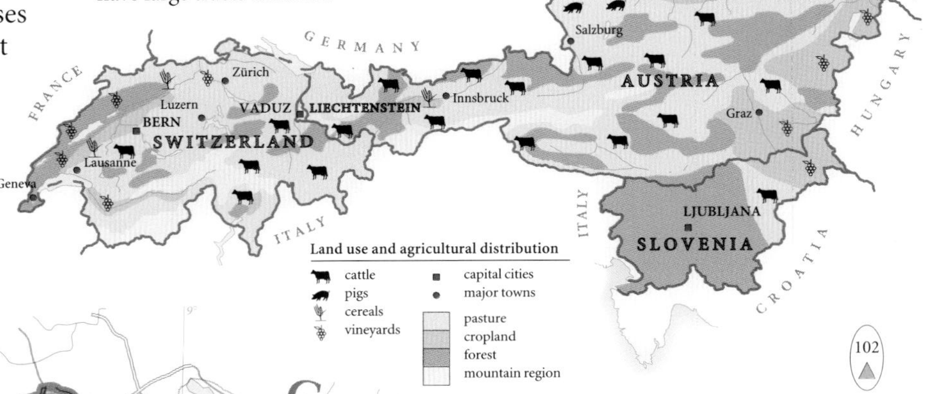

Land use and agricultural distribution

- cattle
- pigs
- cereals
- vineyards
- capital cities
- major towns
- pasture
- cropland
- forest
- mountain region

The Matterhorn, on the Swiss-Italian border, is one of the highest mountains in the Alps, at 14,692 ft (4478 m). The term 'horn' refers to its distinctive peak, formed by three glaciers eroding hollows, known as cirques, in each of its sides.

THE LANDSCAPE

THE ALPS OCCUPY THREE-FIFTHS OF SWITZERLAND, most of southern Austria and the northwest of Slovenia. They were formed by the collision of the African and Eurasian tectonic plates, which began 65 million years ago. Their complex geology is reflected in the differing heights and rock types of the various ranges. The Rhine flows along Liechtenstein's border with Switzerland, creating a broad flood plain in the north and west of Liechtenstein. In the far northeast and east are a number of lowland regions, including the Vienna Basin, Burgenland and the plain of the Danube. Slovenia's major rivers flow across the lower eastern regions; in the west, the rivers flow underground through the limestone Karst region.

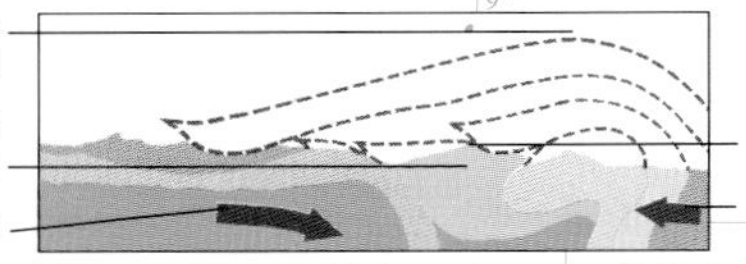

Original height after uplift and folding
Folded strata are overturned creating a *nappe*
Eurasian Plate
Present-day height of Alps
African Plate

The convergence of the African and Eurasian plates compressed and folded huge masses of rock strata. As the plates continued to move together, the folded strata were overturned, creating complex nappes. Much of the rock strata has since been eroded, resulting in the current topography of the Alps.

Constricted as it cuts through ridges in the Alps, the Danube meanders across the lowlands, where uplift combined with river erosion has deepened meanders.

The Vienna Basin lies mainly below 390 ft (120 m). It gradually subsided and filled with sediment as the Alps were uplifted.

Neusiedler See straddles the border of Austria and Hungary; the area around it provides some of the best wine-growing land in Austria.

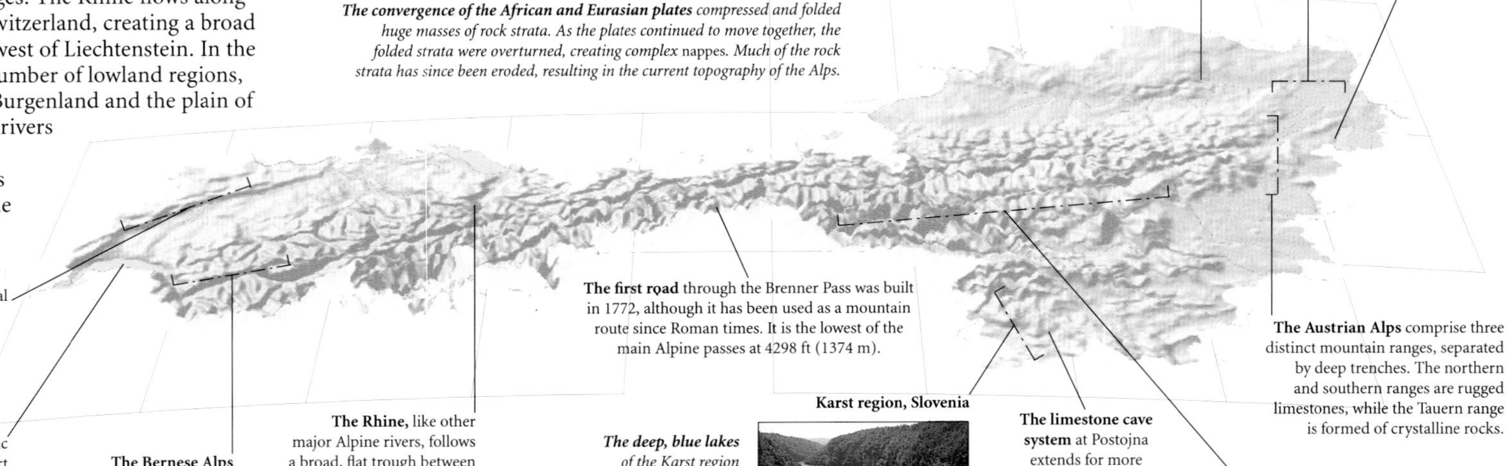

The mountains of the Jura form a natural border between Switzerland and France. Their marine limestones date from over 200 million years ago. When the Alps were formed the Jura were folded into a series of parallel ridges and troughs.

Tectonic activity has resulted in dramatic changes in land height over very short distances. Lake Geneva, lying at 1221 ft (372 m) is only 43 miles (70 km) away from the 15,772 ft (4807 m) peak of Mont Blanc, on the France–Italy border.

The Bernese Alps (*Berner Alpen*) contain the Aletsch, which at 15 miles (24 km) is the longest Alpine glacier.

The Rhine, like other major Alpine rivers, follows a broad, flat trough between the mountains. Along part of its course, the Rhine forms the boundary between Switzerland and Liechtenstein.

The first road through the Brenner Pass was built in 1772, although it has been used as a mountain route since Roman times. It is the lowest of the main Alpine passes at 4298 ft (1374 m).

Karst region, Slovenia

The deep, blue lakes of the Karst region of Slovenia are part of a drainage network which runs largely underground through this limestone area.

The limestone cave system at Postojna extends for more than 10 miles (16 km) and includes caverns reaching 125 ft (40 m) in height and width.

The Austrian Alps comprise three distinct mountain ranges, separated by deep trenches. The northern and southern ranges are rugged limestones, while the Tauern range is formed of crystalline rocks.

The Tauern range in the central Austrian Alps contains the highest mountain in Austria, the towering Grossglockner, rising 12,461 ft (3798 m).

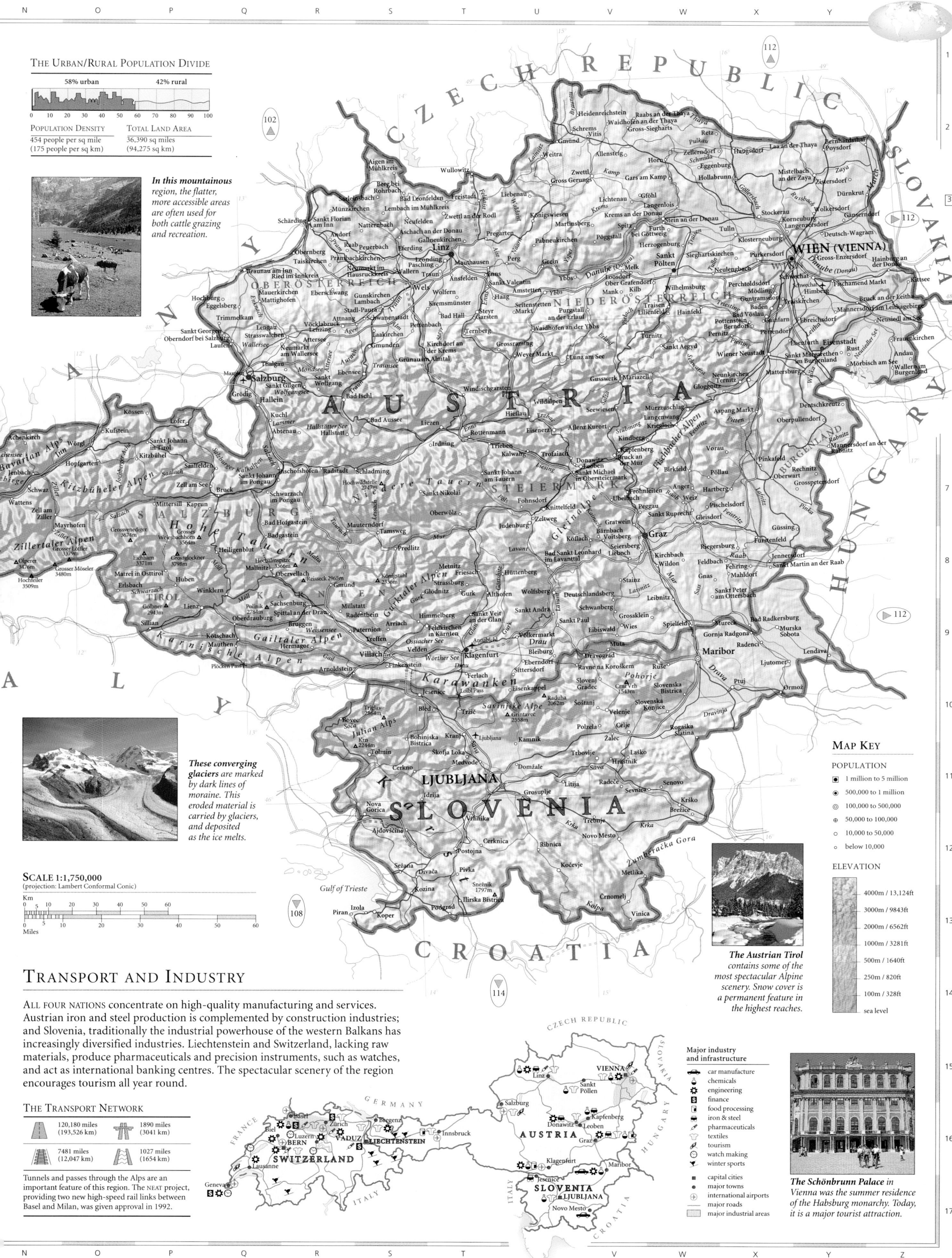

THE URBAN/RURAL POPULATION DIVIDE

58% urban 42% rural

0 10 20 30 40 50 60 70 80 90 100

POPULATION DENSITY | TOTAL LAND AREA
454 people per sq mile | 36,390 sq miles
(175 people per sq km) | (94,275 sq km)

In this mountainous region, the flatter, more accessible areas are often used for both cattle grazing and recreation.

These converging glaciers are marked by dark lines of moraine. This eroded material is carried by glaciers, and deposited as the ice melts.

SCALE 1:1,750,000
(projection: Lambert Conformal Conic)

Km
0 5 10 20 30 40 50 60
Miles
0 5 10 20 30 40 50 60

TRANSPORT AND INDUSTRY

ALL FOUR NATIONS concentrate on high-quality manufacturing and services. Austrian iron and steel production is complemented by construction industries; and Slovenia, traditionally the industrial powerhouse of the western Balkans has increasingly diversified industries. Liechtenstein and Switzerland, lacking raw materials, produce pharmaceuticals and precision instruments, such as watches, and act as international banking centres. The spectacular scenery of the region encourages tourism all year round.

THE TRANSPORT NETWORK

120,180 miles (193,526 km)	1890 miles (3041 km)
7481 miles (12,047 km)	1027 miles (1654 km)

Tunnels and passes through the Alps are an important feature of this region. The NEAT project, providing two new high-speed rail links between Basel and Milan, was given approval in 1992.

The Austrian Tirol contains some of the most spectacular Alpine scenery. Snow cover is a permanent feature in the highest reaches.

MAP KEY

POPULATION

- 1 million to 5 million
- 500,000 to 1 million
- 100,000 to 500,000
- 50,000 to 100,000
- 10,000 to 50,000
- below 10,000

ELEVATION

- 4000m / 13,124ft
- 3000m / 9843ft
- 2000m / 6562ft
- 1000m / 3281ft
- 500m / 1640ft
- 250m / 820ft
- 100m / 328ft
- sea level

Major industry and infrastructure

- car manufacture
- chemicals
- engineering
- finance
- food processing
- iron & steel
- pharmaceuticals
- textiles
- tourism
- watch making
- winter sports
- capital cities
- major towns
- international airports
- major roads
- major industrial areas

The Schönbrunn Palace in Vienna was the summer residence of the Habsburg monarchy. Today, it is a major tourist attraction.

CENTRAL EUROPE

CZECH REPUBLIC, HUNGARY, POLAND, SLOVAKIA

WHEN SLOVAKIA AND THE CZECH REPUBLIC became separate countries in 1993, they joined Hungary and Poland in a new role as independent nation states, following centuries of shifting boundaries and imperial strife. This turbulent history bequeathed the region a rich cultural heritage, shared through the works of its many great writers and composers, and celebrated in the vibrant historic capitals of Prague, Budapest and Warsaw. Having shaken off Soviet domination in 1989, these states are facing up to the challenge of winning commercial investment to modernize outmoded industry, while bearing the severe environmental impact from forty years of large-scale industrialization.

THE LANDSCAPE

THE FORESTED Carpathian Mountains, uplifted with the Alps, lie southeast of the older Bohemian massif, which contains the Sudeten and Krušné Hory (*Erzgebirge*) ranges. They divide the fertile plains of the Danube to the south and the Vistula (*Wisła*), which flows north across vast expanses of glacial deposits into the Baltic Sea.

TRANSPORT AND INDUSTRY

HEAVY INDUSTRY HAS DOMINATED POST-WAR LIFE in Central Europe. Poland has large coal reserves, having inherited the Silesian coalfield from Germany after the Second World War, allowing the export of large quantities of coal, along with other minerals. Hungary specializes in consumer goods and services, while Slovakia's industrial base is still relatively small. The Czech Republic's traditional glassworks and breweries bring some stability to its precarious Soviet-built manufacturing sector.

The Biebrza River has left meanders and oxbow lakes as it flows across low-lying ground.

Gerlachovský Štít, in the Tatra Mountains, is Slovakia's highest mountain, at 8711ft (2655 m).

Carpathian Mountains

Danube River

Meanders form as rivers flow across plains at a low gradient. A steep cliff or bluff, forms on the outside curve, and a gentler slip-off slope on the inside bend.

Slip-off slope

Bluff

Direction of flow

Longshore currents moving east along the Baltic coast have built a 40 mile (65 km) spit composed of material from the Vistula (*Wisła*) River.

Pomerania is a sandy coastal region of glacially-formed lakes stretching west from the Vistula (*Wisła*).

The Great Hungarian Plain formed by the flood plain of the Danube is a mixture of steppe and cultivated land, covering nearly half of Hungary's total area.

Hot mineral springs occur where geothermally heated water wells up through faults and fractures in the rocks of the Sudeten Mountains.

Bohemian Massif

The Slovak Ore Mountains (*Slovenské Rudohorie*) are noted for their mineral resources, including high-grade iron ore.

The Berounka River cuts through the precipitous wooded landscape of the Bohemian massif, banked by a broad flood plain.

Krušné Hory (Erzgebirge)

THE TRANSPORT NETWORK

722 miles (1165 km)	338,659 miles (546,224 km)
28,970 miles (46,727 km)	3822 miles (6165 km)

The huge growth of tourism and business has prompted major investment in the transport infrastructure, with new road-building schemes within and between the main cities of the region.

Major industry and infrastructure

- car manufacture
- chemicals
- engineering
- food processing
- mining
- shipbuilding
- tourism

- capital cities
- major towns
- international airports
- major roads
- major industrial areas

Budapest, the capital of Hungary, straddles the Danube. It comprises the historic towns of Buda, on the west bank, and Pest, which contains the Parliament Building, seen here on the far bank.

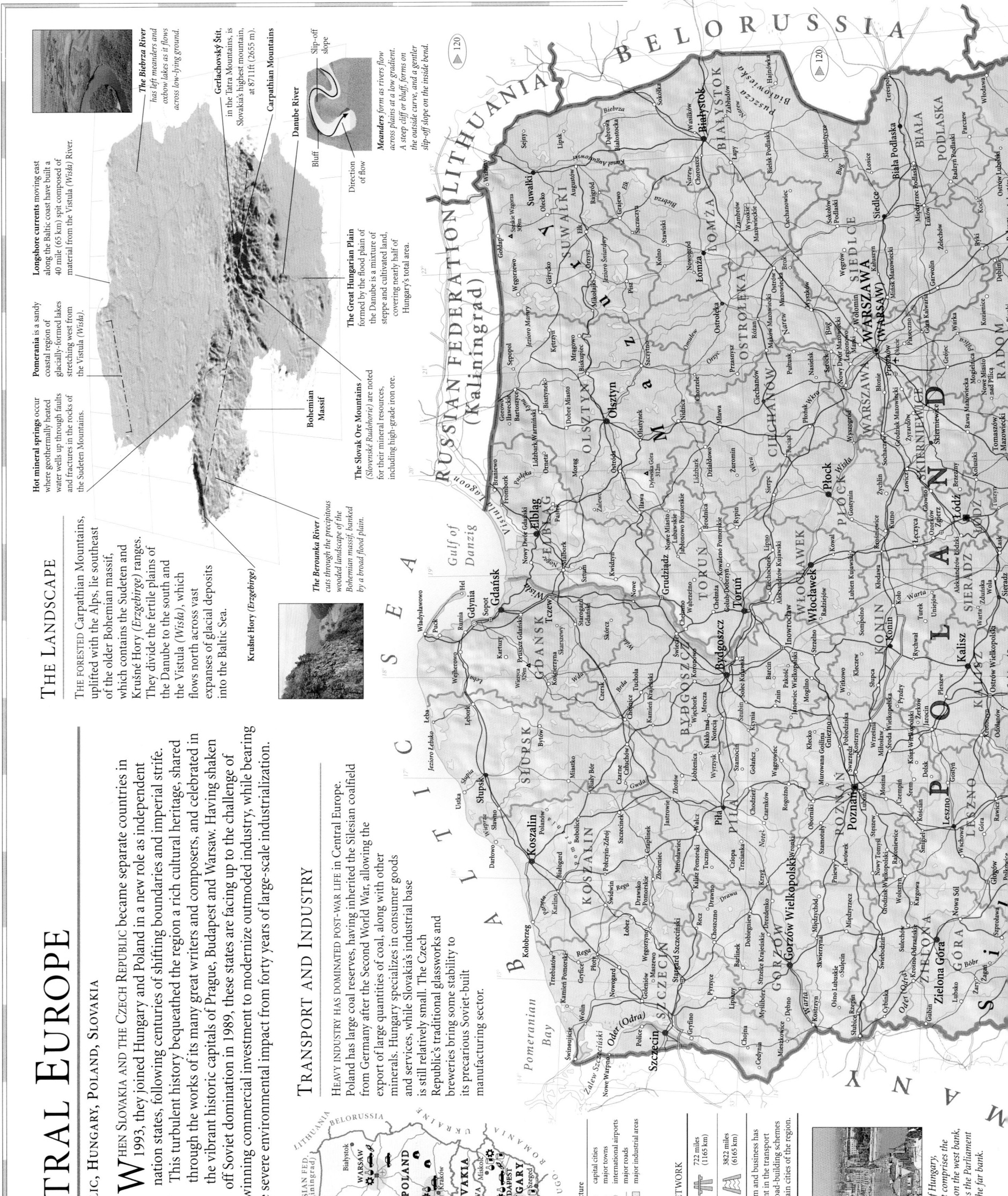

USING THE LAND

Cereals, sugar beet and potatoes are Central Europe's main crops, along with hops for the Czech breweries, sweet peppers for paprika, sunflowers and vines in milder areas. The plains of Poland and Hungary are well-suited to livestock-rearing, while forestry is important in the mountains of Slovakia.

The upper Dunajec River of Poland and eastern Slovakia forms a gorge through the Pieniny range of the Carpathian Mountains.

Hay, used to feed livestock, is one of the major crops grown on the fertile foothills of Slovakia's Tatra Mountains.

THE WESTERN BALKANS

ALBANIA, BOSNIA & HERZEGOVINA, CROATIA, MACEDONIA, YUGOSLAVIA

FOR 46 YEARS THE FEDERATION of Yugoslavia held together the most diverse ethnic region in Europe, along the picturesque mountain hinterland of the Dalmatian coast. Economic collapse resulted in internal tensions. The Serbian government regained central control over the previously autonomous regions of Kosovo and Vojvodina. In June 1991 Croatia and Slovenia (page 110) declared independence and Yugoslavia fragmented into five new nations. Bosnia and Herzegovina was devastated as Serbs and Croats struggled to establish ethnically exclusive territories, while the Bosnian government sought to preserve the country's multi-ethnic character. Albania is slowly emerging from the long isolation imposed by the communist Hoxha regime.

Hot, dry summers and mild winters offer excellent conditions for viticulture in Montenegro. The precipitous Dinaric Alps have kept this region relatively isolated for centuries.

SCALE 1:2,500,000
(projection: Lambert Conformal Conic)

THE LANDSCAPE

THE TISZA, SAVA AND DRAVA RIVERS drain the broad northern lowland, meeting the Danube after it crosses the Hungarian border. In the west, the Dinaric Alps divide the Adriatic Sea from the interior. Mainland valleys and elongated islands run parallel to the steep Dalmatian (*Dalmacija*) coastline, following alternating bands of resistant limestone.

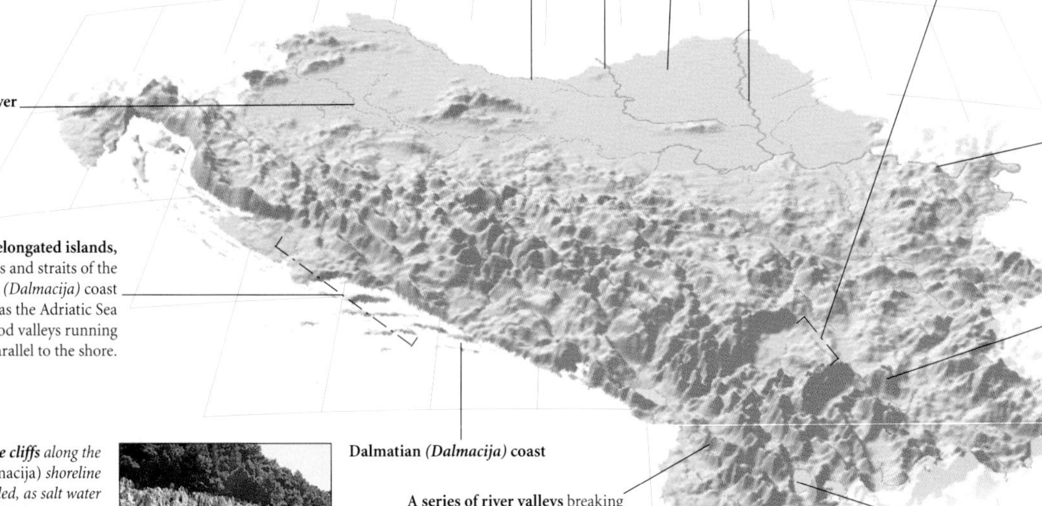

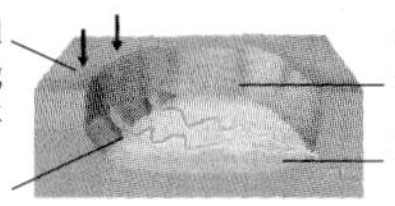

Polijes in the Kosovo region
Sheer limestone walls enclose all sides
Flat polje floor
Underground drainage along joints in the rock
Spring at foot of cliff

Rain and underground water dissolve limestone along massive vertical joints (cracks). This creates poljes: depressions several miles across with steep walls and broad, flat floors.

At Iron Gate (Đerdap), on the border with Romania, the Danube narrows and cuts through foothills of the Balkan and Carpathian mountains, forming the deepest gorge in Europe.

A major earthquake at Skopje, Macedonia, in 1963 killed 1000 people. The whole region lies on an active crustal plate margin.

Lake Ohrid

Lake Ohrid borders Albania and Macedonia. Ohrid is the deepest lake in the Western Balkans, reaching depths of 938 ft (286 m).

Tisza River

Drava River

The river flood plains of the Pannonian Basin are flanked by terraces of gravel and wind-blown glacial deposits known as loess.

At least 70% of the fresh water in the Western Balkans drains eastwards into the Black Sea, mostly via the Danube (Dunav).

Sava River

The elongated islands, promontories and straits of the Dalmatian (Dalmacija) coast were formed as the Adriatic Sea rose to flood valleys running parallel to the shore.

Dalmatian (Dalmacija) coast

A series of river valleys breaking through the Dinaric Alps from the lowlands of western Albania give access to the interior.

Limestone cliffs along the Dalmatian (Dalmacija) shoreline are heavily eroded, as salt water dissolves the rock along existing horizontal cracks, or joints. This tends to form a platform of rock at the foot of the cliff.

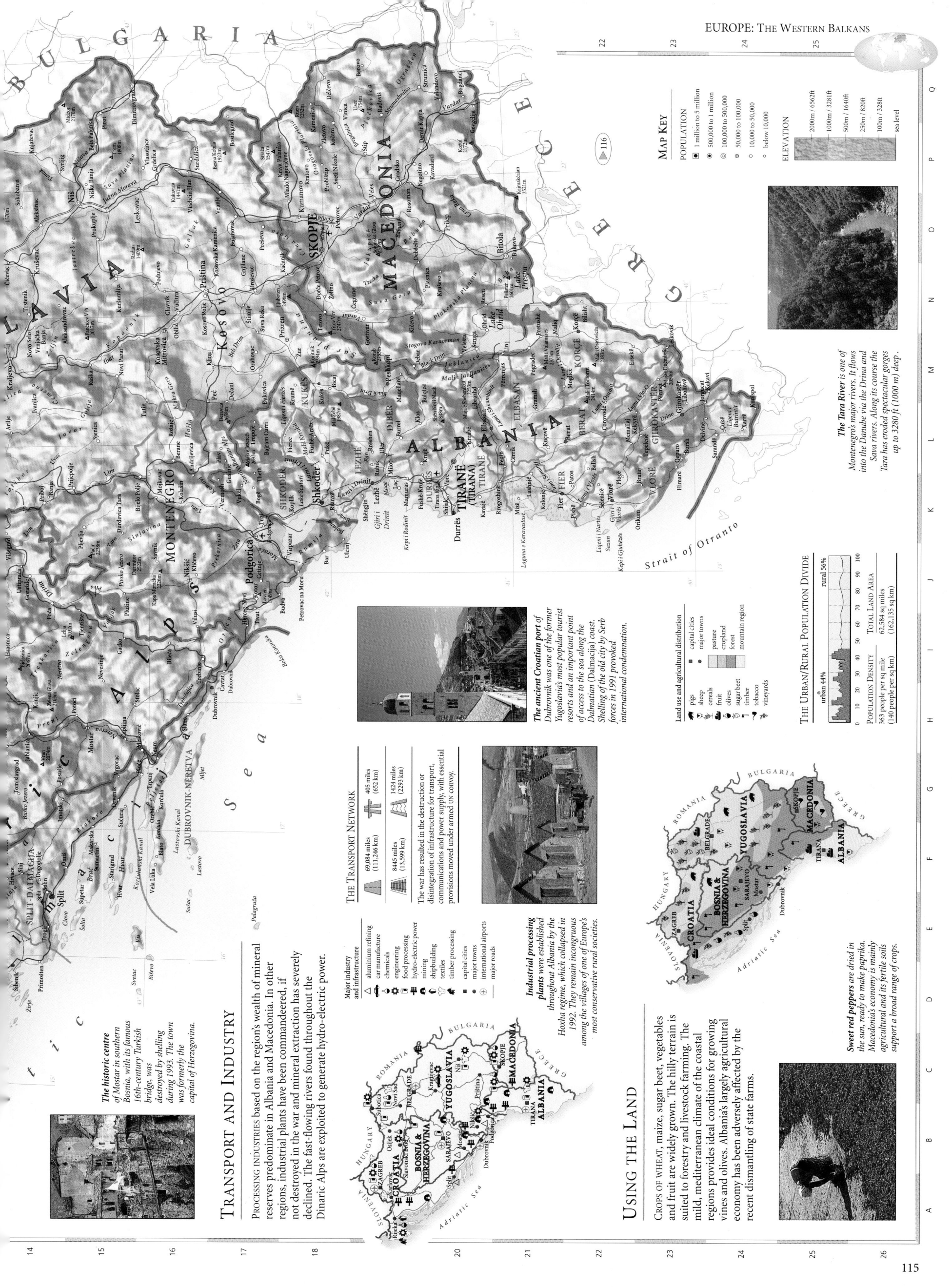

MAP KEY

POPULATION
- 1 million to 5 million
- 500,000 to 1 million
- 100,000 to 500,000
- 50,000 to 100,000
- 10,000 to 50,000
- below 10,000

ELEVATION
- 2000m / 6562ft
- 1000m / 3281ft
- 500m / 1640ft
- 250m / 820ft
- 100m / 328ft
- sea level

The Tara River is one of Montenegro's major rivers. It flows into the Danube via the Drina and Sava rivers. Along its course the Tara has eroded spectacular gorges up to 3280 ft (1000 m) deep.

The ancient Croatian port of Dubrovnik was one of the former Yugoslavia's most popular tourist resorts and an important point of access to the sea along the Dalmatian (Dalmacija) coast. Shelling of the old city by Serb forces in 1991 provoked international condemnation.

The historic centre of Mostar in southern Bosnia, with its famous 16th-century Turkish bridge, was destroyed by shelling during 1993. The town was formerly the capital of Herzegovina.

TRANSPORT AND INDUSTRY

PROCESSING INDUSTRIES based on the region's wealth of mineral reserves predominate in Albania and Macedonia. In other regions, industrial plants have been commandeered, if not destroyed in the war and mineral extraction has severely declined. The fast-flowing rivers found throughout the Dinaric Alps are exploited to generate hydro-electric power.

THE TRANSPORT NETWORK

69,084 miles (111,246 km)	405 miles (652 km)
8445 miles (13,599 km)	1424 miles (2293 km)

The war has resulted in the destruction or disintegration of infrastructure for transport, communications and power supply, with essential provisions moved under armed UN convoy.

Major industry and infrastructure
- aluminium refining
- car manufacture
- chemicals
- engineering
- food processing
- hydro-electric power
- mining
- shipbuilding
- textiles
- timber processing
- capital cities
- major towns
- international airports
- major roads

Industrial processing plants were established throughout Albania by the Hoxha regime, which collapsed in 1992. They remain incongruous among the villages of one of Europe's most conservative rural societies.

Land use and agricultural distribution
- capital cities
- major towns
- pasture
- cropland
- forest
- mountain region
- pigs
- sheep
- cereals
- fruit
- olives
- sugar beet
- timber
- tobacco
- vineyards

THE URBAN/RURAL POPULATION DIVIDE

urban 44% — rural 56%

POPULATION DENSITY	TOTAL LAND AREA
363 people per sq mile (140 people per sq km)	62,584 sq miles (162,135 sq km)

USING THE LAND

CROPS OF WHEAT, maize, sugar beet, vegetables and fruit are widely grown. The hilly terrain is suited to forestry and livestock farming. The mild, mediterranean climate of the coastal regions provides ideal conditions for growing vines and olives. Albania's largely agricultural economy has been adversely affected by the recent dismantling of state farms.

Sweet red peppers are dried in the sun, ready to make paprika. Macedonia's economy is mainly agricultural and its fertile soils support a broad range of crops.

BULGARIA & GREECE

Including EUROPEAN TURKEY

G REECE IS RENOWNED as the original hearth of Western civilization. The rugged terrain and numerous islands have profoundly affected its development, creating a strong agricultural and maritime tradition. In the past 50 years, this formerly rural society has rapidly urbanized, with more than half the population now living in the capital, Athens, and in the northern city of Salonica. Bulgaria, dominated for centuries by the Ottoman Turks, became part of the eastern bloc after the Second World War, only slowly emerging from Soviet influence in 1989. Moves towards democracy have led to some political instability and Bulgaria has been slow to align its economy with the rest of Europe.

THE LANDSCAPE

BULGARIA'S BALKAN MOUNTAINS divide the Danubian Plain (*Dunavska Ravnina*) and Maritsa Basin, meeting the Black Sea in the east along sandy beaches. The steep Rhodope Mountains form a natural barrier with Greece, while the younger Pindus form a rugged central spine which descends into the Aegean Sea to give a vast archipelago of over 2000 islands, the largest of which is Crete.

Mount Olympus is the mythical home of the Greek Gods and, at 9570 ft (2917 m), is the highest mountain in Greece.

Limestone rocks exposed by erosion of metamorphic rocks

Mount Olympus

Ancient metamorphic rock, formed miles below the surface

Mount Olympus is a composite of rocks formed by two major tectonic events. First the older metamorphic rocks were thrust over the limestones, then two million years ago regional warping and subsequent erosion, re-exposed the limestone.

Younger limestones created in shallow seas

The Peloponnese consist of several mountainous peninsulas, linked to the mainland by the Isthmus of Corinth. The Corinth Canal (*Dioryga Korinthou*), built in 1893, cuts through the isthmus, linking the Aegean and Ionian seas.

The Danube, Europe's second longest river, forms most of Bulgaria's northern border. The Danubian Plain (*Dunavska Ravnina*), extending from the southern bank, is extremely fertile.

The Arda River cuts through the Rhodope Mountains in rugged, rocky gorges.

The islands of Crete, Kythira, Karpathos and Rhodes are part of an arc which bends southeastwards from the Peloponnese, forming the southern boundary of the Aegean.

Layers of black volcanic ash still cover the island of Thira. This volcano last erupted 3500 years ago, but still shows signs of volcanic activity.

Balkan Mountains

Maritsa Basin

Rhodope Mountains

Pindus Mountains

Kythira

Corinth Canal (*Dioryga Korinthou*)

Crete

Karpathos

Rhodes

TRANSPORT AND INDUSTRY

SOVIET INVESTMENT introduced heavy industry into Bulgaria, and the processing of agricultural produce, such as tobacco, is important throughout the country. Both countries have substantial shipyards and Greece has one of the world's largest merchant fleets. Many small craft workshops, producing textiles and processed foods, are clustered around Greek cities. The service and construction sectors have profited from the successful tourist industry.

Bulgaria's railways require investment to revive an outdated infrastructure. In Greece, despite a developing road network, ferry-boats remain the most effective form of transport in many areas.

Major industry and infrastructure

- chemicals
- engineering
- food processing
- shipbuilding
- textiles
- tourism
- capital cities
- major towns
- international airports
- major roads
- major industrial areas

THE TRANSPORT NETWORK

103,930 miles (167,630 km)

345 miles (557 km)

345 miles (557 km)

294 miles (474 km)

SCALE 1:2,500,000
(projection: Lambert Conformal Conic)

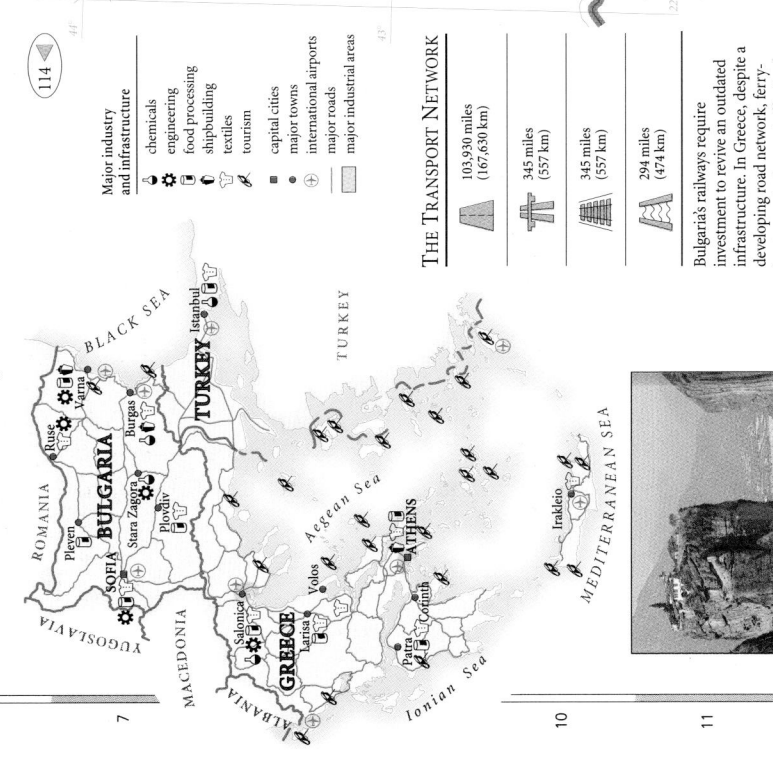

A towering pinnacle at Metéora in central Greece is home to the monastery of Roussanou. The 24 rock towers which dominate the plain of Thessaly (Thessalia) are remnants of an old plateau. Long-term weathering along fissures in the rock has worn away the rest of the plateau.

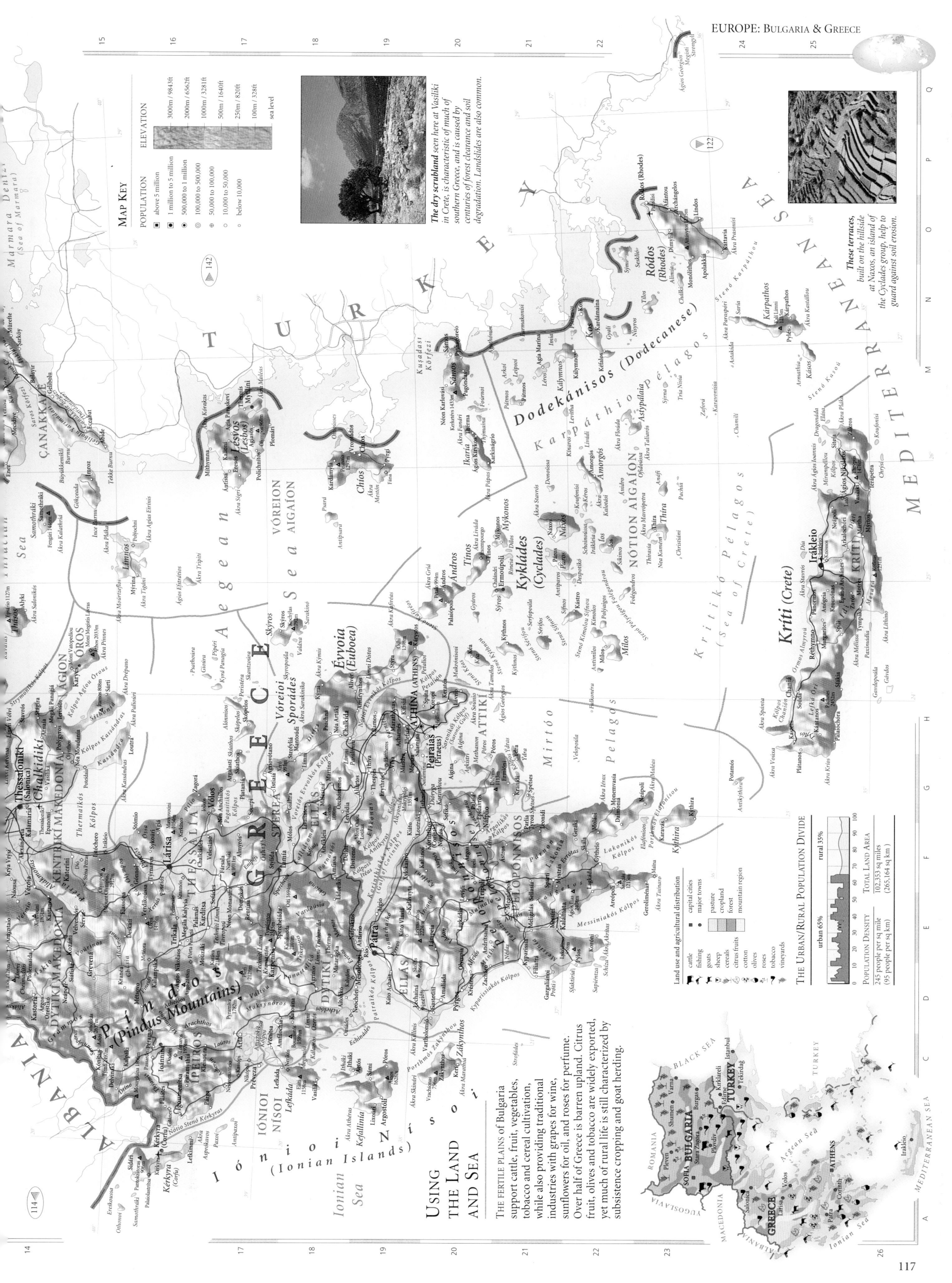

MAP KEY

POPULATION

- above 5 million
- 1 million to 5 million
- 500,000 to 1 million
- 100,000 to 500,000
- 50,000 to 100,000
- 10,000 to 50,000
- below 10,000

ELEVATION

- 3000m / 9843ft
- 2000m / 6562ft
- 1000m / 3281ft
- 500m / 1640ft
- 250m / 820ft
- 100m / 328ft
- sea level

The dry scrubland seen here at Vasiliki in Crete, is characteristic of much of southern Greece, and is caused by centuries of forest clearance and soil degradation. Landslides are also common.

These terraces, built on the hillside at Naxos, an island of the Cyclades group, help to guard against soil erosion.

USING THE LAND AND SEA

THE FERTILE PLAINS of Bulgaria support cattle, fruit, vegetables, tobacco and cereal cultivation, while also providing traditional industries with grapes for wine, sunflowers for oil, and roses for perfume. Citrus fruit, olives and tobacco are widely exported, yet much of Greece is barren upland. Over half of Greece is barren upland. Citrus fruit, olives and tobacco are widely exported, yet much of rural life is still characterized by subsistence cropping and goat herding.

THE URBAN/RURAL POPULATION DIVIDE

urban 65%   rural 35%

POPULATION DENSITY	TOTAL LAND AREA
245 people per sq mile (95 people per sq km)	102,353 sq miles (265,164 sq km)

Land use and agricultural distribution

- cattle
- fishing
- goats
- sheep
- cereals
- citrus fruits
- cotton
- olives
- roses
- tobacco
- vineyards

- capital cities
- major towns
- pasture
- cropland
- forest
- mountain region

ROMANIA, MOLDAVIA & UKRAINE

THE INDUSTRIAL, SOCIAL AND CULTURAL make-up of Romania and the former Soviet states of Moldavia and Ukraine still bear the imprint of their communist past. As part of the USSR, Ukraine was a leading agricultural, industrial and energy producer. These industries, like those in Moldavia and Romania, are now being reoriented more firmly towards Western markets. As a result of shifting borders, and Soviet policy actively encouraging Russian immigration into other Soviet states like Ukraine and Moldavia, all three countries now contain large numbers of foreign nationals. Moldavians and Romanians are still close in terms of language and culture, although Moldavia is striving to remain an independent nation.

USING THE LAND

THE FERTILE BLACK SOILS of Ukraine, often called 'the breadbasket of Europe', have enabled the cultivation of a variety of cereals and vegetables, which are widely exported. Romania and Moldavia also grow cereals, sunflowers and vegetables, and are noted for the quality of their wines.

The fertile lands and tolerant climate of Moldavia are ideally suited to growing grapes for wine.

Land use and agricultural distribution

- cattle
- pigs
- poultry
- sheep
- cereals
- cotton
- sugar beet
- sunflowers
- vineyards

- capital cities
- major towns

- pasture
- cropland
- forest
- wetland

THE URBAN/RURAL POPULATION DIVIDE

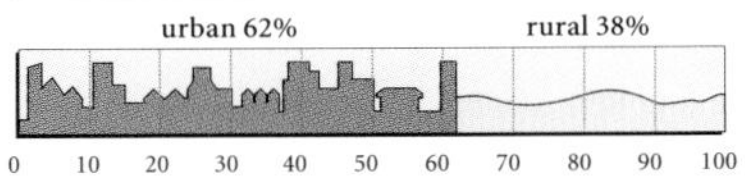

urban 62%   rural 38%

0 10 20 30 40 50 60 70 80 90 100

POPULATION DENSITY
238 people per sq mile
(92 people per sq km)

TOTAL LAND AREA
334,947 sq miles
(867,740 sq km)

Glacial lakes are found throughout the Transylvanian Alps (Carpaţii Meridionali), although the mountains no longer have any permanent snow cover.

TRANSPORT AND INDUSTRY

HEAVY INDUSTRY using local raw materials characterizes much of this region. The industrial heartland of Ukraine, specializing in metal and machine-building industries, is based around its vast mineral reserves in the Donbass region. In Moldavia, food processing draws on produce from its agricultural sector. Romanian industry relies both on local raw materials and imported iron, steel and oil.

Major industry and infrastructure

- car manufacture
- chemicals
- coal
- engineering
- food processing
- mining
- oil & gas
- textiles
- tourism

- capital cities
- major towns
- international airports
- major roads
- major industrial areas

THE TRANSPORT NETWORK

223,834 miles (361,024 km)	70 miles (113 km)		
21,989 miles (35,466 km)	3796 miles (6124 km)		

Increased industrialization has necessitated the upgrading of road and rail networks in all three countries. Modernization has tended to focus only on major cities and industrial areas.

During the 1960s and 1970s, many industries, like this carbon factory, developed using the mineral resources on the flanks of the Transylvanian Alps (Carpaţii Meridionali).

SCALE 1:3,250,000
(projection: Lambert Conformal Conic)

Km
0 10 20 30 40 50 60 70 80 90 100
Miles
0 10 20 30 40 50 60 70 80 90 100

▷ 125
▷ 130
▽ 122
▲ 120

MAP KEY

POPULATION

- ◙ 1 million to 5 million
- ● 500,000 to 1 million
- ◉ 100,000 to 500,000
- ⊕ 50,000 to 100,000
- ○ 10,000 to 50,000
- ∘ below 10,000

ELEVATION

- 2000m / 6562ft
- 1000m / 3281ft
- 500m / 1640ft
- 250m / 820ft
- 100m / 328ft
- sea level

RUSSIAN FEDERATION

RUSSIA

UKRAINE

MOLDAVIA

Black Sea

Sea of Azov

Gulf of Taganrog

CHERNIHIVS'KA · SUMS'KA OBLAST' · POLTAVS'KA OBLAST' · KHARKIVS'KA · LUHANS'KA OBLAST' · KYYIVS'KA OBLAST' · CHERKAS'KA OBLAST' · DNIPROPETROVS'KA · DONETS'KA OBLAST' · KIROVOHRADS'KA OBLAST' · MYKOLAYIVS'KA OBLAST' · ODES'KA OBLAST' · KHERSONS'KA OBLAST' · ZAPORIZ'KA OBLAST' · VINNYTS'KA OBLAST' · REPUBLIKA KRYM · Kryms'kyy Pivostriv

KYYIV (KIEV) · Kharkiv · Donets'k · Dnipropetrovs'k · Zaporizhzhya · Odesa · Chernihiv · Sumy · Poltava · Cherkasy · Kirovohrad · Kryvyy Rih · Mykolayiv · Kherson · Zhytomyr · Vinnytsya · Bila Tserkva · Zhdytomyr · Luhans'k · Makiyivka · Horlivka · Mariupol' · Melitopol' · Berdyans'k · Kerch · Sevastopol' · Simferopol · Yalta · Yevpatoriya · CHIŞINĂU · Tiraspol · Constanța · Tulcea

Dnieper (Dnipro) · Dniester · Danube · Bratul Chilia · Bratul Sulina · Delta Dunării

---

The Swallow's Nest castle

The Swallow's Nest castle at Yalta is one of many tourist resorts on the Crimean (Krym) coast, dubbed the 'Russian riviera'.

THE LANDSCAPE

VAST FLAT LOWLANDS and gently rolling hills cover most of southeastern Europe. In the southwest, the Carpathian Mountains form a gentle arc. To the south of the Carpathian Mountains lies the Danube Plain, across which the Danube River flows to the Black Sea. To the north and east, the hills of Moldavia level out into low plains, running east to the steppes of Ukraine.

Divided into crystalline massifs, the southern arm of the Carpathian Mountains, the Transylvanian Alps (Carpaţii Meridionali), extend 170 miles (274 km) across southwestern Romania.

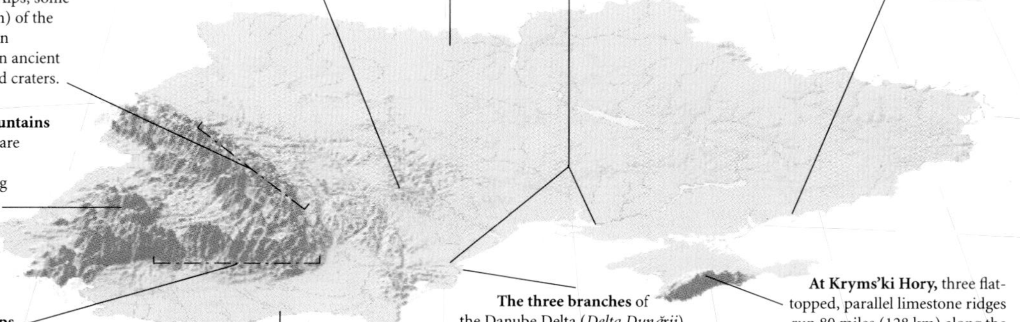

Uplifted and folded at the same time as the Alps, some 250 miles (400 km) of the eastern Carpathian Mountains contain ancient volcanic cones and craters.

The Apuseni Mountains (Munţii Apuşeni) are rich in mineral deposits, including gold and iron ore.

Transylvanian Alps (Carpaţii Meridionali)

The Danube forms a natural border between Romania and Bulgaria.

The Codrii Hills dominate the landscape of central Moldavia; they are intersected by deep, flat valleys and ravines.

Steppe landscape covers two-thirds of Ukraine. These flat, treeless grasslands extend from central Europe to central Asia.

Most of the major rivers in southeastern Europe, like the Danube, the Dniester and Dnieper flow south and east to the Black Sea.

The three branches of the Danube Delta (Delta Dunării) form a triangle of wetlands covering some 1950 sq miles (5050 sq km).

At Kryms'ki Hory, three flat-topped, parallel limestone ridges run 80 miles (128 km) along the southern coast of the Crimean (Krym) Peninsula.

Balkas are common throughout Ukraine. They are large U-shaped valleys, formed during the last Ice Age, which contain narrower, deep valleys. These were incised by a sudden flow of water, following an ice melt.

Water has eroded a new post-glacial valley

Old glaciated valley

Anti-clockwise currents have created the sandspits which fringe the Sea of Azov.

The Baltic States & Belorussia

Belorussia, Estonia, Latvia, Lithuania, Kaliningrad

Occupying Europe's main corridor to Russia, the four distinct cultures of Estonia, Latvia, Lithuania and Belorussia share a history of struggle for nationhood against the interests of more powerful neighbours. As the first republics to declare their independence from the Soviet Union in 1990–91, the Baltic states of Estonia, Latvia and Lithuania have sought an economic role in the EU, while reaffirming their European cultural roots through the church and a strong musical tradition. Meanwhile, Belorussia has shown economic and political allegiance to Russia by joining the Commonwealth of Independent States.

The seaport of Riga is Latvia's capital and the centre of economic and cultural life. With a 34% Russian minority in Latvia, language and the right to national citizenship are key issues.

Using The Land

Across the four nations cattle and pig farming are widespread, together with diverse arable crops, including flax for making linen, potatoes used to produce vodka, cereals and other vegetables. Almost a third of the land is forested; demand for timber has increased the importance of forest management.

Land use and agricultural distribution

- cattle
- pigs
- cereals
- flax
- potatoes
- timber
- capital cities
- major towns

- pasture
- cropland
- forest
- wetland

THE URBAN/RURAL POPULATION DIVIDE

urban 69%   rural 31%

POPULATION DENSITY	TOTAL LAND AREA
127 people per sq mile (49 people per sq km)	145,006 sq miles (375,656 sq km)

A pine forest in northern Belorussia. Conifers in the north give way to hardwood forest further south. Timber mills are supplied with logs floated along the country's many navigable waterways.

The Western Drina River provides hydro-electric power and, during the summer months, access to the Baltic Sea. The lower course of the river freezes from December to April.

MAP KEY

POPULATION
- ◉ 1 million to 5 million
- ◎ 500,000 to 1 million
- ⊕ 100,000 to 500,000
- ○ 50,000 to 100,000
- ○ 10,000 to 50,000
- ○ below 10,000

ELEVATION
- 250m/820ft
- 100m/328ft
- sea level

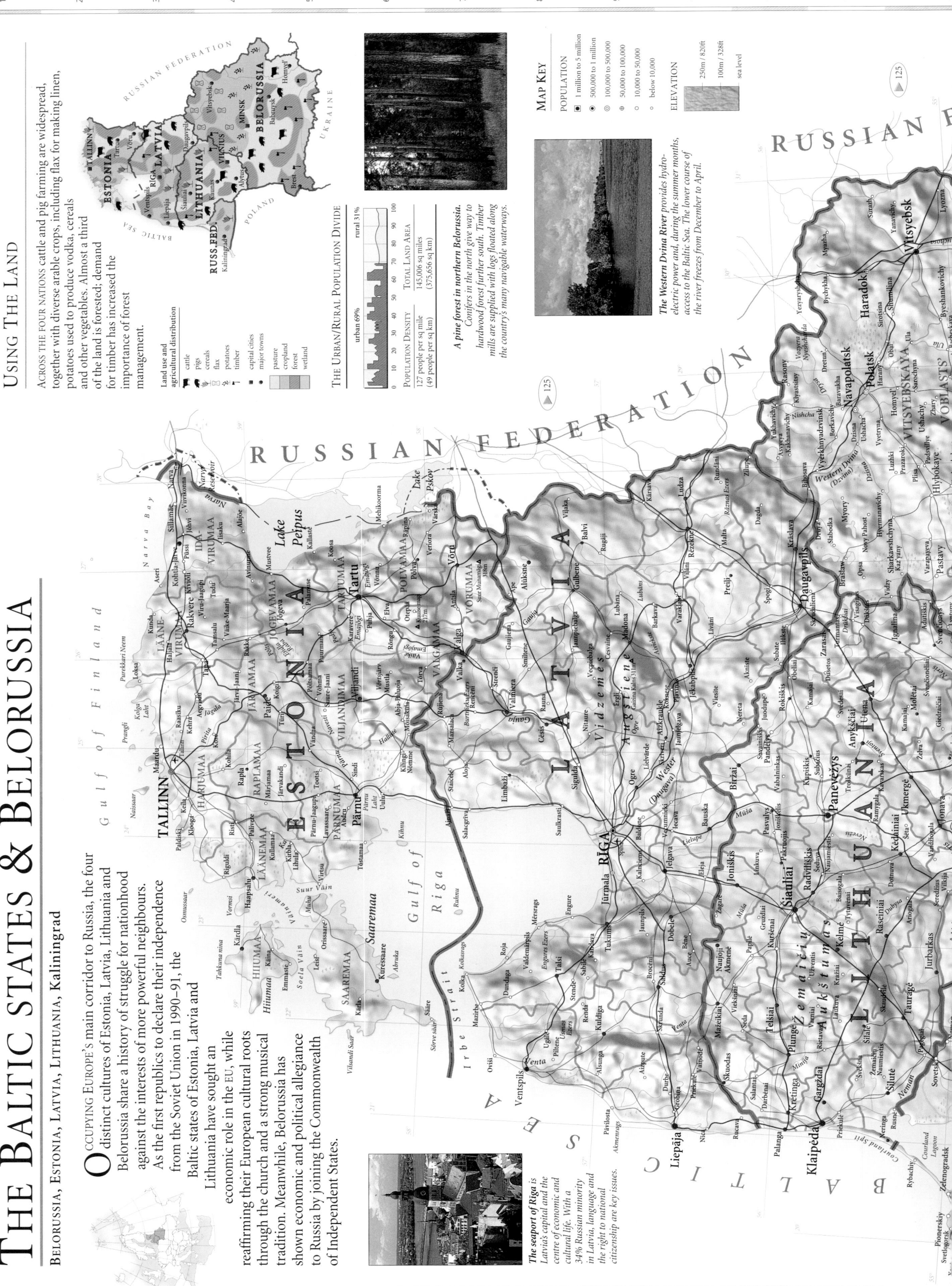

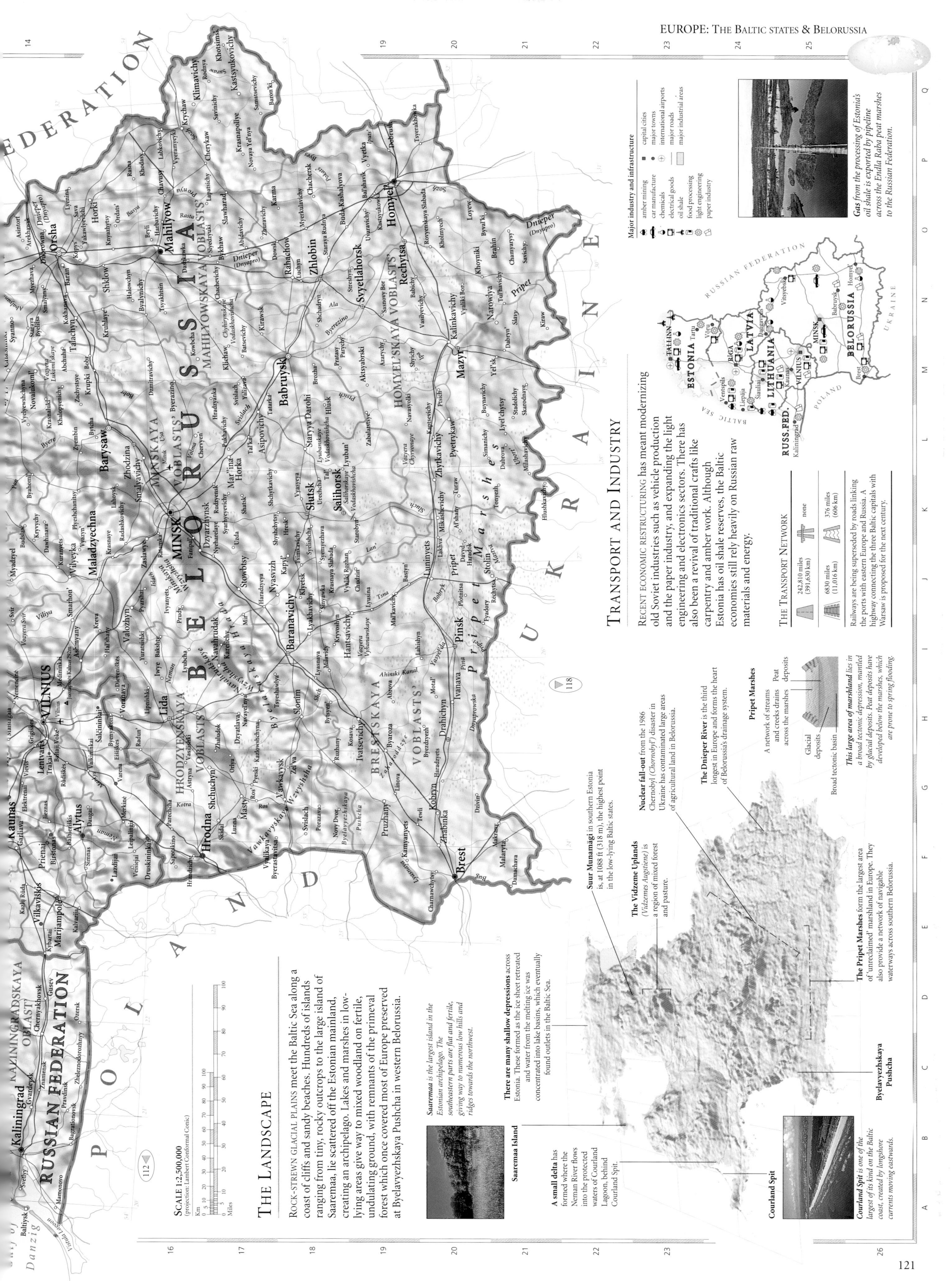

THE LANDSCAPE

ROCK-STREWN GLACIAL PLAINS meet the Baltic Sea along a coast of cliffs and sandy beaches. Hundreds of islands ranging from tiny, rocky outcrops to the large island of Saaremaa, lie scattered off the Estonian mainland, creating an archipelago. Lakes and marshes in low-lying areas give way to mixed woodland on fertile, undulating ground, with remnants of the primeval forest which once covered most of Europe preserved at Byelavyezhskaya Pushcha in western Belorussia.

SCALE 1:2,500,000
(projection: Lambert Conformal Conic)

Saaremaa Island

Courland Spit

Byelavyezhskaya Pushcha

Saaremaa is the largest island in the Estonian archipelago. The southeastern parts are flat and fertile, giving way to numerous low hills and ridges towards the northwest.

There are many shallow depressions across Estonia. These formed as the ice sheet retreated and water from the melting ice was concentrated into lake basins, which eventually found outlets in the Baltic Sea.

A small delta has formed where the Neman River flows into the protected waters of Courland Lagoon, behind Courland Spit.

Courland Spit is one of the largest of its kind on the Baltic coast, created by longshore currents moving eastwards.

Suur Munamägi in southern Estonia is, at 1088 ft (318 m), the highest point in the low-lying Baltic states.

The Vidzeme Uplands (*Vidzemes Augstiene*) is a region of mixed forest and pasture.

Nuclear fall-out from the 1986 Chernobyl (*Chornobyl'*) disaster in Ukraine has contaminated large areas of agricultural land in Belorussia.

The Dnieper River is the third longest in Europe and forms the heart of Belorussia's drainage system.

Pripet Marshes

A network of streams and creeks drains across the marshes

The Pripet Marshes form the largest area of "unreclaimed" marshland in Europe. They also provide a network of navigable waterways across southern Belorussia.

This large area of marshland lies in a broad tectonic depression, mantled by glacial deposits. Peat deposits have developed below the marshes, which are prone to spring flooding.

Peat deposits

Glacial deposits

Broad tectonic basin

TRANSPORT AND INDUSTRY

RECENT ECONOMIC RESTRUCTURING has meant modernizing old Soviet industries such as vehicle production and the paper industry, and expanding the light engineering and electronics sectors. There has also been a revival of traditional crafts like carpentry and amber work. Although Estonia has oil shale reserves, the Baltic economies still rely heavily on Russian raw materials and energy.

Gas from the processing of Estonia's oil shale is exported by pipeline across the Endla Raba peat marshes to the Russian Federation.

Major industry and infrastructure

- amber mining
- car manufacture
- chemicals
- electrical goods
- oil shale
- food processing
- light engineering
- paper industry

- capital cities
- major towns
- international airports
- major roads
- major industrial areas

THE TRANSPORT NETWORK

| 242,810 miles (391,630 km) | none |
| 6830 miles (11,016 km) | 376 miles (606 km) |

Railways which are being superseded by roads linking the ports with eastern Europe and Russia. A highway connecting the three Baltic capitals with Warsaw is proposed for the next century.

ESTONIA
LATVIA
LITHUANIA
BELORUSSIA
RUSS.FED.
RUSSIAN FEDERATION
UKRAINE
POLAND
BALTIC SEA
TALLINN
RIGA
VILNIUS
MINSK
Homyel
Kaliningrad

THE MEDITERRANEAN

THE MEDITERRANEAN SEA stretches over 2500 miles (4000 km) east to west, separating Europe from Africa. At its most westerly point it is connected to the Atlantic Ocean through the Strait of Gibraltar. In the east, the Suez Canal, opened in 1869, gives passage to the Indian Ocean. In the northeast, linked by the Sea of Marmara, lies the Black Sea. The Mediterranean is bordered by 28 states and territories, and more than 100 million people live on its shores and islands. Throughout history, the Mediterranean has been a focal area for many great empires and civilizations, reflected in the variety of cultures found on its shores. Since the 1960s, development along the southern coast of Europe has expanded rapidly to accommodate increasing numbers of tourists and to enable the exploitation of oil and gas reserves. This has resulted in rising levels of pollution, threatening the future of the sea.

TRANSPORT AND INDUSTRY

THE OPENING OF THE SUEZ CANAL in 1869 made the Mediterranean a key shipping route to Asia. Oil and gas reserves, although comparatively small on a world scale, are being explored and exploited off the coasts of Libya, Greece, Italy, Spain and Tunisia. The Mediterranean's greatest natural resources are its miles of beaches and warm sea. Over half the world's income from tourism is generated in the Mediterranean.

Benidorm is one of the most popular resorts on Spain's Costa Blanca. Many of the Mediterranean's coastal resorts have grown up since the 1950s, expanding from small fishing villages to large resorts catering almost exclusively for tourists.

USING THE LAND AND SEA

A QUARTER OF THE FISH SPECIES found in the Mediterranean are economically important. Sardines are the main catch in northern and western regions and aquaculture, including oyster farming, is becoming increasingly important in the eastern Mediterranean. Olives, citrus fruit, cork trees and vines thrive in the mediterranean climate, enjoying hot, dry summers and mild, wet winters. Italy and Spain are world leaders in commercial olive production.

The growing of citrus fruit such as lemons, limes, oranges and grapefruit is common along the coasts surrounding the Mediterranean.

Land use and agricultural distribution

- goats
- sheep
- cereals
- citrus fruits
- cork
- fishing
- olives
- sunflowers
- tobacco
- vineyards
- • major towns

- pasture
- cropland
- forest
- mountain region
- wetland
- desert

THE LANDSCAPE

THE MEDITERRANEAN SEA IS ALMOST TOTALLY LANDLOCKED, joined to the Atlantic Ocean through the Strait of Gibraltar, which is only 8 miles (13 km) wide. Lying on an active plate margin, sea floor movements have formed a variety of basins, troughs and ridges. A submarine ridge running from Tunisia to the island of Sicily divides the Mediterranean into two distinct basins. The western basin is characterized by broad, smooth abyssal (or ocean) plains. In contrast, the eastern basin is dominated by a large ridge system, running east to west.

The narrow Strait of Gibraltar inhibits water exchange between the Mediterranean Sea and the Atlantic Ocean, producing a high degree of salinity and a low tidal range within the Mediterranean. The lack of tides has encouraged the build-up of pollutants in many semi-enclosed bays.

The Dalmatian (Dalmacija) coast has many long, elongated islands running parallel to the mainland. These resulted when rising sea levels drowned valleys running parallel with the coast.

Main surface current

Denser, more saline currents flow back to Atlantic

Dense currents sink below surface

Because the Mediterranean is almost enclosed by land, its circulation is quite different to the oceans. There is one major current which flows in from the Atlantic and moves east. Currents flowing back to the Atlantic are denser and flow below the main current.

The Ionian Basin is the deepest in the Mediterranean, reaching depths of 16,800 ft (5121 m).

Industrial pollution flowing from the Dnieper and Danube rivers has destroyed a large proportion of the fish population that used to inhabit the upper layers of the Black Sea.

The eastern basin of the Mediterranean contains many features which indicate the force of a colliding plate margin, including volcanoes, earthquake zones, ridges and seamounts.

The Atlas Mountains are a range of fold mountains which lie in Morocco and Algeria. They run parallel to the Mediterranean, forming a topographical and climatic divide between the Mediterranean coast and the western Sahara.

The edge of the Eurasian Plate is edged by a continental shelf. In the Mediterranean Sea this is widest at the Ebro Fan where it extends 60 miles (96 km).

Beneath the Strait of Sicily lies a submarine ridge which rises to 1200 ft (360 m) below sea level. It divides the eastern and western basins of the Mediterranean.

An arc of active submarine, island and mainland volcanoes, including Etna and Vesuvius, lie in and around southern Italy. The area is also susceptible to earthquakes and landslides.

The shallow basin of the Aegean contains numerous small islands, many of volcanic origin.

Nutrient flows into the eastern Mediterranean, and sediment flows to the Nile Delta have been severely lowered by the building of the Aswan Dam across the Nile in Eygpt. This is causing the delta to shrink.

Map labels

EUROPE

ATLANTIC OCEAN

Sevastopol'

Marseille   Venice

Nice

Madrid   Barcelona   Rome   Naples   Dubrovnik   BLACK SEA

Valencia   Istanbul   Ankara

Izmir

Oran   Algiers   Athens

Tunis   MEDITERRANEAN SEA   Beirut

Tripoli   Tel Aviv-Yafo

Benghazi   Alexandria

Cairo

AFRICA   ASIA

66

66

76

A Coruña   Cabo Ortegal   Cabo de Peñas   Gijón   Oviedo

Cabo Fisterra

Vigo   Ourense   León

Porto   Valladolid

Vila Nova de Gaia   Douro

Cabo Mondego   Embalse de Almendra

PORTUGAL   Salamanca

LISBOA (LISBON)   Badajoz   Guadiana   SPA

Cabo da Roca   Tagus   Tagus

Setúbal

Cabo Carvoeiro

Golfo de Cádiz   Huelva   Sevilla (Seville)   Córdoba   Jaén

Cabo de São Vicente   Jerez de la Frontera   Granada

Cádiz   Sierra Nevada

Algeciras   GIBRALTAR (to UK)   Málaga

Cap Spartel   Strait of Gibraltar   Ceuta (to Spain)

Tanger   Tétouan   Alborán Sea   Melilla (to Spain)

RABAT   Kénitra   Cabo des Trois Fourches

Casablanca   Salé

Mohammedia   Fès   Meknès

Safi   MOROCCO

Cap Beddouza   Oum er Rbia

Tensift   Beni-Mellal   Jbel Ayachi

Marrakech   Haut   Atlas   Moyen Atlas

Major industry and infrastructure

- fishing port
- oil & gas
- tourism
- major towns
- international airports
- major roads
- major industrial areas

Monte Carlo is just one of the luxurious resorts scattered along the Riviera, which stretches along the coast from Cannes in France to La Spezia in Italy. The region's mild winters and hot summers have attracted wealthy tourists since the early 19th century.

CYPRUS

IN 1974 T... Cyprus wh... of the sou... and a UN f... areas. In ... itself the T... It is only ...

Oxygen in the Black Sea is dissolved only in its upper layers; at depths below 230–300 ft (70–100 m) the sea is 'dead' and can support no lifeforms other than specially-adapted bacteria.

The city of Venice is built on an archipelago of islands and mud-flats in the middle of a lagoon at the head of the Adriatic Sea. The city's numerous canals follow water routes between the original 118 islands.

Cyprus is the third largest Mediterranean island after Sardinia and Sicily. The island is mountainous; containing two main ranges, the Troodos and the Kyrenia mountains .

Both the Dead Sea in Jordan and the Gulf of Aqaba are extensions of the Great Rift Valley which runs through eastern Africa.

The Suez Canal, opened in 1869, extends 100 miles (160 km) from Port Said to the Gulf of Suez.

MALTA

SCALE 1:900,000
(projection: Lambert Conformal Conic)

0 5 10 20 Km

0 20 Miles

Commercial fisheries are found throughout the Mediterranean. Operations have traditionally been small-scale. As elsewhere, high demand has caused a decline in fish stocks.

A *fishing trawler* lies at anchor in the icy waters of Karaginskiy Zaliv, at the northern end of the Kamchatka Peninsula (Poluostrov Kamchatka) in eastern Siberia. The Russian Federation's fishing fleet is the largest in the world and operates worldwide.

The shores of Lake Baikal (Ozero Baykal) are a mixture of forest and the grassy steppe seen here. The lake freezes to a depth of 33 ft (10 m) in winter.

SCALE 1:13,800,000
(projection: Lambert Conformal Conic)

THE RUSSIAN FEDERATION

THE COLD WAR ERA OF GLOBAL RELATIONS was concluded in 1991 with the formal dissolution of the Soviet Union. The Russian Federation declared its separate sovereignty from the foundering communist empire following independence declarations from a number of former Soviet republics. As the leading member of the Commonwealth of Independent States, the Russian Federation has a central role in the development of post-Soviet Eurasia. Crossing 11 time zones, the Russian Federation is almost twice the size of the US, and with more than 150 ethnic minorities and 21 autonomous republics, regionalist dissent within its own territory remains a danger.

Summer beds of moss and lichen scatter a 90% surface cover of ice across the islands of Franz Josef Land (Zemlya Frantsa-Iosifa), the northernmost land in the eastern hemisphere.

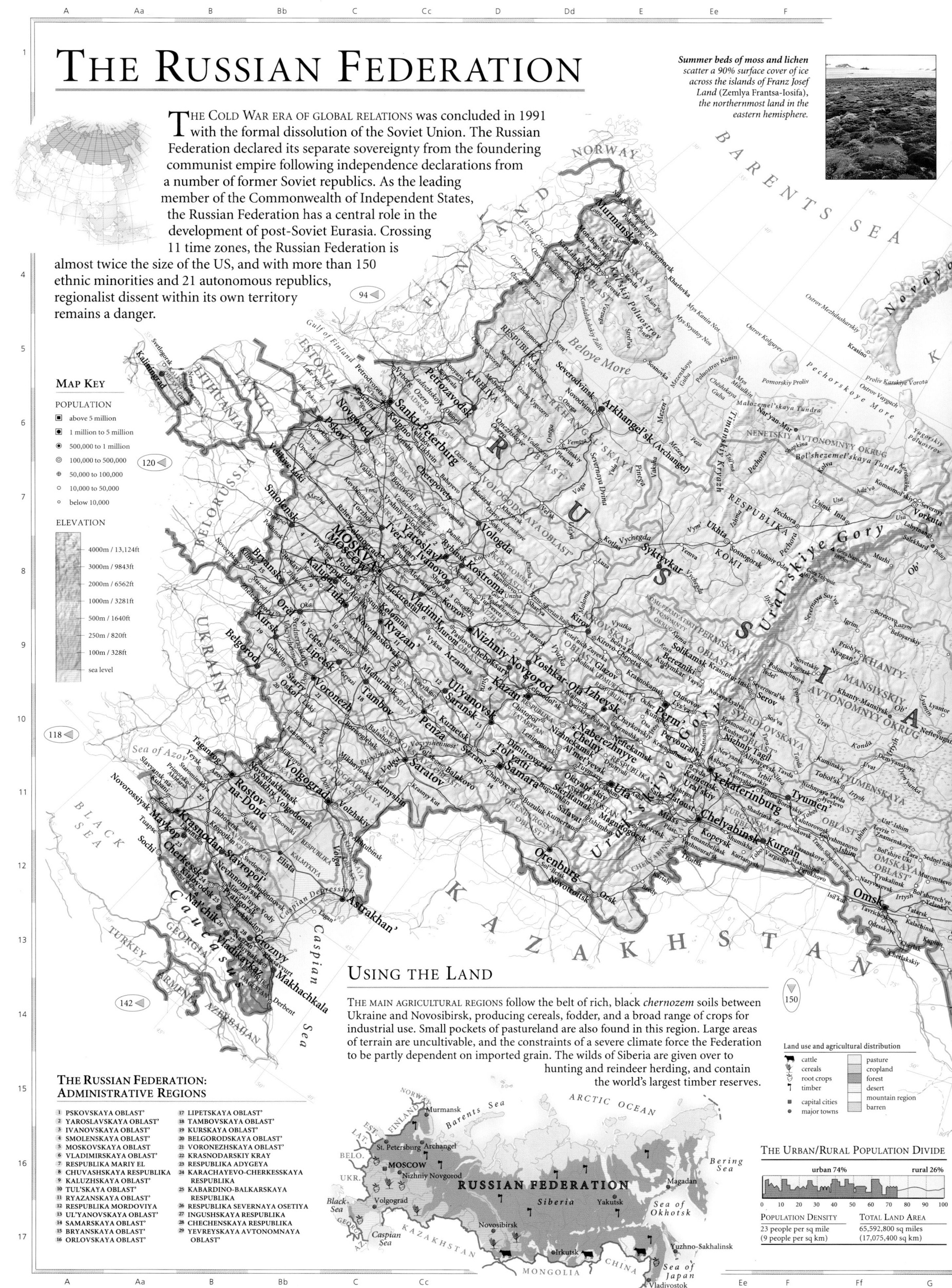

MAP KEY

POPULATION

- ▪ above 5 million
- ▪ 1 million to 5 million
- ⊡ 500,000 to 1 million
- ⊙ 100,000 to 500,000
- ⊕ 50,000 to 100,000
- ○ 10,000 to 50,000
- ∘ below 10,000

ELEVATION

- 4000m / 13,124ft
- 3000m / 9843ft
- 2000m / 6562ft
- 1000m / 3281ft
- 500m / 1640ft
- 250m / 820ft
- 100m / 328ft
- sea level

USING THE LAND

THE MAIN AGRICULTURAL REGIONS follow the belt of rich, black *chernozem* soils between Ukraine and Novosibirsk, producing cereals, fodder, and a broad range of crops for industrial use. Small pockets of pastureland are also found in this region. Large areas of terrain are uncultivable, and the constraints of a severe climate force the Federation to be partly dependent on imported grain. The wilds of Siberia are given over to hunting and reindeer herding, and contain the world's largest timber reserves.

Land use and agricultural distribution

- cattle
- cereals
- root crops
- timber
- capital cities
- major towns
- pasture
- cropland
- forest
- desert
- mountain region
- barren

THE RUSSIAN FEDERATION: ADMINISTRATIVE REGIONS

1. PSKOVSKAYA OBLAST'
2. YAROSLAVSKAYA OBLAST'
3. IVANOVSKAYA OBLAST'
4. SMOLENSKAYA OBLAST'
5. MOSKOVSKAYA OBLAST'
6. VLADIMIRSKAYA OBLAST'
7. RESPUBLIKA MARIY EL
8. CHUVASHSKAYA RESPUBLIKA
9. KALUZHSKAYA OBLAST'
10. TUL'SKAYA OBLAST'
11. RYAZANSKAYA OBLAST'
12. RESPUBLIKA MORDOVIYA
13. UL'YANOVSKAYA OBLAST'
14. SAMARSKAYA OBLAST'
15. BRYANSKAYA OBLAST'
16. ORLOVSKAYA OBLAST'
17. LIPETSKAYA OBLAST'
18. TAMBOVSKAYA OBLAST'
19. KURSKAYA OBLAST'
20. BELGORODSKAYA OBLAST'
21. VORONEZHSKAYA OBLAST'
22. KRASNODARSKIY KRAY
23. RESPUBLIKA ADYGEYA
24. KARACHAYEVO-CHERKESSKAYA RESPUBLIKA
25. KABARDINO-BALKARSKAYA RESPUBLIKA
26. RESPUBLIKA SEVERNAYA OSETIYA
27. INGUSHSKAYA RESPUBLIKA
28. CHECHENSKAYA RESPUBLIKA
29. YEVREYSKAYA AVTONOMNAYA OBLAST'

RUSSIAN FEDERATION

THE URBAN/RURAL POPULATION DIVIDE

urban 74%   rural 26%

POPULATION DENSITY	TOTAL LAND AREA
23 people per sq mile (9 people per sq km)	65,592,800 sq miles (17,075,400 sq km)

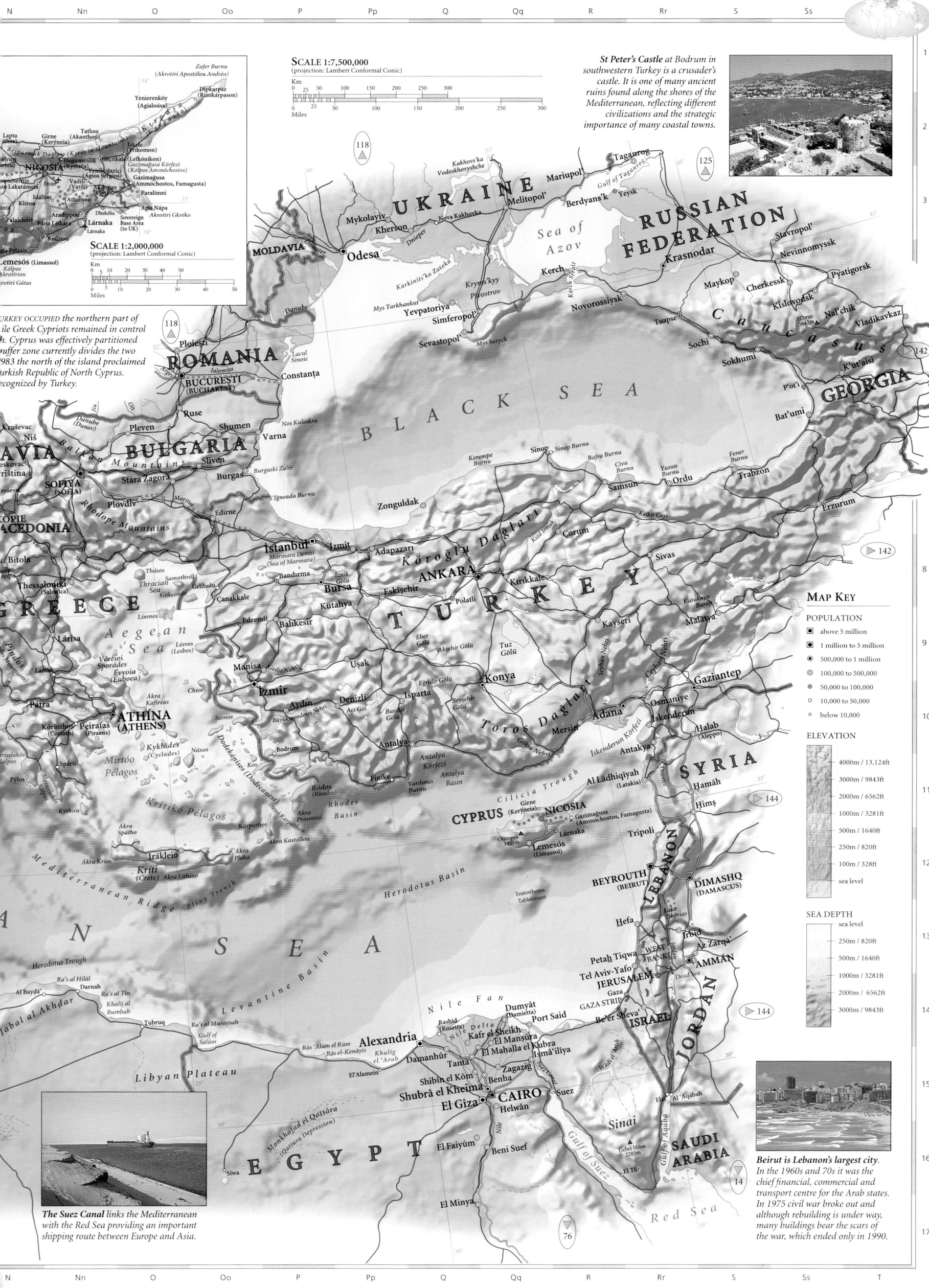

St Peter's Castle at Bodrum in southwestern Turkey is a crusader's castle. It is one of many ancient ruins found along the shores of the Mediterranean, reflecting different civilizations and the strategic importance of many coastal towns.

The Suez Canal links the Mediterranean with the Red Sea providing an important shipping route between Europe and Asia.

Beirut is Lebanon's largest city. In the 1960s and 70s it was the chief financial, commercial and transport centre for the Arab states. In 1975 civil war broke out and although rebuilding is under way, many buildings bear the scars of the war, which ended only in 1990.

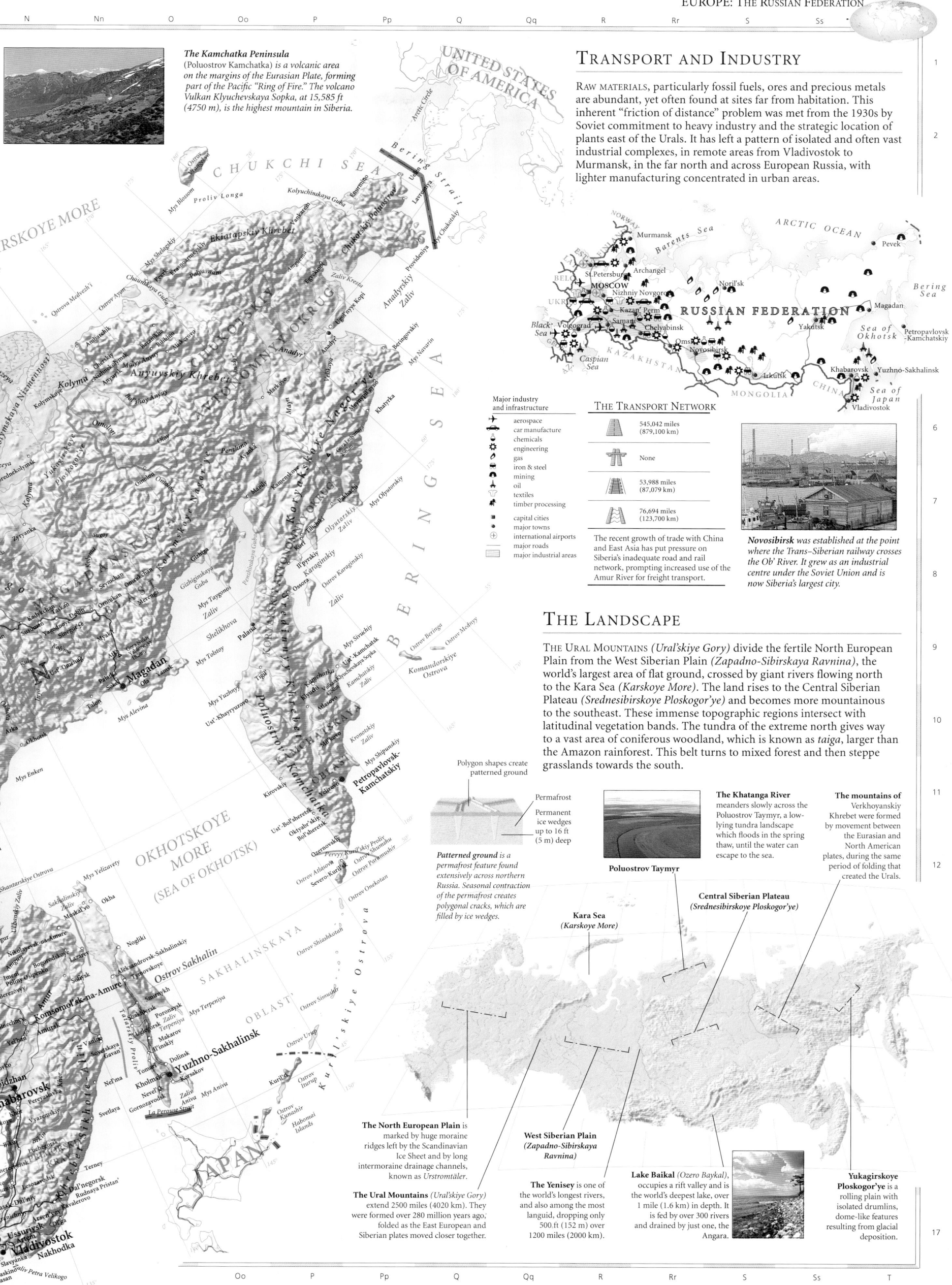

The Kamchatka Peninsula (Poluostrov Kamchatka) *is a volcanic area on the margins of the Eurasian Plate, forming part of the Pacific "Ring of Fire." The volcano Vulkan Klyuchevskaya Sopka, at 15,585 ft (4750 m), is the highest mountain in Siberia.*

TRANSPORT AND INDUSTRY

RAW MATERIALS, particularly fossil fuels, ores and precious metals are abundant, yet often found at sites far from habitation. This inherent "friction of distance" problem was met from the 1930s by Soviet commitment to heavy industry and the strategic location of plants east of the Urals. It has left a pattern of isolated and often vast industrial complexes, in remote areas from Vladivostok to Murmansk, in the far north and across European Russia, with lighter manufacturing concentrated in urban areas.

Major industry and infrastructure

- ✈ aerospace
- 🚗 car manufacture
- ⚗ chemicals
- ⚙ engineering
- ◒ gas
- ⚒ iron & steel
- ⛏ mining
- ◓ oil
- ⚑ textiles
- 🌲 timber processing

- ▪ capital cities
- ▫ major towns
- ⊕ international airports
- ▭ major roads
- ▭ major industrial areas

THE TRANSPORT NETWORK

🛣	545,042 miles (879,100 km)
🛣	None
🚉	53,988 miles (87,079 km)
🚉	76,694 miles (123,700 km)

The recent growth of trade with China and East Asia has put pressure on Siberia's inadequate road and rail network, prompting increased use of the Amur River for freight transport.

Novosibirsk was established at the point where the Trans–Siberian railway crosses the Ob' River. It grew as an industrial centre under the Soviet Union and is now Siberia's largest city.

THE LANDSCAPE

THE URAL MOUNTAINS (Ural'skiye Gory) divide the fertile North European Plain from the West Siberian Plain (Zapadno-Sibirskaya Ravnina), the world's largest area of flat ground, crossed by giant rivers flowing north to the Kara Sea (Karskoye More). The land rises to the Central Siberian Plateau (Srednesibirskoye Ploskogor'ye) and becomes more mountainous to the southeast. These immense topographic regions intersect with latitudinal vegetation bands. The tundra of the extreme north gives way to a vast area of coniferous woodland, which is known as *taiga*, larger than the Amazon rainforest. This belt turns to mixed forest and then steppe grasslands towards the south.

Polygon shapes create patterned ground

Permafrost

Permanent ice wedges up to 16 ft (5 m) deep

Patterned ground is a permafrost feature found extensively across northern Russia. Seasonal contraction of the permafrost creates polygonal cracks, which are filled by ice wedges.

The Khatanga River meanders slowly across the Poluostrov Taymyr, a low-lying tundra landscape which floods in the spring thaw, until the water can escape to the sea.

Poluostrov Taymyr

The mountains of Verkhoyanskiy Khrebet were formed by movement between the Eurasian and North American plates, during the same period of folding that created the Urals.

Central Siberian Plateau (Srednesibirskoye Ploskogor'ye)

Kara Sea (Karskoye More)

The North European Plain is marked by huge moraine ridges left by the Scandinavian Ice Sheet and by long intermoraine drainage channels, known as Urstromtäler.

The Ural Mountains (Ural'skiye Gory) extend 2500 miles (4020 km). They were formed over 280 million years ago, folded as the East European and Siberian plates moved closer together.

West Siberian Plain (Zapadno-Sibirskaya Ravnina)

The Yenisey is one of the world's longest rivers, and also among the most languid, dropping only 500 ft (152 m) over 1200 miles (2000 km).

Lake Baikal (Ozero Baykal), occupies a rift valley and is the world's deepest lake, over 1 mile (1.6 km) in depth. It is fed by over 300 rivers and drained by just one, the Angara.

Yukagirskoye Ploskogor'ye is a rolling plain with isolated drumlins, dome-like features resulting from glacial deposition.

NORTHERN EUROPEAN RUSSIA

Reaching into the Arctic Circle, this region of lakeland, forest and tundra is historically bound to Europe by St Petersburg, the old imperial capital of Tsarist Russia and home to a third of the region's population. Communist rule from Moscow left the north politically marginalized, contributing to the present problems of outmoded industry, poor infrastructure and serious environmental neglect. However, with borders embracing Finland, Norway, the Baltic and the northern sea route to the Atlantic, the region's success in foreign trade is now of prime importance to the Russian economy.

St Peter and Paul Fortress is the oldest building in St Petersburg, founded by Peter the Great in 1703 as a modern, European capital for Russia.

THE LANDSCAPE

The ancient bedrock of the Scandinavian Shield lies exposed across the glacially scoured Khibiny Mountains of the Kola Peninsula (*Kol'skiy Poluostrov*), becoming mantled with till towards the North European Plain. The Valdai Hills (*Valdayskaya Vozvyshennost'*) form an important watershed for the plain's rivers, while thick forest veils a complicated topography of moraines, lakes and ground disturbed by frost action. The Ural Mountains (*Ural'skiye Gory*) form a border with Asia in the east.

The Khibiny Mountains were formed by volcanic intrusions into the Scandinavian Shield, over 570 million years ago.

Kola Peninsula (Kol'skiy Poluostrov)

The Kola Peninsula (Kol'skiy Poluostrov) is part of the Scandinavian Shield, an area of ancient bedrock underlying Scandinavia. Rocks in excess of 2500 million years old are exposed across the peninsula.

Karst features, including sinkholes, lakes and caverns, are found in limestone outcrops across the plain of the Severnaya Dvina and Mezen' rivers.

The low-lying plains of the Pechora, Mezen' and Severnaya Dvina rivers were flooded by the sea while the land was still isostatically depressed following the last Ice Age, a process which has hidden the landforms created by glacial deposition.

Retreating glacier
Meltwater channels
Terminal moraine

Terminal moraines are crescent-shaped ridges of glacial deposits, widely found in central Russia. Detritus is carried by the glacier and deposited at its terminus (snout) as it melts, marking the limit of the ice advance.

Ural Mountains (*Ural'skiye Gory*)

Lake Onega (Onezhskoye Ozero) is the remnant of a body of water which, 12,000 years ago, connected the White Sea (Beloye More) with the Gulf of Finland and the Baltic Sea.

Two of Europe's biggest rivers, the Volga and Western Dvina, rise in the swampy uplands of the Valdai Hills (*Valdayskaya Vozvyshennost'*).

USING THE LAND AND SEA

The cold climate confines agriculture mainly to southern and western provinces, where dairy farming predominates and arable land is given over to fodder crops as well as flax, potatoes, oats and rye. Areas beyond the northern margins of cultivation are used for forestry, hunting, herding and fishing, with some vegetables grown in hothouses around urban areas.

Land use and agricultural distribution
- cattle
- fishing
- reindeer
- timber
- fodder
- major towns
- pasture
- cropland
- forest
- mountain region
- wetland
- tundra
- barren
- ice

THE URBAN/RURAL POPULATION DIVIDE

urban 74%   rural 26%

0 10 20 30 40 50 60 70 80 90 100

POPULATION DENSITY	TOTAL LAND AREA
27 people per sq mile	829,398 sq miles
10 people per sq km	(2,148,700 sq km)

Many rapids are found along the 175 mile (280 km) course of the Suna River.

The Ural Mountains
(Ural'skiye Gory) *form the traditional boundary between Europe and Asia. Elevations rarely exceed 6000 ft (1830 m). The region is extremely barren in the far northern latitudes.*

SCALE 1:5,500,000
(projection: Lambert Conformal Conic)

MAP KEY

POPULATION

- 1 million to 5 million
- 500,000 to 1 million
- 100,000 to 500,000
- 50,000 to 100,000
- 10,000 to 50,000
- below 10,000

ELEVATION

- 1000m / 3281ft
- 500m / 1640ft
- 250m / 820ft
- 100m / 328ft
- sea level

TRANSPORT AND INDUSTRY

THE PORTS OF ST PETERSBURG, Murmansk and Archangel serve a regional economy led by large-scale resource extraction. Nickel, iron ore and apatite are mined in the Kola Peninsula (*Kol'skiy Poluostrov*), and fossil fuels in the Pechora Basin. Paper production is central to Archangel's vast timber industry, while St Petersburg, drawing on ample labour, has become a major manufacturing centre.

Major industry and infrastructure

- chemicals
- coal
- defence
- engineering
- food processing
- hydro-electric power
- mining
- oil & gas
- textiles
- timber processing
- major towns
- international airports
- major roads
- major industrial areas

THE TRANSPORT NETWORK

- 53,700 miles (85,920 km)
- None
- 10,300 miles (16,572 km)
- 12,500 miles (20,000 km)

Railways linking remote industrial centres with the region's ports are the principal means of supply, although the impressive system of canals, linking natural waterways, is used for freight haulage during the summer.

Ice forces the port
at St Petersburg to close in winter, yet Murmansk, on the Barents Sea, remains open, its waters prevented from freezing by warmer ocean currents extending from the North Atlantic Drift.

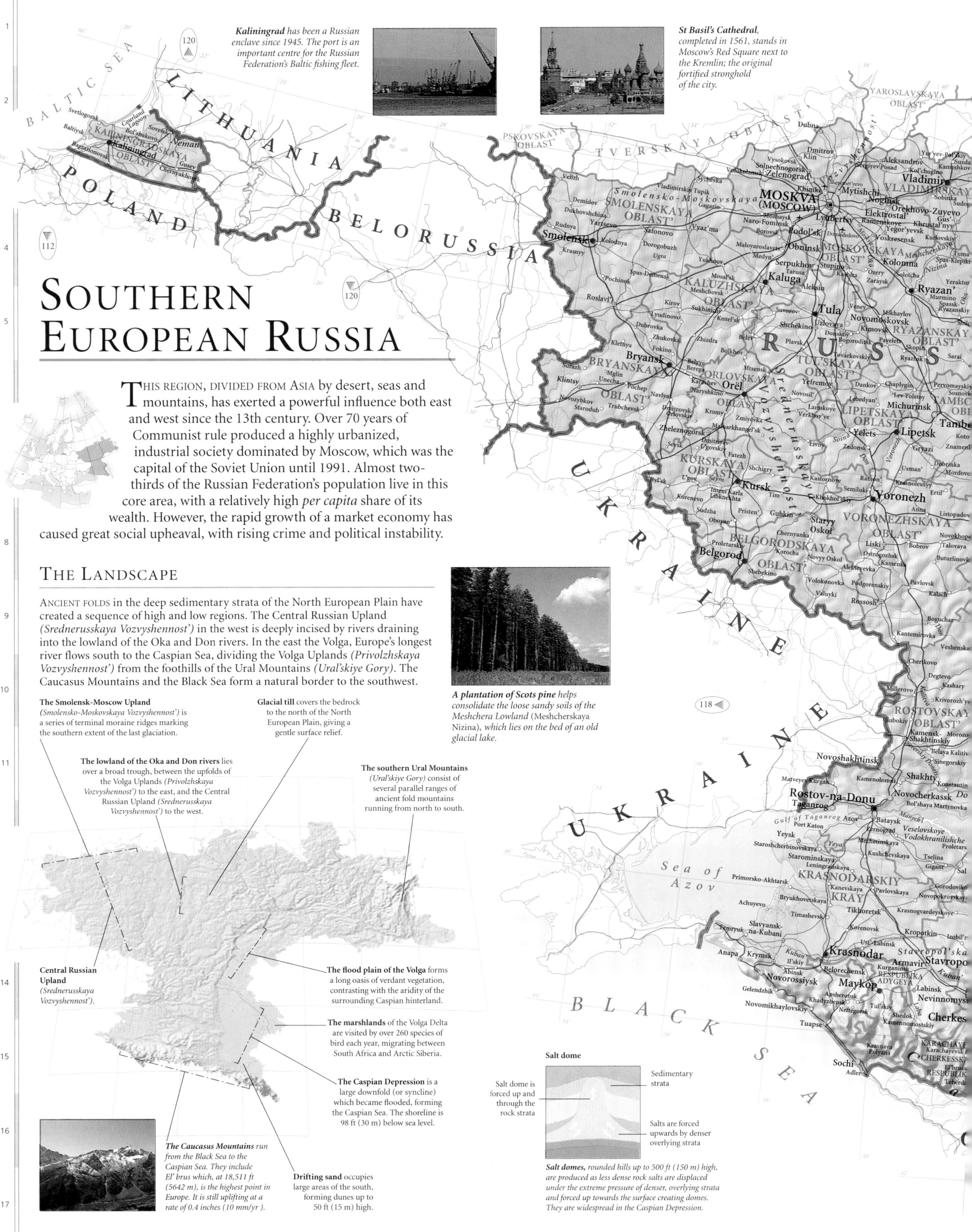

Kaliningrad has been a Russian enclave since 1945. The port is an important centre for the Russian Federation's Baltic fishing fleet.

St Basil's Cathedral, completed in 1561, stands in Moscow's Red Square next to the Kremlin; the original fortified stronghold of the city.

SOUTHERN EUROPEAN RUSSIA

THIS REGION, DIVIDED FROM ASIA by desert, seas and mountains, has exerted a powerful influence both east and west since the 13th century. Over 70 years of Communist rule produced a highly urbanized, industrial society dominated by Moscow, which was the capital of the Soviet Union until 1991. Almost two-thirds of the Russian Federation's population live in this core area, with a relatively high *per capita* share of its wealth. However, the rapid growth of a market economy has caused great social upheaval, with rising crime and political instability.

THE LANDSCAPE

ANCIENT FOLDS in the deep sedimentary strata of the North European Plain have created a sequence of high and low regions. The Central Russian Upland (*Srednerusskaya Vozvyshennost'*) in the west is deeply incised by rivers draining into the lowland of the Oka and Don rivers. In the east the Volga, Europe's longest river flows south to the Caspian Sea, dividing the Volga Uplands (*Privolzhskaya Vozvyshennost'*) from the foothills of the Ural Mountains (*Ural'skiye Gory*). The Caucasus Mountains and the Black Sea form a natural border to the southwest.

A plantation of Scots pine helps consolidate the loose sandy soils of the Meshchera Lowland (*Meshcherskaya Nizina*), which lies on the bed of an old glacial lake.

The Smolensk-Moscow Upland (*Smolensko-Moskovskaya Vozvyshennost'*) is a series of terminal moraine ridges marking the southern extent of the last glaciation.

Glacial till covers the bedrock to the north of the North European Plain, giving a gentle surface relief.

The lowland of the Oka and Don rivers lies over a broad trough, between the upfolds of the Volga Uplands (*Privolzhskaya Vozvyshennost'*) to the east, and the Central Russian Upland (*Srednerusskaya Vozvyshennost'*) to the west.

The southern Ural Mountains (*Ural'skiye Gory*) consist of several parallel ranges of ancient fold mountains running from north to south.

Central Russian Upland (*Srednerusskaya Vozvyshennost'*).

The flood plain of the Volga forms a long oasis of verdant vegetation, contrasting with the aridity of the surrounding Caspian hinterland.

The marshlands of the Volga Delta are visited by over 260 species of bird each year, migrating between South Africa and Arctic Siberia.

The Caspian Depression is a large downfold (or syncline) which became flooded, forming the Caspian Sea. The shoreline is 98 ft (30 m) below sea level.

Salt dome

Sedimentary strata

Salt dome is forced up and through the rock strata

Salts are forced upwards by denser overlying strata

Salt domes, rounded hills up to 500 ft (150 m) high, are produced as less dense rock salts are displaced under the extreme pressure of denser, overlying strata and forced up towards the surface creating domes. They are widespread in the Caspian Depression.

The Caucasus Mountains run from the Black Sea to the Caspian Sea. They include El' brus which, at 18,511 ft (5642 m), is the highest point in Europe. It is still uplifting at a rate of 0.4 inches (10 mm/yr).

Drifting sand occupies large areas of the south, forming dunes up to 50 ft (15 m) high.

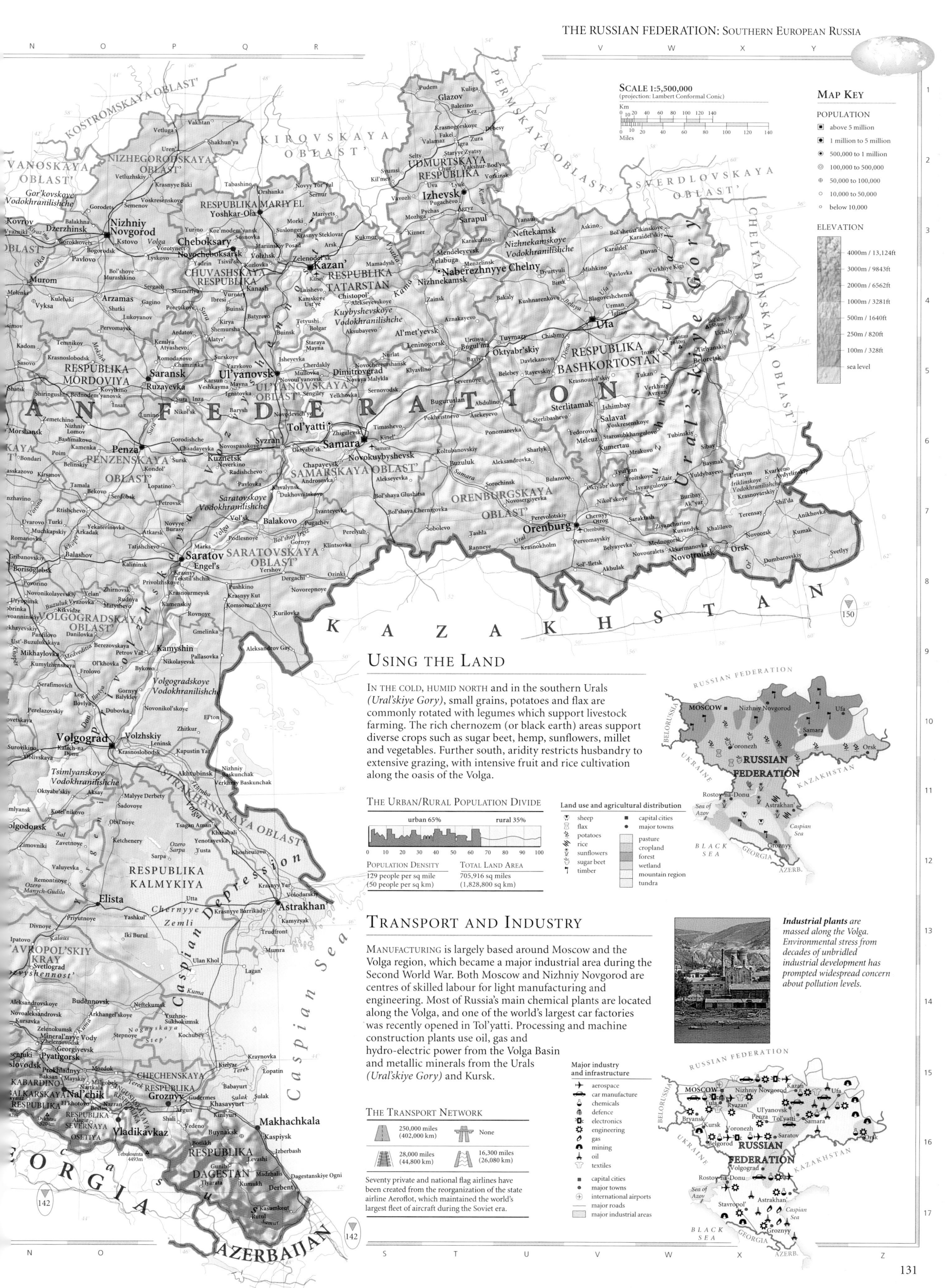

SCALE 1:5,500,000
(projection: Lambert Conformal Conic)

MAP KEY

POPULATION

- above 5 million
- 1 million to 5 million
- 500,000 to 1 million
- 100,000 to 500,000
- 50,000 to 100,000
- 10,000 to 50,000
- below 10,000

ELEVATION

- 4000m / 13,124ft
- 3000m / 9843ft
- 2000m / 6562ft
- 1000m / 3281ft
- 500m / 1640ft
- 250m / 820ft
- 100m / 328ft
- sea level

USING THE LAND

IN THE COLD, HUMID NORTH and in the southern Urals (Ural'skiye Gory), small grains, potatoes and flax are commonly rotated with legumes which support livestock farming. The rich chernozem (or black earth) areas support diverse crops such as sugar beet, hemp, sunflowers, millet and vegetables. Further south, aridity restricts husbandry to extensive grazing, with intensive fruit and rice cultivation along the oasis of the Volga.

THE URBAN/RURAL POPULATION DIVIDE

urban 65%   rural 35%

0 10 20 30 40 50 60 70 80 90 100

POPULATION DENSITY	TOTAL LAND AREA
129 people per sq mile (50 people per sq km)	705,916 sq miles (1,828,800 sq km)

Land use and agricultural distribution

- sheep
- flax
- potatoes
- rice
- sunflowers
- sugar beet
- timber
- capital cities
- major towns
- pasture
- cropland
- forest
- wetland
- mountain region
- tundra

TRANSPORT AND INDUSTRY

MANUFACTURING is largely based around Moscow and the Volga region, which became a major industrial area during the Second World War. Both Moscow and Nizhniy Novgorod are centres of skilled labour for light manufacturing and engineering. Most of Russia's main chemical plants are located along the Volga, and one of the world's largest car factories was recently opened in Tol'yatti. Processing and machine construction plants use oil, gas and hydro-electric power from the Volga Basin and metallic minerals from the Urals (Ural'skiye Gory) and Kursk.

Industrial plants are massed along the Volga. Environmental stress from decades of unbridled industrial development has prompted widespread concern about pollution levels.

Major industry and infrastructure

- aerospace
- car manufacture
- chemicals
- defence
- electronics
- engineering
- gas
- mining
- oil
- textiles
- capital cities
- major towns
- international airports
- major roads
- major industrial areas

THE TRANSPORT NETWORK

250,000 miles (402,000 km)	None
28,000 miles (44,800 km)	16,300 miles (26,080 km)

Seventy private and national flag airlines have been created from the reorganization of the state airline Aeroflot, which maintained the world's largest fleet of aircraft during the Soviet era.

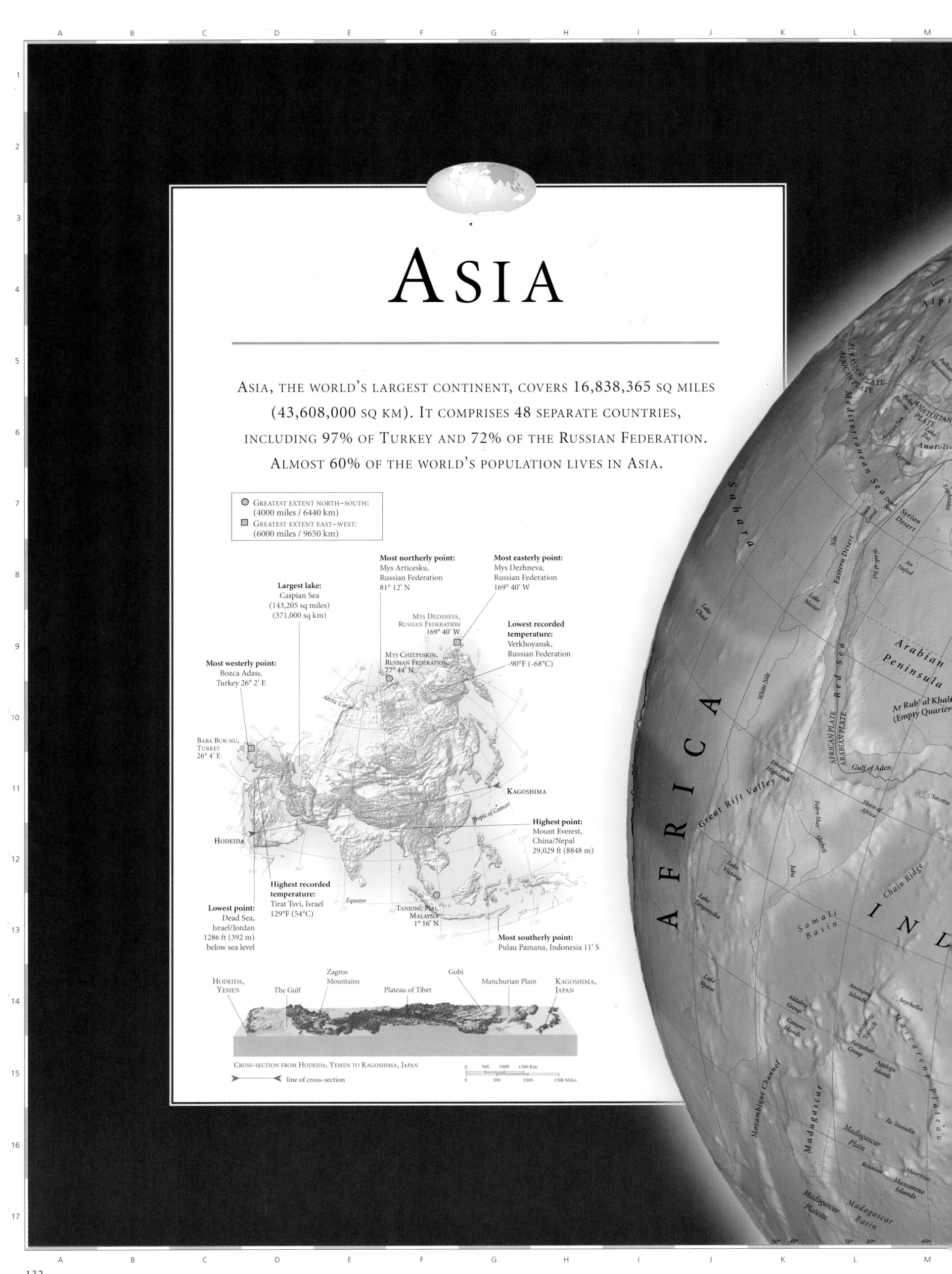

ASIA

ASIA, THE WORLD'S LARGEST CONTINENT, COVERS 16,838,365 SQ MILES
(43,608,000 SQ KM). IT COMPRISES 48 SEPARATE COUNTRIES,
INCLUDING 97% OF TURKEY AND 72% OF THE RUSSIAN FEDERATION.
ALMOST 60% OF THE WORLD'S POPULATION LIVES IN ASIA.

⬤ GREATEST EXTENT NORTH–SOUTH:
(4000 miles / 6440 km)
■ GREATEST EXTENT EAST–WEST:
(6000 miles / 9650 km)

Most northerly point:
Mys Articesku,
Russian Federation
81° 12' N

Most easterly point:
Mys Dezhneva,
Russian Federation
169° 40' W

Largest lake:
Caspian Sea
(143,205 sq miles)
(371,000 sq km)

MYS DEZHNEVA,
RUSSIAN FEDERATION
169° 40' W

**Lowest recorded
temperature:**
Verkhoyansk,
Russian Federation
-90°F (-68°C)

Most westerly point:
Bozca Adası,
Turkey 26° 2' E

MYS CHELYUSKIN,
RUSSIAN FEDERATION,
77° 44' N

BABA BUR-NU,
TURKEY
26° 4' E

Arctic Circle

KAGOSHIMA

Tropic of Cancer

Highest point:
Mount Everest,
China/Nepal
29,029 ft (8848 m)

HODEIDA

**Highest recorded
temperature:**
Tirat Tsvi, Israel
129°F (54°C)

Equator

TANJONG PIAI,
MALAYSIA
1° 16' N

Lowest point:
Dead Sea,
Israel/Jordan
1286 ft (392 m)
below sea level

Most southerly point:
Pulau Pamana, Indonesia 11° S

HODEIDA,
YEMEN

The Gulf

Zagros
Mountains

Plateau of Tibet

Gobi

Manchurian Plain

KAGOSHIMA,
JAPAN

CROSS-SECTION FROM HODEIDA, YEMEN TO KAGOSHIMA, JAPAN

◀ line of cross-section

| 0 | 500 | 1000 | 1500 Km |

| 0 | 500 | 1000 | 1500 Miles |

N O P Q R S T U V W X Y Z

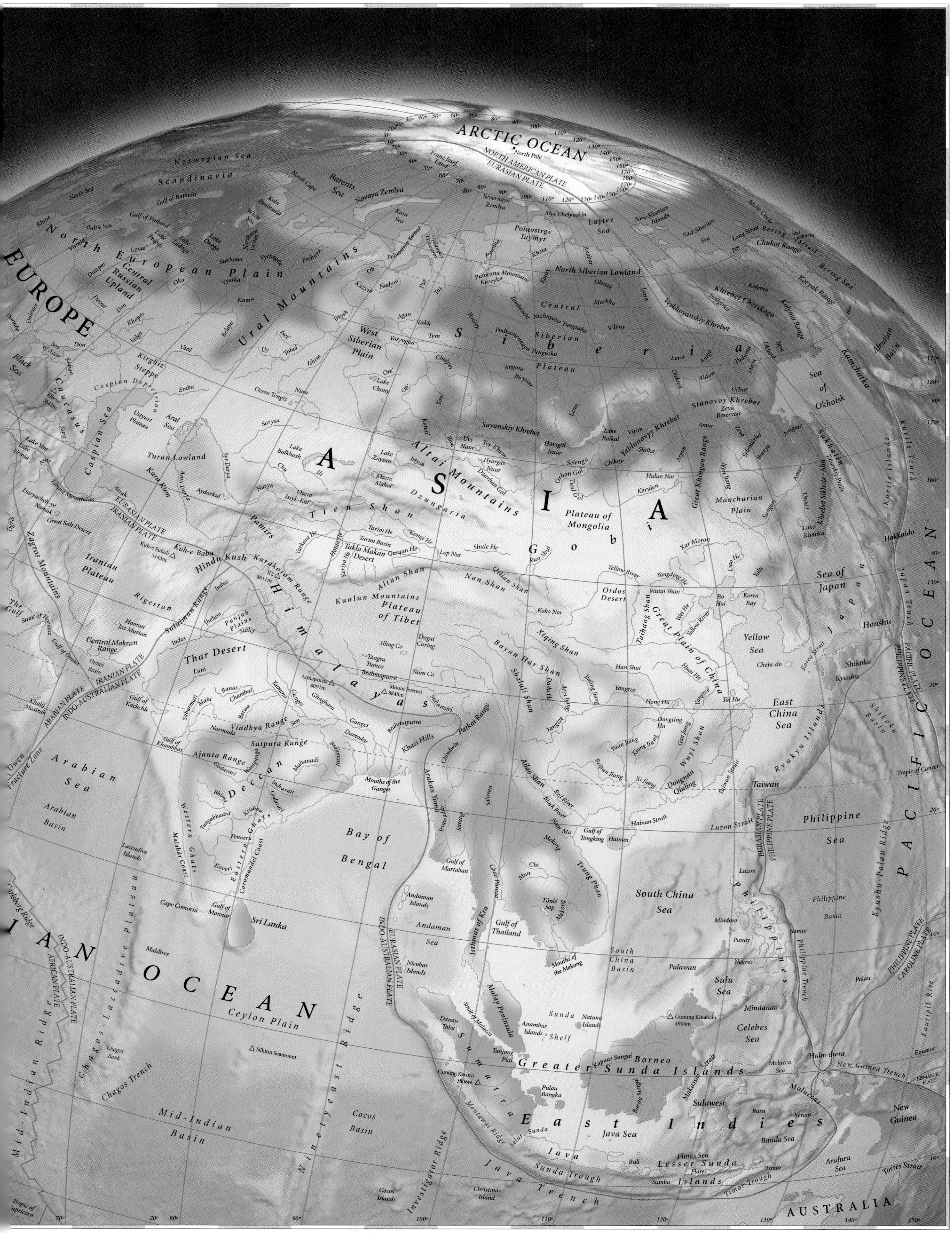
ARCTIC OCEAN
North Pole
NORTH AMERICAN PLATE
EURASIAN PLATE
Franz Josef Land
Severnaya Zemlya
Norwegian Sea
Scandinavia
North Sea
Gulf of Bothnia
Barents Sea
Novaya Zemlya
North Cape
Kola Peninsula
White Sea
Kara Sea
Gulf of Finland
Baltic Sea
Lake Ladoga
Lake Onega
Rhine
Vistula
Lake Peipus
Lovat'
Northern Dvina
North European Plain
Central Russian Upland
Dnieper
Sukhona
Vychegda
Pechora
Poluostrov Yamal
Gydanskiy Poluostrov
Mys Chelyuskin
Poluostrov Taymyr
Laptev Sea
New Siberian Islands
East Siberian Sea
Long Strait
Bering Strait
Chukot Range
Bering Sea
Arctic Circle
EUROPE
Ural Mountains
Oka
Vyatka
Kama
Desna
Don
Dniester
Danube
Khopër
Volga
Belaya
Ob'
Nadym
Pur
Taz
Kazym
Pyasina
Kheta
Anabar
Putorana Mountains
Kureyka
North Siberian Lowland
Olenëk
Markha
Lena
Verkhoyanskiy Khrebet
Kolyma
Indigirka
Khrebet Cherskogo
Kolyma Range
Koryak Range
Kamchatka
Aleutian Basin
Irtysh
Agan
Vakh
West Siberian Plain
Vasyugan
Tym
Yenisey
Central Siberian Plateau
Nizhnyaya Tunguska
Podkamennaya Tunguska
Vilyuy
Siberia
Sea of Azov
Black Sea
Kuban
Caucasus
Elbrus 5642m
Kirghiz Steppe
Caspian Depression
Ural
Uy
Tobol
Ishim
Iset'
Chulym
Angara
Biryusa
Aldan
Amga
Yudoma
Okhotsk
Maya
Uchur
Sea of Okhotsk
Stanovoy Khrebet
Zeya Reservoir
Om'
Lake Chany
Caspian Sea
Emba
Ozero Tengiz
Nura
Tom'
Aral Sea
Ustyurt Plateau
Kura
Sarysu
Lake Van
Lake Urmia
Aras
Sayanskiy Khrebet
Katun'
Biya
Uvs Nuur
Tes-Khem
Hövsgöl Nuur
Lake Baikal
Vitim
Yablonovyy Khrebet
Shilka
Argun
Amur
Zeya
Selemdzha
Bureya
Amgun'
Sakhalin
Tatarskiy Proliv
Kurile Islands
Kurile Trench
Turan Lowland
Syr Darya
Lake Balkhash
Lake Zaysan
Irtysh
ASIA
Altai Mountains
Hyargas Nuur
Dzavhan Gol
Selenga
Chikoy
Orhon Gol
Tuul Gol
Hulun Nur
Kerulen
Great Khingan Range
Nen Jiang
Manchurian Plain
Songhua
Ussuri
Khrebet Sikhote-Alin
Lake Khanka
Hokkaido
Kara Kum
Amu Darya
Chu
Ili
Ozero Alakol'
Aydarkul
Naryn
Ozero Issyk-Kul'
Dzungaria
Elburz Mountains
Daryacheh-ye Namak
Atrak
EURASIAN PLATE
IRANIAN PLATE
Tien Shan
Plateau of Mongolia
Gobi
Tigris
Great Salt Desert
Pamirs
Yarkant He
Hotan He
Tarim He
Tarim Basin
Kongi He
Takla Makan Desert
Qarqan He
Lop Nur
Shule He
Ruo Shui
Xar Moron
Liao He
Yalu
Sea of Japan
Japan Trench
Zagros Mountains
Kuh-e Fuladi 5143m
Kuh-e-Baba
Hindu Kush
Karakoram Range
K2 8611m
Iranian Plateau
Keriya He
Altun Shan
Nan Shan
Qilian Shan
Yellow River
Yongding He
Ordos Desert
Wutai Shan
Bo Hai
Korea Bay
Japan
Honshu
PACIFIC OCEAN
Rigestan
Sulaiman Range
Indus
Kunlun Mountains
Plateau of Tibet
Koko Nor
Taihang Shan
Wei He
Yellow River
Great Plain of China
Yellow Sea
The Gulf
Strait of Hormuz
Hamun Jaz Murian
Jhelum
Punjab Plains
Sutlej
Himalayas
Dogai Coring
Xiqing Shan
Bayan Har Shan
Gulf of Oman
Central Makran Range
Oman Basin
Thar Desert
Luni
Siling Co
Tangra Yumco
Brahmaputra
Nam Co
Shaluli Shan
Dadu He
Min Jiang
Jialing Jiang
Han Shui
Huai He
Cheju-do
Korea Strait
PACIFIC PLATE
PHILIPPINE PLATE
Shikoku
Kyushu
IRANIAN PLATE
ARABIAN PLATE
INDO-AUSTRALIAN PLATE
Khalij Masirah
Gulf of Kachchh
Sabarmati
Mahi
Banas
Chambal
Betwa
Yamuna
Ganges
Annapurna 8091m
Mount Everest 8848m
Ghaghara
Subansiri
Yangtze
Hong Hu
Tai Hu
East China Sea
Shikoku Basin
Vindhya Range
Son
Narmada
Ganges
Damodar
Brahmaputra
Patkai Range
Dongting Hu
Gan Jiang
Owen Fracture Zone
Gulf of Khambhat
Satpura Range
Brahmani
Khasi Hills
Chindwin
Yuan Jiang
Xiang Jiang
Wuyi Shan
Ryukyu Islands
Arabian Sea
Ajanta Range
Wainganga
Godavari
Mahanadi
Deccan
Indravati
Mouths of the Ganges
Arakan Yoma
Ailao Shan
Beipan Jiang
Xi Jiang
Dongnan Qiuling
Taiwan Strait
Taiwan
Tropic of Cancer
Arabian Basin
Bhima
Krishna
Godavari
Tungabhadra
Western Ghats
Eastern Ghats
Penneru
Irrawaddy
Sittang
Salween
Red River
Black River
Nam Ma
Hainan Strait
Gulf of Tongking
Hainan
Luzon Strait
EURASIAN PLATE
PHILIPPINE PLATE
Philippine Sea
Kyushu-Palau Ridge
Bay of Bengal
Malabar Coast
Coromandel Coast
Laccadive Islands
Kaveri
Gulf of Martaban
Mekong
Chao Phraya
Chi
Mun
Trung Phan
Luzon
Philippines
Philippine Trench
Philippine Basin
Cape Comorin
Gulf of Mannar
Sri Lanka
Andaman Islands
Andaman Sea
Isthmus of Kra
Gulf of Thailand
Tônlé Sap
Mekong
South China Sea
Mindoro
Panay
Negros
Maldives
Laccadive Plateau
INDO-AUSTRALIAN PLATE
AFRICAN PLATE
INDIAN OCEAN
EURASIAN PLATE
INDO-AUSTRALIAN PLATE
Nicobar Islands
Mouths of the Mekong
South China Basin
Palawan
Sulu Sea
Mindanao
Palau
PHILIPPINE PLATE
CAROLINE PLATE
Eauripik Rise
Mid-Indian Ridge
Chagos-Laccadive Ridge
Ceylon Plain
Chagos Bank
Nikitin Seamount
Chagos Trench
Ninetyeast Ridge
Malay Peninsula
Strait of Malacca
Danau Toba
Anambas Islands
Natuna Islands
Sunda Shelf
Gunung Kinabalu 4904m
Celebes Sea
Halmahera
Equator
New Guinea Trench
BISMARCK PLATE
Tanjong Piai
Kapuas Sungai
Borneo
Greater Sunda Islands
Makassar Strait
Molucca Sea
Moluccas
Gunung Kerinci 3806m
Sumatra
Pulau Bangka
Barito Sungai
Sulawesi
Buru
Seram
New Guinea
Mid-Indian Basin
Cocos Basin
Mentawai Ridge
Selat Sunda
East Indies
Java Sea
Banda Sea
Investigator Ridge
Java
Bali
Flores Sea
Flores
Lesser Sunda Islands
Sumba
Timor
Timor Trough
Arafura Sea
Torres Strait
Sunda Trough
Java Trench
Cocos Islands
Christmas Island
Tropic of Capricorn
AUSTRALIA

N O P Q R S T U V W X Y Z

ASIAN RESOURCES

ALTHOUGH AGRICULTURE REMAINS THE ECONOMIC MAINSTAY of most Asian countries, the number of people employed in agriculture has steadily declined, as new industries have been developed during the past 30 years. China, Indonesia, Malaysia, Thailand and Turkey have all experienced far-reaching structural change in their economies, while the breakup of the Soviet Union has created a new economic challenge in the Central Asian republics. The countries of The Gulf illustrate the rapid transformation from rural nomadism to modern, urban society which oil wealth has brought to parts of the continent. Asia's most economically dynamic countries, Japan, Singapore, South Korea, and Taiwan, fringe the Pacific Ocean and are known as the Pacific Rim. In contrast, other Southeast Asian countries like Laos and Cambodia remain both economically and industrially underdeveloped.

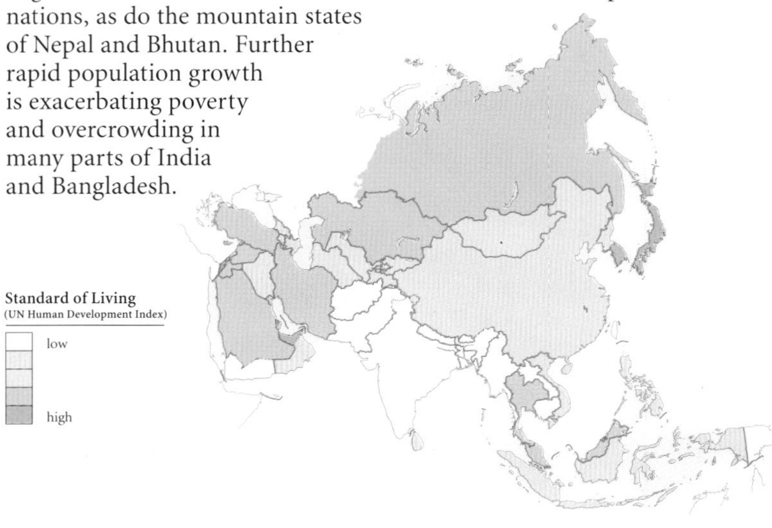

INDUSTRY

JAPANESE INDUSTRY LEADS THE CONTINENT in both productivity and efficiency; electronics, hi-tech industries, car manufacture and shipbuilding are important. In recent years, the so-called economic 'tigers' of the Pacific Rim such as Taiwan and South Korea are now challenging Japan's economic dominance. Heavy industries such as engineering, chemicals, and steel typify the industrial complexes along the corridor created by the Trans-Siberian Railway, the Fergana Valley in Central Asia, and also much of the huge industrial plain of east China. The discovery of oil in The Gulf has brought immense wealth to countries that previously relied on subsistence agriculture on marginal desert land.

Industry

✈ aerospace	🖨 printing & publishing
🍺 brewing	⚓ shipbuilding
🚗 car/vehicle manufacture	sugar processing
cement	tea processing
chemicals	textiles
electronics	timber processing
⚙ engineering	tobacco processing
finance	coal
fish processing	oil
food processing	gas
hi-tech industry	industrial cities
iron & steel	major industrial areas
pharmaceuticals	

STANDARD OF LIVING

DESPITE JAPAN'S HIGH STANDARDS OF LIVING, and Southwest Asia's oil-derived wealth, immense disparities exist across the continent. Afghanistan remains one of the world's most underdeveloped nations, as do the mountain states of Nepal and Bhutan. Further rapid population growth is exacerbating poverty and overcrowding in many parts of India and Bangladesh.

Standard of Living
(UN Human Development Index)

low

high

On a small island at the southern tip of the Malay Peninsula lies Singapore, one of the Pacific Rim's most vibrant economic centres. Multinational banking and finance form the core of the city's wealth.

GNP per capita (US$)

0–499
500–999
1000–4999
5000–9999
10000–19999
20000+

Iron and steel, engineering and shipbuilding typify the heavy industry found in eastern China's industrial cities, especially the nation's leading manufacturing centre, Shanghai.

Traditional industries are still crucial to many rural economies across Asia. Here, on the Vietnamese coast, salt has been extracted from seawater by evaporation and is being loaded into a van to take to market.

ARCTIC OCEAN

PACIFIC OCEAN

Sea of Okhotsk

RUSSIAN FEDERATION

Yakutsk

Yekaterinburg
Chelyabinsk
Magnitogorsk
Omsk
Novosibirsk
Novokuznetsk
Kemerovo
Krasnoyarsk
Bratsk
Irkutsk
Khabarovsk

Trans-Siberian Railway

KAZAKHSTAN
Karaganda
Aral Sea
Alma-Ata
Tashkent
UZBEKISTAN
Farghona
KYRGYZSTAN
Dushanbe
TAJIKISTAN
TURKMENISTAN
Ashgabat

Istanbul
Izmir
Ankara
TURKEY
GEORGIA
Tbilisi
ARMENIA
Yerevan
AZERB.
Baku
CYPRUS
LEBANON
SYRIA
Beirut
Damascus
Tel Aviv-Yafo
ISRAEL
JORDAN
Amman
IRAQ
Baghdad
Kirkuk
Basra
IRAN
Tehran
Isfahan
SAUDI ARABIA
Kuwait
KUWAIT
BAHRAIN
QATAR
Ad Damman
Riyadh
Abu Dhabi
Dubai
U.A.E.
The Gulf
OMAN
Jedda
YEMEN

Red Sea
Gulf of Aden
Gulf of Oman

Caspian Sea

AFGHANISTAN
Rawalpindi
Lahore
PAKISTAN
Karachi

MONGOLIA
Ulan Bator
Urumqi

CHINA
Lanzhou
Chengdu
Chongqing
Kunming
Xi'an
Zhengzhou
Taiyuan
Jinan
Beijing
Tianjin
Shenyang
Harbin
Vladivostok
NORTH KOREA
Pyongyang
SOUTH KOREA
Seoul
Pusan
Qingdao
Dalian
Nanjing
Wuhan
Shanghai
Guangzhou
Hong Kong
Taipei
TAIWAN

JAPAN
Tokyo
Nagoya
Kobe

Delhi
Kanpur
NEPAL
BHUTAN
INDIA
Ahmadabad
Indore
Jamshedpur
BANGLADESH
Dhaka
Calcutta
Nagpur
Bombay
Chittagong
BURMA
Mandalay
Rangoon
Bangalore
Madras
SRI LANKA

Arabian Sea
INDIAN OCEAN

LAOS
Hanoi
VIETNAM
Da Nang
THAILAND
Bangkok
CAMBODIA
Ho Chi Minh City
South China Sea
Manila
PHILIPPINES

Kuala Lumpur
MALAYSIA
BRUNEI
Singapore
SINGAPORE
INDONESIA
Jakarta
Surabaya

ENVIRONMENTAL ISSUES

THE TRANSFORMATION OF UZBEKISTAN by the former Soviet Union into the world's second largest producer of cotton led to the diversion of several major rivers for irrigation. Starved of this water, the Aral Sea diminished in volume by over 50% in 30 years, irreversibly altering the ecology of the area. Heavy industries in eastern China have polluted coastal waters, rivers and urban air, while in Burma, Malaysia and Indonesia, ancient hardwood rainforests are being felled faster than they can regenerate.

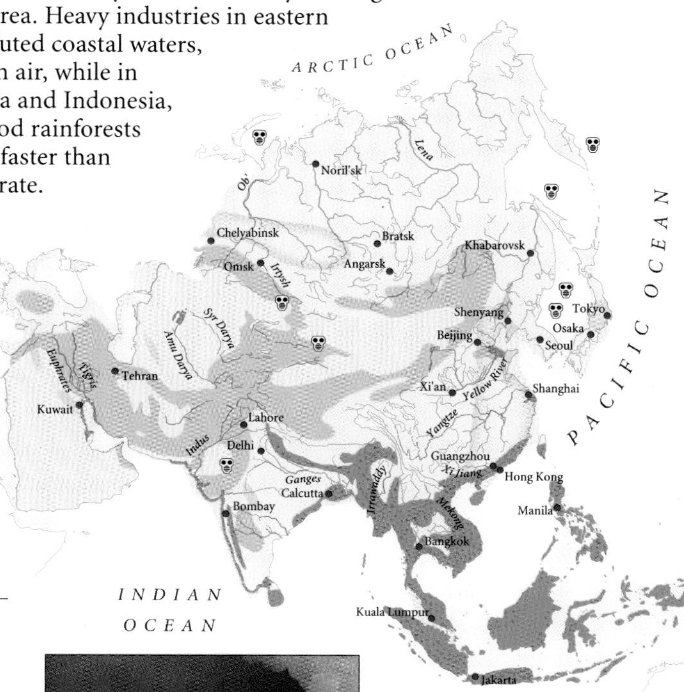

Environmental Issues
- tropical forest
- forest destroyed
- desert
- desertification
- acid rain
- polluted rivers
- marine pollution
- heavy marine pollution
- radioactive contamination
- poor urban air quality

The long-term environmental impact of the Gulf War (1991) is still uncertain. As Iraqi troops left Kuwait, equipment was abandoned to rust and thousands of oil wells were set alight, pouring crude oil into The Gulf.

Although Siberia remains a quintessentially frozen, inhospitable wasteland, vast untapped mineral reserves – especially the oil and gas of the West Siberian Plain – have lured industrial development to the area since the 1950s and 1960s.

MINERAL RESOURCES

AT LEAST 60% OF THE WORLD'S known oil and gas deposits are found in Asia; notably the vast oil fields of The Gulf, and the less-exploited oil and gas fields of the Ob' Basin in west Siberia. Immense coal reserves in Siberia and China have been utilized to support large steel industries. Southeast Asia has some of the world's largest deposits of tin, found in a belt running down the Malay Peninsula to Indonesia.

Mineral Resources
- oil field
- gas field
- coal field
- chromite
- copper
- gold
- iron
- lead
- nickel
- platinum
- tin
- wolfram

USING THE LAND AND SEA

VAST AREAS OF ASIA REMAIN UNCULTIVATED as a result of unsuitable climatic and soil conditions. In favourable areas such as river deltas, farming is intensive. Rice is the staple crop of most Asian countries, grown in paddy fields on waterlogged alluvial plains and terraced hillsides, and often irrigated for higher yields. Across the black earth region of the Eurasian steppe in southern Siberia and Kazakhstan, wheat farming is the dominant activity. Cash crops, like tea in Sri Lanka and dates in the Arabian Peninsula, are grown for export, and provide valuable income. The sovereignty of the rich fishing grounds in the South China Sea is disputed by China, Malaysia, Taiwan, the Philippines and Vietnam, because of potential oil reserves.

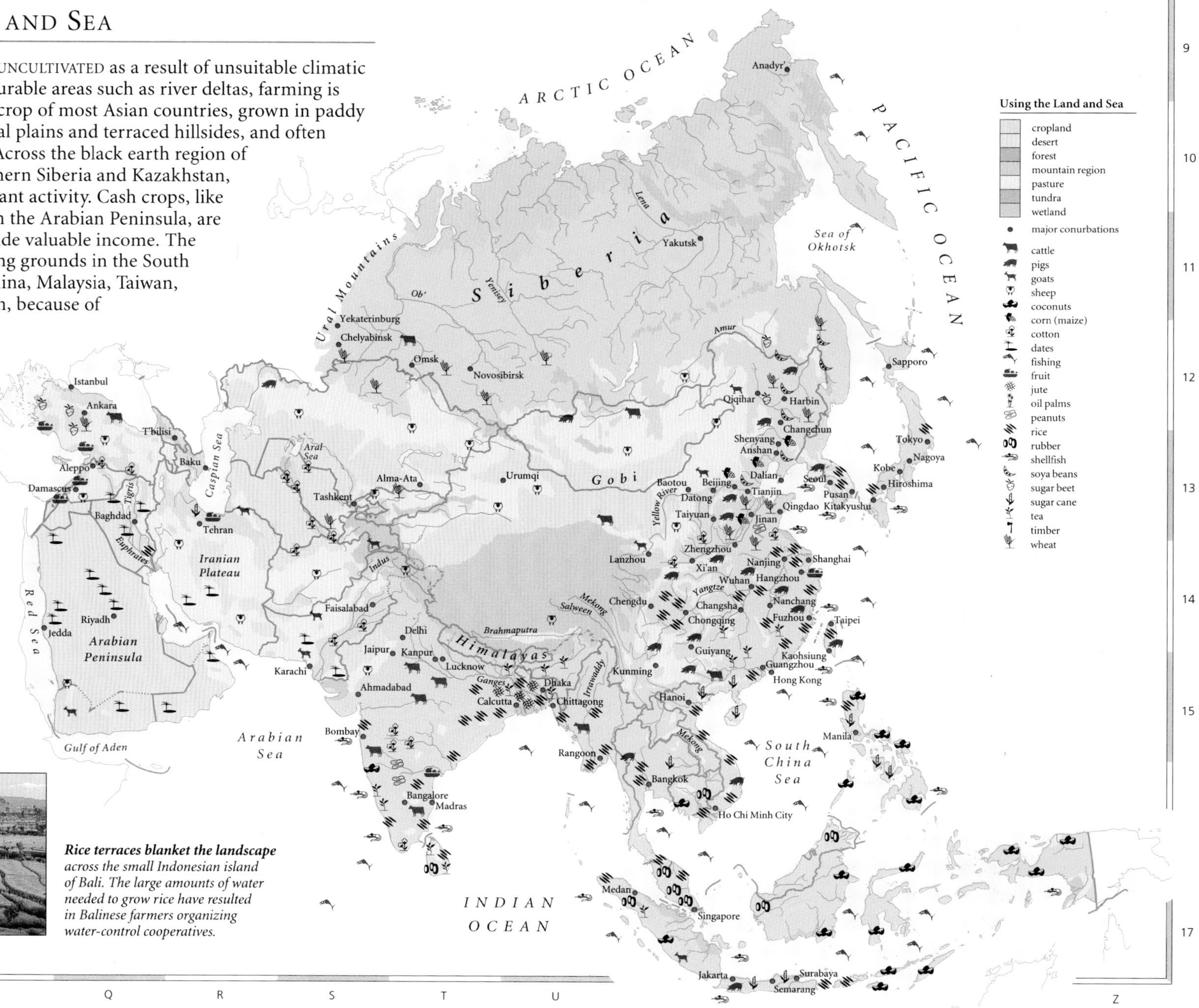

Using the Land and Sea
- cropland
- desert
- forest
- mountain region
- pasture
- tundra
- wetland
- major conurbations
- cattle
- pigs
- goats
- sheep
- coconuts
- corn (maize)
- cotton
- dates
- fishing
- fruit
- jute
- oil palms
- peanuts
- rice
- rubber
- shellfish
- soya beans
- sugar beet
- sugar cane
- tea
- timber
- wheat

Date palms have been cultivated in oases throughout the Arabian Peninsula since antiquity. In addition to the fruit, palms are used for timber, fuel, rope, and for making vinegar, syrup and a liquor known as arrack.

Rice terraces blanket the landscape across the small Indonesian island of Bali. The large amounts of water needed to grow rice have resulted in Balinese farmers organizing water-control cooperatives.

135

SIBERIAN PLATEAU AND PLAIN

THE WEST SIBERIAN PLAIN is one of the largest in the world, and contains a vast system of marshes. The whole area is covered by glacial deposits, underlain by the Angara Shield, a remnant of the ancient continent of Laurasia. The flat relief of the region and thick surface deposits result in poor drainage; this, combined with the freezing and thawing of the extensive permafrost layer leads to the formation of the vast swamps which cover the area. Many of the north-flowing rivers are also frozen for up to half the year.

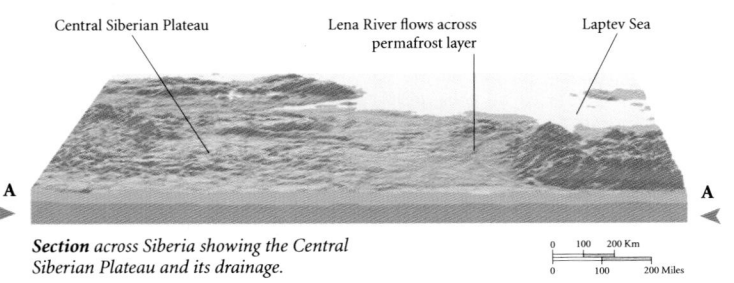

Section across Siberia showing the Central Siberian Plateau and its drainage.

Labels: Central Siberian Plateau; Lena River flows across permafrost layer; Laptev Sea

A — A

THE ARABIAN SHIELD AND IRANIAN PLATEAU

APPROXIMATELY FIVE MILLION YEARS AGO, rifting of the continental crust split the Arabian Plate from the African Plate and flooded the Red Sea. As this rift spread, the Arabian Plate collided with the Eurasian Plate, transforming part of the Tethys seabed into the Zagros Mountains which run northwest-southeast across western Iran.

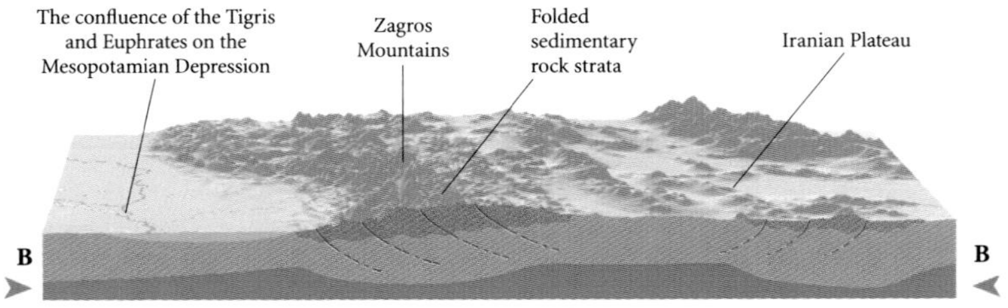

Cross-section through southwestern Asia, showing the Mesopotamian Depression, the folded Zagros Mountains and the Iranian Plateau.

Labels: The confluence of the Tigris and Euphrates on the Mesopotamian Depression; Zagros Mountains; Folded sedimentary rock strata; Iranian Plateau

B — B

THE TURAN BASIN AND KAZAKH UPLANDS

THE TURAN BASIN AND KAZAKH UPLANDS are a complex mixture of mountain foothills, an arid limestone plateau and deserts including the Kyzl Kum and Kara Kum. In the centre of the Turan Lowland – an area of inland drainage – is the desiccated Aral Sea, reduced to a fraction of its former size because of the diversion of its flow into irrigation channels. The only rivers with sufficient water to cross this arid region are the Syr Dayra and Amu Dayra.

THE INDIAN SHIELD AND HIMALAYAN SYSTEM

THE LARGE SHIELD AREA beneath the Indian subcontinent is between 2.5 and 3.5 billion years old. As the floor of the southern Indian Ocean spread, it pushed the Indian Shield north. This was eventually driven beneath the Plateau of Tibet. This process closed up the ancient Tethys Sea and uplifted the world's highest mountain chain, the Himalayas. Much of the uplifted rock strata was from the seabed of the Tethys Sea, partly accounting for the weakness of the rocks and the high levels of erosion found in the Himalayas.

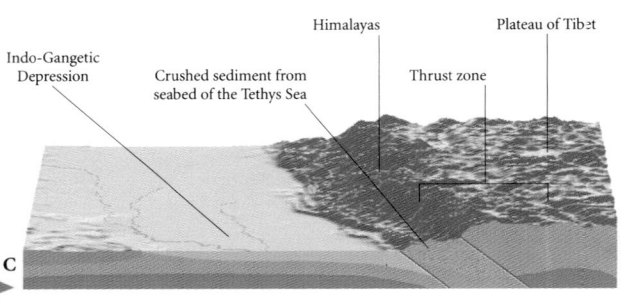

Cross-section through the Himalayas showing thrust faulting of the rock strata.

Labels: Indo-Gangetic Depression; Crushed sediment from seabed of the Tethys Sea; Himalayas; Thrust zone; Plateau of Tibet

C — C

CENTRAL ASIAN PLATEAUX AND BASINS

THE PLATEAU OF TIBET lies north of the Himalayas and covers 965,250 sq miles (2,500,000 sq km); its average elevation is 16,500 ft (5000 m). The region is noted for its extreme aridity. In the south, the Himalayan mountain belt blocks moisture-bearing winds. The pressure from the Indo-Australian Plate against the plateau is causing both uplift and, when combined with the downward force caused by weight of the plateau, extension east and west of the of the more malleable underlying crust. The brittle upper rock layers are extensively faulted.

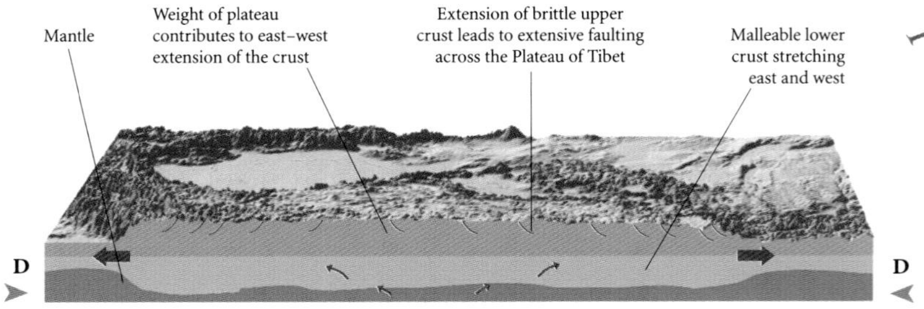

Cross-section across the Plateau of Tibet showing uplift and crustal extension caused by the collision of the Indo-Australian and Eurasian plates.

Labels: Mantle; Weight of plateau contributes to east-west extension of the crust; Extension of brittle upper crust leads to extensive faulting across the Plateau of Tibet; Malleable lower crust stretching east and west

D — D

Map labels: ARCTIC; Franz Josef Land; Kara Sea; Poluostrov Yamal; Gulf of Ob; Nadym; SIBERIA; West Siberian Plain; Ob; Tobol; Ishim; Irtysh; Kirghiz Steppe; Kulunda Steppe; Ozero Zaysan; Kazakh Uplands; Aral Sea; TURAN BASIN & KAZAKH UPLANDS; Ustyurt Plateau; Lake Balkhash; Ili; Kirghiz Range; Chatkal Range; Ozero Issyk-Kul'; Tien Shan; Turan Lowland; Kyzyl Kum; Syr Darya; Turkestan Range; Tarim He; Takla Makan; EUROPE; Ural Mountains; Ural; Black Sea; Sea of Azov; Caspian Sea; Kara Bogaz; ANATOLIAN PLATE; EURASIAN PLATE; Anatolia; Taurus Mountains; Gulf of Antalya; Güney Dogu Toroslar; Caucasus; Kura; Kara Kum; Amu Darya; Pamir; Hindu Kush; Karakoram Range; K2 8611m; Karakoram Pass 5568m; Mediterranean Sea; AFRICA; Syrian Desert; ARABIAN SHIELD & IRANIAN PLATEAU; Euphrates; Tigris; An Nafud; Elburz Mountains; Great Salt Desert; Iranian Plateau; Zagros Mountains; IRANIAN PLATE; Kabul; Khyber Pass 1080m; Indus; Sulaiman Range; Sutlej; Thar Desert; INDIAN SHIELD & HIMALAYAN SYSTEM; Red Sea; AFRICAN PLATE; ARABIAN PLATE; Aş Şummān; Ad Dahnā'; As Summah; Al Biyad; Arabian Peninsula; Ar Rub' al Khālī (Empty Quarter); The Gulf; Strait of Hormuz; Gulf of Oman; Mounts of the Indus; Rann of Kachchh; Gulf of Kachchh; INDO-AUSTRALIAN PLATE; Vindhya Range; Narmada; Satpura Range; Deccan; Krishna; Godavari; Eastern Ghats; Western Ghats; Hadhramaut; Gulf of Aden; ARABIAN PLATE; AFRICAN PLATE; Socotra; Arabian Sea; Gulf of Khambhat; INDIAN OCEAN; Sri Lanka; Gulf of Mannar

Scale bars: 0 100 200 Km / 0 100 200 Miles; 0 50 100 Km / 0 50 100 Miles; 0 50 100 Km / 0 50 100 Miles; 0 200 400 Km / 0 200 400 Miles

PHYSICAL ASIA

THE STRUCTURE OF ASIA can be divided into two distinct regions. The landscape of northern Asia consists of old mountain chains, shields, plateaux and basins, like the Ural Mountains in the west and the Central Siberian Plateau to the east. To the south of this region, are a series of plateaux and basins, including the vast Plateau of Tibet and the Tarim Basin. In contrast, the landscapes of southern Asia are much younger, formed by tectonic activity beginning about 65 million years ago, leading to an almost continuous mountain chain running from Europe, across much of Asia, and culminating in the mighty Himalayan mountain belt, formed when the Indo-Australian Plate collided with the Eurasian Plate. They are still being uplifted today. North of the mountains lies a belt of deserts, including the Gobi and the Takla Makan. In the far south, tectonic activity has formed narrow island arcs, extending over 4000 miles (7000 km). To the west lies the Arabian Shield, once part of the African Plate. As it was rifted apart from Africa, the Arabian Plate collided with the Eurasian Plate, uplifting the Zagros Mountains.

SHAPING THE LANDSCAPE

IN THE NORTH, melting of extensive permafrost leads to typical periglacial features such as thermokarst. In the arid areas wind action transports sand creating extensive dune systems. An active tectonic margin in the south causes continued uplift, and volcanic and seismic activity, but also high rates of weathering and erosion. Across the continent, huge rivers erode and transport vast quantities of sediment depositing it on the plains or forming large deltas.

PERIGLACIATION

[1] Permafrost is widespread across northern Siberia. When ground ice, which makes up a large proportion of the soil layer, melts, it contracts and extensive ground subsidence occurs. Over time this process leads to depressions in the landscape and the gradual movement of soil down slopes. Eventually the accumulation of water in the depressions leads to thermokarstic lakes (left).

PERIGLACIATION: FORMATION OF THERMOKARST

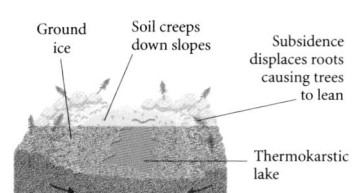

RIVER SYSTEMS

[2] Vast river systems flow across Asia, many originating in the Himalayas and the Plateau of Tibet. Seasonal melting of snow and monsoon rains swell the river flow leading to flooding and erosion. The Yellow River (above) gets its colour from the high level of eroded material from the loess plateau.

RIVER SYSTEMS: EROSION OF THE LOESS PLATEAU BY THE YELLOW RIVER

THE EVOLVING LANDSCAPE

Landscape

- limestone region
- sinking land
- stable land
- uplifting land
- ▲ active volcano
- • • • area of tectonic activity
- – – – limit of permafrost
- → ocean current

TECTONIC ACTIVITY

[7] The Dead Sea (above) lies in a pull-apart basin. The sliding of the African Plate against the Arabian Plate, at unequal rates, led to the sinking of blocks of crust. This depression has been filled by the waters of the Dead Sea and Lake Tiberias (Sea of Galilee). The plates continue to move causing intermittent earthquakes.

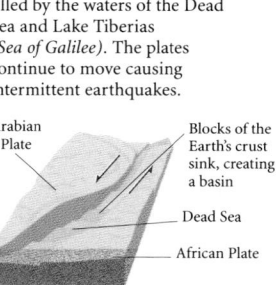

TECTONIC ACTIVITY: THE FORMATION OF A PULL-APART BASIN

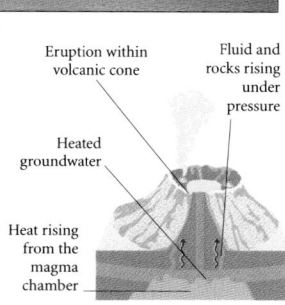

CHEMICAL WEATHERING

[3] Tower karsts are widespread across south China (above) and Vietnam. It is thought the karstic towers were formed under a soil cover, where small depressions in the limestone bedrock began to be weathered by soil water acids, eventually creating larger hollows. This process continued over millions of years, deepening the hollows and leaving steep-sided limestone hills.

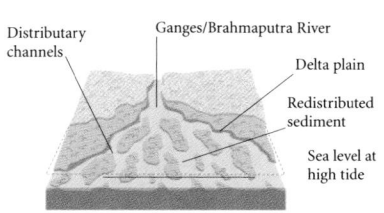

SEDIMENTATION

[6] The Ganges/Brahmaputra is a tide-dominated delta (above). The two rivers transport huge quantities of mountain sediment, which is deposited on the delta plain. This debris is then redistributed by tidal currents, to form extensions to the bars, beach ridges and deltaic deposits.

SEDIMENTATION: THE DESTRUCTION OF A DELTA

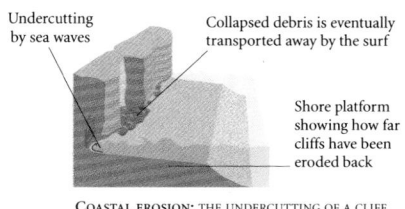

COASTAL EROSION

[5] The erosion of cliffs along the coast of Indonesia (above) and Thailand occurs when waves and currents undermine the base leading to collapse of material. The surf then gradually erodes this material away, exposing the cliff to further undercutting. This process eventually creates shore platforms.

COASTAL EROSION: THE UNDERCUTTING OF A CLIFF

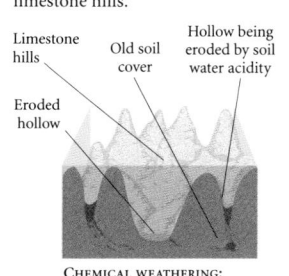

VOLCANIC ACTIVITY

[4] Volcanic eruptions occur frequently across Southeast Asia's island arcs (above). Low-level eruptions occur when groundwater, superheated by underlying magma, becomes pressurized, forcing hot fluid and rocks up through cracks in the volcanic cone. This is known as a phreatic eruption.

VOLCANIC ACTIVITY: A PHREATIC ERUPTION

CHEMICAL WEATHERING: FORMATION OF TOWER KARST

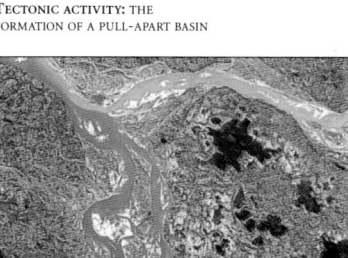

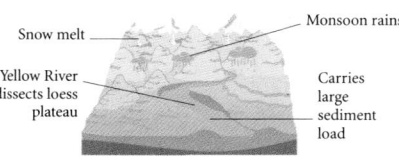

POLITICAL ASIA

ASIA IS THE WORLD'S LARGEST CONTINENT, encompassing many different and discrete realms, from the desert Arab lands of the southwest to the subtropical archipelago of Indonesia; from the vast barren wastes of Siberia to the fertile river valleys of China and South Asia, seats of some of the world's most ancient civilizations. The collapse of the Soviet Union has fragmented the north of the continent into the Siberian portion of the Russian Federation, and the new republics of Central Asia. Strong religious traditions heavily influence the politics of South and Southwest Asia. Hindu and Muslim rivalries threaten to upset the political equilibrium in South Asia where India – in terms of population – remains the world's largest democracy. Communist China is the last great world empire; a population giant, but still relatively closed to the western world, while on its doorstep, the economically progressive and dynamic Pacific Rim countries, led by Japan, continue to assert their worldwide economic force.

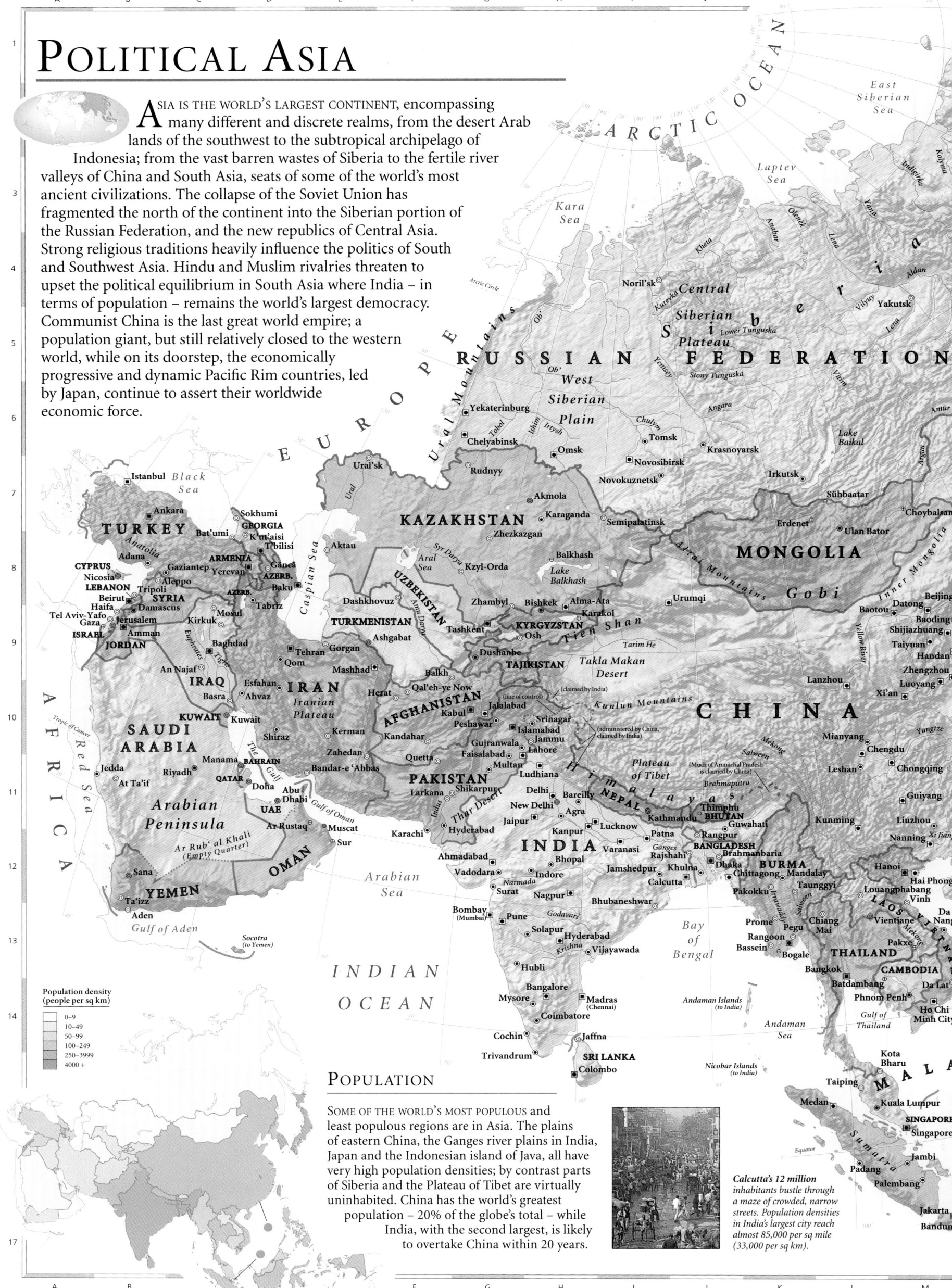

Population density (people per sq km)

- 0–9
- 10–49
- 50–99
- 100–249
- 250–3999
- 4000 +

POPULATION

SOME OF THE WORLD'S MOST POPULOUS and least populous regions are in Asia. The plains of eastern China, the Ganges river plains in India, Japan and the Indonesian island of Java, all have very high population densities; by contrast parts of Siberia and the Plateau of Tibet are virtually uninhabited. China has the world's greatest population – 20% of the globe's total – while India, with the second largest, is likely to overtake China within 20 years.

Calcutta's 12 million inhabitants bustle through a maze of crowded, narrow streets. Population densities in India's largest city reach almost 85,000 per sq mile (33,000 per sq km).

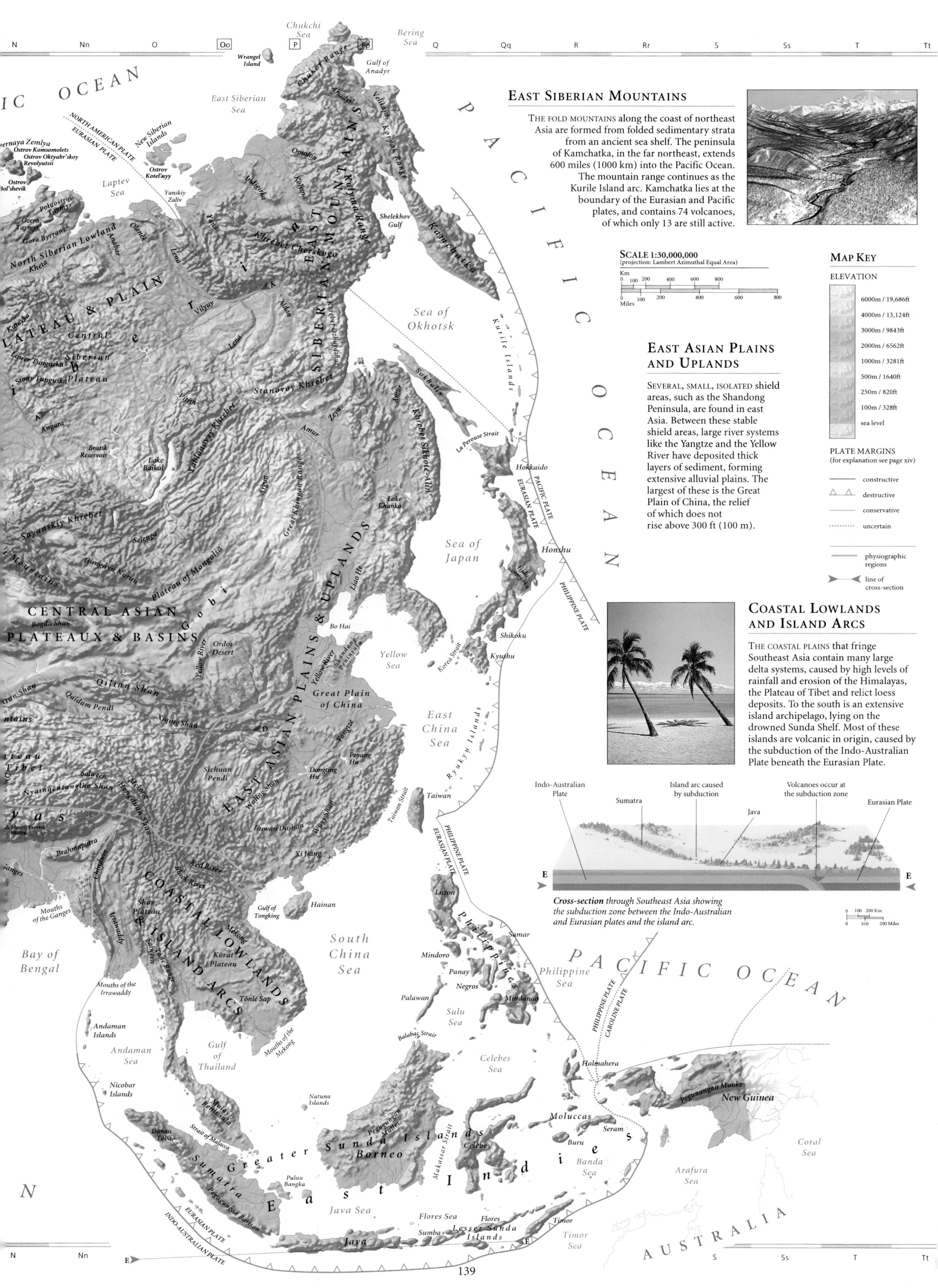

East Siberian Mountains

THE FOLD MOUNTAINS along the coast of northeast Asia are formed from folded sedimentary strata from an ancient sea shelf. The peninsula of Kamchatka, in the far northeast, extends 600 miles (1000 km) into the Pacific Ocean. The mountain range continues as the Kurile Island arc. Kamchatka lies at the boundary of the Eurasian and Pacific plates, and contains 74 volcanoes, of which only 13 are still active.

SCALE 1:30,000,000
(projection: Lambert Azimuthal Equal Area)

East Asian Plains and Uplands

SEVERAL, SMALL, ISOLATED shield areas, such as the Shandong Peninsula, are found in east Asia. Between these stable shield areas, large river systems like the Yangtze and the Yellow River have deposited thick layers of sediment, forming extensive alluvial plains. The largest of these is the Great Plain of China, the relief of which does not rise above 300 ft (100 m).

MAP KEY

ELEVATION

- 6000m / 19,686ft
- 4000m / 13,124ft
- 3000m / 9843ft
- 2000m / 6562ft
- 1000m / 3281ft
- 500m / 1640ft
- 250m / 820ft
- 100m / 328ft
- sea level

PLATE MARGINS
(for explanation see page xiv)

- constructive
- destructive
- conservative
- uncertain
- physiographic regions
- line of cross-section

Coastal Lowlands and Island Arcs

THE COASTAL PLAINS that fringe Southeast Asia contain many large delta systems, caused by high levels of rainfall and erosion of the Himalayas, the Plateau of Tibet and relict loess deposits. To the south is an extensive island archipelago, lying on the drowned Sunda Shelf. Most of these islands are volcanic in origin, caused by the subduction of the Indo-Australian Plate beneath the Eurasian Plate.

Cross-section through Southeast Asia showing the subduction zone between the Indo-Australian and Eurasian plates and the island arc.

TURKEY & THE CAUCASUS

ARMENIA, AZERBAIJAN, GEORGIA, TURKEY

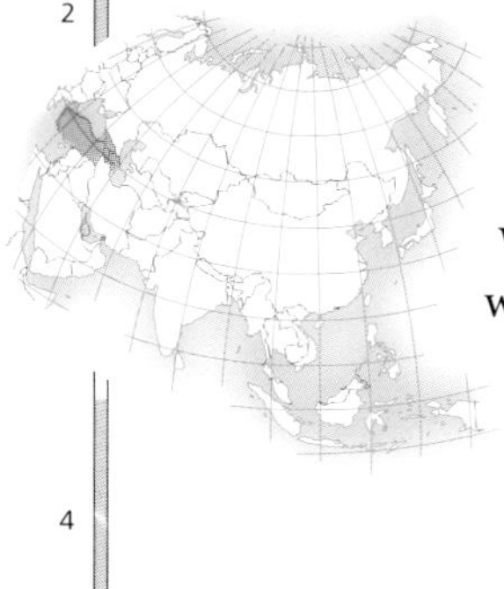

THIS REGION OCCUPIES THE FRAGMENTED JUNCTION between Europe, Asia and the Russian Federation. Sunni Islam provides a common identity for the secular state of Turkey, which the revered leader Kemal Atatürk established from the remnants of the Ottoman Empire after the First World War. Turkey has a broad resource base and expanding trade links with Europe, but the east is relatively undeveloped and strife between the state and a large Kurdish minority has yet to be resolved. Georgia is similarly challenged by ethnic separatism, while the Christian state of Armenia and the mainly Muslim and oil-rich Azerbaijan are locked in conflict over the territory of Nagornyy Karabakh.

TRANSPORT AND INDUSTRY

TURKEY LEADS THE REGION'S well-diversified economy. Petrochemicals, textiles, engineering and food processing are the main industries. Azerbaijan is able to export oil, while the other states rely heavily on hydro-electric power and imported fuel. Georgia produces precision machinery. War and earthquake damage have devastated Armenia's infrastructure.

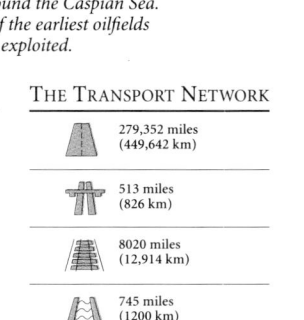

Azerbaijan has substantial oil reserves, located in and around the Caspian Sea. They were some of the earliest oilfields in the world to be exploited.

Major industry and infrastructure

- carpet weaving
- cement
- chemicals
- coal
- engineering
- food processing
- oil
- textiles
- tourism
- vehicle manufacture
- capital cities
- major towns
- international airports
- major roads
- major industrial areas

THE TRANSPORT NETWORK

279,352 miles (449,642 km)	
513 miles (826 km)	
8020 miles (12,914 km)	
745 miles (1200 km)	

Physical and political barriers have severely limited communications between Armenia, Georgia and Azerbaijan. Turkey has a relatively well-developed transport network.

USING THE LAND AND SEA

TURKEY IS LARGELY SELF-SUFFICIENT in food. The irrigated Black Sea coastlands have the world's highest yields of hazelnuts. Tobacco, cotton, sultanas, tea and figs are the region's main cash crops and a great range of fruit and vegetables are grown. Wine grapes are among the labour-intensive crops which allow full use of limited agricultural land in the Caucasus. Sturgeon fishing is particularly important in Azerbaijan.

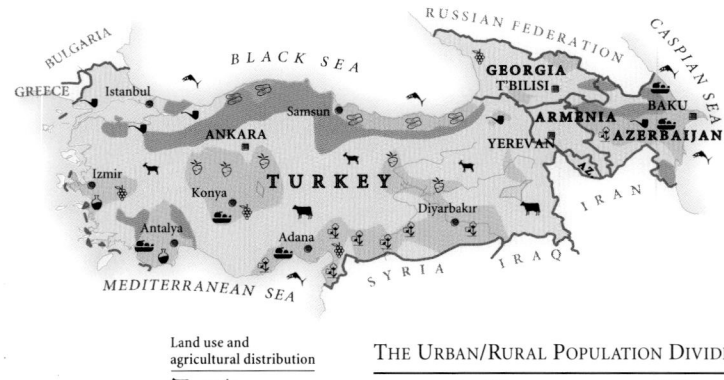

Land use and agricultural distribution

- cattle
- goats
- cotton
- fishing
- fruit
- hazelnuts
- olives
- sugar beet
- tobacco
- vineyards
- capital cities
- major towns
- pasture
- cropland
- forest

THE URBAN/RURAL POPULATION DIVIDE

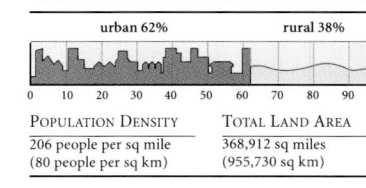

urban 62%   rural 38%

0 10 20 30 40 50 60 70 80 90 100

POPULATION DENSITY	TOTAL LAND AREA
206 people per sq mile (80 people per sq km)	368,912 sq miles (955,730 sq km)

For many centuries, Istanbul has held tremendous strategic importance as a crucial gateway between Europe and Asia. Founded by the Greeks as Byzantium, the city became the centre of the East Roman Empire and was known as Constantinople to the Romans. From the 15th century onwards the city became the centre of the great Ottoman Empire.

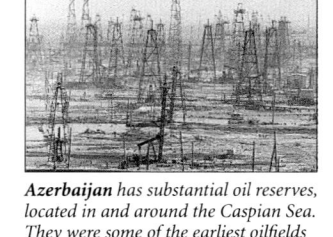
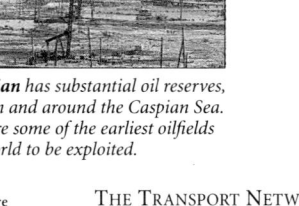

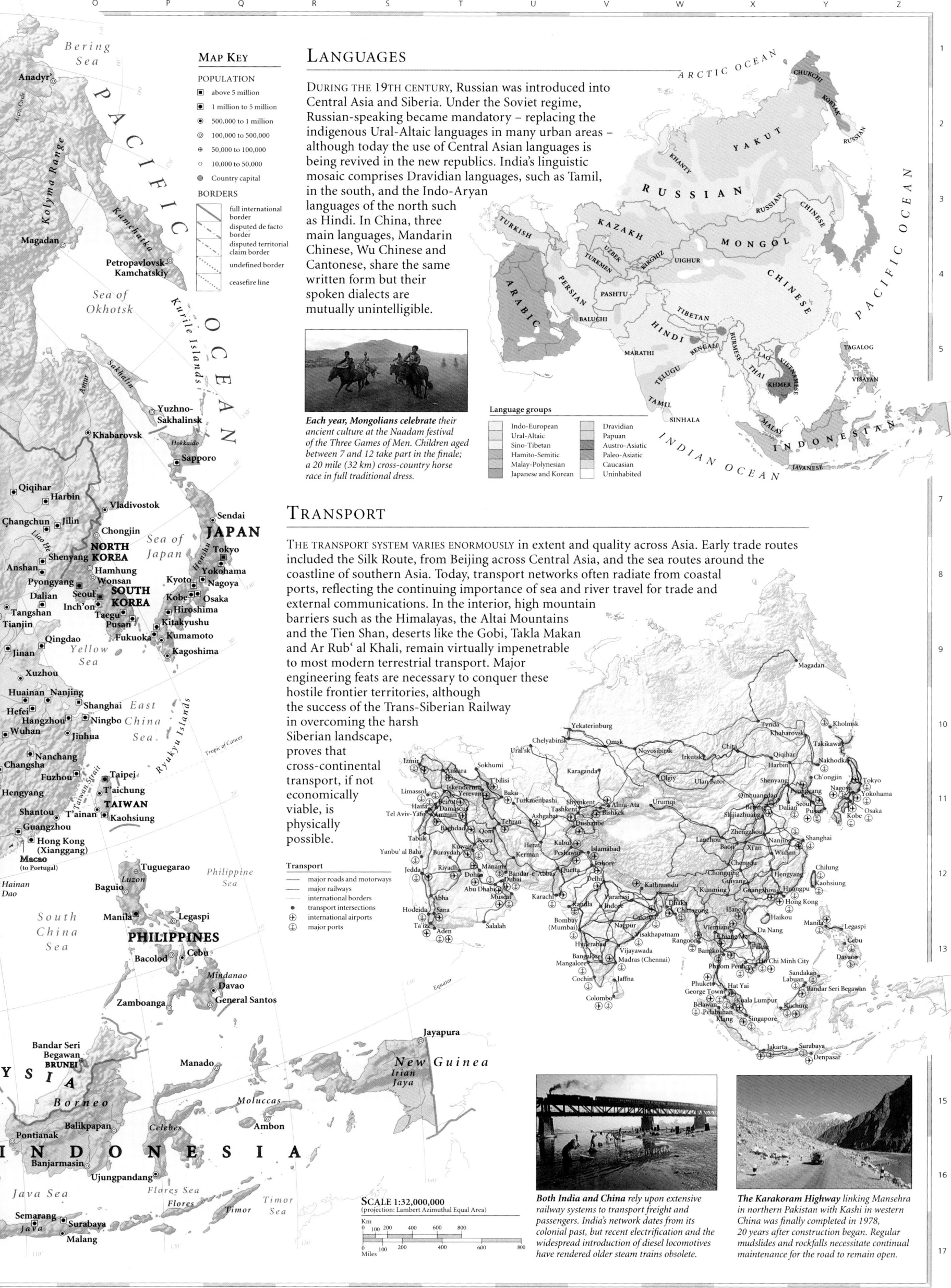

MAP KEY

POPULATION
- ■ above 5 million
- ■ 1 million to 5 million
- ■ 500,000 to 1 million
- ⊕ 100,000 to 500,000
- ⊕ 50,000 to 100,000
- ○ 10,000 to 50,000
- ● Country capital

BORDERS
- full international border
- disputed de facto border
- disputed territorial claim border
- undefined border
- ceasefire line

LANGUAGES

DURING THE 19TH CENTURY, Russian was introduced into Central Asia and Siberia. Under the Soviet regime, Russian-speaking became mandatory – replacing the indigenous Ural-Altaic languages in many urban areas – although today the use of Central Asian languages is being revived in the new republics. India's linguistic mosaic comprises Dravidian languages, such as Tamil, in the south, and the Indo-Aryan languages of the north such as Hindi. In China, three main languages, Mandarin Chinese, Wu Chinese and Cantonese, share the same written form but their spoken dialects are mutually unintelligible.

Each year, Mongolians celebrate their ancient culture at the Naadam festival of the Three Games of Men. Children aged between 7 and 12 take part in the finale; a 20 mile (32 km) cross-country horse race in full traditional dress.

Language groups
- Indo-European
- Ural-Altaic
- Sino-Tibetan
- Hamito-Semitic
- Malay-Polynesian
- Japanese and Korean
- Dravidian
- Papuan
- Austro-Asiatic
- Paleo-Asiatic
- Caucasian
- Uninhabited

TRANSPORT

THE TRANSPORT SYSTEM VARIES ENORMOUSLY in extent and quality across Asia. Early trade routes included the Silk Route, from Beijing across Central Asia, and the sea routes around the coastline of southern Asia. Today, transport networks often radiate from coastal ports, reflecting the continuing importance of sea and river travel for trade and external communications. In the interior, high mountain barriers such as the Himalayas, the Altai Mountains and the Tien Shan, deserts like the Gobi, Takla Makan and Ar Rub' al Khali, remain virtually impenetrable to most modern terrestrial transport. Major engineering feats are necessary to conquer these hostile frontier territories, although the success of the Trans-Siberian Railway in overcoming the harsh Siberian landscape, proves that cross-continental transport, if not economically viable, is physically possible.

Transport
- major roads and motorways
- major railways
- international borders
- ● transport intersections
- ⊕ international airports
- ⊕ major ports

Both India and China rely upon extensive railway systems to transport freight and passengers. India's network dates from its colonial past, but recent electrification and the widespread introduction of diesel locomotives have rendered older steam trains obsolete.

The Karakoram Highway linking Mansehra in northern Pakistan with Kashi in western China was finally completed in 1978, 20 years after construction began. Regular mudslides and rockfalls necessitate continual maintenance for the road to remain open.

SCALE 1:32,000,000
(projection: Lambert Azimuthal Equal Area)

Km
0 100 200 400 600 800

Miles
0 100 200 400 600 800

CLIMATE

THE CLIMATE OF ASIA exhibits marked differences from region to region, with freezing polar conditions in the north, hot and cold deserts in central regions and subtropical conditions throughout the south. Much of this variation can be attributed to enormous mountain barriers and internal depressions found across the continent. Monsoon winds, which reverse semi-annually, cause alternate wet and dry seasons across southern Asia. These air masses moving north from the ocean are stripped of their moisture over the Himalayas causing arid conditions across the Plateau of Tibet. Both the south and east are susceptible to tropical cyclones or typhoons.

Treeless, frozen plains, with permanently frozen soil layers characterize much of Siberia. Even during the summer only the top 2–3 ft (1 m) of soil thaws.

Tundra-like marshes are found alongside vast sand dunes in the Takla Makan Desert in China. In the spring, windstorms of hurricane-force can send dust as high as 13,000 ft (4000 m) in the air.

The Gobi Desert experiences major extremes in climate, with winter temperatures sometimes falling below -40°C (-40°F) and summer temperatures exceeding 45°C (113°F).

Climate

| tundra |
| subarctic |
| cool continental |
| warm humid |
| mediterranean |
| semi-arid |
| arid |
| humid equatorial |
| tropical |

☼ daily hours of sunshine, January
☼ daily hours of sunshine, July
→ cyclone
→ typhoon
→ cold/dry monsoon
→ warm/wet monsoon
→ cold wind

TEMPERATURE

Temperature

	below -30°C (-22°F)		0 to 10°C (32 to 50°F)
	-30 to -20°C (-22 to -4°F)		10 to 20°C (50°F)
	-20 to -10°C (-4 to 14°F)		20 to 30°C (68 to 86°F)
	-10 to 0°C (14 to 32°F)		above 30°C (86°F)

Average January temperature   *Average July temperature*

Tropical cyclones occur principally during late summer and early autumn. The intense winds and heavy rainfall can devastate entire villages.

Through India, the southwest monsoon, which brings heavy rainfall from May to September, accounts for 80% of annual precipitation.

RAINFALL

Rainfall

	0 – 25 mm (0–1 in)
	25–50 mm (1–2 in)
	50–100 mm (2–4 in)
	100–200 mm (4–8 in)
	200–300 mm (8–12 in)
	300–400 mm (12–16 in)
	400–500 mm (16–20 in)
	more than 500 mm (20 in)

Average January rainfall   *Average July rainfall*

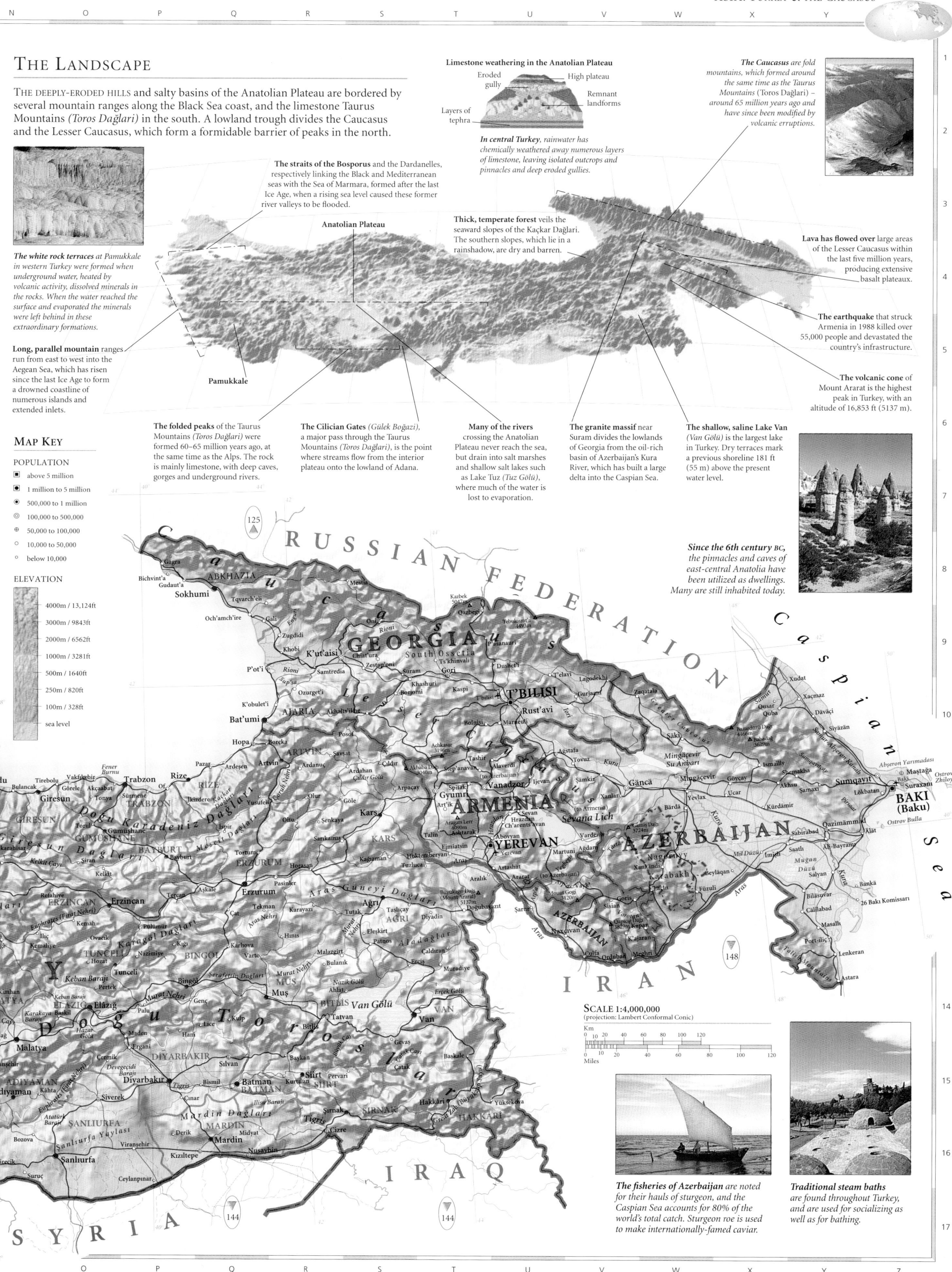

THE LANDSCAPE

THE DEEPLY-ERODED HILLS and salty basins of the Anatolian Plateau are bordered by several mountain ranges along the Black Sea coast, and the limestone Taurus Mountains (*Toros Dağlari*) in the south. A lowland trough divides the Caucasus and the Lesser Caucasus, which form a formidable barrier of peaks in the north.

The white rock terraces at Pamukkale in western Turkey were formed when underground water, heated by volcanic activity, dissolved minerals in the rocks. When the water reached the surface and evaporated the minerals were left behind in these extraordinary formations.

Long, parallel mountain ranges run from east to west into the Aegean Sea, which has risen since the last Ice Age to form a drowned coastline of numerous islands and extended inlets.

The straits of the Bosporus and the Dardanelles, respectively linking the Black and Mediterranean seas with the Sea of Marmara, formed after the last Ice Age, when a rising sea level caused these former river valleys to be flooded.

Anatolian Plateau

Pamukkale

Limestone weathering in the Anatolian Plateau

Eroded gully — High plateau

Layers of tephra — Remnant landforms

In central Turkey, rainwater has chemically weathered away numerous layers of limestone, leaving isolated outcrops and pinnacles and deep eroded gullies.

The Caucasus are fold mountains, which formed around the same time as the Taurus Mountains (*Toros Dağlari*) – around 65 million years ago and have since been modified by volcanic eruptions.

Thick, temperate forest veils the seaward slopes of the Kaçkar Dağlari. The southern slopes, which lie in a rainshadow, are dry and barren.

Lava has flowed over large areas of the Lesser Caucasus within the last five million years, producing extensive basalt plateaux.

The earthquake that struck Armenia in 1988 killed over 55,000 people and devastated the country's infrastructure.

The volcanic cone of Mount Ararat is the highest peak in Turkey, with an altitude of 16,853 ft (5137 m).

The folded peaks of the Taurus Mountains (*Toros Dağlari*) were formed 60–65 million years ago, at the same time as the Alps. The rock is mainly limestone, with deep caves, gorges and underground rivers.

The Cilician Gates (*Gülek Boğazi*), a major pass through the Taurus Mountains (*Toros Dağlari*), is the point where streams flow from the interior plateau onto the lowland of Adana.

Many of the rivers crossing the Anatolian Plateau never reach the sea, but drain into salt marshes and shallow salt lakes such as Lake Tuz (*Tuz Gölü*), where much of the water is lost to evaporation.

The granite massif near Suram divides the lowlands of Georgia from the oil-rich basin of Azerbaijan's Kura River, which has built a large delta into the Caspian Sea.

The shallow, saline Lake Van (*Van Gölü*) is the largest lake in Turkey. Dry terraces mark a previous shoreline 181 ft (55 m) above the present water level.

Since the 6th century BC, the pinnacles and caves of east-central Anatolia have been utilized as dwellings. Many are still inhabited today.

MAP KEY

POPULATION

- ■ above 5 million
- ▣ 1 million to 5 million
- ◉ 500,000 to 1 million
- ◎ 100,000 to 500,000
- ⊕ 50,000 to 100,000
- ○ 10,000 to 50,000
- · below 10,000

ELEVATION

- 4000m / 13,124ft
- 3000m / 9843ft
- 2000m / 6562ft
- 1000m / 3281ft
- 500m / 1640ft
- 250m / 820ft
- 100m / 328ft
- sea level

SCALE 1:4,000,000
(projection: Lambert Conformal Conic)

Km
0 10 20 40 60 80 100 120

Miles
0 10 20 40 60 80 100 120

The fisheries of Azerbaijan are noted for their hauls of sturgeon, and the Caspian Sea accounts for 80% of the world's total catch. Sturgeon roe is used to make internationally-famed caviar.

Traditional steam baths are found throughout Turkey, and are used for socializing as well as for bathing.

THE NEAR EAST

IRAQ, ISRAEL, JORDAN, LEBANON, SYRIA

SOME OF THE WORLD'S OLDEST CIVILIZATIONS developed in this region – the Fertile Crescent – which is venerated by Jews, Muslims and Christians, but torn by competing religious, ethnic and national claims to the land. Turkish Ottoman rule ended with the First World War and the region was divided into areas administered by Britain and France. The UN endorsed calls for a Jewish homeland in what was then Palestine and in 1948 the state of Israel was declared. Hostility towards the Jewish state led to a series of wars but since 1977, and especially since 1993, a peace process between Israel and her neighbours has been evolving. Since independence, Syria has played a leading role in Middle Eastern politics. The once-prosperous state of Lebanon is emerging from a ruinous factional war, while Iraq's great oil wealth has funded military campaigns against Iran and Kuwait, and the stifling of internal dissent, leading to international ostracization.

USING THE LAND AND SEA

WATER SCARCITY limits cropland to the north and to areas watered principally by the Tigris, Euphrates and Jordan rivers. In Israel, new irrigation techniques are allowing cultivation in the arid Negev. Wheat is the chief grain and large areas of scrub support livestock herding. Commercial produce includes dates, tobacco, citrus fruits, olives, grapes and cotton, which is Syria's main export crop. Fishing is still important in the Mediterranean.

THE URBAN/RURAL POPULATION DIVIDE

urban 63%   rural 37%

POPULATION DENSITY
145 people per sq mile
(56 people per sq km)

TOTAL LAND AREA
325,460 sq miles
(843,160 sq km)

Land use and agricultural distribution

- sheep
- cereals
- citrus fruits
- cotton
- dates
- fishing
- rice
- tobacco
- capital cities
- major towns
- pasture
- cropland
- wetland
- desert

TRANSPORT AND INDUSTRY

THE PETROCHEMICAL INDUSTRY is well established, and central to the economies of Syria and Iraq, which was the world's second largest oil exporter before the war with Iran which began in 1980. Lebanon has traditionally been a centre for commerce, while Israel has a well-diversified economy with an expanding tourist industry, despite few natural resources.

THE TRANSPORT NETWORK

62,624 miles (100,844 km)

1000 miles (1600 km)

3897 miles (6275 km)

498 miles (802 km)

Jordan's sea port of Al 'Aqabah is connected to Damascus in Syria by road and rail. This route to the Red Sea provides for large exports of phosphate and trade with states in The Gulf.

Major industry and infrastructure

- car manufacture
- cement
- chemicals
- electronics
- finance
- food processing
- iron & steel
- oil
- oil refining
- textiles
- capital cities
- major towns
- international airports
- major roads
- major industrial areas

The Dome of the Rock in Jerusalem is a magnificent mosque, revered by Muslims. Close by is the Wailing Wall, the city's most sacred Jewish landmark and the Church of the Holy Sepulchre, a famous Christian place of worship.

The city of Petra, carved from spectacular rose-coloured limestone, lies deep within a canyon in southern Jordan. Revenues from the spice trade funded the construction of the city which was built by the Nabatean people in about 400 BC.

Water and wind erosion over thousands of years have created the Canyon of the Oasis at En 'Avedat in the Negev Desert (HaNegev). Extreme diurnal temperature fluctuations, coupled with wind erosion, have caused layers of rock to crack and peel away.

THE LANDSCAPE

THE AL JAZIRAH PLATEAU divides the Euphrates and Tigris rivers, which cross the Mesopotamian plain to reach their confluence in the southeast. The rocky Syrian Desert extends west to the northern extremity of the Great Rift Valley, which runs from the mountains of Lebanon to the Gulf of Aqaba. The River Jordan flows south along this trough into the Dead Sea, divided from the Mediterranean coastal plain by a steep-sided plateau.

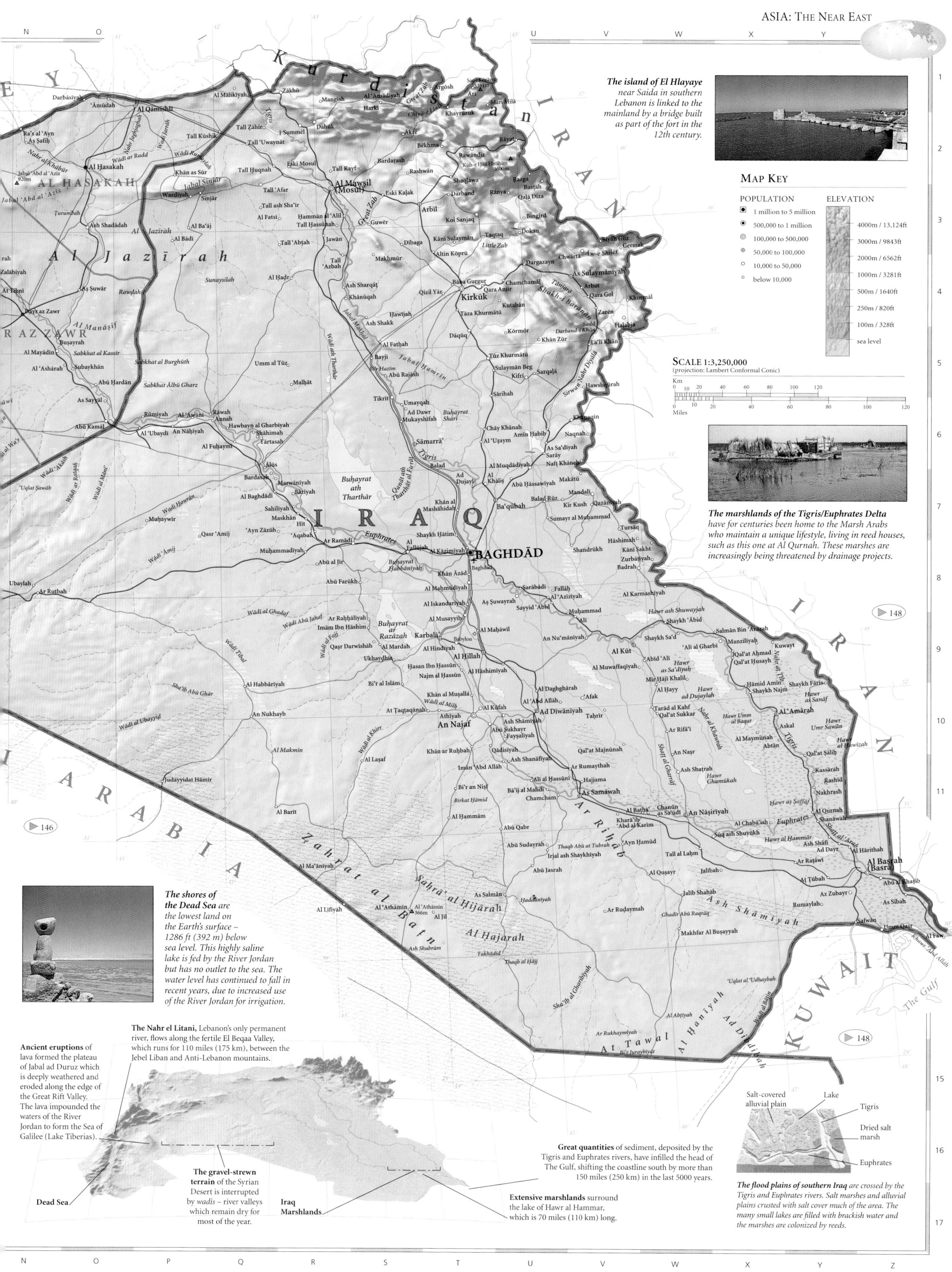

ASIA: THE NEAR EAST

The island of El Hlayaye near Saida in southern Lebanon is linked to the mainland by a bridge built as part of the fort in the 12th century.

MAP KEY

POPULATION

- 1 million to 5 million
- 500,000 to 1 million
- 100,000 to 500,000
- 50,000 to 100,000
- 10,000 to 50,000
- below 10,000

ELEVATION

4000m / 13,124ft
3000m / 9843ft
2000m / 6562ft
1000m / 3281ft
500m / 1640ft
250m / 820ft
100m / 328ft
sea level

SCALE 1:3,250,000
(projection: Lambert Conformal Conic)

The marshlands of the Tigris/Euphrates Delta have for centuries been home to the Marsh Arabs who maintain a unique lifestyle, living in reed houses, such as this one at Al Qurnah. These marshes are increasingly being threatened by drainage projects.

The shores of the Dead Sea are the lowest land on the Earth's surface – 1286 ft (392 m) below sea level. This highly saline lake is fed by the River Jordan but has no outlet to the sea. The water level has continued to fall in recent years, due to increased use of the River Jordan for irrigation.

Ancient eruptions of lava formed the plateau of Jabal ad Duruz which is deeply weathered and eroded along the edge of the Great Rift Valley. The lava impounded the waters of the River Jordan to form the Sea of Galilee (Lake Tiberias).

The Nahr el Litani, Lebanon's only permanent river, flows along the fertile El Beqaa Valley, which runs for 110 miles (175 km), between the Jebel Liban and Anti-Lebanon mountains.

Dead Sea

The gravel-strewn terrain of the Syrian Desert is interrupted by wadis – river valleys which remain dry for most of the year.

Iraq Marshlands

Great quantities of sediment, deposited by the Tigris and Euphrates rivers, have infilled the head of The Gulf, shifting the coastline south by more than 150 miles (250 km) in the last 5000 years.

Extensive marshlands surround the lake of Hawr al Hammar, which is 70 miles (110 km) long.

Salt-covered alluvial plain / Lake / Tigris / Dried salt marsh / Euphrates

The flood plains of southern Iraq are crossed by the Tigris and Euphrates rivers. Salt marshes and alluvial plains crusted with salt cover much of the area. The many small lakes are filled with brackish water and the marshes are colonized by reeds.

145

THE ARABIAN PENINSULA

BAHRAIN, KUWAIT, OMAN, QATAR, SAUDI ARABIA, UNITED ARAB EMIRATES (UAE), YEMEN

HUGE EXPANSES OF DESERT cover much of the Arabian Peninsula, limiting settlement to oases, the mountains along the Red Sea and coastal belts. The most populous area is the fertile highlands of Yemen. The Islamic faith and Arabic language give the region a cultural and religious unity, and the Saudi city of Mecca (Makkah) is Islam's most holy place, visited by over two million pilgrims each year. More than half the world's oil reserves are contained in this region, and the exploitation of oil and gas has brought great wealth, particularly to Saudi Arabia. Yemen and Oman are the least developed of the Arabian states, with large rural populations. Within Saudi Arabia over two-thirds of the people live in urban areas.

USING THE LAND

MOST OF THE ARABIAN PENINSULA is unsuited to settled agriculture, making irrigation and land reclamation projects essential. The narrow coastal plain and isolated oases, commonly amounting to less than 1% of the land area, are used to cultivate grains, coffee and exotic fruits. Goats, sheep and camels are widespread throughout the region.

THE URBAN/RURAL POPULATION DIVIDE

urban 42%   rural 58%

0 10 20 30 40 50 60 70 80 90 100

POPULATION DENSITY
29 people per sq mile
(11 people per sq km)

TOTAL LAND AREA
1,147,856 sq miles
(2,973,720 sq km)

Land use and agricultural distribution

- goats
- sheep
- cereals
- coffee
- dates
- fruit

- ■ capital cities
- ● major towns
- pasture
- cropland
- desert

The fertile soils of Yemen have encouraged settlement of almost all of the land from sea level up to the mountains at 10,000 ft (3050 m). In the higher reaches elaborate terraces have been constructed to facilitate crop cultivation.

THE LANDSCAPE

A PLATEAU MORE THAN 2500 ft (760 m) high extends across much of the Arabian Peninsula. The plateau slopes eastwards from the massive, rifted escarpment along the coast of the Red Sea, to the shallow waters of The Gulf. The interior is characterized by *cuestas* and valleys, drained by a system of *wadis*. A crescent of sand and gravel deserts lies to the east.

The An Nafud Desert is covered with *barchan* dunes varying between 30–100 ft (10–30 m) high. The 'horns' of the crescent-shaped dunes reflect the direction in which they are being moved by the wind.

Inselbergs are dotted over a wide area of the Najd Plateau. These resistant remnants of the ancient basement rock are left standing when the softer weathered rock has been worn away.

Evaporation
Storm surge flooding
Normal level of tidal range
Crusted layer left behind
Salt wedge penetrates inland water

A sabkha is a flat, salt-encrusted plain which occurs near the coast just above the high water mark. Flooding by sea water leads to saturation of the land with saline-rich groundwater. As this evaporates, a cracked layer of sand, cemented together with salt, gypsum and calcium carbonate is left behind.

Few areas in the Arabian Peninsula have rivers flowing through them. Most are drained by ephemeral watercourses called *wadis*.

The Hejaz (*Al Ḥijāz*) and Asir Mountains form part of the same geological region as the highlands of Sudan and Eritrea, to which they were once joined. They were separated when faulting opened the Red Sea, over 50 million years ago.

Across the Najd Plateau the flat relief is broken by *mesas;* steep-sided rock plateaux and *cuestas;* ridges with one steep and one gentle slope.

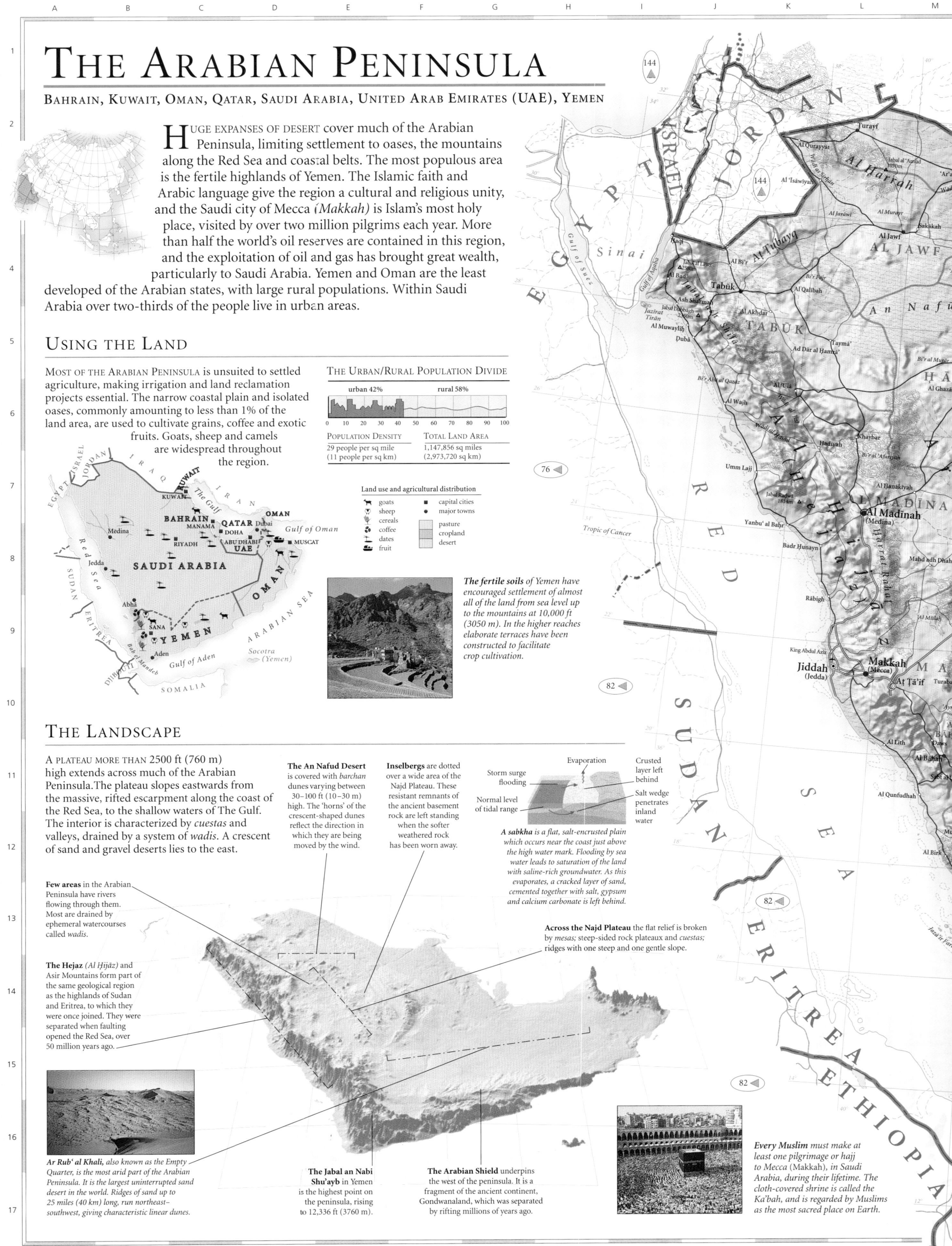

Ar Rub' al Khali, also known as the Empty Quarter, is the most arid part of the Arabian Peninsula. It is the largest uninterrupted sand desert in the world. Ridges of sand up to 25 miles (40 km) long, run northeast–southwest, giving characteristic linear dunes.

The Jabal an Nabi Shu'ayb in Yemen is the highest point on the peninsula, rising to 12,336 ft (3760 m).

The Arabian Shield underpins the west of the peninsula. It is a fragment of the ancient continent, Gondwanaland, which was separated by rifting millions of years ago.

Every Muslim must make at least one pilgrimage or hajj to Mecca (Makkah), in Saudi Arabia, during their lifetime. The cloth-covered shrine is called the Ka'bah, and is regarded by Muslims as the most sacred place on Earth.

TRANSPORT AND INDUSTRY

THE EXTRACTION AND REFINING OF OIL AND GAS are the major industrial activities in the Arabian Peninsula. The region also has an active construction sector, with many Arab cities reflecting the wealth generated by the oil industry. The service sector is dominated by financial and technical institutions, which, like the construction sector, mainly serve the oil industry. Traditional handicrafts such as carpet-weaving are found in rural areas.

Saudi Arabia contains the world's largest oil reserves, lying mainly along The Gulf coast. Each day the region produces 8.3 million barrels of oil. Here, in the desert, excess oil is being burnt off.

THE TRANSPORT NETWORK

🛣	139,180 miles (224,122 km)		373 miles (600 km)
🛤	848 miles (1365 km)		none

Internal surface transport is poorly developed across the peninsula. Along the coast, commercial routes have developed, but connections between bordering states rely on major airports.

Major industry and infrastructure

- cement
- chemicals
- iron & steel
- oil
- oil refining
- food processing
- capital cities
- major towns
- international airports
- major roads
- major industrial areas

MAP KEY

POPULATION

- 1 million to 5 million
- 500,000 to 1 million
- 100,000 to 500,000
- 50,000 to 100,000
- 10,000 to 50,000
- below 10,000

ELEVATION

- 3000m / 9843ft
- 2000m / 6562ft
- 1000m / 3281ft
- 500m / 1640ft
- 250m / 820ft
- 100m / 328ft
- sea level

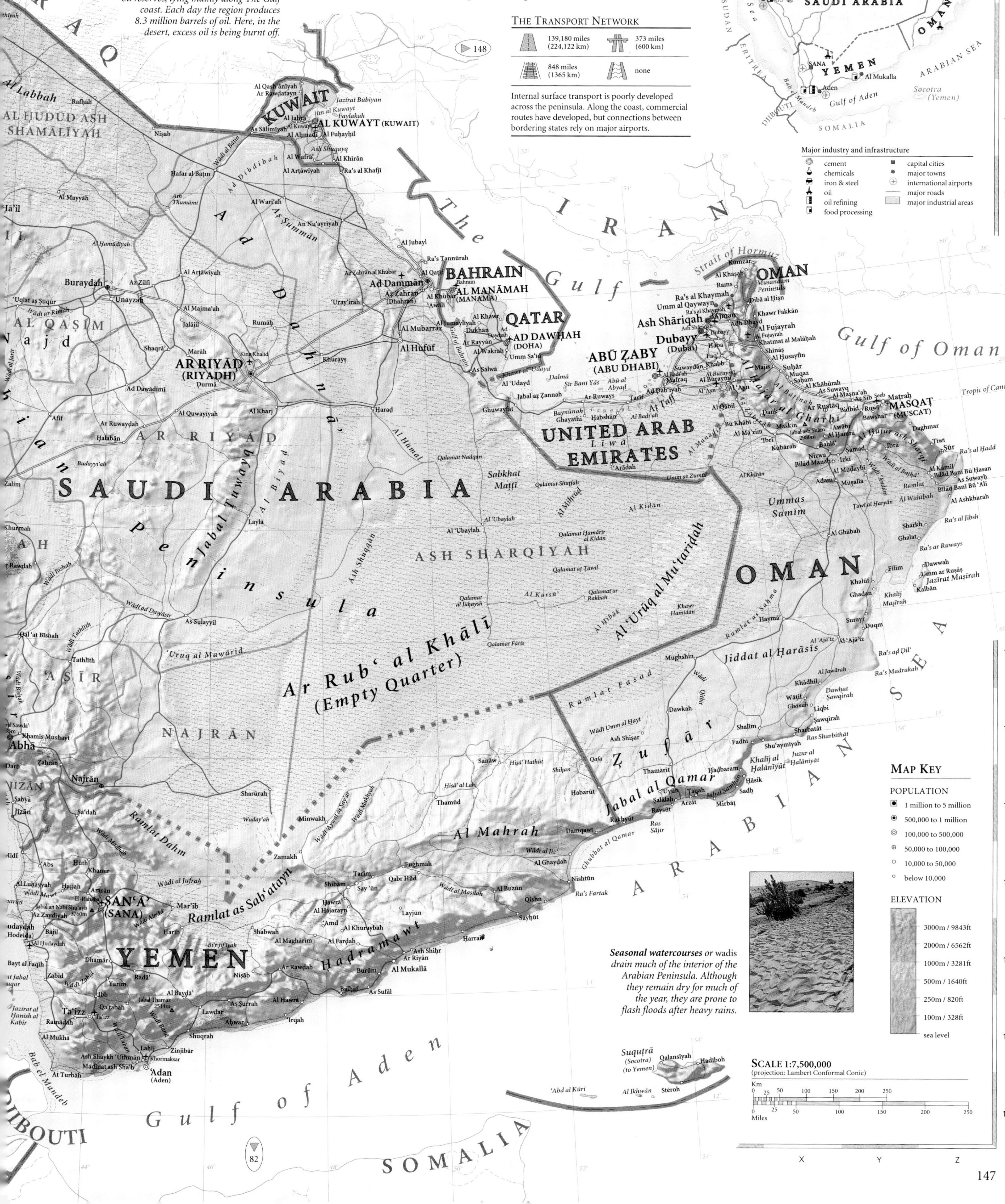

Seasonal watercourses or wadis drain much of the interior of the Arabian Peninsula. Although they remain dry for much of the year, they are prone to flash floods after heavy rains.

SCALE 1:7,500,000
(projection: Lambert Conformal Conic)

Km 0 25 50 75 100 150 200 250
Miles 0 25 50 100 150 200 250

147

IRAN & THE GULF STATES

BAHRAIN, IRAN, KUWAIT, QATAR, UNITED ARAB EMIRATES (UAE)

THE DISCOVERY OF OIL in The Gulf in the 1930s brought great wealth to the surrounding states. The revenue was largely used to modernize industry and infrastructure, initiating great social change in these formerly agrarian countries. Today, over 80% of the people in the Gulf states live in urban areas, and foreign nationals make up a sizeable proportion of the population in Kuwait, Qatar and the United Arab Emirates. The importance of control of the oil reserves has led to a number of territorial disputes, including most recently the Iran–Iraq War and the Gulf War. Islam is practised almost exclusively throughout the region and two distinct strands are found; Sunni Muslims in Qatar, Kuwait and UAE, and Shi'a Muslims in Iran and Bahrain. In 1979 Iran became the world's largest theocracy.

THE LANDSCAPE

THE LAND RISES STEEPLY from the fragmented coastal lowlands bordering The Gulf, to reach Iran's interior plateau, bounded by heavily-eroded mountain chains. An unstable volcanic belt runs northwest to southeast across Iran causing frequent earthquakes. On the sandy west coast of The Gulf, the relief is generally flat, with patches of salt marsh. Bahrain consists of two groups of islands, which are mostly small and rocky.

Pyroclastic layers
Lava flow
Lava flow layers

Qolleh-ye Damavand in the Elburz Mountains is a composite volcano. It comprises layers of lava and pyroclasts – fragmentary rocks which accumulate on the slopes of the volcano after being ejected into the air.

Marine sediments from deep beneath the ancient Tethys Sea have been uplifted to form the Elburz Mountains, which stretch along the shores of the Caspian Sea, northern Iran.

Lava and ash from previous volcanic activity covers a 200-mile (320-km) stretch from the border with Azerbaijan to the Caspian Sea.

Iran's two mountain chains, the Zagros and Elburz, were uplifted at the same time as the Alps in Europe, when the African Plate collided with the Eurasian Plate.

Caspian Sea

Qolleh-ye Damavand

Dominated by a vast, semi-arid interior plateau, most of Iran lies above 1640 ft (500 m). The region is poorly drained with many of its basins remaining dry for months at a time.

The fierce Shamal wind affects much of this region. Every summer it blows dust south from the flood plains of the Tigris and Euphrates, reducing visibility to such an extent that Kuwait International Airport is frequently forced to close.

Prolific springs tapping artesian water make cultivation possible across the north of Bahrain's main island. This provides a sharp contrast to the sandy plains in the south and west.

The oilfields of The Gulf are formed from marine shale deposits lying in sedimentary basins at the margins of the Zagros Mountains.

Autumn winds blowing across The Gulf can reach speeds of up to 95 mph (150 kmph) causing severe storms, squalls and waterspouts.

Numerous islands lie along the southern coast of The Gulf. Some of these are salt domes, created when less dense salts were displaced and forced up to the surface by denser, overlying strata.

The Dasht-e Lut

The Dasht-e Lut covers a large portion of eastern Iran with its dry, wind-eroded plain of scattered sandstone pillars and salty depressions. During the summer, temperatures soar, making it one of the world's hottest, driest places.

USING THE LAND AND SEA

ALONG THE COAST of the Caspian Sea, desalinated water allows fruits and vegetables to be produced, although water shortages and desert soils still limit farming. Sheep are the most important livestock raised in Iran and commercial forests cover the northwest of the country. Shrimp stocks were decimated by pollution during the Gulf War, but fishing remains important for domestic and export markets.

All of the Gulf states have commercial fishing fleets. Before the discovery of oil, fishing was the region's leading industry.

The Kuwait Towers in the centre of Kuwait are symbols of the vast wealth oil has brought to the country. Before 1960, the city had only one main street and was surrounded by a mud wall.

Land use and agricultural distribution
- goats
- sheep
- cereals
- citrus fruits
- cotton
- dates
- fishing
- timber
- capital cities
- major towns
- pasture
- cropland
- forest
- desert
- wetland

THE URBAN/RURAL POPULATION DIVIDE

urban 59%   rural 41%

0 10 20 30 40 50 60 70 80 90 100

POPULATION DENSITY
103 people per sq mile
(40 people per sq km)

TOTAL LAND AREA
642,883 sq miles
(1,665,500 sq km)

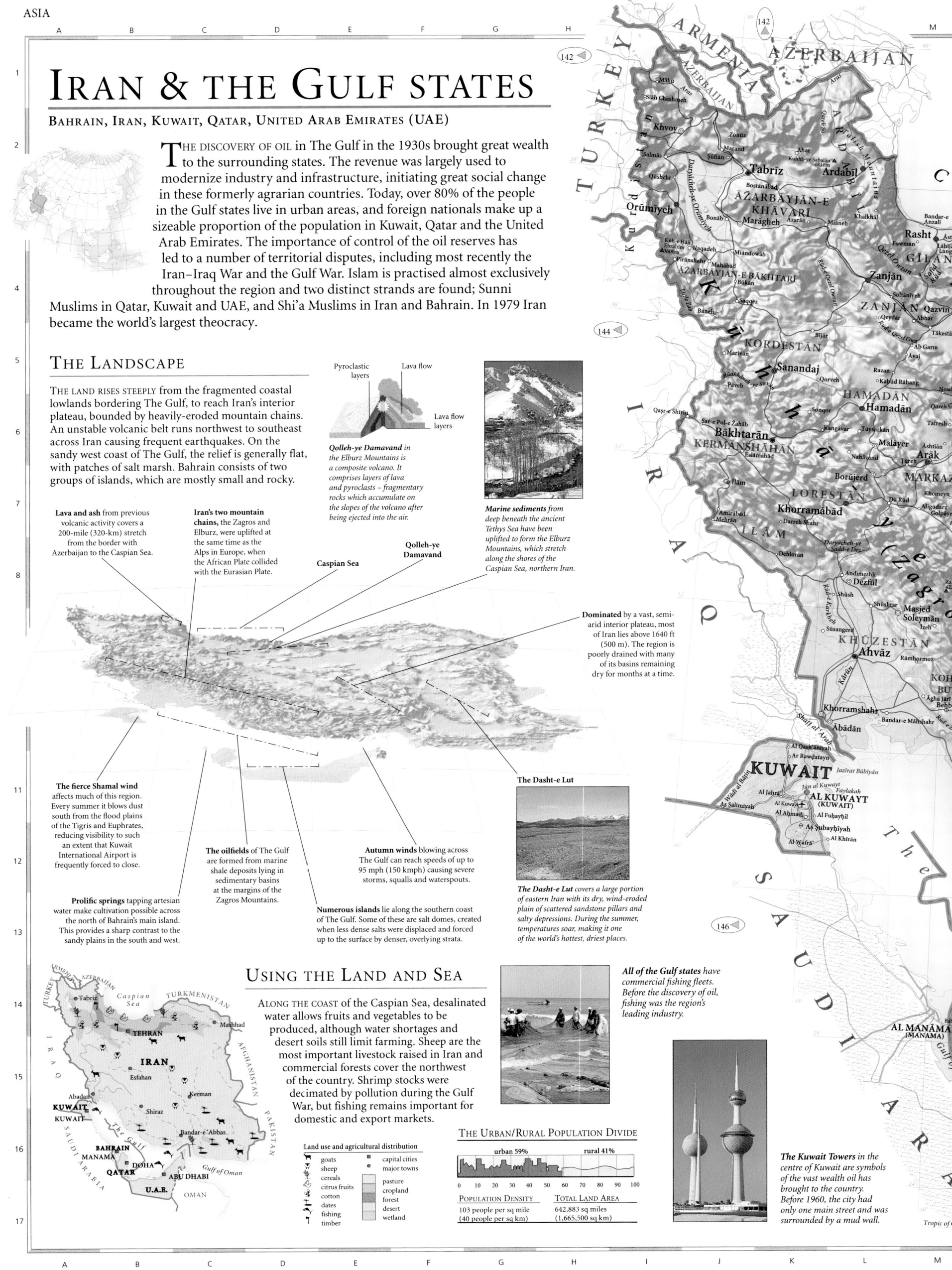

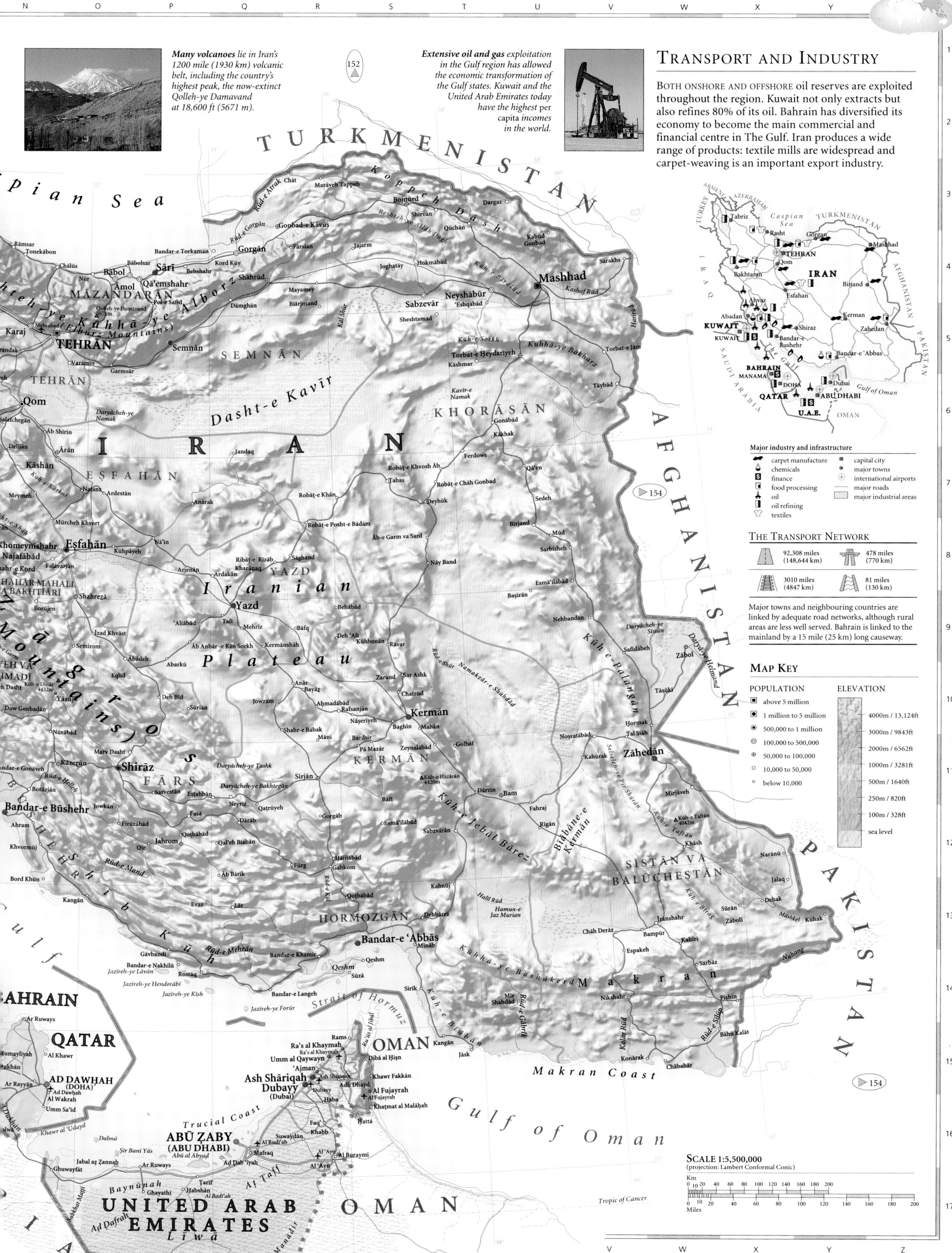

Many volcanoes lie in Iran's 1200 mile (1930 km) volcanic belt, including the country's highest peak, the now-extinct Qolleh-ye Damavand at 18,600 ft (5671 m).

Extensive oil and gas exploitation in the Gulf region has allowed the economic transformation of the Gulf states. Kuwait and the United Arab Emirates today have the highest per capita incomes in the world.

TRANSPORT AND INDUSTRY

BOTH ONSHORE AND OFFSHORE oil reserves are exploited throughout the region. Kuwait not only extracts but also refines 80% of its oil. Bahrain has diversified its economy to become the main commercial and financial centre in The Gulf. Iran produces a wide range of products: textile mills are widespread and carpet-weaving is an important export industry.

Major industry and infrastructure

- carpet manufacture
- chemicals
- finance
- food processing
- oil
- oil refining
- textiles
- capital city
- major towns
- international airports
- major roads
- major industrial areas

THE TRANSPORT NETWORK

92,308 miles (148,644 km)	478 miles (770 km)
3010 miles (4847 km)	81 miles (130 km)

Major towns and neighbouring countries are linked by adequate road networks, although rural areas are less well served. Bahrain is linked to the mainland by a 15 mile (25 km) long causeway.

MAP KEY

POPULATION
- above 5 million
- 1 million to 5 million
- 500,000 to 1 million
- 100,000 to 500,000
- 50,000 to 100,000
- 10,000 to 50,000
- below 10,000

ELEVATION
- 4000m / 13,124ft
- 3000m / 9843ft
- 2000m / 6562ft
- 1000m / 3281ft
- 500m / 1640ft
- 250m / 820ft
- 100m / 328ft
- sea level

SCALE 1:5,500,000
(projection: Lambert Conformal Conic)

149

A B C D E F G H I J K L M

KAZAKHSTAN

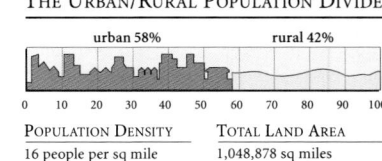

ABUNDANT NATURAL RESOURCES lie in the immense steppe grasslands, deserts and central plateau of the former Soviet republic of Kazakhstan. An intensive programme of industrial and agricultural development to exploit these resources during the Soviet era resulted in catastrophic industrial pollution, including fallout from nuclear testing and the shrinkage of the Aral Sea. Since independence, the government has encouraged foreign investment and liberalized the economy to promote growth. The adoption of Kazakh as the national language is intended to encourage a new sense of national identity in a state where living conditions for the majority remain harsh, both in cramped urban centres and impoverished rural areas.

TRANSPORT AND INDUSTRY

THE SINGLE MOST IMPORTANT INDUSTRY in Kazakhstan is mining, based around extensive oil deposits near the Caspian Sea, the world's largest chromium mine, and vast reserves of iron ore. Recent foreign investment has helped to develop industries including food processing and steel manufacture, and to expand the exploitation of mineral resources. The Russian space programme is still based at Baykonur, near Zhezkazgan in central Kazakhstan.

Major industry and infrastructure

- ▲ chemicals
- ✿ engineering
- 🐟 fish processing
- 🍴 food processing
- ◣ iron & steel
- △ metallurgy
- ⛏ mining
- 🛢 oil
- ■ capital cities
- ● major towns
- ✈ international airports
- — major roads
- ▨ major industrial areas

THE TRANSPORT NETWORK

🛣	103,623 miles (166,864 km)
🛣	none
🚈	8786 miles (14,148 km)
🚈	none

Industrial areas in the north and east are well-connected to Russia. Air and rail links with Germany and China have been established through foreign investment. Better access to Baltic ports is being sought.

125 ◀

An open-cast coal mine in Kazakhstan. Foreign investment is being actively sought by the Kazakh government in order to fully exploit the potential of the country's rich mineral reserves.

MAP KEY

POPULATION

- ▣ 1 million to 5 million
- ◉ 500,000 to 1 million
- ◎ 100,000 to 500,000
- ⊕ 50,000 to 100,000
- ⊙ 10,000 to 50,000
- ∘ below 10,000

ELEVATION

- 4000m / 13,124ft
- 3000m / 9843ft
- 2000m / 6562ft
- 1000m / 3281ft
- 500m / 1640ft
- 250m / 820ft
- 100m / 328ft
- sea level

USING THE LAND AND SEA

THE REARING OF LARGE HERDS of sheep and goats on the steppe grasslands forms the core of Kazakh agriculture. Arable cultivation and cotton-growing in pasture and desert areas was encouraged during the Soviet era, but relative yields are low. The heavy use of fertilizers and the diversion of natural water sources for irrigation has degraded much of the land.

THE URBAN/RURAL POPULATION DIVIDE

urban 58%   rural 42%

0 10 20 30 40 50 60 70 80 90 100

POPULATION DENSITY	TOTAL LAND AREA
16 people per sq mile (6 people per sq km)	1,048,878 sq miles (2,717,300 sq km)

Land use and agricultural distribution

- 🐄 cattle
- 🐐 goats
- 🐑 sheep
- cotton
- 🐟 fishing
- 🌾 wheat
- ■ capital cities
- ● major towns
- pasture
- cropland
- forest
- mountain region
- desert

The nomadic peoples who moved their herds around the steppe grasslands are now largely settled, although echoes of their traditional lifestyle, in particular their superb riding skills, remain.

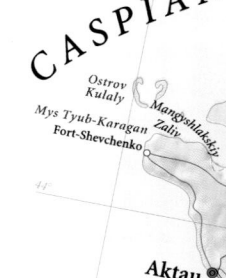

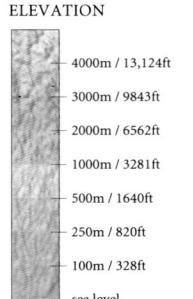

(Map of Kazakhstan with labelled geographic features, cities, and physical regions including:)

RUSSIA · RUSSIAN FEDERATION

Ural'sk · Aktyubinsk · Kustanay · Rudnyy · Atyrau · Aktau

Caspian Sea · Aral Sea · Ustyurt Plateau · Turanskaya Nizmennost'

ZAPADNYY KAZAKHSTAN · AKTYUBINSK · KUSTANAY · Turgayskaya Stolovaya Strana

Caspian Depression · Ryn-Peski · Plato Mangyshlak · MANGISTAU · Sor Metvyy Kultuk · KZYL-ORDA

UZBEKISTAN · TURKMENISTAN

KAZAKH...

SCALE 1:6,250,000
(projection: Lambert Conformal Conic)

Km 0 25 50 100 150 200 250
Miles 0 25 50 100 150 200 250

THE LANDSCAPE

STRETCHING MORE THAN 1250 MILES (2000 km) from the Caspian Sea in the west to China in the east, more than 40% of Kazakhstan is covered by steppe grasslands which give way to barren desert in the south. The land rises eastwards towards the mineral-rich central plateau, to form the Altai Mountains.

1960 1996 2010

Since 1960, the Aral Sea has shrunk by 40%, become extremely saline, and lost all but five of its once-abundant fish species. Factors in this ecological disaster include the excessive use of fertilizers, defoliants and the diversion of its main source rivers for the irrigation of desert lands.

The Caspian Sea is the largest body of inland water in the world.

The desert of Peski Bol'shiye Barsuki is mainly sandy, displaying a number of classic dune formations. Groundwater supports a small amount of vegetation.

A large number of salt lakes fill depressions in the rolling uplands of central Kazakhstan.

The Altai Mountains lie on Kazakhstan's eastern borders with China and the Russian Federation. Cold and largely barren, they are the source of many of the rivers which flow across the steppe.

Altai Mountains

Tien Shan

Khrebet Kanchingiz

Aral Sea

Its waters taken for industry and irrigation, the Syr Darya, one of Kazakhstan's major rivers, now barely reaches the Aral Sea which it used to fill. Like many Kazakh rivers it has been heavily polluted with chemicals and its flow has been restricted by up to 60%.

The waters of Lake Balkhash (*Ozero Balkhash*), unlike those of the Aral Sea, are still able to support a fishing industry.

The central Kazakh Uplands (*Kazakhskiy Melkosopochnik*) contain much of the country's mineral riches. The landscape is largely flat with occasional rocky outcrops and hillocks.

Immense stretches of steppe grasslands characterize much of the Kazakh landscape. These lowland areas have been used for arable cultivation in recent years, although problems with irrigation have meant that much of the land is being allowed to revert to its natural vegetation and pastoral usage.

Rows of pine trees edge this valley near Alma-Ata. The snow-covered slopes in the background are used for skiing.

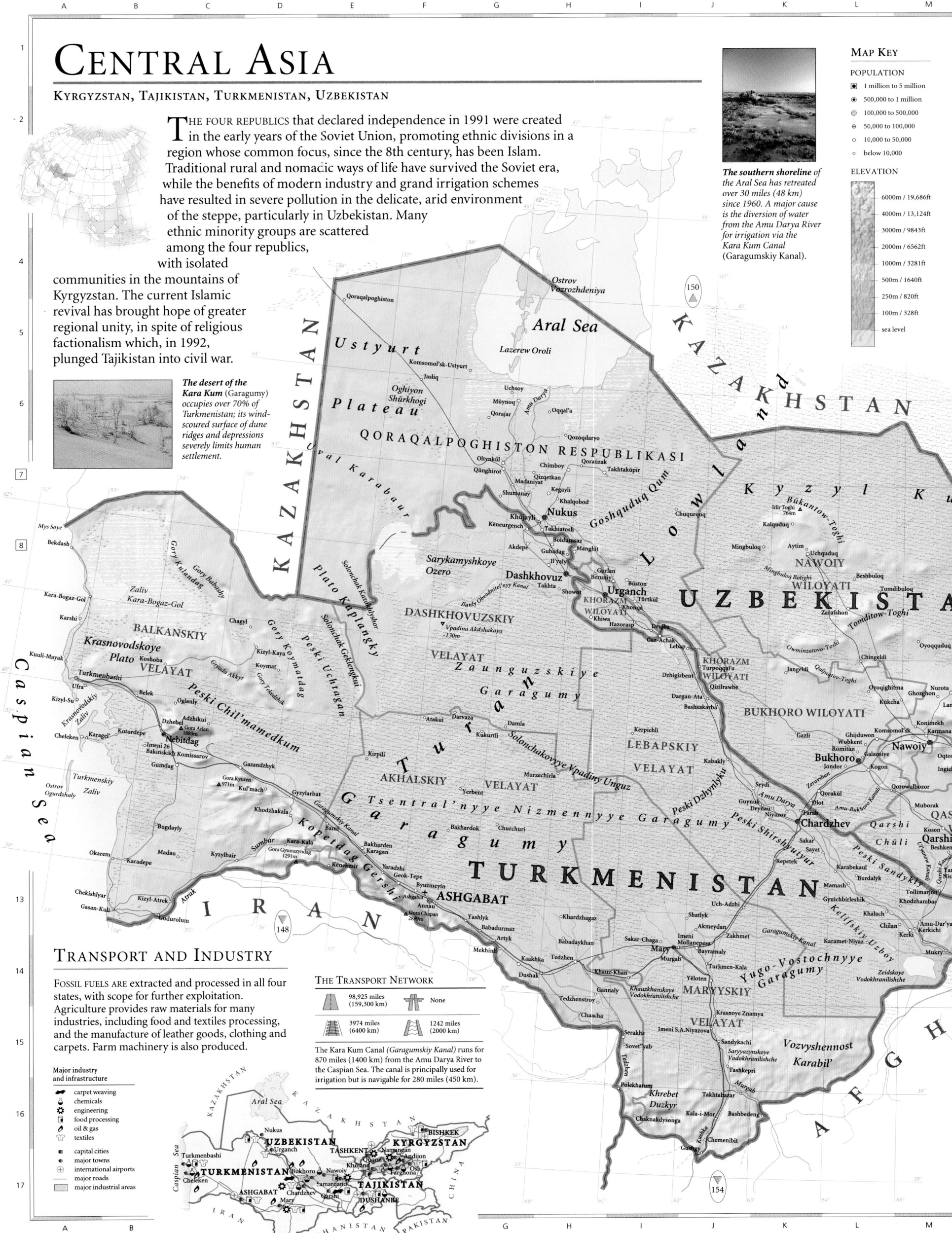

CENTRAL ASIA

KYRGYZSTAN, TAJIKISTAN, TURKMENISTAN, UZBEKISTAN

THE FOUR REPUBLICS that declared independence in 1991 were created in the early years of the Soviet Union, promoting ethnic divisions in a region whose common focus, since the 8th century, has been Islam. Traditional rural and nomadic ways of life have survived the Soviet era, while the benefits of modern industry and grand irrigation schemes have resulted in severe pollution in the delicate, arid environment of the steppe, particularly in Uzbekistan. Many ethnic minority groups are scattered among the four republics, with isolated communities in the mountains of Kyrgyzstan. The current Islamic revival has brought hope of greater regional unity, in spite of religious factionalism which, in 1992, plunged Tajikistan into civil war.

The desert of the Kara Kum (Garagumy) occupies over 70% of Turkmenistan; its wind-scoured surface of dune ridges and depressions severely limits human settlement.

The southern shoreline of the Aral Sea has retreated over 30 miles (48 km) since 1960. A major cause is the diversion of water from the Amu Darya River for irrigation via the Kara Kum Canal (Garagumskiy Kanal).

MAP KEY

POPULATION

- ◉ 1 million to 5 million
- ◎ 500,000 to 1 million
- ⊚ 100,000 to 500,000
- ⊕ 50,000 to 100,000
- ⊙ 10,000 to 50,000
- ○ below 10,000

ELEVATION

- 6000m / 19,686ft
- 4000m / 13,124ft
- 3000m / 9843ft
- 2000m / 6562ft
- 1000m / 3281ft
- 500m / 1640ft
- 250m / 820ft
- 100m / 328ft
- sea level

TRANSPORT AND INDUSTRY

FOSSIL FUELS ARE extracted and processed in all four states, with scope for further exploitation. Agriculture provides raw materials for many industries, including food and textiles processing, and the manufacture of leather goods, clothing and carpets. Farm machinery is also produced.

THE TRANSPORT NETWORK

98,925 miles (159,300 km)	None
3974 miles (6400 km)	1242 miles (2000 km)

The Kara Kum Canal (Garagumskiy Kanal) runs for 870 miles (1400 km) from the Amu Darya River to the Caspian Sea. The canal is principally used for irrigation but is navigable for 280 miles (450 km).

Major industry and infrastructure

- 🐪 carpet weaving
- ⚗ chemicals
- ⚙ engineering
- 🍴 food processing
- ◇ oil & gas
- ⊽ textiles

- ■ capital cities
- ● major towns
- ⊕ international airports
- — major roads
- ▨ major industrial areas

THE LANDSCAPE

THE GREAT TIEN SHAN and Pamir ranges meet in a succession of high mountain chains. These mountains encircle the fertile Fergana Valley and reach west into the desert of the Kyzyl Kum, dividing the Syr Darya and Amu Darya rivers. Sandy steppeland extends to the shores of the Caspian Sea, with the desert of the Kara Kum (Garagumy) in the south. The Amu Darya drains into the Aral Sea in the north.

Salt marshes fill many of the depressions in the Ustyurt Plateau, a barren, rocky tableland about 650 ft (200 m) above sea level.

Some of the world's largest deposits of marine salts are found in Zaliv Kara-Bogaz-Gol. This shallow, saline gulf has an average depth of only 33 ft (10 m), and a very high evaporation rate, producing the salty deposits.

The Kara Kum (Garagumy) is one of the world's largest expanses of sand. Wind action has created a terrain of shifting, crescent-shaped sand dunes known as barchans.

The Amu Darya is the only river in Central Asia with a sufficient volume of water to cross the desert of the Kara Kum (Garagumy) from the Pamirs to the Aral Sea, where it forms a delta largely vegetated by scrub grasses.

A series of major rock faults has created the Fergana Valley, a deep depression surrounded by high mountains. Water from the Syr Darya river and from underground sources supports intensive agriculture, despite minimal rainfall.

Kyzyl Kum

In the heavily-fractured and faulted mountain region, earthquakes are common, caused by the sudden release of tension along active fault lines.

Shock waves travel through ground — Epicentre — Fault

Earthquake zone

Syr Darya

Naryn River

Mount Communism (Qullai Kommunizm), in the northern Pamirs, was so named for being the highest point in the former Soviet Union, rising to 24,590 ft (7495 m).

Qarokŭl

Nestling high in the Pamir range, and fed by glacial meltwater, Qarokŭl is the largest of the lakes in this region.

Bare mountains provide a stark background to the croplands along the Naryn River in Kyrgyzstan. Irrigation is essential for cultivation in this dry region.

Ozero Issyk-Kul' lies at an altitude of 5193 ft (1584 m). The lake remains ice-free throughout the year, due to the slight salinity of the water.

Tien Shan

The Tien Shan extend from China in the east, reaching heights over 24,400 ft (7439 m) and branching into many parallel ranges in the west.

SCALE 1:4,250,000
(projection: Lambert Conformal Conic)

USING THE LAND

CROPLAND OUTSIDE Kyrgyzstan is restricted to irrigated areas such as the Fergana Valley. Central Asia is a leading global producer of cotton, and traditional silk-farming remains widespread. A wide range of fruits, vegetables and grains are grown and livestock raised includes horses, goats and karakul sheep.

Land use and agricultural distribution

cattle	capital cities	
goats	major towns	
sheep	pasture	
cereals	cropland	
cotton	desert	
fruit	wetland	

Plentiful sunshine, rich soils and massive irrigation schemes have made Uzbekistan the world's third largest cotton producer, although water shortages now prevent any further expansion of irrigated land.

THE URBAN/RURAL POPULATION DIVIDE

urban 39%   rural 61%

POPULATION DENSITY	TOTAL LAND AREA
73 people per sq mile	492,961 sq miles
(28 people per sq km)	(1,277,100 sq km)

AFGHANISTAN & PAKISTAN

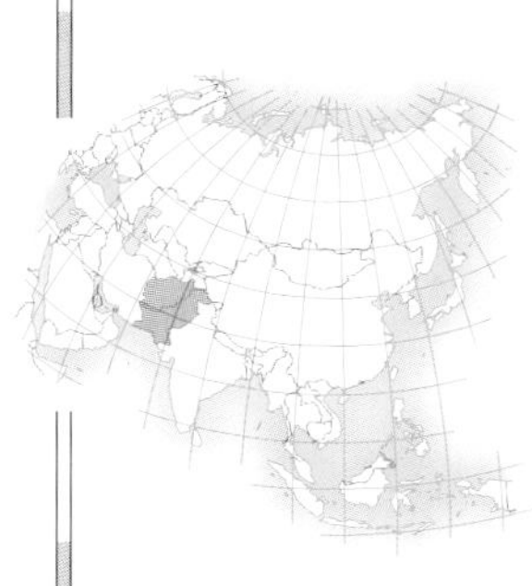

PAKISTAN WAS CREATED by the partition of British India in 1947, becoming the western arm of a new Islamic state for Indian Muslims; the eastern sector, in Bengal, seceded to become the separate country of Bangladesh in 1971. Over half of Pakistan's 122 million people live in the Punjab, at the fertile head of the great Indus Basin. The river sustains a national economy based on irrigated agriculture, including cotton for the vital textiles industry. Afghanistan, a mountainous, landlocked country, with an ancient and independent culture, has been wracked by war since 1979, when calls for help from a beleaguered government led to a Soviet invasion. Despite the Soviet withdrawal, factional strife continues and five million Afghan refugees remain over the border in Pakistan.

The town of Bamian lies high in the Hindu Kush, 250 miles (420 km) west of the Afghan capital, Kabul. It contains two huge statues of Buddha and a number of sanctuaries and cells carved in the rock. In 1222, the ancient city was destroyed by Chinghiz Khan.

TRANSPORT AND INDUSTRY

PAKISTAN IS HIGHLY dependent on the cotton textiles industry, although diversified manufacture is expanding around cities such as Karachi and Lahore. Afghanistan's limited industry is based mainly on the processing of agricultural raw materials and includes traditional crafts such as carpet-making.

Major industry and infrastructure

- carpet weaving
- chemicals
- engineering
- finance
- food processing
- iron & steel
- oil & gas
- textiles
- ■ capital cities
- • major towns
- ✈ international airports
- — major roads
- ▨ major industrial areas

THE TRANSPORT NETWORK

🛣	82,740 miles (133,237 km)
	None
🚆	7855 miles (12,649 km)
	745 miles (1200 km)

The Karakoram Highway was completed after 20 years of construction in 1978. It breaches the Himalayan mountain barrier providing a commercial motor route linking lowland Pakistan and China.

The Karakoram Highway is one of the highest major roads in the world. It took over 24,000 workers almost 20 years to complete.

THE LANDSCAPE

AFGHANISTAN'S TOPOGRAPHY is dominated by the mountains of the Hindu Kush, which spread south and west into numerous mountain spurs. The dry plateau of southwestern Afghanistan extends into Pakistan and the hills which overlook the great Indus Basin. In northern Pakistan the Hindu Kush, Himalayan and Karakoram ranges meet to form one of the world's highest mountain regions.

The arid Hindu Kush makes much of Afghanistan uninhabitable, with over 50% of the land lying above 6500 ft (2000 m).

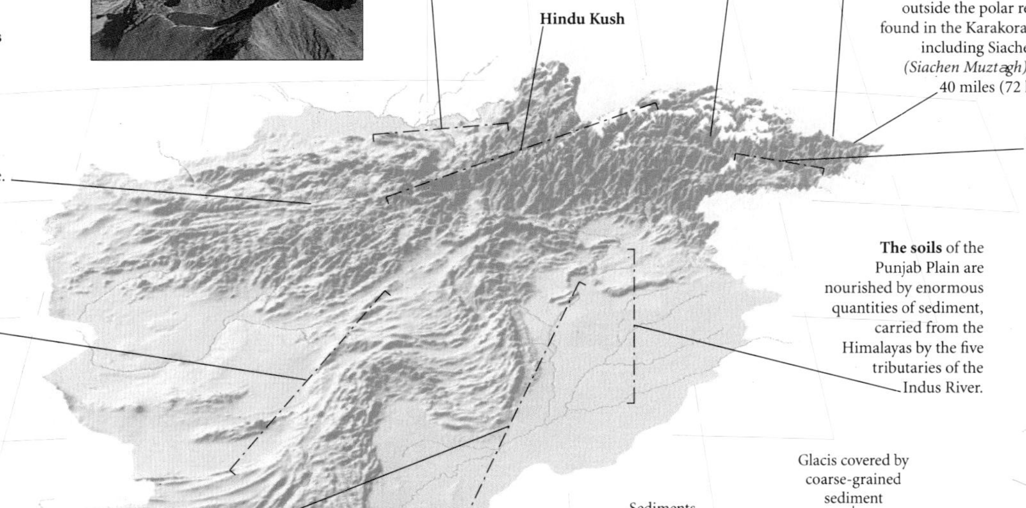

Frequent earthquakes mean that mountain-building processes are continuing in this region, as the Indo-Australian Plate drifts northwards, colliding with the Eurasian Plate.

Mountain chains running southwest from the Hindu Kush into Pakistan form a barrier to the humid winds which blow from the Indian Ocean, creating arid conditions across southern Afghanistan.

The Hunza River rises in the northern Karakoram Range, running for 120 miles (193 km) before joining the Gilgit River.

Hunza River

The plains and foothills which extend from the northern slopes of the Hindu Kush are part of the great grassy steppe lands of Central Asia.

K2 (Mount Godwin Austen), in the Karakoram Range, is the second highest mountain in the world, at an altitude of 28,251 ft (8611 m).

Some of the largest glaciers outside the polar regions are found in the Karakoram Range, including Siachen Glacier (Siachen Muztagh), which is 40 miles (72 km) long.

Hindu Kush

Himalayas

The soils of the Punjab Plain are nourished by enormous quantities of sediment, carried from the Himalayas by the five tributaries of the Indus River.

The Indus Basin is part of the Indus-Ganges lowland, a vast depression which has been filled with layers of sediment over the last 50 million years. These deposits are estimated to be over 16,400 ft (5000 m) deep.

The Indus Delta is prone to heavy flooding and high levels of salinity. It remains a largely uncultivated wilderness area.

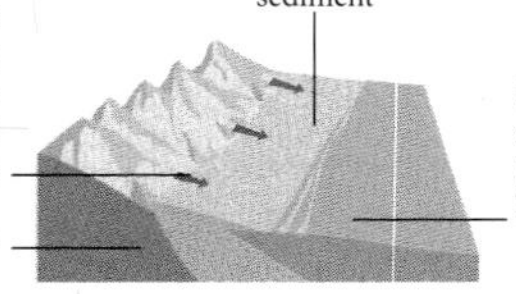

Sediments washed down from mountains accumulate on glacis slopes

Glacis covered by coarse-grained sediment

Fine sediments deposited on salt flats are removed by wind erosion

Bedrock

Glacis are gentle, debris-covered slopes which lead into salt flats or deserts. They typically occur at the base of mountains in arid regions such as Afghanistan.

SCALE 1:4,500,000
(projection: Lambert Conformal Conic)

Km
0 10 20 40 60 80 100 120 140 160 180 200

0 10 20 40 60 80 100 120 140 160 180 200
Miles

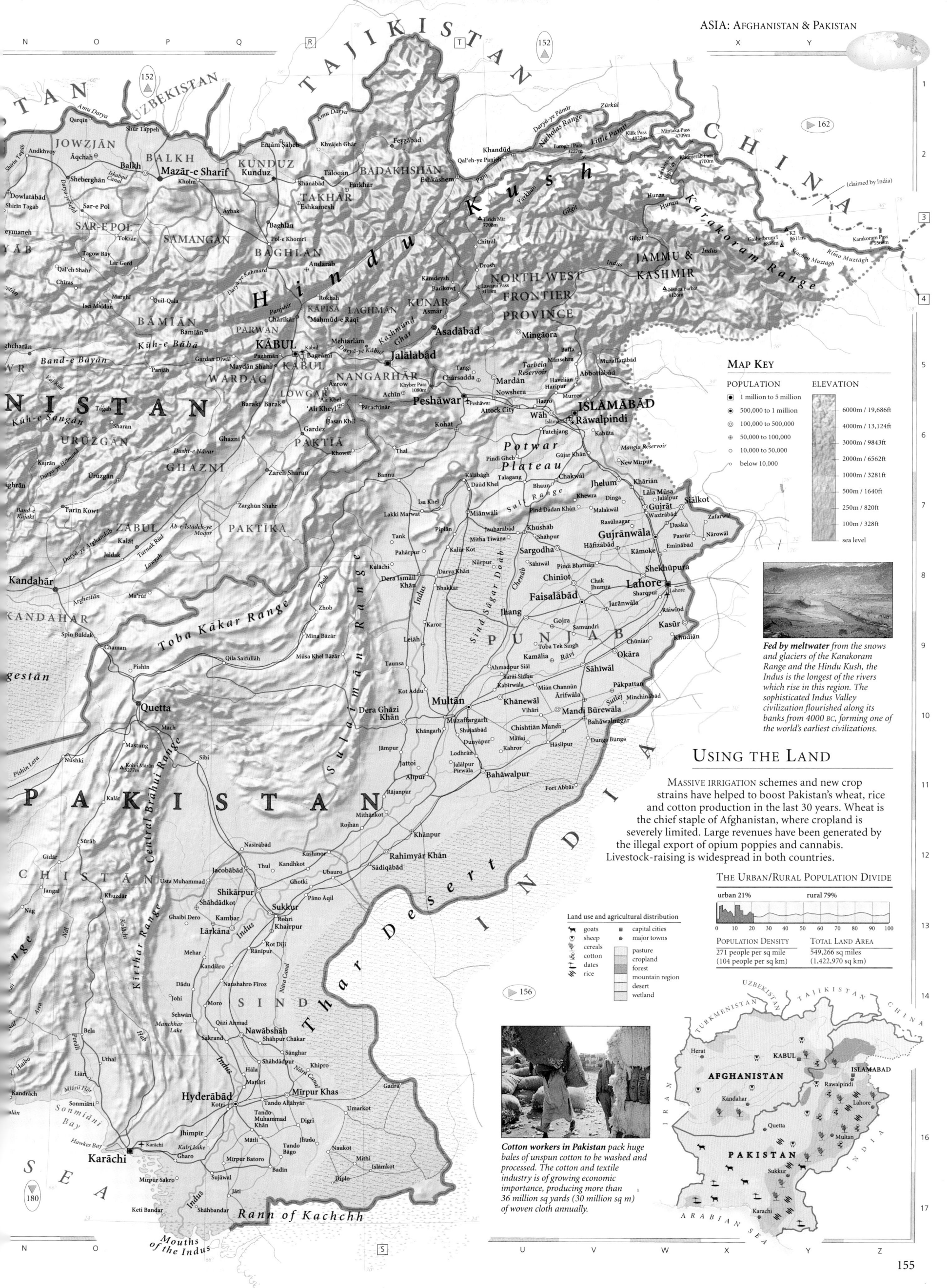

Fed by meltwater from the snows and glaciers of the Karakoram Range and the Hindu Kush, the Indus is the longest of the rivers which rise in this region. The sophisticated Indus Valley civilization flourished along its banks from 4000 BC, forming one of the world's earliest civilizations.

USING THE LAND

MASSIVE IRRIGATION schemes and new crop strains have helped to boost Pakistan's wheat, rice and cotton production in the last 30 years. Wheat is the chief staple of Afghanistan, where cropland is severely limited. Large revenues have been generated by the illegal export of opium poppies and cannabis. Livestock-raising is widespread in both countries.

THE URBAN/RURAL POPULATION DIVIDE

urban 21%   rural 79%

POPULATION DENSITY	TOTAL LAND AREA
271 people per sq mile (104 people per sq km)	549,266 sq miles (1,422,970 sq km)

Land use and agricultural distribution
- goats
- sheep
- cereals
- cotton
- dates
- rice
- capital cities
- major towns
- pasture
- cropland
- forest
- mountain region
- desert
- wetland

Cotton workers in Pakistan pack huge bales of unspun cotton to be washed and processed. The cotton and textile industry is of growing economic importance, producing more than 36 million sq yards (30 million sq m) of woven cloth annually.

MAP KEY

POPULATION
- 1 million to 5 million
- 500,000 to 1 million
- 100,000 to 500,000
- 50,000 to 100,000
- 10,000 to 50,000
- below 10,000

ELEVATION
- 6000m / 19,686ft
- 4000m / 13,124ft
- 3000m / 9843ft
- 2000m / 6562ft
- 1000m / 3281ft
- 500m / 1640ft
- 250m / 820ft
- 100m / 328ft
- sea level

SOUTH ASIA

BANGLADESH, BHUTAN, INDIA, MALDIVES, NEPAL, PAKISTAN, SRI LANKA

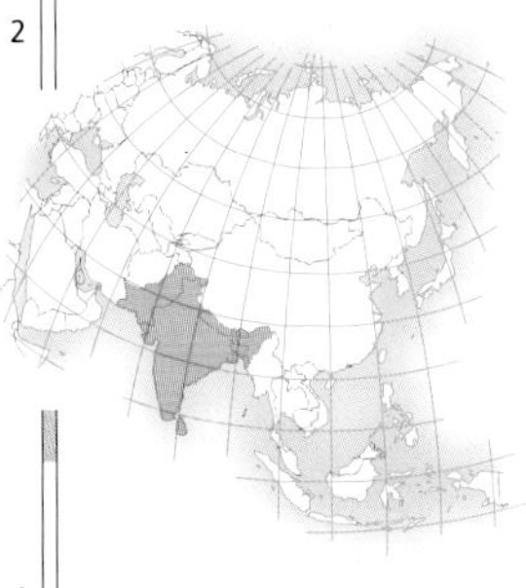

MORE THAN ONE-FIFTH of the world's population lives in the south Asian subcontinent. Great cultural diversity has come from a long succession of foreign invaders, including Hindu Aryans, Islamic Moguls and the British, whose empire incorporated the princely states of the Maharajas and extended to the borders of Nepal and Bhutan in the Himalayas. Half a century after independence, India is the world's largest democracy, and at the current rate of growth, may overtake China as the world's most populous country within the next century. There are points of tension in the region over claims for independence by the Sikhs in the Indian Punjab and the Tamil separatists in Sri Lanka, and the long-standing dispute with Pakistan over Jammu and Kashmir in the north.

THE LANDSCAPE

SOUTH ASIA is effectively isolated from the rest of Asia by desert along the western flank of Pakistan, and a continuous wall of mountains, dominated by the Himalayas, to the north and east. The great basins of the Indus and Ganges separate this mountain fringe from the rolling plateau of the Indian peninsula, which is bordered by a line of coastal hills, the Eastern and Western Ghats.

The towering Karakoram and Hindu Kush ranges, formed at the same time as the Himalayas, dominate Pakistan's northern borders. K2 on the border of northern Pakistan is the second highest mountain on Earth, at 28,252 ft (8611 m).

The Indus River flows more than 1100 miles (1800 km) from southwestern Tibet to its mouth on the Arabian Sea. It has an estimated catchment area of 371,853 sq miles (963,100 sq km).

The coast of western Pakistan is a staircase of folded rock strata caused by successive periods of rapid uplift.

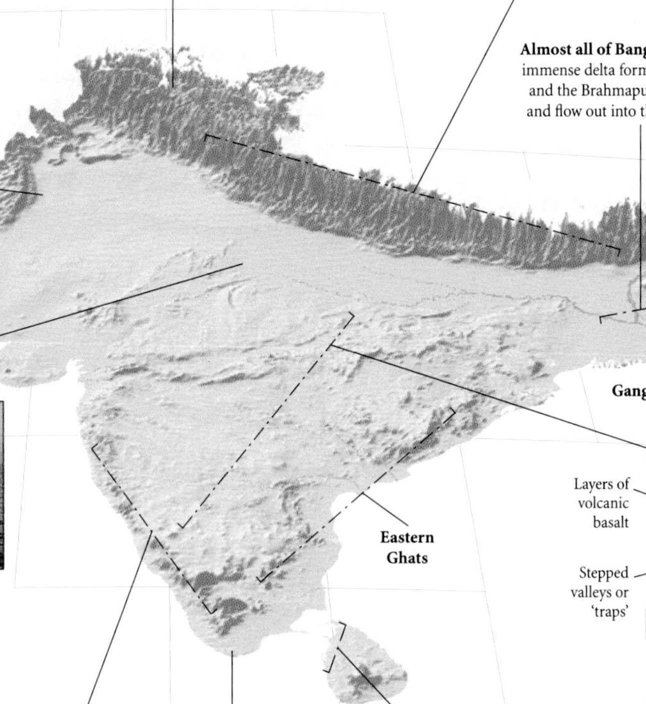

The Himalayas are the highest and most extensive mountain system in the world. They were formed when the Indo-Australian Plate collided with the Eurasian Plate about 40 million years ago, thrusting up huge masses of land and creating a 'ripple' effect, which formed lesser mountain ranges in Tibet and Southeast Asia. Mount Everest is the world's tallest mountain at 29,028 ft (8847 m).

Almost all of Bangladesh lies in the immense delta formed by the Ganges and the Brahmaputra which merge and flow out into the Bay of Bengal.

Ganges Delta

The Indus Valley near Skardu in northern Pakistan has been partially infilled by great quantities of eroded sediment. Most of this is carried from the region's bare slopes by swollen rivers during the spring thaw and mass movement activity.

Deccan Plateau

Layers of volcanic basalt

Stepped valleys or 'traps'

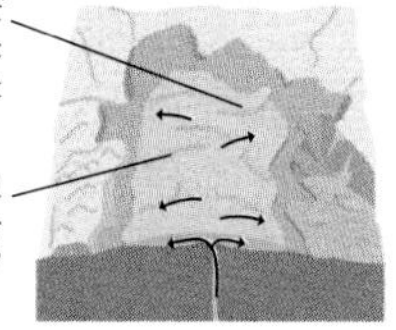

The Deccan Plateau covers an area of more than 123,553 sq miles (320,000 sq km). It is formed of deep layers of volcanic basalt, reaching thicknesses of more than 9800 ft (3000 m) towards the coast. Distinctive stepped valleys cut in the basalt plateau by rivers are known as 'traps'.

Eastern Ghats

Coastal deposition has formed many typical features along the western coast of Sri Lanka. These include spits and bars, sometimes enclosing lagoons.

Trivandrum in southern India normally receives the first of the monsoon rains, which are essential to south Asian agriculture and moderate the extreme summer heat. The monsoon then moves northwards over a period of about two months.

Bharatpur

Rivers flowing from the Himalayas into a broad depression in northern India have formed marshes around Bharatpur. They are now a sanctuary for numerous bird species.

The Western Ghats are formed by a fault scarp which runs unbroken for more than 930 miles (1500 km). They reach their highest point at the southern Cardamon Hills.

156

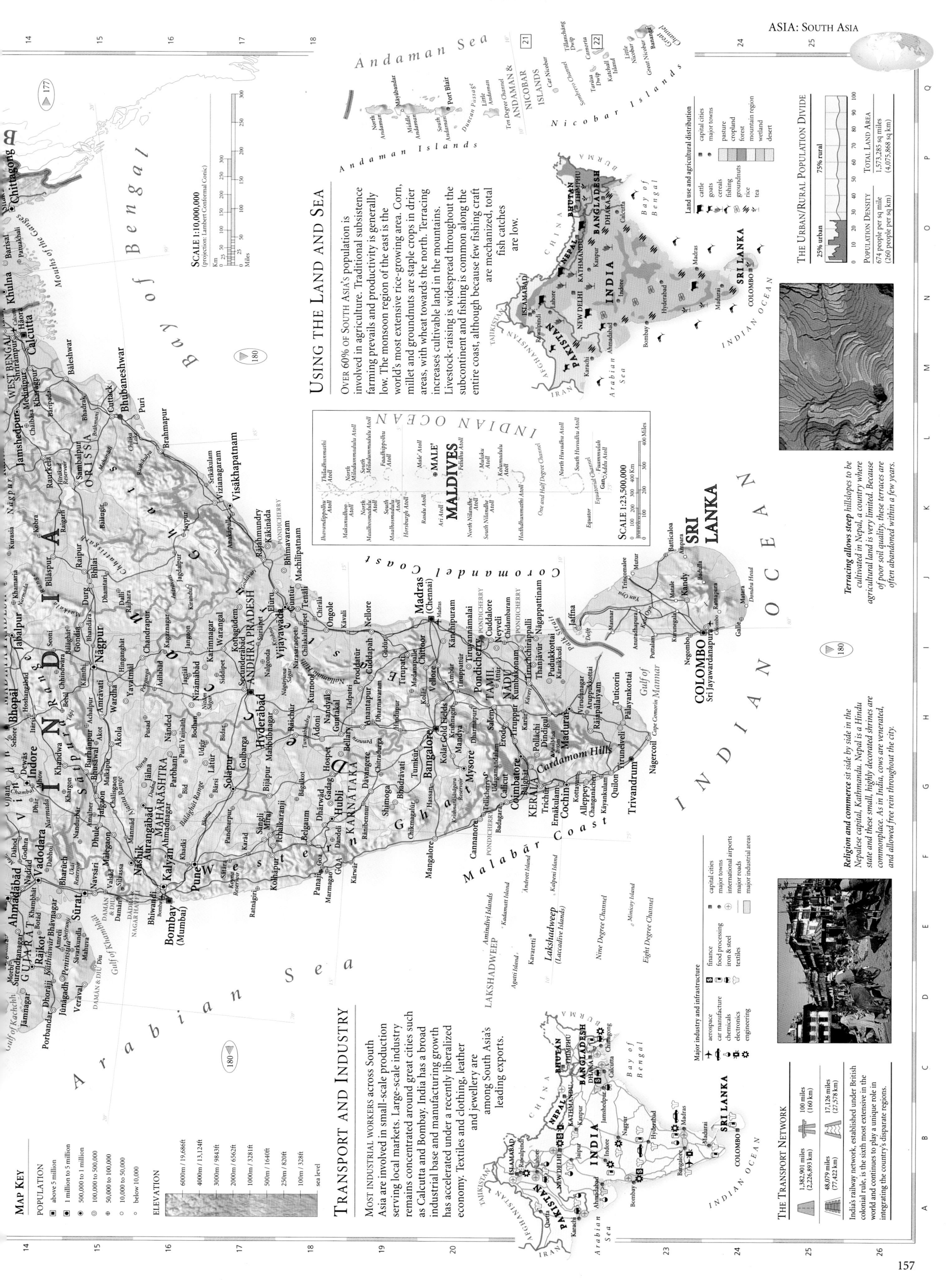

MAP KEY

POPULATION
- above 5 million
- 1 million to 5 million
- 500,000 to 1 million
- 100,000 to 500,000
- 50,000 to 100,000
- 10,000 to 50,000
- below 10,000

ELEVATION
6000m / 19,686ft
4000m / 13,124ft
3000m / 9843ft
2000m / 656oft
1000m / 328oft
500m / 164oft
250m / 82oft
100m / 328ft
sea level

SCALE 1:10,000,000
(projection: Lambert Conformal Conic)

USING THE LAND AND SEA

OVER 60% OF SOUTH ASIA's population is involved in agriculture. Traditional subsistence farming prevails and productivity is generally low. The monsoon region of the east is the world's most extensive rice-growing area. Corn, millet and groundnuts are staple crops in drier areas, with wheat towards the north. Terracing increases cultivable land in the mountains. Livestock-raising is widespread throughout the subcontinent and fishing is common along the entire coast, although because few fishing craft are mechanized, total fish catches are low.

Land use and agricultural distribution
- capital cities
- major towns
- pasture
- cropland
- forest
- mountain region
- wetland
- desert

- cattle
- goats
- cereals
- groundnuts
- rice
- tea

THE URBAN/RURAL POPULATION DIVIDE
25% urban
75% rural

POPULATION DENSITY
674 people per sq mile
(260 people per sq km)

TOTAL LAND AREA
1,573,285 sq miles
(4,075,868 sq km)

Terracing allows steep hillslopes to be cultivated in Nepal, a country where agricultural land is very limited. Because of poor soil quality, these terraces are often abandoned within a few years.

Religion and commerce sit side by side in the Nepalese capital, Kathmandu. Nepal is a Hindu state and these small, highly decorated shrines are commonplace. As in India, cows are venerated, and allowed free rein throughout the city.

TRANSPORT AND INDUSTRY

MOST INDUSTRIAL WORKERS across South Asia are involved in small-scale production serving local markets. Large-scale industry remains concentrated around great cities such as Calcutta and Bombay. India has a broad industrial base and manufacturing growth has accelerated under a recently liberalized economy. Textiles and clothing, leather and jewellery are among South Asia's leading exports.

Major industry and infrastructure
- aerospace
- car manufacture
- chemicals
- electronics
- engineering
- finance
- food processing
- iron & steel
- textiles

- capital cities
- major towns
- international airports
- major roads
- major industrial areas

THE TRANSPORT NETWORK

1,382,901 miles
(2,226,893 km)

100 miles
(160 km)

48,079 miles
(77,422 km)

17,126 miles
(27,578 km)

India's railway network, established under British colonial rule, is the sixth most extensive in the world and continues to play a unique role in integrating the country's disparate regions.

SCALE 1:23,500,000

157

NORTHERN INDIA & THE HIMALAYAN STATES

BANGLADESH, BHUTAN, NEPAL, Arunachal Pradesh,
Assam, Bihar, Chandigarh, Delhi, Haryana,
Himachal Pradesh, Jammu & Kashmir, Manipur,
Meghalaya, Mizoram, Nagaland, Punjab, Rajasthan,
Sikkim, Tripura, Uttar Pradesh, West Bengal

THE GANGES AND BRAHMAPUTRA river basins and the massive mountain barrier of the Himalayas define this region's landscape and have served to reinforce potent cultural and religious differences among its people. Hinduism pervades most aspects of national life and is a growing political force within India, a secular country which also encompasses the centre of Sikhism at Amritsar and the world's largest Muslim minority. Nepal is a crowded mountain state, which faces severe ecological problems from deforestation, while the tiny Himalayan Buddhist kingdom of Bhutan is emerging from long-term isolation, to welcome selected visitors. The Muslim state of Bangladesh, formerly East Pakistan, is one of the world's most densely populated countries and one of the poorest, with more than 120 million people living largely on the massive Ganges/Brahmaputra Delta. Many Bangladeshis live under threat of repeated, catastrophic floods.

The Golden Temple in Amritsar, the most sacred shrine of the Sikh religion, was the scene of violent clashes between Sikh separatists and government forces in 1984.

MAP KEY

POPULATION

- ▣ 1 million to 5 million
- ◉ 500,000 to 1 million
- ⊕ 100,000 to 500,000
- ⊙ 50,000 to 100,000
- ○ 10,000 to 50,000
- ∘ below 10,000

ELEVATION

- 6000m / 19,686ft
- 4000m / 13,124ft
- 3000m / 9843ft
- 2000m / 6562ft
- 1000m / 3281ft
- 500m / 1640ft
- 250m / 820ft
- 100m / 328ft
- sea level

TRANSPORT AND INDUSTRY

TEXTILES, ENGINEERING, chemicals and electronics are leading industries in north India. The plateau of Chota Nagpur provides ore for iron and steel production in the major industrial region northeast of Calcutta. Bangladesh processes jute and Nepal has a small manufacturing sector based on agricultural produce, while Bhutan's limited industry is concentrated in the southern lowland area.

SCALE 1:5,750,000
(projection: Lambert Conformal Conic)

Major industry and infrastructure

⛰ adventure tourism		⬮ oil	
🚗 car manufacture		⛁ tea processing	
⚗ chemicals		⬘ textiles	
coal			
electronics		■ capital cities	
⚙ engineering		• major towns	
finance		✈ international airports	
food processing		major roads	
iron & steel		major industrial areas	
jute processing			

THE TRANSPORT NETWORK

Over 60% of Bangladesh's internal trade is carried by boat. The country has a very disjointed land transport network, with no bridges over the Brahmaputra and few road crossings on the Ganges River.

THE LANDSCAPE

MOST OF THE REGION is drained by the River Ganges, which meets the Brahmaputra in Bangladesh to form an immense delta before flowing into the Bay of Bengal. The Himalayas extend eastwards over 1500 miles (2400 km), from the parallel ranges running through Jammu and Kashmir. The Thar Desert occupies the southwest.

The Indian Punjab lies mainly to the west of the Ganges watershed and its rivers flow into the Indus. Control of this water resource has been a source of great friction with neighbouring Pakistan.

The border between India and Pakistan runs through the Thar Desert, an area of sandy *seif* dunes 50–100 ft (15–30 m) in height. Fossils found in the desert indicate that the dunes, stabilized by vegetation, have been in their current position for about 3000 years.

Sambhar Salt Lake in Rajasthan is India's largest lake. Unlike most of the Himalayan lakes which are glacial in origin – formed in ice-scoured basins or as the result of depositional damming – it is an ephemeral salt lake filled periodically by flash flooding.

The Pir Panjal Range in southwestern Kashmir rises to elevations of 12,500 ft (3810 m). Despite the freezing conditions, settlements and extensive pastures are found above the tree line.

The northern ranges of the Himalayas contain the highest mountains in the world, with average heights of more than 23,000 ft (7000 m) and many peaks higher than 26,000 ft (8000 m).

The Ganges River, sacred to the Hindu people, drains a vast lowland area at the base of the Himalayas. The northern plains are covered by sandy deposits, broken by mud-banks formed when the river floods.

The rapid deforestation of Himalayan valleys has led to acute soil erosion and increased rates of rainwater run-off, both cited as possible causes of the worsening floods downstream in the Ganges/Brahmaputra Delta, although natural rates are high and may be the real cause.

In the last 40 million years, the course of the Brahmaputra has been diverted hundreds of miles to the east by the rising landmass of the Himalayas.

The Khasi Hills are an example of a *horst*, a fractured block of bedrock which has been thrust upwards.

Over half of the great Ganges/Brahmaputra Delta floods each year during the monsoon as rivers, swollen by meltwater from the Himalayas and by excess rainwater, break their banks and fertilize the land with nutrient-rich sediment.

The summit of Machhapuchhre rises to 22,942 ft (6993 m). It is also known as the 'Fish's Tail' because of its distinctive peak.

Debris slides in the middle Himalayas

Soil blocks — Debris fans at base of slope — Slide plain

Soil loss in the middle Himalayas has largely been attributed to debris slides, where large blocks of soil are mobilized by saturation along a slide plane. Once mobile, the soil slides down the slope, gaining speed and thinning to form a fan at the base of the slope.

USING THE LAND

GRAIN PRODUCTION dominates land use. Rice is most widely grown in the east. Irrigation and new crop strains have dramatically increased yields in the Punjab, a major wheat-producing area. River flood plains are intensively farmed and livestock-herding is widespread, particularly in Bhutan. Regional crops include jute in Bangladesh, tea in Assam, cardamom in Sikkim and saffron in Kashmir.

THE URBAN/RURAL POPULATION DIVIDE

urban 22%   rural 78%

0 10 20 30 40 50 60 70 80 90 100

POPULATION DENSITY
728 people per sq mile
(281 people per sq km)

TOTAL LAND AREA
665,104 sq miles
(1,723,068 sq km)

Land use and agricultural distribution

- cattle
- goats
- sheep
- cereals
- jute
- rice
- tea

- capital cities
- major towns
- pasture
- cropland
- forest
- mountain region
- wetland
- desert

An adverse climate, steep slopes and poor soils limit crop cultivation in Bhutan, which is a largely agrarian economy. Rice, corn and wheat are the main staples, although orchards are being established as the soil and climate suit this type of farming.

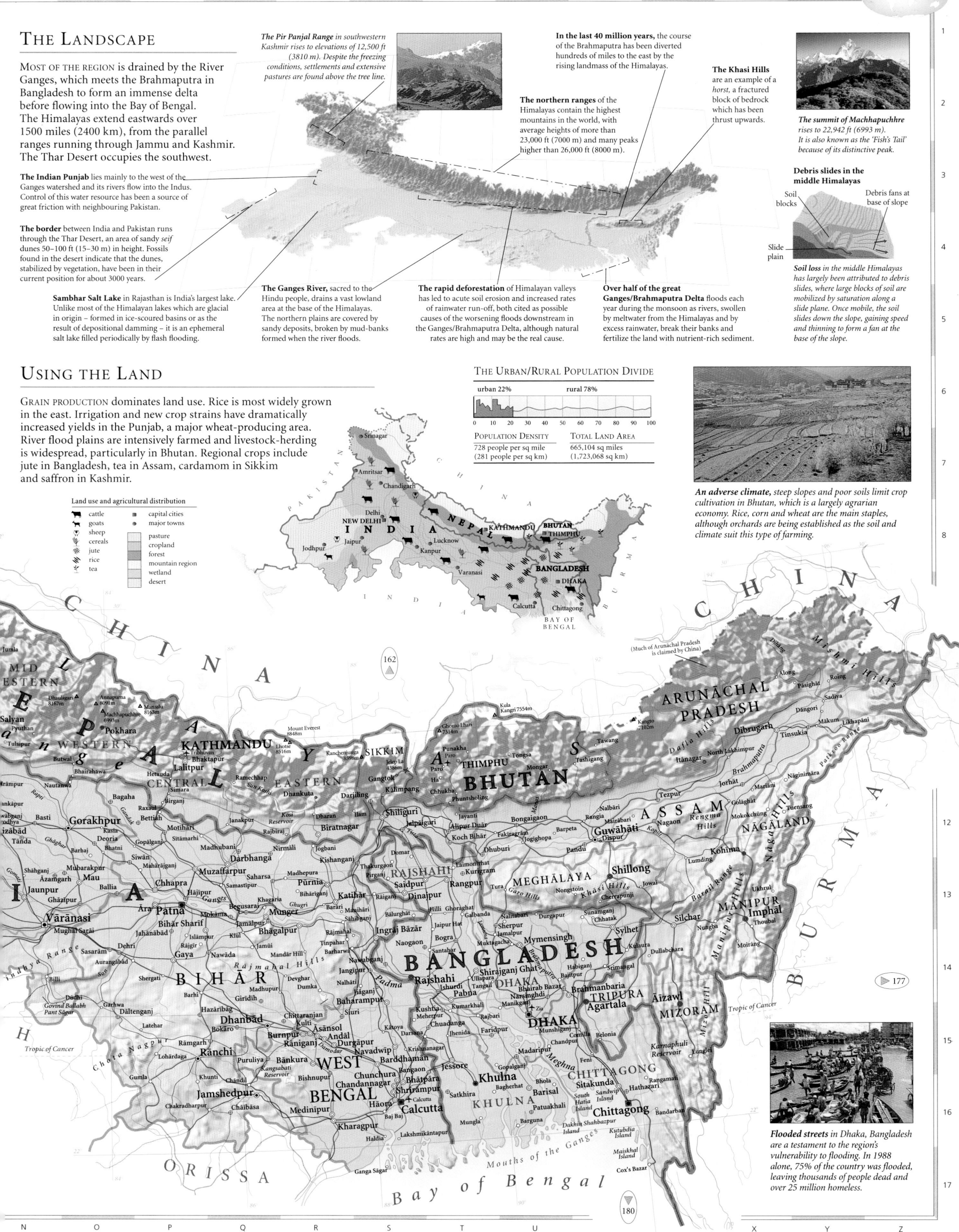

Flooded streets in Dhaka, Bangladesh are a testament to the region's vulnerability to flooding. In 1988 alone, 75% of the country was flooded, leaving thousands of people dead and over 25 million homeless.

SOUTHERN INDIA & SRI LANKA

Sri Lanka, Andhra Pradesh, Dadra & Nagar Haveli, Daman & Diu, Goa, Gujarat, Karnataka, Kerala, Lakshadweep, Madhya Pradesh, Maharashtra, Orissa, Pondicherry, Tamil Nadu

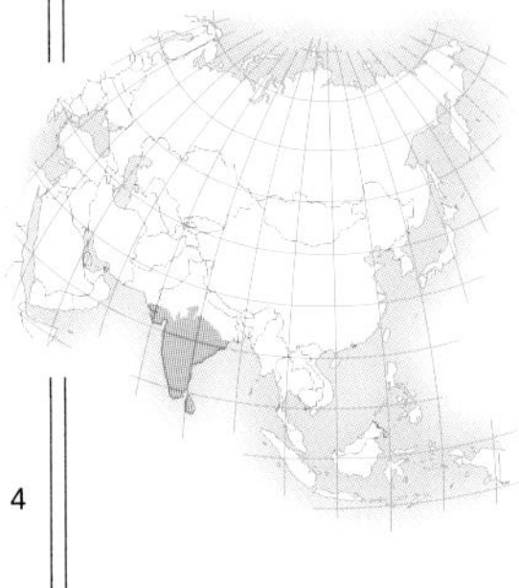

THE UNIQUE AND HIGHLY INDEPENDENT southern states reflect the diverse and decentralized nature of India, which has fourteen official languages. The southern half of the peninsula lay beyond the reach of early invaders from the north and retained the distinct and ancient culture of Dravidian peoples such as the Tamils, whose language is spoken in preference to Hindi throughout southern India. The interior plateau of southern India is less densely populated than the coastal lowlands, where the European colonial imprint is strongest. Urban and industrial growth is accelerating, but southern India's vast population remains predominantly rural. The island of Sri Lanka has two distinct cultural groups; the mainly Buddhist Sinhalese majority, and the Tamil minority whose struggle for a homeland in the northeast has led to prolonged civil war.

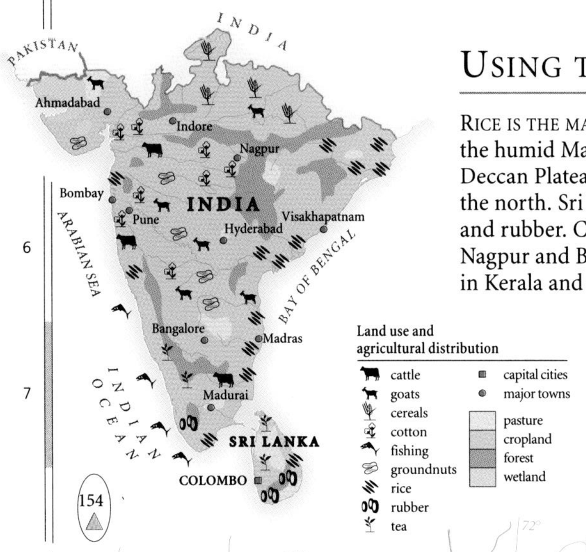

USING THE LAND AND SEA

RICE IS THE MAIN staple in the east, in Sri Lanka and along the humid Malabar Coast. Groundnuts are grown on the Deccan Plateau, with wheat, corn and chickpeas, towards the north. Sri Lanka is a leading exporter of tea, coconuts and rubber. Cotton plantations supply local mills around Nagpur and Bombay. Fishing supports many communities in Kerala and the Laccadive Islands.

Commercial plantations, growing tea, (seen here), cardamom, coffee, coconuts and rubber, occupy about half the agricultural land in Kerala, necessitating food imports for local consumption.

Land use and agricultural distribution

- cattle
- goats
- cereals
- cotton
- fishing
- groundnuts
- rice
- rubber
- tea

■ capital cities
● major towns

pasture
cropland
forest
wetland

THE URBAN/RURAL POPULATION DIVIDE

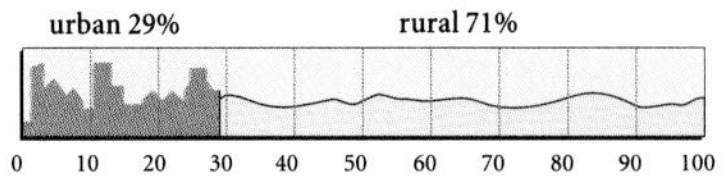

urban 29%   rural 71%

POPULATION DENSITY	TOTAL LAND AREA
650 people per sq mile (251 people per sq km)	698,295 sq miles (1,809,054 sq km)

THE LANDSCAPE

THE UNDULATING DECCAN PLATEAU underlies most of southern India; it slopes gently down towards the east and is largely enclosed by the Ghats coastal hill ranges. The Western Ghats run continuously along the Arabian Sea coast, while the Eastern Ghats are interrupted by rivers which follow the slope of the plateau and flow across broad lowlands into the Bay of Bengal. The plateaux and basins of Sri Lanka's central highlands are surrounded by a broad plain.

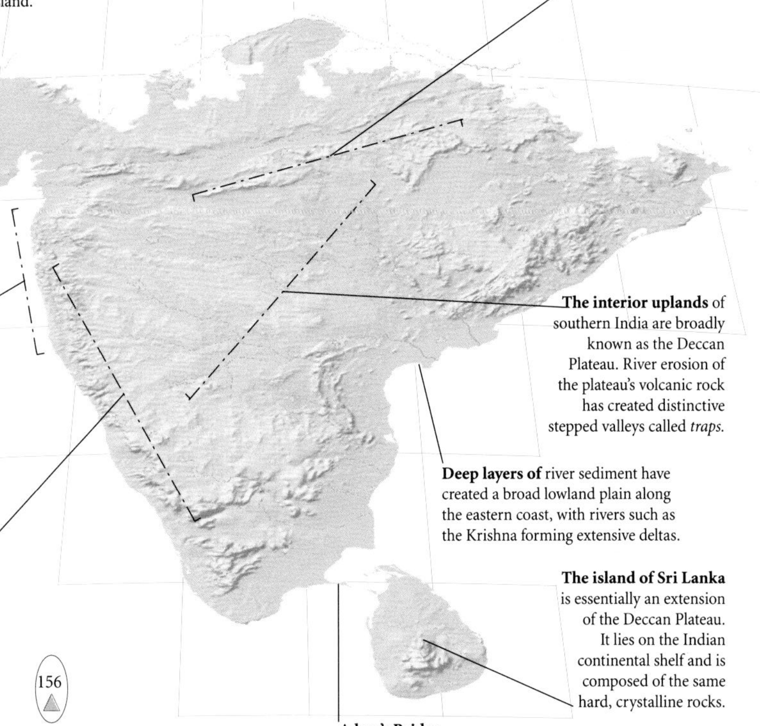

Along the northern boundary of the Deccan Plateau, old basement rocks are interspersed with younger sedimentary strata. This creates spectacular scarplands, cut by numerous waterfalls along the softer sedimentary strata.

The Rann of Kachchh tidal marshes encircle the low-lying Kachchh Peninsula. For several months during the rainy season the water level of the marshes rises and Kachchh becomes an island.

The Konkan coast, which runs between Daman and Goa, is characterized by rocky headlands and bays with crescent-shaped beaches. Flooded river valleys known as *rias* extend inland.

The Western Ghats run north–south marking the western boundary of the Deccan Plateau. Their height rises to the south where their summits reach altitudes of 8000 ft (2500 m).

The interior uplands of southern India are broadly known as the Deccan Plateau. River erosion of the plateau's volcanic rock has created distinctive stepped valleys called *traps*.

Deep layers of river sediment have created a broad lowland plain along the eastern coast, with rivers such as the Krishna forming extensive deltas.

The island of Sri Lanka is essentially an extension of the Deccan Plateau. It lies on the Indian continental shelf and is composed of the same hard, crystalline rocks.

Adam's Bridge

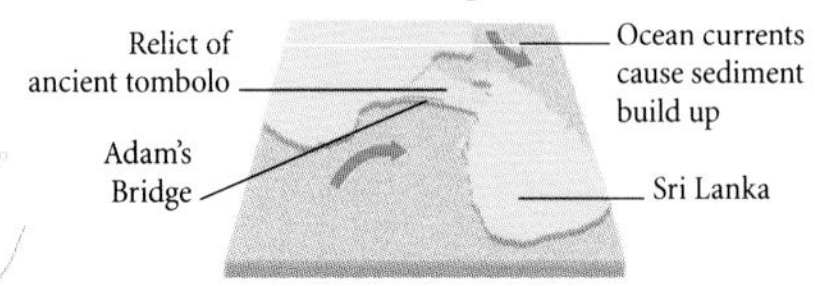

Ocean currents cause sediment build up

Sri Lanka

Relict of ancient tombolo

Adam's Bridge

Adam's Bridge (Rama's Bridge) is a chain of sandy shoals lying about 4 ft (1.2 m) under the sea between India and Sri Lanka. They once formed the world's longest tombolo, or land bridge, before the sea level began to rise several thousand years ago.

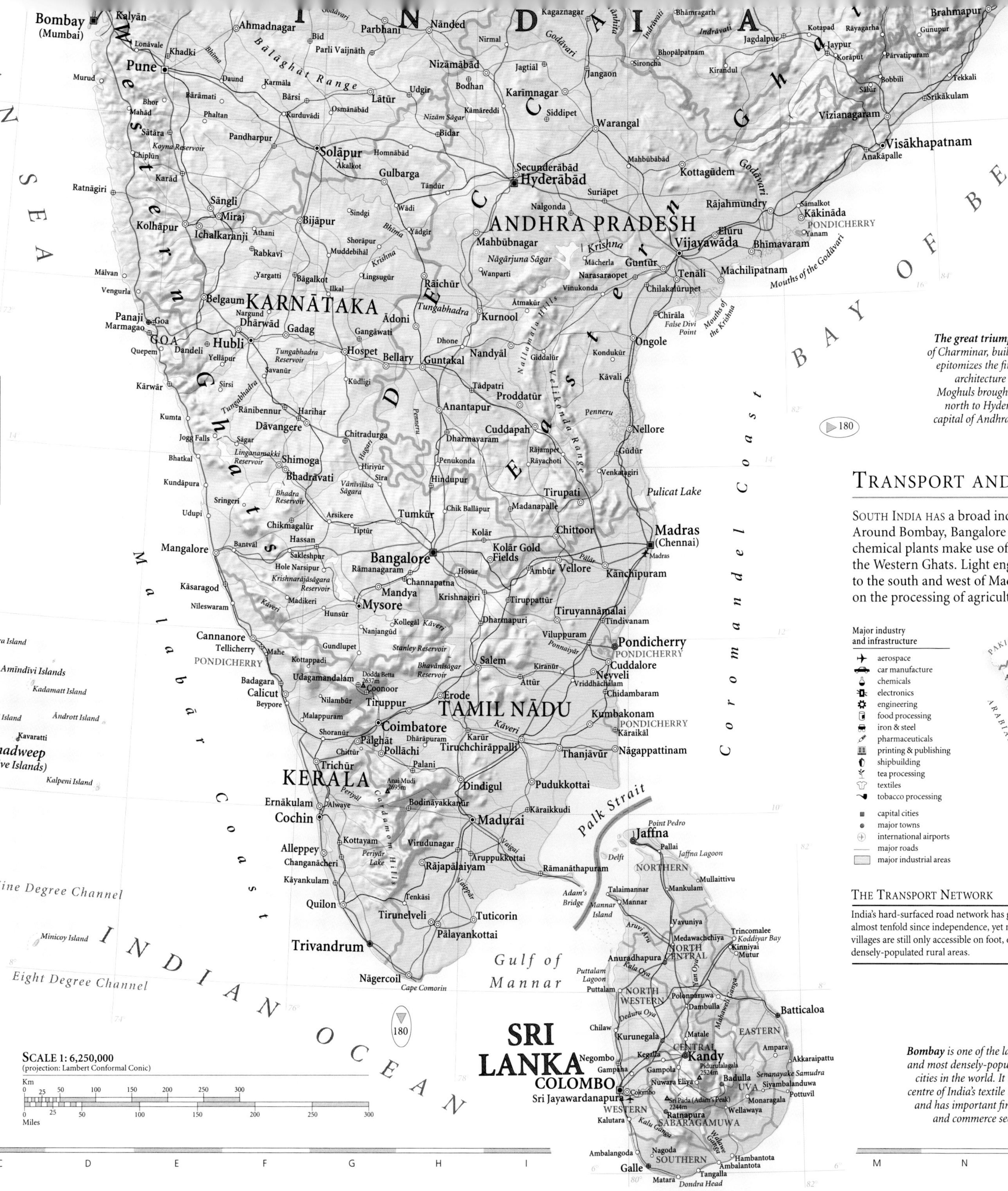

The great triumphal arch of Charminar, built in 1591, epitomizes the fine Islamic architecture which the Moghuls brought from the north to Hyderabad, the capital of Andhra Pradesh.

TRANSPORT AND INDUSTRY

SOUTH INDIA HAS a broad industrial base, with three leading regions. Around Bombay, Bangalore and Ahmadabad, cotton mills and chemical plants make use of cheap hydro-electric power generated in the Western Ghats. Light engineering and textiles are well established to the south and west of Madras. Sri Lanka's industry is based mainly on the processing of agricultural products.

Major industry and infrastructure

- aerospace
- car manufacture
- chemicals
- electronics
- engineering
- food processing
- iron & steel
- pharmaceuticals
- printing & publishing
- shipbuilding
- textiles
- tobacco processing
- tea processing
- capital cities
- major towns
- international airports
- major roads
- major industrial areas

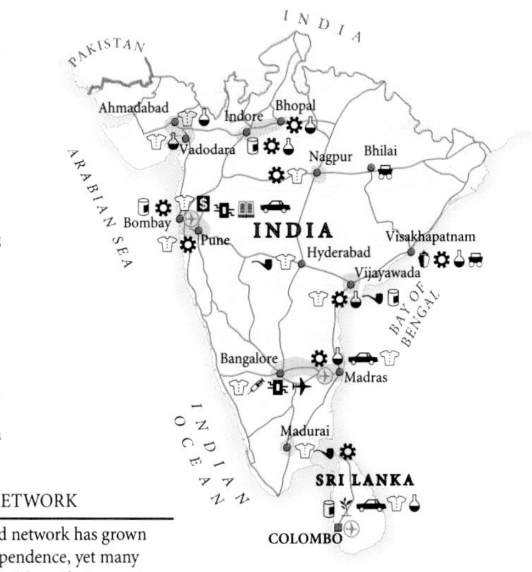

THE TRANSPORT NETWORK

India's hard-surfaced road network has grown almost tenfold since independence, yet many villages are still only accessible on foot, even in densely-populated rural areas.

Bombay is one of the largest and most densely-populated cities in the world. It is the centre of India's textile trade and has important finance and commerce sectors.

180

MAP KEY

POPULATION

- ■ above 5 million
- ■ 1 million to 5 million
- ● 500,000 to 1 million
- ⊕ 100,000 to 500,000
- ⊙ 50,000 to 100,000
- ○ 10,000 to 50,000
- ○ below 10,000

ELEVATION

- 2000m / 6562ft
- 1000m / 3281ft
- 500m / 1640ft
- 250m / 820ft
- 100m / 328ft
- sea level

Sea pencils thrive on the coral reefs around the coast of the Laccadive Islands and Sri Lanka. The reefs support an amazing diversity of marine life, but are increasingly under threat from growing coastal populations.

Local fisheries around Sri Lanka afford great potential for exploitation, but development has been hampered by technological constraints. Most fishermen live on the coastal fringes and operate on a small scale.

SCALE 1:6,250,000
(projection: Lambert Conformal Conic)

Km
Miles

BAY OF BENGAL

CORAL COAST

INDIA

ANDHRA PRADESH

KARNĀTAKA

KERALA

TAMIL NĀDU

GOA

LAKSHADWEEP

Lakshadweep
(Laccadive Islands)

ARABIAN SEA

INDIAN OCEAN

Western Ghats

Balaghat Range

Nallamalai Range

Velikonda Range

Cardamom Hills

Malabar Coast

Coromandel Coast

Gulf of Mannar

Palk Strait

Nine Degree Channel

Eight Degree Channel

SRI LANKA

COLOMBO
Sri Jayawardanapura

NORTHERN
NORTH CENTRAL
NORTH WESTERN
CENTRAL
EASTERN
WESTERN
UVA
SABARAGAMUWA
SOUTHERN

Bombay (Mumbai)

Hyderabad
Secunderabad

Bangalore

Madras (Chennai)

Pondicherry

Trivandrum

MAINLAND EAST ASIA

CHINA, MONGOLIA, NORTH KOREA, SOUTH KOREA, TAIWAN, *Macao (to Portugal)*

CHINA, THE WORLD'S MOST POPULOUS NATION, has an unbroken cultural history, longer than that of any other country, and is rapidly emerging as a leading world power. When Mao Zedong established Communist rule in 1949, China had become a backward feudal empire, stricken by civil war and over a century of European and Japanese incursions. The closed regime withstood the traumas of rapid industrialization, communalized farming and the brutal purges of the Cultural Revolution but, since the 1980s has introduced economic reforms, led by expanded foreign trade. China's population is heavily concentrated in the east and, despite accelerating urban growth, remains predominantly rural. One cultural group, the Han, make up over 90% of the people, while five 'Autonomous Regions' have been established in the south and west for the main ethnic minorities.

TRANSPORT AND INDUSTRY

LARGE-SCALE INDUSTRIAL growth has always been a priority of the Communist government. Metals and machine production, chemicals and engineering are among the leading industries, concentrated in the major cities of the east coast. Textiles and clothing manufacture, the main consumer goods sector, is relatively well dispersed, with a few significant centres such as Shanghai, Beijing and Hong Kong.

Major industry and infrastructure

- car manufacture
- chemicals
- electronics
- engineering
- finance
- food processing
- iron & steel
- shipbuilding
- textiles
- capital cities
- major towns
- international airports
- major roads
- major industrial areas

THE TRANSPORT NETWORK

734,473 miles (1,182,727 km)		1182 miles (1904 km)	
41,798 miles (67,308 km)		70,495 miles (113,519 km)	

Steam trains use China's abundant coal and are still the main form of passenger and goods transport. The rail network is now struggling to meet an ever-growing demand.

Coal is China's most abundant mineral resource. This mine at Fuxin in Liaoning province is used to provide coal for a nearby power station.

THE LANDSCAPE

THE EAST ASIAN LANDMASS is arranged in three distinct levels, the highest of which is the Plateau of Tibet in the southwest. The arid uplands of northwestern China form a barren middle step. The main rivers flow eastward from these two platforms to the East China and South China sea coasts, across a broad region of alluvial lowlands and low hills.

Paektu-san, at 9023 ft (2750 m), is North Korea's highest peak; an extinct volcanic cone now filled by a crater lake.

The loess plateau of northern China is the world's greatest expanse of loess, a loose soil made up of wind-blown material. The plateau has been heavily eroded by tributaries of the Yellow River.

Shifting sand dunes are found in the arid west of the northeast China Plain, while the eastern part of this great expanse is wet and swampy.

River-eroded fine soils

Thick blanket of loess

Because of its very small grain-size, loess has been easily transported and deposited by winds which scour the plains, and in northern China, deposits of loess can be up to 3000 ft (1000 m) thick. Loess-based soils are very fertile, but clearing land for agriculture quickly destabilizes the soil and allows it to be eroded.

The Gobi Desert extends across the Nei Mongol Gaoyuan; a vast saucer-shaped upland surrounded by a rim of higher mountains.

Tarim Basin (*Tarim Pendi*)

Plateau of Tibet

The Plateau of Tibet occupies about a quarter of China's total area. The Yangtze, Mekong, Indus and Brahmaputra rivers all originate in the south and east of the plateau.

The Himalayas extend along the southwestern edge of the Plateau of Tibet, forming a continuous mountain barrier over 1500 miles (2500 km) long.

Warm, humid conditions have caused intensive erosion of south China's karst areas, producing spectacular jagged peaks and vast caves in the limestone.

Paektu-san

North China Plain

The Yangtze is China's longest river and the principal navigable waterway.

Sichuan Pendi

Gansu province, through which the ancient Silk Route passes on its way to the west, is characterized by extensive loess deposits which are terraced and used for crop cultivation.

Although it is over 20 years since his death, the legacy of Chairman Mao Zedong, architect of the Great Proletariat Cultural Revolution, is still very much in evidence across China's landscape. In 1959 Mao launched a 20-year period of industrialization and socio-economic realignment, rejecting western ideals and social codes.

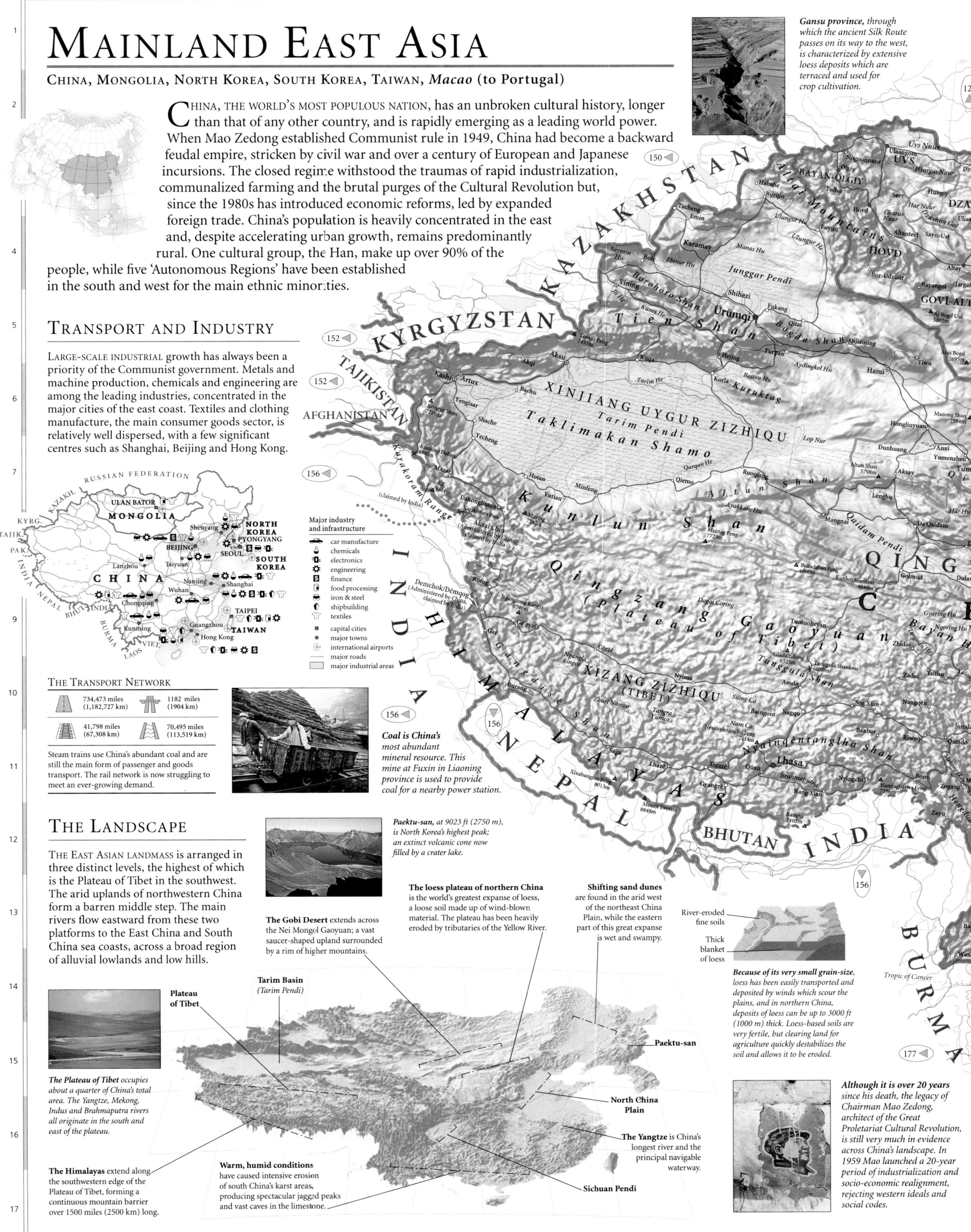

The Great Wall of China remains one of the world's largest-ever construction projects, and is so vast that it is visible from space. Finally completed in AD 214, it runs for over 4000 miles (6400 km) from the Yellow Sea, stretching into Central Asia.

SCALE 1:12,500,000
(projection: Lambert Conformal Conic)

Km
0 25 50   100   150   200   250   300   350   400   450   500

Miles
0   50   100   150   200   250   300   350   400   450   500

MAP KEY

POPULATION

■ above 5 million
▣ 1 million to 5 million
◉ 500,000 to 1 million
◉ 100,000 to 500,000
⊕ 50,000 to 100,000
○ 10,000 to 50,000
∘ below 10,000

ELEVATION

6000m / 19,686ft
4000m / 13,124ft
3000m / 9843ft
2000m / 6562ft
1000m / 3281ft
500m / 1640ft
250m / 820ft
100m / 328ft
sea level

RUSSIAN FEDERATION

MONGOLIA

HOVSGOL
ARHANGAY
HENTIY
ULAANBAATAR
(ULAN BATOR)
DORNOD
TÖV
SÜHBAATAR
ÖVÖRHANGAY
DUNDGOVI
BAYANHONGOR
DORNOGOVI
ÖMNÖGOVI

Gobi

Nei Mongol Gaoyuan

NEI MONGOL ZIZHIQU (INNER MONGOLIA) Da Hingaan Ling

HEILONGJIANG

Harbin
Qiqihar
Daqing
Suihua
Jixi
Mudanjiang

JILIN
Changchun
Jilin

LIAONING
Shenyang
Fushun
Anshan

NORTH KOREA

P'YONGYANG

SOUTH KOREA

SEOUL
(SEOUL)

SEA OF JAPAN

JAPAN

GANSU
NINGXIA
Xining
Lanzhou

C H I N A

HEBEI
BEIJING (PEKING)
BEIJING SHI
Hohhot
Baotou
Datong
Tangshan
TIANJIN SHI
Tianjin
Bo Hai
Bohai Haixia   Bohai Bay
Dalian
Korea Bay
Yantai

SHANXI
Taiyuan
Shijiazhuang

SHANDONG
Jinan
Zibo
Qingdao
Yellow Sea

SHAANXI
Xi'an
Xianyang
HENAN
Luoyang
Zhengzhou
Kaifeng

Xuzhou

JIANGSU
Nanjing
ANHUI
Hefei

SHANGHAI SHI
Shanghai
Wuxi
Suzhou

HUBEI
Wuhan

SICHUAN
Chengdu
CHONGQING SHI
Chongqing

ZHEJIANG
Hangzhou
Ningbo
Wenzhou

EAST CHINA SEA

Mianyang

Leshan
Zigong

GUIZHOU
Guiyang

HUNAN
Changsha

JIANGXI
Nanchang

FUJIAN
Fuzhou
Xiamen

TAIWAN
T'AIPEI
T'aichung
Kaohsiung

Tropic of Cancer

YUNNAN
Kunming

GUANGXI ZHUANGZU ZIZHIQU
Nanning

GUANGDONG
Guangzhou
Shenzhen

Hong Kong (Xianggang)
Zhuhai
MACAO (to Portugal)

VIETNAM
LAOS

Gulf of Tongking

HAINAN
Hainan Dao
Haikou

SOUTH CHINA SEA

USING THE LAND AND SEA

AROUND 90% OF China is unsuitable for cultivation, being either climactically or topographically adverse, or lacking sufficiently fertile soils. Most of the west is used for nomadic herding, while farmland is concentrated in the eastern monsoon region, with rice grown in the tropical and subtropical south. Cereals and soya beans predominate as rainfall and temperatures decline further north.

Land use and agricultural distribution

- pigs
- sheep
- corn (maize)
- cotton
- fishing
- fruit
- rice
- sugar cane
- soya beans

■ capital cities
• major towns

pasture
cropland
forest
mountain region

THE URBAN/RURAL POPULATION DIVIDE

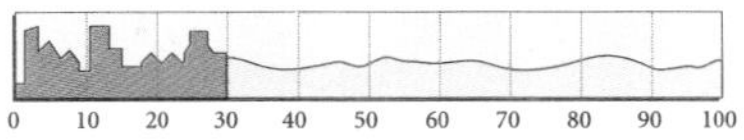

urban 30%   rural 70%

0 10 20 30 40 50 60 70 80 90 100

POPULATION DENSITY
297 people per sq mile
(115 people per sq km)

TOTAL LAND AREA
4,288,672 sq miles
(11,110,550 sq km)

Beijing (formerly Peking), is China's capital city and, with Shanghai, one of its leading industrial and cultural centres. The morning and evening rush-hours are dominated by bicycles, which constitute the bulk of traffic.

RUSSIAN FEDERATION

KAZAKH.
KYRG.
TAJIK.
PAK.
INDIA
NEPAL
BHUTAN
BURMA
LAOS
VIET.

MONGOLIA
ULAN BATOR
Urumqi

C H I N A

Lhasa
Kunming

NORTH KOREA
PYONGYANG
SEOUL
SOUTH KOREA
BEIJING
Shenyang
Harbin

Wuhan
Shanghai

Guangzhou
Macao

TAIPEI
TAIWAN

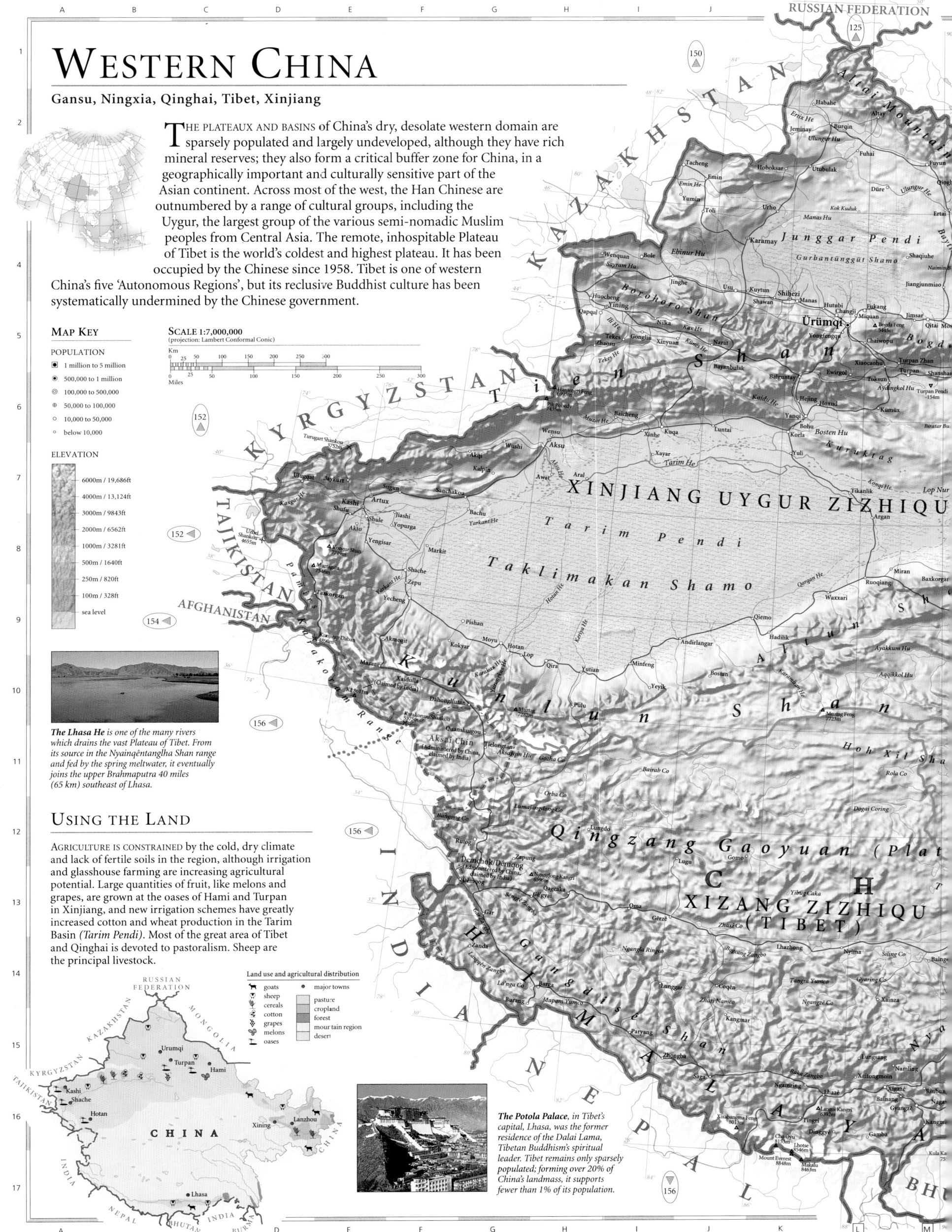

WESTERN CHINA

Gansu, Ningxia, Qinghai, Tibet, Xinjiang

THE PLATEAUX AND BASINS of China's dry, desolate western domain are sparsely populated and largely undeveloped, although they have rich mineral reserves; they also form a critical buffer zone for China, in a geographically important and culturally sensitive part of the Asian continent. Across most of the west, the Han Chinese are outnumbered by a range of cultural groups, including the Uygur, the largest group of the various semi-nomadic Muslim peoples from Central Asia. The remote, inhospitable Plateau of Tibet is the world's coldest and highest plateau. It has been occupied by the Chinese since 1958. Tibet is one of western China's five 'Autonomous Regions', but its reclusive Buddhist culture has been systematically undermined by the Chinese government.

MAP KEY

POPULATION
- ■ 1 million to 5 million
- ● 500,000 to 1 million
- ◉ 100,000 to 500,000
- ⊕ 50,000 to 100,000
- ○ 10,000 to 50,000
- ∘ below 10,000

ELEVATION
- 6000m / 19,686ft
- 4000m / 13,124ft
- 3000m / 9843ft
- 2000m / 6562ft
- 1000m / 3281ft
- 500m / 1640ft
- 250m / 820ft
- 100m / 328ft
- sea level

SCALE 1:7,000,000
(projection: Lambert Conformal Conic)

The Lhasa He is one of the many rivers which drains the vast Plateau of Tibet. From its source in the Nyainqêntanglha Shan range and fed by the spring meltwater, it eventually joins the upper Brahmaputra 40 miles (65 km) southeast of Lhasa.

USING THE LAND

AGRICULTURE IS CONSTRAINED by the cold, dry climate and lack of fertile soils in the region, although irrigation and glasshouse farming are increasing agricultural potential. Large quantities of fruit, like melons and grapes, are grown at the oases of Hami and Turpan in Xinjiang, and new irrigation schemes have greatly increased cotton and wheat production in the Tarim Basin (Tarim Pendi). Most of the great area of Tibet and Qinghai is devoted to pastoralism. Sheep are the principal livestock.

Land use and agricultural distribution
- goats
- sheep
- cereals
- cotton
- grapes
- melons
- oases
- major towns
- pasture
- cropland
- forest
- mountain region
- desert

The Potola Palace, in Tibet's capital, Lhasa, was the former residence of the Dalai Lama, Tibetan Buddhism's spiritual leader. Tibet remains only sparsely populated; forming over 20% of China's landmass, it supports fewer than 1% of its population.

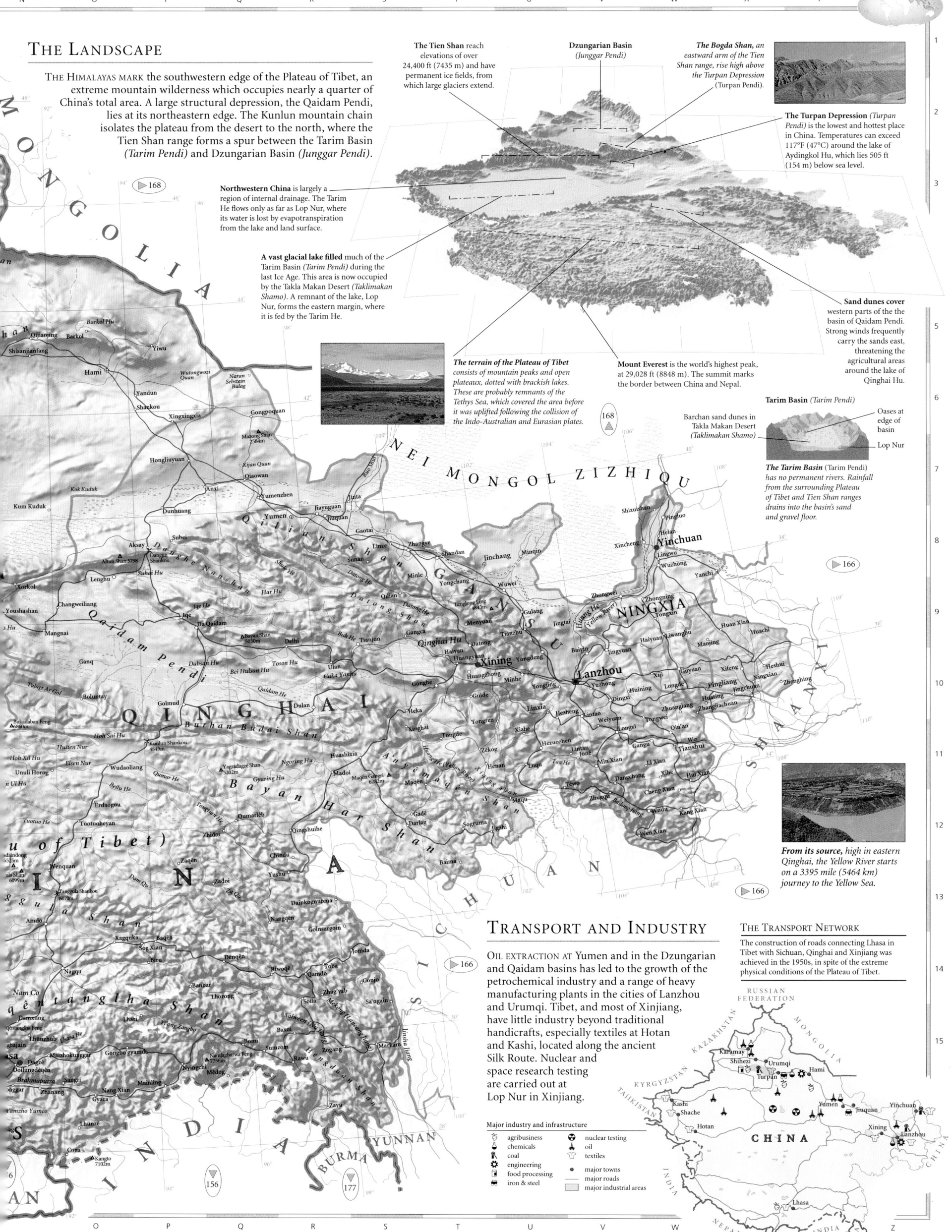

THE LANDSCAPE

THE HIMALAYAS MARK the southwestern edge of the Plateau of Tibet, an extreme mountain wilderness which occupies nearly a quarter of China's total area. A large structural depression, the Qaidam Pendi, lies at its northeastern edge. The Kunlun mountain chain isolates the plateau from the desert to the north, where the Tien Shan range forms a spur between the Tarim Basin (*Tarim Pendi*) and Dzungarian Basin (*Junggar Pendi*).

The Tien Shan reach elevations of over 24,400 ft (7435 m) and have permanent ice fields, from which large glaciers extend.

Dzungarian Basin (*Junggar Pendi*)

The Bogda Shan, an eastward arm of the Tien Shan range, rise high above the Turpan Depression (*Turpan Pendi*).

The Turpan Depression (*Turpan Pendi*) is the lowest and hottest place in China. Temperatures can exceed 117°F (47°C) around the lake of Aydingkol Hu, which lies 505 ft (154 m) below sea level.

Northwestern China is largely a region of internal drainage. The Tarim He flows only as far as Lop Nur, where its water is lost by evapotranspiration from the lake and land surface.

A vast glacial lake filled much of the Tarim Basin (*Tarim Pendi*) during the last Ice Age. This area is now occupied by the Takla Makan Desert (*Taklimakan Shamo*). A remnant of the lake, Lop Nur, forms the eastern margin, where it is fed by the Tarim He.

The terrain of the Plateau of Tibet consists of mountain peaks and open plateaux, dotted with brackish lakes. These are probably remnants of the Tethys Sea, which covered the area before it was uplifted following the collision of the Indo-Australian and Eurasian plates.

Mount Everest is the world's highest peak, at 29,028 ft (8848 m). The summit marks the border between China and Nepal.

Sand dunes cover western parts of the the basin of Qaidam Pendi. Strong winds frequently carry the sands east, threatening the agricultural areas around the lake of Qinghai Hu.

Tarim Basin (*Tarim Pendi*)

Barchan sand dunes in Takla Makan Desert (*Taklimakan Shamo*)

Oases at edge of basin

Lop Nur

The Tarim Basin (Tarim Pendi) has no permanent rivers. Rainfall from the surrounding Plateau of Tibet and Tien Shan ranges drains into the basin's sand and gravel floor.

From its source, high in eastern Qinghai, the Yellow River starts on a 3395 mile (5464 km) journey to the Yellow Sea.

TRANSPORT AND INDUSTRY

OIL EXTRACTION AT Yumen and in the Dzungarian and Qaidam basins has led to the growth of the petrochemical industry and a range of heavy manufacturing plants in the cities of Lanzhou and Urumqi. Tibet, and most of Xinjiang, have little industry beyond traditional handicrafts, especially textiles at Hotan and Kashi, located along the ancient Silk Route. Nuclear and space research testing are carried out at Lop Nur in Xinjiang.

THE TRANSPORT NETWORK

The construction of roads connecting Lhasa in Tibet with Sichuan, Qinghai and Xinjiang was achieved in the 1950s, in spite of the extreme physical conditions of the Plateau of Tibet.

Major industry and infrastructure
- agribusiness
- chemicals
- coal
- engineering
- food processing
- iron & steel
- nuclear testing
- oil
- textiles
- major towns
- major roads
- major industrial areas

EASTERN CHINA

TAIWAN, Anhui, Beijing, Fujian, Guangdong, Guangxi, Guizhou, Hainan, Hebei, Henan, Hubei, Hunan, Jiangsu, Jiangxi, Shaanxi, Shandong, Shanghai, Shanxi, Sichuan, Tianjin, Yunnan, Zhejiang, *Macao* (to Portugal)

THE EAST IS CHINA'S HEARTLAND. Massive industrial development since 1949 has transformed much of the densely populated rural landscape, in a region still prone to flooding and drought. Over 20 cities have populations of over a million, including the giant metropolis of Shanghai and the capital Beijing, which has been China's cultural and political centre since the 13th century. The ethnically diverse southwest and the oil-rich interior provinces of Sichuan and Shaanxi have largely missed out on the remarkable economic growth occurring in designated free-trade areas along the coasts of the South and East China seas. The republic of Taiwan was established in 1949 by Chinese nationalists ousted from the mainland by the victorious Communist forces. Taiwan now has one of the strongest economies in the world but its sovereignty is not recognized by China. Hong Kong provides a major international trade link for China; a 99-year 'lease' period of British control was concluded in 1997.

North of the Qin Ling range in Shaanxi province, is an agriculturally fertile region covered with fine, wind-blown deposits and known as the loess plateau. The loose sediments are vulnerable to water erosion.

USING THE LAND AND SEA

THIS IS A REGION of intensive cultivation. Wheat, millet, sorghum and cotton are the main crops of the Yellow River basin. South from Sichuan, rice becomes the principal crop, grown with wheat, corn and cotton along the Yangtze River. Tea is produced in the hills and sugar cane along the coast of the southeast, where flat land is limited. Pigs and poultry are raised in great numbers.

On the hills above the North China Plain, slopes are terraced to utilize the rich loess soils of the Taihang Shan range.

Land use and agricultural distribution

cattle	■ capital cities
pigs	● major towns
cereals	
corn (maize)	pasture
cotton	cropland
fishing	forest
peanuts	mountain region
rice	wetland
sugar cane	tundra
tea	

MAP KEY

POPULATION
- ■ above 5 million
- ■ 1 million to 5 million
- ◉ 500,000 to 1 million
- ◎ 100,000 to 500,000
- ⊕ 50,000 to 100,000
- ⊙ 10,000 to 50,000
- ○ below 10,000

ELEVATION
- 6000m / 19,686ft
- 4000m / 13,124ft
- 3000m / 9843ft
- 2000m / 6562ft
- 1000m / 3281ft
- 500m / 1640ft
- 250m / 820ft
- 100m / 328ft
- sea level

SCALE 1:7,750,000
(projection: Lambert)

Km
0 25 50   100   150   200   250   300

Miles
0   25 50   100   150   200   250   300

Since the transferral of Hong Kong from the United Kingdom to China, only the Portuguese territory of Macao, with its colonial architecture, bars and casinos, remains as a vestige of Europe's territorial exploits in the Far East. Macao reverts to Chinese rule in 1999.

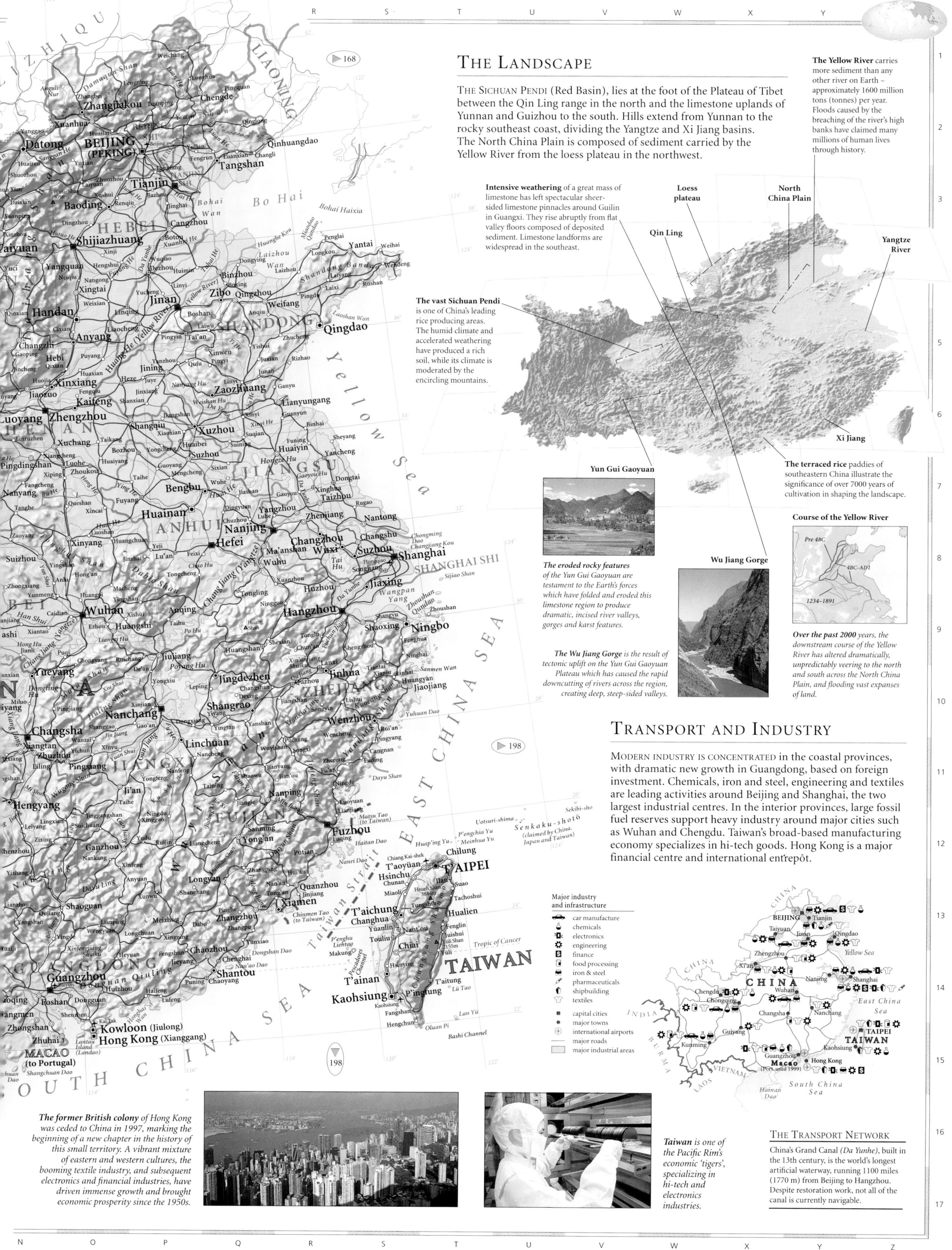

THE LANDSCAPE

THE SICHUAN PENDI (Red Basin), lies at the foot of the Plateau of Tibet between the Qin Ling range in the north and the limestone uplands of Yunnan and Guizhou to the south. Hills extend from Yunnan to the rocky southeast coast, dividing the Yangtze and Xi Jiang basins. The North China Plain is composed of sediment carried by the Yellow River from the loess plateau in the northwest.

The Yellow River carries more sediment than any other river on Earth – approximately 1600 million tons (tonnes) per year. Floods caused by the breaching of the river's high banks have claimed many millions of human lives through history.

Intensive weathering of a great mass of limestone has left spectacular sheer-sided limestone pinnacles around Guilin in Guangxi. They rise abruptly from flat valley floors composed of deposited sediment. Limestone landforms are widespread in the southeast.

Loess plateau

North China Plain

Qin Ling

Yangtze River

The vast Sichuan Pendi is one of China's leading rice producing areas. The humid climate and accelerated weathering have produced a rich soil, while its climate is moderated by the encircling mountains.

Xi Jiang

The terraced rice paddies of southeastern China illustrate the significance of over 7000 years of cultivation in shaping the landscape.

Yun Gui Gaoyuan

The eroded rocky features of the Yun Gui Gaoyuan are testament to the Earth's forces which have folded and eroded this limestone region to produce dramatic, incised river valleys, gorges and karst features.

Wu Jiang Gorge

The Wu Jiang Gorge is the result of tectonic uplift on the Yun Gui Gaoyuan Plateau which has caused the rapid downcutting of rivers across the region, creating deep, steep-sided valleys.

Course of the Yellow River

Pre 4BC

4BC–AD1

1234–1891

Over the past 2000 years, the downstream course of the Yellow River has altered dramatically, unpredictably veering to the north and south across the North China Plain, and flooding vast expanses of land.

TRANSPORT AND INDUSTRY

MODERN INDUSTRY IS CONCENTRATED in the coastal provinces, with dramatic new growth in Guangdong, based on foreign investment. Chemicals, iron and steel, engineering and textiles are leading activities around Beijing and Shanghai, the two largest industrial centres. In the interior provinces, large fossil fuel reserves support heavy industry around major cities such as Wuhan and Chengdu. Taiwan's broad-based manufacturing economy specializes in hi-tech goods. Hong Kong is a major financial centre and international entrepôt.

Major industry and infrastructure

- car manufacture
- chemicals
- electronics
- engineering
- finance
- food processing
- iron & steel
- pharmaceuticals
- shipbuilding
- textiles
- capital cities
- major towns
- international airports
- major roads
- major industrial areas

The former British colony of Hong Kong was ceded to China in 1997, marking the beginning of a new chapter in the history of this small territory. A vibrant mixture of eastern and western cultures, the booming textile industry, and subsequent electronics and financial industries, have driven immense growth and brought economic prosperity since the 1950s.

Taiwan is one of the Pacific Rim's economic 'tigers', specializing in hi-tech and electronics industries.

THE TRANSPORT NETWORK

China's Grand Canal (Da Yunhe), built in the 13th century, is the world's longest artificial waterway, running 1100 miles (1770 m) from Beijing to Hangzhou. Despite restoration work, not all of the canal is currently navigable.

NORTHEASTERN CHINA, MONGOLIA & KOREA

MONGOLIA, NORTH KOREA, SOUTH KOREA, Heilongjiang, Inner Mongolia, Jilin, Liaoning

THIS NORTHERLY REGION has for centuries been a domain of shifting borders and competing colonial powers. Mongolia was the heartland of Chinghiz Khan's vast Mongol empire in the 13th century, while northeastern China was home to the Manchus, China's last ruling dynasty (1644–1911). The mineral and forest wealth of the northeast helped make this China's principal region of heavy industry, although the outdated state factories now face decline. South Korea's state-led market economy has grown dramatically and Seoul is now one of the world's largest cities. The austere communist regime of North Korea has isolated itself from the expanding markets of the Pacific Rim and faces continuing economic stagnation.

The Eurasian steppe stretches from the mouth of the Danube in Europe, to Mongolia. In Mongolia, nomadic people have lived in felt huts called yurts or gers, for thousands of years.

MAP KEY

POPULATION

- above 5 million
- 1 million to 5 million
- 500,000 to 1 million
- 100,000 to 500,000
- 50,000 to 100,000
- 10,000 to 50,000
- below 10,000

ELEVATION

- 4000m / 13,124ft
- 3000m / 9843ft
- 2000m / 6562ft
- 1000m / 3281ft
- 500m / 1640ft
- 250m / 820ft
- 100m / 328ft
- sea level

SCALE 1:7,000,000
(projection: Lambert Conformal Conic)

Km
0 25 50 100 150 200
0 25 50 100 150 200
Miles

THE LANDSCAPE

THE GREAT NORTH CHINA PLAIN is largely enclosed by mountain ranges including the Great and Lesser Khingan Ranges (*Da Hinggan Ling* and *Xiao Hinggan Ling*) in the north, and the Changbai Shan, which extend south into the rugged peninsula of Korea. The broad steppeland plateau of Nei Mongol Gaoyuan borders the southeastern edge of the great cold desert of the Gobi which extends west across the southern reaches of Mongolia. In northwest Mongolia the Altai Mountains and various lesser ranges are interspersed with lakeland basins.

Gobi
Semi-arid zone
Desert zone
Ordos Desert (*Mu Us Shamo*)

Much of Mongolia and Inner Mongolia is a vast desert area. To the south and east, a semi-arid region extends into China proper.

The Gobi Desert stretches from Central Asia, through Mongolia and into China. Bare rock surfaces, rather than sand dunes, typify the cold desert landscape of the Gobi.

Tributaries of the Amur River follow U-shaped valleys through the Great Khingan Range (*Da Hinggan Ling*). These were cut by ice-age glaciers between 3 and 10 million years ago.

Lesser Khingan Range (*Xiao Hinggan Ling*)

Changbai Shan

T'aebaek-sanmaek

The Altai Mountains are the highest and longest of the mountain ranges which extend into Mongolia from the northwest. These mountains provide one of the last refuges for the endangered snow leopard.

The Yellow River sweeps north around the Ordos Desert (*Mu Us Shamo*), bringing water to an otherwise barren region.

Columns of basalt rock protrude in occasional clusters from the flat surface of the eastern Gobi. Their regular, six-sided form was produced when the rock cooled and contracted from its molten state.

Great Khingan Range (*Da Hinggan Ling*)

A crater lake occupies the 9023 ft (2750 m) snowy summit of the extinct volcano Paektu-san, the highest peak in the mountains of the Changbai Shan.

The wooded mountain range of T'aebaek-sanmaek forms the backbone of the Korean peninsula, running north–south along the eastern coastline.

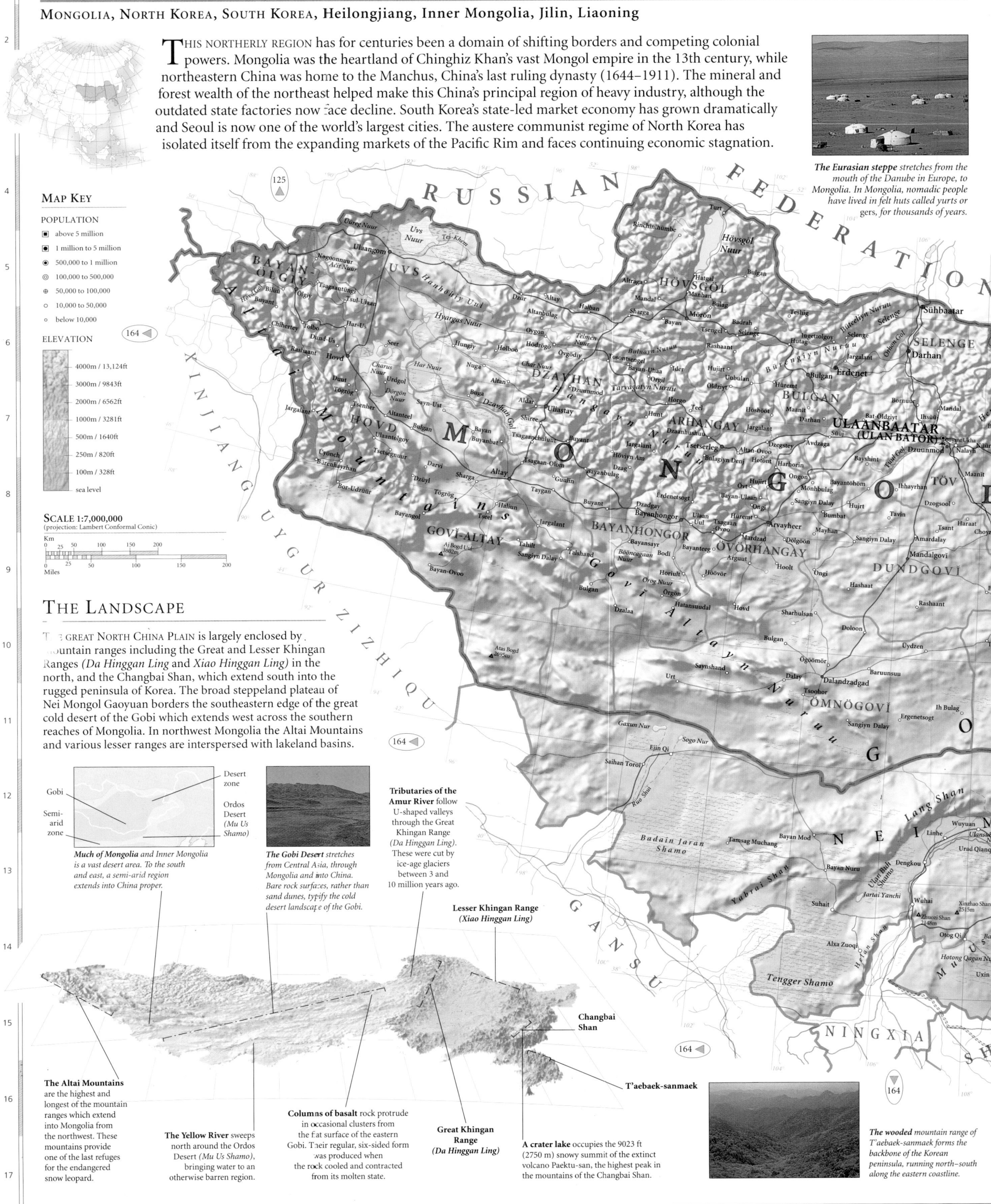

TRANSPORT AND INDUSTRY

NORTH KOREA'S CENTRALLY-PLANNED ECONOMY is strongly oriented towards heavy industry, while South Korea has a broad manufacturing base which includes textiles, steel, electronics, and one of the world's largest shipbuilding industries. Mongolia and Inner Mongolia's great mineral resource potential is largely undeveloped. The heavy industrial region around Shenyang produces iron, steel, chemicals and cement on a massive scale.

Major industry and infrastructure

- car manufacture
- chemicals
- coal
- electronics
- engineering
- finance
- food processing
- iron & steel
- pharmaceuticals
- shipbuilding
- textiles
- capital cities
- major towns
- international airports
- major roads
- major industrial areas

THE TRANSPORT NETWORK

Liaoning has China's most comprehensive railway network, the legacy of the Japanese occupation of Manchuria, earlier this century. The railways are used primarily for freight transport.

Ulan Bator, the Mongolian capital bears many of the hallmarks of Soviet-style central planning, the result of economic and industrial assistance from the Soviet Union following Mongolian independence in 1921.

While North Korea has remained politically and economically isolated from the rest of the world, South Korea has enjoyed immense economic growth. It has benefited considerably from US economic aid in the aftermath of the Korean war of 1950–1953.

USING THE LAND AND SEA

MONGOLIA AND INNER MONGOLIA rely heavily on livestock farming, with only about 1% of the land area cultivated. Northeastern China produces wheat, corn, soya beans and sugar beet. The cool climate limits the range of crops and large upland areas of the northeast remain forested. Rice is the staple food of North and South Korea. The latter has become a leading ocean-fishing nation.

Land use and agricultural distribution

- goats
- pigs
- sheep
- fishing
- corn (maize)
- rice
- soya beans
- sugar beet
- wheat
- capital cities
- major towns
- pasture
- cropland
- forest
- mountain region
- desert

169

JAPAN

IN THE YEARS SINCE THE END of the Second World War, Japan has become the world's most dynamic industrial nation. The country comprises a string of over 4000 islands which lie in a great northeast to southwest arc in the northwest Pacific. Four major islands: Hokkaido, Honshu, Shikoku and Kyushu are home to the great majority of Japan's population of 124 million people, although the mountainous terrain of the central region means that most cities are situated on the coast. A densely populated industrial belt stretches along much of Honshu's southern coast, including Japan's crowded capital, Tokyo. Alongside its spectacular economic growth and the increasing westernization of its cities, Japan still maintains a most singular culture, reflected in its traditional food, formal behavioural codes, unique Shinto religion and the reverence for the emperor, who is officially regarded as a god.

TRANSPORT AND INDUSTRY

JAPAN IS THE WORLD'S second largest market economy, outranked only by the USA. Technological development, particularly of computers, electronic goods, cars and motorcycles is second to none. Japanese industry invests in its workforce, and in long-term research and development to maintain the high standard of its products, and a reputation for innovation. Japanese businesses are now global both in their manufacturing bases and in the distribution of goods.

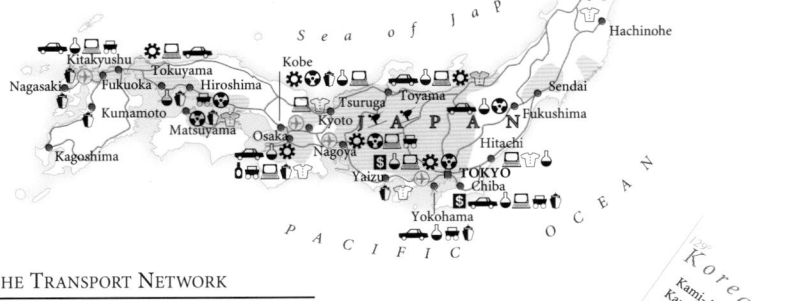

Major industry and infrastructure	
🍶	brewing
🚗	car manufacture
⚗	chemicals
💻	hi-tech industry
⚙	engineering
$	finance
	iron & steel
	research & development
⚓	shipbuilding
	textiles
	winter sports
■	capital cities
●	major towns
⊕	international airports
	major roads
	major industrial areas

THE TRANSPORT NETWORK

🛣	691,076 miles (1,112,844 km)	🛣	2423 miles (3900 km)
🚆	12,577 miles (20,254 km)	🚡	1099 miles (1770 km)

Japanese road construction traditionally lagged behind that of its extensive and technologically advanced railway network. The road network's relative lack of development has led to severe urban congestion, although expressways have now been built in some cities.

USING THE LAND AND SEA

ALTHOUGH ONLY ABOUT 11% OF JAPAN is suitable for cultivation, substantial government support, a favourable climate and intensive farming methods enable the country to be virtually self-sufficient in rice production. Northern Hokkaido, the largest and most productive farming region, has an open terrain and climate similar to that of the US Midwest, and produces over half of Japan's cereal requirements. Farmers are being encouraged to diversify by growing fruit, vegetables and wheat, as well as raising livestock.

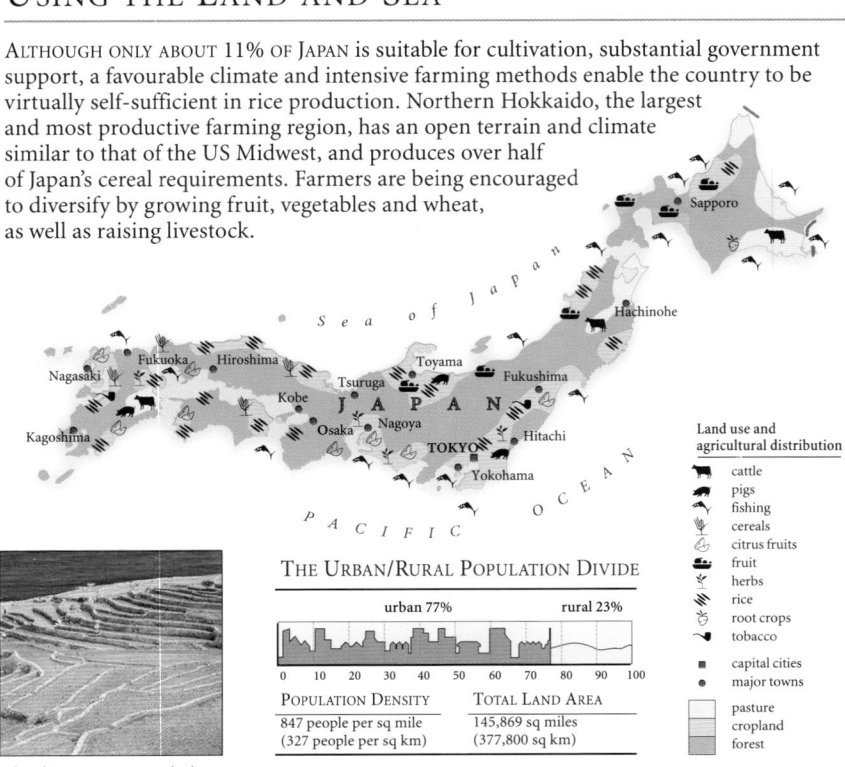

Land use and agricultural distribution	
🐄	cattle
🐖	pigs
🐟	fishing
🌾	cereals
🍊	citrus fruits
🍎	fruit
🌿	herbs
🌾	rice
	root crops
	tobacco
■	capital cities
●	major towns
	pasture
	cropland
	forest

THE URBAN/RURAL POPULATION DIVIDE

urban 77% rural 23%

0 10 20 30 40 50 60 70 80 90 100

POPULATION DENSITY	TOTAL LAND AREA
847 people per sq mile (327 people per sq km)	145,869 sq miles (377,800 sq km)

Cutting terraces maximizes the limited agricultural land, enabling Japan to produce large quantities of rice.

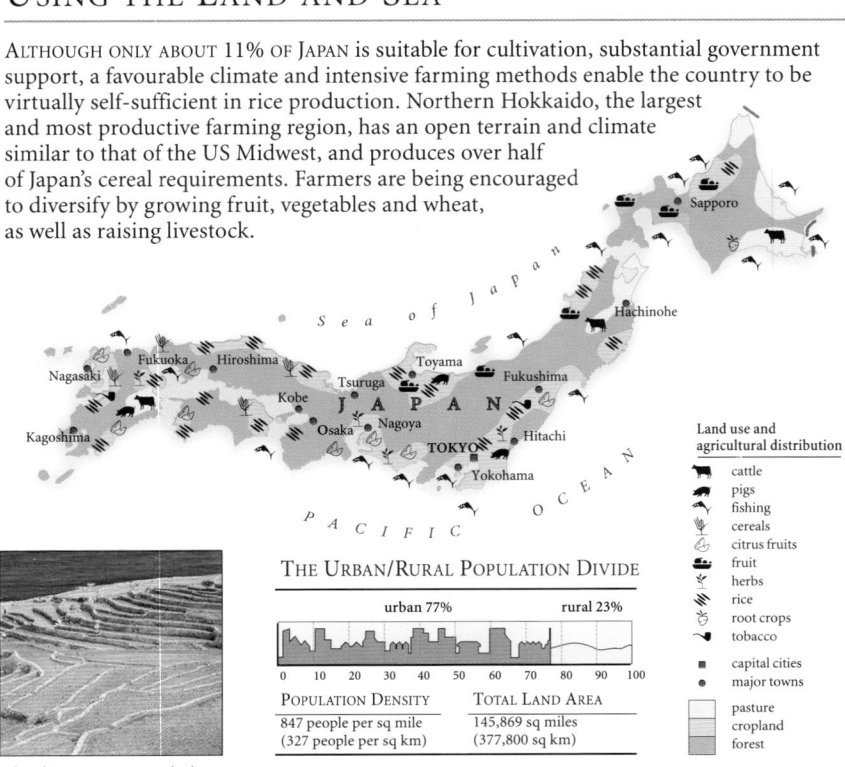

The Kobe earthquake in January 1995 highlighted Japan's vulnerability to earthquakes, despite technological advances. It shattered much of the infrastructure of this important port. More than 5000 people died as buildings and overhead highways collapsed and fires broke out.

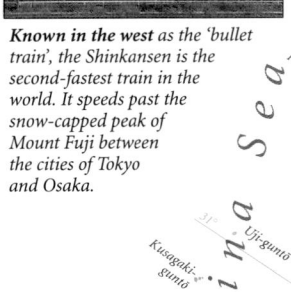

Known in the west as the 'bullet train', the Shinkansen is the second-fastest train in the world. It speeds past the snow-capped peak of Mount Fuji between the cities of Tokyo and Osaka.

A number of new volcanoes have emerged in Japan this century. They exist alongside older cones like this one in Aso-Kuju National Park on Kyushu, now dormant and grass-covered.

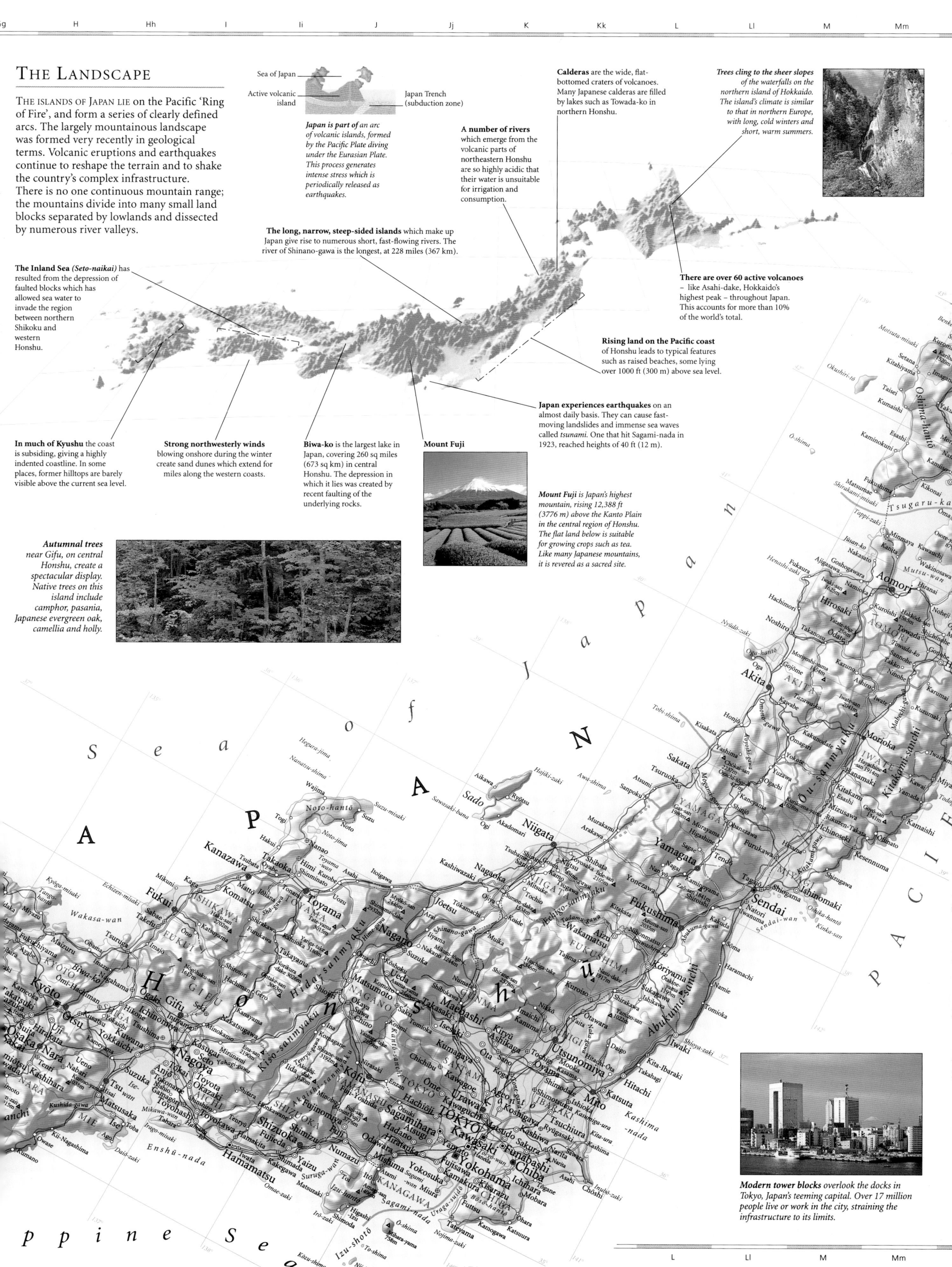

THE LANDSCAPE

THE ISLANDS OF JAPAN LIE on the Pacific 'Ring of Fire', and form a series of clearly defined arcs. The largely mountainous landscape was formed very recently in geological terms. Volcanic eruptions and earthquakes continue to reshape the terrain and to shake the country's complex infrastructure. There is no one continuous mountain range; the mountains divide into many small land blocks separated by lowlands and dissected by numerous river valleys.

Sea of Japan

Active volcanic island

Japan Trench (subduction zone)

Japan is part of an arc of volcanic islands, formed by the Pacific Plate diving under the Eurasian Plate. This process generates intense stress which is periodically released as earthquakes.

Calderas are the wide, flat-bottomed craters of volcanoes. Many Japanese calderas are filled by lakes such as Towada-ko in northern Honshu.

Trees cling to the sheer slopes of the waterfalls on the northern island of Hokkaido. The island's climate is similar to that in northern Europe, with long, cold winters and short, warm summers.

A number of rivers which emerge from the volcanic parts of northeastern Honshu are so highly acidic that their water is unsuitable for irrigation and consumption.

The long, narrow, steep-sided islands which make up Japan give rise to numerous short, fast-flowing rivers. The river of Shinano-gawa is the longest, at 228 miles (367 km).

There are over 60 active volcanoes – like Asahi-dake, Hokkaido's highest peak – throughout Japan. This accounts for more than 10% of the world's total.

The Inland Sea (Seto-naikai) has resulted from the depression of faulted blocks which has allowed sea water to invade the region between northern Shikoku and western Honshu.

Rising land on the Pacific coast of Honshu leads to typical features such as raised beaches, some lying over 1000 ft (300 m) above sea level.

Japan experiences earthquakes on an almost daily basis. They can cause fast-moving landslides and immense sea waves called *tsunami*. One that hit Sagami-nada in 1923, reached heights of 40 ft (12 m).

In much of Kyushu the coast is subsiding, giving a highly indented coastline. In some places, former hilltops are barely visible above the current sea level.

Strong northwesterly winds blowing onshore during the winter create sand dunes which extend for miles along the western coasts.

Biwa-ko is the largest lake in Japan, covering 260 sq miles (673 sq km) in central Honshu. The depression in which it lies was created by recent faulting of the underlying rocks.

Mount Fuji

Mount Fuji is Japan's highest mountain, rising 12,388 ft (3776 m) above the Kanto Plain in the central region of Honshu. The flat land below is suitable for growing crops such as tea. Like many Japanese mountains, it is revered as a sacred site.

Autumnal trees near Gifu, on central Honshu, create a spectacular display. Native trees on this island include camphor, pasania, Japanese evergreen oak, camellia and holly.

Modern tower blocks overlook the docks in Tokyo, Japan's teeming capital. Over 17 million people live or work in the city, straining the infrastructure to its limits.

Malaysia exports a greater tonnage of tropical timber than anywhere else in the world. Much of it comes from Sarawak in Borneo. Although in principle logging is only allowed on a sustainable basis, environmentalists fear that the rainforest in Sarawak will have disappeared by the early 21st century.

This tiny island near Kota Kinabalu, in Sabah, eastern Malaysia, is a part of a designated national park. Thickly forested, it is surrounded by broad, sandy beaches and shallow inland seas.

THAILAND

MALAYSIA

SOUTH CHINA SEA

Kota Bharu
RLIS
Setar
KEDAH
own
Butterworth
NG
Taiping
PERAK
Ipoh
Damar Laut
Bagan Datuk
Pulau Redang
Pasir Puteh
Tasik Temengor
Tasik Kenyir
KELANTAN
Kuala Terengganu
TERENGGANU
Dungun
Cukai
Pulau Tenggul

Kuala Lipis
Merapuh Lama
PAHANG
Karak
Kuantan
Sungai Pahang

Pulau Laut

Pulau Tioman

SARA
Kuala B
Miri
Tanjung Payong
Loaga
Buni
Bintulu
Mukah
Matu
Batang Rajang
Kanowit
Sibu
Sarikei

Kepulauan Anambas
Pulau Siantan
Pulau Jemaja

Kepulauan Natuna
Pulau Natuna Besar

Pulau Midai
Pulau Subi Besar
Pulau Serasan

Natuna Sea

Tanjung Datu
Teluk Datu
Kuching
Kuching
Bau
Serian
Sri Aman
Batang Lupar

B o
Kapuas Mountain

KUALA LUMPUR
KUALA LUMPUR
Klang
Shah Alam
Pelabuhan Klang
NEGERI SEMBILAN
Seremban
SELANGOR
Sungai Bernam
Padang
MELAKA
Melaka
Muar
Batu Pahat
JOHOR
Johor Bahru
SINGAPORE
SINGAPORE
Singapore Strait
Kukup
Kulai

Pemangkat
Singkawang
Sambas
Bengkayang
Perigi
Pinang
Sidas
Sanggau
KALIMANTAN BARAT
Kalimantan

Pegunungan Schwaner

Ka li

Kualakeriau
Semitau
Danau Genali
Danau Luar
Nangaserawai

Palembang
SUMATERA SELATAN

Pulau Bangka
Pangkalpinang

Selat Karimata

KALIMANTAN TENGA

Kali

Bukit Raya
2278m

Tumbangsenamang

Java Sea

JAKARTA
JAKARTA RAYA
Serang
Tangerang
Bekasi
Karawang
Bandung
JAWA BARAT

Semarang
JAWA TENGAH
Surabaya
JAWA TIMUR
Malang
Yogyakarta
YOGYAKARTA

Throughout Southeast Asia, where agricultural land is at a premium, terraces are cut into the slopes to maximize the area available for cultivation. These terraces on the Indonesian island of Bali are used to support rice paddies.

MARITIME SOUTHEAST ASIA

BRUNEI, INDONESIA, MALAYSIA, SINGAPORE

T HE INTRICATE ARC OF ISLANDS which runs from peninsular Malaysia east to Irian Jaya in western New Guinea sustains a huge variety of peoples, languages and cultures. Indonesia is by far the largest country in the region, and 87% of its huge, predominantly Muslim, population is crowded onto Java, the most habitable of Indonesia's 13,677 islands. Malaysia, split between the mainland and the east Malaysian states of Sabah and Sarawak on Borneo, has a diverse population, as well as a fast-growing economy, although the pace of its development is still far outstripped by that of Singapore. This small island nation is the financial and commercial capital of Southeast Asia, and an Asian 'tiger' economy. The Sultanate of Brunei in northern Borneo, one of the world's last princely states, also has an extremely high standard of living, based on its oil revenues.

USING THE LAND AND SEA

RICE IS THE MOST IMPORTANT ARABLE CROP in Indonesia and Malaysia, and both countries manage to meet almost all of their domestic demand. Malaysian rubber accounts for 25% of world production and is the main cash crop, grown on plantations and small farms, along with oil palms and copra. Timber is exported from both Malaysia and Indonesia. Modern agricultural techniques enable Singapore to produce fruit and vegetables despite a shortage of suitable land.

Spiral cuts in the bark of this rubber palm show where it has been tapped. Sophisticated 'cloning' techniques mean that trees which produce consistently high quantities of rubber can be easily reproduced.

THE URBAN/RURAL POPULATION DIVIDE

urban 32%   rural 68%

0 10 20 30 40 50 60 70 80 90 100

POPULATION DENSITY	TOTAL LAND AREA
262 people per sq mile (101 people per sq km)	828,356 sq miles (2,146,000 sq km)

Land use and agricultural distribution

- coconuts
- fishing
- oil palms
- rice
- rubber
- shellfish
- sugar cane
- timber
- capital cities
- major towns
- pasture
- cropland
- forest
- wetland

THE LANDSCAPE

FROM SUMATRA IN THE WEST, the volcanic islands of Indonesia run for nearly 3100 miles (5000 km). The Sunda Shelf, an extension of the Eurasian Plate, lies between Java, Bali, Sumatra, Lombok and Borneo. Their volcanic mountains rise from a base below the sea and they were once joined together by dry land, which has since been submerged by rising sea levels.

Malay Peninsula has a rugged east coast, but the west coast, fronting the Strait of Malacca, has many sheltered beaches and bays. The two coasts are divided by the Banjaran Titiwangsa, which run the length of the peninsula.

The river of Sungai Mahakam cuts through the central highlands of Borneo, the third largest island in the world, with a total area of 292,222 sq miles (757,050 sq km). Although mountainous, Borneo is one of the most stable of the Indonesian islands, with little volcanic activity.

The Sunda Shelf underlies this whole region. It is one of the largest submarine shelves in the world, covering an area of 714,285 sq miles (1,850,000 sq km). During the early Quaternary period, when sea levels were lower, the shelf was exposed.

Borneo / Broad, shallow valleys on sea floor / Malay Peninsula / Present sea level / Sumatra / Drowned rivers / Quaternary sea level, 460 ft (140 m) below present sea level

Gunung Kinabalu is the highest peak in Malaysia, rising 13,455 ft (4101 m).

The four-pronged island of Celebes is the product of complex tectonic activity which ruptured and then reattached small fragments of the Earth's crust to form the island's many peninsulas.

Irian Jaya contains some of the most dense and least explored tropical rainforests in the world, inhabited by many rare species of plants and animals.

The island of Krakatau (Pulau Rakata), lying between Sumatra and Java, was all but destroyed in 1883, when the volcano erupted. The release of gas and dust into the atmosphere disrupted cloud cover and global weather patterns for several years.

Gunung Semeru

The volcano of Gunung Semeru in eastern Java lies on the Pacific 'Rim of Fire'. It is part of the ancient Tennegger volcano and remains highly active.

Indonesia has more than 220 volcanoes, most of which are still active. They are strung out along the island arc from Sumatra through the Lesser Sunda Islands, into the Moluccas and Celebes.

Coral islands such as Timor in eastern Indonesia show evidence of very recent and dramatic movements of the Earth's plates. Reefs in Timor have risen by as much as 4000 ft (1300 m) in the last million years.

The Pegunungan Jayawijaya range in central Irian Jaya contains the world's highest range of limestone mountains, some with peaks more than 16,400 ft (5000 m) high. Heavy rainfall and high temperatures, which promote rapid weathering, have led to the creation of large underground caves and river systems such as the river of Sungai Baliem.

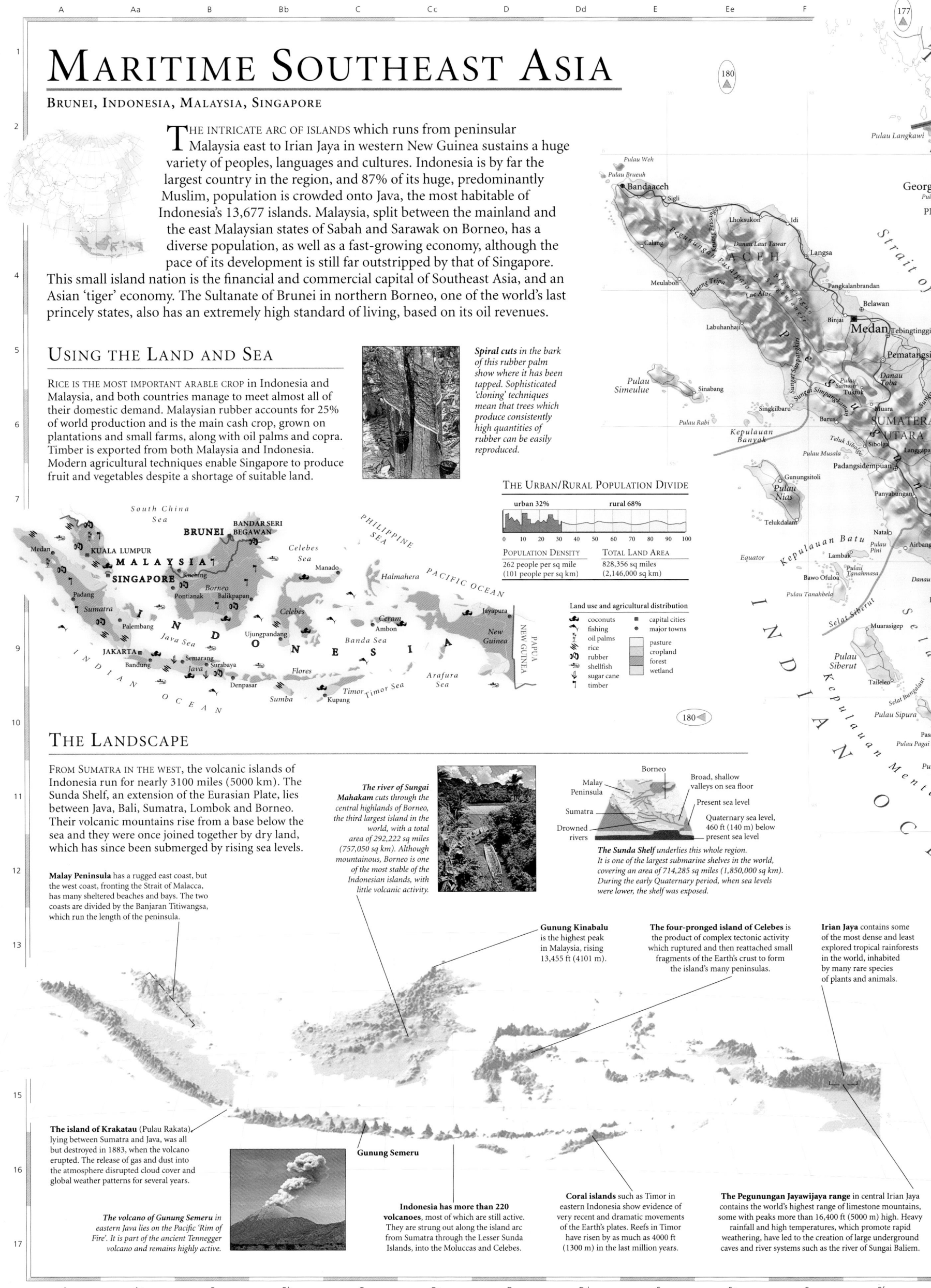

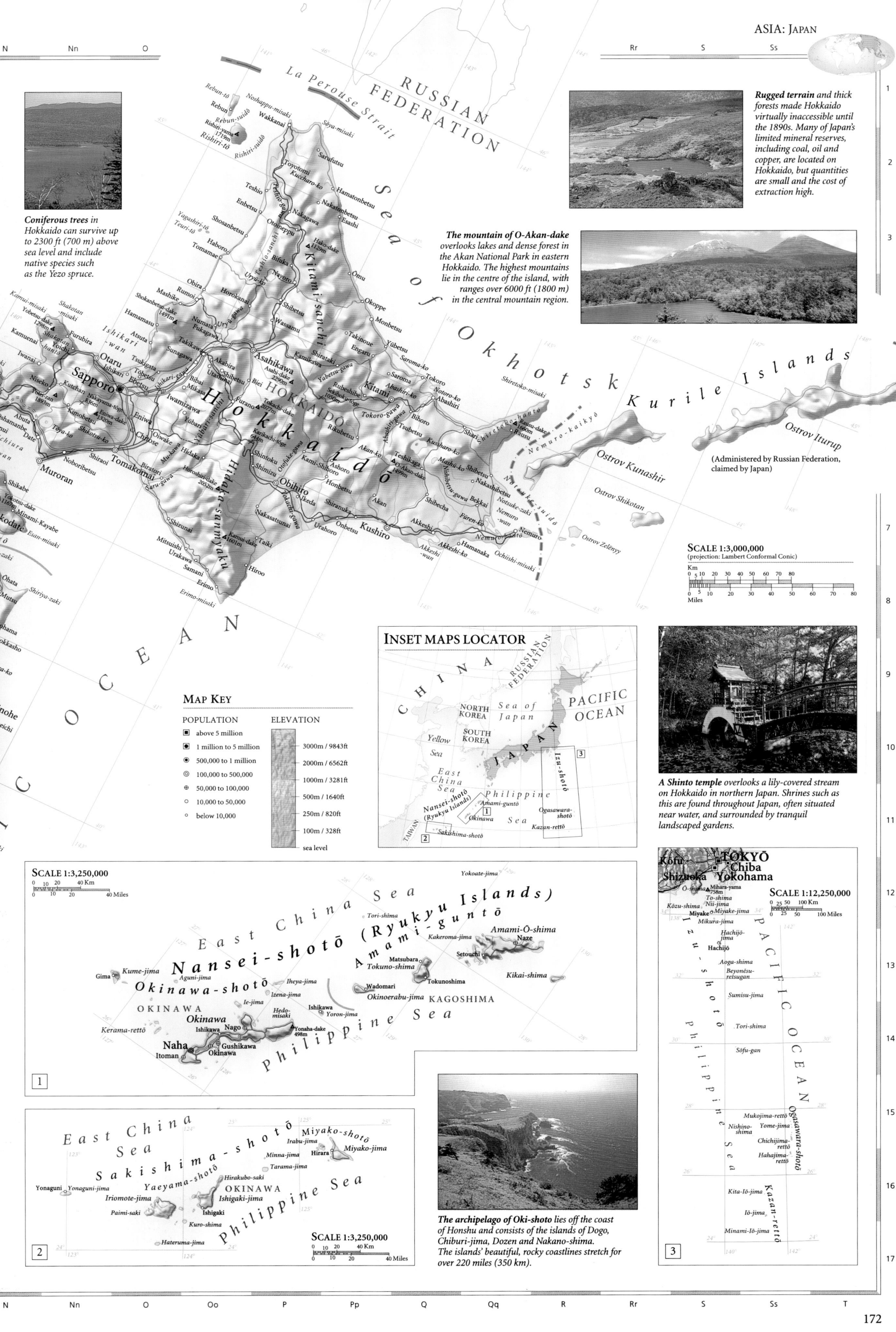

Coniferous trees in Hokkaido can survive up to 2300 ft (700 m) above sea level and include native species such as the Yezo spruce.

Rugged terrain and thick forests made Hokkaido virtually inaccessible until the 1890s. Many of Japan's limited mineral reserves, including coal, oil and copper, are located on Hokkaido, but quantities are small and the cost of extraction high.

The mountain of O-Akan-dake overlooks lakes and dense forest in the Akan National Park in eastern Hokkaido. The highest mountains lie in the centre of the island, with ranges over 6000 ft (1800 m) in the central mountain region.

(Administered by Russian Federation, claimed by Japan)

SCALE 1:3,000,000
(projection: Lambert Conformal Conic)

INSET MAPS LOCATOR

MAP KEY

POPULATION
- ▣ above 5 million
- ▣ 1 million to 5 million
- ◉ 500,000 to 1 million
- ◎ 100,000 to 500,000
- ⊕ 50,000 to 100,000
- ⊕ 10,000 to 50,000
- ○ below 10,000

ELEVATION
- 3000m / 9843ft
- 2000m / 6562ft
- 1000m / 3281ft
- 500m / 1640ft
- 250m / 820ft
- 100m / 328ft
- sea level

A Shinto temple overlooks a lily-covered stream on Hokkaido in northern Japan. Shrines such as this are found throughout Japan, often situated near water, and surrounded by tranquil landscaped gardens.

SCALE 1:3,250,000

SCALE 1:12,250,000

The archipelago of Oki-shoto lies off the coast of Honshu and consists of the islands of Dogo, Chiburi-jima, Dozen and Nakano-shima. The islands' beautiful, rocky coastlines stretch for over 220 miles (350 km).

SCALE 1:3,250,000

PHILIPPINES

PHILIPPINE

198

177

*Sulu
Sea*

Pulau Balambangan

Pulau
Banggi

Tiga Tarok
Teluk
Paitan
Kanibongan

Kudat

Tuaran   Gunung Kinabalu
4101m
Kota Kinabalu   Ranau
Kota Kinabalu
Kuala Penyu
Teluk
Labuk   Sandakan

Sungai Sugut

Sungai Labuk

LABUAN
Pulau Labuan   Kuala Kimanis
Labuan   Tambunan   SABAH
Bandar Seri   Keningau
Begawan   Sungai Kinabatangan

BANDAR
SERI
BEGAWAN   Tenom   Lahad Datu
BRUNEI   Teluk
Lahad Datu
Pulau Timbun Mata
Pulau Bum Bun
Tawau

Pulau Sebatik

*Celebes
Sea*

*Kepulauan
Kawio*

*Kepulauan
Nanusa*

*Pulau
Karakelong*   *Kepulauan
Talaud*

Melanguane
Pulau Salibabu   Damau   *Pulau
Kaburuang*

*Pulau
Sangihe*

Tahuna

Uluq   *Pulau Siau*

*Pulau
Tahulandang*

*Kepulauan
Loloda Utara*   Tanjung Bisoa

Galela   *Pulau
Morotai*
Sopi   Tanjung
Sabatai

Tobelo

Pediwang   Iga   Ta
Aket

Sungai Sembakung

Pulau Mandul
Bunyu   Sebuku Teluk
Pulau Bunyu

Tarakan   *Pulau Tarakan*

Pulau Mapat

Sungai Sesayap

Sungai Sesayap

K

neo

Metulang

KALIMANTAN TIMUR

Gunung Menyapa
2000m

Muarawahau

Sangkulirang   Gunung Antu
780m

Sepasu

Tanjungbatu

Tanjungredeb

Teluk
Pantai

Pulau Maratua

Sungai Kayan

Sungai Berau

Sungai Kayan

Sungai Bahau

Pegunungan Sambaliung

Teluk Sangkulirang

Tolitoli

Salumpaga

Oan   Teluk Bilang

Tompo   *Teluk Dondo*   Leok   Lanu

Gunung Malino
2459m   Pegunungan Paleleh   Lemito

Molosipat

Teluk Palalelch   Teluk Kuandang

Kuandang

Danau
Limboto   Gunung Bulawa
1970m
Gorontalo   Molibagu

Manado
Tomohon   Bitung
Airmadidi
Tondano   Danau Tondano
SULAWESI   Amurang
UTARA

Seraï   *Pulau Bangka*

Teluk Amurang

Teluk Gorontalo

Pulau Mayu

Pulau Karakelong

Ternate
Pulau Ternate   Kusu   Teluk
Soasiu   Kau
Pulau Tidore

Pulau Makian

*Pulau
Halmahera*

Buli   Teluk Buli

Bicoli

*Teluk
Weda*

Mafa

Ha

Longiram

*Danau
Semayang*
Danau Melintang

tan

Tenggarong   Tanjung Ayu

Samarinda
Sangasanga
Lohjanan

Balikpapan

Makassar Strait

Sungai Mahakam

Muaratewe

Danau Jempang

Waru   Teluk Adang

Muarakaman

Dayu

Tanjung

Amuntai

ALIMANTAN
SELATAN   Negara
Rantau
Banjarmasin   Kandangan

Martapura

Pelaihari   Pegunungan Meratus

Pulau Sebuku

Kotabaru

Selat Laut

*Pulau
Laut*

Karambu

*Kepulauan
Balabalangan*

Pulau Karamain

lembo-besar

*Kepulauan
Laut Kecil*

Donggala

Tate

Teluk Tambu

Towera   *Gulf of
Tomini*

Palu
Pakuli

Gimpu   Danau
Lindu

Lambogo

Tambarana

Poso

Pandiri   Tentena

Karosa

Babana

Teluk Palu   Tambu

Teluk Poso

*Kepulauan
Togian*

*Pulau
Batudaka*

Dondo   Toima
*Teluk
Uebonti*   Teku
Bolang   Teluk Poh   Maliki
Luwuk
Tobamawu   Pegunungan Balingara

SULAWESI
TENGAH   Kembani

Baturebe   *Pulau Peleng*

Pelei   *Pulau
Banggai*

Balo

*Kepulauan
Banggai*

Pulau Peleng

Masamba

Danau Poso

Teluk Towori

*Teluk
Tolo*

*Molucca
Sea*

Maluk

*Kepulauan
Bacan*   *Pulau Bacan*

*Pulau
Kasiruta*   *Selat Patinti*
*Pulau
Mandioli*   *Selat Obi*

Pulau Obi

Selat Obi

Pulau Bisa   Sesepe

Kawassi   *Selat Tobalai*

Gani

Maluku

Ceram

*Kepulauan
Gomumu*

Pulau Tuliabu   Penu
Tano
Capalulu
Pulau Mangole
*Kepalauan
Treko*   *Kepalauan Sula*   Sanana
*Pulau
Sanana*

Selat Salat Timpaus

*Sulawesi
(Celebes)*

Mamuju

Malunda   *Teluk Mamuju*

Pegunungan Quarles

SULAWESI
SELATAN   Rantepao

Polewali   Enrekang

Majene   *Teluk
Mandar*

*Sungai
Saddang*   Danau Sidenreng
Parepare   Anabanua
Danan Tempe
Singkang
Sungai Walanae   Watampone

Watu
Wotu   Usu

Saroako   Danau Matana
Mahalona
Danau Towuti

*Pulau Luha
Danau Towuti*

*Kepulauan
Salabangka*

Wiau   Asera

Malamala
Pegunungan
Mekanga

Kendari

Teluk Staring

Pulau Manui

Teluk Bone

Kolaka
*Pulau
Padamarang*   *Pulau Wowoni*

Pulau Wowoni

Teluk
Wiwoni

SULAWESI
TENGGARA

Bugingkalo   Tampo
Lasihao   Raha
Pising   Bonelipu
Selat Kabaena   *Selat Tioro*
*Pulau
Kabaena*   *Pulau
Muna*
Kamaru
Baubau   Teluk
Kolowanawatobo
*Pulau
Buton*

*Pulau
Binongko*   *Kepulauan
Kaledupa*   *Kepulauan
Tukangbesi*

*Kepulauan
Langkesi*

*Kepulauan
Luciparra*

*Kepulauan
Penyu*

Waflia   Gunung Kaubalatmada
2725m   *Pulau Boano*
Namlea   *Pulau
Kelang*
Pulau Buru   Luhu
Tifu   Sungai Apu   *Pulau Mapa*
Elara   Watawa
*Pulau
Ambelau*

Lasahata   Tanjung N
Piru   Pi

Latu   Sap

Ambon
Pulau Ambon   Halong   *Pulau Haruku*

Kepulauan Leas

MALU

MALU

Banda Sea

Maros

Ujungpandang

Takalar

Bulukumba

Jeneponto

Selat Selayar

Benteng   *Pulau Kabia*

*Kepulauan
Macan*

*Pulau
Batata*

*Pulau
Binongko*

I N D O N E S I A

Bali Sea

*Pulau
Kangean*   *Kepulauan
Kangean*

*Kepulauan
Sabalana*

*Kepulauan
Tengah*

*Pulau
Tanahjampea*

Pulau Kalao

Pulau Bonerate

*Kepulauan
Bonerate*

*Flores
Sea*

Pulau Kalaotoa

Kepulauan

Selat Romang

Pulau Wetar   *Pulau Romang*

*Kepulauan
Leti*

*Pulau
Moa*

Bali

Singaraja
wangi   Tejakula   *Kepulauan Alor*
Bayan   *Pulau Lomblen*   *Pulau Alor*
BALI   Karangasem   Kubu   Sanggar   Alas   *Pulau Moyo*   Kalabahi   *Pulau
Kambing*
Denpasar   *Pulau
Lombok*   Taliwang   Sumbawabesar   Dompu   *Pulau
Komodo*   Ruteng   Larantuka   *Selat Alor*
Ngurah Rai   Mataram   *Gunung Api
4949m*   Raba   Pota   Maumere   Jabala
*Nusa
Penida*   Kuta   *Gunung Tukan
1400m*   *Teluk Saleh*   *Pulau
Sangeang*   Bajawa   Endeh   *Kepulauan
Solor*
gara   *Selat Lombok*   *Sumbawa*   *Selat Sape*   Labuhanbajo   *Flores*   *Kepulauan
Pantar*   Dili
NUSA TENGGARA BARAT   Lunyuk   Gerampi   *Selat Sumba*   *Selat Sumba*   *Pulau Pantar*   Manatuto   Lospalos
N (L e s s e r   S u n d a   *Selat Sumba*   *S u n d a   I s l a n d s*   TIMOR TIMUR
Bondokodi   *Pulau Sumba*   Waikabubak   NUSA TENGGARA TIMUR   Gunung Kekneno
2070m   Soe   Maliana
Waingapu   *Savu Sea*   Kefamenanu   Nikiniki
Raing   Sulamu   Toineke   Seui
*Kepulauan
Sawu*   *Pulau Sawu*   Kupang   *Timor Sea*
Pulau Semau   *Pulau Roti*
Selat Raijua   *Pulau Roti*
Raa

USING THE LAND AND SEA

THE FERTILE FLOOD PLAINS of rivers such as the Mekong and Salween, and the humid climate, enable the production of rice throughout the region. Cambodia, Burma and Laos still have substantial forests, producing hardwoods such as teak and rosewood. Cash crops include tropical fruits such as coconuts, bananas and pineapples, rubber, oil palm, sugar cane and the jute substitute, kenaf. Pigs and cattle are the main livestock raised. Large quantities of marine and freshwater fish are caught throughout the region.

Land use and agricultural distribution
- cattle
- pigs
- bananas
- coconuts
- fishing
- oil palms
- rice
- rubber
- sugar cane
- timber
- capital cities
- major towns
- pasture
- cropland
- forest
- mountain region

THE URBAN/RURAL POPULATION DIVIDE

urban 22%   rural 78%

POPULATION DENSITY	TOTAL LAND AREA
253 people per sq mile (98 people per sq km)	733,828 sq miles (1,901,110 sq km)

The Paracel Islands and the Spratly Islands are two strategically sensitive island groups, disputed by several surrounding countries. The Paracels are claimed by China, Taiwan and Vietnam, though only China has actually occupied them. The Spratlys are claimed by China, Taiwan, Vietnam, Malaysia and the Philippines and are particularly important as they lie on oil and gas deposits.

The walled city of Hue, in central Vietnam, was built in the 19th century in the style of a Chinese city. It is the site of a number of religious monuments, including the Thien-Mu Pagoda.

TRANSPORT AND INDUSTRY

SINGAPORE HAS A THRIVING ECONOMY based on international trade and finance. Annual trade through the port is among the highest of any port in the world. Indonesia still depends on natural resources, particularly wood, petroleum and gas, although the economy is rapidly diversifying, with manufactured exports including garments, consumer electronics and footwear; a high-profile aircraft industry has developed at Bandung. In Malaysia, although oil, gas and timber remain important resource-based industries, it has a fast-growing and varied manufacturing sector.

Major industry and infrastructure
- aerospace
- copra processing
- chemicals
- electronics
- engineering
- finance
- food processing
- iron & steel
- oil
- ship building
- timber processing
- textiles
- ▪ capital cities
- ● major towns
- ✈ international airports
- major roads
- major industrial areas

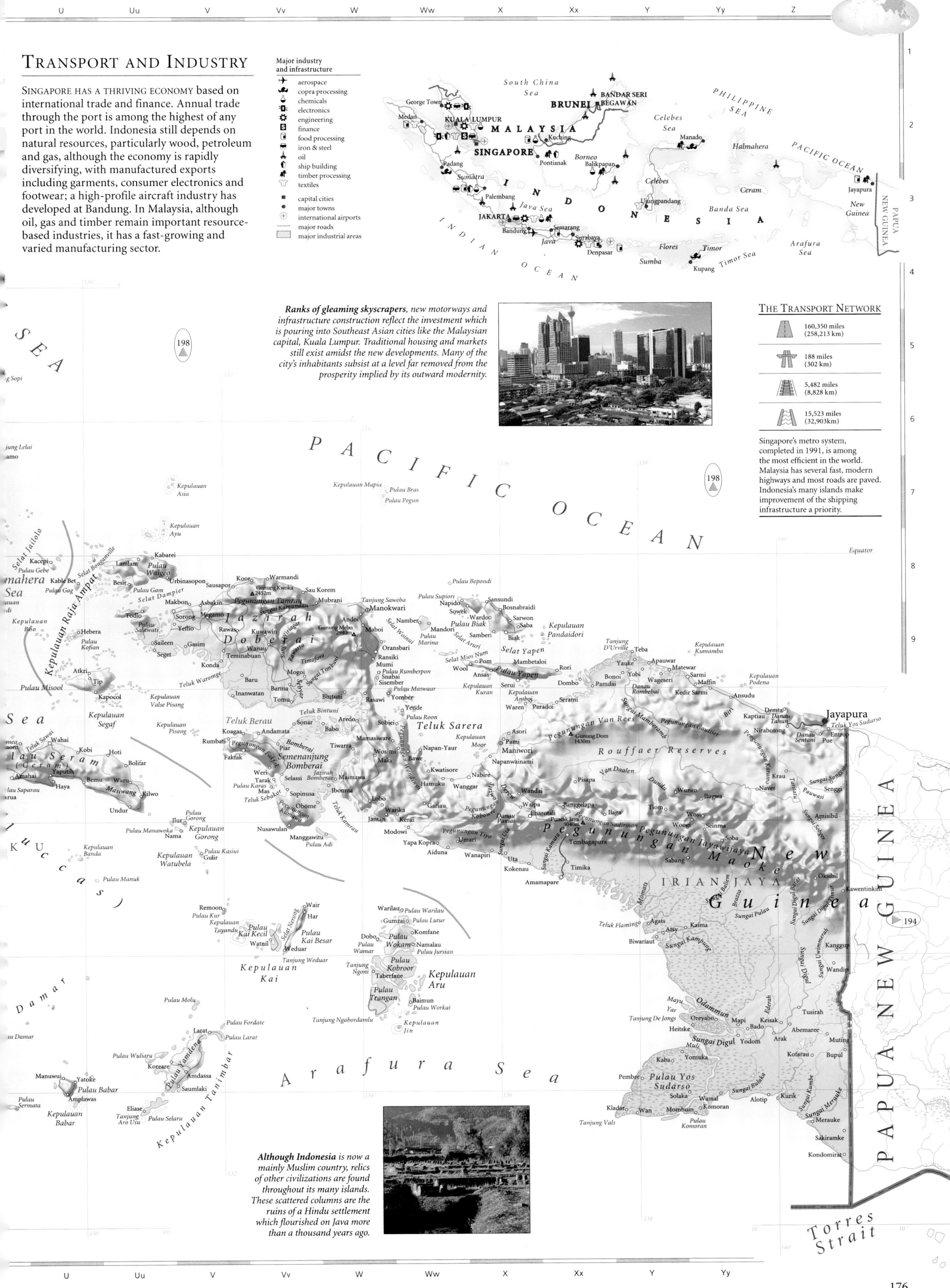

Ranks of gleaming skyscrapers, new motorways and infrastructure construction reflect the investment which is pouring into Southeast Asian cities like the Malaysian capital, Kuala Lumpur. Traditional housing and markets still exist amidst the new developments. Many of the city's inhabitants subsist at a level far removed from the prosperity implied by its outward modernity.

THE TRANSPORT NETWORK

- 160,350 miles (258,213 km)
- 188 miles (302 km)
- 5,482 miles (8,828 km)
- 15,523 miles (32,903km)

Singapore's metro system, completed in 1991, is among the most efficient in the world. Malaysia has several fast, modern highways and most roads are paved. Indonesia's many islands make improvement of the shipping infrastructure a priority.

Although Indonesia is now a mainly Muslim country, relics of other civilizations are found throughout its many islands. These scattered columns are the ruins of a Hindu settlement which flourished on Java more than a thousand years ago.

MAINLAND SOUTHEAST ASIA & THE PHILIPPINES

BURMA, CAMBODIA, LAOS, PHILIPPINES, THAILAND, VIETNAM

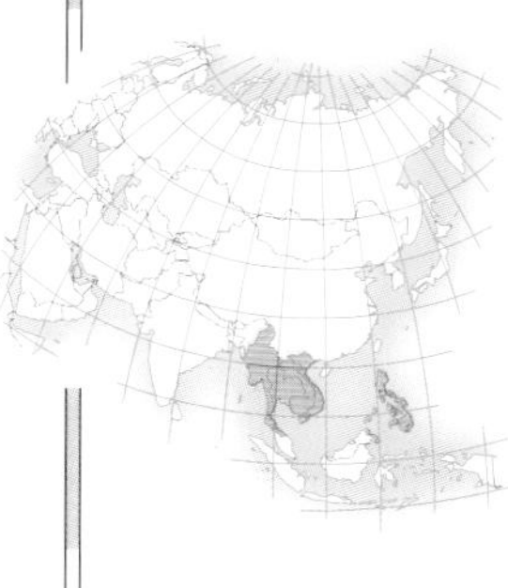

THICKLY FORESTED MOUNTAINS, intercut by the broad valleys of five great rivers characterize the landscape of Southeast Asia's mainland countries. Agriculture remains the main activity for much of the population, which is concentrated in the river flood plains and deltas. Linked ethnic and cultural roots give the region a distinct identity. Most people on the mainland are Theravada Buddhists, and the Philippines is the only predominantly Christian country in Southeast Asia. Foreign intervention began in the 16th century with the opening of the spice trade; Cambodia, Laos and Vietnam were French colonies until the end of the Second World War, Burma was under British control; and the Philippines was controlled by Spain and the USA in the 20th century. Only Thailand was never colonized. Today, Thailand and the Philippines are poised to play a leading role in the economic development of the Pacific Rim, and Laos and Vietnam have begun to mend the devastation of the Vietnam War, and to develop their economies. With continuing political instability and a shattered infrastructure, Cambodia faces an uncertain future, while Burma is seeking investment and the ending of its 30-year isolation from the world community.

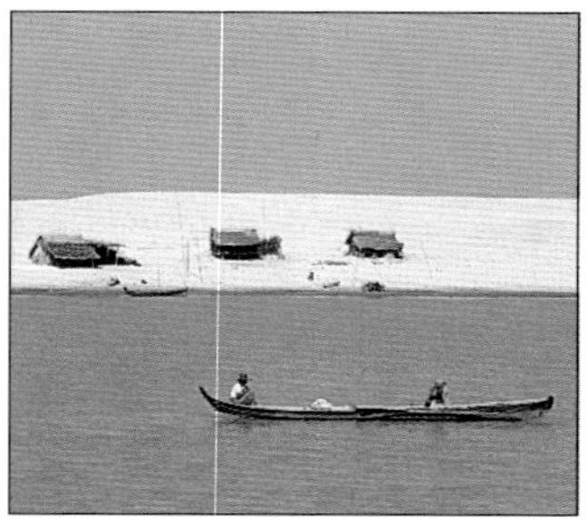

The Irrawaddy River is Burma's vital central artery, watering the ricefields and providing a rich source of fish, as well as an important transport link, particularly for local traffic.

Commercial logging – still widespread in Burma – has now been stopped in Thailand because of over-exploitation of the tropical rainforest.

THE LANDSCAPE

A SERIES OF MOUNTAIN RANGES runs north–south through the mainland, formed as the result of the collision between the Eurasian Plate and the Indian subcontinent, which created the Himalayas. They are interspersed by the valleys of a number of great rivers. On their passage to the sea these rivers have deposited sediment, forming huge, fertile flood plains and deltas. The Philippines' 7000 islands are mountainous and volcanic, with narrow coastal plains.

The Irrawaddy River runs virtually north–south, draining the plains of northern Burma. The Irrawaddy Delta is the country's main rice-growing area.

Hkakabo Razi is the highest point in mainland Southeast Asia. It rises 19,300 ft (5885 m) at the border between China and Burma.

Mountains dominate the Laotian landscape with more than 90% of the land lying more than 600 ft (180 m) above sea level. The mountains of the Chaine Annamitique form the country's eastern border.

Lake Taal on the Philippine island of Luzon lies within the crater of an immense volcano which has erupted twice in the 20th century, first in 1911 and again in 1965, causing the deaths of more than 3200 people.

The Red River Delta in northern Vietnam is fringed to the north by steep-sided, round-topped limestone hills, typical of karst scenery.

Mindanao has five mountain ranges, many of which have large numbers of active volcanoes. Lying just west of the Philippine Trench, which forms the boundary between the colliding Philippine and Eurasian plates, the entire island chain is subject to earthquakes and volcanic activity.

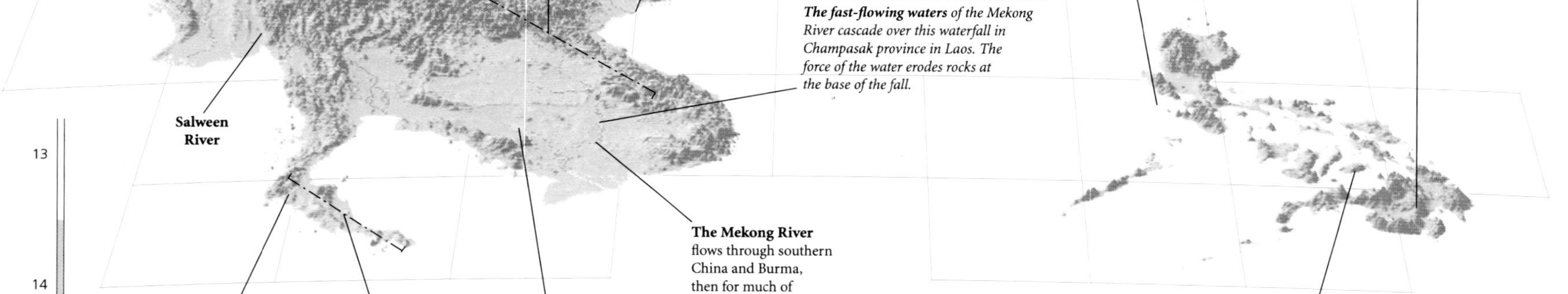

The fast-flowing waters of the Mekong River cascade over this waterfall in Champasak province in Laos. The force of the water erodes rocks at the base of the fall.

Salween River

The Mekong River flows through southern China and Burma, then for much of its length forms the border between Laos and Thailand, flowing through Cambodia before terminating in a vast delta on the southern Vietnamese coast.

Malay Peninsula

Tonle Sap, a freshwater lake, drains into the Mekong Delta via the Mekong River. It is the largest lake in Southeast Asia.

The coastline of the Isthmus of Kra

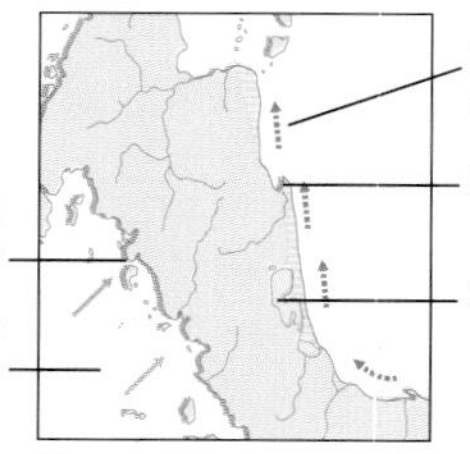

Longshore drift

Spit

Eroded coastline

Lagoon

Wave attack

Bohol

Thailand

The coast of the Isthmus of Kra, in southeast Thailand has many small, precipitous islands like these, formed by chemical erosion on limestone, which is weathered along vertical cracks. The humidity of the climate in Southeast Asia increases the rate of weathering.

The east and west coasts of the Isthmus of Kra differ greatly. The tectonically uplifting west coast is exposed to the harsh south-westerly monsoon and is heavily eroded. On the east coast, longshore currents produce depositional features such as spits and lagoons.

Bohol in the southern Philippines is famous for its so-called 'chocolate hills'. There are more than 1000 of these regular mounds on the island. The hills are limestone in origin, the smoothed remains of an earlier cycle of erosion. Their brown appearance in the dry season gives the hills their name.

BANGLADESH

Bay of Bengal

Andaman Sea

N | Nn | O | Oo | P | Pp | Q | Qq | R | Rr | S | Ss

TRANSPORT AND INDUSTRY

INDUSTRIAL MANUFACTURING has become increasingly important in Thailand, Vietnam and the Philippines in recent years. The assembling of component-based electrical and electronic goods is becoming more common throughout this region, with foreign companies benefiting from low labour costs and the upgrading of technology. The economies of Burma and Cambodia are still based on agricultural produce and the processing of raw materials. Tin is the region's most important metal, and nickel, copper and chromite are also mined, although the quantities produced are not significant on a global scale. Thailand's successful tourist industry is the country's highest earner of foreign exchange.

THE TRANSPORT NETWORK

130,235 miles (209,718 km)		None	
7087 miles (11,413 km)		20,433 miles (32,903 km)	

Transport development has concentrated on the building of road networks. Water and sea transport remain important, although air links have improved, particularly in Thailand and the Philippines.

Major industry and infrastructure

- chemicals
- electronics
- engineering
- finance
- food processing
- iron & steel
- oil & gas
- mining
- shipbuilding
- textiles
- timber processing
- capital cities
- major towns
- international airports
- major roads
- major industrial areas

Opium poppies are destroyed under army supervision in Thailand. This action is part of a government-sponsored initiative to reduce the trade in drugs such as heroin, which is derived from these plants. Drug trafficking is a major problem throughout the region; the area is known as the 'Golden Triangle', and Laos is the third-largest producer of opium poppies in the world.

The terracing of land to restrict soil erosion and create flat surfaces for agriculture is a common practice throughout Southeast Asia, particularly where land is scarce. These terraces are on Luzon in the Philippines.

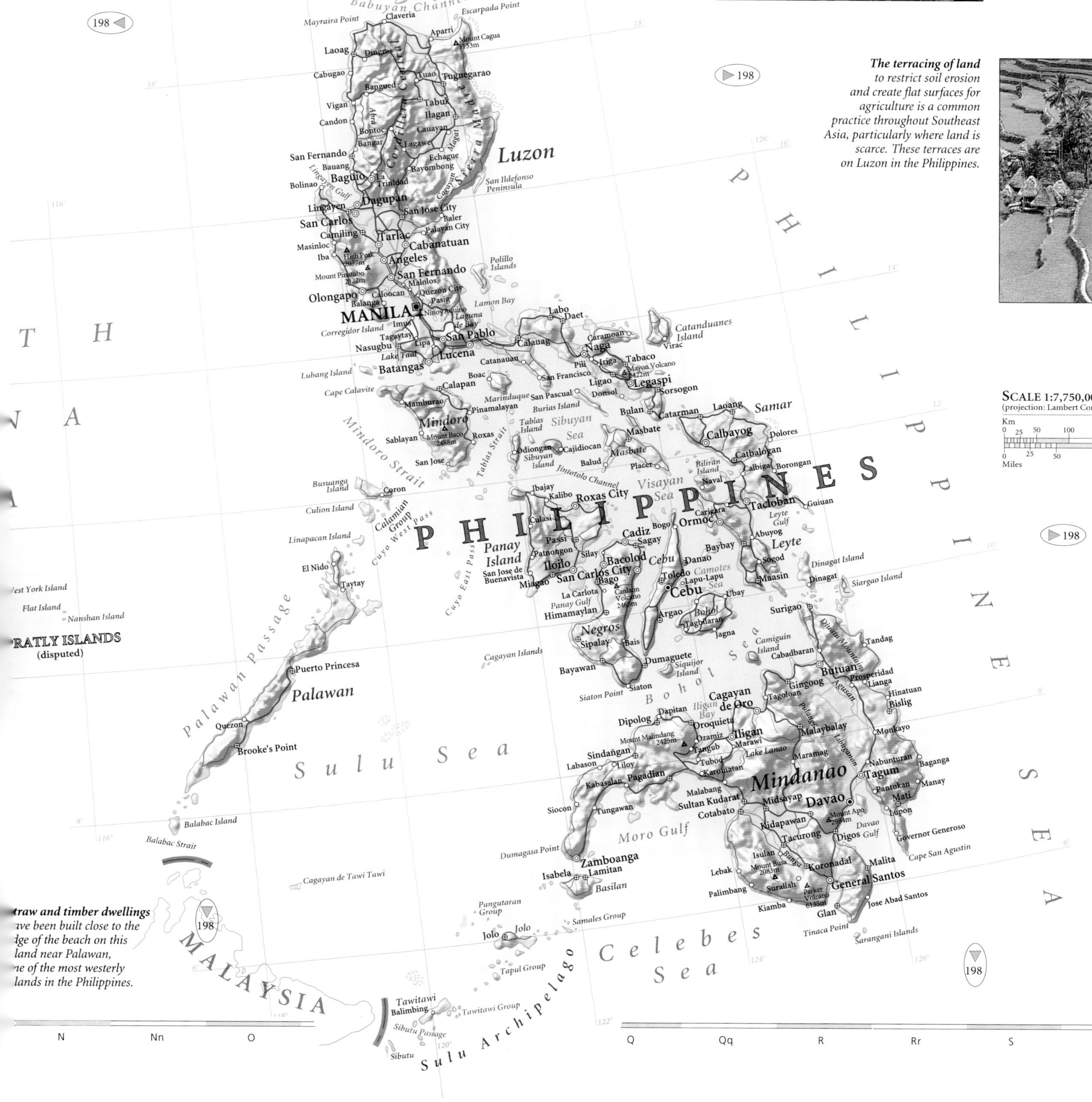

SCALE 1:7,750,000
(projection: Lambert Conformal Conic)

MAP KEY

POPULATION

- above 5 million
- 1 million to 5 million
- 500,000 to 1 million
- 100,000 to 500,000
- 50,000 to 100,000
- 10,000 to 50,000
- below 10,000

ELEVATION

- 4000m / 13,124ft
- 3000m / 9843ft
- 2000m / 6562ft
- 1000m / 3281ft
- 500m / 1640ft
- 250m / 820ft
- 100m / 328ft
- sea level

Straw and timber dwellings have been built close to the edge of the beach on this island near Palawan, one of the most westerly islands in the Philippines.

THE INDIAN OCEAN

DESPITE BEING THE SMALLEST of the three major oceans, the evolution of the Indian Ocean was the most complex. The ocean basin was formed during the break up of the supercontinent Gondwanaland, when the Indian subcontinent moved northeast, Africa moved west and Australia separated from Antarctica. Like the Pacific Ocean, the warm waters of the Indian Ocean are punctuated by coral atolls and islands. About one-fifth of the world's population – over 1000 million people – live on its shores. Those people living along the northern coasts are constantly threatened by flooding and typhoons caused by the monsoon winds.

THE LANDSCAPE

THE INDIAN OCEAN BEGAN FORMING about 150 million years ago, but in its present form it is relatively young, only about 36 million years old. Along the three subterranean mountain chains of its mid-ocean ridge the seafloor is still spreading. The Indian Ocean has fewer trenches than other oceans and only a narrow continental shelf around most of its surrounding land.

Sediments come from Ganges/Brahmaputra river system

Submarine canyons transport sediment to fan – some of these are more than 1500 miles (2500 km) long

Sri Lanka

The Ganges Fan is one of the world's largest submarine accumulations of sediment, extending far beyond Sri Lanka. It is fed by the Ganges/Brahmaputra river system, whose sediment is carried through a network of underwater canyons at the edge of the continental shelf.

The mid-oceanic ridge runs from the Arabian Sea. It diverges east of Madagascar, one arm runs southwest to join the Mid-Atlantic Ridge, the other branches southeast, joining the Pacific-Antarctic Ridge, southeast of Tasmania.

The Ninetyeast Ridge takes its name from the line of longitude it follows. It is the world's longest and straightest under-sea ridge.

Two of the world's largest rivers flow into the Indian Ocean; the Indus and the Ganges/Brahmaputra. Both have deposited enormous fans of sediment.

Indus River

A large proportion of the coast of Thailand, on the Isthmus of Kra, is stabilized by mangrove thickets. They act as an important breeding ground for wildlife.

The Java Trench is the world's longest, it runs 1600 miles (2570 km) from the southwest of Java, but is only 50 miles (80 km) wide.

The relief of Madagascar rises from a low-lying coastal strip in the east, to the central plateau. The plateau is also a major watershed separating Madagascar's three main river basins.

The central group of the Seychelles are mountainous, granite islands. They have a narrow coastal belt and lush, tropical vegetation cloaks the highlands.

The Kerguelen Islands in the Southern Ocean were created by a hot spot in the Earth's crust. The islands were formed in succession as the Antarctic Plate moved slowly over the hot spot.

The circulation in the northern Indian Ocean is controlled by the monsoon winds. Biannually these winds reverse their pattern, causing a reversal in the surface currents and alternative high and low pressure conditions over Asia and Australia.

RESOURCES

MANY OF THE SMALL ISLANDS in the Indian Ocean rely exclusively on tuna-fishing and tourism to maintain their economies. Most fisheries are artisanal, although large-scale tuna-fishing does take place in the Seychelles, Mauritius and the western Indian Ocean. Non-living resources include oil in The Gulf, pearls in the Red Sea and tin from deposits off the shores of Burma, Thailand and Indonesia.

The recent use of large drag nets for tuna-fishing has not only threatened the livelihoods of many small-scale fisheries, but also caused widespread environmental concern about the potential impact on other marine species.

Resources (including wildlife)
- fish
- penguins
- shellfish
- whales
- oil & gas
- tin deposits
- tourism
- major towns
- major ports

SCALE 1:11,000,000
0 25 50   100   150   200 Km
0 25 50   100   150   200 Miles

MADAGASCAR

Nosy Glorieuses
Tanjona Bobaomby
Antsirañana
Tanjona Anorontany
Nosy Be · Ambilobe
Iharaña
AMBANJA · ANTSIRANANA
Analalava
Antsohihy
Sambava
Antalaha
Mahajanga · MAHAJANGA
Maroyoay
Mitsinjo
Soalala
Besalampy
Kandreho
Maintirano
Antsalova
Belo Tsiribihina
Morondava
Mahabo
Mandabe
Beroroha
Tanjona Ankaoa
Morombe · Mangoky
Ankazoabo
Ampanihy
Sakaraha
Betioky
Bekily
Beloha
Ambovombe
Tsiombe
Tanjona Vohimena

ANTANANARIVO
FIANARANTSOA
TOLIARA
Toliara

INDIAN OCEAN

EGYPT
Suez
Yanbu' al Bahr
Tropic of Cancer
SAUDI
Jedda
Red Sea
Port Sudan
SUDAN
ERITREA
Massawa
Hodeida
Aden
DJIBOUTI
Djibouti
ETHIOPIA
KENYA
SOMALIA
Mogadishu
Equator
Lake Victoria
Kismaayo
TANZANIA
Mombasa
Tanga · Pemba
Zanzibar
Dar es Salaam
Mafia
Lake Nyasa
Ruvuma
COMORO
MAYOTTE (to France)
Comoro Basin
Nacala
MOZAMBIQUE
Quelimane
Beira
Limpopo
Tropic of Capricorn
SWAZILAND
Maputo
SOUTH AFRICA
LESOTHO
Durban
Orange River
Cape Town
Mosselbaai
Port Elizabeth
East London
Agulhas Bank
Transkei Basin
Natal Basin
Agulhas Plateau
Agulhas Basin
Atlantic-Indian Ridge
Atlantic-Indian Basin
Prince Edward Islands (to South Africa)
Antarctic Circle

ASIA
Suez · Kuwait
Bombay
Arabian Sea
Bay of Bengal
Rangoon
South China Sea
Singapore
Mombasa
Toamasina
INDIAN OCEAN
Java Sea
Timor Sea
AUSTRALIA
Fremantle
SOUTHERN OCEAN
ANTARCTICA
AFRICA

SCALE 1:4,500,000
0 10 20   40   60   80   100 Km
0 10   20   40   60   80   100 Miles

Grande Comore
Mitsamiouli · Saondzou
Hahaya · Mbéni · Koimbani
Mitsoudjé · Itsandra
Dembéni · Foumbouni
MORONI
COMOROS
Mohéli
Miringoni · Fomboni
Nioumachoua · Ouanani
Anjouan
Moutsamudu · Ouani
Sima · Domoni
Moya · Mramani
MAYOTTE (to France)
Dzaoudzi · Pamandzi
MAMOUDZOU · Bandrélé
Comoro Islands
Mozambique Channel
INDIAN OCEAN

SCALE 1:2,000,000
0 5 10   20   30 Km
0 5 10   20   30 Miles

Inner Islands
Ile Aride
Praslin · Curieuse · Les Sœurs
Cousin · Cousine · Grand Sœur · Félicité
Ile du Nord · La Digue · Marianne
Mount Dauban · Silhouette
SEYCHELLES
Mamelles
Mahé · North Point · Ile aux Récifs
VICTORIA
Morne Seychellois
Sainte Anne · Ile au Cerf · Frégate
Ile Thérèse · Cascade
Anse Boileau · Mahé
Pointe Lazare · Anse Lazare
Quatre Bornes · Pointe Lazare
Pointe Police
INDIAN OCEAN

Coral reefs support an enormous diversity of animal and plant life. Many species of tiny tropical fish, like these squirrel fish, live and feed around the profusion of reefs and atolls in the Indian Ocean.

The steeper eastern side of Madagascar is drained by numerous short, fast-flowing rivers. In contrast, larger, more languid rivers flow across the west. Both erode huge quantities of Madagascar's reddish soil.

There are over 1300 small coral islands in the Maldives, but only about 200 are inhabited. They are based around an ancient submerged volcanic mountain range and all the islands are low-lying, none rising more than 6 ft (1.8 m) above sea level.

SCALE 1:42,000,000
(projection: Mollweide)

Km 0 200 400 600 800 1000
Miles 0 200 400 600 800 1000

1

Map labels

AQ
KUWAIT
Kuwait
IRAN
ASIA
East China Sea
2
Ad Dammām
BAHRAIN
QATAR
Doha
Abu Dhabi
UAE
Mīnā' Qābūs
OMAN
ARABIA
YEMEN
Salālah
Bandar-e 'Abbās
UAE
Dubai
Gulf of Oman
Gwādar
PAKISTAN
Karāchi
Murray Ridge
Indus Fan
Bhāvnagar
Narmada
INDIA
Bombay
Godavari
Krishna
Ganges
Brahmaputra
BANGLADESH
Dhaka
Calcutta
Chittagong
Irrawaddy
BURMA
Mekong
CHINA
Tropic of Cancer
Ryūkyū Islands
TAIWAN
3

The Gulf
Owen Fracture Zone
Andrew Tablemount
Tarot Tablemount
Sharbatat Ridge
Alula-Tarrack Fracture Zone
(to Yemen)
Socotra
Arabian Basin
Arabian Sea
Laccadive Islands (to India)
Mangalore
Madras
Visākhapatnam
Ganges Fan
Bay of Bengal
Rangoon
Salween
LAOS
THAILAND
Gulf of Tongking
VIETNAM
South China Sea
PHILIPPINES
Philippine Sea

Carlsberg Ridge
Chain Ridge
Coco-de-Mer Seamounts
Cochin
Tuticorin
Trincomalee
SRI LANKA
Colombo
CAMBODIA
Gulf of Thailand
Andaman Islands (to India)
Andaman Basin
Andaman Sea
Nicobar Islands (to India)
MALAYSIA
Sulu Sea
Celebes Sea

Somali Basin
Seychelles
Mahé
Madagascar
SEYCHELLES
Amirante Islands
Amirante Basin
Amirante Trench
MALDIVES
Ceylon Plain
Chagos-Laccadive Plateau
Chagos Trench
Chagos Fracture Zone
Chagos Archipelago
Diego Garcia
British Indian Ocean Territory (to UK)
Ninetyeast Ridge
Cocos Basin
Bedawan
Kepulauan
Strait of Malacca
Sumatra
Klang
Singapore
Borneo
INDONESIA
Celebes
Molucca Sea
Ceram Sea
New Guinea
Equator

Farquhar Group
Agalega Islands (to Mauritius)
Saya de Malha Bank
Nazareth Bank
Cargados Carajos Bank
Mascarene Basin
Mascarene Plateau
Nema Fracture Zone
Argo Fracture Zone
Mid-Indian Ridge
Mid-Indian Basin
Osborn Plateau
Investigator Ridge
Java Sea
Java
Bali
Sumbawa
Lombok Basin
Pulau Sumba
Savu
Timor
Java Trench
Java Ridge
Christmas Island (to Australia)
Rao Rise
North Australian Basin
Banda Sea
Timor Sea
Timor Trough
Arafura Sea

INDIAN
Mauritius
Mascarene Islands
Réunion (to France)
Mascarene Plain
Rodrigues (to Mauritius)
Egeria Fracture Zone
Mozambique Ridge
Madagascar Basin
Wharton Basin
Cocos Islands (to Australia)
Gascoyne Plain
Ashmore & Cartier Islands (to Australia)
North Australian Basin
Rowley Shoals
Joseph Bonaparte Gulf
Darwin
Gulf of Carpentaria
Wyndham
Broome

OCEAN
Madagascar Basin
Exmouth Plateau
Cuvier Basin
Shark Bay
Port Hedland
Tropic of Capricorn
9

Batavia Seamount
Golden Draak Seamount
East Indiaman Ridge
Wallaby Plateau
Cuvier Plateau
Perth Basin
Geraldton
AUSTRALIA

Broken Ridge
Ob' Trench
Naturaliste Plateau
Fremantle
Bunbury
Albany
Great Australian Bight
Port Augusta
Darling
Murray
Adelaide
10

Crozet Basin
Amsterdam Fracture Zone
Amsterdam Island
St. Paul Island
Southeast Indian Ridge
Diamantina Fracture Zone
South Australian Basin
Melbourne
King Island
Bass Strait
Tasmania

West Indian Ridge
Southwest Indian Ridge
Crozet Plateau
Crozet Islands
French Southern & Antarctic Territories (to France)
Kerguelen
Kerguelen Plateau
Heard & McDonald Islands (to Australia)
South Australian Plain
Tasman Plateau
12

SOUTHERN OCEAN
South Indian Basin
13

Ob' Tablemount
Lena Tablemount
Banzare Seamounts
Enderby Plain
14

ANTARCTICA
Prydz Bay
Antarctic Circle
15

Captions

The island of Mauritius is volcanic in origin. Its central plateau is bounded by mountains which may once have formed the rim of a volcanic crater.

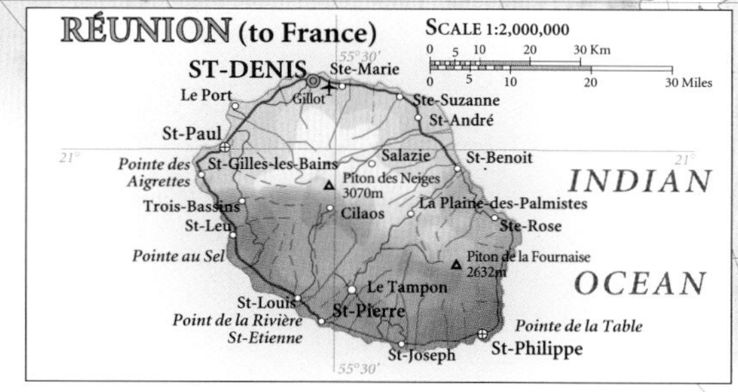

INSET MAP KEY

POPULATION
◉ 500,000 to 1 million
◎ 100,000 to 500,000
⊙ 50,000 to 100,000
○ 10,000 to 50,000
∘ below 10,000

ELEVATION
3000m / 9843ft
2000m / 6562ft
1000m / 3281ft
500m / 1640ft
250m / 820ft
100m / 328ft
sea level

OCEAN MAP KEY

SEA DEPTH
sea level
250m / 820ft
500m / 1640ft
1000m / 3281ft
2000m / 6562ft
3000m / 9843ft

RÉUNION (to France)

SCALE 1:2,000,000
0 5 10 20 30 Km
0 5 10 20 30 Miles

ST-DENIS
Ste-Marie
Le Port
Gillot
Ste-Suzanne
St-Paul
Salazie
Ste-André
Pointe des Aigrettes
St-Gilles-les-Bains
Piton des Neiges 3070m
St-Benoit
Trois-Bassins
Cilaos
La Plaine-des-Palmistes
St-Leu
Ste-Rose
Pointe au Sel
Le Tampon
Piton de la Fournaise 2632m
St-Louis
St-Pierre
Point de la Table
Pointe de la Rivière
St-Étienne
St-Philippe
INDIAN OCEAN

MAURITIUS

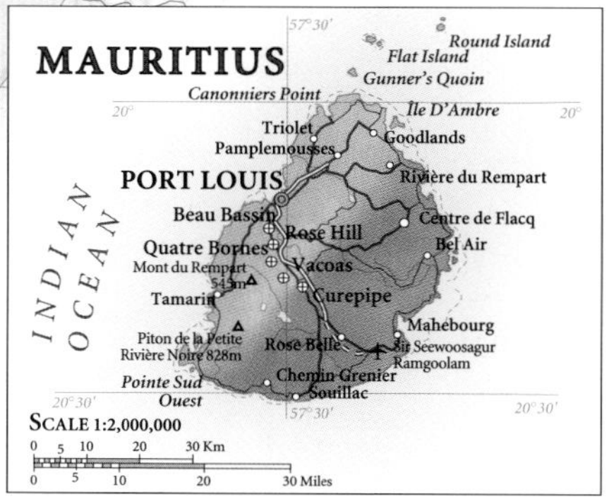

Round Island
Flat Island
Gunner's Quoin
Canonniers Point
Île D'Ambre
Triolet
Pamplemousses
Goodlands
PORT LOUIS
Rivière du Rempart
Beau Bassin
Rose Hill
Centre de Flacq
Quatre Bornes
Bel Air
Mont du Rempart
Vacoas
Piton de la Petite Rivière Noire 828m
Curepipe
Mahébourg
Tamarin
Rose Belle
Chemin Grenier
Seewoosagur Ramgoolam
Pointe Sud Ouest
Souillac
INDIAN OCEAN
SCALE 1:2,000,000
0 5 10 20 30 Km
0 5 10 20 30 Miles
16
17

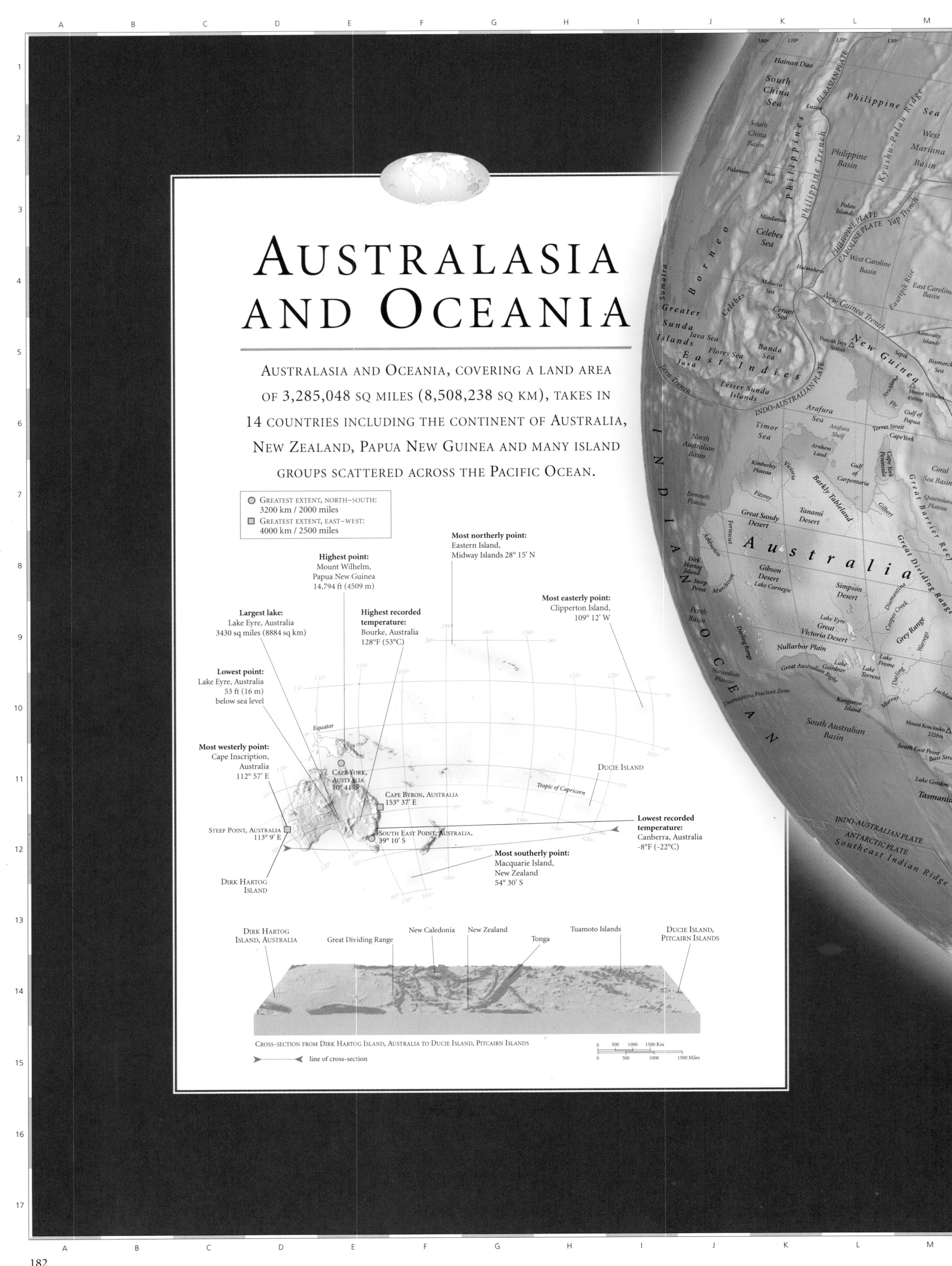

AUSTRALASIA AND OCEANIA

AUSTRALASIA AND OCEANIA, COVERING A LAND AREA
OF 3,285,048 SQ MILES (8,508,238 SQ KM), TAKES IN
14 COUNTRIES INCLUDING THE CONTINENT OF AUSTRALIA,
NEW ZEALAND, PAPUA NEW GUINEA AND MANY ISLAND
GROUPS SCATTERED ACROSS THE PACIFIC OCEAN.

⊙ GREATEST EXTENT, NORTH–SOUTH:
3200 km / 2000 miles
▢ GREATEST EXTENT, EAST–WEST:
4000 km / 2500 miles

Highest point:
Mount Wilhelm,
Papua New Guinea
14,794 ft (4509 m)

Most northerly point:
Eastern Island,
Midway Islands 28° 15' N

Most easterly point:
Clipperton Island,
109° 12' W

Largest lake:
Lake Eyre, Australia
3430 sq miles (8884 sq km)

**Highest recorded
temperature:**
Bourke, Australia
128°F (53°C)

Lowest point:
Lake Eyre, Australia
53 ft (16 m)
below sea level

Most westerly point:
Cape Inscription,
Australia
112° 57' E

CAPE YORK,
AUSTRALIA
10° 41' S

CAPE BYRON, AUSTRALIA
153° 37' E

DUCIE ISLAND

STEEP POINT, AUSTRALIA
113° 9' E

SOUTH EAST POINT, AUSTRALIA,
39° 10' S

**Lowest recorded
temperature:**
Canberra, Australia
-8°F (-22°C)

DIRK HARTOG
ISLAND

Most southerly point:
Macquarie Island,
New Zealand
54° 30' S

DIRK HARTOG
ISLAND, AUSTRALIA

Great Dividing Range

New Caledonia

New Zealand

Tonga

Tuamoto Islands

DUCIE ISLAND,
PITCAIRN ISLANDS

CROSS-SECTION FROM DIRK HARTOG ISLAND, AUSTRALIA TO DUCIE ISLAND, PITCAIRN ISLANDS

line of cross-section

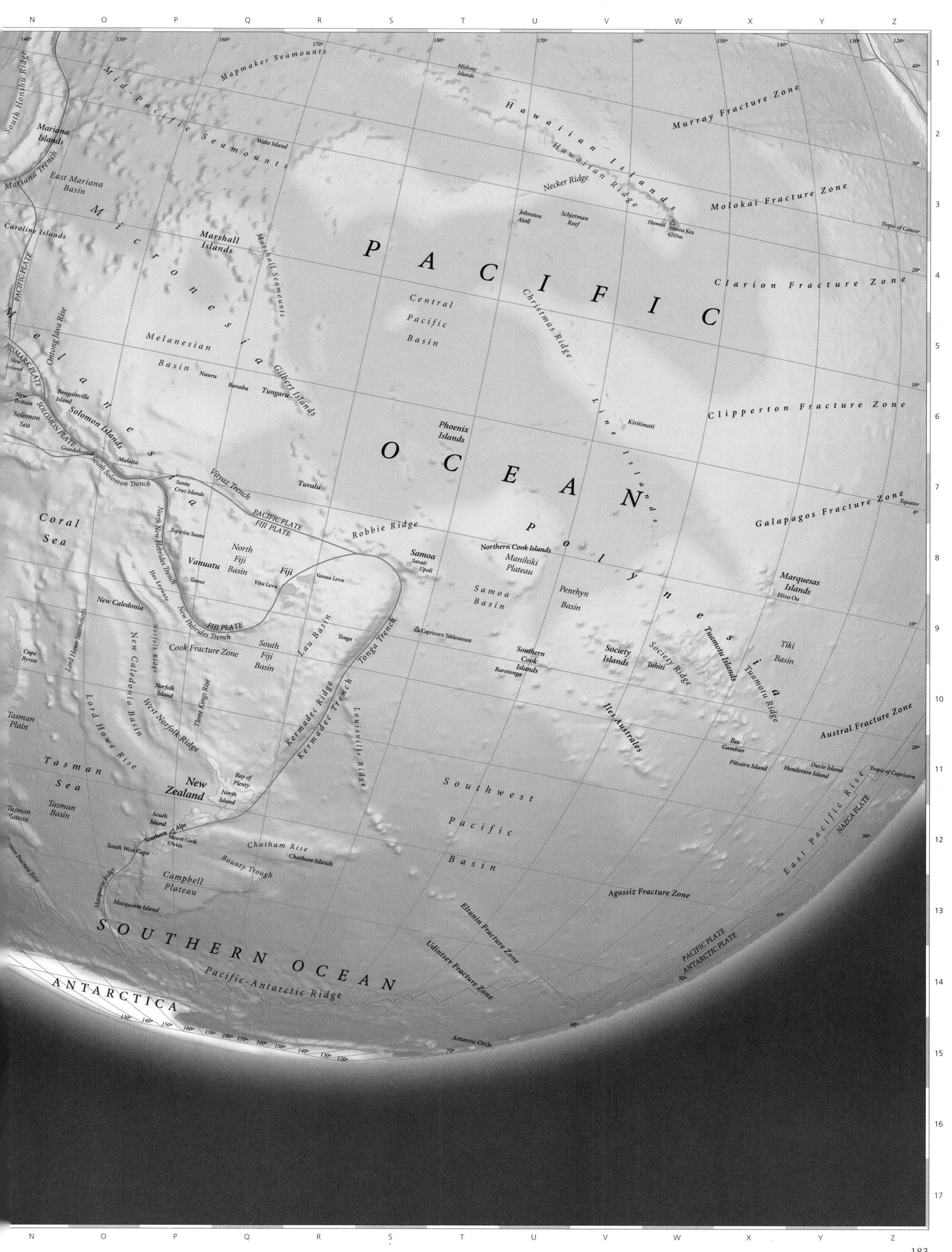

South Honshu Ridge

Mapmaker Seamounts

Midway Islands

Murray Fracture Zone

Hawaiian Islands

Mariana Islands

Mid-Pacific Seamounts

Wake Island

Hawaiian Ridge

Mariana Trench

East Mariana Basin

Necker Ridge

Molokai Fracture Zone

Micronesia

Caroline Islands

PACIFIC PLATE

Marshall Islands

Marshall Seamounts

Johnston Atoll

Schjetman Reef

Hawaii △ Mauna Kea 4205m

Tropic of Cancer

Clarion Fracture Zone

PACIFIC

Central Pacific Basin

Melanesia

Melanesian Basin

Nauru

Banaba

Gilbert Islands

Tungaru

Christmas Ridge

Line Islands

Kiritimati

Clipperton Fracture Zone

Ontong Java Rise

BISMARK PLATE

New Ireland

OCEAN

Phoenix Islands

New Britain

Bougainville Island

Solomon Islands

SOLOMON PLATE

Solomon Sea

Guadalcanal

Malaita

South Solomon Trench

Vityaz Trench

Tuvalu

Santa Cruz Islands

Polynesia

Galapagos Fracture Zone

Equator 0°

Coral Sea

Espiritu Santo

PACIFIC PLATE

FIJI PLATE

Robbie Ridge

Samoa

Savaii

Upoli

Northern Cook Islands

Manihiki Plateau

North New Hebrides Trench

North Fiji Basin

Vanuatu

Fiji

Vanua Levu

Samoa Basin

Penrhyn Basin

Marquesas Islands

Hiva Oa

Tanna

Vitu Levu

Iles Loyaute

New Caledonia

New Hebrides Trench

FIJI PLATE

Capricorn Tablemount

Southern Cook Islands

Society Islands

Tahiti

Society Ridge

Tiki Basin

Tuamotu Islands

Cape Byron

Lord Howe Seamounts

New Caledonia Basin

Norfolk Ridge

Cook Fracture Zone

South Fiji Basin

Lau Basin

Tonga

Rarotonga

Tuamotu Ridge

Tasman Plain

Lord Howe Rise

West Norfolk Ridge

Norfolk Island

Three Kings Rise

Kermadec Ridge

Kermadec Trench

Louisville Ridge

Iles Australes

Iles Gambier

Austral Fracture Zone

Tasman Sea

New Zealand

Bay of Plenty

Southwest

Pitcairn Island

Henderson Island

Ducie Island

Tropic of Capricorn

EAST PACIFIC RISE

NAZCA PLATE

Tasman Plateau

Tasman Basin

South Island

North Island

Southern Alps

Mount Cook 3764m

Chatham Rise

Pacific

South West Cape

Bounty Trough

Chatham Islands

Basin

Agassiz Fracture Zone

Macquarie Ridge

Campbell Plateau

Macquarie Island

SOUTHERN OCEAN

Eltanin Fracture Zone

Udintsev Fracture Zone

PACIFIC PLATE

ANTARCTIC PLATE

ANTARCTICA

Pacific-Antarctic Ridge

Antarctic Circle

POLITICAL AUSTRALASIA AND OCEANIA

Western Australia's mineral wealth has transformed its state capital, Perth, into one of Australia's major cities. Perth is one of the world's most isolated cities – over 2500 miles (4000 km) from the population centres of the eastern seaboard.

VAST EXPANSES OF OCEAN separate this geographically fragmented realm, characterized more by each country's isolation than by any political unity. Australia's and New Zealand's traditional ties with the United Kingdom, as members of the Commonwealth, are now being called into question as Australasian and Oceanian nations are increasingly looking to forge new relationships with neighbouring Asian countries like Japan. External influences have featured strongly in the politics of the Pacific Islands; the various territories of Micronesia were largely under US control until the late 1980s, and France, New Zealand, the USA and the UK still have territories under colonial rule in Polynesia. Nuclear weapons-testing by Western superpowers was widespread during the Cold War period, but has now been discontinued.

POPULATION

DENSITY OF SETTLEMENT in the region is generally low. Australia is one of the least densely populated countries on Earth with over 80% of its population living within 25 miles (40 km) of the coast – mostly in the southeast of the country. New Zealand, and the island groups of Melanesia, Micronesia and Polynesia, are much more densely populated, although many of the smaller islands remain uninhabited.

Population density (people per sq km)

- 0-4
- 5-24
- 25-49
- 50-99
- 100-199
- 200-299
- 300 +

The myriad of small coral islands which are scattered across the Pacific Ocean are often uninhabited, as they offer little shelter from the weather, often no fresh water, and only limited food supplies.

The planes of the Australian Royal Flying Doctor Service are able to cover large expanses of barren land quickly, bringing medical treatment to the most inaccessible and far-flung places.

Map labels:

Northern Mariana Islands (to US)
Mariana Islands
Saipan
Wake Island (to US)
Philippine Sea
Guam (to US)
AGANA
Bikini Atoll
Mi cro ne si
MICRONESIA
Yap
Caroline Islands
Chuuk
Pohnpei PALIKIR
Ralik Chain
Kosrae
Babeldaob OREOR
PALAU
Melane si
NAURU
Equator
PAPUA NEW GUINEA
New Ireland
Wewak
Bismarck Sea
New Britain Rabaul
Solomon Islands
SOLOMON ISLANDS
New Guinea
Madang Ubai
Arawa Bougainville Island
Mount Hagen
Lae
Solomon Sea
New Georgia Islands
HONIARA
Tapini
Guadalcanal
Santa Cruz Islands
PORT MORESBY
VANUATU
Arafura Sea
Torres Strait
Coral Sea
Espiritu Santo Malekula
Efate
PORT-VILA
Darwin
Arnhem Land
Cape York Peninsula
Great Barrier Reef
Coral Sea Islands
New Caledonia (to France)
NOUMÉA
Timor Sea
Joseph Bonaparte Gulf
Katherine
Gulf of Carpentaria
Cairns
Wyndham
Normanton
Townsville
Mackay
PA
Kimberley Plateau
Derby
NORTHERN
Tennant Creek
Hughenden
Great Dividing Range
Broome
Tanami Desert
Mount Isa
QUEENSLAND
Rockhampton
Port Hedland
TERRITORY
Barcaldine
Norfolk Island (to Australia)
Great Sandy Desert
AUSTRALIA
Alice Springs
Simpson Desert
Charleville
Miles
Brisbane
Hamersley Range
Gibson Desert
Cunnamulla
Toowoomba
Grafton
Lake Eyre North
Bourke
Barwon
INDIAN OCEAN
SOUTH AUSTRALIA
Wilcannia
Darling
NEW
Dubbo
Newcastle
Lord Howe Island (to Australia)
Carnarvon
WESTERN AUSTRALIA
Great Victoria Desert
Lake Everard
Lake Gairdner
Port Augusta
SOUTH WALES
Sydney
Campbelltown
Wollongong
Mount Magnet
Lake Torrens
Whyalla
Murray
Wagga Wagga
CANBERRA
AUSTRALIAN CAPITAL TERRITORY
Tropic of Capricorn
Geraldton
Kalgoorlie
Nullarbor Plain
Ceduna
Adelaide
Bendigo
VICTORIA
Tasman Sea
Great Australian Bight
Kangaroo Island
Horsham
Ballarat
Melbourne
Geelong
Perth
Esperance
Mount Gambier
Bass Strait
Launceston
TASMANIA
Albany
Tasmania
Hobart
SOUTHE

LANGUAGES

ENGLISH IS SPOKEN THROUGHOUT New Zealand and Australia, superimposed upon a mosaic of indigenous languages. Many, such as the Papuan dialects and languages – of which there are more than 700 – are only spoken by relatively small numbers of people, although Maori is spoken extensively in parts of New Zealand. In Papua New Guinea, Melanesian Pidgin, derived from English, has become the *lingua franca*. Across Australasia and Oceania, languages can be divided into the many dialects of Austronesian, spoken in Micronesia and Polynesia, and the numerous Papuan languages of Melanesia.

Language groups
Australian
Papuan
Germanic
Malay–Polynesian
Uninhabited

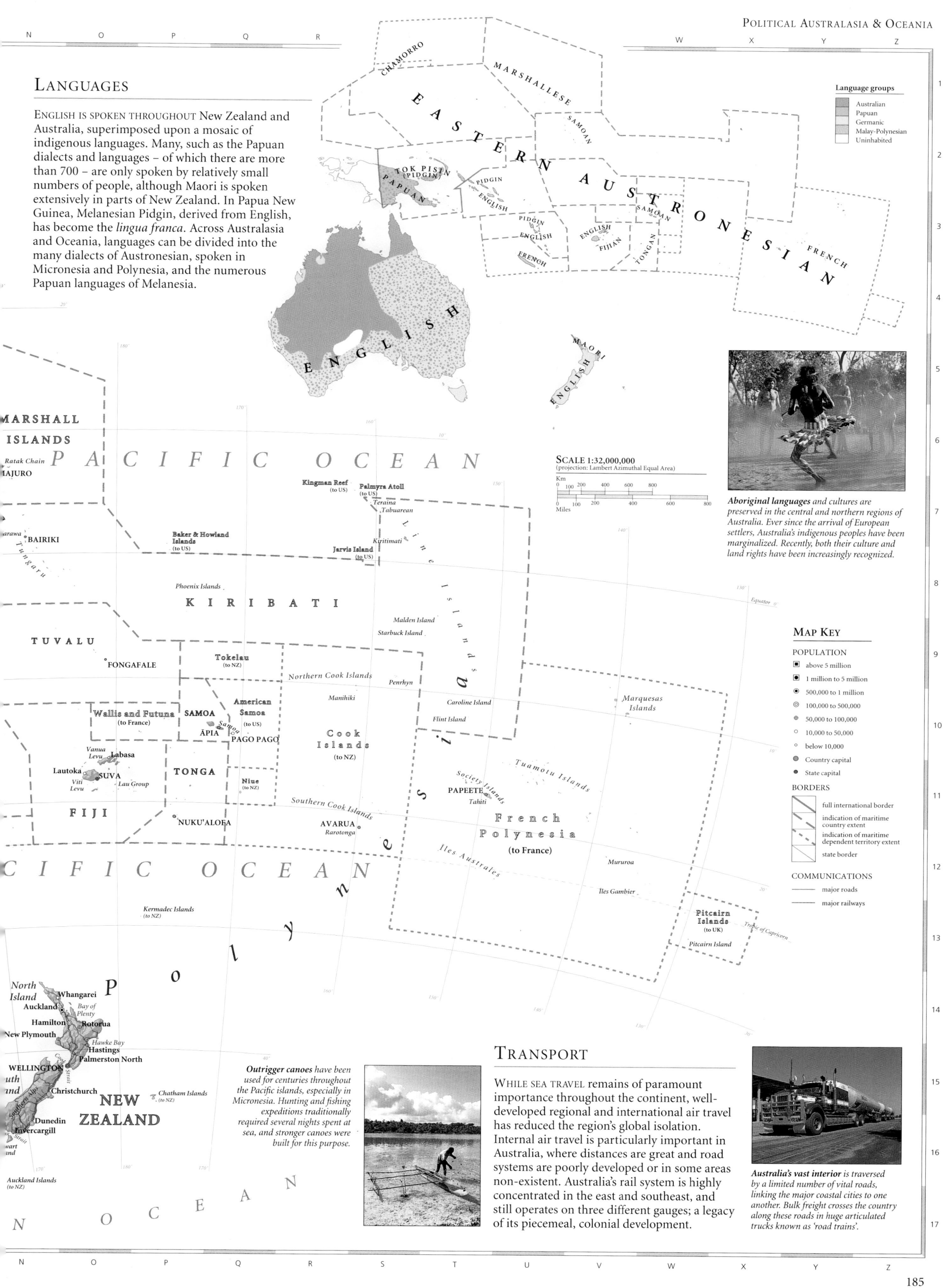

Aboriginal languages and cultures are preserved in the central and northern regions of Australia. Ever since the arrival of European settlers, Australia's indigenous peoples have been marginalized. Recently, both their culture and land rights have been increasingly recognized.

SCALE 1:32,000,000
(projection: Lambert Azimuthal Equal Area)

MAP KEY

POPULATION
- above 5 million
- 1 million to 5 million
- 500,000 to 1 million
- 100,000 to 500,000
- 50,000 to 100,000
- 10,000 to 50,000
- below 10,000
- Country capital
- State capital

BORDERS
- full international border
- indication of maritime country extent
- indication of maritime dependent territory extent
- state border

COMMUNICATIONS
- major roads
- major railways

TRANSPORT

WHILE SEA TRAVEL remains of paramount importance throughout the continent, well-developed regional and international air travel has reduced the region's global isolation. Internal air travel is particularly important in Australia, where distances are great and road systems are poorly developed or in some areas non-existent. Australia's rail system is highly concentrated in the east and southeast, and still operates on three different gauges; a legacy of its piecemeal, colonial development.

Outrigger canoes have been used for centuries throughout the Pacific islands, especially in Micronesia. Hunting and fishing expeditions traditionally required several nights spent at sea, and stronger canoes were built for this purpose.

Australia's vast interior is traversed by a limited number of vital roads, linking the major coastal cities to one another. Bulk freight crosses the country along these roads in huge articulated trucks known as 'road trains'.

AUSTRALASIAN AND OCEANIAN RESOURCES

NATURAL RESOURCES ARE OF MAJOR ECONOMIC IMPORTANCE throughout Australasia and Oceania. Australia in particular is a major world exporter of raw materials such as coal, iron ore and bauxite, while New Zealand's agricultural economy is dominated by sheep-raising. Trade with western Europe has declined significantly in the last 20 years, and the Pacific Rim countries of Southeast Asia are now the main trading partners, as well as a source of new settlers to the region. Australasia and Oceania's greatest resources are its climate and environment; tourism increasingly provides a vital source of income for the whole continent.

The largely unpolluted waters of the Pacific Ocean support rich and varied marine life, much of which is farmed commercially. Here, oysters are gathered for market off the coast of New Zealand's South Island.

Huge flocks of sheep *are a common sight in New Zealand, where they outnumber people by 20 to 1. New Zealand is one of the world's largest exporters of wool and frozen lamb.*

STANDARD OF LIVING

IN MARKED CONTRAST TO ITS NEIGHBOUR, Australia, with one of the world's highest life expectancies and standards of living, Papua New Guinea is one of the world's least developed countries. In addition, high population growth and urbanization rates throughout the Pacific islands contribute to overcrowding. The Aboriginal and Maori people of Australia and New Zealand have been isolated for many years. Recently, their traditional land ownership rights have begun to be legally recognized in an effort to ease their social and economic isolation, and to improve living standards.

Standard of Living
(UN Human Development Index)

low

high

figures unavailable

ENVIRONMENTAL ISSUES

THE PROSPECT OF RISING SEA LEVELS poses a threat to many low-lying islands in the Pacific. Nuclear weapons-testing, once common throughout the region, was finally discontinued in 1996. Australia's ecological balance has been irreversibly altered by the introduction of alien species. Although it has the world's largest underground water reserve, the Great Artesian Basin, the availability of fresh water in Australia remains critical. Periodic droughts combined with over-grazing lead to desertification and increase the risk of devastating bush fires, and occasional flash floods.

Environmental Issues

national parks

tropical forest

forest destroyed

desert

desertification

polluted rivers

radioactive contamination

marine pollution

heavy marine pollution

poor urban air quality

Northern Mariana Islands (to US)

Saipan

Guam (to US)

MICRO

PALAU

Mel

PAPUA NEW GUINEA

New Guinea

Port Moresby

Arafura Sea

Torres Strait

INDIAN OCEAN

Timor Sea

Darwin

Gulf of Carpentaria

Great Barrier Reef

Townsville

AUSTRALIA

Adelaide

Geelo

Perth

SOUTHERN

Bikini Atoll

Eniwetak Atoll

Malden Island

Fangataufa

Coral Sea

PACIFIC OCEAN

INDIAN OCEAN

Murchison

Mackenzie

Darling

Murray

Sydney

Tasman Sea

In 1946 Bikini Atoll, *in the Marshall Islands, was chosen as the site for Operation Crossroads – investigating the effects of atomic bombs upon naval vessels. Further nuclear tests continued until the early 1990s. The long-term environmental effects are unknown.*

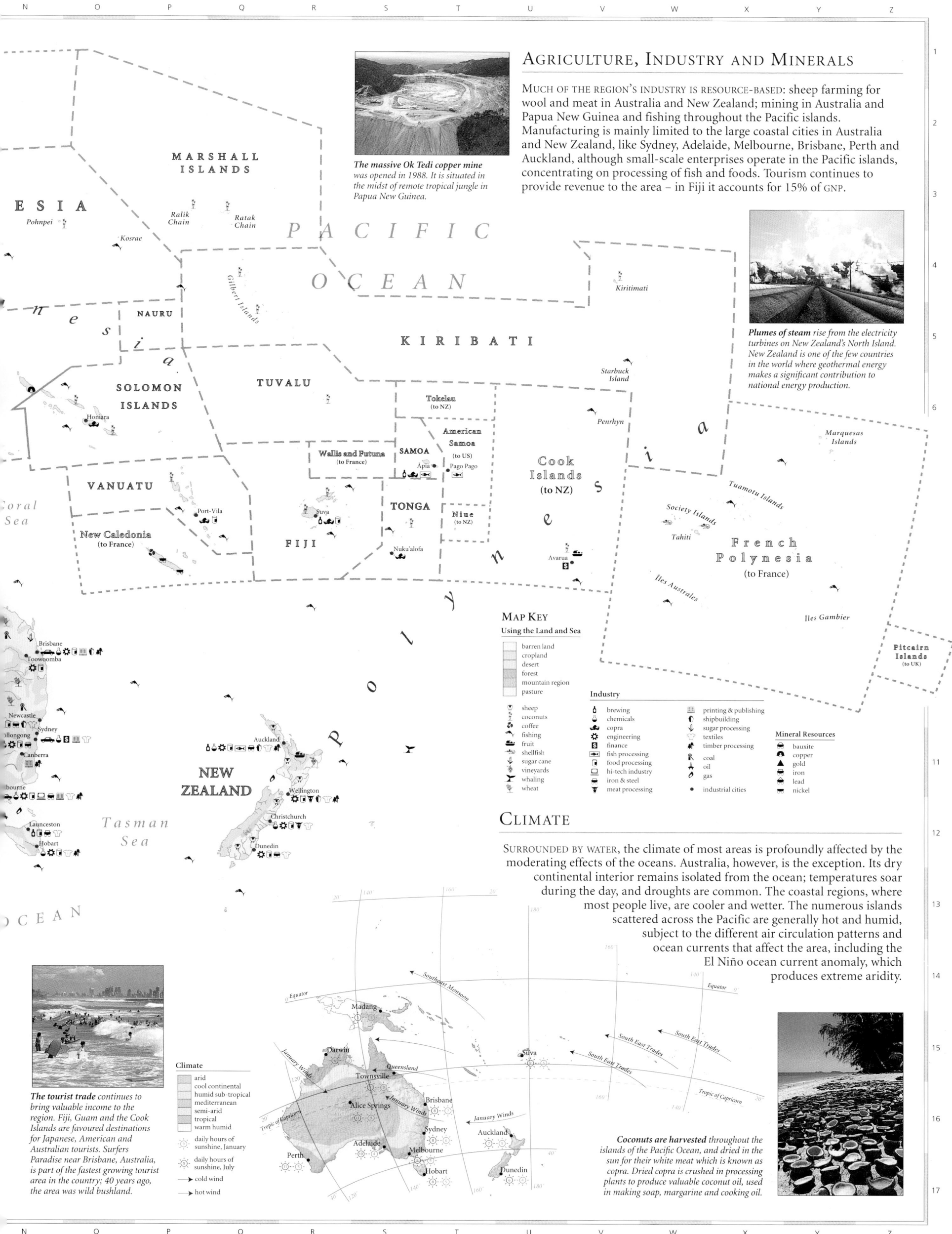

AGRICULTURE, INDUSTRY AND MINERALS

MUCH OF THE REGION'S INDUSTRY IS RESOURCE-BASED: sheep farming for wool and meat in Australia and New Zealand; mining in Australia and Papua New Guinea and fishing throughout the Pacific islands. Manufacturing is mainly limited to the large coastal cities in Australia and New Zealand, like Sydney, Adelaide, Melbourne, Brisbane, Perth and Auckland, although small-scale enterprises operate in the Pacific islands, concentrating on processing of fish and foods. Tourism continues to provide revenue to the area – in Fiji it accounts for 15% of GNP.

The massive Ok Tedi copper mine was opened in 1988. It is situated in the midst of remote tropical jungle in Papua New Guinea.

Plumes of steam rise from the electricity turbines on New Zealand's North Island. New Zealand is one of the few countries in the world where geothermal energy makes a significant contribution to national energy production.

MAP KEY

Using the Land and Sea

barren land
cropland
desert
forest
mountain region
pasture

sheep
coconuts
coffee
fishing
fruit
shellfish
sugar cane
vineyards
whaling
wheat

Industry

brewing
chemicals
copra
engineering
finance
fish processing
food processing
hi-tech industry
iron & steel
meat processing

printing & publishing
shipbuilding
sugar processing
textiles
timber processing
coal
oil
gas
industrial cities

Mineral Resources

bauxite
copper
gold
iron
lead
nickel

CLIMATE

SURROUNDED BY WATER, the climate of most areas is profoundly affected by the moderating effects of the oceans. Australia, however, is the exception. Its dry continental interior remains isolated from the ocean; temperatures soar during the day, and droughts are common. The coastal regions, where most people live, are cooler and wetter. The numerous islands scattered across the Pacific are generally hot and humid, subject to the different air circulation patterns and ocean currents that affect the area, including the El Niño ocean current anomaly, which produces extreme aridity.

Climate

arid
cool continental
humid sub-tropical
mediterranean
semi-arid
tropical
warm humid

daily hours of sunshine, January
daily hours of sunshine, July
cold wind
hot wind

The tourist trade continues to bring valuable income to the region. Fiji, Guam and the Cook Islands are favoured destinations for Japanese, American and Australian tourists. Surfers Paradise near Brisbane, Australia, is part of the fastest growing tourist area in the country; 40 years ago, the area was wild bushland.

Coconuts are harvested throughout the islands of the Pacific Ocean, and dried in the sun for their white meat which is known as copra. Dried copra is crushed in processing plants to produce valuable coconut oil, used in making soap, margarine and cooking oil.

AUSTRALIA

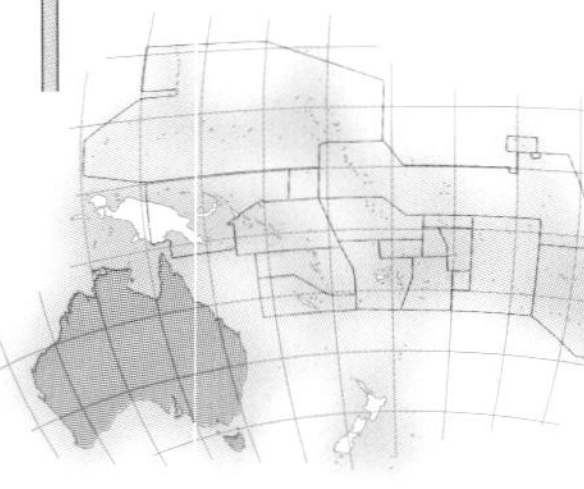

AUSTRALIA IS THE WORLD'S smallest continent, a stable landmass lying between the Indian and Pacific oceans. Previously home only to its aboriginal peoples, since the end of the 18th century immigration has transformed the face of the country. Initially settlers came mainly from western Europe, particularly the UK, and for years Australia remained wedded to its British colonial past. Latterly, more immigrants have come from eastern Europe, and from Asian countries such as Japan, South Korea and Indonesia. Australia is now forging strong trading links with these 'Pacific Rim' countries and its economic future seems to lie with Asia and the Americas, rather than Europe, its traditional partner.

Uluru (Ayers Rock), the world's largest free-standing rock, is a massive outcrop of red sandstone in Australia's desert centre. Wind and sandstorms have ground the rock into the smooth curves seen here. Uluru is revered as a sacred site by many aboriginal peoples.

USING THE LAND

OVER 165 MILLION SHEEP are dispersed in vast herds around the country, contributing to a major export industry. Cattle-ranching is important, particularly in the west. Wheat, and grapes for Australia's wine industry, are grown mainly in the south. Much of the country is desert, unsuitable for agriculture unless irrigation is used.

THE URBAN/RURAL POPULATION DIVIDE

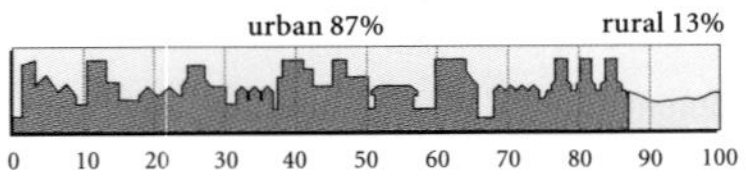

urban 87%   rural 13%

0 10 20 30 40 50 60 70 80 90 100

POPULATION DENSITY	TOTAL LAND AREA
5 people per sq mile (2 people per sq km)	2,967,893 sq miles (7,686,850 sq km)

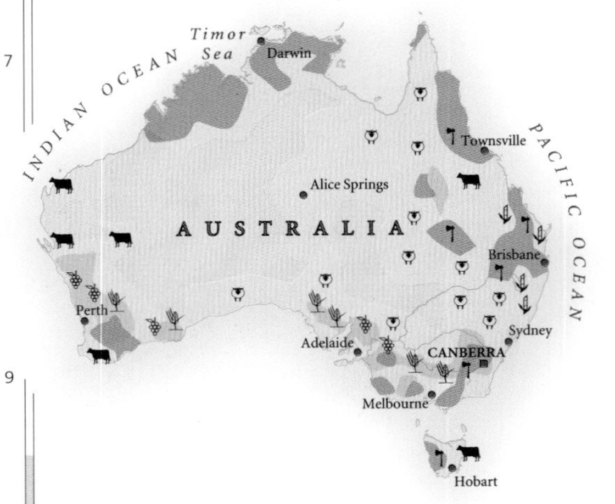

SCALE 1:10,500,000
(projection: Lambert Conformal Conic)

MAP KEY

POPULATION
- 1 million to 5 million
- 500,000 to 1 million
- 100,000 to 500,000
- 50,000 to 100,000
- 10,000 to 50,000
- below 10,000

ELEVATION
- 2000m / 6562ft
- 1000m / 3281ft
- 500m / 1640ft
- 250m / 820ft
- 100m / 328ft
- sea level

Land use and agricultural distribution
- cattle
- sheep
- cereals
- sugar cane
- timber
- vineyards
- capital cities
- major towns
- pasture
- cropland
- forest
- desert
- mountain region

Lines of ripening vines stretch for miles in Barossa Valley, a major wine-growing region near Adelaide.

THE LANDSCAPE

AUSTRALIA CONSISTS OF MANY ERODED PLATEAUX, lying firmly in the middle of the Indo-Australian Plate. It is the world's flattest continent, and the driest, after Antarctica. The coasts tend to be more hilly and fertile, especially in the east. The mountains of the Great Dividing Range form a natural barrier between the eastern coastal areas and the flat, dry plains and desert regions of the Australian 'outback'.

The Great Barrier Reef is the world's largest area of coral islands and reefs. It runs for about 1240 miles (2000 km) along the Queensland coast.

The Pinnacles are a series of rugged sandstone pillars. Their strange shapes have been formed by water and wind erosion.

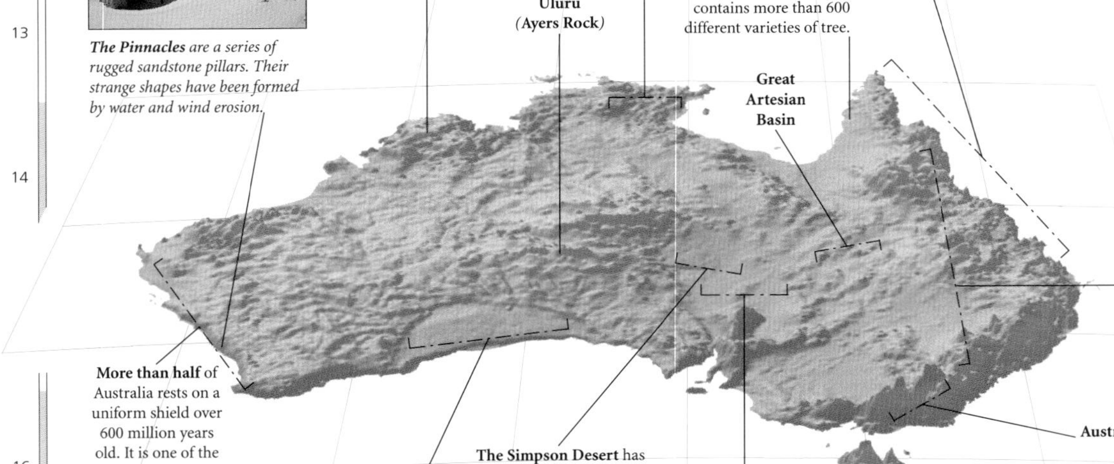

The ancient Kimberley Plateau is the source of some of Australia's richest mineral deposits, including diamonds.

Arnhem Land

Uluru (Ayers Rock)

The tropical rainforest of the Cape York Peninsula contains more than 600 different varieties of tree.

Great Artesian Basin

The Great Dividing Range forms a watershed between east- and west-flowing rivers. Erosion has created deep valleys, gorges and waterfalls where rivers tumble over escarpments on their way to the sea.

More than half of Australia rests on a uniform shield over 600 million years old. It is one of the Earth's original geological plates.

The Simpson Desert has a number of large salt pans, created by the evaporation of past rivers and now sourced by seasonal rains. Some are crusted with gypsum, but most are covered by common salt crystals.

The Nullarbor Plain is a low-lying limestone plateau which is so flat that the Trans-Australian Railway runs through it in a straight line for more than 300 miles (483 km).

The Lake Eyre Basin, lying 51 ft (16 m) below sea level, is one of the largest inland drainage systems in the world, covering an area of more than 500,000 sq miles (1,300,000 sq km).

Australian Alps

Tasmania has the same geological structure as the Australian Alps. During the last period of glaciation, 18,000 years ago, sea levels were some 300 ft (100 m) lower and it was joined to the mainland.

Great Artesian Basin

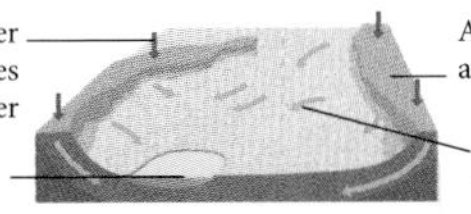

Rainwater replenishes aquifer

Aquifers from which artesian water is obtained

Lake Eyre

Underground water movements

The Great Artesian Basin underlies nearly 20% of the total area of Australia, providing a valuable store of underground water, essential to Australian agriculture. The ephemeral rivers which drain the northern part of the basin have highly braided courses and, in consequence, the area is known as 'channel country'

Map labels

Cape Londonderry, Cape Bougainville, Kalumburu, Bigge Island, Bonaparte Archipelago, Heywood Islands, Adele Island, Mount Hann, Collier Bay, Kimberley, Kupingarri, Plateau, King Leopold Range, Lombadina, King Sound, Derby, Fitzroy Crossing, Fitzroy River, Broome, Great Sandy Desert, Port Hedland, De Grey River, Percival Lakes, Tobin Lake, Dampier Archipelago, Wickham, Whim Creek, Marble Bar, Dampier, Karratha, Roebourne, Barrow Island, Onslow, Fortescue River, Lake Dora, Lake Auld, North West Cape, Hamersley Range, Wittenoom, Exmouth, Ashburton River, Tom Price, Lake Disappointment, Learmonth, Paraburdoo, Mount Meharry 1251m, Newman, Little Sandy Desert, Gibson Desert, Coral Bay, Kenneth Range, Kulmarina Roadhouse, WESTERN, Tropic of Capricorn, Minilya, Mount Augustus 1105m, Waldburg Range, Carnarvon Range, Lake Gregory, Lake Carnegie, Lake Macleod, Gascoyne River, Gascoyne Junction, Robinson Range, Wiluna, Lake Wells, Bernier Island, Carnarvon, Meekatharra, Lake Way, Dorre Island, Shark Bay, Denham, Murchison River, Lake Annean, Lake Austin, AUSTRALIA, Lake Throssell, Dirk Hartog Island, Lake Yeo, Kalbarri, Mount Magnet, Lake Carey, Yalgoo, Leonora, Menzies, Lake Ballard, Lake Rebecca, Mongers Lake, Lake Barlee, Geraldton, Lake Moore, Wubin, Pithara, Kalgoorlie, Coolgardie, Kambalda, Lake Lefroy, Kitchener, Moora, The Pinnacles, Southern Cross, Lake Cowan, Wanneroo, Merredin, Norseman, Balladonia, Gingin, Northam, Lake Johnston, Lake Dundas, Perth, York, Brookton, Tower Peak 594m, Fremantle, Rockingham, Kondinin, Lake Hope, Mandurah, Narrogin, Lake King, Esperance, Collie, Wagin, Bunbury, Katanning, Ravensthorpe, Busselton, Bridgetown, Manjimup, Stirling, Margaret River, Pemberton, Mount Barker, Cape Leeuwin, Augusta, Albany, INDIAN OCEAN, Timor Sea, Darwin, Townsville, Alice Springs, Brisbane, Perth, Sydney, Adelaide, CANBERRA, Melbourne, Hobart, PACIFIC OCEAN

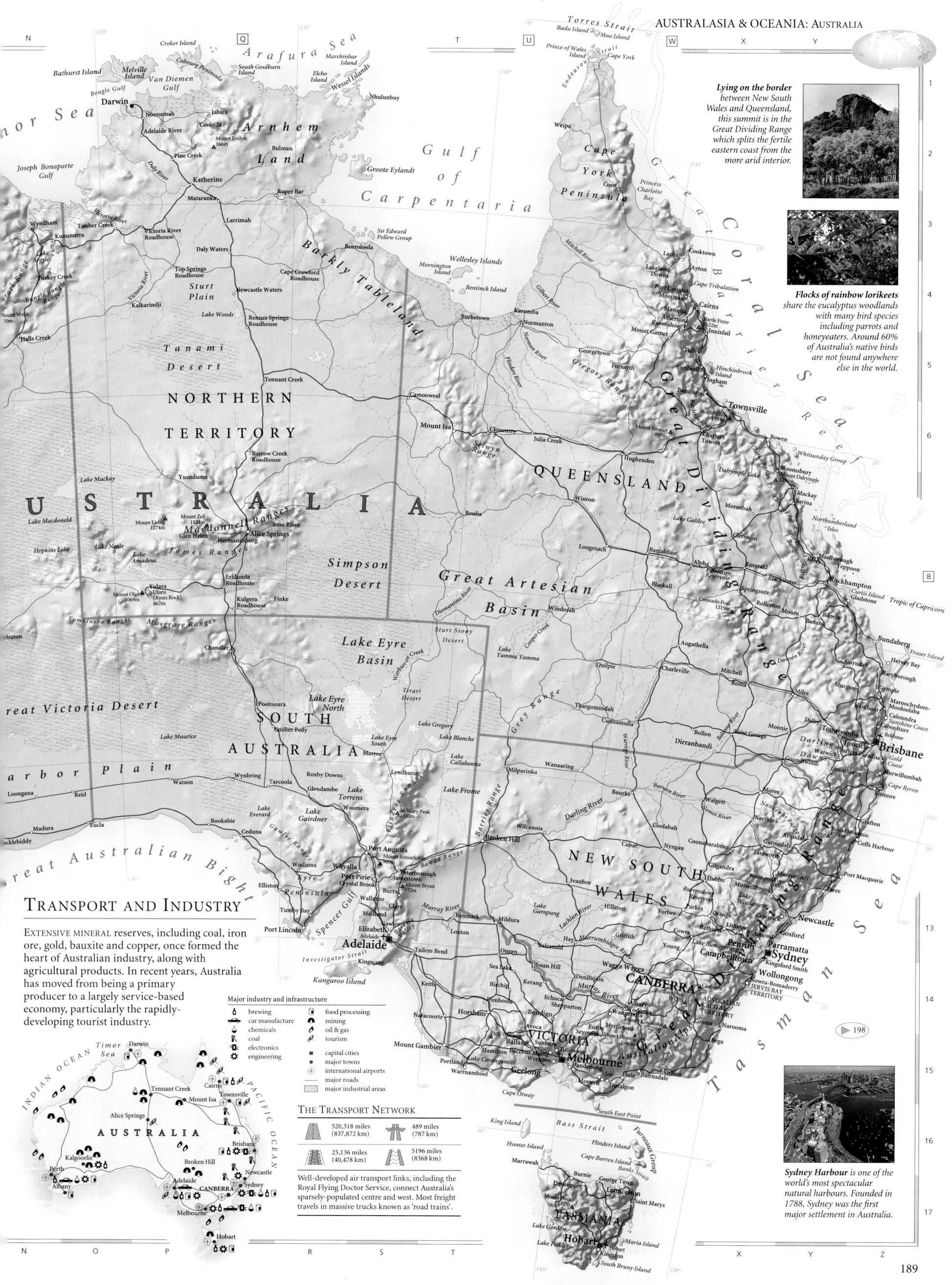

Lying on the border between New South Wales and Queensland, this summit is in the Great Dividing Range which splits the fertile eastern coast from the more arid interior.

Flocks of rainbow lorikeets share the eucalyptus woodlands with many bird species including parrots and honeyeaters. Around 60% of Australia's native birds are not found anywhere else in the world.

TRANSPORT AND INDUSTRY

EXTENSIVE MINERAL reserves, including coal, iron ore, gold, bauxite and copper, once formed the heart of Australian industry, along with agricultural products. In recent years, Australia has moved from being a primary producer to a largely service-based economy, particularly the rapidly-developing tourist industry.

Major industry and infrastructure

- brewing
- car manufacture
- chemicals
- coal
- electronics
- engineering
- food processing
- mining
- oil & gas
- tourism
- ■ capital cities
- □ major towns
- ✈ international airports
- — major roads
- major industrial areas

THE TRANSPORT NETWORK

520,318 miles (837,872 km)	489 miles (787 km)
25,136 miles (40,478 km)	5196 miles (8368 km)

Well-developed air transport links, including the Royal Flying Doctor Service, connect Australia's sparsely-populated centre and west. Most freight travels in massive trucks known as 'road trains'.

Sydney Harbour is one of the world's most spectacular natural harbours. Founded in 1788, Sydney was the first major settlement in Australia.

▶ 198

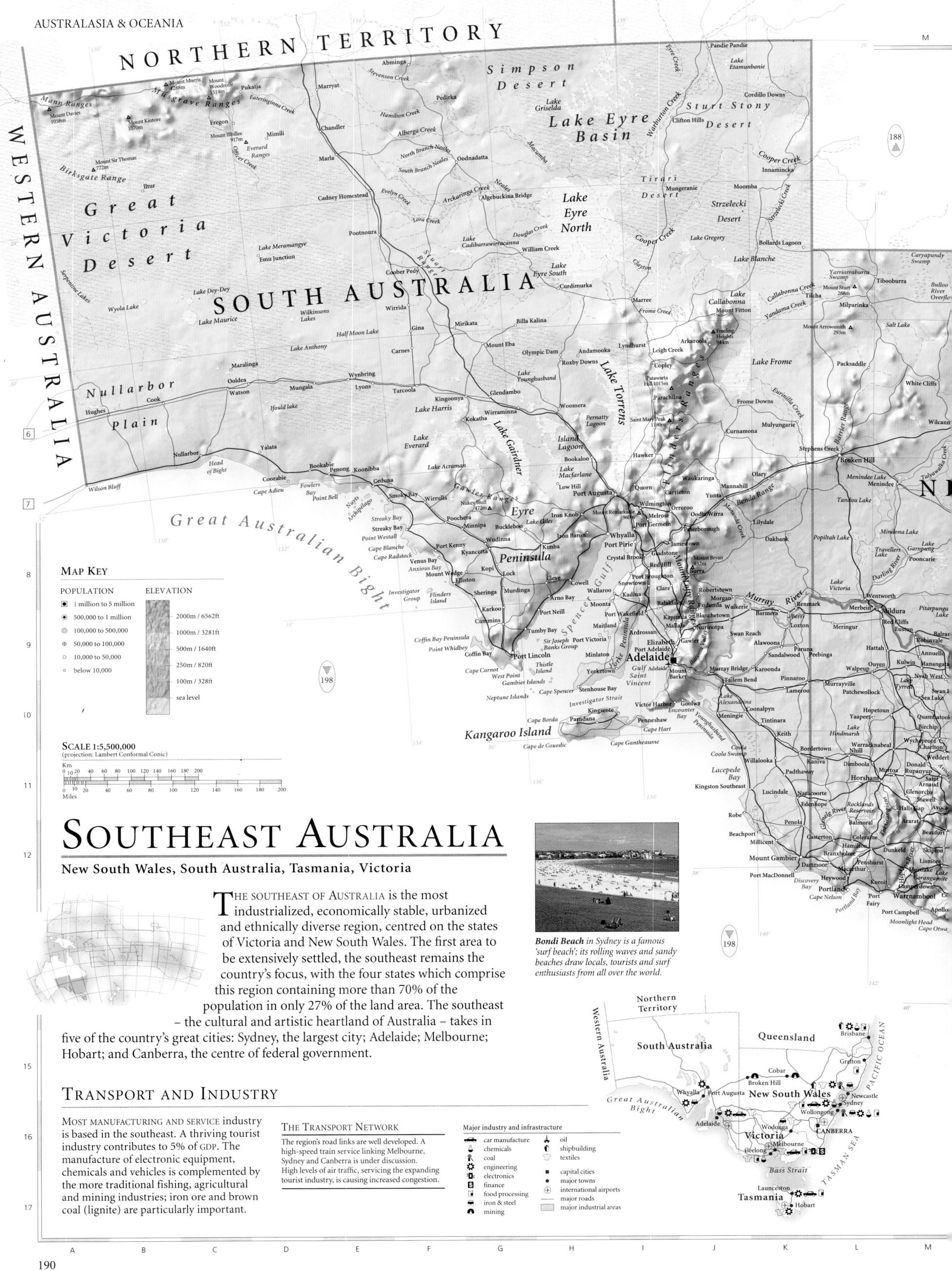

MAP KEY

POPULATION

- ▣ 1 million to 5 million
- ◉ 500,000 to 1 million
- ⊕ 100,000 to 500,000
- ⊕ 50,000 to 100,000
- ○ 10,000 to 50,000
- ○ below 10,000

ELEVATION

- 2000m / 6562ft
- 1000m / 3281ft
- 500m / 1640ft
- 250m / 820ft
- 100m / 328ft
- sea level

SCALE 1:5,500,000
(projection: Lambert Conformal Conic)

SOUTHEAST AUSTRALIA

New South Wales, South Australia, Tasmania, Victoria

THE SOUTHEAST OF AUSTRALIA is the most industrialized, economically stable, urbanized and ethnically diverse region, centred on the states of Victoria and New South Wales. The first area to be extensively settled, the southeast remains the country's focus, with the four states which comprise this region containing more than 70% of the population in only 27% of the land area. The southeast – the cultural and artistic heartland of Australia – takes in five of the country's great cities: Sydney, the largest city; Adelaide; Melbourne; Hobart; and Canberra, the centre of federal government.

Bondi Beach *in Sydney is a famous 'surf beach'; its rolling waves and sandy beaches draw locals, tourists and surf enthusiasts from all over the world.*

TRANSPORT AND INDUSTRY

MOST MANUFACTURING AND SERVICE industry is based in the southeast. A thriving tourist industry contributes to 5% of GDP. The manufacture of electronic equipment, chemicals and vehicles is complemented by the more traditional fishing, agricultural and mining industries; iron ore and brown coal (lignite) are particularly important.

THE TRANSPORT NETWORK

The region's road links are well developed. A high-speed train service linking Melbourne, Sydney and Canberra is under discussion. High levels of air traffic, servicing the expanding tourist industry, is causing increased congestion.

Major industry and infrastructure

- car manufacture
- chemicals
- coal
- engineering
- electronics
- finance
- food processing
- iron & steel
- mining
- oil
- shipbuilding
- textiles
- ■ capital cities
- ■ major towns
- ⊕ international airports
- major roads
- major industrial areas

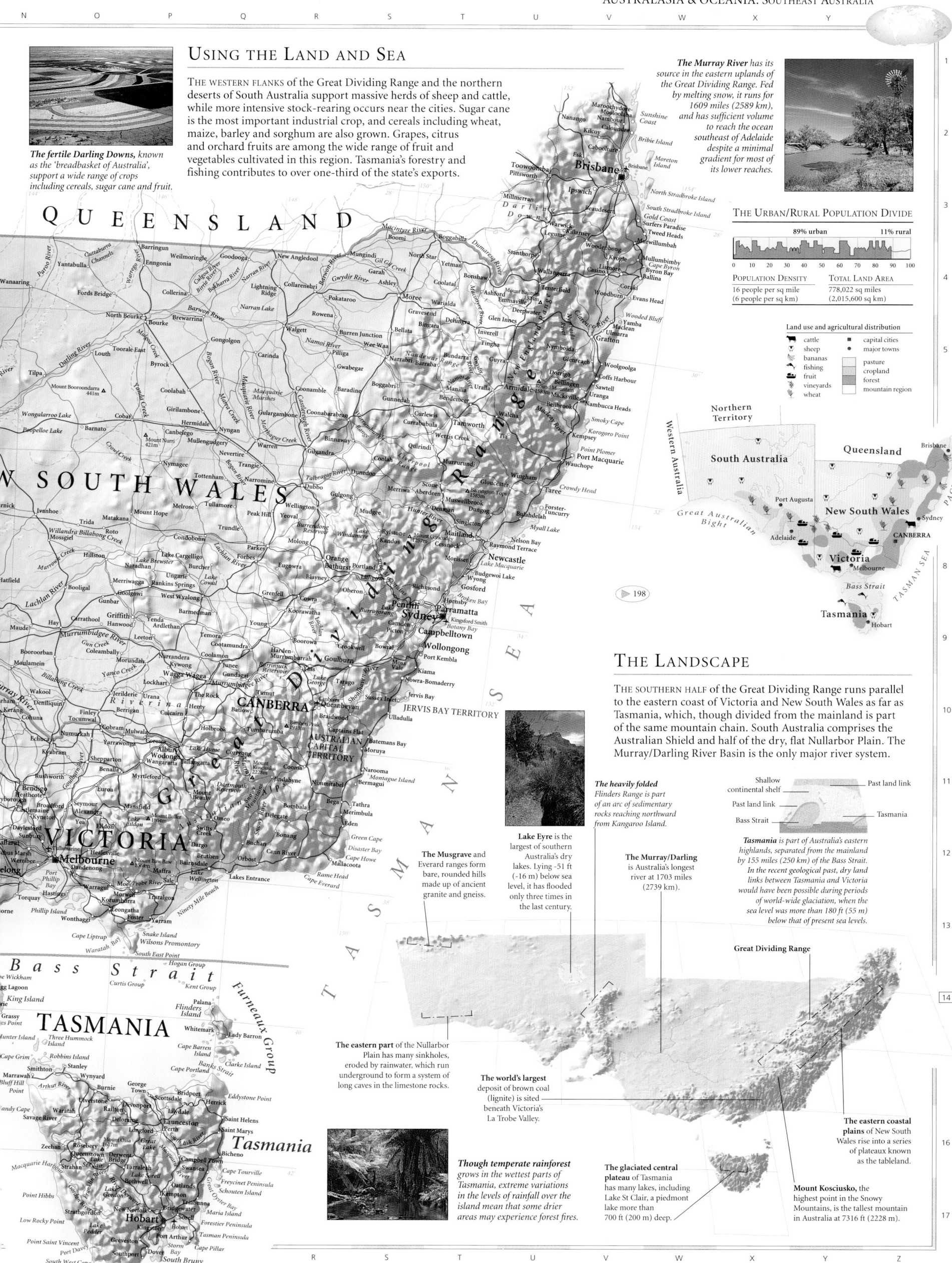

USING THE LAND AND SEA

THE WESTERN FLANKS of the Great Dividing Range and the northern deserts of South Australia support massive herds of sheep and cattle, while more intensive stock-rearing occurs near the cities. Sugar cane is the most important industrial crop, and cereals including wheat, maize, barley and sorghum are also grown. Grapes, citrus and orchard fruits are among the wide range of fruit and vegetables cultivated in this region. Tasmania's forestry and fishing contributes to over one-third of the state's exports.

The fertile Darling Downs, known as the 'breadbasket of Australia', support a wide range of crops including cereals, sugar cane and fruit.

The Murray River has its source in the eastern uplands of the Great Dividing Range. Fed by melting snow, it runs for 1609 miles (2589 km), and has sufficient volume to reach the ocean southeast of Adelaide despite a minimal gradient for most of its lower reaches.

THE URBAN/RURAL POPULATION DIVIDE

89% urban   11% rural

0 10 20 30 40 50 60 70 80 90 100

POPULATION DENSITY	TOTAL LAND AREA
16 people per sq mile (6 people per sq km)	778,022 sq miles (2,015,600 sq km)

Land use and agricultural distribution

- cattle
- sheep
- bananas
- fishing
- fruit
- vineyards
- wheat
- capital cities
- major towns
- pasture
- cropland
- forest
- mountain region

▶ 198

THE LANDSCAPE

THE SOUTHERN HALF of the Great Dividing Range runs parallel to the eastern coast of Victoria and New South Wales as far as Tasmania, which, though divided from the mainland is part of the same mountain chain. South Australia comprises the Australian Shield and half of the dry, flat Nullarbor Plain. The Murray/Darling River Basin is the only major river system.

The heavily folded Flinders Range is part of an arc of sedimentary rocks reaching northward from Kangaroo Island.

Lake Eyre is the largest of southern Australia's dry lakes. Lying -51 ft (-16 m) below sea level, it has flooded only three times in the last century.

The Musgrave and Everard ranges form bare, rounded hills made up of ancient granite and gneiss.

The Murray/Darling is Australia's longest river at 1703 miles (2739 km).

Tasmania is part of Australia's eastern highlands, separated from the mainland by 155 miles (250 km) of the Bass Strait. In the recent geological past, dry land links between Tasmania and Victoria would have been possible during periods of world-wide glaciation, when the sea level was more than 180 ft (55 m) below that of present sea levels.

- Shallow continental shelf
- Past land link
- Past land link
- Bass Strait
- Tasmania

Great Dividing Range

The eastern part of the Nullarbor Plain has many sinkholes, eroded by rainwater, which run underground to form a system of long caves in the limestone rocks.

The world's largest deposit of brown coal (lignite) is sited beneath Victoria's La Trobe Valley.

Though temperate rainforest grows in the wettest parts of Tasmania, extreme variations in the levels of rainfall over the island mean that some drier areas may experience forest fires.

The glaciated central plateau of Tasmania has many lakes, including Lake St Clair, a piedmont lake more than 700 ft (200 m) deep.

Mount Kosciusko, the highest point in the Snowy Mountains, is the tallest mountain in Australia at 7316 ft (2228 m).

The eastern coastal plains of New South Wales rise into a series of plateaux known as the tableland.

NEW ZEALAND

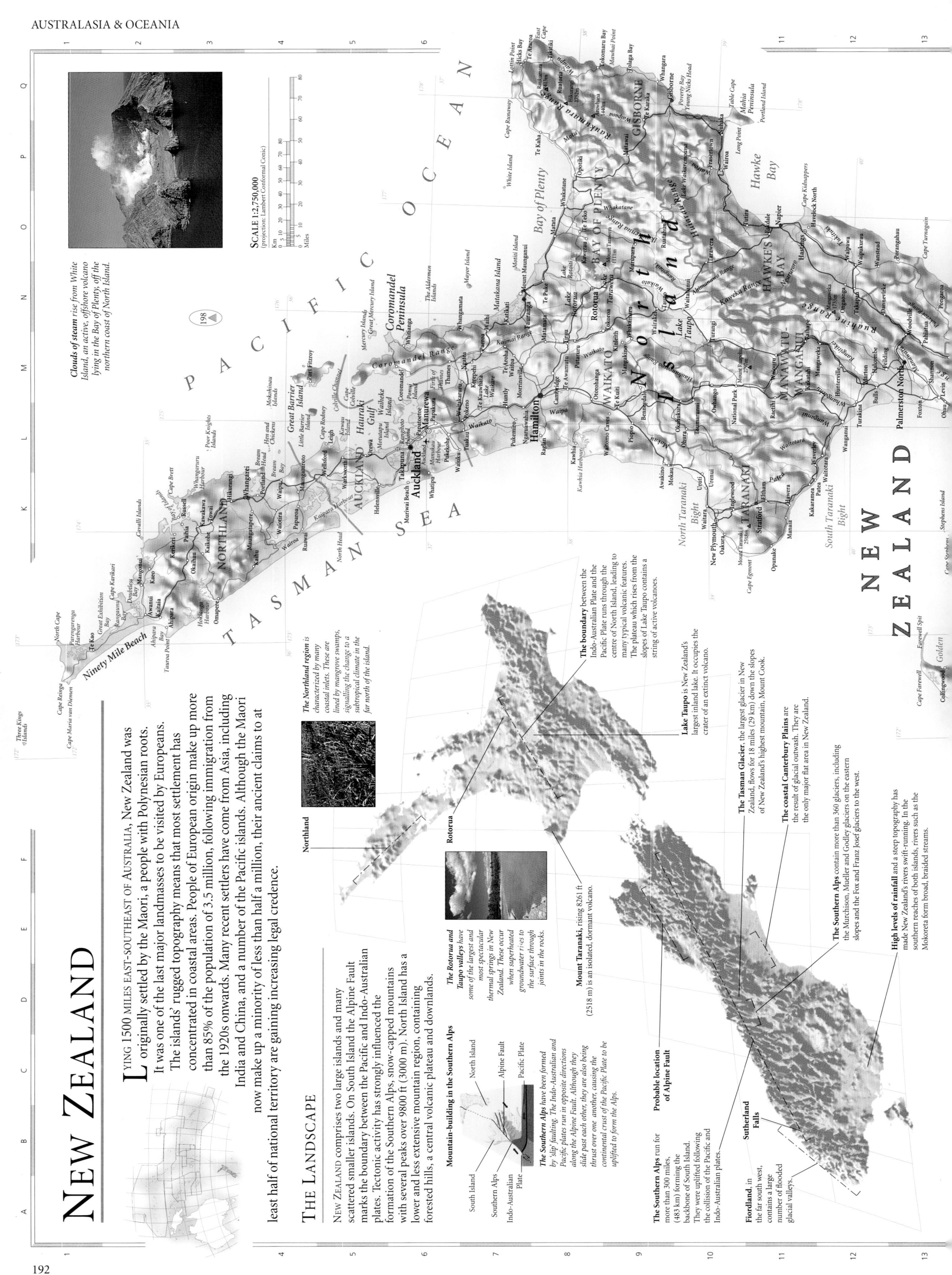

LYING 1500 MILES EAST-SOUTHEAST OF AUSTRALIA, New Zealand was originally settled by the Maori, a people with Polynesian roots. It was one of the last major landmasses to be visited by Europeans. The islands' rugged topography means that most settlement has concentrated in coastal areas. People of European origin make up more than 85% of the population of 3.5 million, following immigration from the 1920s onwards. Many recent settlers have come from Asia, including India and China, and a number of the Pacific islands. Although the Maori now make up a minority of less than half a million, their ancient claims to at least half of national territory are gaining increasing legal credence.

THE LANDSCAPE

NEW ZEALAND comprises two large islands and many scattered smaller islands. On South Island the Alpine Fault marks the boundary between the Pacific and Indo-Australian plates. Tectonic activity has strongly influenced the formation of the Southern Alps, snow-capped mountains with several peaks over 9800 ft (3000 m). North Island has a lower and less extensive mountain region, containing forested hills, a central volcanic plateau and downlands.

Mountain-building in the Southern Alps

North Island
Alpine Fault
Pacific Plate

South Island
Southern Alps
Indo-Australian Plate

The Southern Alps have been formed by slip faulting. The Indo-Australian and Pacific plates run in opposite directions along the Alpine Fault. Although they slide past each other, they are also being thrust over one another, causing the continental crust of the Pacific Plate to be uplifted to form the Alps.

The Southern Alps run for more than 300 miles (483 km) forming the backbone of South Island. They were uplifted following the collision of the Pacific and Indo-Australian plates.

Probable location of Alpine Fault

Fiordland, in the far south west, contains a large number of flooded glacial valleys.

Sutherland Falls

The Northland region is characterized by many coastal inlets. These are lined by mangrove swamps, signalling the change to a subtropical climate in the far north of the island.

Northland

The Rotorua and Taupo valleys have some of the largest and most spectacular thermal springs in New Zealand. These occur when superheated groundwater rises to the surface through joints in the rocks.

Rotorua

Mount Taranaki, rising 8261 ft (2518 m) is an isolated, dormant volcano.

The boundary between the Indo-Australian Plate and the Pacific Plate runs through the centre of North Island, leading to many typical volcanic features. The plateau which rises from the slopes of Lake Taupo contains a string of active volcanoes.

Lake Taupo is New Zealand's largest inland lake. It occupies the crater of an extinct volcano.

The Tasman Glacier, the largest glacier in New Zealand, flows for 18 miles (29 km) down the slopes of New Zealand's highest mountain, Mount Cook.

The coastal Canterbury Plains are the result of glacial outwash. They are the only major flat area in New Zealand.

The Southern Alps contain more than 360 glaciers, including the Murchison, Mueller and Godley glaciers on the eastern slopes and the Fox and Franz Josef glaciers to the west.

High levels of rainfall and a steep topography has made New Zealand's rivers swift-running. In the southern reaches of both islands, rivers such as the Mokoreta form broad, braided streams.

Clouds of steam rise from White Island, an active, offshore volcano lying in the Bay of Plenty, off the northern coast of North Island.

SCALE 1:2,750,000
(projection: Lambert Conformal Conic)

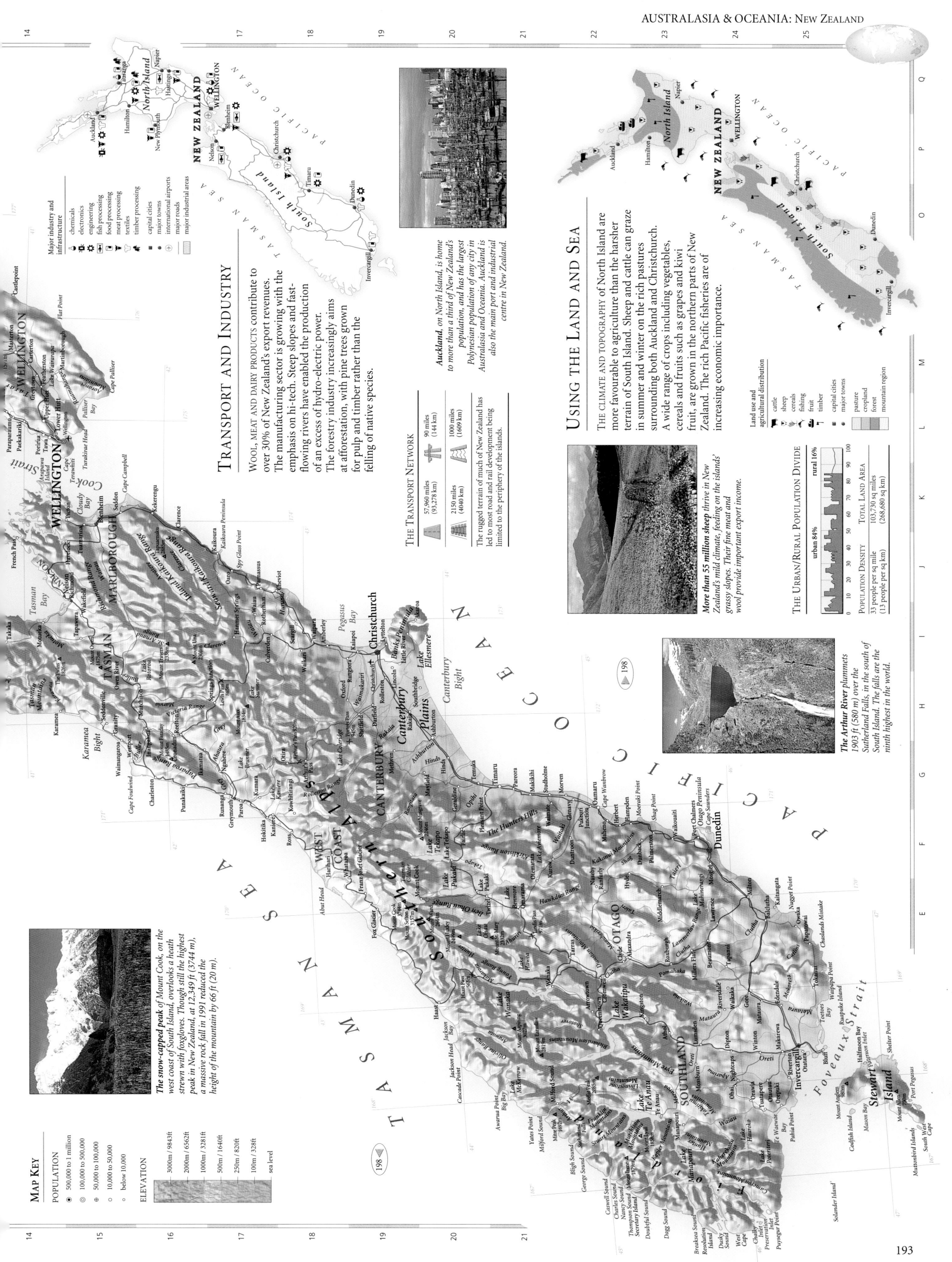

Transport and Industry

WOOL, MEAT AND DAIRY PRODUCTS contribute to over 30% of New Zealand's export revenues. The manufacturing sector is growing with the emphasis on hi-tech. Steep slopes and fast-flowing rivers have enabled the production of an excess of hydro-electric power. The forestry industry increasingly aims at afforestation, with pine trees grown for pulp and timber rather than the felling of native species.

Auckland, on North Island, is home to more than a third of New Zealand's population, and has the largest Polynesian population of any city in Australasia and Oceania. Auckland is also the main port and industrial centre in New Zealand.

The Transport Network

	90 miles (144 km)
	1000 miles (1609 km)
57,960 miles (93,278 km)	
2150 miles (4040 km)	

The rugged terrain of much of New Zealand has led to most road and rail development being limited to the periphery of the islands.

Using the Land and Sea

THE CLIMATE AND TOPOGRAPHY of North Island are more favourable to agriculture than the harsher terrain of South Island. Sheep and cattle can graze in summer and winter on the rich pastures surrounding both Auckland and Christchurch. A wide range of crops including vegetables, cereals and fruits such as grapes and kiwi fruit, are grown in the northern parts of New Zealand. The rich Pacific fisheries are of increasing economic importance.

More than 55 million sheep thrive in New Zealand's mild climate, feeding on the islands' grassy slopes. Their fine meat and wool provide important export income.

The Arthur River plummets 1903 ft (580 m) over the Sutherland Falls, in the south of South Island. The falls are the ninth highest in the world.

The Urban/Rural Population Divide

	urban 84%	rural 16%

POPULATION DENSITY	TOTAL LAND AREA
33 people per sq mile (13 people per sq km)	103,730 sq miles (268,680 sq km)

Land use and agricultural distribution
- cattle
- sheep
- fishing
- fruit
- timber
- capital cities
- major towns
- pasture
- cropland
- forest
- mountain region

The snow-capped peak of Mount Cook, on the west coast of South Island, overlooks a heath strewn with foxgloves. Though still the highest peak in New Zealand, at 12,349 ft (3744 m), a massive rock fall in 1991 reduced the height of the mountain by 66 ft (20 m).

Map Key

POPULATION
- 500,000 to 1 million
- 100,000 to 500,000
- 50,000 to 100,000
- 10,000 to 50,000
- below 10,000

ELEVATION
- 3000m / 9843ft
- 2000m / 6562ft
- 1000m / 3281ft
- 500m / 1640ft
- 250m / 820ft
- 100m / 328ft
- sea level

Major industry and infrastructure
- chemicals
- electronics
- engineering
- fish processing
- food processing
- meat processing
- textiles
- timber processing
- capital cities
- major towns
- international airports
- major roads
- major industrial areas

PAPUA NEW GUINEA & THE SOLOMON ISLANDS

Cut off by inaccessible, largely mountainous terrain, the peoples of Papua New Guinea have maintained a remarkable diversity of language and culture. There are over 750 separate languages, and yet more distinct tribes. Much of the country remains isolated, with many of the indigenous inhabitants of the interior living as hunter-gatherers. To the east of Papua New Guinea, the Solomons form an archipelago of several hundred islands, scattered over an area of 252,897 sq miles (655,000 sq km). The Solomon Islanders, a mainly Melanesian people, live on the six largest islands.

USING THE LAND AND SEA

Most agriculture in Papua New Guinea is at a subsistence level, with more than two-thirds of the land used for rough grazing, particularly for pigs. The tropical rainforest is a rich timber resource. The Solomon Islanders rely heavily on coconuts for export revenue and fishing, mainly for tuna, is a staple industry.

TRANSPORT AND INDUSTRY

Papua New Guinea has substantial mineral resources including the world's largest copper reserves at Panguna on Bougainville Island; gold, and potential oil and natural gas. Political instability on Bougainville and an undeveloped infrastructure deters the investment necessary for exploition of these reserves. The Solomon Islanders rely mainly on copra and timber with some production of palm oil and cocoa. Traditional crafts are made for the tourist market and for export.

Much of Papua New Guinea and the Solomons is inaccessible by road. A network of airstrips serves even remote villages on the islands. The Solomons' airport has been extended to take jumbo jets to improve connections for tourism.

The slopes of this extinct volcano near Talasea on the island of New Britain have been almost entirely colonized by rainforest vegetation.

Major industry and infrastructure
- beverages
- coffee processing
- copra processing
- food processing
- mining
- textiles
- timber processing
- capital cities
- major towns
- international airports
- major roads

Land use and agricultural distribution
- bananas
- cocoa
- coconuts
- fishing
- oil palms
- rubber
- timber
- capital cities
- major towns
- cropland
- forest
- wetland

Over 70% of Papua New Guinea is covered by dense, tropical rainforest, sustained by high levels of rainfall. Uncontrolled logging in the formerly inaccessible rainforest has led to species loss and soil erosion on steep slopes.

THE URBAN/RURAL POPULATION DIVIDE

urban 15%   rural 85%

0 10 20 30 40 50 60 70 80 90 100

POPULATION DENSITY
15 people per sq mile
(6 people per sq km)

TOTAL LAND AREA
290,210 sq miles
(751,840 sq km)

MAP KEY

POPULATION
- ◎ 100,000 to 500,000
- ⊕ 50,000 to 100,000
- ○ 10,000 to 50,000
- ○ below 10,000

ELEVATION
- 4000m / 13,124ft
- 3000m / 9843ft
- 2000m / 6562ft
- 1000m / 3281ft
- 500m / 1640ft
- 250m / 820ft
- 100m / 328ft
- sea level

Huli tribesmen from Southern Highlands Province in Papua New Guinea parade in ceremonial dress, their powdered wigs decorated with exotic plumage and their faces and bodies painted with coloured pigments.

SCALE 1:5,500,000
(projection: Mercator)

MICRONESIA

MARSHALL ISLANDS, MICRONESIA, NAURU, PALAU,
Guam, Northern Mariana Islands, Wake Island

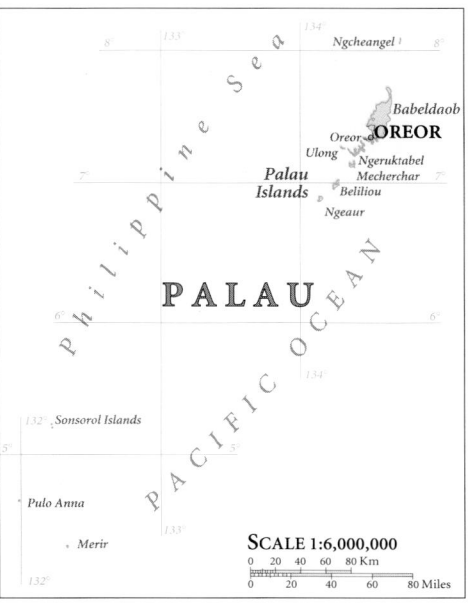

THE MICRONESIAN ISLANDS lie in the western reaches of the Pacific Ocean and are all part of the same volcanic zone. The Federated States of Micronesia is the largest group, with more than 600 atolls and forested volcanic islands in an area of more than 1120 sq miles (2900 sq km). Micronesia is a mixture of former colonies, overseas territories and dependencies. Most of the region still relies on aid and subsidies to sustain economies limited by resources, isolation, and an emigrating population, drawn to New Zealand and Australia by the attractions of a western lifestyle.

PALAU

PALAU IS AN ARCHIPELAGO OF OVER 200 ISLANDS, only eight of which are inhabited. It was the last remaining UN trust territory in the Pacific, controlled by the USA until 1994, when it became independent. The economy operates on a subsistence level, with coconuts and cassava the principal crops. Fishing licences and tourism provide foreign currency.

SCALE 1:750,000

SCALE 1:6,000,000

GUAM (to US)

LYING AT THE SOUTHERN END of the Mariana Islands, Guam is an important US military base and tourist destination. Social and political life is dominated by the indigenous Chamorro, who make up just under half the population, although the increasing prevalence of western culture threatens Guam's traditional social stability.

The tranquillity of these coastal lagoons, at Inarajan in southern Guam, belies the fact that the island lies in a region where typhoons are common.

SCALE 1:825,000

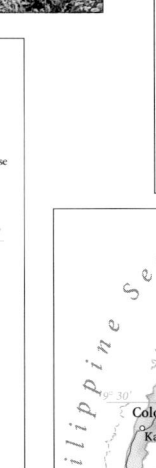

SCALE 1:825,000

NORTHERN MARIANA ISLANDS (to US)

A US COMMONWEALTH TERRITORY, the Northern Marianas comprise the whole of the Mariana archipelago except for Guam. The islands retain their close links with the United States and continue to receive US aid. Tourism, though bringing in much-needed revenue, has speeded the decline of the traditional subsistence economy. Most of the population lives on Saipan.

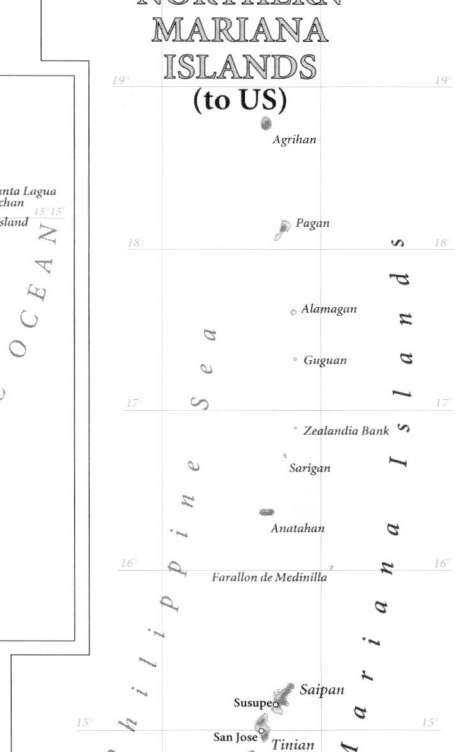

SCALE 1:500,000

The Palau Islands have numerous hidden lakes and lagoons. These sustain their own ecosystems which have developed in isolation. This has produced adaptations in the animals and plants which are often unique to each lake.

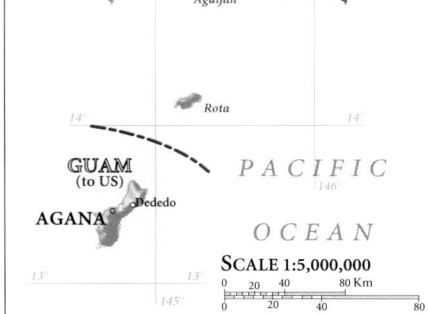

SCALE 1:5,000,000

MICRONESIA

A MIXTURE OF HIGH VOLCANIC ISLANDS and low-lying coral atolls, the Federated States of Micronesia include all the Caroline Islands except Palau. Pohnpei, Kosrae, Chuuk and Yap are the four main island cluster states, each of which has its own language, with English remaining the official language. Nearly half the population is concentrated on Pohnpei, the largest island. Independent since 1979, the islands continue to receive considerable aid from the USA which supplements an economy based primarily on fishing and copra processing.

Ulithi Atoll, lying in the state of Yap, the most westerly part of Micronesia, is a typical coral island, with a series of reefs enclosing a large lagoon.

A B C D E F G H I J K L

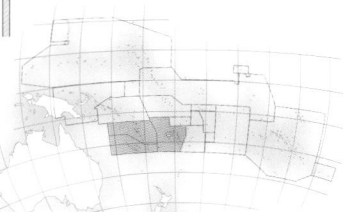

MELANESIA

FIJI, VANUATU, *New Caledonia* (to France)

THREE MAIN ISLAND groups make up the area of southern Melanesia in the southwestern Pacific: the independent countries of Fiji and Vanuatu and the French overseas territory of New Caledonia. The major Melanesian island group, the Solomon Islands, lies to the east of Papua New Guinea (pages 194–95). Most of the larger islands are volcanic in origin; the smaller ones are mainly coral atolls and are largely uninhabited. The economy in all three island groups is increasingly driven by tourism, not necessarily to the benefit of other economic activities.

VANUATU

A STRING OF MOUNTAINOUS VOLCANIC ISLANDS covering more than 800 sq miles (1300 sq km) of the south Pacific, Vanuatu achieved independence from France and the UK in 1980. The majority of the population relies on subsistence fishing and agriculture. Once-important copra and cocoa exports are declining as a result of cost-effective substitutes from elsewhere, and alternatives are being explored. There is further resource potential in the forests and fishing grounds, and beef and arable farming are of growing importance. Tourism, accounting for 40% of GDP, is the fastest-growing sector of the economy, and further expansion is planned.

SCALE 1:6,000,000
(projection: Lambert Conformal Conic)

NEW CALEDONIA (to France)

NEW CALEDONIA, a French overseas territory known as Kanaky by its indigenous peoples, comprises a large main island, 260 miles (418 km) long, and many smaller islands and atolls. Socio-economic inequality, unemployment and the issue of independence have caused tension between the Kanaks and the French-speaking expatriate population. This has resulted in a long history of political violence, although a referendum on independence is promised for 1998. New Caledonia produces 25% of the world's nickel, and improved incomes from tourism and agriculture have benefited the economy.

Much of New Caledonia is volcanic, with relatively high interior plateaux descending to coastal plains. Nickel is the most important mineral resource, but the hills also harbour metallic deposits including chrome, cobalt, iron, gold, silver and copper.

MAP KEY

POPULATION
- ⊕ 50,000 to 100,000
- ○ 10,000 to 50,000
- ○ below 10,000

ELEVATION
- 1000m / 3281ft
- 500m / 1640ft
- 250m / 820ft
- 100m / 328ft
- sea level

FIJI

FIJI IS A VOLCANIC ARCHIPELAGO in the southwestern Pacific consisting of two large islands and 880 smaller islets, and covering a total area of 7054 sq miles (18,270 sq km). The majority of the population lives on the two largest islands. The people are split fairly evenly between Indo-Fijians, who arrived when Fiji was still a British colony, and the indigenous Fijians who have, since 1987, controlled the government. Sugar and copra are the most important crops in a diversified agricultural base and forestry is becoming increasingly important. A relatively varied economy has potential for mineral and hydro-electric exploitation, while Fiji's climate and location on the main Pacific air routes are an impetus to tourism.

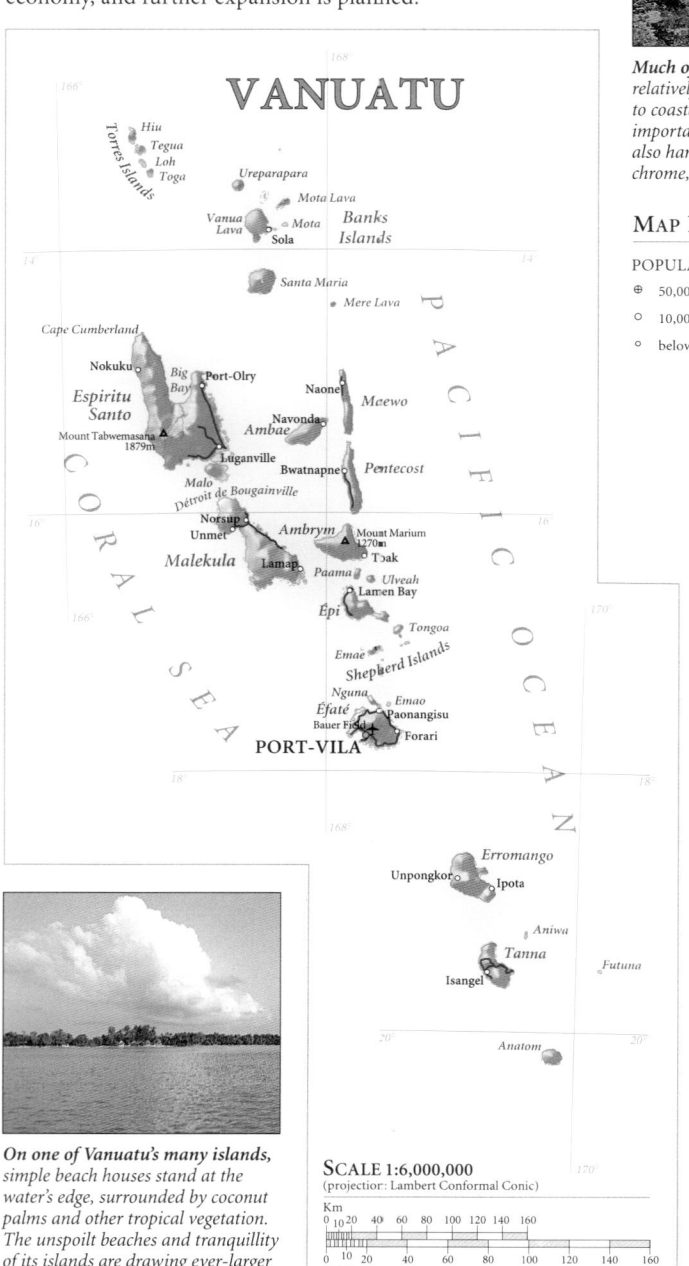

On one of Vanuatu's many islands, simple beach houses stand at the water's edge, surrounded by coconut palms and other tropical vegetation. The unspoilt beaches and tranquillity of its islands are drawing ever-larger numbers of tourists to Vanuatu.

SCALE 1:6,000,000
(projection: Lambert Conformal Conic)

Abaca Eco-tourist Park near Lautoka on the island of Viti Levu in western Fiji is one of a number of projects aimed at combining tourism with awareness about the environment. The government and people of Fiji are keen to protect the unique ecology of the islands and prevent further damage to the coral reefs. Until the recent ending of nuclear testing in the Pacific by Western nations, Fiji lay downwind of some of the main testing sites.

SCALE 1:6,000,000
(projection: Mercator)

A B C D E F G H I J K L M

PACIFIC OCEAN

THE PACIFIC IS THE WORLD'S LARGEST AND DEEPEST OCEAN. It is nearly twice the area of the Atlantic and contains almost three times as much water. The ocean is dotted with islands and surrounded by some of the world's most populous states; over half the world's population lives on its shores. The Pacific is bordered by active plate margins known as the 'Ring of Fire', causing earthquakes and tsunamis, and creating volcanic islands and subterranean mountain chains. The largest underwater mountains break the surface as island arcs. The fisheries of the Pacific are some of the most productive in the world and provide a vital resource for many of the Pacific islands. Since the Second World War there has been a shift in trading patterns, with a considerable growth in trade between the United States and the countries of the Pacific Rim.

INSET MAP KEY

POPULATION
○ below 10,000

ELEVATION
1000m / 3281ft
500m / 1640ft
250m / 820ft
100m / 328ft
sea level

OCEAN MAP KEY

SEA DEPTH
sea level
250m / 820ft
500m / 1640ft
1000m / 3281ft
2000m / 6562ft
3000m / 9843ft
5000m / 16,410ft

SCALE 1:50,000,000
(projection: Mollweide)

AMERICAN SAMOA AND SAMOA

AMERICAN SAMOA AND SAMOA are part of the island archipelago of Polynesia. The two most populous islands are Tutuila in American Samoa and Upolu in Samoa. Although the economies of both these states remain predominantly resource-based, both are expanding their light manufacturing sectors, and the US administration is the primary employer in American Samoa. Tuna fishing is particularly important: 25% of all tuna consumed in the USA is processed and canned in Pago Pago.

Japan is one of the major trading nations within the Pacific, importing iron and steel from Australia, and grain from the USA. The major exports from the 'Pacific Rim' are electronics, precision equipment and motor cars.

SCALE 1:3,000,000

Many of the buildings in Samoa reflect the country's colonial past. Once a colony of New Zealand, Samoa is now an independent state; American Samoa remains an unincorporated territory of the United States.

THE RING OF FIRE

THE ACTIVE PLATE MARGINS surrounding the Pacific have created numerous land and island volcanoes along its border. The actual basin of the Pacific is made up of a number of separate tectonic plates which move away from each other, colliding with other plates. When they collide, the oceanic plates, being thinner, are forced beneath the thicker continental plates, forming deep ocean trenches and high ridges. These collision zones are known as subduction zones and are characterized by intense seismic and volcanic activity.

RESOURCES

MANY OF THE SMALL ISLANDS in the Pacific rely heavily on marine resources to provide valuable export incomes. These fisheries tend to be small-scale and are forced to compete with the large commerical fleets from Japan and the Russian Federation. Although many metallic mineral deposits have been discovered in the Pacific, few are exploited. The major areas of oil and gas extraction are off the coast of Vietnam, along the Kamchatka Peninsula and off the coast of Alaska. The numerous reefs which fringe the islands of the Pacific are harvested for corals.

Farms such as this black pearl oyster farm in Tahiti are widespread throughout the Pacific. The culturing or farming of marine organisms, such as molluscs and crustaceans, has been practised for hundreds of years.

Resources
🐟 fish
🦐 shellfish
🐋 whales
⬦ oil & gas
● major towns
⚓ major ports

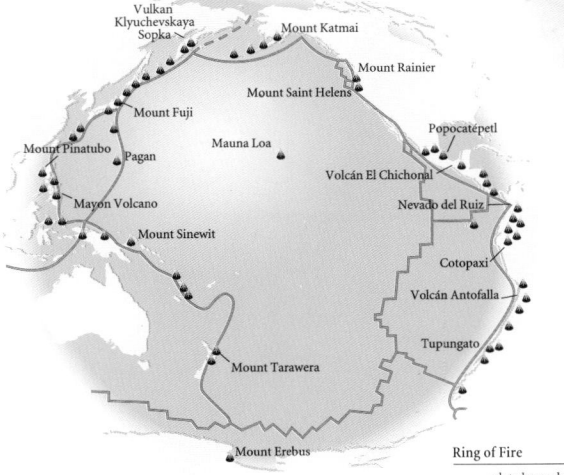

Ring of Fire
— plate boundaries
● major volcanoes

Mayon Volcano in the Philippines is one of many active volcanoes on the Pacific 'Ring of Fire'. It is noted for its perfect conical shape; the base of the cone is 80 miles (130 km) in circumference.

The Hawaiian volcanoes lie in the centre of a plate, not on a plate margin, and are known as intraplate volcanoes. They are associated with hot spots, whereby a plume of hot molten rock rises to the surface as the plate moves over it.

N O P Q R S T U V W X Y

1
2
3
4
5
6
7
8
9
10
11
12
13

The Sepik River drains the lowlands north of the Central Range, flowing eastwards into the Bismarck Sea.

The Bismarck Range is precipitous, rugged and covered in dense vegetation, rising to 14,793 ft (4509 m) at Mount Wilhelm in central Papua New Guinea.

Most of Papua New Guinea's outlying islands, including New Britain, Bougainville Island and New Ireland, are precipitous and of volcanic origin.

The Star Mountains include some of the most remote terrain on Earth. The area is rich in gold and copper.

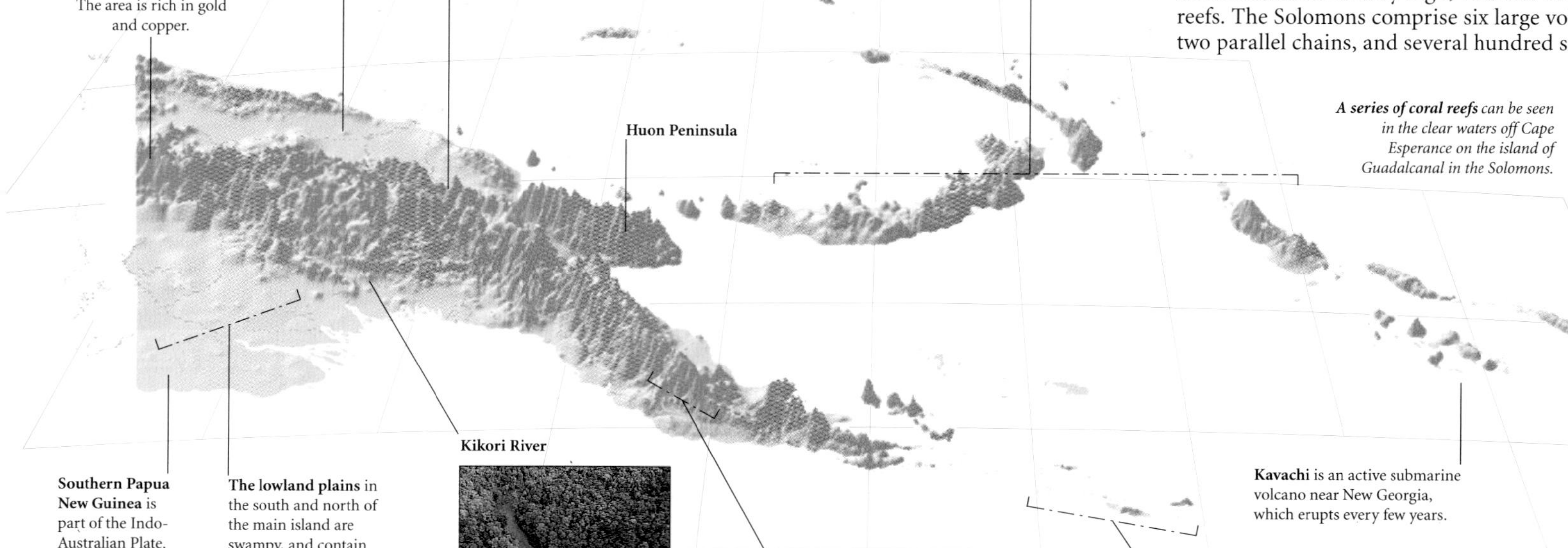

Huon Peninsula

THE LANDSCAPE

THE PLATE MARGIN between the Pacific and Indo-Australian plates runs through the mainland of Papua New Guinea, which is dominated by steep and forested mountain ranges. The 600 or so outer islands are mainly high, volcanic islands, fringed by coral reefs. The Solomons comprise six large volcanic islands which form two parallel chains, and several hundred small islands and atolls.

A series of coral reefs can be seen in the clear waters off Cape Esperance on the island of Guadalcanal in the Solomons.

Cape Esperance

Kikori River

Southern Papua New Guinea is part of the Indo-Australian Plate. New Guinea only became separated physically from Australia about 8000 years ago following the flooding of the Torres Strait.

The lowland plains in the south and north of the main island are swampy, and contain some fertile alluvial soils. This contrasts with the mountainous islands in the rest of Papua New Guinea where soils are generally thin and nutrients are retained in the existing vegetation.

Papua New Guinea's rivers, though fairly short, carry extremely high sediment loads, largely due to soil erosion. This is caused by a combination of very steep slopes and heavy rainfall, and is made worse by forest clearance, particularly 'slash and burn' techniques and road or mine operations.

The Owen Stanley Range contains several of Papua New Guinea's highest peaks, the greatest of which is Mount Victoria at 13,200 ft (4035 m).

Kavachi is an active submarine volcano near New Georgia, which erupts every few years.

The Louisiade Archipelago contains 10 volcanic islands and numerous coral islets. Tagula Island is the largest of the islands, containing the archipelago's highest peak at 2645 ft (806 m).

Huon Peninsula

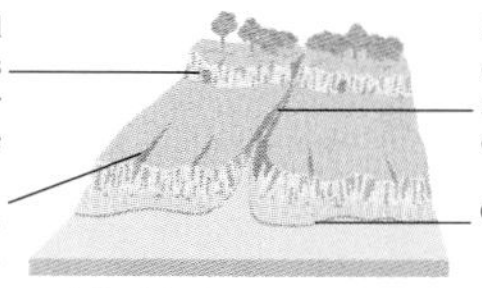

Caves and undercut cliffs mark former shoreline

Stream cuts down through recently exposed land

Former level of beach

Current beach

Uplift of the land in tectonically active regions can lead to former coastlines being lifted beyond the reach of the sea. New cliffs and caves are formed at a lower level, and rivers cut down through the lower land to reach sea level once more.

PACIFIC OCEAN

Duff Islands
Reef Islands
Tinakula
SOLOMON ISLANDS
Nendō Noka
TEMOTU
Lata
Santa Cruz Islands
Utupua
Vanikolo

(same scale as main map)

Lying close to the banks of the Sepik River in northern Papua New Guinea, this building is known as the Spirit House. It is constructed from leaves and twigs, ornately woven and trimmed into geometric patterns. The house is decorated with a mask and topped by a carved statue.

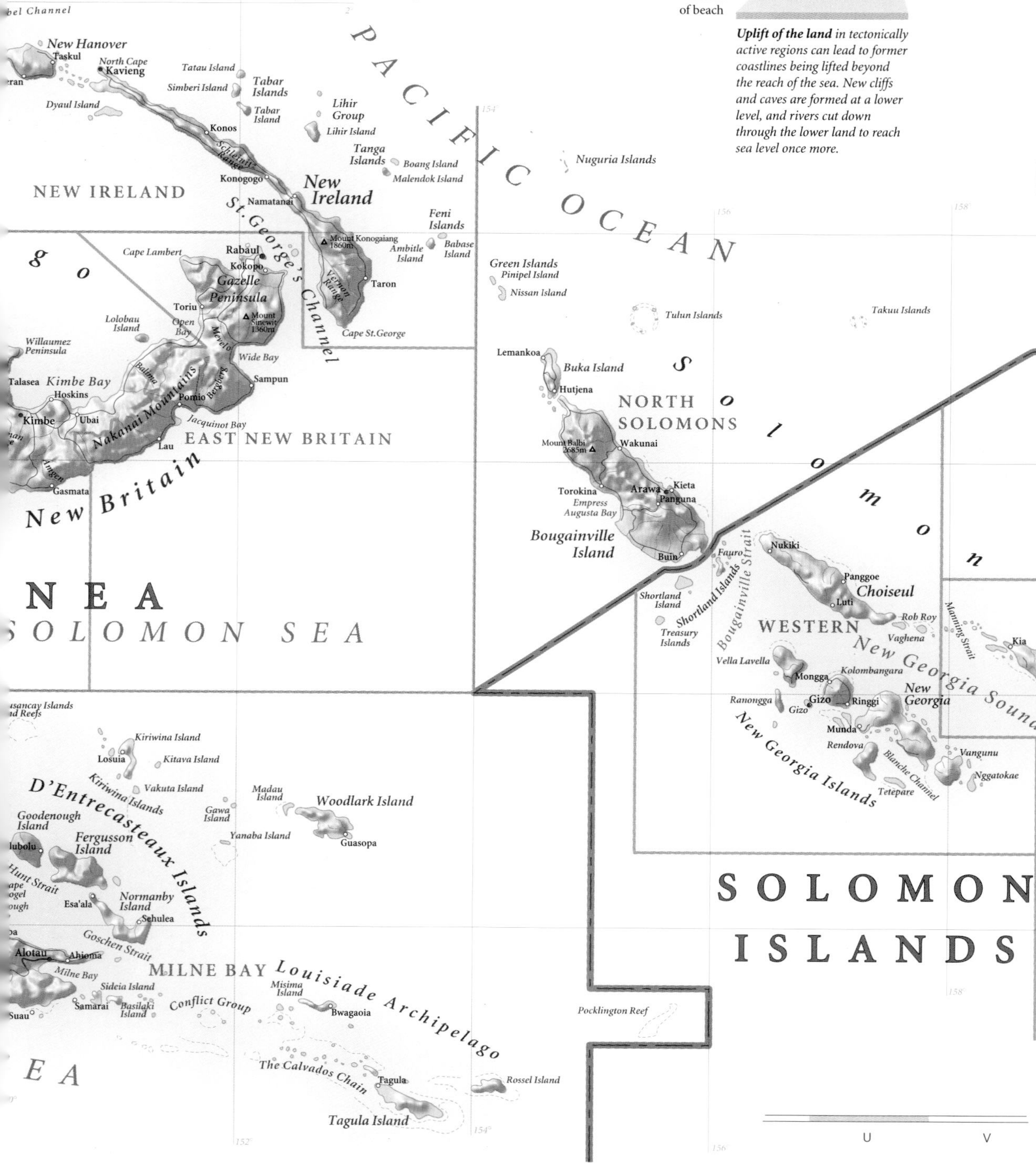

PACIFIC OCEAN

Matthias Group
Emirau Island

Bel Channel

New Hanover
Taskul
North Cape
Kavieng
Dyaul Island
Tatau Island
Simberi Island
Tabar Islands
Tabar Island
Lihir Group
Lihir Island
Tanga Islands
Boang Island
Malendok Island
Nuguria Islands
Konogogo
Namatanai
New Ireland
NEW IRELAND
Konos
Feni Islands
St. George's Channel
Cape Lambert
Rabaul
Kokopo
Gazelle Peninsula
Mount Konogaiang 1800m
Ambitle Island
Babase Island
Taron
Green Islands
Pinipel Island
Nissan Island
Cape St.George
Toriu
Open Bay
Mount Ulawun 1360m
Lolobau Island
Willaumez Peninsula
Talasea
Kimbe Bay
Hoskins
Nakanai Mountains
Wide Bay
Pomio
Sampun
Jacquinot Bay
Lau
EAST NEW BRITAIN
Kimbe
Ubai
Nukumanu Islands
Lemankoa
Buka Island
Hutjena
NORTH SOLOMONS
Tulun Islands
Takuu Islands
Ontong Java Atoll
Wakunai
Mount Balbi 2685m
Torokina
Empress Augusta Bay
Arawa
Kieta
Panguna
Bougainville Island
Buin
Roncador Reef

NEA
SOLOMON SEA
New Britain
Gasmata

S O L O M O N

Fauro
Nukiki
Shortland Island
Shortland Islands
Treasury Islands
Bougainville Strait
Panggoe
Luti
Choiseul
Rob Roy
Vaghena
WESTERN
New Georgia Sound
Kia
Baolo
Isabel
Santa Isabel
Buala
Manning Strait
Vella Lavella
Mongga
Kolombangara
New Georgia
Ranongga
Gizo
Ringgi
Munda
Rendova
Vangunu
Nggatokae
San Jorge
Kaolo
Mount Sasari 1219m
New Georgia Islands
Blanche Channel
Tetepare
Dai Island
MALAITA
Mabu
Kwailibesi
Sikaiana
i s l a n d s
Russell Islands
Yandina
Savo
CENTRAL
Florida Islands
Tulaghi
Tarapaina
Maramasike
Auki
Olomburi
Malaita

D'Entrecasteaux Islands
Losuia
Kiriwina Island
Kitava Island
Kiriwina Islands
Vakuta Island
Madau Island
Woodlark Island
Gawa Island
Yanaba Island
Guasopa
Goodenough Island
Iubolu
Fergusson Island
Hunt Strait
Normanby Island
Esa'ala
Sehulea
Goschen Strait
Alotau
Ahioma
Sideia Island
Samarai
Basilaki Island
Suau
MILNE BAY
Misima Island
Bwagaoia
Louisiade Archipelago
Pocklington Reef

S O L O M O N I S L A N D S

HONIARA
Henderson Field
Tangarare
Guadalcanal
Tambea
Mount Popomanaseu 2330m
Nduindui
Aola
Avuavu
GUADALCANAL
Iron Bottom Sound
Cape Esperance
Apio
Ulawa Island
CENTRAL
MAKIRA
Heuru
Three Sisters Islands
Kirakira
San Cristobal
Hauraha
Star Harbour

The Calvados Chain
Tagula
Rossel Island
Tagula Island

Bellona
Lavanggu
Rennell

198

MARSHALL ISLANDS

A GROUP OF 34 WIDELY-SCATTERED ATOLLS in the central Pacific Ocean, the Marshall Islands include some of the largest atolls in the world, formed from low coral islands with sandy beaches and enclosing vast lagoons. Formerly under US protection as part of the UN Trust Territory of the Pacific Islands, and including the former US nuclear testing sites of Bikini Atoll and Enewetak Atoll, the Marshall Islands became self-governing in 1979. The economy is reliant on US aid and on the rent paid by the USA for its missile base on Kwajalein Atoll.

NAURU

A FORMER BRITISH COLONY, the tiny island of Nauru, with an area of only 8.2 sq miles (21.2 sq km), has been exploited for its substantial phosphate deposits by the UK, Australia and New Zealand. Since independence in 1968, the phosphate industry has made its citizens some of the wealthiest in the world, and scars from the vast mining operation pit the island's landscape. Phosphate reserves are now virtually exhausted and investment overseas will in future form the bulk of Nauru's income.

A series of coral pinnacles stand exposed in the shallow water off the coast of Nauru. Much of the island has an extraordinary 'lunar' landscape, created by years of phosphate extraction.

Majuro Atoll is the Marshall Islands' capital and commercial centre. Almost half the population live on the narrow islands, often in overcrowded conditions.

Traditionally built canoes are still important in Micronesia, used for transport and for fishing. This large canoe, on Satawal, in the state of Yap, needs nearly 20 people to return it to the boathouse.

WAKE ISLAND (to US)

AN UNINCORPORATED TERRITORY of the USA with a tiny population, Wake Island remains strategically important to US forces, and has been used as a base in several conflicts. Formed by the rim of an extinct underwater volcano, it is now used as an emergency airstrip for trans-Pacific flights, and as a stop-over for cargo planes.

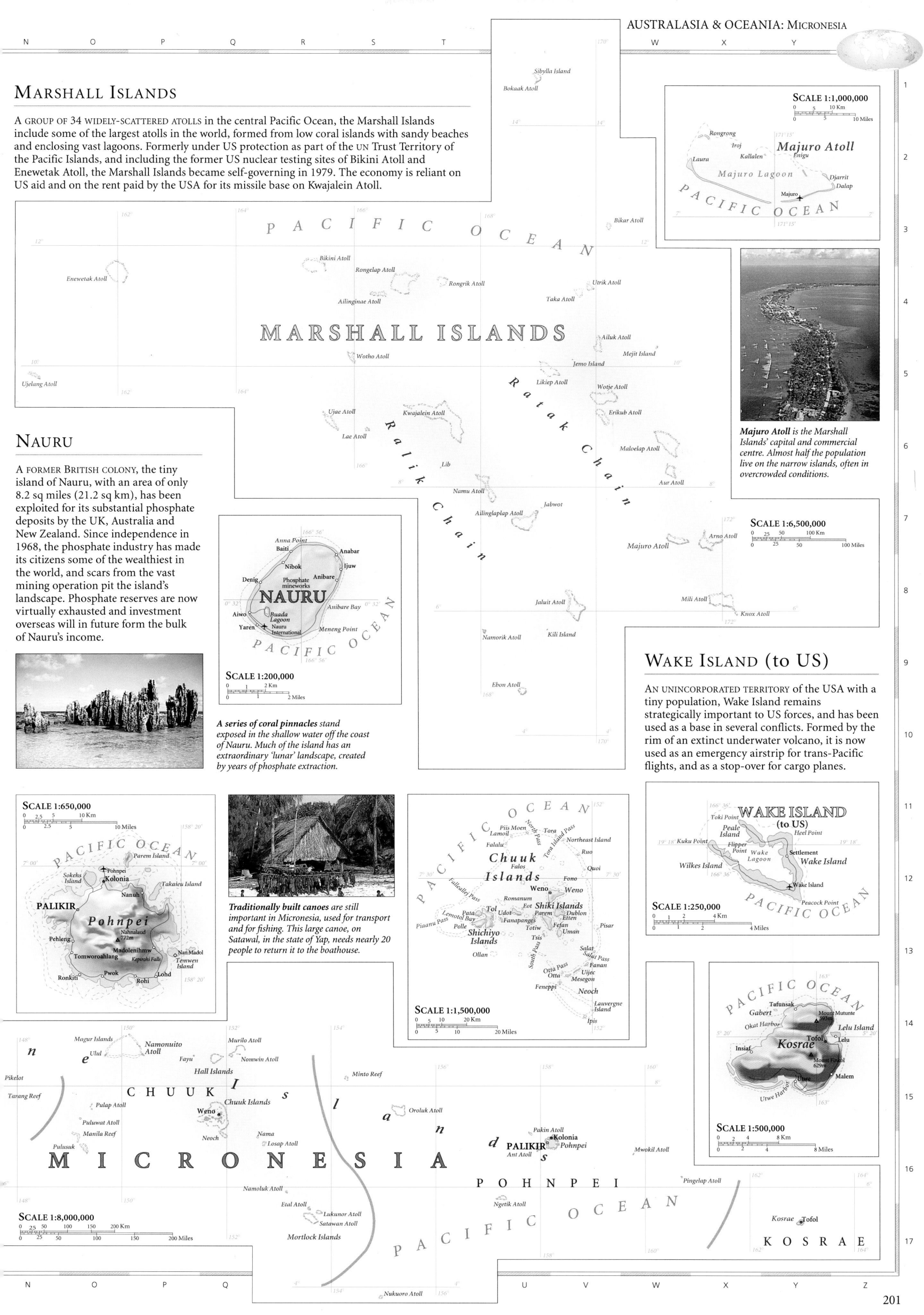

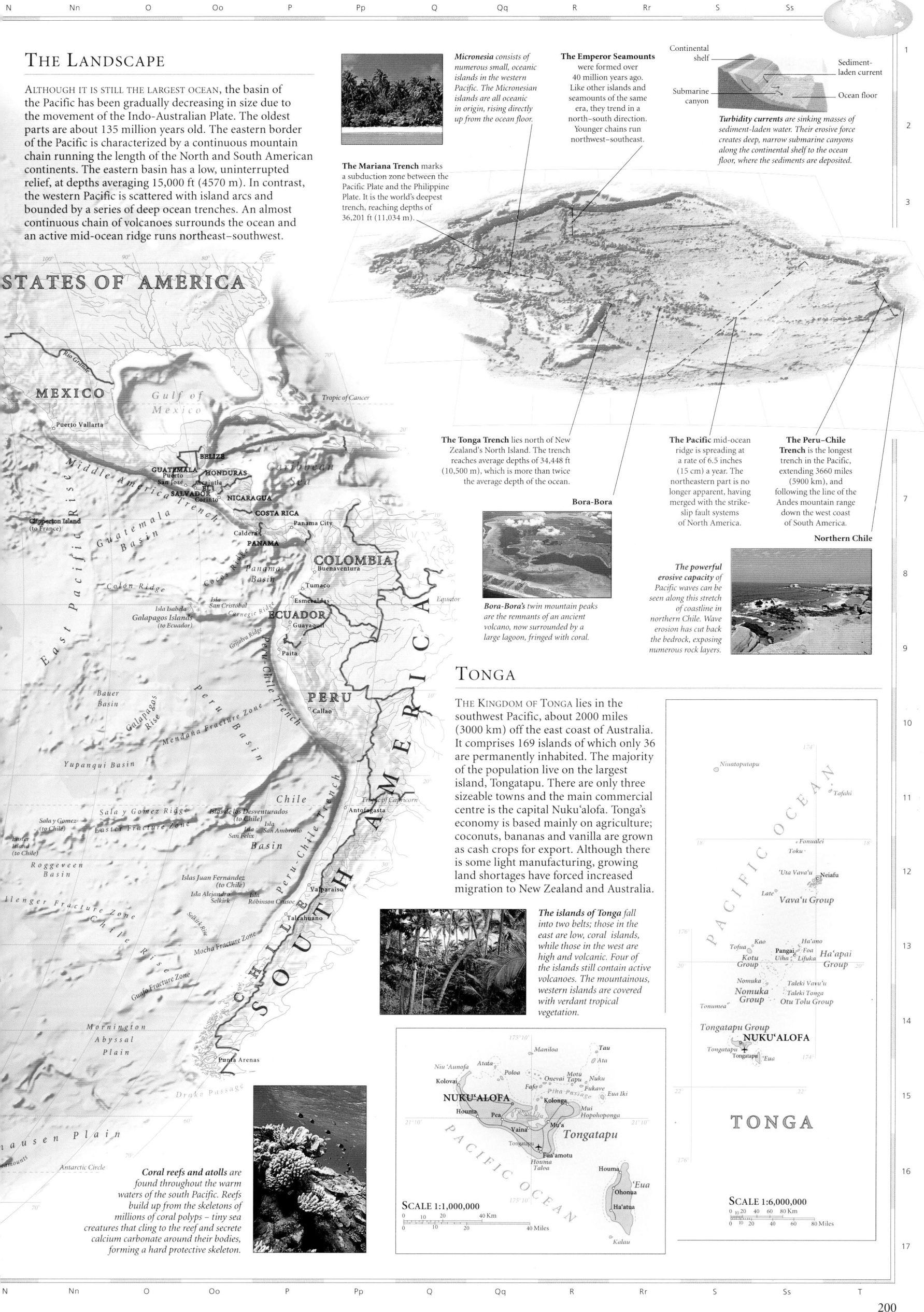

THE LANDSCAPE

ALTHOUGH IT IS STILL THE LARGEST OCEAN, the basin of
the Pacific has been gradually decreasing in size due to
the movement of the Indo-Australian Plate. The oldest
parts are about 135 million years old. The eastern border
of the Pacific is characterized by a continuous mountain
chain running the length of the North and South American
continents. The eastern basin has a low, uninterrupted
relief, at depths averaging 15,000 ft (4570 m). In contrast,
the western Pacific is scattered with island arcs and
bounded by a series of deep ocean trenches. An almost
continuous chain of volcanoes surrounds the ocean and
an active mid-ocean ridge runs northeast–southwest.

Micronesia consists of
numerous small, oceanic
islands in the western
Pacific. The Micronesian
islands are all oceanic
in origin, rising directly
up from the ocean floor.

The Emperor Seamounts
were formed over
40 million years ago.
Like other islands and
seamounts of the same
era, they trend in a
north–south direction.
Younger chains run
northwest–southeast.

Continental
shelf
Sediment-
laden current
Submarine
canyon
Ocean floor

Turbidity currents are sinking masses of
sediment-laden water. Their erosive
force creates deep, narrow submarine canyons
along the continental shelf to the ocean
floor, where the sediments are deposited.

The Mariana Trench marks
a subduction zone between the
Pacific Plate and the Philippine
Plate. It is the world's deepest
trench, reaching depths of
36,201 ft (11,034 m).

The Tonga Trench lies north of New
Zealand's North Island. The trench
reaches average depths of 34,448 ft
(10,500 m), which is more than twice
the average depth of the ocean.

The Pacific mid-ocean
ridge is spreading at
a rate of 6.5 inches
(15 cm) a year. The
northeastern part is no
longer apparent, having
merged with the strike-
slip fault systems
of North America.

**The Peru–Chile
Trench** is the longest
trench in the Pacific,
extending 3660 miles
(5900 km), and
following the line of the
Andes mountain range
down the west coast
of South America.

Bora-Bora

Bora-Bora's twin mountain peaks
are the remnants of an ancient
volcano, now surrounded by a
large lagoon, fringed with coral.

Northern Chile

*The powerful
erosive capacity* of
Pacific waves can be
seen along this stretch
of coastline in
northern Chile. Wave
erosion has cut back
the bedrock, exposing
numerous rock layers.

TONGA

THE KINGDOM OF TONGA lies in the
southwest Pacific, about 2000 miles
(3000 km) off the east coast of Australia.
It comprises 169 islands of which only 36
are permanently inhabited. The majority
of the population live on the largest
island, Tongatapu. There are only three
sizeable towns and the main commercial
centre is the capital Nuku'alofa. Tonga's
economy is based mainly on agriculture;
coconuts, bananas and vanilla are grown
as cash crops for export. Although there
is some light manufacturing, growing
land shortages have forced increased
migration to New Zealand and Australia.

The islands of Tonga fall
into two belts; those in the
east are low, coral islands,
while those in the west are
high and volcanic. Four of
the islands still contain active
volcanoes. The mountainous,
western islands are covered
with verdant tropical
vegetation.

Coral reefs and atolls are
found throughout the warm
waters of the south Pacific. Reefs
build up from the skeletons of
millions of coral polyps – tiny sea
creatures that cling to the reef and
secrete calcium carbonate around
their bodies, forming a hard
protective skeleton.

SCALE 1:1,000,000
SCALE 1:6,000,000

Wave action has eroded this shoreline near Port Campbell in southeastern Australia leaving isolated pinnacles of rock cut off from the main coastline. They are known as the 'Twelve Apostles'.

POLYNESIA

KIRIBATI, TUVALU, *Cook Islands, Easter Island, French Polynesia, Niue,*
Pitcairn Islands, Tokelau, Wallis & Futuna

THE NUMEROUS ISLAND GROUPS OF POLYNESIA lie to the east of Australia, scattered over a vast area in the south Pacific. The islands are a mixture of low-lying coral atolls, some of which enclose lagoons, and the tips of great underwater volcanoes. The populations on the islands are small, and most people are of Polynesian origin, as are the Maori of New Zealand. Local economies remain simple, relying mainly on subsistence crops, mineral deposits – many now exhausted – fishing and tourism.

KIRIBATI

A FORMER BRITISH COLONY, Kiribati became independent in 1979. Banaba's phosphate deposits ran out in 1980, following decades of exploitation by the British. Economic development remains slow and most agriculture is at a subsistence level, though coconuts provide export income, and underwater agriculture is being developed.

With the exception of Banaba all the islands in Kiribati's three groups are low-lying, coral atolls. This aerial view shows the sparsely vegetated islands, intercut by many small lagoons.

TUVALU

A CHAIN of nine coral atolls, 360 miles (579 km) long with a land area of just over 9 sq miles (23 sq km), Tuvalu is one of the world's smallest and most isolated states. As the Ellice Islands, Tuvalu was linked to the Gilbert Islands (now part of Kiribati) as a British colony until independence in 1978. Politically and socially conservative, Tuvaluans live by fishing and subsistence farming.

Funafuti Atoll contains more than 40% of Tuvalu's people, giving it an extremely high population density.

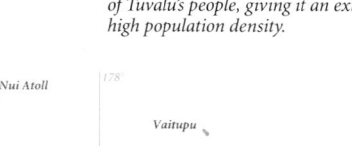

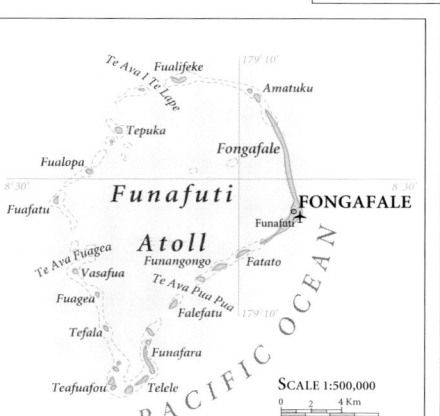

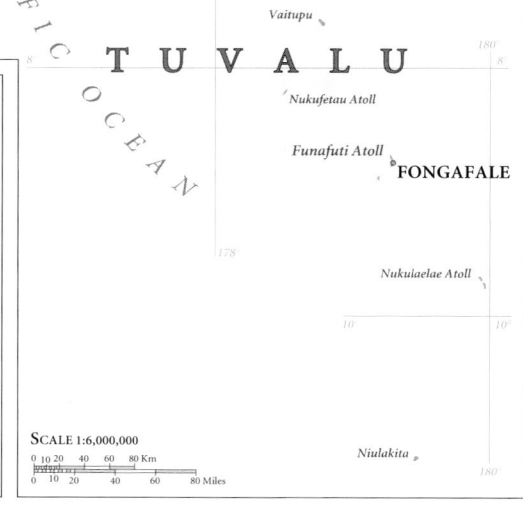

TOKELAU (to New Zealand)

A LOW-LYING CORAL ATOLL, Tokelau is a dependent territory of New Zealand with few natural resources. Although a 1990 cyclone destroyed crops and infrastructure, a tuna cannery and the sale of fishing licences have raised revenue and a catamaran link between the islands has increased their tourism potential. Tokelau's small size and economic weakness makes independence from New Zealand unlikely.

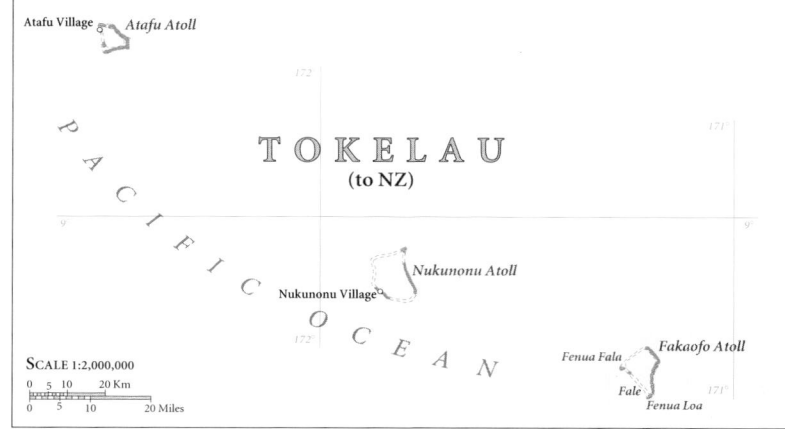

Fishermen cast their nets to catch small fish in the shallow waters off Atafu Atoll, the most westerly island in Tokelau.

WALLIS & FUTUNA (to France)

IN CONTRAST TO OTHER FRENCH overseas territories in the south Pacific, the inhabitants of Wallis and Futuna have shown little desire for greater autonomy. A subsistence economy produces a variety of tropical crops, while foreign currency remittances come from expatriates and from the sale of licences to Japanese and Korean fishing fleets.

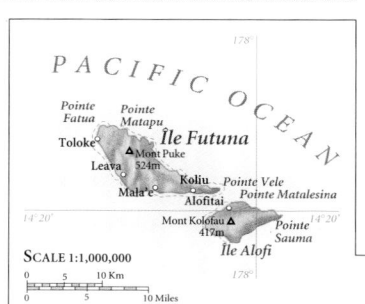

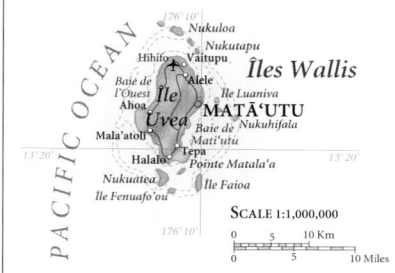

COOK ISLANDS (to New Zealand)

A MIXTURE OF CORAL ATOLLS and volcanic peaks, the Cook Islands achieved self-government in 1965 but exist in free association with New Zealand. A diverse economy includes pearl and giant clam farming, and an ostrich farm, plus tourism and banking. A 1991 friendship treaty with France provides for French surveillance of territorial waters.

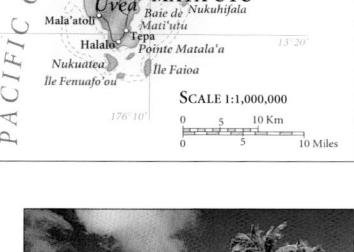

Palm trees fringe the white sands of a beach on Aitutaki in the Southern Cook Islands, where tourism is of increasing economic importance.

NIUE (to New Zealand)

NIUE, the world's largest coral island, is self-governing but exists in free association with New Zealand. Tropical fruits are grown for local consumption; tourism and the sale of postage stamps provide foreign currency. The lack of local job prospects has led more than 10,000 Niueans to emigrate to New Zealand, which has now invested heavily in Niue's economy in the hope of reversing this trend.

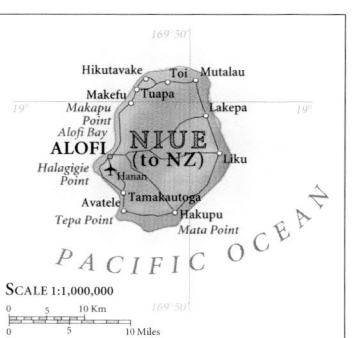

Waves have cut back the original coastline, exposing a sandy beach, near Mutalau in the northeast corner of Niue.

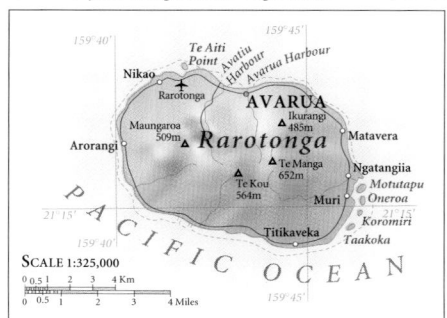

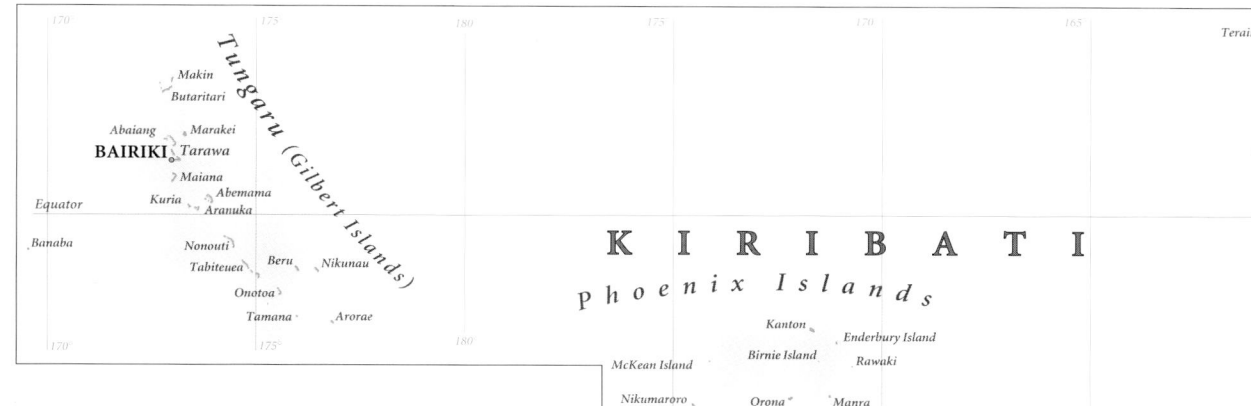

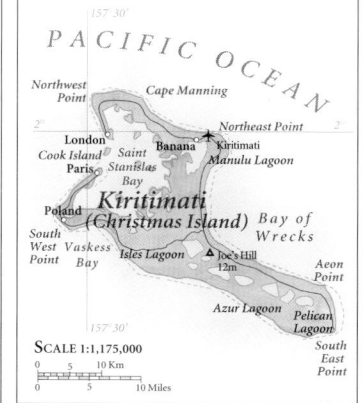

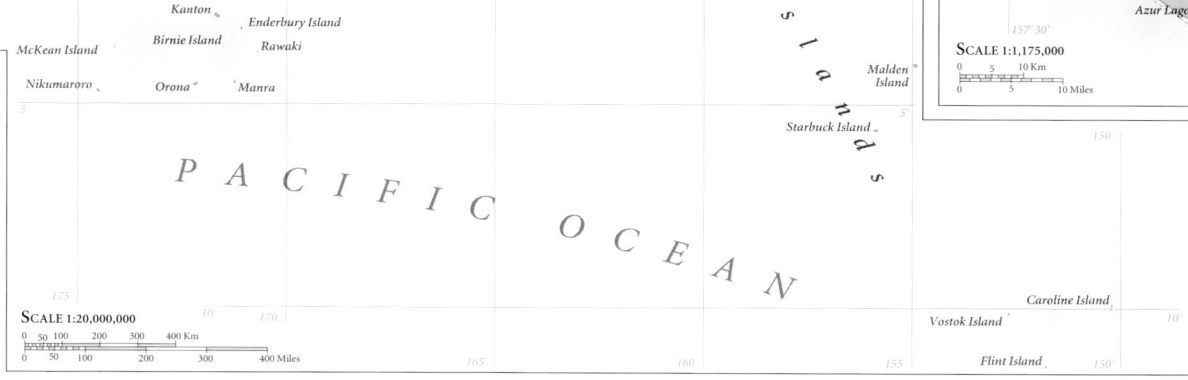

K I R I B A T I

phoenix Islands

Line Islands

SCALE 1:1,175,000

PACIFIC OCEAN

FRENCH POLYNESIA (to France)

THE 130 ISLANDS OF FRENCH POLYNESIA cover 4 million sq miles (10.5 million sq km). Nearly 75% of the people live on Tahiti. The use of Mururoa as a nuclear testing site by the French military transformed the economy, creating many jobs. The end of testing led to calls from the Polynesian majority for greater autonomy from France, the rebuilding of indigenous trade, and a reduction in tourism to stop the erosion of the islands' traditional culture.

SCALE 1:20,000,000

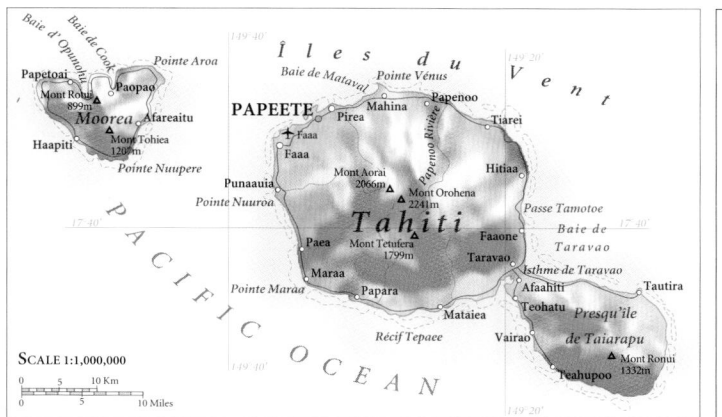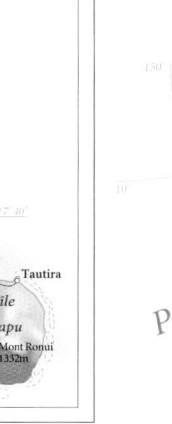

SCALE 1:1,000,000

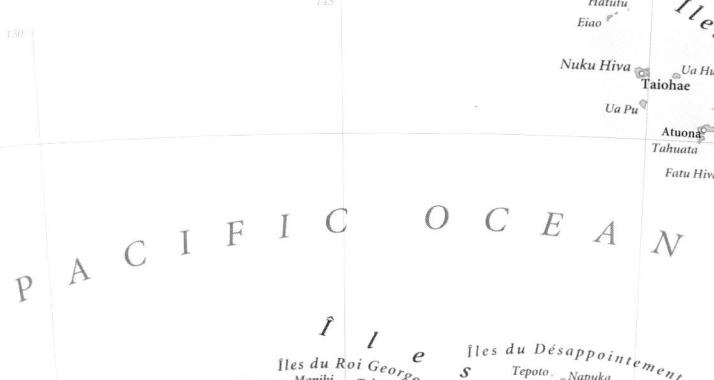

PACIFIC OCEAN

The traditional
Tahitian welcome for visitors, who are greeted by parties of canoes, has become a major tourist attraction.

PITCAIRN ISLANDS (to UK)

BRITAIN'S MOST ISOLATED DEPENDENCY, Pitcairn Island was first populated by mutineers from the HMS *Bounty* in 1790. Emigration is further depleting the already limited gene pool of the island's inhabitants, with associated social and health problems. Barter, fishing and subsistence farming form the basis of the economy although postage stamp sales provide foreign currency earnings, and offshore mineral exploitation may boost the economy in future.

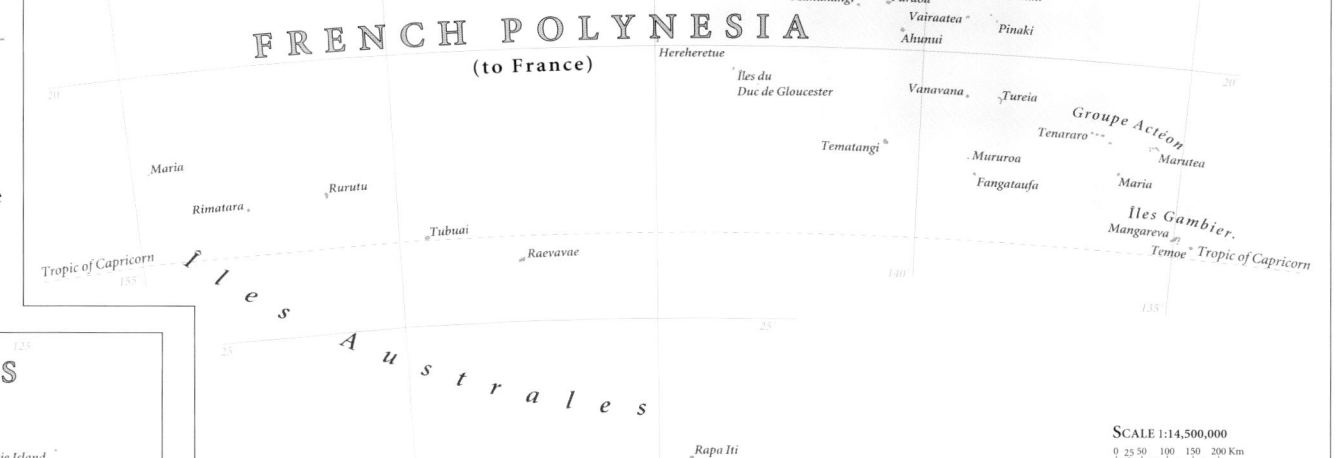

FRENCH POLYNESIA

(to France)

Îles Australes

SCALE 1:14,500,000

PITCAIRN ISLANDS

(to UK)

SCALE 1:10,000,000

PACIFIC OCEAN

The Pitcairn Islanders rely on regular airdrops from New Zealand and periodic visits by supply vessels to provide them with basic commodities.

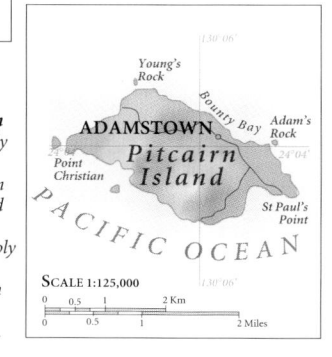

ADAMSTOWN

Pitcairn Island

PACIFIC OCEAN

SCALE 1:125,000

EASTER ISLAND (to Chile)

ONE OF THE MOST EASTERLY ISLANDS in Polynesia, Easter Island *(Isla de Pascua)* – also known as Rapa Nui, is part of Chile. The mainly Polynesian inhabitants support themselves by farming, which is mainly of a subsistence nature, and includes cattle rearing and crops such as sugar cane, bananas, corn, gourds and potatoes. In recent years, tourism has become the most important source of income and the island sustains a small commercial airport.

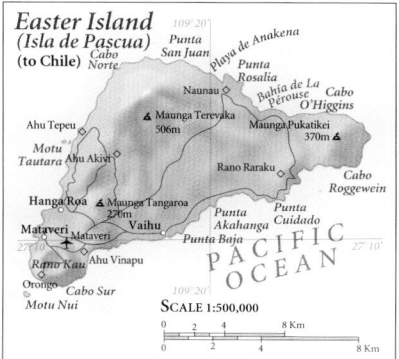

Easter Island
(Isla de Pascua)
(to Chile)

PACIFIC OCEAN

SCALE 1:500,000

The Naunau, a series of huge stone statues overlook Playa de Anakena, on Easter Island. Carved from a soft volcanic rock, they were erected between 400 and 900 years ago.

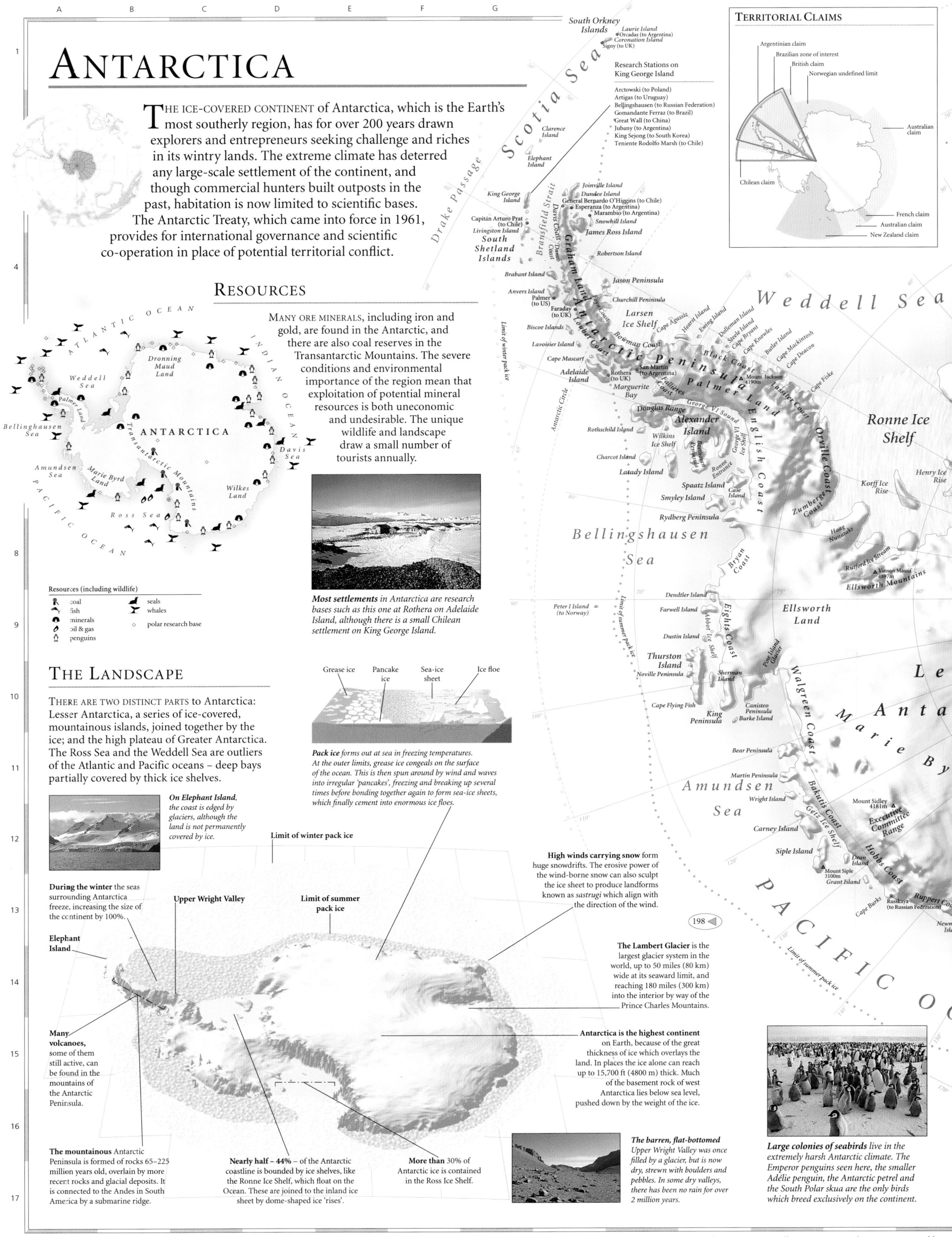

ANTARCTICA

THE ICE-COVERED CONTINENT of Antarctica, which is the Earth's most southerly region, has for over 200 years drawn explorers and entrepreneurs seeking challenge and riches in its wintry lands. The extreme climate has deterred any large-scale settlement of the continent, and though commercial hunters built outposts in the past, habitation is now limited to scientific bases. The Antarctic Treaty, which came into force in 1961, provides for international governance and scientific co-operation in place of potential territorial conflict.

RESOURCES

MANY ORE MINERALS, including iron and gold, are found in the Antarctic, and there are also coal reserves in the Transantarctic Mountains. The severe conditions and environmental importance of the region mean that exploitation of potential mineral resources is both uneconomic and undesirable. The unique wildlife and landscape draw a small number of tourists annually.

Resources (including wildlife)

- coal
- fish
- minerals
- oil & gas
- penguins
- seals
- whales
- polar research base

THE LANDSCAPE

THERE ARE TWO DISTINCT PARTS to Antarctica: Lesser Antarctica, a series of ice-covered, mountainous islands, joined together by the ice; and the high plateau of Greater Antarctica. The Ross Sea and the Weddell Sea are outliers of the Atlantic and Pacific oceans – deep bays partially covered by thick ice shelves.

On Elephant Island, the coast is edged by glaciers, although the land is not permanently covered by ice.

Grease ice | Pancake ice | Sea-ice sheet | Ice floe

Pack ice forms out at sea in freezing temperatures. At the outer limits, grease ice congeals on the surface of the ocean. This is then spun around by wind and waves into irregular 'pancakes', freezing and breaking up several times before bonding together again to form sea-ice sheets, which finally cement into enormous ice floes.

Most settlements in Antarctica are research bases such as this one at Rothera on Adelaide Island, although there is a small Chilean settlement on King George Island.

Research Stations on King George Island

- Arctowski (to Poland)
- Artigas (to Uruguay)
- Bellingshausen (to Russian Federation)
- Comandante Ferraz (to Brazil)
- Great Wall (to China)
- Jubany (to Argentina)
- King Sejong (to South Korea)
- Teniente Rodolfo Marsh (to Chile)

TERRITORIAL CLAIMS

- Argentinian claim
- Brazilian zone of interest
- British claim
- Norwegian undefined limit
- Chilean claim
- Australian claim
- French claim
- Australian claim
- New Zealand claim

During the winter the seas surrounding Antarctica freeze, increasing the size of the continent by 100%.

Limit of winter pack ice

Upper Wright Valley

Limit of summer pack ice

Elephant Island

Many volcanoes, some of them still active, can be found in the mountains of the Antarctic Peninsula.

High winds carrying snow form huge snowdrifts. The erosive power of the wind-borne snow can also sculpt the ice sheet to produce landforms known as *sastrugi* which align with the direction of the wind.

198 ◀

The Lambert Glacier is the largest glacier system in the world, up to 50 miles (80 km) wide at its seaward limit, and reaching 180 miles (300 km) into the interior by way of the Prince Charles Mountains.

Antarctica is the highest continent on Earth, because of the great thickness of ice which overlays the land. In places the ice alone can reach up to 15,700 ft (4800 m) thick. Much of the basement rock of west Antarctica lies below sea level, pushed down by the weight of the ice.

The mountainous Antarctic Peninsula is formed of rocks 65–225 million years old, overlain by more recent rocks and glacial deposits. It is connected to the Andes in South America by a submarine ridge.

Nearly half – 44% – of the Antarctic coastline is bounded by ice shelves, like the Ronne Ice Shelf, which float on the Ocean. These are joined to the inland ice sheet by dome-shaped ice 'rises'.

More than 30% of Antarctic ice is contained in the Ross Ice Shelf.

The barren, flat-bottomed Upper Wright Valley was once filled by a glacier, but is now dry, strewn with boulders and pebbles. In some dry valleys, there has been no rain for over 2 million years.

Large colonies of seabirds live in the extremely harsh Antarctic climate. The Emperor penguins seen here, the smaller Adelie penguin, the Antarctic petrel and the South Polar skua are the only birds which breed exclusively on the continent.

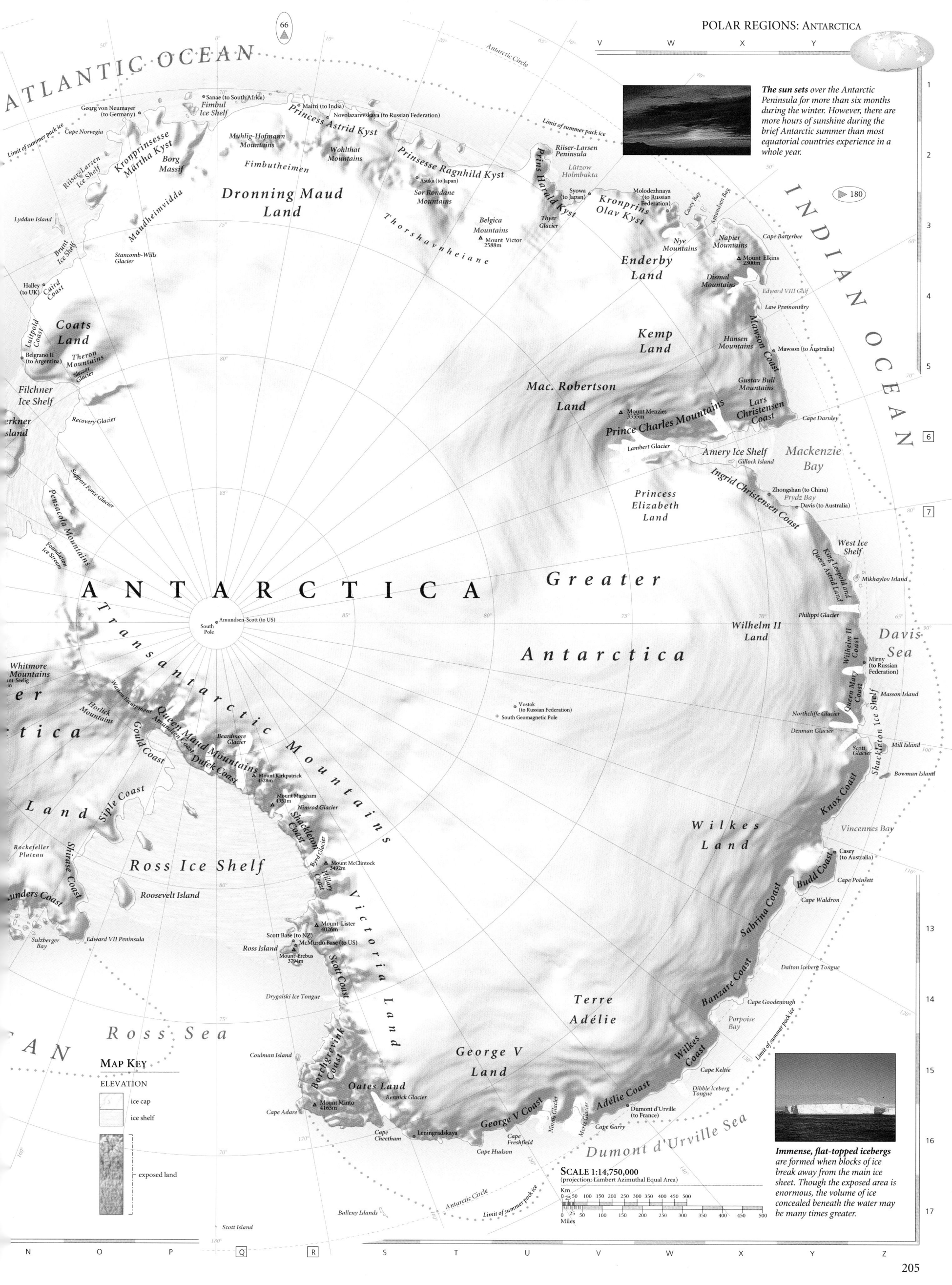

The sun sets over the Antarctic Peninsula for more than six months during the winter. However, there are more hours of sunshine during the brief Antarctic summer than most equatorial countries experience in a whole year.

Immense, flat-topped icebergs are formed when blocks of ice break away from the main ice sheet. Though the exposed area is enormous, the volume of ice concealed beneath the water may be many times greater.

MAP KEY

ELEVATION

ice cap

ice shelf

exposed land

SCALE 1:14,750,000
(projection: Lambert Azimuthal Equal Area)

THE ARCTIC

THREE CONTINENTS, ASIA, NORTH AMERICA AND EUROPE, reach into the Arctic Circle at their northernmost limits, almost entirely encircling the Arctic Ocean. Despite the region's extraordinarily harsh climate, it has been inhabited for thousands of years by peoples such as the European Lapps, the Russian Nenet, and the North American Inuit, who draw a living from fishing, herding and hunting. More recently, particularly in the Russian Arctic, opportunities to exploit oil and other mineral reserves have encouraged immigration. Pollution of the Arctic's unique ecology and damage to the traditional lifestyles of many native peoples have been the unfortunate results of this activity, and international co-operation is needed to safeguard the future of the region.

MAP KEY

POPULATION

- ■ above 5 million
- ◼ 1 million to 5 million
- ◉ 500,000 to 1 million
- ◎ 100,000 to 500,000
- ⊕ 50,000 to 100,000
- ○ 10,000 to 50,000
- ○ below 10,000

SEA DEPTH

- sea level
- 250m / 820ft
- 500m / 1640ft
- 1000m / 3281ft
- 2000m / 6562ft
- 3000m / 9843ft

SCALE 1:21,000,000
(projection: Lambert Azimuthal Equal Area)

Wind-blown snow etches deep patterns in the ice sheet known as sastrugi. They align with the direction of the wind

RESOURCES

LARGE QUANTITIES of coal, oil and natural gas are to be found in the basins of the Arctic Ocean, and in northern Canada, Alaska and the Russian Federation. The cost and difficulty of extraction and, more recently, awareness of damage to the environment, have limited exploitation to coastal regions. The unfrozen waters have stocks of fish including cod, plaice and haddock. Quotas have now been put in place to restrict the number of fish caught annually. Reindeer are herded in large numbers by many of the native Arctic peoples. Most grain and vegetables are imported from elsewhere.

Resources

- coal
- fish
- mining
- oil & gas
- radioactive contamination
- major towns
- major ports

Icebreakers, ships with specially strengthened hulls, designed to break a path through the ice, are used to keep important routes open during the winter, when falling temperatures cause much of the Arctic Ocean to freeze over.

THE LANDSCAPE

THE ARCTIC OCEAN comprises two large ocean basins divided by three submarine ridges, the greatest of which, the Lomonosov Ridge, is a huge underwater mountain range which has an average height of more than 10,000 ft (3000 m). The lands which encircle the Arctic Ocean are underlain by great shield areas of ancient rocks, which were heavily glaciated during the last Ice Age.

Icebergs are constantly broken up and re-shaped by wind and the oceans. This flat-topped iceberg has been undercut, leaving a craggy ice cliff.

A complex and ancient mountain system, extending from the Queen Elizabeth Islands to eastern Greenland was formed more than 245 million years ago.

The Canadian Shield underlies almost all of the Canadian Arctic. It is a very stable plateau of ancient rock, now covered by glacial lakes and sediment, which supports tundra vegetation.

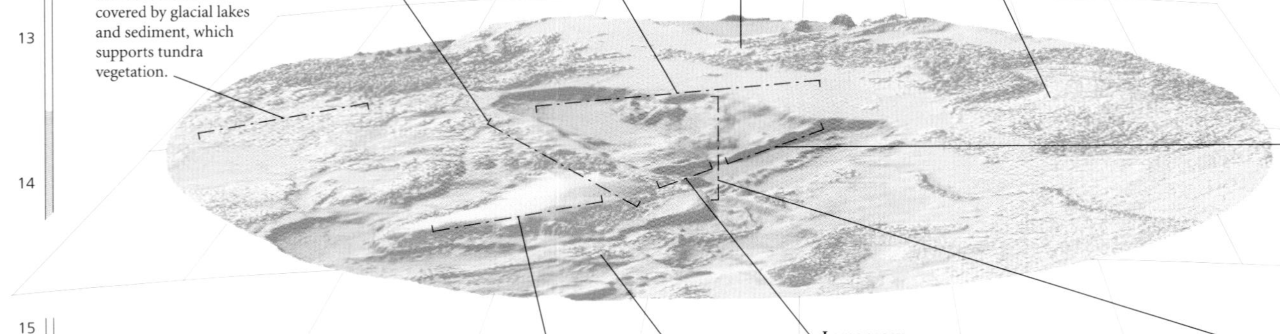

The Arctic Ocean is the world's smallest ocean with a total area of 5,440,000 sq miles (15,100,000 sq km).

At a latitude of more than 75° N, the Arctic Ocean is almost permanently covered by pack-ice, though high winds and the movement of the seas may cause the ice to crack and break up.

In the more southerly reaches of the Arctic, like Siberia, much of the land is covered by permafrost. In the summer, higher temperatures warm the frozen ground, causing a number of typical phenomena. These include solifluction, the fast downhill movement of top soil layers; freeze/thaw activity, which patterns the ground into regular polygonal shapes, and the formation of large domes with a frozen ice core, known as pingos.

Lomonosov Ridge

Lomonosov Ridge

Arctic ice shelf

Much of Greenland is covered by a massive ice sheet more than 650,000 sq miles (1,683,400 sq km) in extent. The weight of the ice has depressed the central land area to form a basin lying more than 1000 ft (300 m) below sea level. Only at the edges of the island is bare rock visible.

Iceland has five major glaciers, sustained by heavy snowfall. Parts of the ice cap cover active volcanoes, such as Bárdharbunga, which periodically erupt causing the melted ice to form a great lake at the glacier margins.

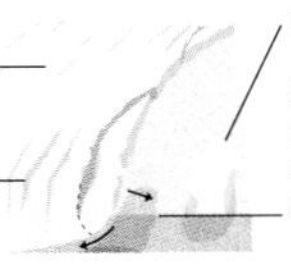

Iceberg

Ice sheet

Sea water melts the edge of the ice sheet

Crevasses occur at the edge of the ice sheet

At the boundary of the Arctic ice shelves, sea water flows under the ice causing melting and forming crevasses on the surface. This eventually weakens blocks of ice which break away as icebergs. This process is known as calving.

Map labels: Bering Sea, NORTH AMERICA, ASIA, ARCTIC OCEAN, EUROPE, ATLANTIC OCEAN, Inuvik, Tiksi, Qaanaaq, Noril'sk, Murmansk, Reykjavík

Right-hand map labels: NORTH AMERICA, CANADA, Great Bear Lake, Great Slave Lake, Coppermine, Mackenzie, Bathurst Inlet, Cambridge Bay, Queen Maud Gulf, King William Island, Booth Peninsula, Nelson, Back, Churchill, Southampton Island, Repulse Bay, Melville Peninsula, Hudson Bay, Coats Island, Mansel Island, Foxe Basin, Prince Charles Island, Ivujivik, Inukjuak, Hudson Strait, Foxe Peninsula, Lake Harbour, Baffin Island, Cumberland Sound, Ungava Bay, Cape Chidley, Davis Strait, Nain, Labrador Sea, Maniitsoq, NUUK, Labrador Basin, Paamiut, Ivittuut, Qaqortoq, Nanortalik, Uummannarsuaq, Eirik Ridge, ATLANTIC

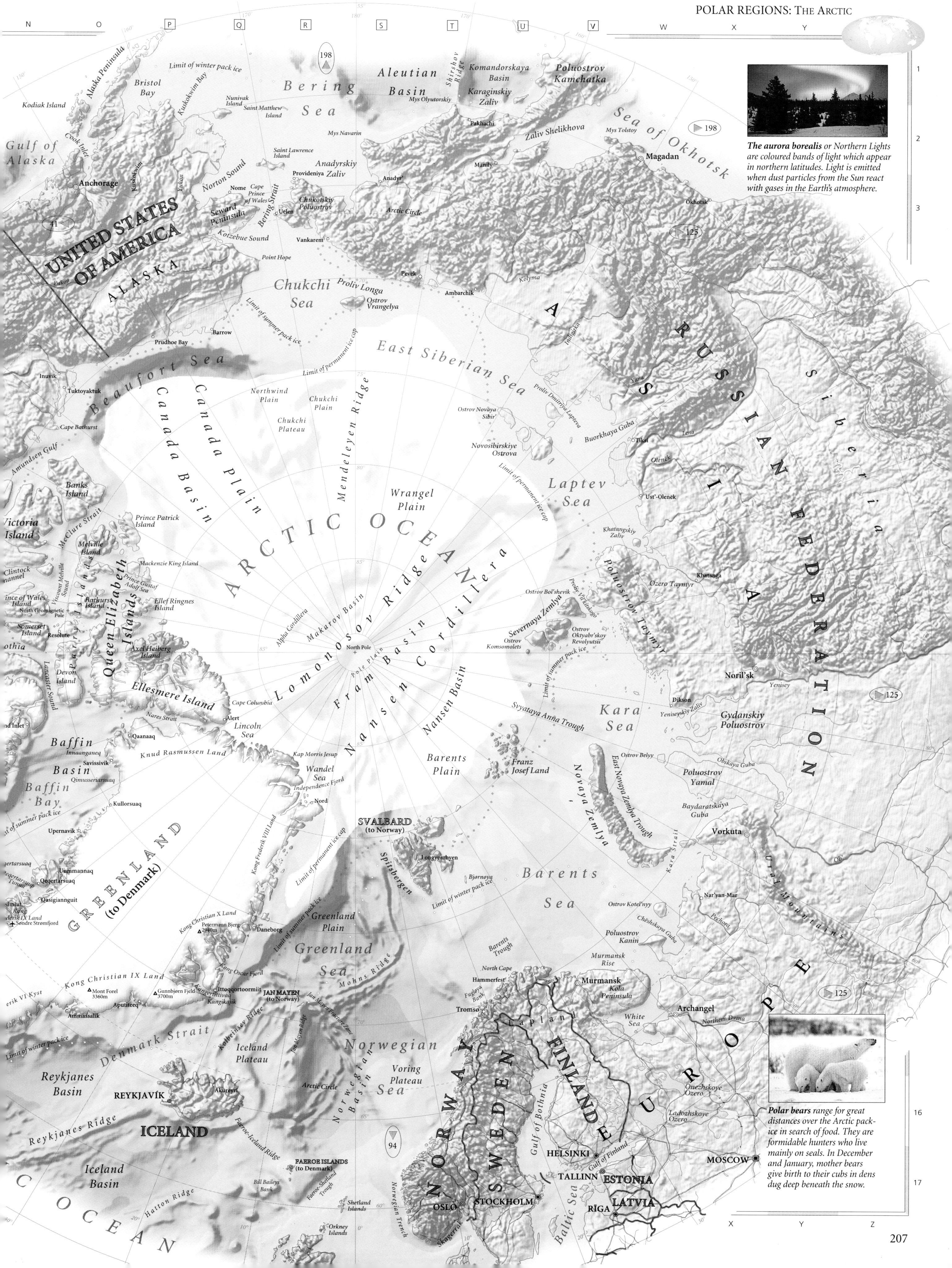

N O P Q R S T U V W X Y

1

2

The aurora borealis or Northern Lights are coloured bands of light which appear in northern latitudes. Light is emitted when dust particles from the Sun react with gases in the Earth's atmosphere.

3

Map labels

Aleutian Basin
Bering Sea
Komandorskaya Basin
Karaginskiy Zaliv
Poluostrov Kamchatka
Shirshov Ridge
Mys Olyutorskiy
Sea of Okhotsk
Pakhachi
Zaliv Shelikhova
Mys Navarin
Mys Tolstoy
Magadan
Okhotsk
Anadyrskiy Zaliv
Manily
Anadyr
Providencia Zaliv
Chukotskiy Poluostrov
Uelen
Arctic Circle

Alaska Peninsula
Bristol Bay
Kuskokwim Bay
Nunivak Island
Saint Matthew Island
Saint Lawrence Island
Kodiak Island
Gulf of Alaska
Cook Inlet
Anchorage
Norton Sound
Nome
Cape Prince of Wales
Seward Peninsula
Bering Strait
UNITED STATES OF AMERICA
ALASKA
Yukon
Kotzebue Sound
Point Hope
Vankarem

Kolyma
Indigirka
RUSSIAN FEDERATION
Siberia
A
Pevek
Ambarchik
Proliv Longa
Ostrov Vrangelya
Chukchi Sea
Barrow
Prudhoe Bay
Beaufort Sea
Limit of winter pack ice
Limit of summer pack ice
Limit of permanent ice cap
Inuvik
Tuktoyaktuk
Cape Bathurst

East Siberian Sea
Proliv Dmitriya Lapteva
Yana
Lena
Ust'-Olenek
Olenek
Buorkhaya Guba
Tiksi
Novosibirskiye Ostrova
Ostrov Novaya Sibir'
Laptev Sea

Amundsen Gulf
Banks Island
Canada Plain
Canada Basin
Northwind Plain
Chukchi Plain
Chukchi Plateau
Mendeleyen Ridge
Wrangel Plain
ARCTIC OCEAN
Victoria Island
McClure Strait
Melville Island
Prince Patrick Island
Mackenzie King Island
Prince Gustaf Adolf Island
Ellef Ringnes Island
Viscount Melville Sound
Makarov Basin
Alpha Cordillera
Khatanga
Ozero Taymyr
Poluostrov Taymyr
Khatangskiy Zaliv
Ostrov Bol'shevik
Proliv Vil'kitskogo
Severnaya Zemlya
Ostrov Oktyabr'skoy Revolyutsii
Ostrov Komsomolets

Clintock Channel
Prince of Wales Island
North Geomagnetic Pole
Somerset Island
Bathurst Island
Queen Elizabeth Islands
Axel Heiberg Island
Resolute
Parry Islands
Lomonosov Ridge
Fram Basin Cordillera
Nansen Cordillera
North Pole
Pole Plain
Nansen Basin
Noril'sk
Yenisey
Dikson
Yeniseyskiy Zaliv
Gydanskiy Poluostrov
FEDERATION
Kara Sea
Svyataya Anna Trough

Devon Island
Ellesmere Island
Cape Columbia
Alert
Lincoln Sea
Nares Strait
Qaanaaq
Innaangneq
Savissivik
Qimusseriarsuaq
Baffin Basin
Baffin Bay
Knud Rasmussen Land
Kap Morris Jesup
Wandel Sea
Independence Fjord
Nord
Barents Plain
Franz Josef Land
Novaya Zemlya
East Novaya Zemlya Trough
Ostrov Belyy
Obskaya Guba
Poluostrov Yamal
Baydaratskaya Guba
Limit of summer pack ice
Vorkuta
Ural Mountains

Kullorsuaq
Upernavik
Uummannaq
Qeqertarsuaq
GREENLAND (to Denmark)
Kong Frederik VIII Land
Kong Christian X Land
Daneborg
Wandel Sea
SVALBARD (to Norway)
Spitsbergen
Longyearbyen
Bjørnøya
Ostrov Kotel'nyy
Chëshskaya Guba
Poluostrov Kanin
Barents Sea
Limit of winter pack ice
Nar'yan-Mar
Pechora

Baffin Bay
Qasigiannguit
Kong Frederik IX Land
Søndre Strømfjord
Petermann Bjerg 2940m
Gunnbjørn Fjeld 3700m
Mont Forel 3360m
Aputiteeq
Ammassalik
Limit of winter pack ice
Kong Oscar Fjord
Ittoqqortoormiit
Kangikajik
Greenland Plain
Greenland Sea
Mohns Ridge
Barents Trough
North Cape
Hammerfest
EUROPE
Lapland
Murmansk Rise
White Sea
Murmansk
Kola Peninsula
Archangel
Northern Dvina
125

JAN MAYEN (to Norway)
Jan Mayen Fracture Zone
Kolbeinsey Ridge
Limit of summer pack ice
Tromsø
Fugløya Bank
Onezhskoye Ozero
Ladozhskoye Ozero

Denmark Strait
Kong Christian IX Land
Erik VI Kyst
Iceland Plateau
Norwegian Sea
Norwegian Basin
Voring Plateau
Arctic Circle
Akureyri
NORWAY
SWEDEN
FINLAND
Gulf of Bothnia

Reykjanes Basin
REYKJAVÍK
ICELAND
Iceland Basin
Reykjanes Ridge
Faeroe-Iceland Ridge
FAEROE ISLANDS (to Denmark)
Bill Baileys Bank
Faeroe-Shetland Trough
Shetland Islands
Orkney Islands
Norwegian Trough
Voring Plateau
HELSINKI
TALLINN
ESTONIA
Gulf of Finland
Baltic Sea
MOSCOW
OSLO
STOCKHOLM
Skagerrak
RIGA
LATVIA
OCEAN

198
94
125
41

16

Polar bears range for great distances over the Arctic pack-ice in search of food. They are formidable hunters who live mainly on seals. In December and January, mother bears give birth to their cubs in dens dug deep beneath the snow.

17

THE TIME ZONES

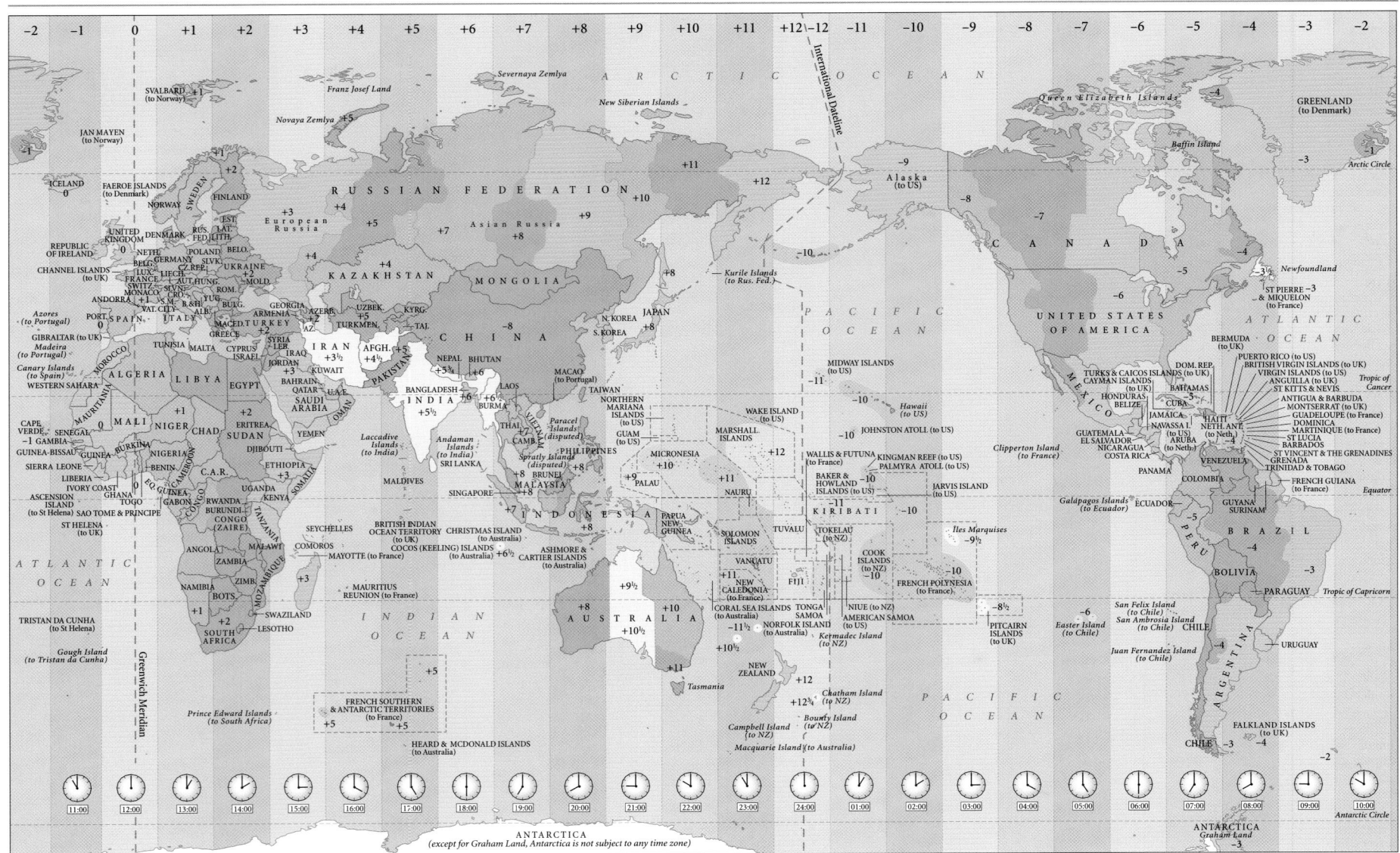

The numbers at the top of the map indicate the number of hours each time zone is ahead or behind Greenwich Mean Time (GMT). The clocks and 24 hour times given at the bottom of the map show the time in each time zone when it is 12:00 hours noon GMT.

COUNTRIES OF THE WORLD

THERE ARE CURRENTLY 192 independent countries in the world – more than at any previous time – and 59 dependencies. Antarctica is the only land area on Earth which is not officially part of, and does not belong to, any one country.

In 1950, the world comprised 82 countries. In the decades following, many more states came into being as they achieved independence from their former colonial rulers. Most recently, the break-up of the Soviet Union in 1991, and Yugoslavia in 1992, swelled the ranks of independent states.

COUNTRY FACTFILE KEY

Formation Date of independence / date current borders were established
Population Total population / population density – based on total *land* area / percentage of urban-based population
Languages An asterisk (*) denotes the official language(s)
Calorie consumption Average number of calories consumed daily per person

---

AFGHANISTAN
Central Asia

Official name Islamic State of Afghanistan
Formation 1919 / 1919
Capital Kabul
Population 20.1 million / 80 people per sq mile (31 people per sq km) / 20%
Total area 251,770 sq miles (652,090 sq km)
Languages Persian*, Pashtu*, Dari, Uzbek, Turkmen
Religions Sunni Muslim 84%, Shi'a Muslim 15%, other 1%
Ethnic mix Pashtun 38%, Tajik 25%, Hazara 19%, Uzbek 6%, other 12%
Government Mujahideen coalition
Currency Afghani = 100 puls
Literacy rate 29%
Calorie consumption 1523 kilocalories

ALBANIA
Southeast Europe

Official name Republic of Albania
Formation 1912 / 1913
Capital Tirana
Population 3.4 million / 321 people per sq mile (124 people per sq km) / 36%
Total area 11,100 sq miles (28,750 sq km)
Languages Albanian*, Greek, Macedonian
Religions Muslim 70%, Greek Orthodox 20%, Roman Catholic 10%
Ethnic mix Albanian 96%, Greek 2%, other (including Macedonian) 2%
Government Multiparty republic
Currency Lek = 100 qindars
Literacy rate 72%
Calorie consumption 2605 kilocalories

ALGERIA
North Africa

Official name Democratic and Popular Republic of Algeria
Formation 1962 / 1962
Capital Algiers
Population 27.9 million / 31 people per sq mile (12 people per sq km) / 53%
Total area 919,590 sq miles (2,381,740 sq km)
Languages Arabic*, Berber, French
Religions Muslim 99%, Christian & Jewish 1%
Ethnic mix Arab and Berber 99%, European 1%
Government Military regime
Currency Dinar = 100 centimes
Literacy rate 57%
Calorie consumption 2897 kilocalories

ANDORRA
Southwest Europe

Official name Principality of Andorra
Formation 1278 / 1278
Capital Andorra la Vella
Population 64,000 / 357 people per sq mile (138 people per sq km) / 94%
Total area 181 sq miles (468 sq km)
Languages Catalan*, Spanish, French, Portuguese
Religions Roman Catholic 86%, other 14%
Ethnic mix Catalan 61%, Spanish Castilian 30%, other 9%
Government Parliamentary democracy
Currency French franc, Spanish peseta
Literacy rate 100%
Calorie consumption 3708 kilocalories

ANGOLA
Southern Africa

Official name Republic of Angola
Formation 1975 / 1975
Capital Luanda
Population 11.1 million / 23 people per sq mile (9 people per sq km) / 30%
Total area 481,551 sq miles (1,246,700 sq km)
Languages Portuguese*, Umbundu, Kimbundu, Kongo
Religions Roman Catholic / Protestant 64%, traditional beliefs 34%, other 2%
Ethnic mix Ovimbundu 37%, Kimbundu 25%, Bakongo 13%, other 25%
Government Multiparty republic
Currency Kwanza = 100 lwei
Literacy rate 42%
Calorie consumption 1839 kilocalories

ANTIGUA & BARBUDA
West Indies

Official name Antigua and Barbuda
Formation 1981 / 1981
Capital St John's
Population 65,000 / 384 people per sq mile (148 people per sq km) / 36%
Total area 170 sq miles (440 sq km)
Languages English*, English Creole
Religions Protestant 87%, Roman Catholic 10%, other 3%
Ethnic mix Black 98%, other 2%
Government Parliamentary democracy
Currency E. Caribbean $ = 100 cents
Literacy rate 96%
Calorie consumption 2458 kilocalories

ARGENTINA
South America

Official name Republic of Argentina
Formation 1816 / 1925
Capital Buenos Aires
Population 34.6 million / 34 people per sq mile (13 people per sq km) / 87%
Total area 1,068,296 sq miles (2,766,890 sq km)
Languages Spanish*, Italian, English German, French, Indian languages
Religions Roman Catholic 90%, Jewish 2%, other 8%
Ethnic mix White 85%, other (including *mestizo* and Indian) 15%
Government Multiparty republic
Currency Peso = 100 centavos
Literacy rate 95%
Calorie consumption 2880 kilocalories

ARMENIA
Southwest Asia

Official name Republic of Armenia
Formation 1991 / 1991
Capital Yerevan
Population 3.6 million / 314 people per sq mile (121 people per sq km) / 68%
Total area 11,505 sq miles (29,000 sq km)
Languages Armenian*, Azerbaijani, Russian, Kurdish
Religions Armenian Apostolic 90%, other Christian and Muslim 10%
Ethnic mix Armenian 93%, Azerbaijani 3%, Russian, Kurdish 4%
Government Multiparty republic
Currency Dram = 100 louma
Literacy rate 99%
Calorie consumption NOT AVAILABLE

AUSTRALIA
Australasia & Oceania

Official name Commonwealth of Australia
Formation 1901 / 1901
Capital Canberra
Population 17.8 million / 5 people per sq mile (2 people per sq km) / 85%
Total area 2,967,893 sq miles (7,686,850 sq km)
Languages English*, Greek, Italian, Malay, Vietnamese, Aboriginal
Religions Protestant 60%, Roman Catholic 26%, other 14%
Ethnic mix Caucasian 95%, Asian 4%, Aboriginal and other 1%
Government Parliamentary democracy
Currency Australian $ = 100 cents
Literacy rate 99%
Calorie consumption 3179 kilocalories

AUSTRIA
Central Europe

Official name Republic of Austria
Formation 1918 / 1945
Capital Vienna
Population 8 million / 251 people per sq mile (97 people per sq km) / 55%
Total area 32,375 sq miles (83,850 sq km)
Languages German*, Croatian, Slovene, Hungarian (Magyar)
Religions Roman Catholic 85%, Protestant 6%, other 9%
Ethnic mix German 99%, other (including Hungarian, Slovene, Croat) 1%
Government Multiparty republic
Currency Schilling = 100 groschen
Literacy rate 99%
Calorie consumption 3497 kilocalories

AZERBAIJAN
Southwest Asia

Official name Azerbaijani Republic
Formation 1991 / 1991
Capital Baku
Population 7.6 million / 228 people per sq mile (88 people per sq km) / 55%
Total area 33,436 sq miles (86,600 sq km)
Languages Azerbaijani*, Russian, Armenian
Religions Muslim 83%, Armenian Apostolic, Russian Orthodox 17%
Ethnic mix Azerbaijani 83%, Russian 6%, Armenian 6%, other 5%
Government Multiparty republic
Currency Manat = 100 gopik
Literacy rate 97%
Calorie consumption NOT AVAILABLE

BAHAMAS
West Indies

Official name Commonwealth of the Bahamas
Formation 1973 / 1973
Capital Nassau
Population 300,000 / 78 people per sq mile (30 people per sq km) / 85%
Total area 5359 sq miles (13,880 sq km)
Languages English*, English Creole
Religions Protestant 76%, Roman Catholic 19%, other 5%
Ethnic mix Black 85%, White 15%
Government Parliamentary democracy
Currency Bahamian $ = 100 cents
Literacy rate 98%
Calorie consumption 2624 kilocalories

BAHRAIN
Southwest Asia

Official name State of Bahrain
Formation 1971 / 1971
Capital Manama
Population 600,000 / 2,286 people per sq mile (882 people per sq km) / 89%
Total area 263 sq miles (680 sq km)
Languages Arabic*, English, Urdu
Religions Muslim (Shi'a majority) 85%, Christian 7%, other 8%
Ethnic mix Arab 73%, South Asian 14%, Persian 8%, other 5%
Government Absolute monarchy (emirate)
Currency Dinar = 1,000 fils
Literacy rate 84%
Calorie consumption NOT AVAILABLE

BANGLADESH
South Asia

Official name People's Republic of Bangladesh
Formation 1971 / 1971
Capital Dhaka
Population 120.4 million / 2330 people per sq mile (899 people per sq km) / 17%
Total area 55,598 sq miles (143,998 sq km)
Languages Bengali*, Urdu, Chakma, Marma, Garo, Khasi
Religions Muslim 83%, Hindu 16%, other 1%
Ethnic mix Bengali 98%, other 2%
Government Multiparty republic
Currency Taka = 100 paisa
Literacy rate 35%
Calorie consumption 2019 kilocalories

BARBADOS
West Indies

Official name Barbados
Formation 1966 / 1966
Capital Bridgetown
Population 300,000 / 1809 people per sq mile (698 people per sq km) / 46%
Total area 166 sq miles (430 sq km)
Languages English*, English Creole
Religions Protestant 94%, Roman Catholic 5%, other 1%
Ethnic mix Black 80%, mixed 15%, White 4%, other 1%
Government Parliamentary democracy
Currency Barbados $ = 100 cents
Literacy rate 99%
Calorie consumption 3207 kilocalories

BELGIUM
Northwest Europe

Official name Kingdom of Belgium
Formation 1830 / 1830
Capital Brussels
Population 10.1 million / 798 people per sq mile (308 people per sq km) / 97%
Total area 12,780 sq miles (33,100 sq km)
Languages French*, Dutch*, German, Flemish
Religions Roman Catholic 75%, other 25%
Ethnic mix Flemish 58%, Walloon 32%, other European 6%, other 4%
Government Constitutional monarchy
Currency Franc = 100 centimes
Literacy rate 99%
Calorie consumption: 3681 kilocalories

BELIZE
Central America

Official name Belize
Formation 1981 / 1981
Capital Belmopan
Population 200,000 /23 people per sq mile (9 people per sq km) / 47%
Total area 8,865 sq miles (22,960 sq km)
Languages English*, English Creole, Spanish
Religions Christian 87%, other 13%
Ethnic mix *mestizo* 44%, Creole 30%, Indian 11%, Garifuna 8%, other 7%
Government Parliamentary democracy
Currency Belizean $ =100 cents
Literacy rate 95%
Calorie consumption 2662 kilocalories

BELORUSSIA
Eastern Europe

Official name Republic of Belarus
Formation 1991 / 1991
Capital Minsk
Population 10.1 million / 127 people per sq mile (49 people per sq km) / 68%
Total area 80,154 sq miles (207,600 sq km)
Languages Belorussian*, Russian
Religions Russian Orthodox 60%, Roman Catholic 8%, other 32%
Ethnic mix Belorussian 78%, Russian 13%, Polish 4%, other 5%
Government Multiparty republic
Currency Rouble = 100 kopeks
Literacy rate 98%
Calorie consumption NOT AVAILABLE

BENIN
West Africa

Official name Republic of Benin
Formation 1960 / 1960
Capital Porto-Novo
Population 5.4 million / 127 people per sq mile (49 people per sq km) / 30%
Total area 43,480 sq miles (112,620 sq km)
Languages French*, Fon, Adja, Yoruba
Religions Traditional beliefs 70%, Muslim 15%, Christian 15%
Ethnic mix Fon 39%, Yoruba 12%, Adja 10%, other 39%
Government Multiparty republic
Currency CFA franc = 100 centimes
Literacy rate 23%
Calorie consumption 2532 kilocalories

BHUTAN
Southeast Asia

Official name Kingdom of Bhutan
Formation 1949 / 1865
Capital Thimphu
Population 1.6 million / 88 people per sq mile (34 people per sq km) / 6%
Total area 18,147 sq miles (47,000 sq km)
Languages Dzongkha*, Nepali, Assamese
Religions Mahayana Buddhist 70%, Hindu 24%, Muslim 5%, other 1%
Ethnic mix Bhutia 61%, Gurung 15%, Assamese 13%, other 11%
Government Constitutional monarchy
Currency Ngultrum = 100 chetrum
Literacy rate 38%
Calorie consumption 2553 kilocalories

BOLIVIA
South America

Official name Republic of Bolivia
Formation 1825 / 1938
Capitals La Paz / Sucre
Population 7.4 million / 18 people per sq mile (7 people per sq km) / 58%
Total area 424,162 sq miles (1,098,580 sq km)
Languages Spanish*, Quechua*, Aymará*
Religions Roman Catholic 95%, other 5%
Ethnic mix Indian 55%, *mestizo* 27%, White 10%, other 8%
Government Multiparty republic
Currency Boliviano = 100 centavos
Literacy rate 83%
Calorie consumption 2094 kilocalories

BOSNIA & HERZEGOVINA
Southeast Europe

Official name Republic of Bosnia and Herzegovina
Formation 1992 / 1992
Capital Sarajevo
Population 3.5 million / 176 people per sq mile (68 people per sq km) / 36%
Total area 19,741 sq miles (51,130 sq km)
Languages Serbian*, Croatian*
Religions Muslim 40%, Orthodox Catholic 31%, other 29%
Ethnic mix Bosnian 44%, Serb 31%, Croat 17%, other 8%
Government Multiparty republic
Currency Dinar = 100 para
Literacy rate 93%
Calorie consumption NOT AVAILABLE

BOTSWANA
Southern Africa

Official name Republic of Botswana
Formation 1966 / 1966
Capital Gaborone
Population 1.5 million / 8 people per sq mile (3 people per sq km) / 25%
Total area 224,600 sq miles (581,730 sq km)
Languages English*, Tswana, Shona, San
Religions Traditional beliefs 50%, Christian 50%
Ethnic mix Tswana 75%, Shona 12%, San 3%, other 10%
Government Multiparty republic
Currency Pula = 100 thebe
Literacy rate 67%
Calorie consumption 2266 kilocalories

BRAZIL
South America

Official name Federative Republic of Brazil
Formation 1822 / 1929
Capital Brasília
Population 161.8 million / 49 people per sq mile (19 people per sq km) / 76%
Total area 3,286,472 sq miles (8,511,970 sq km)
Languages Portuguese*, German, Italian
Religions Roman Catholic 90%, other 10%
Ethnic mix White (Portuguese, Italian, German, Japanese) 55%, mixed 38%, Black 6%, other 1%
Government Multiparty republic
Currency Real = 100 centavos
Literacy rate 80%
Calorie consumption 2824 kilocalories

BRUNEI
Southeast Asia

Official name Sultanate of Brunei
Formation 1984 / 1984
Capital Bandar Seri Begawan
Population 300,000 / 148 people per sq mile (57 people per sq km) / 58%
Total area 2,228 sq miles (5,770 sq km)
Languages Malay*, English, Chinese
Religions Muslim 63%, Buddhist 14%, Christian 10%, other 13%
Ethnic mix Malay 69%, Chinese 18%, other 13%
Government Absolute monarchy
Currency Brunei $ = 100 cents
Literacy rate 89%
Calorie consumption 2745 kilocalories

BULGARIA
Southeast Europe

Official name Republic of Bulgaria
Formation 1908 / 1923
Capital Sofia
Population 8.8 million / 207 people per sq mile (80 people per sq km) / 69%
Total area 42,822 sq miles (110,910 sq km)
Languages Bulgarian*, Turkish, Macedonian, Romany, Armenian
Religions Christian 85%, Muslim 13%, Jewish 1%, other 1%
Ethnic mix Bulgarian 85%, Turkish 9%, Macedonian 3%, Gypsy 3%
Government Multiparty republic
Currency Lev = 100 stoninki
Literacy rate 98%
Calorie consumption 2831 kilocalories

BURKINA
West Africa

Official name Burkina Faso
Formation 1960 / 1960
Capital Ouagadougou
Population 10.3 million / 98 people per sq mile (38 people per sq km) / 22%
Total area 105,870 sq miles (274,200 sq km)
Languages French*, Mossi, Fulani
Religions Traditional beliefs 65%, Muslim 25%, Christian 10%
Ethnic mix Mossi 45%, Mande 10%, Fulani 10%, other 35%
Government Multiparty republic
Currency CFA franc = 100 centimes
Literacy rate 18%
Calorie consumption 2387 kilocalories

BURMA
Southeast Asia

Official name Union of Myanmar
Formation 1948 / 1948
Capital Rangoon
Population 46.5 million / 184 people per sq mile (71 people per sq km) / 25%
Total area 261,200 sq miles (676,550 sq km)
Languages Burmese*, Karen, Mon
Religions Buddhist 89%, Muslim 4%, other 7%
Ethnic mix Burman 68%, Shan 9%, Karen 6%, Rakhine 4%, other 13%
Government Military regime
Currency Kyat = 100 pyas
Literacy rate 81%
Calorie consumption 2598 kilocalories

BURUNDI
Central Africa

Official name Republic of Burundi
Formation 1962 / 1962
Capital Bujumbura
Population 6.4 million / 648 people per sq mile (250 people per sq km) / 7%
Total area 10,750 sq miles (27,830 sq km)
Languages Kirundi*, French*, Swahili
Religions Christian 68%, traditional beliefs 32%
Ethnic mix Hutu 85%, Tutsi 13%, Twa pygmy 1%, other 1%
Government Multiparty republic
Currency Franc = 100 centimes
Literacy rate 50%
Calorie consumption 1941 kilocalories

CAMBODIA
Southeast Asia

Official name Kingdom of Cambodia
Formation 1953 / 1953
Capital Phnom Penh
Population 10.3 million / 150 people per sq mile (58 people per sq km) / 19%
Total area 69,000 sq miles (181,040 sq km)
Languages Khmer*, French, Chinese, Vietnamese
Religions Buddhist 88%, Muslim 2%, other 10%
Ethnic mix Khmer 94%, Chinese 4%, other 2%
Government Constitutional monarchy
Currency Riel = 100 sen
Literacy rate 35%
Calorie consumption 2021 kilocalories

CAMEROON
Central Africa

Official name Republic of Cameroon
Formation 1960 / 1960
Capital Yaoundé
Population 12.5 million / 73 people per sq mile (28 people per sq km) / 42%
Total area 183,570 sq miles (475,440 sq km)
Languages English*, French*, Fang, Bulu, Yaundé, Duala
Religions Traditional beliefs 51%, Christian 33%, Muslim 16%
Ethnic mix Bamileke and Manum 20%, Fang 19%, other 61%
Government Multiparty republic
Currency CFA franc = 100 centimes
Literacy rate 54%
Calorie consumption 1981 kilocalories

CANADA
North America

Official name Canada
Formation 1867 / 1949
Capital Ottawa
Population 29.5 million / 8 people per sq mile (3 people per sq km) / 77%
Total area 3,851,788 sq miles (9,976,140 sq km)
Languages English*, French*, Chinese, Italian, German, Portuguese, Inuit
Religions Roman Catholic 46%, Protestant 30%, other 24%
Ethnic mix British origin 40%, French origin 27%, other 33%
Government Parliamentary state
Currency Canadian $ = 100 cents
Literacy rate 96%
Calorie consumption 3094 kilocalories

CAPE VERDE
Atlantic Ocean

Official Name Republic of Cape Verde
Formation 1975 / 1975
Capital Praia
Population 400,000 / 257 people per sq mile (99 people per sq km) / 49%
Total area 1556 sq miles (4030 sq km)
Languages Portuguese*, Creole
Religions Roman Catholic 98%, Protestant 2%
Ethnic mix Creole (*mestizo*) 71%, Black 28%, White 1%
Government Multiparty republic
Currency Escudo = 100 centavos
Literacy rate 63%
Calorie consumption 2805 kilocalories

CENTRAL AFRICAN REPUBLIC
Central Africa

Official name Central African Republic
Formation 1960 / 1960
Capital Bangui
Population 3.3 million / 13 people per sq mile (5 people per sq km) / 38%
Total area 240,530 sq miles (622,980 sq km)
Languages French*, Sango, Banda, Gbaya
Religions Christian 50%, traditional beliefs 27%, Muslim 15%, other 8%
Ethnic mix Baya 34%, Banda 27%, Mandjia 21%, other 18%
Government Multiparty republic
Currency CFA franc = 100 centimes
Literacy rate 38%
Calorie consumption 1690 kilocalories

CHAD
Central Africa

Official name Republic of Chad
Formation 1960 / 1960
Capital Ndjamena
Population 6.4 million / 19 people per sq mile (5 people per sq km) / 21%
Total area 495,752 sq miles (1,284,000 sq km)
Languages French*, Sara, Maba
Religions Muslim 44%, Christian 33%, traditional beliefs 23%
Ethnic mix Bagirmi, Sara and Kreish 31%, Sudanic Arab 26%, Teda 7%, other 36%
Government Transitional
Currency CFA franc = 100 centimes
Literacy rate 45%
Calorie consumption 1989 kilocalories

CHILE
South America

Official name Republic of Chile
Formation 1818 / 1929
Capital Santiago
Population 14.3 million / 49 people per sq mile (19 people per sq km) / 84%
Total area 292,258 sq miles (756,950 sq km)
Languages Spanish*, Indian languages
Religions Roman Catholic 89%, Protestant 11%
Ethnic mix White and *mestizo* 92%, Indian 6%, other 2%
Government Multiparty republic
Currency Peso = 100 centavos
Literacy rate 94%
Calorie consumption 2582 kilocalories

CHINA
East Asia

Official name People's Republic of China
Formation 1949 / 1950
Capital Beijing
Population 1.2 billion / 340 people per sq mile (131 people per sq km) / 28%
Total area 3,628,166 sq miles (9,396,960 sq km)
Languages Mandarin*, Wu, Cantonese, Hsiang, Min, Hakka, Kan
Religions Confucianist 20%, Buddhist 6%, Taoist 2%, other 72%
Ethnic mix Han 93%, Zhaung 1%, other 6%
Government Single-party republic
Currency Yuan = 10 jiao = 100 fen
Literacy rate 78%
Calorie consumption 2727 kilocalories

COLOMBIA
South America

Official name Republic of Colombia
Formation 1819 / 1922
Capital Bogotá
Population 35.1 million / 88 people per sq mile (34 people per sq km) / 71%
Total area 439,733 sq miles (1,138,910 sq km)
Languages Spanish*, Indian languages, English Creole
Religions Roman Catholic 95%, other 5%
Ethnic mix *mestizo* 58%, White 20%, mixed 14%, other 8%
Government Multiparty republic
Currency Peso = 100 centavos
Literacy rate 87%
Calorie consumption 2677 kilocalories

COMOROS
Indian Ocean

Official name Federal Islamic Republic of the Comoros
Formation 1975 / 1975
Capital Moroni
Population 600,000 / 814 people per sq mile (314 people per sq km) / 29%
Total area 861 sq miles (2230 sq km)
Languages Arabic*, French*, Comoran
Religions Muslim 86%, Roman Catholic 14%
Ethnic mix Comorian 96%, other 4%
Government Islamic republic
Currency Franc = 100 centimes
Literacy rate 48%
Calorie consumption 1897 kilocalories

CONGO
Central Africa

Official name Republic of the Congo
Formation 1960 / 1960
Capital Brazzaville
Population 2.6 million / 21 people per sq km (8 people per sq km) / 56%
Total area 132,040 sq miles (342,000 sq km)
Languages French*, Kongo, Teke, Lingala
Religions Roman Catholic 50%, traditional beliefs 48%, other 2%
Ethnic mix Bakongo 48%, Teke 17%, Mboshi 17%, other 18%
Government Multiparty republic
Currency CFA franc = 100 centimes
Literacy rate 57%
Calorie consumption 2296 kilocalories

CONGO (ZAIRE) *Central Africa*

Official name Democratic Republic of Congo
Formation 1960 / 1960
Capital Kinshasa
Population 43.9 million / 49 people per sq mile (19 people per sq km) / 29%
Total area 905,563 sq miles (2,345,410 sq km)
Languages French*, Kiswahili, Tshiluba, Lingala
Religions Christian 70%, traditional beliefs 20%, Muslim 10%
Ethnic mix Bantu 23%, Hamitic 23%, other 54%
Government Transitional
Currency New zaire = 100 makuta
Literacy rate 77%
Calorie consumption 2060 kilocalories

COSTA RICA
Central America

Official name Republic of Costa Rica
Formation 1821 / 1838
Capital San José
Population 3.4 million / 174 people per sq mile (67 people per sq km) / 48%
Total area 19,730 miles (51,100 sq km)
Languages Spanish*, English Creole, Bribri, Cabecar
Religions Roman Catholic 95%, other 5%
Ethnic mix White / *mestizo* 96%, Black 2%, Indian 2%
Government Multiparty republic
Currency Colón = 100 centimos
Literacy rate 93%
Calorie consumption 2883 kilocalories

CROATIA
Southeast Europe

Official name Republic of Croatia
Formation 1991 / 1991
Capital Zagreb
Population 4.5 million / 207 people per sq mile (80 people per sq km) / 51%
Total area 21,830 sq miles (56,540 sq km)
Languages Croatian*, Serbian, Hungarian (Magyar), Slovenian
Religions Roman Catholic 77%, Eastern Orthodox 11%, Protestant 1%, Muslim 1%, other 10%
Ethnic mix Croat 80%, Serb 12%, Hungarian, Slovenian, other 8%
Government Multiparty republic
Currency Kuna = 100 lipa
Literacy rate 97%
Calorie consumption NOT AVAILABLE

CUBA
West Indies

Official name Republic of Cuba
Formation 1902 / 1898
Capital Havana
Population 10.8 million / 251 people per sq mile (97 people per sq km) / 75%
Total area 42,803 sq miles (110,860 sq km)
Languages Spanish*, English, French
Religions Roman Catholic 85%, other 15%
Ethnic mix White 66%, Afro-European 22%, other 12%
Government Socialist republic
Currency Peso = 100 centavos
Literacy rate 94%
Calorie consumption 2833 kilocalories

CYPRUS
Southeast Europe

Official name Republic of Cyprus
Formation 1960 / 1983
Capital Nicosia
Population 700,000 / 197 people per sq mile (76 people per sq km) / 53%
Total area 3572 sq miles (9251 sq km)
Languages Greek*, Turkish, English
Religions Greek Orthodox 77%, Muslim 18%, other 5%
Ethnic mix Greek 77%, Turkish 18%, other (mainly British) 5%
Government Multiparty republic
Currency Cypriot £ / Turkish lira
Literacy rate 94%
Calorie consumption 3779 kilocalories

CZECH REPUBLIC
Central Europe

Official name Czech Republic
Formation 1993 / 1993
Capital Prague
Population 10.3 million / 339 people per sq mile (131 people per sq km) / 65%
Total area 30,260 sq miles (78,370 sq km)
Languages Czech*, Slovak, Romany, Hungarian (Magyar)
Religions Roman Catholic 44%, Protestant 6%, other Christian 12%, other 38%
Ethnic mix Czech 85%, Moravian 13%, other 2%
Government Multiparty republic
Currency Koruna = 100 halura
Literacy rate 99%
Calorie consumption 3156 kilocalories

DENMARK
Northern Europe

Official name Kingdom of Denmark
Formation AD 960 / 1953
Capital Copenhagen
Population 5.2 million / 319 people per sq mile (123 people per sq km) / 85%
Total area 16,629 sq miles (43,069 sq km)
Languages Danish*, Faeroese, Inuit
Religions Evangelical Lutheran 91%, other Christian 9%
Ethnic mix Danish 96%, Faeroese & Inuit 1%, other 3%
Government Constitutional monarchy
Currency Krone = 100 øre
Literacy rate 100%
Calorie consumption 3664 kilocalories

DJIBOUTI
East Africa

Official name Republic of Djibouti
Formation 1977 / 1977
Capital Djibouti
Population 600,000 / 67 people per sq mile (26 people per sq km) / 81%
Total area 8958 sq miles (23,200 sq km)
Languages Arabic*, French*, Somali, Afar
Religions Christian 87%, other 13%
Ethnic mix Issa 35%, Afar 20%, Gadaboursis and Isaaks 28%, other 17%
Government Single-party republic
Currency Franc = 100 centimes
Literacy rate 43%
Calorie consumption 2338 kilocalories

DOMINICA
West Indies

Official name Commonwealth of Dominica
Formation 1978 / 1978
Capital Roseau
Population 71,000 / 246 people per sq mile (95 people per sq km)/ 57%
Total area 290 sq miles (750 sq km)
Languages English*, French Creole, Carib, Cocoy
Religions Roman Catholic 77%, Protestant 15%, other 8%
Ethnic mix Black 98%, Indian 2%
Government Multiparty republic
Currency E. Caribbean $ = 100 cents
Literacy rate 97%
Calorie consumption 2778 kilocalories

DOMINICAN REPUBLIC
West Indies

Official name Dominican Republic
Formation 1865 / 1865
Capital Santo Domingo
Population 7.8 million / 417 people per sq mile (161 people per sq km) / 62%
Total area 18,815 sq miles (48,730 sq km)
Languages Spanish*, French Creole
Religions Roman Catholic 95%, other 5%
Ethnic mix Afro-European 73%, White 16%, Black 11%
Government Multiparty republic
Currency Peso = 100 centavos
Literacy rate 83%
Calorie consumption 2286 kilocalories

ECUADOR
South America

Official name Republic of Ecuador
Formation 1830 / 1942
Capital Quito
Population 11.5 million / 109 people per sq mile (42 people per sq km) / 56%
Total area 109,483 sq miles (283,560 sq km)
Languages Spanish*, Quechua, other Indian languages
Religions Roman Catholic 95%, other 5%
Ethnic mix *mestizo* 55%, Indian 25%, Black 10%, White 10%
Government Multiparty republic
Currency Sucre = 100 centavos
Literacy rate 87%
Calorie consumption 2583 kilocalories

EGYPT
North Africa

Official name Arab Republic of Egypt
Formation 1936 / 1982
Capital Cairo
Population 62.9 million / 163 people per sq mile (63 people per sq km) / 44%
Total area 386,660 sq miles (1,001,450 sq km)
Languages Arabic*, French, English, Berber, Greek, Armenian
Religions Muslim 94%, other 6%
Ethnic mix Eastern Hamitic 90%, other (including Greek, Armenian) 10%
Government Multiparty republic
Currency Pound = 100 piastres
Literacy rate 48%
Calorie consumption 3335 kilocalories

EL SALVADOR
Central America

Official name Republic of El Salvador
Formation 1856 / 1838
Capital San Salvador
Population 5.8 million / 726 people per sq mile (280 people per sq km) / 44%
Total area 8124 sq miles (21,040 sq km)
Languages Spanish*, Nahua
Religions Roman Catholic 75%, other 25%
Ethnic mix *mestizo* 89%, Indian 10%, White 1%
Government Multiparty republic
Currency Colón = 100 centavos
Literacy rate 73%
Calorie consumption 2663 kilocalories

EQUATORIAL GUINEA
Central Africa

Official name Republic of Equatorial Guinea
Formation 1968 / 1968
Capital Malabo
Population 400,000 / 36 people per sq mile (14 people per sq km) / 39%
Total area 10,830 sq miles (28,050 sq km)
Languages Spanish*, Fang, Bubi
Religions Christian 89%, other 11%
Ethnic mix Fang 72%, Bubi 14%, Duala 3%, other 11%
Government Multiparty republic
Currency CFA franc = 100 centimes
Literacy rate 50%
Calorie consumption NOT AVAILABLE

ERITREA
East Africa

Official name State of Eritrea
Formation 1993 / 1993
Capital Asmara
Population 3.5 million / 96 people per sq mile (37 people per sq km) / 22%
Total area 36,170 sq miles (93,680 sq km)
Languages Tigrinya*, Arabic*, Tigre
Religions Coptic Christian 45%, Muslim 45%, other 10%
Ethnic mix Nine main ethnic groups
Government Provisional military government
Currency Ethiopian birr = 100 cents
Literacy rate 20%
Calorie consumption 1610 kilocalories

ESTONIA
Northeast Europe

Official name Republic of Estonia
Formation 1991 / 1991
Capital Tallinn
Population 1.6 million / 86 people per sq mile (37 people per sq km) / 72%
Total area 17,423 sq miles (45,125 sq km)
Languages Estonian*, Russian
Religions Evangelical Lutheran 98%, Eastern Orthodox, Baptist 2%
Ethnic mix Estonian 62%, Russian 30%, Ukrainian 3%, other 5%
Government Multiparty republic
Currency Kroon = 100 cents
Literacy rate 99%
Calorie consumption NOT AVAILABLE

ETHIOPIA
East Africa

Official name Federal Democratic Republic of Ethiopia
Formation 1903 / 1993
Capital Addis Ababa
Population 55.1 million / 130 people per sq mile (50 people per sq km) / 13%
Total area 435,605 sq miles (1,128,221 sq km)
Languages Amharic*, English, Arabic
Religions Muslim 43%, Christian 37%, traditional beliefs, other 20%,
Ethnic mix Oromo 40%, Amhara and Tigrean 32%, other 28%
Government Multiparty republic
Currency Birr = 100 cents
Literacy rate 24%
Calorie consumption 1610 kilocalories

FIJI
Australasia & Oceania

Official name Sovereign Democratic Republic of Fiji
Formation 1970 / 1970
Capital Suva
Population 800,000 / 114 people per sq mile (44 people per sq km) / 40%
Total area 7,054 sq miles (18,270 sq km)
Languages English*, Fijian, Hindu, Urdu
Religions Christian 52%, Hindu 8%, Muslim 38%, other 2%
Ethnic mix Native Fijian 49%, Indo-Fijian 46%, other 5%
Government Multiparty republic
Currency Fiji $ = 100 cents
Literacy rate 87%
Calorie consumption 3089 kilocalories

FINLAND
Northern Europe

Official name Republic of Finland
Formation 1917 / 1917-1920
Capital Helsinki
Population 5.1 million / 44 people per sq mile (17 people per sq km) / 62%
Total area 130,552 sq miles (338,130 sq km)
Languages Finnish*, Swedish*, Lappish
Religions Evangelical Lutheran 89%, Greek Orthodox 1%, other 10%
Ethnic mix Finnish 93%, Swedish 6%, other (including Sami) 1%
Government Multiparty republic
Currency Markka = 100 pennia
Literacy rate 99%
Calorie consumption 3018 kilocalories

FRANCE
Western Europe

Official name French Republic
Formation 1685 / 1919–1920
Capital Paris
Population 58 million / 272 people per sq mile (105 people per sq km) / 73%
Total area 212,930 sq miles (551,500 sq km)
Languages French*, Provençal, Breton, Catalan, Basque
Religions Roman Catholic 90%, Protestant 2%, Jewish 1%, other 7%
Ethnic mix French 92%, North African 3%, other 5%
Government Multiparty republic
Currency Franc = 100 centimes
Literacy rate 99%
Calorie consumption 3633 kilocalories

GABON
Central Africa

Official name Gabonese Republic
Formation 1960 / 1960
Capital Libreville
Population 1.3 million / 13 people per sq mile (5 people per sq km) / 48%
Total area 103,347 sq miles (267,670 sq km)
Languages French*, Fang, Punu, Sira, Nzebi, Mpongwe
Religions Roman Catholic, other Christian 96%, Muslim 2%, other 2%
Ethnic mix Fang 36%, Mpongwe 15%, Mbete 14%, other 35%
Government Multiparty republic
Currency CFA franc = 100 centimes
Literacy rate 61%
Calorie consumption 2500 kilocalories

GAMBIA
West Africa

Official name Republic of the Gambia
Formation 1965 / 1965
Capital Banjul
Population 1.1 million / 286 people per sq mile (110 people per sq km) / 24%
Total area 4363 sq miles (11,300 sq km)
Languages English*, Mandinka, Fulani, Wolof, Diola, Soninke
Religions Muslim 85%, Christian 9%, traditional beliefs 6%
Ethnic mix Mandinka 41%, Fulani 14%, Wolof 13%, other 32%
Government Military regime
Currency Dalasi = 100 butut
Literacy rate 64%
Calorie consumption 2360 kilocalories

GEORGIA
Southwest Asia

Official name Republic of Georgia
Formation 1991 / 1991
Capital Tbilisi
Population 5.5 million / 206 people per sq mile (79 people per sq km) / 57%
Total area 26,911 sq miles (69,700 sq km)
Languages Georgian*, Russian
Religions Georgian Orthodox 70%, Russian Orthodox 10%, other 20%
Ethnic mix Georgian 69%, Armenian 9%, Russian 6%, other 16%
Government Republic
Currency Coupons
Literacy rate 99%
Calorie consumption NOT AVAILABLE

GERMANY
Northern Europe

Official name Federal Republic of Germany
Formation 1871 / 1990
Capital Berlin
Population 81.6 million / 604 people per sq mile (233 people per sq km) / 86%
Total area 137,800 sq miles (356,910 sq km)
Languages German*, Sorbian, Turkish
Religions Protestant 45%, Roman Catholic 37%, other 18%
Ethnic mix German 92%, other 8%
Government Multiparty republic
Currency Deutsche Mark = 100 pfennigs
Literacy rate 99%
Calorie consumption 3344 kilocalories

GHANA
West Africa

Official name Republic of Ghana
Formation 1957 / 1957
Capital Accra
Population 17.5 million / 197 people per sq mile (76 people per sq km) / 35%
Total area 92,100 sq miles (238,540 sq km)
Languages English*, Akan, Mossi, Ewe
Religions Traditional beliefs 38%, Muslim 30%, Christian 24%, other 8%
Ethnic mix Akan 52%, Mossi 15%, Ewe 12%, Ga 8%, other 13%
Government Multiparty republic
Currency Cedi = 100 pesewas
Literacy rate 61%
Calorie consumption 2199 kilocalories

GREECE
Southeast Europe

Official name Hellenic Republic
Formation 1830 / 1945–1947
Capital Athens
Population 10.5 million / 207 people per sq mile (80 people per sq km) / 64%
Total area 50,961 sq miles (131,990 sq km)
Languages Greek*, Turkish, Albanian, Macedonian
Religions Greek Orthodox 98%, Muslim 1%, other 1%
Ethnic mix Greek 98%, other 2%
Government Multiparty republic
Currency Drachma = 100 lepta
Literacy rate 95%
Calorie consumption 3815 kilocalories

GRENADA
West Indies

Official name Grenada
Formation 1974 / 1974
Capital St. George's
Population 92,000 / 705 people per sq mile (271 people per sq km) / 17%
Total area 131 sq miles (340 sq km)
Languages English*, English Creole
Religions Roman Catholic 68%, Protestant 32%
Ethnic mix Black 84%, Afro-European 13%, South Asian 3%
Government Parliamentary democracy
Currency E. Caribbean $ = 100 cents
Literacy rate 98%
Calorie consumption 2402 kilocalories

GUATEMALA
Central America

Official name Republic of Guatemala
Formation 1838 / 1838
Capital Guatemala City
Population 10.6 million / 255 people per sq mile (98 people per sq km) / 40%
Total area 42,043 sq miles (108,890 sq km)
Languages Spanish*, Quiché, Mam, Kekchí
Religions Christian 99%, other 1%
Ethnic mix Indian 55%, *ladino* (European-Indian, White) 45%
Government Multiparty republic
Currency Quetzal = 100 centavos
Literacy rate 54%
Calorie consumption 2255 kilocalories

GUINEA
West Africa

Official name Republic of Guinea
Formation 1958 / 1958
Capital Conakry
Population 6.7 million / 70 people per sq mile (27 people per sq km) / 28%
Total area 94,926 sq miles (245,860 sq km)
Languages French*, Fulani, Malinke, Soussou, Kissi
Religions Muslim 85%, Christian 8%, traditional beliefs 7%
Ethnic mix Fulani 40%, Malinke 25%, Susu 12%, other 23%
Government Multiparty republic
Currency Franc = 100 centimes
Literacy rate 33%
Calorie consumption 2389 kilocalories

GUINEA-BISSAU
West Africa

Official name Republic of Guinea-Bissau
Formation 1974 / 1974
Capital Bissau
Population 1.1 million / 102 people per sq mile (39 people per sq km) / 21%
Total area 13,940 sq miles (36,120 sq km)
Languages Portuguese*, Balante, Fulani, Malinke
Religions Traditional beliefs 54%, Muslim 38%, Christian 8%
Ethnic mix Balante 27%, Fulani 22%, Malinke 12%, other 39%
Government Multiparty republic
Currency Peso = 100 centavos
Literacy rate 36%
Calorie consumption 2556 kilocalories

GUYANA
South America

Official name Cooperative Republic of Guyana
Formation 1966 / 1966
Capital Georgetown
Population 800,000 / 10 people per sq mile (4 people per sq km) / 35%
Total area 83,000 sq miles (214,970 sq km)
Languages English*, English Creole, Hindi, Tamil, English
Religions Christian 57%, Hindu 33%, Muslim 9%, other 1%
Ethnic mix South Asian 51%, Black and mixed 43%, other 6%
Government Multiparty republic
Currency Guyana $ =100 cents
Literacy rate 98%
Calorie consumption 2384 kilocalories

HAITI
West Indies

Official name Republic of Haiti
Formation 1804 / 1804
Capital Port-au-Prince
Population 7.2 million / 679 people per sq mile (261 people per sq km) / 30%
Total area 10,714 sq miles (27,750 sq km)
Languages French*, French Creole*,
Religions Roman Catholic 80%, Protestant 16%, Voodoo 4%
Ethnic mix Black 95%, Afro-European 5%
Government Multiparty republic
Currency Gourde = 100 centimes
Literacy rate 35%
Calorie consumption 1706 kilocalories

HONDURAS
Central America

Official name Republic of Honduras
Formation 1838 / 1838
Capital Tegucigalpa
Population 5.7 million / 133 people per sq mile (51 people per sq km) / 42%
Total area 43,278 sq miles (112,090 sq km)
Languages Spanish*, English Creole, Garifuna, Indian languages
Religions Roman Catholic 97%, other 3%
Ethnic mix *mestizo* 90%, Indian 7%, Garifuna (Black Carib) 2%, White 1%
Government Multiparty republic
Currency Lempira = 100 centavos
Literacy rate 71%
Calorie consumption 2305 kilocalories

HUNGARY
Central Europe

Official name Republic of Hungary
Formation 1918 / 1945
Capital Budapest
Population 10.1 million / 282 people per sq mile (109 people per sq km) / 63%
Total area 35,919 sq miles (93,030 sq km)
Languages Hungarian (Magyar)*, German, Slovak
Religions Roman Catholic 68%, Protestant 25%, other 7%
Ethnic mix Hungarian (Magyar) 90%, German 2%, other 8%
Government Multiparty republic
Currency Forint = 100 filler
Literacy rate 99%
Calorie consumption 3503 kilocalories

ICELAND
Northwest Europe

Official name Republic of Iceland
Formation 1944 / 1944
Capital Reykjavík
Population 300,000 / 8 people per sq mile (3 people per sq km) / 91%
Total area 39,770 sq miles (103,000 sq km)
Languages Icelandic*, English
Religions Evangelical Lutheran 96%, other Christian 3%, other 1%
Ethnic mix Icelandic (Norwegian-Celtic descent) 98%, other 2%
Government Constitutional republic
Currency Krona = 100 aurar
Literacy rate 100%
Calorie consumption 3058 kilocalories

INDIA
South Asia

Official name Republic of India
Formation 1947 / 1961
Capital New Delhi
Population 935.7 million / 816 people per sq mile (315 people per sq km) / 26%
Total area 1,269,338 sq miles (3,287,590 sq km)
Languages Hindi*, English*, Urdu, Bengali, Marathi, Telugu, Tamil, Bihari
Religions Hindu 83%, Muslim 11%, Christian 2%, Sikh 2%, other 2%
Ethnic mix Indo-Aryan 72%, Dravidian 25%, Mongoloid and other 3%
Government Multiparty republic
Currency Rupee = 100 paisa
Literacy rate 52%
Calorie consumption 2395 kilocalories

INDONESIA
Southeast Asia

Official name Republic of Indonesia
Formation 1949 / 1963
Capital Jakarta
Population 197.6 million / 282 people per sq mile (109 people per sq km) / 33%
Total area 735,555 sq miles (1,904,570 sq km)
Languages Bahasa Indonesia*, 250 (est.) languages or dialects
Religions Muslim 87%, Christian 10%, Hindu 2%, Buddhist 1%
Ethnic mix Javanese 45%, Sundanese 14%, Madurese 8%, other 33%
Government Multiparty republic
Currency Rupiah = 100 sen
Literacy rate 82%
Calorie consumption 2752 kilocalories

IRAN
Southwest Asia

Official name Islamic Republic of Iran
Formation 1906 / 1906
Capital Tehran
Population 67.3 million / 106 people per sq mile (41 people per sq km) / 57%
Total area 636,293 sq miles (1,648,000 sq km)
Languages Farsi (Persian)*, Azerbaijani, Giaki, Mazanderani, Kurdish, Baluchi, Arabic, Turkmen
Religions Shi'a Muslim 95%, Sunni Muslim 4%, other 1%
Ethnic mix Persian 52%, Azerbaijani 24%, Kurdish 9%, other 15%
Government Islamic Republic
Currency Rial = 100 dinars
Literacy rate 72%
Calorie consumption 2860 kilocalories

IRAQ
Southwest Asia

Official name Republic of Iraq
Formation 1932 / 1981
Capital Baghdad
Population 20.4 million / 122 people per sq mile (47 people per sq km) / 73%
Total area 169,235 sq miles (438,320 sq km)
Languages Arabic*, Kurdish, Turkish, Farsi (Persian)
Religions Shi'a Muslim 63%, Sunni Muslim 34%, other 3%
Ethnic mix Arab 79%, Kurdish 16%, Persian 3%, Turkish 2%
Government Single-party republic
Currency Dinar = 1000 fils
Literacy rate 60%
Calorie consumption 2121 kilocalories

IRELAND
Northwest Europe

Official name Republic of Ireland
Formation 1921 / 1922
Capital Dublin
Population 3.6 million / 135 people per sq mile (52 people per sq km) / 57%
Total area 27,155 sq miles (70,280 sq km)
Languages English*, Irish Gaelic*
Religions Roman Catholic 93%, Protestant 5%, other 2%
Ethnic mix Irish 95%, other 5%
Government Multiparty republic
Currency Irish pound = 100 pence
Literacy rate 99%
Calorie consumption 3847 kilocalories

ISRAEL
Southwest Asia

Official name State of Israel
Formation 1948 / 1982
Capital Jerusalem
Population 5.6 million / 713 people per sq mile (275 people per sq km) / 91%
Total area 7992 sq miles (20,700 sq km)
Languages Hebrew*, Arabic, Yiddish
Religions Jewish 83%, Muslim 13%, Christian 2%, other 2%
Ethnic mix Jewish 83%, Arab 17%
Government Multiparty republic
Currency New shekel = 100 agorat
Literacy rate 95%
Calorie consumption 3050 kilocalories

ITALY
Southern Europe

Official name Italian Republic
Formation 1871 / 1954
Capital Rome
Population 57.2 million / 505 people per sq mile (195 people per sq km) / 67%
Total area 116,320 sq miles (301,270 sq km)
Languages Italian*, German, French, Rhaeto-Romanic, Sardinian
Religions Roman Catholic 99%, other 1%
Ethnic mix Italian 98%, other 2%
Government Multiparty republic
Currency Lira = 100 centesimi
Literacy rate 97%
Calorie consumption 3561 kilocalories

IVORY COAST
West Africa

Official name Republic of the Ivory Coast
Formation 1960 / 1960
Capital Yamoussoukro
Population 14.5 million / 117 people per sq mile (45 people per sq km) / 42%
Total area 124,503 sq miles (322,463 sq km)
Languages French*, Akran, Kru, Voltaic
Religions Traditional beliefs 63%, Muslim 25%, Christian 12%
Ethnic mix Baoule 23%, Bété 18%, Kru 17%, Malinke 15%, other 27%
Government Multiparty republic
Currency CFA franc = 100 centimes
Literacy rate 54%
Calorie consumption 2491 kilocalories

JAMAICA
West Indies

Official name Jamaica
Formation 1962 / 1962
Capital Kingston
Population 2.4 million / 577 people per sq mile (222 people per sq km) / 52%
Total area 4243 sq miles (10,990 sq km)
Languages English*, English Creole
Religions Christian 60%, other 40%
Ethnic mix Black 75%, mixed 15%, South Asian 5%, other 5%
Government Parliamentary democracy
Currency Jamaican $ = 100 cents
Literacy rate 98%
Calorie consumption 2607 kilocalories

JAPAN
East Asia

Official name Japan
Formation 1868 / 1945
Capital Tokyo
Population 125.1 million / 834 people per sq mile (322 people per sq km) / 77%
Total area 145,869 sq miles (377,800 sq km)
Languages Japanese*, Korean, Chinese
Religions Shinto and Buddhist 76%, Buddhist 16%, other 8%
Ethnic mix Japanese 99.4%, other 0.6%
Government Constitutional monarchy
Currency Yen = 100 sen
Literacy rate 99%
Calorie consumption 2903 kilocalories

JORDAN
Southwest Asia

Official name Hashemite Kingdom of Jordan
Formation 1946 / 1976
Capital Amman
Population 5.4 million / 159 people per sq mile (61 people per sq km) / 70%
Total area 34,440 sq miles (89,210 sq km)
Languages Arabic*
Religions Muslim 95%, Christian 5%
Ethnic mix Arab 98%, (Palestinian 49%), Armenian 1%, Circassian 1%
Government Constitutional monarchy
Currency Dinar = 1000 fils
Literacy rate 83% Urban
Calorie consumption 3022 kilocalories

KAZAKHSTAN
Central Asia

Official Name Republic of Kazakhstan
Formation 1991 / 1991
Capital Akmola
Population 17.1 million / 16 people per sq mile (6 people per sq km) / 58%
Total area 1,049,150 sq miles (2,717,300 sq km)
Languages Kazakh*, Russian, German
Religions Muslim 47%, other 53% (mostly Russian Orthodox and Lutheran)
Ethnic mix Kazakh 40%, Russian 38%, Ukrainian 6%, other 16%
Government Multiparty republic
Currency Tenge = 100 tein
Literacy rate 97%
Calorie consumption NOT AVAILABLE

KENYA
East Africa

Official name Republic of Kenya
Formation 1963 / 1963
Capital Nairobi
Population 28.3 million / 130 people per sq mile (50 people per sq km) / 25%
Total area 224,081 sq miles (580,370 sq km)
Languages Swahili*, English, Kikuyu, Luo, Kamba
Religions Christian 66%, traditional beliefs 26%, other 8%
Ethnic mix Kikuyu 21%, Luhya 14%, Kamba 11%, other 54%
Government Multiparty republic
Currency Shilling = 100 cents
Literacy rate 69%
Calorie consumption 2075 kilocalories

KIRIBATI
Australasia & Oceania

Official Name Republic of Kiribati
Formation 1979 / 1979
Capital Bairiki
Population 77,000 / 281 people per sq mile (108 people per sq km) / 36%
Total area 274 sq miles (710 sq km)
Languages English*, Kiribati
Religions Roman Catholic 53%, Protestant 40%, other Christian 4%, other 3%
Ethnic mix I-Kiribati 98%, other 2%
Government Multiparty republic
Currency Australian $ = 100 cents
Literacy rate 98%
Calorie consumption 2651 kilocalories

KUWAIT
Southwest Asia

Official name State of Kuwait
Formation 1961 / 1981
Capital Kuwait
Population 1.5 million / 218 people per sq mile (84 people per sq km) / 95%
Total area 6880 sq miles (17,820 sq km)
Languages Arabic*, English
Religions Muslim 92%, Christian 6%, other 2%
Ethnic mix Arab 85%, South Asian 9%, Persian 4%, other 2%
Government Constitutional monarchy
Currency Dinar = 1000 fils
Literacy rate 73%
Calorie consumption 2523 kilocalories

KYRGYZSTAN
Central Asia

Official name Kyrgyz Republic
Formation 1991 / 1991
Capital Bishkek
Population 4.7 million / 62 people per sq mile (24 people per sq km) / 39%
Total area 76,640 sq miles (198,500 sq km)
Languages Kyrgyz*, Russian*, Uzbek
Religions Muslim 65%, other (mostly Russian Orthodox) 35%
Ethnic mix Kyrgyz 52%, Russian 21%, Uzbek 13%, other (mostly Kazakh and Tajik) 14%
Government Multiparty republic
Currency Som =100 teen
Literacy rate 97%
Calorie consumption NOT AVAILABLE

LAOS
Southeast Asia

Official name Lao People's Democratic Republic
Formation 1953 / 1953
Capital Vientiane
Population 4.9 million / 54 people per sq mile (21 people per sq km) / 20%
Total area 91, 428 sq miles (236,800 sq km)
Languages Lao*, Miao, Yao
Religions Buddhist 85%, Christian 2%, other 13%
Ethnic mix Lao Loum 56%, Lao Theung 34%, Lao Soung 10%
Government Single-party republic
Currency Kip = 100 cents
Literacy rate 57%
Calorie consumption 2259 kilocalories

LATVIA
Northeast Europe

Official name Republic of Latvia
Formation 1991 / 1991
Capital Riga
Population 2.6 million / 104 people per sq mile (40 people per sq km) / 72%
Total area 24,938 sq miles (64,589 sq km)
Languages Latvian*, Russian
Religions Evangelical Lutheran 85%, other Christian 15%
Ethnic mix Latvian 52%, Russian 34%, Belorussian 5%, other 9%
Government Multiparty republic
Currency Lats = 100 santimi
Literacy rate 99%
Calorie consumption NOT AVAILABLE

LEBANON
Southwest Asia

Official name Republic of Lebanon
Formation 1944 / 1944
Capital Beirut
Population 3 million / 762 people per sq mile (293 people per sq km) / 86%
Total area 4015 sq miles (10,400 sq km)
Languages Arabic*, French, Armenian, English
Religions Muslim (mainly Shi'a) 57%, Christian (mainly Maronite) 43%
Ethnic mix Arab 93% (Lebanese 83%, Palestinian 10%), other 7%
Government Multiparty republic
Currency Pound = 100 piastres
Literacy rate 91%
Calorie consumption 3317 kilocalories

LESOTHO
Southern Africa

Official name Kingdom of Lesotho
Formation 1966 / 1966
Capital Maseru
Population 2.1 million / 10 people per sq mile (27 people per sq km) / 21%
Total area 11,718 sq miles (30,350 sq km)
Languages English*, Sesotho*, Zulu
Religions Christian 93%, other 7%
Ethnic mix Basotho 99%, other 1%
Government Constitutional monarchy
Currency Loti = 100 lisente
Literacy rate 69%
Calorie consumption 2201 kilocalories

LIBERIA
West Africa

Official name Republic of Liberia
Formation 1847 / 1889–1907
Capital Monrovia
Population 3 million / 80 people per sq mile (27 people per sq km) / 44%
Total area 43,000 sq miles (111,370 sq km)
Languages English*, Kpelle, Bassa, Vai, Kru, Grebo, Kissi, Gola
Religions Traditional beliefs 70%, Muslim 20%, Christian 10%
Ethnic mix Kpelle 20%, Bassa 14%, Americo-Liberians 5%, other 61%
Government Transitional
Currency Liberian $ = 100 cents
Literacy rate 39%
Calorie consumption 1640 kilocalories

LIBYA
North Africa

Official name Socialist People's Libyan Arab Jamahiriya
Formation 1951 / 1951
Capital Tripoli
Population 5.4 million / 8 people per sq mile (3 people per sq km) / 84%
Total area 679,358 sq miles (1,759,540 sq km)
Languages Arabic*, Tuareg
Religions Muslim 97%, other 3%
Ethnic mix Arab and Berber 97%, other 3%
Government Socialist *jamahiriya* (state of the masses)
Currency Dinar = 1000 dirhams
Literacy rate 64%
Calorie consumption 3308 kilocalories

LIECHTENSTEIN
Southeast Europe

Official name Principality of Liechtenstein
Formation 1719 / 1719
Capital Vaduz
Population 30,630 / 495 people per sq mile (191 people per sq km) / 87%
Total area 62 sq miles (160 sq km)
Languages German*, Alemannish, Italian
Religions Roman Catholic 87%, Protestant 8%, other 5%
Ethnic mix Liechtensteiner 63%, Swiss 15%, German 9%, other 13%
Government Constitutional monarchy
Currency Swiss franc = 100 centimes
Literacy rate 100%
Calorie consumption NOT AVAILABLE

LITHUANIA
Northeast Europe

Official name Republic of Lithuania
Formation 1991 / 1991
Capital Vilnius
Population 3.7 million / 148 people per sq mile (57 people per sq km) / 70%
Total area 25,174 sq miles (65,200 sq km)
Languages Lithuanian*, Russian
Religions Roman Catholic 87%, Russian Orthodox 10%, other 3%
Ethnic mix Lithuanian 80%, Russian 9%, Polish 8%, other 3%
Government Multiparty republic
Currency Litas = 100 centas
Literacy rate 98%
Calorie consumption NOT AVAILABLE

LUXEMBOURG
Northwest Europe

Official name Grand Duchy of Luxembourg
Formation 1890 / 1890
Capital Luxembourg
Population 400,000 / 403 people per sq mile (155 people per sq km) / 88%
Total area 998 sq miles (2586 sq km)
Languages Letzeburgish*, French, Portuguese, Italian
Religions Roman Catholic 97%, other 3%
Ethnic mix Luxemburger 72%, Portuguese 9%, Italian 5%, other 14%
Government Constitutional monarchy
Currency Franc = 100 centimes
Literacy rate 99% Urban
Calorie consumption 3681 kilocalories

MACEDONIA
Southeast Europe

Official name Former Yugoslav Republic of Macedonia
Formation 1991 / 1991
Capital Skopje
Population 2.2 million / 223 people per sq mile (86 people per sq km) / 59%
Total area 9,929 sq miles (25,715 sq km)
Languages Macedonian, Serbian, Croatian (no official language)
Religions Christian 80%, Muslim 20%
Ethnic mix Macedonian 67%, Albanian 20%, Turkish 4%, other 9%
Government Multiparty republic
Currency Denar = 100 deni
Literacy rate 89%
Calorie consumption NOT AVAILABLE

MADAGASCAR
Indian Ocean

Official name Democratic Republic of Madagascar
Formation 1960 / 1960
Capital Antananarivo
Population 14.8 million / 65 people per sq mile (25 people per sq km) / 25%
Total area 226,660 sq miles (587,040 sq km)
Languages Malagasy*, French*
Religions Traditional beliefs 52%, Christian 41%, Muslim 7%
Ethnic mix Merina 26%, Betsimisaraka 15%, Betsileo 12%, other 47%
Government Multiparty republic
Currency Franc = 100 centimes
Literacy rate 81%
Calorie consumption 2135 kilocalories

MALAWI
Southern Africa

Official name Republic of Malawi
Formation 1964 / 1964
Capital Lilongwe
Population 11.1 million / 307 people per sq mile (118 people per sq km) / 12%
Total area 45,745 sq miles (118,480 sq km)
Languages English*, Chewa, Lomwe, Yao
Religions Christian 66%, traditional beliefs 18%, other 16%
Ethnic mix Maravi 55%, Lomwe 17%, Yao 13%, other 15%
Government Multiparty republic
Currency Kwacha = 100 tambala
Literacy rate 49%
Calorie consumption 1825 kilocalories

MALAYSIA
Southeast Asia

Official name Malaysia
Formation 1957 / 1965
Capital Kuala Lumpur
Population 20.1 million / 158 people per sq mile (61 people per sq km) / 51%
Total area 127,317 sq miles (329,750 sq km)
Languages Malay*, Chinese, Tamil
Religions Muslim 53%, Buddhist and Confucianist 30%, other 17%
Ethnic mix Malay and Aboriginal 60%, Chinese 30%, Indian 8%, other 2%
Government Federal constitutional monarchy
Currency Ringgit = 100 cents
Literacy rate 78%
Calorie consumption 2888 kilocalories

MALDIVES
Indian Ocean

Official name Republic of Maldives
Formation 1965 / 1965
Capital Male
Population 300,000 / 2591 people per sq mile (1000 people per sq km) / 26%
Total area 116 sq miles (300 sq km)
Languages Divehi (Maldivian)*, Sinhala, Tamil
Religions Sunni Muslim 100%
Ethnic mix Maldivian 99%, other 1%
Government Republic
Currency Rufiyaa = 100 laari
Literacy rate 91%
Calorie consumption 2580 kilocalories

MALI
West Africa

Official name Republic of Mali
Formation 1960 / 1960
Capital Bamako
Population 10.8 million / 24 people per sq mile (9 people per sq km) / 25%
Total area 478,837 sq miles (1,240,190 sq km)
Languages French*, Bambara, Fulani, Senufo, Soninké
Religions Muslim 80%, traditional beliefs 18%, Christian 2%
Ethnic mix Bambara 31%, Fulani 13%, Senufo 12%, other 44%
Government Multiparty republic
Currency CFA franc = 100 centimes
Literacy rate 32%
Calorie consumption 2278 kilocalories

MALTA
Southern Europe

Official name Republic of Malta
Formation 1964 / 1964
Capital Valletta
Population 400,000 / 3239 people per sq mile (1250 people per sq km) / 88%
Total area 124 sq miles (320 sq km)
Languages Maltese*, English*
Religions Roman Catholic 98%, other (mostly Anglican) 2%
Ethnic mix Maltese (mixed Arab, Sicilian, Norman, Spanish, Italian, English) 98%, other 2%
Government Multiparty republic
Currency Lira = 100 cents
Literacy rate 86%
Calorie consumption 3486 kilocalories

MARSHALL ISLANDS
Australasia & Oceania

Official name Republic of the Marshall Islands
Formation 1986 / 1986
Capital Majuro
Population 52,000 / 744 people per sq mile (287 people per sq km) / 28%
Total area 70 sq miles (181 sq km)
Languages English*, Marshallese*
Religions Protestant 80%, Roman Catholic 15%, other 5%
Ethnic mix Marshallese 90%, other Pacific Islanders 10%
Government Republic
Currency US $ = 100 cents
Literacy rate 91%
Calorie consumption NOT AVAILABLE

MAURITANIA
West Africa

Official name Islamic Republic of Mauritania
Formation 1960 / 1960
Capital Nouakchott
Population 2.3 million / 5 people per sq mile (2 people per sq km) / 50%
Total area 395,953 sq miles (1,025,520 sq km)
Languages French*, Hassaniyah Arabic, Wolof
Religions Muslim 100%
Ethnic mix Maure 80%, Wolof 7%, Tukulor 5%, other 8%
Government Multiparty republic
Currency Ouguiya = 5 khoums
Literacy rate 34%
Calorie consumption 2685 kilocalories

MAURITIUS
Indian Ocean

Official name Republic of Mauritius
Formation 1968 / 1968
Capital Port Louis
Population 1.1 million / 1542 people per sq mile (595 people per sq km) / 41%
Total area 718 sq miles (1860 sq km)
Languages English*, French Creole, Hindi, Urdu, Tamil, Chinese
Religions Hindu 52%, Roman Catholic, 26%, Muslim 17%, other 5%
Ethnic mix Creole 55%, South Asian 40%, Chinese 3%, other 2%
Government Multiparty republic
Currency Rupee = 100 cents
Literacy rate 79%
Calorie consumption 2690 kilocalories

MEXICO
North America

Official name United Mexican States
Formation 1836 / 1867
Capital Mexico City
Population 93.7 million / 127 people per sq mile (49 people per sq km) / 74%
Total area 756,061 sq miles (1,958,200 sq km)
Languages Spanish*, Mayan dialects
Religions Roman Catholic 89%, Protestant 6%, other 5%
Ethnic mix *mestizo* 55%, Indian 30%, White 6%, other 9%
Government Multiparty republic
Currency Peso = 100 centavos
Literacy rate 89%
Calorie consumption 3146 kilocalories

MICRONESIA
Australasia & Oceania

Official name Federated States of Micronesia
Formation 1986 / 1986
Capital Palikir
Population 107,000 / 394 people per sq mile (152 people per sq km) / 36%
Total area 1120 sq miles (2900 sq km)
Languages English*, Trukese, Pohnpeian, Mortlockese, Kosrean
Religions Roman Catholic 50%, Protestant 48%, other 2%
Ethnic mix Micronesian 99%, other 1%
Government Republic
Currency US $ = 100 cents
Literacy rate 90%
Calorie consumption NOT AVAILABLE

MOLDAVIA
Southeast Europe

Official name Republic of Moldova
Formation 1991 / 1991
Capital Chişinău
Population 4.4 million / 339 people per sq mile (131 people per sq km) / 49%
Total area 13,000 sq miles (33,700 sq km)
Languages Moldavian*, Russian, Romanian
Religions Romanian Orthodox 98%, Jewish 1%, other 1%
Ethnic mix Moldavian (Romanian) 65%, Ukrainian 14%, Russian 13%, other 8%
Government Multiparty republic
Currency Leu = 100 bani
Literacy rate 96%
Calorie consumption NOT AVAILABLE

MONACO
Southern Europe

Official name Principality of Monaco
Formation 1861 / 1861
Capital Monaco
Population 31,000 / 41,332 people per sq mile (15,897 people per sq km) / 100%
Total area 0.75 sq miles (1.95 sq km)
Languages French*, Italian, Monégasque, English
Religions Roman Catholic 95%, other 5%
Ethnic mix French 47%, Monégasque 17%, Italian 16%, other 20%
Government Constitutional monarchy
Currency French franc = 100 centimes
Literacy rate 99%
Calorie consumption NOT AVAILABLE

MONGOLIA
EastAsia

Official name Mongolia
Formation 1924 / 1911
Capital Ulan Bator
Population 2.4 million / 5 people per sq mile (2 people per sq km) / 59%
Total area 604,247 sq miles (1,565,000 sq km)
Languages Khalkha Mongol*, Turkic, Russian, Chinese
Religions Predominantly Tibetan Buddhist, with a Muslim minority
Ethnic mix Khalkha Mongol 90%, Kazakh 4%, Chinese 2%, other 4%
Government Multiparty republic
Currency Tughrik = 100 möngös
Literacy rate 81%
Calorie consumption 1899 kilocalories

MOROCCO
North Africa

Official name Kingdom of Morocco
Formation 1956 / 1956
Capital Rabat
Population 27 million / 155 people per sq mile (60 people per sq km) / 47%
Total area 269,757 sq miles (698,670 sq km)
Religions Muslim 99%, other 1%
Ethnic mix Arab and Berber 99%, European 1%
Government Constitutional monarchy
Currency Dirham = 100 centimes
Literacy rate 44%
Calorie consumption 2984 kilocalories

MOZAMBIQUE
Southern Africa

Official name Republic of Mozambique
Formation 1975 / 1975
Capital Maputo
Population 16 million / 135 people per sq mile (20 people per sq km) / 30%
Total area 309,493 sq miles (801,590 sq km)
Languages Portuguese*, Makua, Tsonga, Sena, Lomwe
Religions Traditional beliefs 60%, Christian 30%, Muslim 10%
Ethnic mix Makua-Lomwe 47%, Tsonga 23%, Malawi 12%, other 18%
Government Multiparty republic
Currency Metical = 100 centavos
Literacy rate 40%
Calorie consumption 1680 kilocalories

NAMIBIA
Southern Africa

Official name Republic of Namibia
Formation 1990 / 1994
Capital Windhoek
Population 1.5 million / 5 people per sq mile (2 people per sq km) / 34%
Total area 318,260 sq miles (824,290 sq km)
Languages English*, Afrikaans, Ovambo, Kavango, Bergdama
Religions Christian 90%, other 10%
Ethnic mix Ovambo 50%, Kavango 9%, Herero 7%, Damara 7%, other 27%
Government Multiparty republic
Currency Rand = 100 cents
Literacy rate 40%
Calorie consumption 2134 kilocalories

NAURU
Australasia & Oceania

Official name Republic of Nauru
Formation 1968 / 1968
Capital No official capital
Population 10,000 / 1233 people per sq mile (476 people per sq km) / 100%
Total area 8.2 sq miles (21.2 sq km)
Languages Nauruan*, English, Kiribati, Chinese, Tuvaluan
Religions Christian 95%, other 5%
Ethnic mix Nauruan 58%, other Pacific Islanders 26%, Chinese 8%, European 8%
Government Parliamentary democracy
Currency Australian $ = 100 cents
Literacy rate 99%
Calorie consumption NOT AVAILABLE

NEPAL
South Asia

Official name Kingdom of Nepal
Formation 1769 / 1769
Capital Kathmandu
Population 21.4 million / 404 people per sq mile (156 people per sq km) / 12%
Total area 54,363 sq miles (140,800 sq km)
Languages Nepali*, Maithilli, Bhojpuri
Religions Hindu 90%, Buddhist 5%, Muslim 3%, other 2%
Ethnic mix Nepalese 58%, Bihari 19%, Tamang 6%, other 17%
Government Constitutional monarchy
Currency Rupee = 100 paisa
Literacy rate 26%
Calorie consumption 1957 kilocalories

NETHERLANDS
Northwest Europe

Official name Kingdom of the Netherlands
Formation 1815 / 1890
Capitals Amsterdam, The Hague
Population 15.5 million / 1188 people per sq mile (457 people per sq km) / 89%
Total area 14,410 sq miles (37,330 sq km)
Languages Dutch*, Frisian
Religions Roman Catholic 36%, Protestant 27%, other 37%
Ethnic mix Dutch 96%, other 4%
Government Constitutional monarchy
Currency Guilder = 100 cents
Literacy rate 99%
Calorie consumption 3222 kilocalories

NEW ZEALAND
Australasia & Oceania

Official name New Zealand
Formation 1947 / 1947
Capital Wellington
Population 3.6 million / 34 people per sq mile (13 people per sq km) / 86%
Total area 103,730 sq miles (268,680 sq km)
Languages English, Maori
Religions Protestant 62%, Roman Catholic 18%, other 20%
Ethnic mix European 88%, Maori 9%, other 3%
Government Constitutional monarchy
Currency NZ $ = 100 cents
Literacy rate 99%
Calorie consumption 3669 kilocalories

NICARAGUA
Central America

Official name Republic of Nicaragua
Formation 1838 / 1838
Capital Managua
Population 4.4 million / 96 people per sq mile (37 people per sq km) / 62%
Total area 50,193 sq miles (130,000 sq km)
Languages Spanish*, English Creole, Miskito
Religions Roman Catholic 95%, other 5%
Ethnic mix *mestizo* 69%, White 17%, Black 9%, Indian 5%
Government Multiparty republic
Currency Córdoba = 100 pence
Literacy rate 65%
Calorie consumption 2293 kilocalories

NIGER
West Africa

Official name Republic of Niger
Formation 1960 / 1960
Capital Niamey
Population 9.2 million / 18 people per sq mile (7 people per sq km) / 16%
Total area 489,188 sq miles (1,267,000 sq km)
Languages French*, Hausa, Djerma, Fulani, Tuareg, Teda
Religions Muslim 85%, traditional beliefs 14%, Christian 1%
Ethnic mix Hausa 56%, Djerma 22%, Fulani 9%, other 13%
Government Multiparty republic
Currency CFA franc = 100 centimes
Literacy rate 28%
Calorie consumption 2257 kilocalories

NIGERIA
West Africa

Official name Federal Republic of Nigeria
Formation 1960 / 1960
Capital Abuja
Population 111.7 million / 319 people per sq mile (123 people per sq km) / 37%
Total area 356,668 sq miles (923,770 sq km)
Languages English*, Hausa, Yoruba, Ibo
Religions Muslim 50%, Christian 40%, traditional beliefs 10%
Ethnic mix Hausa 21%, Yoruba 20%, Ibo 17%, Fulani 9%, other 33%
Government Military regime
Currency Naira = 100 kobo
Literacy rate 53%
Calorie consumption 2124 kilocalories

NORTH KOREA
East Asia

Official name Democratic People's Republic of Korea
Formation 1948 / 1948
Capital Pyongyang
Population 23.9 million / 515 people per sq mile (198 people per sq km) / 60%
Total area 46,540 sq miles (120,540 sq km)
Languages Korean*, Chinese
Religions Traditional beliefs 16%, Ch'ondogyo 14%, Buddhist 2%, non-religious 68%
Ethnic mix Korean 99%, other 1%
Government Single-party republic
Currency Won = 100 chon
Literacy rate 99%
Calorie consumption 2833 kilocalories

NORWAY
Northern Europe

Official name Kingdom of Norway
Formation 1905 / 1930
Capital Oslo
Population 4.3 million / 36 people per sq mile (14 people per sq km) / 73%
Total area 125,060 sq miles (323,900 sq km)
Languages Norwegian* (Bokmal and *Nynorsk*), Lappish, Finnish
Religions Evangelical Lutheran 88%, other Christian 12%
Ethnic mix Norwegian 95%, Lapp 1%, other 4%
Government Constitutional monarchy
Currency Krone = 100 øre
Literacy rate 99%
Calorie consumption 3244 kilocalories

OMAN
Southwest Asia

Official name Sultanate of Oman
Formation 1650 / 1951
Capital Muscat
Population 2.2 million / 26 people per sq mile (10 people per sq km) / 12%
Total area 82,030 sq miles (212,460 sq km)
Languages Arab*, Baluchi
Religions Ibadi Muslim 75%, other Muslim 11%, Hindu 14%
Ethnic mix Arab 75%, Baluchi 15%, Other 15%
Government Monarchy with Consultative Council
Currency Rial = 1000 baizas
Literacy rate 44%
Calorie consumption 3013 kilocalories

PAKISTAN
South Asia

Official name Islamic Republic of Pakistan
Formation 1947 / 1972
Capital Islamabad
Population 140.5 million / 472 people per sq mile (182 people per sq km) / 33%
Total area 307,374 sq miles (796,100 sq km)
Main languages Urdu*, Punjabi, Sindhi, Pashtu, Baluchi
Religions Sunni Muslim 77%, Shi'a Muslim 20%, Hindu 2%, Christian 1%
Ethnic mix Punjabi 56%, Sindhi 13%, Pashtun 8%, other 23%
Government Multiparty republic
Currency Rupee = 100 paisa
Literacy rate 38% Urban
Calorie consumption 2315 kilocalories

PALAU
Australasia & Oceania

Official name Palau
Formation 1994 / 1994
Capital Oreor
Population 16,200 /83 people per sq mile (32 people per sq km) / 52%
Total area 192 sq miles (497 sq km)
Languages Palauan, English, Sonsorolese-Tobian (no official language)
Religions Christian 70%, traditional beliefs 30%
Ethnic mix Palauan 99%, 1% Other
Government Multiparty republic
Currency US $ = 100 cents
Literacy rate 92%
Calorie consumption NOT AVAILABLE

PANAMA
Central America

Official name Republic of Panama
Formation 1903 / 1914
Capital Panama City
Population 2.6 million / 88 people per sq mile (34 people per sq km) / 52%
Total area 29,761 sq miles (77,080 sq km)
Languages Spanish*, English Creole, Indian languages
Religions Roman Catholic 93%, other 7%
Ethnic mix *mestizo* 70%, Black 14%, White 10%, Indian 6%
Government Multiparty republic
Currency Balboa = 100 centesimos
Literacy rate 91%
Calorie consumption 2242 kilocalories

PAPUA NEW GUINEA
Australasia & Oceania

Official name Independent State of Papua New Guinea
Formation 1975 / 1975
Capital Port Moresby
Population 4.3 million / 23 people per sq mile (9 people per sq km) / 15%
Total area 178,700 sq miles (462, 840 sq km)
Languages Pidgin English*, Motu*, 750 (est.) native languages
Religions Christian 66%, other 34%
Ethnic mix Papuan 85%, other 15%
Government Parliamentary democracy
Currency Kina = 100 toea
Literacy rate 72%
Calorie consumption 2613 kilocalories

PARAGUAY
South America

Official name Paraguay
Formation 1811 / 1938
Capital Asunción
Population 5 million / 34 people per sq mile (13 people per sq km) / 51%
Total area 157,046 sq miles (406,750 sq km)
Languages Spanish*, Guaraní
Religions Roman Catholic 90%, other 10%
Ethnic mix *mestizo* 95%, White 3%, Indian 2%
Government Multiparty republic
Literacy rate 92%
Calorie consumption 2670 kilocalories

PERU
South America

Official name Republic of Peru
Formation 1824 / 1942
Capital Lima
Population 23.8 million / 49 people per sq mile (19 people per sq km) / 71%
Total area 496,223 sq miles (1,285,220 sq km)
Languages Spanish*, Quechua, Aymará
Religions Roman Catholic 95%, other 5%
Ethnic mix Indian 45%, *mestizo* 37%, White 15%, other 3%
Government Multiparty republic
Currency New sol = 100 centimos
Literacy rate 89%
Calorie consumption 1882 kilocalories

PHILIPPINES
Southwest Asia

Official name Republic of the Philippines
Formation 1946 / 1946
Capital Manila
Population 67.6 million / 588 people per sq mile (227 people per sq km) / 51%
Total area 115,831 sq miles (300,000 sq km)
Languages Pilipino*, English, Cebuano, Hiligaynon, Samaran, Bikol
Religions Roman Catholic 83%, Protestant 9%, Muslim 5%, other 3%
Ethnic mix Filipino 96%, Chinese 2%, other 2%
Government Multiparty republic
Currency Peso = 100 centavos
Literacy rate 95%
Calorie consumption 2257 kilocalories

POLAND
Northern Europe

Official name Republic of Poland
Formation 1918 / 1945
Capital Warsaw
Population 38.4 million / 327 people per sq mile (126 people per sq km) / 63%
Total area 120,720 sq miles (312,680 sq km)
Languages Polish*, German
Religions Roman Catholic 95%, other Christian 5%
Ethnic mix Polish 98%, other 2%
Government Multiparty republic
Currency Zloty = 100 groszy
Literacy rate 99%
Calorie consumption 3301 kilocalories

PORTUGAL
Southwest Europe

Official name Republic of Portugal
Formation 1140 / 1640
Capital Lisbon
Population 9.8 million / 277 people per sq mile (107 people per sq km) / 34%
Total area 35,670 sq miles (92,390 sq km)
Languages Portuguese*
Religions Roman Catholic 97%, Protestant 1%, other 2%
Ethnic mix Portuguese 98%, African 1%, other 1%
Government Multiparty republic
Currency Escudo = 100 centavos
Literacy rate 86%
Calorie consumption 3634 kilocalories

QATAR
Southwest Asia

Official name State of Qatar
Formation 1971 / 1971
Capital Doha
Population 600,000 / 143 people per sq mile (55 people per sq km) / 90%
Total area 4247 sq miles (11,000 sq km)
Languages Arabic*, Farsi (Persian), Urdu, Hindi, English
Religions Sunni Muslim 86%, Hindu 10%, Christian 4%
Ethnic mix Arab 40%, South Asian 35%, Persian 12%, other 13%
Government Absolute monarchy
Currency Riyal = 100 dirhams
Literacy rate 79%
Calorie consumption NOT AVAILABLE

ROMANIA
Southeast Europe

Official name Romania
Formation 1947 / 1947
Capital Bucharest
Population 22.8 million /257 people per sq mile (99 people per sq km) / 54%
Total area 91,700 sq miles (237,500 sq km)
Languages Romanian*, Hungarian,
Religions Romanian Orthodox 70%, Roman Catholic 6%, Protestant 6%, other 18%
Ethnic mix Romanian 89%, Hungarian 8%, other (including Gypsy) 3%
Government Multiparty republic
Currency Leu = 100 bani
Literacy rate 97%
Calorie consumption 3051 kilocalories

RUSSIAN FEDERATION
Europe / Asia

Official name Russian Federation
Formation 1991 / 1991
Capital Moscow
Population 147 million /23 people per sq mile (9 people per sq km) / 75%
Total area 6,592,800 sq miles (17,075,400 sq km)
Languages Russian*, Tatar, Ukrainian
Religions Russian Orthodox 80%, other (including Jewish, Muslim) 20%
Ethnic mix Russian 80%, Tatar 4%, Ukrainian 3%, other 13%
Currency Rouble = 100 kopeks
Literacy rate 98%
Calorie consumption NOT AVAILABLE

RWANDA
Central Africa

Official name Rwandese Republic
Formation 1962 / 1962
Capital Kigali
Population 8 million / 788 people per sq mile (304 people per sq km) / 6%
Total area 10,170 sq miles (26,340 sq km)
Languages Kinyarwanda*, French*, Kiswahili, English
Religions Christian 74%, traditional beliefs 25%, other 1%
Ethnic mix Hutu 90%, Tutsi 9%, Twa pygmy 1%
Government Multiparty republic
Currency Franc = 100 centimes
Literacy rate 61%
Calorie consumption 1821 kilocalories

SAINT KITTS & NEVIS
West Indies

Official name Federation of Saint Christopher and Nevis
Formation 1983 / 1983
Capital Basseterre
Population 44,000 / 295 people per sq mile (114 people per sq km) / 41%
Total area 139 sq miles (360 sq km)
Languages English*, English Creole
Religions Protestant 85%, Roman Catholic 10%, other Christian 5%
Ethnic mix Black 95%, mixed 5%
Government Parliamentary democracy
Currency E. Caribbean $ = 100 cents
Literacy rate 97%
Calorie consumption 2419 kilocalories

SAINT LUCIA
West Indies

Official name Saint Lucia
Formation 1979 / 1979
Capital Castries
Population 145,000 / 617 people per sq mile (238 people per sq km) / 47%
Total area 239 sq miles (620 sq km)
Languages English*, French Creole, Hindi, Urdu
Religions Roman Catholic 90%, other 10%
Ethnic mix Black 90%, Afro-European 6%, South Asian 4%
Government Parliamentary democracy
Currency E. Caribbean $ = 100 cents
Literacy rate 93%
Calorie consumption 2588 kilocalories

SAINT VINCENT & THE GRENADINES
West Indies

Official name Saint Vincent and the Grenadines
Formation 1979 / 1979
Capital Kingstown
Population 111,000 / 845 people per sq mile (326 people per sq km) / 43%
Total area 131 sq miles (340 sq km)
Languages English*, English Creole
Religions Protestant 62% Roman Catholic 19%, other 19%
Ethnic mix Black 82%, mixed 14%, White 3%, South Asian 1%
Government Parliamentary democracy
Currency E. Caribbean $ = 100 cents
Literacy rate 84%
Calorie consumption 2347 kilocalories

SAMOA
Australasia & Oceania

Official name Independent State of Samoa
Formation 1962 / 1962
Capital Apia
Population 169,000 / 155 people per sq mile (60 people per sq km) / 21%
Total area 1027 sq miles (2840 sq km)
Languages Samoan*, English*
Religions Protestant 74%, Roman Catholic 26%
Ethnic mix Samoan 93%, other 7%
Government Parliamentary state
Currency Tala = 100 sene
Literacy rate 92%
Calorie consumption 2828 kilocalories

SAN MARINO
Southern Europe

Official name Republic of San Marino
Formation AD 301 / 1862
Capital San Marino
Population 24,000 / 1018 people per sq mile (393 people per sq km) / 90%
Total area 24 sq miles (61 sq km)
Languages Italian*
Religions Roman Catholic 96%, other 4%
Ethnic mix Sammarinese 95%, other 5%
Government Multiparty republic
Currency Italian lira = 100 centesimi
Literacy rate 96%
Calorie consumption 3561 kilocalories

SAO TOME & PRINCIPE
West Africa

Official name Democratic Republic of Sao Tome and Principe
Formation 1975 / 1975
Capital São Tomé
Population 125,000 / 337 people per sq mile (130 people per sq km) / 44%
Total area 372 sq miles (964 sq km)
Languages Portuguese, Portuguese Creole
Religions Roman Catholic 90%, other Christian 10%
Ethnic mix Black 90%, Portuguese and Creole 10%
Government Multiparty republic
Currency Dobra = 100 centimos
Literacy rate 57%
Calorie consumption 2129 kilocalories

SAUDI ARABIA
Southwest Asia

Official name Kingdom of Saudi Arabia
Formation 1932 / 1981
Capital Riyadh
Population 17.9 million / 21 people per sq mile (8 people per sq km) / 78%
Total area 829,995 sq miles (2,149,690 sq km)
Languages Arabic*
Religions Sunni Muslim 85%, Shi'a Muslim 14%, Christian 1%
Ethnic mix Arab 90%, Yemeni 8%, other Arab 1%, other 1%
Government Absolute monarchy
Currency Riyal = 100 malalah
Literacy rate 63%
Calorie consumption 2735 kilocalories

SENEGAL
West Africa

Official name Republic of Senegal
Formation 1960 / 1960
Capital Dakar
Population 8.3 million /111 people per sq mile (43 people per sq km) / 41%
Total area 75,950 sq miles (196,720 sq km)
Languages French*, Wolof, Fulani, Serer
Religions Muslim 92%, traditional beliefs 6%, Christian 2%
Ethnic mix Wolof 46%, Fulani 25%, Serer 16%, other 13%
Government Multiparty republic
Currency CFA franc = 100 centimes
Literacy rate 33%
Calorie consumption 2262 kilocalories

SEYCHELLES
Indian Ocean

Official name Republic of Seychelles
Formation 1976 / 1976
Capital Victoria
Population 73,000 / 700 people per sq mile (270 people per sq km) / 52%
Total area 108 sq miles (280 sq km)
Languages Creole*, French, English
Religions Roman Catholic 90%, other 10%
Ethnic mix Seychellois (mixed African, South Asian and European) 95%, Chinese and South Asian 5%
Government Multiparty republic
Currency Rupee = 100 cents
Literacy rate 58%
Calorie consumption 2287 kilocalories

SIERRA LEONE
West Africa

Official name Republic of Sierra Leone
Formation 1961 / 1961
Capital Freetown
Population 4.5 million / 163 people per sq mile (63 people per sq km) / 34%
Total area 27,699 sq miles (71,740 sq km)
Languages English*, Krio (Creole), Mende, Temne
Religions Traditional beliefs 52%, Muslim 40%, Christian 8%
Ethnic mix Mende 34%, Temne 31%, Limba 9%, Kono 5%, other 21%
Government Military regime
Currency Leone = 100 cents
Literacy rate 31%
Calorie consumption 1694 kilocalorie

SINGAPORE
Southeast Asia

Official name Republic of Singapore
Formation 1965 / 1965
Capital Singapore
Population 2.8 million / 11,894 people per sq mile (4590 people per sq km) / 100%
Total area 239 sq miles (620 sq km)
Languages Malay*, Chinese, Tamil, English
Religions Buddhist 30%, Christian 20%, Muslim 17%, other 33%
Ethnic mix Chinese 76%, Malay 15%, South Asian 7%, other 2%
Government Multiparty democracy
Currency Singapore $ = 100 cents
Literacy rate 91%
Calorie consumption 3128 kilocalories

SLOVAKIA
Central Europe

Official name Slovak Republic
Formation 1993 / 1993
Capital Bratislava
Population 5.4 million / 285 people per sq mile (110 people per sq km) / 57%
Total area 19,100 sq miles (49,500 sq km)
Languages Slovak*, Hungarian (Magyar), Romany, Czech
Religions Roman Catholic 80%, Protestant 12%, other 8%
Ethnic mix Slovak 85%, Hungarian 9%, Czech 1%, other 5%
Government Multiparty republic
Currency Koruna = 100 halierov
Literacy rate 99%
Calorie consumption 3156 kilocalories

SLOVENIA
Central Europe

Official name Republic of Slovenia
Formation 1991 / 1991
Capital Ljubljana
Population 1.9 million / 244 people per sq mile (94 people per sq km) / 62%
Total area 7820 sq miles (20,250 sq km)
Languages Slovene*, Serbian, Croatian
Religions Roman Catholic 96%, Muslim 1%, other 3%
Ethnic mix Slovene 92%, Croat 3%, Serb 1%, other 4%
Government Multiparty republic
Currency Tolar = 100 stotins
Literacy rate 99%
Calorie consumption NOT AVAILABLE

SOLOMON ISLANDS
Australasia & Oceania

Official name Solomon Islands
Formation 1978 / 1978
Capital Honiara
Population 400,000 / 36 people per sq mile (14 people per sq km) / 16%
Total area 111,583 sq miles (289,000 sq km)
Languages English*, 87 (established) native languages
Religions Christian 91%, other 9%
Ethnic mix Melanesian 94%, other 6%
Government Parliamentary democracy
Currency Solomon Is $ = 100 cents
Literacy rate 24%
Calorie consumption 2173 kilocalories

SOMALIA
East Africa

Official name Somali Democratic Republic
Formation 1960 / 1960
Capital Mogadishu
Population 9.3 million / 39 people per sq mile (15 people per sq km) / 25%
Total area 246,200 sq miles (637,660 sq km)
Languages Somali*, Arabic, English
Religions Sunni Muslim 99%, other (including Christian) 1%
Ethnic mix Somali 98%, Bantu, Arab and other 2%
Government Transitional
Currency Shilling = 100 cents
Literacy rate 24%
Calorie consumption 1499 kilocalories

SOUTH AFRICA
Southern Africa

Official name Republic of South Africa
Formation 1910 / 1934
Capitals Pretoria, Cape Town, Bloemfontein
Population 41.5 million / 88 people per sq mile (34 people per sq km) / 50%
Total area 471,443 sq miles (1,221,040 sq km)
Languages Afrikaans*, English, 11 African languages
Religions Protestant 55%, Roman Catholic 9%, Hindu 1%, Muslim 1%, other 34%
Ethnic mix Black 75%, White 14%, mixed 9%, South Asian 2%
Government Multiparty republic
Currency Rand = 100 cents
Literacy rate 82%
Calorie consumption 2695 kilocalories

SOUTH KOREA
East Asia

Official name Republic of Korea
Formation 1948 / 1948
Capital Seoul
Population 45 million / 1,182 people per sq mile (456 people per sq km) / 77%
Total area 38,232 sq miles (99,020 sq km)
Languages Korean*, Chinese
Religions Mahayana Buddhist 47%, Protestant 38%, Roman Catholic 11%, Confucianist 3%, other 1%
Ethnic mix Korean 99.9% other 0.1%
Government Multiparty republic
Currency Won = 100 chon
Literacy rate 97%
Calorie consumption 3285 kilocalories

SPAIN
Southeast Europe

Official name Kingdom of Spain
Formation 1492 / 1713
Capital Madrid
Population 39.6 million / 205 people per sq mile (79 people per sq km) / 76%
Total area 194,900 sq miles (504,780 sq km)
Languages Castilian Spanish*, Catalan*, Galician*, Basque*
Religions Roman Catholic 99%, other 1%
Ethnic mix Castilian Spanish 72%, Catalan 16%, Galician 7%, other 5%
Government Constitutional monarchy
Currency Peseta = 100 céntimos
Literacy rate 95%
Calorie consumption 3708 kilocalories

SRI LANKA
South Asia

Official name Democratic Socialist Republic of Sri Lanka
Formation 1948 / 1948
Capital Colombo
Population 18.4 million / 736 people per sq mile (284 people per sq km) / 22%
Total area 25,332 sq miles (65,610 sq km)
Languages Sinhala*, Tamil, English
Religions Buddhist 70%, Hindu 15%, Christian 8%, Muslim 7%
Ethnic mix Sinhalese 74%, Tamil 18%, other 8%
Government Multiparty republic
Currency Rupee = 100 cents
Literacy rate 90%
Calorie consumption 2273 kilocalories

SUDAN
East Africa

Official name Republic of Sudan
Formation 1956 / 1956
Capital Khartoum
Population 28.1 million / 31 people per sq mile (12 people per sq km) / 23%
Total area 967,493 sq miles (2,505,815 sq km)
Languages Arabic*, Dinka, Nuer, Nubian, Beja, Zande, Bari, Fur
Religions Muslim 70%, traditional beliefs 20%, Christian 5%, other 5%
Ethnic mix Arab 51%, Dinka 13%, Nuba 9%, Beja 7%, other 20%
Government Military regime
Currency Pound = 100 piastres
Literacy rate 46%
Calorie consumption 2202 kilocalories

SURINAM
South America

Official name Republic of Surinam
Formation 1975 / 1975
Capital Paramaribo
Population 400,000 / 5 people per sq mile (2 people per sq km) / 49%
Total area 63,039 sq miles (163,270 sq km)
Languages Dutch*, Pidgin English (Taki-Taki), Hindi, Javanese, Carib
Religions Christian 48%, Hindu 27%, Muslim 20%, other 5%
Ethnic mix South Asian 37%, Creole 31%, Javanese 15%, other 17%
Government Multiparty republic
Currency Guilder = 100 cents
Literacy rate 93%
Calorie consumption 2547 kilocalories

SWAZILAND
Southern Africa

Official name Kingdom of Swaziland
Formation 1968 / 1968
Capital Mbabane
Population 900,000 / 135 people per
sq mile (52 people per sq km) / 29%
Total area 6703 sq miles
(17,360 sq km)
Languages Siswati*, English*, Zulu
Religions Christian 60%, traditional
beliefs 40%
Ethnic mix Swazi 95%, other 5%
Government Executive monarchy
Currency Lilangeni = 100 cents
Literacy rate 77%
Calorie consumption 2706 kilocalories

SWEDEN
Northern Europe

Official name Kingdom of Sweden
Formation 1809 / 1905
Capital Stockholm
Population 8.8 million / 50 people per
sq mile (20 people per sq km) / 83%
Total area 173,730 sq miles (449,960 sq km)
Languages Swedish*, Finnish, Lappish,
Religions Evangelical Lutheran 94%, Roman
Catholic 2%, other 4%
Ethnic mix Swedish 87%, Finnish and
Lapp 1%, other European 12%
Government Constitutional monarchy
Currency Krona = 100 öre
Literacy rate 99%
Calorie consumption 2972 kilocalories

SWITZERLAND
Central Europe

Official name Swiss Confederation
Formation 1815 / 1815
Capital Bern
Population 7.2 million / 469 people per
sq mile (181 people per sq km) / 60%
Total area 15,940 sq miles (41,290 sq km)
Languages German*, French*,
Italian*, Romansch*
Religions Roman Catholic 48%,
Protestant 44%, other 8%
Ethnic mix German 65%, French 18%,
Italian 10%, other 7%
Government Federal republic
Currency Franc = 100 centimes
Literacy rate 99%
Calorie consumption 3379 kilocalories

SYRIA
Southwest Asia

Official name Syrian Arab Republic
Formation 1946 / 1946
Capital Damascus
Population 14.7 million / 207 people per
sq mile (80 people per sq km) / 51%
Total area 71,500 sq miles (185,180 sq km)
Languages Arabic*, French, Kurdish,
Armenian, Circassian, Turkmen
Religions Sunni Muslim 74%,
other Muslim 16%, Christian 10%
Ethnic mix Arab 90%, other 10%
Government Single-party republic
Currency Pound = 100 piastres
Literacy rate 71%

TAIWAN
East Asia

Official name Republic of China
Formation 1949 / 1949
Capital Taipei
Population 20.9 million / 1682 people per sq
mile (649 people per sq km) / 69%
Total area 13,969 sq miles (36,179 sq km)
Languages Mandarin*, Amoy Chinese,
Hakka Chinese
Religions Buddhist, Confucianist,
Taoist 93%, other 7%
Ethnic mix Taiwanese 84%, mainland
Chinese 14%, other 2%
Government Multiparty republic
Currency New Taiwan $ = 100 cents
Literacy rate 94%
Calorie consumption NOT AVAILABLE

TAJIKISTAN
Central Asia

Official name Republic of Tajikistan
Formation 1991 / 1991
Capital Dushanbe
Population 6.1 million / 111 people per
sq mile (43 people per sq km) / 32%
Total area 55,251 sq miles (143,100 sq km)
Main languages Tajik*, Uzbek, Russian
Religions Sunni Muslim 85%,
Shi'a Muslim 5%, other 10%
Ethnic mix Tajik 62%, Uzbek 24%,
Russian 4%, Tatar 2%, other 8%
Government Single-party republic
Currency Tajik rouble = 100 kopeks
Literacy rate 98%
Calorie consumption NOT AVAILABLE

TANZANIA
East Africa

Official name United Republic of Tanzania
Formation 1964 / 1964
Capital Dodoma
Population 29.7 million / 88 people per
sq mile (34 people per sq km) / 22%
Total area 364,900 sq miles (945,090 sq km)
Languages English*, Swahili, Sukuma,
Chagga, Nyamwezi, Hehe, Makonde
Religions Traditional beliefs 42%,
Muslim 31%, Christian 27%
Ethnic mix 120 ethnic Bantu groups
99%, other 1%
Government Single-party republic
Currency Shilling = 100 cents
Literacy rate 68%
Calorie consumption 2018 kilocalories

THAILAND
Southeast Asia

Official name Kingdom of Thailand
Formation 1882 / 1887
Capital Bangkok
Population 58.8 million / 298 people
per sq mile (115 people per sq km) / 19%
Total area 198,116 sq miles (513,120 sq km)
Languages Thai*, Chinese, Malay,
Khmer, Mon, Karen
Religions Buddhist 95%, other 5%
Ethnic mix Thai 75%, Chinese 14%,
Malay 4%, other 7%
Government Constitutional monarchy
Currency Baht = 100 stangs
Literacy rate 94%
Calorie consumption 2432 kilocalories

TOGO
West Africa

Official name Togolese Republic
Formation 1960 / 1960
Capital Lomé
Population 4.1 million / 195 people per
sq mile (75 people per sq km) / 30%
Total area 21,927 sq miles (56,790 sq km)
Languages French*, Ewe, Kabye, Gurma
Religions Traditional beliefs 70%,
Christian 20%, Muslim 10%
Ethnic mix Ewe 43%, Kabye 26%,
Gurma 16%, other 15%
Government Multiparty republic
Currency CFA franc = 100 centimes
Literacy rate 52%
Calorie consumption 2242 kilocalories

TONGA
Australasia & Oceania

Official name Kingdom of Tonga
Formation 1970 / 1970
Capital Nuku'alofa
Population 98,000 / 352 people per
sq mile (136 people per sq km) / 21%
Total area 290 sq miles
(750 sq km)
Languages Tongan*, English
Religions Protestant 82%, Roman
Catholic 18%
Ethnic mix Tongan 98%, other 2%
Government Constitutional monarchy
Currency Pa'anga = 100 seniti
Literacy rate 99%
Calorie consumption 2946 kilocalories

TRINIDAD & TOBAGO
West Indies

Official name Republic of Trinidad and Tobago
Formation 1962 / 1962
Capital Port-of-Spain
Population 1.3 million / 656 people per
sq mile (253 people per sq km) / 70%
Total area 1981 sq miles (5130 sq km)
Languages English*, English Creole, Hindi,
French, Spanish
Religions Christian 58%, Hindu 30%, Muslim
8%, other 4%
Ethnic mix Black 43%, South Asian 40%,
mixed 14%, other 3%
Government Multiparty republic
Currency Trinidad & Tobago $ = 100 cents
Literacy rate 98%
Calorie consumption 2585 kilocalories

TUNISIA
North Africa

Official name Republic of Tunisia
Formation 1956 / 1956
Capital Tunis
Population 8.9 million / 148 people per
sq mile (57 people per sq km) / 56%
Total area 63,170 sq miles (163,610 sq km)
Languages Arabic*, French
Religions Muslim 98%, Christian 1%,
other 1%
Ethnic mix Arab and Berber 98%,
European 1%, other 1%
Government Multiparty republic
Currency Dinar = 1000 millimes
Literacy rate 67%
Calorie consumption 3330 kilocalories

TURKEY
Asia / Europe

Official name Republic of Turkey
Formation 1923 / 1939
Capital Ankara
Population 61.9 million / 207 people
per sq mile (80 people per sq km) / 64%
Total area 300,950 sq miles (779,450 sq km)
Languages Turkish*, Kurdish, Arabic,
Circassian, Armenian
Religions Muslim 99%, other 1%
Ethnic mix Turkish 80%, Kurdish 17%,
other 3%
Government Multiparty republic
Currency Turkish lira = 100 krural
Literacy rate 82%
Calorie consumption 3429 kilocalories

TURKMENISTAN
Central Asia

Official name Turkmenistan
Formation 1991 / 1991
Capital Ashgabat
Population 4.1 million / 21 people per
sq mile (8 people per sq km) / 45%
Total area 188,455 sq miles (488,100 sq km)
Languages Turkmen*, Uzbek, Russian
Religions Muslim 85%, Eastern
Orthodox 10%, other 5%
Ethnic mix Turkmen 72%, Russian 9%,
Uzbek 9%, other 10%
Government Single-party republic
Currency Manat = 100 tenge
Literacy rate 98%
Calorie consumption NOT AVAILABLE

TUVALU
Australasia & Oceania

Official name Tuvalu
Formation 1978 / 1978
Capital Fongafale
Population 9000 / 997 people per
sq mile (346 people per sq km) / 31%
Total area 10 sq miles
(26 sq km)
Languages Tuvaluan*, Kiribati, English
Religions Protestant 97%, other 3%
Ethnic mix Tuvaluan 95% other 5%
Government Constitutional monarchy
Currency Australian $ = 100 cents
Literacy rate 95%
Calorie consumption NOT AVAILABLE

UGANDA
East Africa

Official name Republic of Uganda
Formation 1962 / 1962
Capital Kampala
Population 21.3 million / 277 people per
sq mile (107 people per sq km) / 12%
Total area 91,073 sq miles (235,880 sq km)
Languages English*, Luganda, Nkole, Chiga,
Lango, Acholi, Teso
Religions Christian 66%, traditional
beliefs 18%, Muslim 16%
Ethnic mix Buganda 18%, Banyoro 14%,
Teso 9%, other 59%
Government Multiparty republic
Currency Shilling = 100 cents
Literacy rate 62%
Calorie consumption 2159 kilocalories

UKRAINE
Eastern Europe

Official name Ukraine
Formation 1991 / 1991
Capital Kiev
Population 51.4 million / 220 people per
sq mile (85 people per sq km) / 69%
Total area 223,090 sq miles (603,700 sq km)
Languages Ukrainian*, Russian, Tatar
Religions Mostly Ukrainian Orthodox,
with Roman Catholic, Protestant and
Jewish minorities
Ethnic mix Ukrainian 73%, Russian 22%,
other (including Tatar) 5%
Government Multiparty republic
Currency Karbovanets (coupons)
Literacy rate 98%
Calorie consumption NOT AVAILABLE

UNITED ARAB EMIRATES
Southwest Asia

Official name United Arab Emirates
Formation 1971 / 1971
Capital Abu Dhabi
Population 1.9 million / 9 people per
sq mile (23 people per sq km) / 82%
Total area 32,278 sq miles (83,600 sq km)
Languages Arabic*, Farsi (Persian),
Urdu, Hindi, English
Religions Sunni Muslim 77%,
Shi'a Muslim 19%, other 4%
Ethnic mix South Asian 50%, Emirian 19%,
other Arab 23%, other 8%
Government Federation of monarchs
Currency Dirham = 100 fils
Literacy rate 79%
Calorie consumption 3384 kilocalories

UNITED KINGDOM
Northwest Europe

Official name United Kingdom of Great
Britain and Northern Ireland
Formation 1801 / 1922
Capital London
Population 58.3 million / 625 people per
sq mile (241 people per sq km) / 89%
Total area 94,550 sq miles (244,880 sq km)
Languages English*, Welsh, Scottish, Gaelic
Religions Protestant 52%, Roman
Catholic 9%, Muslim 3%, other 36%
Ethnic mix English 81%, Scottish 10%,
Welsh 2%, other 7%
Government Constitutional monarchy
Currency Pound sterling = 100 pence
Literacy rate 99%
Calorie consumption 3317 kilocalories

UNITED STATES
North America

Official name United States of America
Formation 1787 / 1959
Capital Washington DC
Population 263.3 million / 75 people
per sq mile (29 people per sq km) / 76%
Total area 3,681,760 sq miles (9,372,610 sq km)
Languages English*, Spanish, Italian, German,
French, Polish, Chinese, Greek
Religions Protestant 56%, Roman
Catholic 28%, Jewish 2%, other 14%
Ethnic mix White (including Hispanic) 83%,
Black 13%, other 4%
Government Multiparty republic
Currency US $ = 100 cents
Literacy rate 99%
Calorie consumption 3732 kilocalories

URUGUAY
South America

Official name Oriental Republic of Uruguay
Formation 1828 / 1909
Capital Montevideo
Population 3.2 million / 122 people per
sq mile (18 people per sq km) / 90%
Total area 67,494 sq miles (174,810 sq km)
Languages Spanish*
Religions Roman Catholic 66%,
Protestant 2%, Jewish 2%, other 30%
Ethnic mix European 88%, mestizo 8%
Black 4%
Government Multiparty republic
Currency Peso = 100 centimes
Literacy rate 97%
Calorie consumption 2750 kilocalories

UZBEKISTAN
Central Asia

Official name Republic of Uzbekistan
Formation 1991 / 1991
Capital Tashkent
Population 22.8 million / 132 people per
sq mile (51 people per sq km) / 41%
Total area 439,733 sq miles
(1,138,910 sq km)
Languages Uzbek*, Russian
Religions Muslim 88%, other (mostly Eastern
Orthodox) 12%
Ethnic mix Uzbek 71%, Russian 8%,
Tajik 5%, Kazakh 4%, other 12%
Government Single-party republic
Currency Sum = 100 teen
Literacy rate 97%
Calorie consumption NOT AVAILABLE

VANUATU
Australasia & Oceania

Official name Republic of Vanuatu
Formation 1980 / 1980
Capital Port-Vila
Population 200,000 / 41 people per
sq mile (16 people per sq km) / 19%
Total area 4706 sq miles
(12,190 sq km)
Languages Bislama*, English, French
Religions Protestant 77%, Roman Catholic
15%, traditional beliefs 8%
Ethnic mix Ni-Vanuatu 98%, other 2%
Government Multiparty republic
Currency Vatu = 100 centimes
Literacy rate 70%
Calorie consumption 2739 kilocalories

VATICAN CITY
Southern Europe

Official name Vatican City State
Formation 1929 / 1929
Capital Not applicable
Population 1000 / 5890 people per
sq mile (2273 people per sq km) / 100%
Total area 0.17 sq miles (0.44 sq km)
Languages Italian*, Latin*
Religions Roman Catholic 100%
Ethnic mix Italian 90%, Swiss 10%
(including the Swiss Guard, which
is responsible for papal security)
Government Papal Commission
Currency Italian lira = 100 centesimi
Literacy rate 100%
Calorie consumption 3561 kilocalories

VENEZUELA
South America

Official name Republic of Venezuela
Formation 1830 / 1929
Capital Caracas
Population 21.8 million / 65 people per
sq mile (25 people per sq km) / 91%
Total area 352,143 sq miles (912,050 sq km)
Languages Spanish*, Indian languages
Religions Roman Catholic 96%,
Protestant 2%, other 2%
Ethnic mix mestizo 67%, White 21%,
Black 10%, Indian 2%
Government Multiparty republic
Currency Bolívar = 100 centimos
Literacy rate 91%
Calorie consumption 2618 kilocalories

VIETNAM
Southeast Asia

Official name Socialist Republic of Vietnam
Formation 1976 / 1976
Capital Hanoi
Population 74.5 million / 593 people
per sq mile (229 people per sq km) / 20%
Total area 127,243 sq miles (329,560 sq km)
Languages Vietnamese*, Chinese,
Thai, Khmer, Muong
Religions Buddhist 55%, Roman
Catholic 7%, Muslim 1%, other 37%
Ethnic mix Vietnamese 88%, Chinese 4%,
Thai 2%, other 6%
Government Single-party republic
Currency Dong = 10 hao = 100 xu
Literacy rate 94%
Calorie consumption 2250 kilocalories

YEMEN
Southwest Asia

Official name Republic of Yemen
Formation 1990 / 1990
Capital Sana
Population 14.5 million / 70 people per
sq mile (27 people per sq km) / 31%
Total area 203,849 sq miles (527,970 sq km)
Languages Arabic*, Hindi, Tamil, Urdu
Religions Sunni Muslim 55%, Shi'a
Muslim 42%, other 3%
Ethnic mix Arab 95%, Afro-Arab 3%, South
Asian, African, European 2%
Government Multiparty republic
Currency Rial (North), Dinar (South) –
both are legal currency
Literacy rate 41%
Calorie consumption 2203 kilocalories

YUGOSLAVIA (SERBIA & MONTENEGRO)
Europe

Official name Federal Republic of Yugoslavia
Formation 1992 / 1992
Capital Belgrade
Population 10.8 million / 1088 people per
sq mile (420 people per sq km) / 50%
Total area 9929 sq miles (25,715 sq km)
Languages Serbian*, Croatian, Albanian
Religions Roman Catholic, Eastern Orthodox
65%, Muslim 19%, other 16%
Ethnic mix Serb 63%, Albanian 14%,
Montenegrin 6%, other 17%
Government Multiparty republic
Currency Dinar = 100 para
Literacy rate 93%
Calorie consumption NOT AVAILABLE

ZAMBIA
Southern Africa

Official name Republic of Zambia
Formation 1964 / 1964
Capital Lusaka
Population 9.5 million / 34 people per
sq mile (13 people per sq km) / 42%
Total area 285,992 sq miles (740,720 sq km)
Languages English*, Bemba*, Nyanja*, Tonga,
Kaonde, Lunda
Religions Christian 63%, Traditional
beliefs 35%, other 2%
Ethnic mix Bemba 36%, Maravi 18%,
Tonga 15%, other 31%
Government Multiparty republic
Currency Kwacha = 100 ngwee
Literacy rate 78%
Calorie consumption 1931 kilocalories

ZIMBABWE
Southern Africa

Official name Republic of Zimbabwe
Formation 1980 / 1980
Capital Harare
Population 11.3 million / 75 people
per sq mile (29 people per sq km) / 30%
Total area 150,800 sq miles (390,580 sq km)
Languages English*, Shona, Ndebele
Religions Syncretic (Christian and traditional
beliefs) 50%, Christian 26%,
traditional beliefs 24%
Ethnic mix Shona 71%, Ndebele 16%, other
11%, White, Asian 2%
Government Multiparty republic
Currency Zimbabwe $ = 100 cents
Literacy rate 85%
Calorie consumption 1985 kilocalories

Glossary

THIS GLOSSARY lists all geographical, technical and foreign language terms which appear in the text, followed by a brief definition of the term. Any acronyms used in the text are also listed in full. Terms in italics are for cross-reference and indicate that the word is separately defined in the glossary.

A

Aboriginal The original (*indigenous*) inhabitants of a country or continent. Especially used with reference to Australia.

Abyssal plain A broad *plain* found in the depths of the ocean, more than 10,000 ft (3000 m) below sea level.

Acid rain Rain, sleet, snow or mist which has absorbed waste gases from fossil-fuelled power stations and vehicle exhausts, becoming more acid. It causes severe environmental damage.

Adaptation The gradual evolution of plants and animals so that they become better suited to survive and reproduce in their *environment*.

Afforestation The planting of new forest in areas which were once forested but have been cleared.

Agribusiness A term applied to activities such as the growing of crops, rearing of animals or the manufacture of farm machinery, which eventually leads to the supply of agricultural produce at market.

Air mass A huge, homogeneous mass of air, within which horizontal patterns of temperature and *humidity* are consistent. Air masses are separated by *fronts*.

Alliance An agreement between two or more states, to work together to achieve common purposes.

Alluvial fan A large fan-shaped deposit of fine sediments deposited by a river as it emerges from a narrow, mountain valley onto a broad, open *plain*.

Alluvium Material deposited by rivers. Nowadays usually only applied to finer particles of silt and clay.

Alpine Mountain *environment*, between the *treeline* and the level of permanent snow cover.

Alpine mountains Ranges of mountains formed between 30 and 65 million years ago, by *folding*, in west and central Europe.

Amerindian A term applied to people *indigenous* to North, Central and South America.

Animal husbandry The business of rearing animals.

Antarctic circle The parallel which lies at *latitude* of 66° 32′ S.

Anticline A geological *fold* that forms an arch shape, curving upwards in the rock *strata*.

Anticyclone An area of relatively high atmospheric pressure.

Aquaculture Collective term for the farming of produce derived from the sea, including fish-farming, the cultivation of shellfish, and plants such as seaweed.

Aquifer A body of rock which can absorb water. Also applied to any rock strata that have sufficient porosity to yield *groundwater* through wells or springs.

Arable Land which has been ploughed and is being used, or is suitable, for growing crops.

Archipelago A group or chain of islands.

Arctic Circle The parallel which lies at a *latitude* of 66° 32′ N.

Arête A thin, jagged mountain ridge which divides two adjacent *cirques*, found in regions where *glaciation* has occurred.

Arid Dry. An area of low rainfall, where the rate of *evaporation* may be greater than that of *precipitation*. Often defined as those areas that receive less than one inch (25 mm) of rain a year. In these areas only drought-resistant plants can survive.

Artesian well A naturally occurring source of underground water, stored in an *aquifer*.

Artisanal Small-scale, manual operation, such as fishing, using little or no machinery.

ASEAN Association of Southeast Asian Nations. Established in 1967 to promote economic, social and cultural co-operation. Its members include Brunei, Indonesia, Malaysia, Philippines, Singapore and Thailand.

Aseismic A region where *earthquake* activity has ceased.

Asteroid A minor planet circling the Sun, mainly between the orbits of Mars and Jupiter.

Asthenosphere A zone of hot, partially melted rock, which underlies the *lithosphere*, within the Earth's *crust*.

Atmosphere The envelope of odourless, colourless and tasteless gases surrounding the Earth, consisting of *oxygen* (23%), *nitrogen* (75%), argon (1%), *carbon dioxide* (0.03%), as well as tiny proportions of other gases.

Atmospheric pressure The pressure created by the action of gravity on the gases surrounding the Earth.

Atoll A ring-shaped island or *coral reef* often enclosing a *lagoon* of sea water.

Avalanche The rapid movement of a mass of snow and ice down a steep slope. Similar movements of other materials are described as *rock avalanches* or *landslides* and *sand avalanches*.

B

Badlands A landscape that has been heavily-eroded and dissected by rainwater, and which has little or no vegetation.

Back slope The gentler windward slope of a sand *dune* or gentler slope of a *cuesta*.

Bajos An *alluvial fan* deposited by a river at the base of mountains and hills which encircle *desert* areas.

Bar, coastal An offshore strip of sand or shingle, either above or below the water. Usually parallel to the shore but sometimes crescent-shaped or at an oblique angle.

Barchan A crescent-shaped sand *dune*, formed where wind direction is very consistent. The horns of the crescent point downwind and where there is enough sand the barchan is mobile.

Barrio A Spanish term for the shanty towns – self-built settlements – which are clustered around many South and Central American cities (*see also Favela*).

Basalt Dark, fine-grained *igneous rock*. Formed near the Earth's surface from fast-cooling *lava*.

Base level The level below which flowing water cannot erode the land.

Basement rock A mass of ancient rock often of *Pre-Cambrian age*, covered by a layer of more recent *sedimentary rocks*. Commonly associated with *shield* areas.

Beach Lake or sea shore where waves break and there is an accumulation of loose material – mud, sand, shingle or pebbles.

Bedrock Solid, consolidated and relatively unweathered rock, found on the surface of the land or just below a layer of soil or *weathered* rock.

Biodiversity The quantity of animal or plant species in a given area.

Biomass The total mass of organic matter – plants and animals – in a given area. It is usually measured in kilogrammes per square metre. Plant biomass is proportionally greater than that of animals, except in cities.

Biosphere The zone just above and below the Earth's surface, where all plants and animals live.

Blizzard A severe windstorm with snow and sleet. Visibility is often severely restricted.

Bluff The steep bank of a *meander*, formed by the erosive action of a river.

Boreal forest Tracts of mainly coniferous forest found in northern *latitudes*.

Breccia A type of rock composed of sharp fragments, cemented by a fine-grained material such as clay.

Butte An isolated, flat-topped hill with steep or vertical sides, buttes are the eroded remnants of a former land surface.

C

Caatinga Portuguese (Brazilian) term for thorny woodland growing in areas of pale granitic soils.

CACM Central American Common Market. Established in 1960 to further economic ties between its members, which are Costa Rica, El Salvador, Guatemala, Honduras and Nicaragua.

Calcite Hexagonal crystals of calcium carbonate.

Caldera A huge volcanic vent, often containing a number of smaller vents, and sometimes a crater lake.

Carbon cycle The transfer of carbon to and from the *atmosphere*. This occurs on land through *photosynthesis*. In the sea, *carbon dioxide* is absorbed, some returning to the air and some taken up into the bodies of sea creatures.

Carbon dioxide A colourless, odourless gas (CO_2) which makes up 0.03% of the *atmosphere*.

Carbonation The process whereby rocks are broken down by carbonic acid. Carbon dioxide in the air dissolves in rainwater, forming carbonic acid. *Limestone* terrain can be rapidly eaten away.

Cash crop A single crop grown specifically for export sale, rather than for local use. Typical examples include coffee, tea and citrus fruits.

Cassava A type of grain meal, used to produce tapioca. A staple crop in many parts of Africa.

Castle kopje Hill or rock outcrop, especially in southern Africa, where steep sides, and a summit composed of blocks, give a castle-like appearance.

Cataracts A series of stepped waterfalls created as a river flows over a band of hard, resistant rock.

Causeway A raised route through marshland or a body of water.

CEEAC Economic Community of Central African States. Established in 1983 to promote regional co-operation and if possible, establish a common market between 11 Central African nations.

Chemical weathering The chemical reactions leading to the decomposition of rocks. Types of chemical weathering include *carbonation*, *hydrolysis* and *oxidation*.

Chernozem A fertile soil, also known as 'black earth' consisting of a layer of dark topsoil, rich in decaying vegetation, overlying a lighter chalky layer.

Cirque Armchair-shaped basin, found in mountain regions, with a steep back, or rear, wall and a raised rock lip, often containing a lake (or *tarn*). The cirque floor has been eroded by a *glacier*, while the back wall is eroded both by the *glacier* and by *weathering*.

Climate The average weather conditions in a given area over a period of years, sometimes defined as 30 years or more.

Cold War A period of hostile relations between the USA and the Soviet Union and their allies after the Second World War.

Composite volcano Also known as a strato-volcano, the volcanic cone is composed of alternating deposits of *lava* and *pyroclastic* material.

Compound A substance made up of *elements* chemically combined in a consistent way.

Condensation The process whereby a gas changes into a liquid. For example, water vapour in the *atmosphere* condenses around tiny airborne particles to form droplets of water.

Confluence The point at which two rivers meet.

Conglomerate Rock composed of large, water-worn or rounded pebbles, held together by a natural cement.

Coniferous forest A forest type containing trees which are generally, but not necessarily, *evergreen* and have slender, needle-like leaves and which reproduce by means of seeds contained in a cone.

Continental drift The theory that the continents of today are fragments of one or more prehistoric *supercontinents* which have moved across the Earth's surface, creating ocean basins. The theory has been superseded by a more sophisticated one – *plate tectonics*.

Continental shelf An area of the continental crust, below sea level, which slopes gently. It is separated from the deep ocean by a much more steeply inclined *continental slope*.

Continental slope A steep slope running from the edge of the *continental shelf* to the ocean floor.

Conurbation A vast metropolitan area created by the expansion of towns and cities into a virtually continuous urban area.

Cool continental A rainy *climate* with warm summers [warmest month below 76°F (22°C)] and often severe winters [coldest month below 32°F (0°C)].

Copra The dried, white kernel of a coconut, from which coconut oil is extracted.

Coral reef An underwater barrier created by colonies of the coral polyp. Polyps secrete a protective skeleton of calcium carbonate, and reefs develop as live polyps build on the skeletons of dead generations.

Core The centre of the Earth, consisting of a dense mass of iron and nickel. It is thought that the outer core is molten or liquid, and that the hot inner core is solid due to extremely high pressures.

Coriolis effect A deflecting force caused by the rotation of the Earth. In the northern hemisphere a body, such as an *air mass* or ocean current, is deflected to the right, and in the southern hemisphere to the left. This prevents winds from blowing straight from areas of high to low pressure.

Coulées A US / Canadian term for a ravine formed by river *erosion*.

Craton A large block of the Earth's *crust* which has remained stable for a long period of *geological time*. It is made up of ancient *shield* rocks.

Cretaceous A period of *geological time* beginning about 145 million years ago and lasting until about 65 million years ago.

Crevasse A deep crack in a *glacier*.

Crust The hard, thin outer shell of the Earth. The crust floats on the *mantle*, which is softer and more dense. Under the oceans (oceanic crust) the crust is 3.7–6.8 miles (6–11 km) thick. Continental crust averages 18–24 miles (30–40 km).

Crystalline rock Rocks formed when molten *magma* crystallizes (*igneous rocks*) or when heat or pressure cause re-crystallization (*metamorphic rocks*). Crystalline rocks are distinct from *sedimentary rocks*.

Cuesta A hill which rises into a steep slope on one side but has a gentler gradient on its other slope.

Cyclone An area of low *atmospheric pressure*, occurring where the air is warm and relatively low in density, causing low level winds to spiral. *Hurricanes* and *typhoons* are tropical cyclones.

D

De facto
1 Government or other activity that takes place, or exists in actuality if not by right.
2 A border, which exists in practice, but which is not officially recognized by all the countries it adjoins.

Deciduous forest A forest of trees which shed their leaves annually at a particular time or season. In *temperate* climates the fall of leaves occurs in the Autumn. Some *coniferous* trees, such as the larch, are deciduous. Deciduous vegetation contrasts with *evergreen*, which keeps its leaves for more than a year.

Defoliant Chemical spray used to remove foliage (leaves) from trees.

Deforestation The act of cutting down and clearing large areas of forest for human activities, such as agricultural land or urban development.

Delta Low-lying, fan-shaped area at a river mouth, formed by the *deposition* of successive layers of *sediment*. Slowing as it enters the sea, a river deposits sediment and may, as a result, split into numerous smaller channels, known as *distributaries*.

Denudation The combined effect of *weathering*, *erosion* and *mass movement*, which, over long periods, exposes underlying rocks.

Deposition The laying down of material that has accumulated:
(*1*) after being *eroded* and then transported by physical forces such as wind, ice or water;
(*2*) as organic remains, such as coal and coral;
(*3*) as the result of *evaporation* and chemical *precipitation*.

Depression
1 In climatic terms it is a large low pressure system.
2 A complex *fold*, producing a large valley, which incorporates both a *syncline* and an *anticline*.

Desert An *arid* region of low rainfall, with little vegetation or animal life, which is adapted to the dry conditions. The term is now applied not only to hot tropical and subtropical regions, but to arid areas of the continental interiors and to the ice deserts of the *Arctic* and *Antarctic*.

Desertification The gradual extension of *desert* conditions in *arid* or *semi-arid* regions, as a result of climatic change or human activity, such as over-grazing and *deforestation*.

Despot A ruler with absolute power. Despots are often associated with oppressive regimes.

Detritus Piles of rock deposited by an erosive agent such as a river or *glacier*.

Distributary A minor branch of a river, which does not rejoin the main stream, common at *deltas*.

Diurnal Daily, something that occurs each day. Diurnal temperature refers to the variation in temperature over the course of a full day and night.

Divide A US term describing the area of high ground separating two *drainage basins*.

Donga A steep-sided *gully*, resulting from *erosion* by a river or by floods.

Dormant A term used to describe a *volcano* which is not currently erupting. They differ from extinct volcanoes as dormant volcanoes are still considered likely to erupt in the future.

Drainage basin The area drained by a single river system, its boundary is marked by a *watershed* or *divide*.

Drought A long period of continuously low rainfall.

Drumlin A long, streamlined hillock composed of material deposited by a *glacier*. They often occur in groups known as swarms.

Dune A mound or ridge of sand, shaped, and often moved, by the wind. They are found in hot *deserts* and on low-lying coasts where onshore winds blow across sandy beaches.

Dyke A wall constructed in low-lying areas to contain floodwaters or protect from high tides.

E

Earthflow The rapid movement of soil and other loose surface material down a slope, when saturated by water. Similar to a mudflow but not as fast-flowing, due to a lower percentage of water.

Earthquake Sudden movements of the Earth's *crust*, causing the ground to shake. Frequently occurring at *tectonic plate* margins. The shock, or series of shocks, spreads out from an *epicentre*.

EC The European Community (*see* EU).

Ecosystem A system of living organisms – plants and animals – interacting with their *environment*.

ECOWAS Economic Community of West African States. Established in 1975, it incorporates 16 West African states and aims to promote closer regional and economic co-operation.

Element
1 A constituent of the *climate* – *precipitation*, *humidity*, temperature, *atmospheric pressure* or wind.
2 A substance that cannot be separated into simpler substances by chemical means.

El Niño A climatic phenomenon, the El Niño effect occurs about 14 times each century and leads to major shifts in global air circulation. It is associated with unusually warm currents off the coasts of Peru, Ecuador and Chile. The anomaly can last for up to two years.

Environment The conditions created by the surroundings (both natural and artificial) within which an organism lives. In human geography the word includes the surrounding economic, cultural and social conditions.

Eon (aeon) Traditionally a long, but indefinite, period of *geological time*.

Ephemeral A non-permanent feature, often used in connection with seasonal rivers or lakes in dry areas.

Epicentre The point on the Earth's surface directly above the underground origin – or focus – of an *earthquake*.

Equator The line of *latitude* which lies equidistant between the North and South Poles.

Erg An extensive area of sand *dunes*, particularly in the Sahara Desert.

Erosion The processes which wear away the surface of the land. *Glaciers*, wind, rivers, waves and currents all carry debris which causes *erosion*. Some definitions also include *mass movement* due to gravity as an agent of erosion.

Escarpment A steep slope at the margin of a level, upland surface. In a landscape created by *folding*, escarpments (or scarps) frequently lie behind a more gentle backward slope.

Esker A narrow, winding ridge of sand and gravel deposited by streams of water flowing beneath or at the edge of a *glacier*.

Erratic A rock transported by a *glacier* and deposited some distance from its place of origin.

Eustacy A world-wide fall or rise in ocean levels.

EU The European Union. Established in 1965, it was formerly known as the EEC (European Economic Community) and then the EC (European Community). Its members are Austria, Belgium, Denmark, Finland, France, Germany, Greece, Ireland, Italy, Luxembourg, Netherlands, Portugal, Spain, Sweden and UK. It seeks to establish an integrated European common market and eventual federation.

Evaporation The process whereby a liquid or solid is turned into a gas or vapour. Also refers to the diffusion of water vapour into the *atmosphere* from exposed water surfaces such as lakes and seas.

Evapotranspiration The loss of moisture from the Earth's surface through a combination of *evaporation*, and *transpiration* from the leaves of plants.

Evergreen Plants with long-lasting leaves, which are not shed annually or seasonally.

Exfoliation A kind of *weathering* whereby scale-like flakes of rock are peeled or broken off by the development of salt crystals in water within the rocks. *Groundwater*, which contains dissolved salts, seeps to the surface and evaporates, precipitating a film of salt crystals, which expands causing fine cracks. As these grow, flakes of rock break off.

Extrusive rock *Igneous* rock formed when molten material (*magma*) pours forth at the Earth's surface and cools rapidly. It usually has a glassy texture.

F

Factionalism The actions of one or more minority political group acting against the interests of the majority government.

Fault A fracture or crack in rock, where strains (*tectonic* movement) have caused blocks to move, vertically or laterally, relative to each other.

Fauna Collective name for the animals of a particular period of time, or region.

Favela Brazilian term for the shanty towns or self-built, temporary dwellings which have grown up around the edge of many South and Central American cities.

Ferrel cell A component in the global pattern of air circulation, which rises in the colder *latitudes* (60° N and S) and descends in warmer *latitudes* (30° N and S). The Ferrel cell forms part of the world's three-cell air circulation pattern, with the *Hadley* and Polar cells.

Fissure A deep crack in a rock or a *glacier*.

Fjord A deep, narrow inlet, created when the sea inundates the *U-shaped valley* created by a *glacier*.

Flash flood A sudden, short-lived rise in the water level of a river or stream, or surge of water down a dry river channel, or *wadi*, caused by heavy rainfall.

Flax A plant used to make linen.

Flood plain The broad, flat part of a river valley, adjacent to the river itself, formed by *sediment* deposited during flooding.

Flora The collective name for the plants of a particular period of time or region.

Flow The movement of a river within its banks, particularly in terms of the speed and volume of water.

Fold A bend in the rock *strata* of the Earth's *crust*, resulting from compression.

Fossil The remains, or traces, of a dead organism preserved in the Earth's *crust*.

Fossil dune A *dune* formed in a once-*arid* region which is now wetter. *Dunes* normally move with the wind, but in these cases vegetation makes them stable.

Fossil fuel Fuel – coal, natural gas or oil – composed of the fossilized remains of plants and animals.

Front The boundary between two *air masses*, which contrast sharply in temperature and *humidity*.

Frontal depression An area of low pressure caused by rising warm air. They are generally 600–1200 miles (1000–2000 km) in diameter. Within *depressions* there are both warm and cold fronts.

Frost shattering A form of *weathering* where water freezes in cracks, causing expansion. As temperatures fluctuate and the ice melts and refreezes, it eventually causes the rocks to shatter and fragments of rock to break off.

G

Gaucho South American term for a stock herder or cowboy who works on the grassy *plains* of Paraguay, Uruguay and Argentina.

Geological time-scale The chronology of the Earth's history as revealed in its rocks. Geological time is divided into a number of periods: *eon*, era, period, epoch, age and chron (the shortest). These units are not of uniform length.

Geosyncline A concave fold (*syncline*) or large depression in the Earth's *crust*, extending hundreds of kilometres. This basin contains a deep layer of sediment, especially at its centre, from the land masses around it.

Geothermal energy Heat derived from hot rocks within the Earth's *crust* and resulting in hot springs, steam or hot rocks at the surface. The energy is generated by rock movements, and from the breakdown of radioactive elements occurring under intense pressure.

GDP Gross Domestic Product. The total value of goods and services produced by a country excluding income from foreign countries.

Geyser A jet of steam and hot water that intermittently erupts from vents in the ground in areas that are, or were, *volcanic*. Some geysers occasionally reach heights of 196 ft (60 m).

Ghetto An area of a city or region occupied by an overwhelming majority of people from one racial or religious group, who may be subject to persecution or containment.

Glaciation The growth of *glaciers* and *ice sheets*, and their impact on the landscape.

Glacier A body of ice moving downslope under the influence of gravity and consisting of compacted and frozen snow. A glacier is distinct from an *ice sheet*, which is wider and less confined by features of the landscape.

Glacio-eustacy A world-wide change in the level of the oceans, caused when the formation of *ice sheets* takes up water or when their melting returns water to the ocean. The formation of ice sheets in the *Pleistocene* epoch, for example, caused sea level to drop by about 320 ft (100 m).

Glaciofluvial To do with glacial *meltwater*, the landforms it creates and its processes; *erosion*, transportation and *deposition*. Glaciofluvial effects are more powerful and rapid where they occur within or beneath the *glacier*, rather than beyond its edge.

Glacis A gentle slope or *pediment*.

Global warming An increase in the average temperature of the Earth. At present the *greenhouse effect* is thought to contribute to this.

GNP Gross National Product. The total value of goods and services produced by a country.

Gondwanaland The *supercontinent* thought to have existed over 200 million years ago in the southern hemisphere. Gondwanaland is believed to have comprised today's Africa, Madagascar, Australia, parts of South America, *Antarctica* and the Indian subcontinent.

Graben A block of rock let down between two parallel *faults*. Where the graben occurs within a valley, the structure is known as a *rift valley*.

Grease ice Slicks of ice which form in *Antarctic* seas, when ice crystals are bonded together by wind and wave action.

Greenhouse effect A change in the temperature of the *atmosphere*. Short-wave solar radiation travels through the *atmosphere* unimpeded to the Earth's surface, whereas outgoing, long-wave terrestrial radiation is absorbed by materials that re-radiate it back to the Earth. Radiation trapped in this way, by water vapour, carbon dioxide and other 'greenhouse gases', keeps the Earth warm. As more *carbon dioxide* is released into the atmosphere by the burning of *fossil fuels*, the greenhouse effect may cause a global increase in temperature.

Groundwater Water that has seeped into the pores, cavities and cracks of rocks or into soil and water held in an *aquifer*.

Gully A deep, narrow channel eroded in the landscape by *ephemeral* streams.

Guyot A small, flat-topped submarine mountain, formed as a result of subsidence which occurs during *sea-floor spreading*.

Gypsum A soft mineral *compound* (hydrated calcium sulphate), used as the basis of many forms of plaster, including plaster of Paris.

H

Hadley cell A large-scale component in the global pattern of air circulation. Warm air rises over the *Equator* and blows at high altitude towards the poles, sinking in subtropical regions (30° N and 30° S) and creating high pressure. The air then flows at the surface towards the *Equator* in the form of trade winds. There is one cell in each hemisphere. Named after G Hadley, who published his theory in 1735.

Hamada An Arabic word for a plateau of bare rock in a *desert*.

Hanging valley A tributary valley which ends suddenly, high above the bed of the main valley. The effect is found where the main valley has been more deeply eroded by a *glacier*, than has the tributary valley. A stream in a hanging valley will descend to the floor of the main valley as a waterfall or *cataract*.

Headwards The action of a river eroding back upstream, as opposed to the normal process of downstream *erosion*. Headwards erosion is often associated with *gullying*.

Hoodos Pinnacles of rock which have been worn away by *weathering* in *semi-arid* regions.

Horst A block of the Earth's *crust* which has been left upstanding by the sinking of adjoining blocks along fault lines.

Hot spot A region of the Earth's *crust* where high thermal activity occurs, often leading to volcanic eruptions. Hot spots often occur far from plate boundaries, but their movement is associated with *plate tectonics*.

Humid equatorial Rainy *climate* with no winter, where the coolest month is generally above 64°F (18°C).

Humidity The relative amount of moisture held in the Earth's *atmosphere*.

Hurricane
1 A tropical *cyclone* occurring in the Caribbean and western North Atlantic.
2 A wind of more than 65 knots (75 kmph).

Hydro-electric power Energy produced by harnessing the rapid movement of water down steep mountain slopes to drive turbines to generate electricity.

Hydrolysis The chemical breakdown of rocks in reaction with water, forming new compounds.

I

Ice Age A period in the Earth's history when surface temperatures in the temperate *latitudes* were much lower and *ice sheets* expanded considerably. There have been *ice ages* from *Pre-Cambrian* times onwards. The most recent began two million years ago and ended 10,000 years ago.

Ice cap A permanent dome of ice in highland areas. The term ice cap is often seen as distinct from *ice sheet*, which denotes a much wider covering of ice; and is also used refer to the very extensive polar and Greenland ice caps.

Ice floe A large, flat mass of ice floating free on the ocean surface. It is usually formed after the break-up of winter ice by heavy storms.

Ice sheet A continuous, very thick layer of ice and snow. The term is usually used of ice masses which are continental in extent.

Ice shelf A floating mass of ice attached to the edge of a coast. The seaward edge is usually a sheer cliff up to 100 ft (30 m) high.

Ice wedge Massive blocks of ice up to 6.5 ft (2 m) wide at the top and extending 32 ft (10 m) deep. They are found in cracks in *polygonally-patterned* ground in *periglacial* regions.

Iceberg A large mass of ice in a lake or a sea, which has broken off from a floating *ice sheet* (an *ice shelf*) or from a *glacier*.

Igneous rock Rock formed when molten material, *magma*, from the hot, lower layers of the Earth's *crust*, cools, solidifies and crystallizes, either within the Earth's *crust* (*intrusive*) or on the surface (*extrusive*).

IMF International Monetary Fund. Established in 1944 as a UN agency, it contains 175 members around the world and is concerned with world monetary stability and economic development.

Incised meander A *meander* where the river, following its original course, cuts deeply into *bedrock*. This may occur when a mature, meandering river begins to erode its bed much more vigorously after the surrounding land has been uplifted.

Indigenous People, plants or animals native to a particular region.

Infrastructure The communications and services – roads, railways and telecommunications – necessary for the functioning of a country or region.

Inselberg An isolated, steep-sided hill, rising from a low *plain* in *semi-arid* and *savannah* landscapes. Inselbergs are usually composed of a rock, such as granite, which resists *erosion*.

Interglacial A period of global *climate*, between two *ice ages*, when temperatures rise and *ice sheets* and *glaciers* retreat.

Intraplate volcano A *volcano* which lies in the centre of one of the Earth's *tectonic plates*, rather than, as is more common, at its edge. They are thought to have been formed by a *hot spot*.

Intrusion (intrusive igneous rock) Rock formed when molten material, *magma*, penetrates existing rocks below the Earth's surface before cooling and solidifying. These rocks cool more slowly than extrusive rock and therefore tend to have coarser grains.

Irrigation The artificial supply of agricultural water to dry areas, often involving the creation of canals and the diversion of natural watercourses.

Island arc A curved chain of islands. Typically, such an arc fringes an ocean trench, formed at the margin between two *tectonic plates*. As one plate overrides another, *earthquakes* and volcanic activity are common and the islands themselves are often volcanic cones.

Isostasy The state of equilibrium which the Earth's *crust* maintains as its lighter and heavier parts float on the denser underlying mantle.

Isthmus A narrow strip of land connecting two larger landmasses or islands.

J

Jet stream A narrow belt of westerly winds in the *troposphere*, at altitudes above 39,000 ft (12,000 m). Jet streams tend to blow more strongly in winter and include: the subtropical jet stream; the *polar* front jet stream in mid-*latitudes*; the *Arctic* jet stream; and the polar-night jet stream.

Joint A crack in a rock, formed where blocks of rock have not shifted relative to each other, as is the case with a *fault*. Joints are created by *folding*; by shrinkage in *igneous rock* as it cools or *sedimentary rock* as it dries out; and by the release of pressure in a rock mass when overlying materials are removed by *erosion*.

Jute A plant fibre used to make coarse ropes, sacks and matting.

K

Kame A mound of stratified sand and gravel with steep sides, deposited in a *crevasse* by *meltwater* running over a *glacier*. When the ice retreats, this forms an undulating terrain of hummocks.

Karst A barren *limestone* landscape created by carbonic acid in streams and rainwater, in areas where *limestone* is close to the surface. Typical features include caverns, tower-like hills, *sinkholes* and flat limestone pavements.

Kettle hole A round hollow formed in a glacial deposit by a detached block of glacial ice, which later melted. They can fill with water to form kettle-lakes.

L

Lagoon A shallow stretch of coastal salt-water behind a partial barrier such as a sandbank or *coral reef*. Lagoon is also used to describe the water encircled by an *atoll*.

LAIA Latin American Integration Association. Established in 1980, its members are Argentina, Bolivia, Brazil, Chile, Colombia, Ecuador, Mexico, Paraguay, Peru, Uruguay and Venezuela. It aims to promote economic co-operation between member states.

Landslide The sudden downslope movement of a mass of rock or earth on a slope, caused either by heavy rain; the impact of waves; an *earthquake* or human activity.

Laterite A hard red deposit left by *chemical weathering* in tropical conditions, and consisting mainly of oxides of iron and aluminium.

Latitude The angular distance from the *Equator*, to a given point on the Earth's surface. Imaginary lines of *latitude* running parallel to the Equator encircle the Earth, and are measured in degrees north or south of the Equator. The Equator is 0°, the poles 90° South and North respectively. Also called parallels.

Laurasia In the theory of *continental drift*, the northern part of the great *supercontinent* of *Pangaea*. Laurasia is said to consist of N America, Greenland and all of Eurasia north of the Indian subcontinent.

Lava The molten rock, *magma*, which erupts onto the Earth's surface through a *volcano*, or through a *fault* or crack in the Earth's *crust*. Lava refers to the rock both in its molten and in its later, solidified form.

Leaching The process whereby water dissolves minerals and moves them down through layers of soil or rock.

Levée A raised bank alongside the channel of a river. Levées are either human-made or formed in times of flood when the river overflows its channel, slows and deposits much of its *sediment* load.

Lichen An organism which is the symbiotic product of an algae and a fungus. Lichens form in tight crusts on stones and trees, and are resistant to extreme cold. They are often found in tundra regions.

Lignite Low-grade coal, also known as brown coal. Found in large deposits in eastern Europe.

Limestone A porous *sedimentary* rock formed from carbonate materials.

Lingua franca The language adopted as the common language between speakers whose native languages are different. This is common in former colonial states.

Lithosphere The rigid upper layer of the Earth, comprising the *crust* and the upper part of the *mantle*.

Llanos Vast grassland *plains* of northern South America.

Loess Fine-grained, yellow deposits of unstratified silts and sands. Loess is believed to be wind-carried *sediment* created in the last *Ice Age*. Some deposits may later have been redistributed by rivers. Loess-derived soils are of high quality, fertile and easy to work.

Longitude A division of the Earth which pinpoints how far east or west a given place is from the Prime Meridian (0°) which runs through the Royal Observatory at Greenwich, England (UK). Imaginary lines of longitude are drawn around the world from pole to pole. The world is divided into 360 degrees.

Longshore drift The transport of sand and silt along the coast, carried by waves hitting the beach at an angle.

M

Magma Underground, molten rock, which is very hot and highly charged with gas. It is generated at great pressure, at depths 10 miles (16 km) or more below the Earth's surface. It can issue as *lava* at the Earth's surface or, more often, solidify below the surface as *intrusive igneous rock*.

Mantle The layer of the Earth between the *crust* and the *core*. It is about 1800 miles (2900 km) thick. The uppermost layer of the mantle is the soft, 125-mile (200 km) thick *asthenosphere* on which the more rigid *lithosphere* floats.

Maquiladoras Factories on the Mexico side of the Mexico/US border, which are allowed to import raw materials and components duty-free and use low-cost labour to assemble the goods, finally exporting them for sale in the US.

Market gardening The intensive growing of fruit and vegetables close to large local markets.

Mass movement Downslope movement of weathered materials such as rock, often helped by rainfall or glacial *meltwater*. Mass movement may be a gradual process or rapid, as in a *landslide* or rockfall.

Massif A single very large mountain or an area of mountains with uniform characteristics and clearly-defined boundaries.

Meander A loop-like bend in a river, which is found typically in the lower, mature reaches of a river but can form wherever the valley is wide and the slope gentle.

Mediterranean climate A temperate *climate* of hot, dry summers and warm, damp winters. This is typical of the western fringes of the world's continents in the warm temperate regions between *latitudes* of 30° and 40° (north and south).

Meltwater Water resulting from the melting of a *glacier* or *ice sheet*.

Mesa A broad, flat-topped hill, characteristic of *arid* regions.

Mesosphere A layer of the Earth's *atmosphere*, between the *stratosphere* and the *thermosphere*. Extending from about 25–50 miles (40–80 km) above the surface of the Earth.

Mestizo A person of mixed *Amerindian* and European origin.

Metallurgy The refining and working of metals.

Metamorphic rocks Rocks which have been altered from their original form, in terms of texture, composition and structure by intense heat, pressure, or by the introduction of new chemical substances – or a combination of more than one of these.

Meteor A body of rock, metal or other material, which travels through space at great speeds. Meteors are visible as they enter the Earth's *atmosphere* as shooting stars and fireballs.

Meteorite The remains of a *meteor* that has fallen to Earth.

Meteoroid A *meteor* which is still travelling in space, outside the Earth's *atmosphere*.

Mezzogiorno A term applied to the southern portion of Italy.

Milankovitch hypothesis A theory suggesting that there are a series of cycles which slightly alter the Earth's position when rotating about the Sun. The cycles identified all affect the amount of *radiation* the Earth receives at different *latitudes*. The theory is seen as a key factor in the cause of *ice ages*.

Millet A grain-crop, forming part of the staple diet in much of Africa.

Mistral A strong, dry, cold northerly or north-westerly wind, which blows from the Massif Central of France to the Mediterranean Sea. It is common in winter and its cold blasts can cause crop damage in the Rhône Delta, in France.

Mohorovičić discontinuity (Moho) The structural divide at the margin between the Earth's *crust* and the *mantle*. On average it is 20 miles (35 km) below the continents and 6 miles (10 km) below the oceans. The different densities of the *crust* and the mantle cause *earthquake* waves to accelerate at this point.

Monarchy A form of government in which the head of state is a single hereditary monarch. The monarch may be a mere figurehead, or may retain significant authority.

Monsoon A wind which changes direction bi-annually. The change is caused by the reversal of pressure over landmasses and the adjacent oceans. Because the inflowing moist winds bring rain, the term monsoon is also used to refer to the rains themselves. The term is derived from and most commonly refers to the seasonal winds of south and east Asia.

Montaña Mountain areas along the west coast of South America.

Moraine Debris, transported and deposited by a *glacier* or *ice sheet* in unstratified, mixed, piles of rock, boulders, pebbles and clay.

Mountain-building The formation of *fold* mountains by tectonic activity. Also known as orogeny, mountain-building often occurs on the margin where two *tectonic plates* collide. The periods when most mountain-building occurred are known as orogenic phases and lasted many millions of years.

Mudflow An *avalanche* of mud which occurs when a mass of soil is drenched by rain or melting snow. It is a type of *mass movement*, faster than an *earthflow* because it is lubricated by water.

N

Nappe A mass of rocks which has been overfolded by repeated thrust *faulting*.

NAFTA The North American Free Trade Association. Established in 1994 between Canada, Mexico and the US to set up a free-trade zone.

NASA The North American Space Agency. It is a government body, established in 1958 to develop manned and unmanned space programmes.

NATO The North Atlantic Trade Organization. Established in 1949 to promote mutual defence and co-operation between its members, which are Belgium, Canada, Denmark, France, Germany, Greece, Iceland, Italy, Luxembourg, the Netherlands, Norway, Portugal, Spain, Turkey, UK, and US.

Nitrogen The odourless, colourless gas which makes up 78% of the atmosphere. Within the soil, it is a vital nutrient for plants.

Nomads (nomadic) Wandering communities who move around in search of suitable pasture for their herds of animals.

Nuclear fusion A technique used to create a new nucleus by the merging of two lighter ones, resulting in the release of large quantities of energy.

O

Oasis A fertile area in the midst of a *desert*, usually watered by an underground *aquifer*.

Oceanic ridge A mid-ocean ridge formed, according to the theory of *plate tectonics*, when plates drift apart and hot *magma* pours through to form new oceanic *crust*.

Oligarchy The government of a state by a small, exclusive group of people – such as an elite class or a family group.

Onion-skin weathering The *weathering* away or *exfoliation* of a rock or outcrop by the peeling off of surface layers.

Oriente A flatter region lying to the east of the Andes in South America.

Outwash plain *Glaciofluvial* material (typically clay, sand and gravel) carried beyond an ice sheet by *meltwater* streams, forming a broad, flat deposit.

Oxbow lake A crescent-shaped lake formed on a river *flood plain* when a river erodes the outside bend of a *meander*, making the neck of the *meander* narrower until the river cuts across the neck. The meander is cut off and is dammed off with sediment, creating an oxbow lake. Also known as a cut-off or mortlake.

Oxidation A form of *chemical weathering* where *oxygen* dissolved in water reacts with minerals in rocks – particularly iron – to form oxides. Oxidation causes brown or yellow staining on rocks, and eventually leads to the break down of the rock.

Oxygen A colourless, odourless gas which is one of the main constituents of the Earth's *atmosphere* and is essential to life on Earth.

Ozone layer A layer of enriched *oxygen* (O_3) within the stratosphere, mostly between 18–50 miles (30–80 km) above the Earth's surface. It is vital to the existence of life on Earth because it absorbs harmful shortwave ultraviolet radiation, while allowing beneficial longer wave ultraviolet radiation to penetrate to the Earth's surface.

P

Pacific Rim The name given to the economically-dynamic countries bordering the Pacific Ocean.

Pack ice Ice masses more than 10 ft (3 m) thick which form on the sea surface and are not attached to a landmass.

Pancake ice Thin discs of ice, up to 8 ft (2.4 m) wide which form when slicks of *grease ice* are tossed together by winds and stormy seas.

Pangaea In the theory of continental drift, Pangaea is the original great land mass which, about 190 million years ago, began to split into Gondwanaland in the south and Laurasia in the north, separated by the Tethys Sea.

Pastoralism Grazing of livestock – usually sheep, goats or cattle. Pastoralists in many drier areas have traditionally been *nomadic*.

Parallel *see Latitude.*

Peat Ancient, partially-decomposed vegetation found in wet, boggy conditions where there is little *oxygen*. It is the first stage in the development of coal and is often dried for use as fuel. It is also used to improve soil quality.

Pediment A gently-sloping ramp of *bedrock* below a steeper slope, often found at mountain edges in *desert* areas, but also in other climatic zones. Pediments may include depositional elements such as *alluvial fans*.

Peninsula A thin strip of land surrounded on three of its sides by water. Large examples include Florida and Korea.

Per capita Latin term meaning 'for each person'.

Periglacial Regions on the edges of *ice sheets* or *glaciers* or, more commonly, cold regions experiencing intense frost action, *permafrost* or both. Periglacial climates bring long, freezing winters and short, mild summers.

Permafrost Permanently frozen ground, typical of *Arctic* regions. Although a layer of soil above the permafrost melts in summer, the melted water does not drain through the permafrost.

Permeable rocks Rocks through which water can seep, because they are either porous or cracked.

Pharmaceuticals The manufacture of medicinal drugs.

Phreatic eruption A volcanic eruption which occurs when *lava* combines with *groundwater*, superheating the water and causing a sudden emission of steam at the surface.

Physical weathering (mechanical weathering) The breakdown of rocks by physical, as opposed to chemical, processes. Examples include: changes in pressure or temperature; the effect of windblown sand; the pressure of growing salt crystals in cracks within rock; and the expansion and contraction of water within rock as it freezes and thaws.

Pingo A dome of earth with a core of ice, found in *tundra* regions. Pingos are formed either when *groundwater* freezes and expands, pushing up the land surface, or when trapped, freezing water in a lake expands and pushes up lake *sediments* to form the pingo dome.

Placer A belt of mineral-bearing rock *strata* lying at or close to the Earth's surface, from which minerals can be easily extracted.

Plain A flat, level region of land, often relatively low-lying.

Plateau A highland tract of flat land.

Plate *see Tectonic plates.*

Plate tectonics The study of *tectonic plates*, which helps to explain *continental drift*, mountain formation and volcanic activity. The movement of tectonic plates may be explained by the currents of rock rising and falling from within the Earth's *mantle*, as it heats up and then cools. The boundaries of the plates are known as plate margins and most mountains, *earthquakes* and *volcanoes* occur at these margins. Constructive margins are moving apart; destructive margins are crunching together and conservative margins are sliding past one another.

Pleistocene A period of *geological time* spanning from about 5.2 million years ago to 1.6 million years ago.

Plutonic rock *Igneous* rocks found deep below the surface. They are coarse-grained because they cooled and solidified slowly.

Polar The zones within the *Arctic* and *Antarctic* circles.

Polje A long, broad *depression* found in *karst* (*limestone*) regions.

Polygonal patterning Typical ground patterning, found in areas where the soil is subject to severe frost action, often in *periglacial* regions.

Porosity A measure of how much water can be held within a rock or a soil. Porosity is measured as the percentage of holes or pores in a material, compared to its total volume. For example, the porosity of slate is less than 1%, whereas that of gravel is 25–35%.

Prairies Originally a French word for grassy *plains* with few or no trees.

Pre-Cambrian The earliest period of *geological time* dating from over 570 million years ago.

Precipitation The fall of moisture from the *atmosphere* onto the surface of the Earth, whether as dew, hail, rain, sleet or snow.

Pyramidal peak A steep, isolated mountain summit, formed when the back walls of three or more *cirques* are cut back and move towards each other. The cliffs around such a horned peak, or horn, are divided by sharp *arêtes*. The Matterhorn in the Swiss Alps is an example.

Pyroclasts Fragments of rock ejected during volcanic eruptions.

Q

Quaternary The current period of *geological time*, which started about 1.6 million years ago.

R

Radiation The emission of energy in the form of particles or waves. Radiation from the sun includes heat, light, ultraviolet rays, gamma rays and X-rays. Only some of the solar energy radiated into space reaches the Earth.

Rainforest Dense forests in tropical zones with high rainfall, temperature and *humidity*. Strictly, the term applies to the equatorial rainforest in tropical lowlands with constant rainfall and no seasonal change. The Congo and Amazon basins are examples. The term is applied more loosely to lush forest in other climates. Within rainforests organic life is dense and varied: at least 40% of all plant and animal species are found here and there may be as many as 100 tree species per hectare.

Rainshadow An area which experiences low rainfall, because of its position on the leeward side of a mountain range.

Reg A large area of stony *desert*, where tightly-packed gravel lies on top of clayey sand. A reg is formed where the wind blows away the finer sand.

Remote-sensing Method of obtaining information about the *environment* using unmanned equipment, such as a satellite, which relays the information to a point where it is collected and used.

Resistance The capacity of a rock to resist *denudation*, by processes such as *weathering* and *erosion*.

Ria A flooded *V-shaped river valley* or estuary, flooded by a rise in sea level (*eustacy*) or sinking land. It is shorter than a *fjord* and gets deeper as it meets the sea.

Rift valley A long, narrow depression in the Earth's *crust*, formed by the sinking of rocks between two *faults*.

River channel The trough which contains a river and is moulded by the flow of water within it.

Roche moutonée A rock found in a glaciated valley. The side facing the flow of the *glacier* has been smoothed and rounded, while the other side has been left more rugged because the *glacier*, as it flows over it, has plucked out frozen fragments and carried them away.

Runoff Water draining from a land surface by flowing across it.

S

Sabkha The floor of an isolated *depression* which occurs in an *arid environment* – usually covered by salt deposits and devoid of vegetation.

SADC Southern African Development Community. Established in 1992 to promote economic integration between its member states, which are Angola, Botswana, Lesotho, Malawi, Mauritius, Mozambique, Namibia, South Africa, Swaziland, Tanzania, Zambia and Zimbabwe.

Salt plug A rounded hill produced by the upward doming of rock *strata* caused by the movement of salt or other evaporite deposits under intense pressure.

Sastrugi Ice ridges formed by wind action. They lie parallel to the direction of the wind.

Savannah Open grassland found between the zone of *deserts*, and that of tropical *rainforests* in the tropics and subtropics. Scattered trees and shrubs are found in some kinds of savannah. A savannah *climate* usually has wet and dry seasons.

Scarp *see Escarpment.*

Scree Piles of rock fragments beneath a cliff or rock face, caused by mechanical *weathering*, especially *frost shattering*, where the expansion and contraction of freezing and thawing water within the rock, gradually breaks it up.

Sea-floor spreading The process whereby *tectonic plates* move apart, allowing hot *magma* to erupt and solidify. This forms a new sea floor and, ultimately, widens the ocean.

Seamount An isolated, submarine mountain or hill, probably of volcanic origin.

Season A period of time linked to regular changes in the weather, especially the intensity of solar *radiation*.

Sediment Grains of rock transported and deposited by rivers, sea, ice or wind.

Sedimentary rocks Rocks formed from the debris of pre-existing rocks or of organic material. They are found in many *environments* – on the ocean floor, on beaches, rivers and *deserts*. Organically-formed sedimentary rocks include coal and chalk. Other sedimentary rocks, such as flint, are formed by chemical processes. Most of these rocks contain *fossils*, which can be used to date them.

Seif A sand *dune* which lies parallel to the direction of the prevailing wind. Seifs form steep-sided ridges, sometimes extending for miles.

Seismic activity Movement within the Earth, such as an *earthquake* or *tremor*.

Selva A region of wet forest found in the Amazon Basin.

Semi-arid, semi-desert The *climate* and landscape which lies between *savannah* and *desert* or between savannah and a *mediterranean* climate. In semi-arid conditions there is a little more moisture than in a true *desert*; and more patches of drought-resistant vegetation can survive.

Shale (marine shale) A compacted *sedimentary rock*, with fine-grained particles. Marine shale is formed on the seabed. Fuel such as oil may be extracted from it.

Sheetwash Water which runs downhill in thin sheets without forming channels. It can cause *sheet erosion*.

Sheet erosion The washing away of soil by a thin film or sheet of water, known as *sheetwash*.

Shield A vast stable block of the Earth's *crust*, which has experienced little or no *mountain-building*.

Sierra The Spanish word for mountains.

Sinkhole A circular *depression* in a *limestone* region. They are formed by the collapse of an underground cave system or the *chemical weathering* of the *limestone*.

Sisal A plant-fibre used to make matting.

Slash and burn A farming technique involving the cutting down and burning of scrub forest, to create agricultural land. After a number of seasons this land is abandoned and the process is repeated. This practice is common in Africa and South America.

Slip face The steep leeward side of a sand *dune* or slope. Opposite side to a *back slope*.

Soil A thin layer of rock particles mixed with the remains of dead plants and animals. This occurs naturally on the surface of the Earth and provides a medium for plants to grow.

Soil creep The very gradual downslope movement of rock debris and soil, under the influence of gravity. This is a type of *mass movement*.

Soil erosion The wearing away of soil more quickly than it is replaced by natural processes. Soil can be carried away by wind as well as by water. Human activities, such as over-grazing and the clearing of land for farming, accelerate the process in many areas.

Solar energy Energy derived from the Sun. Solar energy is converted into other forms of energy. For example, the wind and waves, as well as the creation of plant material in photosynthesis, depend on solar energy.

Solifluction A kind of *soil creep*, where water in the surface layer has saturated the soil and rock debris which slips slowly downhill. It often happens where frozen top-layer deposits thaw, leaving frozen layers below them.

Sorghum A type of grass found in South America, similar to sugar cane. When refined it is used to make molasses.

Spit A thin linear deposit of sand or shingle extending from the sea shore. Spits are formed as angled waves shift sand along the beach, eventually extending a ridge of sand beyond a change in the angle of the coast. Spits are common where the coastline bends, especially at estuaries.

Squash A type of edible gourd.

Stack A tall, isolated pillar of rock near a coastline, created as wave action erodes away the adjacent rock.

Stalactite A tapering cylinder of mineral deposit, hanging from the roof of a cave in a *karst* area. It is formed by calcium carbonate, dissolved in water, which drips through the roof of a *limestone* cavern.

Stalagmite A cone of calcium carbonate, similar to a *stalactite*, rising from the floor of a *limestone* cavern and formed when drops of water fall from the roof of a *limestone* cave. If the water has dripped from a *stalactite* above the stalagmite, the two may join to form a continuous pillar.

Staple crop The main crop on which a country is economically and or physically reliant. For example, the major crop grown for large-scale local consumption in South Asia is rice.

Steppe Large areas of dry grassland in the northern hemisphere – particularly found in southeast Europe and central Asia.

Strata The plural of stratum, a distinct, virtually horizontal layer of deposited material, lying parallel to other layers.

Stratosphere A layer of the *atmosphere*, above the *troposphere*, extending from about 7–30 miles (11–50 km) above the Earth's surface. In the lower part of the stratosphere, the temperature is relatively stable and there is little moisture.

Strike-slip fault Occurs where plates move sideways past each other and blocks of rocks move horizontally in relation to each other, not up or down as in normal *faults*.

Subduction zone A region where two *tectonic plates* collide, forcing one beneath the other. Typically, a dense oceanic plate dips below a lighter continental plate, melting in the heat of the *asthenosphere*. This is why the zone is also called a destructive margin (*see Plate tectonics*). These zones are characterized by *earthquakes*, volcanoes, *mountain-building* and the development of oceanic trenches and *island arcs*.

Submarine canyon A steep-sided valley, which extends along the *continental shelf* to the ocean floor. Often formed by *turbidity currents*.

Submarine fan Deposits of silt and *alluvium*, carried by large rivers forming great fan-shaped deposits on the ocean floor.

Subsistence agriculture An agricultural practice, whereby enough food is produced to support the farmer and his dependents, but not providing any surplus to generate an income.

Subtropical A term applied loosely to *climates* which are nearly tropical or tropical for a part of the year – areas north or south of the *tropics* but outside the *temperate zone*.

Supercontinent A large continent that breaks up to form smaller continents or which forms when smaller continents merge. In the theory of *continental drift*, the supercontinents are *Pangaea*, *Gondwanaland* and *Laurasia*.

Sustainable development An approach to development, especially applied to economies across the world which exploit natural resources without destroying them or damaging the *environment*.

Syncline A basin-shaped downfold in rock *strata*, created when the *strata* are compressed, for example where *tectonic plates* collide.

T

Tableland A highland area with a flat or gently undulating surface.

Taiga The belt of *coniferous* forest found in the north of Asia and North America. The conifers are adapted to survive low temperatures and long periods of snowfall.

Tarn A Scottish term for a small mountain lake, usually found at the head of a *glacier*.

Tectonic plates Plates, or tectonic plates, are the rigid slabs which form the Earth's outer shell, the *lithosphere*. Eight big plates and several smaller ones have been identified.

Temperate A moderate *climate* without extremes of temperature, typical of the mid-*latitudes* between the *tropics* and the *polar* circles.

Theocracy A state governed by religious laws – today Iran is the world's largest theocracy.

Thermokarst Subsidence created by the thawing of ground ice in *periglacial* areas, creating depressions.

Thermosphere A layer of the Earth's *atmosphere* which lies above the *mesophere*, about 60–300 miles (100–500 km) above the Earth

Terraces Steps cut into steep slopes to create flat surfaces for cultivating crops. They also help reduce soil *erosion* on unconsolidated slopes. They are most common in heavily-populated parts of Southeast Asia.

Till Unstratified glacial deposits or drift left by a *glacier* or *ice sheet*. Till includes mixtures of clay, sand, gravel and boulders.

Topography The typical shape and features of a given area such as land height and terrain.

Tombolo A large sand *spit* which attaches part of the mainland to an island.

Tornado A violent, spiralling windstorm, with a centre of very low pressure. Wind speeds reach 200 mph (320 kmph) and there is often thunder and heavy rain.

Transform fault In *plate tectonics*, a *fault* of continental scale, occurring where two plates slide past each other, staying close together for example, the San Andreas Fault, USA. The jerky, uneven movement creates *earthquakes* but does not destroy or add to the Earth's *crust*

Transpiration The loss of water vapour through the pores (or stomata) of plants. The process helps to return moisture to the *atmosphere*.

Trap An area of fine-grained *igneous rock* which has been extruded and cooled on the Earth's surface in stages, forming a series of steps or terraces.

Treeline The line beyond which trees cannot grow, dependent on *latitude* and altitude, as well as local factors such as soil.

Tremor A slight *earthquake*.

Trench (oceanic trench) A long, deep trough in the ocean floor, formed, according to the theory of *plate tectonics*, when two plates collide and one dives under the other, creating a *subduction zone*.

Tropics The zone between the *Tropic of Cancer* and the *Tropic of Capricorn* where the *climate* is hot. Tropical climate is also applied to areas rather further north and south of the *Equator* where the climate is similar to that of the true tropics.

Tropic of Cancer A line of *latitude* or imaginary circle round the Earth, lying at 23° 28' N.

Tropic of Capricorn A line of *latitude* or imaginary circle round the Earth, lying at 23° 28' S.

Troposphere The lowest layer of the Earth's *atmosphere*. From the surface, it reaches a height of between 4–10 miles (7–16 km). It is the most turbulent zone of the atmosphere and accounts for the generation of most of the world's weather. The layer above it is called the *stratosphere*.

Tsunami A huge wave created by shock waves from an *earthquake* under the sea. Reaching speeds of up to 600 mph (960 kmph), the wave may increase to heights of 50 ft (15 m) on entering coastal waters; and it can cause great damage.

Tundra The treeless *plains* of the *Arctic Circle*, found south of the *polar* region of permanent ice and snow, and north of the belt of *coniferous* forests known as *taiga*. In this region of long, very cold winters, vegetation is usually limited to mosses, *lichens*, sedges and rushes, although flowers and dwarf shrubs blossom in the brief summer.

Turbidity current An oceanic feature. A turbidity current is a mass of *sediment*-laden water which has substantial erosive power. Turbidity currents are thought to contribute to the formation of *submarine canyons*.

Typhoon A kind of *hurricane* (or tropical cyclone) bringing violent winds and heavy rain, a typhoon can do great damage. They occur in the South China Sea, especially around the Philippines.

U

U-shaped valley A river valley that has been deepened and widened by a *glacier*. They are characteristically flat-bottomed and steep-sided and generally much deeper than river valleys.

UN United Nations. Established in 1945, it contains 184 nations and aims to maintain international peace and security, and promote co-operation over economic, social, cultural and humanitarian problems.

UNICEF United Nations Children's Fund. A UN organization set up to promote family and child related programmes.

Urstromtäler A German word used to describe *meltwater* channels which flowed along the front edge of the advancing *ice sheet* during the last Ice Age, 18,000–20,000 years ago.

V

V-shaped valley A typical valley eroded by a river in its upper course.

Virgin rainforest Tropical *rainforest* in its original state, untouched by human activity such as logging, clearance for agriculture, settlement or road building.

Viticulture The cultivation of grapes for wine.

Volcano An opening or vent in the Earth's *crust* where molten rock, *magma*, erupts. Volcanoes tend to be conical but may also be a crack in the Earth's surface or a hole blasted through a mountain. The magma is accompanied by other materials such as gas, steam and fragments of rock, or *pyroclasts*. They tend to occur on destructive or constructive tectonic*plate* margins.

W–Z

Wadi The dry bed left by a torrent of water. Also classified as a *ephemeral* stream, found in *arid* and *semi-arid* regions, which are subject to sudden and often severe flash flooding.

Warm humid climate A rainy climate with warm summers and mild winters.

Water cycle The continuous circulation of water between the Earth's surface and the *atmosphere*. The processes include *evaporation* and *transpiration* of moisture into the atmosphere, and its return as *precipitation*, some of which flows into lakes and oceans.

Water table The upper level of *groundwater* saturation in permeable rock *strata*.

Watershed The dividing line between one *drainage basin* – an area where all streams flow into a single river system – and another. In the US, watershed also means the whole drainage basin of a single river system – its catchment area.

Waterspout A rotating column of water in the form of cloud, mist and spray which form on open water. Often has the appearance of a small *tornado*.

Weathering The decay and break-up of rocks at or near the Earth's surface, caused by water, wind, heat or ice, organic material or the *atmosphere*. *Physical weathering* includes the effects of frost and temperature changes. Biological weathering includes the effects of plant roots, burrowing animals and the acids produced by animals, especially as they decay after death. *Carbonation* and *hydrolysis* are among many kinds of *chemical weathering*.

GEOGRAPHICAL NAMES

THE FOLLOWING GLOSSARY lists all geographical terms occurring on the maps and in main-entry names in the Index-Gazetteer. These terms may precede, follow or be run together with the proper element of the name; where they precede it the term is reversed for indexing purposes - thus Poluostrov Yamal is indexed as Yamal, Puluostrov.

KEY
Geographical term *Language,* Term

A

Å *Danish, Norwegian,* River
Āb *Persian,* River
Adrar *Berber,* Mountains
Agía, Ágios *Greek,* Saint
Air *Indonesian,* River
Ákra *Greek,* Cape, point
Alpen *German,* Alps
Alt- *German,* Old
Altiplanicie *Spanish,* Plateau
Älve(en) *Swedish,* River
-ån *Swedish,* River
Anse *French,* Bay
'Aqabat *Arabic,* Pass
Archipiélago *Spanish,* Archipelago
Arcipelago *Italian,* Archipelago
Arquipélago *Portuguese,* Archipelago
Arrecife(s) *Spanish,* Reef(s)
Aru *Tamil,* River
Augstiene *Latvian,* Upland
Aukštuma *Lithuanian,* Upland
Aust- *Norwegian,* Eastern
Avtonomnyy Okrug *Russian,* Autonomous district
Āw *Kurdish,* River
'Ayn *Arabic,* Spring, well
'Ayoûn *Arabic,* Wells

B

Baelt *Danish,* Strait
Bahía *Spanish,* Bay
Baḥr *Arabic,* River
Baía *Portuguese,* Bay
Baie *French,* Bay
Bañado *Spanish,* Marshy land
Bandao *Chinese,* Peninsula
Banjaran *Malay,* Mountain range
Barajı *Turkish,* Dam
Barragem *Portuguese,* Reservoir
Bassin *French,* Basin
Batang *Malay,* Stream
Beinn, Ben *Gaelic,* Mountain
-berg *Afrikaans, Norwegian,* Mountain
Besar *Indonesian, Malay,* Big
Birkat, Birket *Arabic,* Lake, well, Cistern
Boğazi *Turkish,* Lake
Boka *Serbo-Croatian,* Bay
Bol'sh-aya, -iye, -oy, -oye *Russian,* Big
Botigh(i) *Uzbek,* Depression basin
-bre(en) *Norwegian,* Glacier
Bredning *Danish,* Bay
Bucht *German,* Bay
Bugt(en) *Danish,* Bay
Buḥayrat *Arabic,* Lake, reservoir
Buḥeiret *Arabic,* Lake
Bukit *Malay,* Mountain
-bukta *Norwegian,* Bay
bukten *Swedish,* Bay
Bulag *Mongolian,* Spring
Bulak *Uighur,* Spring
Burnu *Turkish,* Cape, point
Buuraha *Somali,* Mountains

C

Cabo *Portuguese,* Cape
Caka *Tibetan,* Salt lake
Canal *Spanish,* Channel
Cap *French,* Cape
Capo *Italian,* Cape, headland
Cascada *Portuguese,* Waterfall
Cayo(s) *Spanish,* Islet(s), rock(s)
Cerro *Spanish,* Mountain
Chaîne *French,* Mountain range
Chapada *Portuguese,* Hills, upland
Chau *Cantonese,* Island
Chāy *Turkish,* River
Chhâk *Cambodian,* Bay
Chhu *Tibetan,* River
-chŏsuji *Korean,* Reservoir
Chott *Arabic,* Depression, salt lake
Chŭli *Uzbek,* Grassland, steppe
Ch'ün-tao *Chinese,* Island group
Chuŏr Phnum *Cambodian,* Mountains
Ciudad *Spanish,* City, town
Co *Tibetan,* Lake
Colline(s) *French,* Hill(s)
Cordillera *Spanish,* Mountain range
Costa *Spanish,* Coast
Côte *French,* Coast
Coxilha *Portuguese,* Mountains
Cuchilla *Spanish,* Mountains

D

Daban *Mongolian, Uighur,* Pass
Daği *Azerbaijani, Turkish,* Mountain
Dağlari *Azerbaijani, Turkish,* Mountains
-dake *Japanese,* Peak
-dal(en) *Norwegian,* Valley
Danau *Indonesian,* Lake
Dao *Chinese,* Island
Đao *Vietnamese,* Island
Daryā *Persian,* River
Daryācheh *Persian,* Lake
Dasht *Persian,* Desert, plain
Dawḥat *Arabic,* Bay
Denizi *Turkish,* Sea
Dere *Turkish,* Stream
Desierto *Spanish,* Desert
Dili *Azerbaijani,* Spit
-do *Korean,* Island
Dooxo *Somali,* Valley
Düzü *Azerbaijani,* Steppe
-dwīp *Bengali,* Island

E

-eilanden *Dutch,* Islands
Embalse *Spanish,* Reservoir
Ensenada *Spanish,* Bay
Erg *Arabic,* Dunes
Estany *Catalan,* Lake
Estero *Spanish,* Inlet
Estrecho *Spanish,* Strait
Étang *French,* Lagoon, lake
-ey *Icelandic,* Island
Ezero *Bulgarian, Macedonian,* Lake
Ezers *Latvian,* Lake

F

Feng *Chinese,* Peak
Fjord *Danish,* Fjord
-fjord(en) *Danish, Norwegian, Swedish,* fjord
-fjørdhur *Faeroese,* Fjord
Fleuve *French,* River
Fliegu *Maltese,* Channel
-fljór *Icelandic,* River
-flói *Icelandic,* Bay
Forêt *French,* Forest

G

-gan *Japanese,* Rock
-gang *Korean,* River
Ganga *Hindi, Nepali, Sinhala,* River
Gaoyuan *Chinese,* Plateau
Garagumy *Turkmen,* Sands
-gawa *Japanese,* River
Gebel *Arabic,* Mountain
-gebirge *German,* Mountain range
Ghadīr *Arabic,* Well
Ghubbat *Arabic,* Bay
Gjiri *Albanian,* Bay
Gol *Mongolian,* River
Golfe *French,* Gulf
Golfo *Italian, Spanish,* Gulf
Göl(ü) *Turkish,* Lake
Golyam, -a *Bulgarian,* Big
Gora *Russian, Serbo-Croatian,* Mountain
Góra *Polish,* Mountain
Gory *Russian,* Mountain
Gryada *Russian,* Ridge
Guba *Russian,* Bay
-gundo *Korean,* Island group
Gunung *Malay,* Mountain

H

Ḥadd *Arabic,* Spit
-haehyŏp *Korean,* Strait
Haff *German,* Lagoon
Hai *Chinese,* Bay, lake, sea
Haixia *Chinese,* Strait
Hamada *Arabic,* Plateau
Ḥammādat *Arabic,* Plateau
Hāmūn *Persian,* Lake
-hantō *Japanese,* Peninsula
Har, Haré *Hebrew,* Mountain
Ḥarrat *Arabic,* Lava-field
Hav(et) *Danish, Swedish,* Sea
Hawr *Arabic,* Lake
Hāyk' *Amharic,* Lake
He *Chinese,* River
-hegység *Hungarian,* Mountain range
Heide *German,* Heath, moorland
Helodrano *Malagasy,* Bay
Higashi- *Japanese,* East(ern)
Ḥiṣā' *Arabic,* Well
Hka *Burmese,* River
-ho *Korean,* Lake
Hô *Korean,* Reservoir
Ḥolot *Hebrew,* Dunes
Hora *Belorussian, Czech,* Mountain
Hrada *Belorussian,* Mountain, ridge
Hsi *Chinese,* River
Hu *Chinese,* Lake
Huk *Danish,* Point

I

Île(s) *French,* Island(s)
Ilha(s) *Portuguese,* Island(s)
Ilhéu(s) *Portuguese,* Islet(s)
Imeni *Russian,* In the name of
Inish- *Gaelic,* Island
Insel(n) *German,* Island(s)
Irmaği, Irmak *Turkish,* River
Isla(s) *Spanish,* Island(s)
Isola (Isole) *Italian,* Island(s)

J

Jabal *Arabic,* Mountain
Jāl *Arabic,* Ridge
-järv *Estonian,* Lake
-järvi *Finnish,* Lake
Jazā'ir *Arabic,* Islands
Jazīrat *Arabic,* Island
Jazīreh *Persian,* Island
Jebel *Arabic,* Mountain
Jezero *Serbo-Croatian,* Lake
Jezioro *Polish,* Lake
Jiang *Chinese,* River
-jima *Japanese,* Island
Jižní *Czech,* Southern
-jõgi *Estonian,* River
-joki *Finnish,* River
-jökull *Icelandic,* Glacier
Jūn *Arabic,* Bay
Juzur *Arabic,* Islands

K

Kaikyō *Japanese,* Strait
-kaise *Lappish,* Mountain
Kali *Nepali,* River
Kalnas *Lithuanian,* Mountain
Kalns *Latvian,* Mountain
Kang *Chinese,* Harbour
Kangri *Tibetan,* Mountain(s)
Kaôh *Cambodian,* Island
Kapp *Norwegian,* Cape
Káto *Greek,* Lower
Kavīr *Persian,* Desert
K'edi *Georgian,* Mountain range
Kediet *Arabic,* Mountain
Kepi *Albanian,* Cape, point
Kepulauan *Indonesian, Malay,* Island group
Khalig, Khalīj *Arabic,* Gulf
Khawr *Arabic,* Inlet
Khola *Nepali,* River
Khrebet *Russian,* Mountain range
Ko *Thai,* Island
-ko *Japanese,* Inlet, lake
Kólpos *Greek,* Bay
-kopf *German,* Peak
Körfäzi *Azerbaijani,* Bay
Körfezi *Turkish,* Bay
Kõrgustik *Estonian,* Upland
Kosa *Russian, Ukrainian,* Spit
Koshi *Nepali,* River
Kou *Chinese,* River-mouth
Kowtal *Persian,* Pass
Kray *Russian,* Region, territory
Kryazh *Russian,* Ridge
Kuduk *Uighur,* Well
Kūh(hā) *Persian,* Mountain(s)
-kul' *Russian,* Lake
Kŭl(i) *Tajik, Uzbek,* Lake
-kundo *Korean,* Island group
-kysten *Norwegian,* Coast
Kyun *Burmese,* Island

L

Laaq *Somali,* Watercourse
Lac *French,* Lake
Lacul *Romanian,* Lake
Lagh *Somali,* Stream
Lago *Italian, Portuguese, Spanish,* Lake
Lagoa *Portuguese,* Lagoon
Laguna *Italian, Spanish,* Lagoon, lake
Laht *Estonian,* Bay
Laut *Indonesian,* Bay
Lembalemba *Malagasy,* Plateau
Lerr *Armenian,* Mountain
Lerrnashght'a *Armenian,* Mountain range
Les *Czech,* Forest
Lich *Armenian,* Lake
Liehtao *Chinese,* Island group
Liqeni *Albanian,* Lake
Límni *Greek,* Lake
Ling *Chinese,* Mountain range
Llano *Spanish,* Plain, prairie
Lumi *Albanian,* River
Lyman *Ukrainian,* Estuary

M

Madīnat *Arabic,* City, town
Mae Nam *Thai,* River
-māgi *Estonian,* Hill
Maja *Albanian,* Mountain
Mal *Albanian,* Mountains
Mal-aya, -oye, -yy, *Russian,* Small
-man *Korean,* Bay
Mar *Spanish,* Lake
Marios *Lithuanian,* Lake
Massif *French,* Mountains
Meer *German,* Lake
-meer *Dutch,* Lake
Melkosopochnik *Russian,* Plain
-meri *Estonian,* Sea
Mifraẕ *Hebrew,* Bay
Minami- *Japanese,* South(ern)
-misaki *Japanese,* Cape, point
Monkhafad *Arabic,* Depression
Montagne(s) *French,* Mountain(s)
Montañas *Spanish,* Mountains
Mont(s) *French,* Mountain(s)
Monte *Italian, Portuguese,* Mountain
More *Russian,* Sea
Mörön *Mongolian,* River
Mys *Russian,* Cape, point

N

-nada *Japanese,* Open stretch of water
Nagor'ye *Russian,* Upland
Naḥal *Hebrew,* River
Nahr *Arabic,* River
Nam *Laotian,* River
Namakzār *Persian,* Salt desert
Né-a, -on, -os *Greek,* New
Nedre- *Norwegian,* Lower
-neem *Estonian,* Cape, point
Nehri *Turkish,* River
-nes *Norwegian,* Cape, point
Nevado *Spanish,* Mountain (snow-capped)
Nieder- *German,* Lower
Nishi- *Japanese,* West(ern)
-nísi *Greek,* Island
Nisoi *Greek,* Islands
Nizhn-eye, -iy, -iye, -yaya *Russian,* Lower
Nizmennost' *Russian,* Lowland, plain
Nord *Danish, French, German,* North
Norte *Portuguese, Spanish,* North
Nos *Bulgarian,* Point, spit
Nosy *Malagasy,* Island
Nov-a, -i, *Bulgarian, Serbo-Croatian,* New
Nov-aya, -o, -oye, -yy, -yye *Russian,* New
Now-a, -e, -y *Polish,* New
Nur *Mongolian,* Lake
Nuruu *Mongolian,* Mountains
Nuur *Mongolian,* Lake
Nyzovyna *Ukrainian,* Lowland, plain

O

-ø *Danish,* Island
Ober- *German,* Upper
Oblast' *Russian,* Province
Órmos *Greek,* Bay
Orol(i) *Uzbek,* Island
Øster- *Norwegian,* Eastern
Ostrov(a) *Russian,* Island(s)
Otok *Serbo-Croatian,* Island
Oued *Arabic,* Watercourse
-oy *Faeroese,* Island
-øy(a) *Norwegian,* Island
Oya *Sinhala,* River
Ozero *Russian, Ukrainian,* Lake

P

Passo *Italian,* Pass
Pegunungan *Indonesian, Malay,* Mountain range
Pélagos *Greek,* Sea
Pendi *Chinese,* Basin
Penisola *Italian,* Peninsula
Pertuis *French,* Strait
Peski *Russian,* Sands
Phanom *Thai,* Mountain
Phou *Laotian,* Mountain
Pi *Chinese,* Point
Pic *Catalan, French,* Peak
Pico *Portuguese, Spanish,* Peak
-piggen *Danish,* Peak
Pik *Russian,* Peak
Pivostriv *Ukrainian,* Peninsula
Planalto *Portuguese,* Plateau
Planina, Planini *Bulgarian, Macedonian, Serbo-Croatian,* Mountain range
Plato *Russian,* Plateau
Ploskogor'ye *Russian,* Upland
Poluostrov *Russian,* Peninsula
Ponta *Portuguese,* Point
Porthmós *Greek,* Strait
Pótamos *Greek,* River
Presa *Spanish,* Dam
Prokhod *Bulgarian,* Pass
Proliv *Russian,* Strait
Pulau *Indonesian, Malay,* Island
Pulu *Malay,* Island
Punta *Spanish,* Point
Pushcha *Belorussian,* Forest
Puszcza *Polish,* Forest

Q

Qā' *Arabic,* Depression
Qalamat *Arabic,* Well
Qatorkŭh(i) *Tajik,* Mountain
Qiuling *Chinese,* Hills
Qolleh *Persian,* Mountain
Qu *Tibetan,* Stream
Quan *Chinese,* Well
Qulla(i) *Tajik,* Peak
Qundao *Chinese,* Island group

R

Raas *Somali,* Cape
-rags *Latvian,* Cape
Ramlat *Arabic,* Sands
Ra's *Arabic,* Cape, headland, point
Ravnina *Bulgarian, Russian,* Plain
Récif *French,* Reef
Recife *Portuguese,* Reef
Reka *Bulgarian,* River
Represa (Rep.) *Portuguese, Spanish,* Reservoir
Reshteh *Persian,* Mountain range
Respublika *Russian,* Republic, first-order administrative division
Respublika(si) *Uzbek,* Republic, first-order administrative division
-retsugan *Japanese,* Chain of rocks
-rettō *Japanese,* Island chain
Riacho *Spanish,* Stream
Riban' *Malagasy,* Mountains
Rio *Portuguese,* River
Río *Spanish,* River
Riu *Catalan,* River
Rivier *Dutch,* River
Rivière *French,* River
Rowd *Pashtu,* River
Rt *Serbo-Croatian,* Point
Rūd *Persian,* River
Rūdkhāneh *Persian,* River
Rudohorie *Slovak,* Mountains
Ruisseau *French,* Stream

S

-saar *Estonian,* Island
-saari *Finnish,* Island
Sabkhat *Arabic,* Salt marsh
Sāgar(a) *Hindi,* Lake, reservoir
Ṣaḥrā' *Arabic,* Desert
Saint, Sainte *French,* Saint
Salar *Spanish,* Salt-pan
Salto *Portuguese, Spanish,* Waterfall
Samudra *Sinhala,* Reservoir
-san *Japanese, Korean,* Mountain
-sanchi *Japanese,* Mountains
-sandur *Icelandic,* Beach
Sankt *German, Swedish,* Saint
-sanmaek *Korean,* Mountain range
-sanmyaku *Japanese,* Mountain range
San, Santa, Santo *Italian, Portuguese, Spanish,* Saint
São *Portuguese,* Saint
Sarīr *Arabic,* Desert
Sebkha, Sebkhet *Arabic,* Depression, salt marsh
Sedlo *Czech,* Pass
See *German,* Lake
Selat *Indonesian,* Strait
Selatan *Indonesian,* Southern
-selkä *Finnish,* Lake, ridge
Selseleh *Persian,* Mountain range
Serra *Portuguese,* Mountain
Serranía *Spanish,* Mountain
-seto *Japanese,* Channel, strait
Sever-naya, -noye, -nyy, -o *Russian,* Northern
Sha'īb *Arabic,* Watercourse
Shākh *Kurdish,* Mountain
Shamo *Chinese,* Desert
Shan *Chinese,* Mountain(s)
Shankou *Chinese,* Pass
Shanmo *Chinese,* Mountain range
Shaṭṭ *Arabic,* Distributary
Shet' *Amharic,* River
Shi *Chinese,* Municipality
-shima *Japanese,* Island
Shiqqat *Arabic,* Depression
-shotō *Japanese,* Group of islands
Shuiku *Chinese,* Reservoir
Shŭrkhog(i) *Uzbek,* Salt marsh
Sierra *Spanish,* Mountains
Sint *Dutch,* Saint
-sjø(en) *Norwegian,* Lake
-sjön *Swedish,* Lake
Solonchak *Russian,* Salt lake
Solonchakovyye Vpadiny *Russian,* Salt basin, wetlands
Son *Vietnamese,* Mountain
Sông *Vietnamese,* River
Sør- *Norwegian,* Southern
-spitze *German,* Peak
Star-á, -é *Czech,* Old
Star-aya, -oye, -yy, -yye *Russian,* Old
Stenó *Greek,* Strait
Step' *Russian,* Steppe
Štít *Slovak,* Peak
Stœng *Cambodian,* River
Stolovaya Strana *Russian,* Plateau
Stredné *Slovak,* Middle
Střední *Czech,* Middle
Stretto *Italian,* Strait
Su Anbari *Azerbaijani,* Reservoir
-suidō *Japanese,* Channel, strait
Sund *Swedish,* Sound, strait
Sungai *Indonesian, Malay,* River
Suu *Turkish,* River

T

Tal *Mongolian,* Plain
Tandavan' *Malagasy,* Mountain range
Tangorombohitr' *Malagasy,* Mountain massif
Tanjung *Indonesian, Malay,* Cape, point
Tao *Chinese,* Island
Ṭaraq *Arabic,* Hills
Tassili *Berber,* Mountain, plateau
Tau *Russian,* Mountain(s)
Taungdan *Burmese,* Mountain range
Techníti Límni *Greek,* Reservoir
Tekojärvi *Finnish,* Reservoir
Teluk *Indonesian, Malay,* Bay
Tengah *Indonesian,* Middle
Terara *Amharic,* Mountain
Timur *Indonesian,* Eastern
-tind(an) *Norwegian,* Peak
Tizma(si) *Uzbek,* Mountain range, ridge
-tō *Japanese,* Island
Tog *Somali,* Valley
-tōge *Japanese,* Pass
Togh(i) *Uzbek,* Mountain
Tônlé *Cambodian,* Lake
Top *Dutch,* Peak
-tunturi *Finnish,* Mountain
Ṭurāq *Arabic,* Hills
Tur'at *Arabic,* Channel

U

Udde(n) *Swedish,* Cape, point
'Uqlat *Arabic,* Well
Utara *Indonesian,* Northern
Uul *Mongolian,* Mountains

V

Väin *Estonian,* Strait
Vallée *French,* Valley
-vatn *Icelandic,* Lake
-vatnet *Norwegian,* Lake
Velayat *Turkmen,* Province
-vesi *Finnish,* Lake
Vestre- *Norwegian,* Western
-vidda *Norwegian,* Plateau
-vík *Icelandic,* Bay
-viken *Swedish,* Bay, inlet
Vinh *Vietnamese,* Bay
Víztárloló *Hungarian,* Reservoir
Vodaskhovishcha *Belorussian,* Reservoir
Vodokhranilishche (Vdkhr.) *Russian,* Reservoir
Vodoskhovyshche (Vdskh.) *Ukrainian,* Reservoir
Volcán *Spanish,* Volcano
Vostochn-o, yy *Russian,* Eastern
Vozvyshennost' *Russian,* Upland, plateau
Vozyera *Belorussian,* Lake
Vpadina *Russian,* Depression
Vrchovina *Czech,* Mountains
Vrha *Macedonian,* Peak
Vychodné *Slovak,* Eastern
Vysochyna *Ukrainian,* Upland
Vysočina *Czech,* Upland

W

Waadi *Somali,* Watercourse
Wādī *Arabic* Watercourse
Wāḥat, Wâhat *Arabic,* Oasis
Wald *German,* Forest
Wan *Chinese,* Bay
Way *Indonesian,* River
Webi *Somali,* River
Wenz *Amharic,* River
Wiloyat(i) *Uzbek,* Province
Wyżyna *Polish,* Upland
Wzgórza *Polish,* Upland
Wzvyshsha *Belorussian,* Upland

X

Xé *Laotian,* River
Xi *Chinese,* Stream

Y

-yama *Japanese,* Mountain
Yanchi *Chinese,* Salt lake
Yang *Chinese,* Bay
Yanhu *Chinese,* Salt lake
Yarımadası *Azerbaijani, Turkish,* Peninsula
Yaylası *Turkish,* Plateau
Yazovir *Bulgarian,* Reservoir
Yoma *Burmese,* Mountains
Ytre- *Norwegian,* Outer
Yü *Chinese,* Island
Yunhe *Chinese,* Canal
Yuzhn-o, -yy *Russian,* Southern

Z

-zaki *Japanese,* Cape, point
Zaliv *Bulgarian, Russian,* Bay
-zan *Japanese,* Mountain
Zangbo *Tibetan,* River
Zapadn-aya, -o, -yy *Russian,* Western
Západné *Slovak,* Western
Západní *Czech,* Western
Zatoka *Polish, Ukrainian,* Bay
-zee *Dutch,* Sea
Zemlya *Russian,* Earth, land
Zizhiqu *Chinese,* Autonomous region

25 de Mayo – Abu Zenîma

Index

Glossary of Abbreviations

This glossary provides a comprehensive guide to the abbreviations used in this Atlas, and in the Index.

A
abbrev. abbreviated
AD Anno Domini
Afr. Afrikaans
Alb. Albanian
Amh. Amharic
anc. ancient
approx. approximately
Ar. Arabic
Arm. Armenian
ASEAN Association of South East Asian Nations
ASSR Autonomous Soviet Socialist Republic
Aust. Australian
Az. Azerbaijani
Azerb. Azerbaijan

B
Basq. Basque
BC before Christ
Bel. Belorussian
Ben. Bengali
Ber. Berber
B-H Bosnia-Herzegovina
bn billion (one thousand million)
BP British Petroleum
Bret. Breton
Brit. British
Bul. Bulgarian
Bur. Burmese

C
C central
C. Cape
°C degrees Centigrade
CACM Central America Common Market
Cam. Cambodian
Cant. Cantonese
CAR Central African Republic
Cast. Castilian
Cat. Catalan
CEEAC Central America Common Market
Chin. Chinese
CIS Commonwealth of Independent States
cm centimetre(s)
Cro. Croat
Cz. Czech
Czech Rep. Czech Republic

D
Dan. Danish
Div. Divehi
Dom. Rep. Dominican Republic
Dut. Dutch

E
E east
EC *see* EU
EEC *see* EU
ECOWAS Economic Community of West African States
ECU European Currency Unit
EMS European Monetary System
Eng. English
est estimated
Est. Estonian
EU European Union (previously European Community [EC], European Economic Community [EEC])

F
°F degrees Fahrenheit
Faer. Faeroese
Fij. Fijian
Fin. Finnish
Fr. French
Fris. Frisian
ft foot/feet
FYROM Former Yugoslav Republic of Macedonia

G
g gram(s)
Gael. Gaelic
Gal. Galician
GDP Gross Domestic Product (the total value of goods and services produced by a country excluding income from foreign countries)
Geor. Georgian
Ger. German
Gk Greek
GNP Gross National Product (the total value of goods and services produced by a country)

H
Heb. Hebrew
HEP hydro-electric power
Hind. Hindi
hist. historical
Hung. Hungarian

I
I. Island
Icel. Icelandic
in inch(es)
In. Inuit (Eskimo)
Ind. Indonesian
Intl International
Ir. Irish
Is Islands
It. Italian

J
Jap. Japanese

K
Kaz. Kazakh
kg kilogram(s)
Kir. Kirghiz
km kilometre(s)
km² square kilometre (singular)
Kor. Korean
Kurd. Kurdish

L
L. Lake
LAIA Latin American Integration Association
Lao. Laotian
Lapp. Lappish
Lat. Latin
Latv. Latvian
Liech. Liechtenstein
Lith. Lithuanian
Lux. Luxembourg

M
m million/metre(s)
Mac. Macedonian
Maced. Macedonia
Mal. Malay
Malg. Malagasy
Malt. Maltese
mi. mile(s)
Mong. Mongolian
Mt. Mountain
Mts Mountains

N
N north
NAFTA North American Free Trade Agreement
Nep. Nepali
Neth. Netherlands
Nic. Nicaraguan
Nor. Norwegian
NZ New Zealand

P
Pash. Pashtu
PNG Papua New Guinea
Pol. Polish
Poly. Polynesian
Port. Portuguese
prev. previously

R
Rep. Republic
Res. Reservoir
Rmsch Romansch
Rom. Romanian
Rus. Russian
Russ. Fed. Russian Federation

S
S south
SADC Southern Africa Development Community
SCr. Serbo-Croatian
Sinh. Sinhala
Slvk Slovak
Slvn. Slovene
Som. Somali
Sp. Spanish
St., St Saint
Strs Straits
Swa. Swahili
Swe. Swedish
Switz. Switzerland

T
Taj. Tajik
Th. Thai
Thai. Thailand
Tib. Tibetan
Turk. Turkish
Turkm. Turkmenistan

U
UAE United Arab Emirates
Uigh. Uighur
UK United Kingdom
Ukr. Ukrainian
UN United Nations
Urd. Urdu
US/USA United States of America
USSR Union of Soviet Socialist Republics
Uzb. Uzbek

V
var. variant
Vdkhr. Vodokhranilishche (Russian for reservoir)
Vdskh. Vodoskhovyshche (Ukrainian for reservoir)
Vtn. Vietnamese

W
W west
Wel. Welsh

Y
Yugo. Yugoslavia

THIS INDEX LISTS all the placenames and features shown on the regional and continental maps in this Atlas. Placenames are referenced to the largest scale map on which they appear. The policy followed throughout the Atlas is to use the local spelling or local name at regional level; commonly-used English language names may occasionally be added (in parentheses) where this is an aid to identification e.g. Firenze (Florence). English names, where they exist, have been used for all international features e.g. oceans and country names; they are also used on the continental maps and in the introductory World Today section; these are then fully cross-referenced to the local names found on the regional maps. The index also contains commonly-found alternative names and variant spellings, which are also fully cross-referenced.

All main entry names are those of settlements unless otherwise indicated by the use of italicized definitions or representative symbols, which are keyed at the foot of each page.

1

25 de Mayo *see* Veinticinco de Mayo
143 *Y13* **26 Bakı Komissarı** ***Rus.*** Imeni 26 Bakinskikh Komissarov. SE Azerbaijan
26 Baku Komissarlary Adyndaky *see* Imeni 26 Bakinskikh Komissarov
8 *M16* **100 Mile House** ***var.*** Hundred Mile House. British Columbia, SW Canada

A

Aabenraa *see* Åbenrå
Aabybro *see* Åbybro
103 *C16* **Aachen** ***Dut.*** Aken, ***Fr.*** Aix-la-Chapelle; ***anc.*** Aquae Grani, Aquisgranum. Nordrhein-Westfalen, W Germany
Aaiún *see* Laâyoune
Aakirkeby *see* Åkirkeby
Aalborg *see* Ålborg
Aalborg Bugt *see* Ålborg Bugt
103 *J21* **Aalen** Baden-Württemberg, S Germany
Aalestrup *see* Ålestrup
100 *I11* **Aalsmeer** Noord-Holland, C Netherlands
101 *F18* **Aalst** ***Fr.*** Alost. Oost-Vlaanderen, C Belgium
101 *K18* **Aalst** Noord-Brabant, S Netherlands
100 *O12* **Aalten** Gelderland, E Netherlands
101 *D17* **Aalter** Oost-Vlaanderen, NW Belgium
Aanaar *see* Inari
Aanaarjävri *see* Inarijärvi
95 *M17* **Äänekoski** Keski-Suomi, C Finland
144 *H7* **Aanjar** ***var.*** 'Anjar. C Lebanon
85 *G21* **Aansluit** Northern Cape, N South Africa
Aar *see* Aare
110 *F7* **Aarau** Aargau, N Switzerland
110 *D8* **Aarberg** Bern, W Switzerland
101 *D16* **Aardenburg** Zeeland, SW Netherlands
110 *D8* **Aare** ***var.*** Aar. ≈ W Switzerland
110 *F7* **Aargau** ***Fr.*** Argovie. ◐ *canton* N Switzerland
Aarhus *see* Århus
Aarlen *see* Arlon
Aars *see* Års
101 *I17* **Aarschot** Vlaams Brabant, C Belgium
Aassi, Nahr el *see* Orontes
Aat *see* Ath
166 *G7* **Aba** ***prev.*** Ngawa. Sichuan, C China
79 *V17* **Aba** Abia, S Nigeria
81 *P16* **Aba** Haut-Zaïre, NE Zaire
146 *J6* **Abā al Qazāz, Bi'r** *well* NW Saudi Arabia
Abā as Su'ūd *see* Najrān
61 *G14* **Abacaxis, Rio** ≈ NW Brazil
Abaco Island *see* Great Abaco/Little Abaco
Abaco Island *see* Great Abaco, N Bahamas
148 *K10* **Ābādān** Khūzestān, SW Iran
149 *O10* **Ābādeh** Fārs, C Iran
76 *H8* **Abadla** W Algeria
61 *M20* **Abaeté** Minas Gerais, SE Brazil
169 *Q10* **Abag Qi** ***var.*** Xin Hot. Nei Mongol Zizhiqu, N China
64 *P7* **Abaí** Caazapá, S Paraguay
203 *O2* **Abaiang** ***var.*** Apia; ***prev.*** Charlotte Island. *atoll* Tungaru, W Kiribati
Abaj *see* Abay
79 *U15* **Abaji** Federal Capital District, C Nigeria
39 *O7* **Abajo Peak** ▲ Utah, W USA
79 *V16* **Abakaliki** Enugu, S Nigeria
126 *Hh15* **Abakan** Respublika Khakasiya, S Russian Federation
126 *Hh15* **Abakan** ≈ S Russian Federation
79 *S11* **Abala** Tillabéri, SW Niger
79 *U11* **Abalak** Tahoua, C Niger
121 *N14* **Abalyanka** ***Rus.*** Obolyanka. ≈ N Belorussia
126 *Ii14* **Aban** Krasnoyarskiy Kray, S Russian Federation
149 *P9* **Āb Anbār-e Kān Sorkh** Yazd, C Iran
59 *G16* **Abancay** Apurímac, SE Peru
202 *H2* **Abaokoro** *atoll* Tungaru, W Kiribati
Abariringa *see* Kanton
149 *P10* **Abarkū** Yazd, C Iran
172 *Qq5* **Abashiri** ***var.*** Abasiri. Hokkaidō, NE Japan
172 *Q6* **Abashiri-gawa** ≈ Hokkaidō, NE Japan
172 *Q5* **Abashiri-ko** ◎ Hokkaidō, NE Japan
Abasiri *see* Abashiri
43 *P10* **Abasolo** Tamaulipas, C Mexico
194 *L16* **Abau** Central, S PNG
151 *R10* **Abay** ***var.*** Abaj. Karaganda, C Kazakhstan
83 *I15* **Ābaya Hāyk'** ***Eng.*** Lake Margherita, ***It.*** Abbaia. ◎ SW Ethiopia
Ābay Wenz *see* Blue Nile
126 *Hh15* **Abaza** Respublika Khakasiya, S Russian Federation
Abbaia *see* Ābaya Hāyk'
149 *Q13* **Āb Bārīk** Fārs, S Iran
109 *C18* **Abbasanta** Sardegna, Italy, C Mediterranean Sea
Abbatis Villa *see* Abbeville
32 *M3* **Abbaye, Point** *headland* Michigan, N USA
Abbazia *see* Opatija
Abbé, Lake *see* Abhe, Lake
105 *N2* **Abbeville** ***anc.*** Abbatis Villa. Somme, N France
25 *R7* **Abbeville** Alabama, S USA
25 *U6* **Abbeville** Georgia, SE USA
24 *I9* **Abbeville** Louisiana, S USA
23 *P12* **Abbeville** South Carolina, SE USA
xxxv *J10* **Abbeycwmhir** Powys, C Wales, UK
xxxviii *G14* **Abbey Dore** Herefordshire, W England, UK
xliv *C12* **Abbeydorney** Kerry, SW Ireland
xliv *D12* **Abbeyfeale** ***Ir.*** Mainistir na Féile. Limerick, SW Ireland
xliv *I10* **Abbeyleix** Laois, C Ireland
xl *L7* **Abbey Town** Cumbria, NW England, UK
108 *D8* **Abbiategrasso** Lombardia, NW Italy
95 *I14* **Abborrträsk** Norrbotten, N Sweden
204 *J9* **Abbot Ice Shelf** *ice shelf* Antarctica
xxxvi *L14* **Abbotsbury** Dorset, S England, UK
8 *M17* **Abbotsford** British Columbia, SW Canada
32 *K6* **Abbotsford** Wisconsin, N USA
xxxvii *S8* **Abbots Langley** Hertfordshire, E England, UK
xxxix *R12* **Abbotsley** Cambridgeshire, E England, UK
155 *U5* **Abbottābād** North-West Frontier Province, NW Pakistan
121 *M14* **Abchuha** ***Rus.*** Obchuga. Minskaya Voblasts', NW Belorussia
100 *I10* **Abcoude** Utrecht, C Netherlands
145 *N2* **'Abd al 'Azīz, Jabal** ▲▲ NE Syria
147 *U17* **'Abd al Kūrī** *island* SE Yemen
145 *Z13* **'Abd Allāh, Khawr** *bay* Iraq/Kuwait
131 *U6* **Abdulino** Orenburgskaya Oblast', W Russian Federation
80 *J10* **Abéché** ***var.*** Abécher, Abeshr. Ouaddaï, SE Chad
Abécher *see* Abéché
149 *S8* **Āb-e Garm va Sard** Khorāsān, E Iran
79 *R8* **Abeïbara** Kidal, NE Mali
107 *P5* **Abejar** Castilla-León, N Spain
56 *E9* **Abejorral** Antioquia, W Colombia
Abela *see* Ávila
Abellinum *see* Avellino
94 *Q2* **Abeløya** *island* Kong Karls Land, E Svalbard
82 *I13* **Ābeltī** C Ethiopia
203 *O2* **Abemama** ***var.*** Apamama; ***prev.*** Roger Simpson Island. *atoll* Tungaru, W Kiribati
176 *Yy14* **Abemaree** ***var.*** Abemarre. Irian Jaya, E Indonesia
79 *O16* **Abengourou** E Ivory Coast
97 *G24* **Åbenrå** ***var.*** Aabenraa, ***Ger.*** Apenrade. Sønderjylland, SW Denmark
103 *L22* **Abens** ≈ SE Germany
79 *S16* **Abeokuta** Ogun, SW Nigeria
xxxv *F10* **Aberaeron** Ceredigion, SW Wales, UK
Aberbrothock *see* Arbroath
xxxv *K14* **Abercarn** Caerphilly, S Wales, UK
xlii *N11* **Aberchirder** Aberdeenshire, NE Scotland, UK
Abercorn *see* Mbala
xxxv *H13* **Abercraf** Powys, C Wales, UK
31 *R6* **Abercrombie** North Dakota, N USA
xxxv *I14* **Aberdare** Rhondda Cynon Taff, S Wales, UK
xxxv *E7* **Aberdaron** Gwynedd, NW Wales, UK
xliii *P14* **Aberdeen** ***anc.*** Devana. City of Aberdeen, NE Scotland, UK
191 *T7* **Aberdeen** New South Wales, SE Australia
9 *T15* **Aberdeen** Saskatchewan, S Canada
85 *H25* **Aberdeen** Eastern Cape, S South Africa
23 *X2* **Aberdeen** Maryland, NE USA
25 *N3* **Aberdeen** Mississippi, S USA
23 *T10* **Aberdeen** North Carolina, SE USA
31 *P8* **Aberdeen** South Dakota, N USA
34 *F8* **Aberdeen** Washington, NW USA
xliii *O14* **Aberdeen, City of** ◐ *unitary authority* NE Scotland, UK
15 *K6* **Aberdeen Lake** ◎ Northwest Territories, NE Canada
xlii *M12* **Aberdeenshire** ◐ *unitary authority* NE Scotland, UK
xliii *M19* **Aberdour** Fife, E Scotland, UK
xxxv *G9* **Aberdyfi** Gwynedd, NW Wales, UK
xxxv *J11* **Aberedw** Powys, C Wales, UK
xliii *K16* **Aberfeldy** Perth and Kinross, C Scotland, UK
xxxv *E5* **Aberffraw** Isle of Anglesey, NW Wales, UK
xli *S14* **Aberford** Leeds, N England, UK
xliii *I18* **Aberfoyle** Stirling, C Scotland, UK
xxxv *K13* **Abergavenny** ***anc.*** Gobannium. Monmouthshire, SE Wales, UK
xxxv *I4* **Abergele** Conwy, N Wales, UK
xxxv *G12* **Abergorlech** Carmarthenshire, S Wales, UK
Abergwaun *see* Fishguard
xxxv *H11* **Abergwesyn** Powys, C Wales, UK
xxxv *G8* **Abergynolwyn** Gwynedd, NW Wales, UK
xxxv *I15* **Aberkenfig** Bridgend, S Wales, UK
xliii *N19* **Aberlady** East Lothian, SE Scotland, UK
xxxv *H8* **Aberllefenni** Gwynedd, NW Wales, UK
Abermarre *see* Abemaree
xxxv *J9* **Abermule** Powys, C Wales, UK
27 *N5* **Abernathy** Texas, SW USA
xliii *L18* **Abernethy** Perth and Kinross, C Scotland, UK
xliii *M17* **Abernyte** Perth and Kinross, C Scotland, UK
xxxv *E11* **Aberporth** Ceredigion, W Wales, UK
Abersee *see* Wolfgangsee
xxxv *E7* **Abersoch** Gwynedd, NW Wales, UK
xxxv *K14* **Abersychan** Torfaen, SE Wales, UK
Abertawe *see* Swansea
Aberteifi *see* Cardigan
xxxv *K14* **Abertillery** Blaenau Gwent, SE Wales, UK
34 *I15* **Abert, Lake** ◎ Oregon, NW USA
xliii *L18* **Aberuthven** Perth and Kinross, C Scotland, UK
xxxv *G9* **Aberystwyth** Ceredigion, W Wales, UK
Abeshr *see* Abéché
108 *F10* **Abetone** Toscana, C Italy
129 *V5* **Abez'** Respublika Komi, NW Russian Federation
148 *M5* **Āb Garm** Zanjān, NW Iran
147 *N12* **Abhā** 'Asīr, SW Saudi Arabia
148 *M5* **Abhar** Zanjān, NW Iran
Abhé Bad/Ābhē Bid Hāyk' *see* Abhe, Lake
82 *K12* **Abhe, Lake** ***var.*** Lake Abbé, ***Amh.*** Ābhē Bid Hāyk', ***Som.*** Abhé Bad. ◎ Djibouti/Ethiopia
79 *V17* **Abia** ◐ *state* SE Nigeria
145 *V9* **'Abīd 'Alī** E Iraq
121 *O17* **Abidavichy** ***Rus.*** Obidovichi. Mahilyowskaya Voblasts', E Belorussia
117 *L15* **Abide** Çanakkale, NW Turkey
79 *N17* **Abidjan** S Ivory Coast
Āb-i-Istāda *see* Īstādeh-ye Moqor, Āb-e-
29 *N4* **Abilene** Kansas, C USA
27 *Q7* **Abilene** Texas, SW USA
Abindonia *see* Abingdon
xxxvii *P8* **Abingdon** ***anc.*** Abindonia. Oxfordshire, S England, UK
32 *K12* **Abingdon** Illinois, N USA
23 *P8* **Abingdon** Virginia, NE USA
Abingdon *see* Pinta, Isla
xliii *K22* **Abington** South Lanarkshire, C Scotland, UK
20 *J15* **Abington** Pennsylvania, NE USA
130 *K14* **Abinsk** Krasnodarskiy Kray, SW Russian Federation
39 *R9* **Abiquiu Reservoir** ⊡ New Mexico, SW USA
94 *I10* **Abisko** Norrbotten, N Sweden
10 *G12* **Abitibi** ≈ Ontario, S Canada
10 *H12* **Abitibi, Lake** ◎ Ontario, S Canada
82 *J10* **Ābīy Ādī** N Ethiopia
120 *H6* **Abja-Paluoja** Viljandimaa, S Estonia
143 *Q8* **Abkhazia** ◐ *autonomous republic* NW Georgia
190 *F1* **Abminga** South Australia
77 *W9* **Abnûb** C Egypt
Åbo *see* Turku
Åbo-Björneborg *see* Turku-Pori
158 *G9* **Abohar** Punjab, N India
79 *O17* **Aboisso** SE Ivory Coast
80 *H5* **Abo, Massif d'** ▲▲ NW Chad
79 *R16* **Abomey** S Benin
81 *F16* **Abong Mbang** Est, SE Cameroon
113 *L23* **Abony** Pest, C Hungary
80 *J11* **Abou-Déïa** Salamat, SE Chad
Aboudouhour *see* Abū aḍ Ḍuhūr
Abou Kémal *see* Abū Kamāl
Abou Simbel *see* Abu Simbel
143 *T12* **Abovyan** C Armenia
xliii *N14* **Aboyne** Aberdeenshire, NE Scotland, UK
179 *P8* **Abra** ≈ Luzon, N Philippines
147 *P15* **Abrād, Wādī** *seasonal river* W Yemen
Abraham Bay *see* The Carlton
106 *G10* **Abrantes** ***var.*** Abrántes. Santarém, C Portugal
64 *J4* **Abra Pampa** Jujuy, N Argentina
Abrashlare *see* Brezovo
56 *G7* **Abrego** Norte de Santander, N Colombia
Abrene *see* Pytalovo
42 *C7* **Abreojos, Punta** *headland* W Mexico
67 *J16* **Abrolhos Bank** *undersea feature* W Atlantic Ocean
121 *H19* **Abrova** ***Rus.*** Obrovo. Brestskaya Voblasts', SW Belorussia
118 *G11* **Abrud** ***Ger.*** Gross-Schlatten, ***Hung.*** Abrudbánya. Alba, SW Romania
Abrudbánya *see* Abrud
120 *E6* **Abruka** *island* SW Estonia
109 *J15* **Abruzzese, Appennino** ▲▲ C Italy
109 *J14* **Abruzzi** ◐ *region* C Italy
147 *N14* **'Abs** ***var.*** Sūq 'Abs. W Yemen
35 *T12* **Absaroka Range** ▲▲ Montana/Wyoming, NW USA
143 *Z11* **Abşeron Yarımadası** ***Rus.*** Apsheronskiy Poluostrov. *peninsula* E Azerbaijan
149 *N6* **Āb Shīrīn** Eşfahān, C Iran
145 *X10* **Abtān** SE Iraq
111 *R6* **Abtenau** Salzburg, NW Austria
170 *Dd12* **Abu** Yamaguchi, Honshū, SW Japan
158 *E14* **Ābu** Rājasthān, N India
144 *I4* **Abū aḍ Ḍuhūr** ***Fr.*** Aboudouhour. Idlib, NW Syria
149 *P17* **Abū al Abyaḍ** *island* C UAE
144 *K10* **Abū al Ḥuşayn, Khabrat** ◎ N Jordan
145 *R8* **Abū al Jīr** C Iraq
145 *Y12* **Abū al Khaşīb** ***var.*** Abul Khasib. SE Iraq
145 *U12* **Abū at Tubrah, Thaqb** *well* S Iraq
77 *V11* **Abu Balâs** ▲ SW Egypt
Abu Dhabi *see* Abū Ẓaby
145 *R8* **Abū Farūkh** C Iraq
82 *C12* **Abu Gabra** Southern Darfur, W Sudan
145 *P10* **Abū Ghār, Sha'īb** *dry watercourse* S Iraq
82 *G7* **Abu Hamed** River Nile, N Sudan
145 *O5* **Abū Ḥardān** ***var.*** Hajîne. Dayr az Zawr, E Syria
145 *T7* **Abū Ḥāssawīyah** E Iraq
144 *K10* **Abū Ḥifnah, Wādī** *dry watercourse* N Jordan
79 *V15* **Abuja** ● (Nigeria) Federal Capital District, C Nigeria
145 *R9* **Abū Jahaf, Wādī** *dry watercourse* C Iraq
58 *F12* **Abujao, Río** ≈ E Peru
145 *U12* **Abū Jasrah** S Iraq
145 *O6* **Abū Kamāl** ***Fr.*** Abou Kémal. Dayr az Zawr, E Syria
175 *Q11* **Abuki, Pegunungan** ▲▲ Sulawesi, C Indonesia
171 *Ll14* **Abukuma-gawa** ≈ Honshū, C Japan
171 *Ll15* **Abukuma-sanchi** ▲▲ Honshū, C Japan
Abula *see* Ávila
Abul Khasib *see* Abū al Khaşīb
81 *K16* **Abumombazi** ***var.*** Abumonbazi. Equateur, N Zaire
Abumonbazi *see* Abumombazi
61 *D15* **Abunã** Rondônia, W Brazil
58 *K13* **Abunã, Rio** ***var.*** Río Abuná. ≈ Bolivia/Brazil
144 *G10* **Abū Nuşayr** ***var.*** Abu Nuseir. 'Ammān, W Jordan
Abu Nuseir *see* Abū Nuşayr
145 *T12* **Abū Qabr** S Iraq
144 *K5* **Abū Raḩbah, Jabal** ▲▲ C Syria
145 *S5* **Abū Rajāsh** N Iraq
145 *W13* **Abū Raqrāq, Ghadīr** *well* S Iraq
158 *E14* **Ābu Road** Rājasthān, N India
82 *I6* **Abu Shagara, Ras** *headland* NE Sudan
77 *W12* **Abu Simbel** ***var.*** Abou Simbel, Abū Sunbul. *ancient monument* S Egypt
145 *U12* **Abū Sudayrah** S Iraq
145 *T10* **Abū Şukhayr** S Iraq
Abū Sunbul *see* Abu Simbel
172 *Nn6* **Abuta** Hokkaidō, NE Japan
193 *E18* **Abut Head** *headland* South Island, NZ
82 *E9* **Abu 'Urug** Northern Kordofan, C Sudan
82 *K12* **Ābuyē Mēda** ▲ C Ethiopia
179 *R13* **Abuyog** Leyte, C Philippines
82 *D11* **Abu Zabad** Western Kordofan, C Sudan
Abū Ẓabī *see* Abū Ẓaby
149 *P16* **Abū Ẓaby** ***var.*** Abū Ẓabī, ***Eng.*** Abu Dhabi. ● (UAE) Abū Ẓaby, C UAE
77 *X8* **Abu Zenîma** E Egypt

◆ Country ● Country Capital ◇ Dependent Territory ○ Dependent Territory Capital ◐ Administrative Region ✈ International Airport ▲ Mountain ▲▲ Mountain Range Volcano ≈ River ◎ Lake ⊡ Reservoir

Åby – Akabira

97 N17 **Åby** Östergötland, S Sweden
Abyaḍ, Al Baḥr al *see* White Nile
97 G20 **Åbybro** *var.* Aabybro. Nordjylland, N Denmark
82 D13 **Abyei** Western Kordofan, S Sudan
Abyla *see* Ávila
Abymes *see* les Abymes
Abyssinia *see* Ethiopia
Açâba *see* Assaba
56 F11 **Acacias** Meta, C Colombia
60 L13 **Açailandia** Maranhão, E Brazil
Acaill *see* Achill Island
44 E8 **Acajutla** Sonsonate, W El Salvador
81 D17 **Acalayong** SW Equatorial Guinea
43 N13 **Acámbaro** Guanajuato, C Mexico
56 C6 **Acandí** Chocó, NW Colombia
106 H4 **A Cañiza** *var.* La Cañiza. Galicia, NW Spain
42 J11 **Acaponeta** Nayarit, C Mexico
42 J11 **Acaponeta, Río de** ≈ C Mexico
43 O16 **Acapulco** *var.* Acapulco de Juárez. Guerrero, S Mexico
Acapulco de Juárez *see* Acapulco
57 T13 **Acarai Mountains** *Sp.* Serra Acaraí. ⛰ Brazil/Guyana
Acaraí, Serra *see* Acarai Mountains
60 O13 **Acaraú** Ceará, NE Brazil
56 J6 **Acarigua** Portuguesa, N Venezuela
44 C6 **Acatenango, Volcán de** ⋀ S Guatemala
43 Q15 **Acatlán** *var.* Acatlán de Osorio. Puebla, S Mexico
Acatlán de Osorio *see* Acatlán
43 S15 **Acayucan** *var.* Acayucán. Veracruz-Llave, E Mexico
Accho *see* 'Akko
23 Y5 **Accomac** Virginia, NE USA
79 Q17 **Accra** ● (Ghana) SE Ghana
xli O14 **Accrington** Lancashire, NW England, UK
63 B19 **Acebal** Santa Fe, C Argentina
173 Ee4 **Aceh** *off.* Daerah Istimewa Aceh, *var.* Acheen, Achin, Atchin, Atjeh. ◈ *autonomous district* NW Indonesia
109 M18 **Acerenza** Basilicata, S Italy
109 K17 **Acerra** *anc.* Acerrae. Campania, S Italy
Acerrae *see* Acerra
Ach'asar Lerr *see* Achkasar
xliii C16 **Acha** Argyll and Bute, W Scotland, UK
59 J17 **Achacachi** La Paz, W Bolivia
56 K7 **Achaguas** Apure, C Venezuela
xliii F20 **Achahoish** Argyll and Bute, W Scotland, UK
160 H12 **Achalpur** *prev.* Elichpur, Ellichpur. Mahārāshtra, C India
63 F18 **Achar** Tacuarembó, C Uruguay
117 H19 **Acharnés** *var.* Aharnes; *prev.* Akharnaí. Attikí, C Greece
xlii L7 **Achavanich** Highland, N Scotland, UK
Acheen *see* Aceh
101 K16 **Achel** Limburg, NE Belgium
117 D16 **Achelóos** *var.* Akhelóös, Aspropótamos; *anc.* Achelous. ≈ W Greece
Achelous *see* Achelóos
169 W8 **Acheng** Heilongjiang, NE China
111 N6 **Achenkirch** Tirol, W Austria
103 L24 **Achenpass** *pass* Austria/Germany
111 N7 **Achensee** ◎ W Austria
103 F22 **Achern** Baden-Württemberg, SW Germany
117 C16 **Acherón** ≈ W Greece
79 W11 **Achétinamou** ≈ S Niger
xlii H8 **Achfary** Highland, NW Scotland, UK
158 J12 **Achhnera** Uttar Pradesh, N India
44 C7 **Achiguate, Río** ≈ S Guatemala
xliii D14 **A'Chill** Highland, NW Scotland, UK
xliv B6 **Achill** Mayo, NW Ireland
xliv C6 **Achill Head** *Ir.* Ceann Acla. *headland* W Ireland
xliv C6 **Achill Island** *Ir.* Acaill. *island* W Ireland
xliv C6 **Achill Sound** Mayo, W Ireland
xlii G9 **Achiltibuie** Highland, NW Scotland, UK
102 H11 **Achim** Niedersachsen, NW Germany
155 S5 **Achīn** Nangarhār, E Afghanistan
Achin *see* Aceh
126 Hh14 **Achinsk** Krasnoyarskiy Kray, S Russian Federation
168 E5 **Achit Nuur** ◎ NW Mongolia
143 T11 **Achkasar** *Arm.* Ach'asar Lerr. ▲ Armenia/Georgia
xlii D8 **Achmore** Western Isles, NW Scotland, UK
xliii F17 **Achnacroish** Argyll and Bute, W Scotland, UK
xlii H11 **Achnasheen** Highland, NW Scotland, UK
xlii M12 **Achnastank** Moray, N Scotland, UK
xliii E16 **Achosnich** Highland, NW Scotland, UK
xlii H7 **Achriesgill** Highland, NW Scotland, UK
130 K13 **Achuyevo** Krasnodarskiy Kray, SW Russian Federation
83 F16 **Achwa** *var.* Aswa. ≈ N Uganda
142 E15 **Acıgöl** *salt lake* SW Turkey
109 L24 **Acireale** Sicilia, Italy, C Mediterranean Sea
Aciris *see* Agri
27 N7 **Ackerly** Texas, SW USA
24 M4 **Ackerman** Mississippi, S USA
31 W13 **Ackley** Iowa, C USA
xli R4 **Acklington** Northumberland, N England, UK
46 J5 **Acklins Island** *island* SE Bahamas
Acla, Ceann *see* Achill Head
xliv F6 **Aclare** Sligo, N Ireland
xxxix Y9 **Acle** Norfolk, E England, UK
64 H11 **Aconcagua, Cerro** ▲ W Argentina
Açores/Açores, Arquipélago dos/Açores, Ilhas dos *see* Azores
106 H2 **A Coruña** *Cast.* La Coruña, *Eng.* Corunna; *anc.* Caronium. Galicia, NW Spain
44 L10 **Acoyapa** Chontales, S Nicaragua
108 H13 **Acquapendente** Lazio, C Italy
108 J13 **Acquasanta Terme** Marche, C Italy
108 I13 **Acquasparta** Lazio, C Italy
108 C9 **Acqui Terme e Bagni** Piemonte, NW Italy
Acrae *see* Palazzola Acreide
190 F7 **Acraman, Lake** *salt lake* South Australia
61 A15 **Acre** *off.* Estado do Acre. ◈ *state* W Brazil
Acre *see* 'Akko
61 C16 **Acre, Rio** ≈ W Brazil
109 N20 **Acri** Calabria, SW Italy
Acte *see* Ágion Óros
203 Y12 **Actéon, Groupe** *island group* Îles Tuamotu, SE French Polynesia
xxxvi B7 **Acton** Ealing, SE England, UK
13 P12 **Acton-Vale** Québec, SE Canada
43 P13 **Actopan** *var.* Actopán. Hidalgo, C Mexico
61 P14 **Açu** *var.* Assu. Rio Grande do Norte, E Brazil
Acunum Acusio *see* Montélimar
79 Q17 **Ada** SE Ghana
31 R5 **Ada** Minnesota, N USA
33 R12 **Ada** Ohio, N USA
29 O12 **Ada** Oklahoma, C USA
114 L8 **Ada** Serbia, N Yugoslavia
Ada Bazar *see* Adapazarı
42 D3 **Adair, Bahía de** *bay* NW Mexico
106 M7 **Adaja** ≈ N Spain
40 H17 **Adak Island** *island* Aleutian Islands, Alaska, USA
Adalia *see* Antalya
Adalia, Gulf of *see* Antalya Körfezi
147 X9 **Adam** N Oman
Adama *see* Nazrēt
62 I8 **Adamantina** São Paulo, S Brazil
81 E14 **Adamaoua** *Eng.* Adamawa. ◈ *province* N Cameroon
70 F11 **Adamaoua, Massif d'** *Eng.* Adamawa Highlands. *plateau* NW Cameroon
79 Y14 **Adamawa** ◈ *state* E Nigeria
Adamawa *see* Adamaoua
Adamawa Highlands *see* Adamaoua, Massif d'
108 F6 **Adamello** ▲ N Italy
83 J14 **Ādamī Tulu** C Ethiopia
65 M23 **Adam, Mount** ▲ West Falkland, Falkland Islands
31 R16 **Adams** Nebraska, C USA
20 H8 **Adams** New York, NE USA
31 Q3 **Adams** North Dakota, N USA
161 I23 **Adam's Bridge** *chain of shoals* NW Sri Lanka
34 H10 **Adams, Mount** ▲ Washington, NW USA
Adam's Peak *see* Sri Pada
203 R16 **Adam's Rock** *island* Pitcairn Island, Pitcairn Islands
203 P16 **Adamstown** ○ (Pitcairn Islands) Pitcairn Island, Pitcairn Islands
22 G10 **Adamsville** Tennessee, S USA
27 S9 **Adamsville** Texas, SW USA
147 O17 **'Adan** *Eng.* Aden. SW Yemen
142 K16 **Adana** *var.* Seyhan. Adana, S Turkey
142 K16 **Adana** *var.* Seyhan. ◈ *province* S Turkey
Adâncata *see* Horlivka
175 Nn10 **Adang, Teluk** *bay* Borneo, C Indonesia
142 F11 **Adapazarı** *prev.* Ada Bazar. Sakarya, NW Turkey
82 H8 **Adarama** River Nile, NE Sudan
xliv F11 **Adare** Limerick, SW Ireland
205 Q16 **Adare, Cape** *headland* Antarctica
108 E6 **Adda** *anc.* Addua. ≈ N Italy
82 A13 **Adda** ≈ W Sudan
149 Q17 **Aḍ Ḍab'īyah** Abū Ẓaby, C UAE
149 O18 **Aḍ Ḍafrah** *desert* S UAE
147 Q6 **Ad Dahnā'** *desert* E Saudi Arabia
76 A11 **Ad Dakhla** *var.* Dakhla. SW Western Sahara
Ad Dalanj *see* Dilling
Ad Damar *see* Ed Damer
Ad Damazīn *see* Ed Damazin
Ad Dāmir *see* Ed Damer
181 N2 **Ad Dammām** *desert* NE Saudi Arabia
147 R6 **Ad Dammān** *var.* Dammām. Ash Sharqīyah, NE Saudi Arabia
Ad Dāmūr *see* Damoûr
146 K5 **Ad Dār al Ḥamrā'** Tabūk, NW Saudi Arabia
146 M13 **Ad Darb** Jīzān, SW Saudi Arabia
147 O8 **Ad Dawādimī** Ar Riyāḍ, C Saudi Arabia
149 N16 **Ad Dawḥah** *Eng.* Doha. ● (Qatar) C Qatar
149 N16 **Ad Dawḥah** *Eng.* Doha. ✈ C Qatar
145 S6 **Ad Dawr** N Iraq
145 Y12 **Ad Dayr** *var.* Dayr, Shahbān. E Iraq
xxxviii I8 **Adderley** Shropshire, W England, UK
Addi Arkay *see* Ādī Ārk'ay
145 X15 **Ad Dibdibah** *physical region* Iraq/Kuwait
Aḍ Ḍiffah *see* Libyan Plateau
xli Q13 **Addingham** Bradford, N England, UK
Addis Ababa *see* Ādīs Ābeba
Addison *see* Webster Springs
145 U10 **Ad Dīwānīyah** *var.* Diwaniyah. C Iraq
Addua *see* Adda
157 K22 **Addu Atoll** *atoll* S Maldives
Ad Dujail *see* Ad Dujayl
145 T7 **Ad Dujayl** *var.* Ad Dujail. N Iraq
Ad Duwaym/Ad Duwēm *see* Ed Dueim
101 D16 **Adegem** Oost-Vlaanderen, NW Belgium
25 U7 **Adel** Georgia, SE USA
31 U14 **Adel** Iowa, C USA
190 I9 **Adelaide** South Australia
46 H2 **Adelaide** New Providence, N Bahamas
190 I9 **Adelaide** ✈ South Australia
204 H6 **Adelaide Island** *island* Antarctica
15 K4 **Adelaide Peninsula** *peninsula* Northwest Territories, N Canada
189 P2 **Adelaide River** Northern Territory, N Australia
78 M10 **'Adel Bagrou** Hodh ech Chargui, SE Mauritania
194 I11 **Adelbert Range** ⛰ N PNG
188 K3 **Adele Island** *island* Western Australia
109 O17 **Adelfia** Puglia, SE Italy
205 V16 **Adélie Coast** *physical region* Antarctica
205 V14 **Adélie, Terre** *physical region* Antarctica
Adelnau *see* Odolanów
Adelsberg *see* Postojna
Aden *see* 'Adan
147 Q17 **Aden, Gulf of** *gulf* SW Arabian Sea
79 V10 **Aderbissinat** Agadez, C Niger
Adhaim *see* Al 'Uẓaym
149 R16 **Adh Dhayd** *var.* Al Dhaid. Ash Shāriqah, NE UAE
146 M4 **'Adhfā'** *spring/well* NW Saudi Arabia
144 I13 **'Ādhriyāt, Jabāl al** ⛰ S Jordan
194 L12 **Adi** ≈ New Britain, C PNG
82 I10 **Ādī Ārk'ay** *var.* Addi Arkay. N Ethiopia
190 C7 **Adieu, Cape** *headland* South Australia
108 H8 **Adige** *Ger.* Etsch. ≈ N Italy
82 J10 **Ādīgrat** N Ethiopia
160 I13 **Ādilabād** *var.* Ādilābād. Andhra Pradesh, C India
37 P2 **Adin** California, W USA
176 Vv12 **Adi, Pulau** *island* E Indonesia
20 K8 **Adirondack Mountains** ⛰ New York, NE USA
82 J13 **Ādīs Ābeba** *Eng.* Addis Ababa. ● (Ethiopia) C Ethiopia
82 J13 **Ādīs Ābeba** ✈ C Ethiopia
82 I11 **Ādīs Zemen** NW Ethiopia
Adi Ugri *see* Mendefera
143 N15 **Adıyaman** Adıyaman, SE Turkey
143 N15 **Adıyaman** ◈ *province* S Turkey
118 L11 **Adjud** Vrancea, E Romania
47 T6 **Adjuntas** C Puerto Rico
Adjuntas, Presa de las *see* Vicente Guerrero, Presa
Ādkup *see* Erikub Atoll
130 L15 **Adler** Krasnodarskiy Kray, SW Russian Federation
Adler *see* Orlice
xli N15 **Adlington** Lancashire, NW England, UK
110 G7 **Adliswil** Zürich, NW Switzerland
15 L1 **Admiralty Inlet** *fjord* Baffin Island, Northwest Territories, NE Canada
34 G7 **Admiralty Inlet** *inlet* Washington, NW USA
41 X13 **Admiralty Island** *island* Alexander Archipelago, Alaska, USA
194 K8 **Admiralty Islands** *island group* N PNG
142 B14 **Adnan Menderes** ✈ (İzmir) İzmir, W Turkey
39 V6 **Adobe Creek Reservoir** ⊡ Colorado, C USA
79 T16 **Ado-Ekiti** Ondo, SW Nigeria
Adola *see* Kibre Mengist
63 C23 **Adolfo González Chaues** Buenos Aires, E Argentina
161 H17 **Ādoni** Andhra Pradesh, C India
104 K15 **Adour** *anc.* Aturus. ≈ SW France
Adowa *see* Ādwa
107 O15 **Adra** Andalucía, S Spain
109 L24 **Adrano** Sicilia, Italy, C Mediterranean Sea
76 I9 **Adrar** C Algeria
78 K7 **Adrar** ◈ *region* C Mauritania
76 L11 **Adrar** ⛰ SE Algeria
76 A12 **Adrar Souttouf** ⛰ SW Western Sahara
Adrasman *see* Adrasmon
153 Q10 **Adrasmon** *Rus.* Adrasman. NW Tajikistan
80 K10 **Adré** Ouaddaï, E Chad
108 H9 **Adria** *anc.* Atria, Hadria, Hatria. Veneto, NE Italy
33 R10 **Adrian** Michigan, N USA
31 S11 **Adrian** Minnesota, N USA
29 R5 **Adrian** Missouri, C USA
26 M2 **Adrian** Texas, SW USA
23 S4 **Adrian** West Virginia, NE USA
Adrianople/Adrianopolis *see* Edirne
123 Mm8 **Adriatic Basin** *undersea feature* Adriatic Sea, N Mediterranean Sea
Adriatico, Mare *see* Adriatic Sea
108 L13 **Adriatic Sea** *Alb.* Deti Adriatik, *It.* Mare Adriatico, *SCr.* Jadransko More, *Slvn.* Jadransko Morje. *sea* N Mediterranean Sea
Adriatik, Deti *see* Adriatic Sea
Adua *see* Ādwa
xliv C14 **Adrigole** Cork, S Ireland
Aduana del Sásabe *see* Sásabe
xxxvii T12 **Adur** ≈ SE England, UK
81 O17 **Adusa** Haut-Zaïre, NE Zaire
120 J13 **Adutiškis** Švenčionys, E Lithuania
29 Y7 **Advance** Missouri, C USA
67 D25 **Adventure Sound** *bay* East Falkland, Falkland Islands
82 J10 **Ādwa** *var.* Adowa, *It.* Adua. N Ethiopia
126 M8 **Adycha** ≈ NE Russian Federation
130 L14 **Adygeya, Respublika** ◈ *autonomous republic* SW Russian Federation
152 C11 **Adzhikui** *Turkm.* Ajyguyy. Balkanskiy Velayat, W Turkmenistan
79 N17 **Adzopé** SE Ivory Coast
129 U4 **Adz'va** ≈ NW Russian Federation
129 U5 **Adz'vavom** Respublika Komi, NW Russian Federation
Ædua *see* Autun
117 K19 **Aegean Islands** *island group* Greece/Turkey
Aegean North *see* Vóreion Aigaíon
117 I17 **Aegean Sea** *Gk.* Aigaíon Pélagos, Aigaío Pélagos, *Turk.* Ege Denizi. *sea* NE Mediterranean Sea
Aegean South *see* Nótion Aigaíon
120 H3 **Aegviidu** *Ger.* Charlottenhof. Harjumaa, NW Estonia
Aegyptus *see* Egypt
Aelana *see* Al 'Aqabah
Aelok *see* Ailuk Atoll
Aelōninae *see* Ailinginae Atoll
Aeļōnļapļap *see* Ailinglaplap Atoll
Æmilia *see* Emilia-Romagna
Æmilianum *see* Millau
Aemona *see* Ljubljana
Aenaria *see* Ischia
Aeolian Islands *see* Eolie, Isole
203 Z3 **Aeon Point** *headland* Kiritimati, NE Kiribati
97 G24 **Ærø** *Ger.* Arrö. *island* C Denmark
97 H24 **Ærøskøbing** Fyn, C Denmark
Æsernia *see* Isernia
106 G3 **A Estrada** Galicia, NW Spain
117 C18 **Aetós** Itháki, Iónioi Nísoi, Greece, C Mediterranean Sea
203 Q8 **Afaahiti** Tahiti, W French Polynesia
145 U10 **'Afak** C Iraq
Afanasjevo *see* Afanas'yevo
129 T14 **Afanas'yevo** *var.* Afanasjevo. Kirovskaya Oblast', NW Russian Federation
Afándou *see* Afántou
117 O23 **Afántou** *var.* Afándou. Ródos, Dodekánisos, Greece, Aegean Sea
Afar Depression *see* Danakil Desert
203 O7 **Afareaitu** Moorea, W French Polynesia
146 L7 **'Afariyah, Bi'r al** *well* NW Saudi Arabia
Afars et des Issas, Territoire Français des *see* Djibouti
85 D22 **Affenrücken** Karas, SW Namibia
xlii G13 **Affric, Loch** ◎ NW Scotland, UK
Afghānestān, Dowlat-e Eslāmī-ye *see* Afghanistan
154 M6 **Afghanistan** *off.* Islamic State of Afghanistan, *Per.* Dowlat-e Eslāmī-ye Afghānestān; *prev.* Republic of Afghanistan. ◆ *islamic state* C Asia
Afgoi *see* Afgooye
83 N17 **Afgooye** *It.* Afgoi. Shabeellaha Hoose, S Somalia
147 N8 **'Afīf** Ar Riyāḍ, C Saudi Arabia
79 V17 **Afikpo** Abia, S Nigeria
Afiun Karahissar *see* Afyon
96 H7 **Åfjord** Sør-Trøndelag, C Norway
111 V6 **Aflenz Kurort** Steiermark, E Austria
76 J6 **Aflou** N Algeria
83 L18 **Afmadow** Jubbada Hoose, S Somalia
41 Q14 **Afognak Island** *island* Alaska, USA
106 J2 **A Fonsagrada** Galicia, NW Spain
194 L15 **Afore** Northern, S PNG
61 O15 **Afrânio** Pernambuco, E Brazil
68-69 **Africa** *continent*
70 L11 **Africa, Horn of** *physical region* Ethiopia/Somalia
180 K11 **Africana Seamount** *undersea feature* SW Indian Ocean
88 A14 **African Plate** *tectonic feature*
144 I2 **'Afrīn** Ḥalab, N Syria
142 M15 **Afşin** Kahramanmaraş, C Turkey
100 J7 **Afsluitdijk** *dam* N Netherlands
31 U15 **Afton** Iowa, C USA
31 W9 **Afton** Minnesota, N USA
29 R8 **Afton** Oklahoma, C USA
142 F14 **Afyon** *prev.* Afyonkarahisar. Afyon, W Turkey
142 F14 **Afyon** *var.* Afiun Karahissar, Afyonkarahisar. ◈ *province* W Turkey
Afyonkarahisar *see* Afyon
Agadès *see* Agadez
79 V10 **Agadez** *prev.* Agadès. Agadez, C Niger
79 W8 **Agadez** ◈ *department* N Niger
76 E8 **Agadir** SW Morocco
66 M9 **Agadir Canyon** *undersea feature* SE Atlantic Ocean
151 R12 **Agadyr'** Zhezkazgan, C Kazakhstan
181 O7 **Agalega Islands** *island group* N Mauritius
44 K6 **Agalta, Sierra de** ⛰ E Honduras
126 Gg10 **Agan** ≈ C Russian Federation
196 B16 **Agana** *var.* Agaña. ○ (Guam) NW Guam
196 B15 **Agana Bay** *bay* NW Guam
196 C16 **Agana Field** ✈ (Agana) C Guam
171 Kk13 **Agano-gawa** ≈ Honshū, C Japan
196 B17 **Aga Point** *headland* S Guam
160 G9 **Agar** Madhya Pradesh, C India
83 I14 **Āgaro** W Ethiopia
159 V15 **Agartala** Tripura, NE India
204 I5 **Agassiz, Cape** *headland* Antarctica
183 V13 **Agassiz Fracture Zone** *tectonic feature* S Pacific Ocean
196 B16 **Agat** W Guam
196 B16 **Agat Bay** *bay* W Guam
151 P13 **Agat, Gory** *hill* C Kazakhstan
Agatha *see* Agde
117 M20 **Agathónisi** *island* Dodekánisos, Greece, Aegean Sea
176 Y13 **Agats** Irian Jaya, E Indonesia
161 C21 **Agatti Island** *island* Lakshadweep, India, N Indian Ocean
40 D16 **Agattu Island** *island* Aleutian Islands, Alaska, USA
40 D16 **Agattu Strait** *strait* Aleutian Islands, Alaska, USA
12 B8 **Agawa** ≈ Ontario, S Canada
12 B8 **Agawa Bay** *lake bay* Ontario, S Canada
79 N17 **Agboville** SE Ivory Coast
143 V12 **Ağdam** *Rus.* Agdam. SW Azerbaijan
105 P16 **Agde** *anc.* Agatha. Hérault, S France
105 P16 **Agde, Cap d'** *headland* S France
Agedabia *see* Ajdābiyā
104 L14 **Agen** *anc.* Aginnum. Lot-et-Garonne, SW France
Agendicum *see* Sens
171 K16 **Ageo** Saitama, Honshū, S Japan
111 R5 **Ager** ≈ N Austria
Agere Hiywet *see* Hāgere Hiywet
110 G8 **Ägerisee** ◎ W Switzerland
148 M10 **Āghā Jārī** Khūzestān, SW Iran
xliv I6 **Aghalane** Fermanagh, W Northern Ireland, UK
41 P15 **Aghiyuk Island** *island* Alaska, USA
76 B12 **Aghouinit** SE Western Sahara
Aghri Dagh *see* Büyükağrı Dağı
76 B10 **Aghzoumal, Sebkhet** *var.* Sebjet Agsumal. *salt lake* E Western Sahara
117 F15 **Agiá** *var.* Ayiá. Thessalía, C Greece
42 G7 **Agiabampo, Estero de** *estuary* NW Mexico
124 Nn4 **Agía Fýlaxis** *var.* Ayia Phyla. S Cyprus
Agialoúsa *see* Yenierenköy
117 M21 **Agía Marína** Léros, Dodekánisos, Greece, Aegean Sea
124 Oo3 **Agía Nápa** *var.* Ayia Napa. E Cyprus
117 L16 **Agía Paraskeví** Lésvos, E Greece
117 J15 **Agías Eirínis, Ákra** *headland* Límnos, E Greece
117 L17 **Agiasós** *var.* Ayiásos, Ayiássos. Lésvos, E Greece
Aginnum *see* Agen
126 K16 **Aginskiy Buryatskiy Avtonomnyy Okrug** ◈ *autonomous district* S Russian Federation
126 Kk16 **Aginskoye** Aginskiy Buryatskiy Avtonomnyy Okrug, S Russian Federation
117 I14 **Ágion Óros** *Eng.* Mount Athos. ◈ *monastic republic* NE Greece
117 H14 **Ágion Óros** *var.* Akte, Aktí; *anc.* Acte. *peninsula* NE Greece
116 D13 **Ágios Achílleios** *religious building* Dytikí Makedonía, N Greece
117 J16 **Ágios Efstrátios** *var.* Áyios Evstrátios, Hagios Evstrátios. *island* E Greece
117 H20 **Ágios Geórgios** *island* Kykládes, Greece, Aegean Sea
117 Q23 **Ágios Geórgios** *island* SE Greece
117 E21 **Ágios Ilías** ▲ S Greece
117 K25 **Ágios Ioannis, Ákra** *headland* Kríti, Greece, E Mediterranean Sea
117 L20 **Ágios Kírykos** *var.* Áyios Kírikos. Ikaría, Dodekánisos, Greece, Aegean Sea
117 D16 **Ágios Nikolaos** Thessalía, C Greece
117 K25 **Ágios Nikólaos** *var.* Áyios Nikólaos. Kríti, Greece, E Mediterranean Sea
Ágios Sérgios *see* Yeniboğaziçi
117 H14 **Agíou Órous, Kólpos** *gulf* N Greece
109 K24 **Agira** *anc.* Agyrium. Sicilia, Italy, C Mediterranean Sea
117 G20 **Agkístri** *island* S Greece
116 G12 **Ágkistro** *var.* Angistro. ▲ NE Greece
105 O17 **Agly** ≈ S France
Agnetheln *see* Agnita
12 E10 **Agnew Lake** ◎ Ontario, S Canada
79 O16 **Agnibilékrou** E Ivory Coast
118 I11 **Agnita** *Ger.* Agnetheln, *Hung.* Szentágota. Sibiu, SW Romania
109 K15 **Agnone** Molise, C Italy
171 Hh17 **Ago** Mie, Honshū, SW Japan
108 C8 **Agogna** ≈ N Italy
79 P17 **Agona Swedru** *var.* Swedru. SE Ghana
Agordat *see* Akurdet
Agosta *see* Augusta
105 N15 **Agout** ≈ S France
158 J12 **Āgra** Uttar Pradesh, N India
Agra and Oudh, United Provinces of *see* Uttar Pradesh
Agram *see* Zagreb
107 U5 **Agramunt** Cataluña, NE Spain
107 Q5 **Agreda** Castilla-León, N Spain
143 S13 **Ağrı** *var.* Karaköse; *prev.* Karakılısse. Ağrı, NE Turkey
143 S13 **Ağrı** ◈ *province* NE Turkey
109 N19 **Agri** *anc.* Aciris. ≈ S Italy
Agri Dagi *see* Büyükağrı Dağı
109 J24 **Agrigento** *Gk.* Akragas; *prev.* Girgenti. Sicilia, Italy, C Mediterranean Sea
196 K4 **Agrihan** *island* N Northern Mariana Islands
117 D18 **Agrínio** *prev.* Agrinion. Dytikí Ellás, W Greece
Agrinion *see* Agrínio
117 G17 **Agriovótano** Évvoia, C Greece
109 L18 **Agropoli** Campania, S Italy
131 T3 **Agryz** Udmurtskaya Respublika, NW Russian Federation
143 U11 **Ağstafa** *Rus.* Akstafa. NW Azerbaijan
Agsumal, Sebjet *see* Aghzoumal, Sebkhet
42 J11 **Agua Brava, Laguna** *lagoon* W Mexico
56 F7 **Aguachica** Cesar, N Colombia
61 J20 **Água Clara** Mato Grosso do Sul, SW Brazil
46 D5 **Aguada de Pasajeros** Cienfuegos, C Cuba
56 J5 **Aguada Grande** Lara, N Venezuela
47 S5 **Aguadilla** W Puerto Rico
45 S16 **Aguadulce** Coclé, S Panama
106 L14 **Aguadulce** Andalucía, S Spain
43 O8 **Agualeguas** Nuevo León, NE Mexico
42 L9 **Aguanaval, Río** ≈ C Mexico
44 J5 **Aguán, Río** ≈ N Honduras
27 R16 **Agua Nueva** Texas, SW USA
62 J8 **Aguapeí, Rio** ≈ S Brazil
63 E14 **Aguapey, Río** ≈ NE Argentina
42 G3 **Agua Prieta** Sonora, NW Mexico
106 G5 **A Guardia** *var.* Laguardia, La Guardia. Galicia, NW Spain
58 E6 **Aguarico, Río** ≈ Ecuador/Peru
57 O6 **Aguasay** Monagas, NE Venezuela
42 M12 **Aguascalientes** Aguascalientes, C Mexico
42 L12 **Aguascalientes** ◈ *state* C Mexico
59 I18 **Aguas Calientes, Río** ≈ S Peru
107 R7 **Aguasvivas** ≈ NE Spain
62 J7 **Água Vermelha, Represa de** ⊡ S Brazil
58 E12 **Aguaytía** Ucayali, C Peru
106 I5 **A Gudiña** *var.* La Gudiña. Galicia, NW Spain
106 G7 **Águeda** Aveiro, N Portugal
106 J8 **Águeda** ≈ Portugal/Spain
79 Q8 **Aguelhok** Kidal, NE Mali
79 V12 **Aguié** Maradi, S Niger
196 K8 **Aguijan** *island* S Northern Mariana Islands
106 M14 **Aguilar** *var.* Aguilar de la Frontera. Andalucía, S Spain
106 M3 **Aguilar de Campóo** Castilla-León, N Spain
Aguilar de la Frontera *see* Aguilar
44 F7 **Aguilares** San Salvador, C El Salvador
107 Q14 **Aguilas** Murcia, SE Spain
42 L15 **Aguililla** Michoacán de Ocampo, SW Mexico
85 F26 **Agulhas** *var.* L'Agulhas. Western Cape, SW South Africa
180 J11 **Agulhas Bank** *undersea feature* SW Indian Ocean
180 K11 **Agulhas Basin** *undersea feature* SW Indian Ocean
85 F26 **Agulhas, Cape** *Afr.* Kaap Agulhas. *headland* SW South Africa
Agulhas, Kaap *see* Agulhas, Cape
62 O9 **Agulhas Negras, Pico das** ▲ SE Brazil
180 K11 **Agulhas Plateau** *undersea feature* SW Indian Ocean
172 Oo14 **Aguni-jima** *island* Nansei-shotō, SW Japan
Agurain *see* Salvatierra
179 Rr15 **Agusan** ≈ Mindanao, S Philippines
56 G5 **Agustín Codazzi** *var.* Codazzi. Cesar, N Colombia
Agyrium *see* Agira
76 L12 **Ahaggar** *high plateau region* SE Algeria
Ahal Welayaty *see* Akhalskiy Velayat
148 K2 **Ahar** Āẕarbāyjān-e Khāvarī, NW Iran
Aharnes *see* Acharnés
144 J3 **Aḥaş, Jabal** ▲ NW Syria
144 J3 **Aḥaş, Jebal** ⛰ W Syria
193 G16 **Ahaura** ≈ South Island, NZ
102 E13 **Ahaus** Nordrhein-Westfalen, NW Germany
203 U9 **Ahe** *atoll* Îles Tuamotu, C French Polynesia
xliv I12 **Ahenny** Tipperary, S Ireland
192 N10 **Ahimanawa Range** ⛰ North Island, NZ
121 I19 **Ahinski Kanal** *Rus.* Oginskiy Kanal. *canal* SW Belorussia
195 N16 **Ahioma** SE PNG
192 I2 **Ahipara** Northland, North Island, NZ
192 I2 **Ahipara Bay** *bay* SE Tasman Sea
41 N13 **Ahklun Mountains** ⛰ Alaska, USA
143 R14 **Ahlat** Bitlis, E Turkey
103 F14 **Ahlen** Nordrhein-Westfalen, W Germany
160 D10 **Ahmadābād** *var.* Ahmedabad. Gujarāt, W India
149 R10 **Ahmadābād** Kermān, C Iran
Ahmadi *see* Al Aḥmadī
Ahmad Khel *see* Ḥasan Khēl
161 F14 **Ahmadnagar** *var.* Ahmednagar. Mahārāshtra, W India
155 T9 **Ahmadpur Siāl** Punjab, E Pakistan
79 N5 **Aḥmar, 'Erg el** *desert* N Mali
82 K13 **Ahmar Mountains** ⛰ C Ethiopia
Ahmedabad *see* Ahmadābād
Ahmednagar *see* Ahmadnagar
116 N12 **Ahmetbey** Kırklareli, NW Turkey
12 H12 **Ahmic Lake** ◎ Ontario, S Canada
202 G12 **Ahoa** Île Uvea, E Wallis and Futuna
xliv K3 **Ahoghill** Ballymena, NE Northern Ireland, UK
42 G8 **Ahomé** Sinaloa, C Mexico
23 X8 **Ahoskie** North Carolina, SE USA
103 D17 **Ahr** ≈ W Germany
149 N12 **Ahram** *var.* Ahrom. Būshehr, S Iran
102 J9 **Ahrensburg** Schleswig-Holstein, N Germany
Ahrom *see* Ahram
95 L17 **Ähtäri** Vaasa, W Finland
42 K12 **Ahuacatlán** Nayarit, C Mexico
44 E7 **Ahuachapán** Ahuachapán, W El Salvador
44 A9 **Ahuachapán** ◈ *department* W El Salvador
203 V16 **Ahu Akivi** *var.* Siete Moai. *ancient monument* Easter Island, Chile, E Pacific Ocean
203 W11 **Ahunui** *atoll* Îles Tuamotu, C French Polynesia
193 E20 **Ahuriri** ≈ South Island, NZ
97 L22 **Åhus** Kristianstad, S Sweden
Ahu Tahira *see* Ahu Vinapu
203 V16 **Ahu Tepeu** *ancient monument* Easter Island, Chile, E Pacific Ocean
203 V17 **Ahu Vinapu** *var.* Ahu Tahira. *ancient monument* Easter Island, Chile, E Pacific Ocean
148 L9 **Ahvāz** *var.* Ahwāz; *prev.* Nāsiri. Khūzestān, SW Iran
Ahvenanmaa *see* Åland
147 Q16 **Aḥwar** SW Yemen
Ahwāz *see* Ahvāz
Aibak *see* Āybak
103 K22 **Aichach** Bayern, SE Germany
171 I16 **Aichi** *off.* Aichi-ken, *var.* Aiti. ◈ *prefecture* Honshū, SW Japan
Aïdin *see* Aydın
176 Ww12 **Aiduna** Irian Jaya, E Indonesia
Aidussina *see* Ajdovščina
194 F13 **Aiema** ≈ W PNG
Aifir, Clochán an *see* Giant's Causeway
Aigaíon Pélagos/Aigaío Pélagos *see* Aegean Sea
111 S3 **Aigen im Mülkreis** Oberösterreich, N Austria
117 G20 **Aígina** *var.* Aíyina, Egina. Aígina, C Greece
117 G20 **Aígina** *island* S Greece
117 E18 **Aígio** *var.* Egio; *prev.* Aíyion. Dytikí Ellás, S Greece
110 C10 **Aigle** Vaud, SW Switzerland
105 P14 **Aigoual, Mont** ▲ S France
181 O16 **Aigrettes, Pointe des** *headland* W Réunion
63 G19 **Aiguá** *var.* Aigua. Maldonado, S Uruguay
105 S13 **Aigues** ≈ SE France
105 N10 **Aigurande** Indre, C France
Ai-hun *see* Heihe
171 K11 **Aikawa** Niigata, Sado, C Japan
23 Q13 **Aiken** South Carolina, SE USA
27 N4 **Aiken** Texas, SW USA
166 F13 **Ailao Shan** ⛰ SW China
45 W14 **Ailigandí** San Blas, NE Panama
201 R4 **Ailinginae Atoll** *var.* Aelōninae. *atoll* Ralik Chain, SW Marshall Islands
201 T7 **Ailinglaplap Atoll** *var.* Aelōnlaplap. *atoll* Ralik Chain, S Marshall Islands
Aillionn, Loch *see* Allen, Lough
xliii G23 **Ailsa Craig** *island* SW Scotland, UK
201 V5 **Ailuk Atoll** *var.* Aelok. *atoll* Ratak Chain, NE Marshall Islands
126 Mm12 **Aim** Khabarovskiy Kray, E Russian Federation
105 R11 **Ain** ◈ *department* E France
105 S10 **Ain** ≈ E France
Aïn Aïssa *see* Ayn 'Īsá
120 G7 **Ainaži** *Est.* Heinaste, *Ger.* Hainasch. Limbaži, N Latvia
76 L6 **Aïn Beida** NE Algeria
78 K4 **'Aïn Ben Tili** Tiris Zemmour, N Mauritania
76 J5 **Aïn Defla** *var.* Aïn Eddefla. N Algeria
Aïn Eddefla *see* Aïn Defla
76 L5 **Ain El Bey** ✈ (Constantine) NE Algeria
Ain Īsa *see* Ayn 'Īsá
117 C19 **Aínos** ▲ Kefallinía, Iónioi Nísoi, Greece, C Mediterranean Sea
107 T4 **Ainsa** Aragón, NE Spain
xl M15 **Ainsdale** Sefton, NW England, UK
76 I7 **Aïn Sefra** NW Algeria
31 N13 **Ainsworth** Nebraska, C USA
Aintab *see* Gaziantep
76 H5 **Aïn Témouchent** N Algeria
194 H11 **Aiome** Madang, N PNG
Aïoun el Atrous/Aïoun el Atroûss *see* 'Ayoûn el 'Atroûs
56 E11 **Aipe** Huila, C Colombia
58 D9 **Aipena, Río** ≈ N Peru
59 L19 **Aiquile** Cochabamba, C Bolivia
Aïr *see* Aïr, Massif de l'
196 E10 **Airai** Babeldaob, C Palau
196 E10 **Airai** ✈ (Oreor) Babeldaob, N Palau
173 Ff8 **Airbangis** Sumatera, NW Indonesia
xliii F19 **Aird** Argyll and Bute, W Scotland, UK
xliii K20 **Airdrie** North Lanarkshire, S Scotland, UK
9 Q16 **Airdrie** Alberta, SW Canada
Air du Azbine *see* Aïr, Massif de l'
xli T14 **Aire** ≈ N England, UK
104 K15 **Aire-sur-l'Adour** Landes, SW France
105 O1 **Aire-sur-la-Lys** Pas-de-Calais, N France
16 N2 **Air Force Island** *island* Baffin Island, Northwest Territories, NE Canada
174 L11 **Airhitam, Teluk** *bay* Borneo, C Indonesia
175 Rr7 **Airmadidi** Sulawesi, N Indonesia
79 V8 **Aïr, Massif de l'** *var.* Aïr, Air du Azbine, Asben. ⛰ NC Niger
xli U14 **Airmyn** North Yorkshire, N England, UK
110 G10 **Airolo** Ticino, S Switzerland
xliii K19 **Airth** Falkirk, C Scotland, UK
xli P12 **Airton** North Yorkshire, N England, UK
104 K9 **Airvault** Deux-Sèvres, W France
103 K19 **Aisch** ≈ S Germany
65 G20 **Aisén** *off.* Región Aisén del General Carlos Ibañez del Campo, *var.* Aysen. ◈ *region* S Chile
8 H7 **Aishihik Lake** ◎ Yukon Territory, W Canada
105 P3 **Aisne** ◈ *department* N France
105 R4 **Aisne** ≈ NE France
111 T4 **Aist** ≈ N Austria
116 K13 **Aisými** Anatolikí Makedonía kai Thráki, NE Greece
107 S11 **Aitana** ▲ E Spain
194 F9 **Aitape** *var.* Eitape. Sandaun, NW PNG
xlii I3 **Aith** Orkney Islands, N Scotland, UK
xlii N3 **Aith** Shetland Islands, NE Scotland, UK
Aiti *see* Aichi
31 V6 **Aitkin** Minnesota, N USA
xlii K12 **Aitnoch** Moray, N Scotland, UK
117 D18 **Aitolikó** *var.* Etoliko; *prev.* Aitolikón. Dytikí Ellás, C Greece
Aitolikón *see* Aitolikó
202 L15 **Aitutaki** *island* S Cook Islands
118 H11 **Aiud** *Ger.* Strassburg, *Hung.* Nagyenyed; *prev.* Engeten. Alba, SW Romania
120 I9 **Aiviekste** ≈ C Latvia
201 Q8 **Aiwo** SW Nauru
196 E8 **Aiwokako Passage** *passage* Babeldaob, N Palau
Aix *see* Aix-en-Provence
105 S15 **Aix-en-Provence** *var.* Aix; *anc.* Aquae Sextiae. Bouches-du-Rhône, SE France
Aix-la-Chapelle *see* Aachen
105 T11 **Aix-les-Bains** Savoie, E France
194 E11 **Aiyang, Mount** ▲ NW PNG
Aíyina *see* Aígina
Aíyion *see* Aígio
159 W15 **Āīzawl** Mizoram, NE India
120 H9 **Aizkraukle** Aizkraukle, S Latvia
120 C9 **Aizpute** Liepāja, W Latvia
171 L14 **Aizu-Wakamatsu** *var.* Aizuwakamatu. Fukushima, Honshū, C Japan
Aizuwakamatu *see* Aizu-Wakamatsu
104 E2 **Ajaccio** Corse, France, C Mediterranean Sea
104 E2 **Ajaccio, Golfe d'** *gulf* Corse, France, C Mediterranean Sea
43 Q15 **Ajalpán** Puebla, S Mexico
160 F13 **Ajanta Range** ⛰ C India
143 R10 **Ajaria** ◈ *autonomous republic* SW Georgia
Ajastan *see* Armenia
95 G14 **Ajaureforsen** Västerbotten, N Sweden
193 H17 **Ajax, Mount** ▲ South Island, NZ
168 F9 **Aj Bogd Uul** ▲ SW Mongolia
77 R8 **Ajdābiyā** *var.* Agedabia, Ajdābiyah. NE Libya
Ajdābiyah *see* Ajdābiyā
111 S12 **Ajdovščina** *Ger.* Haidenschaft, *It.* Aidussina. W Slovenia
171 Mm8 **Ajigasawa** Aomori, Honshū, C Japan
Ajjinena *see* El Geneina
113 H23 **Ajka** Veszprém, W Hungary
144 G9 **'Ajlūn** Irbid, N Jordan
144 H9 **'Ajlūn, Jabal** ⛰ W Jordan
149 R15 **'Ajmān** *var.* Ajman, 'Ujmān. 'Ajmān, NE UAE
158 G12 **Ajmer** *var.* Ajmere. Rājasthān, N India
38 J15 **Ajo** Arizona, SW USA
107 N2 **Ajo, Cabo de** *headland* N Spain
38 J16 **Ajo Range** ⛰ Arizona, SW USA
Ajyguyy *see* Adzhikui
Akaba *see* Al 'Aqabah
172 P5 **Akabira** Hokkaidō, NE Japan

◆ Country
● Country Capital
◇ Dependent Territory
○ Dependent Territory Capital
◈ Administrative Region
✈ International Airport
▲ Mountain
⛰ Mountain Range
⋀ Volcano
≈ River
◎ Lake
⊡ Reservoir

AKADOMARI – AL ḤAMŪDĪYAH

171 K12 **Akadomari** Niigata, Sado, C Japan
83 E20 **Akagera** *var.* Kagera. ≈ Rwanda/Tanzania *see also* Kagera
203 W16 **Akahanga, Punta** *headland* Easter Island, Chile, E Pacific Ocean
171 Ii16 **Akaishi-dake** ▲ Honshū, S Japan
171 J16 **Akaishi-sanmyaku** ▲▲ Honshū, S Japan
82 J13 **Āk'ak'i** C Ethiopia
161 G15 **Akalkot** Mahārāshtra, W India
Akamagaseki *see* Shimonoseki
172 Q7 **Akan** Hokkaidō, NE Japan
172 Q6 **Akan-ko** ◎ Hokkaidō, NE Japan
Akanthoú *see* Tatlısu
193 I19 **Akaroa** Canterbury, South Island, NZ
82 E6 **Akasha** Northern, N Sudan
170 G14 **Akashi** *var.* Akasi. Hyōgo, Honshū, SW Japan
145 N7 **'Akāsh, Wādī** *var.* Wādī 'Ukash. *dry watercourse* W Iraq
Akasi *see* Akashi
94 K11 **Äkäsjokisuu** Lappi, N Finland
143 S11 **Akbaba Dağı** ▲ Armenia/Turkey
142 B15 **Akbük Limanı** *bay* W Turkey
131 V8 **Akbulak** Orenburgskaya Oblast', W Russian Federation
143 O11 **Akçaabat** Trabzon, NE Turkey
143 N15 **Akçadağ** Malatya, C Turkey
142 G11 **Akçakoca** Bolu, NW Turkey
Akchakaya, Vpadina *see* Akdzhakaya, Vpadina
78 H7 **Akchâr** *desert* W Mauritania
151 S12 **Akchatau** *Kaz.* Aqshataū. Zhezkazgan, C Kazakhstan
142 L13 **Akdağlar** ▲▲ C Turkey
142 E17 **Ak Dağları** ▲▲ SW Turkey
142 K13 **Akdağmadeni** Yozgat, C Turkey
Akdar, Jebel *see* Akhḑar al Jabal
152 G8 **Akdepe** *prev.* Ak-Tepe, Leninsk, *Turkm.* Lenin. Dashkhovuzskiy Velayat, N Turkmenistan
Ak-Dere *see* Byala
124 O3 **Akdoğan** *Gk.* Lýsi. C Cyprus
126 Hh16 **Ak-Dovurak** Respublika Tyva, S Russian Federation
152 F9 **Akdzhakaya, Vpadina** *var.* Vpadina Akchakaya. *depression* N Turkmenistan
175 Tt7 **Akelamo** Pulau Halmahera, E Indonesia
xli P2 **Akeld** Northumberland, N England, UK
xxxvii Q6 **Akeley** Buckinghamshire, C England, UK
Aken *see* Aachen
Akermanceaster *see* Bath
97 P15 **Åkersberga** Stockholm, C Sweden
97 H15 **Akershus** ◈ *county* S Norway
81 L16 **Aketi** Haut-Zaïre, N Zaire
Akgyr Erezi *see* Gryada Akkyr
152 E12 **Akhalskiy Velayat** *Turkm.* Ahal Welayaty. ◈ *province* C Turkmenistan
143 S10 **Akhalts'ikhe** SW Georgia
Akhangaran *see* Ohangaron
Akharnaí *see* Acharnés
77 R7 **Akhḑar, Al Jabal al** *hill range* NE Libya
Akhelóös *see* Achelóos
41 Q15 **Akhiok** Kodiak Island, Alaska, USA
142 C13 **Akhisar** Manisa, W Turkey
77 X10 **Akhmîm** *anc.* Panopolis. C Egypt
158 H6 **Akhnūr** Jammu and Kashmir, NW India
131 P11 **Akhtuba** ≈ SW Russian Federation
131 P11 **Akhtubinsk** Astrakhanskaya Oblast', SW Russian Federation
Akhtyrka *see* Okhtyrka
170 F15 **Aki** Kōchi, Shikoku, SW Japan
41 N12 **Akiachak** Alaska, USA
41 N12 **Akiak** Alaska, USA
203 X11 **Akiaki** *atoll* Îles Tuamotu, E French Polynesia
10 H9 **Akimiski Island** *island* Northwest Territories, C Canada
142 K17 **Akıncı Burnu** *headland* S Turkey
Akıncılar *see* Selçuk
119 U10 **Akinovka** Zaporiz'ka Oblast', S Ukraine
97 M24 **Åkirkeby** *var.* Aakirkeby. Bornholm, E Denmark
171 M10 **Akita** Akita, Honshū, C Japan
171 M10 **Akita** *off.* Akita-ken. ◈ *prefecture* Honshū, C Japan
78 H8 **Akjoujt** *prev.* Fort-Repoux. Inchiri, W Mauritania
94 H11 **Akkajaure** ◎ N Sweden
Akkala *see* Oqqal'a
161 L25 **Akkaraipattu** Eastern Province, E Sri Lanka
94 H11 **Akkavare** ▲ N Sweden
151 P13 **Akkense** Zhezkazgan, C Kazakhstan
Akkerman *see* Bilhorod-Dnistrovs'kyy
131 W8 **Akkermanovka** Orenburgskaya Oblast', W Russian Federation
172 Qq7 **Akkeshi** Hokkaidō, NE Japan
172 Qq7 **Akkeshi-ko** ◎ Hokkaidō, NE Japan
172 Qq8 **Akkeshi-wan** *bay* NW Pacific Ocean
144 F8 **'Akko** *Eng.* Acre, *Fr.* Saint-Jean-d'Acre; *Bibl.* Accho, Ptolemaïs. Northern, N Israel
151 T14 **Akkol'** *Kaz.* Aqköl. Almaty, SE Kazakhstan
151 Q16 **Akkol'** *Kaz.* Aqköl. Zhambyl, S Kazakhstan
150 M11 **Akkol', Ozero** *prev.* Ozero Zhaman-Akkol'. ◎ C Kazakhstan
100 L6 **Akkrum** Friesland, N Netherlands
150 F12 **Akkystau** *Kaz.* Aqqystaū. Atyrau, SW Kazakhstan
14 Ff3 **Aklavik** Northwest Territories, NW Canada
120 B9 **Akmenrags** *headland* W Latvia
164 E9 **Akmeqit** Xinjiang Uygur Zizhiqu, NW China
152 J14 **Akmeydan** Maryyskiy Velayat, C Turkmenistan
151 Q9 **Akmola** *Kaz.* Aqmola; *prev.* Akmolinsk, Tselinograd. ● (Kazakhstan) Akmola, N Kazakhstan
151 P9 **Akmola** *off.* Akmolinskaya Oblast', *Kaz.* Aqmola Oblysy; *prev.* Tselinogradskaya Oblast. ◈ *province* C Kazakhstan
Akmolinsk/Akmolinskaya Oblast' *see* Akmola
Aknavásár *see* Târgu Ocna
120 I11 **Aknīste** Jēkabpils, S Latvia
170 G14 **Akō** Hyōgo, Honshū, SW Japan
83 G14 **Akobo** Jonglei, SE Sudan
83 G14 **Akobo** *var.* Ākobowenz. ≈ Ethiopia/Sudan
Ākobowenz *see* Akobo
160 H12 **Akola** Mahārāshtra, C India
Akordat *see* Akurdet
79 Q16 **Akosombo Dam** *dam* SE Ghana
160 H12 **Akot** Mahārāshtra, C India
79 N16 **Akoupé** SE Ivory Coast
10 M3 **Akpatok Island** *island* Northwest Territories, E Canada
164 G7 **Akqi** Xinjiang Uygur Zizhiqu, NW China
144 I2 **Akrād, Jabal al** ▲▲ N Syria
Akragas *see* Agrigento
94 H3 **Akranes** Vesturland, W Iceland
145 S2 **Ākrē** *Ar.* 'Aqrah. N Iraq
97 C16 **Åkrehamn** Rogaland, S Norway
79 V9 **Akrérèb** Agadez, C Niger
117 D22 **Akrítas, Ákra** *headland* S Greece
39 V3 **Akron** Colorado, C USA
31 R12 **Akron** Iowa, C USA
33 U12 **Akron** Ohio, N USA
Akrotiri *see* Akrotírion
Akrotiri Bay *see* Akrotírion, Kólpos
124 N4 **Akrotírion** *var.* Akrotiri. *UK air base* S Cyprus
124 Nn4 **Akrotírion, Kólpos** *var.* Akrotiri Bay. *bay* S Cyprus
123 Mm4 **Akrotiri Sovereign Base Area** *UK military installation* S Cyprus
164 F11 **Aksai Chin** *Chin.* Aksayqin. *disputed region* China/India
Aksaj *see* Aksay
142 I15 **Aksaray** Aksaray, C Turkey
142 I15 **Aksaray** ◈ *province* C Turkey
165 P8 **Aksay** *var.* Aksay Kazakzu Zizhixian. Gansu, N China
150 G8 **Aksay** *var.* Aksaj, *Kaz.* Aqsay. Zapadnyy Kazakhstan, NW Kazakhstan
131 O11 **Aksay** Volgogradskaya Oblast', SW Russian Federation
153 W10 **Aksay** *var.* Toxkan He. ≈ China/Kyrgyzstan
Aksay Kazakzu Zizhixian *see* Aksay
Aksayqin *see* Aksai Chin
164 G11 **Aksayqin Hu** ◎ NW China
142 G14 **Akşehir** Konya, W Turkey
142 G14 **Akşehir Gölü** ◎ C Turkey
142 G16 **Akseki** Antalya, SW Turkey
126 L15 **Aksenovo-Zilovskoye** Chitinskaya Oblast', S Russian Federation
126 Kk16 **Aksha** Chitinskaya Oblast', S Russian Federation
151 V11 **Akshatau, Khrebet** ▲▲ E Kazakhstan
153 Y8 **Ak-Shyyrak** Issyk-Kul'skaya Oblast', E Kyrgyzstan
Akstafa *see* Ağstafa
164 H7 **Aksu** Xinjiang Uygur Zizhiqu, NW China
151 R8 **Aksu** *Kaz.* Aqsū. Akmola, N Kazakhstan
151 T8 **Aksu** *var.* Jermak, *Kaz.* Ermak; *prev.* Yermak. Pavlodar, NE Kazakhstan
151 W13 **Aksu** *Kaz.* Aqsū. Taldykorgan, SE Kazakhstan
151 V13 **Aksu** *Kaz.* Aqsū. ≈ SE Kazakhstan
151 X11 **Aksuat** *Kaz.* Aqsūat. Semipalatinsk, E Kazakhstan
151 Y11 **Aksuat** *Kaz.* Aqsūat. Vostochnyy Kazakhstan, SE Kazakhstan
131 S4 **Aksubayevo** Respublika Tatarstan, W Russian Federation
164 H7 **Aksu He** *Rus.* Sary-Dzhaz. ≈ China/Kyrgyzstan *see also* Sary-Dzhaz
82 J10 **Āksum** N Ethiopia
151 O12 **Aktas** *Kaz.* Aqtas. Zhezkazgan, C Kazakhstan
Aktash *see* Oqtosh
153 V9 **Ak-Tash, Gora** ▲ C Kyrgyzstan
151 R10 **Aktau** *Kaz.* Aqtaū. Karaganda, C Kazakhstan
150 E11 **Aktau** *Kaz.* Aqtaū; *prev.* Shevchenko. Mangistau, W Kazakhstan
Aktau, Khrebet *see* Oqtogh, SW Tajikistan
Aktau, Khrebet *see* Oqtow Tizmasi, C Uzbekistan
Akte *see* Ágion Óros
Ak-Tepe *see* Akdepe
153 X7 **Ak-Terek** Issyk-Kul'skaya Oblast', E Kyrgyzstan
Aktí *see* Ágion Óros
164 E8 **Akto** Xinjiang Uygur Zizhiqu, NW China
151 V12 **Aktogay** *Kaz.* Aqtoghay. Semipalatinsk, E Kazakhstan
151 T12 **Aktogay** *Kaz.* Aqtoghay. Zhezkazgan, C Kazakhstan
121 M18 **Aktsyabrski** *Rus.* Oktyabr'skiy; *prev.* Karpilovka. Homyel'skaya Voblasts', SE Belorussia
150 I10 **Aktyubinsk** *Kaz.* Aqtöbe. Aktyubinsk, NW Kazakhstan
150 H11 **Aktyubinsk** *off.* Aktyubinskaya Oblast', *Kaz.* Aqtöbe Oblysy. ◈ *province* W Kazakhstan
153 W7 **Ak-Tyuz** *var.* Aktyuz. Chuyskaya Oblast', N Kyrgyzstan
81 J17 **Akula** Equateur, NW Zaire
170 Bb15 **Akune** Kagoshima, Kyūshū, SW Japan
40 L16 **Akun Island** *island* Aleutian Islands, Alaska, USA
82 J9 **Akurdet** *var.* Agordat, Akordat. C Eritrea
79 T16 **Akure** Ondo, SW Nigeria
94 J2 **Akureyri** Nordhurland Eystra, N Iceland
40 L17 **Akutan** Akutan Island, Alaska, USA
40 K17 **Akutan Island** *island* Aleutian Islands, Alaska, USA
79 V17 **Akwa Ibom** ◈ *state* SE Nigeria
Akyab *see* Sittwe
131 W7 **Ak"yar** Respublika Bashkortostan, W Russian Federation
151 Y11 **Akzhar** *Kaz.* Aqzhar. Vostochnyy Kazakhstan, E Kazakhstan
96 F13 **Ål** Buskerud, S Norway
121 N18 **Ala** *Rus.* Ola. ≈ SE Belorussia
22 H11 **Alabama** *off.* State of Alabama; also known as Camellia State, Heart of Dixie, The Cotton State, Yellowhammer State. ◈ *state* S USA
25 P6 **Alabama River** ≈ Alabama, S USA
25 P4 **Alabaster** Alabama, S USA
145 U10 **Al 'Abd Allāh** *var.* Al Abdullah. S Iraq
Al Abdullah *see* Al 'Abd Allāh
145 W14 **Al Abṭīyah** *well* S Iraq
153 S9 **Ala-Buka** Dzhalal-Abadskaya Oblast', W Kyrgyzstan
194 K15 **Alabule** ≈ C PNG
142 J12 **Alaca** Çorum, N Turkey
142 K10 **Alaçam** Samsun, N Turkey
Alacant *see* Alicante
25 V9 **Alachua** Florida, SE USA
143 S13 **Aladağlar** ▲▲ W Turkey
142 K15 **Ala Dağları** ▲▲ C Turkey
131 O16 **Alagir** Respublika Severnaya Osetiya, SW Russian Federation
108 B6 **Alagna Valsesia** Valle d'Aosta, NW Italy
105 P12 **Alagnon** ≈ C France
61 P16 **Alagoas** *off.* Estado de Alagoas. ◈ *state* E Brazil
61 P17 **Alagoinhas** Bahia, E Brazil
107 R5 **Alagón** Aragón, NE Spain
106 J9 **Alagón** ≈ W Spain
95 K16 **Alahärmä** Vaasa, W Finland
al Ahdar *see* Al Akhḑar
148 K12 **Al Aḩmadī** *var.* Ahmadi. E Kuwait
Al Ain *see* Al 'Ayn
107 Z8 **Alaior** *prev.* Alayor. Menorca, Spain, W Mediterranean Sea
153 T11 **Alai Range** *Rus.* Alayskiy Khrebet. ▲▲ Kyrgyzstan/Tajikistan
Alais *see* Alès
147 X11 **Al 'Ajā'iz** E Oman
147 X11 **Al 'Ajā'iz** *oasis* SE Oman
95 L16 **Alajärvi** Vaasa, W Finland
120 K4 **Alajõe** Ida-Virumaa, NE Estonia
44 M13 **Alajuela** Alajuela, C Costa Rica
44 L12 **Alajuela** *off.* Provincia de Alajuela. ◈ *province* N Costa Rica
45 T14 **Alajuela, Lago** ◎ C Panama
40 M11 **Alakanuk** Alaska, USA
146 K5 **Al Akhḑar** *var.* al Ahdar. Tabūk, NW Saudi Arabia
Alaköl *see* Alakol', Ozero
151 X13 **Alakol', Ozero** *Kaz.* Alaköl. ◎ SE Kazakhstan
128 I5 **Alakurtti** Murmanskaya Oblast', NW Russian Federation
40 F10 **Alalakeiki Channel** *channel* Hawaii, USA, C Pacific Ocean
Al 'Alamayn *see* El 'Alamein
145 R1 **Al 'Amādīyah** N Iraq
196 K5 **Alamagan** *island* C Northern Mariana Islands
145 X10 **Al 'Amārah** *var.* Amara. E Iraq
82 J11 **Ālamat'ā** NE Ethiopia
39 R11 **Alameda** New Mexico, SW USA
124 Pp15 **'Alam el Rûm, Râs** *headland* N Egypt
Alamícamba *see* Alamikamba
44 M8 **Alamikamba** *var.* Alamícamba. Región Autónoma Atlántico Norte, NE Nicaragua
26 K11 **Alamito Creek** ≈ Texas, SW USA
42 M8 **Alamitos, Sierra de los** ▲ NE Mexico
37 X9 **Alamo** Nevada, W USA
22 F9 **Alamo** Tennessee, S USA
43 Q12 **Álamo** Veracruz-Llave, C Mexico
39 S14 **Alamogordo** New Mexico, SW USA
38 J12 **Alamo Lake** ⊠ Arizona, SW USA
42 H7 **Alamos** Sonora, NW Mexico
39 S7 **Alamosa** Colorado, C USA
95 J20 **Åland** *var.* Aland Islands, *Fin.* Ahvenanmaa. ◈ *province* SW Finland
95 J19 **Åland** *Fin.* Ahvenanmaa. *island* SW Finland
90 K9 **Åland** *var.* Aland Islands, *Fin.* Ahvenanmaa. *island group* SW Finland
Aland Islands *see* Åland
Aland Sea *see* Ålands Hav
97 Q14 **Ålands Hav** *var.* Aland Sea. *strait* Baltic Sea/Gulf of Bothnia
45 P16 **Alanje** Chiriquí, SW Panama
27 O2 **Alanreed** Texas, SW USA
142 G17 **Alanya** Antalya, S Turkey
25 U7 **Alapaha River** ≈ Florida/Georgia, SE USA
125 Ee11 **Alapayevsk** Sverdlovskaya Oblast', C Russian Federation
Alappuzha *see* Alleppey
144 F14 **Al 'Aqabah** *var.* Akaba, Aqaba, 'Aqaba; *anc.* Aelana, Elath. Ma'ān, SW Jordan
Al 'Arabīyah as Su'ūdīyah *see* Saudi Arabia
al Araïch *see* Larache
107 Q10 **Alarcón** Castilla-La Mancha, C Spain
107 Q9 **Alarcón, Embalse de** ⊠ C Spain
144 J2 **Al 'Arīmah** *Fr.* Arime. Ḩalab, N Syria
Al 'Arīsh *see* El 'Arîsh
147 R5 **Al Arṭāwīyah** SE Kuwait
147 P6 **Al Arṭāwīyah** Ar Riyāḑ, N Saudi Arabia
175 O16 **Alas** Sumbawa, S Indonesia
Alasca, Golfo de *see* Alaska, Gulf of
142 D14 **Alaşehir** Manisa, W Turkey
145 N5 **Al 'Ashārah** *var.* Ashara. Dayr az Zawr, E Syria
Al Ashkhara *see* Al Ashkharah
147 Z9 **Al Ashkharah** *var.* Al Ashkhara. NE Oman
41 P8 **Alaska** *off.* State of Alaska; also known as Land of the Midnight Sun, The Last Frontier, Seward's Folly; *prev.* Russian America. ◈ *state* NW USA
41 T13 **Alaska, Gulf of** *var.* Golfo de Alasca. *gulf* Canada/USA
41 O15 **Alaska Peninsula** *peninsula* Alaska, USA
41 Q11 **Alaska Range** ▲▲ Alaska, USA
173 Ee4 **Alas, Lae** ≈ Sumatera, NW Indonesia
Al-Asnam *see* Chlef
175 O16 **Alas, Selat** *strait* Nusa Tenggara, C Indonesia
108 B10 **Alassio** Liguria, NW Italy
Alat *see* Olot
143 Y12 **Älät** *Rus.* Alyat; *prev.* Alyaty-Pristan'. SE Azerbaijan
145 S13 **Al 'Athāmīn** S Iraq
41 P7 **Alatna River** ≈ Alaska, USA
109 J15 **Alatri** Lazio, C Italy
Alattio *see* Alta
131 P5 **Alatyr'** Chuvashskaya Respublika, W Russian Federation
58 C7 **Alausí** Chimborazo, C Ecuador
107 O3 **Álava** *Basq.* Araba. ◈ *province* País Vasco, N Spain
143 T11 **Alaverdi** N Armenia
Alavo *see* Alavus
95 N14 **Ala-Vuokki** Oulu, E Finland
95 K17 **Alavus** *Swe.* Alavo. Vaasa, W Finland
Al 'Awābī *see* Awābī
145 P6 **Al 'Awānī** W Iraq
77 U12 **Al Awaynāt** SE Libya
Al Awaynāt *see* Al 'Uwaynāt
xxxv E3 **Alaw, Llyn** *var.* Alaw Reservoir. ◎ NW Wales, UK
190 K9 **Alawoona** South Australia
Alaw Reservoir *see* Alaw, Llyn
Alaykel'/Alay-Kuu *see* Këk-Art
149 R17 **Al 'Ayn** *var.* Al Ain. Abū Ẓaby, E UAE
149 R17 **Al 'Ayn** *var.* Al Ain. ✕ Abū Ẓaby, E UAE
144 G12 **Al 'Aynā** Al Karak, W Jordan
Alayor *see* Alaior
Alayskiy Khrebet *see* Alai Range
127 N7 **Alazeya** ≈ NE Russian Federation
145 U8 **Al 'Azīzīyah** *var.* Aziziya. E Iraq
123 L14 **Al 'Azīzīyah** NW Libya
144 I10 **Al Azraq al Janūbī** Az Zarqā', N Jordan
108 B9 **Alba** *anc.* Alba Pompeia. Piemonte, NW Italy
27 V6 **Alba** Texas, SW USA
118 G11 **Alba** ◈ *county* W Romania
145 P3 **Al Ba'āj** N Iraq
144 J2 **Al Bāb** Ḩalab, N Syria
118 G10 **Albac** *Hung.* Fehérvölgy; *prev.* Álbák. Alba, SW Romania
107 Q11 **Albacete** Castilla-La Mancha, C Spain
107 P11 **Albacete** ◈ *province* Castilla-La Mancha, C Spain
146 I4 **Al Bad'** Tabūk, NW Saudi Arabia
106 L7 **Alba de Tormes** Castilla-León, N Spain
145 P3 **Al Bādī** N Iraq
147 V8 **Al Badī'ah** ✕ (Abū Ẓaby) Abū Ẓaby, C UAE
149 P17 **Al Badī'ah** *var.* Al Bedei'ah. *spring/well* C UAE
145 Q7 **Al Baghdādī** *var.* Khān al Baghdādī. SW Iraq
Al Bāha *see* Al Bāḩah
146 M11 **Al Bāḩah** *var.* Al Bāha. Al Bāḩah, SW Saudi Arabia
146 M11 **Al Bāḩah** *off.* Minṭaqat al Bāḩah. ◈ *province* W Saudi Arabia
Al Baḩrayn *see* Bahrain
107 S11 **Albaida** País Valenciano, E Spain
118 H11 **Alba Iulia** *Ger.* Weissenburg, *Hung.* Gyulafehérvár; *prev.* Bălgrad, Karlsburg, Károly-Fehérvár. Alba, W Romania
Álbák *see* Albac
144 G10 **Al Balqā'** *off.* Muḩāfaẓat al Balqā', *var.* Balqā'. ◈ *governorate* NW Jordan
12 F11 **Alban** Ontario, S Canada
105 O15 **Alban** Tarn, S France
10 K11 **Albanel, Lac** ◎ Québec, SE Canada
115 L20 **Albania** *off.* Republic of Albania, *Alb.* Republika e Shqipërisë, Shqipëria; *prev.* People's Socialist Republic of Albania. ◆ *republic* SE Europe
Albania *see* Aubagne
109 H15 **Albano Laziaie** Lazio, C Italy
188 J14 **Albany** Western Australia
25 S7 **Albany** Georgia, SE USA
33 P13 **Albany** Indiana, N USA
22 L8 **Albany** Kentucky, S USA
31 U7 **Albany** Minnesota, N USA
29 R2 **Albany** Missouri, C USA
20 L10 **Albany** *state capital* New York, NE USA
34 G12 **Albany** Oregon, NW USA
27 Q6 **Albany** Texas, SW USA
10 F10 **Albany** ≈ Ontario, S Canada
Alba Pompeia *see* Alba
Alba Regia *see* Székesfehérvár
144 J6 **Al Bāridah** *var.* Bāridah. Ḩimş, C Syria
145 Q11 **Al Barīt** S Iraq
107 R8 **Albarracín** Aragón, NE Spain
145 Y12 **Al Başrah** *Eng.* Basra; *hist.* Busra, Bussora. SE Iraq
145 V11 **Al Baṭḩā'** SE Iraq
147 X8 **Al Bāṭinah** *var.* Batinah. *coastal region* N Oman
1 H16 **Albatross Plateau** *undersea feature* E Pacific Ocean
Al Batrūn *see* Batroûn
124 Nn14 **Al Bayḑā'** *var.* Beida. NE Libya
147 P16 **Al Bayḑā'** *var.* Al Beida. SW Yemen
Al Bedei'ah *see* Al Badī'ah
Al Beida *see* Al Bayḑā'
23 S10 **Albemarle** *var.* Albermarle. North Carolina, SE USA
Albemarle Island *see* Isabela, Isla
23 N8 **Albemarle Sound** *inlet* W Atlantic Ocean
108 B10 **Albenga** Liguria, NW Italy
106 L8 **Alberche** ≈ C Spain
105 O17 **Albères, Chaîne des** *var.* les Albères, Montes Albères. ▲▲ France/Spain
Albères, Montes *see* Albères, Chaîne des
190 F2 **Alberga Creek** *seasonal river* South Australia
106 G7 **Albergaria-a-Velha** Aveiro, N Portugal
107 S10 **Alberic** País Valenciano, E Spain
Albermarle *see* Albemarle
109 P18 **Alberobello** Puglia, SE Italy
110 J7 **Alberschwende** Vorarlberg, W Austria
105 O3 **Albert** Somme, N France
9 O12 **Alberta** ◈ *province* SW Canada
194 K14 **Albert Edward, Mount** ▲ S PNG
Albert Edward Nyanza *see* Edward, Lake
63 C20 **Alberti** Buenos Aires, E Argentina
113 K23 **Albertirsa** Pest, C Hungary
101 I16 **Albertkanaal** *canal* N Belgium
81 P17 **Albert, Lake** *var.* Albert Nyanza, Lac Mobutu Sese Seko. ◎ Uganda/Zaire
31 V11 **Albert Lea** Minnesota, N USA
83 F16 **Albert Nile** ≈ NW Uganda
Albert Nyanza *see* Albert, Lake
105 T11 **Albertville** Savoie, E France
25 Q2 **Albertville** Alabama, S USA
Albertville *see* Kalemie
105 N15 **Albi** *anc.* Albiga. Tarn, S France
31 W15 **Albia** Iowa, C USA
Albiga *see* Albi
57 X9 **Albina** Marowijne, NE Surinam
85 A15 **Albina, Ponta** *headland* SW Angola
32 M16 **Albion** Illinois, N USA
33 P11 **Albion** Indiana, N USA
31 P14 **Albion** Nebraska, C USA
20 E9 **Albion** New York, NE USA
20 B12 **Albion** Pennsylvania, NE USA
Al Biqā' *see* El Beqaa
146 J4 **Al Bi'r** *var.* Bi'r Ibn Hirmās. Tabūk, NW Saudi Arabia
146 M12 **Al Birk** Makkah, SW Saudi Arabia
147 Q9 **Al Biyāḑ** *desert* C Saudi Arabia
100 H13 **Alblasserdam** Zuid-Holland, SW Netherlands
107 T8 **Albocácer** *var.* Albocasser. País Valenciano, E Spain
Albocasser *see* Albocácer
97 H19 **Ålbæk** Nordjylland, N Denmark
Albona *see* Labin
107 O17 **Alborán, Isla de** *island* S Spain
Alborán, Mar de *see* Alboran Sea
107 N17 **Alboran Sea** *Sp.* Mar de Alborán. *sea* SW Mediterranean Sea
97 G20 **Ålborg** *var.* Aalborg, Ålborg-Nørresundby; *anc.* Alburgum. Nordjylland, N Denmark
97 H21 **Ålborg Bugt** *var.* Aalborg Bugt. *bay* N Denmark
Ålborg-Nørresundby *see* Ålborg
149 O5 **Alborz, Reshteh-ye Kūhhā-ye** *Eng.* Elburz Mountains. ▲▲ N Iran
107 Q14 **Albox** Andalucía, S Spain
xxxviii A13 **Albrighton** Shropshire, W England, UK
103 H23 **Albstadt** Baden-Württemberg, SW Germany
106 G14 **Albufeira** Beja, S Portugal
145 P5 **Ālbū Gharz, Sabkhat** ◎ W Iraq
107 O15 **Albuñol** Andalucía, S Spain
39 Q11 **Albuquerque** New Mexico, SW USA
147 W8 **Al Buraymī** *var.* Buraimi. N Oman
149 R17 **Al Buraymī** *var.* Buraimi. *spring/well* Oman/UAE
Al Burayqah *see* Marsá al Burayqah
Alburgum *see* Ålborg
106 I10 **Alburquerque** Extremadura, W Spain
189 V14 **Albury** New South Wales, SE Australia
191 P11 **Albury-Wodonga** New South Wales/Victoria, SE Australia
147 T14 **Al Buzūn** SE Yemen
95 G17 **Alby** Västernorrland, C Sweden
98 **Albyn, Glen** *see* Mor, Glen
106 G12 **Alcácer do Sal** Setúbal, W Portugal
Alcalá de Chisvert *see* Alcalá de Chivert
107 T8 **Alcalá de Chivert** *var.* Alcalá de Chisvert. País Valenciano, E Spain
106 K14 **Alcalá de Guadaira** Andalucía, S Spain
107 O8 **Alcalá de Henares** *Ar.* Alkal'a; *anc.* Complutum. Madrid, C Spain
106 K16 **Alcalá de los Gazules** Andalucía, S Spain
107 N14 **Alcalá La Real** Andalucía, S Spain
109 I23 **Alcamo** Sicilia, Italy, C Mediterranean Sea
107 T4 **Alcanadre** ≈ NE Spain
107 T8 **Alcanar** Cataluña, NE Spain
106 J5 **Alcañices** Castilla-León, N Spain
107 T7 **Alcañiz** Aragón, NE Spain
106 I9 **Alcántara** Extremadura, W Spain
106 J9 **Alcántara, Embalse de** ⊠ W Spain
107 R13 **Alcantarilla** Murcia, SE Spain
107 P11 **Alcaraz** Castilla-La Mancha, C Spain
107 P12 **Alcaraz, Sierra de** ▲▲ C Spain
106 I12 **Alcarrache** ≈ SW Spain
107 T6 **Alcarràs** Cataluña, NE Spain
107 N14 **Alcaudete** Andalucía, S Spain
Alcázar *see* Ksar-el-Kebir
107 O10 **Alcázar de San Juan** *anc.* Alce. Castilla-La Mancha, C Spain
Alcazarquivir *see* Ksar-el-Kebir
Alce *see* Alcázar de San Juan
59 B17 **Alcebo, Volcán** ⩘ Galapagos Islands, Ecuador, E Pacific Ocean
xxxviii K12 **Alcester** Warwickshire, C England, UK
145 X12 **Al Chabā'ish** *var.* Al Kaba'ish. SE Iraq
119 Y7 **Alchevs'k** *prev.* Kommunarsk, Voroshilovsk. Luhans'ka Oblast', E Ukraine
Alcira *see* Alzira
23 N9 **Alcoa** Tennessee, S USA
106 F9 **Alcobaça** Leiria, C Portugal
107 N8 **Alcobendas** Madrid, C Spain
Alcoi *see* Alcoy
107 P7 **Alcolea del Pinar** Castilla-La Mancha, C Spain
xxxix R11 **Alconbury** Cambridgeshire, E England, UK
106 I11 **Alconchel** Extremadura, W Spain
107 S9 **Alcora** País Valenciano, E Spain
107 N8 **Alcorcón** Madrid, C Spain
107 S7 **Alcorisa** Aragón, NE Spain
63 B19 **Alcorta** Santa Fe, C Argentina
106 H14 **Alcoutim** Faro, S Portugal
35 W15 **Alcova** Wyoming, C USA
107 S11 **Alcoy** *var.* Alcoi. País Valenciano, E Spain
107 Y9 **Alcúdia, Badia d'** *bay* Mallorca, Spain, W Mediterranean Sea
180 M7 **Aldabra Group** *island group* SW Seychelles
145 U10 **Al Daghghārah** C Iraq
42 J5 **Aldama** Chihuahua, N Mexico
43 P11 **Aldama** Tamaulipas, C Mexico
126 Ll12 **Aldan** Respublika Sakha (Yakutiya), NE Russian Federation
126 Mm12 **Aldan** ≈ NE Russian Federation
168 G7 **Aldar** Dzavhan, W Mongolia
al Dar al Baida *see* Rabat
xxxvii O9 **Aldbourne** Wiltshire, S England, UK
xli X13 **Aldbrough** East Riding of Yorkshire, N England, UK
xxxix X12 **Alde** ≈ E England, UK
xxxix Y12 **Aldeburgh** Suffolk, E England, UK
107 P5 **Aldehuela de Calatañazor** Castilla-León, N Spain
Aldeia Nova *see* Aldeia Nova de São Bento
106 H13 **Aldeia Nova de São Bento** *var.* Aldeia Nova. Beja, S Portugal
31 V11 **Alden** Minnesota, N USA
xxxvii O12 **Alderbury** Wiltshire, S England, UK
xl G17 **Alderley Edge** Cheshire, W England, UK
xxxvii Q10 **Aldermaston** Newbury, S England, UK
192 N6 **Aldermen Islands, The** *island group* N NZ
xxxvii W14 **Alderney** *island* Channel Islands
xxxvii R11 **Aldershot** Hampshire, S England, UK
23 R6 **Alderson** West Virginia, NE USA
xxxviii G6 **Aldford** Cheshire, W England, UK
Al Dhaid *see* Adh Dhayd
xl L12 **Aldingham** Cumbria, NW England, UK
xxxviii C14 **Aldridge** Walsall, C England, UK
xxxvii O8 **Aldsworth** Gloucestershire, C England, UK
xli T15 **Aldwick le Street** Doncaster, N England, UK
32 J11 **Aledo** Illinois, N USA
78 H9 **Aleg** Brakna, SW Mauritania
66 Q10 **Alegranza** *island* Islas Canarias, Spain, NE Atlantic Ocean
39 P12 **Alegres Mountain** ▲ New Mexico, SW USA
63 F15 **Alegrete** Rio Grande do Sul, S Brazil
63 C16 **Alejandra** Santa Fe, C Argentina
200 Oo12 **Alejandro Selkirk, Isla** *island* Islas Juan Fernández, Chile, E Pacific Ocean
128 I12 **Alekhovshchina** Leningradskaya Oblast', NW Russian Federation
41 O13 **Aleknagik** Alaska, USA
Aleksandriya *see* Oleksandriya
Aleksandropol' *see* Gyumri
130 L3 **Aleksandrov** Vladimirskaya Oblast', W Russian Federation
115 N14 **Aleksandrovac** Serbia, C Yugoslavia
131 R9 **Aleksandrov Gay** Saratovskaya Oblast', W Russian Federation
131 U6 **Aleksandrovka** Orenburgskaya Oblast', W Russian Federation
Aleksandrovka *see* Oleksandrivka
116 J8 **Aleksandrovo** Loveshka Oblast, N Bulgaria
129 V13 **Aleksandrovsk** Permskaya Oblast', NW Russian Federation
Aleksandrovsk *see* Zaporizhzhya
131 N14 **Aleksandrovskoye** Stavropol'skiy Kray, SW Russian Federation
127 O14 **Aleksandrovsk-Sakhalinskiy** Ostrov Sakhalin, Sakhalinskaya Oblast', SE Russian Federation
112 J10 **Aleksandrów Kujawski** Włocławek, C Poland
112 K12 **Aleksandrów Łódzki** Łódź, C Poland
Alekseevka *see* Alekseyevka
151 Q8 **Alekseyevka** *Kaz.* Alekseevka. Akmola, C Kazakhstan
151 P7 **Alekseyevka** *Kaz.* Alekseevka. Kokshetau, N Kazakhstan
151 Z10 **Alekseyevka** *Kaz.* Alekseevka. Vostochnyy Kazakhstan, E Kazakhstan
131 S7 **Alekseyevka** Samarskaya Oblast', W Russian Federation
126 Jj13 **Alekseyevsk** Irkutskaya Oblast', C Russian Federation
131 R4 **Alekseyevskoye** Respublika Tatarstan, W Russian Federation
130 K5 **Aleksin** Tul'skaya Oblast', W Russian Federation
115 O14 **Aleksinac** Serbia, SE Yugoslavia
202 G11 **Alele** Île Uvea, E Wallis and Futuna
97 N20 **Ålem** Kalmar, S Sweden
104 L6 **Alençon** Orne, N France
60 I12 **Alenquer** Pará, NE Brazil
40 G10 **Alenuihaha Channel** *channel* Hawaii, USA, C Pacific Ocean
Alep/Aleppo *see* Ḩalab
104 F2 **Aléria** Corse, France, C Mediterranean Sea
207 Q11 **Alert** Ellesmere Island, Northwest Territories, N Canada
105 Q14 **Alès** *prev.* Alais. Gard, S France
118 G9 **Aleşd** *Hung.* Élesd. Bihor, SW Romania
108 C9 **Alessandria** *Fr.* Alexandrie. Piemonte, N Italy
97 G21 **Ålestrup** *var.* Aalestrup. Viborg, NW Denmark
96 D9 **Ålesund** Møre og Romsdal, S Norway
110 E10 **Aletschhorn** ▲ SW Switzerland
207 S1 **Aleutian Basin** *undersea feature* Bering Sea
40 H17 **Aleutian Islands** *island group* Alaska, USA
41 P14 **Aleutian Range** ▲▲ Alaska, USA
1 B5 **Aleutian Trench** *undersea feature* S Bering Sea
127 O10 **Alevina, Mys** *headland* E Russian Federation
13 Q6 **Alex** ≈ Québec, SE Canada
30 J3 **Alexander** North Dakota, N USA
41 W14 **Alexander Archipelago** *island group* Alaska, USA
Alexanderbaai *see* Alexander Bay
85 D23 **Alexander Bay** *Afr.* Alexanderbaai. Northern Cape, W South Africa
25 Q5 **Alexander City** Alabama, S USA
204 J6 **Alexander Island** *island* Antarctica
Alexander Range *see* Kirghiz Range
191 O12 **Alexandra** Victoria, SE Australia
193 D22 **Alexandra** Otago, South Island, NZ
117 F14 **Alexándreia** *var.* Alexándria. Kentrikí Makedonía, N Greece
Alexandretta *see* İskenderun
Alexandretta, Gulf of *see* İskenderun Körfezi
xliii H19 **Alexandria** West Dunbartonshire, W Scotland, UK
13 N13 **Alexandria** Ontario, SE Canada
124 Q15 **Alexandria** *Ar.* Al Iskandarīyah. N Egypt
46 J12 **Alexandria** C Jamaica
118 J15 **Alexandria** Teleorman, S Romania
33 P13 **Alexandria** Indiana, N USA
22 M4 **Alexandria** Kentucky, S USA
24 H7 **Alexandria** Louisiana, S USA
31 T7 **Alexandria** Minnesota, N USA
31 Q11 **Alexandria** South Dakota, N USA
23 W4 **Alexandria** Virginia, NE USA
Alexándria *see* Alexándreia
20 I7 **Alexandria Bay** New York, NE USA
Alexandrie *see* Alessandria
190 J10 **Alexandrina, Lake** ◎ South Australia
116 K13 **Alexandroúpoli** *var.* Alexandroúpolis, *Turk.* Dedeagaç, Dedeagach. Anatolikí Makedonía kai Thráki, NE Greece
Alexandroúpolis *see* Alexandroúpoli
8 L15 **Alexis Creek** British Columbia, SW Canada
126 Gg15 **Aleysk** Altayskiy Kray, S Russian Federation
145 S8 **Al Fallūjah** *var.* Falluja. C Iraq
107 R8 **Alfambra** ≈ E Spain
Al Faqa *see* Faq'
147 R15 **Al Farḑah** C Yemen
107 Q4 **Alfaro** La Rioja, N Spain
107 U5 **Alfarràs** Cataluña, NE Spain
Al Fāshir *see* El Fasher
Al Fashn *see* El Fashn
116 M7 **Alfatar** Razgradska Oblast, NE Bulgaria
145 S5 **Al Fatḩah** C Iraq
145 Q3 **Al Fatsī** N Iraq
145 Z13 **Al Fāw** *var.* Fao. SE Iraq
Al Fayyūm *see* El Faiyûm
117 D20 **Alfeiós** *prev.* Alfiós, *anc.* Alpheius, Alpheus. ≈ S Greece
102 I13 **Alfeld** Niedersachsen, C Germany
Alfiós *see* Alfeiós
Alföld *see* Great Hungarian Plain
xxxix S5 **Alford** Lincolnshire, E England, UK
xlii N13 **Alford** Aberdeenshire, NE Scotland, UK
96 C11 **Ålfotbreen** *glacier* S Norway
21 P9 **Alfred** Maine, NE USA
20 F11 **Alfred** New York, NE USA
63 K14 **Alfredo Vagner** Santa Catarina, S Brazil
xxxviii M7 **Alfreton** Derbyshire, C England, UK
xxxvii U13 **Alfriston** East Sussex, SE England, UK
96 M12 **Alfta** Gävleborg, C Sweden
146 K12 **Al Fuḩayḩīl** *var.* Fahaheel. SE Kuwait
145 Q6 **Al Fuḩaymī** C Iraq
149 S16 **Al Fujayrah** *Eng.* Fujairah. Al Fujayrah, NE UAE
149 S16 **Al Fujayrah** *Eng.* Fujairah. ✕ Al Fujayrah, NE UAE
Al Furāt *see* Euphrates
150 I10 **Alga** *Kaz.* Algha. Aktyubinsk, NW Kazakhstan
150 G9 **Algabas** Zapadnyy Kazakhstan, NW Kazakhstan
97 C17 **Ålgård** Rogaland, S Norway
106 G14 **Algarve** *cultural region* S Portugal
190 G3 **Algebuckina Bridge** South Australia
106 K16 **Algeciras** Andalucía, SW Spain
107 S10 **Algemesí** País Valenciano, E Spain
Al-Genain *see* El Geneina
123 I11 **Alger** *var.* Algiers, El Djazaïr, Al Jazair. ● (Algeria) N Algeria
76 H9 **Algeria** *off.* Democratic and Popular Republic of Algeria. ◆ *republic* N Africa
123 J9 **Algerian Basin** *var.* Balearic Plain *undersea feature* W Mediterranean Sea
Algha *see* Alga
144 I4 **Al Ghāb** ◎ NW Syria
147 X10 **Al Ghābah** *var.* Ghaba. C Oman
147 U14 **Al Ghayḑah** E Yemen
146 M6 **Al Ghazālah** Ḩā'il, NW Saudi Arabia
109 B17 **Alghero** Sardegna, Italy, C Mediterranean Sea
97 M20 **Älghult** Kronoberg, S Sweden
Al Ghurdaqah *see* Hurghada
Algiers *see* Alger
107 S10 **Alginet** País Valenciano, E Spain
85 I26 **Algoa Bay** *bay* S South Africa
106 L15 **Algodonales** Andalucía, S Spain
107 N9 **Algodor** ≈ C Spain
Al Golea *see* El Goléa
33 N6 **Algoma** Wisconsin, N USA
31 U12 **Algona** Iowa, C USA
22 L8 **Algood** Tennessee, S USA
107 O2 **Algorta** País Vasco, N Spain
63 E18 **Algorta** Río Negro, W Uruguay
Al Haba *see* Haba
145 Q10 **Al Habbārīyah** S Iraq
Al Hadhar *see* Al Ḩaḑr
145 Q4 **Al Ḩaḑr** *var.* Al Hadhar; *anc.* Hatra. NW Iraq
145 T13 **Al Ḩajarah** *desert* S Iraq
147 W8 **Al Ḩajār al Gharbī** ▲▲ N Oman
147 Y8 **Al Ḩajar ash Sharqī** ▲▲ NE Oman
147 R15 **Al Hajarayn** C Yemen
144 L10 **Al Ḩamād** *desert* Jordan/Saudi Arabia
Al Hamad *see* Syrian Desert
77 N9 **Al Ḩamādah al Ḩamrā'** *var.* Al Ḩamrā'. *desert* NW Libya
107 N15 **Alhama de Granada** Andalucía, S Spain
107 R13 **Alhama de Murcia** Murcia, SE Spain
37 T15 **Alhambra** California, W USA
145 T12 **Al Ḩammām** S Iraq
147 X8 **Al Ḩamrā'** NE Oman
Al Ḩamrā' *see* Al Ḩamādah al Ḩamrā'
147 O6 **Al Ḩamūdīyah** *spring/well* N Saudi Arabia

◆ Country ● Country Capital ◇ Dependent Territory ○ Dependent Territory Capital ◈ Administrative Region ✕ International Airport ▲ Mountain ▲▲ Mountain Range ⩘ Volcano ≈ River ◎ Lake ⊠ Reservoir

Al Ḩanākīyah – Amazonas

146 M7 **Al Ḩanākīyah** Al Madīnah, W Saudi Arabia
145 W14 **Al Ḩanīyah** *escarpment* Iraq/Saudi Arabia
145 Y12 **Al Ḩārithah** SE Iraq
146 L3 **Al Ḩarrah** *desert* NW Saudi Arabia
77 Q10 **Al Harūj al Aswad** *desert* C Libya
Al Hasaifin *see* Al Ḩusayfīn
145 N2 **Al Ḩasakah** *var.* Al Hasijah, El Haseke, *Fr.* Hassetché. Al Ḩasakah, NE Syria
145 O2 **Al Ḩasakah** *off.* Muḩāfaẓat al Ḩasakah, *var.* Al Hasakah, Āl Hasakah, Hasakah, Hassakeh. ◆ *governorate* NE Syria
145 T9 **Al Hāshimīyah** C Iraq
144 G13 **Al Hāshimīyah** Ma'ān, S Jordan
Al Hasijah *see* Al Ḩasakah
106 M15 **Alhaurín el Grande** Andalucía, S Spain
147 Q16 **Al Ḩawrā** S Yemen
145 V10 **Al Ḩayy** *var.* Kut al Hai, Kūt al Ḩayy. E Iraq
147 U11 **Al Ḩibāk** *desert* E Saudi Arabia
144 H8 **Al Hījānah** *var.* Hejanah, Hijanah. Dimashq, W Syria
146 K7 **Al Ḩijāz** *Eng.* Hejaz. *physical region* NW Saudi Arabia
Al Hilbeh *see* 'Ulayyānīyah, Bi'r al
145 T9 **Al Ḩillah** *var.* Hilla. C Iraq
145 T9 **Al Hindīyah** *var.* Hindiya. C Iraq
144 G12 **Al Ḩisā** Aţ Ţafīlah, W Jordan
76 G5 **Al-Hoceïma** *var.* al Hoceima, Al-Hoceima, Alhucemas; *prev.* Villa Sanjurjo. N Morocco
Alhucemas *see* Al-Hoceïma
107 N17 **Alhucemas, Peñon de** *island group* S Spain
147 N15 **Al Ḩudaydah** *Eng.* Hodeida. W Yemen
147 N15 **Al Ḩudaydah** *Eng.* Hodeida. ✕ W Yemen
146 M4 **Al Ḩudūd ash Shamālīyah** *var.* Minţaqat al Ḩudūd ash Shamālīyah, *Eng.* Northern Border Region. ◆ *province* N Saudi Arabia
147 S7 **Al Hufūf** *var.* Hofuf. Ash Sharqīyah, NE Saudi Arabia
al-Hurma *see* Al Khurmah
147 X7 **Al Ḩusayfīn** *var.* Al Hasaifin. N Oman
144 G9 **Al Ḩuşn** *var.* Husn. Irbid, N Jordan
145 U9 **'Alī** E Iraq
106 L10 **Alia** Extremadura, W Spain
149 P9 **'Alīābād** Yazd, C Iran
'Alīābad *see* Qā'emshahr
107 S7 **Aliaga** Aragón, NE Spain
142 B13 **Aliağa** İzmir, W Turkey
Aliákmon *see* Aliákmonas
117 F14 **Aliákmonas** *prev.* Aliákmon, *anc.* Haliacmon. ≈ N Greece
145 W9 **'Alī al Gharbī** E Iraq
145 U11 **'Alī al Ḩassūnī** S Iraq
117 G18 **Alíartos** Stereá Ellás, C Greece
143 Y12 **Äli-Bayramlı** *Rus.* Ali-Bayramly. SE Azerbaijan
Ali-Bayramly *see* Äli-Bayramlı
116 P12 **Alibey Barajı** ⊠ NW Turkey
79 S13 **Alibori** ≈ N Benin
114 M10 **Alibunar** Serbia, NE Yugoslavia
107 S12 **Alicante** *Cat.* Alacant; *Lat.* Lucentum. País Valenciano, SE Spain
107 S12 **Alicante** ◆ *province* País Valenciano, SE Spain
107 S12 **Alicante** ✕ Murcia, E Spain
85 I25 **Alice** Eastern Cape, S South Africa
27 S14 **Alice** Texas, SW USA
85 I25 **Alicedale** Eastern Cape, S South Africa
67 B25 **Alice, Mount** *hill* West Falkland, Falkland Islands
109 P20 **Alice, Punta** *headland* S Italy
189 Q7 **Alice Springs** Northern Territory, C Australia
25 N4 **Aliceville** Alabama, S USA
153 U13 **Alichur** SE Tajikistan
153 U14 **Alichuri Janubí, Qatorkŭhi** *Rus.* Yuzhno-Alichurskiy Khrebet. ⛰ SE Tajikistan
153 U13 **Alichuri Shimolí, Qatorkŭhi** *Rus.* Severo-Alichurskiy Khrebet. ⛰ SE Tajikistan
109 K22 **Alicudi, Isola** *island* Isole Eolie, S Italy
158 J11 **Alīgarh** Uttar Pradesh, N India
148 M7 **Alīgūdarz** Lorestān, W Iran
1 F12 **Alijos, Islas** *island group* California, SW USA
155 R6 **'Alī Kbel** *Pash.* 'Alī Khēl. Paktīkā, E Afghanistan
Ali Khel *see* 'Alī Kheyl, Paktīā, Afghanistan
'Alī Khēl *see* 'Alī Kbel, Paktīkā, Afghanistan
155 R6 **'Alī Kheyl** *var.* Ali Khel, Jajı. Paktīā, SE Afghanistan
147 V17 **Al Ikhwān** *island group* SE Yemen
Aliki *see* Alykí
81 H19 **Alima** ≈ C Congo
Al Imārāt al 'Arabīyah al Muttaḩidah *see* United Arab Emirates
194 M12 **Alimbit** ≈ New Britain, C PNG
117 N23 **Alimía** *island* Dodekánisos, Greece, Aegean Sea
57 V12 **Alimimuni Piek** ▲ S Surinam
81 K15 **Alindao** Basse-Kotto, S Central African Republic
97 J18 **Alingsås** Älvsborg, S Sweden
83 K18 **Alinjugul** *spring/well* E Kenya
155 S11 **Alīpur** Punjab, E Pakistan
159 T12 **Alīpur Duār** West Bengal, NE India
20 B14 **Aliquippa** Pennsylvania, NE USA
82 L12 **'Ali Sabieh** *var.* 'Alī Sabīḩ. S Djibouti
'Alī Sabīḩ *see* 'Ali Sabieh
146 K3 **Al 'Īsāwīyah** Al Jawf, NW Saudi Arabia
106 J10 **Aliseda** Extremadura, W Spain
145 T8 **Al Iskandarīyah** C Iraq
Al Iskandarīyah *see* Alexandria
127 Oo5 **Aliskerovo** Chukotskiy Avtonomnyy Okrug, NE Russian Federation
116 H13 **Alistráti** Kentrikí Makedonía, NE Greece
41 P15 **Alitak Bay** *bay* Kodiak Island, Alaska, USA
Al Ittiḩād *see* Madīnat ash Sha'b
117 H18 **Alivéri** *var.* Alivérion. Évvoia, C Greece
Alivérion *see* Alivéri
Aliwal-Noord *see* Aliwal North
85 I24 **Aliwal North** *Afr.* Aliwal-Noord. Eastern Cape, SE South Africa
124 Nn15 **Al Jabal al Akhḑar** ⛰ NE Libya
144 H13 **Al Jafr** Ma'ān, S Jordan
77 T8 **Al Jaghbūb** NE Libya
148 K11 **Al Jahrā'** *var.* Al Jahrah, Jahra. C Kuwait
Al Jahrah *see* Al Jahrā'
Al Jamāhīrīyah al 'Arabīyah al Lībīyah ash Sha'bīyah al Ishtirākī *see* Libya
146 K3 **Al Jarāwī** *spring/well* NW Saudi Arabia
147 X11 **Al Jawārah** *oasis* SE Oman
146 L3 **Al Jawf** *var.* Jauf. Al Jawf, NW Saudi Arabia
146 L4 **Al Jawf** *off.* Minţaqat al Jawf. ◆ *province* N Saudi Arabia
Al Jawlān *see* Golan Heights
Al Jazair *see* Alger
145 N4 **Al Jazīrah** *physical region* Iraq/Syria
106 F14 **Aljezur** Faro, S Portugal
145 S13 **Al Jīl** S Iraq
144 G11 **Al Jīzah** *var.* Jiza. 'Ammān, N Jordan
Al Jīzah *see* El Gîza
Al Jubail *see* Al Jubayl
147 S6 **Al Jubayl** *var.* Al Jubail. Ash Sharqīyah, NE Saudi Arabia
147 T10 **Āl Juḩaysh, Qalamat** *well* SE Saudi Arabia
149 N15 **Al Jumaylīyah** N Qatar
Al Junaynah *see* El Geneina
106 G13 **Aljustrel** Beja, S Portugal
Al Kaba'ish *see* Al Chabā'ish
Al-Kadhimain *see* Al Kāẓimīyah
Al Kāf *see* El Kef
Alkal'a *see* Alcalá de Henares
37 W4 **Alkali Flat** *salt flat* Nevada, W USA
37 Q1 **Alkali Lake** ◎ Nevada, W USA
147 Z9 **Al Kāmil** NE Oman
144 G11 **Al Karak** *var.* El Kerak, Karak, Kerak; *anc.* Kir Moab, Kir of Moab. Al Karak, W Jordan
144 G12 **Al Karak** *off.* Muḩāfaẓat al Karak. ◆ *governorate* W Jordan
145 W8 **Al Karmashīyah** E Iraq
Al-Kashaniya *see* Al Qash'ānīyah
Al-Kasr al-Kebir *see* Ksar-el-Kebir
145 T8 **Al Kāẓimīyah** *var.* Al-Kadhimain, Kadhimain. C Iraq
101 J18 **Alken** Limburg, NE Belgium
147 X8 **Al Khābūrah** *var.* Khabura. N Oman
Al Khalīl *see* Hebron
145 T7 **Al Khāliş** C Iraq
Al Khaluf *see* Khalūf
xxxvii Y11 **Alkham** Kent, SE England, UK
Al Khārijah *see* El Khârga
147 Q8 **Al Kharj** Ar Riyāḑ, C Saudi Arabia
147 W6 **Al Khaşab** *var.* Khasab. N Oman
Al Khaur *see* Al Khawr
149 N15 **Al Khawr** *var.* Al Khaur, Al Khor. N Qatar
148 K12 **Al Khīrān** *var.* Al Khiran. SE Kuwait
147 W9 **Al Khīrān** *spring/well* NW Oman
Al Khiyām *see* El Khiyam
Al-Khobar *see* Al Khubar
Al Khor *see* Al Khawr
147 S6 **Al Khubar** *var.* Al-Khobar. Ash Sharqīyah, NE Saudi Arabia
77 T11 **Al Khufrah** SE Libya
123 L14 **Al Khums** *var.* Homs, Khoms, Khums. NW Libya
147 R15 **Al Khuraybah** C Yemen
146 M9 **Al Khurmah** *var.* al-Hurma. Makkah, W Saudi Arabia
147 V9 **Al Kidan** *desert* NE Saudi Arabia
100 H9 **Alkmaar** Noord-Holland, NW Netherlands
145 T10 **Al Kūfah** *var.* Kufa. S Iraq
147 T10 **Al Kursū'** *desert* E Saudi Arabia
145 V9 **Al Kūt** *var.* Kūt al 'Amārah, Kut al Imara. E Iraq
Al-Kuwait *see* Al Kuwayt
Al Kuwayr *see* Guwēr
148 K11 **Al Kuwayt** *var.* Al-Kuwait, *Eng.* Kuwait, Kuwait City; *prev.* Qurein. ● (Kuwait) E Kuwait
148 K11 **Al Kuwayt** ✕ C Kuwait
117 G19 **Alkyonidón, Kólpos** *gulf* C Greece
147 N4 **Al Labbah** *physical region* N Saudi Arabia
144 G4 **Al Lādhiqīyah** *Eng.* Latakia, *Fr.* Lattaquié; *anc.* Laodicea, Laodicea ad Mare. Al Lādhiqīyah, W Syria
144 H4 **Al Lādhiqīyah** *off.* Muḩāfaẓat al Lādhiqīyah, *var.* Al Lathqiyah, Latakia, Lattakia. ◆ *governorate* W Syria
21 R2 **Allagash River** ≈ Maine, NE USA
158 M13 **Allahābād** Uttar Pradesh, N India
149 S3 **Allāh Dāgh, Reshteh-ye** ⛰ NE Iran
41 Q8 **Allakaket** Alaska, USA
126 Mm11 **Allakh-Yun'** ≈ NE Russian Federation
9 T15 **Allan** Saskatchewan, S Canada
177 Ff6 **Allanmyo** Magwe, C Burma
85 I22 **Allanridge** Free State, C South Africa
106 H4 **Allariz** Galicia, NW Spain
145 R11 **Al Laşaf** *var.* Al Lussuf. S Iraq
Al Lathqiyah *see* Al Lādhiqīyah
25 S2 **Allatoona Lake** ⊠ Georgia, SE USA
85 J19 **Alldays** Northern, NE South Africa
Alle *see* Łyna
33 P10 **Allegan** Michigan, N USA
19 Qq8 **Allegheny Mountains** ⛰ NE USA
20 E12 **Allegheny Plateau** ⛰ New York/Pennsylvania, NE USA
20 D11 **Allegheny Reservoir** ⊠ New York/Pennsylvania, NE USA
20 E12 **Allegheny River** ≈ New York/Pennsylvania, NE USA
24 K9 **Allemands, Lac des** ◎ Louisiana, S USA
27 U6 **Allen** Texas, SW USA
23 R14 **Allendale** South Carolina, SE USA
xli P7 **Allendale Town** Northumberland, N England, UK
43 N6 **Allende** Coahuila de Zaragoza, NE Mexico
43 O9 **Allende** Nuevo León, NE Mexico
xli P7 **Allenheads** Northumberland, N England, UK
xliv H6 **Allen, Lough** *Ir.* Loch Aillionn. ◎ NW Ireland
193 B26 **Allen, Mount** ▲ Stewart Island, Southland, SW NZ
111 V2 **Allensteig** Niederösterreich, N Austria
Allenstein *see* Olsztyn
20 I14 **Allentown** Pennsylvania, NE USA
161 G23 **Alleppey** *var.* Alappuzha; *prev.* Alleppi. Kerala, SW India
Alleppi *see* Alleppey
102 J12 **Aller** ≈ NW Germany
31 V16 **Allerton** Iowa, C USA
xxxviii E15 **Allesley** Coventry, C England, UK
101 K19 **Alleur** Liège, E Belgium
103 J25 **Allgäuer Alpen** ⛰ Austria/Germany
xxxviii K6 **Allgreave** Cheshire, C England, UK
xxxvii W9 **Allhallows** Kent, SE England, UK
30 J13 **Alliance** Nebraska, C USA
33 U12 **Alliance** Ohio, N USA
105 O10 **Allier** ◆ *department* N France
145 R13 **Al Līfīyah** S Iraq
46 J13 **Alligator Pond** C Jamaica
23 Y9 **Alligator River** ≈ North Carolina, SE USA
31 W12 **Allison** Iowa, C USA
12 G14 **Alliston** Ontario, S Canada
146 L11 **Al Līth** Makkah, SW Saudi Arabia
Al Liwā' *see* Līwā
xliii K19 **Alloa** Clackmannan, C Scotland, UK
xl K8 **Allonby** Cumbria, NW England, UK
105 U14 **Allos** Alpes-de-Haute-Provence, SE France
xliii I22 **Alloway** South Ayrshire, W Scotland, UK
110 D6 **Allschwil** Basel-Land, NW Switzerland
xlii I7 **Alltnacaillich** Highland, NW Scotland, UK
xxxv H14 **Alltwen** Neath Port Talbot, S Wales, UK
xliv D14 **Allua, Lough** ◎ S Ireland
Al Lubnān *see* Lebanon
147 N14 **Al Luḩayyah** W Yemen
12 K12 **Allumettes, Île des** *island* Québec, SE Canada
Al Lussuf *see* Al Laşaf
111 S5 **Alm** ≈ N Austria
13 Q7 **Alma** Québec, SE Canada
29 S10 **Alma** Arkansas, C USA
25 V7 **Alma** Georgia, SE USA
29 P4 **Alma** Kansas, C USA
33 Q8 **Alma** Michigan, N USA
31 O17 **Alma** Nebraska, C USA
32 I7 **Alma** Wisconsin, N USA
145 R12 **Al Ma'ānīyah** S Iraq
Alma-Ata/Alma-Atinskaya Oblast' *see* Almaty
Almacellas *see* Almacelles
107 T5 **Almacelles** *var.* Almacellas. Cataluña, NE Spain
106 F11 **Almada** Setúbal, W Portugal
106 L11 **Almadén** Castilla-La Mancha, C Spain
68 L6 **Almadies, Pointe des** *headland* W Senegal
146 L7 **Al Madīnah** *Eng.* Medina. Al Madīnah, W Saudi Arabia
146 L7 **Al Madīnah** *off.* Minţaqat al Madīnah. ◆ *province* W Saudi Arabia
144 H9 **Al Mafraq** *var.* Mafraq. Al Mafraq, N Jordan
144 J10 **Al Mafraq** *off.* Muḩāfaẓat al Mafraq. ◆ *governorate* NW Jordan
147 R15 **Al Maghārīm** C Yemen
107 N11 **Almagro** Castilla-La Mancha, C Spain
Al Maḩallah al Kubrá *see* El Maḩalla el Kubra
145 T9 **Al Maḩāwīl** *var.* Khān al Maḩāwīl. C Iraq
Al Mahdīyah *see* Mahdia
145 T8 **Al Maḩmūdīyah** *var.* Mahmudiya. C Iraq
147 T14 **Al Mahrah** ⛰ E Yemen
147 P7 **Al Majma'ah** Ar Riyāḑ, C Saudi Arabia
145 Q11 **Al Makmīn** *well* S Iraq
145 Q1 **Al Mālikīyah** *var.* Malkiye. Al Ḩasakah, N Syria
Almalyk *see* Olmaliq
Al Mamlakah al Urdunīyah al Hāshimīyah *see* Jordan
Al Mamlakah *see* Morocco
149 Q18 **Al Manādir** *var.* Al Manadir. *desert* Oman/UAE
148 L15 **Al Manāmah** *Eng.* Manama. ● (Bahrain) N Bahrain
145 O5 **Al Manāşif** ⛰ E Syria
37 O4 **Almanor, Lake** ⊠ California, W USA
107 R11 **Almansa** Castilla-La Mancha, C Spain
Al Manşūrah *see* El Manşûra
106 L3 **Almanza** Castilla-León, N Spain
106 L8 **Almanzor** ▲ W Spain
107 P14 **Almanzora** ≈ SE Spain
145 S9 **Al Mardah** C Iraq
Al-Mariyya *see* Almería
77 R7 **Al Marj** *var.* Barka, *It.* Barce. NE Libya
144 L2 **Al Mashrafah** Ar Raqqah, N Syria
147 X8 **Al Maşna'ah** *var.* Al Muşana'a. NE Oman
107 T9 **Almassora** País Valenciano, E Spain
Almatinskaya Oblast' *see* Almaty
151 U15 **Almaty** *var.* Alma-Ata. Almaty, SE Kazakhstan
151 S14 **Almaty** *off.* Almatinskaya Oblast', *Kaz.* Almaty Oblysy; *prev.* Alma-Atinskaya Oblast'. ◆ *province* SE Kazakhstan
151 U15 **Almaty** ✕ Almaty, SE Kazakhstan
Almaty Oblysy *see* Almaty
al-Mawailih *see* Al Muwayliḩ
145 R3 **Al Mawşil** *Eng.* Mosul. N Iraq
145 N5 **Al Mayādīn** *var.* Mayadin, *Fr.* Meyadine. Dayr az Zawr, E Syria
145 X10 **Al Maymūnah** *var.* Maimuna. SE Iraq
147 N5 **Al Mayyāh** Ḩā'il, N Saudi Arabia
Al Ma'zam *see* Al Ma'zim
107 P6 **Almazán** Castilla-León, N Spain
147 W8 **Al Ma'zim** *var.* Al Ma'zam. NW Oman
126 Kk11 **Almaznyy** Respublika Sakha (Yakutiya), NE Russian Federation
Al Mazra' *see* Al Mazra'ah
144 G11 **Al Mazra'ah** *var.* Al Mazra', Mazra'a. Al Karak, W Jordan
103 G15 **Alme** ≈ W Germany
106 I7 **Almeida** Guarda, N Portugal
106 G10 **Almeirim** Santarém, C Portugal
xxxviii G13 **Almeley** Herefordshire, W England, UK
100 O10 **Almelo** Overijssel, E Netherlands
107 S9 **Almenara** País Valenciano, E Spain
107 P12 **Almenaras** ▲ S Spain
107 P5 **Almenar de Soria** Castilla-León, N Spain
106 J6 **Almendra, Embalse de** ⊠ Castilla-León, NW Spain
106 J11 **Almendralejo** Extremadura, W Spain
100 J10 **Almere** *var.* Almere-stad. Flevoland, C Netherlands
100 J10 **Almere-Buiten** Flevoland, C Netherlands
100 J10 **Almere-Haven** Flevoland, C Netherlands
Almere-stad *see* Almere
107 P15 **Almería** *Ar.* Al-Mariyya; *anc.* Unci, *Lat.* Portus Magnus. Andalucía, S Spain
107 P14 **Almería** ◆ *province* Andalucía, S Spain
107 P15 **Almería, Golfo de** *gulf* S Spain
131 S5 **Al'met'yevsk** Respublika Tatarstan, W Russian Federation
97 L21 **Älmhult** Kronoberg, S Sweden
147 U9 **Al Miḩrāḑ** *desert* NE Saudi Arabia
Al Mīnā' *see* El Mina
106 L17 **Almina, Punta** *headland* Ceuta, Spain, N Africa
Al Minyā *see* El Minya
Al Miqdādīyah *see* Al Muqdādīyah
45 P14 **Almirante** Bocas del Toro, NW Panama
Almirós *see* Almyrós
146 M9 **Al Mislaḩ** *spring/well* W Saudi Arabia
Almissa *see* Omiš
106 G13 **Almodôvar** *var.* Almodóvar. Beja, S Portugal
106 M11 **Almodóvar del Campo** Castilla-La Mancha, C Spain
107 Q9 **Almodóvar del Pinar** Castilla-La Mancha, C Spain
xliii K17 **Almond** ≈ C Scotland, UK
xxxvi L9 **Almondsbury** South Gloucestershire, SW England, UK
33 S9 **Almont** Michigan, N USA
12 L13 **Almonte** Ontario, SE Canada
106 J14 **Almonte** Andalucía, S Spain
106 K9 **Almonte** ≈ W Spain
158 K9 **Almora** Uttar Pradesh, N India
106 M8 **Almorox** Castilla-La Mancha, C Spain
147 S7 **Al Mubarraz** Ash Sharqīyah, E Saudi Arabia
Al Muḑaibī *see* Al Muḑaybī
144 G15 **Al Mudawwarah** Ma'ān, SW Jordan
147 Y9 **Al Muḑaybī** *var.* Al Muḑaibī. NE Oman
Almudébar *see* Almudévar
107 S5 **Almudévar** *var.* Almudébar. Aragón, NE Spain
147 S15 **Al Mukallā** *var.* Mukalla. SE Yemen
147 N16 **Al Mukhā** *Eng.* Mocha. SW Yemen
107 N15 **Almuñécar** Andalucía, S Spain
145 U7 **Al Muqdādīyah** *var.* Al Miqdādīyah. C Iraq
146 L3 **Al Murayr** *spring/well* NW Saudi Arabia
142 M12 **Almus** Tokat, N Turkey
Al Muşana'a *see* Al Maşna'ah
145 T9 **Al Musayyib** *var.* Musaiyib. C Iraq
145 V9 **Al Muwaffaqīyah** S Iraq
144 H10 **Al Muwaqqar** *var.* El Muwaqqar. 'Ammān, W Jordan
146 J5 **Al Muwayliḩ** *var.* al-Mawailih. Tabūk, NW Saudi Arabia
117 F17 **Almyrós** *var.* Almirós. Thessalía, C Greece
117 I24 **Almyroú, Órmos** *bay* Krití, Greece, E Mediterranean Sea
xli Q3 **Aln** ≈ N England, UK
xlii J11 **Alness** Highland, NW Scotland, UK
xli R3 **Alnmouth** Northumberland, N England, UK
Al Nūwfalīyah *see* An Nawfalīyah
xli R3 **Alnwick** Northumberland, N England, UK
Al Obayyid *see* El Obeid
Al Odaid *see* Al 'Udayd
202 B16 **Alofi** ○ (Niue) W Niue
202 A16 **Alofi Bay** *bay* W Niue, C Pacific Ocean
202 E13 **Alofi, Île** *island* S Wallis and Futuna
202 E13 **Alofitai** Île Alofi, W Wallis and Futuna
Aloha State *see* Hawaii
120 G7 **Aloja** Limbaži, N Latvia
159 X10 **Along** Arunāchel Pradesh, NE India
117 H16 **Alónnisos** *island* Vóreioi Sporádes, Greece, Aegean Sea
106 M15 **Álora** Andalucía, S Spain
175 Rr15 **Alor, Kepulauan** *island group* E Indonesia
175 Rr16 **Alor, Pulau** *prev.* Ombai. *island* Kepulauan Alor, E Indonesia
175 R16 **Alor, Selat** *strait* Flores Sea/Savu Sea
173 G2 **Alor Setar** *var.* Alor Star, Alur Setar. Kedah, Peninsular Malaysia
Alost *see* Aalst
160 F9 **Ālot** Madhya Pradesh, C India
195 N16 **Alotau** Milne Bay, SE PNG
176 Yy15 **Alotip** Irian Jaya, E Indonesia
Al Oued *see* El Oued
37 R12 **Alpaugh** California, W USA
Alpen *see* Alps
33 R6 **Alpena** Michigan, N USA
Alpes *see* Alps
105 S14 **Alpes-de-Haute-Provence** ◆ *department* SE France
105 U14 **Alpes-Maritimes** ◆ *department* SE France
189 W8 **Alpha** Queensland, E Australia
207 R9 **Alpha Cordillera** *var.* Alpha Ridge. *undersea feature* Arctic Ocean
Alpha Ridge *see* Alpha Cordillera
Alpheius *see* Alfeiós
101 I15 **Alphen** Noord-Brabant, S Netherlands
100 H11 **Alphen aan den Rijn** *var.* Alphen. Zuid-Holland, C Netherlands
Alpheus *see* Alfeiós
Alpi *see* Alps
106 G10 **Alpiarça** Santarém, C Portugal
26 K10 **Alpine** Texas, SW USA
110 F8 **Alpnach** Unterwalden, W Switzerland
110 D11 **Alps** *Fr.* Alpes, *Ger.* Alpen, *It.* Alpi. ⛰ C Europe
147 W8 **Al Qābil** *var.* Qabil. N Oman
Al Qaḑārif *see* Gedaref
77 P8 **Al Qaddāḩīyah** N Libya
Al Qadmouss *see* Al Qadmūs
Al Qāhirah *see* Cairo
146 K4 **Al Qalībah** Tabūk, NW Saudi Arabia
145 O1 **Al Qāmishlī** *var.* Kamishli, Qamishly. Al Ḩasakah, NE Syria
144 I6 **Al Qaryatayn** *var.* Qaryatayn, *Fr.* Qariateïne. Ḩimş, C Syria
148 K11 **Al Qash'ānīyah** *var.* Al-Kashaniya. NE Kuwait
147 N7 **Al Qaşīm** *off.* Minţaqat Qaşīm, Qassim. ◆ *province* C Saudi Arabia
144 J5 **Al Qaşr** Ḩimş, C Syria
Al Qaşr *see* El Qaşr
Al Qaşrayn *see* Kasserine
147 S6 **Al Qaţīf** Ash Sharqīyah, NE Saudi Arabia
144 G11 **Al Qaţrānah** *var.* El Qatrani, Qatrana. Al Karak, W Jordan
77 P11 **Al Qaţrūn** SW Libya
Al Qayrawān *see* Kairouan
Al-Qsar al-Kbir *see* Ksar-el-Kebir
Al Qubayyāt *see* Qoubaïyât
Al Qudayr *see* Al Qadr
Al Quds/Al Quds ash Sharīf *see* Jerusalem
144 G8 **Al Qunayţirah** *var.* El Kuneitra, El Quneitra, Kuneitra, Qunaytra. Al Qunayţirah, SW Syria
144 G8 **Al Qunayţirah** *off.* Muḩāfaẓat al Qunayţirah, *var.* El Q'unayţirah, Qunaytirah, *Fr.* Kuneitra. ◆ *governorate* SW Syria
146 M11 **Al Qunfudhah** Makkah, SW Saudi Arabia
146 K2 **Al Qurayyāt** Al Jawf, NW Saudi Arabia
145 Y11 **Al Qurnah** *var.* Kurna. SE Iraq
145 V12 **Al Quşayr** S Iraq
144 I6 **Al Quşayr** *var.* El Quseir, Quşayr, *Fr.* Kousseir. Ḩimş, W Syria
Al Quşayr *see* Quseir
144 H7 **Al Quţayfah** *var.* Quţayfah, Qutayfe, Quteife, *Fr.* Kouteifé. Dimashq, W Syria
147 P8 **Al Quwayīyah** Ar Riyāḑ, C Saudi Arabia
Al Quwayr *see* Guwēr
144 F14 **Al Quwayrah** *var.* El Quweira. Ma'ān, SW Jordan
Al Rayyan *see* Ar Rayyān
Al Rbeil *see* Ar Rubayl
xxxviii D12 **Alrewas** Staffordshire, C England, UK
Al Ruweis *see* Ar Ruways
97 G24 **Als** *Ger.* Alsen. *island* SW Denmark
105 U5 **Alsace** *Ger.* Elsass; *anc.* Alsatia. ◆ *region* NE France
xxxviii I7 **Alsager** Cheshire, W England, UK
9 R16 **Alsask** Saskatchewan, S Canada
107 P3 **Alsasua** Navarra, N Spain
Alsatia *see* Alsace
103 C16 **Alsdorf** Nordrhein-Westfalen, W Germany
8 G8 **Alsek** ≈ Canada/USA
Alsen *see* Als
103 F19 **Alsenz** ≈ W Germany
103 H17 **Alsfeld** Hessen, C Germany
121 K20 **Al'shany** *Rus.* Ol'shany. Brestskaya Voblasts', SW Belorussia
xlii F13 **Alsh, Loch** *inlet* NW Scotland, UK
Alsókubin *see* Dolný Kubín
xli O7 **Alston** Cumbria, NW England, UK
120 C9 **Alsunga** Kuldīga, W Latvia
Alt *see* Olt
94 K9 **Alta** *Fin.* Alattio. Finnmark, N Norway
31 T12 **Alta** Iowa, C USA
110 I7 **Altach** Vorarlberg, W Austria
94 K9 **Altaelva** ≈ N Norway
94 J8 **Altafjorden** *fjord* NE Norwegian Sea
64 K10 **Alta Gracia** Córdoba, C Argentina
44 K11 **Alta Gracia** Rivas, SW Nicaragua
56 H4 **Altagracia** Zulia, NW Venezuela
56 M5 **Altagracia de Orituco** Guárico, N Venezuela
Altai *see* Altai Mountains
133 T7 **Altai Mountains** *var.* Altai, *Chin.* Altay Shan, *Rus.* Altay. ⛰ Asia/Europe
25 V6 **Altamaha River** ≈ Georgia, SE USA
60 J13 **Altamira** Pará, NE Brazil
56 D12 **Altamira** Huila, S Colombia
44 M13 **Altamira** Alajuela, N Costa Rica
43 Q11 **Altamira** Tamaulipas, C Mexico
32 L15 **Altamont** Illinois, N USA
29 Q7 **Altamont** Kansas, C USA
34 H16 **Altamont** Oregon, NW USA
22 K10 **Altamont** Tennessee, S USA
25 X11 **Altamonte Springs** Florida, SE USA
109 O17 **Altamura** *anc.* Lupatia. Puglia, SE Italy
42 H9 **Altamura, Isla** *island* C Mexico
168 G7 **Altan** Dzavhan, W Mongolia
168 G6 **Altanbulag** Dzavhan, N Mongolia
Altan Emel *see* Xin Barag Youqi
168 J8 **Altan-Ovoo** Arhangay, C Mongolia
168 E7 **Altanteel** Hovd, W Mongolia
42 F3 **Altar** Sonora, NW Mexico
42 D2 **Altar, Desierto de** *var.* Sonoran Desert. *desert* Mexico/USA *see also* Sonoran Desert
107 Q8 **Alta, Sierra** ▲ N Spain
42 H9 **Altata** Sinaloa, C Mexico
44 D4 **Alta Verapaz** *off.* Departamento de Alta Verapaz. ◆ *department* C Guatemala
109 L18 **Altavilla Silentia** Campania, S Italy
23 T7 **Altavista** Virginia, NE USA
164 L2 **Altay** Xinjiang Uygur Zizhiqu, NW China
168 G5 **Altay** Dzavhan, N Mongolia
168 G8 **Altay** Govĭ-Altay, W Mongolia
Altay *see* Altai Mountains
126 H16 **Altay, Respublika** *var.* Gornyy Altay; *prev.* Gorno-Altayskaya Respublika. ◆ *autonomous republic* S Russian Federation
Altay Shan *see* Altai Mountains
125 G15 **Altayskiy Kray** ◆ *territory* S Russian Federation
Altbetsche *see* Bečej
103 L20 **Altdorf** Bayern, SE Germany
110 G8 **Altdorf** *var.* Altorf. Uri, C Switzerland
107 T11 **Altea** País Valenciano, E Spain
102 L10 **Alte Elde** ≈ N Germany
103 M16 **Altenburg** Thüringen, E Germany
Altenburg *see* București, Romania
Altenburg *see* Baia de Criș, Romania
102 P12 **Alte Oder** ≈ NE Germany
106 H10 **Alter do Chão** Portalegre, C Portugal
94 I10 **Altevatnet** ◎ N Norway
29 V12 **Altheimer** Arkansas, C USA
111 T9 **Althofen** Kärnten, S Austria
116 H7 **Altimir** Oblast Montana, NW Bulgaria
142 K11 **Altınkaya Barajı** ⊠ N Turkey
145 S3 **Altin Köprü** *var.* Altun Kupri. N Iraq
142 E13 **Altıntaş** Kütahya, W Turkey
59 K18 **Altiplano** *physical region* W South America
Altkanischa *see* Kanjiža
105 U7 **Altkirch** Haut-Rhin, NE France
Altlublau *see* Stará Ľubovňa
102 L12 **Altmark** *cultural region* N Germany
Altmoldowa *see* Moldova Veche
xlii I8 **Altnaharra** Highland, NW Scotland, UK
27 W8 **Alto** Texas, SW USA
106 H11 **Alto Alentejo** *physical region* S Portugal
61 I19 **Alto Araguaia** Mato Grosso, C Brazil
60 L12 **Alto Bonito** Pará, NE Brazil
85 O15 **Alto Molócuè** Zambézia, NE Mozambique
xxxvii Q11 **Alton** Hampshire, S England, UK
xxxviii K7 **Alton** Staffordshire, C England, UK
32 K15 **Alton** Illinois, N USA
29 W8 **Alton** Missouri, C USA
9 X17 **Altona** Manitoba, S Canada
xxxvii N10 **Alton Priors** Wiltshire, S England, UK
20 E14 **Altoona** Pennsylvania, NE USA
32 J6 **Altoona** Wisconsin, N USA
64 N3 **Alto Paraguay** *off.* Departamento del Alto Paraguay. ◆ *department* N Paraguay
61 L17 **Alto Paraíso de Goiás** Goiás, S Brazil
64 P6 **Alto Paraná** *off.* Departamento del Alto Paraná. ◆ *department* E Paraguay
Alto Paraná *see* Paraná
61 L15 **Alto Parnaíba** Maranhão, E Brazil
58 H13 **Alto Purús, Río** ≈ E Peru
Altorf *see* Altdorf
65 H19 **Alto Río Senguer** *var.* Alto Río Senguerr. Chubut, S Argentina
43 Q13 **Altotonga** Veracruz-Llave, E Mexico
103 N23 **Altötting** Bayern, SE Germany
Altpasua *see* Stara Pazova
168 I5 **Altraga** Hövsgöl, N Mongolia
xli P17 **Altrincham** Trafford, NW England, UK
Alt-Schwanenburg *see* Gulbene
Altsohl *see* Zvolen
110 I7 **Altstätten** Sankt Gallen, NE Switzerland
44 G1 **Altun Ha** *ruins* Belize, N Belize
Altun Kupri *see* Altin Köprü
164 D8 **Altun Shan** ▲ C China
164 L9 **Altun Shan** *var.* Altyn Tagh. ⛰ NW China
37 P2 **Alturas** California, W USA
28 K12 **Altus** Oklahoma, C USA
28 K11 **Altus Lake** ⊠ Oklahoma, C USA
Altvater *see* Praděd
Altyn Tagh *see* Altun Shan
Alu *see* Shortland Island
al-'Ubaila *see* Al 'Ubaylah
145 O6 **Al 'Ubaydī** W Iraq
147 T9 **Al 'Ubaylah** *var.* al-'Ubaila. Ash Sharqīyah, E Saudi Arabia
147 T9 **Al 'Ubaylah** *spring/well* E Saudi Arabia
Al Ubayyiḑ *see* El Obeid
147 T7 **Al 'Udayd** *var.* Al Odaid. Abū Ẓaby, W UAE
120 J8 **Alūksne** *Ger.* Marienburg. Alūksne, NE Latvia
146 K6 **Al 'Ulā** Al Madīnah, NW Saudi Arabia
181 N4 **Alula-Fartak Trench** *var.* Illaue Fartak Trench. *undersea feature* W Indian Ocean
144 I11 **Al 'Umarī** 'Ammān, E Jordan
33 S13 **Alum Creek Lake** ⊠ Ohio, N USA
65 H15 **Aluminé** Neuquén, C Argentina
97 O14 **Alunda** Uppsala, C Sweden
119 T14 **Alupka** Respublika Krym, S Ukraine
77 P8 **Al 'Uqaylah** N Libya
Al Uqşur *see* Luxor
Al Urdunn *see* Jordan
173 G6 **Alur Panal** *bay* Sumatera, W Indonesia
147 V10 **Al 'Urūq al Mu'tariḑah** *salt lake* SE Saudi Arabia
145 Q7 **Ālūs** C Iraq
119 T13 **Alushta** Respublika Krym, S Ukraine
77 N11 **Al 'Uwaynāt** *var.* Al Awaynāt. SW Libya
145 T6 **Al 'Uẓaym** *var.* Adhaim. E Iraq
xliii K19 **Alva** Clackmannan, C Scotland, UK
28 L8 **Alva** Oklahoma, C USA
106 H8 **Alva** ≈ N Portugal
97 J18 **Älvängen** Älvsborg, S Sweden
12 F14 **Alvanley** Ontario, S Canada
43 S14 **Alvarado** Veracruz-Llave, E Mexico
27 T7 **Alvarado** Texas, SW USA
60 D13 **Alvarães** Amazonas, NW Brazil
42 G6 **Alvaro Obregón, Presa** ⊠ W Mexico
96 H10 **Alvdal** Hedmark, S Norway
96 K12 **Älvdalen** Kopparberg, C Sweden
63 E15 **Alvear** Corrientes, NE Argentina
xxxviii C16 **Alvechurch** Worcestershire, W England, UK
106 F10 **Alverca do Ribatejo** Lisboa, C Portugal
xlii L11 **Alves** Moray, N Scotland, UK
97 L20 **Alvesta** Kronoberg, S Sweden
xxxvi L9 **Alveston** South Gloucestershire, SW England, UK
xxxviii L12 **Alveston** Warwickshire, C England, UK
xlii K13 **Alvie** Highland, NW Scotland, UK
96 D13 **Ålvik** Hordaland, S Norway
27 W12 **Alvin** Texas, SW USA
96 O13 **Älvkarleby** Uppsala, C Sweden
27 S5 **Alvord** Texas, SW USA
95 G18 **Älvros** Jämtland, C Sweden
97 J19 **Älvsborg** ◆ *county* S Sweden
94 J13 **Älvsbyn** Norrbotten, N Sweden
148 K12 **Al Wafrā'** SE Kuwait
146 J6 **Al Wajh** Tabūk, NW Saudi Arabia
149 N16 **Al Wakrah** *var.* Wakra. C Qatar
144 M8 **al Walaj, Sha'īb** *dry watercourse* W Iraq
158 I11 **Alwar** Rājasthān, N India
147 Q5 **Al Wari'ah** Ash Sharqīyah, N Saudi Arabia
161 G22 **Alwaye** Kerala, SW India
xxxv H5 **Alwen, Llyn** ◎ N Wales, UK
168 K14 **Alxa Zuoqi** *var.* Ehen Hudag. Nei Mongol Zizhiqu, N China
Al Yaman *see* Yemen
144 G9 **Al Yarmūk** Irbid, N Jordan
Alyat/Alyaty-Pristan' *see* Älät
117 I14 **Alykí** *var.* Aliki. Thásos, N Greece
xliii M16 **Alyth** Perth and Kinross, C Scotland, UK
121 F14 **Alytus** *Pol.* Olita. Alytus, S Lithuania
103 N23 **Alz** ≈ SE Germany
35 Y11 **Alzada** Montana, NW USA
126 Ii14 **Alzamay** Irkutskaya Oblast', S Russian Federation
101 M25 **Alzette** ≈ S Luxembourg
107 S10 **Alzira** *var.* Alcira ; *anc.* Saetabicula, Suero. País Valenciano, E Spain
Al Zubair *see* Az Zubayr
189 O8 **Amadeus, Lake** *seasonal lake* Northern Territory, C Australia
83 E15 **Amadi** Western Equatoria, SW Sudan
16 Nn3 **Amadjuak Lake** ◎ Baffin Island, Northwest Territories, N Canada
97 J23 **Amager** *island* E Denmark
170 Cc13 **Amagi** Fukuoka, Kyūshū, SW Japan
171 J17 **Amagi-san** ▲ Honshū, S Japan
175 Tt11 **Amahai** *var.* Masohi. Pulau Seram, E Indonesia
40 M16 **Amak Island** *island* Alaska, USA
170 Bb14 **Amakusa-nada** *gulf* Kyūshū, SW Japan
97 J16 **Åmål** Älvsborg, S Sweden
56 E8 **Amalfi** Antioquia, N Colombia
109 L18 **Amalfi** Campania, S Italy
117 D19 **Amaliáda** *var.* Amaliás. Dytikí Ellás, S Greece
Amaliás *see* Amaliáda
160 F12 **Amalner** Mahārāshtra, C India
176 X12 **Amamapare** Irian Jaya, E Indonesia
61 H21 **Amambaí, Serra de** *var.* Cordillera de Amambay, Serra de Amambay. ⛰ Brazil/Paraguay *see also* Amambay, Cordillera de
64 P4 **Amambay** *off.* Departamento del Amambay. ◆ *department* E Paraguay
64 P5 **Amambay, Cordillera de** *var.* Serra de Amambaí, Serra de Amambay. ⛰ Brazil/Paraguay *see also* Amambaí, Serra de
Amambay, Serra de *see* Amambaí, Serra de/Amambay, Cordillera de
172 Q13 **Amami-guntō** *island group* SW Japan
172 Qq13 **Amami-Ō-shima** *island* S Japan
194 E10 **Amanab** Sandaun, NW PNG
108 J13 **Amandola** Marche, C Italy
109 N21 **Amantea** Calabria, SW Italy
203 W10 **Amanu** *island* Îles Tuamotu, C French Polynesia
60 J10 **Amapá** Amapá, NE Brazil
60 J11 **Amapá** *off.* Estado de Amapá; *prev.* Território de Amapá. ◆ *state* NE Brazil
44 H8 **Amapala** Valle, S Honduras
Amara *see* Al 'Amārah
106 H6 **Amarante** Porto, N Portugal
177 G5 **Amarapura** Mandalay, C Burma
168 L9 **Amardalay** Dundgovĭ, C Mongolia
106 I12 **Amareleja** Beja, S Portugal
37 V11 **Amargosa Range** ⛰ California, W USA
27 N2 **Amarillo** Texas, SW USA
Amarinthos *see* Amárynthos
109 K15 **Amaro, Monte** ▲ C Italy
117 H18 **Amárynthos** *var.* Amarinthos. Évvoia, C Greece
Amasia *see* Amasya
142 K12 **Amasya** *anc.* Amasia. Amasya, N Turkey
142 K11 **Amasya** ◆ *province* N Turkey
44 F4 **Amatique, Bahía de** *bay* Gulf of Honduras, W Caribbean Sea
44 D6 **Amatitlán, Lago de** ◎ S Guatemala
109 J14 **Amatrice** Lazio, C Italy
202 C8 **Amatuku** *atoll* C Tuvalu
101 J20 **Amay** Liège, E Belgium
50 F7 **Amazon** *Sp.* Amazonas. ≈ Brazil/Peru
61 C14 **Amazonas** *off.* Estado do Amazonas. ◆ *state* N Brazil
56 G15 **Amazonas** *off.* Comisaria del Amazonas. ◆ *province* SE Colombia
58 C10 **Amazonas** *off.* Departamento de Amazonas. ◆ *department* N Peru

◆ Country ● Country Capital ◇ Dependent Territory ○ Dependent Territory Capital ◆ Administrative Region ✕ International Airport ▲ Mountain ⛰ Mountain Range Volcano ≈ River ◎ Lake ⊠ Reservoir

Amazonas – Anosibe An'Ala

56 M12 **Amazonas** *off.* Territorio Amazonas. ◆ *federal territory* S Venezuela
Amazonas *see* Amazon
50 F7 **Amazon Basin** *basin* N South America
49 V5 **Amazon Fan** *undersea feature* W Atlantic Ocean
60 K11 **Amazon, Mouths of the** *delta* NE Brazil
197 C12 **Ambae** *var.* Aoba, Omba. *island* C Vanuatu
158 I9 **Ambāla** Haryāna, NW India
161 J26 **Ambalangoda** Southern Province, SW Sri Lanka
161 K26 **Ambalantota** Southern Province, S Sri Lanka
180 I6 **Ambalavao** Fianarantsoa, C Madagascar
56 E10 **Ambalema** Tolima, C Colombia
81 E17 **Ambam** Sud, S Cameroon
180 J2 **Ambanja** Antsirañana, N Madagascar
127 O5 **Ambarchik** Respublika Sakha (Yakutiya), NE Russian Federation
64 K9 **Ambargasta, Salinas de** *salt lake* C Argentina
128 J6 **Ambarnyy** Respublika Kareliya, NW Russian Federation
58 C7 **Ambato** Tungurahua, C Ecuador
180 I5 **Ambatolampy** Antananarivo, C Madagascar
180 H4 **Ambatomainty** Mahajanga, W Madagascar
180 J4 **Ambatondrazaka** Toamasina, C Madagascar
175 Ss12 **Ambelau, Pulau** *see* Ambelau, Pulau
103 L20 **Amberg** *var.* Amberg in der Oberpfalz. Bayern, SE Germany
Amberg in der Oberpfalz *see* Amberg
44 H1 **Ambergris Cay** *island* NE Belize
105 S11 **Ambérieu-en-Bugey** Ain, E France
xxxvii S13 **Amberley** West Sussex, SE England, UK
193 I18 **Amberley** Canterbury, South Island, NZ
105 P11 **Ambert** Puy-de-Dôme, C France
Ambianum *see* Amiens
78 J11 **Ambidédi** Kayes, SW Mali
160 M10 **Ambikāpur** Madhya Pradesh, C India
180 J2 **Ambilobe** Antsirañana, N Madagascar
195 Q10 **Ambitle Island** *island* Feni Islands, NE PNG
xli R4 **Amble** Northumberland, N England, UK
xxxviii A15 **Amblecote** Dudley, C England, UK
41 O7 **Ambler** Alaska, USA
xl M10 **Ambleside** Cumbria, NW England, UK
Amblève *see* Amel
Ambo *see* Hāgere Hiywet
180 I8 **Amboasary** Toliara, S Madagascar
180 J4 **Ambodifotatra** *var.* Ambodifototra. Toamasina, E Madagascar
Amboenten *see* Ambunten
180 I5 **Ambohidratrimo** Antananarivo, C Madagascar
180 I6 **Ambohimahasoa** Fianarantsoa, SE Madagascar
180 K3 **Ambohitralanana** Antsirañana, NE Madagascar
176 X10 **Amboi, Kepulauan** *island group* E Indonesia
Amboina *see* Ambon
104 M8 **Amboise** Indre-et-Loire, C France
175 T11 **Ambon** *prev.* Amboina, Amboyna. Pulau Ambon, E Indonesia
175 T12 **Ambon, Pulau** *island* E Indonesia
83 I20 **Amboseli, Lake** ◎ Kenya/Tanzania
180 I6 **Ambositra** Fianarantsoa, SE Madagascar
180 I8 **Ambovombe** Toliara, S Madagascar
37 W14 **Amboy** California, W USA
32 L11 **Amboy** Illinois, N USA
Amboyna *see* Ambon
Ambracia *see* Árta
20 B14 **Ambridge** Pennsylvania, NE USA
Ambrim *see* Ambrym
84 A11 **Ambriz** Bengo, NW Angola
Ambrizete *see* N'Zeto
197 C13 **Ambrym** *var.* Ambrim. *island* C Vanuatu
174 Mm14 **Ambunten** *prev.* Amboenten. Pulau Madura, E Indonesia
194 G10 **Ambunti** East Sepik, NW PNG
161 I20 **Āmbūr** Tamil Nādu, SE India
40 E17 **Amchitka Island** *island* Aleutian Islands, Alaska, USA
40 F17 **Amchitka Pass** *strait* Aleutian Islands, Alaska, USA
xxxix P3 **Amcotts** North Lincolnshire, N England, UK
147 R15 **'Amd** C Yemen
80 J10 **Am Dam** Ouaddaï, E Chad
176 Uu15 **Amdassa** Pulau Yamdena, E Indonesia
129 U1 **Amderma** Nenetskiy Avtonomnyy Okrug, NW Russian Federation
165 N14 **Amdo** Xizang Zizhiqu, W China
42 K13 **Ameca** Jalisco, SW Mexico
43 P14 **Amecameca** *var.* Amecameca de Juárez. México, C Mexico
Amecameca de Juárez *see* Amecameca
63 A20 **Ameghino** Buenos Aires, E Argentina
101 M21 **Amel** *Fr.* Amblève. Liège, E Belgium
100 K4 **Ameland** *Fris.* It Amelân. *island* Waddeneilanden, N Netherlands
Amelân, It *see* Ameland
109 H14 **Amelia** Umbria, C Italy
23 V6 **Amelia Court House** Virginia, NE USA
25 W8 **Amelia Island** *island* Florida, SE USA
20 L12 **Amenia** New York, NE USA
America *see* United States of America
67 M21 **America-Antarctica Ridge** *undersea feature* S Atlantic Ocean
America in Miniature *see* Maryland
62 L9 **Americana** São Paulo, S Brazil
35 Q15 **American Falls** Idaho, NW USA
35 Q15 **American Falls Reservoir** ▣ Idaho, NW USA
38 L3 **American Fork** Utah, W USA
198 D8 **American Samoa** ◇ *US unincorporated territory* W Polynesia
25 S6 **Americus** Georgia, SE USA
100 K12 **Amerongen** Utrecht, C Netherlands
100 K11 **Amersfoort** Utrecht, C Netherlands
xxxvii S8 **Amersham** Buckinghamshire, SE England, UK
32 I5 **Amery** Wisconsin, N USA
205 W6 **Amery Ice Shelf** *ice shelf* Antarctica
31 V13 **Ames** Iowa, C USA
xxxvii O11 **Amesbury** Wiltshire, S England, UK
21 P10 **Amesbury** Massachusetts, NE USA
Amestratus *see* Mistretta
117 F18 **Amfíkleia** *var.* Amfiklia. Stereá Ellás, C Greece
Amfiklia *see* Amfíkleia
117 D17 **Amfilochía** *var.* Amfilokhía. Dytikí Ellás, C Greece
Amfilokhía *see* Amfilochía
116 H13 **Amfípoli** *anc.* Amphipolis. *site of ancient city* Kentrikí Makedonía, NE Greece
117 F18 **Ámfissa** Stereá Ellás, C Greece
126 M11 **Amga** Respublika Sakha (Yakutiya), NE Russian Federation
126 M11 **Amga** ~ NE Russian Federation
Amgalang *see* Xin Barag Zuoqi
195 N12 **Amgen** ~ New Britain, C PNG
127 P4 **Amguema** ~ NE Russian Federation
127 Nn14 **Amgun'** ~ SE Russian Federation
11 P15 **Amherst** Nova Scotia, SE Canada
20 M11 **Amherst** Massachusetts, NE USA
20 D10 **Amherst** New York, NE USA
26 M4 **Amherst** Texas, SW USA
23 U6 **Amherst** Virginia, NE USA
Amherst *see* Kyaikkami
12 C18 **Amherstburg** Ontario, S Canada
23 Q6 **Amherstdale** West Virginia, NE USA
12 K15 **Amherst Island** *island* Ontario, SE Canada
Amida *see* Diyarbakır
30 J6 **Amidon** North Dakota, N USA
105 O3 **Amiens** *anc.* Ambianum, Samarobriva. Somme, N France
145 P8 **'Āmij, Wādī** *var.* Wadi 'Amīq. *dry watercourse* W Iraq
142 L17 **Amik Ovası** ◎ S Turkey
Amilhayt, Wādī *see* Umm al Ḥayt, Wādī
Amíndaion/Amindeo *see* Amýntaio
161 C21 **Amīndīvi Islands** *island group* Lakshadweep, India, N Indian Ocean
145 U6 **Amīn Ḥabīb** E Iraq
85 E20 **Aminuis** Omaheke, E Namibia
'Amīq, Wadi *see* 'Āmij, Wādī
148 J7 **Amīrābād** Īlām, NW Iran
Amirante Bank *see* Amirante Ridge
181 N6 **Amirante Basin** *undersea feature* W Indian Ocean
181 N6 **Amirante Islands** *var.* Amirantes Group. *island group* C Seychelles
181 N7 **Amirante Ridge** *var.* Amirante Bank. *undersea feature* W Indian Ocean
Amirantes Group *see* Amirante Islands
181 N7 **Amirante Trench** *undersea feature* W Indian Ocean
176 Z12 **Amisibil** Irian Jaya, E Indonesia
9 U13 **Amisk Lake** ◎ Saskatchewan, C Canada
Amistad, Presa de la *see* Amistad Reservoir
27 O12 **Amistad Reservoir** *var.* Presa de la Amistad. ▣ Mexico/USA
Amisus *see* Samsun
24 K8 **Amite** *var.* Amite City. Louisiana, S USA
Amite City *see* Amite
29 T12 **Amity** Arkansas, C USA
160 H11 **Amla** *prev.* Amulla. Madhya Pradesh, C India
40 I17 **Amlia Island** *island* Aleutian Islands, Alaska, USA
xxxv F3 **Amlwch** Isle of Anglesey, NW Wales, UK
Ammaia *see* Portalegre
144 H10 **'Ammān** *var.* Amman; *anc.* Philadelphia, *Bibl.* Rabbah Ammon, Rabbath Ammon. ● (Jordan) 'Ammān, NW Jordan
144 H10 **'Ammān** *off.* Muḥāfaẓat 'Ammān. ◆ *governorate* NW Jordan
xxxv G13 **Ammanford** Carmarthenshire, S Wales, UK
95 N14 **Ämmänsaari** Oulu, E Finland
95 H13 **Ammarnäs** Västerbotten, N Sweden
207 O15 **Ammassalik** *var.* Angmagssalik. S Greenland
103 K24 **Ammer** ~ SE Germany
103 K24 **Ammersee** ◎ SE Germany
100 J13 **Ammerzoden** Gelderland, C Netherlands
Ammóchostos *see* Gazimağusa
Ammóchostos, Kólpos *see* Gazimağusa Körfezi
Amnok-kang *see* Yalu
Amoea *see* Portalegre
Amoentai *see* Amuntai
Amoerang *see* Amurang
149 O4 **Āmol** *var.* Amul. Māzandarān, N Iran
117 K21 **Amorgós** Amorgós, Kykládes, Greece, Aegean Sea
117 K22 **Amorgós** *island* Kykládes, Greece, Aegean Sea
25 N3 **Amory** Mississippi, S USA
10 I13 **Amos** Québec, SE Canada
97 G15 **Åmot** Buskerud, S Norway
97 E15 **Åmot** Telemark, S Norway
97 J15 **Åmotfors** Värmland, C Sweden
78 L10 **Amourj** Hodh ech Chargui, SE Mauritania
Amoy *see* Xiamen
180 H7 **Ampanihy** Toliara, SW Madagascar
161 L25 **Ampara** *var.* Amparai. Eastern Province, E Sri Lanka
180 J4 **Amparafaravola** Toamasina, E Madagascar
Amparai *see* Ampara
62 M9 **Amparo** São Paulo, S Brazil
180 J5 **Ampasimanolotra** Toamasina, E Madagascar
59 H17 **Ampato, Nevado** ▲ S Peru
103 L23 **Amper** ~ SE Germany
66 M9 **Ampère Seamount** *undersea feature* E Atlantic Ocean
Amphipolis *see* Amfípoli
178 M10 **Amphitrite Group** *island group* N Paracel Islands
176 U15 **Amplawas** *var.* Emplawas. Pulau Babar, E Indonesia
xli T11 **Ampleforth** North Yorkshire, N England, UK
107 U7 **Amposta** Cataluña, NE Spain
xxxvii S6 **Ampthill** Bedfordshire, C England, UK
13 V7 **Amqui** Québec, SE Canada
147 O14 **'Amrān** W Yemen
Amraoti *see* Amrāvati
160 H12 **Amrāvati** *prev.* Amraoti. Mahārāshtra, C India
160 C11 **Amreli** Gujarāt, W India
110 H6 **Amriswil** Thurgau, NE Switzerland
144 H5 **'Amrīt** *ruins* Ṭarṭūs, W Syria
158 H7 **Amritsar** Punjab, N India
158 J10 **Amroha** Uttar Pradesh, N India
102 G7 **Amrum** *island* NW Germany
95 I15 **Åmsele** Västerbotten, N Sweden
100 I10 **Amstelveen** Noord-Holland, C Netherlands
100 I10 **Amsterdam** ● (Netherlands) Noord-Holland, C Netherlands
20 K10 **Amsterdam** New York, NE USA
181 Q11 **Amsterdam Fracture Zone** *tectonic feature* S Indian Ocean
181 R11 **Amsterdam Island** *island* NE French Southern and Antarctic Territories
111 U4 **Amstetten** Niederösterreich, N Austria
80 J11 **Am Timan** Salamat, SE Chad
152 L12 **Amu-Bukhoro Kanali** *var.* Aral-Bukhorskiy Kanal. *canal* C Uzbekistan
145 O1 **'Āmūdah** *var.* Amude. Al Ḥasakah, N Syria
152 M14 **Amu-Dar'ya** Lebapskiy Velayat, NE Turkmenistan
153 O15 **Amu Darya** *Rus.* Amudar'ya, *Taj.* Dar"yoi Amu, *Turkm.* Amyderya, *Uzb.* Amudaryo; *anc.* Oxus. ~ C Asia
Amudar'ya/Amudaryo/Amu, Dar"yoi *see* Amu Darya
Amude *see* 'Āmūdah
146 L3 **'Amūd, Jabal al** ▲ NW Saudi Arabia
40 J17 **Amukta Island** *island* Aleutian Islands, Alaska, USA
40 I17 **Amukta Pass** *strait* Aleutian Islands, Alaska, USA
Amul *see* Āmol
Amulla *see* Amla
Amundsen Basin *see* Fram Basin
xliii K17 **Amulree** Perth and Kinross, C Scotland, UK
205 X3 **Amundsen Bay** *bay* Antarctica
205 P10 **Amundsen Coast** *physical region* Antarctica
15 H2 **Amundsen Gulf** *gulf* Northwest Territories, N Canada
199 Ll16 **Amundsen Plain** *undersea feature* S Pacific Ocean
205 Q9 **Amundsen-Scott** *US research station* Antarctica
204 J11 **Amundsen Sea** *sea* S Pacific Ocean
96 M12 **Amungen** ◎ C Sweden
175 N10 **Amuntai** *prev.* Amoentai. Borneo, C Indonesia
133 W6 **Amur** *Chin.* Heilong Jiang. ~ China/Russian Federation
175 Rr7 **Amurang** *prev.* Amoerang. Sulawesi, C Indonesia
175 Rr7 **Amurang, Teluk** *bay* Sulawesi, C Indonesia
107 O3 **Amurrio** País Vasco, N Spain
127 Nn15 **Amursk** Khabarovskiy Kray, SE Russian Federation
126 M14 **Amurskaya Oblast'** ◆ *province* SE Russian Federation
82 G7 **'Amur, Wadi** ~ NE Sudan
117 C17 **Amvrakikós Kólpos** *gulf* W Greece
Amvrosiyevka *see* Amvrosiyivka
119 X8 **Amvrosiyivka** *Rus.* Amvrosiyevka. Donets'ka Oblast', SE Ukraine
Amyderya *see* Amu Darya
116 E13 **Amýntaio** *var.* Amindeo; *prev.* Amíndaion. Dytikí Makedonía, N Greece
12 B6 **Amyot** Ontario, S Canada
203 U10 **Anaa** *atoll* Îles Tuamotu, C French Polynesia
Anabanoea *see* Anabanua
175 Pp12 **Anabanua** *prev.* Anabanoea. Sulawesi, C Indonesia
201 R8 **Anabar** NE Nauru
126 K7 **Anabar** ~ NE Russian Federation
An Abhainn Mhór *see* Blackwater
57 O6 **Anaco** Anzoátegui, NE Venezuela
35 Q10 **Anaconda** Montana, NW USA
34 H7 **Anacortes** Washington, NW USA
28 M11 **Anadarko** Oklahoma, C USA
116 N12 **Ana Dere** ~ NW Turkey
106 G8 **Anadia** Aveiro, N Portugal
Anadolu Dağları *see* Doğu Karadeniz Dağları
127 Pp5 **Anadyr'** Chukotskiy Avtonomnyy Okrug, NE Russian Federation
127 P5 **Anadyr'** ~ NE Russian Federation
Anadyr, Gulf of *see* Anadyrskiy Zaliv
133 X4 **Anadyrskiy Khrebet** *var.* Chukot Range. ▲ NE Russian Federation
127 Q4 **Anadyrskiy Zaliv** *Eng.* Gulf of Anadyr. *gulf* NE Russian Federation
117 K22 **Anáfi** *anc.* Anaphe. *island* Kykládes, Greece, Aegean Sea
109 J15 **Anagni** Lazio, C Italy
'Ānah *see* 'Annah
37 T15 **Anaheim** California, W USA
8 L15 **Anahim Lake** British Columbia, SW Canada
40 B8 **Anahola** Kauai, Hawaii, USA, C Pacific Ocean
27 X11 **Anahuac** Texas, SW USA
43 O7 **Anáhuac** Nuevo León, NE Mexico
161 G22 **Anai Mudi** ▲ S India
Anaiza *see* 'Unayzah
161 M15 **Anakāpalle** Andhra Pradesh, E India
203 W15 **Anakena, Playa de** *beach* Easter Island, Chile, E Pacific Ocean
41 Q7 **Anaktuvuk Pass** Alaska, USA
41 Q6 **Anaktuvuk River** ~ Alaska, USA
180 J3 **Analalava** Mahajanga, NW Madagascar
46 F6 **Ana María, Golfo de** *gulf* C Cuba
Anambas Islands *see* Anambas, Kepulauan
174 Ii5 **Anambas, Kepulauan** *var.* Anambas Islands. *island group* W Indonesia
79 U17 **Anambra** ◆ *state* SE Nigeria
31 N4 **Anamoose** North Dakota, N USA
31 Y13 **Anamosa** Iowa, C USA
142 H17 **Anamur** İçel, S Turkey
142 H17 **Anamur Burnu** *headland* S Turkey
170 Ff16 **Anan** Tokushima, Shikoku, SW Japan
160 O12 **Ānandadur** Orissa, E India
161 H18 **Anantapur** Andhra Pradesh, S India
158 H5 **Anantnāg** *var.* Islamabad. Jammu and Kashmir, NW India
Ananyev *see* Anan'yiv
119 O9 **Anan'yiv** *Rus.* Ananyev. Odes'ka Oblast', SW Ukraine
130 J14 **Anapa** Krasnodarskiy Kray, SW Russian Federation
Anaphe *see* Anáfi
61 K18 **Anápolis** Goiás, C Brazil
149 R10 **Anār** Kermān, C Iran
Anár *see* Inari
149 P7 **Anārak** Eşfahān, C Iran
Anar Dara *see* Anār Darreh
154 J7 **Anār Darreh** *var.* Anar Dara. Farāh, W Afghanistan
Anárjohka *see* Inarijoki
xliv C13 **Anascaul** Kerry, SW Ireland
25 X9 **Anastasia Island** *island* Florida, SE USA
196 K7 **Anatahan** *island* C Northern Mariana Islands
132 M6 **Anatolia** *plateau* C Turkey
88 F14 **Anatolian Plate** *tectonic feature* Asia/Europe
116 H13 **Anatolikí Makedonía kai Thráki** *Eng.* Macedonia East and Thrace. ◆ *region* NE Greece
197 D17 **Anatom** *var.* Aneityum; *prev.* Kéamu. *island* S Vanuatu
64 L8 **Añatuya** Santiago del Estero, N Argentina
An Baile Meánach *see* Ballymena
An Bhearú *see* Barrow
An Bhóinn *see* Boyne
An Blascaod Mór *see* Great Blasket Island
An Cabhán *see* Cavan
An Caisleán Nua *see* Newcastle
99 **An Caisleán Riabhach** *see* Castlerea, Ireland
99 **An Caisleán Riabhach** *see* Castlereagh, Northern Ireland, UK
58 C13 **Ancash** *off.* Departamento de Ancash. ◆ *department* W Peru
An Cathair *see* Caher
104 J8 **Ancenis** Loire-Atlantique, NW France
An Chanáil Ríoga *see* Royal Canal
An Cheacha *see* Caha Mountains
41 R11 **Anchorage** Alaska, USA
41 R12 **Anchorage** ✕ Alaska, USA
41 Q13 **Anchor Point** Alaska, USA
An Chorr Chríochach *see* Cookstown
67 M24 **Anchorstack Point** *headland* W Tristan da Cunha
An Clár *see* Clare
An Clochán *see* Clifden
99 **An Clochán Liath** *see* Dunglow
25 U12 **Anclote Keys** *island group* Florida, SE USA
An Cóbh *see* Cobh
59 J17 **Ancohuma, Nevado de** ▲ W Bolivia
An Comar *see* Comber
59 D14 **Ancón** Lima, W Peru
108 J12 **Ancona** Marche, C Italy
xli P1 **Ancroft** Northumberland, N England, UK
xliii O22 **Ancrum** The Borders, S Scotland, UK
Ancuabe *see* Ancuabi
84 Q13 **Ancuabi** *var.* Ancuabe. Cabo Delgado, NE Mozambique
65 F17 **Ancud** *prev.* San Carlos de Ancud. Los Lagos, S Chile
65 G17 **Ancud, Golfo de** *gulf* S Chile
Ancyra *see* Ankara
169 V8 **Anda** Heilongjiang, NE China
59 G16 **Andahuaylas** Apurímac, S Peru
An Daingean *see* Dingle
159 R15 **Āndāl** West Bengal, NE India
96 E9 **Åndalsnes** Møre og Romsdal, S Norway
106 K13 **Andalucía** *Eng.* Andalusia. ◆ *autonomous community* S Spain
25 P7 **Andalusia** Alabama, S USA
Andalusia *see* Andalucía
157 Q21 **Andaman and Nicobar Islands** *var.* Andamans and Nicobars. ◆ *union territory* India, NE Indian Ocean
181 T4 **Andaman Basin** *undersea feature* NE Indian Ocean
157 P19 **Andaman Islands** *island group* India, NE Indian Ocean
181 T4 **Andaman Sea** *sea* NE Indian Ocean
59 K19 **Andamarca** Oruro, C Bolivia
176 V10 **Andamata** Irian Jaya, E Indonesia
190 H5 **Andamooka** South Australia
147 Y9 **'Andām, Wādī** *seasonal river* NE Oman
180 J3 **Andapa** Antsirañana, NE Madagascar
155 R4 **Andarāb** *var.* Banow. Baghlān, NE Afghanistan
Andarbag *see* Andarbogh
153 S13 **Andarbogh** *Rus.* Andarbag, Anderbak. S Tajikistan
111 Z5 **Andau** Burgenland, E Austria
Andaung Pech *see* Bâ Kêv
110 I10 **Andeer** Graubünden, S Switzerland
94 H9 **Andenes** Nordland, C Norway
101 J20 **Andenne** Namur, SE Belgium
79 S11 **Andéramboukane** Gao, E Mali
Anderbak *see* Andarbogh
101 G18 **Anderlecht** Brussels, C Belgium
101 G21 **Anderlues** Hainaut, S Belgium
110 G9 **Andermatt** Uri, C Switzerland
103 E17 **Andernach** *anc.* Antunnacum. Rheinland-Pfalz, SW Germany
196 D15 **Andersen Air Force Base** *air base* NE Guam
41 R9 **Anderson** Alaska, USA
37 N4 **Anderson** California, W USA
33 P13 **Anderson** Indiana, N USA
29 R8 **Anderson** Missouri, C USA
23 P11 **Anderson** South Carolina, SE USA
27 V10 **Anderson** Texas, SW USA
15 Gg3 **Anderson** ~ Northwest Territories, NW Canada
97 K20 **Anderstorp** Jönköping, S Sweden
56 D9 **Andes** Antioquia, W Colombia
49 P7 **Andes** ▲ W South America
31 P12 **Andes, Lake** ◎ South Dakota, N USA
94 H9 **Andfjorden** *fjord* E Norwegian Sea
161 H16 **Andhra Pradesh** ◆ *state* E India
100 J8 **Andijk** Noord-Holland, NW Netherlands
153 S10 **Andijon** *Rus.* Andizhan. Andijon Wiloyati, E Uzbekistan
153 S10 **Andijon Wiloyati** *Rus.* Andizhanskaya Oblast'. ◆ *province* E Uzbekistan
Andikíthira *see* Antikýthira
180 J4 **Andilamena** Toamasina, C Madagascar
148 L8 **Andīmeshk** *var.* Andimishk; *prev.* Salehābād. Khūzestān, SW Iran
Andimishk *see* Andīmeshk
Andipáros *see* Antíparos
Andipaxi *see* Antípaxoi
Andípsara *see* Antípsara
142 L16 **Andırın** Kahramanmaraş, S Turkey
164 J8 **Andirlangar** Xinjiang Uygur Zizhiqu, NW China
Andírrion *see* Antírrio
Ándissa *see* Ántissa
Andizhan *see* Andijon
Andizhanskaya Oblast' *see* Andijon Wiloyati
155 N2 **Andkhvoy** Fāryāb, N Afghanistan
107 Q2 **Andoain** País Vasco, N Spain
176 W9 **Andoi** Irian Jaya, E Indonesia
169 Y15 **Andong** *Jap.* Antō. E South Korea
111 R4 **Andorf** Oberösterreich, N Austria
107 S7 **Andorra** Aragón, NE Spain
107 V4 **Andorra** *off.* Principality of Andorra, *Cat.* Valls d'Andorra, *Fr.* Vallée d'Andorre. ◆ *monarchy* SW Europe
Andorra *see* Andorra la Vella
107 V4 **Andorra la Vella** *var.* Andorra, *Fr.* Andorre la Vielle, *Sp.* Andorra la Vieja. ● (Andorra) C Andorra
Andorra la Vieja *see* Andorra la Vella
Andorra, Valls d'/Andorre, Vallée d' *see* Andorra
Andorre la Vielle *see* Andorra la Vella
xxxvii P11 **Andover** Hampshire, S England, UK
29 N6 **Andover** Kansas, C USA
94 G10 **Andøya** *island* C Norway
62 I8 **Andradina** São Paulo, S Brazil
Andraitx *see* Andratx
41 N10 **Andreafsky River** ~ Alaska, USA
40 H17 **Andreanof Islands** *island group* Aleutian Islands, Alaska, USA
128 H16 **Andreapol'** Tverskaya Oblast', W Russian Federation
xl G10 **Andreas** N Isle of Man
Andreas, Cape *see* Zafer Burnu
Andreevka *see* Andreyevka
23 N10 **Andrews** North Carolina, SE USA
23 T13 **Andrews** South Carolina, SE USA
26 M7 **Andrews** Texas, SW USA
181 N5 **Andrew Tablemount** *var.* Gora Andryu. *undersea feature* W Indian Ocean
151 W13 **Andreyevka** *Kaz.* Andreevka. Taldykorgan, SW Kazakhstan
109 N17 **Andria** Puglia, SE Italy
115 K16 **Andrijevica** Montenegro, SW Yugoslavia
117 E20 **Andrítsaina** Pelopónnisos, S Greece
An Droichead Nua *see* Droichead Nua
Androna *see* Khirbat al Andarīn
Andropov *see* Rybinsk
117 J19 **Ándros** Ándros, Kykládes, Greece, Aegean Sea
117 J20 **Ándros** *island* Kykládes, Greece, Aegean Sea
21 O7 **Androscoggin River** ~ Maine/New Hampshire, NE USA
46 F3 **Andros Island** *island* NW Bahamas
131 R7 **Androsovka** Samarskaya Oblast', W Russian Federation
46 G3 **Andros Town** Andros Island, NW Bahamas
161 D21 **Āndrott Island** *island* Lakshadweep, India, N Indian Ocean
119 N5 **Andrushivka** Zhytomyrs'ka Oblast', N Ukraine
113 K17 **Andrychów** Bielsko-Biała, S Poland
Andryu, Gora *see* Andrew Tablemount
94 I10 **Andselv** Troms, N Norway
81 O17 **Andudu** Haut-Zaïre, NE Zaire
107 N13 **Andújar** *anc.* Illiturgis. Andalucía, SW Spain
84 C12 **Andulo** Bié, W Angola
105 Q14 **Anduze** Gard, S France
An Earagail *see* Errigal
97 L19 **Aneby** Jönköping, S Sweden
Anécho *see* Aného
79 Q9 **Anéfis** Kidal, NE Mali
47 U8 **Anegada** *island* NE British Virgin Islands
63 B25 **Anegada, Bahía** *bay* E Argentina
47 U9 **Anegada Passage** *passage* Anguilla/British Virgin Islands
79 R17 **Aného** *var.* Anécho; *prev.* Petit-Popo. S Togo
Aneityum *see* Anatom
119 N10 **Anenii Noi** *Rus.* Novyye Aneny. C Moldova
194 L12 **Anepmete** New Britain, E PNG
107 U4 **Aneto** ▲ NE Spain
Änew *see* Annau
Änewetak *see* Enewetak Atoll
79 Y8 **Aney** Agadez, NE Niger
99 **An Fheoir** *see* Nore
126 Ii13 **Angara** ~ C Russian Federation
126 J15 **Angarsk** Irkutskaya Oblast', S Russian Federation
95 G17 **Ånge** Västernorrland, C Sweden
Ángel *see* Úhlava
42 D4 **Ángel de la Guarda, Isla** *island* NW Mexico
179 P10 **Angeles** *off.* Angeles City. Luzon, N Philippines
Angeles City *see* Angeles
Angel Falls *see* Ángel, Salto
97 J22 **Ängelholm** Kristianstad, S Sweden
63 A17 **Angélica** Santa Fe, C Argentina
27 W8 **Angelina River** ~ Texas, SW USA
57 Q9 **Ángel, Salto** *Eng.* Angel Falls. *waterfall* E Venezuela
97 M15 **Ängelsberg** Västmanland, C Sweden
37 P8 **Angels Camp** California, W USA
111 W7 **Anger** Steiermark, SE Austria
Angerapp *see* Ozersk
Angerburg *see* Węgorzewo
95 H15 **Ångermanälven** ~ N Sweden
102 P11 **Angermünde** Brandenburg, NE Germany
104 K7 **Angers** *anc.* Juliomagus. Maine-et-Loire, NW France
13 W7 **Angers** ~ Québec, SE Canada
95 J16 **Ångesön** *island* N Sweden
Angistro *see* Ágkistro
116 H13 **Angítis** ~ NE Greece
178 J14 **Ângk Tasaôm** *prev.* Angtassom. Takêv, S Cambodia
xxxv C14 **Angle** Pembrokeshire, SW Wales, UK
193 C25 **Anglem, Mount** ▲ Stewart Island, Southland, SW NZ
xxxv E4 **Anglesey** *island* NW Wales, UK
104 I15 **Anglet** Pyrénées-Atlantiques, SW France
27 W12 **Angleton** Texas, SW USA
Anglia *see* England
12 H9 **Angliers** Québec, SE Canada
Anglo-Egyptian Sudan *see* Sudan
Angmagssalik *see* Ammassalik
xxxvii S13 **Angmering** West Sussex, SE England, UK
178 Ii8 **Ang Nam Ngum** ◎ C Laos
81 N16 **Ango** Haut-Zaïre, N Zaire
85 Q15 **Angoche** Nampula, E Mozambique
65 G14 **Angol** Araucanía, C Chile
33 Q11 **Angola** Indiana, N USA
84 A9 **Angola** *off.* Republic of Angola; *prev.* People's Republic of Angola, Portuguese West Africa. ◆ *republic* SW Africa
67 P15 **Angola Basin** *undersea feature* E Atlantic Ocean
41 X13 **Angoon** Admiralty Island, Alaska, USA
153 O14 **Angor** Surkhondaryo Wiloyati, S Uzbekistan
Angora *see* Ankara
194 H10 **Angoram** East Sepik, NW PNG
42 H8 **Angostura** Sinaloa, C Mexico
Angostura *see* Ciudad Bolívar
43 U17 **Angostura, Presa de la** ▣ SE Mexico
30 J11 **Angostura Reservoir** ▣ South Dakota, N USA
104 L11 **Angoulême** *anc.* Iculisma. Charente, W France
104 K11 **Angoumois** *cultural region* W France
66 O2 **Angra do Heroísmo** Terceira, Azores, Portugal, NE Atlantic Ocean
62 O10 **Angra dos Reis** Rio de Janeiro, SE Brazil
Angra Pequena *see* Lüderitz
153 Q10 **Angren** Toshkent Wiloyati, E Uzbekistan
Angtassom *see* Ângk Tasaôm
178 Hh11 **Ang Thong** *var.* Angthong. Ang Thong, C Thailand
81 M16 **Angu** Haut-Zaïre, N Zaire
107 S5 **Angüés** Aragón, NE Spain
47 U9 **Anguilla** ◇ *UK dependent territory* E West Indies
47 V9 **Anguilla** *island* E West Indies
46 F4 **Anguilla Cays** *islets* SW Bahamas
Angul *see* Anugul
167 N1 **Anguli Nur** ◎ E China
81 O18 **Angumu** Haut-Zaïre, E Zaire
xliii M15 **Angus** ◆ *unitary authority* E Scotland, UK
12 G14 **Angus** Ontario, S Canada
61 K19 **Anhangüera** Goiás, S Brazil
101 I21 **Anhée** Namur, S Belgium
97 I21 **Anholt** *island* C Denmark
166 M11 **Anhua** *prev.* Dongping. Hunan, S China
167 P8 **Anhui** *var.* Anhui Sheng, Anhwei, Wan. ◆ *province* E China
Anhui Sheng/Anhwei *see* Anhui
41 O11 **Aniak** Alaska, USA
41 O12 **Aniak River** ~ Alaska, USA
An Iarmhí *see* Westmeath
201 R8 **Anibare** E Nauru
201 R8 **Anibare Bay** *bay* E Nauru, W Pacific Ocean
Anicium *see* le Puy
117 K22 **Ánidro** *island* Kykládes, Greece, Aegean Sea
79 R15 **Anié** C Togo
79 Q15 **Anié** ~ C Togo
104 J16 **Anie, Pic d'** ▲ SW France
131 Y7 **Anikhovka** Orenburgskaya Oblast', W Russian Federation
12 G9 **Anima Nipissing Lake** ◎ Ontario, S Canada
39 O16 **Animas** New Mexico, SW USA
39 P16 **Animas Peak** ▲ New Mexico, SW USA
39 P16 **Animas Valley** *valley* New Mexico, SW USA
118 F13 **Anina** *Ger.* Steierdorf, *Hung.* Stájerlakanina; *prev.* Ştaierdorf-Anina, Steierdorf-Anina, Steyerlak-Anina. Caraş-Severin, SW Romania
31 U14 **Anita** Iowa, C USA
127 Oo16 **Aniva, Mys** *headland* Ostrov Sakhalin, SE Russian Federation
127 Oo16 **Aniva, Zaliv** *bay* SE Russian Federation
197 E16 **Aniwa** *island* S Vanuatu
95 M19 **Anjalankoski** Kymi, S Finland
'Anjar *see* Aanjar
Anjiangying *see* Luanping
12 B8 **Anjigami Lake** ◎ Ontario, S Canada
171 Hh16 **Anjō** *var.* Anzyô. Aichi, Honshū, SW Japan
104 J8 **Anjou** *cultural region* NW France
180 I13 **Anjouan** *var.* Nzwani, Johanna Island. *island* SE Comoros
180 J4 **Anjozorobe** Antananarivo, C Madagascar
169 W13 **Anju** W North Korea
100 M5 **Anjum** *Fris.* Eanjum. Friesland, N Netherlands
180 G6 **Ankaboa, Tanjona** *headland* W Madagascar
166 L7 **Ankang** *prev.* Xing'an. Shaanxi, C China
142 I12 **Ankara** *prev.* Angora, *anc.* Ancyra. ● (Turkey) Ankara, C Turkey
142 H12 **Ankara** ◆ *province* C Turkey
97 N19 **Ankarsrum** Kalmar, S Sweden
180 H6 **Ankazoabo** Toliara, SW Madagascar
180 I4 **Ankazobe** Antananarivo, C Madagascar
31 V14 **Ankeny** Iowa, C USA
178 Kk11 **An Khê** Gia Lai, C Vietnam
102 O9 **Anklam** Mecklenburg-Vorpommern, NE Germany
82 K13 **Ānkober** C Ethiopia
79 O17 **Ankobra** ~ S Ghana
81 N22 **Ankoro** Shaba, SE Zaire
101 L24 **Anlier, Forêt d'** *forest* SE Belgium
166 I13 **Anlong** Guizhou, S China
An Longfort *see* Longford
178 Ii11 **Ânlong Vêng** Siĕmréab, NW Cambodia
An Lorgain *see* Lurgan
167 N8 **Anlu** Hubei, C China
An Mhí *see* Meath
An Mhuir Cheilteach *see* Celtic Sea
An Muileann gCearr *see* Mullingar
95 F16 **Ånn** Jämtland, C Sweden
130 M8 **Anna** Voronezhskaya Oblast', W Russian Federation
32 L17 **Anna** Illinois, N USA
27 U5 **Anna** Texas, SW USA
76 L5 **Annaba** *prev.* Bône. NE Algeria
An Nabatīyah at Taḥtā *see* Nabatîyé
103 N17 **Annaberg-Buchholz** Sachsen, E Germany
111 T9 **Annabichl** ✕ (Klagenfurt) Kärnten, S Austria
146 M5 **An Nafūd** *desert* NW Saudi Arabia
xliv C6 **Annagh Head** *headland* NW Ireland
145 P6 **'Annah** *var.* 'Ānah. NW Iraq
145 P6 **An Nāḥiyah** W Iraq
145 T10 **An Najaf** *var.* Najaf. S Iraq
23 V5 **Anna, Lake** ▣ Virginia, NE USA
xliv I6 **Annalee** ~ N Ireland
xliv L6 **Annalong** Newry and Mourne, S Northern Ireland, UK
178 Jj9 **Annamitique, Chaîne** ▲ C Laos
xliii M24 **Annan** Dumfries and Galloway, S Scotland, UK
31 U8 **Annandale** Minnesota, N USA
23 W4 **Annandale** Virginia, NE USA
201 Q7 **Anna Point** *headland* N Nauru
23 X3 **Annapolis** *state capital* Maryland, NE USA
196 A10 **Anna, Pulo** *island* S Palau
159 O10 **Annapurna** ▲ C Nepal
An Nāqūrah *see* En Nâqoûra
33 R10 **Ann Arbor** Michigan, N USA
An Nás *see* Naas
145 W12 **An Nāṣirīyah** *var.* Nasiriya. SE Iraq
145 W11 **An Naṣr** E Iraq
xlii G9 **Annat Bay** *bay* NW Scotland, UK
152 F13 **Annau** *Turkm.* Änew. Akhalskiy Velayat, C Turkmenistan
123 Mm16 **An Nawfalīyah** *var.* Al Nūwfalīyah. N Libya
xliii I22 **Annbank** South Ayrshire, W Scotland, UK
21 P10 **Ann, Cape** *headland* Massachusetts, NE USA
188 I10 **Annean, Lake** ◎ Western Australia
Anneciacum *see* Annecy
105 T11 **Annecy** *anc.* Anneciacum. Haute-Savoie, E France
105 T11 **Annecy, Lac d'** ◎ E France
105 T10 **Annemasse** Haute-Savoie, E France
41 Z14 **Annette Island** *island* Alexander Archipelago, Alaska, USA
An Nhon *see* Binh Đinh
An Nīl al Abyaḍ *see* White Nile
An Nīl al Azraq *see* Blue Nile
25 Q3 **Anniston** Alabama, S USA
81 A19 **Annobón** *island* W Equatorial Guinea
105 R12 **Annonay** Ardèche, E France
46 K12 **Annotto Bay** C Jamaica
147 R5 **An Nu'ayrīyah** *var.* Narīya. Ash Sharqīyah, NE Saudi Arabia
190 M9 **Annuello** Victoria, SE Australia
145 Q10 **An Nukhayb** S Iraq
145 U9 **An Nu'mānīyah** E Iraq
Áno Arkhánai *see* Epáno Archánes
117 J25 **Anógeia** *var.* Anogia, Anóyia. Kríti, Greece, E Mediterranean Sea
Anogia *see* Anógeia
31 V8 **Anoka** Minnesota, N USA
An Ómaigh *see* Omagh
180 I1 **Anorontany, Tanjona** *headland* N Madagascar
180 J5 **Anosibe An'Ala** Toamasina, E Madagascar

◆ Country ● Country Capital ◇ Dependent Territory ○ Dependent Territory Capital ◆ Administrative Region ✕ International Airport ▲ Mountain ▲ Mountain Range Volcano ~ River ◎ Lake ▣ Reservoir

Anóyia see Anógeia
An Pointe see Warrenpoint
167 P9 **Anqing** Anhui, E China
167 Q5 **Anqiu** Shandong, E China
99   **An Ráth** see Ráthluirc
  An Ribhéar see Kenmare River
  An Ros see Rush
101 K19 **Ans** Liège, E Belgium
  Anşāb see Niṣāb
176 Ww10 **Ansab** Irian Jaya, E Indonesia
103 J20 **Ansbach** Bayern, SE Germany
  An Sciobairín see Skibbereen
99   **An Scoil** see Skull
  An Seancheann see Old Head of Kinsale
47 Y5 **Anse-Bertrand** Grande Terre, N Guadeloupe
180 H17 **Anse Boileau** Mahé, NE Seychelles
47 S11 **Anse La Raye** NW Saint Lucia
56 D9 **Anserma** Caldas, W Colombia
111 T4 **Ansfelden** Oberösterreich, N Austria
169 U12 **Anshan** Liaoning, NE China
166 J12 **Anshun** Guizhou, S China
63 F17 **Ansina** Tacuarembó, C Uruguay
31 O15 **Ansley** Nebraska, C USA
27 P6 **Anson** Texas, SW USA
79 Q10 **Ansongo** Gao, E Mali
  An Srath Bán see Strabane
23 R5 **Ansted** West Virginia, NE USA
xli T17 **Anston** Rotherham, N England, UK
xliii N18 **Anstruther** Fife, E Scotland, UK
xxxviii M11 **Ansty** Warwickshire, C England, UK
176 Yy10 **Ansudu** Irian Jaya, E Indonesia
59 G15 **Anta** Cusco, S Peru
59 G16 **Antabamba** Apurímac, C Peru
  Antafalva see Kovačica
142 L17 **Antakya** anc. Antioch, Antiochia. Hatay, S Turkey
180 K3 **Antalaha** Antsiraňana, NE Madagascar
142 F17 **Antalya** prev. Adalia, anc. Attaleia, Bibl. Attalia. Antalya, SW Turkey
142 F17 **Antalya ◆** province SW Turkey
142 F16 **Antalya ×** Antalya, SW Turkey
124 Qq11 **Antalya Basin** undersea feature E Mediterranean Sea
  Antalya, Gulf of see Antalya Körfezi
142 F16 **Antalya Körfezi** var. Gulf of Adalia, Eng. Gulf of Antalya. gulf SW Turkey
180 J5 **Antanambao Manampotsy** Toamasina, E Madagascar
180 I5 **Antananarivo** prev. Tananarive. ● (Madagascar) Antananarivo, C Madagascar
180 I4 **Antananarivo ◆** province C Madagascar
180 J5 **Antananarivo ×** Antananarivo, C Madagascar
  An tAonach see Nenagh
204–205 **Antarctica** continent
204 I15 **Antarctic Peninsula** peninsula Antarctica
63 J15 **Antas, Rio das ♣** S Brazil
201 U16 **Ant Atoll** atoll Caroline Islands, E Micronesia
xlii G10 **An Teallach ▲** NW Scotland, UK
99   **An Teampall Mór** see Templemore
  Antep see Gaziantep
106 M15 **Antequera** anc. Anticaria, Antiquaria. Andalucía, S Spain
  Antequera see Oaxaca
39 S5 **Antero Reservoir ☐** Colorado, C USA
28 M7 **Anthony** Kansas, C USA
39 R16 **Anthony** New Mexico, SW USA
190 D5 **Anthony, Lake** salt lake South Australia
76 E8 **Anti-Atlas ▲** SW Morocco
105 U15 **Antibes** anc. Antipolis. Alpes-Maritimes, SE France
105 U15 **Antibes, Cap d'** headland SE France
  Anticaria see Antequera
11 Q11 **Anticosti, Île d'** Eng. Anticosti Island. island Québec, E Canada
  Anticosti Island see Anticosti, Île d'
104 K3 **Antifer, Cap d'** headland N France
32 I6 **Antigo** Wisconsin, N USA
11 Q15 **Antigonish** Nova Scotia, SE Canada
66 P11 **Antigua** Fuerteventura, Islas Canarias, NE Atlantic Ocean
47 X10 **Antigua** island S Antigua and Barbuda, Leeward Islands
  Antigua see Antigua Guatemala
47 W9 **Antigua and Barbuda ◆** commonwealth republic E West Indies
44 C6 **Antigua Guatemala** var. Antigua. Sacatepéquez, SW Guatemala
43 P11 **Antiguo Morelos** var. Antiguo-Morelos. Tamaulipas, C Mexico
117 F19 **Antikyra, Kólpos** gulf C Greece
117 G24 **Antikýthira** var. Andikíthira. island S Greece
144 I7 **Anti-Lebanon** var. Jebel esh Sharqi, Ar. Al Jabal ash Sharqī, Fr. Anti-Liban. ▲ Lebanon/Syria
  Anti-Liban see Anti-Lebanon
117 I22 **Antímilos** island Kykládes, Greece, Aegean Sea
38 L6 **Antimony** Utah, W USA
  An tInbhear Mór see Arklow
32 M10 **Antioch** Illinois, N USA
  Antioch see Antakya
104 I10 **Antioche, Pertuis d'** inlet W France
  Antiochia see Antakya
56 D8 **Antioquia** Antioquia, C Colombia
56 E8 **Antioquia** off. Departamento de Antioquia. ◆ province C Colombia
117 J21 **Antíparos** var. Andíparos. island Kykládes, Greece, Aegean Sea
117 B17 **Antípaxoi** var. Andipaxi. island Iónioi Nísoi, Greece, C Mediterranean Sea
117 J08 **Antíparos** var. Andíparos. island E Greece
  Antiquaria see Antequera

13 N10 **Antique, Lac ☐** Québec, SE Canada
117 E18 **Antírrio** var. Andírrion. Dytikí Ellás, C Greece
117 K16 **Ántissa** var. Ándissa. Lésvos, SE Greece
  An tIúr see Newry
  Antivari see Bar
58 C6 **Antizana ▲** N Ecuador
29 Q13 **Antlers** Oklahoma, C USA
95 J14 **Antnäs** Norrbotten, N Sweden
  Antō see Andong
64 G5 **Antofagasta** Antofagasta, N Chile
64 G6 **Antofagasta** off. Región de Antofagasta. ◆ region N Chile
64 I7 **Antofalla, Salar de** salt lake NW Argentina
101 D20 **Antoing** Hainaut, SW Belgium
26 M5 **Anton** Texas, SW USA
45 S16 **Antón** Coclé, C Panama
39 T11 **Anton Chico** New Mexico, SW USA
62 K12 **Antonina** Paraná, S Brazil
105 O5 **Antony** Hauts-de-Seine, N France
  Antratsit see Antratsyt
119 Y8 **Antratsyt** Rus. Antratsit. Luhans'ka Oblast', E Ukraine
xliv L4 **Antrim** Ir. Aontroim. Antrim, NE Northern Ireland, UK
xliv K4 **Antrim** Ir. Aontroim. ◆ district NE Northern Ireland, UK
xliv L3 **Antrim Mountains ▲** NE Northern Ireland, UK
180 H5 **Antsalova** Mahajanga, W Madagascar
  Antserana see Antsiraňana
  An tSionainn see Shannon
180 J2 **Antsiraňana** var. Antserana; prev. Antsirane, Diégo-Suarez. Antsiraňana, N Madagascar
180 J2 **Antsiraňana ◆** province N Madagascar
  Antsirane see Antsiraňana
  An tSiúir see Suir
120 I7 **Antsla** Ger. Anzen. Võrumaa, SE Estonia
180 J3 **Antsohihy** Mahajanga, NW Madagascar
  An tSláine see Slaney
65 G14 **Antuco, Volcán ▲** C Chile
175 P7 **Antu, Gunung ▲** Borneo, N Indonesia
  An Tullach see Tullow
  An-tung see Dandong
  Antunnacum see Andernach
101 G16 **Antwerp** Eng. Antwerp, Fr. Anvers. Antwerpen, N Belgium
101 H16 **Antwerpen** Eng. Antwerp, Fr. Anvers. ◆ province N Belgium
  An Uaimh see Navan
160 N12 **Anugul** var. Angul. Orissa, E India
158 F9 **Anūpgarh** Rājasthān, NW India
160 K10 **Anūppur** Madhya Pradesh, C India
161 K24 **Anuradhapura** North Central Province, C Sri Lanka
  Anvers see Antwerpen
204 G4 **Anvers Island** island Antarctica
41 N11 **Anvik** Alaska, USA
41 N10 **Anvik River ♣** Alaska, USA
40 F17 **Anvil Peak ▲** Semisopochnoi Island, Alaska, USA
165 P7 **Anxi** Gansu, N China
190 F8 **Anxious Bay** bay South Australia
167 O5 **Anyang** Henan, C China
165 S11 **A'nyêmaqên Shan ▲** C China
120 H12 **Anykščiai** Anykščiai, E Lithuania
167 P13 **Anyuan** Jiangxi, S China
127 O6 **Anyuysk** Chukotskiy Avtonomnyy Okrug, NE Russian Federation
127 Oo5 **Anyuyskiy Khrebet ▲** NE Russian Federation
56 D8 **Anza** Antioquia, C Colombia
  Anzen see Antsla
126 H13 **Anzhero-Sudzhensk** Kemerovskaya Oblast', S Russian Federation
109 J16 **Anzio** Lazio, C Italy
57 O6 **Anzoátegui** off. Estado Anzoátegui. ◆ state NE Venezuela
153 P12 **Anzob** W Tajikistan
  Anzyó see Anjō
  Aoba see Ambae
172 Ss13 **Aoga-shima** island Izu-shotō, SE Japan
169 T12 **Aohan Qi** Nei Mongol Zizhiqu, N China
43 O15 **Aoiz** Navarra, N Spain
193 X16 **Aola** var. Tenaghau. Guadalcanal, C Solomon Islands
178 Gg15 **Ao Luk Nua** Krabi, SW Thailand
  Aomen see Macao
172 N8 **Aomori** Aomori, Honshū, C Japan
172 Mm9 **Aomori** off. Aomori-ken. ◆ prefecture Honshū, C Japan
  Aontroim see Antrim
117 C15 **Aóos** var. Vijosa, Vijosë, Alb. Lumi i Vjosës, Alb./Albania/ Greece see also Vjosës, Lumi i
203 Q7 **Aorai, Mont ▲** Tahiti, W French Polynesia
  Aoraki see Cook, Mount
178 Ii13 **Aôral, Phnum** prev. Phnom Aural. ▲ W Cambodia
  Aorangi see Cook, Mount
193 U13 **Aorangi Mountains ▲** North Island, NZ
192 H13 **Aorere ♣** South Island, NZ
108 A7 **Aosta** anc. Augusta Praetoria. Valle d'Aosta, NW Italy
79 O11 **Aoudoundou, Lac ☐** S Mali
78 K8 **Aoukâr** var. Aouker. plateau C Mauritania
80 J13 **Aouk, Bahr ♣** Central African Republic/Chad
  Aouker see Aoukâr
78 G7 **Aousard** SE Western Sahara
170 G12 **Aoya** Tottori, Honshū, SW Japan
80 H5 **Aozou** Borkou-Ennedi-Tibesti, N Chad
29 S12 **Apache** Oklahoma, C USA
38 L14 **Apache Junction** Arizona, SW USA
26 J9 **Apache Mountains ▲** Texas, SW USA
38 M16 **Apache Peak ▲** Arizona, SW USA
118 H10 **Apahida** Cluj, NW Romania
25 T9 **Apalachee Bay** bay Florida, SE USA

25 T3 **Apalachee River ♣** Georgia, SE USA
25 S10 **Apalachicola** Florida, SE USA
25 S10 **Apalachicola Bay** bay Florida, SE USA
25 R9 **Apalachicola River ♣** Florida, SE USA
  Apam see Apan
  Apamama see Abemama
43 P14 **Apan** var. Apam. Hidalgo, C Mexico
44 J8 **Apanás, Lago de ☐** NW Nicaragua
56 H14 **Apaporis, Río ♣** Brazil/Colombia
193 C23 **Aparima ♣** South Island, NZ
179 P7 **Aparri** Luzon, N Philippines
114 J9 **Apatin** Serbia, NW Yugoslavia
128 I4 **Apatity** Murmanskaya Oblast', NW Russian Federation
57 X9 **Apatou** NW French Guiana
42 M14 **Apatzingán** var. Apatzingán de la Constitución. Michoacán de Ocampo, SW Mexico
176 Y9 **Apauwar** Irian Jaya, E Indonesia
43 O15 **Apaxtla** var. Apaxtla de Castrejón
43 O15 **Apaxtla de Castrejón** var. Apaxtla. Guerrero, S Mexico
120 J7 **Ape** Alūksne, NE Latvia
100 L11 **Apeldoorn** Gelderland, E Netherlands
  Apennines see Appennino
  Apenrade see Åbenrå
59 L17 **Apere, Río ♣** C Bolivia
55 W11 **Apetina** Sipaliwini, SE Surinam
23 V9 **Apex** North Carolina, SE USA
81 M14 **Api** Haut-Zaïre, N Zaire
158 M9 **Api ▲** NW Nepal
  Apia see Abaiang
198 Bb8 **Ápia ●** (Western Samoa) Upolu, SE Western Samoa
62 K11 **Apiaí** São Paulo, S Brazil
175 P16 **Api, Gunung ▲** Pulau Sangeang, S Indonesia
43 O15 **Apipilulco** Guerrero, S Mexico
43 P14 **Apizaco** Tlaxcala, S Mexico
xxxix Q5 **Apley** Lincolnshire, E England, UK
59 J16 **Apo, Río ♣** C Bolivia
59 J16 **Apolo** La Paz, W Bolivia
59 J16 **Apolobamba, Cordillera ▲** Bolivia/Peru
179 Rr16 **Apo, Mount ᙇ** Mindanao, S Philippines
25 W11 **Apopka** Florida, SE USA
25 W11 **Apopka, Lake ☐** Florida, SE USA
61 J19 **Aporé, Rio ♣** C Brazil
32 K2 **Apostle Islands** island group Wisconsin, N USA
  Apostolas Andreas, Cape see Zafer Burnu
  Apóstoles Misiones, NE Argentina
  Apostolou Andréa, Akrotíri see Zafer Burnu
119 S9 **Apostolove** Rus. Apostolovo. Dnipropetrovs'ka Oblast', E Ukraine
  Apostolovo see Apostolove
19 Qq9 **Appalachian Mountains ▲** E USA
97 K14 **Äppelbo** Kopparberg, C Sweden
100 N7 **Appelscha** Fris. Appelskea. Friesland, N Netherlands
  Appelskea see Appelscha
108 G11 **Appennino** Eng. Apennines. ▲ Italy/San Marino
109 L17 **Appennino Napoletano ▲** C Italy
110 I7 **Appenzell** Appenzell, NW Switzerland
110 H7 **Appenzell ◆** canton NE Switzerland
57 V12 **Appikalo** Sipaliwini, S Surinam
100 O5 **Appingedam** Groningen, NE Netherlands
xxxix T7 **Appleby** North Lincolnshire, E England, UK
27 X8 **Appleby** Texas, SW USA
xli O9 **Appleby-in-Westmorland** Cumbria, NW England, UK
xlii F12 **Applecross** Highland, NW Scotland, UK
xxxvi F7 **Appledore** Devon, SW England, UK
xxxvii X12 **Appledore** Kent, SE England, UK
32 K10 **Apple River ♣** Illinois, N USA
32 I5 **Apple River ♣** Wisconsin, N USA
27 W9 **Apple Springs** Texas, SW USA
31 S8 **Appleton** Minnesota, N USA
32 M7 **Appleton** Wisconsin, N USA
29 S5 **Appleton City** Missouri, C USA
37 V14 **Apple Valley** California, W USA
31 V9 **Apple Valley** Minnesota, N USA
23 U6 **Appomattox** Virginia, NE USA
196 B16 **Apra Harbour** harbour W Guam
196 B16 **Apra Heights** W Guam
108 F6 **Aprica, Passo dell'** pass N Italy
109 M13 **Apricena** anc. Hadria Picena. Puglia, SE Italy
128 L14 **Apsheronsk** Krasnodarskiy Kray, SW Russian Federation
  Apsheronskiy Poluostrov see Abşeron Yarimadasi
105 S15 **Apt** anc. Apta Julia. Vaucluse, SE France
  Apta Julia see Apt
40 H12 **Apua Point** headland Hawaii, USA, C Pacific Ocean
62 I10 **Apucarana** Paraná, S Brazil
56 K8 **Apure ◆** state C Venezuela
58 E7 **Apure, Río ♣** C Venezuela
59 F14 **Apurímac off.** Departamento de Apurímac. ◆ department C Peru
59 F15 **Apurímac, Río ♣** S Peru
118 G10 **Apuseni, Munţii ▲** W Romania
207 P15 **Aputiteeq** var. Aputitêq. ● Greenland
  Aputitêq see Aputiteeq
  'Aqaba/'Aqaba see Al 'Aqabah
144 F15 **'Aqaba, Gulf of** var. Gulf of Elat, Ar. Khalīj al 'Aqabah; anc. Sinus Aelaniticus. gulf NE Red Sea
145 R7 **'Aqabah** C Iraq

  'Aqabah, Khalīj al see Aqaba, Gulf of
155 O2 **Aqchah** var. Āqcheh. Jowzjān, N Afghanistan
  Āqcheh see Aqchah
  Aqköl see Akkol'
  Aqmola/Aqmola Oblysy see Akmola
164 L10 **Aqqikkol Hu ☐** NW China
  Aqqystaū see Akkystau
  Aqrah see Akrê
  Aqsay see Aksay
  Aqshataū see Akchatau
  Aqsū see Aksu
  Aqsūat see Aksuat
  Aqtas see Aktas
  Aqtaū see Aktau
  Aqtöbe/Aqtöbe Oblysy see Aktyubinsk
  Aqtoghay see Aktogay
  Aquae Augustae see Dax
  Aquae Calidae/Aquae Solis see Bath
  Aquae Flaviae see Chaves
  Aquae Grani see Aachen
  Aquae Panoniae see Baden
  Aquae Sextiae see Aix-en-Provence
  Aquae Tarbelicae see Dax
38 J11 **Aquarius Mountains ▲** Arizona, SW USA
64 O5 **Aquidabán, Río ♣** E Paraguay
61 H20 **Aquidauana** Mato Grosso do Sul, S Brazil
42 L15 **Aquila** Michoacán de Ocampo, SW Mexico
  Aquila/Aquila degli Abruzzi see L'Aquila
78 J13 **Aquilla** Texas, SW USA
46 L9 **Aquin** S Haiti
  Aquisgranum see Aachen
104 J13 **Aquitaine ◆** region SW France
178 III **Ara ♣** N Spain
107 S4 **Ara** NE Spain
  Araba see Álava
144 G12 **'Arabah, Wādī al** Heb. Ha'Arava. dry watercourse Israel/Jordan
119 U12 **Arabats'ka Strilka, Kosa** spit S Ukraine
119 U12 **Arabats'ka Zatoka** gulf S Ukraine
  'Arab, Baḥr al see Arab, Bahr el
82 C12 **'Arab, Baḥr el** var. Baḥr al 'Arab. ♣ S Sudan
58 E7 **Arabelo, Río ♣** E Peru
181 O4 **Arabian Basin** undersea feature N Arabian Sea
  Arabian Desert see Şaḥrā' el Sharqîya
147 N9 **Arabian Peninsula** peninsula SW Asia
87 P15 **Arabian Plate** tectonic feature Africa/Asia/Europe
147 W14 **Arabian Sea** sea NW Indian Ocean
  Arabicus, Sinus see Red Sea
  'Arabī, Khalīj al see Gulf, The
  Arabistan see Khūzestān
  'Arabīyah as Su'ūdiyah, Al Mamlakah al see Saudi Arabia
  'Arabīyah Jumhūrīyah, Miṣr al see Egypt
144 I9 **'Arab, Jabal al ▲** S Syria
124 Pp14 **'Arab, Khalīg el** Eng. Arabs Gulf. gulf N Egypt
  Arab Republic of Egypt see Egypt
  Arabs Gulf see 'Arab, Khalig el
  'Arab, Shaṭṭ al Eng. Shatt al Arab, Per. Arvand Rūd. ♣ Iran/Iraq
142 J11 **Araç** Kastamonu, N Turkey
61 P16 **Aracaju** state capital Sergipe, E Brazil
60 P13 **Aracataca** Magdalena, N Colombia
60 P13 **Aracati** Ceará, E Brazil
62 J8 **Araçatuba** São Paulo, S Brazil
106 J13 **Aracena** Andalucía, S Spain
117 F20 **Arachnaío ▲** S Greece
117 D16 **Arachthos** var. Arta; prev. Árakhthos, anc. Arachthus. ♣ W Greece
  Arachthus see Árachthos
61 N19 **Aracruz** Minas Gerais, SE Brazil
142 I11 **Araç Çayı ♣** N Turkey
144 I11 **'Arad** Southern, S Israel
118 F7 **Arad** W Romania
118 F7 **Arad ◆** county W Romania
80 J9 **Arada** Biltine, NE Chad
149 P18 **'Arādah** Abū Ẓaby, S UAE
  Aradhippou see Aradippou
124 O3 **Aradippou** var. Aradhippou. SE Cyprus
61 L20 **Araçuaí** Minas Gerais, SE Brazil
  Araxes see Aras
182 K6 **Arafura Sea** Ind. Laut Arafuru. sea W Pacific Ocean
182 L6 **Arafura Shelf** undersea feature C Arafura Sea
  Arafuru, Laut see Arafura Sea
61 J18 **Aragarças** Goiás, C Brazil
61 J18 **Araguaia, Rio ♣** C Brazil
61 J16 **Araguaia, Río** see Araguaia, Rio
106 K4 **Arahal** Andalucía, S Spain
173 JJ13 **Arai** Niigata, Honshū, C Japan
  Arainn Mhór see Aran Island
170 J5 **Arao** Kumamoto, Kyūshū, SW Japan
79 O8 **Araouane** Tombouctou, N Mali
31 N16 **Arapahoe** Nebraska, C USA
59 J16 **Arapa, Laguna ☐** W Peru
193 K14 **Arapawa Island** island C NZ
63 E17 **Arapey Grande, Río ♣** N Uruguay
61 K16 **Arapiraca** Alagoas, E Brazil
146 M3 **'Ar'ar** Ar. Ar'ak's, Az. Araz Nehri, Per. Rūd-e Aras, Rus. Araks; prev. Araxes. ♣ SW Asia
133 N7 **Aras de Alpuente** País Valenciano, E Spain
143 S13 **Aras Güneyi Dağları ▲** NE Turkey
  Aras, Rūd-e see Aras
203 U9 **Aratika** atoll Îles Tuamotu, C French Polynesia
  Aratürük see Yiwu
60 P13 **Arauca** Arauca, NE Colombia
62 B2 **Araçatuba** Intendencia de Arauca. ◆ province NE Colombia
65 G15 **Araucanía off.** Región de la Araucanía. ◆ region C Chile
56 L7 **Arauca, Río ♣** Colombia/Venezuela
65 F14 **Arauco** Bío Bío, C Chile
65 F14 **Arauco, Golfo de** gulf S Chile
56 H8 **Arauquita** Arauca, C Colombia
  Arausio see Orange
159 N19 **Arāvali Range ▲** N India
195 S12 **Arawa** Bougainville Island, NE PNG
193 C20 **Arawata ♣** South Island, NZ
194 L12 **Arawe Islands** island group E PNG
61 L20 **Araxá** Minas Gerais, SE Brazil
  Araxes see Aras
57 R4 **Araya** Sucre, N Venezuela
83 I15 **'Arba Minch'** SW Ethiopia
145 U4 **Arbat** NE Iraq
109 D19 **Arbatax** Sardegna, Italy, C Mediterranean Sea
143 T12 **Aragats, Gora ▲** W Armenia
143 T12 **Aragats Lerr** Rus. Gora Aragats. ▲ W Armenia
34 E14 **Arago, Cape** headland Oregon, NW USA
107 R6 **Aragón ♣** autonomous community E Spain
107 Q4 **Aragón ▲** NE Spain
109 I24 **Aragona** Sicilia, Italy, C Mediterranean Sea
107 Q7 **Aragoncillo ▲** C Spain
57 N6 **Aragua ◆** state N Venezuela
57 N6 **Aragua de Barcelona** Anzoátegui, N Venezuela
57 O6 **Aragua de Maturín** Monagas, NE Venezuela
39 N12 **Araguari** ♣

  Arakawa Niigata, Honshū, C Japan
177 Ff6 **Arakan State** var. Rakhine State. ◆ state W Burma
177 Ff5 **Arakan Yoma ▲** W Burma
171 Kk12 **Arakawa** Niigata, Honshū, C Japan
  Árakhthos see Árachthos
  Araks/Arak's see Aras
164 H7 **Aral** Xinjiang Uygur Zizhiqu, NW China
  Aral see Vose', Tajikistan
152 H5 **Aral-Bukhorskiy Kanal** Amu-Bukhoro Kanali
152 H5 **Aral Sea** Kaz. Aral Tengizi, Rus. Aral'skoye More, Uzb. Orol Dengizi. inland sea Kazakhstan/Uzbekistan
150 L13 **Aral'sk** Kaz. Aral. Kzyl-Orda, SW Kazakhstan
  Aral'skoye More/Aral Tengizi see Aral Sea
43 O10 **Aramberri** Nuevo León, NE Mexico
194 F14 **Aramia ♣** SW PNG
149 N6 **Ārān** var. Goārā. Eşfahān, C Iran
107 N5 **Aranda de Duero** Castilla-León, N Spain
114 M12 **Aranđelovac** prev. Arandjelovac. Serbia, C Yugoslavia
  Arandjelovac see Aranđelovac
xliv F3 **Aran Fawddwy ▲** NW Wales, UK
xliv F3 **Aran Island** Ir. Árainn Mhór. island NW Ireland
xliv C9 **Aran Islands** island group W Ireland
107 N9 **Aranjuez** Madrid, C Spain
84 E20 **Aranos** Hardap, SE Namibia
27 U14 **Aransas Bay** inlet Texas, SW USA
27 T14 **Aransas Pass** Texas, SW USA
203 O3 **Aranuka** prev. Nanouki. atoll Tungaru, W Kiribati
178 Ill **Aranyaprathet** Prachin Buri, S Thailand
  Aranyosasztal see Zlatý Stôl
  Aranyosgyéres see Câmpia Turzii
  Aranyosmarót see Zlaté Moravce
170 Cc14 **Arao** Kumamoto, Kyūshū, SW Japan
79 O8 **Araouane** Tombouctou, N Mali
31 N16 **Arapahoe** Nebraska, C USA
193 K14 **Arapawa Island** island C NZ
63 E17 **Arapey Grande, Río ♣** N Uruguay
61 K16 **Arapiraca** Alagoas, E Brazil
146 M3 **'Ar'ar** Al Ḥudūd ash Shamālīyah, NW Saudi Arabia
56 G15 **Araracuara** Caquetá, S Colombia
63 K15 **Araranguá** Santa Catarina, S Brazil
62 L8 **Araraquara** São Paulo, S Brazil
61 O13 **Araras** Pará, N Brazil
62 H11 **Araras, Serra das ▲** S Brazil
143 U12 **Ararat** Victoria, SE Australia
190 M12 **Ararat, Mount** see Büyükağrı Dağı
146 M3 **'Ar'ar, Wādī** dry watercourse Iraq/Saudi Arabia
143 N7 **Aras** Arm. Arak's, Az. Araz Nehri, Per. Rūd-e Aras, Rus. Araks; prev. Araxes. ♣ SW Asia
107 R9 **Aras de Alpuente** País Valenciano, E Spain
143 S13 **Aras Güneyi Dağları ▲** NE Turkey
  Aras, Rūd-e see Aras
203 U9 **Aratika** atoll Îles Tuamotu, C French Polynesia
  Aratürük see Yiwu
60 P13 **Arauca** Arauca, NE Colombia
56 I8 **Arauca** off. Intendencia de Arauca. ◆ province NE Colombia
65 G15 **Araucanía off.** Región de la Araucanía. ◆ region C Chile
56 L7 **Arauca, Río ♣** Colombia/Venezuela
65 F14 **Arauco** Bío Bío, C Chile
65 F14 **Arauco, Golfo de** gulf S Chile
56 H8 **Arauquita** Arauca, C Colombia
  Arausio see Orange
159 N19 **Arāvali Range ▲** N India
195 S12 **Arawa** Bougainville Island, NE PNG
193 C20 **Arawata ♣** South Island, NZ
194 L12 **Arawe Islands** island group E PNG
61 L20 **Araxá** Minas Gerais, SE Brazil
  Araxes see Aras
57 R4 **Araya** Sucre, N Venezuela
83 I15 **'Arba Minch'** SW Ethiopia
145 U4 **Arbat** NE Iraq
109 D19 **Arbatax** Sardegna, Italy, C Mediterranean Sea
106 I12 **Arbil** see Erbil, Irbil, Kurd. Hawlêr; anc. Arbela. N Iraq
9 X15 **Arborg** Manitoba, S Canada
97 N16 **Arbrå** Gävleborg, C Sweden
56 L5 **Arboletes** Antioquia, NW Colombia
116 J12 **Arbino** Khaskovska Oblast, S Bulgaria
xliii U16 **Arbroath** anc. Aberbrothock. Angus, E Scotland, UK
191 P7 **Arbroath** New South Wales, SE Australia
xxxvii Q7 **Ardley** Oxfordshire, C England, UK
xliii I18 **Ardlui** Argyll and Bute, W Scotland, UK
xliii F19 **Ardlussa** Argyll and Bute, W Scotland, UK
xliii G9 **Ardmair** Highland, N Scotland, UK
105 U12 **Ard Mhacha** see Armagh
104 J13 **Ardmolich** Highland, NW Scotland, UK
28 K13 **Ardmore** New York, NE USA
xliii H14 **Ardmore** Louisiana, S USA
23 J7 **Ardmore** Oklahoma, C USA
25 R4 **Ardmore** Pennsylvania, NE USA
29 O12 **Ardmore** Tennessee, S USA
xliv C8 **Ardmore** Ir. Aird Mhór. SE Ireland

37 U6 **Arc Dome ▲** Nevada, W USA
43 O15 **Arce** Lazio, C Italy
43 O15 **Arcelia** Guerrero, S Mexico
101 M15 **Arcen** Limburg, SE Netherlands
  Archangel see Arkhangel'sk
  Archangel Bay see Cheshskaya Guba
116 F7 **Archar ♣** NW Bulgaria
33 R11 **Archbold** Ohio, N USA
107 R12 **Archena** Murcia, SE Spain
27 R5 **Archer City** Texas, SW USA
xliii H6 **Archidona** Andalucía, S Spain
  Archiemore Highland, N Scotland, UK
67 B25 **Archipiélago de los Canales** ▲ see Falkland Islands
xxxvi D6 **Archway** Islington, SE England, UK
108 G23 **Arcidosso** Toscana, C Italy
108 Q5 **Arcis-sur-Aube** Aube, N France
190 F3 **Arckaringa Creek** seasonal river South Australia
108 G7 **Arco** Trentino-Alto Adige, N Italy
32 M14 **Arcola** Illinois, N USA
107 P6 **Arcos de Jalón** Castilla-León, N Spain
106 K15 **Arcos de la Frontera** Andalucía, S Spain
106 G9 **Arcos de Valdevez** Viana do Castelo, N Portugal
61 P15 **Arcoverde** Pernambuco, E Brazil
104 H5 **Arcovest, Pointe de l'** headland NW France
207 R8 **Arctic Ocean** ocean
14 G4 **Arctic Red River ♣** Northwest Territories/Yukon Territory, NW Canada
  Arctic Red River see Tsiigehtchic
41 S6 **Arctic Village** Alaska, USA
204 H1 **Arctowski** Polish research station South Shetland Islands, Antarctica
116 I12 **Arda ♣** var. Ardhas, Gk. Ardas. ♣ Bulgaria/Greece see also Ardas
148 L2 **Ardabil** var. Ardebil. Ardabil, NW Iran
148 L2 **Ardabil** off. Ostān-e ardabil. ◆ province NW Iran
143 R11 **Ardahan** Kars, NE Turkey
149 N8 **Ardakān** Yazd, C Iran
96 E12 **Årdalstangen** Sogn og Fjordane, S Norway
xliii G17 **Ardanaiseig** Argyll and Bute, W Scotland, UK
143 R11 **Ardanuç** Artvin, NE Turkey
xliv G4 **Ardara** Ir. Ard an Rátha. Donegal, N Ireland
xliii F12 **Ardarroch** Highland, NW Scotland, UK
116 L12 **Ardas ♣** var. Ardhas, Bul. Arda. ♣ Bulgaria/Greece see also Arda
144 II3 **Ard aş Şawwān** var. Ardh es Suwwān. plain S Jordan
143 U12 **Ardatov** Respublika Mordoviya, W Russian Federation
xliii E21 **Ardbeg** Argyll and Bute, W Scotland, UK
12 G3 **Ardberg** Ontario, S Canada
xliii H10 **Ardcharnich** Highland, NW Scotland, UK
  Ardeal see Transylvania
  Ardebil see Ardabil
105 Q13 **Ardèche ♣** C France
105 Q13 **Ardèche ◆** department E France
xliv C7 **Ardee** Ir. Baile Átha Fhirdhia. Louth, NE Ireland
xliii J19 **Arden** Argyll and Bute, W Scotland, UK
xliii O3 **Ardennes ◆** department NE France
101 I21 **Ardennes** physical region Belgium/France
xliii J19 **Ardentinny** Argyll and Bute, W Scotland, UK
xliv M6 **Arderin ▲** C Ireland
xliii I18 **Ardersier** Highland, NW Scotland, UK
143 J19 **Ardeşen** Rize, NE Turkey
149 O7 **Ardestān** var. Ardistan. Eşfahān, C Iran
110 J9 **Ardez** Graubünden, SE Switzerland
xliii F18 **Ardfern** Argyll and Bute, W Scotland, UK
xliii O3 **Ardfert** Kerry, SW Ireland
xliii F20 **Ardgay** Highland, NW Scotland, UK
xliv M6 **Ardglass** Down, SE Northern Ireland, UK
xliv C14 **Ardgroom** Cork, S Ireland
xliii C9 **Ardhasaig** Western Isles, NW Scotland, UK
  Ardhas see Arda/Ardas
  Ardh es Suwwān see Ard aş Şawwān
106 I12 **Ardila, Ribeira de Sp.** Ardilla. ♣ Portugal/Spain see also Ardilla
106 I12 **Ardilla, Cerro la ▲** C Mexico
  Ardilla Port. Ribeira de Ardila. see also Ardila, Ribeira de
9 T17 **Ardill** Saskatchewan, S Canada
116 J8 **Ardino** Khaskovska Oblast, S Bulgaria
  Ardistan see Ardestān
191 P7 **Ardlethan** New South Wales, SE Australia

xliii E16 **Ardnamurchan** peninsula NW Scotland, UK
xliii D15 **Ardnamurchan, Point of** headland NW Scotland, UK
xliv F8 **Ardnasodan** Galway, W Ireland
101 C17 **Ardooie** West-Vlaanderen, W Belgium
xliii G10 **Ardrahan** Galway, W Ireland
xliii F19 **Ardressie** Highland, NW Scotland, UK
xliii H21 **Ardrishaig** Argyll and Bute, W Scotland, UK
190 I9 **Ardrossan** North Ayrshire, W Scotland, UK
xliv M5 **Ardrossan** South Australia
xliv M5 **Ards ◆** district E Northern Ireland, UK
xliv M5 **Ards Peninsula** peninsula E Northern Ireland, UK
xliii J17 **Ardtalnaig** Perth and Kinross, C Scotland, UK
xliii E15 **Ardtoe** Highland, NW Scotland, UK
xliii F18 **Arduaine** Argyll and Bute, W Scotland, UK
118 H9 **Ardusat** Hung. Erdőszáda. Maramureş, N Romania
xliii G12 **Ardvasar** Highland, NW Scotland, UK
xliii H25 **Ardwell** Dumfries and Galloway, SW Scotland, UK
95 J16 **Åre** Jämtland, C Sweden
81 P16 **Arebi** Haut-Zaïre, NE Zaire
176 W10 **Aredo** Irian Jaya, E Indonesia
61 P14 **Areia Branca** Rio Grande do Norte, E Brazil
121 O14 **Arekhawsk** Rus. Orekhovsk. Vitsyebskaya Voblasts', N Belorussia
  Arel see Arlon
  Arelas/Arelate see Arles
44 L13 **Arenal, Embalse de ☐** N Costa Rica
44 L13 **Arenal, Volcán ▲** N Costa Rica
  Arenal Laguna var. Embalse de Arenal. ☐ N Costa Rica
36 K6 **Arena, Point** headland California, W USA
61 H17 **Arenápolis** Mato Grosso, W Brazil
42 G10 **Arena, Punta** headland W Mexico
106 L8 **Arenas de San Pedro** Castilla-León, N Spain
65 I24 **Arenas, Punta de** headland S Argentina
63 B20 **Arenas** Buenos Aires, E Argentina
97 F17 **Arendal** Aust-Agder, S Norway
101 J16 **Arendonk** Antwerpen, N Belgium
xxxv M4 **Arenig Fawr ▲** NW Wales, UK
45 T15 **Arenosa** Panamá, N Panama
107 W3 **Arenys de Mar** Cataluña, NE Spain
117 F22 **Areópoli** prev. Areópolis. Pelopónnisos, S Greece
  Areópolis see Areópoli
59 H18 **Arequipa** Arequipa, SE Peru
59 G17 **Arequipa** off. Departamento de Arequipa. ◆ department SW Peru
106 M7 **Arévalo** Castilla-León, N Spain
108 H12 **Arezzo** anc. Arretium. Toscana, C Italy
107 Q4 **Arga ♣** N Spain
107 R5 **Argaeus** see Erciyes Dağı
117 G17 **Argalastí** Thessalía, C Greece
117 O10 **Argamasilla de Alba** Castilla-La Mancha, C Spain
164 L8 **Argan** Xinjiang Uygur Zizhiqu, NW China
107 N9 **Arganda** Madrid, C Spain
179 Qq14 **Arganil** Coimbra, N Portugal
159 V15 **Argao** Cebu, C Philippines
128 K9 **Arga-Sala ♣** NE Russian Federation
105 T15 **Argens ♣** SE France
108 I7 **Argenta** Emilia-Romagna, N Italy
105 N4 **Argentan** Orne, N France
149 O7 **Argentat** Corrèze, C France
108 A9 **Argentera** Piemonte, NE Italy
64 K13 **Argenteuil** Val-d'Oise, N France
64 K13 **Argentina** off. Republic of Argentina. ◆ republic S South America
  Argentina Basin see Argentine Basin
  Argentine Abyssal Plain see Argentine Plain
67 I19 **Argentine Basin** var. Argentina Basin. undersea feature SW Atlantic Ocean
67 I19 **Argentine Plain** var. Argentine Abyssal Plain. undersea feature SW Atlantic Ocean
  Argentine Rise see Falkland Plateau
65 H22 **Argentino, Lago ☐** S Argentina
104 K8 **Argenton-Château** Deux-Sèvres, W France
104 M9 **Argenton-sur-Creuse** Indre, C France
  Argentoratum see Strasbourg
118 I12 **Argeş ◆** county S Romania
118 I13 **Argeş ♣** S Romania
157 P7 **Arghandāb, Daryā-ye ♣** SE Afghanistan
155 O8 **Arghastān Pash.** Arghestān. ♣ SE Afghanistan
  Arghestān see Arghastān
  Argirocastro see Gjirokastër
82 E7 **Argo** Northern, N Sudan
181 P7 **Argo Fracture Zone** tectonic feature C Indian Ocean
117 E22 **Argolikós Kólpos** gulf S Greece
105 R4 **Argonne** physical region NE France
174 Mm15 **Argopuro, Gunung ▲** Jawa, S Indonesia
117 F20 **Árgos** Pelopónnisos, S Greece
145 S1 **Argosh ▲** N Iraq
117 D14 **Árgos Orestikó** Dytikí Makedonía, N Greece
117 B19 **Argostóli** var. Argostólion. Kefallinía, Iónioi Nísoi, Greece, C Mediterranean Sea
  Argostólion see Argostóli
  Argovie see Aargau
37 O14 **Arguello, Point** headland California, W USA

Argun – Asturias

131 P16 **Argun** Chechenskaya Respublika, SW Russian Federation
163 T2 **Argun** *Chin.* Ergun He, *Rus.* Argun'. ≈ China/Russian Federation
79 T12 **Argungu** Kebbi, NW Nigeria
168 J9 **Arguut** Övörhangay, C Mongolia
189 N3 **Argyle, Lake** *salt lake* Western Australia
98 G12 **Argyll** *cultural region* W Scotland, UK
xliii F18 **Argyll and Bute** ⬖ *unitary authority* W Scotland, UK
Argyrokastron *see* Gjirokastër
168 I7 **Arhangay** ⬖ *province* C Mongolia
Arhangelos *see* Archángelos
97 P14 **Arholma** Stockholm, C Sweden
97 G22 **Århus** *var.* Aarhus. Århus, C Denmark
97 G22 **Århus** ⬖ *county* C Denmark
145 T1 **Ārī** E Iraq
194 M12 **Aria** ≈ New Britain, E PNG
Aria *see* Herāt
170 C13 **Ariake-kai** *bay* NE East China Sea
85 F22 **Ariamsvlei** Karas, SE Namibia
109 L17 **Ariano Irpino** Campania, S Italy
56 F11 **Ariari, Río** ≈ C Colombia
157 K19 **Ari Atoll** *atoll* C Maldives
79 P11 **Aribinda** N Burkina
64 G2 **Arica** *hist.* San Marcos de Arica. Tarapacá, N Chile
56 H16 **Arica** Amazonas, S Colombia
64 G2 **Arica** ✕ Tarapacá, N Chile
170 G16 **Arida** Wakayama, Honshū, SW Japan
116 E13 **Aridaía** *var.* Aridea, Aridhaía. Dytikí Makedonía, N Greece
Aridea *see* Aridaía
180 I15 **Aride, Île** *island* Inner Islands, NE Seychelles
Aridhaía *see* Aridaía
105 N17 **Ariège** ⬖ *department* S France
104 M16 **Ariège** *var.* la Riege. ≈ Andorra/France
118 H11 **Arieş** ≈ W Romania
155 U10 **Ārifwāla** Punjab, E Pakistan
Ariguaní *see* El Difícil
144 G11 **Arīhā** Al Karak, W Jordan
144 I3 **Arīḩā** *var.* Arīhā. Idlib, W Syria
Arīḩā *see* Jericho
39 W4 **Arikaree River** ≈ Colorado/Nebraska, C USA
170 Bb12 **Arikawa** Nagasaki, Nakadōri-jima, SW Japan
xliii C16 **Arileod** Argyll and Bute, W Scotland, UK
114 L13 **Arilje** Serbia, W Yugoslavia
47 U14 **Arima** Trinidad, Trinidad and Tobago
Arime *see* Al 'Arīmah
Ariminum *see* Rimini
xliii D16 **Arinagour** Argyll and Bute, W Scotland, UK
61 H16 **Arinos, Rio** ≈ W Brazil
42 M14 **Ario de Rosales** *var.* Ario de Rosáles. Michoacán de Ocampo, SW Mexico
120 F12 **Ariogala** Raseiniai, C Lithuania
49 T7 **Aripuanã** ≈ W Brazil
61 E15 **Ariquemes** Rondônia, W Brazil
xliii E15 **Arisaig** Highland, NW Scotland, UK
124 Rr15 **'Arîsh, Wâdi el** ≈ NE Egypt
56 K6 **Arismendi** Barinas, C Venezuela
8 J14 **Aristazabal Island** *island* SW Canada
62 F13 **Aristóbulo del Valle** Misiones, NE Argentina
180 I5 **Arivonimamo** ✕ (Antananarivo) Antananarivo, C Madagascar
xlii C9 **Arivruaich** Western Isles, NW Scotland, UK
Arixang *see* Wenquan
107 Q6 **Ariza** Aragón, NE Spain
64 I6 **Arizaro, Salar de** *salt lake* NW Argentina
64 K13 **Arizona** San Luis, C Argentina
38 J12 **Arizona** *off.* State of Arizona; also known as Copper State, Grand Canyon State. ⬖ *state* SW USA
42 G4 **Arizpe** Sonora, NW Mexico
97 J16 **Årjäng** Värmland, C Sweden
149 P8 **Arjenān** Yazd, C Iran
94 I13 **Arjeplog** Norrbotten, N Sweden
56 E5 **Arjona** Bolívar, N Colombia
107 N13 **Arjona** Andalucía, S Spain
127 N11 **Arka** Khabarovskiy Kray, E Russian Federation
24 L2 **Arkabutla Lake** ⊠ Mississippi, S USA
131 O7 **Arkadak** Saratovskaya Oblast', W Russian Federation
29 T13 **Arkadelphia** Arkansas, C USA
xliii G14 **Arkaig, Loch** ◎ NW Scotland, UK
117 J25 **Arkalochóri** *prev.* Arkalohori, Arkalokhórion. Kríti, Greece, E Mediterranean Sea
Arkalohori/Arkalokhórion *see* Arkalochóri
151 O10 **Arkalyk** *Kaz.* Arqalyq. Turgay, C Kazakhstan
29 U10 **Arkansas** *off.* State of Arkansas; also known as The Land of Opportunity. ⬖ *state* S USA
29 W14 **Arkansas City** Arkansas, C USA
29 O7 **Arkansas City** Kansas, C USA
18 Kk10 **Arkansas River** ≈ C USA
190 J5 **Arkaroola** South Australia
Arkhángelos *see* Archángelos
128 L8 **Arkhangel'sk** *Eng.* Archangel. Arkhangel'skaya Oblast', NW Russian Federation
128 L9 **Arkhangel'skaya Oblast'** ⬖ *province* NW Russian Federation
131 O14 **Arkhangel'skoye** Stavropol'skiy Kray, SW Russian Federation
127 N16 **Arkhara** Amurskaya Oblast', S Russian Federation
xliv L11 **Arklow** *Ir.* An tInbhear Mór. Wicklow, SE Ireland
117 M20 **Arkoí** *island* Dodekánisos, Greece, Aegean Sea
29 R11 **Arkoma** Oklahoma, C USA
102 O7 **Arkona, Kap** *headland* NE Germany
97 N17 **Arkösund** Östergötland, S Sweden
126 H4 **Arkticheskogo Instituta, Ostrova** *island* N Russian Federation
97 O15 **Arlanda** ✕ (Stockholm) Stockholm, C Sweden
152 C11 **Arlan, Gora** ▲ W Turkmenistan
107 O5 **Arlanza** ≈ N Spain
107 N5 **Arlanzón** ≈ N Spain
105 R15 **Arles** *var.* Arles-sur-Rhône; *anc.* Arelas, Arelate. Bouches-du-Rhône, SE France
Arles-sur-Rhône *see* Arles
105 O17 **Arles-sur-Tech** Pyrénées-Orientales, S France
31 U9 **Arlington** Minnesota, N USA
31 R15 **Arlington** Nebraska, C USA
34 J11 **Arlington** Oregon, NW USA
31 R10 **Arlington** South Dakota, N USA
22 E10 **Arlington** Tennessee, S USA
27 T6 **Arlington** Texas, SW USA
23 W4 **Arlington** Virginia, NE USA
34 H7 **Arlington** Washington, NW USA
32 M10 **Arlington Heights** Illinois, N USA
79 U8 **Arlit** Agadez, C Niger
101 L24 **Arlon** *Dut.* Aarlen, *Ger.* Arel; *Lat.* Orolaunum. Luxembourg, SE Belgium
29 R7 **Arma** Kansas, C USA
xlii J6 **Armadale** Highland, NW Scotland, UK
xliii E14 **Armadale** Highland, NW Scotland, UK
xliii K20 **Armadale** West Lothian, SE Scotland, UK
xliv K5 **Armagh** *Ir.* Ard Mhacha. Armagh, S Northern Ireland, UK
xliv K5 **Armagh** ⬖ *district* S Northern Ireland, UK
104 K15 **Armagnac** *cultural region* S France
105 Q7 **Armançon** ≈ C France
62 K10 **Armando Laydner, Represa** ⊠ S Brazil
117 M24 **Armathía** *island* SE Greece
xli N7 **Armathwaite** Cumbria, NW England, UK
130 M14 **Armavir** Krasnodarskiy Kray, SW Russian Federation
56 E10 **Armenia** Quindío, W Colombia
143 T12 **Armenia** *off.* Republic of Armenia, *var.* Ajastan, *Arm.* Hayastani Hanrapetut'yun; *prev.* Armenian Soviet Socialist Republic. ◆ *republic* SW Asia
Armenierstadt *see* Gherla
105 O1 **Armentières** Nord, N France
42 K14 **Armería** Colima, SW Mexico
191 T5 **Armidale** New South Wales, SE Australia
xxxviii K9 **Armitage** Staffordshire, C England, UK
31 P11 **Armour** South Dakota, N USA
xliv L2 **Armoy** Moyle, N Northern Ireland, UK
63 B18 **Armstrong** Santa Fe, C Argentina
9 N16 **Armstrong** British Columbia, SW Canada
10 D11 **Armstrong** Ontario, S Canada
31 U11 **Armstrong** Iowa, C USA
27 S16 **Armstrong** Texas, SW USA
xli T15 **Armthorpe** Doncaster, N England, UK
119 S11 **Armyans'k** *Rus.* Armyansk. Respublika Krym, S Ukraine
117 H14 **Arnaía** *var.* Arnea. Kentrikí Makedonía, N Greece
123 Mm3 **Arnaoúti, Akrotíri** *var.* Arnaoútis, Cape Arnaouti. *headland* W Cyprus
Arnaouti, Cape/Arnaoútis *see* Arnaoúti, Akrotíri
10 L4 **Arnaud** ≈ Québec, E Canada
105 Q8 **Arnay-le-Duc** Côte d'Or, C France
Arnea *see* Arnaía
107 Q4 **Arnedo** La Rioja, N Spain
97 I14 **Årnes** Akershus, S Norway
95 E15 **Årnes** Sør-Trøndelag, S Norway
28 K9 **Arnett** Oklahoma, C USA
100 L12 **Arnhem** Gelderland, SE Netherlands
189 Q2 **Arnhem Land** *physical region* Northern Territory, N Australia
108 F11 **Arno** ≈ C Italy
Arņo *see* Arno Atoll
201 W7 **Arno Atoll** *var.* Arņo. *atoll* Ratak Chain, NE Marshall Islands
190 H8 **Arno Bay** South Australia
xxxix N7 **Arnold** Nottinghamshire, C England, UK
37 Q8 **Arnold** California, W USA
29 X5 **Arnold** Missouri, C USA
31 N15 **Arnold** Nebraska, C USA
111 R10 **Arnoldstein** *Slvn.* Pod Klošter. Kärnten, S Austria
105 N9 **Arnon** ≈ C France
47 P14 **Arnos Vale** ✕ (Kingstown) Saint Vincent, SE Saint Vincent and the Grenadines
94 I8 **Arnøy** *island* N Norway
12 L12 **Arnprior** Ontario, SE Canada
103 G15 **Arnsberg** Nordrhein-Westfalen, W Germany
xl M11 **Arnside** Cumbria, NW England, UK
103 K16 **Arnstadt** Thüringen, C Germany
Arnswalde *see* Choszczno
56 K5 **Aroa** Yaracuy, N Venezuela
85 E21 **Aroab** Karas, SE Namibia
117 E19 **Aroania** ▲▲ S Greece
203 O6 **Aroa, Pointe** *headland* Moorea, W French Polynesia
Aroe Islands *see* Aru, Kepulauan
103 H15 **Arolsen** Niedersachsen, C Germany
108 C7 **Arona** Piemonte, NE Italy
21 R3 **Aroostook River** ≈ Canada/USA
Arop Island *see* Long Island
40 M12 **Aropuk Lake** ◎ Alaska, USA
203 P4 **Arorae** *atoll* Tungaru, W Kiribati
202 G16 **Arorangi** Rarotonga, S Cook Islands
110 I9 **Arosa** Graubünden, S Switzerland
106 F4 **Arousa, Ría de** *estuary* E Atlantic Ocean
176 Uu16 **Aro Usu, Tanjung** *headland* Pulau Selaru, SE Indonesia
192 P8 **Arowhana** ▲ North Island, NZ
143 V12 **Arp'a** *Az.* Arpaçay. ≈ Armenia/Azerbaijan
143 S11 **Arpaçay** Kars, NE Turkey
Arpaçay *see* Arp'a
Arqalyq *see* Arkalyk
155 N14 **Arra** ≈ SW Pakistan
Arrabona *see* Győr
Arrah *see* Āra
Ar Rahad *see* Er Rahad
145 R9 **Ar Raḩḩālīyah** C Iraq
62 Q10 **Arraial do Cabo** Rio de Janeiro, SE Brazil
106 H11 **Arraiolos** Évora, S Portugal
145 R8 **Ar Ramādī** *var.* Ramadi, Rumadiya. SW Iraq
144 J6 **Ar Rāmī** Ḩimş, C Syria
Ar Rams *see* Rams
144 H9 **Ar Ramthā** *var.* Ramtha. Irbid, N Jordan
xliii G21 **Arran, Isle of** *island* SW Scotland, UK
144 L3 **Ar Raqqah** *var.* Rakka; *anc.* Nicephorium. Ar Raqqah, N Syria
144 L3 **Ar Raqqah** *off.* Muḩāfaẓat al Raqqah, *var.* Raqqah, *Fr.* Rakka. ⬖ *governorate* N Syria
105 O2 **Arras** *anc.* Nemetocenna. Pas-de-Calais, N France
Ar Raşāfah *see* Ar Ruşāfah
Arrasate *see* Mondragón
144 G12 **Ar Rashādīyah** Aţ Ţafīlah, W Jordan
144 I5 **Ar Rastān** *var.* Rastâne. Ḩimş, W Syria
145 X12 **Ar Raţāwī** E Iraq
104 L15 **Arrats** ≈ S France
147 N10 **Ar Rawḑah** Makkah, S Saudi Arabia
147 Q15 **Ar Rawḑah** S Yemen
148 K11 **Ar Rawḑatayn** *var.* Raudhatain. N Kuwait
149 N16 **Ar Rayyān** *var.* Al Rayyan. C Qatar
104 L17 **Arreau** Hautes-Pyrénées, S France
66 Q11 **Arrecife** *var.* Arrecife de Lanzarote, Puerto Arrecife. Lanzarote, Islas Canarias, NE Atlantic Ocean
Arrecife de Lanzarote *see* Arrecife
45 P6 **Arrecife Edinburgh** *reef* NE Nicaragua
63 C19 **Arrecifes** Buenos Aires, E Argentina
45 O5 **Arrecifes de la Media Luna** *reef* E Honduras
104 F6 **Arrée, Monts d'** ▲▲ NW France
Ar Refā'ī *see* Ar Rifā'ī
Arretium *see* Arezzo
Arriaca *see* Guadalajara
111 S9 **Arriach** Kärnten, S Austria
43 T16 **Arriaga** Chiapas, SE Mexico
43 N12 **Arriaga** San Luis Potosí, C Mexico
145 W10 **Ar Rifā'ī** *var.* Ar Refā'ī. SE Iraq
145 V12 **Ar Riḩāb** *salt flat* S Iraq
106 L2 **Arriondas** Asturias, N Spain
147 R7 **Ar Riyāḑ** *Eng.* Riyadh. ● (Saudi Arabia) Ar Riyāḑ, C Saudi Arabia
147 O8 **Ar Riyāḑ** *off.* Minţaqat ar Riyāḑ. ⬖ *province* C Saudi Arabia
147 S15 **Ar Riyān** S Yemen
Arrö *see* Ærø
xliii H18 **Arrochar** Argyll and Bute, W Scotland, UK
63 H18 **Arroio Grande** Rio Grande do Sul, S Brazil
104 K15 **Arros** ≈ S France
105 Q9 **Arroux** ≈ C France
xxxviii K12 **Arrow** Warwickshire, C England, UK
27 R5 **Arrowhead, Lake** ⊠ Texas, SW USA
xliv G6 **Arrow, Lough** ◎ N Ireland
190 L5 **Arrowsmith, Mount** *hill* New South Wales, SE Australia
193 D21 **Arrowtown** Otago, South Island, NZ
63 D17 **Arroyo Barú** Entre Ríos, E Argentina
106 J10 **Arroyo de la Luz** Extremadura, W Spain
65 J16 **Arroyo de la Ventana** Río Negro, SE Argentina
37 P13 **Arroyo Grande** California, W USA
Ar Ru'ays *see* Ar Ruways
147 R11 **Ar Rub' al Khālī** *Eng.* Empty Quarter, Great Sandy Desert. *desert* SW Asia
145 V13 **Ar Ruḑaymah** S Iraq
63 A16 **Arrufó** Santa Fe, C Argentina
144 I7 **Ar Ruḩaybah** *var.* Ruhaybeh, *Fr.* Rouhaïbé. Dimashq, W Syria
145 V15 **Ar Rukhaymīyah** *well* S Iraq
145 U11 **Ar Rumaythah** *var.* Rumaitha. S Iraq
147 X8 **Ar Rustāq** *var.* Rostak, Rustaq. N Oman
145 N8 **Ar Ruţbah** *var.* Rutba. SW Iraq
146 M3 **Ar Rūthīyah** *spring/well* NW Saudi Arabia
ar-Ruwaida *see* Ar Ruwayḑah
147 O8 **Ar Ruwayḑah** *var.* ar-Ruwaida. Jīzān, C Saudi Arabia
149 N15 **Ar Ruways** *var.* Al Ruweis, Ar Ru'ays, Ruwais. N Qatar
149 O17 **Ar Ruways** *var.* Ar Ru'ays, Ruwaisv. Abū Ẓaby, W UAE
97 G21 **Års** *var.* Aars. Nordjylland, N Denmark
Arsanias *see* Murat Nehri
127 Nn18 **Arsen'yev** Primorskiy Kray, SE Russian Federation
161 G19 **Arsikere** Karnātaka, W India
131 R3 **Arsk** Respublika Tatarstan, W Russian Federation
96 N10 **Årskogen** Gävleborg, C Sweden
124 N3 **Ársos** C Cyprus
96 N13 **Årsunda** Gävleborg, C Sweden
Arta *see* Árachthos
117 C17 **Árta** *anc.* Ambracia. Ípeiros, W Greece
143 T12 **Artashat** S Armenia
42 M15 **Arteaga** Michoacán de Ocampo, SW Mexico
127 Nn18 **Artem** Primorskiy Kray, SE Russian Federation
46 C4 **Artemisa** La Habana, W Cuba
119 W7 **Artemivs'k** Donets'ka Oblast', E Ukraine
126 I14 **Artemovsk** Krasnoyarskiy Kray, S Russian Federation
126 Kk13 **Artemovskiy** Irkutskaya Oblast', C Russian Federation
125 Ee13 **Artemovskiy** Sverdlovskaya Oblast', C Russian Federation
107 U5 **Artesa de Segre** Cataluña, NE Spain
39 U14 **Artesia** New Mexico, SW USA
27 Q14 **Artesia Wells** Texas, SW USA
110 G8 **Arth** Schwyz, C Switzerland
12 F15 **Arthur** Ontario, S Canada
32 M14 **Arthur** Illinois, N USA
30 L14 **Arthur** Nebraska, C USA
31 Q5 **Arthur** North Dakota, N USA
193 B21 **Arthur** ≈ South Island, NZ
20 B13 **Arthur, Lake** ⊠ Pennsylvania, NE USA
191 N15 **Arthur River** ≈ Tasmania, SE Australia
193 G18 **Arthur's Pass** Canterbury, South Island, NZ
193 G17 **Arthur's Pass** *pass* South Island, NZ
46 I3 **Arthur's Town** Cat Island, C Bahamas
xliv J13 **Arthurstown** Wexford, SE Ireland
46 M9 **Artibonite, Rivière de l'** ≈ C Haiti
63 E16 **Artigas** *prev.* San Eugenio, San Eugenio del Cuareim. Artigas, N Uruguay
63 E16 **Artigas** ⬖ *department* N Uruguay
204 H1 **Artigas** *Uruguayan research station* Antarctica
143 T11 **Art'ik** W Armenia
197 G4 **Art, Île** *island* Îles Belep, W New Caledonia
105 O2 **Artois** *cultural region* N France
142 L12 **Artova** Tokat, N Turkey
107 Y9 **Artrutx, Cap d'** *var.* Cabo Dartuch. *headland* Menorca, Spain, W Mediterranean Sea
Artsiz *see* Artsyz
119 N11 **Artsyz** *Rus.* Artsiz. Odes'ka Oblast', SW Ukraine
164 E7 **Artux** Xinjiang Uygur Zizhiqu, NW China
143 R11 **Artvin** Artvin, NE Turkey
143 R11 **Artvin** ⬖ *province* NE Turkey
152 G14 **Artyk** Akhalskiy Velayat, C Turkmenistan
81 Q16 **Aru** Haut-Zaïre, NE Zaire
106 I4 **A Rúa** *var.* La Rúa. Galicia, NW Spain
83 E17 **Arua** NW Uganda
Aruângua *see* Luangwa
47 O15 **Aruba** *var.* Oruba. ◇ *Dutch autonomous region* S West Indies
49 Q4 **Aruba** *island* Aruba, Lesser Antilles
Aru Islands *see* Aru, Kepulauan
176 Ww14 **Aru, Kepulauan** *Eng.* Aru Islands; *prev.* Aroe Islands. *island group* E Indonesia
xxxvii S12 **Arun** ≈ SE England, UK
159 W10 **Arunāchal Pradesh** *prev.* North East Frontier Agency, North East Frontier Agency of Assam. ⬖ *state* NE India
xxxvii S13 **Arundel** West Sussex, SE England, UK
169 U7 **Arun Qi** Nei Mongol Zizhiqu, N China
161 H23 **Aruppukkottai** Tamil Nādu, SE India
176 Ww9 **Aruri, Selat** *strait* Irian Jaya, E Indonesia
83 I20 **Arusha** Arusha, N Tanzania
83 I21 **Arusha** ⬖ *region* E Tanzania
83 I20 **Arusha** ✕ Arusha, N Tanzania
56 C9 **Arusí, Punta** *headland* NW Colombia
174 Ll10 **Arut, Sungai** ≈ Borneo, C Indonesia
161 J23 **Aruvi Aru** ≈ NW Sri Lanka
81 M17 **Aruwimi** *var.* Ituri (upper course). ≈ NE Zaire
Árva *see* Orava
39 T4 **Arvada** Colorado, C USA
xliv I7 **Arvagh** Cavan, N Ireland
Arvand Rūd *see* 'Arab, Shaţţ al
168 J8 **Arvayheer** Övörhangay, C Mongolia
15 L8 **Arviat** *prev.* Eskimo Point. Northwest Territories, C Canada
95 I14 **Arvidsjaur** Norrbotten, N Sweden
97 J15 **Arvika** Värmland, C Sweden
94 J8 **Årviksand** Troms, N Norway
37 S13 **Arvin** California, W USA
151 P7 **Arykbalyk** *Kaz.* Aryqbalyq. Kokshetau, N Kazakhstan
Aryqbalyq *see* Arykbalyk
151 P17 **Arys'** *Kaz.* Arys. Yuzhnyy Kazakhstan, S Kazakhstan
Arys *see* Orzysz
Arys Köli *see* Arys, Ozero
151 O14 **Arys, Ozero** *Kaz.* Arys Köli. ◎ C Kazakhstan
109 D16 **Arzachena** Sardegna, Italy, C Mediterranean Sea
131 O4 **Arzamas** Nizhegorodskaya Oblast', W Russian Federation
147 V13 **Arzāt** S Oman
106 H3 **Arzúa** Galicia, NW Spain
113 A16 **Aš** *Ger.* Asch. Západní Čechy, W Czech Republic
97 H15 **Ås** Akershus, S Norway
97 H20 **Aså** Nordjylland, N Denmark
85 E21 **Asab** Karas, S Namibia
79 U16 **Asaba** Delta, S Nigeria
155 S4 **Asadābād** *var.* Asadābād; *prev.* Chaghasarāy. Kunar, E Afghanistan
144 K3 **Asad, Buḩayrat al** ◎ N Syria
65 H20 **Asador, Pampa del** *plain* S Argentina
171 Kk17 **Asahi** Chiba, Honshū, S Japan
171 J13 **Asahi** Toyama, Honshū, SW Japan
172 Pp5 **Asahi-dake** ▲ Hokkaidō, N Japan
170 Ff13 **Asahi-gawa** ≈ Honshū, SW Japan
172 P5 **Asahikawa** Hokkaidō, N Japan
153 S10 **Asaka** *Rus.* Assake; *prev.* Leninsk. Andijon Wiloyati, E Uzbekistan
79 P17 **Asamankese** SE Ghana
171 Jj15 **Asama-yama** ▲ Honshū, S Japan
196 B15 **Asan** W Guam
196 B15 **Asan Point** *headland* W Guam
159 R15 **Āsānsol** West Bengal, NE India
176 V9 **Asbakin** Irian Jaya, E Indonesia
Asben *see* Aïr, Massif de l'
125 Ee11 **Asbest** Sverdlovskaya Oblast', C Russian Federation
13 Q12 **Asbestos** Québec, SE Canada
31 Y13 **Asbury** Iowa, C USA
20 K15 **Asbury Park** New Jersey, NE USA
43 Z12 **Ascención, Bahiá de la** *bay* NW Caribbean Sea
42 I3 **Ascensión** Chihuahua, N Mexico
67 M14 **Ascension Fracture Zone** *tectonic feature* C Atlantic Ocean
67 G14 **Ascension Island** ◇ *dependency of St.Helena* C Atlantic Ocean
67 N16 **Ascension Island** *island* C Atlantic Ocean
Asch *see* Aš
111 S3 **Aschach an der Donau** Oberösterreich, N Austria
103 H18 **Aschaffenburg** Bayern, SW Germany
103 F14 **Ascheberg** Nordrhein-Westfalen, W Germany
103 L14 **Aschersleben** Sachsen-Anhalt, C Germany
108 G12 **Asciano** Toscana, C Italy
xliii H20 **Ascog** Argyll and Bute, W Scotland, UK
108 J13 **Ascoli Piceno** *anc.* Asculum Picenum. Marche, C Italy
109 M17 **Ascoli Satriano** *anc.* Asculub, Ausculum Apulum. Puglia, SE Italy
110 G11 **Ascona** Ticino, S Switzerland
xxxvii S10 **Ascot** Windsor and Maidenhead, S England, UK
Asculub *see* Ascoli Satriano
Asculum Picenum *see* Ascoli Piceno
82 L11 **Aseb** *var.* Assab, *Amh.* Āseb. SE Eritrea
97 M20 **Åseda** Kronoberg, S Sweden
131 T6 **Asekeyevo** Orenburgskaya Oblast', W Russian Federation
194 J13 **Aseki** Morobe, C PNG
83 J14 **Āsela** *var.* Asella, Aselle, Asselle. C Ethiopia
95 H15 **Åsele** Västerbotten, N Sweden
Asella/Aselle *see* Āsela
96 K12 **Åsen** Kopparberg, C Sweden
116 J11 **Asenovgrad** *prev.* Stanimaka. Plovdivska Oblast, S Bulgaria
175 Q11 **Asera** Sulawesi, C Indonesia
97 E17 **Åseral** Vest-Agder, S Norway
120 J3 **Aseri** *var.* Asserien, *Ger.* Asserin. Ida-Virumaa, NE Estonia
42 J10 **Aserradero** Durango, W Mexico
xxxix O9 **Asfordby** Leicestershire, C England, UK
97 H16 **Åsgårdstrand** Vestfold, S Norway
xxxvii Z10 **Ash** Kent, SE England, UK
xxxvii V10 **Ash** Kent, SE England, UK
xxxvii R11 **Ash** Surrey, SE England, UK
125 E11 **Asha** Chelyabinskaya Oblast', C Russian Federation
Ashara *see* Al 'Ashārah
xliv K8 **Ashbourne** Meath, E Ireland
xxxviii L7 **Ashbourne** Derbyshire, C England, UK
25 T6 **Ashburn** Georgia, SE USA
xxxvi H15 **Ashburton** Devon, SW England, UK
193 G19 **Ashburton** Canterbury, South Island, NZ
193 G19 **Ashburton** ≈ South Island, NZ
188 H8 **Ashburton River** ≈ Western Australia
xxxvii O9 **Ashbury** Oxfordshire, C England, UK
xxxviii L9 **Ashby de la Zouch** Leicestershire, C England, UK
151 V10 **Ashchysu** ≈ E Kazakhstan
8 M16 **Ashcroft** British Columbia, SW Canada
144 E10 **Ashdod** *anc.* Azotos, *Lat.* Azotus. Central, W Israel
29 S14 **Ashdown** Arkansas, C USA
23 T9 **Asheboro** North Carolina, SE USA
9 X15 **Ashern** Manitoba, S Canada
23 P10 **Asheville** North Carolina, SE USA
10 E8 **Asheweig** ≈ Ontario, C Canada
29 V9 **Ash Flat** Arkansas, C USA
xliv L10 **Ashford** Wicklow, E Ireland
xxxvi F12 **Ashford** Devon, SW England, UK
xxxvii X11 **Ashford** Kent, SE England, UK
191 T4 **Ashford** New South Wales, SE Australia
xxxviii L6 **Ashford in the Water** Derbyshire, C England, UK
38 K11 **Ash Fork** Arizona, SW USA
152 F13 **Ashgabat** *prev.* Ashkhabad, Poltoratsk. ● (Turkmenistan) Akhalskiy Velayat, C Turkmenistan
152 F13 **Ashgabat** ✕ Akhalskiy Velayat, C Turkmenistan
29 T7 **Ash Grove** Missouri, C USA
171 K15 **Ashikaga** *var.* Asikaga. Tochigi, Honshū, S Japan
xxxvii X8 **Ashingdon** Essex, E England, UK
xli R4 **Ashington** Northumberland, N England, UK
171 Mm10 **Ashiro** Iwate, Honshū, C Japan
170 E16 **Ashizuri-misaki** *headland* Shikoku, SW Japan
Ashkelon *see* Ashqelon
Ashkhabad *see* Ashgabat
xliii N22 **Ashkirk** The Borders, S Scotland, UK
25 Q4 **Ashland** Alabama, S USA
28 K7 **Ashland** Kansas, C USA
23 P5 **Ashland** Kentucky, S USA
21 S2 **Ashland** Maine, NE USA
24 M1 **Ashland** Mississippi, S USA
29 U4 **Ashland** Missouri, C USA
31 S15 **Ashland** Nebraska, C USA
33 T12 **Ashland** Ohio, N USA
34 G15 **Ashland** Oregon, NW USA
23 W6 **Ashland** Virginia, NE USA
32 K3 **Ashland** Wisconsin, N USA
22 I8 **Ashland City** Tennessee, S USA
xxxviii I8 **Ashley** Staffordshire, C England, UK
191 S4 **Ashley** New South Wales, SE Australia
31 O7 **Ashley** North Dakota, N USA
181 W7 **Ashmore and Cartier Islands** ◇ *Australian external territory* E Indian Ocean
121 I14 **Ashmyany** *Rus.* Oshmyany. Hrodzyenskaya Voblasts', W Belorussia
20 K12 **Ashokan Reservoir** ⊠ New York, NE USA
172 Pp6 **Ashoro** Hokkaidō, NE Japan
144 E10 **Ashqelon** *var.* Ashkelon. Southern, C Israel
Ashraf *see* Behshahr
145 O3 **Ash Shadādah** *var.* Ash Shaddādah, Jisr ash Shadadi, Shaddādī, Shedadi, Tell Shedadi. Al Ḩasakah, NE Syria
Ash Shaddādah *see* Ash Shadādah
145 Y12 **Ash Shāfī** E Iraq
145 R4 **Ash Shakk** *var.* Shaykh. C Iraq
Ash Sham/Ash Shām *see* Dimashq
145 T10 **Ash Shāmīyah** *var.* Shamiya. C Iraq
145 Y13 **Ash Shāmīyah** *var.* Al Bādiyah al Janūbīyah. *desert* S Iraq
145 T11 **Ash Shanāfīyah** *var.* Ash Shināfīyah. S Iraq
144 G13 **Ash Sharāh** *var.* Esh Sharā. ▲▲ W Jordan
149 R16 **Ash Shāriqah** *Eng.* Sharjah. Ash Shāriqah, NE UAE
149 R16 **Ash Shāriqah** *var.* Sharjah. ✕ Ash Shāriqah, NE UAE
146 I4 **Ash Sharmah** *var.* Šarma. Tabūk, NW Saudi Arabia
145 R4 **Ash Sharqāţ** NW Iraq
147 S10 **Ash Sharqīyah** *off.* Al Minţaqah ash Sharqīyah, *Eng.* Eastern Region. ⬖ *province* E Saudi Arabia
145 W11 **Ash Shaţrah** *var.* Shatra. SE Iraq
144 G13 **Ash Shawbak** Ma'ān, W Jordan
144 L5 **Ash Shaykh Ibrāhīm** Ḩimş, C Syria
147 O17 **Ash Shaykh 'Uthmān** SW Yemen
147 S15 **Ash Shiḩr** SE Yemen
Ash Shināfīyah *see* Ash Shanāfīyah
147 V12 **Ash Shişar** *var.* Shisur. SW Oman
145 S13 **Ash Shubrūm** *well* S Iraq
147 R4 **Ash Shuqayq** *var.* As Shageeg. *desert* S Kuwait
147 R10 **Ash Shuqqān** *desert* E Saudi Arabia
77 O9 **Ash Shuwayrif** *var.* Ash Shwayrif. N Libya
Ash Shwayrif *see* Ash Shuwayrif
33 U10 **Ashtabula** Ohio, N USA
31 Q5 **Ashtabula, Lake** ⊠ North Dakota, N USA
143 T12 **Ashtarak** W Armenia
148 M6 **Āshtīān** *var.* Āshtiyān. Markazī, W Iran
Āshtiyān *see* Āshtīān
Ashton *see* Ashton-under-Lyne
35 R13 **Ashton** Idaho, NW USA
xxxvii N8 **Ashton Keynes** Wiltshire, S England, UK
xli P16 **Ashton-under-Lyne** *var.* Ashton. Tameside, NW England, UK
11 O10 **Ashuanipi Lake** ◎ Newfoundland and Labrador, E Canada
13 P6 **Ashuapmushuan** ≈ Québec, SE Canada
25 Q3 **Ashville** Alabama, S USA
33 S14 **Ashville** Ohio, N USA
32 K3 **Ashwabay, Mount** *hill* Wisconsin, N USA
xxxvi F14 **Ashwater** Devon, SW England, UK
xxxvii T6 **Ashwell** Hertfordshire, SE England, UK
xxxix P9 **Ashwell** Rutland, C England, UK
xxxix W10 **Ashwellthorpe** Norfolk, E England, UK
176 Uu7 **Asia, Kepulauan** *island group* E Indonesia
160 N13 **Āsika** Orissa, E India
Asikaga *see* Ashikaga
95 M18 **Asikkala** *var.* Vääksy. Häme, SW Finland
76 G5 **Asilah** N Morocco
'Aşī, Nahr al *see* Orontes
109 B16 **Asinara, Isola** *island* W Italy
126 H13 **Asino** Tomskaya Oblast', C Russian Federation
121 O14 **Asintorf** *Rus.* Osintorf. Vitsyebskaya Voblasts', N Belorussia
121 L17 **Asipovichy** *Rus.* Osipovichi. Mahilyowskaya Voblasts', C Belorussia
147 N12 **'Asīr** *off.* Minţaqat 'Asīr. ⬖ *province* SW Saudi Arabia
146 M11 **'Asīr** *Eng.* Asir. ▲▲ SW Saudi Arabia
145 X10 **Askal** E Iraq
143 P13 **Aşkale** Erzurum, NE Turkey
xl L11 **Askam-in-Furness** Cumbria, NW England, UK
119 T11 **Askaniya-Nova** Khersons'ka Oblast', S Ukraine
xliv E11 **Askeaton** Limerick, SW Ireland
97 H15 **Asker** Akershus, S Norway
xli T15 **Askern** Doncaster, N England, UK
97 L17 **Askersund** Örebro, C Sweden
Askī Kalak *see* Eski Kaļak
97 I15 **Askim** Østfold, S Norway
131 V3 **Askino** Respublika Bashkortostan, W Russian Federation
117 D14 **Áskio** ▲▲ N Greece
xliii G19 **Asknish** Argyll and Bute, W Scotland, UK
158 L9 **Askot** Uttar Pradesh, N India
xli P11 **Askrigg** North Yorkshire, N England, UK
96 C12 **Askvoll** Sogn og Fjordane, S Norway
142 A13 **Aslan Burnu** *headland* W Turkey
142 L16 **Aslantaş Barajı** ⊠ S Turkey
xliv D8 **Asleagh** Mayo, NW Ireland
155 S4 **Asmār** *var.* Bar Kunar. Kunar, E Afghanistan
82 I9 **Asmara** *Amh.* Āsmera. ● (Eritrea) C Eritrea
Āsmera *see* Asmara
97 L21 **Åsnen** ◎ S Sweden
117 F19 **Asopós** ≈ S Greece
176 X10 **Asori** Irian Jaya, E Indonesia
82 G12 **Āsosa** W Ethiopia
34 M10 **Asotin** Washington, NW USA
Aspadana *see* Eşfahān
Aspang *see* Aspang Markt
111 X6 **Aspang Markt** *var.* Aspang. Niederösterreich, E Austria
xl K8 **Aspatria** Cumbria, NW England, UK
107 S12 **Aspe** País Valenciano, E Spain
39 R5 **Aspen** Colorado, C USA
27 P6 **Aspermont** Texas, SW USA
Asphaltites, Lacus *see* Dead Sea
Aspinwall *see* Colón
193 C20 **Aspiring, Mount** ▲ South Island, NZ
117 B16 **Asprókavos, Ákra** *headland* Kérkyra, Iónioi Nísoi, Greece, C Mediterranean Sea
Aspropótamos *see* Achelóos
xl E14 **Aspull** Bolton, NW England, UK
Assab *see* Aseb
78 J10 **Assaba** *var.* Açâba. ⬖ *region* S Mauritania
144 L4 **As Sabkhah** *var.* Sabkha. Ar Raqqah, NE Syria
145 U6 **As Sa'dīyah** E Iraq
Assad, Lake *see* Asad, Buḩayrat al
144 I8 **Aş Şafā** ▲ S Syria
144 I10 **Aş Şafāwī** Al Mafraq, N Jordan
Aş Şaff *see* El Şaff
145 N2 **Aş Şafīḩ** Al Ḩasakah, N Syria
Aş Şaḩrā' al Gharbīyah *see* Sahara el Gharbîya
Aş Şaḩrā' ash Sharqīyah *see* Sahara el Sharqîya
Assake *see* Asaka
As Salamīyah *see* Salamīyah
147 Q4 **As Salimi** *var.* Salemy. SW Kuwait
148 J11 **As Sālimīyah** W Kuwait
69 W7 **'Assal, Lac** ◎ C Djibouti
As Sallūm *see* Salûm
145 T13 **As Salmān** S Iraq
144 G10 **As Salţ** *var.* Salt. Al Balqā', NW Jordan
148 M16 **As Salwā** *var.* Salwa, Salwah. S Qatar
159 V12 **Assam** ⬖ *state* NE India
Assamaka *see* Assamakka
79 T8 **Assamakka** *var.* Assamaka. Agadez, NW Niger
145 U11 **As Samāwah** *var.* Samawa. S Iraq
As Saqia al Hamra *see* Saguia al Hamra
144 J4 **Aş Şā'rān** Ḩamāh, C Syria
144 G9 **Aş Şarīḩ** Irbid, N Jordan
23 Z5 **Assateague Island** *island* Maryland, NE USA
145 O6 **As Sayyāl** *var.* Sayyāl. Dayr az Zawr, E Syria
101 G18 **Asse** Vlaams Brabant, C Belgium
101 D16 **Assebroek** West-Vlaanderen, NW Belgium
Asselle *see* Āsela
109 C20 **Assemini** Sardegna, Italy, C Mediterranean Sea
100 N7 **Assen** Drenthe, NE Netherlands
101 E16 **Assenede** Oost-Vlaanderen, NW Belgium
97 G24 **Assens** Fyn, C Denmark
Asserien/Asserin *see* Aseri
101 I21 **Assesse** Namur, SE Belgium
As Shageeg *see* Ash Shuqayq
147 Y8 **As Sīb** *var.* Seeb. NE Oman
145 Z13 **As Sībah** *var.* Sibah. SE Iraq
xxxix V13 **Assington** Suffolk, E England, UK
9 T17 **Assiniboia** Saskatchewan, S Canada
9 V15 **Assiniboine** ≈ Manitoba, S Canada
9 P16 **Assiniboine, Mount** ▲ Alberta/British Columbia, SW Canada
Assiout *see* Asyût
62 J9 **Assis** São Paulo, S Brazil
108 I13 **Assisi** Umbria, C Italy
Assiut *see* Asyût
Assling *see* Jesenice
Assouan *see* Aswân
Assu *see* Açu
Assuan *see* Aswân
148 K12 **Aş Şubayḩīyah** *var.* Subiyah. S Kuwait
147 R16 **As Sufāl** S Yemen
144 L5 **As Sukhnah** *var.* Sukhne, *Fr.* Soukhné. Ḩimş, C Syria
145 U4 **As Sulaymānīyah** *var.* Sulaimaniya, *Kurd.* Slēmānī. NE Iraq
147 P11 **As Sulayyil** Ar Riyāḑ, S Saudi Arabia
123 M16 **As Sulţān** N Libya
147 Q5 **Aş Şummān** *desert* N Saudi Arabia
147 Q16 **Aş Şurrah** SW Yemen
145 N4 **Aş Şuwār** *var.* Şuwār. Dayr az Zawr, E Syria
144 H9 **As Suwaydā'** *var.* El Suweida, Es Suweida, Suweida, *Fr.* Soueida. As Suwaydā', SW Syria
144 H9 **As Suwaydā'** *off.* Muḩāfaẓat as Suwaydā', *var.* As Suwaydā, Suwaydá, Suweida, *Fr.* Soueida. ⬖ *governorate* S Syria
147 Z9 **As Suwayḩ** NE Oman
147 X8 **As Suwayq** *var.* Suwaik. N Oman
145 T8 **Aş Şuwayrah** *var.* Suwaira. E Iraq
As Suways *see* Suez
xlii H8 **Assynt, Loch** ◎ NW Scotland, UK
Asta Colonia *see* Asti
Astacus *see* İzmit
117 M23 **Astakída** *island* SE Greece
148 M3 **Āstāneh** Gīlān, NW Iran
Asta Pompeia *see* Asti
143 Y14 **Astara** S Azerbaijan
Astarabad *see* Gorgān
101 L15 **Asten** Noord-Brabant, SE Netherlands
Asterābād *see* Gorgān
108 C8 **Asti** *anc.* Asta Colonia, Asta Pompeia, Hasta Colonia, Hasta Pompeia. Piemonte, NW Italy
Astigi *see* Ecija
Astipálaia *see* Astypálaia
154 L16 **Astola Island** *island* SW Pakistan
xxxviii I7 **Aston** Cheshire, W England, UK
xli S17 **Aston** Rotherham, N England, UK
xxxvii R7 **Aston Clinton** Buckinghamshire, C England, UK
158 H4 **Astor** Jammu and Kashmir, NW India
106 K4 **Astorga** *anc.* Asturica Augusta. Castilla-León, N Spain
34 F10 **Astoria** Oregon, NW USA
1 F8 **Astoria Fan** *undersea feature* E Pacific Ocean
97 J22 **Åstorp** Kristianstad, S Sweden
Astrabad *see* Gorgān
131 Q13 **Astrakhan'** Astrakhanskaya Oblast', SW Russian Federation
Astrakhan-Bazar *see* Cälilabad
131 Q11 **Astrakhanskaya Oblast'** ⬖ *province* SW Russian Federation
95 J15 **Åsträsk** Västerbotten, N Sweden
Astrida *see* Butare
67 O22 **Astrid Ridge** *undersea feature* S Atlantic Ocean
194 J11 **Astrolabe Bay** *inlet* N PNG
197 I4 **Astrolabe, Récifs de l'** *reef* C New Caledonia
124 Nn3 **Astromerítis** N Cyprus
117 F20 **Ástros** Pelopónnisos, S Greece
121 G16 **Astryna** *Rus.* Ostryna. Hrodzyenskaya Voblasts', W Belorussia
106 J2 **Asturias** ⬖ *autonomous community* NW Spain

◆ Country
● Country Capital
◇ Dependent Territory
○ Dependent Territory Capital
⬖ Administrative Region
✕ International Airport
▲ Mountain
▲▲ Mountain Range
Volcano
≈ River
◎ Lake
⊠ Reservoir

ASTURIAS – AZUMA-SAN

Asturias *see* Oviedo
Asturica Augusta *see* Astorga
xxxviii C17 **Astwood Bank** Worcestershire, W England, UK
117 L22 **Astypálaia** ***var.*** Astipálaia, ***It.*** Stampalia. *island* Kykládes, Greece, Aegean Sea
198 Aa8 **Āsuisui, Cape** *headland* Savai'i, W Western Samoa
205 S2 **Asuka** *Japanese research station* Antarctica
64 O6 **Asunción** ● (Paraguay) Central, S Paraguay
64 O6 **Asunción** ✕ Central, S Paraguay
196 K3 **Asuncion Island** *island* N Northern Mariana Islands
44 E6 **Asunción Mita** Jutiapa, SE Guatemala
Asunción Nochixtlán *see* Nochixtlán
42 E3 **Asunción, Río** ≈ NW Mexico
97 M18 **Åsunden** ◎ S Sweden
120 K11 **Asvyeya** ***Rus.*** Osveya. Vitsyebskaya Voblasts', N Belorussia
Aswa *see* Achwa
77 X11 **Aswân** ***var.*** Assouan, Assuan; ***anc.*** Syene. SE Egypt
77 X11 **Aswân High Dam** *dam* SE Egypt
77 W9 **Asyût** ***var.*** Assiout, Assiut, Siut; ***anc.*** Lycopolis. C Egypt
200 R15 **Ata** *island* Tongatapu Group, SW Tonga
64 G8 **Atacama** ***off.*** Región de Atacama. ◐ *region* C Chile
Atacama Desert *see* Atacama, Desierto de
64 H4 **Atacama, Desierto de** ***Eng.*** Atacama Desert. *desert* N Chile
64 I6 **Atacama, Puna de** ⛰ NW Argentina
64 I5 **Atacama, Salar de** *salt lake* N Chile
56 E11 **Ataco** Tolima, C Colombia
202 H8 **Atafu Atoll** *island* NW Tokelau
202 H8 **Atafu Village** Atafu Atoll, NW Tokelau
76 K12 **Atakor** ⛰ SE Algeria
79 R14 **Atakora, Chaîne de l'** ***var.*** Atakora Mountains. ⛰ N Benin
Atakora Mountains *see* Atakora, Chaîne de l'
79 R16 **Atakpamé** C Togo
152 F11 **Atakui** Akhalskiy Velayat, C Turkmenistan
60 B13 **Atalaia do Norte** Amazonas, N Brazil
171 J17 **Atami** Shizuoka, Honshū, S Japan
78 I7 **Aṭâr** Adrar, W Mauritania
168 G10 **Atas Bogd** ▲ SW Mongolia
37 P12 **Atascadero** California, W USA
27 S13 **Atascosa River** ≈ Texas, SW USA
151 R11 **Atasu** Zhezkazgan, C Kazakhstan
151 R12 **Atasu** ≈ C Kazakhstan
200 Qq15 **Atata** *island* Tongatapu Group, S Tonga
142 H10 **Atatürk** ✕ (İstanbul) İstanbul, NW Turkey
143 N16 **Atatürk Barajı** ▣ S Turkey
Atax *see* Aude
82 G8 **Atbara** ***var.*** 'Aṭbāra h. River Nile, NE Sudan
82 H8 **Atbara** ***var.*** Nahr 'Aṭbarah. ≈ Eritrea/Sudan
'Aṭbārah/'Aṭbarah, Nahr *see* Atbara
151 P9 **Atbasar** Akmola, N Kazakhstan
At-Bashi *see* At-Bashy
153 W9 **At-Bashy** ***var.*** At-Bashi. Narynskaya Oblast', C Kyrgyzstan
24 I10 **Atchafalaya Bay** *bay* Louisiana, S USA
24 I8 **Atchafalaya River** ≈ Louisiana, S USA
Atchin *see* Aceh
29 Q3 **Atchison** Kansas, C USA
79 P16 **Atebubu** C Ghana
107 Q6 **Ateca** Aragón, NE Spain
42 K11 **Atengo, Río** ≈ C Mexico
Aternum *see* Pescara
109 K15 **Atessa** Abruzzi, C Italy
Ateste *see* Este
101 E19 **Ath** ***var.*** Aat. Hainaut, SW Belgium
9 Q13 **Athabasca** Alberta, SW Canada
9 Q12 **Athabasca** ***var.*** Athabaska. ≈ Alberta, SW Canada
9 R10 **Athabasca, Lake** ◎ Alberta/Saskatchewan, SW Canada
Athabaska *see* Athabasca
117 C16 **Athamánon** ⛰ C Greece
xliv J8 **Athboy** ***Ir.*** Baile Átha Buí. Meath, E Ireland
xliv D12 **Athea** Limerick, SW Ireland
Athenae *see* Athína
xliv F9 **Athenry** ***Ir.*** Baile Átha an Rí. Galway, W Ireland
25 P2 **Athens** Alabama, S USA
25 T3 **Athens** Georgia, SE USA
33 T14 **Athens** Ohio, N USA
22 M10 **Athens** Tennessee, S USA
27 V7 **Athens** Texas, SW USA
Athens *see* Athína
117 B18 **Athéras, Ákra** *headland* Kefallinía, Iónioi Nísoi, Greece, C Mediterranean Sea
xxxvi G12 **Atherington** Devon, SW England, UK
xxxviii E14 **Atherstone** Warwickshire, C England, UK
xli O16 **Atherton** Wigan, NW England, UK
189 W4 **Atherton** Queensland, NE Australia
83 I19 **Athi** ≈ S Kenya
124 O3 **Athiénou** SE Cyprus
117 H19 **Athína** ***Eng.*** Athens; ***prev.*** Athínai, ***anc.*** Athenae. ● (Greece) Attikí, C Greece
Athínai *see* Athína
145 S10 **Athīyah** C Iraq
xliv G8 **Athleague** Roscommon, C Ireland
xliv H8 **Athlone** ***Ir.*** Baile Átha Luain. Westmeath, C Ireland
161 F16 **Athni** Karnātaka, W India
193 C23 **Athol** Southland, South Island, NZ
21 N11 **Athol** Massachusetts, NE USA
117 I15 **Áthos** ▲ NE Greece
Athos, Mount *see* Ágion Óros
Ath Thawrah *see* Madīnat ath Thawrah
147 P5 **Ath Thumāmī** *spring/well* N Saudi Arabia
101 L25 **Athus** Luxembourg, SE Belgium
xliv J10 **Athy** ***Ir.*** Baile Átha Í. Kildare, C Ireland
80 I10 **Ati** Batha, C Chad
83 F16 **Atiak** NW Uganda
59 G17 **Atico** Arequipa, SW Peru
107 O6 **Atienza** Castilla-La Mancha, C Spain
41 Q6 **Atigun Pass** *pass* Alaska, USA
10 B12 **Atikokan** Ontario, S Canada
11 O9 **Atikonak Lac** ◎ Newfoundland and Labrador, E Canada
44 C6 **Atitlán, Lago de** ◎ W Guatemala
202 L16 **Atiu** *island* S Cook Islands
Atjeh *see* Aceh
127 O9 **Atka** Magadanskaya Oblast', E Russian Federation
40 H17 **Atka** Atka Island, Alaska, USA
40 H17 **Atka Island** *island* Aleutian Islands, Alaska, USA
131 O7 **Atkarsk** Saratovskaya Oblast', W Russian Federation
29 U11 **Atkins** Arkansas, C USA
31 O13 **Atkinson** Nebraska, C USA
176 U10 **Atkri** Irian Jaya, E Indonesia
43 O13 **Atlacomulco** ***var.*** Atlacomulco de Fabela. México, C Mexico
Atlacomulco de Fabela *see* Atlacomulco
25 S3 **Atlanta** *state capital* Georgia, SE USA
33 R6 **Atlanta** Michigan, N USA
27 X6 **Atlanta** Texas, SW USA
31 T15 **Atlantic** Iowa, C USA
23 Y10 **Atlantic** North Carolina, SE USA
25 W8 **Atlantic Beach** Florida, SE USA
20 J17 **Atlantic City** New Jersey, NE USA
180 L14 **Atlantic-Indian Basin** *undersea feature* SW Indian Ocean
180 K13 **Atlantic-Indian Ridge** *undersea feature* SW Indian Ocean
56 E4 **Atlántico** ***off.*** Departamento del Atlántico. ◐ *province* NW Colombia
66-67 **Atlantic Ocean** *ocean*
44 K7 **Atlántico Norte, Región Autónoma** ***prev.*** Zelaya Norte. ◐ *autonomous region* NE Nicaragua
44 L10 **Atlántico Sur, Región Autónoma** ***prev.*** Zelaya Sur. ◐ *autonomous region* SE Nicaragua
44 I5 **Atlántida** ◐ *department* N Honduras
79 Y15 **Atlantika Mountains** ⛰ E Nigeria
66 J10 **Atlantis Fracture Zone** *tectonic feature* NW Atlantic Ocean
76 H7 **Atlas Mountains** ⛰ NW Africa
127 Pp13 **Atlasova, Ostrov** *island* SE Russian Federation
127 Pp10 **Atlasovo** Kamchatskaya Oblast', E Russian Federation
123 H13 **Atlas Saharien** ***var.*** Saharan Atlas. ⛰ Algeria/Morocco
Atlas, Tell *see* Atlas Tellien
123 Gg10 **Atlas Tellien** ***Eng.*** Tell Atlas. ⛰ N Algeria
8 I9 **Atlin** British Columbia, W Canada
8 I9 **Atlin Lake** ◎ British Columbia, W Canada
43 P14 **Atlixco** Puebla, S Mexico
96 B11 **Atløyna** *island* S Norway
161 I17 **Ātmakūr** Andhra Pradesh, C India
25 O8 **Atmore** Alabama, S USA
103 J20 **Atmühl** ≈ S Germany
96 H11 **Atna** ≈ S Norway
170 E12 **Atō** Yamaguchi, Honshū, SW Japan
59 L21 **Atocha** Potosí, S Bolivia
29 P12 **Atoka** Oklahoma, C USA
29 O12 **Atoka Lake** ***var.*** Atoka Reservoir. ▣ Oklahoma, C USA
Atoka Reservoir *see* Atoka Lake
35 Q14 **Atomic City** Idaho, NW USA
42 L10 **Atotonilco** Zacatecas, C Mexico
42 M13 **Atotonilco el Alto** ***var.*** Atotonilco. Jalisco, SW Mexico
79 N7 **Atouila, 'Erg** *desert* N Mali
43 N16 **Atoyac** ***var.*** Atoyac de Alvarez. Guerrero, S Mexico
Atoyac de Alvarez *see* Atoyac
43 P15 **Atoyac, Río** ≈ S Mexico
41 O5 **Atqasuk** Alaska, USA
152 C13 **Atrak** ***Per.*** Rūd-e Atrak, ***Rus.*** Atrek, ***Turkm.*** Etrek. ≈ Iran/Turkmenistan
Atrak, Rūd-e *see* Atrak
97 J20 **Ätran** ≈ S Sweden
56 C7 **Atrato, Río** ≈ NW Colombia
Atrek *see* Atrak
109 K14 **Atri** Abruzzi, C Italy
Atria *see* Adria
171 Jj16 **Atsugi** ***var.*** Atugi. Kanagawa, Honshū, S Japan
171 L12 **Atsumi** Yamagata, Honshū, C Japan
172 Oo4 **Atsuta** Hokkaidō, NE Japan
176 Y13 **Atsy** Irian Jaya, E Indonesia
149 Q17 **Aṭ Ṭaff** *desert* C UAE
144 G12 **Aṭ Ṭafīlah** ***var.*** Et Tafila, Tafila. Aṭ Ṭafīlah, W Jordan
144 G12 **Aṭ Ṭafīlah** ***off.*** Muḥāfaẓat aṭ Ṭafīlah. ◐ *governorate* W Jordan
146 L10 **Aṭ Ṭā'if** Makkah, W Saudi Arabia
Attaleia/Attalia *see* Antalya
25 Q3 **Attalla** Alabama, S USA
144 L2 **At Tall al Abyaḍ** ***var.*** Tall al Abyaḍ, Tell Abyad, ***Fr.*** Tell Abiad. Ar Raqqah, N Syria
144 L7 **Aṭ Ṭanf** Ḥimṣ, S Syria
Attapu *see* Samakhixai
145 S10 **At Ṭaqṭaqānah** C Iraq
117 O23 **Attávytos** ▲ Ródos, Dodekánisos, Greece, Aegean Sea
145 V15 **At Tawal** *desert* Iraq/Saudi Arabia
10 G9 **Attawapiskat** Ontario, C Canada
10 F9 **Attawapiskat** ≈ Ontario, S Canada
10 D9 **Attawapiskat Lake** ◎ Ontario, C Canada
At Taybé *see* Ṭayyibah
103 F16 **Attendorn** Nordrhein-Westfalen, W Germany
111 R5 **Attersee** Salzburg, NW Austria
111 R5 **Attersee** ◎ N Austria
101 L24 **Attert** Luxembourg, SE Belgium
144 M4 **At Tibnī** ***var.*** Tibnī. Dayr az Zawr, NE Syria
33 N13 **Attica** Indiana, N USA
20 E10 **Attica** New York, NE USA
Attica *see* Attikí
11 N7 **Attikamagen Lake** ◎ Newfoundland and Labrador, E Canada
117 H20 **Attikí** ***Eng.*** Attica. ◐ *region* C Greece
21 O12 **Attleboro** Massachusetts, NE USA
xxxix W10 **Attleborough** Norfolk, E England, UK
xxxix W9 **Attlebridge** Norfolk, E England, UK
111 R5 **Attnang** Oberösterreich, N Austria
155 U6 **Attock City** Punjab, E Pakistan
Attopeu *see* Samakhixai
27 X8 **Attoyac River** ≈ Texas, SW USA
40 D16 **Attu** Attu Island, Alaska, USA
145 Y12 **Aṭ Ṭūbah** E Iraq
146 K4 **Aṭ Ṭubayq** *plain* Jordan/Saudi Arabia
40 C16 **Attu Island** *island* Aleutian Islands, Alaska, USA
Aṭ Ṭūr *see* El Ṭûr
161 I21 **Āttūr** Tamil Nādu, SE India
147 N17 **At Turbah** SW Yemen
64 I12 **Atuel, Río** ≈ C Argentina
Atugi *see* Atsugi
203 X7 **Atuona** Hiva Oa, NE French Polynesia
Aturus *see* Adour
97 M18 **Åtvidaberg** Östergötland, S Sweden
37 P9 **Atwater** California, W USA
31 T8 **Atwater** Minnesota, N USA
xli X13 **Atwick** East Riding of Yorkshire, N England, UK
28 I2 **Atwood** Kansas, C USA
33 U12 **Atwood Lake** ▣ Ohio, N USA
xxxvi M10 **Atworth** Wiltshire, S England, UK
131 P5 **Atyashevo** Respublika Mordoviya, W Russian Federation
150 F12 **Atyrau** ***prev.*** Gur'yev. Atyrau, W Kazakhstan
150 E11 **Atyrau** ***off.*** Atyrauskaya Oblast', var. ***Kaz.*** Atyraū Oblysy; ***prev.*** Gur'yevskaya Oblast'. ◐ *province* W Kazakhstan
Atyraū Oblysy/Atyrauskaya Oblast' *see* Atyrau
110 J7 **Au** Vorarlberg, NW Austria
194 G8 **Aua Island** *island* NW PNG
105 S16 **Aubagne** ***anc.*** Albania. Bouches-du-Rhône, SE France
101 L25 **Aubange** Luxembourg, SE Belgium
105 Q6 **Aube** ◐ *department* N France
105 R6 **Aube** ≈ N France
101 L19 **Aubel** Liège, E Belgium
105 Q13 **Aubenas** Ardèche, E France
105 O8 **Aubigny-sur-Nère** Cher, C France
105 O13 **Aubin** Aveyron, S France
105 O13 **Aubrac, Monts d'** ⛰ S France
38 J10 **Aubrey Cliffs** *cliff* Arizona, SW USA
25 R5 **Auburn** Alabama, S USA
37 P6 **Auburn** California, W USA
32 K14 **Auburn** Illinois, N USA
33 Q11 **Auburn** Indiana, N USA
22 J7 **Auburn** Kentucky, S USA
21 P8 **Auburn** Maine, NE USA
21 N11 **Auburn** Massachusetts, NE USA
31 S16 **Auburn** Nebraska, C USA
20 H10 **Auburn** New York, NE USA
34 H8 **Auburn** Washington, NW USA
105 N11 **Aubusson** Creuse, C France
120 E10 **Auce** ***Ger.*** Autz. Dobele, SW Latvia
104 L15 **Auch** ***Lat.*** Augusta Auscorum, Elimberrum. Gers, S France
xliii F19 **Auchbraad** Argyll and Bute, W Scotland, UK
xliii O15 **Auchenblae** Aberdeenshire, NE Scotland, UK
xliii H25 **Auchenmaig** Dumfries and Galloway, SW Scotland, UK
79 U16 **Auchi** Edo, S Nigeria
xlii H10 **Auchindrean** Highland, NW Scotland, UK
xliii J22 **Auchinleck** East Ayrshire, W Scotland, UK
xlii N13 **Auchleven** Aberdeenshire, NE Scotland, UK
xlii P12 **Auchnagatt** Aberdeenshire, NE Scotland, UK
xliii K18 **Auchterarder** Perth and Kinross, C Scotland, UK
xliii M18 **Auchtermuchty** Fife, E Scotland, UK
25 T9 **Aucilla River** ≈ Florida/Georgia, SE USA
xlii M6 **Auckengill** Highland, N Scotland, UK
192 L6 **Auckland** Auckland, North Island, NZ
192 K5 **Auckland** ***off.*** Auckland Region. ◐ *region* North Island, NZ
192 L6 **Auckland** ✕ Auckland, North Island, NZ
199 Ii15 **Auckland Islands** *island group* S NZ
105 O16 **Aude** ◐ *department* S France
105 N16 **Aude** ***anc.*** Atax. ≈ S France
Audenarde *see* Oudenaarde
Audern *see* Audru
104 E6 **Audierne** Finistère, NW France
104 E6 **Audierne, Baie d'** *bay* NW France
105 U7 **Audincourt** Doubs, E France
xxxviii I7 **Audlem** Cheshire, W England, UK
xxxviii J7 **Audley** Staffordshire, C England, UK
120 G5 **Audru** ***Ger.*** Audern. Pärnumaa, SW Estonia
31 T14 **Audubon** Iowa, C USA
103 N17 **Aue** Sachsen, E Germany
102 H12 **Aue** ≈ NW Germany
102 L9 **Auerbach** Bayern, SE Germany
103 M17 **Auerbach** Sachsen, E Germany
110 I10 **Auererrhein** ≈ SW Switzerland
103 N17 **Auersberg** ▲ E Germany
189 W9 **Augathella** Queensland, E Australia
xliv J5 **Augher** Dungannon, C Northern Ireland, UK
xliv J5 **Aughnacloy** Dungannon, C Northern Ireland, UK
xliv G9 **Aughrim** Galway, W Ireland
xliv K10 **Aughrim** Wicklow, E Ireland
33 Q12 **Auglaize River** ≈ Ohio, N USA
85 F22 **Augrabies Falls** *waterfall* W South Africa
33 R7 **Au Gres River** ≈ Michigan, N USA
Augsbourg *see* Augsburg
103 K22 **Augsburg** ***Fr.*** Augsbourg; ***anc.*** Augusta Vindelicorum. Bayern, S Germany
Augusta *see* London
188 I14 **Augusta** Western Australia
109 L25 **Augusta** ***It.*** Agosta. Sicilia, Italy, C Mediterranean Sea
29 O6 **Augusta** Arkansas, C USA
25 V3 **Augusta** Georgia, SE USA
29 W11 **Augusta** Kansas, C USA
21 Q7 **Augusta** *state capital* Maine, NE USA
35 Q8 **Augusta** Montana, NW USA
Augusta Auscorum *see* Auch
Augusta Emerita *see* Mérida
Augusta Praetoria *see* Aosta
Augusta Suessionum *see* Soissons
Augusta Trajana *see* Stara Zagora
Augusta Treverorum *see* Trier
Augusta Vangionum *see* Worms
Augusta Vindelicorum *see* Augsburg
97 G24 **Augustenborg** ***Ger.*** Augustenburg. Sønderjylland, SW Denmark
Augustenburg *see* Augustenborg
41 Q13 **Augustine Island** *island* Alaska, USA
12 L9 **Augustines, Lac des** ◎ Québec, SE Canada
Augustobona Tricassium *see* Troyes
Augustodunum *see* Autun
Augustodurum *see* Bayeux
Augustoritum Lemovicensium *see* Limoges
112 O8 **Augustów** ***Rus.*** Avgustov. Suwałki, NE Poland
Augustow Canal *see* Augustowski, Kanał
112 O8 **Augustowski, Kanał** ***Eng.*** Augustow Canal, ***Rus.*** Avgustovskiy Kanal. *canal* NE Poland
188 I9 **Augustus, Mount** ▲ Western Australia
195 X15 **Auki** Malaita, N Solomon Islands
23 W8 **Aulander** North Carolina, SE USA
xlii K11 **Auldearn** Highland, NW Scotland, UK
xliii K24 **Auldgirth** Dumfries and Galloway, SW Scotland, UK
xliii N19 **Auldhame** East Lothian, SE Scotland, UK
188 L7 **Auld, Lake** *salt lake* Western Australia
Aulie Ata/Auliye-Ata *see* Zhambyl
108 E10 **Aulla** Toscana, C Italy
104 F6 **Aulne** ≈ NW France
Aulong *see* Ulong
39 T3 **Ault** Colorado, C USA
xlii F10 **Aultbea** Highland, NW Scotland, UK
105 N3 **Aumale** Seine-Maritime, N France
Auminzatau, Gory *see* Owminzatovo-Toshi
79 T14 **Auna** Niger, W Nigeria
97 H21 **Auning** Århus, C Denmark
198 Cc9 **Aunu'u Island** *island* W American Samoa
85 E20 **Auob** ***var.*** Oup. ≈ Namibia/South Africa
95 K19 **Aura** Turku-Pori, SW Finland
111 R5 **Aurach** ≈ N Austria
Aural, Phnom *see* Aôral, Phnum
159 O14 **Aurangābād** Bihār, N India
160 F13 **Aurangābād** Mahārāshtra, C India
201 V7 **Aur Atoll** *atoll* E Marshall Islands
104 G7 **Auray** Morbihan, NW France
96 G13 **Aurdal** Oppland, S Norway
96 F8 **Aure** Møre og Romsdal, S Norway
31 T12 **Aurelia** Iowa, C USA
Aurelia Aquensis *see* Baden-Baden
Aurelianum *see* Orléans
123 J12 **Aurès, Massif de l'** ⛰ NE Algeria
102 F10 **Aurich** Niedersachsen, NW Germany
105 O13 **Aurillac** Cantal, C France
Aurine, Alpi *see* Zillertaler Alpen
Aurium *see* Ourense
12 H15 **Aurora** Ontario, S Canada
57 S8 **Aurora** NW Guyana
39 T4 **Aurora** Colorado, C USA
32 M11 **Aurora** Illinois, N USA
33 Q15 **Aurora** Indiana, N USA
31 W4 **Aurora** Minnesota, N USA
29 S8 **Aurora** Missouri, C USA
31 P16 **Aurora** Nebraska, C USA
38 J5 **Aurora** Utah, W USA
Aurora *see* San Francisco, Philippines
Aurora *see* Maewo, Vanuatu
96 F10 **Aursjøen** ◎ S Norway
96 I9 **Aursunden** ◎ S Norway
85 D21 **Aus** Karas, SW Namibia
Ausa *see* Vic
12 E16 **Ausable** ≈ Ontario, S Canada
33 O3 **Au Sable Point** *headland* Michigan, N USA
33 S7 **Au Sable Point** *headland* Michigan, N USA
33 R6 **Au Sable River** ≈ Michigan, N USA
59 H16 **Ausangate, Nevado** ▲ C Peru
Auschwitz *see* Oświęcim
Ausculum Apulum *see* Ascoli Satriano
107 Q4 **Ausejo** La Rioja, N Spain
xlii N4 **Auskerry** *island* N Scotland, UK
Aussig *see* Ústí nad Labem
97 F17 **Aust-Agder** ◐ *county* S Norway
94 P2 **Austfonna** *glacier* NE Svalbard
33 P15 **Austin** Indiana, N USA
31 W11 **Austin** Minnesota, N USA
37 U5 **Austin** Nevada, W USA
27 S10 **Austin** *state capital* Texas, S USA
188 J10 **Austin, Lake** *salt lake* Western Australia
33 V11 **Austintown** Ohio, N USA
27 V9 **Austonio** Texas, SW USA
Australes, Archipel des *see* Australes, Îles
Australes et Antarctiques Françaises, Terres *see* French Southern and Antarctic Territories
203 T14 **Australes, Îles** ***var.*** Archipel des Australes, Îles Tubuai, Tubuai Islands, ***Eng.*** Austral Islands. *island group* SW French Polynesia
183 Y11 **Austral Fracture Zone** *tectonic feature* S Pacific Ocean
189 O7 **Australia** ***off.*** Commonwealth of Australia. ◆ *commonwealth republic*
182 M8 **Australia** *continent*
191 Q12 **Australian Alps** ⛰ SE Australia
191 R11 **Australian Capital Territory** ***prev.*** Federal Capital Territory. ◐ *territory* SE Australia
Australie, Bassin Nord de l' *see* North Australian Basin
Austral Islands *see* Australes, Îles
Austrava *see* Ostrov
111 T6 **Austria** ***off.*** Republic of Austria, ***Ger.*** Österreich. ◆ *republic* C Europe
94 K3 **Austurland** ◐ *region* SE Iceland
94 G10 **Austvågøy** *island* C Norway
xli O12 **Austwick** North Yorkshire, N England, UK
60 G13 **Autazes** Amazonas, N Brazil
104 M16 **Auterive** Haute-Garonne, S France
Autesiodorum *see* Auxerre
105 N2 **Authie** ≈ N France
Autissiodorum *see* Auxerre
42 K14 **Autlán** ***var.*** Autlán de Navarro. Jalisco, SW Mexico
Autlán de Navarro *see* Autlán
Autricum *see* Chartres
105 Q9 **Autun** ***anc.*** Ædua, Augustodunum. Saône-et-Loire, C France
Autz *see* Auce
101 H20 **Auvelais** Namur, S Belgium
105 P11 **Auvergne** ◐ *region* C France
104 M12 **Auvézère** ≈ W France
105 P7 **Auxerre** ***anc.*** Autesiodorum, Autissiodorum. Yonne, C France
105 N2 **Auxi-le-Château** Pas-de-Calais, N France
105 S8 **Auxonne** Côte d'Or, C France
57 P9 **Auyan Tebuy** ▲ SE Venezuela
105 O10 **Auzances** Creuse, C France
29 U8 **Ava** Missouri, C USA
148 M5 **Āvaj** Zanjān, W Iran
97 C15 **Avaldsnes** Rogaland, S Norway
105 Q8 **Avallon** Yonne, C France
104 K6 **Avaloirs, Mont des** ▲ NW France
37 S16 **Avalon** Santa Catalina Island, California, W USA
20 J17 **Avalon** New Jersey, NE USA
11 V13 **Avalon Peninsula** *peninsula* Newfoundland, Newfoundland and Labrador, E Canada
62 K10 **Avaré** São Paulo, S Brazil
Avaricum *see* Bourges
202 H16 **Avarua** ○ (Cook Islands) Rarotonga, S Cook Islands
202 H16 **Avarua Harbour** *harbour* Rarotonga, S Cook Islands
Avasfelsőfalu *see* Negrești-Oaș
40 L17 **Avatanak Island** *island* Aleutian Islands, Alaska, USA
202 B16 **Avatele** S Niue
202 H16 **Avatiu** Rarotonga, S Cook Islands
202 H15 **Avatiu Harbour** *harbour* Rarotonga, S Cook Islands
Avdeyevka *see* Avdiyivka
116 J13 **Ávdira** Anatolikí Makedonía kai Thráki, NE Greece
119 X8 **Avdiyivka** ***Rus.*** Avdeyevka. Donets'ka Oblast', SE Ukraine
168 K7 **Avdzaga** C Monogolia
106 G6 **Ave** ≈ N Portugal
xxxvii N10 **Avebury** Wiltshire, S England, UK
106 G7 **Aveiro** ***anc.*** Talabriga. Aveiro, W Portugal
106 G7 **Aveiro** ◐ *district* N Portugal
Avela *see* Ávila
101 D18 **Avelgem** West-Vlaanderen, W Belgium
63 D20 **Avellaneda** Buenos Aires, E Argentina
109 L17 **Avellino** ***anc.*** Abellinum. Campania, S Italy
37 Q12 **Avenal** California, W USA
Avenio *see* Avignon
96 E8 **Averoya** *island* S Norway
109 K17 **Aversa** Campania, S Italy
35 N9 **Avery** Idaho, NW USA
27 W5 **Avery** Texas, SW USA
Aves, Islas de *see* Las Aves, Islas
Avesnes *see* Avesnes-sur-Helpe
105 Q2 **Avesnes-sur-Helpe** ***var.*** Avesnes. Nord, N France
66 G12 **Aves Ridge** *undersea feature* SE Caribbean Sea
97 M14 **Avesta** Kopparberg, C Sweden
xxxvi G16 **Aveton Gifford** Devon, SW England, UK
105 O14 **Aveyron** ◐ *department* S France
105 N14 **Aveyron** ≈ S France
109 J15 **Avezzano** Abruzzi, C Italy
117 D16 **Avgó** ▲ C Greece
Avgustov *see* Augustów
Avgustovskiy Kanal *see* Augustowski, Kanał
xliii G18 **Avich, Loch** ◎ W Scotland, UK
xlii K13 **Aviemore** Highland, N Scotland, UK
193 F21 **Aviemore, Lake** ◎ South Island, NZ
105 R15 **Avignon** ***anc.*** Avenio. Vaucluse, SE France
106 M7 **Ávila** ***var.*** Avila; ***anc.*** Abela, Abula, Abyla, Avela. Castilla-León, C Spain
106 L8 **Ávila** ◐ *province* Castilla-León, C Spain
106 K2 **Avilés** Asturias, NW Spain
120 J4 **Avinurme** ***Ger.*** Awwinorm. Ida-Virumaa, NE Estonia
106 H10 **Avis** Portalegre, C Portugal
97 F22 **Avlum** Ringkøbing, C Denmark
190 M11 **Avoca** Victoria, SE Australia
31 T14 **Avoca** Iowa, C USA
190 M11 **Avoca River** ≈ Victoria, SE Australia
xlii J11 **Avoch** Highland, NW Scotland, UK
109 L25 **Avola** Sicilia, Italy, C Mediterranean Sea
xxxvi L9 **Avon** ≈ C England, UK
xxxvii O13 **Avon** ≈ S England, UK
xxxvi G15 **Avon** ≈ SW England, UK
20 F10 **Avon** New York, NE USA
31 P12 **Avon** South Dakota, N USA
38 K13 **Avondale** Arizona, SW USA
xxxvi K9 **Avonmouth** City of Bristol, SW England, UK
25 X13 **Avon Park** Florida, SE USA
104 J5 **Avranches** Manche, N France
105 O3 **Avre** ≈ N France
195 X16 **Avuavu** ***var.*** Kolotambu. Guadalcanal, C Solomon Islands
Avveel *see* Ivalo, Finland
Avveel *see* Ivalojoki, Finland
Avvil *see* Ivalo
79 O17 **Awaaso** ***var.*** Awaso. SW Ghana
147 X8 **Awābī** ***var.*** Al 'Awābī. NE Oman
170 G15 **Awaji-shima** *island* SW Japan
192 L9 **Awakino** Waikato, North Island, NZ
148 M15 **'Awālī** C Bahrain
101 K19 **Awans** Liège, E Belgium
192 I2 **Awanui** Northland, North Island, NZ
154 M14 **Awārān** Baluchistān, SW Pakistan
83 K16 **Awara Plain** *plain* NE Kenya
82 M13 **Āwarē** E Ethiopia
144 M6 **'Awāriḍ, Wādī** *dry watercourse* E Syria
193 B20 **Awarua Point** *headland* South Island, NZ
83 J14 **Āwasa** S Ethiopia
82 K13 **Āwash** C Ethiopia
82 K12 **Āwash** ***var.*** Hawash. ≈ C Ethiopia
171 Kk11 **Awa-shima** *island* C Japan
Awaso *see* Awaaso
164 H7 **Awat** Xinjiang Uygur Zizhiqu, NW China
193 J15 **Awatere** ≈ South Island, NZ
77 O10 **Awbārī** SW Libya
77 N9 **Awbāri, Idhān** ***var.*** Edeyen d'Oubari. *desert* Algeria/Libya
82 C13 **Aweil** Northern Bahr el Ghazal, SW Sudan
xliii G18 **Awe, Loch** ◎ W Scotland, UK
79 U16 **Awka** Anambra, SW Nigeria
41 O6 **Awuna River** ≈ Alaska, USA
Awwinorm *see* Avinurme
Ax *see* Dax
Axarfjördhur *see* Öxarfjördhur
105 N17 **Axat** Aude, S France
xxxvi K10 **Axbridge** Somerset, SW England, UK
xxxvi K10 **Axe** ≈ SW England, UK
xxxvi J14 **Axe** ≈ SW England, UK
101 F16 **Axel** Zeeland, SW Netherlands
207 P9 **Axel Heiberg Island** ***var.*** Axel Heiburg. *island* Northwest Territories, N Canada
Axel Heiburg *see* Axel Heiberg Island
79 O17 **Axim** S Ghana
116 F13 **Axiós** ***var.*** Vardar. ≈ Greece/FYR Macedonia *see also* Vardar
105 N17 **Ax-les-Thermes** Ariège, S France
xxxvi J13 **Axminster** Devon, SW England, UK
171 Gg14 **Ayabe** Kyōto, Honshū, SW Japan
122 F13 **Ayachi, Jbel** ▲ C Morocco
63 D22 **Ayacucho** Buenos Aires, E Argentina
59 F15 **Ayacucho** Ayacucho, S Peru
59 E16 **Ayacucho** ***off.*** Departamento de Ayacucho. ◐ *department* SW Peru
151 W11 **Ayaguz** ***Kaz.*** Ayaköz; ***prev.*** Sergiopol. Semipalatinsk, E Kazakhstan
151 V12 **Ayaguz** ***Kaz.*** Ayaköz. ≈ E Kazakhstan
Ayakagytma *see* Oyoqighitma
Ayakkuduk *see* Oyoqquduq
164 L10 **Ayakkum Hu** ◎ NW China
Ayaköz *see* Ayaguz
106 H14 **Ayamonte** Andalucía, S Spain
127 N12 **Ayan** Khabarovskiy Kray, E Russian Federation
142 J10 **Ayancık** Sinop, N Turkey
57 S9 **Ayanganna Mountain** ▲ C Guyana
79 U16 **Ayangba** Kogi, C Nigeria
127 P6 **Ayanka** Koryakskiy Avtonomnyy Okrug, E Russian Federation
56 E7 **Ayapel** Córdoba, NW Colombia
142 H12 **Ayaş** Ankara, N Turkey
59 I16 **Ayaviri** Puno, S Peru
155 P3 **Āybak** ***var.*** Aibak, Haibak; ***prev.*** Samangān. Samangān, NE Afghanistan
153 N10 **Aydarkŭl** ***Rus.*** Ozero Aydarkul'. ◎ C Uzbekistan
Aydarkul', Ozero *see* Aydarkŭl
23 W10 **Ayden** North Carolina, SE USA
142 C15 **Aydın** ***var.*** Aïdin; ***anc.*** Tralles. Aydın, SW Turkey
142 C15 **Aydın** ***var.*** Aïdin. ◐ *province* SW Turkey
142 I17 **Aydıncık** İçel, S Turkey
142 C15 **Aydın Dağları** ⛰ W Turkey
164 L6 **Aydingkol Hu** ◎ NW China
131 X7 **Aydyrlinskiy** Orenburgskaya Oblast', W Russian Federation
107 S4 **Ayerbe** Aragón, NE Spain
Ayers Rock *see* Uluru
Ayeyarwady *see* Irrawaddy
Ayiá *see* Agiá
Ayia Napa *see* Agía Nápa
Ayia Phyla *see* Agía Fýlaxis
Ayiásos/Ayiássos *see* Agiasós
Áyios Evstrátios *see* Ágios Efstrátios
Áyios Kírikos *see* Ágios Kírykos
Áyios Nikólaos *see* 3Ágios Nikólaos
Ayios Seryios *see* Yeniboğaziçi
82 I11 **Āykel** NW Ethiopia
126 K10 **Aykhal** Respublika Sakha (Yakutiya), NE Russian Federation
12 J12 **Aylen Lake** ◎ Ontario, SE Canada
xxxvii R7 **Aylesbury** Buckinghamshire, SE England, UK
xxxvii Y10 **Aylesham** Kent, SE England, UK
107 O6 **Ayllón** Castilla-León, N Spain
12 F17 **Aylmer** Ontario, S Canada
12 L12 **Aylmer** Québec, SE Canada
13 R12 **Aylmer, Lac** ◎ Québec, SE Canada
15 J6 **Aylmer Lake** ◎ Northwest Territories, NW Canada
xxxix X8 **Aylsham** Norfolk, E England, UK
151 V14 **Aynabulak** Taldykorgan, SE Kazakhstan
144 K2 **'Ayn al 'Arab** Ḥalab, N Syria
Aynayn *see* 'Aynīn
145 V12 **'Ayn Ḥamūd** S Iraq
xxxix N14 **Aynho** Northamptonshire, C England, UK
153 P12 **Ayní** ***prev.*** Rus. Varzimanor Ayni. W Tajikistan
146 M10 **'Aynīn** ***var.*** Aynayn. *spring/well* SW Saudi Arabia
23 U12 **Aynor** South Carolina, SE USA
145 Q7 **'Ayn Zāzūh** C Iraq
159 N12 **Ayodhya** Uttar Pradesh, N India
127 O5 **Ayon, Ostrov** *island* NE Russian Federation
107 R11 **Ayora** País Valenciano, E Spain
79 Q11 **Ayorou** Tillabéri, W Niger
81 E16 **Ayos** Centre, S Cameroon
78 L5 **'Ayoûn 'Abd el Mâlek** *well* N Mauritania
78 K10 **'Ayoûn el 'Atroûs** ***var.*** Aïoun el Atrous, Aïoun el Atroûss. Hodh el Gharbi, SE Mauritania
xliii I22 **Ayr** South Ayrshire, W Scotland, UK
xliii J22 **Ayr** ≈ W Scotland, UK
xl G10 **Ayre, Point of** *headland* N Isle of Man
xxxv J4 **Ayr, Point of** *headland* N Wales, UK
98 I13 **Ayrshire** *cultural region* SW Scotland, UK
Aysen *see* Aisén
xli Q11 **Aysgarth** North Yorkshire, N England, UK
82 L12 **Āysha** E Ethiopia
152 K8 **Aytim** Nawoiy Wiloyati, N Uzbekistan
xli V11 **Ayton** North Yorkshire, N England, UK
xliii P20 **Ayton** The Borders, S Scotland, UK
189 W4 **Ayton** Queensland, NE Australia
116 M9 **Aytos** Burgaska Oblast, E Bulgaria
176 Uu7 **Ayu, Kepulauan** *island group* E Indonesia
A Yun Pa *see* Cheo Reo
175 O8 **Ayu, Tanjung** *headland* Borneo, N Indonesia
42 K13 **Ayutla** Jalisco, C Mexico
43 P16 **Ayutlá** ***var.*** Ayutla de los Libres. Guerrero, S Mexico
Ayutla de los Libres *see* Ayutlá
178 H11 **Ayutthaya** ***var.*** Phra Nakhon Si Ayutthaya. Phra Nakhon Si Ayutthaya, C Thailand
142 B13 **Ayvalık** Balıkesir, W Turkey
101 L20 **Aywaille** Liège, E Belgium
147 R13 **'Aywat aş Şay'ar, Wādī** *seasonal river* N Yemen
Azaffal *see* Azeffâl
107 T9 **Azahar, Costa del** *coastal region* E Spain
107 S6 **Azaila** Aragón, NE Spain
106 F10 **Azambuja** Lisboa, C Portugal
159 N13 **Āzamgarh** Uttar Pradesh, N India
79 O9 **Azaouâd** *desert* C Mali
79 S10 **Azaouagh, Vallée de l'** ***var.*** Azaouak. ≈ W Niger
Azaouak *see* Azaouagh, Vallée de l'
63 F14 **Azara** Misiones, NE Argentina
148 K3 **Āzarān** Āžarbāyjān-e Khāvarī, N Iran
Azärbaycan/Azärbaycan Respublikası *see* Azerbaijan
148 I4 **Āžarbāyjān-e Bākhtarī** ***off.*** Ostān-e Āžarbāyjān-e Bākhtarī, ***var.*** Āzarbāyjān-e Gharbī, ***Eng.*** West Azerbaijan. ◐ *province* NW Iran
Āžarbāyjān-e Gharbī *see* Āžarbāyjān-e Bākhtarī
148 J3 **Āžarbāyjān-e Khāvarī** ***off.*** Ostān-e Āžarbāyjān-e Khāvarī, ***var.*** Āžarbāyjān-e Sharqī, ***Eng.*** East Azerbaijan. ◐ *province* NW Iran
Āžarbāyjān-e Sharqī *see* Āžarbāyjān-e Khāvarī
79 W13 **Azare** Bauchi, N Nigeria
121 M19 **Azarychy** ***Rus.*** Ozarichi. Homyel'skaya Voblasts', SE Belorussia
104 L8 **Azay-le-Rideau** Indre-et-Loire, C France
144 I2 **A'zāz** Ḥalab, NW Syria
78 H7 **Azeffâl** ***var.*** Azaffal. *desert* Mauritania/Western Sahara
143 V12 **Azerbaijan** ***off.*** Azerbaijani Republic, ***Az.*** Azärbaycan, Azärbaycan Respublikası; ***prev.*** Azerbaijan SSR. ◆ *republic* SE Asia
151 T7 **Azhbulat, Ozero** ◎ NE Kazakhstan
76 F7 **Azilal** C Morocco
Azimabad *see* Patna
21 O6 **Aziscohos Lake** ▣ Maine, NE USA
Azizbekov *see* Vayk'
Azizie *see* Telish
Aziziya *see* Al 'Azīzīyah
131 T4 **Aznakayevo** Respublika Tatarstan, W Russian Federation
58 C8 **Azogues** Cañar, S Ecuador
66 N2 **Azores** ***var.*** Açores, Ilhas dos Açores, ***Port.*** Arquipélago dos Açores. *island group* Portugal, NE Atlantic Ocean
66 L8 **Azores-Biscay Rise** *undersea feature* E Atlantic Ocean
Azotos/Azotus *see* Ashdod
80 K11 **Azoum, Bahr** *seasonal river* SE Chad
130 L12 **Azov** Rostovskaya Oblast', SW Russian Federation
130 J13 **Azov, Sea of** ***Rus.*** Azovskoye More, ***Ukr.*** Azovs'ke More. *sea* NE Black Sea
Azovs'ke More/Azovskoye More *see* Azov, Sea of
Azraq, Bahr el *see* Blue Nile
144 I10 **Azraq, Wāḥat al** *oasis* N Jordan
Āzro *see* Āzrow
76 G6 **Azrou** C Morocco
155 R5 **Āzrow** ***var.*** Āzro. Lowgar, E Afghanistan
39 P8 **Aztec** New Mexico, SW USA
38 M13 **Aztec Peak** ▲ Arizona, SW USA
47 N9 **Azua** ***var.*** Azua de Compostela. S Dominican Republic
Azua de Compostela *see* Azua
106 K12 **Azuaga** Extremadura, W Spain
58 B8 **Azuay** ◐ *province* W Ecuador
170 Bb11 **Azuchi-Ō-shima** *island* SW Japan
107 O11 **Azuer** ≈ C Spain
45 S17 **Azuero, Península de** *peninsula* S Panama
64 I6 **Azufre, Volcán** ***var.*** Volcán Lastarria. ▲ N Chile
118 J12 **Azuga** Prahova, SE Romania
63 C22 **Azul** Buenos Aires, E Argentina
64 I8 **Azul, Cerro** ▲ NW Argentina
58 E12 **Azul, Cordillera** ⛰ C Peru
171 Ll14 **Azuma-san** ▲ Honshū, C Japan

◆ Country
● Country Capital
◇ Dependent Territory
○ Dependent Territory Capital
◐ Administrative Region
✕ International Airport
▲ Mountain
⛰ Mountain Range
Volcano
≈ River
◎ Lake
▣ Reservoir

Azur, Côte d' – Balkanskiy Velayat

105 V15 Azur, Côte d' coastal region SE France
203 Z3 Azur Lagoon ◎ Kiritimati, E Kiribati
'Azza see Gaza
Az Zāb al Kabīr see Great Zab
144 H7 Az Zabdānī var. Zabadani. Dimashq, W Syria
147 W8 Aẓ Ẓāhirah desert NW Oman
147 S6 Aẓ Ẓahrān Eng. Dhahran. Ash Sharqīyah, NE Saudi Arabia
147 R6 Aẓ Ẓahrān al Khubar var. Dhahran Al Khobar. ✈ Ash Sharqīyah, NE Saudi Arabia
Az Zaqāzīq see Zagazig
144 H10 Az Zarqā' var. Zarqa. Az Zarqā', NW Jordan
144 I11 Az Zarqā' off. Muḥāfaẓat az Zarqā', var. Zarqa. ◈ governorate N Jordan
77 O7 Az Zāwiyah var. Zawia. NW Libya
147 N15 Az Zaydīyah W Yemen
76 I11 Azzel Matti, Sebkha var. Sebkra Azz el Matti. salt flat C Algeria
147 P6 Az Zilfī Ar Riyāḍ, N Saudi Arabia
145 Y13 Az Zubayr var. Al Zubair. SE Iraq
Az Zuqur see Jabal Zuuqar, Jazīrat

B

197 H14 Ba prev. Mba. Viti Levu, W Fiji
Ba see Đa Răng
175 R18 Baa Pulau Rote, C Indonesia
197 G5 Baaba, Île island Îles Belep, W New Caledonia
144 H7 Baalbek var. Ba'labakk; anc. Heliopolis. E Lebanon
110 G8 Baar Zug, N Switzerland
83 L17 Baardheere var. Bardere, It. Bardera. Gedo, SW Somalia
82 Q12 Baargaal Bari, NE Somalia
101 I15 Baarle-Hertog Antwerpen, N Belgium
101 I15 Baarle-Nassau Antwerpen, N Belgium
100 J11 Baarn Utrecht, C Netherlands
116 D13 Baba var. Buševa, Gk. Varnoús. ▲ FYR Macedonia/Greece
78 H10 Bababé Brakna, W Mauritania
142 G10 Baba Burnu headland NW Turkey
119 N13 Babadag Tulcea, SE Romania
143 X10 Babadağ Dağı ▲ NE Azerbaijan
Babadayhan see Babadaykhan
152 H14 Babadaykhan Turkm. Babadayhan; prev. Kirovsk. Akhalskiy Velayat, C Turkmenistan
152 G14 Babadurmaz Akhalskiy Velayat, C Turkmenistan
116 M12 Babaeski Kırklareli, NW Turkey
145 T4 Bāba Gurgur N Iraq
58 B7 Babahoyo prev. Bodegas. Los Ríos, C Ecuador
155 P5 Bābā, Kūh-e ⛰ C Afghanistan
175 P10 Babana Sulawesi, C Indonesia
176 U16 Babar, Kepulauan island group E Indonesia
176 U15 Babar, Pulau island Kepulauan Babar, E Indonesia
158 G4 Bābāsar Pass pass India/Pakistan
195 Q10 Babase Island island Feni Islands, NE PNG
152 C9 Babashy ⛰ W Turkmenistan
174 L15 Babat Jawa, S Indonesia
174 I10 Babat Sumatera, W Indonesia
Babatag, Khrebet see Bobotogh, Qatorkŭhi
83 H21 Babati Arusha, NE Tanzania
128 J13 Babayevo Vologodskaya Oblast', NW Russian Federation
131 Q15 Babayurt Respublika Dagestan, SW Russian Federation
35 P6 Babb Montana, NW USA
xxxvi I15 Babbacombe Bay bay SW England, UK
31 X4 Babbitt Minnesota, N USA
196 E9 Babeldaob var. Babeldaop, Babelthuap. island N Palau
Babeldaop see Babeldaob
147 N17 Bab el Mandeb strait Gulf of Aden/Red Sea
Babelthuap see Babeldaob
113 K17 Babia Góra var. Babia Hora. ▲ Czech Republic/Poland
Babia Hora see Babia Góra
Babian Jiang see Black River
Babichi see Babichy
121 N19 Babichy Rus. Babichi. Homyel'skaya Voblasts', SE Belorussia
114 I10 Babina Greda Vukovar-Srijem, E Croatia
8 K13 Babine Lake ◎ British Columbia, SW Canada
176 Vv10 Babo Irian Jaya, E Indonesia
149 O4 Bābol var. Babul, Balfrush, Barfrush; prev. Barfurush. Māzandarān, N Iran
149 O4 Bābolsar var. Babulsar; prev. Meshed-i-Sar. Māzandarān, N Iran
38 L16 Baboquivari Peak ▲ Arizona, SW USA
81 G15 Baboua Nana-Mambéré, W Central African Republic
121 M17 Babruysk Rus. Bobruysk. Mahilyowskaya Voblasts', E Belorussia
Babu see Hexian
Babul see Bābol
Babulsar see Bābolsar
115 O19 Babuna ⛰ C FYR Macedonia
115 O19 Babuna ⛰ C FYR Macedonia
154 K7 Bābūs, Dasht-e Pash. Bebas, Dasht-i. ⛰ W Afghanistan
126 Jj16 Babushkin Respublika Buryatiya, S Russian Federation
179 P7 Babuyan Channel channel N Philippines
179 Pp7 Babuyan Island island N Philippines
145 T9 Babylon site of ancient city C Iraq
114 J9 Bač Ger. Batsch. Serbia, NW Yugoslavia
60 M13 Bacabal Maranhão, E Brazil
43 Y14 Bacalar Quintana Roo, SE Mexico
43 Y14 Bacalar Chico, Boca strait SE Mexico
175 Ss8 Bacan, Kepulauan island group E Indonesia
175 T8 Bacan, Pulau prev. Batjan. island Maluku, E Indonesia
118 L10 Bacău Hung. Bákó. Bacău, NE Romania
118 K11 Bacău ◈ county E Romania
Bắc Bộ, Vinh see Tongking, Gulf of
178 Jj5 Bắc Can Bắc Thai, N Vietnam
105 T5 Baccarat Meurthe-et-Moselle, NE France
191 N12 Bacchus Marsh Victoria, SE Australia
42 H4 Bacerac Sonora, NW Mexico
118 L10 Băceşti Vaslui, E Romania
178 Jj6 Bắc Giang Ha Bắc, N Vietnam
56 I5 Bachaquero Zulia, NW Venezuela
Bacher see Pohorje
120 M13 Bacheykava Rus. Bocheykovo. Vitsyebskaya Voblasts', N Belorussia
42 I5 Bachíniva Chihuahua, N Mexico
164 G8 Bachu Xinjiang Uygur Zizhiqu, NW China
15 J6 Back ≈ Northwest Territories, N Canada
xlii N3 Backaland Orkney Islands, N Scotland, UK
114 K10 Bačka Palanka prev. Palanka. Serbia, NW Yugoslavia
114 K8 Bačka Topola Hung. Topolya; prev. Hung. Bácstopolya. Serbia, N Yugoslavia
97 J17 Bäckefors Älvsborg, S Sweden
Bäckermühle Schulzenmühle see Żywiec
97 L16 Bäckhammar Värmland, C Sweden
114 K9 Bački Petrovac Hung. Petrőcz; prev. Petrovac, Petrovácz. Serbia, NW Yugoslavia
103 I21 Backnang Baden-Württemberg, SW Germany
178 J15 Bạc Liêu var. Vinh Loi. Minh Hai, S Vietnam
178 Jj6 Bắc Ninh Ha Bắc, N Vietnam
42 G4 Bacoachi Sonora, NW Mexico
179 Q13 Bacolod off. Bacolod City. Negros, C Philippines
179 P12 Baco, Mount ▲ Mindoro, N Philippines
113 K25 Bácsalmás Bács-Kiskun, S Hungary
Bácsjózseffalva see Žednik
113 J24 Bács-Kiskun off. Bács-Kiskun Megye. ◈ county S Hungary
Bácsszenttamás see Srbobran
Bácstopolya see Bačka Topola
xxxix Y8 Bacton Norfolk, E England, UK
Bactra see Balkh
xli P15 Bacup Lancashire, NW England, UK
161 F21 Badagara Kerala, SW India
103 M24 Bad Aibling Bayern, SE Germany
168 I13 Badain Jaran Shamo desert N China
106 I11 Badajoz anc. Pax Augusta. Extremadura, W Spain
106 J11 Badajoz ◈ province Extremadura, W Spain
155 S2 Badakhshān ◈ province NE Afghanistan
107 W6 Badalona anc. Baetulo. Cataluña, E Spain
160 O11 Bādāmapāhārh Orissa, E India
158 K8 Badarīnāth ▲ N India
174 J8 Badas, Kepulauan island group W Indonesia
111 S6 Bad Aussee Salzburg, E Austria
33 S8 Bad Axe Michigan, N USA
103 G16 Bad Berleburg Nordrhein-Westfalen, W Germany
103 L17 Bad Blankenburg Thüringen, C Germany
Bad Borseck see Borsec
xxxix N12 Badby Northamptonshire, C England, UK
xlii G7 Badcall Highland, N Scotland, UK
103 G18 Bad Camberg Hessen, W Germany
102 L8 Bad Doberan Mecklenburg-Vorpommern, N Germany
103 N14 Bad Düben Sachsen, E Germany
111 X4 Baden var. Baden bei Wien; anc. Aquae Panoniae, Thermae Pannonicae. Niederösterreich, NE Austria
110 F9 Baden Aargau, N Switzerland
103 G21 Baden-Baden anc. Aurelia Aquensis. Baden-Württemberg, SW Germany
Baden bei Wien see Baden
xlii O12 Badenscoth Aberdeenshire, NE Scotland, UK
103 G22 Baden-Württemberg Fr. Bade-Wurtemberg. ◈ state SW Germany
114 A10 Baderna Istra, NW Croatia
Bade-Wurtemberg see Baden-Württemberg
103 H20 Bad Fredrichshall Baden-Württemberg, S Germany
102 P11 Bad Freienwalde Brandenburg, NE Germany
111 Q8 Badgastein var. Gastein. Salzburg, NW Austria
Badger State see Wisconsin
154 L4 Bādghīs ◈ province NW Afghanistan
111 T5 Bad Hall Oberösterreich, N Austria
103 J14 Bad Harzburg Niedersachsen, C Germany
103 I16 Bad Hersfeld Hessen, C Germany
100 I10 Badhoevedorp Noord-Holland, C Netherlands
111 Q8 Bad Hofgastein Salzburg, NW Austria
Bad Homburg see Bad Homburg vor der Höhe
103 G18 Bad Homburg vor der Höhe var. Bad Homburg. Hessen, W Germany
103 E17 Bad Honnef Nordrhein-Westfalen, W Germany
155 Q17 Badīn Sind, SE Pakistan
23 S10 Badin Lake ⊡ North Carolina, SE USA
42 I8 Badiraguato Sinaloa, C Mexico
111 R6 Bad Ischl Oberösterreich, N Austria
Badjawa see Bajawa
103 J18 Bad Kissingen Bayern, SE Germany
Bad Königswart see Lázně Kynžvart
103 F19 Bad Kreuznach Rheinland-Pfalz, SW Germany
103 F24 Bad Krozingen Baden-Württemberg, SW Germany
103 G16 Bad Laasphe Nordrhein-Westfalen, W Germany
30 J6 Badlands physical region North Dakota, N USA
103 K16 Bad Langensalza Thüringen, C Germany
111 T3 Bad Leonfelden Oberösterreich, N Austria
103 I20 Bad Mergentheim Baden-Württemberg, SW Germany
103 H17 Bad Nauheim Hessen, W Germany
103 E17 Bad Neuenahr-Ahrweiler Rheinland-Pfalz, W Germany
Bad Neustadt see Bad Neustadt an der Saale
103 J18 Bad Neustadt an der Saale var. Bad Neustadt. Berlin, C Germany
Badnur see Betūl
176 Yy15 Bado Irian Jaya, E Indonesia
102 H13 Bad Oeynhausen Nordrhein-Westfalen, NW Germany
102 J9 Bad Oldesloe Schleswig-Holstein, N Germany
79 Q16 Badou C Togo
Bad Polzin see Połczyn-Zdrój
102 H13 Bad Pyrmont Niedersachsen, C Germany
111 X9 Bad Radkersburg Steiermark, SE Austria
145 V8 Badrah E Iraq
168 J6 Badrah Hövsgöl, N Mongolia
103 N24 Bad Reichenhall Bayern, SE Germany
146 K8 Badr Ḥunayn Al Madīnah, W Saudi Arabia
30 M10 Bad River ≈ South Dakota, N USA
32 K4 Bad River ≈ Wisconsin, N USA
102 H13 Bad Salzuflen Nordrhein-Westfalen, NW Germany
103 J16 Bad Salzungen Thüringen, C Germany
111 V8 Bad Sankt Leonhard im Lavanttal Kärnten, S Austria
102 K9 Bad Schwartau Schleswig-Holstein, N Germany
103 L24 Bad Tölz Bayern, SE Germany
189 U1 Badu Island island Queensland, NE Australia
161 K25 Badulla Uva Province, C Sri Lanka
111 X5 Bad Vöslau Niederösterreich, NE Austria
103 I24 Bad Waldsee Baden-Württemberg, S Germany
37 U11 Badwater Basin depression California, W USA
103 J20 Bad Windsheim Bayern, C Germany
103 J23 Bad Wörishofen Bayern, S Germany
102 G10 Bad Zwischenahn Niedersachsen, NW Germany
106 M13 Baena Andalucía, S Spain
Baeterrae/Baeterrae Septimanorum see Béziers
Baetic Cordillera/Baetic Mountains see Béticos, Sistemas
Baetulo see Badalona
59 K18 Baeza Napo, NE Ecuador
107 N13 Baeza Andalucía, S Spain
81 D15 Bafang Ouest, W Cameroon
78 H12 Bafatá C Guinea-Bissau
155 U5 Baffa North-West Frontier Province, NW Pakistan
15 L11 Baffin ◈ district Northwest Territories, NE Canada
207 O11 Baffin Basin undersea feature N Labrador Sea
207 N12 Baffin Bay bay Canada/Greenland
27 T15 Baffin Bay inlet Texas, SW USA
206 M12 Baffin Island island Northwest Territories, NE Canada
81 E15 Bafia Centre, C Cameroon
79 R14 Bafilo NE Togo
78 J12 Bafing headstream W Africa
78 J12 Bafoulabé Kayes, W Mali
81 D15 Bafoussam Ouest, W Cameroon
149 R9 Bāfq Yazd, C Iran
142 L10 Bafra Samsun, N Turkey
142 L10 Bafra Burnu headland N Turkey
149 S12 Bāft Kermān, S Iran
81 N18 Bafwabalinga Haut-Zaïre, NE Zaire
81 N18 Bafwaboli Haut-Zaïre, NE Zaire
81 N17 Bafwasende Haut-Zaïre, NE Zaire
194 J11 Bagabag Island island N PNG
44 K13 Bagaces Guanacaste, NW Costa Rica
159 O12 Bagaha Bihār, N India
161 F16 Bāgalkot Karnātaka, W India
83 J22 Bagamoyo Pwani, E Tanzania
174 Gg4 Bagan Datuk var. Bagan Datok. Perak, Peninsular Malaysia
179 Rr15 Baganga Mindanao, S Philippines
174 Gg6 Bagansiapiapi var. Pasirpangarayan. Sumatera, W Indonesia
Bagaria see Bagheria
79 T11 Bagaroua Tahoua, W Niger
81 I20 Bagata Bandundu, W Zaire
Bagdad see Baghdād
126 Kk15 Bagdarin Respublika Buryatiya, S Russian Federation
63 G17 Bagé Rio Grande do Sul, S Brazil
Bagenalstown see Muine Bheag
105 P16 Bages et de Sigean, Étang de ◎ S France
35 W17 Baggs Wyoming, C USA
160 F11 Bāgh Madhya Pradesh, C India
145 T8 Baghdād var. Bagdad, Eng. Baghdad. ● (Iraq) C Iraq
145 T8 Baghdād ✈ C Iraq
159 T16 Bagherhat Khulna, S Bangladesh
109 J23 Bagheria var. Bagaria. Sicilia, Italy, C Mediterranean Sea
149 S10 Bāghīn Kermān, C Iran
155 Q3 Baghlān Baghlān, NE Afghanistan
155 Q3 Baghlān var. Bāghlān. ◈ province NE Afghanistan
154 M7 Bāghrān Helmand, S Afghanistan
31 T4 Bagley Minnesota, N USA
108 H10 Bagnacavallo Emilia-Romagna, C Italy
104 K16 Bagnères-de-Bigorre Hautes-Pyrénées, S France
104 L17 Bagnères-de-Luchon Hautes-Pyrénées, S France
108 F11 Bagni di Lucca Toscana, C Italy
108 H11 Bagno di Romagna Emilia-Romagna, C Italy
105 R14 Bagnols-sur-Cèze Gard, S France
168 M14 Bag Nur ◎ N China
179 Q13 Bago off. Bago City. Negros, C Philippines
Bago see Pegu
78 M13 Bagoé ≈ Ivory Coast/Mali
Bagrāmē see Bagrāmī
155 R5 Bagrāmī var. Bagrāmē. Kābul, E Afghanistan
121 B14 Bagrationovsk Ger. Preussisch Eylau. Kaliningradskaya Oblast', W Russian Federation
Bagrax see Bohu
Bagrax Hu see Bosten Hu
xxxvii S10 Bagshot Surrey, SE England, UK
58 C10 Bagua Amazonas, NE Peru
179 P9 Baguio off. Baguio City. Luzon, N Philippines
79 V9 Bagzane, Monts ▲ N Niger
Bāḥah, Minṭaqat al see Al Bāḥah
Bahama Islands see Bahamas
46 H3 Bahamas off. Commonwealth of the Bahamas. ◆ commonwealth republic N West Indies
1 L13 Bahamas var. Bahama Islands. island group N West Indies
159 S15 Baharampur prev. Berhampore. West Bengal, NE India
175 Nn6 Bahau, Sungai ≈ Borneo, N Indonesia
155 U10 Bahāwalnagar Punjab, E Pakistan
155 T11 Bahāwalpur Punjab, E Pakistan
142 L16 Bahçe Adana, S Turkey
166 J8 Ba He ≈ C China
Bäherden see Bakharden
61 N16 Bahia off. Estado da Bahia. ◈ state E Brazil
63 B24 Bahía Blanca Buenos Aires, E Argentina
42 L15 Bahía Bufadero Michoacán de Ocampo, SW Mexico
65 J19 Bahía Bustamante Chubut, SE Argentina
42 D5 Bahía de los Ángeles Baja California, NW Mexico
42 C6 Bahía de Tortugas Baja California Sur, W Mexico
44 J4 Bahía, Islas de la Eng. Bay Islands. island group N Honduras
42 E5 Bahía Kino Sonora, NW Mexico
42 E9 Bahía Magdalena var. Puerto Magdalena. Baja California Sur, W Mexico
56 C8 Bahía Solano var. Ciudad Mutis, Solano. Chocó, W Colombia
82 I11 Bahir Dar var. Bahr Dar, Bahrdar Giyorgis. NW Ethiopia
147 X8 Bahlā' var. Bahlah, Bahlat. NW Oman
Bāhla see Bālān
Bahlah/Bahlat see Bahlā'
158 M11 Bahraich Uttar Pradesh, N India
149 M14 Bahrain off. State of Bahrain, Dawlat al Bahrayn, Ar. Al Baḥrayn; prev. Bahrein, anc. Tylos or Tyros. ◆ monarchy SW Asia
148 M14 Bahrain ✈ C Bahrain
148 M15 Bahrain, Gulf of gulf Persian Gulf, NW Arabian Sea
144 I7 Baḥrat Mallāḥah ◎ W Syria
Bahrayn, Dawlat al see Bahrain
Bahr Dar/Bahrdar Giyorgis see Bahir Dar
Bahrein see Bahrain
83 E16 Bahr el Gabel ◈ state S Sudan
83 E19 Bahr ez Zaref ≈ C Sudan
69 R8 Bahr Kameur ≈ N Central African Republic
Bahr Tabariya, Sea of see Tiberias, Lake
149 W15 Bāhū Kalāt Sīstān va Balūchestān, SE Iran
120 N13 Bahushewsk Rus. Bogushëvsk. Vitsyebskaya Voblasts', NE Belorussia
Bai see Tagow Bāy
118 G13 Baia de Aramă Mehedinţi, SW Romania
118 G11 Baia de Criş Ger. Altenburg, Hung. Körösbánya. Hunedoara, SW Romania
85 A16 Baia dos Tigres Namibe, SW Angola
84 A13 Baia Farta Benguela, W Angola
118 H9 Baia Mare Ger. Frauenbach, Hung. Nagybánya; prev. Neustadt. Maramureş, NW Romania
118 H8 Baia Sprie Ger. Mittelstadt, Hung. Felsőbánya. Maramureş, NW Romania
80 G13 Baïbokoum Logone-Oriental, SW Chad
166 F12 Baicao Ling ⛰ SW China
169 U9 Baicheng var. Pai-ch'eng; prev. T'aon-an. Jilin, NE China
164 I6 Baicheng var. Bay. Xinjiang Uygur Zizhiqu, NW China
118 J13 Băicoi Prahova, SE Romania
Baidoa see Baydhabo
13 U6 Baie-Comeau Québec, SE Canada
13 T7 Baie-des-Bacon Québec, SE Canada
13 S8 Baie-des-Rochers Québec, SE Canada
13 U6 Baie-des-Sables Québec, SE Canada
10 K11 Baie-du-Poste Québec, SE Canada
180 H17 Baie Lazare Mahé, NE Seychelles
47 Y5 Baie-Mahault Basse Terre, C Guadeloupe
13 R9 Baie-St-Paul Québec, SE Canada
13 V5 Baie-Trinité Québec, SE Canada
11 T11 Baie Verte Newfoundland, Newfoundland and Labrador, SE Canada
Baiguan see Shangyu
145 U11 Bā'ij al Mahdī S Iraq
Baiji see Bayjī
Baikal, Lake see Baykal, Ozero
Bailādila see Kirandul
Baile an Chaistil see Ballycastle
Baile an Róba see Ballinrobe
Baile an tSratha see Ballintra
Baile Átha an Rí see Athenry
Baile Átha Buí see Athboy
Baile Átha Cliath see Dublin
Baile Átha Fhirdhia see Ardee
Baile Átha Í see Athy
Baile Átha Luain see Athlone
Baile Átha Troim see Trim
Baile Brigín see Balbriggan
Baile Easa Dara see Ballysadare
118 I13 Băile Govora Vâlcea, SW Romania
118 F13 Băile Herculane Ger. Herkulesbad, Hung. Herkulesfürdő. Caraş-Severin, SW Romania
Baile Locha Riach see Loughrea
Baile Mhistéala see Mitchelstown
Baile Monaidh see Ballymoney
xliii D18 Baile Mór Argyll and Bute, W Scotland, UK
107 N12 Bailén Andalucía, S Spain
Baile na hInse see Ballynahinch
Baile na Lorgan see Castleblayney
Baile na Mainistreach see Newtownabbey
Baile na nGallóglach see Millford
Baile Nua na hArda see Newtownards
118 I12 Băile Olăneşti Vâlcea, SW Romania
118 H14 Băileşti Dolj, SW Romania
xliv J7 Bailieborough Cavan, N Ireland
Bailingmiao see Darhan Muminggan Lianheqi
60 K11 Bailique, Ilha island NE Brazil
105 O1 Bailleul Nord, N France
80 H12 Ba Illi Chari-Baguirmi, SW Chad
165 V12 Bailong Jiang ≈ C China
84 C13 Bailundo Port. Vila Teixeira da Silva. Huambo, C Angola
165 T13 Baima var. Sêraitang. Qinghai, C China
176 W14 Baimun Pulau Workai, E Indonesia
194 H14 Baimuru Gulf, S PNG
164 M16 Bainang Xizang Zizhiqu, W China
xli P11 Bainbridge North Yorkshire, N England, UK
25 S8 Bainbridge Georgia, SE USA
175 Pp17 Baing Pulau Sumba, SE Indonesia
164 M14 Baingoin Xizang Zizhiqu, W China
106 G2 Baio Grande Galicia, NW Spain
106 G4 Baiona Galicia, NW Spain
169 V7 Baiquan Heilongjiang, NE China
Bā'ir see Bāyir
164 I11 Bairab Co ◎ W China
27 Q7 Baird Texas, SW USA
41 N7 Baird Mountains ⛰ Alaska, USA
15 Mm2 Baird Peninsula peninsula Baffin Island, Northwest Territories, NE Canada
Baireuth see Bayreuth
202 H3 Bairiki ● (Kiribati) Tarawa, NW Kiribati
169 S11 Bairin Youqi var. Daban. Nei Mongol Zizhiqu, N China
169 S10 Bairin Zuoqi var. Lindong. Nei Mongol Zizhiqu, N China
151 P17 Bairkum Kaz. Bayyrqum. Yuzhnyy Kazakhstan, S Kazakhstan
191 P12 Bairnsdale Victoria, SE Australia
179 Q14 Bais Negros, S Philippines
104 L15 Baïse var. Baise. ≈ S France
169 W11 Baishan prev. Hunjiang. Jilin, NE China
120 F12 Baisogala Radviliškis, C Lithuania
201 Q7 Baiti N Nauru
106 G13 Baixo Alentejo physical region S Portugal
66 P5 Baixo, Ilhéu de island Madeira, Portugal, NE Atlantic Ocean
85 E15 Baixo Longa Cuando Cubango, SE Angola
165 V10 Baiyin Gansu, C China
166 E8 Baiyü Sichuan, C China
167 N14 Baiyun ✈ (Guangzhou) Guangdong, S China
166 K4 Baiyu Shan ⛰ C China
113 J25 Baja Bács-Kiskun, S Hungary
42 C4 Baja California ◈ state NW Mexico
42 C4 Baja California Eng. Lower California. peninsula NW Mexico
42 E9 Baja California Sur ◈ state W Mexico
Bājah see Béja
Bajan see Bayan
203 V16 Baja, Punta headland Easter Island, Chile, E Pacific Ocean
42 B4 Baja, Punta headland NW Mexico
57 R5 Baja, Punta headland NE Venezuela
44 D5 Baja Verapaz off. Departamento de Baja Verapaz. ◈ department C Guatemala
175 Q16 Bajawa prev. Badjawa. Flores, S Indonesia
159 S16 Baj Baj prev. Budge-Budge. West Bengal, E India
147 N15 Bājil W Yemen
191 U4 Bajimba, Mount ▲ New South Wales, SE Australia
114 K13 Bajina Bašta Serbia, W Yugoslavia
159 U14 Bajitpur Dhaka, E Bangladesh
114 K8 Bajmok Serbia, NW Yugoslavia
Bajo Boquete see Boquete
115 L17 Bajram Curri Kukës, N Albania
81 J14 Bakala Ouaka, C Central African Republic
131 T4 Bakaly Respublika Bashkortostan, W Russian Federation
Bakan see Shimonoseki
151 U14 Bakanas Kaz. Baqanas. Almaty, SE Kazakhstan
151 V12 Bakanas Kaz. Baqanas. ≈ E Kazakhstan
151 U14 Bakbakty Kaz. Baqbaqty. Almaty, SE Kazakhstan
126 Gg13 Bakchar Tomskaya Oblast', C Russian Federation
78 I11 Bakel E Senegal
37 W13 Baker California, W USA
24 J8 Baker Louisiana, S USA
35 Y9 Baker Montana, NW USA
34 L12 Baker Oregon, NW USA
199 Jj8 Baker and Howland Islands ◇ US unincorporated territory W Polynesia
38 L12 Baker Butte ▲ Arizona, SW USA
41 X15 Baker Island island Alexander Archipelago, Alaska, USA
15 Kk6 Baker Lake Northwest Territories, N Canada
15 Kk6 Baker Lake ◎ Northwest Territories, N Canada
37 R13 Bakersfield California, W USA
26 M9 Bakersfield Texas, SW USA
23 P9 Bakersville North Carolina, SE USA
xxxviii L6 Bakewell Derbyshire, C England, UK
Bakhābī see Bū Khābī
152 E12 Bakharden Turkm. Bäherden; prev. Bakherden. Akhalskiy Velayat, C Turkmenistan
152 F12 Bakhardok Turkm. Bokurdak. Akhalskiy Velayat, C Turkmenistan
149 U5 Bākharz, Kuhhā-ye ⛰ NE Iran
158 D13 Bākhāsar Rājasthān, NW India
Bakhchisaray see Bakhchysaray
119 T13 Bakhchysaray Rus. Bakhchisaray. Respublika Krym, S Ukraine
Bakherden see Bakharden
119 R3 Bakhmach Chernihivs'ka Oblast', N Ukraine
126 Hh11 Bakhta Krasnoyarskiy Kray, C Russian Federation
148 K6 Bākhtarān prev. Kermānshāh, Qahremānshahr. Kermānshāhān, W Iran
Bākhtarān see Kermānshāhān
149 Q11 Bakhtegān, Daryācheh-ye ◎ C Iran
151 X12 Bakhty Semipalatinsk, E Kazakhstan
143 Z11 Bakı Eng. Baku. ● (Azerbaijan) E Azerbaijan
143 Z11 Bakı ✈ E Azerbaijan
142 C13 Bakır Çayı ≈ W Turkey
94 L1 Bakkafjördhur Austurland, NE Iceland
94 L1 Bakkaflói sea area W Norwegian Sea
83 I15 Bako SW Ethiopia
78 L15 Bako NW Ivory Coast
Bákó see Bacău
113 H23 Bakony Eng. Bakony Mountains, Ger. Bakonywald. ⛰ W Hungary
Bakony Mountains/Bakonywald see Bakony
83 M16 Bakool off. Gobolka Bakool. ◈ region W Somalia
81 L15 Bakouma Mbomou, SE Central African Republic
131 N15 Baksan Kabardino-Balkarskaya Respublika, SW Russian Federation
121 I16 Bakshty Hrodzyenskaya Voblasts', W Belorussia
Baku see Bakı
204 K12 Bakutis Coast physical region Antarctica
Bakwanga see Mbuji-Mayi
151 O15 Bakyrly Yuzhnyy Kazakhstan, S Kazakhstan
xxxv I6 Bala Gwynedd, NW Wales, UK
12 H13 Bala Ontario, S Canada
142 I13 Balâ Ankara, C Turkey
179 O16 Balabac Island island W Philippines
Balabac, Selat see Balabac Strait
175 O1 Balabac Strait var. Selat Balabac. strait Malaysia/Philippines
Ba'labakk see Baalbek
175 O10 Balabalangan, Kepulauan island group N Indonesia
197 H4 Balabio, Île island Province Nord, W New Caledonia
118 I14 Balaci Teleorman, S Romania
145 S7 Balad N Iraq
145 U7 Balad Rūz E Iraq
126 J15 Balagansk Irkutskaya Oblast', S Russian Federation
160 I11 Bālāghāt Madhya Pradesh, C India
161 F14 Bālāghāt Range ⛰ W India
104 E1 Balagne physical region Corse, France, C Mediterranean Sea
107 U5 Balaguer Cataluña, NE Spain
107 S3 Balaïtous var. Pic de Balaïtous. ▲ France/Spain
Balaïtous, Pic de see Balaïtous
131 O3 Balakhna Nizhegorodskaya Oblast', W Russian Federation
126 I14 Balakhta Krasnoyarskiy Kray, S Russian Federation
190 I9 Balaklava South Australia
Balakleya see Balakliya
119 V6 Balakliya Rus. Balakleya. Kharkivs'ka Oblast', E Ukraine
131 Q7 Balakovo Saratovskaya Oblast', W Russian Federation
xxxv H7 Bala Lake ◎ NW Wales, UK
xlii C9 Balallan Western Isles, NW Scotland, UK
85 P14 Balama Cabo Delgado, N Mozambique
175 Nn1 Balambangan, Pulau island East Malaysia
154 L3 Bālā Morghāb Laghmān, NW Afghanistan
158 E11 Bālān prev. Bāhla. Rājasthān, NW India
118 J10 Bălan Hung. Balánbánya. Harghita, C Romania
Balánbánya see Bălan
179 P10 Balanga Luzon, N Philippines
160 M12 Balāngīr prev. Bolangir. Orissa, E India
131 N8 Balashov Saratovskaya Oblast', W Russian Federation
Balasore see Bāleshwar
113 K21 Balassagyarmat Nógrád, N Hungary
31 S10 Balaton Minnesota, N USA
113 H24 Balaton var. Lake Balaton, Ger. Plattensee. ◎ W Hungary
113 I23 Balatonfüred var. Füred. Veszprém, W Hungary
Balaton, Lake see Balaton
118 I11 Bălăuşeri Ger. Bladenmarkt, Hung. Balavásár. Mureş, C Romania
Balavásár see Bălăuşeri
107 Q11 Balazote Castilla-La Mancha, C Spain
Balázsfalva see Blaj
xliii L17 Balbeggie Perth and Kinross, C Scotland, UK
121 F14 Balbieriškis Prienai, S Lithuania
195 S12 Balbi, Mount ▲ Bougainville Island, NE PNG
60 F11 Balbina, Represa ⊡ NW Brazil
xlii J11 Balblair Highland, NW Scotland, UK
45 T15 Balboa Panamá, C Panama
xliv L8 Balbriggan Ir. Baile Brigín. Dublin, E Ireland
Balbunar see Kubrat
83 N17 Balcad Shabeellaha Dhexe, C Somalia
63 D23 Balcarce Buenos Aires, E Argentina
9 U16 Balcarres Saskatchewan, S Canada
116 O8 Balchik Varnenska Oblast, NE Bulgaria
xlii G8 Balchladich Highland, NW Scotland, UK
193 E24 Balclutha Otago, South Island, NZ
xxxvii U12 Balcombe West Sussex, SE England, UK
27 Q12 Balcones Escarpment escarpment Texas, SW USA
20 F14 Bald Eagle Creek ≈ Pennsylvania, NE USA
Baldenburg see Biały Bór
xxxix P7 Balderton Nottinghamshire, C England, UK
23 V12 Bald Head Island island North Carolina, SE USA
29 W10 Bald Knob Arkansas, C USA
32 K17 Bald Knob hill Illinois, N USA
xxxvii T6 Baldock Hertfordshire, E England, UK
Baldohn see Baldone
120 G9 Baldone Ger. Baldohn. Rīga, W Latvia
24 I9 Baldwin Louisiana, S USA
33 P7 Baldwin Michigan, N USA
29 Q4 Baldwin City Kansas, C USA
41 N8 Baldwin Peninsula headland Alaska, USA
20 H9 Baldwinsville New York, NE USA
25 N2 Baldwyn Mississippi, S USA
9 W15 Baldy Mountain ▲ Manitoba, S Canada
35 T7 Baldy Mountain ▲ Montana, NW USA
39 O13 Baldy Peak ▲ Arizona, SW USA
Bâle see Basel
107 X9 Baleares ◈ autonomous community E Spain
107 X11 Baleares, Islas Eng. Balearic Islands. island group Spain, W Mediterranean Sea
Baleares Major see Mallorca
Balearic Islands see Baleares, Islas
Balearic Plain see Algerian Basin
Balearis Minor see Menorca
174 M6 Baleh, Batang ≈ East Malaysia
10 J8 Baleine, Grande Rivière de la ≈ Québec, E Canada
10 K7 Baleine, Petite Rivière de la ≈ Québec, SE Canada
11 N6 Baleine, Rivière à la ≈ Québec, E Canada
101 I16 Balen Antwerpen, N Belgium
179 P9 Baler Luzon, N Philippines
xliii L20 Balerno City of Edinburgh, SE Scotland, UK
xlii A11 Baleshare island NW Scotland, UK
160 P11 Bāleshwar prev. Balasore. Orissa, E India
xliii B17 Balevullin Argyll and Bute, W Scotland, UK
126 L16 Baley Chitinskaya Oblast', S Russian Federation
79 S12 Baléyara Tillabéri, W Niger
131 T1 Balezino Udmurtskaya Respublika, NW Russian Federation
44 J4 Balfate Colón, N Honduras
xlii M4 Balfour Orkney Islands, N Scotland, UK
9 O17 Balfour British Columbia, SW Canada
31 N3 Balfour North Dakota, N USA
xliii J19 Balfron Stirling, C Scotland, UK
Balfrush see Bābol
151 R9 Balgazyn Respublika Tyva, S Russian Federation
9 U16 Balgonie Saskatchewan, S Canada
Bālgrad see Alba Iulia
83 J19 Balguda spring/well S Kenya
164 K6 Balguntay Xinjiang Uygur Zizhiqu, NW China
147 R16 Balḥāf S Yemen
xxxvi D9 Balham Wandsworth, SE England, UK
158 F13 Bāli Rājasthān, N India
175 N15 Bali ◈ province S Indonesia
175 N16 Bali island C Indonesia
175 K16 Balice ✈ (Kraków) Kraków, S Poland
176 Yy13 Baliem, Sungai ≈ Irian Jaya, E Indonesia
142 C12 Balıkesir Balıkesir, W Turkey
142 C12 Balıkesir ◈ province NW Turkey
144 L3 Balīkh, Nahr ≈ N Syria
175 O9 Balikpapan Borneo, C Indonesia
175 O9 Balikpapan, Teluk bay Borneo, C Indonesia
Bali, Laut see Bali Sea
195 O11 Balima ≈ New Britain, C PNG
179 P17 Balimbing Tawitawi, SW Philippines
194 G14 Balimo Western, SW PNG
Bálinc see Balinţ
175 Qq9 Balingara, Pegunungan ⛰ Sulawesi, N Indonesia
103 H23 Balingen Baden-Württemberg, SW Germany
118 F11 Balinţ Hung. Bálinc. Timiş, W Romania
179 Pp6 Balintang Channel channel N Philippines
xlii K10 Balintore Highland, N Scotland, UK
144 K3 Bālis Ḥalab, N Syria
175 N15 Bali Sea Ind. Laut Bali. sea C Indonesia
175 N16 Bali, Selat strait C Indonesia
xlii A12 Balivanich Western Isles, NW Scotland, UK
100 K7 Balk Friesland, N Netherlands
124 O7 Balkan Mountains Bul./SCr. Stara Planina. ⛰ Bulgaria/Yugoslavia
152 B9 Balkanskiy Velayat Turkm. Balkan Welayaty. ◈ province W Turkmenistan

◆ Country ● Country Capital ◇ Dependent Territory ○ Dependent Territory Capital ◈ Administrative Region ✈ International Airport ▲ Mountain ⛰ Mountain Range ▴ Volcano ≈ River ◎ Lake ⊡ Reservoir
227

BALKAN WELAYATY – BARÍKOWŢ

Balkan Welayaty *see* Balkanskiy Velayat
151 P8 **Balkashino** Akmola, N Kazakhstan
155 O2 **Balkh** *anc.* Bactra. Balkh, N Afghanistan
155 P2 **Balkh** ◆ *province* N Afghanistan
151 T13 **Balkhash** *Kaz.* Balqash. Zhezkazgan, SE Kazakhstan
Balkhash, Lake *see* Balkhash, Ozero
151 T13 **Balkhash, Ozero** *Eng.* Lake Balkhash, *Kaz.* Balqash. ◎ SE Kazakhstan
Balla Balla *see* Mbalabala
xliii G16 **Ballachulish** Highland, NW Scotland, UK
188 M12 **Balladonia** Western Australia
xliv L7 **Ballagan Point** *headland* NE Ireland
xliv F7 **Ballaghaderreen** *Ir.* Bealach an Doirín. Roscommon, C Ireland
xliv H10 **Ballaghmore** Laois, C Ireland
94 H10 **Ballangen** Nordland, NW Norway
xliii H24 **Ballantrae** South Ayrshire, W Scotland, UK
191 N12 **Ballarat** Victoria, SE Australia
188 K11 **Ballard, Lake** *salt lake* Western Australia
Ballari *see* Bellary
xl F12 **Ballasalla** S Isle of Man
xliii M14 **Ballater** Aberdeenshire, NE Scotland, UK
xl G11 **Ballaugh** NE Isle of Man
78 L11 **Ballé** Koulikoro, W Mali
42 D7 **Ballenas, Bahía de** *bay* W Mexico
42 D5 **Ballenas, Canal de** *channel* NW Mexico
205 R17 **Balleny Islands** *island group* Antarctica
42 J7 **Balleza** *var.* San Pablo Balleza. Chihuahua, N Mexico
116 M13 **Ballı** Tekirdağ, NW Turkey
159 O13 **Ballia** Uttar Pradesh, N India
xliv E6 **Ballina** *Ir.* Béal an Átha. Mayo, W Ireland
191 V4 **Ballina** New South Wales, SE Australia
xliv G6 **Ballinafad** Sligo, N Ireland
Ballinagh *see* Bellananagh
xliv H6 **Ballinamore** *Ir.* Béal an Átha Móir. Leitrim, NW Ireland
xliv G9 **Ballinasloe** *Ir.* Béal Átha na Sluaighe. Galway, W Ireland
xliv E7 **Ballindine** Mayo, NW Ireland
xliv E12 **Ballingarry** Limerick, SW Ireland
xliv D14 **Ballingeary** Cork, S Ireland
27 P8 **Ballinger** Texas, SW USA
xliii L18 **Ballingry** Fife, E Scotland, UK
xliv F14 **Ballinhassig** Cork, S Ireland
xliii L16 **Ballinluig** Perth and Kinross, C Scotland, UK
xliv E8 **Ballinrobe** *Ir.* Baile an Róba. Mayo, W Ireland
xliv B14 **Ballinskelligs** Kerry, SW Ireland
xliv B14 **Ballinskelligs Bay** *Ir.* Bá na Scealg. *inlet* SW Ireland
xliv F15 **Ballinspittle** Cork, S Ireland
xliv E7 **Ballintober** Mayo, NW Ireland
xliv G7 **Ballintober** Roscommon, C Ireland
xliv G4 **Ballintra** *Ir.* Baile an tSratha. Donegal, NW Ireland
xliii L16 **Ballintuim** Perth and Kinross, C Scotland, UK
xliv J10 **Ballitore** Kildare, E Ireland
xliv J8 **Ballivor** Meath, E Ireland
xliii I19 **Balloch** West Dunbartonshire, W Scotland, UK
xliv J11 **Ballon** Carlow, SE Ireland
105 T7 **Ballon d'Alsace** ▲ NE France
Ballon de Guebwiller *see* Grand Ballon
115 K21 **Ballsh** *var.* Ballshi. Fier, SW Albania
Ballshi *see* Ballsh
100 K4 **Ballum** Friesland, N Netherlands
xliv J6 **Ballybay** *Ir.* Béal Átha Beithe. Monaghan, N Ireland
xliv H4 **Ballybofey** *Ir.* Bealach Féich. Donegal, NW Ireland
xliv D11 **Ballybunnion** Kerry, SW Ireland
xliv L11 **Ballycanew** Wexford, SE Ireland
xliv M4 **Ballycarry** Carrickfergus, E Northern Ireland, UK
xliv E5 **Ballycastle** Mayo, NW Ireland
xliv L2 **Ballycastle** *Ir.* Baile an Chaistil. Moyle, N Northern Ireland, UK
xliv L4 **Ballyclare** *Ir.* Bealach Cláir. Newtownabbey, E Northern Ireland, UK
xliv C8 **Ballyconneely** Galway, W Ireland
99 E16 **Ballyconnell** *Ir.* Béal Átha Conaill. N Ireland
xliv G14 **Ballycotton** Cork, S Ireland
xliv C6 **Ballycroy** Mayo, NW Ireland
xliv D15 **Ballydehob** Cork, S Ireland
xliv D13 **Ballydesmond** Cork, S Ireland
xliv B15 **Ballydonegan** Cork, S Ireland
xliv D12 **Ballyduff** Kerry, SW Ireland
xliv B13 **Ballyferriter** Kerry, SW Ireland
xliv M3 **Ballygalley** Larne, E Northern Ireland, UK
xliv J5 **Ballygawley** Dungannon, C Northern Ireland, UK
xliv M5 **Ballygowan** Ards, E Northern Ireland, UK
xliii D20 **Ballygrant** Argyll and Bute, W Scotland, UK
xliv M5 **Ballyhalbert** Ards, E Northern Ireland, UK
xliii C16 **Ballyhaugh** Argyll and Bute, W Scotland, UK
xliv F7 **Ballyhaunis** *Ir.* Beál Átha hAmhnais. Mayo, W Ireland
xliv C12 **Ballyheige** Kerry, SW Ireland
xliv I1 **Ballyhillin** Donegal, N Ireland
xliv F12 **Ballyhoura Mountains** ▲ S Ireland
xliv I7 **Ballyjamesduff** Cavan, N Ireland
xliv J3 **Ballykelly** Limavady, N Northern Ireland, UK
xliv D14 **Ballylickey** Cork, S Ireland
xliv I2 **Ballyliffin** Donegal, N Ireland
xliv D11 **Ballylongford** Kerry, SW Ireland
xliv J10 **Ballylynan** Laois, C Ireland
xliv H13 **Ballymacarbry** Waterford, S Ireland
xliv H8 **Ballymahon** Longford, C Ireland
xliv L3 **Ballymena** *Ir.* An Baile Meánach. Ballymena, NE Northern Ireland, UK
xliv K3 **Ballymena** ◆ *district* NE Northern Ireland, UK
xliv G7 **Ballymoe** Galway, W Ireland
xliv K2 **Ballymoney** *Ir.* Baile Monaidh. Ballymoney, NE Northern Ireland, UK
xliv K3 **Ballymoney** ◆ *district* N Northern Ireland, UK
xliv H8 **Ballymore** Westmeath, C Ireland
xliv F6 **Ballymote** Sligo, N Ireland
xliv J12 **Ballynabola** Wexford, SE Ireland
xliv I8 **Ballynafid** Westmeath, C Ireland
xliv H13 **Ballynagaul** Waterford, S Ireland
xliv L5 **Ballynahinch** *Ir.* Baile na hInse. Down, SE Northern Ireland, UK
xliv B13 **Ballynana** Kerry, SW Ireland
xliv F11 **Ballyneety** Limerick, SW Ireland
xliv L4 **Ballynure** Newtownabbey, E Northern Ireland, UK
xliv M6 **Ballyquintin Point** *headland* E Northern Ireland, UK
xliv I11 **Ballyragget** Kilkenny, SE Ireland
xliv K4 **Ballyronan** Cookstown, C Northern Ireland, UK
xliv F6 **Ballysadare** *Ir.* Baile Easa Dara. Sligo, NW Ireland
xliv G4 **Ballyshannon** *Ir.* Béal Átha Seanaidh. Donegal, NW Ireland
xliv J13 **Ballyteige Bay** *bay* SE Ireland
xliv F9 **Ballyvaughan** Clare, W Ireland
xliv M5 **Ballywalter** Ards, E Northern Ireland, UK
xliii F13 **Balmacara** Highland, NW Scotland, UK
65 H19 **Balmaceda** Aisén, S Chile
65 G23 **Balmaceda, Cerro** ▲ S Chile
xliii J24 **Balmaclellan** Dumfries and Galloway, SW Scotland, UK
xliii I19 **Balmaha** Stirling, C Scotland, UK
113 N22 **Balmazújváros** Hajdú-Bihar, E Hungary
xliii P13 **Balmedie** Aberdeenshire, NE Scotland, UK
110 E10 **Balmhorn** ▲ SW Switzerland
190 L12 **Balmoral** Victoria, SE Australia
26 K9 **Balmorhea** Texas, SW USA
xli G12 **Balnacra** Highland, NW Scotland, UK
xliii E17 **Balnahard** Argyll and Bute, W Scotland, UK
Balneario Claromecó *see* Claromecó
175 R9 **Balo** Sulawesi, N Indonesia
xliii E17 **Ba, Loch** ◎ W Scotland, UK
xliii H16 **Ba, Loch** ◎ NW Scotland, UK
Balochistān *see* Baluchistān
84 B13 **Balombo** *Port.* Norton de Matos, Vila Norton de Matos. Benguela, W Angola
84 B13 **Balombo** ⁓ W Angola
189 X10 **Balonne River** ⁓ Queensland, E Australia
158 E13 **Bālotra** Rājasthān, N India
Balqā'/Balqā', Muḩāfaẓat al *see* Al Balqā'
Balqash *see* Balkhash/Balkhash, Ozero
xliii J17 **Balquhidder** Stirling, C Scotland, UK
158 M12 **Balrāmpur** Uttar Pradesh, N India
190 M9 **Balranald** New South Wales, SE Australia
xliv K8 **Balrath** Meath, E Ireland
118 H14 **Balş** Olt, S Romania
xxxviii E16 **Balsall** Solihull, C England, UK
12 H11 **Balsam Creek** Ontario, S Canada
32 J5 **Balsam Lake** Wisconsin, N USA
12 I14 **Balsam Lake** ◎ Ontario, SE Canada
61 M14 **Balsas** Maranhão, E Brazil
42 M15 **Balsas, Río** *var.* Río Mexcala. ⁓ S Mexico
45 W16 **Balsas, Río** ⁓ SE Panama
xxxix T3 **Balsham** Cambridgeshire, E England, UK
121 O18 **Bal'shavik** *Rus.* Bol'shevik. Homyel'skaya Voblasts', SE Belorussia
97 O15 **Bålsta** Uppsala, C Sweden
110 E7 **Balsthal** Solothurn, NW Switzerland
119 O8 **Balta** Odes'ka Oblast', SW Ukraine
121 H14 **Baltaji Voke** Vilnius, SE Lithuania
107 N5 **Baltanás** Castilla-León, N Spain
63 E16 **Baltasar Brum** Artigas, N Uruguay
xli J1 **Baltasound** Shetland Islands, NE Scotland, UK
118 M9 **Bălţi** *Rus.* Bel'tsy. N Moldavia
Baltic Port *see* Paldiski
120 B10 **Baltic Sea** *Ger.* Ostee, *Rus.* Baltiskoye More. *sea* N Europe
xliv D15 **Baltimore** Cork, S Ireland
23 X3 **Baltimore** Maryland, NE USA
33 T13 **Baltimore** Ohio, N USA
xliv K10 **Baltinglass** Wicklow, E Ireland
Baltischport/Baltiski *see* Paldiski
Baltiskoye More *see* Baltic Sea
121 A14 **Baltiysk** *Ger.* Pillau. Kaliningradskaya Oblast', W Russian Federation
Baltkrievija *see* Belorussia
xxxvi K11 **Baltonsborough** Somerset, SW England, UK
194 K9 **Baluan Island** *island* N PNG
Balūchestān va Sīstān *see* Sīstān va Balūchestān
154 M12 **Baluchistān** *var.* Balochistān, Beluchistan. ◆ *province* SW Pakistan
179 Q12 **Balud** Masbate, N Philippines
174 Mm6 **Balui, Batang** ⁓ East Malaysia
159 S13 **Bālurghat** West Bengal, NE India
120 J8 **Balvi** Balvi, NE Latvia
194 H12 **Balyer River** Western Highlands, C PNG
153 W7 **Balykchy** *Kir.* Ysyk-Köl; *prev.* Issyk-Kul', Rybach'ye. Issyk-Kul'skaya Oblast', NE Kyrgyzstan
58 B7 **Balzar** Guayas, W Ecuador
110 I8 **Balzers** S Liechtenstein
149 T12 **Bam** Kermān, SE Iran
79 Y13 **Bama** Borno, NE Nigeria
78 L12 **Bamako** ● (Mali) Capital District, SW Mali
79 P10 **Bamba** Gao, C Mali
44 M8 **Bambana, Río** ⁓ NE Nicaragua
81 J15 **Bambari** Ouaka, C Central African Republic
189 W5 **Bambaroo** Queensland, NE Australia
103 K19 **Bamberg** Bayern, SE Germany
23 R14 **Bamberg** South Carolina, SE USA
81 M16 **Bambesa** Haut-Zaïre, N Zaire
78 G11 **Bambey** W Senegal
81 H16 **Bambio** Sangha-Mbaéré, SW Central African Republic
85 I24 **Bamboesberge** ▲ S South Africa
xli R2 **Bamburgh** Northumberland, N England, UK
81 D14 **Bamenda** Nord-Ouest, W Cameroon
8 K17 **Bamfield** Vancouver Island, British Columbia, SW Canada
xxxviii L5 **Bamford** Derbyshire, C England, UK
152 E12 **Bami** *Turkm.* Bamy. Akhalskiy Velayat, C Turkmenistan
155 P4 **Bāmīān** *var.* Bāmiān. Bāmīān, NE Afghanistan
155 O4 **Bāmīān** ◆ *province* C Afghanistan
81 J14 **Bamingui** Bamingui-Bangoran, C Central African Republic
80 J13 **Bamingui** ⁓ N Central African Republic
80 J13 **Bamingui-Bangoran** ◆ *prefecture* N Central African Republic
xli N9 **Bampton** Cumbria, NW England, UK
xxxvi H12 **Bampton** Devon, SW England, UK
xxxvii O8 **Bampton** Oxfordshire, C England, UK
149 V13 **Bampūr** Sīstān va Balūchestān, SE Iran
194 G14 **Bamu** ⁓ SW PNG
Bamy *see* Bami
Bán *see* Bánovce nad Bebravou
83 N17 **Banaadir** *off.* Gobolka Banaadir. ◆ *region* S Somalia
203 N3 **Banaba** *var.* Ocean Island. *island* Tungaru, W Kiribati
61 O14 **Banabuiú, Açude** ◎ NE Brazil
59 O19 **Bañados del Izozog** *salt lake* SE Bolivia
xliv H9 **Banagher** *Ir.* Beannchar. Offaly, C Ireland
81 M17 **Banalia** Haut-Zaïre, N Zaire
78 L12 **Banamba** Koulikoro, W Mali
42 G4 **Banámichi** Sonora, NW Mexico
189 Y9 **Banana** Queensland, E Australia
203 Z2 **Banana** *prev.* Main Camp. Kiritimati, E Kiribati
61 K16 **Bananal, Ilha do** *island* C Brazil
25 Y12 **Banana River** *lagoon* Florida, SE USA
157 Q22 **Bananga** Andaman and Nicobar Islands, India, NE Indian Ocean
Banaras *see* Vārānasi
116 N13 **Banarlı** Tekirdağ, NW Turkey
158 H12 **Banās** ⁓ N India
77 Z11 **Banâs, Râs** *headland* E Egypt
114 N10 **Banatski Karlovac** Serbia, NE Yugoslavia
xliii H15 **Banavie** Highland, NW Scotland, UK
147 P16 **Banā, Wādī** *dry watercourse* SW Yemen
142 E14 **Banaz** Uşak, W Turkey
142 E14 **Banaz Çayı** ⁓ W Turkey
165 P14 **Banbar** Xizang Zizhiqu, W China
xliv L5 **Banbridge** *Ir.* Droichead na Banna. Banbridge, SE Northern Ireland, UK
xliv L5 **Banbridge** ◆ *district* SE Northern Ireland, UK
Ban Bua Yai *see* Bua Yai
xxxvii P6 **Banbury** Oxfordshire, S England, UK
178 H7 **Ban Chiang Dao** Chiang Mai, NW Thailand
xliii O14 **Banchory** Aberdeenshire, NE Scotland, UK
12 J13 **Bancroft** Ontario, SE Canada
35 R15 **Bancroft** Idaho, NW USA
31 U11 **Bancroft** Iowa, C USA
160 I9 **Bānda** Madhya Pradesh, C India
158 L13 **Bānda** Uttar Pradesh, N India
173 E3 **Bandaaceh** *var.* Banda Atjeh; *prev.* Koetaradja, Kutaradja, Kutaraja. Sumatera, W Indonesia
Banda Atjeh *see* Bandaaceh
176 U12 **Banda, Kepulauan** *island group* E Indonesia
Banda, Laut *see* Banda Sea
79 N17 **Bandama** *var.* Bandama Fleuve. ⁓ S Ivory Coast
79 N15 **Bandama Blanc** ⁓ C Ivory Coast
Bandama Fleuve *see* Bandama
Bandar 'Abbās *see* Bandar-e 'Abbās
159 W16 **Bandarban** Chittagong, SE Bangladesh
82 Q13 **Bandarbeyla** *var.* Bender Beila, Bender Beyla. Bari, NE Somalia
149 R14 **Bandar-e 'Abbās** *var.* Bandar 'Abbās; *prev.* Gombroon. Hormozgān, S Iran
148 M3 **Bandar-e Anzalī** Gīlān, NW Iran
149 N12 **Bandar-e Būshehr** *var.* Būshehr, *Eng.* Bushire. Būshehr, S Iran
148 M11 **Bandar-e Gonāveh** *var.* Ganāveh; *prev.* Gonāveh. Būshehr, SW Iran
149 R14 **Bandar-e Khamīr** Hormozgān, S Iran
149 Q14 **Bandar-e Langeh** *var.* Bandar-e Lengeh, Lingeh. Hormozgān, S Iran
Bandar-e Lengeh *see* Bandar-e Langeh
148 L10 **Bandar-e Māhshahr** *var.* Māh-Shahr; *prev.* Bandar-e Ma'shūr. Khūzestān, SW Iran
Bandar-e Ma'shūr *see* Bandar-e Māhshahr
149 O14 **Bandar-e Nakhīlū** Hormozgān, S Iran
Bandar-e Shāh *see* Bandar-e Torkaman
149 P4 **Bandar-e Torkaman** *var.* Bandar-e Torkeman, Bandar-e Torkman; *prev.* Bandar-e Shāh. Māzandarān, N Iran
Bandar-e Torkeman/Bandar-e Torkman *see* Bandar-e Torkaman
Bandar Kassim *see* Boosaaso
174 Ii13 **Bandarlampung** *prev.* Tanjungkarang, Teloekbetoeng, Telukbetung. Sumatera, W Indonesia
Bandar Maharani *see* Muar
Bandar Masulipatnam *see* Machilipatnam
Bandar Penggaram *see* Batu Pahat
175 N3 **Bandar Seri Begawan** *prev.* Brunei Town. ● (Brunei) N Brunei
174 Mm3 **Bandar Seri Begawan** ✈ N Brunei
175 Ss13 **Banda Sea** *var.* Laut Banda. *sea* E Indonesia
106 H5 **Bande** Galicia, NW Spain
61 G15 **Bandeirantes** Mato Grosso, W Brazil
61 N20 **Bandeira, Pico da** ▲ SE Brazil
85 K19 **Bandelierkop** Northern, NE South Africa
64 L8 **Bandera** Santiago del Estero, N Argentina
27 Q11 **Bandera** Texas, SW USA
42 J13 **Banderas, Bahía de** *bay* W Mexico
79 O11 **Bandiagara** Mopti, C Mali
158 I12 **Bāndīkūi** Rājasthān, N India
142 C11 **Bandırma** *var.* Penderma. Balıkesir, NW Turkey
Bandjarmasin *see* Banjarmasin
Bandoeng *see* Bandung
xliv F14 **Bandon** *Ir.* Droicheadna Bandan. Cork, SW Ireland
xliv E14 **Bandon** ⁓ S Ireland
34 E14 **Bandon** Oregon, NW USA
178 J8 **Ban Dong Bang** Nong Khai, E Thailand
178 I6 **Ban Donkon** Oudômxai, N Laos
180 J14 **Bandrélé** SE Mayotte
81 H20 **Bandundu** *prev.* Banningville. Bandundu, W Zaire
81 I21 **Bandundu** *off.* Région de Bandundu. ◆ *region* W Zaire
174 Jj14 **Bandung** *prev.* Bandoeng. Jawa, C Indonesia
118 L15 **Băneasa** Constanţa, SW Romania
148 J4 **Bāneh** Kordestān, N Iran
46 I7 **Banes** Holguín, E Cuba
98 K8 **Banff** *cultural region* NE Scotland, UK
xlii O11 **Banff** Aberdeenshire, NE Scotland, UK
9 P16 **Banff** Alberta, SW Canada
Bánffyhunyad *see* Huedin
79 N14 **Banfora** SW Burkina
161 H19 **Bangalore** Karnātaka, S India
159 S16 **Bangaon** West Bengal, NE India
179 P9 **Bangar** Luzon, N Philippines
81 L15 **Bangassou** Mbomou, SE Central African Republic
194 K12 **Bangeta, Mount** ▲ C PNG
175 Qq10 **Banggai, Kepulauan** *island group* C Indonesia
175 R9 **Banggai, Pulau** *island* Kepulauan Banggai, N Indonesia
176 X11 **Banggelapa** Irian Jaya, E Indonesia
Banggi *see* Banggi, Pulau
175 O1 **Banggi, Pulau** *var.* Banggi. *island* East Malaysia
124 N15 **Banghāzī** *Eng.* Bengazi, Benghazi, *It.* Bengasi. NE Libya
Bang Hieng *see* Xé Banghiang
174 K8 **Bangkai, Tanjung** *var.* Bankai. *headland* Borneo, N Indonesia
174 M14 **Bangkalan** Pulau Madura, C Indonesia
175 S6 **Bangka, Pulau** *island* N Indonesia
174 J10 **Bangka, Pulau** *island* W Indonesia
174 Ii10 **Bangka, Selat** *strait* Sumatera, W Indonesia
175 Rr6 **Bangka, Selat** *var.* Selat Likupang. *strait* Sulawesi, N Indonesia
174 Gg8 **Bangkinang** Sumatera, W Indonesia
174 H10 **Bangko** Sumatera, W Indonesia
Bangkok *see* Krung Thep
Bangkok, Bight of *see* Krung Thep, Ao
159 T14 **Bangladesh** *off.* People's Republic of Bangladesh; *prev.* East Pakistan. ◆ *republic* S Asia
178 Kk13 **Ba Ngoi** Khanh Hoa, S Vietnam
158 K5 **Bangong Co** *var.* Pangong Tso. ◎ China/India *see also* Pangong Tso
xliv M4 **Bangor** *Ir.* Beannchar. North Down, E Northern Ireland, UK
xxxv G5 **Bangor** Gwynedd, NW Wales, UK
21 R6 **Bangor** Maine, NE USA
20 I14 **Bangor** Pennsylvania, NE USA
69 R8 **Bangoran** ⁓ S Central African Republic
xliv D6 **Bangor Erris** Mayo, NW Ireland
xxxv K6 **Bangor-is-y-coed** Wrexham, NE Wales, UK
Bang Phra *see* Trat
Bang Pla Soi *see* Chon Buri
27 Q8 **Bangs** Texas, SW USA
178 H13 **Bang Saphan** *var.* Bang Saphan Yai. Prachuap Khiri Khan, SW Thailand
Bang Saphan Yai *see* Bang Saphan
38 I8 **Bangs, Mount** ▲ Arizona, SW USA
95 E15 **Bangsund** Nord-Trøndelag, C Norway
179 P8 **Bangued** Luzon, N Philippines
81 I15 **Bangui** ● (Central African Republic) Ombella-Mpoko, SW Central African Republic
81 I15 **Bangui** ✈ Ombella-Mpoko, SW Central African Republic
85 N16 **Bangula** Southern, S Malawi
Bangwaketse *see* Southern
84 K12 **Bangweulu, Lake** *var.* Lake Bengweulu. ◎ N Zambia
Banhā *see* Benha
Ban Hat Yai *see* Hat Yai
178 I8 **Ban Hin Heup** Viangchan, C Laos
Ban Houayxay/Ban Houei Sai *see* Houayxay
178 H12 **Ban Hua Hin** *var.* Hua Hin. Prachuap Khiri Khan, SW Thailand
81 L14 **Bani** Haute-Kotto, E Central African Republic
79 N12 **Bani** ⁓ S Mali
47 O9 **Baní** S Dominican Republic
Banias *see* Bāniyās
79 S11 **Bani Bangou** Tillabéri, SW Niger
78 M12 **Banifing** *var.* Ngorolaka. ⁓ Burkina/Mali
79 R13 **Banikoara** N Benin
Banī Mazār *see* Beni Mazâr
116 K8 **Baniski Lom** ⁓ N Bulgaria
23 U7 **Banister River** ⁓ Virginia, NE USA
Banī Suwayf *see* Beni Suef
77 O8 **Banī Walīd** NW Libya
144 H5 **Bāniyās** *var.* Banias, Baniyas, Paneas. Tarţūs, W Syria
115 K14 **Banja** Serbia, W Yugoslavia
Banjak, Kepulauan *see* Banyak, Kepulauan
114 J12 **Banja Koviljača** Serbia, W Yugoslavia
114 G11 **Banja Luka** NW Bosnia and Herzegovina
175 N11 **Banjarmasin** *prev.* Bandjarmasin. Borneo, C Indonesia
Banjoewangi *see* Banyuwangi
78 F11 **Banjul** *prev.* Bathurst. ● (Gambia) W Gambia
78 F11 **Banjul** ✈ W Gambia
Banjuwangi *see* Banyuwangi
Bank *see* Bankä
143 Y13 **Bankä** *Rus.* Bank. SE Azerbaijan
178 Jj11 **Ban Kadian** *var.* Ban Kadiene. Champasak, S Laos
Ban Kadiene *see* Ban Kadian
Bankai *see* Bangkai, Tanjung
178 Gg15 **Ban Kam Phuam** Phangnga, SW Thailand
Ban Kantang *see* Kantang
79 O11 **Bankass** Mopti, S Mali
xliii L24 **Bankend** Dumfries and Galloway, SW Scotland, UK
97 L19 **Bankeryd** Jönköping, S Sweden
85 K16 **Banket** Mashonaland West, N Zimbabwe
xliii L17 **Bankfoot** Perth and Kinross, C Scotland, UK
178 Jj11 **Ban Khamphô** Attapu, S Laos
25 O4 **Bankhead Lake** ⊡ Alabama, S USA
79 Q11 **Bankilaré** Tillabéri, SW Niger
xl M15 **Banks** Lancashire, NW England, UK
xliii M24 **Bankshill** Dumfries and Galloway, SW Scotland, UK
Banks, Îles *see* Banks Islands
8 I14 **Banks Island** *island* British Columbia, SW Canada
15 Hh1 **Banks Island** *island* Banks Island, Northwest Territories, NW Canada
197 C10 **Banks Islands** *Fr.* Îles Banks. *island group* N Vanuatu
25 U8 **Banks Lake** ◎ Georgia, SE USA
34 K8 **Banks Lake** ⊡ Washington, NW USA
193 I19 **Banks Peninsula** *peninsula* South Island, NZ
191 Q15 **Banks Strait** *strait* SW Tasman Sea
Ban Kui Nua *see* Kui Buri
159 R16 **Bānkura** West Bengal, NE India
178 J8 **Ban Lakxao** *var.* Lak Sao. Bolikhamxai, C Laos
178 H17 **Ban Lam Phai** Songkhla, SW Thailand
Ban Mae Sot *see* Mae Sot
Ban Mae Suai *see* Mae Suai
Ban Mak Khaeng *see* Udon Thani
177 G3 **Banmauk** Sagaing, N Burma
Banmo *see* Bhamo
178 Jj10 **Ban Mun-Houamuang** S Laos
xliv K5 **Bann** *var.* Lower Bann, Upper Bann. ⁓ N Northern Ireland, UK
178 Jj10 **Ban Nadou** Salavan, S Laos
178 J10 **Ban Nakala** Savannakhét, S Laos
178 I8 **Ban Nakha** Viangchan, C Laos
178 Jj9 **Ban Nakham** Khammouan, S Laos
178 I8 **Ban Namoun** Xaignabouli, N Laos
178 Hh17 **Ban Nang Sata** Yala, SW Thailand
178 Gg15 **Ban Na San** Surat Thani, SW Thailand
178 Ii7 **Ban Nasi** Xiangkhoang, N Laos
46 I3 **Bannerman Town** Eleuthera Island, C Bahamas
37 V15 **Banning** California, W USA
Banningville *see* Bandundu
xliii K19 **Bannockburn** Stirling, C Scotland, UK
178 Jj11 **Ban Nongsim** Champasak, S Laos
155 S7 **Bannu** *prev.* Edwardesabad. North-West Frontier Province, NW Pakistan
Bañolas *see* Banyoles
58 C7 **Baños** Tungurahua, C Ecuador
Bánovce *see* Bánovce nad Bebravou
113 I19 **Bánovce nad Bebravou** *var.* Bánovce, *Hung.* Bán. Západné Slovensko, W Slovakia
114 I12 **Banovići** E Bosnia and Herzegovina
Banow *see* Andarāb
Ban Pak Phanang *see* Pak Phanang
178 Hh7 **Ban Pan Nua** Lampang, NW Thailand
178 I10 **Ban Phai** Khon Kaen, E Thailand
178 Jj9 **Ban Phou A Douk** Khammouan, C Laos
178 I8 **Ban Phu** Uthai Thani, W Thailand
178 H11 **Ban Pong** Ratchaburi, W Thailand
202 I3 **Banraeaba** Tarawa, W Kiribati
178 Gg11 **Ban Sai Yok** Kanchanaburi, W Thailand
Ban Sattahip/Ban Sattahipp *see* Sattahip
Ban Sichon *see* Sichon
xliv G12 **Bansha** Tipperary, S Ireland
Ban Si Racha *see* Siracha
113 J19 **Banská Bystrica** *Ger.* Neusohl, *Hung.* Besztercebánya. Stredné Slovensko, C Slovakia
178 J8 **Ban Sôppheung** Bolikhamxai, C Laos
Ban Sop Prap *see* Sop Prap
xxxvii T10 **Banstead** Surrey, SE England, UK
158 G15 **Bānswāra** Rājasthān, N India
178 Gg15 **Ban Ta Khun** Surat Thani, SW Thailand
Ban Takua Pa *see* Takua Pa
178 Jj9 **Ban Talak** Khammouan, C Laos
79 R15 **Bantè** W Benin
xliv E13 **Banteer** Cork, S Ireland
178 Ii8 **Ban Thabôk** Bolikhamxai, C Laos
178 Jj10 **Ban Tôp** Savannakhét, S Laos
xliv D14 **Bantry** *Ir.* Beanntraí. Cork, SW Ireland
xliv C15 **Bantry Bay** *Ir.* Bá Bheanntraí. *bay* SW Ireland
174 L15 **Bantul** *prev.* Bantoel. Jawa, C Indonesia
161 F19 **Bantvāl** *var.* Bantwāl. Karnātaka, E India
Bantwāl *see* Bantvāl
116 N9 **Banya** Burgaska Oblast, E Bulgaria
173 Ee6 **Banyak, Kepulauan** *prev.* Kepulauan Banjak. *island group* NW Indonesia
107 U8 **Banya, La** *headland* E Spain
81 E14 **Banyo** Adamaoua, NW Cameroon
107 X4 **Banyoles** *var.* Bañolas. Cataluña, NE Spain
178 H16 **Ban Yong Sata** Trang, SW Thailand
174 Mm16 **Banyuwangi** *var.* Banjuwangi; *prev.* Banjoewangi. Jawa, S Indonesia
205 X14 **Banzare Coast** *physical region* Antarctica
181 Q14 **Banzare Seamounts** *undersea feature* S Indian Ocean
Banzart *see* Bizerte
Baochang *see* Taibus Qi
167 O3 **Baoding** *var.* Pao-ting; *prev.* Tsingyuan. Hebei, E China
Baoebaoe *see* Baubau
Baoi, Ceann *see* Dursey Head
Baoi, Oileán *see* Dursey Island
166 J6 **Baoji** *var.* Pao-chi, Paoki. Shaanxi, C China
195 V14 **Baolo** Santa Isabel, N Solomon Islands
178 K13 **Bao Lôc** Lâm Đông, S Vietnam
169 Z7 **Baoqing** Heilongjiang, NE China
Baoqing *see* Shaoyang
81 H15 **Baoro** Nana-Mambéré, W Central African Republic
166 E12 **Baoshan** *var.* Pao-shan. Yunnan, SW China
169 N13 **Baotou** *var.* Pao-t'ou, Paotow. Nei Mongol Zizhiqu, N China
78 L14 **Baoulé** ⁓ S Mali
78 K12 **Baoulé** ⁓ W Mali
105 O2 **Bapaume** Pas-de-Calais, N France
12 J13 **Baptiste Lake** ◎ Ontario, SE Canada
Baqanas *see* Bakanas
Baqbaqty *see* Bakbakty
165 P14 **Baqên** *var.* Dartang. Xizang Zizhiqu, W China
144 F14 **Bāqir, Jabal** ▲ S Jordan
145 T7 **Ba'qūbah** *var.* Qubba. C Iraq
64 H5 **Baquedano** Antofagasta, N Chile
118 M6 **Bar** Vinnyts'ka Oblast', C Ukraine
115 J18 **Bar** *It.* Antivari. Montenegro, SW Yugoslavia
82 E10 **Bara** Northern Kordofan, C Sudan
83 M18 **Baraawe** *It.* Brava. Shabeellaha Hoose, S Somalia
158 M12 **Bāra Banki** Uttar Pradesh, N India
125 G13 **Barabinsk** Novosibirskaya Oblast', C Russian Federation
32 L8 **Baraboo** Wisconsin, N USA
32 K8 **Baraboo Range** *hill range* Wisconsin, N USA
Baracaldo *see* San Vicente de Barakaldo
13 Y6 **Barachois** Québec, SE Canada
46 J7 **Baracoa** Guantánamo, E Cuba
63 C19 **Baradero** Buenos Aires, E Argentina
191 R6 **Baradine** New South Wales, SE Australia
Baraf Daja Islands *see* Damar, Kepulauan
160 M12 **Baragarh** Orissa, E India
83 I17 **Baragoi** Rift Valley, W Kenya
47 N9 **Barahona** SW Dominican Republic
159 W13 **Barail Range** ▲ NE India
82 I9 **Baraka** *var.* Barka, *Ar.* Khawr Barakah. *seasonal river* Eritrea/Sudan
82 G10 **Barakat** Gezira, C Sudan
Barakī *see* Barakī Barak
Barakī Rajan *see* Barakī Barak
160 N11 **Bārākot** Orissa, E India
Baram *see* Baram, Batang
57 S7 **Barama River** ⁓ N Guyana
161 E14 **Bārāmati** Mahārāshtra, W India
174 Mm4 **Baram, Batang** *var.* Baram, Barram. ⁓ East Malaysia
158 H5 **Bārāmūla** Jammu and Kashmir, NW India
121 N14 **Baran'** Vitsyebskaya Voblasts', NE Belorussia
158 I14 **Bārān** Rājasthān, N India
145 U4 **Barānān, Shākh-i** ▲ E Iraq
121 I17 **Baranavichy** *Pol.* Baranowicze, *Rus.* Baranovichi. Brestskaya Voblasts', SW Belorussia
127 Oo5 **Baranikha** Chukotskiy Avtonomnyy Okrug, NE Russian Federation
118 M4 **Baranivka** Zhytomyrs'ka Oblast', N Ukraine
41 W14 **Baranof Island** *island* Alexander Archipelago, Alaska, USA
Baranovichi/Baranowicze *see* Baranavichy
113 N15 **Baranów Sandomierski** Tarnobrzeg, SE Poland
113 I26 **Baranya** *off.* Baranya Megye. ◆ *county* S Hungary
159 R13 **Barāri** Bihār, NE India
24 L10 **Barataria Bay** *bay* Louisiana, S USA
Barat Daya, Kepulauan *see* Damar, Kepulauan
120 L12 **Baravukha** *Rus.* Borovukha. Vitsyebskaya Voblasts', N Belorussia
56 E11 **Baraya** Huila, C Colombia
61 M21 **Barbacena** Minas Gerais, SE Brazil
56 B13 **Barbacoas** Nariño, SW Colombia
56 L6 **Barbacoas** Aragua, N Venezuela
47 Z13 **Barbados** ◆ *commonwealth republic* SE West Indies
49 S3 **Barbados** *island* Barbados
107 U11 **Barbaria, Cap de** *var.* Cabo de Berberia. *headland* Formentera, E Spain
116 N13 **Barbaros** Tekirdağ, NW Turkey
76 A11 **Barbas, Cap** *headland* S Western Sahara
107 T5 **Barbastro** Aragón, NE Spain
106 K16 **Barbate** ⁓ SW Spain
106 K16 **Barbate de Franco** Andalucía, S Spain
85 K21 **Barberton** Mpumalanga, NE South Africa
33 U12 **Barberton** Ohio, N USA
104 K12 **Barbezieux-St-Hilaire** Charente, W France
xli O11 **Barbon** Cumbria, NW England, UK
56 G9 **Barbosa** Santander, C Colombia
23 N7 **Barbourville** Kentucky, S USA
47 W9 **Barbuda** *island* N Antigua and Barbuda
189 W8 **Barcaldine** Queensland, E Australia
Barcarozsnyó *see* Râşnov
106 I11 **Barcarrota** Extremadura, W Spain
Barcău *see* Berettyó
Barce *see* Al Marj
109 L23 **Barcellona** *var.* Barcellona Pozzo di Gotto. Sicilia, Italy, C Mediterranean Sea
Barcellona Pozzo di Gotto *see* Barcellona
107 W6 **Barcelona** *anc.* Barcino, Barcinona. Cataluña, E Spain
57 N5 **Barcelona** Anzoátegui, NE Venezuela
107 S5 **Barcelona** ◆ *province* Cataluña, NE Spain
107 W6 **Barcelona** ✈ Cataluña, E Spain
105 U14 **Barcelonnette** Alpes-de-Haute-Provence, SE France
60 E12 **Barcelos** Amazonas, N Brazil
106 G5 **Barcelos** Braga, N Portugal
112 I10 **Barcin** *Ger.* Bartschin. Bydgoszcz, C Poland
Barcino/Barcinona *see* Barcelona
Barcoo *see* Cooper Creek
113 H26 **Barcs** Somogy, SW Hungary
143 W11 **Bärdä** *Rus.* Barda. C Azerbaijan
80 H5 **Bardaï** Borkou-Ennedi-Tibesti, N Chad
145 R2 **Bardaraşh** N Iraq
145 Q7 **Bardasah** SW Iraq
159 S16 **Barddhamān** West Bengal, NE India
113 N18 **Bardejov** *Ger.* Bartfeld, *Hung.* Bártfa. Východné Slovensko, NE Slovakia
xli Q10 **Barden** North Yorkshire, N England, UK
107 R4 **Bárdenas Reales** *physical region* N Spain
Bardera/Bardere *see* Baardheere
Bardesīr *see* Bardsīr
94 K3 **Bardharbunga** ▲ C Iceland
Bardhë, Drini i *see* Beli Drim
108 E9 **Bardi** Emilia-Romagna, C Italy
xxxix Q6 **Bardney** Lincolnshire, E England, UK
108 A8 **Bardonecchia** Piemonte, W Italy
xli O6 **Bardon Mill** Northumberland, N England, UK
xl M12 **Bardsea** Cumbria, NW England, UK
xli S13 **Bardsey** Leeds, N England, UK
xxxv D7 **Bardsey Island** *island* NW Wales, UK
xxxv G5 **Bardsey Sound** *sound* NW Wales, UK
149 S11 **Bardsīr** *var.* Bardesīr, Mashīz. Kermān, C Iran
22 L6 **Bardstown** Kentucky, S USA
Barduli *see* Barletta
22 G7 **Bardwell** Kentucky, S USA
158 K11 **Bareilly** *var.* Bareli. Uttar Pradesh, N India
Bareli *see* Bareilly
100 H13 **Barendrecht** Zuid-Holland, SW Netherlands
104 M3 **Barentin** Seine-Maritime, N France
94 N3 **Barentsburg** Spitsbergen, W Svalbard
Barentsevo More/Barents Havet *see* Barents Sea
94 O3 **Barentsøya** *island* E Svalbard
207 T11 **Barents Plain** *undersea feature* N Barents Sea
129 P3 **Barents Sea** *Nor.* Barents Havet, *Rus.* Barentsevo More. *sea* Arctic Ocean
207 U14 **Barents Trough** *undersea feature* SW Barents Sea
82 I9 **Barentu** W Eritrea
104 J3 **Barfleur** Manche, N France
104 J3 **Barfleur, Pointe de** *headland* N France
xxxviii M12 **Barford** Warwickshire, C England, UK
Barfrush/Barfurush *see* Bābol
164 H14 **Barga** Xizang Zizhiqu, W China
107 N9 **Bargas** Castilla-La Mancha, C Spain
83 I15 **Bargē** SW Ethiopia
108 A9 **Barge** Piemonte, NE Italy
xxxv J14 **Bargoed** Caerphilly, S Wales, UK
159 U16 **Barguna** Khulna, S Bangladesh
Bārguşad *see* Vorotan
126 K15 **Barguzin** Respublika Buryatiya, S Russian Federation
159 O13 **Barhaj** Uttar Pradesh, N India
xxxvii Y10 **Barham** Kent, SE England, UK
191 N10 **Barham** New South Wales, SE Australia
158 J12 **Barhan** Uttar Pradesh, N India
21 S7 **Bar Harbor** Mount Desert Island, Maine, NE USA
159 R14 **Barharwa** Bihār, NE India
159 P15 **Barhi** Bihār, N India
109 O17 **Bari** *var.* Bari delle Puglie; *anc.* Barium. Puglia, SE Italy
82 P12 **Bari** *off.* Gobolka Bari. ◆ *region* NE Somalia
178 K14 **Ba Ria** Ba Ria-Vung Tau, S Vietnam
Bāridah *see* Al Bāridah
Bari delle Puglie *see* Bari
Barikot *see* Barīkowţ
155 T4 **Barīkowţ** *var.* Barikot. Kunar, NE Afghanistan

◆ Country ● Country Capital ◇ Dependent Territory ○ Dependent Territory Capital ◆ Administrative Region ✈ International Airport ▲ Mountain ▲ Mountain Range ⛰ Volcano ⁓ River ◎ Lake ⊡ Reservoir

Barillas – Beauvais

44 C4 **Barillas** var. Santa Cruz Barillas. Huehuetenango, W Guatemala
56 J6 **Barinas** Barinas, W Venezuela
56 I7 **Barinas** off. Estado Barinas; prev. Zamora. ◈ state C Venezuela
56 J6 **Barinitas** Barinas, NW Venezuela
160 P11 **Bāripada** Orissa, E India
62 K9 **Bariri** São Paulo, S Brazil
77 W11 **Bâris** S Egypt
158 G14 **Bari Sādri** Rājasthān, N India
159 U16 **Barisal** Khulna, S Bangladesh
173 G7 **Barisan, Pegunungan** ▲▲ Sumatera, W Indonesia
175 N10 **Barito, Sungai** ≈ Borneo, C Indonesia
Barium see Bari
Barka see Baraka
Barka see Al Marj
166 H8 **Barkam** Sichuan, C China
120 J9 **Barkava** Madona, C Latvia
8 M15 **Barkerville** British Columbia, SW Canada
xxxvi G6 **Barking** Barking and Dagenham, SE England, UK
xxxiv L16 **Barking and Dagenham** ◈ London borough SE England, UK
xxxvi G5 **Barkingside** Redbridge, SE England, UK
12 J12 **Bark Lake** ◎ Ontario, SE Canada
22 H7 **Barkley, Lake** ▣ Kentucky/Tennessee, S USA
8 K17 **Barkley Sound** inlet British Columbia, W Canada
85 J24 **Barkly East** Afr. Barkly-Oos. Eastern Cape, SE South Africa
Barkly-Oos see Barkly East
189 S4 **Barkly Tableland** plateau Northern Territory/Queensland, N Australia
Barkly-Wes see Barkly West
85 H22 **Barkly West** Afr. Barkly-Wes. Northern Cape, N South Africa
165 O5 **Barkol** var. Barkol Kazak Zizhixian. Xinjiang Uygur Zizhiqu, NW China
165 O5 **Barkol Hu** ◎ NW China
Barkol Kazak Zizhixian see Barkol
32 J3 **Bark Point** headland Wisconsin, N USA
27 P11 **Barksdale** Texas, SW USA
xxxix P7 **Barkston** Lincolnshire, E England, UK
Bar Kunar see Asmār
xxxvii U6 **Barkway** Hertfordshire, SE England, UK
118 L11 **Bârlad** prev. Bîrlad. Vaslui, E Romania
118 M11 **Bârlad** prev. Bîrlad. ≈ E Romania
xxxviii J8 **Barlaston** City of Stoke-on-Trent, C England, UK
78 D9 **Barlavento, Ilhas de** var. Windward Islands. island group N Cape Verde
xli T14 **Barlby** North Yorkshire, N England, UK
105 R5 **Bar-le-Duc** var. Bar-sur-Ornain. Meuse, NE France
188 K11 **Barlee, Lake** ◎ Western Australia
188 H8 **Barlee Range** ▲▲ Western Australia
xxxviii M9 **Barlestone** Leicestershire, C England, UK
109 N16 **Barletta** anc. Barduli. Puglia, SE Italy
xxxvii U6 **Barley** Hertfordshire, SE England, UK
112 E10 **Barlinek** Ger. Berlinchen. Gorzów, W Poland
29 S11 **Barling** Arkansas, C USA
176 Vv10 **Barma** Irian Jaya, E Indonesia
191 Q9 **Barmedman** New South Wales, SE Australia
Barmen-Elberfeld see Wuppertal
158 D12 **Bārmer** Rājasthān, NW India
190 K9 **Barmera** South Australia
xxxv G8 **Barmouth** Gwynedd, NW Wales, UK
xxxv G8 **Barmouth Bay** bay NW Wales, UK
xli W12 **Barmston** East Riding of Yorkshire, N England, UK
xliv E9 **Barna** Galway, W Ireland
160 F10 **Barnagar** Madhya Pradesh, C India
158 H9 **Barnāla** Punjab, NW India
xli Q9 **Barnard Castle** Durham, N England, UK
191 O6 **Barnato** New South Wales, SE Australia
xliv D5 **Barnatra** Mayo, NW Ireland
126 H14 **Barnaul** Altayskiy Kray, C Russian Federation
111 V8 **Bärnbach** Steiermark, SE Austria
20 K16 **Barnegat** New Jersey, NE USA
xxxvi B8 **Barnes** Richmond upon Thames, SE England, UK
25 S4 **Barnesville** Georgia, SE USA
31 R6 **Barnesville** Minnesota, N USA
33 U13 **Barnesville** Ohio, N USA
xxxvii T8 **Barnet** Barnet, SE England, UK
xxxiv K16 **Barnet** ◈ London borough SE England, UK
100 K11 **Barneveld** var. Barnveld. Gelderland, C Netherlands
xxxix V11 **Barnham** Suffolk, E England, UK
xxxix W9 **Barnham Broom** Norfolk, E England, UK
27 O9 **Barnhart** Texas, SW USA
xxxix V11 **Barningham** Suffolk, E England, UK
xli P13 **Barnoldswick** Lancashire, N England, UK
29 P8 **Barnsdall** Oklahoma, C USA
xli S15 **Barnsley** Barnsley, N England, UK
xxxvii N8 **Barnsley** Gloucestershire, C England, UK
xli R16 **Barnsley** ◈ unitary authority N England, UK
21 Q12 **Barnstable** Massachusetts, NE USA
xxxvi F12 **Barnstaple** Devon, SW England, UK
xxxvi E12 **Barnstaple Bay** bay SW England, UK
Barnveld see Barneveld
23 Q14 **Barnwell** South Carolina, SE USA
69 U8 **Baro** var. Baro Wenz. ≈ Ethiopia/Sudan
79 U15 **Baro** Niger, C Nigeria
Baro see Baro Wenz
Baroda see Vadodara
155 U2 **Baroghil Pass** var. Kowtal-e Barowghīl. pass Afghanistan/Pakistan
121 Q17 **Baron'ki** Rus. Boron'ki. Mahilyowskaya Voblasts', E Belorussia
190 J9 **Barossa Valley** valley South Australia
Baroui see Salisbury
83 H14 **Baro Wenz** var. Baro, Nahr Barū. ≈ Ethiopia/Sudan
159 U12 **Barpeta** Assam, NE India
33 S7 **Barques, Pointe Aux** headland Michigan, N USA
56 I5 **Barquisimeto** Lara, NW Venezuela
xliii I23 **Barr** South Ayrshire, W Scotland, UK
xliii A14 **Barra** island NW Scotland, UK
61 N16 **Barra** Bahia, E Brazil
191 T5 **Barraba** New South Wales, SE Australia
62 L9 **Barra Bonita** São Paulo, S Brazil
66 J12 **Barracuda Fracture Zone** var. Fifteen Twenty Fracture Zone. tectonic feature SW Atlantic Ocean
66 G11 **Barracuda Ridge** undersea feature N Atlantic Ocean
45 N12 **Barra del Colorado** Limón, NE Costa Rica
45 N9 **Barra de Río Grande** Región Autónoma Atlántico Sur, E Nicaragua
84 A11 **Barra do Cuanza** Luanda, NW Angola
62 O9 **Barra do Piraí** Rio de Janeiro, SE Brazil
63 D16 **Barra do Quaraí** Rio Grande do Sul, SE Brazil
61 G14 **Barra do São Manuel** Pará, N Brazil
85 N19 **Barra Falsa, Ponta da** headland S Mozambique
xliii A15 **Barra Head** headland NW Scotland, UK
Barram see Baram, Batang
62 O9 **Barra Mansa** Rio de Janeiro, SE Brazil
59 D14 **Barranca** Lima, W Peru
56 F8 **Barrancabermeja** Santander, N Colombia
56 H4 **Barrancas** La Guajira, N Colombia
56 J6 **Barrancas** Barinas, NW Venezuela
57 Q6 **Barrancas** Monagas, NE Venezuela
56 F6 **Barranco de Loba** Bolívar, N Colombia
106 I12 **Barrancos** Beja, S Portugal
64 N7 **Barranqueras** Chaco, N Argentina
56 E4 **Barranquilla** Atlántico, N Colombia
85 N20 **Barra, Ponta da** headland S Mozambique
107 P11 **Barrax** Castilla-La Mancha, C Spain
21 N11 **Barre** Massachusetts, NE USA
20 M7 **Barre** Vermont, NE USA
61 M17 **Barreiras** Bahia, E Brazil
106 F11 **Barreiro** Setúbal, W Portugal
67 C26 **Barren Island** island S Falkland Islands
22 K7 **Barren River Lake** ▣ Kentucky, S USA
62 L7 **Barretos** São Paulo, S Brazil
xliii I24 **Barrgrennan** Dumfries and Galloway, SW Scotland, UK
xliii I20 **Barrhead** East Renfrewshire, W Scotland, UK
9 P14 **Barrhead** Alberta, SW Canada
xliii H24 **Barrhill** South Ayrshire, W Scotland, UK
12 G14 **Barrie** Ontario, S Canada
9 N16 **Barrière** British Columbia, SW Canada
12 H8 **Barrière, Lac** ◎ Québec, SE Canada
190 L6 **Barrier Range** hill range New South Wales, SE Australia
44 G3 **Barrier Reef** reef E Belize
196 C16 **Barrigada** C Guam
Barrington Island see Santa Fe, Isla
191 T7 **Barrington Tops** ▲ New South Wales, SE Australia
191 O4 **Barringun** New South Wales, SE Australia
xliii F14 **Barrisdale** Highland, NW Scotland, UK
61 K18 **Barro Alto** Goiás, S Brazil
61 N14 **Barro Duro** Piauí, NE Brazil
32 I5 **Barron** Wisconsin, N USA
12 J12 **Barron** ≈ Ontario, SE Canada
63 H15 **Barros Cassal** Rio Grande do Sul, S Brazil
47 P14 **Barrouallie** Saint Vincent, W Saint Vincent and the Grenadines
xliv J12 **Barrow** Ir. An Bhearú. ≈ SE Ireland
xxxix U12 **Barrow** Suffolk, E England, UK
41 O4 **Barrow** Alaska, USA
189 Q6 **Barrow Creek Roadhouse** Northern Territory, N Australia
xli P14 **Barrowford** Lancashire, NW England, UK
xl L12 **Barrow-in-Furness** Cumbria, NW England, UK
188 G7 **Barrow Island** island Western Australia
41 O4 **Barrow, Point** headland Alaska, USA
9 V14 **Barrows** Manitoba, S Canada
xxxix O9 **Barrow upon Soar** Leicestershire, C England, UK
xxxv J16 **Barry** The Vale of Glamorgan, S Wales, UK
12 J12 **Barry's Bay** Ontario, SE Canada
150 K14 **Barsakel'mes, Ostrov** island SW Kazakhstan
Barść Łużyca see Forst
153 S14 **Barsem** S Tajikistan
151 V11 **Barshatas** Semipalatinsk, E Kazakhstan
161 F14 **Bārsi** Mahārāshtra, W India
102 I13 **Barsinghausen** Niedersachsen, C Germany
153 X8 **Barskoon** Issyk-Kul'skaya Oblast', E Kyrgyzstan
102 F10 **Barssel** Niedersachsen, NW Germany
37 U14 **Barstow** California, W USA
26 L8 **Barstow** Texas, SW USA
105 R6 **Bar-sur-Aube** Aube, NE France
Bar-sur-Ornain see Bar-le-Duc
105 Q6 **Bar-sur-Seine** Aube, N France
153 S13 **Bartang** S Tajikistan
153 T13 **Bartang** ≈ SE Tajikistan
Bartenstein see Bartoszyce
Bártfa/Bartfeld see Bardejov
102 N7 **Barth** Mecklenburg-Vorpommern, NE Germany
29 W13 **Bartholomew, Bayou** ≈ Arkansas/Louisiana, S USA
57 T8 **Bartica** N Guyana
142 H10 **Bartın** Zonguldak, N Turkey
189 W4 **Bartle Frere** ▲ Queensland, E Australia
29 P8 **Bartlesville** Oklahoma, C USA
31 P14 **Bartlett** Nebraska, C USA
22 E10 **Bartlett** Tennessee, S USA
27 T9 **Bartlett** Texas, SW USA
38 L13 **Bartlett Reservoir** ▣ Arizona, SW USA
xli R9 **Barton** North Yorkshire, N England, UK
21 N6 **Barton** Vermont, NE USA
xxxvii S6 **Barton-le-Clay** Bedfordshire, C England, UK
xxxix P3 **Barton-upon-Humber** North Lincolnshire, N England, UK
112 L7 **Bartoszyce** Ger. Bartenstein. Olsztyn, N Poland
25 W12 **Bartow** Florida, SE USA
Bartschin see Barcin
176 V10 **Baru** Irian Jaya, E Indonesia
173 G6 **Barumun, Sungai** ≈ Sumatera, W Indonesia
Barū, Nahr see Baro Wenz
174 M16 **Barung, Nusa** island S Indonesia
173 Ff6 **Barus** Sumatera, NW Indonesia
168 L10 **Baruunsuu** Ömnögovĭ, S Mongolia
169 P8 **Baruun-Urt** Sühbaatar, E Mongolia
45 P15 **Barú, Volcán** var. Volcán de Chiriquí. ⊻ W Panama
xlii D7 **Barvas** Western Isles, NW Scotland, UK
101 K21 **Barvaux** Luxembourg, SE Belgium
44 M13 **Barva, Volcán** ⊻ NW Costa Rica
119 W6 **Barvinkove** Kharkivs'ka Oblast', E Ukraine
160 G11 **Barwāh** Madhya Pradesh, C India
Bärwalde Neumark see Mieszkowice
160 F11 **Barwāni** Madhya Pradesh, C India
191 P5 **Barwon River** ≈ New South Wales, SE Australia
121 L15 **Barysaw** Rus. Borisov. Minskaya Voblasts', NE Belorussia
131 Q6 **Barysh** Ul'yanovskaya Oblast', W Russian Federation
119 Q4 **Baryshivka** Kyyivs'ka Oblast', N Ukraine
81 J17 **Basankusu** Equateur, NW Zaire
119 N11 **Basarabeasca** Rus. Bessarabka. SE Moldavia
118 M14 **Basarabi** Constanța, SW Romania
42 H6 **Basaseachic** Chihuahua, NW Mexico
107 O2 **Basauri** País Vasco, N Spain
63 D18 **Basavilbaso** Entre Ríos, E Argentina
xxxviii G9 **Baschurch** Shropshire, W England, UK
81 F21 **Bas-Congo** off. Region du Bas-Congo prev. Bas-Zaïre ◈ region SW Congo (Zaire)
110 E6 **Basel** Eng. Basle, Fr. Bâle. Basel-Stadt, NW Switzerland
110 E7 **Basel** Eng. Basle, Fr. Bâle. ◈ canton NW Switzerland
149 T14 **Bashākerd, Kūhhā-ye** ▲▲ SE Iran
9 Q15 **Bashaw** Alberta, SW Canada
152 K16 **Bashbedeng** Maryyskiy Velayat, S Turkmenistan
85 J24 **Bashee** ≈ S South Africa
167 T15 **Bashi Channel** Chin. Pa-shih Hai-hsia. channel Philippines/Taiwan
Bashkiria see Bashkortostan, Respublika
125 Dd12 **Bashkortostan, Respublika** prev. Bashkiria. ◈ autonomous republic W Russian Federation
131 N6 **Bashmakovo** Penzenskaya Oblast', W Russian Federation
152 J10 **Bashsakarba** Lebapskiy Velayat, NE Turkmenistan
119 R9 **Bashtanka** Mykolayivs'ka Oblast', S Ukraine
195 O17 **Basilaki Island** island SE PNG
xxxvii W9 **Basildon** Essex, E England, UK
24 H8 **Basile** Louisiana, S USA
109 M18 **Basilicata** ◈ region S Italy
35 V13 **Basin** Wyoming, C USA
xxxvii Q11 **Basingstoke** Hampshire, S England, UK
149 U8 **Başīrān** Khorāsān, E Iran
114 B10 **Baška** It. Bescanuova. Primorje-Gorski Kotar, NW Croatia
143 T15 **Başkale** Van, SE Turkey
12 L10 **Baskatong, Réservoir** ▣ Québec, SE Canada
143 O14 **Baskil** Elâzığ, E Turkey
Basle see Basel
xxxviii L6 **Baslow** Derbyshire, C England, UK
160 H9 **Bāsoda** Madhya Pradesh, C India
81 L17 **Basoko** Haut-Zaïre, N Zaire
Basque Country, The see País Vasco
Basra see Al Başrah
105 U5 **Bas-Rhin** ◈ department NE France
Bassam see Grand-Bassam
9 Q16 **Bassano** Alberta, SW Canada
108 H7 **Bassano del Grappa** Veneto, NE Italy
79 Q15 **Bassar** var. Bassari. NW Togo
Bassari see Bassar
180 L9 **Bassas da India** island group W Madagascar
110 D7 **Bassecourt** Jura, W Switzerland
177 Ff8 **Bassein** var. Pathein. Irrawaddy, SW Burma
81 J15 **Basse-Kotto** ◈ prefecture S Central African Republic
107 V5 **Bassella** Cataluña, NE Spain
104 J5 **Basse-Normandie** Eng. Lower Normandy. ◈ region N France
xl L8 **Bassenthwaite** Cumbria, NW England, UK
xl L8 **Bassenthwaite Lake** ◎ NW England, UK
47 Q11 **Basse-Pointe** N Martinique
78 H12 **Basse Santa Su** E Gambia
Basse-Saxe see Niedersachsen
47 X6 **Basse-Terre** ○ (Guadeloupe) Basse Terre, SW Guadeloupe
47 X6 **Basse Terre** island W Guadeloupe
47 V10 **Basseterre** ● (Saint Kitts and Nevis) Saint Kitts, Saint Kitts and Nevis
31 O13 **Bassett** Nebraska, C USA
23 S7 **Bassett** Virginia, NE USA
39 N15 **Bassett Peak** ▲ Arizona, SW USA
78 M10 **Bassikounou** Hodh ech Chargui, SE Mauritania
79 R15 **Bassila** W Benin
Bass, Îlots de see Marotiri
xxxix P6 **Bassingham** Lincolnshire, E England, UK
33 O11 **Bass Lake** Indiana, N USA
xliii N19 **Bass Rock** island E Scotland, UK
191 O14 **Bass Strait** strait SE Australia
102 H11 **Bassum** Niedersachsen, NW Germany
31 X3 **Basswood Lake** ◎ Canada/USA
97 J21 **Båstad** Kristianstad, S Sweden
145 U2 **Baştah** E Iraq
159 N12 **Basti** Uttar Pradesh, N India
104 F1 **Bastia** Corse, France, C Mediterranean Sea
101 L23 **Bastogne** Luxembourg, SE Belgium
xxxix Q9 **Baston** Lincolnshire, E England, UK
24 I5 **Bastrop** Louisiana, S USA
27 T11 **Bastrop** Texas, SW USA
95 J15 **Bastuträsk** Västerbotten, N Sweden
121 J19 **Bastyn'** Rus. Bostyn'. Brestskaya Voblasts', SW Belorussia
Basuo see Dongfang
Basutoland see Lesotho
121 O15 **Basya** ≈ E Belorussia
119 V8 **Basyl'kivka** Dnipropetrovs'ka Oblast', E Ukraine
Bas-Zaïre see Bas-Congo
81 D17 **Bata** NW Equatorial Guinea
81 D17 **Bata** ✕ S Equatorial Guinea
Batae Coritanorum see Leicester
126 M8 **Batagay** Respublika Sakha (Yakutiya), NE Russian Federation
126 Ll8 **Batagay-Alyta** Respublika Sakha (Yakutiya), NE Russian Federation
114 L10 **Batajnica** Serbia, N Yugoslavia
142 H15 **Bataklık Gölü** ◎ S Turkey
116 H11 **Batak, Yazovir** ▣ SW Bulgaria
158 H7 **Batāla** Punjab, N India
106 F9 **Batalha** Leiria, C Portugal
81 N17 **Batama** Haut-Zaïre, NE Zaire
126 Ll10 **Batamay** Respublika Sakha (Yakutiya), NE Russian Federation
174 I7 **Batam, Pulau** island Kepulauan Riau, W Indonesia
166 F9 **Batang** Sichuan, C China
174 Kk14 **Batang** Jawa, C Indonesia
81 I14 **Batangafo** Ouham, NW Central African Republic
179 P11 **Batangas** off. Batangas City. Luzon, N Philippines
Bătania see Battonya
179 Pp6 **Batan Islands** island group N Philippines
62 L8 **Batatais** São Paulo, S Brazil
20 E10 **Batavia** New York, NE USA
Batavia see Jakarta
181 T9 **Batavia Seamount** undersea feature E Indian Ocean
130 L12 **Bataysk** Rostovskaya Oblast', SW Russian Federation
12 B9 **Batchawana** ≈ Ontario, S Canada
12 B9 **Batchawana Bay** Ontario, S Canada
178 Ii12 **Bătdâmbâng** prev. Battambang. Bătdâmbâng, NW Cambodia
81 G20 **Batéké, Plateaux** plateau S Congo
191 S11 **Batemans Bay** New South Wales, SE Australia
23 Q13 **Batesburg** South Carolina, SE USA
30 K12 **Batesland** South Dakota, N USA
29 V10 **Batesville** Arkansas, C USA
33 Q14 **Batesville** Indiana, N USA
24 L2 **Batesville** Mississippi, S USA
27 Q13 **Batesville** Texas, SW USA
xxxvi L10 **Bath** hist. Akermanceaster, anc. Aquae Calidae, Aquae Solis. Bath and North East Somerset, SW England, UK
46 L13 **Bath** E Jamaica
21 Q8 **Bath** Maine, NE USA
20 F11 **Bath** New York, NE USA
Bath see Berkeley Springs
80 I10 **Batha** off. Préfecture du Batha. ◈ prefecture C Chad
80 I10 **Batha** seasonal river C Chad
xxxvi K10 **Bath and North East Somerset** ◈ unitary authority SW England, UK
147 Y8 **Baṭḥā', Wādī al** dry watercourse NE Oman
xliii L20 **Bathgate** West Lothian, SE Scotland, UK
158 H9 **Bathinda** Punjab, NW India
100 M11 **Bathmen** Overijssel, E Netherlands
47 Z14 **Bathsheba** E Barbados
191 R8 **Bathurst** New South Wales, SE Australia
11 O13 **Bathurst** New Brunswick, SE Canada
Bathurst see Banjul
15 Gg2 **Bathurst, Cape** headland Northwest Territories, NW Canada
206 L8 **Bathurst Inlet** Northwest Territories, N Canada
15 J4 **Bathurst Inlet** inlet Northwest Territories, N Canada
189 N1 **Bathurst Island** island Northern Territory, N Australia
207 O9 **Bathurst Island** island Parry Islands, Northwest Territories, N Canada
79 O14 **Batié** SW Burkina
197 J14 **Batiki** prev. Mbatiki. island C Fiji
Batinah see Al Bāṭinah
147 Y9 **Bāṭin, Wādī al** dry watercourse SW Asia
13 P9 **Batiscan** ≈ Québec, SE Canada
142 F16 **Batı Toroslar** ▲▲ SW Turkey
Batjan see Bacan, Pulau
xli R14 **Batley** Kirklees, N England, UK
Batlle y Ordóñez see José Batlle y Ordóñez
191 Q10 **Batlow** New South Wales, SE Australia
143 Q15 **Batman** var. Iluh. Batman, SE Turkey
143 Q15 **Batman** ◈ province SE Turkey
76 L6 **Batna** NE Algeria
Batoe see Batu, Kepulauan
168 K7 **Bat-Öldziyt** Töv, C Mongolia
24 J8 **Baton Rouge** state capital Louisiana, S USA
81 G15 **Batouri** Est, E Cameroon
144 G14 **Baṭrā', Jibāl al** ▲ S Jordan
144 G6 **Batroûn** var. Al Batrūn. N Lebanon
Batsch see Bač
Batsevichi see Batsevichy
121 M17 **Batsevichy** Rus. Batsevichi. Mahilyowskaya Voblasts', E Belorussia
94 M7 **Båtsfjord** Finnmark, N Norway
Battambang see Bătdâmbâng
205 X3 **Batterbee, Cape** headland Antarctica
xxxvi C9 **Battersea** Wandsworth, SE England, UK
161 L24 **Batticaloa** Eastern Province, E Sri Lanka
101 L19 **Battice** Liège, E Belgium
109 L18 **Battipaglia** Campania, S Italy
xxxvii W12 **Battle** East Sussex, SE England, UK
9 R15 **Battle** ≈ Alberta/Saskatchewan, SW Canada
Battle Born State see Nevada
33 Q10 **Battle Creek** Michigan, N USA
29 T7 **Battlefield** Missouri, C USA
9 S15 **Battleford** Saskatchewan, S Canada
31 S6 **Battle Lake** Minnesota, N USA
37 U3 **Battle Mountain** Nevada, W USA
113 M25 **Battonya** Rom. Bătania. Békés, SE Hungary
175 Qq14 **Batuata, Pulau** island C Indonesia
175 Q8 **Batudaka, Pulau** island N Indonesia
173 F8 **Batu, Kepulauan** prev. Batoe. island group W Indonesia
143 Q10 **Bat'umi** W Georgia
174 H6 **Batu Pahat** prev. Bandar Penggaram. Johor, Peninsular Malaysia
175 Q10 **Baturebe** Sulawesi, N Indonesia
126 H13 **Baturino** Tomskaya Oblast', C Russian Federation
119 R3 **Baturyn** Chernihivs'ka Oblast', N Ukraine
144 F10 **Bat Yam** Tel Aviv, C Israel
131 Q4 **Batyrevo** Chuvashskaya Respublika, W Russian Federation
Batys Qazaqstan Oblysy see Zapadnyy Kazakhstan
104 F5 **Batz, Île de** island NW France
174 L7 **Bau** Sarawak, East Malaysia
179 P9 **Bauang** Luzon, N Philippines
175 Qq13 **Baubau** var. Baoebaoe. Pulau Buton, C Indonesia
79 W14 **Bauchi** Bauchi, NE Nigeria
79 W14 **Bauchi** ◈ state C Nigeria
104 H7 **Baud** Morbihan, NW France
31 T2 **Baudette** Minnesota, N USA
200 Nn10 **Bauer Basin** undersea feature E Pacific Ocean
197 C14 **Bauer Field** var. Port Vila. ✕ (Port-Vila) Éfaté, C Vanuatu
11 T9 **Bauld, Cape** headland Newfoundland, Newfoundland and Labrador, E Canada
xxxix R5 **Baumber** Lincolnshire, E England, UK
105 T8 **Baume-les-Dames** Doubs, E France
195 X15 **Baunani** Malaita, N Solomon Islands
103 I15 **Baunatal** Hessen, C Germany
109 D18 **Baunei** Sardegna, Italy, C Mediterranean Sea
59 M15 **Baures, Río** ≈ N Bolivia
62 K9 **Bauru** São Paulo, S Brazil
Baushar see Bawshar
120 G10 **Bauska** Ger. Bauske. Bauska, S Latvia
Bauske see Bauska
103 Q15 **Bautzen** Lus. Budyšin. Sachsen, E Germany
Bauzanum see Bolzano
Bavaria see Bayern
111 N7 **Bavarian Alps** Ger. Bayrische Alpen. ▲▲ Austria/Germany
Bavière see Bayern
42 H4 **Bavispe, Río** ≈ NW Mexico
131 T5 **Bavly** Respublika Tatarstan, W Russian Federation
174 Kk10 **Bawal, Pulau** island N Indonesia
174 Mm10 **Bawan** Borneo, C Indonesia
191 O12 **Baw Baw, Mount** ▲ Victoria, SE Australia
xxxix X9 **Bawburgh** Norfolk, E England, UK
xxxix W8 **Bawdeswell** Norfolk, E England, UK
xxxix Y13 **Bawdsey** Suffolk, E England, UK
175 W11 **Bawe** Irian Jaya, E Indonesia
174 M13 **Bawean, Pulau** island S Indonesia
174 L15 **Bawen** Jawa, S Indonesia
77 V9 **Bawīṭi** N Egypt
79 Q13 **Bawku** N Ghana
178 Gg7 **Bawlakè** Kayah State, C Burma
173 Ff8 **Bawo Ofuloa** Pulau Tanahmasa, W Indonesia
147 Y8 **Bawshar** var. Baushar. NE Oman
xli U16 **Bawtry** Doncaster, N England, UK
Ba Xian see Bazhou
164 M8 **Baxkorgan** Xinjiang Uygur Zizhiqu, W China
25 V6 **Baxley** Georgia, SE USA
165 R15 **Baxoi** Xizang Zizhiqu, W China
31 W14 **Baxter** Iowa, C USA
31 U6 **Baxter** Minnesota, N USA
29 R8 **Baxter Springs** Kansas, C USA
83 M17 **Bay** off. Gobolka Bay. ◈ region SW Somalia
Bay see Baicheng
46 H7 **Bayamo** Granma, E Cuba
47 U5 **Bayamón** E Puerto Rico
169 W8 **Bayan** Heilongjiang, NE China
175 Nn16 **Bayan** prev. Bajan. Pulau Lombok, C Indonesia
168 I6 **Bayan** Arhangay, C Mongolia
169 P7 **Bayan** Dornod, E Mongolia
169 R9 **Bayan** Dornogovĭ, SE Mongolia
168 F7 **Bayan** Govĭ-Altay, W Mongolia
169 O8 **Bayan** Hentiy, C Mongolia
158 I12 **Bayāna** Rājasthān, N India
155 N5 **Bāyān, Band-e** ▲▲ C Afghanistan
168 H8 **Bayanbulag** Bayanhongor, C Mongolia
169 N7 **Bayanbulag** Hentiy, C Mongolia
164 J5 **Bayanbulak** Xinjiang Uygur Zizhiqu, W China
126 Jj15 **Bayanday** Ust'-Ordynskiy Buryatskiy Avtonomnyy Okrug, S Russian Federation
Bayan Gol see Dengkou
168 F8 **Bayangol** Govĭ-Altay, SW Mongolia
165 R12 **Bayan Har Shan** var. Bayan Khar. ▲▲ C China
168 I8 **Bayanhongor** Bayanhongor, C Mongolia
168 H9 **Bayanhongor** ◈ province C Mongolia
Bayan Khar see Bayan Har Shan
173 G3 **Bayan Lepas** ✕ (George Town) Pinang, Peninsular Malaysia
168 K13 **Bayan Mod** Nei Mongol Zizhiqu, N China
168 K13 **Bayan Nuru** Nei Mongol Zizhiqu, N China
169 N12 **Bayan Obo** Nei Mongol Zizhiqu, N China
45 V15 **Bayano, Lago** ◎ E Panama
168 C5 **Bayan-Ölgiy** ◈ province NW Mongolia
168 F9 **Bayan-Ovoo** Govĭ-Altay, SW Mongolia
168 H9 **Bayansayr** Bayanhongor, C Mongolia
165 Q9 **Bayan Shan** ▲ C China
168 J9 **Bayanteeg** Övörhangay, C Mongolia
168 L8 **Bayantöhöm** Töv, C Mongolia
168 H6 **Bayan-Uhaa** Dzavhan, C Mongolia
168 J8 **Bayan-Ulaan** Övörhangay, C Mongolia
Bayan Ul Hot see Xi Ujimqin Qi
30 J14 **Bayard** Nebraska, C USA
39 P15 **Bayard** New Mexico, SW USA
105 T13 **Bayard, Col** pass SE France
169 O8 **Bayasgalant** Sühbaatar, E Mongolia
142 J12 **Bayat** Çorum, N Turkey
179 Q14 **Bayawan** Negros, C Philippines
149 R10 **Bayāẓ** Kermān, C Iran
179 R13 **Baybay** Leyte, C Philippines
23 X10 **Bayboro** North Carolina, SE USA
143 P12 **Bayburt** Bayburt, NE Turkey
143 P12 **Bayburt** ◈ province NE Turkey
33 R8 **Bay City** Michigan, N USA
27 V12 **Bay City** Texas, SW USA
125 G7 **Baydaratskaya Guba** var. Baydarata Bay. bay N Russian Federation
83 M16 **Baydhabo** var. Baydhowa, Isha Baydhabo, It. Baidoa. Bay, SW Somalia
Baydhowa see Baydhabo
xxxvii O9 **Baydon** Wiltshire, S England, UK
103 N21 **Bayerischer Wald** ▲▲ SE Germany
103 K21 **Bayern** Eng. Bavaria, Fr. Bavière. ◈ state SE Germany
153 V9 **Bayetovo** Narynskaya Oblast', C Kyrgyzstan
104 K4 **Bayeux** anc. Augustodurum. Calvados, N France
12 E15 **Bayfield** ≈ Ontario, S Canada
151 O15 **Baygakum** Kaz. Bäygequm. Kzyl-Orda, S Kazakhstan
Bäygequm see Baygakum
142 C14 **Bayındır** İzmir, SW Turkey
144 H12 **Bāyir** var. Bā'ir. Ma'ān, S Jordan
Bay Islands see Bahía, Islas de la
145 R5 **Bayjī** var. Baiji. N Iraq
151 Q16 **Baykadam** Kaz. Bayqadam. Zhambyl, S Kazakhstan
126 K15 **Baykal, Ozero** Eng. Lake Baikal. ◎ S Russian Federation
126 J16 **Baykal'sk** Irkutskaya Oblast', S Russian Federation
143 R15 **Baykan** Siirt, SE Turkey
126 Ii12 **Baykit** Evenkiyskiy Avtonomnyy Okrug, C Russian Federation
151 N12 **Baykonur** Zhezkazgan, C Kazakhstan
164 E7 **Baykurt** Xinjiang Uygur Zizhiqu, W China
12 I9 **Bay, Lac** ◎ Québec, SE Canada
179 Pp11 **Bay, Laguna de** ◎ Luzon, N Philippines
131 W6 **Baymak** Respublika Bashkortostan, W Russian Federation
25 O8 **Bay Minette** Alabama, S USA
149 O17 **Baynūnah** desert W UAE
192 O8 **Bay of Plenty** off. Bay of Plenty Region. ◈ region North Island, NZ
203 Z3 **Bay of Wrecks** bay Kiritimati, E Kiribati
179 P9 **Bayombong** Luzon, N Philippines
104 I15 **Bayonne** anc. Lapurdum. Pyrénées-Atlantiques, SW France
24 H4 **Bayou D'Arbonne Lake** ▣ Louisiana, S USA
25 N9 **Bayou La Batre** Alabama, S USA
Bayou State see Mississippi
Bayqadam see Baykadam
Bayram-Ali see Bayramaly
152 J14 **Bayramaly** prev. Bayram-Ali. Maryyskiy Velayat, S Turkmenistan
103 L19 **Bayreuth** var. Baireuth. Bayern, SE Germany
Bayrische Alpen see Bavarian Alps
Bayrūt see Beyrouth
24 L9 **Bay Saint Louis** Mississippi, S USA
Baysān see Bet She'an
168 L8 **Bayshint** Töv, C Mongolia
12 H13 **Bays, Lake of** ◎ Ontario, S Canada
24 M6 **Bay Springs** Mississippi, S USA
Bay State see Massachusetts
Baysun see Boysun
12 H13 **Baysville** Ontario, S Canada
147 N15 **Bayt al Faqīh** W Yemen
164 M4 **Baytik Shan** ▲▲ China/Mongolia
Bayt Laḥm see Bethlehem
27 W11 **Baytown** Texas, SW USA
175 O9 **Bayur, Tanjung** headland Borneo, N Indonesia
123 Ll16 **Bayy al Kabīr, Wādī** dry watercourse NW Libya
Bayyrqum see Bairkum
107 P14 **Baza** Andalucía, S Spain
143 X10 **Bazardüzü Dağı** Rus. Gora Bazardyuzyu. ▲ N Azerbaijan
Bazardyuzyu, Gora see Bazardüzü Dağı
Bazargic see Dobrich
85 N18 **Bazaruto, Ilha do** island SE Mozambique
104 K14 **Bazas** Gironde, SW France
107 O14 **Baza, Sierra de** ▲ S Spain
166 J8 **Bazhong** Sichuan, C China
167 P3 **Bazhou** prev. Baxian, Ba Xian. Hebei, E China
12 M9 **Bazin** ≈ Québec, SE Canada
Bazin see Pezinok
145 Q7 **Bāzīyah** C Iraq
144 H6 **Bcharré** var. Bcharreh, Bsharrī, Bsherri. NE Lebanon
Bcharreh see Bcharré
30 J5 **Beach** North Dakota, N USA
xxxvii R6 **Beachampton** Buckinghamshire, C England, UK
190 K12 **Beachport** South Australia
xxxvii V13 **Beachy Head** headland SE England, UK
20 K13 **Beacon** New York, NE USA
xxxv J10 **Beacon Hill** hill E Wales, UK
xxxvii R9 **Beaconsfield** Buckinghamshire, C England, UK
xli R2 **Beadnell** Northumberland, N England, UK
xxxvi F13 **Beaford** Devon, SW England, UK
65 J25 **Beagle Channel** channel Argentina/Chile
189 O1 **Beagle Gulf** gulf Northern Territory, N Australia
xli Q1 **Beal** Northumberland, N England, UK
Bealach an Doirín see Ballaghaderreen
Bealach Cláir see Ballyclare
Bealach Féich see Ballybofey
180 J3 **Bealanana** Mahajanga, NE Madagascar
Béal an Átha see Ballina
Béal an Átha Móir see Ballinamore
Béal an Mhuirhead see Belmullet
Béal Átha Beithe see Ballybay
99 **Béal Átha Conaill** see Ballyconnell
Beál Átha hAmhnais see Ballyhaunis
Béal Átha na Sluaighe see Ballinasloe
Béal Átha Seanaidh see Ballyshannon
Bealdovuopmi see Peltovuoma
Béal Feirste see Belfast
Béal Tairbirt see Belturbet
xxxvi K13 **Beaminster** Dorset, S England, UK
Beanna Boirche see Mourne Mountains
99 **Beannchar** see Banagher, Ireland
99 **Beannchar** see Bangor, Northern Ireland, UK
Beanntraí see Bantry
25 N2 **Bear Creek** ≈ Alabama/Mississippi, S USA
32 J13 **Bear Creek** ≈ Illinois, N USA
29 U13 **Bearden** Arkansas, C USA
205 Q10 **Beardmore Glacier** glacier Antarctica
32 K13 **Beardstown** Illinois, N USA
30 L14 **Bear Hill** ▲ Nebraska, C USA
xliv C15 **Bear Island** island S Ireland
Bear Island see Bjørnøya
12 H12 **Bear Lake** Ontario, S Canada
38 M1 **Bear Lake** ◎ Idaho/Utah, NW USA
xxxviii D17 **Bearley** Warwickshire, C England, UK
41 U11 **Bear, Mount** ▲ Alaska, USA
104 J16 **Béarn** cultural region SW France
204 J11 **Bear Peninsula** peninsula Antarctica
xliii J20 **Bearsden** East Dunbartonshire, S Scotland, UK
158 I7 **Beās** ≈ India/Pakistan
107 P3 **Beasain** País Vasco, N Spain
107 O12 **Beas de Segura** Andalucía, S Spain
47 N10 **Beata, Cabo** headland SW Dominican Republic
47 N10 **Beata, Isla** island SW Dominican Republic
66 F11 **Beata Ridge** undersea feature N Caribbean Sea
31 R17 **Beatrice** Nebraska, C USA
85 L16 **Beatrice** Mashonaland East, NE Zimbabwe
xliii L23 **Beattock** Dumfries and Galloway, SW Scotland, UK
9 N11 **Beatton** ≈ British Columbia, W Canada
9 N11 **Beatton River** British Columbia, W Canada
37 V10 **Beatty** Nevada, W USA
23 N6 **Beattyville** Kentucky, S USA
181 X16 **Beau Bassin** W Mauritius
105 R15 **Beaucaire** Gard, S France
12 I8 **Beauchastel, Lac** ◎ Québec, SE Canada
12 I10 **Beauchêne, Lac** ◎ Québec, SE Canada
191 V3 **Beaudesert** Queensland, E Australia
190 M12 **Beaufort** Victoria, SE Australia
23 X11 **Beaufort** North Carolina, SE USA
23 R15 **Beaufort** South Carolina, SE USA
40 M11 **Beaufort Sea** sea Arctic Ocean
Beaufort-Wes see Beaufort West
85 G25 **Beaufort West** Afr. Beaufort-Wes. Western Cape, SW South Africa
105 N7 **Beaugency** Loiret, C France
21 R1 **Beau Lake** ▣ Maine, NE USA
xxxvii P13 **Beaulieu** Hampshire, S England, UK
xxxvii P13 **Beaulieu** ≈ S England, UK
xliii I12 **Beauly** Highland, N Scotland, UK
xliii J12 **Beauly Firth** inlet N Scotland, UK
xxxv G4 **Beaumaris** Isle of Anglesey, NW Wales, UK
101 G21 **Beaumont** Hainaut, S Belgium
193 E23 **Beaumont** Otago, South Island, NZ
24 M7 **Beaumont** Mississippi, S USA
27 X10 **Beaumont** Texas, SW USA
104 M15 **Beaumont-de-Lomagne** Tarn-et-Garonne, S France
104 L6 **Beaumont-sur-Sarthe** Sarthe, NW France
105 R8 **Beaune** Côte d'Or, C France
13 R9 **Beaupré** Québec, SE Canada
104 J8 **Beaupréau** Maine-et-Loire, NW France
101 I22 **Beauraing** Namur, SE Belgium
105 R12 **Beaurepaire** Isère, E France
9 Y16 **Beausejour** Manitoba, S Canada
105 N4 **Beauvais** anc. Bellovacum, Caesaromagus. Oise, N France

◆ Country ● Country Capital ◇ Dependent Territory ○ Dependent Territory Capital ◈ Administrative Region ✕ International Airport ▲ Mountain ▲▲ Mountain Range ⊻ Volcano ≈ River ◎ Lake ▣ Reservoir

BEAUVAL – BEREZAN'

9 S13 **Beauval** Saskatchewan, C Canada
104 I9 **Beauvoir-sur-Mer** Vendée, NW France
41 R8 **Beaver** Alaska, USA
28 J8 **Beaver** Oklahoma, C USA
20 B14 **Beaver** Pennsylvania, NE USA
38 K6 **Beaver** Utah, W USA
8 L9 **Beaver** ≈ British Columbia/Yukon Territory, W Canada
9 S13 **Beaver** ≈ Saskatchewan, C Canada
31 N17 **Beaver City** Nebraska, C USA
8 G6 **Beaver Creek** Yukon Territory, W Canada
33 R14 **Beavercreek** Ohio, N USA
41 S8 **Beaver Creek** ≈ Alaska, USA
28 H3 **Beaver Creek** ≈ Kansas/Nebraska, C USA
30 J5 **Beaver Creek** ≈ Montana/North Dakota, N USA
31 Q14 **Beaver Creek** ≈ Nebraska, C USA
27 Q4 **Beaver Creek** ≈ Texas, SW USA
32 M8 **Beaver Dam** Wisconsin, N USA
32 M8 **Beaver Dam Lake** ◎ Wisconsin, N USA
20 B14 **Beaver Falls** Pennsylvania, NE USA
35 P12 **Beaverhead Mountains** ⛰ Idaho/Montana, NW USA
35 Q12 **Beaverhead River** ≈ Montana, NW USA
67 A25 **Beaver Island** *island* W Falkland Islands
33 P5 **Beaver Island** *island* Michigan, N USA
29 S9 **Beaver Lake** ▣ Arkansas, C USA
9 N13 **Beaverlodge** Alberta, W Canada
20 I8 **Beaver River** ≈ New York, NE USA
28 J8 **Beaver River** ≈ Oklahoma, C USA
20 B13 **Beaver River** ≈ Pennsylvania, NE USA
67 A25 **Beaver Settlement** Beaver Island, W Falkland Islands
Beaver State *see* Oregon
12 H14 **Beaverton** Ontario, S Canada
34 G11 **Beaverton** Oregon, NW USA
158 G12 **Beāwar** Rājasthān, N India
Bebas, Dasht-i *see* Bābūs, Dasht-e
62 L8 **Bebedouro** São Paulo, S Brazil
xl B16 **Bebington** Wirral, NW England, UK
103 I16 **Bebra** Hessen, C Germany
43 W12 **Becal** Campeche, SE Mexico
13 Q11 **Bécancour** ≈ Québec, SE Canada
xxxix Y10 **Beccles** Suffolk, E England, UK
114 L9 **Bečej** *Ger.* Altbetsche, *Hung.* Óbecse, Rácz-Becse; *prev.* Magyar-Becse, Stari Bečej. Serbia, N Yugoslavia
106 I3 **Becerréa** Galicia, NW Spain
76 H7 **Béchar** *prev.* Colomb-Béchar. W Algeria
41 O14 **Becharof Lake** ◎ Alaska, USA
118 H15 **Bechet** *var.* Bechetu. Dolj, SW Romania
Bechetu *see* Bechet
xxxvii U9 **Beckenham** Bromley, SE England, UK
xl K7 **Beckfoot** Cumbria, NW England, UK
xxxvii N10 **Beckhampton** Wiltshire, S England, UK
xxxix P7 **Beckingham** Lincolnshire, E England, UK
xxxix O4 **Beckingham** Nottinghamshire, C England, UK
xxxvi M11 **Beckington** Somerset, SW England, UK
23 R6 **Beckley** West Virginia, NE USA
xxxix U11 **Beck Row** Suffolk, E England, UK
xxxvi F7 **Beckton** Newham, SE England, UK
103 G14 **Beckum** Nordrhein-Westfalen, W Germany
27 X7 **Beckville** Texas, SW USA
37 X4 **Becky Peak** ▲ Nevada, W USA
118 I9 **Beclean** *Hung.* Bethlen; *prev.* Betlen. Bistriţa-Năsăud, N Romania
xxxvi G6 **Becontree** Redbridge, SE England, UK
Bécs *see* Wien
113 H18 **Bečva** *Ger.* Betschau, *Pol.* Beczwa. ≈ E Czech Republic
Beczwa *see* Bečva
xli R11 **Bedale** North Yorkshire, N England, UK
105 P15 **Bédarieux** Hérault, S France
xxxv G6 **Beddgelert** Gwynedd, NW Wales, UK
122 Dd12 **Beddouza, Cap** *headland* W Morocco
82 I13 **Bedelē** W Ethiopia
153 Y8 **Bedel Pass** *Rus.* Pereval Bedel. *pass* China/Kyrgyzstan
Bedel, Pereval *see* Bedel Pass
97 H22 **Beder** Århus, C Denmark
xxxvii S6 **Bedford** Bedfordshire, E England, UK
33 O15 **Bedford** Indiana, N USA
31 U16 **Bedford** Iowa, C USA
22 L4 **Bedford** Kentucky, S USA
20 D15 **Bedford** Pennsylvania, NE USA
23 T6 **Bedford** Virginia, NE USA
xxxix R10 **Bedford Level** *physical region* E England, UK
xxxvii S6 **Bedfordshire** ◐ *county* E England, UK
xli R5 **Bedlington** Northumberland, N England, UK
131 N5 **Bednodem'yanovsk** Penzenskaya Oblast', W Russian Federation
100 N5 **Bedum** Groningen, NE Netherlands
xxxv J14 **Bedwas** Caerphilly, S Wales, UK
xxxviii E15 **Bedworth** Warwickshire, C England, UK
29 V11 **Beebe** Arkansas, C USA
47 T9 **Beef Island** ✕ (Road Town) Tortola, E British Virgin Islands
xli W12 **Beeford** East Riding of Yorkshire, N England, UK
Beehive State *see* Utah
101 L18 **Beek** Limburg, SE Netherlands
101 L18 **Beek** ✕ (Maastricht) Limburg, SE Netherlands
101 K14 **Beek-en-Donk** Noord-Brabant, S Netherlands
xxxvi J14 **Beer** Devon, SW England, UK
144 F13 **Be'ér Menuha** Southern, S Israel
101 D16 **Beernem** West-Vlaanderen, NW Belgium
101 I16 **Beerse** Antwerpen, N Belgium
Beersheba *see* Be'ér Sheva'
144 E11 **Be'ér Sheva'** *var.* Beersheba, *Ar.* Bir es Saba. Southern, S Israel
100 J13 **Beesd** Gelderland, C Netherlands
101 M16 **Beesel** Limburg, SE Netherlands
85 J21 **Beestekraal** North-West, N South Africa
xxxix N8 **Beeston** Nottinghamshire, C England, UK
xliii K24 **Beeswing** Dumfries and Galloway, SW Scotland, UK
xli N11 **Beetham** Cumbria, NW England, UK
204 J7 **Beethoven Peninsula** *peninsula* Alexander Island, Antarctica
Beetstersweach *see* Beetsterzwaag
100 M6 **Beetsterzwaag** *Fris.* Beetstersweach. Friesland, N Netherlands
27 S13 **Beeville** Texas, SW USA
81 J18 **Befale** Equateur, NW Zaire
Befandriana *see* Befandriana Avaratra
180 J3 **Befandriana Avaratra** *var.* Befandriana, Befandriana Nord. Mahajanga, NW Madagascar
Befandriana Nord *see* Befandriana Avaratra
81 K18 **Befori** Equateur, N Zaire
180 I7 **Befotaka** Fianarantsoa, S Madagascar
191 R11 **Bega** New South Wales, SE Australia
104 G5 **Bégard** Côtes d'Armor, NW France
114 M9 **Begejski Kanal** *canal* NE Yugoslavia
151 V9 **Begen'** Semipalatinsk, E Kazakhstan
96 G13 **Begna** ≈ S Norway
Begoml' *see* Byahoml'
Begovat *see* Bekobod
xxxv J9 **Beguildy** Powys, C Wales, UK
159 Q13 **Begusarai** Bihār, NE India
149 R9 **Behābād** Yazd, C Iran
Behagle *see* Laï
57 Z10 **Béhague, Pointe** *headland* E French Guiana
Behar *see* Bihār
148 M10 **Behbahān** *var.* Behbehān. Khūzestān, SW Iran
Behbehān *see* Behbahān
46 G3 **Behring Point** Andros Island, W Bahamas
149 P4 **Behshahr** *prev.* Ashraf. Māzandarān, N Iran
169 V6 **Bei'an** Heilongjiang, NE China
Beibunar *see* Sredishte
Beibu Wan *see* Tongking, Gulf of
Beida *see* Al Bayḑā'
82 H13 **Beigi** W Ethiopia
166 L16 **Beihai** Guangxi Zhuangzu Zizhiqu, S China
165 Q10 **Bei Hulsan Hu** ◎ C China
167 N13 **Bei Jiang** ≈ S China
167 O2 **Beijing** *var.* Pei-ching, *Eng.* Peking; *prev.* Pei-p'ing. *country/municipality capital* (China) Beijing Shi, E China
167 P2 **Beijing** ✕ Beijing Shi, E China
Beijing *see* Beijing Shi
167 O2 **Beijing Shi** *var.* Beijing, Jing, Pei-ching, *Eng.* Peking; *prev.* Pei-p'ing. ◐ *municipality* E China
78 G8 **Beïla** Trarza, W Mauritania
100 N7 **Beilen** Drenthe, NE Netherlands
166 L15 **Beiliu** Guangxi Zhuangzu Zizhiqu, S China
165 O12 **Beilu He** ≈ W China
Beilul *see* Beylul
xliii K15 **Beinn A'Ghlo** ▲ C Scotland, UK
xliii K15 **Beinn Dearg** ▲ C Scotland, UK
xlii H10 **Beinn Dearg** ▲ N Scotland, UK
Beinn MacDuibh *see* Ben Macdui
166 I12 **Beipan Jiang** ≈ S China
169 T12 **Beipiao** Liaoning, NE China
85 N17 **Beira** Sofala, C Mozambique
85 N17 **Beira** ✕ Sofala, C Mozambique
106 I7 **Beira Alta** *former province* N Portugal
106 H9 **Beira Baixa** *former province* C Portugal
106 G8 **Beira Litoral** *former province* N Portugal
Beirut *see* Beyrouth
Beisān *see* Bet She'an
9 Q16 **Beiseker** Alberta, SW Canada
85 K19 **Beitbridge** Matabeleland South, S Zimbabwe
xliii I21 **Beith** North Ayrshire, W Scotland, UK
118 G10 **Beiuş** *Hung.* Belényes. Bihor, NW Romania
169 U12 **Beizhen** Liaoning, NE China
106 H12 **Beja** *anc.* Pax Julia. Beja, SE Portugal
106 G13 **Beja** ◐ *district* S Portugal
76 M5 **Béja** *var.* Bājah. N Tunisia
123 Ii11 **Béjaïa** *var.* Bejaïa, *Fr.* Bougie; *anc.* Saldae. NE Algeria
106 K8 **Béjar** Castilla-León, N Spain
Bejraburi *see* Phetchaburi
Bekaa Valley *see* El Beqaa
Bekabad *see* Bekobod
Békás *see* Bicaz
174 J14 **Bekasi** Jawa, C Indonesia
Bek-Budi *see* Qarshi
152 A8 **Bekdash** Balkanskiy Velayat, NW Turkmenistan
153 T10 **Bek-Dzhar** Oshskaya Oblast', SW Kyrgyzstan
113 N24 **Békés** *Rom.* Bichiş. Békés, SE Hungary
113 M24 **Békés** *off.* Békés Megye. ◐ *county* SE Hungary
113 M24 **Békéscsaba** *Rom.* Bichiş-Ciaba. Békés, SE Hungary
145 S2 **Bēkhma** E Iraq
180 H7 **Bekily** Toliara, S Madagascar
172 Qq7 **Bekkai** Hokkaidō, NE Japan
153 Q11 **Bekobod** *Rus.* Bekabad; *prev.* Begovat. Toshkent Wiloyati, E Uzbekistan
131 O7 **Bekovo** Penzenskaya Oblast', W Russian Federation
Bél *see* Beliu
158 M13 **Bela** Uttar Pradesh, N India
155 N15 **Bela** Baluchistān, SW Pakistan
81 F15 **Bélabo** Est, C Cameroon
114 N10 **Bela Crkva** *Ger.* Weisskirchen, *Hung.* Fehértemplom. Serbia, W Yugoslavia
181 Y16 **Bel Air** *var.* Rivière Sèche. E Mauritius
106 L12 **Belalcázar** Andalucía, S Spain
115 P15 **Bela Palanka** Serbia, SE Yugoslavia
Belarus *see* Belorussia
Belau *see* Palau
61 H21 **Bela Vista** Mato Grosso do Sul, SW Brazil
85 L21 **Bela Vista** Maputo, S Mozambique
173 Ff4 **Belawan** Sumatera, W Indonesia
Bēla Woda *see* Weisswasser
131 U4 **Belaya** ≈ W Russian Federation
127 N7 **Belaya Gora** Respublika Sakha (Yakutiya), NE Russian Federation
130 M11 **Belaya Kalitiva** Rostovskaya Oblast', SW Russian Federation
129 R14 **Belaya Kholunitsa** Kirovskaya Oblast', NW Russian Federation
Belaya Tserkov' *see* Bila Tserkva
79 V11 **Belbédji** Zinder, S Niger
xxxviii B16 **Belbroughton** Worcestershire, W England, UK
112 K13 **Bełchatów** *var.* Belchatow. Piotrków, C Poland
Belcher, Îles *see* Belcher Islands
10 H7 **Belcher Islands** *Fr.* Îles Belcher. *island group* Northwest Territories, SE Canada
xxxix R5 **Belchford** Lincolnshire, E England, UK
107 S6 **Belchite** Aragón, NE Spain
xliv E8 **Belclare** Galway, W Ireland
xliv H5 **Belcoo** Fermanagh, W Northern Ireland, UK
31 O2 **Belcourt** North Dakota, N USA
xliv D5 **Belderg** Mayo, NW Ireland
33 P9 **Belding** Michigan, N USA
131 U5 **Belebey** Respublika Bashkortostan, W Russian Federation
83 N16 **Beledweyne** *var.* Belet Huen, *It.* Belet Uen. Hiiraan, C Somalia
152 B10 **Belek** Balkanskiy Velayat, W Turkmenistan
60 L12 **Belém** *var.* Pará. *state capital* Pará, N Brazil
67 I14 **Belém Ridge** *undersea feature* C Atlantic Ocean
39 R12 **Belen** New Mexico, SW USA
64 I7 **Belén** Catamarca, NW Argentina
56 G9 **Belén** Boyacá, C Colombia
44 J11 **Belén** Rivas, SW Nicaragua
64 O5 **Belén** Concepción, C Paraguay
63 D16 **Belén** Salto, N Uruguay
63 D20 **Belén de Escobar** Buenos Aires, E Argentina
116 J7 **Belene** Loveshka Oblast, N Bulgaria
116 J7 **Belene, Ostrov** *island* N Bulgaria
45 R15 **Belén, Río** ≈ C Panama
Belényes *see* Beiuş
197 G4 **Belep, Îles** *island group* W New Caledonia
106 H3 **Belesar, Embalse de** ▣ NW Spain
Belet Huen/Belet Uen *see* Beledweyne
130 J5 **Belëv** Tul'skaya Oblast', W Russian Federation
xliv L4 **Belfast** *Ir.* Béal Feirste. *political division capital* E Northern Ireland, UK
21 R7 **Belfast** Maine, NE USA
xliv L4 **Belfast International** ✕ Antrim, E Northern Ireland, UK
xliv L4 **Belfast City** ✕ Belfast City, E Northern Ireland, UK
xliv L4 **Belfast City** ◐ *district* E Northern Ireland, UK
xliv M4 **Belfast Lough** *Ir.* Loch Lao. *inlet* E Northern Ireland, UK
30 K5 **Belfield** North Dakota, N USA
xli Q2 **Belford** Northumberland, N England, UK
105 U7 **Belfort** Territoire-de-Belfort, E France
Belgard *see* Białogard
161 E17 **Belgaum** Karnātaka, W India
Belgian Congo *see* Zaire
205 T3 **Belgica Mountains** ⛰ Antarctica
België/Belgique *see* Belgium
101 F20 **Belgium** *off.* Kingdom of Belgium, *Dut.* België, *Fr.* Belgique. ◆ *monarchy* NW Europe
130 J8 **Belgorod** Belgorodskaya Oblast', W Russian Federation
Belgorod-Dnestrovskiy *see* Bilhorod-Dnistrovs'kyy
130 J8 **Belgorodskaya Oblast'** ◐ *province* W Russian Federation
Belgrad *see* Beograd
31 T8 **Belgrade** Minnesota, N USA
35 S11 **Belgrade** Montana, NW USA
Belgrade *see* Beograd
205 N5 **Belgrano II** *Argentinian research station* Antarctica
23 X9 **Belhaven** North Carolina, SE USA
109 I23 **Belice** *anc.* Hypsas. ≈ Sicilia, Italy, C Mediterranean Sea
Belice *see* Belize/Belize City
115 M16 **Beli Drim** *Alb.* Drini i Bardhë. ≈ Albania/Yugoslavia
Beligrad *see* Berat
196 C8 **Beliliou** *prev.* Peleliu. *island* S Palau
116 L8 **Beli Lom, Yazovir** ▣ NE Bulgaria
114 I8 **Beli Manastir** *Hung.* Pélmonostor; *prev.* Monostor. Osijek-Baranja, NE Croatia
104 J13 **Bélin-Béliet** Gironde, SW France
81 F17 **Bélinga** Ogooué-Ivindo, NE Gabon
23 S4 **Belington** West Virginia, NE USA
131 O6 **Belinskiy** Penzenskaya Oblast', W Russian Federation
174 Ii9 **Belinyu** Pulau Bangka, W Indonesia
174 Jj11 **Belitung, Pulau** *island* W Indonesia
118 F10 **Beliu** *Hung.* Bél. Arad, W Romania
116 I9 **Beli Vit** ≈ NW Bulgaria
44 G2 **Belize** *Sp.* Belice; *prev.* British Honduras, Colony of Belize. ◆ *commonwealth republic* Central America
44 F2 **Belize** *Sp.* Belice. ◐ *district* NE Belize
44 G2 **Belize** ≈ Belize/Guatemala
Belize *see* Belize City
44 G2 **Belize City** *var.* Belize, *Sp.* Belice. Belize, NE Belize
44 G2 **Belize City** ✕ Belize, NE Belize
Beljak *see* Villach
41 N16 **Belkofski** Alaska, USA
126 L4 **Bel'kovskiy, Ostrov** *island* Novosibirskiye Ostrova, NE Russian Federation
12 J8 **Bell** ≈ Québec, SE Canada
8 J15 **Bella Bella** British Columbia, SW Canada
104 M10 **Bellac** Haute-Vienne, C France
8 K15 **Bella Coola** British Columbia, SW Canada
xliv D6 **Bellacorick** Mayo, NW Ireland
xliv K3 **Bellaghy** Magherafelt, C Northern Ireland, UK
108 D6 **Bellagio** Lombardia, N Italy
33 P6 **Bellaire** Michigan, N USA
xliv I7 **Bellananagh** *var.* Ballinagh. Cavan, N Ireland
xliv G8 **Bellaneeny** Roscommon, C Ireland
108 D6 **Bellano** Lombardia, N Italy
161 G17 **Bellary** *var.* Ballari. Karnātaka, S India
191 S5 **Bellata** New South Wales, SE Australia
63 D16 **Bella Unión** Artigas, N Uruguay
xliv E7 **Bellavary** Mayo, NW Ireland
63 C14 **Bella Vista** Corrientes, NE Argentina
64 J7 **Bella Vista** Tucumán, N Argentina
64 P4 **Bella Vista** Amambay, C Paraguay
58 B10 **Bellavista** Cajamarca, N Peru
58 D11 **Bellavista** San Martín, N Peru
191 U6 **Bellbrook** New South Wales, SE Australia
29 V5 **Belle** Missouri, C USA
23 Q5 **Belle** West Virginia, NE USA
xliv h5 **Belleek** Fermanagh, W Northern Ireland, UK
33 R13 **Bellefontaine** Ohio, N USA
20 F14 **Bellefonte** Pennsylvania, NE USA
30 J9 **Belle Fourche** South Dakota, N USA
30 J9 **Belle Fourche Reservoir** ▣ South Dakota, N USA
30 K9 **Belle Fourche River** ≈ South Dakota/Wyoming, N USA
105 S10 **Bellegarde-sur-Valserine** Ain, E France
25 Y14 **Belle Glade** Florida, SE USA
104 G8 **Belle Île** *island* NW France
11 T9 **Belle Isle** *island* Belle Isle, Newfoundland and Labrador, E Canada
11 S10 **Belle Isle, Strait of** *strait* Newfoundland and Labrador, E Canada
Bellenz *see* Bellinzona
31 W14 **Belle Plaine** Iowa, C USA
31 V9 **Belle Plaine** Minnesota, N USA
12 I9 **Belleterre** Québec, SE Canada
12 J15 **Belleville** Ontario, SE Canada
105 R10 **Belleville** Rhône, E France
32 K15 **Belleville** Illinois, N USA
29 N3 **Belleville** Kansas, C USA
31 Z13 **Bellevue** Iowa, C USA
31 S15 **Bellevue** Nebraska, C USA
33 S11 **Bellevue** Ohio, N USA
27 S5 **Bellevue** Texas, SW USA
34 H8 **Bellevue** Washington, NW USA
57 Y11 **Bellevue de l'Inini, Montagnes** ⛰ S French Guiana
105 S11 **Belley** Ain, E France
Bellin *see* Kangirsuk
191 V6 **Bellingen** New South Wales, SE Australia
xli P5 **Bellingham** Northumberland, N England, UK
34 H6 **Bellingham** Washington, NW USA
Belling Hausen Mulde *see* Southeast Pacific Basin
204 H2 **Bellingshausen** *Russian research station* South Shetland Islands, Antarctica
Bellingshausen *see* Motu One
Bellingshausen Abyssal Plain *see* Bellingshausen Plain
200 N16 **Bellingshausen Plain** *var.* Bellingshausen Abyssal Plain. *undersea feature* SE Pacific Ocean
204 I8 **Bellingshausen Sea** *sea* Antarctica
100 P6 **Bellingwolde** Groningen, NE Netherlands
110 H11 **Bellinzona** *Ger.* Bellenz. Ticino, S Switzerland
27 T8 **Bellmead** Texas, SW USA
56 E8 **Bello** Antioquia, W Colombia
xliii F22 **Bellochantuy** Argyll and Bute, W Scotland, UK
63 B21 **Bellocq** Buenos Aires, E Argentina
Bello Horizonte *see* Belo Horizonte
195 W17 **Bellona** *var.* Mungiki. *island* S Solomon Islands
Bellovacum *see* Beauvais
190 D7 **Bell, Point** *headland* South Australia
22 F9 **Bells** Tennessee, S USA
27 U5 **Bells** Texas, SW USA
xli Q2 **Bellshill** Northumberland, N England, UK
xliii K20 **Bellshill** North Lanarkshire, C Scotland, UK
94 N3 **Bellsund** *inlet* SW Svalbard
108 H6 **Belluno** Veneto, NE Italy
64 L11 **Bell Ville** Córdoba, C Argentina
85 E26 **Bellville** Western Cape, SW South Africa
27 U11 **Bellville** Texas, SW USA
106 L12 **Belmez** Andalucía, S Spain
31 V12 **Belmond** Iowa, C USA
xli O15 **Belmont** Lancashire, NW England, UK
xlii J1 **Belmont** Shetland Islands, NE Scotland, UK
20 E11 **Belmont** New York, NE USA
23 R10 **Belmont** North Carolina, SE USA
61 O18 **Belmonte** Bahia, E Brazil
106 I8 **Belmonte** Castelo Branco, C Portugal
107 P10 **Belmonte** Castilla-La Mancha, C Spain
44 G2 **Belmopan** ● (Belize) Cayo, C Belize
xliv C5 **Belmullet** *Ir.* Béal an Mhuirhead. Mayo, W Ireland
126 Mm15 **Belogorsk** Amurskaya Oblast', SE Russian Federation
Belogorsk *see* Bilohirs'k
116 F7 **Belogradchik** Oblast Montana, NW Bulgaria
180 H8 **Beloha** Toliara, S Madagascar
61 M20 **Belo Horizonte** *prev.* Bello Horizonte. *state capital* Minas Gerais, SE Brazil
28 M3 **Beloit** Kansas, C USA
32 L9 **Beloit** Wisconsin, N USA
Belokorovichi *see* Bilokorovychi
126 H15 **Belokurikha** Altayskiy Kray, S Russian Federation
128 J8 **Belomorsk** Respublika Kareliya, NW Russian Federation
128 J8 **Belomorsko-Baltiyskiy Kanal** *Eng.* White Sea-Baltic Canal, White Sea Canal. *canal* NW Russian Federation
159 V15 **Belonia** Tripura, NE India
Belopol'ye *see* Bilopillya
107 O4 **Belorado** Castilla-León, N Spain
130 L14 **Belorechensk** Krasnodarskiy Kray, SW Russian Federation
131 W5 **Beloretsk** Respublika Bashkortostan, W Russian Federation
121 H16 **Belorussia** *off.* Republic of Belarus, *var.* Belarus, *Latv.* Baltkrievija; *prev.* Belorussian SSR, *Rus.* Belorusskaya SSR. ◆ *republic* E Europe
Belorussian SSR *see* Belorussia
Belorusskaya Gryada *see* Byelaruskaya Hrada
Belorusskaya SSR *see* Belorussia
Beloshchel'ye *see* Nar'yan-Mar
116 N8 **Beloslav** Varnenska Oblast, NE Bulgaria
Belostok *see* Białystok
180 H5 **Belo Tsiribihina** *var.* Belo-sur-Tsiribihina. Toliara, W Madagascar
Belovár *see* Bjelovar
Belovezhskaya Pushcha *see* Białowieska, Puszcza/Byelavyezhskaya Pushcha
116 H10 **Belovo** Plovdivska Oblast, W Bulgaria
126 H14 **Belovo** Kemerovskaya Oblast', S Russian Federation
Belovodsk *see* Bilovods'k
125 Ff9 **Beloyarskiy** Khanty-Mansiyskiy Avtonomnyy Okrug, N Russian Federation
128 K7 **Beloye More** *Eng.* White Sea. *sea* NW Russian Federation
128 K13 **Beloye, Ozero** ◎ NW Russian Federation
116 J10 **Belozem** Plovdivska Oblast, C Bulgaria
128 K13 **Belozërsk** Vologodskaya Oblast', NW Russian Federation
101 E20 **Belœil** Hainaut, SW Belgium
110 D8 **Belp** Bern, W Switzerland
110 D8 **Belp** ✕ (Bern) Bern, C Switzerland
109 L24 **Belpasso** Sicilia, Italy, C Mediterranean Sea
xxxviii M7 **Belper** Derbyshire, C England, UK
33 U14 **Belpre** Ohio, N USA
xli Q5 **Belsay** Northumberland, N England, UK
100 M8 **Belterwijde** ◎ N Netherlands
xxxix Y10 **Belton** Norfolk, E England, UK
xxxix O4 **Belton** North Lincolnshire, N England, UK
29 R4 **Belton** Missouri, C USA
23 P11 **Belton** South Carolina, SE USA
27 T9 **Belton** Texas, SW USA
27 S9 **Belton Lake** ▣ Texas, SW USA
Bel'tsy *see* Bălţi
xliv I6 **Belturbet** *Ir.* Béal Tairbirt. Cavan, N Ireland
Beluchistan *see* Baluchistān
151 Z9 **Belukha, Gora** ▲ Kazakhstan/Russian Federation
109 M20 **Belvedere Marittimo** Calabria, SW Italy
32 L10 **Belvidere** Illinois, N USA
20 J14 **Belvidere** New Jersey, NE USA
xxxix P8 **Belvoir** Leicestershire, C England, UK
Bely *see* Belyy
131 V8 **Belyayevka** Orenburgskaya Oblast', W Russian Federation
Belynichi *see* Byalynichy
128 H17 **Belyy** *var.* Bely, Beyj. Tverskaya Oblast', W Russian Federation
130 I6 **Belyye Berega** Bryanskaya Oblast', W Russian Federation
126 H5 **Belyy, Ostrov** *island* N Russian Federation
126 H12 **Belyy Yar** Tomskaya Oblast', C Russian Federation
102 N13 **Belzig** Brandenburg, NE Germany
24 K4 **Belzoni** Mississippi, S USA
180 H4 **Bemaraha** *var.* Plateau du Bemaraha. ⛰ W Madagascar
84 B10 **Bembe** Uíge, NW Angola
79 S14 **Bembèrèkè** *var.* Bimbéréké. N Benin
106 K12 **Bembézar** ≈ SW Spain
106 J3 **Bembibre** Castilla-León, N Spain
xxxvii Q14 **Bembridge** Isle of Wight, S England, UK
31 T4 **Bemidji** Minnesota, N USA
100 L12 **Bemmel** Gelderland, SE Netherlands
xli X11 **Bempton** East Riding of Yorkshire, N England, UK
176 U11 **Bemu** Pulau Seram, E Indonesia
Benāb *see* Bonāb
107 T5 **Benabarre** *var.* Benavarn. Aragón, NE Spain
Benaco *see* Garda, Lago di
81 L20 **Bena-Dibele** Kasai Oriental, C Zaire
107 R9 **Benageber, Embalse de** ▣ E Spain
191 O11 **Benalla** Victoria, SE Australia
106 M14 **Benamejí** Andalucía, S Spain
Benares *see* Vārānasi
xlii H7 **Ben Arkle** ▲ NW Scotland, UK
xlii G13 **Ben Attow** ▲ NW Scotland, UK
Benavarn *see* Benabarre
106 F10 **Benavente** Santarém, C Portugal
106 K5 **Benavente** Castilla-León, N Spain
27 S15 **Benavides** Texas, SW USA
xlii B12 **Benbecula** *island* NW Scotland, UK
xliii K17 **Ben Chonzie** ▲ C Scotland, UK
Bencovazzo *see* Benkovac
xliii G17 **Ben Cruachan** ▲ W Scotland, UK
34 H13 **Bend** Oregon, NW USA
190 K7 **Benda Range** ⛰ South Australia
191 T6 **Bendemeer** New South Wales, SE Australia
Bender *see* Tighina
Bender Beila/Bender Beyla *see* Bandarbeyla
Bender Cassim/Bender Qaasim *see* Boosaaso
Bendery *see* Tighina
xliii G17 **Benderloch** Argyll and Bute, W Scotland, UK
191 N11 **Bendigo** Victoria, SE Australia
xliii I17 **Ben Dórain** ▲ W Scotland, UK
120 E10 **Bēne** Dobele, SW Latvia
100 K13 **Beneden-Leeuwen** Gelderland, C Netherlands
103 L24 **Benediktenwand** ▲ S Germany
Benemérita de San Cristóbal *see* San Cristóbal
79 N12 **Bénéna** Ségou, S Mali
180 I7 **Benenitra** Toliara, S Madagascar
Beneschau *see* Benešov
Beneški Zaliv *see* Venice, Gulf of
113 D17 **Benešov** *Ger.* Beneschau. Střední Čechy, W Czech Republic
126 Ll3 **Benetta, Ostrov** *island* Novosibirskiye Ostrova, NE Russian Federation
109 L17 **Benevento** *anc.* Beneventum, Malventum. Campania, S Italy
Beneventum *see* Benevento
181 S3 **Bengal, Bay of** *bay* N Indian Ocean
81 M17 **Bengamisa** Haut-Zaïre, N Zaire
Bengasi *see* Banghāzī
174 Ll15 **Bengawan, Sungai** ≈ Jawa, S Indonesia
Bengazi *see* Banghāzī
167 P7 **Bengbu** *var.* Peng-pu. Anhui, E China
34 L9 **Benge** Washington, NW USA
Benghazi *see* Banghāzī
174 H7 **Bengkalis** Pulau Bengkalis, W Indonesia
174 H6 **Bengkalis, Pulau** *island* W Indonesia
174 Kk7 **Bengkayang** Borneo, C Indonesia
Bengkoelen/Bengkoeloe *see* Bengkulu
174 H12 **Bengkulu** *prev.* Bengkoeloe, Benkoelen, Benkulen. Sumatera, W Indonesia
174 H11 **Bengkulu** *off.* Propinsi Bengkulu; *prev.* Bengkoelen, Benkoelen, Benkulen. ◐ *province* W Indonesia
84 A11 **Bengo** ◐ *province* W Angola
97 J16 **Bengtsfors** Älvsborg, S Sweden
84 B13 **Benguela** *var.* Benguella. Benguela, W Angola
85 A14 **Benguela** ◐ *province* W Angola
Benguella *see* Benguela
Bengweulu, Lake *see* Bangweulu, Lake
124 Qq15 **Benha** *var.* Banhā. N Egypt
198 G6 **Benham Seamount** *undersea feature* W Philippine Sea
xlii I8 **Ben Hee** ▲ NW Scotland, UK
xlii I7 **Ben Hope** ▲ N Scotland, UK
81 P18 **Beni** Nord Kivu, NE Zaire
59 L15 **Beni** *var.* El Beni. ◐ *department* N Bolivia
76 H8 **Beni Abbès** W Algeria
107 T8 **Benicarló** País Valenciano, E Spain
107 T9 **Benicasim** País Valenciano, E Spain
107 T12 **Benidorm** País Valenciano, SE Spain
77 W9 **Beni Mazâr** *var.* Banī Mazār. C Egypt
122 F12 **Beni-Mellal** C Morocco
79 R14 **Benin** *off.* Republic of Benin; *prev.* Dahomey. ◆ *republic* W Africa
79 S17 **Benin, Bight of** *gulf* W Africa
79 U16 **Benin City** Edo, SW Nigeria
xxxix S7 **Benington** Lincolnshire, E England, UK
59 K16 **Beni, Río** ≈ N Bolivia
123 Gg11 **Beni Saf** *var.* Beni-Saf. NW Algeria
107 T11 **Benissa** País Valenciano, E Spain
124 Qq17 **Beni Suef** *var.* Banī Suwayf. N Egypt
9 V15 **Benito** Manitoba, S Canada
Benito *see* Uolo, Río
63 C23 **Benito Juárez** Buenos Aires, E Argentina
43 P14 **Benito Juaréz Internacional** ✕ (México) México, S Mexico
27 P5 **Benjamin** Texas, SW USA
60 B13 **Benjamin Constant** Amazonas, N Brazil
42 F4 **Benjamín Hill** Sonora, NW Mexico
65 F19 **Benjamín, Isla** *island* Archipiélago de los Chonos, S Chile
172 N5 **Benkei-misaki** *headland* Hokkaidō, NE Japan
30 L17 **Benkelman** Nebraska, C USA
xlii J8 **Ben Klibreck** ▲ N Scotland, UK
Benkoelen *see* Bengkulu
114 D13 **Benkovac** *It.* Bencovazzo. Zadar-Knin, S Croatia
Benkulen *see* Bengkulu
xliii J17 **Ben Lawers** ▲ C Scotland, UK
xxxv F4 **Benllech** Isle of Anglesey, NW Wales, UK
xlii I7 **Ben Loyal** ▲ NW Scotland, UK
xliii H17 **Ben Lui** ▲ C Scotland, UK
xliii L14 **Ben Macdui** *var.* Beinn MacDuibh. ▲ C Scotland, UK
xliii I17 **Ben More** ▲ C Scotland, UK
xliii E17 **Ben More** ▲ W Scotland, UK
xlii H8 **Ben More Assynt** ▲ N Scotland, UK
193 E20 **Benmore, Lake** ◎ South Island, NZ
100 L12 **Bennekom** Gelderland, SE Netherlands
23 T11 **Bennettsville** South Carolina, SE USA
xliii H15 **Ben Nevis** ▲ N Scotland, UK
192 M9 **Benneydale** Waikato, North Island, NZ
Bennichab *see* Bennichchâb
78 H8 **Bennichchâb** *var.* Bennichab. Inchiri, W Mauritania
20 L10 **Bennington** Vermont, NE USA
193 E20 **Ben Ohau Range** ⛰ South Island, NZ
85 J21 **Benoni** Gauteng, NE South Africa
180 J2 **Be, Nosy** *var.* Nossi-Bé. *island* NW Madagascar
Bénoué *see* Benue
44 F2 **Benque Viejo del Carmen** Cayo, W Belize
xlii M12 **Ben Rinnes** ▲ N Scotland, UK
103 G19 **Bensheim** Hessen, W Germany
xxxvii Q8 **Benson** Oxfordshire, C England, UK
39 N16 **Benson** Arizona, SW USA
31 S8 **Benson** Minnesota, N USA
23 U10 **Benson** North Carolina, SE USA
175 Pp14 **Benteng** Pulau Selayar, C Indonesia
85 A14 **Bentiaba** Namibe, SW Angola
189 T4 **Bentinck Island** *island* Wellesley Islands, Queensland, N Australia
82 E13 **Bentiu** Wahda, S Sudan
144 G8 **Bent Jbaïl** *var.* Bint Jubayl. S Lebanon
xli T15 **Bentley** Doncaster, N England, UK
xxxvii R11 **Bentley** Hampshire, S England, UK
9 Q15 **Bentley** Alberta, SW Canada
63 I15 **Bento Gonçalves** Rio Grande do Sul, S Brazil
29 Y7 **Benton** Arkansas, C USA
32 L16 **Benton** Illinois, N USA
22 H7 **Benton** Kentucky, S USA
24 G5 **Benton** Louisiana, S USA
29 U12 **Benton** Missouri, C USA
22 M10 **Benton** Tennessee, S USA
33 O10 **Benton Harbor** Michigan, N USA
29 S9 **Bentonville** Arkansas, C USA
xliii M23 **Bentpath** Dumfries and Galloway, SW Scotland, UK
79 V16 **Benue** ◐ *state* SE Nigeria
80 F13 **Benue** *Fr.* Bénoué. ≈ Cameroon/Nigeria
174 Hh6 **Benut** Johor, Peninsular Malaysia
xliii I18 **Ben Venue** ▲ C Scotland, UK
xliii J18 **Ben Vorlich** ▲ C Scotland, UK
xxxix S10 **Benwick** Cambridgeshire, E England, UK
xlii I11 **Ben Wyvis** ▲ NW Scotland, UK
169 V12 **Benxi** *prev.* Pen-ch'i, Penhsihu, Penki. Liaoning, NE China
Benyakoni *see* Byenyakoni
114 K10 **Beočin** Serbia, N Yugoslavia
Beodericsworth *see* Bury St Edmunds
114 M11 **Beograd** *Eng.* Belgrade, *Ger.* Belgrad; *anc.* Singidunum. ● (Yugoslavia) Serbia, N Yugoslavia
114 L11 **Beograd** *Eng.* Belgrade. ✕ Serbia, N Yugoslavia
78 M16 **Béoumi** C Ivory Coast
37 V3 **Beowawe** Nevada, W USA
176 Ww8 **Bepondi, Pulau** *see* Bepondi, Pulau
170 D13 **Beppu** Ōita, Kyūshū, SW Japan
170 Dd14 **Beppu-wan** *bay* SW Japan
197 H15 **Beqa** *prev.* Mbengga. *island* W Fiji
Beqa Barrier Reef *see* Kavukavu Reef
47 Y14 **Bequia** *island* C Saint Vincent and the Grenadines
115 L16 **Berane** *prev.* Ivangrad. Montenegro, SW Yugoslavia
115 L21 **Berat** *var.* Berati, *SCr.* Beligrad. Berat, C Albania
115 L21 **Berat** ◐ *district* C Albania
Berătău *see* Berettyó
Berati *see* Berat
Beraun *see* Berounka, Czech Republic
Beraun *see* Beroun, Czech Republic
175 O6 **Berau, Sungai** ≈ Borneo, N Indonesia
176 V10 **Berau, Teluk** *var.* MacCluer Gulf. *bay* Irian Jaya, E Indonesia
82 G8 **Berber** River Nile, NE Sudan
82 N12 **Berbera** Woqooyi Galbeed, NW Somalia
81 H16 **Berbérati** Mambéré-Kadéï, SW Central African Republic
Berberia, Cabo de *see* Barbaria, Cap de
57 T9 **Berbice River** ≈ NE Guyana
Berchid *see* Berrechid
105 N2 **Berck-Plage** Pas-de-Calais, N France
27 T13 **Berclair** Texas, SW USA
119 W10 **Berda** ≈ SE Ukraine
Berdichev *see* Berdychiv
126 Ll11 **Berdigestyakh** Respublika Sakha (Yakutiya), NE Russian Federation
126 H14 **Berdsk** Novosibirskaya Oblast', C Russian Federation
119 W10 **Berdyans'k** *Rus.* Berdyansk; *prev.* Osipenko. Zaporiz'ka Oblast', SE Ukraine
119 W10 **Berdyans'ka Kosa** *spit* SE Ukraine
119 V10 **Berdyans'ka Zatoka** *gulf* S Ukraine
119 N5 **Berdychiv** *Rus.* Berdichev. Zhytomyrs'ka Oblast', N Ukraine
22 M6 **Berea** Kentucky, S USA
xxxvi F15 **Bere Alston** Devon, SW England, UK
xxxvi F15 **Bere Ferrers** Devon, SW England, UK
Beregovo/Beregszász *see* Berehove
118 G8 **Berehove** *Cz.* Berehovo, *Hung.* Beregszász, *Rus.* Beregovo. Zakarpats'ka Oblast', W Ukraine
Berehovo *see* Berehove
194 J15 **Bereina** Central, S PNG
47 O12 **Berekua** S Dominica
79 O16 **Berekum** W Ghana
77 Y11 **Berenice** *var.* Mînâ Baranîs. SE Egypt
15 L14 **Berens** ≈ Manitoba/Ontario, C Canada
9 X14 **Berens River** Manitoba, C Canada
xxxvi M14 **Bere Regis** Dorset, S England, UK
31 R12 **Beresford** South Dakota, N USA
118 J4 **Berestechko** Volyns'ka Oblast', NW Ukraine
118 M11 **Bereşti** Galaţi, E Romania
119 U6 **Berestova** ≈ E Ukraine
Beretău *see* Berettyó
113 N23 **Berettyó** *Rom.* Barcău; *prev.* Berătău, Beretău. ≈ Hungary/Romania
113 N23 **Berettyóújfalu** Hajdú-Bihar, E Hungary
Berëza/Bereza Kartuska *see* Byaroza
119 Q4 **Berezan'** Kyyivs'ka Oblast', N Ukraine

◆ Country
● Country Capital
◇ Dependent Territory
○ Dependent Territory Capital
◐ Administrative Region
✕ International Airport
▲ Mountain
⛰ Mountain Range
Volcano
≈ River
◎ Lake
▣ Reservoir

Berezanka – Bin Ghanīmah, Jabal

119 Q10 Berezanka Mykolayivs'ka Oblast', S Ukraine
118 J6 Berezhany Pol. Brzeżany. Ternopil's'ka Oblast', W Ukraine
Berezina see Byerezino
Berezino see Byerazino
119 P10 Berezivka Rus. Berezovka. Odes'ka Oblast', SW Ukraine
119 Q2 Berezna Chernihivs'ka Oblast', NE Ukraine
118 L3 Berezne Rivnens'ka Oblast', NW Ukraine
119 R9 Bereznehuvate Mykolayivs'ka Oblast', S Ukraine
129 N10 Bereznik Arkhangel'skaya Oblast', NW Russian Federation
129 U13 Berezniki Permskaya Oblast', NW Russian Federation
Berezovka see Berezivka
125 Ff9 Berezovo Khanty-Mansiyskiy Avtonomnyy Okrug, N Russian Federation
131 O9 Berezovskaya Volgogradskaya Oblast', SW Russian Federation
126 H14 Berezovskiy Kemerovskaya Oblast', S Russian Federation
127 N14 Berezovyy Khabarovskiy Kray, E Russian Federation
85 E25 Berg ≈ W South Africa
Berg see Berg bei Rohrbach
107 V4 Berga Cataluña, NE Spain
97 N20 Berga Kalmar, S Sweden
142 B13 Bergama İzmir, W Turkey
108 E7 Bergamo anc. Bergomum. Lombardia, N Italy
107 P3 Bergara País Vasco, N Spain
111 S3 Berg bei Rohrbach var. Berg. Oberösterreich, N Austria
195 O11 Bergberg ≈ New Britain, C Papau New Guinea
102 I11 Bergen Mecklenburg-Vorpommern, NE Germany
103 O16 Bergen Niedersachsen, NW Germany
100 H8 Bergen Noord-Holland, NW Netherlands
96 C13 Bergen Hordaland, S Norway
Bergen see Mons
57 W9 Berg en Dal Brokopondo, C Surinam
101 G15 Bergen op Zoom Noord-Brabant, S Netherlands
104 L13 Bergerac Dordogne, SW France
101 J16 Bergeyk Noord-Brabant, S Netherlands
103 D16 Bergheim Nordrhein-Westfalen, W Germany
57 X10 Bergi Sipaliwini, E Surinam
103 E16 Bergisch Gladbach Nordrhein-Westfalen, W Germany
103 F14 Bergkamen Nordrhein-Westfalen, W Germany
97 N21 Bergkvara Kalmar, S Sweden
Bergomum see Bergamo
100 K13 Bergse Maas ≈ S Netherlands
97 P15 Bergshamra Stockholm, C Sweden
96 N10 Bergsjö Gävleborg, C Sweden
95 J14 Bergsviken Norrbotten, N Sweden
100 L6 Bergum Fris. Burgum. Friesland, N Netherlands
100 M6 Bergumer Meer ◎ N Netherlands
96 N12 Bergviken ◎ C Sweden
174 I9 Berhala, Selat strait Sumatera, W Indonesia
Berhampore see Baharampur
127 Q9 Beringa, Ostrov island E Russian Federation
101 J17 Beringen Limburg, NE Belgium
41 T12 Bering Glacier glacier Alaska, USA
Beringov Proliv see Bering Strait
127 Q5 Beringovskiy Chukotskiy Avtonomnyy Okrug, NE Russian Federation
199 K2 Bering Sea sea N Pacific Ocean
40 L9 Bering Strait Rus. Beringov Proliv. strait Bering Sea/ Chukchi Sea
Berislav see Beryslav
107 O15 Berja Andalucía, S Spain
96 H9 Berkåk Sør-Trøndelag, S Norway
100 N11 Berkel ≈ Germany/Netherlands
xxxvi L8 Berkeley Gloucestershire, C England, UK
37 N8 Berkeley California, W USA
67 E24 Berkeley Sound sound NE Falkland Islands
23 V2 Berkeley Springs var. Bath. West Virginia, NE USA
xxxvii S8 Berkhamsted Hertfordshire, SE England, UK
205 N6 Berkner Island island Antarctica
116 G8 Berkovitsa Oblast Montana, NW Bulgaria
99 M22 Berkshire cultural region S England, UK
101 H17 Berlaar Antwerpen, N Belgium
Berlanga see Berlanga de Duero
107 P6 Berlanga de Duero var. Berlanga. Castilla-León, N Spain
1 I16 Berlanga Rise undersea feature E Pacific Ocean
101 F17 Berlare Oost-Vlaanderen, NW Belgium
106 E9 Berlenga, Ilha da island C Portugal
94 M7 Berlevåg Finnmark, N Norway
102 O12 Berlin ● (Germany) Berlin, NE Germany
23 Z4 Berlin Maryland, NE USA
21 O7 Berlin New Hampshire, NE USA
20 D16 Berlin Pennsylvania, NE USA
32 L7 Berlin Wisconsin, N USA
102 O12 Berlin ◐ state NE Germany
Berlinchen see Barlinek
33 U12 Berlin Lake ◎ Ohio, N USA
191 R11 Bermagui New South Wales, SE Australia
42 L8 Bermejillo Durango, C Mexico
64 M6 Bermejo (viejo), Río ≈ N Argentina
64 L5 Bermejo, Río ≈ N Argentina
64 I10 Bermejo, Río ≈ W Argentina
107 P2 Bermeo País Vasco, N Spain
106 K6 Bermillo de Sayago Castilla-León, N Spain
108 E6 Bermina, Pizzo Rmsch. Piz Bernina. ▲ Italy/Switzerland see also Bernina, Piz
xxxvi D8 Bermondsey Southwark, SE England, UK
66 A12 Bermuda var. Bermuda Islands, Bermudas; prev. Somers Islands. ◇ UK crown colony NW Atlantic Ocean
1 N11 Bermuda var. Great Bermuda, Long Island, Main Island. island Bermuda
Bermuda Islands see Bermuda
Bermuda-New England Seamount Arc see New England Seamounts
1 N11 Bermuda Rise undersea feature C Sargasso Sea
Bermudas see Bermuda
110 D8 Bern Fr. Berne. ● (Switzerland) Bern, W Switzerland
110 D9 Bern Fr. Berne. ◐ canton W Switzerland
39 R11 Bernalillo New Mexico, SW USA
12 H12 Bernard Lake ◎ Ontario, S Canada
63 B18 Bernardo de Irigoyen Santa Fe, NE Argentina
20 J14 Bernardsville New Jersey, NE USA
65 K14 Bernasconi La Pampa, C Argentina
102 O12 Bernau Brandenburg, NE Germany
104 L4 Bernay Eure, N France
103 L14 Bernburg Sachsen-Anhalt, C Germany
111 X5 Berndorf Niederösterreich, NE Austria
33 Q12 Berne Indiana, N USA
Berne see Bern
110 D10 Berner Alpen var. Berner Oberland, Eng. Bernese Oberland. ⛰ SW Switzerland
xliii A15 Berneray island NW Scotland, UK
xlii B10 Berneray island NW Scotland, UK
Berner Oberland/Bernese Oberland see Berner Alpen
111 Y2 Bernhardsthal Niederösterreich, N Austria
24 H4 Bernice Louisiana, S USA
29 Y8 Bernie Missouri, C USA
188 G9 Bernier Island island Western Australia
Bernina Pass see Bernina, Passo del
110 J10 Bernina, Passo del Eng. Bernina Pass. pass SE Switzerland
110 J10 Bernina, Piz It. Pizzo Bermina. ▲ Italy/Switzerland see also Bermina, Pizzo
xli D12 Bernisdale Highland, NW Scotland, UK
101 E20 Bernissart Hainaut, SW Belgium
103 E18 Bernkastel-Kues Rheinland-Pfalz, W Germany
Beroea see Ḥalab
180 H6 Beroroha Toliara, SW Madagascar
Béroubouay see Gbéroubouè
113 C17 Beroun Ger. Beraun. Střední Čechy, W Czech Republic
113 C16 Berounka Ger. Beraun. ≈ W Czech Republic
115 Q18 Berovo E FYR Macedonia
76 F6 Berrechid var. Berchid. W Morocco
105 R15 Berre, Étang de ◎ SE France
105 S15 Berre-l'Étang Bouches-du-Rhône, SE France
190 K9 Berri South Australia
xlii L8 Berriedale Highland, N Scotland, UK
33 O10 Berrien Springs Michigan, N USA
191 O10 Berrigan New South Wales, SE Australia
xxxvi J11 Berrow Somerset, SW England, UK
105 N9 Berry cultural region C France
37 N7 Berryessa, Lake ◎ California, W USA
46 G2 Berry Islands island group N Bahamas
29 T9 Berryville Arkansas, C USA
23 V3 Berryville Virginia, NE USA
85 D21 Berseba Karas, S Namibia
119 O8 Bershad' Vinnyts'ka Oblast', C Ukraine
30 L3 Berthold North Dakota, N USA
39 T3 Berthoud Colorado, C USA
39 S4 Berthoud Pass pass Colorado, C USA
81 F15 Bertoua Est, E Cameroon
27 S10 Bertram Texas, SW USA
65 G22 Bertrand, Cerro ▲ S Argentina
101 J23 Bertrix Luxembourg, SE Belgium
203 P3 Beru var. Peru. atoll Tungaru, W Kiribati
Beruni see Beruniy
152 I9 Beruniy var. Biruni, Rus. Beruni. Qoraqalpoghiston Respublikasi, W Uzbekistan
60 F13 Beruri Amazonas, NW Brazil
60 K12 Berwick cultural region SE Scotland, UK
20 H14 Berwick Pennsylvania, NE USA
xli P1 Berwick-upon-Tweed Northumberland, N England, UK
119 S10 Beryslav Rus. Berislav. Khersons'ka Oblast', S Ukraine
Berytus see Beyrouth
180 H4 Besalampy Mahajanga, W Madagascar
105 T8 Besançon anc. Besontium, Vesontio. Doubs, E France
105 P10 Besbre ≈ C France
Bescanuova see Baška
Besdan see Bezdan
Besed' see Byesyedz'
153 R10 Beshariq Rus. Besharyk; prev. Kirovo. Farghona Wiloyati, E Uzbekistan
Besharyk see Beshariq
152 L9 Beshbuloq Rus. Beshulak. Nawoiy Wiloyati, N Uzbekistan
Beshenkovichi see Byeshankovichy
152 M13 Beshkent Qashqadaryo Wiloyati, S Uzbekistan
Beshulak see Beshbuloq
176 Uu8 Besir Irian Jaya, E Indonesia
114 L10 Beška Serbia, N Yugoslavia
Beskra see Biskra
131 O16 Beslan Respublika Severnaya Osetiya, SW Russian Federation
115 P16 Besna Kobila ▲ SE Yugoslavia
143 N16 Besni Adıyaman, S Turkey
Besontium see Besançon
124 Nn2 Besparmak Dağları Eng. Kyrenia Mountains. ⛰ N Cyprus
Bessarabka see Basarabeasca
xliv K6 Bessbrook Newry and Mourne, S Northern Ireland, UK
94 O2 Bessels, Kapp headland C Svalbard
25 P4 Bessemer Alabama, S USA
32 K3 Bessemer Michigan, N USA
23 Q10 Bessemer City North Carolina, SE USA
104 M10 Bessines-sur-Gartempe Haute-Vienne, C France
101 K15 Best Noord-Brabant, S Netherlands
27 N9 Best Texas, SW USA
129 O11 Bestuzhevo Arkhangel'skaya Oblast', NW Russian Federation
126 M11 Bestyakh Respublika Sakha (Yakutiya), NE Russian Federation
Beszterce see Bistrița
Besztercebánya see Banská Bystrica
180 I5 Betafo Antananarivo, C Madagascar
106 H2 Betanzos Galicia, NW Spain
106 G2 Betanzos, Ría de estuary NW Spain
81 G15 Bétaré Oya Est, E Cameroon
107 S9 Bétera País Valenciano, E Spain
79 R15 Bétérou C Benin
85 K21 Bethal Mpumalanga, NE South Africa
32 K15 Bethalto Illinois, N USA
85 D21 Bethanie var. Bethanien, Bethany. Karas, S Namibia
Bethanien see Bethanie
29 N10 Bethany Missouri, C USA
29 S2 Bethany Oklahoma, C USA
Bethany see Bethanie
41 N12 Bethel Alaska, USA
21 P7 Bethel Maine, NE USA
23 W9 Bethel North Carolina, SE USA
20 B15 Bethel Park Pennsylvania, NE USA
xxxv G5 Bethesda Gwynedd, NW Wales, UK
23 W3 Bethesda Maryland, NE USA
85 J22 Bethlehem Free State, C South Africa
20 I14 Bethlehem Pennsylvania, NE USA
144 F10 Bethlehem Ar. Bayt Laḥm, Heb. Bet Leḥem. C West Bank
Bethlen see Beclean
xxxvi E7 Bethnal Green Tower Hamlets, SE England, UK
85 I24 Bethulie Free State, C South Africa
105 O1 Béthune Pas-de-Calais, N France
104 M3 Béthune ≈ N France
106 M14 Béticos, Sistemas var. Sistema Penibético, Eng. Baetic Cordillera, Baetic Mountains. ⛰ S Spain
56 I6 Betijoque Trujillo, NW Venezuela
61 M20 Betim Minas Gerais, SE Brazil
202 H3 Betio Tarawa, W Kiribati
180 H7 Betioky Toliara, S Madagascar
Bet Leḥem see Bethlehem
Betlen see Beclean
178 H17 Betong Yala, SW Thailand
81 H16 Bétou La Likouala, N Congo
151 P14 Betpak-Dala Kaz. Betpaqdala. plateau S Kazakhstan
Betpaqdala see Betpak-Dala
xliv D6 Betra Mayo, NW Ireland
180 H7 Betroka Toliara, S Madagascar
Betschau see Bečva
144 G9 Bet She'an Ar. Baysān, Beisān; anc. Scythopolis. Northern, N Israel
13 T6 Betsiamites Québec, SE Canada
13 T6 Betsiamites ≈ Québec, SE Canada
180 I4 Betsiboka ≈ N Madagascar
101 M25 Bettembourg Luxembourg, S Luxembourg
101 M23 Bettendorf Diekirch, NE Luxembourg
31 Z14 Bettendorf Iowa, C USA
77 R13 Bette, Pic var. Bikkū Bīttī, It. Picco Bette. ▲ S Libya
Bette, Picco see Bette, Pic
159 P12 Bettiah Bihār, N India
41 Q7 Bettles Alaska, USA
97 N17 Bettna Södermanland, C Sweden
xlii J6 Bettyhill Highland, N Scotland, UK
160 H11 Betūl prev. Badnur. Madhya Pradesh, C India
160 H9 Betwa ≈ C India
xxxv H5 Betws-y-Coed Conwy, N Wales, UK
103 F16 Betzdorf Rheinland-Pfalz, W Germany
84 C9 Béu Uíge, NW Angola
xxxv E11 Beulah Ceredigion, W Wales, UK
xxxv I11 Beulah Powys, C Wales, UK
33 P6 Beulah Michigan, N USA
30 L5 Beulah North Dakota, N USA
100 M8 Beulakerwijde ◎ N Netherlands
xxxvii W11 Beult ≈ SE England, UK
100 L13 Beuningen Gelderland, SE Netherlands
Beuthen see Bytom
105 N7 Beuvron ≈ C France
101 F16 Beveren Oost-Vlaanderen, N Belgium
23 T9 B.Everett Jordan Reservoir var. Jordan Lake. ⊡ North Carolina, SE USA
xli W13 Beverley East Riding of Yorkshire, E England, UK
Beverley see Beverly
101 J17 Beverlo Limburg, NE Belgium
21 P11 Beverly Massachusetts, NE USA
34 J9 Beverly var. Beverley. Washington, NW USA
37 S15 Beverly Hills California, W USA
103 I14 Beverungen Nordrhein-Westfalen, C Germany
100 H9 Beverwijk Noord-Holland, W Netherlands
xli N6 Bewcastle Cumbria, N England, UK
xxxviii I11 Bewdley Worcestershire, W England, UK
xxxvii W11 Bewl Water ⊡ SE England, UK
110 C10 Bex Vaud, W Switzerland
xxxvii W13 Bexhill var. Bexhill-on-Sea. East Sussex, SE England, UK
Bexhill-on-Sea see Bexhill
xxxiv L16 Bexley ◐ London borough SE England, UK
xxxvi G9 Bexley Bexley, SE England, UK
xxxvi G8 Bexleyheath london borough capital Bexley, SE England, UK
142 E17 Bey Dağları ⛰ SW Turkey
Beyj see Belyy
142 E10 Beykoz İstanbul, NW Turkey
78 K15 Beyla Guinée-Forestière, SE Guinea
143 X12 Beyläqan prev. Zhdanov. SW Azerbaijan
82 L10 Beylul var. Beilul. SE Eritrea
150 H14 Beyneu Kaz. Beyneū. Mangistau, SW Kazakhstan
Beyneū see Beyneu
172 Ss14 Beyonēsu-retsugan Eng. Bayonnaise Rocks. island group SE Japan
142 G12 Beypazarı Ankara, NW Turkey
161 F21 Beypore Kerala, SW India
144 G7 Beyrouth var. Bayrūt, Eng. Beirut; anc. Berytus. ● (Lebanon) W Lebanon
144 G7 Beyrouth ✕ W Lebanon
142 G15 Beyşehir Konya, SW Turkey
142 G15 Beyşehir Gölü ◎ C Turkey
xxxix V12 Beyton Suffolk, E England, UK
110 J7 Bezau Vorarlberg, NW Austria
114 J8 Bezdan Ger. Besdan, Hung. Bezdán. Serbia, NW Yugoslavia
Bezdezh see Byezdzyezh
128 G15 Bezhanitsy Pskovskaya Oblast', W Russian Federation
128 K15 Bezhetsk Tverskaya Oblast', W Russian Federation
105 P16 Béziers anc. Baeterrae, Baeterrae Septimanorum, Julia Beterrae. Hérault, S France
Bezmein see Byuzmeyin
Bezwada see Vijayawāda
160 P12 Bhadrak var. Bhadrakh. Orissa, E India
Bhadrakh see Bhadrak
161 F19 Bhadra Reservoir ⊡ SW India
161 F18 Bhadrāvati Karnātaka, SW India
159 R14 Bhāgalpur Bihār, NE India
Bhairab see Bhairab Bazar
159 U14 Bhairab Bazar var. Bhairab. Dhaka, C Bangladesh
159 O11 Bhairahawa Western, S Nepal
155 S8 Bhakkar Punjab, E Pakistan
159 P11 Bhaktapur Central, C Nepal
178 Gg3 Bhamo var. Banmo. Kachin State, N Burma
Bhāmragad see Bhāmragarh
160 K13 Bhāmragarh var. Bhāmragad. Mahārāshtra, C India
160 J12 Bhandāra Mahārāshtra, C India
Bhārat see India
158 J12 Bharatpur prev. Bhurtpore. Rājasthān, N India
160 D11 Bharūch Gujarāt, W India
161 E18 Bhatkal Karnātaka, W India
159 O13 Bhatni var. Bhatni Junction. Uttar Pradesh, N India
Bhatni Junction see Bhatni
159 S16 Bhātpāra West Bengal, NE India
155 U7 Bhaun Punjab, E Pakistan
Bhaunagar see Bhāvnagar
160 M13 Bhavānipātna Orissa, E India
161 H21 Bhavānisāgar Reservoir ⊡ S India
160 D11 Bhāvnagar prev. Bhaunagar. Gujarāt, W India
Bheanntraí, Bá see Bantry Bay
Bheara, Béal an see Gweebarra Bay
160 K12 Bhilai Madhya Pradesh, C India
158 G13 Bhīlwāra Rājasthān, N India
161 E16 Bhima ≈ S India
161 K16 Bhimavaram Andhra Pradesh, E India
160 I7 Bhind Madhya Pradesh, C India
158 E13 Bhinmāl Rājasthān, N India
Bhir see Bid
160 D13 Bhiwandi Mahārāshtra, W India
158 H10 Bhiwāni Haryāna, N India
158 L13 Bhognīpur Uttar Pradesh, N India
159 U16 Bhola Khulna, S Bangladesh
160 H10 Bhopāl Madhya Pradesh, C India
161 J14 Bhopālpatnam Madhya Pradesh, C India
161 E14 Bhor Mahārāshtra, W India
160 O12 Bhubaneshwar prev. Bhubaneswar, Bhuvaneshwar. Orissa, E India
Bhubaneswar see Bhubaneshwar
160 B9 Bhuj Gujarāt, W India
Bhuket see Phuket
Bhurtpore see Bharatpur
Bhusaval see Bhusāwal
160 G12 Bhusāwal prev. Bhusaval. Mahārāshtra, C India
159 T12 Bhutan off. Kingdom of Bhutan, var. Druk-yul. ◆ monarchy S Asia
Bhuvaneshwar see Bhubaneshwar
149 T15 Bībān, Kūh-e ⛰ S Iran
79 V18 Biafra, Bight of var. Bight of Bonny. bay W Africa
176 X9 Biak Irian Jaya, E Indonesia
176 Ww9 Biak, Pulau island E Indonesia
112 P12 Biała Podlaska Biała Podlaska, E Poland
112 O12 Biała Podlaska off. Województwo Bialskopodlaskie. ◐ province E Poland
112 F7 Białogard Ger. Belgard. Koszalin, NW Poland
Białostockie, Województwo see Białystok
112 P10 Białowieska, Puszcza Bel. Byelavyezhskaya Pushcha, Rus. Belovezhskaya Pushcha. physical region Belorussia/Poland see also Byelavyezhskaya Pushcha
Bialskopodlaskie, Województwo see Biała Podlaska
112 G8 Biały Bór Ger. Baldenburg. Koszalin, NW Poland
112 P9 Białystok Rus. Belostok, Bielostok. Białystok, E Poland
112 O10 Białystok off. Województwo Białostockie, Rus. Belostok, Bielostok. ◐ province E Poland
109 L24 Biancavilla prev. Inessa. Sicilia, Italy, C Mediterranean Sea
Bianco, Monte see Blanc, Mont
78 L15 Biankouma W Ivory Coast
178 Ii7 Bia, Phou var. Pou Bia. ▲ C Laos
Bia, Pou see Bia, Phou
149 R5 Biārjmand Semnān, N Iran
104 I15 Biarritz Pyrénées-Atlantiques, SW France
110 H10 Biasca Ticino, S Switzerland
63 E17 Biassini Salto, N Uruguay
172 Oo5 Bibai Hokkaidō, NE Japan
85 B15 Bibala Port. Vila Arriaga. Namibe, SW Angola
106 I4 Bibéi ≈ NW Spain
Biberach see Biberach an der Riss
103 I23 Biberach an der Riss var. Biberach, Ger. Biberach an der Riß. Baden-Württemberg, S Germany
110 E7 Biberist Solothurn, NW Switzerland
79 O16 Bibiani SW Ghana
114 C13 Bibinje Zadar-Knin, W Croatia
Biblical Gebal see Jbaïl
118 I5 Bibrka Pol. Bóbrka, Rus. Bobrka. L'vivs'ka Oblast', NW Ukraine
xxxvii N8 Bibury Gloucestershire, C England, UK
119 N10 Bic ≈ S Moldavia
115 M18 Bicaj Kukës, NE Albania
118 K10 Bicaz Hung. Békás. Neamţ, NE Romania
xxxviii Q7 Bicester Oxfordshire, C England, UK
191 Q16 Bicheno Tasmania, SE Australia
Bichiș see Békés
Bichiș-Ciaba see Békéscsaba
Bichitra see Phichit
143 P8 Bichvint'a Rus. Pitsunda. NW Georgia
13 T7 Bic, Île du island Québec, SE Canada
xxxix R8 Bicker Lincolnshire, E England, UK
xxxvi H15 Bickington Devon, SW England, UK
xxxvi H13 Bickleigh Devon, SW England, UK
34 J10 Bickleton Washington, NW USA
xxxviii H7 Bickley Moss Cheshire, W England, UK
38 L6 Bicknell Utah, W USA
175 Tt7 Bicoli Pulau Halmahera, E Indonesia
113 J22 Bicske Fejér, C Hungary
161 F14 Bīd prev. Bhir. Mahārāshtra, W India
79 U15 Bida Niger, C Nigeria
161 H15 Bīdar Karnātaka, C India
147 Y8 Bidbid NE Oman
21 P9 Biddeford Maine, NE USA
xxxvii W11 Biddenden Kent, SE England, UK
100 L9 Biddinghuizen Flevoland, C Netherlands
35 X11 Biddle Montana, NW USA
xxxviii J7 Biddulph Staffordshire, C England, UK
xlii H16 Bidean Nam Bian ▲ W Scotland, UK
xxxvi E12 Bideford Devon, SW England, UK
xxxviii K13 Bidford-on-Avon Warwickshire, C England, UK
84 D13 Bié ◐ province C Angola
37 O2 Bieber California, W USA
112 O9 Biebrza ≈ NE Poland
172 P5 Biei Hokkaidō, NE Japan
110 D8 Biel Fr. Bienne. Bern, W Switzerland
102 G13 Bielefeld Nordrhein-Westfalen, NW Germany
110 D8 Bieler See Fr. Lac de Bienne. ◎ W Switzerland
Bielitz/Bielitz-Biala see Bielsko-Biała
108 C7 Biella Piemonte, N Italy
Bielostok see Białystok
Bielskie, Województwo/Bielsko see Bielsko-Biała
113 J17 Bielsko-Biała Ger. Bielitz, Bielitz-Biala. Bielsko-Biała, S Poland
113 J17 Bielsko-Biała off. Województwo Bielskie. ◐ province S Poland
112 P10 Bielsk Podlaski Białystok, E Poland
Bien Bien see Điện Biên
Biên Đông see South China Sea
9 V17 Bienfait Saskatchewan, S Canada
178 Jj14 Biên Hoa Đông Nai, S Vietnam
Bienne see Biel
Bienne, Lac de see Bieler See
10 K8 Bienville, Lac ◎ Québec, C Canada
84 D13 Bié, Planalto do var. Bié Plateau. plateau C Angola
Bié Plateau see Bié, Planalto do
110 B9 Bière Vaud, W Switzerland
100 O4 Bierum Groningen, NE Netherlands
100 I13 Biesbos var. Biesbosch. wetland S Netherlands
Biesbosch see Biesbos
101 H21 Biesme Namur, S Belgium
103 H21 Bietigheim-Bissingen Baden-Württemberg, SW Germany
101 J23 Bièvre Namur, SE Belgium
81 D18 Bifoun Moyen-Ogooué, NW Gabon
172 Pp3 Bifuka Hokkaidō, NE Japan
142 C11 Biga Çanakkale, NW Turkey
142 C13 Bigadiç Balıkesir, W Turkey
28 J7 Big Basin basin Kansas, C USA
193 B20 Big Bay bay South Island, NZ
197 B12 Big Bay bay C Vanuatu
33 O5 Big Bay de Noc ◎ Michigan, N USA
33 N3 Big Bay Point headland Michigan, N USA
35 R10 Big Belt Mountains ⛰ Montana, NW USA
31 N10 Big Bend Dam dam South Dakota, N USA
26 K12 Big Bend National Park national park Texas, S USA
24 K5 Big Black River ≈ Mississippi, S USA
29 O3 Big Blue River ≈ Kansas/Nebraska, C USA
xxxvi G16 Bigbury Bay bay SW England, UK
xxxix Q3 Bigby Lincolnshire, E England, UK
26 M10 Big Canyon ≈ Texas, SW USA
35 N12 Big Creek Idaho, NW USA
25 N8 Big Creek Lake ⊡ Alabama, S USA
25 X15 Big Cypress Swamp wetland Florida, SE USA
41 S9 Big Delta Alaska, USA
32 K6 Big Eau Pleine Reservoir ⊡ Wisconsin, N USA
21 P5 Bigelow Mountain ▲ Maine, NE USA
31 U3 Big Falls Minnesota, N USA
35 P8 Bigfork Montana, NW USA
31 U3 Big Fork River ≈ Minnesota, N USA
xliii J15 Biggar South Lanarkshire, C Scotland, UK
9 S15 Biggar Saskatchewan, S Canada
188 L3 Bigge Island island Western Australia
xxxvii U10 Biggin Hill Bromley, SE England, UK
xxxvii T6 Biggleswade Bedfordshire, C England, UK
37 O5 Biggs California, W USA
34 I11 Biggs Oregon, NW USA
12 K13 Big Gull Lake ◎ Ontario, SE Canada
39 P16 Big Hachet Peak ▲ New Mexico, SW USA
35 P11 Big Hole River ≈ Montana, NW USA
35 V13 Bighorn Basin basin Wyoming, C USA
35 U11 Bighorn Lake ◎ Montana/Wyoming, N USA
35 W13 Bighorn Mountains ⛰ Wyoming, C USA
38 J13 Big Horn Peak ▲ Arizona, SW USA
35 V11 Bighorn River ≈ Montana/ Wyoming, NW USA
16 O5 Big Island island Northwest Territories, NE Canada
41 O16 Big Koniuji Island island Shumagin Islands, Alaska, USA
27 N9 Big Lake Texas, SW USA
21 T5 Big Lake ◎ Maine, NE USA
32 I3 Big Manitou Falls waterfall Wisconsin, N USA
37 R2 Big Mountain ▲ Nevada, W USA
110 G10 Bignasco Ticino, S Switzerland
31 R16 Big Nemaha River ≈ Nebraska, C USA
78 G12 Bignona SW Senegal
Bigorra see Tarbes
Bigosovo see Bihosava
37 S10 Big Pine California, W USA
37 Q14 Big Pine Mountain ▲ California, W USA
29 V6 Big Piney Creek ≈ Missouri, C USA
67 M24 Big Point headland N Tristan da Cunha
33 P8 Big Rapids Michigan, N USA
32 K6 Big Rib River ≈ Wisconsin, N USA
12 L14 Big Rideau Lake ◎ Ontario, SE Canada
9 T14 Big River Saskatchewan, C Canada
29 X5 Big River ≈ Missouri, C USA
33 N7 Big Sable Point headland Michigan, N USA
35 S7 Big Sandy Montana, NW USA
27 W6 Big Sandy Texas, SW USA
39 V5 Big Sandy Creek ≈ Colorado, C USA
31 Q16 Big Sandy Creek ≈ Nebraska, C USA
31 V5 Big Sandy Lake ◎ Minnesota, N USA
38 J11 Big Sandy River ≈ Arizona, SW USA
23 P5 Big Sandy River ≈ S USA
25 V6 Big Satilla Creek ≈ Georgia, SE USA
31 R12 Big Sioux River ≈ Iowa/South Dakota, N USA
37 U7 Big Smoky Valley valley Nevada, W USA
27 N7 Big Spring Texas, SW USA
21 Q5 Big Squaw Mountain ▲ Maine, NE USA
23 O7 Big Stone Gap Virginia, NE USA
31 Q8 Big Stone Lake ◎ Minnesota/ South Dakota, N USA
24 K4 Big Sunflower River ≈ Mississippi, S USA
35 T11 Big Timber Montana, NW USA
10 D8 Big Trout Lake Ontario, C Canada
12 I12 Big Trout Lake ◎ Ontario, SE Canada
37 O2 Big Valley Mountains ⛰ California, W USA
27 Q13 Big Wells Texas, SW USA
12 F11 Bigwood Ontario, S Canada
114 D11 Bihać NW Bosnia and Herzegovina
159 P14 Bihār prev. Behar. ◐ state N India
Bihār see Bihār Sharīf
83 F20 Biharamulo Kagera, NW Tanzania
159 R13 Bihārīganj Bihār, NE India
159 P14 Bihār Sharīf var. Bihār. Bihār, N India
118 F10 Bihor ◐ county NW Romania
172 Q6 Bihoro Hokkaidō, NE Japan
120 K11 Bihosava Rus. Bigosovo. Vitsyebskaya Voblasts', NW Belorussia
Bijagos Archipelago see Bijagós, Arquipélago dos
78 G13 Bijagós, Arquipélago dos var. Bijagos Archipelago. island group W Guinea-Bissau
161 F16 Bijāpur Karnātaka, C India
148 K5 Bījār Kordestān, W Iran
114 J11 Bijeljina NE Bosnia and Herzegovina
115 K15 Bijelo Polje Montenegro, SW Yugoslavia
166 E11 Bijiang prev. Zhiziluo. Yunnan, SW China
166 I11 Bijie Guizhou, S China
158 J10 Bijnor Uttar Pradesh, N India
158 F11 Bīkāner Rājasthān, NW India
201 V3 Bikar Atoll var. Pikaar. atoll Ratak Chain, N Marshall Islands
202 H3 Bikeman atoll Tungaru, W Kiribati
202 I3 Bikenebu Tarawa, W Kiribati
127 Nn16 Bikin Khabarovskiy Kray, SE Russian Federation
127 Nn16 Bikin ≈ SE Russian Federation
201 R3 Bikini Atoll var. Pikinni. atoll Ralik Chain, NW Marshall Islands
85 L17 Bikita Masvingo, E Zimbabwe
Bikkū Bīttī see Bette, Pic
81 I19 Bikoro Equateur, W Zaire
147 Z9 Bilād Banī Bū 'Alī NE Oman
147 Z9 Bilād Banī Bū Ḥasan NE Oman
147 X9 Bilād Manaḥ var. Manaḥ. NE Oman
79 Q12 Bilanga C Burkina
175 Q7 Bilang, Teluk bay Sulawesi, N Indonesia
158 F12 Bilāra Rājasthān, N India
158 K10 Bilāri Uttar Pradesh, N India
144 J5 Bil'ās, Jabal al ▲ C Syria
158 I8 Bilāspur Himāchal Pradesh, N India
160 L11 Bilāspur Madhya Pradesh, C India
173 G6 Bila, Sungai ≈ Sumatera, W Indonesia
143 Y13 Biläsuvar Rus. Bilyasuvar; prev. Pushkino. SE Azerbaijan
119 O5 Bila Tserkva Rus. Belaya Tserkov'. Kyyivs'ka Oblast', N Ukraine
178 H11 Bilauktaung Range var. Thanintari Taungdan. ⛰ Burma/Thailand
107 O2 Bilbao Basq. Bilbo. País Vasco, N Spain
Bilbo see Bilbao
xxxix W13 Bildeston Suffolk, E England, UK
94 H2 Bíldudalur Vestfirdhir, NW Iceland
115 I16 Bileća S Bosnia and Herzegovina
142 E12 Bilecik Bilecik, NW Turkey
142 F12 Bilecik ◐ province NW Turkey
118 E11 Biled Ger. Billed, Hung. Billéd. Timiș, W Romania
113 O15 Biłgoraj Zamość, SE Poland
119 P11 Bilhorod-Dnistrovs'kyy Rus. Belgorod-Dnestrovskiy, Rom. Cetatea Albă; prev. Akkerman, anc. Tyras. Odes'ka Oblast', SW Ukraine
81 M16 Bili Haut-Zaïre, N Zaire
127 Oo5 Bilibino Chukotskiy Avtonomnyy Okrug, NE Russian Federation
178 Gg8 Bilin Mon State, S Burma
179 Qq12 Biliran Island island C Philippines
115 N21 Bilisht var. Bilishti. Korçë, SE Albania
Bilishti see Bilisht
191 N10 Billabong Creek var. Moulamein Creek. seasonal river New South Wales, SE Australia
190 G4 Billa Kalina South Australia
207 Q17 Bill Baileys Bank undersea feature N Atlantic Ocean
Billed/Billéd see Biled
xxxvii W8 Billericay Essex, SE England, UK
xxxix O10 Billesdon Leicestershire, C England, UK
159 N14 Billi Uttar Pradesh, N India
xli N16 Billinge St Helens, NW England, UK
xli S8 Billingham Redcar and Cleveland, N England, UK
xxxix R7 Billinghay Lincolnshire, E England, UK
35 U11 Billings Montana, NW USA
97 J16 Billingsfors Älvsborg, S Sweden
xxxvii S12 Billingshurst West Sussex, SE England, UK
xxxviii I11 Billingsley Shropshire, W England, UK
xxxix Y9 Billockby Norfolk, E England, UK
Bill of Cape Clear, The see Clear, Cape
30 L9 Billsburg South Dakota, N USA
97 F23 Billund Ribe, W Denmark
38 L11 Bill Williams Mountain ▲ Arizona, SW USA
38 I12 Bill Williams River ≈ Arizona, SW USA
79 Y8 Bilma Agadez, NE Niger
79 Y8 Bilma, Grand Erg de desert NE Niger
189 Y9 Biloela Queensland, E Australia
114 G8 Bilo Gora ⛰ N Croatia
119 U13 Bilohirs'k Rus. Belogorsk; prev. Karasubazar. Respublika Krym, S Ukraine
118 M3 Bilokorovychi Rus. Belokorovichi. Zhytomyrs'ka Oblast', N Ukraine
119 X5 Bilokurakine Luhans'ka Oblast', E Ukraine
119 T3 Bilopillya Rus. Belopol'ye. Sums'ka Oblast', NE Ukraine
119 Y6 Bilovods'k Rus. Belovodsk. Luhans'ka Oblast', E Ukraine
24 M9 Biloxi Mississippi, S USA
119 R10 Bilozerka Khersons'ka Oblast', S Ukraine
119 W7 Bilozers'ke Donets'ka Oblast', E Ukraine
xxxviii B14 Bilston Wolverhampton, C England, UK
100 J11 Bilthoven Utrecht, C Netherlands
80 K9 Biltine Biltine, E Chad
80 J9 Biltine off. Préfecture de Biltine. ◐ prefecture E Chad
168 D5 Bilüü Bayan-Ölgiy, W Mongolia
Bilwi see Puerto Cabezas
Bilyasuvar see Biläsuvar
119 O11 Bilyayivka Odes'ka Oblast', SW Ukraine
101 K18 Bilzen Limburg, NE Belgium
Bimbéréké see Bembèrèkè
191 R10 Bimberi Peak ▲ New South Wales, SE Australia
79 Q15 Bimbila E Ghana
81 I15 Bimbo Ombella-Mpoko, SW Central African Republic
46 F2 Bimini Islands island group W Bahamas
160 I9 Bina Madhya Pradesh, C India
149 T4 Bīnālūd, Kūh-e ⛰ NE Iran
xxxix R4 Binbrook Lincolnshire, E England, UK
101 F20 Binche Hainaut, S Belgium
Bindloe Island see Marchena, Isla
85 L16 Bindura Mashonaland Central, NE Zimbabwe
107 T5 Binefar Aragón, NE Spain
85 I16 Binga Matabeleland North, W Zimbabwe
191 T5 Bingara New South Wales, SE Australia
103 F18 Bingen am Rhein Rheinland-Pfalz, SW Germany
28 M11 Binger Oklahoma, C USA
Bingerau see Węgrów
Bin Ghalfān, Jazā'ir see Ḥalāniyāt, Juzur al
xxxix O7 Bingham Nottinghamshire, C England, UK
21 Q6 Bingham Maine, NE USA
20 H11 Binghamton New York, NE USA
Bin Ghanīmah, Jabal see Bin Ghunaymah, Jabal

◆ Country ● Country Capital ◇ Dependent Territory ○ Dependent Territory Capital ◐ Administrative Region ✕ International Airport ▲ Mountain ⛰ Mountain Range Volcano ≈ River ◎ Lake ⊡ Reservoir

Bin Ghunaymah, Jabal – Boerne

77 P11 **Bin Ghunaymah, Jabal** *var.* Jabal Bin Ghanīmah. ⛰ C Libya
145 U3 **Bingird** NE Iraq
xli Q14 **Bingley** Bradford, N England, UK
143 P14 **Bingöl** Bingöl, E Turkey
143 P14 **Bingöl** ◈ *province* E Turkey
167 R6 **Binhai** *var.* Binhai Xian. Dongkan. Jiangsu, E China
Binhai Xian *see* Binhai
xxxix V7 **Binham** Norfolk, E England, UK
178 Kk12 **Binh Đinh** *var.* An Nhon. Binh Đinh, C Vietnam
178 Kk10 **Binh Sơn** *var.* Châu Ô. Quang Ngai, C Vietnam
Binimani *see* Bintimani
173 Ff5 **Binjai** Sumatera, W Indonesia
191 R6 **Binnaway** New South Wales, SE Australia
110 E6 **Binningen** Basel-Land, NW Switzerland
175 R13 **Binongko, Pulau** *island* Kepulauan Tukangbesi, C Indonesia
174 Gg3 **Bintang, Banjaran** ⛰ Peninsular Malaysia
174 I7 **Bintan, Pulau** *island* Kepulauan Riau, W Indonesia
78 J14 **Bintimani** *var.* Binimani. ▲ NE Sierra Leone
Bint Jubayl *see* Bent Jbaïl
174 M5 **Bintulu** Sarawak, East Malaysia
176 Vv10 **Bintuni** *prev.* Steenkool. Irian Jaya, E Indonesia
176 Vv10 **Bintuni, Teluk** *bay* Irian Jaya, E Indonesia
169 W8 **Bin Xian** Heilongjiang, NE China
166 K14 **Binyang** Guangxi Zhuangzu Zizhiqu, S China
167 Q4 **Binzhou** Shandong, E China
65 G14 **Bío Bío** *off.* Región del Bío Bío. ◈ *region* C Chile
65 G14 **Bío Bío, Río** ≈ C Chile
81 C16 **Bioco, Isla de** *var.* Bioko, *Eng.* Fernando Po, *Sp.* Fernando Póo; *prev.* Macías Nguema Biyogo. *island* NW Equatorial Guinea
114 D13 **Biograd na Moru** *It.* Zaravecchia. Zadar-Knin, S Croatia
Bioko *see* Bioco, Isla de
115 F14 **Biokovo** ⛰ S Croatia
Biorra *see* Birr
Bipontium *see* Zweibrücken
149 W13 **Birag, Kūh-e** ⛰ SE Iran
77 O10 **Birāk** *var.* Brak. C Libya
145 S10 **Bi'r al Islām** C Iraq
160 N11 **Biramitrapur** Orissa, E India
145 T11 **Bi'r an Nişf** S Iraq
80 L12 **Birao** Vakaga, NE Central African Republic
164 M6 **Biratar Bulak** *well* NW China
159 R12 **Biratnagar** Eastern, SE Nepal
172 Oo6 **Biratori** Hokkaidō, NE Japan
41 S8 **Birch Creek** Alaska, USA
40 M11 **Birch Creek** ≈ Alaska, USA
9 T14 **Birch Hills** Saskatchewan, S Canada
190 M10 **Birchip** Victoria, SE Australia
31 X4 **Birch Lake** ⊙ Minnesota, N USA
9 Q11 **Birch Mountains** ⛰ Alberta, W Canada
9 V15 **Birch River** Manitoba, S Canada
46 H12 **Birchs Hill** *hill* W Jamaica
41 R11 **Birchwood** Alaska, USA
xliv F11 **Birdhill** Tipperary, S Ireland
xxxviii M6 **Birdholme** Derbyshire, C England, UK
196 I5 **Bird Island** *island* S Northern Mariana Islands
xxxvi M7 **Birdlip** Gloucestershire, C England, UK
xli U12 **Birdsall** North Yorkshire, N England, UK
143 N16 **Birecik** Şanlıurfa, S Turkey
158 M10 **Birendranagar** *var.* Surkhet. Mid Western, W Nepal
Bir es Saba *see* Be'ér Sheva'
76 A12 **Bir-Gandouz** SW Western Sahara
159 P12 **Birganj** Central, C Nepal
xliii O21 **Birgham** The Borders, S Scotland, UK
83 B14 **Biri** ≈ W Sudan
Bi'r Ibn Hirmās *see* Al Bi'r
176 Yy10 **Biri, Sungai** ≈ Irian Jaya, E Indonesia
149 U8 **Birjand** Khorāsān, E Iran
145 T11 **Birkat Ḩāmid** *well* S Iraq
97 F18 **Birkeland** Aust-Agder, S Norway
103 E19 **Birkenfeld** Rheinland-Pfalz, SW Germany
xl B16 **Birkenhead** Wirral, NW England, UK
111 W7 **Birkfeld** Steiermark, SE Austria
190 A2 **Birksgate Range** ⛰ South Australia
Birlad *see* Bârlad
xli R4 **Birling** Northumberland, N England, UK
xxxviii C14 **Birmingham** Birmingham, C England, UK
xxxviii C14 **Birmingham** ◈ *unitary authority* C England, UK
xxxviii D15 **Birmingham** ✕ Birmingham, C England, UK
25 P4 **Birmingham** Alabama, S USA
Bir Mogrein *see* Bîr Mogreïn
78 J4 **Bîr Mogreïn** *var.* Bir Moghrein; *prev.* Fort-Trinquet. Tiris Zemmour, N Mauritania
203 S4 **Birnie Island** *atoll* Phoenix Islands, C Kiribati
Birni-Ngaouré *see* Birnin Gaouré
79 S12 **Birnin Gaouré** *var.* Birni-Ngaouré. Dosso, SW Niger
79 S12 **Birnin Kebbi** Kebbi, NW Nigeria
Birni-Nkonni *see* Birnin Konni
79 T12 **Birnin Konni** *var.* Birni-Nkonni. Tahoua, SW Niger
79 W13 **Birnin Kudu** Jigawa, N Nigeria
127 N16 **Birobidzhan** Yevreyskaya Avtonomnaya Oblast', SE Russian Federation
xliv H10 **Birr** *var.* Parsonstown, *Ir.* Biorra. Offaly, C Ireland
191 P4 **Birrie River** ≈ New South Wales/Queensland, SE Australia
xliii L3 **Birsay** Orkney Islands, N Scotland, UK
110 D7 **Birse** ≈ NW Switzerland
Birsen *see* Biržai
110 E6 **Birsfelden** Basel-Land, NW Switzerland
131 U4 **Birsk** Respublika Bashkortostan, W Russian Federation
121 F14 **Birštonas** Prienai, C Lithuania
xli V3 **Birtley** Gateshead, NE England, UK
xli P5 **Birtley** Northumberland, N England, UK
165 P14 **Biru** Xinjiang Uygur Zizhiqu, W China
Biruni *see* Beruniy
126 Ii14 **Biryusa** ≈ C Russian Federation
126 Ii14 **Biryusinsk** Irkutskaya Oblast', C Russian Federation
120 G10 **Biržai** *Ger.* Birsen. Biržai, NE Lithuania
123 Jj17 **Birżebbuġa** SE Malta
Bisanthe *see* Tekirdağ
175 T9 **Bisa, Pulau** *island* Maluku, E Indonesia
39 N17 **Bisbee** Arizona, SW USA
31 O2 **Bisbee** North Dakota, N USA
Biscaia, Baía de *see* Biscay, Bay of
104 I13 **Biscarrosse et de Parentis, Étang de** ⊙ SW France
106 M1 **Biscay, Bay of** *Sp.* Golfo de Vizcaya, *Port.* Baía de Biscaia. *bay* France/Spain
25 Z16 **Biscayne Bay** *bay* Florida, SE USA
66 M7 **Biscay Plain** *undersea feature* SE Bay of Biscay
109 N17 **Bisceglie** Puglia, SE Italy
Bischoflack *see* Škofja Loka
Bischofsburg *see* Biskupiec
111 Q7 **Bischofshofen** Salzburg, NW Austria
103 P15 **Bischofswerda** Sachsen, E Germany
105 V5 **Bischwiller** Bas-Rhin, NE France
23 T10 **Biscoe** North Carolina, SE USA
204 G5 **Biscoe Islands** *island group* Antarctica
12 E9 **Biscotasi Lake** ⊙ Ontario, S Canada
12 E9 **Biscotasing** Ontario, S Canada
56 J6 **Biscucuy** Portuguesa, NW Venezuela
116 K11 **Biser** Khaskovska Oblast, SE Bulgaria
115 D15 **Biševo** *It.* Busi. *island* SW Croatia
147 N12 **Bīshah, Wādī** *dry watercourse* C Saudi Arabia
xxxviii K13 **Bishampton** Worcestershire, W England, UK
153 U7 **Bishkek** *var.* Pishpek; *prev.* Frunze. ● (Kyrgyzstan) Chuyskaya Oblast', N Kyrgyzstan
153 U7 **Bishkek** ✕ Chuyskaya Oblast', N Kyrgyzstan
159 R16 **Bishnupur** West Bengal, NE India
85 J25 **Bisho** Eastern Cape, S South Africa
37 S9 **Bishop** California, W USA
27 S15 **Bishop** Texas, SW USA
xli R8 **Bishop Auckland** Durham, N England, UK
xliii J20 **Bishopbriggs** East Dunbartonshire, C Scotland, UK
xli S12 **Bishop Monkton** North Yorkshire, N England, UK
xxxvii N10 **Bishops Cannings** Wiltshire, S England, UK
xxxviii G11 **Bishop's Castle** Shropshire, W England, UK
xxxvi L13 **Bishop's Caundle** Dorset, S England, UK
xxxvi M7 **Bishop's Cleeve** Gloucestershire, C England, UK
Bishop's Lynn *see* King's Lynn
xxxvii V7 **Bishop's Stortford** Hertfordshire, E England, UK
xxxv G15 **Bishopston** Swansea, S Wales, UK
xxxvii Q12 **Bishop's Waltham** Hampshire, S England, UK
23 S12 **Bishopville** South Carolina, SE USA
144 M5 **Bishrī, Jabal** ⛰ E Syria
169 U4 **Bishui** Heilongjiang, NE China
83 G17 **Bisina, Lake** *prev.* Lake Salisbury. ⊙ E Uganda
Biskara *see* Biskra
76 L6 **Biskra** *var.* Beskra, Biskara. NE Algeria
112 M8 **Biskupiec** *Ger.* Bischofsburg. Olsztyn, N Poland
xxxvi M8 **Bisley** Gloucestershire, C England, UK
xxxvii S10 **Bisley** Surrey, SE England, UK
179 Rr15 **Bislig** Mindanao, S Philippines
29 X6 **Bismarck** Missouri, C USA
30 M5 **Bismarck** *state capital* North Dakota, N USA
194 K9 **Bismarck Archipelago** *island group* NE PNG
133 Z16 **Bismarck Plate** *tectonic feature* W Pacific Ocean
194 I12 **Bismarck Range** ⛰ N PNG
194 J10 **Bismarck Sea** *sea* W Pacific Ocean
143 P15 **Bismil** Diyarbakır, SE Turkey
45 N6 **Bismuna, Laguna** *lagoon* NE Nicaragua
Bisnulok *see* Phitsanulok
175 T6 **Bisoa, Tanjung** *headland* Pulau Halmahera, N Indonesia
30 K7 **Bison** South Dakota, N USA
95 H17 **Bispfors** Jämtland, C Sweden
78 G13 **Bissau** ● (Guinea-Bissau) W Guinea-Bissau
78 G13 **Bissau** ✕ W Guinea-Bissau
101 M24 **Bissen** Luxembourg, C Luxembourg
78 G12 **Bissorã** W Guinea-Bissau
9 O10 **Bistcho Lake** ⊙ Alberta, W Canada
24 G5 **Bistineau, Lake** ⊡ Louisiana, S USA
Bistrica *see* Ilirska Bistrica
118 I9 **Bistriţa** *Ger.* Bistritz, *Hung.* Beszterce; *prev.* Nösen. Bistriţa-Năsăud, N Romania
118 K10 **Bistriţa** *Ger.* Bistritz. ≈ NE Romania
118 I9 **Bistriţa-Năsăud** ◈ *county* N Romania
Bistritz *see* Bistriţa
Bistritz ober Pernstein *see* Bystřice nad Pernštejnem
158 L11 **Biswān** Uttar Pradesh, N India
112 M7 **Bisztynek** Olsztyn, N Poland
81 E17 **Bitam** Woleu-Ntem, N Gabon
103 D18 **Bitburg** Rheinland-Pfalz, SW Germany
105 U4 **Bitche** Moselle, NE France
80 I11 **Bitkine** Guéra, C Chad
143 R15 **Bitlis** Bitlis, SE Turkey
143 R14 **Bitlis** ◈ *province* E Turkey
Bitoeng *see* Bitung
115 N20 **Bitola** *Turk.* Monastir; *prev.* Bitolj. S FYR Macedonia
Bitolj *see* Bitola
109 O17 **Bitonto** *anc.* Butuntum. Puglia, SE Italy
79 Q13 **Bitou** *var.* Bittou. SE Burkina
161 C20 **Bitra Island** *island* Lakshadweep, India, N Indian Ocean
xxxvi F11 **Bittadon** Devon, SW England, UK
103 M14 **Bitterfeld** Sachsen-Anhalt, E Germany
xxxviii H11 **Bitterley** Shropshire, W England, UK
34 O9 **Bitterroot Range** ⛰ Idaho/Montana, NW USA
35 P10 **Bitterroot River** ≈ Montana, NW USA
109 D18 **Bitti** Sardegna, Italy, C Mediterranean Sea
Bittou *see* Bitou
175 S7 **Bitung** *prev.* Bitoeng. Sulawesi, C Indonesia
62 I12 **Bituruna** Paraná, S Brazil
79 Y13 **Biu** Borno, E Nigeria
Biumba *see* Byumba
171 H14 **Biwa-ko** ⊙ Honshū, SW Japan
176 Y13 **Biwarlaut** Irian Jaya, E Indonesia
29 P10 **Bixby** Oklahoma, C USA
126 H15 **Biya** ≈ S Russian Federation
Biy-Khem *see* Bol'shoy Yenisey
126 H15 **Biysk** Altayskiy Kray, S Russian Federation
170 Ff14 **Bizen** Okayama, Honshū, SW Japan
Bizerta *see* Bizerte
123 K11 **Bizerte** *Ar.* Banzart, *Eng.* Bizerta. N Tunisia
Bizkaia *see* Vizcaya
94 G2 **Bjargtangar** *headland* W Iceland
Bjärnå *see* Perniö
97 K22 **Bjärnum** Kristianstad, S Sweden
95 I16 **Bjästa** Västernorrland, C Sweden
115 I14 **Bjelašnica** ▲ SE Bosnia and Herzegovina
114 C10 **Bjelolasica** ⛰ NW Croatia
114 F8 **Bjelovar** *Hung.* Belovár. Bjelovar-Bilogora, N Croatia
114 F8 **Bjelovar-Bilogora** *off.* Bjelovarsko-Bilogorska Županija. ◈ *province* NE Croatia
Bjelovarsko-Bilogorska Županija *see* Bjelovar-Bilogora
94 H10 **Bjerkvik** Nordland, C Norway
97 G21 **Bjerringbro** Viborg, NW Denmark
Bjeshkët e Namuna *see* North Albanian Alps
97 L14 **Björbo** Kopparberg, C Sweden
97 I15 **Bjørkelangen** Akershus, S Norway
97 O14 **Björklinge** Uppsala, C Sweden
97 I14 **Björksele** Västerbotten, N Sweden
95 I16 **Björna** Västernorrland, C Sweden
97 C14 **Bjørnafjorden** *fjord* S Norway
97 L16 **Björneborg** Värmland, C Sweden
Björneborg *see* Pori
97 E14 **Bjornesfjorden** ⊙ S Norway
94 M9 **Bjørnevatn** Finnmark, N Norway
207 T13 **Bjørnøya** *Eng.* Bear Island. *island* N Norway
95 I15 **Bjurholm** Västerbotten, N Sweden
97 J22 **Bjuv** Malmöhus, S Sweden
78 M12 **Bla** Ségou, W Mali
189 W8 **Blackall** Queensland, E Australia
31 V2 **Black Bay** *lake bay* Minnesota, N USA
29 N9 **Black Bear Creek** ≈ Oklahoma, C USA
xli O14 **Blackburn** Lancashire, N England, UK
xliii O13 **Blackburn** Aberdeenshire, NE Scotland, UK
xliii J20 **Blackburn** West Lothian, S Scotland, UK
xl C14 **Blackburn** ◈ *unitary authority* NW England, UK
47 W10 **Blackburne** ✕ (Plymouth) E Montserrat
41 T11 **Blackburn, Mount** ▲ Alaska, USA
37 N5 **Black Butte Lake** ⊡ California, W USA
204 J5 **Black Coast** *physical region* Antarctica
xliii J23 **Blackcraig Hill** ▲ W Scotland, UK
9 Q16 **Black Diamond** Alberta, SW Canada
20 K11 **Black Dome** ▲ New York, NE USA
115 L18 **Black Drin** *Alb.* Lumi i Drinit të Zi, *SCr.* Crni Drim. ≈ Albania/FYR Macedonia
10 D6 **Black Duck** ≈ Ontario, C Canada
31 U4 **Blackduck** Minnesota, N USA
35 R14 **Blackfoot** Idaho, NW USA
35 P9 **Blackfoot River** ≈ Montana, NW USA
xliii K18 **Blackford** Perth and Kinross, C Scotland, UK
Black Forest *see* Schwarzwald
30 J10 **Blackhawk** South Dakota, N USA
xliv D9 **Black Head** *headland* W Ireland
xxxvi F8 **Blackheath** Lewisham, SE England, UK
30 I10 **Black Hills** ⛰ South Dakota/Wyoming, N USA
xlii J11 **Black Isle** *peninsula* NW Scotland, UK
9 T10 **Black Lake** ⊙ Saskatchewan, C Canada
33 Q5 **Black Lake** ⊙ Michigan, N USA
20 I7 **Black Lake** ⊙ New York, NE USA
24 G6 **Black Lake** ⊡ Louisiana, S USA
xliv H5 **Blacklion** Cavan, N Ireland
xliii H25 **Black Loch** ⊙ Dumfries and Galloway, SW Scotland, UK
28 F7 **Black Mesa** ▲ Oklahoma, C USA
xxxv I15 **Blackmill** Bridgend, S Wales, UK
23 P10 **Black Mountain** North Carolina, SE USA
37 P13 **Black Mountain** ▲ California, W USA
39 Q2 **Black Mountain** ▲ Colorado, C USA
xxxv K12 **Black Mountains** ⛰ SE Wales, UK
38 H10 **Black Mountains** ⛰ Arizona, SW USA
35 Q16 **Black Pine Peak** ▲ Idaho, NW USA
xl M14 **Blackpool** Lancashire, NW England, UK
xl K13 **Blackpool** ◈ *unitary authority* NW England, UK
39 Q14 **Black Range** ⛰ New Mexico, SW USA
46 I12 **Black River** W Jamaica
12 J14 **Black River** ≈ Ontario, SE Canada
133 U12 **Black River** *Chin.* Babian Jiang, Lixian Jiang, *Fr.* Rivière Noire, *Vtn.* Sông Đa. ≈ China/Vietnam
46 I12 **Black River** ≈ W Jamaica
41 T7 **Black River** ≈ Alaska, USA
39 N13 **Black River** ≈ Arizona, SW USA
29 X7 **Black River** ≈ Arkansas/Missouri, C USA
24 I7 **Black River** ≈ Louisiana, S USA
33 S8 **Black River** ≈ Michigan, N USA
33 Q5 **Black River** ≈ Michigan, N USA
20 I8 **Black River** ≈ New York, NE USA
23 T13 **Black River** ≈ South Carolina, SE USA
32 J7 **Black River** ≈ Wisconsin, N USA
32 J7 **Black River Falls** Wisconsin, N USA
37 R3 **Black Rock Desert** *desert* Nevada, W USA
xl E14 **Blackrod** Bolton, NW England, UK
Black Sand Desert *see* Garagumy
23 S7 **Blacksburg** Virginia, NE USA
142 H10 **Black Sea** *var.* Euxine Sea, *Bul.* Cherno More, *Rom.* Marea Neagră, *Rus.* Chernoye More, *Turk.* Karadeniz, *Ukr.* Chorne More. *sea* Asia/Europe
119 Q10 **Black Sea Lowland** *Ukr.* Prychornomors'ka Nyzovyna. *depression* SE Europe
35 S17 **Blacks Fork** ≈ Wyoming, C USA
25 V7 **Blackshear** Georgia, SE USA
25 S6 **Blackshear, Lake** ⊡ Georgia, SE USA
xliv C6 **Blacksod Bay** *Ir.* Cuan an Fhóid Duibh. *inlet* W Ireland
xliv J12 **Blackstairs Mountains** ⛰ SE Ireland
23 V7 **Blackstone** Virginia, NE USA
xxxvii Q7 **Blackthorn** Oxfordshire, C England, UK
79 O14 **Black Volta** *var.* Borongo, Mouhoun, Moun Hou, *Fr.* Volta Noire. ≈ W Africa
25 O5 **Black Warrior River** ≈ Alabama, S USA
xliv J7 **Blackwater** ≈ E Ireland
xliv K12 **Blackwater** Wexford, SE Ireland
xliv H13 **Blackwater** *Ir.* An Abhainn Mhór. ≈ S Ireland
xliv J5 **Blackwater** ≈ Ireland/Northern Ireland, UK
xxxvii X8 **Blackwater** ≈ E England, UK
189 X8 **Blackwater** Queensland, E Australia
xlii H16 **Blackwater Reservoir** ⊡ NW Scotland, UK
29 T4 **Blackwater River** ≈ Missouri, C USA
23 W7 **Blackwater River** ≈ Virginia, NE USA
Blackwater State *see* Nebraska
29 N8 **Blackwell** Oklahoma, C USA
27 P7 **Blackwell** Texas, SW USA
101 J15 **Bladel** Noord-Brabant, S Netherlands
Bladenmarkt *see* Bălăuşeri
xxxv G6 **Blaenau Ffestiniog** Gwynedd, NW Wales, UK
xxxv J13 **Blaenau Gwent** ◈ *unitary authority* SE Wales, UK
xxxv K13 **Blaenavon** Torfaen, SE Wales, UK
xxxvi K10 **Blagdon** North West Somerset, SW England, UK
116 G11 **Blagoevgrad** *prev.* Gorna Dzhumaya. Sofiyska Oblast, W Bulgaria
126 Gg14 **Blagoveshchenka** Altayskiy Kray, S Russian Federation
126 M16 **Blagoveshchensk** Amurskaya Oblast', SE Russian Federation
131 V4 **Blagoveshchensk** Respublika Bashkortostan, W Russian Federation
104 I7 **Blain** Loire-Atlantique, NW France
xxxv K13 **Blaina** Blaenau Gwent, SE Wales, UK
31 V8 **Blaine** Minnesota, N USA
34 H6 **Blaine** Washington, NW USA
9 T15 **Blaine Lake** Saskatchewan, S Canada
31 S14 **Blair** Nebraska, C USA
xliii K15 **Blair Atholl** Perth and Kinross, C Scotland, UK
xliii L16 **Blairgowrie** Perth and Kinross, C Scotland, UK
20 C15 **Blairsville** Pennsylvania, NE USA
118 H11 **Blaj** *Ger.* Blasendorf, *Hung.* Balázsfalva. Alba, SW Romania
66 F9 **Blake-Bahama Ridge** *undersea feature* W Atlantic Ocean
25 S7 **Blakely** Georgia, SE USA
xxxviii G13 **Blakemere** Herefordshire, W England, UK
xxxvi L8 **Blakeney** Gloucestershire, C England, UK
xxxix W7 **Blakeney** Norfolk, E England, UK
xxxix W7 **Blakeney Point** *headland* E England, UK
66 E10 **Blake Plateau** *var.* Blake Terrace. *undersea feature* W Atlantic Ocean
32 M1 **Blake Point** *headland* Michigan, N USA
xxxix O13 **Blakesley** Northamptonshire, C England, UK
Blake Terrace *see* Blake Plateau
63 B24 **Blanca, Bahía** *bay* E Argentina
58 C12 **Blanca, Cordillera** ⛰ W Peru
107 T12 **Blanca, Costa** *physical region* SE Spain
39 S7 **Blanca Peak** ▲ Colorado, C USA
26 I9 **Blanca, Sierra** ▲ Texas, SW USA
123 K11 **Blanc, Cap** *headland* N Tunisia
Blanc, Cap *see* Nouâdhibou, Râs
33 R12 **Blanchard River** ≈ Ohio, N USA
190 E8 **Blanche, Cape** *headland* South Australia
195 U15 **Blanche Channel** *channel* NW Solomon Islands
190 J4 **Blanche, Lake** ⊙ South Australia
33 R14 **Blanchester** Ohio, N USA
190 J9 **Blanchetown** South Australia
47 U13 **Blanchisseuse** Trinidad, Trinidad and Tobago
xli P7 **Blanchland** Northumberland, N England, UK
105 T11 **Blanc, Mont** *It.* Monte Bianco. ▲ France/Italy
27 R11 **Blanco** Texas, SW USA
44 K14 **Blanco, Cabo** *headland* NW Costa Rica
34 D14 **Blanco, Cape** *headland* Oregon, NW USA
64 H10 **Blanco, Río** ≈ W Argentina
58 F10 **Blanco, Río** ≈ NE Peru
13 O9 **Blanc, Réservoir** ⊡ Québec, SE Canada
23 R7 **Bland** Virginia, NE USA
94 I2 **Blanda** ≈ N Iceland
xxxvi M13 **Blandford Forum** Dorset, S England, UK
39 O7 **Blanding** Utah, W USA
xliii J19 **Blanefield** Stirling, C Scotland, UK
107 X5 **Blanes** Cataluña, NE Spain
105 N3 **Blangy-sur-Bresle** Seine-Maritime, N France
113 C18 **Blanice** *Ger.* Blanitz. ≈ SE Czech Republic
Blanitz *see* Blanice
101 C16 **Blankenberge** West-Vlaanderen, NW Belgium
103 D17 **Blankenheim** Nordrhein-Westfalen, W Germany
27 R8 **Blanket** Texas, SW USA
57 O3 **Blanquilla, Isla** *var.* La Blanquilla. *island* N Venezuela
Blanquilla, La *see* Blanquilla, Isla
63 F18 **Blanquillo** Durazno, C Uruguay
113 G18 **Blansko** *Ger.* Blanz. Jižní Morava, SE Czech Republic
85 N15 **Blantyre** *var.* Blantyre-Limbe. Southern, S Malawi
85 N15 **Blantyre** ✕ Southern, S Malawi
Blantyre-Limbe *see* Blantyre
Blanz *see* Blansko
100 J10 **Blaricum** Noord-Holland, C Netherlands
Blasendorf *see* Blaj
xliv A13 **Blasket Islands** *island group* W Ireland
Blatnitsa *see* Durankulak
115 F15 **Blato** *It.* Blatta. Dubrovnik-Neretva, S Croatia
Blatta *see* Blato
110 E10 **Blatten** Valais, SW Switzerland
103 J20 **Blaufelden** Baden-Württemberg, SW Germany
97 E23 **Blåvands Huk** *headland* W Denmark
104 G6 **Blavet** ≈ NW France
xli R6 **Blaydon** Gateshead, NE England, UK
104 J12 **Blaye** Gironde, SW France
191 R8 **Blayney** New South Wales, SE Australia
xxxvi J10 **Bleadon** North West Somerset, SW England, UK
67 D25 **Bleaker Island** *island* SE Falkland Islands
xxxix O7 **Bleasby** Nottinghamshire, C England, UK
111 T10 **Bled** *Ger.* Veldes. NW Slovenia
xxxvii O7 **Bledington** Gloucestershire, C England, UK
101 D20 **Bléharies** Hainaut, SW Belgium
111 U9 **Bleiburg** *Slvn.* Pliberk. Kärnten, S Austria
103 L17 **Bleiloch-Stausee** ⊡ C Germany
100 H12 **Bleiswijk** Zuid-Holland, W Netherlands
97 L22 **Blekinge** ◈ *county* S Sweden
xli N8 **Blencarn** Cumbria, NW England, UK
12 D17 **Blenheim** Ontario, S Canada
193 K15 **Blenheim** Marlborough, South Island, NZ
101 M15 **Blerick** Limburg, SE Netherlands
Blesae *see* Blois
27 V13 **Blessing** Texas, SW USA
xliv K9 **Blessington** Wicklow, E Ireland
xxxvii R6 **Bletchley** Buckinghamshire, SE England, UK
12 I10 **Bleu, Lac** ⊙ Québec, SE Canada
xxxvii Q9 **Blewbury** Oxfordshire, C England, UK
Blibba *see* Blitta
123 I11 **Blida** *var.* El Boulaida, El Bouláida. N Algeria
97 P15 **Blidö** Stockholm, C Sweden
97 K18 **Blidsberg** Älvsborg, S Sweden
xxxix N7 **Blidworth** Nottinghamshire, C England, UK
193 A21 **Bligh Sound** *sound* South Island, NZ
197 H13 **Bligh Water** *strait* NW Fiji
12 D11 **Blind River** Ontario, S Canada
33 R11 **Blissfield** Michigan, N USA
xxxix O13 **Blisworth** Northamptonshire, C England, UK
174 Ll16 **Blitar** Jawa, C Indonesia
79 R15 **Blitta** *prev.* Blibba. C Togo
21 O13 **Block Island** *island* Rhode Island, NE USA
21 O13 **Block Island Sound** *sound* Rhode Island, NE USA
xxxvii O6 **Blockley** Gloucestershire, C England, UK
100 H10 **Bloemendaal** Noord-Holland, W Netherlands
85 H23 **Bloemfontein** *var.* Mangaung. ● (South Africa-judicial capital) Free State, C South Africa
85 I22 **Bloemhof** North-West, NW South Africa
104 M7 **Blois** *anc.* Blesae. Loir-et-Cher, C France
100 L8 **Blokzijl** Overijssel, N Netherlands
97 N20 **Blomstermåla** Kalmar, S Sweden
94 I2 **Blönduós** Nordhurland Vestra, N Iceland
112 L11 **Błonie** Warszawa, C Poland
xliv G2 **Bloody Foreland** *Ir.* Cnoc Fola. *headland* NW Ireland
33 N15 **Bloomfield** Indiana, N USA
31 X16 **Bloomfield** Iowa, C USA
29 Y8 **Bloomfield** Missouri, C USA
39 P9 **Bloomfield** New Mexico, SW USA
27 U7 **Blooming Grove** Texas, SW USA
31 W10 **Blooming Prairie** Minnesota, N USA
32 L13 **Bloomington** Illinois, N USA
33 O15 **Bloomington** Indiana, N USA
31 V9 **Bloomington** Minnesota, N USA
27 U13 **Bloomington** Texas, SW USA
20 H14 **Bloomsburg** Pennsylvania, NE USA
189 X7 **Bloomsbury** Queensland, NE Australia
174 Ll14 **Blora** Jawa, C Indonesia
20 G12 **Blossburg** Pennsylvania, NE USA
27 V5 **Blossom** Texas, SW USA
127 Oo3 **Blossom, Mys** *headland* Wrangel Island, NE Russian Federation
25 R8 **Blountstown** Florida, SE USA
23 P8 **Blountville** Tennessee, S USA
23 Q9 **Blowing Rock** North Carolina, SE USA
xxxvii P6 **Bloxham** Oxfordshire, C England, UK
xxxviii C14 **Bloxwich** Walsall, C England, UK
xli R13 **Blubberhouses** North Yorkshire, N England, UK
110 J8 **Bludenz** Vorarlberg, W Austria
38 L6 **Blue Bell Knoll** ▲ Utah, W USA
25 Y12 **Blue Cypress Lake** ⊙ Florida, SE USA
31 U11 **Blue Earth** Minnesota, N USA
23 Q7 **Bluefield** Virginia, NE USA
23 R7 **Bluefield** West Virginia, NE USA
45 N10 **Bluefields** Región Autónoma Atlántico Sur, SE Nicaragua
45 N10 **Bluefields, Bahía de** *bay* W Caribbean Sea
31 Z14 **Blue Grass** Iowa, C USA
Bluegrass State *see* Kentucky
Blue Hen State *see* Delaware
21 S7 **Blue Hill** Maine, NE USA
31 P16 **Blue Hill** Nebraska, C USA
32 J5 **Blue Hills** *hill range* Wisconsin, N USA
36 L3 **Blue Lake** California, W USA
Blue Law State *see* Connecticut
39 Q6 **Blue Mesa Reservoir** ⊡ Colorado, C USA
29 S12 **Blue Mountain** ▲ Arkansas, C USA
21 O6 **Blue Mountain** ▲ New Hampshire, NE USA
20 K8 **Blue Mountain** ▲ New York, NE USA
20 H15 **Blue Mountain** *ridge* Pennsylvania, NE USA
46 H10 **Blue Mountain Peak** ▲ E Jamaica
191 S8 **Blue Mountains** ⛰ New South Wales, SE Australia
34 L11 **Blue Mountains** ⛰ Oregon/Washington, NW USA
82 G12 **Blue Nile** ◈ *state* E Sudan
82 H12 **Blue Nile** *var.* Abai, Bahr el Azraq, *Amh.* Ābay Wenz, *Ar.* An Nīl al Azraq. ≈ Ethiopia/Sudan
15 Hh4 **Bluenose Lake** ⊙ Northwest Territories, NW Canada
29 O3 **Blue Rapids** Kansas, C USA
25 S1 **Blue Ridge** Georgia, SE USA
19 Q10 **Blue Ridge** *var.* Blue Ridge Mountains. ⛰ North Carolina/Virginia, E USA
25 S1 **Blue Ridge Lake** ⊡ Georgia, SE USA
Blue Ridge Mountains *see* Blue Ridge
9 N15 **Blue River** British Columbia, SW Canada
29 O12 **Blue River** ≈ Oklahoma, C USA
29 R4 **Blue Springs** Missouri, C USA
xliv G4 **Blue Stack Mountains** ⛰ N Ireland
23 R6 **Bluestone Lake** ⊡ West Virginia, NE USA
193 C25 **Bluff** Southland, South Island, NZ
39 O8 **Bluff** Utah, W USA
23 P8 **Bluff City** Tennessee, S USA
67 E24 **Bluff Cove** East Falkland, Falkland Islands
27 S7 **Bluff Dale** Texas, SW USA
191 N15 **Bluff Hill Point** *headland* Tasmania, SE Australia
33 Q12 **Bluffton** Indiana, N USA
33 R12 **Bluffton** Ohio, N USA
27 T7 **Blum** Texas, SW USA
103 G24 **Blumberg** Baden-Württemberg, SW Germany
62 K13 **Blumenau** Santa Catarina, S Brazil
31 N9 **Blunt** South Dakota, N USA
xxxix S11 **Bluntisham** Cambridgeshire, E England, UK
34 H15 **Bly** Oregon, NW USA
41 R13 **Blying Sound** *sound* Alaska, USA
xli R5 **Blyth** Northumberland, N England, UK
xxxix N5 **Blyth** Nottinghamshire, C England, UK
xli R5 **Blyth** ≈ N England, UK
xxxix Y11 **Blyth** ≈ E England, UK
xxxix Y11 **Blythburgh** Suffolk, E England, UK
37 Y16 **Blythe** California, W USA
29 Y9 **Blytheville** Arkansas, C USA
xxxix P4 **Blyton** Lincolnshire, E England, UK
119 V7 **Blyznyuky** Kharkivs'ka Oblast', E Ukraine
78 I15 **Bo** S Sierra Leone
97 G16 **Bø** Telemark, S Norway
179 Pp11 **Boac** Marinduque, N Philippines
44 K10 **Boaco** Boaco, S Nicaragua
44 J10 **Boaco** ◈ *department* C Nicaragua
81 I15 **Boali** Ombella-Mpoko, SW Central African Republic
Boalsert *see* Bolsward
194 K13 **Boana** Morobe, C PNG
195 Q10 **Boang Island** *island* Tanga Islands, NE PNG
33 V12 **Boardman** Ohio, N USA
34 J11 **Boardman** Oregon, NW USA
xliii N18 **Boarhills** Fife, E Scotland, UK
12 F13 **Boat Lake** ⊙ Ontario, S Canada
xliii K13 **Boat of Garten** Highland, NW Scotland, UK
60 F10 **Boa Vista** *state capital* Roraima, NW Brazil
78 D9 **Boa Vista** *island* Ilhas de Barlavento, E Cape Verde
25 O2 **Boaz** Alabama, S USA
166 L15 **Bobai** Guangxi Zhuangzu Zizhiqu, S China
180 J1 **Bobaomby, Tanjona** *Fr.* Cap d'Ambre. *headland* N Madagascar
161 M14 **Bobbili** Andhra Pradesh, E India
108 D9 **Bobbio** Emilia-Romagna, C Italy
12 I14 **Bobcaygeon** Ontario, SE Canada
Bober *see* Bóbr
105 O5 **Bobigny** Seine-St-Denis, N France
79 N13 **Bobo-Dioulasso** SW Burkina
112 G8 **Bobolice** *Ger.* Bublitz. Koszalin, NW Poland
175 T7 **Bobopayo** Pulau Halmahera, E Indonesia
153 P13 **Bobotogh, Qatorkūhi** *Rus.* Khrebet Babatag. ⛰ Tajikistan/Uzbekistan
116 G10 **Bobovdol** Sofiyska Oblast, W Bulgaria
121 M15 **Bobr** Minskaya Voblasts', NW Belorussia
121 M15 **Bobr** ≈ C Belorussia
113 E14 **Bóbr** *Eng.* Bobrawa, *Ger.* Bober. ≈ SW Poland
Bobrawa *see* Bóbr
Bobrik *see* Bobryk
Bobrinets *see* Bobrynets'
Bobrka/Bóbrka *see* Bibrka
130 L8 **Bobrov** Voronezhskaya Oblast', W Russian Federation
119 Q4 **Bobrovytsya** Chernihivs'ka Oblast', N Ukraine
Bobruysk *see* Babruysk
121 J19 **Bobryk** *Rus.* Bobrik. ≈ SW Belorussia
119 Q8 **Bobrynets'** *Rus.* Bobrinets. Kirovohrads'ka Oblast', C Ukraine
12 K14 **Bobs Lake** ⊙ Ontario, SE Canada
56 I6 **Bobures** Zulia, NW Venezuela
44 H1 **Boca Bacalar Chico** *headland* N Belize
114 G11 **Bočac** NW Bosnia and Herzegovina
43 R14 **Boca del Río** Veracruz-Llave, S Mexico
57 O4 **Boca de Pozo** Nueva Esparta, NE Venezuela
61 C15 **Boca do Acre** Amazonas, N Brazil
57 N12 **Boca Mavaca** Amazonas, S Venezuela
81 G14 **Bocaranga** Ouham-Pendé, W Central African Republic
25 Z15 **Boca Raton** Florida, SE USA
45 P14 **Bocas del Toro** Bocas del Toro, NW Panama
45 P15 **Bocas del Toro** *off.* Provincia de Bocas del Toro. ◈ *province* NW Panama
45 P15 **Bocas del Toro, Archipiélago de** *island group* NW Panama
44 I7 **Bocay** Jinotega, N Nicaragua
107 N6 **Boceguillas** Castilla-León, N Spain
Bocheykovo *see* Bacheykava
113 L17 **Bochnia** Tarnów, SE Poland
101 K16 **Bocholt** Limburg, NE Belgium
103 D14 **Bocholt** Nordrhein-Westfalen, W Germany
103 E15 **Bochum** Nordrhein-Westfalen, W Germany
xxxvii V6 **Bocking Churchstreet** Essex, SE England, UK
104 F2 **Bocognano** Corse, France, C Mediterranean Sea
56 I6 **Boconó** Trujillo, NW Venezuela
118 F12 **Bocşa** *Ger.* Bokschen, *Hung.* Boksánbánya. Caraş-Severin, SW Romania
81 H15 **Boda** Lobaye, SW Central African Republic
96 L12 **Böda** Kopparberg, C Sweden
97 O20 **Böda** Kalmar, S Sweden
97 L19 **Bodafors** Jönköping, S Sweden
126 Kk13 **Bodaybo** Irkutskaya Oblast', E Russian Federation
24 G5 **Bodcau, Bayou** *var.* Bodcau Creek. ≈ Louisiana, S USA
Bodcau Creek *see* Bodcau, Bayou
xlii Q12 **Boddam** Aberdeenshire, NE Scotland, UK
xlii I5 **Boddam** Shetland Islands, NE Scotland, UK
46 D8 **Bodden Town** *var.* Boddentown. Grand Cayman, SW Cayman Islands
103 K14 **Bode** ≈ C Germany
xxxv E4 **Bodedern** Isle of Anglesey, NW Wales, UK
36 L7 **Bodega Head** *headland* California, W USA
Bodegas *see* Babahoyo
100 H11 **Bodegraven** Zuid-Holland, C Netherlands
80 H8 **Bodélé** *depression* W Chad
94 J13 **Boden** Norrbotten, N Sweden
Bodensee *see* Constance, Lake, C Europe
xliv G7 **Boderg, Lough** ⊙ C Ireland
67 M15 **Bode Verde Fracture Zone** *tectonic feature* E Atlantic Ocean
xxxv E6 **Bodfuan** Gwynedd, NW Wales, UK
161 H14 **Bodhan** Andhra Pradesh, C India
168 I9 **Bodi** Bayanhongor, C Mongolia
xxxvii W12 **Bodiam** East Sussex, SE England, UK
161 H22 **Bodināyakkanūr** Tamil Nādu, SE India
110 H10 **Bodio** Ticino, S Switzerland
xxxvi D15 **Bodmin** Cornwall, SW England, UK
xxxvi D15 **Bodmin Moor** *moorland* SW England, UK
94 G12 **Bodø** Nordland, C Norway
61 H20 **Bodoquena, Serra da** ⛰ SW Brazil
142 B16 **Bodrum** Muğla, SW Turkey
Bodzafordulό *see* Întorsura Buzăului
101 L14 **Boekel** Noord-Brabant, SE Netherlands
Boeloekoemba *see* Bulukumba
105 Q11 **Boën** Loire, E France
81 K18 **Boende** Equateur, C Zaire
27 R11 **Boerne** Texas, SW USA

◆ Country ● Country Capital ◇ Dependent Territory ○ Dependent Territory Capital ◈ Administrative Region ✕ International Airport ▲ Mountain ⛰ Mountain Range Volcano ≈ River ⊙ Lake ⊡ Reservoir

BOEROE – BOUGHESSA

Boeroe *see* Buru, Pulau
Boetoeng *see* Buton, Pulau
24 I5 **Boeuf River** ≈ Arkansas/Louisiana, S USA
78 H14 **Boffa** Guinée-Maritime, W Guinea
xliv H7 **Bofin, Lough** ◎ N Ireland
Bó Finne, Inis *see* Inishbofin
Boga *see* Bogë
177 Ff9 **Bogale** Irrawaddy, SW Burma
24 L8 **Bogalusa** Louisiana, S USA
79 Q12 **Bogandé** C Burkina
81 I15 **Bogangolo** Ombella-Mpoko, C Central African Republic
191 Q7 **Bogan River** ≈ New South Wales, SE Australia
27 W5 **Bogata** Texas, SW USA
113 D14 **Bogatynia** *Ger.* Reichenau. Jelenia Góra, SW Poland
142 K13 **Boğazlıyan** Yozgat, C Turkey
81 J17 **Bogbonga** Equateur, NW Zaire
164 J14 **Bogcang Zangbo** ≈ W China
164 L5 **Bogda Feng** ▲ NW China
116 I9 **Bogdan** ▲ C Bulgaria
115 Q20 **Bogdanci** SE FYR Macedonia
164 M5 **Bogda Shan** *var.* Po-ko-to Shan. ▲▲ NW China
115 K17 **Bogë** *var.* Boga. Shkodër, N Albania
Bogendorf *see* Łuków
97 G23 **Bogense** Fyn, C Denmark
191 T3 **Boggabilla** New South Wales, SE Australia
191 S6 **Boggabri** New South Wales, SE Australia
xliv E13 **Boggeragh Mountains** ▲▲ S Ireland
194 I10 **Bogia** Madang, N PNG
xxxvii S13 **Bognor Regis** West Sussex, SE England, UK
179 Qq13 **Bogo** Cebu, C Philippines
Bogodukhov *see* Bohodukhiv
189 V15 **Bogong, Mount** ▲ Victoria, SE Australia
174 J14 **Bogor** *Dut.* Buitenzorg. Jawa, C Indonesia
130 L5 **Bogoroditsk** Tul'skaya Oblast', W Russian Federation
131 O3 **Bogorodsk** Nizhegorodskaya Oblast', W Russian Federation
Bogorodskoje *see* Bogorodskoye
127 Nn14 **Bogorodskoye** Khabarovskiy Kray, SE Russian Federation
129 R15 **Bogorodskoye** *var.* Bogorodskoje. Kirovskaya Oblast', NW Russian Federation
56 F10 **Bogotá** *prev.* Santa Fe, Santa Fe de Bogotá. ● (Colombia) Cundinamarca, C Colombia
159 T14 **Bogra** Rajshahi, N Bangladesh
Bogschan *see* Boldu
126 Ii13 **Boguchany** Krasnoyarskiy Kray, C Russian Federation
130 M9 **Boguchar** Voronezhskaya Oblast', W Russian Federation
78 H10 **Bogué** Brakna, SW Mauritania
24 K8 **Bogue Chitto** ≈ Louisiana/Mississippi, S USA
Bogushëvsk *see* Bahushewsk
Boguslav *see* Bohuslav
46 K12 **Bog Walk** C Jamaica
167 Q3 **Bo Hai** *var.* Gulf of Chihli. *gulf* NE China
167 R3 **Bohai Haixia** *strait* NE China
167 Q3 **Bohai Wan** *bay* NE China
113 C17 **Bohemia** *Cz.* Čechy, *Ger.* Böhmen. *cultural and historical region* W Czech Republic
113 B18 **Bohemian Forest** *Cz.* Ceský Les, Šumava, *Ger.* Böhmerwald. ▲▲ C Europe
Bohemian-Moravian Highlands *see* Českomoravská Vrchovina
79 R16 **Bohicon** S Benin
111 S11 **Bohinjska Bistrica** *Ger.* Wocheiner Feistritz. NW Slovenia
Bohkká *see* Pokka
Böhmen *see* Bohemia
Böhmerwald *see* Bohemian Forest
Böhmisch-Krumau *see* Český Krumlov
Böhmisch-Leipa *see* Česká Lípa
Böhmisch-Mährische Höhe *see* Českomoravská Vrchovina
Böhmisch-Trübau *see* Česká Třebová
119 U5 **Bohodukhiv** *Rus.* Bogodukhov. Kharkivs'ka Oblast', E Ukraine
179 Qq14 **Bohol** *island* C Philippines
179 Qq15 **Bohol Sea** *var.* Mindanao Sea. *sea* S Philippines
118 I7 **Bohorodchany** Ivano-Frankivs'ka Oblast', W Ukraine
168 M9 **Böhöt** Dundgovĭ, C Mongolia
164 K6 **Bohu** *var.* Bagrax. Xinjiang Uygur Zizhiqu, NW China
113 I17 **Bohumín** *Ger.* Oderberg; *prev.* Neuoderberg, Nový Bohumín. Severní Morava, E Czech Republic
119 P6 **Bohuslav** *Rus.* Boguslav. Kyyivs'ka Oblast', N Ukraine
60 F11 **Boiaçu** Roraima, N Brazil
109 K16 **Boiano** Molise, C Italy
13 R8 **Boilleau** Québec, SE Canada
61 O17 **Boipeba, Ilha de** *island* SE Brazil
106 G3 **Boiro** Galicia, NW Spain
33 Q5 **Bois Blanc Island** *island* Michigan, N USA
31 R7 **Bois de Sioux River** ≈ Minnesota, N USA
35 N14 **Boise** *var.* Boise City. *state capital* Idaho, NW USA
28 G8 **Boise City** Oklahoma, C USA
35 N14 **Boise River, Middle Fork** ≈ Idaho, NW USA
Bois, Lac des *see* Woods, Lake of the
Bois-le-Duc *see* 's-Hertogenbosch
9 W17 **Boissevain** Manitoba, S Canada
13 T7 **Boisvert, Pointe au** *headland* Québec, SE Canada
102 K10 **Boizenburg** Mecklenburg-Vorpommern, N Germany
Bojador *see* Boujdour
115 K18 **Bojana** *Alb.* Bunë. ≈ Albania/Yugoslavia *see also* Bunë
149 S3 **Bojnūrd** *var.* Bujnurd. Khorāsān, N Iran
174 Ll15 **Bojonegoro** *prev.* Bodjonegoro. Jawa, C Indonesia
201 T1 **Bokaak Atoll** *var.* Bokak, Taongi. *atoll* Ratak Chain, NE Marshall Islands
Bokak *see* Bokaak Atoll
159 Q15 **Bokāro** Bihār, N India
81 I18 **Bokatola** Equateur, NW Zaire
78 H13 **Boké** Guinée-Maritime, W Guinea
Bokhara *see* Bukhoro
191 Q4 **Bokharra River** ≈ New South Wales/Queensland, SE Australia
Bo Kheo *see* Bâ Kêv
97 C16 **Boknafjorden** *fjord* S Norway
80 H11 **Bokoro** Chari-Baguirmi, W Chad
81 K19 **Bokota** Equateur, NW Zaire
178 Gg13 **Bokpyin** Tenasserim, S Burma
Boksánbánya/Bokschen *see* Bocşa
85 F21 **Bokspits** Kgalagadi, SW Botswana
81 K18 **Bokungu** Equateur, C Zaire
Bokurdak *see* Bakhardok
80 G10 **Bol** Lac, W Chad
175 Qq9 **Bolaang** Sulawesi, N Indonesia
78 G13 **Bolama** SW Guinea-Bissau
Bolangir *see* Balāngīr
Bolanos *see* Bolanos, Mount, Guam
Bolaños *see* Bolaños de Calatrava, Spain
107 N11 **Bolaños de Calatrava** *var.* Bolaños. Castilla-La Mancha, C Spain
196 B17 **Bolanos, Mount** *var.* Bolanos. ▲ S Guam
42 L12 **Bolaños, Río** ≈ C Mexico
117 M14 **Bolayır** Çanakkale, NW Turkey
104 L3 **Bolbec** Seine-Maritime, N France
xli S6 **Boldon** South Tyneside, NE England, UK
xxxvii P13 **Boldre** Hampshire, S England, UK
118 L13 **Boldu** *var.* Bogschan. Buzău, SE Romania
152 H8 **Boldumsaz** *prev.* Kalinin, Kalininsk, Porsy. Dashkhovuzskiy Velayat, N Turkmenistan
164 I4 **Bole** *var.* Bortala. Xinjiang Uygur Zizhiqu, NW China
79 O15 **Bole** NW Ghana
81 J19 **Boleko** Equateur, W Zaire
113 E14 **Bolesławiec** *Ger.* Bunzlau. Jelenia Góra, SW Poland
131 R4 **Bolgar** *prev.* Kuybyshev. Respublika Tatarstan, W Russian Federation
79 P14 **Bolgatanga** N Ghana
Bolgrad *see* Bolhrad
119 N12 **Bolhrad** *Rus.* Bolgrad. Odes'ka Oblast', SW Ukraine
169 Y8 **Boli** Heilongjiang, NE China
81 I19 **Bolia** Bandundu, W Zaire
95 J14 **Boliden** Västerbotten, N Sweden
176 Uu11 **Bolifar** Pulau Seram, E Indonesia
179 Oo9 **Bolinao** Luzon, N Philippines
29 T6 **Bolivar** Missouri, C USA
22 F10 **Bolivar** Tennessee, S USA
56 C12 **Bolívar** Cauca, SW Colombia
56 F7 **Bolívar** *off.* Departmento de Bolívar. ◐ *province* N Colombia
58 A13 **Bolívar** ◐ *province* C Ecuador
57 N9 **Bolívar** *off.* Estado Bolívar. ◐ *state* SE Venezuela
27 X12 **Bolivar Peninsula** *headland* Texas, SW USA
56 I6 **Bolívar, Pico** ▲ W Venezuela
59 K17 **Bolivia** *off.* Republic of Bolivia. ◆ *republic* W South America
114 O13 **Boljevac** Serbia, E Yugoslavia
Bolkenhain *see* Bolków
130 J5 **Bolkhov** Orlovskaya Oblast', W Russian Federation
113 F14 **Bolków** *Ger.* Bolkenhain. Jelenia Góra, SW Poland
190 K3 **Bollards Lagoon** South Australia
105 R14 **Bollene** Vaucluse, SE France
xl G16 **Bollin** ≈ Cheshire, C England, UK
xl H17 **Bollington** Cheshire, W England, UK
96 N12 **Bollnäs** Gävleborg, C Sweden
189 W10 **Bollon** Queensland, C Australia
199 Jj14 **Bollons Tablemount** *undersea feature* S Pacific Ocean
95 H17 **Bollstabruk** Västernorrland, C Sweden
Bolluilos de Par del Condado *see* Bollulos Par del Condado
106 J14 **Bollulos Par del Condado** *var.* Bolluilos de Par del Condado. Andalucía, S Spain
97 K21 **Bolmen** ◎ S Sweden
143 T10 **Bolnisi** S Georgia
81 H19 **Bolobo** Bandundu, W Zaire
127 N14 **Bolodek** Khabarovskiy Kray, SE Russian Federation
108 G10 **Bologna** Emilia-Romagna, N Italy
128 I15 **Bologoye** Tverskaya Oblast', W Russian Federation
81 J18 **Bolomba** Equateur, NW Zaire
43 X13 **Bolónchén de Rejón** *var.* Bolonchén de Rejón. Campeche, SE Mexico
126 H14 **Bolotnoye** Novosibirskaya Oblast', C Russian Federation
116 J13 **Boloústra, Ákra** *headland* NE Greece
178 Jj10 **Bolovens, Plateau des** *plateau* S Laos
108 H13 **Bolsena** Lazio, C Italy
109 G14 **Bolsena, Lago di** ◎ C Italy
130 B3 **Bol'shakovo** *Ger.* Kreuzingen; *prev.* Gross-Skaisgirren. Kaliningradskaya Oblast', W Russian Federation
126 J6 **Bol'shaya Balakhnya** ≈ N Russian Federation
Bol'shaya Berëstovitsa *see* Vyalikaya Byerastavitsa
131 S7 **Bol'shaya Chernigovka** Samarskaya Oblast', W Russian Federation
131 S7 **Bol'shaya Glushitsa** Samarskaya Oblast', W Russian Federation
150 H9 **Bol'shaya Khobda** *Kaz.* Ülkenqobda. ≈ Kazakhstan/Russian Federation
126 Jj8 **Bol'shaya Kuonamka** ≈ NE Russian Federation
130 M12 **Bol'shaya Martynovka** Rostovskaya Oblast', SW Russian Federation
126 I13 **Bol'shaya Murta** Krasnoyarskiy Kray, C Russian Federation
129 V4 **Bol'shaya Rogovaya** ≈ NW Russian Federation
129 U7 **Bol'shaya Synya** ≈ NW Russian Federation
151 V9 **Bol'shaya Vladimirovka** Semipalatinsk, E Kazakhstan
125 G13 **Bol'sherech'ye** Omskaya Oblast', C Russian Federation
127 Pp12 **Bol'sheretsk** Kamchatskaya Oblast', E Russian Federation
131 W3 **Bol'sheust'ikinskoye** Respublika Bashkortostan, W Russian Federation
Bol'shevik *see* Bal'shavik
126 Ii3 **Bol'shevik, Ostrov** *island* Severnaya Zemlya, N Russian Federation
129 U4 **Bol'shezemel'skaya Tundra** *physical region* NW Russian Federation
150 J13 **Bol'shiye Barsuki, Peski** *desert* SW Kazakhstan
125 Ff12 **Bol'shiye Uki** Omskaya Oblast', C Russian Federation
127 O6 **Bol'shoy Anyuy** ≈ NE Russian Federation
126 K6 **Bol'shoy Begichev, Ostrov** *island* NE Russian Federation
131 O4 **Bol'shoye Murashkino** Nizhegorodskaya Oblast', W Russian Federation
131 W4 **Bol'shoy Iremel'** ▲ W Russian Federation
131 R7 **Bol'shoy Irgiz** ≈ W Russian Federation
126 M5 **Bol'shoy Lyakhovskiy, Ostrov** *island* NE Russian Federation
126 Ll13 **Bol'shoy Nimnyr** Respublika Sakha (Yakutiya), NE Russian Federation
Bol'shoy Rozhan *see* Vyaliki Rozhan
150 E10 **Bol'shoy Uzen'** *Kaz.* Ülkenözen. ≈ Kazakhstan/Russian Federation
126 Ii15 **Bol'shoy Yenisey** *var.* Biy-Khem. ≈ S Russian Federation
42 K6 **Bolson de Mapimi** ▲▲ NW Mexico
xxxix N6 **Bolsover** Derbyshire, C England, UK
100 K6 **Bolsward** *Fris.* Boalsert. Friesland, N Netherlands
107 T4 **Boltaña** Aragón, NE Spain
xli S11 **Boltby** North Yorkshire, N England, UK
xl E14 **Bolton** *prev.* Bolton-le-Moors. Bolton, NW England, UK
xli O15 **Bolton** ◐ *unitary authority* NW England, UK
12 G15 **Bolton** Ontario, S Canada
23 V12 **Bolton** North Carolina, SE USA
Bolton-le-Moors *see* Bolton
xli N12 **Bolton-le-Sands** Lancashire, NW England, UK
142 G11 **Bolu** Bolu, NW Turkey
142 G11 **Bolu** ◐ *province* NW Turkey
195 N15 **Bolubolu** Goodenough Island, S PNG
94 H1 **Bolungarvík** Vestfirdhir, NW Iceland
165 O10 **Boluntay** Qinghai, W China
xliv A14 **Bolus Head** *headland* SW Ireland
142 F14 **Bolvadin** Afyon, W Turkey
116 M10 **Bolyarovo** *prev.* Pashkeni. Burgaska Oblast, SE Bulgaria
108 G6 **Bolzano** *Ger.* Bozen; *anc.* Bauzanum. Trentino-Alto Adige, N Italy
81 F22 **Boma** Bas-Zaïre, W Zaire
191 R12 **Bombala** New South Wales, SE Australia
106 F10 **Bombarral** Leiria, C Portugal
160 D13 **Bombay** *Guj.* Mumbai. Mahārāshtra, W India
160 D13 **Bombay** ✕ Mahārāshtra, W India
176 Vv11 **Bomberai** ≈ Irian Jaya, E Indonesia
176 Vv11 **Bomberai, Jazirah** *peninsula* Irian Jaya, E Indonesia
176 Vv11 **Bomberai, Semenanjung** *headland* Irian Jaya, E Indonesia
83 F18 **Bombo** S Uganda
81 I17 **Bomboma** Equateur, NW Zaire
61 I14 **Bom Futuro** Pará, N Brazil
165 Q15 **Bomi** *var.* Bowo, Zhamo. Xizang Zizhiqu, W China
81 N17 **Bomili** Haut-Zaïre, NE Zaire
61 N17 **Bom Jesus da Lapa** Bahia, E Brazil
62 Q8 **Bom Jesus do Itabapoana** Rio de Janeiro, SE Brazil
97 C15 **Bømlafjorden** *fjord* S Norway
97 B15 **Bømlo** *island* S Norway
126 M14 **Bomnak** Amurskaya Oblast', SE Russian Federation
81 I17 **Bomongo** Equateur, NW Zaire
63 K14 **Bom Retiro** Santa Catarina, S Brazil
81 L15 **Bomu** *var.* Mbomou, Mbomu, M'Bomu. ≈ Central African Republic/Zaire
148 J3 **Bonāb** *var.* Benāb, Bunab. Āžarbāyjān-e Khāvarī, N Iran
47 Q16 **Bonaire** *island* E Netherlands Antilles
41 U11 **Bona, Mount** ▲ Alaska, USA
194 M16 **Bonando** ≈ SE Papau New Guinea
191 Q12 **Bonang** Victoria, SE Australia
44 L7 **Bonanza** Región Autónoma Atlántico Norte, NE Nicaragua
39 O4 **Bonanza** Utah, W USA
47 O9 **Bonao** C Dominican Republic
188 L3 **Bonaparte Archipelago** *island group* Western Australia
34 K6 **Bonaparte, Mount** ▲ Washington, NW USA
xlii J10 **Bonar Bridge** Highland, NW Scotland, UK
41 N11 **Bonasila Dome** ▲ Alaska, USA
47 T15 **Bonasse** Trinidad, Trinidad and Tobago
13 X7 **Bonaventure** Québec, SE Canada
13 X7 **Bonaventure** ≈ Québec, SE Canada
11 V11 **Bonavista** Newfoundland, Newfoundland and Labrador, SE Canada
11 U11 **Bonavista Bay** *inlet* NW Atlantic Ocean
xliii G17 **Bonawe** Argyll and Bute, W Scotland, UK
123 Kk11 **Bon, Cap** *headland* N Tunisia
xxxv E12 **Boncath** Pembrokeshire, SW Wales, UK
xliii N22 **Bonchester Bridge** The Borders, S Scotland, UK
81 E19 **Bonda** Ogooué-Lolo, C Gabon
131 N6 **Bondari** Tambovskaya Oblast', W Russian Federation
108 G9 **Bondeno** Emilia-Romagna, C Italy
32 L4 **Bond Falls Flowage** ◎ Michigan, N USA
81 L16 **Bondo** Haut-Zaïre, N Zaire
175 P17 **Bondokodi** Pulau Sumba, S Indonesia
79 O15 **Bondoukou** E Ivory Coast
Bondoukui/Bondoukuy *see* Boundoukui
174 Mm15 **Bondowoso** Jawa, C Indonesia
35 S14 **Bondurant** Wyoming, C USA
Bone *see* Watampone, Indonesia
Bône *see* Annaba, Algeria
32 I5 **Bone Lake** ◎ Wisconsin, N USA
175 R12 **Bonelipu** Pulau Buton, C Indonesia
175 Q14 **Bonerate, Kepulauan** *var.* Macan. *island group* C Indonesia
175 Pp15 **Bonerate, Pulau** *island* Kepulauan Bonerate, 234C Indonesia
xliii L19 **Bo'Ness** Falkirk, C Scotland, UK
31 O12 **Bonesteel** South Dakota, N USA
64 I8 **Bonete, Cerro** ▲ N Argentina
175 Pp11 **Bone, Teluk** *bay* Sulawesi, C Indonesia
110 D6 **Bonfol** Jura, NW Switzerland
159 U12 **Bongaigaon** Assam, NE India
81 K17 **Bongandanga** Equateur, NW Zaire
80 L13 **Bongo, Massif des** *var.* Chaîne des Mongos. ▲▲ NE Central African Republic
80 G12 **Bongor** Mayo-Kébbi, SW Chad
79 N16 **Bongouanou** E Ivory Coast
178 Kk11 **Bông Sơn** *var.* Hoai Nhơn. Binh Đinh, C Vietnam
27 U5 **Bonham** Texas, SW USA
Bonhard *see* Bonyhád
105 U6 **Bonhomme, Col du** *pass* NE France
104 F3 **Bonifacio** Corse, France, C Mediterranean Sea
Bonifacio, Bocche de/Bonifacio, Bouches de *see* Bonifacio, Strait of
104 F3 **Bonifacio, Strait of** *Fr.* Bouches de Bonifacio, *It.* Bocche de Bonifacio. *strait* C Mediterranean Sea
25 Q8 **Bonifay** Florida, SE USA
Bonin Islands *see* Ogasawara-shotō
199 H6 **Bonin Trench** *undersea feature* NW Pacific Ocean
25 W15 **Bonita Springs** Florida, SE USA
44 I5 **Bonito, Pico** ▲ N Honduras
103 E17 **Bonn** Nordrhein-Westfalen, W Germany
94 H11 **Bonnåsjøen** Nordland, C Norway
12 J12 **Bonnechere** Ontario, SE Canada
12 J12 **Bonnechere** ≈ Ontario, SE Canada
35 N7 **Bonners Ferry** Idaho, NW USA
29 R4 **Bonner Springs** Kansas, C USA
104 L6 **Bonnétable** Sarthe, NW France
29 X6 **Bonne Terre** Missouri, C USA
8 J5 **Bonnet Plume** ≈ Yukon Territory, NW Canada
104 M6 **Bonneval** Eure-et-Loir, C France
105 T10 **Bonneville** Haute-Savoie, E France
38 J3 **Bonneville Salt Flats** *salt flat* Utah, W USA
79 U18 **Bonny** Rivers, S Nigeria
Bonny, Bight of *see* Biafra, Bight of
xliii K19 **Bonnybridge** Falkirk, C Scotland, UK
39 W4 **Bonny Reservoir** ⊡ Colorado, C USA
xliii M20 **Bonnyrigg** Midlothian, SE Scotland, UK
9 R14 **Bonnyville** Alberta, SW Canada
109 C18 **Bono** Sardegna, Italy, C Mediterranean Sea
176 Xx10 **Bonoi** Irian Jaya, E Indonesia
Bononia *see* Vidin, Bulgaria
Bononia *see* Boulogne-sur-Mer, France
109 B18 **Bonorva** Sardegna, Italy, C Mediterranean Sea
32 M15 **Bonpas Creek** ≈ Illinois, N USA
202 I3 **Bonriki** Tarawa, W Kiribati
191 T4 **Bonshaw** New South Wales, SE Australia
xxxv H9 **Bont-goch** Ceredigion, W Wales, UK
78 I16 **Bonthe** SW Sierra Leone
xxxv H7 **Bont Newydd** Gwynedd, NW Wales, UK
179 P8 **Bontoc** Luzon, N Philippines
194 M16 **Bonua** ≈ S PNG
xxxv J15 **Bonvilston** The Vale of Glamorgan, S Wales, UK
27 Y9 **Bon Wier** Texas, SW USA
113 J25 **Bonyhád** *Ger.* Bonhard. Tolna, S Hungary
Bonzabaai *see* Bonza Bay
85 J25 **Bonza Bay** *Afr.* Bonzabaai. Eastern Cape, S South Africa
190 D7 **Bookabie** South Australia
190 H6 **Bookaloo** South Australia
39 P5 **Book Cliffs** *cliff* Colorado/Utah, W USA
175 Tt9 **Boo, Kepulauan** *island group* E Indonesia
27 P1 **Booker** Texas, SW USA
78 K15 **Boola** Guinée-Forestière, SE Guinea
191 O8 **Booligal** New South Wales, SE Australia
101 G17 **Boom** Antwerpen, N Belgium
45 N6 **Boom** *var.* Boon. Región Autónoma Atlántico Norte, NE Nicaragua
191 S3 **Boomi** New South Wales, SE Australia
Boon *see* Boom
31 V13 **Boone** Iowa, C USA
23 Q8 **Boone** North Carolina, SE USA
29 S11 **Booneville** Arkansas, C USA
23 N6 **Booneville** Kentucky, S USA
25 N2 **Booneville** Mississippi, S USA
23 V3 **Boonsboro** Maryland, NE USA
168 H9 **Böön Tsagaan Nuur** ◎ S Mongolia
36 L6 **Boonville** California, W USA
33 N16 **Boonville** Indiana, N USA
29 U4 **Boonville** Missouri, C USA
20 I9 **Boonville** New York, NE USA
82 M12 **Boorama** Woqooyi Galbeed, NW Somalia
191 O6 **Booroondarra, Mount** *hill* New South Wales, SE Australia
191 N9 **Booroorban** New South Wales, SE Australia
191 R9 **Boorowa** New South Wales, SE Australia
101 H17 **Boortmeerbeek** Vlaams Brabant, C Belgium
82 P11 **Boosaaso** *var.* Bandar Kassim, Bender Qaasim, Bosaso, *It.* Bender Cassim. Bari, N Somalia
21 Q8 **Boothbay Harbor** Maine, NE USA
Boothia Felix *see* Boothia Peninsula
15 Kk2 **Boothia, Gulf of** *gulf* Northwest Territories, NE Canada
15 K2 **Boothia Peninsula** *prev.* Boothia Felix. *peninsula* Northwest Territories, NE Canada
xl K11 **Bootle** Cumbria, NW England, UK
xl B15 **Bootle** Sefton, NW England, UK
81 E18 **Booué** Ogooué-Ivindo, NE Gabon
103 J21 **Bopfingen** Baden-Württemberg, S Germany
103 F18 **Boppard** Rheinland-Pfalz, W Germany
64 M4 **Boquerón** *off.* Departamento de Boquerón. ◐ *department* W Paraguay
45 P15 **Boquete** *var.* Bajo Boquete. Chiriquí, W Panama
42 J6 **Boquilla, Presa de la** ⊡ N Mexico
42 L5 **Boquillas** *var.* Boquillas del Carmen. Coahuila de Zaragoza, NE Mexico
Boquillas del Carmen *see* Boquillas
126 I11 **Bor** Krasnoyarskiy Kray, C Russian Federation
83 F15 **Bor** Jonglei, S Sudan
97 L20 **Bor** Jönköping, S Sweden
142 J15 **Bor** Niğde, S Turkey
114 P12 **Bor** Serbia, E Yugoslavia
203 S10 **Bora-Bora** *island* Îles Sous le Vent, W French Polynesia
178 Ii10 **Borabu** Maha Sarakham, E Thailand
35 P13 **Borah Peak** ▲ Idaho, NW USA
Boralday *see* Burunday
97 J19 **Borås** Älvsborg, S Sweden
149 N11 **Borāzjān** *var.* Borazjān. Būshehr, S Iran
Borazjān *see* Borāzjān
60 G13 **Borba** Amazonas, N Brazil
106 H11 **Borba** Évora, S Portugal
Borbetomagus *see* Worms
57 O7 **Borbón** Bolívar, E Venezuela
61 Q15 **Borborema, Planalto da** *plateau* NE Brazil
118 M14 **Borcea, Braţul** ≈ S Romania
Borchalo *see* Marneuli
205 R15 **Borchgrevink Coast** *physical region* Antarctica
143 Q11 **Borçka** Artvin, NE Turkey
100 N11 **Borculo** Gelderland, E Netherlands
190 G10 **Borda, Cape** *headland* South Australia
104 K13 **Bordeaux** *anc.* Burdigala. Gironde, SW France
9 T15 **Borden** Saskatchewan, S Canada
12 D8 **Borden Lake** ◎ Ontario, S Canada
15 L1 **Borden Peninsula** *peninsula* Baffin Island, Northwest Territories, NE Canada
190 K11 **Bordertown** South Australia
94 H2 **Bordheyri** Vestfirdhir, NW Iceland
108 B11 **Bordighera** Liguria, NW Italy
76 K5 **Bordj-Bou-Arreridj** *var.* Bordj Bou Arreridj, Bordj Bou Arréridj. N Algeria
123 I10 **Bordj El Bahri, Cap de** *headland* N Algeria
76 L10 **Bordj Omar Driss** E Algeria
149 N13 **Bord Khūn** Hormozgān, S Iran
xxxvii R11 **Bordon** Hampshire, S England, UK
153 V7 **Bordunskiy** Chuyskaya Oblast', N Kyrgyzstan
xxxvii T8 **Borehamwood** Hertfordshire, E England, UK
xliii M23 **Boreland** Dumfries and Galloway, SW Scotland, UK
97 M17 **Borensberg** Östergötland, S Sweden
xlii A10 **Boreray** *island* NW Scotland, UK
Borgå *see* Porvoo
94 L2 **Borgarfjördhur** Austurland, NE Iceland
94 H3 **Borgarnes** Vesturland, W Iceland
95 G14 **Børgefjellet** ▲▲ C Norway
100 O7 **Borger** Drenthe, NE Netherlands
27 N2 **Borger** Texas, SW USA
97 N20 **Borgholm** Kalmar, S Sweden
109 N22 **Borgia** Calabria, SW Italy
101 J18 **Borgloon** Limburg, NE Belgium
205 P2 **Borg Massif** ▲▲ Antarctica
24 L9 **Borgne, Lake** ◎ Louisiana, S USA
108 C7 **Borgomanero** Piemonte, NE Italy
108 G10 **Borgo Panigale** ✕ (Bologna) Emilia-Romagna, N Italy
109 J15 **Borgorose** Lazio, C Italy
108 A9 **Borgo San Dlmazzo** Piemonte, N Italy
108 G11 **Borgo San Lorenzo** Toscana, C Italy
108 C7 **Borgosesia** Piemonte, NE Italy
108 E9 **Borgo Val di Taro** Emilia-Romagna, C Italy
108 G6 **Borgo Valsugana** Trentino-Alto Adige, N Italy
xliii J25 **Borgue** Dumfries and Galloway, SW Scotland, UK
xlii L8 **Borgue** Highland, N Scotland, UK
169 O11 **Borhoyn Tal** Dornogovĭ, SE Mongolia
178 Ii8 **Borikhan** *var.* Borikhane. Bolikhamxai, C Laos
Borikhane *see* Borikhan
Borislav *see* Boryslav
131 N8 **Borisoglebsk** Voronezhskaya Oblast', W Russian Federation
Borisov *see* Barysaw
Borisovgrad *see* Pŭrvomay
Borispol' *see* Boryspil'
180 I3 **Boriziny** Mahajanga, NW Madagascar
107 Q5 **Borja** Aragón, NE Spain
Borjas Blancas *see* Les Borges Blanques
143 S10 **Borjomi** *Rus.* Borzhomi. C Georgia
120 L12 **Borkavichy** *Rus.* Borkovichi. Vitsyebskaya Voblasts', N Belorussia
103 H16 **Borken** Hessen, C Germany
103 E14 **Borken** Nordrhein-Westfalen, W Germany
94 H10 **Borkenes** Troms, N Norway
80 H7 **Borkou-Ennedi-Tibesti** *off.* Préfecture du Borkou-Ennedi-Tibesti. ◐ *prefecture* N Chad
Borkovichi *see* Borkavichy
102 E9 **Borkum** *island* NW Germany
83 K17 **Bor, Lagh** *var.* Lak Bor. *dry watercourse* NE Kenya
Bor, Lak *see* Bor, Lagh
97 M14 **Borlänge** Kopparberg, C Sweden
108 C9 **Bormida** ≈ NW Italy
108 F6 **Bormio** Lombardia, N Italy
103 M16 **Borna** Sachsen, E Germany
100 O10 **Borne** Overijssel, E Netherlands
101 F17 **Bornem** Antwerpen, N Belgium
174 M6 **Borneo** *island* Brunei/Indonesia/Malaysia
103 E16 **Bornheim** Nordrhein-Westfalen, W Germany
97 L24 **Bornholm** ◐ *county* E Denmark
97 L24 **Bornholm** *island* E Denmark
79 Y13 **Borno** ◐ *state* NE Nigeria
106 K15 **Bornos** Andalucía, S Spain
168 L7 **Bornuur** Töv, C Mongolia
126 I14 **Borodino** Krasnoyarskiy Kray, S Russian Federation
119 O4 **Borodyanka** Kyyivs'ka Oblast', N Ukraine
126 M10 **Borogontsy** Respublika Sakha (Yakutiya), NE Russian Federation
164 I5 **Borohoro Shan** ▲▲ NW China
79 O13 **Boromo** SW Burkina
37 T13 **Boron** California, W USA
179 R12 **Borongan** Samar, C Philippines
Borongo *see* Black Volta
Boron'ki *see* Baron'ki
Borosjenő *see* Ineu
Borossebes *see* Sebiş
78 L15 **Borotou** NW Ivory Coast
xli S12 **Boroughbridge** North Yorkshire, N England, UK
119 W6 **Borova** Kharkivs'ka Oblast', E Ukraine
116 H8 **Borovan** Oblast Montana, NW Bulgaria
128 I14 **Borovichi** Novgorodskaya Oblast', W Russian Federation
Borovlje *see* Ferlach
114 J9 **Borovo** Vukovar-Srijem, NE Croatia
151 Q7 **Borovoye** *Kaz.* Būrabay. Kokshetau, N Kazakhstan
130 K4 **Borovsk** Kaluzhskaya Oblast', W Russian Federation
125 F12 **Borovskiy** Tyumenskaya Oblast', C Russian Federation
151 N7 **Borovskoy** Kustanay, N Kazakhstan
Borovukha *see* Baravukha
97 L23 **Borrby** Kristianstad, S Sweden
xliv J11 **Borris** Carlow, SE Ireland
xliv H10 **Borris in Ossory** Laois, C Ireland
xliv G10 **Borrisokane** Tipperary, S Ireland
xliv H11 **Borrisoleigh** Tipperary, S Ireland
189 R3 **Borroloola** Northern Territory, N Australia
118 F9 **Bors** Bihor, NW Romania
118 I9 **Borşa** *Hung.* Borsa. Maramureş, N Romania
118 J10 **Borsec** *Ger.* Bad Borseck, *Hung.* Borszék. Harghita, C Romania
94 K8 **Børselv** Finnmark, N Norway
115 L23 **Borsh** *var.* Borshi. Vlorë, S Albania
Borshchev *see* Borshchiv
118 K7 **Borshchiv** *Pol.* Borszczów, *Rus.* Borshchev. Ternopil's'ka Oblast', W Ukraine
Borshi *see* Borsh
113 L20 **Borsod-Abaúj-Zemplén** *off.* Borsod-Abaúj-Zemplén Megye. ◐ *county* NE Hungary
101 E15 **Borssele** Zeeland, SW Netherlands
Borszczów *see* Borshchiv
Borszék *see* Borsec
Bortala *see* Bole
xxxv G9 **Borth** Ceredigion, W Wales, UK
105 O12 **Bort-les-Orgues** Corrèze, C France
Bor u České Lípy *see* Nový Bor
168 E8 **Bor-Udzüür** Hovd, W Mongolia
149 N9 **Borūjen** Chahār Maḩall va Bakhtīārī, C Iran
148 L7 **Borūjerd** *var.* Burujird. Lorestān, W Iran
118 H6 **Boryslav** *Pol.* Borysław, *Rus.* Borislav. L'vivs'ka Oblast', NW Ukraine
Borysław *see* Boryslav
119 P4 **Boryspil'** *Rus.* Borispol'. Kyyivs'ka Oblast', N Ukraine
119 P4 **Boryspil'** *Rus.* Borispol'. ✕ (Kyyiv) Kyyivs'ka Oblast', N Ukraine
Borzhomi *see* Borjomi
119 R3 **Borzna** Chernihivs'ka Oblast', NE Ukraine
126 L16 **Borzya** Chitinskaya Oblast', S Russian Federation
109 B18 **Bosa** Sardegna, Italy, C Mediterranean Sea
114 F10 **Bosanska Dubica** NW Bosnia and Herzegovina
114 G10 **Bosanska Gradiška** N Bosnia and Herzegovina
114 F10 **Bosanska Kostajnica** NW Bosnia and Herzegovina
114 E11 **Bosanska Krupa** NW Bosnia and Herzegovina
114 H10 **Bosanski Brod** N Bosnia and Herzegovina
114 E10 **Bosanski Novi** NW Bosnia and Herzegovina
114 E11 **Bosanski Petrovac** NW Bosnia and Herzegovina
114 I10 **Bosanski Šamac** N Bosnia and Herzegovina
114 E12 **Bosansko Grahovo** W Bosnia and Herzegovina
Bosaso *see* Boosaaso
194 G13 **Bosavi, Mount** ⋏ W PNG
xxxviii I13 **Bosbury** Herefordshire, W England, UK
xxxvi D14 **Boscastle** Cornwall, SW England, UK
166 J14 **Bose** Guangxi Zhuangzu Zizhiqu, S China
xxxvii R13 **Bosham** West Sussex, S England, UK
167 Q5 **Boshan** Shandong, E China
xxxv D14 **Bosherston** Pembrokeshire, SW Wales, UK
115 P16 **Bosilegrad** *prev.* Bosiljgrad. Serbia, SE Yugoslavia
Bosiljgrad *see* Bosilegrad
Bösing *see* Pezinok
100 H12 **Boskoop** Zuid-Holland, C Netherlands
113 G18 **Boskovice** *Ger.* Boskowitz. Jižní Morava, SE Czech Republic
Boskowitz *see* Boskovice
114 I10 **Bosna** ≈ N Bosnia and Herzegovina
176 X9 **Bosnabraidi** Irian Jaya, E Indonesia
114 H12 **Bosnia and Herzegovina** *off.* Republic of Bosnia and Herzegovina. ◆ *republic* SE Europe
81 J16 **Bosobolo** Equateur, NW Zaire
171 K17 **Bōsō-hantō** *peninsula* Honshū, S Japan
Bosora *see* Buşrá ash Shām
Bosphorus/Bosporus *see* İstanbul Boğazı
Bosporus Cimmerius *see* Kerch Strait
Bosporus Thracius *see* İstanbul Boğazı
Bosra *see* Buşrá ash Shām
81 H14 **Bossangoa** Ouham, C Central African Republic
Bossé Bangou *see* Bossey Bangou
81 I15 **Bossembélé** Ombella-Mpoko, C Central African Republic
81 H15 **Bossentélé** Ouham-Pendé, W Central African Republic
79 R12 **Bossey Bangou** *var.* Bossé Bangou. Tillabéri, SW Niger
24 G5 **Bossier City** Louisiana, S USA
85 D20 **Bossiesvlei** Hardap, S Namibia
79 Y11 **Bosso** Diffa, SE Niger
63 F15 **Bossoroca** Rio Grande do Sul, S Brazil
164 J10 **Bostan** Xinjiang Uygur Zizhiqu, W China
148 K3 **Bostānābād** Āžarbāyjān-e Khāvarī, N Iran
164 K6 **Bosten Hu** *var.* Bagrax Hu. ◎ NW China
xxxix S7 **Boston** *prev.* St Botolph's Town. Lincolnshire, E England, UK
21 O11 **Boston** *state capital* Massachusetts, NE USA
8 M17 **Boston Bar** British Columbia, SW Canada
29 T10 **Boston Mountains** ▲▲ Arkansas, C USA
13 P8 **Bostonnais** ≈ Québec, SE Canada
Bostyn' *see* Bastyn'
114 J10 **Bosut** ≈ E Croatia
xxxvi D17 **Boswinger** Cornwall, SW England, UK
160 C11 **Botād** Gujarāt, W India
191 T9 **Botany Bay** *inlet* New South Wales, SE Australia
xxxix W11 **Botesdale** Suffolk, E England, UK
85 G18 **Boteti** *var.* Botletle. ≈ N Botswana
116 J9 **Botev** ▲ C Bulgaria
116 H9 **Botevgrad** *prev.* Orkhaniye. Sofiyska Oblast, W Bulgaria
xl L8 **Bothel** Cumbria, NW England, UK
95 J16 **Bothnia, Gulf of** *Fin.* Pohjanlahti, *Swe.* Bottniska Viken. *gulf* N Baltic Sea
191 P17 **Bothwell** Tasmania, SE Australia
106 H5 **Boticas** Vila Real, N Portugal
57 W10 **Boti-Pasi** Sipaliwini, C Surinam
Botletle *see* Boteti
xxxvii P13 **Botley** Hampshire, S England, UK
131 P16 **Botlikh** Chechenskaya Respublika, SW Russian Federation
119 N10 **Botna** ≈ E Moldavia
118 I9 **Botoşani** *Hung.* Botosány. Botoşani, NE Romania
118 K8 **Botoşani** ◐ *county* NE Romania
Botosány *see* Botoşani
167 P4 **Botou** *prev.* Bozhen. Hebei, E China
101 M20 **Botrange** ▲ E Belgium
109 O21 **Botricello** Calabria, SW Italy
85 I23 **Botshabelo** Free State, C South Africa
95 J15 **Botsmark** Västerbotten, N Sweden
85 G19 **Botswana** *off.* Republic of Botswana. ◆ *republic* S Africa
xxxix P8 **Bottesford** Leicestershire, C England, UK
31 N2 **Bottineau** North Dakota, N USA
Bottniska Viken *see* Bothnia, Gulf of
62 L9 **Botucatu** São Paulo, S Brazil
78 M16 **Bouaflé** C Ivory Coast
79 N16 **Bouaké** *var.* Bwake. C Ivory Coast
81 G14 **Bouar** Nana-Mambéré, W Central African Republic
76 H7 **Bouarfa** NE Morocco
113 B19 **Boubín** ▲ SW Czech Republic
81 I14 **Bouca** Ouham, W Central African Republic
13 T5 **Boucher** ≈ Québec, SE Canada
105 R15 **Bouches-du-Rhône** ◐ *department* SE France
76 C9 **Bou Craa** *var.* Bu Craa. NW Western Sahara
79 O9 **Boû Djébéha** *oasis* C Mali
110 C8 **Boudry** Neuchâtel, W Switzerland
188 L2 **Bougainville, Cape** *headland* Western Australia
67 E24 **Bougainville, Cape** *headland* East Falkland, Falkland Islands
197 B12 **Bougainville, Détroit de** *Eng.* Bougainville Strait. *strait* C Vanuatu
195 S13 **Bougainville Island** *island* NE PNG
195 T13 **Bougainville Strait** *strait* N Solomon Islands
Bougainville Strait *see* Bougainville, Détroit de
176 U8 **Bouganville, Selat** *strait* Irian Jaya, E Indonesia
123 J11 **Bougaroun, Cap** *headland* NE Algeria
79 R8 **Boughessa** Kidal, NE Mali

◆ Country
● Country Capital
◇ Dependent Territory
○ Dependent Territory Capital
◐ Administrative Region
✕ International Airport
▲ Mountain
▲▲ Mountain Range
⋏ Volcano
≈ River
◎ Lake
⊡ Reservoir

BOUGHTON STREET – BROAD SOUND

xxxvii X10 **Boughton Street** Kent, SE England, UK
Bougie see Béjaïa
78 L13 **Bougouni** Sikasso, SW Mali
101 J24 **Bouillon** Luxembourg, SE Belgium
76 K5 **Bouira** var. Bouïra. N Algeria
76 D8 **Bou-Izakarn** SW Morocco
76 B9 **Boujdour** var. Bojador. W Western Sahara
76 G5 **Boukhalef** ✕ (Tanger) N Morocco
Boukombé see Boukoumbé
79 R14 **Boukoumbé** var. Boukombé. C Benin
78 G6 **Boû Lanouâr** Dakhlet Nouâdhibou, W Mauritania
39 T4 **Boulder** Colorado, C USA
35 R10 **Boulder** Montana, NW USA
37 X12 **Boulder City** Nevada, W USA
189 T7 **Boulia** Queensland, C Australia
13 N10 **Boullé** ≈ Québec, SE Canada
104 J9 **Boulogne** ≈ NW France
Boulogne see Boulogne-sur-Mer
104 L16 **Boulogne-sur-Gesse** Haute-Garonne, S France
105 N1 **Boulogne-sur-Mer** var. Boulogne; anc. Bononia, Gesoriacum, Gessoriacum. Pas-de-Calais, N France
197 I7 **Bouloupari** Province Sud, S New Caledonia
79 Q12 **Boulsa** C Burkina
xlii M13 **Boultenstone** Aberdeenshire, NE Scotland, UK
79 W11 **Boultoum** Zinder, C Niger
197 K13 **Bouma** Taveuni, N Fiji
81 G16 **Boumba** ≈ SE Cameroon
78 J9 **Boûmdeïd** var. Boumdeït. Assaba, S Mauritania
Boumdeït see Boûmdeïd
117 C17 **Boumistós** ▲ W Greece
79 O15 **Bouna** NE Ivory Coast
21 P4 **Boundary Bald Mountain** ▲ Maine, NE USA
37 S8 **Boundary Peak** ▲ Nevada, W USA
78 M14 **Boundiali** N Ivory Coast
81 G19 **Boundji** Cuvette, C Congo
79 O13 **Boundoukui** var. Bondoukui, Bondoukuy. W Burkina
38 L2 **Bountiful** Utah, W USA
Bounty Basin see Bounty Trough
203 Q16 **Bounty Bay** bay Pitcairn Island, C Pacific Ocean
199 Jj14 **Bounty Islands** island group S NZ
183 Q13 **Bounty Trough** var. Bounty Basin. undersea feature S Pacific Ocean
197 I6 **Bourail** Province Sud, C New Caledonia
29 V5 **Bourbeuse River** ≈ Missouri, C USA
105 Q9 **Bourbon-Lancy** Saône-et-Loire, C France
33 N11 **Bourbonnais** Illinois, N USA
105 O10 **Bourbonnais** cultural region C France
105 S7 **Bourbonne-les-Bains** Haute-Marne, N France
Bourbon Vendée see la Roche-sur-Yon
76 M8 **Bourdj Messaouda** E Algeria
79 Q10 **Bourem** Gao, C Mali
Bourg see Bourg-en-Bresse
105 N11 **Bourganeuf** Creuse, C France
Bourgas see Burgas
Bourge-en-Bresse see Bourg-en-Bresse
105 S10 **Bourg-en-Bresse** var. Bourg, Bourge-en-Bresse. Ain, E France
105 O8 **Bourges** anc. Avaricum. Cher, C France
105 T11 **Bourget, Lac du** ◎ E France
105 P8 **Bourgogne** Eng. Burgundy. ◈ region E France
105 S11 **Bourgoin-Jallieu** Isère, E France
105 R14 **Bourg-St-Andéol** Ardèche, E France
105 U11 **Bourg-St-Maurice** Savoie, E France
110 C11 **Bourg St.Pierre** Valais, SW Switzerland
78 H8 **Boû Rjeimât** well W Mauritania
191 P5 **Bourke** New South Wales, SE Australia
xxxix Q9 **Bourne** Lincolnshire, E England, UK
xxxvii S8 **Bourne End** Buckinghamshire, C England, UK
xxxvii N14 **Bournemouth** Bournemouth, S England, UK
xxxvii N14 **Bournemouth** ◈ unitary authority S England, UK
xxxviii C15 **Bournville** Birmingham, C England, UK
101 M23 **Bourscheid** Diekirch, NE Luxembourg
xxxvi M12 **Bourton** Dorset, S England, UK
xxxvii O7 **Bourton-on-the-Water** Gloucestershire, C England, UK
76 K6 **Bou Saâda** var. Bou Saada. N Algeria
38 I13 **Bouse Wash** ≈ Arizona, SW USA
105 N10 **Boussac** Creuse, C France
104 M16 **Boussens** Haute-Garonne, S France
80 H12 **Bousso** prev. Fort-Bretonnet. Chari-Baguirmi, S Chad
78 H9 **Boutilimit** Trarza, SW Mauritania
67 D21 **Bouvet Island** ◇ Norwegian dependency S Atlantic Ocean
79 U11 **Bouza** Tahoua, SW Niger
111 R10 **Bovec** Ger. Flitsch, It. Plezzo. NW Slovenia
100 J8 **Bovenkarspel** Noord-Holland, NW Netherlands
31 V5 **Bovey** Minnesota, N USA
xxxvi H15 **Bovey Tracey** Devon, SW England, UK
34 M9 **Bovill** Idaho, NW USA
26 L4 **Bovina** Texas, SW USA
109 M17 **Bovino** Puglia, SE Italy
63 C17 **Bovril** Entre Ríos, E Argentina
xxxvi G13 **Bow** Devon, SW England, UK
xxxvi E7 **Bow** Tower Hamlets, SE England, UK
xlii M5 **Bow** Orkney Islands, N Scotland, UK
30 L2 **Bowbells** North Dakota, N USA
xli W5 **Bowburn** Durham, N England, UK
9 Q16 **Bow City** Alberta, SW Canada
31 O8 **Bowdle** South Dakota, N USA
xl F16 **Bowdon** Cheshire, C England, UK
189 X6 **Bowen** Queensland, NE Australia
xxxvi D5 **Bowe Park** Enfield, SE England, UK
198 B4 **Bowers Ridge** undersea feature S Bering Sea
xlii L6 **Bowertower** Highland, N Scotland, UK
xli Q9 **Bowes** Durham, N England, UK
15 Jj4 **Bowes Point** headland Northwest Territories, N Canada
27 S5 **Bowie** Texas, SW USA
9 R17 **Bow Island** Alberta, SW Canada
Bowkān see Būkān
xli N13 **Bowland, Forest of** forest N England, UK
22 J7 **Bowling Green** Kentucky, S USA
29 V3 **Bowling Green** Missouri, C USA
33 R11 **Bowling Green** Ohio, N USA
23 W5 **Bowling Green** Virginia, NE USA
30 J6 **Bowman** North Dakota, N USA
16 N3 **Bowman Bay** bay NW Atlantic Ocean
204 I5 **Bowman Coast** physical region Antarctica
30 J7 **Bowman-Haley Lake** ⊠ North Dakota, N USA
205 Z11 **Bowman Island** island Antarctica
xliii D20 **Bowmore** Argyll and Bute, W Scotland, UK
xl L6 **Bowness-on-Solway** Cumbria, NW England, UK
xl M10 **Bowness-on-Windermere** Cumbria, NW England, UK
Bowo see Bomi
191 S9 **Bowral** New South Wales, SE Australia
194 K14 **Bowutu Mountains** ▲▲ C PNG
85 I16 **Bowwood** Southern, S Zambia
xxxvi M10 **Box** Wiltshire, S England, UK
30 I12 **Box Butte Reservoir** ⊠ Nebraska, C USA
30 J10 **Box Elder** South Dakota, N USA
xxxix W13 **Boxford** Suffolk, E England, UK
97 M18 **Boxholm** Östergötland, S Sweden
Bo Xian/Boxian see Bozhou
167 Q4 **Boxing** Shandong, E China
101 L14 **Boxmeer** Noord-Brabant, SE Netherlands
101 J14 **Boxtel** Noord-Brabant, S Netherlands
142 J10 **Boyabat** Sinop, N Turkey
56 F9 **Boyacá** off. Departamento de Boyacá. ◈ province C Colombia
119 O4 **Boyarka** Kyyivs'ka Oblast', N Ukraine
24 H7 **Boyce** Louisiana, S USA
35 U11 **Boyd** Montana, NW USA
27 S6 **Boyd** Texas, SW USA
23 V8 **Boydton** Virginia, NE USA
Boyer Ahmadī va Kohkīlūyeh see Kohkīlūyeh va Būyer Aḥmadī
31 T13 **Boyer River** ≈ Iowa, C USA
23 W8 **Boykins** Virginia, NE USA
xliv G6 **Boyle** Ir. Mainistirna Búille. Roscommon, C Ireland
9 Q13 **Boyle** Alberta, SW Canada
xliv K8 **Boyne** Ir. An Bhóinn. ≈ E Ireland
33 Q5 **Boyne City** Michigan, N USA
25 Z14 **Boynton Beach** Florida, SE USA
153 O13 **Boysun** Rus. Baysun. Surkhondaryo Wiloyati, S Uzbekistan
xxxvi E14 **Boyton** Cornwall, SW England, UK
Bozau see Întorsura Buzăului
142 C14 **Boz Dağları** ▲▲ W Turkey
xxxix P12 **Bozeat** Northamptonshire, C England, UK
35 S11 **Bozeman** Montana, NW USA
Bozen see Bolzano
81 J16 **Bozene** Equateur, NW Zaire
167 P7 **Bozhou** var. Boxian, Bo Xian. Anhui, E China
142 H16 **Bozkır** Konya, S Turkey
142 K13 **Bozok Yaylası** plateau C Turkey
81 H14 **Bozoum** Ouham-Pendé, W Central African Republic
143 N16 **Bozova** Sanlıurfa, S Turkey
Bozrah see Buşrá ash Shām
142 E12 **Bozüyük** Bilecik, NW Turkey
108 B9 **Bra** Piemonte, NW Italy
204 G4 **Brabant Island** island Antarctica
xxxvii Y11 **Brabourne** Kent, SE England, UK
115 F15 **Brač** var. Brach, It. Brazza; anc. Brattia. island S Croatia
xlii D12 **Bracadale** Highland, NW Scotland, UK
Bracara Augusta see Braga
109 H15 **Bracciano** Lazio, C Italy
109 H14 **Bracciano, Lago di** ◎ C Italy
12 H13 **Bracebridge** Ontario, S Canada
Brach see Brač
95 G17 **Bräcke** Jämtland, C Sweden
27 P12 **Brackettville** Texas, SW USA
xxxix N14 **Brackley** Northamptonshire, C England, UK
xliv J9 **Bracknagh** Offaly, C Ireland
xxxvii R10 **Bracknell** Bracknell Forest, S England, UK
xxxvii R9 **Bracknell Forest** ◈ unitary authority SE England, UK
xliii K18 **Braco** Perth and Kinross, C Scotland, UK
63 K14 **Braço do Norte** Santa Catarina, S Brazil
118 G11 **Brad** Hung. Brád. Hunedoara, SW Romania
109 N18 **Bradano** ≈ S Italy
25 V13 **Bradenton** Florida, SE USA
xli R14 **Bradford** Bradford, N England, UK
xli Q14 **Bradford** ◈ unitary authority N England, UK
12 H14 **Bradford** Ontario, S Canada
29 W10 **Bradford** Arkansas, C USA
20 D12 **Bradford** Pennsylvania, NE USA
xxxvi L10 **Bradford-on-Avon** Wiltshire, S England, UK
xxxvii Q14 **Brading** Isle of Wight, S England, UK
29 T15 **Bradley** Arkansas, C USA
xxxvi I13 **Bradninch** Devon, SW England, UK
27 P7 **Bradshaw** Texas, SW USA
xxxviii L5 **Bradwell** Derbyshire, C England, UK
xxxvii X8 **Bradwell-on-Sea** Essex, SE England, UK
xxxvi E13 **Bradworthy** Devon, SW England, UK
27 Q9 **Brady** Texas, SW USA
27 Q9 **Brady Creek** ≈ Texas, SW USA
xlii I3 **Brae** Shetland Islands, NE Scotland, UK
xliii M15 **Braedownie** Angus, E Scotland, UK
xliii L14 **Braemar** Aberdeenshire, NE Scotland, UK
118 K8 **Brăești** Botoșani, NW Romania
xlii N3 **Braeswick** Orkney Islands, N Scotland, UK
xli S12 **Brafferton** North Yorkshire, N England, UK
106 G5 **Braga** anc. Bracara Augusta. Braga, NW Portugal
106 G5 **Braga** ◈ district N Portugal
118 J15 **Bragadiru** Teleorman, S Romania
63 C20 **Bragado** Buenos Aires, E Argentina
106 J5 **Bragança** Eng. Braganza; anc. Julio Briga. Bragança, NE Portugal
106 I5 **Bragança** ◈ district N Portugal
62 N9 **Bragança Paulista** São Paulo, S Brazil
Braganza see Bragança
xlii C7 **Bragar** Western Isles, NW Scotland, UK
Bragin see Brahin
31 V7 **Braham** Minnesota, N USA
Brahe see Brda
Brahestad see Raahe
121 O20 **Brahin** Rus. Bragin. Homyel'skaya Voblasts', SE Belorussia
159 U15 **Brahmanbaria** Chittagong, E Bangladesh
160 O12 **Brāhmani** ≈ E India
160 N13 **Brahmapur** Orissa, E India
133 S10 **Brahmaputra** var. Padma, Tsangpo, Ben. Jamuna, Chin. Yarlung Zangbo Jiang, Ind. Bramaputra, Dihang, Siang. ≈ S Asia
xxxv D7 **Braich y Pwll** headland NW Wales, UK
191 R10 **Braidwood** New South Wales, SE Australia
32 M11 **Braidwood** Illinois, N USA
118 M13 **Brăila** Brăila, E Romania
118 L13 **Brăila** ◈ county SE Romania
xxxviii L7 **Brailsford** Derbyshire, C England, UK
101 G19 **Braine-l'Alleud** Walloon Brabant, C Belgium
101 F19 **Braine-le-Comte** Hainaut, SW Belgium
31 U6 **Brainerd** Minnesota, N USA
xxxvii W7 **Braintree** Essex, SE England, UK
xxxvii P12 **Braishfield** Hampshire, S England, UK
xl L9 **Braithwaite** Cumbria, NW England, UK
101 J19 **Braives** Liège, E Belgium
85 H23 **Brak** ≈ C South Africa
Brak see Birāk
101 E18 **Brakel** Oost-Vlaanderen, SW Belgium
100 J13 **Brakel** Gelderland, C Netherlands
78 H9 **Brakna** ◈ region S Mauritania
97 J17 **Brålanda** Älvsborg, S Sweden
Bramaputra see Brahmaputra
xxxvii Q12 **Bramdean** Hampshire, S England, UK
xxxix Y11 **Bramfield** Suffolk, E England, UK
xxxix W13 **Bramford** Suffolk, E England, UK
xl H16 **Bramhall** Stockport, NW England, UK
xli S13 **Bramham** Leeds, N England, UK
xxxvii Q10 **Bramley** Hampshire, S England, UK
97 F23 **Bramming** Ribe, W Denmark
xli N6 **Brampton** Cumbria, NW England, UK
12 G15 **Brampton** Ontario, S Canada
102 F12 **Bramsche** Niedersachsen, NW Germany
xxxvii O12 **Bramshaw** Hampshire, S England, UK
118 J12 **Bran** Ger. Törzburg, Hung. Törcsvár. Brașov, S Romania
xxxix U7 **Brancaster** Norfolk, E England, UK
31 W8 **Branch** Minnesota, N USA
23 R14 **Branchville** South Carolina, SE USA
49 Y6 **Branco, Cabo** headland E Brazil
60 F11 **Branco, Rio** ≈ N Brazil
110 J8 **Brand** Vorarlberg, W Austria
85 B18 **Brandberg** ▲ NW Namibia
97 H14 **Brandbu** Oppland, S Norway
97 F22 **Brande** Ringkøbing, W Denmark
Brandebourg see Brandenburg
102 M12 **Brandenburg** var. Brandenburg an der Havel. Brandenburg, NE Germany
22 K5 **Brandenburg** Kentucky, S USA
102 N12 **Brandenburg** off. Freie und Hansestadt Hamburg, Fr. Brandebourg. ◈ state NE Germany
Brandenburg an der Havel see Brandenburg
xlii M11 **Branderburgh** Moray, N Scotland, UK
xli W13 **Brandesburton** East Riding of Yorkshire, N England, UK
85 I23 **Brandfort** Free State, C South Africa
xliv B12 **Brandon** Kerry, SW Ireland
xli R8 **Brandon** Durham, N England, UK
xxxix U11 **Brandon** Suffolk, E England, UK
9 W16 **Brandon** Manitoba, S Canada
25 V12 **Brandon** Florida, SE USA
24 L6 **Brandon** Mississippi, S USA
xliv B12 **Brandon Bay** bay SW Ireland
xliv B12 **Brandon Head** headland SW Ireland
xliv B12 **Brandon Mountain** Ir. Cnoc Bréanainn. ▲ SW Ireland
xli T11 **Brandsby** North Yorkshire, N England, UK
Brandsen see Coronel Brandsen
97 I14 **Brandval** Hedmark, S Norway
85 F24 **Brandvlei** Northern Cape, W South Africa
25 U9 **Branford** Florida, SE USA
112 K7 **Braniewo** Ger. Braunsberg. Elbląg, N Poland
204 H3 **Bransfield Strait** strait Antarctica
39 U8 **Branson** Colorado, C USA
29 T8 **Branson** Missouri, C USA
xxxix P8 **Branston** Leicestershire, C England, UK
xxxix Q6 **Branston** Lincolnshire, E England, UK
12 G16 **Brantford** Ontario, S Canada
104 L12 **Brantôme** Dordogne, SW France
190 L12 **Branxholme** Victoria, SE Australia
Brasil see Brazil
61 C16 **Brasiléia** Acre, W Brazil
61 K18 **Brasília** ● (Brazil) Distrito Federal, C Brazil
Braslav see Braslaw
120 J12 **Braslaw** Pol. Brasław, Rus. Braslav. Vitsyebskaya Voblasts', N Belorussia
118 J12 **Brașov** Ger. Kronstadt, Hung. Brassó; prev. Orașul Stalin. Brașov, C Romania
118 I12 **Brașov** ◈ county C Romania
176 W7 **Bras, Pulau** island Kepulauan Mapia, E Indonesia
79 U18 **Brass** Rivers, S Nigeria
101 H16 **Brasschaat** var. Brasschaet. Antwerpen, N Belgium
Brasschaet see Brasschaat
175 O4 **Brassey, Banjaran** var. Brassey Range. ▲▲ East Malaysia
Brassey Range see Brassey, Banjaran
xxxviii L7 **Brassington** Derbyshire, C England, UK
Brassó see Brașov
25 T1 **Brasstown Bald** ▲ Georgia, SE USA
115 K22 **Brataj** Vlorë, SW Albania
116 J10 **Bratan** var. Morozov. ▲ C Bulgaria
113 F21 **Bratislava** Ger. Pressburg, Hung. Pozsony. ● (Slovakia) Západné Slovensko, SW Slovakia
116 H10 **Bratiya** ▲ C Bulgaria
126 J14 **Bratsk** Irkutskaya Oblast', C Russian Federation
119 Q8 **Brats'ke** Mykolayivs'ka Oblast', S Ukraine
126 J14 **Bratskoye Vodokhranilishche** Eng. Bratsk Reservoir. ⊠ S Russian Federation
Bratsk Reservoir see Bratskoye Vodokhranilishche
Brattia see Brač
xxxvi F14 **Bratton Clovelly** Devon, SW England, UK
96 D9 **Brattvåg** Møre og Romsdal, S Norway
114 K12 **Bratunac** E Bosnia and Herzegovina
116 J10 **Bratya Daskalovi** prev. Grozdovo. Khaskovska Oblast, C Bulgaria
111 U2 **Braunau** ≈ N Austria
Braunau see Braunau am Inn
111 Q4 **Braunau am Inn** var. Braunau. Oberösterreich, N Austria
Braunsberg see Braniewo
102 J13 **Braunschweig** Eng./Fr. Brunswick. Niedersachsen, N Germany
xxxix N12 **Braunston** Northamptonshire, C England, UK
xxxvi F12 **Braunton** Devon, SW England, UK
Brava see Baraawe
107 Y6 **Brava, Costa** coastal region NE Spain
45 V16 **Brava, Punta** headland E Panama
97 N17 **Bråviken** inlet S Sweden
58 B10 **Bravo, Cerro** ▲ N Peru
Bravo del Norte, Río/Bravo, Río see Grande, Rio
37 X17 **Brawley** California, W USA
xliv L10 **Bray** Ir. Bré. Wicklow, E Ireland
xxxvi G12 **Brayford** Devon, SW England, UK
61 G16 **Brazil** off. Federative Republic of Brazil, Port. Repùblica Federativa do Brasil, Sp. Brasil; prev. United States of Brazil. ◆ federal republic South America
67 K15 **Brazil Basin** var. Brazilian Basin, Brazil'skaya Kotlovina. undersea feature W Atlantic Ocean
Brazilian Basin see Brazil Basin
Brazilian Highlands see Central, Planalto
Brazil'skaya Kotlovina see Brazil Basin
27 U10 **Brazos River** ≈ Texas, SW USA
176 Yy13 **Brazza** ≈ Irian Jaya, E Indonesia
Brazza see Brač
81 G21 **Brazzaville** ● (Congo) Capital District, S Congo
81 G21 **Brazzaville** ✕ Le Pool, S Congo
114 J11 **Brčko** NE Bosnia and Herzegovina
112 H8 **Brda** Ger. Brahe. ≈ N Poland
Bré see Bray
xxxvi B17 **Breage** Cornwall, SW England, UK
193 A23 **Breaksea Sound** sound South Island, NZ
xxxvi L8 **Bream** Gloucestershire, C England, UK
192 L4 **Bream Bay** bay North Island, NZ
192 L4 **Bream Head** headland North Island, NZ
xxxvi J10 **Brean** Somerset, SW England, UK
Bréanainn, Cnoc see Brandon Mountain
47 S6 **Brea, Punta** headland W Puerto Rico
xlii C8 **Breasclete** Western Isles, NW Scotland, UK
24 I9 **Breaux Bridge** Louisiana, S USA
118 J13 **Breaza** Prahova, SE Romania
174 K14 **Brebes** Jawa, C Indonesia
xxxv G12 **Brechfa** Carmarthenshire, S Wales, UK
xliii N16 **Brechin** Angus, E Scotland, UK
101 H15 **Brecht** Antwerpen, N Belgium
39 S4 **Breckenridge** Colorado, C USA
31 R6 **Breckenridge** Minnesota, N USA
27 R6 **Breckenridge** Texas, SW USA
xxxix V10 **Breckland** heathland E England, UK
99 J21 **Brecknock** cultural region SE Wales, UK
65 G25 **Brecknock, Península** headland S Chile
113 G19 **Břeclav** Ger. Lundenburg. Jižní Morava, SE Czech Republic
xxxv J12 **Brecon** Powys, E Wales, UK
xxxv I13 **Brecon Beacons** ▲▲ S Wales, UK
101 I14 **Breda** Noord-Brabant, S Netherlands
97 K20 **Bredaryd** Jönköping, S Sweden
85 F26 **Bredasdorp** Western Cape, SW South Africa
xl H15 **Bredbury** Stockport, NW England, UK
95 H16 **Bredbyn** Västernorrland, N Sweden
xxxvii W12 **Brede** East Sussex, SE England, UK
xxxvii W10 **Bredhurst** Kent, SE England, UK
xxxviii K14 **Bredon** Worcestershire, W England, UK
125 E13 **Bredy** Chelyabinskaya Oblast', C Russian Federation
101 K17 **Bree** Limburg, NE Belgium
69 T15 **Breede** ≈ S South Africa
xxxviii M9 **Breedon on the Hill** Leicestershire, C England, UK
100 I7 **Breezand** Noord-Holland, NW Netherlands
115 P18 **Bregalnica** ≈ E FYR Macedonia
110 I6 **Bregenz** anc. Brigantium. Vorarlberg, W Austria
110 J7 **Bregenzer Wald** ▲▲ W Austria
116 F6 **Bregovo** Oblast Montana, NW Bulgaria
104 H5 **Bréhat, Île de** island NW France
94 H2 **Breidhafjördhur** bay W Iceland
94 L3 **Breidhdalsvík** Austurland, E Iceland
110 H9 **Breil** Ger. Brigels. Graubünden, S Switzerland
94 J8 **Breivikbotn** Finnmark, N Norway
96 I9 **Brekken** Sør-Trøndelag, S Norway
96 G7 **Brekstad** Sør-Trøndelag, S Norway
96 B10 **Bremangerlandet** island S Norway
Brême see Bremen
102 H11 **Bremen** Fr. Brême. Bremen, NW Germany
25 R3 **Bremen** Georgia, SE USA
33 O11 **Bremen** Indiana, N USA
102 H10 **Bremen** off. Freie Hansestadt Bremen, Fr. Brême. ◈ state N Germany
102 G9 **Bremerhaven** Bremen, NW Germany
Bremersdorp see Manzini
34 G8 **Bremerton** Washington, NW USA
102 H10 **Bremervörde** Niedersachsen, NW Germany
27 U9 **Bremond** Texas, SW USA
xxxvi G11 **Brendon** Devon, SW England, UK
xxxvi I12 **Brendon Hills** hill range SW England, UK
27 U10 **Brenham** Texas, SW USA
xxxv I5 **Brenig, Llyn** ◎ N Wales, UK
xlii B8 **Brenish** Western Isles, NW Scotland, UK
110 M8 **Brenner** Tirol, W Austria
Brenner, Col du/Brennero, Passo del see Brenner Pass
110 M8 **Brenner Pass** var. Brenner Sattel, Fr. Col du Brenner, Ger. Brennerpass, It. Passo del Brennero. pass Austria/Italy
Brenner Sattel see Brenner Pass
110 G10 **Brenno** ≈ SW Switzerland
108 F7 **Breno** Lombardia, N Italy
xxxiv K16 **Brent** ◈ London borough SE England, UK
25 O5 **Brent** Alabama, S USA
108 H7 **Brenta** ≈ NE Italy
xxxvii U6 **Brent Pelham** Hertfordshire, SE England, UK
xxxvii V8 **Brentwood** Essex, E England, UK
20 L14 **Brentwood** Long Island, New York, NE USA
108 F7 **Brescia** anc. Brixia. Lombardia, N Italy
101 D15 **Breskens** Zeeland, SW Netherlands
Breslau see Wrocław
108 H5 **Bressanone** Ger. Brixen. Trentino-Alto Adige, N Italy
xlii I4 **Bressay** island NE Scotland, UK
104 K9 **Bressuire** Deux-Sèvres, W France
121 F20 **Brest** Pol. Brześć nad Bugiem, Rus. Brest-Litovsk; prev. Brześć Litewski. Brestskaya Voblasts', SW Belorussia
104 F5 **Brest** Finistère, NW France
Brest-Litovsk see Brest
114 A10 **Brestova** Istra, NW Croatia
Brestskaya Oblast' see Brestskaya Voblasts'
121 G19 **Brestskaya Voblasts'** prev. Rus. Brestskaya Oblast'. ◈ province SW Belorussia
104 G6 **Bretagne** Eng. Brittany; Lat. Britannia Minor. ◈ region NW France
118 G12 **Bretea-Română** Hung. Oláhbrettye; prev. Bretea-Romînă. Hunedoara, W Romania
Bretea-Romînă see Bretea-Română
105 O3 **Breteuil** Oise, N France
104 I10 **Breton, Pertuis** inlet W France
24 L10 **Breton Sound** sound Louisiana, S USA
xlii I3 **Brettabister** Shetland Islands, NE Scotland, UK
192 K2 **Brett, Cape** headland North Island, NZ
103 G21 **Bretten** Baden-Württemberg, SW Germany
101 K15 **Breugel** Noord-Brabant, S Netherlands
108 B6 **Breuil** It. Cervinia. Valle d'Aosta, NW Italy
100 I11 **Breukelen** Utrecht, C Netherlands
23 P10 **Brevard** North Carolina, SE USA
40 L9 **Brevig Mission** Alaska, USA
97 G16 **Brevik** Telemark, S Norway
191 P5 **Brewarrina** New South Wales, SE Australia
21 R6 **Brewer** Maine, NE USA
xxxviii B13 **Brewood** Staffordshire, C England, UK
31 T11 **Brewster** Minnesota, N USA
31 N14 **Brewster** Nebraska, C USA
33 U12 **Brewster** Ohio, N USA
191 O8 **Brewster, Lake** ◎ New South Wales, SE Australia
25 P7 **Brewton** Alabama, S USA
Brezhnev see Naberezhnyye Chelny
111 W12 **Brežice** Ger. Rann. E Slovenia
116 G9 **Breznik** Sofiyska Oblast, W Bulgaria
113 K19 **Brezno** Ger. Bries, Briesen, Hung. Breznóbánya; prev. Brezno nad Hronom. Stredné Slovensko, C Slovakia
Breznóbánya/Brezno nad Hronom see Brezno
118 I12 **Brezoi** Vâlcea, SW Romania
116 J10 **Brezovo** prev. Abrashlare. Plovdivska Oblast, C Bulgaria
81 K14 **Bria** Haute-Kotto, C Central African Republic
xlii L11 **Briach** Moray, N Scotland, UK
105 U13 **Briançon** anc. Brigantio. Hautes-Alpes, SE France
38 K7 **Brian Head** ▲ Utah, W USA
xxxv H11 **Brianne Reservoir, Llyn** ⊠ E Wales, UK
105 O7 **Briare** Loiret, C France
191 V2 **Bribie Island** island Queensland, E Australia
45 O14 **Bribrí** Limón, E Costa Rica
118 L8 **Briceni** var. Brinceni, Rus. Brichany. N Moldavia
Bricgstow see Bristol
Brichany see Briceni
xl G10 **Bride** N Isle of Man
101 M24 **Bridel** Luxembourg, C Luxembourg
xxxvi F14 **Bridestowe** Devon, SW England, UK
xxxvi Y10 **Bridge** Kent, SE England, UK
xliv I3 **Bridgend** Donegal, N Ireland
xliii D20 **Bridgend** Argyll and Bute, W Scotland, UK
xliii G19 **Bridgend** Argyll and Bute, W Scotland, UK
xliii L17 **Bridgend** Perth and Kinross, C Scotland, UK
xxxv I15 **Bridgend** Bridgend, S Wales, UK
xxxv I15 **Bridgend** ◈ unitary authority S Wales, UK
12 I14 **Bridgenorth** Ontario, SE Canada
xliii K19 **Bridge of Allan** Stirling, C Scotland, UK
xlii L12 **Bridge of Avon** Moray, N Scotland, UK
xliii L16 **Bridge of Cally** Perth and Kinross, C Scotland, UK
xliii K25 **Bridge of Dee** Dumfries and Galloway, SW Scotland, UK
xlii P13 **Bridge of Don** City of Aberdeen, NE Scotland, UK
xliii O14 **Bridge of Dye** Aberdeenshire, NE Scotland, UK
xliii L18 **Bridge of Earn** Perth and Kinross, C Scotland, UK
xliii M14 **Bridge of Gairn** Aberdeenshire, NE Scotland, UK
xliii I16 **Bridge of Gaur** Perth and Kinross, C Scotland, UK
xliii H17 **Bridge of Orchy** Argyll and Bute, W Scotland, UK
xliii I20 **Bridge of Weir** Renfrewshire, W Scotland, UK
25 Q1 **Bridgeport** Alabama, S USA
37 R8 **Bridgeport** California, W USA
20 L13 **Bridgeport** Connecticut, NE USA
33 N15 **Bridgeport** Illinois, N USA
30 J14 **Bridgeport** Nebraska, C USA
27 S6 **Bridgeport** Texas, SW USA
23 S3 **Bridgeport** West Virginia, NE USA
27 S5 **Bridgeport, Lake** ⊠ Texas, SW USA
35 U11 **Bridger** Montana, NW USA
20 I17 **Bridgeton** New Jersey, NE USA
xliv K13 **Bridgetown** Wexford, SE Ireland
188 J14 **Bridgetown** Western Australia
47 Y14 **Bridgetown** ● (Barbados) SW Barbados
191 P17 **Bridgewater** Tasmania, SE Australia
11 P16 **Bridgewater** Nova Scotia, SE Canada
21 P12 **Bridgewater** Massachusetts, NE USA
31 Q11 **Bridgewater** South Dakota, N USA
23 U5 **Bridgewater** Virginia, NE USA
xxxviii I10 **Bridgnorth** Shropshire, W England, UK
21 P8 **Bridgton** Maine, NE USA
xxxvi J11 **Bridgwater** Somerset, SW England, UK
xxxvi I11 **Bridgwater Bay** bay SW England, UK
xli X12 **Bridlington** East Riding of Yorkshire, E England, UK
xli X12 **Bridlington Bay** bay E England, UK
xxxvi K14 **Bridport** Dorset, S England, UK
191 P15 **Bridport** Tasmania, SE Australia
105 O5 **Brie** cultural region N France
Brieg see Brzeg
Briel see Brielle
100 G12 **Brielle** var. Briel, Bril, Eng. The Brill. Zuid-Holland, SW Netherlands
110 E9 **Brienz** Bern, C Switzerland
110 E9 **Brienzer See** ◎ SW Switzerland
xli P14 **Brierfield** Lancashire, NW England, UK
Bries/Briesen see Brezno
Brietzig see Brzesko
105 S4 **Briey** Meurthe-et-Moselle, NE France
110 E10 **Brig** Fr. Brigue, It. Briga. Valais, SW Switzerland
Briga see Brig
103 G24 **Brigach** ≈ S Germany
20 K17 **Brigantine** New Jersey, NE USA
Brigantio see Briançon
Brigantium see Bregenz
Brigels see Breil
xxxix Q3 **Brigg** North Lincolnshire, N England, UK
27 S9 **Briggs** Texas, SW USA
38 L1 **Brigham City** Utah, W USA
xli R14 **Brighouse** Calderdale, N England, UK
xxxvii P14 **Brighstone** Isle of Wight, S England, UK
xxxvii Y7 **Brightlingsea** Essex, SE England, UK
xxxvii U13 **Brighton** Brighton and Hove, SE England, UK
12 J15 **Brighton** Ontario, SE Canada
39 T4 **Brighton** Colorado, C USA
32 K15 **Brighton** Illinois, N USA
xxxvii T13 **Brighton and Hove** ◈ unitary authority SE England, UK
105 T16 **Brignoles** Var, W France
xliii J18 **Brig o'Turk** Stirling, C Scotland, UK
xxxix P11 **Brigstock** Northamptonshire, C England, UK
Brigue see Brig
107 O7 **Brihuega** Castilla-La Mancha, C Spain
114 A10 **Brijuni** It. Brioni. island group NW Croatia
78 G12 **Brikama** W Gambia
Bril see Brielle
xxxvii Q7 **Brill** Buckinghamshire, C England, UK
Brill, The see Brielle
103 G15 **Brilon** Nordrhein-Westfalen, W Germany
Brinceni see Briceni
109 Q18 **Brindisi** anc. Brundisium, Brundusium. Puglia, SE Italy
xxxix S5 **Brinkhill** Lincolnshire, E England, UK
29 W11 **Brinkley** Arkansas, C USA
xxxviii M11 **Brinklow** Warwickshire, C England, UK
xxxvii N9 **Brinkworth** Wiltshire, S England, UK
xliv G2 **Brinlack** Donegal, N Ireland
xlii M3 **Brinyan** Orkney Islands, N Scotland, UK
Brioni see Brijuni
105 P12 **Brioude** anc. Brivas. Haute-Loire, C France
Briovera see St-Lô
191 U2 **Brisbane** Queensland, E Australia
191 V2 **Brisbane** ✕ Queensland, E Australia
27 P2 **Briscoe** Texas, SW USA
108 H10 **Brisighella** Emilia-Romagna, C Italy
110 G11 **Brissago** Ticino, S Switzerland
xxxvi L10 **Bristol** anc. Bricgstow. City of Bristol, SW England, UK
20 M12 **Bristol** Connecticut, NE USA
25 R9 **Bristol** Florida, SE USA
21 N9 **Bristol** New Hampshire, NE USA
31 Q8 **Bristol** South Dakota, N USA
23 P8 **Bristol** Tennessee, S USA
20 M8 **Bristol** Vermont, NE USA
41 N14 **Bristol Bay** bay Alaska, USA
xxxv H16 **Bristol Channel** inlet England/Wales, UK
xxxvi K9 **Bristol, City of** ◈ unitary authority SW England, UK
37 W14 **Bristol Lake** ◎ California, W USA
29 P10 **Bristow** Oklahoma, C USA
88 C10 **Britain** var. Great Britain. island UK
Britannia Minor see Bretagne
8 L12 **British Columbia** Fr. Colombie-Britannique. ◈ province SW Canada
British Guiana see Guyana
British Honduras see Belize
181 Q7 **British Indian Ocean Territory** ◇ UK dependent territory C Indian Ocean
88 B9 **British Isles** island group NW Europe
8 I1 **British Mountains** ▲▲ Yukon Territory, NW Canada
British North Borneo see Sabah
British Solomon Islands Protectorate see Solomon Islands
47 S8 **British Virgin Islands** var. Virgin Islands. ◇ UK dependent territory E West Indies
xxxv H14 **Briton Ferry** Neath Port Talbot, S Wales, UK
85 J21 **Brits** North-West, N South Africa
85 H24 **Britstown** Northern Cape, W South Africa
12 F12 **Britt** Ontario, S Canada
31 V12 **Britt** Iowa, C USA
Brittany see Bretagne
31 Q7 **Britton** South Dakota, N USA
Briva Curretia see Brive-la-Gaillarde
Briva Isarae see Pontoise
Brivas see Brioude
Brive see Brive-la-Gaillarde
104 M12 **Brive-la-Gaillarde** prev. Brive, anc. Briva Curretia. Corrèze, C France
107 O4 **Briviesca** Castilla-León, N Spain
Brixen see Bressanone
xxxvi H16 **Brixham** Devon, SW England, UK
Brixia see Brescia
xxxvi D8 **Brixton** Lambeth, SE England, UK
xxxix O12 **Brixworth** Northamptonshire, C England, UK
151 S15 **Brlik** prev. Novotroickoje, Novotroitskoye. Zhambyl, SE Kazakhstan
113 G18 **Brno** Ger. Brünn. Jižní Morava, SE Czech Republic
xlii D8 **Broad Bay** bay NW Scotland, UK
xxxvii N12 **Broad Chalke** Wiltshire, S England, UK
xxxvi I14 **Broad Clyst** Devon, SW England, UK
27 X8 **Broaddus** Texas, SW USA
xliv E12 **Broadford** Limerick, SW Ireland
xlii E13 **Broadford** Highland, N Scotland, UK
191 O12 **Broadford** Victoria, SE Australia
xliv C5 **Broad Haven** inlet NW Ireland
xxxvi I13 **Broadhembury** Devon, SW England, UK
xxxvii N9 **Broad Hinton** Wiltshire, S England, UK
xliii L22 **Broad Law** ▲ S Scotland, UK
xxxvi L14 **Broadmayne** Dorset, S England, UK
25 U3 **Broad River** ≈ Georgia, SE USA
23 N8 **Broad River** ≈ North Carolina/South Carolina, SE USA
xxxv B14 **Broad Sound** sound SW Wales, UK

◆ Country
● Country Capital
◇ Dependent Territory
○ Dependent Territory Capital
◈ Administrative Region
✕ International Airport
▲ Mountain
▲▲ Mountain Range
Volcano
≈ River
◎ Lake
⊠ Reservoir

Broadsound Range – Burley

189 Y8 **Broadsound Range** ▲▲ Queensland, E Australia
xxxvii Z10 **Broadstairs** Kent, SE England, UK
xxxix Y9 **Broads, The** *wetland* E England, UK
xxxvii N13 **Broadstone** Poole, S England, UK
35 X11 **Broadus** Montana, NW USA
xxxvi J13 **Broadway** Somerset, SW England, UK
xxxviii L14 **Broadway** Worcestershire, W England, UK
23 U4 **Broadway** Virginia, NE USA
xxxvi L14 **Broadwey** Dorset, S England, UK
xxxvi K13 **Broadwindsor** Dorset, S England, UK
120 E9 **Brocēni** Saldus, SW Latvia
xlii E12 **Brochel** Highland, NW Scotland, UK
9 U11 **Brochet** Manitoba, C Canada
9 U10 **Brochet, Lac** ◎ Manitoba, C Canada
13 S5 **Brochet, Lac au** ◎ Québec, SE Canada
103 K14 **Brocken** ▲ C Germany
xxxvii O13 **Brockenhurst** Hampshire, S England, UK
xli N8 **Brockleymoor** Cumbria, NW England, UK
21 O12 **Brockton** Massachusetts, NE USA
12 L14 **Brockville** Ontario, SE Canada
20 D13 **Brockway** Pennsylvania, NE USA
Brod/Bród *see* Slavonski Brod
15 Kk1 **Brodeur Peninsula** *peninsula* Baffin Island, Northwest Territories, NE Canada
xliii G21 **Brodick** North Ayrshire, W Scotland, UK
Brod na Savi *see* Slavonski Brod
112 K9 **Brodnica** *Ger.* Buddenbrock. Toruń, N Poland
114 G10 **Brod-Posavina** *off.* Brodsko-Posavska Županija. ◐ *province* NE Croatia
118 J5 **Brody** L'vivs'ka Oblast', NW Ukraine
97 G22 **Brædstrup** Vejle, C Denmark
100 I10 **Broek-in-Waterland** Noord-Holland, C Netherlands
34 L13 **Brogan** Oregon, NW USA
112 N10 **Brok** Ostrołęka, E Poland
29 P9 **Broken Arrow** Oklahoma, C USA
191 T9 **Broken Bay** *bay* New South Wales, SE Australia
31 N15 **Broken Bow** Nebraska, C USA
29 R13 **Broken Bow** Oklahoma, C USA
29 R12 **Broken Bow Lake** ⊡ Oklahoma, C USA
190 L6 **Broken Hill** New South Wales, SE Australia
181 S10 **Broken Ridge** *undersea feature* S Indian Ocean
194 H10 **Broken Water Bay** *bay* W Bismarck Sea
57 W10 **Brokopondo** Brokopondo, NE Surinam
57 W10 **Brokopondo** ◐ *district* C Surinam
Bromberg *see* Bydgoszcz
xxxviii H11 **Bromfield** Shropshire, W England, UK
xxxvii U9 **Bromley** Bromley, SE England, UK
xxxiv L17 **Bromley** ◐ *London borough* SE England, UK
97 L22 **Bromölla** Kristianstad, S Sweden
xli V11 **Brompton** North Yorkshire, N England, UK
xli S11 **Brompton** North Yorkshire, N England, UK
xxxvi I12 **Brompton Ralph** Somerset, SW England, UK
xxxvi H12 **Brompton Regis** Somerset, SW England, UK
xxxviii B16 **Bromsgrove** Worcestershire, W England, UK
xxxviii I12 **Bromyard** Herefordshire, W England, UK
97 G20 **Brønderslev** Nordjylland, N Denmark
108 D8 **Broni** Lombardia, N Italy
8 K11 **Bronlund Peak** ▲ British Columbia, W Canada
95 F14 **Brønnøysund** Nordland, C Norway
25 V10 **Bronson** Florida, SE USA
33 Q11 **Bronson** Michigan, N USA
27 X8 **Bronson** Texas, SW USA
109 L24 **Bronte** Sicilia, Italy, C Mediterranean Sea
27 P8 **Bronte** Texas, SW USA
xxxvii P14 **Brook** Isle of Wight, S England, UK
xxxvi X10 **Brooke** Norfolk, E England, UK
27 Y9 **Brookeland** Texas, SW USA
179 O15 **Brooke's Point** Palawan, W Philippines
29 T3 **Brookfield** Missouri, C USA
24 K7 **Brookhaven** Mississippi, S USA
34 E16 **Brookings** Oregon, NW USA
31 R10 **Brookings** South Dakota, N USA
xxxvii X12 **Brookland** Kent, SE England, UK
31 W14 **Brooklyn** Iowa, C USA
31 U8 **Brooklyn Park** Minnesota, N USA
23 U7 **Brookneal** Virginia, NE USA
9 R16 **Brooks** Alberta, SW Canada
27 V11 **Brookshire** Texas, SW USA
40 L8 **Brooks Mountain** ▲ Alaska, USA
40 M11 **Brooks Range** ▲▲ Alaska, USA
33 O12 **Brookston** Indiana, N USA
25 V11 **Brooksville** Florida, SE USA
25 N4 **Brooksville** Mississippi, S USA
188 J13 **Brookton** Western Australia
33 Q14 **Brookville** Indiana, N USA
20 D13 **Brookville** Pennsylvania, NE USA
33 Q14 **Brookville Lake** ⊡ Indiana, N USA
188 K5 **Broome** Western Australia
39 S4 **Broomfield** Colorado, C USA
xli R4 **Broomhill** Northumberland, N England, UK
xlii G10 **Broom, Loch** *inlet* NW Scotland, UK
Broos *see* Orăştie
xlii K9 **Brora** Highland, N Scotland, UK
xlii J9 **Brora** ≈ N Scotland, UK
xlii K9 **Brora, Loch** ◎ N Scotland, UK
97 F23 **Brørup** Ribe, W Denmark
97 L23 **Brösarp** Kristianstad, S Sweden
xxxviii I10 **Broseley** Shropshire, W England, UK
xliv D12 **Brosna** Kerry, SW Ireland
xliv I9 **Brosna** ≈ Westmeath, C Ireland
118 J9 **Broşteni** Suceava, NE Romania
104 M6 **Brou** Eure-et-Loir, C France
Broucsella *see* Brussel/Bruxelles
xli O9 **Brough** Cumbria, NW England, UK
xlii L6 **Brough** Highland, N Scotland, UK
xlii L3 **Brough Head** *island* N Scotland, UK
xliv L3 **Broughshane** Ballymena, NE Northern Ireland, UK
xli N14 **Broughton** Lancashire, NW England, UK
xxxix P11 **Broughton** Northamptonshire, C England, UK
xxxix P3 **Broughton** North Lincolnshire, N England, UK
xli P13 **Broughton** North Yorkshire, N England, UK
xlii M2 **Broughton** Orkney Islands, N Scotland, UK
xliii L21 **Broughton** The Borders, S Scotland, UK
xxxv K5 **Broughton** Flintshire, N Wales, UK
xxxix N10 **Broughton Astley** Leicestershire, C England, UK
Broughton Bay *see* Tongjosŏn-man
xl L11 **Broughton in Furness** Cumbria, NW England, UK
16 O1 **Broughton Island** Northwest Territories, NE Canada
xlii N3 **Broughtown** Orkney Islands, N Scotland, UK
144 G7 **Broummâna** C Lebanon
24 J9 **Broussard** Louisiana, S USA
100 E13 **Brouwersdam** *dam* SW Netherlands
100 E13 **Brouwershaven** Zeeland, SW Netherlands
119 P4 **Brovary** Kyyivs'ka Oblast', N Ukraine
97 G20 **Brovst** Nordjylland, N Denmark
33 S8 **Brown City** Michigan, N USA
26 M6 **Brownfield** Texas, SW USA
xxxviii C13 **Brownhills** Walsall, C England, UK
35 Q7 **Browning** Montana, NW USA
35 R6 **Brown, Mount** ▲ Montana, NW USA
194 K15 **Brown River** ≈ S PNG
1 M9 **Browns Bank** *undersea feature* NW Atlantic Ocean
33 O14 **Brownsburg** Indiana, N USA
20 J16 **Browns Mills** New Jersey, NE USA
46 J12 **Browns Town** C Jamaica
33 P15 **Brownstown** Indiana, N USA
31 R8 **Browns Valley** Minnesota, N USA
22 K7 **Brownsville** Kentucky, S USA
22 F9 **Brownsville** Tennessee, S USA
27 T17 **Brownsville** Texas, SW USA
57 W10 **Brownsweg** Brokopondo, C Surinam
31 U9 **Brownton** Minnesota, N USA
21 R5 **Brownville Junction** Maine, NE USA
xxxvi D14 **Brown Willy** *hill* SW England, UK
27 R8 **Brownwood** Texas, SW USA
27 R8 **Brownwood Lake** ⊡ Texas, SW USA
xxxvii T8 **Broxbourne** Hertfordshire, E England, UK
xliii L20 **Broxburn** City of Edinburgh, E Scotland, UK
xxxviii H7 **Broxton** Cheshire, W England, UK
106 I9 **Brozas** Extremadura, W Spain
121 M18 **Brozha** Mahilyowskaya Voblasts', E Belorussia
xlii M7 **Bruan** Highland, N Scotland, UK
105 O2 **Bruay-en-Artois** Pas-de-Calais, N France
105 P2 **Bruay-sur-l'Escaut** Nord, N France
12 F13 **Bruce Peninsula** *peninsula* Ontario, S Canada
22 H9 **Bruceton** Tennessee, S USA
27 T9 **Bruceville** Texas, SW USA
103 G21 **Bruchsal** Baden-Württemberg, SW Germany
111 Q7 **Bruck** Salzburg, NW Austria
Bruck *see* Bruck an der Mur
111 Y4 **Bruck an der Leitha** Niederösterreich, NE Austria
111 V7 **Bruck an der Mur** *var.* Bruck. Steiermark, C Austria
103 M24 **Bruckmühl** Bayern, SE Germany
xxxvi J11 **Brue** ≈ SW England, UK
173 Dd3 **Brueuh, Pulau** *island* NW Indonesia
xliv F12 **Bruff** Limerick, SW Ireland
Bruges *see* Brugge
110 F7 **Brugg** Aargau, NW Switzerland
101 C16 **Brugge** *Fr.* Bruges. West-Vlaanderen, NW Belgium
111 R9 **Bruggen** Kärnten, S Austria
103 E16 **Brühl** Nordrhein-Westfalen, W Germany
xliii D20 **Bruichladdich** Argyll and Bute, W Scotland, UK
101 F14 **Bruinisse** Zeeland, SW Netherlands
174 L5 **Bruit, Pulau** *island* East Malaysia
12 K10 **Brûlé, Lac** ◎ Québec, SE Canada
32 M4 **Brule River** ≈ Michigan/Wisconsin, N USA
101 H23 **Brûly** Namur, S Belgium
61 N17 **Brumado** Bahia, E Brazil
100 M11 **Brummen** Gelderland, E Netherlands
96 H13 **Brumunddal** Hedmark, S Norway
xxxix Y9 **Brundall** Norfolk, E England, UK
25 Q6 **Brundidge** Alabama, S USA
Brundisium/Brundusium *see* Brindisi
35 N15 **Bruneau River** ≈ Idaho, NW USA
Bruneck *see* Brunico
174 Mm4 **Brunei** *off.* Sultanate of Brunei, *Mal.* Negara Brunei Darussalam. ◆ *monarchy* SE Asia
175 N3 **Brunei Bay** *var.* Teluk Brunei. *bay* N Brunei
Brunei, Teluk *see* Brunei Bay
Brunei Town *see* Bandar Seri Begawan
108 H5 **Brunico** *Ger.* Bruneck. Trentino-Alto Adige, N Italy
Brünn *see* Brno
193 G17 **Brunner, Lake** ◎ South Island, NZ
101 M18 **Brunssum** Limburg, SE Netherlands
25 W7 **Brunswick** Georgia, SE USA
21 Q8 **Brunswick** Maine, NE USA
23 V3 **Brunswick** Maryland, NE USA
29 T3 **Brunswick** Missouri, C USA
33 T11 **Brunswick** Ohio, N USA
Brunswick *see* Braunschweig
65 H24 **Brunswick, Peninsula** *headland* S Chile
113 H17 **Bruntál** *Ger.* Freudenthal. Severní Morava, E Czech Republic
205 N3 **Brunt Ice Shelf** *ice shelf* Antarctica
xliv F12 **Bruree** Limerick, SW Ireland
Brusa *see* Bursa
39 U3 **Brush** Colorado, C USA
44 M5 **Brus Laguna** Gracias a Dios, E Honduras
62 K13 **Brusque** Santa Catarina, S Brazil
Brussa *see* Bursa
101 E18 **Brussel** *var.* Brussels, *Fr.* Bruxelles, *Ger.* Brüssel; *anc.* Broucsella. ● (Belgium) Brussels, C Belgium *see also* Bruxelles
Brüssel/Brussels *see* Brussel/Bruxelles
119 O5 **Brusyliv** Zhytomyrs'ka Oblast', N Ukraine
191 Q12 **Bruthen** Victoria, SE Australia
xxxvi L12 **Bruton** Somerset, SW England, UK
Bruttium *see* Calabria
Brüx *see* Most
101 E18 **Bruxelles** *var.* Brussels, *Dut.* Brussel, *Ger.* Brüssel; *anc.* Broucsella. ● (Belgium) Brussels, C Belgium *see also* Brussel
56 J7 **Bruzual** Apure, W Venezuela
33 Q11 **Bryan** Ohio, N USA
27 U10 **Bryan** Texas, SW USA
204 J4 **Bryan Coast** *physical region* Antarctica
126 I13 **Bryanka** Krasnoyarskiy Kray, C Russian Federation
119 Y7 **Bryanka** Luhans'ka Oblast', E Ukraine
190 J8 **Bryan, Mount** ▲ South Australia
130 I6 **Bryansk** Bryanskaya Oblast', W Russian Federation
130 H6 **Bryanskaya Oblast'** ◐ *province* W Russian Federation
204 J5 **Bryant, Cape** *headland* Antarctica
29 U8 **Bryant Creek** ≈ Missouri, C USA
38 K8 **Bryce Canyon** *canyon* Utah, W USA
xliii M24 **Brydekirk** Dumfries and Galloway, SW Scotland, UK
121 O15 **Bryli** *Rus.* Bryli. Mahilyowskaya Voblasts', E Belorussia
xxxv H13 **Brynamman** Carmarthenshire, S Wales, UK
xxxv I12 **Bryn Du** *hill* E Wales, UK
97 C17 **Bryne** Rogaland, S Norway
xxxv J13 **Brynmawr** Blaenau Gwent, SE Wales, UK
xxxv F5 **Brynsiencyn** Isle of Anglesey, NW Wales, UK
27 R6 **Bryson** Texas, SW USA
23 N10 **Bryson City** North Carolina, SE USA
12 K11 **Bryson, Lac** ◎ Québec, SE Canada
130 K13 **Bryukhovetskaya** Krasnodarskiy Kray, SW Russian Federation
113 H15 **Brzeg** *Ger.* Brieg; *anc.* Civitas Altae Ripae. Opole, SW Poland
113 G14 **Brzeg Dolny** *Ger.* Dyhernfurth. Wrocław, SW Poland
Brześć Litewski/Brześć nad Bugiem *see* Brest
113 L17 **Brzesko** *Ger.* Brietzig. Tarnów, SE Poland
Brzeżany *see* Berezhany
112 K12 **Brzeziny** Skierniewice, C Poland
Brzostowica Wielka *see* Vyalikaya Byerastavitsa
113 O17 **Brzozów** Krosno, SE Poland
Bsharrī/Bsherri *see* Bcharré
197 I13 **Bua** Vanua Levu, N Fiji
97 J20 **Bua** Halland, S Sweden
84 M13 **Bua** ≈ C Malawi
Bua *see* Čiovo
83 L18 **Bu'aale** *It.* Buale. Jubbada Dhexe, SW Somalia
201 Q8 **Buada Lagoon** *lagoon* Nauru, C Pacific Ocean
195 W14 **Buala** Santa Isabel, E Solomon Islands
Buale *see* Bu'aale
202 H1 **Buariki** *atoll* Tungaru, W Kiribati
178 I10 **Bua Yai** *var.* Ban Bua Yai. Nakhon Ratchasima, E Thailand
77 P8 **Bu'ayrāt al Ḩasūn** *var.* Buwayrāt al Hasūn. C Libya
78 H13 **Buba** S Guinea-Bissau
175 Qq7 **Bubaa** Sulawesi, N Indonesia
83 D20 **Bubanza** NW Burundi
85 K18 **Bubi** *prev.* Bubye. ≈ S Zimbabwe
148 L11 **Būbīyan, Jazīrat** *island* E Kuwait
Bublitz *see* Bobolice
xli U14 **Bubwith** East Riding of Yorkshire, N England, UK
Bubye *see* Bubi
197 J13 **Buca** *prev.* Mbutha. Vanua Levu, N Fiji
142 F16 **Bucak** Burdur, SW Turkey
56 G8 **Bucaramanga** Santander, N Colombia
109 M18 **Buccino** Campania, S Italy
118 K9 **Bucecea** Botoşani, NE Romania
118 J6 **Buchach** *Pol.* Buczacz. Ternopil's'ka Oblast', W Ukraine
191 Q12 **Buchan** Victoria, SE Australia
78 J17 **Buchanan** *prev.* Grand Bassa. SW Liberia
25 R3 **Buchanan** Georgia, SE USA
33 O11 **Buchanan** Michigan, N USA
23 T6 **Buchanan** Virginia, NE USA
27 R10 **Buchanan Dam** Texas, SW USA
27 R10 **Buchanan, Lake** ⊡ Texas, SW USA
xlii Q12 **Buchan Ness** *headland* NE Scotland, UK
11 T12 **Buchans** Newfoundland, Newfoundland and Labrador, SE Canada
xliii K17 **Buchanty** Perth and Kinross, C Scotland, UK
Bucharest *see* Bucureşti
103 H20 **Buchen** Baden-Württemberg, SW Germany
102 I10 **Buchholz in der Nordheide** Niedersachsen, NW Germany
xliii J19 **Buchlyvie** Stirling, C Scotland, UK
110 I8 **Buchs** Aargau, N Switzerland
110 F7 **Buchs** Sankt Gallen, NE Switzerland
xli P11 **Buckden** North Yorkshire, N England, UK
102 H13 **Bückeburg** Niedersachsen, NW Germany
38 K14 **Buckeye** Arizona, SW USA
Buckeye State *see* Ohio
xxxvi G15 **Buckfastleigh** Devon, SW England, UK
23 S4 **Buckhannon** West Virginia, NE USA
xliii M18 **Buckhaven** Fife, E Scotland, UK
27 T9 **Buckholts** Texas, SW USA
xxxvi F5 **Buckhurst Hill** Redbridge, SE England, UK
xlii M11 **Buckie** Moray, NE Scotland, UK
xxxvii Q6 **Buckingham** Buckinghamshire, C England, UK
12 M12 **Buckingham** Québec, SE Canada
23 U6 **Buckingham** Virginia, NE USA
xxxvii Q7 **Buckinghamshire** ◐ *county* SE England, UK
xxxvii O8 **Buckland** Oxfordshire, C England, UK
41 N8 **Buckland** Alaska, USA
xxxvi F12 **Buckland Brewer** Devon, SW England, UK
190 G7 **Buckleboo** South Australia
xxxvii P13 **Bucklers Hard** Hampshire, S England, UK
xxxv K5 **Buckley** Flintshire, N Wales, UK
28 K7 **Bucklin** Kansas, C USA
29 T3 **Bucklin** Missouri, C USA
xxxix R6 **Bucknall** Lincolnshire, E England, UK
xxxviii G12 **Bucknell** Shropshire, W England, UK
xlii P13 **Bucksburn** City of Aberdeen, NE Scotland, UK
xxxvi E12 **Buck's Cross** Devon, SW England, UK
38 I12 **Buckskin Mountains** ▲▲ Arizona, SW USA
21 R7 **Bucksport** Maine, NE USA
xlii M12 **Buck, The** ▲ N Scotland, UK
84 A9 **Buco Zau** Cabinda, NW Angola
Bu Craa *see* Bou Craa
118 K14 **Bucureşti** *Eng.* Bucharest, *Ger.* Bukarest; *prev.* Altenburg, *anc.* Cetatea Damboviţei. ● (Romania) Bucureşti, S Romania
33 S12 **Bucyrus** Ohio, N USA
Buczacz *see* Buchach
96 E9 **Bud** Møre og Romsdal, S Norway
27 S11 **Buda** Texas, SW USA
121 O18 **Buda-Kashalyova** *Rus.* Buda-Koshelëvo. Homyel'skaya Voblasts', SE Belorussia
Buda-Koshelëvo *see* Buda-Kashalyova
177 G4 **Budalin** Sagaing, C Burma
113 J22 **Budapest** *off.* Budapest Főváros, *SCr.* Budimpešta. ● (Hungary) Pest, N Hungary
158 K11 **Budaun** Uttar Pradesh, N India
147 O9 **Budayyi'ah** *oasis* C Saudi Arabia
205 Y12 **Budd Coast** *physical region* Antarctica
Buddenbrock *see* Brodnica
xliii N17 **Buddon Ness** *headland* E Scotland, UK
109 C17 **Budduso** Sardegna, Italy, C Mediterranean Sea
xxxvi E13 **Bude** Cornwall, SW England, UK
24 J7 **Bude** Mississippi, S USA
xxxvi D13 **Bude Bay** *bay* SW England, UK
101 K16 **Budel** Noord-Brabant, SE Netherlands
102 I8 **Büdelsdorf** Schleswig-Holstein, N Germany
131 O14 **Budënnovsk** Stavropol'skiy Kray, SW Russian Federation
118 K14 **Budeşti** Călăraşi, SE Romania
Budgewoi *see* Budgewoi Lake
191 T8 **Budgewoi Lake** *var.* Budgewoi. New South Wales, SE Australia
94 I2 **Búdhardalur** Vesturland, W Iceland
Budimpešta *see* Budapest
81 J16 **Budjala** Equateur, NW Zaire
xxxvi I14 **Budleigh Salterton** Devon, SW England, UK
108 G10 **Budrio** Emilia-Romagna, C Italy
Budslav *see* Budslaw
121 K14 **Budslaw** *Rus.* Budslav. Minskaya Voblasts', N Belorussia
Budua *see* Budva
174 L15 **Budu, Tanjung** *headland* East Malaysia
115 J17 **Budva** *It.* Budua. Montenegro, SW Yugoslavia
Budweis *see* České Budějovice
Budyšin *see* Bautzen
81 D16 **Buea** Sud-Ouest, SW Cameroon
105 S13 **Buëch** ≈ SE France
20 J17 **Buena** New Jersey, NE USA
64 K12 **Buena Esperanza** San Luis, C Argentina
56 C11 **Buenaventura** Valle del Cauca, W Colombia
42 I4 **Buenaventura** Chihuahua, N Mexico
59 M18 **Buena Vista** Santa Cruz, C Bolivia
42 G10 **Buenavista** Baja California Sur, W Mexico
39 S5 **Buena Vista** Colorado, C USA
25 S5 **Buena Vista** Georgia, SE USA
23 T6 **Buena Vista** Virginia, NE USA
46 F5 **Buena Vista, Bahia de** *bay* N Cuba
37 R13 **Buena Vista Lake Bed** ◎ California, W USA
107 P8 **Buendía, Embalse de** ⊡ C Spain
65 F16 **Bueno, Río** ≈ S Chile
64 N12 **Buenos Aires** *hist.* Santa Maria del Buen Aire. ● (Argentina) Buenos Aires, E Argentina
45 O15 **Buenos Aires** Puntarenas, SE Costa Rica
63 C20 **Buenos Aires** *off.* Provincia de Buenos Aires. ◐ *province* E Argentina
65 H19 **Buenos Aires, Lago** *var.* Lago General Carrera. ◎ Argentina/Chile
56 C13 **Buesaco** Nariño, SW Colombia
31 U8 **Buffalo** Minnesota, N USA
28 K8 **Buffalo** Missouri, C USA
20 D10 **Buffalo** New York, NE USA
29 T6 **Buffalo** Oklahoma, C USA
30 J7 **Buffalo** South Dakota, N USA
27 V8 **Buffalo** Texas, SW USA
35 W12 **Buffalo** Wyoming, C USA
31 U11 **Buffalo Center** Iowa, C USA
26 M3 **Buffalo Lake** ⊡ Texas, SW USA
32 K7 **Buffalo Lake** ⊡ Wisconsin, N USA
9 S12 **Buffalo Narrows** Saskatchewan, C Canada
29 U9 **Buffalo River** ≈ Arkansas, C USA
31 R5 **Buffalo River** ≈ Minnesota, N USA
22 I10 **Buffalo River** ≈ Tennessee, S USA
32 J6 **Buffalo River** ≈ Wisconsin, N USA
46 L12 **Buff Bay** E Jamaica
25 T3 **Buford** Georgia, SE USA
30 J3 **Buford** North Dakota, N USA
35 Y17 **Buford** Wyoming, C USA
118 J14 **Buftea** Bucureşti, S Romania
86 I9 **Bug** *Bel.* Zakhodni Buh, *Eng.* Western Bug, *Rus.* Zapadnyy Bug, *Ukr.* Zakhidnyy Buh. ≈ E Europe
56 D11 **Buga** Valle del Cauca, W Colombia
168 F7 **Buga** Dzavhan, W Mongolia
105 O17 **Bugarach, Pic du** ▲ S France
xxxix O12 **Bugbrooke** Northamptonshire, C England, UK
152 B12 **Bugdayly** Balkanskiy Velayat, W Turkmenistan
Buggs Island Lake *see* John H.Kerr Reservoir
Bughotu *see* Santa Isabel
175 Q12 **Bugingkalo** Sulawesi, C Indonesia
Bugingkaro *see* Bungingkolu, Tanjung
66 P6 **Bugio** *island* Madeira, Portugal, NE Atlantic Ocean
xxxvi D16 **Bugle** Cornwall, SW England, UK
94 M8 **Bugøynes** Finnmark, N Norway
129 Q3 **Bugrino** Nenetskiy Avtonomnyy Okrug, NW Russian Federation
131 T5 **Bugul'ma** Respublika Tatarstan, W Russian Federation
Bügür *see* Luntai
131 T6 **Buguruslan** Orenburgskaya Oblast', W Russian Federation
165 R9 **Buh He** ≈ C China
35 O15 **Buhl** Idaho, NW USA
103 F22 **Bühl** Baden-Württemberg, SW Germany
118 K10 **Buhuşi** Bacău, E Romania
Buie d'Istria *see* Buje
xxxv J11 **Builth Wells** Powys, E Wales, UK
195 S13 **Buin** Bougainville Island, NE PNG
110 J9 **Buin, Piz** ▲ Austria/Switzerland
131 Q4 **Buinsk** Chuvashskaya Respublika, W Russian Federation
131 Q4 **Buinsk** Respublika Tatarstan, W Russian Federation
169 R8 **Buir Nur** *Mong.* Buyr Nuur. ◎ China/Mongolia *see also* Buyr Nuur
100 M5 **Buitenpost** *Fris.* Bûtenpost. Friesland, N Netherlands
Buitenzorg *see* Bogor
85 F19 **Buitepos** Omaheke, E Namibia
107 N7 **Buitrago del Lozoya** Madrid, C Spain
Buj *see* Buy
106 M13 **Bujalance** Andalucía, S Spain
115 O17 **Bujanovac** Serbia, SE Yugoslavia
107 S6 **Bujaraloz** Aragón, NE Spain
114 A9 **Buje** *It.* Buie d'Istria. Istra, NW Croatia
Bujnurd *see* Bojnūrd
83 D21 **Bujumbura** *prev.* Usumbura. ● (Burundi) W Burundi
83 D20 **Bujumbura** ✕ W Burundi
126 L15 **Bukachacha** Chitinskaya Oblast', S Russian Federation
165 N11 **Bukadaban Feng** ▲ C China
195 R11 **Buka Island** *island* NE PNG
83 F18 **Bukakata** S Uganda
81 N24 **Bukama** Shaba, SE Zaire
148 J4 **Būkān** *var.* Bowkān. Āzarbāyjān-e Bākhtarī, NW Iran
Bukantau, Gory *see* Bŭkantow-Toghi
152 K8 **Bŭkantow-Toghi** *Rus.* Gory Bukantau. ▲▲ N Uzbekistan
Bukarest *see* Bucureşti
81 O19 **Bukavu** *prev.* Costermansville. Sud Kivu, E Zaire
83 F21 **Bukene** Tabora, NW Tanzania
147 W8 **Bū Khābi** *var.* Bakhābī. NW Oman
Bukhara *see* Bukhoro
Bukharskaya Oblast' *see* Bukhoro Wiloyati
152 L11 **Bukhoro** *var.* Bokhara, *Rus.* Bukhara. Bukhoro Wiloyati, C Uzbekistan
152 J11 **Bukhoro Wiloyati** *Rus.* Bukharskaya Oblast'. ◐ *province* C Uzbekistan
174 I12 **Bukitkemuning** Sumatera, W Indonesia
173 G8 **Bukittinggi** *prev.* Fort de Kock. Sumatera, W Indonesia
113 L21 **Bükk** ▲▲ NE Hungary
83 F19 **Bukoba** Kagera, NW Tanzania
115 N20 **Bukovo** S FYR Macedonia
110 G6 **Bülach** Zürich, NW Switzerland
Bülaevo *see* Bulayevo
168 I6 **Bulag** Hövsgöl, N Mongolia
168 M7 **Bulag** Töv, C Mongolia
168 I8 **Bulagiyn Denj** Arhangay, C Mongolia
191 U7 **Bulahdelah** New South Wales, SE Australia
176 Yy15 **Bulaka, Sungai** ≈ Irian Jaya, E Indonesia
179 Qq12 **Bulan** Luzon, N Philippines
143 N11 **Bulancak** Giresun, N Turkey
158 J10 **Bulandshahr** Uttar Pradesh, N India
143 R14 **Bulanık** Muş, E Turkey
131 V7 **Bulanovo** Orenburgskaya Oblast', W Russian Federation
85 J17 **Bulawayo** *var.* Buluwayo. Matabeleland North, SW Zimbabwe
85 J17 **Bulawayo** ✕ Matabeleland North, SW Zimbabwe
151 Q6 **Bulayevo** *Kaz.* Bŭlaevo. Severnyy Kazakhstan, N Kazakhstan
142 D15 **Buldan** Denizli, SW Turkey
160 G12 **Buldāna** Mahārāshtra, C India
40 E16 **Buldir Island** *island* Aleutian Islands, Alaska, USA
Buldur *see* Burdur
xxxvii O11 **Bulford** Wiltshire, S England, UK
168 H9 **Bulgan** Bayanhongor, C Mongolia
168 K6 **Bulgan** Bulgan, N Mongolia
168 F7 **Bulgan** Hovd, W Mongolia
168 J5 **Bulgan** Hövsgöl, N Mongolia
168 J10 **Bulgan** Ömnögövi, S Mongolia
168 J7 **Bulgan** ◐ *province* N Mongolia
116 H10 **Bulgaria** *off.* Republic of Bulgaria, *Bul.* Bŭlgariya; *prev.* People's Republic of Bulgaria. ◆ *republic* SE Europe
Bŭlgariya *see* Bulgaria
116 L9 **Bŭlgarka** ▲ E Bulgaria
175 T7 **Buli** Pulau Halmahera, E Indonesia
175 Tt7 **Buli, Teluk** *bay* Pulau Halmahera, E Indonesia
166 J13 **Buliu He** ≈ S China
Bullange *see* Büllingen
106 M11 **Bullaque** ≈ C Spain
107 Q13 **Bullas** Murcia, SE Spain
82 M12 **Bullaxaar** Woqooyi Galbeed, NW Somalia
110 C9 **Bulle** Fribourg, SW Switzerland
193 G15 **Buller** ≈ South Island, NZ
191 P12 **Buller, Mount** ▲ Victoria, SE Australia
38 H11 **Bullhead City** Arizona, SW USA
101 N21 **Büllingen** *Fr.* Bullange. Liège, E Belgium
Bullion State *see* Missouri
23 T14 **Bull Island** *island* South Carolina, SE USA
190 M4 **Bulloo River Overflow** *wetland* New South Wales, SE Australia
192 M12 **Bulls** Manawatu-Wanganui, North Island, NZ
23 T14 **Bulls Bay** *bay* South Carolina, SE USA
29 U9 **Bull Shoals Lake** ⊡ Arkansas/Missouri, C USA
xliv I4 **Bull, The** *island* S Ireland
189 Q2 **Bulman** Northern Territory, N Australia
xli U12 **Bulmer** North Yorkshire, N England, UK
168 I6 **Bulnayn Nuruu** ▲▲ N Mongolia
194 H13 **Bulolo** Morobe, C PNG
175 Qq7 **Bulowa, Gunung** ▲ Sulawesi, N Indonesia
Bulqiza *see* Bulqizë
115 L19 **Bulqizë** *var.* Bulqiza. Dibër, C Albania
Bulsar *see* Valsād
175 R7 **Buludawa Keten, Pegunungan** ▲▲ Sulawesi, N Indonesia
175 Pp13 **Bulukumba** *prev.* Boeloekoemba. Sulawesi, C Indonesia
153 O11 **Bulunghur** *Rus.* Bulungur; *prev.* Krasnogvardeysk. Samarqand Wiloyati, C Uzbekistan
81 I21 **Bulungu** Bandundu, SW Zaire
Bulungur *see* Bulunghur
Buluwayo *see* Bulawayo
81 K17 **Bumba** Equateur, N Zaire
124 O15 **Bumbah, Khalij al** *gulf* N Libya
168 K8 **Bumbat** Övörhangay, C Mongolia
83 F19 **Bumbire Island** *island* N Tanzania
175 Oo4 **Bum Bun, Pulau** *island* East Malaysia
83 J17 **Buna** North Eastern, NE Kenya
27 Y10 **Buna** Texas, SW USA
Bunab *see* Bonāb
Bunai *see* M'bunai
153 S13 **Bunay** S Tajikistan
xliv G2 **Bunbeg** Donegal, N Ireland
xxxviii H7 **Bunbury** Cheshire, W England, UK
188 I13 **Bunbury** Western Australia
xliv K13 **Bunclody** Wexford, SE Ireland
xliv I2 **Buncrana** *Ir.* Bun Cranncha. Donegal, NW Ireland
Bun Cranncha *see* Buncrana
189 Z9 **Bundaberg** Queensland, E Australia
191 T5 **Bundarra** New South Wales, SE Australia
102 G13 **Bünde** Nordrhein-Westfalen, NW Germany
158 H13 **Būndi** Rājasthān, N India
194 I12 **Bundi** Madang, N PNG
Bun Dobhráin *see* Bundoran
xliv G5 **Bundoran** *Ir.* Bun Dobhráin. Donegal, NW Ireland
115 K18 **Bunë** *SCr.* Bojana. ≈ Albania/Yugoslavia *see also* Bojana
xliii D18 **Bunessan** Argyll and Bute, W Scotland, UK
179 R16 **Bunga** ≈ Mindanao, S Philippines
173 Ff10 **Bungalaut, Selat** *strait* W Indonesia
xxxix Y10 **Bungay** Suffolk, E England, UK
178 I8 **Bung Kan** Nong Khai, E Thailand
189 N4 **Bungle Bungle Range** ▲▲ Western Australia
84 C10 **Bungo** Uíge, NW Angola
83 G18 **Bungoma** Western, W Kenya
170 Dd15 **Bungo-suidō** *strait* SW Japan
170 Dd13 **Bungo-Takada** Ōita, Kyūshū, SW Japan
102 K8 **Bungsberg** *hill* N Germany
Bungur *see* Bunyu
81 P17 **Bunia** Haut-Zaïre, NE Zaire
37 U6 **Bunker Hill** ▲ Nevada, W USA
24 I7 **Bunkie** Louisiana, S USA
xliv I13 **Bunmahon** Waterford, S Ireland
xliv F10 **Bunnaglass** Galway, W Ireland
25 X10 **Bunnell** Florida, SE USA
107 S10 **Buñol** País Valenciano, E Spain
xliv F11 **Bunratty** Clare, W Ireland
100 K11 **Bunschoten** Utrecht, C Netherlands
xxxvii U6 **Buntingford** Hertfordshire, SE England, UK
142 K14 **Bünyan** Kayseri, C Turkey
175 Oo5 **Bunyu** *var.* Bungur. Borneo, N Indonesia
175 Oo5 **Bunyu, Pulau** *island* N Indonesia
Bunzlau *see* Bolesławiec
Buoddobohki *see* Patoniva
126 Ll6 **Buorkhaya Guba** *bay* N Russian Federation
176 Z15 **Bupul** Irian Jaya, E Indonesia
83 K19 **Bura** Coast, SE Kenya
82 P12 **Buraan** Sanaag, N Somalia
Būrabay *see* Borovoye
Buraida *see* Buraydah
Buraimi *see* Al Buraymī
151 Y11 **Buran** Vostochnyy Kazakhstan, E Kazakhstan
164 G15 **Burang** Xizang Zizhiqu, W China
Burao *see* Burco
144 H8 **Burāq** Dar'ā, S Syria
147 O6 **Buraydah** *var.* Buraida. Al Qaşīm, N Saudi Arabia
xxxviii K6 **Burbage** Derbyshire, C England, UK
xxxvii O10 **Burbage** Wiltshire, S England, UK
37 S15 **Burbank** California, W USA
33 N11 **Burbank** Illinois, N USA
191 Q8 **Burcher** New South Wales, SE Australia
82 N13 **Burco** *var.* Burao, Bur'o. Togdheer, NW Somalia
152 L13 **Burdalyk** Lebapskiy Velayat, E Turkmenistan
189 W6 **Burdekin River** ≈ Queensland, NE Australia
29 O7 **Burden** Kansas, C USA
Burdigala *see* Bordeaux
142 E15 **Burdur** *var.* Buldur. Burdur, SW Turkey
142 E15 **Burdur** *var.* Buldur. ◐ *province* SW Turkey
142 E15 **Burdur Gölü** *salt lake* SW Turkey
57 H21 **Burdwood Bank** *undersea feature* SW Atlantic Ocean
xxxix Y9 **Bure** ≈ E England, UK
82 I12 **Burē** NW Ethiopia
82 H13 **Burē** W Ethiopia
95 J15 **Bureå** Västerbotten, N Sweden
103 G14 **Büren** Nordrhein-Westfalen, W Germany
168 K6 **Bürengiyn Nuruu** ▲▲ N Mongolia
168 E8 **Bürenhayrhan** Hovd, W Mongolia
xxxix V14 **Bures** Essex, E England, UK
Bürewāla *see* Mandi Būrewāla
127 N17 **Bureya** ≈ SE Russian Federation
xxxviii I7 **Burfard** Cheshire, C England, UK
54 J9 **Burfjord** Troms, N Norway
xxxvii O7 **Burford** Oxfordshire, C England, UK
102 L13 **Burg** *var.* Burg an der Ihle, Burg bei Magdeburg. Sachsen-Anhalt, C Germany
Burg an der Ihle *see* Burg
116 N10 **Burgas** *var.* Bourgas. Burgaska Oblast, E Bulgaria
116 N9 **Burgas** ✕ Burgaska Oblast, E Bulgaria
Burgas *see* Burgaska Oblast
116 L9 **Burgaska Oblast** *var.* Burgas. ◐ *province* E Bulgaria
116 N10 **Burgaski Zaliv** *gulf* E Bulgaria
116 M10 **Burgasko Ezero** *lagoon* E Bulgaria
23 V11 **Burgaw** North Carolina, SE USA
Burg bei Magdeburg *see* Burg
110 E8 **Burgdorf** Bern, NW Switzerland
111 Y7 **Burgenland** *off.* Land Burgenland. ◐ *state* SE Austria
11 S13 **Burgeo** Newfoundland, Newfoundland and Labrador, SE Canada
85 I24 **Burgersdorp** Eastern Cape, SE South Africa
85 K20 **Burgersfort** Mpumalanga, NE South Africa
xxxvii T12 **Burgess Hill** West Sussex, SE England, UK
103 N23 **Burghausen** Bayern, SE Germany
xxxix Y9 **Burgh Castle** Norfolk, E England, UK
xlii L11 **Burghead** Moray, N Scotland, UK
xxxvii Q10 **Burghfield** Newbury, S England, UK
xxxix T6 **Burgh le Marsh** Lincolnshire, E England, UK
145 O5 **Burghūth, Sabkhat al** ◎ E Syria
103 M20 **Burglengenfeld** Bayern, SE Germany
43 P9 **Burgos** Tamaulipas, C Mexico
107 N4 **Burgos** Castilla-León, N Spain
107 N4 **Burgos** ◐ *province* Castilla-León, N Spain
Burgstadlberg *see* Hradiště
97 P20 **Burgsvik** Gotland, SE Sweden
Burgum *see* Bergum
Burgundy *see* Bourgogne
165 Q11 **Burhan Budai Shan** ▲▲ C China
142 B12 **Burhaniye** Balıkesir, W Turkey
160 G12 **Burhānpur** Madhya Pradesh, C India
179 Q11 **Burias Island** *island* C Philippines
131 W7 **Buribay** Respublika Bashkortostan, W Russian Federation
45 O17 **Burica, Punta** *headland* Costa Rica/Panama
178 I10 **Buriram** *var.* Buri Ram, Puriramya. Buri Ram, E Thailand
107 S10 **Burjassot** País Valenciano, E Spain
83 N16 **Burka Giibi** Hiiraan, C Somalia
153 X8 **Burkan** ≈ E Kyrgyzstan
27 R4 **Burkburnett** Texas, SW USA
31 O12 **Burke** South Dakota, N USA
8 K15 **Burke Channel** *channel* British Columbia, W Canada
204 J10 **Burke Island** *island* Antarctica
22 L7 **Burkesville** Kentucky, S USA
189 T4 **Burketown** Queensland, NE Australia
27 Q8 **Burkett** Texas, SW USA
27 Y9 **Burkeville** Texas, SW USA
23 V7 **Burkeville** Virginia, NE USA
79 O12 **Burkina** *off.* Burkina Faso; *prev.* Upper Volta. ◆ *republic* W Africa
Burkina Faso *see* Burkina
204 L13 **Burks, Cape** *headland* Antarctica
12 H12 **Burk's Falls** Ontario, S Canada
103 H23 **Burladingen** Baden-Württemberg, S Germany
27 T7 **Burleson** Texas, SW USA
xxxvii O13 **Burley** Hampshire, S England, UK
35 P15 **Burley** Idaho, NW USA

◆ Country ● Country Capital ◇ Dependent Territory ○ Dependent Territory Capital ◐ Administrative Region ✕ International Airport ▲ Mountain ▲▲ Mountain Range Volcano ≈ River ◎ Lake ⊡ Reservoir

BURLIN – CALLABONNA CREEK

150 G8 **Burlin** Zapadnyy Kazakhstan, NW Kazakhstan
12 G16 **Burlington** Ontario, S Canada
39 W4 **Burlington** Colorado, C USA
31 Y15 **Burlington** Iowa, C USA
29 P5 **Burlington** Kansas, C USA
23 T9 **Burlington** North Carolina, SE USA
30 M3 **Burlington** North Dakota, N USA
20 L7 **Burlington** Vermont, NE USA
32 M9 **Burlington** Wisconsin, N USA
29 Q1 **Burlington Junction** Missouri, C USA
xxxviii H8 **Burlton** Shropshire, W England, UK
159 Y14 **Burma** *off.* Union of Myanmar, *var.* Myanmar. ◆ *military dictatorship* SE Asia
8 L17 **Burnaby** British Columbia, SW Canada
119 O12 **Burnas, Ozero** ◎ SW Ukraine
xli V13 **Burnby** East Riding of Yorkshire, N England, UK
xli R11 **Burneston** North Yorkshire, N England, UK
27 S10 **Burnet** Texas, SW USA
37 O3 **Burney** California, W USA
xxxix V7 **Burnham Market** Norfolk, E England, UK
xxxvii X8 **Burnham-on-Crouch** Essex, SE England, UK
xxxvi J11 **Burnham-on-Sea** Somerset, SW England, UK
xlii Q12 **Burnhaven** Aberdeenshire, NE Scotland, UK
191 O16 **Burnie** Tasmania, SE Australia
xli P14 **Burnley** Lancashire, NW England, UK
151 Q16 **Burnoye** Zhambyl, S Kazakhstan
159 R15 **Burnpur** West Bengal, NE India
34 K14 **Burns** Oregon, NW USA
xli Q12 **Burnsall** North Yorkshire, N England, UK
28 K11 **Burns Flat** Oklahoma, C USA
xliii J23 **Burnside** East Ayrshire, W Scotland, UK
22 M7 **Burnside** Kentucky, S USA
15 I15 **Burnside** ≈ Northwest Territories, NW Canada
34 L15 **Burns Junction** Oregon, NW USA
8 L13 **Burns Lake** British Columbia, SW Canada
31 V9 **Burnsville** Minnesota, N USA
23 P9 **Burnsville** North Carolina, SE USA
23 R4 **Burnsville** West Virginia, NE USA
xliii M19 **Burntisland** Fife, E Scotland, UK
12 I13 **Burnt River** ≈ Ontario, SE Canada
12 I11 **Burntroot Lake** ◎ Ontario, SE Canada
xxxviii C13 **Burntwood** Staffordshire, C England, UK
9 W12 **Burntwood** ≈ Manitoba, C Canada
Bur'o *see* Burco
164 L2 **Burqin** Xinjiang Uygur Zizhiqu, NW China
190 J8 **Burra** South Australia
xliii J1 **Burrafirth** Shetland Islands, NE Scotland, UK
191 S9 **Burragorang, Lake** ⊠ New South Wales, SE Australia
xlii I2 **Burravoe** Shetland Islands, NE Scotland, UK
xli N5 **Burray** *island* NE Scotland, UK
115 L19 **Burrel** *var.* Burreli. Dibër, C Albania
Burreli *see* Burrel
xliii M17 **Burrelton** Perth and Kinross, C Scotland, UK
xliv E9 **Burren** Clare, W Ireland
xliv E10 **Burren** *physical region* W Ireland
191 R8 **Burrendong Reservoir** ⊠ New South Wales, SE Australia
191 R5 **Burren Junction** New South Wales, SE Australia
107 T9 **Burriana** País Valenciano, E Spain
191 R10 **Burrinjuck Reservoir** ⊠ New South Wales, SE Australia
38 J12 **Burro Creek** ≈ Arizona, SW USA
42 M5 **Burro, Serranías del** ▲ NW Mexico
xliii I26 **Burrow Head** *headland* SW Scotland, UK
64 K7 **Burruyacú** Tucumán, N Argentina
xxxv F14 **Burry Port** Carmarthenshire, S Wales, UK
142 E12 **Bursa** *var.* Brussa; *prev.* Brusa, *anc.* Prusa. Bursa, NW Turkey
142 D12 **Bursa** *var.* Brusa, Brussa. ◐ *province* NW Turkey
77 Y9 **Būr Safāga** *var.* Būr Safājah. E Egypt
Būr Safājah *see* Būr Safāga
Būr Sa'īd *see* Port Said
xl M15 **Burscough** Lancashire, NW England, UK
83 O14 **Bur Tinle** Mudug, C Somalia
33 Q5 **Burt Lake** ◎ Michigan, N USA
Burtnieks *see* Burtnieku Ezers
120 H7 **Burtnieku Ezers** *var.* Burtnieks. ◎ N Latvia
xl B17 **Burton** Cheshire, W England, UK
33 Q9 **Burton** Michigan, N USA
xli W12 **Burton Agnes** East Riding of Yorkshire, N England, UK
xxxvi K14 **Burton Bradstock** Dorset, S England, UK
xli W11 **Burton Fleming** East Riding of Yorkshire, N England, UK
xli N11 **Burton-in-Kendal** Cumbria, NW England, UK
xxxix O7 **Burton Joyce** Nottinghamshire, C England, UK
xxxix P11 **Burton Latimer** Northamptonshire, C England, UK
xli S12 **Burton Leonard** North Yorkshire, N England, UK
Burton on Trent *see* Burton upon Trent
xli X14 **Burton Pidsea** East Riding of Yorkshire, N England, UK
xliv G3 **Burtonport** Donegal, N Ireland
xxxviii L9 **Burton upon Trent** *var.* Burton on Trent, Burton-upon-Trent. Staffordshire, C England, UK
95 J15 **Burträsk** Västerbotten, N Sweden
151 S14 **Burubaytal** *prev.* Burylbaytal. Zhambyl, SE Kazakhstan
Burujird *see* Borūjerd
Burultokay *see* Fuhai
147 R15 **Burūm** SE Yemen
151 U16 **Burunday** *Kaz.* Boralday. Almaty, SE Kazakhstan
83 D21 **Burundi** *off.* Republic of Burundi; *prev.* Kingdom of Burundi, Urundi. ◆ *republic* C Africa
175 S11 **Buru, Pulau** *prev.* Boeroe. *island* E Indonesia
79 T17 **Burutu** Delta, S Nigeria
xxxviii H7 **Burwardsley** Cheshire, W England, UK
8 G7 **Burwash Landing** Yukon Territory, W Canada
xxxix T12 **Burwell** Cambridgeshire, E England, UK
31 O14 **Burwell** Nebraska, C USA
xlii M5 **Burwick** Orkney Islands, N Scotland, UK
xl G14 **Bury** Bury, NW England, UK
xxxvii S13 **Bury** West Sussex, SE England, UK
xl F14 **Bury** ◐ *unitary authority* NW England, UK
126 K15 **Buryatiya, Respublika** *prev.* Buryatskaya ASSR. ◐ *autonomous republic* S Russian Federation
Buryatskaya ASSR *see* Buryatiya, Respublika
Burylbaytal *see* Burubaytal
119 S3 **Buryn'** Sums'ka Oblast', NE Ukraine
xxxix U12 **Bury St Edmunds** *hist.* Beodericsworth. Suffolk, E England, UK
116 G8 **Bŭrziya** ≈ NW Bulgaria
108 D9 **Busalla** Liguria, NW Italy
179 R17 **Busa, Mount** ▲ Mindanao, S Philippines
Busan *see* Pusan
145 N5 **Buşayrah** Dayr az Zawr, E Syria
Buševa *see* Baba
149 N12 **Būshehr** *off.* Ostān-e Būshehr. ◐ *province* SW Iran
Būshehr/Bushire *see* Bandar-e Būshehr
27 N2 **Bushland** Texas, SW USA
xliv K2 **Bushmills** Moyle, N Northern Ireland, UK
32 J12 **Bushnell** Illinois, N USA
Busi *see* Biševo
83 G18 **Busia** SE Uganda
Busiasch *see* Buziaş
81 K16 **Businga** Equateur, NW Zaire
81 J18 **Busira** ≈ NW Zaire
118 I5 **Bus'k** *Rus.* Busk. L'vivs'ka Oblast', W Ukraine
97 E14 **Buskerud** ◐ *county* S Norway
115 F14 **Buško Jezero** ⊠ SW Bosnia and Herzegovina
113 M15 **Busko-Zdrój** Kielce, SE Poland
Busra *see* Al Başrah, Iraq
Buşrá *see* Buşrá ash Shām, Syria
144 H9 **Buşrá ash Shām** *var.* Bosora, Bosra, Bozrah, Buşrá. Dar'ā, S Syria
188 I13 **Busselton** Western Australia
83 C14 **Busseri** ≈ W Sudan
108 E9 **Busseto** Emilia-Romagna, C Italy
108 A8 **Bussoleno** Piemonte, NE Italy
Bussora *see* Al Başrah
100 J10 **Bussum** Noord-Holland, C Netherlands
43 N7 **Bustamante** Nuevo León, NE Mexico
65 I23 **Bustamante, Punta** *headland* S Argentina
Bustan *see* Bŭston
118 J12 **Buşteni** Prahova, SE Romania
108 D7 **Busto Arsizio** Lombardia, N Italy
153 Q10 **Bŭston** *Rus.* Buston. W Tajikistan
152 I9 **Bŭston** *Rus.* Bustan. Qoraqalpoghiston Respublikasi, W Uzbekistan
179 P12 **Busuanga Island** *island* Calamian Group, W Philippines
102 H8 **Büsum** Schleswig-Holstein, N Germany
81 M16 **Buta** Haut-Zaïre, N Zaire
83 E20 **Butare** *prev.* Astrida. S Rwanda
203 O2 **Butaritari** *atoll* Tungaru, W Kiribati
Butawal *see* Butwal
168 K6 **Büteeliyn Nuruu** ▲ N Mongolia
8 L16 **Bute Inlet** *fjord* British Columbia, W Canada
xliii G20 **Bute, Island of** *island* SW Scotland, UK
81 P18 **Butembo** Nord Kivu, NE Zaire
Bütenpost *see* Buitenpost
109 K25 **Butera** Sicilia, Italy, C Mediterranean Sea
xliii G21 **Bute, Sound of** *sound* W Scotland, UK
101 M20 **Bütgenbach** Liège, E Belgium
Butha Qi *see* Zalantun
177 F5 **Buthidaung** Arakan State, W Burma
63 I16 **Butiá** Rio Grande do Sul, S Brazil
83 F17 **Butiaba** NW Uganda
xxxvi K12 **Butleigh** Somerset, SW England, UK
25 N6 **Butler** Alabama, S USA
25 S5 **Butler** Georgia, SE USA
33 Q11 **Butler** Indiana, N USA
29 R5 **Butler** Missouri, C USA
20 B14 **Butler** Pennsylvania, NE USA
204 K5 **Butler Island** *island* Antarctica
xxxix Y13 **Butley** Suffolk, E England, UK
23 U8 **Butner** North Carolina, SE USA
175 Qq13 **Buton, Pulau** *var.* Pulau Butung; *prev.* Boetoeng. *island* C Indonesia
175 Qq13 **Buton, Selat** *strait* C Indonesia
Bütow *see* Bytów
115 L23 **Butrintit, Liqeni i** ◎ S Albania
25 N3 **Buttahatchee River** ≈ Alabama/Mississippi, S USA
35 Q10 **Butte** Montana, NW USA
31 O12 **Butte** Nebraska, C USA
xli O6 **Butterburn** Cumbria, NW England, UK
xl L9 **Buttermere** Cumbria, NW England, UK
xxxix S7 **Butterwick** Lincolnshire, E England, UK
173 G3 **Butterworth** Pinang, Peninsular Malaysia
85 J25 **Butterworth** *var.* Gcuwa. Eastern Cape, SE South Africa
xliv F11 **Buttevant** Cork, S Ireland
11 O3 **Button Islands** *island group* Northwest Territories, NE Canada
37 R13 **Buttonwillow** California, W USA
179 R14 **Butuan** *off.* Butuan City. Mindanao, S Philippines
Butung, Pulau *see* Buton, Pulau
Butuntum *see* Bitonto
130 M8 **Buturlinovka** Voronezhskaya Oblast', W Russian Federation
159 O11 **Butwal** *var.* Butawal. Western, C Nepal
103 G17 **Butzbach** Hessen, W Germany
102 L9 **Bützow** Mecklenburg-Vorpommern, N Germany
82 N13 **Buuhoodle** Togdheer, N Somalia
83 N16 **Buulobarde** *var.* Buulo Berde. Hiiraan, C Somalia Africa
Buulo Berde *see* Buulobarde
82 P12 **Buuraha Cal Miskaat** ▲ NE Somalia
83 L19 **Buur Gaabo** Jubbada Hoose, S Somalia
101 M22 **Buurgplaatz** ▲ N Luxembourg
Buwayrāt al Hasūn *see* Bu'ayrāt al Ḩasūn
102 I10 **Buxtehude** Niedersachsen, NW Germany
xxxviii K6 **Buxton** Derbyshire, C England, UK
xxxix X8 **Buxton** Norfolk, E England, UK
128 M14 **Buy** *var.* Buj. Kostromskaya Oblast', NW Russian Federation
168 G7 **Buyanbat** Govĭ-Altay, W Mongolia
168 H8 **Buyant** Bayanhongor, C Mongolia
168 D6 **Buyant** Bayan-Ölgiy, W Mongolia
168 H7 **Buyant** Dzavhan, C Mongolia
169 N9 **Buyant** Hentiy, C Mongolia
169 N10 **Buyant-Uhaa** Dornogovĭ, SE Mongolia
168 M7 **Buyant Ukha** ✕ (Ulaanbaatar) Töv, N Mongolia
131 Q16 **Buynaksk** Respublika Dagestan, SW Russian Federation
121 L20 **Buynavichy** *Rus.* Buynovichi. Homyel'skaya Voblasts', SE Belorussia
Buynovichi *see* Buynavichy
78 L16 **Buyo** SW Ivory Coast
78 L16 **Buyo, Lac de** ⊠ W Ivory Coast
169 R7 **Buyr Nuur** *var.* Buir Nur. ◎ China/Mongolia *see also* Buir Nur
143 T13 **Büyükağrı Dağı** *var.* Aghri Dagh, Agri Dagi, Koh I Noh, Masis, *Eng.* Great Ararat, Mount Ararat. ▲ E Turkey
143 R15 **Büyük Çayı** ≈ NE Turkey
116 O13 **Büyük Çekmece** İstanbul, NW Turkey
116 N12 **Büyükkarıştıran** Kırklareli, NW Turkey
117 L14 **Büyükkemikli Burnu** *headland* NW Turkey
142 E15 **Büyükmenderes Nehri** ≈ SW Turkey
Büyükzap Suyu *see* Great Zab
104 M9 **Buzançais** Indre, C France
118 K13 **Buzău** Buzău, SE Romania
118 K13 **Buzău** ◐ *county* SE Romania
118 L12 **Buzău** ≈ E Romania
77 S11 **Buzaymah** *var.* Bzīmah. SE Libya
170 D13 **Buzen** Fukuoka, Kyūshū, SW Japan
118 F12 **Buziaş** *Ger.* Busiasch, *Hung.* Buziásfürdő; *prev.* Buziás. Timiş, W Romania
Buziásfürdő *see* Buziaş
85 M18 **Búzi, Rio** ≈ C Mozambique
119 Q10 **Buz'kyy Lyman** *bay* S Ukraine
Büzmeyin *see* Byuzmeyin
151 O8 **Buzuluk** Turgay, C Kazakhstan
131 T6 **Buzuluk** Orenburgskaya Oblast', W Russian Federation
131 N8 **Buzuluk** ≈ SW Russian Federation
21 P12 **Buzzards Bay** Massachusetts, NE USA
21 P13 **Buzzards Bay** *bay* Massachusetts, NE USA
85 G16 **Bwabata** Caprivi, NE Namibia
195 P17 **Bwagaoia** Misima Island, SE PNG
Bwake *see* Bouaké
197 C12 **Bwatnapne** Pentecost, C Vanuatu
121 K14 **Byahoml'** *Rus.* Begoml'. Vitsyebskaya Voblasts', N Belorussia
116 J8 **Byala** Razgradska Oblast, N Bulgaria
116 N9 **Byala** *prev.* Ak-Dere. Varnenska Oblast, NE Bulgaria
Byala Reka *see* Erydropótamos
116 H8 **Byala Slatina** Oblast Montana, NW Bulgaria
121 N15 **Byalynichy** *Rus.* Belynichi. Mahilyowskaya Voblasts', E Belorussia
121 G19 **Byaroza** *Pol.* Bereza Kartuska, *Rus.* Berëza. Brestskaya Voblasts', SW Belorussia
Bybles *see* Jbail
113 O14 **Bychawa** Lublin, SE Poland
Bychikha *see* Bychykha
120 N11 **Bychykha** *Rus.* Bychikha. Vitsyebskaya Voblasts', NE Belorussia
113 I14 **Byczyna** *Ger.* Pitschen. Opole, SW Poland
Bydgoskie, Województwo *see* Bydgoszcz
112 I10 **Bydgoszcz** *Ger.* Bromberg. Bydgoszcz, W Poland
112 H9 **Bydgoszcz** *off.* Województwo Bydgoskie, *Ger.* Bromberg. ◐ *province* W Poland
121 I17 **Byelaruskaya Hrada** *Rus.* Belorusskaya Gryada. *ridge* N Belorussia
121 G18 **Byelavyezhskaya Pushcha** *Pol.* Puszcza Białowieska, *Rus.* Belovezhskaya Pushcha. *forest* Belorussia/Poland *see also* Białowieska, Puszcza
121 H15 **Byenyakoni** *Rus.* Benyakoni. Hrodzyenskaya Voblasts', W Belorussia
121 M16 **Byerazino** *Rus.* Berezino. Minskaya Voblasts', C Belorussia
120 L13 **Byerazino** *Rus.* Berezino. Vitsyebskaya Voblasts', N Belorussia
121 L14 **Byerezino** *Rus.* Berezina. ≈ C Belorussia
120 M13 **Byeshankovichy** *Rus.* Beshenkovichi. Vitsyebskaya Voblasts', N Belorussia
33 U13 **Byesville** Ohio, N USA
121 P18 **Byesyedz'** *Rus.* Besed'. ≈ SE Belorussia
121 H19 **Byezdzyezh** *Rus.* Bezdezh. Brestskaya Voblasts', SW Belorussia
xxxix N13 **Byfield** Northamptonshire, C England, UK
xxxvii S10 **Byfleet** Surrey, SE England, UK
95 J15 **Bygdeå** Västerbotten, N Sweden
96 F12 **Bygdin** ◎ S Norway
95 J15 **Bygdsiljum** Västerbotten, N Sweden
97 E17 **Bygland** Aust-Agder, S Norway
97 E17 **Byglandsfjord** Aust-Agder, S Norway
121 N16 **Bykhaw** *Rus.* Bykhov. Mahilyowskaya Voblasts', E Belorussia
Bykhov *see* Bykhaw
131 P9 **Bykovo** Volgogradskaya Oblast', SW Russian Federation
126 L6 **Bykovskiy** Respublika Sakha (Yakutiya), NE Russian Federation
xxxv I5 **Bylchau** Conwy, N Wales, UK
205 R12 **Byrd Glacier** *glacier* Antarctica
12 K10 **Byrd, Lac** ◎ Québec, SE Canada
xli O4 **Byrness** Northumberland, N England, UK
191 P5 **Byrock** New South Wales, SE Australia
32 L10 **Byron** Illinois, N USA
191 V4 **Byron Bay** New South Wales, SE Australia
191 V4 **Byron, Cape** *headland* New South Wales, E Australia
65 F21 **Byron, Isla** *island* S Chile
Byron Island *see* Nikunau
67 B24 **Byron Sound** *sound* NW Falkland Islands
126 J5 **Byrranga, Gora** ▲ N Russian Federation
95 J14 **Byske** Västerbotten, N Sweden
113 K18 **Bystrá** ▲ N Slovakia
113 F18 **Bystřice nad Pernštejnem** *Ger.* Bistritz ober Pernstein. Jižní Morava, SE Czech Republic
Bystrovka *see* Kemin
113 G16 **Bystrzyca Kłodzka** *Ger.* Habelschwerdt. Wałbrzych, SW Poland
113 I18 **Bytča** Stredné Slovensko, NW Slovakia
121 L15 **Bytcha** *Rus.* Bytcha. Minskaya Voblasts', NE Belorussia
Byteń/Byten' *see* Bytsyen'
113 J16 **Bytom** *Ger.* Beuthen. Katowice, S Poland
112 H7 **Bytów** *Ger.* Bütow. Słupsk, NW Poland
121 H18 **Bytsyen'** *Pol.* Byteń, *Rus.* Byten'. Brestskaya Voblasts', SW Belorussia
83 E19 **Byumba** *var.* Biumba. N Rwanda
152 F13 **Byuzmeyin** *Turkm.* Büzmeyin; *prev.* Bezmein. Akhalskiy Velayat, C Turkmenistan
121 O20 **Byval'ki** Homyel'skaya Voblasts', SE Belorussia
97 O20 **Byxelkrok** Kalmar, S Sweden
Byzantium *see* İstanbul
Bzīmah *see* Buzaymah

C

64 O6 **Caacupé** Cordillera, S Paraguay
64 P6 **Caaguazú** *off.* Departamento de Caaguazú. ◐ *department* C Paraguay
84 C13 **Caála** *var.* Kaala, Robert Williams, *Port.* Vila Robert Williams. Huambo, C Angola
64 P7 **Caazapá** Caazapá, S Paraguay
64 P7 **Caazapá** *off.* Departamento de Caazapá. ◐ *department* SE Paraguay
83 P15 **Cabaad, Raas** *headland* C Somalia
179 R14 **Cabadbaran** Mindanao, S Philippines
57 N10 **Cabadisocaña** Amazonas, S Venezuela
46 F5 **Cabaiguán** Sancti Spíritus, C Cuba
Caballeria, Cabo *see* Cavalleria, Cap de
39 Q14 **Caballo Reservoir** ⊠ New Mexico, SW USA
42 L6 **Caballos Mesteños, Llano de los** *plain* N Mexico
106 L2 **Cabañaquinta** Asturias, N Spain
44 B9 **Cabañas** ◐ *department* E El Salvador
179 P10 **Cabanatuan** *off.* Cabanatuan City. Luzon, N Philippines
13 T8 **Cabano** Québec, SE Canada
106 L11 **Cabeza del Buey** Extremadura, W Spain
47 V5 **Cabezas de San Juan** *headland* E Puerto Rico
107 N2 **Cabezón de la Sal** Cantabria, N Spain
Cabhán *see* Cavan
63 B23 **Cabildo** Buenos Aires, E Argentina
Cabillonum *see* Chalon-sur-Saône
56 H5 **Cabimas** Zulia, NW Venezuela
84 A9 **Cabinda** *var.* Kabinda. Cabinda, NW Angola
84 A9 **Cabinda** *var.* Kabinda. ◐ *province* NW Angola
35 N7 **Cabinet Mountains** ▲ Idaho/Montana, NW USA
84 B11 **Cabiri** Bengo, NW Angola
65 J20 **Cabo Blanco** Santa Cruz, SE Argentina
84 P13 **Cabo Delgado** *off.* Província de Capo Delgado. ◐ *province* NE Mozambique
12 L9 **Cabonga, Réservoir** ⊠ Québec, SE Canada
29 V7 **Cabool** Missouri, C USA
191 V2 **Caboolture** Queensland, E Australia
Cabora Bassa, Lake *see* Cahora Bassa, Albufeira de
42 F3 **Caborca** Sonora, NW Mexico
Cabo San Lucas *see* San Lucas
29 V11 **Cabot** Arkansas, C USA
12 F12 **Cabot Head** *headland* Ontario, S Canada
16 Ss10 **Cabot Strait** *strait* E Canada
xxxix Q4 **Cabourne** Lincolnshire, E England, UK
Cabo Verde, Ilhas do *see* Cape Verde
106 M14 **Cabra** Andalucía, S Spain
xlii M13 **Cabrach** Moray, N Scotland, UK
109 B19 **Cabras** Sardegna, Italy, C Mediterranean Sea
196 A15 **Cabras Island** *island* W Guam
47 O8 **Cabrera** N Dominican Republic
107 X10 **Cabrera** *anc.* Capraria. *island* Islas Baleares, Spain, W Mediterranean Sea
106 J4 **Cabrera** ≈ NW Spain
107 Q15 **Cabrera, Sierra** ▲ S Spain
9 S16 **Cabri** Saskatchewan, S Canada
107 R10 **Cabriel** ≈ E Spain
56 M7 **Cabruta** Guárico, C Venezuela
179 Oo8 **Cabugao** Luzon, N Philippines
56 G10 **Cabuyaro** Meta, C Colombia
62 I13 **Caçador** Santa Catarina, S Brazil
44 G8 **Cacaguatique, Cordillera** *var.* Cordillera. ▲ NE El Salvador
114 L13 **Čačak** Serbia, C Yugoslavia
57 Y10 **Cacao** NE French Guiana
63 H16 **Caçapava do Sul** Rio Grande do Sul, S Brazil
23 U3 **Cacapon River** ≈ West Virginia, NE USA
109 J23 **Caccamo** Sicilia, Italy, C Mediterranean Sea
109 A17 **Caccia, Capo** *headland* Sardegna, Italy, C Mediterranean Sea
61 G18 **Cáceres** Mato Grosso, W Brazil
106 J10 **Cáceres** *Ar.* Qazris. Extremadura, W Spain
106 J9 **Cáceres** ◐ *province* Extremadura, W Spain
Cachacrou *see* Scotts Head Village
63 C21 **Cacharí** Buenos Aires, E Argentina
28 L12 **Cache** Oklahoma, C USA
8 M16 **Cache Creek** British Columbia, SW Canada
37 N6 **Cache Creek** ≈ California, W USA
39 S3 **Cache La Poudre River** ≈ Colorado, C USA
Cacheo *see* Cacheu
29 W11 **Cache River** ≈ Arkansas, C USA
32 L17 **Cache River** ≈ Illinois, N USA
78 G12 **Cacheu** *var.* Cacheo. W Guinea-Bissau
61 I15 **Cachimbo** Pará, NE Brazil
61 H15 **Cachimbo, Serra do** ▲ C Brazil
84 D13 **Cachingues** Bié, C Angola
56 G7 **Cáchira** Norte de Santander, N Colombia
63 H16 **Cachoeira do Sul** Rio Grande do Sul, S Brazil
61 O20 **Cachoeiro de Itapemirim** Espírito Santo, SE Brazil
84 E12 **Cacolo** Lunda Sul, NE Angola
85 C14 **Caconda** Huíla, C Angola
84 A9 **Cacongo** Cabinda, NW Angola
37 U9 **Cactus Peak** ▲ Nevada, W USA
84 A11 **Cacuaco** Luanda, NW Angola
85 B14 **Cacula** Huíla, SW Angola
69 R12 **Caculuvar** ≈ SW Angola
61 O19 **Caçumba, Ilha** *island* SE Brazil
57 N10 **Cacuri** Amazonas, S Venezuela
83 N17 **Cadale** Shabeellaha Dhexe, E Somalia
107 X4 **Cadaqués** Cataluña, NE Spain
113 J18 **Čadca** *Hung.* Csaca. Stredné Slovensko, N Slovakia
29 P13 **Caddo** Oklahoma, C USA
27 R6 **Caddo** Texas, SW USA
27 X6 **Caddo Lake** ⊠ Louisiana/Texas, SW USA
29 S12 **Caddo Mountains** ▲ Arkansas, C USA
43 O8 **Cadereyta** Nuevo León, NE Mexico
xxxv H8 **Cader Idris** ▲ NW Wales, United Kingdom
190 F3 **Cadibarrawirracanna, Lake** *salt lake* South Australia
12 I7 **Cadillac** Québec, SE Canada
9 T17 **Cadillac** Saskatchewan, S Canada
104 K13 **Cadillac** Gironde, SW France
33 P7 **Cadillac** Michigan, N USA
xl F15 **Cadishead** Salford, NW England, UK
107 V4 **Cadí, Torre de** ▲ NE Spain
179 Q13 **Cadiz** *off.* Cadiz City. Negros, C Philippines
22 H7 **Cadiz** Kentucky, S USA
33 U13 **Cadiz** Ohio, N USA
106 J15 **Cádiz** *anc.* Gades, Gadier, Gadir, Gadire. Andalucía, SW Spain
106 K15 **Cádiz** ◐ *province* Andalucía, SW Spain
106 I15 **Cadiz, Bahía de** *bay* SW Spain
Cadiz City *see* Cadiz
106 H15 **Cádiz, Golfo de** *Eng.* Gulf of Cadiz. *gulf* Portugal/Spain
Cadiz, Gulf of *see* Cádiz, Golfo de
37 X14 **Cadiz Lake** ◎ California, W USA
xxxvii O13 **Cadnam** Hampshire, S England, UK
190 E2 **Cadney Homestead** South Australia
Cadurcum *see* Cahors
85 F17 **Caecae** Ngamiland, NW Botswana
104 K4 **Caen** Calvados, N France
Caene/Caenepolis *see* Qena
Caerdydd *see* Cardiff
Caer Glou *see* Gloucester
xxxv K5 **Caergwrle** Flintshire, NE Wales, UK
Caer Gybi *see* Holyhead
xxxv K14 **Caerleon** Newport, SE Wales, UK
Caerleon *see* Chester
Caer Luel *see* Carlisle
xxxv F5 **Caernarfon** *var.* Caernarvon, Carnarvon. Gwynedd, NW Wales, UK
xxxv D5 **Caernarfon Bay** *bay* NW Wales, UK
99 I19 **Caernarvon** *cultural region* NW Wales, UK
Caernarvon *see* Caernarfon
xxxv J15 **Caerphilly** Caerphilly, S Wales, UK
xxxv J14 **Caerphilly** ◐ *unitary authority* S Wales, UK
xxxv I9 **Caersws** Powys, C Wales, UK
xxxv L14 **Caerwent** Monmouthshire, SE Wales, UK
xxxv J4 **Caerwys** Flintshire, N Wales, UK
Caesaraugusta *see* Zaragoza
Caesarea Mazaca *see* Kayseri
Caesarobriga *see* Talavera de la Reina
Caesarodunum *see* Tours
Caesaromagus *see* Beauvais
Caesena *see* Cesena
61 N17 **Caetité** Bahia, E Brazil
64 J6 **Cafayate** Salta, N Argentina
179 Pp9 **Cagayan** ≈ Luzon, N Philippines
179 R15 **Cagayan de Oro** *off.* Cagayan de Oro City. Mindanao, S Philippines
179 Oo17 **Cagayan de Tawi Tawi** *island* S Philippines
179 Pp14 **Cagayan Islands** *island group* C Philippines
33 O14 **Cagles Mill Lake** ⊠ Indiana, N USA
108 I12 **Cagli** Marche, C Italy
109 C20 **Cagliari** *anc.* Caralis. Sardegna, Italy, C Mediterranean Sea
109 C20 **Cagliari, Golfo di** *gulf* Sardegna, Italy, C Mediterranean Sea
105 U15 **Cagnes-sur-Mer** Alpes-Maritimes, SE France
56 L5 **Cagua** Aragua, N Venezuela
179 Pp8 **Cagua, Mount** ▲ Luzon, N Philippines
56 F13 **Caguán, Río** ≈ SW Colombia
47 U6 **Caguas** E Puerto Rico
25 P5 **Cahaba River** ≈ Alabama, S USA
44 E5 **Cahabón, Río** ≈ C Guatemala
85 B15 **Cahama** Cunene, SW Angola
xliv C14 **Caha Mountains** *Ir.* An Cheacha. ▲ SW Ireland
xliv H12 **Caher** *Ir.* An Cathair. Tipperary, S Ireland
xliv B13 **Cahersiveen** *Ir.* Cathair Saidhbhín. Kerry, SW Ireland
xliv B14 **Caherdaniel** Kerry, SW Ireland
32 K15 **Cahokia** Illinois, N USA
85 L15 **Cahora Bassa, Albufeira de** *var.* Lake Cabora Bassa. ⊠ NW Mozambique
xliv L12 **Cahore Point** *Ir.* Rinn Chathóir. *headland* SE Ireland
104 M14 **Cahors** *anc.* Cadurcum. Lot, S France
58 D9 **Cahuapanas, Río** ≈ N Peru
118 M12 **Cahul** *Rus.* Kagul. S Moldavia
Cahul, Lacul *see* Kahul, Ozero
85 N16 **Caia** Sofala, C Mozambique
61 J19 **Caiapó, Serra do** ▲ C Brazil
46 F5 **Caibarién** Villa Clara, C Cuba
57 O5 **Caicara** Monagas, NE Venezuela
61 P14 **Caicó** Rio Grande do Norte, E Brazil
46 M6 **Caicos Islands** *island group* W Turks and Caicos Islands
46 L5 **Caicos Passage** *strait* Bahamas/Turks and Caicos Islands
167 O9 **Caidian** *prev.* Hanyang. Hubei, C China
Caiffa *see* Ḩefa
188 M12 **Caiguna** Western Australia
Caillí, Ceann *see* Hag's Head
42 J11 **Caimanero, Laguna del** *var.* Laguna del Camaronero. *lagoon* E Pacific Ocean
119 N10 **Căinari** *Rus.* Kaynary. C Moldavia
59 L19 **Caine, Río** ≈ C Bolivia
Caiphas *see* Ḩefa
205 N4 **Caird Coast** *physical region* Antarctica
xliii F19 **Cairnbaan** Argyll and Bute, W Scotland, UK
xliii H18 **Cairndow** Argyll and Bute, W Scotland, UK
xliii L14 **Cairn Gorm** ▲ C Scotland, UK
xliii L14 **Cairngorm Mountains** ▲ C Scotland, UK
xlii N12 **Cairnie** Aberdeenshire, NE Scotland, UK
41 P12 **Cairn Mountain** ▲ Alaska, USA
xliii H24 **Cairnryan** Dumfries and Galloway, SW Scotland, UK
189 W4 **Cairns** Queensland, NE Australia
xliii J23 **Cairnsmore of Carsphairn** ▲ SW Scotland, UK
xliii K22 **Cairn Table** ▲ C Scotland, UK
xliii L15 **Cairnwell, The** ▲ C Scotland, UK
124 Qq16 **Cairo** *Ar.* Al Qāhirah, *var.* El Qâhira. ● (Egypt) N Egypt
25 T8 **Cairo** Georgia, SE USA
32 L17 **Cairo** Illinois, N USA
77 V8 **Cairo** ✕ C Egypt
Caiseal *see* Cashel
Caisleán an Bharraigh *see* Castlebar
Caisleán na Finne *see* Castlefinn
xxxix Z9 **Caister-on-Sea** Norfolk, E England, UK
xxxix Q4 **Caistor** Lincolnshire, E England, UK
98 J6 **Caithness** *cultural region* N Scotland, UK
85 D15 **Caiundo** Cuando Cubango, S Angola
58 C11 **Cajamarca** *prev.* Caxamarca. Cajamarca, NW Peru
58 B11 **Cajamarca** *off.* Departamento de Cajamarca. ◐ *department* N Peru
105 N14 **Cajarc** Lot, S France
179 Q12 **Cajidiocan** Sibuyan Island, C Philippines
44 G6 **Cajón, Represa El** ⊠ NW Honduras
60 N12 **Caju, Ilha do** *island* NE Brazil
Cakaubalavu Reef *see* Kavukavu Reef
165 R10 **Caka Yanhu** ◎ C China
114 E7 **Čakovec** *Ger.* Csakathurn, *Hung.* Csáktornya; *prev. Ger.* Tschakathurn. Medimurje, N Croatia
79 V17 **Calabar** Cross River, S Nigeria
12 K13 **Calabogie** Ontario, SE Canada
56 L6 **Calabozo** Guárico, C Venezuela
109 N20 **Calabria** *anc.* Bruttium. ◐ *region* SW Italy
106 M16 **Calaburra, Punta de** *headland* S Spain
118 G14 **Calafat** Dolj, SW Romania
Calafate *see* El Calafate
107 Q4 **Calahorra** La Rioja, N Spain
105 N1 **Calais** Pas-de-Calais, N France
21 T5 **Calais** Maine, NE USA
Calais, Pas de *see* Dover, Strait of
Calalen *see* Kallalen
64 H4 **Calama** Antofagasta, N Chile
Calamianes *see* Calamian Group
179 P13 **Calamian Group** *var.* Calamianes. *island group* W Philippines
107 R7 **Calamocha** Aragón, NE Spain
31 N14 **Calamus River** ≈ Nebraska, C USA
118 G12 **Călan** *Ger.* Kalan, *Hung.* Pusztakalán. Hunedoara, SW Romania
107 S7 **Calanda** Aragón, NE Spain
173 F4 **Calang** Sumatera, W Indonesia
179 P11 **Calapan** Mindoro, N Philippines
Călăras *see* Călăraşi
118 M9 **Călăraşi** *var.* Călăras, *Rus.* Kalarash. C Moldavia
118 L14 **Călăraşi** Călăraşi, SE Romania
118 K14 **Călăraşi** ◐ *county* SE Romania
56 E10 **Calarca** Quindío, W Colombia
107 Q12 **Calasparra** Murcia, SE Spain
109 I23 **Calatafimi** Sicilia, Italy, C Mediterranean Sea
107 Q6 **Calatayud** Aragón, NE Spain
179 Pp11 **Calauag** Luzon, N Philippines
37 P8 **Calaveras River** ≈ California, W USA
179 Oo11 **Calavite, Cape** *headland* Mindoro, N Philippines
179 Qq12 **Calbayog** *off.* Calbayog City. Samar, C Philippines
179 R12 **Calbiga** Samar, C Philippines
24 G9 **Calcasieu Lake** ◎ Louisiana, S USA
24 H8 **Calcasieu River** ≈ Louisiana, S USA
58 B6 **Calceta** Manabí, W Ecuador
63 B16 **Calchaquí** Santa Fe, C Argentina
64 J6 **Calchaquí, Río** ≈ NW Argentina
60 J10 **Calçoene** Amapá, NE Brazil
159 S16 **Calcutta** West Bengal, NE India
159 S16 **Calcutta** ✕ West Bengal, N India
56 E9 **Caldas** *off.* Departamento de Caldas. ◐ *province* W Colombia
106 F10 **Caldas da Rainha** Leiria, W Portugal
106 G3 **Caldas de Reis** *var.* Caldas de Reyes. Galicia, NW Spain
Caldas de Reyes *see* Caldas de Reis
xl M8 **Caldbeck** Cumbria, NW England, UK
60 F13 **Caldeirão** Amazonas, NW Brazil
xli R15 **Calder** ≈ N England, UK
64 G7 **Caldera** Atacama, N Chile
44 L14 **Caldera** Puntarenas, W Costa Rica
xl K10 **Calder Bridge** Cumbria, NW England, UK
xliii K20 **Caldercruix** North Lanarkshire, C Scotland, UK
xli P15 **Calderdale** ◐ *unitary authority* N England, UK
107 N10 **Calderina** ▲ C Spain
xlii K6 **Calder, Loch** ◎ N Scotland, UK
xliii J21 **Caldermill** South Lanarkshire, C Scotland, UK
xxxv D14 **Caldey Island** *island* SW Wales, UK
xxxv L14 **Caldicot** Monmouthshire, SE Wales, UK
143 T13 **Çaldıran** Van, E Turkey
xli R9 **Caldwell** North Yorkshire, N England, UK
34 M14 **Caldwell** Idaho, NW USA
29 N8 **Caldwell** Kansas, C USA
12 G15 **Caledon** Ontario, S Canada
85 I23 **Caledon** *var.* Mohokare. ≈ Lesotho/South Africa
44 G1 **Caledonia** Corozal, N Belize
12 G16 **Caledonia** Ontario, S Canada
31 X11 **Caledonia** Minnesota, N USA
107 X5 **Calella** *var.* Calella de la Costa. Cataluña, NE Spain
Calella de la Costa *see* Calella
25 P4 **Calera** Alabama, S USA
65 I19 **Caleta Olivia** Santa Cruz, SE Argentina
37 X17 **Calexico** California, W USA
xl F12 **Calf of Man** *island* SW Isle of Man
xlii N3 **Calfsound** Orkney Islands, N Scotland, UK
xli O10 **Calf, The** ▲ NW England, UK
xliii D16 **Calgary** Argyll and Bute, W Scotland, UK
9 Q16 **Calgary** Alberta, SW Canada
9 Q16 **Calgary** ✕ Alberta, SW Canada
39 U5 **Calhan** Colorado, C USA
66 O5 **Calheta** Madeira, Portugal, NE Atlantic Ocean
25 R2 **Calhoun** Georgia, SE USA
22 I6 **Calhoun** Kentucky, S USA
24 M3 **Calhoun City** Mississippi, S USA
23 P12 **Calhoun Falls** South Carolina, SE USA
56 D11 **Cali** Valle del Cauca, W Colombia
29 V9 **Calico Rock** Arkansas, C USA
161 F21 **Calicut** *var.* Kozhikode. Kerala, SW India
37 Y9 **Caliente** Nevada, W USA
29 U5 **California** Missouri, C USA
20 B15 **California** Pennsylvania, NE USA
37 Q12 **California** *off.* State of California; *also known as* El Dorado, The Golden State. ◐ *state* W USA
37 P11 **California Aqueduct** *aqueduct* California, W USA
37 T13 **California City** California, W USA
42 F6 **California, Golfo de** *Eng.* Gulf of California; *prev.* Sea of Cortez. *gulf* W Mexico
California, Gulf of *see* California, Golfo de
143 Y13 **Cälilabad** *Rus.* Dzhalilabad; *prev.* Astrakhan-Bazar. S Azerbaijan
118 I12 **Călimăneşti** Vâlcea, SW Romania
118 J9 **Călimani, Munţii** ▲ N Romania
Calinisc *see* Cupcina
37 X17 **Calipatria** California, W USA
Calisia *see* Kalisz
36 M7 **Calistoga** California, W USA
85 G25 **Calitzdorp** Western Cape, SW South Africa
43 W12 **Calkiní** Campeche, E Mexico
190 K4 **Callabonna Creek** *var.* Tilcha Creek. *seasonal river* New South Wales/South Australia

236
◆ Country ● Country Capital ◇ Dependent Territory ○ Dependent Territory Capital ◐ Administrative Region ✕ International Airport ▲ Mountain ▲ Mountain Range Volcano ≈ River ◎ Lake ⊠ Reservoir

Celtic Shelf – Châtillon-sur-Seine

66 N7 Celtic Shelf undersea feature E Atlantic Ocean
116 L13 Çeltik Gölu ◎ NW Turkey
xxxv E3 Cemaes Isle of Anglesey, NW Wales, UK
xxxv D11 Cemaes Head headland SW Wales, UK
115 M14 Čemerno ▲ C Yugoslavia
xxxv H8 Cemmaes Powys, C Wales, UK
175 Oo16 Cempi, Teluk bay Nusa Tenggara, S Indonesia
107 Q12 Cenajo, Embalse del ⊠ S Spain
107 P4 Cenicero La Rioja, N Spain
108 E9 Ceno ≈ NW Italy
104 K13 Cenon Gironde, SW France
12 K13 Centennial Lake ◎ Ontario, SE Canada
Centennial State see Colorado
39 S7 Center Colorado, C USA
31 Q13 Center Nebraska, C USA
30 M5 Center North Dakota, N USA
27 X8 Center Texas, SW USA
31 W8 Center City Minnesota, N USA
38 L5 Centerfield Utah, W USA
22 K9 Center Hill Lake ⊠ Tennessee, S USA
31 X13 Center Point Iowa, C USA
27 R11 Center Point Texas, SW USA
31 W16 Centerville Iowa, C USA
29 W7 Centerville Missouri, C USA
31 R12 Centerville South Dakota, N USA
22 I9 Centerville Tennessee, S USA
27 V9 Centerville Texas, SW USA
42 M5 Centinela, Picacho del ▲ NE Mexico
108 G9 Cento Emilia-Romagna, N Italy
Centrafricaine, République see Central African Republic
41 S8 Central Alaska, USA
39 P15 Central New Mexico, SW USA
85 H18 Central ◆ district E Botswana
144 E10 Central ◆ district C Israel
83 I19 Central ◆ province C Kenya
84 M13 Central ◆ region C Malawi
159 P12 Central ◆ zone C Nepal
194 J15 Central ◆ province S PNG
65 I21 Central ◆ department C Paraguay
195 W15 Central off. Central Province. ◆ province S Solomon Islands
85 J14 Central ◆ province C Zambia
119 P11 Central ✕ (Odesa) Odes'ka Oblast', SW Ukraine
Central see Centre
81 H14 Central African Republic var. République Centrafricaine, abbrev. CAR; prev. Ubangi-Shari, Oubangui-Chari, Territoire de l'Oubangui-Chari. ◆ republic C Africa
198 G6 Central Basin Trough undersea feature W Pacific Ocean
Central Borneo see Kalimantan Tengah
155 P12 Central Brāhui Range ▲ W Pakistan
Central Celebes see Sulawesi Tengah
31 Y13 Central City Iowa, C USA
22 I6 Central City Kentucky, S USA
31 P15 Central City Nebraska, C USA
50 D6 Central, Cordillera ▲ W Bolivia
56 D11 Central, Cordillera ▲ W Colombia
44 M13 Central, Cordillera ▲ C Costa Rica
47 N9 Central, Cordillera ▲ C Dominican Republic
45 R16 Central, Cordillera ▲ C Panama
179 P8 Central, Cordillera ▲ Luzon, N Philippines
47 S6 Central, Cordillera ▲ Puerto Rico
44 H7 Central District var. Tegucigalpa. ◆ district C Honduras
32 L15 Centralia Illinois, N USA
29 U4 Centralia Missouri, C USA
34 G9 Centralia Washington, NW USA
Central Indian Ridge see Mid-Indian Ridge
Central Java see Jawa Tengah
Central Kalimantan see Kalimantan Tengah
154 L14 Central Makrān Range ▲ W Pakistan
199 J8 Central Pacific Basin undersea feature C Pacific Ocean
61 M19 Central, Planalto var. Brazilian Highlands. ▲ E Brazil
34 F15 Central Point Oregon, NW USA
161 K25 Central Province ◆ province C Sri Lanka
Central Provinces and Berar see Madhya Pradesh
194 G11 Central Range ▲ NW PNG
Central Russian Upland see Srednerusskaya Vozvyshennost'
Central Siberian Plateau/Central Siberian Uplands see Srednesibirskoye Ploskogor'ye
106 K8 Central, Sistema ▲ C Spain
Central Sulawesi see Sulawesi Tengah
37 N3 Central Valley California, W USA
37 P8 Central Valley valley California, W USA
25 Q3 Centre Alabama, S USA
81 E15 Centre Eng. Central. ◆ province C Cameroon
104 M8 Centre ◆ region N France
181 Y16 Centre de Flacq E Mauritius
57 Y9 Centre Spatial Guyanais space station N French Guiana
25 O5 Centreville Alabama, S USA
23 X3 Centreville Maryland, NE USA
24 J7 Centreville Mississippi, S USA
Centum Cellae see Civitavecchia
166 M14 Cenxi Guangxi Zhuangzu Zizhiqu, S China
Ceos see Kéa
Cephaloedium see Cefalù
114 I9 Čepin Hung. Csepén. Osijek-Baranja, E Croatia
174 Ll15 Cepu prev. Tjepoe, Tjepu. Jawa, C Indonesia
Ceram see Seram, Pulau
175 T10 Ceram Sea Ind. Laut Seram. sea E Indonesia
198 G9 Ceram Trough undersea feature W Pacific Ocean
Cerasus see Giresun
38 I10 Cerbat Mountains ▲ Arizona, SW USA
105 P17 Cerbère, Cap headland S France
106 F13 Cercal do Alentejo Setúbal, S Portugal
113 A18 Čerchov Ger. Czerkow. ▲ W Czech Republic
105 O13 Cère ≈ C France
xxxv F10 Ceredigion ◆ unitary authority W Wales, UK
xliii M18 Ceres Fife, E Scotland, UK
63 A16 Ceres Santa Fe, C Argentina
61 K18 Ceres Goiás, C Brazil
Ceresio see Lugano, Lago di
105 O17 Céret Pyrénées-Orientales, S France
56 E6 Cereté Córdoba, NW Colombia
180 I17 Cerf, Île au island Inner Islands, NE Seychelles
101 G22 Cerfontaine Namur, S Belgium
Cergy-Pontoise see Pontoise
109 N16 Cerignola Puglia, SE Italy
Cerigo see Kýthira
105 O9 Cérilly Allier, C France
142 I11 Çerkeş Çankırı, N Turkey
142 D10 Çerkezköy Tekirdağ, NW Turkey
111 T12 Cerknica Ger. Zirknitz. SW Slovenia
111 S11 Cerkno W Slovenia
118 F10 Cermei Hung. Csermő. Arad, W Romania
143 O15 Çermik Dıyarbakır, SE Turkey
114 I10 Cerna Vukovar-Srijem, E Croatia
Cernăuţi see Chernivtsi
118 M14 Cernavodă Constanţa, SW Romania
105 U7 Cernay Haut-Rhin, NE France
xxxvi L13 Cerne Abbas Dorset, S England, UK
Černice see Schwarzach
43 O8 Cerralvo Nuevo León, NE Mexico
42 G9 Cerralvo, Isla island W Mexico
109 L16 Cerreto Sannita Campania, S Italy
xxxv I6 Cerrigydrudion Conwy, N Wales, UK
115 L20 Cërrik var. Cerriku. Elbasan, C Albania
Cerriku see Cërrik
43 O11 Cerritos San Luis Potosí, C Mexico
62 K11 Cerro Azul Paraná, S Brazil
63 F18 Cerro Chato Treinta y Tres, E Uruguay
63 F19 Cerro Colorado Florida, S Uruguay
58 E13 Cerro de Pasco Pasco, C Peru
63 G18 Cerro Largo ◆ department NE Uruguay
63 G14 Cêrro Largo Rio Grande do Sul, S Brazil
44 E7 Cerrón Grande, Embalse ⊠ N El Salvador
65 I14 Cerros Colorados, Embalse ⊠ W Argentina
107 V5 Cervera Cataluña, NE Spain
106 M3 Cervera del Pisuerga Castilla-León, N Spain
107 Q5 Cervera del Río Alhama La Rioja, N Spain
109 H15 Cerveteri Lazio, C Italy
108 H10 Cervia Emilia-Romagna, N Italy
108 J7 Cervignano del Friuli Friuli-Venezia Giulia, NE Italy
109 L17 Cervinara Campania, S Italy
Cervinia see Breuil
108 B6 Cervino, Monte var. Matterhorn. ▲ Italy/Switzerland see also Matterhorn
104 F2 Cervione Corse, France, C Mediterranean Sea
106 I1 Cervo Galicia, NW Spain
56 F5 Cesar off. Departamento del Cesar. ◆ province N Colombia
108 H10 Cesena anc. Caesena. Emilia-Romagna, N Italy
108 I10 Cesenatico Emilia-Romagna, N Italy
120 H8 Cēsis Ger. Wenden. Cēsis, C Latvia
113 D15 Česká Lípa Ger. Böhmisch-Leipa. Severní Čechy, N Czech Republic
Česká Republika see Czech Republic
113 F17 Česká Třebová Ger. Böhmisch-Trübau. Východní Čechy, E Czech Republic
113 D19 České Budějovice Ger. Budweis. Jižní Čechy, SW Czech Republic
113 D19 České Velenice Jižní Čechy, S Czech Republic
113 E18 Českomoravská Vrchovina var. Českomoravská Vysočina, Eng. Bohemian-Moravian Highlands, Ger. Böhmisch-Mährische Höhe. ▲ S Czech Republic
Českomoravská Vysočina see Českomoravská Vrchovina
113 C19 Český Krumlov var. Böhmisch-Krumau, Ger. Krummau. Jižní Čechy, SW Czech Republic
Ceský Les see Bohemian Forest
114 F8 Česma ≈ N Croatia
142 A14 Çeşme İzmir, W Turkey
Cess see Cestos
191 T8 Cessnock New South Wales, SE Australia
78 K17 Cestos var. Cess. ≈ S Liberia
120 I9 Cesvaine Madona, E Latvia
118 G14 Cetate Dolj, SW Romania
Cetatea Albă see Bilhorod-Dnistrovs'kyy
115 J17 Cetinje It. Cettigne. Montenegro, SW Yugoslavia
109 N20 Cetraro Calabria, S Italy
Cette see Sète
196 A17 Cetti Bay bay SW Guam
Cettigne see Cetinje
106 L17 Ceuta var. Sebta. Ceuta, Spain, N Africa
90 C16 Ceuta enclave Spain, N Africa
108 B9 Ceva Piemonte, NE Italy
105 P14 Cévennes ▲ S France
110 G10 Cevio Ticino, S Switzerland
142 K16 Ceyhan Adana, S Turkey
142 K17 Ceyhan Nehri ≈ S Turkey
143 P17 Ceylanpınar Şanlıurfa, SE Turkey
Ceylon see Sri Lanka
181 R6 Ceylon Plain undersea feature N Indian Ocean
Ceyre to the Caribs see Marie-Galante
105 Q14 Cèze ≈ S France
152 H15 Chaacha Turkm. Chäche. Akhalskiy Velayat, S Turkmenistan
131 P6 Chaadayevka Penzenskaya Oblast', W Russian Federation
178 H12 Cha-Am Phetchaburi, SW Thailand
149 W15 Chābahār var. Chāh Bahār, Chahbar. Sīstān va Balūchestān, SE Iran
63 B19 Chabas Santa Fe, C Argentina
105 T10 Chablais physical region E France
63 B20 Chacabuco Buenos Aires, E Argentina
44 K8 Chachagón, Cerro ▲ N Nicaragua
58 C10 Chachapoyas Amazonas, NW Peru
Chäche see Chaacha
121 O18 Chachersk Rus. Chechersk. Homyel'skaya Voblasts', SE Belorussia
121 N16 Chachevichy Rus. Chechevichi. Mahilyowskaya Voblasts', E Belorussia
63 B14 Chaco off. Provincia de Chaco. ◆ province NE Argentina
Chaco see Gran Chaco
64 M6 Chaco Austral physical region N Argentina
64 M3 Chaco Boreal physical region N Paraguay
64 M6 Chaco Central physical region N Argentina
41 Y15 Chacon, Cape headland Prince of Wales Island, Alaska, USA
80 H9 Chad off. Republic of Chad, Fr. Tchad. ◆ republic C Africa
23 U12 Chadbourn North Carolina, SE USA
xl H14 Chadderton Oldham, NW England, UK
xxxviii B16 Chaddesley Corbett Worcestershire, W England, UK
xxxvii P9 Chaddleworth Newbury, S England, UK
85 L14 Chadiza Eastern, E Zambia
69 Q7 Chad, Lake Fr. Lac Tchad. ◎ C Africa
126 J13 Chadobets ≈ C Russian Federation
30 J12 Chadron Nebraska, C USA
Chadyr-Lunga see Ciadîr-Lunga
169 W14 Chaeryŏng SW North Korea
107 P17 Chafarinas, Islas island group S Spain
29 Y7 Chaffee Missouri, C USA
154 L12 Chāgai Hills var. Chāh Gay. ▲ Afghanistan/Pakistan
126 M12 Chagda Respublika Sakha (Yakutiya), NE Russian Federation
xxxvi G14 Chagford Devon, SW England, UK
Chaghasarāy see Asadābād
155 N5 Chaghcharān var. Chakhcharan, Cheghcheran, Qala Āhangarān. Ghowr, C Afghanistan
105 R9 Chagny Saône-et-Loire, C France
181 Q7 Chagos Archipelago var. Oil Islands. island group British Indian Ocean Territory
133 O15 Chagos Bank undersea feature C Indian Ocean
133 O14 Chagos-Laccadive Plateau undersea feature N Indian Ocean
181 Q7 Chagos Trench undersea feature N Indian Ocean
45 T14 Chagres, Río ≈ C Panama
47 U14 Chaguanas Trinidad, Trinidad and Tobago
56 M6 Chaguaramas Guárico, N Venezuela
152 C9 Chagyl Balkanskiy Velayat, NW Turkmenistan
Chahārmahāl and Bakhtiyārī see Chahār Maḩall va Bakhtīārī
148 M9 Chahār Maḩall va Bakhtīārī off. Ostān-e Chahār Maḩall va Bakhtīārī, var. Chahārmahāl and Bakhtiyārī. ◆ province SW Iran
Chāh Bahār/Chahbar see Chābahār
149 V13 Chāh Derāz Sīstān va Balūchestān, SE Iran
Chāh Gay see Chāgai Hills
178 Hh10 Chai Badan Lop Buri, C Thailand
159 Q16 Chāībāsa Bihār, N India
81 E19 Chaillu, Massif du ▲ C Gabon
178 Hh10 Chai Nat var. Chainat, Jainat, Jayanath. Chai Nat, C Thailand
67 M14 Chain Fracture Zone tectonic feature E Atlantic Ocean
181 N5 Chain Ridge undersea feature W Indian Ocean
Chairn, Ceann an see Carnsore Point
164 L5 Chaiwopu Xinjiang Uygur Zizhiqu, W China
178 I10 Chaiyaphum var. Jayabum. Chaiyaphum, C Thailand
64 N10 Chajarí Entre Ríos, E Argentina
44 C5 Chajul Quiché, W Guatemala
85 K16 Chakari Mashonaland West, N Zimbabwe
83 J22 Chake Chake Pemba South, E Tanzania
154 J9 Chakhānsūr Nīmrūz, SW Afghanistan
Chakhānsūr see Nīmrūz
Chakhcharan see Chaghcharān
155 V8 Chak Jhumra var. Jhumra. Punjab, E Pakistan
152 I16 Chaknakdysonga Akhalskiy Velayat, S Turkmenistan
159 P16 Chakradharpur Bihār, N India
158 J8 Chakrāta Uttar Pradesh, N India
155 U7 Chakwāl Punjab, NE Pakistan
59 F17 Chala Arequipa, SW Peru
104 K12 Chalais Charente, W France
110 D10 Chalais Valais, SW Switzerland
117 J20 Chalándri var. Halandri; prev. Khalándrion. prehistoric site Sýros, Kykládes, Greece, Aegean Sea
196 H6 Chalan Kanoa Saipan, S Northern Mariana Islands
196 C16 Chalan Pago C Guam
Chalap Dalam/Chalap Dalan see Chehel Abdālān, Kūh-e
44 F7 Chalatenango Chalatenango, N El Salvador
44 A9 Chalatenango ◆ department NW El Salvador
85 P15 Chalaua Nampula, NE Mozambique
83 I16 Chalbi Desert desert N Kenya
44 D7 Chalchuapa Santa Ana, W El Salvador
Chalcidice see Chalkidikí
Chalcis see Chalkída
xxxvii P14 Chale Isle of Wight, S England, UK
105 N6 Châlette-sur-Loing Loiret, C France
13 X8 Chaleur Bay Fr. Baie des Chaleurs. bay New Brunswick/Québec, E Canada
Chaleurs, Baie des see Chaleur Bay
xxxvii S8 Chalfont St Giles Buckinghamshire, C England, UK
59 G16 Chalhuanca Apurímac, S Peru
160 F12 Chālisgaon Mahārāshtra, C India
117 N23 Chálki island Dodekánisos, Greece, Aegean Sea
117 F16 Chalkiádes Thessalía, C Greece
117 H18 Chalkída var. Halkida; prev. Khalkís, anc. Chalcis. Evvoia, E Greece
117 G14 Chalkidikí var. Khalkidhikí; anc. Chalcidice. peninsula NE Greece
193 A24 Chalky Inlet inlet South Island, NZ
41 S7 Chalkyitsik Alaska, USA
xxxvi G11 Challacombe Devon, SW England, UK
104 I9 Challans Vendée, NW France
59 K19 Challapata Oruro, SW Bolivia
199 H7 Challenger Deep undersea feature W Pacific Ocean
200 Nn12 Challenger Fracture Zone tectonic feature SE Pacific Ocean
199 Ii13 Challenger Plateau undersea feature E Tasman Sea
35 P13 Challis Idaho, NW USA
xliii I24 Challoch Dumfries and Galloway, SW Scotland, UK
xxxvii X10 Challock Kent, SE England, UK
24 L9 Chalmette Louisiana, S USA
128 J11 Chalna Respublika Kareliya, NW Russian Federation
105 Q5 Châlons-en-Champagne prev. Châlons-sur-Marne, hist. Arcae Remorum, anc. Carolopois. Marne, NE France
Châlons-sur-Marne see Châlons-en-Champagne
105 R9 Chalon-sur-Saône anc. Cabillonum. Saône-et-Loire, C France
Chaltel, Cerro see Fitzroy, Monte
149 N4 Chālūs Māzandarān, N Iran
104 M11 Châlus Haute-Vienne, C France
103 N20 Cham Bayern, SE Germany
110 F7 Cham Zug, N Switzerland
39 R8 Chama New Mexico, SW USA
Cha Mai see Thung Song
85 E22 Chamaites Karas, S Namibia
155 O9 Chaman Baluchistān, SW Pakistan
39 R9 Chama, Rio ≈ New Mexico, SW USA
158 I6 Chamba Himāchal Pradesh, N India
83 I25 Chamba Ruvuma, S Tanzania
156 H12 Chambal ≈ C India
9 U16 Chamberlain Saskatchewan, S Canada
31 O11 Chamberlain South Dakota, N USA
21 R3 Chamberlain Lake ◎ Maine, NE USA
41 S5 Chamberlin, Mount ▲ Alaska, USA
39 O11 Chambers Arizona, SW USA
20 F16 Chambersburg Pennsylvania, NE USA
33 N5 Chambers Island island Wisconsin, N USA
105 T11 Chambéry anc. Camberia. Savoie, E France
84 L12 Chambeshi Northern, NE Zambia
84 L12 Chambeshi ≈ NE Zambia
76 M6 Chambi, Jebel var. Jabal ash Sha'nabī. ▲ W Tunisia
13 Q7 Chambord Québec, SE Canada
194 G10 Chambri Lake ◎ W PNG
145 U11 Chamcham S Iraq
145 T4 Chamchamāl N Iraq
42 J14 Chamela Jalisco, SW Mexico
44 G5 Chamelecón, Río ≈ NW Honduras
64 J9 Chamical La Rioja, C Argentina
117 L23 Chamilí island Kykládes, Greece, Aegean Sea
178 Ii13 Châmnar Kaôh Kông, SW Cambodia
158 K9 Chamoli Uttar Pradesh, N India
105 U11 Chamonix-Mont-Blanc Haute-Savoie, E France
160 L11 Chāmpa Madhya Pradesh, C India
8 H8 Champagne Yukon Territory, W Canada
105 Q5 Champagne cultural region N France
Champagne see Campania
105 Q5 Champagne-Ardenne ◆ region N France
105 S9 Champagnole Jura, E France
32 M13 Champaign Illinois, N USA
178 Jj11 Champasak Champasak, S Laos
105 U6 Champ de Feu ▲ NE France
11 O7 Champdoré, Lac ◎ Québec, NE Canada
44 B6 Champerico Retalhuleu, SW Guatemala
110 C11 Champéry Valais, SW Switzerland
20 L6 Champlain New York, NE USA
20 L9 Champlain Canal canal New York, NE USA
13 P13 Champlain, Lac ◎ Québec, SE Canada
20 L7 Champlain, Lake ◎ Canada/USA
105 S7 Champlitte Haute-Saône, E France
43 W13 Champotón Campeche, SE Mexico
106 G10 Chamusca Santarém, C Portugal
121 O20 Chamyarysy Rus. Chemerisy. Homyel'skaya Voblasts', SE Belorussia
131 P5 Chamzinka Respublika Mordoviya, W Russian Federation
Chanáil Mhór, An see Grand Canal
Chanak see Çanakkale
64 G7 Chañaral Atacama, N Chile
106 H13 Chança var. Chanza. ≈ Portugal/Spain
59 D14 Chancay Lima, W Peru
Chan-chiang/Chanchiang see Zhanjiang
41 R7 Chandalar Alaska, USA
41 R6 Chandalar River ≈ Alaska, USA
158 L10 Chandan Chauki Uttar Pradesh, N India
159 S16 Chandannagar prev. Chandernagore. West Bengal, E India
158 K10 Chandausi Uttar Pradesh, N India
24 M10 Chandeleur Islands island group Louisiana, S USA
24 M9 Chandeleur Sound sound N Gulf of Mexico
158 I8 Chandīgarh Punjab, N India
159 Q16 Chāndil Bihār, NE India
190 D2 Chandler South Australia
13 Y7 Chandler Québec, SE Canada
29 O10 Chandler Oklahoma, C USA
27 V7 Chandler Texas, SW USA
41 Q6 Chandler River ≈ Alaska, USA
58 H13 Chandles, Río ≈ E Peru
169 N9 Chandmanī Dornogovĭ, SE Mongolia
12 J13 Chandos Lake ◎ Ontario, SE Canada
159 U15 Chandpur Chittagong, C Bangladesh
160 I13 Chandrapur Mahārāshtra, C India
85 J15 Changa Southern, S Zambia
Changan see Xi'an, Shaanxi, China
Chang'an see Rong'an, Guangxi Zhuangzu Zizhiqu, China
161 G23 Changanācheri Kerala, SW India
85 M19 Changane ≈ S Mozambique
85 M16 Changara Tete, NW Mozambique
169 X11 Changbai var. Changbai Chaoxianzu Zizhixian. Jilin, NE China
Changbai Chaoxianzu Zizhixian see Changbai
169 X11 Changbai Shan ▲ NE China
169 V10 Changchun var. Ch'angch'un, Ch'ang-ch'un; prev. Hsinking. Jilin, NE China
166 M10 Changde Hunan, S China
167 S13 Changhua Jap. Shōka. C Taiwan
174 I7 Changi ✕ (Singapore) E Singapore
164 L5 Changji Xinjiang Uygur Zizhiqu, NW China
163 O13 Chang Jiang var. Yangtze Kiang, Eng. Yangtze. ≈ C China
166 L17 Changjiang prev. Shiliu. Hainan, S China
167 S8 Changjiang Kou delta E China
178 I13 Chang, Ko island S Thailand
167 Q2 Changli Hebei, E China
169 V10 Changling Jilin, NE China
167 N11 Changsha var. Ch'angsha, Ch'ang-sha. Hunan, S China
167 Q10 Changshan Zhejiang, SE China
169 V14 Changshan Qundao island group NE China
167 S8 Changshu var. Ch'ang-shu. Jiangsu, E China
169 V11 Changtu Liaoning, NE China
45 P14 Changuinola Bocas del Toro, NW Panama
165 N9 Changweiliang Qinghai, W China
166 K6 Changwu Shaanxi, C China
169 U13 Changxing Dao island N China
166 M9 Changyang Hubei, C China
169 W14 Changyŏn SW North Korea
167 N5 Changzhi Shanxi, C China
167 R8 Changzhou Jiangsu, E China
117 H24 Chaniá var. Hania, Khaniá, Eng. Canea; anc. Cydonia. Kríti, Greece, E Mediterranean Sea
64 J5 Chañi, Nevado de ▲ NW Argentina
117 H24 Chanión, Kólpos gulf Kríti, Greece, E Mediterranean Sea
Chankiri see Çankırı
32 M11 Channahon Illinois, N USA
161 H20 Channapatna Karnātaka, E India
xxxvii X15 Channel Islands Fr. Îles Normandes. island group S English Channel
37 R16 Channel Islands island group California, W USA
11 S13 Channel-Port aux Basques Newfoundland, Newfoundland and Labrador, SE Canada
Channel, The see English Channel
xxxvii Z11 Channel Tunnel tunnel France/UK
26 M2 Channing Texas, SW USA
Chantabun/Chantaburi see Chanthaburi
106 H3 Chantada Galicia, NW Spain
178 I12 Chanthaburi var. Chantabun, Chantaburi. Chantaburi, S Thailand
105 O4 Chantilly Oise, N France
15 Kk4 Chantrey Inlet inlet Northwest Territories, N Canada
145 V12 Chanūn as Sa'ūdī S Iraq
29 Q6 Chanute Kansas, C USA
125 G13 Chany, Ozero ◎ C Russian Federation
Chanza see Chança
Ch'ao-an/Chaochow see Chaozhou
167 P8 Chao Hu ◎ E China
178 Hh11 Chao Phraya, Mae Nam ≈ C Thailand
169 T8 Chaor He ≈ NE China
Chaouèn see Chefchaouen
167 P14 Chaoyang Guangdong, S China
169 T12 Chaoyang Liaoning, NE China
Chaoyang see Huinan, Jilin, China
Chaoyang see Jiayin, Heilongjiang, China
167 Q14 Chaozhou var. Chaoan, Chao'an, Ch'ao-an; prev. Chaochow. Guangdong, SE China
60 N13 Chapadinha Maranhão, E Brazil
10 K12 Chapais Québec, SE Canada
42 L13 Chapala Jalisco, SW Mexico
42 L13 Chapala, Lago de ◎ C Mexico
152 F13 Chapan, Gora ▲ C Turkmenistan
58 M18 Chapare, Río ≈ C Bolivia
56 E11 Chaparral Tolima, C Colombia
150 F9 Chapayevo Zapadnyy Kazakhstan, NW Kazakhstan
126 Kk12 Chapayevo Respublika Sakha (Yakutiya), NE Russian Federation
131 R6 Chapayevsk Samarskaya Oblast', W Russian Federation
62 H13 Chapecó Santa Catarina, S Brazil
62 I13 Chapecó, Rio ≈ S Brazil
xxxviii K5 Chapel-en-le-Frith Derbyshire, C England, UK
22 J9 Chapel Hill Tennessee, S USA
xxxix T5 Chapel St Leonards Lincolnshire, E England, UK
46 J12 Chapelton C Jamaica
xli S16 Chapeltown Sheffield, N England, UK
12 C8 Chapleau Ontario, SE Canada
12 D7 Chapleau ≈ Ontario, S Canada
9 T16 Chaplin Saskatchewan, S Canada
130 M6 Chaplygin Lipetskaya Oblast', W Russian Federation
119 S11 Chaplynka Khersons'ka Oblast', S Ukraine
15 L3 Chapman, Cape headland Northwest Territories, NE Canada
27 T15 Chapman Ranch Texas, SW USA
Chapman's see Okwa
23 P5 Chapmanville West Virginia, NE USA
30 K15 Chappell Nebraska, C USA
Chapra see Chhapra
58 D9 Chapuli, Río ≈ N Peru
78 I6 Châr well N Mauritania
126 Kk13 Chara Chitinskaya Oblast', S Russian Federation
126 Kk13 Chara ≈ C Russian Federation
56 G8 Charala Santander, C Colombia
43 N10 Charcas San Luis Potosí, C Mexico
27 T13 Charco Texas, SW USA
204 H7 Charcot Island island Antarctica
66 M8 Charcot Seamounts undersea feature E Atlantic Ocean
xxxvi K13 Chard Somerset, SW England, UK
151 P17 Chardara Yuzhnyy Kazakhstan, S Kazakhstan
151 P17 Chardarinskoye Vodokhranilishche ⊠ S Kazakhstan
33 U11 Chardon Ohio, N USA
46 K9 Chardonnières SW Haiti
xxxvi J13 Chardstock Devon, SW England, UK
152 K12 Chardzhev prev. Chardzhou, Chardzhui, Leninsk-Turkmenski, Turkm. Chärjew. Lebapskiy Velayat, E Turkmenistan
Chardzhevskaya Oblast' see Lebapskiy Velayat
Chardzhou/Chardzhui see Chardzhev
104 L11 Charente ◆ department W France
104 J11 Charente ≈ W France
104 J10 Charente-Maritime ◆ department W France
143 U12 Ch'arents'avan C Armenia
80 I12 Chari var. Shari. ≈ Central African Republic/Chad
80 G11 Chari-Baguirmi off. Préfecture du Chari-Baguirmi. ◆ prefecture SW Chad
155 Q4 Chārīkār Parwān, NE Afghanistan
xxxvii X11 Charing Kent, SE England, UK
31 V15 Chariton Iowa, C USA
29 U3 Chariton River ≈ Missouri, C USA
57 T7 Charity NW Guyana
33 R7 Charity Island island Michigan, N USA
Chärjew see Chardzhev
Chärjew Oblasty see Lebapskiy Velayat
Charkhlik/Charkhliq see Ruoqiang
xxxvii P7 Charlbury Oxfordshire, C England, UK
101 G20 Charleroi Hainaut, S Belgium
9 V12 Charles Manitoba, C Canada
13 R10 Charlesbourg Québec, SE Canada
23 Y7 Charles, Cape headland Virginia, NE USA
31 W12 Charles City Iowa, C USA
23 W6 Charles City Virginia, NE USA
105 O5 Charles de Gaulle ✕ (Paris) Seine-et-Marne, N France
10 K1 Charles Island island Northwest Territories, NE Canada
Charles Island see Santa María, Isla
18 Mm5 Charles-Lindbergh ✕ (Minneapolis/Saint Paul) Minnesota, N USA
32 K9 Charles Mound hill Illinois, N USA
193 A22 Charles Sound sound South Island, NZ
193 G15 Charleston West Coast, South Island, NZ
29 Z7 Charleston Arkansas, C USA
32 M14 Charleston Illinois, N USA
24 L3 Charleston Mississippi, S USA
29 S11 Charleston Missouri, C USA
23 T15 Charleston South Carolina, SE USA
23 Q5 Charleston state capital West Virginia, NE USA
12 L14 Charleston Lake ◎ Ontario, SE Canada
37 W11 Charleston Peak ▲ Nevada, W USA
47 W10 Charlestown Nevis, Saint Kitts and Nevis
33 P16 Charlestown Indiana, N USA
20 M9 Charlestown New Hampshire, NE USA
xlii M12 Charlestown of Aberlour Moray, N Scotland, UK
23 V3 Charles Town West Virginia, NE USA
xliv F6 Charlestown Mayo, NW Ireland
189 W9 Charleville Queensland, E Australia
105 R3 Charleville-Mézières Ardennes, N France
33 P5 Charlevoix Michigan, N USA
33 Q6 Charlevoix, Lake ◎ Michigan, N USA
41 T9 Charley River ≈ Alaska, USA
66 J6 Charlie-Gibbs Fracture Zone tectonic feature N Atlantic Ocean
105 Q10 Charlieu Loire, E France
33 Q9 Charlotte Michigan, N USA
23 R10 Charlotte North Carolina, SE USA
22 I8 Charlotte Tennessee, S USA
27 R13 Charlotte Texas, SW USA
23 R10 Charlotte ✕ North Carolina, SE USA
47 T9 Charlotte Amalie prev. Saint Thomas. ○ [Virgin Islands (US)] Saint Thomas, N Virgin Islands (US)
23 U7 Charlotte Court House Virginia, NE USA
25 W14 Charlotte Harbor inlet Florida, SE USA
Charlotte Island see Abaiang
97 J15 Charlottenberg Värmland, C Sweden
Charlottenhof see Aegviidu
23 U5 Charlottesville Virginia, NE USA
Charlotte Town see Roseau, Dominica
Charlotte Town see Gouyave, Grenada
11 Q14 Charlottetown Prince Edward Island, Prince Edward Island, SE Canada
47 Z16 Charlotteville Tobago, Trinidad and Tobago
xxxvi F8 Charlton Greenwich, SE England, UK
xxxvii N9 Charlton Wiltshire, S England, UK
190 M11 Charlton Victoria, SE Australia
10 H10 Charlton Island island Northwest Territories, C Canada
xxxvii N7 Charlton Kings Gloucestershire, C England, UK
xxxvii T11 Charlwood Surrey, SE England, UK
105 T6 Charmes Vosges, NE France
xxxvi K14 Charmouth Dorset, S England, UK
121 F19 Charnawchytsy Rus. Chernavchitsy. Brestskaya Voblasts', SW Belorussia
13 R10 Charny Québec, SE Canada
155 T5 Chārsadda North-West Frontier Province, NW Pakistan
152 M14 Charshanga prev. Charshangy, Turkm. Charshangngy. Lebapskiy Velayat, E Turkmenistan
Charshangngy/Charshangy see Charshanga
151 W10 Charsk Semipalatinsk, E Kazakhstan
189 W6 Charters Towers Queensland, NE Australia
13 R12 Chartierville Québec, SE Canada
104 M6 Chartres anc. Autricum, Civitas Carnutum. Eure-et-Loir, C France
xxxix N12 Charwelton Northamptonshire, C England, UK
151 W15 Charyn Kaz. Sharyn. Almaty, SE Kazakhstan
63 D21 Chascomús Buenos Aires, E Argentina
9 N16 Chase British Columbia, SW Canada
23 U7 Chase City Virginia, NE USA
21 S4 Chase, Mount ▲ Maine, NE USA
120 M13 Chashniki Rus. Chashniki. Vitsyebskaya Voblasts', N Belorussia
117 D15 Chásia ▲ C Greece
31 V9 Chaska Minnesota, N USA
193 D25 Chaslands Mistake headland South Island, NZ
129 R11 Chasovo Respublika Komi, NW Russian Federation
Chasovo see Vazhgort
128 H14 Chastova Novgorodskaya Oblast', NW Russian Federation
149 R3 Chāt Māzandarān, N Iran
Chatak see Chhatak
41 R9 Chatanika Alaska, USA
41 R9 Chatanika River ≈ Alaska, USA
153 T8 Chat-Bazar Talasskaya Oblast', NW Kyrgyzstan
47 Y14 Chateaubelair Saint Vincent, W Saint Vincent and the Grenadines
104 J7 Châteaubriant Loire-Atlantique, NW France
105 Q8 Château-Chinon Nièvre, C France
110 C10 Château d'Oex Vaud, W Switzerland
104 L7 Château-du-Loir Sarthe, NW France
104 M6 Châteaudun Eure-et-Loir, C France
104 K7 Château-Gontier Mayenne, NW France
13 O13 Châteauguay Québec, SE Canada
104 F6 Châteaulin Finistère, NW France
105 N9 Châteaumeillant Cher, C France
104 K11 Châteauneuf-sur-Charente Charente, W France
104 M7 Château-Renault Indre-et-Loire, C France
105 N9 Châteauroux prev. Indreville. Indre, C France
105 T5 Château-Salins Moselle, NE France
105 P4 Château-Thierry Aisne, N France
101 H21 Châtelet Hainaut, S Belgium
Châtelherault see Châtellerault
104 L9 Châtellerault var. Châtelherault. Vienne, W France
31 X10 Chatfield Minnesota, N USA
xxxvii W10 Chatham Kent, SE England, UK
11 O14 Chatham New Brunswick, SE Canada
12 D17 Chatham Ontario, S Canada
32 K14 Chatham Illinois, N USA
23 T7 Chatham Virginia, NE USA
65 F22 Chatham, Isla island S Chile
183 R12 Chatham Island island Chatham Islands, NZ
Chatham Island see San Cristóbal, Isla
Chatham Island Rise see Chatham Rise
199 Jj14 Chatham Islands island group NZ, SW Pacific Ocean
183 Q12 Chatham Rise var. Chatham Island Rise. undersea feature S Pacific Ocean
41 X13 Chatham Strait strait Alaska, USA
Chathóir, Rinn see Cahore Point
104 M9 Châtillon-sur-Indre Indre, C France
105 Q7 Châtillon-sur-Seine Côte d'Or, C France

◆ Country ● Country Capital ◇ Dependent Territory ○ Dependent Territory Capital ◆ Administrative Region ✕ International Airport ▲ Mountain ▲ Mountain Range ▲ Volcano ≈ River ◎ Lake ⊠ Reservoir

Chatkal – Chishmy

153 S8 **Chatkal** Uzb. Chotqol. ≈ Kyrgyzstan/Uzbekistan
153 R9 **Chatkal Range** Rus. Chatkal'skiy Khrebet. ▲▲ Kyrgyzstan/Uzbekistan
Chatkal'skiy Khrebet see Chatkal Range
25 N7 **Chatom** Alabama, S USA
Chatrapur see Chhatrapur
149 S10 **Chatrūd** Kermān, C Iran
25 S2 **Chatsworth** Georgia, SE USA
Chattagām see Chittagong
25 S8 **Chattahoochee** Florida, SE USA
25 R8 **Chattahoochee River** ≈ SE USA
22 L10 **Chattanooga** Tennessee, S USA
xxxix S11 **Chatteris** Cambridgeshire, E England, UK
153 V10 **Chatyr-Kël', Ozero** ◎ C Kyrgyzstan
153 W9 **Chatyr-Tash** Narynskaya Oblast', C Kyrgyzstan
13 R12 **Chaudière** ≈ Québec, SE Canada
178 J14 **Châu Đôc** var. Chauphu, Chau Phu. An Giang, S Vietnam
158 D13 **Chauhtan** prev. Chohtan. Rājasthān, NW India
177 Ff5 **Chauk** Magwe, W Burma
105 R6 **Chaumont** prev. Chaumont-en-Bassigny. Haute-Marne, N France
Chaumont-en-Bassigny see Chaumont
127 O4 **Chaunskaya Guba** bay NE Russian Federation
105 P3 **Chauny** Aisne, N France
Châu Ô see Binh Sơn
Chau Phu see Châu Đôc
104 I5 **Chausey, Îles** island group N France
Chausy see Chavusy
20 C11 **Chautauqua Lake** ◎ New York, NE USA
104 L9 **Chauvigny** Vienne, W France
128 L6 **Chavan'ga** Murmanskaya Oblast', NW Russian Federation
12 K10 **Chavannes, Lac** ◎ Québec, SE Canada
Chavantes, Represa de see Xavantes, Represa de
63 D15 **Chavarría** Corrientes, NE Argentina
Chavash Respubliki see Chuvashskaya Respublika
106 I5 **Chaves** anc. Aquae Flaviae. Vila Real, N Portugal
Chávez, Isla see Santa Cruz, Isla
84 G13 **Chavuma** North Western, NW Zambia
121 O16 **Chavusy** Rus. Chausy. Mahilyowskaya Voblasts', E Belorussia
xxxvi G13 **Chawleigh** Devon, SW England, UK
xxxvii Q11 **Chawton** Hampshire, S England, UK
151 Q16 **Chayan** Yuzhnyy Kazakhstan, S Kazakhstan
153 U8 **Chayek** Narynskaya Oblast', C Kyrgyzstan
145 T6 **Chāy Khānah** E Iraq
129 T16 **Chaykovskiy** Permskaya Oblast', NW Russian Federation
178 K12 **Chbar** Môndól Kiri, E Cambodia
xxxviii K7 **Cheadle** Staffordshire, C England, UK
xli P17 **Cheadle** Stockport, NW England, UK
25 Q4 **Cheaha Mountain** ▲ Alabama, S USA
Cheatharlach see Carlow
23 S2 **Cheat River** ≈ NE USA
113 A16 **Cheb** Ger. Eger. Západní Čechy, W Czech Republic
131 Q3 **Cheboksary** Chuvashskaya Respublika, W Russian Federation
33 Q5 **Cheboygan** Michigan, N USA
Chechaouèn see Chefchaouen
Chechenia see Chechenskaya Respublika
131 O15 **Chechenskaya Respublika** Eng. Chechenia, Chechnia, Rus. Chechnya. ◐ autonomous republic SW Russian Federation
69 N4 **Chech, Erg** desert Algeria/Mali
Chechersk see Chachersk
Chechevichi see Chachevichy
Che-chiang see Zhejiang
Chechnia/Chechnya see Chechenskaya Respublika
169 Y15 **Chech'ŏn** Jap. Teisen. N South Korea
113 L15 **Chęciny** Kielce, S Poland
29 Q10 **Checotah** Oklahoma, C USA
11 R15 **Chedabucto Bay** inlet Nova Scotia, E Canada
xxxvi K11 **Cheddar** Somerset, SW England, UK
xxxviii K7 **Cheddleton** Staffordshire, C England, UK
177 F7 **Cheduba Island** island W Burma
39 T5 **Cheesman Lake** ▣ Colorado, C USA
205 S16 **Cheetham, Cape** headland Antarctica
76 G5 **Chefchaouen** var. Chaouèn, Chechaouèn, Sp. Xauen. N Morocco
Chefoo see Yantai
40 M12 **Chefornak** Alaska, USA
126 Mm15 **Chegdomyn** Khabarovskiy Kray, SE Russian Federation
78 M4 **Chegga** Tiris Zemmour, NE Mauritania
Cheghcheran see Chaghcharān
34 G9 **Chehalis** Washington, NW USA
34 G9 **Chehalis River** ≈ Washington, NW USA
154 M6 **Chehel Abdālān, Kūh-e** var. Chalap Dalam, Pash. Chalap Dalan. ▲▲ C Afghanistan
117 D14 **Cheimaditis, Límni** ◎ N Greece
105 U15 **Cheiron, Mont** ▲ SE France
169 X17 **Cheju** Jap. Saishū. S South Korea
169 Y17 **Cheju** ✕ S South Korea
169 Y17 **Cheju-do** Jap. Saishū; prev. Quelpart. island S South Korea
169 X17 **Cheju-haehyŏp** strait S South Korea
Chekiang see Zhejiang
Chekichler see Chekishlyar
152 B13 **Chekishlyar** Turkm. Chekichler. Balkanskiy Velayat, W Turkmenistan
196 F8 **Chelab** Babeldaob, N Palau
153 N11 **Chelak** Rus. Chelek. Samarqand Wiloyati, C Uzbekistan
34 J7 **Chelan, Lake** ▣ Washington, NW USA
Chelek see Chelak
152 A11 **Cheleken** Balkanskiy Velayat, W Turkmenistan
xl G17 **Chelford** Cheshire, W England, UK
Chélif/Chéliff see Chelif, Oued
76 J5 **Chelif, Oued** var. Chélif, Chéliff, Chellif, Shellif. ≈ N Algeria
150 K12 **Chelkar** Aktyubinsk, W Kazakhstan
Chelkar, Ozero see Shalkar, Ozero
xxxviii M8 **Chellaston** City of Derby, C England, UK
Chellif see Chelif, Oued
113 P14 **Chełm** Rus. Kholm. Chełm, SE Poland
113 P14 **Chełm** off. Województwo Chełmskie, Rus. Kholm. ◐ province SE Poland
xxxvii W7 **Chelmer** ≈ E England, UK
112 I9 **Chełmno** Ger. Culm, Kulm. Toruń, N Poland
xxxvii W8 **Chelmsford** Essex, E England, UK
12 F10 **Chelmsford** Ontario, S Canada
Chełmskie, Województwo see Chełm
112 J9 **Chełmża** Ger. Culmsee, Kulmsee. Toruń, N Poland
xxxvi C8 **Chelsea** Kensington and Chelsea, SE England, UK
29 Q8 **Chelsea** Oklahoma, C USA
20 M8 **Chelsea** Vermont, NE USA
xxxvi M7 **Cheltenham** Gloucestershire, C England, UK
107 R9 **Chelva** País Valenciano, E Spain
125 Ee12 **Chelyabinsk** Chelyabinskaya Oblast', C Russian Federation
125 E12 **Chelyabinskaya Oblast'** ◐ province C Russian Federation
126 Jj4 **Chelyuskin, Mys** headland N Russian Federation
126 H15 **Chemal** Altayskiy Kray, S Russian Federation
43 Y12 **Chemax** Yucatán, SE Mexico
85 N16 **Chemba** Sofala, C Mozambique
84 J13 **Chembe** Luapula, NE Zambia
152 J17 **Chemenibit** Maryyskiy Velayat, S Turkmenistan
Chemerisy see Chamyarysy
118 K7 **Chemerivtsi** Khmel'nyts'ka Oblast', W Ukraine
104 J8 **Chemillé** Maine-et-Loire, NW France
181 X17 **Chemin Grenier** S Mauritius
103 N16 **Chemnitz** prev. Karl-Marx-Stadt. Sachsen, E Germany
Chemulpo see Inch'ŏn
34 H14 **Chemult** Oregon, NW USA
20 G12 **Chemung River** ≈ New York/Pennsylvania, NE USA
155 U8 **Chenāb** ≈ India/Pakistan
41 S9 **Chena Hot Springs** Alaska, USA
20 I11 **Chenango River** ≈ New York, NE USA
174 Gg3 **Chenderoh, Tasik** ◎ Peninsular Malaysia
13 Q11 **Chêne, Rivière du** ≈ Québec, SE Canada
34 L8 **Cheney** Washington, NW USA
28 M6 **Cheney Reservoir** ▣ Kansas, C USA
Chengchiatun see Liaoyuan
Ch'eng-chou/Chengchow see Zhengzhou
167 P1 **Chengde** var. Jehol. Hebei, E China
166 I9 **Chengdu** var. Chengtu, Ch'eng-tu. Sichuan, C China
167 Q14 **Chenghai** Guangdong, S China
Chenghsien see Zhengzhou
166 L17 **Chengmai** Hainan, S China
Chengtu/Ch'eng-tu see Chengdu
165 W12 **Cheng Xian** Gansu, C China
Chenkiang see Zhenjiang
Chennai see Madras
105 R8 **Chenôve** Côte d'Or, C France
Chenstokhov see Częstochowa
166 L11 **Chenxi** Hunan, S China
Chen Xian/Chenxian/Chen Xiang see Chenzhou
167 N12 **Chenzhou** var. Chenxian, Chen Xian, Chen Xiang. Hunan, S China
178 Kk12 **Cheo Reo** var. A Yun Pa. Gia Lai, S Vietnam
116 I11 **Chepelare** Plovdivska Oblast, S Bulgaria
116 I11 **Chepelarska Reka** ≈ S Bulgaria
58 B11 **Chepén** La Libertad, C Peru
64 J10 **Chepes** La Rioja, C Argentina
45 U14 **Chepo** Panamá, C Panama
Chepping Wycombe see High Wycombe
xxxv M14 **Chepstow** Monmouthshire, SE Wales, UK
129 R14 **Cheptsa** ≈ NW Russian Federation
32 K3 **Chequamegon Point** headland Wisconsin, N USA
105 O8 **Cher** ◐ department C France
104 M8 **Cher** ≈ C France
Cherangani Hills see Cherangany Hills
83 H17 **Cherangany Hills** var. Cherangani Hills. ▲▲ W Kenya
23 S11 **Cheraw** South Carolina, SE USA
104 I3 **Cherbourg** anc. Carusbur. Manche, N France
131 R5 **Cherdakly** Ul'yanovskaya Oblast', W Russian Federation
129 U12 **Cherdyn'** Permskaya Oblast', NW Russian Federation
128 J14 **Cherekha** ≈ W Russian Federation
126 J15 **Cheremkhovo** Irkutskaya Oblast', S Russian Federation
126 Hh15 **Cheremushki** Respublika Khakasiya, S Russian Federation
Cheren see Keren
128 K14 **Cherepovets** Vologodskaya Oblast', NW Russian Federation
129 O11 **Cherevkovo** Arkhangel'skaya Oblast', NW Russian Federation
76 I6 **Chergui, Chott ech** salt lake NW Algeria
Cherikov see Cherykaw
xxxvii Q12 **Cheriton** Hampshire, S England, UK
xxxvi H13 **Cheriton Fitzpaine** Devon, SW England, UK
119 P6 **Cherkas'ka Oblast'** var. Cherkasy, Rus. Cherkasskaya Oblast'. ◐ province C Ukraine
Cherkasskaya Oblast' see Cherkas'ka Oblast'
Cherkassy see Cherkasy
119 Q6 **Cherkasy** Rus. Cherkassy. Cherkas'ka Oblast', C Ukraine
Cherkasy see Cherkas'ka Oblast'
130 M15 **Cherkessk** Karachayevo-Cherkesskaya Respublika, SW Russian Federation
125 G13 **Cherlak** Omskaya Oblast', C Russian Federation
125 Ff14 **Cherlakskiy** Omskaya Oblast', C Russian Federation
129 U13 **Chermoz** Permskaya Oblast', NW Russian Federation
Chernavchitsy see Charnawchytsy
129 T3 **Chernaya** Nenetskiy Avtonomnyy Okrug, NW Russian Federation
129 T4 **Chernaya** ≈ NW Russian Federation
Chernigov see Chernihiv
Chernigovskaya Oblast' see Chernihivs'ka Oblast'
119 Q2 **Chernihiv** Rus. Chernigov. Chernihivs'ka Oblast', NE Ukraine
Chernihiv see Chernihivs'ka Oblast'
119 V9 **Chernihivka** Zaporiz'ka Oblast', SE Ukraine
119 P2 **Chernihivs'ka Oblast'** var. Chernihiv, Rus. Chernigovskaya Oblast'. ◐ province NE Ukraine
116 I9 **Cherni Osŭm** ≈ N Bulgaria
118 J8 **Chernivets'ka Oblast'** var. Chernivtsi, Rus. Chernovitskaya Oblast'. ◐ province W Ukraine
116 I9 **Cherni Vit** ≈ NW Bulgaria
116 G10 **Cherni Vrŭkh** ▲ W Bulgaria
118 K8 **Chernivtsi** Ger. Czernowitz, Rom. Cernăuţi, Rus. Chernovtsy. Chernivets'ka Oblast', W Ukraine
118 M7 **Chernivtsi** Vinnyts'ka Oblast', C Ukraine
Chernivtsi see Chernivets'ka Oblast'
Chernobyl' see Chornobyl'
126 Hh15 **Chernogorsk** Respublika Khakasiya, S Russian Federation
Cherno More see Black Sea
Chernomorskoye see Chornomors'ke
151 T7 **Chernoretskoye** Pavlodar, NE Kazakhstan
Chernovitskaya Oblast' see Chernivets'ka Oblast'
Chernovtsy see Chernivtsi
151 U8 **Chernoye** Pavlodar, NE Kazakhstan
Chernoye More see Black Sea
129 U16 **Chernushka** Permskaya Oblast', NW Russian Federation
119 N4 **Chernyakhiv** Rus. Chernyakhov. Zhytomyrs'ka Oblast', N Ukraine
Chernyakhov see Chernyakhiv
121 C14 **Chernyakhovsk** Ger. Insterburg. Kaliningradskaya Oblast', W Russian Federation
130 K8 **Chernyanka** Belgorodskaya Oblast', W Russian Federation
129 V5 **Chernyshëva, Gryada** ▲▲ NW Russian Federation
150 J14 **Chernyshëva, Zaliv** gulf SW Kazakhstan
126 L15 **Chernyshevsk** Chitinskaya Oblast', S Russian Federation
126 K11 **Chernyshevskiy** Respublika Sakha (Yakutiya), NE Russian Federation
131 P13 **Chërnyye Zemli** plain SW Russian Federation
Chërnyy Irtysh see Ertix He
131 V7 **Chernyy Otrog** Orenburgskaya Oblast', W Russian Federation
31 T12 **Cherokee** Iowa, C USA
28 M8 **Cherokee** Oklahoma, C USA
27 R9 **Cherokee** Texas, SW USA
23 O8 **Cherokee Lake** ▣ Tennessee, S USA
Cherokees, Lake O' The see Grand Lake O' The Cherokees
46 H1 **Cherokee Sound** Great Abaco, N Bahamas
159 V13 **Cherrapunji** Meghālaya, NE India
30 L9 **Cherry Creek** ≈ South Dakota, N USA
20 J16 **Cherry Hill** New Jersey, NE USA
29 Q7 **Cherryvale** Kansas, C USA
23 Q10 **Cherryville** North Carolina, SE USA
Cherski Range see Cherskogo, Khrebet
127 O5 **Cherskiy** Respublika Sakha (Yakutiya), NE Russian Federation
126 Mm8 **Cherskogo, Khrebet** var. Cherski Range. ▲▲ NE Russian Federation
Cherso see Cres
130 L10 **Chertkovo** Rostovskaya Oblast', SW Russian Federation
xxxvii S10 **Chertsey** Surrey, SE England, UK
Cherven' see Chervyen'
116 H8 **Cherven Bryag** Loveshka Oblast, NW Bulgaria
118 M4 **Chervonoarmiys'k** Zhytomyrs'ka Oblast', N Ukraine
Chervonograd see Chervonohrad
118 I4 **Chervonohrad** Rus. Chervonograd. L'vivs'ka Oblast', NW Ukraine
119 W6 **Chervonooskil's'ke Vodoskhovyshche** Rus. Krasnooskol'skoye Vodokhranilishche. ▣ NE Ukraine
Chervonoye, Ozero see Chyrvonaye, Vozyera
119 S4 **Chervonozavods'ke** Poltavs'ka Oblast', C Ukraine
121 L16 **Chervyen'** Rus. Cherven'. Minskaya Voblasts', C Belorussia
121 P16 **Cherykaw** Rus. Cherikov. Mahilyowskaya Voblasts', E Belorussia
33 R9 **Chesaning** Michigan, N USA
23 X5 **Chesapeake Bay** inlet NE USA
xxxvii S8 **Chesham** Buckinghamshire, C England, UK
Cheshevlya see Tsyeshawlya
xl H17 **Cheshire** ◐ county C England, UK
129 P5 **Chëshskaya Guba** var. Archangel Bay, Chesha Bay, Dvina Bay. bay NW Russian Federation
xxxvi U8 **Cheshunt** Hertfordshire, SE England, UK
12 F14 **Chesley** Ontario, S Canada
xxxviii B13 **Cheslyn Hay** Staffordshire, C England, UK
23 Q10 **Chesnee** South Carolina, SE USA
xxxviii G6 **Chester** Wel. Caerleon; hist. Legaceaster, Lat. Deva, Devana Castra. Cheshire, C England, UK
37 O4 **Chester** California, W USA
32 K16 **Chester** Illinois, N USA
35 S7 **Chester** Montana, NW USA
20 I16 **Chester** Pennsylvania, NE USA
23 R1 **Chester** South Carolina, SE USA
27 X9 **Chester** Texas, SW USA
23 W6 **Chester** Virginia, NE USA
23 R11 **Chester** West Virginia, NE USA
xxxviii M6 **Chesterfield** Derbyshire, C England, UK
23 S11 **Chesterfield** South Carolina, SE USA
23 W6 **Chesterfield** Virginia, NE USA
199 I10 **Chesterfield, Îles** island group NW New Caledonia
15 Ll6 **Chesterfield Inlet** Northwest Territories, NW Canada
15 L6 **Chesterfield Inlet** inlet Northwest Territories, N Canada
xli R7 **Chester-le-Street** Durham, N England, UK
23 Y3 **Chester River** ≈ Delaware/Maryland, NE USA
xliii O22 **Chesters** The Borders, S Scotland, UK
23 X3 **Chestertown** Maryland, NE USA
21 R4 **Chesuncook Lake** ◎ Maine, NE USA
xxxviii I8 **Cheswardine** Shropshire, W England, UK
32 J5 **Chetek** Wisconsin, N USA
11 R14 **Chéticamp** Nova Scotia, SE Canada
xxxvi L13 **Chetnole** Dorset, S England, UK
29 Q8 **Chetopa** Kansas, C USA
43 Y14 **Chetumal** var. Payo Obispo. Quintana Roo, SE Mexico
Chetumal, Bahia/Chetumal, Bahía de see Chetumal Bay
44 G1 **Chetumal Bay** var. Bahia Chetumal, Bahía de Chetumal. bay Belize/Mexico
8 M13 **Chetwynd** British Columbia, W Canada
40 M11 **Chevak** Alaska, USA
38 M12 **Chevelon Creek** ≈ Arizona, SW USA
193 J17 **Cheviot** Canterbury, South Island, NZ
xliii O23 **Cheviot Hills** hill range England/Scotland, UK
xli P3 **Cheviot, The** ▲ NE England, UK
12 M11 **Chevreuil, Lac du** ◎ Québec, SE Canada
83 I16 **Ch'ew Bahir** var. Lake Stefanie. ◎ Ethiopia/Kenya
34 L7 **Chewelah** Washington, NW USA
xxxvi L10 **Chew Magna** Bath and North East Somerset, SW England, UK
xxxvi L11 **Chewton Mendip** Somerset, SW England, UK
28 K10 **Cheyenne** Oklahoma, C USA
35 Z17 **Cheyenne** state capital Wyoming, C USA
28 L5 **Cheyenne Bottoms** ◎ Kansas, C USA
18 Kk6 **Cheyenne River** ≈ South Dakota/Wyoming, N USA
39 W5 **Cheyenne Wells** Colorado, C USA
110 C9 **Cheyres** Vaud, W Switzerland
Chezdi-Oşorheiu see Târgu Secuiesc
159 P13 **Chhapra** prev. Chapra. Bihār, N India
159 V13 **Chhatak** var. Chatak. Chittagong, NE Bangladesh
160 J9 **Chhatarpur** Madhya Pradesh, C India
160 N13 **Chhatrapur** prev. Chatrapur. Orissa, E India
160 L12 **Chhattīsgarh** plain C India
160 I11 **Chhindwāra** Madhya Pradesh, C India
Chhlong see Phumĭ Chhlong
Chhuk see Phumĭ Chhuk
159 T12 **Chhukha** SW Bhutan
167 S14 **Chiai** var. Chia-i, Chiayi, Kiayi, Jiayi, Jap. Kagi. C Taiwan
Chia-mu-ssu see Jiamusi
85 B15 **Chiange** Port. Vila de Almoster. Huíla, SW Angola
Chiang-hsi see Jiangxi
167 S12 **Chiang Kai-shek** ✕ (T'aipei) N Taiwan
178 I8 **Chiang Khan** Loei, E Thailand
178 H7 **Chiang Mai** var. Chiangmai, Chiengmai, Kiangmai. Chiang Mai, NW Thailand
178 H7 **Chiang Mai** ✕ Chiang Mai, NW Thailand
178 Hh6 **Chiang Rai** var. Chianpai, Chienrai, Muang Chiang Rai. Chiang Rai, NW Thailand
Chiang-su see Jiangsu
Chianning/Chian-ning see Nanjing
Chianpai see Chiang Rai
108 G12 **Chianti** cultural region C Italy
Chiapa see Chiapa de Corzo
43 U16 **Chiapa de Corzo** var. Chiapa. Chiapas, SE Mexico
43 V16 **Chiapas** ◐ state SE Mexico
108 J12 **Chiaravalle** Marche, C Italy
109 N22 **Chiaravalle Centrale** Calabria, SW Italy
108 E7 **Chiari** Lombardia, N Italy
110 H12 **Chiasso** Ticino, S Switzerland
143 S9 **Chiat'ura** C Georgia
43 P15 **Chiautla** var. Chiautla de Tapia. Puebla, S Mexico
Chiautla de Tapia see Chiautla
108 D10 **Chiavari** Liguria, NW Italy
108 E6 **Chiavenna** Lombardia, N Italy
Chiayi see Chiai
Chiazza see Piazza Armerina
172 Ss12 **Chiba** var. Tiba. Chiba, Honshū, S Japan
171 K17 **Chiba** off. Chiba-ken, var. Tiba. ◐ prefecture Honshū, S Japan
85 M18 **Chibabava** Sofala, C Mozambique
85 B15 **Chibia** Port. João de Almeida, Vila João de Almeida. Huíla, SW Angola
85 M18 **Chiboma** Sofala, C Mozambique
84 J12 **Chibondo** Luapula, N Zambia
84 K11 **Chibote** Luapula, NE Zambia
10 K12 **Chibougamau** Québec, SE Canada
170 Ff11 **Chiburi-jima** island Oki-shotō, SW Japan
85 M20 **Chibuto** Gaza, S Mozambique
33 N11 **Chicago** Illinois, N USA
33 N11 **Chicago Heights** Illinois, N USA
13 W6 **Chic-Chocs, Monts** Eng. Shickshock Mountains. ▲▲ Québec, SE Canada
41 W13 **Chichagof Island** island Alexander Archipelago, Alaska, USA
59 K20 **Chichas, Cordillera de** ▲▲ SW Bolivia
43 X12 **Chichén-Itzá, Ruinas** ruins Yucatán, SE Mexico
xxxvii R13 **Chichester** West Sussex, SE England, UK
171 Jj16 **Chichibu** var. Titibu. Saitama, Honshū, S Japan
44 C5 **Chichicastenango** Quiché, W Guatemala
44 I9 **Chichigalpa** Chinandega, NW Nicaragua
Ch'i-ch'i-ha-erh see Qiqihar
172 T16 **Chichijima-rettō** Eng. Beechy Group. island group SE Japan
56 K4 **Chichiriviche** Falcón, N Venezuela
41 R11 **Chickaloon** Alaska, USA
22 L10 **Chickamauga Lake** ▣ Tennessee, S USA
25 N7 **Chickasawhay River** ≈ Mississippi, S USA
28 M11 **Chickasha** Oklahoma, C USA
41 T9 **Chicken** Alaska, USA
xxxvi L14 **Chickerell** Dorset, S England, UK
106 J16 **Chiclana de la Frontera** Andalucía, S Spain
58 B11 **Chiclayo** Lambayeque, NW Peru
37 N5 **Chico** California, W USA
85 L15 **Chicoa** Tete, NW Mozambique
85 M20 **Chicomo** Gaza, S Mozambique
20 M11 **Chicopee** Massachusetts, NE USA
65 I19 **Chico, Río** ≈ SE Argentina
65 I21 **Chico, Río** ≈ S Argentina
29 W14 **Chicot, Lake** ◎ Arkansas, C USA
13 R7 **Chicoutimi** Québec, SE Canada
13 Q8 **Chicoutimi** ≈ Québec, SE Canada
85 L19 **Chicualacuala** Gaza, SW Mozambique
85 B14 **Chicuma** Benguela, C Angola
161 J21 **Chidambaram** Tamil Nādu, SE India
xxxvii S11 **Chiddingfold** Surrey, SE England, UK
xxxvi K14 **Chideock** Dorset, S England, UK
206 K13 **Chidley, Cape** headland Newfoundland and Labrador, E Canada
103 N24 **Chiemsee** ◎ SE Germany
Chiengmai see Chiang Mai
Chienrai see Chiang Rai
108 B8 **Chieri** Piemonte, NW Italy
108 F8 **Chiese** ≈ N Italy
109 K14 **Chieti** var. Teate. Abruzzi, C Italy
xxxvii P9 **Chieveley** Newbury, S England, UK
101 E19 **Chièvres** Hainaut, SW Belgium
169 S12 **Chifeng** var. Ulanhad. Nei Mongol Zizhiqu, N China
84 F13 **Chifumage** ≈ E Angola
84 M13 **Chifunda** Eastern, NE Zambia
151 S14 **Chiganak** var. Čiganak. Zhambyl, SE Kazakhstan
41 P15 **Chiginagak, Mount** ▲ Alaska, USA
Chigirin see Chyhyryn
43 P13 **Chignahuapan** Puebla, S Mexico
41 O15 **Chignik** Alaska, USA
85 M19 **Chigombe** ≈ S Mozambique
56 D7 **Chigorodó** Antioquia, NW Colombia
85 M19 **Chigubo** Gaza, S Mozambique
xxxvi G5 **Chigwell** Essex, SE England, UK
168 D6 **Chihertey** Bayan-Ölgiy, W Mongolia
Chih-fu see Yantai
Chihli see Hebei
Chihli, Gulf of see Bo Hai
42 J6 **Chihuahua** Chihuahua, NW Mexico
42 I6 **Chihuahua** ◐ state N Mexico
151 O15 **Chiili** Kzyl-Orda, S Kazakhstan
28 M7 **Chikaskia River** ≈ Kansas/Oklahoma, C USA
161 H19 **Chik Ballāpur** Karnātaka, W India
128 G15 **Chikhachevo** Pskovskaya Oblast', W Russian Federation
161 F19 **Chikmagalūr** Karnātaka, W India
133 V7 **Chikoy** ≈ C Russian Federation
85 J15 **Chikumbi** Lusaka, C Zambia
84 M13 **Chikwa** Eastern, NE Zambia
Chikwana see Chikwawa
85 N15 **Chikwawa** var. Chikwana. Southern, S Malawi
161 J16 **Chilakalūrupet** Andhra Pradesh, E India
152 L14 **Chilan** Lebapskiy Velayat, E Turkmenistan
Chilapa see Chilapa de Alvarez
43 P16 **Chilapa de Alvarez** var. Chilapa. Guerrero, S Mexico
161 J25 **Chilaw** North Western Province, W Sri Lanka
59 D15 **Chilca** Lima, W Peru
25 Q4 **Childersburg** Alabama, S USA
27 P4 **Childress** Texas, SW USA
xxxviii I8 **Child's Ercall** Shropshire, W England, UK
65 G14 **Chile** off. Republic of Chile. ◆ republic SW South America
49 R10 **Chile Basin** undersea feature E Pacific Ocean
65 H20 **Chile Chico** Aisén, W Chile
64 I9 **Chilecito** La Rioja, NW Argentina
64 H12 **Chilecito** Mendoza, W Argentina
85 L14 **Chilembwe** Eastern, E Zambia
200 O13 **Chile Rise** undersea feature SE Pacific Ocean
xxxvii Y10 **Chilham** Kent, SE England, UK
119 N13 **Chilia Braţul** ≈ SE Romania
Chilia-Nouă see Kiliya
151 V15 **Chilik** Almaty, SE Kazakhstan
151 V15 **Chilik** ≈ SE Kazakhstan
160 O13 **Chilika Lake** var. Chilka Lake. ◎ E India
84 J13 **Chililabombwe** Copperbelt, C Zambia
Chi-lin see Jilin
Chilka Lake see Chilika Lake
8 H9 **Chilkoot Pass** pass British Columbia, W Canada
Chill Ala, Cuan see Killala Bay
64 G13 **Chillán** Bío Bío, C Chile
63 C22 **Chillar** Buenos Aires, E Argentina
xxxvi F14 **Chillaton** Devon, SW England, UK
Chill Chiaráin, Cuan see Kilkieran Bay
32 K12 **Chillicothe** Illinois, N USA
29 S3 **Chillicothe** Missouri, C USA
33 S14 **Chillicothe** Ohio, N USA
27 Q4 **Chillicothe** Texas, SW USA
8 M17 **Chilliwack** British Columbia, SW Canada
Chill Mhantáin, Ceann see Wicklow Head
Chill Mhantáin, Sléibhte see Wicklow Mountains
110 C10 **Chillon** Vaud, W Switzerland
152 C11 **Chil'mamedkum, Peski** Turkm. Chilmämetgum. desert W Turkmenistan
Chilmämetgum see Chil'mamedkum, Peski
65 F17 **Chiloé, Isla de** var. Isla Grande de Chiloé. island W Chile
34 H15 **Chiloquin** Oregon, NW USA
43 O16 **Chilpancingo** var. Chilpancingo de los Bravos. Guerrero, S Mexico
Chilpancingo de los Bravos see Chilpancingo
xxxvii R8 **Chiltern Hills** hill range S England, UK
32 M7 **Chilton** Wisconsin, N USA
84 F11 **Chiluage** Lunda Sul, NE Angola
84 N12 **Chilumba** prev. Deep Bay. Northern, N Malawi
167 T12 **Chilung** var. Keelung, Jap. Kirun, Kirun'; prev. Sp. Santissima Trinidad. N Taiwan
85 N15 **Chilwa, Lake** var. Lago Chirua, Lake Shirwa. ◎ SE Malawi
178 J10 **Chi, Mae Nam** ≈ E Thailand
44 C6 **Chimaltenango** Chimaltenango, C Guatemala
44 A2 **Chimaltenango** off. Departamento de Chimaltenango. ◐ department S Guatemala
45 V15 **Chimán** Panamá, E Panama
85 M17 **Chimanimani** prev. Mandidzudzure, Melsetter. Manicaland, E Zimbabwe
101 G22 **Chimay** Hainaut, S Belgium
39 S10 **Chimayo** New Mexico, SW USA
Chimbay see Chimboy
58 A13 **Chimborazo** ◐ province C Ecuador
58 C7 **Chimborazo** ▲ C Ecuador
58 C12 **Chimbote** Ancash, W Peru
152 H7 **Chimboy** Rus. Chimbay. Qoraqalpoghiston Respublikasi, NW Uzbekistan
194 H12 **Chimbu** ◐ province C PNG
56 F6 **Chimichagua** Cesar, N Colombia
Chimishliya see Cimişlia
Chimkent see Shymkent
Chimkentskaya Oblast' see Yuzhnyy Kazakhstan
30 I14 **Chimney Rock** rock Nebraska, C USA
85 M17 **Chimoio** Manica, C Mozambique
84 K11 **Chimpembe** Northern, NE Zambia
43 O8 **China** Nuevo León, NE Mexico
162 M9 **China** off. People's Republic of China, Chin. Chung-hua Jen-min Kung-ho-kuo, Zhonghua Renmin Gongheguo; prev. Chinese Empire. ◆ republic E Asia
21 Q7 **China Lake** ◎ Maine, NE USA
44 F8 **Chinameca** San Miguel, E El Salvador
Chi-nan/Chinan see Jinan
44 H9 **Chinandega** Chinandega, NW Nicaragua
44 H9 **Chinandega** ◐ department NW Nicaragua
China, People's Republic of see China
China, Republic of see Taiwan
26 J11 **Chinati Mountains** ▲▲ Texas, SW USA
Chinaz see Chinoz
59 E15 **Chincha Alta** Ica, SW Peru
9 N11 **Chinchaga** ≈ Alberta, SW Canada
Chin-chiang see Quanzhou
Chinchilla see Chinchilla de Monte Aragón
107 Q11 **Chinchilla de Monte Aragón** var. Chinchilla. Castilla-La Mancha, C Spain
56 D10 **Chinchiná** Caldas, W Colombia
107 O8 **Chinchón** Madrid, C Spain
43 Z14 **Chinchorro, Banco** island SE Mexico
Chin-chou/Chinchow see Jinzhou
23 Z5 **Chincoteague** Assateague Island, Virginia, NE USA
85 O17 **Chinde** Zambézia, NE Mozambique
169 X17 **Chin-do** Jap. Chin-tō. island SW South Korea
165 R13 **Chindu** Qinghai, C China
177 G2 **Chindwin** ≈ N Burma
Chinese Empire see China
152 L10 **Chingeldi** Rus. Chingildi. Nawoiy Wiloyati, N Uzbekistan
Ch'ing Hai see Qinghai Hu
Chinghai see Qinghai
Chingildi see Chingeldi
150 H9 **Chingirlau** Kaz. Shyngghyrlaū. Zapadnyy Kazakhstan, W Kazakhstan
84 J13 **Chingola** Copperbelt, C Zambia
Ching-Tao/Ch'ing-tao see Qingdao
84 C13 **Chinguar** Huambo, C Angola
78 I7 **Chinguetti** var. Chinguetti. Adrar, C Mauritania
169 Z16 **Chinhae** Jap. Chinkai. S South Korea
177 Ff4 **Chin Hills** ▲▲ W Burma
85 K16 **Chinhoyi** prev. Sinoia. Mashonaland West, N Zimbabwe
Chinhsien see Jinzhou
41 Q14 **Chiniak, Cape** headland Kodiak Island, Alaska, USA
12 G10 **Chiniguchi Lake** ◎ Ontario, S Canada
155 U8 **Chiniot** Punjab, NE Pakistan
169 Y16 **Chinju** Jap. Shinshū. S South Korea
Chinkai see Chinhae
80 M13 **Chinko** ≈ E Central African Republic
39 O9 **Chinle** Arizona, SW USA
167 R13 **Chinmen Tao** var. Jinmen Dao, Quemoy. island W Taiwan
Chinnchâr see Shinshār
Chinnereth see Tiberias, Lake
xxxvii R8 **Chinnor** Oxfordshire, C England, UK
171 J15 **Chino** var. Tino. Nagano, Honshū, S Japan
104 L8 **Chinon** Indre-et-Loire, C France
35 T7 **Chinook** Montana, NW USA
Chinook State see Washington
199 Jj3 **Chinook Trough** undersea feature N Pacific Ocean
38 K11 **Chino Valley** Arizona, SW USA
153 P10 **Chinoz** Rus. Chinaz. Toshkent Wiloyati, E Uzbekistan
84 L12 **Chinsali** Northern, NE Zambia
177 F4 **Chin State** ◐ state W Burma
Chinsura see Chunchura
Chin-tō see Chin-do
56 E6 **Chinú** Córdoba, NW Colombia
101 K24 **Chiny, Forêt de** forest SE Belgium
85 M15 **Chioco** Tete, NW Mozambique
108 H8 **Chioggia** anc. Fossa Claudia. Veneto, NE Italy
116 H12 **Chionótrypa** ▲ NE Greece
117 L18 **Chíos** var. Hios, Khíos, It. Scio, Turk. Sakiz-Adasi. Chíos, E Greece
117 K18 **Chíos** var. Khíos. island E Greece
85 M14 **Chipata** prev. Fort Jameson. Eastern, E Zambia
85 C14 **Chipindo** Huíla, C Angola
25 R8 **Chipley** Florida, SE USA
161 D15 **Chiplūn** Mahārāshtra, W India
83 H22 **Chipogolo** Dodoma, C Tanzania
25 R8 **Chipola River** ≈ Florida, SE USA
xxxix U12 **Chippenham** Cambridgeshire, E England, UK
xxxvi M9 **Chippenham** Wiltshire, S England, UK
32 J6 **Chippewa Falls** Wisconsin, N USA
32 J4 **Chippewa, Lake** ▣ Wisconsin, N USA
33 Q8 **Chippewa River** ≈ Michigan, N USA
32 I6 **Chippewa River** ≈ Wisconsin, N USA
xxxvii N6 **Chipping Campden** Gloucestershire, C England, UK
xxxvii O7 **Chipping Norton** Oxfordshire, C England, UK
xxxvii V8 **Chipping Ongar** Essex, SE England, UK
xxxvi M9 **Chipping Sodbury** South Gloucestershire, SW England, UK
Chipping Wycombe see High Wycombe
116 G8 **Chiprovtsi** Montana, NW Bulgaria
21 T4 **Chiputneticook Lakes** lakes Canada/USA
58 D13 **Chiquián** Ancash, W Peru
43 Y11 **Chiquilá** Quintana Roo, SE Mexico
44 E6 **Chiquimula** Chiquimula, SE Guatemala
44 A3 **Chiquimula** off. Departamento de Chiquimula. ◐ department SE Guatemala
44 D7 **Chiquimulilla** Santa Rosa, S Guatemala
56 F9 **Chiquinquirá** Boyacá, C Colombia
161 J17 **Chīrāla** Andhra Pradesh, E India
155 N4 **Chīras** Ghowr, N Afghanistan
158 H11 **Chirāwa** Rājasthān, N India
xxxviii G10 **Chirbury** Shropshire, W England, UK
Chirchik see Chirchiq
153 Q9 **Chirchiq** Rus. Chirchik. Toshkent Wiloyati, E Uzbekistan
153 P10 **Chirchiq** ≈ E Uzbekistan
Chire see Shire
85 L18 **Chiredzi** Masvingo, SE Zimbabwe
26 K8 **Chireno** Texas, SW USA
79 X7 **Chirfa** Agadez, NE Niger
39 O16 **Chiricahua Mountains** ▲▲ Arizona, SW USA
39 O16 **Chiricahua Peak** ▲ Arizona, SW USA
56 F6 **Chiriguaná** Cesar, N Colombia
41 P15 **Chirikof Island** island Alaska, USA
45 P16 **Chiriquí** off. Provincia de Chiriquí. ◐ province SW Panama
45 P17 **Chiriquí, Golfo de** Eng. Chiriqui Gulf. gulf SW Panama
45 P15 **Chiriquí Grande** Bocas del Toro, W Panama
Chiriqui Gulf see Chiriquí, Golfo de
45 P15 **Chiriquí, Laguna de** lagoon NW Panama
45 O16 **Chiriquí Viejo, Río** ≈ W Panama
Chiriquí, Volcán de see Barú, Volcán
xxxv K6 **Chirk** Wrexham, NE Wales, UK
xliii P20 **Chirnside** The Borders, S Scotland, UK
85 N15 **Chiromo** Southern, S Malawi
116 J10 **Chirpan** Khaskovska Oblast, C Bulgaria
45 N14 **Chirripó Atlántico, Río** ≈ E Costa Rica
Chirripó, Cerro see Chirripó Grande, Cerro
45 N14 **Chirripó Grande, Cerro** var. Cerro Chirripó. ▲ SE Costa Rica
45 N13 **Chirripó, Río** var. Río Chirripó del Pacífico. ≈ NE Costa Rica
Chirua, Lago see Chilwa, Lake
85 J15 **Chirundu** Southern, S Zambia
31 W8 **Chisago City** Minnesota, N USA
85 J14 **Chisamba** Central, C Zambia
41 T10 **Chisana** Alaska, USA
84 I13 **Chisasa** North Western, NW Zambia
10 I9 **Chisasibi** Québec, C Canada
44 D4 **Chisec** Alta Verapaz, C Guatemala
131 U5 **Chishmy** Respublika Bashkortostan, W Russian Federation

Chisholm – Clayton

31 V4 **Chisholm** Minnesota, N USA
155 U10 **Chishtiān Mandi** Punjab, E Pakistan
166 I11 **Chishui He** ≈ C China
Chisimaio/Chisimayu *see* Kismaayo
119 N10 **Chişinău** *Rus.* Kishinev. ● (Moldavia) C Moldavia
119 N10 **Chişinău** ✕ S Moldavia
Chişinău-Criş *see* Chişineu-Criş
118 F10 **Chişineu-Criş** *Hung.* Kişjenő; *prev.* Chişinău-Criş. Arad, W Romania
85 K14 **Chisomo** Central, C Zambia
108 A8 **Chisone** ≈ NW Italy
26 K12 **Chisos Mountains** ▲▲ Texas, SW USA
41 T10 **Chistochina** Alaska, USA
131 R4 **Chistopol'** Respublika Tatarstan, W Russian Federation
151 O8 **Chistopol'ye** Kokshetau, N Kazakhstan
xxxvi B8 **Chiswick** Hounslow, SE England, UK
126 Kk16 **Chita** Chitinskaya Oblast', S Russian Federation
85 B16 **Chitado** Cunene, SW Angola
Chitaldroog/Chitaldrug *see* Chitradurga
85 C15 **Chitanda** ≈ S Angola
Chitangwiza *see* Chitungwiza
84 F10 **Chitato** Lunda Norte, NE Angola
85 C14 **Chitembo** Bié, C Angola
41 T11 **Chitina** Alaska, USA
41 T11 **Chitina River** ≈ Alaska, USA
126 Kk14 **Chitinskaya Oblast'** ◈ *province* S Russian Federation
84 M11 **Chitipa** Northern, NW Malawi
172 Oo6 **Chitose** *var.* Titose. Hokkaidō, NE Japan
161 G18 **Chitradurga** *prev.* Chitaldroog, Chitaldrug. Karnātaka, W India
155 T3 **Chitrāl** North-West Frontier Province, NW Pakistan
45 S16 **Chitré** Herrera, S Panama
159 V16 **Chittagong** *Ben.* Chāttagām. Chittagong, SE Bangladesh
159 U16 **Chittagong** ◈ *division* E Bangladesh
159 Q15 **Chittaranjan** West Bengal, NE India
158 G14 **Chittaurgarh** Rājasthān, N India
xxxvii N11 **Chitterne** Wiltshire, S England, UK
xxxvi G12 **Chittlehampton** Devon, SW England, UK
161 I19 **Chittoor** Andhra Pradesh, E India
161 G21 **Chittūr** Kerala, SW India
85 K16 **Chitungwiza** *prev.* Chitangwiza. Mashonaland East, NE Zimbabwe
64 H4 **Chíuchíu** Antofagasta, N Chile
84 F12 **Chiumbe** *var.* Tshiumbe. ≈ Angola/Zaire
85 F15 **Chiume** Moxico, E Angola
84 K13 **Chiundaponde** Northern, NE Zambia
108 H13 **Chiusi** Toscana, C Italy
56 J5 **Chivacoa** Yaracuy, N Venezuela
108 B8 **Chivasso** Piemonte, NW Italy
85 L17 **Chivhu** *prev.* Enkeldoorn. Midlands, C Zimbabwe
63 C20 **Chivilcoy** Buenos Aires, E Argentina
84 N12 **Chiweta** Northern, N Malawi
44 D4 **Chixoy, Río** *var.* Río Negro, Río Salinas. ≈ Guatemala/Mexico
84 H13 **Chizela** North Western, NW Zambia
129 O5 **Chizha** Nenetskiy Avtonomnyy Okrug, NW Russian Federation
170 G13 **Chizu** Tottori, Honshū, SW Japan
Chkalov *see* Orenburg
76 J5 **Chlef** *var.* Ech Cheliff, Ech Chleff; *prev.* Al-Asnam, El Asnam, Orléansville. NW Algeria
117 G18 **Chlómo** ▲ C Greece
113 M15 **Chmielnik** Kielce, S Poland
178 J11 **Chŏâm Khsant** Preăh Vihéar, N Cambodia
64 G10 **Choapa, Río** *var.* Choapo. ≈ C Chile
Choapas *see* Las Choapas
Choarta *see* Chwārtā
85 H17 **Chobe** ◈ *district* NE Botswana
69 T13 **Chobe** ≈ N Botswana
xxxvii S10 **Chobham** Surrey, SE England, UK
12 K8 **Chochocouane** ≈ Québec, SE Canada
112 E13 **Chocianów** *Ger.* Kotzenan. Legnica, SW Poland
56 C9 **Chocó** *off.* Departamento del Chocó. ◈ *province* W Colombia
37 X16 **Chocolate Mountains** ▲▲ California, W USA
23 W9 **Chocowinity** North Carolina, SE USA
29 N10 **Choctaw** Oklahoma, C USA
25 Q8 **Choctawhatchee Bay** *bay* Florida, SE USA
25 Q8 **Choctawhatchee River** ≈ Florida, SE USA
Chodau *see* Chodov
169 V14 **Chŏ-do** *island* SW North Korea
Chodorów *see* Khodoriv
113 A16 **Chodov** *Ger.* Chodau. Západní Čechy, W Czech Republic
112 G10 **Chodzież** Piła, NW Poland
65 J15 **Choele Choel** Río Negro, C Argentina
85 L14 **Chofombo** Tete, NW Mozambique
Chohtan *see* Chauhtan
9 U14 **Choiceland** Saskatchewan, C Canada
xlii J8 **Choire, Loch** ◎ NW Scotland, UK
195 U13 **Choiseul** *var.* Lauru. *island* NW Solomon Islands
65 M23 **Choiseul Sound** *sound* East Falkland, Falkland Islands
42 H7 **Choix** Sinaloa, C Mexico
112 D10 **Chojna** Szczecin, W Poland
112 H8 **Chojnice** *Ger.* Konitz. Bydgoszcz, NW Poland
113 F14 **Chojnów** *Ger.* Hainau, Haynau. Legnica, W Poland
171 Ll11 **Chōkai-san** ▲ Honshū, C Japan
178 I11 **Chok Chai** Nakhon Ratchasima, C Thailand
82 I12 **Ch'ok'ē** *var.* Choke Mountains. ▲▲ NW Ethiopia
27 R13 **Choke Canyon Lake** ⊠ Texas, SW USA
Choke Mountains *see* Ch'ok'ē
151 T15 **Chokpar** *Kaz.* Shoqpar. Zhambyl, S Kazakhstan
153 W7 **Chok-Tal** *var.* Choktal. Issyk-Kul'skaya Oblast', E Kyrgyzstan
Chókué *see* Chokwé
126 Mm6 **Chokurdakh** Respublika Sakha (Yakutiya), NE Russian Federation
85 L20 **Chokwé** *var.* Chókué. Gaza, S Mozambique
196 F8 **Chol** Babeldaob, N Palau
166 E8 **Chola Shan** ▲▲ C China
xxxvii O11 **Cholderton** Wiltshire, S England, UK
104 J8 **Cholet** Maine-et-Loire, NW France
65 H17 **Cholila** Chubut, W Argentina
xli P6 **Chollerford** Northumberland, N England, UK
xli P6 **Chollerton** Northumberland, N England, UK
Cholo *see* Thyolo
153 V8 **Cholpon** Narynskaya Oblast', C Kyrgyzstan
153 X7 **Cholpon-Ata** Issyk-Kul'skaya Oblast', E Kyrgyzstan
xxxvii Q9 **Cholsey** Oxfordshire, C England, UK
43 P14 **Cholula** Puebla, S Mexico
44 I8 **Choluteca** Choluteca, S Honduras
44 H8 **Choluteca** ◈ *department* S Honduras
44 G6 **Choluteca, Río** ≈ SW Honduras
85 I15 **Choma** Southern, S Zambia
159 T11 **Chomo Lhari** ▲ NW Bhutan
178 H7 **Chom Thong** Chiang Mai, NW Thailand
113 B15 **Chomutov** *Ger.* Komotau. Severní Čechy, NW Czech Republic
126 K12 **Chona** ≈ C Russian Federation
169 X15 **Ch'ŏnan** *Jap.* Tenan. W South Korea
178 Hh12 **Chon Buri** *prev.* Bang Pla Soi. Chon Buri, S Thailand
58 B6 **Chone** Manabí, W Ecuador
169 W13 **Ch'ŏngch'ŏn-gang** ≈ W North Korea
169 Y11 **Ch'ŏngjin** NE North Korea
169 W13 **Chŏngju** W North Korea
167 S8 **Chongming Dao** *island* E China
166 J10 **Chongqing** *var.* Ch'ung-ching, Ch'ung-ch'ing, Chungking, Pahsien, Tchongking, Yuzhou. Sichuan, C China
166 J10 **Chongqing Shi** *var.* Chongqing, Chungking ◈ *municipality* C China
Chŏngup *see* Chŏnju
167 O10 **Chongyang** Hubei, C China
169 Y16 **Chŏnju** *prev.* Chŏngup, *Jap.* Seiyu. SW South Korea
169 Y15 **Chŏnju** *Jap.* Zenshū. SW South Korea
Chonnacht *see* Connaught
169 Q9 **Chonogol** Sühbaatar, E Mongolia
65 F19 **Chonos, Archipiélago de los** *island group* S Chile
44 K10 **Chontales** ◈ *department* S Nicaragua
178 Jj14 **Chơn Thanh** Sông Be, S Vietnam
164 K17 **Cho Oyu** *var.* Qowowuyag. ▲ China/Nepal *see also* Qowowuyag
118 G7 **Chop** *Cz.* Čop, *Hung.* Csap. Zakarpats'ka Oblast', W Ukraine
23 Y3 **Choptank River** ≈ Maryland, NE USA
xli Q7 **Chopwell** Gateshead, NE England, UK
Chorcaí, Cuan *see* Cork Harbour
45 P15 **Chorcha, Cerro** ▲ W Panama
Chorku *see* Chorkŭh
153 R11 **Chorkŭh** *Rus.* Chorku. N Tajikistan
xli N15 **Chorley** Lancashire, NW England, UK
Chorne More *see* Black Sea
119 R5 **Chornobay** Cherkas'ka Oblast', C Ukraine
119 O3 **Chornobyl'** *Rus.* Chernobyl'. Kyyivs'ka Oblast', N Ukraine
119 R12 **Chornomors'ke** *Rus.* Chernomorskoye. Respublika Krym, S Ukraine
119 R4 **Chornukhy** Poltavs'ka Oblast', C Ukraine
Chorokh/Chorokhi *see* Çoruh Nehri
112 O9 **Choroszcz** Białystok, NE Poland
118 K6 **Chortkiv** *Rus.* Chortkov. Ternopil's'ka Oblast', W Ukraine
Chortkov *see* Chortkiv
Chorum *see* Çorum
112 M9 **Chorzele** Ostrołęka, NE Poland
113 J16 **Chorzów** *Ger.* Königshütte; *prev.* Królewska Huta. Katowice, S Poland
169 W12 **Ch'osan** N North Korea
Chōsen-kaikyō *see* Korea Strait
171 Kk17 **Chōshi** *var.* Tyôsi. Chiba, Honshū, S Japan
65 H14 **Chos Malal** Neuquén, W Argentina
Chosŏn-minjujuŭi-inmin-kanghwaguk *see* North Korea
112 E9 **Choszczno** *Ger.* Arnswalde. Gorzów, W Poland
159 O15 **Chota Nāgpur** *plateau* N India
35 R8 **Choteau** Montana, NW USA
Chotqol *see* Chatkal
12 M8 **Chouart** ≈ Québec, SE Canada
78 I7 **Choûm** Adrar, C Mauritania
29 Q9 **Chouteau** Oklahoma, C USA
23 X8 **Chowan River** ≈ North Carolina, SE USA
37 Q10 **Chowchilla** California, W USA
169 P7 **Choybalsan** Dornod, E Mongolia
168 M9 **Choyr** Dornogovĭ, C Mongolia
xxxix T10 **Christchurch** Cambridgeshire, E England, UK
xxxvii O14 **Christchurch** Dorset, S England, UK
193 I19 **Christchurch** Canterbury, South Island, NZ
193 I18 **Christchurch** ✕ Canterbury, South Island, NZ
46 J12 **Christiana** C Jamaica
85 H22 **Christiana** Free State, C South Africa
117 J23 **Christiáni** *island* Kykládes, Greece, Aegean Sea
Christiania *see* Oslo
12 G13 **Christian Island** *island* Ontario, S Canada
203 P16 **Christian, Point** *headland* Pitcairn Island, Pitcairn Islands
40 M11 **Christian River** ≈ Alaska, USA
Christiansand *see* Kristiansand
23 S7 **Christiansburg** Virginia, NE USA
97 G23 **Christiansfeld** Sønderjylland, SW Denmark
Christianshåb *see* Qasigiannguit
41 X14 **Christian Sound** *inlet* Alaska, USA
47 T9 **Christiansted** Saint Croix, S Virgin Islands (US)
Christiansund *see* Kristiansund
27 R13 **Christine** Texas, SW USA
181 U7 **Christmas Island** ◇ *Australian external territory* E Indian Ocean
133 T17 **Christmas Island** *island* E Indian Ocean
Christmas Island *see* Kiritimati
199 K8 **Christmas Ridge** *undersea feature* C Pacific Ocean
32 L16 **Christopher** Illinois, N USA
27 P9 **Christoval** Texas, SW USA
113 F17 **Chrudim** Východní Čechy, C Czech Republic
117 K25 **Chrýsi** *island* SE Greece
123 Mm3 **Chrysochoú, Kólpos** *var.* Khrysokhou Bay. *bay* E Mediterranean Sea
116 I13 **Chrysoúpoli** *var.* Hrisoupoli; *prev.* Khrisoúpolis. Anatolikí Makedonía kai Thráki, NE Greece
113 K16 **Chrzanów** *var.* Chrzanow, *Ger.* Zaumgarten. Katowice, S Poland
133 Q7 **Chu** *Kaz.* Shū. ≈ Kazakhstan/Kyrgyzstan
44 C5 **Chuacús, Sierra de** ▲▲ W Guatemala
159 S15 **Chuadanga** Khulna, W Bangladesh
Chuan *see* Sichuan
Ch'uan-chou *see* Quanzhou
41 O11 **Chuathbaluk** Alaska, USA
194 I12 **Chuave** Chimbu, W PNG
Chubek *see* Moskva
65 I17 **Chubut** *off.* Provincia de Chubut. ◈ *province* S Argentina
65 I17 **Chubut, Río** ≈ SE Argentina
45 V15 **Chucanti, Cerro** ▲ E Panama
Ch'u-chiang *see* Shaoguan
45 W15 **Chucunaque, Río** ≈ E Panama
Chudin *see* Chudzin
xxxvi H14 **Chudleigh** Devon, SW England, UK
118 M5 **Chudniv** Zhytomyrs'ka Oblast', N Ukraine
128 H13 **Chudovo** Novgorodskaya Oblast', W Russian Federation
Chudskoye Ozero *see* Peipus, Lake
121 J18 **Chudzin** *Rus.* Chudin. Brestskaya Voblasts', SW Belorussia
41 Q13 **Chugach Islands** *island group* Alaska, USA
41 S11 **Chugach Mountains** ▲▲ Alaska, USA
170 Ee12 **Chūgoku-sanchi** ▲▲ Honshū, SW Japan
Chuguyev *see* Chuhuyiv
119 V5 **Chuhuyiv** *var.* Chuguyev. Kharkivs'ka Oblast', E Ukraine
63 H19 **Chuí** Rio Grande do Sul, S Brazil
Chuí *see* Chuy
151 S15 **Chu-Iliyskiye Gory** *Kaz.* Shū-Ile Taūlary. ▲▲ S Kazakhstan
Chukai *see* Cukai
Chukchi Avtonomnyy Okrug *see* Chukotskiy Avtonomnyy Okrug
Chukchi Peninsula *see* Chukotskiy Poluostrov
207 R6 **Chukchi Plain** *undersea feature* Arctic Ocean
207 R6 **Chukchi Plateau** *undersea feature* Arctic Ocean
207 R4 **Chukchi Sea** *Rus.* Chukotskoye More. *sea* Arctic Ocean
129 N14 **Chukhloma** Kostromskaya Oblast', NW Russian Federation
Chukotka *see* Chukotskiy Avtonomnyy Okrug
Chukot Range *see* Anadyrskiy Khrebet
127 Oo5 **Chukotskiy Avtonomnyy Okrug** *var.* Chukchi Avtonomnyy Okrug, Chukotka. ◈ *autonomous district* NE Russian Federation
127 Q4 **Chukotskiy, Mys** *headland* NE Russian Federation
127 Pp4 **Chukotskiy Poluostrov** *Eng.* Chukchi Peninsula. *peninsula* NE Russian Federation
Chukotskoye More *see* Chukchi Sea
Chukurkak *see* Chuqurqoq
151 P15 **Chulakkurgan** Yuzhnyy Kazakhstan, S Kazakhstan
37 U17 **Chula Vista** California, W USA
126 Ll13 **Chul'man** Respublika Sakha (Yakutiya), NE Russian Federation
xxxvi G13 **Chulmleigh** Devon, SW England, UK
58 B9 **Chulucanas** Piura, NW Peru
126 Gg14 **Chulym** Novosibirskaya Oblast', C Russian Federation
126 H13 **Chulym** ≈ C Russian Federation
158 K6 **Chumar** Jammu and Kashmir, N India
116 K9 **Chumerna** ▲ C Bulgaria
127 N13 **Chumikan** Khabarovskiy Kray, E Russian Federation
178 I9 **Chum Phae** Khon Kaen, C Thailand
178 Gg14 **Chumphon** *var.* Jumporn. Chumphon, SW Thailand
178 Hh10 **Chumsaeng** *var.* Chum Saeng. Nakhon Sawan, C Thailand
126 H14 **Chumysh** ≈ S Russian Federation
126 Ii13 **Chuna** ≈ C Russian Federation
167 R9 **Chun'an** *var.* Pailing. Zhejiang, SE China
167 S13 **Chunan** N Taiwan
169 Y14 **Ch'unch'ŏn** *Jap.* Shunsen. N South Korea
159 S16 **Chunchura** *prev.* Chinsura. West Bengal, NE India
151 W15 **Chundzha** Almaty, SE Kazakhstan
Ch'ung-ch'ing/Ch'ung-ching *see* Chongqing
Chung-hua Jen-min Kung-ho-kuo *see* China
169 Y15 **Ch'ungju** *Jap.* Chūshū. C South Korea
Chungking *see* Chongqing, Chongqing Shi
167 T14 **Chungyang Shanmo** *Chin.* Taiwan Shan. ▲▲ C Taiwan
155 V9 **Chūniān** Punjab, E Pakistan
126 Ii14 **Chunskiy** Irkutskaya Oblast', S Russian Federation
126 J11 **Chunya** ≈ C Russian Federation
128 J6 **Chupa** Respublika Kareliya, NW Russian Federation
129 P8 **Chuprovo** Respublika Komi, NW Russian Federation
59 G17 **Chuquibamba** Arequipa, SW Peru
64 H4 **Chuquicamata** Antofagasta, N Chile
59 L21 **Chuquisaca** ◈ *department* S Bolivia
Chuquisaca *see* Sucre
152 I8 **Chuqurqoq** *Rus.* Chukurkak. Qoraqalpoghiston Respublikasi, NW Uzbekistan
131 T2 **Chur** Udmurtskaya Respublika, NW Russian Federation
110 I9 **Chur** *Fr.* Coire, *It.* Coira, *Rmsch.* Cuera, Quera; *anc.* Curia Rhaetorum. Graubünden, E Switzerland
126 M11 **Churapcha** Respublika Sakha (Yakutiya), NE Russian Federation
9 V16 **Churchbridge** Saskatchewan, S Canada
xxxvi M7 **Churchdown** Gloucestershire, C England, UK
xxxviii J9 **Church Eaton** Staffordshire, C England, UK
xli T14 **Church Fenton** North Yorkshire, N England, UK
23 O8 **Church Hill** Tennessee, S USA
9 X9 **Churchill** Manitoba, C Canada
9 X10 **Churchill** ≈ Manitoba/Saskatchewan, C Canada
11 P9 **Churchill** ≈ Newfoundland and Labrador, E Canada
9 Y9 **Churchill, Cape** *headland* Manitoba, C Canada
11 P9 **Churchill Falls** Newfoundland and Labrador, E Canada
9 S12 **Churchill Lake** ◎ Saskatchewan, C Canada
21 Q3 **Churchill Lake** ⊠ Maine, NE USA
204 I5 **Churchill Peninsula** *peninsula* Antarctica
xxxviii H6 **Church Minshull** Cheshire, W England, UK
24 H8 **Church Point** Louisiana, S USA
31 O3 **Churchs Ferry** North Dakota, N USA
xxxv K9 **Church Stoke** Powys, C Wales, UK
xxxviii H10 **Church Stretton** Shropshire, W England, UK
xliv K13 **Churchtown** Wexford, SE Ireland
xliv J13 **Churchtown** Wexford, SE Ireland
152 G12 **Churchuri** Akhalskiy Velayat, C Turkmenistan
23 T5 **Churchville** Virginia, NE USA
158 G10 **Chūru** Rājasthān, NW India
56 J4 **Churuguara** Falcón, N Venezuela
150 J12 **Chushkakul, Gory** ▲▲ SW Kazakhstan
Chūshū *see* Ch'ungju
39 O9 **Chuska Mountains** ▲▲ Arizona/New Mexico, SW USA
Chu, Sông *see* Sam, Nam
125 Ee11 **Chusovaya** ≈ W Russian Federation
129 V14 **Chusovoy** Permskaya Oblast', NW Russian Federation
153 R10 **Chust** Namangan Wiloyati, E Uzbekistan
Chust *see* Khust
13 U6 **Chute-aux-Outardes** Québec, SE Canada
119 U5 **Chutove** Poltavs'ka Oblast', C Ukraine
201 O15 **Chuuk** *var.* Truk. ◈ *state* C Micronesia
201 P15 **Chuuk Islands** *var.* Hogoley Islands; *prev.* Truk Islands. *island group* Caroline Islands, C Micronesia
Chuvashia *see* Chuvashskaya Respublika
131 P4 **Chuvashskaya Respublika** *var.* Chavash Respubliki, *Eng.* Chuvashia. ◈ *autonomous republic* W Russian Federation
Chuwārtah *see* Chwārtā
Chu Xian/Chuxian *see* Chuzhou
166 G13 **Chuxiong** Yunnan, SW China
153 V7 **Chuy** Chuyskaya Oblast', N Kyrgyzstan
63 H19 **Chuy** *var.* Chuí. Rocha, E Uruguay
126 K12 **Chuya** Respublika Sakha (Yakutiya), NE Russian Federation
Chüy Oblasty *see* Chuyskaya Oblast'
153 U8 **Chuyskaya Oblast'** *Kir.* Chüy Oblasty. ◈ *province* N Kyrgyzstan
167 Q7 **Chuzhou** *var.* Chuxian, Chu Xian. Anhui, E China
145 U3 **Chwārtā** *var.* Choarta, Chuwārtah. NE Iraq
xxxv F6 **Chwilog** Gwynedd, NW Wales, UK
121 N16 **Chyhirynskaye Vodaskhovishcha** ⊠ E Belorussia
119 R6 **Chyhyryn** *Rus.* Chigirin. Cherkas'ka Oblast', N Ukraine
Chyrvonaya Slabada *see* Krasnaya Slabada
121 L19 **Chyrvonaye, Vozyera** *Rus.* Ozero Chervonoye. ◎ SE Belorussia
178 K12 **Ch, Srê** Gia Lai, C Vietnam
119 N11 **Ciadîr-Lunga** *var.* Ceadâr-Lunga, *Rus.* Chadyr-Lunga. S Moldavia
174 K15 **Ciamis** *prev.* Tjiamis. Jawa, C Indonesia
174 J14 **Cianjur** *prev.* Tjiandjoer. Jawa, C Indonesia
62 H10 **Cianorte** Paraná, S Brazil
Ciarraí *see* Kerry
114 N13 **Ćićevac** Serbia, E Yugoslavia
197 K14 **Cicia** *prev.* Thithia. *island* Lau Group, E Fiji
107 P4 **Cidacos** ≈ N Spain
142 I10 **Cide** Kastamonu, N Turkey
112 L10 **Ciechanów** *prev.* Zichenau. Ciechanów, C Poland
112 L10 **Ciechanów** *off.* Województwo Ciechanowskie. ◈ *province* C Poland
112 O10 **Ciechanowiec** *Ger.* Rudelstadt. Łomża, E Poland
Ciechanowskie, Województwo *see* Ciechanów
112 J10 **Ciechocinek** Włocławek, C Poland
46 F6 **Ciego de Ávila** Ciego de Ávila, C Cuba
56 F4 **Ciénaga** Magdalena, N Colombia
56 E6 **Ciénaga de Oro** Córdoba, NW Colombia
46 E5 **Cienfuegos** Cienfuegos, C Cuba
106 F4 **Cíes, Illas** *island group* NW Spain
113 P16 **Cieszanów** Przemyśl, SE Poland
113 J17 **Cieszyn** *Cz.* Těšín, *Ger.* Teschen. Bielsko-Biała, S Poland
107 R12 **Cieza** Murcia, SE Spain
142 F13 **Çifteler** Eskişehir, W Turkey
107 P7 **Cifuentes** Castilla-La Mancha, C Spain
Čiganak *see* Chiganak
107 P9 **Cigüela** ≈ C Spain
142 H14 **Cihanbeyli** Konya, C Turkey
142 H14 **Cihanbeyli Yaylası** *plateau* C Turkey
106 L10 **Cíjara, Embalse de** ⊠ C Spain
174 K15 **Cikalong** Jawa, S Indonesia
174 Ii14 **Cikawung** Jawa, S Indonesia
197 K12 **Cikobia** *prev.* Thikombia. *island* N Fiji
174 K15 **Cilacap** *prev.* Tjilatjap. Jawa, C Indonesia
181 O16 **Cilaos** C Réunion
xxxv J5 **Cilcain** Flintshire, N Wales, UK
xxxv G11 **Cilcennin** Ceredigion, W Wales, UK
143 S11 **Çıldır** Kars, NE Turkey
143 S11 **Çıldır Gölü** ◎ NE Turkey
174 K14 **Ciledug** *prev.* Tjiledoeg. Jawa, SW Indonesia
xxxv E12 **Cilgerran** Pembrokeshire, SW Wales, UK
166 M10 **Cili** Hunan, S China
124 R12 **Cilicia Trough** *undersea feature* E Mediterranean Sea
Cill Airne *see* Killarney
Cill Chainnigh *see* Kilkenny
Cill Chaoi *see* Kilkee
Cill Choca *see* Kilcock
Cill Dara *see* Kildare
107 N3 **Cilleruelo de Bezana** Castilla-León, N Spain
Cilli *see* Celje
Cill Mhantáin *see* Wicklow
Cill Rois *see* Kilrush
xxxv H12 **Cilycwm** Carmarthenshire, S Wales, UK
28 J6 **Cimarron** Kansas, C USA
39 T9 **Cimarron** New Mexico, SW USA
28 M9 **Cimarron River** ≈ Kansas/Oklahoma, C USA
119 N11 **Cimişlia** *Rus.* Chimishliya. S Moldavia
Cîmpia Turzii *see* Câmpia Turzii
Cîmpina *see* Câmpina
Cîmpulung *see* Câmpulung
Cîmpulung Moldovenesc *see* Câmpulung Moldovenesc
143 P15 **Çınar** Dıyarbakır, SE Turkey
56 J8 **Cinaruco, Río** ≈ Colombia/Venezuela
Cina Selatan, Laut *see* South China Sea
107 T5 **Cinca** ≈ NE Spain
114 G13 **Cincar** ▲ SW Bosnia and Herzegovina
33 Q15 **Cincinnati** Ohio, N USA
22 M4 **Cincinnati** ✕ Kentucky, S USA
Cinco de Outubro *see* Xá-Muteba
xxxvi L7 **Cinderford** Gloucestershire, C England, UK
142 C15 **Çine** Aydın, SW Turkey
101 J21 **Ciney** Namur, SE Belgium
106 H6 **Cinfães** Viseu, N Portugal
108 J12 **Cingoli** Marche, C Italy
43 U16 **Cintalapa** *var.* Cintalapa de Figueroa. Chiapas, SE Mexico
Cintalapa de Figueroa *see* Cintalapa
104 E1 **Cinto, Monte** ▲ Corse, France, C Mediterranean Sea
Cintra *see* Sintra
107 Q5 **Cintruénigo** Navarra, N Spain
Cionn tSáile *see* Kinsale
118 K13 **Ciorani** Prahova, SE Romania
115 E14 **Čiovo** *It.* Bua. *island* S Croatia
174 J14 **Cipanas** Jawa, S Indonesia
Cipiúr *see* Kippure
65 I15 **Cipolletti** Río Negro, C Argentina
123 L8 **Circeo, Capo** *headland* C Italy
41 S8 **Circle** *var.* Circle City. Alaska, USA
35 X8 **Circle** Montana, NW USA
Circle City *see* Circle
33 S14 **Circleville** Ohio, N USA
38 K6 **Circleville** Utah, W USA
174 K14 **Cirebon** *prev.* Tjirebon. Jawa, S Indonesia
xxxvii N8 **Cirencester** *anc.* Corinium, Corinium Dobunorum. Gloucestershire, C England, UK
Cirkvenica *see* Crikvenica
109 O20 **Ciro** Calabria, SW Italy
109 O20 **Cirò Marina** Calabria, S Italy
104 K14 **Ciron** ≈ SW France
Cirquenizza *see* Crikvenica
27 R7 **Cisco** Texas, SW USA
118 I12 **Cisnădie** *Ger.* Heltau, *Hung.* Nagydisznód. Sibiu, SW Romania
65 G18 **Cisnes, Río** ≈ S Chile
27 T11 **Cistern** Texas, SW USA
106 L3 **Cistierna** Castilla-León, N Spain
174 Ii14 **Citeureup** Jawa, S Indonesia
Citharista *see* la Ciotat
Citlaltépetl *see* Orizaba, Volcán Pico de
57 X10 **Citron** NW French Guiana
25 N7 **Citronelle** Alabama, S USA
37 O7 **Citrus Heights** California, W USA
108 H7 **Cittadella** Veneto, NE Italy
108 H13 **Città della Pieve** Umbria, C Italy
108 H12 **Città di Castello** Umbria, C Italy
109 I14 **Cittaducale** Lazio, C Italy
109 N22 **Cittanova** Calabria, SW Italy
Cittavecchia *see* Starigrad
118 G10 **Ciucea** *Hung.* Csucsa. Cluj, NW Romania
118 M13 **Ciucurova** Tulcea, SE Romania
43 N5 **Ciudad Acuña** *var.* Villa Acuña. Coahuila de Zaragoza, NE Mexico
43 N15 **Ciudad Altamirano** Guerrero, S Mexico
44 G7 **Ciudad Barrios** San Miguel, NE El Salvador
56 I7 **Ciudad Bolívar** Barinas, NW Venezuela
57 N7 **Ciudad Bolívar** *prev.* Angostura. Bolívar, E Venezuela
42 K6 **Ciudad Camargo** Chihuahua, N Mexico
42 E8 **Ciudad Constitución** Baja California Sur, W Mexico
Ciudad Cortés *see* Cortés
43 V17 **Ciudad Cuauhtémoc** Chiapas, SE Mexico
44 J9 **Ciudad Darío** *var.* Dario. Matagalpa, W Nicaragua
Ciudad de Dolores Hidalgo *see* Dolores Hidalgo
44 C6 **Ciudad de Guatemala** *Eng.* Guatemala City; *prev.* Santiago de los Caballeros. ● (Guatemala) Guatemala, C Guatemala
Ciudad del Carmen *see* Carmen
64 Q6 **Ciudad del Este** *prev.* Cuidad Presidente Stroessner, Presidente Stroessner, Puerto Presidente Stroessner. Alto Paraná, SE Paraguay
64 K5 **Ciudad de Libertador General San Martín** *var.* Libertador General San Martín. Jujuy, C Argentina
Ciudad Delicias *see* Delicias
43 O11 **Ciudad del Maíz** San Luis Potosí, C Mexico
Ciudad de México *see* México
56 J7 **Ciudad de Nutrias** Barinas, NW Venezuela
Ciudad de Panamá *see* Panamá
57 P7 **Ciudad Guayana** *prev.* San Tomé de Guayana, Santo Tomé de Guayana. Bolívar, NE Venezuela
42 K14 **Ciudad Guzmán** Jalisco, SW Mexico
43 V17 **Ciudad Hidalgo** Chiapas, SE Mexico
43 N14 **Ciudad Hidalgo** Michoacán de Ocampo, SW Mexico
42 J3 **Ciudad Juárez** Chihuahua, N Mexico
42 L8 **Ciudad Lerdo** Durango, C Mexico
43 Q11 **Ciudad Madero** *var.* Villa Cecilia. Tamaulipas, C Mexico
43 P11 **Ciudad Mante** Tamaulipas, C Mexico
44 F2 **Ciudad Melchor de Mencos** *var.* Melchor de Mencos. Petén, NE Guatemala
43 P8 **Ciudad Miguel Alemán** Tamaulipas, C Mexico
Ciudad Mutis *see* Bahía Solano
42 G6 **Ciudad Obregón** Sonora, NW Mexico
56 I5 **Ciudad Ojeda** Zulia, NW Venezuela
57 P7 **Ciudad Piar** Bolívar, E Venezuela
Ciudad Porfirio Díaz *see* Piedras Negras
Ciudad Quesada *see* Quesada
107 N11 **Ciudad Real** Castilla-La Mancha, C Spain
107 N11 **Ciudad Real** ◈ *province* Castilla-La Mancha, C Spain
106 J7 **Ciudad-Rodrigo** Castilla-León, N Spain
44 A6 **Ciudad Tecún Umán** San Marcos, SW Guatemala
Ciudad Trujillo *see* Santo Domingo
43 P12 **Ciudad Valles** San Luis Potosí, C Mexico
43 O10 **Ciudad Victoria** Tamaulipas, C Mexico
44 C6 **Ciudad Vieja** Suchitepéquez, S Guatemala
118 L8 **Ciuhuru** *var.* Reuţel. ≈ N Moldavia
Ciutadella *see* Ciutadella de Menorca
107 Z8 **Ciutadella de Menorca** *var.* Ciutadella. Menorca, Spain, W Mediterranean Sea
142 L11 **Civa Burnu** *headland* N Turkey
108 J7 **Cividale del Friuli** Friuli-Venezia Giulia, NE Italy
109 H14 **Civita Castellana** Lazio, C Italy
108 J12 **Civitanova Marche** Marche, C Italy
Civitas Altae Ripae *see* Brzeg
Civitas Carnutum *see* Chartres
Civitas Eburovicum *see* Évreux
Civitas Nemetum *see* Speyer
109 G15 **Civitavecchia** *anc.* Centum Cellae, Trajani Portus. Lazio, C Italy
104 L10 **Civray** Vienne, W France
142 E14 **Çivril** Denizli, W Turkey
167 O5 **Cixian** Hebei, E China
143 R16 **Cizre** Şırnak, SE Turkey
xliii H19 **Clachaig** Argyll and Bute, W Scotland, UK
xliii F21 **Clachan** Argyll and Bute, W Scotland, UK
xlii A11 **Clachan-a-Luib** Western Isles, NW Scotland, UK
xliii G19 **Clachan of Glendaruel** Argyll and Bute, W Scotland, UK
xliii F18 **Clachan-Seil** Argyll and Bute, W Scotland, UK
xlii G8 **Clachtoll** Highland, NW Scotland, UK
xliii K19 **Clackmannan** Clackmannan, C Scotland, UK
xliii K18 **Clackmannan** ◈ *unitary authority* C Scotland, UK
Clacton *see* Clacton-on-Sea
xxxvii Y7 **Clacton-on-Sea** *var.* Clacton. Essex, E England, UK
xliii H18 **Cladich** Argyll and Bute, W Scotland, UK
xxxv H10 **Claerwen Reservoir** ⊠ E Wales, UK
xliii F16 **Claggan** Highland, NW Scotland, UK
24 H5 **Claiborne, Lake** ⊠ Louisiana, S USA
104 L10 **Clain** ≈ W France
9 Q11 **Claire, Lake** ◎ Alberta, C Canada
27 O6 **Clairemont** Texas, SW USA
36 M3 **Clair Engle Lake** ⊠ California, W USA
20 B15 **Clairton** Pennsylvania, NE USA
34 F7 **Clallam Bay** Washington, NW USA
105 P8 **Clamecy** Nièvre, C France
xliv K9 **Clane** Kildare, E Ireland
xxxvii O8 **Clanfield** Oxfordshire, C England, UK
25 P5 **Clanton** Alabama, S USA
xliii G20 **Claonaig** Argyll and Bute, W Scotland, UK
xxxvi D9 **Clapham** Lambeth, SE England, UK
xli O12 **Clapham** North Yorkshire, N England, UK
99 E18 **Clara** *Ir.* Clóirtheach. C Ireland
63 D17 **Clara** Entre Ríos, E Argentina
31 T9 **Clara City** Minnesota, N USA
63 D23 **Claraz** Buenos Aires, E Argentina
xxxv D13 **Clarbeston** Pembrokeshire, SW Wales, UK
Clár Chlainne Mhuiris *see* Claremorris
xxxix V13 **Clare** Suffolk, E England, UK
xliv E10 **Clare** *Ir.* An Clár. ◈ *county* W Ireland
xliv F8 **Clare** ≈ W Ireland
190 I8 **Clare** South Australia
xliv E10 **Clarecastle** Clare, W Ireland
xliv H10 **Clareen** Offaly, C Ireland
xliv E9 **Claregalway** Galway, W Ireland
xliv C7 **Clare Island** *Ir.* Cliara. *island* W Ireland
46 J12 **Claremont** C Jamaica
31 W10 **Claremont** Minnesota, N USA
21 N9 **Claremont** New Hampshire, NE USA
29 Q9 **Claremore** Oklahoma, C USA
xliv E7 **Claremorris** *Ir.* Clár Chlainne Mhuiris. Mayo, W Ireland
193 J16 **Clarence** Canterbury, South Island, NZ
193 J16 **Clarence** ≈ South Island, NZ
67 F15 **Clarence Bay** *bay* Ascension Island, C Atlantic Ocean
65 H25 **Clarence, Isla** *island* S Chile
204 H2 **Clarence Island** *island* South Shetland Islands, Antarctica
191 V5 **Clarence River** ≈ New South Wales, SE Australia
46 J5 **Clarence Town** Long Island, C Bahamas
29 W12 **Clarendon** Arkansas, C USA
27 O3 **Clarendon** Texas, SW USA
11 U12 **Clarenville** Newfoundland, Newfoundland and Labrador, SE Canada
9 Q17 **Claresholm** Alberta, SW Canada
xliv F9 **Clarinbridge** Galway, W Ireland
31 T16 **Clarinda** Iowa, C USA
57 N5 **Clarines** Anzoátegui, NE Venezuela
31 V12 **Clarion** Iowa, C USA
20 C13 **Clarion** Pennsylvania, NE USA
199 L7 **Clarion Fracture Zone** *tectonic feature* NE Pacific Ocean
20 D13 **Clarion River** ≈ Pennsylvania, NE USA
31 Q9 **Clark** South Dakota, N USA
38 K11 **Clarkdale** Arizona, SW USA
13 W4 **Clarke City** Québec, SE Canada
191 Q15 **Clarke Island** *island* Furneaux Group, Tasmania, SE Australia
189 X6 **Clarke Range** ▲▲ Queensland, E Australia
25 T2 **Clarkesville** Georgia, SE USA
31 S9 **Clarkfield** Minnesota, N USA
35 N7 **Clark Fork** Idaho, NW USA
35 N8 **Clark Fork** ≈ Idaho/Montana, NW USA
41 Q12 **Clark, Lake** ◎ Alaska, USA
37 W12 **Clark Mountain** ▲ California, W USA
39 S3 **Clark Peak** ▲ Colorado, C USA
12 D14 **Clark, Point** *headland* Ontario, S Canada
23 S3 **Clarksburg** West Virginia, NE USA
24 K2 **Clarksdale** Mississippi, S USA
35 U12 **Clarks Fork Yellowstone River** ≈ Montana/Wyoming, NW USA
25 V3 **Clarks Hall Lake** ◎ Georgia/South Carolina, SE USA
23 P13 **Clarks Hill Lake** *var.* J.Storm Thurmond Reservoir. ⊠ Georgia/South Carolina, SE USA
31 R14 **Clarkson** Nebraska, C USA
41 O13 **Clarks Point** Alaska, USA
20 I13 **Clarks Summit** Pennsylvania, NE USA
34 M10 **Clarkston** Washington, NW USA
46 J12 **Clark's Town** C Jamaica
29 T10 **Clarksville** Arkansas, C USA
33 P13 **Clarksville** Indiana, N USA
22 I8 **Clarksville** Tennessee, S USA
27 W5 **Clarksville** Texas, SW USA
23 U8 **Clarksville** Virginia, NE USA
23 U11 **Clarkton** North Carolina, SE USA
63 C24 **Claromecó** *var.* Balneario Claromecó. Buenos Aires, E Argentina
xlii J10 **Clashmore** Highland, NW Scotland, UK
xlii G8 **Clashnessie** Highland, NW Scotland, UK
xliii J24 **Clatteringshaws Loch** ◎ SW Scotland, UK
27 N3 **Claude** Texas, SW USA
xliv J3 **Claudy** Londonderry, NW Northern Ireland, UK
xli N12 **Claughton** Lancashire, NW England, UK
Clausentum *see* Southampton
xxxviii D17 **Claverdon** Warwickshire, C England, UK
179 P7 **Claveria** Luzon, N Philippines
101 J20 **Clavier** Liège, E Belgium
xxxvi E13 **Clawton** Devon, SW England, UK
25 W6 **Claxton** Georgia, SE USA
23 R4 **Clay** West Virginia, NE USA
29 N3 **Clay Center** Kansas, C USA
31 P16 **Clay Center** Nebraska, C USA
xxxviii M6 **Clay Cross** Derbyshire, C England, UK
xxxix W13 **Claydon** Suffolk, E England, UK
xl G11 **Clay Head** *headland* C Isle of Man
23 Y2 **Claymont** Delaware, NE USA
xxxix P7 **Claypole** Lincolnshire, E England, UK
38 M14 **Claypool** Arizona, SW USA
25 R6 **Clayton** Alabama, S USA
25 T1 **Clayton** Georgia, SE USA

◆ Country
● Country Capital
◇ Dependent Territory
○ Dependent Territory Capital
◈ Administrative Region
✕ International Airport
▲ Mountain
▲▲ Mountain Range
Volcano
≈ River
◎ Lake
⊠ Reservoir

CLAYTON – CONCA

24 J5 **Clayton** Louisiana, S USA
29 Q12 **Clayton** Missouri, C USA
39 V9 **Clayton** New Mexico, SW USA
23 V9 **Clayton** North Carolina, SE USA
29 X5 **Clayton** Oklahoma, C USA
xli O14 **Clayton-le-Moors** Lancashire, NW England, UK
190 I4 **Clayton River** *seasonal river* South Australia
23 R7 **Claytor Lake** ⊞ Virginia, NE USA
xliii E15 **Cleadale** Highland, NW Scotland, UK
29 P13 **Clear Boggy Creek** ≈ Oklahoma, C USA
xliv C15 **Clear, Cape** *var.* The Bill of Cape Clear, *Ir.* Ceann Cléire. *headland* SW Ireland
38 M12 **Clear Creek** ≈ Arizona, SW USA
41 S12 **Cleare, Cape** *headland* Montague Island, Alaska, USA
20 E13 **Clearfield** Pennsylvania, NE USA
38 L2 **Clearfield** Utah, W USA
27 Q6 **Clear Fork Brazos River** ≈ Texas, SW USA
33 T12 **Clear Fork Reservoir** ⊞ Ohio, N USA
9 N12 **Clear Hills** ▲ Alberta, SW Canada
xliv D15 **Clear Island** *island* S Ireland
31 V12 **Clear Lake** Iowa, C USA
31 R9 **Clear Lake** South Dakota, N USA
36 M6 **Clear Lake** ◎ California, W USA
24 G6 **Clear Lake** ⊞ Louisiana, S USA
36 M6 **Clearlake** California, W USA
37 P1 **Clear Lake Reservoir** ⊞ California, W USA
9 N16 **Clearwater** British Columbia, SW Canada
25 U12 **Clearwater** Florida, SE USA
9 R12 **Clearwater** ≈ Alberta/Saskatchewan, C Canada
29 W7 **Clearwater Lake** ⊞ Missouri, C USA
35 N10 **Clearwater Mountains** ▲ Idaho, NW USA
35 N10 **Clearwater River** ≈ Idaho, NW USA
31 S4 **Clearwater River** ≈ Minnesota, N USA
xliii A14 **Cleat** Western Isles, NW Scotland, UK
xl K9 **Cleator Moor** Cumbria, NW England, UK
27 T7 **Cleburne** Texas, SW USA
xli R14 **Cleckheaton** Kirklees, N England, UK
34 I9 **Cle Elum** Washington, NW USA
xxxviii H11 **Clee St Margaret** Shropshire, W England, UK
xxxix R3 **Cleethorpes** North East Lincolnshire, E England, UK
Cléire, Ceann *see* Clear, Cape
23 O11 **Clemson** South Carolina, SE USA
23 Q4 **Clendenin** West Virginia, NE USA
xxxviii I11 **Cleobury Mortimer** Shropshire, W England, UK
28 M9 **Cleo Springs** Oklahoma, C USA
Clerk Island *see* Onotoa
189 X8 **Clermont** Queensland, E Australia
13 S8 **Clermont** Québec, SE Canada
105 O4 **Clermont** Oise, N France
31 X12 **Clermont** Iowa, C USA
105 P11 **Clermont-Ferrand** Puy-de-Dôme, C France
105 Q15 **Clermont-l'Hérault** Hérault, S France
101 M22 **Clervaux** Diekirch, N Luxembourg
108 G6 **Cles** Trentino-Alto Adige, N Italy
190 H8 **Cleve** South Australia
Cleve *see* Kleve
xxxvi K10 **Clevedon** North West Somerset, SW England, UK
25 T2 **Cleveland** Georgia, SE USA
24 K3 **Cleveland** Mississippi, S USA
33 T11 **Cleveland** Ohio, N USA
29 O9 **Cleveland** Oklahoma, C USA
22 L10 **Cleveland** Tennessee, S USA
27 W10 **Cleveland** Texas, SW USA
33 N7 **Cleveland** Wisconsin, N USA
33 O4 **Cleveland Cliffs Basin** ◎ Michigan, N USA
33 U11 **Cleveland Heights** Ohio, N USA
xli T10 **Cleveland Hills** *hill range* N England, UK
35 P6 **Cleveland, Mount** ▲ Montana, NW USA
xl M13 **Cleveleys** Lancashire, NW England, UK
Cleves *see* Kleve
xliv C7 **Clew Bay** *Ir.* Cuan Mó. *inlet* W Ireland
25 Y14 **Clewiston** Florida, SE USA
Cliara *see* Clare Island
xli N9 **Cliburn** Cumbria, NW England, UK
xxxvii Q11 **Cliddesden** Hampshire, S England, UK
xliv C8 **Clifden** *Ir.* An Clochán. Galway, W Ireland
xxxvii W9 **Cliffe** Kent, SE England, UK
xxxviii G13 **Clifford** Herefordshire, W England, UK
39 O14 **Clifton** Arizona, SW USA
20 K14 **Clifton** New Jersey, NE USA
27 S8 **Clifton** Texas, SW USA
23 S6 **Clifton Forge** Virginia, NE USA
190 I1 **Clifton Hills** South Australia
xxxviii I12 **Clifton upon Teme** Worcestershire, W England, UK
9 S17 **Climax** Saskatchewan, S Canada
23 O8 **Clinch River** ≈ Tennessee/Virginia, S USA
27 P12 **Cline** Texas, SW USA
23 N10 **Clingmans Dome** ▲ North Carolina/Tennessee, SE USA
26 H8 **Clint** Texas, SW USA
8 M16 **Clinton** British Columbia, SW Canada
12 E15 **Clinton** Ontario, S Canada
29 U10 **Clinton** Arkansas, C USA
32 L10 **Clinton** Illinois, N USA
31 Z14 **Clinton** Iowa, C USA
22 G7 **Clinton** Kentucky, S USA
24 J8 **Clinton** Louisiana, S USA
21 N11 **Clinton** Massachusetts, NE USA
33 R10 **Clinton** Michigan, N USA
24 K5 **Clinton** Mississippi, S USA
29 S5 **Clinton** Missouri, C USA
23 V10 **Clinton** North Carolina, SE USA
28 L10 **Clinton** Oklahoma, C USA
23 Q12 **Clinton** South Carolina, SE USA
22 M9 **Clinton** Tennessee, S USA
15 J7 **Clinton-Colden Lake** ◎ Northwest Territories, NW Canada
8 H5 **Clinton Creek** Yukon Territory, NW Canada
32 L13 **Clinton Lake** ⊞ Illinois, N USA
29 Q4 **Clinton Lake** ⊞ Kansas, N USA
23 T11 **Clio** South Carolina, SE USA
199 IJ7 **Clipperton Fracture Zone** *tectonic feature* E Pacific Ocean
200 N7 **Clipperton Island** ◇ *French dependency of French Polynesia* E Pacific Ocean
48 K6 **Clipperton Island** *island* E Pacific Ocean
1 F16 **Clipperton Seamounts** *undersea feature* E Pacific Ocean
xxxix O11 **Clipston** Northamptonshire, C England, UK
xlii C9 **Clisham** ▲ NW Scotland, UK
104 J8 **Clisson** Loire-Atlantique, NW France
xli O13 **Clitheroe** Lancashire, NW England, UK
xxxviii H9 **Clive** Shropshire, W England, UK
xlii J1 **Clivocast** Shetland Islands, NE Scotland, UK
64 K7 **Clodomira** Santiago del Estero, N Argentina
xliv H3 **Cloghan** Donegal, N Ireland
xliv H9 **Cloghan** Offaly, C Ireland
xliv G12 **Clogheen** Tipperary, S Ireland
xliv I5 **Clogher** Dungannon, C Northern Ireland, UK
xliv L7 **Clogher Head** *headland* E Ireland
xliv L7 **Clogherhead** Louth, NE Ireland
xliv M5 **Cloghy** Ards, E Northern Ireland, UK
xliv L3 **Clog Mills** Ballymena, NE Northern Ireland, UK
Cloich na Coillte *see* Clonakilty
Clóirtheach *see* Clara
xlii P12 **Clola** Aberdeenshire, NE Scotland, UK
xliv E15 **Clonakilty** *Ir.* Cloich na Coillte. Cork, SW Ireland
xliv E15 **Clonakilty Bay** *bay* S Ireland
xliv I9 **Clonaslee** Laois, C Ireland
xliv F8 **Clonberg** Galway, W Ireland
xliv D8 **Clonbur** Galway, W Ireland
189 T6 **Cloncurry** Queensland, C Australia
xliv K9 **Clondalkin** *Ir.* Cluain Dolcáin. Dublin, E Ireland
xliv I13 **Clonea Bay** *bay* S Ireland
xliv I5 **Clones** *Ir.* Cluain Eois. Monaghan, N Ireland
xliv G9 **Clonfert** Galway, W Ireland
xliv H9 **Clonmacnoise** Offaly, C Ireland
xliv H12 **Clonmel** *Ir.* Cluain Meala. Tipperary, S Ireland
xliv K12 **Clonroche** Wexford, SE Ireland
xliv J6 **Clontibret** Monaghan, NE Ireland
xliv E8 **Cloonboo** Galway, W Ireland
xliv F11 **Cloonlara** Clare, W Ireland
xliv G10 **Cloonoon** Galway, W Ireland
xliv F9 **Cloonymorris** Galway, W Ireland
xxxvii S6 **Clophill** Bedfordshire, C England, UK
102 G11 **Cloppenburg** Niedersachsen, NW Germany
31 W6 **Cloquet** Minnesota, N USA
39 S14 **Cloudcroft** New Mexico, SW USA
35 W12 **Cloud Peak** ▲ Wyoming, C USA
193 K14 **Cloudy Bay** *inlet* S outh Island, NZ
xli W10 **Cloughton** North Yorkshire, N England, UK
xliii M15 **Clova** Angus, E Scotland, UK
xxxvi E12 **Clovelly** Devon, SW England, UK
xliii N21 **Clovenfords** The Borders, S Scotland, UK
23 R10 **Clover** South Carolina, SE USA
36 M6 **Cloverdale** California, W USA
22 J5 **Cloverport** Kentucky, S USA
37 Q10 **Clovis** California, W USA
39 W12 **Clovis** New Mexico, SW USA
xxxix N5 **Clowne** Derbyshire, C England, UK
xxxviii J11 **Clows Top** Worcestershire, W England, UK
12 K13 **Cloyne** Ontario, SE Canada
Cluain Dolcáin *see* Clondalkin
Cluain Eois *see* Clones
Cluainín *see* Manorhamilton
Cluain Meala *see* Clonmel
xlii G13 **Cluanie, Loch** ◎ NW Scotland, UK
118 H10 **Cluj** ◆ *county* NW Romania
Cluj *see* Cluj-Napoca
118 H10 **Cluj-Napoca** *Ger.* Klausenburg, *Hung.* Kolozsvár; *prev.* Cluj. Cluj, NW Romania
xxxviii G11 **Clun** Shropshire, W England, UK
xliii H14 **Clunes** Highland, NW Scotland, UK
xxxviii G11 **Clungunford** Shropshire, W England, UK
Clunia *see* Feldkirch
105 R10 **Cluny** Saône-et-Loire, C France
105 T10 **Cluses** Haute-Savoie, E France
108 E7 **Clusone** Lombardia, N Italy
27 W12 **Clute** Texas, SW USA
193 D23 **Clutha** ≈ South Island, NZ
xxxvi L10 **Clutton** Bath and North East Somerset, SW England, UK
99 J18 **Clwyd** *cultural region* NE Wales, UK
xxxv J4 **Clwyd** ≈ N Wales, UK
xxxv J4 **Clwydian Range** ▲ N Wales, UK
xxxv H14 **Clydach** Swansea, S Wales, UK
xxxv I14 **Clydach Vale** Rhondda Cynon Taff, S Wales, UK
xliii K22 **Clyde** ≈ W Scotland, UK
193 D22 **Clyde** Otago, South Island, NZ
29 N3 **Clyde** Kansas, C USA
31 P2 **Clyde** North Dakota, N USA
33 S11 **Clyde** Ohio, N USA
27 Q7 **Clyde** Texas, SW USA
12 K13 **Clyde** ≈ Ontario, SE Canada
xliii I20 **Clydebank** West Dunbartonshire, W Scotland, UK
xliii H20 **Clyde, Firth of** *inlet* S Scotland, UK
35 S11 **Clyde Park** Montana, NW USA
xxxv F6 **Clynnog-fawr** Gwynedd, NW Wales, UK
xxxv K11 **Clyro** Powys, C Wales, UK
xxxvi I13 **Clyst** ≈ SW England, UK
xxxvi I14 **Clyst St Mary** Devon, SW England, UK
xxxv I9 **Clywedog, Llyn** *var.* Clywedog Reservoir. ⊞ E Wales, UK
Clywedog Reservoir *see* Clywedog, Llyn
106 I7 **Côa** ≈ N Portugal
37 W16 **Coachella** California, W USA
37 W16 **Coachella Canal** *canal* California, W USA
xliv E14 **Coachford** Cork, S Ireland
42 I9 **Coacoyole** Durango, C Mexico
27 N7 **Coahoma** Texas, SW USA
8 K8 **Coal** ≈ Yukon Territory, NW Canada
xliii K21 **Coalburn** South Lanarkshire, C Scotland, UK
42 L14 **Coalcomán** *var.* Coalcomán de Matamoros. Michoacán de Ocampo, S Mexico
Coalcomán de Matamoros *see* Coalcomán
41 T8 **Coal Creek** Alaska, USA
9 Q17 **Coaldale** Alberta, SW Canada
29 P12 **Coalgate** Oklahoma, C USA
37 P11 **Coalinga** California, W USA
xliv K4 **Coalisland** Dungannon, C Northern Ireland, UK
8 L9 **Coal River** British Columbia, W Canada
23 Q6 **Coal River** ≈ West Virginia, NE USA
xxxviii M9 **Coalville** Leicestershire, C England, UK
38 M2 **Coalville** Utah, W USA
60 E13 **Coari** Amazonas, N Brazil
61 D14 **Coari, Rio** ≈ NW Brazil
83 J20 **Coast** ◆ *province* SE Kenya
Coast *see* Pwani
14 F11 **Coast Mountains** *Fr.* Chaîne Côtière. ▲ Canada/USA
17 F3 **Coast Ranges** ▲ W USA
xliii K20 **Coatbridge** North Lanarkshire, S Scotland, UK
44 B6 **Coatepeque** Quezaltenango, SW Guatemala
20 H16 **Coatesville** Pennsylvania, NE USA
13 Q13 **Coaticook** Québec, SE Canada
15 Mm6 **Coats Island** *island* Northwest Territories, NE Canada
205 O4 **Coats Land** *physical region* Antarctica
43 T14 **Coatzacoalcos** *var.* Quetzalcoalco; *prev.* Puerto México. Veracruz-Llave, E Mexico
43 S14 **Coatzacoalcos, Río** ≈ SE Mexico
118 M15 **Cobadin** Constanţa, SW Romania
12 H9 **Cobalt** Ontario, S Canada
44 D5 **Cobán** Alta Verapaz, C Guatemala
191 O6 **Cobar** New South Wales, SE Australia
20 F12 **Cobb Hill** ▲ Pennsylvania, NE USA
1 D8 **Cobb Seamount** *undersea feature* E Pacific Ocean
12 K12 **Cobden** Ontario, SE Canada
xliv G14 **Cobh** *Ir.* An Cóbh; *prev.* Cove of Cork, Queenstown. Cork, SW Ireland
59 J14 **Cobija** Pando, NW Bolivia
Coblence/Coblenz *see* Koblenz
20 J10 **Cobleskill** New York, NE USA
12 I15 **Cobourg** Ontario, SE Canada
189 P1 **Cobourg Peninsula** *headland* Northern Territory, N Australia
191 O10 **Cobram** Victoria, SE Australia
84 N13 **Cóbuè** Niassa, N Mozambique
103 K18 **Coburg** Bayern, SE Germany
21 Q5 **Coburn Mountain** ▲ Maine, NE USA
Coca *see* Puerto Francisco de Orellana
59 H18 **Cocachacra** Arequipa, SW Peru
61 J17 **Cocalinho** Mato Grosso, W Brazil
Cocanada *see* Kākināda
107 S11 **Cocentaina** País Valenciano, E Spain
59 L18 **Cochabamba** *hist.* Oropeza. Cochabamba, C Bolivia
59 K18 **Cochabamba** ◆ *department* C Bolivia
59 L18 **Cochabamba, Cordillera de** ▲ C Bolivia
103 E18 **Cochem** Rheinland-Pfalz, W Germany
39 R6 **Cochetopa Hills** ▲ Colorado, C USA
161 G22 **Cochin** *var.* Kochi. Kerala, SW India
46 D5 **Cochinos, Bahía de** *Eng.* Bay of Pigs. *bay* SE Cuba
39 O16 **Cochise Head** ▲ Arizona, SW USA
25 U5 **Cochran** Georgia, SE USA
9 P16 **Cochrane** Alberta, SW Canada
10 G12 **Cochrane** Ontario, S Canada
65 G20 **Cochrane** Aisén, S Chile
9 U10 **Cochrane** ≈ Manitoba/Saskatchewan, C Canada
Cochrane, Lago *see* Pueyrredón, Lago
Cocibolca *see* Nicaragua, Lago de
Cockade State *see* Maryland
46 M6 **Cockburn Harbour** South Caicos, S Turks and Caicos Islands
12 C11 **Cockburn Island** *island* Ontario, S Canada
xliii O20 **Cockburnspath** The Borders, S Scotland, UK
46 J3 **Cockburn Town** San Salvador, E Bahamas
47 N6 **Cockburn Town** ○ (Turks & Caicos Islands) Grand Turk Island, S Turks & Caicos Islands
xliii N19 **Cockenzie and Port Seton** East Lothian, SE Scotland, UK
xli N13 **Cockerham** Lancashire, NW England, UK
xl K8 **Cockermouth** Cumbria, NW England, UK
23 X2 **Cockeysville** Maryland, NE USA
xxxix V12 **Cockfield** Suffolk, E England, UK
xxxvii R12 **Cocking** West Sussex, SE England, UK
189 N12 **Cocklebiddy** Western Australia
xxxix U9 **Cockley Cley** Norfolk, E England, UK
46 I12 **Cockpit Country, The** *physical region* W Jamaica
xxxviii H8 **Cockshutt** Shropshire, W England, UK
45 S16 **Coclé** *off.* Provincia de Coclé. ◆ *province* C Panama
45 S15 **Coclé del Norte** Colón, C Panama
25 Y12 **Cocoa** Florida, SE USA
25 Y12 **Cocoa Beach** Florida, SE USA
81 D17 **Cocobeach** Estuaire, NW Gabon
46 G5 **Coco, Cayo** *island* C Cuba
157 Q19 **Coco Channel** *strait* Andaman Sea/Bay of Bengal
181 N6 **Coco-de-Mer Seamounts** *undersea feature* W Indian Ocean
38 K10 **Coconino Plateau** *plain* Arizona, SW USA
45 N6 **Coco, Río** *var.* Río Wanki, Segoviao Wangkí. ≈ Honduras/Nicaragua
181 T8 **Cocos (Keeling) Islands** ◇ *Australian external territory* E Indian Ocean
181 T7 **Cocos Basin** *undersea feature* E Indian Ocean
196 B17 **Cocos Island** *island* S Guam
Cocos Island Ridge *see* Cocos Ridge
133 S17 **Cocos Islands** *island group* E Indian Ocean
1 G15 **Cocos Plate** *tectonic feature*
200 Oo8 **Cocos Ridge** *var.* Cocos Island Ridge. *undersea feature* E Pacific Ocean
42 K13 **Cocula** Jalisco, SW Mexico
109 D17 **Coda Cavallo, Capo** *headland* Sardegna, Italy, C Mediterranean Sea
60 E13 **Codajás** Amazonas, N Brazil
Codazzi *see* Agustín Codazzi
21 Q12 **Cod, Cape** *headland* Massachusetts, NE USA
193 B25 **Codfish Island** *island* SW NZ
xxxvii N11 **Codford St Peter** Wiltshire, S England, UK
108 H9 **Codigoro** Emilia-Romagna, N Italy
11 P5 **Cod Island** *island* Newfoundland and Labrador, E Canada
118 J12 **Codlea** *Ger.* Zeiden, *Hung.* Feketehalom. Braşov, C Romania
60 M13 **Codó** Maranhão, E Brazil
108 E8 **Codogno** Lombardia, N Italy
118 M10 **Codrii** *hill range* C Moldavia
47 W9 **Codrington** Barbuda, Antigua and Barbuda
108 J7 **Codroipo** Friuli-Venezia Giulia, NE Italy
xxxviii J10 **Codsall** Staffordshire, C England, UK
30 M12 **Cody** Nebraska, C USA
35 U12 **Cody** Wyoming, C USA
23 P7 **Coeburn** Virginia, NE USA
xxxv K5 **Coedpoeth** Wrexham, NE Wales, UK
56 E10 **Coello** Tolima, W Colombia
Coemba *see* Cuemba
189 V2 **Coen** Queensland, NE Australia
103 E14 **Coesfeld** Nordrhein-Westfalen, W Germany
34 M8 **Coeur d'Alene** Idaho, NW USA
34 M8 **Coeur d'Alene Lake** ⊞ Idaho, NW USA
100 O8 **Coevorden** Drenthe, NE Netherlands
8 H6 **Coffee Creek** Yukon Territory, W Canada
32 L15 **Coffeen Lake** ⊞ Illinois, N USA
24 L3 **Coffeeville** Mississippi, S USA
29 Q8 **Coffeyville** Kansas, C USA
190 G9 **Coffin Bay** South Australia
190 F9 **Coffin Bay Peninsula** *peninsula* South Australia
191 V5 **Coffs Harbour** New South Wales, SE Australia
107 R10 **Cofrentes** País Valenciano, E Spain
xxxvii W7 **Coggeshall** Essex, SE England, UK
Cogîlnic *see* Kohyl'nyk
104 K11 **Cognac** *anc.* Compniacum. Charente, W France
108 B7 **Cogne** Valle d'Aosta, NW Italy
105 U16 **Cogolin** Var, SE France
107 O7 **Cogolludo** Castilla-La Mancha, C Spain
Cohalm *see* Rupea
20 F11 **Cohocton River** ≈ New York, NE USA
20 L10 **Cohoes** New York, NE USA
191 N10 **Cohuna** Victoria, SE Australia
45 P17 **Coiba, Isla de** *island* SW Panama
xliii F9 **Coigeach, Rubha** *headland* NW Scotland, UK
65 H23 **Coig, Río** ≈ S Argentina
65 G19 **Coihaique** *var.* Coyhaique. Aisén, S Chile
161 G21 **Coimbatore** Tamil Nādu, S India
106 G8 **Coimbra** *anc.* Conimbria, Conimbriga. Coimbra, W Portugal
106 G8 **Coimbra** ◆ *district* N Portugal
106 L15 **Coín** Andalucía, S Spain
59 J20 **Coipasa, Laguna** ◎ W Bolivia
59 J20 **Coipasa, Salar de** *salt lake* W Bolivia
Coira/Coire *see* Chur
Coirib, Loch *see* Corrib, Lough
56 K6 **Cojedes** *off.* Estado Cojedes. ◆ *state* N Venezuela
44 F7 **Cojutepeque** Cuscatlán, C El Salvador
35 S16 **Cokeville** Wyoming, C USA
xliii I9 **Colaboll** Highland, NW Scotland, UK
190 M13 **Colac** Victoria, SE Australia
61 O20 **Colatina** Espírito Santo, SE Brazil
29 O13 **Colbert** Oklahoma, C USA
102 L12 **Colbitz-Letzinger Heide** *heathland* N Germany
xl F12 **Colby** S Isle of Man
28 I3 **Colby** Kansas, C USA
59 H17 **Colca, Río** ≈ SW Peru
xxxvii X7 **Colchester** *hist.* Colneceaste, *anc.* Camulodunum. Essex, E England, UK
21 N13 **Colchester** Connecticut, NE USA
xlii J7 **Coldbackie** Highland, N Scotland, UK
40 M16 **Cold Bay** Alaska, USA
xliii P20 **Coldingham** The Borders, S Scotland, UK
xli T11 **Cold Kirby** North Yorkshire, N England, UK
9 R14 **Cold Lake** Alberta, SW Canada
9 R13 **Cold Lake** ◎ Alberta/Saskatchewan, S Canada
xxxvii W8 **Cold Norton** Essex, SE England, UK
31 U8 **Cold Spring** Minnesota, N USA
27 W10 **Coldspring** Texas, SW USA
xliii P21 **Coldstream** The Borders, SE Scotland, UK
9 N17 **Coldstream** British Columbia, SW Canada
12 H13 **Coldwater** Ontario, S Canada
28 K7 **Coldwater** Kansas, C USA
33 Q10 **Coldwater** Michigan, N USA
27 N1 **Coldwater Creek** ≈ Oklahoma/Texas, SW USA
24 K2 **Coldwater River** ≈ Mississippi, S USA
191 O9 **Coleambally** New South Wales, SE Australia
21 O6 **Colebrook** New Hampshire, NE USA
29 T5 **Cole Camp** Missouri, C USA
41 T6 **Coleen River** ≈ Alaska, USA
xxxvi L8 **Coleford** Gloucestershire, C England, UK
9 P17 **Coleman** Alberta, SW Canada
27 Q8 **Coleman** Texas, SW USA
Çölemerik *see* Hakkâri
85 K22 **Colenso** KwaZulu/Natal, E South Africa
xliv K2 **Coleraine** *Ir.* Cúil Raithin. Coleraine, N Northern Ireland, UK
xliv J2 **Coleraine** ◆ *district* N Northern Ireland, UK
190 L12 **Coleraine** Victoria, SE Australia
193 G18 **Coleridge, Lake** ◎ South Island, NZ
85 H24 **Colesberg** Northern Cape, C South Africa
xxxvi N7 **Colesbourne** Gloucestershire, C England, UK
xxxviii D15 **Coleshill** Warwickshire, C England, UK
24 H7 **Colfax** Louisiana, S USA
34 L9 **Colfax** Washington, NW USA
32 J6 **Colfax** Wisconsin, N USA
65 I19 **Colhué Huapí, Lago** ◎ S Argentina
47 Z6 **Colibris, Pointe des** *headland* Grande Terre, E Guadeloupe
108 D6 **Colico** Lombardia, N Italy
101 E14 **Colijnsplaat** Zeeland, SW Netherlands
42 L14 **Colima** Colima, S Mexico
42 K14 **Colima** ◆ *state* SW Mexico
42 L14 **Colima, Nevado de** ⚠ C Mexico
61 M14 **Colinas** Maranhão, E Brazil
xliii G20 **Colintraive** Argyll and Bute, W Scotland, UK
xliii C16 **Coll** *island* W Scotland, UK
107 N7 **Collado Villalba** *var.* Villalba. Madrid, C Spain
191 R4 **Collarenebri** New South Wales, SE Australia
39 P5 **Collbran** Colorado, C USA
108 G12 **Colle di Val d'Elsa** Toscana, C Italy
41 R9 **College** Alaska, USA
34 K10 **College Place** Washington, NW USA
27 U10 **College Station** Texas, SW USA
191 P4 **Collerina** New South Wales, SE Australia
188 I13 **Collie** Western Australia
188 L4 **Collier Bay** *bay* Western Australia
22 F10 **Collierville** Tennessee, S USA
xlii P12 **Collieston** Aberdeenshire, NE Scotland, UK
xxxvi E15 **Colliford Reservoir** ⊞ SW England, UK
xliii L24 **Collin** Dumfries and Galloway, SW Scotland, UK
108 F11 **Collina, Passo della** *pass* C Italy
xli S13 **Collingham** Leeds, N England, UK
xxxix P6 **Collingham** Nottinghamshire, C England, UK
12 G14 **Collingwood** Ontario, S Canada
192 I13 **Collingwood** Tasman, South Island, NZ
194 M15 **Collingwood Bay** *bay* SE PNG
24 L7 **Collins** Mississippi, S USA
32 K15 **Collinsville** Illinois, N USA
29 P9 **Collinsville** Oklahoma, C USA
22 H10 **Collinwood** Tennessee, S USA
Collipo *see* Leiria
65 G14 **Collipulli** Araucanía, C Chile
xliv K7 **Collon** Louth, NE Ireland
xliv F6 **Collooney** *Ir.* Cúil Mhuine. Sligo, NW Ireland
31 R10 **Colman** South Dakota, N USA
105 U6 **Colmar** *Ger.* Kolmar. Haut-Rhin, NE France
106 M15 **Colmenar** Andalucía, S Spain
Colmenar *see* Colmenar de Oreja
107 O9 **Colmenar de Oreja** *var.* Colmenar. Madrid, C Spain
107 N7 **Colmenar Viejo** Madrid, C Spain
27 X9 **Colmesneil** Texas, SW USA
xliii H24 **Colmonell** South Ayrshire, W Scotland, UK
Cöln *see* Köln
xlii M13 **Colnabaichin** Aberdeenshire, NE Scotland, UK
xli P13 **Colne** Lancashire, NW England, UK
xxxvii X7 **Colne** ≈ SE England, UK
Colneceaste *see* Colchester
42 C3 **Colnett** Baja California, NW Mexico
61 G15 **Colniza** Mato Grosso, W Brazil
Cologne *see* Köln
44 B6 **Colomba** Quezaltenango, SW Guatemala
Colomb-Béchar *see* Béchar
56 E11 **Colombia** Huila, C Colombia
56 G10 **Colombia** *off.* Republic of Colombia. ◆ *republic* N South America
66 E12 **Colombian Basin** *undersea feature* SW Caribbean Sea
Colombie-Britannique *see* British Columbia
13 T6 **Colombier** Québec, SE Canada
161 J25 **Colombo** ● (Sri Lanka) Western Province, W Sri Lanka
161 J25 **Colombo** ✕ Western Province, SW Sri Lanka
31 N11 **Colome** South Dakota, N USA
63 D18 **Colon** Entre Ríos, E Argentina
63 B19 **Colón** Buenos Aires, E Argentina
46 D5 **Colón** Matanzas, C Cuba
45 T14 **Colón** *prev.* Aspinwall. Colón, C Panama
44 K5 **Colón** ◆ *department* NE Honduras
45 S15 **Colón** *off.* Provincia de Colón. ◆ *province* N Panama
59 A16 **Colón, Archipiélago de** *var.* Islas de los Galápagos, *Eng.* Galapagos Islands, Tortoise Islands. *island group* Ecuador, E Pacific Ocean
46 K5 **Colonel Hill** Crooked Island, SE Bahamas
42 B3 **Colonet, Cabo** *headland* NW Mexico
196 G14 **Colonia** Yap, W Micronesia
63 D19 **Colonia** ◆ *department* SW Uruguay
Colonia *see* Kolonia, Micronesia
Colonia *see* Colonia del Sacramento, Uruguay
Colonia Agrippina *see* Köln
63 D20 **Colonia del Sacramento** *var.* Colonia. Colonia, SW Uruguay
64 L8 **Colonia Dora** Santiago del Estero, N Argentina
Colonia Julia Fanestris *see* Fano
23 W5 **Colonial Beach** Virginia, NE USA
23 V6 **Colonial Heights** Virginia, NE USA
200 Oo8 **Colón Ridge** *undersea feature* E Pacific Ocean
xliii D19 **Colonsay** *island* W Scotland, UK
59 K22 **Colorada, Laguna** ◎ SW Bolivia
39 R6 **Colorado** *off.* State of Colorado; also known as Centennial State, Silver State. ◆ *state* C USA
65 H22 **Colorado, Cerro** ▲ S Argentina
27 O7 **Colorado City** Texas, SW USA
38 M7 **Colorado Plateau** *plateau* W USA
63 A24 **Colorado, Río** ≈ E Argentina
45 N12 **Colorado, Río** ≈ NE Costa Rica
Colorado, Río *see* Colorado River
18 Hh10 **Colorado River** *var.* Río Colorado. ≈ Mexico/USA
18 Ll15 **Colorado River** ≈ Texas, SW USA
37 W15 **Colorado River Aqueduct** *aqueduct* California, W USA
46 A4 **Colorados, Archipiélago de los** *island group* NW Cuba
64 J9 **Colorados, Desagües de los** ◎ W Argentina
39 T5 **Colorado Springs** Colorado, C USA
42 L11 **Colotlán** Jalisco, SW Mexico
xlii N12 **Colpy** Aberdeenshire, NE Scotland, UK
59 L19 **Colquechaca** Potosí, C Bolivia
25 S7 **Colquitt** Georgia, SE USA
xxxix P8 **Colsterworth** Lincolnshire, E England, UK
xxxix O8 **Colston Bassett** Nottinghamshire, C England, UK
xxxix X8 **Coltishall** Norfolk, E England, UK
31 R11 **Colton** South Dakota, N USA
34 M10 **Colton** Washington, NW USA
37 P8 **Columbia** California, W USA
32 K16 **Columbia** Illinois, N USA
22 L7 **Columbia** Kentucky, S USA
24 J6 **Columbia** Louisiana, S USA
23 W3 **Columbia** Maryland, NE USA
24 L7 **Columbia** Mississippi, S USA
29 U4 **Columbia** Missouri, C USA
23 Y9 **Columbia** North Carolina, SE USA
20 G16 **Columbia** Pennsylvania, NE USA
23 Q12 **Columbia** *state capital* South Carolina, SE USA
22 I9 **Columbia** Tennessee, S USA
1 F9 **Columbia** ≈ Canada/USA
34 K9 **Columbia Basin** *basin* Washington, NW USA
207 Q7 **Columbia, Cape** *headland* Ellesmere Island, Northwest Territories, NE Canada
33 Q12 **Columbia City** Indiana, N USA
23 W3 **Columbia, District of** ◆ *federal district* NE USA
35 P7 **Columbia Falls** Montana, NW USA
9 O15 **Columbia Icefield** *icefield* Alberta/British Columbia, S Canada
9 O15 **Columbia, Mount** ▲ Alberta/British Columbia, SW Canada
9 N15 **Columbia Mountains** ▲ British Columbia, SW Canada
25 P4 **Columbiana** Alabama, S USA
33 V12 **Columbiana** Ohio, N USA
34 M14 **Columbia Plateau** *plateau* Idaho/Oregon, NW USA
31 P7 **Columbia Road Reservoir** ⊞ South Dakota, N USA
67 K16 **Columbia Seamount** *undersea feature* C Atlantic Ocean
85 D25 **Columbine, Cape** *headland* SW South Africa
107 U9 **Columbretes, Islas** *island group* E Spain
25 R5 **Columbus** Georgia, SE USA
33 P14 **Columbus** Indiana, N USA
29 R7 **Columbus** Kansas, C USA
25 N4 **Columbus** Mississippi, S USA
35 U11 **Columbus** Montana, NW USA
31 Q15 **Columbus** Nebraska, C USA
39 Q16 **Columbus** New Mexico, SW USA
23 P10 **Columbus** North Carolina, SE USA
30 K2 **Columbus** North Dakota, N USA
33 S13 **Columbus** *state capital* Ohio, N USA
27 U11 **Columbus** Texas, SW USA
32 L8 **Columbus** Wisconsin, N USA
33 R12 **Columbus Grove** Ohio, N USA
31 Y15 **Columbus Junction** Iowa, C USA
46 J3 **Columbus Point** *headland* Cat Island, C Bahamas
37 T8 **Columbus Salt Marsh** *salt marsh* Nevada, W USA
37 N6 **Colusa** California, W USA
xliii K25 **Colvend** Dumfries and Galloway, SW Scotland, UK
34 L7 **Colville** Washington, NW USA
192 M5 **Colville, Cape** *headland* North Island, NZ
192 M5 **Colville Channel** *channel* North Island, NZ
41 P6 **Colville River** ≈ Alaska, USA
xli P5 **Colwell** Northumberland, N England, UK
xxxv H4 **Colwyn Bay** Conwy, N Wales, UK
xxxvi J14 **Colyford** Devon, SW England, UK
xxxvi J14 **Colyton** Devon, SW England, UK
108 H9 **Comacchio** *var.* Commachio; *anc.* Comactium. Emilia-Romagna, N Italy
108 H9 **Comacchio, Valli di** *lagoon* Adriatic Sea, N Mediterranean Sea
Comactium *see* Comacchio
43 V17 **Comalapa** Chiapas, SE Mexico
43 U15 **Comalcalco** Tabasco, SE Mexico
65 H16 **Comallo** Río Negro, SW Argentina
28 M12 **Comanche** Oklahoma, C USA
27 R8 **Comanche** Texas, SW USA
204 H2 **Comandante Ferraz** *Brazilian research station* Antarctica
64 N6 **Comandante Fontana** Formosa, N Argentina
65 I22 **Comandante Luis Peidra Buena** Santa Cruz, S Argentina
61 O18 **Comandatuba** Bahia, SE Brazil
118 K11 **Comăneşti** *Hung.* Kománfalva. Bacău, SW Romania
59 M19 **Comarapa** Santa Cruz, C Bolivia
118 I13 **Comarnic** Prahova, SE Romania
44 H6 **Comayagua** Comayagua, W Honduras
44 H6 **Comayagua** ◆ *department* W Honduras
44 I6 **Comayagua, Montañas de** ▲ C Honduras
23 R15 **Combahee River** ≈ South Carolina, SE USA
64 G10 **Combarbalá** Coquimbo, C Chile
105 S7 **Combeaufontaine** Haute-Saône, E France
xxxvi G11 **Combe Martin** Devon, SW England, UK
xliv M5 **Comber** *Ir.* An Comar. Ards, E Northern Ireland, UK
xxxix S12 **Comberton** Cambridgeshire, E England, UK
xxxvi J13 **Combe St Nicholas** Somerset, SW England, UK
101 K20 **Comblain-au-Pont** Liège, E Belgium
104 I6 **Combourg** Ille-et-Vilaine, NW France
46 M9 **Comendador** *prev.* Elías Piña. W Dominican Republic
xliv H12 **Comeragh Mountains** ▲ S Ireland
Comer See *see* Como, Lago di
27 R11 **Comfort** Texas, SW USA
159 V15 **Comilla** *Ben.* Kumillā. Chittagong, E Bangladesh
101 B18 **Comines** Hainaut, W Belgium
123 J16 **Comino** *Malt.* Kemmuna. *island* C Malta
109 D18 **Comino, Capo** *headland* Sardegna, Italy, C Mediterranean Sea
109 K25 **Comiso** Sicilia, Italy, C Mediterranean Sea
43 V16 **Comitán** *var.* Comitán de Domínguez. Chiapas, SE Mexico
Comitán de Domínguez *see* Comitán
Commachio *see* Comacchio
Commander Islands *see* Komandorskiye Ostrova
105 O10 **Commentry** Allier, C France
25 T2 **Commerce** Georgia, SE USA
29 R8 **Commerce** Oklahoma, C USA
27 V5 **Commerce** Texas, SW USA
39 T4 **Commerce City** Colorado, C USA
105 S5 **Commercy** Meuse, NE France
57 W9 **Commewijne** *var.* Commewyne. ◆ *district* NE Surinam
Commewyne *see* Commewijne
13 P8 **Commissaires, Lac des** ◎ Québec, SE Canada
66 A12 **Commissioner's Point** *headland* W Bermuda
15 Ll3 **Committee Bay** *bay* Northwest Territories, N Canada
108 D7 **Como** *anc.* Comum. Lombardia, N Italy
65 J19 **Comodoro Rivadavia** Chubut, SE Argentina
108 D6 **Como, Lago di** *var.* Lario, *Eng.* Lake Como, *Ger.* Comer See. ◎ N Italy
Como, Lake *see* Como, Lago di
42 E7 **Comondú** Baja California Sur, W Mexico
118 F12 **Comorâşte** *Hung.* Komornok. Caraş-Severin, SW Romania
Comores, République Fédérale Islamique des *see* Comoros
161 G24 **Comorin, Cape** *headland* SE India
180 M8 **Comoro Basin** *undersea feature* SW Indian Ocean
70 K14 **Comoro Islands** *island group* W Indian Ocean
180 H13 **Comoros** *off.* Federal Islamic Republic of the Comoros, *Fr.* République Fédérale Islamique des Comores. ◆ *republic* W Indian Ocean
8 L17 **Comox** Vancouver Island, British Columbia, SW Canada
105 O4 **Compiègne** Oise, N France
Complutum *see* Alcalá de Henares
Compniacum *see* Cognac
42 K12 **Compostela** Nayarit, C Mexico
Compostella *see* Santiago
62 L11 **Comprida, Ilha** *island* S Brazil
xxxvii R12 **Compton** West Sussex, SE England, UK
119 N11 **Comrat** *Rus.* Komrat. S Moldavia
xliii K17 **Comrie** Perth and Kinross, C Scotland, UK
27 O11 **Comstock** Texas, SW USA
33 P9 **Comstock Park** Michigan, N USA
199 Kk3 **Comstock Seamount** *undersea feature* N Pacific Ocean
Comum *see* Como
165 N17 **Cona** Xizang Zizhiqu, W China
78 H14 **Conakry** ● (Guinea) Conakry, SW Guinea
78 H14 **Conakry** ✕ Conakry, SW Guinea
Conamara *see* Connemara
Conca *see* Cuenca

◆ Country
● Country Capital
◇ Dependent Territory
○ Dependent Territory Capital
◆ Administrative Region
✕ International Airport
▲ Mountain
▲ Mountain Range
⚠ Volcano
≈ River
◎ Lake
⊞ Reservoir

● COUNTRY ● COUNTRY CAPITAL ◇ DEPENDENT TERRITORY ◈ DEPENDENT TERRITORY CAPITAL ▲ ADMINISTRATIVE REGION ✕ INTERNATIONAL AIRPORT ▲ MOUNTAIN ▲ MOUNTAIN RANGE ☒ VOLCANO ◿ RIVER ◉ LAKE ⊞ RESERVOIR

CRANBOURNE CHASE – DAHLAC ARCHIPELAGO

xxxvii N12 **Cranbourne Chase** *hill range* S England, UK
xxxvii W11 **Cranbrook** Kent, SE England, UK
9 P17 **Cranbrook** British Columbia, SW Canada
32 M5 **Crandon** Wisconsin, N USA
34 K14 **Crane** Oregon, NW USA
26 M9 **Crane** Texas, SW USA
Crane *see* The Crane
27 S8 **Cranfills Gap** Texas, SW USA
xxxix P11 **Cranford St John** Northamptonshire, C England, UK
xxxvii S11 **Cranleigh** Surrey, SE England, UK
xliii O20 **Cranshaws** The Borders, S Scotland, UK
21 O12 **Cranston** Rhode Island, NE USA
Cranz *see* Zelenogradsk
61 L15 **Craolândia** Tocantins, E Brazil
104 J7 **Craon** Mayenne, NW France
xliii G19 **Crarae** Argyll and Bute, W Scotland, UK
205 V16 **Crary, Cape** *headland* Antarctica
Crasna *see* Kraszna
34 G14 **Crater Lake** ◎ Oregon, NW USA
194 I13 **Crater Mount** ▲ C PNG
35 P14 **Craters of the Moon National Monument** *national park* Idaho, NW USA
61 O14 **Crateús** Ceará, E Brazil
xliii O14 **Crathes** Aberdeenshire, NE Scotland, UK
xliii M14 **Crathie** Aberdeenshire, NE Scotland, UK
Crathis *see* Crati
xli S10 **Crathorne** North Yorkshire, N England, UK
109 N20 **Crati** *anc.* Crathis. ≈ S Italy
xliv F9 **Craughwell** Galway, W Ireland
9 U16 **Craven** Saskatchewan, S Canada
xxxviii H11 **Craven Arms** Shropshire, W England, UK
56 I8 **Cravo Norte** Arauca, E Colombia
xliii L22 **Crawford** South Lanarkshire, C Scotland, UK
30 J12 **Crawford** Nebraska, C USA
27 T8 **Crawford** Texas, SW USA
9 O17 **Crawford Bay** British Columbia, SW Canada
xliii K22 **Crawfordjohn** South Lanarkshire, C Scotland, UK
67 M19 **Crawford Seamount** *undersea feature* S Atlantic Ocean
33 O13 **Crawfordsville** Indiana, N USA
25 S9 **Crawfordville** Florida, SE USA
xxxvii P11 **Crawley** Hampshire, S England, UK
xxxvii T11 **Crawley** West Sussex, SE England, UK
xlii E12 **Crawlin Islands** *island group* NW Scotland, UK
35 S10 **Crazy Mountains** ▲▲ Montana, NW USA
xlii A12 **Creagorry** Western Isles, NW Scotland, UK
xxxviii H13 **Credenhill** Herefordshire, W England, UK
xxxvi H13 **Crediton** Devon, SW England, UK
xliii I24 **Cree** ≈ SW Scotland, UK
9 T11 **Cree** ≈ Saskatchewan, C Canada
39 R7 **Creede** Colorado, C USA
xliv D11 **Creegh** Clare, W Ireland
42 I6 **Creel** Chihuahua, N Mexico
9 S11 **Cree Lake** ◎ Saskatchewan, C Canada
xliv H2 **Creeslough** Donegal, N Ireland
xliii I25 **Creetown** Dumfries and Galloway, SW Scotland, UK
xliv J4 **Creggan** Omagh, W Northern Ireland, UK
xliv C7 **Cregganbaun** Mayo, NW Ireland
9 V13 **Creighton** Saskatchewan, C Canada
31 Q13 **Creighton** Nebraska, C USA
105 O4 **Creil** Oise, N France
108 E8 **Crema** Lombardia, N Italy
108 E8 **Cremona** Lombardia, N Italy
Creole State *see* Louisiana
114 M10 **Crepaja** *Hung.* Cserépalja. Serbia, N Yugoslavia
105 O4 **Crépy-en-Valois** Oise, N France
114 B10 **Cres** *It.* Cherso. Primorje-Gorski Kotar, NW Croatia
114 A11 **Cres** *It.* Cherso; *anc.* Crexa. *island* W Croatia
34 H14 **Crescent** Oregon, NW USA
36 K1 **Crescent City** California, W USA
25 W10 **Crescent City** Florida, SE USA
178 M10 **Crescent Group** *island group* C Paracel Islands
25 W10 **Crescent Lake** ◎ Florida, SE USA
31 X11 **Cresco** Iowa, C USA
63 B18 **Crespo** Entre Ríos, E Argentina
56 E5 **Crespo** ✕ (Cartagena) Bolívar, NW Colombia
xxxviii H10 **Cressage** Shropshire, W England, UK
105 R13 **Crest** Drôme, E France
39 R5 **Crested Butte** Colorado, C USA
33 S12 **Crestline** Ohio, N USA
9 O17 **Creston** British Columbia, SW Canada
31 U15 **Creston** Iowa, C USA
35 V16 **Creston** Wyoming, C USA
39 S7 **Crestone Peak** ▲ Colorado, C USA
25 P8 **Crestview** Florida, SE USA
123 Gg10 **Cretan Trough** *undersea feature* Aegean Sea, C Mediterranean Sea
31 R16 **Crete** Nebraska, C USA
Crete *see* Kríti
105 O5 **Créteil** Val-de-Marne, N France
Crete, Sea of/Creticum, Mare *see* Kritikó Pélagos
xliii F20 **Cretshengan** Argyll and Bute, W Scotland, UK
107 X4 **Creus, Cap de** *headland* NE Spain
105 N10 **Creuse** ◈ *department* C France
104 L9 **Creuse** ≈ C France
105 T4 **Creutzwald** Moselle, NE France
107 S12 **Crevillente** País Valenciano, E Spain
xxxviii I7 **Crewe** Cheshire, C England, UK
23 V7 **Crewe** Virginia, NE USA
xxxvi K13 **Crewkerne** Somerset, SW England, UK
Crexa *see* Cres
xliii I17 **Crianlarich** Stirling, C Scotland, UK
xxxv G11 **Cribyn** Ceredigion, W Wales, UK
45 Q15 **Cricamola, Río** ≈ NW Panama
xxxv F6 **Criccieth** Gwynedd, NW Wales, UK
xxxviii M7 **Crich** Derbyshire, C England, UK
63 K14 **Criciúma** Santa Catarina, S Brazil
xxxix N11 **Crick** Northamptonshire, C England, UK
xxxv K13 **Crickhowell** Powys, C Wales, UK
xxxvii N8 **Cricklade** Wiltshire, S England, UK
xxxvi B6 **Cricklewood** Brent, SE England, UK
xliii K17 **Crieff** Perth and Kinross, C Scotland, UK
114 B10 **Crikvenica** *It.* Cirquenizza; *prev.* Cirkvenica, Crjkvenica. Primorje-Gorski Kotar, NW Croatia
Crimea/Crimean Oblast *see* Krym, Respublika
103 M16 **Crimmitschau** *var.* Krimmitschau. Sachsen, E Germany
xlii P11 **Crimond** Aberdeenshire, NE Scotland, UK
xliii F19 **Crinan** Argyll and Bute, W Scotland, UK
xxxix X9 **Cringleford** Norfolk, E England, UK
118 G11 **Crişcior** *Hung.* Kristyor. Hunedoara, W Romania
23 Y5 **Crisfield** Maryland, NE USA
33 P3 **Crisp Point** *headland* Michigan, N USA
61 L19 **Cristalina** Goiás, C Brazil
46 J7 **Cristal, Sierra del** ▲▲ E Cuba
45 T14 **Cristóbal** Colón, C Panama
56 F4 **Cristóbal Colón, Pico** ▲ N Colombia
Cristur/Cristuru Săcuiesc *see* Cristuru Secuiesc
118 I11 **Cristuru Secuiesc** *prev.* Cristur, Cristuru Săcuiesc, Sitaş Cristuru, *Ger.* Kreutz, *Hung.* Székelykeresztúr, Szitás-Keresztúr. Harghita, C Romania
118 F10 **Crişul Alb** *var.* Weisse Kreisch, *Ger.* Weisse Körös, *Hung.* Fehér-Körös. ≈ Hungary/Romania
118 F10 **Crişul Negru** *Ger.* Schwarze Körös, *Hung.* Fekete-Körös. ≈ Hungary/Romania
118 G10 **Crişul Repede** *var.* Schnelle Kreisch, *Ger.* Schnelle Körös, *Hung.* Sebes-Körös. ≈ Hungary/Romania
119 N10 **Criuleni** *Rus.* Kriulyany. C Moldavia
Crivadia Vulcanului *see* Vulcan
Crjkvenica *see* Crikvenica
115 O17 **Crna Gora** ▲▲ FYR Macedonia/Yugoslavia
Crna Gora *see* Montenegro
115 O20 **Crna Reka** ≈ S FYR Macedonia
Crni Drim *see* Black Drin
111 V10 **Crni Vrh** ▲ NE Slovenia
111 V13 **Črnomelj** *Ger.* Tschernembl. SE Slovenia
xliv D7 **Croagh Patrick** *Ir.* Cruach Phádraig. ▲ W Ireland
114 D9 **Croatia** *off.* Republic of Croatia, *Ger.* Kroatien, *SCr.* Hrvatska. ◆ *republic* SE Europe
Croce, Picco di *see* Wilde Kreuzspitze
13 P8 **Croche** ≈ Québec, SE Canada
175 Nn3 **Crocker, Banjaran** *var.* Crocker Range. ▲▲ East Malaysia
Crocker Range *see* Crocker, Banjaran
27 V9 **Crockett** Texas, SW USA
xxxvii U11 **Crockham Hill** Kent, SE England, UK
69 V14 **Crocodile** *var.* Krokodil. ≈ N South Africa
Crocodile *see* Limpopo
22 I7 **Crofton** Kentucky, S USA
31 Q12 **Crofton** Nebraska, C USA
xli R9 **Croft-on-Tees** Darlington, N England, UK
xliii F17 **Croggan** Argyll and Bute, W Scotland, UK
Croia *see* Krujë
105 R16 **Croisette, Cap** *headland* SE France
104 G8 **Croisic, Pointe du** *headland* NW France
105 S13 **Croix Haute, Col de la** *pass* E France
13 U5 **Croix, Pointe à la** *headland* Québec, SE Canada
12 F13 **Croker, Cape** *headland* Ontario, S Canada
189 P1 **Croker Island** *island* Northern Territory, N Australia
xlii J11 **Cromarty** Highland, N Scotland, UK
xlii J11 **Cromarty Firth** *inlet* N Scotland, UK
101 M21 **Crombach** Liège, E Belgium
xlii L13 **Cromdale** Highland, NW Scotland, UK
xxxix X7 **Cromer** Norfolk, E England, UK
xlii D9 **Cromore** Western Isles, NW Scotland, UK
193 D22 **Cromwell** Otago, South Island, NZ
193 H16 **Cronadun** West Coast, South Island, NZ
xxxvii R11 **Crondall** Hampshire, S England, UK
xli R8 **Crook** Durham, N England, UK
41 O11 **Crooked Creek** Alaska, USA
46 K5 **Crooked Island** *island* SE Bahamas
46 J5 **Crooked Island Passage** *channel* SE Bahamas
34 I13 **Crooked River** ≈ Oregon, NW USA
xli P2 **Crookham** Northumberland, N England, UK
xliv C15 **Crookhaven** Cork, S Ireland
31 R4 **Crookston** Minnesota, N USA
30 I10 **Crooks Tower** ▲ South Dakota, N USA
xliv E14 **Crookstown** Cork, S Ireland
33 T14 **Crooksville** Ohio, N USA
191 R9 **Crookwell** New South Wales, SE Australia
xliv F12 **Croom** Limerick, SW Ireland
xxxvii P6 **Cropredy** Oxfordshire, C England, UK
xl G11 **Crosby** C Isle of Man
xl B15 **Crosby** *var.* Great Crosby. Sefton, NW England, UK
12 L14 **Crosby** Ontario, SE Canada
31 U6 **Crosby** Minnesota, N USA
30 K2 **Crosby** North Dakota, N USA
xli N9 **Crosby Ravensworth** Cumbria, NW England, UK
27 O5 **Crosbyton** Texas, SW USA
xliv E8 **Cross** Mayo, NW Ireland
79 V16 **Cross** ≈ Cameroon/Nigeria
xliii F21 **Crossaig** Argyll and Bute, W Scotland, UK
25 U10 **Cross City** Florida, SE USA
Crossen *see* Krosno Odrzańskie
29 V14 **Crossett** Arkansas, C USA
xli O8 **Cross Fell** ▲ N England, UK
9 P16 **Crossfield** Alberta, SW Canada
xliii K21 **Crossford** South Lanarkshire, C Scotland, UK
xliv M5 **Crossgar** Down, E Northern Ireland, UK
xxxv G13 **Cross Hands** Carmarthenshire, S Wales, UK
xliv G14 **Crosshaven** Cork, S Ireland
23 Q12 **Cross Hill** South Carolina, SE USA
xliii I23 **Crosshill** South Ayrshire, W Scotland, UK
21 U6 **Cross Island** *island* Maine, NE USA
9 X13 **Cross Lake** Manitoba, C Canada
24 F5 **Cross Lake** ⊠ Louisiana, S USA
xliv K6 **Crossmaglen** Newry and Mourne, S Northern Ireland, UK
38 I12 **Crossman Peak** ▲ Arizona, SW USA
xliii K24 **Crossmichael** Dumfries and Galloway, SW Scotland, UK
xliv E6 **Crossmolina** Mayo, NW Ireland
27 Q7 **Cross Plains** Texas, SW USA
79 V17 **Cross River** ◈ *state* SE Nigeria
22 L9 **Crossville** Tennessee, S USA
xl M11 **Crosthwaite** Cumbria, NW England, UK
xli N15 **Croston** Lancashire, NW England, UK
33 S8 **Croswell** Michigan, N USA
12 K13 **Crotch Lake** ◎ Ontario, SE Canada
Croton/Crotona *see* Crotone
109 O21 **Crotone** *var.* Cotrone; *anc.* Croton, Crotona. Calabria, SW Italy
xxxvii X8 **Crouch** ≈ E England, UK
xxxvi D6 **Crouch End** Haringey, SE England, UK
xxxix N14 **Croughton** Northamptonshire, C England, UK
35 V11 **Crow Agency** Montana, NW USA
xxxvii V12 **Crowborough** East Sussex, SE England, UK
191 U7 **Crowdy Head** *headland* New South Wales, SE Australia
27 Q4 **Crowell** Texas, SW USA
xxxix R9 **Crowland** Lincolnshire, E England, UK
191 O6 **Crowl Creek** *seasonal river* New South Wales, SE Australia
xxxix O3 **Crowle** North Lincolnshire, N England, UK
xxxviii K13 **Crowle** Worcestershire, W England, UK
24 H9 **Crowley** Louisiana, S USA
37 S9 **Crowley, Lake** ⊠ California, W USA
29 X10 **Crowleys Ridge** *hill range* Arkansas, C USA
194 J11 **Crown Island** *island* N Papau New Guinea
33 N11 **Crown Point** Indiana, N USA
39 P10 **Crownpoint** New Mexico, SW USA
35 R10 **Crow Peak** ▲ Montana, NW USA
9 P17 **Crowsnest Pass** *pass* Alberta/British Columbia, SW Canada
xxxvii R10 **Crowthorne** Bracknell Forest, S England, UK
31 T6 **Crow Wing River** ≈ Minnesota, N USA
xxxix Q3 **Croxton** North Lincolnshire, N England, UK
xlii K12 **Croy** Highland, NW Scotland, UK
xxxvi F11 **Croyde** Devon, SW England, UK
xxxvii U10 **Croydon** Croydon, SE England, UK
xxxiv L17 **Croydon** ◈ *London borough* SE England, UK
181 P11 **Crozet Basin** *undersea feature* S Indian Ocean
181 O12 **Crozet Islands** *island group* French Southern and Antarctic Territories
181 N12 **Crozet Plateau** *var.* Crozet Plateaus. *undersea feature* SW Indian Ocean
Crozet Plateaus *see* Crozet Plateau
104 E6 **Crozon** Finistère, NW France
Cruacha Dubha, Na *see* Macgillycuddy's Reeks
Cruach Phádraig *see* Croagh Patrick
118 M14 **Crucea** Constanţa, SE Romania
46 E5 **Cruces** Cienfuegos, C Cuba
109 O20 **Crucoli Torretta** Calabria, SW Italy
xlii P12 **Cruden Bay** Aberdeenshire, NE Scotland, UK
xxxviii I9 **Crudgington** Shropshire, W England, UK
xxxvii N8 **Crudwell** Wiltshire, S England, UK
43 P9 **Cruillas** Tamaulipas, C Mexico
66 K9 **Cruiser Tablemount** *undersea feature* E Atlantic Ocean
xlii C8 **Crulivig** Western Isles, NW Scotland, UK
xliv L4 **Crumlin** Antrim, NE Northern Ireland, UK
xl L9 **Crummock Water** ◎ NW England, UK
xliv E10 **Crusheen** Clare, W Ireland
63 G14 **Cruz Alta** Rio Grande do Sul, S Brazil
46 G8 **Cruz, Cabo** *headland* S Cuba
62 N9 **Cruzeiro** São Paulo, S Brazil
62 H10 **Cruzeiro do Oeste** Paraná, S Brazil
61 A15 **Cruzeiro do Sul** Acre, W Brazil
xxxv E12 **Crymych** Pembrokeshire, SW Wales, UK
xxxv H14 **Crynant** Neath Port Talbot, S Wales, UK
25 U11 **Crystal Bay** *bay* Florida, SE USA
190 I8 **Crystal Brook** South Australia
9 X17 **Crystal City** Manitoba, S Canada
29 X5 **Crystal City** Missouri, C USA
27 P13 **Crystal City** Texas, SW USA
32 M4 **Crystal Falls** Michigan, N USA
25 Q8 **Crystal Lake** Florida, SE USA
33 O6 **Crystal Lake** ◎ Michigan, N USA
25 V11 **Crystal River** Florida, SE USA
39 Q5 **Crystal River** ≈ Colorado, C USA
24 K6 **Crystal Springs** Mississippi, S USA
Csaca *see* Čadca
Csakathurn/Csáktornya *see* Čakovec
Csap *see* Chop
Csepén *see* Čepin
Cserépalja *see* Crepaja
Csermő *see* Cermei
Csíkszereda *see* Miercurea-Ciuc
113 L24 **Csongrád** Csongrád, SE Hungary
113 L24 **Csongrád** *off.* Csongrád Megye. ◈ *county* SE Hungary
113 H22 **Csorna** Győr-Moson-Sopron, NW Hungary
Csucsa *see* Ciucea
113 G25 **Csurgó** Somogy, SW Hungary
Csurog *see* Čurug
56 L5 **Cúa** Miranda, N Venezuela
84 C11 **Cuale** Malanje, NW Angola
69 T12 **Cuando** *var.* Kwando. ≈ S Africa
85 E15 **Cuando Cubango** *var.* Kuando-Kubango. ◈ *province* SE Angola
85 E16 **Cuangar** Cuando Cubango, S Angola
84 D11 **Cuango** Lunda Norte, NE Angola
84 C10 **Cuango** Uíge, NW Angola
84 C10 **Cuango** *var.* Kwango. ≈ Angola/Zaire *see also* Kwango
Cuan, Loch *see* Strangford Lough
84 C12 **Cuanza** *var.* Kwanza. ≈ C Angola
84 B11 **Cuanza Norte** *var.* Kuanza Norte. ◈ *province* NE Angola
84 B12 **Cuanza Sul** *var.* Kuanza Sul. ◈ *province* NE Angola
63 E16 **Cuareim, Río** *var.* Rio Quaraí. ≈ Brazil/Uruguay *see also* Quaraí, Rio
85 D15 **Cuatir** ≈ S Angola
42 M7 **Cuatro Ciénegas** *var.* Cuatro Ciénegas de Carranza. Coahuila de Zaragoza, NE Mexico
Cuatro Ciénegas de Carranza *see* Cuatro Ciénegas
42 I6 **Cuauhtémoc** Chihuahua, N Mexico
43 P14 **Cuautla** Morelos, S Mexico
106 H12 **Cuba** Beja, S Portugal
29 W6 **Cuba** Missouri, C USA
39 R10 **Cuba** New Mexico, SW USA
46 E6 **Cuba** *off.* Republic of Cuba. ◆ *republic* W West Indies
49 O2 **Cuba** *island* W West Indies
84 B13 **Cubal** Benguela, W Angola
85 C15 **Cubango** *var.* Kuvango, *Port.* Vila Artur de Paiva, Vila da Ponte. Huíla, SW Angola
85 D16 **Cubango** *var.* Kavango, Kavengo, Kubango, Okavango, Okavanggo. ≈ S Africa *see also* Okavango
56 H8 **Cubará** Boyacá, N Colombia
xxxviii F16 **Cubbington** Warwickshire, C England, UK
142 I12 **Çubuk** Ankara, N Turkey
85 D14 **Cuchi** Cuando Cubango, C Angola
44 C5 **Cuchumatanes, Sierra de los** ▲▲ W Guatemala
xxxvii U12 **Cuckfield** West Sussex, SE England, UK
Cuculaya, Rio *see* Kukalaya, Rio
84 E12 **Cucumbi** *prev.* Trás-os-Montes. Lunda Sul, NE Angola
56 G7 **Cúcuta** *var.* San José de Cúcuta. Norte de Santander, N Colombia
33 N9 **Cudahy** Wisconsin, N USA
161 J21 **Cuddalore** Tamil Nādu, SE India
161 I18 **Cuddapah** Andhra Pradesh, S India
xli S15 **Cudworth** Barnsley, N England, UK
106 M6 **Cuéllar** Castilla-León, N Spain
84 D13 **Cuemba** *var.* Coemba. Bié, C Angola
58 B8 **Cuenca** Azuay, S Ecuador
107 Q9 **Cuenca** *anc.* Conca. Castilla-La Mancha, C Spain
107 P9 **Cuenca** ◈ *province* Castilla-La Mancha, C Spain
42 L9 **Cuencamé** *var.* Cuencamé de Ceniceros. Durango, C Mexico
Cuencamé de Ceniceros *see* Cuencamé
107 Q8 **Cuenca, Serrania de** ▲▲ C Spain
Cuera *see* Chur
107 P5 **Cuerda del Pozo, Embalse de la** ⊠ N Spain
43 O14 **Cuernavaca** Morelos, S Mexico
27 T12 **Cuero** Texas, SW USA
46 I7 **Cueto** Holguín, E Cuba
43 Q13 **Cuetzalán** *var.* Cuetzalán del Progreso. Puebla, S Mexico
Cuetzalán del Progreso *see* Cuetzalán
107 Q14 **Cuevas de Almanzora** Andalucía, S Spain
107 T8 **Cuevas de Vinromá** País Valenciano, E Spain
xxxvii U8 **Cuffley** Hertfordshire, E England, UK
118 H12 **Cugir** *Hung.* Kudzsir. Alba, SW Romania
61 H18 **Cuiabá** *prev.* Cuyabá. *state capital* Mato Grosso, SW Brazil
61 H19 **Cuiabá, Rio** ≈ SW Brazil
43 R15 **Cuicatlán** *var.* San Juan Bautista Cuicatlán. Oaxaca, SE Mexico
203 W16 **Cuidado, Punta** *headland* Easter Island, Chile, E Pacific Ocean
Cuidad Presidente Stroessner *see* Ciudad del Este
Cúige *see* Connaught
Cúige Laighean *see* Leinster
99 **Cúige Mumhan** *see* Munster
100 L13 **Cuijck** Noord-Brabant, SE Netherlands
Cúil an tSúdaire *see* Portarlington
44 D7 **Cuilapa** Santa Rosa, S Guatemala
44 B5 **Cuilco, Río** ≈ W Guatemala
Cúil Mhuine *see* Collooney
Cúil Raithin *see* Coleraine
85 C14 **Cuima** Huambo, C Angola
85 E16 **Cuito** *var.* Kwito. ≈ SE Angola
85 E15 **Cuíto Cuanavale** Cuando Cubango, E Angola
43 N14 **Cuitzeo, Lago de** ◎ C Mexico
29 W4 **Cuivre River** ≈ Missouri, C USA
Çuka *see* Çukë
174 Hh4 **Cukai** *var.* Chukai, Kemaman. Terengganu, Peninsular Malaysia
115 L23 **Çukë** *var.* Çuka. Vlorë, S Albania
Cularo *see* Grenoble
179 Pp13 **Culasi** Panay Island, C Philippines
35 Y7 **Culbertson** Montana, NW USA
30 M16 **Culbertson** Nebraska, C USA
191 P10 **Culcairn** New South Wales, SE Australia
xliv J2 **Culdaff** Donegal, N Ireland
47 W5 **Culebra** *var.* Dewey. E Puerto Rico
47 W6 **Culebra, Isla de** *island* E Puerto Rico
39 T8 **Culebra Peak** ▲ Colorado, C USA
106 J5 **Culebra, Sierra de la** ▲▲ NW Spain
100 J12 **Culemborg** Gelderland, C Netherlands
143 V14 **Culfa** *Rus.* Dzhul'fa. SW Azerbaijan
xli N8 **Culgaith** Cumbria, NW England, UK
191 P4 **Culgoa River** ≈ New South Wales/Queensland, SE Australia
42 I9 **Culiacán** *var.* Culiacán Rosales, Culiacán-Rosales. Sinaloa, C Mexico
Culiacán-Rosales/Culiacán Rosales *see* Culiacán
179 P13 **Culion Island** *island* Calamian Group, W Philippines
107 P14 **Cúllar-Baza** Andalucía, S Spain
xlii N11 **Cullen** Moray, N Scotland, UK
107 S10 **Cullera** País Valenciano, E Spain
xliv E6 **Cullin, Lough** ◎ NW Ireland
xlii I1 **Cullivoe** Shetland Islands, NE Scotland, UK
25 P3 **Cullman** Alabama, S USA
xxxvi I13 **Cullompton** Devon, SW England, UK
110 B10 **Cully** Vaud, W Switzerland
xliv K3 **Cullybackey** Ballymena, NE Northern Ireland, UK
Culm *see* Chełmno
xliv I3 **Culmore** Donegal, N Ireland
Culmsee *see* Chełmża
xxxvi I13 **Culmstock** Devon, SW England, UK
23 V4 **Culpeper** Virginia, NE USA
xliii L19 **Culross** Fife, E Scotland, UK
xlii H4 **Culswick** Shetland Islands, NE Scotland, UK
xliii L22 **Culter Fell** ▲ C Scotland, UK
xliii P14 **Cults** City of Aberdeen, NE Scotland, UK
Culpepper Island *see* Darwin, Isla
193 I17 **Culverden** Canterbury, South Island, NZ
xxxix N13 **Culworth** Northamptonshire, C England, UK
57 N5 **Cumaná** Sucre, NE Venezuela
57 O5 **Cumanacoa** Sucre, NE Venezuela
56 C13 **Cumbal, Nevado de** *elevation* S Colombia
23 O7 **Cumberland** Kentucky, S USA
23 U2 **Cumberland** Maryland, NE USA
23 V6 **Cumberland** Virginia, NE USA
197 A11 **Cumberland, Cape** *var.* Cape Nahoi. *headland* Espiritu Santo, N Vanuatu
9 V14 **Cumberland House** Saskatchewan, C Canada
25 W8 **Cumberland Island** *island* Georgia, SE USA
22 L7 **Cumberland, Lake** ⊠ Kentucky, S USA
16 O1 **Cumberland Peninsula** *peninsula* Baffin Island, Northwest Territories, NE Canada
1 K11 **Cumberland Plateau** *plateau* E USA
32 L1 **Cumberland Point** *headland* Michigan, N USA
23 O7 **Cumberland River** ≈ Kentucky/Tennessee, S USA
16 O2 **Cumberland Sound** *inlet* Baffin Island, Northwest Territories, NE Canada
xliii K20 **Cumbernauld** North Lanarkshire, S Scotland, UK
xl L8 **Cumbria** ◈ *county* NW England, UK
xl L9 **Cumbrian Mountains** ▲▲ NW England, UK
xlii O11 **Cuminestown** Aberdeenshire, NE Scotland, UK
xl M7 **Cummersdale** Cumbria, NW England, UK
xliii L24 **Cummertrees** Dumfries and Galloway, SW Scotland, UK
25 S2 **Cumming** Georgia, SE USA
Cummin in Pommern *see* Kamień Pomorski
190 G9 **Cummins** South Australia
xliii J22 **Cumnock** East Ayrshire, W Scotland, UK
xxxvii P8 **Cumnor** Oxfordshire, C England, UK
42 G4 **Cumpas** Sonora, NW Mexico
142 H16 **Çumra** Konya, C Turkey
xli N7 **Cumrew** Cumbria, NW England, UK
65 G15 **Cunco** Araucanía, C Chile
56 E9 **Cundinamarca** *off.* Departamento de Cundinamarca. ◈ *province* C Colombia
43 U15 **Cunduacán** Tabasco, SE Mexico
85 C16 **Cunene** ◈ *province* S Angola
85 A16 **Cunene** *var.* Kunene. ≈ Angola/ Namibia *see also* Kunene
108 A9 **Cuneo** *Fr.* Coni. Piemonte, NW Italy
85 E15 **Cunjamba** Cuando Cubango, E Angola
189 V10 **Cunnamulla** Queensland, E Australia
94 K8 **Cuokkarašša** ▲ N Norway
108 B7 **Cuorgne** Piemonte, NE Italy
xliii M18 **Cupar** Fife, E Scotland, UK
118 L8 **Cupcina** *Rus.* Kupchino; *prev.* Calinisc, Kalinisk. N Moldavia
56 C8 **Cupica** Chocó, W Colombia
56 C8 **Cupica, Golfo de** *gulf* W Colombia
114 N13 **Ćuprija** Serbia, E Yugoslavia
Cura *see* Villa de Cura
47 P16 **Curaçao** *island* Netherlands Antilles
58 H13 **Curanja, Río** ≈ E Peru
58 F7 **Curaray, Rio** ≈ Ecuador/Peru
118 K14 **Curcani** Călăraşi, SE Romania
190 H4 **Curdimurka** South Australia
105 P7 **Cure** ≈ C France
181 Y16 **Curepipe** C Mauritius
57 R6 **Curiapo** Delta Amacuro, NE Venezuela
Curia Rhaetorum *see* Chur
64 G12 **Curicó** Maule, C Chile
Curieta *see* Krk
180 I15 **Curieuse** *island* Inner Islands, NE Seychelles
61 C16 **Curitiba** Acre, W Brazil
62 K12 **Curitiba** *prev.* Curytiba. *state capital* Paraná, S Brazil
62 J13 **Curitibanos** Santa Catarina, S Brazil
191 S6 **Curlewis** New South Wales, SE Australia
190 J6 **Curnamona** South Australia
85 A15 **Curoca** ≈ SW Angola
191 T6 **Currabubula** New South Wales, SE Australia
xliv J9 **Curragh, The** *physical region* E Ireland
61 Q14 **Currais Novos** Rio Grande do Norte, E Brazil
xliv B14 **Currane, Lough** ◎ SW Ireland
37 W7 **Currant** Nevada, W USA
37 W6 **Currant Mountain** ▲ Nevada, W USA
46 H2 **Current** Eleuthera Island, C Bahamas
29 W8 **Current River** ≈ Arkansas/Missouri, C USA
xliii M20 **Currie** City of Edinburgh, SE Scotland, UK
190 M14 **Currie** Tasmania, SE Australia
23 Y8 **Currituck** North Carolina, SE USA
23 Y8 **Currituck Sound** *sound* North Carolina, SE USA
41 R11 **Curry** Alaska, USA
Curtbunar *see* Tervel
118 I13 **Curtea de Argeş** *var.* Curtea-de-Arges. Argeş, S Romania
118 E10 **Curtici** *Ger.* Kurtitsch, *Hung.* Kürtös. Arad, W Romania
30 M16 **Curtis** Nebraska, C USA
106 H2 **Curtis-Estación** Galicia, NW Spain
191 O14 **Curtis Group** *island group* Tasmania, SE Australia
189 Y8 **Curtis Island** *island* Queensland, SE Australia
60 K11 **Curuá, Ilha do** *island* NE Brazil
49 U7 **Curuá, Rio** ≈ N Brazil
61 A14 **Curuçá, Rio** ≈ NW Brazil
114 L9 **Čurug** *Hung.* Csurog. Serbia, N Yugoslavia
63 D16 **Curuzú Cuatiá** Corrientes, NE Argentina
61 M19 **Curvelo** Minas Gerais, SE Brazil
20 E14 **Curwensville** Pennsylvania, NE USA
32 M3 **Curwood, Mount** ▲ Michigan, N USA
Curytiba *see* Curitiba
Curzola *see* Korčula
44 A10 **Cuscatlán** ◈ *department* C El Salvador
59 H15 **Cusco** *var.* Cuzco. Cusco, C Peru
59 H15 **Cusco** *off.* Departamento de Cusco; *var.* Cuzco. ◈ *department* C Peru
xliv C6 **Cushcamcarragh** ▲ NW Ireland
xliv L3 **Cushendall** Moyle, N Northern Ireland, UK
xliv L2 **Cushendun** Moyle, N Northern Ireland, UK
29 O9 **Cushing** Oklahoma, C USA
27 W8 **Cushing** Texas, SW USA
42 I6 **Cusihuiriachic** Chihuahua, N Mexico
105 P10 **Cusset** Allier, C France
25 S6 **Cusseta** Georgia, SE USA
30 J10 **Custer** South Dakota, N USA
Cüstrin *see* Kostrzyn
35 Q7 **Cut Bank** Montana, NW USA
Cutch, Gulf of *see* Kachchh, Gulf of
25 S6 **Cuthbert** Georgia, SE USA
9 S15 **Cut Knife** Saskatchewan, S Canada
25 Y16 **Cutler Ridge** Florida, SE USA
24 K10 **Cut Off** Louisiana, S USA
65 I15 **Cutral-Có** Neuquén, C Argentina
xliv F10 **Cutra, Lough** ◎ W Ireland
109 O21 **Cutro** Calabria, SW Italy
191 O4 **Cuttaburra Channels** *seasonal river* New South Wales, SE Australia
160 O12 **Cuttack** Orissa, E India
85 C15 **Cuvelai** Cunene, SW Angola
81 G18 **Cuvette** *var.* Région de la Cuvette. ◈ *province* C Congo
181 V9 **Cuvier Basin** *undersea feature* E Indian Ocean
181 U9 **Cuvier Plateau** *undersea feature* E Indian Ocean
84 B12 **Cuvo** ≈ W Angola
102 H9 **Cuxhaven** Niedersachsen, NW Germany
Cuyabá *see* Cuiabá
179 Pp13 **Cuyo East Pass** *passage* C Philippines
179 P13 **Cuyo West Pass** *passage* C Philippines
Cuyuni, Río *see* Cuyuni River
57 S8 **Cuyuni River** *var.* Río Cuyuni. ≈ Guyana/Venezuela
Cuzco *see* Cusco
xxxv K13 **Cwmbran** *Wel.* Cwmbrân. Torfaen, SW Wales, UK
30 K15 **C.W.McConaughy, Lake** ⊠ Nebraska, C USA
xxxv F13 **Cwmffrwd** Carmarthenshire, S Wales, UK
83 D20 **Cyangugu** SW Rwanda
112 D11 **Cybinka** *Ger.* Ziebingen. Zielona Góra, W Poland
Cyclades *see* Kykládes
Cydonia *see* Chaniá
xxxv I5 **Cyffylliog** Denbighshire, N Wales, UK
Cymru *see* Wales
22 M5 **Cynthiana** Kentucky, S USA
xxxv I6 **Cynwyd** Denbighshire, N Wales, UK
xxxv F12 **Cynwyl Elfed** Carmarthenshire, S Wales, UK
9 S17 **Cypress Hills** ▲▲ Alberta/Saskatchewan, SW Canada
Cypro-Syrian Basin *see* Cyprus Basin
123 Mm1 **Cyprus** *off.* Republic of Cyprus, *Gk.* Kypros, *Turk.* Kıbrıs, Kıbrıs Cumhuriyeti. ◆ *republic* E Mediterranean Sea
86 L14 **Cyprus** *Gk.* Kypros, *Turk.* Kıbrıs. *island* E Mediterranean Sea
123 Gg10 **Cyprus Basin** *var.* Cypro-Syrian Basin. *undersea feature* E Mediterranean Sea
Cythera *see* Kýthira
Cythnos *see* Kýthnos
112 F9 **Czaplinek** *Ger.* Tempelburg. Koszalin, NW Poland
Czarna Woda *see* Wda
112 G8 **Czarne** Słupsk, NW Poland
112 G10 **Czarnków** Piła, NW Poland
113 E17 **Czech Republic** *Cz.* Česká Republika. ◆ *republic* C Europe
Czegléd *see* Cegléd
112 G12 **Czempiń** Poznań, W Poland
Czenstochau *see* Częstochowa
Czerkow *see* Čerchov
Czernowitz *see* Chernivtsi
112 I8 **Czersk** Bydgoszcz, NW Poland
113 J15 **Częstochowa** *Ger.* Czenstochau, Tschenstochau, *Rus.* Chenstokhov. Częstochowa, S Poland
113 J15 **Częstochowa** *off.* Województwo częstochowskie, *Ger.* Czenstochau, Tschenstochau, *Rus.* Chenstokhov. ◈ *province* S Poland
Częstochowskie, Województwo *see* Częstochowa
112 F10 **Człopa** *Ger.* Schloppe. Piła, W Poland
112 H8 **Człuchów** *Ger.* Schlochau. Słupsk, NW Poland

D

169 V9 **Da'an** *var.* Dalai. Jilin, NE China
13 S10 **Daaquam** Québec, SE Canada
Daawo, Webi *see* Dawa Wenz
56 I4 **Dabajuro** Falcón, NW Venezuela
79 N15 **Dabakala** NE Ivory Coast
Daban *see* Bairin Youqi
113 K23 **Dabas** Pest, C Hungary
166 L8 **Daba Shan** ▲▲ C China
146 J5 **Dabbāgh, Jabal** ▲ NW Saudi Arabia
56 D8 **Dabeiba** Antioquia, NW Colombia
166 L17 **Daben** Hainan, S China
160 E11 **Dabhoi** Gujarāt, W India
167 P8 **Dabie Shan** ▲▲ C China
78 J13 **Dabola** Haute-Guinée, C Guinea
79 N17 **Dabou** S Ivory Coast
112 P8 **Dąbrowa Białostocka** Białystok, NE Poland
113 M16 **Dąbrowa Tarnowska** Tarnów, SE Poland
121 M20 **Dabryn'** *Rus.* Dobryn'. Homyel'skaya Voblasts', SE Belorussia
165 P10 **Dabsan Hu** ◎ C China
167 Q13 **Dabu** *prev.* Huliao. Guangdong, S China
118 H15 **Dăbuleni** Dolj, SW Romania
Dacca *see* Dhaka
103 L23 **Dachau** Bayern, SE Germany
166 K8 **Dachuan** *prev.* Daxian, Da Xian. Sichuan, C China
Dacia Bank *see* Dacia Seamount
66 M10 **Dacia Seamount** *var.* Dacia Bank. *undersea feature* E Atlantic Ocean
39 T3 **Dacono** Colorado, C USA
xl M8 **Dacre** Cumbria, NW England, UK
Đăc Tô *see* Đak Tô
Dacura *see* Dákura
25 W12 **Dade City** Florida, SE USA
158 L10 **Dadeldhura** *var.* Dandeldhura. Far Western, W Nepal
25 Q5 **Dadeville** Alabama, S USA
105 N15 **Dadou** ≈ S France
160 D12 **Dādra and Nagar Haveli** ◈ *union territory* W India
155 P14 **Dādu** Sind, SE Pakistan
178 K11 **Da Du Boloc** Kon Tum, C Vietnam
166 G9 **Dadu He** ≈ C China
Daegu *see* Taegu
Daerah Istimewa Aceh *see* Aceh
179 Q11 **Daet** Luzon, N Philippines
166 I11 **Dafang** Guizhou, S China
159 W11 **Dafla Hills** ▲▲ NE India
9 U15 **Dafoe** Saskatchewan, S Canada
78 G10 **Dagana** N Senegal
Dagana *see* Dahana, Tajikistan
Dagana *see* Massakory, Chad
120 K11 **Dagda** Krāslava, SE Latvia
Dagden *see* Hiiumaa
Dagden-Sund *see* Soela Väin
xxxvii V9 **Dagenham** Barking and Dagenham, SE England, UK
131 P16 **Dagestan, Respublika** *prev.* Dagestanskaya ASSR, *Eng.* Daghestan. ◈ *autonomous republic* SW Russian Federation
Dagestanskaya ASSR *see* Dagestan, Respublika
131 R17 **Dagestanskiye Ogni** Respublika Dagestan, SW Russian Federation
193 A23 **Dagg Sound** *sound* South Island, NZ
Daghestan *see* Dagestan, Respublika
147 Y8 **Daghmar** NE Oman
Dağlıq Qarabağ *see* Nagornyy Karabakh
xxxvii S7 **Dagnall** Buckinghamshire, C England, UK
Dagö *see* Hiiumaa
56 D11 **Dagua** Valle del Cauca, W Colombia
166 H11 **Daguan** Yunnan, SW China
179 P9 **Dagupan** *off.* Dagupan City. Luzon, N Philippines
165 N16 **Dagzê** Xizang Zizhiqu, W China
153 Q13 **Dahana** *Rus.* Dagana, Dakhana. SW Tajikistan
169 V10 **Dahei Shan** ▲▲ N China
169 T7 **Da Hinggan Ling** *Eng.* Great Khingan Range. ▲▲ NE China
Dahlac Archipelago *see* Dahlak Archipelago

◆ Country
● Country Capital
◇ Dependent Territory
○ Dependent Territory Capital
◈ Administrative Region
✕ International Airport
▲ Mountain
▲▲ Mountain Range
Volcano
≈ River
◎ Lake
⊠ Reservoir

DAHLAK ARCHIPELAGO – DEGGENDORF

82 K9 **Dahlak Archipelago** *var.* Dahlac Archipelago. *island group* E Eritrea
25 T2 **Dahlonega** Georgia, SE USA
103 O14 **Dahme** Brandenburg, E Germany
102 O13 **Dahme** ≈ E Germany
147 O14 **Dahm, Ramlat** *desert* NW Yemen
160 E10 **Dāhod** *prev.* Dohad. Gujarāt, W India
Dahomey *see* Benin
164 G10 **Dahongliutan** Xinjiang Uygur Zizhiqu, NW China
Dahra *see* Dara
145 R2 **Dahūk** *var.* Dohuk, *Kurd.* Dihōk. N Iraq
118 J15 **Daia** Giurgiu, S Romania
171 L15 **Daigo** Ibaraki, Honshū, S Japan
169 O13 **Dai Hai** ◎ N China
Daihoku *see* T'aipei
195 X14 **Dai Island** *island* N Solomon Islands
177 G8 **Daik-u** Pegu, SW Burma
144 H9 **Dā'īl** Dar'ā, S Syria
178 Kk12 **Đai Lanh** Khanh Hoa, S Vietnam
xliii H23 **Dailly** South Ayrshire, W Scotland, UK
167 Q13 **Daimao Shan** ▲▲ SE China
xliii I16 **Daimh, Loch an** ◎ C Scotland, UK
107 N11 **Daimiel** Castilla-La Mancha, C Spain
117 F22 **Daimoniá** Pelopónnisos, S Greece
Dainan *see* T'ainan
xliv I9 **Daingean** Offaly, C Ireland
27 W6 **Daingerfield** Texas, SW USA
Daingin, Bá an *see* Dingle Bay
165 R13 **Dainkognubma** Xizang Zizhiqu, W China
171 Hh17 **Daiō-zaki** *headland* Honshū, SW Japan
Dairbhre *see* Valencia Island
63 B22 **Daireaux** Buenos Aires, E Argentina
Dairen *see* Dalian
xliii N18 **Dairsie** Fife, E Scotland, UK
77 W9 **Dairûṭ** *var.* Dayrūṭ. C Egypt
170 Ff12 **Dai-sen** ▲ Kyūshū, SW Japan
27 X10 **Daisetta** Texas, SW USA
199 Gg5 **Daitō-jima** *island group* SW Japan
199 Gg5 **Daitō Ridge** *undersea feature* N Philippine Sea
167 N3 **Daixian** *var.* Dai Xian. Shanxi, C China
167 Q12 **Daiyun Shan** ▲▲ SE China
46 M8 **Dajabón** NW Dominican Republic
166 G8 **Dajin Chuan** ≈ C China
154 J6 **Dak** ◎ W Afghanistan
78 F11 **Dakar** ● (Senegal) W Senegal
78 F11 **Dakar** ✕ W Senegal
178 K11 **Đak Glây** Kon Tum, C Vietnam
Dakhana *see* Dahana
159 U16 **Dakhin Shahbazpur Island** *island* S Bangladesh
Dakhla *see* Ad Dakhla
78 F7 **Dakhlet Nouâdhibou** ◈ *region* NW Mauritania
Đak Lap *see* Kiên Đưc
178 K13 **Đak Nông** Đăc Lăc, S Vietnam
79 U11 **Dakoro** Maradi, S Niger
31 U12 **Dakota City** Iowa, C USA
31 R13 **Dakota City** Nebraska, C USA
115 M17 **Đakovica** *var.* Djakovica, *Alb.* Gjakovë. Serbia, S Yugoslavia
114 I10 **Đakovo** *var.* Djakovo, *Hung.* Diakovár. Osijek-Baranja, E Croatia
Dakshin *see* Deccan
178 K11 **Đak Tô** *var.* Đăc Tô. Kon Tum, C Vietnam
45 N7 **Dákura** *var.* Dacura. Región Autónoma Atlántico Norte, NE Nicaragua
97 I14 **Dal** Akershus, S Norway
84 E12 **Dala** Lunda Sul, E Angola
110 J8 **Dalaas** Vorarlberg, W Austria
78 I13 **Dalaba** Moyenne-Guinée, W Guinea
Dalai *see* Da'an
Dalain Hob *see* Ejin Qi
Dalai Nor *see* Hulun Nur
169 Q11 **Dalai Nur** *salt lake* N China
Dala-Jarna *see* Järna
97 M14 **Dalälven** ≈ C Sweden
142 D16 **Dalaman** Muğla, SW Turkey
142 C16 **Dalaman** ✕ Muğla, SW Turkey
142 D16 **Dalaman Çayı** ≈ SW Turkey
168 K11 **Dalandzadgad** Ömnögovĭ, S Mongolia
97 D17 **Dalane** *physical region* S Norway
201 Z2 **Dalap-Uliga-Djarrit** *var.* Delap-Uliga-Darrit, D-U-D. *island group* Ratak Chain, SE Marshall Islands
96 L13 **Dalarna** *prev. Eng.* Dalecarlia. *cultural region* C Sweden
97 P16 **Dalarö** Stockholm, C Sweden
178 Kk13 **Đa Lat** Lâm Đông, S Vietnam
xliii G18 **Dalavich** Argyll and Bute, W Scotland, UK
168 J11 **Dalay** Ömnögovĭ, S Mongolia
154 L12 **Dālbandin** *var.* Dāl Bandin. Baluchistān, SW Pakistan
xliii K25 **Dalbeattie** Dumfries and Galloway, SW Scotland, UK
97 J17 **Dalbosjön** *lake bay* S Sweden
xl F12 **Dalby** W Isle of Man
189 Y10 **Dalby** Queensland, E Australia
xlii H13 **Dalchreichart** Highland, NW Scotland, UK
xxxv C14 **Dale** Pembrokeshire, SW Wales, UK
96 D13 **Dale** Hordaland, S Norway
96 C12 **Dale** Sogn og Fjordane, S Norway
34 K12 **Dale** Oregon, NW USA
27 T11 **Dale** Texas, SW USA
Dalecarlia *see* Dalarna
23 W4 **Dale City** Virginia, NE USA
22 L8 **Dale Hollow Lake** ▣ Kentucky/Tennessee, S USA
100 O8 **Dalen** Drenthe, NE Netherlands
97 E15 **Dalen** Telemark, S Norway
xlii H3 **Dale of Walls** Shetland Islands, NE Scotland, UK
177 F4 **Daletme** Chin State, W Burma
25 Q7 **Daleville** Alabama, S USA
100 M9 **Dalfsen** Overijssel, E Netherlands
xliii L16 **Dalguise** Perth and Kinross, C Scotland, UK
xlii K7 **Dalhalvaig** Highland, N Scotland, UK
26 M1 **Dalhart** Texas, SW USA
11 O13 **Dalhousie** New Brunswick, SE Canada
158 I6 **Dalhousie** Himāchal Pradesh, N India
166 F12 **Dali** *var.* Xiaguan. Yunnan, SW China
Dali *see* Idálion
169 U14 **Dalian** *var.* Dairen, Dalien, Lüda, Ta-lien, *Rus.* Dalny. Liaoning, NE China
107 O15 **Dalías** Andalucía, S Spain
xlii A13 **Daliburgh** Western Isles, NW Scotland, UK
Dalien *see* Dalian
Dalijan *see* Delījān
114 J9 **Dalj** *Hung.* Dalja. Osijek-Baranja, E Croatia
Dalja *see* Dalj
xliii M20 **Dalkeith** Midlothian, SE Scotland, UK
xliv L9 **Dalkey** Dublin, E Ireland
xlii L11 **Dallas** Moray, N Scotland, UK
34 F12 **Dallas** Oregon, NW USA
27 U6 **Dallas** Texas, SW USA
27 T7 **Dallas-Fort Worth** ✕ Texas, SW USA
160 K12 **Dalli Rājhara** Madhya Pradesh, C India
41 X15 **Dall Island** *island* Alexander Archipelago, Alaska, USA
40 M12 **Dall Lake** ◎ Alaska, USA
79 S12 **Dallol Bosso** *seasonal river* W Niger
147 U7 **Dalmā** *island* W UAE
115 E14 **Dalmacija** *Eng.* Dalmatia, *Ger.* Dalmatien, *It.* Dalmazia. *cultural region* S Croatia
xliii H17 **Dalmally** Argyll and Bute, W Scotland, UK
Dalmatia/Dalmatien/Dalmazia *see* Dalmacija
xliii I23 **Dalmellington** East Ayrshire, W Scotland, UK
127 Nn17 **Dal'negorsk** Primorskiy Kray, SE Russian Federation
127 Nn17 **Dal'nerechensk** Primorskiy Kray, SE Russian Federation
Dalny *see* Dalian
78 M16 **Daloa** C Ivory Coast
166 J11 **Dalou Shan** ▲▲ S China
xliii I21 **Dalry** North Ayrshire, W Scotland, UK
xliii I22 **Dalrymple** South Ayrshire, W Scotland, UK
189 X7 **Dalrymple Lake** ◎ Queensland, E Australia
12 H14 **Dalrymple Lake** ◎ Ontario, S Canada
189 X7 **Dalrymple, Mount** ▲ Queensland, E Australia
95 K20 **Dalsbruk** *Fin.* Taalintehdas. Turku-Pori, SW Finland
97 K19 **Dalsjöfors** Älvsborg, S Sweden
97 J17 **Dals Långed** *var.* Långed. Älvsborg, S Sweden
xl M7 **Dalston** Cumbria, NW England, UK
159 O15 **Dāltenganj** *prev.* Daltonganj. Bihār, N India
xliii L24 **Dalton** Dumfries and Galloway, SW Scotland, UK
25 R2 **Dalton** Georgia, SE USA
Daltonganj *see* Dāltenganj
205 X14 **Dalton Iceberg Tongue** *ice feature* Antarctica
xl L12 **Dalton-in-Furness** Cumbria, NW England, UK
94 J1 **Dalvík** Nordhurland Eystra, N Iceland
xliii J15 **Dalwhinnie** Highland, NW Scotland, UK
xxxvi J13 **Dalwood** Devon, SW England, UK
37 N8 **Daly City** California, W USA
189 P2 **Daly River** ≈ Northern Territory, N Australia
189 Q3 **Daly Waters** Northern Territory, N Australia
121 F20 **Damachava** *var.* Damachova, *Pol.* Domaczewo, *Rus.* Domachëvo. Brestskaya Voblasts', SW Belorussia
Damachova *see* Damachava
79 W11 **Damagaram Takaya** Zinder, S Niger
160 D12 **Damān** Damān and Diu, W India
160 B12 **Damān and Diu** ◈ *union territory* W India
77 V7 **Damanhûr** *anc.* Hermopolis Parva. N Egypt
Damão *see* Damān
167 O1 **Damaqun Shan** ▲▲ E China
81 I15 **Damara** Ombella-Mpoko, S Central African Republic
85 D18 **Damaraland** *physical region* C Namibia
175 T15 **Damar, Kepulauan** *var.* Baraf Daja Islands, Kepulauan Barat Daya. *island group* C Indonesia
174 Gg4 **Damar Laut** Perak, Peninsular Malaysia
175 Tt15 **Damar, Pulau** *island* Maluku, E Indonesia
Damas *see* Dimashq
79 Y12 **Damasak** Borno, NE Nigeria
Damasco *see* Dimashq
23 Q8 **Damascus** Virginia, NE USA
Damascus *see* Dimashq
79 X13 **Damaturu** Yobe, NE Nigeria
175 Ss4 **Damau** Pulau Kaburuang, N Indonesia
149 O5 **Damāvand, Qolleh-ye** ▲ N Iran
84 B10 **Damba** Uíge, NW Angola
116 M12 **Dambaslar** Tekirdağ, NW Turkey
118 J13 **Dâmbovița** *prev.* Dîmbovița. ◈ *county* SE Romania
118 J13 **Dâmbovița** *prev.* Dîmbovița. ≈ S Romania
181 Y15 **D'Ambre, Île** *island* NE Mauritius
161 K24 **Dambulla** Central Province, C Sri Lanka
46 K9 **Dame-Marie** SW Haiti
46 J9 **Dame Marie, Cap** *headland* SW Haiti
xxxvii N12 **Damerham** Hampshire, S England, UK
149 Q4 **Dāmghān** Semnān, N Iran
Damietta *see* Dumyât
144 G10 **Dāmiyā** Al Balqā', NW Jordan
152 G11 **Damla** Dashkhovuzskiy Velayat, N Turkmenistan
Dammām *see* Ad Dammān
102 G12 **Damme** Niedersachsen, NW Germany
159 R15 **Dāmodar** ≈ NE India
160 J9 **Damoh** Madhya Pradesh, C India
79 P15 **Damongo** NW Ghana
144 G7 **Damoûr** *var.* Ad Dāmūr. W Lebanon
175 Pp7 **Dampal, Teluk** *bay* Sulawesi, C Indonesia
xlii F12 **Damph, Loch** ◎ NW Scotland, UK
188 H7 **Dampier** Western Australia
188 H6 **Dampier Archipelago** *island group* Western Australia
176 Uu9 **Dampier, Selat** *strait* Irian Jaya, E Indonesia
194 L12 **Dampier Strait** *strait* NE PNG
147 U14 **Damqawt** *var.* Damqut. E Yemen
165 O13 **Dam Qu** ≈ C China
Damqut *see* Damqawt
178 Ii13 **Dâmrei, Chuŏr Phmun** *Fr.* Chaîne de l'Éléphant. ▲▲ SW Cambodia
110 C7 **Damvant** Jura, NW Switzerland
Damwâld *see* Damwoude
100 L5 **Damwoude** *Fris.* Damwâld. Friesland, N Netherlands
165 N15 **Damxung** Xizang Zizhiqu, W China
82 K11 **Danakil Desert** *var.* Afar Depression, Danakil Plain. *desert* E Africa
Danakil Plain *see* Danakil Desert
37 R8 **Dana, Mount** ▲ California, W USA
78 L16 **Danané** W Ivory Coast
178 Kk10 **Đă Nâng** *prev.* Tourane. Quang Nam-Đa Năng, C Vietnam
179 Qq13 **Danao** *var.* Danao City. Cebu, C Philippines
166 G9 **Danba** Sichuan, C China
Danborg *see* Daneborg
xxxvii W8 **Danbury** Essex, SE England, UK
20 L13 **Danbury** Connecticut, NE USA
27 W12 **Danbury** Texas, SW USA
37 X15 **Danby Lake** ◎ California, W USA
204 H4 **Danco Coast** *physical region* Antarctica
84 B11 **Dande** ≈ NW Angola
Dandeldhura *see* Dadeldhura
161 E17 **Dandeli** Karnātaka, W India
191 O12 **Dandenong** Victoria, SE Australia
169 V13 **Dandong** *var.* Tan-tung; *prev.* An-tung. Liaoning, NE China
207 Q14 **Daneborg** *var.* Danborg. N Greenland
27 V12 **Danevang** Texas, SW USA
Dänew *see* Deynau
12 L12 **Danford Lake** Québec, SE Canada
21 T4 **Danforth** Maine, NE USA
39 P3 **Danforth Hills** ▲▲ Colorado, C USA
Dangara *see* Danghara
165 V12 **Dangchang** Gansu, C China
Dangchengwan *see* Subei
84 B10 **Dange** Uíge, NW Angola
Dangerous Archipelago *see* Tuamotu, Îles
85 E26 **Danger Point** *headland* SW South Africa
153 Q13 **Danghara** *Rus.* Dangara. SW Tajikistan
165 P8 **Danghe Nanshan** ▲▲ W China
82 I12 **Dangila** *var.* Dānglā. NW Ethiopia
165 P8 **Dangjin Shankou** *pass* N China
Dangla *see* Tanggula Shan
Dānglā *see* Dangila, NW Ethiopia
Dangme Chu *see* Manās
159 Y11 **Dāngori** Assam, NE India
Dang Raek, Phanom/Dangrek, Chaîne des *see* Dângrêk, Chuŏr Phnum
178 Ii11 **Dângrêk, Chuŏr Phnum** *var.* Phanom Dang Raek, Phanom Dong Rak, *Fr.* Chaîne des Dangrek. ▲▲ Cambodia/Thailand
44 G3 **Dangriga** *prev.* Stann Creek. Stann Creek, E Belize
167 P6 **Dangshan** Anhui, E China
35 T15 **Daniel** Wyoming, C USA
85 H22 **Daniëlskuil** Northern Cape, N South Africa
21 N12 **Danielson** Connecticut, NE USA
128 M15 **Danilov** Yaroslavskaya Oblast', W Russian Federation
131 O9 **Danilovka** Volgogradskaya Oblast', SW Russian Federation
Danish West Indies *see* Virgin Islands (US)
166 L7 **Dan Jiang** ≈ C China
166 M7 **Danjiangkou Shuiku** ▣ C China
147 W8 **Ḍank** *var.* Dhank. NW Oman
158 J7 **Dankhar** Himāchal Pradesh, N India
130 L6 **Dankov** Lipetskaya Oblast', W Russian Federation
44 J7 **Danlí** El Paraíso, S Honduras
Danmark *see* Denmark
Danmarksstraedet *see* Denmark Strait
97 O14 **Dannemora** Uppsala, C Sweden
20 L6 **Dannemora** New York, NE USA
102 K11 **Dannenberg** Niedersachsen, N Germany
192 N12 **Dannevirke** Manawatu-Wanganui, North Island, NZ
23 U8 **Dan River** ≈ Virginia, NE USA
178 Hh9 **Dan Sai** Loei, C Thailand
20 F10 **Dansville** New York, NE USA
Dantzig *see* Gdańsk
88 E12 **Danube** *Bul.* Dunav, *Cz.* Dunaj, *Ger.* Donau, *Hung.* Duna, *Rom.* Dunărea. ≈ C Europe
Danubian Plain *see* Dunavska Ravnina
177 Ff8 **Danubyu** Irrawaddy, SW Burma
Danum *see* Doncaster
21 P11 **Danvers** Massachusetts, NE USA
29 T11 **Danville** Arkansas, C USA
33 N13 **Danville** Illinois, N USA
33 O14 **Danville** Indiana, N USA
31 Y15 **Danville** Iowa, C USA
22 M6 **Danville** Kentucky, S USA
20 G14 **Danville** Pennsylvania, NE USA
23 T6 **Danville** Virginia, NE USA
166 L17 **Danxian** *var.* Dan Xian, Nada. Hainan, S China
Danzig *see* Gdańsk
Danziger Bucht *see* Danzig, Gulf of
112 J6 **Danzig, Gulf of** *var.* Gulf of Gdańsk, *Ger.* Danziger Bucht, *Pol.* Zakota Gdańska, *Rus.* Gdan'skaya Bukhta. *gulf* N Poland
166 F10 **Daocheng** Sichuan, C China
Daokou *see* Huaxian
106 H7 **Dão, Rio** ≈ N Portugal
Daosa *see* Dausa
79 Y7 **Dao Timmi** Agadez, NE Niger
166 M13 **Daoxian** *var.* Dao Xian. Hunan, S China
79 Q14 **Dapaong** N Togo
25 N8 **Daphne** Alabama, S USA
179 Qq15 **Dapitan** Mindanao, S Philippines
165 P9 **Da Qaidam** Qinghai, C China
169 V8 **Daqing** Heilongjiang, NE China
169 O13 **Daqing Shan** ▲▲ N China
Daqm *see* Duqm
145 T5 **Dāqūq** *var.* Tāwūq. N Iraq
78 G10 **Dara** *var.* Dahra. NW Senegal
144 H9 **Dar'ā** *var.* Der'a, *Fr.* Déraa. Dar'ā, SW Syria
144 H8 **Dar'ā** *off.* Muḥāfaẓat Dar'ā, *var.* Dará, Derá, Derrá. ◈ *governorate* S Syria
149 Q12 **Dārāb** Fārs, S Iran
118 K8 **Darabani** Botoșani, NW Romania
Daraj *see* Dirj
148 M8 **Dārān** Eşfahān, W Iran
178 Kk12 **Đa Răng, Sông** *var.* Ba. ≈ S Vietnam
126 Kk16 **Darasun** Chitinskaya Oblast', S Russian Federation
Daraut-Kurgan *see* Daroot-Korgon
79 W13 **Darazo** Bauchi, E Nigeria
145 S3 **Darband** N Iraq
145 V4 **Darband-i Khān, Sadd** *dam* NE Iraq
145 N1 **Darbāsīyah** *var.* Derbisīye. Al Ḥasakah, N Syria
120 C11 **Darbėnai** Kretinga, NW Lithuania
159 Q13 **Darbhanga** Bihār, N India
40 M9 **Darby, Cape** *headland* Alaska, USA
114 I9 **Darda** *Hung.* Dárda. Osijek-Baranja, E Croatia
29 T11 **Dardanelle** Arkansas, C USA
29 S11 **Dardanelle, Lake** ▣ Arkansas, C USA
Dardanelles *see* Çanakkale Boğazı
Dardanelli *see* Çanakkale
Dar-el-Beida *see* Casablanca
142 M14 **Darende** Malatya, C Turkey
83 J22 **Dar es Salaam** Dar es Salaam, E Tanzania
83 J22 **Dar es Salaam** ✕ Pwani, E Tanzania
xli S16 **Darfield** Barnsley, N England, UK
193 H18 **Darfield** Canterbury, South Island, NZ
108 F7 **Darfo** Lombardia, N Italy
82 B10 **Darfur** *var.* Darfur Massif. *cultural region* W Sudan
Darfur Massif *see* Darfur
152 J10 **Dargan-Ata** *var.* Darganata. Lebapskiy Velayat, NE Turkmenistan
Darganata *see* Dargan-Ata
149 T3 **Dargaz** *var.* Darreh Gaz; *prev.* Moḥammadābād. Khorāsān, NE Iran
145 U4 **Dargazayn** NE Iraq
191 P12 **Dargo** Victoria, SE Australia
168 K7 **Darhan** Bulgan, C Mongolia
169 N8 **Darhan** Hentiy, C Mongolia
168 L6 **Darhan** Selenge, N Mongolia
169 N12 **Darhan Muminggan Lianheqi** *var.* Bailingmiao. Nei Mongol Zizhiqu, N China
25 W7 **Darien** Georgia, SE USA
45 W16 **Darién** *off.* Provincia del Darién. ◈ *province* SE Panama
Darién, Golfo del *see* Darien, Gulf of
45 X14 **Darien, Gulf of** *Sp.* Golfo del Darién. *gulf* S Caribbean Sea
Darien, Isthmus of *see* Panamá, Istmo de
44 K9 **Dariense, Cordillera** ▲▲ C Nicaragua
45 W15 **Darién, Serranía del** ▲▲ Colombia/Panama
Dario *see* Ciudad Darío
Dariorigum *see* Vannes
Dariv *see* Darvi
Darj *see* Dirj
Darjeeling *see* Darjiling
159 S12 **Darjiling** *prev.* Darjeeling. West Bengal, NE India
Darkehnen *see* Ozersk
165 S12 **Darlag** Qinghai, C China
191 T3 **Darling Downs** *hill range* Queensland, E Australia
30 M2 **Darling, Lake** ▣ North Dakota, N USA
188 I12 **Darling Range** ▲▲ Western Australia
190 L8 **Darling River** ≈ New South Wales, SE Australia
xli W7 **Darlington** Darlington, N England, UK
xli R9 **Darlington** ◈ *unitary authority* N England, UK
23 T12 **Darlington** South Carolina, SE USA
32 K9 **Darlington** Wisconsin, N USA
112 G7 **Darłowo** Koszalin, NW Poland
103 G19 **Darmstadt** Hessen, SW Germany
77 S7 **Darnah** *var.* Dérna. NE Libya
105 S6 **Darney** Vosges, NE France
190 M7 **Darnick** New South Wales, SE Australia
205 Y6 **Darnley, Cape** *headland* Antarctica
107 R7 **Daroca** Aragón, NE Spain
153 S11 **Daroot-Korgon** *var.* Daraut-Kurgan. Oshskaya Oblast', SW Kyrgyzstan
63 A23 **Darragueira** *var.* Darregueira. Buenos Aires, E Argentina
Darregueira *see* Darragueira
Darreh Gaz *see* Dargaz
148 K7 **Darreh Shahr** *var.* Darreh-ye Shahr. Īlām, W Iran
Darreh-ye Shahr *see* Darreh Shahr
34 I7 **Darrington** Washington, NW USA
27 P1 **Darrouzett** Texas, SW USA
159 S15 **Darsana** *var.* Darshana. Khulna, N Bangladesh
Darshana *see* Darsana
102 M7 **Darss** *peninsula* NE Germany
102 M7 **Darsser Ort** *headland* NE Germany
xxxvi H15 **Dart** ≈ SW England, UK
Dartang *see* Baqên
xxxvii V9 **Dartford** Kent, SE England, UK
xxxvi H15 **Dartington** Devon, SW England, UK
xxxvi G15 **Dartmoor** *moorland* SW England, UK
190 L12 **Dartmoor** Victoria, SE Australia
xxxvi H16 **Dartmouth** Devon, SW England, UK
11 Q15 **Dartmouth** Nova Scotia, SE Canada
13 Y6 **Dartmouth** ≈ Québec, SE Canada
191 Q11 **Dartmouth Reservoir** ◎ Victoria, SE Australia
xli S15 **Darton** Barnsley, N England, UK
xliv G5 **Dartry Mountains** ▲▲ N Ireland
Dartuch, Cabo *see* Artrutx, Cap d'
194 G15 **Daru** Western, SW PNG
114 G9 **Daruvar** *Hung.* Daruvár. Bjelovar-Bilogora, NE Croatia
152 F10 **Darvaza** *Turkm.* Derweze. Akhalskiy Velayat, C Turkmenistan
Darvaza *see* Darwoza
Darvazskiy Khrebet *see* Darvoz, Qatorkŭhi
xliii J21 **Darvel** East Ayrshire, W Scotland, UK
168 F8 **Darvi** *var.* Dariv. Govĭ-Altay, W Mongolia
154 L9 **Darvīshān** *var.* Darweshan, Garmser. Helmand, S Afghanistan
153 R13 **Darvoz, Qatorkŭhi** *Rus.* Darvazskiy Khrebet. ▲▲ C Tajikistan
xli O15 **Darwen** Lancashire, NW England, UK
Darweshan *see* Darvīshān
65 J15 **Darwin** Río Negro, S Argentina
189 O1 **Darwin** *prev.* Palmerston, Port Darwin. *territory capital* Northern Territory, N Australia
67 D24 **Darwin** *var.* Darwin Settlement. East Falkland, Falkland Islands
64 H8 **Darwin, Cordillera** ▲▲ N Chile
59 B17 **Darwin, Volcán** ☗ Galapagos Islands, Ecuador, E Pacific Ocean
153 O10 **Darwoza** *Rus.* Darvaza. Jizzakh Wiloyati, C Uzbekistan
155 S8 **Darya Khān** Punjab, E Pakistan
151 O15 **Dar'yalyktakyr, Ravnina** *plain* S Kazakhstan
149 T11 **Dārzīn** Kermān, S Iran
166 L8 **Dashennongjia** ▲ C China
Dashhowuz *see* Dashkhovuz
Dashhowuz Welayaty *see* Dashkhovuzskiy Velayat
121 O16 **Dashkawka** *Rus.* Dashkovka. Mahilyowskaya Voblasts', E Belorussia
152 H8 **Dashkhovuz** *Turkm.* Dashhowuz; *prev.* Tashauz. Dashkhovuzskiy Velayat, N Turkmenistan
Dashkhovuz *see* Dashkhovuzskiy Velayat
152 E9 **Dashkhovuzskiy Velayat** *var.* Dashkhovuz, *Turkm.* Dashhowuz Welayaty. ◈ *province* N Turkmenistan
Dashköpri *see* Tashkepri
Dashkovka *see* Dashkawka
154 J15 **Dasht** ≈ SW Pakistan
Dashtidzhum *see* Dashtijum
153 R13 **Dashtijum** *Rus.* Dashtidzhum. SW Tajikistan
155 W7 **Daska** Punjab, NE Pakistan
Đa, Sông *see* Black River
79 R15 **Dassa** *var.* Dassa-Zoumé. S Benin
Dassa-Zoumé *see* Dassa
31 U8 **Dassel** Minnesota, N USA
158 H3 **Dastegil Sar** *var.* Disteghil Sār. ▲ N India
142 C16 **Datça** Muğla, SW Turkey
172 Nn6 **Date** Hokkaidō, NE Japan
160 I8 **Datia** *prev.* Duttia. Madhya Pradesh, C India
165 T10 **Datong** Qinghai, C China
167 N2 **Datong** *var.* Tatung, Ta-t'ung. Shanxi, C China
165 S9 **Datong He** ≈ C China
165 S9 **Datong Shan** ▲▲ C China
174 Kk6 **Datu, Tanjung** *headland* Indonesia/Malaysia
Daua *see* Dawa Wenz
180 H16 **Dauban, Mount** ▲ Silhouette, NE Seychelles
155 T7 **Dāūd Khel** Punjab, E Pakistan
121 G15 **Daugai** Alytus, S Lithuania
Daugava *see* Western Dvina
120 J11 **Daugavpils** *Ger.* Dünaburg; *prev.* Rus. Dvinsk. *municipality* Daugvapils, SE Latvia
Dauka *see* Dawkah
Daulatabad *see* Malāyer
103 D18 **Daun** Rheinland-Pfalz, W Germany
161 E14 **Daund** *prev.* Dhond. Mahārāshtra, W India
178 Gg12 **Daung Kyun** *island* S Burma
9 W15 **Dauphin** Manitoba, S Canada
105 S13 **Dauphiné** *cultural region* E France
25 N9 **Dauphin Island** *island* Alabama, S USA
9 X15 **Dauphin River** Manitoba, S Canada
79 V12 **Daura** Katsina, N Nigeria
158 H12 **Dausa** *prev.* Daosa. Rājasthān, N India
Dauwa *see* Dawwah
xlii L12 **Dava** Moray, N Scotland, UK
xliii F22 **Davaar** *island* W Scotland, UK
143 Y10 **Däväçi** *Rus.* Divichi. NE Azerbaijan
161 F18 **Dāvangere** Karnātaka, W India
179 Rr16 **Davao** *off.* Davao City. Mindanao, S Philippines
179 Rr16 **Davao Gulf** *gulf* Mindanao, S Philippines
13 Q11 **Daveluyville** Québec, SE Canada
xxxviii I6 **Davenham** Cheshire, W England, UK
31 Z14 **Davenport** Iowa, C USA
34 L8 **Davenport** Washington, NW USA
xxxix N12 **Daventry** Northamptonshire, C England, UK
45 P16 **David** Chiriquí, W Panama
13 O11 **David** ≈ Québec, SE Canada
31 R15 **David City** Nebraska, C USA
David-Gorodok *see* Davyd-Haradok
9 T16 **Davidson** Saskatchewan, S Canada
23 R10 **Davidson** North Carolina, SE USA
28 K12 **Davidson** Oklahoma, C USA
41 S6 **Davidson Mountains** ▲▲ Alaska, USA
180 M8 **Davie Ridge** *undersea feature* W Indian Ocean
190 A1 **Davies, Mount** ▲ South Australia
xliii M23 **Davington** Dumfries and Galloway, SW Scotland, UK
xlii J12 **Daviot** Highland, NW Scotland, UK
37 O7 **Davis** California, W USA
29 N12 **Davis** Oklahoma, C USA
205 Y7 **Davis** *Australian research station* Antarctica
204 H3 **Davis Coast** *physical region* Antarctica
20 C16 **Davis, Mount** ▲ Pennsylvania, NE USA
26 K9 **Davis Mountains** ▲▲ Texas, SW USA
205 Z9 **Davis Sea** *sea* Antarctica
67 O20 **Davis Seamounts** *undersea feature* S Atlantic Ocean
206 M13 **Davis Strait** *strait* Baffin Bay/Labrador Sea
131 U5 **Davlekanovo** Respublika Bashkortostan, W Russian Federation
110 J9 **Davos** *Rmsch.* Tavau. Graubünden, E Switzerland
121 J20 **Davyd-Haradok** *Pol.* Dawidgródek, *Rus.* David-Gorodok. Brestskaya Voblasts', SW Belorussia
169 U12 **Dawa** Liaoning, NE China
147 O11 **Dawāsir, Wādī ad** *dry watercourse* S Saudi Arabia
83 K15 **Dawa Wenz** *var.* Daua, Webi Daawo. ≈ E Africa
Dawaymah, Birkat ad *see* Umm al Baqar, Hawr
Dawei *see* Tavoy
121 K14 **Dawhinava** *Rus.* Dolginovo. Minskaya Voblasts', N Belorussia
Dawidgródek *see* Davyd-Haradok
147 V12 **Dawkah** *var.* Dauka. SW Oman
Dawlat Qaṭar *see* Qatar
xxxviii I10 **Dawley** Shropshire, W England, UK
xxxvi I15 **Dawlish** Devon, SW England, UK
26 M3 **Dawn** Texas, SW USA
xliv F3 **Dawros Head** *headland* N Ireland
146 M11 **Daws** Al Bāḥah, SW Saudi Arabia
8 H5 **Dawson** *var.* Dawson City. Yukon Territory, NW Canada
25 S6 **Dawson** Georgia, SE USA
31 S9 **Dawson** Minnesota, N USA
Dawson City *see* Dawson
9 N13 **Dawson Creek** British Columbia, W Canada
8 H7 **Dawson Range** ▲▲ Yukon Territory, W Canada
189 Y9 **Dawson River** ≈ Queensland, E Australia
8 J15 **Dawsons Landing** British Columbia, SW Canada
22 I7 **Dawson Springs** Kentucky, S USA
25 S2 **Dawsonville** Georgia, SE USA
166 G8 **Dawu** Sichuan, C China
Dawu *see* Maqên
Dawukou *see* Shizuishan
147 Y10 **Dawwah** *var.* Dauwa. W Oman
104 J15 **Dax** *var.* Ax; *anc.* Aquae Augustae, Aquae Tarbelicae. Landes, SW France
Da Xian/Daxian *see* Dachuan
166 G9 **Daxue Shan** ▲▲ C China
166 G12 **Dayao** Yunnan, SW China
Dayishan *see* Gaoyou
191 N12 **Daylesford** Victoria, SE Australia
37 U10 **Daylight Pass** *pass* California, W USA
63 D17 **Daymán, Río** ≈ N Uruguay
Dayr *see* Ad Dayr
144 G10 **Dayr 'Allā** *var.* Deir 'Alla. Al Balqā', N Jordan
145 N4 **Dayr az Zawr** *var.* Deir ez Zor. Dayr az Zawr, E Syria
144 M5 **Dayr az Zawr** *off.* Muḥāfaẓat Dayr az Zawr, *var.* Dayr Az-Zor. ◈ *governorate* E Syria
Dayr Az-Zor *see* Dayr az Zawr
Dayrūṭ *see* Dairûṭ
9 Q15 **Daysland** Alberta, SW Canada
33 R14 **Dayton** Ohio, N USA
22 L10 **Dayton** Tennessee, S USA
27 W11 **Dayton** Texas, SW USA
34 L10 **Dayton** Washington, NW USA
25 X10 **Daytona Beach** Florida, SE USA
175 N10 **Dayu** Borneo, C Indonesia
167 O13 **Dayu Ling** ▲▲ S China
167 R7 **Da Yunhe** *Eng.* Grand Canal. *canal* E China
167 S11 **Dayu Shan** *island* SE China
166 J9 **Dazhu** Sichuan, C China
166 J9 **Dazu** Sichuan, C China
85 H24 **De Aar** Northern Cape, C South Africa
204 K5 **Deacon, Cape** *headland* Antarctica
41 R5 **Deadhorse** Alaska, USA
35 T12 **Dead Indian Peak** ▲ Wyoming, C USA
25 R9 **Dead Lake** ◎ Florida, SE USA
46 J4 **Deadman's Cay** Long Island, C Bahamas
144 G11 **Dead Sea** *var.* Bahret Lut, Lacus Asphaltites, *Ar.* Al Baḥr al Mayyit, Baḥrat Lūt, *Heb.* Yam HaMelaḥ. *salt lake* Israel/Jordan
30 J9 **Deadwood** South Dakota, N USA
xxxvii Z10 **Deal** Kent, SE England, UK
85 I22 **Dealesville** Free State, C South Africa
Dealnu *see* Tana/Teno
167 P10 **De'an** Jiangxi, S China
xxxvi L8 **Dean, Forest of** *forest* C England, UK
64 K9 **Deán Funes** Córdoba, C Argentina
204 L12 **Dean Island** *island* Antarctica
33 S10 **Dearborn** Michigan, N USA
29 R3 **Dearborn** Missouri, C USA
xl K8 **Dearham** Cumbria, NW England, UK
34 K9 **Deary** Idaho, NW USA
34 M9 **Deary** Washington, NW USA
8 J10 **Dease** ≈ British Columbia, W Canada
8 J10 **Dease Lake** British Columbia, W Canada
37 U11 **Death Valley** California, W USA
37 U11 **Death Valley** *valley* California, W USA
104 L4 **Deauville** Calvados, N France
119 X7 **Debal'tseve** *Rus.* Debal'tsevo. Donets'ka Oblast', SE Ukraine
Debal'tsevo *see* Debal'tseve
115 M19 **Debar** *Ger.* Dibra, *Turk.* Debre. W FYR Macedonia
41 O9 **Debauch Mountain** ▲ Alaska, USA
De Behagle *see* Laï
xxxix X13 **Deben** ≈ E England, UK
xxxix X12 **Debenham** Suffolk, E England, UK
27 X7 **De Berry** Texas, SW USA
131 T2 **Debesy** Udmurtskaya Respublika, NW Russian Federation
113 N16 **Dębica** Tarnów, SE Poland
De Bildt *see* De Bilt
100 J11 **De Bilt** *var.* De Bildt. Utrecht, C Netherlands
127 O9 **Debin** Magadanskaya Oblast', E Russian Federation
112 N13 **Dęblin** *Rus.* Ivangorod. Lublin, E Poland
112 D10 **Dębno** Gorzów, W Poland
41 S10 **Deborah, Mount** ▲ Alaska, USA
35 N8 **De Borgia** Montana, NW USA
Debra Birhan *see* Debre Birhan
Debra Marcos *see* Debre Mark'os
Debra Tabor *see* Debre Tabor
Debre *see* Debar
82 J13 **Debre Birhan** *var.* Debra Birhan. C Ethiopia
113 N22 **Debrecen** *Ger.* Debreczin, *Rom.* Debreţin; *prev.* Debreczen. Hajdú-Bihar, E Hungary
Debreczen/Debreczin *see* Debrecen
82 I12 **Debre Mark'os** *var.* Debra Marcos. NW Ethiopia
115 N19 **Debrešte** SW FYR Macedonia
82 J11 **Debre Tabor** *var.* Debra Tabor. NW Ethiopia
Debreţin *see* Debrecen
82 J13 **Debre Zeyt** C Ethiopia
115 L16 **Dečani** Serbia, S Yugoslavia
25 P2 **Decatur** Alabama, S USA
25 S3 **Decatur** Georgia, SE USA
32 L13 **Decatur** Illinois, N USA
33 Q12 **Decatur** Indiana, N USA
24 M5 **Decatur** Mississippi, S USA
31 S14 **Decatur** Nebraska, C USA
27 S6 **Decatur** Texas, SW USA
22 H9 **Decaturville** Tennessee, S USA
105 O13 **Decazeville** Aveyron, S France
161 H17 **Deccan** *Hind.* Dakshin. *plateau* C India
12 J8 **Decelles, Réservoir** ▣ Québec, SE Canada
10 K2 **Déception** Québec, NE Canada
166 G11 **Dechang** Sichuan, C China
113 C15 **Děčín** *Ger.* Tetschen. Severní Čechy, NW Czech Republic
105 P9 **Decize** Nièvre, C France
100 I6 **De Cocksdorp** Noord-Holland, NW Netherlands
31 X11 **Decorah** Iowa, C USA
xxxvii P6 **Deddington** Oxfordshire, C England, UK
Dedeagaç/Dedeagach *see* Alexandroúpoli
196 C15 **Dededo** N Guam
100 N9 **Dedemsvaart** Overijssel, E Netherlands
21 O11 **Dedham** Massachusetts, NE USA
65 H19 **Dedo, Cerro** ▲ SW Argentina
79 O13 **Dédougou** W Burkina
128 G15 **Dedovichi** Pskovskaya Oblast', W Russian Federation
169 V6 **Dedu** *var.* Qingshan. Heilongjiang, NE China
161 J24 **Deduru Oya** ≈ W Sri Lanka
85 N14 **Dedza** Central, S Malawi
85 N14 **Dedza Mountain** ▲ C Malawi
99 J19 **Dee** *Wel.* Afon Dyfrdwy. ≈ England/Wales, UK
xxxv K4 **Dee** *Wel.* Afon Dyfrdwy. ≈ England/Wales, UK
xliii J25 **Dee** ≈ S Scotland, UK
xliii N14 **Dee** ≈ NE Scotland, UK
xliv E11 **Deel** ≈ W Ireland
Deep Bay *see* Chilumba
23 T3 **Deep Creek Lake** ▣ Maryland, NE USA
38 J4 **Deep Creek Range** ▲▲ Utah, W USA
29 P10 **Deep Fork** ≈ Oklahoma, C USA
xxxix Q9 **Deeping St Nicholas** Lincolnshire, E England, UK
12 J11 **Deep River** Ontario, SE Canada
23 T10 **Deep River** ≈ North Carolina, SE USA
191 U4 **Deepwater** New South Wales, SE Australia
xliv I8 **Deeravaragh, Lough** ◎ C Ireland
33 S14 **Deer Creek Lake** ◎ Ohio, N USA
25 Z15 **Deerfield Beach** Florida, SE USA
41 N8 **Deering** Alaska, USA
40 M16 **Deer Island** *island* Alaska, USA
21 S7 **Deer Isle** *island* Maine, NE USA
11 S11 **Deer Lake** Newfoundland, Newfoundland and Labrador, SE Canada
101 D18 **Deerlijk** West-Vlaanderen, W Belgium
35 Q10 **Deer Lodge** Montana, NW USA
34 L8 **Deer Park** Washington, NW USA
31 U5 **Deer River** Minnesota, N USA
Deés *see* Dej
xxxviii J13 **Defford** Worcestershire, W England, UK
33 R11 **Defiance** Ohio, N USA
25 Q8 **De Funiak Springs** Florida, SE USA
97 L23 **Degeberga** Kristianstad, S Sweden
106 H12 **Degebe, Ribeira** ≈ S Portugal
82 M13 **Degeh Bur** SE Ethiopia
13 U9 **Dégelis** Québec, SE Canada
79 U17 **Degema** Rivers, S Nigeria
97 L16 **Degerfors** Örebro, C Sweden
200 N16 **De Gerlache Seamounts** *undersea feature* SE Pacific Ocean
103 N21 **Deggendorf** Bayern, SE Germany

◆ Country
● Country Capital
◇ Dependent Territory
○ Dependent Territory Capital
◈ Administrative Region
✕ International Airport
▲ Mountain
▲▲ Mountain Range
☗ Volcano
≈ River
◎ Lake
▣ Reservoir

DEĞIRMENLIK – DINGLE

124 Nn2 **Değirmenlik** *Gk.* Kythréa. N Cyprus
82 I11 **Degoma** NW Ethiopia
De Gordyk *see* Gorredijk
29 T12 **De Gray Lake** ⊟ Arkansas, C USA
188 J6 **De Grey River** ≈ Western Australia
130 M10 **Degtevo** Rostovskaya Oblast', SW Russian Federation
149 X13 **Dehak** Sīstān va Balūchestān, SE Iran
149 R9 **Deh 'Alī** Kermān, C Iran
149 S13 **Dehbārez** *var.* Rūdān. Hormozgān, S Iran
149 P10 **Deh Bīd** Fārs, C Iran
148 M10 **Deh Dasht** Kohkīlūyeh va Būyer Aḥmadī, SW Iran
77 N8 **Dehibat** SE Tunisia
Dehli *see* Delhi
148 K8 **Dehlorān** Īlām, W Iran
153 N13 **Dehqonobod** *Rus.* Dekhkanabad. Qashqadaryo Wiloyati, S Uzbekistan
158 J9 **Dehra Dūn** Uttar Pradesh, N India
159 O14 **Dehri** Bihār, N India
154 K10 **Deh Shū** *var.* Deshu. Helmand, S Afghanistan
xxxv G5 **Deiniolen** Gwynedd, NW Wales, UK
101 D17 **Deinze** Oost-Vlaanderen, NW Belgium
Deir 'Alla *see* Dayr 'Allā
Deir ez Zor *see* Dayr az Zawr
Deirgeirt, Loch *see* Derg, Lough
118 H9 **Dej** *Hung.* Dés; *prev.* Deés. Cluj, NW Romania
97 K15 **Deje** Värmland, C Sweden
176 Y14 **De Jongs, Tanjung** *headland* Irian Jaya, SE Indonesia
De Jouwer *see* Joure
32 M10 **De Kalb** Illinois, N USA
24 M5 **De Kalb** Mississippi, S USA
27 W5 **De Kalb** Texas, SW USA
Dekéleia *see* Dhekélia
81 K20 **Dekese** Kasai Occidental, C Zaire
Dekhkanabad *see* Dehqonobod
81 I14 **Dékoa** Kémo, 247C Central African Republic
100 H6 **De Koog** Noord-Holland, NW Netherlands
xxxvi D14 **Delabole** Cornwall, SW England, UK
32 M9 **Delafield** Wisconsin, N USA
63 C23 **De La Garma** Buenos Aires, E Argentina
12 K10 **Delahey, Lac** ◎ Québec, SE Canada
82 E11 **Delami** Southern Kordofan, C Sudan
25 X11 **De Land** Florida, SE USA
37 R12 **Delano** California, W USA
31 V8 **Delano** Minnesota, N USA
38 K6 **Delano Peak** ▲ Utah, W USA
Delap-Uliga-Darrit *see* Dalap-Uliga-Djarrit
154 L7 **Delārām** Farāh, SW Afghanistan
40 F17 **Delarof Islands** *island group* Aleutian Islands, Alaska, USA
32 M9 **Delavan** Wisconsin, N USA
33 S13 **Delaware** Ohio, N USA
20 I17 **Delaware** *off.* State of Delaware; also known as Blue Hen State, Diamond State, First State. ◈ *state* NE USA
20 I17 **Delaware Bay** *bay* NE USA
26 J8 **Delaware Mountains** ▲▲ Texas, SW USA
20 I12 **Delaware River** ≈ NE USA
29 Q3 **Delaware River** ≈ Kansas, C USA
20 J14 **Delaware Water Gap** *valley* New Jersey/Pennsylvania, NE USA
103 G14 **Delbrück** Nordrhein-Westfalen, W Germany
9 Q15 **Delburne** Alberta, SW Canada
180 M12 **Del Cano Rise** *undersea feature* SW Indian Ocean
115 Q18 **Delčevo** NE FYR Macedonia
Delcommune, Lac *see* Nzilo, Lac
100 O10 **Delden** Overijssel, E Netherlands
191 R12 **Delegate** New South Wales, SE Australia
De Lemmer *see* Lemmer
110 D7 **Delémont** *Ger.* Delsberg. Jura, NW Switzerland
27 R7 **De Leon** Texas, SW USA
117 F18 **Delfoí** Stereá Ellás, C Greece
xlii P13 **Delfrigs** Aberdeenshire, NE Scotland, UK
100 G12 **Delft** Zuid-Holland, W Netherlands
161 J23 **Delft** *island* NW Sri Lanka
100 O5 **Delfzijl** Groningen, NE Netherlands
1 E9 **Delgada Fan** *undersea feature* NE Pacific Ocean
44 F7 **Delgado** San Salvador, SW El Salvador
84 Q12 **Delgado, Cabo** *headland* N Mozambique
82 E6 **Delgo** Northern, N Sudan
165 R10 **Delhi** *var.* Delingha. Qinghai, C China
158 I10 **Delhi** *var.* Dehli, *Hind.* Dilli; *hist.* Shahjahanabad. Delhi, N India
24 J5 **Delhi** Louisiana, S USA
20 J11 **Delhi** New York, NE USA
158 I10 **Delhi** ◈ *union territory* NW India
142 J17 **Deli Burnu** *headland* S Turkey
57 X10 **Délices** C French Guiana
142 J12 **Delice Çayı** ≈ C Turkey
42 J6 **Delicias** *var.* Ciudad Delicias. Chihuahua, N Mexico
149 N7 **Delījān** *var.* Dalijan, Dilijan. Markazī, W Iran
114 P12 **Deli Jovan** ▲ E Yugoslavia
Déli-Kárpátok *see* Carpaţii Meridionali
15 H6 **Déline** *prev.* Fort Franklin. Northwest Territories, NW Canada
Delingha *see* Delhi
13 Q7 **Delisle** Québec, SE Canada
9 T15 **Delisle** Saskatchewan, S Canada
103 M15 **Delitzsch** Sachsen, E Germany
35 Q12 **Dell** Montana, NW USA
26 I7 **Dell City** Texas, SW USA
105 U7 **Delle** Territoire-de-Belfort, E France
38 J9 **Dellenbaugh, Mount** ▲ Arizona, SW USA
31 R11 **Dell Rapids** South Dakota, N USA
23 Y4 **Delmar** Maryland, NE USA
20 K11 **Delmar** New York, NE USA
102 G11 **Delmenhorst** Niedersachsen, NW Germany
114 C9 **Delnice** Primorje-Gorski Kotar, NW Croatia
39 R7 **Del Norte** Colorado, C USA
41 N6 **De Long Mountains** ▲▲ Alaska, USA
191 P16 **Deloraine** Tasmania, SE Australia
9 W17 **Deloraine** Manitoba, S Canada
xliv D8 **Delphi** Mayo, NW Ireland
33 O12 **Delphi** Indiana, N USA
33 Q12 **Delphos** Ohio, N USA
25 Z15 **Delray Beach** Florida, SE USA
27 O12 **Del Rio** Texas, SW USA
Delsberg *see* Delémont
96 N11 **Delsbo** Gävleborg, C Sweden
39 P6 **Delta** Colorado, C USA
38 K5 **Delta** Utah, W USA
79 T17 **Delta** ◈ *state* S Nigeria
57 Q6 **Delta Amacuro** *off.* Territorio Delta Amacuro. ◈ *federal district* NE Venezuela
41 S9 **Delta Junction** Alaska, USA
25 X11 **Deltona** Florida, SE USA
191 T5 **Delungra** New South Wales, SE Australia
160 C12 **Delvāda** Gujarāt, W India
63 B21 **Del Valle** Buenos Aires, E Argentina
xliv J8 **Delvin** Westmeath, C Ireland
Delvina *see* Delvinë
117 C15 **Delvinákí** *var.* Dhelvinákion; *prev.* Pogónion. Ípeiros, W Greece
115 L23 **Delvinë** *var.* Delvina, *It.* Delvino. Vlorë, S Albania
Delvino *see* Delvinë
118 I7 **Delyatyn** Ivano-Frankivs'ka Oblast', W Ukraine
131 U5 **Dëma** ≈ W Russian Federation
107 O5 **Demanda, Sierra de la** ▲▲ W Spain
41 T5 **Demarcation Point** *headland* Alaska, USA
81 K21 **Demba** Kasai Occidental, C Zaire
180 H13 **Dembéni** Grande Comore, NW Comoros
81 M15 **Dembia** Mbomou, SE Central African Republic
Dembidollo *see* Dembī Dolo
82 H13 **Dembī Dolo** *var.* Dembidollo. W Ethiopia
158 K6 **Demchok** *var.* Dêmqog. China/India *see also* Dêmqog
158 L6 **Demchok** *var.* Dêmqog. *disputed region* China/India *see also* Dêmqog
100 I12 **De Meern** Utrecht, C Netherlands
101 I17 **Demer** ≈ C Belgium
66 H12 **Demerara Plain** *undersea feature* W Atlantic Ocean
66 H12 **Demerara Plateau** *undersea feature* W Atlantic Ocean
57 T9 **Demerara River** ≈ NE Guyana
130 H3 **Demidov** Smolenskaya Oblast', W Russian Federation
39 Q15 **Deming** New Mexico, SW USA
34 H6 **Deming** Washington, NW USA
60 E10 **Demini, Rio** ≈ NW Brazil
142 D13 **Demirci** Manisa, W Turkey
115 P19 **Demir Kapija** *prev.* Železna Vrata. SE FYR Macedonia
116 N11 **Demirköy** Kırklareli, NW Turkey
102 N9 **Demmin** Mecklenburg-Vorpommern, NE Germany
25 O5 **Demopolis** Alabama, S USA
33 N11 **Demotte** Indiana, N USA
164 F13 **Dêmqog** *var.* Demchok. China/India *see also* Demchok
158 L6 **Dêmqog** *var.* Demchok. *disputed region* China/India *see also* Demchok
176 Yy10 **Demta** Irian Jaya, E Indonesia
125 G11 **Dem'yanka** ≈ C Russian Federation
128 H15 **Demyansk** Novgorodskaya Oblast', W Russian Federation
125 Ff11 **Dem'yanskoye** Tyumenskaya Oblast', C Russian Federation
105 P2 **Denain** Nord, N France
41 S10 **Denali** Alaska, USA
Denali *see* McKinley, Mount
83 M14 **Denan** SE Ethiopia
Denau *see* Denow
xxxv I5 **Denbigh** *Wel.* Dinbych. Denbighshire, NE Wales, UK
xxxv I5 **Denbighshire** ◈ *unitary authority* N Wales, UK
100 I6 **Den Burg** Noord-Holland, NW Netherlands
xli R15 **Denby Dale** Kirklees, N England, UK
101 F18 **Dender** *Fr.* Dendre. ≈ W Belgium
101 F18 **Denderleeuw** Oost-Vlaanderen, NW Belgium
101 F17 **Dendermonde** *Fr.* Termonde. Oost-Vlaanderen, NW Belgium
Dendre *see* Dender
204 I9 **Dendtler Island** *island* Antarctica
100 P10 **Denekamp** Overijssel, E Netherlands
79 W12 **Dengas** Zinder, S Niger
Dêngkagoin *see* Têwo
168 L13 **Dengkou** *var.* Bayan Gol. Nei Mongol Zizhiqu, N China
165 Q14 **Dêngqên** Xizang Zizhiqu, W China
Deng Xian *see* Dengzhou
166 M7 **Dengzhou** *prev.* Deng Xian. Henan, C China
Dengzhou *see* Penglai
Den Haag *see* 's-Gravenhage
100 N9 **Den Ham** Overijssel, E Netherlands
188 H10 **Denham** Western Australia
46 J12 **Denham, Mount** ▲ C Jamaica
24 J8 **Denham Springs** Louisiana, S USA
xliii N16 **Denhead** Aberdeenshire, NE Scotland, UK
xlii P11 **Denhead** Angus, E Scotland, UK
100 I7 **Den Helder** Noord-Holland, NW Netherlands
xliii N22 **Denholm** The Borders, S Scotland, UK
107 T11 **Dénia** País Valenciano, E Spain
201 Q8 **Denig** W Nauru
191 N10 **Deniliquin** New South Wales, SE Australia
31 T14 **Denison** Iowa, C USA
27 U5 **Denison** Texas, SW USA
142 D15 **Denizli** Denizli, SW Turkey
142 D15 **Denizli** ◈ *province* SW Turkey
Denjong *see* Sikkim
191 S7 **Denman** New South Wales, SE Australia
205 Y10 **Denman Glacier** *glacier* Antarctica
23 R14 **Denmark** South Carolina, SE USA
97 G23 **Denmark** *off.* Kingdom of Denmark, *Dan.* Danmark; *anc.* Hafnia. ◆ *monarchy* N Europe
94 H1 **Denmark Strait** *var.* Danmarksstraedet. *strait* Greenland/Iceland
47 T11 **Dennery** E Saint Lucia
xliii K19 **Denny** Falkirk, C Scotland, UK
100 I7 **Den Oever** Noord-Holland, NW Netherlands
153 O13 **Denow** *Rus.* Denau. Surkhondaryo Wiloyati, S Uzbekistan
175 N16 **Denpasar** *prev.* Paloe. Bali, C Indonesia
xli Q15 **Denshaw** Oldham, NW England, UK
xli O11 **Dent** Cumbria, NW England, UK
xli O11 **Dent** ≈ NW England, UK
118 E12 **Denta** Timiş, W Romania
xxxix P8 **Denton** Lincolnshire, E England, UK
xl H15 **Denton** Tameside, NW England, UK
23 Y3 **Denton** Maryland, NE USA
27 T6 **Denton** Texas, SW USA
195 O15 **D'Entrecasteaux Islands** *island group* SE PNG
39 T4 **Denver** *state capital* Colorado, C USA
18 K8 **Denver** ✕ Colorado, C USA
26 L6 **Denver City** Texas, SW USA
158 J9 **Deoband** Uttar Pradesh, N India
Deoghar *see* Devghar
160 E13 **Deolāli** Mahārāshtra, W India
160 I10 **Deori** Madhya Pradesh, C India
159 O12 **Deoria** Uttar Pradesh, N India
101 A17 **De Panne** West-Vlaanderen, W Belgium
xxxix U12 **Depden** Suffolk, E England, UK
56 M5 **Dependencia Federal** *off.* Territorio Dependencia Federal. ◈ *federal dependency* N Venezuela
Dependencia Federal, Territorio *see* Dependencia Federal
32 M7 **De Pere** Wisconsin, N USA
20 D10 **Depew** New York, NE USA
101 E17 **De Pinte** Oost-Vlaanderen, NW Belgium
27 V5 **Deport** Texas, SW USA
xxxvi E8 **Deptford** Lewisham, SE England, UK
126 M7 **Deputatskiy** Respublika Sakha (Yakutiya), NE Russian Federation
29 S13 **De Queen** Arkansas, C USA
24 G8 **De Quincy** Louisiana, S USA
83 J20 **Dera** *spring/well* S Kenya
Der'a/Derá/Déraa *see* Dar'ā
155 S10 **Dera Ghāzi Khān** *var.* Dera Ghāzikhān. Punjab, C Pakistan
155 S8 **Dera Ismāīl Khān** North-West Frontier Province, C Pakistan
115 L16 **Đeravica** ▲ S Yugoslavia
118 L6 **Derazhnya** Khmel'nyts'ka Oblast', W Ukraine
131 R17 **Derbent** Respublika Dagestan, SW Russian Federation
153 N13 **Derbent** Surkhondaryo Wiloyati, S Uzbekistan
Derbisīye *see* Darbāsīyah
81 M15 **Derbissaka** Mbomou, SE Central African Republic
xxxviii M8 **Derby** City of Derby, C England, UK
188 L4 **Derby** Western Australia
29 N7 **Derby** Kansas, C USA
xxxviii M8 **Derby, City of** ◈ *unitary authority* C England, UK
xxxviii L6 **Derbyshire** ◈ *county* C England, UK
114 O11 **Đerdap** *physical region* E Yugoslavia
Dereli *see* Gónnoi
176 X11 **Derew** ≈ Irian Jaya, E Indonesia
xliv I4 **Derg** ≈ Ireland/Northern Ireland, UK
131 R8 **Dergachi** Saratovskaya Oblast', W Russian Federation
Dergachi *see* Derhachi
xliv F10 **Derg, Lough** *Ir.* Loch Deirgeirt. ◎ W Ireland
xliv H4 **Derg, Lough** ◎ N Ireland
119 V5 **Derhachi** *Rus.* Dergachi. Kharkivs'ka Oblast', E Ukraine
24 G8 **De Ridder** Louisiana, S USA
143 P16 **Derik** Mardin, SE Turkey
85 E20 **Derm** Hardap, C Namibia
150 M14 **Dermentobe** *prev.* Dyurmen'tyube. Kzyl-Orda, S Kazakhstan
29 W14 **Dermott** Arkansas, C USA
Dérna *see* Darnah
Dernberg, Cape *see* Dolphin Head
24 J11 **Dernieres, Isles** *island group* Louisiana, S USA
Dernis *see* Drniš
xxxvii W14 **Déroute, Passage de la** *strait* Channel Islands/France
Derrá *see* Dar'ā
xliv C14 **Derreendarragh** Kerry, SW Ireland
Derry *see* Londonderry
xliv G2 **Derrybeg** Donegal, N Ireland
xliv H5 **Derrygonnelly** Fermanagh, W Northern Ireland, UK
xliv K2 **Derrykeighan** Ballymoney, N Northern Ireland, UK
xliv I6 **Derrylin** Fermanagh, W Northern Ireland, UK
xliv H6 **Derrynacreeve** Cavan, N Ireland
xliv G3 **Derryveagh Mountains** ▲▲ N Ireland
xxxix U8 **Dersingham** Norfolk, E England, UK
Dertona *see* Tortona
Dertosa *see* Tortosa
82 H8 **Derudeb** Red Sea, NE Sudan
xliii D16 **Dervaig** Argyll and Bute, W Scotland, UK
114 H10 **Derventa** N Bosnia and Herzegovina
xl L8 **Derwent** ≈ NW England, UK
xli U13 **Derwent** ≈ N England, UK
191 O16 **Derwent Bridge** Tasmania, SE Australia
xxxviii L4 **Derwent Reservoir** ⊟ C England, UK
xli Q7 **Derwent Reservoir** ⊟ N England, UK
191 O17 **Derwent, River** ≈ Tasmania, SE Australia
Derweze *see* Darvaza
Deržavinsk *see* Derzhavinsk
151 O9 **Derzhavinsk** *var.* Deržavinsk. Turgay, C Kazakhstan
Dés *see* Dej
59 J18 **Desaguadero** Puno, S Peru
59 J18 **Desaguadero, Río** ≈ Bolivia/Peru
203 W9 **Désappointement, Îles du** *island group* Îles Tuamotu, C French Polynesia
29 W11 **Des Arc** Arkansas, C USA
12 C10 **Desbarats** Ontario, S Canada
xxxix P11 **Desborough** Northamptonshire, C England, UK
64 H13 **Descabezado Grande, Volcán** ⛰ C Chile
42 B2 **Descanso** Baja California, NW Mexico
104 L9 **Descartes** Indre-et-Loire, C France
9 T13 **Deschambault Lake** ◎ Saskatchewan, C Canada
Deschnaer Koppe *see* Velká Deštná
34 I11 **Deschutes River** ≈ Oregon, NW USA
82 J12 **Desē** *var.* Dese, *It.* Dessie. N Ethiopia
65 I20 **Deseado, Río** ≈ S Argentina
108 F8 **Desenzano del Garda** Lombardia, N Italy
38 K3 **Deseret Peak** ▲ Utah, W USA
65 J19 **Deserta Grande** *island* Madeira, Portugal, NE Atlantic Ocean
66 P6 **Desertas, Ilhas** *island group* Madeira, Portugal, NE Atlantic Ocean
37 X16 **Desert Center** California, W USA
37 V15 **Desert Hot Springs** California, W USA
12 K10 **Désert, Lac** ◎ Québec, SE Canada
38 J2 **Desert Peak** ▲ Utah, W USA
xxxix N12 **Desford** Leicestershire, C England, UK
33 R11 **Deshler** Ohio, N USA
Deshu *see* Deh Shū
Desiderii Fanum *see* St-Dizier
108 D7 **Desio** Lombardia, N Italy
117 E15 **Deskáti** *var.* Dheskáti. Dytikí Makedonía, N Greece
30 L2 **Des Lacs River** ≈ North Dakota, N USA
29 X6 **Desloge** Missouri, C USA
9 Q12 **Desmarais** Alberta, W Canada
30 Q10 **De Smet** South Dakota, N USA
31 V14 **Des Moines** *state capital* Iowa, C USA
19 N8 **Des Moines River** ≈ C USA
119 P4 **Desna** ≈ Russian Federation/Ukraine
118 G14 **Desnăţui** ≈ S Romania
65 F24 **Desolación, Isla** *island* S Chile
31 V14 **De Soto** Iowa, C USA
25 Q4 **De Soto Falls** *waterfall* Alabama, S USA
85 I25 **Despatch** Eastern Cape, S South Africa
107 N12 **Despeñaperros, Desfiladero de** *pass* S Spain
33 N10 **Des Plaines** Illinois, N USA
117 J21 **Despotikó** *island* Kykládes, Greece, Aegean Sea
114 N12 **Despotovac** Serbia, E Yugoslavia
103 M14 **Dessau** Sachsen-Anhalt, E Germany
Desse *see* Desē
101 J16 **Dessel** Antwerpen, N Belgium
Dessie *see* Desē
Destêrro *see* Florianópolis
25 P9 **Destin** Florida, SE USA
Deštná *see* Velká Deštná
200 O11 **Desventurados, Islas de los** *island group* W Chile
105 N1 **Desvres** Pas-de-Calais, N France
118 E12 **Deta** *Ger.* Detta. Timiş, W Romania
103 H14 **Detmold** Nordrhein-Westfalen, W Germany
33 S10 **Detroit** Michigan, N USA
27 W5 **Detroit** Texas, SW USA
33 S10 **Detroit** ✕ Canada/USA
31 S6 **Detroit Lakes** Minnesota, N USA
33 S10 **Detroit Metropolitan** ✕ Michigan, N USA
Detta *see* Deta
178 J11 **Det Udom** Ubon Ratchathani, E Thailand
113 K20 **Detva** *Hung.* Gyeva. Stredné Slovensko, C Slovakia
160 G13 **Deūlgaon Rāja** Mahārāshtra, C India
101 L15 **Deurne** Noord-Brabant, SE Netherlands
101 H16 **Deurne** ✕ (Antwerpen) Antwerpen, N Belgium
Deutsch-Brod *see* Havlíčkův Brod
Deutschendorf *see* Poprad
Deutsch-Eylau *see* Iława
111 Y6 **Deutschkreutz** Burgenland, E Austria
Deutsch Krone *see* Wałcz
Deutschland/Deutschland, Bundesrepublik *see* Germany
111 V9 **Deutschlandsberg** Steiermark, SE Austria
Deutsch-Südwestafrika *see* Namibia
111 Y3 **Deutsch-Wagram** Niederösterreich, E Austria
Deux-Ponts *see* Zweibrücken
12 I11 **Deux Rivieres** Ontario, SE Canada
104 K9 **Deux-Sèvres** ◈ *department* W France
Deva *see* Chester
118 G11 **Deva** *Ger.* Diemrich, *Hung.* Déva. Hunedoara, W Romania
Devana *see* Aberdeen
Devana Castra *see* Chester
Đevđelija *see* Gevgelija
142 L12 **Deveci Dağları** ▲▲ N Turkey
143 P15 **Devegeçidi Barajı** ⊟ SE Turkey
142 K15 **Develi** Kayseri, C Turkey
100 M11 **Deventer** Overijssel, E Netherlands
13 O10 **Devenyns, Lac** ◎ Québec, SE Canada
xlii N12 **Deveron** ≈ NE Scotland, UK
159 R14 **Devghar** *prev.* Deoghar. Bihār, NE India
xxxv H10 **Devil's Bridge** Ceredigion, W Wales, UK
29 R10 **Devil's Den** *plateau* Arkansas, C USA
37 R7 **Devils Gate** *pass* California, W USA
32 J2 **Devils Island** *island* Apostle Islands, Wisconsin, N USA
Devil's Island *see* Diable, Île du
31 P3 **Devils Lake** North Dakota, N USA
33 R10 **Devils Lake** ◎ Michigan, N USA
31 O3 **Devils Lake** ◎ North Dakota, N USA
37 W13 **Devils Playground** *desert* California, W USA
27 O11 **Devils River** ≈ Texas, SW USA
35 Y12 **Devils Tower** ▲ Wyoming, C USA
116 I11 **Devin** *prev.* Dovlen. Plovdivska Oblast, SW Bulgaria
27 R12 **Devine** Texas, SW USA
xxxvii N10 **Devizes** Wiltshire, S England, UK
158 H13 **Devli** Rājasthān, N India
Devne *see* Devnya
116 N8 **Devnya** *prev.* Devne. Varnenska Oblast, NE Bulgaria
33 U14 **Devola** Ohio, N USA
Devoll *see* Devollit, Lumi i
115 M21 **Devollit, Lumi i** *var.* Devoll. ≈ SE Albania
xxxvi G14 **Devon** ◈ *county* SW England, UK
9 Q14 **Devon** Alberta, SW Canada
207 N10 **Devon Island** *prev.* North Devon Island. *island* Parry Islands, Northwest Territories, NE Canada
191 O16 **Devonport** Tasmania, SE Australia
142 H11 **Devrek** Zonguldak, N Turkey
160 G10 **Dewās** Madhya Pradesh, C India
De Westerein *see* Zwaagwesteinde
29 P8 **Dewey** Oklahoma, C USA
Dewey *see* Culebra
100 M8 **De Wijk** Drenthe, NE Netherlands
29 W12 **De Witt** Arkansas, C USA
31 Z14 **De Witt** Iowa, C USA
31 R16 **De Witt** Nebraska, C USA
xli R15 **Dewsbury** Kirklees, N England, UK
167 Q10 **Dexing** Jiangxi, S China
29 Y8 **Dexter** Missouri, C USA
39 U14 **Dexter** New Mexico, SW USA
166 I8 **Deyang** Sichuan, C China
190 C4 **Dey-Dey, Lake** *salt lake* South Australia
149 S7 **Deyhūk** Khorāsān, E Iran
152 K12 **Deynau** *var.* Dyanev, *Turkm.* Dänew. Lebapskiy Velayat, NE Turkmenistan
148 L8 **Dezfūl** *var.* Dizful. Khūzestān, SW Iran
133 X4 **Dezhneva, Mys** *headland* NE Russian Federation
167 P4 **Dezhou** Shandong, E China
Dezh Shāhpūr *see* Marīvān
Dhahran *see* Aẓ Ẓahrān
Dhahran Al Khobar *see* Aẓ Ẓahrān al Khubar
159 U14 **Dhaka** *prev.* Dacca. ● (Bangladesh) Dhaka, C Bangladesh
159 T15 **Dhaka** ◈ *division* C Bangladesh
Dhali *see* Idálion
147 O15 **Dhamār** W Yemen
160 K12 **Dhamtari** Madhya Pradesh, C India
159 Q15 **Dhanbād** Bihār, NE India
158 L10 **Dhangadhi** *var.* Dhangarhi. Far Western, W Nepal
Dhangarhi *see* Dhangadhi
Dhank *see* Ḍank
159 R12 **Dhankuta** Eastern, E Nepal
158 I6 **Dhaola Dhār** ▲▲ NE India
160 F10 **Dhār** Madhya Pradesh, C India
159 R12 **Dharan** *var.* Dharan Bazar. Eastern, E Nepal
161 H21 **Dhārāpuram** Tamil Nādu, SE India
161 H20 **Dharmapuri** Tamil Nādu, SE India
161 H18 **Dharmavaram** Andhra Pradesh, E India
160 M11 **Dharmjaygarh** Madhya Pradesh, C India
Dharmsāla *see* Dharmshāla
158 I7 **Dharmshāla** *prev.* Dharmsāla. Himāchal Pradesh, N India
161 F17 **Dhārwād** *prev.* Dharwar. Karnātaka, SW India
Dharwar *see* Dhārwād
159 O10 **Dhaulāgiri** ▲ C Nepal
83 L18 **Dheere Laaq** *var.* Lak Dera, *It.* Lach Dera. *seasonal river* Kenya/Somalia
124 O3 **Dhekéleia Sovereign Base Area** *UK military installation* E Cyprus
124 O3 **Dhekéleia** *Eng.* Dhekelia. *Gk.* Dekéleia. *UK air base* SE Cyprus
Dhelvinákion *see* Delvinákí
115 M22 **Dhëmbelit, Majae** ▲ S Albania
160 O12 **Dhenkānāl** Orissa, E India
Dheskáti *see* Deskáti
144 G11 **Dhibān** 'Ammān, NW Jordan
Dhidhimótikhon *see* Didymóteicho
Dhíkti Ori *see* Díkti
144 I12 **Dhirwah, Wādī adh** *dry watercourse* C Jordan
Dhístomon *see* Dístomo
Dhodhekánisos *see* Dodekánisos
Dhodhóni *see* Dodóni
Dhofar *see* Ẓufār
Dhomokós *see* Domokós
Dhond *see* Daund
161 H17 **Dhone** Andhra Pradesh, C India
160 B11 **Dhorāji** Gujarāt, W India
Dhráma *see* Dráma
160 C10 **Dhrāngadhra** Gujarāt, W India
Dhrepanon, Akra *see* Drépano, Ákra
159 T13 **Dhuburi** Assam, NE India
160 F12 **Dhule** *prev.* Dhulia. Mahārāshtra, C India
Dhulia *see* Dhule
Dhūn Dealgan, Cuan *see* Dundalk Bay
Dhún Droma, Cuan *see* Dundrum Bay
Dhún na nGall, Bá *see* Donegal Bay
Dhū Shaykh *see* Qazānīyah
82 Q13 **Dhuudo** Bari, NE Somalia
83 N15 **Dhuusa Marreeb** *var.* Dusa Marreb, *It.* Dusa Mareb. Galguduud, C Somalia
117 J24 **Día** *island* SE Greece
57 Y9 **Diable, Île du** *var.* Devil's Island. *island* N French Guiana
13 N12 **Diable, Rivière du** ≈ Québec, SE Canada
37 N8 **Diablo, Mount** ▲ California, W USA
37 O9 **Diablo Range** ▲▲ California, W USA
26 I8 **Diablo, Sierra** ▲▲ Texas, SW USA
47 O11 **Diablotins, Morne** ▲ N Dominica
79 N11 **Diafarabé** Mopti, C Mali
79 N11 **Diaka** ≈ SW Mali
Diakovár *see* Đakovo
78 I12 **Dialakoto** S Senegal
63 B18 **Diamante** Entre Ríos, E Argentina
64 I12 **Diamante, Río** ≈ C Argentina
61 M19 **Diamantina** Minas Gerais, SE Brazil
61 N17 **Diamantina, Chapada** ▲▲ E Brazil
181 U11 **Diamantina Fracture Zone** *tectonic feature* E Indian Ocean
189 T8 **Diamantina River** ≈ Queensland/South Australia
40 D9 **Diamond Head** *headland* Oahu, Hawaii, USA, C Pacific Ocean
39 P2 **Diamond Peak** ▲ Colorado, C USA
37 W5 **Diamond Peak** ▲ Nevada, W USA
Diamond State *see* Delaware
78 J11 **Diamou** Kayes, SW Mali
97 I23 **Dianalund** Vestsjælland, C Denmark
67 G25 **Diana's Peak** ▲ C Saint Helena
166 M16 **Dianbai** Guangdong, S China
166 G13 **Dian Chi** ◎ SW China
108 B10 **Diano Marina** Liguria, NW Italy
79 R13 **Diapaga** E Burkina
Diarbekr *see* Diyarbakır
109 J15 **Diavolo, Passo del** *pass* C Italy
63 B18 **Díaz** Santa Fe, C Argentina
147 W6 **Dibā al Ḥiṣn** *var.* Dibāh, Dibba. Ash Shāriqah, NE UAE
145 S3 **Dībaga** N Iraq
Dibāh *see* Dibā al Ḥiṣn
81 L22 **Dibaya** Kasai Occidental, S Zaire
Dibba *see* Dibā al Ḥiṣn
205 W15 **Dibble Iceberg Tongue** *ice feature* Antarctica
115 L19 **Dibër** ◈ *district* E Albania
85 I20 **Dibete** Central, SE Botswana
27 W9 **Diboll** Texas, SW USA
Dibra *see* Debar
159 X11 **Dibrugarh** Assam, NE India
56 G4 **Dibulla** La Guajira, N Colombia
27 O5 **Dickens** Texas, SW USA
21 R2 **Dickey** Maine, NE USA
32 K9 **Dickeyville** Wisconsin, N USA
30 K5 **Dickinson** North Dakota, N USA
1 E6 **Dickins Seamount** *undersea feature* NE Pacific Ocean
29 O13 **Dickson** Oklahoma, C USA
22 I9 **Dickson** Tennessee, S USA
Dicle *see* Tigris
Dicsőszentmárton *see* Târnăveni
100 M12 **Didam** Gelderland, E Netherlands
169 Y8 **Didao** Heilongjiang, NE China
xxxvii P9 **Didcot** Oxfordshire, C England, UK
78 L12 **Didiéni** Koulikoro, W Mali
Didimo *see* Dídymo
Didimotiho *see* Didymóteicho
83 K17 **Didimtu** *spring/well* NE Kenya
69 U9 **Didinga Hills** ▲ S Sudan
9 Q16 **Didsbury** Alberta, SW Canada
158 G11 **Didwāna** Rājasthān, N India
117 G20 **Dídymo** *var.* Didimo. ▲ S Greece
116 L12 **Didymóteicho** *var.* Dhidhimótikhon, Didimotiho. Anatolikí Makedonía kai Thráki, NE Greece
105 S13 **Die** Drôme, E France
79 O13 **Diébougou** SW Burkina
Diedenhofen *see* Thionville
9 S16 **Diefenbaker, Lake** ⊟ Saskatchewan, S Canada
64 H7 **Diego de Almagro** Atacama, N Chile
65 F23 **Diego de Almagro, Isla** *island* S Chile
63 A20 **Diego de Alvear** Santa Fe, C Argentina
181 Q7 **Diego Garcia** *island* S British Indian Ocean Territory
Diégo-Suarez *see* Antsirañana
101 M23 **Diekirch** Diekirch, C Luxembourg
101 L23 **Diekirch** ◈ *district* N Luxembourg
78 K11 **Diéma** Kayes, W Mali
103 H15 **Diemel** ≈ W Germany
100 I10 **Diemen** Noord-Holland, C Netherlands
Diemrich *see* Deva
178 I6 **Điên Biên** *var.* Bien Bien, Dien Bien Phu. Lai Châu, N Vietnam
Dien Bien Phu *see* Điên Biên
178 Jj8 **Điên Châu** Nghê An, N Vietnam
101 K18 **Diepenbeek** Limburg, NE Belgium
100 N11 **Diepenheim** Overijssel, E Netherlands
100 M10 **Diepenveen** Overijssel, E Netherlands
102 G12 **Diepholz** Niedersachsen, NW Germany
104 M3 **Dieppe** Seine-Maritime, N France
100 M12 **Dieren** Gelderland, E Netherlands
29 S13 **Dierks** Arkansas, C USA
101 J17 **Diest** Vlaams Brabant, C Belgium
110 F7 **Dietikon** Zürich, NW Switzerland
105 R13 **Dieulefit** Drôme, E France
105 T5 **Dieuze** Moselle, NE France
121 H15 **Dieveniškės** Šalčininkai, SE Lithuania
100 N7 **Diever** Drenthe, NE Netherlands
103 F17 **Diez** Rheinland-Pfalz, W Germany
79 Y12 **Diffa** Diffa, SE Niger
79 Y10 **Diffa** ◈ *department* SE Niger
101 L25 **Differdange** Luxembourg, SW Luxembourg
xxxix Q7 **Digby** Lincolnshire, E England, UK
11 O16 **Digby** Nova Scotia, SE Canada
xlii D11 **Digg** Highland, NW Scotland, UK
28 J5 **Dighton** Kansas, C USA
Dignano d'Istria *see* Vodnjan
105 T14 **Digne** *var.* Digne-les-Bains. Alpes-de-Haute-Provence, SE France
Digne-les-Bains *see* Digne
Digoel *see* Digul, Sungai
105 Q10 **Digoin** Saône-et-Loire, C France
179 Rr16 **Digos** Mindanao, S Philippines
155 Q16 **Digri** Sind, SE Pakistan
176 Z13 **Digul Barat, Sungai** ≈ Irian Jaya, E Indonesia
176 Z14 **Digul, Sungai** *prev.* Digoel. ≈ Irian Jaya, E Indonesia
176 Z13 **Digul Timur, Sungai** ≈ Irian Jaya, E Indonesia
Dihang *see* Brahmaputra
159 X10 **Dihang** ≈ NE India
Dihōk *see* Dahūk
83 L17 **Diinsoor** Bay, S Somalia
Dijlah *see* Tigris
101 H17 **Dijle** ≈ C Belgium
105 R8 **Dijon** *anc.* Dibio. Côte d'Or, C France
95 H14 **Dikanäs** Västerbotten, N Sweden
82 L12 **Dikhil** SW Djibouti
142 B13 **Dikili** İzmir, W Turkey
101 B17 **Diksmuide** *var.* Dixmuide, *Fr.* Dixmude. West-Vlaanderen, W Belgium
126 Hh6 **Dikson** Taymyrskiy (Dolgano-Nenetskiy) Avtonomnyy Okrug, N Russian Federation
117 K25 **Díkti** *var.* Dhíkti Ori. ▲▲ Kríti, Greece, E Mediterranean Sea
79 Z13 **Dikwa** Borno, NE Nigeria
83 J15 **Dila** S Ethiopia
101 G18 **Dilbeek** Vlaams Brabant, C Belgium
175 S16 **Dili** *var.* Dilli, Dilly. Timor, C Indonesia
79 Y11 **Dilia** *var.* Dillia. ≈ SE Niger
Dilijan *see* Delījān
178 K13 **Di Linh** Lâm Đông, S Vietnam
103 G16 **Dillenburg** Hessen, W Germany
27 Q13 **Dilley** Texas, SW USA
Dilli *see* Delhi, India
Dilli *see* Dili, Indonesia
Dillia *see* Dilia
82 E11 **Dilling** *var.* Ad Dalanj. Southern Kordofan, C Sudan
103 D20 **Dillingen** Saarland, SW Germany
Dillingen *see* Dillingen an der Donau
103 J22 **Dillingen an der Donau** *var.* Dillingen. Bayern, S Germany
41 O13 **Dillingham** Alaska, USA
35 Q12 **Dillon** Montana, NW USA
23 T12 **Dillon** South Carolina, SE USA
33 T13 **Dillon Lake** ◎ Ohio, N USA
Dilly *see* Dili
Dilman *see* Salmās
81 K24 **Dilolo** Shaba, S Zaire
117 J20 **Dílos** *island* Kykládes, Greece, Aegean Sea
147 Y11 **Ḍil', Ra's aḍ** *headland* E Oman
31 R5 **Dilworth** Minnesota, N USA
144 H7 **Dimashq** *var.* Ash Shām, Esh Sham, *Eng.* Damascus, *Fr.* Damas, *It.* Damasco. ● (Syria) Dimashq, SW Syria
144 I8 **Dimashq** *off.* Muḥāfaẓat Dimashq, *var.* Damascus, *Ar.* Ash Sham, Ash Shām, Damasco, Esh Sham, *Fr.* Damas. ◈ *governorate* S Syria
144 I7 **Dimashq** ✕ Dimashq, S Syria
81 L21 **Dimbelenge** Kasai Occidental, C Zaire
79 N16 **Dimbokro** E Ivory Coast
190 L11 **Dimboola** Victoria, SE Australia
Dîmboviţa *see* Dâmboviţa
Dimitrov *see* Dymytrov
116 K11 **Dimitrovgrad** Khaskovska Oblast, S Bulgaria
131 R5 **Dimitrovgrad** Ul'yanovskaya Oblast', W Russian Federation
115 Q15 **Dimitrovgrad** *prev.* Caribrod. Serbia, SE Yugoslavia
Dimitrovo *see* Pernik
Dimlang *see* Vogel Peak
26 M3 **Dimmitt** Texas, SW USA
116 F7 **Dimovo** Oblast Montana, NW Bulgaria
61 A16 **Dimpolis** Acre, W Brazil
117 O23 **Dimyliá** Ródos, Dodekánisos, Greece, Aegean Sea
179 R13 **Dinagat** Dinagat Island, S Philippines
179 Rr13 **Dinagat Island** *island* S Philippines
159 S13 **Dinajpur** Rajshahi, NW Bangladesh
104 I6 **Dinan** Côtes d'Armor, NW France
101 I21 **Dinant** Namur, S Belgium
142 E15 **Dinar** Afyon, SW Turkey
114 F13 **Dinara** ▲ W Croatia
Dinara *see* Dinaric Alps
104 I5 **Dinard** Ille-et-Vilaine, NW France
114 F13 **Dinaric Alps** *var.* Dinara. ▲▲ Bosnia and Herzegovina/Croatia
149 N10 **Dīnār, Kūh-e** ▲ C Iran
xxxv E7 **Dinas** Gwynedd, NW Wales, UK
xxxv D12 **Dinas** Pembrokeshire, SW Wales, UK
xxxv H8 **Dinas-Mawddwy** Gwynedd, NW Wales, UK
xxxv J15 **Dinas Powys** The Vale of Glamorgan, S Wales, UK
Dinbych *see* Denbigh
161 H22 **Dindigul** Tamil Nādu, SE India
85 M19 **Dindiza** Gaza, S Mozambique
155 V7 **Dinga** Punjab, E Pakistan
81 H21 **Dinga** Bandundu, SW Zaire
164 L16 **Dingyê** Xizang Zizhiqu, W China
xliv B13 **Dingle** *Ir.* An Daingean. Kerry, SW Ireland

◆ Country ● Country Capital ◇ Dependent Territory ○ Dependent Territory Capital ◈ Administrative Region ✕ International Airport ▲ Mountain ▲▲ Mountain Range ⛰ Volcano ≈ River ◎ Lake ⊟ Reservoir

Dingle Bay – Dragalina

xliv B13 **Dingle Bay** *Ir.* Bá an Daingin. *bay* SW Ireland
20 I13 **Dingmans Ferry** Pennsylvania, NE USA
103 N22 **Dingofling** Bayern, SE Germany
179 P8 **Dingras** Luzon, N Philippines
78 J13 **Dinguiraye** Haute-Guinée, N Guinea
xlii I11 **Dingwall** Highland, N Scotland, UK
165 V10 **Dingxi** Gansu, C China
167 Q7 **Dingyuan** Anhui, E China
167 O3 **Dingzhou** *prev.* Ding Xian. Hebei, E China
178 K6 **Đinh Lập** Lang Sơn, N Vietnam
178 K14 **Đinh Quan** Đông Nai, S Vietnam
102 E13 **Dinkel** ∽ Germany/Netherlands
103 J21 **Dinkelsbühl** Bayern, S Germany
xliii N14 **Dinnet** Aberdeenshire, NE Scotland, UK
xli T17 **Dinnington** Rotherham, N England, UK
103 D14 **Dinslaken** Nordrhein-Westfalen, W Germany
xxxvii N12 **Dinton** Wiltshire, S England, UK
37 R11 **Dinuba** California, W USA
23 W7 **Dinwiddie** Virginia, NE USA
100 N13 **Dinxperlo** Gelderland, E Netherlands
117 F14 **Dió** *anc.* Dium. *site of ancient city* Kentrikí Makedonía, N Greece
Diófás *see* Nucet
78 M12 **Dioïla** Koulikoro, W Mali
117 G19 **Dióryga Korinthou** *Eng.* Corinth Canal. *canal* S Greece
78 G12 **Diouloulou** SW Senegal
79 N11 **Dioura** Mopti, W Mali
78 G11 **Diourbel** W Senegal
158 L10 **Dipayal** Far Western, W Nepal
124 Oo2 **Dipkarpaz** *Gk.* Rizokarpaso, Rizokárpason. NE Cyprus
155 R17 **Diplo** Sind, SE Pakistan
179 Qq15 **Dipolog** *var.* Dipolog City. Mindanao, S Philippines
xliii F21 **Dippen** Argyll and Bute, W Scotland, UK
xliii G22 **Dippin** North Ayrshire, W Scotland, UK
193 C23 **Dipton** Southland, South Island, NZ
79 O10 **Diré** Tombouctou, C Mali
82 L13 **Dirē Dawa** E Ethiopia
Dirfis *see* Dírfys
117 H18 **Dírfys** *var.* Dirfis. ▲▲ Évvioa, C Greece
77 N9 **Dirj** *var.* Daraj, Darj. W Libya
188 G10 **Dirk Hartog Island** *island* Western Australia
79 Y8 **Dirkou** Agadez, NE Niger
xliii N19 **Dirleton** East Lothian, SE Scotland, UK
189 X11 **Dirranbandi** Queensland, E Australia
83 O16 **Dirri** Galguduud, C Somalia
Dirschau *see* Tczew
39 N6 **Dirty Devil River** ∽ Utah, W USA
34 E10 **Disappointment, Cape** *headland* Washington, NW USA
188 L8 **Disappointment, Lake** *salt lake* Western Australia
191 R12 **Disaster Bay** *bay* New South Wales, SE Australia
46 J11 **Discovery Bay** C Jamaica
190 K13 **Discovery Bay** *inlet* SE Australia
69 Y15 **Discovery II Fracture Zone** *tectonic feature* SW Indian Ocean
Discovery Seamount/Discovery Seamounts *see* Discovery Tablemount
67 O19 **Discovery Tablemount** *var.* Discovery Seamount, Discovery Seamounts. *undersea feature* SW Indian Ocean
110 G9 **Disentis** *Rmsch.* Mustér. Graubünden, S Switzerland
xli S12 **Dishforth** North Yorkshire, N England, UK
41 O10 **Dishna River** ∽ Alaska, USA
205 X4 **Dismal Mountains** ▲▲ Antarctica
30 M14 **Dismal River** ∽ Nebraska, C USA
Disna *see* Dzisna
101 L19 **Dison** Liège, E Belgium
159 V12 **Dispur** Assam, NE India
13 R11 **Disraeli** Québec, SE Canada
xxxix W11 **Diss** Norfolk, E England, UK
xl K9 **Distington** Cumbria, NW England, UK
117 F18 **Dístomo** *prev.* Dhístomon. Stereá Ellás, C Greece
117 H18 **Dístos, Límni** ◎ Évvoia, C Greece
61 L18 **Distrito Federal** *Eng.* Federal District. ◐ *federal district* C Brazil
43 P14 **Distrito Federal** ◐ *federal district* S Mexico
56 L4 **Distrito Federal** *off.* Territorio Distrito Federal. ◐ *federal district* N Venezuela
Distrito Federal, Territorio *see* Distrito Federal
xxxix Y10 **Ditchingham** Norfolk, E England, UK
xxxvii U12 **Ditchling** East Sussex, SE England, UK
118 J10 **Ditrău** *Hung.* Ditró. Harghita, C Romania
Ditró *see* Ditrău
xxxvi H16 **Dittisham** Devon, SW England, UK
xxxviii I11 **Ditton Priors** Shropshire, W England, UK
160 B12 **Diu** Damān and Diu, W India
179 Rr14 **Diuata Mountains** ▲▲ Mindanao, S Philippines
Dium *see* Dió
111 S13 **Divača** SW Slovenia
104 K5 **Dives** ∽ N France
Divichi *see* Däväçi
35 Q11 **Divide** Montana, NW USA
Divin *see* Dzivin
85 N18 **Divinhe** Sofala, E Mozambique
61 L20 **Divinópolis** Minas Gerais, SE Brazil
126 I14 **Divnogorsk** Krasnoyarskiy Kray, S Russian Federation
131 N13 **Divnoye** Stavropol'skiy Kray, SW Russian Federation
78 M17 **Divo** S Ivory Coast
Divodurum Mediomatricum *see* Metz
143 N13 **Divriği** Sivas, C Turkey
Diwaniyah *see* Ad Dīwānīyah
12 J10 **Dix Milles, Lac** ◎ Québec, SE Canada
12 M8 **Dix Milles, Lac des** ◎ Québec, SE Canada
Dixmude/Dixmuide *see* Diksmuide
37 N7 **Dixon** California, W USA
32 L10 **Dixon** Illinois, N USA
22 I6 **Dixon** Kentucky, S USA
29 V6 **Dixon** Missouri, C USA
39 S9 **Dixon** New Mexico, SW USA
41 Y15 **Dixon Entrance** *strait* Canada/USA
20 D14 **Dixonville** Pennsylvania, NE USA
143 T13 **Diyadin** Ağrı, E Turkey
145 V5 **Diyālá, Nahr** *var.* Rudkhaneh-ye Sīrvān, Sirwan. ∽ Iran/Iraq *see also* Sīrvān, Rudkhaneh-ye
143 P15 **Diyarbakır** *var.* Diarbekr; *anc.* Amida. Dıyarbakır, SE Turkey
143 P15 **Diyarbakır** *var.* Diarbekr. ◐ *province* SE Turkey
Dizful *see* Dezfūl
81 F16 **Dja** ∽ SE Cameroon
Djadié *see* Zadié
79 X7 **Djado** Agadez, NE Niger
79 X6 **Djado, Plateau du** ▲▲ NE Niger
Djailolo *see* Halmahera, Pulau
Djajapura *see* Jayapura
Djakarta *see* Jakarta
Djakovica *see* Đakovica
Djakovo *see* Đakovo
81 G20 **Djambala** Plateaux, C Congo
Djambi *see* Jambi
Djambi *see* Hari, Batang, Sumatera, W Indonesia
76 M9 **Djanet** E Algeria
76 M11 **Djanet** *prev.* Fort Charlet. SE Algeria
Djatiwangi *see* Jatiwangi
Djaul *see* Dyaul Island
Djawa *see* Jawa
Djéblé *see* Jablah
80 I10 **Djédaa** Batha, C Chad
76 J6 **Djelfa** *var.* El Djelfa. N Algeria
81 M14 **Djéma** Haut-Mbomou, E Central African Republic
Djeneponto *see* Jeneponto
79 N12 **Djenné** *var.* Jenné. Mopti, C Mali
Djérablous *see* Jarābulus
Djerba *see* Jerba, Île de
81 F15 **Djérem** ∽ C Cameroon
Djevdjelija *see* Gevgelija
79 P11 **Djibo** N Burkina
82 L12 **Djibouti** *var.* Jibuti. ● (Djibouti) E Djibouti
82 L12 **Djibouti** *off.* Republic of Djibouti, *var.* Jibuti; *prev.* French Somaliland, French Territory of the Afars and Issas, *Fr.* Côte Française des Somalis, Territoire Français des Afars et des Issas. ◆ *republic* E Africa
82 L12 **Djibouti** ✕ C Djibouti
Djidjel/Djidjelli *see* Jijel
57 W10 **Djoemoe** Sipaliwini, C Surinam
Djokjakarta *see* Yogyakarta
81 K21 **Djoku-Punda** Kasai Occidental, S Zaire
81 K18 **Djolu** Equateur, N Zaire
Djorče Petrov *see* Đorče Petrov
81 F17 **Djoua** ∽ Congo/Gabon
79 R14 **Djougou** W Benin
81 F16 **Djoum** Sud, S Cameroon
80 I8 **Djourab, Erg du** *dunes* N Chad
81 P17 **Djugu** Haut-Zaïre, NE Zaire
Djumbir *see* Ďumbier
94 L3 **Djúpivogur** Austurland, SE Iceland
96 L13 **Djura** Kopparberg, C Sweden
Djurdjevac *see* Đurđevac
85 G18 **D'Kar** Ghanzi, NW Botswana
207 U6 **Dmitriya Lapteva, Proliv** *strait* N Russian Federation
130 J7 **Dmitriyev-L'govskiy** Kurskaya Oblast', W Russian Federation
Dmitriyevsk *see* Makiyivka
130 K3 **Dmitrov** Moskovskaya Oblast', W Russian Federation
Dmitrovichi *see* Dzmitravichy
130 J6 **Dmitrovsk-Orlovskiy** Orlovskaya Oblast', W Russian Federation
119 R3 **Dmytrivka** Chernihivs'ka Oblast', N Ukraine
Dnepr *see* Dnieper
Dneprodzerzhinsk *see* Dniprodzerzhyns'k
Dneprodzerzhinskoye Vodokhranilishche *see* Dniprodzerzhyns'ke Vodoskhovyshche
Dnepropetrovsk *see* Dnipropetrovs'k
Dnepropetrovskaya Oblast' *see* Dnipropetrovs'ka Oblast'
Dneprorudnoye *see* Dniprorudne
Dneprovskiy Liman *see* Dniprovs'kyy Lyman
Dneprovsko-Bugskiy Kanal *see* Dnyaprowska-Buhski, Kanal
Dnestr *see* Dniester
Dnestrovskiy Liman *see* Dnistrovs'kyy Lyman
88 H11 **Dnieper** *Bel.* Dnyapro, *Rus.* Dnepr, *Ukr.* Dnipro. ∽ E Europe
119 P3 **Dnieper Lowland** *Bel.* Prydnyaprowskaya Nizina, *Ukr.* Prydniprovs'ka Nyzovyna. *lowlands* Belorussia/Ukraine
118 M8 **Dniester** *Rom.* Nistru, *Rus.* Dnestr, *Ukr.* Dnister; *anc.* Tyras. ∽ Moldavia/Ukraine
Dnipro *see* Dnieper
119 T7 **Dniprodzerzhyns'k** *Rus.* Dneprodzerzhinsk; *prev.* Kamenskoye. Dnipropetrovs'ka Oblast', E Ukraine
119 T7 **Dniprodzerzhyns'ke Vodoskhovyshche** *Rus.* Dneprodzerzhinskoye Vodokhranilishche. ⊠ C Ukraine
119 U7 **Dnipropetrovs'k** *Rus.* Dnepropetrovsk; *prev.* Yekaterinoslav. Dnipropetrovs'ka Oblast', E Ukraine
119 U8 **Dnipropetrovs'k** ✕ Dnipropetrovs'ka Oblast', S Ukraine
Dnipropetrovs'k *see* Dnipropetrovs'ka Oblast'
119 T7 **Dnipropetrovs'ka Oblast'** *var.* Dnipropetrovs'k, *Rus.* Dnepropetrovskaya Oblast'. ◐ *province* E Ukraine
119 U9 **Dniprorudne** *Rus.* Dneprorudnoye. Zaporiz'ka Oblast', SE Ukraine
119 Q11 **Dniprovs'kyy Lyman** *Rus.* Dneprovskiy Liman. *bay* S Ukraine
Dnister *see* Dniester
119 O11 **Dnistrovs'kyy Lyman** *Rus.* Dnestrovskiy Liman. *inlet* S Ukraine
128 G14 **Dno** Pskovskaya Oblast', W Russian Federation
Dnyapro *see* Dnieper
121 H20 **Dnyaprowska-Buhski, Kanal** *Rus.* Dneprovsko-Bugskiy Kanal. *canal* SW Belorussia
11 O14 **Doaktown** New Brunswick, SE Canada
80 H13 **Doba** Logone-Oriental, S Chad
120 E9 **Dobele** *Ger.* Doblen. Dobele, W Latvia
103 N16 **Döbeln** Sachsen, E Germany
176 Vv9 **Doberai, Jazirah** *Dut.* Vogelkop. *peninsula* Irian Jaya, E Indonesia
112 F10 **Dobiegniew** *Ger.* Woldenberg Neumark. Gorzów, W Poland
Doblen *see* Dobele
83 K18 **Dobli** *spring/well* SW Somalia
176 W13 **Dobo** Pulau Wamar, E Indonesia
114 H11 **Doboj** N Bosnia and Herzegovina
112 L8 **Dobre Miasto** *Ger.* Guttstadt. Olsztyn, N Poland
116 N7 **Dobrich** *Rom.* Bazargic; *prev.* Tolbukhin. Varnenska Oblast, NE Bulgaria
130 M8 **Dobrinka** Lipetskaya Oblast', W Russian Federation
130 M7 **Dobrinka** Volgogradskaya Oblast', SW Russian Federation
Dobrla Vas *see* Eberndorf
113 I15 **Dobrodzień** *Ger.* Guttentag. Częstochowa, S Poland
Dobrogea *see* Dobruja
119 W7 **Dobropillya** *Rus.* Dobropol'ye. Donets'ka Oblast', SE Ukraine
Dobropol'ye *see* Dobropillya
119 P8 **Dobrovelychkivka** Kirovohrads'ka Oblast', C Ukraine
Dobrudja/Dobrudzha *see* Dobruja
116 O7 **Dobruja** *var.* Dobrudja, *Bul.* Dobrudzha, *Rom.* Dobrogea. *physical region* Bulgaria/Romania
121 P19 **Dobrush** Homyel'skaya Voblasts', SE Belorussia
129 U14 **Dobryanka** Permskaya Oblast', NW Russian Federation
119 P2 **Dobryanka** Chernihivs'ka Oblast', N Ukraine
Dobryn' *see* Dabryn'
23 R8 **Dobson** North Carolina, SE USA
xxxvi E15 **Dobwalls** Cornwall, SW England, UK
61 N20 **Doce, Rio** ∽ SE Brazil
xxxix U8 **Docking** Norfolk, E England, UK
95 I16 **Docksta** Västernorrland, C Sweden
43 N10 **Doctor Arroyo** Nuevo León, NE Mexico
64 L4 **Doctor Pedro P. Peña** Boquerón, W Paraguay
175 T7 **Dodaga** Pulau Halmahera, E Indonesia
161 G21 **Dodda Betta** ▲ S India
xxxix S10 **Doddington** Cambridgeshire, E England, UK
xxxvii X10 **Doddington** Kent, SE England, UK
xli P2 **Doddington** Northumberland, N England, UK
Dodecanese *see* Dodekánisos
117 M22 **Dodekánisos** *var.* Nóties Sporádes, *Eng.* Dodecanese; *prev.* Dhodhekánisos. *island group* SE Greece
28 J6 **Dodge City** Kansas, C USA
32 K9 **Dodgeville** Wisconsin, N USA
xxxv K5 **Dodleston** Flintshire, N England, UK
xxxvi D17 **Dodman Point** *headland* SW England, UK
83 J14 **Dodola** S Ethiopia
83 H22 **Dodoma** ● (Tanzania) Dodoma, C Tanzania
83 H22 **Dodoma** ◐ *region* C Tanzania
117 C16 **Dodóni** *var.* Dhodhóni. *site of ancient city* Ípeiros, W Greece
35 U7 **Dodson** Montana, NW USA
27 P3 **Dodson** Texas, SW USA
100 M12 **Doesburg** Gelderland, E Netherlands
100 N12 **Doetinchem** Gelderland, E Netherlands
164 L12 **Dogai Coring** *var.* Lake Montcalm. ◎ W China
143 N15 **Doğanşehir** Malatya, C Turkey
xxxix R6 **Dogdyke** Lincolnshire, E England, UK
86 E9 **Dogger Bank** *undersea feature* C North Sea
25 S10 **Dog Island** *island* Florida, SE USA
12 C7 **Dog Lake** ◎ Ontario, S Canada
108 B9 **Dogliani** Piemonte, NE Italy
170 G11 **Dōgo** *island* Oki-shotō, SW Japan
Do Gonbadān *see* Dow Gonbadān
79 S12 **Dogondoutchi** Dosso, SW Niger
Dōgo-san *see* Dōgo-yama
170 F13 **Dōgo-yama** *var.* Dōgo-san. ▲ Kyūshū, SW Japan
Dogrular *see* Pravda
143 T13 **Doğubayazıt** Ağrı, E Turkey
143 P12 **Doğu Karadeniz Dağları** *var.* Anadolu Dağları. ▲▲ NE Turkey
Doha *see* Ad Dawḥah
Dohad *see* Dāhod
Dohuk *see* Dahūk
165 N16 **Doilungdêqên** Xizang Zizhiqu, W China
116 F12 **Doïranis, Límnis** *Bul.* Ezero Doyransko. ◎ N Greece
Doire *see* Londonderry
101 H22 **Doische** Namur, S Belgium
61 P17 **Dois de Julho** ✕ (Salvador) Bahia, NE Brazil
62 H12 **Dois Vizinhos** Paraná, S Brazil
82 H10 **Doka** Gedaref, E Sudan
Doka *see* Kéita, Bahr
145 T3 **Dokan** *var.* Dūkān. E Iraq
96 H13 **Dokka** Oppland, S Norway
100 L5 **Dokkum** Friesland, N Netherlands
100 L5 **Dokkumer Ee** ∽ N Netherlands
78 K13 **Doko** Haute-Guinée, NE Guinea
Dokshitsy *see* Dokshytsy
120 K13 **Dokshytsy** *Rus.* Dokshitsy. Vitsyebskaya Voblasts', N Belorussia
119 X8 **Dokuchayevs'k** *var.* Dokuchayevsk. Donets'ka Oblast', SE Ukraine
Dolak, Pulau *see* Yos Sudarso, Pulau
31 P9 **Doland** South Dakota, N USA
xxxv J8 **Dolanog** Powys, C Wales, UK
65 J18 **Dolavón** Chaco, S Argentina
13 P6 **Dolbeau** Québec, SE Canada
104 I5 **Dol-de-Bretagne** Ille-et-Vilaine, NW France
66 J13 **Doldrums Fracture Zone** *tectonic feature* W Atlantic Ocean
105 S8 **Dôle** Jura, E France
xxxv J9 **Dolfor** Powys, C Wales, UK
xxxv H5 **Dolgarrog** Conwy, N Wales, UK
xxxv H7 **Dolgellau** Gwynedd, NW Wales, UK
Dolginovo *see* Dawhinava
Dolgi, Ostrov *see* Dolgiy, Ostrov
129 U2 **Dolgiy, Ostrov** *var.* Ostrov Dolgi. *island* NW Russian Federation
168 J9 **Dölgöön** Övörhangay, C Mongolia
109 C20 **Dolianova** Sardegna, Italy, C Mediterranean Sea
Dolina *see* Dolyna
127 Oo15 **Dolinsk** Ostrov Sakhalin, Sakhalinskaya Oblast', SE Russian Federation
Dolinskaya *see* Dolyns'ka
81 F21 **Dolisie** *prev.* Loubomo. Le Niari, S Congo
118 G14 **Dolj** ◐ *county* SW Romania
xliv G11 **Dolla** Tipperary, S Ireland
xliii L18 **Dollar** Clackmannan, C Scotland, UK
100 P5 **Dollard** *bay* NW Germany
204 J5 **Dolleman Island** *island* Antarctica
116 I8 **Dolni Dŭbnik** Loveshka Oblast, NW Bulgaria
116 F8 **Dolni Lom** Oblast Montana, NW Bulgaria
Dolnja Lendava *see* Lendava
116 K9 **Dolno Panicherevo** *var.* Panicherevo. Khaskovska Oblast, C Bulgaria
113 K18 **Dolný Kubín** *Hung.* Alsókubin. Stredné Slovensko, N Slovakia
108 H8 **Dolo** Veneto, NE Italy
Dolomites/Dolomiti *see* Dolomitiche, Alpi
108 H6 **Dolomitiche, Alpi** *var.* Dolomiti, *Eng.* Dolomites. ▲▲ NE Italy
Dolonnur *see* Duolun
168 K10 **Doloon** Ömnögövĭ, S Mongolia
63 D19 **Dolores** Buenos Aires, E Argentina
44 E3 **Dolores** Petén, N Guatemala
179 R12 **Dolores** Samar, C Philippines
107 S12 **Dolores** País Valenciano, E Spain
63 E21 **Dolores** Soriano, SW Uruguay
43 N12 **Dolores Hidalgo** *var.* Ciudad de Dolores Hidalgo. Guanajuato, C Mexico
15 Hh3 **Dolphin and Union Strait** *strait* Northwest Territories, N Canada
67 D23 **Dolphin, Cape** *headland* East Falkland, Falkland Islands
46 H12 **Dolphin Head** *hill* W Jamaica
85 B21 **Dolphin Head** *var.* Cape Dernberg. *headland* SW Namibia
xliii L21 **Dolphinton** The Borders, S Scotland, UK
112 G12 **Dolsk** *Ger.* Dolzig. Poznań, W Poland
xxxvi F13 **Dolton** Devon, SW England, UK
178 J8 **Đô Lương** Nghê An, N Vietnam
xxxv H6 **Dolwyddelan** Conwy, N Wales, UK
118 I6 **Dolyna** *Rus.* Dolina. Ivano-Frankivs'ka Oblast', W Ukraine
119 R8 **Dolyns'ka** *Rus.* Dolinskaya. Kirovohrads'ka Oblast', S Ukraine
Dolzig *see* Dolsk
Domachëvo/Domaczewo *see* Damachava
119 P9 **Domanivka** Mykolayivs'ka Oblast', S Ukraine
159 S13 **Domar** Rajshahi, N Bangladesh
110 I9 **Domat/Ems** Graubünden, SE Switzerland
113 A18 **Domažlice** *Ger.* Taus. Západní Čechy, SW Czech Republic
131 X8 **Dombarovskiy** Orenburgskaya Oblast', W Russian Federation
96 G10 **Dombås** Oppland, S Norway
85 M17 **Dombe** Manica, C Mozambique
84 A13 **Dombe Grande** Benguela, C Angola
105 R10 **Dombes** *physical region* E France
176 Xx10 **Dombo** Irian Jaya, E Indonesia
113 I25 **Dombóvár** Tolna, S Hungary
101 D14 **Domburg** Zeeland, SW Netherlands
60 L13 **Dom Eliseu** Pará, NE Brazil
Domel Island *see* Letsôk-aw Kyun
105 O11 **Dôme, Puy de** ▲ C France
38 H13 **Dome Rock Mountains** ▲▲ Arizona, SW USA
Domesnes, Cape *see* Kolkasrags
64 G8 **Domeyko** Atacama, N Chile
64 H5 **Domeyko, Cordillera** ▲▲ N Chile
104 K5 **Domfront** Orne, N France
176 Xx10 **Dom, Gunung** ▲ Irian Jaya, E Indonesia
47 X11 **Dominica** *off.* Commonwealth of Dominica. ◆ *republic* E West Indies
49 S3 **Dominica** *island* Dominica
Dominica Channel *see* Martinique Passage
45 N15 **Dominical** Puntarenas, SE Costa Rica
47 Q8 **Dominican Republic** ◆ *republic* C West Indies
47 X11 **Dominica Passage** *passage* E Caribbean Sea
101 K14 **Dommel** ∽ S Netherlands
83 O14 **Domo** SE Ethiopia
130 L4 **Domodedovo** ✕ (Moskva) Moskovskaya Oblast', W Russian Federation
108 C6 **Domodossola** Piemonte, NE Italy
117 F17 **Domokós** *var.* Dhomokós. Stereá Ellás, C Greece
180 I14 **Domoni** Anjouan, SE Comoros
63 G16 **Dom Pedrito** Rio Grande do Sul, S Brazil
Dompoe *see* Dompu
175 Oo16 **Dompu** *prev.* Dompoe. Sumbawa, C Indonesia
Domschale *see* Domžale
64 H13 **Domuyo, Volcán** ⋀ W Argentina
111 U11 **Domžale** *Ger.* Domschale. C Slovenia
xli U14 **Don** ∽ N England, UK
xlii O13 **Don** ∽ NE Scotland, UK
131 O10 **Don** *var.* Duna, Tanais. ∽ SW Russian Federation
xliv M4 **Donaghadee** Ards, E Northern Ireland, UK
190 M11 **Donald** Victoria, SE Australia
24 J9 **Donaldsonville** Louisiana, S USA
25 S8 **Donalsonville** Georgia, SE USA
Donau *see* Danube
103 G23 **Donaueschingen** Baden-Württemberg, SW Germany
103 K22 **Donaumoos** *wetland* S Germany
103 K22 **Donauwörth** Bayern, S Germany
111 U7 **Donawitz** Steiermark, SE Austria
119 X7 **Donbass** *industrial region* Russian Federation/Ukraine
106 K11 **Don Benito** Extremadura, W Spain
xli T16 **Doncaster** *anc.* Danum. Doncaster, N England, UK
xli T15 **Doncaster** ◐ *unitary authority* N England, UK
46 K12 **Don Christophers Point** *headland* C Jamaica
57 V9 **Donderkamp** Sipaliwini, NW Surinam
84 B12 **Dondo** Cuanza Norte, NW Angola
175 Q9 **Dondo** Sulawesi, N Indonesia
85 N17 **Dondo** Sofala, C Mozambique
175 Pp7 **Dondo, Teluk** *bay* Sulawesi, N Indonesia
161 K26 **Dondra Head** *headland* S Sri Lanka
Dondușani *see* Dondușeni
118 M8 **Dondușeni** *var.* Dondușani, *Rus.* Dondyushany. N Moldavia
Dondyushany *see* Dondușeni
xliv G4 **Donegal** *Ir.* Dún na nGall. Donegal, NW Ireland
xliv H3 **Donegal** *Ir.* Dún na nGall. ◐ *county* NW Ireland
xliv H4 **Donegal Bay** *Ir.* Bá Dhún na nGall. *bay* NW Ireland
xliv C11 **Donegal Point** *headland* W Ireland
86 K10 **Donets** ∽ Russian Federation/Ukraine
119 X8 **Donets'k** *Rus.* Donetsk; *prev.* Stalino. Donets'ka Oblast', E Ukraine
119 W8 **Donets'k** ✕ Donets'ka Oblast', E Ukraine
Donets'k *see* Donets'ka Oblast'
119 W8 **Donets'ka Oblast'** *var.* Donets'k, *Rus.* Donetskaya Oblast'; *prev.* Rus. Stalinskaya Oblast'. ◐ *province* SE Ukraine
Donetskaya Oblast' *see* Donets'ka Oblast'
69 P8 **Donga** ∽ Cameroon/Nigeria
163 O13 **Dongchuan** Yunnan, SW China
101 I14 **Dongen** Noord-Brabant, S Netherlands
166 K17 **Dongfang** *var.* Basuo. Hainan, S China
169 Z7 **Dongfanghong** Heilongjiang, NE China
169 W11 **Dongfeng** Jilin, NE China
175 P9 **Donggala** Sulawesi, C Indonesia
169 V13 **Donggou** Liaoning, NE China
167 O14 **Dongguan** Guangdong, S China
178 K9 **Đông Ha** Quang Tri, C Vietnam
Dong Hai *see* East China Sea
166 M16 **Donghai Dao** *island* S China
178 Jj9 **Đông Hơi** Quang Binh, C Vietnam
110 H10 **Dongio** Ticino, S Switzerland
Dongkan *see* Binhai
166 L11 **Dongkou** Hunan, S China
Dongliao *see* Liaoyuan
Dong-nai *see* Đông Nai, Sông
178 K13 **Đông Nai, Sông** *var.* Dong-nai, Dong Noi, Donnai. ∽ S Vietnam
167 O14 **Dongnan Qiuling** *plateau* SE China
169 Y9 **Dongning** Heilongjiang, NE China
Dong Noi *see* Đông Nai, Sông
85 C14 **Dongo** Huíla, C Angola
82 E7 **Dongola** *var.* Donqola, Dunqulah. Northern, N Sudan
81 I17 **Dongou** La Likouala, NE Congo
178 Jj13 **Đông Phu** Sông Be, S Vietnam
Dong Rak, Phanom *see* Dângrêk, Chuŏr Phnum
167 Q14 **Dongshan Dao** *island* SE China
169 N14 **Dongsheng** Nei Mongol Zizhiqu, N China
167 R7 **Dongtai** Jiangsu, E China
167 N10 **Dongting Hu** *var.* Tung-t'ing Hu. ◎ S China
167 P10 **Dongxiang** Jiangxi, S China
167 Q4 **Dongying** Shandong, E China
xxxix R8 **Donington** Lincolnshire, E England, UK
29 X8 **Doniphan** Missouri, C USA
8 G7 **Donjek** ∽ Yukon Territory, W Canada
114 E11 **Donji Lapac** Zadar-Knin, C Croatia
114 H8 **Donji Miholjac** Osijek-Baranja, NE Croatia
114 P12 **Donji Milanovac** Serbia, E Yugoslavia
114 G12 **Donji Vakuf** C Bosnia and Herzegovina
100 M6 **Donkerbroek** Friesland, N Netherlands
178 Hh11 **Don Muang** ✕ (Krung Thep) Nonthaburi, C Thailand
27 S17 **Donna** Texas, SW USA
13 Q10 **Donnacona** Québec, SE Canada
Donnai *see* Đông Nai, Sông
31 Y16 **Donnellson** Iowa, C USA
9 O13 **Donnelly** Alberta, W Canada
103 F19 **Donnersberg** ▲ W Germany
xxxviii I9 **Donnington** Shropshire, W England, UK
Donoso *see* Miguel de la Borda
107 P2 **Donostia-San Sebastián** País Vasco, N Spain
xliv F13 **Donoughmore** Cork, S Ireland
117 K21 **Donoússa** *island* Kykládes, Greece, Aegean Sea
37 P8 **Don Pedro Reservoir** ⊠ California, W USA
Donqola *see* Dongola
130 L5 **Donskoy** Tul'skaya Oblast', W Russian Federation
179 Q11 **Donsol** Luzon, N Philippines
xliv C6 **Dooagh** Mayo, NW Ireland
xliv C6 **Doogort** *var.* Dugort. Mayo, NW Ireland
xliv C6 **Doohooma** Mayo, NW Ireland
83 L16 **Doolow** SE Ethiopia
xliv G11 **Doon** Limerick, SW Ireland
xliv D11 **Doonbeg** ∽ W Ireland
41 Q7 **Doonerak, Mount** ▲ Alaska, USA
xliii I23 **Doon, Loch** ◎ W Scotland, UK
100 J12 **Doorn** Utrecht, C Netherlands
Doornik *see* Tournai
33 N6 **Door Peninsula** *peninsula* Wisconsin, N USA
82 P13 **Dooxo Nugaaleed** *var.* Nogal Valley. *valley* E Somalia
xli N13 **Dophinholme** Lancashire, NW England, UK
166 G8 **Do Qu** ∽ C China
108 B7 **Dora Baltea** *anc.* Duria Major. ∽ NW Italy
188 K7 **Dora, Lake** *salt lake* Western Australia
108 A8 **Dora Riparia** *anc.* Duria Minor. ∽ NW Italy
Dorbiljin *see* Emin
169 V8 **Dorbod** *var.* Dorbod Mongolzu Zizhixian, Talkang. Heilongjiang, NE China
Dorbod Mongolzu Zizhixian *see* Dorbod
115 N18 **Đorče Petrov** *var.* Djorče Petrov, Gorče Petrov. N FYR Macedonia
xxxvi M14 **Dorchester** *anc.* Durnovaria. Dorset, S England, UK
xxxvii Q8 **Dorchester** Oxfordshire, C England, UK
12 F16 **Dorchester** Ontario, S Canada
15 Mm4 **Dorchester, Cape** *headland* Baffin Island, Northwest Territories, NE Canada
85 D19 **Dordabis** Khomas, C Namibia
104 L12 **Dordogne** ◐ *department* SW France
105 N12 **Dordogne** ∽ W France
100 H13 **Dordrecht** *var.* Dordt, Dort. Zuid-Holland, SW Netherlands
Dordt *see* Dordrecht
105 P11 **Dore** ∽ C France
9 S13 **Doré Lake** Saskatchewan, C Canada
105 O12 **Dore, Monts** ▲▲ C France
xlii J12 **Dores** Highland, NW Scotland, UK
103 M23 **Dorfen** Bayern, SE Germany
109 D18 **Dorgali** Sardegna, Italy, C Mediterranean Sea
168 F7 **Dörgön Nuur** ◎ NW Mongolia
79 Q12 **Dori** N Burkina
85 E24 **Doring** ∽ S South Africa
xxxvii T11 **Dorking** Surrey, SE England, UK
103 E16 **Dormagen** Nordrhein-Westfalen, W Germany
105 P4 **Dormans** Marne, N France
xli Y6 **Dormanstown** Redcar and Cleveland, N England, UK
110 E6 **Dornach** Solothurn, NW Switzerland
Dorna Watra *see* Vatra Dornei
110 J7 **Dornbirn** Vorarlberg, W Austria
xlii F13 **Dornie** Highland, NW Scotland, UK
xlii J10 **Dornoch** Highland, N Scotland, UK
xlii J10 **Dornoch Firth** *inlet* N Scotland, UK
169 P7 **Dornod** ◐ *province* E Mongolia
169 N10 **Dornogovĭ** ◐ *province* SE Mongolia
79 P10 **Doro** Tombouctou, S Mali
118 L14 **Dorobanțu** Călărași, S Romania
113 J22 **Dorog** Komárom-Esztergom, N Hungary
130 I4 **Dorogobuzh** Smolenskaya Oblast', W Russian Federation
118 K8 **Dorohoi** Botoșani, NE Romania
95 H15 **Dorotea** Västerbotten, N Sweden
Dorpat *see* Tartu
188 G10 **Dorre Island** *island* Western Australia
xxxviii D16 **Dorridge** Solihull, C England, UK
191 U5 **Dorrigo** New South Wales, SE Australia
37 N1 **Dorris** California, W USA
xxxvi L13 **Dorset** ◐ *county* S England, UK
12 H13 **Dorset** Ontario, SE Canada
103 E14 **Dorsten** Nordrhein-Westfalen, W Germany
xxxviii G13 **Dorstone** Herefordshire, W England, UK
Dort *see* Dordrecht
103 F15 **Dortmund** Nordrhein-Westfalen, W Germany
102 F12 **Dortmund-Ems-Kanal** *canal* W Germany
142 L17 **Dörtyol** Hatay, S Turkey
148 L7 **Do Rūd** *var.* Dow Rūd, Durud. Lorestān, W Iran
81 O15 **Doruma** Haut-Zaïre, N Zaire
13 O12 **Dorval** ✕ (Montréal) Québec, SE Canada
47 T5 **Dos Bocas, Lago** ◎ C Puerto Rico
106 K14 **Dos Hermanas** Andalucía, S Spain
Dospad Dagh *see* Rhodope Mountains
37 P10 **Dos Palos** California, W USA
116 I11 **Dospat** Plovdivska Oblast, SW Bulgaria
116 H11 **Dospat, Yazovir** ⊠ SW Bulgaria
102 M11 **Dosse** ∽ NE Germany
79 S12 **Dosso** Dosso, SW Niger
79 S12 **Dosso** ◐ *department* SW Niger
150 G12 **Dossor** Atyrau, SW Kazakhstan
153 V9 **Dostuk** Narynskaya Oblast', C Kyrgyzstan
151 X13 **Dostyk** *prev.* Druzhba. Taldykorgan, SE Kazakhstan
25 R7 **Dothan** Alabama, S USA
41 T9 **Dot Lake** Alaska, USA
120 F12 **Dotnuva** Kėdainiai, C Lithuania
101 D19 **Dottignies** Hainaut, W Belgium
105 P2 **Douai** *prev.* Douay, *anc.* Duacum. Nord, N France
12 L9 **Douaire, Lac** ◎ Québec, SE Canada
81 D16 **Douala** *var.* Duala. Littoral, W Cameroon
81 D16 **Douala** ✕ Littoral, W Cameroon
104 F6 **Douarnenez** Finistère, NW France
104 E6 **Douarnenez, Baie de** *bay* NW France
Douay *see* Douai
27 O6 **Double Mountain Fork Brazos River** ∽ Texas, SW USA
25 O3 **Double Springs** Alabama, S USA
105 T8 **Doubs** ◐ *department* E France
110 C8 **Doubs** ∽ France/Switzerland
193 A22 **Doubtful Sound** *sound* South Island, NZ
192 J2 **Doubtless Bay** *bay* North Island, NZ
27 X9 **Doucette** Texas, SW USA
104 K8 **Doué-la-Fontaine** Maine-et-Loire, NW France
79 O11 **Douentza** Mopti, S Mali
xliii G21 **Dougarie** North Ayrshire, W Scotland, UK
xliv F14 **Douglas** Cork, S Ireland
xl G12 **Douglas** ○ (Isle of Man) E Isle of Man
xliii K22 **Douglas** South Lanarkshire, C Scotland, UK
67 D24 **Douglas** East Falkland, Falkland Islands
85 H23 **Douglas** Northern Cape, C South Africa
41 X13 **Douglas** Alexander Archipelago, Alaska, USA
39 O17 **Douglas** Arizona, SW USA
25 U7 **Douglas** Georgia, SE USA
35 Y15 **Douglas** Wyoming, C USA
8 J14 **Douglas Channel** *channel* British Columbia, W Canada
190 G3 **Douglas Creek** *seasonal river* South Australia
33 P5 **Douglas Lake** ◎ Michigan, N USA
23 O9 **Douglas Lake** ⊠ Tennessee, S USA
41 Q13 **Douglas, Mount** ▲ Alaska, USA
204 I6 **Douglas Range** ▲▲ Alexander Island, Antarctica
xliii N16 **Douglastown** Angus, E Scotland, UK
124 N10 **Doukáto, Ákra** *headland* Lefkáda, W Greece
105 O2 **Doullens** Somme, N France
Douma *see* Dūmā
81 F15 **Doumé** Est, E Cameroon
xlii M4 **Dounby** Orkney Islands, N Scotland, UK
xliii J18 **Doune** Stirling, C Scotland, UK
xlii K6 **Dounreay** Highland, NW Scotland, UK
101 E21 **Dour** Hainaut, S Belgium
61 K18 **Dourada, Serra** ▲▲ S Brazil
61 I21 **Dourados** Mato Grosso do Sul, S Brazil
105 N5 **Dourdan** Essonne, N France
106 I6 **Douro** *Sp.* Duero. ∽ Portugal/Spain *see also* Duero
106 G6 **Douro Litoral** *former province* N Portugal
Douvres *see* Dover
104 K15 **Douze** ∽ SW France
xxxviii K5 **Dove Holes** Derbyshire, C England, UK
xxxvii Z11 **Dover** *Fr.* Douvres; *Lat.* Dubris Portus. Kent, SE England, UK
191 P17 **Dover** Tasmania, SE Australia
19 Rr8 **Dover** *state capital* Delaware, NE USA
21 P9 **Dover** New Hampshire, NE USA
20 J14 **Dover** New Jersey, NE USA
33 U12 **Dover** Ohio, N USA
22 H8 **Dover** Tennessee, S USA
xxxviii L8 **Doveridge** Derbyshire, C England, UK
xxxvii Z12 **Dover, Strait of** *var.* Straits of Dover, *Fr.* Pas de Calais. *strait* England, UK/France
Dover, Straits of *see* Dover, Strait of
Dovlen *see* Devin
96 G11 **Dovre** Oppland, S Norway
96 G10 **Dovrefjell** *plateau* S Norway
Dovsk *see* Dowsk
85 M14 **Dowa** Central, C Malawi
33 O10 **Dowagiac** Michigan, N USA
149 N10 **Dow Gonbadān** *var.* Do Gonbadān, Gonbadān. Kohkīlūyeh va Būyer Aḩmadī, SW Iran
154 M2 **Dowlatābād** Fāryāb, N Afghanistan
xliv M5 **Down** ◐ *district* SE Northern Ireland, UK
35 R16 **Downey** Idaho, NW USA
xli P2 **Downham** Northumberland, N England, UK
xxxix T10 **Downham Market** Norfolk, E England, UK
xliii P14 **Downies** Aberdeenshire, NE Scotland, UK
37 P5 **Downieville** California, W USA
xliv M5 **Downpatrick** *Ir.* Dún Pádraig. Down, SE Northern Ireland, UK
28 M3 **Downs** Kansas, C USA
20 J12 **Downsville** New York, NE USA
xxxvii O12 **Downton** Wiltshire, S England, UK
xliv H6 **Dowra** Leitrim, N Ireland
Dow Rūd *see* Do Rūd
31 V12 **Dows** Iowa, C USA
121 O17 **Dowsk** *Rus.* Dovsk. Homyel'skaya Voblasts', SE Belorussia
37 Q4 **Doyle** California, W USA
20 I15 **Doylestown** Pennsylvania, NE USA
Doyransko, Ezero *see* Doïranis, Límnis
116 I8 **Doyrentsi** Loveshka Oblast, N Bulgaria
170 Ff11 **Dōzen** *island* Oki-shotō, SW Japan
12 K9 **Dozois, Réservoir** ⊠ Québec, SE Canada
76 D9 **Drâa** *seasonal river* S Morocco
Drâa, Hammada du *see* Dra, Hamada du
Drabble *see* José Enrique Rodó
119 Q5 **Drabiv** Cherkas'ka Oblast', C Ukraine
Drable *see* José Enrique Rodó
105 S13 **Drac** ∽ E France
Drač/Draç *see* Durrës
62 I8 **Dracena** São Paulo, S Brazil
100 M6 **Drachten** Friesland, N Netherlands
94 H11 **Drag** Nordland, C Norway
118 L14 **Dragalina** Călărași, SE Romania

◆ Country
● Country Capital
◇ Dependent Territory
○ Dependent Territory Capital
◐ Administrative Region
✕ International Airport
▲ Mountain
▲▲ Mountain Range
⋀ Volcano
∽ River
◎ Lake
⊠ Reservoir

♦ COUNTRY ◇ DEPENDENT TERRITORY ♦ ADMINISTRATIVE REGION ▲ MOUNTAIN ⋆ VOLCANO ◉ LAKE
● COUNTRY CAPITAL ○ DEPENDENT TERRITORY CAPITAL × INTERNATIONAL AIRPORT ▲ MOUNTAIN RANGE ♒ RIVER ☒ RESERVOIR

DYSERTH – EKEREM

xxxv I4 **Dyserth** Denbighshire, N Wales, UK
Dysna see Dzisna
117 D18 **Dytikí Elláś** *Eng.* Greece West. ◐ *region* C Greece
117 C14 **Dytikí Makedonía** *Eng.* Macedonia West. ◐ *region* N Greece
Dyurmen'tyube *see* Dermentobe
131 U4 **Dyurtyuli** Respublika Bashkortostan, W Russian Federation
Dyushambe *see* Dushanbe
168 I7 **Dzaanhushuu** Arhangay, C Mongolia
Dza Chu *see* Mekong
168 I8 **Dzadgay** Bayanhongor, C Mongolia
168 H8 **Dzag** Bayanhongor, C Mongolia
168 H10 **Dzalaa** Bayanhongor, C Mongolia
180 J14 **Dzaoudzi** E Mayotte
Dzaudzhikau *see* Vladikavkaz
168 G7 **Dzavhan** ◐ *province* NW Mongolia
168 G7 **Dzavhan Gol** ~ NW Mongolia
168 J7 **Dzegstey** Arhangay, C Mongolia
131 O3 **Dzerzhinsk** Nizhegorodskaya Oblast', W Russian Federation
Dzerzhinsk *see* Dzyarzhynsk, Belorussia
Dzerzhinsk *see* Dzerzhyns'k, Ukraine
Dzerzhinskiy *see* Nar'yan-Mar
151 W13 **Dzerzhinskoye** Taldykorgan, SE Kazakhstan
119 X7 **Dzerzhyns'k** *Rus.* Dzerzhinsk. Donets'ka Oblast', SE Ukraine
118 M5 **Dzerzhyns'k** Zhytomyrs'ka Oblast', N Ukraine
Dzhailgan *see* Jayilgan
151 N14 **Dzhalagash** *Kaz.* Zhalashash. Kzyl-Orda, S Kazakhstan
153 T10 **Dzhalal-Abad** *Kir.* Jalal-Abad. Dzhalal-Abadskaya Oblast', W Kyrgyzstan
153 S9 **Dzhalal-Abadskaya Oblast'** *Kir.* Jalal-Abad Oblasty. ◐ *province* W Kyrgyzstan
Dzhalilabad *see* Cälilabad
126 Ll15 **Dzhalinda** Amurskaya Oblast', SE Russian Federation
150 G9 **Dzhambeyty** *Kaz.* Zhympity. Zapadnyy Kazakhstan, W Kazakhstan
Dzhambul/Dzhambulskaya Oblast' *see* Zhambyl
Dzhankel'dy *see* Jangeldi
119 T12 **Dzhankoy** Respublika Krym, S Ukraine
151 V14 **Dzhansugurov** *Kaz.* Zhansügirov. Taldykorgan, SE Kazakhstan
153 R9 **Dzhany-Bazar** *var.* Yangibazar. Dzhalal-Abadskaya Oblast', W Kyrgyzstan
150 D9 **Dzhanybek** *Kaz.* Zhänibek. Zapadnyy Kazakhstan, W Kazakhstan
126 L8 **Dzhardzhan** Respublika Sakha (Yakutiya), NE Russian Federation
Dzharkurgan *see* Jarqürghon
119 S11 **Dzharylhats'ka Zatoka** *gulf* S Ukraine
Dzhayilgan *see* Jayilgan
152 B11 **Dzhebel** *Turkm.* Jebel. Balkanskiy Velayat, W Turkmenistan
153 T14 **Dzhelandy** SE Tajikistan
153 Y7 **Dzhergalan** *Kir.* Jyrgalan. Issyk-Kul'skaya Oblast', NE Kyrgyzstan
150 L8 **Dzhetygara** *Kaz.* Zhetiqara. Kustanay, NW Kazakhstan
Dzhezkazgan/Dzhezkazganskaya Oblast' *see* Zhezkazgan
152 J10 **Dzhigirbent** *Turkm.* Jigerbent. Lebapskiy Velayat, NE Turkmenistan
Dzhirgatal' *see* Jirgatol
Dzhizak *see* Jizzakh
Dzhizakskaya Oblast' *see* Jizzakh Wiloyati
127 N12 **Dzhugdzhur, Khrebet** ▲▲ E Russian Federation
Dzhul'fa *see* Culfa
Dzhuma *see* Juma
151 W14 **Dzhungarskiy Alatau** ▲▲ China/Kazakhstan
150 M14 **Dzhusaly** *Kaz.* Zholsaly. Kzyl-Orda, SW Kazakhstan
152 J12 **Dzhynlykum, Peski** *desert* E Turkmenistan
112 L9 **Działdowo** Ciechanów, C Poland
113 L16 **Działoszyce** Kielce, S Poland
43 X11 **Dzidzantún** Yucatán, E Mexico
113 G15 **Dzierżoniów** *Ger.* Reichenbach. Wałbrzych, SW Poland
43 X11 **Dzilam de Bravo** Yucatán, E Mexico
120 L12 **Dzisna** *Rus.* Disna. Vitsyebskaya Voblasts', N Belorussia
120 K12 **Dzisna** *Lith.* Dysna, *Rus.* Disna. ~ Belorussia/Lithuania
121 G20 **Dzivin** *Rus.* Divin. Brestskaya Voblasts', SW Belorussia
121 M15 **Dzmitravichy** *Rus.* Dmitrovichi. Minskaya Voblasts', C Belorussia
168 M8 **Dzogsool** Töv, C Mongolia
133 S8 **Dzungaria** *var.* Sungaria, Zungaria. *physical region* W China
Dzungarian Basin *see* Junggar Pendi
168 G5 **Dzür** Dzavhan, W Mongolia
169 Q8 **Dzüünbulag** Dornod, E Mongolia
169 O8 **Dzüünbulag** Sühbaatar, E Mongolia
168 H7 **Dzuunmod** Dzavhan, C Mongolia
168 L8 **Dzuunmod** Töv, C Mongolia
Dzüün Soyonï Nuruu *see* Eastern Sayans
168 F8 **Dzüyl** Govĭ-Altay, SW Mongolia
Dzvina *see* Western Dvina
121 J16 **Dzyarzhynsk** *Rus.* Dzerzhinsk; *prev.* Kaydanovo. Minskaya Voblasts', C Belorussia
121 H17 **Dzyatlava** *Pol.* Zdzięciół, *Rus.* Dyatlovo. Hrodzyenskaya Voblasts', W Belorussia

E

Éadan Doire *see* Edenderry
E *see* Hubei
39 W6 **Eads** Colorado, C USA
39 O13 **Eagar** Arizona, SW USA
41 T8 **Eagle** Alaska, USA
11 S8 **Eagle** ~ Newfoundland and Labrador, E Canada
8 I3 **Eagle** ~ Yukon Territory, NW Canada
31 T7 **Eagle Bend** Minnesota, N USA
30 M8 **Eagle Butte** South Dakota, N USA
31 V12 **Eagle Grove** Iowa, C USA
21 R2 **Eagle Lake** Maine, NE USA
27 U11 **Eagle Lake** Texas, SW USA
10 A11 **Eagle Lake** ◎ Ontario, S Canada
37 P3 **Eagle Lake** ◎ California, W USA
21 R3 **Eagle Lake** ◎ Maine, NE USA
31 Y3 **Eagle Mountain** ▲ Minnesota, N USA
27 T6 **Eagle Mountain Lake** ⊡ Texas, SW USA
39 S9 **Eagle Nest Lake** ⊡ New Mexico, SW USA
27 P13 **Eagle Pass** Texas, SW USA
67 C25 **Eagle Passage** *passage* SW Atlantic Ocean
37 R8 **Eagle Peak** ▲ California, W USA
37 Q2 **Eagle Peak** ▲ California, W USA
39 P13 **Eagle Peak** ▲ New Mexico, SW USA
8 I4 **Eagle Plain** Yukon Territory, NW Canada
34 G15 **Eagle Point** Oregon, NW USA
195 N17 **Eagle Point** *headland* SE PNG
41 R11 **Eagle River** Alaska, USA
32 M2 **Eagle River** Michigan, N USA
32 L4 **Eagle River** Wisconsin, N USA
23 S6 **Eagle Rock** Virginia, NE USA
xliii J21 **Eaglesham** East Renfrewshire, W Scotland, UK
38 J13 **Eagletail Mountains** ▲▲ Arizona, SW USA
178 Kk12 **Ea Hleo** Đắc Lắc, S Vietnam
178 Kk12 **Ea Kar** Đắc Lắc, S Vietnam
xxxvi A7 **Ealing** Ealing, SE England, UK
xxxiv K16 **Ealing** ◐ *London borough* SE England, UK
Eanjum *see* Anjum
Eanodat *see* Enontekiö
xli P13 **Earby** Lancashire, NW England, UK
10 B10 **Ear Falls** Ontario, C Canada
xxxix S11 **Earith** Cambridgeshire, E England, UK
29 X10 **Earle** Arkansas, C USA
xxxvi R9 **Earley** Reading, S England, UK
37 R12 **Earlimart** California, W USA
22 I6 **Earlington** Kentucky, S USA
xxxix P12 **Earls Barton** Northamptonshire, C England, UK
xxxvii W6 **Earls Colne** Essex, SE England, UK
xliii N18 **Earlsferry** Fife, E Scotland, UK
xxxvi C9 **Earlsfield** Wandsworth, SE England, UK
xxxix N10 **Earl Shilton** Leicestershire, C England, UK
xliii N21 **Earlston** The Borders, S Scotland, UK
xxxix W12 **Earl Stonham** Suffolk, E England, UK
12 H8 **Earlton** Ontario, S Canada
31 T13 **Early** Iowa, C USA
xliii K17 **Earn** ~ N Scotland, UK
xliii J17 **Earn, Loch** ◎ C Scotland, UK
193 C21 **Earnslaw, Mount** ▲ South Island, NZ
26 M4 **Earth** Texas, SW USA
xxxvii R12 **Easebourne** West Sussex, SE England, UK
xli W4 **Easington** Durham, N England, UK
xli Y14 **Easington** East Riding of Yorkshire, N England, UK
xli X4 **Easington Colliery** Durham, N England, UK
xli T12 **Easingwold** North Yorkshire, N England, UK
xliv F5 **Easky** Sligo, N Ireland
23 P11 **Easley** South Carolina, SE USA
East *see* Est
East Açores Fracture Zone *see* East Azores Fracture Zone
xli P7 **East Allen** ~ N England, UK
xxxix V11 **East Anglia** *physical region* E England, UK
13 Q12 **East Angus** Québec, SE Canada
East Antarctica *see* Greater Antarctica
20 E10 **East Aurora** New York, NE USA
East Australian Basin *see* Tasman Basin
xliii I22 **East Ayrshire** ◐ *unitary authority* SW Scotland, UK
East Azerbaijan *see* Āzarbāyjān-e Khāvarī
66 L9 **East Azores Fracture Zone** *var.* East Açores Fracture Zone. *tectonic feature* E Atlantic Ocean
24 M11 **East Bay** *bay* Louisiana, S USA
xxxix W14 **East Bergholt** Suffolk, E England, UK
27 V11 **East Bernard** Texas, SW USA
31 V8 **East Bethel** Minnesota, N USA
East Borneo *see* Kalimantan Timur
xxxvii V13 **Eastbourne** East Sussex, SE England, UK
xxxvi J11 **East Brent** Somerset, SW England, UK
xxxix O7 **East Bridgford** Nottinghamshire, C England, UK
13 R11 **East-Broughton** Québec, SE Canada
46 M6 **East Caicos** *island* E Turks and Caicos Islands
192 R7 **East Cape** *headland* North Island, NZ
182 M4 **East Caroline Basin** *undersea feature* SW Pacific Ocean
xxxvii P9 **East Challow** Oxfordshire, C England, UK
198 G5 **East China Sea** *Chin.* Dong Hai. *sea* W Pacific Ocean
xxxvi L13 **East Chinnock** Somerset, SW England, UK
xxxvii X9 **Eastchurch** Kent, SE England, UK
xxxvii P13 **East Cowes** Isle of Wight, S England, UK
xlii J13 **East Croachy** Highland, NW Scotland, UK
xxxvii V13 **East Dean** East Sussex, SE England, UK
xxxix W9 **East Dereham** Norfolk, E England, UK
32 J9 **East Dubuque** Illinois, N USA
xliii I19 **East Dunbartonshire** ◐ *unitary authority* C Scotland, UK
9 S17 **Eastend** Saskatchewan, S Canada
xlii J11 **Easter Ardross** Highland, NW Scotland, UK
xliii M14 **Easter Balmoral** Aberdeenshire, NE Scotland, UK
200 Nn11 **Easter Fracture Zone** *tectonic feature* E Pacific Ocean
Easter Island *see* Pascua, Isla de
83 J18 **Eastern** ◐ *province* Kenya
159 Q12 **Eastern** ◐ *zone* E Nepal
84 L13 **Eastern** ◐ *province* E Zambia
85 H24 **Eastern Cape** *off.* Eastern Cape Province, *Afr.* Oos-Kaap. ◐ *province* SE South Africa
Eastern Desert *see* Sahara el Sharqîya
83 F15 **Eastern Equatoria** ◐ *state* SE Sudan
Eastern Euphrates *see* Murat Nehri
161 J17 **Eastern Ghats** ▲▲ SE India
194 I13 **Eastern Highlands** ◐ *province* C PNG
161 K25 **Eastern Province** ◐ *province* E Sri Lanka
Eastern Region *see* Ash Sharqīyah
126 I15 **Eastern Sayans** *Mong.* Dzüün Soyonï Nuruu, *Rus.* Vostochnyy Sayan. ▲▲ Mongolia/Russian Federation
Eastern Scheldt *see* Oosterschelde
Eastern Sierra Madre *see* Madre Oriental, Sierra
Eastern Transvaal *see* Mpumalanga
xlii I4 **Easter Quarff** Shetland Islands, NE Scotland, UK
xlii H4 **Easter Skeld** Shetland Islands, NE Scotland, UK
9 W14 **Easterville** Manitoba, C Canada
Easterwâlde *see* Oosterwolde
65 M23 **East Falkland** *var.* Soledad. *island* E Falkland Islands
21 P12 **East Falmouth** Massachusetts, NE USA
East Fayu *see* Fayu
East Flanders *see* Oost-Vlaanderen
41 S6 **East Fork Chandalar River** ~ Alaska, USA
31 U12 **East Fork Des Moines River** ~ Iowa/Minnesota, C USA
East Frisian Islands *see* Ostfriesische Inseln
xli P8 **Eastgate** Durham, N England, UK
20 K10 **East Glenville** New York, NE USA
xxxvii O10 **East Grafton** Wiltshire, S England, UK
31 R4 **East Grand Forks** Minnesota, N USA
xxxvii U11 **East Grinstead** West Sussex, SE England, UK
xxxix O12 **East Haddon** Northamptonshire, C England, UK
xxxix Q3 **East Halton** North Lincolnshire, N England, UK
xxxvi F7 **East Ham** Newham, SE England, UK
xxxvii P8 **East Hanney** Oxfordshire, C England, UK
xxxix W11 **East Harling** Norfolk, E England, UK
20 M12 **East Hartford** Connecticut, NE USA
20 M13 **East Haven** Connecticut, NE USA
xxxvii T10 **East Horsley** Surrey, SE England, UK
xxxvii P9 **East Ilsley** Newbury, S England, UK
181 T9 **East Indiaman Ridge** *undersea feature* E Indian Ocean
133 V16 **East Indies** *island group* SE Asia
xxxvi M8 **Eastington** Gloucestershire, C England, UK
East Java *see* Jawa Timur
33 Q6 **East Jordan** Michigan, N USA
East Kalimantan *see* Kalimantan Timur
East Kazakhstan *see* Vostochnyy Kazakhstan
xxxix S6 **East Keal** Lincolnshire, E England, UK
xliii J20 **East Kilbride** South Lanarkshire, S Scotland, UK
xxxvii M11 **East Knoyle** Wiltshire, S England, UK
27 R7 **Eastland** Texas, SW USA
33 Q9 **East Lansing** Michigan, N USA
37 X11 **East Las Vegas** Nevada, W USA
xxxix N8 **East Leake** Nottinghamshire, C England, UK
xxxvii P12 **Eastleigh** Hampshire, S England, UK
xliii N19 **East Linton** East Lothian, SE Scotland, UK
33 V12 **East Liverpool** Ohio, N USA
85 J25 **East London** *Afr.* Oos-Londen; *prev.* Emonti, Port Rex. Eastern Cape, S South Africa
xxxvi E16 **East Looe** Cornwall, SW England, UK
xliii N20 **East Lothian** ◐ *unitary authority* SE Scotland, UK
10 J10 **Eastmain** Québec, E Canada
10 I10 **Eastmain** ~ Québec, C Canada
13 P13 **Eastman** Québec, SE Canada
25 U6 **Eastman** Georgia, SE USA
183 O3 **East Mariana Basin** *undersea feature* W Pacific Ocean
xxxix O5 **East Markham** Nottinghamshire, C England, UK
xxxvii Q12 **East Meon** Hampshire, S England, UK
32 K11 **East Moline** Illinois, N USA
195 O12 **East New Britain** ◐ *province* E PNG
31 T15 **East Nishnabotna River** ~ Iowa, C USA
xxxvii I14 **Eastnor** Herefordshire, W England, UK
xxxix P10 **East Norton** Rutland, C England, UK
207 V12 **East Novaya Zemlya Trough** *var.* Novaya Zemlya Trough. *undersea feature* W Kara Sea
East Nusa Tenggara *see* Nusa Tenggara Timur
xxxvi L15 **Easton** Dorset, S England, UK
xxxvii P12 **Easton** Hampshire, S England, UK
23 X4 **Easton** Maryland, NE USA
20 I14 **Easton** Pennsylvania, NE USA
xxxix Q10 **Easton on the Hill** Northamptonshire, C England, UK
200 N8 **East Pacific Rise** *undersea feature* E Pacific Ocean
East Pakistan *see* Bangladesh
33 V12 **East Palestine** Ohio, N USA
32 L12 **East Peoria** Illinois, N USA
25 S3 **East Point** Georgia, SE USA
21 U6 **Eastport** Maine, NE USA
29 Z8 **East Prairie** Missouri, C USA
xxxvi H17 **East Prawle** Devon, SW England, UK
21 O12 **East Providence** Rhode Island, NE USA
xxxix V8 **East Raynham** Norfolk, E England, UK
xliii I21 **East Renfrewshire** ◐ *unitary authority* C Scotland, UK
22 L11 **East Ridge** Tennessee, S USA
xli U13 **East Riding of Yorkshire** ◐ *unitary authority* N England, UK
xliii M24 **Eastriggs** Dumfries and Galloway, SW Scotland, UK
xli U14 **Eastrington** East Riding of Yorkshire, N England, UK
20 F9 **East Rochester** New York, NE USA
xxxix V8 **East Rudham** Norfolk, E England, UK
xxxvii Z10 **Eastry** Kent, SE England, UK
32 K15 **East Saint Louis** Illinois, N USA
xliii N20 **East Saltoun** East Lothian, SE Scotland, UK
67 K21 **East Scotia Basin** *undersea feature* SE Scotia Sea
East Sea *see* Japan, Sea of
194 F11 **East Sepik** ◐ *province* NW PNG
181 N4 **East Sheba Ridge** *undersea feature* W Arabian Sea
xxxvi A8 **East Sheen** Richmond upon Thames, SE England, UK
East Siberian Sea *see* Vostochno-Sibirskoye More
20 I14 **East Stroudsburg** Pennsylvania, NE USA
xxxvii U12 **East Sussex** ◐ *county* SE England, UK
East Tasmanian Rise/East Tasmania Plateau/East Tasmania Rise *see* East Tasman Plateau
199 Hh13 **East Tasman Plateau** *var.* East Tasmanian Rise, East Tasmania Plateau, East Tasmania Rise. *undersea feature* SW Tasman Sea
66 L7 **East Thulean Rise** *undersea feature* N Atlantic Ocean
East Timor *see* Timor Timur
xxxix S6 **Eastville** Lincolnshire, E England, UK
23 Y6 **Eastville** Virginia, NE USA
37 R7 **East Walker River** ~ California/Nevada, W USA
xxxvii R13 **East Wittering** West Sussex, SE England, UK
xli Q11 **East Witton** North Yorkshire, N England, UK
xxxix N7 **Eastwood** Nottinghamshire, C England, UK
190 D1 **Eateringinna Creek** ~ South Australia
39 T3 **Eaton** Colorado, C USA
13 Q12 **Eaton** ~ Québec, SE Canada
9 S16 **Eatonia** Saskatchewan, S Canada
33 Q10 **Eaton Rapids** Michigan, N USA
25 U4 **Eatonton** Georgia, SE USA
34 H9 **Eatonville** Washington, NW USA
32 J6 **Eau Claire** Wisconsin, N USA
Eau Claire, Lac à L' *see* St.Clair, Lake
10 J7 **Eau Claire, Lac à l'** ◎ Québec, SE Canada
32 L6 **Eau Claire River** ~ Wisconsin, N USA
196 J16 **Eauripik Atoll** *atoll* Caroline Islands, C Micronesia
199 H8 **Eauripik Rise** *undersea feature* W Pacific Ocean
104 K15 **Eauze** Gers, S France
43 P11 **Ébano** San Luis Potosí, C Mexico
xxxv J13 **Ebbw Vale** Blaenau Gwent, SE Wales, UK
xli Q7 **Ebchester** Durham, N England, UK
81 E17 **Ebebiyin** NE Equatorial Guinea
97 H22 **Ebeltoft** Århus, C Denmark
111 X5 **Ebenfurth** Niederösterreich, E Austria
20 D14 **Ebensburg** Pennsylvania, NE USA
111 S5 **Ebensee** Oberösterreich, N Austria
103 H20 **Eberbach** Baden-Württemberg, SW Germany
124 Q9 **Eber Gölü** *salt lake* C Turkey
111 U9 **Eberndorf** *Slvn.* Dobrla Vas. Kärnten, S Austria
111 R4 **Eberschwang** Oberösterreich, N Austria
102 O11 **Eberswalde-Finow** Brandenburg, E Germany
Ebesfalva *see* Dumbrăveni
172 Oo5 **Ebetsu** *var.* Ebetu. Hokkaidō, NE Japan
Ebetu *see* Ebetsu
Ebinayon *see* Evinayong
164 I4 **Ebinur Hu** ◎ NW China
144 I3 **Ebla** *Ar.* Tell Mardikh. *site of ancient city* Idlib, NW Syria
Eblana *see* Dublin
110 H7 **Ebnat** Sankt Gallen, NE Switzerland
109 L18 **Eboli** Campania, S Italy
81 E16 **Ebolowa** Sud, S Cameroon
81 N21 **Ebombo** Kasai Oriental, C Zaire
201 T9 **Ebon Atoll** *var.* Epoon. *atoll* Ralik Chain, S Marshall Islands
Ebora *see* Évora
Eboracum/Eburacum *see* York
Eborodunum *see* Yverdon
103 J19 **Ebrach** Bayern, C Germany
111 X5 **Ebreichsdorf** Niederösterreich, E Austria
107 S6 **Ebro** ~ NE Spain
107 N3 **Ebro, Embalse del** ⊡ N Spain
123 Hh8 **Ebro Fan** *undersea feature* W Mediterranean Sea
Ebusus *see* Eivissa
101 F20 **Écaussinnes-d'Enghien** Hainaut, SW Belgium
Ecbatana *see* Hamadān
xliii M24 **Ecclefechan** Dumfries and Galloway, SW Scotland, UK
xli O16 **Eccles** Salford, NW England, UK
xliii O21 **Eccles** The Borders, S Scotland, UK
23 Q6 **Eccles** West Virginia, NE USA
xli S16 **Ecclesfield** Sheffield, N England, UK
xxxviii J8 **Eccleshall** Staffordshire, C England, UK
xxxviii G6 **Eccleston** Cheshire, W England, UK
xli N15 **Eccleston** Lancashire, NW England, UK
117 L14 **Eceabat** Çanakkale, NW Turkey
179 P9 **Echague** Luzon, N Philippines
Ech Cheliff/Ech Chleff *see* Chlef
Echeng *see* Ezhou
171 Kk13 **Echigo-sanmyaku** ▲▲ Honshū, C Japan
117 C18 **Echinádes** *island group* W Greece
116 J12 **Echínos** *var.* Ehinos, Ekhínos. Anatolikí Makedonía kai Thráki, NE Greece
171 H13 **Echizen-misaki** *headland* Honshū, SW Japan
Echmiadzin *see* Ejmiatsin
15 Hh5 **Echo Bay** Northwest Territories, NW Canada
37 Y11 **Echo Bay** Nevada, W USA
38 L9 **Echo Cliffs** *cliff* Arizona, SW USA
12 C10 **Echo Lake** ◎ Ontario, S Canada
37 Q7 **Echo Summit** ▲ California, W USA
12 L8 **Échouani, Lac** ◎ Québec, SE Canada
xlii O13 **Echt** Aberdeenshire, NE Scotland, UK
101 L17 **Echt** Limburg, SE Netherlands
103 H22 **Echterdingen** ✕ (Stuttgart) Baden-Württemberg, SW Germany
101 N24 **Echternach** Grevenmacher, E Luxembourg
191 N11 **Echuca** Victoria, SE Australia
106 L14 **Ecija** *anc.* Astigi. Andalucía, SW Spain
Eckengraf *see* Viesīte
102 I7 **Eckernförde** Schleswig-Holstein, N Germany
102 J7 **Eckernförder Bucht** *inlet* N Germany
xliii O22 **Eckford** The Borders, S Scotland, UK
xxxviii M5 **Eckington** Derbyshire, C England, UK
104 L7 **Écommoy** Sarthe, NW France
12 L10 **Écorce, Lac de l'** ◎ Québec, SE Canada
13 Q8 **Écorces, Rivière aux** ~ Québec, SE Canada
58 C7 **Ecuador** *off.* Republic of Ecuador. ◆ *republic* NW South America
82 L10 **Ed** *var.* Edd. SE Eritrea
97 I17 **Ed** Älvsborg, S Sweden
100 I9 **Edam** Noord-Holland, C Netherlands
xlii N3 **Eday** *island* NE Scotland, UK
27 S17 **Edcouch** Texas, SW USA
Edd *see* Ed
82 C11 **Ed Da'ein** Southern Darfur, W Sudan
82 G11 **Ed Damazin** *var.* Ad Damazīn. Blue Nile, E Sudan
82 G8 **Ed Damer** *var.* Ad Dāmir, Ad Damar. River Nile, NE Sudan
82 E8 **Ed Debba** Northern, N Sudan
xlii J10 **Edderton** Highland, NW Scotland, UK
xliii N21 **Eddleston** The Borders, S Scotland, UK
xlii G8 **Eddrachillis Bay** *bay* NW Scotland, UK
82 F10 **Ed Dueim** *var.* Ad Duwaym, Ad Duwēm. White Nile, C Sudan
191 Q16 **Eddystone Point** *headland* Tasmania, SE Australia
xxxvi F17 **Eddystone Rocks** *rocks* SW England, UK
31 W15 **Eddyville** Iowa, C USA
22 H7 **Eddyville** Kentucky, S USA
100 L12 **Ede** Gelderland, C Netherlands
79 T16 **Ede** Osun, SW Nigeria
81 D16 **Edéa** Littoral, SW Cameroon
113 M20 **Edelény** Borsod-Abaúj-Zemplén, NE Hungary
xl M6 **Eden** ~ NW England, UK
191 R12 **Eden** New South Wales, SE Australia
23 T8 **Eden** North Carolina, SE USA
27 P9 **Eden** Texas, SW USA
xxxvii V11 **Edenbridge** Kent, SE England, UK
85 I23 **Edenburg** Free State, C South Africa
193 D24 **Edendale** Southland, South Island, NZ
xliv J9 **Edenderry** *Ir.* Éadan Doire. Offaly, C Ireland
xxxix Q9 **Edenham** Lincolnshire, E England, UK
190 L11 **Edenhope** Victoria, SE Australia
xxxviii L6 **Edensor** Derbyshire, C England, UK
23 X8 **Edenton** North Carolina, SE USA
103 G16 **Eder** ~ NW Germany
176 Yy14 **Ederah** ~ Irian Jaya, E Indonesia
xliv I4 **Ederny** Fermanagh, W Northern Ireland, UK
103 H15 **Edersee** ◎ W Germany
Edessa *see* Şanlıurfa
116 E13 **Édessa** *var.* Édhessa. Kentrikí Makedonía, N Greece
Edfu *see* Idfu
31 P16 **Edgar** Nebraska, C USA
21 P13 **Edgartown** Martha's Vineyard, Massachusetts, NE USA
41 X13 **Edgecumbe, Mount** ▲ Baranof Island, Alaska, USA
23 Q13 **Edgefield** South Carolina, SE USA
31 P6 **Edgeley** North Dakota, N USA
30 I11 **Edgemont** South Dakota, N USA
94 O3 **Edgeøya** *island* S Svalbard
29 Q4 **Edgerton** Kansas, C USA
31 S10 **Edgerton** Minnesota, N USA
23 X3 **Edgewood** Maryland, NE USA
27 V6 **Edgewood** Texas, SW USA
xli O15 **Edgeworth** Lancashire, NW England, UK
xliv H7 **Edgeworthstown** Longford, C Ireland
xxxviii I9 **Edgmond** Shropshire, W England, UK
xxxvi A5 **Edgware** Harrow, SE England, UK
Édhessa *see* Édessa
31 V9 **Edina** Minnesota, N USA
29 U2 **Edina** Missouri, C USA
27 S17 **Edinburg** Texas, SW USA
xliii M20 **Edinburgh** *national region capital* City of Edinburgh, S Scotland, UK
xliii L20 **Edinburgh** ✕ City of Edinburgh, S Scotland, UK
67 M24 **Edinburgh** *var.* Settlement of Edinburgh. ○ (Tristan da Cunha) NW Tristan da Cunha
33 P14 **Edinburgh** Indiana, N USA
xliii L20 **Edinburgh, City of** ◐ *unitary authority* E Scotland, UK
118 L8 **Edineţ** *var.* Edineţi, *Rus.* Yedintsy. NW Moldavia
Edineţi *see* Edineţ
Edingen *see* Enghien
142 B9 **Edirne** *Eng.* Adrianople; *anc.* Adrianopolis, Hadrianopolis. Edirne, NW Turkey
142 B11 **Edirne** ◐ *province* NW Turkey
20 K15 **Edison** New Jersey, NE USA
23 S15 **Edisto Island** South Carolina, SE USA
23 R14 **Edisto River** ~ South Carolina, SE USA
35 S10 **Edith, Mount** ▲ Montana, NW USA
29 N10 **Edmond** Oklahoma, C USA
34 H8 **Edmonds** Washington, NW USA
xxxvi D5 **Edmonton** Enfield, SE England, UK
9 Q14 **Edmonton** Alberta, SW Canada
22 K7 **Edmonton** Kentucky, S USA
9 Q14 **Edmonton** ✕ Alberta, SW Canada
31 P3 **Edmore** North Dakota, N USA
11 N13 **Edmundston** New Brunswick, SE Canada
27 U12 **Edna** Texas, SW USA
41 X14 **Edna Bay** Kosciusko Island, Alaska, USA
79 U16 **Edo** ◐ *state* S Nigeria
108 F6 **Edolo** Lombardia, N Italy
66 L6 **Edoras Bank** *undersea feature* C Atlantic Ocean
142 B12 **Edremit** Balıkesir, NW Turkey
142 B12 **Edremit Körfezi** *gulf* NW Turkey
97 P14 **Edsbro** Stockholm, C Sweden
97 N18 **Edsbruk** Kalmar, S Sweden
96 M12 **Edsbyn** Gävleborg, C Sweden
9 O14 **Edson** Alberta, SW Canada
64 K13 **Eduardo Castex** La Pampa, C Argentina
60 F12 **Eduardo Gomes** ✕ (Manaus) Amazonas, NW Brazil
Edwardesabad *see* Bannu
69 U9 **Edward, Lake** *var.* Albert Edward Nyanza, Edward Nyanza, Lac Idi Amin, Lake Rutanzige. ◎ Uganda/Zaire
Edward Nyanza *see* Edward, Lake
24 K5 **Edwards** Mississippi, S USA
27 O10 **Edwards Plateau** *plain* Texas, SW USA
32 J11 **Edwards River** ~ Illinois, N USA
32 K15 **Edwardsville** Illinois, N USA
205 O13 **Edward VII Peninsula** *peninsula* Antarctica
xxxix N6 **Edwinstowe** Nottinghamshire, C England, UK
xliii N15 **Edzell** Angus, E Scotland, UK
205 X4 **Edward VIII Gulf** *bay* Antarctica
8 J11 **Edziza, Mount** ▲ British Columbia, W Canada
41 N12 **Eek** Alaska, USA
101 D16 **Eeklo** *var.* Eekloo. Oost-Vlaanderen, NW Belgium
Eekloo *see* Eeklo
41 N12 **Eek River** ~ Alaska, USA
100 N6 **Eelde** Drenthe, NE Netherlands
36 L5 **Eel River** ~ California, W USA
33 P12 **Eel River** ~ Indiana, N USA
Eems *see* Ems
100 O4 **Eemshaven** Groningen, NE Netherlands
100 O5 **Eems Kanaal** *canal* NE Netherlands
100 M11 **Eerbeek** Gelderland, E Netherlands
101 C17 **Eernegem** West-Vlaanderen, W Belgium
101 J15 **Eersel** Noord-Brabant, S Netherlands
Eesti Vabariik *see* Estonia
197 C14 **Éfaté** *Fr.* Vaté; *prev.* Sandwich Island. *island* C Vanuatu
111 S4 **Eferding** Oberösterreich, N Austria
32 M15 **Effingham** Illinois, N USA
119 N15 **Eforie-Nord** Constanţa, SE Romania
119 N15 **Eforie Sud** Constanţa, E Romania
99 **Efyrnwy, Afon** *see* Vyrnwy
169 N7 **Eg** Hentiy, N Mongolia
107 P4 **Ega** ~ NE Spain
109 G23 **Egadi, Isole** *island group* S Italy
37 X6 **Egan Range** ▲▲ Nevada, W USA
12 K12 **Eganville** Ontario, SE Canada
Ege Denizi *see* Aegean Sea
41 O14 **Egegik** Alaska, USA
113 L21 **Eger** *Ger.* Erlau. Heves, NE Hungary
Eger *see* Cheb, Czech Republic
Eger *see* Ohre, Czech Republic/Germany
181 P8 **Egeria Fracture Zone** *tectonic feature* W Indian Ocean
97 C17 **Egersund** Rogaland, S Norway
110 J7 **Egg** Vorarlberg, NW Austria
103 H14 **Egge-gebirge** ▲ C Germany
111 Q4 **Eggelsberg** Oberösterreich, N Austria
111 W2 **Eggenburg** Niederösterreich, NE Austria
103 N22 **Eggenfelden** Bayern, SE Germany
20 J17 **Egg Harbor City** New Jersey, NE USA
67 G25 **Egg Island** *island* W Saint Helena
191 N14 **Egg Lagoon** Tasmania, SE Australia
xli X7 **Egglescliffe** Stockton-on-Tees, N England, UK
xxxvii S10 **Egham** Surrey, SE England, UK
101 I20 **Éghezée** Namur, C Belgium
xlii M3 **Egilsay** *island* N Scotland, UK
94 L2 **Egilsstadhir** Austurland, E Iceland
Egina *see* Aígina
Egindibulaq *see* Yegindybulak
Egio *see* Aígio
105 N12 **Égletons** Corrèze, C France
xli Q3 **Eglingham** Northumberland, N England, UK
xliv J3 **Eglinton** Londonderry, NW Northern Ireland, UK
xxxvi E17 **Egloskerry** Cornwall, SW England, UK
xxxv H5 **Eglwysbach** Conwy, N Wales, UK
xxxv H9 **Eglwys Fach** Ceredigion, W Wales, UK
xxxv D12 **Eglwyswrw** Pembrokeshire, SW Wales, UK
100 H9 **Egmond aan Zee** Noord-Holland, NW Netherlands
Egmont *see* Taranaki, Mount
192 J10 **Egmont, Cape** *headland* North Island, NZ
Egoli *see* Johannesburg
xl K9 **Egremont** Cumbria, NW England, UK
142 I15 **Eğridir Gölü** ◎ W Turkey
Egri Palanka *see* Kriva Palanka
xli V9 **Egton** North Yorkshire, N England, UK
97 G23 **Egtved** Vejle, C Denmark
127 Pp4 **Egvekinot** Chukotskiy Avtonomnyy Okrug, NE Russian Federation
77 V9 **Egypt** *off.* Arab Republic of Egypt, *Ar.* Jumhūrīyah Miṣr al 'Arabīyah; *prev.* United Arab Republic, *anc.* Aegyptus. ◆ *republic* NE Africa
32 L17 **Egypt, Lake Of** ⊡ Illinois, N USA
Ehen Hudag *see* Alxa Zuoqi
170 E15 **Ehime** *off.* Ehime-ken. ◐ *prefecture* Shikoku, SW Japan
103 I23 **Ehingen** Baden-Württemberg, S Germany
Ehinos *see* Echínos
23 R14 **Ehrhardt** South Carolina, SE USA
110 K7 **Ehrwald** Tirol, W Austria
203 W6 **Eiao** *island* Îles Marquises, NE French Polynesia
107 P2 **Eibar** País Vasco, N Spain
100 O11 **Eibergen** Gelderland, E Netherlands
111 V9 **Eibiswald** Steiermark, SE Austria
111 P8 **Eichham** ▲ SW Austria
103 J15 **Eichsfeld** *hill range* C Germany
103 L21 **Eichstätt** Bayern, SE Germany
102 H8 **Eider** ~ N Germany
96 E13 **Eidfjord** Hordaland, S Norway
96 D13 **Eidfjorden** *fjord* S Norway
96 F9 **Eidsvåg** Møre og Romsdal, S Norway
97 I15 **Eidsvoll** Akershus, S Norway
94 N2 **Eidsvollfjellet** ▲ NW Svalbard
Eier-Berg *see* Suur Munamägi
103 D18 **Eifel** *plateau* W Germany
110 E9 **Eiger** ▲ C Switzerland
xliii E15 **Eigg** *island* W Scotland, UK
xliii D15 **Eigg, Sound of** *strait* NW Scotland, UK
161 D24 **Eight Degree Channel** *channel* India/Maldives
46 G1 **Eight Mile Rock** Grand Bahama Island, N Bahamas
204 J9 **Eights Coast** *physical region* Antarctica
188 K6 **Eighty Mile Beach** *beach* Western Australia
101 L18 **Eijsden** Limburg, SE Netherlands
97 G15 **Eikeren** ◎ S Norway
Eil *see* Eyl
Eilat *see* Elat
191 O12 **Eildon** Victoria, SE Australia
191 O12 **Eildon, Lake** ◎ Victoria, SE Australia
82 E8 **Eilei** Northern Kordofan, C Sudan
103 N15 **Eilenburg** Sachsen, E Germany
xliii G15 **Eil, Loch** *inlet* NW Scotland, UK
96 H13 **Eina** Oppland, S Norway
103 I14 **Einbeck** Niedersachsen, C Germany
101 K15 **Eindhoven** Noord-Brabant, S Netherlands
110 G8 **Einsiedeln** Schwyz, NE Switzerland
Eipel *see* Ipel'
Éire *see* Ireland, Republic of
Éireann, Muir *see* Irish Sea
Eirik Outer Ridge *see* Eirik Ridge
66 I6 **Eirik Ridge** *var.* Eirik Outer Ridge. *undersea feature* E Labrador Sea
94 I3 **Eiríksjökull** ▲ C Iceland
61 B14 **Eirunepé** Amazonas, N Brazil
101 L17 **Eisden** Limburg, NE Belgium
85 F18 **Eiseb** ~ Botswana/Namibia
Eisen *see* Yŏngch'ŏn
103 J16 **Eisenach** Thüringen, C Germany
Eisenburg *see* Vasvár
111 U6 **Eisenerz** Steiermark, SE Austria
102 Q13 **Eisenhüttenstadt** Brandenburg, E Germany
111 U10 **Eisenkappel** *Slvn.* Železna Kapela. Kärnten, S Austria
Eisenmarkt *see* Hunedoara
111 Y5 **Eisenstadt** Burgenland, E Austria
Eishū *see* Yŏngju
121 H15 **Eišiškes** Šalčininkai, SE Lithuania
103 L15 **Eisleben** Sachsen-Anhalt, C Germany
202 I3 **Eita** Tarawa, W Kiribati
Eitape *see* Aitape
107 V11 **Eivissa** *var.* Iviza, *Cast.* Ibiza; *anc.* Ebusus. Eivissa, Spain, W Mediterranean Sea
107 V10 **Eivissa** *var.* Iviza, *Cast.* Ibiza; *anc.* Ebusus. *island* Islas Baleares, Spain, W Mediterranean Sea
107 R4 **Ejea de los Caballeros** Aragón, NE Spain
42 E8 **Ejido Insurgentes** Baja California Sur, W Mexico
168 I12 **Ejin Qi** *var.* Dalain Hob. Nei Mongol Zizhiqu, N China
Ejmiadzin *see* Ejmiatsin
143 T12 **Ejmiatsin** *var.* Ejmiadzin, Etchmiadzin, *Rus.* Echmiadzin. W Armenia
79 P16 **Ejura** C Ghana
43 R16 **Ejutla** *var.* Ejutla de Crespo. Oaxaca, SE Mexico
Ejutla de Crespo *see* Ejutla
35 Y10 **Ekalaka** Montana, NW USA
Ekapa *see* Cape Town
Ekaterinodar *see* Krasnodar
95 L20 **Ekenäs** *Fin.* Tammisaari. Uusimaa, SW Finland
Ekerem *see* Okarem

◆ Country ● Country Capital ◇ Dependent Territory ○ Dependent Territory Capital ◐ Administrative Region ✕ International Airport ▲ Mountain ▲▲ Mountain Range Volcano ~ River ◎ Lake ⊡ Reservoir
249

EKETAHUNA – ENTERPRISE

192 M13 **Eketahuna** Manawatu-Wanganui, North Island, NZ
Ekhínos see Echínos
127 P3 **Ekiatapskiy Khrebet** ▲▲ NE Russian Federation
151 T8 **Ekibastuz** Pavlodar, NE Kazakhstan
127 N14 **Ekimchan** Amurskaya Oblast', SE Russian Federation
97 O15 **Ekoln** ◎ C Sweden
82 I7 **Ekowit** Red Sea, NE Sudan
97 L19 **Eksjö** Jönköping, S Sweden
95 I15 **Ekträsk** Västerbotten, N Sweden
41 O13 **Ekuk** Alaska, USA
10 F9 **Ekwan** ≈ Ontario, C Canada
41 O13 **Ekwok** Alaska, USA
177 G6 **Ela** Mandalay, C Burma
El Aaiun see El Ayoun
83 N15 **Ēl Ābrēd** E Ethiopia
117 F22 **Elafónisos** *island* S Greece
117 F22 **Elafonísou, Porthmós** *strait* S Greece
El-Aïoun see El Ayoun
77 U8 **El 'Alamein** *var.* Al 'Alamayn. N Egypt
43 Q12 **El Alazán** Veracruz-Llave, C Mexico
59 J18 **El Alto** *var.* La Paz. ✕ (La Paz) La Paz, W Bolivia
Elam see Īlām
El Amparo see El Amparo de Apure
56 I8 **El Amparo de Apure** *var.* El Amparo. Apure, C Venezuela
xxxv I10 **Elan Village** Powys, C Wales, UK
175 Ss12 **Elara** Pulau Ambelau, E Indonesia
El Araïch/El Araïche see Larache
42 D6 **El Arco** Baja California, NW Mexico
77 X7 **El 'Arîsh** *var.* Al 'Arīsh. NE Egypt
117 L25 **Elása** *island* SE Greece
El Asnam see Chlef
Elassón see Elassóna
117 E15 **Elassóna** *prev.* Elassón. Thessalía, C Greece
107 N2 **El Astillero** Cantabria, N Spain
144 F14 **Elat** *var.* Eilat, Elath. Southern, S Israel
Elat, Gulf of see Aqaba, Gulf of
Elath see Elat, Israel
Elath see Al 'Aqabah, Jordan
117 C17 **Eláti** ▲ Lefkáda, Iónioi Nísoi, Greece, C Mediterranean Sea
196 L16 **Elato Atoll** *atoll* Caroline Islands, C Micronesia
82 C7 **El'Atrun** Northern Darfur, NW Sudan
76 H6 **El Ayoun** *var.* El Aaiun, El-Aïoun, La Youne. NE Morocco
143 N14 **Elâzığ** *var.* Elâziz. Elâzığ, E Turkey
143 O14 **Elâzığ** *var.* Elâziz. ◐ *province* C Turkey
Elâziz see Elâzığ
25 Q7 **Elba** Alabama, S USA
108 E13 **Elba, Isola d'** *island* Archipelago Toscano, C Italy
56 F6 **El Banco** Magdalena, N Colombia
El Barco see O Barco
106 L8 **El Barco de Ávila** Castilla-León, N Spain
El Barco de Valdeorras see O Barco
144 H7 **El Barouk, Jabal** ▲ C Lebanon
115 L20 **Elbasan** *var.* Elbasani. Elbasan, C Albania
115 L20 **Elbasan** ◐ *district* C Albania
Elbasani see Elbasan
56 K6 **El Baúl** Cojedes, C Venezuela
88 D10 **Elbe** *Cz.* Labe. ≈ Czech Republic/Germany
102 L13 **Elbe-Havel-Kanal** *canal* E Germany
102 K9 **Elbe-Lübeck-Kanal** *canal* N Germany
El Beni see Beni
144 H7 **El Beqaa** *var.* Al Biqā', Bekaa Valley. *valley* E Lebanon
27 R6 **Elbert** Texas, SW USA
39 R5 **Elbert, Mount** ▲ Colorado, C USA
25 U3 **Elberton** Georgia, SE USA
102 K11 **Elbe-Seiten-Kanal** *canal* N Germany
104 M4 **Elbeuf** Seine-Maritime, N France
Elbing see Elbląg
142 M15 **Elbistan** Kahramanmaraş, S Turkey
112 K7 **Elbląg** *var.* Elblag, *Ger.* Elbing. Elbląg, N Poland
112 J7 **Elbląg** *off.* Województwo Elbląskie, *Ger.* Elbing. ◐ *province* N Poland
Elbląskie, Województwo see Elbląg
45 N10 **El Bluff** Región Autónoma Atlántico Sur, SE Nicaragua
65 H17 **El Bolsón** Río Negro, W Argentina
107 P11 **El Bonillo** Castilla-La Mancha, C Spain
El Boulaida/El Boulaïda see Blida
9 T16 **Elbow** Saskatchewan, S Canada
31 S7 **Elbow Lake** Minnesota, N USA
131 N16 **El'brus** *var.* Gora El'brus. ▲ SW Russian Federation
El'brus, Gora see El'brus
130 M15 **El'brusskiy** Karachayevo-Cherkesskaya Respublika, SW Russian Federation
83 D14 **El Buhayrat** *var.* Lakes State. ◐ *state* S Sudan
El Bur see Ceel Buur
100 L10 **Elburg** Gelderland, E Netherlands
107 O6 **El Burgo de Osma** Castilla-León, C Spain
Elburz Mountains see Alborz, Reshteh-ye Kūhhā-ye
37 V17 **El Cajon** California, W USA
65 H22 **El Calafate** *var.* Calafate. Santa Cruz, S Argentina
57 Q8 **El Callao** Bolívar, E Venezuela
27 U12 **El Campo** Texas, SW USA
56 I7 **El Cantón** Barinas, W Venezuela
37 Q8 **El Capitan** ▲ California, W USA
56 H5 **El Carmelo** Zulia, NW Venezuela
64 J5 **El Carmen** Jujuy, NW Argentina
56 E5 **El Carmen de Bolívar** Bolívar, NW Colombia
57 O8 **El Casabe** Bolívar, SE Venezuela
44 M12 **El Castillo de La Concepción** Río San Juan, SE Nicaragua
El Cayo see San Ignacio
37 X17 **El Centro** California, W USA
57 N6 **El Chaparro** Anzoátegui, NE Venezuela
107 S12 **Elche** *var.* Elx-Elche; *anc.* Ilici, *Lat.* Illicis. País Valenciano, E Spain
107 Q12 **Elche de la Sierra** Castilla-La Mancha, C Spain
43 U15 **El Chichonal, Volcán** ⛰ SE Mexico
42 C2 **El Chinero** Baja California, NW Mexico
189 R1 **Elcho Island** *island* Wessel Islands, Northern Territory, N Australia
65 H18 **El Corcovado** Chubut, SW Argentina
107 R12 **Elda** País Valenciano, E Spain
102 M10 **Elde** ≈ NE Germany
100 L12 **Elden** Gelderland, E Netherlands
83 J16 **El Der** *spring/well* S Ethiopia
El Dere see Ceel Dheere
42 E3 **El Desemboque** Sonora, NW Mexico
56 F5 **El Difícil** *var.* Ariguaní. Magdalena, N Colombia
126 Mm11 **El'dikan** Respublika Sakha (Yakutiya), NE Russian Federation
El Djazaïr see Alger
El Djelfa see Djelfa
31 X15 **Eldon** Iowa, C USA
29 U5 **Eldon** Missouri, C USA
56 E13 **El Doncello** Caquetá, S Colombia
31 W13 **Eldora** Iowa, C USA
62 G12 **Eldorado** Misiones, NE Argentina
42 I9 **El Dorado** Sinaloa, C Mexico
29 U14 **El Dorado** Arkansas, C USA
32 M17 **Eldorado** Illinois, N USA
29 O6 **El Dorado** Kansas, C USA
28 K12 **Eldorado** Oklahoma, C USA
27 O9 **Eldorado** Texas, SW USA
57 Q8 **El Dorado** Bolívar, E Venezuela
56 F10 **El Dorado** ✕ (Bogotá) Cundinamarca, C Colombia
El Dorado see California
29 O6 **El Dorado Lake** ▣ Kansas, C USA
29 S6 **El Dorado Springs** Missouri, C USA
83 H18 **Eldoret** Rift Valley, W Kenya
xliii I24 **Eldrick** South Ayrshire, W Scotland, UK
31 Z14 **Eldridge** Iowa, C USA
97 J21 **Eldsberga** Halland, S Sweden
27 R4 **Electra** Texas, SW USA
39 Q7 **Electra Lake** ▣ Colorado, C USA
40 B8 **Eleele** *Haw.* 'Ele'ele. Kauai, Hawaii, USA, C Pacific Ocean
Elefantes see Olifants
117 H19 **Elefsína** *prev.* Elevsís. Attikí, C Greece
117 G19 **Eléftheres** *anc.* Eleutherae. *site of ancient city* Attikí/Stereá Ellás, C Greece
116 I13 **Eleftheroúpoli** *prev.* Elevtheroúpolis. Anatolikí Makedonía kai Thráki, NE Greece
76 F10 **El Eglab** ▲ SW Algeria
120 F10 **Eleja** Jelgava, C Latvia
Elek see Ilek
121 G14 **Elektrėnai** Kaišiadorys, SE Lithuania
130 L3 **Elektrostal'** Moskovskaya Oblast', W Russian Federation
83 H15 **Elemi Triangle** *disputed region* Kenya/Sudan
56 G16 **El Encanto** Amazonas, S Colombia
39 R14 **Elephant Butte Reservoir** ▣ New Mexico, SW USA
Éléphant, Chaîne de l' see Dâmrei, Chuŏr Phnum
204 G2 **Elephant Island** *island* South Shetland Islands, Antarctica
Elephant River see Olifants
El Escorial see San Lorenzo de El Escorial
Élesd see Aleşd
116 F11 **Eleshnitsa** ≈ W Bulgaria
143 S13 **Eleşkirt** Ağrı, E Turkey
44 F5 **El Estor** Izabal, E Guatemala
Eleutherae see Eléftheres
46 I2 **Eleuthera Island** *island* N Bahamas
39 S5 **Elevenmile Canyon Reservoir** ▣ Colorado, C USA
29 W8 **Eleven Point River** ≈ Arkansas/Missouri, C USA
Elevsís see Elefsína
Elevtheroúpolis see Eleftheroúpoli
77 W8 **El Faiyûm** *var.* Al Fayyūm. N Egypt
82 B10 **El Fasher** *var.* Al Fāshir. Northern Darfur, W Sudan
77 W8 **El Fashn** *var.* Al Fashn. C Egypt
El Ferrol/El Ferrol del Caudillo see Ferrol
41 W13 **Elfin Cove** Chichagof Island, Alaska, USA
107 W4 **El Fluvià** ≈ NE Spain
xxxviii D13 **Elford** Staffordshire, C England, UK
42 H7 **El Fuerte** Sinaloa, W Mexico
82 D11 **El Fula** Western Kordofan, C Sudan
El Gedaref see Gedaref
82 A10 **El Geneina** *var.* Ajjinena, Al-Genain, Al Junaynah. Western Darfur, W Sudan
xlii L11 **Elgin** Moray, NE Scotland, UK
32 M10 **Elgin** Illinois, N USA
31 P14 **Elgin** Nebraska, C USA
37 Y9 **Elgin** Nevada, W USA
30 L6 **Elgin** North Dakota, N USA
28 M12 **Elgin** Oklahoma, C USA
27 T10 **Elgin** Texas, SW USA
127 N9 **El'ginskiy** Respublika Sakha (Yakutiya), NE Russian Federation
77 W8 **El Gîza** *var.* Al Jīzah, Gîza, Gizeh. N Egypt
xlii E13 **Elgol** Highland, NW Scotland, UK
76 J8 **El Goléa** *var.* Al Golea. C Algeria
42 D2 **El Golfo de Santa Clara** Sonora, NW Mexico
83 G18 **Elgon, Mount** ▲ E Uganda
96 I10 **Elgpiggen** ▲ S Norway
107 T4 **El Grado** Aragón, NE Spain
42 L6 **El Guaje, Laguna** ▣ NE Mexico
56 H6 **El Guayabo** Zulia, W Venezuela
79 O6 **El Guettâra** *oasis* N Mali
xxxvii Y11 **Elham** Kent, SE England, UK
78 J6 **El Ḥammâmi** *desert* N Mauritania
78 M5 **El Ḥank** *cliff* N Mauritania
El Haseke see Al Ḥasakah
82 H10 **El Hawata** Gedaref, E Sudan
El Higo see Higos
176 Uu16 **Eliase** Pulau Selaru, E Indonesia
Elías Piña see Comendador
27 R6 **Eliasville** Texas, SW USA
Elichpur see Achalpur
39 V13 **Elida** New Mexico, SW USA
xliii N18 **Elie** Fife, E Scotland, UK
117 F18 **Elikónas** ▲ C Greece
69 T10 **Elila** ≈ W Zaire
41 N9 **Elim** Alaska, USA
Elimberrum see Auch
Eliocroca see Lorca
63 B16 **Elisa** Santa Fe, C Argentina
Elisabethstedt see Dumbrăveni
Élisabethville see Lubumbashi
131 O13 **Elista** Respublika Kalmykiya, SW Russian Federation
190 I9 **Elizabeth** South Australia
23 Q3 **Elizabeth** West Virginia, NE USA
21 Q9 **Elizabeth, Cape** *headland* Maine, NE USA
23 Y8 **Elizabeth City** North Carolina, SE USA
22 P8 **Elizabethton** Tennessee, S USA
32 M17 **Elizabethtown** Illinois, N USA
22 K6 **Elizabethtown** Kentucky, S USA
20 L7 **Elizabethtown** New York, NE USA
23 U11 **Elizabethtown** North Carolina, SE USA
20 G15 **Elizabethtown** Pennsylvania, NE USA
76 E6 **El-Jadida** *prev.* Mazagan. W Morocco
El Jafr see Jafr, Qā' al
82 F11 **El Jebelein** White Nile, E Sudan
112 N8 **Ełk** *Ger.* Lyck. Suwałki, NE Poland
112 O8 **Ełk** ≈ NE Poland
31 Y12 **Elkader** Iowa, C USA
82 G9 **El Kamlin** Gezira, C Sudan
35 N11 **Elk City** Idaho, NW USA
28 K10 **Elk City** Oklahoma, C USA
29 P7 **Elk City Lake** ▣ Kansas, C USA
36 M5 **Elk Creek** California, W USA
30 J10 **Elk Creek** ≈ South Dakota, N USA
76 M5 **El Kef** *var.* Al Kāf, Le Kef. NW Tunisia
76 F7 **El Kelâa Srarhna** *var.* Kal al Sraghna. C Morocco
El Kerak see Al Karak
9 P17 **Elkford** British Columbia, SW Canada
El Khalil see Hebron
82 E7 **El Khandaq** Northern, N Sudan
77 W10 **El Khârga** *var.* Al Khārijah. C Egypt
33 P11 **Elkhart** Indiana, N USA
28 H7 **Elkhart** Kansas, C USA
27 V8 **Elkhart** Texas, SW USA
32 M7 **Elkhart Lake** ◎ Wisconsin, N USA
El Khartûm see Khartoum
39 Q3 **Elkhead Mountains** ▲▲ Colorado, C USA
20 I12 **Elk Hill** ▲ Pennsylvania, NE USA
144 G8 **El Khiyam** *var.* Al Khiyām, Khiam. S Lebanon
31 S15 **Elkhorn** Nebraska, C USA
32 M9 **Elkhorn** Wisconsin, N USA
31 R14 **Elkhorn River** ≈ Nebraska, C USA
131 O16 **El'khotovo** Respublika Severnaya Osetiya, SW Russian Federation
116 L10 **Elkhovo** *prev.* Kizilagach. Burgaska Oblast, SE Bulgaria
23 R8 **Elkin** North Carolina, SE USA
23 S4 **Elkins** West Virginia, NE USA
205 X3 **Elkins, Mount** ▲ Antarctica
12 G8 **Elk Lake** Ontario, S Canada
110 L7 **Elk Lake** ◎ Michigan, N USA
20 F12 **Elkland** Pennsylvania, NE USA
37 W3 **Elko** Nevada, W USA
El Kôm see Al Kawm
9 R14 **Elk Point** Alberta, SW Canada
31 R12 **Elk Point** South Dakota, N USA
31 V8 **Elk River** Minnesota, N USA
22 J10 **Elk River** ≈ Alabama/Tennessee, S USA
23 R4 **Elk River** ≈ West Virginia, NE USA
22 J7 **Elkton** Kentucky, S USA
23 Y2 **Elkton** Maryland, NE USA
31 R10 **Elkton** South Dakota, N USA
22 I10 **Elkton** Tennessee, S USA
23 U5 **Elkton** Virginia, NE USA
El Kuneitra see Al Qunayṭirah
83 L15 **El Kure** SE Ethiopia
82 D12 **El Lagowa** Western Kordofan, C Sudan
41 S12 **Ellamar** Alaska, USA
xli Q15 **Elland** Calderdale, N England, UK
xliii F20 **Ellary** Argyll and Bute, W Scotland, UK
Ellás see Greece
xxxviii L7 **Ellastone** Staffordshire, C England, UK
25 S6 **Ellaville** Georgia, SE USA
207 P9 **Ellef Ringnes Island** *island* Northwest Territories, N Canada
31 V10 **Ellendale** Minnesota, N USA
31 P7 **Ellendale** North Dakota, N USA
38 M6 **Ellen, Mount** ▲ Utah, W USA
34 I9 **Ellensburg** Washington, NW USA
20 K12 **Ellenville** New York, NE USA
Ellep see Lib
23 T10 **Ellerbe** North Carolina, SE USA
xxxviii G8 **Ellesmere** Shropshire, W England, UK
207 P10 **Ellesmere Island** *island* Queen Elizabeth Islands, Northwest Territories, N Canada
193 H19 **Ellesmere, Lake** ◎ South Island, NZ
xl C17 **Ellesmere Port** Cheshire, C England, UK
33 O14 **Ellettsville** Indiana, N USA
101 E19 **Ellezelles** Hainaut, SW Belgium
15 Jj4 **Ellice** ≈ Northwest Territories, NE Canada
Ellice Islands see Tuvalu
Ellichpur see Achalpur
23 W3 **Ellicott City** Maryland, NE USA
25 S2 **Ellijay** Georgia, SE USA
xli R2 **Ellingham** Northumberland, N England, UK
29 W7 **Ellington** Missouri, C USA
28 L5 **Ellinwood** Kansas, C USA
85 J24 **Elliot** Eastern Cape, SE South Africa
12 D10 **Elliot Lake** Ontario, S Canada
189 X6 **Elliot, Mount** ▲ Queensland, E Australia
23 T5 **Elliott Knob** ▲ Virginia, NE USA
28 K4 **Ellis** Kansas, C USA
190 F8 **Elliston** South Australia
24 M7 **Ellisville** Mississippi, S USA
107 V5 **El Llobregat** ≈ NE Spain
xlii P12 **Ellon** Aberdeenshire, NE Scotland, UK
Ellore see Elūru
23 S13 **Elloree** South Carolina, SE USA
xli V14 **Elloughton** East Riding of Yorkshire, N England, UK
28 M4 **Ellsworth** Kansas, C USA
21 S7 **Ellsworth** Maine, NE USA
32 I6 **Ellsworth** Wisconsin, N USA
28 M11 **Ellsworth, Lake** ▣ Oklahoma, C USA
204 K9 **Ellsworth Land** *physical region* Antarctica
204 L9 **Ellsworth Mountains** ▲▲ Antarctica
103 J21 **Ellwangen** Baden-Württemberg, S Germany
20 B14 **Ellwood City** Pennsylvania, NE USA
110 H8 **Elm** Glarus, NE Switzerland
34 G9 **Elma** Washington, NW USA
124 Qq15 **El Maḥalla el Kubra** *var.* Al Maḥallah al Kubrá, Mahalla el Kubra. N Egypt
76 E9 **El Mahbas** *var.* Mahbés. SW Western Sahara
65 H17 **El Maitén** Chubut, W Argentina
142 E16 **Elmalı** Antalya, SW Turkey
82 G10 **El Manaqil** Gezira, C Sudan
56 M12 **El Mango** Amazonas, S Venezuela
77 W7 **El Manṣûra** *var.* Al Manṣūrah, Manṣūra. N Egypt
57 P8 **El Manteco** Bolívar, E Venezuela
31 O16 **Elm Creek** Nebraska, C USA
xxxvii U6 **Elmdon** Essex, SE England, UK
El Mediyya see Médéa
79 V9 **Elméki** Agadez, C Niger
110 K7 **Elmen** Tirol, W Austria
20 J16 **Elmer** New Jersey, NE USA
144 G6 **El Mina** *var.* Al Mīnā'. N Lebanon
77 W9 **El Minya** *var.* Al Minyā, Minya. C Egypt
12 F15 **Elmira** Ontario, S Canada
20 G11 **Elmira** New York, NE USA
38 K13 **El Mirage** Arizona, SW USA
31 O7 **Elm Lake** ▣ South Dakota, N USA
El Moján see San Rafael
107 N7 **El Molar** Madrid, C Spain
78 L7 **El Mrâyer** *well* C Mauritania
78 L5 **El Mreiti** *well* N Mauritania
78 L8 **El Mreyyé** *desert* E Mauritania
31 P8 **Elm River** ≈ North Dakota/South Dakota, N USA
102 I9 **Elmshorn** Schleswig-Holstein, N Germany
xxxix W12 **Elmswell** Suffolk, E England, UK
82 D12 **El Muglad** Western Kordofan, C Sudan
El Muwaqqar see Al Muwaqqar
12 G14 **Elmvale** Ontario, S Canada
32 K12 **Elmwood** Illinois, N USA
28 J8 **Elmwood** Oklahoma, C USA
105 P17 **Elne** *anc.* Illiberis. Pyrénées-Orientales, S France
56 F11 **El Nevado, Cerro** *elevation* C Colombia
179 Oo13 **El Nido** Palawan, W Philippines
64 I12 **El Nihuil** Mendoza, W Argentina
77 W7 **El Nouzha** ✕ (Alexandria) N Egypt
82 E10 **El Obeid** *var.* Al Obayyid, Al Ubayyid. Northern Kordofan, C Sudan
43 O13 **El Oro** México, S Mexico
58 B8 **El Oro** ◐ *province* SW Ecuador
63 B19 **Elortondo** Santa Fe, C Argentina
56 J8 **Elorza** Apure, C Venezuela
El Ouâdi see El Oued
76 L7 **El Oued** *var.* Al Oued, El Ouâdi, El Wad. NE Algeria
38 L15 **Eloy** Arizona, SW USA
57 Q7 **El Palmar** Bolívar, E Venezuela
42 K8 **El Palmito** Durango, W Mexico
57 P7 **El Pao** Bolívar, E Venezuela
56 K5 **El Pao** Cojedes, N Venezuela
44 J7 **El Paraíso** El Paraíso, S Honduras
44 I7 **El Paraíso** ◐ *department* SE Honduras
32 L12 **El Paso** Illinois, N USA
26 G8 **El Paso** Texas, SW USA
26 G8 **El Paso** ✕ Texas, SW USA
107 U7 **El Perello** Cataluña, NE Spain
xliv G7 **Elphin** Roscommon, C Ireland
xlii H9 **Elphin** Highland, NW Scotland, UK
57 P5 **El Pilar** Sucre, NE Venezuela
44 F7 **El Pital, Cerro** ▲ El Salvador/Honduras
37 Q9 **El Portal** California, W USA
42 J3 **El Porvenir** Chihuahua, N Mexico
45 U14 **El Porvenir** San Blas, N Panama
107 W6 **El Prat de Llobregat** Cataluña, NE Spain
44 H5 **El Progreso** Yoro, NW Honduras
44 A2 **El Progreso** *off.* Departamento de El Progreso. ◐ *department* C Guatemala
El Progreso see Guastatoya
106 L9 **El Puente del Arzobispo** Castilla-La Mancha, C Spain
106 J15 **El Puerto de Santa María** Andalucía, S Spain
64 I8 **El Puesto** Catamarca, NW Argentina
El Qâhira see Cairo
77 V10 **El Qaṣr** *var.* Al Qaṣr. C Egypt
El Qatrani see Al Qaṭrānah
42 I10 **El Quelite** Sinaloa, C Mexico
64 G9 **Elqui, Río** ≈ N Chile
El Quneitra see Al Qunayṭirah
El Quseir see Al Quṣayr
El Quweira see Al Quwayrah
147 O15 **El-Rahaba** ✕ (Ṣan'ā') W Yemen
44 M10 **El Rama** Región Autónoma Atlántico Sur, SE Nicaragua
45 W16 **El Real** *var.* El Real de Santa María. Darién, SE Panama
El Real de Santa María see El Real
28 M10 **El Reno** Oklahoma, C USA
xliii I25 **Elrig** Dumfries and Galloway, SW Scotland, UK
42 K9 **El Rodeo** Durango, C Mexico
106 J13 **El Ronquillo** Andalucía, S Spain
9 S16 **Elrose** Saskatchewan, S Canada
32 K8 **Elroy** Wisconsin, N USA
27 S17 **Elsa** Texas, SW USA
77 W8 **El Şaff** *var.* Aş Şaff. N Egypt
42 J10 **El Salto** Durango, C Mexico
44 D8 **El Salvador** *off.* Republica de El Salvador. ◆ *republic* Central America
56 K7 **El Samán de Apure** Apure, C Venezuela
12 D7 **Elsas** Ontario, S Canada
Elsass see Alsace
42 J5 **El Sáuz** Chihuahua, N Mexico
29 W4 **Elsberry** Missouri, C USA
xli P4 **Elsdon** Northumberland, N England, UK
47 P9 **El Seibo** *var.* Santa Cruz de El Seibo, Santa Cruz del Seibo. E Dominican Republic
44 B7 **El Semillero Barra Nahualate** Escuintla, SW Guatemala
Elsene see Ixelles
165 N11 **Elsen Nur** ◎ C China
38 L6 **Elsinore** Utah, W USA
Elsinore see Helsingør
101 L18 **Elsloo** Limburg, SE Netherlands
63 G13 **El Soberbio** Misiones, NE Argentina
57 N6 **El Socorro** Guárico, C Venezuela
56 L6 **El Sombrero** Guárico, N Venezuela
100 L10 **Elspeet** Gelderland, E Netherlands
xliii L21 **Elsrickle** South Lanarkshire, C Scotland, UK
100 L12 **Elst** Gelderland, E Netherlands
xxxvii R11 **Elstead** Surrey, SE England, UK
103 O15 **Elsterwerda** Brandenburg, E Germany
xxxvii S8 **Elstree** Hertfordshire, SE England, UK
42 J4 **El Sueco** Chihuahua, N Mexico
El Suweida see As Suwaydā'
El Suweis see Suez
xl M14 **Elswick** Lancashire, NW England, UK
xxxix S12 **Elsworth** Cambridgeshire, E England, UK
56 D12 **El Tambo** Cauca, SW Colombia
183 T13 **Eltanin Fracture Zone** *tectonic feature* SE Pacific Ocean
107 X5 **El Ter** ≈ NE Spain
xxxvi G9 **Eltham** Greenwich, SE England, UK
192 K11 **Eltham** Taranaki, North Island, NZ
57 O6 **El Tigre** Anzoátegui, NE Venezuela
El Tigrito see San José de Guanipa
xxxix R12 **Eltisley** Cambridgeshire, E England, UK
56 J5 **El Tocuyo** Lara, N Venezuela
xxxix Q10 **Elton** Cambridgeshire, E England, UK
131 Q10 **El'ton** Volgogradskaya Oblast', SW Russian Federation
34 K10 **Eltopia** Washington, NW USA
63 A18 **El Trébol** Santa Fe, C Argentina
42 J13 **El Tuito** Jalisco, SW Mexico
77 X8 **El Ṭûr** *var.* Aṭ Ṭūr. NE Egypt
161 K16 **Elūru** *prev.* Ellore. Andhra Pradesh, E India
120 H13 **Elva** *Ger.* Elwa. Tartumaa, SE Estonia
39 R9 **El Vado Reservoir** ▣ New Mexico, SW USA
45 S15 **El Valle** Coclé, C Panama
xliii L22 **Elvanfoot** South Lanarkshire, C Scotland, UK
106 I11 **Elvas** Portalegre, C Portugal
56 K7 **El Venado** Apure, C Venezuela
107 V6 **El Vendrell** Cataluña, NE Spain
96 I13 **Elverum** Hedmark, S Norway
44 I9 **El Viejo** Chinandega, NW Nicaragua
56 G7 **El Viejo, Cerro** ▲ C Colombia
56 H6 **El Vigía** Mérida, NW Venezuela
107 Q4 **El Villar de Arnedo** La Rioja, N Spain
xli U13 **Elvington** York, N England, UK
61 A14 **Elvira** Amazonas, W Brazil
Elwa see Elva
El Wad see El Oued
83 K17 **El Wak** North Eastern, NE Kenya
35 R7 **Elwell, Lake** ▣ Montana, NW USA
33 P13 **Elwood** Indiana, N USA
29 R3 **Elwood** Kansas, C USA
31 N16 **Elwood** Nebraska, C USA
xxxviii I6 **Elworth** Cheshire, C England, UK
Elx-Elche see Elche
xxxix T11 **Ely** Cambridgeshire, E England, UK
xxxv J15 **Ely** Cardiff, S Wales, UK
xxxv J15 **Ely** ≈ SE Wales, UK
31 X4 **Ely** Minnesota, N USA
37 X6 **Ely** Nevada, W USA
xxxix S10 **Ely, Isle of** *physical region* E England, UK
El Yopal see Yopal
33 T11 **Elyria** Ohio, N USA
47 S9 **El Yunque** ▲ E Puerto Rico
103 F23 **Elz** ≈ SW Germany
197 C14 **Emae** *island* Shepherd Islands, C Vanuatu
120 I5 **Emajõgi** *Ger.* Embach. ≈ SE Estonia
Emāmrūd see Shāhrūd
155 Q2 **Emām Ṣāheb** *var.* Emam Saheb, Hazarat Imam. Kunduz, NE Afghanistan
Emāmshahr see Shāhrūd
97 M20 **Emån** ≈ S Sweden
197 D14 **Emao** *island* C Vanuatu
150 H11 **Emba** *Kaz.* Embi. Aktyubinsk, W Kazakhstan
150 H12 **Emba** *Kaz.* Zhem. ≈ W Kazakhstan
Embach see Emajõgi
64 K5 **Embarcación** Salta, N Argentina
32 M15 **Embarras River** ≈ Illinois, N USA
Embi see Emba
xli R3 **Embleton** Northumberland, N England, UK
xlii K10 **Embo** Highland, N Scotland, UK
xli Q13 **Embsay** North Yorkshire, N England, UK
83 I19 **Embu** Eastern, C Kenya
102 E10 **Emden** Niedersachsen, NW Germany
31 Q4 **Emerado** North Dakota, N USA
189 X8 **Emerald** Queensland, E Australia
Emerald Isle see Montserrat
59 J15 **Emero, Río** ≈ W Bolivia
9 Y17 **Emerson** Manitoba, S Canada
31 T15 **Emerson** Iowa, C USA
31 R13 **Emerson** Nebraska, C USA
38 M5 **Emery** Utah, W USA
Emesa see Ḥimş
142 E13 **Emet** Kütahya, W Turkey
194 G12 **Emeti** Western, SW PNG
37 V3 **Emigrant Pass** *pass* Nevada, W USA
80 I6 **Emi Koussi** ▲ N Chad
Emilia see Emilia-Romagna
43 V15 **Emiliano Zapata** Chiapas, SE Mexico
108 E9 **Emilia-Romagna** *prev.* Emilia, *anc.* Æmilia. ◐ *region* N Italy
164 J3 **Emin** *var.* Dorbiljin. Xinjiang Uygur Zizhiqu, NW China
155 W8 **Emīnābād** Punjab, E Pakistan
22 I5 **Eminence** Kentucky, S USA
29 W7 **Eminence** Missouri, C USA
116 N9 **Emine, Nos** *headland* E Bulgaria
164 J3 **Emin He** ≈ NW China
195 N8 **Emirau Island** *island* N PNG
142 F13 **Emirdağ** Afyon, W Turkey
97 M21 **Emmaboda** Kalmar, S Sweden
120 E5 **Emmaste** Hiiumaa, W Estonia
20 I15 **Emmaus** Pennsylvania, NE USA
191 U4 **Emmaville** New South Wales, SE Australia
110 E8 **Emme** ≈ W Switzerland
100 L8 **Emmeloord** Flevoland, N Netherlands
100 O8 **Emmen** Drenthe, NE Netherlands
110 F8 **Emmen** Luzern, C Switzerland
103 F23 **Emmendingen** Baden-Württemberg, SW Germany
100 P8 **Emmer-Compascuum** Drenthe, NE Netherlands
103 D14 **Emmerich** Nordrhein-Westfalen, W Germany
31 U12 **Emmetsburg** Iowa, C USA
34 M14 **Emmett** Idaho, NW USA
40 M10 **Emmonak** Alaska, USA
xxxix T9 **Emneth** Norfolk, E England, UK
xliv I10 **Emo** Laois, C Ireland
Emona see Ljubljana
Emonti see East London
26 L12 **Emory Peak** ▲ Texas, SW USA
42 F6 **Empalme** Sonora, NW Mexico
85 L23 **Empangeni** KwaZulu/Natal, E South Africa
63 C14 **Empedrado** Corrientes, NE Argentina
199 I13 **Emperor Seamounts** *undersea feature* NW Pacific Ocean
199 J3 **Emperor Trough** *undersea feature* N Pacific Ocean
xxxix Q9 **Empingham** Rutland, C England, UK
37 R4 **Empire** Nevada, W USA
Empire State of the South see Georgia
Emplawas see Amplawas
108 F11 **Empoli** Toscana, C Italy
29 P5 **Emporia** Kansas, C USA
23 W7 **Emporia** Virginia, NE USA
20 E13 **Emporium** Pennsylvania, NE USA
195 S12 **Empress Augusta Bay** *inlet* Bougainville Island, PNG
Empty Quarter see Ar Rub' al Khālī
102 E10 **Ems** *Dut.* Eems. ≈ NW Germany
102 F13 **Emsdetten** Nordrhein-Westfalen, NW Germany
Ems-Hunte Canal see Küstenkanal
102 F10 **Ems-Jade-Kanal** *canal* NW Germany
102 F11 **Emsland** *cultural region* NW Germany
xxxvii R13 **Emsworth** West Sussex, SE England, UK
190 D3 **Emu Junction** South Australia
169 T3 **Emur He** ≈ NE China
57 R8 **Encanto Landing** NW Guyana
95 F16 **Enafors** Jämtland, C Sweden
96 N11 **Enånger** Gävleborg, C Sweden
xlii G9 **Enard Bay** *bay* NW Scotland, UK
Enareträsk see Inarijärvi
176 X12 **Enarotali** Irian Jaya, E Indonesia
171 I15 **Ena-san** ▲ Honshū, S Japan
144 E12 **'En 'Avedat** *well* S Israel
172 P2 **Enbetsu** Hokkaidō, NE Japan
63 H16 **Encantadas, Serra das** ▲ S Brazil
42 E7 **Encantado, Cerro** ▲ NW Mexico
64 P7 **Encarnación** Itapúa, S Paraguay
42 M12 **Encarnación de Díaz** Jalisco, SW Mexico
79 O17 **Enchi** SW Ghana
27 Q14 **Encinal** Texas, SW USA
37 U17 **Encinitas** California, W USA
27 S16 **Encino** Texas, SW USA
56 H6 **Encontrados** Zulia, NW Venezuela
190 I10 **Encounter Bay** *inlet* South Australia
63 F15 **Encruzilhada** Rio Grande do Sul, S Brazil
63 H16 **Encruzilhada do Sul** Rio Grande do Sul, S Brazil
113 M20 **Encs** Borsod-Abaúj-Zemplén, NE Hungary
199 M3 **Endeavour Seamount** *undersea feature* N Pacific Ocean
189 V1 **Endeavour Strait** *strait* Queensland, NE Australia
175 Q16 **Endeh** Flores, S Indonesia
97 G23 **Endelave** *island* C Denmark
203 T4 **Enderbury Island** *atoll* Phoenix Islands, C Kiribati
9 N16 **Enderby** British Columbia, SW Canada
205 W4 **Enderby Land** *physical region* Antarctica
181 N14 **Enderby Plain** *undersea feature* S Indian Ocean
31 Q6 **Enderlin** North Dakota, N USA
Endersdorf see Jędrzejów
30 K16 **Enders Reservoir** ▣ Nebraska, C USA
20 H11 **Endicott** New York, NE USA
41 P7 **Endicott Mountains** ▲▲ Alaska, USA
120 I5 **Endla Raba** *wetland* C Estonia
xxxviii J7 **Endon** Staffordshire, C England, UK
119 T9 **Enerhodar** Zaporiz'ka Oblast', SE Ukraine
59 F14 **Ene, Río** ≈ C Peru
201 N4 **Enewetak Atoll** *var.* Ānewetak, Eniwetok. *atoll* Ralik Chain, W Marshall Islands
116 L13 **Enez** Edirne, NW Turkey
xliv J8 **Enfield** Meath, E Ireland
xxxvii U8 **Enfield** Enfield, SE England, UK
xxxiv K15 **Enfield** ◐ *London borough* SE England, UK
23 W8 **Enfield** North Carolina, SE USA
194 G12 **Enga** ◐ *province* W PNG
47 Q9 **Engaño, Cabo** *headland* E Dominican Republic
172 Q5 **Engaru** Hokkaidō, NE Japan
144 F11 **'En Gedi** Southern, E Israel
110 F9 **Engelberg** Unterwalden, C Switzerland
23 Y9 **Engelhard** North Carolina, SE USA
131 P8 **Engel's** Saratovskaya Oblast', W Russian Federation
103 G24 **Engen** Baden-Württemberg, SW Germany
Engeten see Aiud
174 H13 **Enggano, Pulau** *island* W Indonesia
82 J8 **Enghershatu** ▲ N Eritrea
101 F19 **Enghien** *Dut.* Edingen. Hainaut, SW Belgium
99 M20 **England** *Lat.* Anglia. *national region* UK
29 V12 **England** Arkansas, C USA
15 L2 **Englefield, Cape** *headland* Northwest Territories, NE Canada
12 H8 **Englehart** Ontario, S Canada
39 T4 **Englewood** Colorado, C USA
33 O16 **English** Indiana, N USA
41 Q13 **English Bay** Alaska, USA
English Bazar see Ingrāj Bāzār
99 N25 **English Channel** *var.* The Channel, *Fr.* la Manche. *channel* NW Europe
204 J7 **English Coast** *physical region* Antarctica
107 S11 **Enguera** País Valenciano, E Spain
120 E8 **Engure** Tukums, W Latvia
120 E8 **Engures Ezers** ◎ NW Latvia
143 R9 **Enguri** *Rus.* Inguri. ≈ NW Georgia
Engyum see Gangi
28 M9 **Enid** Oklahoma, C USA
24 L3 **Enid Lake** ▣ Mississippi, S USA
201 Y2 **Enigu** *island* Ratak Chain, SE Marshall Islands
Enikale Strait see Kerch Strait
153 Z8 **Enil'chek** Issyk-Kul'skaya Oblast', E Kyrgyzstan
117 F17 **Enipéfs** ≈ C Greece
172 O6 **Eniwa** Hokkaidō, NE Japan
172 O6 **Eniwa-dake** ⛰ Hokkaidō, NE Japan
Eniwetok see Enewetak Atoll
Enkeldoorn see Chivhu
127 Nn11 **Enken, Mys** *headland* NE Russian Federation
100 J8 **Enkhuizen** Noord-Holland, NW Netherlands
111 Q4 **Enknach** ≈ N Austria
97 N15 **Enköping** Uppsala, C Sweden
109 K24 **Enna** *var.* Castrogiovanni, Henna. Sicilia, Italy, C Mediterranean Sea
82 D11 **En Nahud** Western Kordofan, C Sudan
144 F8 **En Nâqoûra** *var.* An Nāqūrah. SW Lebanon
En Nazira see Nazerat
80 K8 **Ennedi** *plateau* E Chad
xliv I8 **Ennell, Lough** ◎ C Ireland
103 E15 **Ennepetal** Nordrhein-Westfalen, W Germany
xl K9 **Ennerdale Water** ◎ NW England, UK
191 P4 **Enngonia** New South Wales, SE Australia
xliv E10 **Ennis** *Ir.* Inis. Clare, W Ireland
35 R11 **Ennis** Montana, NW USA
27 U7 **Ennis** Texas, SW USA
xliv K12 **Enniscorthy** *Ir.* Inis Córthaidh. Wexford, SE Ireland
xliv E14 **Enniskean** Cork, S Ireland
xliv L10 **Enniskerry** Wicklow, E Ireland
xliv I5 **Enniskillen** *var.* Inniskilling, *Ir.* Inis Ceithleann. Fermanagh, SW Northern Ireland, UK
xliv E10 **Ennistimon** *Ir.* Inis Díomáin. Clare, W Ireland
111 T4 **Enns** Oberösterreich, N Austria
111 T4 **Enns** ≈ C Austria
95 O16 **Eno** Pohjois-Karjala, SE Finland
26 M5 **Enochs** Texas, SW USA
95 N17 **Enonkoski** Mikkeli, SE Finland
94 K10 **Enontekiö** *Lapp.* Eanodat. Lappi, N Finland
23 Q11 **Enoree** South Carolina, SE USA
23 P11 **Enoree River** ≈ South Carolina, SE USA
20 M6 **Enosburg Falls** Vermont, NE USA
175 P11 **Enrekang** Sulawesi, C Indonesia
47 N10 **Enriquillo** SW Dominican Republic
47 N9 **Enriquillo, Lago** ◎ SW Dominican Republic
100 L9 **Ens** Flevoland, N Netherlands
xlii B10 **Ensay** *island* NW Scotland, UK
100 P11 **Enschede** Overijssel, E Netherlands
42 B2 **Ensenada** Baja California, NW Mexico
103 E20 **Ensheim** ✕ (Saarbrücken) Saarland, W Germany
166 L9 **Enshi** Hubei, C China
171 Hh17 **Enshū-nada** *gulf* SW Japan
25 O8 **Ensley** Florida, SE USA
Enso see Svetogorsk
xxxvii P7 **Enstone** Oxfordshire, C England, UK
83 F18 **Entebbe** S Uganda
83 F18 **Entebbe** ✕ C Uganda
103 M18 **Entenbühl** ▲ Czech Republic/Germany
100 N10 **Enter** Overijssel, E Netherlands
xliii K23 **Enterkinfoot** Dumfries and Galloway, SW Scotland, UK
25 Q7 **Enterprise** Alabama, S USA

◆ Country ● Country Capital ◇ Dependent Territory ○ Dependent Territory Capital ◐ Administrative Region ✕ International Airport ▲ Mountain ▲▲ Mountain Range ⛰ Volcano ≈ River ◎ Lake ▣ Reservoir

F

◆ COUNTRY ◇ DEPENDENT TERRITORY ◆ ADMINISTRATIVE REGION ▲ MOUNTAIN ⧫ VOLCANO ⊚ LAKE
● COUNTRY CAPITAL ○ DEPENDENT TERRITORY CAPITAL ✈ INTERNATIONAL AIRPORT ▲ MOUNTAIN RANGE ♂ RIVER ⊠ RESERVOIR

251

FAHAHEEL – FIONN LOCH

Fahaheel *see* Al Fuḩayḩīl
Fahlun *see* Falun
149 *U12* **Fahraj** Kermān, SE Iran
66 *P5* **Faial** Madeira, Portugal, NE Atlantic Ocean
66 *N2* **Faial** *var.* Ilha do Faial. *island* Azores, Portugal, NE Atlantic Ocean
Faial, Ilha do *see* Faial
110 *G10* **Faido** Ticino, S Switzerland
Faifo *see* Hôi An
Failaka Island *see* Faylakah
xl *H14* **Failsworth** Tameside, NW England, UK
202 *G12* **Faioa, Île** *island* N Wallis and Futuna
189 *W8* **Fairbairn Reservoir** ⊞ Queensland, E Australia
41 *R9* **Fairbanks** Alaska, USA
23 *U12* **Fair Bluff** North Carolina, SE USA
33 *R14* **Fairborn** Ohio, N USA
xxxv *G8* **Fairbourne** Gwynedd, NW Wales, UK
25 *S3* **Fairburn** Georgia, SE USA
32 *M12* **Fairbury** Illinois, N USA
31 *Q17* **Fairbury** Nebraska, C USA
31 *T9* **Fairfax** Minnesota, N USA
29 *O8* **Fairfax** Oklahoma, C USA
23 *R14* **Fairfax** South Carolina, SE USA
37 *N8* **Fairfield** California, W USA
35 *O14* **Fairfield** Idaho, NW USA
32 *M16* **Fairfield** Illinois, N USA
31 *X15* **Fairfield** Iowa, C USA
35 *R8* **Fairfield** Montana, NW USA
33 *Q14* **Fairfield** Ohio, N USA
27 *U8* **Fairfield** Texas, SW USA
xxxvii *O8* **Fairford** Gloucestershire, C England, UK
29 *T7* **Fair Grove** Missouri, C USA
21 *P12* **Fairhaven** Massachusetts, NE USA
xliv *L2* **Fair Head** *headland* N Northern Ireland, UK
25 *N8* **Fairhope** Alabama, S USA
xlii *P1* **Fair Isle** *island* NE Scotland, UK
xliii *H21* **Fairlie** North Ayrshire, W Scotland, UK
193 *F20* **Fairlie** Canterbury, South Island, NZ
xxxvii *W13* **Fairlight** East Sussex, SE England, UK
xxxvi *I14* **Fairmile** Devon, SW England, UK
31 *U11* **Fairmont** Minnesota, N USA
31 *Q16* **Fairmont** Nebraska, C USA
23 *S3* **Fairmont** West Virginia, NE USA
33 *P13* **Fairmount** Indiana, N USA
20 *H10* **Fairmount** New York, NE USA
31 *R7* **Fairmount** North Dakota, N USA
xxxvii *P12* **Fair Oak** Hampshire, S England, UK
39 *S5* **Fairplay** Colorado, C USA
20 *F9* **Fairport** New York, NE USA
9 *O12* **Fairview** Alberta, W Canada
28 *L9* **Fairview** Oklahoma, C USA
38 *L4* **Fairview** Utah, W USA
37 *T6* **Fairview Peak** ▲ Nevada, W USA
196 *H14* **Fais** *atoll* Caroline Islands, W Micronesia
155 *U8* **Faisalābād** *prev.* Lyallpur. Punjab, NE Pakistan
Faisaliya *see* Fayşalīyah
30 *L8* **Faith** South Dakota, N USA
159 *N12* **Faizābād** Uttar Pradesh, N India
Faizabad/Faizābād *see* Feyẕābād
47 *S9* **Fajardo** E Puerto Rico
145 *R9* **Fajj, Wādī al** *dry watercourse* S Iraq
146 *K4* **Fajr, Bi'r** *well* NW Saudi Arabia
203 *W10* **Fakahina** *atoll* Îles Tuamotu, C French Polynesia
202 *L10* **Fakaofo Atoll** *island* SE Tokelau
203 *U10* **Fakarava** *atoll* Îles Tuamotu, C French Polynesia
131 *T2* **Fakel** Udmurtskaya Respublika, NW Russian Federation
xxxix *V8* **Fakenham** Norfolk, E England, UK
176 *V11* **Fakfak** Irian Jaya, E Indonesia
176 *V11* **Fakfak, Pegunungan** ▲▲ Irian Jaya, E Indonesia
159 *T12* **Fakīragrām** Assam, NE India
116 *M10* **Fakiyska Reka** ≈ SE Bulgaria
97 *J24* **Fakse** Storstrøm, SE Denmark
97 *J24* **Fakse Bugt** *bay* SE Denmark
97 *J24* **Fakse Ladeplads** Storstrøm, SE Denmark
169 *V11* **Faku** Liaoning, NE China
xxxvi *C16* **Fal** ≈ SW England, UK
xliii *N20* **Fala** Midlothian, SE Scotland, UK
78 *J14* **Falaba** N Sierra Leone
104 *K5* **Falaise** Calvados, N France
116 *H12* **Falakró** ▲▲ NE Greece
201 *T12* **Falalu** *island* Chuuk, C Micronesia
177 *Ff4* **Falam** Chin State, W Burma
149 *N8* **Falāvarjān** Eşfahān, C Iran
118 *M11* **Fălciu** Vaslui, E Romania
56 *I4* **Falcón** *off.* Estado Falcón. ◈ *state* NW Venezuela
108 *J12* **Falconara Marittima** Marche, C Italy
Falcone, Capo del *see* Falcone, Punta del
109 *A16* **Falcone, Punta del** *var.* Capo del Falcone. *headland* Sardegna, Italy, C Mediterranean Sea
9 *Y16* **Falcon Lake** Manitoba, S Canada
Falcon Lake *see* Falcón, Presa/Falcon Reservoir
43 *O7* **Falcón, Presa** *var.* Falcon Lake, Falcon Reservoir. ⊞ Mexico/USA *see also* Falcon Reservoir
27 *Q16* **Falcon Reservoir** *var.* Falcon Lake, Presa Falcón. ⊞ Mexico/USA *see also* Falcón, Presa
xxxix *Q5* **Faldingworth** Lincolnshire, E England, UK
202 *L10* **Fale** *island* Fakaofo Atoll, SE Tokelau
198 *Aa7* **Faleālupo** Savai'i, NW Western Samoa
202 *B10* **Falefatu** *island* Funafuti Atoll, C Tuvalu
198 *Aa7* **Fālelima** Savai'i, NW Western Samoa
97 *N18* **Falerum** Östergötland, S Sweden
Faleshty *see* Făleşti
118 *M9* **Făleşti** *Rus.* Faleshty. NW Moldavia
xxxvi *L8* **Falfield** South Gloucestershire, SW England, UK
27 *S15* **Falfurrias** Texas, SW USA
9 *O13* **Falher** Alberta, W Canada
Falkenau an der Eger *see* Sokolov
97 *J21* **Falkenberg** Halland, S Sweden
Falkenberg *see* Niemodlin
Falkenburg in Pommern *see* Złocieniec
102 *N12* **Falkensee** Brandenburg, NE Germany
xliii *K19* **Falkirk** Falkirk, C Scotland, UK
xliii *K19* **Falkirk** ◈ *unitary authority* C Scotland, UK
xliii *M18* **Falkland** Fife, E Scotland, UK
67 *I20* **Falkland Escarpment** *undersea feature* SW Atlantic Ocean
65 *K24* **Falkland Islands** *var.* Falklands, Islas Malvinas. ◇ *UK dependent territory* SW Atlantic Ocean
49 *W14* **Falkland Islands** *island group* SW Atlantic Ocean
67 *I20* **Falkland Plateau** *var.* Argentine Rise. *undersea feature* SW Atlantic Ocean
Falklands *see* Falkland Islands
65 *M23* **Falkland Sound** *var.* Estrecho de San Carlos. *strait* C Falkland Islands
Falknov nad Ohří *see* Sokolov
117 *H21* **Falkonéra** *island* S Greece
97 *K18* **Falköping** Skaraborg, S Sweden
145 *U8* **Fallāḩ** E Iraq
37 *U16* **Fallbrook** California, W USA
201 *U12* **Falleallej Pass** *passage* Chuuk Islands, C Micronesia
95 *J14* **Fällfors** Västerbotten, N Sweden
204 *I6* **Fallières Coast** *physical region* Antarctica
102 *I11* **Fallingbostel** Niedersachsen, NW Germany
xliv *C6* **Fallmore** Mayo, NW Ireland
35 *X9* **Fallon** Montana, NW USA
37 *S5* **Fallon** Nevada, W USA
21 *O12* **Fall River** Massachusetts, NE USA
29 *P6* **Fall River Lake** ⊞ Kansas, C USA
37 *O3* **Fall River Mills** California, W USA
23 *W4* **Falls Church** Virginia, NE USA
31 *S17* **Falls City** Nebraska, C USA
27 *S12* **Falls City** Texas, SW USA
Falluja *see* Al Fallūjah
79 *S12* **Falmey** Dosso, SW Niger
xxxvi *C17* **Falmouth** Cornwall, SW England, UK
47 *W10* **Falmouth** Antigua, Antigua and Barbuda
46 *J11* **Falmouth** W Jamaica
22 *M4* **Falmouth** Kentucky, S USA
21 *P13* **Falmouth** Massachusetts, NE USA
23 *W5* **Falmouth** Virginia, NE USA
xxxvi *C17* **Falmouth Bay** *bay* SW England, UK
201 *U12* **Falos** *island* Chuuk, C Micronesia
85 *E26* **False Bay** *Afr.* Valsbaai. *bay* SW South Africa
161 *K17* **False Divi Point** *headland* E India
40 *M16* **False Pass** Unimak Island, Alaska, USA
160 *P12* **False Point** *headland* E India
107 *U6* **Falset** Cataluña, NE Spain
97 *I25* **Falster** *island* SE Denmark
97 *J23* **Falsterbo** Malmöhus, S Sweden
xli *O5* **Falstone** Northumberland, N England, UK
118 *K9* **Fălticeni** *Hung.* Falticsén. Suceava, NE Romania
Falticsén *see* Fălticeni
96 *M13* **Falun** *var.* Fahlun. Kopparberg, C Sweden
Famagusta *see* Gazimağusa
Famagusta Bay *see* Gazimağusa Körfezi
64 *I8* **Famatina** La Rioja, NW Argentina
101 *J21* **Famenne** *physical region* SE Belgium
115 *D22* **Fan** *var.* Fani. ≈ N Albania
79 *X15* **Fan** ≈ E Nigeria
78 *M12* **Fana** Koulikoro, SW Mali
117 *K19* **Fána** *ancient harbour* Chíos, SE Greece
xliv *I2* **Fanad Head** *headland* N Ireland
201 *V13* **Fanan** *island* Chuuk, C Micronesia
201 *U12* **Fanapanges** *island* Chuuk, C Micronesia
117 *L20* **Fanári, Ákra** *headland* Ikaría, Dodekánisos, Greece, Aegean Sea
xxxv *H13* **Fan Brycheiniog** *var.* Camarthen Van. ▲ E Wales, UK
47 *Q13* **Fancy** Saint Vincent, Saint Vincent and the Grenadines
180 *I5* **Fandriana** Fianarantsoa, SE Madagascar
178 *H6* **Fang** Chiang Mai, NW Thailand
82 *E13* **Fangak** Jonglei, SE Sudan
203 *W10* **Fangatau** *atoll* Îles Tuamotu, C French Polynesia
203 *X12* **Fangataufa** *island* Îles Tuamotu, SE French Polynesia
200 *Qq15* **Fanga Uta** *bay* S Tonga
167 *N7* **Fangcheng** Henan, C China
166 *K15* **Fangchenggang** *var.* Fangcheng Gezu Zizhixian; *prev.* Fangcheng. Guangxi Zhuangzu Zizhiqu, S China
xli *U13* **Fangfoss** East Riding of Yorkshire, N England, UK
167 *S15* **Fangshan** S Taiwan
169 *X8* **Fangzheng** Heilongjiang, NE China
Fani *see* Fan
121 *K16* **Fanipal'** *Rus.* Fanipol'. Minskaya Voblasts', C Belorussia
Fanipol' *see* Fanipal'
xlii *H11* **Fannich, Loch** ◎ NW Scotland, UK
27 *T13* **Fannin** Texas, SW USA
Fanning Island *see* Tabuaeran
96 *G8* **Fannrem** Sør-Trøndelag, S Norway
108 *I11* **Fano** *anc.* Colonia Julia Fanestris, Fanum Fortunae. Marche, C Italy
97 *E23* **Fanø** *island* W Denmark
178 *Ii5* **Fan Si Pan** ▲ N Vietnam
Fanum Fortunae *see* Fano
Fao *see* Al Fāw
147 *W7* **Faq'** *var.* Al Faqa. Dubayy, E UAE
152 *K12* **Farab** *Turkm.* Farap. Lebapskiy Velayat, NE Turkmenistan
204 *H5* **Faraday** *UK research station* Antarctica
193 *G16* **Faraday, Mount** ▲ South Island, NZ
81 *P16* **Faradje** Haut-Zaïre, NE Zaire
Faradofay *see* Tôlañaro
180 *I7* **Farafangana** Fianarantsoa, SE Madagascar
154 *J7* **Farāh** *var.* Farah, Fararud. Farāh, W Afghanistan
154 *K7* **Farāh** ◈ *province* W Afghanistan
154 *J7* **Farāh Rūd** ≈ W Afghanistan
xlii *H6* **Faraid Head** *headland* NW Scotland, UK
196 *K7* **Farallon de Medinilla** *island* C Northern Mariana Islands
196 *J2* **Farallon de Pajaros** *var.* Uracas. *island* N Northern Mariana Islands
78 *J14* **Faranah** Haute-Guinée, S Guinea
Farap *see* Farab
Fararud *see* Farāh
146 *M13* **Farasān, Jazā'ir** *island group* SW Saudi Arabia
180 *I5* **Faratsiho** Antananarivo, C Madagascar
196 *K15* **Faraulep Atoll** *atoll* Caroline Islands, C Micronesia
xxxix *R10* **Farcet** Cambridgeshire, E England, UK
101 *H20* **Farciennes** Hainaut, S Belgium
107 *O14* **Fardes** ≈ S Spain
xliv *H8* **Fardrum** Westmeath, C Ireland
203 *S10* **Fare** Huahine, W French Polynesia
xxxvii *Q13* **Fareham** Hampshire, S England, UK
41 *P11* **Farewell** Alaska, USA
192 *H13* **Farewell, Cape** *headland* South Island, NZ
Farewell, Cape *see* Uummannarsuaq
192 *I13* **Farewell Spit** *spit* South Island, NZ
97 *I17* **Färgelanda** Älvsborg, S Sweden
153 *S10* **Farghona** *Rus.* Fergana; *prev.* Novyy Margilan. Farghona Wiloyati, E Uzbekistan
Farghona Valley *see* Fergana Valley
153 *R10* **Farghona Wiloyati** *Rus.* Ferganskaya Oblast'. ◈ *province* E Uzbekistan
Farghona, Wodii/Farghona Wodiysi *see* Fergana Valley
25 *V8* **Fargo** Georgia, SE USA
31 *R5* **Fargo** North Dakota, N USA
31 *V10* **Faribault** Minnesota, N USA
158 *J11* **Farīdabād** Haryāna, N India
158 *H8* **Farīdkot** Punjab, NW India
159 *T15* **Faridpur** Dhaka, C Bangladesh
124 *N16* **Fārigh, Wādī al** ≈ N Libya
180 *I4* **Farihy Alaotra** ◎ C Madagascar
96 *M11* **Färila** Gävleborg, C Sweden
106 *E9* **Farilhões** *island* C Portugal
78 *G12* **Farim** NW Guinea-Bissau
xxxvii *O8* **Faringdon** Oxfordshire, C England, UK
Farish *see* Forish
147 *T11* **Fāris, Qalamat** *well* SE Saudi Arabia
97 *N21* **Färjestaden** Kalmar, S Sweden
155 *R2* **Farkhār** Takhār, NE Afghanistan
153 *Q14* **Farkhor** *Rus.* Parkhar. SW Tajikistan
118 *F12* **Fârliug** *prev.* Fîrliug, *Hung.* Furluk. Caraş-Severin, SW Romania
117 *M21* **Farmakonísi** *island* Dodekánisos, Greece, Aegean Sea
32 *M13* **Farmer City** Illinois, N USA
xxxv *G11* **Farmers** Carmarthenshire, S Wales, UK
33 *N14* **Farmersburg** Indiana, N USA
27 *U6* **Farmersville** Texas, SW USA
24 *H5* **Farmerville** Louisiana, S USA
31 *X16* **Farmington** Iowa, C USA
21 *Q6* **Farmington** Maine, NE USA
31 *V9* **Farmington** Minnesota, N USA
29 *X6* **Farmington** Missouri, C USA
21 *O9* **Farmington** New Hampshire, NE USA
39 *P9* **Farmington** New Mexico, SW USA
38 *L2* **Farmington** Utah, W USA
xlii *N11* **Farmtown** Moray, N Scotland, UK
23 *W9* **Farmville** North Carolina, SE USA
23 *U6* **Farmville** Virginia, NE USA
xxxvii *S10* **Farnborough** Hampshire, S England, UK
xli *R2* **Farne Islands** *island group* N England, UK
xxxix *Y12* **Farnham** Suffolk, E England, UK
xxxvii *R11* **Farnham** Surrey, S England, UK
xxxvii *V10* **Farningham** Kent, SE England, UK
xxxix *O6* **Farnsfield** Nottinghamshire, C England, UK
xli *O16* **Farnworth** Bolton, NW England, UK
8 *J7* **Faro** Yukon Territory, W Canada
106 *G14* **Faro** Faro, S Portugal
106 *G14* **Faro** ◈ *district* S Portugal
106 *G14* **Faro** ✈ Faro, S Portugal
80 *F13* **Faro** ≈ Cameroon/Nigeria
97 *Q18* **Fårö** Gotland, SE Sweden
Faroe Bank Channel *see* Faroe Gap
Faro, Punta del *see* Peloro, Capo
97 *Q18* **Fårösund** Gotland, SE Sweden
181 *N7* **Farquhar Group** *island group* S Seychelles
xliv *D13* **Farranfore** Kerry, SW Ireland
xlii *H12* **Farrar** ≈ NW Scotland, UK
20 *B13* **Farrell** Pennsylvania, NE USA
158 *K11* **Farrukhābād** Uttar Pradesh, N India
149 *P11* **Fārs** *off.* Ostān-e Fārs; *anc.* Persis. ◈ *province* S Iran
117 *F16* **Fársala** Thessalía, C Greece
149 *R4* **Fārsīān** Māzandarān, N Iran
Fars, Khalīj-e *see* Gulf, The
97 *G21* **Farsø** Nordjylland, N Denmark
97 *D18* **Farsund** Vest-Agder, S Norway
147 *U14* **Fartak, Ra's** *headland* E Yemen
xxxix *N13* **Farthinghoe** Northamptonshire, C England, UK
62 *H13* **Fartura, Serra da** ▲▲ S Brazil
Farvel, Kap *see* Uummannarsuaq
26 *L4* **Farwell** Texas, SW USA
204 *I9* **Farwell Island** *island* Antarctica
158 *L9* **Far Western** ◈ *zone* W Nepal
154 *M3* **Fāryāb** ◈ *province* N Afghanistan
149 *P12* **Fasā** Fārs, S Iran
147 *U12* **Fasad, Ramlat** *desert* SW Oman
109 *P17* **Fasano** Puglia, SE Italy
94 *L3* **Fáskrúdhsfjördhur** Austurland, E Iceland
119 *O5* **Fastiv** *Rus.* Fastov. Kyyivs'ka Oblast', NW Ukraine
xliv *C15* **Fastnet Rock** *Ir.* Carraig Aonair. *island* SW Ireland
Fastov *see* Fastiv
202 *C9* **Fatato** *island* Funafuti Atoll, C Tuvalu
158 *K12* **Fatehgarh** Uttar Pradesh, N India
155 *U6* **Fatehjang** Punjab, E Pakistan
158 *G11* **Fatehpur** Rājasthān, N India
158 *L13* **Fatehpur** Uttar Pradesh, N India
130 *J7* **Fatezh** Kurskaya Oblast', W Russian Federation
78 *G11* **Fatick** W Senegal
106 *G9* **Fátima** Santarém, W Portugal
142 *M11* **Fatsa** Ordu, N Turkey
Fatshan *see* Foshan
202 *D12* **Fatua, Pointe** *var.* Pointe Nord. *headland* Île Futuna, S Wallis and Futuna
203 *X7* **Fatu Hiva** *island* Îles Marquises, NE French Polynesia
Fatunda *see* Fatundu
81 *H21* **Fatundu** *var.* Fatunda. Bandundu, W Zaire
xliii *K20* **Fauldhouse** West Lothian, SE Scotland, UK
31 *O8* **Faulkton** South Dakota, N USA
118 *L13* **Făurei** *prev.* Filimon Sîrbu. Brăila, SE Romania
195 *T13* **Fauro** *island* Shortland Islands, NW Solomon Islands
94 *G12* **Fauske** Nordland, C Norway
9 *P13* **Faust** Alberta, W Canada
101 *L23* **Fauvillers** Luxembourg, SE Belgium
109 *J24* **Favara** Sicilia, Italy, C Mediterranean Sea
Faventia *see* Faenza
xxxvii *X10* **Faversham** Kent, SE England, UK
109 *G23* **Favignana, Isola** *island* Isole Egadi, S Italy
xxxvii *P13* **Fawley** Hampshire, S England, UK
10 *D8* **Fawn** ≈ Ontario, SE Canada
Faxa Bay *see* Faxaflói
94 *H3* **Faxaflói** *Eng.* Faxa Bay. *bay* W Iceland
xli *V14* **Faxfleet** East Riding of Yorkshire, N England, UK
80 *I7* **Faya** *prev.* Faya-Largeau, Largeau. Borkou-Ennedi-Tibesti, N Chad
Faya-Largeau *see* Faya
197 *J5* **Fayaoué** Province des Îles Loyauté, C New Caledonia
144 *M5* **Fayḑāt** *hill range* E Syria
25 *O3* **Fayette** Alabama, S USA
31 *X12* **Fayette** Iowa, C USA
24 *J6* **Fayette** Mississippi, S USA
29 *U4* **Fayette** Missouri, C USA
29 *S9* **Fayetteville** Arkansas, C USA
23 *U10* **Fayetteville** North Carolina, SE USA
22 *J10* **Fayetteville** Tennessee, S USA
27 *U11* **Fayetteville** Texas, SW USA
23 *R5* **Fayetteville** West Virginia, NE USA
147 *R4* **Faylakah** *var.* Failaka Island. *island* E Kuwait
145 *T10* **Fayşalīyah** *var.* Faisaliya. S Iraq
201 *P15* **Fayu** *var.* East Fayu. *island* Hall Islands, C Micronesia
xxxviii *D14* **Fazeley** Staffordshire, C England, UK
158 *G8* **Fāzilka** Punjab, NW India
Fdérick *see* Fdérik
78 *I6* **Fdérik** *var.* Fdérick, *Fr.* Fort Gouraud. Tiris Zemmour, NW Mauritania
Feabhail, Loch *see* Foyle, Lough
xliv *D12* **Feale** ≈ SW Ireland
23 *V12* **Fear, Cape** *headland* Bald Head Island, North Carolina, SE USA
xliii *J16* **Fearnan** Perth and Kinross, C Scotland, UK
xlii *F11* **Fearnmore** Highland, NW Scotland, UK
37 *O6* **Feather River** ≈ California, W USA
193 *M14* **Featherston** Wellington, North Island, NZ
xli *S15* **Featherstone** Wakefield, N England, UK
104 *L3* **Fécamp** Seine-Maritime, N France
xxxviii *K12* **Feckenham** Worcestershire, W England, UK
Fédala *see* Mohammedia
63 *D17* **Federación** Entre Ríos, E Argentina
63 *D17* **Federal** Entre Ríos, E Argentina
79 *T15* **Federal Capital District** ◈ *capital territory* C Nigeria
Federal Capital Territory *see* Australian Capital Territory
Federal District *see* Distrito Federal
23 *Y4* **Federalsburg** Maryland, NE USA
76 *M6* **Fedjaj, Chott el** *var.* Chott el Fejaj, Shaṭṭ al Fijāj. *salt lake* C Tunisia
96 *B13* **Fedje** *island* S Norway
150 *M7* **Fedorovka** Kustanay, N Kazakhstan
131 *U6* **Fedorovka** Respublika Bashkortostan, W Russian Federation
Fëdory *see* Fyadory
119 *U11* **Fedotova Kosa** *spit* SE Ukraine
xliv *D6* **Feeagh, Lough** ◎ NW Ireland
xliv *J3* **Feeny** Limavady, N Northern Ireland, UK
xli *Q10* **Feetham** North Yorkshire, N England, UK
201 *V13* **Fefan** *atoll* Chuuk Islands, C Micronesia
113 *O21* **Fehérgyarmat** Szabolcs-Szatmár-Bereg, E Hungary
Fehér-Körös *see* Crişul Alb
Fehértemplom *see* Bela Crkva
Fehérvölgy *see* Albac
102 *L7* **Fehmarn** *island* N Germany
Fehmarnbelt *see* Femerbælt
111 *X8* **Fehring** Steiermark, SE Austria
61 *B15* **Feijó** Acre, W Brazil
192 *M12* **Feilding** Manawatu-Wanganui, North Island, NZ
Feira *see* Feira de Santana
61 *O17* **Feira de Santana** *var.* Feira. Bahia, E Brazil
111 *X7* **Feistritz** ≈ SE Austria
Feistritz *see* Ilirska Bistrica
167 *P8* **Feixi** *prev.* Shangpaihe. Anhui, E China
Fejaj, Chott el *see* Fedjaj, Chott el
113 *I23* **Fejér** *off.* Fejér Megye. ◈ *county* W Hungary
97 *I24* **Fejø** *island* SE Denmark
142 *K15* **Feke** Adana, S Turkey
Feketehalom *see* Codlea
Fekete-Körös *see* Crişul Negru
Felaniche *see* Felanitx
111 *T3* **Feldaist** ≈ N Austria
111 *W8* **Feldbach** Steiermark, SE Austria
103 *F24* **Feldberg** ▲ SW Germany
118 *J12* **Feldioara** *Ger.* Marienburg, *Hung.* Földvár. Braşov, C Romania
110 *I7* **Feldkirch** *anc.* Clunia. Vorarlberg, W Austria
111 *S9* **Feldkirchen in Kärnten** *Slvn.* Trg. Kärnten, S Austria
Félegyháza *see* Kiskunfélegyháza
198 *B8* **Feleolo** ✈ (Āpia) Upolu, C Western Samoa
106 *H6* **Felgueiras** Porto, N Portugal
Felicitas Julia *see* Lisboa
180 *J16* **Félicité** *island* Inner Islands, NE Seychelles
157 *K20* **Felidhu Atoll** *atoll* C Maldives
43 *Y13* **Felipe Carrillo Puerto** Quintana Roo, SE Mexico
xxxix *X14* **Felixstowe** Suffolk, E England, UK
105 *N11* **Felletin** Creuse, C France
Fellin *see* Viljandi
xli *V3* **Felling** Gateshead, NE England, UK
Felsőbánya *see* Baia Sprie
Felsőmuzslya *see* Mužlja
Felsővisó *see* Vişeu de Sus
xli *R4* **Felton** Northumberland, N England, UK
37 *N10* **Felton** California, W USA
108 *H7* **Feltre** Veneto, NE Italy
xxxix *U10* **Feltwell** Norfolk, E England, UK
97 *H25* **Femerbælt** *Ger.* Fehmarnbelt. *strait* Denmark/Germany
97 *I24* **Femø** *island* SE Denmark
96 *I10* **Femunden** ◎ S Norway
xliv *H6* **Fenagh** Leitrim, N Ireland
106 *H2* **Fene** Galicia, NW Spain
12 *I14* **Fenelon Falls** Ontario, SE Canada
201 *U13* **Feneppi** *atoll* Chuuk Islands, C Micronesia
143 *O11* **Fener Burnu** *headland* N Turkey
117 *J14* **Fengári** ▲ Samothráki, E Greece
169 *V13* **Fengcheng** *var.* Feng-cheng, Fenghwangcheng. Liaoning, NE China
166 *K11* **Fenggang** *prev.* Longquan. Guizhou, S China
167 *S9* **Fenghua** Zhejiang, SE China
Fenghwangcheng *see* Fengcheng
166 *L9* **Fengjie** Sichuan, C China
166 *M14* **Fengkai** *prev.* Jiankou. Guangdong, S China
167 *T13* **Fenglin** *Jap.* Hōrin. C Taiwan
167 *P1* **Fengning** *prev.* Dagezhen. Hebei, E China
166 *E13* **Fengqing** Yunnan, SW China
167 *O6* **Fengqiu** Henan, C China
167 *Q2* **Fengrun** Hebei, E China
169 *T4* **Fengshui Shan** ▲ NE China
167 *P14* **Fengshun** Guangdong, S China
Fengtien *see* Liaoning, China
Fengtien *see* Shenyang, China
166 *J7* **Fengxian** *var.* Feng Xian; *prev.* Shuangshipu. Shaanxi, C China
Fengxiang *see* Luobei
169 *P13* **Fengzhen** Nei Mongol Zizhiqu, N China
166 *M6* **Fen He** ≈ C China
159 *V15* **Feni** Chittagong, E Bangladesh
195 *Q10* **Feni Islands** *island group* NE PNG
40 *H17* **Fenimore Pass** *strait* Aleutian Islands, Alaska, USA
86 *B9* **Feni Ridge** *undersea feature* N Atlantic Ocean
xliv *C12* **Fenit** Kerry, SW Ireland
Fennern *see* Vändra
32 *J9* **Fennimore** Wisconsin, N USA
180 *J4* **Fenoarivo** Toamasina, E Madagascar
97 *I24* **Fensmark** Storstrøm, SE Denmark
xxxix *S9* **Fens, The** *wetland* E England, UK
33 *R9* **Fenton** Michigan, N USA
202 *K10* **Fenua Fala** *island* SE Tokelau
202 *F12* **Fenuafo'ou, Île** *island* E Wallis and Futuna
202 *L10* **Fenua Loa** *island* Fakaofo Atoll, E Tokelau
xliii *I21* **Fenwick** East Ayrshire, W Scotland, UK
xli *Q2* **Fenwick** Northumberland, N England, UK
166 *M4* **Fenyang** Shanxi, C China
xxxvi *C17* **Feock** Cornwall, SW England, UK
119 *U13* **Feodosiya** *var.* Kefe, *It.* Kaffa; *anc.* Theodosia. Respublika Krym, S Ukraine
xliv *B12* **Feohanagh** Kerry, SW Ireland
xliii *E20* **Feolin Ferry** Argyll and Bute, W Scotland, UK
96 *I10* **Feragen** ◎ S Norway
xliv *H9* **Ferbane** Offaly, C Ireland
76 *L5* **Fer, Cap de** *headland* NE Algeria
33 *O16* **Ferdinand** Indiana, N USA
Ferdinand *see* Montana, Bulgaria
Ferdinand *see* Mihail Kogălniceanu, Romania
Ferdinandsberg *see* Oţelu Roşu
149 *T7* **Ferdows** *var.* Firdaus; *prev.* Tūn. Khorāsān, E Iran
105 *Q5* **Fère-Champenoise** Marne, N France
Ferencz-Jósef Csúcs *see* Gerlachovský Štít
109 *J16* **Ferentino** Lazio, C Italy
116 *L13* **Féres** Anatolikí Makedonía kai Thráki, NE Greece
Fergana *see* Farghona
153 *S10* **Fergana Valley** *var.* Farghona Valley, *Rus.* Ferganskaya Dolina, *Taj.* Wodii Farghona, *Uzb.* Farghona Wodiysi. *basin* Tajikistan/Uzbekistan
Ferganskaya Dolina *see* Fergana Valley
Ferganskaya Oblast' *see* Farghona Wiloyati
153 *U9* **Ferganskiy Khrebet** ▲▲ C Kyrgyzstan
12 *F15* **Fergus** Ontario, S Canada
31 *S6* **Fergus Falls** Minnesota, N USA
195 *N15* **Fergusson Island** *var.* Kaluwawa. *island* SE PNG
113 *K22* **Ferihegy** ✈ (Budapest) Budapest, C Hungary
Ferizaj *see* Uroševac
79 *N14* **Ferkessédougou** N Ivory Coast
111 *T10* **Ferlach** *Slvn.* Borovlje. Kärnten, S Austria
xliv *H5* **Fermanagh** ◈ *district* SW Northern Ireland, UK
108 *J13* **Fermo** *anc.* Firmum Picenum. Marche, C Italy
106 *J6* **Fermoselle** Castilla-León, N Spain
xliv *G13* **Fermoy** *Ir.* Mainistir Fhear Maí. Cork, SW Ireland
25 *W8* **Fernandina Beach** Amelia Island, Florida, SE USA
59 *A17* **Fernandina, Isla** *var.* Narborough Island. *island* Galapagos Islands, Ecuador, E Pacific Ocean
49 *Y5* **Fernando de Noronha** *island* E Brazil
Fernando Po/Fernando Póo *see* Bioco, Isla de
62 *J7* **Fernandópolis** São Paulo, S Brazil
106 *M13* **Fernán Núñez** Andalucía, S Spain
85 *Q14* **Fernão Veloso, Baia de** *bay* NE Mozambique
36 *K3* **Ferndale** California, W USA
34 *H6* **Ferndale** Washington, NW USA
xxxvii *N13* **Ferndown** Dorset, S England, UK
xlii *K12* **Ferness** Highland, NW Scotland, UK
xxxvii *R12* **Fernhurst** West Sussex, SE England, UK
9 *P17* **Fernie** British Columbia, SW Canada
37 *R5* **Fernley** Nevada, W USA
xliv *K11* **Ferns** Wexford, SE Ireland
Ferozepore *see* Fīrozpur
109 *N18* **Ferrandina** Basilicata, S Italy
108 *G9* **Ferrara** *anc.* Forum Alieni. Emilia-Romagna, N Italy
123 *H11* **Ferrat, Cap** *headland* NW Algeria
109 *D20* **Ferrato, Capo** *headland* Sardegna, Italy, C Mediterranean Sea
106 *G12* **Ferreira do Alentejo** Beja, S Portugal
58 *B11* **Ferreñafe** Lambayeque, W Peru
110 *C12* **Ferret** Valais, SW Switzerland
104 *I13* **Ferret, Cap** *headland* W France
24 *I6* **Ferriday** Louisiana, S USA
Ferro *see* Hierro
109 *D16* **Ferro, Capo** *headland* Sardegna, Italy, C Mediterranean Sea
106 *H2* **Ferrol** *var.* El Ferrol; *prev.* El Ferrol del Caudillo. Galicia, NW Spain
58 *B12* **Ferrol, Península de** *peninsula* W Peru
38 *M5* **Ferron** Utah, W USA
23 *S7* **Ferrum** Virginia, NE USA
xliv *L11* **Ferrybank** Wicklow, E Ireland
xli *R8* **Ferryhill** Durham, N England, UK
25 *O8* **Ferry Pass** Florida, SE USA
Ferryville *see* Menzel Bourguiba
31 *S4* **Fertile** Minnesota, N USA
Fertő *see* Neusiedler See
100 *L5* **Ferwerd** *Fris.* Ferwert. Friesland, N Netherlands
Ferwert *see* Ferwerd
76 *G6* **Fès** *Eng.* Fez. N Morocco
81 *I22* **Feshi** Bandundu, SW Zaire
31 *O4* **Fessenden** North Dakota, N USA
Festenberg *see* Twardogóra
29 *X5* **Festus** Missouri, C USA
118 *M14* **Feteşti** Ialomiţa, SE Romania
xliv *H12* **Fethard** Tipperary, S Ireland
xliv *J13* **Fethard** Wexford, SE Ireland
142 *D17* **Fethiye** Muğla, SW Turkey
xlii *J2* **Fetlar** *island* NE Scotland, UK
97 *I15* **Fetsund** Akershus, S Norway
xliii *O15* **Fettercairn** Aberdeenshire, NE Scotland, UK
10 *L5* **Feuilles, Lac aux** ◎ Québec, E Canada
10 *L5* **Feuilles, Rivière aux** ≈ Québec, E Canada
101 *M23* **Feulen** Diekirch, C Luxembourg
105 *Q11* **Feurs** Loire, E France
97 *F18* **Fevik** Aust-Agder, S Norway
126 *Mm14* **Fevral'sk** Amurskaya Oblast', SE Russian Federation
xli *R13* **Fewston** North Yorkshire, N England, UK
155 *S2* **Feyẕābād** *var.* Faizabad, Faizābād, Feyzābād, Fyzabad. Badakhshān, NE Afghanistan
Fez *see* Fès
xxxv *H6* **Ffestiniog** Gwynedd, NW Wales, UK
xxxv *F11* **Ffostrasol** Ceredigion, W Wales, UK
Fhóid Duibh, Cuan an *see* Blacksod Bay
64 *I8* **Fiambalá** Catamarca, NW Argentina
180 *I6* **Fianarantsoa** Fianarantsoa, C Madagascar
180 *H6* **Fianarantsoa** ◈ *province* SE Madagascar
80 *G12* **Fianga** Mayo-Kébbi, SW Chad
Ficce *see* Fichē
82 *J12* **Fichē** *It.* Ficce. C Ethiopia
103 *N17* **Fichtelberg** ▲ Czech Republic/Germany
103 *M18* **Fichtelgebirge** ▲▲ SE Germany
103 *M19* **Fichtelnaab** ≈ SE Germany
108 *E9* **Fidenza** Emilia-Romagna, N Italy
115 *K21* **Fier** *var.* Fieri. Fier, SW Albania
115 *K21* **Fier** ◈ *district* W Albania
Fieri *see* Fier
Fierza *see* Fierzë
115 *L17* **Fierzë** *var.* Fierza. Shkodër, N Albania
115 *L17* **Fierzës, Liqeni i** ◎ N Albania
110 *F10* **Fiesch** Valais, SW Switzerland
108 *G11* **Fiesole** Toscana, C Italy
144 *G12* **Fīfah** Aţ Ţafīlah, W Jordan
xliii *M18* **Fife** *var.* Kingdom of Fife. ◈ *unitary authority* E Scotland, UK
Fife, Kingdom of *see* Fife
xliii *O18* **Fife Ness** *headland* E Scotland, UK
Fifteen Twenty Fracture Zone *see* Barracuda Fracture Zone
105 *N13* **Figeac** Lot, S France
97 *N19* **Figeholm** Kalmar, SE Sweden
Figig *see* Figuig
85 *J18* **Figtree** Matabeleland South, SW Zimbabwe
106 *F8* **Figueira da Foz** Coimbra, W Portugal
107 *X4* **Figueres** Cataluña, E Spain
76 *H7* **Figuig** *var.* Figig. E Morocco
Fijāj, Shaṭṭ al *see* Fedjaj, Chott el
197 *J14* **Fiji** *off.* Sovereign Democratic Republic of Fiji, *Fij.* Viti. ◆ *republic* SW Pacific Ocean
197 *J13* **Fiji** *island group* SW Pacific Ocean
183 *Q8* **Fiji Plate** *tectonic feature*
107 *P14* **Filabres, Sierra de los** ▲▲ SE Spain
85 *K18* **Filabusi** Matabeleland South, S Zimbabwe
44 *K13* **Filadelfia** Guanacaste, W Costa Rica
113 *K20* **Fil'akovo** *Hung.* Fülek. Stredné Slovensko, S Slovakia
205 *N5* **Filchner Ice Shelf** *ice shelf* Antarctica
12 *J11* **Fildegrand** ≈ Québec, SE Canada
35 *O15* **Filer** Idaho, NW USA
Filevo *see* Vŭrbitsa
xli *W11* **Filey** North Yorkshire, N England, UK
xli *W11* **Filey Bay** *bay* N England, UK
118 *H14* **Filiaşi** Dolj, SW Romania
117 *B16* **Filiátes** Ípeiros, W Greece
117 *D21* **Filiatrá** Pelopónnisos, S Greece
109 *K22* **Filicudi, Isola** *island* Isole Eolie, S Italy
147 *Y10* **Filim** E Oman
Filimon Sîrbu *see* Făurei
79 *S11* **Filingué** Tillabéri, W Niger
116 *K13* **Filiourí** ≈ NE Greece
116 *I13* **Fílippoi** *anc.* Philippi. *site of ancient city* Anatolikí Makedonía kai Thráki, NE Greece
97 *L15* **Filipstad** Värmland, C Sweden
110 *I9* **Filisur** Graubünden, S Switzerland
96 *E12* **Fillefjell** ▲▲ S Norway
37 *R14* **Fillmore** California, W USA
38 *K5* **Fillmore** Utah, W USA
xxxviii *E15* **Fillongley** Warwickshire, C England, UK
12 *J10* **Fils, Lac du** ◎ Québec, SE Canada
xxxvi *L9* **Filton** South Gloucestershire, SW England, UK
142 *H11* **Filyos Çayı** ≈ N Turkey
205 *Q1* **Fimbul Ice Shelf** *ice shelf* Antarctica
205 *Q2* **Fimbutheimen** *physical region* Antarctica
108 *G9* **Finale Emilia** Emilia-Romagna, C Italy
108 *C10* **Finale Ligure** Liguria, NW Italy
107 *P14* **Fiñana** Andalucía, S Spain
180 *I6* **Finandrahana** Fianarantsoa, SE Madagascar
xliii *N16* **Finavon** Angus, E Scotland, UK
23 *S6* **Fincastle** Virginia, NE USA
xxxix *U9* **Fincham** Norfolk, E England, UK
xxxvii *V6* **Finchingfield** Essex, SE England, UK
xxxvi *C5* **Finchley** Barnet, SE England, UK
101 *M25* **Findel** ✈ (Luxembourg) Luxembourg, C Luxembourg
xlii *L11* **Findhorn** Moray, N Scotland, UK
xlii *K12* **Findhorn** ≈ N Scotland, UK
33 *R12* **Findlay** Ohio, N USA
xlii *N11* **Findochty** Moray, N Scotland, UK
xxxvii *T13* **Findon** West Sussex, SE England, UK
xxxix *P11* **Finedon** Northamptonshire, C England, UK
xliii *D17* **Fingal's Cave** *cave* W Scotland, UK
20 *G11* **Finger Lakes** *lakes* New York, NE USA
85 *L14* **Fingoè** Tete, NW Mozambique
142 *E17* **Finike** Antalya, SW Turkey
104 *F6* **Finistère** ◈ *department* NW France
194 *J12* **Finisterre, Mount** ▲ C PNG
194 *J12* **Finisterre Range** ▲▲ N PNG
189 *Q8* **Finke** Northern Territory, N Australia
111 *S10* **Finkenstein** Kärnten, S Austria
201 *Y15* **Finkol, Mount** *var.* Mount Crozer. ▲ Kosrae, E Micronesia
95 *L17* **Finland** *off.* Republic of Finland, *Fin.* Suomen Tasavalta, Suomi. ◆ *republic* N Europe
128 *F12* **Finland, Gulf of** *Est.* Soome Laht, *Fin.* Suomenlahti, *Ger.* Finnischer Meerbusen, *Rus.* Finskiy Zaliv, *Swe.* Finska Viken. *gulf* E Baltic Sea
8 *L11* **Finlay** ≈ British Columbia, W Canada
191 *O10* **Finley** New South Wales, SE Australia
31 *Q4* **Finley** North Dakota, N USA
xliv *I4* **Finn** ≈ Ireland/Northern Ireland, UK
xxxix *W12* **Finningham** Suffolk, E England, UK
xli *U16* **Finningley** Doncaster, N England, UK
Finnischer Meerbusen *see* Finland, Gulf of
94 *K9* **Finnmark** ◈ *county* N Norway
94 *K9* **Finnmarksvidda** *physical region* N Norway
94 *I9* **Finnsnes** Troms, N Norway
xxxvi *D7* **Finsbury** Islington, SE England, UK
194 *K13* **Finschhafen** Morobe, C PNG
96 *E13* **Finse** Hordaland, S Norway
Finska Viken/Finskiy Zaliv *see* Finland, Gulf of
97 *M17* **Finspång** Östergötland, S Sweden
110 *F10* **Finsteraarhorn** ▲ Swtizerland
103 *O14* **Finsterwalde** Brandenburg, E Germany
xlii *M4* **Finstown** Orkney Islands, N Scotland, UK
xliv *I5* **Fintona** Omagh, W Northern Ireland, UK
xliv *H3* **Fintown** Donegal, N Ireland
xliii *J19* **Fintry** Stirling, C Scotland, UK
xlii *G10* **Fionn Loch** ◎ NW Scotland, UK

◆ Country ● Country Capital ◇ Dependent Territory ○ Dependent Territory Capital ◈ Administrative Region ✈ International Airport ▲ Mountain ▲▲ Mountain Range Volcano ≈ River ◎ Lake ⊞ Reservoir

FIONNPHORT – FRASER

xliii D18 **Fionnphort** Argyll and Bute, W Scotland, UK
193 A23 **Fiordland** *physical region* South Island, NZ
108 E9 **Fiorenzuola d'Arda** Emilia-Romagna, C Italy
Firat Nehri *see* Euphrates
Firdaus *see* Ferdows
20 M14 **Fire Island** *island* New York, NE USA
108 G11 **Firenze** *Eng.* Florence; *anc.* Florentia. Toscana, C Italy
108 G10 **Firenzuola** Toscana, C Italy
12 C6 **Fire River** Ontario, S Canada
Firling *see* Fårliug
63 B19 **Firmat** Santa Fe, C Argentina
105 Q12 **Firminy** Loire, E France
Firmum Picenum *see* Fermo
158 J12 **Fīrozābād** Uttar Pradesh, N India
158 G8 **Firozpur** *var.* Ferozepore. Punjab, NW India
First State *see* Delaware
149 O12 **Fīrūzābād** Fārs, S Iran
Fischamend *see* Fischamend Markt
111 Y4 **Fischamend Markt** *var.* Fischamend. Niederösterreich, NE Austria
111 W6 **Fischbacher Alpen** ▲▲ E Austria
Fischhausen *see* Primorsk
85 D21 **Fish** *var.* Vis. ∼ S Namibia
85 F24 **Fish** *Afr.* Vis. ∼ SW South Africa
xxxvii P14 **Fishbourne** Isle of Wight, S England, UK
9 X15 **Fisher Branch** Manitoba, S Canada
9 X15 **Fisher River** Manitoba, S Canada
21 N13 **Fishers Island** *island* New York, NE USA
39 U8 **Fishers Peak** ▲ Colorado, C USA
15 M6 **Fisher Strait** *strait* Northwest Territories, N Canada
xxxv C12 **Fishguard** *Wel.* Abergwaun. Pembrokeshire, SW Wales, UK
xxxv C11 **Fishguard Bay** *bay* SW Wales, UK
xli U15 **Fishlake** Doncaster, N England, UK
21 R2 **Fish River Lake** ◎ Maine, NE USA
204 K6 **Fiske, Cape** *headland* Antarctica
105 P4 **Fismes** Marne, N France
106 F3 **Fisterra, Cabo** *headland* NW Spain
21 N11 **Fitchburg** Massachusetts, NE USA
xlii H5 **Fitful Head** *headland* NE Scotland, UK
97 C14 **Fitjar** Hordaland, S Norway
198 Bb8 **Fito** ▲ Upolu, C Western Samoa
25 U6 **Fitzgerald** Georgia, SE USA
188 M5 **Fitzroy Crossing** Western Australia
65 G21 **Fitzroy, Monte** *var.* Cerro Chaltel. ▲ S Argentina
189 Y8 **Fitzroy River** ∼ Queensland, E Australia
188 L5 **Fitzroy River** ∼ Western Australia
12 E12 **Fitzwilliam Island** *island* Ontario, S Canada
109 J15 **Fiuggi** Lazio, C Italy
Fiume *see* Rijeka
109 H15 **Fiumicino** Lazio, C Italy
Fiumicino *see* Leonardo da Vinci
xxxvi E14 **Fivelanes** Cornwall, SW England, UK
xliv I5 **Fivemiletown** Dungannon, C Northern Ireland, UK
xxxvii T12 **Five Oaks** West Sussex, SE England, UK
108 E10 **Fivizzano** Toscana, C Italy
81 O21 **Fizi** Sud Kivu, E Zaire
Fizuli *see* Füzuli
94 I11 **Fjällåsen** Norrbotten, N Sweden
97 G20 **Fjerritslev** Nordjylland, N Denmark
F.J.S. *see* Franz Josef Strauss
97 L16 **Fjugesta** Örebro, C Sweden
Fladstrand *see* Frederikshavn
39 V5 **Flagler** Colorado, C USA
25 X10 **Flagler Beach** Florida, SE USA
38 L11 **Flagstaff** Arizona, SW USA
67 H24 **Flagstaff Bay** *bay* Saint Helena, C Atlantic Ocean
21 P5 **Flagstaff Lake** ◎ Maine, NE USA
96 E13 **Flåm** Sogn og Fjordane, S Norway
13 O8 **Flamand** ∼ Québec, SE Canada
32 J5 **Flambeau River** ∼ Wisconsin, N USA
xli X12 **Flamborough** East Riding of Yorkshire, N England, UK
xli X12 **Flamborough Head** *headland* E England, UK
102 N13 **Fläming** *hill range* NE Germany
18 I7 **Flaming Gorge Reservoir** ◻ Utah/Wyoming, NW USA
176 Xx13 **Flamingo, Teluk** *bay* N Arafura Sea
101 B18 **Flanders** *Dut.* Vlaanderen, *Fr.* Flandre. *cultural region* Belgium/France
Flandre *see* Flanders
31 R10 **Flandreau** South Dakota, N USA
xlii A8 **Flannan Isles** *island group* NW Scotland, UK
xxxviii K6 **Flash** Staffordshire, C England, UK
30 M6 **Flasher** North Dakota, N USA
95 G15 **Flåsjön** ◎ N Sweden
41 O11 **Flat** Alaska, USA
14 G7 **Flat** ∼ Northwest Territories, NW Canada
94 H1 **Flateyri** Vestfirdhir, Nw Iceland
35 P8 **Flathead Lake** ◎ Montana, NW USA
xxxvi I10 **Flat Holm** *island* S England, UK
181 Y15 **Flat Island** *Fr.* Île Plate. *island* N Mauritius
179 N14 **Flat Island** *island* NE Spratly Islands
27 T11 **Flatonia** Texas, SW USA
193 M14 **Flat Point** *headland* North Island, NZ
29 X6 **Flat River** Missouri, C USA
33 P8 **Flat River** ∼ Michigan, N USA
33 P14 **Flatrock River** ∼ Indiana, N USA
34 E6 **Flattery, Cape** *headland* Washington, NW USA
66 B12 **Flatts Village** *var.* The Flatts Village. C Bermuda
110 H7 **Flawil** Sankt Gallen, NE Switzerland
xli U12 **Flaxton** North Yorkshire, N England, UK
xxxvii R10 **Fleet** Hampshire, S England, UK
xl L13 **Fleetwood** Lancashire, NW England, UK
20 H15 **Fleetwood** Pennsylvania, NE USA
97 D18 **Flekkefjord** Vest-Agder, S Norway
23 N5 **Flemingsburg** Kentucky, S USA
20 J15 **Flemington** New Jersey, NE USA
66 I7 **Flemish Cap** *undersea feature* NW Atlantic Ocean
97 N16 **Flen** Södermanland, C Sweden
102 I6 **Flensburg** Schleswig-Holstein, N Germany
102 J6 **Flensburger Förde** *inlet* Denmark/Germany
104 K5 **Flers** Orne, N France
97 C14 **Flesland** ✕ (Bergen) Hordaland, S Norway
Flessingue *see* Vlissingen
23 P10 **Fletcher** North Carolina, SE USA
33 R6 **Fletcher Pond** ◎ Michigan, N USA
104 L15 **Fleurance** Gers, S France
110 B8 **Fleurier** Neuchâtel, W Switzerland
101 H20 **Fleurus** Hainaut, S Belgium
105 N7 **Fleury-les-Aubrais** Loiret, C France
100 K10 **Flevoland** ◐ *province* C Netherlands
Flickertail State *see* North Dakota
xl K8 **Flimby** Cumbria, NW England, UK
110 H9 **Flims** Glarus, NE Switzerland
190 F8 **Flinders Island** *island* Investigator Group, South Australia
191 P14 **Flinders Island** *island* Furneaux Group, Tasmania, SE Australia
190 I6 **Flinders Ranges** ▲▲ South Australia
189 U5 **Flinders River** ∼ Queensland, NE Australia
9 V13 **Flin Flon** Manitoba, C Canada
xl B17 **Flint** Flintshire, NE Wales, UK
33 R9 **Flint** Michigan, N USA
xxxix O7 **Flintham** Nottinghamshire, C England, UK
29 O7 **Flint Hills** *hill range* Kansas, C USA
203 Y6 **Flint Island** *island* Line Islands, E Kiribati
25 S4 **Flint River** ∼ Georgia, SE USA
33 R9 **Flint River** ∼ Michigan, N USA
xxxv J5 **Flintshire** ◐ *unitary authority* N Wales, UK
201 X12 **Flipper Point** *headland* C Wake Island
96 I13 **Flisa** Hedmark, S Norway
96 J13 **Flisa** ∼ S Norway
126 Hh4 **Flissingskiy, Mys** *headland* Novaya Zemlya, NW Russian Federation
Flitsch *see* Bovec
xxxvii S6 **Flitwick** Bedfordshire, C England, UK
107 U6 **Flix** Cataluña, NE Spain
xxxix P3 **Flixborough** North Lincolnshire, N England, UK
97 J19 **Floda** Älvsborg, S Sweden
xlii D11 **Flodigarry** Highland, NW Scotland, UK
103 O16 **Flöha** ∼ E Germany
27 O4 **Flomot** Texas, SW USA
31 V5 **Floodwood** Minnesota, N USA
32 M15 **Flora** Illinois, N USA
105 P14 **Florac** Lozère, S France
25 Q8 **Florala** Alabama, S USA
105 S4 **Florange** Moselle, NE France
Floreana, Isla *see* Santa María, Isla
25 O2 **Florence** Alabama, S USA
38 L14 **Florence** Arizona, SW USA
39 T6 **Florence** Colorado, C USA
29 O5 **Florence** Kansas, C USA
22 M4 **Florence** Kentucky, S USA
34 E13 **Florence** Oregon, NW USA
23 T12 **Florence** South Carolina, SE USA
27 S9 **Florence** Texas, SW USA
Florence *see* Firenze
56 E13 **Florencia** Caquetá, S Colombia
101 H21 **Florennes** Namur, S Belgium
Florentia *see* Firenze
65 J18 **Florentino Ameghino, Embalse** ◻ S Argentina
101 J24 **Florenville** Luxembourg, SE Belgium
44 E3 **Flores** Petén, N Guatemala
63 E19 **Flores** ◐ *department* S Uruguay
175 Pp16 **Flores** *island* Nusa Tenggara, C Indonesia
66 M1 **Flores** *island* Azores, Portugal, NE Atlantic Ocean
Floreshty *see* Florești
Flores, Lago de *see* Petén Itzá, Lago
Flores, Laut *see* Flores Sea
175 P15 **Flores Sea** *Ind.* Laut Flores. *sea* C Indonesia
118 M8 **Florești** *Rus.* Floreshty. N Moldavia
27 S12 **Floresville** Texas, SW USA
61 N14 **Floriano** Piauí, E Brazil
63 K14 **Florianópolis** *prev.* Destêrro. *state capital* Santa Catarina, S Brazil
46 G6 **Florida** Camagüey, C Cuba
63 F19 **Florida** Florida, S Uruguay
63 F19 **Florida** ◐ *department* S Uruguay
25 U9 **Florida** *off.* State of Florida; also known as Peninsular State, Sunshine State. ◐ *state* SE USA
25 Y17 **Florida Bay** *bay* Florida, SE USA
56 G8 **Floridablanca** Santander, N Colombia
195 X15 **Florida Islands** *island group* C Solomon Islands
25 Y17 **Florida Keys** *island group* Florida, SE USA
39 Q16 **Florida Mountains** ▲▲ New Mexico, SW USA
66 D10 **Florida, Straits of** *strait* Atlantic Ocean/Gulf of Mexico
116 D13 **Flórina** *var.* Phlórina. Dytikí Makedonía, N Greece
29 X4 **Florissant** Missouri, C USA
96 C11 **Florø** Sogn og Fjordane, S Norway
xlii M5 **Flotta** *island* N Scotland, UK
117 L22 **Floúda, Ákra** *headland* Astypálaia, Kykládes, Greece, Aegean Sea
23 S7 **Floyd** Virginia, NE USA
27 N4 **Floydada** Texas, SW USA
Flüela Wisshorn *see* Weisshorn
100 K7 **Fluessen** ◎ N Netherlands
107 S5 **Flúmen** ∼ NE Spain
109 C20 **Flumendosa** ∼ Sardegna, Italy, C Mediterranean Sea
33 R9 **Flushing** Michigan, N USA
Flushing *see* Vlissingen
27 O6 **Fluvanna** Texas, SW USA
194 F14 **Fly** ∼ Indonesia/PNG
204 I10 **Flying Fish, Cape** *headland* Thurston Island, Antarctica
Flylân *see* Vlieland
200 Ss13 **Foa** *island* Ha'apai Group, C Tonga
9 U15 **Foam Lake** Saskatchewan, S Canada
115 J14 **Foča** SE Bosnia and Herzegovina
xlii M11 **Fochabers** Moray, N Scotland, UK
118 L12 **Focșani** Vrancea, E Romania
Fogaras/Fogarasch *see* Făgăraș
109 M16 **Foggia** Puglia, SE Italy
Foggo *see* Faggo
78 D10 **Fogo** *island* Ilhas de Sotavento, SW Cape Verde
11 U11 **Fogo Island** *island* Newfoundland and Labrador, E Canada
111 U7 **Fohnsdorf** Steiermark, SE Austria
102 G7 **Föhr** *island* NW Germany
106 F14 **Fóia** ▲ S Portugal
12 I10 **Foins, Lac aux** ◎ Québec, SE Canada
105 N17 **Foix** Ariège, S France
130 I5 **Fokino** Bryanskaya Oblast', W Russian Federation
Fola, Cnoc *see* Bloody Foreland
96 E13 **Folarskardnuten** ▲ S Norway
94 G11 **Folda** *fjord* C Norway
95 F14 **Foldereid** Nord-Trøndelag, C Norway
95 E14 **Foldfjorden** *fjord* C Norway
Földvár *see* Feldioara
117 J22 **Folégandros** *island* Kykládes, Greece, Aegean Sea
25 O9 **Foley** Alabama, S USA
31 U7 **Foley** Minnesota, N USA
12 E7 **Foleyet** Ontario, S Canada
97 D14 **Folgefonni** *glacier* S Norway
108 I13 **Foligno** Umbria, C Italy
xxxvii Y11 **Folkestone** Kent, SE England, UK
xxxix Q8 **Folkingham** Lincolnshire, E England, UK
25 W8 **Folkston** Georgia, SE USA
96 H10 **Folldal** Hedmark, S Norway
27 P1 **Follett** Texas, SW USA
108 F13 **Follonica** Toscana, C Italy
23 T15 **Folly Beach** South Carolina, SE USA
xxxvi F14 **Folly Gate** Devon, SW England, UK
37 O7 **Folsom** California, W USA
118 M12 **Foltești** Galați, E Romania
180 H14 **Fomboni** Mohéli, S Comoros
20 K10 **Fonda** New York, NE USA
9 S10 **Fond-du-Lac** Saskatchewan, C Canada
32 M8 **Fond du Lac** Wisconsin, N USA
9 T10 **Fond-du-Lac** ∼ Saskatchewan, C Canada
202 C9 **Fongafale** *var.* Funafuti. ● (Tuvalu) Funafuti Atoll, SE Tuvalu
202 G8 **Fongafale** *atoll* C Tuvalu
109 C18 **Fonni** Sardegna, Italy, C Mediterranean Sea
201 V12 **Fono** *island* Chuuk, C Micronesia
56 G4 **Fonseca** La Guajira, N Colombia
Fonseca, Golfo de *see* Fonseca, Gulf of
44 H8 **Fonseca, Gulf of** *Sp.* Golfo de Fonseca. *gulf* Central America
105 O6 **Fontainebleau** Seine-et-Marne, N France
65 G19 **Fontana, Lago** ◎ W Argentina
23 N10 **Fontana Lake** ◻ North Carolina, SE USA
109 L24 **Fontanarossa** ✕ (Catania) Sicilia, Italy, C Mediterranean Sea
9 N11 **Fontas** ∼ British Columbia, W Canada
60 D12 **Fonte Boa** Amazonas, N Brazil
104 J10 **Fontenay-le-Comte** Vendée, NW France
35 T16 **Fontenelle Reservoir** ◻ Wyoming, C USA
xliv I10 **Fontstown** Kildare, E Ireland
200 Ss12 **Fonualei** *island* Vava'u Group, N Tonga
113 H24 **Fonyód** Somogy, W Hungary
Foochow *see* Fuzhou
41 Q10 **Foraker, Mount** ▲ Alaska, USA
197 D14 **Forari** Éfaté, C Vanuatu
105 U4 **Forbach** Moselle, NE France
191 Q8 **Forbes** New South Wales, SE Australia
79 T17 **Forcados** Delta, S Nigeria
105 S14 **Forcalquier** Alpes-de-Haute-Provence, SE France
103 K19 **Forchheim** Bayern, SE Germany
xli P2 **Ford** Northumberland, N England, UK
xliii G18 **Ford** Argyll and Bute, W Scotland, UK
176 V14 **Fordate, Pulau** *island* Kepulauan Tanimbar, E Indonesia
37 R13 **Ford City** California, W USA
97 D11 **Førde** Sogn og Fjordane, S Norway
xliii L19 **Fordell** Fife, E Scotland, UK
xxxix U11 **Fordham** Cambridgeshire, E England, UK
xxxix T10 **Fordham** Norfolk, E England, UK
xxxvii O13 **Fordingbridge** Hampshire, S England, UK
xliii O15 **Fordoun** Aberdeenshire, NE Scotland, UK
33 N4 **Ford River** ∼ Michigan, N USA
191 O4 **Fords Bridge** New South Wales, SE Australia
22 J6 **Fordsville** Kentucky, S USA
29 U13 **Fordyce** Arkansas, C USA
78 I14 **Forécariah** Guinée-Maritime, SW Guinea
xxxvii N14 **Foreland, The** *headland* SW England, UK
207 O14 **Forel, Mont** ▲ SE Greenland
9 R17 **Foremost** Alberta, SW Canada
12 D16 **Forest** Ontario, S Canada
24 L5 **Forest** Mississippi, S USA
33 S12 **Forest** Ohio, N USA
31 V11 **Forest City** Iowa, C USA
23 Q10 **Forest City** North Carolina, SE USA
xxxvi F6 **Forest Gate** Newham, SE England, UK
34 G11 **Forest Grove** Oregon, NW USA
xli N10 **Forest Hall** Cumbria, NW England, UK
xxxvi E9 **Forest Hill** Lewisham, SE England, UK
191 P17 **Forestier Peninsula** *peninsula* Tasmania, SE Australia
31 V8 **Forest Lake** Minnesota, N USA
25 S3 **Forest Park** Georgia, SE USA
31 Q3 **Forest River** ∼ North Dakota, N USA
xxxvii U11 **Forest Row** East Sussex, SE England, UK
13 T6 **Forestville** Québec, SE Canada
105 Q11 **Forez, Monts du** ▲▲ C France
xliii N16 **Forfar** Angus, E Scotland, UK
28 J8 **Forgan** Oklahoma, C USA
Forge du Sud *see* Dudelange
103 J24 **Forggensee** ◎ S Germany
153 N10 **Forish** *Rus.* Farish. Jizzakh Wiloyati, C Uzbekistan
22 F9 **Forked Deer River** ∼ Tennessee, S USA
34 F7 **Forks** Washington, NW USA
94 N2 **Forlandsundet** *sound* W Svalbard
108 H10 **Forlì** *anc.* Forum Livii. Emilia-Romagna, N Italy
31 Q7 **Forman** North Dakota, N USA
xl L16 **Formby** Sefton, NW England, UK
107 V11 **Formentera** *anc.* Ophiusa, *Lat.* Frumentum. *island* Islas Baleares, Spain, W Mediterranean Sea
Formentor, Cabo de *see* Formentor, Cap de
107 Y9 **Formentor, Cap de** *var.* Cabo de Formentor, Cape Formentor. *headland* Mallorca, Spain, W Mediterranean Sea
Formentor, Cape *see* Formentor, Cap de
109 J16 **Formia** Lazio, C Italy
64 O7 **Formosa** Formosa, NE Argentina
64 M6 **Formosa** *off.* Provincia de Formosa. ◐ *province* NE Argentina
Formosa/Formo'sa *see* Taiwan
61 I17 **Formosa, Serra** ▲ C Brazil
Formosa Strait *see* Taiwan Strait
97 H15 **Fornebu** ✕ (Oslo) Akershus, S Norway
27 U6 **Forney** Texas, SW USA
97 H21 **Fornæs** *headland* C Denmark
108 E9 **Fornovo di Taro** Emilia-Romagna, C Italy
119 T14 **Foros** Respublika Krym, S Ukraine
Føroyar *see* Faeroe Islands
xlii L11 **Forres** Moray, NE Scotland, UK
29 X11 **Forrest City** Arkansas, C USA
41 Y15 **Forrester Island** *island* Alexander Archipelago, Alaska, USA
27 N7 **Forsan** Texas, SW USA
189 V5 **Forsayth** Queensland, NE Australia
97 L19 **Forserum** Jönköping, S Sweden
97 K15 **Forshaga** Värmland, C Sweden
xlii K7 **Forsinard** Highland, N Scotland, UK
95 L19 **Forssa** Häme, SW Finland
103 Q14 **Forst** *Lus.* Baršć Łužyca. Brandenburg, E Germany
191 U7 **Forster-Tuncurry** New South Wales, SE Australia
25 T4 **Forsyth** Georgia, SE USA
29 T8 **Forsyth** Missouri, C USA
35 W10 **Forsyth** Montana, NW USA
155 U11 **Fort Abbās** Punjab, E Pakistan
10 G10 **Fort Albany** Ontario, C Canada
58 L13 **Fortaleza** Pando, N Bolivia
60 P13 **Fortaleza** *prev.* Ceará. *state capital* Ceará, NE Brazil
61 D16 **Fortaleza** Rondônia, W Brazil
58 C13 **Fortaleza, Río** ∼ W Peru
Fort-Archambault *see* Sarh
23 U3 **Fort Ashby** West Virginia, NE USA
xliii I14 **Fort Augustus** Highland, N Scotland, UK
Fort-Bayard *see* Zhanjiang
35 S8 **Fort Benton** Montana, NW USA
37 Q1 **Fort Bidwell** California, W USA
36 L5 **Fort Bragg** California, W USA
33 N16 **Fort Branch** Indiana, N USA
Fort-Bretonnet *see* Bousso
35 T17 **Fort Bridger** Wyoming, C USA
Fort-Cappolani *see* Tidjikja
Fort Charlet *see* Djanet
Fort-Chimo *see* Kuujjuaq
9 R10 **Fort Chipewyan** Alberta, C Canada
Fort Cobb Lake *see* Fort Cobb Reservoir
28 L11 **Fort Cobb Reservoir** *var.* Fort Cobb Lake. ◻ Oklahoma, C USA
39 T3 **Fort Collins** Colorado, C USA
12 K12 **Fort-Coulonge** Québec, SE Canada
Fort-Crampel *see* Kaga Bandoro
Fort-Dauphin *see* Tôlañaro
26 K10 **Fort Davis** Texas, SW USA
39 O10 **Fort Defiance** Arizona, SW USA
47 Q12 **Fort-de-France** *prev.* Fort-Royal. ○ (Martinique) W Martinique
47 P12 **Fort-de-France, Baie de** *bay* W Martinique
Fort de Kock *see* Bukittinggi
25 P6 **Fort Deposit** Alabama, S USA
31 U13 **Fort Dodge** Iowa, C USA
11 S10 **Forteau** Québec, E Canada
108 E11 **Forte dei Marmi** Toscana, C Italy
12 H17 **Fort Erie** Ontario, S Canada
188 H7 **Fortescue River** ∼ Western Australia
xliii L18 **Forteviot** Perth and Kinross, C Scotland, UK
21 S2 **Fort Fairfield** Maine, NE USA
Fort-Foureau *see* Kousséri
10 A11 **Fort Frances** Ontario, S Canada
Fort Franklin *see* Déljne
25 R7 **Fort Gaines** Georgia, SE USA
39 T8 **Fort Garland** Colorado, C USA
23 P5 **Fort Gay** West Virginia, NE USA
xlii J11 **Fort George** Highland, NW Scotland, UK
Fort George *see* La Grande Rivière
29 Q10 **Fort Gibson** Oklahoma, C USA
29 Q9 **Fort Gibson Lake** ◻ Oklahoma, C USA
15 Gg5 **Fort Good Hope** *var.* Good Hope. Northwest Territories, NW Canada
25 V4 **Fort Gordon** Georgia, SE USA
Fort Gouraud *see* Fdérik
xliii J19 **Forth** ∼ C Scotland, UK
xliii K20 **Forth** South Lanarkshire, C Scotland, UK
Fort Hall *see* Murang'a
26 H8 **Fort Hancock** Texas, SW USA
Fort Hertz *see* Putao
xliii N19 **Forth, Firth of** *estuary* E Scotland, UK
12 L14 **Forthton** Ontario, SE Canada
12 M8 **Fortier** ∼ Québec, SE Canada
xliii J16 **Fortingall** Perth and Kinross, C Scotland, UK
Fortín General Eugenio Garay *see* General Eugenio A. Garay
Fort Jameson *see* Chipata
Fort Johnston *see* Mangochi
21 R1 **Fort Kent** Maine, NE USA
Fort-Lamy *see* Ndjamena
25 Z15 **Fort Lauderdale** Florida, SE USA
23 R11 **Fort Lawn** South Carolina, SE USA
15 Gg9 **Fort Liard** *var.* Liard. Northwest Territories, W Canada
46 M8 **Fort-Liberté** NE Haiti
23 N9 **Fort Loudoun Lake** ◻ Tennessee, S USA
39 T3 **Fort Lupton** Colorado, C USA
9 R12 **Fort MacKay** Alberta, C Canada
9 Q17 **Fort Macleod** *var.* MacLeod. Alberta, SW Canada
31 Y16 **Fort Madison** Iowa, C USA
Fort Manning *see* Mchinji
27 P9 **Fort McKavett** Texas, SW USA
9 R12 **Fort McMurray** Alberta, C Canada
14 Ff3 **Fort McPherson** *var.* McPherson. Northwest Territories, NW Canada
23 R11 **Fort Mill** South Carolina, SE USA
Fort-Millot *see* Ngouri
39 U3 **Fort Morgan** Colorado, C USA
25 W14 **Fort Myers** Florida, SE USA
25 W15 **Fort Myers Beach** Florida, SE USA
8 M10 **Fort Nelson** British Columbia, W Canada
8 M10 **Fort Nelson** ∼ British Columbia, W Canada
15 Gg6 **Fort Norman** *var.* Norman. Northwest Territories, NW Canada
25 Q2 **Fort Payne** Alabama, S USA
35 W7 **Fort Peck** Montana, NW USA
35 V8 **Fort Peck Lake** ◻ Montana, NW USA
25 Y13 **Fort Pierce** Florida, SE USA
31 N10 **Fort Pierre** South Dakota, N USA
83 E18 **Fort Portal** SW Uganda
15 Hh8 **Fort Providence** *var.* Providence. Northwest Territories, W Canada
9 U16 **Fort Qu'Appelle** Saskatchewan, S Canada
Fort-Repoux *see* Akjoujt
15 I8 **Fort Resolution** *var.* Resolution. Northwest Territories, W Canada
35 T13 **Fortress Mountain** ▲ Wyoming, C USA
xlii J11 **Fortrose** Highland, NW Scotland, UK
Fort Rosebery *see* Mansa
Fort-Rousset *see* Owando
Fort-Royal *see* Fort-de-France
10 I10 **Fort Rupert** *prev.* Rupert House. Québec, SE Canada
14 G12 **Fort St.James** British Columbia, SW Canada
9 N12 **Fort St.John** British Columbia, W Canada
Fort Sandeman *see* Zhob
9 Q14 **Fort Saskatchewan** Alberta, SW Canada
29 R6 **Fort Scott** Kansas, C USA
10 E6 **Fort Severn** Ontario, C Canada
33 R12 **Fort Shawnee** Ohio, N USA
150 E14 **Fort-Shevchenko** Mangistau, W Kazakhstan
Fort-Sibut *see* Sibut
15 H8 **Fort Simpson** *var.* Simpson. Northwest Territories, W Canada
15 I9 **Fort Smith** *district capital* Northwest Territories, W Canada
29 R10 **Fort Smith** Arkansas, C USA
15 I7 **Fort Smith** ◐ *district* Northwest Territories, NW Canada
39 T13 **Fort Stanton** New Mexico, SW USA
26 L9 **Fort Stockton** Texas, SW USA
39 U12 **Fort Sumner** New Mexico, SW USA
28 K8 **Fort Supply** Oklahoma, C USA
28 K8 **Fort Supply Lake** ◻ Oklahoma, C USA
31 O10 **Fort Thompson** South Dakota, N USA
Fort-Trinquet *see* Bîr Mogreïn
107 R12 **Fortuna** Murcia, SE Spain
36 K3 **Fortuna** California, W USA
30 J2 **Fortuna** North Dakota, N USA
xxxvi L15 **Fortuneswell** Dorset, S England, UK
25 T5 **Fort Valley** Georgia, SE USA
9 P11 **Fort Vermilion** Alberta, W Canada
Fort Victoria *see* Masvingo
33 P13 **Fortville** Indiana, N USA
25 P9 **Fort Walton Beach** Florida, SE USA
33 P12 **Fort Wayne** Indiana, N USA
xliii H15 **Fort William** Highland, N Scotland, UK
27 T6 **Fort Worth** Texas, SW USA
30 M7 **Fort Yates** North Dakota, N USA
41 S7 **Fort Yukon** Alaska, USA
Forum Alieni *see* Ferrara
Forum Julii *see* Fréjus
Forum Livii *see* Forlì
149 Q15 **Forūr, Jazīreh-ye** *island* S Iran
xxxix S8 **Fosdyke** Lincolnshire, E England, UK
96 H7 **Fosen** *physical region* S Norway
167 N14 **Foshan** *var.* Fatshan, Fo-shan, Namhoi. Guangdong, S China
Fossa Claudia *see* Chioggia
108 B9 **Fossano** Piemonte, NW Italy
101 H21 **Fosses-la-Ville** Namur, S Belgium
34 J12 **Fossil** Oregon, NW USA
Foss Lake *see* Foss Reservoir
108 I11 **Fossombrone** Marche, C Italy
28 K10 **Foss Reservoir** *var.* Foss Lake. ◻ Oklahoma, C USA
31 S4 **Fosston** Minnesota, N USA
191 O13 **Foster** Victoria, SE Australia
9 T12 **Foster Lakes** ◎ Saskatchewan, C Canada
33 S12 **Fostoria** Ohio, N USA
xxxix R4 **Fotherby** Lincolnshire, E England, UK
xlii N4 **Foubister** Orkney Islands, N Scotland, UK
81 D19 **Fougamou** Ngounié, C Gabon
104 J6 **Fougères** Ille-et-Vilaine, NW France
Fou-hsin *see* Fuxin
29 S14 **Fouke** Arkansas, C USA
xlii G4 **Foula** *island* NE Scotland, UK
67 D24 **Foul Bay** *bay* East Falkland, Falkland Islands
xxxvii X8 **Foulness Island** *island* SE England, UK
xli P13 **Foulridge** Lancashire, NW England, UK
xxxix W8 **Foulsham** Norfolk, E England, UK
193 F15 **Foulwind, Cape** *headland* South Island, NZ
81 E15 **Foumban** Ouest, NW Cameroon
180 H13 **Foumbouni** Grande Comore, NW Comoros
205 N8 **Foundation Ice Stream** *glacier* Antarctica
39 T6 **Fountain** Colorado, C USA
38 L4 **Fountain Green** Utah, W USA
23 P11 **Fountain Inn** South Carolina, SE USA
29 S11 **Fourche LaFave River** ∼ Arkansas, C USA
35 Z13 **Four Corners** Wyoming, C USA
xxxv J8 **Four Crosses** Powys, C Wales, UK
105 Q2 **Fourmies** Nord, N France
40 J17 **Four Mountains, Islands of** *island group* Aleutian Islands, Alaska, USA
181 P17 **Fournaise, Piton de la** ▲ SE Réunion
12 J8 **Fournière, Lac** ◎ Québec, SE Canada
117 L20 **Foúrnoi** *island* Dodekánisos, Greece, Aegean Sea
66 K13 **Four North Fracture Zone** *tectonic feature* W Atlantic Ocean
Fouron-Saint-Martin *see* Sint-Martens-Voeren
32 L3 **Fourteen Mile Point** *headland* Michigan, N USA
78 I13 **Fouta Djallon** *var.* Futa Jallon. ▲▲ W Guinea
193 C25 **Foveaux Strait** *strait* S NZ
xxxvi D16 **Fowey** Cornwall, SW England, UK
xxxvi D15 **Fowey** ∼ SW England, UK
37 Q11 **Fowler** California, W USA
39 U6 **Fowler** Colorado, C USA
33 N12 **Fowler** Indiana, N USA
190 D7 **Fowlers Bay** *bay* South Australia
27 R13 **Fowlerton** Texas, SW USA
148 M3 **Fowman** *var.* Fuman, Fumen. Gīlān, NW Iran
xxxviii I14 **Fownhope** Herefordshire, W England, UK
67 C25 **Fox Bay East** West Falkland, Falkland Islands
67 C25 **Fox Bay West** West Falkland, Falkland Islands
12 J14 **Foxboro** Ontario, SE Canada
9 O14 **Fox Creek** Alberta, W Canada
xl F12 **Foxdale** S Isle of Man
66 G5 **Foxe Basin** *sea* Northwest Territories, N Canada
66 G5 **Foxe Channel** *channel* Northwest Territories, N Canada
97 I16 **Foxen** ◎ C Sweden
16 N4 **Foxe Peninsula** *peninsula* Baffin Island, Northwest Territories, NE Canada
xliv E6 **Foxford** Mayo, NW Ireland
193 E19 **Fox Glacier** West Coast, South Island, NZ
xli W11 **Foxholes** North Yorkshire, N England, UK
40 L17 **Fox Islands** *island* Aleutian Islands, Alaska, USA
32 M10 **Fox Lake** Illinois, N USA
9 V12 **Fox Mine** Manitoba, C Canada
37 R3 **Fox Mountain** ▲ Nevada, W USA
67 E25 **Fox Point** *headland* East Falkland, Falkland Islands
32 M11 **Fox River** ∼ Illinois/Wisconsin, N USA
32 L7 **Fox River** ∼ Wisconsin, N USA
192 L13 **Foxton** Manawatu-Wanganui, North Island, NZ
9 S16 **Fox Valley** Saskatchewan, S Canada
9 W16 **Foxwarren** Manitoba, S Canada
xlii I13 **Foyers** Highland, NW Scotland, UK
xliv I3 **Foyle** ∼ Ireland/Northern Ireland, UK
xliv J2 **Foyle, Lough** *Ir.* Loch Feabhail. *inlet* N Ireland
204 H5 **Foyn Coast** *physical region* Antarctica
xliv E11 **Foynes** Limerick, SW Ireland
106 I2 **Foz** Galicia, NW Spain
62 I12 **Foz do Areia, Represa de** ◻ S Brazil
61 A16 **Foz do Breu** Acre, W Brazil
85 A16 **Foz do Cunene** Namibe, SW Angola
62 G12 **Foz do Iguaçu** Paraná, S Brazil
60 C12 **Foz do Mamoriá** Amazonas, NW Brazil
107 T6 **Fraga** Aragón, NE Spain
46 F5 **Fragoso, Cayo** *island* C Cuba
63 G18 **Fraile Muerto** Cerro Largo, NE Uruguay
101 H21 **Fraire** Namur, S Belgium
101 L21 **Fraiture, Baraque de** *hill* SE Belgium
Frakštát *see* Hlohovec
207 S10 **Fram Basin** *var.* Amundsen Basin. *undersea feature* Arctic Ocean
101 F20 **Frameries** Hainaut, S Belgium
21 O11 **Framingham** Massachusetts, NE USA
xxxix X12 **Framlingham** Suffolk, E England, UK
xxxvi L14 **Frampton** Dorset, S England, UK
xxxvi L8 **Frampton on Severn** Gloucestershire, C England, UK
xli V14 **Framwellgate Moor** Durham, N England, UK
62 L7 **Franca** São Paulo, S Brazil
197 G4 **Français, Récif des** *reef* W New Caledonia
109 K14 **Francavilla al Mare** Abruzzi, C Italy
109 P18 **Francavilla Fontana** Puglia, SE Italy
104 M8 **France** *off.* French Republic, It./Sp. Francia; *prev.* Gaul, Gaule, *Lat.* Gallia. ◆ *republic* W Europe
47 O8 **Francés Viejo, Cabo** *headland* NE Dominican Republic
81 F19 **Franceville** *var.* Massoukou, Masuku. Haut-Ogooué, E Gabon
81 F19 **Franceville** ✕ Haut-Ogooué, E Gabon
Francfort *see* Frankfurt am Main
105 T8 **Franche-Comté** ◐ *region* E France
Francia *see* France
31 O11 **Francis Case, Lake** ◻ South Dakota, N USA
62 H12 **Francisco Beltrão** Paraná, S Brazil
Francisco I. Madero *see* Villa Madero
63 A21 **Francisco Madero** Buenos Aires, E Argentina
44 H6 **Francisco Morazán** *prev.* Tegucigalpa. ◐ *department* C Honduras
85 J18 **Francistown** North East, NE Botswana
Franconian Forest *see* Frankenwald
Franconian Jura *see* Fränkische Alb
100 K6 **Franeker** *Fris.* Frjentsjer. Friesland, N Netherlands
Frankenalb *see* Fränkische Alb
103 H16 **Frankenberg** Hessen, C Germany
103 J20 **Frankenhöhe** *hill range* C Germany
33 R8 **Frankenmuth** Michigan, N USA
103 F20 **Frankenstein** *hill* W Germany
Frankenstein/Frankenstein in Schlesien *see* Ząbkowice Śląskie
103 G20 **Frankenthal** Rheinland-Pfalz, W Germany
103 L18 **Frankenwald** *Eng.* Franconian Forest. ▲▲ C Germany
46 J12 **Frankfield** C Jamaica
12 J14 **Frankford** Ontario, SE Canada
33 O13 **Frankfort** Indiana, N USA
29 O3 **Frankfort** Kansas, C USA
22 L5 **Frankfort** *state capital* Kentucky, S USA
Frankfort on the Main *see* Frankfurt am Main
Frankfurt *see* Słubice, Poland
Frankfurt *see* Frankfurt am Main, Germany
103 G18 **Frankfurt am Main** *var.* Frankfurt, *Fr.* Francfort; *prev. Eng.* Frankfort on the Main. Hessen, SW Germany
102 Q12 **Frankfurt an der Oder** Brandenburg, E Germany
103 L21 **Fränkische Alb** *var.* Frankenalb, *Eng.* Franconian Jura. ▲▲ S Germany
103 I18 **Fränkische Saale** ∼ C Germany
103 L19 **Fränkische Schweiz** *hill range* C Germany
25 R4 **Franklin** Georgia, SE USA
33 P14 **Franklin** Indiana, N USA
22 J7 **Franklin** Kentucky, S USA
24 I9 **Franklin** Louisiana, S USA
31 O17 **Franklin** Nebraska, C USA
23 N10 **Franklin** North Carolina, SE USA
20 C13 **Franklin** Pennsylvania, NE USA
22 J9 **Franklin** Tennessee, S USA
27 U9 **Franklin** Texas, SW USA
23 X7 **Franklin** Virginia, NE USA
23 T4 **Franklin** West Virginia, NE USA
32 M9 **Franklin** Wisconsin, N USA
15 H2 **Franklin Bay** *inlet* Northwest Territories, N Canada
34 K7 **Franklin D.Roosevelt Lake** ◻ Washington, NW USA
37 W4 **Franklin Lake** ◎ Nevada, W USA
193 B22 **Franklin Mountains** ▲▲ South Island, NZ
41 R5 **Franklin Mountains** ▲▲ Alaska, USA
41 N4 **Franklin, Point** *headland* Alaska, USA
191 O17 **Franklin River** ∼ Tasmania, SE Australia
15 K2 **Franklin Strait** *strait* Northwest Territories, N Canada
24 K8 **Franklinton** Louisiana, S USA
23 U9 **Franklinton** North Carolina, SE USA
Frankstadt *see* Frenštát pod Radhoštěm
27 V7 **Frankston** Texas, SW USA
35 U12 **Frannie** Wyoming, C USA
13 U5 **Franquelin** Québec, SE Canada
13 U5 **Franquelin** ∼ Québec, SE Canada
85 C18 **Fransfontein** Kunene, NW Namibia
95 H17 **Fränsta** Västernorrland, C Sweden
xxxvii V11 **Frant** East Sussex, SE England, UK
126 H1 **Frantsa-Iosifa, Zemlya** *Eng.* Franz Josef Land. *island group* N Russian Federation
193 E18 **Franz Josef Glacier** West Coast, South Island, NZ
Franz Josef Land *see* Frantsa-Iosifa, Zemlya
Franz-Josef Spitze *see* Gerlachovský Štít
103 L23 **Franz Josef Strauss** *abbrev.* F.J.S. ✕ (München) Bayern, SE Germany
109 A19 **Frasca, Capo della** *headland* Sardegna, Italy, C Mediterranean Sea
109 I15 **Frascati** Lazio, C Italy
9 N14 **Fraser** ∼ British Columbia, SW Canada

◆ Country
● Country Capital
◇ Dependent Territory
○ Dependent Territory Capital
◐ Administrative Region
✕ International Airport
▲ Mountain
▲▲ Mountain Range
Volcano
∼ River
◎ Lake
◻ Reservoir

FRASERBURG – GANTSEVICHI

85 G24 **Fraserburg** Western Cape, SW South Africa
xlii P11 **Fraserburgh** Aberdeenshire, NE Scotland, UK
189 Z9 **Fraser Island** *var.* Great Sandy Island. *island* Queensland, E Australia
8 L14 **Fraser Lake** British Columbia, SW Canada
8 L15 **Fraser Plateau** *plateau* British Columbia, SW Canada
192 P10 **Frasertown** Hawke's Bay, North Island, NZ
101 E19 **Frasnes-lez-Buissenal** Hainaut, SW Belgium
110 I7 **Frastanz** Vorarlberg, NW Austria
12 B8 **Frater** Ontario, S Canada
Frauenbach *see* Baia Mare
Frauenburg *see* Saldus, Latvia
Frauenburg *see* Frombork, Poland
110 H6 **Frauenfeld** Thurgau, NE Switzerland
111 Z5 **Frauenkirchen** Burgenland, E Austria
63 D19 **Fray Bentos** Río Negro, W Uruguay
63 F19 **Fray Marcos** Florida, S Uruguay
31 S6 **Frazee** Minnesota, N USA
106 M5 **Frechilla** Castilla-León, N Spain
xl M14 **Freckleton** Lancashire, NW England, UK
32 I4 **Frederic** Wisconsin, N USA
97 G23 **Fredericia** Vejle, C Denmark
23 W3 **Frederick** Maryland, NE USA
28 L12 **Frederick** Oklahoma, C USA
31 P7 **Frederick** South Dakota, N USA
31 X12 **Fredericksburg** Iowa, C USA
27 R10 **Fredericksburg** Texas, SW USA
23 W5 **Fredericksburg** Virginia, NE USA
41 X13 **Frederick Sound** *sound* Alaska , USA
29 X6 **Fredericktown** Missouri, C USA
62 H13 **Frederico Westphalen** Rio Grande do Sul, S Brazil
11 O15 **Fredericton** New Brunswick, SE Canada
97 I22 **Frederiksborg** *off.* Frederiksborgs Amt. ◈ *county* E Denmark
Frederikshåb *see* Paamiut
97 H19 **Frederikshavn** *prev.* Fladstrand. Nordjylland, N Denmark
97 J22 **Frederikssund** Frederiksborg, E Denmark
47 T9 **Frederiksted** Saint Croix, S Virgin Islands (US)
97 I22 **Frederiksværk** *var.* Frederiksværk og Hanehoved. Frederiksborg, E Denmark
Frederiksværk og Hanehoved *see* Frederiksværk
56 E9 **Fredonia** Antioquia, W Colombia
38 K8 **Fredonia** Arizona, SW USA
29 P7 **Fredonia** Kansas, C USA
20 C11 **Fredonia** New York, NE USA
37 P4 **Fredonyer Pass** *pass* California, W USA
95 I15 **Fredrika** Västerbotten, N Sweden
97 L14 **Fredriksberg** Kopparberg, C Sweden
Fredrikshald *see* Halden
Fredrikshamn *see* Hamina
97 H16 **Fredrikstad** Østfold, S Norway
32 K16 **Freeburg** Illinois, N USA
20 K15 **Freehold** New Jersey, NE USA
20 H14 **Freeland** Pennsylvania, NE USA
190 J5 **Freeling Heights** ▲ South Australia
37 Q7 **Freel Peak** ▲ California, W USA
16 T7 **Freels, Cape** *headland* Newfoundland, Newfoundland and Labrador, E Canada
31 Q11 **Freeman** South Dakota, N USA
46 G1 **Freeport** Grand Bahama Island, N Bahamas
32 L10 **Freeport** Illinois, N USA
27 W12 **Freeport** Texas, SW USA
46 G1 **Freeport** ✕ Grand Bahama Island, N Bahamas
27 R14 **Freer** Texas, SW USA
85 I22 **Free State** *off.* Free State Province; *prev.* Orange Free State, *Afr.* Oranje Vrystaat. ◈ *province* C South Africa
Free State *see* Maryland
78 G15 **Freetown** ● (Sierra Leone) W Sierra Leone
180 J16 **Frégate** *island* Inner Islands, NE Seychelles
106 J12 **Fregenal de la Sierra** Extremadura, W Spain
190 C2 **Fregon** South Australia
104 H5 **Fréhel, Cap** *headland* NW France
96 F8 **Frei** Møre og Romsdal, S Norway
103 O16 **Freiberg** Sachsen, E Germany
103 O16 **Freiberger Mulde** ≈ E Germany
Freiburg *see* Freiburg im Breisgau, Germany
Freiburg *see* Fribourg, Switzerland
103 F23 **Freiburg im Breisgau** *var.* Freiburg, *Fr.* Fribourg-en-Brisgau. Baden-Württemberg, SW Germany
Freiburg in Schlesien *see* Świebodzice
Freie Hansestadt Bremen *see* Bremen
Freie und Hansestadt Hamburg *see* Brandenburg
103 L22 **Freising** Bayern, SE Germany
111 T3 **Freistadt** Oberösterreich, N Austria
Freistadtl *see* Hlohovec
103 O16 **Freital** Sachsen, E Germany
Freiwaldau *see* Jeseník
106 J6 **Freixo de Espada à Cinta** Bragança, N Portugal
105 U15 **Fréjus** *anc.* Forum Julii. Var, SE France
188 I13 **Fremantle** Western Australia
xxxvi F12 **Fremington** Devon, SW England, UK
37 N9 **Fremont** California, W USA
33 Q11 **Fremont** Indiana, N USA
31 W15 **Fremont** Iowa, C USA
33 P8 **Fremont** Michigan, N USA
31 R15 **Fremont** Nebraska, C USA
33 S11 **Fremont** Ohio, N USA
35 T14 **Fremont Peak** ▲ Wyoming, C USA
38 M6 **Fremont River** ≈ Utah, W USA
23 O9 **French Broad River** ≈ Tennessee, S USA
23 N5 **Frenchburg** Kentucky, S USA
20 C12 **French Creek** ≈ Pennsylvania, NE USA
34 K15 **Frenchglen** Oregon, NW USA
57 Y10 **French Guiana** *var.* Guiana, Guyane. ◇ *French overseas department* N South America
French Guinea *see* Guinea
33 O15 **French Lick** Indiana, N USA
xliv G7 **Frenchpark** Roscommon, C Ireland
193 J14 **French Pass** Marlborough, South Island, NZ
203 T11 **French Polynesia** ◇ *French overseas territory* C Polynesia
French Republic *see* France
12 F11 **French River** ≈ Ontario, S Canada
French Somaliland *see* Djibouti
181 P12 **French Southern and Antarctic Territories** *Fr.* Terres Australes et Antarctiques Françaises. ◇ *French overseas territory* S Indian Ocean
French Sudan *see* Mali
French Territory of the Afars and Issas *see* Djibouti
French Togoland *see* Togo
76 J6 **Frenda** NW Algeria
xxxvii R11 **Frensham** Surrey, SE England, UK
113 I18 **Frenštát pod Radhoštěm** *Ger.* Frankstadt. Severní Morava, E Czech Republic
78 M17 **Fresco** S Ivory Coast
205 U16 **Freshfield, Cape** *headland* Antarctica
xliv I11 **Freshford** Kilkenny, SE Ireland
xxxvii P14 **Freshwater** Isle of Wight, S England, UK
42 L10 **Fresnillo** *var.* Fresnillo de González Echeverría. Zacatecas, C Mexico
Fresnillo de González Echeverría *see* Fresnillo
37 Q10 **Fresno** California, W USA
xxxix X11 **Fressingfield** Suffolk, E England, UK
xlii M6 **Freswick** Highland, N Scotland, UK
Freu, Cabo del *see* Freu, Cap des
107 Y9 **Freu, Cap des** *var.* Cabo del Freu. *headland* Mallorca, Spain, W Mediterranean Sea
103 G22 **Freudenstadt** Baden-Württemberg, SW Germany
Freudenthal *see* Bruntál
191 Q17 **Freycinet Peninsula** *peninsula* Tasmania, SE Australia
78 H14 **Fria** Guinée-Maritime, W Guinea
85 A17 **Fria, Cape** *headland* NW Namibia
37 Q10 **Friant** California, W USA
64 K8 **Frías** Santiago del Estero, N Argentina
110 D9 **Fribourg** *Ger.* Freiburg. Fribourg, W Switzerland
110 C9 **Fribourg** *Ger.* Freiburg. ◈ *canton* W Switzerland
Fribourg-en-Brisgau *see* Freiburg im Breisgau
xxxix T9 **Friday Bridge** Cambridgeshire, E England, UK
34 G7 **Friday Harbor** San Juan Islands, Washington, NW USA
xli V12 **Fridaythorpe** East Riding of Yorkshire, N England, UK
194 F11 **Frieda** ≈ NW PNG
Friedau *see* Ormož
103 K23 **Friedberg** Bayern, S Germany
103 H18 **Friedberg** Hessen, W Germany
Friedeberg Neumark *see* Strzelce Krajeńskie
Friedek-Mistek *see* Frýdek-Místek
Friedland *see* Pravdinsk
103 I24 **Friedrichshafen** Baden-Württemberg, S Germany
Friedrichstadt *see* Jaunjelgava
31 Q16 **Friend** Nebraska, C USA
Friendly Islands *see* Tonga
57 V9 **Friendship** Coronie, N Surinam
32 L7 **Friendship** Wisconsin, N USA
111 T8 **Friesach** Kärnten, S Austria
Friesche Eilanden *see* Frisian Islands
103 F22 **Friesenheim** Baden-Württemberg, SW Germany
Friesische Inseln *see* Frisian Islands
100 K6 **Friesland** ◈ *province* N Netherlands
xxxvii Y7 **Frinton-on-Sea** Essex, SE England, UK
62 Q10 **Frio, Cabo** *headland* SE Brazil
xliii N16 **Friockheim** Angus, E Scotland, UK
26 M3 **Friona** Texas, SW USA
44 L12 **Frío, Río** ≈ N Costa Rica
27 R13 **Frio River** ≈ Texas, SW USA
xliii E17 **Frisa, Loch** ◎ W Scotland, UK
101 M25 **Frisange** Luxembourg, S Luxembourg
Frisches Haff *see* Vistula Lagoon
38 J6 **Frisco Peak** ▲ Utah, W USA
86 F9 **Frisian Islands** *Dut.* Friesche Eilanden, *Ger.* Friesische Inseln. *island group* N Europe
xxxix S6 **Friskney** Lincolnshire, E England, UK
20 L12 **Frissell, Mount** ▲ Connecticut, NE USA
97 J19 **Fristad** Älvsborg, S Sweden
27 N2 **Fritch** Texas, SW USA
97 J19 **Fritsla** Älvsborg, S Sweden
103 H16 **Fritzlar** Hessen, C Germany
108 H6 **Friuli-Venezia Giulia** ◈ *region* NE Italy
xl K9 **Frizington** Cumbria, NW England, UK
Frjentsjer *see* Franeker
206 L13 **Frobisher Bay** *inlet* Baffin Island, Northwest Territories, NE Canada
Frobisher Bay *see* Iqaluit
9 S12 **Frobisher Lake** ◎ Saskatchewan, C Canada
xl D17 **Frodsham** Cheshire, W England, UK
96 G7 **Frohavet** *sound* C Norway
Frohenbruck *see* Veselí nad Lužnicí
111 V7 **Frohnleiten** Steiermark, SE Austria
101 G22 **Froidchapelle** Hainaut, S Belgium
131 O9 **Frolovo** Volgogradskaya Oblast', SW Russian Federation
112 K7 **Frombork** *Ger.* Frauenburg. Elbląg, N Poland
xxxvi M11 **Frome** Somerset, SW England, UK
xxxvi M14 **Frome** ≈ S England, UK
190 I4 **Frome Creek** *seasonal river* South Australia
190 J6 **Frome Downs** South Australia
190 J5 **Frome, Lake** *salt lake* South Australia
xxxv I6 **Frongoch** Gwynedd, NW Wales, UK
Fronicken *see* Wronki
106 H10 **Fronteira** Portalegre, C Portugal
42 M7 **Frontera** Coahuila de Zaragoza, NE Mexico
43 U14 **Frontera** Tabasco, SE Mexico
42 G3 **Fronteras** Sonora, NW Mexico
105 Q16 **Frontignan** Hérault, S France
56 D8 **Frontino** Antioquia, NW Colombia
23 V4 **Front Royal** Virginia, NE USA
109 J16 **Frosinone** *anc.* Frusino. Lazio, C Italy
109 K16 **Frosolone** Molise, C Italy
27 U7 **Frost** Texas, SW USA
23 U2 **Frostburg** Maryland, NE USA
25 X13 **Frostproof** Florida, SE USA
Frostviken *see* Kvarnbergsvattnet
97 M15 **Frövi** Örebro, C Sweden
xxxvii O10 **Froxfield** Wiltshire, S England, UK
96 F7 **Frøya** *island* W Norway
39 P5 **Fruita** Colorado, C USA
30 J9 **Fruitdale** South Dakota, N USA
25 W11 **Fruitland Park** Florida, SE USA
Frumentum *see* Formentera
153 S11 **Frunze** Oshskaya Oblast', SW Kyrgyzstan
Frunze *see* Bishkek
119 O9 **Frunzivka** Odes'ka Oblast', SW Ukraine
Frusino *see* Frosinone
110 E9 **Frutigen** Bern, W Switzerland
113 I17 **Frýdek-Místek** *Ger.* Friedek-Mistek. Severní Morava, SE Czech Republic
200 Qq16 **Fua'amotu** Tongatapu, S Tonga
202 A9 **Fuafatu** *island* Funafuti Atoll, C Tuvalu
202 A9 **Fuagea** *island* Funafuti Atoll, C Tuvalu
202 B8 **Fualifeke** *atoll* C Tuvalu
202 A8 **Fualopa** *island* Funafuti Atoll, C Tuvalu
157 K22 **Fuammulah** *var.* Gnaviyani Atoll. *atoll* S Maldives
167 R11 **Fu'an** Fujian, SE China
Fu-chien *see* Fujian
Fu-chou *see* Fuzhou
170 F13 **Fuchū** *var.* Hutyû. Hiroshima, Honshū, SW Japan
166 M13 **Fuchuan** Guangxi Zhuangzu Zizhiqu, S China
172 N11 **Fudai** Iwate, Honshū, C Japan
xliii A14 **Fuday** *island* NW Scotland, UK
167 S11 **Fuding** Fujian, SE China
83 J20 **Fudua** *spring/well* S Kenya
106 M16 **Fuengirola** Andalucía, S Spain
106 J12 **Fuente de Cantos** Extremadura, W Spain
106 J11 **Fuente del Maestre** Extremadura, W Spain
106 L12 **Fuente Obejuna** Andalucía, S Spain
106 L6 **Fuentesaúco** Castilla-León, N Spain
64 O3 **Fuerte Olimpo** *var.* Olimpo. Alto Paraguay, NE Paraguay
42 H8 **Fuerte, Río** ≈ C Mexico
66 Q11 **Fuerteventura** *island* Islas Canarias, Spain, NE Atlantic Ocean
147 S14 **Fughmah** *var.* Faghman, Fugma. C Yemen
94 M2 **Fuglehuken** *headland* W Svalbard
207 T15 **Fugløya Bank** *undersea feature* E Norwegian Sea
Fugma *see* Fughmah
83 K16 **Fugugo** *spring/well* NE Kenya
164 L2 **Fuhai** *var.* Burultokay. Xinjiang Uygur Zizhiqu, NW China
167 P10 **Fu He** ≈ S China
Fuhkien *see* Fujian
102 J9 **Fuhlsbüttel** ✕ (Hamburg) Hamburg, N Germany
103 L14 **Fuhne** ≈ C Germany
Fu-hsin *see* Fuxin
Fujairah *see* Al Fujayrah
171 J17 **Fuji** *var.* Huzi. Shizuoka, Honshū, S Japan
167 Q12 **Fujian** *var.* Fu-chien, Fuhkien, Fujian Sheng, Fukien, Min. ◈ *province* SE China
166 I9 **Fu Jiang** ≈ C China
Fujian Sheng *see* Fujian
171 Ii17 **Fujieda** *var.* Huzieda. Shizuoka, Honshū, S Japan
Fuji, Mount/Fujiyama *see* Fuji-san
169 Y7 **Fujin** Heilongjiang, NE China
171 J16 **Fujinomiya** *var.* Huzinomiya. Shizuoka, Honshū, S Japan
171 J16 **Fuji-san** *var.* Fujiyama, *Eng.* Mount Fuji. ▲ Honshū, SE Japan
171 Jj17 **Fujisawa** *var.* Huzisawa. Kanagawa, Honshū, S Japan
171 J16 **Fuji-Yoshida** *var.* Huziyosida. Yamanashi, Honshū, S Japan
172 Oo4 **Fukagawa** *var.* Hukagawa. Hokkaidō, NE Japan
164 L5 **Fukang** Xinjiang Uygur Zizhiqu, W China
171 M8 **Fukaura** Aomori, Honshū, C Japan
200 R15 **Fukave** *island* Tongatapu Group, S Tonga
Fukien *see* Fujian
171 Gg14 **Fukuchiyama** *var.* Hukutiyama. Kyōto, Honshū, SW Japan
170 B12 **Fukue** *var.* Hukue. Nagasaki, Fukue-jima, SW Japan
170 B12 **Fukue-jima** *island* Gotō-rettō, SW Japan
171 Hh13 **Fukui** *var.* Hukui. Fukui, Honshū, SW Japan
171 Hh14 **Fukui** *off.* Fukui-ken, *var.* Hukui. ◈ *prefecture* Honshū, SW Japan
170 C12 **Fukuoka** *var.* Hukuoka; *hist.* Najima. Fukuoka, Kyūshū, SW Japan
170 Cc13 **Fukuoka** *off.* Fukuoka-ken, *var.* Hukuoka. ◈ *prefecture* Kyūshū, SW Japan
171 L13 **Fukushima** *var.* Hukusima. Fukushima, Honshū, C Japan
171 Mm7 **Fukushima** Hokkaidō, NE Japan
171 Kk14 **Fukushima** *off.* Fukushima-ken, *var.* Hukusima. ◈ *prefecture* Honshū, C Japan
170 F14 **Fukuyama** *var.* Hukuyama. Hiroshima, Honshū, SW Japan
78 G13 **Fulacunda** C Guinea-Bissau
133 P8 **Fūlādī, Kūh-e** ▲ E Afghanistan
197 K16 **Fulaga** *island* Lau Group, E Fiji
xxxix T12 **Fulbourn** Cambridgeshire, E England, UK
103 I17 **Fulda** Hessen, C Germany
31 S10 **Fulda** Minnesota, N USA
103 I16 **Fulda** ≈ C Germany
Fülek *see* Fil'akovo
xli T13 **Fulford** York, N England, UK
xxxvi C8 **Fulham** Hammersmith and Fulham, SE England, UK
Fulin *see* Hanyuan
166 K10 **Fuling** Sichuan, C China
37 T15 **Fullerton** California, SE USA
31 P15 **Fullerton** Nebraska, C USA
110 M8 **Fulpmes** Tirol, W Austria
xxxix S4 **Fulstow** Lincolnshire, E England, UK
22 G8 **Fulton** Kentucky, S USA
25 N2 **Fulton** Mississippi, S USA
29 V4 **Fulton** Missouri, C USA
20 H9 **Fulton** New York, NE USA
xli N14 **Fulwood** Lancashire, NW England, UK
xli S17 **Fulwood** Sheffield, N England, UK
Fuman/Fumen *see* Fowman
105 R3 **Fumay** Ardennes, N France
104 M13 **Fumel** Lot-et-Garonne, SW France
171 K17 **Funabashi** *var.* Hunabasi. Chiba, Honshū, S Japan
202 B10 **Funafara** *atoll* C Tuvalu
202 C9 **Funafuti** ✕ Funafuti Atoll, C Tuvalu
Funafuti *see* Fongafale
202 F8 **Funafuti Atoll** *atoll* C Tuvalu
202 B9 **Funangongo** *atoll* C Tuvalu
95 F17 **Funäsdalen** Jämtland, C Sweden
66 O6 **Funchal** Madeira, Portugal, NE Atlantic Ocean
66 P5 **Funchal** ✕ Madeira, Portugal, NE Atlantic Ocean
56 F5 **Fundación** Magdalena, N Colombia
106 I8 **Fundão** *var.* Fundáo. Castelo Branco, C Portugal
11 O16 **Fundy, Bay of** *bay* Canada/USA
Fünen *see* Fyn
56 C13 **Fúnes** Nariño, SW Colombia
Fünfkirchen *see* Pécs
85 M19 **Funhalouro** Inhambane, S Mozambique
167 R6 **Funing** Jiangsu, E China
166 I14 **Funing** Yunnan, SW China
166 M7 **Funiu Shan** ⛰ C China
79 U13 **Funtua** Katsina, N Nigeria
xlii J2 **Funzie** Shetland Islands, NE Scotland, UK
167 R12 **Fuqing** Fujian, SE China
85 M14 **Furancungo** Tete, NW Mozambique
172 P5 **Furano** *var.* Hurano. Hokkaidō, NE Japan
118 I15 **Furculeşti** Teleorman, S Romania
Füred *see* Balatonfüred
172 Qq7 **Fūren-ko** ◎ Hokkaidō, NE Japan
149 R12 **Fūrg** Fārs, S Iran
Furluk *see* Fârliug
Fūrmanov *see* Furmanovka
151 S15 **Furmanovka** *Kaz.* Fūrmanov. Zhambyl, S Kazakhstan
150 E9 **Furmanovo** Zapadnyy Kazakhstan, W Kazakhstan
xliii G18 **Furnace** Argyll and Bute, W Scotland, UK
61 L20 **Furnas, Represa de** ⊠ SE Brazil
191 Q14 **Furneaux Group** *island group* Tasmania, SE Australia
Furnes *see* Veurne
166 J10 **Furong Jiang** ≈ S China
144 I5 **Furqlus** Ḥimṣ, W Syria
102 F12 **Fürstenau** Niedersachsen, NW Germany
111 X8 **Fürstenfeld** Steiermark, SE Austria
103 L23 **Fürstenfeldbruck** Bayern, S Germany
102 P12 **Fürstenwalde** Brandenburg, NE Germany
103 K20 **Fürth** Bayern, S Germany
111 W3 **Furth bei Göttweig** Niederösterreich, NW Austria
172 O4 **Furubira** Hokkaidō, NE Japan
96 L12 **Furudal** Kopparberg, C Sweden
171 Ii14 **Furukawa** Gifu, Honshū, SW Japan
171 M12 **Furukawa** *var.* Hurukawa. Miyagi, Honshū, C Japan
56 F10 **Fusagasugá** Cundinamarca, C Colombia
Fusan *see* Pusan
Fushë-Arëzi/Fushë-Arrësi *see* Fushë-Arrëz
115 L18 **Fushë-Arrëz** *var.* Fushë-Arëzi, Fushë-Arrësi. Shkodër, N Albania
Fushë-Kruja *see* Fushë-Krujë
115 K19 **Fushë-Krujë** *var.* Fushë-Kruja. Durrës, C Albania
169 V12 **Fushun** *var.* Fou-shan, Fu-shun. Liaoning, NE China
Fusin *see* Fuxin
110 G10 **Fusio** Ticino, S Switzerland
169 X11 **Fusong** Jilin, NE China
103 K24 **Füssen** Bayern, S Germany
166 K15 **Fusui** *prev.* Funan. Guangxi Zhuangzu Zizhiqu, S China
Futa Jallon *see* Fouta Djallon
65 G18 **Futaleufú** Los Lagos, S Chile
114 K10 **Futog** Serbia, NW Yugoslavia
171 K17 **Futtsu** *var.* Huttu. Chiba, Honshū, S Japan
197 E16 **Futuna** *island* S Vanuatu
202 D12 **Futuna, Île** *island* S Wallis and Futuna
167 Q11 **Futun Xi** ≈ SE China
166 L5 **Fuxian** *var.* Fu Xian. Shaanxi, C China
Fuxian *see* Wafangdian
166 G13 **Fuxian Hu** ⊠ SW China
169 U12 **Fuxin** *var.* Fou-hsin, Fu-hsin, Fusin. Liaoning, NE China
Fuxing *see* Wangmo
167 P7 **Fuyang** Anhui, E China
167 O4 **Fuyang He** ≈ E China
169 U7 **Fuyu** Heilongjiang, NE China
Fuyu/Fu-yü *see* Songyuan
169 Z6 **Fuyuan** Heilongjiang, NE China
164 M3 **Fuyun** *var.* Koktokay. Xinjiang Uygur Zizhiqu, NW China
113 L22 **Füzesabony** Heves, E Hungary
167 R12 **Fuzhou** *var.* Foochow, Fu-chou. Fujian, SE China
Fuzhou *see* Linchuan
143 W13 **Füzuli** *Rus.* Fizuli. SW Azerbaijan
121 I20 **Fyadory** *Rus.* Fëdory. Brestskaya Voblasts', SW Belorussia
xxxvii V8 **Fyfield** Essex, SE England, UK
97 G24 **Fyn** *off.* Fyns Amt, *var.* Fünen. ◈ *county* C Denmark
97 G23 **Fyn** *Ger.* Fünen. *island* C Denmark
xliii G19 **Fyne, Loch** *inlet* W Scotland, UK
97 E16 **Fyresvatnet** ◎ S Norway
FYR Macedonia/ FYROM *see* Macedonia, FYR
Fyzabad *see* Feyẕābād
xlii O12 **Fyvie** Aberdeenshire, NE Scotland, UK

G

83 O14 **Gaalkacyo** *var.* Galka'yo, *It.* Galcaio. Mudug, C Somalia
Gabakly *see* Kabakly
116 H8 **Gabare** Oblast Montana, NW Bulgaria
104 K15 **Gabas** ≈ SW France
37 T7 **Gabbs** Nevada, W USA
84 B12 **Gabela** Cuanza Sul, W Angola
Gaberones *see* Gaborone
201 X14 **Gabert** *island* Caroline Islands, E Micronesia
76 M7 **Gabès** *var.* Qābis. E Tunisia
76 M6 **Gabès, Golfe de** *Ar.* Khalīj Qābis. *gulf* E Tunisia
Gablonz an der Neisse *see* Jablonec nad Nisou
Gablös *see* Cavalese
81 E18 **Gabon** *off.* Gabonese Republic. ◆ *republic* C Africa
85 I20 **Gaborone** *prev.* Gaberones. ● (Botswana) South East, SE Botswana
85 I20 **Gaborone** ✕ South East, SE Botswana
106 K8 **Gabriel y Galán, Embalse de** ⊠ W Spain
149 U15 **Gābrīk, Rūd-e** ≈ SE Iran
116 J9 **Gabrovo** Loveshka Oblast, C Bulgaria
78 H12 **Gabú** *prev.* Nova Lamego. E Guinea-Bissau
31 O6 **Gackle** North Dakota, N USA
115 I15 **Gacko** S Bosnia and Herzegovina
161 F17 **Gadag** Karnātaka, W India
95 G15 **Gäddede** Jämtland, C Sweden
165 S12 **Gadê** Qinghai, C China
Gades/Gadier/Gadir/Gadire *see* Cádiz
107 P15 **Gádor, Sierra de** ⛰ S Spain
155 S15 **Gadra** Sind, SE Pakistan
25 Q3 **Gadsden** Alabama, S USA
38 H15 **Gadsden** Arizona, SW USA
Gadyach *see* Hadyach
81 H15 **Gadzi** Mambéré-Kadéï, SW Central African Republic
118 J13 **Găeşti** Dâmboviţa, S Romania
109 J17 **Gaeta** Lazio, C Italy
109 J17 **Gaeta, Golfo di** *var.* Gulf of Gaeta. *gulf* C Italy
196 L14 **Gaferut** *atoll* Caroline Islands, W Micronesia
23 Q10 **Gaffney** South Carolina, SE USA
Gäfle *see* Gävle
Gäfleborg *see* Gävleborg
76 M6 **Gafsa** *var.* Qafṣah. W Tunisia
Gafurov *see* Ghafurov
130 J3 **Gagarin** Smolenskaya Oblast', W Russian Federation
153 O10 **Gagarin** Jizzakh Wiloyati, C Uzbekistan
103 G21 **Gaggenau** Baden-Württemberg, SW Germany
196 F16 **Gagil Tamil** *var.* Gagil-Tomil. *island* Caroline Islands, W Micronesia
Gagil-Tomil *see* Gagil Tamil
131 O4 **Gagino** Nizhegorodskaya Oblast', W Russian Federation
109 Q19 **Gagliano del Capo** Puglia, SE Italy
96 L13 **Gagnef** Kopparberg, C Sweden
78 M17 **Gagnoa** C Ivory Coast
11 N10 **Gagnon** Québec, E Canada
Gago Coutinho *see* Lumbala N'Guimbo
175 Tt8 **Gag, Pulau** *island* E Indonesia
143 P8 **Gagra** NW Georgia
33 S13 **Gahanna** Ohio, N USA
149 R13 **Gahkom** Hormozgān, S Iran
Gahnpa *see* Ganta
59 Q19 **Gaíba, Laguna** ◎ E Bolivia
159 T13 **Gaibanda** *var.* Gaibandah. Rajshahi, NW Bangladesh
Gaibandah *see* Gaibanda
Gaibhlte, Cnoc Mór na n *see* Galtymore Mountain
111 R9 **Gail** ≈ S Austria
103 I21 **Gaildorf** Baden-Württemberg, S Germany
xxxviii B13 **Gailey** Staffordshire, C England, UK
105 N15 **Gaillac** *var.* Gaillac-sur-Tarn. Tarn, S France
Gaillac-sur-Tarn *see* Gaillac
Gaillimh *see* Galway
Gaillimhe, Cuan na *see* Galway Bay
111 Q9 **Gailtaler Alpen** ⛰ S Austria
65 J17 **Gaimán** Chaco, S Argentina
22 K8 **Gainesboro** Tennessee, S USA
25 V10 **Gainesville** Florida, SE USA
25 T2 **Gainesville** Georgia, SE USA
29 U8 **Gainesville** Missouri, C USA
27 T5 **Gainesville** Texas, SW USA
111 X5 **Gainfarn** Niederösterreich, NE Austria
xxxix O4 **Gainsborough** Lincolnshire, E England, UK
190 G6 **Gairdner, Lake** *salt lake* South Australia
xlii F10 **Gairloch** Highland, NW Scotland, UK
xliii H15 **Gairlochy** Highland, NW Scotland, UK
xlii M4 **Gairsay** *island* N Scotland, UK
94 L8 **Gaissane** ⛰ N Norway
45 T15 **Gaital, Cerro** ▲ C Panama
23 W3 **Gaithersburg** Maryland, NE USA
169 U13 **Gaizhou** Liaoning, NE China
Gaiziņ *see* Gaizina Kalns
120 I9 **Gaizina Kalns** *var.* Gaiziņ. ▲ E Latvia
Gajac *see* Villeneuve-sur-Lot
174 L15 **Gajahmungkur, Danau** ◎ Jawa, S Indonesia
41 S10 **Gakona** Alaska, USA
Galaassiya *see* Galaosiye
Ğalāğıl *see* Jalājil
Galam, Pulau *see* Gelam, Pulau
64 J6 **Galán, Cerro** ▲ NW Argentina
113 H21 **Galanta** *Hung.* Galánta. Západné Slovensko, SW Slovakia
152 L11 **Galaosiye** *Rus.* Galaassiya. Bukhoro Wiloyati, C Uzbekistan
59 B17 **Galápagos** *off.* Provincia de Galápagos. ◈ *province* Ecuador, E Pacific Ocean
199 M9 **Galapagos Fracture Zone** *tectonic feature* E Pacific Ocean
200 O10 **Galapagos Rise** *undersea feature* E Pacific Ocean
xliii N21 **Galashiels** The Borders, SE Scotland, UK
118 M12 **Galaţi** *Ger.* Galatz. Galaţi, E Romania
118 L12 **Galaţi** ◈ *county* E Romania
109 Q19 **Galatina** Puglia, SE Italy
109 Q19 **Galatone** Puglia, SE Italy
Galatz *see* Galaţi
23 R8 **Galax** Virginia, NE USA
Galaymor *see* Kala-i-Mor
xliv G12 **Galbally** Limerick, SW Ireland
Galcaio *see* Gaalkacyo
66 P11 **Gáldar** Gran Canaria, Islas Canarias, Spain NE Atlantic Ocean
96 F11 **Galdhøpiggen** ▲ S Norway
42 I4 **Galeana** Chihuahua, N Mexico
43 O9 **Galeana** Nuevo León, NE Mexico
62 P9 **Galeão** ✕ (Rio de Janeiro) Rio de Janeiro, SE Brazil
175 T6 **Galela** Pulau Halmahera, E Indonesia
41 O9 **Galena** Alaska, USA
32 K10 **Galena** Illinois, N USA
29 R7 **Galena** Kansas, C USA
29 T8 **Galena** Missouri, C USA
47 V15 **Galeota Point** *headland* Trinidad, Trinidad and Tobago
107 P13 **Galera** Andalucía, S Spain
47 Y16 **Galera Point** *headland* Trinidad, Trinidad and Tobago
58 A5 **Galera, Punta** *headland* NW Ecuador
32 K12 **Galesburg** Illinois, N USA
32 J7 **Galesville** Wisconsin, N USA
20 F12 **Galeton** Pennsylvania, NE USA
xli N13 **Galgate** Lancashire, NW England, UK
118 H9 **Gâlgău** *Hung.* Galgó; *prev.* Gîlgău. Sălaj, NW Romania
Galgó *see* Gâlgău
Galgóc *see* Hlohovec
83 N15 **Galguduud** *off.* Gobolka Galguduud. ◈ *region* E Somalia
143 Q9 **Gali** W Georgia
129 N14 **Galich** Kostromskaya Oblast', NW Russian Federation
116 H7 **Galiche** Oblast Montana, NW Bulgaria
106 H3 **Galicia** *anc.* Gallaecia. ◈ *autonomous community* NW Spain
66 M8 **Galicia Bank** *undersea feature* E Atlantic Ocean
Galilee *see* HaGalil
189 W7 **Galilee, Lake** ◎ Queensland, NE Australia
Galilee, Sea of *see* Tiberias, Lake
108 E11 **Galileo Galilei** ✕ (Pisa) Toscana, C Italy
33 S12 **Galion** Ohio, N USA
Galka'yo *see* Gaalkacyo
82 H11 **Gallabat** Gedaref, E Sudan
Gallaecia *see* Galicia
108 C7 **Gallarate** Lombardia, NW Italy
29 S2 **Gallatin** Missouri, C USA
22 J8 **Gallatin** Tennessee, S USA
35 R11 **Gallatin Peak** ▲ Montana, NW USA
35 R12 **Gallatin River** ≈ Montana/ Wyoming,NW USA
161 J26 **Galle** *prev.* Point de Galle. Southern Province, SW Sri Lanka
107 S5 **Gállego** ≈ NE Spain
200 N9 **Gallego Rise** *undersea feature* E Pacific Ocean
Gallegos *see* Río Gallegos
65 H23 **Gallegos, Río** ≈ Argentina/Chile
xliv E15 **Galley Head** *headland* S Ireland
Gallia *see* France
24 K10 **Galliano** Louisiana, S USA
116 G13 **Gallikós** ≈ N Greece
39 S12 **Gallinas Peak** ▲ New Mexico, SW USA
56 H3 **Gallinas, Punta** *headland* NE Colombia
39 T11 **Gallinas River** ≈ New Mexico, SW USA
109 Q19 **Gallipoli** Puglia, SE Italy
Gallipoli *see* Gelibolu
Gallipoli Peninsula *see* Gelibolu Yarımadası
33 T15 **Gallipolis** Ohio, N USA
94 J12 **Gällivare** Norrbotten, N Sweden
111 T4 **Gallneukirchen** Oberösterreich, N Austria
107 Q7 **Gallo** ≈ C Spain
95 G17 **Gällö** Jämtland, C Sweden
109 I23 **Gallo, Capo** *headland* Sicilia, Italy, C Mediterranean Sea
39 P13 **Gallo Mountains** ⛰ New Mexico, SW USA
20 G8 **Galloo Island** *island* New York, NE USA
xliii H26 **Galloway, Mull of** *headland* S Scotland, UK .
39 P10 **Gallup** New Mexico, SW USA
107 R5 **Gallur** Aragón, NE Spain
Gâlma *see* Guelma
xliii E15 **Galmisdale** Highland, NW Scotland, UK
xliii I21 **Galston** East Ayrshire, W Scotland, UK
37 O8 **Galt** California, W USA
76 C10 **Galtat-Zemmour** C Western Sahara
97 G22 **Galten** Århus, C Denmark
xliv G12 **Galtymore Mountain** *Ir.* Cnoc Mór na nGaibhlte. ▲ S Ireland
xliv G12 **Galty Mountains** *Ir.* Na Gaibhlte. ⛰ S Ireland
32 K11 **Galva** Illinois, N USA
27 X12 **Galveston** Texas, SW USA
27 W11 **Galveston Bay** *inlet* Texas, SW USA
27 W12 **Galveston Island** *island* Texas, SW USA
63 B18 **Gálvez** Santa Fe, C Argentina
xliv E9 **Galway** *Ir.* Gaillimh. Galway, W Ireland
xliv F8 **Galway** *Ir.* Gaillimh. ◈ *county* W Ireland
xliv E9 **Galway** ✕ Galway, W Ireland
xliv D9 **Galway Bay** *Ir.* Cuan na Gaillimhe. *bay* W Ireland
85 F18 **Gam** Otjozondjupa, NE Namibia
194 G14 **Gama** ≈ SW PNG
171 Hh16 **Gamagōri** Aichi, Honshū, SW Japan
56 F7 **Gamarra** Cesar, N Colombia
Gámas *see* Kaamanen
164 L17 **Gamba** Xizang Zizhiqu, W China
79 P14 **Gambaga** NE Ghana
82 G13 **Gambēla** W Ethiopia
40 K10 **Gambell** Saint Lawrence Island, Alaska, USA
78 E12 **Gambia** *off.* Republic of The Gambia, The Gambia. ◆ *republic* W Africa
78 I12 **Gambia** *Fr.* Gambie. ≈ W Africa
66 K12 **Gambia Plain** *undersea feature* E Atlantic Ocean
Gambie *see* Gambia
33 T13 **Gambier** Ohio, N USA
203 Y13 **Gambier, Îles** *island group* E French Polynesia
190 G10 **Gambier Islands** *island group* South Australia
xli N8 **Gamblesby** Cumbria, NW England, UK
81 H19 **Gamboma** Plateaux, E Congo
81 G16 **Gamboula** Mambéré-Kadéï, SW Central African Republic
39 P10 **Gamerco** New Mexico, SW USA
143 V12 **Gamiş Dağı** ▲ W Azerbaijan
Gamlakarleby *see* Kokkola
97 N18 **Gamleby** Kalmar, S Sweden
xxxix R13 **Gamlingay** Cambridgeshire, E England, UK
Gammelstad *see* Gammelstaden
95 J14 **Gammelstaden** *var.* Gammelstad. Norrbotten, N Sweden
Gammouda *see* Sidi Bouzid
161 J25 **Gampaha** Western Province, W Sri Lanka
161 K25 **Gampola** Central Province, C Sri Lanka
176 Uu8 **Gam, Pulau** *island* E Indonesia
178 Jj5 **Gâm, Sông** ≈ N Vietnam
xxxix O5 **Gamston** Nottinghamshire, C England, UK
94 L7 **Gamvik** Finnmark, N Norway
156 H13 **Gan** Addu Atoll, C Maldives
Gan *see* Gansu, China
Gan *see* Jiangxi, China
Ganaane *see* Juba
39 O10 **Ganado** Arizona, SW USA
27 U12 **Ganado** Texas, SW USA
12 L14 **Gananoque** Ontario, SE Canada
Ganāveh *see* Bandar-e Gonāveh
143 V11 **Gäncä** *Rus.* Gyandzha; *prev.* Kirovabad, Yelisavetpol. W Azerbaijan
Ganchi *see* Ghonchí
Gand *see* Gent
84 B13 **Ganda** *var.* Mariano Machado, *Port.* Vila Mariano Machado. Benguela, W Angola
81 L22 **Gandajika** Kasai Oriental, S Zaire
159 O12 **Gandak** *Nep.* Nārāyāni. ≈ India/Nepal
11 U11 **Gander** Newfoundland, Newfoundland and Labrador, SE Canada
11 U11 **Gander** ✕ Newfoundland, Newfoundland and Labrador, E Canada
102 G11 **Ganderkesee** Niedersachsen, NW Germany
107 T7 **Gandesa** Cataluña, NE Spain
160 B10 **Gāndhīdhām** Gujarāt, W India
160 D10 **Gāndhīnagar** Gujarāt, W India
160 F9 **Gāndhi Sāgar** ◎ C India
107 T11 **Gandía** País Valenciano, E Spain
165 O10 **Gang** Qinghai, W China
158 G9 **Gangānagar** Rājasthān, NW India
158 I12 **Gangāpur** Rājasthān, N India
159 S17 **Ganga Sāgar** West Bengal, NE India
Gangavathi *see* Gangāwati
161 G17 **Gangāwati** *var.* Gangavathi. Karnātaka, C India
165 S9 **Gangca** *var.* Shaliuhe. Qinghai, C China
164 H14 **Gangdisê Shan** *Eng.* Kailas Range. ⛰ W China
105 Q15 **Ganges** Hérault, S France
159 P13 **Ganges** *Ben.* Padma. ≈ Bangladesh/India *see also* Padma
Ganges Cone *see* Ganges Fan
181 S3 **Ganges Fan** *var.* Ganges Cone. *undersea feature* N Bay of Bengal
159 U17 **Ganges, Mouths of the** *delta* Bangladesh/India
109 K23 **Gangi** *anc.* Engyum. Sicilia, Italy, C Mediterranean Sea
158 K8 **Gangotri** Uttar Pradesh, N India
Gangra *see* Çankırı
159 S11 **Gangtok** Sikkim, N India
165 W11 **Gangu** Gansu, C China
169 U5 **Gan He** ≈ NE China
175 T9 **Gani** Pulau Halmahera, E Indonesia
167 O12 **Gan Jiang** ≈ S China
152 H15 **Gannaly** Akhalskiy Velayat, S Turkmenistan
169 U7 **Gannan** Heilongjiang, NE China
105 P10 **Gannat** Allier, C France
35 T14 **Gannett Peak** ▲ Wyoming, C USA
31 O10 **Gannvalley** South Dakota, N USA
111 Y3 **Gänserndorf** Niederösterreich, NE Austria
Gansos, Lago dos *see* Goose Lake
165 T9 **Gansu** *var.* Gan, Gansu Sheng, Kansu. ◈ *province* N China
Gansu Sheng *see* Gansu
78 K16 **Ganta** *var.* Gahnpa. NE Liberia
190 H11 **Gantheaume, Cape** *headland* South Australia
Gantsevichi *see* Hantsavichy

◆ Country
● Country Capital
◇ Dependent Territory
○ Dependent Territory Capital
◈ Administrative Region
✕ International Airport
▲ Mountain
⛰ Mountain Range
Volcano
≈ River
◎ Lake
⊠ Reservoir

Ganu Mór – Giáltra

xlii H7 **Ganu Mór** ▲ NW Scotland, UK
167 Q6 **Ganyu** var. Qingkou. Jiangsu, E China
150 D12 **Ganyushkino** Atyrau, SW Kazakhstan
167 O12 **Ganzhou** Jiangxi, S China
79 Q10 **Gao** Gao, E Mali
79 R10 **Gao** ◈ region SE Mali
167 O10 **Gao'an** Jiangxi, S China
167 N5 **Gaoping** Shanxi, C China
165 S8 **Gaotai** Gansu, N China
Gaoth Dobhair see Gweedore
79 O14 **Gaoua** SW Burkina
78 I13 **Gaoual** Moyenne-Guinée, N Guinea
Gaoxiong see Kaohsiung
167 R7 **Gaoyou** var. Dayishan. Jiangsu, E China
167 R7 **Gaoyou Hu** ◎ E China
166 M15 **Gaozhou** Guangdong, S China
105 T13 **Gap** anc. Vapincum. Hautes-Alpes, SE France
164 G13 **Gar** var. Gar Xincun. Xizang Zizhiqu, W China
Garabekevyul/Garabekewül see Karabekaul
Garabogazköl see Kara-Bogaz-Gol
45 V16 **Garachiné** Darién, SE Panama
45 V16 **Garachiné, Punta** headland SE Panama
Garagan see Karagan
56 G10 **Garagoa** Boyacá, C Colombia
Garagöl see Karagel'
Garagum see Garagumy
Garagum Kanaly see Garagumskiy Kanal
152 E12 **Garagumskiy Kanal** var. Kara Kum Canal, Karakumskiy Kanal, Turkm. Garagum Kanaly. canal C Turkmenistan
152 F12 **Garagumy** var. Qara Qum, Eng. Black Sand Desert, Kara Kum, Turkm. Garagum; prev. Peski Karakumy. desert C Turkmenistan
191 S4 **Garah** New South Wales, SE Australia
66 O11 **Garajonay** ▲ Gomera, Islas Canarias, Spain NE Atlantic Ocean
116 M8 **Gara Khitrino** Varnenska Oblast, NE Bulgaria
78 L13 **Garalo** Sikasso, SW Mali
xliv F6 **Gara, Lough** ◎ N Ireland
Garam see Hron
Garamäbnyyaz see Karamet-Niyaz
Garamszentkereszt see Žiar nad Hronom
79 Q13 **Garango** S Burkina
61 Q15 **Garanhuns** Pernambuco, E Brazil
196 H5 **Garapan** Saipan, S Northern Mariana Islands
Gárassavon see Kaaresuvanto
80 J13 **Garba** Bamingui-Bangoran, N Central African Republic
83 L16 **Garbahaarrey** It. Garba Harre. Gedo, SW Somalia
Garba Harre see Garbahaarrey
83 J18 **Garba Tula** Eastern, C Kenya
29 N9 **Garber** Oklahoma, C USA
36 L4 **Garberville** California, W USA
xxxix W11 **Garboldisham** Norfolk, E England, UK
102 I12 **Garbsen** Niedersachsen, N Germany
62 K9 **Garça** São Paulo, S Brazil
106 L10 **García de Solá, Embalse de** ▣ C Spain
105 Q14 **Gard** ◈ department S France
105 Q14 **Gard** ∿ S France
108 F7 **Garda, Lago di** var. Benaco, Eng. Lake Garda, Ger. Gardasee. ◎ NE Italy
Garda, Lake see Garda, Lago di
Gardan Diwal see Gardan Diwāl
155 Q5 **Gardan Diwāl** var. Gardan Diwal. Wardag, C Afghanistan
105 S15 **Gardanne** Bouches-du-Rhône, SE France
Gardasee see Garda, Lago di
102 L12 **Gardelegen** Sachsen-Anhalt, C Germany
12 B10 **Garden** ∿ Ontario, S Canada
25 N6 **Garden City** Georgia, SE USA
28 I6 **Garden City** Kansas, C USA
29 S5 **Garden City** Missouri, C USA
27 N8 **Garden City** Texas, SW USA
25 P3 **Gardendale** Alabama, S USA
33 P5 **Garden Island** island Michigan, N USA
24 M11 **Garden Island Bay** bay Louisiana, S USA
33 O5 **Garden Peninsula** peninsula Michigan, N USA
Garden State see New Jersey
xlii O11 **Gardenstown** Aberdeenshire, NE Scotland, UK
97 I14 **Gardermoen** Akershus, S Norway
Gardeyz see Gardēz
155 Q6 **Gardēz** var. Gardeyz, Gordiaz. Paktiā, E Afghanistan
95 G14 **Gardiken** ◎ N Sweden
21 Q7 **Gardiner** Maine, NE USA
35 S12 **Gardiner** Montana, NW USA
21 N13 **Gardiners Island** island New York, NE USA
Gardner Island see Nikumaroro
21 T6 **Gardner Lake** ◎ Maine, NE USA
37 Q6 **Gardnerville** Nevada, W USA
Gardo see Qardho
108 F7 **Gardone Val Trompia** Lombardia, N Italy
Garegegasnjárga see Karigasniemi
xliii H19 **Garelochead** Argyll and Bute, W Scotland, UK
40 F17 **Gareloi Island** island Aleutian Islands, Alaska, USA
108 B10 **Garessio** Piemonte, NE Italy
34 M9 **Garfield** Washington, NW USA
33 U11 **Garfield Heights** Ohio, N USA
xli S14 **Garforth** Leeds, N England, UK
Gargaliani see Gargaliánoi
117 D21 **Gargaliánoi** var. Gargaliani. Pelopónnisos, S Greece
109 N15 **Gargano, Promontorio del** headland SE Italy
110 J8 **Gargellen** Graubünden, W Switzerland
95 I14 **Gargnäs** Västerbotten, N Sweden
xli P13 **Gargrave** North Yorkshire, N England, UK
120 C11 **Gargždai** Gargždai, W Lithuania
160 J13 **Garhchiroli** Mahārāshtra, C India
159 O15 **Garhwa** Bihār, N India
176 Ww11 **Gariau** Irian Jaya, E Indonesia
85 E24 **Garies** Northern Cape, W South Africa
83 K19 **Garissa** Coast, E Kenya
23 V11 **Garland** North Carolina, SE USA
27 T6 **Garland** Texas, SW USA
38 L1 **Garland** Utah, W USA
108 D8 **Garlasco** Lombardia, N Italy
121 F14 **Garliava** Kaunas, S Lithuania
xliii I25 **Garlieston** Dumfries and Galloway, SW Scotland, UK
Garm see Gharm
148 M9 **Garm, Āb-e** var. Rūd-e Khersān. ∿ SW Iran
103 K25 **Garmisch-Partenkirchen** Bayern, S Germany
149 O5 **Garmsār** prev. Qishlaq. Semnān, N Iran
Garmser see Darvīshān
xliv K6 **Garnagh** Armagh, S Northern Ireland, UK
31 V12 **Garner** Iowa, C USA
23 U9 **Garner** North Carolina, SE USA
29 Q5 **Garnett** Kansas, C USA
101 M25 **Garnich** Luxembourg, SW Luxembourg
190 M8 **Garnpung, Lake** salt lake New South Wales, SE Australia
Garoe see Garoowe
Garoet see Garut
159 U13 **Gāro Hills** hill range NE India
104 K13 **Garonne** anc. Garumna. ∿ S France
82 P13 **Garoowe** var. Garoe. Nugaal, N Somalia
80 F12 **Garoua** var. Garua. Nord, N Cameroon
81 G14 **Garoua Boulaï** Est, E Cameroon
79 O10 **Garou, Lac** ◎ C Mali
194 M11 **Garove Island** island Witu Islands, C PNG
97 L16 **Garphyttan** Örebro, C Sweden
xlii E8 **Garrabost** Western Isles, NW Scotland, UK
xxxv G6 **Garreg** Gwynedd, NW Wales, UK
31 R11 **Garretson** South Dakota, N USA
33 Q11 **Garrett** Indiana, N USA
xli O8 **Garrigill** Cumbria, NW England, UK
xliv G5 **Garrison** Fermanagh, W Northern Ireland, UK
35 Q10 **Garrison** Montana, NW USA
30 M4 **Garrison** North Dakota, N USA
27 X8 **Garrison** Texas, SW USA
30 L4 **Garrison Dam** dam North Dakota, N USA
xliv L3 **Garron Point** headland E Northern Ireland, UK
106 J9 **Garrovillas** Extremadura, W Spain
xliii K17 **Garrow** Perth and Kinross, C Scotland, UK
xliii J15 **Garry** ∿ C Scotland, UK
Garrygala see Kara-Kala
15 Jj6 **Garry Lake** ◎ Northwest Territories, N Canada
xliii G14 **Garry, Loch** ◎ NW Scotland, UK
xliv G14 **Garryvoe** Cork, S Ireland
Gars see Gars am Kamp
111 W3 **Gars am Kamp** var. Gars. Niederösterreich, NE Austria
83 K20 **Garsen** Coast, S Kenya
Garshy see Karshi
12 F10 **Garson** Ontario, S Canada
xli N13 **Garstang** Lancashire, NW England, UK
111 T5 **Garsten** Oberösterreich, N Austria
xl C16 **Garston** Liverpool, NW England, UK
Gartar see Qianning
104 M10 **Gartempe** ∿ C France
xlii H3 **Garth** Shetland Islands, NE Scotland, UK
xxxv I11 **Garth** Powys, C Wales, UK
xxxix P3 **Garthorpe** North Lincolnshire, N England, UK
xliii I19 **Gartocharn** West Dunbartonshire, W Scotland, UK
Gartog see Markam
xli X14 **Garton** East Riding of Yorkshire, N England, UK
xli V12 **Garton-on-the-Wolds** East Riding of Yorkshire, N England, UK
Garua see Garoua
85 D21 **Garub** Karas, SW Namibia
Garumna see Garonne
174 Jj15 **Garut** prev. Garoet. Jawa, C Indonesia
xliv K3 **Garvagh** Coleraine, N Northern Ireland, UK
xliii N20 **Garvald** East Lothian, SE Scotland, UK
xliii D19 **Garvard** Argyll and Bute, W Scotland, UK
xlii I11 **Garve** Highland, NW Scotland, UK
xliii E18 **Garvellachs** island group W Scotland, UK
193 C20 **Garvie Mountains** ▲▲ South Island, NZ
112 N12 **Garwolin** Siedlce, E Poland
27 U12 **Garwood** Texas, SW USA
Gar Xincun see Gar
33 N11 **Gary** Indiana, N USA
27 X7 **Gary** Texas, SW USA
170 E12 **Garyū-san** ▲ Kyūshū, SW Japan
164 G13 **Gar Zangbo** ∿ W China
166 F8 **Garzê** Sichuan, C China
56 E12 **Garzón** Huila, S Colombia
152 B13 **Gasan-Kuli** var. Esenguly. Balkanskiy Velayat, W Turkmenistan
33 P13 **Gas City** Indiana, N USA
104 K15 **Gascogne** Eng. Gascony. cultural region S France
Gascogne, Golfe de see Gascony, Gulf of
28 V5 **Gasconade River** ∿ Missouri, C USA
Gascony see Gascogne
104 H15 **Gascony, Gulf of** var. Golfe de Gascogne. gulf France/Spain
188 H9 **Gascoyne Junction** Western Australia
181 V8 **Gascoyne Plain** undersea feature E Indian Ocean
188 H9 **Gascoyne River** ∿ Western Australia
199 I12 **Gascoyne Tablemount** undersea feature N Tasman Sea
69 U6 **Gash** var. Nahr al Qāsh. ∿ W Sudan
155 X3 **Gasherbrum** ▲ NE Pakistan
165 N9 **Gas Hu** ◎ C China
79 X12 **Gashua** Yobe, NE Nigeria
176 Uu9 **Gasim** Irian Jaya, E Indonesia
195 N12 **Gasmata** New Britain, E PNG
25 V14 **Gasparilla Island** island Florida, SE USA
174 Jj11 **Gaspar, Selat** strait W Indonesia
13 Y6 **Gaspé** Québec, SE Canada
13 Z6 **Gaspé, Cap de** headland Québec, SE Canada
13 X6 **Gaspé, Péninsule de** var. Péninsule de la Gaspésie. peninsula Québec, SE Canada
Gaspésie, Péninsule de la see Gaspé, Péninsule de
171 Ll12 **Gas-san** ▲ Honshū, C Japan
79 W15 **Gassol** Taraba, E Nigeria
Gastein see Badgastein
23 R10 **Gastonia** North Carolina, SE USA
23 V8 **Gaston, Lake** ▣ North Carolina/Virginia, SE USA
117 D19 **Gastoúni** Dytikí Ellás, S Greece
65 I17 **Gastre** Chubut, S Argentina
Gat see Ghāt
107 P15 **Gata, Cabo de** headland S Spain
Gata, Cape see Gátas, Akrotíri
107 T11 **Gata de Gorgos** País Valenciano, E Spain
118 E12 **Gătaia** Ger. Gataja, Hung. Gátalja; prev. Gáttája. Timiș, W Romania
Gataja/Gátalja see Gătaia
124 Nn4 **Gátas, Akrotíri** var. Cape Gata. headland S Cyprus
106 J8 **Gata, Sierra de** ▲▲ W Spain
128 G13 **Gatchina** Leningradskaya Oblast', NW Russian Federation
23 P8 **Gate City** Virginia, NE USA
xliii J25 **Gatehouse of Fleet** Dumfries and Galloway, SW Scotland, UK
xli V2 **Gateshead** Gateshead, NE England, UK
xli V3 **Gateshead** ◈ unitary authority NE England, UK
15 Jj2 **Gateshead Island** island Northwest Territories, N Canada
23 X8 **Gatesville** North Carolina, SE USA
27 S8 **Gatesville** Texas, SW USA
12 L12 **Gatineau** Québec, SE Canada
12 L11 **Gatineau** ∿ Ontario/Québec, SE Canada
xl G16 **Gatley** Manchester, NW England, UK
23 N9 **Gatlinburg** Tennessee, S USA
Gatooma see Kadoma
Gáttája see Gătaia
45 T14 **Gatún, Lago** ▣ C Panama
61 N14 **Gaturiano** Piauí, NE Brazil
xxxvii T11 **Gatwick** ✕ (London) SE England, UK
197 J15 **Gau** prev. Ngau. island C Fiji
Gaua see Santa Maria
106 L16 **Gaucín** Andalucía, S Spain
Gauhāti see Guwāhāti
120 I8 **Gauja** Ger. Aa. ∿ Estonia/Latvia
120 I7 **Gaujiena** Alūksne, NE Latvia
Gaul/Gaule see France
96 H9 **Gauldalen** valley S Norway
23 R5 **Gauley River** ∿ West Virginia, NE USA
101 D19 **Gaurain-Ramecroix** Hainaut, SW Belgium
97 F15 **Gausta** ▲ S Norway
85 J21 **Gauteng** off. Gauteng Province; prev. Pretoria-Witwatersrand-Vereeniging. ◈ province NE South Africa
Gauteng see Germiston, South Africa
Gauteng see Johannesburg, South Africa
176 Y10 **Gauttier, Pegunungan** ▲▲ Irian Jaya, E Indonesia
149 P14 **Gāvbandī** Hormozgān, S Iran
117 H25 **Gavdopoúla** island SE Greece
117 H26 **Gávdos** island SE Greece
104 K16 **Gave de Pau** var. Gave-de-Pay. ∿ SW France
Gave-de-Pay see Gave de Pau
104 J16 **Gave d'Oloron** ∿ SW France
101 E18 **Gavere** Oost-Vlaanderen, NW Belgium
96 N13 **Gävle** var. Gäfle; prev. Gefle. Gävleborg, C Sweden
96 M11 **Gävleborg** var. Gäfleborg, Gefleborg. ◈ county C Sweden
96 O13 **Gävlebukten** bay C Sweden
128 L16 **Gavrilov-Yam** Yaroslavskaya Oblast', W Russian Federation
195 P15 **Gawa Island** island SE Papau New Guinea
190 I9 **Gawler** South Australia
190 G7 **Gawler Ranges** hill range South Australia
Gawso see Goaso
168 H11 **Gaxun Nur** ◎ N China
159 P14 **Gaya** Bihār, N India
79 S13 **Gaya** Dosso, SW Niger
Gaya see Kyjov
33 Q6 **Gaylord** Michigan, N USA
31 U9 **Gaylord** Minnesota, N USA
189 Y9 **Gayndah** Queensland, E Australia
129 T12 **Gayny** Komi-Permyatskiy Avtonomnyy Okrug, NW Russian Federation
Gaysin see Haysyn
xxxix U9 **Gayton** Norfolk, E England, UK
Gayvorno see Hayvoron
144 E11 **Gaza** Ar. Ghazzah, Heb. 'Azza. NE Gaza Strip
85 L20 **Gaza** off. Província de Gaza. ◈ province SW Mozambique
152 I9 **Gaz-Achak** Turkm. Gazojak. Lebapskiy Velayat, NE Turkmenistan
Gazalkent see Ghazalkent
152 C11 **Gazandzhyk** Turkm. Gazanjyk; prev. Kazandzhik. Balkanskiy Velayat, W Turkmenistan
Gazanjyk see Gazandzhyk
79 V12 **Gazaoua** Maradi, S Niger
144 E11 **Gaza Strip** Ar. Qitā' Ghazzah. disputed region SW Asia
195 P11 **Gazelle Peninsula** headland New Britain, E PNG
197 J5 **Gazelle, Récif de la** reef C New Caledonia
Gazgan see Ghozghon
Gazi Antep see Gaziantep
142 M16 **Gaziantep** var. Gazi Antep; prev. Aintab, Antep. Gaziantep, S Turkey
142 M17 **Gaziantep** var. Gazi Antep. ◈ province S Turkey
116 M13 **Gaziköy** Tekirdağ, NW Turkey
124 O3 **Gazimağusa** var. Famagusta, Gk. Ammóchostos. E Cyprus
124 Nn2 **Gazimağusa Körfezi** var. Famagusta Bay, Gk. Kólpos Ammóchostos. bay E Cyprus
152 K11 **Gazli** Bukhoro Wiloyati, C Uzbekistan
Gazojak see Gaz-Achak
81 K15 **Gbadolite** Equateur, NW Zaire
78 K16 **Gbanga** var. Gbarnga. N Liberia
Gbarnga see Gbanga
79 S14 **Gbéroubouè** var. Béroubouay. N Benin
79 W16 **Gboko** Benue, S Nigeria
Gcuwa see Butterworth
112 I7 **Gdańsk** Fr. Dantzig, Ger. Danzig. Gdańsk, N Poland
112 J7 **Gdańsk** off. Województwo Gdańskie, Fr. Dantzig, Ger. Danzig. ◈ province N Poland
Gdan'skaya Bukhta/Gdańsk, Gulf of see Danzig, Gulf of
Gdańska, Zakota see Danzig, Gulf of
Gdańskie, Województwo see Gdańsk
Gdingen see Gdynia
128 F13 **Gdov** Pskovskaya Oblast', W Russian Federation
112 I6 **Gdynia** Ger. Gdingen. Gdańsk, N Poland
xlii D11 **Geary** Highland, NW Scotland, UK
28 M10 **Geary** Oklahoma, C USA
Geavvú see Kevo
78 H12 **Gêba, Rio** ∿ C Guinea-Bissau
175 T8 **Gebe, Pulau** island E Indonesia
142 E11 **Gebze** Kocaeli, NW Turkey
124 O2 **Geçitkale** Gk. Lefkonico, Lefkónikon. NE Cyprus
82 H10 **Gedaref** var. Al Qaḍārif, El Gedaref. Gedaref, E Sudan
82 H10 **Gedaref** ◈ state E Sudan
xxxix P11 **Geddington** Northamptonshire, C England, UK
82 B11 **Gedid Ras el Fil** Southern Darfur, W Sudan
101 I23 **Gedinne** Namur, SE Belgium
142 E13 **Gediz** Kütahya, W Turkey
142 C14 **Gediz Nehri** ∿ W Turkey
83 N14 **Gedlegubē** SE Ethiopia
xxxix S8 **Gedney Drove End** Lincolnshire, E England, UK
xxxix S9 **Gedney Hill** Lincolnshire, E England, UK
83 L17 **Gedo** off. Gobolka Gedo. ◈ region SW Somalia
97 I25 **Gedser** Storstrøm, SE Denmark
101 I16 **Geel** var. Gheel. Antwerpen, N Belgium
191 N13 **Geelong** Victoria, SE Australia
Ge'e'mu see Golmud
101 I14 **Geertruidenberg** Noord-Brabant, S Netherlands
102 H10 **Geeste** ∿ NW Germany
102 J10 **Geesthacht** Schleswig-Holstein, N Germany
xliv G6 **Geevagh** Sligo, N Ireland
191 P17 **Geeveston** Tasmania, SE Australia
Gefle see Gävle
Gefleborg see Gävleborg
164 G13 **Gê'gyai** Xizang Zizhiqu, W China
79 X12 **Geidam** Yobe, NE Nigeria
9 T11 **Geikie** ∿ Saskatchewan, C Canada
96 F13 **Geilo** Buskerud, S Norway
96 E10 **Geiranger** Møre og Romsdal, S Norway
103 I22 **Geislingen** var. Geislingen an der Steige. Baden-Württemberg, SW Germany
Geislingen an der Steige see Geislingen
83 F20 **Geita** Mwanza, NW Tanzania
97 G15 **Geithus** Buskerud, S Norway
166 H14 **Gejiu** var. Kochiu. Yunnan, S China
Gëkdepe see Geok-Tepe
152 E9 **Geklengkui, Solonchak** var. Solonchak Goklenkuy. salt marsh NW Turkmenistan
83 D14 **Gel** ∿ W Sudan
109 K25 **Gela** prev. Terranova di Sicilia. Sicilia, Italy, C Mediterranean Sea
Geladaindong see Gladaindong
83 N14 **Geladī** SE Ethiopia
174 Kk11 **Gelam, Pulau** var. Pulau Galam. island N Indonesia
100 L11 **Gelderland** prev. Eng. Guelders. ◈ province E Netherlands
100 J13 **Geldermalsen** Gelderland, C Netherlands
103 D14 **Geldern** Nordrhein-Westfalen, W Germany
101 K15 **Geldrop** Noord-Brabant, SE Netherlands
101 L17 **Geleen** Limburg, SE Netherlands
130 K14 **Gelendzhik** Krasnodarskiy Kray, SW Russian Federation
Gelib see Jilib
142 B11 **Gelibolu** Eng. Gallipoli. Çanakkale, NW Turkey
117 L14 **Gelibolu Yarımadası** Eng. Gallipoli Peninsula. peninsula NW Turkey
Gelinting, Teluk see Geliting, Teluk
175 Qq16 **Geliting, Teluk** var. Teluk Gelinting. bay Nusa Tenggara, S Indonesia
xxxv J14 **Gelligaer** Caerphilly, S Wales, UK
83 O14 **Gellinsor** Mudug, C Somalia
103 H18 **Gelnhausen** Hessen, C Germany
103 E14 **Gelsenkirchen** Nordrhein-Westfalen, W Germany
xliii K25 **Gelston** Dumfries and Galloway, SW Scotland, UK
85 C20 **Geluk** Hardap, SW Namibia
101 H20 **Gembloux** Namur, Belgium
194 I12 **Gembogl** Chimbu, C PNG
81 J16 **Gemena** Equateur, NW Zaire
101 L14 **Gemert** Noord-Brabant, SE Netherlands
142 E11 **Gemlik** Bursa, NW Turkey
Gem of the Mountains see Idaho
108 J6 **Gemona del Friuli** Friuli-Venezia Giulia, NE Italy
Gem State see Idaho
Genale Wenz see Juba
174 Ll7 **Genali, Danau** ◎ Borneo, N Indonesia
101 G19 **Genappe** Walloon Brabant, C Belgium
143 P14 **Genç** Bingöl, E Turkey
Genck see Genk
100 M9 **Genemuiden** Overijssel, E Netherlands
65 K14 **General Acha** La Pampa, C Argentina
63 C21 **General Alvear** Buenos Aires, E Argentina
64 I12 **General Alvear** Mendoza, W Argentina
63 B20 **General Arenales** Buenos Aires, E Argentina
63 D21 **General Belgrano** Buenos Aires, E Argentina
204 H3 **General Bernardo O'Higgins** Chilean research station Antarctica
43 O8 **General Bravo** Nuevo León, NE Mexico
64 M7 **General Capdevila** Chaco, N Argentina
General Carrera, Lago see Buenos Aires, Lago
43 N9 **General Cepeda** Coahuila de Zaragoza, NE Mexico
65 K15 **General Conesa** Río Negro, E Argentina
63 G18 **General Enrique Martínez** Treinta y Tres, E Uruguay
64 L3 **General Eugenio A. Garay** var. Fortín General Eugenio Garay; prev. Yrendagüé. Nueva Asunción, NW Paraguay
63 C18 **General Galarza** Entre Ríos, E Argentina
63 E22 **General Guido** Buenos Aires, E Argentina
General José F.Uriburu see Zárate
63 E22 **General Juan Madariaga** Buenos Aires, E Argentina
43 O16 **General Juan N Alvarez** ✕ (Acapulco) Guerrero, S Mexico
63 B22 **General La Madrid** Buenos Aires, E Argentina
63 E21 **General Lavalle** Buenos Aires, E Argentina
General Machado see Camacupa
64 I8 **General Manuel Belgrano, Cerro** ▲ W Argentina
43 O8 **General Mariano Escobero** ✕ (Monterrey) Nuevo León, NE Mexico
63 B20 **General O'Brien** Buenos Aires, E Argentina
64 K13 **General Pico** La Pampa, C Argentina
64 M7 **General Pinedo** Chaco, N Argentina
63 B20 **General Pinto** Buenos Aires, E Argentina
63 E22 **General Pirán** Buenos Aires, E Argentina
45 N15 **General, Río** ∿ S Costa Rica
65 I15 **General Roca** Río Negro, C Argentina
179 Rr17 **General Santos** off. General Santos City. Mindanao, S Philippines
43 O9 **General Terán** Nuevo León, NE Mexico
116 N7 **General Toshevo** Rom. I.G.Duca, prev. Casim, Kasimköj. Varnenska Oblast, NE Bulgaria
63 B20 **General Viamonte** Buenos Aires, E Argentina
63 A20 **General Villegas** Buenos Aires, E Argentina
Gênes see Genova
20 E11 **Genesee River** ∿ New York/Pennsylvania, N USA
32 K11 **Geneseo** Illinois, N USA
20 F10 **Geneseo** New York, NE USA
59 L14 **Geneshuaya, Río** ∿ N Bolivia
25 Q8 **Geneva** Alabama, S USA
32 M10 **Geneva** Illinois, N USA
31 Q16 **Geneva** Nebraska, C USA
20 G10 **Geneva** New York, NE USA
33 U10 **Geneva** Ohio, NE USA
Geneva see Genève
110 B10 **Geneva, Lake** Fr. Lac de Genève, Lac Léman, le Léman, Ger. Genfer See. ◎ France/Switzerland
110 A10 **Genève** Eng. Geneva, Ger. Genf, It. Ginevra. Genève, SW Switzerland
110 A11 **Genève** Eng. Geneva, Ger. Genf, It. Ginevra. ◈ canton SW Switzerland
110 A10 **Genève** var. Geneva. ✕ Vaud, SW Switzerland
Genève, Lac de see Geneva, Lake
Genf see Genève
Genfer See see Geneva, Lake
169 S5 **Gen He** ∿ NE China
Genichesk see Heniches'k
106 L14 **Genil** ∿ S Spain
101 K18 **Genk** var. Genck. Limburg, NE Belgium
170 Cc12 **Genkai-nada** gulf Kyūshū, SW Japan
109 C19 **Gennargentu, Monti del** ▲ Sardegna, Italy, C Mediterranean Sea
101 M14 **Gennep** Limburg, SE Netherlands
32 M10 **Genoa** Illinois, N USA
31 Q15 **Genoa** Nebraska, C USA
Genoa see Genova
Genoa, Gulf of see Genova, Golfo di
108 D10 **Genova** Eng. Genoa, Fr. Gênes; anc. Genua. Liguria, NW Italy
108 D10 **Genova, Golfo di** Eng. Gulf of Genoa. gulf NW Italy
59 C17 **Genovesa, Isla** var. Tower Island. island Galapagos Islands, Ecuador, E Pacific Ocean
Genshū see Wŏnju
101 E17 **Gent** Eng. Ghent, Fr. Gand. Oost-Vlaanderen, NW Belgium
174 J15 **Genteng** Jawa, C Indonesia
102 M12 **Genthin** Sachsen-Anhalt, E Germany
29 R9 **Gentry** Arkansas, C USA
Genua see Genova
109 I15 **Genzano di Roma** Lazio, C Italy
Geokchay see Göyçay
152 F13 **Geok-Tepe** var. Gëkdepe, Turkm. Gökdepe. Akhalskiy Velayat, C Turkmenistan
126 Gg1 **Georga, Zemlya** Eng. George Land. island Zemlya Frantsa-Iosifa, N Russian Federation
85 G26 **George** Western Cape, S South Africa
31 S11 **George** Iowa, C USA
11 O5 **George** ∿ Newfoundland and Labrador/Québec, E Canada
xxxvi F11 **Georgeham** Devon, SW England, UK
67 C25 **George Island** island S Falkland Islands
191 R10 **George, Lake** ◎ New South Wales, SE Australia
83 E18 **George, Lake** ◎ SW Uganda
25 W10 **George, Lake** ◎ Florida, SE USA
20 L8 **George, Lake** ▣ New York, NE USA
George Land see Georga, Zemlya
Georgenburg see Jurbarkas
George River see Kangiqsualujjuaq
66 G8 **Georges Bank** undersea feature W Atlantic Ocean
193 A21 **George Sound** sound South Island, NZ
67 F15 **Georgetown** ○ (Ascension Island) NW Ascension Island
189 V5 **Georgetown** Queensland, NE Australia
191 P15 **George Town** Tasmania, SE Australia
46 I4 **George Town** Great Exuma Island, C Bahamas
46 D8 **George Town** var. Georgetown. ○ (Cayman Islands) Grand Cayman, SW Cayman Islands
78 H12 **Georgetown** E Gambia
57 T8 **Georgetown** ● (Guyana) N Guyana
173 Ff3 **George Town** var. Penang, Pinang. Pinang, Peninsular Malaysia
47 Y14 **Georgetown** Saint Vincent, Saint Vincent and the Grenadines
23 Y4 **Georgetown** Delaware, NE USA
25 R6 **Georgetown** Georgia, SE USA
22 M5 **Georgetown** Kentucky, S USA
23 T13 **Georgetown** South Carolina, SE USA
27 S10 **Georgetown** Texas, SW USA
57 T8 **Georgetown** ✕ N Guyana
205 U16 **George V Coast** physical region Antarctica
205 T15 **George V Land** physical region Antarctica
204 J7 **George VI Ice Shelf** ice shelf Antarctica
204 J6 **George VI Sound** sound Antarctica
27 S14 **George West** Texas, SW USA
143 R9 **Georgia** off. Republic of Georgia, Geor. Sak'art'velo, Rus. Gruzinskaya SSR, Gruziya; prev. Georgian SSR. ◆ republic SW Asia
25 S5 **Georgia** off. State of Georgia; also known as Empire State of the South, Peach State. ◈ state SE USA
12 F12 **Georgian Bay** lake bay Ontario, S Canada
8 L17 **Georgia, Strait of** strait British Columbia, W Canada
Georgi Dimitrov see Kostenets
Georgi Dimitrov, Yazovir see Koprinka, Yazovir
116 M9 **Georgi Traykov, Yazovir** ▣ NE Bulgaria
Georgiu-Dezh see Liski
151 W10 **Georgiyevka** Semipalatinsk, E Kazakhstan
151 T6 **Georgiyevka** Zhambyl, SE Kazakhstan
131 N15 **Georgiyevsk** Stavropol'skiy Kray, SW Russian Federation
102 G13 **Georgsmarienhütte** Niedersachsen, NW Germany
205 O1 **Georg von Neumayer** German research station Antarctica
103 M16 **Gera** Thüringen, E Germany
103 K16 **Gera** ∿ C Germany
101 E19 **Geraardsbergen** Oost-Vlaanderen, SW Belgium
117 F21 **Geráki** Pelopónnisos, S Greece
29 W5 **Gerald** Missouri, C USA
49 V8 **Geral de Goiás, Serra** ▲▲ E Brazil
193 G20 **Geraldine** Canterbury, South Island, NZ
188 H11 **Geraldton** Western Australia
10 E11 **Geraldton** Ontario, S Canada
62 J12 **Geral, Serra** ▲▲ S Brazil
175 P16 **Gerampi** Sumbawa, S Indonesia
105 U6 **Gérardmer** Vosges, NE France
Gerasa see Jarash
Gerdauen see Zheleznodorozhnyy
41 Q11 **Gerdine, Mount** ▲ Alaska, USA
142 H11 **Gerede** Bolu, N Turkey
142 H11 **Gerede Çayı** ∿ N Turkey
154 M8 **Gereshk** Helmand, SW Afghanistan
103 L24 **Geretsried** Bayern, S Germany
107 P14 **Gérgal** Andalucía, S Spain
194 K13 **Gerhards, Cape** headland C PNG
30 I14 **Gering** Nebraska, C USA
37 R3 **Gerlach** Nevada, W USA
Gerlachfalvi Csúcs/Gerlachovka see Gerlachovský Štít
113 L18 **Gerlachovský Štít** var. Gerlachovka, Ger. Gerlsdorfer Spitze, Hung. Gerlachfalvi Csúcs; prev. Stalinov Štít, Ger. Franz-Josef Spitze, Hung. Ferencz-Jósef Csúcs. ▲ N Slovakia
110 E8 **Gerlafingen** Solothurn, NW Switzerland
Gerlsdorfer Spitze see Gerlachovský Štít
145 V3 **Germak** E Iraq
German East Africa see Tanzania
Germanicopolis see Çankırı
Germanicum, Mare/German Ocean see North Sea
Germanovichi see Hyermanavichy
German Southwest Africa see Namibia
22 E10 **Germantown** Tennessee, S USA
103 I15 **Germany** off. Federal Republic of Germany, Ger. Bundesrepublik Deutschland, Deutschland. ◆ federal republic N Europe
103 L23 **Germering** Bayern, SE Germany
85 J21 **Germiston** var. Gauteng. Gauteng, NE South Africa
Gernika see Gernika-Lumo
107 P2 **Gernika-Lumo** var. Gernika, Guernica, Guernica y Lumo. País Vasco, N Spain
171 Ii15 **Gero** Gifu, Honshū, SW Japan
117 F22 **Geroliménas** Pelopónnisos, S Greece
107 W5 **Gerona** ◈ province Cataluña, NE Spain
Gerona see Girona
101 H21 **Gerpinnes** Hainaut, S Belgium
xxxvii S9 **Gerrards Cross** Buckinghamshire, C England, UK
104 L15 **Gers** ◈ department S France
104 L14 **Gers** ∿ S France
Gerunda see Girona
142 K10 **Gerze** Sinop, N Turkey
164 I13 **Gêrzê** Xizang Zizhiqu, W China
Gesoriacum/Gessoriacum see Boulogne-sur-Mer
101 J21 **Gesves** Namur, SE Belgium
95 J20 **Geta** Åland, SW Finland
107 N8 **Getafe** Madrid, C Spain
97 J21 **Getinge** Halland, S Sweden
20 F16 **Gettysburg** Pennsylvania, NE USA
31 N8 **Gettysburg** South Dakota, N USA
204 K12 **Getz Ice Shelf** ice shelf Antarctica
143 S15 **Gevaş** Van, SE Turkey
Gevgeli see Gevgelija
115 Q20 **Gevgelija** var. Đevđelija, Djevdjelija, Turk. Gevgeli. SE FYR Macedonia
105 T10 **Gex** Ain, E France
94 I3 **Geysir** physical region SW Iceland
142 F11 **Geyve** Sakarya, NW Turkey
82 G10 **Gezira** ◈ state E Sudan
111 V3 **Gföhl** Niederösterreich, N Austria
85 H22 **Ghaap Plateau** Afr. Ghaapplato. plateau C South Africa
Ghaapplato see Ghaap Plateau
Ghaba see Al Ghābah
144 J8 **Ghāb, Tall** ▲ SE Syria
145 Q9 **Ghadaf, Wādī al** dry watercourse C Iraq
Ghadamès see Ghadāmis
76 M9 **Ghadāmis** var. Ghadamès, Rhadames. W Libya
147 Y10 **Ghadan** E Oman
77 O10 **Ghaddūwah** C Libya
153 Q11 **Ghafurov** Rus. Gafurov; prev. Sovetabad. NW Tajikistan
159 N12 **Ghāghara** ∿ S Asia
155 P13 **Ghaibi Dero** Sind, SE Pakistan
147 Y10 **Ghalat** E Oman
153 O11 **Ghallaorol** Jizzakh Wiloyati, C Uzbekistan
145 W11 **Ghamūkah, Hawr** ◎ S Iraq
79 P15 **Ghana** off. Republic of Ghana. ◆ republic W Africa
147 X12 **Ghānah** spring/well S Oman
Ghanongga see Ranongga
Ghansi/Ghansiland see Ghanzi
85 F18 **Ghanzi** var. Khanzi. Ghanzi, W Botswana
85 G19 **Ghanzi** var. Ghansi, Ghansiland, Khanzi. ◈ district C Botswana
69 T14 **Ghanzi** var. Knanzi. ∿ Botswana/South Africa
Ghap'an see Kapan
144 F13 **Gharandal** Ma'ān, SW Jordan
Gharbt, Jabal al see Liban, Jebel
76 K7 **Ghardaïa** N Algeria
145 U14 **Gharibīyah, Sha'īb al** ∿ S Iraq
153 R12 **Gharm** Rus. Garm. C Tajikistan
155 P17 **Gharo** Sind, SE Pakistan
145 W10 **Gharrāf, Shaṭṭ al** ∿ S Iraq
Gharvān see Gharyān
77 O7 **Gharyān** var. Gharvān. NW Libya
76 M11 **Ghāt** var. Gat. SW Libya
Ghawdex see Gozo
147 U8 **Ghayathi** Abū Ẓaby, W UAE
Ghazāl, Baḥr al see Ghazal, Bahr el
80 H9 **Ghazal, Bahr el** var. Soro. seasonal river C Chad
82 E13 **Ghazal, Bahr el** var. Baḥr al Ghazāl. ∿ S Sudan
153 Q9 **Ghazalkent** Rus. Gazalkent. Toshkent Wiloyati, E Uzbekistan
76 H6 **Ghazaouet** NW Algeria
158 J10 **Ghāziābād** Uttar Pradesh, N India
159 O13 **Ghāzīpur** Uttar Pradesh, N India
155 Q6 **Ghaznī** var. Ghazni. Ghaznī, E Afghanistan
155 P7 **Ghaznī** ◈ province SE Afghanistan
Ghazzah see Gaza
Gheel see Geel
Ghelîzâne see Relizane
Ghent see Gent
Gheorghe Brațul see Sfântu Gheorghe, Brațul
Gheorghe Gheorghiu-Dej see Onești
118 J10 **Gheorgheni** prev. Gheorghieni, Sînt-Miclăuș, Ger. Niklasmarkt, Hung. Gyergyószentmiklós. Harghita, C Romania
Gheorghieni see Gheorgheni
118 H10 **Gherla** Ger. Neuschliss, Hung. Szamosújvár; prev. Armenierstadt. Cluj, NW Romania
Gheweifat see Ghuwayfāt
152 L11 **Ghijduwon** Rus. Gizhduvan. Bukhoro Wiloyati, C Uzbekistan
Ghilan see Gīlān
109 C18 **Ghilarza** Sardegna, Italy, C Mediterranean Sea
Ghilizane see Relizane
Ghimbi see Gīmbī
Ghiriș see Câmpia Turzii
104 F2 **Ghisonaccia** Corse, France, C Mediterranean Sea
Ghizo see Gizo
153 Q11 **Ghonchí** Rus. Ganchi. NW Tajikistan
Ghor see Ghowr
159 T13 **Ghoraghat** Rajshahi, NW Bangladesh
155 R13 **Ghotki** Sind, SE Pakistan
154 M5 **Ghowr** var. Ghor. ◈ province C Afghanistan
152 M10 **Ghozghon** Rus. Gazgan. Nawoiy Wiloyati, C Uzbekistan
153 T13 **Ghŭdara** var. Gudara, Rus. Kudara. SE Tajikistan
159 R13 **Ghugri** ∿ N India
153 S14 **Ghund** Rus. Gunt. ∿ SE Tajikistan
Ghurdaqah see Hurghada
154 J5 **Ghūrīān** Herāt, W Afghanistan
147 T8 **Ghuwayfāt** var. Gheweifat. Abū Ẓaby, W UAE
123 Mm17 **Ghuzayyil, Sabkhat** salt lake N Libya
153 N13 **Ghuzor** Rus. Guzar. Qashqadaryo Wiloyati, S Uzbekistan
117 G17 **Giáltra** Évvoia, C Greece

◆ Country
● Country Capital
◇ Dependent Territory
○ Dependent Territory Capital
◈ Administrative Region
✕ International Airport
▲ Mountain
▲▲ Mountain Range
Volcano
∿ River
◎ Lake
▣ Reservoir

GIAMAME – GORHAM

Giamame see Jamaame
116 F13 Giannitsá var. Yiannitsá. Kentrikí Makedonía, N Greece
109 F14 Giannutri, Isola di island Archipelago Toscano, C Italy
xliv K2 Giant's Causeway Ir. Clochán an Aifir. lava flow N Northern Ireland, UK
178 J15 Gia Rai Minh Hai, S Vietnam
109 L24 Giarre Sicilia, Italy, C Mediterranean Sea
46 I7 Gibara Holguín, E Cuba
31 O16 Gibbon Nebraska, C USA
34 K11 Gibbon Oregon, NW USA
35 P11 Gibbonsville Idaho, NW USA
66 A13 Gibb's Hill hill S Bermuda
94 I9 Gibostad Troms, N Norway
106 I14 Gibraleón Andalucía, S Spain
106 L16 Gibraltar ○ (Gibraltar) S Gibraltar
106 L16 Gibraltar ◇ UK dependent territory SW Europe
Gibraltar, Détroit de/Gibraltar, Estrecho de see Gibraltar, Strait of
106 J17 Gibraltar, Strait of Fr. Détroit de Gibraltar, Sp. Estrecho de Gibraltar. strait Atlantic Ocean/Mediterranean Sea
33 S11 Gibsonburg Ohio, N USA
32 M13 Gibson City Illinois, N USA
188 L8 Gibson Desert desert Western Australia
8 L17 Gibsons British Columbia, SW Canada
155 N12 Gīdār Baluchistān, SW Pakistan
161 I17 Giddalūr Andhra Pradesh, E India
27 U10 Giddings Texas, SW USA
29 Y8 Gideon Missouri, C USA
83 I15 Gīdolē SW Ethiopia
120 H13 Giedraičiai Molėtai, E Lithuania
105 O7 Gien Loiret, C France
103 G17 Giessen Hessen, W Germany
100 O6 Gieten Drenthe, NE Netherlands
xliii J20 Giffnock East Renfrewshire, C Scotland, UK
xliii N20 Gifford East Lothian, SE Scotland, UK
25 Y13 Gifford Florida, SE USA
15 I11 Gifford ≈ Baffin Island, Northwest Territories, NE Canada
102 J12 Gifhorn Niedersachsen, N Germany
9 P13 Gift Lake Alberta, W Canada
171 Hh15 Gifu var. Gihu. Gifu, Honshū, SW Japan
171 I14 Gifu off. Gifu-ken, var. Gihu. ◐ prefecture Honshū, SW Japan
130 M13 Gigant Rostovskaya Oblast', SW Russian Federation
42 E8 Giganta, Sierra de la ▲ W Mexico
56 E12 Gigante Huila, S Colombia
116 I7 Gigen Loveshka Oblast, NW Bulgaria
Giggiga see Jijiga
xli O12 Giggleswick North Yorkshire, N England, UK
xliii E21 Gigha Island island SW Scotland, UK
xliii F21 Gigha, Sound of strait W Scotland, UK
xliii A14 Gighay island NW Scotland, UK
109 E14 Giglio, Isola del island Archipelago Toscano, C Italy
Gihu see Gifu
106 L2 Gijón Asturias, NW Spain
81 D20 Gikongoro SW Rwanda
38 K14 Gila Bend Arizona, SW USA
38 J14 Gila Bend Mountains ▲ Arizona, SW USA
39 N14 Gila Mountains ▲ Arizona, SW USA
38 I15 Gila Mountains ▲ Arizona, SW USA
148 M4 Gīlān off. Ostān-e Gīlān; var. Ghilan, Guilan. ◐ province NW Iran
Gilani see Gnjilane
38 L14 Gila River ≈ Arizona, SW USA
31 W4 Gilbert Minnesota, N USA
Gilbert Islands see Tungaru
8 L16 Gilbert, Mount ▲ British Columbia, SW Canada
189 U4 Gilbert River ≈ Queensland, NE Australia
1 C6 Gilbert Seamounts undersea feature NE Pacific Ocean
xl K8 Gilcrux Cumbria, NW England, UK
35 S7 Gildford Montana, NW USA
85 P15 Gilé Zambézia, NE Mozambique
32 K4 Gile Flowage ◎ Wisconsin, N USA
190 G7 Giles, Lake salt lake South Australia
77 U12 Gilf Kebir Plateau Ar. Haḍabat al Jilf al Kabīr. plateau SW Egypt
xliv K5 Gilford Banbridge, SE Northern Ireland, UK
191 R6 Gilgandra New South Wales, SE Australia
Gilgău see Gâlgău
83 I19 Gilgil Rift Valley, SW Kenya
191 S4 Gil Gil Creek ≈ New South Wales, SE Australia
155 V3 Gilgit Jammu and Kashmir, NE Pakistan
155 V3 Gilgit ≈ N Pakistan
9 X11 Gillam Manitoba, C Canada
97 J22 Gilleleje Frederiksborg, E Denmark
32 K14 Gillespie Illinois, N USA
29 W13 Gillett Arkansas, C USA
35 X12 Gillette Wyoming, C USA
xxxvi M12 Gillingham Dorset, S England, UK
xxxvii W10 Gillingham Kent, SE England, UK
xli R10 Gilling West North Yorkshire, N England, UK
xliv G5 Gill, Lough ◎ N Ireland
205 X6 Gillock Island island Antarctica
181 O16 Gillot ✕ (St-Denis) N Réunion
67 H25 Gill Point headland E Saint Helena
32 M12 Gilman Illinois, N USA
27 W6 Gilmer Texas, SW USA
xliii K17 Gilmerton Perth and Kinross, C Scotland, UK
xxxix N11 Gilmorton Leicestershire, C England, UK
Gilolo see Halmahera, Pulau
83 G14 Gilo Wenz ≈ SW Ethiopia
37 O10 Gilroy California, W USA
xli N6 Gilsland Cumbria, NW England, UK
194 H12 Giluwe, Mount ▲ W PNG
xxxv K13 Gilwern Monmouthshire, SE Wales, UK
126 M14 Gilyuy ≈ SE Russian Federation
101 I14 Gilze Noord-Brabant, S Netherlands
172 O14 Gima Okinawa, Kume-jima, SW Japan
82 H13 Gīmbī It. Ghimbi. W Ethiopia
47 T12 Gimie, Mount ▲ C Saint Lucia
9 X16 Gimli Manitoba, S Canada
Gimma see Jīma
97 O14 Gimo Uppsala, C Sweden
104 L15 Gimone ≈ S France
Gimpoe see Gimpu
175 Pp9 Gimpu prev. Gimpoe. Sulawesi, C Indonesia
190 F5 Gina South Australia
Ginevra see Genève
101 J19 Gingelom Limburg, NE Belgium
188 I12 Gingin Western Australia
179 R14 Gingoog Mindanao, S Philippines
83 K14 Gīnīr S Ethiopia
Giohar see Jawhar
109 O17 Gioia del Colle Puglia, SE Italy
109 M22 Gioia, Golfo di gulf S Italy
Giona see Gkióna
117 I16 Gioúra island Vóreioi Sporádes, Greece, Aegean Sea
109 O17 Giovinazzo Puglia, SE Italy
Gipeswic see Ipswich
Gipuzkoa see Guipúzcoa
Giran see Ilan
32 K14 Girard Illinois, N USA
29 R7 Girard Kansas, C USA
27 O6 Girard Texas, SW USA
56 E10 Girardot Cundinamarca, C Colombia
180 M7 Giraud Seamount undersea feature SW Indian Ocean
85 A15 Giraul ≈ SW Angola
xlii P13 Girdle Ness headland NE Scotland, UK
143 N11 Giresun var. Kerasunt; anc. Cerasus, Pharnacia. Giresun, NE Turkey
143 N12 Giresun var. Kerasunt. ◐ province NE Turkey
143 N12 Giresun Dağları ▲ N Turkey
77 X10 Girga var. Girgeh, Jirjā. C Egypt
Girgeh see Girga
Girgenti see Agrigento
194 H10 Girgir, Cape headland NW PNG
159 Q15 Girīdīh Bihār, NE India
191 P6 Girilambone New South Wales, SE Australia
Girin see Jilin
124 R12 Girne Gk. Kerýneia, Kyrenia. N Cyprus
107 X5 Girona var. Gerona; anc. Gerunda. Cataluña, NE Spain
104 J12 Gironde ◐ department SW France
104 J11 Gironde estuary SW France
107 V5 Gironella Cataluña, NE Spain
105 N15 Girou ≈ S France
xliii H23 Girvan South Ayrshire, W Scotland, UK
26 M9 Girvin Texas, SW USA
192 Q9 Gisborne Gisborne, North Island, NZ
192 P9 Gisborne off. Gisborne District. ◐ unitary authority North Island, NZ
xli P13 Gisburn Lancashire, NW England, UK
Giseifu see Üijŏngbu
Gisenye see Gisenyi
83 D19 Gisenyi var. Gisenye. NW Rwanda
97 K20 Gislaved Jönköping, S Sweden
105 N4 Gisors Eure, N France
Gissar see Hisor
153 P12 Gissar Range Rus. Gissarskiy Khrebet. ▲ Tajikistan/Uzbekistan
Gissarskiy Khrebet see Gissar Range
101 B16 Gistel West-Vlaanderen, W Belgium
110 F9 Giswil Unterwalden, C Switzerland
117 B16 Gitánes ancient monument Ípeiros, W Greece
83 E20 Gitarama C Rwanda
83 E20 Gitega C Burundi
Githio see Gýtheio
110 H11 Giubiasco Ticino, S Switzerland
108 K13 Giulianova Abruzzi, C Italy
Giulie, Alpi see Julian Alps
Giumri see Gyumri
118 M13 Giurgeni Ialomița, SE Romania
118 J15 Giurgiu Giurgiu, S Romania
118 J14 Giurgiu ◐ county SE Romania
97 F22 Give Vejle, C Denmark
105 R2 Givet Ardennes, N France
105 R11 Givors Rhône, E France
85 K19 Giyani Northern, NE South Africa
82 I13 Giyon C Ethiopia
Giza/Gizeh see El Gîza
77 V8 Giza, Pyramids of ancient monument N Egypt
Gizhduvan see Ghijduwon
127 Oo8 Gizhiga Magadanskaya Oblast', E Russian Federation
127 Oo8 Gizhiginskaya Guba bay E Russian Federation
195 T14 Gizo Gizo, NW Solomon Islands
195 T14 Gizo var. Ghizo. island NW Solomon Islands
112 N7 Giżycko Ger. Lötzen. Suwałki, NE Poland
Gizymałv see Hrymayliv
Gjakovë see Đakovica
96 F12 Gjende ◎ S Norway
97 F17 Gjerstad Aust-Agder, S Norway
Gjilan see Gnjilane
Gjinokastër see Gjirokastër
115 L23 Gjirokastër var. Gjirokastra; prev. Gjinokastër, Gk. Argyrokastron, It. Argirocastro. Gjirokastër, S Albania
115 L22 Gjirokastër ◐ district S Albania
Gjirokastra see Gjirokastër
15 K3 Gjoa Haven King William Island, Northwest Territories, NW Canada
96 H13 Gjøvik Oppland, S Norway
115 J22 Gjuhëzës, Kepi i headland SW Albania
Gjurgjevac see Đurđevac
117 E18 Gkióna var. Giona. ▲ C Greece
124 Oo3 Gkréko, Akrotíri var. Cape Greco, Pidálion. headland E Cyprus
101 I18 Glabbeek-Zuurbemde Vlaams Brabant, C Belgium
11 R14 Glace Bay Cape Breton Island, Nova Scotia, SE Canada
9 O16 Glacier British Columbia, SW Canada
41 W12 Glacier Bay inlet Alaska, USA
34 I7 Glacier Peak ▲ Washington, NW USA
23 Q7 Glade Spring Virginia, NE USA
xxxv K11 Gladestry Powys, C Wales, UK
27 W7 Gladewater Texas, SW USA
189 Y8 Gladstone Queensland, E Australia
190 I8 Gladstone South Australia
9 X16 Gladstone Manitoba, S Canada
33 O5 Gladstone Michigan, N USA
29 R4 Gladstone Missouri, C USA
33 Q7 Gladwin Michigan, N USA
97 J15 Glafsfjorden ◎ C Sweden
xli U10 Glaisdale North Yorkshire, N England, UK
94 H2 Gláma physical region NW Iceland
86 F7 Glåma ≈ SE Norway
xliii M16 Glamis Angus, E Scotland, UK
114 F13 Glamoč W Bosnia and Herzegovina
99 J22 Glamorgan cultural region S Wales, UK
97 G24 Glamsbjerg Fyn, C Denmark
179 Rr17 Glan Mindanao, S Philippines
97 M17 Glan ◎ S Sweden
111 T9 Glan ≈ SE Austria
103 F19 Glan ≈ W Germany
xxxv H13 Glanaman Carmarthenshire, S Wales, UK
xliv D12 Glanaruddery Mountains hill range W Ireland
165 N13 Glandaindong var. Gêladaindong. ▲ C China
xli Q3 Glanton Northumberland, N England, UK
Glaris see Glarus
110 H9 Glarner Alpen Eng. Glarus Alps. ▲ E Switzerland
110 H8 Glarus Glarus, E Switzerland
110 H9 Glarus Fr. Glaris. ◐ canton C Switzerland
Glarus Alps see Glarner Alpen
xlii H11 Glascarnoch, Loch ◎ NW Scotland, UK
29 N3 Glasco Kansas, C USA
xliii M14 Glascorrie Aberdeenshire, NE Scotland, UK
xliii G16 Glasdrum Argyll and Bute, W Scotland, UK
xliii J20 Glasgow City of Glasgow, S Scotland, UK
xliii I20 Glasgow ✕ Renfrewshire, W Scotland, UK
22 K7 Glasgow Kentucky, S USA
29 T4 Glasgow Missouri, C USA
35 W7 Glasgow Montana, NW USA
23 T6 Glasgow Virginia, NE USA
xliii J20 Glasgow, City of ◐ unitary authority C Scotland, UK
xxxv G6 Glaslyn ≈ NW Wales, UK
9 S14 Glaslyn Saskatchewan, S Canada
20 I16 Glassboro New Jersey, NE USA
xliii J26 Glasserton Dumfries and Galloway, SW Scotland, UK
xlii I11 Glass, Loch ◎ NW Scotland, UK
26 L10 Glass Mountains ▲ Texas, SW USA
xl M13 Glasson Lancashire, NW England, UK
xxxvi K11 Glastonbury Somerset, SW England, UK
Glatz see Kłodzko
103 N16 Glauchau Sachsen, E Germany
Glavn'a Morava see Velika Morava
115 N16 Glavnik Serbia, S Yugoslavia
131 T1 Glazov Udmurtskaya Respublika, NW Russian Federation
Głda see Gwda
111 U8 Gleinalpe ▲ SE Austria
111 W8 Gleisdorf Steiermark, SE Austria
Gleiwitz see Gliwice
xxxix V13 Glemsford Suffolk, E England, UK
xliii E21 Glenacardoch Point headland W Scotland, UK
41 S11 Glenallen Alaska, USA
xliv D5 Glenamoy Mayo, NW Ireland
104 F7 Glénan, Îles island group NW France
xliv L3 Glenariff Moyle, N Northern Ireland, UK
xliv L3 Glenarm Larne, E Northern Ireland, UK
xliv L5 Glenavy Lisburn, E Northern Ireland, UK
193 G21 Glenavy Canterbury, South Island, NZ
xliii E16 Glenbeg Highland, NW Scotland, UK
xliv C13 Glenbeigh Kerry, SW Ireland
8 H5 Glenboyle Yukon Territory, NW Canada
23 X3 Glen Burnie Maryland, NE USA
38 L8 Glen Canyon canyon Utah, W USA
38 L8 Glen Canyon Dam dam Arizona, SW USA
xliii L24 Glencaple Dumfries and Galloway, SW Scotland, UK
32 K15 Glen Carbon Illinois, N USA
xliii H16 Glen Coe valley N Scotland, UK
12 E17 Glencoe Ontario, S Canada
85 K22 Glencoe KwaZulu/Natal, E South Africa
31 U9 Glencoe Minnesota, N USA
xliv F4 Glencolumbkille Donegal, N Ireland
xliii G16 Glencoe Highland, NW Scotland, UK
38 K13 Glendale Arizona, SW USA
37 S15 Glendale California, W USA
xliv J11 Glendalough Wicklow, E Ireland
190 G5 Glendambo South Australia
xliii L18 Glendevon Perth and Kinross, C Scotland, UK
35 Y8 Glendive Montana, NW USA
35 Y15 Glendo Wyoming, C USA
xliii I13 Glendoebeg Highland, NW Scotland, UK
57 S10 Glendor Mountains ▲ C Guyana
xliii K18 Gleneagles Perth and Kinross, C Scotland, UK
xliii D21 Glenegedale Argyll and Bute, W Scotland, UK
xlii F13 Glenelg Highland, NW Scotland, UK
190 K12 Glenelg River ≈ South Australia/Victoria, SE Australia
xlii L12 Glenernie Moray, N Scotland, UK
xliii L18 Glenfarg Perth and Kinross, C Scotland, UK
xxxix N9 Glenfield Leicestershire, C England, UK
31 P4 Glenfield North Dakota, N USA
xliii G15 Glenfinnan Highland, NW Scotland, UK
27 V12 Glen Flora Texas, SW USA
12 J2 Glengad Head headland N Ireland
xliv D14 Glengarriff Cork, S Ireland
189 P7 Glen Helen Northern Territory, N Australia
191 U5 Glen Innes New South Wales, SE Australia
xlii M13 Glenkindie Aberdeenshire, NE Scotland, UK
33 P6 Glen Lake ◎ Michigan, N USA
xliii H25 Glenluce Dumfries and Galloway, SW Scotland, UK
8 I7 Glenlyon Peak ▲ Yukon Territory, W Canada
xlii I13 Glen Mor valley NW Scotland, UK
xliv F8 Glennamaddy Galway, W Ireland
39 N16 Glenn, Mount ▲ Arizona, SW USA
35 N15 Glenns Ferry Idaho, NW USA
25 W6 Glennville Georgia, SE USA
8 J10 Glenora British Columbia, W Canada
190 M11 Glenorchy Victoria, SE Australia
191 V5 Glenreagh New South Wales, SE Australia
35 X15 Glenrock Wyoming, C USA
xliii M18 Glenrothes Fife, E Scotland, UK
20 L9 Glens Falls New York, NE USA
xxxix Q4 Glentham Lincolnshire, E England, UK
xliv G3 Glenties Ir. Na Gleannta. Donegal, NW Ireland
30 L5 Glen Ullin North Dakota, N USA
23 R4 Glenville West Virginia, NE USA
29 T12 Glenwood Arkansas, C USA
31 S15 Glenwood Iowa, C USA
31 T7 Glenwood Minnesota, N USA
38 L5 Glenwood Utah, W USA
32 I5 Glenwood City Wisconsin, N USA
39 Q4 Glenwood Springs Colorado, C USA
xlii I3 Gletness Shetland Islands, NE Scotland, UK
110 F10 Gletsch Valais, S Switzerland
Glevum see Gloucester
31 U14 Glidden Iowa, C USA
xliv D11 Glin Limerick, SW Ireland
114 E9 Glina Sisak-Moslavina, NE Croatia
96 F11 Glittertind ▲ S Norway
113 J16 Gliwice Ger. Gleiwitz. Katowice, S Poland
38 M14 Globe Arizona, SW USA
Globino see Hlobyne
111 T6 Glockturm ▲ SW Austria
118 L9 Glodeni Rus. Glodyany. N Moldavia
111 S9 Glödnitz Kärnten, S Austria
Glodyany see Glodeni
Glogau see Głogów
111 W6 Gloggnitz Niederösterreich, E Austria
112 F13 Głogów Ger. Glogau, Glogow. Legnica, W Poland
113 I16 Głogówek Ger. Oberglogau. Opole, SW Poland
94 G12 Glomfjord Nordland, C Norway
96 I12 Glomma var. Glommen. ≈ S Norway
Glommen see Glomma
95 I14 Glommersträsk Norrbotten, N Sweden
180 I1 Glorieuses, Nosy island group N Madagascar
67 C25 Glorious Hill hill East Falkland, Falkland Islands
40 J12 Glory of Russia Cape headland Saint Matthew Island, Alaska, USA
xxxviii K4 Glossop Derbyshire, C England, UK
24 J7 Gloster Mississippi, S USA
xxxvi M7 Gloucester hist. Caer Glou, Lat. Glevum. Gloucestershire, C England, UK
191 U7 Gloucester New South Wales, SE Australia
194 L12 Gloucester New Britain, E PNG
21 P10 Gloucester Massachusetts, NE USA
23 X6 Gloucester Virginia, NE USA
xxxvi L7 Gloucestershire ◐ county C England, UK
xlii I1 Gloup Shetland Islands, NE Scotland, UK
33 T14 Glouster Ohio, N USA
44 H3 Glovers Reef reef E Belize
20 K10 Gloversville New York, NE USA
112 K12 Głowno Łódź, C Poland
113 H16 Głubczyce Ger. Leobschütz. Opole, SW Poland
130 L11 Glubokiy Rostovskaya Oblast', SW Russian Federation
151 W9 Glubokoye Vostochnyy Kazakhstan, E Kazakhstan
Glubokoye see Hlybokaye
113 H16 Głuchołazy Ger. Ziegenhais. Opole, SW Poland
102 I9 Glückstadt Schleswig-Holstein, N Germany
Glukhov see Hlukhiv
xli Q13 Glusburn North Yorkshire, N England, UK
Glushkevichi see Hlushkavichy
Glusk/Glussk see Hlusk
Glybokaya see Hlyboka
xxxv J6 Glyn Ceiriog Wrexham, NE Wales, UK
xxxvii U13 Glyndebourne East Sussex, SE England, UK
xxxv J6 Glyndyfrdwy Denbighshire, N Wales, UK
97 F21 Glyngøre Viborg, NW Denmark
xxxv I13 Glyn-Neath Neath Port Talbot, S Wales, UK
131 Q9 Gmelinka Volgogradskaya Oblast', SW Russian Federation
111 U2 Gmünd Kärnten, S Austria
111 R8 Gmünd Niederösterreich, N Austria
Gmünd see Schwäbisch Gmünd
111 S5 Gmunden Oberösterreich, N Austria
Gmundner See see Traunsee
96 N10 Gnarp Gävleborg, C Sweden
111 W8 Gnas Steiermark, SE Austria
Gnesen see Gniezno
97 O16 Gnesta Södermanland, C Sweden
112 H11 Gniezno Ger. Gnesen. Poznań, C Poland
115 O17 Gnjilane var. Gilani, Alb. Gjilan. Serbia, S Yugoslavia
xxxviii J9 Gnosall Staffordshire, C England, UK
97 K20 Gnosjö Jönköping, S Sweden
161 E17 Goa prev. Old Goa, Vela Goa, Velha Goa. Goa, W India
161 E17 Goa var. Old Goa. ◐ state W India
44 H7 Goascorán, Río ≈ El Salvador/ Honduras
79 O16 Goaso var. Gawso. W Ghana
xliii G21 Goat Fell ▲ W Scotland, UK
83 K14 Goba It. Gobbà. S Ethiopia
85 C20 Gobabed Erongo, W Namibia
85 E19 Gobabis Omaheke, E Namibia
Gobannium see Abergavenny
66 M7 Goban Spur undersea feature NW Atlantic Ocean
Gobbà see Goba
65 H21 Gobernador Gregores Santa Cruz, S Argentina
63 F14 Gobernador Ingeniero Virasoro Corrientes, NE Argentina
168 L12 Gobi desert China/Mongolia
170 G16 Gobō Wakayama, Honshū, SW Japan
103 D14 Goch Nordrhein-Westfalen, W Germany
85 E20 Gochas Hardap, S Namibia
xxxvii S11 Godalming Surrey, SE England, UK
161 I14 Godāvari var. Godavari. ≈ C India
161 L16 Godāvari, Mouths of the delta E India
13 V5 Godbout Québec, SE Canada
13 U5 Godbout ≈ Québec, SE Canada
13 U5 Godbout Est ≈ Québec, SE Canada
29 N6 Goddard Kansas, C USA
12 E15 Goderich Ontario, S Canada
Godhavn see Qeqertarsuaq
160 E10 Godhra Gujarāt, W India
Göding see Hodonín
xxxix R11 Godmanchester Cambridgeshire, E England, UK
xxxvi L14 Godmanstone Dorset, S England, UK
113 K22 Gödöllő Pest, N Hungary
64 H11 Godoy Cruz Mendoza, W Argentina
9 Y11 Gods ≈ Manitoba, C Canada
xxxvii Q14 Godshill Isle of Wight, S England, UK
9 Y13 Gods Lake Manitoba, C Canada
9 X13 Gods Lake ◎ Manitoba, C Canada
xxxvii U11 Godstone Surrey, SE England, UK
Godthaab/Godthåb see Nuuk
Godwin Austen, Mount see K2
Goede Hoop, Kaap de see Good Hope, Cape of
Goedgegun see Nhlangano
Goeie Hoop, Kaap die see Good Hope, Cape of
11 O7 Goélands, Lac aux ◎ Québec, SE Canada
100 E13 Goeree island SW Netherlands
101 F15 Goes Zeeland, SW Netherlands
Goettingen see Göttingen
21 O10 Goffstown New Hampshire, NE USA
12 E8 Gogama Ontario, S Canada
170 Ee12 Gō-gawa ≈ Honshū, SW Japan
32 L3 Gogebic, Lake ◎ Michigan, N USA
32 K3 Gogebic Range hill range Michigan/Wisconsin, N USA
143 V13 Gogi, Mount Arm. Gogi Lerr, Az. Küküdağ. ▲ Armenia/Azerbaijan
xxxv H10 Goginan Ceredigion, W Wales, UK
128 F12 Gogland, Ostrov island NW Russian Federation
113 I15 Gogolin Opole, SW Poland
Gogonou see Gogounou
79 S14 Gogounou var. Gogonou. N Benin
158 I10 Gohāna Haryāna, N India
61 K18 Goianésia Goiás, C Brazil
61 K18 Goiânia prev. Goyania. state capital Goiás, C Brazil
61 K18 Goiás Goiás, C Brazil
61 J18 Goiás off. Estado de Goiás; prev. Goiaz, Goyaz. ◐ state C Brazil
Goiaz see Goiás
xliii H19 Goil, Loch inlet W Scotland, UK
165 R14 Goinsargoin Xizang Zizhiqu, W China
62 H10 Goio-Erê Paraná, SW Brazil
101 I15 Goirle Noord-Brabant, S Netherlands
106 H8 Góis Coimbra, N Portugal
171 Gg16 Gojō var. Gozyô. Nara, Honshū, SW Japan
171 M10 Gojōme Akita, Honshū, NW Japan
155 U9 Gojra Punjab, E Pakistan
170 D15 Gokase-gawa ≈ Kyūshū, SW Japan
142 A11 Gökçeada var. Imroz Adası, Gk. Imbros. island NW Turkey
Gökçeada see Imroz
Gökdepe see Geok-Tepe
142 I10 Gökırmak ≈ N Turkey
Goklenkuy, Solonchak see Geklengkui, Solonchak
142 C16 Gökova Körfezi gulf SW Turkey
142 K15 Göksu ≈ S Turkey
142 L15 Göksun Kahramanmaraş, C Turkey
142 I17 Göksu Nehri ≈ S Turkey
85 J16 Gokwe Midlands, NW Zimbabwe
96 F13 Gol Buskerud, S Norway
159 X12 Golāghāt Assam, NE India
xliv G2 Gola Island island N Ireland
112 H10 Gołańcz Piła, W Poland
144 G8 Golan Heights Ar. Al Jawlān, Heb. HaGolan. ▲ SW Syria
Golārā see Ārān
Golaya Pristan see Hola Prystan'
149 T11 Golbāf Kermān, C Iran
142 M15 Gölbaşı Adıyaman, S Turkey
111 P9 Gölbner ▲ SW Austria
xli Q15 Golcar Kirklees, N England, UK
32 M17 Golconda Illinois, N USA
37 T3 Golconda Nevada, W USA
142 E11 Gölcük Kocaeli, NW Turkey
110 I7 Goldach Sankt Gallen, NE Switzerland
112 N7 Gołdap Ger. Goldap. Suwałki, NE Poland
34 E15 Gold Beach Oregon, NW USA
Goldberg see Złotoryja
xxxv L15 Goldcliff Newport, SE Wales, UK
70 D12 Gold Coast coastal region S Ghana
191 V3 Gold Coast cultural region Queensland, E Australia
41 R10 Gold Creek Alaska, USA
xliv G12 Golden Tipperary, S Ireland
9 O16 Golden British Columbia, SW Canada
39 T4 Golden Colorado, C USA
192 I13 Golden Bay bay South Island, NZ
29 R7 Golden City Missouri, C USA
34 I11 Goldendale Washington, NW USA
Goldener Tisch see Zlatý Stôl
46 L13 Golden Grove E Jamaica
12 J12 Golden Lake ◎ Ontario, SE Canada
24 K10 Golden Meadow Louisiana, S USA
47 V10 Golden Rock ✕ (Basseterre) Saint Kitts, Saint Kitts and Nevis
Golden State, The see California
85 K16 Golden Valley Mashonaland West, N Zimbabwe
xxxvi B6 Golders Green Barnet, SE England, UK
37 U9 Goldfield Nevada, W USA
Goldingen see Kuldīga
Goldmarkt see Zlatna
8 K17 Gold River Vancouver Island, British Columbia, SW Canada
23 V10 Goldsboro North Carolina, SE USA
26 M8 Goldsmith Texas, SW USA
27 R8 Goldthwaite Texas, SW USA
143 R11 Göle Kars, NE Turkey
Golema Ada see Ostrovo
116 H9 Golema Planina ▲ W Bulgaria
116 F9 Golemi Vrŭkh ▲ W Bulgaria
112 D8 Goleniów Ger. Gollnow. Szczecin, NW Poland
37 Q16 Goleta California, W USA
45 O16 Golfito Puntarenas, SE Costa Rica
27 T13 Goliad Texas, SW USA
115 L14 Golija ▲ SW Yugoslavia
115 O16 Goljak ▲ SE Yugoslavia
142 M12 Gölköy Ordu, N Turkey
Gollel see Lavumisa
111 X3 Göllersbach ≈ NE Austria
Gollnow see Goleniów
Golmo see Golmud
165 P10 Golmud var. Ge'e'mu, Golmo, Chin. Ko-erh-mu. Qinghai, C China
104 F1 Golo ≈ Corse, France, C Mediterranean Sea
Golovanevsk see Holovanivs'k
Golovchin see Halowchyn
41 N9 Golovin Alaska, USA
148 M7 Golpāyegān var. Gulpaigan. Eşfahān, W Iran
Golshan see Ṭabas
Gol'shany see Hal'shany
xlii K9 Golspie Highland, N Scotland, UK
114 O11 Golubac Serbia, NE Yugoslavia
112 J9 Golub-Dobrzyń Toruń, N Poland
151 S7 Golubovka Pavlodar, N Kazakhstan
84 B11 Golungo Alto Cuanza Norte, NW Angola
116 M8 Golyama Kamchiya ≈ E Bulgaria
116 L8 Golyama Reka ≈ N Bulgaria
116 H11 Golyama Syutkya ▲ SW Bulgaria
116 I12 Golyam Perelik ▲ S Bulgaria
116 I11 Golyam Persenk ▲ S Bulgaria
125 F12 Golyshmanovo Tyumenskaya Oblast', C Russian Federation
81 P19 Goma Nord Kivu, NE Zaire
171 Gg16 Gomadan-zan ▲ Honshū, SW Japan
Gomati see Gumti
79 X14 Gombe Bauchi, E Nigeria
69 U10 Gombe var. Igombe. ≈ E Tanzania
79 Y14 Gombi Adamawa, E Nigeria
Gombroon see Bandar-e 'Abbās
Gomel' see Homyel'
Gomel'skaya Oblast' see Homyel'skaya Voblasts'
66 N11 Gomera island Islas Canarias, Spain, NE Atlantic Ocean
42 I5 Gómez Farias Chihuahua, N Mexico
42 L8 Gómez Palacio Durango, C Mexico
164 J13 Gomo Xizang Zizhiqu, W China
175 T11 Gomumu, Pulau see Gomumu, Pulau
149 T6 Gonābād var. Gunabad. Khorāsān, NE Iran
46 L8 Gonaïves var. Les Gonaïves. N Haiti
126 M13 Gonam ≈ NE Russian Federation
46 L9 Gonâve, Canal de la var. Canal de Sud. channel N Caribbean Sea
46 K9 Gonâve, Golfe de la gulf N Caribbean Sea
Gonāveh see Bandar-e Gonāveh
46 K9 Gonâve, Île de la island C Haiti
Gonbadān see Dow Gonbadān
149 Q3 Gonbad-e Kāvūs var. Gunbad-i-Qawus. Māzandarān, N Iran
158 M12 Gonda Uttar Pradesh, N India
Gondar see Gonder
82 I11 Gonder var. Gondar. NW Ethiopia
80 J13 Gondey Moyen-Chari, S Chad
160 J12 Gondia Mahārāshtra, C India
106 G6 Gondomar Porto, NW Portugal
142 C12 Gönen Balıkesir, W Turkey
142 C12 Gönen Çayı ≈ NW Turkey
xlii I3 Gonfirth Shetland Islands, NE Scotland, UK
165 O15 Gongbo'gyamda Xizang Zizhiqu, W China
165 N16 Gonggar Xizang Zizhiqu, W China
166 G9 Gongga Shan ▲ C China
165 T10 Gonghe Qinghai, C China
164 I5 Gongliu var. Tokkuztara. Xinjiang Uygur Zizhiqu, NW China
79 W14 Gongola ≈ E Nigeria
Gongoleh State see Jonglei
191 P5 Gongolgon New South Wales, SE Australia
165 Q6 Gongpoquan Gansu, N China
166 I10 Gongxian var. Gong Xian. Sichuan, C China
Gongzhuling see Huaide
165 S14 Gonjo Xizang Zizhiqu, W China
109 B20 Gonnesa Sardegna, Italy, C Mediterranean Sea
Gonni/Gónnos see Gónnoi
117 F15 Gónnoi var. Gonni, Gónnos; prev. Dereli. Thessalía, C Greece
172 N9 Gonohe Aomori, Honshū, C Japan
170 Cc11 Gōnoura Nagasaki, Iki, SW Japan
37 O11 Gonzales California, W USA
24 J9 Gonzales Louisiana, S USA
27 T12 Gonzales Texas, SW USA
43 P11 González Tamaulipas, C Mexico
23 V6 Goochland Virginia, NE USA
195 N16 Goodenough Bay inlet SE PNG
205 X14 Goodenough, Cape headland Antarctica
195 N15 Goodenough Island var. Morata. island SE PNG
Good Hope see Fort Good Hope
41 N8 Goodhope Bay bay Alaska, USA
85 D26 Good Hope, Cape of Afr. Kaap de Goede Hoop, Kaap die Goeie Hoop. headland SW South Africa
Good Hope, Cape of see Yamsursba, Tanjung
8 K10 Good Hope Lake British Columbia, W Canada
85 E23 Goodhouse Northern Cape, W South Africa
35 O15 Gooding Idaho, NW USA
28 H3 Goodland Kansas, C USA
181 Y15 Goodlands NW Mauritius
22 J8 Goodlettsville Tennessee, S USA
41 N13 Goodnews Alaska, USA
27 O3 Goodnight Texas, SW USA
191 Q4 Goodooga New South Wales, SE Australia
xxxvi L7 Goodrich Gloucestershire, C England, UK
31 N4 Goodrich North Dakota, N USA
27 W10 Goodrich Texas, SW USA
31 X10 Goodview Minnesota, N USA
28 H8 Goodwell Oklahoma, C USA
xxxv C17 Goodwick Pembrokeshire, SW Wales, UK
xli U14 Goole East Riding of Yorkshire, E England, UK
191 O8 Goolgowi New South Wales, SE Australia
190 I10 Goolwa South Australia
189 Y11 Goondiwindi Queensland, E Australia
xxxvi C16 Goonhavern Cornwall, SW England, UK
100 O11 Goor Overijssel, E Netherlands
Goose Bay see Happy Valley-Goose Bay
35 V13 Gooseberry Creek ≈ Wyoming, C USA
23 S14 Goose Creek South Carolina, SE USA
65 M23 Goose Green East Falkland, Falkland Islands
17 G6 Goose Lake var. Lago dos Gansos. ◎ California/Oregon, W USA
31 Q4 Goose River ≈ North Dakota, N USA
159 T16 Gopalganj Dhaka, S Bangladesh
159 O12 Gopālganj Bihār, N India
Gopher State see Minnesota
103 I22 Göppingen Baden-Württemberg, SW Germany
112 G13 Góra Ger. Guhrau. Leszno, W Poland
112 M12 Góra Kalwaria Warszawa, C Poland
159 O12 Gorakhpur Uttar Pradesh, N India
Gorany see Harany
115 J14 Goražde SE Bosnia and Herzegovina
Gorbovichi see Harbavichy
Gorče Petrov see Đorče Petrov
1 E9 Gorda Ridges undersea feature NE Pacific Ocean
Gordiaz see Gardēz
80 K12 Gordil Vakaga, N Central African Republic
xliii O21 Gordon The Borders, S Scotland, UK
25 U5 Gordon Georgia, SE USA
30 K12 Gordon Nebraska, C USA
27 R7 Gordon Texas, SW USA
xlii K9 Gordonbush Highland, N Scotland, UK
30 L13 Gordon Creek ≈ Nebraska, C USA
65 I25 Gordon, Isla island S Chile
191 O17 Gordon, Lake ◎ Tasmania, SE Australia
191 O17 Gordon River ≈ Tasmania, SE Australia
xlii N11 Gordonstown Aberdeenshire, NE Scotland, UK
23 V5 Gordonsville Virginia, NE USA
82 H13 Gorē W Ethiopia
193 D24 Gore Southland, South Island, NZ
80 H13 Goré Logone-Oriental, S Chad
12 D11 Gore Bay Manitoulin Island, Ontario, S Canada
xliii M20 Gorebridge Midlothian, SE Scotland, UK
27 Q5 Goree Texas, SW USA
143 O11 Görele Giresun, NE Turkey
21 N6 Gore Mountain ▲ Vermont, NE USA
41 R13 Gore Point headland Alaska, USA
39 R4 Gore Range ▲ Colorado, C USA
xliv L11 Gorey Ir. Guaire. Wexford, SE Ireland
xxxvii X17 Gorey Jersey, Channel Islands
149 R12 Gorgāb Kermān, S Iran
149 Q4 Gorgān var. Astarabad, Astrabad, Gurgan; prev. Asterābād, anc. Hyrcania. Māzandarān, N Iran
149 Q4 Gorgān, Rūd-e ≈ N Iran
78 I10 Gorgol ◐ region S Mauritania
108 D12 Gorgona, Isola di island Archipelago Toscano, C Italy
21 P8 Gorham Maine, NE USA

◆ Country ● Country Capital ◇ Dependent Territory ○ Dependent Territory Capital ◐ Administrative Region ✕ International Airport ▲ Mountain ▲ Mountain Range Volcano ≈ River ◎ Lake ⊡ Reservoir

GORI – GREAT SHELFORD

143 T10 **Gori** C Georgia
100 I13 **Gorinchem** var. Gorkum. Zuid-Holland, C Netherlands
xxxvii Q9 **Goring** Oxfordshire, C England, UK
xxxvii T13 **Goring-by-Sea** West Sussex, SE England, UK
143 V13 **Goris** SE Armenia
128 K16 **Goritsy** Tverskaya Oblast', W Russian Federation
108 J7 **Gorizia** Ger. Görz. Friuli-Venezia Giulia, NE Italy
118 G13 **Gorj** ◈ county SW Romania
Gorjanci see Žumberačka Gora
Görkau see Jirkov
Gorki see Horki
Gor'kiy see Nizhniy Novgorod
Gor'kiy Reservoir see Gor'kovskoye Vodokhranilishche
125 D9 **Gor'kovskoye Vodokhranilishche** Eng. Gor'kiy Reservoir. ⊠ W Russian Federation
Gorkum see Gorinchem
xxxix Z9 **Gorleston-on-Sea** Norfolk, E England, UK
97 I23 **Gørlev** Vestsjælland, E Denmark
113 M17 **Gorlice** Nowy Sącz, S Poland
103 Q15 **Görlitz** Sachsen, E Germany
Görlitz see Zgorzelec
Gorlovka see Horlivka
27 R7 **Gorman** Texas, SW USA
23 T3 **Gormania** West Virginia, NE USA
xliii C20 **Gorm, Loch** ◎ W Scotland, UK
Gorna Dzhumaya see Blagoevgrad
116 K8 **Gorna Oryakhovitsa** Loveshka Oblast, N Bulgaria
116 J8 **Gorna Studena** Loveshka Oblast, N Bulgaria
Gornja Mužlja see Mužlja
111 X9 **Gornja Radgona** Ger. Oberradkersburg. NE Slovenia
114 M13 **Gornji Milanovac** Serbia, C Yugoslavia
114 G13 **Gornji Vakuf** SW Bosnia and Herzegovina
126 H15 **Gorno-Altaysk** Respublika Altay, S Russian Federation
Gorno-Altayskaya Respublika see Altay, Respublika
126 K13 **Gorno-Chuyskiy** Irkutskaya Oblast', C Russian Federation
129 V14 **Gornozavodsk** Permskaya Oblast', NW Russian Federation
127 O16 **Gornozavodsk** Ostrov Sakhalin, Sakhalinskaya Oblast', SE Russian Federation
126 Gg15 **Gornyak** Altayskiy Kray, S Russian Federation
131 R8 **Gornyy** Saratovskaya Oblast', W Russian Federation
Gornyy Altay see Altay, Respublika
131 O10 **Gornyy Balykley** Volgogradskaya Oblast', SW Russian Federation
82 I13 **Goroch'an** ▲ W Ethiopia
Gorodenka see Horodenka
131 O3 **Gorodets** Nizhegorodskaya Oblast', W Russian Federation
Gorodets see Haradzyets
Gorodeya see Haradzyeya
131 P6 **Gorodishche** Penzenskaya Oblast', W Russian Federation
Gorodishche see Horodyshche
Gorodnya see Horodnya
Gorodok see Haradok
Gorodok/Gorodok Yagellonski see Horodok
130 M13 **Gorodovikovsk** Respublika Kalmykiya, SW Russian Federation
194 I12 **Goroka** Eastern Highlands, C PNG
Gorokhov see Horokhiv
131 N3 **Gorokhovets** Vladimirskaya Oblast', W Russian Federation
79 Q11 **Gorom-Gorom** NE Burkina
176 V12 **Gorong, Kepulauan** island group E Indonesia
85 M17 **Gorongosa** Sofala, C Mozambique
176 Uu12 **Gorong, Pulau** island Kepulauan Gorong, E Indonesia
175 R8 **Gorontalo** Sulawesi, C Indonesia
175 Qq8 **Gorontalo, Teluk** bay Sulawesi, C Indonesia
Gorontalo, Teluk see Tomini, Gulf of
112 L7 **Górowo Iławeckie** Ger. Landsberg. Olsztyn, N Poland
xxxvi D17 **Gorran Haven** Cornwall, SW England, UK
100 M7 **Gorredijk** Fris. De Gordyk. Friesland, N Netherlands
86 C14 **Gorringe Ridge** undersea feature E Atlantic Ocean
xxxv G14 **Gorseinon** Swansea, S Wales, UK
xlii M4 **Gorseness** Orkney Islands, N Scotland, UK
100 M11 **Gorssel** Gelderland, E Netherlands
xliv F10 **Gort** Galway, W Ireland
xliv H2 **Gortahork** Donegal, N Ireland
xliv F6 **Gorteen** Sligo, N Ireland
xliv I4 **Gortin** Omagh, W Northern Ireland, UK
111 T8 **Görtschitz** ⟿ S Austria
Goryn see Horyn'
Görz see Gorizia
112 E10 **Gorzów** off. Województwo Gorzowskie. ◈ province W Poland
Gorzowskie, Województwo see Gorzów
112 E10 **Gorzów Wielkopolski** Ger. Landsberg, Landsberg an der Warthe. Gorzów, W Poland
xxxix R8 **Gosberton** Lincolnshire, E England, UK
110 G9 **Göschenen** Uri, C Switzerland
195 N16 **Goschen Strait** strait SE PNG
171 Kk13 **Gosen** Niigata, Honshū, C Japan
191 T8 **Gosford** New South Wales, SE Australia
xl K10 **Gosforth** Cumbria, NW England, UK
xli V2 **Gosforth** Newcastle upon Tyne, NE England, UK
33 P11 **Goshen** Indiana, N USA
20 K13 **Goshen** New York, NE USA
Goshoba see Koshoba
171 Mm8 **Goshogawara** var. Gosyogawara. Aomori, Honshū, C Japan
152 I8 **Goshquduq Qum** var. Tosquduq Qumlari, Rus. Peski Taskuduk. desert W Uzbekistan
103 J14 **Goslar** Niedersachsen, C Germany
29 Y9 **Gosnell** Arkansas, C USA
114 C11 **Gospić** Lika-Senj, C Croatia
xxxvii Q13 **Gosport** Hampshire, S England, UK
96 D9 **Gossa** island S Norway
110 H7 **Gossau** Sankt Gallen, NE Switzerland
101 G20 **Gosselies** var. Goss'lies. Hainaut, S Belgium
79 P10 **Gossi** Tombouctou, C Mali
Goss'lies see Gosselies
115 N18 **Gostivar** W FYR Macedonia
Gostomel' see Hostomel'
112 G12 **Gostyń** var. Gostyn. Leszno, W Poland
112 K11 **Gostynin** Płock, C Poland
Gosyogawara see Goshogawara
97 J18 **Göta Älv** ⟿ S Sweden
97 N17 **Göta kanal** canal S Sweden
97 K18 **Götaland** cultural region S Sweden
97 H17 **Göteborg** Eng. Gothenburg. Göteborg och Bohus, S Sweden
97 H17 **Göteborg och Bohus** var. Göteborg and Bohus. ◈ county S Sweden
79 X16 **Gotel Mountains** ⛰ E Nigeria
97 K17 **Götene** Skaraborg, S Sweden
Gotera see San Francisco
103 K16 **Gotha** Thüringen, C Germany
xxxix N8 **Gotham** Nottinghamshire, C England, UK
31 N15 **Gothenburg** Nebraska, C USA
Gothenburg see Göteborg
79 R12 **Gothèye** Tillabéri, SW Niger
Gothland see Gotland
97 P19 **Gotland** var. Gothland, Gottland. ◈ county SE Sweden
97 O18 **Gotland** island SE Sweden
170 B12 **Gotō-rettō** island group SW Japan
116 H12 **Gotse Delchev** prev. Nevrokop. Sofiyska Oblast, SW Bulgaria
97 P17 **Gotska Sandön** island SE Sweden
170 Ee12 **Gōtsu** var. Gôtu. Shimane, Honshū, SW Japan
103 I15 **Göttingen** var. Goettingen. Niedersachsen, C Germany
Gottland see Gotland
95 I16 **Gottne** Västernorrland, C Sweden
Gottschee see Kočevje
Gottwaldov see Zlín
Gôtu see Gōtsu
Goturdepe see Koturdepe
110 I7 **Götzis** Vorarlberg, NW Austria
100 H12 **Gouda** Zuid-Holland, C Netherlands
xxxvii W11 **Goudhurst** Kent, SE England, UK
78 I11 **Goudiri** var. Goudiry. E Senegal
Goudiry see Goudiri
79 X12 **Goudoumaria** Diffa, S Niger
13 R9 **Gouffre, Rivière du** ⟿ Québec, SE Canada
67 M19 **Gough Fracture Zone** tectonic feature S Atlantic Ocean
67 M19 **Gough Island** island Tristan da Cunha, S Atlantic Ocean
13 N8 **Gouin, Réservoir** ⊠ Québec, SE Canada
12 B10 **Goulais River** Ontario, S Canada
191 R9 **Goulburn** New South Wales, SE Australia
191 O11 **Goulburn River** ⟿ Victoria, SE Australia
205 O10 **Gould Coast** physical region Antarctica
Goulimime see Guelmime
116 F13 **Gouménissa** Kentrikí Makedonía, N Greece
79 O10 **Goundam** Tombouctou, NW Mali
80 H12 **Goundi** Moyen-Chari, S Chad
80 G12 **Gounou-Gaya** Mayo-Kébbi, SW Chad
79 O12 **Gourci** var. Gourcy. NW Burkina
Gourcy see Gourci
104 M13 **Gourdon** Lot, S France
79 W11 **Gouré** Zinder, SE Niger
104 G6 **Gourin** Morbihan, NW France
79 P10 **Gourma-Rharous** Tombouctou, C Mali
105 N4 **Gournay-en-Bray** Seine-Maritime, N France
80 J6 **Gouro** Borkou-Ennedi-Tibesti, N Chad
xliii H20 **Gourock** Inverclyde, W Scotland, UK
106 H8 **Gouveia** Guarda, N Portugal
20 I7 **Gouverneur** New York, NE USA
101 L21 **Gouvy** Luxembourg, E Belgium
47 R14 **Gouyave** var. Charlotte Town. NW Grenada
Goverla, Gora see Hoverla, Hora
61 N20 **Governador Valadares** Minas Gerais, SE Brazil
179 Rr16 **Governor Generoso** Mindanao, S Philippines
46 I2 **Governor's Harbour** Eleuthera Island, C Bahamas
168 F9 **Govĭ-Altay** ◈ province SW Mongolia
168 I10 **Govĭ Altayn Nuruu** ⛰ S Mongolia
160 L9 **Govind Ballabh Pant Sāgar** ⊠ C India
158 I7 **Govind Sagar** ⊠ NE India
153 N14 **Govurdak** Turkm. Gowurdak; prev. Guardak. Lebapskiy Velayat, E Turkmenistan
20 D11 **Gowanda** New York, NE USA
154 I10 **Gowd-e Zereh, Dasht-e** var. Guad-i-Zirreh. marsh SW Afghanistan
xxxv F14 **Gower** peninsula S Wales, UK
12 F8 **Gowganda** Ontario, S Canada
12 G8 **Gowganda Lake** ◎ Ontario, S Canada
xliv H7 **Gowna, Lough** ◎ N Ireland
xliv J11 **Gowran** Kilkenny, SE Ireland
31 U13 **Gowrie** Iowa, C USA
Gowurdak see Govurdak
xxxix Q3 **Goxhill** North Lincolnshire, N England, UK
63 C15 **Goya** Corrientes, NE Argentina
Goyania see Goiânia
143 X11 **Göyçay** Rus. Geokchay. C Azerbaijan
Goymat see Koymat
Goymatdag see Koymatdag, Gory
142 F12 **Göynük** Bolu, NW Turkey
172 N12 **Goyō-san** ▲ Honshū, C Japan
80 K11 **Goz Beïda** Ouaddaï, SE Chad
164 H11 **Gozha Co** ◎ W China
123 J15 **Gozo** Malt. Ghawdex. island N Malta
82 H9 **Göz Regeb** Kassala, NE Sudan
Gozyō see Gojō
85 H25 **Graaff-Reinet** Eastern Cape, S South Africa
Graasten see Gråsten
78 L17 **Grabo** SW Ivory Coast
114 P11 **Grabovica** Serbia, E Yugoslavia
112 I13 **Grabów nad Prosną** Kalisz, C Poland
110 I8 **Grabs** Sankt Gallen, NE Switzerland
114 D12 **Gračac** Zadar-Knin, C Croatia
114 I11 **Gračanica** NE Bosnia and Herzegovina
12 L11 **Gracefield** Québec, SE Canada
101 K19 **Grâce-Hollogne** Liège, E Belgium
25 R8 **Graceville** Florida, SE USA
31 R8 **Graceville** Minnesota, N USA
44 G6 **Gracias** Lempira, W Honduras
Gracias see Lempira
44 L5 **Gracias a Dios** ◈ department E Honduras
45 O6 **Gracias a Dios, Cabo de** headland Honduras/Nicaragua
66 O2 **Graciosa** var. Ilha Graciosa. island Azores, Portugal, NE Atlantic Ocean
66 Q11 **Graciosa** island Islas Canarias, Spain, NE Atlantic Ocean
Graciosa, Ilha see Graciosa
114 I11 **Gradačac** N Bosnia and Herzegovina
61 J15 **Gradaús, Serra dos** ⛰ C Brazil
106 L3 **Gradefes** Castilla-León, N Spain
Gradizhsk see Hradyz'k
108 J7 **Grado** Friuli-Venezia Giulia, NE Italy
106 K2 **Grado** Asturias, N Spain
115 P19 **Gradsko** C FYR Macedonia
39 V11 **Grady** New Mexico, SW USA
114 E8 **Grad Zagreb** ◈ province NC Croatia
31 T12 **Graettinger** Iowa, C USA
xxxix R12 **Grafham Water** ◎ E England, UK
103 M23 **Grafing** Bayern, SE Germany
27 S6 **Graford** Texas, SW USA
191 V5 **Grafton** New South Wales, SE Australia
31 Q3 **Grafton** North Dakota, N USA
23 S3 **Grafton** West Virginia, NE USA
23 T9 **Graham** North Carolina, SE USA
27 R6 **Graham** Texas, SW USA
Graham Bell Island see Greem-Bell, Ostrov
8 I13 **Graham Island** island Queen Charlotte Islands, British Columbia, SW Canada
21 S6 **Graham Lake** ◎ Maine, NE USA
204 H4 **Graham Land** physical region Antarctica
39 N15 **Graham, Mount** ▲ Arizona, SW USA
Grahamstad see Grahamstown
85 I25 **Grahamstown** Afr. Grahamstad. Eastern Cape, S South Africa
xliv J12 **Graiguenamanagh** Kilkenny, SE Ireland
xxxvii X9 **Grain** Kent, SE England, UK
70 C12 **Grain Coast** coastal region S Liberia
174 Mm16 **Grajagan** Jawa, S Indonesia
174 Mm16 **Grajagan, Teluk** bay Jawa, S Indonesia
60 L14 **Grajaú** Maranhão, E Brazil
60 M13 **Grajaú, Rio** ⟿ NE Brazil
112 O8 **Grajewo** Łomża, NE Poland
97 F24 **Gram** Sønderjylland, SW Denmark
105 N13 **Gramat** Lot, S France
24 H5 **Grambling** Louisiana, S USA
117 C14 **Grámmos** ⛰ Albania/Greece
xliii J15 **Grampian Mountains** ⛰ C Scotland, UK
190 L12 **Grampians, The** ⛰ Victoria, SE Australia
xxxvi C16 **Grampound** Cornwall, SW England, UK
100 O9 **Gramsbergen** Overijssel, E Netherlands
xlii A12 **Gramsdale** Western Isles, NW Scotland, UK
115 L21 **Gramsh** var. Gramshi. Elbasan, C Albania
Gramshi see Gramsh
Gran see Hron, Slovakia
Gran see Esztergom, N Hungary
56 F11 **Granada** Meta, C Colombia
44 J10 **Granada** Granada, SW Nicaragua
107 N14 **Granada** Andalucía, S Spain
39 W6 **Granada** Colorado, C USA
44 J11 **Granada** ◈ department SW Nicaragua
107 N14 **Granada** ◈ province Andalucía, S Spain
65 I21 **Gran Antiplanicie Central** plain S Argentina
xliv I7 **Granard** Ir. Gránard. Longford, C Ireland
65 J20 **Gran Bajo** basin S Argentina
65 J16 **Gran Bajo del Gualicho** basin E Argentina
65 I21 **Gran Bajo de San Julián** basin SE Argentina
27 S7 **Granbury** Texas, SW USA
13 P12 **Granby** Québec, SE Canada
29 S8 **Granby** Missouri, C USA
39 S3 **Granby, Lake** ⊠ Colorado, C USA
66 O12 **Gran Canaria** var. Grand Canary. island Islas Canarias, Spain, NE Atlantic Ocean
49 T11 **Gran Chaco** var. Chaco. lowland plain South America
47 R14 **Grand Anse** SW Grenada
Grand-Anse see Portsmouth
46 G1 **Grand Bahama Island** island N Bahamas
Grand Balé see Tui
105 U7 **Grand Ballon** Ger. Ballon de Guebwiller. ▲ NE France
11 T13 **Grand Bank** Newfoundland, Newfoundland and Labrador, SE Canada
66 I7 **Grand Banks of Newfoundland** undersea feature NW Atlantic Ocean
Grand Bassa see Buchanan
79 N17 **Grand-Bassam** var. Bassam. SE Ivory Coast
12 E16 **Grand Bend** Ontario, S Canada
78 L17 **Grand-Bérébi** var. Grand-Béréby. SW Ivory Coast
Grand-Béréby see Grand-Bérébi
47 X11 **Grand-Bourg** Marie-Galante, SE Guadeloupe
46 M6 **Grand Caicos** var. Middle Caicos. island C Turks and Caicos Islands
12 K12 **Grand Calumet, Île du** island Québec, SE Canada
xliv J9 **Grand Canal** Ir. An Chanáil Mhór. canal C Ireland
Grand Canary see Gran Canaria
38 K10 **Grand Canyon** Arizona, SW USA
38 J9 **Grand Canyon** canyon Arizona, SW USA
Grand Canyon State see Arizona
46 D8 **Grand Cayman** island SW Cayman Islands
9 R14 **Grand Centre** Alberta, SW Canada
78 L17 **Grand Cess** SE Liberia
110 D12 **Grand Combin** ▲ S Switzerland
34 K8 **Grand Coulee** Washington, NW USA
34 J8 **Grand Coulee** valley Washington, NW USA
47 X5 **Grand Cul-de-Sac Marin** bay N Guadeloupe
Grand Duchy of Luxembourg see Luxembourg
65 I22 **Grande, Bahía** bay S Argentina
9 N14 **Grande Cache** Alberta, W Canada
105 U12 **Grande Casse** ▲ E France
180 G12 **Grande Comore** var. Njazidja, Great Comoro. island NW Comoros
63 G18 **Grande, Cuchilla** hill range E Uruguay
47 S5 **Grande de Añasco, Río** ⟿ W Puerto Rico
Grande de Chiloé, Isla see Chiloé, Isla de
60 J12 **Grande de Gurupá, Ilha** river island NE Brazil
59 K21 **Grande de Lipez, Río** ⟿ SW Bolivia
47 U6 **Grande de Loíza, Río** ⟿ E Puerto Rico
47 T5 **Grande de Manatí, Río** ⟿ C Puerto Rico
44 L9 **Grande de Matagalpa, Río** ⟿ C Nicaragua
42 K12 **Grande de Santiago, Río** var. Santiago. ⟿ C Mexico
45 O15 **Grande de Térraba, Río** var. Río Térraba. ⟿ SE Costa Rica
10 J9 **Grande Deux, Réservoir la** ⊠ Québec, E Canada
62 O10 **Grande, Ilha** island SE Brazil
9 O13 **Grande Prairie** Alberta, W Canada
76 I8 **Grand Erg Occidental** desert W Algeria
76 L9 **Grand Erg Oriental** desert Algeria/Tunisia
61 J20 **Grande, Rio** ⟿ S Brazil
2 F15 **Grande, Rio** var. Río Bravo, Sp. Río Bravo del Norte, Bravo del Norte. ⟿ Mexico/USA
59 M18 **Grande, Río** ⟿ C Bolivia
13 Y7 **Grande-Rivière** Québec, SE Canada
13 Y6 **Grande Rivière** ⟿ Québec, SE Canada
46 M8 **Grande-Rivière-du-Nord** N Haiti
64 K9 **Grande, Salina** var. Gran Salitral. salt lake C Argentina
13 S7 **Grandes-Bergeronnes** Québec, SE Canada
49 W6 **Grande, Serra** ⛰ W Brazil
42 K4 **Grande, Sierra** ⛰ N Mexico
105 S12 **Grandes Rousses** ⛰ E France
65 K17 **Grandes, Salinas** salt lake E Argentina
47 Y5 **Grande Terre** island E West Indies
13 X5 **Grande-Vallée** Québec, SE Canada
47 Y5 **Grande Vigie, Pointe de la** headland Grande Terre, N Guadeloupe
11 N14 **Grand Falls** New Brunswick, SE Canada
11 T11 **Grand Falls** Newfoundland, Newfoundland and Labrador, SE Canada
26 L9 **Grandfalls** Texas, SW USA
23 P9 **Grandfather Mountain** ▲ North Carolina, SE USA
28 L13 **Grandfield** Oklahoma, C USA
9 N17 **Grand Forks** British Columbia, SW Canada
31 R4 **Grand Forks** North Dakota, N USA
33 O9 **Grand Haven** Michigan, N USA
Grandichi see Hrandzichy
31 P15 **Grand Island** Nebraska, C USA
33 O3 **Grand Island** island Michigan, N USA
24 K10 **Grand Isle** Louisiana, S USA
67 A23 **Grand Jason** island Jason Islands, NW Falkland Islands
39 P5 **Grand Junction** Colorado, C USA
22 F10 **Grand Junction** Tennessee, S USA
12 J9 **Grand-Lac-Victoria** Québec, SE Canada
12 J9 **Grand lac Victoria** ◎ Québec, SE Canada
79 N17 **Grand-Lahou** var. Grand Lahu. S Ivory Coast
Grand Lahu see Grand-Lahou
39 S3 **Grand Lake** Colorado, C USA
11 S11 **Grand Lake** ◎ Newfoundland, Newfoundland and Labrador, E Canada
24 G9 **Grand Lake** ◎ Louisiana, S USA
33 R5 **Grand Lake** ◎ Michigan, N USA
33 Q13 **Grand Lake** ⊠ Ohio, N USA
29 R9 **Grand Lake O' The Cherokees** var. Lake O' The Cherokees. ⊠ Oklahoma, C USA
33 Q9 **Grand Ledge** Michigan, N USA
104 I8 **Grand-Lieu, Lac de** ◎ NW France
21 U6 **Grand Manan Channel** channel Canada/USA
11 O15 **Grand Manan Island** island New Brunswick, SE Canada
31 Y4 **Grand Marais** Minnesota, N USA
13 P10 **Grand-Mère** Québec, SE Canada
39 P5 **Grand Mesa** ⛰ Colorado, C USA
110 C10 **Grand Muveran** ▲ W Switzerland
106 G12 **Grândola** Setúbal, S Portugal
Grand Paradis see Gran Paradiso
197 G4 **Grand Passage** passage N New Caledonia
79 R16 **Grand-Popo** S Benin
31 Z3 **Grand Portage** Minnesota, N USA
27 T6 **Grand Prairie** Texas, SW USA
9 W14 **Grand Rapids** Manitoba, C Canada
33 P9 **Grand Rapids** Michigan, N USA
31 V5 **Grand Rapids** Minnesota, N USA
197 G5 **Grand Récif de Koumac** reef W New Caledonia
197 J8 **Grand Récif Sud** reef S New Caledonia
12 L10 **Grand-Remous** Québec, SE Canada
12 F15 **Grand River** ⟿ Ontario, S Canada
33 P9 **Grand River** ⟿ Michigan, N USA
29 T3 **Grand River** ⟿ Missouri, C USA
30 M7 **Grand River** ⟿ South Dakota, N USA
47 Q11 **Grand' Rivière** N Martinique
34 F11 **Grand Ronde** Oregon, NW USA
34 L11 **Grand Ronde River** ⟿ Oregon/Washington, NW USA
Grand-Saint-Bernard, Col du see Great Saint Bernard Pass
27 V6 **Grand Saline** Texas, SW USA
57 X10 **Grand-Santi** W French Guiana
Grandsee see Grandson
110 B9 **Grandson** prev. Grandsee. Vaud, W Switzerland
180 J16 **Grand Sœur** island Les Sœurs, NE Seychelles
35 S14 **Grand Teton** ▲ Wyoming, C USA
33 P5 **Grand Traverse Bay** lake bay Michigan, N USA
xliii K16 **Grandtully** Perth and Kinross, C Scotland, UK
47 N6 **Grand Turk Island** island SE Turks and Caicos Islands
xxxix O12 **Grand Union Canal** canal SE England, UK
105 S13 **Grand Veymont** ▲ E France
9 W15 **Grandview** Manitoba, S Canada
29 R4 **Grandview** Missouri, C USA
38 I10 **Grand Wash Cliffs** cliff Arizona, SW USA
12 J8 **Granet, Lac** ◎ Québec, SE Canada
97 L14 **Grangärde** Kopparberg, C Sweden
xliv G5 **Grange** Sligo, N Ireland
xxxvi G5 **Grange Hill** Essex, SE England, UK
46 H12 **Grange Hill** W Jamaica
xliii K19 **Grangemouth** Falkirk, C Scotland, UK
xl M11 **Grange-over-Sands** Cumbria, NW England, UK
27 T10 **Granger** Texas, SW USA
34 J10 **Granger** Washington, NW USA
35 T17 **Granger** Wyoming, C USA
Granges see Grenchen
97 L14 **Grängesberg** Kopparberg, C Sweden
xli Y6 **Grangetown** Redcar and Cleveland, N England, UK
35 N11 **Grangeville** Idaho, NW USA
8 K13 **Granisle** British Columbia, SW Canada
32 K15 **Granite City** Illinois, N USA
31 S9 **Granite Falls** Minnesota, N USA
23 Q9 **Granite Falls** North Carolina, SE USA
38 K12 **Granite Mountain** ▲ Arizona, SW USA
35 T12 **Granite Peak** ▲ Montana, NW USA
37 T2 **Granite Peak** ▲ Nevada, W USA
38 J3 **Granite Peak** ▲ Utah, W USA
Granite State see New Hampshire
109 H24 **Granitola, Capo** headland Sicilia, Italy, C Mediterranean Sea
193 H15 **Granity** West Coast, South Island, NZ
Gran Lago see Nicaragua, Lago de
65 J18 **Gran Laguna Salada** ◎ S Argentina
Gran Malvina see West Falkland
97 L18 **Gränna** Jönköping, S Sweden
107 W5 **Granollers** var. Granollérs. Cataluña, NE Spain
108 A7 **Gran Paradiso** Fr. Grand Paradis. ▲ NW Italy
Gran Pilastro see Hochfeiler
Gran Salitral see Grande, Salina
Gran San Bernardo, Passo di see Great Saint Bernard Pass
Gran Santiago see Santiago
109 J14 **Gran Sasso d'Italia** ⛰ C Italy
102 N11 **Gransee** Brandenburg, NE Germany
30 L15 **Grant** Nebraska, C USA
29 R1 **Grant City** Missouri, C USA
xxxix P8 **Grantham** Lincolnshire, E England, UK
67 D24 **Grantham Sound** sound East Falkland, Falkland Islands
204 K13 **Grant Island** island Antarctica
47 Z14 **Grantley Adams** ✈ (Bridgetown) SE Barbados
37 S7 **Grant, Mount** ▲ Nevada, W USA
xlii L13 **Grantown-on-Spey** Highland, N Scotland, UK
37 W8 **Grant Range** ⛰ Nevada, W USA
39 Q11 **Grants** New Mexico, SW USA
32 J4 **Grantsburg** Wisconsin, N USA
xliii O20 **Grantshouse** The Borders, S Scotland, UK
34 F15 **Grants Pass** Oregon, NW USA
38 K3 **Grantsville** Utah, W USA
23 R4 **Grantsville** West Virginia, NE USA
104 I5 **Granville** Manche, N France
9 V12 **Granville Lake** ◎ Manitoba, C Canada
27 V8 **Grapeland** Texas, SW USA
27 T6 **Grapevine** Texas, SW USA
xxxix Q4 **Grasby** Lincolnshire, E England, UK
85 K20 **Graskop** Mpumalanga, NE South Africa
xl M10 **Grasmere** Cumbria, NW England, UK
97 P14 **Gräsö** Uppsala, C Sweden
95 I19 **Gräsö** island C Sweden
105 U15 **Grasse** Alpes-Maritimes, SE France
20 E14 **Grassflat** Pennsylvania, NE USA
xli Q12 **Grassington** North Yorkshire, N England, UK
35 U9 **Grassrange** Montana, NW USA
20 J6 **Grass River** ⟿ New York, NE USA
37 P6 **Grass Valley** California, W USA
191 N14 **Grassy** Tasmania, SE Australia
30 K4 **Grassy Butte** North Dakota, N USA
23 R5 **Grassy Knob** ▲ West Virginia, NE USA
97 G24 **Gråsten** var. Graasten. Sønderjylland, SW Denmark
97 J18 **Grästorp** Skaraborg, S Sweden
xxxvii O11 **Grateley** Hampshire, S England, UK
Gratianopolis see Grenoble
111 V8 **Gratwein** Steiermark, SE Austria
Gratz see Graz
110 I9 **Graubünden** Fr. Grisons, It. Grigioni. ◈ canton SE Switzerland
Graudenz see Grudziądz
105 N15 **Graulhet** Tarn, S France
107 T4 **Graus** Aragón, NE Spain
63 I16 **Gravataí** Rio Grande do Sul, S Brazil
100 L13 **Grave** Noord-Brabant, SE Netherlands
9 T17 **Gravelbourg** Saskatchewan, S Canada
105 N1 **Gravelines** Nord, N France
xxxviii G10 **Gravels** Shropshire, W England, UK
Graven see Grez-Doiceau
12 H13 **Gravenhurst** Ontario, S Canada
35 O10 **Grave Peak** ▲ Idaho, NW USA
104 I11 **Grave, Pointe de** headland W France
xxxvii V9 **Gravesend** Kent, SE England, UK
191 S4 **Gravesend** New South Wales, SE Australia
109 N17 **Gravina di Puglia** Eng. Gravina in Puglia. Puglia, SE Italy
Gravina in Puglia see Gravina di Puglia
105 S8 **Gray** Haute-Saône, E France
25 T4 **Gray** Georgia, SE USA
34 F9 **Grayland** Washington, NW USA
41 N10 **Grayling** Alaska, USA
33 Q6 **Grayling** Michigan, N USA
xli N10 **Grayrigg** Cumbria, NW England, UK
xxxvii V9 **Grays** Essex, SE England, UK
34 F9 **Grays Harbor** inlet Washington, NW USA
22 O5 **Grayson** Kentucky, S USA
39 S4 **Grays Peak** ▲ Colorado, C USA
32 M16 **Grayville** Illinois, N USA
111 V8 **Graz** prev. Gratz. Steiermark, SE Austria
106 L15 **Grazalema** Andalucía, S Spain
115 P15 **Grdelica** Serbia, SE Yugoslavia
46 H1 **Great Abaco** var. Abaco Island. island N Bahamas
Great Admiralty Island see Manus Island
Great Alfold see Great Hungarian Plain
Great Ararat see Büyükağrı Dağı
189 U8 **Great Artesian Basin** lowlands Queensland, C Australia
197 I15 **Great Astrolabe Reef** reef Kadavu, SW Fiji
189 O12 **Great Australian Bight** bight S Australia
xli T9 **Great Ayton** North Yorkshire, N England, UK
xxxvii W8 **Great Baddow** Essex, SE England, UK
66 E11 **Great Bahama Bank** undersea feature E Gulf of Mexico
xxxvii V6 **Great Bardfield** Essex, SE England, UK
xxxvii S5 **Great Barford** Bedfordshire, E England, UK
192 M4 **Great Barrier Island** island N NZ
189 X4 **Great Barrier Reef** reef Queensland, NE Australia
20 L11 **Great Barrington** Massachusetts, NE USA
1 F10 **Great Basin** basin W USA
15 H5 **Great Bear Lake** Fr. Grand Lac de l'Ours. ◎ Northwest Territories, NW Canada
xxxvii O10 **Great Bedwyn** Wiltshire, S England, UK
Great Belt see Storebælt
28 L5 **Great Bend** Kansas, C USA
Great Bermuda see Bermuda
xlii B8 **Great Bernera** island NW Scotland, UK
xliv A13 **Great Blasket Island** Ir. An Blascaod Mór. island SW Ireland
xxxvii R6 **Great Brickhill** Buckinghamshire, C England, UK
Great Britain see Britain
xli T10 **Great Broughton** North Yorkshire, N England, UK
xl E17 **Great Budworth** Cheshire, W England, UK
xli W7 **Great Burdon** Darlington, N England, UK
xxxix S5 **Great Carlton** Lincolnshire, E England, UK
157 Q23 **Great Channel** channel Andaman Sea/Indian Ocean
xxxvii V6 **Great Chesterford** Essex, SE England, UK
xxxix R3 **Great Coates** North East Lincolnshire, E England, UK
177 F10 **Great Coco Island** island SW Burma
Great Crosby see Crosby
23 X7 **Great Dismal Swamp** wetland North Carolina/Virginia, SE USA
35 V16 **Great Divide Basin** basin Wyoming, C USA
189 W7 **Great Dividing Range** ⛰ NE Australia
12 D12 **Great Duck Island** island Ontario, S Canada
xxxvii V7 **Great Dunmow** Essex, SE England, UK
xl M14 **Great Eccleston** Lancashire, NW England, UK
Great Elder Reservoir see Waconda Lake
205 V8 **Greater Antarctica** var. East Antarctica. physical region Antarctica
46 G8 **Greater Antilles** island group West Indies
133 V16 **Greater Sunda Islands** var. Sunda Islands. island group Indonesia
Greater Warsaw see Warszawa
xxxix S12 **Great Eversden** Cambridgeshire, E England, UK
192 I1 **Great Exhibition Bay** inlet North Island, NZ
46 H4 **Great Exuma Island** island C Bahamas
35 R8 **Great Falls** Montana, NW USA
23 R11 **Great Falls** South Carolina, SE USA
86 F9 **Great Fisher Bank** undersea feature C North Sea
xxxix Q11 **Great Gidding** Cambridgeshire, E England, UK
98 **Great Glen** see Mor, Glen
xxxix S12 **Great Gransden** Cambridgeshire, E England, UK
Great Grimsby see Grimsby
46 I4 **Great Guana Cay** island C Bahamas
xli O14 **Great Harwood** Lancashire, NW England, UK
66 I5 **Great Hellefiske Bank** undersea feature N Atlantic Ocean
xxxix V10 **Great Hockham** Norfolk, E England, UK
113 L24 **Great Hungarian Plain** var. Great Alfold, Plain of Hungary, Hung. Alföld. plain SE Europe
46 L7 **Great Inagua** var. Inagua Islands. island S Bahamas
Great Indian Desert see Thar Desert
85 G25 **Great Karoo** var. Great Karroo, High Veld, Afr. Groot Karoo, Hoë Karoo. plateau region S South Africa
Great Karroo see Great Karoo
Great Kei see Groot-Kei
Great Khingan Range see Da Hinggan Ling
12 E11 **Great La Cloche Island** island Ontario, S Canada
191 P16 **Great Lake** ◎ Tasmania, SE Australia
Great Lake see Tônlé Sap
16 O16 **Great Lakes** lakes Ontario, Canada/USA
Great Lakes State see Michigan
xxxix Q3 **Great Limber** Lincolnshire, E England, UK
xxxviii J13 **Great Malvern** Worcestershire, W England, UK
192 M5 **Great Mercury Island** island N NZ
Great Meteor Seamount see Great Meteor Tablemount
66 K10 **Great Meteor Tablemount** var. Great Meteor Seamount. undersea feature E Atlantic Ocean
33 Q14 **Great Miami River** ⟿ Ohio, N USA
xxxvii R8 **Great Missenden** Buckinghamshire, C England, UK
xli O14 **Great Mitton** Lancashire, NW England, UK
157 Q24 **Great Nicobar** island Nicobar Islands, India, NE Indian Ocean
xxxvii Y6 **Great Oakley** Essex, SE England, UK
69 T4 **Great Oasis, The** var. Khârga Oasis. oasis S Egypt
xxxvii T7 **Great Offley** Hertfordshire, SE England, UK
xxxv H4 **Great Ormes Head** headland N Wales, UK
xl M7 **Great Orton** Cumbria, NW England, UK
xxxix T10 **Great Ouse** var. Ouse. ⟿ E England, UK
191 Q17 **Great Oyster Bay** bay Tasmania, SE Australia
46 I13 **Great Pedro Bluff** headland W Jamaica
23 T12 **Great Pee Dee River** ⟿ North Carolina/South Carolina, SE USA
133 W9 **Great Plain of China** plain E China
2 F12 **Great Plains** var. High Plains. plains Canada/USA
39 W6 **Great Plains Reservoirs** ⊠ Colorado, C USA
21 Q13 **Great Point** headland Nantucket Island, Massachusetts, NE USA
xxxix P8 **Great Ponton** Lincolnshire, E England, UK
70 I13 **Great Rift Valley** var. Rift Valley. depression Asia/Africa
xxxvii O7 **Great Rissington** Gloucestershire, C England, UK
83 I23 **Great Ruaha** ⟿ S Tanzania
xxxix V9 **Great Ryburgh** Norfolk, E England, UK
20 K10 **Great Sacandaga Lake** ⊠ New York, NE USA
110 C12 **Great Saint Bernard Pass** Fr. Col du Grand-Saint-Bernard, It. Passo di Gran San Bernardo. pass Italy/Switzerland
46 F1 **Great Sale Cay** island N Bahamas
Great Salt Desert see Kavīr, Dasht-e
38 K1 **Great Salt Lake** salt lake Utah, W USA
38 J3 **Great Salt Lake Desert** plain Utah, W USA
28 M8 **Great Salt Plains Lake** ⊠ Oklahoma, C USA
xxxvii V6 **Great Sampford** Essex, SE England, UK
77 T9 **Great Sand Sea** desert Egypt/Libya
188 L6 **Great Sandy Desert** desert Western Australia
Great Sandy Desert see Ar Rub' al Khālī
Great Sandy Island see Fraser Island
197 I13 **Great Sea Reef** reef Vanua Levu, N Fiji
xxxvii P9 **Great Shefford** Newbury, S England, UK
xxxix T13 **Great Shelford** Cambridgeshire, E England, UK

◆ Country ● Country Capital ◇ Dependent Territory ○ Dependent Territory Capital ◈ Administrative Region ✈ International Airport ▲ Mountain ⛰ Mountain Range Volcano ⟿ River ◎ Lake ⊠ Reservoir

GREAT SITKIN ISLAND – GUINÉE-BISSAU

40 H17 Great Sitkin Island island Aleutian Islands, Alaska, USA
15 I8 Great Slave Lake Fr. Grand Lac des Esclaves. ◎ Northwest Territories, NW Canada
23 O10 Great Smoky Mountains ⛰ North Carolina/Tennessee, SE USA
8 L11 Great Snow Mountain ▲ British Columbia, W Canada
xxxvii N9 Great Somerford Wiltshire, S England, UK
66 A12 Great Sound bay Bermuda, NW Atlantic Ocean
xxxix R12 Great Staughton Cambridgeshire, E England, UK
xxxvii Y12 Greatstone-on-Sea Kent, SE England, UK
xxxvii P7 Great Tew Oxfordshire, C England, UK
xxxvi F12 Great Torrington Devon, SW England, UK
188 M10 Great Victoria Desert desert South Australia/Western Australia
xxxvii X9 Great Wakering Essex, SE England, UK
204 H2 Great Wall Chinese research station South Shetland Islands, Antarctica
xxxvii W7 Great Waltham Essex, SE England, UK
21 T7 Great Wass Island island Maine, NE USA
xxxvii N11 Great Wishford Wiltshire, S England, UK
xxxviii I12 Great Witley Worcestershire, W England, UK
xxxix Z9 Great Yarmouth var. Yarmouth. Norfolk, E England, UK
xxxvii V6 Great Yeldham Essex, SE England, UK
145 S1 Great Zab Ar. Az Zāb al Kabīr, Kurd. Zē-i Bādīnān, Turk. Büyükzap Suyu. ≈ Iraq/Turkey
97 I17 Grebbestad Göteborg och Bohus, S Sweden
Grebenka see Hrebinka
44 M13 Grecia Alajuela, C Costa Rica
63 E18 Greco Río Negro, W Uruguay
Greco, Cape see Gkréko, Akrotíri
106 L8 Gredos, Sierra de ⛰ W Spain
20 F9 Greece New York, NE USA
117 E17 Greece off. Hellenic Republic, Gk. Ellás; anc. Hellas. ◆ republic SE Europe
Greece Central see Stereá Ellás
Greece West see Dytikí Ellás
39 T3 Greeley Colorado, C USA
31 P14 Greeley Nebraska, C USA
126 Hh1 Greem-Bell, Ostrov Eng. Graham Bell Island. island Zemlya Frantsa-Iosifa, N Russian Federation
32 M6 Green Bay Wisconsin, N USA
33 N6 Green Bay lake bay Michigan/Wisconsin, N USA
23 S5 Greenbrier River ≈ West Virginia, NE USA
31 S2 Greenbush Minnesota, N USA
191 R12 Green Cape headland New South Wales, SE Australia
xliv J2 Greencastle Donegal, N Ireland
xliv L6 Greencastle Newry and Mourne, S Northern Ireland, UK
33 O14 Greencastle Indiana, N USA
20 F16 Greencastle Pennsylvania, NE USA
29 T2 Green City Missouri, C USA
23 O9 Greeneville Tennessee, S USA
37 O11 Greenfield California, W USA
33 P14 Greenfield Indiana, N USA
31 U15 Greenfield Iowa, C USA
20 M11 Greenfield Massachusetts, NE USA
29 S7 Greenfield Missouri, C USA
33 S14 Greenfield Ohio, N USA
22 G8 Greenfield Tennessee, S USA
32 M9 Greenfield Wisconsin, N USA
xxxvi A7 Greenford Ealing, SE England, UK
29 T9 Green Forest Arkansas, C USA
xli O5 Greenhaugh Northumberland, N England, UK
xli N6 Greenhead Northumberland, N England, UK
39 T7 Greenhorn Mountain ▲ Colorado, C USA
Green Island see Lü Tao
xliv M4 Greenisland Carrickfergus, E Northern Ireland, UK
195 R10 Green Islands var. Nissan Islands. island group NE PNG
9 S14 Green Lake Saskatchewan, C Canada
32 L8 Green Lake ◎ Wisconsin, N USA
207 O14 Greenland Dan. Grønland, Inuit Kalaallit Nunaat. ◇ Danish external territory NE North America
86 D4 Greenland island NE North America
207 R13 Greenland Plain undersea feature N Greenland Sea
94 J1 Greenland Sea sea Arctic Ocean
xliii O21 Greenlaw The Borders, S Scotland, UK
xliii K18 Greenloaning Perth and Kinross, C Scotland, UK
xliii K22 Green Lowther ▲ C Scotland, UK
39 R4 Green Mountain Reservoir ⊡ Colorado, C USA
20 M8 Green Mountains ⛰ Vermont, NE USA
Green Mountain State see Vermont
xliii H19 Greenock Inverclyde, W Scotland, UK
xl M11 Greenodd Cumbria, NW England, UK
xliv L13 Greenore Point headland SE Ireland
41 T5 Greenough, Mount ▲ Alaska, USA
194 E10 Green River Sandaun, NW PNG
39 N5 Green River Utah, W USA
35 U17 Green River Wyoming, C USA
18 I7 Green River ≈ W USA
32 K11 Green River ≈ Illinois, N USA
22 J7 Green River ≈ Kentucky, S USA
30 K5 Green River ≈ North Dakota, N USA
39 N6 Green River ≈ Utah, W USA
35 T16 Green River ≈ Wyoming, C USA
22 L7 Green River Lake ⊡ Kentucky, S USA
25 O5 Greensboro Alabama, S USA
25 U3 Greensboro Georgia, SE USA
23 T9 Greensboro North Carolina, SE USA
33 P14 Greensburg Indiana, N USA
28 K6 Greensburg Kansas, C USA
22 L7 Greensburg Kentucky, S USA
20 C15 Greensburg Pennsylvania, NE USA
39 O13 Greens Peak ▲ Arizona, SW USA
23 V12 Green Swamp wetland North Carolina, SE USA
23 O4 Greenup Kentucky, S USA
38 M16 Green Valley Arizona, SW USA
78 K17 Greenville var. Sino, Sinoe. SE Liberia
25 P6 Greenville Alabama, S USA
25 T8 Greenville Florida, SE USA
25 S4 Greenville Georgia, SE USA
32 L15 Greenville Illinois, N USA
22 I7 Greenville Kentucky, S USA
21 R4 Greenville Maine, NE USA
33 P9 Greenville Michigan, N USA
24 J4 Greenville Mississippi, S USA
23 W9 Greenville North Carolina, SE USA
33 Q13 Greenville Ohio, N USA
21 O12 Greenville Rhode Island, NE USA
23 P11 Greenville South Carolina, SE USA
27 U6 Greenville Texas, SW USA
xxxiv L16 Greenwich ◐ London borough SE England, UK
xxxvii U9 Greenwich hist. Grenawic. Greenwich, SE England, UK
33 T12 Greenwich Ohio, N USA
29 S11 Greenwood Arkansas, C USA
33 O14 Greenwood Indiana, N USA
24 K4 Greenwood Mississippi, S USA
23 P12 Greenwood South Carolina, SE USA
23 Q12 Greenwood, Lake ⊡ South Carolina, SE USA
23 P11 Greer South Carolina, SE USA
29 V10 Greers Ferry Lake ⊡ Arkansas, C USA
29 S13 Greeson, Lake ⊡ Arkansas, C USA
xxxix P9 Greetham Rutland, C England, UK
31 O12 Gregory South Dakota, N USA
190 J3 Gregory, Lake salt lake South Australia
188 J9 Gregory Lake ◎ W Australia
189 V5 Gregory Range ⛰ Queensland, E Australia
Greifenberg/Greifenberg in Pommern see Gryfice
Greifenhagen see Gryfino
102 O8 Greifswald Mecklenburg-Vorpommern, NE Germany
102 O8 Greifswalder Bodden bay NE Germany
111 U4 Grein Oberösterreich, N Austria
103 M17 Greiz Thüringen, C Germany
Gremicha/Gremiha see Gremikha
128 M4 Gremikha var. Gremicha, Gremiha. Murmanskaya Oblast', NW Russian Federation
129 V14 Gremyachinsk Permskaya Oblast', NW Russian Federation
97 H21 Grenå var. Grenaa. Århus, C Denmark
Grenaa see Grenå
24 L3 Grenada Mississippi, S USA
47 W15 Grenada ◆ commonwealth republic SE West Indies
49 S4 Grenada island Grenada
49 R4 Grenada Basin undersea feature W Atlantic Ocean
24 L3 Grenada Lake ⊡ Mississippi, S USA
47 Y14 Grenadines, The island group Grenada/St Vincent and the Grenadines
Grenawic see Greenwich
110 D7 Grenchen Fr. Granges. Solothurn, NW Switzerland
191 Q9 Grenfell New South Wales, SE Australia
9 V16 Grenfell Saskatchewan, S Canada
94 J1 Grenivík Nordhurland Eystra, N Iceland
105 S12 Grenoble anc. Cularo, Gratianopolis. Isère, E France
30 J2 Grenora North Dakota, N USA
xli S16 Grenoside Sheffield, N England, UK
94 N8 Grense-Jakobselv Finnmark, N Norway
47 S14 Grenville E Grenada
xxxv K5 Gresford Wrexham, NE Wales, UK
34 G11 Gresham Oregon, NW USA
Gresk see Hresk
108 B7 Gressoney-St-Jean Valle d'Aosta, NW Italy
xli Q9 Greta Bridge Durham, N England, UK
xliii M24 Gretna Dumfries and Galloway, SW Scotland, UK
24 K9 Gretna Louisiana, S USA
23 T7 Gretna Virginia, NE USA
xliii M24 Gretna Green Dumfries and Galloway, SW Scotland, UK
xxxix P10 Gretton Northamptonshire, C England, UK
100 F13 Grevelingen inlet S North Sea
102 F13 Greven Nordrhein-Westfalen, NW Germany
117 D15 Grevená Dytikí Makedonía, N Greece
103 D16 Grevenbroich Nordrhein-Westfalen, W Germany
101 N24 Grevenmacher Grevenmacher, E Luxembourg
101 M24 Grevenmacher ◐ district E Luxembourg
102 K9 Grevesmühlen Mecklenburg-Vorpommern, N Germany
193 H16 Grey ≈ South Island, NZ
xliv M5 Greyabbey Ards, E Northern Ireland, UK
35 V12 Greybull Wyoming, C USA
35 U13 Greybull River ≈ Wyoming, C USA
67 A24 Grey Channel sound Falkland Islands
Greyerzer See see Gruyère, Lac de la
11 T10 Grey Islands island group Newfoundland and Labrador, E Canada
20 L10 Greylock, Mount ▲ Massachusetts, NE USA
193 G17 Greymouth West Coast, South Island, NZ
189 U10 Grey Range ⛰ New South Wales/Queensland, E Australia
xl M8 Greystoke Cumbria, NW England, UK
xliv L10 Greystones Ir. Na Clocha Liatha. Wicklow, E Ireland
193 M14 Greytown Wellington, North Island, NZ
85 K23 Greytown KwaZulu/Natal, E South Africa
Greytown see San Juan del Norte
101 H19 Grez-Doiceau Dut. Graven. Walloon Brabant, C Belgium
117 J19 Griá, Ákra headland Ándros, Kykládes, Greece, Aegean Sea
131 N8 Gribanovskiy Voronezhskaya Oblast', W Russian Federation
80 I13 Gribingui ≈ N Central African Republic
37 O6 Gridley California, W USA
85 G23 Griekwastad Northern Cape, C South Africa
25 S4 Griffin Georgia, SE USA
191 O9 Griffith New South Wales, SE Australia
12 F13 Griffith Island island Ontario, S Canada
23 W10 Grifton North Carolina, SE USA
Grigioni see Graubünden
121 H14 Grigiškes Trakai, SE Lithuania
119 N10 Grigoriopol C Moldova
153 X7 Grigor'yevka Issyk-Kul'skaya Oblast', E Kyrgyzstan
200 Oo9 Grijalva Ridge undersea feature E Pacific Ocean
43 U15 Grijalva, Río var. Tabasco. ≈ Guatemala/Mexico
100 N5 Grijpskerk Groningen, NE Netherlands
85 C22 Grillenthal Karas, SW Namibia
81 J15 Grimari Ouaka, C Central African Republic
Grimaylov see Hrymayliv
101 G18 Grimbergen Vlaams Brabant, C Belgium
191 N15 Grim, Cape headland Tasmania, SE Australia
xlii A11 Griminish Point headland NW Scotland, UK
xlii I2 Grimister Shetland Islands, NE Scotland, UK
102 N8 Grimmen Mecklenburg-Vorpommern, NE Germany
xxxix S5 Grimoldby Lincolnshire, E England, UK
xxxix R3 Grimsby prev. Great Grimsby. North East Lincolnshire, E England, UK
12 G16 Grimsby Ontario, S Canada
94 J1 Grímsey var. Grimsey. island N Iceland
9 O12 Grimshaw Alberta, W Canada
97 F18 Grimstad Aust-Agder, S Norway
xxxix U8 Grimston Norfolk, E England, UK
94 H4 Grindavík Reykjanes, W Iceland
110 F9 Grindelwald Bern, S Switzerland
xli O13 Grindleton Lancashire, NW England, UK
97 F23 Grindsted Ribe, W Denmark
31 W14 Grinnell Iowa, C USA
111 U10 Grintavec ▲ N Slovenia
190 H1 Griselda, Lake salt lake South Australia
Grisons see Graubünden
97 P14 Grisslehamn Stockholm, C Sweden
31 T15 Griswold Iowa, C USA
xlii N4 Gritley Orkney Islands, N Scotland, UK
xl L11 Grizebeck Cumbria, NW England, UK
104 M1 Griz Nez, Cap headland N France
114 P13 Grljan Serbia, E Yugoslavia
114 E11 Grmeč ⛰ NW Bosnia and Herzegovina
101 H16 Grobbendonk Antwerpen, N Belgium
Grobin see Grobiņa
120 C10 Grobiņa Ger. Grobin. Liepāja, W Latvia
85 K20 Groblersdal Mpumalanga, NE South Africa
85 G23 Groblershoop Northern Cape, W South Africa
Gródek Jagielloński see Horodok
111 Q6 Grödig Salzburg, W Austria
113 H15 Grodków Opole, SW Poland
Grodnenskaya Oblast' see Hrodzyenskaya Voblasts'
Grodno see Hrodna
112 L12 Grodzisk Mazowiecki Warszawa, C Poland
112 F12 Grodzisk Wielkopolski Poznań, W Poland
Grodzyanka see Hradzyanka
100 O12 Groenlo Gelderland, E Netherlands
85 E22 Groenrivier Karas, SE Namibia
27 U8 Groesbeck Texas, SW USA
100 L13 Groesbeek Gelderland, SE Netherlands
xliii F21 Grogport Argyll and Bute, W Scotland, UK
104 G7 Groix, Îles de island group NW France
112 M12 Grójec Radom, C Poland
67 K15 Gröll Seamount undersea feature C Atlantic Ocean
102 E13 Gronau var. Gronau in Westfalen. Nordrhein-Westfalen, NW Germany
Gronau in Westfalen see Gronau
95 F15 Grong Nord-Trøndelag, C Norway
97 N22 Grönhögen Kalmar, S Sweden
100 N5 Groningen Groningen, NE Netherlands
57 W9 Groningen Saramacca, N Surinam
100 N5 Groningen ◐ province NE Netherlands
Grønland see Greenland
110 H11 Grono Graubünden, S Switzerland
97 M20 Grönskåra Kalmar, S Sweden
27 O2 Groom Texas, SW USA
37 W9 Groom Lake ◎ Nevada, W USA
85 H25 Groot ≈ S South Africa
189 S2 Groote Eylandt island Northern Territory, N Australia
100 M6 Grootegast Groningen, NE Netherlands
85 D17 Grootfontein Otjozondjupa, N Namibia
85 E22 Groot Karasberge ⛰ S Namibia
Groot Karoo see Great Karoo
85 J25 Groot-Kei Eng. Great Kei. ≈ S South Africa
xlii C10 Grosebay Western Isles, NW Scotland, UK
47 T10 Gros Islet N Saint Lucia
16 L8 Gros-Morne NW Haiti
11 S11 Gros Morne ▲ Newfoundland, Newfoundland and Labrador, E Canada
105 R9 Grosne ≈ C France
47 S12 Gros Piton ▲ SW Saint Lucia
Grossa, Isola see Dugi Otok
Grossbetschkerek see Zrenjanin
Grosse Isper see Grosse Ysper
Grosse Kokel see Târnava Mare
103 M21 Grosse Laaber var. Grosse Laber. ≈ SE Germany
Grosse Laber see Grosse Laaber
Grosse Morava see Velika Morava
103 O15 Grossenhain Sachsen, E Germany
111 Y4 Grossenzersdorf Niederösterreich, NE Austria
103 O21 Grosser Arber ▲ SE Germany
103 K17 Grosser Beerberg ▲ C Germany
103 G18 Grosser Feldberg ▲ W Germany
111 O8 Grosser Löffler It. Monte Lovello. ▲ Austria/Italy
111 N8 Grosser Möseler var. Mesule. ▲ Austria/Italy
102 J8 Grosser Plöner See ◎ N Germany
103 O21 Grosser Rachel ▲ SE Germany
Grosser Sund see Suur Väin
13 V6 Grosses-Roches Québec, SE Canada
111 P8 Grosses Weiesbachhorn var. Wiesbachhorn. ▲ W Austria
108 F13 Grosseto Toscana, C Italy
103 M22 Grosse Vils ≈ SE Germany
111 U4 Grosse Ysper var. Grosse Isper. ≈ N Austria
103 G19 Gross-Gerau Hessen, W Germany
111 U3 Gross Gerungs Niederösterreich, N Austria
111 P8 Grossglockner ▲ W Austria
Grosskanizsa see Nagykanizsa
Gross-Karol see Carei
Grosskikinda see Kikinda
111 W9 Grossklein Steiermark, SE Austria
Grosskoppe see Velká Deštná
Grossmeseritsch see Velké Meziříčí
Grossmichel see Michalovce
103 H19 Grossostheim Bayern, C Germany
111 X7 Grosspetersdorf Burgenland, SE Austria
111 T5 Grossraming Oberösterreich, C Austria
103 P14 Grossräschen Brandenburg, E Germany
Grossrauschenbach see Revúca
Gross-Sankt-Johannis see Suure-Jaani
Gross-Schlatten see Abrud
111 V2 Gross-Siegharts Niederösterreich, N Austria
Gross-Skaisgirren see Bol'shakovo
Gross-Steffelsdorf see Rimavská Sobota
Gross Strehlitz see Strzelce Opolskie
111 O8 Grossvenediger ▲ W Austria
Grosswardein see Oradea
Gross Wartenberg see Syców
111 U11 Grosuplje C Slovenia
101 H17 Grote Nete ≈ N Belgium
96 E10 Grotli Oppland, S Norway
21 N13 Groton Connecticut, NE USA
31 P8 Groton South Dakota, N USA
109 P18 Grottaglie Puglia, SE Italy
109 L17 Grottaminarda Campania, S Italy
108 K13 Grottammare Marche, C Italy
23 U5 Grottoes Virginia, NE USA
Grou see Grouw
11 N10 Groulx, Monts ⛰ Québec, E Canada
12 E7 Groundhog ≈ Ontario, S Canada
38 J1 Grouse Creek Utah, W USA
38 J1 Grouse Creek Mountains ⛰ Utah, W USA
100 L6 Grouw Fris. Grou. Friesland, N Netherlands
xxxvii Y10 Grove Kent, SE England, UK
29 R8 Grove Oklahoma, C USA
33 S13 Grove City Ohio, N USA
20 B13 Grove City Pennsylvania, NE USA
25 O6 Grove Hill Alabama, S USA
xxxvi F9 Grove Park Lewisham, SE England, UK
35 S15 Grover Wyoming, C USA
37 P13 Grover City California, W USA
27 Y11 Groves Texas, SW USA
21 O7 Groveton New Hampshire, NE USA
27 W9 Groveton Texas, SW USA
38 J15 Growler Mountains ⛰ Arizona, SW USA
Grozdovo see Bratya Daskalovi
xxxvii W16 Groznez Point headland Jersey, Channel Islands
131 P16 Groznyy Chechenskaya Respublika, SW Russian Federation
Grubeshov see Hrubieszów
114 G9 Grubišno Polje Bjelovar-Bilogora, NE Croatia
Grudovo see Sredets
112 J9 Grudziądz Ger. Graudenz. Toruń, N Poland
xlii I9 Gruids Highland, NW Scotland, UK
xlii F10 Gruinard Bay bay NW Scotland, UK
27 R17 Grulla var. La Grulla. Texas, SW USA
42 K14 Grullo Jalisco, SW Mexico
69 Y10 Grumeti ≈ N Tanzania
97 K16 Grums Värmland, C Sweden
111 S5 Grünau im Almtal Oberösterreich, N Austria
103 H17 Grünberg Hessen, W Germany
Grünberg/Grünberg in Schlesien see Zielona Góra
Grünberg in Schlesien see Zielona Góra
94 H3 Grundarfjördhur Vestfirdhir, W Iceland
xxxix X13 Grundisburgh Suffolk, E England, UK
23 P7 Grundy Virginia, NE USA
31 W13 Grundy Center Iowa, C USA
Grüneberg see Zielona Góra
xlii H4 Gruting Shetland Islands, NE Scotland, UK
27 N1 Gruver Texas, SW USA
110 C9 Gruyère, Lac de la Ger. Greyerzer See. ◎ SW Switzerland
110 C9 Gruyères Fribourg, W Switzerland
120 E11 Gruzdiai Šiauliai, N Lithuania
Gruzinskaya SSR/Gruziya see Georgia
152 C10 Gryada Akkyr Turkm. Akgyr Erezi. hill range NW Turkmenistan
130 L7 Gryazi Lipetskaya Oblast', W Russian Federation
128 M14 Gryazovets Vologodskaya Oblast', NW Russian Federation
113 M17 Grybów Nowy Sącz, SE Poland
96 M13 Grycksbo Kopparberg, C Sweden
112 E8 Gryfice Ger. Greifenberg, Greifenberg in Pommern. Szczecin, NW Poland
112 D9 Gryfino Ger. Greifenhagen. Szczecin, NW Poland
94 H9 Gryllefjord Troms, N Norway
97 L15 Grythyttan Örebro, C Sweden
110 D10 Gstaad Bern, W Switzerland
45 P14 Guabito Bocas del Toro, NW Panama
46 G7 Guacanayabo, Golfo de gulf S Cuba
42 I7 Guachochi Chihuahua, N Mexico
106 J11 Guadajira ≈ SW Spain
106 M13 Guadajoz ≈ S Spain
42 L13 Guadalajara Jalisco, C Mexico
107 O8 Guadalajara Ar. Wad Al-Hajarah; anc. Arriaca. Castilla-La Mancha, C Spain
107 O7 Guadalajara ◐ province Castilla-La Mancha, C Spain
106 K12 Guadalcanal Andalucía, S Spain
195 W16 Guadalcanal off. Guadalcanal Province. ◐ province C Solomon Islands
195 W16 Guadalcanal island C Solomon Islands
107 O12 Guadalén ≈ S Spain
107 R13 Guadalentín ≈ SE Spain
106 K15 Guadalete ≈ SW Spain
107 O13 Guadalimar ≈ S Spain
107 P12 Guadalmena ≈ S Spain
106 L11 Guadalmez ≈ W Spain
107 S7 Guadalope ≈ E Spain
106 K13 Guadalquivir ≈ W Spain
106 J14 Guadalquivir, Marismas del var. Las Marismas. wetland SW Spain
42 M11 Guadalupe Zacatecas, C Mexico
59 E16 Guadalupe Ica, W Peru
106 L10 Guadalupe Extremadura, W Spain
38 L14 Guadalupe Arizona, SW USA
37 P13 Guadalupe California, W USA
199 Mm5 Guadalupe island NW Mexico
Guadalupe see Canelones
42 J3 Guadalupe Bravos Chihuahua, N Mexico
42 A4 Guadalupe, Isla island NW Mexico
39 U15 Guadalupe Mountains ⛰ New Mexico/Texas, SW USA
26 J8 Guadalupe Peak ▲ Texas, SW USA
27 R11 Guadalupe River ≈ SW USA
106 K10 Guadalupe, Sierra de ⛰ W Spain
42 K9 Guadalupe Victoria Durango, C Mexico
42 I8 Guadalupe y Calvo Chihuahua, N Mexico
107 N7 Guadarrama Madrid, C Spain
107 N7 Guadarrama ≈ C Spain
106 M7 Guadarrama, Puerto de pass C Spain
107 N9 Guadarrama, Sierra de ⛰ C Spain
107 Q9 Guadazaón ≈ C Spain
47 X10 Guadeloupe ◇ French overseas department E West Indies
49 S3 Guadeloupe island group E West Indies
47 W10 Guadeloupe Passage passage E Caribbean Sea
106 H13 Guadiana ≈ Portugal/Spain
107 O13 Guadiana Menor ≈ S Spain
107 Q8 Guadiela ≈ C Spain
107 O14 Guadix Andalucía, S Spain
Guad-i-Zirreh see Gowd-e Zereh, Dasht-e
200 O13 Guafo Fracture Zone tectonic feature SE Pacific Ocean
65 F18 Guafo, Isla island S Chile
44 I6 Guaimaca Francisco Morazán, C Honduras
56 J12 Guainía off. Comisaría del Guainía. ◐ province E Colombia
56 K12 Guainía, Río ≈ Colombia/Venezuela
57 O9 Guaiquinima, Cerro elevation SE Venezuela
64 O7 Guairá off. Departamento del Guairá. ◐ department S Paraguay
62 G10 Guaíra Paraná, S Brazil
62 L7 Guaíra São Paulo, S Brazil
Guaire see Gorey
65 F18 Guaiteca, Isla island S Chile
46 G6 Guajaba, Cayo headland C Cuba
61 D16 Guajará-Mirim Rondônia, W Brazil
Guajira see La Guajira
56 H3 Guajira, Península de la peninsula N Colombia
44 J6 Gualaco Olancho, C Honduras
36 L7 Gualala California, W USA
44 E5 Gualán Zacapa, C Guatemala
63 C19 Gualeguay Entre Ríos, E Argentina
63 D18 Gualeguaychú Entre Ríos, E Argentina
63 C18 Gualeguay, Río ≈ E Argentina
65 K16 Gualicho, Salina del salt lake E Argentina
196 B15 Guam ◇ US unincorporated territory W Pacific Ocean
65 F19 Guamblin, Isla island Archipiélago de los Chonos, S Chile
63 A22 Guaminí Buenos Aires, E Argentina
42 H8 Guamúchil Sinaloa, C Mexico
56 H4 Guana var. Misión de Guana. Zulia, NW Venezuela
46 C4 Guanabacoa La Habana, W Cuba
44 K13 Guanacaste off. Provincia de Guanacaste. ◐ province NW Costa Rica
44 K12 Guanacaste, Cordillera de ⛰ NW Costa Rica
42 J8 Guanaceví Durango, C Mexico
46 A5 Guanahacabibes, Golfo de gulf W Cuba
44 K4 Guanaja, Isla de island Islas de la Bahía, N Honduras
46 C4 Guanajay La Habana, W Cuba
43 N12 Guanajuato Guanajuato, C Mexico
42 M12 Guanajuato ◐ state C Mexico
56 J6 Guanare Portuguesa, N Venezuela
56 K7 Guanare, Río ≈ W Venezuela
56 J6 Guanarito Portuguesa, NW Venezuela
166 M3 Guancen Shan ⛰ C China
64 I9 Guandacol La Rioja, W Argentina
46 A5 Guane Pinar del Río, W Cuba
167 N14 Guangdong var. Guangdong Sheng, Kuang-tung, Kwangtung, Yue. ◐ province S China
Guangdong Sheng see Guangdong
Guanghua see Laohekou
Guangju see Kwangju
166 I13 Guangnan Yunnan, SW China
Guangxi see Guangxi Zhuangzu Zizhiqu
166 K14 Guangxi Zhuangzu Zizhiqu var. Guangxi, Gui, Kuang-hsi, Kwangsi, Eng. Kwangsi Chuang Autonomous Region. ◐ autonomous region S China
166 J8 Guangyuan var. Kuang-yuan, Kwangyuan. Sichuan, C China
167 N14 Guangzhou var. Kuang-chou, Kwangchow, Eng. Canton. Guangdong, S China
61 N19 Guanhães Minas Gerais, SE Brazil
166 I12 Guanling var. Guanling Bouyeizu Miaozu Zizhixian. Guizhou, S China
Guanling Bouyeizu Miaozu Zizhixian see Guanling
57 N5 Guanta Anzoátegui, NE Venezuela
46 J8 Guantánamo Guantánamo, SE Cuba
166 H9 Guanxian var. Guan Xian. Sichuan, C China
167 Q6 Guanyun Jiangsu, E China
56 C12 Guapí Cauca, SW Colombia
45 N13 Guápiles Limón, NE Costa Rica
63 I15 Guaporé Rio Grande do Sul, S Brazil
49 S8 Guaporé, Rio var. Río Iténez. ≈ Bolivia/Brazil see also Iténez, Río
58 B7 Guaranda Bolívar, C Ecuador
62 H11 Guaraniaçu Paraná, S Brazil
61 O20 Guarapari Espírito Santo, SE Brazil
62 I12 Guarapuava Paraná, S Brazil
62 J10 Guararapes São Paulo, S Brazil
107 S4 Guara, Sierra de ⛰ NE Spain
62 N10 Guaratinguetá São Paulo, S Brazil
106 I7 Guarda Guarda, N Portugal
106 I7 Guarda ◐ district N Portugal
Guardak see Govurdak
106 M3 Guardo Castilla-León, N Spain
106 K11 Guareña Extremadura, W Spain
62 J11 Guaricana, Pico ▲ S Brazil
56 L6 Guárico off. Estado Guárico. ◐ state N Venezuela
46 J7 Guarico, Punta headland E Cuba
56 L7 Guárico, Río ≈ C Venezuela
62 M10 Guarujá São Paulo, SE Brazil
63 L22 Guarulhos ✕ (São Paulo) São Paulo, S Brazil
45 R17 Guarumal Veraguas, S Panama
Guasapa see Guasopa
42 H8 Guasave Sinaloa, C Mexico
56 I8 Guasdualito Apure, C Venezuela
57 Q7 Guasipati Bolívar, E Venezuela
195 Q15 Guasopa var. Guasapa. Woodlark Island, SE PNG
108 F9 Guastalla Emilia-Romagna, C Italy
44 D6 Guastatoya var. El Progreso. El Progreso, C Guatemala
44 D5 Guatemala off. Republic of Guatemala. ◆ republic Central America
44 A2 Guatemala off. Departamento de Guatemala. ◐ department S Guatemala
200 O7 Guatemala Basin undersea feature E Pacific Ocean
Guatemala City see Guatemala, Ciudad de
47 V14 Guatuaro Point headland Trinidad, Trinidad and Tobago
194 G14 Guavi ≈ SW PNG
56 G13 Guaviare off. Comisaría Guaviare. ◐ province S Colombia
56 J11 Guaviare, Río ≈ E Colombia
63 E15 Guaviraví Corrientes, NE Argentina
56 G12 Guayabero, Río ≈ SW Colombia
47 U6 Guayama E Puerto Rico
44 J7 Guayambre, Río ≈ S Honduras
Guayanas, Macizo de las see Guiana Highlands
47 V6 Guayanés, Punta headland E Puerto Rico
44 J6 Guayape, Río ≈ C Honduras
58 B7 Guayaquil var. Santiago de Guayaquil. Guayas, SW Ecuador
Guayaquil see Simon Bolivar
58 A8 Guayaquil, Golfo de var. Gulf of Guayaquil. gulf SW Ecuador
Guayaquil, Gulf of see Guayaquil, Golfo de
58 A7 Guayas ◐ province W Ecuador
64 N7 Guaycurú, Río ≈ NE Argentina
42 F6 Guaymas Sonora, NW Mexico
47 U5 Guaynabo E Puerto Rico
82 H12 Guba NW Ethiopia
152 H8 Gubadag Turkm. Tel'man; prev. Tel'mansk. Dashkhovuzskiy Velayat, N Turkmenistan
129 T1 Guba Dolgaya Nenetskiy Avtonomnyy Okrug, NW Russian Federation
129 V13 Gubakha Permskaya Oblast', NW Russian Federation
108 I12 Gubbio Umbria, C Italy
102 Q13 Guben var. Wilhelm-Pieck-Stadt. Brandenburg, E Germany
Guben see Gubin
112 D12 Gubin Ger. Guben. Zielona Góra, W Poland
130 K8 Gubkin Belgorodskaya Oblast', W Russian Federation
Gudara see Ghŭdara
107 S8 Gúdar, Sierra de ⛰ E Spain
143 P8 Gudaut'a NW Georgia
96 G12 Gudbrandsdalen valley S Norway
97 G21 Gudenå var. Gudenaa. ≈ C Denmark
Gudenaa see Gudenå
131 P16 Gudermes Chechenskaya Respublika, SW Russian Federation
161 J18 Gūdūr Andhra Pradesh, E India
152 B13 Gudurolum Balkanskiy Velayat, W Turkmenistan
96 D13 Gudvangen Sogn og Fjordane, S Norway
105 U7 Guebwiller Haut-Rhin, NE France
Guéckédou see Guékédou
12 K8 Guéguen, Lac ◎ Québec, SE Canada
78 J15 Guékédou var. Guéckédou. Guinée-Forestière, S Guinea
43 R16 Guelatao Oaxaca, SE Mexico
Guelders see Gelderland
80 G11 Guélengdeng Mayo-Kébbi, W Chad
76 L5 Guelma var. Gâlma. NE Algeria
76 D8 Guelmime var. Goulimime. SW Morocco
12 G15 Guelph Ontario, S Canada
104 I7 Guémené-Penfao Loire-Atlantique, NW France
104 I7 Guer Morbihan, NW France
80 I11 Guéra off. Préfecture du Guéra. ◐ prefecture S Chad
104 H8 Guérande Loire-Atlantique, NW France
80 K9 Guéréda Biltine, E Chad
105 N10 Guéret Creuse, C France
Guernica/Guernica y Lumo see Gernika-Lumo
xxxiv H16 Guernsey off. Bailiwick of Guernsey. ◇ UK crown dependency NW Europe
xxxvii V15 Guernsey island Channel Islands, NW Europe
35 Z15 Guernsey Wyoming, C USA
78 J10 Guérou Assaba, S Mauritania
27 R16 Guerra Texas, SW USA
43 O15 Guerrero ◐ state S Mexico
42 D6 Guerrero Negro Baja California Sur, NW Mexico
xxxvii W12 Guestling Green East Sussex, SE England, UK
105 P9 Gueugnon Saône-et-Loire, C France
78 M17 Guéyo S Ivory Coast
109 L15 Guglionesi Molise, C Italy
196 K5 Guguan island C Northern Mariana Islands
Guhrau see Góra
Gui see Guangxi Zhuangzu Zizhiqu
Guiana see French Guiana
49 V4 Guiana Basin undersea feature W Atlantic Ocean
50 G6 Guiana Highlands var. Macizo de las Guayanas. ⛰ N South America
Guiba see Juba
104 I7 Guichen Ille-et-Vilaine, NW France
63 E18 Guichón Paysandú, W Uruguay
79 U12 Guidan-Roumji Maradi, S Niger
Guidder see Guider
165 T10 Guide Qinghai, C China
80 F12 Guider var. Guidder. Nord, N Cameroon
78 I11 Guidimaka ◐ region S Mauritania
79 W12 Guidimouni Zinder, S Niger
78 G10 Guier, Lac de var. Lac de Guiers. ◎ N Senegal
166 L14 Guigang prev. Guixian, Gui Xian. Guangxi Zhuangzu Zizhiqu, S China
78 L16 Guiglo W Ivory Coast
56 L5 Güigüe Carabobo, N Venezuela
85 M20 Guijá Gaza, S Mozambique
44 E7 Güija, Lago de ◎ El Salvador/Guatemala
106 K8 Guijuelo Castilla-León, N Spain
Guilan see Gīlān
xxxvii S11 Guildford Surrey, SE England, UK
21 R5 Guildford Maine, NE USA
21 O7 Guildhall Vermont, NE USA
xliii L17 Guildtown Perth and Kinross, C Scotland, UK
105 R13 Guilherand Ardèche, E France
166 L13 Guilin var. Kuei-lin, Kweilin. Guangxi Zhuangzu Zizhiqu, S China
10 J6 Guillaume-Delisle, Lac ◎ Québec, NE Canada
105 U13 Guillestre Hautes-Alpes, SE France
xxxv K8 Guilsfield Powys, C Wales, UK
106 H6 Guimarães var. Guimaráes. Braga, N Portugal
60 D11 Guimarães Rosas, Pico ▲ NW Brazil
25 N3 Guin Alabama, S USA
Güina see Wina
78 I14 Guinea off. Republic of Guinea, var. Guinée; prev. French Guinea, People's Revolutionary Republic of Guinea. ◆ republic W Africa
66 N13 Guinea Basin undersea feature E Atlantic Ocean
78 E12 Guinea-Bissau off. Republic of Guinea-Bissau, Fr. Guinée-Bissau, Port. Guiné-Bissau; prev. Portuguese Guinea. ◆ republic W Africa
68 K7 Guinea Fracture Zone tectonic feature E Atlantic Ocean
66 O13 Guinea, Gulf of Fr. Golfe de Guinée. gulf E Atlantic Ocean
Guiné-Bissau see Guinea-Bissau
Guinée see Guinea
Guinée-Bissau see Guinea-Bissau

◆ Country ● Country Capital ◇ Dependent Territory ○ Dependent Territory Capital ◐ Administrative Region ✕ International Airport ▲ Mountain ⛰ Mountain Range Volcano ≈ River ◎ Lake ⊡ Reservoir

GUINÉE-FORESTIÈRE – HAMILTON

78 K15 **Guinée-Forestière** ◐ *state* SE Guinea
Guinée, Golfe de *see* Guinea, Gulf of
78 H13 **Guinée-Maritime** ◐ *state* W Guinea
46 C4 **Güines** La Habana, W Cuba
104 G5 **Guingamp** Côtes d'Armor, NW France
107 P3 **Guipúzcoa** *Basq.* Gipuzkoa. ◐ *province* País Vasco, N Spain
46 C5 **Güira de Melena** La Habana, W Cuba
76 G8 **Guir, Hamada du** *desert* Algeria/Morocco
57 P5 **Güiria** Sucre, NE Venezuela
xli T9 **Guisborough** Redcar and Cleveland, N England, UK
xli R13 **Guiseley** Leeds, N England, UK
166 L14 **Gui Shui** ≈ S China
xxxix W8 **Guist** Norfolk, E England, UK
106 H2 **Guitiriz** Galicia, NW Spain
79 N17 **Guitri** S Ivory Coast
179 R13 **Guiuan** Samar, C Philippines
Gui Xian/Guixian *see* Guigang
166 J12 **Guiyang** *var.* Kuei-Yang, Kuei-yang, Kueyang, Kweiyang; *prev.* Kweichu. Guizhou, S China
166 J12 **Guizhou** *var.* Guizhou Sheng, Kuei-chou, Kweichow, Qian. ◐ *province* S China
Guizhou Sheng *see* Guizhou
104 J13 **Gujan-Mestras** Gironde, SW France
160 B10 **Gujarāt** *var.* Gujerat. ◐ *state* W India
155 V6 **Gūjar Khān** Punjab, E Pakistan
Gujerat *see* Gujarāt
155 V7 **Gujrānwāla** Punjab, NE Pakistan
155 V7 **Gujrāt** Punjab, E Pakistan
165 U9 **Gulang** Gansu, C China
191 R6 **Gulargambone** New South Wales, SE Australia
161 G15 **Gulbarga** Karnātaka, C India
120 J8 **Gulbene** *Ger.* Alt-Schwanenburg. Gulbene, NE Latvia
153 U10 **Gul'cha** *Kir.* Gülchö. Oshskaya Oblast', SW Kyrgyzstan
Gülchö *see* Gul'cha
181 T10 **Gulden Draak Seamount** *undersea feature* E Indian Ocean
142 J16 **Gülek Boğazı** *var.* Cilician Gates. *pass* S Turkey
194 I14 **Gulf** ◐ *province* S PNG
25 O9 **Gulf Breeze** Florida, SE USA
25 V13 **Gulfport** Florida, SE USA
24 M9 **Gulfport** Mississippi, S USA
25 O9 **Gulf Shores** Alabama, S USA
147 T5 **Gulf, The** *var.* Persian Gulf, *Ar.* Khalīj al 'Arabī, *Per.* Khalīj-e Fars. *gulf* SW Asia
191 R7 **Gulgong** New South Wales, SE Australia
166 I11 **Gulin** Sichuan, C China
176 V12 **Gulir** Pulau Kasiui, E Indonesia
Gulistan *see* Guliston
153 P10 **Guliston** *Rus.* Gulistan. Sirdaryo Wiloyati, E Uzbekistan
169 T6 **Guliya Shan** ▲ NE China
Gulja *see* Yining
41 S11 **Gulkana** Alaska, USA
xliii N19 **Gullane** East Lothian, SE Scotland, UK
9 S17 **Gull Lake** Saskatchewan, S Canada
33 P10 **Gull Lake** ◎ Michigan, N USA
31 T6 **Gull Lake** ◎ Minnesota, N USA
97 L16 **Gullspång** Skaraborg, S Sweden
158 H5 **Gulmarg** Jammu and Kashmir, NW India
Gulpaigan *see* Golpāyegān
101 L18 **Gulpen** Limburg, SE Netherlands
151 S13 **Gul'shad** *Kaz.* Gulshat. Zhezkazgan, E Kazakhstan
Gulshat *see* Gul'shad
83 F17 **Gulu** N Uganda
116 K10 **Gŭlŭbovo** Khaskovska Oblast, C Bulgaria
116 I7 **Gulyantsi** Loveshka Oblast, NW Bulgaria
Gulyaypole *see* Hulyaypole
Guma *see* Pishan
81 K16 **Gumba** Equateur, NW Zaire
Gumbinnen *see* Gusev
83 H24 **Gumbiro** Ruvuma, S Tanzania
152 B11 **Gumdag** *prev.* Kum-Dag. Balkanskiy Velayat, W Turkmenistan
79 W12 **Gumel** Jigawa, N Nigeria
107 N5 **Gumiel de Hizán** Castilla-León, N Spain
194 I12 **Gumine** *var.* Gumire. Chimbu, C PNG
Gumire *see* Gumine
159 P16 **Gumla** Bihār, N India
Gumma *see* Gunma
103 F16 **Gummersbach** Nordrhein-Westfalen, W Germany
79 T13 **Gummi** Sokoto, NW Nigeria
Gumpolds *see* Humpolec
159 N13 **Gumti** *var.* Gomati. ≈ N India
Gümülcine/Gümüljina *see* Komotiní
Gümüşane *see* Gümüşhane
143 O12 **Gümüşhane** *var.* Gümüşane, Gumushkhane. Gümüşhane, NE Turkey
143 O12 **Gümüşhane** *var.* Gümüşane, Gumushkhane. ◐ *province* NE Turkey
Gumushkhane *see* Gümüşhane
176 W13 **Gumzai** Pulau Kola, E Indonesia
160 H9 **Guna** Madhya Pradesh, C India
Gunabad *see* Gonābād
Gunbad-i-Qawus *see* Gonbad-e Kāvūs
191 O9 **Gunbar** New South Wales, SE Australia
xli U14 **Gunby** East Riding of Yorkshire, N England, UK
191 O9 **Gun Creek** *seasonal river* New South Wales, SE Australia
191 Q10 **Gundagai** New South Wales, SE Australia
81 K17 **Gundji** Equateur, N Zaire
161 G20 **Gundlupet** Karnātaka, W India
142 G16 **Gündoğmuş** Antalya, S Turkey
143 O14 **Güney Doğu Toroslar** ▲▲ SE Turkey
81 J21 **Gungu** Bandundu, SW Zaire
131 P17 **Gunib** Respublika Dagestan, SW Russian Federation
114 J11 **Gunja** Vukovar-Srijem, E Croatia
33 P9 **Gun Lake** ◎ Michigan, N USA
171 Jj15 **Gunma** *off.* Gunma-ken, *var.* Gumma. ◐ *prefecture* Honshū, S Japan
207 P15 **Gunnbjørn Fjeld** *var.* Gunnbjörns Bjerge. ▲ C Greenland
191 S6 **Gunnedah** New South Wales, SE Australia
xxxvi A8 **Gunnersbury** Hounslow, SE England, UK
181 Y15 **Gunner's Quoin** *var.* Coin de Mire. *island* N Mauritius
xxxvi F15 **Gunnislake** Cornwall, SW England, UK
39 R6 **Gunnison** Colorado, C USA
38 L5 **Gunnison** Utah, W USA
39 P5 **Gunnison River** ≈ Colorado, C USA
xlii I4 **Gunnista** Shetland Islands, NE Scotland, UK
23 X2 **Gunpowder River** ≈ Maryland, NE USA
Güns *see* Kőszeg
Gunsan *see* Kunsan
111 S4 **Gunskirchen** Oberösterreich, N Austria
Gunt *see* Ghund
161 H17 **Guntakal** Andhra Pradesh, C India
25 Q2 **Guntersville** Alabama, S USA
25 Q2 **Guntersville Lake** ⊠ Alabama, S USA
111 X4 **Guntramsdorf** Niederösterreich, E Austria
161 J16 **Guntūr** *var.* Guntur. Andhra Pradesh, SE India
173 F7 **Gunungsitoli** Pulau Nias, W Indonesia
161 M14 **Gunupur** Orissa, E India
xxxvi B17 **Gunwalloe** Cornwall, SW England, UK
103 J23 **Günz** ≈ S Germany
Gunzan *see* Kunsan
103 J22 **Günzburg** Bayern, S Germany
103 K21 **Gunzenhausen** Bayern, S Germany
167 P7 **Guoyang** Anhui, E China
118 G11 **Gurahonț** *Hung.* Honctő. Arad, W Romania
Gurahumora *see* Gura Humorului
118 K9 **Gura Humorului** *Ger.* Gurahumora. Suceava, NE Romania
164 K4 **Gurbantünggüt Shamo** *desert* W China
158 H7 **Gurdāspur** Punjab, N India
29 T13 **Gurdon** Arkansas, C USA
Gurdzhaani *see* Gurjaani
Gurgan *see* Gorgān
158 I10 **Gurgaon** Haryāna, N India
61 M15 **Gurguéia, Rio** ≈ NE Brazil
57 Q7 **Guri, Embalse de** ⊠ E Venezuela
143 V10 **Gurjaani** *Rus.* Gurdzhaani. E Georgia
111 T8 **Gurk** Kärnten, S Austria
111 T9 **Gurk** *Slvn.* Krka. ≈ S Austria
Gurkfeld *see* Krško
116 K9 **Gurkovo** *prev.* Kolupchii. Khaskovska Oblast, C Bulgaria
111 S9 **Gurktaler Alpen** ▲▲ S Austria
152 H8 **Gurlan** *Rus.* Gurlen. Khorazm Wiloyati, W Uzbekistan
Gurlen *see* Gurlan
85 M16 **Guro** Manica, C Mozambique
142 M14 **Gürün** Sivas, C Turkey
61 K16 **Gurupi** Tocantins, C Brazil
60 L12 **Gurupi, Rio** ≈ NE Brazil
158 E14 **Guru Sikhar** ▲ NW India
Gur'yev/Gur'yevskaya Oblast' *see* Atyrau
79 U13 **Gusau** Sokoto, N Nigeria
130 C3 **Gusev** *Ger.* Gumbinnen. Kaliningradskaya Oblast', W Russian Federation
152 J17 **Gushgy** *prev.* Kushka. Maryyskiy Velayat, S Turkmenistan
Gushiago *see* Gushiegu
79 Q14 **Gushiegu** *var.* Gushiago. NE Ghana
172 P15 **Gushikawa** Okinawa, Okinawa, SW Japan
115 L16 **Gusinje** Montenegro, SW Yugoslavia
126 Jj16 **Gusinoozersk** Respublika Buryatiya, S Russian Federation
130 M4 **Gus'-Khrustal'nyy** Vladimirskaya Oblast', W Russian Federation
109 B19 **Guspini** Sardegna, Italy, C Mediterranean Sea
111 X8 **Güssing** Burgenland, SE Austria
111 V6 **Gusswerk** Steiermark, E Austria
94 O2 **Gustav Adolf Land** *physical region* NE Svalbard
205 X5 **Gustav Bull Mountains** ▲▲ Antarctica
41 W13 **Gustavus** Alaska, USA
94 O1 **Gustav V Land** *physical region* NE Svalbard
37 P9 **Gustine** California, W USA
27 R8 **Gustine** Texas, SW USA
102 M9 **Güstrow** Mecklenburg-Vorpommern, NE Germany
97 N18 **Gusum** Östergötland, S Sweden
Guta/Gúta *see* Kolárovo
Gutenstein *see* Ravne na Koroškem
xlii I1 **Gutcher** Shetland Islands, NE Scotland, UK
103 G14 **Gütersloh** Nordrhein-Westfalen, W Germany
29 N10 **Guthrie** Oklahoma, C USA
27 P5 **Guthrie** Texas, SW USA
31 U14 **Guthrie Center** Iowa, C USA
43 Q13 **Gutiérrez Zamora** Veracruz-Llave, E Mexico
Gutta *see* Kolárovo
31 Y12 **Guttenberg** Iowa, C USA
Guttentag *see* Dobrodzień
Guttstadt *see* Dobre Miasto
168 G8 **Guulin** Govĭ-Altay, C Mongolia
159 V12 **Guwāhāti** *prev.* Gauhāti. Assam, NE India
145 R3 **Guwēr** *var.* Al Kuwayr, Al Quwayr, Quwair. N Iraq
Guwlumayak *see* Kuuli-Mayak
57 R9 **Guyana** *off.* Cooperative Republic of Guyana; *prev.* British Guiana. ◆ *republic* N South America
23 P5 **Guyandotte River** ≈ West Virginia, NE USA
Guyane *see* French Guiana
xxxix S9 **Guyhirn** Cambridgeshire, E England, UK
Guyi *see* Sanjiang
28 H8 **Guymon** Oklahoma, C USA
152 K12 **Guynuk** Lebapskiy Velayat, NE Turkmenistan
23 O9 **Guyot, Mount** ▲ North Carolina/Tennessee, SE USA
191 U5 **Guyra** New South Wales, SE Australia
165 W10 **Guyuan** Ningxia, N China
Guzar *see* Ghuzor
124 N3 **Güzelyurt** *Gk.* Mórfou, Morphou. W Cyprus
124 N2 **Güzelyurt Körfezi** *var.* Morfou Bay, Morphou Bay, *Gk.* Kólpos Mórfou. *bay* W Cyprus
42 I3 **Guzmán** Chihuahua, N Mexico
121 B14 **Gvardeysk** *Ger.* Tapaiu. Kaliningradskaya Oblast', W Russian Federation
Gvardeyskoye *see* Hvardiys'ke
191 R5 **Gwabegar** New South Wales, SE Australia
154 J16 **Gwādar** *var.* Gwadur. Baluchistān, SW Pakistan
154 J16 **Gwādar East Bay** *bay* SW Pakistan
154 J16 **Gwādar West Bay** *bay* SW Pakistan
Gwadur *see* Gwādar
85 J17 **Gwai** Matabeleland North, W Zimbabwe
xxxv F4 **Gwalchmai** Isle of Anglesey, NW Wales, UK
160 I7 **Gwalior** Madhya Pradesh, C India
85 J18 **Gwanda** Matabeleland South, SW Zimbabwe
81 N15 **Gwane** Haut-Zaïre, N Zaire
85 I17 **Gwayi** ≈ W Zimbabwe
112 G8 **Gwda** *var.* Głda, *Ger.* Küddow. ≈ NW Poland
xliv F3 **Gweebarra Bay** *Ir.* Béal an Bheara. *inlet* W Ireland
xliv G2 **Gweedore** *Ir.* Gaoth Dobhair. Donegal, NW Ireland
Gwelo *see* Gweru
99 K21 **Gwent** *cultural region* S Wales, UK
85 K17 **Gweru** *prev.* Gwelo. Midlands, C Zimbabwe
31 Q7 **Gwinner** North Dakota, N USA
79 Y13 **Gwoza** Borno, NE Nigeria
Gwy *see* Wye
xxxv J6 **Gwyddelwern** Denbighshire, N Wales, UK
191 R4 **Gwydir River** ≈ New South Wales, SE Australia
xxxv G7 **Gwynedd** ◐ *unitary authority* NW Wales, UK
xxxv H5 **Gwytherin** Conwy, N Wales, UK
165 O16 **Gyaca** Xizang Zizhiqu, W China
Gya'gya *see* Saga
117 M22 **Gyalí** *var.* Yialí. *island* Dodekánisos, Greece, Aegean Sea
Gyandzha *see* Gäncä
164 M16 **Gyangzê** Xizang Zizhiqu, W China
164 L14 **Gyaring Co** ◎ W China
165 Q12 **Gyaring Hu** ◎ C China
117 I20 **Gyáros** *var.* Yioúra. *island* Kykládes, Greece, Aegean Sea
126 Hh7 **Gyda** Yamalo-Nenetskiy Avtonomnyy Okrug, N Russian Federation
126 H7 **Gydanskiy Poluostrov** *Eng.* Gyda Peninsula. *peninsula* N Russian Federation
Gyda Peninsula *see* Gydanskiy Poluostrov
Gyéres *see* Câmpia Turzii
Gyergyószentmiklós *see* Gheorgheni
Gyergyótölgyes *see* Tulgheș
Gyertyámos *see* Cărpiniș
Gyeva *see* Detva
Gyigang *see* Zayü
97 I23 **Gyldenløves Høy** *hill range* C Denmark
189 Z10 **Gympie** Queensland, E Australia
177 Ff7 **Gyobingauk** Pegu, SW Burma
113 M23 **Gyomaendrőd** Békés, SE Hungary
Gyömbér *see* Ďumbier
113 L22 **Gyöngyös** Heves, NE Hungary
113 H22 **Győr** *Ger.* Raab; *Lat.* Arrabona. Győr-Moson-Sopron, NW Hungary
113 G22 **Győr-Moson-Sopron** *off.* Győr-Moson-Sopron Megye. ◐ *county* NW Hungary
9 X15 **Gypsumville** Manitoba, S Canada
10 M4 **Gyrfalcon Islands** *island group* Northwest Territories, NE Canada
97 N14 **Gysinge** Gävleborg, C Sweden
117 F22 **Gýtheio** *var.* Githio; *prev.* Yíthion. Pelopónnisos, S Greece
152 L13 **Gyuichbirleshik** Lebapskiy Velayat, E Turkmenistan
113 N24 **Gyula** *Rom.* Jula. Békés, SE Hungary
Gyulafehérvár *see* Alba Iulia
Gyulovo *see* Roza
143 T11 **Gyumri** *var.* Giumri, *Rus.* Kumayri; *prev.* Aleksandropol', Leninakan. W Armenia
152 D13 **Gyunuzyndag, Gora** ▲ W Turkmenistan
152 D12 **Gyzylarbat** *prev.* Kizyl-Arvat. Balkanskiy Velayat, W Turkmenistan
Gyzylbaydak *see* Krasnoye Znamya
Gyzyletrek *see* Kizyl-Atrek
Gyzylgaya *see* Kizyl-Kaya
Gyzylsu *see* Kizyl-Su

H

159 T12 **Ha** W Bhutan
Haabai *see* Ha'apai Group
101 H17 **Haacht** Vlaams Brabant, C Belgium
111 T4 **Haag** Niederösterreich, NE Austria
204 L8 **Haag Nunataks** ▲▲ Antarctica
94 N2 **Haakon VII Land** *physical region* NW Svalbard
100 O11 **Haaksbergen** Overijssel, E Netherlands
101 E14 **Haamstede** Zeeland, SW Netherlands
200 Ss13 **Ha'ano** *island* Ha'apai Group, C Tonga
200 Ss13 **Ha'apai Group** *var.* Haabai. *island group* C Tonga
95 L15 **Haapajärvi** Oulu, C Finland
95 L17 **Haapamäki** Keski-Suomi, C Finland
95 L15 **Haapavesi** Oulu, C Finland
203 N7 **Haapiti** Moorea, W French Polynesia
120 F4 **Haapsalu** *Ger.* Hapsal. Läänemaa, W Estonia
Ha'Arava *see* 'Arabah, Wādī al
Haarby *see* Hårby
100 H10 **Haarlem** *prev.* Harlem. Noord-Holland, W Netherlands
193 D19 **Haast** West Coast, South Island, NZ
193 C20 **Haast** ≈ South Island, NZ
193 D20 **Haast Pass** *pass* South Island, NZ
200 R16 **Ha'atua** 'Eau, E Tonga
155 P15 **Hab** ≈ SW Pakistan
147 W7 **Haba** *var.* Al Haba. Dubayy, NE UAE
164 K2 **Habahe** *var.* Kaba. Xinjiang Uygur Zizhiqu, NW China
147 U13 **Ḩabarūt** *var.* Habrut. SW Oman
83 J18 **Habaswein** North Eastern, NE Kenya
101 L24 **Habay-la-Neuve** Luxembourg, SE Belgium
145 S8 **Ḩabbānīyah, Buḩayrat** ◎ C Iraq
Habelschwerdt *see* Bystrzyca Kłodzka
159 V14 **Habiganj** Chittagong, NE Bangladesh
169 Q12 **Habirag** Nei Mongol Zizhiqu, N China
97 L19 **Habo** Skaraborg, S Sweden
127 P16 **Habomai Islands** *island group* Kuril'skiye Ostrova, SE Russian Federation
172 P3 **Haboro** Hokkaidō, NE Japan
159 S16 **Habra** West Bengal, NE India
xxxix Q3 **Habrough** North East Lincolnshire, E England, UK
Habrut *see* Ḩabarūt
149 P17 **Ḩabshān** Abū Ẓaby, C UAE
56 E14 **Hacha** Putumayo, S Colombia
172 Ss13 **Hachijō** Tōkyō, Hachijō-jima, SE Japan
172 Ss13 **Hachijō-jima** *var.* Hatizyô Zima. *island* Izu-shotō, SE Japan
171 I14 **Hachiman** Gifu, Honshū, SW Japan
171 M9 **Hachimori** Akita, Honshū, C Japan
172 N10 **Hachinohe** Aomori, Honshū, C Japan
171 Jj16 **Hachiōji** *var.* Hatiôzi. Tōkyō, Honshū, S Japan
95 G17 **Hackås** Jämtland, C Sweden
20 K14 **Hackensack** New Jersey, NE USA
xxxvii Z10 **Hacklinge** Kent, SE England, UK
xli V10 **Hackness** North Yorkshire, N England, UK
xxxvi E6 **Hackney** Hackney, SE England, UK
xxxiv L16 **Hackney** ◐ *London borough* SE England, UK
Hadama *see* Nazrēt
171 J16 **Hadano** Kanagawa, Honshū, S Japan
147 W13 **Ḩadbaram** S Oman
145 U13 **Ḩaddānīyah** *well* S Iraq
xxxvii R8 **Haddenham** Buckinghamshire, C England, UK
xxxix T11 **Haddenham** Cambridgeshire, E England, UK
xliii N19 **Haddington** East Lothian, SE Scotland, UK
xxxix Y10 **Haddiscoe** Norfolk, E England, UK
147 Z8 **Ḩadd, Ra's al** *headland* NE Oman
Haded *see* Xadeed
79 W12 **Hadejia** Jigawa, N Nigeria
79 W12 **Hadejia** ≈ N Nigeria
144 F9 **Hadera** Haifa, C Israel
Hadersleben *see* Haderslev
97 G24 **Haderslev** *Ger.* Hadersleben. Sønderjylland, SW Denmark
157 J21 **Hadhdhunmathi Atoll** *var.* Haddummati Atoll, Laamu Atoll. *atoll* S Maldives
Hadhramaut *see* Ḩaḑramawt
147 W17 **Hadīboh** Suquṭrā, SE Yemen
164 K9 **Hadilik** Xinjiang Uygur Zizhiqu, W China
142 H16 **Hadım** Konya, S Turkey
146 K7 **Hadīyah** Al Madīnah, W Saudi Arabia
xxxvii W9 **Hadleigh** Essex, SE England, UK
xxxix W13 **Hadleigh** Suffolk, E England, UK
xxxviii I9 **Hadley** Shropshire, W England, UK
15 J1 **Hadley Bay** *bay* Victoria Island, Northwest Territories, N Canada
xxxviii H9 **Hadnall** Shropshire, W England, UK
178 Jj6 **Ha Đông** *var.* Hadong. Ha Tây, N Vietnam
147 R15 **Ḩaḑramawt** *Eng.* Hadhramaut. ▲▲ S Yemen
Hadria *see* Adria
Hadrianopolis *see* Edirne
xli O6 **Hadrian's Wall** *ancient wall* N England, UK
Hadria Picena *see* Apricena
97 G22 **Hadsten** Århus, C Denmark
97 G21 **Hadsund** Nordjylland, N Denmark
119 S4 **Hadyach** *Rus.* Gadyach. Poltavs'ka Oblast', NE Ukraine
114 I13 **Hadžići** SE Bosnia and Herzegovina
xxxviii B17 **Hadzor** Worcestershire, W England, UK
169 W14 **Haeju** S North Korea
Haerbin/Haerhpin/Ha-erh-pin *see* Harbin
147 P5 **Ḩafar al Bāţin** Ash Sharqīyah, N Saudi Arabia
9 T15 **Hafford** Saskatchewan, S Canada
142 M13 **Hafik** Sivas, N Turkey
155 V8 **Hāfizābād** Punjab, E Pakistan
94 H4 **Hafnarfjördhur** Reykjanes, W Iceland
Hafnia *see* København, Denmark
Hafnia *see* Denmark
Hafren *see* Severn
Hafun *see* Xaafuun
Hafun, Ras *see* Xaafuun, Raas
82 G10 **Hag 'Abdullah** Sinnar, E Sudan
83 K18 **Hagadera** North Eastern, E Kenya
144 G8 **HaGalil** *Eng.* Galilee. ▲▲ N Israel
12 G10 **Hagar** Ontario, S Canada
161 G18 **Hagari** *var.* Vedāvati. ≈ W India
102 M13 **Hagelberg** *hill* NE Germany
41 N14 **Hagemeister Island** *island* Alaska, USA
103 F15 **Hagen** Nordrhein-Westfalen, W Germany
102 K10 **Hagenow** Mecklenburg-Vorpommern, N Germany
8 K15 **Hagensborg** British Columbia, SW Canada
82 I13 **Hāgere Hiywet** *var.* Agere Hiywet, Ambo. C Ethiopia
35 O15 **Hagerman** Idaho, NW USA
39 U14 **Hagerman** New Mexico, SW USA
23 V2 **Hagerstown** Maryland, NE USA
12 G16 **Hagersville** Ontario, S Canada
104 J15 **Hagetmau** Landes, SW France
97 K14 **Hagfors** Värmland, C Sweden
xl M6 **Haggbeck** Cumbria, NW England, UK
95 G16 **Häggenås** Jämtland, C Sweden
170 Dd12 **Hagi** Yamaguchi, Honshū, SW Japan
178 J5 **Ha Giang** Ha Giang, N Vietnam
Hagios Evstrátios *see* Ágios Efstrátios
xxxviii B15 **Hagley** Worcestershire, W England, UK
HaGolan *see* Golan Heights
105 T4 **Hagondange** Moselle, NE France
xliv D10 **Hag's Head** *Ir.* Ceann Caillí. *headland* W Ireland
104 I3 **Hague, Cap de la** *headland* N France
105 V5 **Haguenau** Bas-Rhin, NE France
172 T16 **Hahajima-rettō** *island group* SE Japan
13 R8 **Há Há , Lac** ◎ Québec, SE Canada
180 H13 **Hahaya** ✕ (Moroni) Grande Comore, NW Comoros
24 K9 **Hahnville** Louisiana, S USA
85 E22 **Haib** Karas, S Namibia
Haibak *see* Āybak
155 N15 **Haibo** ≈ SW Pakistan
169 U12 **Haicheng** Liaoning, NE China
Haida *see* Nový Bor
Haidarabad *see* Hyderābād
Haidenschaft *see* Ajdovščina
178 Jj6 **Hai Dương** Hai Hưng, N Vietnam
144 F9 **Haifa** ◐ *district* NW Israel
Haifa *see* Hefa
Haifa, Bay of *see* Hefa, Mifraz
167 P14 **Haifeng** Guangdong, S China
Haifong *see* Hai Phong
167 P3 **Hai He** ≈ E China
Haikang *see* Leizhou
166 L17 **Haikou** *var.* Hai-k'ou, Hoihow, *Fr.* Hoï-Hao. Hainan, S China
146 M6 **Ḩā'il** Ḩā'il, NW Saudi Arabia
147 N5 **Ḩā'il** *off.* Minţaqah Ḩā'il. ◐ *province* N Saudi Arabia
Hai-la-erh *see* Hailar
169 S6 **Hailar** *var.* Hai-la-erh; *prev.* Hulun. Nei Mongol Zizhiqu, N China
169 S6 **Hailar He** ≈ NE China
35 P14 **Hailey** Idaho, NW USA
12 H9 **Haileybury** Ontario, S Canada
169 X9 **Hailin** Heilongjiang, NE China
Ḩā'il, Minţaqah *see* Ḩā'il
Hailong *see* Meihekou
xxxvii V13 **Hailsham** East Sussex, SE England, UK
95 K14 **Hailuoto** *Swe.* Karlö. *island* W Finland
Haima *see* Haymā'
Haimen *see* Jiaojiang
166 M17 **Hainan** *var.* Hainan Sheng, Qiong. ◐ *province* S China
166 K17 **Hainan Dao** *island* S China
Hainan Sheng *see* Hainan
Hainan Strait *see* Qiongzhou Haixia
Hainasch *see* Ainaži
Hainau *see* Chojnów
101 E20 **Hainaut** ◐ *province* SW Belgium
Hainburg *see* Hainburg an der Donau
111 Z4 **Hainburg an der Donau** *var.* Hainburg. Niederösterreich, NE Austria
41 W12 **Haines** Alaska, USA
34 L12 **Haines** Oregon, NW USA
25 W12 **Haines City** Florida, SE USA
8 H8 **Haines Junction** Yukon Territory, W Canada
111 W4 **Hainfeld** Niederösterreich, NE Austria
103 N16 **Hainichen** Sachsen, E Germany
178 K6 **Hai Phong** *var.* Haifong, Haiphong. N Vietnam
167 S12 **Haitan Dao** *island* SE China
46 K8 **Haiti** *off.* Republic of Haiti. ◆ *republic* C West Indies
37 T11 **Haiwee Reservoir** ⊠ California, W USA
82 I7 **Haiya** Red Sea, NE Sudan
165 T10 **Haiyan** Qinghai, W China
166 M13 **Haiyang Shan** ▲▲ S China
165 V10 **Haiyuan** Ningxia, N China
Hajda *see* Nový Bor
113 M22 **Hajdú-Bihar** *off.* Hajdú-Bihar Megye. ◐ *county* E Hungary
113 N22 **Hajdúböszörmény** Hajdú-Bihar, E Hungary
113 N22 **Hajdúhadház** Hajdú-Bihar, E Hungary
113 N21 **Hajdúnánás** Hajdú-Bihar, E Hungary
113 N22 **Hajdúszoboszló** Hajdú-Bihar, E Hungary
148 I3 **Ḩājī Ebrāhīm, Kūh-e** ▲ Iran/Iraq
171 Kk11 **Hajiki-zaki** *headland* Sado, C Japan
Hajîne *see* Abū Ḩardān
159 P13 **Hājīpur** Bihār, N India
147 N14 **Ḩajjah** W Yemen
145 U11 **Hajjama** S Iraq
149 R12 **Ḩājjīābād** Hormozgān, C Iran
145 U14 **Ḩājj, Thaqb al** *well* S Iraq
115 L16 **Hajla** ▲▲ SW Yugoslavia
112 P10 **Hajnówka** *Ger.* Hermhausen. Białystok, E Poland
177 Ff4 **Haka** Chin State, W Burma
Hakapehi *see* Punaauia
Hakâri *see* Hakkâri
143 T16 **Hakkâri** *var.* Çölemerik, Hakâri. Hakkâri, SE Turkey
143 T16 **Hakkâri** *var.* Hakkari. ◐ *province* SE Turkey
94 J12 **Hakkas** Norrbotten, N Sweden
171 Gg16 **Hakken-zan** ▲ Honshū, SW Japan
172 N9 **Hakkōda-san** ▲ Honshū, C Japan
172 Pp3 **Hako-dake** ▲ Hokkaidō, NE Japan
172 N7 **Hakodate** Hokkaidō, NE Japan
171 Ii12 **Hakui** Ishikawa, Honshū, SW Japan
202 B16 **Hakupu** SE Niue
171 I14 **Haku-san** ▲ Honshū, SW Japan
Hal *see* Halle
155 Q15 **Hāla** Sind, SE Pakistan
144 J3 **Ḩalab** *Eng.* Aleppo, *Fr.* Alep; *anc.* Beroea. Ḩalab, NW Syria
144 J3 **Ḩalab** *off.* Muḩāfaẓat Ḩalab, *var.* Aleppo, Halab. ◐ *governorate* NW Syria
144 J3 **Ḩalab** ✕ Ḩalab, NW Syria
147 O8 **Ḩalabān** *var.* Halibān. Ar Riyāḑ, C Saudi Arabia
145 V4 **Ḩalabja** NE Iraq
202 A16 **Halagigie Point** *headland* W Niue
77 Z11 **Halaib** SE Egypt
202 G12 **Halalo** Île Uvea, N Wallis and Futuna
Halandri *see* Chalándri
147 X13 **Ḩalānīyāt, Juzur al** *var.* Jazā'ir Bin Ghalfān, *Eng.* Kuria Muria Islands. *island group* S Oman
147 W13 **Ḩalānīyāt, Khalīj al** *Eng.* Kuria Muria Bay. *bay* S Oman
Halas *see* Kiskunhalas
40 G11 **Halawa** *Haw.* Hālawa. Hawaii, USA, C Pacific Ocean
40 F9 **Halawa, Cape** *headland* Molokai, Hawaii, USA, C Pacific Ocean
168 H6 **Halban** Hövsgöl, N Mongolia
103 K14 **Halberstadt** Sachsen-Anhalt, C Germany
192 M12 **Halcombe** Manawatu-Wanganui, North Island, NZ
97 I16 **Halden** *prev.* Fredrikshald. Østfold, S Norway
102 L13 **Haldensleben** Sachsen-Anhalt, C Germany
Háldi *see* Halti
159 S17 **Haldia** West Bengal, NE India
158 K10 **Haldwāni** Uttar Pradesh, N India
xli O17 **Hale** Trafford, NW England, UK
40 F10 **Haleakala** *crater* Maui, Hawaii, USA, C Pacific Ocean
27 N4 **Hale Center** Texas, SW USA
101 J18 **Halen** Limburg, NE Belgium
xxxix Y10 **Hales** Norfolk, E England, UK
xxxviii B15 **Halesowen** Dudley, C England, UK
xxxix Y11 **Halesworth** Suffolk, E England, UK
25 O2 **Haleyville** Alabama, S USA
79 O17 **Half Assini** SW Ghana
37 R8 **Half Dome** ▲ California, W USA
193 C25 **Halfmoon Bay** *var.* Oban. Stewart Island, Southland, NZ
190 E5 **Half Moon Lake** *salt lake* South Australia
xxxviii M13 **Halford** Warwickshire, C England, UK
169 R7 **Halhgol** Dornod, E Mongolia
Haliacmon *see* Aliákmonas
Halibān *see* Ḩalabān
12 I13 **Haliburton** Ontario, SE Canada
12 I12 **Haliburton Highlands** *var.* Madawaska Highlands. *hill range* Ontario, SE Canada
xli Q14 **Halifax** Calderdale, N England, UK
11 Q15 **Halifax** Nova Scotia, SE Canada
23 W8 **Halifax** North Carolina, SE USA
23 U7 **Halifax** Virginia, NE USA
11 Q15 **Halifax** ✕ Nova Scotia, SE Canada
149 T13 **Halīl Rūd** *seasonal river* SE Iran
144 I6 **Ḩalīmah** ▲ Lebanon/Syria
168 G8 **Haliun** Govĭ-Altay, W Mongolia
120 I3 **Haljala** *Ger.* Halljal. Lääne-Virumaa, N Estonia
41 Q4 **Halkett, Cape** *headland* Alaska, USA
Halkida *see* Chalkída
xlii L6 **Halkirk** Highland, N Scotland, UK
13 X7 **Hall** ≈ Québec, SE Canada
Hall *see* Schwäbisch Hall
95 H15 **Hälla** Västerbotten, N Sweden
xlii K7 **Halladale** ≈ N Scotland, UK
97 J21 **Halland** ◐ *county* S Sweden
25 Z15 **Hallandale** Florida, SE USA
97 K22 **Hallandsås** *physical region* S Sweden
xxxix P10 **Hallaton** Leicestershire, C England, UK
15 M2 **Hall Beach** Northwest Territories, N Canada
xl L10 **Hall Dunnerdale** Cumbria, NW England, UK
101 G19 **Halle** *Fr.* Hal. Vlaams Brabant, C Belgium
103 M15 **Halle** *var.* Halle an der Saale. Sachsen-Anhalt, C Germany
Halle an der Saale *see* Halle
37 W3 **Halleck** Nevada, W USA
97 L15 **Hällefors** Örebro, C Sweden
97 N16 **Hälleforsnäs** Södermanland, C Sweden
111 Q6 **Hallein** Salzburg, N Austria
103 L15 **Halle-Neustadt** Sachsen-Anhalt, C Germany
27 U12 **Hallettsville** Texas, SW USA
205 N4 **Halley** *UK research station* Antarctica
30 L4 **Halliday** North Dakota, N USA
39 S2 **Halligan Reservoir** ⊠ Colorado, C USA
102 G7 **Halligen** *island group* N Germany
96 G13 **Hallingdal** *valley* S Norway
40 J12 **Hall Island** *island* Alaska, USA
Hall Island *see* Maiana
201 P15 **Hall Islands** *island group* C Micronesia
120 H6 **Halliste** ≈ S Estonia
Halljal *see* Haljala
95 I15 **Hällnäs** Västerbotten, N Sweden
31 R2 **Hallock** Minnesota, N USA
xxxviii J13 **Hallow** Worcestershire, W England, UK
16 Oo3 **Hall Peninsula** *peninsula* Baffin Island, Northwest Territories, NE Canada
22 F9 **Halls** Tennessee, S USA
xxxvi H17 **Hallsands** Devon, SW England, UK
97 M16 **Hallsberg** Örebro, C Sweden
189 N5 **Halls Creek** Western Australia
190 L12 **Halls Gap** Victoria, SE Australia
97 N15 **Hallstahammar** Västmanland, C Sweden
111 R6 **Hallstatt** Salzburg, W Austria
111 R6 **Hallstatter See** ◎ C Austria
97 P14 **Hallstavik** Stockholm, C Sweden
27 X7 **Hallsville** Texas, SW USA
105 P1 **Halluin** Nord, N France
xxxvi D14 **Hallworthy** Cornwall, SW England, UK
Halmahera, Laut *see* Halmahera Sea
175 T7 **Halmahera, Pulau** *prev.* Djailolo, Gilolo, Jailolo. *island* E Indonesia
175 Tt8 **Halmahera Sea** *Ind.* Laut Halmahera. *sea* E Indonesia
97 J21 **Halmstad** Halland, S Sweden
175 T11 **Halong** Pulau Ambon, E Indonesia
121 N15 **Halowchyn** *Rus.* Golovchin. Mahilyowskaya Voblasts', E Belorussia
97 H20 **Hals** Nordjylland, N Denmark
96 F8 **Halsa** Møre og Romsdal, S Norway
xli X14 **Halsham** East Riding of Yorkshire, N England, UK
121 I15 **Hal'shany** *Rus.* Gol'shany. Hrodzyenskaya Voblasts', W Belorussia
Hälsingborg *see* Helsingborg
31 R5 **Halstad** Minnesota, N USA
xxxvii W6 **Halstead** Essex, SE England, UK
29 N6 **Halstead** Kansas, C USA
101 G15 **Halsteren** Noord-Brabant, S Netherlands
95 L16 **Halsua** Vaasa, W Finland
103 E14 **Haltern** Nordrhein-Westfalen, W Germany
xxxix R6 **Haltham** Lincolnshire, E England, UK
94 J9 **Halti** *var.* Haltiatunturi, *Lapp.* Háldi. ▲ Finland/Norway
Haltiatunturi *see* Halti
xl D16 **Halton** ◐ *unitary authority* NW England, UK
xli O6 **Haltwhistle** Northumberland, N England, UK
xxxix Y9 **Halvergate** Norfolk, E England, UK
xxxvi H16 **Halwell** Devon, SW England, UK
xxxvi F13 **Halwill** Devon, SW England, UK
118 J6 **Halych** Ivano-Frankivs'ka Oblast', W Ukraine
Halycus *see* Platani
xxxvi A9 **Ham** Richmond upon Thames, SE England, UK
xlii G4 **Ham** Shetland Islands, NE Scotland, UK
105 P3 **Ham** Somme, N France
Hama *see* Ḩamāh
170 Ee12 **Hamada** Shimane, Honshū, SW Japan
148 L6 **Hamadān** *anc.* Ecbatana. Hamadān, W Iran
148 L6 **Hamadān** *off.* Ostān-e Hamadān. ◐ *province* W Iran
144 I5 **Ḩamāh** *var.* Hama; *anc.* Epiphania, *Bibl.* Hamath. Ḩamāh, W Syria
144 I5 **Ḩamāh** *off.* Muḩāfaẓat Ḩamāh, *var.* Hama. ◐ *governorate* C Syria
171 I17 **Hamakita** Shizuoka, Honshū, S Japan
172 O4 **Hamamasu** Hokkaidō, NE Japan
171 I17 **Hamamatsu** *var.* Hamamatu. Shizuoka, Honshū, S Japan
Hamamatu *see* Hamamatsu
172 Qq7 **Hamanaka** Hokkaidō, NE Japan
171 I17 **Hamana-ko** ◎ Honshū, S Japan
96 I13 **Hamar** *prev.* Storhammer. Hedmark, S Norway
147 U10 **Ḩamārīr al Kidan, Qalamat** *well* E Saudi Arabia
170 G12 **Hamasaka** Hyōgo, Honshū, SW Japan
Hamath *see* Ḩamāh
172 Pp2 **Hamatonbetsu** Hokkaidō, NE Japan
161 K26 **Hambantota** Southern Province, SE Sri Lanka
194 G10 **Hambili** ≈ NW PNG
xxxvii Q12 **Hambledon** Hampshire, S England, UK
xli T14 **Hambleton** North Yorkshire, N England, UK
Hambourg *see* Hamburg
102 J9 **Hamburg** Hamburg, N Germany
29 V14 **Hamburg** Arkansas, C USA
31 S16 **Hamburg** Iowa, C USA
20 D10 **Hamburg** New York, NE USA
102 I10 **Hamburg** *Fr.* Hambourg. ◐ *state* N Germany
154 K5 **Hamdam Āb, Dasht-e** *Pash.* Dasht-i Hamdamab. ▲▲ W Afghanistan
Hamdamab, Dasht-i *see* Hamdam Āb, Dasht-e
20 M13 **Hamden** Connecticut, NE USA
146 K6 **Ḩamḑ, Wādī al** *dry watercourse* W Saudi Arabia
95 L18 **Häme** *Swe.* Tavastehus. ◐ *province* C Finland
95 K18 **Hämeenkyrö** Häme, SW Finland
95 L19 **Hämeenlinna** *Swe.* Tavastehus. Häme, SW Finland
HaMelah, Yam *see* Dead Sea
Hamelin *see* Hameln
102 I13 **Hameln** *Eng.* Hamelin. Niedersachsen, N Germany
188 I8 **Hamersley Range** ▲▲ Western Australia
169 Y12 **Hamgyŏng-sanmaek** ▲▲ N North Korea
169 X13 **Hamhŭng** C North Korea
165 O6 **Hami** *var.* Ha-mi, *Uigh.* Kumul, Qomul. Xinjiang Uygur Zizhiqu, NW China
145 X10 **Ḩamīd Amīn** E Iraq
147 W11 **Hamīdān, Khawr** *oasis* SE Saudi Arabia
144 H5 **Ḩamīdīyah** *var.* Hamîdîyé. Tarṭūs, W Syria
116 L12 **Hamidiye** Edirne, NW Turkey
Hamîdîyé *see* Ḩamīdīyah
xliii J20 **Hamilton** South Lanarkshire, S Scotland, UK
190 L12 **Hamilton** Victoria, SE Australia
66 B12 **Hamilton** ○ (Bermuda) C Bermuda
12 G16 **Hamilton** Ontario, S Canada
192 M7 **Hamilton** Waikato, North Island, NZ
25 N3 **Hamilton** Alabama, S USA
40 M10 **Hamilton** Alaska, USA
32 J13 **Hamilton** Illinois, N USA
29 S3 **Hamilton** Missouri, C USA
35 P10 **Hamilton** Montana, NW USA
27 S8 **Hamilton** Texas, SW USA

◆ Country
● Country Capital
◇ Dependent Territory
○ Dependent Territory Capital
◐ Administrative Region
✕ International Airport
▲ Mountain
▲▲ Mountain Range
⛰ Volcano
≈ River
◎ Lake
⊠ Reservoir

HAMILTON – HAYWARD

12 G16 **Hamilton** ✕ Ontario, S Canada
26 I6 **Hamilton Bank** *undersea feature* SE Labrador Sea
190 E1 **Hamilton Creek** *seasonal river* South Australia
11 R8 **Hamilton Inlet** *inlet* Newfoundland and Labrador, E Canada
29 T12 **Hamilton, Lake** ▣ Arkansas, C USA
37 W6 **Hamilton, Mount** ▲ Nevada, W USA
77 S8 **Ḩamīm, Wādī al** ≈ NE Libya
95 N19 **Hamina** *Swe.* Fredrikshamn. Kymi, S Finland
9 W16 **Hamiota** Manitoba, S Canada
158 L13 **Hamīrpur** Uttar Pradesh, N India
Hamïs Musait *see* Khamīs Mushayt
23 T11 **Hamlet** North Carolina, SE USA
27 P6 **Hamlin** Texas, SW USA
23 P5 **Hamlin** West Virginia, NE USA
33 O7 **Hamlin Lake** ◎ Michigan, N USA
103 F14 **Hamm** *var.* Hamm in Westfalen. Nordrhein-Westfalen, W Germany
Ḩammāmāt, Khalīj al *see* Hammamet, Golfe de
77 N5 **Hammamet, Golfe de** *Ar.* Khalīj al Ḩammāmāt. *gulf* NE Tunisia
145 R3 **Ḩammān al 'Alīl** N Iraq
145 X12 **Ḩammār, Hawr al** ◎ SE Iraq
95 J20 **Hammarland** Åland, SW Finland
95 H16 **Hammarstrand** Jämtland, C Sweden
95 O17 **Hammaslahti** Pohjois-Karjala, SE Finland
101 F17 **Hamme** Oost-Vlaanderen, NW Belgium
102 H10 **Hamme** ≈ NW Germany
97 G22 **Hammel** Århus, C Denmark
103 I18 **Hammelburg** Bayern, C Germany
101 H18 **Hamme-Mille** Walloon Brabant, C Belgium
102 H10 **Hamme-Oste-Kanal** *canal* NW Germany
95 G16 **Hammerdal** Jämtland, C Sweden
94 K8 **Hammerfest** Finnmark, N Norway
xxxvi A7 **Hammersmith** *London borough capital* Hammersmith and Fulham, SE England, UK
xxxiv K16 **Hammersmith and Fulham** ◈ *London borough* SE England, UK
103 D14 **Hamminkeln** Nordrhein-Westfalen, W Germany
Hamm in Westfalen *see* Hamm
28 K10 **Hammon** Oklahoma, C USA
33 N11 **Hammond** Indiana, N USA
24 K8 **Hammond** Louisiana, S USA
xlii I3 **Hamnavoe** Shetland Islands, NE Scotland, UK
xlii I4 **Hamnavoe** Shetland Islands, NE Scotland, UK
101 K20 **Hamoir** Liège, E Belgium
101 J21 **Hamois** Namur, SE Belgium
101 K16 **Hamont** Limburg, NE Belgium
193 F22 **Hampden** Otago, South Island, NZ
21 R6 **Hampden** Maine, NE USA
xxxvii P11 **Hampshire** ◈ *county* S England, UK
xxxvi C6 **Hampstead** Camden, SE England, UK
xli R12 **Hampsthwaite** North Yorkshire, N England, UK
11 O15 **Hampton** New Brunswick, SE Canada
29 U14 **Hampton** Arkansas, C USA
31 V12 **Hampton** Iowa, C USA
21 P10 **Hampton** New Hampshire, NE USA
23 R14 **Hampton** South Carolina, SE USA
23 P8 **Hampton** Tennessee, S USA
23 X7 **Hampton** Virginia, NE USA
96 L11 **Hamra** Gävleborg, C Sweden
82 D10 **Hamrat esh Sheikh** Northern Kordofan, C Sudan
145 S5 **Ḩamrīn, Jabal** ▲▲ N Iraq
123 Jj16 **Hamrun** C Malta
xli U5 **Hamsterley** Durham, N England, UK
xxxvii X11 **Hamstreet** Kent, SE England, UK
178 K14 **Ham Thuận Nam** Binh Thuân, S Vietnam
176 Ww11 **Hamuku** Irian Jaya, E Indonesia
Hāmūn, Daryācheh-ye *see* Şāberī, Hāmūn-e/Sīstān, Daryācheh-ye
Hamwih *see* Southampton
40 G10 **Hana** *Haw.* Hāna. Maui, Hawaii, USA, C Pacific Ocean
23 S14 **Hanahan** South Carolina, SE USA
40 B8 **Hanalei** Kauai, Hawaii, USA, C Pacific Ocean
178 Kk10 **Ha Nam** Quang Nam-Đa Nãng, C Vietnam
171 Mm11 **Hanamaki** Iwate, Honshū, C Japan
40 F10 **Hanamanioa, Cape** *headland* Maui, Hawaii, USA, C Pacific Ocean
202 B16 **Hanan** ✕ (Alofi) SW Niue
103 H18 **Hanau** Hessen, W Germany
15 J7 **Hanbury** ≈ Northwest Territories, NW Canada
Hânceşti *see* Hînceşti
8 M15 **Hanceville** British Columbia, SW Canada
25 P3 **Hanceville** Alabama, S USA
Hancewicze *see* Hantsavichy
166 L6 **Hancheng** Shaanxi, C China
23 V2 **Hancock** Maryland, NE USA
32 M3 **Hancock** Michigan, N USA
31 S8 **Hancock** Minnesota, N USA
20 I12 **Hancock** New York, NE USA
82 Q12 **Handa** Bari, NE Somalia
xlii G7 **Handa Island** *island* NW Scotland, UK
167 O5 **Handan** *var.* Han-tan. Hebei, E China
xxxvii T12 **Handcross** West Sussex, SE England, UK
97 P16 **Handen** Stockholm, C Sweden
83 J22 **Handeni** Tanga, E Tanzania
xl G16 **Handforth** Cheshire, W England, UK
39 Q7 **Handies Peak** ▲ Colorado, C USA
113 J19 **Handlová** *Ger.* Krickerhäu, *Hung.* Nyitrabánya; *prev. Ger.* Kriegerhaj. Stredné Slovensko, C Slovakia
xli S17 **Handsworth** Rotherham, N England, UK
171 K17 **Haneda** ✕ (Tōkyō) Tōkyō, Honshū, S Japan
144 F13 **HaNegev** *Eng.* Negev. *desert* S Israel
37 Q11 **Hanford** California, W USA
203 V16 **Hanga Roa** Easter Island, Chile, E Pacific Ocean
168 H7 **Hangayn Nuruu** ▲▲ C Mongolia
Hang-chou/Hangchow *see* Hangzhou
97 K20 **Hånger** Jönköping, S Sweden
Hangö *see* Hanko
167 R9 **Hangzhou** *var.* Hang-chou, Hangchow. Zhejiang, SE China
168 F5 **Hanhöhiy Uul** ▲▲ NW Mongolia
Hanhowuz *see* Khauz-Khan
143 P15 **Hani** Diyarbakır, SE Turkey
Hania *see* Chaniá
147 R11 **Ḩanish al Kabir, Jazīrat al** *island* SW Yemen
Hanka, Lake *see* Khanka, Lake
95 M17 **Hankasalmi** Keski-Suomi, C Finland
31 R7 **Hankinson** North Dakota, N USA
95 K20 **Hanko** *Swe.* Hangö. Uusimaa, SW Finland
Han-kou/Han-k'ou/Hankow *see* Wuhan
38 M6 **Hanksville** Utah, W USA
158 K6 **Hanle** Jammu and Kashmir, NW India
xxxviii J7 **Hanley** City of Stoke-on-Trent, C England, UK
193 I17 **Hanmer Springs** Canterbury, South Island, NZ
9 R16 **Hanna** Alberta, SW Canada
29 V3 **Hannibal** Missouri, C USA
xxxvii Q10 **Hannington** Hampshire, S England, UK
188 M3 **Hann, Mount** ▲ Western Australia
102 I12 **Hannover** *Eng.* Hanover. Niedersachsen, NW Germany
101 J19 **Hannut** Liège, C Belgium
97 L22 **Hanöbukten** *bay* S Sweden
178 Jj6 **Ha Nôi** *Eng.* Hanoi, *Fr.* Ha noï. ● (Vietnam) N Vietnam
12 F14 **Hanover** Ontario, S Canada
33 P15 **Hanover** Indiana, N USA
20 G16 **Hanover** Pennsylvania, NE USA
23 W6 **Hanover** Virginia, NE USA
Hanover *see* Hannover
65 G23 **Hanover, Isla** *island* S Chile
Hanselbeck *see* Érd
205 X5 **Hansen Mountains** ▲▲ Antarctica
166 M8 **Han Shui** ≈ C China
158 H10 **Hānsi** Haryāna, NW India
xxxvii R6 **Hanslope** Milton Keynes, C England, UK
97 F20 **Hanstholm** Viborg, NW Denmark
Han-tan *see* Handan
164 H6 **Hantengri Feng** *var.* Pik Khan-Tengri. ▲ China/Kazakhstan *see also* Khan-Tengri, Pik
121 I18 **Hantsavichy** *Pol.* Hancewicze, *Rus.* Gantsevichi. Brestskaya Voblasts', SW Belorussia
16 N2 **Hantzsch** ≈ Baffin Island, Northwest Territories, NE Canada
158 G9 **Hanumāngarh** Rājasthān, NW India
xxxvi A7 **Hanwell** Ealing, SE England, UK
191 O9 **Hanwood** New South Wales, SE Australia
Hanyang *see* Caidian
Hanyang *see* Wuhan
166 H10 **Hanyuan** *var.* Fulin. Sichuan, C China
166 J7 **Hanzhong** Shaanxi, C China
203 W11 **Hao** *atoll* Îles Tuamotu, C French Polynesia
159 S16 **Hāora** *prev.* Howrah. West Bengal, NE India
80 K8 **Haouach, Ouadi** *dry watercourse* E Chad
Haoûârine *see* Ḩawārin
94 K13 **Haparanda** Norrbotten, N Sweden
xxxix Y8 **Happisburgh** Norfolk, E England, UK
27 N3 **Happy** Texas, SW USA
36 M1 **Happy Camp** California, W USA
11 Q9 **Happy Valley-Goose Bay** *prev.* Goose Bay. Newfoundland and Labrador, E Canada
Hapsal *see* Haapsalu
158 J10 **Hāpur** Uttar Pradesh, N India
144 F12 **HaQatan, HaMakhtesh** ▲ S Israel
146 I4 **Ḩaql** Tabūk, NW Saudi Arabia
176 Vv13 **Har** Pulau Kai Besar, E Indonesia
168 M8 **Haraat** Dundgovĭ, C Mongolia
Haradh *see* Ḩaraḑ
120 N12 **Haradok** *Rus.* Gorodok. Vitsyebskaya Voblasts', N Belorussia
94 J13 **Harads** Norrbotten, N Sweden
121 G19 **Haradzyets** *Rus.* Gorodets. Brestskaya Voblasts', SW Belorussia
121 J17 **Haradzyeya** *Rus.* Gorodeya. Minskaya Voblasts', C Belorussia
203 V10 **Haraiki** *atoll* Îles Tuamotu, C French Polynesia
171 Ll14 **Haramachi** Fukushima, Honshū, E Japan
120 M12 **Harany** *Rus.* Gorany. Vitsyebskaya Voblasts', N Belorussia
85 L16 **Harare** *prev.* Salisbury. ● (Zimbabwe) Mashonaland East, NE Zimbabwe
85 L16 **Harare** ✕ Mashonaland East, NE Zimbabwe
80 J10 **Haraz-Djombo** Batha, C Chad
121 O16 **Harbavichy** *Rus.* Gorbovichi. Mahilyowskaya Voblasts', E Belorussia
78 J16 **Harbel** W Liberia
169 W8 **Harbin** *var.* Haerbin, Ha-erh-pin, Kharbin; *prev.* Haerhpin, Pingkiang, Pinkiang. Heilongjiang, NE China
33 S7 **Harbor Beach** Michigan, N USA
xli P4 **Harbottle** Northumberland, N England, UK
11 T13 **Harbour Breton** Newfoundland, Newfoundland and Labrador, E Canada
67 D25 **Harbours, Bay of** *bay* East Falkland, Falkland Islands
xxxviii H12 **Harbury** Warwickshire, C England, UK
xxxix O8 **Harby** Leicestershire, C England, UK
xxxix P6 **Harby** Nottinghamshire, C England, UK
97 G24 **Hårby** *var.* Haarby. Fyn, C Denmark
38 I13 **Harcuvar Mountains** ▲▲ Arizona, SW USA
110 I7 **Hard** Vorarlberg, NW Austria
160 H11 **Harda** Madhya Pradesh, C India
97 D14 **Hardanger** *physical region* S Norway
97 D14 **Hardangerfjorden** *fjord* S Norway
96 E13 **Hardangerjøkulen** *glacier* S Norway
97 E14 **Hardangervidda** *plateau* S Norway
85 D20 **Hardap** ◈ *district* S Namibia
23 R15 **Hardeeville** South Carolina, SE USA
100 L5 **Hardegarijp** *Fris.* Hurdegaryp. Friesland, N Netherlands
100 O9 **Hardenberg** Overijssel, E Netherlands
191 Q9 **Harden-Murrumburrah** New South Wales, SE Australia
100 K10 **Harderwijk** Gelderland, C Netherlands
32 J14 **Hardin** Illinois, N USA
35 V11 **Hardin** Montana, NW USA
25 R5 **Harding, Lake** ▣ Alabama/Georgia, SE USA
22 J6 **Hardinsburg** Kentucky, S USA
100 I13 **Hardinxveld-Giessendam** Zuid-Holland, C Netherlands
9 R15 **Hardisty** Alberta, SW Canada
158 L12 **Hardoi** Uttar Pradesh, N India
xli P10 **Hardrow** North Yorkshire, N England, UK
25 U4 **Hardwick** Georgia, SE USA
29 W9 **Hardy** Arkansas, C USA
96 D10 **Hareid** Møre og Romsdal, S Norway
15 Gg5 **Hare Indian** ≈ Northwest Territories, NW Canada
101 D18 **Harelbeke** *var.* Harlebeke. West-Vlaanderen, W Belgium
Harem *see* Ḩārim
102 E11 **Haren** Niedersachsen, NW Germany
100 N6 **Haren** Groningen, NE Netherlands
83 L13 **Hārer** E Ethiopia
xli S13 **Harewood** Leeds, N England, UK
97 P14 **Harg** Uppsala, C Sweden
Hargeisa *see* Hargeysa
82 M13 **Hargeysa** *var.* Hargeisa. Woqooyi Galbeed, NW Somalia
118 J10 **Harghita** ◈ *county* NE Romania
27 S17 **Hargill** Texas, SW USA
168 J8 **Harhorin** Övörhangay, C Mongolia
165 Q9 **Har Hu** ◎ C China
Hariana *see* Haryāna
147 P15 **Ḩarīb** W Yemen
174 I9 **Hari, Batang** *prev.* Djambi. ≈ Sumatera, W Indonesia
158 J9 **Haridwār** *prev.* Hardwar. Uttar Pradesh, N India
161 F18 **Harihar** Karnātaka, W India
193 F18 **Harihari** West Coast, South Island, NZ
144 I3 **Ḩārim** *var.* Harem. Idlib, W Syria
170 G14 **Harima-nada** *sea* S Japan
xxxiv K16 **Haringey** ◈ *London borough* SE England, UK
100 F13 **Haringvliet** *channel* SW Netherlands
100 F13 **Haringvlietdam** *dam* SW Netherlands
155 U5 **Haripur** North-West Frontier Province, NW Pakistan
154 J4 **Harīrūd** *var.* Tedzhen, *Turkm.* Tejen. ≈ Afghanistan/Iran *see also* Tedzhen
96 J11 **Härjåhågnen** *Swe.* Härjahågnen, Härjehågna. ▲ Norway/Sweden
95 K18 **Harjavalta** Turku-Pori, SW Finland
Härjehågna *see* Härjåhågnen
120 G4 **Harjumaa** *off.* Harju Maakond. ◈ *province* NW Estonia
23 X11 **Harkers Island** North Carolina, SE USA
145 S1 **Harki** N Iraq
31 T14 **Harlan** Iowa, C USA
23 O7 **Harlan** Kentucky, S USA
31 N17 **Harlan County Lake** ▣ Nebraska, C USA
118 L9 **Hârlău** *var.* Hîrlău. Iaşi, NE Romania
Harlebeke *see* Harelbeke
xxxv G7 **Harlech** Gwynedd, NW Wales, UK
35 U7 **Harlem** Montana, NW USA
Harlem *see* Haarlem
xxxvi B7 **Harlesden** Brent, SE England, UK
xxxix X11 **Harleston** Norfolk, E England, UK
97 G22 **Harlev** Århus, C Denmark
100 K6 **Harlingen** *Fris.* Harns. Friesland, N Netherlands
27 T17 **Harlingen** Texas, SW USA
xxxvii U7 **Harlow** Essex, E England, UK
35 T10 **Harlowton** Montana, NW USA
96 N11 **Harmånger** Gävleborg, C Sweden
100 I11 **Harmelen** Utrecht, C Netherlands
31 X11 **Harmony** Minnesota, N USA
xxxix P6 **Harmston** Lincolnshire, E England, UK
34 J14 **Harney Basin** *basin* Oregon, NW USA
0 F9 **Harney Basin** ▲▲ Oregon, NW USA
34 J14 **Harney Lake** ◎ Oregon, NW USA
30 J10 **Harney Peak** ▲ South Dakota, N USA
xxxvii N12 **Harnham** Wiltshire, S England, UK
95 H17 **Härnösand** *var.* Hernösand. Västernorrland, C Sweden
Harns *see* Harlingen
168 F6 **Har Nuur** ◎ NW Mongolia
107 P4 **Haro** La Rioja, N Spain
42 F6 **Haro, Cabo** *headland* NW Mexico
xxxvii S5 **Harold** Bedfordshire, C England, UK
xlii J1 **Haroldswick** Shetland Islands, NE Scotland, UK
96 D9 **Harøy** *island* S Norway
xxxvii S7 **Harpenden** Hertfordshire, E England, UK
78 L18 **Harper** *var.* Cape Palmas. NE Liberia
28 M7 **Harper** Kansas, C USA
34 L13 **Harper** Oregon, NW USA
27 Q10 **Harper** Texas, SW USA
37 U13 **Harper Lake** *salt flat* California, W USA
41 T9 **Harper, Mount** ▲ Alaska, USA
xxxix U8 **Harpley** Norfolk, E England, UK
97 J21 **Harplinge** Halland, S Sweden
38 J13 **Harquahala Mountains** ▲▲ Arizona, SW USA
147 T15 **Ḩarrah** SE Yemen
10 H11 **Harricana** ≈ Québec, SE Canada
xxxvii W10 **Harrietsham** Kent, SE England, UK
22 M9 **Harriman** Tennessee, S USA
11 R11 **Harrington Harbour** Québec, E Canada
66 B12 **Harrington Sound** *bay* Bermuda, NW Atlantic Ocean
xxxix P10 **Harringworth** Northamptonshire, C England, UK
xliii D14 **Harris** Highland, NW Scotland, UK
xlii C10 **Harris** *physical region* NW Scotland, UK
29 X10 **Harrisburg** Arkansas, C USA
32 M17 **Harrisburg** Illinois, N USA
31 I14 **Harrisburg** Nebraska, C USA
34 F12 **Harrisburg** Oregon, NW USA
20 G15 **Harrisburg** *state capital* Pennsylvania, NE USA
190 F6 **Harris, Lake** ◎ South Australia
25 W11 **Harris, Lake** ◎ Florida, SE USA
85 J22 **Harrismith** Free State, E South Africa
29 T9 **Harrison** Arkansas, C USA
33 Q7 **Harrison** Michigan, N USA
30 I12 **Harrison** Nebraska, C USA
41 Q5 **Harrison Bay** *inlet* Alaska, USA
24 I6 **Harrisonburg** Louisiana, S USA
23 U4 **Harrisonburg** Virginia, NE USA
11 R7 **Harrison, Cape** *headland* Newfoundland and Labrador, E Canada
29 R5 **Harrisonville** Missouri, C USA
Harris Ridge *see* Lomonosov Ridge
199 K3 **Harris Seamount** *undersea feature* N Pacific Ocean
xliii B10 **Harris, Sound of** *strait* NW Scotland, UK
33 R6 **Harrisville** Michigan, N USA
23 R3 **Harrisville** West Virginia, NE USA
22 M6 **Harrodsburg** Kentucky, S USA
xli S12 **Harrogate** North Yorkshire, N England, UK
27 Q4 **Harrold** Texas, SW USA
xxxvii T8 **Harrow** Harrow, SE England, UK
xxxiv K16 **Harrow** ◈ *London borough* SE England, UK
29 S5 **Harry S.Truman Reservoir** ▣ Missouri, C USA
102 G13 **Harsewinkel** Nordrhein-Westfalen, W Germany
118 M14 **Hârşova** *prev.* Hîrşova. Constanţa, SE Romania
94 H10 **Harstad** Troms, N Norway
xxxix S13 **Harston** Cambridgeshire, E England, UK
xli S8 **Hart** Hartlepool, N England, UK
33 O8 **Hart** Michigan, N USA
26 M4 **Hart** Texas, SW USA
8 I5 **Hart** ≈ Yukon Territory, NW Canada
85 F23 **Hartbees** ≈ C South Africa
111 X7 **Hartberg** Steiermark, SE Austria
xli Q5 **Hartburn** Northumberland, N England, UK
190 I10 **Hart, Cape** *headland* South Australia
97 E14 **Hårteigen** ▲ S Norway
xxxix Y12 **Hartest** Suffolk, E England, UK
xlii L22 **Hart Fell** ▲ SW Scotland, UK
xl E17 **Hartford** Cheshire, C England, UK
25 Q7 **Hartford** Alabama, S USA
29 R11 **Hartford** Arkansas, C USA
20 M12 **Hartford** *state capital* Connecticut, NE USA
22 J6 **Hartford** Kentucky, S USA
33 P10 **Hartford** Michigan, N USA
31 R11 **Hartford** South Dakota, N USA
32 M8 **Hartford** Wisconsin, N USA
33 P13 **Hartford City** Indiana, N USA
xxxviii L6 **Hartington** Derbyshire, C England, UK
31 Q13 **Hartington** Nebraska, C USA
95 G15 **Hartkjølen** ▲ C Norway
xxxvi E12 **Hartland** Devon, SW England, UK
11 N14 **Hartland** New Brunswick, SE Canada
xxxvi D12 **Hartland Point** *headland* SW England, UK
xxxviii A16 **Hartlebury** Worcestershire, W England, UK
xli Y5 **Hartlepool** Hartlepool, N England, UK
xli X5 **Hartlepool** ◈ *unitary authority* NE England, UK
xli T8 **Hartlepool Bay** *bay* N England, UK
31 T12 **Hartley** Iowa, C USA
26 M1 **Hartley** Texas, SW USA
xxxvii R10 **Hartley Wintney** Hampshire, S England, UK
34 J15 **Hart Mountain** ▲ Oregon, NW USA
181 U10 **Hartog Ridge** *undersea feature* W Indian Ocean
95 M18 **Hartola** Mikkeli, S Finland
xxxvi M7 **Hartpury** Gloucestershire, C England, UK
69 U14 **Harts** *var.* Hartz. ≈ South Africa
25 P2 **Hartselle** Alabama, S USA
25 S3 **Hartsfield Atlanta** ✕ Georgia, SE USA
29 Q11 **Hartshorne** Oklahoma, C USA
23 S12 **Hartsville** South Carolina, SE USA
22 K8 **Hartsville** Tennessee, S USA
29 U7 **Hartville** Missouri, C USA
25 U2 **Hartwell** Georgia, SE USA
23 O11 **Hartwell Lake** ▣ Georgia/South Carolina, SE USA
Hartz *see* Harts
Harunabad *see* Eslāmābād
168 E6 **Har-Us Gol** ◎ Hovd, W Mongolia
168 E6 **Har Us Nuur** ◎ NW Mongolia
32 M10 **Harvard** Illinois, N USA
31 P16 **Harvard** Nebraska, C USA
39 R5 **Harvard, Mount** ▲ Colorado, C USA
33 N11 **Harvey** Illinois, N USA
31 N4 **Harvey** North Dakota, N USA
xxxviii K13 **Harvington** Worcestershire, W England, UK
xxxvii P9 **Harwell** Oxfordshire, C England, UK
xxxvii Y6 **Harwich** Essex, E England, UK
xli V10 **Harwood Dale** North Yorkshire, N England, UK
158 H10 **Haryāna** *var.* Hariana. ◈ *state* N India
147 Y9 **Ḩaryān, Ţawī al** *spring/well* NE Oman
103 J14 **Harz** ▲▲ C Germany
Hasakah *see* Al Ḩasakah
171 M12 **Hasama** Miyagi, Honshū, C Japan
142 J15 **Hasan Dağı** ▲ C Turkey
145 T9 **Ḩasan Ibn Ḩassūn** C Iraq
155 R6 **Ḩasan Khēl** *var.* Ahmad Khel. Paktīā, SE Afghanistan
102 F12 **Hase** ≈ NW Germany
Haselberg *see* Krasnoznamensk
102 F12 **Haselünne** Niedersachsen, NW Germany
168 K9 **Hashaat** Dundgovĭ, C Mongolia
Hashemite Kingdom of Jordan *see* Jordan
145 V8 **Hāshimah** E Iraq
171 Gg16 **Hashimoto** *var.* Hasimoto. Wakayama, Honshū, SW Japan
147 W13 **Ḩāsik** S Oman
155 U10 **Hāsilpur** Punjab, E Pakistan
Hasimoto *see* Hashimoto
Hasiyee *see* Ḩisyah
29 Q10 **Haskell** Oklahoma, C USA
27 Q6 **Haskell** Texas, SW USA
116 M11 **Hasköy** Edirne, NW Turkey
97 L24 **Hasle** Bornholm, E Denmark
xxxvii S12 **Haslemere** Surrey, SE England, UK
xli O15 **Haslingden** Lancashire, NW England, UK
104 I16 **Hasparren** Pyrénées-Atlantiques, SW France
Hassakeh *see* Al Ḩasakah
161 G19 **Hassan** Karnātaka, W India
38 J13 **Hassayampa River** ≈ Arizona, SW USA
103 J18 **Hassberge** *hill range* C Germany
96 N10 **Hassela** Gävleborg, C Sweden
101 J18 **Hasselt** Limburg, NE Belgium
100 M9 **Hasselt** Overijssel, E Netherlands
Hassetché *see* Al Ḩasakah
103 J18 **Hassfurt** Bayern, C Germany
76 L9 **Hassi Bel Guebbour** E Algeria
76 L8 **Hassi Messaoud** E Algeria
97 K22 **Hässleholm** Kristianstad, S Sweden
Hasta Colonia/Hasta Pompeia *see* Asti
xxxvii W13 **Hastings** East Sussex, SE England, UK
191 O13 **Hastings** Victoria, SE Australia
192 O11 **Hastings** Hawke's Bay, North Island, NZ
33 P9 **Hastings** Michigan, N USA
31 W9 **Hastings** Minnesota, N USA
31 P16 **Hastings** Nebraska, C USA
97 K22 **Hästveda** Kristianstad, S Sweden
94 J8 **Hasvik** Finnmark, N Norway
39 V6 **Haswell** Colorado, C USA
168 I10 **Hatansuudal** Bayanhongor, C Mongolia
169 P9 **Hatavch** Sühbaatar, E Mongolia
142 K17 **Hatay** ◈ *province* S Turkey
39 R15 **Hatch** New Mexico, SW USA
38 K7 **Hatch** Utah, W USA
xxxvi J12 **Hatch Beauchamp** Somerset, SW England, UK
22 F9 **Hatchie River** ≈ Tennessee, S USA
118 G12 **Haţeg** *Ger.* Wallenthal, *Hung.* Hátszeg; *prev.* Hatzeg, Hötzing. Hunedoara, SW Romania
172 Oo17 **Hateruma-jima** *island* Yaeyama-shotō, SW Japan
xli U15 **Hatfield** Doncaster, N England, UK
xxxviii I12 **Hatfield** Herefordshire, W England, UK
xxxvii T7 **Hatfield** Hertfordshire, E England, UK
191 N8 **Hatfield** New South Wales, SE Australia
xxxvii V7 **Hatfield Broad Oak** Essex, SE England, UK
xxxvii W7 **Hatfield Peverel** Essex, SE England, UK
168 J5 **Hatgal** Hövsgöl, N Mongolia
159 V16 **Hathazari** Chittagong, SE Bangladesh
xxxvi F13 **Hatherleigh** Devon, SW England, UK
xxxix N9 **Hathern** Leicestershire, C England, UK
xxxvi N8 **Hatherop** Gloucestershire, C England, UK
xxxviii L5 **Hathersage** Derbyshire, C England, UK
147 T13 **Hathūt, Hişā'** *oasis* NE Yemen
178 Ii14 **Ha Tiên** Kiên Giang, S Vietnam
178 Jj8 **Ha Tinh** Ha Tinh, N Vietnam
Hatiôzi *see* Hachiōji
144 F12 **Hatira, Haré** *hill range* S Israel
178 J6 **Hat Lot** Sơn La, N Vietnam
47 P16 **Hato Airport** ✕ (Willemstad) Curaçao, SW Netherlands Antilles
56 H9 **Hato Corozal** Casanare, C Colombia
Hato del Volcán *see* Volcán
47 P9 **Hato Mayor** E Dominican Republic
Hatra *see* Al Ḩaḑr
Hatria *see* Adria
Hátszeg *see* Haţeg
149 R16 **Hattā** Dubayy, NE UAE
190 L9 **Hattah** Victoria, SE Australia
100 M9 **Hattem** Gelderland, E Netherlands
23 Z10 **Hatteras** Hatteras Island, North Carolina, SE USA
23 Rr10 **Hatteras, Cape** *headland* North Carolina, SE USA
23 Z9 **Hatteras Island** *island* North Carolina, SE USA
66 F10 **Hatteras Plain** *undersea feature* W Atlantic Ocean
95 G14 **Hattfjelldal** Troms, N Norway
24 M7 **Hattiesburg** Mississippi, S USA
xxxviii L8 **Hatton** Derbyshire, C England, UK
xlii P12 **Hatton** Aberdeenshire, NE Scotland, UK
31 Q4 **Hatton** North Dakota, N USA
Hatton Bank *see* Hatton Ridge
66 L6 **Hatton Ridge** *var.* Hatton Bank. *undersea feature* N Atlantic Ocean
203 W6 **Hatutu** *island* Îles Marquises, NE French Polynesia
113 K22 **Hatvan** Heves, NE Hungary
178 H17 **Hat Yai** *var.* Ban Hat Yai. Songkhla, SW Thailand
Hatzeg *see* Haţeg
Hatzfeld *see* Jimbolia
82 N13 **Haud** *plateau* Ethiopia/Somalia
97 D18 **Hauge** Rogaland, S Norway
97 C15 **Haugesund** Rogaland, S Norway
xxxix W12 **Haughley** Suffolk, E England, UK
xxxviii J9 **Haughton** Staffordshire, C England, UK
111 X2 **Haugsdorf** Niederösterreich, NE Austria
192 M9 **Hauhungaroa Range** ▲▲ North Island, NZ
97 E15 **Haukeligrend** Telemark, S Norway
95 L14 **Haukipudas** Oulu, C Finland
95 M17 **Haukivesi** ◎ SE Finland
95 M17 **Haukivuori** Mikkeli, SE Finland
Hauptkanal *see* Havelländ Grosse
195 Z17 **Hauraha** San Cristobal, SE Solomon Islands
192 L5 **Hauraki Gulf** *gulf* North Island, NZ
193 B24 **Hauroko, Lake** ◎ South Island, NZ
178 Jj15 **Hâu, Sông** ≈ S Vietnam
94 N12 **Hautajärvi** Lappi, NE Finland
76 F7 **Haut Atlas** *Eng.* High Atlas. ▲▲ C Morocco
81 M17 **Haut-Congo** *off.* Région du Haut-Congo *prev.* Haut-Zaïre ◈ *region* NE Congo (Zaire)
104 F1 **Haute-Corse** ◈ *department* Corse, France, C Mediterranean Sea
104 L16 **Haute-Garonne** ◈ *department* S France
78 J13 **Haute-Guinée** ◈ *state* NE Guinea
81 K14 **Haute-Kotto** ◈ *prefecture* E Central African Republic
105 P12 **Haute-Loire** ◈ *department* C France
105 R6 **Haute-Marne** ◈ *department* N France
104 M3 **Haute-Normandie** ◈ *region* N France
13 U6 **Hauterive** Québec, SE Canada
105 T13 **Hautes-Alpes** ◈ *department* SE France
105 S7 **Haute-Saône** ◈ *department* E France
105 T10 **Haute-Savoie** ◈ *department* E France
101 M20 **Hautes Fagnes** *Ger.* Hohes Venn. ▲ E Belgium
104 K16 **Hautes-Pyrénées** ◈ *department* S France
101 L23 **Haute Sûre, Lac de la** ▣ NW Luxembourg
104 M11 **Haute-Vienne** ◈ *department* C France
21 S8 **Haut, Isle au** *island* Maine, NE USA
81 M14 **Haut-Mbomou** ◈ *préfecture* SE Central African Republic
105 Q2 **Hautmont** Nord, N France
81 F19 **Haut-Ogooué** *off.* Province du Haut-Ogooué, *var.* Le Haut-Ogooué. ◈ *province* SE Gabon
Haut-Ogooué, Le *see* Haut-Ogooué
105 U7 **Haut-Rhin** ◈ *department* NE France
76 I6 **Hauts Plateaux** *plateau* Algeria/Morocco
Haut-Zaïre *see* Haut-Congo
40 D9 **Hauula** *Haw.* Hau'ula. Oahu, Hawaii, USA, C Pacific Ocean
103 O22 **Hauzenberg** Bayern, SE Germany
32 K13 **Havana** Illinois, N USA
Havana *see* La Habana
xxxvii R13 **Havant** Hampshire, S England, UK
37 Y14 **Havasu, Lake** ▣ Arizona/California, W USA
97 J23 **Havdrup** Roskilde, E Denmark
102 N10 **Havel** ≈ NE Germany
101 J21 **Havelange** Namur, SE Belgium
102 M11 **Havelberg** Sachsen-Anhalt, NE Germany
155 U5 **Haveliān** North-West Frontier Province, NW Pakistan
102 N12 **Havelländ Grosse** *var.* Hauptkanal. *canal* NE Germany
12 J14 **Havelock** Ontario, SE Canada
193 J14 **Havelock** Marlborough, South Island, NZ
23 X11 **Havelock** North Carolina, SE USA
192 O11 **Havelock North** Hawke's Bay, North Island, NZ
100 M8 **Havelte** Drenthe, NE Netherlands
29 N6 **Haven** Kansas, C USA
xxxv C13 **Haverfordwest** Pembrokeshire, SW Wales, UK
xxxix U13 **Haverhill** Suffolk, E England, UK
21 O10 **Haverhill** Massachusetts, NE USA
xl K11 **Haverigg** Cumbria, NW England, UK
xxxiv M16 **Havering** ◈ *London borough* SE England, UK
95 G17 **Haverö** Västernorrland, C Sweden
113 I17 **Havířov** Severní Morava, E Czech Republic
113 E17 **Havlíčkův Brod** *Ger.* Deutsch-Brod; *prev.* Německý Brod. Východní Čechy, C Czech Republic
94 K7 **Havøysund** Finnmark, N Norway
35 T7 **Havre** Montana, NW USA
Havre *see* le Havre
101 F20 **Havré** Hainaut, S Belgium
11 P11 **Havre-St-Pierre** Québec, E Canada
142 B10 **Havsa** Edirne, NW Turkey
40 D8 **Hawaii** *off.* State of Hawaii; also known as Aloha State, Paradise of the Pacific. ◈ *state* USA, C Pacific Ocean
40 G12 **Hawaii** *Haw.* Hawai'i. *island* Hawaiian Islands, USA, C Pacific Ocean
199 K5 **Hawaiian Islands** *prev.* Sandwich Islands. *island group* Hawaii, USA, C Pacific Ocean
199 Jj6 **Hawaiian Ridge** *undersea feature* N Pacific Ocean
199 Kk6 **Hawaiian Trough** *undersea feature* N Pacific Ocean
xxxv K5 **Hawarden** Flintshire, N Wales, UK
31 R12 **Hawarden** Iowa, C USA
Hawash *see* Āwash
145 P6 **Hawbayn al Gharbiyah** C Iraq
193 D21 **Hawea, Lake** ◎ South Island, NZ
192 K11 **Hawera** Taranaki, North Island, NZ
xli P11 **Hawes** North Yorkshire, N England, UK
22 J5 **Hawesville** Kentucky, S USA
xli N9 **Haweswater** ◎ NW England, UK
40 G11 **Hawi** *Haw.* Hāwī. Hawaii, USA, C Pacific Ocean
xliii N22 **Hawick** The Borders, SE Scotland, UK
145 S4 **Ḩawījah** C Iraq
145 Y10 **Ḩawīzah, Hawr al** ◎ S Iraq
193 E21 **Hawkdun Range** ▲▲ South Island, NZ
192 P10 **Hawke Bay** *bay* North Island, NZ
190 I6 **Hawker** South Australia
192 N11 **Hawke's Bay** *off.* Hawkes Bay Region. ◈ *region* North Island, NZ
155 O16 **Hawkes Bay** *bay* SE Pakistan
13 N12 **Hawkesbury** Ontario, SE Canada
Hawkeye State *see* Iowa
xxxvi W12 **Hawkhurst** Kent, SE England, UK
25 T5 **Hawkinsville** Georgia, SE USA
12 B7 **Hawk Junction** Ontario, S Canada
23 N10 **Haw Knob** ▲ North Carolina/Tennessee, SE USA
23 Q9 **Hawksbill Mountain** ▲ North Carolina, SE USA
35 Z16 **Hawk Springs** Wyoming, C USA
Hawlêr *see* Arbīl
31 S5 **Hawley** Minnesota, N USA
27 P7 **Hawley** Texas, SW USA
xli T11 **Hawnby** North Yorkshire, N England, UK
xli Q14 **Haworth** Bradford, N England, UK
147 R14 **Ḩawrā'** C Yemen
145 P7 **Ḩawrān, Wadi** *dry watercourse* W Iraq
23 T9 **Haw River** ≈ North Carolina, SE USA
145 U5 **Hawshqūrah** E Iraq
37 S7 **Hawthorne** Nevada, W USA
xli T12 **Haxby** York, N England, UK
xxxix O4 **Haxey** North Lincolnshire, N England, UK
39 W3 **Haxtun** Colorado, C USA
191 N9 **Hay** New South Wales, SE Australia
9 O10 **Hay** ≈ W Canada
176 U11 **Haya** Pulau Seram, E Indonesia
172 N11 **Hayachine-san** ▲ Honshū, C Japan
105 S4 **Hayange** Moselle, NE France
HaYarden *see* Jordan
Hayastani Hanrapetut'yun *see* Armenia
Hayasui-seto *see* Hōyo-kaikyō
41 N9 **Haycock** Alaska, USA
38 M14 **Hayden** Arizona, SW USA
39 Q3 **Hayden** Colorado, C USA
xl D15 **Haydock** St Helens, NW England, UK
xli P6 **Haydon Bridge** Northumberland, N England, UK
30 M10 **Hayes** South Dakota, N USA
9 X13 **Hayes** ≈ Manitoba, C Canada
15 Kk11 **Hayes** ≈ Northwest Territories, NE Canada
30 M16 **Hayes Center** Nebraska, C USA
41 S10 **Hayes, Mount** ▲ Alaska, USA
23 N11 **Hayesville** North Carolina, SE USA
xxxviii K5 **Hayfield** Derbyshire, C England, UK
37 X10 **Hayford Peak** ▲ Nevada, W USA
36 M3 **Hayfork** California, W USA
Hayir, Qasr al *see* Ḩayr al Gharbī, Qaşr al
169 P8 **Haylaastay** Sühbaatar, E Mongolia
12 I12 **Hay Lake** ◎ Ontario, SE Canada
xxxvi M16 **Hayle** Cornwall, SW England, UK
xxxvi M16 **Hayle** ≈ SW England, UK
147 X11 **Haymā'** *var.* Haima. C Oman
142 H13 **Haymana** Ankara, C Turkey
144 J7 **Ḩaymūr, Jabal** ▲▲ W Syria
Haynau *see* Chojnów
24 G4 **Haynesville** Louisiana, S USA
25 P6 **Hayneville** Alabama, S USA
xxxv K12 **Hay-on-Wye** Powys, E Wales, UK
116 M12 **Hayrabolu** Tekirdağ, NW Turkey
142 C10 **Hayrabolu Deresi** ≈ NW Turkey
144 J6 **Ḩayr al Gharbī, Qaşr al** *var.* Qasr al Hayir, Qasr al Hir al Gharbi. *ruins* Ḩimş, C Syria
144 L5 **Ḩayr ash Sharqī, Qaşr al** *var.* Qasr al Hir Ash Sharqī. *ruins* Ḩimş, C Syria
15 Hh9 **Hay River** Northwest Territories, W Canada
28 K4 **Hays** Kansas, C USA
30 K12 **Hay Springs** Nebraska, C USA
67 H25 **Haystack, The** ▲ NE Saint Helena
29 N7 **Haysville** Kansas, C USA
119 O7 **Haysyn** *Rus.* Gaysin. Vinnyts'ka Oblast', C Ukraine
29 Y9 **Hayti** Missouri, C USA
31 Q9 **Hayti** South Dakota, N USA
xli V13 **Hayton** East Riding of Yorkshire, N England, UK
xxxix O5 **Hayton** Nottinghamshire, C England, UK
119 O8 **Hayvoron** *Rus.* Gayvorno. Kirovohrads'ka Oblast', C Ukraine
37 N9 **Hayward** California, W USA

◆ Country ● Country Capital ◇ Dependent Territory ○ Dependent Territory Capital ◈ Administrative Region ✕ International Airport ▲ Mountain ▲▲ Mountain Range Volcano ≈ River ◎ Lake ▣ Reservoir

◆ COUNTRY   ◇ DEPENDENT TERRITORY   ◆ ADMINISTRATIVE REGION   ▲ MOUNTAIN   🌋 VOLCANO   ⊗ LAKE
● COUNTRY CAPITAL   ○ DEPENDENT TERRITORY CAPITAL   ✕ INTERNATIONAL AIRPORT   ▲ MOUNTAIN RANGE   ≈ RIVER   ▨ RESERVOIR

HINDSHOLM – HOUDENG-GOEGNIES

97 H23 **Hindsholm** island C Denmark
155 S4 **Hindu Kush** Per. Hendū Kosh. ▲ Afghanistan/Pakistan
161 H19 **Hindupur** Andhra Pradesh, E India
9 O12 **Hines Creek** Alberta, W Canada
25 W6 **Hinesville** Georgia, SE USA
160 I12 **Hinganghāt** Mahārāshtra, C India
xxxix W10 **Hingham** Norfolk, E England, UK
155 N15 **Hingol** ~ SW Pakistan
160 H13 **Hingoli** Mahārāshtra, C India
143 R13 **Hınıs** Erzurum, E Turkey
94 O2 **Hinlopenstretet** strait N Svalbard
94 G10 **Hinnøya** island C Norway
170 D15 **Hinokage** Miyazaki, Kyūshū, SW Japan
170 F11 **Hino-misaki** headland Honshū, SW Japan
110 H10 **Hinterrhein** ~ SW Switzerland
xxxix W13 **Hintlesham** Suffolk, E England, UK
9 O14 **Hinton** Alberta, SW Canada
28 M10 **Hinton** Oklahoma, C USA
23 R6 **Hinton** West Virginia, NE USA
Hios see Chíos
43 N8 **Hipolito** Coahuila de Zaragoza, NE Mexico
Hipponium see Vibo Valentia
170 C12 **Hirado** Nagasaki, Hirado-shima, SW Japan
170 C12 **Hirado-shima** island SW Japan
171 Gg15 **Hirakata** Ōsaka, Honshū, SW Japan
172 P17 **Hirakubo-saki** headland Ishigaki-jima, SW Japan
160 M11 **Hirākud Reservoir** ⊠ E India
Hir al Gharbi, Qasr al see Ḩayr al Gharbī, Qaşr al
172 N9 **Hiranai** Aomori, Honshū, N Japan
172 Pp16 **Hirara** Okinawa, Miyako-jima, SW Japan
Qasr al Hir Ash Sharqī see Ḩayr ash Sharqī, Qaşr al
170 F12 **Hirata** Shimane, Honshū, SW Japan
171 Jj17 **Hiratsuka** var. Hiratuka. Kanagawa, Honshū, S Japan
Hiratuka see Hiratsuka
142 I13 **Hirfanlı Barajı** ⊠ C Turkey
161 G18 **Hiriyūr** Karnātaka, W India
Hîrlău see Hârlău
154 K10 **Hirmand, Rūd-e** var. Daryā-ye Helmand. ~ Afghanistan/Iran see also Helmand, Daryā-ye
Hirmil see Hermel
xxxv I7 **Hirnant** Powys, C Wales, UK
172 P8 **Hiroo** Hokkaidō, NE Japan
171 Mm9 **Hirosaki** Aomori, Honshū, C Japan
170 E13 **Hiroshima** var. Hirosima. Hiroshima, Honshū, SW Japan
170 Ee13 **Hiroshima** off. Hiroshima-ken, var. Hirosima. ◐ prefecture Honshū, SW Japan
Hirosima see Hiroshima
Hirschberg/Hirschberg im Riesengebirge/Hirschberg in Schlesien see Jelenia Góra
105 Q3 **Hirson** Aisne, N France
Hirşova see Hârşova
97 G19 **Hirtshals** Nordjylland, N Denmark
xxxv I14 **Hirwaun** Rhondda Cynon Taff, S Wales, UK
171 H16 **Hisai** Mie, Honshū, SW Japan
158 H10 **Hisār** Haryāna, NW India
194 J15 **Hisiu** Central, SW PNG
153 P13 **Hisor** Rus. Gissar. W Tajikistan
Hispalis see Sevilla
Hispana/Hispania see Spain
46 M7 **Hispaniola** island Dominion Republic/Haiti
66 F11 **Hispaniola Basin** var. Hispaniola Trough. undersea feature SW Atlantic Ocean
Hispaniola Trough see Hispaniola Basin
xxxix S12 **Histon** Cambridgeshire, E England, UK
Historium see Vasto
145 R7 **Hīt** SW Iraq
170 D14 **Hita** Ōita, Kyūshū, SW Japan
171 L16 **Hitachi** var. Hitati. Ibaraki, Honshū, S Japan
171 L15 **Hitachi-Ōta** var. Hitatiôta. Ibaraki, Honshū, S Japan
Hitati see Hitachi
Hitatiôta see Hitachi-Ōta
xxxix W13 **Hitcham** Suffolk, E England, UK
xxxvii T6 **Hitchin** Hertfordshire, E England, UK
xxxvi F9 **Hither Green** Lewisham, SE England, UK
203 Q7 **Hitiaa** Tahiti, W French Polynesia
170 Cc15 **Hitoyoshi** var. Hitoyosi. Kumamoto, Kyūshū, SW Japan
Hitoyosi see Hitoyoshi
96 F7 **Hitra** prev. Hitteren. island S Norway
Hitteren see Hitra
197 B10 **Hiu** island Torres Islands, N Vanuatu
171 K14 **Hiuchiga-take** ▲ Honshū, C Japan
170 Ee14 **Hiuchi-nada** gulf S Japan
203 X7 **Hiva Oa** island Îles Marquises, N French Polynesia
22 M10 **Hiwassee Lake** ⊠ North Carolina, SE USA
22 M10 **Hiwassee River** ~ SE USA
97 H20 **Hjallerup** Nordjylland, N Denmark
97 M16 **Hjälmaren** Eng. Lake Hjalmar. ⊚ C Sweden
Hjalmar, Lake see Hjälmaren
97 C14 **Hjellestad** Hordaland, S Norway
97 D16 **Hjelmeland** Rogaland, S Norway
96 G10 **Hjerkinn** Oppland, S Norway
97 L18 **Hjo** Skaraborg, S Sweden
97 G19 **Hjørring** Nordjylland, N Denmark
178 H1 **Hkakabo Razi** ▲ Burma/China
178 H1 **Hkring Bum** ▲ N Burma
85 L21 **Hlathikulu** var. Hlatikulu. S Swaziland
Hlatikulu see Hlathikulu
Hliboka see Hlyboka
113 F17 **Hlinsko** var. Hlinsko v Čechách. Východní Čechy, C Czech Republic
Hlinsko v Čechách see Hlinsko
119 S6 **Hlobyne** Rus. Globino. Poltavs'ka Oblast', NE Ukraine
113 H20 **Hlohovec** Ger. Freistadtl, Hung. Galgóc; prev. Frakštát. Západné Slovensko, W Slovakia
85 J23 **Hlotse** var. Leribe. NW Lesotho
113 I17 **Hlučín** Ger. Hultschin, Pol. Hulczyn. Severní Morava, E Czech Republic
119 S2 **Hlukhiv** Rus. Glukhov. Sums'ka Oblast', NE Ukraine
121 K21 **Hlushkavichy** Rus. Glushkevichi. Homyel'skaya Voblasts', SE Belorussia
121 L18 **Hlusk** Rus. Glusk, Glussk. Mahilyowskaya Voblasts', E Belorussia
118 K8 **Hlyboka** Ger. Hliboka, Rus. Glybokaya. Chernivets'ka Oblast', W Ukraine
120 K13 **Hlybokaye** Rus. Glubokoye. Vitsyebskaya Voblasts', N Belorussia
79 Q16 **Ho** SE Ghana
178 Jj6 **Hoa Binh** Hoa Binh, N Vietnam
85 E20 **Hoachanas** Hardap, C Namibia
Hoai Nhơn see Bông Sơn
178 Jj8 **Hoa Lac** Quang Binh, C Vietnam
178 J5 **Hoang Liên Sơn** ▲ N Vietnam
85 B17 **Hoanib** ~ NW Namibia
35 S15 **Hoback Peak** ▲ Wyoming, C USA
191 P17 **Hobart** prev. Hobarton, Hobart Town. state capital Tasmania, SE Australia
28 L11 **Hobart** Oklahoma, C USA
191 P17 **Hobart** ✕ Tasmania, SE Australia
Hobarton/Hobart Town see Hobart
39 W14 **Hobbs** New Mexico, SW USA
204 L12 **Hobbs Coast** physical region Antarctica
25 Z14 **Hobe Sound** Florida, SE USA
Hobicaurikány see Uricani
82 E12 **Hobo** Huila, S Colombia
101 G16 **Hoboken** Antwerpen, N Belgium
164 K3 **Hoboksar** var. Hoboksar Mongol Zizhixian. Xinjiang Uygur Zizhiqu, NW China
Hoboksar Mongol Zizhixian see Hoboksar
97 G21 **Hobro** Nordjylland, N Denmark
23 X10 **Hobucken** North Carolina, SE USA
97 O20 **Hoburgen** headland SE Sweden
83 P15 **Hobyo** It. Obbia. Mudug, E Somalia
111 R8 **Hochalmspitze** ▲ SW Austria
111 Q4 **Hochburg** Oberösterreich, N Austria
110 F8 **Hochdorf** Luzern, N Switzerland
111 N8 **Hochfeiler** It. Gran Pilastro. ▲ Austria/Italy
178 Jj14 **Ho Chi Minh** var. Ho Chi Minh City; prev. Saigon. S Vietnam
Ho Chi Minh City see Hô Chi Minh
110 I7 **Höchst** Vorarlberg, NW Austria
Höchstadt see Höchstadt an der Aisch
103 K19 **Höchstadt an der Aisch** var. Höchstadt. Bayern, C Germany
110 I9 **Hochwilde** It. L'Altissima. ▲ Austria/Italy
111 S7 **Hochwildstelle** ▲ C Austria
33 T14 **Hocking River** ~ Ohio, N USA
xxxix U10 **Hockwold cum Wilton** Norfolk, E England, UK
Hoctúm see Hoctún
43 X12 **Hoctún** var. Hoctúm. Yucatán, E Mexico
xli O13 **Hodder** ~ NW England, UK
xxxvii U8 **Hoddesdon** Hertfordshire, SE England, UK
Hodeida see Al Ḩudaydah
22 K6 **Hodgenville** Kentucky, S USA
9 T17 **Hodgeville** Saskatchewan, S Canada
78 L9 **Hodh ech Chargui** ◐ region E Mauritania
Hodh el Garbi see Hodh el Gharbi
78 J10 **Hodh el Gharbi** var. Hodh el Garbi. ◐ region S Mauritania
113 L25 **Hódmezővásárhely** Csongrád, SE Hungary
76 J6 **Hodna, Chott El** var. Chott el-Hodna, Ar. Shatt al-Hodna. salt lake N Algeria
Hodna, Shatt al- see Hodna, Chott El
xxxviii I8 **Hodnet** Shropshire, W England, UK
113 G19 **Hodonín** Ger. Göding. Jižní Morava, SE Czech Republic
168 G6 **Hödrögö** Dzavhan, N Mongolia
Hodság/Hodschag see Odžaci
41 R7 **Hodzana River** ~ Alaska, USA
Hoei see Huy
101 H19 **Hoeilaart** Vlaams Brabant, C Belgium
Hoë Karoo see Great Karoo
100 F12 **Hoek van Holland** Eng. Hook of Holland. Zuid-Holland, W Netherlands
100 L11 **Hoenderloo** Gelderland, E Netherlands
101 L18 **Hoensbroek** Limburg, SE Netherlands
169 Y11 **Hoeryŏng** NE North Korea
101 K18 **Hoeselt** Limburg, NE Belgium
100 K11 **Hoevelaken** Gelderland, C Netherlands
Hoey see Huy
103 M18 **Hof** Bayern, SE Germany
Höfðhakaupstadhur see Skagaströnd
Hofei see Hefei
103 G18 **Hofheim am Taunus** Hessen, W Germany
Hofmarkt see Odorheiu Secuiesc
94 L3 **Höfn** Austurland, SE Iceland
96 N13 **Hofors** Gävleborg, C Sweden
94 J6 **Hofsjökull** glacier C Iceland
94 J1 **Hofsós** Nordhurland Vestra, N Iceland
170 Dd13 **Hōfu** Yamaguchi, Honshū, SW Japan
Hofuf see Al Hufūf
97 J22 **Höganäs** Malmöhus, S Sweden
191 P14 **Hogan Group** island group Tasmania, SE Australia
25 R4 **Hogansville** Georgia, SE USA
41 P8 **Hogatza River** ~ Alaska, USA
30 I14 **Hogback Mountain** ▲ Nebraska, C USA
97 G14 **Høgevarde** ▲ S Norway
Högfors see Karkkila
33 P5 **Hog Island** island Michigan, N USA
23 Y6 **Hog Island** island Virginia, NE USA
Hogoley Islands see Chuuk Islands
97 N20 **Högsby** Kalmar, S Sweden
38 K1 **Hogup Mountains** ▲ Utah, W USA
103 E17 **Hohe Acht** ▲ W Germany
Hohenelbe see Vrchlabí
110 I7 **Hohenems** Vorarlberg, W Austria
Hohenmauth see Vysoké Mýto
Hohensalza see Inowrocław
Hohenstadt see Zábřeh
Hohenstein in Ostpreussen see Olsztynek
22 I9 **Hohenwald** Tennessee, S USA
103 L17 **Hohenwarte-Stausee** ⊠ C Germany
Hohes Venn see Hautes Fagnes
111 Q8 **Hohe Tauern** ▲ W Austria
169 O13 **Hohhot** var. Huhehot, Huhuohaote, Mong. Kukukhoto; prev. Kweisui, Kwesui. Nei Mongol Zizhiqu, N China
105 U6 **Hohneck** ▲ NE France
79 Q16 **Hohoe** E Ghana
170 D12 **Hōhoku** Yamaguchi, Honshū, SW Japan
165 O11 **Hoh Sai Hu** ⊚ C China
165 N11 **Hoh Xil Hu** ⊚ C China
164 L11 **Hoh Xil Shan** ▲ W China
178 Kk10 **Hôi An** prev. Faifo. Quang Nam-Đa Nâng, C Vietnam
Hoï-Hao/Hoihow see Haikou
83 F17 **Hoima** W Uganda
28 L5 **Hoisington** Kansas, C USA
Hojagala see Khodzhakala
Hojambaz see Khodzhambas
97 H23 **Højby** Fyn, C Denmark
97 F24 **Højer** Sønderjylland, SW Denmark
170 Ee14 **Hōjō** var. Hôzyô. Ehime, Shikoku, SW Japan
192 J3 **Hokianga Harbour** inlet SE Tasman Sea
193 F17 **Hokitika** West Coast, South Island, NZ
172 P5 **Hokkai-dō** ◐ territory Hokkaidō, NE Japan
172 Oo5 **Hokkaidō** prev. Ezo, Yeso, Yezo. island NE Japan
97 G15 **Hokksund** Buskerud, S Norway
149 S4 **Hokmābād** Khorāsān, N Iran
Hokō see P'ohang
Hoko-guntō/Hoko-shotō see P'enghu Liehtao
143 T12 **Hoktemberyan** Rus. Oktemberyan. SW Armenia
96 F13 **Hol** Buskerud, S Norway
119 R11 **Hola Prystan'** Rus. Golaya Pristan. Khersons'ka Oblast', S Ukraine
xxxix S8 **Holbeach** Lincolnshire, E England, UK
xxxix S9 **Holbeach St Johns** Lincolnshire, E England, UK
xxxix S8 **Holbeach St Matthew** Lincolnshire, E England, UK
xxxix S8 **Holbeck Marsh** physical region E England, UK
97 I23 **Holbæk** Vestsjælland, E Denmark
168 G6 **Holboo** Dzavhan, W Mongolia
xxxvi D7 **Holborn** Camden, SE England, UK
xxxix X13 **Holbrook** Suffolk, E England, UK
191 P10 **Holbrook** New South Wales, SE Australia
39 N11 **Holbrook** Arizona, SW USA
xxxvi I12 **Holcombe Rogus** Devon, SW England, UK
xli O13 **Holden** Lancashire, NW England, UK
29 S5 **Holden** Missouri, C USA
38 K5 **Holden** Utah, W USA
29 O11 **Holdenville** Oklahoma, C USA
31 O16 **Holdrege** Nebraska, C USA
37 X3 **Hole in the Mountain Peak** ▲ Nevada, W USA
161 G20 **Hole Narsipur** Karnātaka, W India
113 H18 **Holešov** Ger. Holleschau. Jižní Morava, E Czech Republic
47 N14 **Holetown** prev. Jamestown. W Barbados
xxxvi I11 **Holford** Somerset, SW England, UK
33 Q12 **Holgate** Ohio, N USA
46 I7 **Holguín** Holguín, SE Cuba
25 V12 **Holiday** Florida, SE USA
41 O12 **Holitna River** ~ Alaska, USA
96 J13 **Höljes** Värmland, C Sweden
111 X3 **Hollabrunn** Niederösterreich, NE Austria
38 L3 **Holladay** Utah, W USA
xlii M2 **Holland** Orkney Islands, N Scotland, UK
9 X16 **Holland** Manitoba, S Canada
33 O9 **Holland** Michigan, N USA
27 T9 **Holland** Texas, SW USA
Holland see Netherlands
24 K4 **Hollandale** Mississippi, S USA
Hollandia see Jayapura
xxxvii Y7 **Holland-on-Sea** Essex, SE England, UK
Hollandsch Diep see Hollands Diep
101 H14 **Hollands Diep** var. Hollandsch Diep. channel SW Netherlands
xlii O2 **Hollandstoun** Orkney Islands, N Scotland, UK
Holleschau see Holešov
xxxix Y13 **Hollesley** Suffolk, E England, UK
27 R5 **Holliday** Texas, SW USA
20 E15 **Hollidaysburg** Pennsylvania, NE USA
xl I15 **Hollingworth** Tameside, NW England, UK
23 S6 **Hollins** Virginia, NE USA
28 J12 **Hollis** Oklahoma, C USA
37 O10 **Hollister** California, W USA
29 T8 **Hollister** Missouri, C USA
95 M19 **Hollola** Häme, S Finland
xxxvi C6 **Holloway** Islington, SE England, UK
100 K4 **Hollum** Friesland, N Netherlands
97 J23 **Höllviksnäs** Malmöhus, S Sweden
39 W6 **Holly** Colorado, C USA
33 R9 **Holly** Michigan, N USA
23 S14 **Holly Hill** South Carolina, SE USA
xli Y14 **Hollym** East Riding of Yorkshire, N England, UK
xliv E7 **Hollymount** Mayo, NW Ireland
23 W11 **Holly Ridge** North Carolina, SE USA
24 L1 **Holly Springs** Mississippi, S USA
xliv K10 **Hollywood** Wicklow, E Ireland
25 Z15 **Hollywood** Florida, SE USA
xliii M23 **Holm** Dumfries and Galloway, SW Scotland, UK
15 I2 **Holman** Victoria Island, Northwest Territories, N Canada
94 I2 **Hólmavík** Vestfirdhir, NW Iceland
xxxix R10 **Holme** Cambridgeshire, E England, UK
32 J7 **Holmen** Wisconsin, N USA
xxxix U7 **Holme next the Sea** Norfolk, E England, UK
xli U13 **Holme on Spalding Moor** East Riding of Yorkshire, N England, UK
xxxviii I6 **Holmes Chapel** Cheshire, W England, UK
25 R8 **Holmes Creek** ~ Alabama/Florida, SE USA
97 H16 **Holmestrand** Vestfold, S Norway
xli R15 **Holmfirth** Kirklees, N England, UK
95 J16 **Holmön** island N Sweden
97 E22 **Holmsland Klit** beach W Denmark
95 J16 **Holmsund** Västerbotten, N Sweden
97 Q18 **Holmudden** headland SE Sweden
194 L15 **Holnicote Bay** headland SW PNG
144 F10 **Holon** Tel Aviv, C Israel
119 P8 **Holovanivs'k** Rus. Golovanevsk. Kirovohrads'ka Oblast', C Ukraine
97 F21 **Holstebro** Ringkøbing, W Denmark
97 F23 **Holsted** Ribe, W Denmark
31 T13 **Holstein** Iowa, C USA
Holsteinborg/Holsteinsborg/Holstenborg/Holstensborg see Sisimiut
23 O8 **Holston River** ~ Tennessee, S USA
xxxvi E13 **Holsworthy** Devon, SW England, UK
xxxix W7 **Holt** Norfolk, E England, UK
xxxv L5 **Holt** Wrexham, NE Wales, UK
33 Q9 **Holt** Michigan, N USA
100 N10 **Holten** Overijssel, E Netherlands
29 P3 **Holton** Kansas, C USA
29 U5 **Holts Summit** Missouri, C USA
37 X17 **Holtville** California, W USA
100 L5 **Holwerd** Fris. Holwert. Friesland, N Netherlands
Holwert see Holwerd
41 O11 **Holy Cross** Alaska, USA
xliv H11 **Holycross** Tipperary, S Ireland
39 R4 **Holy Cross, Mount Of The** ▲ Colorado, C USA
xxxv E4 **Holyhead** Wel. Caer Gybi. Isle of Anglesey, NW Wales, UK
xxxv E4 **Holyhead Bay** bay NW Wales, UK
xli Q1 **Holy Island** Northumberland, N England, UK
xli Q1 **Holy Island** island NE England, UK
xliii H23 **Holy Island** island W Scotland, UK
xxxv D4 **Holy Island** island NW Wales, UK
39 W3 **Holyoke** Colorado, C USA
20 M11 **Holyoke** Massachusetts, NE USA
xxxv L13 **Holywell** Dorset, S England, UK
xl A17 **Holywell** Flintshire, N Wales, UK
xliii L24 **Holywood** Dumfries and Galloway, SW Scotland, UK
103 I14 **Holzminden** Niedersachsen, C Germany
83 G19 **Homa Bay** Nyanza, W Kenya
Homāyūnshahr see Khomeynishahr
79 P11 **Hombori** Mopti, S Mali
103 E20 **Homburg** Saarland, SW Germany
16 Nn1 **Home Bay** bay Baffin Bay, Northwest Territories, NE Canada
Homenau see Humenné
41 Q13 **Homer** Alaska, USA
24 H4 **Homer** Louisiana, S USA
20 H10 **Homer** New York, NE USA
25 V7 **Homerville** Georgia, SE USA
25 Y16 **Homestead** Florida, SE USA
29 O9 **Hominy** Oklahoma, C USA
96 H8 **Hommelvik** Sør-Trøndelag, S Norway
97 C16 **Hommersåk** Rogaland, S Norway
161 H15 **Homnābād** Karnātaka, C India
24 J7 **Homochitto River** ~ Mississippi, S USA
85 N20 **Homoine** Inhambane, SE Mozambique
114 O12 **Homoljske Planine** ▲ E Yugoslavia
Homonna see Humenné
Homs see Al Khums, Libya
Homs see Ḩimş, Syria
121 P19 **Homyel'** Rus. Gomel'. Homyel'skaya Voblasts', SE Belorussia
120 L12 **Homyel'** Vitsyebskaya Voblasts', N Belorussia
121 L19 **Homyel'skaya Voblasts'** prev. Rus. Gomel'skaya Oblast'. ◐ province SE Belorussia
Honan see Henan, China
Honan see Luoyang, China
172 Pp6 **Honbetsu** Hokkaidō, NE Japan
Honctő see Gurahonţ
56 E9 **Honda** Tolima, C Colombia
85 D24 **Hondeklip** Afr. Hondeklipbaai. Northern Cape, W South Africa
Hondeklipbaai see Hondeklip
9 Q13 **Hondo** Alberta, W Canada
170 C14 **Hondo** Kumamoto, Shimo-jima, SW Japan
27 Q12 **Hondo** Texas, SW USA
44 G1 **Hondo** ~ Central America
Hondo see Honshū
44 G6 **Honduras** off. Republic of Honduras. ◆ republic Central America
Honduras, Golfo de see Honduras, Gulf of
44 H4 **Honduras, Gulf of** Sp. Golfo de Honduras. gulf W Caribbean Sea
9 V12 **Hone** Manitoba, C Canada
23 P12 **Honea Path** South Carolina, SE USA
97 H14 **Hønefoss** Buskerud, S Norway
33 S12 **Honey Creek** ~ Ohio, N USA
27 V5 **Honey Grove** Texas, SW USA
37 Q4 **Honey Lake** ⊚ California, W USA
104 L4 **Honfleur** Calvados, N France
Hon Gai see Hông Gai
167 O8 **Hong'an** prev. Huang'an. Hubei, C China
Hongay see Hông Gai
178 K6 **Hông Gai** var. Hon Gai, Hongay. Quang Ninh, N Vietnam
167 O15 **Honghai Wan** bay N South China Sea
Hông Hà, Sông see Red River
167 O7 **Hong He** ~ C China
167 N9 **Hong Hu** ⊚ C China
166 L11 **Hongjiang** Hunan, S China
167 O15 **Hong Kong** Chin. Xianggang. S China
165 P7 **Hongliuyuan** Gansu, N China
169 O9 **Hongor** Dornogovĭ, SE Mongolia
167 S8 **Hongqiao** ✕ (Shanghai) Shanghai Shi, E China
166 K14 **Hongshui He** ~ S China
166 M5 **Hongtong** Shanxi, C China
170 G16 **Hongū** Wakayama, Honshū, SW Japan
Honguedo, Détroit d' see Honguedo Passage
13 Y5 **Honguedo Passage** var. Honguedo Strait, Fr. Détroit d'Honguedo. strait Québec, E Canada
Honguedo Strait see Honguedo Passage
Hongwan see Sunan
169 X13 **Hongwŏn** E North Korea
166 H7 **Hongyuan** prev. Hurama. Sichuan, C China
167 Q7 **Hongze Hu** var. Hung-tse Hu. ⊚ E China
195 W16 **Honiara** ● (Solomon Islands) Guadalcanal, C Solomon Islands
xxxix W9 **Honingham** Norfolk, E England, UK
xxxix P7 **Honington** Lincolnshire, E England, UK
xxxix V11 **Honington** Suffolk, E England, UK
xxxvi J13 **Honiton** Devon, SW England, UK
171 Ll11 **Honjō** var. Honzyô. Akita, Honshū, C Japan
95 K18 **Honkajoki** Turku-Pori, SW Finland
171 Ii16 **Honkawane** Shizuoka, Honshū, S Japan
94 K7 **Honningsvåg** Finnmark, N Norway
97 I19 **Hönö** Göteborg och Bohus, S Sweden
40 G11 **Honokaa** Haw. Honoka'a. Hawaii, USA, C Pacific Ocean
40 G11 **Honokohau** Haw. Honokōhau. Hawaii, USA, C Pacific Ocean
40 D9 **Honolulu** ◐ Oahu, Hawaii, USA, C Pacific Ocean
40 H11 **Honomu** Haw. Honomū. Hawaii, USA, C Pacific Ocean
107 P10 **Honrubia** Castilla-La Mancha, C Spain
171 I15 **Honshū** var. Hondo, Honsyû. island SW Japan
Honsyû see Honshū
Honte see Westerschelde
Honzyô see Honjō
xxxvii W9 **Hoo** Kent, SE England, UK
15 Ii5 **Hood** ~ Northwest Territories, NW Canada
Hood Island see Española, Isla
34 H11 **Hood, Mount** ▲ Oregon, NW USA
194 K16 **Hood Point** headland S PNG
34 H11 **Hood River** Oregon, NW USA
100 H10 **Hoofddorp** Noord-Holland, W Netherlands
101 G15 **Hoogerheide** Noord-Brabant, S Netherlands
100 N8 **Hoogeveen** Drenthe, NE Netherlands
100 O6 **Hoogezand-Sappemeer** Groningen, NE Netherlands
100 J8 **Hoogkarspel** Noord-Holland, NW Netherlands
100 N5 **Hoogkerk** Groningen, NE Netherlands
100 G13 **Hoogvliet** Zuid-Holland, SW Netherlands
xli U14 **Hook** East Riding of Yorkshire, N England, UK
xxxvii R10 **Hook** Hampshire, S England, UK
28 I8 **Hooker** Oklahoma, C USA
xliv J13 **Hook Head** Ir. Rinn Duáin. headland SE Ireland
xxxvii P6 **Hook Norton** Oxfordshire, C England, UK
Hook of Holland see Hoek van Holland
168 I9 **Hoolt** Övörhangay, C Mongolia
41 W13 **Hoonah** Chichagof Island, Alaska, USA
40 L11 **Hooper Bay** Alaska, USA
33 N13 **Hoopeston** Illinois, N USA
97 K22 **Höör** Malmöhus, S Sweden
100 I9 **Hoorn** Noord-Holland, NW Netherlands
20 L10 **Hoosic River** ~ New York, NE USA
Hoosier State see Indiana
37 Y11 **Hoover Dam** dam Arizona/Nevada, W USA
168 I9 **Höövör** Övörhangay, C Mongolia
143 Q11 **Hopa** Artvin, NE Turkey
20 J14 **Hopatcong** New Jersey, NE USA
xxxviii L5 **Hope** Derbyshire, C England, UK
xxxv K5 **Hope** Flintshire, N Wales, UK
8 M17 **Hope** British Columbia, SW Canada
41 R12 **Hope** Alaska, USA
29 T14 **Hope** Arkansas, C USA
33 P14 **Hope** Indiana, N USA
31 Q5 **Hope** North Dakota, N USA
xxxviii H10 **Hope Bowdler** Shropshire, W England, UK
11 Q7 **Hopedale** Newfoundland and Labrador, NE Canada
Hopeh/Hopei see Hebei
188 K13 **Hope, Lake** salt lake Western Australia
43 X13 **Hopelchén** Campeche, SE Mexico
xlii L11 **Hopeman** Moray, N Scotland, UK
23 U11 **Hope Mills** North Carolina, SE USA
191 O7 **Hope, Mount** New South Wales, SE Australia
94 P4 **Hopen** island SE Svalbard
207 Q4 **Hope, Point** headland Alaska, USA
10 M3 **Hopes Advance, Cap** headland Québec, NE Canada
xxxvi H15 **Hope's Nose** headland SW England, UK
190 L10 **Hopetoun** Victoria, SE Australia
85 H23 **Hopetown** Northern Cape, W South Africa
xxxviii H13 **Hope under Dinmore** Herefordshire, W England, UK
23 W6 **Hopewell** Virginia, NE USA
111 O7 **Hopfgarten im Brixental** Tirol, W Austria
189 N8 **Hopkins Lake** salt lake Western Australia
190 M12 **Hopkins River** ~ Victoria, SE Australia
22 I7 **Hopkinsville** Kentucky, S USA
36 M6 **Hopland** California, W USA
xxxix Z10 **Hopton** Norfolk, E England, UK
97 G24 **Hoptrup** Sønderjylland, SW Denmark
34 F9 **Hoquiam** Washington, NW USA
31 R6 **Horace** North Dakota, N USA
143 R12 **Horasan** Erzurum, NE Turkey
103 G22 **Horb am Neckar** Baden-Württemberg, S Germany
97 K23 **Hörby** Malmöhus, S Sweden
45 P16 **Horconcitos** Chiriquí, W Panama
97 C14 **Hordaland** ◐ county S Norway
xli X4 **Horden** Durham, N England, UK
118 H13 **Horezu** Vâlcea, SW Romania
110 G7 **Horgen** Zürich, N Switzerland
168 I7 **Horgo** Arhangay, C Mongolia
Hörin see Fenglin
169 O13 **Horinger** Nei Mongol Zizhiqu, N China
168 I9 **Horiult** Bayanhongor, C Mongolia
9 U17 **Horizon** Saskatchewan, S Canada
199 J10 **Horizon Bank** undersea feature S Pacific Ocean
199 Jj11 **Horizon Deep** undersea feature W Pacific Ocean
97 L14 **Hörken** Örebro, S Sweden
121 O15 **Horki** Rus. Gorki. Mahilyowskaya Voblasts', E Belorussia
xxxvii U11 **Horley** Surrey, SE England, UK
205 O10 **Horlick Mountains** ▲ Antarctica
119 X7 **Horlivka** Rom. Adâncata, Rus. Gorlovka. Donets'ka Oblast', E Ukraine
149 V11 **Ḩormak** Sīstān va Balūchestān, SE Iran
149 R13 **Hormozgān** off. Ostān-e Hormozgān. ◐ province S Iran
Hormoz, Tangeh-ye see Hormuz, Strait of
147 W6 **Hormuz, Strait of** var. Strait of Ormuz, Per. Tangeh-ye Hormoz. strait Iran/Oman
111 W2 **Horn** Niederösterreich, NE Austria
97 M18 **Horn** Östergötland, S Sweden
15 Hh8 **Horn** ~ Northwest Territories, NW Canada
Hornád see Hernád
15 H3 **Hornaday** ~ Northwest Territories, NW Canada
94 H13 **Hornavan** ⊚ N Sweden
xli N12 **Hornby** Lancashire, NW England, UK
67 C24 **Hornby Mountains** hill range West Falkland, Falkland Islands
Horn, Cape see Hornos, Cabo de
xxxix R6 **Horncastle** Lincolnshire, E England, UK
97 N14 **Horndal** Kopparberg, C Sweden
xxxvii Q13 **Horndean** Hampshire, S England, UK
95 I16 **Hörnefors** Västerbotten, N Sweden
20 F11 **Hornell** New York, NE USA
Horné Nové Mesto see Kysucké Nové Mesto
10 F12 **Hornepayne** Ontario, S Canada
xliv H2 **Horn Head** headland N Ireland
96 D10 **Hornindalsvatnet** ⊚ S Norway
103 G22 **Hornisgrinde** ▲ SW Germany
24 M9 **Horn Island** island Mississippi, S USA
65 J26 **Hornos, Cabo de** Eng. Cape Horn. headland S Chile
119 S10 **Hornostayivka** Khersons'ka Oblast', S Ukraine
191 T9 **Hornsby** New South Wales, SE Australia
xxxvii W12 **Horns Cross** East Sussex, SE England, UK
xli X13 **Hornsea** East Riding of Yorkshire, E England, UK
xxxvi C5 **Hornsey** Haringey, SE England, UK
96 O11 **Hornslandet** peninsula C Sweden
97 H22 **Hornslet** Århus, C Denmark
94 O4 **Hornsundtind** ▲ S Svalbard
Horochów see Horokhiv
118 J7 **Horodenka** Rus. Gorodenka. Ivano-Frankivs'ka Oblast', W Ukraine
119 Q2 **Horodnya** Rus. Gorodnya. Chernihivs'ka Oblast', NE Ukraine
118 K6 **Horodok** Khmel'nyts'ka Oblast', W Ukraine
118 H5 **Horodok** Pol. Gródek Jagielloński, Rus. Gorodok, Gorodok Yagellonski. L'vivs'ka Oblast', NW Ukraine
119 Q6 **Horodyshche** Rus. Gorodishche. Cherkas'ka Oblast', C Ukraine
172 P4 **Horokanai** Hokkaidō, NE Japan
118 J4 **Horokhiv** Pol. Horochów, Rus. Gorokhov. Volyns'ka Oblast', NW Ukraine
172 P7 **Horoshiri-dake** var. Horosiri Dake. ▲ Hokkaidō, N Japan
Horosiri Dake see Horoshiri-dake
113 C17 **Hořovice** Ger. Horowitz. Střední Čechy, W Czech Republic
Horowitz see Hořovice
169 T9 **Horqin Youyi Zhongqi** Nei Mongol Zizhiqu, N China
169 U11 **Horqin Zuoyi Houqi** Nei Mongol Zizhiqu, N China
169 T9 **Horqin Zuoyi Zhongqi** Nei Mongol Zizhiqu, N China
64 O5 **Horqueta** Concepción, C Paraguay
57 O12 **Horqueta Minas** Amazonas, S Venezuela
xxxvi F15 **Horrabridge** Devon, SW England, UK
97 J20 **Horred** Älvsborg, S Sweden
157 J19 **Horsburgh Atoll** atoll N Maldives
22 K7 **Horse Cave** Kentucky, S USA
39 V6 **Horse Creek** ~ Colorado, C USA
29 S6 **Horse Creek** ~ Missouri, C USA
20 G11 **Horseheads** New York, NE USA
xli Q11 **Horsehouse** North Yorkshire, N England, UK
xliv H9 **Horseleap** Westmeath, C Ireland
39 P13 **Horse Mount** ▲ New Mexico, SW USA
97 G22 **Horsens** Vejle, C Denmark
67 F25 **Horse Pasture Point** headland W Saint Helena
35 N13 **Horseshoe Bend** Idaho, NW USA
38 L13 **Horseshoe Reservoir** ⊠ Arizona, SW USA
66 M9 **Horseshoe Seamounts** undersea feature E Atlantic Ocean
xxxix Y8 **Horsey** Norfolk, E England, UK
xxxix X9 **Horsford** Norfolk, E England, UK
xxxvii T12 **Horsham** West Sussex, SE England, UK
190 L11 **Horsham** Victoria, SE Australia
xxxvi M8 **Horsley** Gloucestershire, C England, UK
101 M15 **Horst** Limburg, SE Netherlands
66 N2 **Horta** Faial, Azores, Portugal, NE Atlantic Ocean
97 H16 **Horten** Vestfold, S Norway
113 M23 **Hortobágy-Berettyó** ~ E Hungary
29 Q3 **Horton** Kansas, C USA
15 H3 **Horton** ~ Northwest Territories, NW Canada
xli P12 **Horton in Ribblesdale** North Yorkshire, N England, UK
97 J23 **Hørve** Vestsjælland, E Denmark
97 L22 **Hörvik** Blekinge, S Sweden
144 E11 **Ḩorvot Ḩaluza** ruins Southern, S Israel
xli O15 **Horwich** Bolton, NW England, UK
12 E7 **Horwood Lake** ⊚ Ontario, S Canada
118 K4 **Horyn'** Rus. Goryn. ~ NW Ukraine
83 I14 **Hosa'ina** var. Hosseina, It. Hosanna. SW Ethiopia
Hosanna see Hosa'ina
103 H18 **Hösbach** Bayern, C Germany
Hose Mountains see Hose, Pegunungan
174 Mm6 **Hose, Pegunungan** var. Hose Mountains. ▲ East Malaysia
154 L15 **Hoshāb** Baluchistān, SW Pakistan
160 H10 **Hoshangābād** Madhya Pradesh, C India
118 L4 **Hoshcha** Rivnens'ka Oblast', NW Ukraine
158 I7 **Hoshiārpur** Punjab, NW India
168 J7 **Höshööt** Arhangay, C Mongolia
101 M23 **Hosingen** Diekirch, NE Luxembourg
195 N12 **Hoskins** New Britain, E PNG
161 G17 **Hospet** Karnātaka, C India
106 K4 **Hospital de Orbigo** Castilla-León, N Spain
Hospitalet see L'Hospitalet de Llobregat
94 N13 **Hossa** Oulu, E Finland
Hosseina see Hosa'ina
Hosszúmezjő see Câmpulung Moldovenesc
65 I25 **Hoste, Isla** island S Chile
119 O4 **Hostomel'** Rus. Gostomel'. Kyyivs'ka Oblast', N Ukraine
161 H20 **Hosūr** Tamil Nādu, SE India
xlii I5 **Hoswick** Shetland Islands, NE Scotland, UK
178 H8 **Hot** Chiang Mai, NW Thailand
164 G10 **Hotan** var. Khotan, Chin. Ho-t'ien. Xinjiang Uygur Zizhiqu, NW China
164 H9 **Hotan He** ~ NW China
85 G22 **Hotazel** Northern Cape, N South Africa
39 Q5 **Hotchkiss** Colorado, C USA
37 V7 **Hot Creek Range** ▲ Nevada, W USA
Hote see Hoti
xli V14 **Hotham** East Riding of Yorkshire, N England, UK
176 U11 **Hoti** var. Hote. Pulau Seram, E Indonesia
Ho-t'ien see Hotan
Hotin see Khotyn
95 H15 **Hoting** Jämtland, C Sweden
168 L14 **Hotong Qagan Nur** ⊚ N China
168 J8 **Hotont** Arhangay, C Mongolia
29 T12 **Hot Springs** Arkansas, C USA
30 J11 **Hot Springs** South Dakota, N USA
23 S5 **Hot Springs** Virginia, NE USA
37 Q4 **Hot Springs Peak** ▲ California, W USA
29 T12 **Hot Springs Village** Arkansas, C USA
Hotspur Bank see Hotspur Seamount
67 J16 **Hotspur Seamount** var. Hotspur Bank. undersea feature C Atlantic Ocean
15 Hh6 **Hottah Lake** ⊚ Northwest Territories, NW Canada
46 K9 **Hotte, Massif de la** ▲ SW Haiti
101 K21 **Hotton** Luxembourg, SE Belgium
Hötzing see Hațeg
197 I6 **Houaïlou** Province Nord, C New Caledonia
76 K5 **Houari Boumediène** ✕ (Alger) N Algeria
178 Hh6 **Houayxay** var. Ban Houayxay, Ban Houei Sai. Bokèo, N Laos
xlii J2 **Houbie** Shetland Islands, NE Scotland, UK
105 N5 **Houdan** Yvelines, N France
101 F20 **Houdeng-Goegnies** var. Houdeng-Gœgnies. Hainaut, S Belgium

◆ Country ● Country Capital ◇ Dependent Territory ○ Dependent Territory Capital ◐ Administrative Region ✕ International Airport ▲ Mountain ▲ Mountain Range ▲ Volcano ~ River ⊚ Lake ⊠ Reservoir

104 K14 **Houeillès** Lot-et-Garonne, SW France
101 L22 **Houffalize** Luxembourg, SE Belgium
xl M7 **Houghton** Cumbria, NW England, UK
32 M3 **Houghton** Michigan, N USA
33 Q7 **Houghton Lake** Michigan, N USA
33 Q7 **Houghton Lake** ◎ Michigan, N USA
xli S7 **Houghton-le-Spring** Sunderland, NE England, UK
21 T3 **Houlton** Maine, NE USA
166 M5 **Houma** Shanxi, C China
200 Q15 **Houma** 'Eua, C Tonga
200 R16 **Houma** Tongatapu, S Tonga
24 J10 **Houma** Louisiana, S USA
200 Qq16 **Houma Taloa** *headland* Tongatapu, S Tonga
79 O13 **Houndé** SW Burkina
xxxvii S9 **Hounslow** Hounslow, SE England, UK
xxxiv K16 **Hounslow** ◐ *London borough* SE England, UK
xliii F14 **Hourn, Loch** *inlet* NW Scotland, UK
104 J12 **Hourtin-Carcans, Lac d'** ◎ SW France
38 J5 **House Range** ▲▲ Utah, W USA
8 K13 **Houston** British Columbia, SW Canada
41 R11 **Houston** Alaska, USA
31 X10 **Houston** Minnesota, N USA
24 M3 **Houston** Mississippi, S USA
29 V7 **Houston** Missouri, C USA
27 W11 **Houston** Texas, SW USA
27 W11 **Houston** ✕ Texas, SW USA
100 J12 **Houten** Utrecht, C Netherlands
101 K17 **Houthalen** Limburg, NE Belgium
xlii M4 **Houton** Orkney Islands, N Scotland, UK
101 I22 **Houyet** Namur, SE Belgium
97 H22 **Hov** Århus, C Denmark
97 L17 **Hova** Skaraborg, S Sweden
168 E6 **Hovd** *var.* Khovd. Hovd, W Mongolia
168 J10 **Hovd** Övörhangay, C Mongolia
168 E7 **Hovd** ◐ *province* W Mongolia
168 C5 **Hovd Gol** ≈ NW Mongolia
xxxvii T13 **Hove** Brighton and Hove, SE England, UK
31 N8 **Hoven** South Dakota, N USA
118 I8 **Hoverla, Hora** *Rus.* Gora Goverla. ▲ W Ukraine
xxxix X9 **Hoveton** Norfolk, E England, UK
xli U11 **Hovingham** North Yorkshire, N England, UK
168 H8 **Hövîyn Am** Bayanhongor, C Mongolia
97 M21 **Hovmantorp** Kronoberg, S Sweden
169 N11 **Hövsgöl** Dornogovĭ, SE Mongolia
168 I5 **Hövsgöl** ◐ *province* N Mongolia
Hovsgol, Lake *see* Hövsgöl Nuur
168 J5 **Hövsgöl Nuur** *var.* Lake Hovsgol. ◎ N Mongolia
80 L9 **Howa, Ouadi** *var.* Wādi Howar. ≈ Chad/Sudan *see also* Howar, Wādi
29 P7 **Howard** Kansas, C USA
31 Q10 **Howard** South Dakota, N USA
27 N10 **Howard Draw** *valley* Texas, SW USA
31 U8 **Howard Lake** Minnesota, N USA
82 B8 **Howar, Wādi** *var.* Ouadi Howa. ≈ Chad/Sudan *see also* Howa, Ouadi
xli U14 **Howden** East Riding of Yorkshire, N England, UK
27 U5 **Howe** Texas, SW USA
191 R12 **Howe, Cape** *headland* New South Wales/Victoria, SE Australia
33 R9 **Howell** Michigan, N USA
31 Q9 **Howes** South Dakota, N USA
xliii M20 **Howgate** Midlothian, SE Scotland, UK
xli R3 **Howick** Northumberland, N England, UK
85 K23 **Howick** KwaZulu/Natal, E South Africa
Howrah *see* Hāora
xliv L9 **Howth** Dublin, E Ireland
29 W9 **Hoxie** Arkansas, C USA
28 J3 **Hoxie** Kansas, C USA
xxxix X11 **Hoxne** Suffolk, E England, UK
103 I14 **Höxter** Nordrhein-Westfalen, W Germany
164 K6 **Hoxud** Xinjiang Uygur Zizhiqu, NW China
xlii L5 **Hoy** *island* N Scotland, UK
45 S17 **Hoya, Cerro** ▲ S Panama
96 D12 **Høyanger** Sogn og Fjordane, S Norway
103 P15 **Hoyerswerda** Sachsen, E Germany
xl A16 **Hoylake** Wirral, NW England, UK
170 Dd15 **Hōyo-kaikyō** *var.* Hayasui-seto. *strait* SW Japan
106 J8 **Hoyos** Extremadura, W Spain
31 W5 **Hoyt Lakes** Minnesota, N USA
89 V2 **Hoyvík** Streymoy, N Faeroe Islands
143 O14 **Hozat** Tunceli, E Turkey
Hôzyô *see* Hōjō
113 F16 **Hradec Králové** *Ger.* Königgrätz. Východní Čechy, NE Czech Republic
113 B16 **Hradiště** *Ger.* Burgstadlberg. ▲ NW Czech Republic
119 R6 **Hradyz'k** *Rus.* Gradizhsk. Poltavs'ka Oblast', NE Ukraine
121 M16 **Hradzyanka** *Rus.* Grodzyanka. Mahilyowskaya Voblasts', E Belorussia
121 F16 **Hrandzichy** *Rus.* Grandichi. Hrodzyenskaya Voblasts', W Belorussia
113 H18 **Hranice** *Ger.* Mährisch-Weisskirchen. Severní Morava, E Czech Republic
114 I13 **Hrasnica** SE Bosnia and Herzegovina
111 V11 **Hrastnik** C Slovenia
143 U12 **Hrazdan** *Rus.* Razdan. C Armenia
143 T12 **Hrazdan** *var.* Zanga, *Rus.* Razdan. ≈ C Armenia
119 R5 **Hrebinka** *Rus.* Grebenka. Poltavs'ka Oblast', NE Ukraine
121 K17 **Hresk** *Rus.* Gresk. Minskaya Voblasts', C Belorussia
Hrisoupoli *see* Chrysoúpoli
121 F16 **Hrodna** *Pol.* Grodno. Hrodzyenskaya Voblasts', W Belorussia
121 F16 **Hrodzyenskaya Voblasts'** *prev. Rus.* Grodnenskaya Oblast'. ◐ *province* W Belorussia
113 J21 **Hron** *Ger.* Gran, *Hung.* Garam. ≈ C Slovakia
113 Q14 **Hrubieszów** *Rus.* Grubeshov. Zamość, SE Poland
114 F13 **Hrvace** Split-Dalmacija, SE Croatia
Hrvatska *see* Croatia
Hrvatska Kostajnica *see* Kostajnica
118 K6 **Hrymayliv** *Pol.* Gizymałów, *Rus.* Grimaylov. Ternopil's'ka Oblast', W Ukraine
178 H4 **Hsenwi** Shan State, E Burma
Hsia-men *see* Xiamen
Hsiang-t'an *see* Xiangtan
Hsi Chiang *see* Xi Jiang
178 Gg6 **Hsihseng** Shan State, C Burma
167 S13 **Hsinchu** *municipality* N Taiwan
Hsing-k'ai Hu *see* Khanka, Lake
Hsining/Hsi-ning *see* Xining
Hsinking *see* Changchun
Hsin-yang *see* Xinyang
167 S14 **Hsinying** *var.* Sinying, *Jap.* Shinei. C Taiwan
178 Gg4 **Hsipaw** Shan State, E Burma
Hsu-chou *see* Xuzhou
167 S13 **Hsüeh Shan** ▲ N Taiwan
Hu *see* Shanghai Shi
85 B18 **Huab** ≈ W Namibia
59 M21 **Huacaya** Chuquisaca, S Bolivia
59 J19 **Huachacalla** Oruro, SW Bolivia
165 X9 **Huachi** *var.* Rouyuanchengzi. Gansu, C China
59 N16 **Huachi, Laguna** ◎ N Bolivia
59 D14 **Huacho** Lima, W Peru
169 Y8 **Huachuan** Heilongjiang, NE China
169 P12 **Huade** Nei Mongol Zizhiqu, N China
169 W10 **Huadian** Jilin, NE China
58 E13 **Huagaruncho, Cordillera** ▲▲ C Peru
Hua Hin *see* Ban Hua Hin
203 S10 **Huahine** *island* Îles Sous le Vent, W French Polynesia
Huahua, Río *see* Wawa, Río
178 Ii9 **Huai** ≈ E Thailand
167 P6 **Huaibei** Anhui, E China
169 V10 **Huaide** *var.* Gongzhuling. Jilin, NE China
163 T10 **Huai He** ≈ C China
167 I11 **Huaihua** Hunan, S China
167 N14 **Huaiji** Guangdong, S China
167 O2 **Huailai** *prev.* Shacheng. Hebei, E China
167 P7 **Huainan** *var.* Huai-nan, Hwainan. Anhui, E China
167 N2 **Huairen** Shanxi, C China
167 O7 **Huaiyang** Henan, C China
167 Q7 **Huaiyin** *var.* Qingjiang. Jiangsu, E China
178 Gg16 **Huai Yot** Trang, SW Thailand
43 Q15 **Huajuapan** *var.* Huajuapan de León. Oaxaca, SE Mexico
Huajuapan de León *see* Huajuapan
43 O9 **Hualahuises** Nuevo León, NE Mexico
38 I11 **Hualapai Mountains** ▲▲ Arizona, SW USA
38 I11 **Hualapai Peak** ▲ Arizona, SW USA
64 J7 **Hualfín** Catamarca, N Argentina
167 T13 **Hualien** *var.* Hwalien, *Jap.* Karen. C Taiwan
58 E10 **Huallaga, Río** ≈ N Peru
58 C11 **Huamachuco** La Libertad, C Peru
43 Q14 **Huamantla** Tlaxcala, S Mexico
84 C13 **Huambo** *Port.* Nova Lisboa. Huambo, C Angola
84 B13 **Huambo** ◐ *province* C Angola
43 P15 **Huamuxtitlán** Guerrero, S Mexico
65 H17 **Huancache, Sierra** ▲▲ SW Argentina
59 I17 **Huancané** Puno, SE Peru
59 F16 **Huancapi** Ayacucho, C Peru
59 E15 **Huancavelica** Huancavelica, SW Peru
59 E15 **Huancavelica** *off.* Departamento de Huancavelica. ◐ *department* W Peru
59 E14 **Huancayo** Junín, C Peru
59 K20 **Huanchaca, Cerro** ▲ S Bolivia
58 C12 **Huandoy, Nevado** ▲ W Peru
167 O8 **Huangchuan** Henan, C China
Huang Hai *see* Yellow Sea
163 Q8 **Huang He** *var.* Yellow River. ≈ C China
167 Q4 **Huanghe Kou** *delta* E China
166 L5 **Huangling** Shaanxi, C China
167 O9 **Huangpi** Hubei, C China
167 P9 **Huangqi Hai** ◎ N China
167 Q9 **Huang Shan** ▲ Anhui, E China
167 Q9 **Huangshan** *var.* Tunxi. Anhui, E China
167 O9 **Huangshi** *var.* Huang-shih, Hwangshih. Hubei, C China
Huang-shih *see* Huangshi
166 L5 **Huangtu Gaoyuan** *plateau* C China
63 B22 **Huanguelén** Buenos Aires, E Argentina
167 S10 **Huangyan** Zhejiang, SE China
165 S10 **Huangyuan** Qinghai, C China
165 T10 **Huangzhong** Qinghai, C China
169 W12 **Huanren** Liaoning, NE China
59 F15 **Huanta** Ayacucho, C Peru
58 E13 **Huánuco** Huánuco, C Peru
58 D13 **Huánuco** *off.* Departamento de Huánuco. ◐ *department* C Peru
59 L19 **Huanuni** Oruro, W Bolivia
165 X9 **Huan Xian** Gansu, C China
167 S12 **Huap'ing Yu** *island* N Taiwan
64 H3 **Huara** Tarapacá, N Chile
59 D14 **Huaral** Lima, W Peru
Huarás *see* Huaraz
58 D13 **Huaraz** *var.* Huarás. Ancash, W Peru
59 I16 **Huari Huari, Río** ≈ S Peru
58 C13 **Huarmey** Ancash, W Peru
42 H4 **Huasabas** Sonora, NW Mexico
58 D8 **Huasaga, Río** ≈ Ecuador/Peru
178 H16 **Hua Sai** Nakhon Si Thammarat, SW Thailand
58 D12 **Huascarán, Nevado** ▲ W Peru
64 G8 **Huasco** Atacama, N Chile
64 G8 **Huasco, Río** ≈ C Chile
165 S11 **Huashikia** Qinghai, W China
42 G7 **Huatabampo** Sonora, NW Mexico
165 W10 **Huating** Gansu, C China
178 Jj7 **Huatt, Phou** ▲ N Vietnam
43 Q14 **Huatusco** *var.* Huatusco de Chicuellar. Veracruz-Llave, C Mexico
Huatusco de Chicuellar *see* Huatusco
43 P13 **Huauchinango** Puebla, S Mexico
Huaunta *see* Wounta
43 R15 **Huautla** *var.* Huautla de Jiménez. Oaxaca, SE Mexico
Huautla de Jiménez *see* Huautla
167 O5 **Huaxian** *var.* Daokou, Hua Xian. Henan, C China
31 V13 **Hubbard** Iowa, C USA
27 U8 **Hubbard** Texas, SW USA
27 Q6 **Hubbard Creek Lake** ◎ Texas, SW USA
33 R6 **Hubbard Lake** ◎ Michigan, N USA
xxxix R7 **Hubbert's Bridge** Lincolnshire, E England, UK
166 M9 **Hubei** *var.* E, Hubei Sheng, Hupeh, Hupei. ◐ *province* C China
Hubei Sheng *see* Hubei
111 P8 **Huben** Tirol, W Austria
33 R13 **Huber Heights** Ohio, N USA
161 F17 **Hubli** Karnātaka, SW India
169 X12 **Huch'ang** N North Korea
xxxix N7 **Hucknall** Nottinghamshire, C England, UK
xli R15 **Huddersfield** Kirklees, N England, UK
97 O16 **Huddinge** Stockholm, C Sweden
96 N11 **Hudiksvall** Gävleborg, C Sweden
31 W13 **Hudson** Iowa, C USA
21 O11 **Hudson** Massachusetts, NE USA
33 Q11 **Hudson** Michigan, N USA
32 H6 **Hudson** Wisconsin, N USA
9 V14 **Hudson Bay** Saskatchewan, S Canada
10 G6 **Hudson Bay** *bay* NE Canada
205 T16 **Hudson, Cape** *headland* Antarctica
Hudson, Détroit d' *see* Hudson Strait
29 Q9 **Hudson, Lake** ▣ Oklahoma, C USA
20 K9 **Hudson River** ≈ New Jersey/New York, NE USA
8 M12 **Hudson's Hope** British Columbia, W Canada
10 L2 **Hudson Strait** *Fr.* Détroit d'Hudson. *strait* Northwest Territories/Québec, NE Canada
Huđūd ash Shamālīyah, Minṭaqat al *see* Al Ḥudūd ash Shamālīyah
Hudur *see* Xuddur
178 K9 **Huê** Thua Thiên-Huê, C Vietnam
106 J7 **Huebra** ≈ W Spain
26 H8 **Hueco Mountains** ▲▲ Texas, SW USA
118 G10 **Huedin** *Hung.* Bánffyhunyad. Cluj, NW Romania
42 J10 **Huehueto, Cerro** ▲ C Mexico
44 B5 **Huehuetenango** Huehuetenango, W Guatemala
44 B4 **Huehuetenango** *off.* Departamento de Huehuetenango. ◐ *department* W Guatemala
42 L11 **Huejuquilla** Jalisco, SW Mexico
43 P12 **Huejutla** *var.* Huejutla de Reyes. Hidalgo, C Mexico
Huejutla de Reyes *see* Huejutla
104 G6 **Huelgoat** Finistère, NW France
107 O13 **Huelma** Andalucía, S Spain
106 I14 **Huelva** *anc.* Onuba. Andalucía, SW Spain
106 I13 **Huelva** ◐ *province* Andalucía, SW Spain
106 J13 **Huelva** ≈ SW Spain
107 Q14 **Huércal-Overa** Andalucía, S Spain
39 Q9 **Huerfano Mountain** ▲ New Mexico, SW USA
39 T7 **Huerfano River** ≈ Colorado, C USA
107 S12 **Huertas, Cabo** *headland* SE Spain
107 R6 **Huerva** ≈ N Spain
107 S4 **Huesca** *anc.* Osca. Aragón, NE Spain
107 T4 **Huesca** ◐ *province* Aragón, NE Spain
107 P13 **Huéscar** Andalucía, S Spain
43 N15 **Huetamo** *var.* Huetamo de Núñez. Michoacán de Ocampo, SW Mexico
Huetamo de Núñez *see* Huetamo
107 P8 **Huete** Castilla-La Mancha, C Spain
25 P4 **Hueytown** Alabama, S USA
30 L16 **Hugh Butler Lake** ▣ Nebraska, C USA
189 V6 **Hughenden** Queensland, NE Australia
190 A6 **Hughes** South Australia
41 P8 **Hughes** Alaska, USA
29 X11 **Hughes** Arkansas, C USA
27 W6 **Hughes Springs** Texas, SW USA
xxxvi I7 **HughTown** Isles of Scilly, SW England, UK
39 V5 **Hugo** Colorado, C USA
29 Q13 **Hugo** Oklahoma, C USA
29 Q13 **Hugo Lake** ▣ Oklahoma, C USA
28 H7 **Hugoton** Kansas, C USA
Huhehot/Huhohaote *see* Hohhot
167 R13 **Hui'an** Fujian, SE China
192 O9 **Huiarau Range** ▲▲ North Island, NZ
85 D22 **Huib-Hoch Plateau** *plateau* S Namibia
43 O13 **Huichapan** Hidalgo, C Mexico
Huicheng *see* Shexian
169 W13 **Hŭich'ŏn** C North Korea
56 E12 **Huila** *off.* Departamento del Huila. ◐ *province* S Colombia
85 B15 **Huíla** ◐ *province* SW Angola
56 D11 **Huila, Nevado del** *elevation* C Colombia
85 B15 **Huíla Plateau** *plateau* S Angola
166 G12 **Huili** Sichuan, C China
167 P4 **Huimin** Shandong, E China
169 W11 **Huinan** *var.* Chaoyang. Jilin, NE China
64 K12 **Huinca Renancó** Córdoba, C Argentina
165 V10 **Huining** Gansu, C China
xxxvi I12 **Huish Champflower** Somerset, SW England, UK
166 J12 **Huishui** Guizhou, S China
104 L6 **Huisne** ≈ NW France
100 L12 **Huissen** Gelderland, SE Netherlands
165 N11 **Huiten Nur** ◎ C China
95 K19 **Huittinen** Turku-Pori, SW Finland
43 O15 **Huitzuco** *var.* Huitzuco de los Figueroa. Guerrero, S Mexico
Huitzuco de los Figueroa *see* Huitzuco
165 W11 **Hui Xian** Gansu, C China
43 V17 **Huixtla** Chiapas, SE Mexico
166 H12 **Huize** Yunnan, SW China
100 J10 **Huizen** Noord-Holland, C Netherlands
167 O14 **Huizhou** Guangdong, S China
168 J6 **Hujirt** Arhangay, C Mongolia
168 J8 **Hujirt** Övörhangay, C Mongolia
168 K8 **Hujrt** Töv, C Mongolia
Hukagawa *see* Fukagawa
Hüksan-chedo *see* Hüksan-gundo
169 W17 **Hüksan-gundo** *var.* Hüksan-chedo. *island group* SW South Korea
Hukue *see* Fukue
Hukui *see* Fukui
85 G20 **Hukuntsi** Kgalagadi, SW Botswana
Hukuoka *see* Fukuoka
Hukusima *see* Fukushima
Hukutiyama *see* Fukuchiyama
Hukuyama *see* Fukuyama
169 W8 **Hulan** Heilongjiang, NE China
169 W8 **Hulan He** ≈ NE China
33 Q4 **Hulbert Lake** ◎ Michigan, N USA
Hulczyn *see* Hlučín
169 Z8 **Hulin** Heilongjiang, NE China
169 S9 **Hulingol** *prev.* Huolin Gol. Nei Mongol Zizhiqu, N China
xli W13 **Hull** ≈ N England, UK
Hull *see* Kingston upon Hull
12 L12 **Hull** Québec, SE Canada
31 S12 **Hull** Iowa, C USA
xxxvi M9 **Hullavington** Wiltshire, S England, UK
Hull Island *see* Orona
101 F16 **Hulst** Zeeland, SW Netherlands
169 Q7 **Hulstay** Dornod, NE Mongolia
Hultschin *see* Hlučín
97 M19 **Hultsfred** Kalmar, S Sweden
Hulun *see* Hailar
Hu-lun Ch'ih *see* Hulun Nur
169 Q6 **Hulun Nur** *var.* Hu-lun Ch'ih; *prev.* Dalai Nor. ◎ NE China
Hulwan/Hulwân *see* Helwân
119 V8 **Hulyaypole** *Rus.* Gulyaypole. Zaporiz'ka Oblast', SE Ukraine
169 V4 **Huma** Heilongjiang, NE China
47 V6 **Humacao** E Puerto Rico
169 U4 **Huma He** ≈ NE China
64 J5 **Humahuaca** Jujuy, N Argentina
61 E14 **Humaitá** Amazonas, N Brazil
64 N7 **Humaitá** Ñeembucú, S Paraguay
85 H26 **Humansdorp** Eastern Cape, S South Africa
29 S6 **Humansville** Missouri, C USA
42 I8 **Humaya, Río** ≈ C Mexico
85 C16 **Humbe** Cunene, SW Angola
xli W14 **Humber** *estuary* E England, UK
99 N17 **Humberside** *cultural region* E England, UK
xxxix R4 **Humberston** North East Lincolnshire, E England, UK
Humberto *see* Umberto
27 W11 **Humble** Texas, SW USA
9 U15 **Humboldt** Saskatchewan, S Canada
31 U12 **Humboldt** Iowa, C USA
29 Q6 **Humboldt** Kansas, C USA
31 S17 **Humboldt** Nebraska, C USA
37 S3 **Humboldt** Nevada, W USA
22 G9 **Humboldt** Tennessee, S USA
36 K3 **Humboldt Bay** *bay* California, W USA
37 S4 **Humboldt Lake** ◎ Nevada, W USA
197 J7 **Humboldt, Mont** ▲ S New Caledonia
37 S4 **Humboldt River** ≈ Nevada, W USA
37 T5 **Humboldt Salt Marsh** *wetland* Nevada, W USA
191 P11 **Hume, Lake** ◎ New South Wales/Victoria, SE Australia
113 N19 **Humenné** *Ger.* Homenau, *Hung.* Homonna. Východné Slovensko, E Slovakia
31 V15 **Humeston** Iowa, C USA
56 J5 **Humocaro Bajo** Lara, N Venezuela
31 Q14 **Humphrey** Nebraska, C USA
37 S9 **Humphreys, Mount** ▲ California, W USA
38 L11 **Humphreys Peak** ▲ Arizona, SW USA
113 E17 **Humpolec** *Ger.* Gumpolds, Humpoletz. Jižní Čechy, C Czech Republic
Humpoletz *see* Humpolec
95 K19 **Humppila** Häme, SW Finland
34 F8 **Humptulips** Washington, NW USA
44 H7 **Humuya, Río** ≈ W Honduras
77 P9 **Hūn** N Libya
Hunabasi *see* Funabashi
94 I1 **Húnaflói** *bay* NW Iceland
166 M11 **Hunan** *var.* Hunan Sheng, Xiang. ◐ *province* S China
Hunan Sheng *see* Hunan
169 Y10 **Hunchun** Jilin, NE China
97 I22 **Hundested** Frederiksborg, E Denmark
xxxix U13 **Hundon** Suffolk, E England, UK
Hundred Mile House *see* 100 Mile House
118 G12 **Hunedoara** *Ger.* Eisenmarkt, *Hung.* Vajdahunyad. Hunedoara, SW Romania
118 G12 **Hunedoara** ◐ *county* W Romania
103 I17 **Hünfeld** Hessen, C Germany
113 H23 **Hungary** *off.* Republic of Hungary, *Ger.* Ungarn, *Hung.* Magyarország, *Rom.* Ungaria, *SCr.* Mađarska, *Ukr.* Uhorshchyna; *prev.* Hungarian People's Republic. ◆ *republic* C Europe
Hungary, Plain of *see* Great Hungarian Plain
xxxvii P10 **Hungerford** Newbury, S England, UK
168 F6 **Hungiy** Dzavhan, W Mongolia
169 X13 **Hŭngnam** E North Korea
xliv C14 **Hungry Hill** ▲ SW Ireland
35 P8 **Hungry Horse Reservoir** ▣ Montana, NW USA
Hungt'ou *see* Lan Yü
Hung-tse Hu *see* Hongze Hu
178 Jj6 **Hưng Yên** Hai Hưng, N Vietnam
xlii D11 **Hunish, Rubha** *headland* NW Scotland, UK
Hunjiang *see* Baishan
xli W11 **Hunmanby** North Yorkshire, N England, UK
97 I18 **Hunnebostrand** Göteborg och Bohus, S Sweden
103 E19 **Hunsrück** ▲▲ W Germany
xxxix U7 **Hunstanton** Norfolk, E England, UK
161 G20 **Hunsūr** Karnātaka, E India
168 I7 **Hunt** Arhangay, C Mongolia
102 G12 **Hunte** ≈ NW Germany
31 Q5 **Hunter** North Dakota, N USA
27 S11 **Hunter** Texas, SW USA
193 D20 **Hunter** ≈ South Island, NZ
191 N15 **Hunter Island** *island* Tasmania, SE Australia
20 K11 **Hunter Mountain** ▲ New York, NE USA
193 B23 **Hunter Mountains** ▲▲ South Island, NZ
191 S7 **Hunter River** ≈ New South Wales, SE Australia
34 L7 **Hunters** Washington, NW USA
193 F20 **Hunters Hills, The** *hill range* South Island, NZ
192 M12 **Hunterville** Manawatu-Wanganui, North Island, NZ
33 N16 **Huntingburg** Indiana, N USA
xxxix R12 **Huntingdon** Cambridgeshire, E England, UK
20 E15 **Huntingdon** Pennsylvania, NE USA
22 G9 **Huntingdon** Tennessee, S USA
99 O20 **Huntingdonshire** *cultural region* C England, UK
33 P12 **Huntington** Indiana, N USA
34 L13 **Huntington** Oregon, NW USA
27 X9 **Huntington** Texas, SW USA
38 M5 **Huntington** Utah, W USA
23 P5 **Huntington** West Virginia, NE USA
37 T16 **Huntington Beach** California, W USA
37 W4 **Huntington Creek** ≈ Nevada, W USA
xxxvi L7 **Huntley** Gloucestershire, C England, UK
xlii N12 **Huntly** Aberdeenshire, NE Scotland, UK
192 L7 **Huntly** Waikato, North Island, NZ
8 K8 **Hunt, Mount** ▲ Yukon Territory, NW Canada
xxxvi J11 **Huntspill** Somerset, SW England, UK
12 H12 **Huntsville** Ontario, S Canada
25 P2 **Huntsville** Alabama, S USA
29 S9 **Huntsville** Arkansas, C USA
29 U3 **Huntsville** Missouri, C USA
22 M8 **Huntsville** Tennessee, S USA
27 V10 **Huntsville** Texas, SW USA
38 L2 **Huntsville** Utah, W USA
43 W12 **Hunucmá** Yucatán, SE Mexico
155 W3 **Hunza** *var.* Karīmābād. Jammu and Kashmir, NE Pakistan
155 W3 **Hunza** ≈ NE Pakistan
Hunze *see* Oostermoers Vaart
164 H4 **Huocheng** *var.* Shuiding. Xinjiang Uygur Zizhiqu, NW China
167 N6 **Huojia** Henan, C China
Huolin Gol *see* Hulingol
197 F3 **Huon** *reef* N New Caledonia
194 K13 **Huon Gulf** *gulf* E PNG
194 K13 **Huon Peninsula** *headland* C PNG
Huoshao Dao *see* Lü Tao
Huoshao Tao *see* Lan Yü
Hupeh/Hupei *see* Hubei
Hurano *see* Furano
97 H14 **Hurdalssjøen** ◎ S Norway
12 E13 **Hurd, Cape** *headland* Ontario, S Canada
Hurdegaryp *see* Hardegarijp
xl H17 **Hurdsfield** Cheshire, C England, UK
31 N4 **Hurdsfield** North Dakota, N USA
168 J7 **Hüremt** Bulgan, C Mongolia
168 J8 **Hüremt** Övörhangay, C Mongolia
77 X9 **Hurghada** *var.* Al Ghurdaqah, Ghurdaqah. E Egypt
69 V9 **Huri Hills** ▲ NW Kenya
39 P15 **Hurley** New Mexico, SW USA
32 K4 **Hurley** Wisconsin, N USA
xliii I21 **Hurlford** East Ayrshire, W Scotland, UK
23 Y4 **Hurlock** Maryland, NE USA
xxxvii N13 **Hurn** Dorset, S England, UK
31 P10 **Huron** South Dakota, N USA
33 S6 **Huron, Lake** ◎ Canada/USA
33 N3 **Huron Mountains** *hill range* Michigan, N USA
38 J8 **Hurricane** Utah, W USA
23 P5 **Hurricane** West Virginia, NE USA
38 J8 **Hurricane Cliffs** *cliff* Arizona, SW USA
25 V6 **Hurricane Creek** ≈ Georgia, SE USA
96 E12 **Hurrungane** ▲ S Norway
xxxvii P12 **Hursley** Hampshire, S England, UK
xxxvii P11 **Hurstbourne Priors** Hampshire, S England, UK
xxxvii P11 **Hurstbourne Tarrant** Hampshire, S England, UK
xxxvii U12 **Hurstpierpoint** West Sussex, SE England, UK
103 E16 **Hürth** Nordrhein-Westfalen, W Germany
Hurukawa *see* Furukawa
193 I17 **Hurunui** ≈ South Island, NZ
97 F21 **Hurup** Viborg, NW Denmark
xli R9 **Hurworth-on-Tees** Darlington, N England, UK
119 T14 **Hurzuf** Respublika Krym, S Ukraine
Huş *see* Huşi
94 K1 **Húsavík** Nordhurland Eystra, NE Iceland
xxxix O11 **Husbands Bosworth** Leicestershire, C England, UK
xlii B9 **Hushinish** Western Isles, NW Scotland, UK
118 M10 **Huşi** *var.* Huş. Vaslui, E Romania
97 L19 **Huskvarna** Jönköping, S Sweden
41 P8 **Huslia** Alaska, USA
Husn *see* Al Ḥuṣn
97 C15 **Husnes** Hordaland, S Norway
96 D8 **Hustadvika** *sea area* S Norway
Husté *see* Khust
102 H7 **Husum** Schleswig-Holstein, N Germany
95 I16 **Husum** Västernorrland, C Sweden
118 K6 **Husyatyn** Ternopil's'ka Oblast', W Ukraine
Huszt *see* Khust
168 K6 **Hutag** Bulgan, N Mongolia
28 M6 **Hutchinson** Kansas, C USA
31 U9 **Hutchinson** Minnesota, N USA
25 Y13 **Hutchinson Island** *island* Florida, SE USA
38 L11 **Hutch Mountain** ▲ Arizona, SW USA
147 O14 **Ḥūth** NW Yemen
195 R11 **Hutjena** Buka Island, NE PNG
111 T8 **Hüttenberg** Kärnten, S Austria
27 T10 **Hutto** Texas, SW USA
xxxix T5 **Huttoft** Lincolnshire, E England, UK
xli W13 **Hutton Cranswick** East Riding of Yorkshire, N England, UK
xli S10 **Hutton Rudby** North Yorkshire, N England, UK
Huttu *see* Futtsu
110 E8 **Huttwil** Bern, W Switzerland
164 K5 **Hutubi** Xinjiang Uygur Zizhiqu, NW China
167 N4 **Hutuo He** ≈ C China
Hutyû *see* Fuchū
193 E20 **Huxley, Mount** ▲ South Island, NZ
101 J20 **Huy** *Dut.* Hoei, Hoey. Liège, E Belgium
xl C16 **Huyton** Knowsley, NW England, UK
167 R8 **Huzhou** *var.* Wuxing. Zhejiang, SE China
Huzi *see* Fuji
Huzieda *see* Fujieda
Huzinomiya *see* Fujinomiya
Huzisawa *see* Fujisawa
Huziyosida *see* Fuji-Yoshida
94 I2 **Hvammstangi** Nordhurland Vestra, N Iceland
94 K4 **Hvannadalshnúkur** ▲ S Iceland
115 E15 **Hvar** *It.* Lesina. Split-Dalmacija, S Croatia
115 F15 **Hvar** *It.* Lesina; *anc.* Pharus. *island* S Croatia
119 T13 **Hvardiys'ke** *Rus.* Gvardeyskoye. Respublika Krym, S Ukraine
94 I4 **Hveragerdhi** Sudhurland, SW Iceland
97 E22 **Hvide Sande** Ringkøbing, W Denmark
94 I3 **Hvítá** ≈ C Iceland
97 G15 **Hvittingfoss** Buskerud, S Norway
94 I4 **Hvolsvöllur** Sudhurland, SW Iceland
Hwach'ŏn-chŏsuji *see* P'aro-ho
Hwainan *see* Huainan
Hwalien *see* Hualien
85 I16 **Hwange** *prev.* Wankie. Matabeleland North, W Zimbabwe
Hwang-Hae *see* Yellow Sea
Hwangshih *see* Huangshi
85 L17 **Hwedza** Mashonaland East, E Zimbabwe
65 G20 **Hyades, Cerro** ▲ S Chile
21 Q12 **Hyannis** Massachusetts, NE USA
30 L13 **Hyannis** Nebraska, C USA
168 F6 **Hyargas Nuur** ◎ NW Mongolia
Hybla/Hybla Major *see* Paternò
41 Y14 **Hydaburg** Prince of Wales Island, Alaska, USA
xli P16 **Hyde** Tameside, NW England, UK
193 F22 **Hyde** Otago, South Island, NZ
23 O7 **Hyden** Kentucky, S USA
20 K12 **Hyde Park** New York, NE USA
41 Z14 **Hyder** Alaska, USA
161 I15 **Hyderābād** *var.* Haidarabad. Andhra Pradesh, C India
155 Q16 **Hyderābād** *var.* Haidarabad. Sind, SE Pakistan
105 T16 **Hyères** Var, SE France
105 T16 **Hyères, Îles d'** *island group* S France
120 K12 **Hyermanavichy** *Rus.* Germanovichi. Vitsyebskaya Voblasts', N Belorussia
169 X12 **Hyesan** NE North Korea
8 K8 **Hyland** ≈ Yukon Territory, NW Canada
97 K20 **Hyltebruk** Halland, S Sweden
xliii K21 **Hyndford Bridge** South Lanarkshire, C Scotland, UK
20 D16 **Hyndman** Pennsylvania, NE USA
35 P14 **Hyndman Peak** ▲ Idaho, NW USA
xliii B17 **Hynish** Argyll and Bute, W Scotland, UK
170 G13 **Hyōgo** *off.* Hyōgo-ken. ◐ *prefecture* Honshū, SW Japan
170 G13 **Hyōno-sen** ▲ Kyūshū, SW Japan
Hypanis *see* Kuban'
Hypsas *see* Belice
Hyrcania *see* Gorgān
38 L1 **Hyrum** Utah, W USA
95 N14 **Hyrynsalmi** Oulu, C Finland
35 V10 **Hysham** Montana, NW USA
xxxvii P13 **Hythe** Hampshire, S England, UK
xxxvii Y11 **Hythe** Kent, SE England, UK
9 N13 **Hythe** Alberta, W Canada
170 D15 **Hyūga** Miyazaki, Kyūshū, SW Japan
Hyvinge *see* Hyvinkää
95 L19 **Hyvinkää** *Swe.* Hyvinge. Uusimaa, S Finland

I

118 J9 **Iacobeni** *Ger.* Jakobeny. Suceava, NE Romania
Iader *see* Zadar
180 I7 **Iakora** Fianarantsoa, SE Madagascar
194 H12 **Ialibu** Southern Highlands, W PNG
118 K14 **Ialomiţa** *var.* Jalomitsa. ◐ *county* SE Romania
118 K14 **Ialomiţa** ≈ SE Romania
119 N10 **Ialoveni** *Rus.* Yaloveny. C Moldavia
119 N11 **Ialpug** *var.* Ialpugul Mare, *Rus.* Yalpug. ≈ Moldavia/Ukraine
Ialpugul Mare *see* Ialpug
25 T8 **Iamonia, Lake** ◎ Florida, SE USA
118 L13 **Ianca** Brăila, SE Romania
118 M10 **Iaşi** *Ger.* Jassy. Iaşi, NE Romania
118 L9 **Iaşi** *Ger.* Jassy, Yassy. ◐ *county* NE Romania
116 J13 **Íasmos** Anatolikí Makedonía kai Thráki, NE Greece
24 H6 **Iatt, Lake** ▣ Louisiana, S USA
60 B11 **Iauretê** Amazonas, NW Brazil
179 Oo10 **Iba** Luzon, N Philippines
79 S16 **Ibadan** Oyo, SW Nigeria
56 E10 **Ibagué** Tolima, C Colombia
62 J10 **Ibaiti** Paraná, S Brazil
179 Pp12 **Ibajay** Panay Island, C Philippines
38 J4 **Ibapah Peak** ▲ Utah, W USA
115 M15 **Ibar** *Alb.* Ibër. ≈ C Yugoslavia
170 F14 **Ibara** Okayama, Honshū, SW Japan
171 Kk16 **Ibaraki** *off.* Ibaraki-ken. ◐ *prefecture* Honshū, S Japan
58 C5 **Ibarra** *var.* San Miguel de Ibarra. Imbabura, N Ecuador
Ibaşfalău *see* Dumbrăveni
147 O16 **Ibb** W Yemen
102 F13 **Ibbenbüren** Nordrhein-Westfalen, NW Germany
81 H16 **Ibenga** ≈ N Congo
Ibër *see* Ibar
59 I14 **Iberia** Madre de Dios, E Peru
Iberia *see* Spain
68 M1 **Iberian Basin** *undersea feature* E Atlantic Ocean
Iberian Mountains *see* Ibérico, Sistema
86 D12 **Iberian Peninsula** *physical region* Portugal/Spain
66 M8 **Iberian Plain** *undersea feature* E Atlantic Ocean
Ibérica, Cordillera *see* Ibérico, Sistema
107 P6 **Ibérico, Sistema** *var.* Cordillera Ibérica, *Eng.* Iberian Mountains. ▲▲ NE Spain
10 K7 **Iberville Lac d'** ◎ Québec, NE Canada
79 T14 **Ibeto** Niger, W Nigeria
79 W15 **Ibi** Taraba, C Nigeria
107 S11 **Ibi** País Valenciano, E Spain
61 L20 **Ibiá** Minas Gerais, SE Brazil
63 F15 **Ibicuí, Rio** ≈ S Brazil
63 C19 **Ibicuy** Entre Ríos, E Argentina
63 F16 **Ibirapuitã** ≈ S Brazil
Ibiza *see* Eivissa
144 J4 **Ibn Wardān, Qaşr** *ruins* Ḥamāh, C Syria
Ibo *see* Sassandra
196 E9 **Ibobang** Babeldaob, N Palau
176 Vv11 **Ibonma** Irian Jaya, E Indonesia
61 N17 **Ibotirama** Bahia, E Brazil
147 Y8 **Ibrā** NE Oman
131 Q4 **Ibresi** Chuvashskaya Respublika, W Russian Federation
147 X8 **'Ibrī** NW Oman
xxxvii O13 **Ibsley** Hampshire, S England, UK
xxxviii M9 **Ibstock** Leicestershire, C England, UK
170 Bb16 **Ibusuki** Kagoshima, Kyūshū, SW Japan
59 E16 **Ica** Ica, SW Peru
59 E16 **Ica** *off.* Departamento de Ica. ◐ *department* SW Peru
60 C11 **Içana** Amazonas, NW Brazil
Icaria *see* Ikaría
60 B13 **Içá, Rio** *var.* Río Putumayo. ≈ NW South America *see also* Putumayo, Río
142 I17 **İçel** *var.* Ichili. ◐ *province* S Turkey
94 I3 **Iceland** *off.* Republic of Iceland, *Dan.* Island, *Icel.* Ísland. ◆ *republic* N Atlantic Ocean
88 B6 **Iceland** *island* N Atlantic Ocean
66 L5 **Iceland Basin** *undersea feature* N Atlantic Ocean
Icelandic Plateau *see* Iceland Plateau
207 Q15 **Iceland Plateau** *var.* Icelandic Plateau. *undersea feature* Greenland Sea
161 E16 **Ichalkaranji** Mahārāshtra, W India
170 Cc15 **Ichifusa-yama** ▲ Kyūshū, SW Japan
171 K17 **Ichihara** *var.* Itihara. Chiba, Honshū, S Japan
Ichili *see* İçel
171 I15 **Ichinomiya** *var.* Itinomiya. Aichi, Honshū, SW Japan
171 Mm12 **Ichinoseki** *var.* Itinoseki. Iwate, Honshū, C Japan
119 R3 **Ichnya** Chernihivs'ka Oblast', NE Ukraine
59 L17 **Ichoa, Río** ≈ C Bolivia
I-ch'un *see* Yichun
xxxix U11 **Icklingham** Suffolk, E England, UK
Iconium *see* Konya
Iculisma *see* Angoulême
41 U12 **Icy Bay** *inlet* Alaska, USA
41 N5 **Icy Cape** *headland* Alaska, USA
41 W13 **Icy Strait** *strait* Alaska, USA
29 R13 **Idabel** Oklahoma, C USA
31 T13 **Ida Grove** Iowa, C USA
79 U16 **Idah** Kogi, S Nigeria
35 N13 **Idaho** *off.* State of Idaho; also known as Gem of the Mountains, Gem State. ◐ *state* NW USA
35 N14 **Idaho City** Idaho, NW USA
35 R14 **Idaho Falls** Idaho, NW USA
124 Nn3 **Idálion** *var.* Dali, Dhali. C Cyprus
27 N5 **Idalou** Texas, SW USA
106 I9 **Idanha-a-Nova** Castelo Branco, C Portugal
103 E19 **Idar-Oberstein** Rheinland-Pfalz, SW Germany
120 J3 **Ida-Virumaa** *off.* Ida-Viru Maakond. ◐ *province* NE Estonia
xxxvi H15 **Ideford** Devon, SW England, UK
128 J8 **Idel'** Respublika Kareliya, NW Russian Federation
81 C15 **Idenao** Sud-Ouest, SW Cameroon
Idenburg-rivier *see* Taritatu, Sungai
Idensalmi *see* Iisalmi
168 I6 **Ider** Hövsgöl, C Mongolia
77 X10 **Idfu** *var.* Edfu. SE Egypt
Ídhi Óros *see* Ídi
Ídhra *see* Ýdra
173 F3 **Idi** Sumatera, W Indonesia
117 I25 **Ídi** *var.* Ídhi Óros. ▲ Kríti, Greece, E Mediterranean Sea
Idi Amin, Lac *see* Edward, Lake

◆ COUNTRY ◇ DEPENDENT TERRITORY ◈ ADMINISTRATIVE REGION ▲ MOUNTAIN ▼ VOLCANO ◎ LAKE
● COUNTRY CAPITAL ○ DEPENDENT TERRITORY CAPITAL ✈ INTERNATIONAL AIRPORT ▲ MOUNTAIN RANGE ≈ RIVER ☐ RESERVOIR

IRATI – JAMANXIM, RIO

62 J12 **Irati** Paraná, S Brazil
107 R3 **Irati** ↝ N Spain
129 T8 **Irayël'** Respublika Komi, NW Russian Federation
45 N13 **Irazú, Volcán** ▲ C Costa Rica
Irbenskiy Zaliv/Irbes Šaurums *see* Irbe Strait
120 D7 **Irbe Strait** *Est.* Kura Kurk, *Latv.* Irbes Šaurums, *Rus.* Irbenskiy Zaliv; *prev. Est.* Irbe Väin. *strait* Estonia/Latvia
Irbe Väin *see* Irbe Strait
144 G9 **Irbid** Irbid, N Jordan
144 G9 **Irbid** *off.* Muḥāfaẓat Irbid. ◆ *governorate* N Jordan
Irbil *see* Arbil
125 F11 **Irbit** Sverdlovskaya Oblast', C Russian Federation
xxxix P12 **Irchester** Northamptonshire, C England, UK
111 S6 **Irdning** Steiermark, SE Austria
81 I18 **Irebu** Equateur, W Zaire
xl L8 **Ireby** Cumbria, NW England, UK
Ireland *see* Ireland, Republic of
86 C9 **Ireland** *Lat.* Hibernia. *island* Ireland/UK
66 A12 **Ireland Island North** *island* W Bermuda
66 A12 **Ireland Island South** *island* W Bermuda
xliv F8 **Ireland, Republic of** *off.* Republic of Ireland, *var.* Ireland, *Ir.* Éire. ◆ *republic* NW Europe
129 V15 **Iren'** ↝ NW Russian Federation
193 A22 **Irene, Mount** ▲ South Island, NZ
Irgalem *see* Yirga 'Alem
150 L11 **Irgiz** Aktyubinsk, C Kazakhstan
Irian *see* New Guinea
Irian Barat *see* Irian Jaya
176 Y13 **Irian Jaya** *var.* Irian Barat, West Irian, West New Guinea; *prev.* Dutch New Guinea, Netherlands New Guinea. ◆ *province* E Indonesia
80 K9 **Iriba** Biltine, NE Chad
179 Q11 **Iriga** Luzon, N Philippines
131 X7 **Iriklinskoye Vodokhranilishche** ▣ W Russian Federation
83 H23 **Iringa** Iringa, C Tanzania
83 H23 **Iringa** ◆ *region* S Tanzania
172 O17 **Iriomote-jima** *island* Sakishima-shotō, SW Japan
44 L4 **Iriona** Colón, NE Honduras
49 U7 **Iriri** ↝ N Brazil
60 I13 **Iriri, Rio** ↝ C Brazil
Iris *see* Yeşilırmak
37 W9 **Irish, Mount** ▲ Nevada, W USA
99 H17 **Irish Sea** *Ir.* Muir Éireann. *sea* C British Isles
145 U12 **Irjal ash Shaykhīyah** S Iraq
153 U11 **Irkeshtam** Oshskaya Oblast', SW Kyrgyzstan
126 J16 **Irkut** ↝ S Russian Federation
126 Jj16 **Irkutsk** Irkutskaya Oblast', S Russian Federation
126 Jj13 **Irkutskaya Oblast'** ◆ *province* S Russian Federation
Irlir, Gora *see* Irlir Toghi
152 K8 **Irlir Toghi** *var.* Gora Irlir. ▲ N Uzbekistan
Irminger Basin *see* Reykjanes Basin
23 R12 **Irmo** South Carolina, SE USA
104 E6 **Iroise** *sea* NW France
201 X2 **Iroj** *var.* Eroj. *island* Ratak Chain, SE Marshall Islands
xxxvi L9 **Iron Acton** South Gloucestershire, SW England, UK
190 H7 **Iron Baron** South Australia
195 X15 **Iron Bottom Sound** *sound* C Solomon Islands
12 C10 **Iron Bridge** Ontario, S Canada
xxxviii I10 **Ironbridge** The Wrekin, W England, UK
22 H10 **Iron City** Tennessee, S USA
12 I13 **Irondale** ↝ Ontario, SE Canada
190 H7 **Iron Knob** South Australia
xliv I8 **Iron, Lough** ◎ C Ireland
32 M5 **Iron Mountain** Michigan, N USA
xliv H6 **Iron Mountains** ▲ N Ireland
32 M4 **Iron River** Michigan, N USA
32 J3 **Iron River** Wisconsin, N USA
29 X6 **Ironton** Missouri, C USA
33 S15 **Ironton** Ohio, N USA
32 K4 **Ironwood** Michigan, N USA
10 H12 **Iroquois Falls** Ontario, S Canada
33 N12 **Iroquois River** ↝ Illinois/Indiana, N USA
171 Ii18 **Irō-zaki** *headland* Honshū, S Japan
Irpen' *see* Irpin'
119 O4 **Irpin'** *Rus.* Irpen'. Kyyivs'ka Oblast', N Ukraine
119 O4 **Irpin'** *Rus.* Irpen'. ↝ N Ukraine
147 Q16 **'Irqah** SW Yemen
177 Ff8 **Irrawaddy** *var.* Ayeyarwady. ◆ *division* SW Burma
177 G6 **Irrawaddy** *var.* Ayeyarwady. ↝ W Burma
177 Ff9 **Irrawaddy, Mouths of the** *delta* SW Burma
119 N4 **Irsha** ↝ N Ukraine
118 H7 **Irshava** Zakarpats'ka Oblast', W Ukraine
109 N18 **Irsina** Basilicata, S Italy
Irtish *see* Irtysh
xli W11 **Irton** North Yorkshire, N England, UK
133 R5 **Irtysh** *var.* Irtish, *Kaz.* Ertis. ↝ C Asia
151 S7 **Irtyshsk** *Kaz.* Ertis. Pavlodar, NE Kazakhstan
81 P17 **Irumu** Haut-Zaïre, E Zaire
107 Q2 **Irún** País Vasco, N Spain
Iruñea *see* Pamplona
107 Q3 **Irurzun** Navarra, N Spain
xliii I21 **Irvine** North Ayrshire, W Scotland, UK
23 N6 **Irvine** Kentucky, S USA
xliv I5 **Irvinestown** Fermanagh, W Northern Ireland, UK
27 T6 **Irving** Texas, SW USA
22 K5 **Irvington** Kentucky, S USA
Isaak *see* Iisaku
30 L8 **Isabel** South Dakota, N USA
195 W14 **Isabel** *off.* Isabel Province. ◆ *province* N Solomon Islands
179 Q17 **Isabela** Basilan Island, SW Philippines
47 S5 **Isabela** W Puerto Rico
47 N8 **Isabela, Cabo** *headland* NW Dominican Republic
59 A18 **Isabela, Isla** *var.* Albemarle Island. *island* Galapagos Islands, Ecuador, E Pacific Ocean
42 I12 **Isabela, Isla** *island* C Mexico
44 K9 **Isabella, Cordillera** ▲ NW Nicaragua
37 S12 **Isabella Lake** ▣ California, W USA
33 N2 **Isabelle, Point** *headland* Michigan, N USA
Isabel Segunda *see* Vieques
118 M13 **Isaccea** Tulcea, E Romania
94 H1 **Ísafjardardjúp** *inlet* NW Iceland
94 H1 **Ísafjördhur** Vestfirdhir, NW Iceland
170 C13 **Isahaya** Nagasaki, Kyūshū, SW Japan
155 S7 **Īsa Khel** Punjab, E Pakistan
180 H7 **Isalo** *var.* Massif de L'Isalo. ▲ SW Madagascar
Isalo, Massif de L' *see* Isalo
81 K20 **Isandja** Kasai Occidental, C Zaire
197 D16 **Isangel** Tanna, S Vanuatu
81 M18 **Isangi** Haut-Zaïre, C Zaire
103 L24 **Isar** ↝ Austria/Germany
103 M23 **Isar-Kanal** *canal* SE Germany
Isbarta *see* Isparta
xlii M4 **Isbister** Orkney Islands, N Scotland, UK
xli I2 **Isbister** Shetland Islands, NE Scotland, UK
Isca Damnoniorum *see* Exeter
109 K18 **Ischia** *var.* Isola d'Ischia; *anc.* Aenaria. Campania, S Italy
109 J18 **Ischia, Isola d'** *island* S Italy
56 B12 **Iscuandé** *var.* Santa Bárbara. Nariño, SW Colombia
171 Hh16 **Ise** Mie, Honshū, SW Japan
102 J12 **Ise** ↝ N Germany
97 I23 **Isefjord** *fjord* E Denmark
Iseghem *see* Izegem
199 Jj17 **Iselin Seamount** *undersea feature* S Pacific Ocean
Isenhof *see* Püssi
108 E7 **Iseo** Lombardia, N Italy
105 U12 **Iseran, Col de l'** *pass* E France
105 S12 **Isère** ◆ *department* E France
105 S12 **Isère** ↝ E France
103 F15 **Iserlohn** Nordrhein-Westfalen, W Germany
109 K16 **Isernia** *var.* Æsernia. Molise, C Italy
171 Jj15 **Isesaki** Gunma, Honshū, S Japan
133 Q5 **Iset'** ↝ C Russian Federation
171 Hh16 **Ise-wan** *bay* S Japan
79 S15 **Iseyin** Oyo, W Nigeria
Isfahan *see* Eşfahān
153 Q11 **Isfana** Oshskaya Oblast', SW Kyrgyzstan
153 R11 **Isfara** N Tajikistan
155 O4 **Isfi Maidān** Ghowr, N Afghanistan
94 O3 **Isfjorden** *fjord* W Svalbard
Isha Baydhabo *see* Baydhabo
129 V11 **Isherim, Gora** ▲ NW Russian Federation
131 Q5 **Isheyevka** Ul'yanovskaya Oblast', W Russian Federation
172 Oo17 **Ishigaki** Okinawa, Ishigaki-jima, SW Japan
172 P17 **Ishigaki-jima** *var.* Isigaki Zima. *island* Sakishima-shotō, SW Japan
172 O5 **Ishikari** Hokkaidō, NE Japan
172 Oo5 **Ishikari-gawa** *var.* Isikari Gawa. ↝ Hokkaidō, NE Japan
172 O4 **Ishikari-wan** *bay* Hokkaidō, NE Japan
171 L14 **Ishikawa** Fukushima, Honshū, C Japan
172 Oo14 **Ishikawa** *var.* Isikawa. Okinawa, Okinawa, SW Japan
171 I13 **Ishikawa** *off.* Ishikawa-ken, *var.* Isikawa. ◆ *prefecture* Honshū, SW Japan
125 Ff12 **Ishim** Tyumenskaya Oblast', C Russian Federation
133 R6 **Ishim** *Kaz.* Esil. ↝ Kazakhstan/Russian Federation
131 V6 **Ishimbay** Respublika Bashkortostan, W Russian Federation
151 O9 **Ishimskoye** Turgay, C Kazakhstan
171 M13 **Ishinomaki** *var.* Isinomaki. Miyagi, Honshū, C Japan
171 Kk16 **Ishioka** *var.* Isioka. Ibaraki, Honshū, S Japan
170 Ee15 **Ishizuchi-san** ▲ Shikoku, SW Japan
Ishkashim *see* Ishkoshim
Ishkashimskiy Khrebet *see* Ishkoshim, Qatorkŭhi
153 S15 **Ishkoshim** *Rus.* Ishkashim. S Tajikistan
153 S15 **Ishkoshim, Qatorkŭhi** *Rus.* Ishkashimskiy Khrebet. ▲ SE Tajikistan
33 N4 **Ishpeming** Michigan, N USA
153 N11 **Ishtikhon** *Rus.* Ishtykhan. Samarqand Wiloyati, C Uzbekistan
Ishtykhan *see* Ishtikhon
159 T15 **Ishurdi** Rajshahi, W Bangladesh
63 G17 **Isidoro Noblia** Cerro Largo, NE Uruguay
104 J4 **Isigny-sur-Mer** Calvados, N France
Isikari Gawa *see* Ishikari-gawa
Isikawa *see* Ishikawa
142 C11 **Işıklar Dağı** ▲ NW Turkey
109 C19 **Isili** Sardegna, Italy, C Mediterranean Sea
125 Ff13 **Isil'kul'** Omskaya Oblast', C Russian Federation
Isinomaki *see* Ishinomaki
Isioka *see* Ishioka
83 I18 **Isiolo** Eastern, C Kenya
81 O16 **Isiro** Haut-Zaïre, NE Zaire
94 P2 **Isispynten** *headland* NE Svalbard
126 Ll11 **Isit** Respublika Sakha (Yakutiya), NE Russian Federation
155 O2 **Iskabad Canal** *canal* N Afghanistan
153 Q9 **Iskandar** *Rus.* Iskander. Toshkent Wiloyati, E Uzbekistan
Iskander *see* Iskandar
Iskăr *see* Iskür
124 O2 **Iskele** *var.* Trikomo, *Gk.* Tríkomon. E Cyprus
142 K17 **İskenderun** *Eng.* Alexandretta. Hatay, S Turkey
144 H2 **İskenderun Körfezi** *Eng.* Gulf of Alexandretta. *gulf* S Turkey
142 J11 **İskilip** Çorum, N Turkey
Iski-Nauket *see* Eski-Nookat
126 Gg14 **Iskitim** Novosibirskaya Oblast', C Russian Federation
116 J11 **Iskra** *prev.* Popovo. Khaskovska Oblast, S Bulgaria
116 G10 **Iskŭr** *var.* Iskăr. ↝ NW Bulgaria
116 H10 **Iskŭr, Yazovir** *prev.* Yazovir Stalin. ▣ W Bulgaria
xliii L17 **Isla** ↝ C Scotland, UK
43 S15 **Isla** Veracruz-Llave, SE Mexico
121 J15 **Islach** *Rus.* Isloch'. ↝ C Belorussia
106 H14 **Isla Cristina** Andalucía, S Spain
Isla de León *see* San Fernando
155 U6 **Islāmābād** ● (Pakistan) Federal Capital Territory Islāmābād, NE Pakistan
155 V6 **Islāmābād** ✕ Federal Capital Territory Islāmābād, NE Pakistan
Islamabad *see* Anantnāg
155 R17 **Islāmkot** Sind, SE Pakistan
25 Y17 **Islamorada** Florida Keys, Florida, SE USA
159 P14 **Islāmpur** Bihār, N India
Islam Qala *see* Eslām Qal'eh
Island/Ísland *see* Iceland
20 K16 **Island Beach** *spit* New Jersey, NE USA
21 S4 **Island Falls** Maine, NE USA
190 H6 **Island Lagoon** ◎ South Australia
9 Y13 **Island Lake** ◎ Manitoba, C Canada
31 W5 **Island Lake Reservoir** ▣ Minnesota, N USA
35 R13 **Island Park** Idaho, NW USA
21 N6 **Island Pond** Vermont, NE USA
192 K2 **Islands, Bay of** *inlet* North Island, NZ
105 R7 **Is-sur-Tille** Côte d'Or, C France
44 J3 **Islas de la Bahía** ◆ *department* N Honduras
67 L20 **Islas Orcadas Rise** *undersea feature* S Atlantic Ocean
xliii D21 **Islay** *island* SW Scotland, UK
118 I15 **Islaz** Teleorman, S Romania
31 V7 **Isle** Minnesota, N USA
104 M12 **Isle** ↝ W France
xxxix U11 **Isleham** Cambridgeshire, E England, UK
xxxv E4 **Isle of Anglesey** ◆ *unitary authority* NW Wales, UK
xl G12 **Isle of Man** ◇ *UK crown dependency* NW Europe
xliii L26 **Isle of Whithorn** Dumfries and Galloway, SW Scotland, UK
xxxvii P14 **Isle of Wight** ◆ *unitary authority* S England, UK
23 X7 **Isle of Wight** Virginia, NE USA
203 Y3 **Isles Lagoon** ◎ Kiritimati, E Kiribati
39 R11 **Isleta Pueblo** New Mexico, SW USA
xxxiv L16 **Islington** ◆ *London borough* SE England, UK
xxxvi D7 **Islington** *London borough capital* Islington, SE England, UK
xxxvii P7 **Islip** Oxfordshire, C England, UK
Isloch' *see* Islach
63 E19 **Ismael Cortinas** Flores, S Uruguay
Ismailia *see* Ismâ'ilîya
77 W7 **Ismâ'ilîya** *var.* Ismailia. N Egypt
Ismid *see* İzmit
77 X10 **Isna** *var.* Esna. SE Egypt
95 K18 **Isojoki** Vaasa, W Finland
84 M12 **Isoka** Northern, NE Zambia
Isola d'Ischia *see* Ischia
Isola d'Istria *see* Izola
Isonzo *see* Soča
13 U4 **Isoukustouc** ↝ Québec, SE Canada
142 F15 **Isparta** *var.* Isbarta. Isparta, SW Turkey
142 F15 **Isparta** *var.* Isbarta. ◆ *province* SW Turkey
116 M7 **Isperih** *prev.* Kemanlar. Razgradska Oblast, NE Bulgaria
109 L26 **Ispica** Sicilia, Italy, C Mediterranean Sea
154 J14 **Ispikān** Baluchistān, SW Pakistan
143 Q12 **İspir** Erzurum, NE Turkey
144 E12 **Israel** *off.* State of Israel, *var.* Medinat Israel, *Heb.* Yisrael, Yisra'el. ◆ *republic* SW Asia
Issa *see* Vis
57 S9 **Issano** C Guyana
78 M16 **Issia** SW Ivory Coast
Issiq Köl *see* Issyk-Kul', Ozero
105 P11 **Issoire** Puy-de-Dôme, C France
105 N9 **Issoudun** *anc.* Uxellodunum. Indre, C France
83 H22 **Issuna** Singida, C Tanzania
Issyk *see* Yesik
Issyk-Kul' *see* Balykchy
153 X7 **Issyk-Kul', Ozero** *var.* Issiq Köl, *Kir.* Ysyk-Köl. ◎ E Kyrgyzstan
153 X7 **Issyk-Kul'skaya Oblast'** *Kir.* Ysyk-Köl Oblasty. ◆ *province* E Kyrgyzstan
155 Q7 **Istādeh-ye Moqor, Āb-e-** *var.* Āb-i-Istāda. ◎ SE Afghanistan
142 D11 **İstanbul** *Bul.* Tsarigrad, *Eng.* Istanbul; *prev.* Constantinople, *anc.* Byzantium. İstanbul, NW Turkey
116 P12 **İstanbul** ◆ *province* NW Turkey
116 P12 **İstanbul Boğazı** *var.* Bosporus Thracius, *Eng.* Bosphorus, Bosporus, *Turk.* Karadeniz Boğazı. *strait* NW Turkey
Istarska Županija *see* Istra
117 G19 **Isthmía** Pelopónnisos, S Greece
117 G17 **Istiaía** Évvoia, C Greece
56 D9 **Istmina** Chocó, W Colombia
25 W13 **Istokpoga, Lake** ◎ Florida, SE USA
114 A9 **Istra** *off.* Istarska županija. ◆ *province* NW Croatia
114 I10 **Istra** *Eng.* Istria, *Ger.* Istrien. *cultural region* NW Croatia
105 R15 **Istres** Bouches-du-Rhône, SE France
Istria/Istrien *see* Istra
179 R16 **Isulan** Mindanao, S Philippines
194 I11 **Isumrud Strait** *strait* NE PNG
131 V7 **Isyangulovo** Respublika Bashkortostan, W Russian Federation
64 O6 **Itá** Central, S Paraguay
61 O17 **Itaberaba** Bahia, E Brazil
61 M20 **Itabira** *prev.* Presidente Vargas. Minas Gerais, SE Brazil
61 O18 **Itabuna** Bahia, E Brazil
61 J18 **Itacaiu** Mato Grosso, S Brazil
60 G12 **Itacoatiara** Amazonas, N Brazil
56 D9 **Itagüí** Antioquia, W Colombia
62 D13 **Itá Ibaté** Corrientes, NE Argentina
62 G11 **Itaipú, Represa de** ▣ Brazil/Paraguay
60 H13 **Itaituba** Pará, NE Brazil
62 K13 **Itajaí** Santa Catarina, S Brazil
Italia/Italiana, Republica/Italian Republic, The *see* Italy
Italian Somaliland *see* Somalia
27 T7 **Italy** Texas, SW USA
108 G12 **Italy** *off.* The Italian Republic, *It.* Italia, Repubblica Italiana. ◆ *republic* S Europe
61 O19 **Itamaraju** Bahia, E Brazil
61 C14 **Itamarati** Amazonas, W Brazil
61 M19 **Itambé, Pico de** ▲ SE Brazil
171 Gg15 **Itami** ✕ (Ōsaka) Ōsaka, Honshū, SW Japan
117 H15 **Ítamos** ▲ N Greece
159 W11 **Itānagar** Arunāchal Pradesh, NE India
Itany *see* Litani
61 N19 **Itaobim** Minas Gerais, SE Brazil
61 P15 **Itaparica, Represa de** ▣ E Brazil
60 M13 **Itapecuru-Mirim** Maranhão, E Brazil
62 Q8 **Itaperuna** Rio de Janeiro, SE Brazil
61 O18 **Itapetinga** Bahia, E Brazil
62 L10 **Itapetininga** São Paulo, S Brazil
62 K10 **Itapeva** São Paulo, S Brazil
49 W6 **Itapicuru, Rio** ↝ NE Brazil
60 O13 **Itapipoca** Ceará, E Brazil
62 M9 **Itapira** São Paulo, S Brazil
62 K8 **Itápolis** São Paulo, S Brazil
62 K10 **Itaporanga** São Paulo, S Brazil
64 P7 **Itapúa** *off.* Departamento de Itapúa. ◆ *department* SE Paraguay
61 E15 **Itapuã do Oeste** Rondônia, W Brazil
63 E15 **Itaqui** Rio Grande do Sul, S Brazil
62 K10 **Itararé** São Paulo, S Brazil
62 K10 **Itararé, Rio** ↝ S Brazil
160 H11 **Itārsi** Madhya Pradesh, C India
27 T7 **Itasca** Texas, SW USA
Itassi *see* Vieille Case
62 D13 **Itatí** Corrientes, NE Argentina
62 K10 **Itatinga** São Paulo, S Brazil
xxxvii P12 **Itchen** ↝ S England, UK
117 F18 **Itéas, Kólpos** *gulf* C Greece
59 N15 **Iténez, Río** *var.* Rio Guaporé. ↝ Bolivia/Brazil *see also* Guaporé, Rio
56 H11 **Iteviate, Río** ↝ C Colombia
102 I13 **Ith** *hill range* C Germany
33 Q8 **Ithaca** Michigan, N USA
20 H11 **Ithaca** New York, NE USA
117 C18 **Itháki** Itháki, Iónioi Nísoi, Greece, C Mediterranean Sea
117 C18 **Itháki** *island* Iónioi Nísoi, Greece, C Mediterranean Sea
It Hearrenfean *see* Heerenveen
Ithiara *see* Ichihara
81 L17 **Itimbiri** ↝ N Zaire
Itinomiya *see* Ichinomiya
Itinoseki *see* Ichinoseki
41 Q5 **Itkilik River** ↝ Alaska, USA
171 J17 **Itō** Shizuoka, Honshū, S Japan
171 J13 **Itoigawa** Niigata, Honshū, C Japan
13 R6 **Itomamo, Lac** ◎ Québec, SE Canada
172 Oo15 **Itoman** Okinawa, SW Japan
104 M5 **Iton** ↝ N France
59 M16 **Itonamas, Río** ↝ NE Bolivia
Itoupé, Mont *see* Sommet Tabulaire
Itseqqortoormiit *see* Ittoqqortoormiit
24 K4 **Itta Bena** Mississippi, S USA
109 B17 **Ittiri** Sardegna, Italy, C Mediterranean Sea
207 Q14 **Ittoqqortoormiit** *var.* Itseqqortoormiit, *Dan.* Scoresbysund, *Eng.* Scoresby Sound. C Greenland
62 M10 **Itu** São Paulo, S Brazil
178 Mm14 **Itu Aba Island** *island* W Spratly Islands
56 D8 **Ituango** Antioquia, NW Colombia
61 A14 **Ituí, Rio** ↝ NW Brazil
81 O20 **Itula** Sud Kivu, E Zaire
61 K19 **Itumbiara** Goiás, C Brazil
57 T9 **Ituni** E Guyana
43 X13 **Iturbide** Campeche, SE Mexico
Ituri *see* Aruwimi
127 Pp16 **Iturup, Ostrov** *island* Kuril'skiye Ostrova, SE Russian Federation
62 L7 **Ituverava** São Paulo, S Brazil
61 C15 **Ituxi, Rio** ↝ W Brazil
63 E14 **Ituzaingó** Corrientes, NE Argentina
103 K18 **Itz** ↝ C Germany
102 I9 **Itzehoe** Schleswig-Holstein, N Germany
25 N2 **Iuka** Mississippi, S USA
62 I11 **Ivaiporã** Paraná, S Brazil
62 I11 **Ivaí, Rio** ↝ S Brazil
94 L10 **Ivalo** *Lapp.* Avveel, Avvil. Lappi, N Finland
94 L10 **Ivalojoki** *Lapp.* Avveel. ↝ N Finland
121 H20 **Ivanava** *Pol.* Janów, Janów Poleski, *Rus.* Ivanovo. Brestskaya Voblasts', SW Belorussia
Ivangorod *see* Dęblin
Ivangrad *see* Berane
191 N7 **Ivanhoe** New South Wales, SE Australia
31 S9 **Ivanhoe** Minnesota, N USA
12 D8 **Ivanhoe** ↝ Ontario, S Canada
114 E8 **Ivanić-Grad** Sisak-Moslavina, N Croatia
119 T10 **Ivanivka** Khersons'ka Oblast', S Ukraine
119 P10 **Ivanivka** Odes'ka Oblast', SW Ukraine
115 L14 **Ivanjica** Serbia, C Yugoslavia
114 G11 **Ivanjska** NW Bosnia and Herzegovina
113 H21 **Ivanka** ✕ (Bratislava) Západné Slovensko, SW Slovakia
119 O3 **Ivankiv** *Rus.* Ivankov. Kyyivs'ka Oblast', N Ukraine
Ivankov *see* Ivankiv
41 O15 **Ivanof Bay** Alaska, USA
118 J7 **Ivano-Frankivs'k** *Ger.* Stanislau, *Pol.* Stanisławów, *Rus.* Ivano-Frankovsk; *prev.* Stanislav. Ivano-Frankivs'ka Oblast', W Ukraine
Ivano-Frankivs'k *see* Ivano-Frankivs'ka Oblast'
118 I7 **Ivano-Frankivs'ka Oblast'** *var.* Ivano-Frankivs'k, *Rus.* Ivano-Frankovskaya Oblast'; *prev.* Stanislavskaya Oblast'. ◆ *province* W Ukraine
Ivano-Frankovsk *see* Ivano-Frankivs'k
Ivano-Frankovskaya Oblast' *see* Ivano-Frankivs'ka Oblast'
128 M16 **Ivanovo** Ivanovskaya Oblast', W Russian Federation
Ivanovo *see* Ivanava
125 A16 **Ivanovskaya Oblast'** ◆ *province* W Russian Federation
37 X12 **Ivanpah Lake** ◎ California, W USA
114 E7 **Ivanšćica** ▲ NE Croatia
116 M8 **Ivanski** Varnenska Oblast, NE Bulgaria
131 R7 **Ivanteyevka** Saratovskaya Oblast', W Russian Federation
Ivantsevichi/Ivatsevichi *see* Ivatsevichy
118 I4 **Ivanychi** Volyns'ka Oblast', NW Ukraine
121 H18 **Ivatsevichy** *Pol.* Iwacewicze, *Rus.* Ivantsevichi, Ivatsevichi. Brestskaya Voblasts', SW Belorussia
116 L12 **Ivaylovgrad** Khaskovska Oblast, S Bulgaria
116 K11 **Ivaylovgrad, Yazovir** ▣ S Bulgaria
125 F10 **Ivdel'** Sverdlovskaya Oblast', C Russian Federation
Ivenets *see* Iwyanyets
118 L12 **Iveşti** Galaţi, E Romania
Ivigtut *see* Ivittuut
81 F18 **Ivindo** ↝ Congo/Gabon
xxxvii S7 **Ivinghoe** Buckinghamshire, C England, UK
61 I21 **Ivinheima** Mato Grosso do Sul, SW Brazil
206 M15 **Ivittuut** *var.* Ivigtut. S Greenland
Iviza *see* Eivissa
180 I6 **Ivohibe** Fianarantsoa, SE Madagascar
Ivoire, Côte d' *see* Ivory Coast
194 I14 **Ivori** ↝ S PNG
78 L15 **Ivory Coast** *off.* Republic of the Ivory Coast, *Fr.* Côte d'Ivoire, République de la Côte d'Ivoire. ◆ *republic* W Africa
70 C12 **Ivory Coast** *Fr.* Côte d'Ivoire. *coastal region* S Ivory Coast
97 L22 **Ivösjön** ◎ S Sweden
108 B7 **Ivrea** *anc.* Eporedia. Piemonte, NW Italy
10 J2 **Ivujivik** Québec, NE Canada
121 J16 **Ivyanyets** *Rus.* Ivenets. Minskaya Voblasts', C Belorussia
xxxvi G16 **Ivybridge** Devon, SW England, UK
Iv'ye *see* Iwye
Iwacewicze *see* Ivatsevichy
172 N11 **Iwaizumi** Iwate, Honshū, NE Japan
171 Ll15 **Iwaki** Fukushima, Honshū, N Japan
171 Mm9 **Iwaki-san** ▲ Honshū, C Japan
170 E13 **Iwakuni** Yamaguchi, Honshū, SW Japan
172 Oo5 **Iwamizawa** Hokkaidō, NE Japan
172 Nn5 **Iwanai** Hokkaidō, NE Japan
171 Ll13 **Iwanuma** Miyagi, Honshū, C Japan
171 I17 **Iwata** Shizuoka, Honshū, S Japan
172 N10 **Iwate** Iwate, Honshū, N Japan
171 Mm11 **Iwate** *off.* Iwate-ken. ◆ *prefecture* Honshū, C Japan
171 Mm10 **Iwate-san** ▲ Honshū, C Japan
Iwje *see* Iwye
79 S16 **Iwo** Oyo, SW Nigeria
Iwojima *see* Iō-jima
121 I16 **Iwye** *Pol.* Iwje, *Rus.* Iv'ye. Hrodzyenskaya Voblasts', W Belorussia
44 C4 **Ixcán, Río** ↝ Guatemala/Mexico
101 G18 **Ixelles** *Dut.* Elsene. Brussels, C Belgium
59 J16 **Ixiamas** La Paz, NW Bolivia
43 O13 **Ixmiquilpan** *var.* Ixmiquilpán. Hidalgo, C Mexico
85 K23 **Ixopo** KwaZulu/Natal, E South Africa
Ixtaccíhuatl, Volcán *see* Iztaccíhuatl, Volcán
42 M16 **Ixtapa** Guerrero, S Mexico
43 S16 **Ixtepec** Oaxaca, SE Mexico
42 K12 **Ixtlán** *var.* Ixtlán del Río. Nayarit, C Mexico
Ixtlán del Río *see* Ixtlán
xxxix V11 **Ixworth** Suffolk, E England, UK
125 F12 **Iyevlevo** Tyumenskaya Oblast', C Russian Federation
170 E14 **Iyo** Ehime, Shikoku, SW Japan
170 F15 **Iyomishima** *var.* Iyomisima. Ehime, Shikoku, SW Japan
Iyomisima *see* Iyomishima
170 Dd14 **Iyo-nada** *sea* S Japan
44 E4 **Izabal** *off.* Departamento de Izabal. ◆ *department* E Guatemala
44 F5 **Izabal, Lago de** *prev.* Golfo Dulce. ◎ E Guatemala
149 O9 **Īzad Khvāst** Fārs, C Iran
43 X12 **Izamal** Yucatán, SE Mexico
131 Q16 **Izberbash** Respublika Dagestan, SW Russian Federation
101 C18 **Izegem** *prev.* Iseghem. West-Vlaanderen, W Belgium
148 M9 **Īzeh** Khūzestān, SW Iran
172 P14 **Izena-jima** *island* Nansei-shotō, SW Japan
116 N10 **Izgrev** Burgaska Oblast, SE Bulgaria
131 T2 **Izhevsk** *prev.* Ustinov. Udmurtskaya Respublika, NW Russian Federation
129 S7 **Izhma** Respublika Komi, NW Russian Federation
129 S7 **Izhma** ↝ NW Russian Federation
147 X8 **Izkī** NE Oman
Izmail *see* Izmayil
119 N13 **Izmayil** *Rus.* Izmail. Odes'ka Oblast', SW Ukraine
142 B14 **İzmir** *prev.* Smyrna. İzmir, W Turkey
142 C14 **İzmir** *prev.* Smyrna. ◆ *province* W Turkey
142 E11 **İzmit** *var.* Ismid; *anc.* Astacus. Kocaeli, NW Turkey
106 M14 **Iznájar** Andalucía, S Spain
106 M14 **Iznajar, Embalse de** ▣ S Spain
107 N14 **Iznalloz** Andalucía, S Spain
142 E11 **İznik** Bursa, NW Turkey
142 E12 **İznik Gölü** ◎ NW Turkey
130 M14 **Izobil'nyy** Stavropol'skiy Kray, SW Russian Federation
111 S13 **Izola** *It.* Isola d'Istria. SW Slovenia
144 H9 **Izra'** *var.* Ezra, Ezraa. Dar'ā, S Syria
43 P14 **Iztaccíhuatl, Volcán** *var.* Volcán Ixtaccíhuatal. ⛰ S Mexico
44 C7 **Iztapa** Escuintla, SE Guatemala
Izúcar de Matamoros *see* Matamoros
171 J17 **Izu-hantō** *peninsula* Honshū, S Japan
170 C11 **Izuhara** Nagasaki, Tsushima, SW Japan
170 C15 **Izumi** Kagoshima, Kyūshū, SW Japan
171 Gg15 **Izumiōtsu** Ōsaka, Honshū, SW Japan
171 Gg15 **Izumi-Sano** Ōsaka, Honshū, SW Japan
170 F12 **Izumo** Shimane, Honshū, SW Japan
Izu Shichito *see* Izu-shotō
172 Ss13 **Izu-shotō** *var.* Izu Shichito. *island group* S Japan
199 H4 **Izu Trench** *undersea feature* NW Pacific Ocean
126 I4 **Izvestiy TsIK, Ostrova** *island* N Russian Federation
116 G10 **Izvor** Sofiyska Oblast, W Bulgaria
118 L5 **Izyaslav** Khmel'nyts'ka Oblast', W Ukraine
119 W6 **Izyum** Kharkivs'ka Oblast', E Ukraine

J

95 M18 **Jaala** Kymi, S Finland
146 J5 **Jabal ash Shifā** *desert* NW Saudi Arabia
147 U8 **Jabal az Ẓannah** *var.* Jebel Dhanna. Abū Ẓaby, W UAE
144 E11 **Jabaliya** *var.* Jabāliyah. NE Gaza Strip
Jabāliyah *see* Jabaliya
107 N11 **Jabalón** ↝ C Spain
160 J10 **Jabalpur** *prev.* Jubbulpore. Madhya Pradesh, C India
147 N15 **Jabal Zuuqar, Jazīrat** *var.* Az Zuqur. *island* SW Yemen
Jabat *see* Jabwot
144 J3 **Jabbūl, Sabkhat al** *salt flat* NW Syria
189 P1 **Jabiru** Northern Territory, N Australia
144 H4 **Jablah** *var.* Jeble, *Fr.* Djéblé. Al Lādhiqīyah, W Syria
114 C11 **Jablanac** Lika-Senj, W Croatia
115 H14 **Jablanica** SW Bosnia and Herzegovina
115 M20 **Jablanica** *Alb.* Mali i Jabllanicës, *var.* Malet e Jabllanicës. ▲ Albania/FYR Macedonia *see also* Jabllanicës, Mali i
Jabllanicës, Malet e *see* Jablanica/Jabllanicës, Mali i
115 M20 **Jabllanicës, Mali i** *var.* Malet e Jabllanicës, *Mac.* Jablanica. ▲ Albania/FYR Macedonia *see also* Jablanica
113 E15 **Jablonec nad Nisou** *Ger.* Gablonz an der Neisse. Severní Čechy, N Czech Republic
Jabłonków/Jablunkau *see* Jablunkov
112 J9 **Jabłonowo Pomorskie** Toruń, N Poland
113 J17 **Jablunkov** *Ger.* Jablunkau, *Pol.* Jabłonków. Severní Morava, E Czech Republic
61 Q15 **Jaboatão** Pernambuco, E Brazil
62 L8 **Jaboticabal** São Paulo, S Brazil
201 U7 **Jabwot** *var.* Jabat, Jebat, Jōwat. *island* Ralik Chain, S Marshall Islands
107 S4 **Jaca** Aragón, NE Spain
44 B4 **Jacaltenango** Huehuetenango, W Guatemala
61 G14 **Jacaré-a-Canga** Pará, NE Brazil
62 N10 **Jacareí** São Paulo, S Brazil
61 I18 **Jaciara** Mato Grosso, W Brazil
61 E15 **Jaciparaná** Rondônia, W Brazil
21 P5 **Jackman** Maine, NE USA
37 X1 **Jackpot** Nevada, W USA
22 M8 **Jacksboro** Tennessee, S USA
27 S6 **Jacksboro** Texas, SW USA
25 N7 **Jackson** Alabama, S USA
37 P7 **Jackson** California, W USA
25 T4 **Jackson** Georgia, SE USA
23 O6 **Jackson** Kentucky, S USA
24 J8 **Jackson** Louisiana, S USA
33 Q10 **Jackson** Michigan, N USA
31 T11 **Jackson** Minnesota, N USA
24 K5 **Jackson** *state capital* Mississippi, S USA
29 Y7 **Jackson** Missouri, C USA
23 W8 **Jackson** North Carolina, SE USA
33 T15 **Jackson** Ohio, NE USA
22 G9 **Jackson** Tennessee, S USA
35 S14 **Jackson** Wyoming, C USA
193 C19 **Jackson Bay** *bay* South Island, NZ
194 K16 **Jackson Field** ✕ (Port Moresby) Central/National Capital District, S PNG
193 C20 **Jackson Head** *headland* South Island, NZ
25 S8 **Jackson, Lake** ◎ Florida, SE USA
35 S13 **Jackson Lake** ◎ Wyoming, C USA
204 J6 **Jackson, Mount** ▲ Antarctica
39 U3 **Jackson Reservoir** ◎ Colorado, C USA
25 Q3 **Jacksonville** Alabama, S USA
29 V11 **Jacksonville** Arkansas, C USA
25 W8 **Jacksonville** Florida, SE USA
32 K14 **Jacksonville** Illinois, N USA
23 W11 **Jacksonville** North Carolina, SE USA
27 W7 **Jacksonville** Texas, SW USA
25 X9 **Jacksonville Beach** Florida, SE USA
46 L9 **Jacmel** *var.* Jaquemel. S Haiti
Jacob *see* Nkayi
155 Q12 **Jacobābād** Sind, SE Pakistan
57 T11 **Jacobs Ladder Falls** *waterfall* S Guyana
47 O11 **Jaco, Pointe** *headland* N Dominica
13 Q9 **Jacques-Cartier** ↝ Québec, SE Canada
11 P11 **Jacques-Cartier, Détroit de** *var.* Jacques-Cartier Passage. *strait* Gulf of St. Lawrence/St. Lawrence River
13 W6 **Jacques-Cartier, Mont** ▲ Québec, SE Canada
Jacques-Cartier Passage *see* Jacques-Cartier, Détroit de
195 O12 **Jacquinot Bay** *inlet* New Britain, PNG
63 H16 **Jacuí, Rio** ↝ S Brazil
62 L11 **Jacupiranga** São Paulo, S Brazil
Jaddoûa *see* Jaddū'ah
102 G10 **Jade** ↝ NW Germany
102 G10 **Jadebusen** *bay* NW Germany
Jadotville *see* Likasi
Jadransko More/Jadransko Morje *see* Adriatic Sea
107 O7 **Jadraque** Castilla-La Mancha, C Spain
58 C10 **Jaén** Cajamarca, N Peru
107 N13 **Jaén** Andalucía, SW Spain
107 N13 **Jaén** ◆ *province* Andalucía, S Spain
161 J23 **Jaffna** Northern Province, N Sri Lanka
161 K23 **Jaffna Lagoon** *lagoon* N Sri Lanka
21 N10 **Jaffrey** New Hampshire, NE USA
144 H13 **Jafr, Qā' al** *var.* El Jafr. *salt pan* S Jordan
158 J9 **Jagādhri** Haryāna, N India
120 H4 **Jägala** *var.* Jägala Jõgi, *Ger.* Jaggowal. ↝ NW Estonia
Jägala Jõgi *see* Jägala
Jagannath *see* Puri
161 L14 **Jagdalpur** Madhya Pradesh, C India
169 U5 **Jagdaqi** Nei Mongol Zizhiqu, N China
Jägerndorf *see* Krnov
Jaggowal *see* Jägala
145 O2 **Jaghjaghah, Nahr** ↝ N Syria
179 Qq14 **Jagna** Bohol, C Philippines
114 N13 **Jagodina** *prev.* Svetozarevo. Serbia, C Yugoslavia
114 K12 **Jagodnja** ▲ W Yugoslavia
103 I20 **Jagst** ↝ SW Germany
161 I14 **Jagtiāl** Andhra Pradesh, C India
63 H18 **Jaguarão** Rio Grande do Sul, S Brazil
63 H18 **Jaguarão, Rio** *var.* Río Yaguarón. ↝ Brazil/Uruguay
62 K11 **Jaguariaíva** Paraná, S Brazil
46 D5 **Jagüey Grande** Matanzas, W Cuba
159 P14 **Jahānābād** Bihār, N India
Jahra *see* Al Jahrā'
149 P12 **Jahrom** *var.* Jahrum. Fārs, S Iran
Jahrum *see* Jahrom
Jailolo *see* Halmahera, Pulau
175 Tt8 **Jailolo, Selat** *strait* E Indonesia
Jainat *see* Chai Nat
Jainti *see* Jayanti
158 H12 **Jaipur** *prev.* Jeypore. Rājasthān, N India
159 T14 **Jaipur Hat** Rajshahi, NW Bangladesh
158 D11 **Jaisalmer** Rājasthān, NW India
160 O12 **Jājapur** Orissa, E India
149 R4 **Jājarm** Khorāsān, NE Iran
114 G12 **Jajce** W Bosnia and Herzegovina
Jajı *see* 'Ali Kheyl
85 D17 **Jakalsberg** Otjozondjupa, N Namibia
174 J14 **Jakarta** *prev.* Djakarta, *Dut.* Batavia. ● (Indonesia) Jawa, C Indonesia
8 I8 **Jakes Corner** Yukon Territory, W Canada
158 H9 **Jākhal** Haryāna, NW India
Jakobeny *see* Iacobeni
95 K16 **Jakobstad** *Fin.* Pietarsaari. Vaasa, W Finland
Jakobstadt *see* Jēkabpils
115 O18 **Jakupica** ▲ C FYR Macedonia
39 W15 **Jal** New Mexico, SW USA
147 P7 **Jalājil** *var.* Ğalāğıl. Ar Riyāḍ, C Saudi Arabia
Jalal-Abad *see* Dzhalal-Abad, Dzhalal-Abadskaya Oblast', W Kyrgyzstan
155 S5 **Jalālābād** *var.* Jalalabad, Jelalabad. Nangarhār, E Afghanistan
Jalal-Abad Oblasty *see* Dzhalal-Abadskaya Oblast'
155 V7 **Jalālpur** Punjab, E Pakistan
155 T11 **Jalālpur Pīrwāla** Punjab, E Pakistan
158 H8 **Jalandhar** *prev.* Jullundur. Punjab, N India
44 J7 **Jalán, Río** ↝ S Honduras
44 E6 **Jalapa** Jalapa, C Guatemala
44 J7 **Jalapa** Nueva Segovia, NW Nicaragua
44 A3 **Jalapa** *off.* Departamento de Jalapa. ◆ *department* SE Guatemala
44 E6 **Jalapa, Río** ↝ SE Guatemala
149 X13 **Jālaq** Sīstān va Balūchestān, SE Iran
95 K17 **Jalasjärvi** Vaasa, W Finland
155 O8 **Jaldak** Zābul, SE Afghanistan
62 J7 **Jales** São Paulo, S Brazil
160 P11 **Jaleshwar** *var.* Jaleswar. Orissa, NE India
Jaleswar *see* Jaleshwar
160 F12 **Jalgaon** Mahārāshtra, C India
145 W12 **Jalībah** S Iraq
145 W13 **Jalīb Shahāb** S Iraq
79 X15 **Jalingo** Taraba, E Nigeria
42 K13 **Jalisco** ◆ *state* SW Mexico
160 G13 **Jālna** Mahārāshtra, W India
Jalomitsa *see* Ialomiţa
107 R5 **Jalón** ↝ N Spain
158 E13 **Jālor** Rājasthān, N India
114 K11 **Jalovik** Serbia, W Yugoslavia
42 L12 **Jalpa** Zacatecas, C Mexico
159 S12 **Jalpāiguri** West Bengal, NE India
43 O12 **Jalpán** *var.* Jalpan. Querétaro de Arteaga, C Mexico
69 P2 **Jalta** *island* N Tunisia
77 S9 **Jālū** *var.* Jūlā. NE Libya
201 U8 **Jaluit Atoll** *var.* Jālwōj. *atoll* Ralik Chain, S Marshall Islands
Jālwōj *see* Jaluit Atoll
83 L18 **Jamaame** *It.* Giamame; *prev.* Margherita. Jubbada Hoose, S Somalia
79 W13 **Jamaare** ↝ NE Nigeria
46 G9 **Jamaica** ◆ *commonwealth republic* W West Indies
49 P3 **Jamaica** *island* W West Indies
46 I9 **Jamaica Channel** *channel* Haiti/Jamaica
159 T14 **Jamalpur** Dhaka, N Bangladesh
159 Q14 **Jamālpur** Bihār, NE India
174 I6 **Jamaluang** *var.* Jemaluang. Johor, Peninsular Malaysia
61 I14 **Jamanxim, Rio** ↝ C Brazil

◆ Country ● Country Capital ◇ Dependent Territory ○ Dependent Territory Capital ◆ Administrative Region ✕ International Airport ▲ Mountain ▲ Mountain Range ⛰ Volcano ↝ River ◎ Lake ▣ Reservoir

58 B8 **Jambeli, Canal de** channel S Ecuador
101 I20 **Jambes** Namur, SE Belgium
174 Hh9 **Jambi** var. Telanaipura; prev. Djambi. Sumatera, W Indonesia
174 H9 **Jambi** off. Propinsi Jambi, var. Djambi. ♦ province W Indonesia
Jamden see Yamdena, Pulau
10 H8 **James Bay** bay Ontario/ Québec, E Canada
65 F19 **James, Isla** island Archipiélago de los Chonos, S Chile
189 Q8 **James Ranges** ▲ Northern Territory, C Australia
31 P8 **James River** ♒ North Dakota/South Dakota, N USA
21 X7 **James River** ♒ Virginia, NE USA
204 H4 **James Ross Island** island Antarctica
190 I8 **Jamestown** South Australia
67 G25 **Jamestown** ♦ (Saint Helena) NW Saint Helena
37 P8 **Jamestown** California, W USA
22 L7 **Jamestown** Kentucky, S USA
20 D11 **Jamestown** New York, NE USA
31 P5 **Jamestown** North Dakota, N USA
22 L8 **Jamestown** Tennessee, S USA
13 N10 **Jamet** ♒ Québec, SE Canada
43 Q17 **Jamiltepec** var. Santiago Jamiltepec. Oaxaca, SE Mexico
97 F20 **Jammerbugten** bay Skagerrak, E North Sea
158 H6 **Jammu** var. Jummoo. Jammu and Kashmir, NW India
158 I5 **Jammu and Kashmir.** Jammu-Kashmir, Kashmir. ♦ state NW India
155 V4 **Jammu and Kashmir** disputed region India/Pakistan
160 B10 **Jāmnagar** prev. Navanagar. Gujarāt, W India
155 S11 **Jāmpur** Punjab, E Pakistan
95 L18 **Jämsä** Keski-Suomi, C Finland
95 L18 **Jämsänkoski** Keski-Suomi, C Finland
159 Q16 **Jamshedpur** Bihār, NE India
96 K9 **Jämtland** ♦ county C Sweden
159 Q14 **Jamūi** Bihār, NE India
159 T14 **Jamuna** ♒ N Bangladesh
Jamuna see Brahmaputra
Jamundé see Nhamundá, Rio
56 D11 **Jamundí** Valle del Cauca, SW Colombia
159 Q12 **Janakpur** Central, C Nepal
61 N18 **Janaúba** Minas Gerais, SE Brazil
60 K11 **Janaucu, Ilha** island NE Brazil
149 Q7 **Jandaq** Eşfahān, C Iran
66 Q11 **Jandia, Punta de** headland Fuerteventura, Islas Canarias, Spain, NE Atlantic Ocean
61 N14 **Jandiatuba, Rio** ♒ NW Brazil
107 N12 **Jándula** ♒ S Spain
31 V10 **Janesville** Minnesota, N USA
32 L9 **Janesville** Wisconsin, N USA
155 N13 **Jangal** Baluchistān, SW Pakistan
85 N20 **Jangamo** Inhambane, SE Mozambique
161 J14 **Jangaon** Andhra Pradesh, C India
152 K10 **Jangeldi** Rus. Dzhankel'dy. Bukhoro Wiloyati, C Uzbekistan
159 S14 **Jangipur** West Bengal, NE India
Janina see Ioánnina
Janischken see Joniškis
114 J11 **Janja** NE Bosnia and Herzegovina
Jankovac see Jánoshalma
207 Q15 **Jan Mayen** ♦ Norwegian dependency N Atlantic Ocean
86 D5 **Jan Mayen** island N Atlantic Ocean
207 R15 **Jan Mayen Fracture Zone** tectonic feature Greenland Sea/Norwegian Sea
207 R15 **Jan Mayen Ridge** undersea feature Greenland Sea/ Norwegian Sea
42 H3 **Janos** Chihuahua, N Mexico
113 K25 **Jánoshalma** SCr. Jankovac. Bács-Kiskun, S Hungary
Janów see Ivanava, Belorussia
112 H10 **Janowiec Wielkopolski** Ger. Janowitz. Bydgoszcz, C Poland
Janowitz see Janowiec Wielkopolski
113 O15 **Janów Lubelski** Tarnobrzeg, SE Poland
Janów Poleski see Ivanava
85 H25 **Jansenville** Eastern Cape, S South Africa
176 W12 **Jantan** Irian Jaya, E Indonesia
60 D12 **Januária** Minas Gerais, SE Brazil
Janūbīyah, Al Bādīyah al see Ash Shāmīyah
104 I7 **Janzé** Ille-et-Vilaine, NW France
160 F10 **Jaora** Madhya Pradesh, C India
171 H12 **Japan** var. Nippon, Jap. Nihon. ♦ monarchy E Asia
133 Y9 **Japan** island group E Asia
199 H3 **Japan Basin** undersea feature N Sea of Japan
133 Y8 **Japan, Sea of** var. East Sea, Rus. Yapanskoye More. sea NW Pacific Ocean
199 H4 **Japan Trench** undersea feature NW Pacific Ocean
Japen see Yapen, Pulau
60 A15 **Japiim** var. Máncio Lima. Acre, W Brazil
60 D12 **Japurá** Amazonas, N Brazil
60 C12 **Japurá, Rio** var. Río Caquetá, Yapurá. ♒ Brazil/Colombia see also Caquetá, Río
45 W17 **Jaqué** Darién, SE Panama
Jaquemel see Jacmel
Jarablos see Jarābulus
144 K2 **Jarābulus** var. Jarablus, Jerablus, Fr. Djérablous. Halab, N Syria
62 K13 **Jaraguá do Sul** Santa Catarina, S Brazil
106 K9 **Jaraicejo** Extremadura, W Spain
106 K9 **Jaráiz de la Vera** Extremadura, W Spain
107 O7 **Jarama** ♒ C Spain
65 I20 **Jaramillo** Santa Cruz, SE Argentina
Jarandilla de la Vera see Jarandilla de la Vega
106 K8 **Jarandilla de la Vega** var. Jarandilla de la Vera. Extremadura, W Spain
155 V9 **Jarānwāla** Punjab, NE India
144 G9 **Jarash** var. Jerash; anc. Gerasa. Irbid, NW Jordan
96 N13 **Järbo** Gävleborg, C Sweden

Jardan see Jordan
46 F7 **Jardines de la Reina, Archipiélago de** island group C Cuba
168 J7 **Jargalant** Arhangay, C Mongolia
168 I8 **Jargalant** Bayanhongor, C Mongolia
168 D7 **Jargalant** Bayan-Ölgiy, W Mongolia
168 K6 **Jargalant** Bulgan, N Mongolia
168 G9 **Jargalant** Govi-Altay, W Mongolia
60 I11 **Jari, Rio** var. Jary. ♒ N Brazil
147 N7 **Jarīr, Wādī al** dry watercourse C Saudi Arabia
Jarja see Yur'ya
96 L13 **Järna** var. Dala-Jarna. Kopparberg, C Sweden
97 O16 **Järna** Stockholm, C Sweden
104 H12 **Jarnac** Charente, W France
113 F16 **Jarocin** Kalisz, C Poland
Jaroslau see Jarosław
113 O16 **Jarosław** Ger. Jaroslau, Rus. Yaroslav. Przemyśl, SE Poland
95 F16 **Järpen** Jämtland, C Sweden
153 O14 **Jarqürghon** Rus. Dzharkurgan. Surkhondaryo Wiloyati, S Uzbekistan
145 P2 **Jarrāh, Wadi** dry watercourse NE Syria
xli W2 **Jarrow** South Tyneside, NE England, UK
Jars, Plain of see Xiangkhoang, Plateau de
113 H14 **Jartai Yanchi** ♦ N China
61 G16 **Jaru** Rondônia, W Brazil
169 T10 **Jarud Qi** Nei Mongol Zizhiqu, N China
120 I4 **Järva-Jaani** Ger. Sankt-Johannis. Järvamaa, N Estonia
120 G5 **Järvakandi** Ger. Jerwakant. Raplamaa, NW Estonia
120 H4 **Järvamaa** off. Järva Maakond. ♦ province N Estonia
95 L19 **Järvenpää** Uusimaa, S Finland
12 G17 **Jarvis** Ontario, S Canada
185 R8 **Jarvis Island** ☐ US unincorporated territory C Pacific Ocean
96 M11 **Järvsö** Gävleborg, C Sweden
Jary see Jari, Rio
114 M9 **Jaša Tomić** Serbia, NE Yugoslavia
114 D12 **Jasenice** Zadar-Knin, S Croatia
144 I11 **Jashshat al 'Adlah, Wādī al** dry watercourse E Jordan
79 Q16 **Jasikan** E Ghana
149 T15 **Jāsk** Hormozgān, SE Iran
152 F6 **Jasliq** Rus. Zhaslyk. Qoraqalpoghiston Respublikasi, NW Uzbekistan
113 N17 **Jasło** Krosno, SE Poland
9 U16 **Jasmin** Saskatchewan, S Canada
67 A23 **Jason Islands** island group NW Falkland Islands
204 I4 **Jason Peninsula** peninsula Antarctica
33 N15 **Jasonville** Indiana, N USA
9 O15 **Jasper** Alberta, SW Canada
12 L13 **Jasper** Ontario, S Canada
23 O3 **Jasper** Alabama, S USA
29 T9 **Jasper** Arkansas, C USA
25 U8 **Jasper** Florida, SE USA
33 N16 **Jasper** Indiana, N USA
31 R1 **Jasper** Minnesota, N USA
29 S7 **Jasper** Missouri, C USA
22 K2 **Jasper** Tennessee, S USA
27 Y9 **Jasper** Texas, SW USA
9 O15 **Jasper National Park** national park Alberta/British Columbia, SW Canada
Jassy see Iaşi
115 N14 **Jastrebac** ▲ SE Yugoslavia
114 D9 **Jastrebarsko** Grad Zagreb, N Croatia
112 G9 **Jastrowie** Ger. Jastrow. Piła, NW Poland
113 J17 **Jastrzębie-Zdrój** Katowice, S Poland
113 L22 **Jászapáti** Jász-Nagykun-Szolnok, E Hungary
113 L22 **Jászberény** Jász-Nagykun-Szolnok, E Hungary
113 L23 **Jász-Nagykun-Szolnok** off. Jász-Nagykun-Szolnok Megye. ♦ county E Hungary
61 J19 **Jataí** Goiás, C Brazil
60 G12 **Jatapu, Serra do** ▲ N Brazil
43 W16 **Jatate, Río** ♒ SE Mexico
113 J17 **Jāti** Sind, SE Pakistan
46 F6 **Jatibonico** Sancti Spíritus, C Cuba
174 K14 **Jatiluhur, Danau** ☐ Jawa, S Indonesia
Jativa see Xátiva
174 K14 **Jatiwangi** prev. Djatiwangi. Jawa, C Indonesia
155 S11 **Jattoi** Punjab, E Pakistan
62 L9 **Jaú** São Paulo, S Brazil
60 F11 **Jauaperi, Rio** ♒ N Brazil
101 I19 **Jauche** Walloon Brabant, C Belgium
Jauer see Jawor
Jauf see Al Jawf
155 U7 **Jauharābād** Punjab, E Pakistan
59 E14 **Jauja** Junín, C Peru
45 O10 **Jaumave** Tamaulipas, C Mexico
120 H10 **Jaunjelgava** Ger. Friedrichstadt. Aizkraukle, S Latvia
120 I8 **Jaunlatgale** see Pytalovo
120 E9 **Jaunpils** Tukums, C Latvia
159 N13 **Jaunpur** Uttar Pradesh, N India
31 N8 **Java** South Dakota, N USA
Java see Jawa
107 R9 **Javalambre** ▲ E Spain
181 V7 **Java Ridge** undersea feature E Indian Ocean
61 A14 **Javari, Rio** var. Yavarí. ♒ Brazil/Peru
168 J7 **Javarthushuu** Dornod, NE Mongolia
174 Kk13 **Java Sea** Ind. Laut Jawa. sea W Indonesia
181 U7 **Java Trench** var. Sunda Trench. undersea feature E Indian Ocean
107 T11 **Jávea** var. Xábia. País Valenciano, E Spain
169 Q7 **Javhlant** Hentiy, E Mongolia
175 P13 **Javin** Tirol, W Austria
175 P13 **Javor** ▲ Bosnia and Herzegovina/Yugoslavia
115 L14 **Javorie** Hung. Jávoros. ▲ S Slovakia

Jávoros see Javorie
95 J14 **Jävre** Norrbotten, N Sweden
174 K14 **Jawa, Laut** see Java Sea
174 J15 **Jawa** Eng. Java; prev. Djawa. island C Indonesia
174 J15 **Jawa Barat** off. Propinsi Jawa Barat, Eng. West Java. ♦ province S Indonesia
174 Kk15 **Jawa Tengah** off. Propinsi Jawa Tengah, Eng. Central Java. ♦ province S Indonesia
174 Ll15 **Jawa Timur** off. Propinsi Jawa Timur, Eng. East Java. ♦ province S Indonesia
83 N17 **Jawhar** var. Jowhar, It. Giohar. Shabeellaha Dhexe, S Somalia
113 F14 **Jawor** Ger. Jauer. Legnica, SW Poland
Jaworów see Yavoriv
113 J16 **Jaworzno** Katowice, S Poland
29 Q7 **Jay** Oklahoma, C USA
174 G6 **Jaya, Puncak** prev. Puntjak Carstensz, Puntjak Sukarno. ▲ Irian Jaya, E Indonesia
176 Z10 **Jayapura** var. Djajapura, Dut. Hollandia; prev. Kotabaru, Sukarnapura. Irian Jaya, E Indonesia
176 Y12 **Jayawijaya, Pegunungan** ▲ Irian Jaya, E Indonesia
Jay Dairen see Dalian
153 S12 **Jayilgan** Rus. Dzhailgan, Dzhayilgan. C Tajikistan
161 L14 **Jaypur** var. Jeypore, Jeypur. Orissa, E India
27 O6 **Jayton** Texas, SW USA
149 U13 **Jazā Murīān, Hāmūn** ☐ SE Iran
144 M4 **Jazr** ar Raqqah, C Syria
144 G6 **Jbaïl** var. Jebeil, Jubayl, Jubeil; anc. Biblical Gebal, Byblos. W Lebanon
21 O7 **J.B.Thomas, Lake** ☐ Texas, SW USA
37 X12 **Jean** Nevada, W USA
46 L8 **Jeanerette** Louisiana, S USA
46 L8 **Jean-Rabel** NW Haiti
149 T12 **Jebāl Bārez, Kūh-e** ▲ SE Iran
79 T15 **Jebba** Kwara, W Nigeria
Jebeil see Jbaïl
118 E12 **Jebel** Hung. Széphely; prev. Hung. Zsebely. Timiş, W Romania
Jebel see Dzhebel
Jebel, Bahr el see White Nile
Jebel Dhanna see Jabal az Zannah
Jeble see Jablah
113 L15 **Jędrzejów** Ger. Endersdorf. Kielce, S Poland
102 K12 **Jeetze** var. Jeetzel. ♒ C Germany
Jeetzel see Jeetze
31 U14 **Jefferson** Iowa, C USA
23 Q8 **Jefferson** North Carolina, SE USA
29 S7 **Jefferson** Texas, SW USA
32 L9 **Jefferson** Wisconsin, N USA
35 R10 **Jefferson City** Montana, NW USA
23 N9 **Jefferson City** Tennessee, S USA
29 U5 **Jefferson City** state capital Missouri, C USA
37 U7 **Jefferson, Mount** ▲ Nevada, W USA
34 H7 **Jefferson, Mount** ▲ Oregon, NW USA
23 N5 **Jeffersontown** Kentucky, S USA
33 P16 **Jeffersonville** Indiana, N USA
37 V15 **Jeffrey City** Wyoming, C USA
79 T13 **Jega** Kebbi, NW Nigeria
Jehol see Chengde
64 P5 **Jejui-Guazú, Río** ♒ E Paraguay
120 I10 **Jēkabpils** Ger. Jakobstadt. S Latvia
25 W7 **Jekyll Island** island Georgia, SE USA
174 L11 **Jelai, Sungai** ♒ Borneo, N Indonesia
Jelalabad see Jalālābād
113 H14 **Jelcz-Laskowice** Wrocław, SW Poland
112 F13 **Jelenia Góra** Ger. Hirschberg, Hirschberg im Riesengebirge, Hirschberg in Schlesien. Jelenia Góra, SW Poland
112 F13 **Jelenia Góra** Ger. Hirschberg. ♦ province SW Poland
Jeleniogórskie, Województwo see Jelenia Góra
159 S11 **Jelep La** pass N India
120 F9 **Jelgava** Ger. Mitau. C Latvia
114 L13 **Jelica** ▲ C Yugoslavia
22 M8 **Jellico** Tennessee, S USA
97 G22 **Jelling** Vejle, C Denmark
174 I15 **Jemaja, Pulau** island W Indonesia
101 I20 **Jemappes** Hainaut, S Belgium
174 M16 **Jember** var. Djember. Jawa, S Indonesia
39 R10 **Jemez Pueblo** New Mexico, SW USA
164 K2 **Jeminay** Xinjiang Uygur Zizhiqu, NW China
201 U5 **Jemo Island** atoll Ratak Chain, C Marshall Islands
175 Nn8 **Jempang, Danau** ☐ Borneo, N Indonesia
103 L16 **Jena** Thüringen, C Germany
23 N8 **Jena** Louisiana, S USA
110 I8 **Jenaz** Graubünden, SW Switzerland
111 N7 **Jenbach** Tirol, W Austria
175 P13 **Jenepcote** Djenepcote. Sulawesi, C Indonesia
141 U9 **Jenin** N West Bank
23 N9 **Jenkins** Kentucky, S USA
29 P9 **Jenks** Oklahoma, C USA
167 S9 **Jenné** see Djenné

111 X8 **Jennersdorf** Burgenland, SE Austria
24 I20 **Jennings** Louisiana, S USA
15 J4 **Jenny Lind Island** island Northwest Territories, N Canada
25 Y13 **Jensen Beach** Florida, SE USA
15 M2 **Jens Munk Island** island Northwest Territories, NE Canada
61 O17 **Jequié** Bahia, E Brazil
61 O18 **Jequitinhonha, Rio** ♒ E Brazil
76 M10 **Jerada** NE Morocco
Jerash see Jarash
46 K9 **Jérémie** SW Haiti
42 L11 **Jerez de García Salinas** var. Jerez. Zacatecas, C Mexico
106 J15 **Jerez de la Frontera** var. Jerez; prev. Xeres. Andalucía, SW Spain
106 I12 **Jerez de los Caballeros** Extremadura, W Spain
144 G10 **Jericho** Ar. Arīḥā, Heb. Yeriḥo. E West Bank
76 M7 **Jerid, Chott el** var. Shaṭṭ al Jarīd. salt lake SW Tunisia
191 O10 **Jerilderie** New South Wales, SE Australia
94 K11 **Jerisjärvi** ☐ NW Finland
Jermak see Yermak
82 L13 **Jerome** Idaho, NW USA
33 S8 **Jerome** Idaho, NW USA
107 S12 **Jijona** var. Xixona. País Valenciano, E Spain
xxxiv I16 **Jersey** ♦ UK crown dependency NW Europe
xxxvii X16 **Jersey** anc. Caesarea. island Channel Islands, NW Europe
83 L18 **Jersey City** New Jersey, NE USA
20 F13 **Jersey Shore** Pennsylvania, NE USA
32 K7 **Jerseyville** Illinois, N USA
106 K8 **Jerte** ♒ W Spain
144 F10 **Jerusalem** Ar. Al Quds, Al Quds ash Sharīf, Heb. Yerushalayim; anc. Hierosolyma. ● (Israel) Jerusalem, NE Israel
144 G10 **Jerusalem** ♦ district E Israel
191 S10 **Jervis Bay** New South Wales, SE Australia
191 S10 **Jervis Bay Territory** ♦ territory SE Australia
Jerwakant see Järvakandi
111 U10 **Jesenice** Ger. Assling. NW Slovenia
113 H16 **Jeseník** Ger. Freiwaldau. Severní Morava, E Czech Republic
Jesi see Iesi
108 I8 **Jesolo** var. Iesolo. Veneto, NE Italy
Jesselton see Kota Kinabalu
97 J15 **Jessheim** Akershus, S Norway
159 T15 **Jessore** Khulna, S Bangladesh
25 W6 **Jesup** Georgia, SE USA
43 S15 **Jesús Carranza** Veracruz-Llave, SE Mexico
64 K10 **Jesús María** Córdoba, C Argentina
42 K7 **Jiménez** Chihuahua, N Mexico
43 N5 **Jiménez** Coahuila de Zaragoza, NE Mexico
43 N9 **Jiménez** var. Santander Jiménez. Tamaulipas, C Mexico
42 K7 **Jiménez del Teul** Zacatecas, C Mexico
79 Y14 **Jimeta** Adamawa, E Nigeria
83 K14 **Jimma** var. Jima. Oromo, SW Ethiopia
46 M9 **Jimaní** W Dominican Republic
118 E11 **Jimbolia** Ger. Hatzfeld, Hung. Zsombolya. Timiş, W Romania
106 K16 **Jimena de la Frontera** Andalucía, S Spain
42 K7 **Jiménez** Chihuahua, N Mexico

(continued in subsequent column with Ji– and Jia– entries)

Jiayi see Chiai
169 X6 **Jiayin** var. Chaoyang. Heilongjiang, NE China
165 R8 **Jiayu** Hunan, S China
144 M4 **Jibli** Ar Raqqah, N Syria
118 H9 **Jibou** Hung. Zsibó. Sălaj, NW Romania
147 Z9 **Jibuti** see Djibouti
113 E15 **Jičín** Ger. Jitschin. Východní Čechy, N Czech Republic
146 K10 **Jiddah** Eng. Jedda. Makkah, W Saudi Arabia
147 W11 **Jiddat al Ḥarāsīs** desert C Oman
Jiesjavrre see Iešjávri
166 M4 **Jieshou** Anhui, E China
167 P4 **Jieyang** Guangdong, S China
121 F14 **Jieznas** Prienai, S Lithuania
147 P15 **Jifa, Bi'r** var. Bi'r Jifa'. well C Yemen
79 W13 **Jigawa** ♦ state N Nigeria
Jigerbent see Dzhigirbent
46 J5 **Jiguaní** Granma, E Cuba
46 I7 **Jiguaní** prev. Xigazê. Xizang Zizhiqu, W China
113 E18 **Jih-k'a-tse** var. Xigazê
113 E18 **Jihlava** Ger. Iglau, Pol. Iglawa. Jižní Morava, S Czech Republic
113 E18 **Jihlava** var. Igel; Ger. Iglawa. ♒ S Czech Republic
76 K8 **Jihočeský Kraj** see Jižní Čechy
Jihomoravský Kraj see Jižní Morava
76 K8 **Jijel** var. Djidjel; prev. Djidjelli. NE Algeria
82 L13 **Jijiga** It. Giggiga. E Ethiopia
118 L9 **Jijia** ♒ N Romania
107 S12 **Jijona** var. Xixona. País Valenciano, E Spain
xxxiv I16 **Jilf al Kabir, Haḍabat al** see Gilf Kebir Plateau
83 L18 **Jilib** It. Gelib. Jubbada Dhexe, S Somalia
169 W10 **Jilin** var. Chi-lin, Girin, Kirin; prev. Yungki, Yunki. Jilin, NE China
169 W11 **Jilin Hada Ling** ▲ NE China
169 W11 **Jilin** var. Chi-lin, Girin, Ji, Jilin Sheng, Kirin. ♦ province NE China
169 S4 **Jilin Sheng** see Jilin
169 He **Jiliu He** ♒ NE China
191 Q11 **Jindabyne** New South Wales, SE Australia
113 O18 **Jindřichův Hradec** Ger. Neuhaus. Jižní Čechy, S Czech Republic
167 P5 **Jing** see Beijing Shi, China
161 K11 **Jing** see Jinghe, China
160 F10 **Jingchuan** Gansu, N China
167 O10 **Jingdezhen** Jiangxi, S China
167 P3 **Jinggangshan** Jiangxi, S China
167 P3 **Jinghai** Tianjin Shi, E China
164 K6 **Jinghe** var. Jing. Xinjiang Uygur Zizhiqu, NW China
158 U12 **Jinghong** var. Yunjinghong. Yunnan, SW China
167 P13 **Jingmen** Hubei, C China
169 X10 **Jingpo Hu** ☐ NE China
166 M8 **Jing Shan** ▲ C China
159 W10 **Jingtai** var. Yitiaoshan. Gansu, C China
166 L12 **Jingxi** Guangxi Zhuangzu Zizhiqu, S China
Jing Xian see Jingzhou
167 N7 **Jing Xian** Anhui, E China
165 V10 **Jingyuan** Gansu, C China
167 O11 **Jinhua** Zhejiang, SE China
167 N3 **Jining** Nei Mongol Zizhiqu, N China
167 P5 **Jining** Shandong, E China
83 G18 **Jinja** S Uganda
167 R13 **Jin Jiang** ♒ S China
167 O11 **Jinjiang** var. Qingyang. Fujian, SE China
176 W14 **Jin, Kepulauan** island group E Indonesia
167 N15 **Jinmen Dao** var. Chin-men Tao
166 L12 **Jinotega** Jinotega, NW Nicaragua
44 J7 **Jinotega** ♦ department NW Nicaragua
44 K7 **Jinotepe** Carazo, SW Nicaragua
167 O11 **Jinping** prev. Sanjiang. Guizhou, S China
166 L13 **Jinping** Yunnan, SW China
167 O11 **Jinsha** Guizhou, S China
164 J12 **Jinsha Jiang** ♒ SW China
165 N3 **Jinta** Gansu, N China
167 Q12 **Jintotolo Channel** channel C Philippines
167 N11 **Jinxi** Liaoning, NE China
167 T13 **Jinxi** Jiangxi, S China
167 O11 **Jinxian** Jiangxi, S China
167 N3 **Jinxiang** Shandong, E China
167 R13 **Jinzhai** prev. Meishan. Anhui, E China
167 O6 **Jinzhou** var. Chin-chou, Chinchow; prev. Chinhsien. Liaoning, NE China

Jiayi/Ji– continuation:
169 X6 **Jiayi** see Chiai
169 T12 **Jishou** Hunan, S China
147 T9 **Jisr ash Shadadi** see Ash Shadādī
118 I14 **Jitaru** Olt, S Romania
118 H14 **Jitin** var. Schil, Schyl, Hung. Zsil, Zsily. ♒ S Romania
118 H4 **Jitschin** see Jičín
169 Y7 **Jixi** Heilongjiang, NE China
169 Y7 **Jixi** Anhui, E China
169 T13 **Jixian** Heilongjiang, NE China
164 M5 **Jīzān** see Al Jīzah
146 J5 **Jīzān** var. Qīzān. Jīzān, SW Saudi Arabia
147 N13 **Jīzān** var. Minṭaqat Jīzān. ♦ province SW Saudi Arabia
146 K6 **Jizl, Wādī** dry watercourse W Saudi Arabia
147 X11 **Jīz'** var. Jiz. NE Yemen
147 X11 **Jīz', Wādī** dry watercourse E Yemen
153 N10 **Jizzakh** Rus. Dzhizak. Jizzakh, E Uzbekistan
153 N10 **Jizzakh Wiloyati** Rus. Dzhizakskaya Oblast'. ♦ province C Uzbekistan
62 J11 **Joaçaba** Santa Catarina, S Brazil
78 F11 **Joal-Fadiout** var. Joal. W Senegal
78 F11 **Joal-Fadiout** W Senegal
62 O6 **João Barrosa** Boa Vista, E Cape Verde
85 J21 **João de Almeida** see Chibia
61 Q16 **João Pessoa** prev. Paraíba. state capital Paraíba, E Brazil
27 X7 **Joaquim V.González** Salta, N Argentina
64 L9 **Joaquín V.González** Salta, N Argentina
Joazeiro see Juazeiro
111 O7 **Jochberger Ache** ♒ W Austria
94 K12 **Jock** Norrbotten, N Sweden
44 L6 **Jocón** Yoro, N Honduras
107 O13 **Jódar** Andalucía, S Spain
158 F12 **Jodhpur** Rājasthān, NW India
101 I19 **Jodoigne** Walloon Brabant, C Belgium
97 D22 **Jægerspris** Frederiksborg, E Denmark
95 L17 **Joensuu** Pohjois-Karjala, SE Finland
165 R8 **Jōetsu** var. Zyôetu. Niigata, Honshū, C Japan
85 J21 **Jofane** Inhambane, S Mozambique
161 E14 **Jog** waterfall W India
159 P14 **Jögeva** Ger. Laisholm. Jõgevamaa, E Estonia
120 I5 **Jögevamaa** off. Jõgeva Maakond. ♦ province E Estonia
149 U12 **Joghatāy** Khorāsān, NE Iran
158 I7 **Jogindarnagar** Himāchal Pradesh, N India
Jogjakarta see Yogyakarta
163 O13 **Johana** Toyama, Honshū, SW Japan
85 J21 **Johannesburg** var. Egoli, Erautini, Gauteng, abbrev. Jo'burg. Gauteng, NE South Africa
37 S11 **Johannesburg** California, W USA
85 J21 **Johannesburg** ✈ Gauteng, NE South Africa
Johannisburg see Pisz
44 J7 **Johi Village** S Guyana
35 N13 **John Day** Oregon, NW USA
34 H11 **John Day River** ♒ Oregon, NW USA
20 J4 **John F Kennedy** ✈ (New York) Long Island, New York, NE USA
23 N7 **John H.Kerr Reservoir** var. Buggs Island Lake, Kerr Lake. ☐ North Carolina/Virginia, SE USA
35 Q7 **John Martin Reservoir** ☐ Colorado, C USA
xlii M6 **John o'Groats** Highland, N Scotland, UK
29 P3 **John Redmond Reservoir** ☐ Kansas, C USA
8 J6 **John River** ♒ Alaska, USA
xliii O15 **Johnshaven** Aberdeenshire, NE Scotland, UK
29 N2 **Johnson** Kansas, C USA
20 L7 **Johnson** Vermont, NE USA
20 D13 **Johnsonburg** Pennsylvania, NE USA
20 H11 **Johnson City** New York, NE USA
23 P8 **Johnson City** Tennessee, S USA
27 R11 **Johnson City** Texas, SW USA
37 S12 **Johnsondale** California, W USA
37 S12 **Johnsons Crossing** Yukon Territory, W Canada
23 T13 **Johnsonville** South Carolina, SE USA
33 O13 **Johnston** South Carolina, SE USA
xxxv C13 **Johnston** Pembrokeshire, SW Wales, UK
199 K6 **Johnston Atoll** ☐ US unincorporated territory C Pacific Ocean
183 O3 **Johnston Atoll** atoll C Pacific Ocean

xliii I20 **Johnstone** Renfrewshire, W Scotland, UK
188 K10 **Johnston, Lake** salt lake Western Australia
xiv J11 **Johnstown** Kilkenny, SE Ireland
33 S3 **Johnstown** Ohio, N USA
20 D15 **Johnstown** Pennsylvania, NE USA
174 H8 **Johor** var. Johore. ♦ state Peninsular Malaysia
174 H8 **Johor Baharu** see Johor Bahru
174 I6 **Johor Bahru** var. Johor Baharu, Johore Bahru. Johor, Peninsular Malaysia
Johore see Johor
Johore Bahru see Johor Bahru
120 K3 **Jõhvi** Ger. Jewe. Ida-Virumaa, NE Estonia
105 P7 **Joigny** Yonne, C France
63 **Joinvile** see Joinville
62 K13 **Joinville** var. Joinville. Santa Catarina, S Brazil
105 R6 **Joinville** Haute-Marne, N France
204 H3 **Joinville Island** island Antarctica
43 O17 **Jojutla** var. Jojutla de Juárez. Morelos, S Mexico
Jojutla de Juárez see Jojutla
94 I12 **Jokkmokk** Norrbotten, N Sweden
94 K2 **Jökulsá á Dal** ♒ E Iceland
94 K2 **Jökulsá á Fjöllum** ♒ NE Iceland
Jokyakarta see Yogyakarta
32 M10 **Joliet** Illinois, N USA
13 O11 **Joliette** Québec, SE Canada
96 Pp17 **Jolo** Jolo, SW Philippines
Jølstervatnet ☐ S Norway
174 Ll15 **Jombang** prev. Djombang. Jawa, S Indonesia
58 A6 **Jome, Punta de** headland W Ecuador
106 D6 **Jomda** Xizang Zizhiqu, W China
120 G3 **Jonava** Pol. Janów. Jonava, C Lithuania
152 L11 **Jondor** Rus. Zhondor. Bukhoro Wiloyati, C Uzbekistan
165 Y9 **Jonê** Gansu, C China
29 X9 **Jonesboro** Arkansas, C USA
32 L15 **Jonesboro** Georgia, SE USA
32 L12 **Jonesboro** Illinois, N USA
24 H5 **Jonesboro** Louisiana, S USA
21 T6 **Jonesport** Maine, NE USA
1 J4 **Jones Sound** channel Northwest Territories, N Canada
24 J5 **Jonesville** Louisiana, S USA
33 Q10 **Jonesville** Michigan, N USA
23 Q11 **Jonesville** South Carolina, SE USA
83 F14 **Jonglei** Jonglei, SE Sudan
83 F14 **Jonglei** var. Gongoleh State. ♦ state SE Sudan
83 F14 **Jonglei Canal** canal S Sudan
120 F11 **Joniškis** Ger. Janischken. Joniškis, N Lithuania
97 L19 **Jönköping** Jönköping, S Sweden
97 K20 **Jönköping** ♦ county S Sweden
43 V15 **Jonuta** Tabasco, SE Mexico
104 K12 **Jonzac** Charente-Maritime, W France
29 R9 **Joplin** Missouri, C USA
35 M13 **Joppa** Texas, SW USA
25 X5 **Joshua** Texas, SW USA
37 V15 **Joshua Tree** California, W USA
35 N9 **Jos Plateau** plateau C Nigeria
96 G11 **Josselin** Morbihan, NW France
Jos Sudarso see Yos Sudarso, Pulau
96 G11 **Jostedalsbreen** glacier S Norway
96 F12 **Jotunheimen** ▲ S Norway
144 G9 **Joünié** var. Junīyah. W Lebanon
27 V9 **Jourdanton** Texas, SW USA
100 I7 **Joure** Fris. De Jouwer. Friesland, N Netherlands
23 **Joutsa** Keski-Suomi, C Finland
95 N18 **Joutseno** Kymi, SE Finland

Joutsijärvi – Kamchatskaya Oblast'

94 M12 **Joutsijärvi** Lappi, NE Finland
110 A9 **Joux, Lac de** ◎ W Switzerland
46 D5 **Jovellanos** Matanzas, W Cuba
159 V13 **Jowai** Meghālaya, NE India
Jōwat see Jabwot
Jowhar see Jawhar
149 O12 **Jowkān** Fārs, S Iran
149 Q10 **Jowzam** Kermān, C Iran
155 N2 **Jowzjān** ◈ province N Afghanistan
Józseffalva see Žabalj
J.Storm Thurmond Reservoir see Clarks Hill Lake
47 T6 **Juana Díaz** C Puerto Rico
42 L9 **Juan Aldama** Zacatecas, C Mexico
1 E9 **Juan de Fuca Plate** tectonic feature
34 F7 **Juan de Fuca, Strait of** strait Canada/USA
Juan Fernandez Islands see Juan Fernández, Islas
200 Oo12 **Juan Fernández, Islas** Eng. Juan Fernandez Islands. island group W Chile
57 O4 **Juangriego** Nueva Esparta, NE Venezuela
58 D11 **Juanjuí** var. Juanjuy. San Martín, N Peru
Juanjuy see Juanjuí
95 N16 **Juankoski** Kuopio, C Finland
Juan Lacaze see Juan L.Lacaze
63 E20 **Juan L.Lacaze** var. Juan Lacaze, Puerto Sauce; prev. Sauce. Colonia, SW Uruguay
64 L5 **Juan Solá** Salta, N Argentina
65 F21 **Juan Stuven, Isla** island S Chile
61 H16 **Juará** Mato Grosso, W Brazil
43 N7 **Juárez** var. Villa Juárez. Coahuila de Zaragoza, NE Mexico
42 C2 **Juárez, Sierra de** ▲ NW Mexico
61 O15 **Juazeiro** prev. Joazeiro. Bahia, E Brazil
61 P14 **Juazeiro do Norte** Ceará, E Brazil
83 F15 **Juba** var. Jūbā. Bahr el Gabel, S Sudan
83 L17 **Juba** Amh. Genalē Wenz, It. Guiba, Som. Ganaane, Webi Jubba. ≈ Ethiopia/Somalia
204 H2 **Jubany** Argentinian research station Antarctica
Jubayl see Jbail
83 L18 **Jubbada Dhexe** off. Gobolka Jubbada Dhexe. ◈ region SW Somalia
83 K18 **Jubbada Hoose** ◈ region SW Somalia
Jubba, Webi see Juba
Jubbulpore see Jabalpur
Jubeil see Jbail
76 B9 **Juby, Cap** headland SW Morocco
107 R10 **Júcar** var. Jucar. ≈ C Spain
42 L12 **Juchipila** Zacatecas, C Mexico
43 S16 **Juchitán** var. Juchitán de Zaragosa. Oaxaca, SE Mexico
Juchitán de Zaragosa see Juchitán
144 G11 **Judaea** cultural region Israel/West Bank
144 F11 **Judaean Hills** Heb. Haré Yehuda. hill range E Israel
144 H8 **Judaydah** Fr. Jdaïdé. Dimashq, W Syria
145 P11 **Judayyidat Hāmir** S Iraq
111 U8 **Judenburg** Steiermark, C Austria
35 T8 **Judith River** ≈ Montana, NW USA
29 V11 **Judsonia** Arkansas, C USA
147 P14 **Jufrah, Wādī al** dry watercourse NW Yemen
Jugoslavija/Jugoslavija, Savezna Republika see Yugoslavia
44 K10 **Juigalpa** Chontales, S Nicaragua
167 T13 **Juishui** C Taiwan
102 E9 **Juist** island NW Germany
61 M21 **Juiz de Fora** Minas Gerais, SE Brazil
64 J5 **Jujuy** off. Provincia de Jujuy. ◈ province N Argentina
Jujuy see San Salvador de Jujuy
94 J11 **Jukkasjärvi** Norrbotten, N Sweden
Jula see Gyula, Hungary
Jūlā see Jālū, Libya
39 W2 **Julesburg** Colorado, C USA
Julia Beterrae see Béziers
59 I17 **Juliaca** Puno, SE Peru
189 U6 **Julia Creek** Queensland, C Australia
37 V17 **Julian** California, W USA
100 H7 **Julianadorp** Noord-Holland, NW Netherlands
111 S11 **Julian Alps** Ger. Julische Alpen, It. Alpi Giulie, Slvn. Julijske Alpe. ▲ Italy/Slovenia
57 V11 **Juliana Top** ▲ C Surinam
Julianehåb see Qaqortoq
Julijske Alpe see Julian Alps
42 J6 **Julimes** Chihuahua, N Mexico
Julio Briga see Bragança, Portugal
Juliobriga see Logroño, Spain
63 G15 **Júlio de Castilhos** Rio Grande do Sul, S Brazil
Juliomagus see Angers
Julische Alpen see Julian Alps
Jullundur see Jalandhar
153 N11 **Juma** Rus. Dzhuma. Samarqand Wiloyati, C Uzbekistan
167 O3 **Juma He** ≈ E China
83 L18 **Jumboo** Jubbada Hoose, S Somalia
37 Y11 **Jumbo Peak** ▲ Nevada, W USA
107 R12 **Jumilla** Murcia, SE Spain
159 N10 **Jumla** Mid Western, NW Nepal
Jummoo see Jammu
Jumna see Yamuna
Jumporn see Chumphon
32 K5 **Jump River** ≈ Wisconsin, N USA
160 B11 **Jūnāgadh** var. Junagarh. Gujarāt, W India
Junagarh see Jūnāgadh
167 Q6 **Junan** prev. Shizilu. Shandong, E China
64 G11 **Juncal, Cerro** ▲ C Chile
27 Q10 **Junction** Texas, SW USA
38 K6 **Junction** Utah, W USA
29 O4 **Junction City** Kansas, C USA
34 F13 **Junction City** Oregon, NW USA
62 M10 **Jundiaí** São Paulo, S Brazil
194 E13 **June** ≈ W PNG
41 X12 **Juneau** state capital Alaska, USA
32 M8 **Juneau** Wisconsin, N USA
107 U6 **Juneda** Cataluña, NE Spain
191 Q9 **Junee** New South Wales, SE Australia
37 R8 **June Lake** California, W USA
Jungbunzlau see Mladá Boleslav
164 L4 **Junggar Pendi** Eng. Dzungarian Basin. basin NW China
101 N24 **Junglinster** Grevenmacher, C Luxembourg
20 F14 **Juniata River** ≈ Pennsylvania, NE USA
63 B20 **Junín** Buenos Aires, E Argentina
59 E14 **Junín** Junín, C Peru
59 F14 **Junín** off. Departamento de Junín. ◈ department C Peru
65 H15 **Junín de los Andes** Neuquén, W Argentina
59 D14 **Junín, Lago de** ◎ C Peru
Junīyah see Joûnié
Junkseylon see Phuket
166 I11 **Junlian** Sichuan, C China
27 Q11 **Juno** Texas, SW USA
94 J11 **Junosuando** Norrbotten, N Sweden
95 H16 **Junsele** Västernorrland, C Sweden
Junten see Sunch'ŏn
34 L14 **Juntura** Oregon, NW USA
95 N14 **Juntusranta** Oulu, E Finland
120 H11 **Juodupė** Rokiškis, NE Lithuania
121 H14 **Juozapinės Kalnas** ▲ SE Lithuania
101 K19 **Juprelle** Liège, E Belgium
83 D13 **Jur** ≈ C Sudan
xiii E19 **Jura** island SW Scotland, UK
105 S9 **Jura** ◈ department E France
110 C7 **Jura** ◈ canton NW Switzerland
110 B8 **Jura** var. Jura Mountains. ▲ France/Switzerland
Juraciszki see Yuratsishki
56 C8 **Juradó** Chocó, NW Colombia
Jura Mountains see Jura
xliii E20 **Jura, Paps of** ▲ W Scotland, UK
xliii E20 **Jura, Sound of** strait W Scotland, UK
145 V15 **Juraybīyāt, Bi'r** well S Iraq
120 E13 **Jurbarkas** Ger. Georgenburg, Jurburg. Jurbarkas, W Lithuania
101 F20 **Jurbise** Hainaut, SW Belgium
Jurburg see Jurbarkas
xl G10 **Jurby West** NW Isle of Man
120 F9 **Jūrmala** Rīga, C Latvia
176 Ww13 **Jursian, Pulau** island E Indonesia
60 D13 **Juruá** Amazonas, NW Brazil
50 F7 **Juruá, Rio** var. Río Yuruá. ≈ Brazil/Peru
61 G16 **Juruena** Mato Grosso, W Brazil
61 G16 **Juruena** ≈ W Brazil
171 Mm8 **Jūsan-ko** ◎ Honshū, C Japan
27 O6 **Justiceburg** Texas, SW USA
Justinianopolis see Kirşehir
64 K11 **Justo Daract** San Luis, C Argentina
60 C14 **Jutaí** Amazonas, W Brazil
60 C13 **Jutaí, Rio** ≈ NW Brazil
102 N13 **Jüterbog** Brandenburg, E Germany
44 E6 **Jutiapa** Jutiapa, S Guatemala
44 A3 **Jutiapa** off. Departamento de Jutiapa. ◈ department SE Guatemala
44 J6 **Juticalpa** Olancho, C Honduras
84 I13 **Jutila** North Western, NW Zambia
Jutland see Jylland
86 F8 **Jutland Bank** undersea feature SE North Sea
95 N16 **Juuka** Pohjois-Karjala, E Finland
95 N17 **Juva** Mikkeli, SE Finland
Juvavum see Salzburg
46 A6 **Juventud, Isla de la** var. Isla de Pinos, Eng. Isle of Youth; prev. The Isle of the Pines. island W Cuba
Ju Xian see Juxian
167 Q5 **Juxian** var. Ju Xian. Shandong, E China
167 P6 **Juye** Shandong, E China
115 O15 **Južna Morava** Ger. Südliche Morava. ≈ SE Yugoslavia
97 I23 **Jyderup** Vestsjælland, E Denmark
97 F22 **Jylland** Eng. Jutland. peninsula W Denmark
Jyrgalan see Dzhergalan
95 M17 **Jyväskylä** Keski-Suomi, C Finland

K

155 X3 **K2** Chin. Qogir Feng, Eng. Mount Godwin Austen. ▲ China/Pakistan
40 D9 **Kaaawa** Haw. Ka'a'awa. Oahu, Hawaii, USA, C Pacific Ocean
83 G16 **Kaabong** NE Uganda
Kaaden see Kadaň
57 V9 **Kaaimanston** Sipaliwini, N Surinam
152 G14 **Kaakhka** var. Kaka. Akhalskiy Velayat, S Turkmenistan
Kaala see Caála
197 H5 **Kaala-Gomen** Province Nord, W New Caledonia
94 L9 **Kaamanen** Lapp. Gámas. Lappi, N Finland
Kaapstad see Cape Town
Kaarasjoki see Karasjok
Kaaresuanto see Karesuando
94 J10 **Kaaresuvanto** Lapp. Gárassavon. Lappi, N Finland
95 K19 **Kaarina** Turku-Pori, SW Finland
101 I14 **Kaatsheuvel** Noord-Brabant, S Netherlands
95 N16 **Kaavi** Kuopio, C Finland
Ka'a'wa see Kaaawa
176 Y15 **Kaba** Irian Jaya, E Indonesia
Kaba see Habahe
175 Q13 **Kabaena, Pulau** island C Indonesia
175 Q13 **Kabaena, Selat** strait Sulawesi, C Indonesia
152 J11 **Kabakly** Turkm. Gabakly. Lebapskiy Velayat, NE Turkmenistan
78 J14 **Kabala** N Sierra Leone
83 E19 **Kabale** SW Uganda
57 U10 **Kabalebo Rivier** ≈ W Surinam
81 N22 **Kabalo** Shaba, SE Zaire
81 O21 **Kabambare** Maniema, E Zaire
197 K15 **Kabara** prev. Kambara. island Lau Group, E Fiji
Kabardino-Balkaria see Kabardino-Balkarskaya Respublika
130 M15 **Kabardino-Balkarskaya Respublika** Eng. Kabardino-Balkaria. ◈ autonomous republic SW Russian Federation
81 O19 **Kabare** Sud Kivu, E Zaire
176 Uu8 **Kabarei** Irian Jaya, E Indonesia
179 Q16 **Kabasalan** Mindanao, S Philippines
79 U15 **Kabba** Kogi, S Nigeria
94 I13 **Kåbdalis** Norrbotten, N Sweden
144 M6 **Kabd aş Şārim** hill range E Syria
12 B7 **Kabenung Lake** ◎ Ontario, S Canada
31 W3 **Kabetogama Lake** ◎ Minnesota, N USA
Kabia, Pulau see Kabin, Pulau
81 M22 **Kabinda** Kasai Oriental, SE Zaire
Kabinda see Cabinda
175 P13 **Kabin, Pulau** var. Pulau Kabia. island W Indonesia
175 R16 **Kabir** Pulau Pantar, S Indonesia
155 T10 **Kabīrwāla** Punjab, E Pakistan
176 U8 **Kable Bet** Irian Jaya, E Indonesia
80 I13 **Kabo** Ouham, NW Central African Republic
Kābol see Kābul
85 H14 **Kabompo** North Western, W Zambia
85 H14 **Kabompo** ≈ W Zambia
81 M22 **Kabongo** Shaba, SE Zaire
123 Kk12 **Kaboudia, Rass** headland E Tunisia
128 J14 **Kabozha** Novgorodskaya Oblast', W Russian Federation
149 U4 **Kabūd Gonbad** Khorāsān, NE Iran
148 L5 **Kabūd Rāhang** Hamadān, W Iran
84 L12 **Kabuko** Northern, NE Zambia
155 Q5 **Kābul** var. Kabul, Per. Kābol. ● (Afghanistan) Kābul, E Afghanistan
155 Q5 **Kābul** Eng. Kabul, Per. Kābol. ◈ province E Afghanistan
155 Q5 **Kābul** ✕ Kābul, E Afghanistan
155 R5 **Kabul** var. Daryā-ye Kābul. ≈ Afghanistan/Pakistan see also Kābul, Daryā-ye
155 S5 **Kābul, Daryā-ye** var. Kabul. ≈ Afghanistan/Pakistan see also Kabul
81 O25 **Kabunda** Shaba, SE Zaire
175 Ss4 **Kaburuang, Pulau** island Kepulauan Talaud, N Indonesia
82 G8 **Kabushiya** River Nile, NE Sudan
85 J14 **Kabwe** Central, C Zambia
194 K12 **Kabwum** Morobe, C PNG
115 N17 **Kačanik** Serbia, S Yugoslavia
176 U8 **Kacepi** Pulau Gebe, E Indonesia
120 F13 **Kačerginė** Kaunas, C Lithuania
119 S13 **Kacha** Respublika Krym, S Ukraine
160 A10 **Kachchh, Gulf of** var. Gulf of Cutch, Gulf of Kutch. gulf W India
160 I11 **Kachchhīdhāna** Madhya Pradesh, C India
155 Q11 **Kachchh, Rann of** var. Rann of Kachh, Rann of Kutch. salt marsh India/Pakistan
41 Q13 **Kachemak Bay** bay Alaska, USA
Kachh, Rann of see Kachchh, Rann of
79 V14 **Kachia** Kaduna, C Nigeria
178 Gg2 **Kachin State** ◈ state N Burma
151 T7 **Kachiry** Pavlodar, NE Kazakhstan
126 Jj15 **Kachug** Irkutskaya Oblast', S Russian Federation
143 Q11 **Kaçkar Dağları** ▲ NE Turkey
161 C21 **Kadamatt Island** island Lakshadweep, India, N Indian Ocean
113 B15 **Kadaň** Ger. Kaaden. Severní Čechy, NW Czech Republic
178 Gg12 **Kadan Kyun** prev. King Island. island Mergui Archipelago, S Burma
197 I16 **Kadavu** prev. Kandavu. island S Fiji
197 I15 **Kadavu Passage** channel S Fiji
81 G16 **Kadéï** ≈ Cameroon/Central African Republic
Kadhimain see Al Kāẓimīyah
Kadijica see Kadiytsa
116 M13 **Kadıköy Barajı** ⊡ NW Turkey
190 I8 **Kadina** South Australia
142 H15 **Kadınhanı** Konya, C Turkey
78 M14 **Kadiolo** Sikasso, S Mali
142 L16 **Kadirli** Adana, S Turkey
116 G11 **Kadiytsa** Mac. Kadijica. ▲ Bulgaria/FYR Macedonia
30 L10 **Kadoka** South Dakota, N USA
131 N5 **Kadom** Ryazanskaya Oblast', W Russian Federation
85 K16 **Kadoma** prev. Gatooma. Mashonaland West, C Zimbabwe
82 E12 **Kadugli** Southern Kordofan, S Sudan
79 V14 **Kaduna** Kaduna, C Nigeria
79 V14 **Kaduna** ◈ state C Nigeria
79 V15 **Kaduna** ≈ N Nigeria
128 K14 **Kaduy** Vologodskaya Oblast', NW Russian Federation
160 E13 **Kadwa** ≈ W India
127 Nn9 **Kadykchan** Magadanskaya Oblast', E Russian Federation
Kadzharan see K'ajaran
129 T7 **Kadzherom** Respublika Komi, NW Russian Federation
153 X8 **Kadzhi-Say** Kir. Kajisay. Issyk-Kul'skaya Oblast', NE Kyrgyzstan
78 I10 **Kaédi** Gorgol, S Mauritania
80 G12 **Kaélé** Extrême-Nord, N Cameroon
40 C9 **Kaena Point** headland Oahu, Hawaii, USA, C Pacific Ocean
192 J2 **Kaeo** Northland, North Island, NZ
169 X14 **Kaesŏng** var. Kaesŏng-si. S North Korea
Kaesŏng-si see Kaesŏng
Kaewieng see Kavieng
81 L24 **Kafakumba** Shaba, S Zaire
Kafan see Kapan
79 V14 **Kafanchan** Kaduna, C Nigeria
Kaffa see Feodosiya
78 G11 **Kaffrine** C Senegal
Kafiau see Kofiau, Pulau
117 I19 **Kafiréas, Ákra** headland Évvoia, C Greece
117 I19 **Kafiréos, Stenó** strait Évvoia/Kykládes, Greece, Aegean Sea
Kafirnigan see Kofarnihon
Kafo see Kafu
Kafr ash Shaykh/Kafrel Sheik see Kafr el Sheikh
77 W7 **Kafr el Sheikh** var. Kafr ash Shaykh, Kafrel Sheik. N Egypt
83 F17 **Kafu** var. Kafo. ≈ W Uganda
85 J15 **Kafue** Lusaka, SE Zambia
85 I14 **Kafue** ≈ C Zambia
69 T13 **Kafue Flats** plain C Zambia
171 I13 **Kaga** Ishikawa, Honshū, SW Japan
81 J14 **Kaga Bandoro** prev. Fort-Crampel. Nana-Grébizi, C Central African Republic
83 E18 **Kagadi** W Uganda
40 H17 **Kagalaska Island** island Aleutian Islands, Alaska, USA
Kagan see Kogon
Kaganovichabad see Kolkhozobod
Kagarlyk see Kaharlyk
170 F15 **Kagawa** off. Kagawa-ken. ◈ prefecture Shikoku, SW Japan
160 J13 **Kagaznagar** Andhra Pradesh, C India
95 J14 **Kåge** Västerbotten, N Sweden
83 E19 **Kagera** var. Ziwa Magharibi, Eng. West Lake. ◈ region NW Tanzania
83 E19 **Kagera** var. Akagera. ≈ Rwanda/Tanzania see also Akagera
78 L5 **Kâgheţ** var. Karet. physical region N Mauritania
Kagi see Chiai
143 S12 **Kağızman** Kars, NE Turkey
196 I6 **Kagman Point** headland Saipan, S Northern Mariana Islands
170 Bb15 **Kagoshima** var. Kagosima. Kagoshima, Kyūshū, SW Japan
172 Qq14 **Kagoshima** off. Kagoshima-ken, var. Kagosima. ◈ prefecture Kyūshū, SW Japan
170 Bb16 **Kagoshima-wan** bay SW Japan
Kagosima see Kagoshima
194 H12 **Kagua** Southern Highlands, W PNG
Kagul see Cahul
Kagul, Ozero see Kahul, Ozero
40 B8 **Kahala Point** headland Kauai, Hawaii, USA, C Pacific Ocean
40 G12 **Kahaluu** Haw. Kahalu'u. Hawaii, USA, C Pacific Ocean
83 F21 **Kahama** Shinyanga, NW Tanzania
119 P5 **Kaharlyk** Rus. Kagarlyk. Kyyivs'ka Oblast', N Ukraine
174 Mm10 **Kahayan, Sungai** ≈ Borneo, C Indonesia
81 I22 **Kahemba** Bandundu, SW Zaire
193 A23 **Kaherekoau Mountains** ▲ South Island, NZ
149 W14 **Kahīrī** var. Kūhīrī. Sīstān va Balūchestān, SE Iran
103 L16 **Kahla** Thüringen, C Germany
103 G15 **Kahler Asten** ▲ W Germany
155 Q4 **Kahmard, Daryā-ye** prev. Darya-i-Surkhab. ≈ NE Afghanistan
149 T13 **Kahnūj** Kermān, SE Iran
29 V1 **Kahoka** Missouri, C USA
40 E10 **Kahoolawe** island Hawaii, USA, C Pacific Ocean
142 M16 **Kahramanmaraş** var. Kahraman Maraş, Maraş, Marash. Kahramanmaraş, S Turkey
142 L15 **Kahramanmaraş** var. Kahraman Maraş, Maraş, Marash. ◈ province C Turkey
155 T11 **Kahror** var. Kahror Pakka. Punjab, E Pakistan
Kahror Pakka see Kahror
143 N15 **Kâhta** Adıyaman, S Turkey
40 D8 **Kahuku** Oahu, Hawaii, USA, C Pacific Ocean
40 D8 **Kahuku Point** headland Oahu, Hawaii, USA, C Pacific Ocean
118 M12 **Kahul, Ozero** var. Lacul Cahul, Rus. Ozero Kagul. ◎ Moldavia/Ukraine
149 V11 **Kahūrak** Sīstān va Balūchestān, SE Iran
192 G13 **Kahurangi Point** headland South Island, NZ
155 V6 **Kahūta** Punjab, E Pakistan
79 S14 **Kaiama** Kwara, W Nigeria
194 J12 **Kaiapit** Morobe, C PNG
193 I18 **Kaiapoi** Canterbury, South Island, NZ
38 K9 **Kaibab Plateau** plain Arizona, SW USA
171 Gg14 **Kaibara** Hyōgo, Honshū, SW Japan
176 Vv13 **Kai Besar, Pulau** island Kepulauan Kai, E Indonesia
38 L9 **Kaibito Plateau** plain Arizona, SW USA
164 K6 **Kaidu He** var. Karaxahar. ≈ NW China
57 S10 **Kaieteur Falls** waterfall C Guyana
167 O6 **Kaifeng** Henan, C China
192 J3 **Kaihu** Northland, North Island, NZ
176 V13 **Kai Kecil, Pulau** island Kepulauan Kai, E Indonesia
176 V14 **Kai, Kepulauan** prev. Kei Islands. island group Maluku, SE Indonesia
192 J3 **Kaikohe** Northland, North Island, NZ
193 J16 **Kaikoura** Canterbury, South Island, NZ
193 J16 **Kaikoura Peninsula** peninsula South Island, NZ
Kailas Range see Gangdisê Shan
166 K12 **Kaili** Guizhou, S China
40 F10 **Kailua** Maui, Hawaii, USA, C Pacific Ocean
40 G11 **Kailua** var. Kailua-Kona, Kona. Hawaii, USA, C Pacific Ocean
Kailua-Kona see Kailua
194 E13 **Kaim** ≈ W PNG
176 Y13 **Kaima** Irian Jaya, E Indonesia
192 M7 **Kaimai Range** ▲ North Island, NZ
116 E13 **Kaïmaktsalán** ▲ Greece/FYR Macedonia
193 C20 **Kaimanawa Mountains** ▲ North Island, NZ
120 F4 **Käina** Ger. Keins; prev. Keina. Hiiumaa, W Estonia
111 V7 **Kainach** ≈ SE Austria
170 G16 **Kainan** Tokushima, Shikoku, SW Japan
170 Ff16 **Kainan** Wakayama, Honshū, SW Japan
194 J12 **Kainantu** Eastern Highlands, C PNG
153 U7 **Kaindy** Kir. Kayyngdy. Chuyskaya Oblast', N Kyrgyzstan
79 T14 **Kainji Dam** dam W Nigeria
Kainji Lake see Kainji Reservoir
79 T14 **Kainji Reservoir** var. Kainji Lake. ⊡ W Nigeria
194 J14 **Kaintiba** var. Kamina. Gulf, S PNG
94 K12 **Kainulaisjärvi** Norrbotten, N Sweden
192 K5 **Kaipara Harbour** harbour North Island, NZ
158 I10 **Kairāna** Uttar Pradesh, N India
194 F11 **Kairiru Island** island NW PNG
76 M6 **Kairouan** var. Al Qayrawān. E Tunisia
Kaisaria see Kayseri
103 F20 **Kaiserslautern** Rheinland-Pfalz, SW Germany
120 G13 **Kaišiadorys** Kaišiadorys, S Lithuania
192 I2 **Kaitaia** Northland, North Island, NZ
167 O15 **Kai Tak** ✕ (Hong Kong) S China
193 E24 **Kaitangata** Otago, South Island, NZ
158 I9 **Kaithal** Haryāna, NW India
174 J11 **Kait, Tanjung** headland Sumatera, W Indonesia
40 E9 **Kaiwi Channel** channel Hawaii, USA, C Pacific Ocean
166 K9 **Kaixian** var. Kai Xian. Sichuan, C China
169 V11 **Kaiyuan** var. K'ai-yüan. Liaoning, NE China
166 H14 **Kaiyuan** Yunnan, SW China
41 O9 **Kaiyuh Mountains** ▲ Alaska, USA
95 M15 **Kajaani** Swe. Kajana. Oulu, C Finland
155 N7 **Kajakī, Band-e** ◎ C Afghanistan
Kajan see Kayan, Sungai
Kajana see Kajaani
143 V13 **K'ajaran** Rus. Kadzharan. SE Armenia
Kajisay see Kadzhi-Say
115 O20 **Kajmakčalan** ▲ S FYR Macedonia
Kajnar see Kaynar
155 N6 **Kajrān** Urūzgān, C Afghanistan
155 N5 **Kaj Rūd** ≈ C Afghanistan
Kaka see Kaakhka
10 C12 **Kakabeka Falls** Ontario, S Canada
85 F23 **Kakamas** Northern Cape, W South Africa
83 H18 **Kakamega** Western, W Kenya
114 H13 **Kakanj** C Bosnia and Herzegovina
193 F22 **Kakanui Mountains** ▲ South Island, NZ
192 K11 **Kakaramea** Taranaki, North Island, NZ
78 J16 **Kakata** C Liberia
192 M11 **Kakatahi** Manawatu-Wanganui, North Island, NZ
115 M23 **Kakavi** Gjirokastër, S Albania
153 O14 **Kakaydi** Surkhondaryo Wiloyati, S Uzbekistan
170 Ee13 **Kake** Hiroshima, Honshū, SW Japan
41 X13 **Kake** Kupreanof Island, Alaska, USA
175 R12 **Kakea** Pulau Wowoni, C Indonesia
171 Ii17 **Kakegawa** Shizuoka, Honshū, S Japan
172 Qq13 **Kakeromajima** Kagoshima, SW Japan
149 T6 **Kākhk** var. Kākhk. Khorāsān, E Iran
120 L11 **Kakhanavichy** Rus. Kokhanovichi. Vitsyebskaya Voblasts', N Belorussia
41 P13 **Kakhonak** Alaska, USA
119 S10 **Kakhovka** Khersons'ka Oblast', S Ukraine
119 U9 **Kakhovs'ka Vodoskhovyshche** Rus. Kakhovskoye Vodokhranilishche. ⊡ SE Ukraine
Kakhovskoye Vodokhranilishche see Kakhovs'ka Vodoskhovyshche
119 T11 **Kakhovs'kyy Kanal** canal S Ukraine
Kakia see Khakhea
161 L16 **Kākināda** prev. Cocanada. Andhra Pradesh, E India
Käkisalmi see Priozersk
170 G14 **Kakogawa** Hyōgo, Honshū, SW Japan
83 F18 **Kakoge** C Uganda
151 O7 **Kak, Ozero** ◎ N Kazakhstan
Ka-Krem see Malyy Yenisey
Kakshaal-Too, Khrebet see Kokshaal-Tau
41 S5 **Kaktovik** Alaska, USA
171 Ll13 **Kakuda** Miyagi, Honshū, C Japan
171 M11 **Kakunodate** Akita, Honshū, C Japan
Kalaallit Nunaat see Greenland
155 T7 **Kālābāgh** Punjab, E Pakistan
175 Rr16 **Kalabahi** Pulau Alor, S Indonesia
196 I5 **Kalabera** Saipan, S Northern Mariana Islands
85 G14 **Kalabo** Western, W Zambia
130 M9 **Kalach** Voronezhskaya Oblast', W Russian Federation
125 G13 **Kalachinsk** Omskaya Oblast', C Russian Federation
131 N10 **Kalach-na-Donu** Volgogradskaya Oblast', SW Russian Federation
177 F5 **Kaladan** ≈ W Burma
12 K14 **Kaladar** Ontario, SE Canada
40 G13 **Ka Lae** var. South Cape, South Point. headland Hawaii, USA, C Pacific Ocean
85 G19 **Kalahari Desert** desert Southern Africa
40 B8 **Kalaheo** Haw. Kalāheo. Kauai, Hawaii, USA, C Pacific Ocean
152 J16 **Kala-i-Mor** Turkm. Galaymor. Maryyskiy Velayat, S Turkmenistan
95 K15 **Kalajoki** Oulu, W Finland
Kalak see Eski Kaļak
Kal al Sraghna see El Kelâa Srarhna
34 G10 **Kalama** Washington, NW USA
Kalámai see Kalámata
117 G14 **Kalamariá** Kentrikí Makedonía, N Greece
117 E21 **Kalámata** prev. Kalámai. Pelopónnisos, S Greece
33 P10 **Kalamazoo** Michigan, N USA
33 P9 **Kalamazoo River** ≈ Michigan, N USA
Kalambaka see Kalampáka
119 S13 **Kalamits'ka Zatoka** Rus. Kalamitskiy Zaliv. gulf S Ukraine
Kalamitskiy Zaliv see Kalamits'ka Zatoka
117 H18 **Kálamos** Attikí, C Greece
117 C18 **Kálamos** island Iónioi Nísoi, Greece, C Mediterranean Sea
117 D15 **Kalampáka** var. Kalambaka. Thessalía, C Greece
Kalan see Călan, Romania
Kalan see Tunceli, Turkey
119 S11 **Kalanchak** Khersons'ka Oblast', S Ukraine
175 Pp15 **Kalao, Pulau** island Kepulauan Bonerate, W Indonesia
175 Q15 **Kalaotoa, Pulau** island W Indonesia
161 J24 **Kala Oya** ≈ NW Sri Lanka
Kalarash see Călăraşi
95 H17 **Kälarne** Jämtland, C Sweden
149 V15 **Kalar Rūd** ≈ SE Iran
178 Ii9 **Kalasin** var. Muang Kalasin. Kalasin, E Thailand
155 O8 **Kalāt** Per. Qalāt. Zābul, S Afghanistan
155 O11 **Kalāt** var. Kelat, Khelat. Balūchistān, SW Pakistan
117 J14 **Kalathriá, Ákra** headland Samothráki, NE Greece
200 R17 **Kalau** island Tongatapu Group, SE Tonga
40 E9 **Kalaupapa** Molokai, Hawaii, USA, C Pacific Ocean
131 N13 **Kalaus** ≈ SW Russian Federation
Kalávrita see Kalávryta
117 E19 **Kalávryta** var. Kalávrita. Dytikí Ellás, S Greece
147 Y10 **Kalbān** W Oman
188 H11 **Kalbarri** Western Australia
151 X10 **Kalbinskiy Khrebet** Kaz. Qalba Zhotasy. ▲ E Kazakhstan
150 G10 **Kaldygayty** ≈ W Kazakhstan
142 I12 **Kalecik** Ankara, N Turkey
175 R13 **Kaledupa, Pulau** island Kepulauan Tukangbesi, C Indonesia
81 O19 **Kalehe** Sud Kivu, E Zaire
81 P22 **Kalemie** prev. Albertville. Shaba, SE Zaire
177 Ff3 **Kalemyo** Sagaing, W Burma
84 H12 **Kalene Hill** North Western, NW Zambia
Kale Sultanie see Çanakkale
128 I7 **Kalevala** Respublika Kareliya, NW Russian Federation
177 Ff3 **Kalewa** Sagaing, C Burma
Kalgan see Zhangjiakou
41 Q12 **Kalgin Island** island Alaska, USA
188 L12 **Kalgoorlie** Western Australia
Kali see Sārda
117 E17 **Kaliakoúda** ▲ C Greece
116 O8 **Kaliakra, Nos** headland NE Bulgaria
117 F19 **Kaliánoi** Pelopónnisos, S Greece
179 Q13 **Kalibo** Panay Island, C Philippines
117 N24 **Kalí Límni** ▲ Kárpathos, SE Greece
81 N20 **Kalima** Maniema, E Zaire
174 M8 **Kalimantan** Eng. Indonesian Borneo. geopolitical region Borneo, C Indonesia
174 L8 **Kalimantan Barat** off. Propinsi Kalimantan Barat, Eng. West Borneo, West Kalimantan. ◈ province N Indonesia
174 Mm11 **Kalimantan Selatan** off. Propinsi Kalimantan Selatan, Eng. South Borneo, South Kalimantan. ◈ province N Indonesia
174 M9 **Kalimantan Tengah** off. Propinsi Kalimantan Tengah, Eng. Central Borneo, Central Kalimantan. ◈ province N Indonesia
175 N7 **Kalimantan Timur** off. Propinsi Kalimantan Timur, Eng. East Borneo, East Kalimantan. ◈ province N Indonesia
Kálimnos see Kálymnos
159 S12 **Kālimpang** West Bengal, NE India
Kalinin see Tver', Russian Federation
Kalinin see Boldumsaz, Turkmenistan
Kalininabad see Kalininobod
130 B3 **Kaliningrad** Kaliningradskaya Oblast', W Russian Federation
Kaliningrad see Kaliningradskaya Oblast'
130 A3 **Kaliningradskaya Oblast'** var. Kaliningrad. ◈ province and enclave W Russian Federation
Kalinino see Tashir
153 P14 **Kalininobod** Rus. Kalininabad. SW Tajikistan
131 O8 **Kalininsk** Saratovskaya Oblast', W Russian Federation
Kalininsk see Boldumsaz
Kalinisk see Cupcina
121 M19 **Kalinkavichy** Rus. Kalinkovichi. Homyel'skaya Voblasts', SE Belorussia
Kalinkovichi see Kalinkavichy
83 G18 **Kaliro** SE Uganda
Kalisch/Kalisch/Kalish/Kaliskie, Województwo see Kalisz
35 O7 **Kalispell** Montana, NW USA
112 I13 **Kalisz** Ger. Kalisch, Rus. Kalish; anc. Calisia. Kalisz, C Poland
112 H13 **Kalisz** off. Województwo Kaliskie, Ger. Kalisch. ◈ province C Poland
112 F9 **Kalisz Pomorski** Ger. Kallies. Koszalin, NW Poland
130 M10 **Kalitva** ≈ SW Russian Federation
83 F21 **Kaliua** Tabora, C Tanzania
94 K13 **Kalix** Norrbotten, N Sweden
94 K12 **Kalixälven** ≈ N Sweden
94 J11 **Kalixfors** Norrbotten, N Sweden
151 T8 **Kalkaman** Pavlodar, NE Kazakhstan
Kalkandelen see Tetovo
189 O4 **Kalkarindji** Northern Territory, N Australia
33 P6 **Kalkaska** Michigan, N USA
95 F16 **Kall** Jämtland, C Sweden
201 X2 **Kallalen** var. Calalen. island Ratak Chain, SE Marshall Islands
120 J5 **Kallaste** Ger. Krasnogor. Tartumaa, SE Estonia
95 N16 **Kallavesi** ◎ SE Finland
117 F17 **Kallídromo** ▲ C Greece
Kallies see Kalisz Pomorski
97 M22 **Kallinge** Blekinge, S Sweden
117 L16 **Kalloní** Lésvos, E Greece
95 F16 **Kallsjön** ◎ C Sweden
97 N21 **Kalmar** var. Calmar. Kalmar, S Sweden
97 M19 **Kalmar** var. Calmar. ◈ county S Sweden
97 N20 **Kalmarsund** strait S Sweden
154 L16 **Kalmat, Khor** Eng. Kalmat Lagoon. lagoon SW Pakistan
Kalmat Lagoon see Kalmat, Khor
119 X9 **Kal'mius** ≈ E Ukraine
101 H15 **Kalmthout** Antwerpen, N Belgium
Kalmykia/Kalmykiya-Khal'mg Tangch, Respublika see Kalmykiya, Respublika
131 O12 **Kalmykiya, Respublika** var. Respublika Kalmykiya-Khal'mg Tangch, Eng. Kalmykia; prev. Kalmytskaya ASSR. ◈ autonomous republic SW Russian Federation
Kalmytskaya ASSR see Kalmykiya, Respublika
120 F9 **Kalnciems** Jelgava, C Latvia
116 L10 **Kalnitsa** ≈ SE Bulgaria
113 J24 **Kalocsa** Bács-Kiskun, S Hungary
116 J9 **Kalofer** Plovdivska Oblast, C Bulgaria
40 E10 **Kalohi Channel** channel C Pacific Ocean
85 I16 **Kalomo** Southern, S Zambia
31 X14 **Kalona** Iowa, C USA
117 K22 **Kalotási, Ákra** headland Amorgós, Kykládes, Greece, Aegean Sea
158 J8 **Kalpa** Himāchal Pradesh, N India
117 C15 **Kalpáki** Ípeiros, W Greece
161 C22 **Kalpeni Island** island Lakshadweep, India, N Indian Ocean
158 K13 **Kālpi** Uttar Pradesh, N India
164 G7 **Kalpin** Xinjiang Uygur Zizhiqu, NW China
152 K8 **Kalquduq** Rus. Kulkuduk. Nawoiy Wiloyati, N Uzbekistan
155 P16 **Kalri Lake** ◎ SE Pakistan
149 R5 **Kāl Shūr** N Iran
41 N11 **Kalskag** Alaska, USA
41 O9 **Kaltag** Alaska, USA
110 H7 **Kaltbrunn** Sankt Gallen, NE Switzerland
Kaltdorf see Pruszków
79 X14 **Kaltungo** Bauchi, E Nigeria
130 K4 **Kaluga** Kaluzhskaya Oblast', W Russian Federation
161 J26 **Kalu Ganga** ≈ S Sri Lanka
84 J13 **Kalulushi** Copperbelt, C Zambia
188 M2 **Kalumburu** Western Australia
97 H23 **Kalundborg** Vestsjælland, E Denmark
84 K11 **Kalungwishi** ≈ N Zambia
155 T8 **Kalūr Kot** Punjab, E Pakistan
118 I6 **Kalush** Pol. Kałusz. Ivano-Frankivs'ka Oblast', W Ukraine
Kałusz see Kalush
112 N11 **Kałuszyn** Siedlce, E Poland
161 J26 **Kalutara** Western Province, SW Sri Lanka
Kaluwawa see Fergusson Island
130 I5 **Kaluzhskaya Oblast'** ◈ province W Russian Federation
121 E14 **Kalvarija** Pol. Kalwaria. Marijampolė, S Lithuania
95 K15 **Kälviä** Vaasa, W Finland
111 U6 **Kalwang** Steiermark, E Austria
Kalwaria see Kalvarija
160 D13 **Kalyān** Mahārāshtra, W India
128 K16 **Kalyazin** Tverskaya Oblast', W Russian Federation
117 D18 **Kalydón** anc. Calydon. site of ancient city Dytikí Ellás, C Greece
117 M21 **Kálymnos** var. Kálimnos. Kálymnos, Dodekánisos, Greece, Aegean Sea
117 M21 **Kálymnos** var. Kálimnos. island Dodekánisos, Greece, Aegean Sea
119 O5 **Kalynivka** Kyyivs'ka Oblast', N Ukraine
119 N6 **Kalynivka** Vinnyts'ka Oblast', C Ukraine
44 M10 **Kama** var. Cama. Región Autónoma Atlántico Sur, SE Nicaragua
125 E9 **Kama** ≈ NW Russian Federation
172 N12 **Kamaishi** var. Kamaisi. Iwate, Honshū, C Japan
Kamaisi see Kamaishi
120 H13 **Kamajai** Molėtai, E Lithuania
120 H11 **Kamajai** Rokiškis, NE Lithuania
171 Jj17 **Kamakura** Kanagawa, Honshū, S Japan
155 U9 **Kamālia** Punjab, NE Pakistan
85 I14 **Kamalondo** North Western, NW Zambia
142 I13 **Kaman** Kirşehir, C Turkey
81 O20 **Kamanyola** Sud Kivu, E Zaire
147 N14 **Kamarān** island W Yemen
57 R9 **Kamarang** W Guyana
161 I14 **Kāmāreddi** var. Kamareddy. Andhra Pradesh, C India
Kamareddy see Kāmāreddi
Kama Reservoir see Kamskoye Vodokhranilishche
154 K13 **Kamarod** Baluchistān, SW Pakistan
175 R13 **Kamaru** Pulau Buton, C Indonesia
153 N12 **Kamashi** Qashqadaryo Wiloyati, S Uzbekistan
79 S13 **Kamba** Kebbi, NW Nigeria
Kambaeng Petch see Kamphaeng Phet
188 L12 **Kambalda** Western Australia
155 P13 **Kambar** var. Qambar. Sind, SE Pakistan
Kambara see Kabara
78 I14 **Kambia** W Sierra Leone
175 S16 **Kambing, Pulau** island S Indonesia
Kambos see Kámpos
81 N25 **Kambove** Shaba, SE Zaire
Kambryk see Cambrai
127 Pp10 **Kamchatka** ≈ E Russian Federation
Kamchatka see Kamchatka, Poluostrov
Kamchatka Basin see Komandorskaya Basin
127 P11 **Kamchatka, Poluostrov** Eng. Kamchatka. peninsula E Russian Federation
127 Pp11 **Kamchatskaya Oblast'** ◈ province E Russian Federation

◆ Country ● Country Capital ◇ Dependent Territory ○ Dependent Territory Capital ◈ Administrative Region ✕ International Airport ▲ Mountain ▲ Mountain Range ⚠ Volcano ≈ River ◎ Lake ⊡ Reservoir

KAMCHATSKIY ZALIV – KARPATY

127 *Pp10* **Kamchatskiy Zaliv** *gulf* E Russian Federation
116 *N9* **Kamchiya** ≈ E Bulgaria
116 *L9* **Kamchiya, Yazovir** ◎ E Bulgaria
Kamdesh *see* Kāmdeysh
155 *T4* **Kāmdeysh** *var.* Kamdesh. Kunar, E Afghanistan
170 *Ee14* **Kamega-mori** ▲ Shikoku, SW Japan
120 *M13* **Kamen'** *Rus.* Kamen'. Vitsyebskaya Voblasts', N Belorussia
Kamenets *see* Kamyanyets
Kamenets-Podol'skaya Oblast' *see* Khmel'nyts'ka Oblast'
Kamenets-Podol'skiy *see* Kam"yanets'-Podil's'kyy
115 *Q18* **Kamenica** NE FYR Macedonia
114 *A11* **Kamenjak, Rt** *headland* NW Croatia
150 *F8* **Kamenka** Zapadnyy Kazakhstan, NW Kazakhstan
129 *O6* **Kamenka** Arkhangel'skaya Oblast', NW Russian Federation
130 *L8* **Kamenka** Penzenskaya Oblast', W Russian Federation
131 *O6* **Kamenka** Voronezhskaya Oblast', W Russian Federation
Kamenka *see* Camenca, Moldavia
Kamenka *see* Kam"yanka, Ukraine
Kamenka-Bugskaya *see* Kam"yanka-Buz'ka
Kamenka Dneprovskaya *see* Kam"yanka-Dniprovs'ka
Kamen Kashirskiy *see* Kamin'-Kashyrs'kyy
126 *Gg14* **Kamen'-na-Obi** Altayskiy Kray, S Russian Federation
130 *L15* **Kamennomostskiy** Respublika Adygeya, SW Russian Federation
130 *L11* **Kamenolomni** Rostovskaya Oblast', SW Russian Federation
131 *P8* **Kamenskiy** Saratovskaya Oblast', W Russian Federation
127 *P7* **Kamenskoye** Koryakskiy Avtonomnyy Okrug, E Russian Federation
Kamenskoye *see* Dniprodzerzhyns'k
130 *L11* **Kamensk-Shakhtinskiy** Rostovskaya Oblast', SW Russian Federation
125 *Ee11* **Kamensk-Ural'skiy** Sverdlovskaya Oblast', C Russian Federation
103 *P15* **Kamenz** Sachsen, E Germany
171 *Gg14* **Kameoka** Kyōto, Honshū, SW Japan
xliii *G20* **Kames** Argyll and Bute, W Scotland, UK
130 *M3* **Kameshkovo** Vladimirskaya Oblast', W Russian Federation
171 *H15* **Kameyama** Mie, Honshū, SW Japan
170 *Cc10* **Kami-Agata** Nagasaki, Tsushima, SW Japan
35 *N10* **Kamiah** Idaho, NW USA
Kamień Koszyrski *see* Kamin'-Kashyrs'kyy
112 *H9* **Kamień Krajeński** *Ger.* Kamin in Westpreussen. Bydgoszcz, NW Poland
113 *F15* **Kamienna Góra** *Ger.* Landeshut, Landeshut in Schlesien. Jelenia Góra, SW Poland
112 *D8* **Kamień Pomorski** *Ger.* Cummin in Pommern. Szczecin, NW Poland
172 *N7* **Kamiiso** Hokkaidō, NE Japan
81 *L22* **Kamiji** Kasai Oriental, S Zaire
172 *Pp5* **Kamikawa** Hokkaidō, NE Japan
170 *Bb15* **Kami-Koshiki-jima** *island* SW Japan
81 *M23* **Kamina** Shaba, S Zaire
Kamina *see* Kaintiba
44 *C6* **Kaminaljuyú** *ruins* Guatemala, C Guatemala
Kamin in Westpreussen *see* Kamień Krajeński
118 *J2* **Kamin'-Kashyrs'kyy** *Pol.* Kamień Koszyrski, *Rus.* Kamen Kashirskiy. Volyns'ka Oblast', NW Ukraine
172 *N6* **Kaminokuni** Hokkaidō, NE Japan
171 *Ll13* **Kaminoyama** Yamagata, Honshū, C Japan
171 *Ii14* **Kamioka** Gifu, Honshū, SW Japan
41 *Q13* **Kamishak Bay** *bay* Alaska, USA
172 *Pp6* **Kami-Shihoro** Hokkaidō, NE Japan
Kamishli *see* Al Qāmishlī
Kamissar *see* Kamsar
170 *Cc10* **Kami-Tsushima** Nagasaki, Tsushima, SW Japan
81 *O20* **Kamituga** Sud Kivu, E Zaire
170 *B17* **Kamiyaku** Kagoshima, Yaku-shima, SW Japan
9 *N16* **Kamloops** British Columbia, SW Canada
109 *G25* **Kamma** Sicilia, Italy, C Mediterranean Sea
199 *Ii4* **Kammu Seamount** *undersea feature* N Pacific Ocean
111 *U11* **Kamnik** *Ger.* Stein. C Slovenia
Kamniške Alpe *see* Savinjske Alpe
171 *Kk13* **Kamo** Niigata, Honshū, C Japan
171 *K17* **Kamogawa** Chiba, Honshū, S Japan
155 *W8* **Kāmoke** Punjab, E Pakistan
84 *L13* **Kamoto** Eastern, E Zambia
111 *V3* **Kamp** ≈ N Austria
83 *F18* **Kampala** ● (Uganda) S Uganda
174 *H8* **Kampar, Sungai** ≈ Sumatera, W Indonesia
174 *Ii10* **Kampa, Teluk** *bay* Pulau Bangka, W Indonesia
100 *L9* **Kampen** Overijssel, E Netherlands
81 *N20* **Kampene** Maniema, E Zaire
31 *Q9* **Kampeska, Lake** ◎ South Dakota, N USA
178 *Gg9* **Kamphaeng Phet** *var.* Kambaeng Petch. Kamphaeng Phet, W Thailand
Kampo *see* Campo, Cameroon
Kampo *see* Ntem, Cameroon/Equatorial Guinea
178 *J13* **Kâmpóng Cham** *prev.* Kompong Cham. Kâmpóng Cham, C Cambodia
178 *J13* **Kâmpóng Chhnăng** *prev.* Kompong. Kâmpóng Chhnăng, C Cambodia
178 *Ii12* **Kâmpóng Khleăng** *prev.* Kompong Kleang. Siĕmréab, NW Cambodia
178 *I14* **Kâmpóng Saôm** *prev.* Kompong Som, Sihanoukville. Kâmpóng Saôm, SW Cambodia
178 *J13* **Kâmpóng Spoe** *prev.* Kompong Speu. Kâmpóng Spœ, S Cambodia
124 *N3* **Kámpos** *var.* Kambos. NW Cyprus
178 *Ii14* **Kâmpôt** Kâmpôt, SW Cambodia
Kamptee *see* Kāmthi
79 *O14* **Kampti** SW Burkina
Kampuchea *see* Cambodia
174 *Ll5* **Kampung Sirik** Sarawak, East Malaysia
176 *Y13* **Kampung, Sungai** ≈ Irian Jaya, E Indonesia
176 *Vv12* **Kamrau, Teluk** *bay* Irian Jaya, E Indonesia
9 *V15* **Kamsack** Saskatchewan, S Canada
78 *H13* **Kamsar** *var.* Kamissar. Guinée-Maritime, W Guinea
131 *R4* **Kamskoye Ust'ye** Respublika Tatarstan, W Russian Federation
129 *U14* **Kamskoye Vodokhranilishche** *var.* Kama Reservoir. ▣ NW Russian Federation
160 *I12* **Kāmthi** *prev.* Kamptee. Mahārāshtra, C India
Kamuela *see* Waimea
172 *Nn5* **Kamuenai** Hokkaidō, NE Japan
172 *P7* **Kamui-dake** ▲ Hokkaidō, NE Japan
172 *Nn4* **Kamui-misaki** *headland* Hokkaidō, NE Japan
45 *O15* **Kámuk, Cerro** ▲ SE Costa Rica
176 *Vv9* **Kamundan, Sungai** ≈ Irian Jaya, E Indonesia
176 *X12* **Kamura, Sungai** ≈ Irian Jaya, E Indonesia
118 *K7* **Kam"yanets'-Podil's'kyy** *Rus.* Kamenets-Podol'skiy. Khmel'nyts'ka Oblast', W Ukraine
119 *Q6* **Kam"yanka** *Rus.* Kamenka. Cherkas'ka Oblast', C Ukraine
118 *I5* **Kam"yanka-Buz'ka** *Rus.* Kamenka-Bugskaya. L'vivs'ka Oblast', NW Ukraine
119 *T9* **Kam"yanka-Dniprovs'ka** *Rus.* Kamenka Dneprovskaya. Zaporiz'ka Oblast', SE Ukraine
121 *F19* **Kamyanyets** *Rus.* Kamenets. Brestskaya Voblasts', SW Belorussia
131 *P9* **Kamyshin** Volgogradskaya Oblast', SW Russian Federation
125 *Ee11* **Kamyshlov** Sverdlovskaya Oblast', C Russian Federation
131 *Q13* **Kamyzyak** Astrakhanskaya Oblast', SW Russian Federation
10 *K8* **Kanaaupscow** ≈ Québec, C Canada
38 *K8* **Kanab** Utah, W USA
38 *K9* **Kanab Creek** ≈ Arizona/Utah, SW USA
197 *J13* **Kanacea** *prev.* Kanathea. Taveuni, N Fiji
197 *K14* **Kanacea** *island* Lau Group, E Fiji
40 *G17* **Kanaga Island** *island* Aleutian Islands, Alaska, USA
40 *G17* **Kanaga Volcano** ▲ Kanaga Island, Alaska, USA
171 *J17* **Kanagawa** *off.* Kanagawa-ken. ◐ *prefecture* Honshū, S Japan
11 *Q8* **Kanairiktok** ≈ Newfoundland and Labrador, E Canada
Kanaky *see* New Caledonia
81 *K22* **Kananga** *prev.* Luluabourg. Kasai Occidental, S Zaire
Kananur *see* Cannanore
Kanara *see* Karnātaka
38 *J7* **Kanarraville** Utah, W USA
131 *Q4* **Kanash** Chuvashskaya Respublika, W Russian Federation
Kanathea *see* Kanacea
23 *Q4* **Kanawha River** ≈ West Virginia, NE USA
171 *I15* **Kanayama** Gifu, Honshū, SW Japan
171 *I12* **Kanazawa** Ishikawa, Honshū, SW Japan
177 *G4* **Kanbalu** Sagaing, C Burma
177 *Ff8* **Kanbe** Yangon, SW Burma
178 *H11* **Kanchanaburi** Kanchanaburi, W Thailand
Kānchenjunga *see* Kangchenjunga
151 *V11* **Kanchingiz, Khrebet** ▲▲ E Kazakhstan
161 *J19* **Kānchīpuram** *prev.* Conjeeveram. Tamil Nādu, SE India
155 *N8* **Kandahār** *Per.* Qandahār. Kandahār, S Afghanistan
155 *N9* **Kandahār** *Per.* Qandahār. ◐ *province* SE Afghanistan
Kandalakša *see* Kandalaksha
128 *I5* **Kandalaksha** *var.* Kandalakša, *Fin.* Kantalahti. Murmanskaya Oblast', NW Russian Federation
Kandalaksha Gulf/Kandalakshskaya Guba *see* Kandalakshskiy Zaliv
128 *K6* **Kandalakshskiy Zaliv** *var.* Kandalakshskaya Guba, *Eng.* Kandalaksha Gulf. *bay* NW Russian Federation
Kandalangodi *see* Kandalengoti
85 *G17* **Kandalengoti** *var.* Kandalangodi. Ngamiland, NW Botswana
175 *N10* **Kandangan** Borneo, C Indonesia
Kandau *see* Kandava
120 *E8* **Kandava** *Ger.* Kandau. Tukums, W Latvia
Kandavu *see* Kadavu
79 *R14* **Kandé** *var.* Kanté. NE Togo
103 *F23* **Kandel** ▲ SW Germany
194 *G12* **Kandep** Enga, W PNG
155 *R12* **Kandhkot** Sind, SE Pakistan
79 *S13* **Kandi** N Benin
155 *P14* **Kandiāro** Sind, SE Pakistan
142 *F11* **Kandıra** Kocaeli, NW Turkey
191 *S8* **Kandos** New South Wales, SE Australia
154 *M16* **Kandrāch** *var.* Kanrach. Baluchistān, SW Pakistan
180 *I4* **Kandreho** Mahajanga, C Madagascar
194 *M12* **Kandrian** New Britain, E PNG
Kandukur *see* Kondukūr
161 *K25* **Kandy** Central Province, C Sri Lanka
20 *D12* **Kane** Pennsylvania, NE USA
66 *I11* **Kane Fracture Zone** *tectonic feature* NW Atlantic Ocean
Kanëka *see* Kanëvka
80 *G9* **Kanem** *off.* Préfecture du Kanem. ◐ *prefecture* W Chad
40 *D9* **Kaneohe** *Haw.* Kāne'ohe. Oahu, Hawaii, USA, C Pacific Ocean
Kanestron, Akra *see* Palioúri, Ákra
Kanëv *see* Kaniv
128 *M5* **Kanëvka** *var.* Kanëka. Murmanskaya Oblast', NW Russian Federation
130 *K13* **Kanevskaya** Krasnodarskiy Kray, SW Russian Federation
Kanevskoye Vodokhranilishche *see* Kanivs'ke Vodoskhovyshche
171 *Ll12* **Kaneyama** Yamagata, Honshū, C Japan
85 *G20* **Kang** Kgalagadi, C Botswana
78 *L13* **Kangaba** Koulikoro, SW Mali
142 *M13* **Kangal** Sivas, C Turkey
149 *O13* **Kangān** Būshehr, S Iran
149 *S15* **Kangān** Hormozgān, SE Iran
173 *G2* **Kangar** Perlis, Peninsular Malaysia
78 *L13* **Kangaré** Sikasso, S Mali
190 *F10* **Kangaroo Island** *island* South Australia
95 *M17* **Kangasniemi** Mikkeli, SE Finland
148 *K6* **Kangāvar** *var.* Kangāwar. Kermānshāhān, W Iran
Kangāwar *see* Kangāvar
159 *S11* **Kangchenjunga** *var.* Kānchenjunga. ▲ NE India
166 *G9* **Kangding** Sichuan, C China
175 *Nn14* **Kangean, Kepulauan** *island group* S Indonesia
175 *N14* **Kangean, Pulau** *island* Kepulauan Kangean, S Indonesia
69 *U8* **Kangen** *var.* Kengen. ≈ SE Sudan
207 *Q15* **Kangertittivaq** *Dan.* Scoresby Sund. *fjord* E Greenland
178 *H2* **Kangfang** Kachin State, N Burma
176 *Z13* **Kanggup** Irian Jaya, E Indonesia
169 *X12* **Kanggye** N North Korea
207 *P15* **Kangikajik** *var.* Kap Brewster. *headland* E Greenland
11 *N5* **Kangiqsualujjuaq** *prev.* George River, Port-Nouveau-Québec. Québec, E Canada
10 *L2* **Kangiqsujuaq** *prev.* Maricourt, Wakeham Bay. Québec, NE Canada
10 *M4* **Kangirsuk** *prev.* Bellin, Payne. Québec, E Canada
164 *J15* **Kangmar** Xizang Zizhiqu, W China
164 *M16* **Kangmar** Xizang Zizhiqu, W China
169 *Y14* **Kangnŭng** *Jap.* Kōryō. NE South Korea
81 *D18* **Kango** Estuaire, NW Gabon
158 *I7* **Kāngra** Himāchal Pradesh, NW India
159 *Q16* **Kangsabati Reservoir** ▣ N India
165 *O17* **Kangto** ▲ China/India
165 *W12* **Kang Xian** *var.* Zuitaizi. Gansu, C China
177 *Ff4* **Kani** Sagaing, C Burma
78 *M15* **Kani** NW Ivory Coast
81 *M23* **Kaniama** Shaba, S Zaire
Kanibadam *see* Konibodom
175 *O2* **Kanibongan** Sabah, East Malaysia
193 *F17* **Kaniere** West Coast, South Island, NZ
193 *G17* **Kaniere, Lake** ◎ South Island, NZ
196 *E17* **Kanifaay** Yap, W Micronesia
129 *O4* **Kanin Kamen'** ▲▲ NW Russian Federation
129 *N3* **Kanin Nos** Nenetskiy Avtonomnyy Okrug, NW Russian Federation
129 *N3* **Kanin Nos, Mys** *headland* NW Russian Federation
129 *O5* **Kanin, Poluostrov** *peninsula* NW Russian Federation
145 *V8* **Kānī Sakht** E Iraq
145 *T3* **Kānī Sulaymān** N Iraq
172 *N8* **Kanita** Aomori, Honshū, C Japan
119 *Q5* **Kaniv** *Rus.* Kanëv. Cherkas'ka Oblast', C Ukraine
190 *K11* **Kaniva** Victoria, SE Australia
119 *Q5* **Kanivs'ke Vodoskhovyshche** *Rus.* Kanevskoye Vodokhranilishche. ▣ C Ukraine
114 *L8* **Kanjiža** *Ger.* Altkanischa, *Hung.* Magyarkanizsa, Ókanizsa; *prev.* Stara Kanjiža. Serbia, N Yugoslavia
95 *K18* **Kankaanpää** Turku-Pori, SW Finland
32 *M12* **Kankakee** Illinois, N USA
33 *O11* **Kankakee River** ≈ Illinois/Indiana, N USA
78 *K14* **Kankan** Haute-Guinée, E Guinea
160 *K13* **Kānker** Madhya Pradesh, C India
78 *J10* **Kankossa** Assaba, S Mauritania
178 *Gg13* **Kanmaw Kyun** *var.* Kisseraing, Kithareng. *island* Mergui Archipelago, S Burma
170 *E13* **Kanmuri-yama** ▲ Kyūshū, SW Japan
23 *R10* **Kannapolis** North Carolina, SE USA
95 *L16* **Kannonkoski** Keski-Suomi, C Finland
Kannur *see* Cannanore
95 *K15* **Kannus** Vaasa, W Finland
79 *V13* **Kano** Kano, N Nigeria
79 *V13* **Kano** ◐ *state* N Nigeria
79 *V13* **Kano** ✕ Kano, N Nigeria
170 *F14* **Kan'onji** *var.* Kanonzi. Kagawa, Shikoku, SW Japan
Kanonzi *see* Kan'onji
28 *M5* **Kanopolis Lake** ▣ Kansas, C USA
38 *K5* **Kanosh** Utah, W USA
174 *Ll6* **Kanowit** Sarawak, East Malaysia
170 *Bb17* **Kanoya** Kagoshima, Kyūshū, SW Japan
158 *L13* **Kānpur** *Eng.* Cawnpore. Uttar Pradesh, N India
Kanrach *see* Kandrāch
171 *Gg15* **Kansai** ✕ (Ōsaka) Ōsaka, Honshū, SW Japan
29 *R9* **Kansas** Oklahoma, C USA
28 *L5* **Kansas** *off.* State of Kansas; also known as Jayhawker State, Sunflower State. ◐ *state* C USA
29 *R4* **Kansas City** Kansas, C USA
29 *R4* **Kansas City** Missouri, C USA
29 *R3* **Kansas City** ✕ Missouri, C USA
29 *P4* **Kansas River** ≈ Kansas, C USA
126 *I14* **Kansk** Krasnoyarskiy Kray, S Russian Federation
Kansu *see* Gansu
153 *V7* **Kant** Chuyskaya Oblast', N Kyrgyzstan
Kantalahti *see* Kandalaksha
178 *Gg16* **Kantang** *var.* Ban Kantang. Trang, SW Thailand
117 *H25* **Kántanos** Kríti, Greece, E Mediterranean Sea
79 *R12* **Kantchari** E Burkina
Kanté *see* Kandé
Kantemir *see* Cantemir
130 *L9* **Kantemirovka** Voronezhskaya Oblast', W Russian Federation
178 *J11* **Kantharalak** Si Sa Ket, E Thailand
Kantipur *see* Kathmandu
41 *Q9* **Kantishna River** ≈ Alaska, USA
171 *K16* **Kantō** *physical region* Honshū, SW Japan
203 *S3* **Kanton** *var.* Abariringa, Canton Island; *prev.* Mary Island. *atoll* Phoenix Islands, C Kiribati
171 *Jj15* **Kantō-sanchi** ▲▲ Honshū, S Japan
xliv *E13* **Kanturk** *Ir.* Ceann Toirc. Cork, SW Ireland
57 *T11* **Kanuku Mountains** ▲▲ S Guyana
171 *Kk15* **Kanuma** Tochigi, Honshū, S Japan
85 *H20* **Kanye** Southern, SE Botswana
85 *H17* **Kanyu** Ngamiland, C Botswana
177 *G7* **Kanyutkwin** Pegu, C Burma
81 *M24* **Kanzenze** Shaba, SE Zaire
200 *Ss13* **Kao** *island* Kotu Group, W Tonga
167 *S14* **Kaohsiung** *var.* Gaoxiong, *Jap.* Takao, Takow. S Taiwan
167 *S14* **Kaohsiung** ✕ S Taiwan
Kaokaona *see* Kirakira
85 *B17* **Kaoko Veld** ▲▲ N Namibia
78 *G11* **Kaolack** *var.* Kaolak. W Senegal
Kaolak *see* Kaolack
Kaolan *see* Lanzhou
195 *W15* **Kaolo** San Jorge, N Solomon Islands
85 *H14* **Kaoma** Western, W Zambia
40 *B8* **Kapaa** *Haw.* Kapa'a. Kauai, Hawaii, USA, C Pacific Ocean
115 *J16* **Kapa Moračka** ▲ SW Yugoslavia
143 *V13* **Kapan** *Rus.* Kafan; *prev.* Ghap'an. SE Armenia
84 *L13* **Kapandashila** Northern, NE Zambia
81 *L23* **Kapanga** Shaba, S Zaire
151 *U15* **Kapchagay** *Kaz.* Kapshaghay. Almaty, SE Kazakhstan
151 *V15* **Kapchagayskoye Vodokhranilishche** *Kaz.* Qapshagay Böyeni. ▣ SE Kazakhstan
101 *F15* **Kapelle** Zeeland, SW Netherlands
101 *G16* **Kapellen** Antwerpen, N Belgium
97 *P15* **Kapellskär** Stockholm, C Sweden
83 *H18* **Kapenguria** Rift Valley, W Kenya
111 *V6* **Kapfenberg** Steiermark, C Austria
85 *J14* **Kapiri Mposhi** Central, C Zambia
155 *R4* **Kāpīsā** ◐ *province* E Afghanistan
10 *G10* **Kapiskau** ≈ Ontario, C Canada
192 *K13* **Kapiti Island** *island* C NZ
80 *K9* **Kapka, Massif du** ▲▲ E Chad
Kaplamada *see* Kaubalatmada, Gunung
24 *H9* **Kaplan** Louisiana, S USA
152 *E9* **Kaplangky, Plato** *ridge* Turkmenistan/Uzbekistan
113 *D19* **Kaplice** *Ger.* Kaplitz. Jižní Čechy, S Czech Republic
Kaplitz *see* Kaplice
Kapoche *see* Capoche
176 *U10* **Kapocol** Irian Jaya, E Indonesia
178 *Gg14* **Kapoe** Ranong, SW Thailand
Kapoeas *see* Kapuas, Sungai
83 *G15* **Kapoeta** Eastern Equatoria, SE Sudan
113 *I25* **Kapos** ≈ S Hungary
113 *H25* **Kaposvár** Somogy, SW Hungary
96 *H13* **Kapp** Oppland, S Norway
102 *I7* **Kappeln** Schleswig-Holstein, N Germany
Kaproncza *see* Koprivnica
111 *P7* **Kaprun** Salzburg, C Austria
Kapshaghay *see* Kapchagay
Kapstad *see* Cape Town
Kapsukas *see* Marijampolė
176 *Yy10* **Kaptiau** Irian Jaya, E Indonesia
121 *L19* **Kaptsevichy** *Rus.* Koptsevichi. Homyel'skaya Voblasts', SE Belorussia
Kapuas Hulu, Banjaran/Kapuas Hulu, Pegunungan *see* Kapuas Mountains
174 *M7* **Kapuas Mountains** *Ind.* Banjaran Kapuas Hulu, Pegunungan Kapuas Hulu. ▲▲ Indonesia/Malaysia
174 *Kk8* **Kapuas, Sungai** ≈ Borneo, N Indonesia
175 *N10* **Kapuas, Sungai** *prev.* Kapoeas. ≈ Borneo, C Indonesia
190 *J9* **Kapunda** South Australia
158 *H8* **Kapūrthala** Punjab, N India
174 *L14* **Kapur Utara, Pegugungan** ▲▲ Jawa, S Indonesia
10 *G12* **Kapuskasing** Ontario, S Canada
12 *D6* **Kapuskasing** ≈ Ontario, S Canada
131 *P11* **Kapustin Yar** Astrakhanskaya Oblast', SW Russian Federation
84 *K11* **Kaputa** Northern, NE Zambia
113 *G22* **Kapuvár** Győr-Moson-Sopron, NW Hungary
Kapydzhik, Gora *see* Qapiciğ Dağı
121 *J17* **Kapyl'** *Rus.* Kopyl'. Minskaya Voblasts', C Belorussia
45 *N9* **Kara** *var.* Cara. Región Autónoma Atlántico Sur, E Nicaragua
79 *R14* **Kara** *var.* Lama-Kara. NE Togo
79 *Q14* **Kara** ≈ N Togo
153 *U7* **Kara-Balta** Chuyskaya Oblast', N Kyrgyzstan
150- *G11* **Karabau** Atyrau, W Kazakhstan
152 *E7* **Karabaur', Uval** *Kaz.* Korabavur Pastligi, *Uzb.* Qorabowur Kirlari. *physical region* Kazakhstan/Uzbekistan
152 *L13* **Karabekaul** *var.* Garabekevyul, *Turkm.* Garabekewül. Lebapskiy Velayat, E Turkmenistan
152 *K15* **Karabil', Vozvyshennost'** ▲▲ S Turkmenistan
152 *A9* **Kara-Bogaz-Gol** *Turkm.* Garabogazköl. Balkanskiy Velayat, NW Turkmenistan
152 *B9* **Kara-Bogaz-Gol, Zaliv** *bay* NW Turkmenistan
151 *R15* **Karaboget** *Kaz.* Qaraböget. Zhambyl, S Kazakhstan
142 *H11* **Karabük** Zonguldak, N Turkey
126 *Ii13* **Karabula** Krasnoyarskiy Kray, C Russian Federation
151 *V14* **Karabulak** *Kaz.* Qarabulaq. Taldykorgan, SE Kazakhstan
151 *Y11* **Karabulak** *Kaz.* Qarabulaq. Vostochnyy Kazakhstan, E Kazakhstan
151 *Q17* **Karabulak** *Kaz.* Qarabulaq. Yuzhnyy Kazakhstan, S Kazakhstan
142 *C17* **Kara Burnu** *headland* SW Turkey
150 *K10* **Karabutak** *Kaz.* Qarabutaq. Aktyubinsk, W Kazakhstan
142 *D12* **Karacabey** Bursa, NW Turkey
116 *O12* **Karacaköy** İstanbul, NW Turkey
116 *M12* **Karacaoğlan** Kırklareli, NW Turkey
Karachay-Cherkessia *see* Karachayevo-Cherkesskaya Respublika
130 *L15* **Karachayevo-Cherkesskaya Respublika** *Eng.* Karachay-Cherkessia. ◐ *autonomous republic* SW Russian Federation
130 *M15* **Karachayevsk** Karachayevo-Cherkesskaya Respublika, SW Russian Federation
130 *J6* **Karachev** Bryanskaya Oblast', W Russian Federation
155 *O16* **Karāchi** Sind, SE Pakistan
155 *O16* **Karāchi** ✕ Sind, S Pakistan
Karácsonkő *see* Piatra-Neamț
161 *E15* **Karād** Mahārāshtra, W India
142 *H16* **Karadağ** ▲ S Turkey
153 *T10* **Karadar'ya** *Uzb.* Qoradaryo. ≈ Kyrgyzstan/Uzbekistan
Karadeniz *see* Black Sea
Karadeniz Boğazı *see* İstanbul Boğazı
152 *B13* **Karadepe** Balkanskiy Velayat, W Turkmenistan
Karadzhar *see* Qorajar
Karaferiye *see* Véroia
152 *E13* **Karagan** *Turkm.* Garagan. Akhalskiy Velayat, C Turkmenistan
151 *R10* **Karaganda** *Kaz.* Qaraghandy. Karaganda, C Kazakhstan
151 *R10* **Karaganda** *off.* Karagandinskaya Oblast', *Kaz.* Qaraghandy Oblysy. ◐ *province* C Kazakhstan
Karagandinskaya Oblast' *see* Karaganda
151 *T10* **Karagayly** *Kaz.* Qaraghayly. Karaganda, C Kazakhstan
152 *A11* **Karagel'** *Turkm.* Garagöl. Balkanskiy Velayat, W Turkmenistan
127 *Pp8* **Karaginskiy, Ostrov** *island* E Russian Federation
207 *T1* **Karaginskiy Zaliv** *bay* E Russian Federation
143 *P13* **Karagöl Dağları** ▲▲ NE Turkey
116 *L13* **Karahisar** Edirne, NW Turkey
131 *V3* **Karaidel'** Respublika Bashkortostan, W Russian Federation
131 *V3* **Karaidel'skiy** Respublika Bashkortostan, W Russian Federation
116 *L13* **Karaidemir Barajı** ▣ NW Turkey
161 *J21* **Kāraikāl** Pondicherry, SE India
161 *I22* **Kāraikkudi** Tamil Nādu, SE India
151 *Y11* **Kara Irtysh** *Rus.* Chërnyy Irtysh. ≈ NE Kazakhstan
149 *N5* **Karaj** Tehrān, N Iran
174 *H5* **Karak** Pahang, Peninsular Malaysia
Karak *see* Al Karak
153 *T11* **Kara-Kabak** Oshskaya Oblast', SW Kyrgyzstan
152 *D12* **Kara-Kala** *var.* Garrygala. Balkanskiy Velayat, W Turkmenistan
Karakala *see* Oqqal'a
Karakalpakstan, Respublika *see* Qoraqalpoghiston Respublikasi
Karakalpakya *see* Qoraqalpoghiston
Karakax *see* Moyu
164 *G10* **Karakax He** ≈ NW China
124 *S9* **Karakaya Barajı** ▣ C Turkey
175 *Ss4* **Karakelang, Pulau** *island* N Indonesia
Karakılısse *see* Ağrı
Karak, Muḥāfaẓat al *see* Al Karak
Kara-Köl *see* Kara-Kul'
153 *Y7* **Karakol** *prev.* Przheval'sk. Issyk-Kul'skaya Oblast', NE Kyrgyzstan
153 *X8* **Karakol** *var.* Karakolka. Issyk-Kul'skaya Oblast', NE Kyrgyzstan
Karakolka *see* Karakol
155 *W2* **Karakoram Highway** *road* China/Pakistan
155 *Z3* **Karakoram Pass** *Chin.* Karakoram Shankou. *pass* C Asia
158 *I3* **Karakoram Range** ▲▲ C Asia
Karakoram Shankou *see* Karakoram Pass
Karaköse *see* Ağrı
151 *P14* **Karakoyyn, Ozero** *Kaz.* Qaraqoyyn. ◎ C Kazakhstan
85 *F19* **Karakubis** Ghanzi, W Botswana
153 *T9* **Kara-Kul'** *Kir.* Kara-Köl. Dzhalal-Abadskaya Oblast', W Kyrgyzstan
Karakul' *see* Qarokŭl, Tajikistan
Karakul' *see* Qorakŭl, Uzbekistan
153 *U10* **Kara-Kul'dzha** Oshskaya Oblast', SW Kyrgyzstan
131 *T3* **Karakulino** Udmurtskaya Respublika, NW Russian Federation
Karakul', Ozero *see* Qarokŭl
Kara Kum *see* Garagumy
Kara Kum Canal/Karakumskiy Kanal *see* Garagumskiy Kanal
Karakumy, Peski *see* Garagumy
85 *E17* **Karakuwisa** Okavango, NE Namibia
126 *Jj14* **Karam** Irkutskaya Oblast', S Russian Federation
Karamai *see* Karamay
175 *N13* **Karamain, Pulau** *island* N Indonesia
142 *I16* **Karaman** Karaman, S Turkey
142 *H16* **Karaman** ◐ *province* S Turkey
116 *M8* **Karamandere** ≈ NE Bulgaria
164 *J4* **Karamay** *var.* Karamai, Kelamayi, *prev. Chin.* K'o-la-ma-i. Xinjiang Uygur Zizhiqu, NW China
175 *Nn11* **Karambu** Borneo, N Indonesia
193 *H14* **Karamea** West Coast, South Island, NZ
193 *H14* **Karamea** ≈ South Island, NZ
193 *G15* **Karamea Bight** *gulf* South Island, NZ
152 *L14* **Karamet-Niyaz** *Turkm.* Garamäbnyyaz. Lebapskiy Velayat, E Turkmenistan
164 *K10* **Karamiran He** ≈ NW China
176 *Yy11* **Karamor, Pengunungan** ▲▲ Irian Jaya, E Indonesia
153 *S11* **Karamyk** Oshskaya Oblast', SW Kyrgyzstan
175 *Nn16* **Karangasem** Bali, S Indonesia
160 *H12* **Kāranja** Mahārāshtra, C India
158 *F9* **Karanpur** *var.* Karanpura. Rājasthān, NW India
Karanpura *see* Karanpur
Karánsebes/Karansebesch *see* Caransebeş
151 *T14* **Karaoy** *Kaz.* Qaraoy. Almaty, SE Kazakhstan
116 *N7* **Karapelit** *Rom.* Stejarul. Varnenska Oblast, NE Bulgaria
142 *I15* **Karapınar** Konya, C Turkey
85 *D22* **Karas** ◐ *district* S Namibia
153 *Y8* **Kara-Say** Issyk-Kul'skaya Oblast', NE Kyrgyzstan
85 *E22* **Karasburg** Karas, S Namibia
Kara Sea *see* Karskoye More
94 *L9* **Karasjok** *Fin.* Kaarasjoki. Finnmark, N Norway
94 *K9* **Karašjokka** ≈ N Norway
Kara Strait *see* Karskiye Vorota, Proliv
Kara Su *see* Mesta/Néstos
151 *N8* **Karasu** *Kaz.* Qarasū. Kustanay, N Kazakhstan
142 *F11* **Karasu** Sakarya, NW Turkey
Karasubazar *see* Bilohirs'k
125 *G14* **Karasuk** Novosibirskaya Oblast', C Russian Federation
151 *U13* **Karatal** *Kaz.* Qaratal. ≈ SE Kazakhstan
142 *K17* **Karataş** Adana, S Turkey
151 *Q16* **Karatau** *Kaz.* Qaratau. Zhambyl, S Kazakhstan
Karatau *see* Karatau, Khrebet
151 *P16* **Karatau, Khrebet** *var.* Karatau, *Kaz.* Qaratau. ▲▲ S Kazakhstan
150 *G13* **Karaton** *Kaz.* Qaraton. Atyrau, W Kazakhstan
170 *C12* **Karatsu** *var.* Karatu. Saga, Kyūshū, SW Japan
Karatu *see* Karatsu
126 *Hh7* **Karaul** Taymyrskiy (Dolgano-Nenetskiy) Avtonomnyy Okrug, N Russian Federation
Karaulbazar *see* Qorowulbozor
Karauzyak *see* Qoraŭzak
117 *D16* **Karáva** ▲ C Greece
Karavanke *see* Karawanken
117 *F22* **Karavás** Kýthira, S Greece
115 *J20* **Karavastasë, Laguna e** *var.* Kënet' e Karavastas, Kravasta Lagoon. *lagoon* W Albania
Karavastas, Kënet' e *see* Karavastasë, Laguna e
120 *I5* **Karavere** Tartumaa, E Estonia
117 *L23* **Karavonísia** *island* Kykládes, Greece, Aegean Sea
174 *Jj14* **Karawang** *prev.* Krawang. Jawa, C Indonesia
111 *T10* **Karawanken** *Slvn.* Karavanke. ▲▲ Austria/Yugoslavia
Karaxahar *see* Kaidu He
143 *R13* **Karayazı** Erzurum, NE Turkey
151 *Q12* **Karazhal** Zhezkazgan, C Kazakhstan
145 *S9* **Karbalā'** *var.* Kerbala, Kerbela. S Iraq
96 *L11* **Kårböle** Gävleborg, C Sweden
113 *M23* **Karcag** Jász-Nagykun-Szolnok, E Hungary
Kardak *see* Imia
116 *N7* **Kardam** Varnenska Oblast, NE Bulgaria
117 *M22* **Kardámaina** Kos, Dodekánisos, Greece, Aegean Sea
Kardamila *see* Kardámyla
117 *L18* **Kardámyla** *var.* Kardamila, Kardhámila. Chíos, E Greece
Kardeljevo *see* Ploče
Kardh *see* Qardho
Kardhámila *see* Kardámyla
Kardhítsa *see* Kardítsa
117 *E16* **Kardítsa** *var.* Kardhítsa. Thessalía, C Greece
120 *E4* **Kärdla** *Ger.* Kertel. Hiiumaa, W Estonia
Karelia *see* Kareliya, Respublika
121 *I16* **Karelichy** *Pol.* Korelicze, *Rus.* Korelichi. Hrodzyenskaya Voblasts', W Belorussia
128 *I10* **Kareliya, Respublika** *prev.* Karel'skaya ASSR, *Eng.* Karelia. ◐ *autonomous republic* NW Russian Federation
Karel'skaya ASSR *see* Kareliya, Respublika
83 *E22* **Karema** Rukwa, W Tanzania
Karen *see* Hualien
85 *I14* **Karenda** Central, C Zambia
178 *Gg8* **Karen State** *var.* Kawthule State, Kayin State. ◐ *state* S Burma
94 *J10* **Karesuando** *Lapp.* Kaaresuanto. Norrbotten, N Sweden
Karet *see* Kâgheț
Kareyz-e-Elyās/Kārez Iliās *see* Kārīz-e Elyās
126 *Gg12* **Kargasok** Tomskaya Oblast', C Russian Federation
126 *Gg14* **Kargat** Novosibirskaya Oblast', C Russian Federation
142 *J11* **Kargı** Çorum, N Turkey
158 *I5* **Kargil** Jammu and Kashmir, NW India
Kargilik *see* Yecheng
128 *L11* **Kargopol'** Arkhangel'skaya Oblast', NW Russian Federation
112 *F12* **Kargowa** *Ger.* Unruhstadt. Zielona Góra, W Poland
79 *X13* **Kari** Bauchi, E Nigeria
85 *J15* **Kariba** Mashonaland West, N Zimbabwe
85 *J16* **Kariba, Lake** ▣ Zambia/Zimbabwe
172 *Nn5* **Kariba-yama** ▲ Hokkaidō, NE Japan
85 *C19* **Karibib** Erongo, C Namibia
Karies *see* Karyés
94 *L9* **Karigasniemi** *Lapp.* Garegegasnjárga. Lappi, N Finland
172 *P6* **Karikachi-tōge** *pass* Hokkaidō, NE Japan
192 *J2* **Karikari, Cape** *headland* North Island, NZ
Karīmābād *see* Hunza
174 *K10* **Karimata, Kepulauan** *island group* N Indonesia
174 *K9* **Karimata, Pulau** *island* Kepulauan Karimata, N Indonesia
174 *K10* **Karimata, Selat** *strait* W Indonesia
161 *I14* **Karīmnagar** Andhra Pradesh, C India
194 *I13* **Karimui** Chimbu, C PNG
174 *L13* **Karimunjawa, Pulau** *island* S Indonesia
82 *N12* **Karin** Woqooyi Galbeed, N Somalia
Kariot *see* Ikaría
95 *L20* **Karis** *Fin.* Karjaa. Uusimaa, SW Finland
Káristos *see* Kárystos
154 *J4* **Kārīz-e Elyās** *var.* Kareyz-e-Elyās, Kārez Iliās. Herāt, NW Afghanistan
Karjaa *see* Karis
151 *T10* **Karkaralinsk** *Kaz.* Qarqaraly. Karaganda, E Kazakhstan
194 *J11* **Karkar Island** *island* N PNG
149 *N7* **Karkas, Kūh-e** ▲▲ C Iran
148 *K8* **Karkheh, Rūd-e** ≈ SW Iran
117 *L20* **Karkinágrio** Ikaría, Dodekánisos, Greece, Aegean Sea
119 *R12* **Karkinits'ka Zatoka** *Rus.* Karkinitskiy Zaliv. *gulf* S Ukraine
Karkinitskiy Zaliv *see* Karkinits'ka Zatoka
95 *L19* **Karkkila** *Swe.* Högfors. Uusimaa, S Finland
95 *M19* **Kärkölä** Häme, S Finland
190 *G9* **Karkoo** South Australia
Karkūk *see* Kirkūk
120 *D5* **Kärla** *Ger.* Kergel. Saaremaa, W Estonia
Karleby *see* Kokkola
112 *F7* **Karlino** *Ger.* Körlin an der Persante. Koszalin, NW Poland
143 *Q13* **Karlıova** Bingöl, E Turkey
119 *U6* **Karlivka** Poltavs'ka Oblast', C Ukraine
Karl-Marx-Stadt *see* Chemnitz
Karlö *see* Hailuoto
114 *C11* **Karlobag** *It.* Carlopago. Lika-Senj, W Croatia
114 *D9* **Karlovac** *Ger.* Karlstadt, *Hung.* Károlyváros. Karlovac, C Croatia
114 *C10* **Karlovac** *off.* Karlovačka Županija. ◐ *province* C Croatia
Karlovačka Županija *see* Karlovac
116 *J9* **Karlovo** *prev.* Levskigrad. Plovdivska Oblast, C Bulgaria
113 *A16* **Karlovy Vary** *Ger.* Karlsbad; *prev. Eng.* Carlsbad. Západní Čechy, W Czech Republic
Karlsbad *see* Karlovy Vary
97 *L17* **Karlsborg** Skaraborg, S Sweden
Karlsburg *see* Alba Iulia
97 *L22* **Karlshamn** Blekinge, S Sweden
97 *L16* **Karlskoga** Örebro, C Sweden
97 *M22* **Karlskrona** Blekinge, S Sweden
103 *G21* **Karlsruhe** *var.* Carlsruhe. Baden-Württemberg, SW Germany
97 *K16* **Karlstad** Värmland, C Sweden
31 *R3* **Karlstad** Minnesota, N USA
103 *I18* **Karlstadt** Bayern, C Germany
Karlstadt *see* Karlovac
41 *Q14* **Karluk** Kodiak Island, Alaska, USA
Karluk *see* Qarluq
121 *O17* **Karma** *Rus.* Korma. Homyel'skaya Voblasts', SE Belorussia
161 *F14* **Karmāla** Mahārāshtra, W India
152 *M11* **Karmana** Nawoiy Wiloyati, C Uzbekistan
144 *G8* **Karmi'él** *var.* Carmiel. Northern, N Israel
97 *B16* **Karmøy** *island* S Norway
158 *I9* **Karnāl** Haryāna, N India
159 *W15* **Karnaphuli Reservoir** ▣ NE India
161 *F17* **Karnātaka** *var.* Kanara; *prev.* Maisur, Mysore. ◐ *state* W India
27 *S13* **Karnes City** Texas, SW USA
111 *P9* **Karnische Alpen** *It.* Alpi Carniche. ▲▲ Austria/Italy
116 *M9* **Karnobat** Burgaska Oblast, E Bulgaria
111 *Q9* **Kärnten** *off.* Land Kärnten, *Eng.* Carinthi, *Slvn.* Koroška. ◐ *state* S Austria
Karnul *see* Kurnool
85 *K16* **Karoi** Mashonaland West, N Zimbabwe
Karol *see* Carei
Károly-Fehérvár *see* Alba Iulia
Károlyváros *see* Karlovac
179 *Qq15* **Karomatan** Mindanao, S Philippines
84 *M12* **Karonga** Northern, N Malawi
153 *W10* **Karool-Tëbë** Narynskaya Oblast', C Kyrgyzstan
190 *J9* **Karoonda** South Australia
155 *S9* **Karor** Punjab, E Pakistan
175 *P10* **Karosa** Sulawesi, C Indonesia
Karpasía/Karpas Peninsula *see* Kırpaşa
Karpaten *see* Carpathian Mountains
117 *L22* **Karpáthio Pélagos** *sea* Dodekánisos, Greece, Aegean Sea
117 *N24* **Kárpathos** Kárpathos, SE Greece
117 *N24* **Kárpathos** *It.* Scarpanto; *anc.* Carpathos, Carpathus. *island* SE Greece
Karpathos Strait *see* Karpathou, Stenó
117 *N24* **Karpathou, Stenó** *var.* Karpathos Strait, Scarpanto Strait. *strait* Dodekánisos, Greece, Aegean Sea
Karpaty *see* Carpathian Mountains

◆ Country
● Country Capital
◇ Dependent Territory
○ Dependent Territory Capital
◐ Administrative Region
✕ International Airport
▲ Mountain
▲▲ Mountain Range
▲ Volcano
≈ River
◎ Lake
▣ Reservoir

Karpenísi – Keowee, Lake

117 E17 **Karpenísi** *prev.* Karpenísion. Stereá Ellás, C Greece
Karpenísion *see* Karpenísi
Karpilovka *see* Aktsyabrski
129 O8 **Karpogory** Arkhangel'skaya Oblast', NW Russian Federation
188 I7 **Karratha** Western Australia
143 S12 **Kars** *var.* Qars. Kars, NE Turkey
143 S12 **Kars** *var.* Qars. ◐ *province* NE Turkey
151 O12 **Karsakpay** *Kaz.* Qarsaqbay. Zhezkazgan, C Kazakhstan
95 L15 **Kärsämäki** Oulu, C Finland
Karsau *see* Kārsava
120 K9 **Kārsava** *Ger.* Karsau; *prev. Rus.* Korsovka. Ludza, E Latvia
152 A9 **Karshi** *Turkm.* Garshy. Balkanskiy Velayat, NW Turkmenistan
Karshi *see* Qarshi
Karshinskaya Step *see* Qarshi Chŭli
Karshinskiy Kanal *see* Qarshi Kanali
86 I5 **Karskiye Vorota, Proliv** *Eng.* Kara Strait. *strait* N Russian Federation
126 Gg5 **Karskoye More** *Eng.* Kara Sea. *sea* Arctic Ocean
95 L17 **Karstula** Keski-Suomi, C Finland
131 Q5 **Karsun** Ul'yanovskaya Oblast', W Russian Federation
125 E12 **Kartaly** Chelyabinskaya Oblast', C Russian Federation
20 E13 **Karthaus** Pennsylvania, NE USA
112 I7 **Kartuzy** Gdańsk, NW Poland
172 N10 **Karumai** Iwate, Honshū, C Japan
189 U4 **Karumba** Queensland, NE Australia
148 L10 **Kārūn** *var.* Rūd-e Kārūn. ⚟ SW Iran
94 K13 **Karungi** Norrbotten, N Sweden
94 K13 **Karunki** Lappi, N Finland
Kārūn, Rūd-e *see* Kārūn
161 H21 **Karūr** Tamil Nādu, SE India
95 K17 **Karvia** Turku-Pori, SW Finland
113 J17 **Karviná** *Ger.* Karwin, *Pol.* Karwina; *prev.* Nová Karvinná. Severní Morava, E Czech Republic
161 E17 **Kārwār** Karnātaka, W India
110 M7 **Karwendelgebirge** ▲ Austria/Germany
Karwin/Karwina *see* Karviná
117 I14 **Karyés** *var.* Karies. Ágion Óros, N Greece
126 Kk16 **Karymskoye** Chitinskaya Oblast', S Russian Federation
117 I19 **Kárystos** *var.* Káristos. Évvoia, C Greece
142 E17 **Kaş** Antalya, SW Turkey
41 Y14 **Kasaan** Prince of Wales Island, Alaska, USA
170 G14 **Kasai** Hyōgo, Honshū, SW Japan
81 K21 **Kasai** *var.* Cassai, Kassai. ⚟ Angola/Zaire
81 K22 **Kasai Occidental** *off.* Région Kasai Occidental. ◐ *region* S Zaire
81 L21 **Kasai Oriental** *off.* Région Kasai Oriental. ◐ *region* C Zaire
81 L24 **Kasaji** Shaba, S Zaire
171 Kk16 **Kasama** Ibaraki, Honshū, S Japan
84 L12 **Kasama** Northern, N Zambia
Kasan *see* Koson
85 H16 **Kasane** Chobe, NE Botswana
83 E23 **Kasanga** Rukwa, W Tanzania
81 G21 **Kasangulu** Bas-Zaïre, W Zaire
Kasansay *see* Kosonsoy
161 E20 **Kāsaragod** Kerala, SW India
Kasargen *see* Kasari
120 F13 **Kasari** *var.* Kasari Jõgi, *Ger.* Kasargen. ⚟ W Estonia
Kasari Jõgi *see* Kasari
15 K9 **Kasba Lake** ◎ Northwest Territories, NE Canada
Kaschau *see* Košice
170 Bb16 **Kaseda** Kagoshima, Kyūshū, SW Japan
85 I14 **Kasempa** North Western, NW Zambia
81 O24 **Kasenga** Shaba, SE Zaire
81 P17 **Kasenye** *var.* Kasenyi. Haut-Zaïre, NE Zaire
Kasenyi *see* Kasenye
83 E18 **Kasese** SW Uganda
81 O19 **Kasese** Maniema, E Zaire
158 J11 **Kāsganj** Uttar Pradesh, N India
149 U4 **Kashaf Rūd** ⚟ NE Iran
149 N7 **Kāshān** Eşfahān, C Iran
130 M10 **Kashary** Rostovskaya Oblast', SW Russian Federation
41 O12 **Kashegelok** Alaska, USA
Kashgar *see* Kashi
164 E7 **Kashi** *Chin.* Kaxgar, K'o-shih, *Uigh.* Kashgar. Xinjiang Uygur Zizhiqu, NW China
171 Gg16 **Kashihara** *var.* Kasihara. Nara, Honshū, SW Japan
171 Kk17 **Kashima** Ibaraki, Honshū, S Japan
170 C13 **Kashima** *var.* Kasima. Saga, Kyūshū, SW Japan
171 L16 **Kashima-nada** *gulf* S Japan
128 K15 **Kashin** Tverskaya Oblast', W Russian Federation
158 K10 **Kāshīpur** Uttar Pradesh, N India
130 L4 **Kashira** Moskovskaya Oblast', W Russian Federation
171 K17 **Kashiwa** *var.* Kasiwa. Chiba, Honshū, S Japan
171 Jj13 **Kashiwazaki** *var.* Kasiwazaki. Niigata, Honshū, C Japan
Kashkadar'inskaya Oblast' *see* Qashqadaryo Wiloyati
149 T5 **Kāshmar** *var.* Turshiz; *prev.* Solṭānābād, Torshiz. Khorāsān, NE Iran
Kashmir *see* Jammu and Kashmir
155 R12 **Kashmor** Sind, SE Pakistan
155 S5 **Kashmūnd Ghar** *Eng.* Kashmund Range. ▲ E Afghanistan
Kashmund Range *see* Kashmūnd Ghar
Kasi *see* Vārānasi
159 O12 **Kasia** Uttar Pradesh, N India
41 N12 **Kasigluk** Alaska, USA
Kasihara *see* Kashihara
41 R12 **Kasilof** Alaska, USA
Kasima *see* Kashima
Kasimkõj *see* General Toshevo
130 M4 **Kasimov** Ryazanskaya Oblast', W Russian Federation
81 P18 **Kasindi** Nord Kivu, E Zaire
175 Ss8 **Kasiruta, Pulau** *island* Kepulauan Bacan, E Indonesia
84 M12 **Kasitu** ⚟ N Malawi
176 V12 **Kasiui, Pulau** *island* Kepulauan Watubela, E Indonesia
Kasiwa *see* Kashiwa
Kasiwazaki *see* Kashiwazaki
32 L14 **Kaskaskia River** ⚟ Illinois, N USA
95 J17 **Kaskinen** *Swe.* Kaskö. Vaasa, W Finland
Kaskö *see* Kaskinen
Kas Kong *see* Kŏng, Kaôh
9 O17 **Kaslo** British Columbia, SW Canada
Kásmark *see* Kežmarok
174 M10 **Kasongan** Borneo, C Indonesia
81 N21 **Kasongo** Maniema, E Zaire
81 H22 **Kasongo-Lunda** Bandundu, SW Zaire
117 M24 **Kásos** *island* S Greece
Kasos Strait *see* Kasou, Stenó
117 M25 **Kasou, Stenó** *var.* Kasos Strait. *strait* Dodekánisos/Kríti, Greece, Aegean Sea
143 T10 **Kaspi** C Georgia
116 M8 **Kaspichan** Varnenska Oblast, NE Bulgaria
Kaspiy Mangy Oypaty *see* Caspian Depression
131 Q16 **Kaspiysk** Respublika Dagestan, SW Russian Federation
Kaspiyskiy *see* Lagan'
Kaspiyskoye More/Kaspiy Tengizi *see* Caspian Sea
Kassa *see* Košice
Kassai *see* Kasai
82 I9 **Kassala** Kassala, E Sudan
82 H9 **Kassala** ◐ *state* NE Sudan
117 G15 **Kassándra** *prev.* Pallíni; *anc.* Pallene. *peninsula* NE Greece
117 G15 **Kassándras, Ákra** *headland* N Greece
117 H15 **Kassándras, Kólpos** *var.* Kólpos Toronaíos. *gulf* N Greece
145 Y11 **Kassārah** E Iraq
103 I15 **Kassel** *prev.* Cassel. Hessen, C Germany
76 M6 **Kasserine** *var.* Al Qaşrayn. W Tunisia
12 J14 **Kasshabog Lake** ◎ Ontario, SE Canada
145 O5 **Kassīr, Sabkhat al** ◎ E Syria
31 W10 **Kasson** Minnesota, N USA
117 C17 **Kassópi** *site of ancient city* Ípeiros, W Greece
117 N24 **Kastállou, Ákra** *headland* Kárpathos, SE Greece
142 I11 **Kastamonu** *var.* Castamoni, Kastamuni. Kastamonu, N Turkey
142 I10 **Kastamonu** *var.* Kastamuni. ◐ *province* N Turkey
Kastamuni *see* Kastamonu
117 E14 **Kastaneá** Kentrikí Makedonía, N Greece
117 H24 **Kastélli** Kríti, Greece, E Mediterranean Sea
Kastellórizon *see* Megísti
97 N21 **Kastlösa** Kalmar, S Sweden
117 D14 **Kastoría** Dytikí Makedonía, N Greece
130 K7 **Kastornoye** Kurskaya Oblast', W Russian Federation
117 I21 **Kástro** Sífnos, Kykládes, Greece, Aegean Sea
97 J23 **Kastrup** ✕ (København) København, E Denmark
121 Q17 **Kastsyukovichy** *Rus.* Kostyukovichi. Mahilyowskaya Voblasts', E Belorussia
121 O18 **Kastsyukowka** *Rus.* Kostyukovka. Homyel'skaya Voblasts', SE Belorussia
170 Cc12 **Kasuga** Fukuoka, Kyūshū, SW Japan
171 I15 **Kasugai** Aichi, Honshū, SW Japan
83 E21 **Kasulu** Kigoma, W Tanzania
171 Gg13 **Kasumi** Hyōgo, Honshū, SW Japan
171 Kk16 **Kasumiga-ura** ◎ Honshū, S Japan
131 R17 **Kasumkent** Respublika Dagestan, SW Russian Federation
84 M13 **Kasungu** Central, C Malawi
155 W9 **Kasūr** Punjab, E Pakistan
85 G14 **Kataba** Western, W Zambia
21 R4 **Katahdin, Mount** ▲ Maine, NE USA
81 M20 **Katako-Kombe** Kasai Oriental, C Zaire
41 T12 **Katalla** Alaska, USA
Katana *see* Qaţanā
81 L24 **Katanga** *off.* Region du Katanga *prev.* Shaba ◐ region SE Congo (Zaire)
126 J12 **Katanga** ⚟ C Russian Federation
160 J11 **Katāngi** Madhya Pradesh, C India
188 J13 **Katanning** Western Australia
Katawaz *see* Zarghūn Shahr
157 Q22 **Katchall Island** *island* Nicobar Islands, India, NE Indian Ocean
117 F14 **Kateríni** Kentrikí Makedonía, N Greece
119 P7 **Katerynopil'** Cherkas'ka Oblast', C Ukraine
178 Gg3 **Katha** Sagaing, N Burma
189 P2 **Katherine** Northern Territory, N Australia
160 B11 **Kāthiāwār Peninsula** *peninsula* W India
159 P11 **Kathmandu** *prev.* Kantipur. ● (Nepal) Central, C Nepal
158 H7 **Kathua** Jammu and Kashmir, NW India
78 L12 **Kati** Koulikoro, SW Mali
159 R13 **Katihār** Bihār, NE India
192 N7 **Katikati** Bay of Plenty, North Island, NZ
85 H16 **Katima Mulilo** Caprivi, NE Namibia
79 N15 **Katiola** C Ivory Coast
203 V10 **Katiu** *atoll* Îles Tuamotu, C French Polynesia
119 N12 **Katlabukh, Ozero** ◎ SW Ukraine
41 P14 **Katmai, Mount** ▲ Alaska, USA
160 J9 **Katni** Madhya Pradesh, C India
117 D19 **Káto Achaïa** *var.* Kato Ahaia, Káto Akhaía. Dytikí Ellás, S Greece
Kato Ahaia/Káto Akhaía *see* Káto Achaïa
124 Nn3 **Kato Lakatámeia** *var.* Kato Lakatamia. C Cyprus
Kato Lakatamia *see* Kato Lakatámeia
81 N22 **Katompi** Shaba, SE Zaire
85 K14 **Katondwe** Lusaka, C Zambia
116 H12 **Káto Nevrokópi** *prev.* Káto Nevrokópion. Anatolikí Makedonía kai Thráki, NE Greece
Káto Nevrokópion *see* Káto Nevrokópi
83 E18 **Katonga** ⚟ S Uganda
117 F15 **Káto Ólympos** ▲ C Greece
117 D17 **Katoúna** Dytikí Ellás, C Greece
117 E19 **Káto Vlasiá** Dytikí Makedonía, S Greece
113 J16 **Katowice** *Ger.* Kattowitz. Katowice, S Poland
113 J16 **Katowice** *off.* Województwo Katowickie, *Ger.* Kattowitz. ◐ *province* S Poland
Katowickie, Województwo *see* Katowice
159 S15 **Kātoya** West Bengal, NE India
142 E16 **Katrancık Dağı** ▲ SW Turkey
97 N16 **Katrineholm** Södermanland, C Sweden
xliii I18 **Katrine, Loch** ◎ C Scotland, UK
79 V12 **Katsina** Katsina, N Nigeria
79 U12 **Katsina** ◐ *state* N Nigeria
69 P8 **Katsina Ala** ⚟ S Nigeria
170 C11 **Katsumoto** Nagasaki, Iki, SW Japan
171 L16 **Katsuta** *var.* Katuta. Ibaraki, Honshū, S Japan
171 K17 **Katsuura** *var.* Katuura. Chiba, Honshū, S Japan
171 I14 **Katsuyama** *var.* Katuyama. Fukui, Honshū, SW Japan
170 Ff13 **Katsuyama** Okayama, Honshū, SW Japan
Kattakurgan *see* Kattaqŭrghon
153 N11 **Kattaqŭrghon** *Rus.* Kattakurgan. Samarqand Wiloyati, C Uzbekistan
117 O23 **Kattavía** Ródos, Dodekánisos, Greece, Aegean Sea
97 I21 **Kattegat** *Dan.* Kattegatt. *strait* N Europe
Kattegatt *see* Kattegat
97 P19 **Katthammarsvik** Gotland, SE Sweden
Kattowitz *see* Katowice
127 N17 **Katun'** ⚟ S Russian Federation
Katuta *see* Katsuta
Katuura *see* Katsuura
Katuyama *see* Katsuyama
Katwijk *see* Katwijk aan Zee
100 G11 **Katwijk aan Zee** *var.* Katwijk. Zuid-Holland, W Netherlands
40 B8 **Kauai** *Haw.* Kaua'i. *island* Hawaiian Islands, Hawaii, USA, C Pacific Ocean
40 C8 **Kauai Channel** *channel* Hawaii, USA, C Pacific Ocean
175 Ss11 **Kaubalatmada, Gunung** *var.* Kaplamada. ▲ Pulau Buru, E Indonesia
203 U10 **Kauehi** *atoll* Îles Tuamotu, C French Polynesia
Kauen *see* Kaunas
103 K24 **Kaufbeuren** Bayern, S Germany
27 U7 **Kaufman** Texas, SW USA
103 I15 **Kaufungen** Hessen, C Germany
95 K17 **Kauhajoki** Vaasa, W Finland
95 K16 **Kauhava** Vaasa, W Finland
32 M7 **Kaukauna** Wisconsin, N USA
94 L11 **Kaukonen** Lappi, N Finland
40 A8 **Kaulakahi Channel** *channel* Hawaii, USA, C Pacific Ocean
40 E9 **Kaunakakai** Molokai, Hawaii, USA, C Pacific Ocean
40 F12 **Kauna Point** *headland* Hawaii, USA, C Pacific Ocean
120 F13 **Kaunas** *Ger.* Kauen, *Pol.* Kowno; *prev. Rus.* Kovno. Kaunas, C Lithuania
194 H10 **Kaup** East Sepik, NW PNG
79 U12 **Kaura Namoda** Sokoto, NW Nigeria
Kaushany *see* Căuşeni
95 K16 **Kaustinen** Vaasa, W Finland
175 T7 **Kau, Teluk** *bay* Pulau Halmahera, E Indonesia
101 M23 **Kautenbach** Diekirch, NE Luxembourg
94 K10 **Kautokeino** Finnmark, N Norway
Kavadar *see* Kavadarci
115 P19 **Kavadarci** *Turk.* Kavadar. C FYR Macedonia
Kavaja *see* Kavajë
115 K20 **Kavajë** *It.* Cavaia, Kavaja. Tiranë, W Albania
116 M13 **Kavak Çayı** ⚟ NW Turkey
Kavakli *see* Topolovgrad
116 I13 **Kavála** *prev.* Kaválla. Anatolikí Makedonía kai Thráki, NE Greece
116 I13 **Kaválas, Kólpos** *gulf* Aegean Sea, NE Mediterranean Sea
127 Nn17 **Kavalerovo** Primorskiy Kray, SE Russian Federation
161 J17 **Kāvali** Andhra Pradesh, E India
Kaválla *see* Kavála
Kavango *see* Cubango/Okavango
161 C21 **Kavaratti** Lakshadweep, SW India
116 O8 **Kavarna** Varnenska Oblast, NE Bulgaria
120 G12 **Kavarskas** Anykščiai, E Lithuania
78 I13 **Kavendou** ▲ C Guinea
Kavengo *see* Cubango/Okavango
161 F20 **Kāveri** *var.* Cauvery. ⚟ S India
195 N9 **Kavieng** *var.* Kaewieng. NE PNG
85 H16 **Kavimba** Chobe, NE Botswana
85 I16 **Kavingu** Southern, S Zambia
149 Q6 **Kavīr, Dasht-e** *var.* Great Salt Desert. *salt pan* N Iran
Kavirondo Gulf *see* Winam Gulf
Kavkaz *see* Caucasus
97 K23 **Kävlinge** Malmöhus, S Sweden
197 I15 **Kavukavu Reef** *var.* Beqa Barrier Reef, Cakaubalavu Reef. *reef* Viti Levu, SW Fiji
84 G12 **Kavungo** Moxico, E Angola
171 M10 **Kawabe** Akita, Honshū, C Japan
171 K15 **Kawagoe** Saitama, Honshū, S Japan
171 K16 **Kawaguchi** *var.* Kawaguti. Saitama, Honshū, S Japan
Kawaguti *see* Kawaguchi
172 N11 **Kawai** Iwate, Honshū, C Japan
40 A8 **Kawaihoa Point** *headland* Niihau, Hawaii, USA, C Pacific Ocean
192 K3 **Kawakawa** Northland, North Island, NZ
84 I13 **Kawama** North Western, NW Zambia
84 K11 **Kawambwa** Luapula, N Zambia
170 F14 **Kawanoe** Ehime, Shikoku, SW Japan
160 K11 **Kawardha** Madhya Pradesh, C India
12 I14 **Kawartha Lakes** ◎ Ontario, SE Canada
171 K17 **Kawasaki** Kanagawa, Honshū, S Japan
175 T9 **Kawassi** Pulau Obi, E Indonesia
172 N8 **Kawauchi** Aomori, Honshū, C Japan
192 L5 **Kawau Island** *island* N NZ
192 N10 **Kaweka Range** ▲ North Island, NZ
Kawelecht *see* Puhja
176 Z13 **Kawentinkim** Irian Jaya, E Indonesia
192 O8 **Kawerau** Bay of Plenty, North Island, NZ
192 L8 **Kawhia** Waikato, North Island, NZ
192 K8 **Kawhia Harbour** *inlet* North Island, NZ
37 V8 **Kawich Peak** ▲ Nevada, W USA
37 V9 **Kawich Range** ▲ Nevada, W USA
12 G12 **Kawigamog Lake** ◎ Ontario, S Canada
175 Rr3 **Kawio, Kepulauan** *island group* N Indonesia
178 Gg9 **Kawkareik** Karen State, S Burma
29 O8 **Kaw Lake** ⊠ Oklahoma, C USA
177 G3 **Kawlin** Sagaing, N Burma
Kawm Umbū *see* Kôm Ombo
Kawthule State *see* Karen State
Kaxgar *see* Kashi
164 D7 **Kaxgar He** ⚟ NW China
164 J5 **Kax He** ⚟ NW China
79 P12 **Kaya** C Burkina
178 Gg7 **Kayah State** ◐ *state* C Burma
126 J7 **Kayak** Taymyrskiy (Dolgano-Nenetskiy) Avtonomnyy Okrug, N Russian Federation
41 T12 **Kayak Island** *island* Alaska, USA
116 M11 **Kayalıköy Barajı** ⊠ NW Turkey
177 G8 **Kayan** Yangon, SW Burma
161 G23 **Kāyankulam** Kerala, SW India
175 N6 **Kayan, Sungai** *prev.* Kajan. ⚟ Borneo, C Indonesia
150 F14 **Kaydak, Sor** *salt flat* SW Kazakhstan
Kaydanovo *see* Dzyarzhynsk
39 N9 **Kayenta** Arizona, SW USA
78 J11 **Kayes** Kayes, W Mali
78 J11 **Kayes** ◐ *region* SW Mali
Kayin State *see* Karen State
151 U10 **Kaynar** *var.* Kajnar. Semipalatinsk, E Kazakhstan
Kaynary *see* Căinari
85 H15 **Kayoya** Western, W Zambia
Kayrakkum *see* Qayroqqum
Kayrakkumskoye Vodokhranilishche *see* Qayroqqum, Obanbori
142 K14 **Kayseri** *var.* Kaisaria; *anc.* Caesarea Mazaca, Mazaca. Kayseri, C Turkey
142 K14 **Kayseri** *var.* Kaisaria. ◐ *province* C Turkey
38 L2 **Kaysville** Utah, W USA
126 Hh8 **Kayyerkan** Taymyrskiy (Dolgano-Nenetskiy) Avtonomnyy Okrug, N Russian Federation
Kayyngdy *see* Kaindy
12 L11 **Kazabazua** Québec, SE Canada
12 L12 **Kazabazua** ⚟ Québec, SE Canada
126 M7 **Kazach'ye** Respublika Sakha (Yakutiya), NE Russian Federation
Kazakdar'ya *see* Qozoqdaryo
152 E9 **Kazakhlyshor, Solonchak** *var.* Solonchak Shorkazakhly. *salt marsh* NW Turkmenistan
Kazakhskaya SSR/Kazakh Soviet Socialist Republic *see* Kazakhstan
151 R9 **Kazakhskiy Melkosopochnik** *Eng.* Kazakh Uplands, Kirghiz Steppe, *Kaz.* Saryarqa. *uplands* C Kazakhstan
150 L12 **Kazakhstan** *off.* Republic of Kazakhstan, *var.* Kazakstan, *Kaz.* Qazaqstan, Qazaqstan Respublikasy; *prev.* Kazakh Soviet Socialist Republic, *Rus.* Kazakhskaya SSR. ◆ *republic* C Asia
Kazakh Uplands *see* Kazakhskiy Melkosopochnik
Kazakstan *see* Kazakhstan
150 L14 **Kazalinsk** Kzyl-Orda, S Kazakhstan
131 R4 **Kazan'** Respublika Tatarstan, W Russian Federation
131 R4 **Kazan'** ✕ Respublika Tatarstan, W Russian Federation
15 K8 **Kazan** ⚟ Northwest Territories, NW Canada
Kazandzhik *see* Gazandzhyk
119 R8 **Kazanka** Mykolayivs'ka Oblast', S Ukraine
Kazanketken *see* Qizqetkan
Kazanlik *see* Kazanlŭk
116 J9 **Kazanlŭk** *prev.* Kazanlik. Khaskovska Oblast, C Bulgaria
172 T17 **Kazan-rettō** *Eng.* Volcano Islands. *island group* SE Japan
119 T9 **Kazanskoye** Tyumenskaya Oblast', C Russian Federation
119 V12 **Kazantip, Mys** *headland* S Ukraine
153 U9 **Kazarman** Narynskaya Oblast', C Kyrgyzstan
Kazatin *see* Kozyatyn
Kazbegi *see* Kazbek
Kazbegi *see* Qazbegi
143 T9 **Kazbek** *var.* Kazbegi, *Geor.* Mqinvartsveri. ▲ N Georgia
84 M13 **Kazembe** Eastern, NE Zambia
149 N11 **Kāzerūn** Fārs, S Iran
129 R12 **Kazhym** Respublika Komi, NW Russian Federation
Kazi Ahmad *see* Qāzi Ahmad
Kazi Magomed *see* Qazimämmäd
142 H16 **Kazımkarabekir** Karaman, S Turkey
113 M20 **Kazincbarcika** Borsod-Abaúj-Zemplén, NE Hungary
121 H17 **Kazlowshchyna** *Pol.* Kozlowszczyzna, *Rus.* Kozlovshchina. Hrodzyenskaya Voblasts', W Belorussia
121 E14 **Kazlų Rūda** Marijampolė, S Lithuania
150 E9 **Kaztalovka** Zapadnyy Kazakhstan, W Kazakhstan
81 K22 **Kazumba** Kasai Occidental, S Zaire
171 Mm10 **Kazuno** Akita, Honshū, C Japan
Kazvin *see* Qazvīn
120 J12 **Kaz'yany** *Rus.* Koz'yany. Vitsyebskaya Voblasts', NW Belorussia
125 Ff9 **Kazym** ⚟ N Russian Federation
112 H10 **Kcynia** *Ger.* Exin. Bydgoszcz, W Poland
117 I20 **Kéa** Kéa, Kykládes, Greece, Aegean Sea
117 I20 **Kéa** *prev.* Kéos, *anc.* Ceos. *island* Kykládes, Greece, Aegean Sea
40 H11 **Keaau** *Haw.* Kea'au. Hawaii, USA, C Pacific Ocean
xliv G6 **Keadew** Roscommon, C Ireland
xliv K5 **Keady** Armagh, S Northern Ireland, UK
40 F11 **Keahole Point** *headland* Hawaii, USA, C Pacific Ocean
40 G12 **Kealakekua** Hawaii, USA, C Pacific Ocean
40 H11 **Kea, Mauna** ▲ Hawaii, USA, C Pacific Ocean
39 N10 **Keams** Arizona, SW USA
Kéamu *see* Anatom
31 O16 **Kearney** Nebraska, C USA
38 L3 **Kearns** Utah, W USA
117 H20 **Kéas, Stenó** *strait* SE Greece
143 O14 **Keban Barajı** *dam* C Turkey
143 O14 **Keban Barajı** ⊠ C Turkey
79 S13 **Kebbi** ◐ *state* NW Nigeria
78 G10 **Kébémèr** NW Senegal
76 M7 **Kebili** *var.* Qibilī. C Tunisia
144 H4 **Kebir, Nahr el** ⚟ NW Syria
82 A10 **Kebkabiya** Northern Darfur, W Sudan
94 I11 **Kebnekaise** ▲ N Sweden
83 M14 **K'ebrī Dehar** SE Ethiopia
154 K15 **Kech** ⚟ SW Pakistan
8 K10 **Kechika** ⚟ British Columbia, W Canada
113 K23 **Kecskemét** Bács-Kiskun, C Hungary
174 Gg2 **Kedah** ◐ *state* Peninsular Malaysia
120 F12 **Kėdainiai** Kėdainiai, C Lithuania
Kedder *see* Kehra
11 N13 **Kedgwick** New Brunswick, SE Canada
174 L15 **Kediri** Jawa, C Indonesia
176 Y10 **Kedir Sarmi** Irian Jaya, E Indonesia
169 V7 **Kedong** Heilongjiang, NE China
78 I12 **Kédougou** SE Senegal
126 Gg13 **Kedrovyy** Tomskaya Oblast', C Russian Federation
113 H16 **Kędzierzyn-Kozle** *Ger.* Heydebrech. Opole, SW Poland
xxxix R3 **Keelby** Lincolnshire, E England, UK
14 G6 **Keele** ⚟ Northwest Territories, NW Canada
8 K6 **Keele Peak** ▲ Yukon Territory, NW Canada
Keelung *see* Chilung
21 N10 **Keene** New Hampshire, NE USA
101 H17 **Keerbergen** Vlaams Brabant, C Belgium
85 E21 **Keetmanshoop** Karas, S Namibia
10 A11 **Keewatin** Ontario, S Canada
31 V4 **Keewatin** Minnesota, N USA
15 K7 **Keewatin** *off.* District of Keewatin. ◐ *district* Northwest Territories, NE Canada
117 B18 **Kefallinía** *var.* Kefallonía. *island* Iónioi Nísoi, Greece, C Mediterranean Sea
Kefallonía *see* Kefallinía
117 M22 **Kéfalos** Kos, Dodekánisos, Greece, Aegean Sea
175 Rr17 **Kefamenanu** Timor, C Indonesia
144 F10 **Kefar Sava** Central, C Israel
Kefe *see* Feodosiya
79 V15 **Keffi** Plateau, C Nigeria
94 H4 **Keflavik** ✕ (Reykjavík) Reykjanes, W Iceland
94 H4 **Keflavík** Reykjanes, W Iceland
Kegalee *see* Kegalla
161 J25 **Kegalla** *var.* Kegalee, Kegalle. Sabaragamuwa Province, C Sri Lanka
Kegalle *see* Kegalla
152 H7 **Kegayli** *Rus.* Kegeyli. Qoraqalpoghiston Respublikasi, W Uzbekistan
Kegel *see* Keila
151 W16 **Kegen** Almaty, SE Kazakhstan
Kegeyli *see* Kegayli
xxxix N8 **Kegworth** Leicestershire, C England, UK
103 F22 **Kehl** Baden-Württemberg, SW Germany
120 H3 **Kehra** *Ger.* Kedder. Harjumaa, NW Estonia
119 U6 **Kehychivka** Kharkivs'ka Oblast', E Ukraine
xli Q13 **Keighley** Bradford, N England, UK
Kei Islands *see* Kai, Kepulauan
Keijō *see* Sŏul
120 G3 **Keila** *Ger.* Kegel. Harjumaa, NW Estonia
Keilberg *see* Klínovec
xliii F19 **Keillmore** Argyll and Bute, W Scotland, UK
85 F23 **Keimoes** Northern Cape, W South Africa
Keina/Keinis *see* Käina
xliii K23 **Keir Mill** Dumfries and Galloway, SW Scotland, UK
176 Yy14 **Keisak** Irian Jaya, E Indonesia
Keishū *see* Kyŏngju
xlii M6 **Keiss** Highland, N Scotland, UK
79 T11 **Keïta** Tahoua, C Niger
80 J12 **Kéïta, Bahr** *var.* Doka. ⚟ S Chad
95 M16 **Keitele** ◎ C Finland
xlii M11 **Keith** Moray, NE Scotland, UK
190 K10 **Keith** South Australia
xliii N15 **Keithock** Angus, E Scotland, UK
28 K3 **Keith Sebelius Lake** ⊠ Kansas, C USA
34 G11 **Keizer** Oregon, NW USA
40 A8 **Kekaha** Kauai, Hawaii, USA, C Pacific Ocean
153 U10 **Këk-Art** *prev.* Alaykel', Alay-Kuu. Oshskaya Oblast', SW Kyrgyzstan
153 W10 **Këk-Aygyr** *var.* Keyagyr. Narynskaya Oblast', C Kyrgyzstan
153 V9 **Këk-Dzhar** Narynskaya Oblast', C Kyrgyzstan
12 L8 **Kekek** ⚟ Québec, SE Canada
193 K15 **Kekerengu** Canterbury, South Island, NZ
113 L21 **Kékes** ▲ N Hungary
175 Rr17 **Kekneno, Gunung** ▲ Timor, S Indonesia
153 S9 **Këk-Tash** *Kir.* Kök-Tash. Dzhalal-Abadskaya Oblast', W Kyrgyzstan
83 M15 **K'elafo** SE Ethiopia
175 O6 **Kelai, Sungai** ⚟ Borneo, N Indonesia
Kelamayi *see* Karamay
Kelang *see* Klang
174 H3 **Kelantan** ◐ *state* Peninsular Malaysia
Kelantan *see* Kelantan, Sungai
174 H3 **Kelantan, Sungai** *var.* Kelantan. ⚟ Peninsular Malaysia
Kelat *see* Kalāt
Këlcyra *see* Këlcyrë
115 L22 **Këlcyrë** *var.* Këlcyra. Gjirokastër, S Albania
xli P10 **Keld** North Yorkshire, N England, UK
xxxix O6 **Kelham** Nottinghamshire, C England, UK
152 L14 **Kelifskiy Uzboy** *salt marsh* E Turkmenistan
143 O12 **Kelkit** Gümüşhane, NE Turkey
142 M12 **Kelkit Çayı** ⚟ N Turkey
xliii N17 **Kellas** Angus, E Scotland, UK
79 W11 **Kellé** Zinder, S Niger
81 G18 **Kéllé** Cuvette, W Congo
151 P7 **Kellerovka** Kokshetau, N Kazakhstan
15 H1 **Kellett, Cape** *headland* Banks Island, Northwest Territories, NW Canada
33 S11 **Kelleys Island** *island* Ohio, N USA
35 N8 **Kellogg** Idaho, NW USA
94 M12 **Kelloselkä** Lappi, N Finland
xliv I6 **Kells** Kilkenny, S Ireland
xliv J7 **Kells** *Ir.* Ceanannas. Meath, E Ireland
120 E12 **Kelmė** Kelmė, C Lithuania
101 M19 **Kelmis** *var.* La Calamine. Liège, E Belgium
80 H12 **Kélo** Tandjilé, SW Chad
85 I14 **Kelongwa** North Western, NW Zambia
9 N17 **Kelowna** British Columbia, SW Canada
9 X12 **Kelsey** Manitoba, C Canada
36 M6 **Kelseyville** California, W USA
xliii O21 **Kelso** The Borders, SE Scotland, UK
34 G10 **Kelso** Washington, NW USA
205 W15 **Keltie, Cape** *headland* Antarctica
Keltsy *see* Kielce
xliii L19 **Kelty** Fife, E Scotland, UK
174 Hh6 **Keluang** *var.* Kluang. Johor, Peninsular Malaysia
174 I8 **Kelume** Pulau Lingga, W Indonesia
xxxvii W7 **Kelvedon** Essex, SE England, UK
xxxvii V8 **Kelvedon Hatch** Essex, SE England, UK
9 U15 **Kelvington** Saskatchewan, S Canada
128 J7 **Kem'** Respublika Kareliya, NW Russian Federation
128 I7 **Kem'** ⚟ NW Russian Federation
143 O13 **Kemah** Erzincan, E Turkey
143 N13 **Kemaliye** Erzincan, C Turkey
Kemaman *see* Cukai
Kemanlar *see* Isperikh
8 K14 **Kemano** British Columbia, SW Canada
Kemarat *see* Khemmarat
175 Qq9 **Kembani** Pulau Peleng, N Indonesia
xxxvii N8 **Kemble** Gloucestershire, C England, UK
142 F17 **Kemer** Antalya, SW Turkey
126 H14 **Kemerovo** *prev.* Shcheglovsk. Kemerovskaya Oblast', C Russian Federation
126 H14 **Kemerovskaya Oblast'** ◐ *province* S Russian Federation
94 L13 **Kemi** Lappi, NW Finland
94 M12 **Kemijärvi** *Swe.* Kemiträsk. Lappi, N Finland
94 M12 **Kemijärvi** ◎ N Finland
94 L13 **Kemijoki** ⚟ NW Finland
153 V7 **Kemin** *prev.* Bystrovka. Chuyskaya Oblast', N Kyrgyzstan
94 L13 **Keminmaa** Lappi, NW Finland
Kemins Island *see* Nikumaroro
Kemiö *see* Kimito
Kemiträsk *see* Kemijärvi
131 P5 **Kemlya** Respublika Mordoviya, W Russian Federation
101 B18 **Kemmel** West-Vlaanderen, W Belgium
35 S16 **Kemmerer** Wyoming, C USA
Kemmuna *see* Comino
xlii O13 **Kemnay** Aberdeenshire, NE Scotland, UK
80 I13 **Kémo** ◐ *prefecture* S Central African Republic
27 U7 **Kemp** Texas, SW USA
95 L14 **Kempele** Oulu, C Finland
103 D15 **Kempen** Nordrhein-Westfalen, W Germany
27 Q5 **Kemp, Lake** ◎ Texas, SW USA
205 W5 **Kemp Land** *physical region* Antarctica
27 S9 **Kempner** Texas, SW USA
46 H3 **Kemp's Bay** Andros Island, W Bahamas
xxxviii J13 **Kempsey** Worcestershire, W England, UK
191 U6 **Kempsey** New South Wales, SE Australia
xxxvii S6 **Kempston** Bedfordshire, E England, UK
103 J24 **Kempten** Bayern, S Germany
13 N9 **Kempt, Lac** ◎ Québec, SE Canada
191 P17 **Kempton** Tasmania, SE Australia
160 J9 **Ken** ⚟ C India
41 R12 **Kenai** Alaska, USA
1 D5 **Kenai Mountains** ▲ Alaska, USA
41 R12 **Kenai Peninsula** *peninsula* Alaska, USA
23 V11 **Kenansville** North Carolina, SE USA
124 Pp15 **Kenâyis, Râs el-** *headland* N Egypt
xli N11 **Kendal** Cumbria, NW England, UK
25 Y16 **Kendall** Florida, SE USA
15 L6 **Kendall, Cape** *headland* Northwest Territories, E Canada
20 J15 **Kendall Park** New Jersey, NE USA
33 Q11 **Kendallville** Indiana, N USA
175 Qq12 **Kendari** Sulawesi, C Indonesia
174 L10 **Kendawangan** Borneo, C Indonesia
174 L15 **Kendeng, Pegunungan** ▲ Jawa, S Indonesia
160 O12 **Kendrāpara** *var.* Kendrāparha. Orissa, E India
Kendrāparha *see* Kendrāpara
160 O11 **Kendujhargarh** *prev.* Keonjihargarh. Orissa, E India
27 S13 **Kenedy** Texas, SW USA
152 E13 **Kënekesir** *Turkm.* Könekesir. Balkanskiy Velayat, W Turkmenistan
78 J15 **Kenema** SE Sierra Leone
31 P16 **Kenesaw** Nebraska, C USA
152 G8 **Këneurgench** *Turkm.* Köneürgench; *prev.* Kunya-Urgench. Dashkhovuzskiy Velayat, N Turkmenistan
xxxv H15 **Kenfig** Bridgend, S Wales, UK
81 H21 **Kenge** Bandundu, SW Zaire
Kengen *see* Kangen
178 Hh5 **Keng Tung** *var.* Kentung. Shan State, E Burma
85 F23 **Kenhardt** Northern Cape, W South Africa
78 J12 **Kéniéba** Kayes, W Mali
xxxviii E16 **Kenilworth** Warwickshire, C England, UK
Kenimekh *see* Konimekh
175 Nn3 **Keningau** Sabah, East Malaysia
76 F6 **Kénitra** *prev.* Port-Lyautey. NW Morocco
xliii J24 **Ken, Loch** ◎ SW Scotland, UK
23 V9 **Kenly** North Carolina, SE USA
xliv D14 **Kenmare** *Ir.* Neidín. Kerry, S Ireland
30 L2 **Kenmare** North Dakota, N USA
xliv B14 **Kenmare River** *Ir.* An Ribhéar. *inlet* NE Atlantic Ocean
xliii K16 **Kenmore** Perth and Kinross, C Scotland, UK
20 D10 **Kenmore** New York, NE USA
xliii F20 **Kennacraig** Argyll and Bute, W Scotland, UK
27 W8 **Kennard** Texas, SW USA
31 N10 **Kennebec** South Dakota, N USA
21 Q7 **Kennebec River** ⚟ Maine, NE USA
21 P9 **Kennebunk** Maine, NE USA
41 R13 **Kennedy Entrance** *strait* Alaska, USA
177 Ff3 **Kennedy Peak** ▲ W Burma
24 K9 **Kenner** Louisiana, S USA
xxxvii O10 **Kennet** ⚟ S England, UK
xxxvii O10 **Kennet and Avon Canal** *canal* S England, UK
xlii N12 **Kennethmont** Aberdeenshire, NE Scotland, UK
188 I8 **Kenneth Range** ▲ Western Australia
29 Y9 **Kennett** Missouri, C USA
20 I16 **Kennett Square** Pennsylvania, NE USA
34 K10 **Kennewick** Washington, NW USA
xxxvi H14 **Kennford** Devon, SW England, UK
xxxix W11 **Kenninghall** Norfolk, E England, UK
xxxvii X11 **Kennington** Kent, SE England, UK
xxxvi D8 **Kennington** Lambeth, SE England, UK
10 E11 **Kenogami** ⚟ Ontario, S Canada
13 Q7 **Kénogami, Lac** ◎ Québec, SE Canada
12 G8 **Kenogami Lake** Ontario, S Canada
12 F7 **Kenogamissi Lake** ◎ Ontario, S Canada
8 I6 **Keno Hill** Yukon Territory, NW Canada
10 A11 **Kenora** Ontario, S Canada
33 N9 **Kenosha** Wisconsin, N USA
xlii D12 **Kensaleyre** Highland, NW Scotland, UK
xxxvi C7 **Kensington** *London borough capital* Kensington and Chelsea, SE England, UK
11 P14 **Kensington** Prince Edward Island, SE Canada
28 L3 **Kensington** Kansas, C USA
xxxiv K16 **Kensington and Chelsea** *var.* Royal Borough of Kensington and Chelsea. ◐ *London borough* SE England, UK
xxxvii W11 **Kent** ◐ *county* SE England, UK
xl M10 **Kent** ⚟ NW England, UK
34 H8 **Kent** Oregon, NW USA
26 J9 **Kent** Texas, SW USA
34 H11 **Kent** Washington, NW USA
151 P16 **Kentau** Yuzhnyy Kazakhstan, S Kazakhstan
xxxix U11 **Kentford** Suffolk, E England, UK
191 P14 **Kent Group** *island group* Tasmania, SE Australia
xxxvi G11 **Kentisbury** Devon, SW England, UK
xxxvi C6 **Kentish Town** Camden, SE England, UK
33 N12 **Kentland** Indiana, N USA
xxxvi A6 **Kenton** Harrow, SE England, UK
33 R12 **Kenton** Ohio, N USA
15 J4 **Kent Peninsula** *peninsula* Northwest Territories, N Canada
117 F14 **Kentrikí Makedonía** *Eng.* Macedonia Central. ◐ *region* N Greece
22 J6 **Kentucky** *off.* Commonwealth of Kentucky; also known as The Bluegrass State. ◐ *state* C USA
22 H8 **Kentucky Lake** ⊠ Kentucky/Tennessee, S USA
Kentung *see* Keng Tung
11 P15 **Kentville** Nova Scotia, SE Canada
24 K8 **Kentwood** Louisiana, S USA
33 P9 **Kentwood** Michigan, N USA
83 H17 **Kenya** *off.* Republic of Kenya. ◆ *republic* E Africa
Kenya, Mount *see* Kirinyaga
174 Hh3 **Kenyir, Tasik** *var.* Tasek Kenyir. ◎ Peninsular Malaysia
31 W10 **Kenyon** Minnesota, N USA
31 Y16 **Keokuk** Iowa, C USA
xlii H6 **Keoldale** Highland, NW Scotland, UK
Keonjihargarh *see* Kendujhargarh
Kéos *see* Kéa
31 X16 **Keosauqua** Iowa, C USA
31 X15 **Keota** Iowa, C USA
23 O11 **Keowee, Lake** ⊠ South Carolina, SE USA

◆ Country
● Country Capital
◇ Dependent Territory
○ Dependent Territory Capital
◐ Administrative Region
✕ International Airport
▲ Mountain
▲ Mountain Range
⛰ Volcano
⚟ River
◎ Lake
⊠ Reservoir

KEPA – KILKEE

128 I7 **Kepa** *var.* Kepe. Respublika Kareliya, NW Russian Federation
Kepe *see* Kepa
201 O13 **Kepirohi Falls** *waterfall* Pohnpei, E Micronesia
193 B22 **Kepler Mountains** ▲ South Island, NZ
113 I14 **Kępno** Kalisz, C Poland
67 C24 **Keppel Island** *island* N Falkland Islands
Keppel Island *see* Niuatoputapu
67 C23 **Keppel Sound** *sound* N Falkland Islands
142 D12 **Kepsut** Balıkesir, NW Turkey
176 W12 **Kerai** Irian Jaya, E Indonesia
Kerak *see* Al Karak
161 F22 **Kerala** ◆ *state* S India
194 H10 **Keram** ≈ N PNG
172 O14 **Kerama-rettō** *island group* SW Japan
191 N10 **Kerang** Victoria, SE Australia
Kerasunt *see* Giresun
117 H19 **Keratéa** *var.* Keratea. Attikí, C Greece
95 M19 **Kerava** *Swe.* Kervo. Uusimaa, S Finland
Kerbala/Kerbela *see* Karbalā'
34 F15 **Kerby** Oregon, NW USA
119 W12 **Kerch** *Rus.* Kerch'. Respublika Krym, SE Ukraine
Kerchens'ka Protska/Kerchenskiy Proliv *see* Kerch Strait
119 V13 **Kerchens'kyy Pivostriv** *peninsula* S Ukraine
124 R4 **Kerch Strait** *var.* Bosporus Cimmerius, Enikale Strait, *Rus.* Kerchenskiy Proliv, *Ukr.* Kerchens'ka Protska. *strait* Black Sea/Sea of Azov
158 K8 **Kerdārnāth** Uttar Pradesh, N India
Kerdilio *see* Kerdýlio
116 H13 **Kerdýlio** *var.* Kerdilio. ▲ N Greece
194 J14 **Kerema** Gulf, S PNG
Keremitlik *see* Lyulyakovo
142 I9 **Kerempe Burnu** *headland* N Turkey
82 J9 **Keren** *var.* Cheren. C Eritrea
27 U7 **Kerens** Texas, SW USA
192 M6 **Kerepehi** Waikato, North Island, NZ
151 P10 **Kerey, Ozero** ◎ C Kazakhstan
Kergel *see* Kärla
181 Q12 **Kerguelen** *island* C French Southern and Antarctic Territories
181 Q13 **Kerguelen Plateau** *undersea feature* S Indian Ocean
117 C20 **Kerí** Zákynthos, Iónioi Nísoi, Greece, C Mediterranean Sea
83 H19 **Kericho** Rift Valley, W Kenya
192 K2 **Kerikeri** Northland, North Island, NZ
95 O17 **Kerimäki** Mikkeli, SE Finland
174 Gg10 **Kerinci, Danau** ◎ Sumatera, W Indonesia
174 Gg9 **Kerinci, Gunung** ▲ Sumatera, W Indonesia
Keriya *see* Yutian
100 J9 **Kerkbuurt** Noord-Holland, C Netherlands
100 J13 **Kerkdriel** Gelderland, C Netherlands
77 N6 **Kerkenah, Îles de** *var.* Kerkenna Islands, *Ar.* Juzur Qarqannah. *island group* E Tunisia
Kerkenna Islands *see* Kerkenah, Îles de
117 M20 **Kerketévs** ▲ Sámos, Dodekánisos, Greece, Aegean Sea
31 T8 **Kerkhoven** Minnesota, N USA
152 M14 **Kerki** Lebapskiy Velayat, E Turkmenistan
152 M14 **Kerkichi** Lebapskiy Velayat, E Turkmenistan
117 F16 **Kerkíneo** *prehistoric site* Thessalía, C Greece
116 G12 **Kerkinitis, Límni** ◎ N Greece
Kérkira *see* Kérkyra
101 M18 **Kerkrade** Limburg, SE Netherlands
Kerkuk *see* Kirkūk
117 B16 **Kerkyra** ✕ Kérkyra, Iónioi Nísoi, Greece, C Mediterranean Sea
117 B16 **Kérkyra** *var.* Kérkira, *Eng.* Corfu. Kérkyra, Iónioi Nísoi, Greece, C Mediterranean Sea
117 A16 **Kérkyra** *var.* Kérkira, *Eng.* Corfu. *island* Iónioi Nísoi, Greece, C Mediterranean Sea
199 Jj12 **Kermadec Islands** *island group* NZ, SW Pacific Ocean
183 R10 **Kermadec Ridge** *undersea feature* SW Pacific Ocean
183 R11 **Kermadec Trench** *undersea feature* SW Pacific Ocean
149 S10 **Kermān** *var.* Kirman; *anc.* Carmana. Kermān, C Iran
149 R11 **Kermān** *off.* Ostān-e Kermān, *var.* Kirman; *anc.* Carmania. ◆ *province* SE Iran
149 U12 **Kermān, Bīābān-e** *var.* Kerman Desert. *desert* SE Iran
149 Q9 **Kermānshāh** Yazd, C Iran
Kermānshāh *see* Bākhtarān
148 J6 **Kermānshāhān** *off.* Ostān-e Kermānshāhān; *prev.* Bākhtarān. ◆ *province* W Iran
116 L10 **Kermen** Burgaska Oblast, E Bulgaria
26 L8 **Kermit** Texas, SW USA
23 P6 **Kermit** West Virginia, NE USA
23 S9 **Kernersville** North Carolina, SE USA
37 S12 **Kern River** ≈ California, W USA
37 S12 **Kernville** California, W USA
117 K21 **Kéros** *island* Kykládes, Greece, Aegean Sea
78 K14 **Kérouané** Haute-Guinée, SE Guinea
103 D16 **Kerpen** Nordrhein-Westfalen, W Germany
152 I11 **Kerpichli** Lebapskiy Velayat, NE Turkmenistan
xliii F17 **Kerrera** *island* W Scotland, UK
26 M1 **Kerrick** Texas, SW USA
Kerr Lake *see* John H.Kerr Reservoir
9 S15 **Kerrobert** Saskatchewan, S Canada
27 Q11 **Kerrville** Texas, SW USA
xxxv J9 **Kerry** Powys, C Wales, UK
xliv C13 **Kerry** *Ir.* Ciarraí. ◆ *county* SW Ireland
xliv C12 **Kerry Head** *headland* SW Ireland
Kerrykeel *see* Carrowkeel
23 S11 **Kershaw** South Carolina, SE USA
Kertel *see* Kärdla
97 H23 **Kerteminde** Fyn, C Denmark
169 Q7 **Kerulen** *Chin.* Herlen He, *Mong.* Herlen Gol. ≈ China/Mongolia
Kervo *see* Kerava
Kerýneia *see* Girne
10 H11 **Kesagami Lake** ◎ Ontario, SE Canada
95 O17 **Kesälahti** Pohjois-Karjala, SE Finland
142 B11 **Keşan** Edirne, NW Turkey
171 Mm12 **Kesennuma** Miyagi, Honshū, C Japan
xliv H4 **Kesh** Fermanagh, W Northern Ireland, UK
169 V7 **Keshan** Heilongjiang, NE China
32 M6 **Keshena** Wisconsin, N USA
142 I13 **Keskin** Kırıkkale, C Turkey
95 L17 **Keski-Suomi** *Swe.* Mellersta Finland. ◆ *province* C Finland
Késmárk *see* Kežmarok
xxxix Z11 **Kessingland** Suffolk, E England, UK
128 I6 **Kesten'ga** *var.* Kest Enga. Respublika Kareliya, NW Russian Federation
100 K12 **Kesteren** Gelderland, C Netherlands
xl L9 **Keswick** Cumbria, NW England, UK
12 H14 **Keswick** Ontario, S Canada
113 H24 **Keszthely** Zala, SW Hungary
126 Hh13 **Ket'** ≈ C Russian Federation
79 R17 **Keta** SE Ghana
174 Kk10 **Ketapang** Borneo, C Indonesia
131 O12 **Ketchenery** *prev.* Sovetskoye. Respublika Kalmykiya, SW Russian Federation
41 Y14 **Ketchikan** Revillagigedo Island, Alaska, USA
35 O14 **Ketchum** Idaho, NW USA
Kete/Kete Krakye *see* Kete-Krachi
79 Q15 **Kete-Krachi** *var.* Kete, Kete Krakye. E Ghana
100 L9 **Ketelmeer** *channel* E Netherlands
155 P17 **Keti Bandar** Sind, SE Pakistan
151 W16 **Ketmen', Khrebet** ▲ SE Kazakhstan
79 S16 **Kétou** SE Benin
112 M7 **Kętrzyn** *Ger.* Rastenburg. Olsztyn, NE Poland
xxxix P11 **Kettering** Northamptonshire, C England, UK
33 R14 **Kettering** Ohio, N USA
20 F13 **Kettle Creek** ≈ Pennsylvania, NE USA
34 L7 **Kettle Falls** Washington, NW USA
12 D16 **Kettle Point** *headland* Ontario, S Canada
31 V6 **Kettle River** ≈ Minnesota, N USA
xli P12 **Kettlewell** North Yorkshire, N England, UK
xxxix Q10 **Ketton** Rutland, C England, UK
194 E12 **Ketu** ≈ W PNG
20 G10 **Keuka Lake** ◎ New York, NE USA
Keupriya *see* Primorsko
95 L17 **Keuruu** Keski-Suomi, C Finland
Kevevára *see* Kovin
94 L9 **Kevo** *Lapp.* Geavvú. Lappi, N Finland
46 M6 **Kew** North Caicos, N Turks and Caicos Islands
32 K11 **Kewanee** Illinois, N USA
33 N7 **Kewaunee** Wisconsin, N USA
32 M3 **Keweenaw Bay** ◎ Michigan, N USA
33 N2 **Keweenaw Peninsula** *peninsula* Michigan, N USA
33 N2 **Keweenaw Point** *headland* Michigan, N USA
31 N12 **Keya Paha River** ≈ Nebraska/South Dakota, N USA
Keyaygyr *see* Këk-Aygyr
25 Z16 **Key Biscayne** Florida, SE USA
28 G8 **Keyes** Oklahoma, C USA
xli X14 **Keyingham** East Riding of Yorkshire, N England, UK
25 Y17 **Key Largo** Key Largo, Florida, SE USA
xliv G6 **Key, Lough** ◎ C Ireland
xxxvi L10 **Keynsham** Bath and North East Somerset, SW England, UK
23 U3 **Keyser** West Virginia, NE USA
29 O9 **Keystone Lake** ⊠ Oklahoma, C USA
38 L16 **Keystone Peak** ▲ Arizona, SW USA
Keystone State *see* Pennsylvania
23 U7 **Keysville** Virginia, NE USA
29 T3 **Keytesville** Missouri, C USA
25 W17 **Key West** Florida Keys, Florida, SE USA
xxxix N8 **Keyworth** Nottinghamshire, C England, UK
131 T1 **Kez** Udmurtskaya Respublika, NW Russian Federation
Kezdivásárhely *see* Târgu Secuiesc
126 J13 **Kezhma** Krasnoyarskiy Kray, C Russian Federation
113 L18 **Kežmarok** *Ger.* Käsmark, *Hung.* Késmárk. Východné Slovensko, NE Slovakia
85 F20 **Kgalagadi** ◆ *district* SW Botswana
85 I20 **Kgatleng** ◆ *district* SE Botswana
196 F8 **Kgkeklau** Babeldaob, N Palau
129 R6 **Khabarikha** *var.* Chabaricha. Respublika Komi, NW Russian Federation
127 N16 **Khabarovsk** Khabarovskiy Kray, SE Russian Federation
126 Mm12 **Khabarovskiy Kray** ◆ *territory* E Russian Federation
147 W7 **Khabb** Abū Ẓaby, E UAE
Khabour, Nahr al *see* Khābūr, Nahr al
Khabura *see* Al Khābūrah
145 N2 **Khābūr, Nahr al** *var.* Nahr al Khabour. ≈ Syria/Turkey
Khachmas *see* Xaçmaz
82 B12 **Khadari** ≈ W Sudan
147 X12 **Khādhil** *var.* Khudal. SE Oman
161 E14 **Khadki** *prev.* Kirkee. Mahārāshtra, W India
130 L14 **Khadyzhensk** Krasnodarskiy Kray, SW Russian Federation
116 N9 **Khadzhiyska Reka** ≈ E Bulgaria
119 P10 **Khadzhybeys'kyy Lyman** ◎ SW Ukraine
144 K3 **Khafsah** Ḥalab, N Syria
158 M13 **Khāga** Uttar Pradesh, N India
159 Q13 **Khagaria** Bihār, NE India
155 Q13 **Khairpur** Sind, SE Pakistan
126 Hh15 **Khakasiya, Respublika** *prev.* Khakasskaya Avtonomnaya Oblast', *Eng.* Khakassia. ◆ *autonomous republic* C Russian Federation
Khakassia/Khakasskaya Avtonomnaya Oblast' *see* Khakasiya, Respublika
178 H9 **Kha Khaeng, Khao** ▲ W Thailand
85 G20 **Khakhea** *var.* Kakia. Southern, S Botswana
152 L13 **Khalach** Lebapskiy Velayat, E Turkmenistan
Khalándrion *see* Chalándri
131 W7 **Khalilovo** Orenburgskaya Oblast', W Russian Federation
Khalkabad *see* Khalqobod
148 L3 **Khalkhāl** *prev.* Herowābād. Ardabīl, NW Iran
Khalkidhikí *see* Chalkidikí
Khalkís *see* Chalkída
129 W3 **Khal'mer-Yu** Respublika Komi, NW Russian Federation
121 M14 **Khalopyenichy** *Rus.* Kholopenichi. Minskaya Voblasts', NE Belorussia
152 H7 **Khalqobod** *Rus.* Khalkabad. Qoraqalpoghiston Respublikasi, W Uzbekistan
Khalturin *see* Orlov
147 Y10 **Khalūf** *var.* Al Khaluf. E Oman
160 K10 **Khamaria** Madhya Pradesh, C India
160 D11 **Khambhāt** Gujarāt, W India
160 C12 **Khambhāt, Gulf of** *Eng.* Gulf of Cambay. *gulf* W India
178 K10 **Khâm Đưc** Quang Nam-Đa Năng, C Vietnam
160 G12 **Khāmgaon** Mahārāshtra, C India
147 O14 **Khamir** *var.* Khamr. W Yemen
147 N12 **Khamīs Mushayt** *var.* Hamïs Musait. 'Asīr, SW Saudi Arabia
126 L10 **Khampa** Respublika Sakha (Yakutiya), NE Russian Federation
Khamr *see* Khamir
85 C19 **Khan** ≈ W Namibia
155 Q2 **Khānābād** Kunduz, NE Afghanistan
Khân Abou Châmâte/Khan Abou Ech Cham *see* Khān Abū Shāmāt
144 I7 **Khān Abū Shāmāt** *var.* Khân Abou Châmâte, Khan Abou Ech Cham. Dimashq, W Syria
Khān al Baghdādī *see* Al Baghdādī
Khān al Mahāwīl *see* Al Maḥāwīl
145 T7 **Khān al Mashāhidah** C Iraq
145 T10 **Khān al Muṣallá** S Iraq
145 U6 **Khānaqīn** E Iraq
145 T11 **Khān ar Ruḥbah** S Iraq
145 P2 **Khān as Sūr** N Iraq
145 T8 **Khān Āzād** C Iraq
160 N13 **Khandaparha** *prev.* Khandpara. Orissa, E India
Khandpara *see* Khandaparha
155 T2 **Khandūd** *var.* Khandud, Wakhan. Badakhshān, NE Afghanistan
160 G11 **Khandwa** Madhya Pradesh, C India
126 Mm10 **Khandyga** Respublika Sakha (Yakutiya), NE Russian Federation
155 T10 **Khānewāl** Punjab, NE Pakistan
155 S10 **Khāngarh** Punjab, E Pakistan
Khanh Hung *see* Soc Trăng
Khaniá *see* Chaniá
Khanka *see* Khonqa
169 Z8 **Khanka, Lake** *var.* Hsing-k'ai Hu, Lake Hanka, *Chin.* Xingkai Hu, *Rus.* Ozero Khanka. ◎ China/Russian Federation
Khanka, Ozero *see* Khanka, Lake
Khankendi *see* Xankändi
Khanlar *see* Xanlar
126 Kk10 **Khannya** ≈ NE Russian Federation
155 S12 **Khānpur** Punjab, SE Pakistan
155 S12 **Khānpur** Punjab, E Pakistan
144 I4 **Khān Shaykhūn** *var.* Khan Sheikhun. Idlib, NW Syria
Khan Sheikhun *see* Khān Shaykhūn
151 S15 **Khantau** Zhambyl, S Kazakhstan
151 W16 **Khan Tengri, Pik** ▲ SE Kazakhstan
178 J9 **Khanthabouli** *prev.* Savannakhét. Savannakhét, S Laos
125 Ff10 **Khanty-Mansiysk** *prev.* Ostyako-Voguls'k. Khanty-Mansiyskiy Avtonomnyy Okrug, C Russian Federation
129 V8 **Khanty-Mansiyskiy Avtonomnyy Okrug** ◆ *autonomous district* C Russian Federation
145 R4 **Khānūqah** C Iraq
144 E11 **Khān Yūnis** *var.* Khān Yūnus. S Gaza Strip
Khān Yūnus *see* Khān Yūnis
Khanzi *see* Ghanzi
145 U5 **Khān Zūr** E Iraq
178 H10 **Khao Laem Reservoir** ⊠ W Thailand
126 Kk17 **Khapcheranga** Chitinskaya Oblast', S Russian Federation
131 Q12 **Kharabali** Astrakhanskaya Oblast', SW Russian Federation
159 R16 **Kharagpur** West Bengal, NE India
145 V11 **Kharā'ib 'Abd al Karīm** S Iraq
149 Q8 **Harānaq** Yazd, C Iran
Kharbin *see* Harbin
152 H13 **Khardzhagaz** Akhalskiy Velayat, C Turkmenistan
Khārga Oasis *see* Great Oasis, The
160 F11 **Khargon** Madhya Pradesh, C India
155 V7 **Khāriān** Punjab, NE Pakistan
119 X8 **Kharisyz'k** Donets'ka Oblast', E Ukraine
119 V5 **Kharkiv** *Rus.* Khar'kov. Kharkivs'ka Oblast', NE Ukraine
119 V5 **Kharkiv** ✕ Kharkivs'ka Oblast', E Ukraine
Kharkiv *see* Kharkivs'ka Oblast'
119 U5 **Kharkivs'ka Oblast'** *var.* Kharkiv, *Rus.* Khar'kovskaya Oblast'. ◆ *province* E Ukraine
Khar'kov *see* Kharkiv
Khar'kovskaya Oblast' *see* Kharkivs'ka Oblast'
128 L3 **Kharlovka** Murmanskaya Oblast', NW Russian Federation
116 K11 **Kharmanli** Khaskovska Oblast, S Bulgaria
116 K11 **Kharmanliyska Reka** ≈ S Bulgaria
128 M13 **Kharovsk** Vologodskaya Oblast', NW Russian Federation
82 F9 **Khartoum** *var.* El Khartûm, Khartum. ● (Sudan) Khartoum, C Sudan
82 F9 **Khartoum** ◆ *state* NE Sudan
82 F9 **Khartoum** ✕ Khartoum, C Sudan
82 F9 **Khartoum North** Khartoum, C Sudan
119 X8 **Khartsyz'k** *Rus.* Khartsyzsk. Donets'ka Oblast', SE Ukraine
Khartsyzsk *see* Khartsyz'k
Khartum *see* Khartoum
Khasab *see* Al Khaṣab
127 N18 **Khasan** Primorskiy Kray, SE Russian Federation
131 P16 **Khasavyurt** Respublika Dagestan, SW Russian Federation
149 W12 **Khāsh** *prev.* Vāsht. Sīstān va Balūchestān, SE Iran
154 K8 **Khāsh, Dasht-e** *Eng.* Khash Desert. *desert* SW Afghanistan
Khash Desert *see* Khāsh, Dasht-e
Khashim Al Qirba/Khashm al Qirbah *see* Khashm el Girba
82 H9 **Khashm el Girba** *var.* Khashim Al Qirba, Khashm al Qirbah. Kassala, E Sudan
144 G14 **Khashsh, Jabal al** ▲ S Jordan
143 S10 **Khashuri** C Georgia
159 V13 **Khāsi Hills** *hill range* NE India
116 K11 **Khaskovo** Khaskovska Oblast, S Bulgaria
Khaskovo *see* Khaskovska Oblast
116 J11 **Khaskovska Oblast** *var.* Khaskovo. ◆ *province* S Bulgaria
126 J7 **Khatanga** Taymyrskiy (Dolgano-Nenetskiy) Avtonomnyy Okrug, N Russian Federation
126 J7 **Khatanga** ≈ N Russian Federation
Khatanga, Gulf of *see* Khatangskiy Zaliv
126 Jj6 **Khatangskiy Zaliv** *var.* Gulf of Khatanga. *bay* N Russian Federation
147 W7 **Khatmat al Malāḥah** N Oman
149 S16 **Khaṭmat al Malāḥah** Ash Shāriqah, E UAE
Khātoūniyé *see* Khātūnīyah
127 Q6 **Khatyrka** Chukotskiy Avtonomnyy Okrug, NE Russian Federation
152 I14 **Khauz-Khan** *Turkm.* Hanhowuz. Akhalskiy Velayat, S Turkmenistan
152 I14 **Khauzkhanskoye Vodokhranilishche** ⊠ S Turkmenistan
Khavaling *see* Khovaling
Khavast *see* Khowos
145 W10 **Khawrah, Nahr al** ≈ S Iraq
Khawr Barakah *see* Baraka
147 W7 **Khawr Fakkān** *var.* Khor Fakkan. Ash Shāriqah, NE UAE
146 L6 **Khaybar** Al Madīnah, NW Saudi Arabia
Khaybar, Kowtal-e *see* Khyber Pass
153 S11 **Khaydarkan** *var.* Khaydarken. Oshskaya Oblast', SW Kyrgyzstan
Khaydarken *see* Khaydarkan
129 U2 **Khaypudyrskaya Guba** *bay* NW Russian Federation
145 S1 **Khayrūzuk** E Iraq
Khazar, Baḥr-e/Khazar, Daryā-ye *see* Caspian Sea
Khazarosp *see* Hazorasp
Khazretishi, Khrebet *see* Hazratishoh, Qatorkŭhi
Khelat *see* Kalāt
76 F6 **Khemisset** NW Morocco
178 J10 **Khemmarat** *var.* Kemarat. Ubon Ratchathani, E Thailand
76 L6 **Khenchela** *var.* Khenchla. NE Algeria
Khenchla *see* Khenchela
76 G7 **Khénifra** C Morocco
Khersān, Rūd-e *see* Garm, Āb-e
119 R10 **Kherson** Khersons'ka Oblast', S Ukraine
Kherson *see* Khersons'ka Oblast'
119 S14 **Khersones, Mys** *Rus.* Mys Khersonesskiy. *headland* S Ukraine
Khersonesskiy, Mys *see* Khersones, Mys
119 R10 **Khersons'ka Oblast'** *var.* Kherson, *Rus.* Khersonskaya Oblast'. ◆ *province* S Ukraine
Khersonskaya Oblast' *see* Khersons'ka Oblast'
126 J7 **Kheta** Taymyrskiy (Dolgano-Nenetskiy) Avtonomnyy Okrug, N Russian Federation
126 J7 **Kheta** ≈ N Russian Federation
178 Jj8 **Khe Ve** Quang Binh, C Vietnam
155 U7 **Khewra** Punjab, E Pakistan
Khiam *see* El Khiyam
128 J4 **Khibiny** ▲ NW Russian Federation
126 K16 **Khilok** Chitinskaya Oblast', S Russian Federation
126 K16 **Khilok** ≈ S Russian Federation
130 K3 **Khimki** Moskovskaya Oblast', W Russian Federation
153 S12 **Khingov** *Rus.* Obi-Khingou. ≈ C Tajikistan
Khíos *see* Chíos
155 R15 **Khipro** Sind, SE Pakistan
145 S10 **Khirr, Wādī al** *dry watercourse* S Iraq
116 I10 **Khisarya** Plovdivska Oblast, C Bulgaria
Khiva *see* Khiwa
152 H9 **Khiwa** *Rus.* Khiva. Khorazm Wiloyati, W Uzbekistan
178 H9 **Khlong Khlung** Kamphaeng Phet, W Thailand
178 Gg16 **Khlong Thom** Krabi, SW Thailand
178 I12 **Khlung** Chantaburi, S Thailand
Khmel'nik *see* Khmil'nyk
Khmel'nitskaya Oblast' *see* Khmel'nyts'ka Oblast'
Khmel'nitskiy *see* Khmel 'nyts'kyy
118 K5 **Khmel'nyts'ka Oblast'** *var.* Khmel'nyts'kyy, *Rus.* Khmel'nitskaya Oblast'; *prev.* Kamenets-Podol'skaya Oblast'. ◆ *province* NW Ukraine
118 L6 **Khmel 'nyts'kyy** *Rus.* Khmel'nitskiy; *prev.* Proskurov. Khmel'nyts'ka Oblast', W Ukraine
Khmel'nyts'kyy *see* Khmel'nyts'ka Oblast'
118 M6 **Khmil'nyk** *Rus.* Khmel'nik. Vinnyts'ka Oblast', C Ukraine
143 R9 **Khobi** W Georgia
121 P15 **Khodasy** *Rus.* Khodosy. Mahilyowskaya Voblasts', E Belorussia
118 I6 **Khodoriv** *Pol.* Chodorów, *Rus.* Khodorov. L'vivs'ka Oblast', NW Ukraine
Khodorov *see* Khodoriv
Khodosy *see* Khodasy
152 D12 **Khodzhakala** *Turkm.* Hojagala. Balkanskiy Velayat, W Turkmenistan
152 M13 **Khodzhambas** *Turkm.* Hojambaz. Lebapskiy Velayat, E Turkmenistan
Khodzhent *see* Khŭjand
Khodzheyli *see* Khŭjayli
Khoi *see* Khvoy
Khojend *see* Khŭjand
Khokand *see* Qŭqon
130 L8 **Khokhol'skiy** Voronezhskaya Oblast', W Russian Federation
178 Hh10 **Khok Samrong** Lop Buri, C Thailand
155 P2 **Kholm** *var.* Tashqurghan, *Pash.* Khulm. Balkh, N Afghanistan
128 H15 **Kholm** Novgorodskaya Oblast', W Russian Federation
Kholm *see* Chełm
Kholmech' *see* Kholmyech
127 Oo16 **Kholmsk** Ostrov Sakhalin, Sakhalinskaya Oblast', SE Russian Federation
121 O19 **Kholmyech** *Rus.* Kholmech'. Homyel'skaya Voblasts', SE Belorussia
Kholopenichi *see* Khalopyenichy
85 D19 **Khomas** ◆ *district* C Namibia
85 D19 **Khomas Hochland** *var.* Khomasplato. *plateau* C Namibia
Khomasplato *see* Khomas Hochland
Khomein *see* Khomeyn
148 M7 **Khomeyn** *var.* Khomein, Khumain. Markazī, W Iran
149 N8 **Khomeynīshahr** *prev.* Homāyūnshahr. Eşfahān, C Iran
Khoms *see* Al Khums
Khong Sedone *see* Muang Khôngxédôn
178 I9 **Khon Kaen** *var.* Muang Khon Kaen. Khon Kaen, E Thailand
152 I9 **Khonqa** *Rus.* Khanka. Khorazm Wiloyati, W Uzbekistan
178 I9 **Khon San** Khon Kaen, E Thailand
127 N8 **Khonuu** Respublika Sakha (Yakutiya), NE Russian Federation
131 N8 **Khopër** *var.* Khoper. ≈ SW Russian Federation
127 Nn16 **Khor** Khabarovskiy Kray, SE Russian Federation
127 Nn16 **Khor** ≈ SE Russian Federation
149 S6 **Khorāsān** *off.* Ostān-e Khorāsān, *var.* Khorassan, Khurasan. ◆ *province* NE Iran
Khorassan *see* Khorāsān
Khorat *see* Nakhon Ratchasima
152 H9 **Khorazm Wiloyati** *Rus.* Khorezmskaya Oblast'. ◆ *province* W Uzbekistan
160 O13 **Khordha** *prev.* Khurda. Orissa, E India
129 U4 **Khorey-Ver** Nenetskiy Avtonomnyy Okrug, NW Russian Federation
Khorezmskaya Oblast' *see* Khorazm Wiloyati
Khor Fakkan *see* Khawr Fakkān
151 W15 **Khorgos** Taldykorgan, SE Kazakhstan
126 K16 **Khorinsk** Respublika Buryatiya, S Russian Federation
85 C18 **Khorixas** Kunene, NW Namibia
147 O17 **Khormaksar** *var.* Aden. ✕ ('Adan) SW Yemen
Khormal *see* Khurmāl
Khormuj *see* Khvormūj
Khorog *see* Khorugh
119 S5 **Khorol** Poltavs'ka Oblast', NE Ukraine
148 L7 **Khorramābād** *var.* Khurramabad. Lorestān, W Iran
148 K10 **Khorramshahr** *var.* Khurramshahr, Muhammerah; *prev.* Mohammerah. Khūzestān, SW Iran
153 S14 **Khorugh** *Rus.* Khorog. S Tajikistan
131 Q12 **Khosheutovo** Astrakhanskaya Oblast', SW Russian Federation
Khotan *see* Hotan
Khotimsk *see* Khotsimsk
Khotin *see* Khotyn
121 R16 **Khotsimsk** *Rus.* Khotimsk. Mahilyowskaya Voblasts', E Belorussia
118 K7 **Khotyn** *Rom.* Hotin, *Rus.* Khotin. Chernivets'ka Oblast', W Ukraine
76 F7 **Khouribga** C Morocco
153 Q13 **Khovaling** *Rus.* Khavaling. SW Tajikistan
Khovd *see* Hovd
153 P11 **Khowos** *var.* Ursat'yevskaya, *Rus.* Khavast. Sirdaryo Wiloyati, E Uzbekistan
155 R6 **Khowst** Paktīā, E Afghanistan
Khoy *see* Khvoy
121 N20 **Khoyniki** *Rus.* Khoyniki. Homyel'skaya Voblasts', SE Belorussia
Khozretishi, Khrebet *see* Hazratishoh, Qatorkŭhi
Khrisoúpolis *see* Chrysoúpoli
126 Mm6 **Khroma** ≈ NE Russian Federation
150 J10 **Khromtau** *Kaz.* Khromtaū. Aktyubinsk, W Kazakhstan
Khrysokhou Bay *see* Chrysochoú, Kólpos
119 O7 **Khrystynivka** Cherkas'ka Oblast', C Ukraine
178 J10 **Khuang Nai** Ubon Ratchathani, E Thailand
Khudal *see* Khādhil
Khudat *see* Xudat
155 W9 **Khudiān** Punjab, E Pakistan
Khudzhand *see* Khŭjand
153 O13 **Khufar** Surkhondaryo Wiloyati, S Uzbekistan
85 G21 **Khuis** Kgalagadi, SW Botswana
153 Q11 **Khŭjand** *var.* Khodzhent, Khojend, *Rus.* Khudzhand; *prev.* Leninabad, *Taj.* Leninobod. N Tajikistan
152 H8 **Khŭjayli** *Rus.* Khodzheyli. Qoraqalpoghiston Respublikasi, W Uzbekistan
178 Ii11 **Khukhan** Si Sa Ket, E Thailand
Khulm *see* Kholm
159 T16 **Khulna** Khulna, SW Bangladesh
159 T16 **Khulna** ◆ *division* SW Bangladesh
Khumain *see* Khomeyn
Khums *see* Al Khums
155 W2 **Khunjerāb Pass** *Chin.* Kunjirap Daban. *pass* China/Pakistan *see also* Kunjirap Daban
159 P16 **Khunti** Bihār, N India
178 Gg7 **Khun Yuam** Mae Hong Son, NW Thailand
Khurais *see* Khurayş
Khurasan *see* Khorāsān
147 R7 **Khurayş** *var.* Khurais. Ash Sharqīyah, C Saudi Arabia
Khurda *see* Khordha
158 J11 **Khurja** Uttar Pradesh, N India
145 V4 **Khurmāl** *var.* Khormal. NE Iraq
Khurramabad *see* Khorramābād
Khurramshahr *see* Khorramshahr
155 U7 **Khushāb** Punjab, NE Pakistan
118 H8 **Khust** *Cz.* Chust, Husté, *Hung.* Huszt. Zakarpats'ka Oblast', W Ukraine
82 D11 **Khuwei** Western Kordofan, C Sudan
155 O13 **Khuzdār** Baluchistān, SW Pakistan
148 L9 **Khūzestān** *off.* Ostān-e Khūzestān, *var.* Khuzistan; *prev.* Arabistan, *anc.* Susiana. ◆ *province* SW Iran
126 Jj15 **Khuzhir** Respublika Buryatiya, S Russian Federation
Khuzistan *see* Khūzestān
155 R2 **Khvājeh Ghār** *var.* Khwajaghar, Khwaja-i-Ghar. Takhār, NE Afghanistan
131 Q7 **Khvalynsk** Saratovskaya Oblast', W Russian Federation
149 N12 **Khvormūj** *var.* Khormuj. Būshehr, S Iran
148 I2 **Khvoy** *var.* Khoi, Khoy. Āzarbāyjān-e Bākhtarī, NW Iran
Khwajaghar/Khwaja-i-Ghar *see* Khvājeh Ghār
155 S5 **Khyber Pass** *var.* Kowtal-e Khaybar. *pass* Afghanistan/Pakistan
195 V14 **Kia** Santa Isabel, N Solomon Islands
191 S10 **Kiama** New South Wales, SE Australia
179 R17 **Kiamba** Mindanao, S Philippines
81 O22 **Kiambi** Shaba, SE Zaire
29 Q12 **Kiamichi Mountains** ▲ Oklahoma, C USA
29 Q12 **Kiamichi River** ≈ Oklahoma, C USA
12 M10 **Kiamika, Réservoir** ⊠ Québec, SE Canada
Kiamusze *see* Jiamusi
41 N7 **Kiana** Alaska, USA
Kiangmai *see* Chiang Mai
Kiang-ning *see* Nanjing
Kiangsi *see* Jiangxi
Kiangsu *see* Jiangsu
95 M14 **Kiantajärvi** ◎ E Finland
117 F19 **Kiáto** *prev.* Kiáton. Pelopónnisos, S Greece
Kiáton *see* Kiáto
Kiayi *see* Chiai
69 T9 **Kibali** *var.* Uele (upper course). ≈ NE Zaire
81 E20 **Kibangou** Le Niari, SW Congo
Kibarty *see* Kybartai
94 M8 **Kiberg** Finnmark, N Norway
97 F22 **Kibæk** Ringkøbing, W Denmark
81 N20 **Kibombo** Maniema, E Zaire
83 E20 **Kibondo** Kigoma, NW Tanzania
83 J15 **Kibre Mengist** *var.* Adola. S Ethiopia
Kıbrıs/Kıbrıs Cumhuriyeti *see* Cyprus
83 E20 **Kibungo** *var.* Kibungu. SE Rwanda
Kibungu *see* Kibungo
xxxix P10 **Kibworth Harcourt** Leicestershire, C England, UK
115 N19 **Kičevo** SW FYR Macedonia
129 P13 **Kichmengskiy Gorodok** Vologodskaya Oblast', NW Russian Federation
32 J8 **Kickapoo River** ≈ Wisconsin, N USA
9 P16 **Kicking Horse Pass** *pass* Alberta/British Columbia, SW Canada
79 R9 **Kidal** Kidal, C Mali
79 Q8 **Kidal** ◆ *region* NE Mali
179 R16 **Kidapawan** Mindanao, S Philippines
xxxviF8 **Kidbrooke** Greenwich, SE England, UK
xxxviii A16 **Kidderminster** Worcestershire, C England, UK
78 I11 **Kidira** E Senegal
xxxvii P8 **Kidlington** Oxfordshire, C England, UK
192 O11 **Kidnappers, Cape** *headland* North Island, NZ
xxxviii J7 **Kidsgrove** Staffordshire, C England, UK
xxxv F14 **Kidwelly** Carmarthenshire, S Wales, UK
102 J8 **Kiel** Schleswig-Holstein, N Germany
113 L15 **Kielce** *Rus.* Keltsy. Kielce, SE Poland
113 L15 **Kielce** *off.* Województwo Kieleckie, *Rus.* Keltsy. ◆ *province* SE Poland
xli N4 **Kielder** Northumberland, N England, UK
xli N5 **Kielder Forest** *forest* N England, UK
xli O5 **Kielder Water** ◎ N England, UK
Kieleckie, Województwo *see* Kielce
102 K7 **Kieler Bucht** *bay* N Germany
102 J7 **Kieler Förde** *inlet* N Germany
178 K13 **Kiên Đưc** *var.* Đak Lap. Đăc Lăc, S Vietnam
81 N24 **Kienge** Shaba, SE Zaire
195 S12 **Kieta** Bougainville Island, NE PNG
102 Q12 **Kietz** Brandenburg, NE Germany
Kiev *see* Kyyiv
Kiev Reservoir *see* Kyyivs'ke Vodoskhovyshche
78 J10 **Kiffa** Assaba, S Mauritania
117 H19 **Kifisiá** Attikí, C Greece
117 F18 **Kifisós** ≈ C Greece
145 U5 **Kifrī** N Iraq
83 D20 **Kigali** ● (Rwanda) C Rwanda
83 E20 **Kigali** ✕ C Rwanda
143 P13 **Kiği** Bingöl, E Turkey
83 E21 **Kigoma** Kigoma, W Tanzania
83 E21 **Kigoma** ◆ *region* W Tanzania
40 F10 **Kihei** *Haw.* Kihei. Maui, Hawaii, USA, C Pacific Ocean
95 K17 **Kihniö** Häme, SW Finland
120 F6 **Kihnu** *var.* Kihnu Saar, *Ger.* Kühnö. *island* SW Estonia
Kihnu Saar *see* Kihnu
40 A8 **Kii Landing** Niihau, Hawaii, USA, C Pacific Ocean
95 L14 **Kiiminki** Oulu, C Finland
171 H16 **Kii-Nagashima** *var.* Nagashima. Mie, Honshū, SW Japan
171 Gg16 **Kii-sanchi** ▲ Honshū, SW Japan
94 L11 **Kiistala** Lappi, N Finland
170 Ff16 **Kii-suidō** *strait* S Japan
172 R14 **Kikai-shima** *var.* Kikaiga-shima. *island* Nansei-shotō, SW Japan
114 M8 **Kikinda** *Ger.* Grosskikinda, *Hung.* Nagykikinda; *prev.* Velika Kikinda. Serbia, N Yugoslavia
Kikládhes *see* Kykládes
172 N7 **Kikonai** Hokkaidō, NE Japan
194 H14 **Kikori** Gulf, S PNG
194 G13 **Kikori** ≈ W PNG
170 Cc14 **Kikuchi** *var.* Kikuti. Kumamoto, Kyūshū, SW Japan
Kikuti *see* Kikuchi
131 N8 **Kikvidze** Volgogradskaya Oblast', SW Russian Federation
12 I10 **Kikwissi, Lac** ◎ Québec, SE Canada
81 I21 **Kikwit** Bandundu, W Zaire
97 K15 **Kil** Värmland, C Sweden
96 N12 **Kilafors** Gävleborg, C Sweden
40 B8 **Kilauea** *Haw.* Kilauea. Kauai, Hawaii, USA, C Pacific Ocean
40 H12 **Kilauea Caldera** *crater* Hawaii, USA, C Pacific Ocean
111 V4 **Kilb** Niederösterreich, C Austria
xliv C11 **Kilbaha** Clare, W Ireland
xliii I20 **Kilbarchan** Renfrewshire, W Scotland, UK
xliv I9 **Kilbeggan** Westmeath, C Ireland
xliii F20 **Kilberry** Argyll and Bute, W Scotland, UK
xliii I20 **Kilbirnie** North Ayrshire, W Scotland, UK
xliii F22 **Kilbrannan Sound** *sound* W Scotland, UK
xlii A13 **Kilbride** Argyll and Bute, W Scotland, UK
xliii F17 **Kilbride** Western Isles, NW Scotland, UK
xliv F14 **Kilbrittain** Cork, S Ireland
41 O12 **Kilbuck Mountains** ▲ Alaska, USA
xxxvi B7 **Kilburn** Brent, SE England, UK
xliii H21 **Kilchattan** Argyll and Bute, W Scotland, UK
xliii D19 **Kilchattan** Argyll and Bute, W Scotland, UK
xliii F22 **Kilchenzie** Argyll and Bute, W Scotland, UK
xliii E16 **Kilchoan** Highland, NW Scotland, UK
xliii D20 **Kilchoman** Argyll and Bute, W Scotland, UK
169 Y12 **Kilchu** NE North Korea
xliv K9 **Kilcock** *Ir.* Cill Choca. Kildare, E Ireland
xliv I7 **Kilcogy** Cavan, N Ireland
xliv F10 **Kilcolgan** Galway, W Ireland
xliv H12 **Kilcommon** Tipperary, S Ireland
xliv G9 **Kilconnell** Galway, W Ireland
xliv H9 **Kilcormac** Offaly, C Ireland
191 V2 **Kilcoy** Queensland, E Australia
xliii H19 **Kilcreggan** Argyll and Bute, W Scotland, UK
xliv C15 **Kilcrohane** Cork, S Ireland
xliv K10 **Kilcullen** Kildare, E Ireland
xliii F21 **Kildalloig** Argyll and Bute, W Scotland, UK
xliv K9 **Kildare** *Ir.* Cill Dara. Kildare, E Ireland
xliv J9 **Kildare** *Ir.* Cill Dara. ◆ *county* E Ireland
128 K2 **Kil'din, Ostrov** *island* NW Russian Federation
xlii K8 **Kildonan** Highland, N Scotland, UK
xliii G22 **Kildonan** North Ayrshire, W Scotland, UK
xliv F13 **Kildorrery** Cork, S Ireland
xliv E10 **Kilfenora** Clare, W Ireland
xliii G19 **Kilfinan** Argyll and Bute, W Scotland, UK
xliv D14 **Kilgarvan** Kerry, SW Ireland
xxxv D14 **Kilgetty** Pembrokeshire, SW Wales, UK
27 W7 **Kilgore** Texas, SW USA
xli W12 **Kilham** East Riding of Yorkshire, N England, UK
Kilien Mountains *see* Qilian Shan
116 K9 **Kilifarevo** Loveshka Oblast, C Bulgaria
83 K20 **Kilifi** Coast, SE Kenya
201 U9 **Kili Island** *var.* Kōle. *island* Ralik Chain, S Marshall Islands
155 V2 **Kilik Pass** *pass* Afghanistan/China
Kilimane *see* Quelimane
83 I21 **Kilimanjaro** ◆ *region* E Tanzania
83 I20 **Kilimanjaro** *var.* Uhuru Peak. ▲ NE Tanzania
Kilimbangara *see* Kolombangara
Kilinailau Islands *see* Tulun Islands
83 K23 **Kilindoni** Pwani, E Tanzania
120 H6 **Kilingi-Nõmme** *Ger.* Kurkund. Pärnumaa, SW Estonia
142 M17 **Kilis** Gaziantep, S Turkey
119 N12 **Kiliya** *Rom.* Chilia-Nouă. Odes'ka Oblast', SW Ukraine
xliv D11 **Kilkee** *Ir.* Cill Chaoi. Clare, W Ireland

● Country ◇ Dependent Territory ◆ Administrative Region ▲ Mountain ⛰ Volcano ◎ Lake
● Country Capital ◇ Dependent Territory Capital ✕ International Airport ▲ Mountain Range ≈ River ⊠ Reservoir

Kilkeel – Klamath River

xliv L6 **Kilkeel** Newry and Mourne, S Northern Ireland, UK
xliv F6 **Kilkelly** Mayo, NW Ireland
xliv I11 **Kilkenny** ***Ir.*** Cill Chainnigh. Kilkenny, S Ireland
xliv I11 **Kilkenny** ***Ir.*** Cill Chainnigh. ◐ *county* S Ireland
xxxvi E13 **Kilkhampton** Cornwall, SW England, UK
xliv D9 **Kilkieran** Galway, W Ireland
xliv C9 **Kilkieran Bay** ***Ir.*** Cuan Chill Chiaráin. *bay* W Ireland
xliv D12 **Kilkinlea** Kerry, SW Ireland
116 G13 **Kilkís** Kentrikí Makedonía, N Greece
xliv F11 **Kilkishen** Clare, W Ireland
xliv D14 **Killabunane** Kerry, SW Ireland
xliv E11 **Killadysert** Clare, W Ireland
xliv K3 **Killagan** Ballymoney, N Northern Ireland, UK
xliv E5 **Killala** Mayo, NW Ireland
xliv E5 **Killala Bay** ***Ir.*** Cuan Chill Ala. *inlet* NW Ireland
xliv F11 **Killaloe** Clare, W Ireland
9 R15 **Killam** Alberta, SW Canada
xliv D13 **Killarney** ***Ir.*** Cill Airne. Kerry, SW Ireland
191 U3 **Killarney** Queensland, E Australia
9 W17 **Killarney** Manitoba, S Canada
12 E11 **Killarney** Ontario, S Canada
30 K4 **Killdeer** North Dakota, N USA
30 J4 **Killdeer Mountains** ▲▲ North Dakota, N USA
47 V15 **Killdeer River** ≈ Trinidad, Trinidad and Tobago
xliv I3 **Killea** Donegal, N Ireland
xliv I3 **Killea** Londonderry, NW Northern Ireland, UK
xliii F21 **Killean** Argyll and Bute, W Scotland, UK
xliv D9 **Killeany** Galway, W Ireland
xliii J19 **Killearn** Stirling, C Scotland, UK
xliv K6 **Killeen** Newry and Mourne, S Northern Ireland, UK
27 S9 **Killeen** Texas, SW USA
xliv I9 **Killeigh** Offaly, C Ireland
xliv I11 **Killenaule** Tipperary, S Ireland
41 P6 **Killik River** ≈ Alaska, USA
xliv D11 **Killimer** Clare, W Ireland
xliv G9 **Killimor** Galway, W Ireland
xliii J17 **Killin** Stirling, C Scotland, UK
16 P4 **Killinek Island** *island* Northwest Territories, NE Canada
xliv L9 **Killiney Bay** *bay* E Ireland
Killini *see* Kyllíni
117 C19 **Killínis, Ákra** *headland* S Greece
xliv F12 **Killmallock** Limerick, SW Ireland
xliv C13 **Killorglin** Kerry, SW Ireland
xliv G4 **Killybegs** ***Ir.*** Na Cealla Beaga. Donegal, NW Ireland
xliv M5 **Killyleagh** Down, E Northern Ireland, UK
xliv L10 **Kilmacanoge** Wicklow, E Ireland
xliii I20 **Kilmacolm** Inverclyde, W Scotland, UK
xliv H3 **Kilmacrenan** Donegal, N Ireland
xliv I12 **Kilmaganny** Kilkenny, SE Ireland
xliii J18 **Kilmahog** Stirling, C Scotland, UK
Kilmain *see* Quelimane
xliv E8 **Kilmaine** Mayo, NW Ireland
xlii D11 **Kilmaluag** Highland, NW Scotland, UK
xliv I11 **Kilmanagh** Kilkenny, SE Ireland
xliii M17 **Kilmany** Fife, E Scotland, UK
xliii I21 **Kilmarnock** East Ayrshire, W Scotland, UK
23 X6 **Kilmarnock** Virginia, NE USA
xliii F19 **Kilmartin** Argyll and Bute, W Scotland, UK
xliii I21 **Kilmaurs** East Ayrshire, W Scotland, UK
xliii F18 **Kilmelford** Argyll and Bute, W Scotland, UK
129 S16 **Kil'mez'** Kirovskaya Oblast', NW Russian Federation
131 S2 **Kil'mez'** Udmurtskaya Respublika, NW Russian Federation
129 R16 **Kil'mez'** ≈ NW Russian Federation
xliv L11 **Kilmichael Point** *peninsula* E Ireland
xliv F13 **Kilmona** Cork, S Ireland
xliv K13 **Kilmore Quay** Wexford, SE Ireland
xliii F20 **Kilmory** Argyll and Bute, W Scotland, UK
xliii D14 **Kilmory** Highland, NW Scotland, UK
xlii D11 **Kilmuir** Highland, NW Scotland, UK
xlii J11 **Kilmuir** Highland, NW Scotland, UK
xliv C9 **Kilmurvy** Galway, W Ireland
xliv K12 **Kilnamanagh** Wexford, SE Ireland
xliii F18 **Kilninver** Argyll and Bute, W Scotland, UK
xli Y15 **Kilnsea** East Riding of Yorkshire, N England, UK
69 V11 **Kilombero** ≈ S Tanzania
xliii D19 **Kiloran** Argyll and Bute, W Scotland, UK
94 J10 **Kilpisjarvi** Lappi, N Finland
xliv K3 **Kilrea** Coleraine, N Northern Ireland, UK
xliii N18 **Kilrenny** Fife, E Scotland, UK
xliv D9 **Kilronan** Galway, W Ireland
xliv D11 **Kilrush** ***Ir.*** Cill Rois. Clare, W Ireland
xxxix N12 **Kilsby** Northamptonshire, C England, UK
xliii J19 **Kilsyth** North Lanarkshire, C Scotland, UK
xliv J12 **Kiltealy** Wexford, SE Ireland
xliv E6 **Kiltimagh** Mayo, NW Ireland
xliv F9 **Kiltullagh** Galway, W Ireland
81 O24 **Kilwa** Shaba, SE Zaire
Kilwa *see* Kilwa Kivinje
83 J24 **Kilwa Kivinje** ***var.*** Kilwa. Lindi, SE Tanzania
83 J24 **Kilwa Masoko** Lindi, SE Tanzania
xliii I21 **Kilwinning** North Ayrshire, W Scotland, UK
176 Uu11 **Kilwo** Pulau Seram, E Indonesia
116 P12 **Kilyos** İstanbul, NW Turkey
39 V8 **Kim** Colorado, C USA
175 N3 **Kimanis, Teluk** *bay* Sabah, East Malaysia
190 H8 **Kimba** South Australia
30 I15 **Kimball** Nebraska, C USA
31 O11 **Kimball** South Dakota, N USA
81 I21 **Kimbao** Bandundu, SW Zaire
195 N12 **Kimbe** New Britain, E PNG
195 N11 **Kimbe Bay** *inlet* New Britain, E PNG
9 P17 **Kimberley** British Columbia, SW Canada
85 H23 **Kimberley** Northern Cape, C South Africa
188 M4 **Kimberley Plateau** *plateau* Western Australia
35 P15 **Kimberly** Idaho, NW USA
xxxix Q12 **Kimbolton** Cambridgeshire, E England, UK
169 Y12 **Kimch'aek** ***prev.*** Sŏngjin. E North Korea
169 Y15 **Kimch'ŏn** C South Korea
169 Z16 **Kim Hae** ***var.*** Pusan. ✕ (Pusan) SE South Korea
Kími *see* Kými
95 K20 **Kimito** ***Swe.*** Kemiö. Turku-Pori, SW Finland
xxxvi M14 **Kimmeridge** Dorset, S England, UK
172 O6 **Kimobetsu** Hokkaidō, NE Japan
117 I21 **Kímolos** *island* Kykládes, Greece, Aegean Sea
117 I21 **Kímolou Sífnou, Stenó** *strait* Kykládes, Greece, Aegean Sea
130 L5 **Kimovsk** Tul'skaya Oblast', W Russian Federation
169 X15 **Kimpo** ✕ (Sŏul) NW South Korea
Kimpolung *see* Câmpulung Moldovenesc
xxxvii T7 **Kimpton** Hertfordshire, SE England, UK
128 K16 **Kimry** Tverskaya Oblast', W Russian Federation
81 H21 **Kimvula** Bas-Zaïre, SW Zaire
175 Nn2 **Kinabalu, Gunung** ▲ East Malaysia
Kinabatangan *see* Kinabatangan, Sungai
175 Oo3 **Kinabatangan, Sungai** ***var.*** Kinabatangan. ≈ East Malaysia
117 L21 **Kínaros** *island* Kykládes, Greece, Aegean Sea
9 O15 **Kinbasket Lake** ⊡ British Columbia, SW Canada
xlii K8 **Kinbrace** Highland, N Scotland, UK
xliii K19 **Kincardine** Fife, E Scotland, UK
xlii J10 **Kincardine** Highland, NW Scotland, UK
98 K10 **Kincardine** *cultural region* E Scotland, UK
12 E14 **Kincardine** Ontario, S Canada
xliv G3 **Kincaslough** Donegal, N Ireland
xliii K14 **Kincraig** Highland, NW Scotland, UK
81 K21 **Kinda** Kasai Occidental, SE Zaire
81 M24 **Kinda** Shaba, SE Zaire
177 Ff3 **Kindat** Sagaing, N Burma
111 V6 **Kindberg** Steiermark, C Austria
24 H8 **Kinder** Louisiana, S USA
100 H13 **Kinderdijk** Zuid-Holland, SW Netherlands
xxxviii K5 **Kinder Scout** ▲ C England, UK
9 S16 **Kindersley** Saskatchewan, S Canada
78 I14 **Kindia** Guinée-Maritime, SW Guinea
66 B11 **Kindley Field** *air base* E Bermuda
31 R6 **Kindred** North Dakota, N USA
81 N20 **Kindu** ***prev.*** Kindu-Port-Empain. Maniema, C Zaire
Kindu-Port-Empain *see* Kindu
131 S6 **Kinel'** Samarskaya Oblast', W Russian Federation
129 N15 **Kineshma** Ivanovskaya Oblast', W Russian Federation
xxxviii M13 **Kineton** Warwickshire, C England, UK
King *see* King William's Town
146 K10 **King Abdul Aziz** ✕ (Makkah) Makkah, W Saudi Arabia
23 X6 **King and Queen Court House** Virginia, NE USA
xliii H20 **Kingarth** Argyll and Bute, W Scotland, UK
King Charles Islands *see* Kong Karls Land
King Christian IX Land *see* Kong Christian IX Land
King Christian X Land *see* Kong Christian X Land
37 O11 **King City** California, W USA
29 R2 **King City** Missouri, C USA
40 M16 **King Cove** Alaska, USA
28 M10 **Kingfisher** Oklahoma, C USA
King Frederik VI Coast *see* Kong Frederik VI Kyst
King Frederik VIII Land *see* Kong Frederik VIII Land
67 B24 **King George Bay** *bay* West Falkland, Falkland Islands
204 G3 **King George Island** ***var.*** King George Land. *island* South Shetland Islands, Antarctica
10 I6 **King George Islands** *island group* Northwest Territories, C Canada
King George Land *see* King George Island
xliii M19 **Kinghorn** Fife, E Scotland, UK
128 G13 **Kingisepp** Leningradskaya Oblast', NW Russian Federation
191 N14 **King Island** *island* Tasmania, SE Australia
8 J15 **King Island** *island* British Columbia, SW Canada
King Island *see* Kadan Kyun
Kingissepp *see* Kuressaare
147 Q7 **King Khalid** ✕ (Ar Riyāḍ) Ar Riyāḍ, C Saudi Arabia
37 S2 **King Lear Peak** ▲ Nevada, W USA
205 Y8 **King Leopold and Queen Astrid Land** *physical region* Antarctica
188 M4 **King Leopold Ranges** ▲▲ Western Australia
38 I11 **Kingman** Arizona, SW USA
28 M6 **Kingman** Kansas, C USA
199 K7 **Kingman Reef** ◇ *US territory* C Pacific Ocean
81 N20 **Kingombe** Maniema, E Zaire
190 F5 **Kingoonya** South Australia
204 J10 **King Peninsula** *peninsula* Antarctica
41 P13 **King Salmon** Alaska, USA
xliii N18 **Kingsbarns** Fife, E Scotland, UK
37 Q6 **Kings Beach** California, W USA
xxxvi G16 **Kingsbridge** Devon, SW England, UK
xxxviii L9 **King's Bromley** Staffordshire, C England, UK
37 R11 **Kingsburg** California, W USA
xxxviii D14 **Kingsbury** Warwickshire, C England, UK
xxxvi A5 **Kingsbury** Brent, SE England, UK
xxxvi K12 **Kingsbury Episcopi** Somerset, SW England, UK
xxxviii H14 **Kings Caple** Herefordshire, W England, UK
xxxvii Q10 **Kingsclere** Hampshire, S England, UK
xxxix Q10 **King's Cliffe** Northamptonshire, C England, UK
190 I10 **Kingscote** South Australia
King's County *see* Offaly
xliv J7 **Kingscourt** Cavan, N Ireland
204 H2 **King Sejong** *South Korean research station* Antarctica
191 T9 **Kingsford Smith** ✕ (Sydney) New South Wales, SE Australia
9 P17 **Kingsgate** British Columbia, SW Canada
xxxvi H15 **Kingskerswell** Devon, SW England, UK
xxxviii H12 **Kingsland** Herefordshire, W England, UK
25 W8 **Kingsland** Georgia, SE USA
xxxviii K7 **Kingsley** Staffordshire, C England, UK
31 S13 **Kingsley** Iowa, C USA
xxxix T9 **King's Lynn** ***var.*** Bishop's Lynn, Kings Lynn, Lynn, Lynn Regis. Norfolk, E England, UK
xxxvii V15 **King's Mills** Guernsey, Channel Islands
23 Q10 **Kings Mountain** North Carolina, SE USA
xliii M21 **Kings Muir** The Borders, S Scotland, UK
xxxvii X11 **Kingsnorth** Kent, SE England, UK
xxxviii C16 **Kings Norton** Birmingham, C England, UK
xxxvi G13 **King's Nympton** Devon, SW England, UK
188 K4 **King Sound** *sound* Western Australia
39 N2 **Kings Peak** ▲ Utah, W USA
23 O8 **Kingsport** Tennessee, S USA
37 R11 **Kings River** ≈ California, W USA
xxxvii P12 **King's Somborne** Hampshire, S England, UK
xxxix N14 **King's Sutton** Northamptonshire, C England, UK
xxxviii H14 **Kings Thorn** Herefordshire, W England, UK
xxxix O12 **Kingsthorpe** Northamptonshire, C England, UK
xlii M11 **Kingston** Moray, N Scotland, UK
191 P17 **Kingston** Tasmania, SE Australia
12 K14 **Kingston** Ontario, SE Canada
46 K13 **Kingston** ● (Jamaica) E Jamaica
193 C22 **Kingston** Otago, South Island, NZ
21 P12 **Kingston** Massachusetts, NE USA
29 S3 **Kingston** Missouri, C USA
20 K12 **Kingston** New York, NE USA
33 S14 **Kingston** Ohio, N USA
21 O13 **Kingston** Rhode Island, NE USA
22 M9 **Kingston** Tennessee, S USA
xxxvii P8 **Kingston Bagpuize** Oxfordshire, C England, UK
xxxviii H14 **Kingstone** Herefordshire, W England, UK
37 W12 **Kingston Peak** ▲ California, W USA
xxxvi K10 **Kingston Seymour** North West Somerset, SW England, UK
190 J11 **Kingston Southeast** South Australia
xli W14 **Kingston upon Hull** ***var.*** Hull. City of Kingston upon Hull, E England, UK
xli W13 **Kingston upon Hull, City of** ◐ *unitary authority* N England, UK
xxxvii T9 **Kingston upon Thames** Kingston upon Thames, SE England, UK
xxxiv K17 **Kingston upon Thames** ***var.*** Kingston-upon-Thames. ◐ *London borough* SE England, UK
Kingstown *see* Dún Laoghaire
47 P14 **Kingstown** ● (Saint Vincent and the Grenadines) Saint Vincent, Saint Vincent and the Grenadines
23 T13 **Kingstree** South Carolina, SE USA
66 L8 **Kings Trough** *undersea feature* E Atlantic Ocean
12 C18 **Kingsville** Ontario, S Canada
27 S15 **Kingsville** Texas, SW USA
xxxvi H16 **Kingswear** Devon, SW England, UK
xxxviii B15 **Kingswinford** Dudley, C England, UK
xxxvi L10 **Kingswood** South Gloucestershire, SW England, UK
xxxv K8 **Kingswood** Powys, C Wales, UK
xxxvii P11 **Kings Worthy** Hampshire, S England, UK
xxxviii G13 **Kington** Herefordshire, W England, UK
xliii J14 **Kingussie** Highland, NW Scotland, UK
23 W6 **King William** Virginia, NE USA
15 K3 **King William Island** *island* Northwest Territories, N Canada Arctic Ocean
85 I25 **King William's Town** ***var.*** King, Kingwilliamstown. Eastern Cape, S South Africa
23 T3 **Kingwood** West Virginia, NE USA
142 C13 **Kınık** İzmir, W Turkey
81 G21 **Kinkala** Le Pool, S Congo
171 Mm14 **Kinka-san** *headland* Honshū, C Japan
192 M8 **Kinleith** Waikato, North Island, NZ
xliii D14 **Kinloch** Highland, NW Scotland, UK
xliii I18 **Kinlochard** Stirling, C Scotland, UK
xlii H7 **Kinlochbervie** Highland, NW Scotland, UK
xliii G15 **Kinlocheil** Highland, NW Scotland, UK
xlii G11 **Kinlochewe** Highland, NW Scotland, UK
xliii G14 **Kinloch Hourn** Highland, NW Scotland, UK
xliii H16 **Kinlochleven** Highland, NW Scotland, UK
xliii J16 **Kinloch Rannoch** Perth and Kinross, C Scotland, UK
xliii F17 **Kinlochspelve** Argyll and Bute, W Scotland, UK
xlii L11 **Kinloss** Moray, N Scotland, UK
97 J19 **Kinna** Älvsborg, S Sweden
xlii P11 **Kinnaird Head** ***var.*** Kinnairds Head. *headland* NE Scotland, UK
97 K20 **Kinnared** Halland, S Sweden
xliv J8 **Kinnegad** Westmeath, C Ireland
Kinneret, Yam *see* Tiberias, Lake
xxxviii G9 **Kinnerley** Shropshire, W England, UK
xliv H10 **Kinnitty** Offaly, C Ireland
161 K24 **Kinniyai** Eastern Province, NE Sri Lanka
95 L16 **Kinnula** Keski-Suomi, C Finland
12 I8 **Kinojévis** ≈ Québec, SE Canada
170 G16 **Kino-kawa** ≈ Honshū, SW Japan
9 U11 **Kinoosao** Saskatchewan, C Canada
101 L17 **Kinrooi** Limburg, NE Belgium
xliii L18 **Kinross** Perth and Kinross, C Scotland, UK
98 J11 **Kinross** *cultural region* C Scotland, UK
xliv F14 **Kinsale** ***Ir.*** Cionn tSáile. Cork, SW Ireland
xliv H14 **Kinsalebeg** Waterford, S Ireland
97 D14 **Kinsarvik** Hordaland, S Norway
81 G21 **Kinshasa** ***prev.*** Léopoldville. ● (Zaire) Kinshasa, W Zaire
81 G21 **Kinshasa** ***off.*** Ville de Kinshasa, ***var.*** Kinshasa City. ◐ *region* SW Zaire
81 G21 **Kinshasa** ✕ Kinshasa, SW Zaire
Kinshasa City *see* Kinshasa
119 U9 **Kins'ka** ≈ SE Ukraine
28 K6 **Kinsley** Kansas, C USA
23 W10 **Kinston** North Carolina, SE USA
79 P15 **Kintampo** W Ghana
xxxvii P10 **Kintbury** Newbury, S England, UK
xlii O13 **Kintore** Aberdeenshire, NE Scotland, UK
190 B1 **Kintore, Mount** ▲ South Australia
xliii E21 **Kintour** Argyll and Bute, W Scotland, UK
xliii F22 **Kintyre** *peninsula* W Scotland, UK
xliii E23 **Kintyre, Mull of** *headland* W Scotland, UK
177 G4 **Kin-u** Sagaing, C Burma
10 G8 **Kinushseo** ≈ Ontario, C Canada
9 P13 **Kinuso** Alberta, W Canada
xliv E9 **Kinvarra** Galway, W Ireland
xxxviii A15 **Kinver** Staffordshire, C England, UK
160 I13 **Kinwat** Mahārāshtra, C India
83 F16 **Kinyeti** ▲ S Sudan
103 I17 **Kinzig** ≈ SW Germany
197 J13 **Kioa** *island* N Fiji
Kioga, Lake *see* Kyoga, Lake
28 M8 **Kiowa** Kansas, C USA
29 P12 **Kiowa** Oklahoma, C USA
Kiparissía *see* Kyparissía
12 H10 **Kipawa, Lac** ◎ Québec, SE Canada
83 G24 **Kipengere Range** ▲▲ SW Tanzania
83 E23 **Kipili** Rukwa, W Tanzania
83 K20 **Kipini** Coast, SE Kenya
xli R10 **Kiplin** North Yorkshire, N England, UK
9 V16 **Kipling** Saskatchewan, S Canada
40 M13 **Kipnuk** Alaska, USA
xli T14 **Kippax** Leeds, N England, UK
xliii J19 **Kippen** Stirling, C Scotland, UK
xliv K9 **Kippure** ***Ir.*** Cipiúr. ▲ E Ireland
81 N25 **Kipushi** Shaba, SE Zaire
195 Y17 **Kirakira** ***var.*** Kaokaona. San Cristobal, SE Solomon Islands
161 K14 **Kirandul** ***var.*** Bailādila. Madhya Pradesh, C India
161 I21 **Kīranūr** Tamil Nādu, SE India
121 N21 **Kiraw** ***Rus.*** Kirovo. Homyel'skaya Voblasts', SE Belorussia
121 M17 **Kirawsk** ***Rus.*** Kirovsk; ***prev.*** Startsy. Mahilyowskaya Voblasts', E Belorussia
120 F5 **Kirbla** Läänemaa, W Estonia
27 Y9 **Kirbyville** Texas, SW USA
116 M12 **Kırcasalih** Edirne, NW Turkey
111 W8 **Kirchbach** ***var.*** Kirchbach in Steiermark. Steiermark, SE Austria
Kirchbach in Steiermark *see* Kirchbach
110 H7 **Kirchberg** Sankt Gallen, NE Switzerland
111 S5 **Kirchdorf an der Krems** Oberösterreich, N Austria
Kirchheim *see* Kirchheim unter Teck
103 I22 **Kirchheim unter Teck** ***var.*** Kirchheim. Baden-Württemberg, SW Germany
Kirdzhali *see* Kŭrdzhali
126 Jj14 **Kirenga** ≈ S Russian Federation
126 Jj13 **Kirensk** Irkutskaya Oblast', C Russian Federation
Kirghizia *see* Kyrgyzstan
151 S16 **Kirghiz Range** ***Rus.*** Kirgizskiy Khrebet; ***prev.*** Alexander Range. ▲▲ Kazakhstan/Kyrgyzstan
Kirghiz SSR *see* Kyrgyzstan
Kirghiz Steppe *see* Kazakhskiy Melkosopochnik
Kirgizskaya SSR *see* Kyrgyzstan
Kirgizskiy Khrebet *see* Kirghiz Range
81 I19 **Kiri** Bandundu, W Zaire
Kiriath-Arba *see* Hebron
203 R3 **Kiribati** ***off.*** Republic of Kiribati. ◆ *republic* C Pacific Ocean
142 L17 **Kırıkhan** Hatay, S Turkey
142 I13 **Kırıkkale** Kırıkkale, C Turkey
142 C10 **Kırıkkale** ◐ *province* C Turkey
128 L13 **Kirillov** Vologodskaya Oblast', NW Russian Federation
Kirin *see* Jilin
83 I18 **Kirinyaga** ***prev.*** Mount Kenya. ⛰ C Kenya
128 H13 **Kirishi** ***var.*** Kirisi. Leningradskaya Oblast', NW Russian Federation
170 C16 **Kirishima-yama** ▲ Kyūshū, SW Japan
Kirisi *see* Kirishi
203 Y2 **Kiritimati** ✕ Kiritimati, E Kiribati
203 Y2 **Kiritimati** ***prev.*** Christmas Island. *atoll* Line Islands, E Kiribati
195 O15 **Kiriwina Island** ***Eng.*** Trobriand Island. *island* SE PNG
195 O15 **Kiriwina Islands** ***var.*** Trobriand Islands. *island group* S PNG
xlii I4 **Kirkabister** Shetland Islands, NE Scotland, UK
xl L7 **Kirkbampton** Cumbria, NW England, UK
xliii L25 **Kirkbean** Dumfries and Galloway, SW Scotland, UK
xl L7 **Kirkbride** Cumbria, NW England, UK
xli V12 **Kirkburn** East Riding of Yorkshire, N England, UK
xli R15 **Kirkburton** Kirklees, N England, UK
xl C15 **Kirkby** Knowsley, NW England, UK
xxxix N7 **Kirkby in Ashfield** Nottinghamshire, C England, UK
xli N11 **Kirkby Lonsdale** Cumbria, NW England, UK
xli P12 **Kirkby Malham** North Yorkshire, N England, UK
xli R11 **Kirkby Malzeard** North Yorkshire, N England, UK
xli U11 **Kirkbymoorside** North Yorkshire, N England, UK
xli O9 **Kirkby Stephen** Cumbria, NW England, UK
xliii M19 **Kirkcaldy** Fife, E Scotland, UK
xli N6 **Kirkcambeck** Cumbria, NW England, UK
xliii K22 **Kirkconnel** Dumfries and Galloway, SW Scotland, UK
xliii I25 **Kirkcowan** Dumfries and Galloway, SW Scotland, UK
xliii J25 **Kirkcudbright** Dumfries and Galloway, S Scotland, UK
99 I14 **Kirkcudbright** *cultural region* S Scotland, UK
Kirkee *see* Khadki
94 M8 **Kirkenes** ***var.*** Kirkkoniemi. Finnmark, N Norway
97 I14 **Kirkenær** Hedmark, S Norway
xliii K24 **Kirkgunzeon** Dumfries and Galloway, SW Scotland, UK
xl M14 **Kirkham** Lancashire, NW England, UK
xli O7 **Kirkhaugh** Northumberland, N England, UK
xlii I12 **Kirkhill** Highland, NW Scotland, UK
xlii A11 **Kirkibost** *island* NW Scotland, UK
xliii I25 **Kirkinner** Dumfries and Galloway, SW Scotland, UK
xliii J20 **Kirkintilloch** East Dunbartonshire, C Scotland, UK
94 J4 **Kirkjubæjarklaustur** Sudhurland, S Iceland
Kirk-Kilissa *see* Kırklareli
Kirkkoniemi *see* Kirkenes
95 L20 **Kirkkonummi** ***Swe.*** Kyrkslätt. Uusimaa, S Finland
xl K9 **Kirkland** Cumbria, NW England, UK
xliii K23 **Kirkland** Dumfries and Galloway, SW Scotland, UK
12 G7 **Kirkland Lake** Ontario, S Canada
142 C9 **Kırklareli** ***prev.*** Kirk-Kilissa. Kırklareli, NW Turkey
142 I13 **Kırklareli** ◐ *province* NW Turkey
xli Q14 **Kirklees** ◐ *unitary authority* N England, UK
xliii L20 **Kirkliston** City of Edinburgh, SE Scotland, UK
193 F20 **Kirkliston Range** ▲▲ South Island, NZ
xliii H26 **Kirkmaiden** Dumfries and Galloway, SW Scotland, UK
xl G11 **Kirk Michael** W Isle of Man
xliii L16 **Kirkmichael** Perth and Kinross, C Scotland, UK
xliii I23 **Kirkmichael** South Ayrshire, W Scotland, UK
xliii K21 **Kirkmuirhill** South Lanarkshire, C Scotland, UK
xli P2 **Kirknewton** Northumberland, N England, UK
xliii G24 **Kirkolm** Dumfries and Galloway, SW Scotland, UK
xli N8 **Kirkoswald** Cumbria, NW England, UK
xliii H23 **Kirkoswald** South Ayrshire, W Scotland, UK
xliii K24 **Kirkpatrick Durham** Dumfries and Galloway, SW Scotland, UK
12 D10 **Kirkpatrick Lake** ◎ Ontario, S Canada
205 Q11 **Kirkpatrick, Mount** ▲ Antarctica
xl M9 **Kirkstone Pass** *pass* NW England, UK
29 U2 **Kirksville** Missouri, C USA
xliii O14 **Kirkton of Durris** Aberdeenshire, NE Scotland, UK
xliii M16 **Kirkton of Glenisla** Angus, E Scotland, UK
xliii M16 **Kirkton of Kingoldrum** Angus, E Scotland, UK
xliii M18 **Kirkton of Largo** Fife, E Scotland, UK
xlii O13 **Kirkton of Skene** Aberdeenshire, NE Scotland, UK
145 T4 **Kirkūk** ***var.*** Karkūk, Kerkuk. N Iraq
145 U7 **Kir Kush** E Iraq
xlii M4 **Kirkwall** Orkney Islands, NE Scotland, UK
xli Q5 **Kirkwhelpington** Northumberland, N England, UK
85 H25 **Kirkwood** Eastern Cape, S South Africa
29 X5 **Kirkwood** Missouri, C USA
Kirman *see* Kermān
Kir Moab/ Kir of Moab *see* Al Karak
130 I5 **Kirov** Kaluzhskaya Oblast', W Russian Federation
129 R14 **Kirov** ***prev.*** Vyatka. Kirovskaya Oblast', NW Russian Federation
Kīrov *see* Kirovskiy, Kazakhstan
Kīrov *see* Kirova, Taldykorgan, Kazakhstan
151 U13 **Kirova** ***Kaz.*** Kīrov. Taldykorgan, SE Kazakhstan
Kirovabad *see* Gäncä, Azerbaijan
Kirovabad *see* Panj, Tajikistan
Kirovakan *see* Vanadzor
Kirovo *see* Kiraw, Belorussia
Kirovo/Kirovograd *see* Kirovohrad, Ukraine
Kirovo *see* Beshariq, Uzbekistan
129 R14 **Kirovo-Chepetsk** Kirovskaya Oblast', NW Russian Federation
Kirovogradskaya Oblast'/Kirovohrad *see* Kirovohrads'ka Oblast'
119 R7 **Kirovohrad** ***Rus.*** Kirovograd; ***prev.*** Kirovo, Yelizavetgrad, Zinov'yevsk. Kirovohrads'ka Oblast', C Ukraine
119 P7 **Kirovohrads'ka Oblast'** ***var.*** Kirovohrad, ***Rus.*** Kirovogradskaya Oblast'. ◐ *province* C Ukraine
128 J4 **Kirovsk** Murmanskaya Oblast', NW Russian Federation
Kirovsk *see* Kirawsk, Belorussia
Kirovsk *see* Babadaykhan, Turkmenistan
119 X7 **Kirovs'k** Luhans'ka Oblast', E Ukraine
125 Dd9 **Kirovskaya Oblast'** ◐ *province* NW Russian Federation
119 X8 **Kirov'ske** Donets'ka Oblast', E Ukraine
119 U13 **Kirovs'ke** ***Rus.*** Kirovskoye. Respublika Krym, S Ukraine
151 V14 **Kirovskiy** ***Kaz.*** Kīrov. Taldykorgan, SE Kazakhstan
127 P12 **Kirovskiy** Kamchatskaya Oblast', E Russian Federation
Kirovskoye *see* Kyzyl-Adyr
Kirovskoye *see* Kirovs'ke
124 Oo2 **Kırpaşa** ***var.*** Karpas Peninsula, ***Gk.*** Karpasía. *peninsula* NE Cyprus
152 E11 **Kirpili** Akhalskiy Velayat, C Turkmenistan
xliii M16 **Kirriemuir** Angus, E Scotland, UK
129 S13 **Kirs** Kirovskaya Oblast', NW Russian Federation
131 N7 **Kirsanov** Tambovskaya Oblast', W Russian Federation
142 J14 **Kirşehir** ***anc.*** Justinianopolis. Kirşehir, C Turkey
142 I13 **Kirşehir** ◐ *province* C Turkey
155 P4 **Kīrthar Range** ▲▲ S Pakistan
39 P9 **Kirtland** New Mexico, SW USA
xliii M24 **Kirtlebridge** Dumfries and Galloway, SW Scotland, UK
xxxvii P7 **Kirtlington** Oxfordshire, C England, UK
xxxix S7 **Kirton** Lincolnshire, E England, UK
xxxix O6 **Kirton** Nottinghamshire, C England, UK
xxxix X13 **Kirton** Suffolk, E England, UK
xxxix P4 **Kirton in Lindsey** North Lincolnshire, N England, UK
Kirun/Kirun' *see* Chilung
94 J11 **Kiruna** Norrbotten, N Sweden
81 M18 **Kirundu** Haut-Zaïre, NE Zaire
28 L3 **Kirwin Reservoir** ⊡ Kansas, C USA
131 Q4 **Kirya** Chuvashskaya Respublika, W Russian Federation
171 K15 **Kiryū** Gunma, Honshū, S Japan
97 M18 **Kisa** Östergötland, S Sweden
171 Ll11 **Kisakata** Akita, Honshū, C Japan
Kisalföld *see* Little Alföld
81 L18 **Kisangani** ***prev.*** Stanleyville. Haut-Zaïre, NE Zaire
41 N12 **Kisaralik River** ≈ Alaska, USA
171 K17 **Kisarazu** Chiba, Honshū, S Japan
113 I22 **Kisbér** Komárom-Esztergom, NW Hungary
9 V17 **Kisbey** Saskatchewan, S Canada
126 H14 **Kiselevsk** Kemerovskaya Oblast', S Russian Federation
159 R13 **Kishanganj** Bihār, NE India
158 G12 **Kishangarh** Rājasthān, N India
Kishegyes *see* Mali Iđoš
79 S15 **Kishi** Oyo, W Nigeria
Kishinev *see* Chişinău
Kishiözen *see* Malyy Uzen'
171 Gg15 **Kishiwada** ***var.*** Kisiwada. Ōsaka, Honshū, SW Japan
149 P14 **Kīsh, Jazīreh-ye** ***var.*** Qeys. *island* S Iran
158 I6 **Kishtwār** Jammu and Kashmir, NW India
83 H19 **Kisii** Nyanza, SW Kenya
83 J23 **Kisiju** Pwani, E Tanzania
Kisiwada *see* Kishiwada
Kisjenő *see* Chişineu-Criş
40 E17 **Kiska Island** *island* Aleutian Islands, Alaska, USA
Kiskapus *see* Copşa Mică
113 M22 **Kiskörei-víztároló** ⊡ E Hungary
Kis-Küküllo *see* Târnava Mică
113 L24 **Kiskunfélegyháza** ***var.*** Félegyháza. Bács-Kiskun, C Hungary
113 K25 **Kiskunhalas** ***var.*** Halas. Bács-Kiskun, S Hungary
113 K24 **Kiskunmajsa** Bács-Kiskun, S Hungary
131 N15 **Kislovodsk** Stavropol'skiy Kray, SW Russian Federation
83 L18 **Kismaayo** ***var.*** Chisimayu, Kismayu, ***It.*** Chisimaio. Jubbada Hoose, S Somalia
Kismayu *see* Kismaayo
171 Ii15 **Kiso-sanmyaku** ▲▲ Honshū, S Japan
Kisseraing *see* Kanmaw Kyun
78 K14 **Kissidougou** Guinée-Forestière, S Guinea
25 X12 **Kissimmee** Florida, SE USA
25 X12 **Kissimmee, Lake** ◎ Florida, SE USA
25 X13 **Kissimmee River** ≈ Florida, SE USA
9 V13 **Kississing Lake** ◎ Manitoba, C Canada
113 L24 **Kistelek** Csongrád, SE Hungary
Kistna *see* Krishna
113 M23 **Kisújszállás** Jász-Nagykun-Szolnok, E Hungary
170 F12 **Kisuki** Shimane, Honshū, SW Japan
83 H18 **Kisumu** ***prev.*** Port Florence. Nyanza, W Kenya
Kisutzaneustadtl *see* Kysucké Nové Mesto
113 O20 **Kisvárda** ***Ger.*** Kleinwardein. Szabolcs-Szatmár-Bereg, E Hungary
83 J24 **Kiswere** Lindi, SE Tanzania
Kiszucaújhely *see* Kysucké Nové Mesto
78 K12 **Kita** Kayes, W Mali
Kitab *see* Kitob
172 N5 **Kitahiyama** Hokkaidō, NE Japan
171 L15 **Kita-Ibaraki** Ibaraki, Honshū, S Japan
172 Ss17 **Kita-Iō-jima** ***Eng.*** San Alessandro. *island* SE Japan
171 Mm11 **Kitakami** Iwate, Honshū, C Japan
171 M13 **Kitakami-gawa** ≈ Honshū, C Japan
172 N11 **Kitakami-sanchi** ▲▲ Honshū, C Japan
171 L13 **Kitakata** Fukushima, Honshū, C Japan
170 D12 **Kitakyūshū** ***var.*** Kitakyûsyû. Fukuoka, Kyūshū, SW Japan
Kitakyûsyû *see* Kitakyūshū
83 H18 **Kitale** Rift Valley, W Kenya
172 Q5 **Kitami** Hokkaidō, NE Japan
172 Pp4 **Kitami-sanchi** ▲▲ Hokkaidō, NE Japan
171 Kk17 **Kita-ura** ◎ Honshū, S Japan
195 O15 **Kitava Island** *island* Kiriwina Islands, SE PNG
39 W5 **Kit Carson** Colorado, C USA
188 M12 **Kitchener** Western Australia
12 F16 **Kitchener** Ontario, S Canada
95 O17 **Kitee** Pohjois-Karjala, SE Finland
83 G16 **Kitgum** N Uganda
Kithareng *see* Kanmaw Kyun
Kíthira *see* Kýthira
Kíthnos *see* Kýthnos
15 J3 **Kitikmeot** ◐ *district* Northwest Territories, N Canada
8 J13 **Kitimat** British Columbia, SW Canada
94 L11 **Kitinen** ≈ N Finland
153 N12 **Kitob** ***Rus.*** Kitab. Qashqadaryo Wiloyati, S Uzbekistan
118 K7 **Kitsman'** ***Ger.*** Kotzman, ***Rom.*** Cozmeni, ***Rus.*** Kitsman. Chernivets'ka Oblast', W Ukraine
170 Dd14 **Kitsuki** ***var.*** Kituki. Ōita, Kyūshū, SW Japan
20 C14 **Kittanning** Pennsylvania, NE USA
21 P10 **Kittery** Maine, NE USA
94 L11 **Kittilä** Lappi, N Finland
111 Z4 **Kittsee** Burgenland, E Austria
83 J19 **Kitui** Eastern, S Kenya
Kituki *see* Kitsuki
83 G22 **Kitunda** Tabora, C Tanzania
8 K13 **Kitwanga** British Columbia, SW Canada
84 J13 **Kitwe** ***var.*** Kitwe-Nkana. Copperbelt, C Zambia
Kitwe-Nkana *see* Kitwe
111 O7 **Kitzbühel** Tirol, W Austria
111 O7 **Kitzbüheler Alpen** ▲▲ W Austria
103 J19 **Kitzingen** Bayern, SE Germany
159 Q14 **Kiul** Bihār, NE India
194 E12 **Kiunga** Western, SW PNG
95 M16 **Kiuruvesi** Kuopio, C Finland
40 M7 **Kivalina** Alaska, USA
94 L13 **Kivalo** *ridge* C Finland
118 J3 **Kivertsi** ***Pol.*** Kiwerce, ***Rus.*** Kivertsy. Volyns'ka Oblast', NW Ukraine
Kivertsy *see* Kivertsi
95 L16 **Kivijärvi** Keski-Suomi, C Finland
97 L23 **Kivik** Kristianstad, S Sweden
120 J3 **Kiviõli** Ida-Virumaa, NE Estonia
Kivu, Lac *see* Kivu, Lake
69 U10 **Kivu, Lake** ***Fr.*** Lac Kivu. ◎ Rwanda/Zaire
194 G15 **Kiwai Island** *island* SW PNG
41 N8 **Kiwalik** Alaska, USA
Kiwerce *see* Kivertsi
Kiyev *see* Kyyiv
151 R10 **Kiyevka** Karaganda, C Kazakhstan
Kiyevskaya Oblast' *see* Kyyivs'ka Oblast'
Kiyevskoye Vodokhranilishche *see* Kyyivs'ke Vodoskhovyshche
142 D10 **Kıyıköy** Kırklareli, NW Turkey
151 O9 **Kiyma** Turgay, C Kazakhstan
129 V13 **Kizel** Permskaya Oblast', NW Russian Federation
129 O12 **Kizema** ***var.*** Kizëma. Arkhangel'skaya Oblast', NW Russian Federation
Kizilagach *see* Elkhovo
142 H12 **Kızılcahamam** Ankara, N Turkey
142 J10 **Kızıl Irmak** ≈ C Turkey
Kızılkoca *see* Şefaatli
Kizil Kum *see* Kyzyl Kum
143 P16 **Kızıltepe** Mardin, SE Turkey
Ki Zil Uzen *see* Qezel Owzan
131 Q16 **Kizilyurt** Respublika Dagestan, SW Russian Federation
131 Q15 **Kizlyar** Respublika Dagestan, SW Russian Federation
131 S3 **Kizner** Udmurtskaya Respublika, NW Russian Federation
Kizyl-Arvat *see* Gyzylarbat
152 B13 **Kizyl-Atrek** ***Turkm.*** Gyzyletrek. Balkanskiy Velayat, W Turkmenistan
152 D10 **Kizyl-Kaya** ***Turkm.*** Gyzylgaya. Balkanskiy Velayat, NW Turkmenistan
152 A10 **Kizyl-Su** ***Turkm.*** Gyzylsu. Balkanskiy Velayat, W Turkmenistan
97 H16 **Kjerkøy** *island* S Norway
Kjølen *see* Kölen
94 L7 **Kjøllefjord** Finnmark, N Norway
94 H11 **Kjøpsvik** Nordland, C Norway
174 Ii9 **Klabat, Teluk** *bay* Pulau Bangka, W Indonesia
114 I12 **Kladanj** E Bosnia and Herzegovina
176 Xx16 **Kladar** Irian Jaya, E Indonesia
113 C16 **Kladno** Střední Čechy, NW Czech Republic
114 P11 **Kladovo** Serbia, E Yugoslavia
178 Hh12 **Klaeng** Rayong, S Thailand
111 T9 **Klagenfurt** ***Slvn.*** Celovec. Kärnten, S Austria
120 B11 **Klaipėda** ***Ger.*** Memel. Klaipėda, NW Lithuania
174 M15 **Klakah** Jawa, C Indonesia
36 L2 **Klamath** California, W USA
34 H16 **Klamath Falls** Oregon, NW USA
36 M1 **Klamath Mountains** ▲▲ California/Oregon, W USA
36 L2 **Klamath River** ≈ California/Oregon, W USA

◆ Country
● Country Capital
◇ Dependent Territory
○ Dependent Territory Capital
◐ Administrative Region
✕ International Airport
▲ Mountain
▲▲ Mountain Range
⛰ Volcano
≈ River
◎ Lake
⊡ Reservoir

KLANG – KORLIKI

174 Gg5 **Klang** var. Kelang; prev. Port Swettenham. Selangor, Peninsular Malaysia
96 J13 **Klarälven** Norway/Sweden
113 B15 **Klášterec nad Ohří** Ger. Klösterle an der Eger. Severní Čechy, NW Czech Republic
174 L15 **Klaten** Jawa, C Indonesia
113 B18 **Klatovy** Ger. Klattau. Západní Čechy, SW Czech Republic
Klattau see Klatovy
Klausenburg see Cluj-Napoca
41 Y14 **Klawock** Prince of Wales Island, Alaska, USA
100 P8 **Klazienaveen** Drenthe, NE Netherlands
Kleck see Klyetsk
112 H11 **Kłecko** Poznań, W Poland
112 I11 **Kleczew** Konin, C Poland
8 L15 **Kleena Kleene** British Columbia, SW Canada
85 D20 **Klein Aub** Hardap, C Namibia
Kleine Donau see Mosoni-Duna
103 O14 **Kleine Elster** E Germany
Kleine Kokel see Târnava Mică
101 I16 **Kleine Nete** N Belgium
Kleines Ungarisches Tiefland see Little Alföld
85 E22 **Klein Karas** Karas, S Namibia
Kleinkopisch see Copşa Mică
Klein-Marien see Väike-Maarja
Kleinschlatten see Zlatna
85 D23 **Kleinsee** Northern Cape, W South Africa
Kleinwardein see Kisvárda
117 C16 **Kleisoúra** Ípeiros, W Greece
97 C17 **Klepp** Rogaland, S Norway
85 I22 **Klerksdorp** North-West, N South Africa
130 I5 **Kletnya** Bryanskaya Oblast', W Russian Federation
Kletsk see Klyetsk
103 D14 **Kleve** Eng. Cleves, Fr. Clèves; prev. Cleve. Nordrhein-Westfalen, W Germany
115 J16 **Kličevo** Montenegro, SW Yugoslavia
121 M16 **Klichaw** Rus. Klichev. Mahilyowskaya Voblasts', E Belorussia
Klichev see Klichaw
121 Q16 **Klimavichy** Rus. Klimovichi. Mahilyowskaya Voblasts', E Belorussia
116 M7 **Kliment** Varnenska Oblast, NE Bulgaria
Klimovichi see Klimavichy
95 G14 **Klimpfjäll** Västerbotten, N Sweden
130 K3 **Klin** Moskovskaya Oblast', W Russian Federation
115 M16 **Klina** Serbia, S Yugoslavia
113 B15 **Klínovec** Ger. Keilberg. ▲ NW Czech Republic
97 P19 **Klintehamn** Gotland, SE Sweden
131 R8 **Klintsovka** Saratovskaya Oblast', W Russian Federation
130 H6 **Klintsy** Bryanskaya Oblast', W Russian Federation
97 K22 **Klippan** Kristianstad, S Sweden
94 G13 **Klippen** Västerbotten, N Sweden
124 Nn3 **Klírou** W Cyprus
116 I9 **Klisura** Plovdivska Oblast, C Bulgaria
97 F20 **Klitmøller** Viborg, NW Denmark
114 F11 **Ključ** NW Bosnia and Herzegovina
113 J14 **Kłobuck** Częstochowa, S Poland
112 J11 **Kłodawa** Konin, C Poland
113 G16 **Kłodzko** Ger. Glatz. Wałbrzych, SW Poland
97 I14 **Kløfta** Akershus, S Norway
114 P12 **Kločevac** Serbia, E Yugoslavia
120 G3 **Klooga** Ger. Lodensee. Harjumaa, NW Estonia
101 F15 **Kloosterzande** Zeeland, SW Netherlands
115 L19 **Klos** var. Klosi. Dibër, C Albania
Klosi see Klos
Klösterle an der Eger see Klášterec nad Ohří
111 X3 **Klosterneuburg** Niederösterreich, NE Austria
110 J9 **Klosters** Graubünden, SE Switzerland
110 G7 **Kloten** Zürich, N Switzerland
110 G7 **Kloten** ✕ (Zürich) Zürich, N Switzerland
102 K12 **Klötze** Sachsen-Anhalt, C Germany
10 K3 **Klotz, Lac** ◎ Québec, NE Canada
103 O15 **Klotzsche** ✕ (Dresden) Sachsen, E Germany
8 H7 **Kluane Lake** ◎ Yukon Territory, W Canada
Kluang see Keluang
113 I14 **Kluczbork** Ger. Kreuzburg, Kreuzburg in Oberschlesien. Opole, SW Poland
41 W12 **Klukwan** Alaska, USA
Klyastitsy see Klyastsitsy
120 L11 **Klyastsitsy** Rus. Klyastitsy. Vitsyebskaya Voblasts', N Belorussia
131 T5 **Klyavlino** Samarskaya Oblast', W Russian Federation
86 K9 **Klyaz'in** W Russian Federation
131 N3 **Klyaz'ma** W Russian Federation
121 J17 **Klyetsk** Pol. Kleck, Rus. Kletsk. Minskaya Voblasts', SW Belorussia
153 S8 **Klyuchevka** Talasskaya Oblast', NW Kyrgyzstan
127 Pp10 **Klyuchevskaya Sopka, Vulkan** E Russian Federation
127 Pp10 **Klyuchi** Kamchatskaya Oblast', E Russian Federation
97 D17 **Knaben** Vest-Agder, S Norway
Knanzi see Ghanzi
xxxvii S10 **Knaphill** Surrey, SE England, UK
97 K21 **Knäred** Halland, S Sweden
xli T12 **Knaresborough** North Yorkshire, N England, UK
xli O7 **Knarsdale** Northumberland, N England, UK
xli S11 **Knayton** North Yorkshire, N England, UK
xxxvii T7 **Knebworth** Hertfordshire, SE England, UK
xxxix O6 **Kneesall** Nottinghamshire, C England, UK
116 H8 **Knezha** Oblast Montana, NW Bulgaria
27 O9 **Knickerbocker** Texas, SW USA
30 K5 **Knife River** North Dakota, N USA
8 K16 **Knight Inlet** inlet British Columbia, W Canada
41 S12 **Knight Island** island Alaska, USA
xxxv K10 **Knighton** Powys, E Wales, UK
37 O7 **Knights Landing** California, W USA
xliv B13 **Knightstown** Kerry, SW Ireland
114 E13 **Knin** Zadar-Knin, S Croatia
27 Q12 **Knippal** Texas, SW USA
111 U7 **Knittelfeld** Steiermark, C Austria
xxxviii L7 **Kniveton** Derbyshire, C England, UK
97 O15 **Knivsta** Uppsala, C Sweden
115 P14 **Knjaževac** Serbia, E Yugoslavia
29 S4 **Knob Noster** Missouri, C USA
xliv E7 **Knock** Mayo, NW Ireland
xlii N11 **Knock** Moray, N Scotland, UK
xlii D8 **Knock** Western Isles, NW Scotland, UK
xliv H14 **Knockadoon Head** headland S Ireland
xliv E11 **Knockalough** Clare, W Ireland
xlii H9 **Knockan** Highland, NW Scotland, UK
xlii L13 **Knockandhu** Moray, N Scotland, UK
xliv G8 **Knockcroghery** Roscommon, C Ireland
xliii G22 **Knockenkelly** North Ayrshire, W Scotland, UK
xliv F12 **Knocklong** Limerick, SW Ireland
xliv G13 **Knockmealdown Mountains** ▲ S Ireland
xliv I12 **Knocktopher** Kilkenny, SE Ireland
101 D15 **Knokke-Heist** West-Vlaanderen, NW Belgium
97 H20 **Knøsen** hill N Denmark
Knosós see Knossos
117 J25 **Knossos** Gk. Knosós. prehistoric site Kríti, Greece, E Mediterranean Sea
27 N7 **Knott** Texas, SW USA
xli S14 **Knottingley** Wakefield, N England, UK
xxxviii D16 **Knowle** Solihull, C England, UK
204 K5 **Knowles, Cape** headland Antarctica
xl C15 **Knowsley** Knowsley, NW England, UK
xl M17 **Knowsley** ◐ unitary authority NW England, UK
33 O11 **Knox** Indiana, N USA
31 O3 **Knox** North Dakota, N USA
20 C13 **Knox** Pennsylvania, NE USA
201 X8 **Knox Atoll** var. Ņadikdik, Narikrik. atoll Ratak Chain, SE Marshall Islands
8 H13 **Knox, Cape** headland Graham Island, British Columbia, SW Canada
27 P5 **Knox City** Texas, SW USA
205 Y11 **Knox Coast** physical region Antarctica
33 T12 **Knox Lake** ▣ Ohio, N USA
25 T5 **Knoxville** Georgia, SE USA
32 K12 **Knoxville** Illinois, N USA
31 W15 **Knoxville** Iowa, C USA
23 N9 **Knoxville** Tennessee, S USA
207 P11 **Knud Rasmussen Land** physical region N Greenland
Knüll see Knüllgebirge
103 I16 **Knüllgebirge** var. Knüll. ▲ C Germany
xl F17 **Knutsford** Cheshire, W England, UK
Knyazhevo see Sredishte
Knyazhitsy see Knyazhytsy
121 O15 **Knyazhytsy** Rus. Knyazhitsy. Mahilyowskaya Voblasts', E Belorussia
85 G26 **Knysna** Western Cape, SW South Africa
176 V10 **Koagas** Irian Jaya, E Indonesia
83 J22 **Koani** Zanzibar South, E Tanzania
Koartac see Quaqtaq
174 J10 **Koba** Pulau Bangka, W Indonesia
170 C16 **Kobayashi** var. Kobayasi. Miyazaki, Kyūshū, SW Japan
Kobayasi see Kobayashi
171 Gg14 **Kōbe** Hyōgo, Honshū, SW Japan
Kobelyaki see Kobelyaky
119 T6 **Kobelyaky** Rus. Kobelyaki. Poltavs'ka Oblast', NE Ukraine
97 J22 **København** Eng. Copenhagen; anc. Hafnia. ● (Denmark) Sjælland, København, E Denmark
97 J23 **København** off. Københavns Amt. ◐ county E Denmark
78 K10 **Kobenni** Hodh el Gharbi, S Mauritania
176 U11 **Kobi** Pulau Seram, E Indonesia
103 F17 **Koblenz** prev. Coblenz, Fr. Coblence, anc. Confluentes. Rheinland-Pfalz, W Germany
110 F6 **Koblenz** Aargau, N Switzerland
176 Ww11 **Kobowre, Pegunungan** ▲ Irian Jaya, E Indonesia
160 L11 **Kobra** Madhya Pradesh, C India
Kobrin see Kobryn
176 W14 **Kobroor, Pulau** island Kepulauan Aru, E Indonesia
121 G19 **Kobryn** Pol. Kobryn, Rus. Kobrin. Brestskaya Voblasts', SW Belorussia
41 O7 **Kobuk** Alaska, USA
41 O7 **Kobuk River** Alaska, USA
143 Q10 **K'obulet'i** W Georgia
126 Ll10 **Kobyay** Respublika Sakha (Yakutiya), NE Russian Federation
142 E11 **Kocaeli** ◐ province NW Turkey
115 P18 **Kočani** NE FYR Macedonia
114 K12 **Koceljevo** Serbia, W Yugoslavia
111 U12 **Kočevje** Ger. Gottschee. S Slovenia
159 T12 **Koch Bihār** West Bengal, NE India
126 J10 **Kochechum** N Russian Federation
103 I20 **Kocher** SW Germany
129 T13 **Kochevo** Komi-Permyatskiy Avtonomnyy Okrug, NW Russian Federation
170 Ee15 **Kōchi** var. Kôti. Kōchi, Shikoku, SW Japan
170 Ee15 **Kōchi** off. Kōchi-ken, var. Kôti. ◐ prefecture Shikoku, SW Japan
Kochi see Cochin
Kochiu see Gejiu
Kochkor see Kochkorka
153 V8 **Kochkorka** Kir. Kochkor. Narynskaya Oblast', C Kyrgyzstan
129 V5 **Kochmes** Respublika Komi, NW Russian Federation
131 P15 **Kochubey** Respublika Dagestan, SW Russian Federation
117 I17 **Kochýlas** ▲ Skýros, Vóreioi Sporádes, Greece, Aegean Sea
112 O13 **Kock** Lublin, E Poland
83 J19 **Kodacho** spring/well S Kenya
161 K24 **Koddiyar Bay** bay NE Sri Lanka
41 Q14 **Kodiak** Kodiak Island, Alaska, USA
41 Q14 **Kodiak Island** island Alaska, USA
160 B12 **Kodīnār** Gujarāt, W India
128 M9 **Kodino** Arkhangel'skaya Oblast', NW Russian Federation
126 Ii13 **Kodinsk** Krasnoyarskiy Kray, C Russian Federation
82 F12 **Kodok** Upper Nile, SE Sudan
119 N8 **Kodyma** Odes'ka Oblast', SW Ukraine
101 B17 **Koekelare** West-Vlaanderen, W Belgium
Koeln see Köln
Koepang see Kupang
Ko-erh-mu see Golmud
101 J17 **Koersel** Limburg, NE Belgium
85 E21 **Koës** Karas, SE Namibia
Koetai see Mahakam, Sungai
Koetaradja see Bandaaceh
38 I14 **Kofa Mountains** ▲ Arizona, SW USA
176 Z15 **Kofarau** Irian Jaya, E Indonesia
153 P13 **Kofarnihon** Rus. Kofarnikhon; prev. Ordzhonikidzeabad, Taj. Orjonikidzeobod, Yangi-Bazar. W Tajikistan
153 P14 **Kofarnihon** Rus. Kafirnigan. SW Tajikistan
Kofarnikhon see Kofarnihon
116 M11 **Kofçaz** Kırklareli, NW Turkey
176 U9 **Kofiau, Pulau** var. Kafiau. island Kepulauan Raja Ampat, E Indonesia
117 J25 **Kófinas** ▲ Kríti, Greece, E Mediterranean Sea
124 Nn4 **Kofínou** var. Kophinou. S Cyprus
111 V8 **Köflach** Steiermark, SE Austria
79 Q17 **Koforidua** SE Ghana
170 Ff12 **Kōfu** Tottori, Honshū, SW Japan
171 J15 **Kōfu** var. Kôhu. Yamanashi, Honshū, S Japan
171 K16 **Koga** Ibaraki, Honshū, S Japan
83 F22 **Koga** Tabora, C Tanzania
Kogălniceanu see Mihail Kogălniceanu
11 P6 **Kogaluk** Newfoundland and Labrador, E Canada
10 J4 **Kogaluk** Québec, NE Canada
126 Gg10 **Kogalym** Khanty-Mansiyskiy Avtonomnyy Okrug, C Russian Federation
97 J23 **Køge** Roskilde, E Denmark
97 J23 **Køge Bugt** bay E Denmark
79 U16 **Kogi** ◐ state C Nigeria
152 L11 **Kogon** Rus. Kagan. Bukhoro Wiloyati, C Uzbekistan
169 Y17 **Kŏgŭm-do** island S South Korea
Kőhalom see Rupea
155 T6 **Kohāt** North-West Frontier Province, NW Pakistan
120 G4 **Kohila** Ger. Koil. Raplamaa, NW Estonia
159 X13 **Kohīma** Nāgāland, E India
Koh I Noh see Büyükağrı Dağı
148 L10 **Kohkīlūyeh va Būyer Aḩmadī** off. Ostān-e Kohklūyeh va Būyer Aḩmadi, var. Boyer Ahmadī va Kohkīlūyeh. ◐ province SW Iran
Kohsān see Kūhestān
120 J3 **Kohtla-Järve** Ida-Virumaa, NE Estonia
Kôhu see Kōfu
119 N10 **Kohyl'nyk** Rom. Cogîlnic. Moldavia/Ukraine
171 K13 **Koide** Niigata, Honshū, C Japan
8 G7 **Koidern** Yukon Territory, W Canada
78 J15 **Koidu** E Sierra Leone
120 I4 **Koigi** Järvamaa, C Estonia
Koil see Kohila
180 H13 **Koimbani** Grande Comore, NW Comoros
145 T3 **Koi Sanjaq** var. Koysanjaq, Küysanjaq. N Iraq
95 O16 **Koitere** ◎ E Finland
Koivisto see Primorsk
169 Z16 **Kŏje-do** Jap. Kyōsai-tō. island S South Korea
82 J13 **K'ok'a Hāyk'** ◎ C Ethiopia
Kokand see Qŭqon
190 F6 **Kokatha** South Australia
Kokcha see Kŭkcha
Kokchetav/Kokchetavskaya Oblast' see Kokshetau
95 K18 **Kokemäenjoki** SW Finland
176 X12 **Kokenau** var. Kokonau. Irian Jaya, E Indonesia
85 E22 **Kokerboom** Karas, SE Namibia
121 N14 **Kokhanava** Rus. Kokhanovo. Vitsyebskaya Voblasts', NE Belorussia
Kokhanovichi see Kakhanavichy
Kokhanovo see Kokhanava
Kök-Janggak see Kok-Yangak
95 K16 **Kokkola** Swe. Karleby; prev. Swe. Gamlakarleby. Vaasa, W Finland
164 L3 **Kok Kuduk** well N China
120 H9 **Koknese** Aizkraukle, C Latvia
79 T13 **Koko** Kebbi, W Nigeria
194 K15 **Kokoda** Northern, S PNG
78 K12 **Kokofata** Kayes, W Mali
41 N6 **Kokolik River** Alaska, USA
33 O13 **Kokomo** Indiana, N USA
Kokonau see Kokenau
Koko Nor see Qinghai Hu, China
Koko Nor see Qinghai, China
195 P10 **Kokopo** var. Kopopo; prev. Herbertshöhe. New Britain, E PNG
151 X10 **Kokpekti** Kaz. Kökpekti. Semipalatinsk, E Kazakhstan
151 X11 **Kokpekti** E Kazakhstan
41 P9 **Kokrines** Alaska, USA
41 P9 **Kokrines Hills** ▲ Alaska, USA
151 P17 **Koksaray** Yuzhnyy Kazakhstan, S Kazakhstan
153 X9 **Kokshaal-Tau** Rus. Khrebet Kakshaal-Too. ▲ China/Kyrgyzstan
151 P7 **Kokshetau** Kaz. Kökshetaū; prev. Kokchetav. Kokshetau, N Kazakhstan
151 P7 **Kokshetau** off. Kokshetauskaya Oblast', Kaz. Kökshetaū Oblysy; prev. Kokchetavskaya Oblast'. ◐ province N Kazakhstan
Kökshetaū Oblysy/Kokshetauskaya Oblast' see Kokshetau
101 A17 **Koksijde** West-Vlaanderen, W Belgium
10 M5 **Koksoak** Québec, E Canada
85 K24 **Kokstad** KwaZulu/Natal, E South Africa
151 W15 **Koktal** Kaz. Köktal. Taldykorgan, SE Kazakhstan
151 Q12 **Koktas** C Kazakhstan
Kök-Tash see Këk-Tash
Koktokay see Fuyun
170 C16 **Kokubu** Kagoshima, Kyūshū, SW Japan
126 L15 **Kokuy** Chitinskaya Oblast', S Russian Federation
153 T9 **Kok-Yangak** Kir. Kök-Janggak. Dzhalal-Abadskaya Oblast', W Kyrgyzstan
164 F9 **Kokyar** Xinjiang Uygur Zizhiqu, W China
155 O13 **Kolāchi** var. Kulachi. SW Pakistan
78 J15 **Kolahun** N Liberia
175 Q12 **Kolaka** Sulawesi, C Indonesia
Kolam see Quilon
K'o-la-ma-i see Karamay
Kola Peninsula see Kol'skiy Poluostrov
161 H19 **Kolār** Karnātaka, E India
161 H19 **Kolār Gold Fields** Karnātaka, E India
94 K11 **Kolari** Lappi, NW Finland
113 I21 **Kolárovo** Ger. Gutta; prev. Guta, Hung. Gúta. Západné Slovensko, SW Slovakia
115 K16 **Kolašin** Montenegro, SW Yugoslavia
158 F11 **Kolāyat** Rājasthān, NW India
97 N15 **Kolbäck** Västmanland, C Sweden
Kolbcha see Kowbcha
207 Q15 **Kolbeinsey Ridge** undersea feature Denmark Strait/Norwegian Sea
Kolberg see Kołobrzeg
97 H15 **Kolbotn** Akershus, S Norway
113 N16 **Kolbuszowa** Rzeszów, SE Poland
130 L3 **Kol'chugino** Vladimirskaya Oblast', W Russian Federation
78 H12 **Kolda** S Senegal
97 G23 **Kolding** Vejle, C Denmark
81 M17 **Kole** Haut-Zaïre, N Zaire
81 K20 **Kole** Kasai Oriental, SW Zaire
Kōle see Kili Island
86 F6 **Kölen** Nor. Kjølen. ▲ Norway/Sweden
Kolepom, Pulau see Yos Sudarso, Pulau
120 H3 **Kolga Laht** Ger. Kolko-Wiek. bay N Estonia
129 Q3 **Kolguyev, Ostrov** island NW Russian Federation
161 E16 **Kolhāpur** Mahārāshtra, SW India
157 K21 **Kolhumadulu Atoll** var. Kolumadulu Atoll, Thaa Atoll. atoll S Maldives
95 O16 **Koli** var. Kolinkylä. Pohjois-Karjala, E Finland
41 O13 **Koliganek** Alaska, USA
113 E16 **Kolín** Ger. Kolin. Střední Čechy, C Czech Republic
Kolinkylä see Koli
202 E12 **Koliu** Île Futuna, W Wallis and Futuna
120 E7 **Kolka** Talsi, NW Latvia
120 E7 **Kolkasrags** prev. Eng. Cape Domesnes. headland NW Latvia
Kolkhozabad see Kolkhozobod
153 P14 **Kolkhozobod** Rus. Kolkhozabad; prev. Kaganovichabad, Tugalan. SW Tajikistan
Kolki/Kołki see Kolky
Kolko-Wiek see Kolga Laht
118 K3 **Kolky** Pol. Kołki, Rus. Kolki. Volyns'ka Oblast', NW Ukraine
Kollam see Quilon
161 G20 **Kollegāl** Karnātaka, W India
100 M5 **Kollum** Friesland, N Netherlands
Kolmar see Colmar
103 E16 **Köln** var. Koeln, Eng./Fr. Cologne; prev. Cöln, anc. Colonia Agrippina, Oppidum Ubiorum. Nordrhein-Westfalen, W Germany
112 N9 **Kolno** Łomża, NE Poland
112 J12 **Koło** Konin, C Poland
40 B8 **Koloa** Haw. Kōloa. Kauai, Hawaii, USA, C Pacific Ocean
112 E7 **Kołobrzeg** Ger. Kolberg. Koszalin, NW Poland
130 H4 **Kolodnya** Smolenskaya Oblast', W Russian Federation
202 E13 **Kolofau, Mont** Île Alofi, S Wallis and Futuna
129 O14 **Kologriv** Kostromskaya Oblast', NW Russian Federation
78 L12 **Kolokani** Koulikoro, W Mali
79 N13 **Koloko** W Burkina
195 U14 **Kolombangara** var. Kilimbangara, Nduke. island New Georgia Islands, NW Solomon Islands
Kolomea see Kolomyya
130 L4 **Kolomna** Moskovskaya Oblast', W Russian Federation
118 J7 **Kolomyya** Ger. Kolomea. Ivano-Frankivs'ka Oblast', W Ukraine
78 M13 **Kolondiéba** Sikasso, SW Mali
200 R15 **Kolonga** Tongatapu, S Tonga
201 U16 **Kolonia** var. Colonia. Pohnpei, E Micronesia
Kolonja see Kolonjë
115 K21 **Kolonjë** var. Kolonja. Fier, C Albania
Kolonjë see Ersekë
Kolotambu see Avuavu
200 Q15 **Kolovai** Tongatapu, S Tonga
175 R13 **Kolowanawatobo, Teluk** bay Pulau Buton, C Indonesia
Kolozsvár see Cluj-Napoca
114 C9 **Kolpa** Ger. Kulpa, SCr. Kupa. Croatia/Slovenia
126 H12 **Kolpashevo** Tomskaya Oblast', C Russian Federation
128 H13 **Kolpino** Leningradskaya Oblast', NW Russian Federation
102 M10 **Kölpinsee** ◎ NE Germany
128 K5 **Kol'skiy Poluostrov** Eng. Kola Peninsula. peninsula NW Russian Federation
131 T6 **Koltubanovskiy** Orenburgskaya Oblast', W Russian Federation
114 L11 **Kolubara** C Yugoslavia
Kolupchii see Gurkovo
112 K13 **Koluszki** Piotrków, C Poland
129 T6 **Kolva** NW Russian Federation
95 E14 **Kolvereid** Nord-Trøndelag, W Norway
154 L15 **Kolwa** Baluchistān, SW Pakistan
81 M24 **Kolwezi** Shaba, S Zaire
127 Nn7 **Kolyma** NE Russian Federation
Kolyma Lowland see Kolymskaya Nizmennost'
Kolyma Range/Kolymskiy, Khrebet see Kolymskoye Nagor'ye
127 Nn6 **Kolymskaya Nizmennost'** Eng. Kolyma Lowland. lowlands NE Russian Federation
127 Nn6 **Kolymskoye** Respublika Sakha (Yakutiya), NE Russian Federation
127 N17 **Kolymskoye Nagor'ye** var. Khrebet Kolymskiy, Eng. Kolyma Range. ▲ E Russian Federation
127 N17 **Kolyuchinskaya Guba** bay NE Russian Federation
151 W15 **Kol'zhat** Almaty, SE Kazakhstan
116 G8 **Kom** ▲ NW Bulgaria
82 I13 **Koma** C Ethiopia
79 X12 **Komadugu Gana** NE Nigeria
171 Ii15 **Komagane** Nagano, Honshū, S Japan
81 P17 **Komanda** Haut-Zaïre, NE Zaire
207 U1 **Komandorskaya Basin** var. Kamchatka Basin. undersea feature SW Bering Sea
129 Pp9 **Komandorskiye Ostrova** Eng. Commander Islands. island group E Russian Federation
Kománfalva see Comăneşti
113 I22 **Komárno** Ger. Komorn, Hung. Komárom. Západné Slovensko, SW Slovakia
113 I22 **Komárom** Komárom-Esztergom, NW Hungary
Komárom see Komárno
113 I22 **Komárom-Esztergom** off. Komárom-Esztergom Megye. ◐ county N Hungary
171 I13 **Komatsu** var. Komatu. Ishikawa, Honshū, SW Japan
170 Ff15 **Komatsushima** Tokushima, Shikoku, SW Japan
Komatu see Komatsu
85 D17 **Kombat** Otjozondjupa, N Namibia
Kombissiguiri see Kombissiri
79 P13 **Kombissiri** var. Kombissiguiri. C Burkina
196 E10 **Komebail Lagoon** lagoon N Palau
83 F20 **Kome Island** island N Tanzania
Komeyo see Wandai
176 W13 **Komfane** Pulau Wokam, E Indonesia
119 P10 **Kominternivs'ke** Odes'ka Oblast', SW Ukraine
129 R12 **Komi-Permyatskiy Avtonomnyy Okrug** ◐ autonomous district W Russian Federation
129 R8 **Komi, Respublika** ◐ autonomous republic NW Russian Federation
113 I25 **Komló** Baranya, SW Hungary
Kommunarsk see Alchevs'k
153 S12 **Kommunizm, Qullai** ▲ E Tajikistan
194 G12 **Komo** Southern Highlands, W PNG
175 P16 **Komodo** Pulau Komodo, S Indonesia
175 P16 **Komodo, Pulau** island Nusa Tenggara, S Indonesia
79 N15 **Komoé** var. Komoé Fleuve. E Ivory Coast
Komoé Fleuve see Komoé
77 X11 **Kôm Ombo** var. Kawm Umbū. SE Egypt
81 F20 **Komono** La Lékoumou, SW Congo
176 Y16 **Komoran** Irian Jaya, E Indonesia
176 Y16 **Komoran, Pulau** island E Indonesia
Komorn see Komárno
Komornok see Comorâşte
171 J14 **Komoro** Nagano, Honshū, S Japan
Komosolabad see Komsomolobod
Komotau see Chomutov
116 K13 **Komotiní** var. Gümüljina, Turk. Gümülcine. Anatolikí Makedonía kai Thráki, NE Greece
115 K16 **Komovi** ▲ SW Yugoslavia
119 R8 **Kompaniyivka** Kirovohrads'ka Oblast', C Ukraine
194 H12 **Kompiam** Enga, W PNG
Kompong see Kâmpóng Chhnăng
Kompong Cham see Kâmpóng Cham
Kompong Kleang see Kâmpóng Khleăng
Kompong Som see Kâmpóng Saôm
Kompong Speu see Kâmpóng Spoe
Kompong Thom see Kâmpóng Thum
Komrat see Comrat
Komsomol see Komsomol'skiy, Atyrau, Kazakhstan
Komsomol see Komsomolets, Kustanay, Kazakhstan
150 L7 **Komsomolets** Kaz. Komsomol. Kustanay, N Kazakhstan
126 Ii2 **Komsomolets, Ostrov** island Severnaya Zemlya, N Russian Federation
150 F13 **Komsomolets, Zaliv** lake gulf SW Kazakhstan
153 Q12 **Komsomolobod** Rus. Komosolabad. C Tajikistan
128 M16 **Komsomol'sk** Ivanovskaya Oblast', W Russian Federation
119 S6 **Komsomol's'k** Poltavs'ka Oblast', C Ukraine
152 M11 **Komsomol'sk** Nawoiy Wiloyati, N Uzbekistan
150 G12 **Komsomol'skiy** Kaz. Komsomol. Atyrau, W Kazakhstan
129 W4 **Komsomol'skiy** Respublika Komi, NW Russian Federation
127 Nn15 **Komsomol'sk-na-Amure** Khabarovskiy Kray, SE Russian Federation
Komsomol'sk-na-Ustyurte see Komsomol'sk-Ustyurt
150 K10 **Komsomol'skoye** Aktyubinsk, NW Kazakhstan
131 Q8 **Komsomol'skoye** Saratovskaya Oblast', W Russian Federation
152 G6 **Komsomol'sk-Ustyurt** Rus. Komsomol'sk-na-Ustyurte. Qoraqalpoghiston Respublikasi, NW Uzbekistan
151 P10 **Kon** C Kazakhstan
Kona see Kailua
128 K16 **Konakovo** Tverskaya Oblast', W Russian Federation
149 V15 **Konārak** Sīstān va Balūchestān, SE Iran
Konarhā see Kunar
29 O11 **Konawa** Oklahoma, C USA
176 V9 **Konda** Irian Jaya, E Indonesia
125 Ff11 **Konda** C Russian Federation
160 L13 **Kondagaon** Madhya Pradesh, C India
12 K10 **Kondiaronk, Lac** ◎ Québec, SE Canada
188 J13 **Kondinin** Western Australia
83 H21 **Kondoa** Dodoma, C Tanzania
131 P6 **Kondol'** Penzenskaya Oblast', W Russian Federation
116 N10 **Kondolovo** Burgaska Oblast, SE Bulgaria
176 Z16 **Kondomirat** Irian Jaya, E Indonesia
128 J10 **Kondopoga** Respublika Kareliya, NW Russian Federation
Kondoz see Kunduz
161 J17 **Kondukūr** var. Kandukur. Andhra Pradesh, E India
Kondūz see Kunduz
197 H6 **Koné** Province Nord, W New Caledonia
Könekesir see Kënekesir
Köneürgench see Këneurgench
79 N15 **Kong** N Ivory Coast
41 S5 **Kongakut River** Alaska, USA
207 O14 **Kong Christian IX Land** Eng. King Christian IX Land. physical region SE Greenland
207 P13 **Kong Christian X Land** Eng. King Christian X Land. physical region E Greenland
207 N13 **Kong Frederik IX Land** Eng. King Frederik IX Land. physical region SW Greenland
207 Q12 **Kong Frederik VIII Land** Eng. King Frederik VIII Land. physical region NE Greenland
207 N15 **Kong Frederik VI Kyst** Eng. King Frederik VI Coast. physical region SE Greenland
178 I13 **Kŏng, Kaôh** prev. Kas Kong. island SW Cambodia
94 P2 **Kong Karls Land** Eng. King Charles Islands. island group SE Svalbard
83 G14 **Kong Kong** SE Sudan
Kongo see Congo
85 G16 **Kongola** Caprivi, NE Namibia
81 N21 **Kongolo** Shaba, E Zaire
83 F14 **Kongor** Jonglei, SE Sudan
207 Q14 **Kong Oscar Fjord** fjord E Greenland
79 P12 **Kongoussi** N Burkina
97 G15 **Kongsberg** Buskerud, S Norway
94 Q2 **Kongsøya** island Kong Karls Land, E Svalbard
97 I14 **Kongsvinger** Hedmark, S Norway
178 Jj11 **Kông, Tônle** Lao. Xê Kong. Cambodia/Laos
164 E8 **Kongur Shan** ▲ NW China
83 I22 **Kongwa** Dodoma, C Tanzania
Kong, Xê see Kông, Tônle
Konia see Konya
153 R11 **Konibodom** Rus. Kanibadam. N Tajikistan
113 K15 **Koniecpol** Częstochowa, S Poland
Konieh see Konya
Königgrätz see Hradec Králové
Königinhof an der Elbe see Dvůr Králové nad Labem
103 K23 **Königsbrunn** Bayern, S Germany
Königshütte see Chorzów
103 O24 **Königssee** ◎ SE Germany
111 S8 **Königstuhl** ▲ S Austria
111 U3 **Konigswiesen** Oberösterreich, N Austria
103 E17 **Königswinter** Nordrhein-Westfalen, W Germany
152 M11 **Konimekh** Rus. Kenimekh. Nawoiy Wiloyati, N Uzbekistan
112 I12 **Konin** Ger. Kuhnau. Konin, C Poland
112 I12 **Konin** off. Województwo Konińskie. ◐ province C Poland
Koninkrijk der Nederlanden see Netherlands
Konińskie, Województwo see Konin
115 L24 **Konispol** var. Konispoli. Vlorë, S Albania
Konispoli see Konispol
117 C15 **Kónitsa** Ípeiros, W Greece
Konitz see Chojnice
110 D8 **Köniz** Bern, W Switzerland
115 H14 **Konjic** S Bosnia and Herzegovina
94 J10 **Könkämäälven** Finland/Sweden
161 D14 **Konkan** W India
85 D22 **Konkiep** S Namibia
78 I14 **Konkouré** W Guinea
79 O11 **Konna** Mopti, S Mali
195 P10 **Konogaiang, Mount** ▲ New Ireland, NE PNG
195 P10 **Konogogo** New Ireland, NE PNG
110 E9 **Konolfingen** Bern, W Switzerland
79 P16 **Konongo** C Ghana
195 O9 **Konos** New Ireland, NE PNG
128 M12 **Konosha** Arkhangel'skaya Oblast', NW Russian Federation
119 R3 **Konotop** Sums'ka Oblast', NE Ukraine
164 L7 **Konqi He** NW China
113 L14 **Końskie** Kielce, S Poland
Konstantinovka see Kostyantynivka
130 M11 **Konstantinovsk** Rostovskaya Oblast', SW Russian Federation
103 H24 **Konstanz** var. Constanz, Eng. Constance; hist. Kostnitz, anc. Constantia. Baden-Württemberg, S Germany
Konstanza see Constanţa
79 T14 **Kontagora** Niger, W Nigeria
80 E13 **Kontcha** Nord, N Cameroon
101 G17 **Kontich** Antwerpen, N Belgium
95 O16 **Kontiolahti** Pohjois-Karjala, SE Finland
95 M15 **Kontiomäki** Oulu, C Finland
178 K11 **Kơn Tum** var. Kontum. Kon Tum, C Vietnam
Konur see Sulakyurt
142 H15 **Konya** var. Konieh; prev. Konia, anc. Iconium. Konya, C Turkey
142 H15 **Konya** var. Konia, Konieh. ◐ province C Turkey
151 W15 **Konyrolen** Taldykorgan, SE Kazakhstan
83 I19 **Konza** Eastern, S Kenya
100 I9 **Koog aan den Zaan** Noord-Holland, C Netherlands
190 E7 **Koonibba** South Australia
33 O11 **Koontz Lake** Indiana, N USA
176 V8 **Koor** Irian Jaya, E Indonesia
191 R9 **Koorawatha** New South Wales, SE Australia
120 J5 **Koosa** Tartumaa, E Estonia
35 N7 **Kootenai** var. Kootenay. Canada/USA see also Kootenay
9 P17 **Kootenay** var. Kootenai. Canada/USA see also Kootenai
85 F24 **Kootjieskolk** Northern Cape, W South Africa
115 M15 **Kopaonik** ▲ S Yugoslavia
Kopar see Koper
94 K1 **Kópasker** Nordhurland Eystra, N Iceland
94 H4 **Kópavogur** Reykjanes, W Iceland
111 S13 **Koper** It. Capodistria; prev. Kopar. SW Slovenia
97 C16 **Kopervik** Rogaland, S Norway
Kopetdag, Khrebet see Koppeh Dāgh
125 Ee12 **Kopeysk** Kurganskaya Oblast', C Russian Federation
Kophinou see Kofínou
190 G8 **Kopi** South Australia
Kopiago see Lake Copiago
159 W12 **Kopili** NE India
97 M15 **Köping** Västmanland, C Sweden
115 K17 **Koplik** var. Kopliku. Shkodër, NW Albania
Kopliku see Koplik
Kopopo see Kokopo
96 I11 **Koppang** Hedmark, S Norway
97 L15 **Kopparberg** Örebro, C Sweden
96 J12 **Kopparberg** ◐ county C Sweden
149 S3 **Koppeh Dāgh** var. Khrebet Kopetdag. ▲ Iran/Turkmenistan
Koppename see Coppename Rivier
97 J15 **Koppom** Värmland, C Sweden
Kopreinitz see Koprivnica
116 K9 **Koprinka, Yazovir** prev. Yazovir Georgi Dimitrov. ▣ C Bulgaria
114 F7 **Koprivnica** Ger. Kopreinitz, Hung. Kaproncza. Koprivnica-Križevci, N Croatia
114 F8 **Koprivnica-Križevci** off. Koprivničko-Križevačka Županija. ◐ province N Croatia
113 I17 **Kopřivnice** Ger. Nesselsdorf. Severní Morava, E Czech Republic
Köprülü see Veles
Koptsevichi see Kaptsevichy
Kopyl' see Kapyl'
121 O14 **Kopys'** Rus. Kopys'. Vitsyebskaya Voblasts', NE Belorussia
115 M18 **Korab** ▲ Albania/FYR Macedonia
Korabavur Pastligi see Karabaur', Uval
83 M14 **K'orahē** SE Ethiopia
117 L16 **Kórakas, Ákra** headland Lésvos, E Greece
114 D9 **Korana** C Croatia
161 L14 **Korāput** Orissa, E India
Korat see Nakhon Ratchasima
178 Ii9 **Korat Plateau** plateau E Thailand
145 T1 **Kōrāwa, Sar-i** ▲ NE Iraq
103 H15 **Korbach** Hessen, C Germany
Korça see Korçë
115 M21 **Korçë** var. Korça, Gk. Korytsa, It. Corriza; prev. Koritsa. Korçë, SE Albania
115 M21 **Korçë** ◐ district SE Albania
115 G15 **Korčula** It. Curzola. Dubrovnik-Neretva, S Croatia
115 F15 **Korčula** It. Curzola; anc. Corcyra Nigra. island S Croatia
115 F15 **Korčulanski Kanal** channel S Croatia
148 J5 **Kordestān** off. Ostān-e Kordestān, var. Kurdestan. ◐ province W Iran
149 P4 **Kord Kūy** var. Kurd Kui. Māzandarān, N Iran
169 V13 **Korea Bay** bay China/North Korea
Korea, Democratic People's Republic of see North Korea
176 Uu15 **Koreare** Pulau Yamdena, E Indonesia
Korea, Republic of see South Korea
169 Z17 **Korea Strait** Jap. Chōsen-kaikyō, Kor. Taehan-haehyŏp. channel Japan/South Korea
Korelichi/Korelicze see Karelichy
82 J11 **Korem** N Ethiopia
79 U11 **Korén Adoua** C Niger
130 I7 **Korenevo** Kurskaya Oblast', W Russian Federation
130 L13 **Korenovsk** Krasnodarskiy Kray, SW Russian Federation
118 L4 **Korets'** Pol. Korzec, Rus. Korets. Rivnens'ka Oblast', NW Ukraine
127 Pp8 **Korf** Koryakskiy Avtonomnyy Okrug, E Russian Federation
204 L7 **Korff Ice Rise** ice cap Antarctica
94 G13 **Korgen** Troms, N Norway
153 R9 **Korgon-Dĕbĕ** Dzhalal-Abadskaya Oblast', W Kyrgyzstan
78 M14 **Korhogo** N Ivory Coast
117 F19 **Korinthiakós Kólpos** Eng. Gulf of Corinth; anc. Corinthiacus Sinus. gulf C Greece
117 F19 **Kórinthos** Eng. Corinth; anc. Corinthus. Pelopónnisos, S Greece
115 M18 **Koritnik** ▲ S Yugoslavia
Koritsa see Korçë
171 L14 **Kōriyama** Fukushima, Honshū, C Japan
142 E16 **Korkuteli** Antalya, SW Turkey
164 K6 **Korla** Chin. K'u-erh-lo. Xinjiang Uygur Zizhiqu, NW China
126 H11 **Korliki** Khanty-Mansiyskiy Avtonomnyy Okrug, C Russian Federation

◆ Country
● Country Capital
◇ Dependent Territory
○ Dependent Territory Capital
◐ Administrative Region
✕ International Airport
▲ Mountain
▲ Mountain Range
Volcano
River
◎ Lake
▣ Reservoir

Körlin an der Persante – Kryzhopil'

Körlin an der Persante *see* Karlino
Korma *see* Karma
12 *D8* **Kormak** Ontario, S Canada
Kormakiti, Akrotíri/Kormakiti, Cape/Kormakítis *see* Koruçam Burnu
113 *G23* **Körmend** Vas, W Hungary
145 *T5* **Kōrmōr** E Iraq
114 *C13* **Kornat** *It.* Incoronata. *island* W Croatia
Korneshty *see* Corneşti
111 *X3* **Korneuburg** Niederösterreich, NE Austria
151 *P7* **Korneyevka** Severnyy Kazakhstan, N Kazakhstan
97 *I17* **Kornsjø** Østfold, S Norway
79 *O11* **Koro** Mopti, S Mali
197 *J14* **Koro** *island* C Fiji
194 *F12* **Koroba** Southern Highlands, W PNG
130 *K8* **Korocha** Belgorodskaya Oblast', W Russian Federation
142 *H12* **Köroğlu Dağları** ▲▲ C Turkey
191 *V6* **Korogoro Point** *headland* New South Wales, SE Australia
83 *J21* **Korogwe** Tanga, E Tanzania
190 *L13* **Koroit** Victoria, SE Australia
197 *H15* **Korolevu** Viti Levu, W Fiji
202 *I17* **Koromiri** *island* S Cook Islands
179 *R16* **Koronadal** Mindanao, S Philippines
117 *E22* **Koróni** Pelopónnisos, S Greece
116 *G13* **Korónia, Límni** ◎ N Greece
112 *I9* **Koronowo** *Ger.* Krone an der Brahe. Bydgoszcz, NW Poland
119 *R2* **Korop** Chernihivs'ka Oblast', N Ukraine
117 *H19* **Koropí** Attikí, C Greece
Koror *see* Oreor
Kőrös *see* Križevci
113 *L23* **Körös** ≈ E Hungary
Körösbánya *see* Baia de Criş
197 *J14* **Koro Sea** *sea* C Fiji
Koroška *see* Kärnten
119 *N3* **Korosten'** Zhytomyrs'ka Oblast', NW Ukraine
Korostyshev *see* Korostyshiv
119 *N4* **Korostyshiv** *Rus.* Korostyshev. Zhytomyrs'ka Oblast', N Ukraine
129 *V3* **Korotaikha** ≈ NW Russian Federation
126 *H9* **Korotchayevo** Yamalo-Nenetskiy Avtonomnyy Okrug, N Russian Federation
80 *I8* **Koro Toro** Borkou-Ennedi-Tibesti, N Chad
41 *N16* **Korovin Island** *island* Shumagin Islands, Alaska, USA
197 *I14* **Korovou** Viti Levu, W Fiji
95 *M17* **Korpilahti** Keski-Suomi, C Finland
94 *K12* **Korpilombolo** Norrbotten, N Sweden
127 *Oo16* **Korsakov** Ostrov Sakhalin, Sakhalinskaya Oblast', SE Russian Federation
95 *J16* **Korsholm** *Fin.* Mustasaari. Vaasa, W Finland
97 *I23* **Korsør** Vestsjælland, E Denmark
Korsovka *see* Kārsava
119 *P6* **Korsun'-Shevchenkivs'kyy** *Rus.* Korsun'-Shevchenkovskiy. Cherkas'ka Oblast', C Ukraine
Korsun'-Shevchenkovskiy *see* Korsun'-Shevchenkivs'kyy
101 *C17* **Kortemark** West-Vlaanderen, W Belgium
101 *H18* **Kortenberg** Vlaams Brabant, C Belgium
101 *K18* **Kortessem** Limburg, NE Belgium
101 *E14* **Kortgene** Zeeland, SW Netherlands
82 *F8* **Korti** Northern, N Sudan
101 *C18* **Kortrijk** *Fr.* Courtrai. West-Vlaanderen, W Belgium
124 *N2* **Koruçam Burnu** *var.* Cape Kormakiti, Kormakítis, *Gk.* Akrotíri Kormakíti. *headland* N Cyprus
191 *O13* **Korumburra** Victoria, SE Australia
Koryak Range *see* Koryakskoye Nagor'ye
127 *P8* **Koryakskiy Avtonomnyy Okrug** ◐ *autonomous district* E Russian Federation
Koryakskiy Khrebet *see* Koryakskoye Nagor'ye
127 *Pp7* **Koryakskoye Nagor'ye** *var.* Koryakskiy Khrebet, *Eng.* Koryak Range. ▲▲ NE Russian Federation
129 *P11* **Koryazhma** Arkhangel'skaya Oblast', NW Russian Federation
Kōryō *see* Kangnŭng
Korytsa *see* Korçë
119 *Q2* **Koryukivka** Chernihivs'ka Oblast', N Ukraine
Korzec *see* Korets'
117 *N21* **Kos** Kos, Dodekánisos, Greece, Aegean Sea
117 *M21* **Kos** *It.* Coo; *anc.* Cos. *island* Dodekánisos, Greece, Aegean Sea
129 *T12* **Kosa** Komi-Permyatskiy Avtonomnyy Okrug, NW Russian Federation
129 *T13* **Kosa** ≈ NW Russian Federation
170 *C11* **Kō-saki** *headland* Nagasaki, Tsushima, SW Japan
169 *X13* **Kosan** SE North Korea
121 *H18* **Kosava** *Rus.* Kosovo. Brestskaya Voblasts', SW Belorussia
Kosch *see* Kose
150 *G12* **Koschagyl** *Kaz.* Qosshaghyl. Atyrau, W Kazakhstan
112 *G12* **Kościan** *Ger.* Kosten. Leszno, W Poland
112 *I7* **Kościerzyna** Gdańsk, NW Poland
24 *L4* **Kosciusko** Mississippi, S USA
191 *R11* **Kosciusko, Mount** ▲ New South Wales, SE Australia
120 *H4* **Kose** *Ger.* Kosch. Harjumaa, NW Estonia
116 *G6* **Koshava** Oblast Montana, NW Bulgaria
153 *U9* **Kosh-Dëbë** *var.* Koshtebë. Narynskaya Oblast', C Kyrgyzstan
171 *K16* **Koshigaya** *var.* Kosigaya. Saitama, Honshū, S Japan
K'o-shih *see* Kashi
170 *B15* **Koshikijima-rettō** *var.* Kosikizima Rettô. *island group* SW Japan
151 *W13* **Koshkarkol', Ozero** ◎ SE Kazakhstan
32 *L9* **Koshkonong, Lake** ◎ Wisconsin, N USA
152 *B10* **Koshoba** *Turkm.* Goshoba. Balkanskiy Velayat, NW Turkmenistan
171 *J14* **Kōshoku** *var.* Kôsyoku. Nagano, Honshū, S Japan
Koshtebë *see* Kosh-Dëbë
Kōshū *see* Kwangju
113 *N19* **Košice** *Ger.* Kaschau, *Hung.* Kassa. Východné Slovensko, E Slovakia
Kosigaya *see* Koshigaya
Kosikizima Rettô *see* Koshikijima-rettō
159 *R12* **Kosi Reservoir** ⊡ E Nepal
118 *J8* **Kosiv** Ivano-Frankivs'ka Oblast', W Ukraine
151 *O11* **Koskol'** Zhezkazgan, C Kazakhstan
129 *Q9* **Koslan** Respublika Komi, NW Russian Federation
Köslin *see* Koszalin
152 *M12* **Koson** *Rus.* Kasan. Qashqadaryo Wiloyati, S Uzbekistan
169 *Y13* **Kosŏng** SE North Korea
153 *S9* **Kosonsoy** *Rus.* Kasansay. Namangan Wiloyati, E Uzbekistan
115 *M16* **Kosovo** *prev.* Autonomous Province of Kosovo and Metohija. *cultural region* S Yugoslavia
Kosovo *see* Kosava
Kosovo and Metohija, Autonomous Province of *see* Kosovo
115 *N16* **Kosovo Polje** Serbia, S Yugoslavia
115 *O16* **Kosovska Kamenica** Serbia, SE Yugoslavia
115 *M16* **Kosovska Mitrovica** *Alb.* Mitrovicë; *prev.* Mitrovica, Titova Mitrovica. Serbia, S Yugoslavia
201 *X17* **Kosrae** ◐ *state* E Micronesia
201 *Y14* **Kosrae** *prev.* Kusaie. *island* Caroline Islands, E Micronesia
27 *U9* **Kosse** Texas, SW USA
111 *P6* **Kössen** Tirol, W Austria
78 *M16* **Kossou, Lac de** ◎ C Ivory Coast
Kossukavak *see* Krumovgrad
114 *F10* **Kostajnica** *var.* Hrvatska Kostajnica. Sisak-Moslavina, C Croatia
Kostamus *see* Kostomuksha
Kosten *see* Kościan
116 *H10* **Kostenets** *prev.* Georgi Dimitrov. Sofiyska Oblast, W Bulgaria
82 *F10* **Kosti** White Nile, C Sudan
Kostnitz *see* Konstanz
128 *H7* **Kostomuksha** *Fin.* Kostamus. Respublika Kareliya, NW Russian Federation
118 *K3* **Kostopil'** *Rus.* Kostopol'. Rivnens'ka Oblast', NW Ukraine
Kostopol' *see* Kostopil'
128 *M15* **Kostroma** Kostromskaya Oblast', NW Russian Federation
129 *N14* **Kostroma** ≈ NW Russian Federation
129 *N14* **Kostromskaya Oblast'** ◐ *province* NW Russian Federation
112 *D11* **Kostrzyn** *Ger.* Cüstrin, Küstrin. Gorzów, W Poland
112 *H11* **Kostrzyn** Poznań, C Poland
119 *X7* **Kostyantynivka** *Rus.* Konstantinovka. Donets'ka Oblast', SE Ukraine
Kostyukovichi *see* Kastsyukovichy
Kostyukovka *see* Kastsyukowka
Kōsyoku *see* Kōshoku
129 *U6* **Kos'yu** Respublika Komi, NW Russian Federation
129 *U6* **Kos'yu** ≈ NW Russian Federation
112 *F7* **Koszalin** *Ger.* Köslin. Koszalin, NW Poland
112 *F8* **Koszalin** *off.* Województwo Koszalińskie, *Ger.* Köslin. ◐ *province* NW Poland
Koszalińskie, Województwo *see* Koszalin
113 *F22* **Kőszeg** *Ger.* Güns. Vas, W Hungary
158 *H13* **Kota** *prev.* Kotah. Rājasthān, N India
174 *H9* **Kota Baru** Sumatera, W Indonesia
175 *Nn11* **Kotabaru** Pulau Laut, C Indonesia
Kotabaru *see* Jayapura
174 *H2* **Kota Bharu** *var.* Kota Baharu, Kota Bahru. Kelantan, Peninsular Malaysia
Kotaboemi *see* Kotabumi
174 *Ii12* **Kotabumi** *prev.* Kotaboemi. Sumatera, W Indonesia
155 *S10* **Kot Addu** Punjab, E Pakistan
Kotah *see* Kota
175 *Nn2* **Kota Kinabalu** *prev.* Jesselton. Sabah, East Malaysia
175 *Nn2* **Kota Kinabalu** ✕ Sabah, East Malaysia
94 *M12* **Kotala** Lappi, N Finland
Kotamobagoe *see* Kotamobagu
175 *Rr7* **Kotamobagu** *prev.* Kotamobagoe. Sulawesi, C Indonesia
161 *L14* **Kotapad** *var.* Kotapārh. Orissa, E India
Kotapārh *see* Kotapad
178 *Gg17* **Ko Ta Ru Tao** *island* SW Thailand
174 *L11* **Kotawaringin, Teluk** *bay* Borneo, C Indonesia
155 *Q13* **Kot Diji** Sind, SE Pakistan
158 *K9* **Kotdwāra** Uttar Pradesh, N India
129 *Q14* **Kotel'nich** Kirovskaya Oblast', NW Russian Federation
131 *N12* **Kotel'nikovo** Volgogradskaya Oblast', SW Russian Federation
126 *Ll4* **Kotel'nyy, Ostrov** *island* Novosibirskiye Ostrova, N Russian Federation
119 *T5* **Kotel'va** Poltavs'ka Oblast', C Ukraine
103 *M14* **Köthen** *var.* Cöthen. Sachsen-Anhalt, C Germany
Kōti *see* Kōchi
83 *G17* **Kotido** NE Uganda
95 *N19* **Kotka** Kymi, S Finland
129 *P11* **Kotlas** Arkhangel'skaya Oblast', NW Russian Federation
40 *M10* **Kotlik** Alaska, USA
79 *Q17* **Kotoka** ✕ (Accra) S Ghana
Kotonu *see* Cotonou
115 *J17* **Kotor** *It.* Cattaro. Montenegro, SW Yugoslavia
Kotor *see* Kotoriba
114 *F7* **Kotoriba** *Hung.* Kotor. Međimurje, N Croatia
115 *I17* **Kotorska, Boka** *It.* Bocche di Cattaro. *bay* Montenegro, SW Yugoslavia
114 *H11* **Kotorsko** N Bosnia and Herzegovina
114 *G11* **Kotor Varoš** N Bosnia and Herzegovina
Koto Sho/Kotosho *see* Lan Yü
130 *M7* **Kotovsk** Tambovskaya Oblast', W Russian Federation
119 *O9* **Kotovs'k** *Rus.* Kotovsk. Odes'ka Oblast', SW Ukraine
Kotovsk *see* Hînceşti
121 *G16* **Kotra** *Rus.* Kotra. ≈ W Belorussia
155 *P16* **Kotri** Sind, SE Pakistan
111 *Q9* **Kötschach** Kärnten, S Austria
161 *K15* **Kottagūdem** Andhra Pradesh, E India
161 *F21* **Kottappadi** Kerala, SW India
161 *G23* **Kottayam** Kerala, SW India
Kottbus *see* Cottbus
Kotte *see* Sri Jayawardanapura
81 *K15* **Kotto** ≈ Central African Republic/Zaire
200 *S13* **Kotu Group** *island group* W Tonga
152 *B11* **Koturdepe** *Turkm.* Goturdepe. Balkanskiy Velayat, W Turkmenistan
126 *J9* **Kotuy** ≈ N Russian Federation
85 *M16* **Kotwa** Mashonaland East, NE Zimbabwe
41 *N7* **Kotzebue** Alaska, USA
41 *M7* **Kotzebue Sound** *inlet* Alaska, USA
Kotzenan *see* Chocianów
Kotzman *see* Kitsman'
79 *R14* **Kouandé** NW Benin
81 *J15* **Kouango** Ouaka, S Central African Republic
79 *O13* **Koudougou** C Burkina
100 *K7* **Koudum** Friesland, N Netherlands
117 *L25* **Koufonísi** *island* SE Greece
117 *K21* **Koufonísi** *island* Kykládes, Greece, Aegean Sea
40 *M8* **Kougarok Mountain** ▲ Alaska, USA
81 *E20* **Kouilou** ≈ S Congo
16 *N3* **Koukdjuak** ≈ Baffin Island, Northwest Territories, NE Canada
124 *N4* **Koúklia** SW Cyprus
81 *E19* **Koulamoutou** Ogooué-Lolo, C Gabon
78 *L12* **Koulikoro** Koulikoro, SW Mali
78 *L11* **Koulikoro** ◐ *region* SW Mali
197 *H5* **Koumac** Province Nord, W New Caledonia
171 *J15* **Koumi** Nagano, Honshū, S Japan
80 *I13* **Koumra** Moyen-Chari, S Chad
Kounadougou *see* Koundougou
78 *M15* **Kounahiri** C Ivory Coast
78 *I12* **Koundâra** Moyenne-Guinée, NW Guinea
79 *N13* **Koundougou** *var.* Kounadougou. C Burkina
78 *H11* **Koungheul** C Senegal
151 *T13* **Kounradskiy** Zhezkazgan, SE Kazakhstan
27 *X10* **Kountze** Texas, SW USA
79 *Q13* **Koupéla** C Burkina
79 *N13* **Kouri** Sikasso, SW Mali
57 *Y9* **Kourou** N French Guiana
116 *J12* **Kouroú** ≈ NE Greece
78 *K14* **Kouroussa** Haute-Guinée, C Guinea
Kousseir *see* Al Quşayr
80 *G11* **Kousséri** *prev.* Fort-Foureau. Extrême-Nord, NE Cameroon
Kouteifé *see* Al Quţayfah
78 *M13* **Koutiala** Sikasso, S Mali
78 *M14* **Kouto** NW Ivory Coast
95 *M19* **Kouvola** Kymi, S Finland
81 *G18* **Kouyou** ≈ C Congo
114 *M10* **Kovačica** *Hung.* Antafalva; *prev.* Kovacsicza. Serbia, N Yugoslavia
Kovacsicza *see* Kovačica
Kővárhosszúfalu *see* Satulung
Kovászna *see* Covasna
128 *I4* **Kovdor** Murmanskaya Oblast', NW Russian Federation
128 *I5* **Kovdozero, Ozero** ◎ NW Russian Federation
118 *J3* **Kovel'** *Pol.* Kowel. Volyns'ka Oblast', NW Ukraine
114 *M11* **Kovin** *Hung.* Kevevára; *prev.* Temes-Kubin. Serbia, NE Yugoslavia
Kovno *see* Kaunas
131 *N3* **Kovrov** Vladimirskaya Oblast', W Russian Federation
131 *O5* **Kovylkino** Respublika Mordoviya, W Russian Federation
112 *J11* **Kowal** Włocławek, C Poland
112 *J9* **Kowalewo Pomorskie** *Ger.* Schönsee. Toruń, N Poland
Kowasna *see* Covasna
121 *M16* **Kowbcha** *Rus.* Kolbcha. Mahilyowskaya Voblasts', E Belorussia
Koweit *see* Kuwait
Kowel *see* Kovel'
193 *F17* **Kowhitirangi** West Coast, South Island, NZ
167 *O15* **Kowloon** *Chin.* Jiulong. Hong Kong, S China
Kowno *see* Kaunas
165 *N7* **Kox Kuduk** *well* NW China
142 *D16* **Köyceğiz** Muğla, SW Turkey
129 *N6* **Koyda** Arkhangel'skaya Oblast', NW Russian Federation
152 *D10* **Koymat** *Turkm.* Goymat. Balkanskiy Velayat, NW Turkmenistan
152 *D10* **Koymatdag, Gory** *Turkm.* Goymatdag. *hill range* NW Turkmenistan
161 *E15* **Koyna Reservoir** ⊡ W India
171 *M11* **Koyoshi-gawa** ≈ Honshū, C Japan
Koysanjaq *see* Koi Sanjaq
Koytash *see* Qŭytosh
41 *N9* **Koyuk** Alaska, USA
41 *N9* **Koyuk River** ≈ Alaska, USA
41 *O9* **Koyukuk** Alaska, USA
41 *O9* **Koyukuk River** ≈ Alaska, USA
142 *J13* **Kozaklı** Nevşehir, C Turkey
170 *F13* **Kōzan** Hiroshima, Honshū, SW Japan
142 *K16* **Kozan** Adana, S Turkey
117 *E14* **Kozáni** Dytikí Makedonía, N Greece
114 *F10* **Kozara** ▲▲ NW Bosnia and Herzegovina
119 *P3* **Kozelets'** *Rus.* Kozelets. Chernihivs'ka Oblast', NE Ukraine
119 *S6* **Kozel'shchyna** Poltavs'ka Oblast', C Ukraine
130 *J5* **Kozel'sk** Kaluzhskaya Oblast', W Russian Federation
Kozhikode *see* Calicut
129 *V9* **Kozhimiz, Gora** ▲ NW Russian Federation
128 *L9* **Kozhozero, Ozero** ◎ NW Russian Federation
129 *T7* **Kozhva** *var.* Kozya. Respublika Komi, NW Russian Federation
129 *T7* **Kozhva** ≈ NW Russian Federation
129 *U6* **Kozhym** Respublika Komi, NW Russian Federation
112 *N13* **Kozienice** Radom, C Poland
111 *S13* **Kozina** SW Slovenia
116 *H7* **Kozloduy** Oblast Montana, NW Bulgaria
131 *Q3* **Kozlovka** Chuvashskaya Respublika, W Russian Federation
Kozlovshchina/Kozlowszczyzna *see* Kazlowshchyna
131 *P3* **Koz'modem'yansk** Respublika Mariy El, W Russian Federation
118 *J6* **Kozova** Ternopil's'ka Oblast', W Ukraine
115 *P20* **Kožuf** ▲ S FYR Macedonia
172 *S13* **Kōzu-shima** *island* E Japan
Kozya *see* Kozhva
Koz'yany *see* Kaz'yany
119 *N5* **Kozyatyn** *Rus.* Kazatin. Vinnyts'ka Oblast', C Ukraine
79 *Q16* **Kpalimé** *var.* Palimé. SW Togo
79 *Q16* **Kpandu** E Ghana
101 *F15* **Krabbendijke** Zeeland, SW Netherlands
178 *Gg16* **Krabi** *var.* Muang Krabi. Krabi, SW Thailand
178 *Gg14* **Kra Buri** Ranong, SW Thailand
178 *Jj13* **Krâchéh** *prev.* Kratie. Krâchéh, E Cambodia
97 *G17* **Kragerø** Telemark, S Norway
114 *M13* **Kragujevac** Serbia, C Yugoslavia
Krainburg *see* Kranj
178 *Gg14* **Kra, Isthmus of** *isthmus* Malaysia/Thailand
114 *D12* **Krajina** *cultural region* SW Croatia
Krakatau, Pulau *see* Rakata, Pulau
Krakau *see* Kraków
113 *L16* **Kraków** *Eng.* Cracow, *Ger.* Krakau; *anc.* Cracovia. Kraków, S Poland
113 *K16* **Kraków** *off.* Województwo Krakowskie, *Eng.* Cracow, *Ger.* Krakau. ◐ *province* S Poland
102 *L9* **Krakower See** ◎ NE Germany
Krakowskie, Województwo *see* Kraków
178 *Ii12* **Krâlănh** Siĕmréab, NW Cambodia
47 *Q16* **Kralendijk** Bonaire, E Netherlands Antilles
114 *B10* **Kraljevica** *It.* Porto Re. Primorje-Gorski Kotar, NW Croatia
114 *M13* **Kraljevo** *prev.* Rankovićevo. Serbia, C Yugoslavia
Kralup an der Moldau *see* Kralupy nad Vltavou
113 *C16* **Kralupy nad Vltavou** *Ger.* Kralup an der Moldau. Střední Čechy, NW Czech Republic
119 *W7* **Kramators'k** *Rus.* Kramatorsk. Donets'ka Oblast', SE Ukraine
Kramatorsk *see* Kramators'k
95 *H17* **Kramfors** Västernorrland, C Sweden
117 *D15* **Kranéa** Dytikí Makedonía, N Greece
110 *M7* **Kranebitten** ✕ (Innsbruck) Tirol, W Austria
117 *G20* **Kranídi** Pelopónnisos, S Greece
111 *T11* **Kranj** *Ger.* Krainburg. NW Slovenia
117 *F16* **Krannón** *battleground* Thessalía, C Greece
Kranz *see* Zelenogradsk
114 *D7* **Krapina** Krapina-Zagorje, N Croatia
114 *E8* **Krapina** ≈ N Croatia
114 *D8* **Krapina-Zagorje** *off.* Krapinsko-Zagorska Županija. ◐ *province* N Croatia
116 *L7* **Krapinets** ≈ NE Bulgaria
113 *I15* **Krapkowice** *Ger.* Krappitz. Opole, SW Poland
Krappitz *see* Krapkowice
129 *O12* **Krasavino** Vologodskaya Oblast', NW Russian Federation
125 *Ff5* **Krasino** Novaya Zemlya, Arkhangel'skaya Oblast', N Russian Federation
127 *N18* **Kraskino** Primorskiy Kray, SE Russian Federation
120 *J11* **Krāslava** Krāslava, SE Latvia
121 *M14* **Krasnaluki** *Rus.* Krasnoluki. Vitsyebskaya Voblasts', N Belorussia
121 *P17* **Krasnapollye** *Rus.* Krasnopol'ye. Mahilyowskaya Voblasts', E Belorussia
130 *L15* **Krasnaya Polyana** Krasnodarskiy Kray, SW Russian Federation
121 *J18* **Krasnaya Slabada** *var.* Chyrvonaya Slabada, *Rus.* Krasnaya Sloboda. Minskaya Voblasts', S Belorussia
Krasnaya Sloboda *see* Krasnaya Slabada
121 *J15* **Krasnaye** *Rus.* Krasnoye. Minskaya Voblasts', C Belorussia
113 *O14* **Kraśnik** *Ger.* Kratznick. Lublin, E Poland
113 *O14* **Kraśnik Fabryczny** Lublin, SE Poland
119 *O9* **Krasni Okny** Odes'ka Oblast', SW Ukraine
151 *P7* **Krasnoarmeysk** Kokshetau, N Kazakhstan
131 *P8* **Krasnoarmeysk** Saratovskaya Oblast', W Russian Federation
Krasnoarmeysk *see* Krasnoarmiys'k
127 *Oo4* **Krasnoarmeyskiy** Chukotskiy Avtonomnyy Okrug, NE Russian Federation
119 *W7* **Krasnoarmiys'k** *Rus.* Krasnoarmeysk. Donets'ka Oblast', SE Ukraine
129 *P11* **Krasnoborsk** Arkhangel'skaya Oblast', NW Russian Federation
130 *K14* **Krasnodar** *prev.* Ekaterinodar, Yekaterinodar. Krasnodarskiy Kray, SW Russian Federation
130 *K13* **Krasnodarskiy Kray** ◐ *territory* SW Russian Federation
119 *Z7* **Krasnodon** Luhans'ka Oblast', E Ukraine
Krasnogor *see* Kallaste
131 *T2* **Krasnogorskoye** *Latv.* Sarkaņi. Udmurtskaya Respublika, NW Russian Federation
Krasnograd *see* Krasnohrad
Krasnogvardeysk *see* Bulungh'ur
130 *M13* **Krasnogvardeyskoye** Stavropol'skiy Kray, SW Russian Federation
Krasnogvardeyskoye *see* Krasnohvardiys'ke
119 *U6* **Krasnohrad** *Rus.* Krasnograd. Kharkivs'ka Oblast', E Ukraine
119 *S12* **Krasnohvardiys'ke** *Rus.* Krasnogvardeyskoye. Respublika Krym, S Ukraine
126 *L16* **Krasnokamensk** Chitinskaya Oblast', S Russian Federation
129 *U14* **Krasnokamsk** Permskaya Oblast', W Russian Federation
131 *U8* **Krasnokholm** Orenburgskaya Oblast', W Russian Federation
119 *U5* **Krasnokuts'k** *Rus.* Krasnokutsk. Kharkivs'ka Oblast', E Ukraine
130 *L7* **Krasnolesnyy** Voronezhskaya Oblast', W Russian Federation
Krasnoluki *see* Krasnaluki
Krasnoosol'skoye Vodokhranilishche *see* Chervonooskil's'ke Vodoskhovyshche
119 *S11* **Krasnoperekops'k** *Rus.* Krasnoperekopsk. Respublika Krym, S Ukraine
119 *U4* **Krasnopillya** Sums'ka Oblast', NE Ukraine
Krasnopol'ye *see* Krasnapollye
126 *H9* **Krasnosel'kup** Yamalo-Nenetskiy Avtonomnyy Okrug, N Russian Federation
128 *L5* **Krasnoshchel'ye** Murmanskaya Oblast', NW Russian Federation
131 *T2* **Krasnoslobodsk** Respublika Mordoviya, W Russian Federation
131 *O5* **Krasnoslobodsk** Volgogradskaya Oblast', SW Russian Federation
Krasnostav *see* Krasnystaw
125 *F10* **Krasnotur'insk** Sverdlovskaya Oblast', C Russian Federation
125 *E11* **Krasnoufimsk** Sverdlovskaya Oblast', C Russian Federation
125 *Ee10* **Krasnoural'sk** Sverdlovskaya Oblast', C Russian Federation
131 *V5* **Krasnousol'skiy** Respublika Bashkortostan, W Russian Federation
129 *U12* **Krasnovishersk** Permskaya Oblast', NW Russian Federation
Krasnovodsk *see* Turkmenbashi
152 *A10* **Krasnovodskiy Zaliv** *Turkm.* Krasnowodsk Aylagy. *lake gulf* W Turkmenistan
152 *B10* **Krasnovodskoye Plato** *Turkm.* Krasnowodsk Platosy. *plateau* NW Turkmenistan
Krasnowodsk Aylagy *see* Krasnovodskiy Zaliv
Krasnowodsk Platosy *see* Krasnovodskoye Plato
126 *Hh14* **Krasnoyarsk** Krasnoyarskiy Kray, S Russian Federation
131 *X7* **Krasnoyarskiy** Orenburgskaya Oblast', W Russian Federation
126 *I12* **Krasnoyarskiy Kray** ◐ *territory* C Russian Federation
126 *I14* **Krasnoyarskoye Vodokhranilishche** ⊡ S Russian Federation
Krasnoye *see* Krasnaye
152 *J15* **Krasnoye Znamya** *Turkm.* Gyzylbaydak. Maryyskiy Velayat, S Turkmenistan
129 *R11* **Krasnozatonskiy** Respublika Komi, NW Russian Federation
120 *D13* **Krasnoznamensk** *prev.* Lasdehnen, *Ger.* Haselberg. Kaliningradskaya Oblast', W Russian Federation
119 *R11* **Krasnoznam"yans'kyy Kanal** *canal* S Ukraine
113 *P14* **Krasnystaw** *Rus.* Krasnostav. Chełm, SE Poland
130 *H4* **Krasnyy** Smolenskaya Oblast', W Russian Federation
131 *P2* **Krasnyye Baki** Nizhegorodskaya Oblast', W Russian Federation
131 *Q13* **Krasnyye Barrikady** Astrakhanskaya Oblast', SW Russian Federation
128 *K15* **Krasnyy Kholm** Tverskaya Oblast', W Russian Federation
131 *Q8* **Krasnyy Kut** Saratovskaya Oblast', W Russian Federation
Krasnyy Liman *see* Krasnyy Lyman
119 *Y7* **Krasnyy Luch** *prev.* Krindachevka. Luhans'ka Oblast', E Ukraine
119 *X6* **Krasnyy Lyman** *Rus.* Krasnyy Liman. Donets'ka Oblast', SE Ukraine
131 *R3* **Krasnyy Steklovar** Respublika Mariy El, W Russian Federation
131 *P8* **Krasnyy Tekstil'shchik** Saratovskaya Oblast', W Russian Federation
131 *R13* **Krasnyy Yar** Astrakhanskaya Oblast', SW Russian Federation
Krassóvár *see* Caraşova
118 *L5* **Krasyliv** Khmel'nyts'ka Oblast', W Ukraine
113 *O21* **Kraszna** *Rom.* Crasna. ≈ Hungary/Romania
Kratie *see* Krâchéh
194 *I13* **Kratke Range** ▲▲ C PNG
115 *P17* **Kratovo** NE FYR Macedonia
Kratznick *see* Kraśnik
176 *Yy11* **Krau** Irian Jaya, E Indonesia
178 *Ii13* **Krâvanh, Chuŏr Phnum** *Eng.* Cardamom Mountains, *Fr.* Chaîne des Cardamomes. ▲▲ W Cambodia
Kravasta Lagoon *see* Karavastasë, Laguna e
Krawang *see* Karawang
Kraxatau *see* Rakata, Pulau
131 *Q15* **Kraynovka** Respublika Dagestan, SW Russian Federation
120 *D12* **Kražiai** Kelmė, C Lithuania
29 *P11* **Krebs** Oklahoma, C USA
103 *D15* **Krefeld** Nordrhein-Westfalen, W Germany
Kreisstadt *see* Krosno Odrzańskie
117 *D17* **Kremastón, Technití Límni** ⊡ C Greece
Kremenchug *see* Kremenchuk
Kremenchugskoye Vodokhranilishche/Kremenchuk Reservoir *see* Kremenchuts'ke Vodoskhovyshche
119 *S6* **Kremenchuk** *Rus.* Kremenchug. Poltavs'ka Oblast', NE Ukraine
119 *R6* **Kremenchuts'ke Vodoskhovyshche** *Eng.* Kremenchuk Reservoir, *Rus.* Kremenchugskoye Vodokhranilishche. ⊡ C Ukraine
118 *K5* **Kremenets'** *Pol.* Krzemieniec, *Rus.* Kremenets. Ternopil's'ka Oblast', W Ukraine
Kremennaya *see* Kreminna
119 *X6* **Kreminna** *Rus.* Kremennaya. Luhans'ka Oblast', E Ukraine
39 *R4* **Kremmling** Colorado, C USA
111 *V3* **Krems** ≈ NE Austria
Krems *see* Krems an der Donau
111 *W3* **Krems an der Donau** *var.* Krems. Niederösterreich, N Austria
Kremsier *see* Kroměříž
111 *S4* **Kremsmünster** Oberösterreich, N Austria
40 *M17* **Krenitzin Islands** *island* Aleutian Islands, Alaska, USA
Kresena *see* Kresna
116 *G11* **Kresna** *var.* Kresena. Sofiyska Oblast, SW Bulgaria
114 *O12* **Krespoljin** Serbia, E Yugoslavia
27 *N4* **Kress** Texas, SW USA
127 *Pp4* **Kresta, Zaliv** *bay* E Russian Federation
117 *D20* **Kréstena** *prev.* Selinoús. Dytikí Ellás, S Greece
128 *H14* **Kresttsy** Novgorodskaya Oblast', W Russian Federation
126 *Kk11* **Krestyakh** Respublika Sakha (Yakutiya), NE Russian Federation
Kretikon Delagos *see* Kritikó Pélagos
120 *C11* **Kretinga** *Ger.* Krottingen. Kretinga, NW Lithuania
Kreutz *see* Cristuru Secuiesc
Kreuz *see* Križevci, Croatia
Kreuz *see* Risti, Estonia
Kreuzburg/Kreuzburg in Oberschlesien *see* Kluczbork
Kreuzingen *see* Bol'shakovo
110 *H6* **Kreuzlingen** Thurgau, NE Switzerland
103 *K25* **Kreuzspitze** ▲ S Germany
103 *F16* **Kreuztal** Nordrhein-Westfalen, W Germany
121 *I15* **Kreva** *Rus.* Krevo. Hrodzyenskaya Voblasts', W Belorussia
Krevo *see* Kreva
Kría Vrísi *see* Krýa Vrýsi
81 *D16* **Kribi** Sud, SW Cameroon
Krichëv *see* Krychaw
Krickerhäu/Kriegerhaj *see* Handlová
111 *W6* **Krieglach** Steiermark, E Austria
110 *F8* **Kriens** Luzern, W Switzerland
Krimmitschau *see* Crimmitschau
100 *H12* **Krimpen aan den IJssel** Zuid-Holland, SW Netherlands
Krindachevka *see* Krasnyy Luch
117 *G25* **Kríos, Ákra** *headland* Kríti, Greece, E Mediterranean Sea
161 *J16* **Krishna** *prev.* Kistna. ≈ C India
161 *H20* **Krishnagiri** Tamil Nādu, SE India
161 *K17* **Krishna, Mouths of the** *delta* SE India
159 *S15* **Krishnanagar** West Bengal, N India
161 *G20* **Krishnarājāsāgara Reservoir** ⊡ W India
97 *N19* **Kristdala** Kalmar, S Sweden
Kristiania *see* Oslo
97 *E18* **Kristiansand** *var.* Christiansand. Vest-Agder, S Norway
97 *L22* **Kristianstad** Kristianstad, S Sweden
97 *J22* **Kristianstad** ◐ *county* S Sweden
96 *F8* **Kristiansund** *var.* Christiansund. Møre og Romsdal, S Norway
Kristiinankaupunki *see* Kristinestad
95 *I14* **Kristineberg** Västerbotten, N Sweden
97 *L16* **Kristinehamn** Värmland, C Sweden
95 *J17* **Kristinestad** *Fin.* Kristiinankaupunki. Vaasa, W Finland
Kristyor *see* Crişcior
117 *J25* **Kríti** *Eng.* Crete. ◐ *region* Greece, Aegean Sea
117 *J24* **Kríti** *Eng.* Crete. *island* Greece, Aegean Sea
117 *J23* **Kritikó Pélagos** *var.* Kretikon Delagos, *Eng.* Sea of Crete; *anc.* Mare Creticum. *sea* Greece, Aegean Sea
Kriulyany *see* Criuleni
114 *I12* **Krivaja** ≈ NE Bosnia and Herzegovina
Krivaja *see* Mali Idoš
115 *P17* **Kriva Palanka** *Turk.* Eğri Palanka. NE FYR Macedonia
Krivichi *see* Kryvychy
116 *H8* **Krivodol** Oblast Montana, NW Bulgaria
130 *M10* **Krivorozh'ye** Rostovskaya Oblast', SW Russian Federation
Krivoshin *see* Kryvoshyn
Krivoy Rog *see* Kryvyy Rih
114 *F7* **Križevci** *Ger.* Kreuz, *Hung.* Kőrös. Varaždin, NE Croatia
114 *B10* **Krk** *It.* Veglia. Primorje-Gorski Kotar, NW Croatia
114 *B10* **Krk** *It.* Veglia; *anc.* Curieta. *island* NW Croatia
111 *V12* **Krka** ≈ SE Slovenia
Krka *see* Gurk
111 *R11* **Krn** ▲ NW Slovenia
113 *H16* **Krnov** *Ger.* Jägerndorf. Severní Morava, E Czech Republic
Kroatien *see* Croatia
97 *G14* **Krøderen** Buskerud, S Norway
97 *G14* **Krøderen** ◎ S Norway
Kroi *see* Krui
97 *N17* **Krokek** Östergötland, S Sweden
Krokodil *see* Crocodile
95 *G16* **Krokom** Jämtland, C Sweden
119 *S2* **Krolevets'** *Rus.* Krolevets. Sums'ka Oblast', NE Ukraine
Królewska Huta *see* Chorzów
113 *H18* **Kroměříž** *Ger.* Kremsier. Jižní Morava, E Czech Republic
100 *I9* **Krommenie** Noord-Holland, C Netherlands
130 *J6* **Kromy** Orlovskaya Oblast', W Russian Federation
103 *L18* **Kronach** Bayern, E Germany
Krone an der Brahe *see* Koronowo
178 *I13* **Krŏng Kaôh Kŏng** Kaôh Kŏng, SW Cambodia
97 *K21* **Kronoberg** ◐ *county* S Sweden
127 *Pp11* **Kronotskiy Zaliv** *bay* E Russian Federation
205 *O2* **Kronprinsesse Märtha Kyst** *physical region* Antarctica
205 *V3* **Kronprins Olav Kyst** *physical region* Antarctica
128 *G12* **Kronshtadt** Leningradskaya Oblast', NW Russian Federation
Kronstadt *see* Braşov
85 *I22* **Kroonstad** Free State, C South Africa
126 *Kk13* **Kropotkin** Irkutskaya Oblast', C Russian Federation
130 *L14* **Kropotkin** Krasnodarskiy Kray, SW Russian Federation
Krośnieńskie, Województwo *see* Krosno
112 *J11* **Krośniewice** Płock, C Poland
113 *N17* **Krosno** *Ger.* Krossen. Krosno, SE Poland
113 *N17* **Krosno** *off.* Województwo Krośnieńskie. ◐ *province* SE Poland
112 *E12* **Krosno Odrzańskie** *Ger.* Crossen, Kreisstadt. Zielona Góra, W Poland
Krossen *see* Krosno
Krotoschin *see* Krotoszyn
112 *H13* **Krotoszyn** *Ger.* Krotoschin. Kalisz, C Poland
Krottingen *see* Kretinga
Krousón *see* Krousónas
117 *J25* **Krousónas** *prev.* Krousón, Kroussón. Kríti, Greece, E Mediterranean Sea
Kroussón *see* Krousónas
Krraba *see* Krrabë
115 *L20* **Krrabë** *var.* Krraba. Tiranë, C Albania
115 *L17* **Krrabit, Mali i** ▲▲ N Albania
111 *W12* **Krško** *Ger.* Gurkfeld; *prev.* Videm-Krško. E Slovenia
85 *K19* **Kruger National Park** *national park* Northern, N South Africa
85 *J21* **Krugersdorp** Gauteng, NE South Africa
40 *D16* **Krugloi Point** *headland* Agattu Island, Alaska, USA
Krugloye *see* Kruhlaye
121 *N15* **Kruhlaye** *Rus.* Krugloye. Mahilyowskaya Voblasts', E Belorussia
174 *I13* **Krui** *var.* Kroi. Sumatera, SW Indonesia
101 *G16* **Kruibeke** Oost-Vlaanderen, N Belgium
85 *G25* **Kruidfontein** Western Cape, SW South Africa
101 *F15* **Kruiningen** Zeeland, SW Netherlands
Kruja *see* Krujë
115 *L19* **Krujë** *var.* Kruja, *It.* Croia. Durrës, C Albania
Krulevshchina *see* Krulewshchyna
120 *K13* **Krulewshchyna** *Rus.* Krulevshchina. Vitsyebskaya Voblasts', N Belorussia
27 *T6* **Krum** Texas, SW USA
103 *J23* **Krumbach** Bayern, S Germany
115 *M17* **Krumë** Kukës, NE Albania
Krummau *see* Český Krumlov
116 *K12* **Krumovgrad** *prev.* Kossukavak. Khaskovska Oblast, S Bulgaria
116 *K12* **Krumovitsa** ≈ S Bulgaria
116 *L10* **Krumovo** Burgaska Oblast, SE Bulgaria
178 *Hh11* **Krung Thep** *var.* Krung Thep Mahanakhon, *Eng.* Bangkok. ● (Thailand) Bangkok, C Thailand
178 *Hh12* **Krung Thep, Ao** *var.* Bight of Bangkok. *bay* S Thailand
Krung Thep Mahanakhon *see* Krung Thep
121 *M15* **Krupki** *Rus.* Krupki. Minskaya Voblasts', C Belorussia
97 *G24* **Kruså** *var.* Krusaa. Sønderjylland, SW Denmark
Krusaa *see* Kruså
15 *I4* **Krusenstern, Cape** *headland* Northwest Territories, NW Canada
115 *N14* **Kruševac** Serbia, C Yugoslavia
115 *N19* **Kruševo** SW FYR Macedonia
113 *A15* **Krušné Hory** *Eng.* Ore Mountains, *Ger.* Erzgebirge. ▲▲ Czech Republic/Germany *see also* Erzgebirge
41 *W13* **Kruzof Island** *island* Alexander Archipelago, Alaska, USA
116 *F13* **Krýa Vrýsi** *var.* Kría Vrísi. Kentrikí Makedonía, N Greece
121 *P16* **Krychaw** *Rus.* Krichëv. Mahilyowskaya Voblasts', E Belorussia
66 *K11* **Krylov Seamount** *undersea feature* E Atlantic Ocean
Krym *see* Krym, Respublika
119 *S13* **Krym, Respublika** *var.* Krym, *Eng.* Crimea, Crimean Oblast; *prev. Rus.* Krymskaya ASSR, Krymskaya Oblast'. ◐ *province* SE Ukraine
130 *K14* **Krymsk** Krasnodarskiy Kray, SW Russian Federation
Krymskaya ASSR/Krymskaya Oblast' *see* Krym, Respublika
119 *T13* **Kryms'ki Hory** ▲▲ S Ukraine
119 *T13* **Kryms'kyy Pivostriv** *peninsula* S Ukraine
113 *M18* **Krynica** *Ger.* Tannenhof. Nowy Sącz, S Poland
119 *P8* **Kryve Ozero** Odes'ka Oblast', SW Ukraine
121 *I18* **Kryvoshyn** *Rus.* Krivoshin. Brestskaya Voblasts', SW Belorussia
121 *K14* **Kryvychy** *Rus.* Krivichi. Minskaya Voblasts', C Belorussia
119 *S8* **Kryvyy Rih** *Rus.* Krivoy Rog. Dnipropetrovs'ka Oblast', SE Ukraine
119 *N8* **Kryzhopil'** Vinnyts'ka Oblast', C Ukraine

◆ Country ● Country Capital ◇ Dependent Territory ○ Dependent Territory Capital ◐ Administrative Region ✕ International Airport ▲ Mountain ▲▲ Mountain Range Volcano ≈ River ◎ Lake ⊡ Reservoir

KRZEMIENIEC – KYZYL-SUU

Krzemieniec *see* Kremenets'
113 *J14* **Krzepice** Częstochowa, S Poland
112 *F10* **Krzyż** Piła, W Poland
Ksar al Kabir *see* Ksar-el-Kebir
Ksar al Soule *see* Er-Rachidia
76 *J5* **Ksar El Boukhari** N Algeria
76 *G5* **Ksar-el-Kebir** *var.* Alcázar, Ksar al Kabir, Ksar-el-Kébir, ***Ar.*** Al-Kasr al-Kebir, Al-Qsar al-Kbir, ***Sp.*** Alcazarquivir. NW Morocco
112 *H12* **Książ Wielkopolski** ***Ger.*** Xions. Poznań, W Poland
131 *O3* **Kstovo** Nizhegorodskaya Oblast', W Russian Federation
174 *Mm4* **Kuala Belait** W Brunei
Kuala Dungun *see* Dungun
174 *M7* **Kualakerian** Borneo, C Indonesia
174 *M10* **Kualakuayan** Borneo, C Indonesia
174 *H4* **Kuala Lipis** Pahang, Peninsular Malaysia
174 *H5* **Kuala Lumpur** ● (Malaysia) Kuala Lumpur, Peninsular Malaysia
Kuala Pelabohan Kelang *see* Pelabuhan Klang
175 *Nn3* **Kuala Penyu** Sabah, East Malaysia
40 *E9* **Kualapuu** ***Haw.*** Kualapu'u. Molokai, Hawaii, USA, C Pacific Ocean
173 *G6* **Kuala, Sungai** ~ Sumatera, W Indonesia
174 *Hh3* **Kuala Terengganu** *var.* Kuala Trengganu. Terengganu, Peninsular Malaysia
174 *Hh9* **Kualatungkal** Sumatera, W Indonesia
175 *O3* **Kuamut, Sungai** ~ East Malaysia
175 *Qq7* **Kuandang** Sulawesi, N Indonesia
175 *Qq7* **Kuandang, Teluk** *bay* Sulawesi, N Indonesia
169 *V12* **Kuandian** Liaoning, NE China
Kuando-Kubango *see* Cuando Cubango
Kuang-chou *see* Guangzhou
Kuang-hsi *see* Guangxi Zhuangzu Zizhiqu
Kuang-tung *see* Guangdong
Kuang-yuan *see* Guangyuan
174 *Hh4* **Kuantan** Pahang, Peninsular Malaysia
Kuantan, Batang *see* Indragiri, Sungai
Kuanza Norte *see* Cuanza Norte
Kuanza Sul *see* Cuanza Sul
Kuba *see* Quba
125 *Aa12* **Kuban'** *var.* Hypanis. ~ SW Russian Federation
Kubango *see* Cubango/Okavango
147 *X8* **Kubārah** NW Oman
95 *H16* **Kubbe** Västernorrland, C Sweden
82 *A11* **Kubbum** Southern Darfur, W Sudan
128 *L13* **Kubenskoye, Ozero** ◎ NW Russian Federation
170 *Ee16* **Kubokawa** Kōchi, Shikoku, SW Japan
116 *L7* **Kubrat** ***prev.*** Balbunar. Razgradska Oblast, NE Bulgaria
175 *Oo15* **Kubu** Sumbawa, S Indonesia
114 *O13* **Kučajske Planine** ▲▲ E Yugoslavia
172 *Pp2* **Kuccharo-ko** ◎ Hokkaidō, N Japan
114 *O11* **Kučevo** Serbia, NE Yugoslavia
Kuchan *see* Qūchān
174 *L6* **Kuching** ***prev.*** Sarawak. Sarawak, East Malaysia
174 *L7* **Kuching** ✕ Sarawak, East Malaysia
170 *Aa17* **Kuchinoerabu-jima** *island* Nansei-shotō, SW Japan
170 *C13* **Kuchinotsu** Nagasaki, Kyūshū, SW Japan
111 *Q6* **Kuchl** Salzburg, NW Austria
154 *L9* **Kūchnay Darweyshān** Helmand, S Afghanistan
Kuchurgan *see* Kuchurhan
119 *O9* **Kuchurhan** ***Rus.*** Kuchurgan. ~ NE Ukraine
Kuçova *see* Kuçovë
115 *L21* **Kuçovë** *var.* Kuçova; ***prev.*** Qyteti Stalin. Berat, C Albania
142 *D11* **Küçük Çekmece** İstanbul, NW Turkey
170 *Dd13* **Kudamatsu** *var.* Kudamatu. Yamaguchi, Honshū, SW Japan
Kudamatu *see* Kudamatsu
Kudara *see* Ghŭdara
175 *O1* **Kudat** Sabah, East Malaysia
Küddow *see* Gwda
161 *G17* **Kūdligi** Karnātaka, W India
Kudowa *see* Kudowa-Zdrój
113 *F16* **Kudowa-Zdrój** ***Ger.*** Kudowa. Wałbrzych, SW Poland
119 *P9* **Kudryavtsivka** Mykolayivs'ka Oblast', S Ukraine
174 *L14* **Kudus** ***prev.*** Koedoes. Jawa, C Indonesia
129 *T13* **Kudymkar** Komi-Permyatskiy Avtonomnyy Okrug, NW Russian Federation
Kudzsir *see* Cugir
Kuei-chou *see* Guizhou
Kuei-lin *see* Guilin
Kuei-yang *see* Guiyang
K'u-erh-lo *see* Korla
Kueyang *see* Guiyang
Kufa *see* Al Kūfah
142 *E14* **Küfiçayı** ~ C Turkey
111 *O6* **Kufstein** Tirol, W Austria
151 *V14* **Kugaly** ***Kaz.*** Qoghaly. Taldykorgan, SE Kazakhstan
149 *Y13* **Kūhak** Sīstān va Balūchestān, SE Iran
149 *R9* **Kūhbonān** Kermān, C Iran
154 *J5* **Kūhestān** *var.* Kohsān. Herāt, W Afghanistan
95 *N15* **Kuhmo** Oulu, E Finland
95 *L18* **Kuhmoinen** Keski-Suomi, C Finland
Kuhnau *see* Konin
Kühnö *see* Kihnu
149 *O8* **Kūhpāyeh** Eşfahān, C Iran
178 *H13* **Kui Buri** *var.* Ban Kui Nua. Prachuap Khiri Khan, SW Thailand
Kuibyshev *see* Kuybyshevskoye Vodokhranilishche
84 *D13* **Kuito** ***Port.*** Silva Porto. Bié, C Angola
41 *X14* **Kuiu Island** *island* Alexander Archipelago, Alaska, USA
94 *L13* **Kuivaniemi** Oulu, C Finland
79 *V14* **Kujama** Kaduna, C Nigeria
172 *N10* **Kuji** *var.* Kuzi. Iwate, Honshū, C Japan
Kujto, Ozero *see* Kuyto, Ozero
Kujū-renzan *see* Kujū-san
170 *D14* **Kujū-san** *var.* Kujū-renzan. ▲ Kyūshū, SW Japan
45 *N7* **Kukalaya, Rio** *var.* Rio Cuculaya, Rio Kukulaya. ~ NE Nicaragua
115 *O16* **Kukavica** *var.* Vlajna. ▲ SE Yugoslavia
152 *M10* **Kŭkcha** ***Rus.*** Kokcha. Bukhoro Wiloyati, C Uzbekistan
115 *M18* **Kukës** *var.* Kukësi. Kukës, NE Albania
115 *L18* **Kukës** ◐ *district* NE Albania
Kukësi *see* Kukës
194 *J14* **Kukipi** Gulf, S PNG
131 *S3* **Kukmor** Respublika Tatarstan, W Russian Federation
Kukong *see* Shaoguan
41 *N6* **Kukpowruk River** ~ Alaska, USA
40 *M6* **Kukpuk River** ~ Alaska, USA
Kukukhoto *see* Hohhot
Kukulaya, Rio *see* Kukalaya, Rio
174 *Hh7* **Kukup** Johor, Peninsular Malaysia
201 *W12* **Kuku Point** *headland* NW Wake Island
152 *G11* **Kukurtli** Akhalskiy Velayat, C Turkmenistan
Kūl *see* Kūl, Rūd-e
116 *F7* **Kula** Oblast Montana, NW Bulgaria
142 *D14* **Kula** Manisa, W Turkey
114 *K9* **Kula** Serbia, NW Yugoslavia
155 *S8* **Kulāchi** North-West Frontier Province, NW Pakistan
Kulachi *see* Kolāchi
150 *F11* **Kulagino** ***Kaz.*** Kūlagīno. Atyrau, W Kazakhstan
174 *Hh6* **Kulai** Johor, Peninsular Malaysia
116 *M7* **Kulak** ~ NE Bulgaria
159 *T11* **Kula Kangri** *var.* Kulhakangri. ▲ Bhutan/China
150 *E13* **Kulaly, Ostrov** *island* SW Kazakhstan
153 *V9* **Kulanak** Narynskaya Oblast', C Kyrgyzstan
152 *B8* **Kulandag** ▲▲ W Turkmenistan
159 *V14* **Kulaura** Chittagong, NE Bangladesh
120 *D9* **Kuldīga** ***Ger.*** Goldingen. Kuldīga, W Latvia
Kuldja *see* Yining
Kul'dzhuktau, Gory *see* Quljuqtov-Toghi
131 *N4* **Kulebaki** Nizhegorodskaya Oblast', W Russian Federation
114 *E11* **Kulen Vakuf** NW Bosnia and Herzegovina
189 *Q9* **Kulgera Roadhouse** Northern Territory, N Australia
Kulhakangri *see* Kula Kangri
131 *T1* **Kuliga** Udmurtskaya Respublika, NW Russian Federation
Kulkuduk *see* Kalquduq
120 *G4* **Kullamaa** Läänemaa, W Estonia
207 *O12* **Kullorsuaq** *var.* Kuvdlorssuak. C Greenland
31 *O6* **Kulm** North Dakota, N USA
Kulm *see* Chełmno
152 *D12* **Kul'mach** Balkanskiy Velayat, W Turkmenistan
103 *L18* **Kulmbach** Bayern, SE Germany
Kulmsee *see* Chełmża
153 *Q14* **Kŭlob** ***Rus.*** Kulyab. SW Tajikistan
94 *M13* **Kuloharju** Lappi, N Finland
129 *N7* **Kuloy** Arkhangel'skaya Oblast', NW Russian Federation
129 *N7* **Kuloy** ~ NW Russian Federation
143 *Q14* **Kulp** Dıyarbakır, SE Turkey
Kulpa *see* Kolpa
79 *P14* **Kulpawn** ~ N Ghana
149 *R13* **Kūl, Rūd-e** *var.* Kūl. ~ S Iran
150 *G12* **Kul'sary** ***Kaz.*** Qulsary. Atyrau, W Kazakhstan
159 *R15* **Kulti** West Bengal, NE India
95 *G14* **Kultsjön** ◎ N Sweden
142 *I14* **Kulu** Konya, W Turkey
127 *Nn10* **Kulu** ~ E Russian Federation
125 *G14* **Kulunda** Altayskiy Kray, S Russian Federation
151 *T7* **Kulunda Steppe** ***Kaz.*** Qulyndy Zhazyghy, ***Rus.*** Kulundinskaya Ravnina. *grassland* Kazakhstan/Russian Federation
Kulundinskaya Ravnina *see* Kulunda Steppe
190 *M9* **Kulwin** Victoria, SE Australia
Kulyab *see* Kŭlob
119 *Q3* **Kulykivka** Chernihivs'ka Oblast', N Ukraine
Kum *see* Qom
170 *Ee15* **Kuma** Ehime, Shikoku, SW Japan
131 *P14* **Kuma** ~ SW Russian Federation
Kumafa *see* Kumawa, Pegunungan
171 *K15* **Kumagaya** Saitama, Honshū, S Japan
172 *N6* **Kumaishi** Hokkaidō, NE Japan
174 *Ll11* **Kumai, Teluk** *bay* Borneo, C Indonesia
131 *Y7* **Kumak** Orenburgskaya Oblast', W Russian Federation
176 *Y9* **Kumamba, Kepulauan** *island group* E Indonesia
170 *Cc14* **Kumamoto** Kumamoto, Kyūshū, SW Japan
170 *C14* **Kumamoto** ***off.*** Kumamoto-ken. ◐ *prefecture* Kyūshū, SW Japan
171 *Gg17* **Kumano** Mie, Honshū, SW Japan
Kumanova *see* Kumanovo
115 *O17* **Kumanovo** ***Turk.*** Kumanova. N FYR Macedonia
193 *G17* **Kumara** West Coast, South Island, NZ
188 *J8* **Kumarina Roadhouse** Western Australia
159 *T15* **Kumarkhali** Khulna, W Bangladesh
79 *P16* **Kumasi** ***prev.*** Coomassie. C Ghana
176 *Vv11* **Kumawa, Pegunungan** *var.* Kumafa. ▲▲ Irian Jaya, E Indonesia
Kumayri *see* Gyumri
81 *D15* **Kumba** Sud-Ouest, W Cameroon
116 *N13* **Kumbağ** Tekirdağ, NW Turkey
161 *J21* **Kumbakonam** Tamil Nādu, SE India
176 *Z16* **Kumbe, Sungai** ~ Irian Jaya, E Indonesia
Kum-Dag *see* Gumdag
172 *O14* **Kume-jima** *island* Nansei-shotō, SW Japan
131 *V6* **Kumertau** Respublika Bashkortostan, W Russian Federation
125 *F11* **Kuminskiy** Khanty-Mansiyskiy Avtonomnyy Okrug, C Russian Federation
37 *R4* **Kumiva Peak** ▲ Nevada, W USA
165 *N8* **Kum Kuduk** *well* NW China
165 *N7* **Kumkuduk** Xinjiang Uygur Zizhiqu, W China
Kumkurgan *see* Qumqurghon
97 *M16* **Kumla** Örebro, C Sweden
142 *E17* **Kumluca** Antalya, SW Turkey
102 *N9* **Kummerower See** ◎ NE Germany
79 *X14* **Kumo** Bauchi, E Nigeria
151 *O13* **Kumola** ~ C Kazakhstan
178 *H1* **Kumon Range** ▲▲ N Burma
126 *K14* **Kumora** Respublika Buryatiya, S Russian Federation
85 *F22* **Kums** Karas, SE Namibia
161 *E18* **Kumta** Karnātaka, W India
164 *L6* **Kümük** Xinjiang Uygur Zizhiqu, W China
40 *H12* **Kumukahi, Cape** *headland* Hawaii, USA, C Pacific Ocean
131 *Q17* **Kumukh** Respublika Dagestan, SW Russian Federation
Kumul *see* Hami
131 *N9* **Kumylzhenskaya** Volgogradskaya Oblast', SW Russian Federation
147 *W6* **Kumzār** N Oman
155 *S4* **Kunar** ***Per.*** Konarhā. ◐ *province* E Afghanistan
Kunashiri *see* Kunashir, Ostrov
127 *P16* **Kunashir, Ostrov** *var.* Kunashiri. *island* Kuril'skiye Ostrova, SE Russian Federation
120 *I3* **Kunda** Lääne-Virumaa, NE Estonia
158 *M13* **Kunda** Uttar Pradesh, N India
161 *E19* **Kundāpura** *var.* Coondapoor. Karnātaka, W India
81 *O24* **Kundelungu, Monts** ▲▲ S Zaire
Kundert *see* Hernád
194 *I12* **Kundiawa** Chimbu, W PNG
Kundla *see* Sāvarkundla
174 *Hh7* **Kundur, Pulau** *island* W Indonesia
155 *Q2* **Kunduz** *var.* Kondoz, Kundūz, Qondūz, ***Per.*** Kondūz. Kunduz, NE Afghanistan
155 *Q2* **Kunduz** ***Per.*** Kondūz. ◐ *province* NE Afghanistan
Kuneitra *see* Al Qunayṭirah
85 *B18* **Kunene** ◐ *district* NE Namibia
85 *A16* **Kunene** *var.* Cunene. ~ Angola/Namibia *see also* Cunene
Künes *see* Xinyuan
164 *J5* **Künes He** ~ NW China
97 *I19* **Kungälv** Göteborg och Bohus, S Sweden
153 *W7* **Kungei Ala-Tau** ***Rus.*** Khrebet Kyungëy Ala-Too, ***Kir.*** Küngöy Ala-Too. ▲▲ Kazakhstan/Kyrgyzstan
Küngöy Ala-Too *see* Kungei Ala-Tau
Kungrad *see* Qŭnghirot
97 *J19* **Kungsbacka** Halland, S Sweden
97 *I18* **Kungshamn** Göteborg och Bohus, S Sweden
97 *M16* **Kungsör** Västmanland, C Sweden
81 *J16* **Kungu** Equateur, NW Zaire
129 *V15* **Kungur** Permskaya Oblast', NW Russian Federation
177 *G9* **Kungyangon** Yangon, SW Burma
113 *M22* **Kunhegyes** Jász-Nagykun-Szolnok, E Hungary
178 *H5* **Kunhing** Shan State, E Burma
170 *Cc15* **Kunimi-dake** ▲ Kyūshū, SW Japan
164 *D9* **Kunjirap Daban** *var.* Khūnjerāb Pass. *pass* China/Pakistan *see also* Khūnjerāb Pass
Kunlun Mountains *see* Kunlun Shan
164 *H10* **Kunlun Shan** ***Eng.*** Kunlun Mountains. ▲▲ NW China
165 *P11* **Kunlun Shankou** *pass* C China
166 *G13* **Kunming** *var.* K'un-ming; ***prev.*** Yunnan. Yunnan, SW China
172 *N6* **Kunnui** Hokkaidō, NE Japan
169 *X16* **Kunsan** *var.* Gunsan, ***Jap.*** Gunzan. W South Korea
113 *L24* **Kunszentmárton** Jász-Nagykun-Szolnok, E Hungary
113 *J23* **Kunszentmiklós** Bács-Kiskun, C Hungary
189 *N3* **Kununurra** Western Australia
Kunya-Urgench *see* Këneurgench
Kunyé *see* Pins, Île des
174 *Mm8* **Kunyi** Borneo, C Indonesia
103 *I20* **Künzelsau** Baden-Württemberg, S Germany
167 *S10* **Kuocang Shan** ▲▲ SE China
128 *H5* **Kuoloyarvi** *var.* Luolajarvi. Murmanskaya Oblast', NW Russian Federation
95 *N16* **Kuopio** Kuopio, C Finland
95 *M16* **Kuopio** ◐ *province* C Finland
95 *K17* **Kuortane** Vaasa, W Finland
95 *M18* **Kuortti** Mikkeli, S Finland
Kupa *see* Kolpa
175 *R17* **Kupang** ***prev.*** Koepang. Timor, C Indonesia
41 *Q5* **Kuparuk River** ~ Alaska, USA
Kupchino *see* Cupcina
194 *L16* **Kupiano** Central, S PNG
188 *M4* **Kupingarri** Western Australia
125 *G14* **Kupino** Novosibirskaya Oblast', C Russian Federation
120 *H11* **Kupiškis** Kupiškis, NE Lithuania
116 *L13* **Küplü** Edirne, NW Turkey
41 *X13* **Kupreanof Island** *island* Alexander Archipelago, Alaska, USA
41 *O16* **Kupreanof Point** *headland* Alaska, USA
114 *G13* **Kupres** SW Bosnia and Herzegovina
119 *W5* **Kup"yans'k** ***Rus.*** Kupyansk. Kharkivs'ka Oblast', E Ukraine
119 *W5* **Kup"yans'k-Vuzlovyy** Kharkivs'ka Oblast', E Ukraine
164 *I6* **Kuqa** Xinjiang Uygur Zizhiqu, NW China
Kür *see* Kura
143 *W11* **Kura** ***Az.*** Kür, ***Geor.*** Mtkvari, ***Turk.*** Kura Nehri. ~ SW Asia
57 *R8* **Kuracki** NW Guyana
170 *Ee13* **Kurahashi-jima** *island* SW Japan
Kura Kurk *see* Irbe Strait
153 *Q10* **Kurama Range** ***Rus.*** Kuraminskiy Khrebet. ▲▲ Tajikistan/Uzbekistan
Kuraminskiy Khrebet *see* Kurama Range
Kura Nehri *see* Kura
176 *Ww10* **Kuran, Kepulauan** *island group* E Indonesia
121 *J14* **Kuranyets** ***Rus.*** Kurenets. Minskaya Voblasts', C Belorussia
170 *Ff14* **Kurashiki** *var.* Kurasiki. Okayama, Honshū, SW Japan
160 *L10* **Kurasia** Madhya Pradesh, C India
Kurasiki *see* Kurashiki
170 *G12* **Kurayoshi** *var.* Kurayosi. Tottori, Honshū, SW Japan
Kurayosi *see* Kurayoshi
169 *X6* **Kurbin He** ~ NE China
151 *X10* **Kurchum** ***Kaz.*** Kürshim. Vostochnyy Kazakhstan, E Kazakhstan
151 *Y10* **Kurchum** ~ E Kazakhstan
143 *X11* **Kürdämir** ***Rus.*** Kyurdamir. C Azerbaijan
Kurdestan *see* Kordestān
145 *S1* **Kurdistan** *cultural region* SW Asia
Kurd Kui *see* Kord Kūy
161 *F15* **Kurduvādi** Mahārāshtra, W India
116 *J11* **Kŭrdzhali** *var.* Kirdzhali. Khaskovska Oblast, S Bulgaria
116 *J11* **Kŭrdzhali, Yazovir** ⊡ S Bulgaria
170 *Ee13* **Kure** Hiroshima, Honshū, SW Japan
199 *J5* **Kure Atoll** *var.* Ocean Island. *atoll* Hawaiian Islands, Hawaii, USA, C Pacific Ocean
142 *J10* **Küre Dağları** ▲▲ N Turkey
Kurenets *see* Kuranyets
120 *E6* **Kuressaare** ***Ger.*** Arensburg; ***prev.*** Kingissepp. Saaremaa, W Estonia
126 *I9* **Kureyka** Krasnoyarskiy Kray, N Russian Federation
126 *I9* **Kureyka** ~ N Russian Federation
151 *P10* **Kurgal'dzhin, Ozero** ◎ C Kazakhstan
151 *Q10* **Kurgal'dzhinskiy** ***Kaz.*** Qorghazhyn. Akmola, C Kazakhstan
125 *F12* **Kurgan** Kurganskaya Oblast', C Russian Federation
130 *L14* **Kurganinsk** Krasnodarskiy Kray, SW Russian Federation
125 *Ee12* **Kurganskaya Oblast'** ◐ *province* C Russian Federation
Kurgan-Tyube *see* Qŭrghonteppa
203 *O2* **Kuria** ***prev.*** Woodle Island. *island* Tungaru, W Kiribati
Kuria Muria Bay *see* Ḥalānīyāt, Khalīj al
Kuria Muria Islands *see* Ḥalāniyāt, Juzur al
159 *T13* **Kurigram** Rajshahi, N Bangladesh
176 *Yy16* **Kurik** Irian Jaya, E Indonesia
95 *K17* **Kurikka** Vaasa, W Finland
171 *M12* **Kurikoma-yama** ▲ Honshū, C Japan
199 *Hh3* **Kurile Basin** *undersea feature* NW Pacific Ocean
Kurile Islands *see* Kuril'skiye Ostrova
Kurile-Kamchatka Depression *see* Kurile Trench
199 *Hh3* **Kurile Trench** *var.* Kurile-Kamchatka Depression. *undersea feature* NW Pacific Ocean
131 *Q9* **Kurilovka** Saratovskaya Oblast', W Russian Federation
127 *P15* **Kuril'sk** Kuril'skiye Ostrova, Sakhalinskaya Oblats', SE Russian Federation
127 *Pp15* **Kuril'skiye Ostrova** ***Eng.*** Kurile Islands. *island group* SE Russian Federation
44 *M9* **Kurinwas, Río** ~ E Nicaragua
Kurisches Haff *see* Courland Lagoon
Kurkund *see* Kilingi-Nõmme
130 *M4* **Kurlovskiy** Vladimirskaya Oblast', W Russian Federation
82 *G12* **Kurmuk** Blue Nile, SE Sudan
Kurna *see* Al Qurnah
161 *H17* **Kurnool** *var.* Karnul. Andhra Pradesh, S India
171 *J13* **Kurobe** Toyama, Honshū, SW Japan
170 *Cc13* **Kurogi** Fukuoka, Kyūshū, SW Japan
171 *Mm9* **Kuroishi** *var.* Kuroisi. Aomori, Honshū, C Japan
Kuroisi *see* Kuroishi
171 *Kk14* **Kuroiso** Tochigi, Honshū, S Japan
172 *N5* **Kuromatsunai** Hokkaidō, NE Japan
172 *Oo17* **Kuro-shima** *island* SW Japan
171 *H16* **Kuroso-yama** ▲ Honshū, SW Japan
193 *F21* **Kurow** Canterbury, South Island, NZ
176 *Uu13* **Kur, Pulau** *island* E Indonesia
131 *N15* **Kursavka** Stavropol'skiy Kray, SW Russian Federation
120 *E11* **Kuršėnai** Šiauliai, N Lithuania
Kürshim *see* Kurchum
Kurshskaya Kosa/Kuršių Nerija *see* Courland Spit
130 *J7* **Kursk** Kurskaya Oblast', W Russian Federation
130 *I7* **Kurskaya Oblast'** ◐ *province* W Russian Federation
Kurskiy Zaliv *see* Courland Lagoon
115 *N15* **Kuršumlija** Serbia, S Yugoslavia
143 *R15* **Kurtalan** Siirt, SE Turkey
125 *Ee12* **Kurtamysh** Kurganskaya Oblast', C Russian Federation
Kurtbunar *see* Tervel
Kurt-Dere *see* Vŭlchidol
Kurtitsch/Kürtös *see* Curtici
151 *U15* **Kurtty** ~ SE Kazakhstan
95 *L18* **Kuru** Häme, SW Finland
82 *C13* **Kuru** ~ W Sudan
116 *M13* **Kuru Dağı** ▲▲ NW Turkey
164 *L7* **Kuruktag** ▲▲ NW China
85 *G22* **Kuruman** Northern Cape, N South Africa
69 *T14* **Kuruman** ~ W South Africa
170 *Cc13* **Kurume** Fukuoka, Kyūshū, SW Japan
126 *K15* **Kurumkan** Respublika Buryatiya, S Russian Federation
161 *J25* **Kurunegala** North Western Province, C Sri Lanka
57 *T10* **Kurupukari** C Guyana
129 *U10* **Kur"ya** Respublika Komi, NW Russian Federation
150 *E15* **Kuryk** ***prev.*** Yeraliyev. Mangistau, SW Kazakhstan
142 *B15* **Kuşadası** Aydın, SW Turkey
117 *M19* **Kuşadası Körfezi** *gulf* SW Turkey
170 *Aa16* **Kusagaki-guntō** *island* SW Japan
Kusaie *see* Kosrae
151 *T12* **Kusak** ~ C Kazakhstan
Kusary *see* Qusar
178 *Hh8* **Ku Sathan, Doi** ▲ NW Thailand
171 *H15* **Kusatsu** *var.* Kusatu. Shiga, Honshū, SW Japan
Kusatu *see* Kusatsu
144 *F11* **Kuseifa** Southern, C Israel
142 *C12* **Kuş Gölü** ◎ NW Turkey
130 *L12* **Kushchevskaya** Krasnodarskiy Kray, SW Russian Federation
171 *H16* **Kushida-gawa** ~ Honshū, SW Japan
170 *Bb15* **Kushikino** *var.* Kusikino. Kagoshima, Kyūshū, SW Japan
170 *C17* **Kushima** *var.* Kusima. Miyazaki, Kyūshū, SW Japan
170 *G17* **Kushimoto** Wakayama, Honshū, SW Japan
172 *Q7* **Kushiro** *var.* Kusiro. Hokkaidō, NE Japan
154 *K4* **Kūshk** Herāt, W Afghanistan
152 *J17* **Kushka** ~ S Turkmenistan
Kushka *see* Gushgy
151 *N8* **Kushmurun** ***Kaz.*** Qusmuryn. Kustanay, N Kazakhstan
151 *N8* **Kushmurun, Ozero** ***Kaz.*** Qusmuryn. ◎ N Kazakhstan
131 *U4* **Kushnarenkovo** Respublika Bashkortostan, W Russian Federation
Kushrabat *see* Qŭshrabot
159 *T15* **Kushtia** Khulna, W Bangladesh
125 *Ee10* **Kushva** Sverdlovskaya Oblast', C Russian Federation
Kusikino *see* Kushikino
Kusima *see* Kushima
Kusiro *see* Kushiro
40 *M13* **Kuskokwim Bay** *bay* Alaska USA
41 *P11* **Kuskokwim Mountains** ▲▲ Alaska, USA
41 *N12* **Kuskokwim River** ~ Alaska, USA
110 *G7* **Küsnacht** Zürich, N Switzerland
172 *Qq6* **Kussharo-ko** *var.* Kussyaro. ◎ Hokkaidō, NE Japan
Küssnacht *see* Küssnacht am Rigi
110 *F8* **Küssnacht am Rigi** *var.* Küssnacht. Schwyz, C Switzerland
Kussyaro *see* Kussharo-ko
150 *M7* **Kustanay** ***Kaz.*** Qostanay. Kustanay, N Kazakhstan
150 *L8* **Kustanay** ***off.*** Kustanayskaya Oblast', ***Kaz.*** Qostanay Oblysy. ◐ *province* N Kazakhstan
Kustanayskaya Oblast' *see* Kustanay
Küstence/Küstendje *see* Constanța
102 *F11* **Küstenkanal** *var.* Ems-Hunte Canal. *canal* NW Germany
Küstrin *see* Kostrzyn
175 *T7* **Kusu** Pulau Halmahera, E Indonesia
175 *Nn16* **Kuta** Pulau Lombok, S Indonesia
145 *T4* **Kutabān** N Iraq
142 *E13* **Kütahya** ***prev.*** Kutaia. Kütahya, W Turkey
142 *E13* **Kütahya** *var.* Kutaia. ◐ *province* W Turkey
Kutai *see* Mahakam, Sungai
Kutaia *see* Kütahya
143 *R9* **K'ut'aisi** W Georgia
Kūt al 'Amārah *see* Al Kūt
Kut al Hai/Kūt al Ḥayy *see* Al Ḥayy
Kut al Imara *see* Al Kūt
126 *M12* **Kutana** Respublika Sakha (Yakutiya), NE Russian Federation
Kutaradja/Kutaraja *see* Bandaaceh
172 *Nn5* **Kutchan** Hokkaidō, NE Japan
Kutch, Gulf of *see* Kachchh, Gulf of
Kutch, Rann of *see* Kachchh, Rann of
114 *F9* **Kutina** Sisak-Moslavina, NE Croatia
114 *H9* **Kutjevo** Požega-Slavonija, NE Croatia
113 *E17* **Kutná Hora** ***Ger.*** Kuttenberg. Střední Čechy, C Czech Republic
112 *K12* **Kutno** Płock, C Poland
Kuttenberg *see* Kutná Hora
81 *I20* **Kutu** Bandundu, W Zaire
159 *V17* **Kutubdia Island** *island* SE Bangladesh
82 *B10* **Kutum** Northern Darfur, W Sudan
153 *Y7* **Kuturgu** Issyk-Kul'skaya Oblast', E Kyrgyzstan
10 *M5* **Kuujjuaq** ***prev.*** Fort-Chimo. Québec, E Canada
10 *I7* **Kuujjuarapik** Québec, C Canada
152 *A10* **Kuuli-Mayak** ***Turkm.*** Guwlumayak. Balkanskiy Velayat, NW Turkmenistan
120 *I6* **Kuulse magi** ▲ S Estonia
94 *N13* **Kuusamo** Oulu, E Finland
95 *M19* **Kuusankoski** Kymi, S Finland
131 *W7* **Kuvandyk** Orenburgskaya Oblast', W Russian Federation
Kuvango *see* Cubango
Kuvasay *see* Quwasoy
Kuvdlorssuak *see* Kullorsuaq
128 *I16* **Kuvshinovo** Tverskaya Oblast', W Russian Federation
147 *Q4* **Kuwait** ***off.*** State of Kuwait, *var.* Dawlat al Kuwait, Koweit, Kuweit. ◆ *monarchy* SW Asia
Kuwait *see* Al Kuwayt
Kuwait Bay *see* Kuwayt, Jūn al
Kuwait City *see* Al Kuwayt
Kuwait, Dawlat al *see* Kuwait
Kuwajleen *see* Kwajalein Atoll
171 *H15* **Kuwana** Mie, Honshū, SW Japan
176 *V9* **Kuwawin** Irian Jaya, E Indonesia
145 *X9* **Kuwayt** E Iraq
148 *K11* **Kuwayt, Jūn al** *var.* Kuwait Bay. *bay* E Kuwait
Kuweit *see* Kuwait
119 *P10* **Kuyal'nyts'kyy Lyman** ◎ SW Ukraine
125 *G13* **Kuybyshev** Novosibirskaya Oblast', C Russian Federation
Kuybyshev *see* Bolgar, Respublika Tatarstan, Russian Federation
Kuybyshev *see* Samara
119 *W9* **Kuybysheve** ***Rus.*** Kuybyshevo. Zaporiz'ka Oblast', SE Ukraine
Kuybyshevo *see* Kuybysheve
Kuybyshev Reservoir *see* Kuybyshevskoye Vodokhranilishche
Kuybyshevskaya Oblast' *see* Samarskaya Oblast'
151 *O7* **Kuybyshevskiy** Kokshetau, N Kazakhstan
131 *R4* **Kuybyshevskoye Vodokhranilishche** *var.* Kuibyshev, ***Eng.*** Kuybyshev Reservoir. ⊡ W Russian Federation
127 *N9* **Kuydusun** Respublika Sakha (Yakutiya), NE Russian Federation
129 *U16* **Kuyeda** Permskaya Oblast', NW Russian Federation
Kūysanjaq *see* Koi Sanjaq
128 *I7* **Kuyto, Ozero** *var.* Ozero Kujto. ◎ NW Russian Federation
164 *J4* **Kuytun** Xinjiang Uygur Zizhiqu, NW China
126 *J15* **Kuytun** Irkutskaya Oblast', S Russian Federation
126 *Ii12* **Kuyumba** Evenkiyskiy Avtonomnyy Okrug, C Russian Federation
57 *S12* **Kuyuwini Landing** S Guyana
Kuzi *see* Kuji
40 *M9* **Kuzitrin River** ~ Alaska, USA
131 *P6* **Kuznetsk** Penzenskaya Oblast', W Russian Federation
118 *K3* **Kuznetsovs'k** Rivnens'ka Oblast', NW Ukraine
128 *K6* **Kuzomen'** Murmanskaya Oblast', NW Russian Federation
172 *N10* **Kuzumaki** Iwate, Honshū, C Japan
94 *H9* **Kvaløya** *island* N Norway
94 *K8* **Kvalsund** Finnmark, N Norway
96 *G11* **Kvam** Oppland, S Norway
131 *X7* **Kvarkeno** Orenburgskaya Oblast', W Russian Federation
95 *G15* **Kvarnbergsvattnet** *var.* Frostviken. ◎ N Sweden
114 *A11* **Kvarner** *var.* Carnaro, ***It.*** Quarnero. *gulf* W Croatia
114 *B11* **Kvarnerićka Vrata** *channel* W Croatia
41 *O14* **Kvichak Bay** *bay* Alaska, USA
94 *H12* **Kvikkjokk** Norrbotten, N Sweden
97 *D17* **Kvina** ~ S Norway
94 *Q1* **Kvitøya** *island* NE Svalbard
97 *F16* **Kvitseid** Telemark, S Norway
97 *H24* **Kværndrup** Fyn, C Denmark
81 *H20* **Kwa** ~ W Zaire
79 *Q15* **Kwadwokurom** C Ghana
195 *X14* **Kwailibesi** Malaita, N Solomon Islands
201 *S6* **Kwajalein Atoll** *var.* Kuwajleen. *atoll* Ralik Chain, C Marshall Islands
57 *W9* **Kwakoegron** Brokopondo, N Surinam
83 *J21* **Kwale** Coast, S Kenya
79 *U17* **Kwale** Delta, S Nigeria
81 *H20* **Kwamouth** Bandundu, W Zaire
Kwando *see* Cuando
Kwangchow *see* Guangzhou
Kwangchu *see* Kwangju
169 *X16* **Kwangju** ***off.*** Kwangju-gwangyŏksi, *var.* Guangju, Kwangchu, ***Jap.*** Kōshū. SW South Korea
81 *H20* **Kwango** ***Port.*** Cuango. ~ Angola/Zaire *see also* Cuango
Kwangsi/Kwangsi Chuang Autonomous Region *see* Guangxi Zhuangzu Zizhiqu
Kwangtung *see* Guangdong
Kwangyuan *see* Guangyuan
83 *F17* **Kwania, Lake** ◎ C Uganda
Kwanza *see* Cuanza
79 *S15* **Kwara** ◐ *state* SW Nigeria
176 *Ww11* **Kwatisore** Irian Jaya, E Indonesia
85 *K22* **KwaZulu/Natal** ***off.*** KwaZulu/Natal Province; ***prev.*** Natal. ◐ *province* E South Africa
Kweichow *see* Guizhou
Kweichu *see* Guiyang
Kweilin *see* Guilin
Kweisui *see* Hohhot
Kweiyang *see* Guiyang
85 *K17* **Kwekwe** ***prev.*** Que Que. Midlands, C Zimbabwe
85 *G20* **Kweneng** ◐ *district* S Botswana
Kwesui *see* Hohhot
41 *N12* **Kwethluk** Alaska, USA
41 *N12* **Kwethluk River** ~ Alaska, USA
112 *J8* **Kwidzyń** ***Ger.*** Marienwerder. Elbląg, N Poland
40 *M13* **Kwigillingok** Alaska, USA
194 *K16* **Kwikila** Central, S PNG
81 *I20* **Kwilu** ~ W Zaire
Kwito *see* Cuito
176 *V8* **Kwoka, Gunung** ▲ Irian Jaya, E Indonesia
80 *I12* **Kyabé** Moyen-Chari, S Chad
191 *O11* **Kyabram** Victoria, SE Australia
178 *Gg9* **Kyaikkami** ***prev.*** Amherst. Mon State, S Burma
177 *Ff9* **Kyaiklat** Irrawaddy, SW Burma
177 *G8* **Kyaikto** Mon State, S Burma
126 *Jj16* **Kyakhta** Respublika Buryatiya, S Russian Federation
190 *G8* **Kyancutta** South Australia
177 *Ff7* **Kyangin** Irrawaddy, SW Burma
178 *Jj8* **Ky Anh** Ha Tinh, N Vietnam
177 *Ff5* **Kyaukpadaung** Mandalay, C Burma
177 *F6* **Kyaukpyu** Arakan State, W Burma
177 *G5* **Kyaukse** Mandalay, C Burma
177 *Ff8* **Kyaunggon** Irrawaddy, SW Burma
121 *E14* **Kybartai** ***Pol.*** Kibarty. Vilkaviškis, S Lithuania
158 *I7* **Kyelang** Himāchal Pradesh, NW India
113 *G19* **Kyjov** ***Ger.*** Gaya. Jižní Morava, SE Czech Republic
117 *J21* **Kykládes** *var.* Kikládhes, ***Eng.*** Cyclades. *island group* SE Greece
27 *S11* **Kyle** Texas, SW USA
xlii *F13* **Kyleakin** Highland, NW Scotland, UK
xlii *F13* **Kyle of Lochalsh** Highland, N Scotland, UK
xlii *H8* **Kylestrome** Highland, NW Scotland, UK
103 *D18* **Kyll** ~ W Germany
117 *F19* **Kyllíni** *var.* Killini. ▲▲ S Greece
117 *H18* **Kými** ***prev.*** Kími. Évvoia, C Greece
95 *N18* **Kymi** ***Swe.*** Kymmene. ◐ *province* SE Finland
95 *M19* **Kymijoki** ~ S Finland
117 *H18* **Kýmis, Ákra** *headland* Évvoia, C Greece
Kymmene *see* Kymi
129 *W14* **Kyn** Permskaya Oblast', NW Russian Federation
191 *N12* **Kyneton** Victoria, SE Australia
83 *G17* **Kyoga, Lake** *var.* Lake Kioga. ◎ C Uganda
171 *H13* **Kyōga-misaki** *headland* Honshū, SW Japan
191 *V4* **Kyogle** New South Wales, SE Australia
169 *W15* **Kyŏnggi-man** *bay* NW South Korea
169 *Z16* **Kyŏngju** ***Jap.*** Keishū. SE South Korea
Kyŏngsŏng *see* Sŏul
Kyōsai-tō *see* Kŏje-do
83 *F19* **Kyotera** S Uganda
171 *H15* **Kyōto** Kyōto, Honshū, SW Japan
171 *H14* **Kyōto** ***off.*** Kyōto-fu, *var.* Kyōto Hu. ◐ *urban prefecture* Honshū, SW Japan
Kyōto-fu/Kyōto Hu *see* Kyōto
117 *D21* **Kyparissía** *var.* Kiparissía. Pelopónnisos, S Greece
117 *D20* **Kyparissiakós Kólpos** *gulf* S Greece
Kyperounda *see* Kyperoúnta
124 *N3* **Kyperoúnta** *var.* Kyperounda. C Cyprus
Kypros *see* Cyprus
117 *H16* **Kyrá Panagía** *island* Vóreioi Sporádes, Greece, Aegean Sea
Kyrenia *see* Girne
Kyrenia Mountains *see* Beşparmak Dağları
Kyrgyz Republic *see* Kyrgyzstan
153 *U9* **Kyrgyzstan** ***off.*** Kyrgyz Republic, *var.* Kirghizia; ***prev.*** Kirgizskaya SSR, Kirghiz SSR, Republic of Kyrgyzstan. ◆ *republic* C Asia
102 *M11* **Kyritz** Brandenburg, NE Germany
Kyrkslätt *see* Kirkkonummi
96 *G8* **Kyrksæterøra** Sør-Trøndelag, S Norway
129 *U8* **Kyrta** Respublika Komi, NW Russian Federation
125 *Ee12* **Kyshtym** Chelyabinskaya Oblast', S Russian Federation
113 *J18* **Kysucké Nové Mesto** ***prev.*** Horné Nové Mesto, ***Ger.*** Kisutzaneustadtl, Oberneustadtl, ***Hung.*** Kiszucaújhely. Stredné Slovensko, N Slovakia
119 *N12* **Kytay, Ozero** ◎ SW Ukraine
117 *F23* **Kýthira** *var.* Kíthira, It.Cerigo; ***Lat.*** Cythera. Kýthira, S Greece
117 *F23* **Kýthira** *var.* Kíthira, ***It.*** Cerigo; ***Lat.*** Cythera. *island* S Greece
117 *I20* **Kýthnos** Kýthnos, Kykládes, Greece, Aegean Sea
117 *I20* **Kýthnos** *var.* Kíthnos, Thermiá, ***It.*** Termia; ***anc.*** Cythnos. *island* Kykládes, Greece, Aegean Sea
117 *I20* **Kýthnou, Stenó** *strait* Kykládes, Greece, Aegean Sea
Kythréa *see* Değirmenlik
Kyungëy Ala-Too, Khrebet *see* Kungei Ala-Tau
Kyurdamir *see* Kürdämir
152 *C11* **Kyuren, Gora** ▲ W Turkmenistan
172 *C15* **Kyūshū** *var.* Kyûsyû. *island* SW Japan
199 *Gg6* **Kyushu-Palau Ridge** *var.* Kyusyu-Palau Ridge. *undersea feature* W Pacific Ocean
170 *Cc15* **Kyūshū-sanchi** ▲▲ Kyūshū, SW Japan
116 *F10* **Kyustendil** ***anc.*** Pautalia. Sofiyska Oblast, W Bulgaria
Kyûsyû *see* Kyūshū
Kyusyu-Palau Ridge *see* Kyushu-Palau Ridge
126 *L7* **Kyusyur** Respublika Sakha (Yakutiya), NE Russian Federation
191 *P10* **Kywong** New South Wales, SE Australia
119 *P4* **Kyyiv** ***Eng.*** Kiev, ***Rus.*** Kiyev. ● (Ukraine) Kyyivs'ka Oblast', N Ukraine
Kyyiv *see* Kyyivs'ka Oblast'
119 *O4* **Kyyivs'ka Oblast'** *var.* Kyyiv, ***Rus.*** Kiyevskaya Oblast'. ◐ *province* N Ukraine
119 *P3* **Kyyivs'ke Vodoskhovyshche** ***Eng.*** Kiev Reservoir, ***Rus.*** Kiyevskoye Vodokhranilishche. ⊡ N Ukraine
95 *L16* **Kyyjärvi** Keski-Suomi, C Finland
126 *I16* **Kyzyl** Respublika Tyva, C Russian Federation
153 *S8* **Kyzyl-Adyr** ***prev.*** Kirovskoye. Talasskaya Oblast', NW Kyrgyzstan
151 *V14* **Kyzylagash** Taldykorgan, SE Kazakhstan
152 *C13* **Kyzylbair** Balkanskiy Velayat, W Turkmenistan
Kyzyl-Dzhiik, Pereval *see* Uzbel Shankou
151 *S7* **Kyzylkak, Ozero** ◎ NE Kazakhstan
151 *X11* **Kyzylkesek** Semipalatinsk, E Kazakhstan
153 *S10* **Kyzyl-Kiya** ***Kir.*** Kyzyl-Kyya. Oshskaya Oblast', SW Kyrgyzstan
150 *L11* **Kyzylkol', Ozero** ◎ C Kazakhstan
139 *Ll8* **Kyzyl Kum** *var.* Kizil Kum, Qizil Qum, ***Uzb.*** Qizilqum. *desert* Kazakhstan/Uzbekistan
Kyzyl-Kyya *see* Kyzyl-Kiya
Kyzylrabat *see* Qizilrawbe
Kyzylrabot *see* Qizilrabot
Kyzylsu *see* Kyzyl-Suu
153 *X7* **Kyzyl-Suu** ***prev.*** Pokrovka. Issyk-Kul'skaya Oblast', NE Kyrgyzstan
153 *S12* **Kyzyl-Suu** *var.* Kyzylsu. ~ Kyrgyzstan/Tajikistan

◆ COUNTRY
● COUNTRY CAPITAL
◇ DEPENDENT TERRITORY
○ DEPENDENT TERRITORY CAPITAL
◐ ADMINISTRATIVE REGION
✕ INTERNATIONAL AIRPORT
▲ MOUNTAIN
▲▲ MOUNTAIN RANGE
VOLCANO
~ RIVER
◎ LAKE
⊡ RESERVOIR

KYZYL-TUU – LANETT

153 X8 **Kyzyl-Tuu** Issyk-Kul'skaya Oblast', E Kyrgyzstan
151 Q12 **Kyzylzhar** *Kaz.* Qyzylzhar. Zhezkazgan, C Kazakhstan
151 N15 **Kzyl-Orda** *var.* Qizil Orda, *Kaz.* Qyzylorda; *prev.* Perovsk. Kzyl-Orda, S Kazakhstan
150 L14 **Kzyl-Orda** *off.* Kzyl-Ordinskaya Oblast', *Kaz.* Qyzylorda Oblysy. ◐ *province* S Kazakhstan
Kzyl-Ordinskaya Oblast' *see* Kzyl-Orda
151 R7 **Kzyltu** *Kaz.* Qyzyltū. Kokshetau, N Kazakhstan

L

111 X2 **Laa an der Thaya** Niederösterreich, NE Austria
65 K15 **La Adela** La Pampa, SE Argentina
Laagen *see* Numedalslågen
111 S5 **Laakirchen** Oberösterreich, N Austria
Laaland *see* Lolland
106 I11 **La Albuera** Extremadura, W Spain
107 O7 **La Alcarria** *physical region* C Spain
106 K14 **La Algaba** Andalucía, S Spain
107 P9 **La Almarcha** Castilla-La Mancha, C Spain
107 R6 **La Almunia de Doña Godina** Aragón, NE Spain
43 N5 **La Amistad, Presa** ▣ NW Mexico
120 F4 **Läänemaa** *off.* Lääne Maakond. ◐ *province* NW Estonia
120 I3 **Lääne-Virumaa** *off.* Lääne-Viru Maakond. ◐ *province* NE Estonia
64 J9 **La Antigua, Salina** *salt lake* W Argentina
101 E17 **Laarne** Oost-Vlaanderen, NW Belgium
82 O13 **Laas Caanood** Nugaal, N Somalia
43 O9 **La Ascensión** Nuevo León, NE Mexico
82 N12 **Laas Dhaareed** Woqooyi Galbeed, N Somalia
57 O4 **La Asunción** Nueva Esparta, NE Venezuela
Laatokka *see* Ladozhskoye Ozero
102 I13 **Laatzen** Niedersachsen, NW Germany
40 E9 **Laau Point** *headland* Molokai, Hawaii, USA, C Pacific Ocean
44 D6 **La Aurora** ✕ (Ciudad de Guatemala) Guatemala, C Guatemala
76 C9 **Laâyoune** *var.* Aaiún. ○ (Western Sahara) NW Western Sahara
130 L14 **Laba** ⤳ SW Russian Federation
42 M6 **La Babia** Coahuila de Zaragoza, NE Mexico
13 R7 **La Baie** Québec, SE Canada
175 R16 **Labala** Pulau Lomblen, S Indonesia
64 K8 **La Banda** Santiago del Estero, N Argentina
La Banda Oriental *see* Uruguay
106 K4 **La Bañeza** Castilla-León, N Spain
42 M13 **La Barca** Jalisco, SW Mexico
42 K14 **La Barra de Navidad** Jalisco, C Mexico
197 J13 **Labasa** *prev.* Lambasa. Vanua Levu, N Fiji
xliv E11 **Labasheeda** Clare, W Ireland
179 Q15 **Labason** Mindanao, S Philippines
104 H8 **La Baule-Escoublac** Loire-Atlantique, NW France
Labe *see* Elbe
78 I13 **Labé** Moyenne-Guinée, NW Guinea
25 X14 **La Belle** Florida, SE USA
13 N11 **Labelle** Québec, SE Canada
8 H7 **Laberge, Lake** ◎ Yukon Territory, W Canada
Labes *see* Łobez
Labiau *see* Polessk
114 A10 **Labin** *It.* Albona. Istra, NW Croatia
130 L14 **Labinsk** Krasnodarskiy Kray, SW Russian Federation
107 X5 **La Bisbal d'Empordà** Cataluña, NE Spain
121 P16 **Labkovichy** *Rus.* Lobkovichi. Mahilyowskaya Voblasts', E Belorussia
13 S4 **La Blache, Lac de** ◎ Québec, SE Canada
179 Q11 **Labo** Luzon, N Philippines
Laboehanbadjo *see* Labuhanbajo
Laborca *see* Laborec
113 N18 **Laborec** *Hung.* Laborca. ⤳ E Slovakia
110 D11 **La Borgne** ⤳ S Switzerland
47 T12 **Laborie** SW Saint Lucia
81 F21 **La Bouenza** ◐ *province* S Congo
104 J14 **Labouheyre** Landes, SW France
64 L12 **Laboulaye** Córdoba, C Argentina
11 Q7 **Labrador** *cultural region* Newfoundland and Labrador, SW Canada
66 I6 **Labrador Basin** *var.* Labrador Sea Basin. *undersea feature* Labrador Sea
11 N9 **Labrador City** Newfoundland and Labrador, E Canada
11 Q5 **Labrador Sea** *sea* NW Atlantic Ocean
Labrador Sea Basin *see* Labrador Basin
Labrang *see* Xiahe
56 G9 **Labranzagrande** Boyacá, C Colombia
47 U15 **La Brea** Trinidad, Trinidad and Tobago
61 D14 **Lábrea** Amazonas, N Brazil
13 S6 **Labrieville** Québec, SE Canada
104 K14 **Labrit** Landes, SW France
110 C9 **La Broye** ⤳ SW Switzerland
105 N15 **Labruguière** Tarn, S France
174 I8 **Labu** Pulau Singkep, W Indonesia
175 N3 **Labuan** *var.* Victoria. Labuan, East Malaysia
175 N3 **Labuan** ◐ *federal territory* East Malaysia
Labuan *see* Labuan, Pulau
175 N3 **Labuan, Pulau** *var.* Labuan. *island* East Malaysia
175 Pp16 **Labuhanbajo** *prev.* Laboehanbadjo. Flores, S Indonesia
173 G6 **Labuhanbilik** Sumatera, N Indonesia
173 Ee5 **Labuhanhaji** Sumatera, W Indonesia
Labuk *see* Labuk, Sungai
Labuk Bay *see* Labuk, Teluk
175 O2 **Labuk, Sungai** *var.* Labuk. ⤳ East Malaysia
175 Oo2 **Labuk, Teluk** *var.* Labuk Bay, Telukan Labuk. *bay* S Sulu Sea
Labuk, Telukan *see* Labuk, Teluk
177 Ff9 **Labutta** Irrawaddy, SW Burma
125 G8 **Labytnangi** Yamalo-Nenetskiy Avtonomnyy Okrug, N Russian Federation
80 F10 **Lac** *off.* Préfecture du Lac. ◐ *prefecture* W Chad
115 K19 **Laç** *var.* Laci. Lezhë, C Albania
59 K19 **Lacajahuira, Rio** ⤳ W Bolivia
La Calamine *see* Kelmis
64 G11 **La Calera** Valparaíso, C Chile
11 P11 **Lac-Allard** Québec, E Canada
106 L13 **La Campana** Andalucía, S Spain
104 J12 **Lacanau** Gironde, SW France
44 C2 **Lacandón, Sierra del** ▲ Guatemala/Mexico
La Cañiza *see* A Cañiza
43 W16 **Lacantún, Río** ⤳ SE Mexico
105 Q3 **la Capelle** Aisne, N France
114 K10 **Laćarak** Serbia, NW Yugoslavia
64 L11 **La Carlota** Córdoba, C Argentina
179 Q13 **La Carlota** Negros, S Philippines
106 L13 **La Carlota** Andalucía, S Spain
107 N12 **La Carolina** Andalucía, S Spain
105 O15 **Lacaune** Tarn, S France
13 P7 **Lac-Bouchette** Québec, SE Canada
Laccadive Islands/Laccadive Minicoy and Amindivi Islands, the *see* Lakshadweep
9 Y16 **Lac du Bonnet** Manitoba, S Canada
32 L4 **Lac du Flambeau** Wisconsin, N USA
xxxix R3 **Laceby** North East Lincolnshire, E England, UK
13 P8 **Lac-Édouard** Québec, SE Canada
44 J4 **La Ceiba** Atlántida, N Honduras
56 E9 **La Ceja** Antioquia, W Colombia
190 J11 **Lacepede Bay** *bay* South Australia
34 G9 **Lacey** Washington, NW USA
105 P12 **la Chaise-Dieu** Haute-Loire, C France
116 G13 **Lachanás** Kentrikí Makedonía, N Greece
128 L11 **Lacha, Ozero** ◎ NW Russian Federation
105 O8 **la Charité-sur-Loire** Nièvre, C France
105 N9 **la Châtre** Indre, C France
110 C8 **La Chaux-de-Fonds** Neuchâtel, W Switzerland
Lach Dera *see* Dheere Laaq
110 G8 **Lachen** Schwyz, C Switzerland
191 Q8 **Lachlan River** ⤳ New South Wales, SE Australia
45 T15 **La Chorrera** Panamá, C Panama
13 V7 **Lac-Humqui** Québec, SE Canada
13 N12 **Lachute** Québec, SE Canada
Lachyn *see* Laçın
Laci *see* Laç
143 W13 **Laçın** *Rus.* Lachyn. SW Azerbaijan
105 S16 **la Ciotat** *anc.* Citharista. Bouches-du-Rhône, SE France
20 D10 **Lackawanna** New York, NE USA
9 Q13 **Lac La Biche** Alberta, SW Canada
15 Hh7 **Lac La Martre** Northwest Territories, W Canada
13 R12 **Lac-Mégantic** *var.* Mégantic. Québec, SE Canada
Lacobriga *see* Lagos
xxxvi M10 **Lacock** Wiltshire, S England, UK
42 G5 **La Colorada** Sonora, NW Mexico
9 Q15 **Lacombe** Alberta, SW Canada
32 L12 **Lacon** Illinois, N USA
45 P16 **La Concepción** *var.* Concepción. Chiriquí, W Panama
56 H5 **La Concepción** Zulia, NW Venezuela
56 H5 **La Concepción** Zulia, NW Venezuela
109 C19 **Laconi** Sardegna, Italy, C Mediterranean Sea
21 O9 **Laconia** New Hampshire, NE USA
63 H19 **La Coronilla** Rocha, E Uruguay
La Coruña *see* A Coruña
106 G2 **La Coruña** ◐ *province* Galicia, NW Spain
105 O11 **la Courtine** Creuse, C France
104 J16 **Lacq** Pyrénées-Atlantiques, SW France
13 P9 **La Croche** Québec, SE Canada
31 X3 **la Croix, Lac** ◎ Canada/USA
28 K5 **La Crosse** Kansas, C USA
23 V7 **La Crosse** Virginia, NE USA
34 L9 **La Crosse** Washington, NW USA
32 J7 **La Crosse** Wisconsin, N USA
56 C13 **La Cruz** Nariño, SW Colombia
44 K12 **La Cruz** Guanacaste, NW Costa Rica
42 I10 **La Cruz** Sinaloa, W Mexico
63 F19 **La Cruz** Florida, S Uruguay
44 M9 **La Cruz de Río Grande** Región Autónoma Atlántico Sur, E Nicaragua
56 J4 **La Cruz de Taratara** Falcón, N Venezuela
13 Q10 **Lac-St-Charles** Québec, SE Canada
42 M6 **La Cuesta** Coahuila de Zaragoza, NE Mexico
59 A17 **La Cumbra, Volcán** ⛰ Galapagos Islands, Ecuador, E Pacific Ocean
158 J5 **Ladākh Range** ▲ NE India
28 I5 **Ladder Creek** ⤳ Kansas, C USA
47 X10 **la Désirade** *atoll* E Guadeloupe
Lādhiqīyah, Muḥāfaẓat al *see* Al Lādhiqīyah
85 F25 **Ladismith** Western Cape, SW South Africa
158 G11 **Lādnūn** Rājasthān, NW India
Ladoga, Lake *see* Ladozhskoye Ozero
117 E19 **Ládon** ⤳ S Greece
56 E9 **La Dorada** Caldas, C Colombia
128 H11 **Ladozhskoye Ozero** *Eng.* Lake Ladoga, *Fin.* Laatokka. ◎ NW Russian Federation
39 R12 **Ladron Peak** ▲ New Mexico, SW USA
128 J11 **Ladva-Vetka** Respublika Kareliya, NW Russian Federation
xliii M8 **Ladybank** Fife, E Scotland, UK
191 Q15 **Lady Barron** Tasmania, SE Australia
12 G9 **Lady Evelyn Lake** ◎ Ontario, S Canada
25 W11 **Lady Lake** Florida, SE USA
8 L17 **Ladysmith** Vancouver Island, British Columbia, SW Canada
85 J22 **Ladysmith** KwaZulu/Natal, E South Africa
32 J5 **Ladysmith** Wisconsin, N USA
151 P9 **Ladyzhenka** Akmola, C Kazakhstan
194 K13 **Lae** Morobe, W PNG
201 R6 **Lae Atoll** *atoll* Ralik Chain, W Marshall Islands
42 C3 **La Encantada, Cerro de** ▲ NW Mexico
96 E12 **Lærdalsøyri** Sogn og Fjordane, S Norway
57 N11 **La Esmeralda** Amazonas, S Venezuela
44 G7 **La Esperanza** Intibucá, SW Honduras
32 K8 **La Farge** Wisconsin, N USA
25 R5 **Lafayette** Alabama, S USA
39 T4 **Lafayette** Colorado, C USA
25 R2 **La Fayette** Georgia, SE USA
33 O13 **Lafayette** Indiana, N USA
24 I9 **Lafayette** Louisiana, S USA
22 K8 **Lafayette** Tennessee, S USA
21 N7 **Lafayette, Mount** ▲ New Hampshire, NE USA
La Fe *see* Santa Fé
105 P3 **la Fère** Aisne, N France
104 L6 **la Ferté-Bernard** Sarthe, NW France
104 K5 **la Ferté-Macé** Orne, N France
105 N7 **la Ferté-St-Aubin** Loiret, C France
105 P5 **la Ferté-sous-Jouarre** Seine-et-Marne, N France
79 V15 **Lafia** Plateau, C Nigeria
79 T15 **Lafiagi** Kwara, W Nigeria
9 T17 **Lafleche** Saskatchewan, S Canada
104 K7 **la Flèche** Sarthe, NW France
111 X7 **Lafnitz** *Hung.* Lapines. ⤳ Austria/Hungary
197 I6 **La Foa** Province Sud, S New Caledonia
22 M8 **La Follette** Tennessee, S USA
13 N12 **Lafontaine** Québec, SE Canada
24 K10 **Lafourche, Bayou** ⤳ Louisiana, S USA
64 K6 **La Fragua** Santiago del Estero, N Argentina
56 H7 **La Fría** Táchira, NW Venezuela
106 J7 **La Fuente de San Esteban** Castilla-León, N Spain
194 G11 **Lagaip** ⤳ W PNG
63 B15 **La Gallareta** Santa Fe, C Argentina
131 Q14 **Lagan'** *prev.* Kaspiyskiy. Respublika Kalmykiya, SW Russian Federation
97 L20 **Lagan** Kronoberg, S Sweden
97 K21 **Lågan** ⤳ S Sweden
94 L2 **Lagarfljót** *var.* Lögurinn. ◎ E Iceland
39 R7 **La Garita Mountains** ▲ Colorado, C USA
179 P9 **Lagawe** Luzon, N Philippines
80 F13 **Lagdo** Nord, N Cameroon
80 F13 **Lagdo, Lac de** ◎ N Cameroon
102 H13 **Lage** Nordrhein-Westfalen, W Germany
96 H12 **Lågen** ⤳ S Norway
63 J14 **Lages** Santa Catarina, S Brazil
xliii E20 **Lagg** Argyll and Bute, W Scotland, UK
xliii G22 **Lagg** North Ayrshire, W Scotland, UK
xliii H14 **Laggan** Highland, N Scotland, UK
xliii J14 **Laggan** Highland, N Scotland, UK
xliii D21 **Laggan Bay** *bay* W Scotland, UK
xliii I14 **Laggan, Loch** ◎ N Scotland, UK
155 R4 **Laghmān** ◐ *province* E Afghanistan
76 J6 **Laghouat** N Algeria
xliv E9 **Laghtgeorge** Galway, W Ireland
xliv H4 **Laghy** Donegal, N Ireland
107 Q10 **La Gineta** Castilla-La Mancha, C Spain
117 E21 **Lagkáda** *var.* Langada. Pelopónnisos, S Greece
116 G13 **Lagkadás** *var.* Langades, Langadhás. Kentrikí Makedonía, N Greece
117 E20 **Lagkádia** *var.* Langádhia, Langadia. Pelopónnisos, S Greece
56 F6 **La Gloria** Cesar, N Colombia
43 O7 **La Gloria** Nuevo León, NE Mexico
94 N3 **Lågneset** *headland* W Svalbard
106 G14 **Lagoa** Faro, S Portugal
La Goagira *see* La Guajira
63 I14 **Lagoa Vermelha** Rio Grande do Sul, S Brazil
143 V10 **Lagodekhi** SE Georgia
44 C7 **La Gomera** Escuintla, S Guatemala
Lagone *see* Logone
109 M19 **Lagonegro** Basilicata, S Italy
65 G16 **Lago Ranco** Los Lagos, S Chile
79 S16 **Lagos** Lagos, SW Nigeria
106 F14 **Lagos** *anc.* Lacobriga. Faro, S Portugal
79 S16 **Lagos** ◐ *state* SW Nigeria
42 M12 **Lagos de Moreno** Jalisco, SW Mexico
Lagosta *see* Lastovo
76 A12 **Laguira** SW Western Sahara
94 O1 **Lågøya** *island* N Svalbard
34 L11 **La Grande** Oregon, NW USA
105 Q14 **la Grande-Combe** Gard, S France
10 K9 **La Grande Rivière** *var.* Fort George. ⤳ Québec, SE Canada
25 R4 **La Grange** Georgia, SE USA
33 P11 **Lagrange** Indiana, N USA
22 L5 **La Grange** Kentucky, S USA
29 V2 **La Grange** Missouri, C USA
23 V10 **La Grange** North Carolina, SE USA
27 U11 **La Grange** Texas, SW USA
107 N7 **La Granja** Castilla-León, N Spain
57 Q9 **La Gran Sabana** *grassland* E Venezuela
56 H7 **La Grita** Táchira, NW Venezuela
La Grulla *see* Grulla
13 R11 **La Guadeloupe** Québec, SE Canada
66 F12 **La Guaira** Distrito Federal, N Venezuela
56 G4 **La Guajira** *off.* Departamento de La Guajira, *var.* Guajira, La Goagira. ◐ *province* NE Colombia
196 I4 **Lagua Lichan, Punta** *headland* Saipan, S Northern Mariana Islands
20 K14 **La Guardia** ✕ (New York) Long Island, New York, NE USA
La Guardia/Laguardia *see* A Guardia
107 P4 **Laguardia** País Vasco, N Spain
La Gudiña *see* A Gudiña
105 O9 **la Guerche-sur-l'Aubois** Cher, C France
105 O13 **Laguiole** Aveyron, S France
L'Agulhas *see* Agulhas
63 K14 **Laguna** Santa Catarina, S Brazil
39 Q11 **Laguna** New Mexico, SW USA
37 T16 **Laguna Beach** California, W USA
37 Y17 **Laguna Dam** *dam* Arizona/California, W USA
42 L7 **Laguna El Rey** Coahuila de Zaragoza, N Mexico
37 V17 **Laguna Mountains** ▲ California, W USA
63 B17 **Laguna Paiva** Santa Fe, C Argentina
64 H3 **Lagunas** Tarapacá, N Chile
58 E9 **Lagunas** Loreto, N Peru
59 M20 **Lagunillas** Santa Cruz, SE Bolivia
56 H6 **Lagunillas** Mérida, NW Venezuela
46 C4 **La Habana** *var.* Havana. ● (Cuba) Ciudad de La Habana, W Cuba
175 Oo3 **Lahad Datu** Sabah, East Malaysia
175 Oo3 **Lahad Datu, Teluk** *var.* Telukan Lahad Datu, Teluk Darvel, Teluk Datu; *prev.* Darvel Bay. *bay* Sabah, East Malaysia
40 F10 **Lahaina** Maui, Hawaii, USA, C Pacific Ocean
174 Hh12 **Lahat** Sumatera, W Indonesia
La Haye *see* 's-Gravenhage
Lahej *see* Laḥij
64 G9 **La Higuera** Coquimbo, N Chile
147 S13 **Laḥī, Ḥisā' al** *spring/well* NE Yemen
147 O16 **Laḥij** *var.* Laḥj, *Eng.* Lahej. SW Yemen
148 M3 **Lāhījān** Gīlān, NW Iran
xliv D10 **Lahinch** Clare, W Ireland
121 I19 **Lahishyn** *Pol.* Lohiszyn, *Rus.* Logishin. Brestskaya Voblasts', SW Belorussia
Laḥj *see* Laḥij
103 F18 **Lahn** ⤳ W Germany
Lähn *see* Wleń
97 J21 **Laholm** Halland, S Sweden
97 J21 **Laholmsbukten** *bay* S Sweden
37 R6 **Lahontan Reservoir** ▣ Nevada, W USA
155 W8 **Lahore** Punjab, NE Pakistan
155 W8 **Lahore** ✕ Punjab, E Pakistan
57 Q6 **La Horqueta** Delta Amacuro, NE Venezuela
121 K15 **Lahoysk** *Rus.* Logoysk. Minskaya Voblasts', C Belorussia
103 F22 **Lahr** Baden-Württemberg, S Germany
95 M19 **Lahti** *Swe.* Lahtis. Häme, S Finland
Lahtis *see* Lahti
42 M14 **La Huacana** Michoacán de Ocampo, SW Mexico
42 K14 **La Huerta** Jalisco, SW Mexico
80 H12 **Laï** *prev.* Behagle, De Behagle. Tandjilé, S Chad
194 G12 **Laiagam** Enga, W PNG
Laibach *see* Ljubljana
178 Ii5 **Lai Châu** Lai Châu, N Vietnam
xlii F10 **Laide** Highland, NW Scotland, UK
xliii I16 **Laidon, Loch** ◎ C Scotland, UK
40 D9 **Laie** *Haw.* Lā'ie. Oahu, Hawaii, USA, C Pacific Ocean
104 L5 **l'Aigle** Orne, N France
105 Q7 **Laignes** Côte d'Or, C France
95 K17 **Laihia** Vaasa, W Finland
Laila *see* Laylā
85 F25 **Laingsburg** Western Cape, SW South Africa
111 U2 **Lainsitz** *Cz.* Lužnice. ⤳ Austria/Czech Republic
xlii I9 **Lairg** Highland, N Scotland, UK
83 I17 **Laisamis** Eastern, N Kenya
Laisberg *see* Leisi
131 R4 **Laishevo** Respublika Tatarstan, W Russian Federation
Laisholm *see* Jõgeva
94 H13 **Laisvall** Norrbotten, N Sweden
95 K19 **Laitila** Turku-Pori, SW Finland
167 P5 **Laiwu** Shandong, E China
167 R4 **Laixi** *var.* Shuiji. Shandong, E China
167 R4 **Laiyang** Shandong, E China
167 O3 **Laiyuan** Hebei, E China
167 R4 **Laizhou** *var.* Ye Xian. Shandong, E China
167 Q4 **Laizhou Wan** *var.* Laichow Bay. *bay* E China
39 S8 **La Jara** Colorado, C USA
63 I15 **Lajeado** Rio Grande do Sul, S Brazil
114 L12 **Lajkovac** Serbia, C Yugoslavia
113 K23 **Lajosmizse** Bács-Kiskun, C Hungary
Lajta *see* Leitha
42 I6 **La Junta** Chihuahua, N Mexico
39 V7 **La Junta** Colorado, C USA
94 J13 **Lakatrāsk** Norrbotten, N Sweden
Lak Dera *see* Dheere Laaq
Lakeamu *see* Lakekamu
31 P12 **Lake Andes** South Dakota, N USA
24 H9 **Lake Arthur** Louisiana, S USA
197 L15 **Lakeba** *prev.* Lakemba. *island* Lau Group, E Fiji
197 L14 **Lakeba Passage** *channel* E Fiji
31 S10 **Lake Benton** Minnesota, N USA
25 V9 **Lake Butler** Florida, SE USA
191 P8 **Lake Cargelligo** New South Wales, SE Australia
24 G9 **Lake Charles** Louisiana, S USA
29 X9 **Lake City** Arkansas, C USA
39 Q7 **Lake City** Colorado, C USA
25 V9 **Lake City** Florida, SE USA
31 U13 **Lake City** Iowa, C USA
33 P7 **Lake City** Michigan, N USA
31 W9 **Lake City** Minnesota, N USA
23 T13 **Lake City** South Carolina, SE USA
31 Q7 **Lake City** South Dakota, N USA
22 M8 **Lake City** Tennessee, S USA
194 F12 **Lake Copiago** *var.* Kopiago. Southern Highlands, W PNG
8 L17 **Lake Cowichan** Vancouver Island, British Columbia, SW Canada
31 U10 **Lake Crystal** Minnesota, N USA
27 T6 **Lake Dallas** Texas, SW USA
xl L9 **Lake District** *physical region* NW England, UK
20 D10 **Lake Erie Beach** New York, NE USA
31 T11 **Lakefield** Minnesota, N USA
27 V6 **Lake Fork Reservoir** ◎ Texas, SW USA
32 M9 **Lake Geneva** Wisconsin, N USA
20 L9 **Lake George** New York, NE USA
16 O4 **Lake Harbour** Baffin Island, Northwest Territories, NE Canada
38 I12 **Lake Havasu City** Arizona, SW USA
27 W12 **Lake Jackson** Texas, SW USA
194 J14 **Lakekamu** *var.* Lakeamu. ⤳ S PNG
188 K13 **Lake King** Western Australia
194 F12 **Lake Kutubu** ◎ W PNG
25 V12 **Lakeland** Florida, SE USA
25 U7 **Lakeland** Georgia, SE USA
189 W4 **Lakeland Downs** Queensland, NE Australia
9 P16 **Lake Louise** Alberta, SW Canada
Lakemba *see* Lakeba
31 V11 **Lake Mills** Iowa, C USA
41 Q10 **Lake Minchumina** Alaska, USA
Lakemti *see* Nek'emtē
194 E13 **Lake Murray** Western, SW PNG
xxxix U11 **Lakenheath** Suffolk, E England, UK
33 R9 **Lake Orion** Michigan, N USA
202 B16 **Lakepa** NE Niue
31 T11 **Lake Park** Iowa, C USA
20 K7 **Lake Placid** New York, NE USA
20 K9 **Lake Pleasant** New York, NE USA
36 M6 **Lakeport** California, W USA
31 Q10 **Lake Preston** South Dakota, N USA
24 J5 **Lake Providence** Louisiana, S USA
193 E20 **Lake Pukaki** Canterbury, South Island, NZ
191 Q12 **Lakes Entrance** Victoria, SE Australia
39 N12 **Lakeside** Arizona, SW USA
37 V17 **Lakeside** California, W USA
25 S9 **Lakeside** Florida, SE USA
30 K13 **Lakeside** Nebraska, C USA
34 E13 **Lakeside** Oregon, NW USA
23 W6 **Lakeside** Virginia, NE USA
Lakes State *see* El Buhayrat
Lake State *see* Michigan
193 F20 **Lake Tekapo** Canterbury, South Island, NZ
23 O10 **Lake Toxaway** North Carolina, SE USA
31 T13 **Lake View** Iowa, C USA
34 I16 **Lakeview** Oregon, NW USA
27 O3 **Lakeview** Texas, SW USA
29 W14 **Lake Village** Arkansas, C USA
25 W12 **Lake Wales** Florida, SE USA
39 T4 **Lakewood** Colorado, C USA
20 K15 **Lakewood** New Jersey, NE USA
20 C11 **Lakewood** New York, NE USA
33 T11 **Lakewood** Ohio, N USA
25 Y13 **Lakewood Park** Florida, SE USA
25 Z14 **Lake Worth** Florida, SE USA
158 H4 **Lake Wular** ◎ NE India
128 H11 **Lakhdenpokh'ya** Respublika Kareliya, NW Russian Federation
158 L11 **Lakhīmpur** Uttar Pradesh, N India
160 J11 **Lakhnādon** Madhya Pradesh, C India
Lakhnau *see* Lucknow
160 A9 **Lakhpat** Gujarāt, W India
121 K19 **Lakhva** *Rus.* Lakhva. Brestskaya Voblasts', SW Belorussia
28 I6 **Lakin** Kansas, C USA
155 S7 **Lakki Marwat** North-West Frontier Province, NW Pakistan
117 F21 **Lakonía** *historical region* S Greece
117 F22 **Lakonikós Kólpos** *gulf* S Greece
78 M17 **Lakota** S Ivory Coast
31 U11 **Lakota** Iowa, C USA
31 P3 **Lakota** North Dakota, N USA
Lak Sao *see* Ban Lakxao
94 L8 **Laksefjorden** *fjord* N Norway
94 K8 **Lakselv** Finnmark, N Norway
161 B21 **Lakshadweep** *prev.* the Laccadive, Minicoy and Amindivi Islands. ◐ *union territory* India, N Indian Ocean
161 C22 **Lakshadweep** *Eng.* Laccadive Islands. *island group* India, N Indian Ocean
159 S17 **Lakshmikāntapur** West Bengal, NE India
114 G11 **Laktaši** N Bosnia and Herzegovina
155 V7 **Lāla Mūsa** Punjab, NE Pakistan
la Laon *see* Laon
116 M11 **Lalapaşa** Edirne, NW Turkey
85 P14 **Lalaua** Nampula, N Mozambique
107 S10 **L'Alcúdia** *var.* L'Alcudia. País Valenciano, E Spain
81 F20 **La Lékoumou** ◐ *province* SW Congo
xxxv I15 **Laleston** Bridgend, S Wales, UK
44 E8 **La Libertad** La Libertad, SW El Salvador
44 E3 **La Libertad** Petén, N Guatemala
44 H6 **La Libertad** Comayagua, SW Honduras
42 E4 **La Libertad** *var.* Puerto Libertad. Sonora, NW Mexico
44 K10 **La Libertad** Chontales, S Nicaragua
44 A9 **La Libertad** ◐ *department* SW El Salvador
58 B11 **La Libertad** *off.* Departamento de La Libertad. ◐ *department* W Peru
64 G11 **La Ligua** Valparaíso, C Chile
145 U5 **La'li Khān** E Iraq
81 H16 **La Likouala** ◐ *province* NE Congo
106 H3 **Lalín** Galicia, NW Spain
104 L13 **Lalinde** Dordogne, SW France
106 K16 **La Línea** *var.* La Línea de la Concepción. Andalucía, S Spain
La Línea de la Concepción *see* La Línea
158 J14 **Lalitpur** Uttar Pradesh, N India
159 P11 **Lalitpur** Central, C Nepal
158 K10 **Lālkua** Uttar Pradesh, N India
9 R12 **La Loche** Saskatchewan, C Canada
104 M6 **la Loupe** Eure-et-Loir, C France
101 G20 **La Louvière** Hainaut, S Belgium
L'Altissima *see* Hochwilde
106 L14 **La Luisiana** Andalucía, S Spain
39 S14 **La Luz** New Mexico, SW USA
109 D16 **la Maddalena** Sardegna, Italy, C Mediterranean Sea
64 J7 **La Madrid** Tucumán, N Argentina
Lama-Kara *see* Kara
175 R16 **Lamakera, Selat** *strait* Nusa Tenggara, S Indonesia
13 S8 **La Malbaie** Québec, SE Canada
178 Jj10 **Lamam** Xékong, S Laos
107 P10 **La Mancha** *physical region* C Spain
la Manche *see* English Channel
197 C13 **Lamap** Malekula, C Vanuatu
39 W6 **Lamar** Colorado, C USA
29 S7 **Lamar** Missouri, C USA
23 S12 **Lamar** South Carolina, SE USA
109 C19 **La Marmora, Punta** ▲ Sardegna, Italy, C Mediterranean Sea
15 H7 **La Martre, Lac** ◎ Northwest Territories, NW Canada
58 D10 **Lamas** San Martín, N Peru
44 I5 **La Masica** Atlántida, NW Honduras
105 R12 **Lamastre** Ardèche, E France
La Matepec *see* Santa Ana, Volcán de
46 I7 **La Maya** Santiago de Cuba, E Cuba
111 S5 **Lambach** Oberösterreich, N Austria
173 Ff8 **Lambak** Pulau Pini, W Indonesia
104 H5 **Lamballe** Côtes d'Armor, NW France
81 D18 **Lambaréné** Moyen-Ogooué, W Gabon
Lambasa *see* Labasa
175 Q12 **Lambasina Besar, Pulau** *island* C Indonesia
58 B11 **Lambayeque** Lambayeque, W Peru
58 A10 **Lambayeque** *off.* Departamento de Lambayeque. ◐ *department* NW Peru
xliv L8 **Lambay Island** *Ir.* Reachrainn. *island* E Ireland
xxxvii V11 **Lamberhurst** Kent, SE England, UK
195 O10 **Lambert, Cape** *headland* New Britain, E PNG
205 W6 **Lambert Glacier** *glacier* Antarctica
31 T10 **Lamberton** Minnesota, N USA
29 X4 **Lambert-Saint Louis** ✕ Missouri, C USA
33 R11 **Lambertville** Michigan, N USA
20 J15 **Lambertville** New Jersey, NE USA
xxxvi D8 **Lambeth** Lambeth, SE England, UK
xxxiv L16 **Lambeth** ◐ *London borough* SE England, UK
xli O7 **Lambley** Northumberland, N England, UK
175 Pp9 **Lambogo** Sulawesi, N Indonesia
xxxvii O9 **Lambourn** Newbury, S England, UK
108 D8 **Lambro** ⤳ N Italy
15 H2 **Lambton, Cape** *headland* Banks Island, Northwest Territories, NW Canada
35 W11 **Lame Deer** Montana, NW USA
106 H6 **Lamego** Viseu, N Portugal
197 C13 **Lamen Bay** Épi, C Vanuatu
47 X6 **Lamentin** Basse Terre, N Guadeloupe
Lamentin *see* le Lamentin
190 K10 **Lameroo** South Australia
56 F10 **La Mesa** Cundinamarca, C Colombia
37 U17 **La Mesa** California, W USA
39 R16 **La Mesa** New Mexico, SW USA
27 N6 **Lamesa** Texas, SW USA
109 N21 **Lamezia** Calabria, SE Italy
197 I15 **Lami** Viti Levu, C Fiji
117 F17 **Lamía** Stereá Ellás, C Greece
179 Q17 **Lamitan** Basilan Island, SW Philippines
197 J14 **Lamiti** Gau, C Fiji
176 Uu8 **Lamlam** Irian Jaya, E Indonesia
196 B16 **Lamlam, Mount** ▲ SW Guam
xliii G22 **Lamlash** North Ayrshire, W Scotland, UK
111 Q6 **Lammer** ⤳ E Austria
193 E23 **Lammerlaw Range** ▲ South Island, NZ
xliii N20 **Lammermuir Hills** ▲ SE Scotland, UK
97 L20 **Lammhult** Kronoberg, S Sweden
95 L18 **Lammi** Häme, SW Finland
201 U11 **Lamoil** *island* Chuuk, C Micronesia
37 W3 **Lamoille** Nevada, W USA
20 M7 **Lamoille River** ⤳ Vermont, NE USA
32 J13 **La Moine River** ⤳ Illinois, N USA
179 Pp10 **Lamon Bay** *bay* Luzon, N Philippines
31 V16 **Lamoni** Iowa, C USA
37 R13 **Lamont** California, W USA
29 N8 **Lamont** Oklahoma, C USA
56 E13 **La Montañita** *var.* Montañita. Caquetá, S Colombia
45 N8 **La Mosquitia** *var.* Miskito Coast, *Eng.* Mosquito Coast. *coastal region* E Nicaragua
104 I9 **la Mothe-Achard** Vendée, NW France
196 L15 **Lamotrek Atoll** *atoll* Caroline Islands, C Micronesia
31 P6 **La Moure** North Dakota, N USA
178 H8 **Lampang** *var.* Muang Lampang. Lampang, NW Thailand
178 Ii9 **Lam Pao Reservoir** ▣ E Thailand
27 S9 **Lampasas** Texas, SW USA
27 S9 **Lampasas River** ⤳ Texas, SW USA
43 N7 **Lampazos** *var.* Lampazos de Naranjo. Nuevo León, NE Mexico
Lampazos de Naranjo *see* Lampazos
117 E19 **Lámpeia** Dytikí Ellás, S Greece
103 G19 **Lampertheim** Hessen, W Germany
xxxv G11 **Lampeter** Ceredigion, SW Wales, UK
178 H7 **Lamphun** *var.* Lampun, Muang Lamphun. Lamphun, NW Thailand
xxxix O11 **Lamport** Northamptonshire, C England, UK
9 X10 **Lamprey** Manitoba, C Canada
Lampun *see* Lamphun
174 I13 **Lampung** *off.* Propinsi Lampung. ◐ *province* SW Indonesia
174 Ii13 **Lampung, Teluk** *bay* Sumatera, SW Indonesia
130 K6 **Lamskoye** Lipetskaya Oblast', W Russian Federation
83 K20 **Lamu** Coast, SE Kenya
45 N14 **La Muerte, Cerro** ▲ C Costa Rica
105 S13 **la Mure** Isère, E France
39 S10 **Lamy** New Mexico, SW USA
121 J18 **Lan'** *Rus.* Lan'. ⤳ C Belorussia
40 E10 **Lānaʻi** *Haw.* Lāna'i. *island* Hawaii, USA, C Pacific Ocean
40 E10 **Lanai City** Lanai, Hawaii, USA, C Pacific Ocean
101 L18 **Lanaken** Limburg, NE Belgium
179 R15 **Lanao, Lake** *var.* Lake Sultan Alonto. ◎ Mindanao, S Philippines
xliii K21 **Lanark** South Lanarkshire, S Scotland, UK
98 I13 **Lanark** *cultural region* C Scotland, UK
106 L9 **La Nava de Ricomalillo** Castilla-La Mancha, C Spain
178 Gg13 **Lanbi Kyun** *prev.* Sullivan Island. *island* Mergui Archipelago, S Burma
Lancang Jiang *see* Mekong
xli N14 **Lancashire** ◐ *county* N England, UK
xli N12 **Lancaster** Lancashire, NW England, UK
13 N13 **Lancaster** Ontario, SE Canada
37 T14 **Lancaster** California, W USA
22 M6 **Lancaster** Kentucky, S USA
29 U1 **Lancaster** Missouri, C USA
21 O7 **Lancaster** New Hampshire, NE USA
20 D10 **Lancaster** New York, NE USA
33 T14 **Lancaster** Ohio, N USA
20 H16 **Lancaster** Pennsylvania, NE USA
23 R11 **Lancaster** South Carolina, SE USA
27 U7 **Lancaster** Texas, SW USA
23 X5 **Lancaster** Virginia, NE USA
32 J9 **Lancaster** Wisconsin, N USA
207 N10 **Lancaster Sound** *sound* Northwest Territories, N Canada
xli R7 **Lanchester** Durham, N England, UK
Lan-chou/Lan-chow/Lanchow *see* Lanzhou
109 K14 **Lanciano** Abruzzi, C Italy
113 O16 **Łańcut** Rzeszów, SE Poland
174 Kk8 **Landak, Sungai** ⤳ Borneo, N Indonesia
Landao *see* Lantau Island
Landau *see* Landau an der Isar, Bayern, Germany
Landau *see* Landau in der Pfalz, Rheinland-Pfalz, Germany
103 N22 **Landau an der Isar** *var.* Landau. Bayern, SE Germany
103 F20 **Landau in der Pfalz** *var.* Landau. Rheinland-Pfalz, SW Germany
Land Burgenland *see* Burgenland
110 K8 **Landeck** Tirol, W Austria
101 J19 **Landen** Vlaams Brabant, C Belgium
35 U15 **Lander** Wyoming, C USA
104 F5 **Landerneau** Finistère, NW France
97 K20 **Landeryd** Halland, S Sweden
104 J15 **Landes** ◐ *department* SW France
Landeshut/Landeshut in Schlesien *see* Kamienna Góra
107 R9 **Landete** Castilla-La Mancha, C Spain
xxxvi B17 **Landewednack** Cornwall, SW England, UK
101 M18 **Landgraaf** Limburg, SE Netherlands
104 F5 **Landivisiau** Finistère, NW France
Land of Enchantment *see* New Mexico
Land of Opportunity *see* Arkansas
Land of Steady Habits *see* Connecticut
Land of the Midnight Sun *see* Alaska
110 I8 **Landquart** Graubünden, SE Switzerland
110 J9 **Landquart** ⤳ Austria/Switzerland
23 P10 **Landrum** South Carolina, SE USA
Landsberg *see* Górowo Iławeckie, Olsztyn, Poland
Landsberg *see* Gorzów Wielkopolski, Gorzów, Poland
103 K23 **Landsberg am Lech** Bayern, S Germany
Landsberg an der Warthe *see* Gorzów Wielkopolski
xxxvi L16 **Land's End** *headland* SW England, UK
103 M22 **Landshut** Bayern, SE Germany
Landskron *see* Lanškroun
97 J22 **Landskrona** Malmöhus, S Sweden
100 I10 **Landsmeer** Noord-Holland, C Netherlands
97 J19 **Landvetter** ✕ (Göteborg) Göteborg och Bohus, S Sweden
Landwarów *see* Lentvaris
xliv H8 **Lanesborough** Roscommon, C Ireland
25 R5 **Lanett** Alabama, S USA

◆ COUNTRY
● COUNTRY CAPITAL
◇ DEPENDENT TERRITORY
○ DEPENDENT TERRITORY CAPITAL
◐ ADMINISTRATIVE REGION
✕ INTERNATIONAL AIRPORT
▲ MOUNTAIN
▲ MOUNTAIN RANGE
⛰ VOLCANO
⤳ RIVER
◎ LAKE
▣ RESERVOIR

◆ **Country**
● **Country Capital**
◇ **Dependent Territory**
◉ **Dependent Territory Capital**
◊ **Administrative Region**
✕ **International Airport**
▲ **Mountain**
▲ **Mountain Range**
☒ **Volcano**
☒ **River**
◉ **Lake**
☒ **Reservoir**

LEBANON, MOUNT – LIBERTAD

Lebanon, Mount *see* Liban, Jebel
152 J10 **Lebap** Lebapskiy Velayat, NE Turkmenistan
152 H11 **Lebapskiy Velayat** *Turkm.* Lebap Welayaty; *prev.* Rus. Chardzhevskaya Oblast', *Turkm.* Chärjew Oblasty. ◐ *province* E Turkmenistan
Lebap Welayaty *see* Lebapskiy Velayat
Lebasee *see* Łebsko, Jezioro
101 F17 **Lebbeke** Oost-Vlaanderen, NW Belgium
37 S14 **Lebec** California, W USA
Lebedin *see* Lebedyn
126 Ll12 **Lebedinyy** Respublika Sakha (Yakutiya), NE Russian Federation
130 L6 **Lebedyan'** Lipetskaya Oblast', W Russian Federation
119 T4 **Lebedyn** *Rus.* Lebedin. Sums'ka Oblast', NE Ukraine
10 I12 **Lebel-sur-Quévillon** Québec, SE Canada
94 L8 **Lebesby** Finnmark, N Norway
104 M9 **le Blanc** Indre, C France
29 P5 **Lebo** Kansas, C USA
81 L15 **Lebo** Haut-Zaïre, N Zaire
112 H6 **Lębork** *var.* Lębórk, *Ger.* Lauenburg, Lauenburg in Pommern. Słupsk, NW Poland
105 O17 **le Boulou** Pyrénées-Orientales, S France
110 A9 **Le Brassus** Vaud, W Switzerland
106 J15 **Lebrija** Andalucía, S Spain
112 G6 **Łebsko, Jezioro** *Ger.* Lebasee; *prev.* Jezioro Łeba. ◎ N Poland
65 F14 **Lebu** Bío Bío, C Chile
151 U8 **Lebyazh'ye** Pavlodar, NE Kazakhstan
106 F6 **Leça da Palmeira** Porto, N Portugal
105 U15 **le Cannet** Alpes-Maritimes, SE France
Le Cap *see* Cap-Haïtien
xliv G8 **Lecarrow** Roscommon, C Ireland
105 P2 **le Cateau-Cambrésis** Nord, N France
109 Q18 **Lecce** Puglia, SE Italy
108 D7 **Lecco** Lombardia, N Italy
31 V10 **Le Center** Minnesota, N USA
110 J7 **Lech** Vorarlberg, W Austria
103 K22 **Lech** ↝ Austria/Germany
117 D19 **Lechainá** *var.* Lehena, Lekhainá. Dytikí Ellás, S Greece
104 J11 **le Château d'Oléron** Charente-Maritime, W France
105 Q3 **le Chesne** Ardennes, N France
105 R13 **le Cheylard** Ardèche, E France
xxxvii O8 **Lechlade** Gloucestershire, C England, UK
110 K7 **Lechtaler Alpen** ▲ W Austria
102 H6 **Leck** Schleswig-Holstein, N Germany
xlii H10 **Leckmelm** Highland, NW Scotland, UK
12 L9 **Lecointre, Lac** ◎ Québec, SE Canada
24 H7 **Lecompte** Louisiana, S USA
105 Q9 **le Creusot** Saône-et-Loire, C France
Lecumberri *see* Lekunberri
112 P13 **Łęczna** Lublin, E Poland
112 J12 **Łęczyca** *Ger.* Lentschiza, *Rus.* Lenchitsa. Płock, C Poland
102 F10 **Leda** ↝ NW Germany
xxxviii I14 **Ledbury** Herefordshire, W England, UK
101 F17 **Lede** Oost-Vlaanderen, NW Belgium
106 K6 **Ledesma** Castilla-León, N Spain
47 Q12 **le Diamant** SW Martinique
180 J16 **Le Digue** *island* Inner Islands, NE Seychelles
xlii H9 **Ledmore** Highland, NW Scotland, UK
105 Q10 **le Donjon** Allier, C France
104 M10 **le Dorat** Haute-Vienne, C France
Ledo Salinarius *see* Lons-le-Saunier
9 Q14 **Leduc** Alberta, SW Canada
127 Pp7 **Ledyanaya, Gora** ▲ E Russian Federation
xliv E14 **Lee** *Ir.* An Laoi. ↝ SW Ireland
xxxviii H10 **Leebotwood** Shropshire, W England, UK
31 U5 **Leech Lake** ◎ Minnesota, N USA
28 K10 **Leedey** Oklahoma, C USA
xli R14 **Leeds** Leeds, N England, UK
xli R14 **Leeds** ◐ *unitary authority* N England, UK
25 P4 **Leeds** Alabama, S USA
31 O3 **Leeds** North Dakota, N USA
xxxvi B17 **Leedstown** Cornwall, SW England, UK
xxxviii K7 **Leek** Staffordshire, C England, UK
100 N6 **Leek** Groningen, NE Netherlands
xliv D8 **Leenane** Galway, W Ireland
101 K15 **Leende** Noord-Brabant, SE Netherlands
102 F10 **Leer** Niedersachsen, NW Germany
100 J13 **Leerdam** Zuid-Holland, C Netherlands
100 K12 **Leersum** Utrecht, C Netherlands
25 W11 **Leesburg** Florida, SE USA
23 V3 **Leesburg** Virginia, NE USA
29 R4 **Lees Summit** Missouri, C USA
24 G7 **Leesville** Louisiana, S USA
27 S12 **Leesville** Texas, SW USA
33 U13 **Leesville Lake** ▣ Ohio, N USA
Leesville Lake *see* Smith Mountain Lake
191 P9 **Leeton** New South Wales, SE Australia
100 L6 **Leeuwarden** *Fris.* Ljouwert. Friesland, N Netherlands
188 I14 **Leeuwin, Cape** *headland* Western Australia
37 R8 **Lee Vining** California, W USA
47 V8 **Leeward Islands** *island group* E West Indies
Leeward Islands *see* Vent, Îles Sous le, W French Polynesia
Leeward Islands *see* Sotavento, Ilhas de, Cape Verde
81 G20 **Léfini** ↝ SE Congo
Léfka *see* Lefke
117 C17 **Lefkáda** *prev.* Levkás. Lefkáda, Iónioi Nísoi, Greece, C Mediterranean Sea
117 B17 **Lefkáda** *It.* Santa Maura; *prev.* Levkás, *anc.* Leucas. *island* Iónioi Nísoi, Greece, C Mediterranean Sea
117 H25 **Lefká Óri** ▲ Kríti, Greece, E Mediterranean Sea
124 N3 **Lefke** *Gk.* Léfka. W Cyprus
117 B16 **Lefkímmi** *var.* Levkímmi. Kérkyra, Iónioi Nísoi, Greece, C Mediterranean Sea
Lefkonico/Lefkónikon *see* Geçitkale
Lefkoşa/Lefkosía *see* Nicosia
27 O2 **Lefors** Texas, SW USA
47 R12 **le François** E Martinique
188 L12 **Lefroy, Lake** *salt lake* Western Australia
Legaceaster *see* Chester
107 N8 **Leganés** Madrid, C Spain
179 Q11 **Legaspi** *off.* Legaspi City. Luzon, N Philippines
xxxix S5 **Legbourne** Lincolnshire, E England, UK
Leghorn *see* Livorno
112 M11 **Legionowo** Warszawa, C Poland
101 K24 **Léglise** Luxembourg, SE Belgium
108 G8 **Legnago** Lombardia, NE Italy
108 D7 **Legnano** Veneto, NE Italy
113 F14 **Legnica** *Ger.* Liegnitz. Legnica, W Poland
113 E14 **Legnica** *off.* Województwo Legnickie, *Ger.* Liegnitz. ◐ *province* W Poland
Legnickie, Województwo *see* Legnica
37 Q9 **Le Grand** California, W USA
105 Q15 **le Grau-du-Roi** Gard, S France
191 U3 **Legume** New South Wales, SE Australia
104 L4 **le Havre** *Eng.* Havre; *prev.* le Havre-de-Grâce. Seine-Maritime, N France
le Havre-de-Grâce *see* le Havre
Lehena *see* Lechainá
38 L3 **Lehi** Utah, W USA
20 I14 **Lehighton** Pennsylvania, NE USA
31 O6 **Lehr** North Dakota, N USA
40 A8 **Lehua Island** *island* Hawaiian Islands, Hawaii, USA, C Pacific Ocean
155 S9 **Leiāh** Punjab, NE Pakistan
111 W9 **Leibnitz** Steiermark, SE Austria
xxxix N9 **Leicester** *Lat.* Batae Coritanorum. City of Leicester, C England, UK
xxxviii M9 **Leicester, City of** ◐ *unitary authority* C England, UK
xxxviii E13 **Leicestershire** ◐ *county* C England, UK
100 H11 **Leiden** *prev.* Leyden, *anc.* Lugdunum Batavorum. Zuid-Holland, W Netherlands
100 H11 **Leiderdorp** Zuid-Holland, W Netherlands
100 G11 **Leidschendam** Zuid-Holland, W Netherlands
101 D18 **Leie** *Fr.* Lys. ↝ Belgium/France
Leifear *see* Lifford
xxxvi M7 **Leigh** Gloucestershire, C England, UK
xxxvii V11 **Leigh** Kent, SE England, UK
xli O16 **Leigh** Wigan, NW England, UK
192 L4 **Leigh** Auckland, North Island, NZ
190 I5 **Leigh Creek** South Australia
xliv J11 **Leighlinbridge** Carlow, SE Ireland
25 O2 **Leighton** Alabama, S USA
xxxvii S7 **Leighton Buzzard** Bedfordshire, E England, UK
Léim an Bhradáin *see* Leixlip
Léim an Mhadaidh *see* Limavady
Léime, Ceann *see* Loop Head, Ireland
Léime, Ceann *see* Slyne Head, Ireland
103 G20 **Leimen** Baden-Württemberg, SW Germany
102 I13 **Leine** ↝ NW Germany
103 J15 **Leinefelde** Thüringen, C Germany
Léin, Loch *see* Leane, Lough
xliv H11 **Leinster** *Ir.* Cúige Laighean. *province* E Ireland
xliv J11 **Leinster, Mount** *Ir.* Stua Laighean. ▲ SE Ireland
xxxviii G11 **Leintwardine** Herefordshire, W England, UK
121 F15 **Leipalingis** Lazdijai, S Lithuania
94 J12 **Leipojärvi** Norrbotten, N Sweden
33 R12 **Leipsic** Ohio, N USA
Leipsic *see* Leipzig
117 M20 **Leipsoí** *island* Dodekánisos, Greece, Aegean Sea
103 M15 **Leipzig** *Pol.* Lipsk; *hist.* Leipsic, *anc.* Lipsia. Sachsen, E Germany
103 M15 **Leipzig Halle** ✈ Sachsen, E Germany
106 G9 **Leiria** *anc.* Collipo. Leiria, C Portugal
106 F9 **Leiria** ◐ *district* C Portugal
xlii I6 **Leirinmore** Highland, NW Scotland, UK
97 C15 **Leirvik** Hordaland, S Norway
120 E5 **Leisi** *Ger.* Laisberg. Saaremaa, W Estonia
xxxix Y12 **Leiston** Suffolk, E England, UK
106 J3 **Leitariegos, Puerto de** *pass* NW Spain
22 J6 **Leitchfield** Kentucky, S USA
111 Y5 **Leitha** *Hung.* Lajta. ↝ Austria/Hungary
xxxvii T11 **Leith Hill** *hill* SE England, UK
Leitir Ceanainn *see* Letterkenny
Leitmeritz *see* Litoměřice
Leitomischl *see* Litomyšl
xliv G6 **Leitrim** Leitrim, N Ireland
xliv G6 **Leitrim** *Ir.* Liatroim. ◐ *county* NW Ireland
117 F18 **Leivádia** *prev.* Levádhia. Stereá Ellás, C Greece
Leix *see* Laois
xliv K9 **Leixlip** *Eng.* Salmon Leap, *Ir.* Léim an Bhradáin. Kildare, E Ireland
66 N8 **Leixões** Porto, N Portugal
167 N12 **Leiyang** Hunan, S China
166 L16 **Leizhou** *var.* Haikang. Guangdong, S China
166 L16 **Leizhou Bandao** *var.* Luichow Peninsula. *peninsula* S China
100 H13 **Lek** ↝ SW Netherlands
116 I13 **Lekánis** ▲ NE Greece
180 H13 **Le Kartala** ▲ Grande Comore, NW Comoros
Le Kef *see* El Kef
81 G20 **Lékéti, Monts de la** ▲ S Congo
Lekhainá *see* Lechainá
116 H8 **Lekhchevo** Oblast Montana, NW Bulgaria
94 G11 **Leknes** Nordland, C Norway
81 E21 **Le Kouilou** ◐ *province* SW Congo
96 L13 **Leksand** Kopparberg, C Sweden
128 H8 **Leksozero, Ozero** ◎ NW Russian Federation
107 Q3 **Lekunberri** *var.* Lecumberri. Navarra, N Spain
175 Tt6 **Lelai, Tanjung** *headland* Pulau Halmahera, N Indonesia
47 Q12 **le Lamentin** *var.* Lamentin. C Martinique
47 Q12 **le Lamentin** ✈ (Fort-de-France) C Martinique
33 P6 **Leland** Michigan, N USA
24 J4 **Leland** Mississippi, S USA
97 J16 **Lelång** *var.* Lelången. ◎ S Sweden
Lelången *see* Lelång
xxxvi M16 **Lelant** Cornwall, SW England, UK
Lel'chitsy *see* Lyel'chytsy
le Léman *see* Geneva, Lake
27 O3 **Lelia Lake** Texas, SW USA
115 I14 **Lelija** ▲ SE Bosnia and Herzegovina
110 C8 **Le Locle** Neuchâtel, W Switzerland
201 Y14 **Lelu** Kosrae, E Micronesia
Lelu *see* Lelu Island
201 Y14 **Lelu Island** *var.* Lelu. *island* Kosrae, E Micronesia
57 W9 **Lelydorp** Wanica, N Surinam
100 K9 **Lelystad** Flevoland, C Netherlands
65 K25 **Le Maire, Estrecho de** *strait* S Argentina
174 Hh7 **Lemang** Pulau Rangsang, W Indonesia
195 R11 **Lemankoa** Buka Island, NE PNG
Léman, Lac *see* Geneva, Lake
104 L6 **le Mans** Sarthe, NW France
31 S12 **Le Mars** Iowa, C USA
174 I11 **Lematan, Air** ↝ Sumatera, W Indonesia
111 S3 **Lembach Im Mühlkreis** Oberösterreich, N Austria
103 G23 **Lemberg** ▲ SW Germany
Lemberg *see* L'viv
Lemdiyya *see* Médéa
124 Qq12 **Lemesós** *var.* Limassol. SW Cyprus
102 H13 **Lemgo** Nordrhein-Westfalen, W Germany
35 P13 **Lemhi Range** ▲ Idaho, NW USA
16 Oo2 **Lemieux Islands** *island group* Northwest Territories, NE Canada
175 Q7 **Lemito** Sulawesi, N Indonesia
94 L10 **Lemmenjoki** *Lapp.* Leammi. ↝ NE Finland
100 L7 **Lemmer** *Fris.* De Lemmer. Friesland, N Netherlands
30 L7 **Lemmon** South Dakota, N USA
38 M15 **Lemmon, Mount** ▲ Arizona, SW USA
Lemnos *see* Límnos
33 O14 **Lemon, Lake** ◎ Indiana, N USA
104 J5 **le Mont St-Michel** *castle* Manche, N France
37 Q11 **Lemoore** California, W USA
201 T13 **Lemotol Bay** *bay* Chuuk Islands, C Micronesia
47 Y5 **le Moule** *var.* Moule. Grande Terre, NE Guadeloupe
Lemovices *see* Limoges
Le Moyen-Ogooué *see* Moyen-Ogooué
10 M6 **le Moyne, Lac** ◎ Québec, E Canada
95 L18 **Lempäälä** Häme, SW Finland
44 E7 **Lempa, Río** ↝ Central America
44 F7 **Lempira** *prev.* Gracias. ◐ *department* SW Honduras
xlii D9 **Lemreway** Western Isles, NW Scotland, UK
Lemsalu *see* Limbaži
109 N17 **Le Murge** ▲ SE Italy
129 V6 **Lemva** ↝ NW Russian Federation
97 F21 **Lemvig** Ringkøbing, W Denmark
xliv I13 **Lemybrien** Waterford, S Ireland
177 Ff8 **Lemyethna** Irrawaddy, SW Burma
32 K10 **Lena** Illinois, N USA
133 V4 **Lena** ↝ NE Russian Federation
181 N13 **Lena Tablemount** *undersea feature* S Indian Ocean
Lenchitsa *see* Łęczyca
61 N17 **Lençóis** Bahia, E Brazil
62 K9 **Lençóis Paulista** São Paulo, S Brazil
xliii H23 **Lendalfoot** South Ayrshire, W Scotland, UK
178 Mm15 **Len Dao** *island* S Spratly Islands
111 Y9 **Lendava** *Ger.* Unterlimbach; *prev.* Dolnja Lendava. NE Slovenia
85 F20 **Lendepas** Hardap, SE Namibia
128 H9 **Lendery** Respublika Kareliya, NW Russian Federation
Lendum *see* Lens
xliv I8 **Lene, Lough** ◎ C Ireland
29 R4 **Lenexa** Kansas, C USA
111 Q5 **Lengau** Oberösterreich, N Austria
151 Q17 **Lenger** Yuzhnyy Kazakhstan, S Kazakhstan
165 O9 **Lenghu** Qinghai, C China
165 T9 **Lenglong Ling** ▲ N China
110 D7 **Lengnau** Bern, W Switzerland
166 M12 **Lengshuitan** Hunan, S China
xxxvii X10 **Lenham** Kent, SE England, UK
97 M20 **Lenhovda** Kronoberg, S Sweden
81 E20 **Le Niari** ◐ *province* SW Congo
Lenin *see* Leninskoye, Kazakhstan
Lenin *see* Akdepe, Turkmenistan
Leninabad *see* Khŭjand
Leninakan *see* Gyumri
Lenina, Pik *see* Lenin Peak
119 V12 **Lenine** *Rus.* Lenino. Respublika Krym, S Ukraine
Leningor *see* Leninogorsk
153 Q13 **Leningrad** *Rus.* Leningradskiy; *prev.* Mŭ'minobod, *Rus.* Muminabad. SW Tajikistan
Leningrad *see* Sankt-Peterburg
130 L13 **Leningradskaya** Krasnodarskiy Kray, SW Russian Federation
205 S16 **Leningradskaya** *Russian research station* Antarctica
128 H12 **Leningradskaya Oblast'** ◐ *province* NW Russian Federation
Leningradskiy *see* Leningrad
Lenino *see* Lyenina, Belorussia
Lenino *see* Lenine, Ukraine
Leninobod *see* Khŭjand
151 X9 **Leninogorsk** *Kaz.* Leningor. Vostochnyy Kazakhstan, E Kazakhstan
131 T5 **Leninogorsk** Respublika Tatarstan, W Russian Federation
153 T12 **Lenin Peak** *Rus.* Pik Lenina, *Taj.* Qullai Lenin. ▲ Kyrgyzstan/Tajikistan
153 S8 **Leninpol'** Talasskaya Oblast', NW Kyrgyzstan
Lenin, Qullai *see* Lenin Peak
131 P11 **Leninsk** Volgogradskaya Oblast', SW Russian Federation
Leninsk *see* Akdepe, Turkmenistan
Leninsk *see* Asaka, Uzbekistan
151 T8 **Leninskiy** Pavlodar, E Kazakhstan
126 H14 **Leninsk-Kuznetskiy** Kemerovskaya Oblast', S Russian Federation
151 N7 **Leninskoye** *Kaz.* Lenin. Kustanay, N Kazakhstan
129 P15 **Leninskoye** Kirovskaya Oblast', NW Russian Federation
Leninsk-Turkmenski *see* Chardzhev
Leninváros *see* Tiszaújváros
Lenkoran' *see* Länkäran
103 F15 **Lenne** ↝ W Germany
103 G16 **Lennestadt** Nordrhein-Westfalen, W Germany
31 R11 **Lennox** South Dakota, N USA
65 J25 **Lennox, Isla** *Eng.* Lennox Island. *island* S Chile
Lennox Island *see* Lennox, Isla
xliii J19 **Lennoxtown** East Dunbartonshire, C Scotland, UK
23 Q9 **Lenoir** North Carolina, SE USA
22 M9 **Lenoir City** Tennessee, S USA
110 C7 **Le Noirmont** Jura, NW Switzerland
12 L9 **Lenôtre, Lac** ◎ Québec, SE Canada
31 U15 **Lenox** Iowa, C USA
105 O2 **Lens** *anc.* Lendum, Lentium. Pas-de-Calais, N France
126 Kk12 **Lensk** Respublika Sakha (Yakutiya), NE Russian Federation
113 F24 **Lenti** Zala, SW Hungary
Lentia *see* Linz
95 N14 **Lentiira** Oulu, E Finland
109 L25 **Lentini** *anc.* Leontini. Sicilia, Italy, C Mediterranean Sea
Lentium *see* Lens
Lentschiza *see* Łęczyca
95 N15 **Lentua** ◎ E Finland
121 H14 **Lentvaris** *Pol.* Landwarów. Trakai, SE Lithuania
110 F7 **Lenzburg** Aargau, N Switzerland
xliii J20 **Lenzie** East Dunbartonshire, C Scotland, UK
111 R5 **Lenzing** Oberösterreich, N Austria
79 P13 **Léo** SW Burkina
111 V7 **Leoben** Steiermark, C Austria
Leobschütz *see* Głubczyce
46 L9 **Léogâne** S Haiti
175 Q7 **Leok** Sulawesi, N Indonesia
31 O7 **Leola** South Dakota, N USA
xxxviii I13 **Leominster** Herefordshire, W England, UK
21 N11 **Leominster** Massachusetts, NE USA
31 V16 **Leon** Iowa, C USA
42 M12 **León** *var.* León de los Aldamas. Guanajuato, C Mexico
44 I10 **León** León, NW Nicaragua
106 L4 **León** Castilla-León, NW Spain
44 I9 **León** ◐ *department* W Nicaragua
106 K4 **León** ◐ *province* Castilla-León, NW Spain
León *see* Cotopaxi
104 I15 **Léon** Landes, SW France
27 V9 **Leona** Texas, SW USA
188 K11 **Leonara** Western Australia
27 U5 **Leonard** Texas, SW USA
Leonard Murray Mountains *see* Murray Range
109 H15 **Leonardo da Vinci** *prev.* Fiumicino. ✈ (Roma) Lazio, C Italy
23 X5 **Leonardtown** Maryland, NE USA
27 Q13 **Leona River** ↝ Texas, SW USA
43 Z11 **Leona Vicario** Quintana Roo, SE Mexico
103 H21 **Leonberg** Baden-Württemberg, SW Germany
64 M3 **León, Cerro** ▲ NW Paraguay
León de los Aldamas *see* León
111 T4 **Leonding** Oberösterreich, N Austria
109 I14 **Leonessa** Lazio, C Italy
109 K24 **Leonforte** Sicilia, Italy, C Mediterranean Sea
191 O13 **Leongatha** Victoria, SE Australia
117 F21 **Leonídio** Pelopónnisos, S Greece
106 J4 **León, Montes de** ▲ NW Spain
27 S8 **Leon River** ↝ Texas, SW USA
Leontini *see* Lentini
Léopold II, Lac *see* Mai-Ndombe, Lac
101 J17 **Leopoldsburg** Limburg, NE Belgium
Léopoldville *see* Kinshasa
28 I5 **Leoti** Kansas, C USA
118 M11 **Leova** *Rus.* Leovo. SW Moldavia
Leovo *see* Leova
104 G8 **le Palais** Morbihan, NW France
29 X10 **Lepanto** Arkansas, C USA
174 J11 **Lepar, Pulau** *island* W Indonesia
106 I14 **Lepe** Andalucía, S Spain
Lepel' *see* Lyepyel'
85 I19 **Lephepe** Kweneng, SE Botswana
167 Q10 **Leping** Jiangxi, S China
Lépontiennes, Alpes/Lepontine, Alpi *see* Lepontine Alps
110 G10 **Lepontine Alps** *Fr.* Alpes Lépontiennes, *It.* Alpi Lepontine. ▲ Italy/Switzerland
81 G20 **Le Pool** ◐ *province* S Congo
181 O16 **le Port** NW Réunion
105 N1 **le Portel** Pas-de-Calais, N France
95 N17 **Leppävirta** Kuopio, C Finland
47 Q11 **le Prêcheur** NW Martinique
Lepsi *see* Lepsy
151 V13 **Lepsy** *Kaz.* Lepsi. Taldykorgan, SE Kazakhstan
151 V13 **Lepsy** *Kaz.* Lepsi. ↝ SE Kazakhstan
Le Puglie *see* Puglia
105 Q12 **le Puy** *prev.* le Puy-en-Velay, *hist.* Anicium, Podium Anicensis. Haute-Loire, C France
le Puy-en-Velay *see* le Puy
Le Raizet *see* le Raizet
47 X11 **le Raizet** *var.* Le Raizet. ✈ (Pointe-à-Pitre) Grande Terre, C Guadeloupe
109 J24 **Lercara Friddi** Sicilia, Italy, C Mediterranean Sea
80 G12 **Léré** Mayo-Kébbi, SW Chad
Leribe *see* Hlotse
108 E10 **Lerici** Liguria, NW Italy
56 I14 **Lérida** Vaupés, SE Colombia
107 U5 **Lérida** ◐ *province* Cataluña, NE Spain
Lérida *see* Lleida
107 N5 **Lerma** Castilla-León, N Spain
42 M13 **Lerma, Río** ↝ C Mexico
117 F20 **Lérna** *prehistoric site* Pelopónnisos, S Greece
47 R11 **le Robert** E Martinique
117 M21 **Léros** *island* Dodekánisos, Greece, Aegean Sea
32 L13 **Le Roy** Illinois, N USA
29 Q6 **Le Roy** Kansas, C USA
31 W11 **Le Roy** Minnesota, N USA
20 E10 **Le Roy** New York, NE USA
Lerrnayin Gharabakh *see* Nagornyy Karabakh
97 J19 **Lerum** Älvsborg, S Sweden
xlii J14 **Lerwick** Shetland Islands, NE Scotland, UK
47 Y6 **les Abymes** *var.* Abymes. Grande Terre, C Guadeloupe
les Albères *see* Albères, Chaîne des
104 M4 **les Andelys** Eure, N France
47 Q12 **les Anses-d'Arlets** SW Martinique
107 U6 **Les Borges Blanques** *var.* Borjas Blancas. Cataluña, NE Spain
Lesbos *see* Lésvos
Les Cayes *see* Cayes
33 Q4 **Les Cheneaux Islands** *island* Michigan, N USA
105 T12 **les Écrins** ▲ E France
110 C10 **Le Sépey** Vaud, W Switzerland
13 T7 **Les Escoumins** Québec, SE Canada
Les Gonaïves *see* Gonaïves
Lesh/Leshi *see* Lezhë
166 H9 **Leshan** Sichuan, C China
110 D11 **Les Haudères** Valais, SW Switzerland
104 J9 **les Herbiers** Vendée, NW France
129 O8 **Leshukonskoye** Arkhangel'skaya Oblast', NW Russian Federation
Lesina *see* Hvar
109 M15 **Lesina, Lago di** ◎ SE Italy
116 K13 **Lesítse** ▲ NE Greece
96 G10 **Lesja** Oppland, S Norway
97 L15 **Lesjöfors** Värmland, C Sweden
113 O18 **Lesko** Krosno, SE Poland
115 O15 **Leskovac** Serbia, SE Yugoslavia
115 M22 **Leskovik** *var.* Leskoviku. Korçë, S Albania
Leskoviku *see* Leskovik
xlii N13 **Leslie** Aberdeenshire, NE Scotland, UK
xliii M18 **Leslie** Fife, E Scotland, UK
35 P14 **Leslie** Idaho, NW USA
33 Q10 **Leslie** Michigan, N USA
xliii K21 **Lesmahagow** South Lanarkshire, C Scotland, UK
Leśna/Lesnaya *see* Lyasnaya
104 F5 **Lesneven** Finistère, NW France
114 J11 **Lešnica** Serbia, W Yugoslavia
129 S13 **Lesnoy** Kirovskaya Oblast', NW Russian Federation
126 I13 **Lesosibirsk** Krasnoyarskiy Kray, C Russian Federation
85 J23 **Lesotho** *off.* Kingdom of Lesotho; *prev.* Basutoland. ◆ *monarchy* S Africa
127 Nn17 **Lesozavodsk** Primorskiy Kray, SE Russian Federation
104 J12 **Lesparre-Médoc** Gironde, SW France
110 C8 **Les Ponts-de-Martel** Neuchâtel, W Switzerland
104 I9 **les Sables-d'Olonne** Vendée, NW France
111 S7 **Lessach** *var.* Lessachbach. ↝ E Austria
Lessachbach *see* Lessach
47 W11 **les Saintes** *var.* Îles des Saintes. *island group* S Guadeloupe
76 L5 **Les Salines** ✈ (Annaba) NE Algeria
101 J22 **Lesse** ↝ SE Belgium
97 M20 **Lessebo** Kronoberg, S Sweden
104 G4 **les Sept Îles** *island group* NW France
204 M10 **Lesser Antarctica** *var.* West Antarctica. *physical region* Antarctica
47 P15 **Lesser Antilles** *island group* E West Indies
143 T10 **Lesser Caucasus** *Rus.* Malyy Kavkaz. ▲ SW Asia
Lesser Khingan Range *see* Xiao Hinggan Ling
9 P13 **Lesser Slave Lake** ◎ Alberta, W Canada
Lesser Sunda Islands *see* Nusa Tenggara
101 E19 **Lessines** Hainaut, SW Belgium
105 R16 **les Stes-Maries-de-la-Mer** Bouches-du-Rhône, SE France
12 G15 **Lester B.Pearson** *var.* Toronto. ✈ (Toronto) Ontario, S Canada
31 U9 **Lester Prairie** Minnesota, N USA
95 L16 **Lestijärvi** Vaasa, W Finland
L'Estuaire *see* Estuaire
31 U9 **Le Sueur** Minnesota, N USA
110 B8 **Les Verrières** Neuchâtel, W Switzerland
117 L17 **Lésvos** *anc.* Lesbos. *island* E Greece
xliii G25 **Leswalt** Dumfries and Galloway, SW Scotland, UK
112 G12 **Leszno** *Ger.* Lissa. Leszno, W Poland
112 G13 **Leszno** *off.* Województwo Leszyńskie, *Ger.* Lissa. ◐ *province* W Poland
Leszyńskie, Województwo *see* Leszno
85 L20 **Letaba** Northern, NE South Africa
181 P17 **le Tampon** SW Réunion
xxxvii T6 **Letchworth** Hertfordshire, E England, UK
113 G25 **Letenye** Zala, SW Hungary
xliii N16 **Letham** Angus, E Scotland, UK
9 Q17 **Lethbridge** Alberta, SW Canada
57 S11 **Lethem** S Guyana
85 H18 **Letiahau** ↝ W Botswana
56 J18 **Leticia** Amazonas, S Colombia
175 T15 **Leti, Kepulauan** *island group* E Indonesia
85 I18 **Letlhakane** Central, C Botswana
85 H20 **Letlhakeng** Kweneng, SE Botswana
116 J8 **Letnitsa** Loveshka Oblast, N Bulgaria
105 N1 **le Touquet-Paris-Plage** Pas-de-Calais, N France
177 G8 **Letpadan** Pegu, SW Burma
177 Ff6 **Letpan** Arakan State, W Burma
104 M2 **le Tréport** Seine-Maritime, N France
178 Gg13 **Letsôk-aw Kyun** *var.* Letsutan Island; *prev.* Domel Island. *island* Mergui Archipelago, S Burma
Letsutan Island *see* Letsôk-aw Kyun
xliv H3 **Letterkenny** *Ir.* Leitir Ceanainn. Donegal, NW Ireland
xliv D9 **Lettermore** Galway, W Ireland
xliv D9 **Lettermullan** Galway, W Ireland
xxxv C12 **Letterston** Pembrokeshire, SW Wales, UK
Lettland *see* Latvia
xlii L12 **Lettoch** Highland, NW Scotland, UK
118 M6 **Letychiv** Khmel'nyts'ka Oblast', W Ukraine
Lëtzebuerg *see* Luxembourg
118 H14 **Leu** Dolj, SW Romania
Leucas *see* Lefkáda
105 P17 **Leucate** Aude, S France
105 P17 **Leucate, Étang de** ◎ S France
xliii N17 **Leuchars** Fife, E Scotland, UK
110 E10 **Leuk** Valais, SW Switzerland
110 E10 **Leukerbad** Valais, SW Switzerland
Leusden *see* Leusden-Centrum
100 K11 **Leusden-Centrum** *var.* Leusden. Utrecht, C Netherlands
Leutensdorf *see* Litvínov
Leutschau *see* Levoča
101 H18 **Leuven** *Fr.* Louvain, *Ger.* Löwen. Vlaams Brabant, C Belgium
101 I20 **Leuze** Namur, C Belgium
Leuze *see* Leuze-en-Hainaut
101 E19 **Leuze-en-Hainaut** *var.* Leuze. Hainaut, SW Belgium
Léva *see* Levice
Levádhia *see* Leivádia
94 L8 **Levajok** *var.* Leevvajok. Finnmark, N Norway
38 L4 **Levan** Utah, W USA
95 E16 **Levanger** Nord-Trøndelag, C Norway
124 P14 **Levantine Basin** *undersea feature* E Mediterranean Sea
108 D10 **Levanto** Liguria, W Italy
109 H23 **Levanzo, Isola di** *island* Isole Egadi, S Italy
131 Q17 **Levashi** Respublika Dagestan, SW Russian Federation
26 M5 **Levelland** Texas, SW USA
41 P13 **Levelock** Alaska, USA
xli W13 **Leven** East Riding of Yorkshire, N England, UK
xliii M18 **Leven** Fife, E Scotland, UK
xliii L18 **Leven, Loch** ◎ C Scotland, UK
xli N11 **Levens** Cumbria, NW England, UK
xlii I5 **Levenwick** Shetland Islands, NE Scotland, UK
xlii B10 **Leverburgh** Western Isles, NW Scotland, UK
103 E16 **Leverkusen** Nordrhein-Westfalen, W Germany
113 J21 **Levice** *Ger.* Lewentz, Lewenz, *Hung.* Léva. Západné Slovensko, SW Slovakia
108 G6 **Levico Terme** Trentino-Alto Adige, N Italy
117 E20 **Levídi** Pelopónnisos, S Greece
105 P14 **le Vigan** Gard, S France
192 L13 **Levin** Manawatu-Wanganui, North Island, NZ
13 R10 **Lévis** *var.* Levis. Québec, SE Canada
23 P6 **Levisa Fork** ↝ Kentucky/Virginia, S USA
117 L21 **Levitha** *island* Kykládes, Greece, Aegean Sea
20 L14 **Levittown** Long Island, New York, NE USA
20 J15 **Levittown** Pennsylvania, NE USA
Levkás *see* Lefkáda
Levkímmi *see* Lefkímmi
113 L19 **Levoča** *Ger.* Leutschau, *Hung.* Locse. Východné Slovensko, NE Slovakia
Lévrier, Baie du *see* Nouâdhibou, Dakhlet
105 N9 **Levroux** Indre, C France
116 J8 **Levski** Loveshka Oblast, N Bulgaria
Levskigrad *see* Karlovo
130 L6 **Lev Tolstoy** Lipetskaya Oblast', W Russian Federation
197 I14 **Levuka** Ovalau, C Fiji
xxxvi E14 **Lewannick** Cornwall, SW England, UK
177 G6 **Lewe** Mandalay, C Burma
Lewentz/Lewenz *see* Levice
xxxvii U13 **Lewes** East Sussex, SE England, UK
23 Z4 **Lewes** Delaware, NE USA
31 Q12 **Lewis And Clark Lake** ▣ Nebraska/South Dakota, N USA
20 G14 **Lewisburg** Pennsylvania, NE USA
22 J10 **Lewisburg** Tennessee, S USA
23 S6 **Lewisburg** West Virginia, NE USA
xli E6 **Lewis, Butt of** *headland* NW Scotland, UK
xxxiv L16 **Lewisham** ◐ *London borough* SE England, UK
xxxvi E8 **Lewisham** Lewisham, SE England, UK
xlii C8 **Lewis, Isle of** *island* NW Scotland, UK
37 U4 **Lewis, Mount** ▲ Nevada, W USA
193 H16 **Lewis Pass** *pass* South Island, NZ
35 P7 **Lewis Range** ▲ Montana, NW USA
25 O3 **Lewis Smith Lake** ▣ Alabama, S USA
34 M10 **Lewiston** Idaho, NW USA
21 P7 **Lewiston** Maine, NE USA
31 X10 **Lewiston** Minnesota, N USA
20 D9 **Lewiston** New York, NE USA
38 L1 **Lewiston** Utah, W USA
32 K13 **Lewistown** Illinois, N USA
35 T9 **Lewistown** Montana, NW USA
29 T14 **Lewisville** Arkansas, C USA
27 T6 **Lewisville** Texas, SW USA
27 T6 **Lewisville, Lake** ▣ Texas, SW USA
Le Woleu-Ntem *see* Woleu-Ntem
xxxvi F14 **Lewtrenchard** Devon, SW England, UK
25 U3 **Lexington** Georgia, SE USA
22 M5 **Lexington** Kentucky, S USA
24 L4 **Lexington** Mississippi, S USA
29 S4 **Lexington** Missouri, C USA
31 N16 **Lexington** Nebraska, C USA
22 J9 **Lexington** North Carolina, SE USA
29 N11 **Lexington** Oklahoma, C USA
23 R12 **Lexington** South Carolina, SE USA
22 G9 **Lexington** Tennessee, S USA
27 T10 **Lexington** Texas, SW USA
23 T6 **Lexington** Virginia, NE USA
23 X5 **Lexington Park** Maryland, NE USA
xli Q11 **Leyburn** North Yorkshire, N England, UK
Leyden *see* Leiden
xli N15 **Leyland** Lancashire, NW England, UK
104 J14 **Leyre** ↝ SW France
xxxvii Y10 **Leysdown-on-sea** Kent, SE England, UK
179 R13 **Leyte** *island* C Philippines
179 R13 **Leyte Gulf** *gulf* E Philippines
xxxvi E6 **Leyton** Waltham Forest, SE England, UK
xxxvi E6 **Leytonstone** Waltham Forest, SE England, UK
113 O16 **Leżajsk** Rzeszów, SE Poland
Lezha *see* Lezhë
115 K18 **Lezhë** *var.* Lezha; *prev.* Lesh, Leshi. Lezhë, NW Albania
115 K18 **Lezhë** ◐ *district* NW Albania
105 O16 **Lézignan-Corbières** Aude, S France
130 J7 **L'gov** Kurskaya Oblast', W Russian Federation
xlii M11 **Lhanbryde** Moray, N Scotland, UK
165 P15 **Lhari** Xizang Zizhiqu, W China
165 N16 **Lhasa** *var.* La-sa, Lassa. Xizang Zizhiqu, W China
165 O15 **Lhasa He** ↝ W China
164 K16 **Lhazê** Xizang Zizhiqu, W China
164 K14 **Lhazhong** Xizang Zizhiqu, W China
173 F3 **Lhoksukon** Sumatera, W Indonesia
165 Q15 **Lhorong** Xizang Zizhiqu, W China
107 W6 **L'Hospitalet de Llobregat** *var.* Hospitalet. Cataluña, NE Spain
159 R11 **Lhotse** ▲ China/Nepal
165 N17 **Lhozhag** Xizang Zizhiqu, W China
165 O16 **Lhünzê** Xizang Zizhiqu, W China
165 N15 **Lhünzhub** *var.* Poindo. Xizang Zizhiqu, W China
178 H8 **Li** Lamphun, NW Thailand
Liancheng *see* Qinglong
179 Rr14 **Lianga** Mindanao, S Philippines
167 P12 **Liangcheng** Fujian, SE China
166 K9 **Liangping** Sichuan, C China
Liangzhou *see* Wuwei
167 O9 **Liangzi Hu** ▣ C China
167 R12 **Lianjiang** Fujian, SE China
166 L15 **Lianjiang** Guangdong, S China
167 O13 **Lianping** Guangdong, S China
Lian Xian *see* Lianzhou
166 M11 **Lianyuan** *prev.* Lantian. Hunan, S China
167 Q6 **Lianyungang** *var.* Xinpu. Jiangsu, E China
167 N13 **Lianzhou** *var.* Linxian; *prev.* Lian Xian. Guangdong, S China
Liao *see* Liaoning
167 P5 **Liaocheng** Shandong, E China
169 U13 **Liaodong Bandao** *var.* Liaotung Peninsula. *peninsula* NE China
169 T13 **Liaodong Wan** *Eng.* Gulf of Lantung, Gulf of Liaotung. *gulf* NE China
169 U11 **Liao He** ↝ NE China
169 W12 **Liao Ling** ▲ NE China
169 U12 **Liaoning** *var.* Liao, Liaoning Sheng, Shengking; *hist.* Fengtien, Shenking. ◐ *province* NE China
Liaoning Sheng *see* Liaoning
Liaotung, Gulf of *see* Liaodong Wan
Liaotung Peninsula *see* Liaodong Bandao
169 V12 **Liaoyang** *var.* Liao-yang. Liaoning, NE China
169 V11 **Liaoyuan** *var.* Dongliao, Shuang-liao, *Jap.* Chengchiatun. Jilin, NE China
169 U12 **Liaozhong** Liaoning, NE China
Liaqatabad *see* Piplān
8 M10 **Liard** ↝ W Canada
Liard *see* Fort Liard
8 L10 **Liard River** British Columbia, W Canada
155 O15 **Liāri** Baluchistān, SW Pakistan
xlii G11 **Liathach** ▲ NW Scotland, UK
Liatroim *see* Leitrim
201 S6 **Lib** *var.* Ellep. *island* Ralik Chain, C Marshall Islands
Liban *see* Lebanon
144 H6 **Liban, Jebel** *Ar.* Jabal al Gharbt, Jabal Lubnān, *Eng.* Mount Lebanon. ▲ C Lebanon
xxxv I12 **Libanus** Powys, C Wales, UK
Libau *see* Liepāja
xliii L21 **Libberton** South Lanarkshire, C Scotland, UK
35 N7 **Libby** Montana, NW USA
81 I16 **Libenge** Equateur, NW Zaire
28 I7 **Liberal** Kansas, C USA
29 R7 **Liberal** Missouri, C USA
Liberalitas Julia *see* Évora
113 D15 **Liberec** *Ger.* Reichenberg. Severní Čechy, N Czech Republic
44 K12 **Liberia** Guanacaste, NW Costa Rica
78 K17 **Liberia** *off.* Republic of Liberia. ◆ *republic* W Africa
63 D16 **Libertad** Corrientes, NE Argentina
63 E20 **Libertad** San José, S Uruguay
56 K6 **Libertad** Barinas, NW Venezuela
56 J7 **Libertad** Cojedes, N Venezuela

◆ Country
● Country Capital
◇ Dependent Territory
○ Dependent Territory Capital
◐ Administrative Region
✈ International Airport
▲ Mountain
▲ Mountain Range
⛰ Volcano
↝ River
◎ Lake
▣ Reservoir

LIBERTADOR – LLANGEFNI

64 G12 **Libertador** *off.* Región del Libertador General Bernardo O'Higgins. ⬗ *region* C Chile
Libertador General San Martín *see* Ciudad de Libertador General San Martín
22 L6 **Liberty** Kentucky, S USA
24 J7 **Liberty** Mississippi, S USA
29 R4 **Liberty** Missouri, C USA
20 J12 **Liberty** New York, NE USA
23 T9 **Liberty** North Carolina, SE USA
Libian Desert *see* Libyan Desert
101 J23 **Libin** Luxembourg, SE Belgium
166 K13 **Libo** Guizhou, S China
Libohova *see* Libohovë
115 L23 **Libohovë** *var.* Libohova. Gjirokastër, S Albania
83 K18 **Liboi** North Eastern, E Kenya
104 K13 **Libourne** Gironde, SW France
101 K23 **Libramont** Luxembourg, SE Belgium
115 M20 **Librazhd** *var.* Librazhdi. Elbasan, E Albania
Librazhdi *see* Librazhd
81 C18 **Libreville** ● (Gabon) Estuaire, NW Gabon
179 Rr15 **Libuganon** ≈ Mindanao, S Philippines
77 P10 **Libya** *off.* Socialist People's Libyan Arab Jamahiriya, *Ar.* Al Jamāhīrīyah al 'Arabīyah al Lībīyah ash Sha'bīyah al Ishtirākīyah; *prev.* Libyan Arab Republic. ◆ *islamic state* N Africa
77 T11 **Libyan Desert** *var.* Libian Desert, *Ar.* Aş Şahrā' al Lībīyah. *desert* N Africa
77 T8 **Libyan Plateau** *var.* Ad Diffah. *plateau* Egypt/Libya
Lībīyah, Aş Şahrā' al *see* Libyan Desert
64 G12 **Licantén** Maule, C Chile
109 J25 **Licata** *anc.* Phintias. Sicilia, Italy, C Mediterranean Sea
143 P14 **Lice** Diyarbakır, SE Turkey
xxxviii C13 **Lichfield** Staffordshire, C England, UK
85 N14 **Lichinga** Niassa, N Mozambique
111 V3 **Lichtenau** Niederösterreich, N Austria
85 I21 **Lichtenburg** North-West, N South Africa
103 K18 **Lichtenfels** Bayern, SE Germany
100 O12 **Lichtenvoorde** Gelderland, E Netherlands
Lichtenwald *see* Sevnica
101 C17 **Lichtervelde** West-Vlaanderen, W Belgium
166 L9 **Lichuan** Hubei, C China
29 V7 **Licking** Missouri, C USA
22 M4 **Licking River** ≈ Kentucky, S USA
114 C11 **Lički Osik** Lika-Senj, C Croatia
Ličko-Senjska Županija *see* Lika-Senj
109 K19 **Licosa, Punta** *headland* S Italy
121 H16 **Lida** *Rus.* Lida. Hrodzyenskaya Voblasts', W Belorussia
95 H17 **Liden** Västernorrland, C Sweden
xxxix U12 **Lidgate** Suffolk, E England, UK
31 R7 **Lidgerwood** North Dakota, N USA
Lidhorikíon *see* Lidoríki
97 K21 **Lidhult** Kronoberg, S Sweden
97 P16 **Lidingö** Stockholm, C Sweden
97 K17 **Lidköping** Skaraborg, S Sweden
Lido di Iesolo *see* Lido di Jesolo
108 I8 **Lido di Jesolo** *var.* Lido di Iesolo. Veneto, NE Italy
109 H15 **Lido di Ostia** Lazio, C Italy
Lidokhorikion *see* Lidoríki
117 E18 **Lidoríki** *prev.* Lidhorikíon, Lidokhorikion. Stereá Ellás, C Greece
112 K9 **Lidzbark** Ciechanów, N Poland
112 L7 **Lidzbark Warmiński** *Ger.* Heilsberg. Olsztyn, N Poland
111 U3 **Liebenau** Oberösterreich, N Austria
189 P7 **Liebig, Mount** ▲ Northern Territory, C Australia
111 V8 **Lieboch** Steiermark, SE Austria
110 I8 **Liechtenstein** *off.* Principality of Liechtenstein. ◆ *principality* C Europe
101 F18 **Liedekerke** Vlaams Brabant, C Belgium
101 K19 **Liège** *Dut.* Luik, *Ger.* Lüttich. Liège, E Belgium
101 K20 **Liège** *Dut.* Luik. ⬗ *province* E Belgium
Liegnitz *see* Legnica
95 O16 **Lieksa** Pohjois-Karjala, E Finland
120 F10 **Lielupe** ≈ Latvia/Lithuania
120 G9 **Lielvārde** Ogre, C Latvia
178 Kk14 **Liên Hương** *var.* Tuy Phong. Binh Thuân, S Vietnam
Liên Nghia *see* Đưc Trong
111 P9 **Lienz** Tirol, W Austria
120 B10 **Liepāja** *Ger.* Libau. Liepāja, W Latvia
101 H17 **Lier** *Fr.* Lierre. Antwerpen, N Belgium
97 H15 **Lierbyen** Buskerud, S Norway
101 L21 **Lierneux** Liège, E Belgium
Lierre *see* Lier
103 D18 **Lieser** ≈ W Germany
111 U7 **Liesing** ≈ E Austria
110 E6 **Liestal** Basel-Land, N Switzerland
Lietuva *see* Lithuania
Lievenhof *see* Līvāni
105 O2 **Liévin** Pas-de-Calais, N France
12 M9 **Lièvre, Rivière du** ≈ Québec, SE Canada
111 T6 **Liezen** Steiermark, C Austria
xliv K9 **Liffey** ≈ E Ireland
xliv I3 **Lifford** *Ir.* Leifear. Donegal, NW Ireland
197 K5 **Lifou** *island* Îles Loyauté, E New Caledonia
xxxvi F14 **Lifton** Devon, SW England, UK
200 Ss13 **Lifuka** *island* Ha'apai Group, C Tonga
179 Q11 **Ligao** Luzon, N Philippines
Liger *see* Loire
xxxvi B16 **Ligger Bay** *var.* Perran Bay. *bay* SW England, UK
44 H2 **Lighthouse Reef** *reef* E Belize
191 Q4 **Lightning Ridge** New South Wales, SE Australia
105 N9 **Lignières** Cher, C France
105 S5 **Ligny-en-Barrois** Meuse, NE France
85 P15 **Ligonha** ≈ NE Mozambique
33 P11 **Ligonier** Indiana, N USA
83 I25 **Ligunga** Ruvuma, S Tanzania
108 D9 **Ligure, Appennino** *Eng.* Ligurian Mountains. ⛰ NW Italy
Ligure, Mar *see* Ligurian Sea
108 C9 **Liguria** ⬗ *region* NW Italy
Ligurian Mountains *see* Ligure, Appennino
123 K6 **Ligurian Sea** *Fr.* Mer Ligurienne, *It.* Mar Ligure. *sea* N Mediterranean Sea
Ligurienne, Mer *see* Ligurian Sea
195 P9 **Lihir Group** *island group* NE PNG
195 P9 **Lihir Island** *island* Lihir Group, N PNG
40 B8 **Lihue** *Haw.* Līhu'e. Kauai, Hawaii, USA, C Pacific Ocean
120 F5 **Lihula** *Ger.* Leal. Läänemaa, W Estonia
128 I2 **Liinakhamari** *var.* Linacmamari. Murmanskaya Oblast', NW Russian Federation
Liivi Laht *see* Riga, Gulf of
166 F11 **Lijiang** *var.* Dayan, Lijiang Naxizu Zizhixian. Yunnan, SW China
114 C11 **Lika-Senj** *off.* Ličko-Senjska Županija. ⬗ *province* W Croatia
81 N25 **Likasi** *prev.* Jadotville. Shaba, SE Zaire
81 L16 **Likati** Haut-Zaïre, N Zaire
8 M15 **Likely** British Columbia, SW Canada
159 Y11 **Likhapāni** Assam, NE India
128 J16 **Likhoslavl'** Tverskaya Oblast', W Russian Federation
201 U5 **Likiep Atoll** *atoll* Ratak Chain, C Marshall Islands
97 D18 **Liknes** Vest-Agder, S Norway
81 H18 **Likouala** ≈ N Congo
81 H18 **Likouala aux Herbes** ≈ E Congo
202 B16 **Liku** E Niue
Likupang, Selat *see* Bangka, Selat
29 Y8 **Lilbourn** Missouri, C USA
104 E1 **l'Île-Rousse** Corse, France, C Mediterranean Sea
111 W5 **Lilienfeld** Niederösterreich, NE Austria
167 N11 **Liling** Hunan, S China
97 J18 **Lilla Edet** Älvsborg, S Sweden
105 P1 **Lille** *var.* l'Isle, *Dut.* Rijssel, *Flem.* Ryssel; *prev.* Lisle, *anc.* Insula. Nord, N France
97 G24 **Lillebælt** *var.* Lille Bælt, *Eng.* Little Belt. *strait* S Denmark
104 L3 **Lillebonne** Seine-Maritime, N France
96 H12 **Lillehammer** Oppland, S Norway
105 O1 **Lillers** Pas-de-Calais, N France
97 F18 **Lillesand** Aust-Agder, S Norway
97 I15 **Lillestrøm** Akershus, S Norway
95 F18 **Lillhärdal** Jämtland, C Sweden
xliii N22 **Lilliesleaf** The Borders, S Scotland, UK
23 U10 **Lillington** North Carolina, SE USA
107 O9 **Lillo** Castilla-La Mancha, C Spain
8 M16 **Lillooet** British Columbia, SW Canada
85 M14 **Lilongwe** ● (Malawi) Central, W Malawi
85 M14 **Lilongwe** ✈ Central, W Malawi
85 M14 **Lilongwe** ≈ W Malawi
179 Q15 **Liloy** Mindanao, S Philippines
Lilybaeum *see* Marsala
190 J7 **Lilydale** South Australia
191 P16 **Lilydale** Tasmania, SE Australia
115 J14 **Lim** ≈ Bosnia and Herzegovina/Yugoslavia
59 D15 **Lima** ● (Peru) Lima, W Peru
96 K13 **Lima** Kopparberg, C Sweden
33 R12 **Lima** Ohio, NE USA
59 D14 **Lima** ⬗ *department* W Peru
Lima *see* Jorge Chávez International
106 G5 **Lima** ≈ N Portugal
Lima *see* Limia
113 L17 **Limanowa** Nowy Sącz, S Poland
174 I8 **Limas** Pulau Sebangka, W Indonesia
Limassol *see* Lemesós
xliv J3 **Limavady** *Ir.* Léim an Mhadaidh. Limavady, NW Northern Ireland, UK
xliv J3 **Limavady** ⬗ *district* N Northern Ireland, UK
65 J14 **Limay Mahuida** La Pampa, C Argentina
65 H15 **Limay, Río** ≈ W Argentina
103 N16 **Limbach-Oberfrohna** Sachsen, E Germany
83 F22 **Limba Limba** ≈ C Tanzania
109 C17 **Limbara, Monte** ▲ Sardegna, Italy, C Mediterranean Sea
120 G7 **Limbaži** *Est.* Lemsalu. Limbaži, N Latvia
46 M8 **Limbé** N Haiti
175 Qq7 **Limboto, Danau** ◎ Sulawesi, N Indonesia
101 L19 **Limbourg** Liège, E Belgium
101 K17 **Limburg** ⬗ *province* NE Belgium
101 L16 **Limburg** ⬗ *province* SE Netherlands
103 F17 **Limburg an der Lahn** Hessen, W Germany
96 K13 **Limedsforsen** Kopparberg, C Sweden
62 L9 **Limeira** São Paulo, S Brazil
xliv F11 **Limerick** *Ir.* Luimneach. Limerick, SW Ireland
xliv E12 **Limerick** *Ir.* Luimneach. ⬗ *county* SW Ireland
21 S2 **Limestone** Maine, NE USA
27 U9 **Limestone, Lake** ◎ Texas, SW USA
41 P12 **Lime Village** Alaska, USA
97 F20 **Limfjorden** *fjord* N Denmark
97 J23 **Limhamn** Malmöhus, S Sweden
106 H5 **Limia** *Port.* Lima. ≈ NW Spain
95 L14 **Liminka** Oulu, C Finland
Limín Vathéos *see* Sámos
117 G17 **Límni** Évvoia, C Greece
117 J15 **Límnos** *anc.* Lemnos. *island* E Greece
104 M11 **Limoges** *anc.* Augustoritum Lemovicensium, Lemovices. Haute-Vienne, C France
39 U5 **Limon** Colorado, C USA
45 O13 **Limón** *var.* Puerto Limón. Limón, E Costa Rica
44 K4 **Limón** Colón, NE Honduras
45 N13 **Limón** *off.* Provincia de Limón. ⬗ *province* E Costa Rica
108 A10 **Limone Piemonte** Piemonte, NE Italy
Limones *see* Valdéz
Limonum *see* Poitiers
105 N11 **Limousin** ⬗ *region* C France
105 N16 **Limoux** Aude, S France
85 L19 **Limpopo** *var.* Crocodile. ≈ S Africa
166 K17 **Limu Ling** ⛰ S China
115 M20 **Lin** *var.* Lini. Elbasan, E Albania
Linacmamari *see* Liinakhamari
179 P13 **Linapacan Island** *island* W Philippines
64 G13 **Linares** Maule, C Chile
56 C13 **Linares** Nariño, SW Colombia
43 O9 **Linares** Nuevo León, NE Mexico
107 N12 **Linares** Andalucía, S Spain
109 G15 **Linaro, Capo** *headland* C Italy
108 D8 **Linate** ✈ (Milano) Lombardia, N Italy
166 F13 **Lincang** Yunnan, SW China
167 P11 **Linchuan** *var.* Fuzhou. Jiangxi, S China
xxxix Q6 **Lincoln** *anc.* Lindum, Lindum Colonia. Lincolnshire, E England, UK
63 B20 **Lincoln** Buenos Aires, E Argentina
193 H19 **Lincoln** Canterbury, South Island, NZ
37 O6 **Lincoln** California, W USA
32 L13 **Lincoln** Illinois, N USA
28 M4 **Lincoln** Kansas, C USA
21 S5 **Lincoln** Maine, NE USA
29 T5 **Lincoln** Missouri, C USA
31 R16 **Lincoln** *state capital* Nebraska, C USA
34 F11 **Lincoln City** Oregon, NW USA
xxxix Q6 **Lincoln Edge** *ridge* E England, UK
178 M10 **Lincoln Island** *island* E Paracel Islands
207 Q11 **Lincoln Sea** *sea* Arctic Ocean
xxxix Q6 **Lincolnshire** ⬗ *county* E England, UK
23 R10 **Lincolnton** North Carolina, SE USA
27 V7 **Lindale** Texas, SW USA
103 I25 **Lindau** *var.* Lindau am Bodensee. Bayern, S Germany
Lindau am Bodensee *see* Lindau
126 L9 **Linde** ≈ NE Russian Federation
57 T9 **Linden** E Guyana
25 O6 **Linden** Alabama, S USA
22 H9 **Linden** Tennessee, S USA
27 X6 **Linden** Texas, SW USA
20 J16 **Lindenwold** New Jersey, NE USA
97 M15 **Lindesberg** Örebro, C Sweden
97 D18 **Lindesnes** *headland* S Norway
Líndhos *see* Líndos
83 K24 **Lindi** Lindi, SE Tanzania
83 J24 **Lindi** ⬗ *region* SE Tanzania
81 N17 **Lindi** ≈ NE Zaire
169 V7 **Lindian** Heilongjiang, NE China
193 E21 **Lindis Pass** *pass* South Island, NZ
85 J22 **Lindley** Free State, C South Africa
97 J19 **Lindome** Göteborg och Bohus, S Sweden
Lindong *see* Bairin Zuoqi
117 O23 **Líndos** *var.* Líndhos. Ródos, Dodekánisos, Greece, Aegean Sea
12 I14 **Lindsay** Ontario, SE Canada
37 R11 **Lindsay** California, W USA
35 X8 **Lindsay** Montana, NW USA
29 N11 **Lindsay** Oklahoma, C USA
29 N5 **Lindsborg** Kansas, C USA
97 N21 **Lindsdal** Kalmar, S Sweden
175 Pp9 **Lindu, Danau** ◎ Sulawesi, N Indonesia
Lindum/Lindum Colonia *see* Lincoln
203 W3 **Line Islands** *island group* E Kiribati
Linëvo *see* Linova
166 M5 **Linfen** *var.* Lin-fen. Shanxi, C China
161 F18 **Linganamakki Reservoir** ⊠ SW India
166 L17 **Lingao** Hainan, S China
179 Oo9 **Lingayen** Luzon, N Philippines
179 Oo9 **Lingayen Gulf** *gulf* Luzon, N Philippines
166 M6 **Lingbao** *var.* Guolüezhen. Henan, C China
96 N12 **Lingbo** Gävleborg, C Sweden
Lingeh *see* Bandar-e Langeh
xxxviii G12 **Lingen** Herefordshire, W England, UK
102 E12 **Lingen** *var.* Lingen an der Ems. Niedersachsen, NW Germany
Lingen an der Ems *see* Lingen
xxxvii U11 **Lingfield** Surrey, SE England, UK
174 Ii8 **Lingga, Kepulauan** *island group* W Indonesia
174 I8 **Lingga, Pulau** *island* Kepulauan Lingga, W Indonesia
12 J14 **Lingham Lake** ◎ Ontario, SE Canada
96 M13 **Linghed** Kopparberg, C Sweden
35 Z15 **Lingle** Wyoming, C USA
20 G15 **Linglestown** Pennsylvania, NE USA
81 K18 **Lingomo II** Equateur, NW Zaire
166 L15 **Lingshan** Guangxi Zhuangzu Zizhiqu, S China
166 L17 **Lingshui** Hainan, S China
161 G16 **Lingsugūr** Karnātaka, C India
109 L23 **Linguaglossa** Sicilia, Italy, C Mediterranean Sea
78 H10 **Linguère** N Senegal
165 W8 **Lingwu** Ningxia, N China
Lingxi *see* Yongshun
167 O12 **Lingxian** *var.* Ling Xian. Hunan, S China
169 S12 **Lingyuan** Liaoning, NE China
169 U4 **Linhai** Heilongjiang, NE China
167 S10 **Linhai** *var.* Taizhou. Zhejiang, SE China
61 O20 **Linhares** Espírito Santo, SE Brazil
168 M13 **Linhe** Nei Mongol Zizhiqu, N China
Lini *see* Lin
145 S1 **Līnik, Chiyā-ē** ⛰ N Iraq
97 M18 **Linköping** Östergötland, S Sweden
169 Y8 **Linkou** Heilongjiang, NE China
xlii L4 **Linksness** Orkney Islands, N Scotland, UK
120 F11 **Linkuva** Pakruojis, N Lithuania
xliii L20 **Linlithgow** West Lothian, SE Scotland, UK
29 V5 **Linn** Missouri, C USA
27 S16 **Linn** Texas, SW USA
29 T2 **Linneus** Missouri, C USA
xliii F16 **Linnhe, Loch** *inlet* W Scotland, UK
121 G19 **Linova** *Rus.* Linëvo. Brestskaya Voblasts', SW Belorussia
167 O5 **Linqing** Shandong, E China
167 N6 **Linruzhen** Henan, C China
62 K8 **Lins** São Paulo, S Brazil
95 F17 **Linsell** Jämtland, C Sweden
166 J9 **Linshui** Sichuan, C China
xxxvii R6 **Linslade** Bedfordshire, C England, UK
46 K12 **Linstead** C Jamaica
165 U11 **Lintan** Gansu, N China
165 V11 **Lintao** Gansu, C China
13 S12 **Lintère** ≈ Québec, SE Canada
110 H8 **Linth** ≈ NW Switzerland
110 H8 **Linthal** Glarus, NE Switzerland
xxxix T13 **Linton** Cambridgeshire, E England, UK
xli Q12 **Linton** North Yorkshire, N England, UK
33 N15 **Linton** Indiana, N USA
31 N6 **Linton** North Dakota, N USA
169 R11 **Linxi** Nei Mongol Zizhiqu, N China
165 U11 **Linxia** *var.* Linxia Huizu Zizhizhou. Gansu, C China
Linxia Huizu Zizhizhou *see* Linxia
Linxian *see* Lianzhou
167 Q6 **Linyi** Shandong, S China
167 P4 **Linyi** Shandong, E China
166 M6 **Linyi** Shanxi, C China
111 T4 **Linz** *anc.* Lentia. Oberösterreich, N Austria
165 S8 **Linze** *var.* Shahepu. Gansu, N China
46 J13 **Lionel Town** C Jamaica
105 Q16 **Lion, Golfe du** *Eng.* Gulf of Lion, Gulf of Lions; *anc.* Sinus Gallicus. *gulf* S France
Lion, Gulf of/Lions, Gulf of *see* Lion, Golfe du
85 K16 **Lions Den** Mashonaland West, N Zimbabwe
12 F13 **Lion's Head** Ontario, S Canada
Lios Ceannúir, Bá *see* Liscannor Bay
Lios Mór *see* Lismore
Lios na gCearrbhach *see* Lisburn
Lios Tuathail *see* Listowel
81 G17 **Liouesso** La Sangha, N Congo
Liozno *see* Lyozna
179 P11 **Lipa** *off.* Lipa City. Luzon, N Philippines
27 S7 **Lipan** Texas, SW USA
Lipari Islands/Lipari, Isole *see* Eolie, Isole
109 L22 **Lipari, Isola** *island* Isole Eolie, S Italy
118 L8 **Lipcani** *Rus.* Lipkany. N Moldavia
95 N17 **Liperi** Pohjois-Karjala, SE Finland
130 L7 **Lipetsk** Lipetskaya Oblast', W Russian Federation
130 K6 **Lipetskaya Oblast'** ⬗ *province* W Russian Federation
59 K22 **Lipez, Cordillera de** ⛰ SW Bolivia
xxxvii R12 **Liphook** Hampshire, S England, UK
112 E10 **Lipiany** *Ger.* Lippehne. Szczecin, W Poland
114 G9 **Lipik** Požega-Slavonija, NE Croatia
128 L12 **Lipin Bor** Vologodskaya Oblast', NW Russian Federation
166 L12 **Liping** Guizhou, S China
Lipkany *see* Lipcani
121 H15 **Lipnishki** *Rus.* Lipnishki. Hrodzyenskaya Voblasts', W Belorussia
112 J10 **Lipno** Włocławek, C Poland
118 F11 **Lipova** *Hung.* Lippa. Arad, W Romania
Lipovets *see* Lypovets'
Lippa *see* Lipova
103 E14 **Lippe** ≈ W Germany
Lippehne *see* Lipiany
103 G14 **Lippstadt** Nordrhein-Westfalen, W Germany
27 P1 **Lipscomb** Texas, SW USA
Lipsia/Lipsk *see* Leipzig
112 P7 **Lipsk** Suwałki, NE Poland
Liptau-Sankt-Nikolaus/Liptószentmiklós *see* Liptovský Mikuláš
113 K19 **Liptovský Mikuláš** *Ger.* Liptau-Sankt-Nikolaus, *Hung.* Liptószentmiklós. Stredné Slovensko, N Slovakia
191 O13 **Liptrap, Cape** *headland* Victoria, SE Australia
166 L13 **Lipu** Guangxi Zhuangzu Zizhiqu, S China
147 X12 **Liqbi** S Oman
83 G17 **Lira** N Uganda
59 F15 **Lircay** Huancavelica, C Peru
109 J15 **Liri** ≈ C Italy
150 M8 **Lisakovsk** Kustanay, NW Kazakhstan
81 K17 **Lisala** Equateur, N Zaire
xliv I5 **Lisbellaw** Fermanagh, W Northern Ireland, UK
106 F11 **Lisboa** *Eng.* Lisbon; *anc.* Felicitas Julia, Olisipo. ● (Portugal) Lisboa, W Portugal
106 F10 **Lisboa** ⬗ *Eng.* Lisbon. *district* C Portugal
21 N7 **Lisbon** New Hampshire, NE USA
31 Q6 **Lisbon** North Dakota, N USA
Lisbon *see* Lisboa
21 Q8 **Lisbon Falls** Maine, NE USA
xliv L5 **Lisburn** *Ir.* Lios na gCearrbhach. Lisburn, E Northern Ireland, UK
xliv L5 **Lisburn** ⬗ *district* E Northern Ireland, UK
40 L6 **Lisburne, Cape** *headland* Alaska, USA
xliv D10 **Liscannor Bay** *Ir.* Bá Lios Ceannúir. *inlet* W Ireland
xliv D7 **Liscarney** Mayo, NW Ireland
xliv F12 **Liscarroll** Cork, S Ireland
xliv E10 **Lisdoonvarna** Clare, W Ireland
115 Q18 **Lisec** ▲ E FYR Macedonia
166 F13 **Lishe Jiang** ≈ SW China
166 M4 **Lishi** Shanxi, C China
169 V10 **Lishu** Jilin, NE China
167 R10 **Lishui** Zhejiang, SE China
199 Jj5 **Lisianski Island** *island* Hawaiian Islands, Hawaii, USA, C Pacific Ocean
Lisichansk *see* Lysychans'k
104 L4 **Lisieux** *anc.* Noviomagus. Calvados, N France
xxxvi E15 **Liskeard** Cornwall, SW England, UK
130 L8 **Liski** *prev.* Georgiu-Dezh. Voronezhskaya Oblast', W Russian Federation
Lisle/l'Isle *see* Lille
105 N4 **l'Isle-Adam** Val-d'Oise, N France
105 R15 **l'Isle-sur-la-Sorgue** Vaucluse, SE France
13 S9 **L'Islet** Québec, SE Canada
xliv H13 **Lismore** *Ir.* Lios Mór. Waterford, S Ireland
190 M12 **Lismore** Victoria, SE Australia
xliv I5 **Lisnaskea** Fermanagh, W Northern Ireland, UK
xxxvii R12 **Liss** Hampshire, S England, UK
Lissa *see* Vis, Croatia
Lissa *see* Leszno, Poland
100 H11 **Lisse** Zuid-Holland, W Netherlands
97 D18 **Lista** *peninsula* S Norway
97 D18 **Listafjorden** *fjord* S Norway
205 R13 **Lister, Mount** ▲ Antarctica
130 M8 **Listopadovka** Voronezhskaya Oblast', W Russian Federation
xliv D12 **Listowel** *Ir.* Lios Tuathail. Kerry, SW Ireland
12 F15 **Listowel** Ontario, S Canada
166 L14 **Litang** Guangxi Zhuangzu Zizhiqu, S China
166 F9 **Litang** Sichuan, C China
166 F10 **Litang Qu** ≈ C China
57 X12 **Litani** *var.* Itany. ≈ French Guiana/Surinam
144 G8 **Lītani, Nahr el** *var.* Nahr al Litant. ≈ C Lebanon
Litant, Nahr al *see* Līṭani, Nahr el
Litauen *see* Lithuania
xxxix V9 **Litcham** Norfolk, E England, UK
32 K14 **Litchfield** Illinois, N USA
31 U8 **Litchfield** Minnesota, N USA
38 K13 **Litchfield Park** Arizona, SW USA
xl M16 **Litherland** Sefton, NW England, UK
191 S8 **Lithgow** New South Wales, SE Australia
117 I26 **Líthino, Ákra** *headland* Kríti, Greece, E Mediterranean Sea
120 D12 **Lithuania** *off.* Republic of Lithuania, *Ger.* Litauen, *Lith.* Lietuva, *Pol.* Litwa, *Rus.* Litva; *prev.* Lithuanian SSR, *Rus.* Litovskaya SSR. ◆ *republic* NE Europe
Lithuanian SSR *see* Lithuania
111 U11 **Litija** *Ger.* Littai. C Slovenia
20 H15 **Lititz** Pennsylvania, NE USA
117 F15 **Litóchoro** *var.* Litohoro, Litókhoron. Kentrikí Makedonía, N Greece
Litohoro/Litókhoron *see* Litóchoro
113 C15 **Litoměřice** *Ger.* Leitmeritz. Severní Čechy, N Czech Republic
113 F17 **Litomyšl** *Ger.* Leitomischl. Východní Čechy, NE Czech Republic
113 G17 **Litovel** *Ger.* Littau. Severní Morava, E Czech Republic
127 Nn15 **Litovko** Khabarovskiy Kray, SE Russian Federation
Litovskaya SSR *see* Lithuania
Littai *see* Litija
Littau *see* Litovel
46 G1 **Little Abaco** *var.* Abaco Island. *island* N Bahamas
113 I21 **Little Alföld** *Ger.* Kleines Ungarisches Tiefland, *Hung.* Kisalföld, *Slvk.* Podunajská Rovina. *plain* Hungary/Slovakia
157 Q20 **Little Andaman** *island* Andaman Islands, India, NE Indian Ocean
28 M5 **Little Arkansas River** ≈ Kansas, C USA
192 L4 **Little Barrier Island** *island* N NZ
Little Belt *see* Lillebælt
40 M11 **Little Black River** ≈ Alaska, USA
29 O2 **Little Blue River** ≈ Kansas/Nebraska, C USA
xli P15 **Littleborough** Rochdale, NW England, UK
xxxix Q9 **Little Bytham** Lincolnshire, E England, UK
46 D8 **Little Cayman** *island* E Cayman Islands
9 X11 **Little Churchill** ≈ Manitoba, C Canada
177 Ee10 **Little Coco Island** *island* SW Burma
38 L10 **Little Colorado River** ≈ Arizona, SW USA
12 E11 **Little Current** Manitoulin Island, Ontario, S Canada
10 E11 **Little Current** ≈ Ontario, S Canada
xxxvi G13 **Little Dart** ≈ SW England, UK
40 L8 **Little Diomede Island** *island* Alaska, USA
xxxix T10 **Little Downham** Cambridgeshire, E England, UK
46 I4 **Little Exuma** *island* C Bahamas
31 U7 **Little Falls** Minnesota, N USA
20 J10 **Little Falls** New York, NE USA
xlii K9 **Littleferry** Highland, N Scotland, UK
26 M5 **Littlefield** Texas, SW USA
31 V3 **Littlefork** Minnesota, N USA
31 V3 **Little Fork River** ≈ Minnesota, N USA
9 N16 **Little Fort** British Columbia, SW Canada
9 Y14 **Little Grand Rapids** Manitoba, C Canada
xxxvii S13 **Littlehampton** West Sussex, SE England, UK
37 T2 **Little Humboldt River** ≈ Nevada, W USA
46 K6 **Little Inagua** *var.* Inagua Islands. *island* S Bahamas
23 Q4 **Little Kanawha River** ≈ West Virginia, NE USA
85 F25 **Little Karoo** *plateau* S South Africa
41 O16 **Little Koniuji Island** *island* Shumagin Islands, Alaska, USA
xl F14 **Little Lever** Bolton, NW England, UK
46 H12 **Little London** W Jamaica
11 R10 **Little Mecatina** *Fr.* Rivière du Petit Mécatina. ≈ Newfoundland and Labrador/Québec, E Canada
xlii C11 **Little Minch, The** *strait* NW Scotland, UK
xxxvii S8 **Little Missenden** Buckinghamshire, C England, UK
29 T13 **Little Missouri River** ≈ Arkansas, USA
30 J7 **Little Missouri River** ≈ NW USA
30 J3 **Little Muddy River** ≈ North Dakota, N USA
157 Q22 **Little Nicobar** *island* Nicobar Islands, India, NE Indian Ocean
29 R6 **Little Osage River** ≈ Missouri, C USA
xxxix U11 **Little Ouse** ≈ E England, UK
155 V2 **Little Pamir** *Pash.* Pāmīr-e Khord, *Rus.* Malyy Pamir. ⛰ Afghanistan/Tajikistan
23 U12 **Little Pee Dee River** ≈ North Carolina/South Carolina, SE USA
xxxix T10 **Littleport** Cambridgeshire, E England, UK
29 V10 **Little Red River** ≈ Arkansas, C USA
Little Rhody *see* Rhode Island
193 I19 **Little River** Canterbury, South Island, NZ
23 U12 **Little River** South Carolina, SE USA
29 Y9 **Little River** ≈ Arkansas/Missouri, C USA
29 R13 **Little River** ≈ Arkansas/Oklahoma, USA
25 T7 **Little River** ≈ Georgia, SE USA
24 H6 **Little River** ≈ Louisiana, S USA
27 T10 **Little River** ≈ Texas, SW USA
29 V12 **Little Rock** *state capital* Arkansas, C USA
33 N8 **Little Sable Point** *headland* Michigan, N USA
105 U11 **Little Saint Bernard Pass** *Fr.* Col du Petit St-Bernard, *It.* Colle di Piccolo San Bernardo. *pass* France/Italy
38 K7 **Little Salt Lake** ◎ Utah, W USA
188 K8 **Little Sandy Desert** *desert* Western Australia
31 S13 **Little Sioux River** ≈ Iowa, C USA
40 E17 **Little Sitkin Island** *island* Aleutian Islands, Alaska, USA
9 O13 **Little Smoky** Alberta, W Canada
9 O14 **Little Smoky** ≈ Alberta, W Canada
39 P3 **Little Snake River** ≈ Colorado, C USA
66 A12 **Little Sound** *bay* Bermuda, NW Atlantic Ocean
39 T4 **Littleton** Colorado, C USA
21 N7 **Littleton** New Hampshire, NE USA
20 D11 **Little Valley** New York, NE USA
32 M15 **Little Wabash River** ≈ Illinois, N USA
xxxix V8 **Little Walsingham** Norfolk, E England, UK
12 D10 **Little White River** ≈ Ontario, S Canada
30 M12 **Little White River** ≈ South Dakota, N USA
27 R5 **Little Wichita River** ≈ Texas, SW USA
148 I4 **Little Zab** *Ar.* Nahraz Zāb aş Şaghīr, *Kurd.* Zē-i Kōya, *Per.* Rūdkhāneh-ye Zāb-e Kūchek. ≈ Iran/Iraq
xxxvi L14 **Litton Cheney** Dorset, S England, UK
81 D15 **Littoral** ⬗ *province* W Cameroon
Littoria *see* Latina
Litva/Litwa *see* Lithuania
113 B15 **Litvínov** *Ger.* Leutensdorf. Severní Čechy, NW Czech Republic
118 M6 **Lityn** Vinnyts'ka Oblast', C Ukraine
Liu-chou/Liuchow *see* Liuzhou
169 W11 **Liuhe** Jilin, NE China
Liukang Tenggaya, Kepulauan *see* Sabalana, Kepulauan
85 Q15 **Liúpo** Nampula, NE Mozambique
85 G14 **Liuwa Plain** *plain* W Zambia
166 L13 **Liuzhou** *var.* Liu-chou, Liuchow. Guangxi Zhuangzu Zizhiqu, S China
118 H8 **Livada** *Hung.* Sárköz. Satu Mare, NW Romania
117 J20 **Liváda, Ákra** *headland* Tínos, Kykládes, Greece, Aegean Sea
117 L21 **Livádi** *island* Kykládes, Greece, Aegean Sea
Livanátai *see* Livanátes
117 G18 **Livanátes** *prev.* Livanátai. Stereá Ellás, C Greece
120 I10 **Līvāni** *Ger.* Lievenhof. Preiļi, SE Latvia
67 E25 **Lively Island** *island* SE Falkland Islands
67 D25 **Lively Sound** *sound* SE Falkland Islands
41 R8 **Livengood** Alaska, USA
108 I7 **Livenza** ≈ NE Italy
37 O6 **Live Oak** California, W USA
25 U9 **Live Oak** Florida, SE USA
37 O9 **Livermore** California, W USA
22 I6 **Livermore** Kentucky, S USA
21 Q7 **Livermore Falls** Maine, NE USA
26 J10 **Livermore, Mount** ▲ Texas, SW USA
xl B16 **Liverpool** Liverpool, NW England, UK
xl M16 **Liverpool** ⬗ *unitary authority* NW England, UK
11 P16 **Liverpool** Nova Scotia, SE Canada
xl L16 **Liverpool Bay** *bay* England/Wales, UK
191 S7 **Liverpool Range** ⛰ New South Wales, SE Australia
xliii L20 **Livingston** West Lothian, C Scotland, UK
25 N5 **Livingston** Alabama, S USA
37 P9 **Livingston** California, W USA
24 J8 **Livingston** Louisiana, S USA
35 S11 **Livingston** Montana, NW USA
22 L8 **Livingston** Tennessee, S USA
27 W9 **Livingston** Texas, SW USA
44 F4 **Livingston** Izabal, E Guatemala
85 I16 **Livingstone** *var.* Maramba. Southern, S Zambia
193 B22 **Livingstone Mountains** ⛰ South Island, NZ
82 K13 **Livingstone Mountains** ⛰ S Tanzania
84 N12 **Livingstonia** Northern, N Malawi
204 G4 **Livingston Island** *island* Antarctica
27 W9 **Livingston, Lake** ⊠ Texas, SW USA
114 F13 **Livno** SW Bosnia and Herzegovina
130 K7 **Livny** Orlovskaya Oblast', W Russian Federation
95 M14 **Livojoki** ≈ C Finland
33 R10 **Livonia** Michigan, N USA
108 E11 **Livorno** *Eng.* Leghorn. Toscana, C Italy
Livramento *see* Santana do Livramento
147 U8 **Līwā** *var.* Al Liwā'. *oasis region* S UAE
83 I24 **Liwale** Lindi, SE Tanzania
165 W9 **Liwangbu** Ningxia, N China
85 N15 **Liwonde** Southern, S Malawi
165 V11 **Li Xian** Gansu, C China
166 H8 **Lixian** *var.* Li Xian; *prev.* Zagunao. Sichuan, C China
Lixian Jiang *see* Black River
117 B18 **Lixoúri** *prev.* Lixoúrion. Kefallinía, Iónioi Nísoi, Greece, C Mediterranean Sea
Lixoúrion *see* Lixoúri
Lixus *see* Larache
xxxvi B17 **Lizard** Cornwall, SW England, UK
35 U15 **Lizard Head Peak** ▲ Wyoming, C USA
xxxvi B17 **Lizard Point** *headland* SW England, UK
114 L12 **Ljig** Serbia, C Yugoslavia
Ljouwert *see* Leeuwarden
Ljubelj *see* Loibl Pass
111 U11 **Ljubljana** *Ger.* Laibach, *It.* Lubiana; *anc.* Aemona, Emona. ● (Slovenia) C Slovenia
111 T11 **Ljubljana** ✈ C Slovenia
115 N17 **Ljuboten** ▲ S Yugoslavia
97 P19 **Ljugarn** Gotland, SE Sweden
86 G7 **Ljungan** ≈ N Sweden
95 F17 **Ljungan** ≈ C Sweden
97 K21 **Ljungby** Kronoberg, S Sweden
97 M17 **Ljungsbro** Östergötland, S Sweden
97 I18 **Ljungskile** Göteborg och Bohus, S Sweden
96 M11 **Ljusdal** Gävleborg, C Sweden
96 M11 **Ljusnan** ≈ C Sweden
96 N12 **Ljusne** Gävleborg, C Sweden
97 P15 **Ljusterö** Stockholm, C Sweden
111 X9 **Ljutomer** *Ger.* Luttenberg. NE Slovenia
65 G15 **Llaima, Volcán** ▲ S Chile
xxxv G7 **Llanaber** Gwynedd, NW Wales, UK
xxxv F6 **Llanaelhaearn** Gwynedd, NW Wales, UK
xxxv J7 **Llanarmon Dyffryn Ceiriog** Wrexham, NE Wales, UK
xxxv F11 **Llanarth** Ceredigion, W Wales, UK
xxxv J4 **Llanasa** Flintshire, N Wales, UK
xxxv J10 **Llanbadarn Fynydd** Powys, C Wales, UK
xxxv G7 **Llanbedr** Gwynedd, NW Wales, UK
xxxv E7 **Llanbedrog** Gwynedd, NW Wales, UK
xxxv G5 **Llanberis** Gwynedd, NW Wales, UK
xxxv J10 **Llanbister** Powys, C Wales, UK
xxxv E13 **Llanboidy** Carmarthenshire, S Wales, UK
xxxv I8 **Llanbrynmair** Powys, C Wales, UK
107 X4 **Llançà** *var.* Llansá. Cataluña, NE Spain
xxxv G13 **Llanddarog** Carmarthenshire, S Wales, UK
xxxv I6 **Llandderfel** Gwynedd, NW Wales, UK
xxxv G11 **Llanddewi-Brefi** Ceredigion, W Wales, UK
xxxv J10 **Llanddewi Ystradenni** Powys, C Wales, UK
xxxv F13 **Llandefaelog** Carmarthenshire, S Wales, UK
xxxv G13 **Llandeilo** Carmarthenshire, S Wales, UK
xxxv I9 **Llandinam** Powys, C Wales, UK
xxxv H12 **Llandovery** Carmarthenshire, S Wales, UK
xxxv I6 **Llandrillo** Denbighshire, N Wales, UK
xxxv J11 **Llandrindod Wells** Powys, E Wales, UK
xxxv H4 **Llandudno** Conwy, N Wales, UK
xxxv F5 **Llandwrog** Gwynedd, NW Wales, UK
xxxv G13 **Llandybie** Carmarthenshire, S Wales, UK
xxxv J9 **Llandyssil** Powys, C Wales, UK
xxxv F12 **Llandysul** Ceredigion, W Wales, UK
xxxv G8 **Llanegryn** Gwynedd, NW Wales, UK
xxxv J6 **Llanelidan** Denbighshire, N Wales, UK
xxxv G14 **Llanelli** *prev.* Llanelly. Carmarthenshire, SW Wales, UK
xxxv H7 **Llanelltyd** Gwynedd, NW Wales, UK
Llanelly *see* Llanelli
xxxv F4 **Llanerchymedd** Isle of Anglesey, NW Wales, UK
106 M2 **Llanes** Asturias, N Spain
xxxv E4 **Llanfachraeth** Isle of Anglesey, NW Wales, UK
xxxv E4 **Llanfaelog** Isle of Anglesey, NW Wales, UK
xxxv E4 **Llanfaethlu** Isle of Anglesey, NW Wales, UK
xxxv J8 **Llanfair Caereinion** Powys, C Wales, UK
xxxv G11 **Llanfair Clydogau** Ceredigion, W Wales, UK
xxxv G4 **Llanfairfechan** Conwy, N Wales, UK
xxxv I5 **Llanfair Talhaiarn** Conwy, N Wales, UK
xxxv J7 **Llanfechain** Powys, C Wales, UK
xxxv I12 **Llanfihangel Nant Bran** Powys, C Wales, UK
xxxv J11 **Llanfihangel-nant-Melan** Powys, C Wales, UK
xxxv J7 **Llanfihangel-yng-Ngwynfa** Powys, C Wales, UK
xxxv G8 **Llanfihangel-y-pennant** Gwynedd, NW Wales, UK
xxxv E12 **Llanfrynach** Pembrokeshire, SW Wales, UK
xxxv J7 **Llanfyllin** Powys, C Wales, UK
xxxv G12 **Llanfynydd** Carmarthenshire, S Wales, UK
xxxv J12 **Llanfyrnach** Powys, C Wales, UK
xxxv I8 **Llangadfan** Powys, C Wales, UK
xxxv H12 **Llangadog** Carmarthenshire, S Wales, UK
xxxv F4 **Llangefni** Isle of Anglesey, NW Wales, UK

◆ Country ● Country Capital ◇ Dependent Territory ○ Dependent Territory Capital ⬗ Administrative Region ✈ International Airport ▲ Mountain ⛰ Mountain Range Volcano ≈ River ◎ Lake ⊠ Reservoir

LLANGERNYW – LÓVUA

xxxv H5 **Llangernyw** Conwy, N Wales, UK
xxxv E13 **Llanglydwen** Carmarthenshire, S Wales, UK
xxxv G4 **Llangoed** Isle of Anglesey, NW Wales, UK
xxxv J6 **Llangollen** Denbighshire, NE Wales, UK
xxxv J12 **Llangorse** Powys, C Wales, UK
xxxv I7 **Llangower** Gwynedd, NW Wales, UK
xxxv E11 **Llangranog** Ceredigion, W Wales, UK
xxxv K10 **Llangunllo** Powys, C Wales, UK
xxxv I10 **Llangurig** Powys, C Wales, UK
xxxv I6 **Llangwm** Conwy, N Wales, UK
xxxv G11 **Llangybi** Ceredigion, W Wales, UK
xxxv J13 **Llangynidr** Powys, C Wales, UK
xxxv E13 **Llangynin** Carmarthenshire, S Wales, UK
xxxv J7 **Llangynog** Powys, C Wales, UK
xxxv I15 **Llanharan** Rhondda Cynon Taff, S Wales, UK
xxxv I15 **Llanharry** Rhondda Cynon Taff, S Wales, UK
xxxv I9 **Llanidloes** Powys, C Wales, UK
xxxv G10 **Llanilar** Ceredigion, W Wales, UK
xxxv J8 **Llanllugan** Powys, C Wales, UK
xxxv F6 **Llanllyfni** Gwynedd, NW Wales, UK
xxxv F14 **Llanmadoc** Swansea, S Wales, UK
xxxv G13 **Llannon** Carmarthenshire, S Wales, UK
27 R10 **Llano** Texas, SW USA
xxxv G10 **Llanon** Ceredigion, W Wales, UK
27 Q10 **Llano River** ≈ Texas, SW USA
56 I9 **Llanos** *physical region* Colombia/Venezuela
65 G16 **Llanquihue, Lago** ◎ S Chile
xxxv J5 **Llanrhaeadr** Denbighshire, N Wales, UK
xxxv J7 **Llanrhaeadr-ym-Mochnant** Powys, C Wales, UK
xxxv G14 **Llanrhidian** Swansea, S Wales, UK
xxxv G10 **Llanrhystud** Ceredigion, W Wales, UK
xxxv C12 **Llanrian** Pembrokeshire, SW Wales, UK
xxxv H5 **Llanrwst** Conwy, N Wales, UK
Llansá *see* Llançà
xxxv I5 **Llansannan** Conwy, N Wales, UK
xxxv G12 **Llansawel** Carmarthenshire, S Wales, UK
xxxv J7 **Llansilin** Powys, C Wales, UK
xxxv F13 **Llansteffan** Carmarthenshire, S Wales, UK
xxxv K12 **Llanthony** Monmouthshire, SE Wales, UK
xxxv L14 **Llantrisant** Monmouthshire, SE Wales, UK
xxxv J15 **Llantrisant** Rhondda Cynon Taff, S Wales, UK
xxxv I16 **Llantwit Major** The Vale of Glamorgan, S Wales, UK
xxxv I7 **Llanuwchllyn** Gwynedd, NW Wales, UK
xxxv K13 **Llanvihangel Gobion** Monmouthshire, SE Wales, UK
xxxv I7 **Llanwddyn** Powys, C Wales, UK
xxxv F11 **Llanwenog** Ceredigion, W Wales, UK
xxxv I9 **Llanwnog** Powys, C Wales, UK
xxxv H12 **Llanwrda** Carmarthenshire, S Wales, UK
xxxv H8 **Llanwrin** Powys, C Wales, UK
xxxv I10 **Llanwrthwl** Powys, C Wales, UK
xxxv I11 **Llanwrtyd Wells** Powys, C Wales, UK
xxxv G12 **Llanybydder** Carmarthenshire, S Wales, UK
xxxv D13 **Llanycefn** Pembrokeshire, SW Wales, UK
xxxv D12 **Llanychaer Bridge** Pembrokeshire, SW Wales, UK
xxxv I7 **Llanymawddwy** Gwynedd, NW Wales, UK
xxxv D13 **Llawhaden** Pembrokeshire, SW Wales, UK
xxxv G10 **Lledrod** Ceredigion, W Wales, UK
107 U5 **Lleida** *Cast.* Lérida; *anc.* Ilerda. Cataluña, NE Spain
Llera de Canales *see* Llera
106 K12 **Llerena** Extremadura, W Spain
xxxv E7 **Lleyn Peninsula** *peninsula* NW Wales, UK
107 S9 **Lliria** País Valenciano, E Spain
xxxv F6 **Llithfaen** Gwynedd, NW Wales, UK
107 W4 **Llivia** Cataluña, NE Spain
xxxv J4 **Lloc** Flintshire, N Wales, UK
107 O3 **Llodio** País Vasco, N Spain
107 X5 **Lloret de Mar** Cataluña, NE Spain
Llorri *see* Tossal de l'Orri
8 L11 **Lloyd George, Mount** ▲ British Columbia, W Canada
9 R14 **Lloydminster** Alberta/Saskatchewan, SW Canada
xxxv F11 **Llwyndafydd** Ceredigion, W Wales, UK
xxxv G8 **Llwyngwril** Gwynedd, NW Wales, UK
xxxv J12 **Llyswen** Powys, C Wales, UK
Lluchmayor *see* Llucmajor
38 L6 **Loa** Utah, W USA
174 Mm4 **Loagan Bunut** ◎ East Malaysia
178 Mm14 **Loaita Island** *island* W Spratly Islands
40 G12 **Loa, Mauna** ▲ Hawaii, USA, C Pacific Ocean
Loanda *see* Luanda
81 J22 **Loange** ≈ S Zaire
81 E21 **Loango** Le Kouilou, S Congo
xliii M20 **Loanhead** Midlothian, SE Scotland, UK
108 B10 **Loano** Liguria, NW Italy
64 H4 **Loa, Río** ≈ N Chile
85 I20 **Lobatse** *var.* Lobatsi. Kgatleng, SE Botswana
Lobatsi *see* Lobatse
103 Q15 **Löbau** Sachsen, E Germany
81 H16 **Lobaye** ◆ *prefecture* SW Central African Republic
81 I16 **Lobaye** ≈ SW Central African Republic
101 G21 **Lobbes** Hainaut, S Belgium
63 D23 **Lobería** Buenos Aires, E Argentina
112 F8 **Łobez** *Ger.* Labes. Szczecin, NW Poland
84 A13 **Lobito** Benguela, W Angola
Lobkovichi *see* Labkovichy
Lob Nor *see* Lop Nur
176 W11 **Lobo** Irian Jaya, E Indonesia
106 J11 **Lobón** Extremadura, W Spain
63 D20 **Lobos** Buenos Aires, E Argentina
42 E4 **Lobos, Cabo** *headland* NW Mexico
42 F6 **Lobos, Isla** *island* NW Mexico
Lobositz *see* Lovosice
Lobsens *see* Łobżenica
Loburi *see* Lop Buri
112 H9 **Łobżenica** *Ger.* Lobsens. Koszalin, W Poland
110 G11 **Locarno** *Ger.* Luggarus. Ticino, S Switzerland
xliii F15 **Lochailort** Highland, NW Scotland, UK
xliii F16 **Lochaline** Highland, NW Scotland, UK
xliii H25 **Lochans** Dumfries and Galloway, SW Scotland, UK
xliii L24 **Locharbriggs** Dumfries and Galloway, SW Scotland, UK
xliii H17 **Lochawe** Argyll and Bute, W Scotland, UK
xlii A13 **Lochboisdale** Western Isles, NW Scotland, UK
xliii E17 **Lochbuie** Argyll and Bute, W Scotland, UK
xlii F12 **Lochcarron** Highland, NW Scotland, UK
xliii M22 **Lochcraig Head** ▲ S Scotland, UK
xliii F17 **Lochdon** Argyll and Bute, W Scotland, UK
xlii H10 **Lochdrum** Highland, NW Scotland, UK
xliii J17 **Lochearnhead** Stirling, C Scotland, UK
100 N11 **Lochem** Gelderland, E Netherlands
xlii J12 **Lochend** Highland, NW Scotland, UK
104 M8 **Loches** Indre-et-Loire, C France
Loch Garman *see* Wexford
xliii M19 **Lochgelly** Fife, E Scotland, UK
xliii G19 **Lochgilphead** Argyll and Bute, W Scotland, UK
xliii H18 **Lochgoilhead** Argyll and Bute, W Scotland, UK
xlii G8 **Lochinver** Highland, N Scotland, UK
xlii H11 **Lochluichart** Highland, NW Scotland, UK
xliii L24 **Lochmaben** Dumfries and Galloway, SW Scotland, UK
xlii B11 **Lochmaddy** Western Isles, NW Scotland, UK
xliii M14 **Lochnagar** ▲ C Scotland, UK
xliii G21 **Lochranza** North Ayrshire, W Scotland, UK
101 E17 **Lochristi** Oost-Vlaanderen, NW Belgium
xliii I21 **Lochwinnoch** Renfrewshire, W Scotland, UK
xliii H14 **Lochy, Loch** ◎ N Scotland, UK
190 G8 **Lock** South Australia
xliii L24 **Lockerbie** Dumfries and Galloway, S Scotland, UK
29 S13 **Lockesburg** Arkansas, C USA
191 P10 **Lockhart** New South Wales, SE Australia
27 S11 **Lockhart** Texas, SW USA
20 F13 **Lock Haven** Pennsylvania, NE USA
27 N4 **Lockney** Texas, SW USA
102 O12 **Löcknitz** ≈ NE Germany
20 E9 **Lockport** New York, NE USA
178 Jj13 **Lôc Ninh** Sông Be, S Vietnam
109 N23 **Locri** Calabria, SW Italy
Locse *see* Levoča
29 T2 **Locust Creek** ≈ Missouri, C USA
25 P3 **Locust Fork** ≈ Alabama, S USA
29 Q9 **Locust Grove** Oklahoma, C USA
96 E11 **Lodalskåpa** ▲ S Norway
xxxix Y10 **Loddon** Norfolk, E England, UK
191 N10 **Loddon River** ≈ Victoria, SE Australia
Lodensee *see* Klooga
105 P15 **Lodève** *anc.* Luteva. Hérault, S France
128 I12 **Lodeynoye Pole** Leningradskaya Oblast', NW Russian Federation
35 V11 **Lodge Grass** Montana, NW USA
30 J15 **Lodgepole Creek** ≈ Nebraska/Wyoming, C USA
155 T11 **Lodhrān** Punjab, E Pakistan
108 D8 **Lodi** Lombardia, NW Italy
37 O8 **Lodi** California, W USA
33 T12 **Lodi** Ohio, N USA
94 H10 **Lødingen** Nordland, C Norway
81 L20 **Lodja** Kasai Oriental, C Zaire
39 O3 **Lodore, Canyon of** *canyon* Colorado, C USA
107 Q4 **Lodosa** Navarra, N Spain
83 H16 **Lodwar** Rift Valley, NW Kenya
112 K13 **Łódź** *Rus.* Lodz. Łódź, C Poland
112 K13 **Łódź** *off.* Województwo Łódzkie, *Rus.* Lodz. ◆ *province* C Poland
Łódzkie, Województwo *see* Łódź
178 I8 **Loei** *var.* Loey, Muang Loei. Loei, C Thailand
100 I11 **Loenen** Utrecht, C Netherlands
178 J9 **Loeng Nok Tha** Yasothon, E Thailand
85 F24 **Loeriesfontein** Northern Cape, W South Africa
97 H20 **Læsø** *island* N Denmark
Loewoek *see* Luwuk
Loey *see* Loei
78 J16 **Lofa** ≈ N Liberia
111 P6 **Lofer** Salzburg, C Austria
94 F11 **Lofoten** *var.* Lofoten Islands. *island group* C Norway
Lofoten Islands *see* Lofoten
97 N18 **Loftahammar** Kalmar, S Sweden
xli U9 **Loftus** Redcar and Cleveland, N England, UK
131 O10 **Log** Volgogradskaya Oblast', SW Russian Federation
79 S12 **Loga** Dosso, SW Niger
31 S14 **Logan** Iowa, C USA
28 K3 **Logan** Kansas, C USA
33 T14 **Logan** Ohio, N USA
38 L1 **Logan** Utah, W USA
23 P6 **Logan** West Virginia, NE USA
37 Y10 **Logandale** Nevada, W USA
21 O11 **Logan International** ✕ (Boston) Massachusetts, NE USA
9 N16 **Logan Lake** British Columbia, SW Canada
25 Q4 **Logan Martin Lake** ⊠ Alabama, S USA
8 G8 **Logan, Mount** ▲ Yukon Territory, W Canada
34 I7 **Logan, Mount** ▲ Washington, NW USA
35 P7 **Logan Pass** *pass* Montana, NW USA
33 O12 **Logansport** Indiana, N USA
24 F6 **Logansport** Louisiana, S USA
Logar *see* Lowgar
69 R11 **Loge** ≈ NW Angola
xliii N14 **Logie Coldstone** Aberdeenshire, NE Scotland, UK
xxxv E13 **Login** Carmarthenshire, S Wales, UK
Logishin *see* Lahishyn
Log na Coille *see* Lugnaquillia Mountain
80 G11 **Logone** *var.* Lagone. ≈ Cameroon/Chad
80 G13 **Logone-Occidental** *off.* Préfecture du Logone-Occidental. ◆ *prefecture* SW Chad
80 H13 **Logone Occidental** ≈ SW Chad
80 G13 **Logone-Oriental** *off.* Préfecture du Logone-Oriental. ◆ *prefecture* SW Chad
80 H13 **Logone Oriental** ≈ SW Chad
Logone Oriental *see* Pendé
L'Ogooué-Ivindo *see* Ogooué-Ivindo
L'Ogooué-Lolo *see* Ogooué-Lolo
L'Ogooué-Maritime *see* Ogooué-Maritime
Logoysk *see* Lahoysk
107 P4 **Logroño** *anc.* Vareia, *Lat.* Juliobriga. La Rioja, N Spain
106 L10 **Logrosán** Extremadura, W Spain
97 G20 **Løgstør** Nordjylland, N Denmark
97 H22 **Løgten** Århus, C Denmark
97 F24 **Løgumkloster** Sønderjylland, SW Denmark
Lögurinn *see* Lagarfljót
197 B10 **Loh** *island* Torres Islands, N Vanuatu
159 P15 **Lohārdaga** Bihār, N India
158 H10 **Lohāru** Haryāna, N India
103 D15 **Lohausen** ✕ (Düsseldorf) Nordrhein-Westfalen, W Germany
201 O14 **Lohd** Pohnpei, E Micronesia
194 I14 **Lohiki** ≈ S PNG
94 L12 **Lohiniva** Lappi, N Finland
Lohiszyn *see* Lahishyn
95 L20 **Lohja** *var.* Lojo. Uusimaa, S Finland
175 O8 **Lohjanan** Borneo, C Indonesia
27 Q9 **Lohn** Texas, SW USA
102 G12 **Lohne** Niedersachsen, NW Germany
Lohr *see* Lohr am Main
103 I18 **Lohr am Main** *var.* Lohr. Bayern, C Germany
111 T10 **Loibl Pass** *Ger.* Loiblpass, *Slvn.* Ljubelj. *pass* Austria/Slovenia
178 Gg6 **Loi-Kaw** Kayah State, C Burma
95 K19 **Loimaa** Turku-Pori, SW Finland
105 O6 **Loing** ≈ C France
178 Ii6 **Loi, Phou** ▲ N Laos
104 L7 **Loir** ≈ C France
105 Q11 **Loire** ◆ *department* E France
104 M7 **Loire** *var.* Liger. ≈ C France
104 I7 **Loire-Atlantique** ◆ *department* NW France
105 O7 **Loiret** ◆ *department* C France
104 M8 **Loir-et-Cher** ◆ *department* C France
103 L24 **Loisach** ≈ SE Germany
58 B9 **Loja** Loja, S Ecuador
106 M14 **Loja** Andalucía, S Spain
58 B9 **Loja** ◆ *province* S Ecuador
Lojo *see* Lohja
118 J4 **Lokachi** Volyns'ka Oblast', NW Ukraine
81 M20 **Lokandu** Maniema, C Zaire
94 M11 **Lokan Tekojärvi** ◎ NE Finland
143 Z11 **Lökbatan** *Rus.* Lokbatan. E Azerbaijan
101 F17 **Lokeren** Oost-Vlaanderen, NW Belgium
Lokhvitsa *see* Lokhvytsya
119 S4 **Lokhvytsya** *Rus.* Lokhvitsa. Poltavs'ka Oblast', NE Ukraine
83 H17 **Lokichar** Rift Valley, NW Kenya
83 G16 **Lokichokio** Rift Valley, NW Kenya
83 H16 **Lokitaung** Rift Valley, NW Kenya
94 M11 **Lokka** Lappi, N Finland
96 G8 **Løkken Verk** Sør-Trøndelag, S Norway
128 G16 **Loknya** Pskovskaya Oblast', W Russian Federation
79 V15 **Loko** Plateau, S Nigeria
79 U15 **Lokoja** Kogi, C Nigeria
83 H17 **Lokori** Rift Valley, W Kenya
79 R16 **Lokossa** S Benin
120 I3 **Loksa** *Ger.* Loxa. Harjumaa, NW Estonia
16 P3 **Loks Land** *island* Northwest Territories, NE Canada
82 C13 **Lol** ≈ S Sudan
78 K15 **Lola** Guinée-Forestière, SE Guinea
37 Q5 **Lola, Mount** ▲ California, W USA
83 H20 **Loliondo** Arusha, NE Tanzania
97 H25 **Lolland** *prev.* Laaland. *island* S Denmark
195 O11 **Lolobau Island** *island* E PNG
175 T6 **Loloda Utara, Kepulauan** *island group* E Indonesia
81 E16 **Lolodorf** Sud, SW Cameroon
116 G7 **Lom** *prev.* Lom-Palanka. Oblast Montana, NW Bulgaria
116 G7 **Lom** ≈ NW Bulgaria
81 M19 **Lomami** ≈ C Zaire
59 F17 **Lomas** Arequipa, SW Peru
65 I23 **Lomas, Bahía** *bay* S Chile
63 D20 **Lomas de Zamora** Buenos Aires, E Argentina
63 D20 **Loma Verde** Buenos Aires, E Argentina
188 K4 **Lombadina** Western Australia
108 E6 **Lombardia** *Eng.* Lombardy. ◆ *region* N Italy
Lombardy *see* Lombardia
104 M15 **Lombez** Gers, S France
175 R15 **Lomblen, Pulau** *island* Nusa Tenggara, S Indonesia
181 W7 **Lombok Basin** *undersea feature* E Indian Ocean
175 Nn16 **Lombok, Pulau** *island* Nusa Tenggara, C Indonesia
175 Nn16 **Lombok, Selat** *strait* S Indonesia
79 Q16 **Lomé** ● (Togo) S Togo
79 Q16 **Lomé** ✕ S Togo
81 L19 **Lomela** Kasai Oriental, C Zaire
27 R9 **Lometa** Texas, SW USA
81 F16 **Lomié** Est, SE Cameroon
32 M8 **Lomira** Wisconsin, N USA
97 K23 **Lomma** Malmöhus, S Sweden
101 J16 **Lommel** Limburg, N Belgium
xliii I19 **Lomond, Loch** ◎ C Scotland, UK
207 R9 **Lomonosov Ridge** *var.* Harris Ridge, *Rus.* Khrebet Lomonsova. *undersea feature* Arctic Ocean
Lomonsova, Khrebet *see* Lomonosov Ridge
Lom-Palanka *see* Lom
Lomphat *see* Lumphăt
37 P14 **Lompoc** California, W USA
178 Hh9 **Lom Sak** *var.* Muang Lom Sak. Phetchabun, C Thailand
112 N9 **Łomża** *Rus.* Lomzha. Łomża, NE Poland
112 N9 **Łomża** *off.* Województwo Łomżyńskie, *Rus.* Lomzha. ◆ *province* NE Poland
Lomzha/Łomżyńskie, Województwo *see* Łomża
Lonaula *see* Lonāvale
161 D14 **Lonāvale** *prev.* Lonaula. Mahārāshtra, W India
65 G15 **Loncoche** Araucanía, C Chile
65 H14 **Loncopue** Neuquén, W Argentina
101 G17 **Londerzeel** Vlaams Brabant, C Belgium
Londinium *see* London
xxxvii U9 **London** *anc.* Augusta, *Lat.* Londinium. ● (UK) SE England, UK
12 E16 **London** Ontario, S Canada
203 Y2 **London** Kiritimati, E Kiribati
23 N7 **London** Kentucky, S USA
33 S13 **London** Ohio, NE USA
27 Q10 **London** Texas, SW USA
xxxvi G7 **London City** ✕ City of London, SE England, UK
xxxiv L16 **London, City of** ◆ *London borough* SE England, UK
xliv I3 **Londonderry** *var.* Derry, *Ir.* Doire. Londonderry, NW Northern Ireland, UK
xliv I3 **Londonderry** ◆ *district* NW Northern Ireland, UK
188 M2 **Londonderry, Cape** *headland* Western Australia
65 H25 **Londonderry, Isla** *island* S Chile
45 O7 **Londres, Cayos** *reef* NE Nicaragua
62 I10 **Londrina** Paraná, S Brazil
29 N13 **Lone Grove** Oklahoma, C USA
12 E12 **Lonely Island** *island* Ontario, S Canada
37 T8 **Lone Mountain** ▲ Nevada, W USA
27 V6 **Lone Oak** Texas, SW USA
37 T11 **Lone Pine** California, W USA
Lone Star State *see* Texas
85 D14 **Longa** Cuando Cubango, C Angola
84 B12 **Longa** ≈ W Angola
85 E15 **Longa** ≈ SE Angola
169 W11 **Longang Shan** ▲▲ NE China
207 S4 **Longa, Proliv** *Eng.* Long Strait. *strait* NE Russian Federation
xxxvi K10 **Long Ashton** North West Somerset, SW England, UK
46 J13 **Long Bay** *bay* W Jamaica
23 V13 **Long Bay** *bay* North Carolina/South Carolina, E USA
37 T16 **Long Beach** California, W USA
24 M9 **Long Beach** Mississippi, S USA
20 L14 **Long Beach** Long Island, New York, NE USA
34 F9 **Long Beach** Washington, NW USA
20 K16 **Long Beach Island** *island* New Jersey, NE USA
xli V2 **Longbenton** North Tyneside, NE England, UK
67 M25 **Longbluff** *headland* SW Tristan da Cunha
25 U13 **Longboat Key** *island* Florida, SE USA
20 K15 **Long Branch** New Jersey, NE USA
xxxviii C16 **Longbridge** Birmingham, C England, UK
xxxvi M11 **Longbridge Deverill** Wiltshire, S England, UK
xxxix O12 **Long Buckby** Northamptonshire, C England, UK
46 J5 **Long Cay** *island* SE Bahamas
167 P14 **Longchuan** *prev.* Laolong. Guangdong, S China
Longchuan Jiang *see* Shweli
34 K12 **Long Creek** Oregon, NW USA
xxxvii Q8 **Long Crendon** Buckinghamshire, C England, UK
165 W10 **Longde** Ningxia, N China
xxxix N8 **Long Eaton** Derbyshire, C England, UK
xliv H7 **Longford** *Ir.* An Longfort. Longford, C Ireland
xxxviii M11 **Longford** Coventry, C England, UK
xxxviii L8 **Longford** Derbyshire, C England, UK
xliv H7 **Longford** *Ir.* An Longfort. ◆ *county* C Ireland
191 P16 **Longford** Tasmania, SE Australia
xliii O20 **Longformacus** The Borders, S Scotland, UK
xli Q4 **Longframlington** Northumberland, N England, UK
xlii M5 **Longhope** Orkney Islands, N Scotland, UK
xli Q4 **Longhorsley** Northumberland, N England, UK
xli R3 **Longhoughton** Northumberland, N England, UK
167 P1 **Longhua** Hebei, E China
175 Nn8 **Longiram** Borneo, C Indonesia
46 J4 **Long Island** *island* C Bahamas
10 H8 **Long Island** *island* Northwest Territories, C Canada
194 K11 **Long Island** *var.* Arop Island. *island* N PNG
20 L14 **Long Island** *island* New York, NE USA
Long Island *see* Bermuda
20 M14 **Long Island Sound** *sound* NE USA
166 K13 **Long Jiang** ≈ S China
169 U7 **Longjiang** Heilongjiang, NE China
169 Y10 **Longjing** *var.* Yanji. Jilin, NE China
167 R4 **Longkou** Shandong, E China
10 E11 **Longlac** Ontario, S Canada
21 S1 **Long Lake** ◎ Maine, NE USA
33 O6 **Long Lake** ◎ Michigan, N USA
33 R5 **Long Lake** ◎ Michigan, N USA
31 N6 **Long Lake** ◎ North Dakota, N USA
32 J4 **Long Lake** ⊠ Wisconsin, N USA
101 K23 **Longlier** Luxembourg, SE Belgium
166 I13 **Longlin** *var.* Longlin Gezu Zizhixian. Guangxi Zhuangzu Zizhiqu, S China
xliii H19 **Long, Loch** *inlet* W Scotland, UK
xli T13 **Long Marston** North Yorkshire, N England, UK
xxxviii L13 **Long Marston** Warwickshire, C England, UK
xxxix V13 **Long Melford** Suffolk, E England, UK
39 T3 **Longmont** Colorado, C USA
xxxviii H10 **Long Mynd, The** *hill range* W England, UK
xxxvi L7 **Longney** Gloucestershire, C England, UK
xliii N19 **Longniddry** East Lothian, SE Scotland, UK
xxxviii K6 **Longnor** Staffordshire, C England, UK
31 N13 **Long Pine** Nebraska, C USA
Longping *see* Luodian
12 F17 **Long Point** *headland* Ontario, S Canada
12 K15 **Long Point** *headland* Ontario, SE Canada
192 P10 **Long Point** *headland* North Island, NZ
32 L2 **Long Point** *headland* Michigan, N USA
12 G17 **Long Point Bay** *lake bay* Ontario, S Canada
31 T7 **Long Prairie** Minnesota, N USA
xli P12 **Long Preston** North Yorkshire, N England, UK
11 S11 **Long Range Mountains** *hill range* Newfoundland, Newfoundland and Labrador, E Canada
67 H25 **Long Range Point** *headland* SE Saint Helena
189 V8 **Longreach** Queensland, E Australia
166 H7 **Longriba** Sichuan, C China
xli N14 **Longridge** Lancashire, NW England, UK
166 L10 **Longshan** Hunan, S China
xlii P12 **Longside** Aberdeenshire, NE Scotland, UK
39 S3 **Longs Peak** ▲ Colorado, C USA
Long Strait *see* Longa, Proliv
xxxix X10 **Long Stratton** Norfolk, E England, UK
xxxix S8 **Long Sutton** Lincolnshire, E England, UK
xxxvi K12 **Long Sutton** Somerset, SW England, UK
xli N14 **Longton** Lancashire, NW England, UK
xl M6 **Longtown** Cumbria, NW England, UK
xxxviii G14 **Longtown** Herefordshire, W England, UK
104 K8 **Longué** Maine-et-Loire, NW France
11 P11 **Longue-Pointe** Québec, E Canada
105 S4 **Longuyon** Meurthe-et-Moselle, NE France
27 W7 **Longview** Texas, SW USA
34 G10 **Longview** Washington, NW USA
67 H25 **Longwood** C Saint Helena
27 P7 **Longworth** Texas, SW USA
105 S3 **Longwy** Meurthe-et-Moselle, NE France
165 V11 **Longxi** Gansu, C China
178 J14 **Long Xuyên** *var.* Longxuyen. An Giang, S Vietnam
167 Q13 **Longyan** Fujian, SE China
94 O3 **Longyearbyen** ○ (Svalbard) Spitsbergen, W Svalbard
166 J15 **Longzhou** Guangxi Zhuangzu Zizhiqu, S China
102 F12 **Löningen** Niedersachsen, NW Germany
29 V11 **Lonoke** Arkansas, C USA
97 L21 **Lönsboda** Kristianstad, S Sweden
105 S9 **Lons-le-Saunier** *anc.* Ledo Salinarius. Jura, E France
33 O15 **Loogootee** Indiana, N USA
33 Q9 **Looking Glass River** ≈ Michigan, N USA
23 X11 **Lookout, Cape** *headland* North Carolina, SE USA
41 O6 **Lookout Ridge** *ridge* Alaska, USA
189 N11 **Loongana** Western Australia
101 I14 **Loon op Zand** Noord-Brabant, S Netherlands
xliv C11 **Loop Head** *Ir.* Ceann Léime. *headland* W Ireland
111 V4 **Loosdorf** Niederösterreich, NE Austria
xxxvii W10 **Loose** Kent, SE England, UK
164 G10 **Lop** Xinjiang Uygur Zizhiqu, NW China
114 J11 **Lopare** NE Bosnia and Herzegovina
Lopatichi *see* Lapatsichy
131 Q15 **Lopatin** Respublika Dagestan, SW Russian Federation
131 P7 **Lopatino** Penzenskaya Oblast', W Russian Federation
178 Hh10 **Lop Buri** *var.* Loburi. Lop Buri, C Thailand
27 R16 **Lopeno** Texas, SW USA
Lopevi *see* Ulveah
81 C18 **Lopez, Cap** *headland* W Gabon
100 I12 **Lopik** Utrecht, C Netherlands
Lop Nor *see* Lop Nur
164 M7 **Lop Nur** *var.* Lob Nor, Lop Nor, Lo-pu Po. *seasonal lake* NW China
Lopnur *see* Yuli
81 K17 **Lopori** ≈ NW Zaire
100 O5 **Loppersum** Groningen, NE Netherlands
94 I8 **Lopphavet** *sound* N Norway
Lo-pu Po *see* Lop Nur
Lora *see* Lowrah
190 F3 **Lora Creek** *seasonal river* South Australia
106 K13 **Lora del Río** Andalucía, S Spain
154 M11 **Lora, Hāmūn-i** *wetland* SW Pakistan
33 T11 **Lorain** Ohio, N USA
27 O7 **Loraine** Texas, SW USA
33 R13 **Loramie, Lake** ⊠ Ohio, N USA
107 Q13 **Lorca** *Ar.* Lurka; *anc.* Eliocroca, *Lat.* Illur co. Murcia, S Spain
199 I12 **Lord Howe Island** *island* E Australia
Lord Howe Island *see* Ontong Java Atoll
183 O10 **Lord Howe Rise** *undersea feature* SW Pacific Ocean
199 I12 **Lord Howe Seamounts** *undersea feature* W Pacific Ocean
39 P15 **Lordsburg** New Mexico, SW USA
194 K8 **Lorengau** *var.* Lorungau. Manus Island, N PNG
27 N5 **Lorenzo** Texas, SW USA
148 K7 **Lorestān** *off.* Ostān-e Lorestān, *var.* Luristan. ◆ *province* W Iran
59 M17 **Loreto** Beni, N Bolivia
108 J12 **Loreto** Marche, C Italy
42 F8 **Loreto** Baja California Sur, W Mexico
42 M11 **Loreto** Zacatecas, C Mexico
58 E9 **Loreto** *off.* Departamento de Loreto. ◆ *department* NE Peru
83 K18 **Lorian Swamp** *swamp* E Kenya
56 E6 **Lorica** Córdoba, NW Colombia
104 G7 **Lorient** *prev.* l'Orient. Morbihan, NW France
113 K22 **Lőrinci** Heves, NE Hungary
12 G11 **Loring** Ontario, S Canada
35 V6 **Loring** Montana, NW USA
105 R13 **Loriol-sur-Drôme** Drôme, E France
23 U12 **Loris** South Carolina, SE USA
59 I18 **Loriscota, Laguna** ◎ S Peru
191 N13 **Lorne** Victoria, SE Australia
xliii E18 **Lorn, Firth of** *inlet* W Scotland, UK
Loro Sae *see* Timor Timur
103 F24 **Lörrach** Baden-Württemberg, S Germany
105 T5 **Lorraine** ◆ *region* NE France
Lorungau *see* Lorengau
96 L11 **Los** Gävleborg, C Sweden
37 P14 **Los Alamos** California, W USA
39 S10 **Los Alamos** New Mexico, SW USA
44 F5 **Los Amates** Izabal, E Guatemala
37 S15 **Los Angeles** California, W USA
37 S15 **Los Angeles** ✕ California, W USA
65 G14 **Los Ángeles** Bío Bío, C Chile
37 T13 **Los Angeles Aqueduct** *aqueduct* California, W USA
Losanna *see* Lausanne
65 H20 **Los Antiguos** Santa Cruz, SW Argentina
201 Q16 **Losap Atoll** *atoll* C Micronesia
37 P10 **Los Banos** California, W USA
106 K16 **Los Barrios** Andalucía, S Spain
64 L5 **Los Blancos** Salta, N Argentina
44 L12 **Los Chiles** Alajuela, NW Costa Rica
107 O2 **Los Corrales de Buelna** Cantabria, N Spain
27 T17 **Los Fresnos** Texas, SW USA
37 N9 **Los Gatos** California, W USA
112 O11 **Łosice** Biała Podlaska, E Poland
114 B11 **Lošinj** *Ger.* Lussin, *It.* Lussino. *island* W Croatia
Los Jardines *see* Ngetik Atoll
65 G15 **Los Lagos** Los Lagos, C Chile
65 F17 **Los Lagos** *off.* Región de los Lagos. ◆ *region* C Chile
Loslau *see* Wodzisław Śląski
66 N11 **Los Llanos** *var.* Los Llanos de Aridane. La Palma, Islas Canarias, Spain, NE Atlantic Ocean
Los Llanos de Aridane *see* Los Llanos
39 R11 **Los Lunas** New Mexico, SW USA
65 I16 **Los Menucos** Río Negro, C Argentina
42 H8 **Los Mochis** Sinaloa, C Mexico
37 N4 **Los Molinos** California, W USA
106 M9 **Los Navalmorales** Castilla-La Mancha, C Spain
27 S15 **Los Olmos Creek** ≈ Texas, SW USA
Losonc/Losontz *see* Lučenec
178 Jj5 **Lô, Sông** *Chin.* Panlong Jiang. ≈ China/Vietnam
46 B5 **Los Palacios** Pinar del Río, W Cuba
106 K14 **Los Palacios y Villafranca** Andalucía, S Spain
175 Ss16 **Lospalos** Timor, S Indonesia
39 R12 **Los Pinos Mountains** ▲▲ New Mexico, SW USA
39 R11 **Los Ranchos De Albuquerque** New Mexico, SW USA
42 M14 **Los Reyes** Michoacán de Ocampo, SW Mexico
58 B7 **Los Ríos** ◆ *province* C Ecuador
66 O11 **Los Rodeos** ✕ (Santa Cruz de Ternerife) Tenerife, Islas Canarias, Spain, NE Atlantic Ocean
56 L4 **Los Roques, Islas** *island group* N Venezuela
45 S17 **Los Santos** Los Santos, S Panama
45 S17 **Los Santos** *off.* Provincia de Los Santos. ◆ *province* S Panama
Los Santos *see* Los Santos de Maimona
106 J12 **Los Santos de Maimona** *var.* Los Santos. Extremadura, W Spain
100 P10 **Losser** Overijssel, E Netherlands
xlii L11 **Lossiemouth** Moray, NE Scotland, UK
63 B14 **Los Tábanos** Santa Fe, C Argentina
56 J4 **Los Taques** Falcón, N Venezuela
12 G11 **Lost Channel** Ontario, S Canada
56 L5 **Los Teques** Miranda, N Venezuela
37 Q12 **Lost Hills** California, W USA
38 I7 **Lost Peak** ▲ Utah, W USA
35 P11 **Lost Trail Pass** *pass* Montana, NW USA
xxxvi D16 **Lostwithiel** Cornwall, SW England, UK
195 N15 **Losuia** Kiriwina Island, SE PNG
64 G10 **Los Vilos** Coquimbo, C Chile
107 N10 **Los Yébenes** Castilla-La Mancha, C Spain
105 N13 **Lot** ◆ *department* S France
105 N13 **Lot** ≈ S France
65 F14 **Lota** Bío Bío, C Chile
83 G15 **Lotagipi Swamp** *wetland* Kenya/Sudan
104 K14 **Lot-et-Garonne** ◆ *department* SW France
85 K21 **Lothair** Mpumalanga, NE South Africa
35 R7 **Lothair** Montana, NW USA
xlii K9 **Lothmore** Highland, N Scotland, UK
81 L20 **Loto** Kasai Oriental, C Zaire
198 B8 **Lotofagā** Upolu, SE Western Samoa
110 E10 **Lötschbergtunnel** *tunnel* Valais, SW Switzerland
27 T9 **Lott** Texas, SW USA
128 H3 **Lotta** *var.* Lutto. ≈ Finland/Russian Federation
192 Q7 **Lottin Point** *headland* North Island, NZ
Lötzen *see* Giżycko
Loualaba *see* Lualaba
178 I6 **Louangnamtha** *var.* Luong Nam Tha. Louang Namtha, N Laos
178 I7 **Louangphabang** *var.* Louangphrabang, Luang Prabang. Louangphabang, N Laos
Louangphrabang *see* Louangphabang
204 H5 **Loubet Coast** *physical region* Antarctica
Loubomo *see* Dolisie
Louch *see* Loukhi
104 H6 **Loudéac** Côtes d'Armor, NW France
166 M11 **Loudi** Hunan, S China
81 F21 **Loudima** La Bouenza, S Congo
22 M9 **Loudon** Tennessee, S USA
33 T12 **Loudonville** Ohio, N USA
104 L8 **Loudun** Vienne, W France
104 K7 **Loué** Sarthe, NW France
78 G10 **Louga** NW Senegal
xxxix N9 **Loughborough** Leicestershire, C England, UK
xliv L5 **Loughbrickland** Banbridge, SE Northern Ireland, UK
xliv F9 **Loughrea** *Ir.* Baile Locha Riach. Galway, W Ireland
105 S9 **Louhans** Saône-et-Loire, C France
23 P5 **Louisa** Kentucky, S USA
23 V5 **Louisa** Virginia, NE USA
23 V9 **Louisburg** North Carolina, SE USA
xliv C7 **Louisburgh** Mayo, NW Ireland
27 U12 **Louise** Texas, SW USA
13 P11 **Louiseville** Québec, SE Canada
195 Q17 **Louisiade Archipelago** *island group* SE PNG
29 W3 **Louisiana** Missouri, C USA
24 G8 **Louisiana** *off.* State of Louisiana; also known as Creole State, Pelican State. ◆ *state* S USA
194 K9 **Lou Island** *island* N PNG
85 K19 **Louis Trichardt** Northern, NE South Africa
25 V4 **Louisville** Georgia, SE USA
32 M15 **Louisville** Illinois, N USA
22 K5 **Louisville** Kentucky, S USA
24 M4 **Louisville** Mississippi, S USA
31 S15 **Louisville** Nebraska, C USA
199 Jj12 **Louisville Ridge** *undersea feature* S Pacific Ocean
128 J6 **Loukhi** *var.* Louch. Respublika Kareliya, NW Russian Federation
81 H19 **Loukoléla** Cuvette, E Congo
106 G14 **Loulé** Faro, S Portugal
113 C16 **Louny** *Ger.* Laun. Severní Čechy, NW Czech Republic
31 O15 **Loup City** Nebraska, C USA
31 P15 **Loup River** ≈ Nebraska, C USA
13 S9 **Loup, Rivière du** ≈ Québec, SE Canada
10 K7 **Loups Marins, Lacs des** *lakes* Québec, NE Canada
104 K16 **Lourdes** Hautes-Pyrénées, S France
Lourenço Marques *see* Maputo
106 F11 **Loures** Lisboa, C Portugal
106 F10 **Lourinhã** Lisboa, C Portugal
117 C16 **Loúros** ≈ W Greece
106 G8 **Lousã** Coimbra, N Portugal
166 M10 **Lou Shui** ≈ C China
xliv K7 **Louth** Louth, NE Ireland
xxxix S5 **Louth** Lincolnshire, E England, UK
xliv K7 **Louth** *Ir.* Lú. ◆ *county* NE Ireland
191 O5 **Louth** New South Wales, SE Australia
xliv K5 **Louthgall** Armagh, S Northern Ireland, UK
117 H15 **Loutrá** Kentrikí Makedonía, N Greece
117 G19 **Loutráki** Pelopónnisos, S Greece
Louvain *see* Leuven
101 H19 **Louvain-la Neuve** Walloon Brabant, C Belgium
12 J8 **Louvicourt** Québec, SE Canada
104 M4 **Louviers** Eure, N France
32 K14 **Lou Yaeger, Lake** ⊠ Illinois, N USA
95 J15 **Lövånger** Västerbotten, N Sweden
128 J14 **Lovat'** ≈ NW Russian Federation
115 J17 **Lovćen** ▲ S Yugoslavia
116 I8 **Lovech** Loveshka Oblast, NW Bulgaria
Lovech *see* Loveshka Oblast
27 V9 **Lovelady** Texas, SW USA
39 T3 **Loveland** Colorado, C USA
35 U12 **Lovell** Wyoming, C USA
Lovello, Monte *see* Grosser Löffler
37 S4 **Lovelock** Nevada, W USA
108 E7 **Lovere** Lombardia, N Italy
116 I8 **Loveshka Oblast** *var.* Lovech. ◆ *province* N Bulgaria
32 L10 **Loves Park** Illinois, N USA
28 M2 **Lovewell Reservoir** ⊠ Kansas, C USA
95 M19 **Loviisa** *Swe.* Lovisa. Uusimaa, S Finland
39 V15 **Loving** New Mexico, SW USA
23 U6 **Lovingston** Virginia, NE USA
39 V14 **Lovington** New Mexico, SW USA
Lovisa *see* Loviisa
113 C15 **Lovosice** *Ger.* Lobositz. Severní Čechy, NW Czech Republic
128 K4 **Lovozero** Murmanskaya Oblast', NW Russian Federation
128 K4 **Lovozero, Ozero** ◎ NW Russian Federation
114 B9 **Lovran** *It.* Laurana. Primorje-Gorski Kotar, NW Croatia
118 E11 **Lovrin** *Ger.* Lowrin. Timiș, W Romania
84 E10 **Lóvua** Lunda Norte, NE Angola
84 G12 **Lóvua** Moxico, E Angola

◆ Country
● Country Capital
◇ Dependent Territory
○ Dependent Territory Capital
◆ Administrative Region
✕ International Airport
▲ Mountain
▲▲ Mountain Range
Volcano
≈ River
◎ Lake
⊠ Reservoir

Low Bay – Maassluis

67 D25 Low Bay *bay* East Falkland, Falkland Islands
15 M6 Low, Cape *headland* Northwest Territories, E Canada
xxxix O7 Lowdham Nottinghamshire, C England, UK
35 N10 Lowell Idaho, NW USA
21 O10 Lowell Massachusetts, NE USA
Löwen *see* Leuven
Löwenberg in Schlesien *see* Lwówek Śląski
Lower Austria *see* Niederösterreich
Lower Bann *see* Bann
Lower California *see* Baja California
Lower Danube *see* Niederösterreich
xlii F11 Lower Diabaig Highland, NW Scotland, UK
xxxvii P7 Lower Heyford Oxfordshire, C England, UK
193 L14 Lower Hutt Wellington, North Island, NZ
41 N11 Lower Kalskag Alaska, USA
37 O1 Lower Klamath Lake ◎ California, W USA
37 Q2 Lower Lake ◎ California/Nevada, W USA
xliv I5 Lower Lough Erne ◎ SW Northern Ireland, UK
Lower Lusatia *see* Niederlausitz
Lower Normandy *see* Basse-Normandie, France
8 K9 Lower Post British Columbia, W Canada
31 T4 Lower Red Lake ◎ Minnesota, N USA
Lower Rhine *see* Neder Rijn
Lower Saxony *see* Niedersachsen
Lower Tunguska *see* Nizhnyaya Tunguska
xxxix Z10 Lowestoft Suffolk, E England, UK
xl K9 Loweswater Cumbria, NW England, UK
155 Q5 Lowgar *var.* Logar. ◐ *province* E Afghanistan
xli N10 Lowgill Cumbria, NW England, UK
xl M7 Low Hesket Cumbria, NW England, UK
190 H7 Low Hill South Australia
xli Q2 Lowick Northumberland, N England, UK
112 K12 Łowicz Skierniewice, C Poland
35 N13 Lowman Idaho, NW USA
155 P8 Lowrah *var.* Lora. ≈ SE Afghanistan
Lowrin *see* Lovrin
191 N17 Low Rocky Point *headland* Tasmania, SE Australia
20 I8 Lowville New York, NE USA
Loxa *see* Loksa
190 K9 Loxton South Australia
83 G21 Loya Tabora, C Tanzania
32 K6 Loyal Wisconsin, N USA
xlii I7 Loyal, Loch ◎ N Scotland, UK
20 G13 Loyalsock Creek ≈ Pennsylvania, NE USA
37 Q5 Loyalton California, W USA
Lo-yang *see* Luoyang
197 J6 Loyauté, Îles *island group* S New Caledonia
Loyev *see* Loyew
121 O20 Loyew *Rus.* Loyev. Homyel'skaya Voblasts', SE Belorussia
xliii G14 Loyne, Loch ◎ NW Scotland, UK
129 S13 Loyno Kirovskaya Oblast', NW Russian Federation
105 P13 Lozère ◐ *department* S France
105 Q14 Lozère, Mont ▲ S France
114 J11 Loznica Serbia, W Yugoslavia
119 V7 Lozova *Rus.* Lozovaya. Kharkivs'ka Oblast', E Ukraine
Lozovaya *see* Lozova
107 N7 Lozoyuela Madrid, C Spain
Lœvvajok *see* Levajok
Lu *see* Shandong, China
Lú *see* Louth
84 F12 Luacano Moxico, E Angola
81 N21 Lualaba *Fr.* Loualaba. ≈ SE Zaire
85 H14 Luampa Western, NW Zambia
85 I15 Luampa Kuta Western, W Zambia
167 P8 Lu'an Anhui, E China
106 K2 Luanco Asturias, N Spain
84 A11 Luanda *var.* Loanda, *Port.* São Paulo de Loanda. ● (Angola) Luanda, NW Angola
84 A11 Luanda ◐ *province* NW Angola
84 A11 Luanda ✈ Luanda, NW Angola
84 D12 Luando ≈ C Angola
Luang *see* Tapi, Mae Nam
85 G14 Luanginga *var.* Luanguinga. ≈ Angola/Zambia
178 Gg15 Luang, Khao ▲ SW Thailand
Luang Prabang *see* Louangphabang
178 I8 Luang Prabang Range *Th.* Thiukhaoluang Phrahang. ⛰ Laos/Thailand
178 H16 Luang, Thale *lagoon* S Thailand
Luangua, Rio *see* Luangwa
84 E11 Luangue ≈ NE Angola
Luanguinga *see* Luanginga
85 K15 Luangwa *var.* Aruângua. Lusaka, C Zambia
85 K14 Luangwa *var.* Aruângua, Rio Luangua. ≈ Mozambique/Zambia
167 Q2 Luan He ≈ E China
202 G11 Luaniva, Île *island* E Wallis and Futuna
167 P2 Luanping *var.* Anjiangying. Hebei, E China
84 J13 Luanshya Copperbelt, C Zambia
64 K13 Luan Toro La Pampa, C Argentina
167 Q2 Luanxian *var.* Luan Xian. Hebei, E China
84 J12 Luapula ◐ *province* N Zambia
85 O25 Luapula ≈ Zaire/Zambia
106 J2 Luarca Asturias, N Spain
174 Ll7 Luar, Danau ◎ Borneo, N Indonesia
81 L25 Luashi Shaba, S Zaire
84 G12 Luau *Port.* Vila Teixeira de Sousa. Moxico, NE Angola
81 C16 Luba *prev.* San Carlos. Isla de Bioco, NW Equatorial Guinea
44 F4 Lubaantun *ruins* Toledo, S Belize
113 P16 Lubaczów *var.* Lúbaczów. Przemyśl, SE Poland
Lubale *see* Lubalo
84 E11 Lubalo Lunda Norte, NE Angola
84 E11 Lubalo *var.* Lubale. ≈ Angola/Zaire
120 J9 Lubāna Madona, E Latvia
Lubānas Ezers *see* Lubāns
179 P11 Lubang Island *island* N Philippines
85 B15 Lubango *Port.* Sá da Bandeira. Huíla, SW Angola
120 J9 Lubāns *var.* Lubānas Ezers. ◎ E Latvia
81 M21 Lubao Kasai Oriental, C Zaire
112 O13 Lubartów *Ger.* Qumälisch. Lublin, E Poland
102 G13 Lübbecke Nordrhein-Westfalen, NW Germany
102 O13 Lübben Brandenburg, E Germany
103 P14 Lübbenau Brandenburg, E Germany
27 N5 Lubbock Texas, SW USA
xlii H9 Lubcroy Highland, NW Scotland, UK
Lubcz *see* Lyubcha
21 U6 Lubec Maine, NE USA
102 K9 Lübeck Schleswig-Holstein, N Germany
102 K8 Lübecker Bucht *bay* N Germany
81 M21 Lubefu Kasai Oriental, C Zaire
113 O14 Lubelska, Wyżyna *plateau* SE Poland
Lubelskie, Województwo *see* Lublin
Lüben *see* Lubin
150 H9 Lubenka Zapadnyy Kazakhstan, W Kazakhstan
81 P18 Lubero Nord Kivu, E Zaire
81 L22 Lubi ≈ S Zaire
Lubiana *see* Ljubljana
112 J11 Lubień Kujawski Włocławek, C Poland
69 T11 Lubilandji ≈ S Zaire
112 F13 Lubin *Ger.* Lüben. Legnica, W Poland
113 O14 Lublin *Rus.* Lyublin. Lublin, E Poland
112 O13 Lublin *off.* Województwo Lubelskie, *Rus.* Lyublin. ◐ *province* E Poland
113 J15 Lubliniec Częstochowa, S Poland
xliii J18 Lubnaig, Loch ◎ C Scotland, UK
Lubnān, Jabal *see* Liban, Jebel
119 R5 Lubny Poltavs'ka Oblast', NE Ukraine
Luboml' *see* Lyuboml'
112 G11 Luboń *Ger.* Peterhof. Poznań, W Poland
112 D12 Lubsko *Ger.* Sommerfeld. Zielona Góra, W Poland
81 N24 Lubudi Shaba, SE Zaire
174 Hh11 Lubuklinggau Sumatera, W Indonesia
81 N25 Lubumbashi *prev.* Élisabethville. Shaba, SE Zaire
85 I14 Lubungu Central, C Zambia
81 N18 Lubutu Maniema, E Zaire
Luca *see* Lucca
84 C11 Lucala ≈ W Angola
xliv K9 Lucan *Ir.* Leamhcán. Dublin, E Ireland
12 E16 Lucan Ontario, S Canada
Lucanian Mountains *see* Lucano, Appennino
109 M18 Lucano, Appennino *Eng.* Lucanian Mountains. ⛰ S Italy
84 F11 Lucapa *var.* Lukapa. Lunda Norte, NE Angola
31 V15 Lucas Iowa, C USA
63 C18 Lucas González Entre Ríos, E Argentina
67 C25 Lucas Point *headland* West Falkland, Falkland Islands
33 S15 Lucasville Ohio, N USA
108 F11 Lucca *anc.* Luca. Toscana, C Italy
xxxvi H11 Luccombe Somerset, SW England, UK
46 H12 Lucea W Jamaica
xliii H26 Luce Bay *inlet* SW Scotland, UK
24 M8 Lucedale Mississippi, S USA
179 Pp11 Lucena *off.* Lucena City. Luzon, N Philippines
106 M14 Lucena Andalucía, S Spain
107 S8 Lucena del Cid País Valenciano, E Spain
113 D15 Lučenec *Ger.* Losontz, *Hung.* Losonc. Stredné Slovensko, S Slovakia
Lucentum *see* Alicante
109 M16 Lucera Puglia, SE Italy
Lucerna/Lucerne *see* Luzern
Lucerne, Lake of *see* Vierwaldstätter See
42 J4 Lucero Chihuahua, N Mexico
127 Nn17 Luchegorsk Primorskiy Kray, SE Russian Federation
107 Q13 Luchena ≈ SE Spain
84 N13 Lucheringo *var.* Luchulingo. ≈ N Mozambique
Luchesa *see* Luchosa
Luchin *see* Luchyn
120 N13 Luchosa *Rus.* Luchesa. ≈ N Belorussia
Luchow *see* Hefei
102 K11 Lüchow Mecklenburg-Vorpommern, N Germany
Luchulingo *see* Lucheringo
121 N17 Luchyn *Rus.* Luchin. Homyel'skaya Voblasts', SE Belorussia
57 U11 Lucie Rivier ≈ W Surinam
190 K11 Lucindale South Australia
175 T13 Lucipara, Kepulauan *island group* E Indonesia
85 A14 Lucira Namibe, SW Angola
Łuck *see* Luts'k
103 O14 Luckau Brandenburg, E Germany
102 N13 Luckenwalde Brandenburg, E Germany
12 E15 Lucknow Ontario, S Canada
158 L12 Lucknow *var.* Lakhnau. Uttar Pradesh, N India
104 J10 Luçon Vendée, NW France
46 I7 Lucrecia, Cabo *headland* E Cuba
84 F13 Lucusse Moxico, E Angola
Lüda *see* Dalian
116 M9 Luda Kamchiya ≈ E Bulgaria
Ludasch *see* Luduş
116 I10 Luda Yana ≈ C Bulgaria
xxxix R4 Ludborough Lincolnshire, E England, UK
114 F7 Ludbreg Varaždin, N Croatia
31 P7 Ludden North Dakota, N USA
103 F15 Lüdenscheid Nordrhein-Westfalen, W Germany
85 C21 Lüderitz *prev.* Angra Pequena. Karas, SW Namibia
xxxix R4 Ludford Lincolnshire, E England, UK
xxxvii O11 Ludgershall Wiltshire, S England, UK
xxxvi A17 Ludgvan Cornwall, SW England, UK
xxxix Y9 Ludham Norfolk, E England, UK
158 H8 Ludhiāna Punjab, N India
33 O7 Ludington Michigan, N USA
xxxviii H11 Ludlow Shropshire, W England, UK
37 W14 Ludlow California, W USA
30 J7 Ludlow South Dakota, N USA
20 M9 Ludlow Vermont, NE USA
116 L7 Ludogorie *physical region* NE Bulgaria
25 W6 Ludowici Georgia, SE USA
Ludsan *see* Ludza
118 I10 Luduş *Ger.* Ludasch, *Hung.* Marosludas. Mureş, C Romania
97 M14 Ludvika Kopparberg, C Sweden
103 H21 Ludwigsburg Baden-Württemberg, SW Germany
102 O13 Ludwigsfelde Brandenburg, NE Germany
103 G20 Ludwigshafen *var.* Ludwigshafen am Rhein. Rheinland-Pfalz, W Germany
Ludwigshafen am Rhein *see* Ludwigshafen
103 L20 Ludwigskanal *canal* SE Germany
102 L10 Ludwigslust Mecklenburg-Vorpommern, N Germany
120 K10 Ludza *Ger.* Ludsan. Ludza, E Latvia
81 K21 Luebo Kasai Occidental, SW Zaire
27 Q6 Lueders Texas, SW USA
81 N20 Lueki Maniema, C Zaire
84 F10 Luembe *var.* Lubembe. ≈ Angola/Zaire
84 E13 Luena *var.* Lwena, *Port.* Luso. Moxico, E Angola
81 M24 Luena Shaba, SE Zaire
85 K12 Luena Northern, NE Zambia
84 F13 Luena ≈ E Angola
85 F16 Luengue ≈ SE Angola
69 V13 Luenha ≈ W Mozambique
85 G15 Lueti ≈ Angola/Zambia
166 J7 Lüeyang Shaanxi, C China
167 P14 Lufeng Guangdong, S China
81 N24 Lufira ≈ SE Zaire
81 N25 Lufira, Lac de Retenue de la *var.* Lac Tshangalele. ◎ SE Zaire
27 W8 Lufkin Texas, SW USA
84 L11 Lufubu ≈ N Zambia
128 G14 Luga Leningradskaya Oblast', NW Russian Federation
128 G13 Luga ≈ NW Russian Federation
Luganer See *see* Lugano, Lago di
110 H11 Lugano *Ger.* Lauis. Ticino, S Switzerland
110 H12 Lugano, Lago di *var.* Ceresio, *Ger.* Luganer See. ◎ S Switzerland
Lugansk *see* Luhans'k
197 B12 Luganville Espiritu Santo, C Vanuatu
Lugdunum *see* Lyon
Lugdunum Batavorum *see* Leiden
85 O15 Lugela Zambézia, NE Mozambique
85 O16 Lugela ≈ C Mozambique
84 P13 Lugenda, Rio ≈ N Mozambique
Luggarus *see* Locarno
Lugh Ganana *see* Luuq
xliv K10 Lugnaquillia Mountain *Ir.* Log na Coille. ▲ E Ireland
108 H10 Lugo Emilia-Romagna, N Italy
106 I3 Lugo *anc.* Lugus Augusti. Galicia, NW Spain
106 I3 Lugo ◐ *province* Galicia, NW Spain
23 R12 Lugoff South Carolina, SE USA
118 F12 Lugoj *Ger.* Lugosch, *Hung.* Lugos. Timiş, W Romania
Lugos/Lugosch *see* Lugoj
151 S16 Lugovoy *var.* Lugovoye. Zhambyl, S Kazakhstan
Lugovoye *see* Lugovoy
164 I13 Lugu Xizang Zizhiqu, W China
Lugus Augusti *see* Lugo
Luguvallium/Luguvallum *see* Carlisle
119 Y7 Luhans'k *Rus.* Lugansk; *prev.* Voroshilovgrad. Luhans'ka Oblast', E Ukraine
119 Y7 Luhans'k ✈ Luhans'ka Oblast', E Ukraine
119 X6 Luhans'ka Oblast' *var.* Luhans'k; *prev.* Voroshilovgrad, *Rus.* Voroshilovgradskaya Oblast'. ◐ *province* E Ukraine
167 Q7 Luhe Jiangsu, E China
175 T11 Luhu Pulau Seram, E Indonesia
166 G8 Luhuo *var.* Zhaggo. Sichuan, C China
118 M3 Luhyny Zhytomyrs'ka Oblast', N Ukraine
85 G15 Lui ≈ W Zambia
85 G16 Luiana ≈ SE Angola
85 L15 Luia, Rio *var.* Ruya. ≈ Mozambique/Zimbabwe
xlii H11 Luichart, Loch ◎ NW Scotland, UK
Luichow Peninsula *see* Leizhou Bandao
Luik *see* Liège
84 C13 Luimbale Huambo, C Angola
Luimneach *see* Limerick
xliii F18 Luing *island* W Scotland, UK
108 D6 Luino Lombardia, N Italy
84 E13 Luio ≈ E Angola
94 L11 Luiro ≈ NE Finland
81 N25 Luishia Shaba, SE Zaire
61 M19 Luislândia do Oeste Minas Gerais, SE Brazil
42 K5 Luis L.León, Presa ⊟ N Mexico
Luis Muñoz Marín *see* Carolina
205 N5 Luitpold Coast *physical region* Antarctica
81 K22 Luiza Kasai Occidental, S Zaire
63 D20 Luján Buenos Aires, E Argentina
81 N24 Lukafu Shaba, SE Zaire
Lukapa *see* Lucapa
114 I11 Lukavac NE Bosnia and Herzegovina
81 I20 Lukenie ≈ C Zaire
xliv I12 Lukeswell Kilkenny, SE Ireland
81 H19 Lukolela Equateur, W Zaire
121 M14 Lukoml'skaye, Vozyera *Rus.* Ozero Lukoml'skoye. ◎ N Belorussia
Lukoml'skoye, Ozero *see* Lukoml'skaye, Vozyera
116 I8 Lukovit Loveshka Oblast, NW Bulgaria
112 O12 Łuków *Ger.* Bogendorf. Siedlce, E Poland
131 O4 Lukoyanov Nizhegorodskaya Oblast', W Russian Federation
81 N22 Lukuga ≈ SE Zaire
81 F21 Lukula Bas-Zaïre, SW Zaire
85 G14 Lukulu Western, NW Zambia
201 R17 Lukunor Atoll *atoll* Mortlock Islands, C Micronesia
84 J12 Lukwesa Luapula, NE Zambia
95 K14 Luleå Norrbotten, N Sweden
94 J13 Luleälven ≈ N Sweden
142 C10 Lüleburgaz Kırklareli, NW Turkey
166 M4 Lüliang Shan ⛰ C China
81 O21 Lulimba Maniema, E Zaire
24 K9 Luling Louisiana, S USA
27 T11 Luling Texas, SW USA
xliv J9 Lullymore Kildare, E Ireland
81 I18 Lulonga ≈ NW Zaire
81 K22 Lulua ≈ S Zaire
Luluabourg *see* Kananga
198 D18 Luma Ta'ū, E American Samoa
174 M16 Lumajang Jawa, C Indonesia
164 G12 Lumajangdong Co ◎ W China
84 G13 Lumbala Kaquengue Moxico, E Angola
85 F14 Lumbala N'Guimbo *var.* Nguimbo, *Port.* Gago Coutinho, Vila Gago Coutinho. Moxico, E Angola
23 T11 Lumber River ≈ North Carolina/South Carolina, SE USA
Lumber State *see* Maine
24 L8 Lumberton Mississippi, S USA
23 U11 Lumberton North Carolina, SE USA
107 R4 Lumbier Navarra, N Spain
85 Q15 Lumbo Nampula, NE Mozambique
128 M4 Lumbovka Murmanskaya Oblast', NW Russian Federation
106 J7 Lumbrales Castilla-León, N Spain
159 W13 Lumding Assam, NE India
84 F12 Lumege *var.* Lumeje. Moxico, E Angola
Lumeje *see* Lumege
194 F10 Lumi Sandaun, NW PNG
101 J17 Lummen Limburg, NE Belgium
95 J20 Lumparland Åland, SW Finland
xliii N14 Lumphanan Aberdeenshire, NE Scotland, UK
178 K12 Lumphăt *prev.* Lomphat. Rôtânôkiri, NE Cambodia
xliii N13 Lumsden Aberdeenshire, NE Scotland, UK
9 U16 Lumsden Saskatchewan, S Canada
193 C23 Lumsden Southland, South Island, NZ
174 J11 Lumut, Tanjung *headland* Sumatera, W Indonesia
163 P4 Lün Töv, C Mongolia
166 H13 Lunan *var.* Lunan Yizu Zizhixian. Yunnan, SW China
xliii O16 Lunan Bay *bay* E Scotland, UK
Lunan Yizu Zizhixian *see* Lunan
118 I13 Lunca Corbului Argeş, S Romania
xli V13 Lund East Riding of Yorkshire, N England, UK
97 K23 Lund Malmöhus, S Sweden
37 X6 Lund Nevada, W USA
84 D11 Lunda Norte ◐ *province* NE Angola
84 E12 Lunda Sul ◐ *province* NE Angola
84 M13 Lundazi Eastern, NE Zambia
97 G16 Lunde Telemark, S Norway
Lundenburg *see* Břeclav
97 C17 Lundevatnet ◎ S Norway
Lundi *see* Runde
xxxvi D11 Lundy *island* SW England, UK
xli N10 Lune ≈ NW England, UK
102 J10 Lüneburg Niedersachsen, N Germany
102 J11 Lüneburger Heide *heathland* NW Germany
105 Q15 Lunel Hérault, S France
103 F14 Lünen Nordrhein-Westfalen, W Germany
11 P16 Lunenburg Nova Scotia, SE Canada
23 V7 Lunenburg Virginia, NE USA
105 T5 Lunéville Meurthe-et-Moselle, NE France
85 I14 Lunga ≈ C Zambia
Lunga, Isola *see* Dugi Otok
164 H12 Lungdo Xizang Zizhiqu, W China
164 I14 Lunggar Xizang Zizhiqu, W China
78 I15 Lungi ✈ (Freetown) W Sierra Leone
Lungkiang *see* Qiqihar
Lungleh *see* Lunglei
159 W15 Lunglei *prev.* Lungleh. Mizoram, NE India
164 L15 Lungsang Xizang Zizhiqu, W China
84 E13 Lungué-Bungo *var.* Lungwebungu. ≈ Angola/Zambia *see also* Lungwebungu
85 G14 Lungwebungu *var.* Lungué-Bungo. ≈ Angola/Zambia *see also* Lungué-Bungo
158 F12 Lūni Rājasthān, N India
158 F12 Lūni ≈ N India
Luninets *see* Luninyets
37 S7 Luning Nevada, W USA
Łuniniec *see* Luninyets
131 P6 Lunino Penzenskaya Oblast', W Russian Federation
121 J19 Luninyets *Pol.* Łuniniec, *Rus.* Luninets. Brestskaya Voblasts', SW Belorussia
158 F10 Lūnkaransar Rājasthān, NW India
xlii I3 Lunna Shetland Islands, NE Scotland, UK
121 G17 Lunna *Pol.* Łunna, *Rus.* Lunna. Hrodzyenskaya Voblasts', W Belorussia
78 I15 Lunsar W Sierra Leone
85 K14 Lunsemfwa ≈ C Zambia
164 I6 Luntai *var.* Bügür. Xinjiang Uygur Zizhiqu, NW China
100 K11 Lunteren Gelderland, C Netherlands
175 O16 Lunyuk Sumbawa, S Indonesia
111 U5 Lunz am See Niederösterreich, C Austria
169 Y7 Luobei *var.* Fengxiang. Heilongjiang, NE China
166 J13 Luodian *var.* Longping. Guizhou, S China
166 M15 Luoding Guangdong, S China
166 M6 Luo He ≈ C China
166 L5 Luo He ≈ C China
167 N7 Luohe Henan, C China
Luolajarvi *see* Kuoloyarvi
Luong Nam Tha *see* Louangnamtha
166 L13 Luoqing Jiang ≈ S China
167 O8 Luoshan Henan, C China
167 O12 Luoxiao Shan ⛰ S China
167 N6 Luoyang *var.* Honan, Lo-yang. Henan, C China
167 R12 Luoyuan Fujian, SE China
81 F21 Luozi Bas-Zaïre, W Zaire
85 J17 Lupane Matabeleland North, W Zimbabwe
166 I12 Lupanshui *prev.* Shuicheng. Guizhou, S China
174 Ll7 Lupar, Batang ≈ East Malaysia
Lupatia *see* Altamura
118 G12 Lupeni *Hung.* Lupény. Hunedoara, SW Romania
Lupény *see* Lupeni
84 N13 Lupiliche Niassa, N Mozambique
85 E14 Lupire Cuando Cubango, E Angola
179 Rr16 Lupon Mindanao, S Philippines
81 L22 Luputa Kasai Oriental, S Zaire
123 Jj17 Luqa ✈ (Valletta) S Malta
165 U11 Luqu Gansu, C China
47 U5 Luquillo, Sierra de ⛰ E Puerto Rico
28 L4 Luray Kansas, C USA
23 U4 Luray Virginia, NE USA
105 T7 Lure Haute-Saône, E France
84 D11 Luremo Lunda Norte, NE Angola
xliv L5 Lurgan *Ir.* An Lorgain. Craigavon, S Northern Ireland, UK
xxxvii S12 Lurgashall West Sussex, SE England, UK
59 K18 Luribay La Paz, W Bolivia
85 Q14 Lúrio Nampula, NE Mozambique
85 P14 Lúrio, Rio ≈ NE Mozambique
Luristan *see* Lorestān
Lurka *see* Lorca
85 J15 Lusaka ● (Zambia) Lusaka, SE Zambia
85 J15 Lusaka ◐ *province* C Zambia
85 J15 Lusaka ✈ Lusaka, C Zambia
81 L21 Lusambo Kasai Oriental, C Zaire
195 N14 Lusancay Islands and Reefs *island group* SE PNG
81 I21 Lusanga Bandundu, SW Zaire
81 N21 Lusangi Maniema, E Zaire
Lusatian Mountains *see* Lausitzer Bergland
Lushnja *see* Lushnjë
115 K21 Lushnjë *var.* Lushnja. Fier, C Albania
83 J21 Lushoto Tanga, E Tanzania
104 L10 Lusignan Vienne, W France
xliv L8 Lusk Dublin, E Ireland
35 Z15 Lusk Wyoming, C USA
xlii C10 Luskentyre Western Isles, NW Scotland, UK
Luso *see* Luena
xliii I19 Luss Argyll and Bute, W Scotland, UK
104 L10 Lussac-les-Châteaux Vienne, W France
Lussin/Lussino *see* Lošinj
Lussinpiccolo *see* Mali Lošinj
xlii D12 Lusta Highland, NW Scotland, UK
110 I7 Lustenau Vorarlberg, W Austria
xxxvi H14 Lustleigh Devon, SW England, UK
167 T14 Lü Tao *var.* Huoshao Dao, Lütao, *Eng.* Green Island. *island* SE Taiwan
Lūt, Baḩrat/Lut, Bahret *see* Dead Sea
24 K9 Lutcher Louisiana, S USA
149 T9 Lūt, Dasht-e *var.* Kavīr-e Lūt. *desert* E Iran
85 F14 Lutembo Moxico, E Angola
Lutetia/Lutetia Parisiorum *see* Paris
Luteva *see* Lodève
12 G15 Luther Lake ◎ Ontario, S Canada
195 U13 Luti Choiseul Island, NW Solomon Islands
Lūt, Kavīr-e *see* Lūt, Dasht-e
xxxvii T7 Luton Luton, E England, UK
xxxvii S7 Luton ◐ *unitary authority* C England, UK
xxxvii T7 Luton ✈ (London) Luton, SE England, UK
110 B10 Lutry Vaud, SW Switzerland
15 Ii8 Łutselk'e *prev.* Snowdrift. Northwest Territories, W Canada
31 Y4 Lutsen Minnesota, N USA
118 J4 Luts'k *Pol.* Łuck, *Rus.* Lutsk. Volyns'ka Oblast', NW Ukraine
Luttenberg *see* Ljutomer
xxxix N11 Lutterworth Leicestershire, C England, UK
Lüttich *see* Liège
85 G25 Luttig Western Cape, SW South Africa
Lutto *see* Lotta
xxxix S8 Lutton Lincolnshire, E England, UK
xxxix R10 Lutton Northamptonshire, C England, UK
84 E13 Lutuai Moxico, E Angola
119 Y7 Lutuhyne Luhans'ka Oblast', E Ukraine
176 Ww13 Lutur, Pulau *island* Kepulauan Aru, E Indonesia
25 V12 Lutz Florida, SE USA
Lutzow-Holm Bay *see* Lützow Holmbukta
205 V2 Lützow Holmbukta *var.* Lutzow-Holm Bay. *bay* Antarctica
83 L16 Luuq *It.* Lugh Ganana. Gedo, SW Somalia
94 M12 Luusua Lappi, NE Finland
25 Q6 Luverne Alabama, S USA
31 S11 Luverne Minnesota, N USA
81 O22 Luvua ≈ SE Zaire
84 F13 Luvuei Moxico, E Angola
83 H24 Luwego ≈ S Tanzania
84 K12 Luwingu Northern, NE Zambia
175 Qq9 Luwuk *prev.* Loewoek. Sulawesi, C Indonesia
25 N3 Luxapallila Creek ≈ Alabama/Mississippi, S USA
xxxvi H11 Luxborough Somerset, SW England, UK
101 M25 Luxembourg ● (Luxembourg) Luxembourg, S Luxembourg
101 M25 Luxembourg *off.* Grand Duchy of Luxembourg, *var.* Lëtzebuerg, Luxemburg. ◆ *monarchy* NW Europe
101 J23 Luxembourg ◐ *province* SE Belgium
101 L24 Luxembourg ◐ *district* S Luxembourg
33 N6 Luxemburg Wisconsin, N USA
Luxemburg *see* Luxembourg
105 U7 Luxeuil-les-Bains Haute-Saône, E France
166 E13 Luxi *prev.* Mangshi. Yunnan, SW China
84 E10 Luxico ≈ Angola/Zaire
77 X10 Luxor *Ar.* Al Uqşur. E Egypt
77 X10 Luxor ✈ C Egypt
166 M4 Luya Shan ⛰ C China
104 J15 Luy de Béarn ≈ SW France
104 J15 Luy de France ≈ SW France
129 P12 Luza Kirovskaya Oblast', NW Russian Federation
129 Q12 Luza ≈ NW Russian Federation
106 I16 Luz, Costa de la *coastal region* SW Spain
113 K20 Luže *var.* Lausche. ▲ Czech Republic/Germany *see also* Lausche
110 F8 Luzern *Fr.* Lucerne, *It.* Lucerna. Lucerne, C Switzerland
110 E8 Luzern *Fr.* Lucerne. ◐ *canton* C Switzerland
166 L13 Luzhai Guangxi Zhuangzu Zizhiqu, S China
120 K12 Luzhki *Rus.* Luzhki. Vitsyebskaya Voblasts', N Belorussia
166 I10 Luzhou Sichuan, C China
Lužická Nisa *see* Neisse
Lužické Hory *see* Lausitzer Bergland
Lužnice *see* Lainsitz
179 Pp9 Luzon *island* N Philippines
179 Oo6 Luzon Strait *strait* Philippines/Taiwan
118 I5 L'viv *Ger.* Lemberg, *Pol.* Lwów, *Rus.* L'vov. L'vivs'ka Oblast', W Ukraine
L'viv *see* L'vivs'ka Oblast'
118 I4 L'vivs'ka Oblast' *var.* L'viv, *Rus.* L'vovskaya Oblast'. ◐ *province* NW Ukraine
L'vov *see* L'viv
L'vovskaya Oblast' *see* L'vivs'ka Oblast'
Lwena *see* Luena
Lwów *see* L'viv
112 F11 Lwówek *Ger.* Neustadt bei Pinne. Poznań, W Poland
113 E14 Lwówek Śląski *Ger.* Löwenberg in Schlesien. Jelenia Góra, SW Poland
121 I18 Lyakhavichy *Rus.* Lyakhovichi. Brestskaya Voblasts', SW Belorussia
Lyakhovichi *see* Lyakhavichy
193 B22 Lyall, Mount ▲ South Island, NZ
Lyallpur *see* Faisalābād
125 G10 Lyamin ≈ C Russian Federation
Lyangar *see* Langar
125 G10 Lyantor Khanty-Mansiyskiy Avtonomnyy Okrug, C Russian Federation
128 H11 Lyaskelya Respublika Kareliya, NW Russian Federation
121 I18 Lyasnaya *Rus.* Lesnaya. Brestskaya Voblasts', SW Belorussia
121 F19 Lyasnaya *Pol.* Leśna, *Rus.* Lesnaya. ≈ SW Belorussia
xlii I8 Lybster Highland, N Scotland, UK
128 H15 Lychkovo Novgorodskaya Oblast', W Russian Federation
Lyck *see* Ełk
95 I15 Lycksele Västerbotten, N Sweden
20 G13 Lycoming Creek ≈ Pennsylvania, NE USA
Lycopolis *see* Asyūt
xxxvii X12 Lydd Kent, SE England, UK
205 N3 Lyddan Island *island* Antarctica
85 K20 Lydenburg Mpumalanga, NE South Africa
xxxvi F14 Lydford Devon, SW England, UK
xxxviii G11 Lydham Shropshire, W England, UK
xxxvi L8 Lydney Gloucestershire, C England, UK
121 L20 Lyel'chytsy *Rus.* Lel'chitsy. Homyel'skaya Voblasts', SE Belorussia
121 P14 Lyenina *Rus.* Lenino. Mahilyowskaya Voblasts', E Belorussia
120 L13 Lyepyel' *Rus.* Lepel'. Vitsyebskaya Voblasts', N Belorussia
27 S17 Lyford Texas, SW USA
97 E17 Lygna ≈ S Norway
20 G14 Lykens Pennsylvania, NE USA
117 E21 Lykódimo ▲ S Greece
xxxvi J15 Lyme Bay *bay* S England, UK
xxxvi K14 Lyme Regis Dorset, S England, UK
xxxvii Y11 Lyminge Kent, SE England, UK
xxxvii P14 Lymington Hampshire, S England, UK
xl E16 Lymm Cheshire, W England, UK
xxxvii Y11 Lympne Kent, SE England, UK
112 L7 Łyna *Ger.* Alle. ≈ N Poland
31 P12 Lynch Nebraska, C USA
22 I10 Lynchburg Tennessee, S USA
23 T6 Lynchburg Virginia, NE USA
23 T12 Lynches River ≈ South Carolina, SE USA
34 H6 Lynden Washington, NW USA
xxxvii O13 Lyndhurst Hampshire, S England, UK
190 I5 Lyndhurst South Australia
29 Q5 Lyndon Kansas, C USA
21 N7 Lyndonville Vermont, NE USA
xxxvii N9 Lyneham Wiltshire, S England, UK
xlii M5 Lyness Orkney Islands, N Scotland, UK
xxxix W9 Lyng Norfolk, E England, UK
97 D18 Lyngdal Vest-Agder, S Norway
94 I9 Lyngen *inlet* Arctic Ocean
97 G17 Lyngør Aust-Agder, S Norway
94 I9 Lyngseidet Troms, N Norway
xxxvi E15 Lynher ≈ SW England, UK
xxxvi G11 Lynmouth Devon, SW England, UK
Lynn/Lynn Regis *see* King's Lynn
21 P11 Lynn Massachusetts, NE USA
25 R9 Lynn Haven Florida, SE USA
9 V11 Lynn Lake Manitoba, C Canada
xxxvi G11 Lynton Devon, SW England, UK
120 I13 Lyntupy *Rus.* Lyntupy. Vitsyebskaya Voblasts', NW Belorussia
105 R11 Lyon *Eng.* Lyons; *anc.* Lugdunum. Rhône, E France
15 H3 Lyon, Cape *headland* Northwest Territories, NW Canada
xliii I17 Lyon, Loch ◎ C Scotland, UK
20 K6 Lyon Mountain ▲ New York, NE USA
105 Q11 Lyonnais, Monts du ⛰ C France
67 N25 Lyon Point *headland* SE Tristan da Cunha
190 E5 Lyons South Australia
39 T3 Lyons Colorado, C USA
25 V6 Lyons Georgia, SE USA
28 M5 Lyons Kansas, C USA
31 R14 Lyons Nebraska, C USA
20 G10 Lyons New York, NE USA
Lyons *see* Lyon
120 O13 Lyozna *Rus.* Liozno. Vitsyebskaya Voblasts', NE Belorussia
119 S4 Lypova Dolyna Sums'ka Oblast', NE Ukraine
119 N6 Lypovets' *Rus.* Lipovets. Vinnyts'ka Oblast', C Ukraine
Lys *see* Leie
113 I18 Lysá Hora ▲ E Czech Republic
97 D16 Lysefjorden *fjord* S Norway
97 I18 Lysekil Göteborg och Bohus, S Sweden
Lýsi *see* Akdoğan
35 V14 Lysite Wyoming, C USA
131 P3 Lyskovo Nizhegorodskaya Oblast', W Russian Federation
110 D8 Lyss Bern, W Switzerland
97 H22 Lystrup Århus, C Denmark
129 V14 Lys'va Permskaya Oblast', NW Russian Federation
119 P6 Lysyanka Cherkas'ka Oblast', C Ukraine
119 X6 Lysychans'k *Rus.* Lisichansk. Luhans'ka Oblast', E Ukraine
xl M14 Lytham St Anne's Lancashire, NW England, UK
xli V9 Lythe North Yorkshire, N England, UK
xlii M5 Lythes Orkney Islands, N Scotland, UK
193 I19 Lyttelton Canterbury, South Island, NZ
8 M17 Lytton British Columbia, SW Canada
121 L18 Lyuban' *Rus.* Lyuban'. Minskaya Voblasts', S Belorussia
121 L18 Lyubanskaye Vodaskhovishcha ⊟ C Belorussia
118 M5 Lyubar Zhytomyrs'ka Oblast', N Ukraine
Lyubashëvka *see* Lyubashivka
119 O8 Lyubashivka *Rus.* Lyubashëvka. Odes'ka Oblast', SW Ukraine
121 I16 Lyubcha *Pol.* Lubcz, *Rus.* Lyubcha. Hrodzyenskaya Voblasts', W Belorussia
130 L4 Lyubertsy Moskovskaya Oblast', W Russian Federation
118 K2 Lyubeshiv Volyns'ka Oblast', NW Ukraine
128 M14 Lyubim Yaroslavskaya Oblast', NW Russian Federation
116 K11 Lyubimets Khaskovska Oblast, S Bulgaria
Lyublin *see* Lublin
118 I3 Lyuboml' *Pol.* Luboml. Volyns'ka Oblast', NW Ukraine
Lyubotin *see* Lyubotyn
119 U5 Lyubotyn *Rus.* Lyubotin. Kharkivs'ka Oblast', E Ukraine
130 I5 Lyudinovo Kaluzhskaya Oblast', W Russian Federation
131 T2 Lyuk Udmurtskaya Respublika, NW Russian Federation
116 M9 Lyulyakovo *prev.* Keremitlik. Burgaska Oblast, E Bulgaria
121 I18 Lyusina *Rus.* Lyusino. Brestskaya Voblasts', SW Belorussia
Lyusino *see* Lyusina

M

144 G9 Ma'ād Irbid, N Jordan
Maalahti *see* Malax
xliv D8 Maam Cross Galway, W Ireland
xliv D8 Maamturk Mountains ⛰ W Ireland
Maale *see* Male'
144 G13 Ma'ān Ma'ān, SW Jordan
144 H13 Ma'ān *off.* Muḩāfaẓat Ma'ān, *var.* Ma'an, Ma'ān. ◐ *governorate* S Jordan
95 M16 Maaninka Kuopio, C Finland
168 K7 Maanĭt Bulgan, C Mongolia
168 M8 Maanĭt Töv, C Mongolia
95 N15 Maanselkä Oulu, C Finland
167 Q8 Ma'anshan Anhui, E China
196 F16 Maap *island* Caroline Islands, W Micronesia
120 H3 Maardu *Ger.* Maart. Harjumaa, NW Estonia
Ma'aret-en-Nu'man *see* Ma'arrat an Nu'mān
101 K16 Maarheeze Noord-Brabant, SE Netherlands
Maarianhamina *see* Mariehamn
144 I4 Ma'arrat an Nu'mān *var.* Ma'aret-en-Nu'man, *Fr.* Maarret enn Naamâne. Idlib, NW Syria
Maarret enn Naamâne *see* Ma'arrat an Nu'mān
100 I11 Maarssen Utrecht, C Netherlands
Maart *see* Maardu
xliv G3 Maas Donegal, N Ireland
101 L17 Maas *Fr.* Meuse. ≈ W Europe *see also* Meuse
101 M15 Maasbree Limburg, SE Netherlands
101 L17 Maaseik *prev.* Maeseyck. Limburg, NE Belgium
179 R13 Maasin Leyte, C Philippines
101 L17 Maasmechelen Limburg, NE Belgium
100 G12 Maassluis Zuid-Holland, SW Netherlands

◆ Country ● Country Capital ◇ Dependent Territory ○ Dependent Territory Capital ◐ Administrative Region ✈ International Airport ▲ Mountain ⛰ Mountain Range Volcano ≈ River ◎ Lake ⊟ Reservoir

Maastricht – Malacca

101 L18 **Maastricht** var. Maestricht; anc. Traietum ad Mosam, Traiectum Tungorum. Limburg, SE Netherlands
191 N18 **Maatsuyker Group** island group Tasmania, SE Australia
Maba see Qujiang
85 L20 **Mabalane** Gaza, S Mozambique
27 V7 **Mabank** Texas, SW USA
172 N10 **Mabechi-gawa** var. Mabuchi-gawa. ⟿ Honshū, C Japan
xxxix T5 **Mablethorpe** Lincolnshire, E England, UK
176 W9 **Maboi** Irian Jaya, E Indonesia
85 M19 **Mabote** Inhambane, S Mozambique
34 J10 **Mabton** Washington, NW USA
Mabuchi-gawa see Mabechi-gawa
85 H20 **Mabutsane** Southern, S Botswana
65 G19 **Macá, Cerro** ▲ S Chile
62 Q9 **Macaé** Rio de Janeiro, SE Brazil
84 N13 **Macaloge** Niassa, N Mozambique
Macan see Bonerate, Kepulauan
167 N15 **Macao** Chin. Aomen, Port. Macau. ◇ Portugese special territory E Asia
106 H9 **Mação** Santarém, C Portugal
60 J11 **Macapá** state capital Amapá, N Brazil
45 S17 **Macaracas** Los Santos, S Panama
57 P6 **Macare, Caño** ⟿ NE Venezuela
57 Q6 **Macareo, Caño** ⟿ NE Venezuela
Macarsca see Makarska
MacArthur see Ormoc
190 L12 **Macarthur** Victoria, SE Australia
58 C7 **Macas** Morona Santiago, SE Ecuador
Macassar see Ujungpandang
61 Q14 **Macau** Rio Grande do Norte, E Brazil
Macau see Macao
Macău see Makó, Hungary
67 E24 **Macbride Head** headland East Falkland, Falkland Islands
25 V9 **Macclenny** Florida, SE USA
xl H17 **Macclesfield** Cheshire, C England, UK
198 F6 **Macclesfield Bank** undersea feature N South China Sea
MacCluer Gulf see Berau, Teluk
189 N7 **Macdonald, Lake** salt lake Western Australia
189 Q7 **Macdonnell Ranges** ▲ Northern Territory, C Australia
xlii O11 **Macduff** Aberdeenshire, NE Scotland, UK
106 I6 **Macedo de Cavaleiros** Bragança, N Portugal
Macedonia Central see Kentrikí Makedonía
Macedonia East and Thrace see Anatolikí Makedonía kai Thráki
116 E12 **Macedonia, FYR** off. the Former Yugoslav Republic of Macedonia, var. Macedonia, Mac. Makedonija, abbrev. FYR Macedonia, FYROM. ◆ republic SE Europe
Macedonia West see Dytikí Makedonía
61 Q16 **Maceió** state capital Alagoas, E Brazil
78 K15 **Macenta** Guinée-Forestière, SE Guinea
108 J12 **Macerata** Marche, C Italy
9 S11 **MacFarlane** ⟿ Saskatchewan, C Canada
190 H7 **Macfarlane, Lake** var. Lake Mcfarlane. ◎ South Australia
xliv C13 **Macgillycuddy's Reeks** var. Macgillicuddy's Reeks Mountains, Ir. Na Cruacha Dubha. ▲ SW Ireland
9 X16 **MacGregor** Manitoba, S Canada
155 O10 **Mach** Baluchistān, SW Pakistan
58 C6 **Machachi** Pichincha, C Ecuador
85 M19 **Machaila** Gaza, S Mozambique
Machaire Fíolta see Magherafelt
Machaire Rátha see Maghera
83 I19 **Machakos** Eastern, S Kenya
58 B8 **Machala** El Oro, SW Ecuador
85 J19 **Machaneng** Central, SE Botswana
85 M18 **Machanga** Sofala, E Mozambique
xliii F23 **Macharioch** Argyll and Bute, W Scotland, UK
82 G13 **Machar Marshes** wetland SE Sudan
104 I8 **Machecoul** Loire-Atlantique, NW France
167 O8 **Macheng** Hubei, C China
161 J16 **Mācherla** Andhra Pradesh, C India
159 O11 **Machhapuchhre** ▲ C Nepal
21 T6 **Machias** Maine, NE USA
21 R3 **Machias River** ⟿ Maine, NE USA
21 T6 **Machias River** ⟿ Maine, NE USA
66 P5 **Machico** Madeira, Portugal, NE Atlantic Ocean
161 K16 **Machilīpatnam** var. Bandar Masulipatnam. Andhra Pradesh, E India
56 G5 **Machiques** Zulia, NW Venezuela
xliii F22 **Machrihanish** Argyll and Bute, W Scotland, UK
59 G15 **Machupicchu** Cusco, C Peru
xxxv H8 **Machynlleth** Powys, C Wales, UK
85 M20 **Macia** var. Vila de Macia. Gaza, S Mozambique
Macías Nguema Biyogo see Bioco, Isla de
118 M13 **Măcin** Tulcea, SE Romania
191 T4 **Macintyre River** ⟿ New South Wales/Queensland, SE Australia
189 Y7 **Mackay** Queensland, NE Australia
189 O7 **Mackay, Lake** salt lake Northern Territory/Western Australia
8 M13 **Mackenzie** British Columbia, W Canada
15 Gg6 **Mackenzie** ⟿ Northwest Territories, NW Canada
205 Y6 **Mackenzie Bay** bay Antarctica
8 J1 **Mackenzie Bay** bay NW Canada
2 D8 **Mackenzie Delta** delta Northwest Territories, NW Canada
207 P8 **Mackenzie King Island** island Queen Elizabeth Islands, Northwest Territories, N Canada
14 G5 **Mackenzie Mountains** ▲ Northwest Territories, NW Canada
33 Q5 **Mackinac, Straits Of** ◎ Michigan, N USA
204 K5 **Mackintosh, Cape** headland Antarctica
9 R15 **Macklin** Saskatchewan, S Canada
191 V6 **Macksville** New South Wales, SE Australia
191 V5 **Maclean** New South Wales, SE Australia
85 J24 **Maclear** Eastern Cape, SE South Africa
191 U6 **Macleay River** ⟿ New South Wales, SE Australia
MacLeod see Fort Macleod
188 G9 **Macleod, Lake** ◎ Western Australia
8 I6 **Macmillan** ⟿ Yukon Territory, NW Canada
32 J12 **Macomb** Illinois, N USA
109 B18 **Macomer** Sardegna, Italy, C Mediterranean Sea
84 Q13 **Macomia** Cabo Delgado, NE Mozambique
25 T5 **Macon** Georgia, SE USA
25 N4 **Macon** Mississippi, S USA
29 U3 **Macon** Missouri, C USA
105 R10 **Mâcon** anc. Matisco, Matisco Ædourum. Saône-et-Loire, C France
24 J6 **Macon, Bayou** ⟿ Arkansas/Louisiana, S USA
84 G13 **Macondo** Moxico, E Angola
85 M16 **Macossa** Manica, C Mozambique
9 T12 **Macoun Lake** ◎ Saskatchewan, C Canada
32 K14 **Macoupin Creek** ⟿ Illinois, N USA
Macouria see Tonate
85 N18 **Macovane** Inhambane, SE Mozambique
191 N17 **Macquarie Harbour** inlet Tasmania, SE Australia
199 Ii15 **Macquarie Island** island NZ, SW Pacific Ocean
191 T8 **Macquarie, Lake** lagoon New South Wales, SE Australia
191 Q6 **Macquarie Marshes** wetland New South Wales, SE Australia
183 O13 **Macquarie Ridge** undersea feature SW Pacific Ocean
191 Q6 **Macquarie River** ⟿ New South Wales, SE Australia
191 P17 **Macquarie River** ⟿ Tasmania, SE Australia
205 V5 **Mac. Robertson Land** physical region Antarctica
xliv E14 **Macroom** Ir. Maigh Chromtha. Cork, SW Ireland
44 G5 **Macuelizo** Santa Bárbara, NW Honduras
190 G2 **Macumba River** ⟿ South Australia
59 I16 **Macusani** Puno, S Peru
58 E8 **Macusari, Río** ⟿ N Peru
43 U15 **Macuspana** Tabasco, SE Mexico
144 G10 **Ma'dabā** var. Mādabā, Madeba; anc. Medeba. 'Ammān, NW Jordan
180 G2 **Madagascar** off. Democratic Republic of Madagascar, Malg. Madagasikara; prev. Malagasy Republic. ◆ republic W Indian Ocean
180 I5 **Madagascar** island W Indian Ocean
132 L17 **Madagascar Basin** undersea feature W Indian Ocean
132 L16 **Madagascar Plain** undersea feature W Indian Ocean
69 Y14 **Madagascar Plateau** var. Madagascar Ridge, Madagascar Rise, Rus. Madagaskarskiy Khrebet. undersea feature W Indian Ocean
Madagascar Ridge/Madagascar Rise see Madagascar Plateau
Madagasikara see Madagascar
Madagaskarskiy Khrebet see Madagascar Plateau
66 N2 **Madalena** Pico, Azores, Portugal, NE Atlantic Ocean
79 Y6 **Madama** Agadez, NE Niger
116 J12 **Madan** Plovdivska Oblast, S Bulgaria
161 I19 **Madanapalle** Andhra Pradesh, E India
194 I11 **Madang** Madang, N PNG
194 I11 **Madang** ◐ province N PNG
152 G7 **Madaniyat** Rus. Madeniyet. Qoraqalpoghiston Respublikasi, W Uzbekistan
Madanīyīn see Médenine
79 U11 **Madaoua** Tahoua, SW Niger
Madaras see Vtáčnik
159 U15 **Madaripur** Dhaka, C Bangladesh
79 U12 **Madarounfa** Maradi, S Niger
Madarsko see Hungary
152 B13 **Madau** Turkm. Madaw. Balkanskiy Velayat, W Turkmenistan
195 P15 **Madau Island** island SE PNG
Madaw see Madau
21 S1 **Madawaska** Maine, NE USA
12 J13 **Madawaska** ⟿ Ontario, SE Canada
Madawaska Highlands see Haliburton Highlands
177 G4 **Madaya** Mandalay, C Burma
109 K17 **Maddaloni** Campania, S Italy
31 O3 **Maddock** North Dakota, N USA
101 I14 **Made** Noord-Brabant, S Netherlands
Madeba see Ma'dabā
66 L9 **Madeira** var. Ilha de Madeira. island Madeira, Portugal, NE Atlantic Ocean
Madeira, Ilha de see Madeira
66 O5 **Madeira Islands** Port. Região Autoónoma da Madeira. ◐ autonomous region Madeira, Portugal, NE Atlantic Ocean
66 L9 **Madeira Plain** undersea feature E Atlantic Ocean
66 L9 **Madeira Ridge** undersea feature E Atlantic Ocean
61 F14 **Madeira, Rio** Sp. Río Madera. ⟿ Bolivia/Brazil see also Madera, Río
103 J25 **Mädelegabel** ▲ Austria/Germany
13 X6 **Madeleine** ⟿ Québec, SE Canada
13 X5 **Madeleine, Cap de la** headland Québec, SE Canada
11 Q13 **Madeleine, Îles de la** Eng. Magdalen Islands. island group Québec, E Canada
xxxviii I7 **Madeley** Staffordshire, C England, UK
31 U10 **Madelia** Minnesota, N USA
37 P3 **Madeline** California, W USA
32 K3 **Madeline Island** island Apostle Islands, Wisconsin, N USA
143 O15 **Maden** Elâziğ, SE Turkey
151 V12 **Madeniyet** Semipalatinsk, E Kazakhstan
Madeniyet see Madaniyat
42 H5 **Madera** Chihuahua, N Mexico
37 Q10 **Madera** California, W USA
58 L13 **Madera, Río** Port. Rio Madeira. ⟿ Bolivia/Brazil see also Madeira, Rio
108 D6 **Madesimo** Lombardia, N Italy
147 O14 **Madhāb, Wādī** dry watercourse NW Yemen
159 R13 **Madhepura** prev. Madhipure. Bihār, NE India
Madhipure see Madhepura
159 Q13 **Madhubani** Bihār, N India
159 Q15 **Madhupur** Bihār, NE India
158 K15 **Madhya Pradesh** prev. Central Provinces and Berar. ◐ state C India
59 K15 **Madidi, Río** ⟿ W Bolivia
161 F20 **Madikeri** prev. Mercara. Karnātaka, W India
29 O13 **Madill** Oklahoma, C USA
81 G21 **Madimba** Bas-Zaïre, SW Zaire
144 M4 **Ma'din** Ar Raqqah, C Syria
Madīnah, Minṭaqat al see Al Madīnah
78 M14 **Madinani** NW Ivory Coast
147 O17 **Madīnat ash Sha'b** prev. Al Ittiḥād. SW Yemen
144 K3 **Madīnat ath Thawrah** var. Ath Thawrah. Ar Raqqah, N Syria Asia
181 O6 **Madingley Rise** undersea feature W Indian Ocean
81 E21 **Madingo-Kayes** Le Kouilou, S Congo
81 F21 **Madingou** La Bouenza, S Congo
Madioen see Madiun
25 U8 **Madison** Florida, SE USA
25 T3 **Madison** Georgia, SE USA
33 P15 **Madison** Indiana, N USA
29 P6 **Madison** Kansas, C USA
21 Q6 **Madison** Maine, NE USA
31 S9 **Madison** Minnesota, N USA
24 K5 **Madison** Mississippi, S USA
31 Q14 **Madison** Nebraska, C USA
31 R10 **Madison** South Dakota, N USA
23 V5 **Madison** Virginia, NE USA
23 Q5 **Madison** West Virginia, NE USA
32 L9 **Madison** state capital Wisconsin, N USA
23 T6 **Madison Heights** Virginia, NE USA
22 M10 **Madisonville** Kentucky, S USA
22 I6 **Madisonville** Tennessee, S USA
27 V9 **Madisonville** Texas, SW USA
174 Ll15 **Madiun** prev. Madioen. Jawa, C Indonesia
Madjene see Majene
12 J14 **Madoc** Ontario, SE Canada
Madoera see Madura, Pulau
83 J18 **Mado Gashi** North Eastern, E Kenya
165 R11 **Madoi** Qinghai, C China
201 O13 **Madolenihmw** Pohnpei, E Micronesia
120 I9 **Madona** Ger. Modohn. Madona, E Latvia
109 J23 **Madonie** ▲ Sicilia, Italy, C Mediterranean Sea
147 Y11 **Madrakah, Ra's** headland E Oman
161 J19 **Madras** var. Chennai. Tamil Nādu, S India
34 I12 **Madras** Oregon, NW USA
161 J19 **Madras** ✕ Tamil Nādu, S India
Madras see Tamil Nādu
59 H14 **Madre de Dios** off. Departamento de Madre de Dios. ◐ department E Peru
65 F22 **Madre de Dios, Isla** island S Chile
59 J14 **Madre de Dios, Río** ⟿ Bolivia/Peru
27 T16 **Madre, Laguna** ◎ Texas, SW USA
43 Q9 **Madre, Laguna** lagoon NE Mexico
39 Q12 **Madre Mount** ▲ New Mexico, SW USA
107 N8 **Madrid** ● (Spain) Madrid, C Spain
31 V14 **Madrid** Iowa, C USA
107 N7 **Madrid** ◐ autonomous community C Spain
107 N10 **Madridejos** Castilla-La Mancha, C Spain
106 L7 **Madrigal de las Altas Torres** Castilla-León, N Spain
106 K10 **Madrigalejo** Extremadura, W Spain
36 L3 **Mad River** ⟿ California, W USA
44 J8 **Madriz** ◐ department NW Nicaragua
106 K10 **Madroñera** Extremadura, W Spain
189 N12 **Madura** Western Australia
Madura see Madurai
161 H22 **Madurai** prev. Madura, Mathurai. Tamil Nādu, S India
174 M15 **Madura, Pulau** prev. Madoera. island C Indonesia
174 Mm15 **Madura, Selat** strait C Indonesia
131 Q17 **Madzhalis** Respublika Dagestan, SW Russian Federation
116 K12 **Madzharovo** Khaskovska Oblast, S Bulgaria
85 M14 **Madzimoyo** Eastern, E Zambia
171 K15 **Maebashi** var. Maebasi, Mayebashi. Gunma, Honshū, S Japan
Maebasi see Maebashi
178 Hh6 **Mae Chan** Chiang Rai, NW Thailand
178 Gg7 **Mae Hong Son** var. Maehongson, Muai To. Mae Hong Son, NW Thailand
Mae Nam Khong see Mekong
178 Hh7 **Mae Nam Nan** ⟿ NW Thailand
178 H10 **Mae Nam Tha Chin** ⟿ W Thailand
178 Hh7 **Mae Nam Yom** ⟿ W Thailand
xxxv G6 **Maentwrog** Gwynedd, NW Wales, UK
178 H7 **Mae Sariang** Mae Hong Son, NW Thailand
39 O3 **Maeser** Utah, W USA
Maeseyck see Maaseik
178 Gg9 **Mae Sot** var. Ban Mae Sot. Tak, W Thailand
xxxv I14 **Maesteg** Bridgend, S Wales, UK
Maestricht see Maastricht
178 H7 **Mae Suai** var. Ban Mae Suai. Chiang Rai, NW Thailand
178 H7 **Mae Tho, Doi** ▲ NW Thailand
180 I4 **Maevatanana** Mahajanga, C Madagascar
197 C12 **Maewo** prev. Aurora. island C Vanuatu
175 T8 **Mafa** Pulau Halmahera, E Indonesia
85 I23 **Mafeteng** W Lesotho
101 J21 **Maffe** Namur, SE Belgium
176 Y10 **Maffin** Irian Jaya, E Indonesia
191 P12 **Maffra** Victoria, SE Australia
83 K23 **Mafia** island E Tanzania
83 J23 **Mafia Channel** sea waterway E Tanzania
85 I21 **Mafikeng** North-West, N South Africa
62 J12 **Mafra** Santa Catarina, S Brazil
106 F10 **Mafra** Lisboa, C Portugal
149 Q17 **Mafraq** Abū Ẓaby, C UAE
Mafraq/Mafraq, Muḥāfaẓat al see Al Mafraq
127 O10 **Magadan** Magadanskaya Oblast', E Russian Federation
127 Nn8 **Magadanskaya Oblast'** ◐ province E Russian Federation
110 G11 **Magadino** Ticino, S Switzerland
65 G23 **Magallanes** off. Región de Magallanes y de la Antártica Chilena. ◐ region S Chile
Magallanes see Punta Arenas
Magallanes, Estrecho de see Magellan, Strait of
12 I10 **Maganasipi, Lac** ◎ Québec, SE Canada
56 F6 **Magangué** Bolívar, N Colombia
Magareva see Mangareva
79 V12 **Magaria** Zinder, S Niger
194 M16 **Magarida** Central, SW PNG
179 Pp9 **Magat** ⟿ Luzon, N Philippines
29 T11 **Magazine Mountain** ▲ Arkansas, C USA
78 I15 **Magburaka** C Sierra Leone
126 M14 **Magdagachi** Amurskaya Oblast', SE Russian Federation
64 O12 **Magdalena** Buenos Aires, E Argentina
59 M15 **Magdalena** Beni, N Bolivia
42 F4 **Magdalena** Sonora, NW Mexico
39 Q13 **Magdalena** New Mexico, SW USA
56 F5 **Magdalena** off. Departamento del Magdalena. ◐ province N Colombia
42 E9 **Magdalena, Bahía** bay W Mexico
65 G19 **Magdalena, Isla** island Archipiélago de los Chonos, S Chile
42 D8 **Magdalena, Isla** island W Mexico
49 P6 **Magdalena, Río** ⟿ C Colombia
42 F4 **Magdalena, Río** ⟿ NW Mexico
Magdalen Islands see Madeleine, Îles de la
102 L13 **Magdeburg** Sachsen-Anhalt, C Germany
24 L6 **Magee** Mississippi, S USA
xliv M4 **Magee, Island** island E Northern Ireland, UK
174 Kk15 **Magelang** Jawa, C Indonesia
199 J7 **Magellan Rise** undersea feature C Pacific Ocean
65 H24 **Magellan, Strait of** Sp. Estrecho de Magallanes. strait Argentina/Chile
108 D7 **Magenta** Lombardia, NW Italy
Magerøy see Magerøya
94 K7 **Magerøya** var. Magerøy. island N Norway
170 B17 **Mage-shima** island Nansei-shotō, SW Japan
110 G11 **Maggia** Ticino, S Switzerland
110 G10 **Maggia** ⟿ SW Switzerland
Maggiore, Lago see Maggiore, Lake
108 C6 **Maggiore, Lake** It. Lago Maggiore. ◎ Italy/Switzerland
46 I12 **Maggotty** W Jamaica
78 I10 **Maghama** Gorgol, S Mauritania
xliv K3 **Maghera** Ir. Machaire Rátha. Magherafelt, C Northern Ireland, UK
xliv F10 **Maghera** hill W Ireland
xliv K3 **Magherafelt** Ir. Machaire Fíolta. Magherafelt, C Northern Ireland, UK
xliv K4 **Magherafelt** ◐ district C Northern Ireland, UK
xliv L5 **Magheralin** Craigavon, C Northern Ireland, UK
xl M16 **Maghull** Sefton, NW England, UK
196 H6 **Magicienne Bay** bay Saipan, S Northern Mariana Islands
107 O13 **Magina** ▲ S Spain
83 H24 **Magingo** Ruvuma, S Tanzania
126 Jj14 **Magistral'nyy** Irkutskaya Oblast', S Russian Federation
114 H11 **Maglaj** N Bosnia and Herzegovina
109 Q19 **Maglie** Puglia, SE Italy
38 L2 **Magna** Utah, W USA
Magnesia see Manisa
12 G12 **Magnetawan** ⟿ Ontario, S Canada
125 Dd12 **Magnitogorsk** Chelyabinskaya Oblast', C Russian Federation
29 T14 **Magnolia** Arkansas, C USA
24 K7 **Magnolia** Mississippi, S USA
27 V10 **Magnolia** Texas, SW USA
Magnolia State see Mississippi
97 J15 **Magnor** Hedmark, S Norway
197 K14 **Mago** prev. Mango. island Lau Group, E Fiji
85 L15 **Màgoé** Tete, NW Mozambique
13 Q13 **Magog** Québec, SE Canada
85 J15 **Magoye** Southern, S Zambia
43 Q12 **Magozal** Veracruz-Llave, C Mexico
12 B7 **Magpie** ⟿ Ontario, S Canada
9 Q17 **Magrath** Alberta, SW Canada
107 R10 **Magro** ⟿ E Spain
78 I9 **Magta' Lahjar** var. Magta Lahjar, Magta' Lahjar, Magtá Lahjar. Brakna, SW Mauritania
85 L20 **Magude** Maputo, S Mozambique
xliv I6 **Maguiresbridge** Fermanagh, W Northern Ireland, UK
79 Y12 **Magumeri** Borno, NE Nigeria
201 O14 **Magur Islands** island group Caroline Islands, C Micronesia
Magway see Magwe
177 Ff6 **Magwe** var. Magway. Magwe, W Burma
177 Ff6 **Magwe** var. Magway. ◐ division C Burma
Magyar-Becse see Bečej
Magyarkanizsa see Kanjiža
Magyarország see Hungary
Magyarzsombor see Zimbor
148 J4 **Mahābād** var. Mehabad; prev. Sāūjbulāgh. Āẕarbāyjān-e Bākhtarī, NW Iran
180 H5 **Mahabo** Toliara, W Madagascar
Maha Chai see Samut Sakhon
161 D14 **Mahād** Mahārāshtra, W India
83 N17 **Mahadday Weyne** Shabeellaha Dhexe, C Somalia
81 Q17 **Mahagi** Haut-Zaïre, NE Zaire
Mahāil see Muhāyil
180 I4 **Mahajamba** seasonal river NW Madagascar
158 G10 **Mahājan** Rājasthān, NW India
180 I3 **Mahajanga** var. Majunga. Mahajanga, NW Madagascar
180 I3 **Mahajanga** ◐ province W Madagascar
180 I3 **Mahajanga** ✕ Mahajanga, NW Madagascar
175 N7 **Mahakam, Sungai** var. Koetai, Kutai. ⟿ Borneo, C Indonesia
85 I19 **Mahalapye** var. Mahalatswe. Central, SE Botswana
Mahalatswe see Mahalapye
Mahalla el Kubra see El Maḥalla el Kubra
175 Q10 **Mahalona** Sulawesi, C Indonesia
Mahameru see Semeru, Gunung
149 S11 **Mahān** Kermān, E Iran
160 N12 **Mahanādi** ⟿ E India
180 J5 **Mahanoro** Toamasina, E Madagascar
159 P13 **Mahārājganj** Bihār, N India
160 G13 **Mahārāshtra** ◐ state W India
Mahasaragam see Maha Sarakham
180 I4 **Mahavavy** seasonal river N Madagascar
161 K24 **Mahaweli Ganga** ⟿ C Sri Lanka
Mahbés see El Mahbas
161 J15 **Mahbūbābād** Andhra Pradesh, E India
161 H16 **Mahbūbnagar** Andhra Pradesh, C India
146 M8 **Mahd adh Dhahab** Al Madīnah, W Saudi Arabia
57 S9 **Mahdia** C Guyana
77 N6 **Mahdia** var. Al Mahdīyah, Mehdia. NE Tunisia
161 F20 **Mahe** Fr. Mahé; prev. Mayyali. Pondicherry, SW India
180 I16 **Mahé** ✕ Mahé, NE Seychelles
180 H16 **Mahé** island Inner Islands, NE Seychelles
181 Y17 **Mahebourg** SE Mauritius
158 I11 **Mahendragarh** Haryāna, N India
158 L10 **Mahendranagar** Far Western, W Nepal
83 I23 **Mahenge** Morogoro, SE Tanzania
193 F22 **Maheno** Otago, South Island, NZ
160 D9 **Mahesāna** Gujarāt, W India
160 F11 **Maheshwar** Madhya Pradesh, C India
157 F14 **Mahi** ⟿ N India
192 Q10 **Mahia Peninsula** peninsula North Island, NZ
121 O16 **Mahilyow** Rus. Mogilëv. Mahilyowskaya Voblasts', E Belarus
121 M16 **Mahilyowskaya Voblasts'** prev. Rus. Mogilëvskaya Oblast'. ◐ province E Belarus
203 P7 **Mahina** Tahiti, W French Polynesia
193 E23 **Mahinerangi, Lake** ◎ South Island, NZ
85 L22 **Mahlabatini** KwaZulu/Natal, E South Africa
177 G5 **Mahlaing** Mandalay, C Burma
111 X8 **Mahldorf** Steiermark, SE Austria
Mahmūd-e 'Erāqī see Maḥmūd-e Rāqī
155 R4 **Maḥmūd-e Rāqī** var. Mahmūd-e 'Erāqī. Kāpīsā, NE Afghanistan
Mahmudiya see Al Maḥmūdīyah
31 S5 **Mahnomen** Minnesota, N USA
158 K14 **Mahoba** Uttar Pradesh, N India
107 Z9 **Mahón** Cat. Maó, Eng. Port Mahon; anc. Portus Magonis. Menorca, Spain, W Mediterranean Sea
83 J22 **Mahonda** Zanzibar North, E Tanzania
20 D14 **Mahoning Creek Lake** ⊠ Pennsylvania, NE USA
107 Q10 **Mahora** Castilla-La Mancha, C Spain
Mähren see Moravia
Mährisch-Budwitz see Moravské Budějovice
Mährisch-Kromau see Moravský Krumlov
Mährisch-Neustadt see Uničov
Mährisch-Schönberg see Šumperk
Mährisch-Trübau see Moravská Třebová
Mährisch-Weisskirchen see Hranice
Māh-Shahr see Bandar-e Māhshahr
81 N19 **Mahulu** Maniema, E Zaire
160 C12 **Mahuva** Gujarāt, W India
116 N11 **Mahya Dağı** ▲ NW Turkey
107 T6 **Maials** var. Mayals. Cataluña, NE Spain
203 O2 **Maiana** prev. Hall Island. atoll Tungaru, W Kiribati
203 S11 **Maiao** var. Tapuaemanu, Tubuai-Manu. island Îles du Vent, W French Polynesia
56 H4 **Maicao** La Guajira, N Colombia
Mai Ceu/Mai Chio see Maych'ew
105 U8 **Maîche** Doubs, E France
xxxvi B7 **Maida Vale** Westminster, SE England, UK
xxxvi L11 **Maiden Bradley** Wiltshire, S England, UK
xxxvii R9 **Maidenhead** Windsor and Maidenhead, S England, UK
xxxvi L13 **Maiden Newton** Dorset, S England, UK
xliii H23 **Maidens** South Ayrshire, W Scotland, UK
xliv M3 **Maidens, The** island group E Northern Ireland, UK
xxxvii W10 **Maidstone** Kent, SE England, UK
9 S15 **Maidstone** Saskatchewan, S Canada
79 Y13 **Maiduguri** Borno, NE Nigeria
110 I8 **Maienfeld** Sankt Gallen, NE Switzerland
118 J12 **Măieruș** Hung. Szászmagyarós. Brașov, C Romania
Maigh Chromtha see Macroom
Maigh Eo see Mayo
57 N9 **Maigualida, Sierra** ▲ S Venezuela
xliv F11 **Maigue** ⟿ W Ireland
160 K9 **Maihar** Madhya Pradesh, C India
160 K11 **Maikala Range** ▲ C India
69 T10 **Maiko** ⟿ W Zaire
Mailand see Milano
158 L11 **Mailāni** Uttar Pradesh, N India
155 U10 **Māilsi** Punjab, E Pakistan
153 R8 **Maimak** Talasskaya Oblast', NW Kyrgyzstan
Maimāna see Meymaneh
Maimansingh see Mymensingh
176 Vv11 **Maimawa** Irian Jaya, E Indonesia
Maimuna see Al Maymūnah
103 G18 **Main** ⟿ C Germany
117 F22 **Maïna** ancient monument Pelopónnisos, S Greece
117 E20 **Maínalo** ▲ S Greece
103 L22 **Mainburg** Bayern, SE Germany
Main Camp see Banana
12 E12 **Main Channel** lake channel Ontario, S Canada
81 I20 **Mai-Ndombe, Lac** prev. Lac Léopold II. ◎ W Zaire
103 K20 **Main-Donau-Kanal** canal SE Germany
21 R6 **Maine** off. State of Maine; also known as Lumber State, Pine Tree State. ◐ state NE USA
104 K6 **Maine** cultural region NW France
104 J7 **Maine-et-Loire** ◐ department NW France
20 Q9 **Maine, Gulf of** gulf NE USA
79 X12 **Mainé-Soroa** Diffa, SE Niger
178 Gg1 **Maingkwan** var. Mungkawn. Kachin State, N Burma
Main Island see Bermuda
Mainistir Fhear Maí see Fermoy
Mainistirna Búille see Boyle
Mainistir na Corann see Midleton
Mainistir na Féile see Abbeyfeale
xlii L4 **Mainland** island Orkney, N Scotland, UK
xlii I3 **Mainland** island Shetland, NE Scotland, UK
165 P16 **Mainling** Xizang Zizhiqu, W China
158 K12 **Mainpuri** Uttar Pradesh, N India
105 N5 **Maintenon** Eure-et-Loir, C France
180 H4 **Maintirano** Mahajanga, W Madagascar
95 M15 **Mainua** Oulu, C Finland
103 G18 **Mainz** Fr. Mayence. Rheinland-Pfalz, SW Germany
78 I9 **Maio** var. Vila do Maio. Maio, S Cape Verde
78 E10 **Maio** var. Mayo. island Ilhas de Sotavento, SE Cape Verde
64 G12 **Maipo, Río** ⟿ C Chile
64 H12 **Maipo, Volcán** ▲ W Argentina
63 E22 **Maipú** Buenos Aires, E Argentina
64 I11 **Maipú** Mendoza, E Argentina
64 H11 **Maipú** Santiago, C Chile
56 L5 **Maiquetía** Distrito Federal, N Venezuela
110 I10 **Maira** It. Mera. ⟿ Italy/Switzerland
108 A9 **Maira** ⟿ NW Italy
159 V12 **Mairābari** Assam, NE India
46 K7 **Maisí** Guantánamo, E Cuba
120 H13 **Maišiagala** Vilnius, SE Lithuania
159 V17 **Maiskhal Island** island SE Bangladesh
178 Gg13 **Mai Sombun** Chumphon, SW Thailand
Maisur see Karnātaka, India
Maisur see Mysore, India
191 T8 **Maitland** New South Wales, SE Australia
190 I9 **Maitland** South Australia
12 F15 **Maitland** ⟿ Ontario, S Canada
205 R1 **Maitri** Indian research station Antarctica
165 N15 **Maizhokunggar** Xizang Zizhiqu, W China
45 O10 **Maíz, Islas del** var. Corn Islands. island group SE Nicaragua
171 H14 **Maizuru** Kyōto, Honshū, SW Japan
56 F6 **Majagual** Sucre, N Colombia
43 Z13 **Majahual** Quintana Roo, E Mexico
Majardah, Wādī see Medjerda, Oued/Mejerda
Mājeej see Mejit Island
175 P11 **Majene** prev. Madjene. Sulawesi, C Indonesia
45 V15 **Majé, Serranía de** ▲ E Panama
114 I11 **Majevica** ▲ NE Bosnia and Herzegovina
83 H15 **Maji** SW Ethiopia
147 X7 **Majis** NW Oman
Majorca see Mallorca
Mājro see Majuro Atoll
Majunga see Mahajanga
201 Y3 **Majuro** ✕ Majuro, SE Marshall Islands
201 Y2 **Majuro Atoll** var. Mājro. atoll Ratak Chain, SE Marshall Islands
201 X2 **Majuro Lagoon** lagoon Majuro Atoll, SE Marshall Islands
78 H11 **Maka** C Senegal
81 F20 **Makabana** Le Niari, SW Congo
40 D9 **Makaha** Haw. Mākaha. Oahu, Hawaii, USA, C Pacific Ocean
40 B8 **Makahuena Point** headland Kauai, Hawaii, USA, C Pacific Ocean
40 D9 **Makakilo City** Oahu, Hawaii, USA, C Pacific Ocean
85 H18 **Makalamabedi** Central, C Botswana
Makale see Mek'elē
164 K17 **Makalu** Chin. Makaru Shan. ▲ China/Nepal
83 G23 **Makampi** Mbeya, S Tanzania
151 X12 **Makanchi** Kaz. Maqanshy. Semipalatinsk, E Kazakhstan
44 M8 **Makantaka** Región Autónoma Atlántico Norte, NE Nicaragua
202 B16 **Makapu Point** headland W Niue
193 C24 **Makarewa** Southland, South Island, NZ
119 O4 **Makariv** Kyyivs'ka Oblast', N Ukraine
193 D20 **Makarora** ⟿ South Island, NZ
127 Oo15 **Makarov** Ostrov Sakhalin, Sakhalinskaya Oblast', SE Russian Federation
207 R9 **Makarov Basin** undersea feature Arctic Ocean
199 Hh4 **Makarov Seamount** undersea feature W Pacific Ocean
115 F15 **Makarska** It. Macarsca. Split-Dalmacija, SE Croatia
Makaru Shan see Makalu
129 O15 **Makar'yev** Kostromskaya Oblast', NW Russian Federation
84 L11 **Makasa** Northern, NE Zambia
Makasar see Ujungpandang
Makasar, Selat see Makassar Straits
Makassar see Ujungpandang
198 Ff8 **Makassar Straits** Ind. Selat Makasar. strait C Indonesia
150 G12 **Makat** Kaz. Maqat. Atyrau, SW Kazakhstan
203 T10 **Makatea** island Îles Tuamotu, C French Polynesia
145 U7 **Makātū** E Iraq
180 H6 **Makay** var. Massif du Makay. ▲ SW Madagascar
116 J12 **Makaza** pass Bulgaria/Greece
176 Uu9 **Makbon** Irian Jaya, E Indonesia
Makedonija see Macedonia, FYR
202 B16 **Makefu** W Niue
203 V10 **Makemo** atoll Îles Tuamotu, C French Polynesia
78 I15 **Makeni** C Sierra Leone
Makenzen see Orlyak
Makeyevka see Makiyivka
131 Q16 **Makhachkala** prev. Petrovsk-Port. Respublika Dagestan, SW Russian Federation
150 F11 **Makhambet** Atyrau, W Kazakhstan
Makharadze see Ozurget'i
145 W13 **Makhfar Al Buṣayyah** S Iraq
145 R4 **Makhmūr** N Iraq
144 I11 **Makhrūq, Wadi al** dry watercourse E Jordan
145 R4 **Makhūl, Jabal** ▲ C Iraq
147 R13 **Makhyah, Wādī** dry watercourse N Yemen
176 W11 **Maki** Irian Jaya, E Indonesia
175 Ss8 **Makian, Pulau** island Maluku, E Indonesia
193 G21 **Makikihi** Canterbury, South Island, NZ
203 O2 **Makin** prev. Pitt Island. atoll Tungaru, W Kiribati
83 I20 **Makindu** Eastern, S Kenya
151 Q8 **Makinsk** Akmola, N Kazakhstan
195 Y17 **Makira** off. Makira Province. ◐ province SE Solomon Islands
Makira see San Cristobal
119 X8 **Makiyivka** Rus. Makeyevka; prev. Dmitriyevsk. Donets'ka Oblast', E Ukraine
146 L10 **Makkah** Eng. Mecca. Makkah, W Saudi Arabia
146 M10 **Makkah** var. Minṭaqat Makkah. ◐ province W Saudi Arabia
11 R7 **Makkovik** Newfoundland and Labrador, NE Canada
100 K6 **Makkum** Friesland, N Netherlands
Mako see Makung
113 M25 **Makó** Rom. Macău. Csongrád, SE Hungary
12 G9 **Makobe Lake** ◎ Ontario, S Canada
197 I14 **Makogai** island C Fiji
81 F18 **Makokou** Ogooué-Ivindo, NE Gabon
83 G23 **Makongolosi** Mbeya, S Tanzania
83 E19 **Makota** SW Uganda
81 G18 **Makoua** Cuvette, C Congo
112 M10 **Maków Mazowiecki** Ostrołęka, E Poland
113 K17 **Maków Podhalański** Bielsko-Biała, S Poland
149 V14 **Makran** cultural region Iran/Pakistan
158 G12 **Makrāna** Rājasthān, N India
149 U15 **Makran Coast** coastal region SE Iran
121 F20 **Makrany** Rus. Mokrany. Brestskaya Voblasts', SW Belarus
Makrinoros see Makrynóros
117 H20 **Makrónisosi** island Kykládes, Greece, Aegean Sea
117 D17 **Makrynóros** var. Makrinoros. ▲ C Greece
117 G19 **Makryplági** ▲ C Greece
Maksamaa see Maxmo
128 J15 **Maksatikha** var. Maksatha, Maksaticha. Tverskaya Oblast', W Russian Federation
160 G10 **Maksi** Madhya Pradesh, C India
148 I1 **Mākū** Āẕarbāyjān-e Bākhtarī, NW Iran
159 Y11 **Mākum** Assam, NE India
Makun see Makung
167 R14 **Makung** prev. Mako, Makun. W Taiwan
170 Bb16 **Makurazaki** Kagoshima, Kyūshū, SW Japan
79 V15 **Makurdi** Benue, C Nigeria
125 F12 **Makushino** Kurganskaya Oblast', C Russian Federation
40 L17 **Makushin Volcano** ⛰ Unalaska Island, Alaska, USA
85 K16 **Makwiro** Mashonaland West, N Zimbabwe
Mala see Mallow, Ireland
59 D15 **Mala** Lima, W Peru
Mala see Malaita, Solomon Islands
95 I14 **Malå** Västerbotten, N Sweden
202 G12 **Mala'atoli** Île Uvea, E Wallis and Futuna
179 Qq15 **Malabang** Mindanao, S Philippines
161 E21 **Malabār Coast** coast SW India
81 C16 **Malabo** prev. Santa Isabel. ● (Equatorial Guinea) Isla de Bioco, NW Equatorial Guinea
81 C16 **Malabo** ✕ Isla de Bioco, N Equatorial Guinea
Malacca see Málaga
Malacca see Melaka

◆ Country
● Country Capital
◇ Dependent Territory
○ Dependent Territory Capital
◐ Administrative Region
✕ International Airport
▲ Mountain
▲ Mountain Range
⛰ Volcano
⟿ River
◎ Lake
⊠ Reservoir

MALACCA, STRAIT OF – MAPAT, PULAU

173 G4 **Malacca, Strait of** *Ind.* Selat Malaka. *strait* Indonesia/Malaysia
Malacca *see* Malacky
113 G20 **Malacky** *Hung.* Malacka. Západné Slovensko, W Slovakia
35 R16 **Malad City** Idaho, NW USA
119 Q4 **Mala Divytsya** Chernihivs'ka Oblast', N Ukraine
121 J15 **Maladzyechna** *Pol.* Molodeczno, *Rus.* Molodechno. Minskaya Voblasts', C Belorussia
202 D12 **Malaee** Île Futuna, N Wallis and Futuna
39 V15 **Malaga** New Mexico, SW USA
56 G8 **Málaga** Santander, C Colombia
106 M15 **Málaga** *anc.* Malaca. Andalucía, S Spain
106 L15 **Málaga** ◐ *province* Andalucía, S Spain
106 M15 **Málaga** ✕ Andalucía, S Spain
Malagasy Republic *see* Madagascar
107 N10 **Malagón** Castilla-La Mancha, C Spain
xliv L8 **Malahide** *Ir.* Mullach Íde. Dublin, E Ireland
Málainn *see* Malin
195 Y14 **Malaita** *off.* Malaita Province. ◐ *province* N Solomon Islands
195 Y15 **Malaita** *var.* Mala. *island* N Solomon Islands
82 F13 **Malakal** Upper Nile, S Sudan
114 C10 **Mala Kapela** ▲▲ NW Croatia
27 V7 **Malakoff** Texas, SW USA
Malakula *see* Malekula
155 V7 **Malakwāl** *var.* Mālikwāla. Punjab, E Pakistan
194 J12 **Malalamai** Madang, W PNG
194 J14 **Malalaua** Gulf, S PNG
175 Q11 **Malamala** Sulawesi, C Indonesia
174 M15 **Malang** Jawa, C Indonesia
85 O14 **Malanga** Niassa, N Mozambique
Malange *see* Malanje
94 I9 **Malangen** *sound* N Norway
84 C11 **Malanje** *var.* Malange. Malanje, NW Angola
84 C11 **Malanje** *var.* Malange. ◐ *province* N Angola
154 M16 **Malān, Rās** *headland* SW Pakistan
79 S13 **Malanville** NE Benin
Malapane *see* Ozimek
161 F21 **Malappuram** Kerala, SW India
45 T17 **Mala, Punta** *headland* S Panama
97 N16 **Mälaren** ◎ C Sweden
64 H13 **Malargüe** Mendoza, W Argentina
12 J8 **Malartic** Québec, SE Canada
121 F20 **Malaryta** *Pol.* Maloryta, *Rus.* Malorita. Brestskaya Voblasts', SW Belorussia
65 J19 **Malaspina** Chubut, SE Argentina
41 U12 **Malaspina Glacier** *glacier* Alaska, USA
143 N15 **Malatya** *anc.* Melitene. Malatya, SE Turkey
142 M14 **Malatya** ◐ *province* C Turkey
119 Q7 **Mala Vyska** *Rus.* Malaya Viska. Kirovohrads'ka Oblast', S Ukraine
85 M14 **Malawi** *off.* Republic of Malaŵi; *prev.* Nyasaland, Nyasaland Protectorate. ◆ *republic* S Africa
Malawi, Lake *see* Nyasa, Lake
95 J17 **Malax** *Fin.* Maalahti. Vaasa, W Finland
128 H14 **Malaya Vishera** Novgorodskaya Oblast', W Russian Federation
Malaya Viska *see* Mala Vyska
179 R15 **Malaybalay** Mindanao, S Philippines
148 L6 **Malāyer** *prev.* Daulatabad. Hamadān, W Iran
174 Gg3 **Malay Peninsula** *peninsula* Malaysia/Thailand
174 I3 **Malaysia** *var.* Federation of Malaysia; *prev.* the separate territories of Federation of Malaya, Sarawak and Sabah (North Borneo) and Singapore. ◆ *monarchy* SE Asia
143 R14 **Malazgirt** Muş, E Turkey
13 R8 **Malbaie** ↝ Québec, SE Canada
79 T12 **Malbaza** Tahoua, S Niger
112 J7 **Malbork** *Ger.* Marienburg, Marienburg in Westpreussen. Elbląg, N Poland
xxxvi G17 **Malborough** Devon, SW England, UK
102 N9 **Malchin** Mecklenburg-Vorpommern, N Germany
102 M9 **Malchiner See** ◎ NE Germany
xlii P1 **Malcom's Head** *headland* NE Scotland, UK
Mālda *see* Māldah
101 D16 **Maldegem** Oost-Vlaanderen, NW Belgium
100 L13 **Malden** Gelderland, SE Netherlands
21 O11 **Malden** Massachusetts, NE USA
29 Y8 **Malden** Missouri, C USA
203 X4 **Malden Island** *prev.* Independence Island. *atoll* E Kiribati
181 Q6 **Maldives** *off.* Maldivian Divehi, Republic of Maldives. ◆ *republic* N Indian Ocean
Maldivian Divehi *see* Maldives
xxxvii W8 **Maldon** Essex, E England, UK
63 G20 **Maldonado** Maldonado, S Uruguay
63 G20 **Maldonado** ◐ *department* S Uruguay
43 P17 **Maldonado, Punta** *headland* S Mexico
157 K19 **Male'** *Div.* Maale ● (Maldives) Male' Atoll, C Maldives
108 G6 **Malè** Trentino-Alto Adige, N Italy
78 K13 **Maléa** *var.* Maléya. Haute-Guinée, NE Guinea
117 G22 **Maléas, Ákra** *headland* S Greece
117 L17 **Maléas, Ákra** *headland* Lésvos, E Greece
157 K19 **Male' Atoll** *var.* Kaafu Atoll. *atoll* C Maldives
Malebo, Pool *see* Stanley Pool
160 E12 **Mālegaon** Mahārāshtra, W India
83 F15 **Malek** Jonglei, S Sudan
197 B13 **Malekula** *var.* Malakula; *prev.* Mallicolo. *island* W Vanuatu
201 Y15 **Malem** Kosrae, E Micronesia
85 O15 **Malema** Nampula, N Mozambique
81 N23 **Malemba-Nkulu** Shaba, SE Zaire
195 Q10 **Malendok Island** *island* Tanga Islands, NE PNG
128 K9 **Malen'ga** Respublika Kareliya, NW Russian Federation
97 M20 **Målerås** Kalmar, S Sweden
105 O6 **Malesherbes** Loiret, C France
117 G18 **Malesína** Stereá Ellás, E Greece
Maléya *see* Maléa
131 O15 **Malgobek** Chechenskaya Respublika, SW Russian Federation
107 X5 **Malgrat de Mar** Cataluña, NE Spain
82 C9 **Malha** Northern Darfur, W Sudan
xli P12 **Malham** North Yorkshire, N England, UK
145 Q5 **Malḥāt** C Iraq
34 K14 **Malheur Lake** ◎ Oregon, NW USA
34 L14 **Malheur River** ↝ Oregon, NW USA
78 I13 **Mali** Moyenne-Guinée, NW Guinea
79 O9 **Mali** *off.* Republic of Mali, *Fr.* République du Mali; *prev.* French Sudan, Sudanese Republic. ◆ *republic* W Africa
175 S16 **Maliana** Timor, S Indonesia
178 H1 **Mali Hka** ↝ N Burma
Mali Idjoš *see* Mali Idoš
114 K8 **Mali Idoš** *var.* Mali Idjoš, *Hung.* Kishegyes; *prev.* Krivaja. Serbia, N Yugoslavia
114 K9 **Mali Kanal** *canal* N Yugoslavia
175 R8 **Maliku** Sulawesi, N Indonesia
Malik, Wadi al *see* Milk, Wadi el
Mālikwāla *see* Malakwāl
178 Gg12 **Mali Kyun** *var.* Tavoy Island. *island* Mergui Archipelago, S Burma
97 M19 **Målilla** Kalmar, S Sweden
114 B11 **Mali Lošinj** *It.* Lussinpiccolo. Primorje-Gorski Kotar, W Croatia
xliv I2 **Malin** *Ir.* Málainn. Donegal, NW Ireland
Malin *see* Malyn
179 Q15 **Malindang, Mount** ▲ Mindanao, S Philippines
83 K20 **Malindi** Coast, SE Kenya
Malines *see* Mechelen
xliv I1 **Malin Head** *Ir.* Cionn Mhálanna. *headland* NW Ireland
xliv F4 **Malin More** Donegal, N Ireland
175 Pp7 **Malino, Gunung** ▲ Sulawesi, N Indonesia
115 M21 **Maliq** *var.* Maliqi. Korçë, SE Albania
Maliqi *see* Maliq
179 Rr16 **Malita** Mindanao, S Philippines
160 G12 **Malkāpur** Mahārāshtra, C India
142 B10 **Malkara** Tekirdağ, NW Turkey
121 J19 **Mal'kavichy** *Rus.* Mal'kovichi. Brestskaya Voblasts', SW Belorussia
Malkiye *see* Al Mālikīyah
116 L11 **Malko Sharkovo, Yazovir** ▣ SE Bulgaria
116 N11 **Malko Tŭrnovo** Burgaska Oblast, SE Bulgaria
Mal'kovichi *see* Mal'kavichy
191 R12 **Mallacoota** Victoria, SE Australia
xliii F14 **Mallaig** Highland, N Scotland, UK
190 J9 **Mallala** South Australia
77 W9 **Mallawi** C Egypt
107 R5 **Mallén** Aragón, NE Spain
108 F5 **Malles Venosta** Trentino-Alto Adige, N Italy
Mallicolo *see* Malekula
111 Q8 **Mallnitz** Salzburg, S Austria
107 W9 **Mallorca** *Eng.* Majorca; *anc.* Baleares Major. *island* Islas Baleares, Spain, W Mediterranean Sea
xliv F13 **Mallow** *Ir.* Mala. Cork, SW Ireland
xxxv I8 **Mallwyd** Gwynedd, NW Wales, UK
95 E15 **Malm** Nord-Trøndelag, C Norway
97 L19 **Malmbäck** Jönköping, S Sweden
94 J12 **Malmberget** Norrbotten, N Sweden
101 M20 **Malmédy** Liège, E Belgium
xxxvi M9 **Malmesbury** Wiltshire, S England, UK
85 E25 **Malmesbury** Western Cape, SW South Africa
97 N16 **Malmköping** Södermanland, C Sweden
97 K23 **Malmo** ✕ Malmöhus, S Sweden
97 K23 **Malmö** Malmöhus, S Sweden
97 K23 **Malmöhus** ◐ *county* S Sweden
47 Q16 **Malmok** *headland* Bonaire, S Netherlands Antilles
97 M18 **Malmslätt** Östergötland, S Sweden
129 R16 **Malmyzh** Kirovskaya Oblast', NW Russian Federation
58 A10 **Mal Nomre, Punta** *headland* NW Peru
197 B12 **Malo** *island* W Vanuatu
130 J7 **Maloarkhangel'sk** Orlovskaya Oblast', W Russian Federation
Maloelap *see* Maloelap Atoll
201 V6 **Maloelap Atoll** *var.* Maļoeļap. *atoll* E Marshall Islands
Maloenda *see* Malunda
110 I10 **Maloja** Graubünden, S Switzerland
84 L12 **Malole** Northern, NE Zambia
197 H13 **Malolo** *island* Mamanuca Group, W Fiji
197 H13 **Malolo Barrier Reef** *var.* Ro Ro Reef. *reef* W Fiji
179 P10 **Malolos** Luzon, N Philippines
20 K6 **Malone** New York, NE USA
81 K25 **Malonga** Shaba, S Zaire
113 L15 **Małopolska** *plateau* S Poland
Malorita/Maloryta *see* Malaryta
128 K9 **Maloshuyka** Arkhangel'skaya Oblast', NW Russian Federation
116 G10 **Mal'ovitsa** ▲ W Bulgaria
151 V15 **Malovodnoye** Almaty, SE Kazakhstan
96 C10 **Måløy** Sogn og Fjordane, S Norway
130 K4 **Maloyaroslavets** Kaluzhskaya Oblast', W Russian Federation
125 F6 **Malozemel'skaya Tundra** *physical region* NW Russian Federation
106 J10 **Malpartida de Cáceres** Extremadura, W Spain
106 K9 **Malpartida de Plasencia** Extremadura, W Spain
xxxviii H7 **Malpas** Cheshire, W England, UK
108 C7 **Malpensa** ✕ (Milano) Lombardia, N Italy
78 J6 **Malqteïr** *desert* N Mauritania
120 I10 **Malta** Rēzekne, SE Latvia
35 V7 **Malta** Montana, NW USA
123 Jj14 **Malta** *off.* Republic of Malta. ◆ *republic* C Mediterranean Sea
111 R8 **Malta** *var.* Maltabach. ↝ S Austria
123 L11 **Malta** *island* Malta, C Mediterranean Sea
Maltabach *see* Malta
Malta, Canale di *see* Malta Channel
123 L12 **Malta Channel** *It.* Canale di Malta. *strait* Italy/Malta
85 D20 **Maltahöhe** Hardap, SW Namibia
xli T16 **Maltby** Rotherham, N England, UK
xxxix S5 **Maltby le Marsh** Lincolnshire, E England, UK
xli U11 **Malton** North Yorkshire, N England, UK
175 T11 **Maluku** *off.* Propinsi Maluku, *Dut.* Molukken, *Eng.* Moluccas. ◐ *province* E Indonesia
175 Ss9 **Maluku** *Dut.* Molukken, *Eng.* Moluccas; *prev.* Spice Islands. *island group* E Indonesia
Maluku, Laut *see* Molucca Sea
79 V13 **Malumfashi** Katsina, N Nigeria
175 P11 **Malunda** *prev.* Maloenda. Sulawesi, C Indonesia
96 K13 **Malung** Kopparberg, C Sweden
96 K13 **Malungsfors** Kopparberg, C Sweden
195 X14 **Maluu** *var.* Malu'u. Malaita, N Solomon Islands
161 D16 **Mālvan** Mahārāshtra, W India
Malventum *see* Benevento
29 U12 **Malvern** Arkansas, C USA
31 S15 **Malvern** Iowa, C USA
46 I13 **Malvern** ▲ W Jamaica
xxxviii I13 **Malvern Hills** *hill range* W England, UK
xxxviii J13 **Malvern Link** Worcestershire, W England, UK
Malvinas, Islas *see* Falkland Islands
119 N4 **Malyn** *Rus.* Malin. Zhytomyrs'ka Oblast', N Ukraine
127 O5 **Malyy Anyuy** ↝ NE Russian Federation
131 O11 **Malyye Derbety** Respublika Kalmykiya, SW Russian Federation
Malyy Kavkaz *see* Lesser Caucasus
126 M5 **Malyy Lyakhovskiy, Ostrov** *island* NE Russian Federation
Malyy Pamir *see* Little Pamir
126 Jj4 **Malyy Taymyr, Ostrov** *island* Severnaya Zemlya, N Russian Federation
150 E10 **Malyy Uzen'** *Kaz.* Kishiözen. ↝ Kazakhstan/Russian Federation
126 I16 **Malyy Yenisey** *var.* Ka-Krem. ↝ S Russian Federation
126 K13 **Mama** Irkutskaya Oblast', C Russian Federation
131 S3 **Mamadysh** Respublika Tatarstan, W Russian Federation
119 N14 **Mamaia** Constanța, E Romania
197 G14 **Mamanuca Group** *island group* Yasawa Group, W Fiji
152 L13 **Mamash** Lebapskiy Velayat, E Turkmenistan
176 W11 **Mamasiware** Irian Jaya, E Indonesia
194 L14 **Mambare** ↝ S PNG
81 O17 **Mambasa** Haut-Zaïre, NE Zaire
176 Xx10 **Mamberamo, Sungai** ↝ Irian Jaya, E Indonesia
81 G15 **Mambéré** ↝ SW Central African Republic
81 G15 **Mambéré-Kadéï** ◐ *prefecture* SW Central African Republic
176 X9 **Mambetaloi** Irian Jaya, E Indonesia
Mambij *see* Manbij
81 H18 **Mambili** ↝ W Congo
85 N18 **Mambone** *var.* Nova Mambone. Inhambane, E Mozambique
179 P11 **Mamburao** Mindoro, N Philippines
180 I16 **Mamelles** *island* Inner Islands, NE Seychelles
101 M25 **Mamer** Luxembourg, SW Luxembourg
104 L6 **Mamers** Sarthe, NW France
81 D15 **Mamfe** Sud-Ouest, W Cameroon
151 P6 **Mamlyutka** Severnyy Kazakhstan, N Kazakhstan
38 M15 **Mammoth** Arizona, SW USA
35 S12 **Mammoth Hot Springs** Wyoming, C USA
Mamoedjoe *see* Mamuju
121 A14 **Mamonovo** *Ger.* Heiligenbeil. Kaliningradskaya Oblast', W Russian Federation
59 L14 **Mamoré, Rio** ↝ Bolivia/Brazil
78 I14 **Mamou** Moyenne-Guinée, W Guinea
24 H8 **Mamou** Louisiana, S USA
180 I14 **Mamoudzou** ○ (Mayotte) C Mayotte
180 I3 **Mampikony** Mahajanga, N Madagascar
79 P16 **Mampong** C Ghana
112 M7 **Mamry, Jezioro** *Ger.* Mauersee. ◎ NE Poland
175 P10 **Mamuju** *prev.* Mamoedjoe. Sulawesi, S Indonesia
175 Oo10 **Mamuju, Teluk** *bay* Sulawesi, C Indonesia
85 F19 **Mamuno** Ghanzi, W Botswana
115 K19 **Mamuras** *var.* Mamurasi, Mamurras. Lezhë, C Albania
Mamurasi/Mamurras *see* Mamuras
78 L16 **Man** W Ivory Coast
57 X9 **Mana** NW French Guiana
58 A6 **Manabí** ◐ *province* W Ecuador
44 G4 **Manabique, Punta** *var.* Cabo Tres Puntas. *headland* E Guatemala
56 G11 **Manacacías, Río** ↝ C Colombia
60 F13 **Manacapuru** Amazonas, N Brazil
175 Rr6 **Manado** *prev.* Menado. Sulawesi, C Indonesia
xxxv J8 **Manafon** Powys, C Wales, UK
196 H5 **Managaha** *island* S Northern Mariana Islands
101 G20 **Manage** Hainaut, S Belgium
44 J10 **Managua** ● (Nicaragua) Managua, W Nicaragua
44 J10 **Managua** ◐ *department* W Nicaragua
44 J10 **Managua** ✕ Managua, W Nicaragua
44 J10 **Managua, Lago de** *var.* Xolotlán. ◎ W Nicaragua
Manah *see* Bilād Manaḥ
20 K16 **Manahawkin** New Jersey, NE USA
192 K11 **Manaia** Taranaki, North Island, NZ
180 J6 **Manakara** Fianarantsoa, SE Madagascar
158 J7 **Manāli** Himāchal Pradesh, NW India
133 U12 **Ma, Nam** *Vtn.* Sông Mã. ↝ Laos/Vietnam
Manama *see* Al Manāmah
194 I10 **Manam Island** *island* N PNG
69 Y13 **Mananara** ↝ SE Madagascar
190 M9 **Manangatang** Victoria, SE Australia
180 J6 **Mananjary** Fianarantsoa, SE Madagascar
78 L14 **Manankoro** Sikasso, SW Mali
78 J12 **Manantali, Lac de** ▣ W Mali
Manáos *see* Manaus
193 B23 **Manapouri** Southland, South Island, NZ
193 B23 **Manapouri, Lake** ◎ South Island, NZ
60 F13 **Manaquiri** Amazonas, NW Brazil
Manar *see* Mannar
164 K5 **Manas** Xinjiang Uygur Zizhiqu, NW China
159 U12 **Manās** *var.* Dangme Chu. ↝ Bhutan/India
153 R8 **Manas, Gora** ▲ Kyrgyzstan/Uzbekistan
164 K3 **Manas Hu** ◎ NW China
159 P10 **Manaslu** ▲ C Nepal
39 S8 **Manassa** Colorado, C USA
23 W4 **Manassas** Virginia, NE USA
47 T5 **Manatí** C Puerto Rico
175 S16 **Manatuto** Timor, C Indonesia
194 L14 **Manau** Northern, S PNG
56 H4 **Manaure** La Guajira, N Colombia
60 F12 **Manaus** *prev.* Manáos. *state capital* Amazonas, NW Brazil
142 G17 **Manavgat** Antalya, SW Turkey
192 M13 **Manawatu** ↝ North Island, NZ
192 L11 **Manawatu-Wanganui** *off.* Manawatu-Wanganui Region. ◐ *region* North Island, NZ
176 Uu12 **Manawoka, Pulau** *island* Kepulauan Gorong, E Indonesia
179 Rr16 **Manay** Mindanao, S Philippines
144 K2 **Manbij** *var.* Mambij, *Fr.* Membidj. Ḥalab, N Syria
107 N13 **Mancha Real** Andalucía, S Spain
104 I4 **Manche** ◐ *department* N France
xl G15 **Manchester** *Lat.* Mancunium. Manchester, NW England, UK
xli P16 **Manchester** ◐ *unitary authority* NW England, UK
99 L18 **Manchester** ✕ NW England, UK
25 S5 **Manchester** Georgia, SE USA
31 Y13 **Manchester** Iowa, C USA
23 N7 **Manchester** Kentucky, S USA
21 O10 **Manchester** New Hampshire, NE USA
22 K10 **Manchester** Tennessee, S USA
20 M9 **Manchester** Vermont, NE USA
xl E16 **Manchester Canal** *canal* NW England, UK
155 P15 **Manchhar Lake** ◎ SE Pakistan
Man-chou-li *see* Manzhouli
133 X7 **Manchurian Plain** *plain* NE China
Máncio Lima *see* Japiim
Mancunium *see* Manchester
154 J15 **Mand** Baluchistān, SW Pakistan
Mand *see* Mand, Rūd-e
83 H25 **Manda** Iringa, SW Tanzania
180 H6 **Mandabe** Toliara, W Madagascar
168 I5 **Mandal** Hövsgöl, N Mongolia
168 L7 **Mandal** Töv, C Mongolia
97 E18 **Mandal** Vest-Agder, S Norway
177 G5 **Mandalay** Mandalay, C Burma
177 G6 **Mandalay** ◐ *division* C Burma
168 L9 **Mandalgovi** Dundgovĭ, C Mongolia
145 V7 **Mandalī** E Iraq
97 E18 **Mandalselva** ↝ S Norway
30 M5 **Mandan** North Dakota, N USA
Mandargiri Hill *see* Mandār Hill
159 R14 **Mandār Hill** *prev.* Mandargiri Hill. Bihār, NE India
175 P11 **Mandar, Teluk** *bay* Sulawesi, C Indonesia
109 C19 **Mandas** Sardegna, Italy, C Mediterranean Sea
Mandasor *see* Mandsaur
83 L16 **Mandera** North Eastern, NE Kenya
35 V13 **Manderson** Wyoming, C USA
46 J12 **Mandeville** C Jamaica
24 K9 **Mandeville** Louisiana, S USA
158 I7 **Mandi** Himāchal Pradesh, NW India
78 K14 **Mandiana** Haute-Guinée, E Guinea
155 U10 **Mandi Būrewāla** *var.* Būrewāla. Punjab, E Pakistan
158 G9 **Mandi Dabwāli** Haryāna, NW India
Mandidzudzure *see* Chimanimani
85 M15 **Mandié** Manica, NW Mozambique
85 N14 **Mandimba** Niassa, N Mozambique
175 Ss9 **Mandioli, Pulau** *island* Kepulauan Bacan, E Indonesia
59 Q19 **Mandioré, Laguna** ◎ E Bolivia
160 I10 **Mandla** Madhya Pradesh, C India
85 M20 **Mandlakazi** *var.* Manjacaze. Gaza, S Mozambique
97 E24 **Mandø** *var.* Manø. *island* W Denmark
176 Ww9 **Mandori** Irian Jaya, E Indonesia
Mandoúdhion/Mandoudi *see* Mantoúdi
117 G19 **Mándra** Attikí, C Greece
180 J7 **Mandrare** ↝ S Madagascar
116 M10 **Mandra, Yazovir** *salt lake* SE Bulgaria
109 L23 **Mandrazzi, Portella** *pass* Sicilia, Italy, C Mediterranean Sea
180 J3 **Mandritsara** Mahajanga, N Madagascar
149 O13 **Mand, Rūd-e** *var.* Mand. ↝ S Iran
160 F9 **Mandsaur** *prev.* Mandasor. Madhya Pradesh, C India
160 F11 **Māndu** Madhya Pradesh, C India
175 Oo5 **Mandul, Pulau** *island* N Indonesia
85 G15 **Mandundu** Western, W Zambia
188 I13 **Mandurah** Western Australia
109 P18 **Manduria** Puglia, SE Italy
161 G20 **Mandya** Karnātaka, C India
79 P12 **Mané** C Burkina
xxxix S10 **Manea** Cambridgeshire, E England, UK
108 E8 **Manerbio** Lombardia, NW Italy
Manevichi *see* Manevychi
118 K3 **Manevychi** *Pol.* Maniewicze, *Rus.* Manevichi. Volyns'ka Oblast', NW Ukraine
109 N16 **Manfredonia** Puglia, SE Italy
109 N16 **Manfredonia, Golfo di** *gulf* Adriatic Sea, N Mediterranean Sea
79 P13 **Manga** C Burkina
61 L16 **Mangabeiras, Chapada das** ▲▲ E Brazil
81 J20 **Mangai** Bandundu, W Zaire
202 L17 **Mangaia** *island group* S Cook Islands
192 M9 **Mangakino** Waikato, North Island, NZ
118 M15 **Mangalia** *anc.* Callatis. Constanța, SE Romania
80 J11 **Mangalmé** Guéra, SE Chad
161 E19 **Mangalore** Karnātaka, W India
203 Y13 **Mangareva** *var.* Magareva. *island* Îles Tuamotu, SE French Polynesia
85 I23 **Mangaung** Free State, C South Africa
Mangaung *see* Bloemfontein
160 K9 **Mangawān** Madhya Pradesh, C India
192 M11 **Mangaweka** Manawatu-Wanganui, North Island, NZ
192 N11 **Mangaweka** ▲ North Island, NZ
81 P17 **Mangbwalu** Haut-Zaïre, NE Zaire
xliv D13 **Mangerton Mountain** ▲ SW Ireland
103 L24 **Mangfall** ↝ S Germany
174 K11 **Manggar** Pulau Belitung, W Indonesia
176 Vv12 **Manggawitu** Irian Jaya, E Indonesia
152 H8 **Manghit** *Rus.* Mangit. Qoraqalpoghiston Respublikasi, W Uzbekistan
177 G2 **Mangin Range** ▲▲ N Burma
145 R1 **Mangish** N Iraq
150 F15 **Mangistau** *Kaz.* Mangqystaū Oblysy; *prev.* Mangyshlaskaya. ◐ *province* SW Kazakhstan
Mangit *see* Manghit
56 A13 **Manglares, Cabo** *headland* SW Colombia
155 V6 **Mangla Reservoir** ▣ NE Pakistan
165 N9 **Mangnai** *var.* Lao Mangnai. Qinghai, C China
Mango *see* Mago, Fiji
Mango *see* Sansanné-Mango, Togo
Mangoche *see* Mangochi
85 N14 **Mangochi** *var.* Mangoche; *prev.* Fort Johnston. Southern, SE Malawi
79 N14 **Mangodara** SW Burkina
180 H6 **Mangoky** ↝ W Madagascar
175 S10 **Mangole, Pulau** *island* Kepulauan Sula, E Indonesia
192 J2 **Mangonui** Northland, North Island, NZ
xxxvi L9 **Mangotsfield** South Gloucestershire, SW England, UK
Mangqystaū Oblysy *see* Mangistau
Mangqystaū Shyghanghy *see* Mangyshlakskiy Zaliv
106 H7 **Mangualde** Viseu, N Portugal
63 H18 **Mangueira, Lagoa** ◎ S Brazil
79 X6 **Manguéni, Plateau du** ▲ NE Niger
28 K11 **Mangum** Oklahoma, C USA
81 O18 **Manguredjipa** Nord Kivu, E Zaire
85 L16 **Mangwendi** Mashonaland East, E Zimbabwe
150 F15 **Mangyshlak, Plato** *plateau* SW Kazakhstan
150 E14 **Mangyshlakskiy Zaliv** *Kaz.* Mangqystaū Shyghanghy. *gulf* SW Kazakhstan
Mangyshlaskaya *see* Mangistau
168 I5 **Manhan** Hövsgöl, N Mongolia
29 O4 **Manhattan** Kansas, C USA
101 L21 **Manhay** Luxembourg, SE Belgium
85 L21 **Manhiça** *prev.* Vila de Manhiça. Maputo, S Mozambique
85 L21 **Manhoca** Maputo, S Mozambique
61 N20 **Manhuaçu** Minas Gerais, SE Brazil
149 R11 **Mānī** Kermān, C Iran
56 H10 **Maní** Casanare, C Colombia
58 A6 **Manía, Bahía de** *bay* W Ecuador
85 M17 **Manica** *var.* Vila de Manica. Manica, W Mozambique
85 M17 **Manica** *off.* Província de Manica. ◐ *province* W Mozambique
85 L17 **Manicaland** ◐ *province* E Zimbabwe
13 U5 **Manic Deux, Réservoir** ▣ Québec, SE Canada
Manich *see* Manych
61 F14 **Manicoré** Amazonas, N Brazil
11 N11 **Manicouagan** Québec, SE Canada
11 N11 **Manicouagan** ↝ Québec, SE Canada
13 U6 **Manicouagan, Péninsule de** *peninsula* Québec, SE Canada
11 N11 **Manicouagan, Réservoir** ◎ Québec, SE Canada
13 T4 **Manic Trois, Réservoir** ▣ Québec, SE Canada
81 M20 **Maniema** *off.* Région du Maniema. ◐ *region* E Zaire
Maniewicze *see* Manevychi
166 F8 **Maniganggo** Sichuan, C China
9 Y15 **Manigotagan** Manitoba, S Canada
159 R13 **Manihāri** Bihār, N India
203 U9 **Manihi** *island* Îles Tuamotu, C French Polynesia
202 L13 **Manihiki** *atoll* N Cook Islands
183 U8 **Manihiki Plateau** *undersea feature* C Pacific Ocean
206 M14 **Maniitsoq** *var.* Manitsoq, *Dan.* Sukkertoppen. S Greenland
159 T15 **Manikganj** Dhaka, C Bangladesh
158 M14 **Mānikpur** Uttar Pradesh, N India
179 P11 **Manila** *off.* City of Manila. ● (Philippines) Luzon, N Philippines
29 Y9 **Manila** Arkansas, C USA
201 N16 **Manila Reef** *reef* W Micronesia
191 T6 **Manilla** New South Wales, SE Australia
200 Qq14 **Maniloa** *island* Tongatapu Group, S Tonga
127 P7 **Manily** Koryakskiy Avtonomnyy Okrug, E Russian Federation
176 Ww9 **Manim, Pulau** *island* E Indonesia
173 Ff8 **Maninjau, Danau** ◎ Sumatera, W Indonesia
159 W13 **Manipur** ◐ *state* NE India
159 X14 **Manipur Hills** *hill range* E India
142 C14 **Manisa** *var.* Manissa; *prev.* Saruhan, *anc.* Magnesia. Manisa, W Turkey
142 C13 **Manisa** *var.* Manissa. ◐ *province* W Turkey
xl G11 **Man, Isle of** *island* British Isles
Manissa *see* Manisa
33 O7 **Manistee** Michigan, N USA
33 P7 **Manistee River** ↝ Michigan, N USA
33 O4 **Manistique** Michigan, N USA
33 P4 **Manistique Lake** ◎ Michigan, N USA
9 W13 **Manitoba** ◐ *province* S Canada
9 X16 **Manitoba, Lake** ◎ Manitoba, S Canada
9 X17 **Manitou** Manitoba, S Canada
33 N2 **Manitou Island** *island* Michigan, N USA
12 H11 **Manitou Lake** ◎ Ontario, SE Canada
10 G15 **Manitoulin Island** *island* Ontario, S Canada
39 T5 **Manitou Springs** Colorado, C USA
12 G12 **Manitouwabing Lake** ◎ Ontario, S Canada
12 E12 **Manitouwadge** Ontario, S Canada
10 G15 **Manitowaning** Manitoulin Island, Ontario, S Canada
12 B7 **Manitowik Lake** ◎ Ontario, S Canada
33 N7 **Manitowoc** Wisconsin, N USA
Manitsoq *see* Maniitsoq
145 O7 **Mānī', Wādī al** *dry watercourse* W Iraq
10 J14 **Maniwaki** Québec, SE Canada
176 X11 **Maniwori** Irian Jaya, E Indonesia
56 E10 **Manizales** Caldas, W Colombia
114 F11 **Manjača** ▲ NW Bosnia and Herzegovina
Manjacaze *see* Mandlakazi
188 J14 **Manjimup** Western Australia
111 V4 **Mank** Niederösterreich, C Austria
81 I17 **Mankanza** Equateur, NW Zaire
159 N12 **Mankāpur** Uttar Pradesh, N India
28 M3 **Mankato** Kansas, C USA
31 U10 **Mankato** Minnesota, N USA
119 O7 **Man'kivka** Cherkas'ka Oblast', C Ukraine
78 M15 **Mankono** C Ivory Coast
9 T17 **Mankota** Saskatchewan, S Canada
161 K23 **Mankulam** Northern Province, N Sri Lanka
41 Q9 **Manley Hot Springs** Alaska, USA
20 H10 **Manlius** New York, NE USA
107 W5 **Manlleu** Cataluña, NE Spain
31 V11 **Manly** Iowa, C USA
160 E13 **Manmād** Mahārāshtra, W India
190 J7 **Mannahill** South Australia
161 J23 **Mannar** *var.* Manar. Northern Province, NW Sri Lanka
161 I24 **Mannar, Gulf of** *gulf* India/Sri Lanka
161 J23 **Mannar Island** *island* N Sri Lanka
Mannersdorf *see* Mannersdorf am Leithagebirge
111 Y5 **Mannersdorf am Leithagebirge** *var.* Mannersdorf. Niederösterreich, E Austria
111 Y6 **Mannersdorf an der Rabnitz** Burgenland, E Austria
103 G20 **Mannheim** Baden-Württemberg, SW Germany
9 O12 **Manning** Alberta, W Canada
31 T14 **Manning** Iowa, C USA
30 K5 **Manning** North Dakota, N USA
23 S13 **Manning** South Carolina, SE USA
203 Y2 **Manning, Cape** *headland* Kiritimati, NE Kiribati
195 V13 **Manning Strait** *strait* NW Solomon Islands
23 S3 **Mannington** West Virginia, NE USA
xxxvii Y6 **Manningtree** Essex, SE England, UK
190 A1 **Mann Ranges** ▲▲ South Australia
109 C19 **Mannu** ↝ Sardegna, Italy, C Mediterranean Sea
9 R14 **Mannville** Alberta, SW Canada
78 J15 **Mano** ↝ Liberia/Sierra Leone
Manø *see* Mandø
41 O13 **Manokotak** Alaska, USA
176 W9 **Manokwari** Irian Jaya, E Indonesia
81 N22 **Manono** Shaba, SE Zaire
27 T10 **Manor** Texas, SW USA
xxxv D14 **Manorbier** Pembrokeshire, SW Wales, UK
xliv G5 **Manorhamilton** *Ir.* Cluainín. Leitrim, NW Ireland
xxxvi F6 **Manor Park** Newham, SE England, UK
105 S15 **Manosque** Alpes-de-Haute-Provence, SE France
10 L11 **Manouane, Lac** ◎ Québec, SE Canada
169 W12 **Manp'o** *var.* Manp'ojin. NW North Korea
Manp'ojin *see* Manp'o
203 T4 **Manra** *prev.* Sydney Island. *atoll* Phoenix Islands, C Kiribati
107 V5 **Manresa** Cataluña, NE Spain
158 H9 **Mānsa** Punjab, NW India
84 J12 **Mansa** *prev.* Fort Rosebery. Luapula, N Zambia
78 G12 **Mansa Konko** C Gambia
13 Q11 **Manseau** Québec, SE Canada
155 U5 **Mānsehra** North-West Frontier Province, NW Pakistan
15 Mm6 **Mansel Island** *island* Northwest Territories, NE Canada
xli N11 **Mansergh** Cumbria, NW England, UK
xxxix N6 **Mansfield** Nottinghamshire, C England, UK
191 O12 **Mansfield** Victoria, SE Australia
29 S11 **Mansfield** Arkansas, C USA
24 G6 **Mansfield** Louisiana, S USA
21 O12 **Mansfield** Massachusetts, NE USA
33 T12 **Mansfield** Ohio, N USA
20 G12 **Mansfield** Pennsylvania, NE USA
20 M7 **Mansfield, Mount** ▲ Vermont, NE USA
61 M16 **Mansidão** Bahia, E Brazil
104 L11 **Mansle** Charente, W France
78 G12 **Mansôa** C Guinea-Bissau
49 V8 **Manso, Rio** ↝ C Brazil
Manṣūra *see* El Manṣūra
Mansurabad *see* Mehrān, Rūd-e
58 A6 **Manta** Manabí, W Ecuador
59 F14 **Mantaro, Río** ↝ C Peru
37 O8 **Manteca** California, W USA
56 J7 **Mantecal** Apure, C Venezuela
33 N11 **Manteno** Illinois, N USA
23 Y9 **Manteo** Roanoke Island, North Carolina, SE USA
Mantes-Gassicourt *see* Mantes-la-Jolie
105 N5 **Mantes-la-Jolie** *prev.* Mantes-Gassicourt, Mantes-sur-Seine, *anc.* Medunta. Yvelines, N France
Mantes-sur-Seine *see* Mantes-la-Jolie
38 L5 **Manti** Utah, W USA
Mantinea *see* Mantíneia
117 F20 **Mantíneia** *anc.* Mantinea. *site of ancient city* Pelopónnisos, S Greece
61 M21 **Mantiqueira, Serra da** ▲▲ S Brazil
xxxix P9 **Manton** Rutland, C England, UK
31 W10 **Mantorville** Minnesota, N USA
117 G17 **Mantoúdi** *var.* Mandoudi; *prev.* Mandoúdhion. Évvoia, C Greece
Mantoue *see* Mantova
108 F8 **Mantova** *Eng.* Mantua, *Fr.* Mantoue. Lombardia, NW Italy
95 M19 **Mäntsälä** Uusimaa, S Finland
95 L17 **Mänttä** Häme, SW Finland
Mantua *see* Mantova
129 O14 **Manturovo** Kostromskaya Oblast', NW Russian Federation
95 M18 **Mäntyharju** Mikkeli, SE Finland
94 M13 **Mäntyjärvi** Lappi, N Finland
202 L16 **Manuae** *island* S Cook Islands
203 Q10 **Manuae** *atoll* Îles Sous le Vent, W French Polynesia
198 Dd8 **Manua Islands** *island group* E American Samoa
42 L5 **Manuel Benavides** Chihuahua, N Mexico
63 D21 **Manuel J.Cobo** Buenos Aires, E Argentina
60 M12 **Manuel Luís, Recife** *reef* E Brazil
63 F15 **Manuel Viana** Rio Grande do Sul, S Brazil
61 I14 **Manuel Zinho** Pará, N Brazil
203 V11 **Manuhangi** *atoll* Îles Tuamotu, C French Polynesia
193 E22 **Manuherikia** ↝ South Island, NZ
175 R11 **Manui, Pulau** *island* N Indonesia
Manukau *see* Manurewa
192 L6 **Manukau Harbour** *harbour* North Island, NZ
174 K14 **Manuk, Ci** ↝ Jawa, S Indonesia
176 U12 **Manuk, Pulau** *island* Maluku, E Indonesia
203 Z2 **Manulu Lagoon** ◎ Kiritimati, E Kiribati
190 J7 **Manunda Creek** *seasonal river* South Australia
59 K15 **Manupari, Río** ↝ N Bolivia
192 L6 **Manurewa** *var.* Manukau. Auckland, North Island, NZ
59 K15 **Manurimi, Río** ↝ NW Bolivia
194 I8 **Manus** ◐ *province* N PNG
194 J8 **Manus Island** *var.* Great Admiralty Island. *island* N PNG
176 U15 **Manuwui** Pulau Babar, E Indonesia
31 Q3 **Manvel** North Dakota, N USA
35 Z14 **Manville** Wyoming, C USA
24 G6 **Many** Louisiana, S USA
83 H21 **Manyara, Lake** ◎ NE Tanzania
130 L12 **Manych** *var.* Manich. ↝ SW Russian Federation
131 N13 **Manych-Gudilo, Ozero** *salt lake* SW Russian Federation
85 H14 **Manyinga** North Western, NW Zambia
107 O11 **Manzanares** Castilla-La Mancha, C Spain
46 H7 **Manzanillo** Granma, E Cuba
42 K14 **Manzanillo** Colima, SW Mexico
42 K14 **Manzanillo, Bahía** *bay* SW Mexico
39 S11 **Manzano Mountains** ▲▲ New Mexico, SW USA
39 R12 **Manzano Peak** ▲ New Mexico, SW USA
169 R6 **Manzhouli** *var.* Man-chou-li. Nei Mongol Zizhiqu, N China
Manzil Bū Ruqaybah *see* Menzel Bourguiba
145 X9 **Manziliyah** E Iraq
85 L21 **Manzini** *prev.* Bremersdorp. C Swaziland
85 L21 **Manzini** ✕ (Mbabane) C Swaziland
80 G10 **Mao** Kanem, W Chad
47 N8 **Mao** NW Dominican Republic
Maó *see* Mahón
Maoemere *see* Maumere
165 W9 **Maojing** Gansu, N China
176 Xx12 **Maoke, Pegunungan** *Dut.* Sneeuw-gebergte, *Eng.* Snow Mountains. ▲▲ Irian Jaya, E Indonesia
Maol Réidh, Caoc *see* Mweelrea
166 M15 **Maoming** Guangdong, S China
166 H8 **Maoxian** *var.* Mao Xian; *prev.* Fengyizhen. Sichuan, C China
85 L19 **Mapai** Gaza, SW Mozambique
164 H15 **Mapam Yumco** ◎ W China
85 J15 **Mapanza** Southern, S Zambia
56 J4 **Mapararí** Falcón, N Venezuela
43 U17 **Mapastepec** Chiapas, SE Mexico
175 O5 **Mapat, Pulau** *island* N Indonesia

◆ Country ● Country Capital ◇ Dependent Territory ○ Dependent Territory Capital ◐ Administrative Region ✕ International Airport ▲ Mountain ▲▲ Mountain Range Volcano ↝ River ◎ Lake ▣ Reservoir

MAPI – MASON CITY

176 Yy14 **Mapi** Irian Jaya, E Indonesia
176 Vv7 **Mapia, Kepulauan** *island group* E Indonesia
42 L8 **Mapimí** Durango, C Mexico
85 N19 **Mapinhane** Inhambane, SE Mozambique
57 N7 **Mapire** Monagas, NE Venezuela
9 S17 **Maple Creek** Saskatchewan, S Canada
33 Q9 **Maple River** Michigan, N USA
31 P7 **Maple River** North Dakota/South Dakota, N USA
31 S13 **Mapleton** Iowa, C USA
31 U10 **Mapleton** Minnesota, N USA
31 R5 **Mapleton** North Dakota, N USA
34 F13 **Mapleton** Oregon, NW USA
38 L3 **Mapleton** Utah, W USA
199 Ii5 **Mapmaker Seamounts** *undersea feature* N Pacific Ocean
194 G10 **Maprik** East Sepik, NW PNG
85 L21 **Maputo** *prev.* Lourenço Marques. ● (Mozambique) Maputo, S Mozambique
85 L21 **Maputo** ◆ *province* S Mozambique
85 L21 **Maputo** ✕ Maputo, S Mozambique
69 V14 **Maputo** S Mozambique
Maqanshy *see* Makanchi
Maqat *see* Makat
115 K19 **Maqë** NW Albania
115 M19 **Maqellarë** Dibër, C Albania
165 S12 **Maqên** *var.* Dawu. Qinghai, C China
165 S11 **Maqên Gangri** ▲ C China
165 U12 **Maqu** Gansu, C China
106 M9 **Maqueda** Castilla-La Mancha, C Spain
84 B9 **Maquela do Zombo** Uíge, NW Angola
65 I16 **Maquinchao** Río Negro, C Argentina
31 Z13 **Maquoketa** Iowa, C USA
31 Y13 **Maquoketa River** Iowa, C USA
12 F13 **Mar** Ontario, S Canada
97 F14 **Mår** ◎ S Norway
83 G19 **Mara** ◆ *region* N Tanzania
203 P8 **Maraa** Tahiti, W French Polynesia
60 D12 **Maraã** Amazonas, NW Brazil
203 O8 **Maraa, Pointe** *headland* Tahiti, W French Polynesia
61 K14 **Marabá** Pará, NE Brazil
56 H5 **Maracaibo** Zulia, NW Venezuela
Maracaibo, Gulf of *see* Venezuela, Golfo de
56 H5 **Maracaibo, Lago de** *var.* Lake Maracaibo. *inlet* NW Venezuela
Maracaibo, Lake *see* Maracaibo, Lago de
60 K10 **Maracá, Ilha de** *island* NE Brazil
61 H20 **Maracaju, Serra de** ▲ S Brazil
60 I11 **Maracanaquará, Planalto** ▲ NE Brazil
56 L5 **Maracay** Aragua, N Venezuela
Marada *see* Marādah
77 R9 **Marādah** *var.* Marada. N Libya
79 U12 **Maradi** Maradi, S Niger
79 U11 **Maradi** ◆ *department* S Niger
83 E21 **Maragarazi** *var.* Muragarazi. Burundi/Tanzania
Maragha *see* Marāgheh
148 J3 **Marāgheh** *var.* Maragha. Āzarbāyjān-e Khāvarī, NW Iran
147 P7 **Marāh** *var.* Marrāt. Ar Riyāḑ, C Saudi Arabia
57 N11 **Marahuaca, Cerro** ▲ S Venezuela
29 R5 **Marais des Cygnes River** Kansas/Missouri, C USA
60 L11 **Marajó, Baía de** *bay* N Brazil
61 K12 **Marajó, Ilha de** *island* N Brazil
203 O2 **Marakei** *atoll* Tungaru, W Kiribati
Marakesh *see* Marrakech
83 I18 **Maralal** Rift Valley, C Kenya
85 G21 **Maraleng** Kgalagadi, S Botswana
151 U8 **Maraldy, Ozero** ◎ NE Kazakhstan
190 C5 **Maralinga** South Australia
179 R15 **Maramag** Mindanao, S Philippines
Máramarossziget *see* Sighetu Marmaţiei
195 Y16 **Maramasike** *var.* Small Malaita. *island* N Solomon Islands
Maramba *see* Livingstone
204 H3 **Marambio** *Argentinian research station* Antarctica
118 H9 **Maramureş** ◆ *county* NW Romania
38 L15 **Marana** Arizona, SW USA
107 P7 **Maranchón** Castilla-La Mancha, C Spain
148 J2 **Marand** *var.* Merend. Āzarbāyjān-e Khāvarī, NW Iran
Marandellas *see* Marondera
60 L13 **Maranhão** *off.* Estado do Maranhão. ◆ *state* E Brazil
106 H10 **Maranhão, Barragem do** ⊡ C Portugal
155 O11 **Mārān, Koh-i** ▲ SW Pakistan
108 J7 **Marano, Laguna di** *lagoon* NE Italy
58 E9 **Marañón, Río** N Peru
104 J10 **Marans** Charente-Maritime, W France
85 M20 **Marão** Inhambane, S Mozambique
193 B23 **Mararoa** South Island, NZ
Maraş/Marash *see* Kahramanmaraş
109 M19 **Maratea** Basilicata, S Italy
106 G11 **Marateca** Setúbal, S Portugal
117 B20 **Marathiá, Ákra** *headland* Zákynthos, Iónioi Nísoi, Greece, C Mediterranean Sea
10 E12 **Marathon** Ontario, S Canada
25 Y17 **Marathon** Florida Keys, Florida, SE USA
26 L10 **Marathon** Texas, SW USA
Marathón *see* Marathónas
117 H19 **Marathónas** *prev.* Marathón. Attikí, C Greece
175 Oo6 **Maratua, Pulau** *island* N Indonesia
61 O18 **Maraú** Bahia, SE Brazil
149 R3 **Marāveh Tappeh** Māzandarān, N Iran
26 L11 **Maravillas Creek** Texas, SW USA
194 J13 **Marawaka** Eastern Highlands, C PNG
179 R15 **Marawi** Mindanao, S Philippines
xxxvi L16 **Marazion** Cornwall, SW England, UK
Marbat *see* Mirbāţ
106 L15 **Marbella** Andalucía, S Spain
188 J7 **Marble Bar** Western Australia
38 L9 **Marble Canyon** *canyon* Arizona, SW USA
27 S10 **Marble Falls** Texas, SW USA
29 Y7 **Marble Hill** Missouri, C USA
35 T15 **Marbleton** Wyoming, C USA
Marburg *see* Maribor
Marburg *see* Marburg an der Lahn, Germany
103 H16 **Marburg an der Lahn** *hist.* Marburg. Hessen, W Germany
113 H23 **Marcal** W Hungary
44 G7 **Marcala** La Paz, SW Honduras
113 H24 **Marcali** Somogy, SW Hungary
85 A16 **Marca, Ponta da** *headland* SW Angola
61 I16 **Marcelândia** Mato Grosso, W Brazil
29 T3 **Marceline** Missouri, C USA
62 I13 **Marcelino Ramos** Rio Grande do Sul, S Brazil
57 Y12 **Marcel, Mont** ▲ S French Guiana
xxxix S10 **March** Cambridgeshire, E England, UK
111 Z3 **March** *var.* Morava. C Europe *see also* Morava
108 I12 **Marche** *Eng.* Marches. ◆ *region* C Italy
105 N11 **Marche** *cultural region* C France
101 J21 **Marche-en-Famenne** Luxembourg, SE Belgium
106 K14 **Marchena** Andalucía, S Spain
59 B17 **Marchena, Isla** *var.* Bindloe Island. *island* Galapagos Islands, Ecuador, E Pacific Ocean
Marches *see* Marche
101 J20 **Marchin** Liège, E Belgium
189 S1 **Marchinbar Island** *island* Wessel Islands, Northern Territory, N Australia
64 L9 **Mar Chiquita, Laguna** ◎ C Argentina
105 Q10 **Marcigny** Saône-et-Loire, C France
25 W16 **Marco** Florida, SE USA
Marcodurum *see* Düren
61 O15 **Marcolândia** Pernambuco, E Brazil
108 I8 **Marco Polo** ✕ (Venezia) Veneto, NE Italy
Marcq *see* Mark
118 M8 **Mărculeşti** *Rus.* Markuleshty. N Moldavia
31 S12 **Marcus** Iowa, C USA
41 S11 **Marcus Baker, Mount** ▲ Alaska, USA
199 Hh5 **Marcus Island** *var.* Minami Tori Shima. *island* E Japan
20 K8 **Marcy, Mount** ▲ New York, NE USA
155 T5 **Mardān** North-West Frontier Province, N Pakistan
65 N14 **Mar del Plata** Buenos Aires, E Argentina
xxxvii W11 **Marden** Kent, SE England, UK
143 Q16 **Mardin** Mardin, SE Turkey
143 Q16 **Mardin** ◆ *province* SE Turkey
143 Q16 **Mardin Dağları** ▲ SE Turkey
168 J9 **Mardzad** Övörhangay, C Mongolia
197 L6 **Maré** *island* Îles Loyauté, E New Caledonia
Marea Neagră *see* Black Sea
107 Z8 **Mare de Déu del Toro** ▲ Menorca, Spain, W Mediterranean Sea
189 W4 **Mareeba** Queensland, NE Australia
xlii F11 **Maree, Loch** ◎ N Scotland, UK
Mareeq *see* Mereeg
Marek *see* Dupnitsa
78 J11 **Maréna** Kayes, W Mali
202 I2 **Marenanuka** *atoll* Tungaru, W Kiribati
31 X14 **Marengo** Iowa, C USA
104 J11 **Marennes** Charente-Maritime, W France
109 G23 **Marettimo, Isola** *island* Isole Egadi, S Italy
26 K10 **Marfa** Texas, SW USA
59 P17 **Marfil, Laguna** ◎ E Bolivia
xxxv H15 **Margam** Neath Port Talbot, S Wales, UK
Margarets *see* Marhanets'
27 Q4 **Margaret** Texas, SW USA
188 I14 **Margaret River** Western Australia
194 G12 **Margarima** Southern Highlands, W PNG
57 N4 **Margarita, Isla de** *island* N Venezuela
117 I25 **Margarítes** Kríti, Greece, E Mediterranean Sea
xxxvii Z9 **Margate** *prev.* Mergate. Kent, SE England, UK
25 Z15 **Margate** Florida, SE USA
Margelan *see* Marghilon
105 P13 **Margeride, Montagnes de la** ▲ C France
Margherita *see* Jamaame
109 N16 **Margherita di Savoia** Puglia, SE Italy
Margherita, Lake *see* Ābaya Hāyk'
83 E18 **Margherita Peak** *Fr.* Pic Marguerite. ▲ Uganda/Zaire
155 O4 **Marghī** Bāmīān, N Afghanistan
153 S10 **Marghilon** *var.* Margelan, *Rus.* Margilan. Farghona Wiloyati, E Uzbekistan
118 G9 **Marghita** *Hung.* Margitta. Bihor, NW Romania
Margilan *see* Marghilon
118 K8 **Marginea** Suceava, NE Romania
Margitta *see* Marghita
xliii G22 **Margnaheglish** North Ayrshire, W Scotland, UK
154 K9 **Mārgow, Dasht-e** *desert* SW Afghanistan
101 L18 **Margraten** Limburg, SE Netherlands
8 M15 **Marguerite** British Columbia, SW Canada
204 I6 **Marguerite Bay** *bay* Antarctica
Marguerite, Pic *see* Margherita Peak
xxxix U9 **Marham** Norfolk, E England, UK
xxxvi E13 **Marhamchurch** Cornwall, SW England, UK
119 T9 **Marhanets'** *Rus.* Marganets. Dnipropetrovs'ka Oblast', E Ukraine
xxxix R10 **Marholm** Cambridgeshire, E England, UK
194 E15 **Mari** Western, SW PNG
203 R12 **Maria** *island* Îles Australes, SW French Polynesia
203 Y12 **Maria** *atoll* Groupe Actéon, SE French Polynesia
42 I12 **María Cleofas, Isla** *island* C Mexico
64 H4 **María Elena** *var.* Oficina María Elena. Antofagasta, N Chile
97 G21 **Mariager** Århus, C Denmark
63 C22 **María Ignacia** Buenos Aires, E Argentina
191 P17 **Maria Island** *island* Tasmania, SE Australia
42 H12 **María Madre, Isla** *island* C Mexico
42 I12 **María Magdalena, Isla** *island* C Mexico
199 H6 **Mariana Islands** *island group* Guam/Northern Mariana Islands
183 N3 **Mariana Trench** *var.* Challenger Deep. *undersea feature* W Pacific Ocean
159 X12 **Mariāni** Assam, NE India
29 X11 **Marianna** Arkansas, C USA
25 R8 **Marianna** Florida, SE USA
180 J16 **Marianne** *island* Inner Islands, NE Seychelles
97 M19 **Mariannelund** Jönköping, S Sweden
63 D15 **Mariano I.Loza** Corrientes, NE Argentina
Mariano Machado *see* Ganda
113 A16 **Mariánské Lázně** *Ger.* Marienbad. Západní Čechy, W Czech Republic
Máriaradna *see* Radna
35 S7 **Marias River** Montana, NW USA
Maria-Theresiopel *see* Subotica
Máriatölgyes *see* Dubnica nad Váhom
192 H1 **Maria van Diemen, Cape** *headland* North Island, NZ
111 V5 **Mariazell** Steiermark, E Austria
147 P15 **Mar'ib** W Yemen
97 I25 **Maribo** Storstrøm, S Denmark
111 W9 **Maribor** *Ger.* Marburg. NE Slovenia
Marica *see* Maritsa
37 R13 **Maricopa** California, W USA
Maricourt *see* Kangiqsujuaq
83 D15 **Maridi** Western Equatoria, SW Sudan
204 M11 **Marie Byrd Land** *physical region* Antarctica
199 Ll16 **Marie Byrd Seamount** *undersea feature* N Amundsen Sea
47 X11 **Marie-Galante** *var.* Ceyre to the Carib. *island* SE Guadeloupe
47 Y6 **Marie-Galante, Canal de** *channel* S Guadeloupe
95 J20 **Mariehamn** *Fin.* Maarianhamina. Åland, SW Finland
46 C4 **Mariel** La Habana, W Cuba
101 H22 **Mariembourg** Namur, S Belgium
Marienbad *see* Mariánské Lázně
Marienburg *see* Alūksne, Latvia
Marienburg *see* Malbork, Poland
Marienburg *see* Feldioara, Romania
Marienburg in Westpreussen *see* Malbork
Marienhausen *see* Viļaka
85 D20 **Mariental** Hardap, SW Namibia
20 D13 **Marienville** Pennsylvania, NE USA
Marienwerder *see* Kwidzyń
60 C12 **Marié, Rio** NW Brazil
97 K17 **Mariestad** Skaraborg, S Sweden
25 S3 **Marietta** Georgia, SE USA
33 U14 **Marietta** Ohio, N USA
29 N13 **Marietta** Oklahoma, C USA
83 H18 **Marigat** Rift Valley, W Kenya
105 S16 **Marignane** Bouches-du-Rhône, SE France
Marignano *see* Melegnano
47 O11 **Marigot** NE Dominica
126 Hh14 **Mariinsk** Kemerovskaya Oblast', S Russian Federation
131 Q3 **Mariinskiy Posad** Respublika Mariy El, W Russian Federation
121 E14 **Marijampolė** *prev.* Kapsukas. Marijampolė, S Lithuania
116 G12 **Marikostenovo** Sofiyska Oblast, SW Bulgaria
62 J9 **Marília** São Paulo, S Brazil
84 D11 **Marimba** Malanje, NW Angola
145 T1 **Marī Mīlā** E Iraq
106 G4 **Marín** Galicia, NW Spain
37 N10 **Marina** California, W USA
Marina di Catanzaro *see* Catanzaro Marina
Mar'ina Gorka *see* Mar"ina Horka
121 L17 **Mar"ina Horka** *Rus.* Mar'ina Gorka. Minskaya Voblasts', C Belorussia
179 Pp11 **Marinduque** *island* C Philippines
33 S9 **Marine City** Michigan, N USA
33 N6 **Marinette** Wisconsin, N USA
62 I10 **Maringá** Paraná, S Brazil
85 N16 **Maringuè** Sofala, C Mozambique
106 F9 **Marinha Grande** Leiria, C Portugal
109 I15 **Marino** Lazio, C Italy
61 A15 **Mário Lobão** Acre, W Brazil
25 O5 **Marion** Alabama, S USA
29 Y11 **Marion** Arkansas, C USA
32 L17 **Marion** Illinois, N USA
33 P13 **Marion** Indiana, N USA
31 X13 **Marion** Iowa, C USA
29 O5 **Marion** Kansas, C USA
22 H6 **Marion** Kentucky, S USA
23 P9 **Marion** North Carolina, SE USA
33 S12 **Marion** Ohio, N USA
23 T12 **Marion** South Carolina, SE USA
23 Q7 **Marion** Virginia, NE USA
29 O5 **Marion Lake** Kansas, C USA
23 S13 **Marion, Lake** ⊡ South Carolina, SE USA
29 S8 **Marionville** Missouri, C USA
57 N7 **Maripa** Bolívar, E Venezuela
57 X11 **Maripasoula** W French Guiana
37 Q9 **Mariposa** California, W USA
63 G19 **Mariscala** Lavalleja, S Uruguay
64 M4 **Mariscal Estigarribia** Boquerón, NW Paraguay
58 C6 **Mariscal Sucre** *var.* Quito. ✕ (Quito) Pichincha, C Ecuador
32 K16 **Marissa** Illinois, N USA
105 U14 **Maritime Alps** *Fr.* Alpes Maritimes, *It.* Alpi Marittime. ▲ France/Italy
Maritimes, Alpes *see* Maritime Alps
Maritime Territory *see* Primorskiy Kray
116 K11 **Maritsa** *var.* Marica, *Gk.* Évros, *Turk.* Meriç; *anc.* Hebrus. SW Europe *see also* Évros/Meriç
Maritsa *see* Simeonovgrad
Marittime, Alpi *see* Maritime Alps
Maritzburg *see* Pietermaritzburg
197 C13 **Marium, Mount** ▲ Ambrym, C Vanuatu
119 X9 **Mariupol'** *prev.* Zhdanov. Donets'ka Oblast', SE Ukraine
57 Q6 **Mariusa, Caño** NE Venezuela
148 J5 **Marīvān** *prev.* Dezh Shāhpūr. Kordestān, W Iran
125 A16 **Mariy El, Respublika** *prev.* Mariyskaya ASSR. ◆ *autonomous republic* W Russian Federation
131 R3 **Mariyets** Respublika Mariy El, W Russian Federation
Mariyskaya ASSR *see* Mariy El, Respublika
120 G4 **Märjamaa** *Ger.* Merjama. Raplamaa, NW Estonia
xxxvi K11 **Mark** Somerset, SW England, UK
101 I15 **Mark** *Fr.* Marcq. Belgium/Netherlands
83 N17 **Marka** *var.* Merca. Shabeellaha Hoose, S Somalia
151 Z10 **Markakol', Ozero** *Kaz.* Marqaköl. ◎ E Kazakhstan
78 M12 **Markala** Ségou, W Mali
165 S15 **Markam** *var.* Gartog. Xizang Zizhiqu, W China
97 K21 **Markaryd** Kronoberg, S Sweden
148 L7 **Markazī** *off.* Ostān-e Markazī. ◆ *province* W Iran
12 F14 **Markdale** Ontario, S Canada
29 X10 **Marked Tree** Arkansas, C USA
100 N11 **Markelo** Overijssel, E Netherlands
100 J9 **Markermeer** ◎ C Netherlands
xxxviii M10 **Market Bosworth** Leicestershire, C England, UK
xxxix R9 **Market Deeping** Lincolnshire, E England, UK
xxxviii I8 **Market Drayton** Shropshire, W England, UK
xxxix O10 **Market Harborough** Leicestershire, C England, UK
xliv K5 **Markethill** Armagh, S Northern Ireland, UK
xxxix Q5 **Market Rasen** Lincolnshire, E England, UK
xli V13 **Market Weighton** East Riding of Yorkshire, N England, UK
xxxix N9 **Markfield** Leicestershire, C England, UK
126 Kk10 **Markha** NE Russian Federation
10 H16 **Markham** Ontario, S Canada
27 V12 **Markham** Texas, SW USA
194 J13 **Markham** C PNG
205 Q11 **Markham, Mount** ▲ Antarctica
112 M11 **Marki** Warszawa, C Poland
164 F8 **Markit** Xinjiang Uygur Zizhiqu, NW China
119 Y5 **Markivka** *Rus.* Markovka. Luhans'ka Oblast', E Ukraine
37 Q7 **Markleeville** California, W USA
100 L8 **Marknesse** Flevoland, N Netherlands
81 H14 **Markounda** *var.* Marcounda. Ouham, NW Central African Republic
Markovka *see* Markivka
127 P6 **Markovo** Chukotskiy Avtonomnyy Okrug, NE Russian Federation
131 P8 **Marks** Saratovskaya Oblast', W Russian Federation
24 K2 **Marks** Mississippi, S USA
xxxvi L10 **Marksbury** Bath and North East Somerset, SW England, UK
24 I7 **Marksville** Louisiana, S USA
103 I19 **Marktheidenfeld** Bayern, C Germany
103 J24 **Marktoberdorf** Bayern, S Germany
103 M18 **Marktredwitz** Bayern, E Germany
Markt-Übelbach *see* Übelbach
29 V3 **Mark Twain Lake** ⊡ Missouri, C USA
Markuleshty *see* Mărculeşti
xxxvii S7 **Markyate** Hertfordshire, E England, UK
103 E14 **Marl** Nordrhein-Westfalen, W Germany
190 E2 **Marla** South Australia
xxxvii O10 **Marlborough** Wiltshire, S England, UK
189 Y8 **Marlborough** Queensland, E Australia
193 I15 **Marlborough** *off.* Marlborough District. ◆ *unitary authority* South Island, NZ
105 P3 **Marle** Aisne, N France
33 S8 **Marlette** Michigan, N USA
27 T9 **Marlin** Texas, SW USA
23 S5 **Marlinton** West Virginia, NE USA
xxxv C14 **Marloes** Pembrokeshire, SW Wales, UK
xxxvii R9 **Marlow** Buckinghamshire, C England, UK
28 M12 **Marlow** Oklahoma, C USA
161 E17 **Marmagao** Goa, W India
Marmanda *see* Marmande
104 L13 **Marmande** *anc.* Marmanda. Lot-et-Garonne, SW France
142 C11 **Marmara** Balıkesir, NW Turkey
142 D11 **Marmara Denizi** *Eng.* Sea of Marmara. *sea* NW Turkey
116 N13 **Marmaraereğlisi** Tekirdağ, NW Turkey
Marmara, Sea of *see* Marmara Denizi
142 C16 **Marmaris** Muğla, SW Turkey
30 J6 **Marmarth** North Dakota, N USA
23 Q5 **Marmet** West Virginia, NE USA
108 H5 **Marmolada, Monte** ▲ N Italy
106 M13 **Marmolejo** Andalucía, S Spain
12 J14 **Marmora** Ontario, SE Canada
41 Q14 **Marmot Bay** *bay* Alaska, USA
105 Q4 **Marne** ◆ *department* N France
105 Q4 **Marne** N France
143 U10 **Marneuli** *prev.* Borchalo, Sarvani. S Georgia
80 I13 **Maro** Moyen-Chari, S Chad
56 L12 **Maroa** Amazonas, S Venezuela
180 J3 **Maroantsetra** Toamasina, NE Madagascar
203 W11 **Marokau** *atoll* Îles Tuamotu, C French Polynesia
180 J5 **Marolambo** Toamasina, E Madagascar
180 J2 **Maromokotro** ▲ N Madagascar
85 L16 **Marondera** *prev.* Marandellas. Mashonaland East, NE Zimbabwe
57 X9 **Maroni** *Dut.* Marowijne. French Guiana/Surinam
191 V2 **Maroochydore-Mooloolaba** Queensland, E Australia
175 P13 **Maros** Sulawesi, C Indonesia
118 H11 **Maros** *var.* Mureş, Mureşul, *Ger.* Marosch, Mieresch. Hungary/Romania *see also* Mureş
Marosch *see* Maros/Mureş
Maroshévíz *see* Topliţa
Marosillye *see* Ilia
Marosludas *see* Luduş
Marosújvár/Marosújvárakna *see* Ocna Mureş
Marosvásárhely *see* Târgu Mureş
203 V14 **Marotiri** *var.* Îlots de Bass, Morotiri. *island group* Îles Australes, SW French Polynesia
80 G12 **Maroua** Extrême-Nord, N Cameroon
57 X12 **Marouini Rivier** SE Surinam
180 I3 **Marovoay** Mahajanga, NW Madagascar
57 W9 **Marowijne** ◆ *district* NE Surinam
Marowijne *see* Maroni
xli Q17 **Marple** Stockport, NW England, UK
Marqaköl *see* Markakol', Ozero
199 M9 **Marquesas Fracture Zone** *tectonic feature* E Pacific Ocean
Marquesas Islands *see* Marquises, Îles
25 W17 **Marquesas Keys** *island group* Florida, SE USA
31 Y12 **Marquette** Iowa, C USA
33 N3 **Marquette** Michigan, N USA
105 N1 **Marquise** Pas-de-Calais, N France
203 X7 **Marquises, Îles** *Eng.* Marquesas Islands. *island group* N French Polynesia
191 Q6 **Marra Creek** New South Wales, SE Australia
82 B10 **Marra Hills** *plateau* W Sudan
82 B11 **Marra, Jebel** ▲ W Sudan
76 E7 **Marrakech** *var.* Marakesh, *Eng.* Marrakesh; *prev.* Morocco. W Morocco
Marrakesh *see* Marrakech
Marrāt *see* Marāh
191 N15 **Marrawah** Tasmania, SE Australia
190 I4 **Marree** South Australia
83 L17 **Marrehan** ▲ SW Somalia
85 N17 **Marromeu** Sofala, C Mozambique
106 J17 **Marroquí, Punta** *headland* SW Spain
191 N8 **Marrowie Creek** *seasonal river* New South Wales, SE Australia
85 O14 **Marrupa** Niassa, N Mozambique
190 D1 **Marryat** South Australia
77 Y10 **Marsa 'Alam** SE Egypt
77 R8 **Marsá al Burayqah** *var.* Al Burayqah. N Libya
83 J17 **Marsabit** Eastern, N Kenya
109 H23 **Marsala** *anc.* Lilybaeum. Sicilia, Italy, C Mediterranean Sea
123 Jj17 **Marsaxlokk Bay** *bay* SE Malta
67 G15 **Mars Bay** *bay* Ascension Island, C Atlantic Ocean
103 H15 **Marsberg** Nordrhein-Westfalen, W Germany
xli Q15 **Marsden** Kirklees, N England, UK
9 R15 **Marsden** Saskatchewan, S Canada
100 H7 **Marsdiep** *strait* NW Netherlands
105 R16 **Marseille** *Eng.* Marseilles; *anc.* Massilia. Bouches-du-Rhône, SE France
Marseille-Marignane *see* Provence
32 M11 **Marseilles** Illinois, N USA
Marseilles *see* Marseille
78 J16 **Marshall** W Liberia
41 N11 **Marshall** Alaska, USA
29 U9 **Marshall** Arkansas, C USA
33 N14 **Marshall** Illinois, N USA
33 Q10 **Marshall** Michigan, N USA
31 S9 **Marshall** Minnesota, N USA
29 T4 **Marshall** Missouri, C USA
23 O9 **Marshall** North Carolina, SE USA
27 X6 **Marshall** Texas, SW USA
201 S4 **Marshall Islands** *off.* Republic of the Marshall Islands. ◆ *republic* W Pacific Ocean
183 Q3 **Marshall Islands** *island group* W Pacific Ocean
199 Ii7 **Marshall Seamounts** *undersea feature* SW Pacific Ocean
31 W13 **Marshalltown** Iowa, C USA
xli N13 **Marshaw** Lancashire, NW England, UK
xxxix S4 **Marshchapel** Lincolnshire, E England, UK
xxxvi M9 **Marshfield** South Gloucestershire, SW England, UK
21 P12 **Marshfield** Massachusetts, NE USA
29 T7 **Marshfield** Missouri, C USA
32 K6 **Marshfield** Wisconsin, N USA
xxxvi D14 **Marshgate** Cornwall, SW England, UK
xxxvii Q7 **Marsh Gibbon** Buckinghamshire, C England, UK
46 H1 **Marsh Harbour** Great Abaco, W Bahamas
21 S3 **Mars Hill** Maine, NE USA
23 P9 **Mars Hill** North Carolina, SE USA
24 H10 **Marsh Island** *island* Louisiana, S USA
23 S11 **Marshville** North Carolina, SE USA
xli Z6 **Marske-by-the-Sea** Redcar and Cleveland, N England, UK
13 W5 **Marsoui** Québec, SE Canada
13 R8 **Mars, Rivière à** Québec, SE Canada
97 O15 **Märsta** Stockholm, C Sweden
97 H24 **Marstal** Fyn, C Denmark
xxxvi L12 **Marston Magna** Somerset, SW England, UK
97 I19 **Marstrand** Göteborg och Bohus, S Sweden
27 U8 **Mart** Texas, SW USA
178 Gg9 **Martaban** *var.* Moktama. Mon State, S Burma
177 G9 **Martaban, Gulf of** *gulf* S Burma
109 Q19 **Martano** Puglia, SE Italy
Martapoera *see* Martapura
175 N11 **Martapura** *prev.* Martapoera. Borneo, C Indonesia
101 L23 **Martelange** Luxembourg, SE Belgium
116 L7 **Marten** Razgradska Oblast, N Bulgaria
12 H10 **Marten River** Ontario, S Canada
9 T15 **Martensville** Saskatchewan, S Canada
Marteskirch *see* Târnăveni
Martes Tolosane *see* Martres-Tolosane
117 K25 **Mártha** Kríti, Greece, E Mediterranean Sea
191 Q6 **Marthaguy Creek** New South Wales, SE Australia
xxxix Y9 **Martham** Norfolk, E England, UK
21 P13 **Martha's Vineyard** *island* Massachusetts, NE USA
110 C11 **Martigny** Valais, SW Switzerland
105 R16 **Martigues** Bouches-du-Rhône, SE France
xxxvii N12 **Martin** Hampshire, S England, UK
113 J19 **Martin** *Ger.* Sankt Martin, *Hung.* Turócszentmárton; *prev.* Turčiansky Svätý Martin. Stredné Slovensko, NW Slovakia
30 L11 **Martin** South Dakota, N USA
22 G8 **Martin** Tennessee, S USA
107 S7 **Martín** E Spain
109 P18 **Martina Franca** Puglia, SE Italy
193 M14 **Martinborough** Wellington, North Island, NZ
27 S11 **Martindale** Texas, SW USA
37 N8 **Martinez** California, W USA
25 V3 **Martinez** Georgia, SE USA
43 Q13 **Martínez de La Torre** Veracruz-Llave, E Mexico
xxxvi G11 **Martinhoe** Devon, SW England, UK
47 Y12 **Martinique** ◇ *French overseas department* E West Indies
1 O15 **Martinique** *island* E West Indies
Martinique Channel *see* Martinique Passage
47 X12 **Martinique Passage** *var.* Dominica Channel, Martinique Channel. *channel* Dominica/Martinique
25 Q5 **Martin Lake** ⊡ Alabama, S USA
117 G18 **Martíno** *prev.* Martínon. Stereá Ellás, C Greece
Martínon *see* Martíno
204 J11 **Martin Peninsula** *peninsula* Antarctica
41 S5 **Martin Point** *headland* Alaska, USA
111 V3 **Martinsberg** Niederösterreich, NE Austria
23 V3 **Martinsburg** West Virginia, NE USA
33 V13 **Martins Ferry** Ohio, N USA
Martinskirch *see* Târnăveni
33 O14 **Martinsville** Indiana, N USA
23 S8 **Martinsville** Virginia, NE USA
67 K16 **Martin Vaz, Ilhas** *island group* E Brazil
xxxix X13 **Martlesham** Suffolk, E England, UK
xxxviii I12 **Martley** Worcestershire, W England, UK
xxxvi K12 **Martock** Somerset, SW England, UK
Martök *see* Martuk
xxxix P5 **Marton** Lincolnshire, E England, UK
xli S10 **Marton** North Yorkshire, N England, UK
192 M12 **Marton** Manawatu-Wanganui, North Island, NZ
107 N13 **Martos** Andalucía, S Spain
104 M16 **Martres-Tolosane** *var.* Martes Tolosane. Haute-Garonne, S France
94 M11 **Martti** Lappi, NE Finland
150 I9 **Martuk** *Kaz.* Martök. Aktyubinsk, NW Kazakhstan
143 U12 **Martuni** E Armenia
60 L11 **Marudá** Pará, E Brazil
175 O2 **Marudu, Teluk** *bay* East Malaysia
155 O8 **Ma'rūf** Kandahār, SE Afghanistan
170 F14 **Marugame** Kagawa, Shikoku, SW Japan
193 H16 **Maruia** South Island, NZ
100 M6 **Marum** Groningen, NE Netherlands
81 P23 **Marungu** SE Zaire
203 Y12 **Marutea** *atoll* Groupe Actéon, C French Polynesia
149 O11 **Marv Dasht** *var.* Mervdasht. Fārs, S Iran
105 P13 **Marvejols** Lozère, S France
29 X12 **Marvell** Arkansas, C USA
38 L6 **Marvine, Mount** ▲ Utah, W USA
145 Q7 **Marwānīyah** C Iraq
158 F13 **Mārwār** *var.* Marwar Junction. Rājasthān, N India
Marwar Junction *see* Mārwār
9 R14 **Marwayne** Alberta, SW Canada
xxxvi F12 **Marwood** Devon, SW England, UK
152 I14 **Mary** *prev.* Merv. Maryyskiy Velayat, S Turkmenistan
Mary *see* Maryyskiy Velayat
xlii I11 **Marybank** Highland, NW Scotland, UK
Maryborough *see* Portlaoise
189 Z9 **Maryborough** Queensland, E Australia
190 M11 **Maryborough** Victoria, SE Australia
85 G23 **Marydale** Northern Cape, W South Africa
119 W8 **Mar"yinka** Donets'ka Oblast', E Ukraine
Mary Island *see* Kanton
xliii O15 **Marykirk** Aberdeenshire, NE Scotland, UK
23 W4 **Maryland** *off.* State of Maryland; *also known as* America in Miniature, Cockade State, Free State, Old Line State. ◆ *state* NE USA
27 P7 **Maryneal** Texas, SW USA
xl K8 **Maryport** Cumbria, NW England, UK
xliii H26 **Maryport** Dumfries and Galloway, SW Scotland, UK
11 U13 **Marystown** Newfoundland, Newfoundland and Labrador, SE Canada
38 K6 **Marysvale** Utah, W USA
37 O6 **Marysville** California, W USA
29 O3 **Marysville** Kansas, C USA
33 S13 **Marysville** Michigan, N USA
33 S9 **Marysville** Ohio, NE USA
34 H7 **Marysville** Washington, NW USA
xxxvi F14 **Mary Tavy** Devon, SW England, UK
29 R2 **Maryville** Missouri, C USA
23 N9 **Maryville** Tennessee, S USA
Mary Welayaty *see* Maryyskiy Velayat
xlii N14 **Marywell** Aberdeenshire, NE Scotland, UK
xlii O16 **Marywell** Angus, E Scotland, UK
152 I15 **Maryyskiy Velayat** *var.* Mary, *Turkm.* Mary Welayaty. ◆ *province* S Turkmenistan
Marzūq *see* Murzuq
176 V11 **Mas** Irian Jaya, E Indonesia
44 J11 **Masachapa** *var.* Puerto Masachapa. Managua, W Nicaragua
83 G19 **Masai Mara National Reserve** *reserve* C Kenya
83 I21 **Masai Steppe** *grassland* NW Tanzania
83 F19 **Masaka** SW Uganda
175 N13 **Masalembo Besar, Pulau** *island* S Indonesia
143 Y13 **Masallı** *Rus.* Masally. S Azerbaijan
Masally *see* Masallı
175 Pp10 **Masamba** Sulawesi, C Indonesia
Masampo *see* Masan
169 Y16 **Masan** *prev.* Masampo. S South Korea
Masandam Peninsula *see* Musandam Peninsula
83 J25 **Masasi** Mtwara, SE Tanzania
Masawa *see* Massawa
44 J10 **Masaya** Masaya, W Nicaragua
44 J10 **Masaya** ◆ *department* W Nicaragua
179 Q12 **Masbate** Masbate, N Philippines
179 Qq12 **Masbate** *island* C Philippines
76 I6 **Mascara** *var.* Mouaskar. NW Algeria
181 O7 **Mascarene Basin** *undersea feature* W Indian Ocean
181 O9 **Mascarene Islands** *island group* W Indian Ocean
181 N9 **Mascarene Plain** *undersea feature* W Indian Ocean
181 O7 **Mascarene Plateau** *undersea feature* W Indian Ocean
204 H5 **Mascart, Cape** *headland* Adelaide Island, Antarctica
64 J10 **Mascasín, Salinas de** *salt lake* C Argentina
42 K13 **Mascota** Jalisco, C Mexico
13 O12 **Mascouche** Québec, SE Canada
128 I9 **Masel'gskaya** Respublika Kareliya, NW Russian Federation
85 J23 **Maseru** ● (Lesotho) W Lesotho
85 J23 **Maseru** ✕ W Lesotho
Mashaba *see* Mashava
xli R11 **Masham** North Yorkshire, N England, UK
166 K14 **Mashan** Guangxi Zhuangzu Zizhiqu, S China
85 K17 **Mashava** *prev.* Mashaba. Masvingo, SE Zimbabwe
149 U4 **Mashhad** *var.* Meshed. Khorāsān, NE Iran
172 Oo4 **Mashike** Hokkaidō, NE Japan
Mashiz *see* Bardsīr
155 N14 **Mashkai** SW Pakistan
149 X13 **Māshkel** *var.* Rūd-i Māshkel, Rūd-e Māshkīd. Iran/Pakistan
154 K12 **Māshkel, Hāmūn-i** *salt marsh* SW Pakistan
Māshkel, Rūd-i/Māshkīd, Rūd-e *see* Māshkel
85 K15 **Mashonaland Central** ◆ *province* N Zimbabwe
85 K16 **Mashonaland East** ◆ *province* NE Zimbabwe
85 J16 **Mashonaland West** ◆ *province* NW Zimbabwe
Mashtagi *see* Maştağa
172 Qq6 **Mashū-ko** *var.* Masyû Ko. ◎ Hokkaidō, NE Japan
147 S14 **Masīlah, Wādī al** *dry watercourse* SE Yemen
81 I21 **Masi-Manimba** Bandundu, SW Zaire
83 F17 **Masindi** W Uganda
83 I19 **Masinga Reservoir** ⊡ S Kenya
179 Oo10 **Masinloc** Luzon, N Philippines
Masīra *see* Maşīrah, Jazīrat
Masīra, Gulf of *see* Maşīrah, Khalīj
147 Y10 **Maşīrah, Jazīrat** *var.* Masīra. *island* E Oman
147 Y10 **Maşīrah, Khalīj** *var.* Gulf of Masira. *bay* E Oman
Masis *see* Büyükağrı Dağı
81 O19 **Masisi** Nord Kivu, E Zaire
176 U11 **Masiwang** Pulau Seram, E Indonesia
Masjed-e Soleymān *see* Masjed Soleymān
148 L9 **Masjed Soleymān** *var.* Masjed-e Soleymān, Masjid-i Sulaiman. Khūzestān, SW Iran
Masjid-i Sulaiman *see* Masjed Soleymān
Maskat *see* Masqaţ
145 Q7 **Maskhān** C Iraq
147 X8 **Maskin** *var.* Miskin. NW Oman
xliv D8 **Mask, Lough** *Ir.* Loch Measca. ◎ W Ireland
116 N10 **Maslen Nos** *headland* E Bulgaria
180 K3 **Masoala, Tanjona** *headland* NE Madagascar
Masohi *see* Amahai
33 Q9 **Mason** Michigan, N USA
33 R14 **Mason** Ohio, N USA
27 Q10 **Mason** Texas, SW USA
23 P4 **Mason** West Virginia, NE USA
193 B25 **Mason Bay** *bay* Stewart Island, NZ
32 K13 **Mason City** Illinois, N USA
31 V12 **Mason City** Iowa, C USA

◆ Country
● Country Capital
◇ Dependent Territory
○ Dependent Territory Capital
◆ Administrative Region
✕ International Airport
▲ Mountain
▲ Mountain Range
Volcano
River
◎ Lake
⊡ Reservoir

Mā, Sông – Medora

Mā, Sông *see* Ma, Nam
20 B16 **Masontown** Pennsylvania, NE USA
147 Y8 **Masqaṭ** *var.* Maskat, *Eng.* Muscat. ● (Oman) NE Oman
108 E10 **Massa** Toscana, C Italy
20 M11 **Massachusetts** *off.* Commonwealth of Massachusetts; also known as Bay State, Old Bay State, Old Colony State. ◈ *state* NE USA
21 P11 **Massachusetts Bay** *bay* Massachusetts, NE USA
37 R2 **Massacre Lake** ◎ Nevada, W USA
109 O18 **Massafra** Puglia, SE Italy
110 G11 **Massagno** Ticino, S Switzerland
80 G11 **Massaguet** Chari-Baguirmi, W Chad
Massakori *see* Massakory
80 G10 **Massakory** *var.* Massakori; *prev.* Dagana. Chari-Baguirmi, W Chad
80 H11 **Massalassef** Chari-Baguirmi, SW Chad
108 F13 **Massa Marittima** Toscana, C Italy
84 B11 **Massangano** Cuanza Norte, NW Angola
85 M18 **Massangena** Gaza, S Mozambique
82 J9 **Massawa** *var.* Masawa, *Amh.* Mits'iwa. E Eritrea
82 K9 **Massawa Channel** *channel* E Eritrea
20 J6 **Massena** New York, NE USA
80 H11 **Massenya** Chari-Baguirmi, SW Chad
8 I13 **Masset** Graham Island, British Columbia, SW Canada
104 L16 **Masseube** Gers, S France
12 E11 **Massey** Ontario, S Canada
105 P12 **Massiac** Cantal, C France
105 P12 **Massif Central** *plateau* C France
Massilia *see* Marseille
33 U12 **Massillon** Ohio, N USA
79 N12 **Massina** Ségou, W Mali
85 N19 **Massinga** Inhambane, SE Mozambique
85 L20 **Massingir** Gaza, SW Mozambique
205 Z10 **Masson Island** *island* Antarctica
Massoukou *see* Franceville
143 Z11 **Maştağa** *Rus.* Mashtagi, Mastaga. E Azerbaijan
Mastanli *see* Momchilgrad
192 M13 **Masterton** Wellington, North Island, NZ
20 M14 **Mastic** Long Island, New York, NE USA
155 O10 **Mastung** Baluchistān, SW Pakistan
121 J20 **Mastva** *Rus.* Mostva. ≈ SW Belorussia
121 G17 **Masty** *Rus.* Mosty. Hrodzyenskaya Voblasts', W Belorussia
170 E12 **Masuda** Shimane, Honshū, SW Japan
94 J11 **Masugnsbyn** Norrbotten, N Sweden
Masuku *see* Franceville
85 K17 **Masvingo** *prev.* Fort Victoria, Nyanda, Victoria. Masvingo, SE Zimbabwe
85 K18 **Masvingo** *prev.* Victoria. ◈ *province* SE Zimbabwe
176 W10 **Maswaar, Pulau** *island* East Indies
144 H5 **Maşyāf** *Fr.* Misiaf. Ḥamāh, C Syria
Masyû Ko *see* Mashū-ko
112 E9 **Maszewo** Szczecin, NW Poland
85 I17 **Matabeleland North** ◈ *province* W Zimbabwe
85 J18 **Matabeleland South** ◈ *province* S Zimbabwe
84 O13 **Mataca** Niassa, N Mozambique
197 G13 **Matacawa Levu** *island* Yasawa Group, NW Fiji
12 G8 **Matachewan** Ontario, S Canada
81 F22 **Matadi** Bas-Zaïre, W Zaire
27 O4 **Matador** Texas, SW USA
44 J9 **Matagalpa** Matagalpa, C Nicaragua
44 K9 **Matagalpa** ◈ *department* W Nicaragua
10 I12 **Matagami** Québec, S Canada
27 U13 **Matagorda** Texas, SW USA
27 U13 **Matagorda Bay** *inlet* Texas, SW USA
27 U14 **Matagorda Island** *island* Texas, SW USA
27 V13 **Matagorda Peninsula** *headland* Texas, SW USA
203 Q8 **Mataiea** Tahiti, W French Polynesia
203 T9 **Mataiva** *atoll* Îles Tuamotu, C French Polynesia
191 O7 **Matakana** New South Wales, SE Australia
192 N7 **Matakana Island** *island* NE NZ
85 C15 **Matala** Huíla, SW Angola
202 G12 **Matala'a Pointe** *headland* Île Uvea, N Wallis and Futuna
161 K25 **Matale** Central Province, C Sri Lanka
202 E12 **Matalesina, Pointe** *headland* Île Alofi, W Wallis and Futuna
78 I10 **Matam** NE Senegal
192 M8 **Matamata** Waikato, North Island, NZ
79 V12 **Matamey** Zinder, S Niger
42 L8 **Matamoros** Coahuila de Zaragoza, NE Mexico
43 P15 **Matamoros** *var.* Izúcar de Matamoros. Puebla, S Mexico
43 Q8 **Matamoros** Tamaulipas, C Mexico
175 Q10 **Matana, Danau** ◎ Sulawesi, C Indonesia
77 S13 **Ma'ṭan as Sārah** SE Libya
84 J12 **Matanda** Luapula, N Zambia
83 J24 **Matandu** ≈ S Tanzania
13 V6 **Matane** Québec, SE Canada
13 V6 **Matane** ≈ Québec, SE Canada
79 S12 **Matankari** Dosso, SW Niger
41 R11 **Matanuska River** ≈ Alaska, USA
56 G7 **Matanza** Santander, N Colombia
46 D4 **Matanzas** Matanzas, NW Cuba
13 V7 **Matapédia** ≈ Québec, SE Canada
13 V6 **Matapédia, Lac** ◎ Québec, SE Canada
202 B17 **Mata Point** *headland* SE Niue
202 D12 **Matapu, Pointe** *headland* Île Futuna, W Wallis and Futuna
64 G12 **Mataquito, Río** ≈ C Chile
161 K26 **Matara** Southern Province, S Sri Lanka
117 D18 **Matarágka** *var.* Matarånga. Dytikí Ellás, C Greece
175 Nn16 **Mataram** Pulau Lombok, C Indonesia
Matarånga *see* Matarágka
189 Q3 **Mataranka** Northern Territory, N Australia
107 W6 **Mataró** *anc.* Illuro. Cataluña, E Spain
192 O8 **Matata** Bay of Plenty, North Island, NZ
198 Cc8 **Matātula, Cape** *headland* Tutuila, W American Samoa
193 D24 **Mataura** Southland, South Island, NZ
193 D24 **Mataura** ≈ South Island, NZ
Mata Uta *see* Matā'utu
202 G11 **Matā'utu** *var.* Mata Uta. ○ (Wallis and Futuna) Île Uvea, Wallis and Futuna
198 B8 **Matāutu** Upolu, C Western Samoa
202 G12 **Matā'utu, Baie de** *bay* Île Uvea, Wallis and Futuna
203 P7 **Mataval, Baie de** *bay* Tahiti, W French Polynesia
202 I16 **Matavera** Rarotonga, S Cook Islands
203 V16 **Mataveri** Easter Island, Chile, E Pacific Ocean
203 V17 **Mataveri** ✕ (Easter Island) Easter Island, Chile, E Pacific Ocean
192 P9 **Matawai** Gisborne, North Island, NZ
13 O10 **Matawin** ≈ Québec, SE Canada
151 V13 **Matay** Taldykorgan, SE Kazakhstan
12 K8 **Matchi-Manitou, Lac** ◎ Québec, SE Canada
43 O10 **Matehuala** San Luis Potosí, C Mexico
47 V13 **Matelot** Trinidad, Trinidad and Tobago
85 M15 **Matenge** Tete, NW Mozambique
109 O18 **Matera** Basilicata, S Italy
113 O21 **Mátészalka** Szabolcs-Szatmár-Bereg, E Hungary
176 Y10 **Matewar** Irian Jaya, E Indonesia
95 H17 **Matfors** Västernorrland, C Sweden
104 K11 **Matha** Charente-Maritime, W France
1 F15 **Mathematicians Seamounts** *undersea feature* E Pacific Ocean
23 X6 **Mathews** Virginia, NE USA
27 S14 **Mathis** Texas, SW USA
xxxv C12 **Mathry** Pembrokeshire, SW Wales, UK
158 J11 **Mathura** *prev.* Muttra. Uttar Pradesh, N India
Mathurai *see* Madurai
179 Rr16 **Mati** Mindanao, S Philippines
Matianus *see* Orūmīyeh, Daryācheh-ye
Matiara *see* Matiāri
155 Q15 **Matiāri** *var.* Matiara. Sind, SE Pakistan
43 S16 **Matías Romero** Oaxaca, SE Mexico
45 O13 **Matina** Limón, E Costa Rica
12 D10 **Matinenda Lake** ◎ Ontario, S Canada
21 R8 **Matinicus Island** *island* Maine, NE USA
Matisco/Matisco Ædourum *see* Mâcon
xxxix X8 **Matlaske** Norfolk, E England, UK
155 Q16 **Mātli** Sind, SE Pakistan
xxxviii M6 **Matlock** Derbyshire, C England, UK
xxxviii L6 **Matlock Bath** Derbyshire, C England, UK
61 F18 **Mato Grosso** *prev.* Vila Bela da Santissima Trindade. Mato Grosso, W Brazil
61 G17 **Mato Grosso** *off.* Estado de Mato Grosso; *prev.* Matto Grosso. ◈ *state* W Brazil
62 H8 **Mato Grosso do Sul** *off.* Estado de Mato Grosso do Sul. ◈ *state* S Brazil
61 I18 **Mato Grosso, Planalto de** *plateau* C Brazil
106 G6 **Matosinhos** *prev.* Matozinhos. Porto, NW Portugal
57 Z10 **Matoury** NE French Guiana
Matozinhos *see* Matosinhos
113 L21 **Mátra** ⛰ N Hungary
147 Y8 **Maṭraḥ** *var.* Mutrah. NE Oman
118 L12 **Mătrașești** Vrancea, E Romania
110 M8 **Matrei Am Brenner** Tirol, W Austria
111 P8 **Matrei in Osttirol** Tirol, W Austria
78 I15 **Matru** SW Sierra Leone
77 U7 **Maṭrûḥ** *var.* Mersa Maṭrûḥ; *anc.* Paraetonium. NW Egypt
172 Q13 **Matsubara** *var.* Matubara. Kagoshima, Tokuno-shima, SW Japan
171 K16 **Matsudo** *var.* Matudo. Chiba, Honshū, S Japan
170 F11 **Matsue** *var.* Matsuye, Matue. Shimane, Honshū, SW Japan
171 Mm7 **Matsumae** Hokkaidō, NE Japan
171 J14 **Matsumoto** *var.* Matumoto. Nagano, Honshū, S Japan
171 H16 **Matsusaka** *var.* Matsuzaka, Matusaka. Mie, Honshū, SW Japan
167 S12 **Matsu Tao** *Chin.* Mazu Dao. *island* NW Taiwan
Matsutō *see* Mattō
170 C12 **Matsuura** *var.* Matuura. Nagasaki, Kyūshū, SW Japan
170 Ee14 **Matsuyama** *var.* Matuyama. Ehime, Shikoku, SW Japan
Matsuye *see* Matsue
Matsuzaka *see* Matsusaka
171 J17 **Matsuzaki** Shizuoka, Honshū, S Japan
12 F8 **Mattagami** ≈ Ontario, S Canada
12 F8 **Mattagami Lake** ◎ Ontario, S Canada
64 K12 **Mattaldi** Córdoba, C Argentina
23 Y9 **Mattamuskeet, Lake** ◎ North Carolina, SE USA
23 W6 **Mattaponi River** ≈ Virginia, NE USA
12 I11 **Mattawa** Ontario, SE Canada
12 I11 **Mattawa** ≈ Ontario, SE Canada
21 S5 **Mattawamkeag** Maine, NE USA
21 S4 **Mattawamkeag Lake** ◎ Maine, NE USA
110 D11 **Matterhorn** *It.* Monte Cervino. ▲ Italy/Switzerland *see also* Cervino, Monte
37 W1 **Matterhorn** ▲ Nevada, W USA
34 L12 **Matterhorn** *var.* Sacajawea Peak. ▲ Oregon, NW USA
37 R8 **Matterhorn Peak** ▲ California, W USA
111 Y5 **Mattersburg** Burgenland, E Austria
110 E11 **Matter Vispa** ≈ S Switzerland
57 R7 **Matthews Ridge** N Guyana
46 K7 **Matthew Town** Great Inagua, S Bahamas
111 Q4 **Mattighofen** Oberösterreich, NW Austria
109 N16 **Mattinata** Puglia, SE Italy
147 T9 **Maṭṭī, Sabkhat** *salt flat* Saudi Arabia/UAE
20 M14 **Mattituck** Long Island, New York, NE USA
171 I13 **Mattō** *var.* Matsutō. Ishikawa, Honshū, SW Japan
Matto Grosso *see* Mato Grosso
32 M14 **Mattoon** Illinois, N USA
59 L16 **Mattos, Río** ≈ C Bolivia
Mattu *see* Metu
174 Ll5 **Matu** Sarawak, East Malaysia
59 E14 **Matucana** Lima, W Peru
Matudo *see* Matsudo
Matue *see* Matsue
197 J16 **Matuku** *island* S Fiji
114 B9 **Matulji** Primorje-Gorski Kotar, NW Croatia
Matumoto *see* Matsumoto
57 P5 **Maturín** Monagas, NE Venezuela
Matusaka *see* Matsusaka
Matuura *see* Matsuura
Matuyama *see* Matsuyama
130 K11 **Matveyev Kurgan** Rostovskaya Oblast', SW Russian Federation
131 O8 **Matyshevo** Volgogradskaya Oblast', SW Russian Federation
159 O13 **Mau** *var.* Maunāth Bhanjan. Uttar Pradesh, N India
85 O14 **Maúa** Niassa, N Mozambique
104 M17 **Maubermé, Pic de** *var.* Tuc de Moubermé, *Sp.* Pico Mauberme; *prev.* Tuc de Maubermé. ▲ France/Spain *see also* Moubermé, Tuc de
Maubermé, Pico *see* Maubermé, Pic de/ Moubermé, Tuc de
Maubermé, Tuc de *see* Maubermé, Pic de/ Moubermé, Tuc de
105 Q2 **Maubeuge** Nord, N France
177 Ff8 **Maubin** Irrawaddy, SW Burma
xliii I22 **Mauchline** East Ayrshire, W Scotland, UK
xlii P12 **Maud** Aberdeenshire, NE Scotland, UK
158 L13 **Maudaha** Uttar Pradesh, N India
191 N9 **Maude** New South Wales, SE Australia
205 P3 **Maudheimvidda** *physical region* Antarctica
67 N22 **Maud Rise** *undersea feature* S Atlantic Ocean
111 Q4 **Mauerkirchen** Oberösterreich, NW Austria
Mauersee *see* Mamry, Jezioro
xl H11 **Maughold** E Isle of Man
196 K2 **Maug Islands** *island group* N Northern Mariana Islands
105 Q15 **Mauguio** Hérault, S France
199 Kk6 **Maui** *island* Hawaii, USA, C Pacific Ocean
202 M16 **Mauke** *atoll* S Cook Islands
64 G13 **Maule** *off.* Región del Maule. ◈ *region* C Chile
104 J9 **Mauléon** Deux-Sèvres, W France
104 J16 **Mauléon-Licharre** Pyrénées-Atlantiques, SW France
64 G13 **Maule, Río** ≈ C Chile
65 G17 **Maullín** Los Lagos, S Chile
Maulmain *see* Moulmein
xliv D8 **Maum** Galway, W Ireland
33 R11 **Maumee** Ohio, N USA
33 Q12 **Maumee River** ≈ Indiana/Ohio, N USA
29 U11 **Maumelle** Arkansas, C USA
29 T11 **Maumelle, Lake** ⊠ Arkansas, C USA
175 Qq16 **Maumere** *prev.* Maoemere. Flores, S Indonesia
85 G17 **Maun** Ngamiland, C Botswana
Maunāth Bhanjan *see* Mau
Maunawai *see* Waimea
202 H16 **Maungaroa** ▲ Rarotonga, S Cook Islands
192 K3 **Maungatapere** Northland, North Island, NZ
192 K4 **Maungaturoto** Northland, North Island, NZ
203 R10 **Maupiti** *var.* Maurua. *island* Îles Sous le Vent, W French Polynesia
158 K14 **Mau Rānīpur** Uttar Pradesh, N India
24 K9 **Maurepas, Lake** ◎ Louisiana, S USA
105 T16 **Maures** ⛰ SE France
105 O12 **Mauriac** Cantal, C France
Maurice *see* Mauritius
67 J20 **Maurice Ewing Bank** *undersea feature* SW Atlantic Ocean
190 C4 **Maurice, Lake** *salt lake* South Australia
20 I17 **Maurice River** ≈ New Jersey, NE USA
27 Y10 **Mauriceville** Texas, SW USA
100 K12 **Maurik** Gelderland, C Netherlands
78 H8 **Mauritania** *off.* Islamic Republic of Mauritania, *Ar.* Mūrītānīyah. ◆ *republic* W Africa
181 W15 **Mauritius** *off.* Republic of Mauritius, *Fr.* Maurice. ◆ *republic* W Indian Ocean
132 M17 **Mauritius** *island* W Indian Ocean
181 N9 **Mauritius Trench** *undersea feature* W Indian Ocean
104 H6 **Mauron** Morbihan, NW France
105 N13 **Maurs** Cantal, C France
Maurua *see* Maupiti
Maury Mid-Ocean Channel *see* Maury Seachannel
66 L6 **Maury Seachannel** *var.* Maury Mid-Ocean Channel. *undersea feature* N Atlantic Ocean
32 K8 **Mauston** Wisconsin, N USA
111 R8 **Mauterndorf** Salzburg, NW Austria
111 T4 **Mauthausen** Oberösterreich, N Austria
111 Q9 **Mauthen** Kärnten, S Austria
85 F15 **Mavinga** Cuando Cubango, SE Angola
85 M17 **Mavita** Manica, W Mozambique
117 K22 **Mavrópetra, Ákra** *headland* Thíra, Kykládes, Greece, Aegean Sea
117 F16 **Mavrovoúni** ▲ C Greece
xl K7 **Mawbray** Cumbria, NW England, UK
xxxvi C17 **Mawgan** Cornwall, SW England, UK
192 Q8 **Mawhai Point** *headland* North Island, NZ
177 Ff3 **Mawlaik** Sagaing, C Burma
Mawlamyine *see* Moulmein
xxxvi C17 **Mawnan Smith** Cornwall, SW England, UK
147 N14 **Mawr, Wādī** *dry watercourse* NW Yemen
205 X5 **Mawson** *Australian research station* Antarctica
205 X5 **Mawson Coast** *physical region* Antarctica
30 M4 **Max** North Dakota, N USA
43 W12 **Maxcanú** Yucatán, SE Mexico
Maxesibebi *see* Mount Ayliff
111 Q5 **Maxglan** ✕ (Salzburg) Salzburg, W Austria
95 K16 **Maxmo** *Fin.* Maksamaa. Vaasa, W Finland
23 T11 **Maxton** North Carolina, SE USA
27 R8 **May** Texas, SW USA
194 E10 **May** ≈ NW PNG
127 N17 **Maya** ≈ E Russian Federation
157 Q19 **Māyābandar** Andaman a nd Nicobar Islands, India, E Indian Ocean
Mayadin *see* Al Mayādīn
46 L5 **Mayaguana** *island* SE Bahamas
46 L5 **Mayaguana Passage** *passage* SE Bahamas
47 S6 **Mayagüez** W Puerto Rico
47 R6 **Mayagüez, Bahía de** *bay* W Puerto Rico
Mayals *see* Maials
81 G20 **Mayama** Le Pool, SE Congo
39 V8 **Maya, Mesa De** ▲ Colorado, C USA
149 R4 **Mayamey** Semnān, N Iran
44 F3 **Maya Mountains** *Sp.* Montañas Mayas. ⛰ Belize/Guatemala
46 I7 **Mayarí** Holguín, E Cuba
Mayas, Montañas *see* Maya Mountains
xliii I23 **Maybole** South Ayrshire, W Scotland, UK
20 I17 **May, Cape** *headland* New Jersey, NE USA
82 J11 **Maych'ew** *var.* Mai Chio, *It.* Mai Ceu. N Ethiopia
144 I2 **Maydān Ikbiz** Ḥalab, N Syria
155 Q5 **Maydān Shahr** Wardag, E Afghanistan
82 O12 **Maydh** Sanaag, N Somalia
Maydī *see* Mīdī
Mayebashi *see* Maebashi
Mayence *see* Mainz
104 K6 **Mayenne** Mayenne, NW France
104 J6 **Mayenne** ◈ *department* NW France
104 J7 **Mayenne** ≈ N France
38 K12 **Mayer** Arizona, SW USA
24 J4 **Mayersville** Mississippi, S USA
9 P14 **Mayerthorpe** Alberta, SW Canada
23 S12 **Mayesville** South Carolina, SE USA
xxxvi C7 **Mayfair** Westminster, SE England, UK
xxxvii V12 **Mayfield** East Sussex, SE England, UK
xxxviii L7 **Mayfield** Staffordshire, C England, UK
193 G19 **Mayfield** Canterbury, South Island, NZ
35 N14 **Mayfield** Idaho, NW USA
22 G7 **Mayfield** Kentucky, S USA
38 L5 **Mayfield** Utah, W USA
168 K9 **Mayhan** Övörhangay, C Mongolia
39 T14 **Mayhill** New Mexico, SW USA
xliii O18 **May, Isle of** *island* E Scotland, UK
151 T9 **Maykain** *Kaz.* Mayqayyng. Pavlodar, NE Kazakhstan
130 L14 **Maykop** Respublika Adygeya, SW Russian Federation
Maylibash *see* Maylybas
Mayli-Say *see* Mayluu-Suu
153 T9 **Mayluu-Suu** *prev.* Mayli-Say, *Kir.* Mayly-Say. Dzhalal-Abadskaya Oblast', W Kyrgyzstan
150 L14 **Maylybas** *prev.* Maylibash. Kzyl-Orda, S Kazakhstan
Mayly-Say *see* Mayluu-Suu
Maymana *see* Meymaneh
178 Gg5 **Maymyo** Mandalay, C Burma
127 P6 **Mayn** ≈ NE Russian Federation
131 Q5 **Mayna** Ul'yanovskaya Oblast', W Russian Federation
23 N8 **Maynardville** Tennessee, S USA
xliv K9 **Maynooth** Kildare, E Ireland
12 J13 **Maynooth** Ontario, SE Canada
xliv E7 **Mayo** *Ir.* Maigh Eo. ◈ *county* W Ireland
8 I6 **Mayo** Yukon Territory, NW Canada
25 U9 **Mayo** Florida, SE USA
Mayo *see* Maio
80 G12 **Mayo-Kébbi** *off.* Préfecture du Mayo-Kébbu, *var.* Mayo-Kébi. ◈ *prefecture* SW Chad
Mayo-Kébi *see* Mayo-Kébbi
81 F19 **Mayoko** Le Niari, SW Congo
179 Q11 **Mayon Volcano** ▲ Luzon, N Philippines
63 A24 **Mayor Buratovich** Buenos Aires, E Argentina
106 L4 **Mayorga** Castilla-León, N Spain
192 N6 **Mayor Island** *island* NE NZ
Mayor Pablo Lagerenza *see* Capitán Pablo Lagerenza
Mayor, Puig *see* Major, Puig
181 I14 **Mayotte** ◇ *French territorial collectivity* E Africa
Mayoumba *see* Mayumba
46 J13 **May Pen** C Jamaica
Mayqayyng *see* Maykain
179 P7 **Mayraira Point** *headland* Luzon, N Philippines
111 N8 **Mayrhofen** Tirol, W Austria
194 F10 **May River** East Sepik, NW PNG
126 Mm15 **Mayskiy** Amurskaya Oblast', SE Russian Federation
131 O15 **Mayskiy** Kabardino-Balkarskaya Respublika, SW Russian Federation
151 U9 **Mayskoye** Pavlodar, NE Kazakhstan
20 J17 **Mays Landing** New Jersey, NE USA
23 N4 **Maysville** Kentucky, S USA
29 R2 **Maysville** Missouri, C USA
176 Y14 **Mayu** *channel* Irian Jaya, E Indonesia
81 D20 **Mayumba** *var.* Mayoumba. Nyanga, S Gabon
175 Ss7 **Mayu, Pulau** *island* Maluku, E Indonesia
33 S8 **Mayville** Michigan, N USA
20 C11 **Mayville** New York, NE USA
31 Q4 **Mayville** North Dakota, N USA
126 M11 **Mayya** Respublika Sakha (Yakutiya), NE Russian Federation
Mayyali *see* Mahe
Mayyit, Al Baḥr al *see* Dead Sea
85 J15 **Mazabuka** Southern, S Zambia
Mazaca *see* Kayseri
Mazagan *see* El-Jadida
34 J7 **Mazama** Washington, NW USA
105 O15 **Mazamet** Tarn, S France
149 O4 **Māzandarān** *off.* Ostān-e Māzandarān. ◈ *province* N Iran
162 F7 **Mazar** Xinjiang Uygur Zizhiqu, NW China
109 H24 **Mazara del Vallo** Sicilia, Italy, C Mediterranean Sea
155 O2 **Mazār-e Sharīf** *var.* Mazār-i Sharif. Balkh, N Afghanistan
Mazār-i Sharif *see* Mazār-e Sharīf
107 R13 **Mazarrón** Murcia, SE Spain
107 R14 **Mazarrón, Golfo de** *gulf* SE Spain
57 S9 **Mazaruni River** ≈ N Guyana
44 B6 **Mazatenango** Suchitepéquez, SW Guatemala
42 I10 **Mazatlán** Sinaloa, C Mexico
38 L12 **Mazatzal Mountains** ⛰ Arizona, SW USA
120 D10 **Mažeikiai** Mažeikiai, NW Lithuania
120 D7 **Mazirbe** Talsi, NW Latvia
42 G5 **Mazocahui** Sonora, NW Mexico
59 I18 **Mazocruz** Puno, S Peru
Mazoe, Rio *see* Mazowe
81 N21 **Mazomeno** Maniema, E Zaire
165 Q6 **Mazong Shan** ▲ N China
85 L16 **Mazowe** *var.* Rio Mazoe. ≈ Mozambique/Zimbabwe
Mazra'a *see* Al Mazra'ah
144 G6 **Mazraat Kfar Debiâne** C Lebanon
120 H7 **Mazsalaca** *Est.* Väike-Salatsi, *Ger.* Salisburg. Valmiera, N Latvia
112 L9 **Mazury** *physical region* NE Poland
121 M20 **Mazyr** *Rus.* Mozyr'. Homyel'skaya Voblasts', SE Belorussia
109 K25 **Mazzarino** Sicilia, Italy, C Mediterranean Sea
Mba *see* Ba
85 L21 **Mbabane** ● (Swaziland) NW Swaziland
Mbacké *see* Mbaké
79 N16 **Mbahiakro** E Ivory Coast
81 I16 **Mbaïki** *var.* M'Baiki. Lobaye, SW Central African Republic
81 F14 **Mbakaou, Lac de** ◎ C Cameroon
78 G11 **Mbaké** *var.* Mbacké. W Senegal
84 L11 **Mbala** *prev.* Abercorn. Northern, NE Zambia
85 J18 **Mbalabala** *prev.* Balla Balla. Matabeleland South, SW Zimbabwe
83 G18 **Mbale** E Uganda
81 E16 **Mbalmayo** *var.* M'Balmayo. Centre, S Cameroon
83 H25 **Mbamba Bay** Ruvuma, S Tanzania
81 I18 **Mbandaka** *prev.* Coquilhatville. Equateur, NW Zaire
84 B9 **M'Banza Congo** *var.* Mbanza Congo; *prev.* São Salvador, São Salvador do Congo. Zaire, NW Angola
81 G21 **Mbanza-Ngungu** Bas-Zaïre, W Zaire
69 V11 **Mbarangandu** ≈ E Tanzania
83 E19 **Mbarara** SW Uganda
81 L15 **Mbari** ≈ SE Central African Republic
83 I24 **Mbarika Mountains** ⛰ S Tanzania
Mbatiki *see* Batiki
80 F13 **Mbé** Nord, N Cameroon
83 J24 **Mbemkuru** *var.* Mbwemkuru. ≈ S Tanzania
Mbengga *see* Beqa
180 H13 **Mbéni** Grande Comore, NW Comoros
85 K18 **Mberengwa** Midlands, S Zimbabwe
83 G24 **Mbeya** Mbeya, SW Tanzania
83 G23 **Mbeya** ◈ *region* S Tanzania
81 E19 **Mbigou** Ngounié, C Gabon
Mbilua *see* Vella Lavella
81 F19 **Mbinda** Le Niari, SW Congo
81 D17 **Mbini** W Equatorial Guinea
Mbini *see* Uolo, Río
85 L18 **Mbizi** Masvingo, SE Zimbabwe
83 G23 **Mbogo** Mbeya, W Tanzania
81 N15 **Mboki** Haut-Mbomou, SE Central African Republic
81 G18 **Mbomo** Cuvette, NW Congo
81 L15 **Mbomou** ◈ *prefecture* SE Central African Republic
Mbomou/M'Bomu/Mbomu *see* Bomu
78 F11 **Mbour** W Senegal
78 I10 **Mbout** Gorgol, S Mauritania
81 J14 **Mbrès** *var.* Mbrés. Nana-Grébizi, C Central African Republic
81 L22 **Mbuji-Mayi** *prev.* Bakwanga. Kasai Oriental, S Zaire
194 J9 **M'buke Islands** *island group* N PNG
83 H21 **Mbulu** Arusha, N Tanzania
194 K8 **M'bunai** *var.* Bunai. Manus Island, N PNG
64 N8 **Mburucuyá** Corrientes, NE Argentina
Mbutha *see* Buca
Mbwemkuru *see* Mbemkuru
83 G21 **Mbwikwe** Singida, C Tanzania
11 O15 **McAdam** New Brunswick, SE Canada
27 O5 **McAdoo** Texas, SW USA
37 V2 **McAfee Peak** ▲ Nevada, W USA
29 P11 **McAlester** Oklahoma, C USA
27 S17 **McAllen** Texas, SW USA
23 S11 **McBee** South Carolina, SE USA
9 N14 **McBride** British Columbia, SW Canada
26 M9 **McCamey** Texas, SW USA
35 R15 **McCammon** Idaho, NW USA
37 X11 **McCarran** ✕ (Las Vegas) Nevada, W USA
41 T11 **McCarthy** Alaska, USA
32 M5 **McCaslin Mountain** *hill* Wisconsin, N USA
27 O2 **McClellan Creek** ≈ Texas, SW USA
23 T14 **McClellanville** South Carolina, SE USA
15 Jj2 **McClintock Channel** *channel* Northwest Territories, N Canada
205 R12 **McClintock, Mount** ▲ Antarctica
37 N2 **McCloud** California, W USA
37 N3 **McCloud River** ≈ California, W USA
37 Q9 **McClure, Lake** ⊠ California, W USA
207 O8 **McClure Strait** *strait* Northwest Territories, N Canada
31 N4 **McClusky** North Dakota, N USA
23 T11 **McColl** South Carolina, SE USA
24 K7 **McComb** Mississippi, S USA
20 E16 **McConnellsburg** Pennsylvania, NE USA
33 T14 **McConnelsville** Ohio, N USA
30 M17 **McCook** Nebraska, C USA
23 P13 **McCormick** South Carolina, SE USA
9 W16 **McCreary** Manitoba, S Canada
29 W11 **McCrory** Arkansas, C USA
27 T10 **McDade** Texas, SW USA
25 O8 **McDavid** Florida, SE USA
37 T1 **McDermitt** Nevada, W USA
25 S4 **McDonough** Georgia, SE USA
38 L12 **McDowell Mountains** ⛰ Arizona, SW USA
22 H8 **McEwen** Tennessee, S USA
37 R12 **McFarland** California, W USA
Mcfarlane, Lake *see* Macfarlane, Lake
29 P12 **McGee Creek Lake** ⊠ Oklahoma, C USA
29 W13 **McGehee** Arkansas, C USA
37 X5 **Mcgill** Nevada, W USA
12 K11 **McGillivray, Lac** ◎ Québec, SE Canada
41 P10 **Mcgrath** Alaska, USA
27 T8 **McGregor** Texas, SW USA
35 O12 **McGuire, Mount** ▲ Idaho, NW USA
85 M14 **Mchinji** *prev.* Fort Manning. Central, W Malawi
30 M7 **McIntosh** South Dakota, N USA
16 O3 **McKeand** ≈ Baffin Island, Northwest Territories, NE Canada
203 R4 **McKean Island** *island* Phoenix Islands, C Kiribati
32 J13 **McKee Creek** ≈ Illinois, N USA
20 C15 **Mckeesport** Pennsylvania, NE USA
23 V7 **McKenney** Virginia, NE USA
22 G8 **McKenzie** Tennessee, S USA
193 B20 **McKerrow, Lake** ◎ South Island, NZ
41 Q10 **McKinley, Mount** *var.* Denali. ▲ Alaska, USA
41 R10 **McKinley Park** Alaska, USA
36 K3 **McKinleyville** California, W USA
27 U6 **McKinney** Texas, SW USA
28 I5 **McKinney, Lake** ◎ Kansas, C USA
30 M7 **McLaughlin** South Dakota, N USA
27 O2 **McLean** Texas, SW USA
32 M16 **Mcleansboro** Illinois, N USA
9 O13 **McLennan** Alberta, W Canada
12 L9 **McLennan, Lac** ◎ Québec, SE Canada
8 M13 **McLeod Lake** British Columbia, W Canada
29 N10 **McLoud** Oklahoma, C USA
34 G15 **McLoughlin, Mount** ▲ Oregon, NW USA
39 U15 **McMillan, Lake** ⊠ New Mexico, SW USA
34 G11 **McMinnville** Oregon, NW USA
22 K9 **McMinnville** Tennessee, S USA
205 R13 **McMurdo** *US research station* Antarctica
26 H9 **McNary** Texas, SW USA
39 N13 **Mcnary** Arizona, SW USA
29 N5 **McPherson** Kansas, C USA
McPherson *see* Fort McPherson
25 U6 **McRae** Georgia, SE USA
31 P4 **McVille** North Dakota, N USA
85 J25 **Mdantsane** Eastern Cape, SE South Africa
178 Jj6 **Me** Ninh Binh, N Vietnam
28 J7 **Meade** Kansas, C USA
41 O5 **Meade River** ≈ Alaska, USA
xlii I7 **Meadie, Loch** ◎ NW Scotland, UK
37 Y11 **Mead, Lake** ⊠ Arizona/ Nevada, W USA
26 M5 **Meadow** Texas, SW USA
9 S14 **Meadow Lake** Saskatchewan, C Canada
37 Y10 **Meadow Valley Wash** ≈ Nevada, W USA
24 J7 **Meadville** Mississippi, S USA
20 B12 **Meadville** Pennsylvania, NE USA
12 F14 **Meaford** Ontario, S Canada
Meáin, Inis *see* Inishmaan
106 G8 **Mealhada** Aveiro, N Portugal
xlii I8 **Meall Nom Con** ▲ NW Scotland, UK
xl L8 **Mealsgate** Cumbria, NW England, UK
11 R8 **Mealy Mountains** ⛰ Newfoundland and Labrador, E Canada
9 O10 **Meander River** Alberta, W Canada
34 E11 **Meares, Cape** *headland* Oregon, NW USA
49 V6 **Mearim, Rio** ≈ NE Brazil
Measca, Loch *see* Mask, Lough
xxxviii F13 **Measham** Leicestershire, C England, UK
xliv J8 **Meath** *Ir.* An Mhí. ◈ *county* E Ireland
9 T14 **Meath Park** Saskatchewan, S Canada
105 O5 **Meaux** Seine-et-Marne, N France
xlii C9 **Meavaig** Western Isles, NW Scotland, UK
23 T9 **Mebane** North Carolina, SE USA
176 W9 **Mebo, Gunung** ▲ Irian Jaya, E Indonesia
96 I8 **Mebonden** Sør-Trøndelag, S Norway
84 A10 **Mebridege** ≈ NW Angola
37 W16 **Mecca** California, W USA
Mecca *see* Makkah
31 Y14 **Mechanicsville** Iowa, C USA
20 L10 **Mechanicville** New York, NE USA
101 H17 **Mechelen** *Eng.* Mechlin, *Fr.* Malines. Antwerpen, C Belgium
196 C8 **Mecherchar** *var.* Eil Malk. *island* Palau Islands, Palau
103 D17 **Mechernich** Nordrhein-Westfalen, W Germany
130 L12 **Mechetinskaya** Rostovskaya Oblast', SW Russian Federation
116 J11 **Mechka** ≈ S Bulgaria
Mechlin *see* Mechelen
63 D23 **Mechongué** Buenos Aires, E Argentina
117 L14 **Mecidiye** Edirne, NW Turkey
103 I24 **Meckenbeuren** Baden-Württemberg, S Germany
102 L8 **Mecklenburger Bucht** *bay* N Germany
102 M10 **Mecklenburgische Seenplatte** *wetland* NE Germany
102 L9 **Mecklenburg-Vorpommern** ◈ *state* NE Germany
85 Q15 **Meconta** Nampula, NE Mozambique
113 I25 **Mecsek** ⛰ SW Hungary
85 P14 **Mecubúri** ≈ N Mozambique
85 Q14 **Mecúfi** Cabo Delgado, NE Mozambique
84 O13 **Mecula** Niassa, N Mozambique
173 Ff5 **Medan** Sumatera, E Indonesia
63 A24 **Médanos** *var.* Medanos. Buenos Aires, E Argentina
63 C19 **Médanos** Entre Ríos, E Argentina
161 K24 **Medawachchiya** North Central Province, N Sri Lanka
xxxix P10 **Medbourne** Leicestershire, C England, UK
108 C8 **Mede** Lombardia, N Italy
76 J5 **Médéa** *var.* El Mediyya, Lemdiyya. N Algeria
Medeba *see* Ma'dabā
56 E8 **Medellín** Antioquia, NW Colombia
102 H9 **Medem** ≈ NW Germany
100 J8 **Medemblik** Noord-Holland, NW Netherlands
77 N7 **Médenine** *var.* Madanīyīn. SE Tunisia
78 G9 **Mederdra** Trarza, SW Mauritania
Medeshamstede *see* Peterborough
44 F4 **Medesto Mendez** Izabal, NE Guatemala
21 O11 **Medford** Massachusetts, NE USA
29 N8 **Medford** Oklahoma, C USA
34 G15 **Medford** Oregon, NW USA
32 K6 **Medford** Wisconsin, N USA
41 P10 **Medfra** Alaska, USA
118 M14 **Medgidia** Constanța, SE Romania
Medgyes *see* Mediaș
62 G11 **Medianeira** Paraná, S Brazil
31 Y15 **Mediapolis** Iowa, C USA
118 I11 **Mediaș** *Ger.* Mediasch, *Hung.* Medgyes. Sibiu, C Romania
43 S15 **Medias Aguas** Veracruz-Llave, SE Mexico
Mediasch *see* Mediaș
108 G10 **Medicina** Emilia-Romagna, C Italy
35 X16 **Medicine Bow** Wyoming, C USA
39 S2 **Medicine Bow Mountains** ⛰ Colorado/Wyoming, C USA
35 X16 **Medicine Bow River** ≈ Wyoming, C USA
9 R17 **Medicine Hat** Alberta, SW Canada
28 L7 **Medicine Lodge** Kansas, C USA
28 L7 **Medicine Lodge River** ≈ Kansas/Oklahoma, C USA
114 E7 **Međimurje** *off.* Međimurska Županija. ◈ *province* N Croatia
Međimurska Županija *see* Međimurje
56 G10 **Medina** Cundinamarca, C Colombia
20 E9 **Medina** New York, NE USA
31 O5 **Medina** North Dakota, N USA
33 T11 **Medina** Ohio, N USA
27 Q11 **Medina** Texas, SW USA
Medina *see* Al Madīnah
123 Ll12 **Medina Bank** *undersea feature* C Mediterranean Sea
107 P6 **Medinaceli** Castilla-León, N Spain
106 L6 **Medina del Campo** Castilla-León, N Spain
106 L5 **Medina de Ríoseco** Castilla-León, N Spain
Médina Gonassé *see* Médina Gounas
78 H12 **Médina Gounas** *var.* Médina Gonassé. S Senegal
27 S12 **Medina River** ≈ Texas, SW USA
106 K16 **Medina Sidonia** Andalucía, S Spain
Medinat Israel *see* Israel
121 H14 **Medininkai** Vilnius, SE Lithuania
159 R16 **Medinīpur** West Bengal, NE India
Mediolanum *see* Saintes, France
Mediolanum *see* Milano, Italy
Mediomatrica *see* Metz
124 O13 **Mediterranean Ridge** *undersea feature* C Mediterranean Sea
123 L11 **Mediterranean Sea** *Fr.* Mer Méditerranée. *sea* Africa/Asia/Europe
Méditerranée, Mer *see* Mediterranean Sea
81 N17 **Medje** Haut-Zaïre, NE Zaire
123 K11 **Medjerda, Oued** *var.* Mejerda, Wādī Majardah. ≈ Algeria/ Tunisia *see also* Mejerda
116 G7 **Medkovets** Oblast Montana, NW Bulgaria
95 J15 **Medle** Västerbotten, N Sweden
131 W7 **Mednogorsk** Orenburgskaya Oblast', W Russian Federation
127 Qq9 **Mednyy, Ostrov** *island* E Russian Federation
104 J12 **Médoc** *cultural region* SW France
165 Q16 **Mêdog** Xizang Zizhiqu, W China
30 J5 **Medora** North Dakota, N USA

◆ Country
● Country Capital
◇ Dependent Territory
○ Dependent Territory Capital
◈ Administrative Region
✕ International Airport
▲ Mountain
⛰ Mountain Range
▲ Volcano
≈ River
◎ Lake
⊠ Reservoir

MÉDOUNEU – MIASS

81 E17 **Médouneu** Woleu-Ntem, N Gabon
xxxvii Q11 **Medstead** Hampshire, S England, UK
108 I7 **Meduna** ≈ NE Italy
Medunta *see* Mantes-la-Jolie
Medvedica *see* Medveditsa
128 J16 **Medveditsa** *var.* Medvedica. ≈ W Russian Federation
131 O9 **Medveditsa** ≈ SW Russian Federation
114 E8 **Medvednica** ▲▲ NE Croatia
129 R15 **Medvedok** Kirovskaya Oblast', NW Russian Federation
127 Nn5 **Medvezh'i, Ostrova** *island group* NE Russian Federation
128 J9 **Medvezh'yegorsk** Respublika Kareliya, NW Russian Federation
111 T11 **Medvode** *Ger.* Zwischenwässern. NW Slovenia
xxxvii V11 **Medway** ≈ SE England, UK
130 J4 **Medyn'** Kaluzhskaya Oblast', W Russian Federation
188 J10 **Meekatharra** Western Australia
39 Q4 **Meeker** Colorado, C USA
11 T12 **Meelpaeg Lake** ◎ Newfoundland, Newfoundland and Labrador, E Canada
Meenen *see* Menen
103 M16 **Meerane** Sachsen, E Germany
103 D15 **Meerbusch** Nordrhein-Westfalen, W Germany
100 I12 **Meerkerk** Zuid-Holland, C Netherlands
101 L18 **Meerssen** *var.* Mersen. Limburg, SE Netherlands
158 J10 **Meerut** Uttar Pradesh, N India
35 U13 **Meeteetse** Wyoming, C USA
101 K17 **Meeuwen** Limburg, NE Belgium
83 J16 **Mēga** S Ethiopia
83 J16 **Mēga Escarpment** *escarpment* S Ethiopia
Megála Kalívia *see* Megála Kalývia
117 E16 **Megála Kalývia** *var.* Megála Kalívia. Thessalía, C Greece
117 H14 **Megáli Panagiá** *var.* Megáli Panayía. Kentrikí Makedonía, N Greece
Megáli Panayía *see* Megáli Panagiá
Megáli Préspa, Límni *see* Prespa, Lake
116 K12 **Megálo Livádi** ▲ Bulgaria/Greece
117 E20 **Megalópoli** *prev.* Megalópolis. Pelopónnisos, S Greece
Megalópolis *see* Megalópoli
176 V9 **Megamo** Irian Jaya, E Indonesia
117 C18 **Meganísi** *island* Iónioi Nísoi, Greece, C Mediterranean Sea
Meganom, Mys *see* Mehanom, Mys
Mégantic *see* Lac-Mégantic
13 R12 **Mégantic, Mont** ▲ Québec, SE Canada
117 G19 **Mégara** Attikí, C Greece
27 R5 **Megargel** Texas, SW USA
100 K13 **Megen** Noord-Brabant, S Netherlands
159 U13 **Meghālaya** ◈ *state* NE India
159 U16 **Meghna** ≈ S Bangladesh
143 V14 **Meghri** *Rus.* Megri. SE Armenia
126 Gg11 **Megion** Khanty-Mansiyskiy Avtonomnyy Okrug, C Russian Federation
117 Q23 **Megísti** *var.* Kastellórizon. *island* SE Greece
Megri *see* Meghri
Mehabad *see* Mahābād
118 F13 **Mehadia** *Hung.* Mehádia. Caraș-Severin, SW Romania
94 L7 **Mehamn** Finnmark, N Norway
119 U13 **Mehanom, Mys** *Rus.* Mys Meganom. *headland* S Ukraine
155 P14 **Mehar** Sind, SE Pakistan
188 J8 **Meharry, Mount** ▲ Western Australia
Mehdia *see* Mahdia
118 G14 **Mehedinți** ◈ *county* SW Romania
159 S15 **Meherpur** Khulna, W Bangladesh
23 W8 **Meherrin River** ≈ North Carolina/Virginia, SE USA
Meheso *see* Mī'ēso
203 T11 **Mehetia** *island* Îles du Vent, W French Polynesia
120 K6 **Mehikoorma** Tartumaa, E Estonia
Me Hka *see* Nmai Hka
149 N5 **Mehrabad** ✈ (Tehrān) Tehrān, N Iran
148 J7 **Mehrān** Īlām, W Iran
149 Q14 **Mehrān, Rūd-e** *prev.* Mansurabad. ≈ W Iran
149 Q9 **Mehrīz** Yazd, C Iran
155 R5 **Mehtarlām** *var.* Mehtar Lām, Meterlam, Methariam, Metharlam. Laghmān, E Afghanistan
105 N8 **Mehun-sur-Yèvre** Cher, C France
xxxv E13 **Meidrim** Carmarthenshire, S Wales, UK
xxxv J8 **Meifod** Powys, C Wales, UK
81 G14 **Meiganga** Adamaoua, NE Cameroon
xliii M16 **Meigle** Perth and Kinross, C Scotland, UK
166 H10 **Meigu** Sichuan, C China
169 W11 **Meihekou** *var.* Hailong. Jilin, NE China
101 L15 **Meijel** Limburg, SE Netherlands
xliii L17 **Meikleour** Perth and Kinross, C Scotland, UK
177 G5 **Meiktila** Mandalay, C Burma
Meilbhe, Loch *see* Melvin, Lough
110 G7 **Meilen** Zürich, N Switzerland
Meilu *see* Wuchuan
167 T12 **Meinhua Yu** *island* N Taiwan
103 J17 **Meiningen** Thüringen, C Germany
110 F9 **Meiringen** Bern, S Switzerland
103 O15 **Meissen** *var.* Meißen. Sachsen, E Germany
103 I15 **Meissner** ▲ C Germany
101 K25 **Meix-devant-Virton** Luxembourg, SE Belgium
Mei Xian *see* Meizhou
167 P13 **Meizhou** *var.* Meixian, Mei Xian. Guangdong, S China
69 P2 **Mejerda** *var.* Oued Medjerda, Wādī Majardah. ≈ Algeria/Tunisia *see also* Medjerda, Oued
44 F7 **Mejicanos** San Salvador, C El Salvador
Méjico *see* Mexico
64 G5 **Mejillones** Antofagasta, N Chile
201 V5 **Mejit Island** *var.* Mājeej. *island* Ratak Chain, NE Marshall Islands
81 F17 **Mékambo** Ogooué-Ivindo, NE Gabon
82 J10 **Mek'elē** *var.* Makale. N Ethiopia
76 I10 **Mekerrhane, Sebkha** *var.* Sebkha Meqerghane, Sebkra Mekerrhane. *salt flat* C Algeria
Mekerrhane, Sebkra *see* Mekerrhane, Sebkha
78 G10 **Mékhé** NW Senegal
152 G14 **Mekhinli** Akhalskiy Velayat, C Turkmenistan
13 P9 **Mékinac, Lac** ◎ Québec, SE Canada
Meklong *see* Samut Songhram
76 G6 **Meknès** N Morocco
133 U12 **Mekong** *var.* Lan-ts'ang Chiang, *Cam.* Mékôngk, *Chin.* Lancang Jiang, *Lao.* Mènam Khong, *Th.* Mae Nam Khong, *Tib.* Dza Chu, *Vtn.* Sông Tiên Giang. ≈ SE Asia
Mekongga, Pegunungan *see* Mengkoka, Pegunungan
Mékôngk *see* Mekong
178 K15 **Mekong, Mouths of the** *delta* S Vietnam
40 L12 **Mekoryuk** Nunivak Island, Alaska, USA
79 R14 **Mékrou** ≈ N Benin
174 H6 **Melaka** *var.* Malacca. Melaka, Peninsular Malaysia
174 H6 **Melaka** *var.* Malacca. ◈ *state* Peninsular Malaysia
Melaka, Selat *see* Malacca, Strait of
183 O6 **Melanesia** *island group* W Pacific Ocean
183 P5 **Melanesian Basin** *undersea feature* W Pacific Ocean
175 Ss4 **Melanguane** Pulau Karakelang, N Indonesia
174 Ll8 **Melawi, Sungai** ≈ Borneo, N Indonesia
xxxviii M8 **Melbourne** Derbyshire, C England, UK
191 N12 **Melbourne** *state capital* Victoria, SE Australia
29 V9 **Melbourne** Arkansas, C USA
25 Y12 **Melbourne** Florida, SE USA
31 W14 **Melbourne** Iowa, C USA
94 G10 **Melbu** Nordland, C Norway
Melchor de Mencos *see* Ciudad Melchor de Mencos
65 F19 **Melchor, Isla** *island* Archipiélago de los Chonos, S Chile
42 M9 **Melchor Ocampo** Zacatecas, C Mexico
xxxix S13 **Meldreth** Cambridgeshire, E England, UK
12 C11 **Meldrum Bay** Manitoulin Island, Ontario, S Canada
Meleda *see* Mljet
108 D8 **Melegnano** *prev.* Marignano. Lombardia, N Italy
196 F9 **Melekeok** *var.* Melekeiok. Babeldaob, N Palau
114 L9 **Melenci** *Hung.* Melencze. Serbia, N Yugoslavia
Melencze *see* Melenci
131 N4 **Melenki** Vladimirskaya Oblast', W Russian Federation
131 V6 **Meleuz** Respublika Bashkortostan, W Russian Federation
10 L6 **Mélèzes, Rivière aux** ≈ Québec, C Canada
80 I11 **Melfi** Guéra, S Chad
109 M17 **Melfi** Basilicata, S Italy
9 U14 **Melfort** Saskatchewan, S Canada
106 H4 **Melgaço** Viana do Castelo, N Portugal
107 N4 **Melgar de Fernamental** Castilla-León, N Spain
76 L6 **Melghir, Chott** *var.* Chott Melrhir. *salt lake* E Algeria
96 H8 **Melhus** Sør-Trøndelag, S Norway
106 H3 **Melide** Galicia, NW Spain
Meligalá *see* Meligalás
117 E21 **Meligalás** *prev.* Meligalá. Pelopónnisos, S Greece
62 L12 **Mel, Ilha do** *island* S Brazil
122 G11 **Melilla** *anc.* Rusaddir, Russadir. Melilla, Spain, N Africa
73 N1 **Melilla** *enclave* Spain, N Africa
65 G18 **Melimoyu, Monte** ▲ S Chile
175 N8 **Melintang, Danau** ◎ Borneo, N Indonesia
119 U7 **Melioratyvne** Dnipropetrovs'ka Oblast', E Ukraine
64 G11 **Melipilla** Santiago, C Chile
117 I25 **Mélissa, Ákra** *headland* Kríti, Greece, E Mediterranean Sea
15 Kk16 **Melita** Manitoba, S Canada
Melita *see* Mljet
Melitene *see* Malatya
109 M23 **Melito di Porto Salvo** Calabria, SW Italy
119 U10 **Melitopol'** Zaporiz'ka Oblast', SE Ukraine
111 V4 **Melk** Niederösterreich, NE Austria
xxxvi M10 **Melksham** Wiltshire, S England, UK
97 K15 **Mellan-Fryken** ◎ C Sweden
101 E17 **Melle** Oost-Vlaanderen, NW Belgium
102 G13 **Melle** Niedersachsen, NW Germany
xliv H13 **Melleray, Mount** ▲ S Ireland
Mellersta Finland *see* Keski-Suomi
97 J17 **Mellerud** Älvsborg, S Sweden
104 K10 **Melle-sur-Bretonne** Deux-Sèvres, W France
31 P8 **Mellette** South Dakota, N USA
123 J16 **Mellieha** E Malta
xli N12 **Melling** Lancashire, NW England, UK
xxxix W11 **Mellis** Suffolk, E England, UK
82 B10 **Mellit** Northern Darfur, W Sudan
77 N7 **Mellita** ✈ SE Tunisia
65 G21 **Mellizo Sur, Cerro** ▲ S Chile
xxxvi L11 **Mells** Somerset, SW England, UK
102 G9 **Mellum** *island* NW Germany
xli N8 **Melmerby** Cumbria, NW England, UK
85 L22 **Melmoth** KwaZulu/Natal, E South Africa
113 D16 **Mělník** *Ger.* Melnik. Střední Čechy, NW Czech Republic
126 H13 **Mel'nikovo** Tomskaya Oblast', C Russian Federation
63 G18 **Melo** Cerro Largo, NE Uruguay
Melodunum *see* Melun
Melrhir, Chott *see* Melghir, Chott
xliii N21 **Melrose** The Borders, S Scotland, UK
191 P7 **Melrose** New South Wales, SE Australia
190 I7 **Melrose** South Australia
31 T7 **Melrose** Minnesota, N USA
35 Q11 **Melrose** Montana, NW USA
39 V12 **Melrose** New Mexico, SW USA
110 I8 **Mels** Sankt Gallen, NE Switzerland
xlii M5 **Melsetter** Orkney Islands, N Scotland, UK
Melsetter *see* Chimanimani
xli R9 **Melsonby** North Yorkshire, N England, UK
35 V9 **Melstone** Montana, NW USA
103 I16 **Melsungen** Hessen, C Germany
94 L12 **Meltaus** Lappi, NW Finland
xli Q15 **Meltham** Kirklees, N England, UK
xxxix W8 **Melton Constable** Norfolk, E England, UK
xxxix P9 **Melton Mowbray** Leicestershire, C England, UK
84 Q13 **Meluco** Cabo Delgado, NE Mozambique
105 O5 **Melun** *anc.* Melodunum. Seine-et-Marne, N France
82 F12 **Melut** Upper Nile, SE Sudan
xlii F10 **Melvaig** Highland, NW Scotland, UK
29 P5 **Melvern Lake** ⊡ Kansas, C USA
xlii K6 **Melvich** Highland, N Scotland, UK
9 V16 **Melville** Saskatchewan, S Canada
Melville Bay/Melville Bugt *see* Qimusseriarsuaq
47 O11 **Melville Hall** ✈ (Dominica) NE Dominica
189 O1 **Melville Island** *island* Northern Territory, N Australia
207 O8 **Melville Island** *island* Parry Islands, Northwest Territories, NW Canada
16 R7 **Melville, Lake** ◎ Newfoundland and Labrador, E Canada
15 Ll2 **Melville Peninsula** *peninsula* Northwest Territories, NE Canada
Melville Sound *see* Viscount Melville Sound
27 Q9 **Melvin** Texas, SW USA
xliv G5 **Melvin, Lough** *Ir.* Loch Meilbhe. ◎ S Northern Ireland, UK/Ireland
174 M9 **Memala** Borneo, C Indonesia
115 L22 **Memaliaj** Gjirokastër, S Albania
85 Q14 **Memba** Nampula, NE Mozambique
85 Q14 **Memba, Baia de** *inlet* NE Mozambique
Membidj *see* Manbij
Memel *see* Neman, NE Europe
Memel *see* Klaipėda, Lithuania
103 J23 **Memmingen** Bayern, S Germany
29 U1 **Memphis** Missouri, C USA
22 E10 **Memphis** Tennessee, S USA
27 P3 **Memphis** Texas, SW USA
22 E10 **Memphis** ✈ Tennessee, S USA
13 Q13 **Memphrémagog, Lac** *var.* Lake Memphremagog. ◎ Canada/USA *see also* Memphremagog, Lake
21 N6 **Memphremagog, Lake** *var.* Lac Memphrémagog. ◎ Canada/USA *see also* Memphrémagog, Lac
xlii P11 **Memsie** Aberdeenshire, NE Scotland, UK
119 Q2 **Mena** Chernihivs'ka Oblast', NE Ukraine
29 S12 **Mena** Arkansas, C USA
Menaam *see* Menaldum
Menado *see* Manado
108 D6 **Menaggio** Lombardia, N Italy
31 T6 **Menahga** Minnesota, N USA
xxxv G4 **Menai Bridge** Isle of Anglesey, NW Wales, UK
xxxv F5 **Menai Strait** *strait* NW Wales, UK
79 R10 **Ménaka** Goa, E Mali
100 K5 **Menaldum** *Fris.* Menaam. Friesland, N Netherlands
Mènam Khong *see* Mekong
76 E7 **Menara** ✈ (Marrakech) C Morocco
27 Q9 **Menard** Texas, SW USA
199 M14 **Menard Fracture Zone** *tectonic feature* E Pacific Ocean
32 M7 **Menasha** Wisconsin, N USA
Mencezi Garagum *see* Tsentral'nyye Nizmennyye Garagumy
200 O10 **Mendaña Fracture Zone** *tectonic feature* E Pacific Ocean
174 M10 **Mendawai, Sungai** ≈ Borneo, C Indonesia
105 P13 **Mende** *anc.* Mimatum. Lozère, S France
83 J14 **Mendebo** ▲▲ C Ethiopia
82 J9 **Mendefera** *prev.* Adi Ugri. S Eritrea
207 S7 **Mendeleyev Ridge** *undersea feature* Arctic Ocean
131 T3 **Mendeleyevsk** Respublika Tatarstan, W Russian Federation
103 F15 **Menden** Nordrhein-Westfalen, W Germany
24 L6 **Mendenhall** Mississippi, S USA
40 L13 **Mendenhall, Cape** *headland* Nunivak Island, Alaska, USA
43 P9 **Méndez** *var.* Villa de Méndez. Tamaulipas, C Mexico
82 H13 **Mendī** W Ethiopia
194 G12 **Mendi** Southern Highlands, W PNG
xxxvi K11 **Mendip Hills** *var.* Mendips. *hill range* S England, UK
Mendips *see* Mendip Hills
xxxix W12 **Mendlesham** Suffolk, E England, UK
36 L6 **Mendocino** California, W USA
36 J3 **Mendocino, Cape** *headland* California, W USA
0 B8 **Mendocino Fracture Zone** *tectonic feature* NE Pacific Ocean
37 P10 **Mendota** California, W USA
32 L11 **Mendota** Illinois, N USA
32 K8 **Mendota, Lake** ◎ Wisconsin, N USA
64 I11 **Mendoza** Mendoza, W Argentina
64 I12 **Mendoza** *off.* Provincia de Mendoza. ◈ *province* W Argentina
110 H12 **Mendrisio** Ticino, S Switzerland
174 Hh7 **Mendung** Pulau Mendol, W Indonesia
56 I5 **Mene de Mauroa** Falcón, NW Venezuela
56 I5 **Mene Grande** Zulia, NW Venezuela
142 B14 **Menemen** İzmir, W Turkey
101 C18 **Menen** *var.* Meenen, *Fr.* Menin. West-Vlaanderen, W Belgium
169 Q8 **Menengiyn Tal** *plain* E Mongolia
201 R9 **Meneng Point** *headland* SW Nauru
94 L10 **Menesjärvi** *Lapp.* Menešjávri. Lappi, N Finland
Menešjávri *see* Menesjärvi
109 I24 **Menfi** Sicilia, Italy, C Mediterranean Sea
167 P7 **Mengcheng** Anhui, E China
166 F15 **Menghai** Yunnan, SW China
175 Q11 **Mengkoka, Pegunungan** *var.* Pegunungan Mekongga. ▲▲ Sulawesi, C Indonesia
166 F15 **Mengla** Yunnan, SW China
67 F24 **Menguera Point** *headland* East Falkland, Falkland Islands
166 M13 **Mengzhu Ling** ▲▲ S China
166 H14 **Mengzi** Yunnan, SW China
Menin *see* Menen
190 L7 **Menindee** New South Wales, SE Australia
190 L7 **Menindee Lake** ◎ New South Wales, SE Australia
190 J10 **Meningie** South Australia
105 O5 **Mennecy** Essonne, N France
31 Q12 **Menno** South Dakota, N USA
116 H13 **Menoíkio** ▲▲ NE Greece
33 N5 **Menominee** Michigan, N USA
32 M5 **Menominee River** ≈ Michigan/Wisconsin, N USA
32 M8 **Menomonee Falls** Wisconsin, N USA
32 I6 **Menomonie** Wisconsin, N USA
85 D14 **Menongue** *var.* Vila Serpa Pinto, *Port.* Serpa Pinto. Cuando Cubango, C Angola
123 Ii8 **Menorca** *Eng.* Minorca; *anc.* Balearis Minor. *island* Islas Baleares, Spain, W Mediterranean Sea
107 S13 **Menor, Mar** *lagoon* SE Spain
xli Q13 **Menston** Leeds, N England, UK
41 S10 **Mentasta Lake** ◎ Alaska, USA
41 S10 **Mentasta Mountains** ▲▲ Alaska, USA
173 Ff10 **Mentawai, Kepulauan** *island group* W Indonesia
173 G10 **Mentawai, Selat** *strait* W Indonesia
174 Ii10 **Mentok** Pulau Bangka, W Indonesia
105 V15 **Menton** *It.* Mentone. Alpes-Maritimes, SE France
26 K8 **Mentone** Texas, SW USA
Mentone *see* Menton
33 U11 **Mentor** Ohio, N USA
175 Nn7 **Menyapa, Gunung** ▲ Borneo, N Indonesia
165 T9 **Menyuan** *var.* Menyuan Huizu Zizhixian. Qinghai, C China
Menyuan Huizu Zizhixian *see* Menyuan
76 M5 **Menzel Bourguiba** *var.* Manzil Bū Ruqaybah; *prev.* Ferryville. N Tunisia
142 M15 **Menzelet Barajı** ⊡ C Turkey
131 T4 **Menzelinsk** Respublika Tatarstan, W Russian Federation
188 K11 **Menzies** Western Australia
205 V6 **Menzies, Mount** ▲ Antarctica
xxxvii Q12 **Meon** ≈ S England, UK
xxxvii Q12 **Meonstoke** Hampshire, S England, UK
xxxvii W10 **Meopham** Kent, SE England, UK
42 J6 **Meoqui** Chihuahua, N Mexico
xxxix T11 **Mepal** Cambridgeshire, E England, UK
85 N14 **Meponda** Niassa, NE Mozambique
100 M8 **Meppel** Drenthe, NE Netherlands
102 E12 **Meppen** Niedersachsen, NW Germany
Meqerghane, Sebkha *see* Mekerrhane, Sebkha
107 T6 **Mequinenza, Embalse de** ⊡ NE Spain
32 M8 **Mequon** Wisconsin, N USA
Mera *see* Maira
190 D3 **Meramangye, Lake** *salt lake* South Australia
29 W5 **Meramec River** ≈ Missouri, C USA
Meran *see* Merano
174 H10 **Merangin** ≈ Sumatera, W Indonesia
108 G5 **Merano** *Ger.* Meran. Trentino-Alto Adige, N Italy
174 H4 **Merapuh Lama** Pahang, Peninsular Malaysia
108 D7 **Merate** Lombardia, N Italy
175 Nn11 **Meratus, Pegunungan** ▲▲ Borneo, N Indonesia
176 Z16 **Merauke** Irian Jaya, E Indonesia
176 Z16 **Merauke, Sungai** ≈ Irian Jaya, E Indonesia
190 L9 **Merbein** Victoria, SE Australia
101 F21 **Merbes-le-Château** Hainaut, S Belgium
Merca *see* Marka
56 C13 **Mercaderes** Cauca, SW Colombia
Mercara *see* Madikeri
37 P9 **Merced** California, W USA
63 C20 **Mercedes** Buenos Aires, E Argentina
63 D15 **Mercedes** Corrientes, NE Argentina
64 J11 **Mercedes** *prev.* Villa Mercedes. San Luis, C Argentina
63 D19 **Mercedes** Soriano, SW Uruguay
27 S17 **Mercedes** Texas, SW USA
37 R9 **Merced Peak** ▲ California, W USA
37 P9 **Merced River** ≈ California, W USA
20 B13 **Mercer** Pennsylvania, NE USA
101 G18 **Merchtem** Vlaams Brabant, C Belgium
13 O13 **Mercier** Québec, SE Canada
27 Q9 **Mercury** Texas, SW USA
192 M5 **Mercury Islands** *island group* N NZ
xxxvi M12 **Mere** Wiltshire, S England, UK
21 O9 **Meredith** New Hampshire, NE USA
67 B25 **Meredith, Cape** *headland* West Falkland, Falkland Islands
39 V6 **Meredith, Lake** ◎ Colorado, C USA
27 N2 **Meredith, Lake** ⊡ Texas, SW USA
83 O16 **Mereeg** *var.* Mareeq, *It.* Meregh. Galguduud, E Somalia
119 V5 **Merefa** Kharkivs'ka Oblast', E Ukraine
Meregh *see* Mereeg
197 C11 **Mere Lava** *island* Banks Islands, N Vanuatu
101 E17 **Merelbeke** Oost-Vlaanderen, NW Belgium
Merend *see* Marand
127 Oo9 **Merenga** Magadanskaya Oblast', E Russian Federation
178 K12 **Mereuch** Môndól Kiri, E Cambodia
xxxvii V10 **Mereworth** Kent, SE England, UK
Mergate *see* Margate
150 F9 **Mergenevo** Zapadnyy Kazakhstan, NW Kazakhstan
178 Gg12 **Mergui** Tenasserim, S Burma
177 G12 **Mergui Archipelago** *island group* S Burma
116 L12 **Meriç** Edirne, NW Turkey
116 L12 **Meriç** *Bul.* Maritsa, *Gk.* Évros; *anc.* Hebrus. ≈ SE Europe *see also* Évros/Maritsa
43 X12 **Mérida** Yucatán, SW Mexico
106 J11 **Mérida** *anc.* Augusta Emerita. Extremadura, W Spain
56 I6 **Mérida** Mérida, W Venezuela
56 H7 **Mérida** *off.* Estado Mérida. ◈ *state* W Venezuela
xxxviii E15 **Meriden** Solihull, C England, UK
20 M13 **Meriden** Connecticut, NE USA
24 M5 **Meridian** Mississippi, S USA
27 S8 **Meridian** Texas, SW USA
104 J13 **Mérignac** Gironde, SW France
104 J13 **Mérignac** ✈ (Bordeaux) Gironde, SW France
95 J18 **Merikarvia** Turku-Pori, SW Finland
191 R12 **Merimbula** New South Wales, SE Australia
190 L9 **Meringur** Victoria, SE Australia
Merín, Laguna *see* Mirim Lagoon
99 I19 **Merioneth** *cultural region* W Wales, UK
196 A11 **Merir** *island* Palau Islands, N Palau
196 B17 **Merizo** SW Guam
Merjama *see* Märjamaa
151 S16 **Merke** Zhambyl, S Kazakhstan
27 P7 **Merkel** Texas, SW USA
121 F15 **Merkinė** Varėna, S Lithuania
101 G16 **Merksem** Antwerpen, N Belgium
101 I15 **Merksplas** Antwerpen, N Belgium
Merkulovichi *see* Myerkulavichy
121 G15 **Merkys** ≈ S Lithuania
34 F15 **Merlin** Oregon, NW USA
63 C20 **Merlo** Buenos Aires, E Argentina
144 G8 **Meron, Haré** ▲ N Israel
76 K6 **Merouane, Chott** *salt lake* NE Algeria
82 F7 **Merowe** Northern, N Sudan
188 J12 **Merredin** Western Australia
xliii I24 **Merrick** ▲ S Scotland, UK
34 H16 **Merrill** Oregon, NW USA
32 L5 **Merrill** Wisconsin, N USA
33 N11 **Merrillville** Indiana, N USA
21 O10 **Merrimack River** ≈ Massachusetts/New Hampshire, NE USA
30 L12 **Merriman** Nebraska, C USA
xxxvi K13 **Merriott** Somerset, SW England, UK
9 N17 **Merritt** British Columbia, SW Canada
25 Y12 **Merritt Island** Florida, SE USA
25 Y11 **Merritt Island** *island* Florida, SE USA
30 M12 **Merritt Reservoir** ⊡ Nebraska, C USA
191 S7 **Merriwa** New South Wales, SE Australia
191 O8 **Merriwagga** New South Wales, SE Australia
24 G8 **Merryville** Louisiana, S USA
82 K9 **Mersa Fatma** E Eritrea
104 M7 **Mer St-Aubin** Loir-et-Cher, C France
Mersa Maṭrûḥ *see* Maṭrûḥ
101 M24 **Mersch** Luxembourg, C Luxembourg
103 M15 **Merseburg** Sachsen-Anhalt, C Germany
Mersen *see* Meerssen
xl M17 **Mersey** ≈ NW England, UK
142 J17 **Mersin** İçel, S Turkey
174 I6 **Mersing** Johor, Peninsular Malaysia
120 E8 **Mērsrags** Talsi, NW Latvia
158 G12 **Merta** *var.* Merta City. Rājasthān, N India
Merta City *see* Merta
158 F12 **Merta Road** Rājasthān, N India
xxxv I12 **Merthyr Cynog** Powys, C Wales, UK
xxxv J13 **Merthyr Tydfil** Merthyr Tydfil, S Wales, UK
xxxv J14 **Merthyr Tydfil** ◈ *unitary authority* S Wales, UK
106 H13 **Mértola** Beja, S Portugal
xxxvi F13 **Merton** Devon, SW England, UK
xxxvii T9 **Merton** Merton, SE England, UK
xxxiv K17 **Merton** ◈ *London borough* SE England, UK
205 V16 **Mertz Glacier** *glacier* Antarctica
101 M24 **Mertzig** Diekirch, C Luxembourg
27 O9 **Mertzon** Texas, SW USA
83 I18 **Meru** Eastern, C Kenya
105 N4 **Méru** Oise, N France
83 I20 **Meru, Mount** ▲ NE Tanzania
Merv *see* Mary
Mervdasht *see* Marv Dasht
xliii O22 **Mervinslaw** The Borders, S Scotland, UK
142 K11 **Merzifon** Amasya, N Turkey
103 D20 **Merzig** Saarland, SW Germany
38 L14 **Mesa** Arizona, SW USA
31 V4 **Mesabi Range** ▲▲ Minnesota, N USA
56 H6 **Mesa Bolívar** Mérida, NW Venezuela
109 Q18 **Mesagne** Puglia, SE Italy
41 P12 **Mesa Mountain** ▲ Alaska, USA
117 J25 **Mesará** *lowland* Kríti, Greece, E Mediterranean Sea
39 S14 **Mescalero** New Mexico, SW USA
103 G15 **Meschede** Nordrhein-Westfalen, W Germany
143 Q12 **Mescit Dağları** ▲▲ NE Turkey
201 V13 **Mesegon** *island* Chuuk, C Micronesia
Meseritz *see* Międzyrzecz
56 F11 **Mesetas** Meta, C Colombia
xxxvi G12 **Meshaw** Devon, SW England, UK
Meshchera Lowland *see* Meshcherskaya Nizina
130 M4 **Meshcherskaya Nizina** *Eng.* Meshchera Lowland. *basin* W Russian Federation
130 J5 **Meshchovsk** Kaluzhskaya Oblast', W Russian Federation
129 R9 **Meshchura** Respublika Komi, NW Russian Federation
Meshed *see* Mashhad
Meshed-i-Sar *see* Bābolsar
82 E13 **Meshra'er Req** Warab, S Sudan
39 R15 **Mesilla** New Mexico, SW USA
110 H10 **Mesocco** *Ger.* Misox. Ticino, S Switzerland
117 D18 **Mesolóngi** *prev.* Mesolóngion. Dytikí Ellás, W Greece
Mesolóngion *see* Mesolóngi
12 E8 **Mesomikenda Lake** ◎ Ontario, S Canada
63 D15 **Mesopotamia** *var.* Mesopotamia Argentina. *physical region* NE Argentina
Mesopotamia Argentina *see* Mesopotamia
37 Y10 **Mesquite** Nevada, W USA
84 Q13 **Messalo, Rio** *var.* Mualo. ≈ NE Mozambique
Messana/Messene *see* Messina
101 L25 **Messancy** Luxembourg, SE Belgium
109 M23 **Messina** *var.* Messana, Messene; *anc.* Zancle. Sicilia, Italy, C Mediterranean Sea
85 K19 **Messina** Northern, NE South Africa
Messina, Strait of *see* Messina, Stretto di
109 M23 **Messina, Stretto di** *Eng.* Strait of Messina. *strait* SW Italy
xxxix P4 **Messingham** North Lincolnshire, N England, UK
117 E21 **Messíni** Pelopónnisos, S Greece
117 E21 **Messinía** *peninsula* S Greece
117 E22 **Messiniakós Kólpos** *gulf* S Greece
126 H8 **Messoyakha** ≈ N Russian Federation
116 H11 **Mesta** *Gk.* Néstos, *Turk.* Kara Su. ≈ Bulgaria/Greece *see also* Néstos
Mestghanem *see* Mostaganem
143 R8 **Mestia** *var.* Mestiya. N Georgia
Mestiya *see* Mestia
117 K18 **Mestón, Ákra** *headland* Chíos, E Greece
108 H8 **Mestre** Veneto, NE Italy
61 M16 **Mestre, Espigão** ▲▲ E Brazil
174 Ii11 **Mesuji** ≈ Sumatera, W Indonesia
Mesule *see* Grosser Möseler
8 J10 **Meszah Peak** ▲ British Columbia, W Canada
56 G11 **Meta** *off.* Departamento del Meta. ◈ *province* C Colombia
13 Q8 **Metabetchouane** ≈ Québec, SE Canada
16 O4 **Meta Incognita Peninsula** *peninsula* Baffin Island, Northwest Territories, NE Canada
24 K9 **Metairie** Louisiana, S USA
34 M6 **Metaline Falls** Washington, NW USA
64 K6 **Metán** Salta, N Argentina
84 N13 **Metangula** Niassa, N Mozambique
44 E7 **Metapán** Santa Ana, NW El Salvador
56 K9 **Meta, Río** ≈ Colombia/Venezuela
108 I11 **Metauro** ≈ C Italy
82 H11 **Metema** NW Ethiopia
117 D15 **Metéora** *religious building* Thessalía, C Greece
67 O20 **Meteor Rise** *undersea feature* SW Indian Ocean
195 N9 **Meteran** New Hanover, NE PNG
Meterlam/Methariam/Metharlam *see* Mehtarlām
xxxix X11 **Metfield** Suffolk, E England, UK
117 G20 **Methanon** *peninsula* S Greece
xxxix Q6 **Metheringham** Lincolnshire, E England, UK
xliii M18 **Methil** Fife, E Scotland, UK
xlii O12 **Methlick** Aberdeenshire, NE Scotland, UK
34 J6 **Methow River** ≈ Washington, NW USA
21 O10 **Methuen** Massachusetts, NE USA
xliii L17 **Methven** Perth and Kinross, C Scotland, UK
193 G19 **Methven** Canterbury, South Island, NZ
xxxix U10 **Methwold** Norfolk, E England, UK
Metis *see* Metz
115 G15 **Metković** Dubrovnik-Neretva, SE Croatia
41 Y14 **Metlakatla** Annette Island, Alaska, USA
111 V13 **Metlika** *Ger.* Möttling. SE Slovenia
111 T8 **Metnitz** Kärnten, S Austria
29 W12 **Meto, Bayou** ≈ Arkansas, C USA
174 Ii13 **Metro** Sumatera, W Indonesia
32 M17 **Metropolis** Illinois, N USA
Metropolitan *see* Santiago
37 N8 **Metropolitan Oakland** ✈ California, W USA
117 D15 **Métsovo** *prev.* Métsovon. Ípeiros, C Greece
Métsovon *see* Métsovo
25 V5 **Metter** Georgia, SE USA
101 H21 **Mettet** Namur, S Belgium
103 D20 **Mettlach** Saarland, SW Germany
Mettu *see* Metu
82 H13 **Metu** *var.* Mattu, Mettu. W Ethiopia
175 N7 **Metulang** Borneo, N Indonesia
144 G8 **Metulla** Northern, N Israel
150 G14 **Metvyy Kultuk, Sor** *salt flat* SW Kazakhstan
105 T4 **Metz** *anc.* Divodurum Mediomatricum, Mediomatrica, Metis. Moselle, NE France
103 H22 **Metzingen** Baden-Württemberg, S Germany
173 E4 **Meulaboh** Sumatera, W Indonesia
101 D18 **Meulebeke** West-Vlaanderen, W Belgium
105 U6 **Meurthe** ≈ NE France
105 S5 **Meurthe-et-Moselle** ◈ *department* NE France
105 S4 **Meuse** ◈ *department* NE France
86 F10 **Meuse** *Dut.* Maas. ≈ W Europe *see also* Maas
xxxvi D16 **Mevagissey** Cornwall, SW England, UK
195 O11 **Mevelo** ≈ New Britain, C Papau New Guinea
xliv M4 **Mew Island** *island* E Northern Ireland, UK
xli S16 **Mexborough** Doncaster, N England, UK
Mexcala, Río *see* Balsas, Río
27 U8 **Mexia** Texas, SW USA
60 K11 **Mexiana, Ilha** *island* NE Brazil
42 C1 **Mexicali** Baja California, NW Mexico
28 K8 **Mexico** Missouri, C USA
20 H9 **Mexico** New York, NE USA
27 P15 **Mexico** *off.* United Mexican States, *var.* Méjico, México, *Sp.* Estados Unidos Mexicanos. ◆ *federal republic* N Central America
43 O14 **México** *var.* Ciudad de México, *Eng.* Mexico City. ● (Mexico) México, C Mexico
43 O13 **México** ◈ *state* S Mexico
1 J13 **Mexico Basin** *var.* Sigsbee Deep. *undersea feature* C Gulf of Mexico
Mexico City *see* México
México, Golfo de *see* Mexico, Gulf of
46 B4 **Mexico, Gulf of** *Sp.* Golfo de México. *gulf* W Atlantic Ocean
Meyadine *see* Al Mayādīn
41 Y14 **Meyers Chuck** Etolin Island, Alaska, USA
154 M3 **Meymaneh** *var.* Maimāna, Maymana. Fāryāb, NW Afghanistan
149 N7 **Meymeh** Eşfahān, C Iran
127 Pp6 **Meynypil'gyno** Chukotskiy Avtonomnyy Okrug, NE Russian Federation
110 A10 **Meyrin** Genève, SW Switzerland
177 Ff8 **Mezaligon** Irrawaddy, SW Burma
43 O15 **Mezcala** Guerrero, S Mexico
116 H8 **Mezdra** Oblast Montana, NW Bulgaria
105 P16 **Mèze** Hérault, S France
129 O6 **Mezen'** Arkhangel'skaya Oblast', NW Russian Federation
129 P8 **Mezen'** ≈ NW Russian Federation
Mezen, Bay of *see* Mezenskaya Guba
105 Q13 **Mézenc, Mont** ▲ C France
129 O8 **Mezenskaya Guba** *var.* Bay of Mezen. *bay* NW Russian Federation
125 Bb7 **Mezha** ≈ W Russian Federation
Mezha *see* Myazha
126 Hh15 **Mezhdurechensk** Kemerovskaya Oblast', S Russian Federation
125 F4 **Mezhdusharskiy, Ostrov** *island* Novaya Zemlya, N Russian Federation
Mezhëvo *see* Myezhava
Mezhgor'ye *see* Mizhhir"ya
119 V8 **Mezhova** Dnipropetrovs'ka Oblast', E Ukraine
8 J12 **Meziadin Junction** British Columbia, W Canada
113 G16 **Mezileské Sedlo** *var.* Przełęcz Międzyleska. ≈ Czech Republic/Poland
104 L14 **Mézin** Lot-et-Garonne, SW France
113 M24 **Mezőberény** Békés, SE Hungary
113 M25 **Mezőhegyes** Békés, SE Hungary
113 M25 **Mezőkovácsháza** Békés, SE Hungary
113 M21 **Mezőkövesd** Borsod-Abaúj-Zemplén, NE Hungary
Mezőtelegd *see* Tileagd
113 M23 **Mezőtúr** Jász-Nagykun-Szolnok, E Hungary
42 K10 **Mezquital** Durango, C Mexico
108 G6 **Mezzolombardo** Trentino-Alto Adige, N Italy
84 L13 **Mfuwe** Northern, N Zambia
123 J16 **Mġarr** Gozo, N Malta
130 H6 **Mglin** Bryanskaya Oblast', W Russian Federation
Mhálanna, Cionn *see* Malin Head
xlii I13 **Mhor, Loch** ◎ NW Scotland, UK
160 G10 **Mhow** Madhya Pradesh, C India
Miadzioł Nowy *see* Myadzyel
179 Q13 **Miagao** Panay Island, C Philippines
43 R17 **Miahuatlán** *var.* Miahuatlán de Porfirio Díaz. Oaxaca, SE Mexico
Miahuatlán de Porfirio Díaz *see* Miahuatlán
106 K10 **Miajadas** Extremadura, W Spain
Miajlar *see* Myājlār
38 M14 **Miami** Arizona, SW USA
25 Z16 **Miami** Florida, SE USA
29 R8 **Miami** Oklahoma, C USA
27 O2 **Miami** Texas, SW USA
25 Z16 **Miami** ✈ Florida, SE USA
25 Z16 **Miami Beach** Florida, SE USA
25 Y15 **Miami Canal** *canal* Florida, SE USA
33 R14 **Miamisburg** Ohio, N USA
155 U10 **Miān Channūn** Punjab, E Pakistan
148 J4 **Mīāndowāb** *var.* Mianduab, Miyāndoāb. Āzarbāyjān-e Bākhtarī, NW Iran
180 H5 **Miandrivazo** Toliara, C Madagascar
Mianduab *see* Mīāndowāb
148 K3 **Mīāneh** *var.* Miyāneh. Āzarbāyjān-e Khāvarī, NW Iran
155 O16 **Miāni Hōr** *lagoon* S Pakistan
166 G10 **Mianning** Sichuan, C China
155 T7 **Miānwāli** Punjab, NE Pakistan
166 J7 **Mianxian** *var.* Mian Xian. Shaanxi, C China
166 I8 **Mianyang** Sichuan, C China
Mianyang *see* Xiantao
167 R3 **Miaodao Qundao** *island group* E China
167 S13 **Miaoli** N Taiwan
125 E12 **Miass** Chelyabinskaya Oblast', C Russian Federation

◆ Country
● Country Capital
◇ Dependent Territory
○ Dependent Territory Capital
◈ Administrative Region
✈ International Airport
▲ Mountain
▲▲ Mountain Range
Volcano
≈ River
◎ Lake
⊡ Reservoir

MIASTKO – MITÈMBONI

112 G8 **Miastko** *Ger.* Rummelsburg in Pommern. Słupsk, NW Poland
Miava *see* Myjava
9 O15 **Mica Creek** British Columbia, SW Canada
166 J7 **Micang Shan** ▲▲ C China
xxxviii G14 **Michaelchurch Escley** Herefordshire, W England, UK
194 I12 **Michael, Mount** ▲ C PNG
Mi Chai *see* Nong Khai
113 O19 **Michalovce** *Ger.* Grossmichel, *Hung.* Nagymihály. Východné Slovensko, E Slovakia
101 M20 **Michel, Baraque** *hill* E Belgium
xxxvii P11 **Micheldever** Hampshire, S England, UK
41 S5 **Michelson, Mount** ▲ Alaska, USA
47 P9 **Miches** E Dominican Republic
32 M4 **Michigamme, Lake** ◎ Michigan, N USA
32 M4 **Michigamme Reservoir** ⊡ Michigan, N USA
33 N4 **Michigamme River** ≈ Michigan, N USA
33 O7 **Michigan** *off.* State of Michigan; also known as Great Lakes State, Lake State, Wolverine State. ◐ *state* N USA
33 O11 **Michigan City** Indiana, N USA
33 O8 **Michigan, Lake** ◎ N USA
33 P2 **Michipicoten Bay** *lake bay* Ontario, N Canada
12 A8 **Michipicoten Island** *island* Ontario, S Canada
12 B7 **Michipicoten River** Ontario, S Canada
Michurin *see* Tsarevo
130 M6 **Michurinsk** Tambovskaya Oblast', W Russian Federation
xli P9 **Mickleton** Durham, N England, UK
xxxvii N6 **Mickleton** Gloucestershire, C England, UK
Mico, Punta/Mico, Punto *see* Monkey Point
44 L10 **Mico, Río** ≈ SE Nicaragua
47 T12 **Micoud** SE Saint Lucia
201 N16 **Micronesia** *off.* Federated States of Micronesia. ◆ *federation* W Pacific Ocean
183 P4 **Micronesia** *island group* W Pacific Ocean
174 Jj5 **Midai, Pulau** *island* Kepulauan Natuna, W Indonesia
Mid-Atlantic Cordillera *see* Mid-Atlantic Ridge
67 M17 **Mid-Atlantic Ridge** *var.* Mid-Atlantic Cordillera, Mid-Atlantic Rise, Mid-Atlantic Swell. *undersea feature* Atlantic Ocean
xlii M3 **Midbea** Orkney Islands, N Scotland, UK
Mid-Atlantic Rise/ Mid-Atlantic Swell *see* Mid-Atlantic Ridge
101 E15 **Middelburg** Zeeland, SW Netherlands
85 H24 **Middelburg** Eastern Cape, S South Africa
85 K21 **Middelburg** Mpumalanga, NE South Africa
97 G23 **Middelfart** Fyn, C Denmark
100 G13 **Middelharnis** Zuid-Holland, SW Netherlands
101 B16 **Middelkerke** West-Vlaanderen, W Belgium
100 I9 **Middenbeemster** Noord-Holland, C Netherlands
100 I8 **Middenmeer** Noord-Holland, NW Netherlands
37 Q2 **Middle Alkali Lake** ◎ California, W USA
200 Nn6 **Middle America Trench** *undersea feature* E Pacific Ocean
157 P19 **Middle Andaman** *island* Andaman Islands, India, NE Indian Ocean
Middle Atlas *see* Moyen Atlas
xxxvii P7 **Middle Barton** Oxfordshire, C England, UK
23 R3 **Middlebourne** West Virginia, NE USA
25 W9 **Middleburg** Florida, SE USA
Middleburg Island *see* 'Eua
Middle Caicos *see* Grand Caicos
27 N8 **Middle Concho River** ≈ Texas, SW USA
Middle Congo *see* Congo
41 R6 **Middle Fork Chandalar River** ≈ Alaska, USA
41 Q7 **Middle Fork Koyukuk River** ≈ Alaska, USA
35 O12 **Middle Fork Salmon River** ≈ Idaho, NW USA
xli Q11 **Middleham** North Yorkshire, N England, UK
9 T15 **Middle Lake** Saskatchewan, S Canada
30 L13 **Middle Loup River** ≈ Nebraska, C USA
193 E22 **Middlemarch** Otago, South Island, NZ
33 T15 **Middleport** Ohio, N USA
31 U14 **Middle Raccoon River** ≈ Iowa, C USA
31 R3 **Middle River** ≈ Minnesota, N USA
23 N8 **Middlesboro** Kentucky, S USA
xli Y6 **Middlesbrough** Middlesborough, N England, UK
xli Y7 **Middlesbrough** ◐ *unitary authority* N England, UK
99 N22 **Middlesex** *cultural region* SE England, UK
44 G3 **Middlesex** Stann Creek, C Belize
xli Q11 **Middlesmoor** North Yorkshire, N England, UK
xli N11 **Middleton** Cumbria, NW England, UK
xxxix U9 **Middleton** Norfolk, E England, UK
xl G14 **Middleton** Rochdale, NW England, UK
11 P15 **Middleton** Nova Scotia, SE Canada
22 F10 **Middleton** Tennessee, S USA
32 L9 **Middleton** Wisconsin, N USA
xxxix N13 **Middleton Cheney** Northamptonshire, C England, UK
xli P8 **Middleton in Teesdale** Durham, N England, UK
41 S13 **Middleton Island** *island* Alaska, USA
xxxvii S13 **Middleton-on-Sea** West Sussex, SE England, UK
xli V13 **Middleton-on-the-Wolds** East Riding of Yorkshire, N England, UK
xliv J5 **Middletown** Armagh, S Northern Ireland, UK
xxxv K8 **Middletown** Powys, C Wales, UK
36 M7 **Middletown** California, W USA
23 Y2 **Middletown** Delaware, NE USA
20 K15 **Middletown** New Jersey, NE USA
20 K13 **Middletown** New York, NE USA
33 R14 **Middletown** Ohio, N USA
20 G15 **Middletown** Pennsylvania, NE USA
xxxviii M13 **Middle Tysoe** Warwickshire, C England, UK
xxxvii O11 **Middle Wallop** Hampshire, S England, UK
xxxviii I6 **Middlewich** Cheshire, W England, UK
xli I6 **Midfield** Highland, N Scotland, UK
xxxvii R12 **Midhurst** West Sussex, SE England, UK
147 N14 **Midi** *var.* Maydī. NW Yemen
105 O16 **Midi, Canal du** *canal* S France
104 K17 **Midi de Bigorre, Pic du** ▲ S France
104 K17 **Midi d'Ossau, Pic du** ▲ SW France
181 R7 **Mid-Indian Basin** *undersea feature* N Indian Ocean
181 P7 **Mid-Indian Ridge** *var.* Central Indian Ridge. *undersea feature* C Indian Ocean
105 N14 **Midi-Pyrénées** ◐ *region* S France
27 N8 **Midkiff** Texas, SW USA
12 G13 **Midland** Ontario, S Canada
33 R8 **Midland** Michigan, N USA
30 M10 **Midland** South Dakota, N USA
26 M8 **Midland** Texas, SW USA
85 K17 **Midlands** ◐ *province* C Zimbabwe
xliv G14 **Midleton** *Ir.* Mainistir na Corann. Cork, SW Ireland
xliii M20 **Midlothian** ◐ *unitary authority* S Scotland, UK
27 T7 **Midlothian** Texas, SW USA
180 I7 **Midongy** Fianarantsoa, S Madagascar
104 K15 **Midou** ≈ SW France
199 Ii6 **Mid-Pacific Mountains** *var.* Mid-Pacific Seamounts. *undersea feature* NW Pacific Ocean
Mid-Pacific Seamounts *see* Mid-Pacific Mountains
179 R16 **Midsayap** Mindanao, S Philippines
xxxvi L10 **Midsomer Norton** Bath and North East Somerset, SW England, UK
38 L3 **Midway** Utah, W USA
199 Jj5 **Midway Islands** ◇ *US territory* C Pacific Ocean
35 X14 **Midwest** Wyoming, C USA
29 N10 **Midwest City** Oklahoma, C USA
158 M10 **Mid Western** ◐ *zone* W Nepal
100 P5 **Midwolda** Groningen, NE Netherlands
143 Q16 **Midyat** Mardin, SE Turkey
xlii I2 **Mid Yell** Shetland Islands, NE Scotland, UK
116 F8 **Midzhur** *SCr.* Midžor. ▲ Bulgaria/Yugoslavia *see also* Midžor
115 Q14 **Midžor** *Bul.* Midzhur. ▲ Bulgaria/Yugoslavia *see also* Midzhur
171 Hh16 **Mie** *off.* Mie-ken. ◐ *prefecture* Honshū, SW Japan
113 L16 **Miechów** Kielce, S Poland
112 F11 **Międzychód** *Ger.* Mitteldorf. Gorzów, W Poland
Międzyleska, Przełęcz *see* Mezileské Sedlo
112 O12 **Międzyrzec Podlaski** Biała Podlaska, E Poland
112 E11 **Międzyrzecz** *Ger.* Meseritz. Gorzów, W Poland
Mie-ken *see* Mie
104 L16 **Miélan** Gers, S France
113 N16 **Mielec** Rzeszów, SE Poland
97 L21 **Mien** ◎ S Sweden
43 O8 **Mier** Tamaulipas, C Mexico
118 J11 **Miercurea-Ciuc** *Ger.* Szeklerburg, *Hung.* Csíkszereda. Harghita, C Romania
106 K2 **Mieres** Asturias, NW Spain
Mieresch *see* Maros/Mureș
101 K15 **Mierlo** Noord-Brabant, SE Netherlands
43 O10 **Mier y Noriega** Nuevo León, NE Mexico
Mies *see* Stříbro
82 K13 **Mī'ēso** *var.* Meheso, Miesso. C Ethiopia
Miesso *see* Mī'ēso
112 D10 **Mieszkowice** *Ger.* Bärwalde Neumark. Szczecin, W Poland
20 G14 **Mifflinburg** Pennsylvania, NE USA
20 F14 **Mifflintown** Pennsylvania, NE USA
43 R15 **Miguel Alemán, Presa** ⊡ SE Mexico
42 L9 **Miguel Asua** *var.* Miguel Auza. Zacatecas, C Mexico
Miguel Auza *see* Miguel Asua
45 S15 **Miguel de la Borda** *var.* Donoso. Colón, C Panama
43 N13 **Miguel Hidalgo** ✕ (Guadalajara) Jalisco, SW Mexico
42 H7 **Miguel Hidalgo, Presa** ⊡ W Mexico
118 J14 **Mihăilești** Giurgiu, S Romania
118 M14 **Mihail Kogălniceanu** *var.* Kogălniceanu; *prev.* Caramurat, Ferdinand. Constanța, SE Romania
119 N14 **Mihai Viteazu** Constanța, SE Romania
142 G12 **Mihalıççık** Eskişehir, NW Turkey
170 Ee13 **Mihara** Hiroshima, Honshū, SW Japan
171 Jj17 **Mihara-yama** (volcano) Miyako-jima, SE Japan
107 S8 **Mijares** ≈ E Spain
100 I11 **Mijdrecht** Utrecht, C Netherlands
172 Oo5 **Mikasa** Hokkaidō, NE Japan
Mikashevichi *see* Mikashevichy
121 K19 **Mikashevichy** *Pol.* Mikaszewicze, *Rus.* Mikashevichi. Brestskaya Voblasts', SW Belorussia
Mikaszewicze *see* Mikashevichy
171 Hh16 **Mikawa-wan** *bay* S Japan
Mikhailovgrad *see* Montana, Oblast
130 L5 **Mikhaylov** Ryazanskaya Oblast', W Russian Federation
Mikhaylovgrad *see* Montana/Montana, Oblast
205 Z8 **Mikhaylov Island** *island* Antarctica
151 T6 **Mikhaylovka** Pavlodar, N Kazakhstan
131 N9 **Mikhaylovka** Volgogradskaya Oblast', SW Russian Federation
Mikhaylovka *see* Mykhaylivka
170 G14 **Miki** Hyōgo, Honshū, SW Japan
83 K24 **Mikindani** Mtwara, SE Tanzania
95 N18 **Mikkeli** *Swe.* Sankt Michel. Mikkeli, SE Finland
95 N18 **Mikkeli** *Swe.* Sankt Michel, St.Michel. ◐ *province* C Finland
112 M8 **Mikołajki** *Ger.* Nikolaiken. Suwałki, NE Poland
Míkonos *see* Mýkonos
116 I9 **Mikre** Loveshka Oblast, C Bulgaria
116 C13 **Mikrí Préspa, Límni** ◎ N Greece
129 P4 **Mikulkin, Mys** *headland* NW Russian Federation
83 I23 **Mikumi** Morogoro, SE Tanzania
129 R10 **Mikun'** Respublika Komi, NW Russian Federation
171 Hh13 **Mikuni** Fukui, Honshū, SW Japan
171 Jj14 **Mikuni-tōge** *pass* Honshū, C Japan
172 Ss13 **Mikura-jima** *island* E Japan
31 V7 **Milaca** Minnesota, N USA
64 J10 **Milagro** La Rioja, C Argentina
58 B7 **Milagro** Guayas, SW Ecuador
33 P4 **Milakokia Lake** ◎ Michigan, N USA
32 J1 **Milan** Illinois, N USA
33 R10 **Milan** Michigan, N USA
29 T2 **Milan** Missouri, C USA
39 Q11 **Milan** New Mexico, SW USA
22 G9 **Milan** Tennessee, S USA
Milan *see* Milano
97 F15 **Miland** Telemark, S Norway
85 N15 **Milange** Zambézia, NE Mozambique
108 D8 **Milano** *Eng.* Milan, *Ger.* Mailand; *anc.* Mediolanum. Lombardia, N Italy
27 U10 **Milano** Texas, SW USA
142 C15 **Milas** Muğla, SW Turkey
121 K21 **Milashavichy** *Rus.* Milashevichi. Homyel'skaya Voblasts', SE Belorussia
Milashevichi *see* Milashavichy
121 I18 **Milavidy** *Rus.* Milovidy. Brestskaya Voblasts', SW Belorussia
109 L23 **Milazzo** *anc.* Mylae. Sicilia, Italy, C Mediterranean Sea
31 R8 **Milbank** South Dakota, N USA
xxxvi L12 **Milborne Port** Somerset, SW England, UK
xli Q5 **Milbourne** Northumberland, N England, UK
21 T7 **Milbridge** Maine, NE USA
102 L11 **Milde** ≈ C Germany
xxxix U11 **Mildenhall** Suffolk, E England, UK
12 F14 **Mildmay** Ontario, S Canada
190 L9 **Mildura** Victoria, SE Australia
143 X12 **Mil Düzü** *Rus.* Mil'skaya Ravnina, Mil'skaya Step'. *physical region* C Azerbaijan
166 H13 **Mile** Yunnan, SW China
Mile *see* Mili Atoll
xxxvii X6 **Mile End** Essex, SE England, UK
189 Y10 **Miles** Queensland, E Australia
27 P8 **Miles** Texas, SW USA
35 X9 **Miles City** Montana, NW USA
xliv G11 **Milestone** Tipperary, S Ireland
9 U17 **Milestone** Saskatchewan, S Canada
109 N22 **Mileto** Calabria, SW Italy
109 K16 **Miletto, Monte** ▲ C Italy
xli P2 **Milfield** Northumberland, N England, UK
xxxvii S11 **Milford** Surrey, SE England, UK
Milford *see* Milford Haven
20 M13 **Milford** Connecticut, NE USA
23 Y3 **Milford** *var.* Milford City. Delaware, NE USA
31 T11 **Milford** Iowa, C USA
21 S6 **Milford** Maine, NE USA
31 R16 **Milford** Nebraska, C USA
21 O10 **Milford** New Hampshire, NE USA
20 I13 **Milford** Pennsylvania, NE USA
27 T7 **Milford** Texas, SW USA
38 K6 **Milford** Utah, W USA
Milford City *see* Milford
xxxv C14 **Milford Haven** *prev.* Milford. Pembrokeshire, SW Wales, UK
xxxv C14 **Milford Haven** *inlet* SW Wales, UK
29 O4 **Milford Lake** ⊡ Kansas, C USA
193 B21 **Milford Sound** Southland, South Island, NZ
193 B21 **Milford Sound** *inlet* South Island, NZ
Milhau *see* Millau
Milh, Bahr al *see* Razāzah, Buhayrat ar
145 T10 **Milh, Wādī al** *dry watercourse* S Iraq
201 W8 **Mili Atoll** *var.* Mile. *atoll* Ratak Chain, SE Marshall Islands
112 H13 **Milicz** Wrocław, SW Poland
109 L25 **Militello in Val di Catania** Sicilia, Italy, C Mediterranean Sea
127 Pp11 **Mil'kovo** Kamchatskaya Oblast', E Russian Federation
9 R17 **Milk River** Alberta, SW Canada
46 J13 **Milk River** ≈ C Jamaica
35 W7 **Milk River** ≈ Montana, NW USA
82 D9 **Milk, Wadi el** *var.* Wadi al Malik. ≈ C Sudan
101 L14 **Mill** Noord-Brabant, SE Netherlands
105 P14 **Millau** *var.* Milhau; *anc.* Æmilianum. Aveyron, S France
xxxvi F16 **Millbrook** Cornwall, SW England, UK
12 I14 **Millbrook** Ontario, SE Canada
25 U4 **Milledgeville** Georgia, SE USA
12 C12 **Mille Lacs, Lac des** ◎ Ontario, S Canada
31 V6 **Mille Lacs Lake** ◎ Minnesota, N USA
25 V4 **Millen** Georgia, SE USA
31 O9 **Miller** South Dakota, N USA
32 K5 **Miller Dam Flowage** ⊡ Wisconsin, N USA
41 U12 **Miller, Mount** ▲ Alaska, USA
130 L10 **Millerovo** Rostovskaya Oblast', SW Russian Federation
39 N17 **Miller Peak** ▲ Arizona, SW USA
33 T12 **Millersburg** Ohio, N USA
20 G15 **Millersburg** Pennsylvania, NE USA
193 D23 **Millers Flat** Otago, South Island, NZ
27 Q8 **Millersview** Texas, SW USA
108 B10 **Millesimo** Piemonte, NE Italy
15 Mm15 **Milles Lacs, Lac des** ◎ Ontario, SW Canada
27 Q13 **Millett** Texas, SW USA
105 N11 **Millevaches, Plateau de** *plateau* C France
xliv I2 **Millford** *Ir.* Baile na nGallóglach. Donegal, NW Ireland
xxxvi B5 **Mill Hill** Barnet, SE England, UK
190 K12 **Millicent** South Australia
100 M13 **Millingen aan den Rijn** Gelderland, SE Netherlands
22 E10 **Millington** Tennessee, S USA
21 R4 **Millinocket** Maine, NE USA
21 R4 **Millinocket Lake** ◎ Maine, NE USA
205 Z11 **Mill Island** *island* Antarctica
xliv M4 **Millisle** Ards, E Northern Ireland, UK
191 T3 **Millmerran** Queensland, E Australia
xliii P15 **Mill of Uras** Aberdeenshire, NE Scotland, UK
xl L11 **Millom** Cumbria, NW England, UK
xliii H21 **Millport** North Ayrshire, W Scotland, UK
111 R9 **Millstatt** Kärnten, S Austria
xliv E13 **Millstreet** Cork, S Ireland
xliii M24 **Milltown** Dumfries and Galloway, SW Scotland, UK
xliv D10 **Milltown Malbay** *Ir.* Sráid na Cathrach. Clare, W Ireland
20 J17 **Millville** New Jersey, NE USA
xxxvi E8 **Millwall** Tower Hamlets, SE England, UK
29 S13 **Millwood Lake** ⊡ Arkansas, C USA
Milne Bank *see* Milne Seamounts
195 O17 **Milne Bay** ◐ *province* SE PNG
195 N17 **Milne Bay** *bay* SE PNG
66 J8 **Milne Seamounts** *var.* Milne Bank. *undersea feature* N Atlantic Ocean
xliii J20 **Milngavie** East Dunbartonshire, C Scotland, UK
31 Q6 **Milnor** North Dakota, N USA
xl H13 **Milnrow** Rochdale, NW England, UK
xli N11 **Milnthorpe** Cumbria, NW England, UK
21 R5 **Milo** Maine, NE USA
117 I22 **Mílos** Mílos, Kykládes, Greece, Aegean Sea
117 I22 **Mílos** *island* Kykládes, Greece, Aegean Sea
112 H11 **Miłosław** Poznań, C Poland
115 K19 **Milot** *var.* Miloti. Lezhë, C Albania
Miloti *see* Milot
xlii C12 **Milovaig** Highland, NW Scotland, UK
119 Z5 **Milove** Luhans'ka Oblast', E Ukraine
Milovidy *see* Milavidy
190 L4 **Milparinka** New South Wales, SE Australia
37 N9 **Milpitas** California, W USA
Mil'skaya Ravnina/Mil'skaya Step' *see* Mil Düzü
xlii H11 **Milton** Highland, NW Scotland, UK
xlii J12 **Milton** Highland, NW Scotland, UK
12 G15 **Milton** Ontario, S Canada
193 E24 **Milton** Otago, South Island, NZ
23 Y4 **Milton** Delaware, NE USA
25 P8 **Milton** Florida, SE USA
20 G14 **Milton** Pennsylvania, NE USA
20 L7 **Milton** Vermont, NE USA
xxxvi F15 **Milton Abbot** Devon, SW England, UK
xxxvii S5 **Milton Ernest** Bedfordshire, C England, UK
34 K11 **Milton-Freewater** Oregon, NW USA
xxxvii R6 **Milton Keynes** Milton Keynes, SE England, UK
xxxvii R5 **Milton Keynes** ◐ *unitary authority* C England, UK
xliii J19 **Milton of Campsie** East Dunbartonshire, C Scotland, UK
29 N3 **Miltonvale** Kansas, C USA
167 N10 **Miluo** Hunan, S China
xxxvi I12 **Milverton** Somerset, SW England, UK
32 M9 **Milwaukee** Wisconsin, N USA
Milyang *see* Miryang
Mimatum *see* Mende
39 Q15 **Mimbres Mountains** ▲▲ New Mexico, SW USA
190 D2 **Mimili** South Australia
104 J14 **Mimizan** Landes, SW France
Mimmaya *see* Minmaya
81 E19 **Mimongo** Ngounié, C Gabon
Min *see* Fujian
37 T7 **Mina** Nevada, W USA
149 S14 **Mīnāb** Hormozgān, SE Iran
Mina Baranis *see* Berenice
155 R9 **Mīna Bāzār** Baluchistān, SW Pakistan
170 C15 **Minamata** Kumamoto, Kyūshū, SW Japan
172 Ss17 **Minami-Iō-jima** *Eng.* San Augustine. *island* SE Japan
172 Nn7 **Minami-Kayabe** Hokkaidō, NE Japan
170 B17 **Minamitane** Kagoshima, Tanega-shima, SW Japan
Minami Tori Shima *see* Marcus Island
64 J4 **Mina Pirquitas** Jujuy, NW Argentina
181 O3 **Mīnā' Qābūs** NE Oman
63 F19 **Minas** Lavalleja, S Uruguay
11 P15 **Minas Basin** *bay* Nova Scotia, SE Canada
63 F17 **Minas de Corrales** Rivera, NE Uruguay
46 A5 **Minas de Matahambre** Pinar del Río, W Cuba
106 J13 **Minas de Ríotinto** Andalucía, S Spain
62 K7 **Minas Gerais** *off.* Estado de Minas Gerais. ◐ *state* E Brazil
44 E5 **Minas, Sierra de las** ▲▲ E Guatemala
43 T15 **Minatitlán** Veracruz-Llave, E Mexico
177 Ff6 **Minbu** Magwe, W Burma
155 V10 **Minchinābād** Punjab, E Pakistan
65 G17 **Minchinmávida, Volcán** ▲ S Chile
xlii E9 **Minch, The** *var.* North Minch. *strait* NW Scotland, UK
108 F8 **Mincio** *anc.* Mincius. ≈ N Italy
Mincius *see* Mincio
28 M11 **Minco** Oklahoma, C USA
179 Rr16 **Mindanao** *island* S Philippines
Mindanao Sea *see* Bohol Sea
103 J23 **Mindel** ≈ S Germany
103 J23 **Mindelheim** Bayern, S Germany
Mindello *see* Mindelo
78 C9 **Mindelo** *var.* Mindello; *prev.* Porto Grande. São Vicente, N Cape Verde
12 I13 **Minden** Ontario, SE Canada
102 H13 **Minden** *anc.* Minthun. Nordrhein-Westfalen, NW Germany
24 G5 **Minden** Louisiana, S USA
31 O16 **Minden** Nebraska, C USA
37 Q6 **Minden** Nevada, W USA
190 L8 **Mindona Lake** *seasonal lake* New South Wales, SE Australia
179 Pp12 **Mindoro** *island* N Philippines
179 P12 **Mindoro Strait** *strait* W Philippines
165 S9 **Mine** Gansu, N China
170 Dd12 **Mine** Yamaguchi, Honshū, SW Japan
xliv H14 **Mine Head** *Ir.* Mionn Ard. *headland* S Ireland
xxxvi I11 **Minehead** Somerset, SW England, UK
61 J19 **Mineiros** Goiás, C Brazil
27 V6 **Mineola** Texas, SW USA
27 S13 **Mineral** Texas, SW USA
131 N15 **Mineral'nyye Vody** Stavropol'skiy Kray, SW Russian Federation
32 K9 **Mineral Point** Wisconsin, N USA
27 S6 **Mineral Wells** Texas, SW USA
38 K6 **Minersville** Utah, W USA
33 U12 **Minerva** Ohio, N USA
109 N17 **Minervino Murge** Puglia, SE Italy
105 O16 **Minervois** *physical region* S France
xxxvii N9 **Minety** Wiltshire, S England, UK
164 I10 **Minfeng** *var.* Niya. Xinjiang Uygur Zizhiqu, NW China
81 O25 **Minga** Shaba, SE Zaire
143 W11 **Mingäçevir** *Rus.* Mingechaur, Mingechevir. C Azerbaijan
143 W11 **Mingäçevir Su Anbarı** *Rus.* Mingechaurskoye Vodokhranilishche, Mingechevirskoye Vodokhranilishche. ⊡ NW Azerbaijan
177 G8 **Mingaladon** ✕ (Yangon) Yangon, SW Burma
11 P11 **Mingan** Québec, E Canada
155 U5 **Mingāora** *var.* Mingora, Mongora. North-West Frontier Province, N Pakistan
xlii A13 **Mingary** Western Isles, NW Scotland, UK
152 K8 **Mingbuloq** *Rus.* Mynbulak. Nawoiy Wiloyati, N Uzbekistan
152 K9 **Mingbuloq Botighi** *Rus.* Vpadina Mynbulak. *depression* N Uzbekistan
Mingechaur/Mingechevir *see* Mingäçevir
Mingechaurskoye Vodokhranilishche/Mingechevirskoye Vodokhranilishche *see* Mingäçevir Su Anbarı
177 Ff4 **Mingin** Sagaing, C Burma
107 Q10 **Minglanilla** Castilla-La Mancha, C Spain
33 V13 **Mingo Junction** Ohio, N USA
Mingora *see* Mingāora
169 V7 **Mingshui** Heilongjiang, NE China
Mingteke Daban *see* Mintaka Pass
xliii A15 **Mingulay** *island* NW Scotland, UK
85 Q14 **Minguri** Nampula, NE Mozambique
165 U10 **Minhe** *var.* Shangchuankou. Qinghai, C China
177 Ff6 **Minhla** Magwe, W Burma
178 J15 **Minh Lương** Kiên Giang, S Vietnam
106 G5 **Minho** *Sp.* Miño. ≈ Portugal/Spain *see also* Miño
106 G5 **Minho** *former province* N Portugal
161 C24 **Minicoy Island** *island* SW India
35 P15 **Minidoka** Idaho, NW USA
120 C11 **Minija** ≈ W Lithuania
188 G9 **Minilya** Western Australia
12 E8 **Minisinakwa Lake** ◎ Ontario, S Canada
47 T12 **Ministre Point** *headland* S Saint Lucia
9 V15 **Minitonas** Manitoba, S Canada
Minius *see* Miño
167 R12 **Min Jiang** ≈ SE China
166 H10 **Min Jiang** ≈ C China
190 H9 **Minlaton** South Australia
172 N8 **Minmaya** *var.* Mimmaya. Aomori, Honshū, C Japan
79 U14 **Minna** Niger, C Nigeria
172 Pp16 **Minna-jima** *island* Sakishima-shotō, SW Japan
29 N4 **Minneapolis** Kansas, C USA
31 U9 **Minneapolis** Minnesota, N USA
15 Kk15 **Minnedosa** Manitoba, S Canada
28 J7 **Minneola** Kansas, C USA
31 S7 **Minnesota** *off.* State of Minnesota; also known as Gopher State, New England of the West, North Star State. ◐ *state* N USA
31 S9 **Minnesota River** ≈ Minnesota/South Dakota, N USA
31 V9 **Minnetonka** Minnesota, N USA
31 O3 **Minnewaukan** North Dakota, N USA
190 F7 **Minnipa** South Australia
106 H2 **Miño** Galicia, NW Spain
106 G5 **Miño** *var.* Mino, Minius, *Port.* Minho. ≈ Portugal/Spain *see also* Minho
171 Ii16 **Minobu** Yamanashi, Honshū, S Japan
32 L4 **Minocqua** Wisconsin, N USA
171 I15 **Minokamo** Gifu, Honshū, SW Japan
32 L12 **Minonk** Illinois, N USA
Minorca *see* Menorca
30 M3 **Minot** North Dakota, N USA
165 U8 **Minqin** Gansu, N China
121 J16 **Minsk** ● (Belorussia) Minskaya Voblasts', C Belorussia
121 L16 **Minsk** ✕ Minskaya Voblasts', C Belorussia
Minskaya Oblast' *see* Minskaya Voblasts'
121 K16 **Minskaya Voblasts'** *prev. Rus.* Minskaya Oblast'. ◐ *province* C Belorussia
121 J16 **Minskaya Wzvyshsha** ▲▲ C Belorussia
112 N12 **Mińsk Mazowiecki** *var.* Nowo-Minsk. Siedlce, E Poland
xxxvii O13 **Minstead** Hampshire, S England, UK
xxxvii X9 **Minster** Kent, SE England, UK
xxxvii Z10 **Minster** Kent, SE England, UK
33 Q13 **Minster** Ohio, N USA
xxxviii G10 **Minsterley** Shropshire, W England, UK
81 F15 **Minta** Centre, C Cameroon
155 W2 **Mintaka Pass** *Chin.* Mingteke Daban. *pass* China/Pakistan
117 D20 **Mínthi** ▲ S Greece
Minthun *see* Minden
xlii P11 **Mintlaw** Aberdeenshire, NE Scotland, UK
11 O14 **Minto** New Brunswick, SE Canada
8 H6 **Minto** Yukon Territory, W Canada
41 R9 **Minto** Alaska, USA
31 Q3 **Minto** North Dakota, N USA
10 K6 **Minto, Lac** ◎ Québec, C Canada
205 R16 **Minto, Mount** ▲ Antarctica
9 U17 **Minton** Saskatchewan, S Canada
201 R15 **Minto Reef** *atoll* Caroline Islands, C Micronesia
39 R4 **Minturn** Colorado, C USA
109 J16 **Minturno** Lazio, C Italy
126 Hh15 **Minusinsk** Krasnoyarskiy Kray, S Russian Federation
110 G11 **Minusio** Ticino, S Switzerland
81 E17 **Minvoul** Woleu-Ntem, N Gabon
147 R13 **Minwakh** N Yemen
165 V11 **Min Xian** *var.* Minxian. Gansu, C China
Minya *see* El Minya
33 R6 **Mio** Michigan, N USA
Mionn Ard *see* Mine Head
Miosnum, Pulau *see* Num, Pulau
176 Ww9 **Mios Num, Selat** *strait* Irian Jaya, E Indonesia
164 L5 **Miquan** Xinjiang Uygur Zizhiqu, NW China
121 I17 **Mir** Hrodzyenskaya Voblasts', W Belorussia
108 H8 **Mira** Veneto, NE Italy
106 G13 **Mira** ≈ S Portugal
10 K15 **Mirabel** *var.* Montreal. ✕ (Montréal) Québec, SE Canada
62 Q8 **Miracema** Rio de Janeiro, SE Brazil
56 G9 **Miraflores** Boyacá, C Colombia
42 G10 **Miraflores** Baja California Sur, W Mexico
46 L9 **Miragoâne** S Haiti
161 E16 **Miraj** Mahārāshtra, W India
63 E23 **Miramar** Buenos Aires, E Argentina
105 R15 **Miramas** Bouches-du-Rhône, SE France
104 K12 **Mirambeau** Charente-Maritime, W France
104 L13 **Miramont-de-Guyenne** Lot-et-Garonne, SW France
117 L25 **Mirampéllou Kólpos** *gulf* Kríti, Greece, E Mediterranean Sea
164 L8 **Miran** Xinjiang Uygur Zizhiqu, NW China
56 M5 **Miranda** *off.* Estado Miranda. ◐ *state* N Venezuela
Miranda de Corvo *see* Miranda do Corvo
107 O3 **Miranda de Ebro** La Rioja, N Spain
106 G8 **Miranda do Corvo** *var.* Miranda de Corvo. Coimbra, N Portugal
106 J6 **Miranda do Douro** Bragança, N Portugal
104 L15 **Mirande** Gers, S France
106 I6 **Mirandela** Bragança, N Portugal
27 R15 **Mirando City** Texas, SW USA
108 G9 **Mirandola** Emilia-Romagna, N Italy
62 I8 **Mirandópolis** São Paulo, S Brazil
62 K8 **Mirassol** São Paulo, S Brazil
106 J3 **Miravalles** ▲ NW Spain
44 L12 **Miravalles, Volcán** (volcano) NW Costa Rica
147 W13 **Mirbāṭ** *var.* Marbat. S Oman
46 M9 **Mirebalais** C Haiti
105 T6 **Mirecourt** Vosges, NE France
105 N16 **Mirepoix** Ariège, S France
xli R15 **Mirfield** Kirklees, N England, UK
Mirgorod *see* Myrhorod
145 W10 **Mīr Ḥājī Khalīl** E Iraq
174 Mm4 **Miri** Sarawak, East Malaysia
79 W12 **Miria** Zinder, S Niger
190 F5 **Mirikata** South Australia
56 K4 **Mirimire** Falcón, N Venezuela
63 H18 **Mirim Lagoon** *var.* Lake Mirim, *Sp.* Laguna Merín. *lagoon* Brazil/Uruguay
Mirim, Lake *see* Mirim Lagoon
Mírina *see* Mýrina
180 H14 **Miringoni** Mohéli, S Comoros
149 W11 **Mīrjāveh** Sīstān va Balūchestān, SE Iran
205 Z9 **Mirny** *Russian research station* Antarctica
126 Kk11 **Mirnyy** Respublika Sakha (Yakutiya), NE Russian Federation
Mironovka *see* Myronivka
112 F9 **Mirosławiec** Piła, NW Poland
Mirovo *see* Vrattsa
102 N10 **Mirow** Mecklenburg-Vorpommern, N Germany
158 G6 **Mirpur** Jammu and Kashmir, NW India
Mirpur *see* New Mirpur
155 P17 **Mirpur Batoro** Sind, SE Pakistan
155 Q16 **Mirpur Khās** Sind, SE Pakistan
155 P17 **Mirpur Sakro** Sind, SE Pakistan
149 T14 **Mīr Shahdād** Hormozgān, S Iran
Mirtoan Sea *see* Mirtóo Pélagos
117 G21 **Mirtóo Pélagos** *Eng.* Mirtoan Sea; *anc.* Myrtoum Mare. *sea* S Greece
169 Z16 **Miryang** *var.* Milyang, *Jap.* Mitsuō. SE South Korea
Mirzachirla *see* Murzechirla
170 Dd14 **Misaki** Ehime, Shikoku, SW Japan
43 Q13 **Misantla** Veracruz-Llave, E Mexico
172 N9 **Misawa** Aomori, Honshū, C Japan
59 G14 **Mishagua, Río** ≈ C Peru
169 Z8 **Mishan** Heilongjiang, NE China
33 O11 **Mishawaka** Indiana, N USA
41 N6 **Misheguk Mountain** ▲ Alaska, USA
171 Jj17 **Mishima** *var.* Misima. Shizuoka, Honshū, S Japan
170 Dd11 **Mi-shima** *island* SW Japan
131 V4 **Mishkino** Respublika Bashkortostan, W Russian Federation
159 Y10 **Mishmi Hills** *hill range* NE India
167 N11 **Mi Shui** ≈ S China
Misiaf *see* Maşyāf
109 J23 **Misilmeri** Sicilia, Italy, C Mediterranean Sea
Misima *see* Mishima
195 P17 **Misima Island** *island* SE PNG
Misión de Guana *see* Guana
62 F13 **Misiones** *off.* Provincia de Misiones. ◐ *province* NE Argentina
64 P8 **Misiones** *off.* Departamento de las Misiones. ◐ *department* S Paraguay
Misión San Fernando *see* San Fernando
Miskin *see* Maskin
Miskito Coast *see* La Mosquitia
45 O7 **Miskitos, Cayos** *island group* NE Nicaragua
113 M21 **Miskolc** Borsod-Abaúj-Zemplén, NE Hungary
175 Tt10 **Misool, Pulau** *island* Maluku, E Indonesia
Misox *see* Mesocco
31 Y3 **Misquah Hills** *hill range* Minnesota, N USA
77 P7 **Miṣrātah** *var.* Misurata. NW Libya
123 Ll15 **Miṣrātah, Rās** *headland* N Libya
12 C7 **Missanabie** Ontario, S Canada
60 E10 **Missão Catrimani** Roraima, N Brazil
12 D6 **Missinaibi** ≈ Ontario, S Canada
12 C7 **Missinaibi Lake** ◎ Ontario, S Canada
9 T13 **Missinipe** Saskatchewan, C Canada
30 M11 **Mission** South Dakota, N USA
27 S17 **Mission** Texas, SW USA
10 F10 **Missisa Lake** ◎ Ontario, C Canada
20 M6 **Missisquoi Bay** *lake bay* Canada/USA
12 C10 **Mississagi** ≈ Ontario, S Canada
12 G15 **Mississauga** Ontario, S Canada
33 P12 **Mississinewa Lake** ⊡ Indiana, N USA
33 P12 **Mississinewa River** ≈ Indiana/Ohio, N USA
24 K4 **Mississippi** *off.* State of Mississippi; also known as Bayou State, Magnolia State. ◐ *state* SE USA
12 K13 **Mississippi** ≈ Ontario, SE Canada
24 M10 **Mississippi Delta** *delta* Louisiana, S USA
49 N1 **Mississippi Fan** *undersea feature* N Gulf of Mexico
12 L13 **Mississippi Lake** ◎ Ontario, SE Canada
1 J11 **Mississippi River** ≈ C USA
24 M9 **Mississippi Sound** *sound* Alabama/Mississippi, S USA
35 P9 **Missoula** Montana, NW USA
29 T5 **Missouri** *off.* State of Missouri; also known as Bullion State, Show Me State. ◐ *state* C USA
27 V11 **Missouri City** Texas, SW USA
1 J10 **Missouri River** ≈ C USA
13 Q6 **Mistassibi** ≈ Québec, SE Canada
13 P6 **Mistassini** Québec, SE Canada
13 P6 **Mistassini** ≈ Québec, SE Canada
10 J11 **Mistassini, Lac** ◎ Québec, SE Canada
111 Y3 **Mistelbach an der Zaya** Niederösterreich, NE Austria
109 L24 **Misterbianco** Sicilia, Italy, C Mediterranean Sea
97 N19 **Mistérhult** Kalmar, S Sweden
xxxix O4 **Misterton** Nottinghamshire, C England, UK
xxxvi K13 **Misterton** Somerset, SW England, UK
59 H17 **Misti, Volcán** ▲ S Peru
Mistras *see* Mystrás
109 K23 **Mistretta** *anc.* Amestratus. Sicilia, Italy, C Mediterranean Sea
170 C14 **Misumi** Kumamoto, Kyūshū, SW Japan
170 Ee12 **Misumi** Shimane, Honshū, SW Japan
Misurata *see* Miṣrātah
85 O14 **Mitande** Niassa, N Mozambique
42 J13 **Mita, Punta de** *headland* C Mexico
57 W12 **Mitaraka, Massif du** ▲ NE South America
Mitau *see* Jelgava
189 X9 **Mitchell** Queensland, E Australia
12 E15 **Mitchell** Ontario, S Canada
30 I13 **Mitchell** Nebraska, C USA
34 J12 **Mitchell** Oregon, NW USA
31 P11 **Mitchell** South Dakota, N USA
25 P5 **Mitchell Lake** ⊡ Alabama, S USA
33 P7 **Mitchell, Lake** ◎ Michigan, N USA
23 P9 **Mitchell, Mount** ▲ North Carolina, SE USA
189 V3 **Mitchell River** ≈ Queensland, NE Australia
xliv G12 **Mitchelstown** *Ir.* Baile Mhistéala. Cork, SW Ireland
12 M9 **Mitchinamécus, Lac** ◎ Québec, SE Canada
Mitèmboni *see* Mitemele, Río

◆ Country ● Country Capital ◇ Dependent Territory ○ Dependent Territory Capital ◐ Administrative Region ✕ International Airport ▲ Mountain ▲▲ Mountain Range (volcano) Volcano ≈ River ◎ Lake ⊡ Reservoir

MITEMELE, RÍO – MONTICELLO

81 D17 Mitemele, Río var. Mitèmboni, Temboni, Utamboni. ≈ S Equatorial Guinea
xli R5 Mitford Northumberland, N England, UK
155 S12 Mithānkot Punjab, E Pakistan
155 T7 Mitha Tiwāna Punjab, E Pakistan
155 R17 Mithi Sind, SE Pakistan
Míthimna see Míthymna
Mi Tho see My Tho
117 L16 Míthymna var. Míthimna. Lésvos, E Greece
202 L16 Mitiaro island S Cook Islands
Mitilíni see Mytilíni
13 U7 Mitis ≈ Québec, SE Canada
43 R16 Mitla Oaxaca, SE Mexico
171 Kk16 Mito Ibaraki, Honshū, S Japan
94 N2 Mitra, Kapp headland W Svalbard
192 M13 Mitre ▲ North Island, NZ
193 B21 Mitre Peak ▲ South Island, NZ
41 O15 Mitrofania Island island Alaska, USA
Mitrovica/Mitrowitz see Sremska Mitrovica, Serbia, Yugoslavia
Mitrovica/Mitrovicë see Kosovska Mitrovica, Serbia, Yugoslavia
180 H12 Mitsamiouli Grande Comore, NW Comoros
180 I3 Mitsinjo Mahajanga, NW Madagascar
Mits'iwa see Massawa
180 H13 Mitsoudjé Grande Comore, NW Comoros
172 Oo7 Mitsuishi Hokkaidō, NE Japan
171 K13 Mitsuke var. Mituke. Niigata, Honshū, C Japan
Mitsuō see Miryang
170 Cc10 Mitsushima Nagasaki, Tsushima, SW Japan
102 G12 Mittellandkanal canal NW Germany
110 J7 Mittelberg Vorarlberg, NW Austria
Mitteldorf see Międzychód
Mittelstadt see Baia Sprie
Mitterburg see Pazin
111 P7 Mittersill Salzburg, NW Austria
103 N16 Mittweida Sachsen, E Germany
56 J13 Mitú Vaupés, SE Colombia
Mituke see Mitsuke
Mitumba, Chaine des/Mitumba Range see Mitumba, Monts
81 O22 Mitumba, Monts var. Chaîne des Mitumba, Mitumba Range. ▲▲ E Zaire
81 N23 Mitwaba Shaba, SE Zaire
81 E18 Mitzic Woleu-Ntem, N Gabon
84 K11 Miueru Wantipa, Lake ◎ N Zambia
171 Jj17 Miura Kanagawa, Honshū, S Japan
171 M13 Miyagi off. Miyagi-ken. ◈ prefecture Honshū, C Japan
144 M7 Miyāh, Wādī al dry watercourse E Syria
172 Ss13 Miyake Tōkyō, Miyako-jima, SE Japan
172 N11 Miyako Iwate, Honshū, C Japan
172 Q16 Miyako-jima island Sakishima-shotō, SW Japan
170 C16 Miyakonojō var. Miyakonzyô. Miyazaki, Kyūshū, SW Japan
Miyakonzyô see Miyakonojō
172 Pp16 Miyako-shotō island group SW Japan
150 G11 Miyaly Atyrau, W Kazakhstan
Miyāndoāb see Miāndowāb
Miyāneh see Miāneh
170 C15 Miyanojō Kagoshima, Kyūshū, SW Japan
170 Cc16 Miyazaki Miyazaki, Kyūshū, SW Japan
170 C15 Miyazaki off. Miyazaki-ken. ◈ prefecture Kyūshū, SW Japan
171 H13 Miyazu Kyōto, Honshū, SW Japan
Miyory see Myory
170 F13 Miyoshi var. Miyosi. Hiroshima, Honshū, SW Japan
Miyosi see Miyoshi
Miza see Mizë
83 H14 Mīzan Teferī SW Ethiopia
Mizda see Mizdah
77 O8 Mizdah var. Mizda. NW Libya
115 K20 Mizë var. Miza. Fier, W Albania
xliv C15 Mizen Head Ir. Carn Uí Néid. headland SW Ireland
118 H7 Mizhhir"ya Rus. Mezhgor'ye. Zakarpats'ka Oblast', W Ukraine
166 L4 Mizhi Shaanxi, C China
118 K13 Mizil Prahova, SE Romania
116 H7 Miziya Oblast Montana, NW Bulgaria
159 W15 Mizo Hills hill range E India
159 W15 Mizoram ◈ state NE India
144 F12 Mizpé Ramon Southern, S Israel
59 L19 Mizque Cochabamba, C Bolivia
59 M19 Mizque, Río ≈ C Bolivia
171 I15 Mizunami Gifu, Honshū, SW Japan
171 Mm12 Mizusawa Iwate, Honshū, C Japan
97 M18 Mjölby Östergötland, S Sweden
97 G15 Mjøndalen Buskerud, S Norway
97 J19 Mjörn ◎ S Sweden
96 I13 Mjøsa var. Mjøsen. ◎ S Norway
Mjøsen see Mjøsa
83 G21 Mkalama Singida, C Tanzania
83 K23 Mkata ≈ C Tanzania
85 K14 Mkushi Central, C Zambia
85 L22 Mkuze KwaZulu/Natal, E South Africa
83 J22 Mkwaja Tanga, E Tanzania
113 D16 Mladá Boleslav Ger. Jungbunzlau. Střední Čechy, N Czech Republic
114 M12 Mladenovac Serbia, C Yugoslavia
116 L11 Mladinovo Khaskovska Oblast, SE Bulgaria
115 O17 Mlado Nagoričane N FYR Macedonia
Mlanje see Mulanje
114 N12 Mlava ≈ E Yugoslavia
112 L9 Mława Ciechanów, C Poland
115 G16 Mljet It. Meleda; anc. Melita. island S Croatia
118 K4 Mlyniv Rivnens'ka Oblast', NW Ukraine
85 I21 Mmabatho North-West, N South Africa
85 I19 Mmashoro Central, E Botswana
46 J7 Moa Holguín, E Cuba
78 J15 Moa ≈ Guinea/Sierra Leone
39 O6 Moab Utah, W USA
189 V1 Moa Island island Queensland, NE Australia
197 J15 Moala island S Fiji
85 L21 Moamba Maputo, SW Mozambique
81 F19 Moanda var. Mouanda. Haut-Ogooué, SE Gabon
175 T16 Moa, Pulau island Kepulauan Leti, E Indonesia
xliv H9 Moate Westmeath, C Ireland
85 M15 Moatize Tete, NW Mozambique
81 P22 Moba Shaba, E Zaire
171 K17 Mobara Chiba, Honshū, S Japan
Mobay see Montego Bay
81 K15 Mobaye Basse-Kotto, S Central African Republic
81 K15 Mobayi-Mbongo Equateur, NW Zaire
27 P2 Mobeetie Texas, SW USA
29 U3 Moberly Missouri, C USA
25 N8 Mobile Alabama, S USA
25 N9 Mobile Bay bay Alabama, S USA
25 N8 Mobile River ≈ Alabama, S USA
31 N8 Mobridge South Dakota, N USA
Mobutu Sese Seko, Lac see Albert, Lake
47 N8 Moca N Dominican Republic
Moçâmedes see Namibe
178 J6 Môc Châu Sơn La, N Vietnam
197 L15 Moce island Lau Group, E Fiji
Mocha see Al Mukhā
200 Oo13 Mocha Fracture Zone tectonic feature SE Pacific Ocean
65 F14 Mocha, Isla island C Chile
58 C12 Moche, Río ≈ W Peru
178 J14 Môc Hoa Long An, S Vietnam
xliii I25 Mochrum Dumfries and Galloway, SW Scotland, UK
85 I20 Mochudi Kgatleng, SE Botswana
84 Q13 Mocímboa da Praia var. Vila de Mocímboa da Praia. Cabo Delgado, N Mozambique
96 L13 Mockfjärd Kopparberg, C Sweden
23 R9 Mocksville North Carolina, SE USA
34 F8 Moclips Washington, NW USA
84 C13 Môco var. Morro de Môco. ▲ W Angola
56 D13 Mocoa Putumayo, SW Colombia
62 M8 Mococa São Paulo, S Brazil
Môco, Morro de see Môco
42 H8 Mocorito Sinaloa, C Mexico
42 J4 Moctezuma Chihuahua, N Mexico
43 N11 Moctezuma San Luis Potosí, C Mexico
42 G4 Moctezuma Sonora, NW Mexico
43 P12 Moctezuma, Río ≈ C Mexico
Mó, Cuan see Clew Bay
85 O16 Mocuba Zambézia, NE Mozambique
105 U12 Modane Savoie, E France
xxxvi G16 Modbury Devon, SW England, UK
108 F9 Modena anc. Mutina. Emilia-Romagna, N Italy
38 I7 Modena Utah, W USA
37 O9 Modesto California, W USA
109 L25 Modica anc. Motyca. Sicilia, Italy, C Mediterranean Sea
81 K17 Modjamboli Equateur, N Zaire
111 X4 Mödling Niederösterreich, NE Austria
Modohn see Madona
169 N8 Modot Hentiy, C Mongolia
176 W12 Modowi Irian Jaya, E Indonesia
114 I12 Modračko Jezero ⊡ NE Bosnia and Herzegovina
114 I10 Modriča N Bosnia and Herzegovina
191 O13 Moe Victoria, SE Australia
Moearatewe see Muaratewe
Moei, Mae Nam see Thaungyin
xxxv F4 Moelfre Isle of Anglesey, NW Wales, UK
xxxv H8 Moelfre hill E Wales, UK
96 H13 Moelv Hedmark, S Norway
94 I10 Moen Troms, N Norway
Moen see Weno, Micronesia
Möen see Møn, Denmark
Moena see Muna, Pulau
38 M10 Moenkopi Wash ≈ Arizona, SW USA
193 F22 Moeraki Point headland South Island, NZ
101 F16 Moerbeke Oost-Vlaanderen, NW Belgium
101 H14 Moerdijk Noord-Brabant, S Netherlands
Moero, Lac see Mweru, Lake
103 D15 Moers var. Mörs. Nordrhein-Westfalen, W Germany
Moesi see Musi, Air
Moeskroen see Mouscron
xliii L23 Moffat Dumfries and Galloway, S Scotland, UK
193 C22 Moffat Peak ▲ South Island, NZ
158 H8 Moga Punjab, N India
81 N19 Moga Sud Kivu, E Zaire
Mogadiscio/Mogadishu see Muqdisho
Mogador see Essaouira
106 J6 Mogadouro Bragança, N Portugal
171 Ll12 Mogami-gawa ≈ Honshū, C Japan
178 Gg2 Mogaung Kachin State, N Burma
112 L13 Mogielnica Radom, C Poland
Mogilëv see Mahilyow
Mogilev-Podol'skiy see Mohyliv-Podil's'kyy
Mogilëvskaya Oblast' see Mahilyowskaya Voblasts'
112 I11 Mogilno Bydgoszcz, C Poland
62 L9 Mogi-Mirim var. Moji-Mirim. São Paulo, S Brazil
85 Q15 Mogincual Nampula, NE Mozambique
116 E13 Moglenítsas ≈ N Greece
108 H8 Mogliano Veneto Veneto, NE Italy
115 M21 Mogliçë Korçë, SE Albania
126 L15 Mogocha Chitinskaya Oblast', S Russian Federation
126 H13 Mogochin Tomskaya Oblast', C Russian Federation
82 F13 Mogogh Jonglei, SE Sudan
176 Vv10 Mogoi Irian Jaya, E Indonesia
178 Gg4 Mogok Mandalay, C Burma
39 P14 Mogollon Mountains ▲▲ New Mexico, SW USA
38 M12 Mogollon Rim cliff Arizona, SW USA
63 E23 Mogotes, Punta headland E Argentina
44 J8 Mogotón ▲ NW Nicaragua
106 I14 Moguer Andalucía, S Spain
113 J26 Mohács Baranya, SW Hungary
193 C20 Mohaka ≈ North Island, NZ
30 M2 Mohall North Dakota, N USA
Moḥammadābād see Dargaz
76 F6 Mohammedia prev. Fédala. NW Morocco
76 F6 Mohammed V × (Casablanca) W Morocco
Mohammerah see Khorramshahr
38 H10 Mohave, Lake ⊡ Arizona/Nevada, W USA
38 I12 Mohave Mountains ▲▲ Arizona, SW USA
38 I15 Mohawk Mountains ▲▲ Arizona, SW USA
20 J10 Mohawk River ≈ New York, NE USA
169 T3 Mohe Heilongjiang, NE China
97 L20 Moheda Kronoberg, S Sweden
180 H13 Mohéli var. Mwali, Mohilla, Mohila, Fr. Moili. island S Comoros
xliv D10 Moher, Cliffs of cliff W Ireland
40 K12 Mohican, Cape headland Nunivak Island, Alaska, USA
xliv H7 Mohill Leitrim, N Ireland
Mohn see Muhu
103 G15 Möhne ≈ W Germany
103 G15 Möhne-Stausee ⊡ W Germany
94 P2 Mohn, Kapp headland NW Svalbard
207 S14 Mohns Ridge undersea feature Greenland Sea/Norwegian Sea
59 I17 Moho Puno, SW Peru
Mohokare see Caledon
97 L17 Moholm Skaraborg, S Sweden
38 J11 Mohon Peak ▲ Arizona, SW USA
83 J23 Mohoro Pwani, E Tanzania
Mohra see Moravice
Mohrungen see Morąg
118 M7 Mohyliv-Podil's'kyy Rus. Mogilev-Podol'skiy. Vinnyts'ka Oblast', C Ukraine
97 D17 Moi Rogaland, S Norway
197 I6 Moindou Province Sud, C New Caledonia
118 K11 Moineşti Hung. Mojnest. Bacău, E Romania
Móinteach Mílic see Mountmellick
xliv L5 Moira Craigavon, C Northern Ireland, UK
12 J14 Moira ≈ Ontario, SE Canada
94 G13 Mo i Rana Nordland, C Norway
159 X14 Moirāng Manipur, NE India
117 J25 Moíres Kríti, Greece, E Mediterranean Sea
120 H6 Mõisaküla Ger. Moiseküll. Viljandimaa, S Estonia
Moiseküll see Mõisaküla
13 W4 Moisie Québec, E Canada
13 W3 Moisie ≈ Québec, SE Canada
104 M14 Moissac Tarn-et-Garonne, S France
80 I13 Moïssala Moyen-Chari, S Chad
57 O7 Moitaco Bolívar, E Venezuela
97 P15 Möja Stockholm, C Sweden
107 Q14 Mojácar Andalucía, S Spain
37 T13 Mojave California, W USA
37 V13 Mojave Desert plain California, W USA
37 V13 Mojave River ≈ California, W USA
Moji-Mirim see Mogi-Mirim
115 K15 Mojkovac Montenegro, SW Yugoslavia
Mojnest see Moineşti
174 Ll15 Mojokerto prev. Modjokerto. Jawa, C Indonesia
Môka see Mooka
159 Q13 Mokāma prev. Mokameh, Mukama. Bihār, N India
Mokameh see Mokāma
81 O25 Mokambo Shaba, SE Zaire
40 D9 Mokapu Point headland Oahu, Hawaii, USA, C Pacific Ocean
192 M9 Mokau Waikato, North Island, NZ
192 L9 Mokau ≈ North Island, NZ
37 P7 Mokelumne River ≈ California, W USA
85 J23 Mokhotlong NE Lesotho
Mokil Atoll see Mwokil Atoll
97 N14 Möklinta Västmanland, C Sweden
192 L4 Mokohinau Islands island group N NZ
159 X12 Mokokchūng Nāgāland, NE India
80 F12 Mokolo Extrême-Nord, N Cameroon
193 D24 Mokoreta ≈ South Island, NZ
169 X17 Mokp'o Jap. Moppo. SW South Korea
115 L16 Mokra Gora ▲▲ S Yugoslavia
Mokrany see Makrany
131 O5 Moksha ≈ W Russian Federation
Moktama see Martaban
79 T14 Mokwa Niger, W Nigeria
101 J16 Mol prev. Moll. Antwerpen, N Belgium
109 O17 Mola di Bari Puglia, SE Italy
Molai see Moláoi
43 P13 Molango Hidalgo, C Mexico
117 F22 Moláoi var. Molai. Pelopónnisos, S Greece
43 Z12 Molas del Norte, Punta var. Punta Molas. headland SE Mexico
Molas, Punta see Molas del Norte, Punta
107 R11 Molatón ▲ C Spain
xlii D13 Mol-chlach Highland, NW Scotland, UK
xxxv J5 Mold Flintshire, NE Wales, UK
Moldau see Moldova
Moldau see Vltava, Czech Republic
118 L9 Moldavia off. Republic of Moldova, var. Moldova; prev. Moldavian SSR, Rus. Moldavskaya SSR. ◆ republic SE Europe
Moldavia see Moldova
Moldavian SSR/Moldavskaya SSR see Moldavia
96 E9 Molde Møre og Romsdal, S Norway
Moldotau, Khrebet see Moldo-Too, Khrebet
153 V9 Moldo-Too, Khrebet prev. Khrebet Moldotau. ▲▲ C Kyrgyzstan
118 K9 Moldova ≈ N Romania
118 K9 Moldova Eng. Moldavia, Ger. Moldau. former province NE Romania
Moldova see Moldavia
118 F13 Moldova Nouă Ger. Neumoldowa, Hung. Újmoldova. Caraş-Severin, SW Romania
Moldova, Republic of see Moldavia
118 F13 Moldova Veche Ger. Altmoldowa, Hung. Ómoldova. Caraş-Severin, SW Romania
Moldoveanul see Vârful Moldoveanu
xxxvii T11 Mole ≈ SE England, UK
85 I20 Molepolole Kweneng, SE Botswana
46 L8 Môle-St-Nicolas NW Haiti
120 H13 Molėtai Molėtai, E Lithuania
109 O17 Molfetta Puglia, SE Italy
175 R8 Molibagu Sulawesi, N Indonesia
65 G12 Molina Maule, C Chile
107 Q7 Molina de Aragón Castilla-La Mancha, C Spain
107 R13 Molina de Segura Murcia, SE Spain
32 J11 Moline Illinois, N USA
29 P7 Moline Kansas, C USA
81 P23 Moliro Shaba, SE Zaire
109 K16 Molise ◈ region S Italy
97 K15 Molkom Värmland, C Sweden
Moll see Mol
111 Q9 Möll ≈ S Austria
xxxvi H12 Molland Devon, SW England, UK
97 J22 Mölle Malmöhus, S Sweden
59 H18 Mollendo Arequipa, SW Peru
107 U5 Mollerussa Cataluña, NE Spain
110 H8 Mollis Glarus, NE Switzerland
97 J19 Mölndal Göteborg och Bohus, S Sweden
97 J19 Mölnlycke Göteborg och Bohus, S Sweden
119 U9 Molochans'k Rus. Molochansk. Zaporiz'ka Oblast', SE Ukraine
119 U10 Molochna Rus. Molochnaya. ≈ S Ukraine
Molochnaya see Molochna
119 U10 Molochnyy Lyman bay N Black Sea
Molodechno/Molodeczno see Maladzyechna
205 V3 Molodezhnaya Russian research station Antarctica
128 J14 Mologa ≈ NW Russian Federation
40 E9 Molokai Haw. Moloka'i. island Hawaii, USA, C Pacific Ocean
183 X3 Molokai Fracture Zone tectonic feature NE Pacific Ocean
128 K15 Molokovo Tverskaya Oblast', W Russian Federation
129 Q14 Moloma ≈ NW Russian Federation
191 R8 Molong New South Wales, SE Australia
85 H21 Molopo seasonal river Botswana/South Africa
117 F17 Mólos Stereá Ellás, C Greece
175 Q7 Molosipat Sulawesi, N Indonesia
Molotov see Severodvinsk, Arkhangel'skaya Oblast', Russian Federation
Molotov see Perm', Permskaya Oblast', Russian Federation
81 G17 Moloundou Est, SE Cameroon
105 U5 Molsheim Bas-Rhin, NE France
15 L12 Molson Lake ◎ Manitoba, C Canada
Moluccas see Maluku
175 Rr8 Molucca Sea Ind. Laut Maluku. sea E Indonesia
Molukken see Maluku
85 O15 Molumbo Zambézia, N Mozambique
176 Uu14 Molu, Pulau island Maluku, E Indonesia
85 P16 Moma Nampula, NE Mozambique
127 N17 Moma ≈ NE Russian Federation
176 Xx13 Momats ≈ Irian Jaya, E Indonesia
44 J11 Mombacho, Volcán ⛰ SW Nicaragua
83 K21 Mombasa Coast, SE Kenya
83 J21 Mombasa × Coast, SE Kenya
Mombetsu see Monbetsu
176 Y16 Mombum Irian Jaya, E Indonesia
116 J12 Momchilgrad prev. Mastanli. Khaskovska Oblast, S Bulgaria
101 F23 Momignies Hainaut, S Belgium
56 E6 Momil Córdoba, NW Colombia
44 I10 Momotombo, Volcán ⛰ W Nicaragua
58 B5 Mompiche, Ensenada de bay NW Ecuador
81 K18 Mompono Equateur, NW Zaire
56 F6 Mompós Bolívar, NW Colombia
97 J24 Møn prev. Möen. island SE Denmark
38 L4 Mona Utah, W USA
Mona, Canal de la see Mona Passage
xlii A11 Monach Islands island group NW Scotland, UK
105 V14 Monaco var. Monaco-Ville; anc. Monoecus. ● (Monaco) S Monaco
105 V14 Monaco off. Principality of Monaco. ◆ monarchy W Europe
Monaco see München
Monaco Basin see Canary Basin
Monaco-Ville see Monaco
xliii J14 Monadhliath Mountains ▲▲ N Scotland, UK
57 O6 Monagas off. Estado Monagas. ◈ state NE Venezuela
xliv J5 Monaghan Ir. Muineachán. Monaghan, N Ireland
xliv J6 Monaghan Ir. Muineachán. ◈ county N Ireland
45 S16 Monagrillo Herrera, S Panama
26 L8 Monahans Texas, SW USA
47 Q9 Mona, Isla island W Puerto Rico
47 Q9 Mona Passage Sp. Canal de la Mona. channel Dominican Republic/Puerto Rico
45 O14 Mona, Punta headland E Costa Rica
161 K25 Monaragala Uva Province, SE Sri Lanka
35 S9 Monarch Montana, NW USA
14 Ff14 Monarch Mountain ▲ British Columbia, SW Canada
xlii H12 Monar, Loch ◎ NW Scotland, UK
xliv J9 Monasterevin Kildare, E Ireland
Monasterio see Monesterio
Monasterzyska see Monastyrys'ka
Monastir see Bitola
Monastyriska see Monastyrys'ka
119 O7 Monastyryshche Cherkas'ka Oblast', C Ukraine
118 J6 Monastyrys'ka Pol. Monasterzyska, Rus. Monastyriska. Ternopil's'ka Oblast', W Ukraine
81 E15 Monatélé Centre, SW Cameroon
172 Q4 Monbetsu var. Mombetsu, Monbetu. Hokkaidō, NE Japan
Monbetu see Monbetsu
108 B8 Moncalieri Piemonte, NW Italy
106 G4 Monção Viana do Castelo, N Portugal
107 Q5 Moncayo ▲ N Spain
107 Q5 Moncayo, Sierra del ▲▲ N Spain
128 J4 Monchegorsk Murmanskaya Oblast', NW Russian Federation
103 D15 Mönchengladbach prev. München-Gladbach. Nordrhein-Westfalen, W Germany
106 F14 Monchique Faro, S Portugal
106 G14 Monchique, Serra de ▲▲ S Portugal
23 S14 Moncks Corner South Carolina, SE USA
43 N7 Monclova Coahuila de Zaragoza, NE Mexico
Moncorvo see Torre de Moncorvo
11 P14 Moncton New Brunswick, SE Canada
106 G8 Mondego ≈ N Portugal
106 F8 Mondego, Cabo headland N Portugal
106 I2 Mondoñedo Galicia, NW Spain
101 N25 Mondorf-les-Bains Grevenmacher, SE Luxembourg
104 M7 Mondoubleau Loir-et-Cher, C France
32 J6 Mondovi Wisconsin, N USA
108 B9 Mondovì Piemonte, NW Italy
107 P3 Mondragón var. Arrasate. País Vasco, N Spain
109 J17 Mondragone Campania, S Italy
111 R5 Mondsee ◎ N Austria
126 J16 Mondy Respublika Buryatiya, S Russian Federation
117 G22 Monemvasía Pelopónnisos, S Greece
20 B15 Monessen Pennsylvania, NE USA
106 J12 Monesterio var. Monasterio. Extremadura, W Spain
12 L8 Monet Québec, SE Canada
29 S8 Monett Missouri, C USA
29 X9 Monette Arkansas, C USA
12 G11 Monetville Ontario, S Canada
xliv H10 Moneygall Offaly, C Ireland
xliv K4 Moneymore Cookstown, C Northern Ireland, UK
108 J7 Monfalcone Friuli-Venezia Giulia, NE Italy
106 H10 Monforte Portalegre, C Portugal
106 I4 Monforte Galicia, NW Spain
83 I24 Monga Lindi, SE Tanzania
81 L16 Monga Haut-Zaïre, N Zaire
83 F15 Mongalla Bahr el Gabel, S Sudan
159 U11 Mongar E Bhutan
178 K6 Mong Cai Quang Ninh, N Vietnam
188 I11 Mongers Lake salt lake Western Australia
195 U14 Mongga Kolombangara Island, NW Solomon Islands
178 Hh6 Möng Hpayak Shan State, E Burma
Monghyr see Munger
108 B10 Mongioie ▲ NW Italy
178 Gg5 Möng Küng Shan State, E Burma
Mongla see Mungla
196 C15 Mongmong C Guam
178 Gg6 Möng Nai Shan State, E Burma
80 I11 Mongo Guéra, C Chad
78 I14 Mongo ≈ N Sierra Leone
169 I8 Mongolia Mong. Mongol Uls. ◆ republic E Asia
133 V8 Mongolia, Plateau of plateau E Mongolia
Mongolküre see Zhaosu
Mongol Uls see Mongolia
81 E17 Mongomo E Equatorial Guinea
79 Y12 Mongonu var. Monguno. Borno, NE Nigeria
Mongora see Mingāora
80 K11 Mongororo Ouaddaï, SE Chad
Mongos, Chaîne des see Bongo, Massif des
81 I16 Mongoumba Lobaye, SW Central African Republic
Mongrove, Punta see Cayacal, Punta
85 G15 Mongu Western, W Zambia
78 I10 Monguel Gorgol, SW Mauritania
Monguno see Mongonu
178 H4 Möng Yai Shan State, E Burma
178 Hh5 Möng Yang Shan State, E Burma
178 H3 Möng Yu Shan State, E Burma
168 K8 Mönhbulag Övörhangay, C Mongolia
Mönh Sarĭdag see Munku-Sardyk, Gora
194 L15 Moni ≈ S Papau New Guinea
xliii K23 Moniaive Dumfries and Galloway, SW Scotland, UK
xliii N17 Monifieth Angus, E Scotland, UK
xliii N17 Monikie Angus, E Scotland, UK
117 I15 Moní Megístis Lávras monastery Kentrikí Makedonía, N Greece
117 F18 Moní Osíou Loúkas monastery Stereá Ellás, C Greece
56 F9 Moniquirá Boyacá, C Colombia
105 Q12 Monistrol-sur-Loire Haute-Loire, C France
37 V7 Monitor Range ▲▲ Nevada, W USA
117 I14 Moní Vatopedíou monastery Kentrikí Makedonía, N Greece
179 Rr15 Monkayo Mindanao, S Philippines
Monkchester see Newcastle upon Tyne
85 N14 Monkey Bay Southern, SE Malawi
45 N11 Monkey Point var. Punta Mico, Punte Mono, Punto Mico. headland SE Nicaragua
Monkey River see Monkey River Town
44 G3 Monkey River Town var. Monkey River. Toledo, SE Belize
xxxviii H13 Monkland Herefordshire, W England, UK
12 M13 Monkland Ontario, SE Canada
81 J19 Monkoto Equateur, NW Zaire
xxxvii I12 Monk's Gate West Sussex, SE England, UK
xxxvi I11 Monksilver Somerset, SW England, UK
xliii I22 Monkton South Ayrshire, W Scotland, UK
xxxv L13 Monmouth Wel. Trefynwy. Monmouthshire, SE Wales, UK
32 J12 Monmouth Illinois, N USA
34 F12 Monmouth Oregon, NW USA
xxxv K13 Monmouthshire ◈ unitary authority SE Wales, UK
100 I10 Monnickendam Noord-Holland, C Netherlands
79 R15 Mono ≈ C Togo
Monoecus see Monaco
37 R8 Mono Lake ◎ California, W USA
117 O23 Monólithos Ródos, Dodekánisos, Greece, Aegean Sea
21 Q12 Monomoy Island island Massachusetts, NE USA
33 O12 Monon Indiana, N USA
31 Y12 Monona Iowa, C USA
32 J9 Monona Wisconsin, N USA
20 B15 Monongahela Pennsylvania, NE USA
20 B16 Monongahela River ≈ NE USA
109 P17 Monopoli Puglia, SE Italy
Mono, Punte see Monkey Point
113 K23 Monor Pest, C Hungary
Monostor see Beli Manastir
80 K8 Monou Borkou-Ennedi-Tibesti, NE Chad
107 S12 Monóvar País Valenciano, E Spain
107 R7 Monreal del Campo Aragón, NE Spain
109 I23 Monreale Sicilia, Italy, C Mediterranean Sea
xliii I26 Monreith Dumfries and Galloway, SW Scotland, UK
25 T3 Monroe Georgia, SE USA
31 W14 Monroe Iowa, C USA
24 I5 Monroe Louisiana, S USA
33 S10 Monroe Michigan, N USA
20 K13 Monroe New York, NE USA
23 S11 Monroe North Carolina, SE USA
38 L6 Monroe Utah, W USA
34 H7 Monroe Washington, NW USA
32 J9 Monroe Wisconsin, N USA
29 V3 Monroe City Missouri, C USA
33 O15 Monroe Lake ⊡ Indiana, N USA
25 O7 Monroeville Alabama, S USA
20 C15 Monroeville Pennsylvania, NE USA
78 J16 Monrovia ● (Liberia) W Liberia
78 J16 Monrovia × W Liberia
107 T7 Monroyo Aragón, NE Spain
101 F20 Mons Dut. Bergen. Hainaut, S Belgium
106 I8 Monsanto Castelo Branco, C Portugal
108 H8 Monselice Veneto, NE Italy
178 Gg9 Mon State ◈ state S Burma
100 G12 Monster Zuid-Holland, W Netherlands
97 N20 Mönsterås Kalmar, S Sweden
103 F17 Montabaur Rheinland-Pfalz, W Germany
108 G8 Montagnana Veneto, NE Italy
37 N1 Montague California, W USA
27 S5 Montague Texas, SW USA
191 S11 Montague Island island New South Wales, SE Australia
41 S12 Montague Island island Alaska, USA
41 S13 Montague Strait strait N Gulf of Alaska
104 J8 Montaigu Vendée, NW France
Montaigu see Scherpenheuvel
107 S7 Montalbán Aragón, NE Spain
108 G13 Montalcino Toscana, C Italy
106 H5 Montalegre Vila Real, N Portugal
116 G8 Montana prev. Ferdinand, Mikhaylovgrad. Oblast Montana, NW Bulgaria
110 D10 Montana Valais, SW Switzerland
41 R11 Montana Alaska, USA
35 T9 Montana off. State of Montana; also known as Mountain State, Treasure State. ◈ state NW USA
Montana see Montana, Oblast
116 G8 Montana, Oblast var. Montana; prev. Mikhailovgrad, Mikhaylovgrad. ◈ province NW Bulgaria
106 J10 Montánchez Extremadura, W Spain
Montañita see La Montañita
13 Q8 Mont-Apica Québec, SE Canada
106 G10 Montargil Portalegre, C Portugal
106 G10 Montargil, Barragem de ⊡ C Portugal
105 O7 Montargis Loiret, C France
105 O4 Montataire Oise, N France
104 M14 Montauban Tarn-et-Garonne, S France
21 N14 Montauk Long Island, New York, NE USA
21 N14 Montauk Point headland Long Island, New York, NE USA
105 Q7 Montbard Côte d'Or, C France
105 U7 Montbéliard Doubs, E France
27 W11 Mont Belvieu Texas, SW USA
107 U6 Montblanc var. Montblanch. Cataluña, NE Spain
Montblanch see Montblanc
105 Q11 Montbrison Loire, E France
Montcalm, Lake see Dogai Coring
105 Q9 Montceau-les-Mines Saône-et-Loire, C France
105 U12 Mont Cenis, Col du pass E France
104 K15 Mont-de-Marsan Landes, SW France
105 O3 Montdidier Somme, N France
197 J7 Mont-Dore Province Sud, S New Caledonia
22 K10 Monteagle Tennessee, S USA
59 M20 Monteagudo Chuquisaca, S Bolivia
43 R16 Monte Albán ruins Oaxaca, S Mexico
107 R11 Montealegre del Castillo Castilla-La Mancha, C Spain
61 N18 Monte Azul Minas Gerais, SE Brazil
12 M12 Montebello Québec, SE Canada
108 H7 Montebelluna Veneto, NE Italy
62 G13 Montecarlo Misiones, NE Argentina
63 D16 Monte Caseros Corrientes, NE Argentina
62 J13 Monte Castelo Santa Catarina, S Brazil
108 F11 Montecatini Terme Toscana, C Italy
44 H7 Montecillos, Cordillera de ▲▲ W Honduras
64 I12 Monte Comén Mendoza, W Argentina
46 M8 Monte Cristi var. San Fernando de Monte Cristi. NW Dominican Republic
60 C13 Monte Cristo Amazonas, W Brazil
109 E14 Montecristo, Isola di island Archipelago Toscano, C Italy
Monte Croce Carnico, Passo di see Plöcken Pass
60 J12 Monte Dourado Pará, NE Brazil
42 L11 Monte Escobedo Zacatecas, C Mexico
108 I13 Montefalco Umbria, C Italy
109 H14 Montefiascone Lazio, C Italy
107 N14 Montefrío Andalucía, S Spain
46 I11 Montego Bay var. Mobay. W Jamaica
Montego Bay see Sangster
106 J8 Montehermoso Extremadura, W Spain
106 F10 Montejunto, Serra de ▲ C Portugal
Monteleone di Calabria see Vibo Valentia
56 E7 Montelíbano Córdoba, NW Colombia
105 R13 Montélimar anc. Acunum Acusio, Montilium Adhemari. Drôme, E France
106 K15 Montellano Andalucía, S Spain
37 Y2 Montello Nevada, W USA
32 L8 Montello Wisconsin, N USA
65 J18 Montemayor, Meseta de plain SE Argentina
43 O9 Montemorelos Nuevo León, NE Mexico
106 G11 Montemor-o-Novo Évora, S Portugal
106 G8 Montemor-o-Velho var. Montemor-o-Vélho. Coimbra, N Portugal
106 H7 Montemuro, Serra de ▲ N Portugal
104 K12 Montendre Charente-Maritime, W France
63 I15 Montenegro Rio Grande do Sul, S Brazil
115 J16 Montenegro Serb. Crna Gora. ◈ republic SW Yugoslavia
64 G10 Monte Patria Coquimbo, N Chile
47 O9 Monte Plata E Dominican Republic
85 P14 Montepuez Cabo Delgado, N Mozambique
85 P14 Montepuez ≈ N Mozambique
108 G13 Montepulciano Toscana, C Italy
64 L6 Monte Quemado Santiago del Estero, N Argentina
105 O6 Montereau-Faut-Yonne anc. Condate. Seine-St-Denis, N France
37 N11 Monterey California, W USA
22 L9 Monterey Tennessee, S USA
23 T5 Monterey Virginia, NE USA
Monterey see Monterrey
37 N10 Monterey Bay bay California, W USA
56 D6 Montería Córdoba, NW Colombia
59 N18 Montero Santa Cruz, C Bolivia
64 J7 Monteros Tucumán, C Argentina
106 I5 Monterrei Galicia, NW Spain
43 O8 Monterrey var. Monterey. Nuevo León, NE Mexico
34 F9 Montesano Washington, NW USA
109 M19 Montesano sulla Marcellana Campania, S Italy
109 N16 Monte Sant' Angelo Puglia, SE Italy
61 O16 Monte Santo Bahia, E Brazil
109 D18 Monte Santu, Capo di headland Sardegna, Italy, C Mediterranean Sea
61 M19 Montes Claros Minas Gerais, SE Brazil
109 K14 Montesilvano Marina Abruzzi, C Italy
25 P4 Montevallo Alabama, S USA
108 G12 Montevarchi Toscana, C Italy
31 S9 Montevideo Minnesota, N USA
63 F20 Montevideo ● (Uruguay) Montevideo, S Uruguay
39 S7 Monte Vista Colorado, C USA
25 T5 Montezuma Georgia, SE USA
31 W14 Montezuma Iowa, C USA
28 J6 Montezuma Kansas, C USA
105 U12 Montgenèvre, Col de pass France/Italy
xxxv K9 Montgomery Powys, E Wales, UK
99 K19 Montgomery cultural region E Wales, UK
25 Q5 Montgomery state capital Alabama, S USA
31 V9 Montgomery Minnesota, N USA
20 G13 Montgomery Pennsylvania, NE USA
23 Q5 Montgomery West Virginia, NE USA
Montgomery see Sāhīwāl
29 V4 Montgomery City Missouri, C USA
37 S8 Montgomery Pass pass Nevada, W USA
104 K12 Montguyon Charente-Maritime, W France
110 C10 Monthey Valais, SW Switzerland
29 V13 Monticello Arkansas, C USA
25 T4 Monticello Florida, SE USA
25 T8 Monticello Georgia, SE USA
32 M13 Monticello Illinois, N USA
33 O12 Monticello Indiana, N USA
31 Y13 Monticello Iowa, C USA
22 L7 Monticello Kentucky, S USA
31 V8 Monticello Minnesota, N USA

◆ Country ● Country Capital ◇ Dependent Territory ○ Dependent Territory Capital ◈ Administrative Region × International Airport ▲ Mountain ▲▲ Mountain Range ⛰ Volcano ≈ River ◎ Lake ⊡ Reservoir

Monticello – Mozambique, Canal de

24 K7 **Monticello** Mississippi, S USA
29 V2 **Monticello** Missouri, C USA
20 J12 **Monticello** New York, NE USA
39 O7 **Monticello** Utah, W USA
108 F8 **Montichiari** Lombardia, N Italy
104 M12 **Montignac** Dordogne, SW France
101 G21 **Montignies-le-Tilleul** var. Montigny-le-Tilleul. Hainaut, S Belgium
12 J8 **Montigny, Lac de** ◎ Québec, SE Canada
105 S6 **Montigny-le-Roi** Haute-Marne, N France
Montigny-le-Tilleul see Montignies-le-Tilleul
45 R16 **Montijo** Veraguas, S Panama
106 F11 **Montijo** Setúbal, W Portugal
106 J11 **Montijo** Extremadura, W Spain
Montilium Adhemari see Montélimar
106 M13 **Montilla** Andalucía, S Spain
104 L3 **Montivilliers** Seine-Maritime, N France
13 U7 **Mont-Joli** Québec, SE Canada
12 M10 **Mont-Laurier** Québec, SE Canada
13 X5 **Mont-Louis** Québec, SE Canada
105 N17 **Mont-Louis** var. Mont Louis. Pyrénées-Orientales, S France
105 O10 **Montluçon** Allier, C France
13 R10 **Montmagny** Québec, SE Canada
105 S3 **Montmédy** Meuse, NE France
105 P5 **Montmirail** Marne, N France
13 R9 **Montmorency** ≈ Québec, SE Canada
104 M10 **Montmorillon** Vienne, W France
109 J14 **Montorio al Vomano** Abruzzi, C Italy
106 M13 **Montoro** Andalucía, S Spain
35 S16 **Montpelier** Idaho, NW USA
31 P6 **Montpelier** North Dakota, N USA
20 M7 **Montpelier** state capital Vermont, NE USA
105 Q15 **Montpellier** Hérault, S France
104 L12 **Montpon-Ménestérol** Dordogne, SW France
xliii M18 **Montrave** Fife, E Scotland, UK
12 G8 **Montreal** ≈ Ontario, S Canada
12 C8 **Montreal** ≈ Ontario, S Canada
Montreal see Mirabel
10 K15 **Montréal** Eng. Montreal. Québec, SE Canada
9 T14 **Montreal Lake** ◎ Saskatchewan, C Canada
12 B9 **Montreal River** Ontario, S Canada
105 N2 **Montreuil** Pas-de-Calais, N France
104 K8 **Montreuil-Bellay** Maine-et-Loire, NW France
110 C10 **Montreux** Vaud, SW Switzerland
110 B9 **Montricher** Vaud, W Switzerland
xliii O16 **Montrose** Angus, E Scotland, UK
29 W14 **Montrose** Arkansas, C USA
39 Q6 **Montrose** Colorado, C USA
31 Y16 **Montrose** Iowa, C USA
20 H12 **Montrose** Pennsylvania, NE USA
23 X5 **Montross** Virginia, NE USA
13 O12 **Mont-St-Hilaire** Québec, SE Canada
105 S3 **Mont-St-Martin** Meurthe-et-Moselle, NE France
47 V10 **Montserrat** var. Emerald Isle. ◇ UK dependent territory E West Indies
107 V5 **Montserrat** ▲ NE Spain
106 M7 **Montuenga** Castilla-León, N Spain
101 M19 **Montzen** Liège, E Belgium
39 N8 **Monument Valley** valley Arizona/Utah, SW USA
xlii O13 **Monymusk** Aberdeenshire, NE Scotland, UK
177 G4 **Monywa** Sagaing, C Burma
108 D7 **Monza** Lombardia, N Italy
85 J15 **Monze** Southern, S Zambia
107 T5 **Monzón** Aragón, NE Spain
27 T9 **Moody** Texas, SW USA
100 L13 **Mook** Limburg, SE Netherlands
171 Kk15 **Mooka** var. Mōka. Tochigi, Honshū, S Japan
190 K3 **Moomba** South Australia
12 G13 **Moon** ≈ Ontario, S Canada
Moon see Muhu
189 Y10 **Moonie** Queensland, E Australia
198 B10 **Moonless Mountains** undersea feature E Pacific Ocean
190 L13 **Moonlight Head** headland Victoria, SE Australia
Moon-Sund see Väinameri
190 H8 **Moonta** South Australia
Moor see Mór
188 I12 **Moora** Western Australia
100 H12 **Moordrecht** Zuid-Holland, C Netherlands
35 T9 **Moore** Montana, NW USA
29 N11 **Moore** Oklahoma, C USA
27 R12 **Moore** Texas, SW USA
203 S10 **Moorea** island Îles du Vent, W French Polynesia
23 U3 **Moorefield** West Virginia, NE USA
25 X14 **Moore Haven** Florida, SE USA
188 J11 **Moore, Lake** ◎ Western Australia
21 N7 **Moore Reservoir** ⊠ New Hampshire/Vermont, NE USA
46 G1 **Moores Island** island N Bahamas
23 R10 **Mooresville** North Carolina, SE USA
31 R5 **Moorhead** Minnesota, N USA
24 K4 **Moorhead** Mississippi, S USA
176 Ww10 **Moor, Kepulauan** island group E Indonesia
xxxvi K11 **Moorlinch** Somerset, SW England, UK
101 F18 **Moorsel** Oost-Vlaanderen, C Belgium
101 C18 **Moorslede** West-Vlaanderen, W Belgium
20 L8 **Moosalamoo, Mount** ▲ Vermont, NE USA
103 M22 **Moosburg** Bayern, SE Germany
35 S14 **Moose** Wyoming, C USA
10 H11 **Moose** ≈ Ontario, S Canada
10 H10 **Moose Factory** Ontario, S Canada
21 Q4 **Moosehead Lake** ◎ Maine, NE USA
9 U16 **Moose Jaw** Saskatchewan, S Canada
9 V14 **Moose Lake** Manitoba, C Canada
31 W6 **Moose Lake** Minnesota, N USA
21 P6 **Mooselookmeguntic Lake** ◎ Maine, NE USA
41 R12 **Moose Pass** Alaska, USA
21 P5 **Moose River** ≈ Maine, NE USA
20 J9 **Moose River** ≈ New York, NE USA
9 V16 **Moosomin** Saskatchewan, S Canada
10 H10 **Moosonee** Ontario, SE Canada
21 N12 **Moosup** Connecticut, NE USA
85 N16 **Mopeia** Zambézia, NE Mozambique
Mopelia see Maupihaa
85 H18 **Mopipi** Central, C Botswana
Moppo see Mokp'o
79 N11 **Mopti** Mopti, C Mali
79 O11 **Mopti** ◐ region S Mali
59 H18 **Moquegua** Moquegua, SE Peru
59 H18 **Moquegua** off. Departamento de Moquegua. ◐ department S Peru
113 I23 **Mór** Ger. Moor. Fejér, C Hungary
80 G11 **Mora** Extrême-Nord, N Cameroon
106 G11 **Mora** Évora, S Portugal
107 N9 **Mora** Castilla-La Mancha, C Spain
96 L12 **Mora** Kopparberg, C Sweden
31 V7 **Mora** Minnesota, N USA
39 T10 **Mora** New Mexico, SW USA
115 J17 **Morača** ≈ SW Yugoslavia
158 K10 **Morādābād** Uttar Pradesh, N India
107 U6 **Móra d'Ebre** var. Mora de Ebro. Cataluña, NE Spain
Mora de Ebro see Móra d'Ebre
107 S8 **Mora de Rubielos** Aragón, NE Spain
180 H4 **Morafenobe** Mahajanga, W Madagascar
112 K8 **Morąg** Ger. Mohrungen. Olsztyn, N Poland
113 L25 **Mórahalom** Csongrád, S Hungary
107 N11 **Moral de Calatrava** Castilla-La Mancha, C Spain
65 G19 **Moraleda, Canal** strait SE Pacific Ocean
56 J3 **Morales** Bolívar, N Colombia
56 D12 **Morales** Cauca, SW Colombia
44 F5 **Morales** Izabal, E Guatemala
180 J5 **Moramanga** Toamasina, E Madagascar
29 Q6 **Moran** Kansas, C USA
27 Q7 **Moran** Texas, SW USA
189 X7 **Moranbah** Queensland, NE Australia
46 L13 **Morant Bay** E Jamaica
xliii F14 **Morar** Highland, NW Scotland, UK
xliii F14 **Morar, Loch** ◎ N Scotland, UK
Morata see Goodenough Island
107 Q12 **Moratalla** Murcia, SE Spain
110 C8 **Morat, Lac de** Ger. Murtensee. ◎ W Switzerland
86 I11 **Morava** var. March. ≈ C Europe see also March
Morava see Moravia, Czech Republic
Morava see Velika Morava, Yugoslavia
31 W15 **Moravia** Iowa, C USA
113 F18 **Moravia** Cz. Morava, Ger. Mähren. cultural region E Czech Republic
113 H17 **Moravice** Ger. Mohra. ≈ NE Czech Republic
Moravicza see Moraviţa
113 G17 **Moravská Třebová** Ger. Mährisch-Trübau. Východní Čechy, E Czech Republic
113 E19 **Moravské Budějovice** Ger. Mährisch-Budwitz. Jižní Morava, SE Czech Republic
113 F19 **Moravský Krumlov** Ger. Mährisch-Kromau. Jižní Morava, SE Czech Republic
xlii I11 **Moray** ◐ unitary authority N Scotland, UK
Morawitza see Moraviţa
xlii K11 **Moray Firth** inlet N Scotland, UK
44 B10 **Morazán** ◐ department NE El Salvador
160 C10 **Morbi** Gujarāt, W India
104 G7 **Morbihan** ◐ department NW France
Mörbisch see Mörbisch am See
111 Y5 **Mörbisch am See** var. Mörbisch. Burgenland, E Austria
97 N21 **Mörbylånga** Kalmar, S Sweden
104 J14 **Morcenx** Landes, SW France
xxxvi G13 **Morchard Bishop** Devon, SW England, UK
Morcheh Khort see Mürcheh Khvort
15 L16 **Morden** Manitoba, S Canada
xxxviii H14 **Mordiford** Herefordshire, W England, UK
Mordovia see Mordoviya, Respublika
131 N5 **Mordoviya, Respublika** prev. Mordovskaya ASSR, Eng. Mordovia, Mordvinia. ◐ autonomous republic W Russian Federation
130 M7 **Mordovo** Tambovskaya Oblast', W Russian Federation
Mordovskaya ASSR/ Mordvinia see Mordoviya, Respublika
Moreau see Pelopónnisos
30 K8 **Moreau River** ≈ South Dakota, N USA
xliii O22 **Morebattle** The Borders, S Scotland, UK
xl M12 **Morecambe** Lancashire, NW England, UK
xl M12 **Morecambe Bay** inlet NW England, UK
191 S4 **Moree** New South Wales, SE Australia
194 E15 **Morehead** Western, SW PNG
23 N5 **Morehead** Kentucky, S USA
194 E15 **Morehead** ≈ SW PNG
23 X11 **Morehead City** North Carolina, SE USA
29 Y8 **Morehouse** Missouri, C USA
110 E10 **Mörel** Valais, SW Switzerland
56 D13 **Morelia** Caquetá, S Colombia
43 N14 **Morelia** Michoacán de Ocampo, S Mexico
107 T7 **Morella** País Valenciano, E Spain
xlii H8 **More, Loch** ◎ NW Scotland, UK
42 I7 **Morelos** Chihuahua, N Mexico
43 O15 **Morelos** ◐ state S Mexico
160 H7 **Morena** Madhya Pradesh, C India
106 L12 **Morena, Sierra** ▲▲ S Spain
39 O14 **Morenci** Arizona, SW USA
33 R11 **Morenci** Michigan, N USA
118 J13 **Moreni** Dâmboviţa, S Romania
96 D9 **Møre og Romsdal** ◐ county S Norway
14 Ee12 **Moresby Island** island Queen Charlotte Islands, British Columbia, SW Canada
xxxvi M14 **Moreton** Dorset, S England, UK
xxxvii V8 **Moreton** Essex, SE England, UK
xxxvi H14 **Moretonhampstead** Devon, SW England, UK
xxxvii O6 **Moreton-in-Marsh** Gloucestershire, C England, UK
191 W2 **Moreton Island** island Queensland, E Australia
105 O3 **Moreuil** Somme, N France
xxxvi E13 **Morewenstow** Cornwall, SW England, UK
37 V7 **Morey Peak** ▲ Nevada, W USA
129 U4 **More-Yu** ≈ NW Russian Federation
105 T9 **Morez** Jura, E France
xxxv E6 **Morfa Nefyn** Gwynedd, NW Wales, UK
Mórfou see Güzelyurt
Morfou Bay/Mórfou, Kólpos see Güzelyurt Körfezi
190 J8 **Morgan** South Australia
25 S7 **Morgan** Georgia, SE USA
27 S8 **Morgan** Texas, SW USA
24 J10 **Morgan City** Louisiana, S USA
22 H6 **Morganfield** Kentucky, S USA
37 O10 **Morgan Hill** California, W USA
23 Q9 **Morganton** North Carolina, SE USA
22 J7 **Morgantown** Kentucky, S USA
23 S2 **Morgantown** West Virginia, NE USA
110 B10 **Morges** Vaud, SW Switzerland
Morghāb, Daryā-ye see Murgab
xlii I13 **Mor, Glen** var. Glen Albyn, Great Glen. valley N Scotland, UK
105 T5 **Morhange** Moselle, NE France
164 M5 **Mori** var. Mori Kazak Zizhixian. Xinjiang Uygur Zizhiqu, NW China
172 Nn6 **Mori** Hokkaidō, NE Japan
37 Y6 **Moriah, Mount** ▲ Nevada, W USA
39 S11 **Moriarty** New Mexico, SW USA
56 J12 **Morichal** Guainía, E Colombia
194 H14 **Morigio Island** island S PNG
Mori Kazak Zizhixian see Mori
169 U7 **Morin Dawa** var. Morin Dawa Daurzu Zizhiqi. Nei Mongol Zizhiqu, N China
Morin Dawa Daurzu Zizhiqi see Morin Dawa
15 I13 **Morinville** Alberta, SW Canada
171 Mm11 **Morioka** Iwate, Honshū, C Japan
191 T8 **Morisset** New South Wales, SE Australia
171 Mm10 **Moriyoshi-yama** ▲ Honshū, C Japan
94 K13 **Morjärv** Norrbotten, N Sweden
131 R3 **Morki** Respublika Mariy El, W Russian Federation
126 K10 **Morkoka** ≈ NE Russian Federation
104 F5 **Morlaix** Finistère, NW France
xl K14 **Morley** Leeds, N England, UK
97 M20 **Mörlunda** Kalmar, S Sweden
109 N19 **Mormanno** Calabria, SW Italy
38 L11 **Mormon Lake** ◎ Arizona, SW USA
37 Y10 **Mormon Peak** ▲ Nevada, W USA
Mormon State see Utah
47 Y5 **Morne-à-l'Eau** Grande Terre, N Guadeloupe
31 Y15 **Morning Sun** Iowa, C USA
200 O14 **Mornington Abyssal Plain** undersea feature SE Pacific Ocean
65 F22 **Mornington, Isla** island S Chile
189 T4 **Mornington Island** island Wellesley Islands, Queensland, N Australia
117 E18 **Mórnos** ≈ C Greece
155 P14 **Moro** Sind, SE Pakistan
34 I11 **Moro** Oregon, NW USA
194 K14 **Morobe** Morobe, C PNG
194 J14 **Morobe** ◐ province C PNG
33 N12 **Morocco** Indiana, N USA
76 E8 **Morocco** off. Kingdom of Morocco, Ar. Al Mamlakah. ◆ monarchy N Africa
Morocco see Marrakech
83 I22 **Morogoro** Morogoro, E Tanzania
83 H24 **Morogoro** ◐ region SE Tanzania
179 Qq16 **Moro Gulf** gulf S Philippines
43 N13 **Moroleón** Guanajuato, C Mexico
180 H6 **Morombe** Toliara, W Madagascar
46 G5 **Morón** Ciego de Ávila, C Cuba
56 K5 **Morón** Carabobo, N Venezuela
Morón see Morón de la Frontera
169 N8 **Mörön** Hentiy, C Mongolia
168 I6 **Mörön** Hövsgöl, N Mongolia
58 D8 **Morona, Río** ≈ N Peru
58 C8 **Morona Santiago** ◐ province E Ecuador
180 H5 **Morondava** Toliara, W Madagascar
106 K14 **Morón de la Frontera** var. Morón. Andalucía, S Spain
180 G13 **Moroni** ● (Comoros) Grande Comore, NW Comoros
175 T6 **Morotai, Pulau** island Maluku, E Indonesia
175 T6 **Morotai, Selat** strait Maluku, E Indonesia
Morotiri see Marotiri
83 H17 **Moroto** NE Uganda
Morozov see Bratan
130 M11 **Morozovsk** Rostovskaya Oblast', SW Russian Federation
xli R5 **Morpeth** Northumberland, N England, UK
Morphou see Güzelyurt
Morphou Bay see Güzelyurt Körfezi
30 I13 **Morrill** Nebraska, C USA
29 U11 **Morrilton** Arkansas, C USA
9 Q16 **Morrin** Alberta, SW Canada
192 M7 **Morrinsville** Waikato, North Island, NZ
9 X16 **Morris** Manitoba, S Canada
32 M11 **Morris** Illinois, N USA
31 S8 **Morris** Minnesota, N USA
12 M13 **Morrisburg** Ontario, SE Canada
207 R11 **Morris Jesup, Kap** headland N Greenland
190 B1 **Morris, Mount** ▲ South Australia
32 K10 **Morrison** Illinois, N USA
xxxv H14 **Morriston** Swansea, S Wales, UK
38 K13 **Morristown** Arizona, SW USA
20 J14 **Morristown** New Jersey, NE USA
23 O8 **Morristown** Tennessee, S USA
44 L11 **Morrito** Río San Juan, SW Nicaragua
37 P13 **Morro Bay** California, W USA
97 L22 **Mörrum** Blekinge, S Sweden
85 N16 **Morrumbala** Zambézia, NE Mozambique
85 N20 **Morrumbene** Inhambane, SE Mozambique
97 F21 **Mors** island NW Denmark
Mörs see Moers
27 N1 **Morse** Texas, SW USA
131 N6 **Morshansk** Tambovskaya Oblast', W Russian Federation
104 L5 **Mortagne-au-Perche** Orne, N France
104 J8 **Mortagne-sur-Sèvre** Vendée, NW France
106 G8 **Mortágua** Viseu, N Portugal
104 J5 **Mortain** Manche, N France
108 C8 **Mortara** Lombardia, N Italy
xxxvi F11 **Mortehoe** Devon, SW England, UK
61 J17 **Mortes, Rio das** ≈ C Brazil
xxxviii H12 **Mortimer's Cross** Herefordshire, W England, UK
xxxvi B8 **Mortlake** Richmond upon Thames, SE England, UK
190 M12 **Mortlake** Victoria, SE Australia
Mortlock Group see Takuu Islands
201 Q17 **Mortlock Islands** prev. Nomoi Islands. island group C Micronesia
xxxix Q8 **Morton** Lincolnshire, E England, UK
xxxix O4 **Morton** Lincolnshire, E England, UK
31 T9 **Morton** Minnesota, N USA
24 L5 **Morton** Mississippi, S USA
26 M5 **Morton** Texas, SW USA
34 H9 **Morton** Washington, NW USA
1 D7 **Morton Seamount** undersea feature NE Pacific Ocean
47 U15 **Moruga** Trinidad, Trinidad and Tobago
191 P9 **Morundah** New South Wales, SE Australia
Moruroa see Mururoa
191 S11 **Moruya** New South Wales, SE Australia
xxxvi L16 **Morvah** Cornwall, SW England, UK
105 Q8 **Morvan** physical region C France
xliii M14 **Morven** ▲ NE Scotland, UK
xlii K8 **Morven** ▲ N Scotland, UK
193 G21 **Morven** Canterbury, South Island, NZ
xxxviii I10 **Morville** Shropshire, W England, UK
191 O13 **Morwell** Victoria, SE Australia
129 N6 **Morzhovets, Ostrov** island NW Russian Federation
106 G4 **Mos** Galicia, NW Spain
130 J4 **Mosal'sk** Kaluzhskaya Oblast', W Russian Federation
103 H20 **Mosbach** Baden-Württemberg, SW Germany
97 E18 **Mosby** Vest-Agder, S Norway
35 V9 **Mosby** Montana, NW USA
34 M9 **Moscow** Idaho, NW USA
22 F10 **Moscow** Tennessee, S USA
Moscow see Moskva
103 D19 **Mosel** Fr. Moselle. ≈ W Europe see also Moselle
105 T4 **Moselle** ◐ department NE France
105 T6 **Moselle** Ger. Mosel. ≈ W Europe see also Mosel
34 K9 **Moses Lake** ◎ Washington, NW USA
85 I18 **Mosetse** Central, E Botswana
94 H4 **Mosfellsbær** Sudhurland, SW Iceland
193 F23 **Mosgiel** Otago, South Island, NZ
128 M11 **Mosha** ≈ NW Russian Federation
83 I20 **Moshi** Kilimanjaro, NE Tanzania
112 G12 **Mosina** Poznań, W Poland
32 L6 **Mosinee** Wisconsin, N USA
94 F13 **Mosjøen** Nordland, C Norway
127 Nn13 **Moskal'vo** Ostrov Sakhalin, Sakhalinskaya Oblast', SE Russian Federation
94 I13 **Moskosel** Norrbotten, N Sweden
130 K4 **Moskovskaya Oblast'** ◐ province W Russian Federation
Moskovskiy see Moskva
130 J3 **Moskva** Eng. Moscow. ● (Russian Federation) Gorod Moskva, W Russian Federation
153 Q14 **Moskva** Rus. Moskovskiy; prev. Chubek. SW Tajikistan
130 L4 **Moskva** ≈ W Russian Federation
85 I20 **Mosomane** Kgatleng, SE Botswana
Moson and Magyaróvár see Mosonmagyaróvár
113 H21 **Mosoni-Duna** Ger. Kleine Donau. ≈ NW Hungary
113 H21 **Mosonmagyaróvár** Ger. Wieselburg-Ungarisch-Altenburg; prev. Moson and Magyaróvár, Ger. Wieselburg and Ungarisch-Altenburg. Győr-Moson-Sopron, NW Hungary
Mospino see Mospyne
119 X8 **Mospyne** Rus. Mospino. Donets'ka Oblast', E Ukraine
56 B12 **Mosquera** Nariño, SW Colombia
39 U10 **Mosquero** New Mexico, SW USA
Mosquito Coast see La Mosquitia
33 U11 **Mosquito Creek Lake** ⊠ Ohio, N USA
Mosquito Gulf see Mosquitos, Golfo de los
25 X11 **Mosquito Lagoon** wetland Florida, SE USA
45 N10 **Mosquito, Punta** headland E Nicaragua
45 W14 **Mosquito, Punta** headland NE Panama
45 Q15 **Mosquitos, Golfo de los** Eng. Mosquito Gulf. gulf N Panama
97 H16 **Moss** Østfold, S Norway
Mossâmedes see Namibe
xli I2 **Mossbank** Shetland Islands, NE Scotland, UK
24 G8 **Moss Bluff** Louisiana, S USA
193 C23 **Mossburn** Southland, South Island, NZ
85 G26 **Mosselbaai** var. Mosselbai, Eng. Mossel Bay. Western Cape, SW South Africa
Mosselbai/Mossel Bay see Mosselbaai
81 F20 **Mossendjo** Le Niari, SW Congo
191 N8 **Mossgiel** New South Wales, SE Australia
103 H22 **Mössingen** Baden-Württemberg, S Germany
xliv L4 **Mossley** Newtownabbey, E Northern Ireland, UK
xl H14 **Mossley** Tameside, NW England, UK
189 W4 **Mossman** Queensland, NE Australia
61 P14 **Mossoró** Rio Grande do Norte, NE Brazil
25 N9 **Moss Point** Mississippi, S USA
xlii M11 **Mosstodloch** Moray, N Scotland, UK
191 S9 **Moss Vale** New South Wales, SE Australia
34 G9 **Mossyrock** Washington, NW USA
113 B15 **Most** Ger. Brüx. Severní Čechy, NW Czech Republic
123 Jj16 **Mosta** var. Musta. C Malta
76 I5 **Mostaganem** var. Mestghanem. NW Algeria
115 H14 **Mostar** S Bosnia and Herzegovina
63 J17 **Mostardas** Rio Grande do Sul, S Brazil
118 K14 **Mostiştea** ≈ S Romania
Mostva see Mastva
Mosty see Masty
xxxv J4 **Mostyn** Flintshire, N Wales, UK
118 H5 **Mostys'ka** L'vivs'ka Oblast', W Ukraine
Mosul see Al Mawşil
97 F15 **Møsvatnet** ◎ S Norway
82 J12 **Mot'a** Amhara, N Ethiopia
197 C10 **Mota** island Banks Islands, N Vanuatu
81 H16 **Motaba** ≈ N Congo
107 O10 **Mota del Cuervo** Castilla-La Mancha, C Spain
106 L5 **Mota del Marqués** Castilla-León, N Spain
44 F5 **Motagua, Río** ≈ Guatemala/Honduras
121 H19 **Motal'** Brestskaya Voblasts', SW Belorussia
97 L17 **Motala** Östergötland, S Sweden
197 C10 **Mota Lava** island Banks Islands, N Vanuatu
203 X7 **Motane** var. Mohotani. island Îles Marquises, NE French Polynesia
158 K13 **Moth** Uttar Pradesh, N India
Mother of Presidents/ Mother of States see Virginia
xliii K20 **Motherwell** North Lanarkshire, C Scotland, UK
159 P12 **Motīhāri** Bihār, N India
107 Q10 **Motilla del Palancar** Castilla-La Mancha, C Spain
192 N7 **Motiti Island** island NE NZ
67 E25 **Motley Island** island SE Falkland Islands
85 J19 **Motloutse** ≈ E Botswana
43 V17 **Motozintla de Mendoza** Chiapas, SE Mexico
107 N15 **Motril** Andalucía, S Spain
118 G13 **Motru** Gorj, SW Romania
171 Mm5 **Motsuta-misaki** headland Hokkaidō, NE Japan
30 L6 **Mott** North Dakota, N USA
xxxvi F9 **Mottingham** Bromley, SE England, UK
Möttling see Metlika
109 O18 **Mottola** Puglia, SE Italy
192 P8 **Motu** ≈ North Island, NZ
193 I14 **Motueka** Tasman, South Island, NZ
193 I14 **Motueka** ≈ South Island, NZ
Motu Iti see Tupai
43 X12 **Motul** var. Motul de Felipe Carrillo Puerto. Yucatán, SE Mexico
Motul de Felipe Carrillo Puerto see Motul
203 U17 **Motu Nui** island Easter Island, Chile, E Pacific Ocean
203 Q10 **Motu One** var. Bellingshausen. atoll Îles Sous le Vent, W French Polynesia
202 I16 **Motutapu** island E Cook Islands
200 R15 **Motu Tapu** island Tongatapu Group, S Tonga
192 L5 **Motutapu Island** island N NZ
Motyca see Modica
126 I13 **Motygino** Krasnoyarskiy Kray, C Russian Federation
Mouanda see Moanda
Mouaskar see Mascara
107 U3 **Moubermé, Tuc de** Fr. Pic de Maubermé, Sp. Pico Maubermé; prev. Tuc de Maubermé. ▲ France/Spain see also Maubermé, Pic de
47 N7 **Mouchoir Passage** passage SE Turks and Caicos Islands
78 I9 **Moudjéria** Tagant, SW Mauritania
110 C9 **Moudon** Vaud, W Switzerland
Mouhoun see Black Volta
81 E19 **Mouila** Ngounié, C Gabon
81 K14 **Mouka** Haute-Kotto, C Central African Republic
Moukden see Shenyang
191 N10 **Moulamein** New South Wales, SE Australia
Moulamein Creek see Billabong Creek
76 F6 **Moulay-Bousselham** NW Morocco
Moule see le Moule
82 M11 **Moulhoulé** N Djibouti
105 P9 **Moulins** Allier, C France
178 Gg9 **Moulmein** var. Maulmain, Mawlamyine. Mon State, S Burma
177 F9 **Moulmeingyun** Irrawaddy, SW Burma
76 G6 **Moulouya** var. Mulucha, Muluya, Mulwiya. seasonal river NE Morocco
xxxix R8 **Moulton** Lincolnshire, E England, UK
xxxix P12 **Moulton** Northamptonshire, C England, UK
xxxix U12 **Moulton** Suffolk, E England, UK
25 O2 **Moulton** Alabama, S USA
31 W16 **Moulton** Iowa, C USA
27 T11 **Moulton** Texas, SW USA
25 T7 **Moultrie** Georgia, SE USA
23 S14 **Moultrie, Lake** ⊠ South Carolina, SE USA
24 K3 **Mound Bayou** Mississippi, S USA
32 L17 **Mound City** Illinois, N USA
29 R6 **Mound City** Kansas, C USA
29 Q2 **Mound City** Missouri, C USA
31 N7 **Mound City** South Dakota, N USA
80 H13 **Moundou** Logone-Occidental, SW Chad
29 P10 **Mounds** Oklahoma, C USA
23 R2 **Moundsville** West Virginia, NE USA
178 Ii12 **Moŭng Roessei** Bătdâmbâng, W Cambodia
Moun Hou see Black Volta
14 G5 **Mountain** ≈ Northwest Territories, NW Canada
39 S12 **Mountainair** New Mexico, SW USA
xxxv J14 **Mountain Ash** Rhondda Cynon Taff, S Wales, UK
37 V1 **Mountain City** Nevada, W USA
23 Q8 **Mountain City** Tennessee, S USA
29 U7 **Mountain Grove** Missouri, C USA
29 U9 **Mountain Home** Arkansas, C USA
35 N15 **Mountain Home** Idaho, NW USA
27 Q11 **Mountain Home** Texas, SW USA
31 W4 **Mountain Iron** Minnesota, N USA
31 T10 **Mountain Lake** Minnesota, N USA
25 S3 **Mountain Park** Georgia, SE USA
37 W12 **Mountain Pass** pass California, W USA
29 T12 **Mountain Pine** Arkansas, C USA
41 Y14 **Mountain Point** Annette Island, Alaska, USA
Mountain State see Montana, USA
Mountain State see West Virginia, USA
29 V7 **Mountain View** Arkansas, C USA
40 H12 **Mountain View** Hawaii, USA, C Pacific Ocean
29 V10 **Mountain View** Missouri, C USA
40 M11 **Mountain Village** Alaska, USA
23 R8 **Mount Airy** North Carolina, SE USA
85 K24 **Mount Ayliff** Xh. Maxesibebi. Eastern Cape, SE South Africa
31 U16 **Mount Ayr** Iowa, C USA
190 J9 **Mount Barker** South Australia
188 J14 **Mount Barker** Western Australia
191 P11 **Mount Beauty** Victoria, SE Australia
xliv F8 **Mount Bellew** Galway, W Ireland
12 E16 **Mount Brydges** Ontario, S Canada
33 N16 **Mount Carmel** Illinois, N USA
32 K10 **Mount Carroll** Illinois, N USA
33 S9 **Mount Clemens** Michigan, N USA
193 E19 **Mount Cook** Canterbury, South Island, NZ
85 L16 **Mount Darwin** Mashonaland Central, NE Zimbabwe
21 S7 **Mount Desert Island** island Maine, NE USA
25 W11 **Mount Dora** Florida, SE USA
190 G5 **Mount Eba** South Australia
27 W8 **Mount Enterprise** Texas, SW USA
xxxvii W12 **Mountfield** East Sussex, SE England, UK
190 J4 **Mount Fitton** South Australia
85 J24 **Mount Fletcher** Eastern Cape, SE South Africa
12 F15 **Mount Forest** Ontario, S Canada
190 K12 **Mount Gambier** South Australia
189 W5 **Mount Garnet** Queensland, NE Australia
23 P6 **Mount Gay** West Virginia, NE USA
33 S12 **Mount Gilead** Ohio, N USA
194 H12 **Mount Hagen** Western Highlands, C PNG
xliv J4 **Mount Hamilton** Strabane, W Northern Ireland, UK
20 J16 **Mount Holly** New Jersey, NE USA
23 R10 **Mount Holly** North Carolina, SE USA
29 T12 **Mount Ida** Arkansas, C USA
189 T6 **Mount Isa** Queensland, C Australia
23 U4 **Mount Jackson** Virginia, NE USA
20 D12 **Mount Jewett** Pennsylvania, NE USA
xxxvi C16 **Mountjoy** Cornwall, SW England, UK
20 L13 **Mount Kisco** New York, NE USA
20 B15 **Mount Lebanon** Pennsylvania, NE USA
190 J8 **Mount Lofty Ranges** ▲▲ South Australia
188 J10 **Mount Magnet** Western Australia
192 N7 **Mount Maunganui** Bay of Plenty, North Island, NZ
xliv I10 **Mountmellick** Ir. Móinteach Mílic. Laois, C Ireland
32 L10 **Mount Morris** Illinois, N USA
33 R9 **Mount Morris** Michigan, N USA
20 F10 **Mount Morris** New York, NE USA
20 B16 **Mount Morris** Pennsylvania, NE USA
32 K15 **Mount Olive** Illinois, N USA
23 V10 **Mount Olive** North Carolina, SE USA
23 N4 **Mount Olivet** Kentucky, S USA
31 Y15 **Mount Pleasant** Iowa, C USA
33 Q8 **Mount Pleasant** Michigan, N USA
20 C15 **Mount Pleasant** Pennsylvania, NE USA
23 T14 **Mount Pleasant** South Carolina, SE USA
22 I9 **Mount Pleasant** Tennessee, S USA
27 W6 **Mount Pleasant** Texas, SW USA
38 L4 **Mount Pleasant** Utah, W USA
65 N23 **Mount Pleasant** ✈ (Stanley) East Falkland, Falkland Islands
xliv I10 **Mountrath** Laois, C Ireland
xxxvi M17 **Mount's Bay** inlet SW England, UK
xliv F10 **Mountshannon** Clare, W Ireland
37 N2 **Mount Shasta** California, W USA
xxxix N9 **Mountsorrel** Leicestershire, C England, UK
32 J13 **Mount Sterling** Illinois, N USA
23 N5 **Mount Sterling** Kentucky, S USA
xliv G8 **Mount Talbot** Roscommon, C Ireland
20 E15 **Mount Union** Pennsylvania, NE USA
25 V6 **Mount Vernon** Georgia, SE USA
32 L16 **Mount Vernon** Illinois, N USA
22 M6 **Mount Vernon** Kentucky, S USA
29 S7 **Mount Vernon** Missouri, C USA
33 T13 **Mount Vernon** Ohio, N USA
34 H7 **Mount Vernon** Oregon, NW USA
27 W6 **Mount Vernon** Texas, SW USA
34 K13 **Mount Vernon** Washington, NW USA
22 L5 **Mount Washington** Kentucky, S USA
190 F8 **Mount Wedge** South Australia
32 L14 **Mount Zion** Illinois, N USA
189 Y9 **Moura** Queensland, NE Australia
60 F12 **Moura** Amazonas, NW Brazil
106 H12 **Moura** Beja, S Portugal
106 I12 **Mourão** Évora, S Portugal
78 L11 **Mourdiah** Koulikoro, W Mali
80 K7 **Mourdi, Dépression du** desert lowland Chad/Sudan
104 J16 **Mourenx** Pyrénées-Atlantiques, SW France
Mourgana see Mourgkána
117 C15 **Mourgkána** var. Mourgana. ▲ Albania/Greece
xliv I4 **Mourne** ≈ W Northern Ireland, UK
xliv L6 **Mourne Mountains** Ir. Beanna Boirche. ▲▲ SE Northern Ireland, UK
117 I15 **Moúrtzeflos, Ákra** headland Límnos, E Greece
101 C19 **Mouscron** Dut. Moeskroen. Hainaut, W Belgium
xxxvi M16 **Mousehole** Cornwall, SW England, UK
Mouse River see Souris River
80 H10 **Moussoro** Kanem, W Chad
xliii L24 **Mouswald** Dumfries and Galloway, SW Scotland, UK
105 T11 **Moûtiers** Savoie, E France
180 J14 **Moutsamoudou** var. Mutsamudu. Anjouan, SE Comoros
76 K11 **Mouydir, Monts de** ▲▲ S Algeria
81 F20 **Mouyondzi** La Bouenza, S Congo
117 E16 **Mouzáki** prev. Mouzákion. Thessalía, C Greece
Mouzákion see Mouzáki
xliv J2 **Moville** Donegal, N Ireland
31 S13 **Moville** Iowa, C USA
xxxviii J7 **Mow Cop** Staffordshire, C England, UK
84 E13 **Moxico** ◐ province E Angola
xliv K5 **Moy** Dungannon, C Northern Ireland, UK
xlii J12 **Moy** Highland, NW Scotland, UK
xliii I15 **Moy** Highland, NW Scotland, UK
xliv E6 **Moy** ≈ NW Ireland
180 I14 **Moya** Anjouan, SE Comoros
42 L12 **Moyahua** Zacatecas, C Mexico
83 J16 **Moyalē** S Ethiopia
78 I15 **Moyamba** W Sierra Leone
xliv C8 **Moyard** Galway, W Ireland
xliv E9 **Moycullen** Galway, W Ireland
76 G7 **Moyen Atlas** Eng. Middle Atlas. ▲▲ N Morocco
80 H13 **Moyen-Chari** off. Préfecture du Moyen-Chari. ◐ prefecture S Chad
Moyen-Congo see Congo
85 J24 **Moyeni** var. Quthing. SW Lesotho
78 H13 **Moyenne-Guinée** ◐ state NW Guinea
81 D18 **Moyen-Ogooué** off. Province du Moyen-Ogooué, var. Le Moyen-Ogooué. ◐ province C Gabon
105 S4 **Moyeuvre-Grande** Moselle, NE France
xliv K5 **Moygashel** Dungannon, C Northern Ireland, UK
35 N7 **Moyie Springs** Idaho, NW USA
xliv L2 **Moyle** ◐ district N Northern Ireland, UK
xxxv D12 **Moylgrove** Pembrokeshire, SW Wales, UK
xliii I15 **Moy, Loch** ◎ NW Scotland, UK
xliv F8 **Moylough** Galway, W Ireland
83 F16 **Moyo** NW Uganda
58 D10 **Moyobamba** San Martín, NW Peru
175 O16 **Moyo, Pulau** island S Indonesia
80 H10 **Moyto** Chari-Baguirmi, W Chad
164 G9 **Moyu** var. Karakax. Xinjiang Uygur Zizhiqu, NW China
126 Jj9 **Moyyero** ≈ N Russian Federation
151 Q15 **Moyynkum, Peski** Kaz. Moyynqum. desert S Kazakhstan
Moyynqum see Moyynkum, Peski
151 S12 **Moyynty** Zhezkazgan, C Kazakhstan
151 S12 **Moyynty** ≈ C Kazakhstan
Mozambika, Lakandranon' i see Mozambique Channel
85 M18 **Mozambique** off. Republic of Mozambique; prev. People's Republic of Mozambique, Portuguese East Africa. ◆ republic S Africa
Mozambique Basin see Natal Basin
Mozambique, Canal de see Mozambique Channel

288
◆ Country ● Country Capital ◇ Dependent Territory ○ Dependent Territory Capital ◐ Administrative Region ✈ International Airport ▲ Mountain ▲▲ Mountain Range Volcano ≈ River ◎ Lake ⊠ Reservoir

MOZAMBIQUE CHANNEL – MYDROILYN

85 P17 **Mozambique Channel** *Fr.* Canal de Mozambique, *Mal.* Lakandranon' i Mozambika. *strait* W Indian Ocean
180 L11 **Mozambique Escarpment** *var.* Mozambique Scarp. *undersea feature* SW Indian Ocean
180 L10 **Mozambique Plateau** *var.* Mozambique Rise. *undersea feature* SW Indian Ocean
Mozambique Rise *see* Mozambique Plateau
Mozambique Scarp *see* Mozambique Escarpment
131 O15 **Mozdok** Respublika Severnaya Osetiya, SW Russian Federation
59 K17 **Mozetenes, Serranías de** ▲▲ C Bolivia
130 J4 **Mozhaysk** Moskovskaya Oblast', W Russian Federation
131 T3 **Mozhga** Udmurtskaya Respublika, NW Russian Federation
Mozyr' *see* Mazyr
81 P22 **Mpala** Shaba, E Zaire
81 G19 **Mpama** ∽ C Congo
83 E22 **Mpanda** Rukwa, W Tanzania
84 L11 **Mpande** Northern, NE Zambia
85 J18 **Mphoengs** Matabeleland South, SW Zimbabwe
83 F18 **Mpigi** S Uganda
84 L13 **Mpika** Northern, NE Zambia
85 J14 **Mpima** Central, C Zambia
84 J13 **Mpongwe** Copperbelt, C Zambia
84 K11 **Mporokoso** Northern, N Zambia
81 H20 **Mpouya** Plateaux, SE Congo
79 P16 **Mpraeso** C Ghana
84 L11 **Mpulungu** Northern, N Zambia
85 K21 **Mpumalanga** *prev.* Eastern Transvaal, *Afr.* Oos-Transvaal. ◈ *province* NE South Africa
85 D16 **Mpungu** Okavango, N Namibia
83 I22 **Mpwapwa** Dodoma, C Tanzania
Mqinvartsveri *see* Kazbek
112 M8 **Mrągowo** *Ger.* Sensburg. Olsztyn, NE Poland
131 V6 **Mrakovo** Respublika Bashkortostan, W Russian Federation
114 F12 **Mrkonjić Grad** W Bosnia and Herzegovina
112 H9 **Mrocza** Bydgoszcz, NW Poland
128 I14 **Msta** ∽ NW Russian Federation
Mtkvari *see* Kura
Mtoko *see* Mutoko
130 K6 **Mtsensk** Orlovskaya Oblast', W Russian Federation
83 K24 **Mtwara** Mtwara, SE Tanzania
83 J25 **Mtwara** ◈ *region* SE Tanzania
106 G14 **Mu** ▲ S Portugal
200 Qq15 **Mu'a** Tongatapu, S Tonga
Muai To *see* Mae Hong Son
85 P16 **Mualama** Zambézia, NE Mozambique
Mualo *see* Messalo, Rio
81 E22 **Muanda** Bas-Zaïre, SW Zaire
Muang Chiang Rai *see* Chiang Rai
178 J6 **Muang Ham** Houaphan, N Laos
178 J9 **Muang Hinboun** Khammouan, C Laos
Muang Kalasin *see* Kalasin
Muang Khammouan *see* Thakhèk
178 Jj11 **Muang Không** Champasak, S Laos
178 Jj10 **Muang Khôngxédôn** *var.* Khong Sedone. Salavan, S Laos
Muang Khon Kaen *see* Khon Kaen
178 Ii6 **Muang Khoua** Phôngsali, N Laos
Muang Krabi *see* Krabi
Muang Lampang *see* Lampang
Muang Lamphun *see* Lamphun
Muang Loei *see* Loei
Muang Lom Sak *see* Lom Sak
Muang Nakhon Sawan *see* Nakhon Sawan
178 I6 **Muang Namo** Oudômxai, N Laos
Muang Nan *see* Nan
178 Ii6 **Muang Ngoy** Louangphabang, N Laos
178 I5 **Muang Ou Tai** Phôngsali, N Laos
Muang Pak Lay *see* Pak Lay
Muang Pakxan *see* Pakxan
178 Jj10 **Muang Pakxong** Champasak, S Laos
178 Jj9 **Muang Phalan** *var.* Muang Phalane. Savannakhét, S Laos
Muang Phalane *see* Muang Phalan
Muang Phan *see* Phan
Muang Phayao *see* Phayao
Muang Phichit *see* Phichit
178 Jj9 **Muang Phin** Savannakhét, S Laos
Muang Phitsanulok *see* Phitsanulok
Muang Phrae *see* Phrae
Muang Roi Et *see* Roi Et
Muang Sakon Nakhon *see* Sakon Nakhon
Muang Samut Prakan *see* Samut Prakan
178 I6 **Muang Sing** Louang Namtha, N Laos
Muang Ubon *see* Ubon Ratchathani
Muang Uthai Thani *see* Uthai Thani
178 I7 **Muang Vangviang** Viangchan, C Laos
Muang Xaignabouri *see* Xaignabouli
Muang Xay *see* Xai
178 Jj9 **Muang Xépôn** *var.* Sepone. Savannakhét, S Laos
174 H6 **Muar** *var.* Bandar Maharani. Johor, Peninsular Malaysia
173 Ff6 **Muara** Sumatera, W Indonesia
174 Hh11 **Muarabeliti** Sumatera, W Indonesia
174 H9 **Muarabungo** Sumatera, W Indonesia
174 I11 **Muaraenim** Sumatera, W Indonesia
174 Mm8 **Muarajuloi** Borneo, C Indonesia
175 Nn9 **Muarakaman** Borneo, C Indonesia
173 Ff9 **Muarasigep** Pulau Siberut, W Indonesia
174 Hh9 **Muaratembesi** Sumatera, W Indonesia
175 N9 **Muaratewe** *var.* Muarateweh; *prev.* Moearatewe. Borneo, C Indonesia
Muarateweh *see* Muaratewe
175 O7 **Muarawahau** Borneo, N Indonesia
xliii F21 **Muasdale** Argyll and Bute, W Scotland, UK
144 G13 **Mubārak, Jabal** ▲ S Jordan
159 N13 **Mubārakpur** Uttar Pradesh, N India
Mubarek *see* Muborak
83 F18 **Mubende** SW Uganda
79 Y14 **Mubi** Adamawa, NE Nigeria
152 M12 **Muborak** *Rus.* Mubarek. Qashqadaryo Wiloyati, S Uzbekistan
176 Vv9 **Mubrani** Irian Jaya, E Indonesia
xxxvii U7 **Much Hadham** Hertfordshire, SE England, UK
69 U12 **Muchinga Escarpment** *escarpment* NE Zambia
131 N7 **Muchkapskiy** Tambovskaya Oblast', W Russian Federation
xxxviii I14 **Much Marcle** Herefordshire, W England, UK
xxxviii I10 **Much Wenlock** Shropshire, W England, UK
xliii D15 **Muck** *island* W Scotland, UK
xlii H3 **Muckle Roe** *island* NE Scotland, UK
xliv J6 **Muckno Lough** ◎ NE Ireland
xliv D13 **Muckross** Kerry, SW Ireland
84 Q13 **Mucojo** Cabo Delgado, N Mozambique
84 F12 **Muconda** Lunda Sul, NE Angola
56 I10 **Muco, Río** ∽ E Colombia
85 O16 **Mucubela** Zambézia, NE Mozambique
44 J5 **Mucupina, Monte** ▲ N Honduras
142 J14 **Mucur** Kirşehir, C Turkey
149 U8 **Mūd** Khorāsān, E Iran
169 Y9 **Mudanjiang** *var.* Mu-tan-chiang. Heilongjiang, NE China
169 Y9 **Mudan Jiang** ∽ NE China
142 D11 **Mudanya** Bursa, NW Turkey
30 K8 **Mud Butte** South Dakota, N USA
161 G16 **Muddebihāl** Karnātaka, C India
29 P12 **Muddy Boggy Creek** ∽ Oklahoma, C USA
38 M6 **Muddy Creek** ∽ Utah, W USA
39 V7 **Muddy Creek Reservoir** ⊡ Colorado, C USA
35 W15 **Muddy Gap** Wyoming, C USA
37 Y11 **Muddy Peak** ▲ Nevada, W USA
191 R7 **Mudgee** New South Wales, SE Australia
31 S3 **Mud Lake** ◎ Minnesota, N USA
31 P7 **Mud Lake Reservoir** ⊡ South Dakota, N USA
178 Gg9 **Mudon** Mon State, S Burma
83 O14 **Mudug** *off.* Gobolka Mudug. ◈ *region* NE Somalia
83 O14 **Mudug** *var.* Mudugh. *plain* N Somalia
Mudugh *see* Mudug
85 Q15 **Muecate** Nampula, NE Mozambique
84 Q13 **Mueda** Cabo Delgado, NE Mozambique
44 L10 **Muelle de los Bueyes** Región Autónoma Atlántico Sur, SE Nicaragua
Muenchen *see* München
85 M14 **Muende** Tete, NW Mozambique
27 T5 **Muenster** Texas, SW USA
Muenster *see* Münster
45 O6 **Muerto, Cayo** *reef* NE Nicaragua
43 T17 **Muerto, Mar** *lagoon* SE Mexico
66 F11 **Muertos Trough** *undersea feature* N Caribbean Sea
85 H14 **Mufaya Kuta** Western, NW Zambia
84 J13 **Mufulira** Copperbelt, C Zambia
167 O10 **Mufu Shan** ▲▲ C China
Mugalzhar Taūlary *see* Mugodzhary, Gory
143 Y12 **Muğan Düzü** *Rus.* Muganskaya Ravnina, Muganskaya Step'. *physical region* S Azerbaijan
Muganskaya Ravnina/Muganskaya Step' *see* Muğan Düzü
108 K8 **Múggia** Friuli-Venezia Giulia, NE Italy
159 N14 **Mughal Sarāi** Uttar Pradesh, N India
Mughla *see* Muğla
147 W11 **Mughshin** *var.* Muqshin. S Oman
153 S12 **Mughsu** *Rus.* Muksu. ∽ C Tajikistan
170 Ff16 **Mugi** Tokushima, Shikoku, SW Japan
142 C16 **Muğla** *var.* Mughla. Muğla, SW Turkey
142 C16 **Muğla** *var.* Mughla. ◈ *province* SW Turkey
150 J11 **Mugodzhary, Gory** *Kaz.* Mugalzhar Taūlary. ▲▲ W Kazakhstan
85 O15 **Mugulama** Zambézia, NE Mozambique
145 U9 **Muḥammad** E Iraq
145 R8 **Muḥammadīyah** C Iraq
82 I6 **Muhammad Qol** Red Sea, NE Sudan
77 Y9 **Muhammad, Râs** *headland* E Egypt
Muhammerah *see* Khorramshahr
146 M12 **Muhāyil** *var.* Mahāil. 'Asīr, SW Saudi Arabia
145 O7 **Muḥaywīr** W Iraq
103 H21 **Mühlacker** Baden-Württemberg, SW Germany
Mühlbach *see* Sebeş
Mühldorf *see* Mühldorf am Inn
103 N23 **Mühldorf am Inn** *var.* Mühldorf. Bayern, SE Germany
103 J15 **Mühlhausen** *var.* Mühlhausen in Thüringen. Thüringen, C Germany
Mühlhausen in Thüringen *see* Mühlhausen
205 Q2 **Mühlig-Hofmann Mountains** ▲▲ Antarctica
95 L14 **Muhos** Oulu, C Finland
144 K6 **Mūḥ, Sabkhat al** ◎ C Syria
120 E5 **Muhu** *Ger.* Mohn, Moon. *island* W Estonia
83 F19 **Muhutwe** Kagera, NW Tanzania
Muhu Väin *see* Väinameri
100 J10 **Muiden** Noord-Holland, C Netherlands
xlii J9 **Muie** Highland, NW Scotland, UK
200 R15 **Mui Hopohoponga** *headland* Tongatapu, S Tonga
171 K14 **Muika** *var.* Muikamachi. Niigata, Honshū, C Japan
Muikamachi *see* Muika
Muinchille *see* Cootehill
Muineachán *see* Monaghan
xliv J11 **Muine Bheag** *Eng.* Bagenalstown. Carlow, SE Ireland
xliii N17 **Muirdrum** Angus, E Scotland, UK
xliii J20 **Muirhead** Angus, E Scotland, UK
xliii M17 **Muirhead** North Lanarkshire, C Scotland, UK
xliii J22 **Muirkirk** East Ayrshire, W Scotland, UK
xlii I12 **Muir of Ord** Highland, NW Scotland, UK
58 B5 **Muisne** Esmeraldas, NW Ecuador
85 P14 **Muite** Nampula, NE Mozambique
43 Z11 **Mujeres, Isla** *island* E Mexico
118 G7 **Mukacheve** *Hung.* Munkács, *Rus.* Mukachevo. Zakarpats'ka Oblast', W Ukraine
Mukachevo *see* Mukacheve
174 Ll5 **Mukah** Sarawak, East Malaysia
Mukalla *see* Al Mukallā
Mukama *see* Mokāma
Mukāshafa/Mukashshafah *see* Mukayshīfah
172 Oo6 **Mu-kawa** ∽ Hokkaidō, NE Japan
145 S6 **Mukayshīfah** *var.* Mukāshafa, Mukashshafah. N Iraq
178 J9 **Mukdahan** Mukdahan, E Thailand
Mukden *see* Shenyang
172 Ss16 **Mukojima-rettō** *Eng.* Parry group. *island group* SE Japan
152 M14 **Mukry** Lebapskiy Velayat, E Turkmenistan
Muksu *see* Mughsu
159 U14 **Muktagacha** Dhaka, N Bangladesh
84 K13 **Mukuku** Central, C Zambia
84 K11 **Mukupa Kaoma** Northern, NE Zambia
83 I18 **Mukutan** Rift Valley, W Kenya
85 F16 **Mukwe** Caprivi, NE Namibia
107 R13 **Mula** Murcia, SE Spain
157 K20 **Mulaku Atoll** *var.* Meemu Atoll. *atoll* C Maldives
85 J15 **Mulalika** Lusaka, C Zambia
169 X8 **Mulan** Heilongjiang, NE China
85 N15 **Mulanje** *var.* Mlanje. Southern, S Malawi
42 H5 **Mulatos** Sonora, NW Mexico
25 P3 **Mulberry Fork** ∽ Alabama, S USA
41 P12 **Mulchatna River** ∽ Alaska, USA
129 W4 **Mul'da** Respublika Komi, NW Russian Federation
103 M14 **Mulde** ∽ E Germany
xliii A14 **Muldoanich** *island* NW Scotland, UK
29 R10 **Muldrow** Oklahoma, C USA
42 E7 **Mulegé** Baja California Sur, W Mexico
110 I10 **Mulegns** Graubünden, S Switzerland
81 M21 **Mulenda** Kasai Oriental, C Zaire
26 M4 **Muleshoe** Texas, SW USA
85 O15 **Mulevala** Zambézia, NE Mozambique
191 P5 **Mulgoa Creek** *seasonal river* New South Wales, SE Australia
107 O15 **Mulhacén** *var.* Cerro de Mulhacén. ▲ S Spain
Mulhacén, Cerro de *see* Mulhacén
Mülhausen *see* Mulhouse
103 E24 **Mülheim** Baden-Württemberg, SW Germany
103 E15 **Mülheim** *var.* Mulheim an der Ruhr. Nordrhein-Westfalen, W Germany
Mulheim an der Ruhr *see* Mülheim
105 U7 **Mulhouse** *Ger.* Mülhausen. Haut-Rhin, NE France
166 G11 **Muli** *var.* Bowa, Muli Zangzu Zizhixian. Sichuan, C China
176 Y15 **Muli** *channel* Irian Jaya, E Indonesia
169 Y9 **Muling** Heilongjiang, NE China
xliv F11 **Mulkear** ∽ W Ireland
Mullach Íde *see* Malahide
xliv E12 **Mullaghareirk Mountains** *hill range* W Ireland
xliv K10 **Mullaghcleevaun** ▲ E Ireland
xliv G5 **Mullaghmore** Sligo, N Ireland
Mullaitivu *see* Mullaittivu
161 K23 **Mullaittivu** *var.* Mullaitivu. Northern Province, N Sri Lanka
xliv H6 **Mullan** Fermanagh, W Northern Ireland, UK
35 N8 **Mullan** Idaho, NW USA
xlii H13 **Mullardoch, Loch** ◎ NW Scotland, UK
30 M13 **Mullen** Nebraska, C USA
191 Q6 **Mullengudgery** New South Wales, SE Australia
23 Q6 **Mullens** West Virginia, NE USA
Müller-gerbergte *see* Muller, Pegunungan
174 Mm7 **Muller, Pegunungan** *Dut.* Müller-gerbergte. ▲▲ Borneo, C Indonesia
194 F12 **Muller Range** ▲▲ W PNG
33 Q5 **Mullett Lake** ◎ Michigan, N USA
xlii M2 **Mull Head** *headland* N Scotland, UK
20 J16 **Mullica River** ∽ New Jersey, NE USA
27 R8 **Mullin** Texas, SW USA
xliv I12 **Mullinavat** Kilkenny, SE Ireland
xliv I8 **Mullingar** *Ir.* An Muileann gCearr. Westmeath, C Ireland
23 T12 **Mullins** South Carolina, SE USA
xxxvi B17 **Mullion** Cornwall, SW England, UK
xliii E17 **Mull, Isle of** *island* W Scotland, UK
131 R5 **Mullovka** Ul'yanovskaya Oblast', W Russian Federation
97 K19 **Mullsjö** Skaraborg, S Sweden
xliii E16 **Mull, Sound of** *strait* NW Scotland, UK
191 V4 **Mullumbimby** New South Wales, SE Australia
85 H15 **Mulobezi** Western, SW Zambia
85 C15 **Mulondo** Huíla, SW Angola
85 G15 **Mulonga Plain** *plain* W Zambia
81 N23 **Mulongo** Shaba, SE Zaire
xliv D7 **Mulrany** Mayo, NW Ireland
155 T10 **Multān** Punjab, E Pakistan
95 L17 **Multia** Keski-Suomi, C Finland
Mulucha *see* Moulouya
85 J14 **Mulungushi** Central, C Zambia
85 K14 **Mulungwe** Central, C Zambia
Muluya *see* Moulouya
29 N7 **Mulvane** Kansas, C USA
191 O10 **Mulwala** New South Wales, SE Australia
Mulwiya *see* Moulouya
190 K6 **Mulyungarie** South Australia
Mumbai *see* Bombay
85 D14 **Mumbué** Bié, C Angola
194 J13 **Mumeng** Morobe, C PNG
176 W9 **Mumi** Irian Jaya, E Indonesia
Muminabad/Mŭ'minobod *see* Leningrad
131 Q13 **Mumra** Astrakhanskaya Oblast', SW Russian Federation
43 X12 **Muna** Yucatán, SE Mexico
126 Kk9 **Muna** ∽ NE Russian Federation
158 C12 **Munābāo** Rājasthān, NW India
Munamägi *see* Suur Munamägi
175 Qq13 **Muna, Pulau** *prev.* Moena. *island* C Indonesia
175 Qq13 **Muna, Selat** *strait* Sulawesi, C Indonesia
103 L18 **Münchberg** Bayern, E Germany
103 L23 **München** *var.* Muenchen, *Eng.* Munich, *It.* Monaco. Bayern, SE Germany
München-Gladbach *see* Mönchengladbach
110 E6 **Münchenstein** Basel-Land, NW Switzerland
8 L10 **Muncho Lake** British Columbia, W Canada
33 P13 **Muncie** Indiana, N USA
20 G13 **Muncy** Pennsylvania, NE USA
195 U14 **Munda** New Georgia, NW Solomon Islands
9 Q14 **Mundare** Alberta, SW Canada
27 Q5 **Munday** Texas, SW USA
33 N10 **Mundelein** Illinois, N USA
103 I15 **Münden** Niedersachsen, C Germany
xxxix X7 **Mundesley** Norfolk, E England, UK
xxxix V10 **Mundford** Norfolk, E England, UK
107 Q12 **Mundo** ∽ S Spain
194 L11 **Mundua Island** *island* Witu Islands, C PNG
84 B12 **Munenga** Cuanza Sul, NW Angola
107 P11 **Munera** Castilla-La Mancha, C Spain
22 E9 **Munford** Tennessee, S USA
22 K7 **Munfordville** Kentucky, S USA
190 D5 **Mungala** South Australia
85 M16 **Mungári** Manica, C Mozambique
81 O16 **Mungbere** Haut-Zaïre, NE Zaire
159 Q13 **Munger** *prev.* Monghyr. Bihār, NE India
190 I2 **Mungeranie** South Australia
Mu Nggava *see* Rennell
174 K6 **Mungguresak, Tanjung** *headland* Borneo, N Indonesia
Mungiki *see* Bellona
191 R4 **Mungindi** New South Wales, SE Australia
Mungkawn *see* Maingkwan
159 T16 **Mungla** *var.* Mongla. Khulna, S Bangladesh
84 C13 **Mungo** Huambo, W Angola
xliv F11 **Mungret** Limerick, SW Ireland
196 F16 **Munguuy Bay** *bay* Yap, W Micronesia
84 E13 **Munhango** Bié, C Angola
197 L14 **Munia** *island* Lau Group, E Fiji
Munich *see* München
107 S7 **Muniesa** Aragón, NE Spain
33 O4 **Munising** Michigan, N USA
Munkács *see* Mukacheve
97 I17 **Munkedal** Göteborg och Bohus, S Sweden
97 K15 **Munkfors** Värmland, C Sweden
126 J16 **Munku-Sardyk, Gora** *var.* Mönh Sarĭdag. ▲ Mongolia/Russian Federation
101 E18 **Munkzwalm** Oost-Vlaanderen, NW Belgium
xlii J11 **Munlochy** Highland, NW Scotland, UK
178 J10 **Mun, Mae Nam** ∽ E Thailand
159 U15 **Munshiganj** Dhaka, C Bangladesh
110 D8 **Münsingen** Bern, W Switzerland
xliv D13 **Munster** *Ir.* Cúige Mumhan. *province* S Ireland
105 U6 **Munster** Haut-Rhin, NE France
102 J11 **Munster** Niedersachsen, NW Germany
102 F13 **Münster** *var.* Muenster, Münster in Westfalen. Nordrhein-Westfalen, W Germany
110 F10 **Münster** Valais, S Switzerland
Münsterberg in Schlesien *see* Ziębice
Münster in Westfalen *see* Münster
102 E13 **Münsterland** *cultural region* NW Germany
102 F13 **Münster-Osnabruck** ✕ Nordrhein-Westfalen, NW Germany
33 R4 **Munuscong Lake** ◎ Michigan, N USA
85 K17 **Munyati** ∽ C Zimbabwe
111 R3 **Münzkirchen** Oberösterreich, N Austria
94 K11 **Muodoslompolo** Norrbotten, N Sweden
94 M13 **Muojärvi** ◎ NE Finland
178 Jj6 **Mương Khên** Hoa Binh, N Vietnam
Muong Sai *see* Xai
178 I7 **Muong Xiang Ngeun** *var.* Xieng Ngeun. Louangphabang, N Laos
94 K11 **Muonio** Lappi, N Finland
Muonioälv/Muoniojoki *see* Muonionjoki
94 K11 **Muonionjoki** *var.* Muoniojoki, *Swe.* Muonioälv. ∽ Finland/Sweden
85 N17 **Mupa** ∽ C Mozambique
85 E16 **Mupini** Okavango, NE Namibia
82 F8 **Muqaddam, Wadi** ∽ N Sudan
144 K9 **Muqāṭ** Al Mafraq, E Jordan
147 X7 **Muqaz** N Oman
83 N17 **Muqdisho** *Eng.* Mogadishu, *It.* Mogadiscio. ● (Somalia) Banaadir, S Somalia
83 N17 **Muqdisho** ✕ Banaadir, E Somalia
Muqshin *see* Mughshin
111 T8 **Mur** *SCr.* Mura. ∽ C Europe
Mura *see* Mur
143 T14 **Muradiye** Van, E Turkey
Muragarazi *see* Maragarazi
171 L12 **Murakami** Niigata, Honshū, C Japan
65 G22 **Murallón, Cerro** ▲ S Argentina
83 E20 **Muramvya** C Burundi
83 I19 **Murang'a** *prev.* Fort Hall. Central, SW Kenya
83 H16 **Murangering** Rift Valley, NW Kenya
Murapara *see* Murupara
146 M5 **Murār, Bi'r al** *well* NW Saudi Arabia
129 Q13 **Murashi** Kirovskaya Oblast', NW Russian Federation
105 O12 **Murat** Cantal, C France
116 N12 **Muratlı** Tekirdağ, NW Turkey
143 R14 **Murat Nehri** *var.* Eastern Euphrates; *anc.* Arsanias. ∽ NE Turkey
109 D20 **Muravera** Sardegna, Italy, C Mediterranean Sea
171 Ll12 **Murayama** Yamagata, Honshū, C Japan
124 Oo15 **Muraysah, Ra's al** *headland* N Libya
106 I6 **Murça** Vila Real, N Portugal
82 Q11 **Murcanyo** Bari, NE Somalia
149 N8 **Mūrcheh Khvort** *var.* Morcheh Khort. Eşfahān, C Iran
193 H15 **Murchison** Tasman, South Island, NZ
193 B22 **Murchison Mountains** ▲▲ South Island, NZ
188 I10 **Murchison River** ∽ Western Australia
107 R13 **Murcia** Murcia, SE Spain
107 Q13 **Murcia** ◈ *autonomous community* SE Spain
105 O13 **Mur-de-Barrez** Aveyron, S France
190 G8 **Murdinga** South Australia
30 M10 **Murdo** South Dakota, N USA
13 X6 **Murdochville** Québec, SE Canada
111 W9 **Mureck** Steiermark, SE Austria
116 M13 **Mürefte** Tekirdağ, NW Turkey
118 I10 **Mureş** ◈ *county* N Romania
86 J11 **Mureş** *var.* Maros, Mureşul, *Ger.* Marosch, Mieresch. ∽ Hungary/Romania *see also* Maros
Mureşul *see* Maros/Mureş
104 M16 **Muret** Haute-Garonne, S France
29 T13 **Murfreesboro** Arkansas, C USA
23 W8 **Murfreesboro** North Carolina, SE USA
22 J9 **Murfreesboro** Tennessee, S USA
152 I14 **Murgab** *prev.* Murgap. Maryyskiy Velayat, S Turkmenistan
152 J16 **Murgab** *var.* Murghab, *Pash.* Daryā-ye Morghāb, *Turkm.* Murgap Deryasy. ∽ Afghanistan/Turkmenistan
Murgab *see* Murghob
Murgap/Murgap Deryasy *see* Murgab
116 H9 **Murgash** ▲ W Bulgaria
Murghab *see* Murgab
153 U13 **Murghob** *Rus.* Murgab. SE Tajikistan
153 U13 **Murghob** *Rus.* Murgab. ∽ SE Tajikistan
189 Z10 **Murgon** Queensland, E Australia
202 I16 **Muri** Rarotonga, S Cook Islands
110 F7 **Muri** Aargau, W Switzerland
110 D8 **Muri** *var.* Muri bei Bern. Bern, W Switzerland
106 K3 **Murias de Paredes** Castilla-León, N Spain
Muri bei Bern *see* Muri
84 F11 **Muriege** Lunda Sul, NE Angola
201 P14 **Murilo Atoll** *atoll* Hall Islands, C Micronesia
Mūrītānīyah *see* Mauritania
102 N10 **Müritz** *var.* Müritzee. ◎ NE Germany
Müritzee *see* Müritz
102 L10 **Müritz-Elde-Kanal** *canal* N Germany
192 K6 **Muriwai Beach** Auckland, North Island, NZ
94 J13 **Murjek** Norrbotten, N Sweden
128 J3 **Murmansk** Murmanskaya Oblast', NW Russian Federation
128 I4 **Murmanskaya Oblast'** ◈ *province* NW Russian Federation
207 V14 **Murmansk Rise** *undersea feature* SW Barents Sea
128 J3 **Murmashi** Murmanskaya Oblast', NW Russian Federation
130 M5 **Murmino** Ryazanskaya Oblast', W Russian Federation
103 K24 **Murnau** Bayern, SE Germany
104 E3 **Muro, Capo di** *headland* Corse, France, C Mediterranean Sea
109 M18 **Muro Lucano** Basilicata, S Italy
131 N4 **Murom** Vladimirskaya Oblast', W Russian Federation
125 G13 **Muromtsevo** Omskaya Oblast', C Russian Federation
172 Nn6 **Muroran** Hokkaidō, NE Japan
106 G3 **Muros** Galicia, NW Spain
106 F3 **Muros e Noia, Ría de** *estuary* NW Spain
170 F16 **Muroto** Kōchi, Shikoku, SW Japan
170 F16 **Muroto-zaki** *headland* Shikoku, SW Japan
118 L7 **Murovani Kurylivtsi** Vinnyts'ka Oblast', C Ukraine
112 G11 **Murowana Goślina** Poznań, W Poland
34 M14 **Murphy** Idaho, NW USA
23 N10 **Murphy** North Carolina, SE USA
37 P8 **Murphys** California, W USA
32 L17 **Murphysboro** Illinois, N USA
31 V15 **Murray** Iowa, C USA
22 H8 **Murray** Kentucky, S USA
190 J10 **Murray Bridge** South Australia
183 X2 **Murray Fracture Zone** *tectonic feature* NE Pacific Ocean
194 E13 **Murray, Lake** ◎ SW PNG
23 P12 **Murray, Lake** ⊡ South Carolina, SE USA
8 K8 **Murray, Mount** ▲ Yukon Territory, NW Canada
194 H13 **Murray Range** *var.* Leonard Murray Mountains. ▲▲ W PNG
Murray Range *see* Murray Ridge
181 O3 **Murray Ridge** *var.* Murray Range. *undersea feature* N Arabian Sea
191 N10 **Murray River** ∽ SE Australia
190 K10 **Murrayville** Victoria, SE Australia
155 U5 **Murree** Punjab, E Pakistan
103 I21 **Murrhardt** Baden-Württemberg, S Germany
xliv E9 **Murroogh** Clare, W Ireland
xxxix S9 **Murrow** Cambridgeshire, E England, UK
191 O9 **Murrumbidgee River** ∽ New South Wales, SE Australia
85 P15 **Murrupula** Nampula, NE Mozambique
191 T7 **Murrurundi** New South Wales, SE Australia
111 X9 **Murska Sobota** *Ger.* Olsnitz. NE Slovenia
160 G12 **Murtajāpur** *prev.* Murtazapur. Mahārāshtra, C India
79 S16 **Murtala Muhammed** ✕ (Lagos) Ogun, SW Nigeria
Murtazapur *see* Murtajāpur
110 C8 **Murten** Neuchâtel, W Switzerland
Murtensee *see* Morat, Lac de
190 L11 **Murtoa** Victoria, SE Australia
xli S7 **Murton** Durham, N England, UK
94 N13 **Murtovaara** Oulu, E Finland
Murua Island *see* Woodlark Island
161 D14 **Murud** Mahārāshtra, W India
192 O9 **Murupara** *var.* Murapara. Bay of Plenty, North Island, NZ
203 X12 **Mururoa** *var.* Moruroa. *atoll* Îles Tuamotu, SE French Polynesia
Murviedro *see* Sagunto
160 J9 **Murwāra** Madhya Pradesh, N India
191 V4 **Murwillumbah** New South Wales, SE Australia
152 H11 **Murzechirla** *prev.* Mirzachirla. Akhalskiy Velayat, C Turkmenistan
Murzuk *see* Murzuq
77 O11 **Murzuq** *var.* Marzūq, Murzuk. SW Libya
Murzuq, Edeyin *see* Murzuq, Idhān
77 N11 **Murzuq, Ḩamādat** *plateau* W Libya
77 O11 **Murzuq, Idhān** *var.* Edeyin Murzuq. *desert* SW Libya
111 W6 **Mürzzuschlag** Steiermark, E Austria
143 Q14 **Muş** *var.* Mush. Muş, E Turkey
143 Q14 **Muş** *var.* Mush. ◈ *province* E Turkey
194 L16 **Musa** ∽ S PNG
120 G11 **Mūša** ∽ Latvia/Lithuania
77 X8 **Mûsa, Gebel** ▲ NE Egypt
Musaiyib *see* Al Musayyib
Musa Khel *see* Mūsa Khel Bāzār
155 R9 **Mūsa Khel Bāzār** *var.* Musa Khel. Baluchistān, SW Pakistan
116 H10 **Musala** ▲ W Bulgaria
173 F6 **Musala, Pulau** *island* W Indonesia
85 I15 **Musale** Southern, S Zambia
147 Y9 **Muşalla** NE Oman
147 W6 **Musandam Peninsula** *Ar.* Masandam Peninsula. *peninsula* N Oman
Musay'īd *see* Umm Sa'īd
xxxvi J14 **Musbury** Devon, SW England, UK
Muscat *see* Masqaṭ
Muscat and Oman *see* Oman
31 Y14 **Muscatine** Iowa, C USA
Muscat Sīb Airport *see* Seeb
33 O15 **Muscatuck River** ∽ Indiana, N USA
194 G10 **Muschu Island** *island* NW PNG
32 K8 **Muscoda** Wisconsin, N USA
193 F19 **Musgrave, Mount** ▲ South Island, NZ
189 P9 **Musgrave Ranges** ▲▲ South Australia
Mush *see* Muş
144 H12 **Mushayyish, Qaşr al** *castle* Ma'ān, C Jordan
xliv E13 **Musheramore** ▲ S Ireland
81 H20 **Mushie** Bandundu, W Zaire
174 I11 **Musi, Air** *prev.* Moesi. ∽ Sumatera, W Indonesia
199 K5 **Musicians Seamounts** *undersea feature* N Pacific Ocean
56 D8 **Musinga, Alto** ▲ NW Colombia
31 T2 **Muskeg Bay** *lake bay* Minnesota, N USA
33 O8 **Muskegon** Michigan, N USA
33 O8 **Muskegon Heights** Michigan, N USA
33 P8 **Muskegon River** ∽ Michigan, N USA
33 T14 **Muskingum River** ∽ Ohio, N USA
97 P16 **Muskö** Stockholm, C Sweden
Muskogean *see* Tallahassee
29 Q10 **Muskogee** Oklahoma, C USA
12 H13 **Muskoka, Lake** ◎ Ontario, S Canada
82 H8 **Musmar** Red Sea, NE Sudan
85 K14 **Musofu** Central, C Zambia
83 G19 **Musoma** Mara, N Tanzania
84 L13 **Musoro** Central, C Zambia
194 M8 **Mussau Island** *island* NE PNG
xliii M20 **Musselburgh** East Lothian, SE Scotland, UK
100 P7 **Musselkanaal** Groningen, NE Netherlands
35 V9 **Musselshell River** ∽ Montana, NW USA
84 C12 **Mussende** Cuanza Sul, NW Angola
104 L12 **Mussidan** Dordogne, SW France
101 L25 **Musson** Luxembourg, SE Belgium
158 J9 **Mussoorie** Uttar Pradesh, N India
Musta *see* Mosta
158 M13 **Mustafābād** Uttar Pradesh, N India
142 D12 **Mustafakemalpaşa** Bursa, NW Turkey
Mustafa-Pasha *see* Svilengrad
83 M15 **Mustahīl** SE Ethiopia
26 M7 **Mustang Draw** *valley* Texas, SW USA
27 T14 **Mustang Island** *island* Texas, SW USA
Mustasaari *see* Korsholm
Mustér *see* Disentis
65 I19 **Musters, Lago** ◎ S Argentina
47 Y14 **Mustique** *island* C Saint Vincent and the Grenadines
120 I6 **Mustla** Viljandimaa, S Estonia
xli W11 **Muston** North Yorkshire, N England, UK
120 J4 **Mustvee** *Ger.* Tschorna. Jõgevamaa, E Estonia
44 L9 **Musún, Cerro** ▲ NE Nicaragua
191 T7 **Muswellbrook** New South Wales, SE Australia
xxxvi C5 **Muswell Hill** Haringey, SE England, UK
113 M18 **Muszyna** Nowy Sącz, SE Poland
142 I17 **Mut** İçel, S Turkey
77 V10 **Mût** *var.* Mut. C Egypt
111 V9 **Muta** N Slovenia
202 B15 **Mutalau** N Niue
Mu-tan-chiang *see* Mudanjiang
84 I13 **Mutanda** North Western, NW Zambia
61 O17 **Mutá, Ponta do** *headland* E Brazil
85 L17 **Mutare** *var.* Mutari; *prev.* Umtali. Manicaland, E Zimbabwe
Mutari *see* Mutare
56 D8 **Mutatá** Antioquia, NW Colombia
xliii K18 **Muthill** Perth and Kinross, C Scotland, UK
Mutina *see* Modena
176 Z15 **Muting** Irian Jaya, E Indonesia
85 L16 **Mutoko** *prev.* Mtoko. Mashonaland East, NE Zimbabwe
83 J20 **Mutomo** Eastern, S Kenya
126 J12 **Mutoray** Evenkiyskiy Avtonomnyy Okrug, C Russian Federation
Mutrah *see* Maţraḩ
81 M24 **Mutshatsha** Shaba, S Zaire
172 Nn8 **Mutsu** *var.* Mutu. Aomori, Honshū, N Japan
172 N8 **Mutsu-wan** *bay* N Japan
110 E6 **Muttenz** Basel-Land, NW Switzerland
193 A26 **Muttonbird Islands** *island group* SW NZ
xliv D10 **Mutton Island** *island* W Ireland
Mutu *see* Mutsu
85 O15 **Mutuáli** Nampula, N Mozambique
84 D13 **Mutumbo** Bié, C Angola
201 Y14 **Mutunte, Mount** *var.* Mount Buache. ▲ Kosrae, E Micronesia
161 K24 **Mutur** Eastern Province, E Sri Lanka
94 L13 **Muurola** Lappi, NW Finland
168 M14 **Mu Us Shamo** *var.* Ordos Desert. *desert* N China
84 B11 **Muxima** Bengo, NW Angola
128 I8 **Muyezerskiy** Respublika Kareliya, NW Russian Federation
83 E20 **Muyinga** NE Burundi
44 K9 **Muy Muy** Matagalpa, C Nicaragua
Muynak *see* Mŭynoq
152 G6 **Mŭynoq** *Rus.* Muynak. Qoraqalpoghiston Respublikasi, NW Uzbekistan
81 N22 **Muyumba** Shaba, SE Zaire
155 V5 **Muzaffarābād** Jammu and Kashmir, NE Pakistan
155 S10 **Muzaffargarh** Punjab, E Pakistan
158 J9 **Muzaffarnagar** Uttar Pradesh, N India
159 P13 **Muzaffarpur** Bihār, N India
164 H6 **Muzat He** ∽ W China
85 L15 **Muze** Tete, NW Mozambique
125 Ff8 **Muzhi** Yamalo-Nenetskiy Avtonomnyy Okrug, N Russian Federation
104 H7 **Muzillac** Morbihan, NW France
Muzkol, Khrebet *see* Muzqŭl, Qatorkŭhi
114 L9 **Mužlja** *Hung.* Felsőmuzslya; *prev.* Gornja Mužlja. Serbia, N Yugoslavia
56 F9 **Muzo** Boyacá, C Colombia
85 J15 **Muzoka** Southern, S Zambia
41 Y15 **Muzon, Cape** *headland* Dall Island, Alaska, USA
42 M6 **Múzquiz** Coahuila de Zaragoza, NE Mexico
153 U13 **Muzqŭl, Qatorkŭhi** *Rus.* Khrebet Muzkol. ▲▲ SE Tajikistan
164 G10 **Muztag** ▲ NW China
164 D8 **Muztagata** ▲ NW China
85 K17 **Mvuma** *prev.* Umvuma. Midlands, C Zimbabwe
84 L13 **Mwanya** Eastern, E Zambia
83 G20 **Mwanza** Mwanza, NW Tanzania
81 N23 **Mwanza** Shaba, SE Zaire
83 F20 **Mwanza** ◈ *region* N Tanzania
84 M13 **Mwase Lundazi** Eastern, E Zambia
xliv C7 **Mweelrea** *Ir.* Caoc Maol Réidh. ▲ W Ireland
81 K21 **Mweka** Kasai Occidental, C Zaire
84 K12 **Mwenda** Luapula, N Zambia
81 L22 **Mwene-Ditu** Kasai Oriental, S Zaire
85 L18 **Mwenezi** ∽ S Zimbabwe
81 O20 **Mwenga** Sud Kivu, E Zaire
84 K11 **Mweru, Lake** *var.* Lac Moero. ◎ Zaire/Zambia
84 H13 **Mwinilunga** North Western, NW Zambia
201 V16 **Mwokil Atoll** *var.* Mokil Atoll. *atoll* Caroline Islands, E Micronesia
Myadel' *see* Myadzyel
120 J13 **Myadzyel** *Pol.* Miadzioł Nowy, *Rus.* Myadel'. Minskaya Voblasts', N Belorussia
158 C12 **Myājlār** *var.* Miajlar. Rājasthān, NW India
127 O9 **Myakit** Magadanskaya Oblast', E Russian Federation
25 W13 **Myakka River** ∽ Florida, SE USA
128 L14 **Myaksa** Vologodskaya Oblast', NW Russian Federation
191 U8 **Myall Lake** ◎ New South Wales, SE Australia
177 Ff7 **Myanaung** Irrawaddy, SW Burma
Myanmar/Myanmar, Union of *see* Burma
177 F9 **Myaungmya** Irrawaddy, SW Burma
120 N11 **Myazha** *Rus.* Mezha. Vitsyebskaya Voblasts', NE Belorussia
xlii L7 **Mybster** Highland, N Scotland, UK
xxxv H12 **Myddfai** Carmarthenshire, S Wales, UK
xxxviii H9 **Myddle** Shropshire, W England, UK
xxxv F11 **Mydroilyn** Ceredigion, W Wales, UK

◆ COUNTRY
● COUNTRY CAPITAL
◇ DEPENDENT TERRITORY
○ DEPENDENT TERRITORY CAPITAL
◈ ADMINISTRATIVE REGION
✕ INTERNATIONAL AIRPORT
▲ MOUNTAIN
▲▲ MOUNTAIN RANGE
VOLCANO
∽ RIVER
◎ LAKE
⊡ RESERVOIR

MYERKULAVICHY – NARYMSKIY KHREBET

121 O18 Myerkulavichy Rus. Merkulovichi. Homyel'skaya Voblasts', SE Belorussia
121 N14 Myezhava Rus. Mezhëvo. Vitsyebskaya Voblasts', NE Belorussia
177 Ff5 Myingyan Mandalay, C Burma
177 G5 Myinmu Sagaing, C Burma
178 Gg2 Myitkyina Kachin State, N Burma
177 G5 Myittha Mandalay, C Burma
113 H19 Myjava Hung. Miava. Západné Slovensko, W Slovakia
Myjeldino see Myyëldino
119 U9 Mykhaylivka Rus. Mikhaylovka. Zaporiz'ka Oblast', SE Ukraine
118 I5 Mykolayiv L'vivs'ka Oblast', W Ukraine
119 Q10 Mykolayiv Rus. Nikolayev. Mykolayivs'ka Oblast', S Ukraine
119 Q10 Mykolayiv ✈ Mykolayivs'ka Oblast', S Ukraine
Mykolayiv see Mykolayivs'ka Oblast'
119 P9 Mykolayivka Odes'ka Oblast', SW Ukraine
119 S13 Mykolayivka Respublika Krym, S Ukraine
119 P9 Mykolayivs'ka Oblast' var. Mykolayiv, Rus. Nikolayevskaya Oblast'. ◈ province S Ukraine
117 J20 Mýkonos Mýkonos, Kykládes, Greece, Aegean Sea
117 K20 Mýkonos var. Míkonos. island Kykládes, Greece, Aegean Sea
129 R7 Myla Respublika Komi, NW Russian Federation
Mylae see Milazzo
95 M19 Myllykoski Kymi, S Finland
159 U14 Mymensingh var. Maimansingh; prev. Nasirābād. Dhaka, N Bangladesh
95 K19 Mynämäki Turku-Pori, SW Finland
151 S14 Mynaral Kaz. Myngaral. Zhambyl, S Kazakhstan
Mynbulak see Mingbuloq
Mynbulak, Vpadina see Mingbuloq Botighi
Myngaral see Mynaral
177 F5 Myohaung Arakan State, W Burma
169 W13 Myohyang-sanmaek ▲▲ C North Korea
171 Jj13 Myōkō-san ▲ Honshū, S Japan
85 J15 Myooye Central, C Zambia
120 K12 Myory prev. Miyory. Vitsyebskaya Voblasts', N Belorussia
94 J4 Mýrdalsjökull glacier S Iceland
94 G10 Myre Nordland, C Norway
119 S5 Myrhorod Rus. Mirgorod. Poltavs'ka Oblast', NE Ukraine
117 J15 Mýrina var. Mírina. Límnos, SE Greece
119 P5 Myronivka Rus. Mironovka. Kyyivs'ka Oblast', N Ukraine
23 U13 Myrtle Beach South Carolina, SE USA
34 F14 Myrtle Creek Oregon, NW USA
191 P11 Myrtleford Victoria, SE Australia
34 E14 Myrtle Point Oregon, NW USA
117 K25 Mýrtos Kríti, Greece, E Mediterranean Sea
Myrtoum Mare see Mirtóo Pélagos
95 G17 Myrviken Jämtland, C Sweden
97 I15 Mysen Østfold, S Norway
128 L15 Myshkin Yaroslavskaya Oblast', NW Russian Federation
113 K17 Myślenice Kraków, S Poland
112 D10 Myślibórz Gorzów, W Poland
161 G20 Mysore var. Maisur. Karnātaka, W India
Mysore see Karnātaka
117 F21 Mystrás var. Mistras. Pelopónnisos, S Greece
129 T12 Mysy Komi-Permyatskiy Avtonomnyy Okrug, NW Russian Federation
113 K15 Myszków Częstochowa, S Poland
178 Jj14 My Tho var. Mi Tho. Tiên Giang, S Vietnam
Mytilene see Mytilíni
117 L17 Mytilíni var. Mitilíni; anc. Mytilene. Lésvos, E Greece
130 K3 Mytishchi Moskovskaya Oblast', W Russian Federation
39 N3 Myton Utah, W USA
94 K2 Mývatn ◎ C Iceland
129 T11 Myyëldino var. Myjeldino. Respublika Komi, NW Russian Federation
84 M13 Mzimba Northern, NW Malawi
84 M12 Mzuzu Northern, N Malawi

N

103 M19 Naab ≈ SE Germany
100 G12 Naaldwijk Zuid-Holland, W Netherlands
40 G12 Naalehu var. Nā'ālehu. Hawaii, USA, C Pacific Ocean
95 K19 Naantali Swe. Nådendal. Turku-Pori, SW Finland
100 J10 Naarden Noord-Holland, C Netherlands
111 U4 Naarn ≈ N Austria
xliv K9 Naas Ir. An Nás, Nás na Ríogh. Kildare, C Ireland
xlii F10 Naast Highland, NW Scotland, UK
94 M9 Näätämöjoki Lapp. Njávdám. ≈ NE Finland
85 E23 Nababeep var. Nababiep. Northern Cape, W South Africa
Nababiep see Nababeep
Nabadwip see Navadwīp
171 H16 Nabari Mie, Honshū, SW Japan
Nabatié/Nabatiyet et Tahta see Nabatīyé
144 G8 Nabatīyé var. An Nabatiyah at Taḥtā, Nabatié, Nabatiyet et Tahta. SW Lebanon
Nabatiyet et Tahta see Nabatīyé
197 I13 Nabavatu Vanua Levu, N Fiji
202 I2 Nabeina island Tungaru, W Kiribati
131 T4 Naberezhnyye Chelny prev. Brezhnev. Respublika Tatarstan, W Russian Federation
41 T10 Nabesna Alaska, USA
41 T10 Nabesna River ≈ Alaska, USA
77 N5 Nabeul var. Nābul. NE Tunisia
158 I9 Nābha Punjab, NW India
176 Ww11 Nabire Irian Jaya, E Indonesia
147 O15 Nabī Shu'ayb, Jabal an ▲ W Yemen
197 I13 Nabiti Vanua Levu, N Fiji
144 F10 Nablus var. Nābulus, Heb. Shekhem; anc. Neapolis, Bibl. Shechem. N West Bank
197 I13 Nabouwalu Vanua Levu, N Fiji
Nābul see Nabeul
Nābulus see Nablus
197 J13 Nabuna Vanua Levu, N Fiji
179 Rr15 Nabunturan Mindanao, S Philippines
xli T13 Naburn York, N England, UK
85 Q14 Nacala Nampula, NE Mozambique
44 H8 Nacaome Valle, S Honduras
Na Cealla Beaga see Killybegs
Na-ch'ii see Nagqu
171 Gg17 Nachikatsuura var. Nachi-Katsuura. Wakayama, Honshū, SE Japan
83 J24 Nachingwea Lindi, SE Tanzania
113 F16 Náchod Východní Čechy, NE Czech Republic
Na Clocha Liatha see Greystones
42 G3 Naco Sonora, NW Mexico
27 X8 Nacogdoches Texas, SW USA
42 G4 Nacozari de García Sonora, NW Mexico
xxxix X13 Nacton Suffolk, E England, UK
197 H13 Nacula prev. Nathula. island Yasawa Group, NW Fiji
xliv E13 Nad Cork, S Ireland
Nada see Danxian
79 O14 Nadawli NW Ghana
106 I3 Nadela Galicia, NW Spain
Nådendal see Naantali
150 M7 Nadezhdinka prev. Nadezhdinskiy. Kustanay, N Kazakhstan
Nadezhdinskiy see Nadezhdinka
Nadgan see Nadqān, Qalamat
197 H14 Nadi prev. Nandi. Viti Levu, W Fiji
197 H14 Nadi prev. Nandi. ✈ Viti Levu, W Fiji
160 D10 Nadiād Gujarāt, W India
Nadikdik see Knox Atoll
118 E11 Nădlac Ger. Nadlak, Hung. Nagylak. Arad, W Romania
Nadlak see Nădlac
76 H6 Nador prev. Villa Nador. NE Morocco
147 S9 Nadqān, Qalamat var. Nadgan. well E Saudi Arabia
113 N22 Nádudvar Hajdú-Bihar, E Hungary
123 J16 Nadur Gozo, N Malta
197 J13 Naduri prev. Nanduri. Vanua Levu, N Fiji
118 I7 Nadvirna Pol. Nadwórna, Rus. Nadvornaya. Ivano-Frankivs'ka Oblast', W Ukraine
128 J8 Nadvoitsy Respublika Kareliya, NW Russian Federation
Nadvornaya/Nadwórna see Nadvirna
126 Gg9 Nadym Yamalo-Nenetskiy Avtonomnyy Okrug, N Russian Federation
126 Gg9 Nadym ≈ C Russian Federation
194 J13 Nadzab Morobe, C PNG
79 X13 Nafada Bauchi, E Nigeria
110 H8 Näfels Glarus, NE Switzerland
xli W12 Nafferton East Riding of Yorkshire, N England, UK
117 E18 Náfpaktos var. Návpaktos. Dytikí Ellás, C Greece
117 F20 Náfplio prev. Návplion. Pelopónnisos, S Greece
145 U6 Naft Khāneh E Iraq
155 N13 Nāg Baluchistān, SW Pakistan
179 Q11 Naga off. Naga City; prev. Nueva Caceres. Luzon, N Philippines
Nagaarzê see Nagarzê
10 F11 Nagagami ≈ Ontario, S Canada
170 E14 Nagahama Ehime, Shikoku, SW Japan
171 Hh14 Nagahama Shiga, Honshū, SW Japan
159 X12 Nāga Hills ▲▲ NE India
171 Jj13 Nagai Yamagata, Honshū, C Japan
Na Gaibhlte see Galty Mountains
41 N16 Nagai Island island Shumagin Islands, Alaska, USA
159 X12 Nāgāland ◈ state NE India
171 Jj13 Nagano Nagano, Honshū, S Japan
171 J14 Nagano off. Nagano-ken. ◈ prefecture Honshū, S Japan
171 K13 Nagaoka Niigata, Honshū, C Japan
159 W12 Nagaon prev. Nowgong. Assam, NE India
161 J21 Nāgappattinam var. Negapatam, Negapattinam. Tamil Nādu, SE India
Nagara Nayok see Nakhon Nayok
Nagara Panom see Nakhon Phanom
Nagara Pathom see Nakhon Pathom
Nagara Sridharmaraj see Nakhon Si Thammarat
Nagara Svarga see Nakhon Sawan
161 H16 Nāgārjuna Sāgar ⊡ E India
44 I10 Nagarote León, SW Nicaragua
164 M16 Nagarzê var. Nagaarzê. Xizang Zizhiqu, W China
170 Bb13 Nagasaki Nagasaki, Kyūshū, SW Japan
170 Bb12 Nagasaki off. Nagasaki-ken. ◈ prefecture Kyūshū, SW Japan
170 Bb14 Naga-shima island SW Japan
170 Dd13 Naga-shima island SW Japan
Nagashima see Kii-Nagashima
170 Dd12 Nagato Yamaguchi, Honshū, SW Japan
158 F11 Nāgaur Rājasthān, NW India
160 F10 Nāgda Madhya Pradesh, C India
100 L8 Nagele Flevoland, N Netherlands
161 H24 Nāgercoil Tamil Nādu, SE India
159 X12 Nāginimāra Nāgāland, NE India
Na Gleannta see Glenties
xliv F13 Nagles Mountains ▲▲ S Ireland
172 P14 Nago Okinawa, Okinawa, SW Japan
160 K9 Nāgod Madhya Pradesh, C India
161 J26 Nagoda Southern Province, S Sri Lanka
103 G22 Nagold Baden-Württemberg, SW Germany
Nagorno-Karabakhskaya Avtonomnaya Oblast see Nagornyy Karabakh
126 Ll13 Nagornyy Respublika Sakha (Yakutiya), NE Russian Federation
143 V12 Nagornyy Karabakh var. Nagorno-Karabakhskaya Avtonomnaya Oblast, Arm. Lernayin Gharabakh, Az. Dağliq Qarabağ. former autonomous region SW Azerbaijan
129 R13 Nagorsk Kirovskaya Oblast', NW Russian Federation
171 Hh15 Nagoya Aichi, Honshū, SW Japan
160 I12 Nāgpur Mahārāshtra, C India
162 K10 Nagqu Chin. Na-ch'ii; prev. Hei-ho. Xizang Zizhiqu, W China
158 J8 Nāg Tibba Range ▲▲ N India
47 O8 Nagua NE Dominican Republic
113 H25 Nagyatád Somogy, SW Hungary
Nagybánya see Baia Mare
Nagybecskerek see Zrenjanin
Nagydisznód see Cisnădie
Nagyenyed see Aiud
113 N21 Nagykálló Szabolcs-Szatmár-Bereg, E Hungary
113 G25 Nagykanizsa Ger. Grosskanizsa. Zala, SW Hungary
Nagykároly see Carei
113 K22 Nagykáta Pest, C Hungary
Nagykikinda see Kikinda
113 K23 Nagykőrös Pest, C Hungary
Nagy-Küküllő see Târnava Mare
Nagylak see Nădlac
Nagymihály see Michalovce
Nagyrőce see Revúca
Nagysomkút see Şomcuta Mare
Nagysurány see Šurany
Nagyszalonta see Salonta
Nagyszeben see Sibiu
Nagyszentmiklós see Sânnicolau Mare
Nagyszöllös see Vynohradiv
Nagyszombat see Trnava
Nagytapolcsány see Topoľčany
Nagyvárad see Oradea
172 Oo15 Naha Okinawa, Okinawa, SW Japan
158 J8 Nāhan Himāchal Pradesh, NW India
Nahang, Rūd-e see Nihing
Nahariya see Nahariyya
144 F8 Nahariyya var. Nahariya. Northern, N Israel
148 L6 Nahāvand var. Nehavend. Hamadān, W Iran
103 F19 Nahe ≈ SW Germany
Na h-Iarmhidhe see Westmeath
201 O13 Nahnalaud ▲ Pohnpei, E Micronesia
Nahoi, Cape see Cumberland, Cape
65 H16 Nahuel Huapi, Lago ◎ W Argentina
25 W7 Nahunta Georgia, SE USA
42 J6 Naica Chihuahua, N Mexico
9 U15 Naicam Saskatchewan, S Canada
xxxvi K10 Nailsea North West Somerset, SW England, UK
xxxvi M8 Nailsworth Gloucestershire, C England, UK
169 T11 Naiman Qi Nei Mongol Zizhiqu, N China
164 M4 Naimin Bulak spring NW China
11 P6 Nain Newfoundland and Labrador, NE Canada
149 P8 Nā'īn Eşfahān, C Iran
158 K10 Naini Tāl Uttar Pradesh, N India
160 J11 Nainpur Madhya Pradesh, C India
197 J14 Nairai island C Fiji
xlii I8 Nairn Highland, N Scotland, UK
98 I8 Nairn cultural region NE Scotland, UK
83 I19 Nairobi ● (Kenya) Nairobi Area, S Kenya
83 I19 Nairobi ✈ Nairobi Area, S Kenya
84 P13 Nairoto Cabo Delgado, NE Mozambique
120 G3 Naissaar island N Estonia
Naissus see Niš
197 K13 Naitaba var. Naitauba; prev. Naitamba. island Lau Group, E Fiji
Naitamba/Naitauba see Naitaba
83 I19 Naivasha Rift Valley, SW Kenya
83 H19 Naivasha, Lake ◎ SW Kenya
Najaf see An Najaf
149 N8 Najafābād var. Nejafabad. Eşfahān, C Iran
147 N7 Najd var. Nejd. cultural region C Saudi Arabia
107 O4 Nájera La Rioja, N Spain
107 P4 Najerilla ≈ N Spain
158 J9 Najībābād Uttar Pradesh, N India
Najima see Fukuoka
169 Y11 Najin NE North Korea
145 T9 Najm al Ḩassūn C Iraq
147 O13 Najrān var. Abā as Su'ūd. Najrān, S Saudi Arabia
147 P12 Najrān off. Minţaqat al Najrān. ◈ province S Saudi Arabia
170 Bb12 Nakadōri-jima island Gotō-rettō, SW Japan
172 Pp3 Nakagawa Hokkaidō, NE Japan
171 Kk15 Naka-gawa ≈ Honshū, S Japan
40 F9 Nakalele Point headland Maui, Hawaii, USA, C Pacific Ocean
170 D12 Nakama Fukuoka, Kyūshū, SW Japan
Nakambé see White Volta
Nakamti see Nek'emtē
170 E15 Nakamura Kōchi, Shikoku, SW Japan
195 O12 Nakanai Mountains ▲▲ New Britain, E PNG
171 Jj14 Nakano Nagano, Honshū, S Japan
170 Ff11 Nakano-shima island Oki-shotō, SW Japan
170 Ff12 Nakano-umi var. Naka-umi. ◎ Honshū, SW Japan
171 Mm8 Nakasato Aomori, Honshū, C Japan
172 P7 Nakasatsunai Hokkaidō, NE Japan
172 Qq7 Nakashibetsu Hokkaidō, NE Japan
83 F18 Nakasongola C Uganda
172 Pp3 Nakatonbetsu Hokkaidō, NE Japan
170 D13 Nakatsu var. Nakatu. Ōita, Kyūshū, SW Japan
171 I15 Nakatsugawa var. Nakatugawa. Gifu, Honshū, SW Japan
Nakatu see Nakatsu
Nakatugawa see Nakatsugawa
Naka-umi see Nakano-umi
172 O5 Nakayama-tōge pass Hokkaidō, NE Japan
Nakdong see Naktong-gang
Nakel see Nakło nad Notecią
82 J8 Nakfa N Eritrea
Nakhichevan' see Naxçıvan
127 Nn18 Nakhodka Primorskiy Kray, SE Russian Federation
126 H8 Nakhodka Yamalo-Nenetskiy Avtonomnyy Okrug, N Russian Federation
Nakhon Navok see Nakhon Nayok
178 Hh11 Nakhon Nayok var. Nagara Nayok, Nakhon Navok. Nakhon Nayok, C Thailand
178 H11 Nakhon Pathom var. Nagara Pathom, Nakorn Pathom. Nakhon Pathom, W Thailand
178 J9 Nakhon Phanom var. Nagara Panom. Nakhon Phanom, E Thailand
178 Hh10 Nakhon Ratchasima var. Khorat, Korat. Nakhon Ratchasima, E Thailand
178 H10 Nakhon Sawan var. Muang Nakhon Sawan, Nagara Svarga. Nakhon Sawan, W Thailand
178 H15 Nakhon Si Thammarat var. Nagara Sridharmaraj, Nakhon Sithamnaraj. Nakhon Si Thammarat, SW Thailand
Nakhon Sithamnaraj see Nakhon Si Thammarat
145 Y11 Nakhrash SE Iraq
8 I9 Nakina British Columbia, W Canada
112 H9 Nakło nad Notecią Ger. Nakel. Bydgoszcz, W Poland
41 P13 Naknek Alaska, USA
158 H8 Nakodar Punjab, NW India
84 M11 Nakonde Northern, NE Zambia
Nakorn Pathom see Nakhon Pathom
97 H24 Nakskov Storstrøm, SE Denmark
169 Y15 Naktong-gang var. Nakdong, Jap. Rakutō-kō. ≈ C South Korea
83 H18 Nakuru Rift Valley, SW Kenya
9 O17 Nakusp British Columbia, SW Canada
155 N15 Nāl ≈ W Pakistan
168 M7 Nalayh Töv, C Mongolia
159 V12 Nalbari Assam, NE India
65 G19 Nalcayec, Isla island Archipiélago de los Chonos, S Chile
131 N15 Nal'chik Kabardino-Balkarskaya Respublika, SW Russian Federation
161 I16 Nalgonda Andhra Pradesh, C India
159 S14 Nalhāti West Bengal, NE India
159 U14 Nalitabari Dhaka, N Bangladesh
161 I17 Nallamala Hills ▲▲ E India
142 G12 Nallıhan Ankara, NW Turkey
106 K2 Nalón ≈ NW Spain
178 Gg3 Nalong Kachin State, N Burma
77 N8 Nālūt NW Libya
176 Uu12 Nama Pulau Manawoka, E Indonesia
201 Q16 Nama island C Micronesia
85 O16 Namacurra Zambézia, NE Mozambique
196 F9 Namai Bay bay Babeldaob, N Palau
31 W2 Namakan Lake ◎ Canada/USA
149 O6 Namak, Daryācheh-ye marsh N Iran
149 T6 Namak, Kavīr-e salt pan NE Iran
178 H6 Namaklwe Shan State, E Burma
Namaksār, Kowl-e/Namakzār, Daryācheh-ye see Namakzar
154 I5 Namakzar Pash. Daryācheh-ye Namakzār, Kowl-e Namaksār. marsh Afghanistan/Iran
176 W13 Namalau Pulau Jursian, E Indonesia
83 I20 Namanga Rift Valley, S Kenya
153 S10 Namangan Namangan Wiloyati, E Uzbekistan
Namanganskaya Oblast' see Namangan Wiloyati
153 R10 Namangan Wiloyati Rus. Namanganskaya Oblast'. ◈ province E Uzbekistan
85 Q14 Namapa Nampula, NE Mozambique
85 C21 Namaqualand physical region S Namibia
83 G18 Namasagali C Uganda
195 P10 Namatanai New Ireland, NE PNG
85 I14 Nambala Central, C Zambia
83 J23 Nambanje Lindi, SE Tanzania
176 Ww9 Namber Irian Jaya, E Indonesia
85 G16 Nambiya Ngamiland, N Botswana
191 V2 Nambour Queensland, E Australia
191 V6 Nambucca Heads New South Wales, SE Australia
165 N15 Nam Co ◎ W China
178 I5 Nâm Cum Lai Châu, N Vietnam
Namdik see Namorik Atoll
178 Jj6 Nam Định Nam Ha, N Vietnam
175 Tt11 Namea, Tanjung headland Pulau Seram, E Indonesia
101 I20 Namêche Namur, SE Belgium
32 J4 Namekagon Lake ◎ Wisconsin, N USA
196 F10 Namekakl Passage passage Babeldaob, N Palau
Namen see Namur
85 P15 Nametil Nampula, NE Mozambique
169 X14 Nam-gang ≈ C North Korea
169 Y16 Nam-gang ≈ S South Korea
169 Y17 Namhae-do Jap. Nankai-tō. island S South Korea
Namhoi see Foshan
85 C19 Namib Desert desert W Namibia
85 A15 Namibe Port. Moçâmedes, Mossâmedes. Namibe, SW Angola
85 A15 Namibe ◈ province SE Angola
85 C18 Namibia off. Republic of Namibia, var. South West Africa, Afr. Suidwes-Afrika, Ger. Deutsch-Südwestafrika; prev. German Southwest Africa, South-West Africa. ◆ republic S Africa
67 O17 Namibia Plain undersea feature S Atlantic Ocean
171 Ll14 Namie Fukushima, Honshū, C Japan
171 Mm8 Namioka Aomori, Honshū, C Japan
42 I5 Namiquipa Chihuahua, N Mexico
165 P15 Namjagbarwa Feng ▲ W China
175 Ss11 Namlea Pulau Buru, E Indonesia
164 L16 Namling Xizang Zizhiqu, W China
Namnetes see Nantes
178 I8 Nam Ngum ≈ C Laos
Namo see Namu Atoll
191 R5 Namoi River ≈ New South Wales, SE Australia
201 Q17 Namoluk Atoll atoll Mortlock Islands, C Micronesia
201 O15 Namonuito Atoll atoll Caroline Islands, C Micronesia
201 T9 Namorik Atoll var. Namdik. atoll Ralik Chain, S Marshall Islands
178 I6 Nam Ou ≈ N Laos
34 M14 Nampa Idaho, NW USA
78 M11 Nampala Ségou, W Mali
169 W14 Namp'o SW North Korea
85 P15 Nampula Nampula, NE Mozambique
85 P15 Nampula off. Província de Nampula. ◈ province NE Mozambique
169 W13 Namsan-ni NW North Korea
Namslau see Namysłów
95 E15 Namsos Nord-Trøndelag, C Norway
95 F14 Namsskogan Nord-Trøndelag, C Norway
126 M10 Namsty Respublika Sakha (Yakutiya), NE Russian Federation
178 H6 Nam Teng ≈ E Burma
178 I6 Nam Tha ≈ N Laos
178 Gg4 Namtu Shan State, E Burma
8 J15 Namu British Columbia, SW Canada
201 T7 Namu Atoll var. Namo. atoll Ralik Chain, C Marshall Islands
197 K15 Namuka-i-lau island Lau Group, E Fiji
85 O15 Namuli, Mont ▲ NE Mozambique
85 P14 Namuno Cabo Delgado, N Mozambique
101 I20 Namur Dut. Namen. Namur, SE Belgium
101 H21 Namur Dut. Namen. ◈ province S Belgium
85 D17 Namutoni Kunene, N Namibia
169 Y16 Namwŏn Jap. Nangen. S South Korea
178 Mm14 Namyit Island island S Spratly Islands
113 H14 Namysłów Ger. Namslau. Opole, SW Poland
178 Hh7 Nan var. Muang Nan. Nan, NW Thailand
81 G15 Nana ≈ W Central African Republic
172 Nn7 Nanae Hokkaidō, NE Japan
81 I14 Nana-Grébizi ◈ prefecture N Central African Republic
8 L17 Nanaimo Vancouver Island, British Columbia, SW Canada
40 C9 Nanakuli Haw. Nānākuli. Oahu, Hawaii, USA, C Pacific Ocean
81 G15 Nana-Mambéré ◈ prefecture W Central African Republic
167 R13 Nan'an Fujian, SE China
191 U2 Nanango Queensland, E Australia
171 Ii12 Nanao Ishikawa, Honshū, SW Japan
167 Q14 Nan'ao Dao island S China
171 Ii11 Nanatsu-shima island SW Japan
58 F8 Nanay, Río ≈ NE Peru
166 J8 Nanbu Sichuan, C China
169 X7 Nancha Heilongjiang, NE China
167 P10 Nanchang var. Nan-ch'ang, Nanch'ang-hsien. Jiangxi, S China
Nanch'ang-hsien see Nanchang
167 P11 Nancheng Jiangxi, S China
Nan-ching see Nanjing
166 J9 Nanchong Sichuan, C China
166 J10 Nanchuan Sichuan, C China
105 T5 Nancy Meurthe-et-Moselle, NE France
193 A22 Nancy Sound sound South Island, NZ
158 L9 Nanda Devi ▲ NW India
44 J11 Nandaime Granada, SW Nicaragua
166 K13 Nandan Guangxi Zhuangzu Zizhiqu, S China
161 H14 Nānded Mahārāshtra, C India
170 G15 Nanden Hyōgo, Awaji-shima, SW Japan
191 S5 Nandewar Range ▲▲ New South Wales, SE Australia
Nandi see Nadi
166 E13 Nanding He ≈ China/Vietnam
Nándorhgy see Oţelu Roşu
160 E11 Nandurbār Mahārāshtra, W India
Nanduri see Naduri
161 I17 Nandyāl Andhra Pradesh, E India
167 P11 Nanfeng Jiangxi, S China
Nang see Nang Xian
81 E15 Nanga Eboko Centre, C Cameroon
Nangamesi, Teluk see Waingapu, Teluk
155 W4 Nanga Parbat ▲ India/Pakistan
174 L8 Nangapinoh Borneo, C Indonesia
155 R5 Nangarhār ◈ province E Afghanistan
174 M8 Nangaserawai var. Nangah Serawai. Borneo, C Indonesia
174 L9 Nangatayap Borneo, C Indonesia
Nangen see Namwŏn
105 P5 Nangis Seine-et-Marne, N France
169 X13 Nangnim-sanmaek ▲▲ C North Korea
167 O4 Nangong Hebei, E China
165 Q14 Nangqên Qinghai, C China
178 I11 Nang Rong Buri Ram, E Thailand
165 O16 Nang Xian var. Nang. Xizang Zizhiqu, W China
Nan Hai see South China Sea
166 L8 Nan He ≈ C China
166 F12 Nanhua Yunnan, SW China
Naniwa see Ōsaka
161 G20 Nanjangūd Karnātaka, W India
167 Q8 Nanjing var. Nan-ching, Nanking; prev. Chianning, Chian-ning, Kiang-ning. Jiangsu, E China
Nankai-tō see Namhae-do
167 O12 Nankang Jiangxi, S China
Nanking see Nanjing
170 F15 Nankoku Kōchi, Shikoku, SW Japan
167 N13 Nan Ling ▲▲ S China
166 L15 Nanliu Jiang ≈ S China
201 P13 Nan Madol ruins Temwen Island, E Micronesia
166 K15 Nanning var. Nan-ning; prev. Yung-ning. Guangxi Zhuangzu Zizhiqu, S China
206 M15 Nanortalik S Greenland
Nanouki see Aranuka
166 H13 Nanpan Jiang ≈ S China
158 M11 Nānpāra Uttar Pradesh, N India
167 Q12 Nanping var. Nan-p'ing; prev. Yenping. Fujian, SE China
166 I7 Nanping Sichuan, C China
167 R12 Nanri Dao island SE China
172 Q13 Nansei-shotō Eng. Ryukyu Islands. island group SW Japan
Nansei Syotō Trench see Ryukyu Trench
207 T10 Nansen Basin undersea feature Arctic Ocean
207 T10 Nansen Cordillera var. Arctic-Mid Oceanic Ridge, Nansen Ridge. undersea feature Arctic Ocean
Nansen Ridge see Nansen Cordillera
133 T9 Nan Shan ▲▲ C China
179 Nn14 Nanshan Island island E Spratly Islands
Nansha Qundao see Spratly Islands
10 K3 Nantais, Lac ◎ Québec, NE Canada
105 N5 Nanterre Hauts-de-Seine, N France
104 I8 Nantes Bret. Naoned; anc. Condivincum, Namnetes. Loire-Atlantique, NW France
12 G17 Nanticoke Ontario, S Canada
20 H13 Nanticoke Pennsylvania, NE USA
23 Y4 Nanticoke River ≈ Delaware/Maryland, NE USA
xxxv J10 Nantmel Powys, C Wales, UK
xxxv G6 Nantmor Gwynedd, NW Wales, UK
9 Q17 Nanton Alberta, SW Canada
167 S8 Nantong Jiangsu, E China
167 S13 Nant'ou W Taiwan
105 S10 Nantua Ain, E France
21 Q13 Nantucket Nantucket Island, Massachusetts, NE USA
21 Q13 Nantucket Island island Massachusetts, NE USA
21 Q13 Nantucket Sound sound Massachusetts, NE USA
84 P13 Nantulo Cabo Delgado, N Mozambique
xxxviii H7 Nantwich Cheshire, W England, UK
201 O12 Nanuh Pohnpei, E Micronesia
197 K13 Nanuku Passage channel NE Fiji
202 D6 Nanumaga var. Nanumanga. atoll NW Tuvalu
Nanumanga see Nanumaga
202 D5 Nanumea Atoll atoll NW Tuvalu
61 O19 Nanuque Minas Gerais, SE Brazil
175 Ss4 Nanusa, Kepulauan island group N Indonesia
169 U4 Nanweng He ≈ NE China
166 I10 Nanxi Sichuan, C China
167 N10 Nanxian var. Nan Xian. Hunan, S China
167 N7 Nanyang var. Nan-yang. Henan, C China
167 P6 Nanyang Hu ◎ E China
171 L13 Nan'yō Yamagata, Honshū, C Japan
83 I18 Nanyuki Central, C Kenya
166 M8 Nanzhang Hubei, C China
107 T11 Nao, Cabo de La headland E Spain
10 M9 Naococane, Lac ◎ Québec, E Canada
159 S14 Naogaon Rajshahi, NW Bangladesh
Naokot see Naukot
197 C12 Naone Maewo, C Vanuatu
Naoned see Nantes
117 E14 Náousa Kentrikí Makedonía, N Greece
37 N8 Napa California, W USA
41 O11 Napaimiut Alaska, USA
41 N12 Napakiak Alaska, USA
126 H7 Napalkovo Yamalo-Nenetskiy Avtonomnyy Okrug, N Russian Federation
12 I16 Napanee Ontario, SE Canada
176 Ww11 Napanwainami Irian Jaya, E Indonesia
176 W11 Napan-Yaur Irian Jaya, E Indonesia
41 N12 Napaskiak Alaska, USA
178 J5 Na Phac Cao Bang, N Vietnam
176 Ww9 Napido Irian Jaya, E Indonesia
192 O11 Napier Hawke's Bay, North Island, NZ
205 X3 Napier Mountains ▲▲ Antarctica
13 O13 Napierville Québec, SE Canada
25 W15 Naples Florida, SE USA
27 W5 Naples Texas, SW USA
Naples see Napoli
166 I14 Napo Guangxi Zhuangzu Zizhiqu, S China
58 D6 Napo ◈ province NE Ecuador
31 O6 Napoleon North Dakota, N USA
33 R11 Napoleon Ohio, N USA
Napoléon-Vendée see la Roche-sur-Yon
24 J9 Napoleonville Louisiana, S USA
109 K17 Napoli Eng. Naples, Ger. Neapel; anc. Neapolis. Campania, S Italy
109 J18 Napoli, Golfo di gulf S Italy
59 F7 Napo, Río ≈ Ecuador/Peru
203 W9 Napuka island Îles Tuamotu, C French Polynesia
148 J3 Naqadeh Āžarbāyjān-e Bākhtarī, NW Iran
145 U6 Naqnah E Iraq
Nar see Nera
171 H15 Nara Nara, Honshū, SW Japan
78 L11 Nara Koulikoro, W Mali
171 Gg16 Nara off. Nara-ken. ◈ prefecture Honshū, SW Japan
155 R14 Nāra Canal irrigation canal S Pakistan
190 K11 Naracoorte South Australia
191 P8 Naradhan New South Wales, SE Australia
Naradhivas see Narathiwat
58 B8 Naranjal Guayas, W Ecuador
59 Q19 Naranjos Santa Cruz, E Bolivia
43 Q12 Naranjos Veracruz-Llave, E Mexico
165 Q6 Naran Sebstein Bulag spring NW China
149 X12 Narānū Sīstān va Balūchestān, SE Iran
170 Bb12 Narao Nagasaki, Nakadōri-jima, SW Japan
161 J16 Narasaraopet Andhra Pradesh, E India
164 J5 Narat Xinjiang Uygur Zizhiqu, W China
178 Hh17 Narathiwat var. Naradhivas. Narathiwat, SW Thailand
39 V10 Nara Visa New Mexico, SW USA
Nārāyāni see Gandak
Narbada see Narmada
xxxv D13 Narberth Pembrokeshire, SW Wales, UK
Narbo Martius see Narbonne
105 P16 Narbonne anc. Narbo Martius. Aude, S France
xxxix N10 Narborough Leicestershire, C England, UK
xxxix U9 Narborough Norfolk, E England, UK
Narborough Island see Fernandina, Isla
106 J2 Narcea ≈ NW Spain
158 J9 Narendranagar Uttar Pradesh, N India
Nares Abyssal Plain see Nares Plain
66 G11 Nares Plain var. Nares Abyssal Plain. undersea feature NW Atlantic Ocean
207 P10 Nares Strait Dan. Nares Stræde. strait Canada/Greenland
Nares Stræde see Nares Strait
112 O9 Narew ≈ E Poland
Narew see Naraw
161 F17 Nargund Karnātaka, W India
85 D20 Narib Hardap, S Namibia
Narikrik see Knox Atoll
xliv G3 Narin Donegal, N Ireland
56 B13 Nariño off. Departamento de Nariño. ◈ province SW Colombia
171 Kk17 Narita Chiba, Honshū, S Japan
171 Kk17 Narita ✈ (Tōkyō) Chiba, Honshū, S Japan
Narıya see An Nu'ayrīyah
158 J8 Nārkanda Himāchal Pradesh, NW India
95 L13 Narkaus Lappi, NW Finland
160 E11 Narmada var. Narbada. ≈ C India
158 H11 Narnaul var. Nārnaul. Haryāna, N India
109 I14 Narni Umbria, C Italy
109 J24 Naro Sicilia, Italy, C Mediterranean Sea
Narodichi see Narodychi
129 V7 Narodnaya, Gora ▲ NW Russian Federation
119 N3 Narodychi Rus. Narodichi. Zhytomyrs'ka Oblast', N Ukraine
130 J4 Naro-Fominsk Moskovskaya Oblast', W Russian Federation
83 H19 Narok Rift Valley, SW Kenya
106 H2 Narón Galicia, NW Spain
191 S11 Narooma New South Wales, SE Australia
Narova see Narva
Narovlya see Narowlya
155 W8 Narowāl Punjab, E Pakistan
121 N20 Narowlya Rus. Narovlya. Homyel'skaya Voblasts', SE Belorussia
95 J17 Närpes Fin. Närpiö. Vaasa, W Finland
Närpiö see Närpes
191 S5 Narrabri New South Wales, SE Australia
191 P9 Narrandera New South Wales, SE Australia
191 Q4 Narran Lake ◎ New South Wales, SE Australia
191 Q4 Narran River ≈ New South Wales/Queensland, SE Australia
188 J13 Narrogin Western Australia
191 Q7 Narromine New South Wales, SE Australia
23 R6 Narrows Virginia, NE USA
206 M15 Narsarsuaq ✈ S Greenland
160 I10 Narsimhapur Madhya Pradesh, C India
Narsingdi see Narsinghdi
159 U15 Narsinghdi var. Narsingdi. Dhaka, C Bangladesh
160 H9 Narsinghgarh Madhya Pradesh, C India
169 Q11 Nart Nei Mongol Zizhiqu, N China
Nartës, Gjol i/Nartës, Laguna e see Nartës, Liqeni i
115 J22 Nartës, Liqeni i var. Gjol i Nartës, Laguna e Nartës. ◎ SW Albania
117 F17 Narthákí ▲ C Greece
131 O15 Nartkala Kabardino-Balkarskaya Respublika, SW Russian Federation
170 Ff15 Naruto Tokushima, Shikoku, SW Japan
120 K3 Narva Ida-Virumaa, NE Estonia
120 K4 Narva prev. Narova. ≈ Estonia/Russian Federation
120 K3 Narva Bay Est. Narva Laht, Ger. Narwa-Bucht, Rus. Narvskiy Zaliv. bay Estonia/Russian Federation
Narva Laht see Narva Bay
128 F13 Narva Reservoir Est. Narva Veehoidla, Rus. Narvskoye Vodokhranilishche. ⊡ Estonia/Russian Federation
Narva Veehoidla see Narva Reservoir
94 H10 Narvik Nordland, C Norway
Narvskiy Zaliv see Narva Bay
Narvskoye Vodokhranilishche see Narva Reservoir
Narwa-Bucht see Narva Bay
158 I9 Narwāna Haryāna, NW India
129 R4 Nar'yan-Mar prev. Beloshchel'ye, Dzerzhinskiy. Nenetskiy Avtonomnyy Okrug, NW Russian Federation
126 H12 Narym Tomskaya Oblast', C Russian Federation
151 Y10 Narymskiy Khrebet Kaz. Naryn Zhotasy. ▲▲ E Kazakhstan

◆ Country ● Country Capital ◇ Dependent Territory ○ Dependent Territory Capital ◈ Administrative Region ✈ International Airport ▲ Mountain ▲▲ Mountain Range ⩑ Volcano ≈ River ◎ Lake ⊡ Reservoir

NARYN – NEWARK LAKE

153 W9 **Naryn** Narynskaya Oblast', C Kyrgyzstan
153 U8 **Naryn** ≈ Kyrgyzstan/Uzbekistan
151 W16 **Narynkol** *Kaz.* Narynqol. Almaty, SE Kazakhstan
Naryn Oblasty *see* Narynskaya Oblast'
Narynqol *see* Narynkol
153 V9 **Narynskaya Oblast'** *Kir.* Naryn Oblasty. ◐ *province* C Kyrgyzstan
Naryn Zhotasy *see* Narymskiy Khrebet
130 J6 **Naryshkino** Orlovskaya Oblast', W Russian Federation
97 L14 **Nås** Kopparberg, C Sweden
94 G13 **Nasa** ▲ C Norway
95 H16 **Näsåker** Västernorrland, C Sweden
197 J14 **Nasau** Koro, C Fiji
118 I9 **Năsăud** *Ger.* Nussdorf, *Hung.* Naszód. Bistriţa-Năsăud, N Romania
105 P13 **Nasbinals** Lozère, S France
Na Sceirí *see* Skerries
Nase *see* Naze
xxxix O11 **Naseby** Northamptonshire, C England, UK
193 E22 **Naseby** Otago, South Island, NZ
149 R10 **Nāşerīyeh** Kermān, C Iran
27 X5 **Nash** Texas, SW USA
160 E13 **Nāshik** *prev.* Nāsik. Mahārāshtra, W India
58 E7 **Nashiño, Río** ≈ Ecuador/Peru
31 W12 **Nashua** Iowa, C USA
35 W7 **Nashua** Montana, NW USA
21 O10 **Nashua** New Hampshire, NE USA
29 S13 **Nashville** Arkansas, C USA
25 U7 **Nashville** Georgia, SE USA
32 L16 **Nashville** Illinois, N USA
33 O14 **Nashville** Indiana, N USA
23 V9 **Nashville** North Carolina, SE USA
22 J8 **Nashville** *state capital* Tennessee, S USA
22 J9 **Nashville** ✈ Tennessee, S USA
66 H10 **Nashville Seamount** *undersea feature* NW Atlantic Ocean
114 H9 **Našice** Požega-Slavonija, NE Croatia
112 M11 **Nasielsk** Ciechanów, C Poland
95 K18 **Näsijärvi** ◎ SW Finland
Nāsik *see* Nāshik
82 G13 **Nasir** Upper Nile, SE Sudan
155 Q12 **Nasīrābād** Baluchistān, SW Pakistan
154 J15 **Nasīrābād** Baluchistān, SW Pakistan
Nasīrābād *see* Mymensingh
Nasir, Buhayrat/Nâşir, Buheiret *see* Nasser, Lake
Nāsiri *see* Ahvāz
Nasiriya *see* An Nāşirīyah
Nás na Ríogh *see* Naas
109 L23 **Naso** Sicilia, Italy, C Mediterranean Sea
Nasratabad *see* Zābol
8 J11 **Nass** ≈ British Columbia, SW Canada
79 V15 **Nassarawa** Plateau, C Nigeria
46 H2 **Nassau** ● (Bahamas) New Providence, N Bahamas
46 H2 **Nassau** ✈ New Providence, C Bahamas
202 J13 **Nassau** *island* N Cook Islands
25 W8 **Nassau Sound** *sound* Florida, SE USA
110 L7 **Nassereith** Tirol, W Austria
82 F5 **Nasser, Lake** *var.* Buhayrat Nasir, Buḩayrat Nāşir, Buḩeiret Nâşir. ◎ Egypt/Sudan
97 L19 **Nässjö** Jönköping, S Sweden
101 K22 **Nassogne** Luxembourg, SE Belgium
10 J6 **Nastapoka Islands** *island group* Northwest Territories, C Canada
95 M19 **Nastola** Häme, S Finland
171 L14 **Nasu-dake** ▲ Honshū, S Japan
179 P11 **Nasugbu** Luzon, N Philippines
96 N11 **Näsviken** Gävleborg, C Sweden
Naszód *see* Năsăud
85 I17 **Nata** Central, NE Botswana
56 E11 **Natagaima** Tolima, C Colombia
61 Q14 **Natal** Rio Grande do Norte, E Brazil
173 Ff8 **Natal** Sumatera, N Indonesia
Natal *see* KwaZulu/Natal
181 L10 **Natal Basin** *var.* Mozambique Basin. *undersea feature* W Indian Ocean
27 R12 **Natalia** Texas, SW USA
69 W15 **Natal Valley** *undersea feature* SW Indian Ocean
Natanya *see* Netanya
149 O7 **Naţanz** Eşfahān, C Iran
11 Q11 **Natashquan** Québec, E Canada
11 Q10 **Natashquan** ≈ Newfoundland and Labrador/Québec, E Canada
24 J7 **Natchez** Mississippi, S USA
24 G6 **Natchitoches** Louisiana, S USA
110 E10 **Naters** Valais, S Switzerland
Nathanya *see* Netanya
94 O3 **Nathorst Land** *physical region* W Svalbard
Nathula *see* Nacula
194 J15 **National Capital District** ◐ *province* S PNG
37 U17 **National City** California, W USA
192 M10 **National Park** Manawatu-Wanganui, North Island, NZ
79 R14 **Natitingou** NW Benin
42 B5 **Natividad, Isla** *island* W Mexico
xli N11 **Natland** Cumbria, NW England, UK
Natore *see* Nator
171 M13 **Natori** Miyagi, Honshū, C Japan
20 C14 **Natrona Heights** Pennsylvania, NE USA
83 H20 **Natron, Lake** ◎ Kenya/Tanzania
177 Ff7 **Nattalin** Pegu, C Burma
94 J12 **Nattavaara** Norrbotten, N Sweden
111 S3 **Natternbach** Oberösterreich, N Austria
97 M22 **Nättraby** Blekinge, S Sweden
174 K4 **Natuna Besar, Pulau** *island* Kepulauan Natuna, W Indonesia
Natuna Islands *see* Natuna, Kepulauan
174 Jj5 **Natuna, Kepulauan** *var.* Natuna Islands. *island group* W Indonesia
174 J6 **Natuna, Laut** *sea* W Indonesia
Natur *see* Nator
23 N6 **Natural Bridge** *tourist site* Kentucky, C USA
181 V11 **Naturaliste Fracture Zone** *tectonic feature* E Indian Ocean
182 J10 **Naturaliste Plateau** *undersea feature* E Indian Ocean
Nau *see* Nov
105 O14 **Naucelle** Aveyron, S France
85 D20 **Nauchas** Hardap, C Namibia
110 K9 **Nauders** Tirol, W Austria
Naugard *see* Nowogard
120 F12 **Naujamiestis** Panevėžys, C Lithuania
120 E10 **Naujoji Akmenė** Akmenė, NW Lithuania
155 R16 **Naukot** *var.* Naokot. Sind, SE Pakistan
103 L16 **Naumburg** *var.* Naumburg an der Saale. Sachsen-Anhalt, C Germany
Naumburg am Queis *see* Nowogrodziec
Naumburg an der Saale *see* Naumburg
203 W15 **Naunau** *ancient monument* Easter Island, Chile, E Pacific Ocean
144 G10 **Nā'ūr** 'Ammān, W Jordan
201 Q8 **Nauru** *off.* Republic of Nauru; *prev.* Pleasant Island. ◆ *republic* W Pacific Ocean
183 P5 **Nauru** *island* W Pacific Ocean
201 Q9 **Nauru International** ✈ S Nauru
Nausari *see* Navsāri
21 Q12 **Nauset Beach** *beach* Massachusetts, NE USA
Naushahra *see* Nowshera
155 P14 **Naushahro Fīroz** Sind, SE Pakistan
Naushara *see* Nowshera
197 I14 **Nausori** Viti Levu, W Fiji
58 F9 **Nauta** Loreto, N Peru
159 O12 **Nautanwa** Uttar Pradesh, N India
43 R13 **Nautla** Veracruz-Llave, E Mexico
Nauzad *see* Now Zād
43 N6 **Nava** Coahuila de Zaragoza, NE Mexico
Navabad *see* Navobod
106 L6 **Nava del Rey** Castilla-León, N Spain
159 S15 **Navadwīp** *prev.* Nabadwip. West Bengal, NE India
197 J14 **Navaga** Koro, W Fiji
106 M9 **Navahermosa** Castilla-La Mancha, C Spain
121 I16 **Navahrudak** *Pol.* Nowogródek, *Rus.* Novogrudok. Hrodzyenskaya Voblasts', W Belorussia
121 I16 **Navahrudskaye Wzvyshsha** ▲▲ W Belorussia
38 M8 **Navajo Mount** ▲ Utah, W USA
39 Q9 **Navajo Reservoir** ⊡ New Mexico, SW USA
179 Qq12 **Naval** Biliran Island, C Philippines
106 K9 **Navalmoral de la Mata** Extremadura, W Spain
106 K10 **Navalvillar de Pelea** Extremadura, W Spain
xliv K8 **Navan** *Ir.* An Uaimh. Meath, E Ireland
Navanagar *see* Jāmnagar
120 L12 **Navapolatsk** *Rus.* Novopolotsk. Vitsyebskaya Voblasts', N Belorussia
155 P6 **Nāvar, Dasht-e** *Pash.* Dasht-i-Nawar. *desert* C Afghanistan
127 Q5 **Navarin, Mys** *headland* NE Russian Federation
65 I25 **Navarino, Isla** *island* S Chile
107 Q4 **Navarra** *Eng./Fr.* Navarre. ◐ *autonomous community* N Spain
Navarre *see* Navarra
107 P4 **Navarrete** La Rioja, N Spain
63 C20 **Navarro** Buenos Aires, E Argentina
107 O12 **Navas de San Juan** Andalucía, S Spain
27 V10 **Navasota** Texas, SW USA
27 U9 **Navasota River** ≈ Texas, SW USA
46 I9 **Navassa Island** ◇ *US unincorporated territory* C West Indies
121 L19 **Navasyolki** *Rus.* Novosëlki. Homyel'skaya Voblasts', SE Belorussia
121 H17 **Navayel'nya** *Pol.* Nowojelnia, *Rus.* Novoyel'nya. Hrodzyenskaya Voblasts', W Belorussia
xxxix Q6 **Navenby** Lincolnshire, E England, UK
176 Yy11 **Naver** Nauru Jaya, E Indonesia
xlii J8 **Naver, Loch** ◎ NW Scotland, UK
120 H5 **Navesti** ≈ C Estonia
106 J2 **Navia** Asturias, N Spain
106 J2 **Navia** ≈ NW Spain
61 I21 **Naviraí** Mato Grosso do Sul, SW Brazil
197 G14 **Naviti** *island* Yasawa Group, NW Fiji
130 I6 **Navlya** Bryanskaya Oblast', W Russian Federation
197 J13 **Navoalevu** Vanua Levu, N Fiji
153 P12 **Navobod** *Rus.* Navabad, Novabad. C Tajikistan
153 P13 **Navobod** *Rus.* Navabad. W Tajikistan
Navoi *see* Nawoiy
Navoiyskaya Oblast' *see* Nawoiy Wiloyati
42 G7 **Navojoa** Sonora, NW Mexico
42 H9 **Navolat** *var.* Navolato. Sinaloa, C Mexico
Navolato *see* Navolat
197 C12 **Navonda** Ambae, C Vanuatu
Návpaktos *see* Náfpaktos
Návplion *see* Náfplio
79 P14 **Navrongo** N Ghana
160 D12 **Navsāri** *var.* Nausari. Gujarāt, W India
197 I15 **Navua** Viti Levu, W Fiji
144 H8 **Nawá** Dar'ā, S Syria
Nawabashah *see* Nawābshāh
159 S14 **Nawabganj** Rajshahi, NW Bangladesh
159 S14 **Nawābganj** Uttar Pradesh, N India
155 Q15 **Nawābshāh** *var.* Nawabashah. Sind, S Pakistan
159 P14 **Nawāda** Bihār, N India
158 H11 **Nawalgarh** Rājasthān, N India
Nawāl, Sabkhat an *see* Noual, Sebkhet en
Nawar, Dasht-i- *see* Nāvar, Dasht-e
178 Gg4 **Nawnghkio** *var.* Nawngkio. Shan State, C Burma
Nawngkio *see* Nawnghkio
152 M11 **Nawoiy** *Rus.* Navoi. Nawoiy Wiloyati, C Uzbekistan
152 K8 **Nawoiy Wiloyati** *Rus.* Navoiyskaya Oblast'. ◐ *province* N Uzbekistan
143 U13 **Naxçıvan** *Rus.* Nakhichevan'. SW Azerbaijan
166 I10 **Naxi** Sichuan, C China
117 K21 **Náxos** *var.* Naxos. Náxos, Kykládes, Greece, Aegean Sea
117 K21 **Náxos** *island* Kykládes, Greece, Aegean Sea
42 J11 **Nayarit** ◐ *state* C Mexico
197 K14 **Nayau** *island* Lau Group, E Fiji
149 S8 **Nāy Band** Khorāsān, E Iran
xxxix W14 **Nayland** Suffolk, E England, UK
172 Pp4 **Nayoro** Hokkaidō, NE Japan
106 F9 **Nazaré** *var.* Nazare. Leiria, C Portugal
26 M4 **Nazareth** Texas, SW USA
Nazareth *see* Nazerat
181 O8 **Nazareth Bank** *undersea feature* W Indian Ocean
126 Hh14 **Nazarovo** Krasnoyarskiy Kray, S Russian Federation
42 K9 **Nazas** Durango, C Mexico
59 F16 **Nazca** Ica, S Peru
1 L17 **Nazca Plate** *tectonic feature*
200 Oo11 **Nazca Ridge** *undersea feature* E Pacific Ocean
172 R13 **Naze** *var.* Nase. Kagoshima, Amami-ōshima, SW Japan
144 G9 **Nazerat** *Ar.* En Nazira, *Eng.* Nazareth. Northern, N Israel
143 R14 **Nazik Gölü** ◎ E Turkey
142 C15 **Nazilli** Aydın, SW Turkey
143 P14 **Nazimiye** Tunceli, E Turkey
126 Gg11 **Nazino** Tomskaya Oblast', C Russian Federation
Nazinon *see* Red Volta
8 L15 **Nazko** British Columbia, SW Canada
131 O16 **Nazran'** Ingushskaya Respublika, SW Russian Federation
82 J13 **Nazrēt** *var.* Adama, Hadama. C Ethiopia
Nazwāh *see* Nizwá
125 Ff13 **Nazyvayevsk** Omskaya Oblast', C Russian Federation
84 J13 **Nchanga** Copperbelt, C Zambia
84 J11 **Nchelenge** Luapula, N Zambia
Ncheu *see* Ntcheu
Ndaghamcha, Sebkra de *see* Te-n-Dghâmcha, Sebkhet
83 G21 **Ndala** Tabora, C Tanzania
84 B11 **N'Dalatando** *Port.* Salazar, Vila Salazar. Cuanza Norte, NW Angola
79 S14 **Ndali** C Benin
83 E18 **Ndeke** SW Uganda
80 J13 **Ndélé** Bamingui-Bangoran, N Central African Republic
81 E19 **Ndendé** Ngounié, S Gabon
81 E20 **Ndindi** Nyanga, S Gabon
80 G11 **Ndjamena** *var.* N'Djamena; *prev.* Fort-Lamy. ● (Chad) Chari-Baguirmi, W Chad
80 G11 **Ndjamena** ✈ Chari-Baguirmi, W Chad
81 D18 **Ndjolé** Moyen-Ogooué, W Gabon
84 J13 **Ndola** Copperbelt, C Zambia
Ndrhamcha, Sebkha de *see* Te-n-Dghâmcha, Sebkhet
81 L15 **Ndu** Haut-Zaïre, N Zaire
83 H21 **Nduguti** Singida, C Tanzania
195 X16 **Nduindui** Guadalcanal, C Solomon Islands
Nduke *see* Kolombangara
117 F16 **Néa Anchiálos** *var.* Nea Anhialos, Néa Ankhíalos. Thessalía, C Greece
Nea Anhialos/Néa Ankhíalos *see* Néa Anchiálos
117 H18 **Néa Artáki** Évvoia, C Greece
xliv K5 **Neagh, Lough** ◎ E Northern Ireland, UK
34 F7 **Neah Bay** Washington, NW USA
117 J22 **Nea Kaméni** *island* Kykládes, Greece, Aegean Sea
xliv E8 **Neale** Mayo, NW Ireland
189 O8 **Neale, Lake** ◎ Northern Territory, C Australia
190 G2 **Neales River** *seasonal river* South Australia
117 G14 **Néa Moudanía** *var.* Néa Moudhaniá. Kentrikí Makedonía, N Greece
Néa Moudhaniá *see* Néa Moudanía
118 K10 **Neamţ** ◐ *county* NE Romania
Neapel *see* Napoli
xlii I3 **Neap** Shetland Islands, NE Scotland, UK
117 D14 **Neápoli** *prev.* Neápolis. Dytikí Makedonía, N Greece
117 K25 **Neápoli** Kríti, Greece, E Mediterranean Sea
117 G22 **Neápoli** Pelopónnisos, S Greece
Neapolis *see* Napoli, Italy
Neapolis *see* Nablus, West Bank
Neápolis *see* Neápoli, Greece
40 D16 **Near Islands** *island group* Aleutian Islands, Alaska, USA
xxxvi A6 **Neasden** Brent, SE England, UK
xxxv H14 **Neath** Neath Port Talbot, S Wales, UK
xxxv H14 **Neath Port Talbot** ◐ *unitary authority* S Wales, UK
116 H13 **Néa Zíchni** *var.* Néa Zíkhni; *prev.* Néa Zíkhna. Kentrikí Makedonía, NE Greece
Néa Zíkhna/Néa Zíkhni *see* Néa Zíchni
44 C5 **Nebaj** Quiché, W Guatemala
79 P13 **Nebbou** S Burkina
152 B11 **Nebitdag** Balkanskiy Velayat, W Turkmenistan
56 M13 **Neblina, Pico da** ▲ NW Brazil
128 I13 **Nebolchi** Novgorodskaya Oblast', W Russian Federation
38 L4 **Nebo, Mount** ▲ Utah, W USA
30 L14 **Nebraska** *off.* State of Nebraska; also known as Blackwater State, Cornhusker State, Tree Planters State. ◐ *state* C USA
31 S16 **Nebraska City** Nebraska, C USA
109 K23 **Nebrodi, Monti** *var.* Monti Caronie. ▲▲ Sicilia, Italy, C Mediterranean Sea
8 L14 **Nechako** ≈ British Columbia, SW Canada
31 Q2 **Neche** North Dakota, N USA
27 V8 **Neches** Texas, SW USA
27 W8 **Neches River** ≈ Texas, SW USA
103 H20 **Neckar** ≈ SW Germany
103 H20 **Neckarsulm** Baden-Württemberg, SW Germany
199 K5 **Necker Island** *island* C British Virgin Islands
183 U3 **Necker Ridge** *undersea feature* N Pacific Ocean
63 D23 **Necochea** Buenos Aires, E Argentina
xxxix V7 **Necton** Norfolk, E England, UK
106 H2 **Neda** Galicia, NW Spain
117 E20 **Nédas** ≈ S Greece
27 Y11 **Nederland** Texas, SW USA
Nederland *see* Netherlands
100 K12 **Neder Rijn** *Eng.* Lower Rhine. ≈ C Netherlands
101 L16 **Nederweert** Limburg, SE Netherlands
97 G16 **Nedre Tokke** ◎ S Norway
Nedrigaylov *see* Nedryhayliv
119 S3 **Nedryhayliv** *Rus.* Nedrigaylov. Sums'ka Oblast', NE Ukraine
100 O11 **Neede** Gelderland, E Netherlands
xxxix W12 **Needham Market** Suffolk, E England, UK
35 T13 **Needle Mountain** ▲ Wyoming, C USA
37 Y14 **Needles** California, W USA
xxxvii O14 **Needles, The** *rocks* Isle of Wight, S England, UK
64 O7 **Ñeembucú** *off.* Departamento de Ñeembucú. ◐ *department* SW Paraguay
32 M7 **Neenah** Wisconsin, N USA
9 W16 **Neepawa** Manitoba, S Canada
101 K16 **Neerpelt** Limburg, NE Belgium
76 M6 **Nefta** ✈ W Tunisia
130 L15 **Neftegorsk** Krasnodarskiy Kray, SW Russian Federation
131 U3 **Neftekamsk** Respublika Bashkortostan, W Russian Federation
131 O14 **Neftekumsk** Stavropol'skiy Kray, SW Russian Federation
125 G11 **Nefteyugansk** Khanty-Mansiyskiy Avtonomnyy Okrug, C Russian Federation
Neftezavodsk *see* Seydi
xxxv E6 **Nefyn** Gwynedd, NW Wales, UK
84 C10 **Negage** *var.* N'Gage. Uíge, NW Angola
Negapatam/Negapattinam *see* Nāgappattinam
175 N16 **Negara** Bali, Indonesia
175 N10 **Negara** Borneo, C Indonesia
Negara Brunei Darussalam *see* Brunei
33 N4 **Negaunee** Michigan, N USA
83 J15 **Negēlē** *var.* Negelli, *It.* Neghelli. S Ethiopia
Negelli *see* Negēlē
Negeri Pahang Darul Makmur *see* Pahang
Negeri Selangor Darul Ehsan *see* Selangor
174 H5 **Negeri Sembilan** *var.* Negri Sembilan. ◐ *state* Peninsular Malaysia
94 P3 **Negerpynten** *headland* S Svalbard
Negev *see* HaNegev
Neghelli *see* Negēlē
118 I12 **Negoiu** *var.* Negoiul. ▲ S Romania
Negoiul *see* Negoiu
84 P13 **Negomane** *var.* Negomano. Cabo Delgado, N Mozambique
Negomano *see* Negomane
161 J25 **Negombo** Western Province, SW Sri Lanka
Negoreloye *see* Nyeharelaye
114 P12 **Negotin** Serbia, E Yugoslavia
115 P19 **Negotino** C FYR Macedonia
106 G3 **Negreira** Galicia, NW Spain
118 L10 **Negreşti** Vaslui, E Romania
Negreşti *see* Negreşti-Oaş
118 H8 **Negreşti-Oaş** *Hung.* Avasfelsőfalu; *prev.* Negreşti. Satu Mare, NE Romania
46 H12 **Negril** W Jamaica
Negri Sembilan *see* Negeri Sembilan
65 K15 **Negro, Río** ≈ E Argentina
64 N7 **Negro, Río** ≈ NE Argentina
59 N17 **Negro, Río** ≈ E Bolivia
64 O5 **Negro, Río** ≈ C Paraguay
50 F6 **Negro, Río** ≈ N South America
63 E18 **Negro, Río** ≈ Brazil/Uruguay
Negro, Río *see* Sico Tinto, Río, Honduras
Negro, Río *see* Chixoy, Río, Guatemala/Mexico
179 Q14 **Negros** *island* C Philippines
118 M15 **Negru Vodă** Constanţa, SE Romania
11 P13 **Neguac** New Brunswick, SE Canada
12 B7 **Negwazu, Lake** ◎ Ontario, S Canada
Négyfalu *see* Săcele
34 F10 **Nehalem** Oregon, NW USA
34 F10 **Nehalem River** ≈ Oregon, NW USA
Nehavend *see* Nahāvand
149 V9 **Nehbandān** Khorāsān, E Iran
169 V6 **Nehe** Heilongjiang, NE China
200 Ss12 **Neiafu** 'Uta Vava'u, N Tonga
47 N9 **Neiba** *var.* Neyba. SW Dominican Republic
Néid, Carn Uí *see* Mizen Head
94 M9 **Neiden** Finnmark, N Norway
Neidín *see* Kenmare
Néifinn *see* Nephin
105 S10 **Neige, Crêt de la** ▲ E France
181 O16 **Neiges, Piton des** ▲ C Réunion
13 R9 **Neiges, Rivière des** ≈ Québec, SE Canada
166 I10 **Neijiang** Sichuan, C China
32 K6 **Neillsville** Wisconsin, N USA
Nei Mongol Zizhiqu/Nei Mongol *see* Nei Mongol Zizhiqu
169 Q10 **Nei Mongol Gaoyuan** *plateau* NE China
169 O12 **Nei Mongol Zizhiqu** *var.* Nei Mongol, *Eng.* Inner Mongolia, Inner Mongolian Autonomous Region; *prev.* Nei Monggol Zizhiqu. ◐ *autonomous region* N China
167 O4 **Neiqiu** Hebei, E China
Neiriz *see* Neyrīz
103 Q16 **Neisse** *Cz.* Lužická Nisa, *Ger.* Lausitzer Neisse, *Pol.* Nisa, Nysa Łużycka. ≈ C Europe
Neisse *see* Nysa
56 E11 **Neiva** Huila, S Colombia
166 M7 **Neixiang** Henan, C China
Nejafabad *see* Najafābād
9 V9 **Nejanilini Lake** ◎ Manitoba, C Canada
Nejd *see* Najd
82 I13 **Nek'emtē** *var.* Lakemti, Nakamti. W Ethiopia
130 M9 **Nekhayevskiy** Volgogradskaya Oblast', SW Russian Federation
32 K7 **Nekoosa** Wisconsin, N USA
97 M24 **Neksø** Bornholm, E Denmark
117 C16 **Nekyomanteío** *ancient monument* Épeiros, W Greece
106 H7 **Nelas** Viseu, N Portugal
128 H16 **Nelidovo** Tverskaya Oblast', W Russian Federation
31 P13 **Neligh** Nebraska, C USA
127 N12 **Nel'kan** Khabarovskiy Kray, E Russian Federation
94 M10 **Nellim** *var.* Nellimö, *Lapp.* Njellim. Lappi, N Finland
Nellimö *see* Nellim
161 J18 **Nellore** Andhra Pradesh, E India
127 O16 **Nel'ma** Khabarovskiy Kray, SE Russian Federation
xli P14 **Nelson** Lancashire, NW England, UK
63 B17 **Nelson** Santa Fe, C Argentina
9 O17 **Nelson** British Columbia, SW Canada
193 I14 **Nelson** Nelson, South Island, NZ
31 P17 **Nelson** Nebraska, C USA
193 J14 **Nelson** ◐ *unitary authority* South Island, NZ
9 X12 **Nelson** ≈ Manitoba, C Canada
191 U8 **Nelson Bay** New South Wales, SE Australia
190 K13 **Nelson, Cape** *headland* Victoria, SE Australia
194 M15 **Nelson, Cape** *headland* S PNG
65 G23 **Nelson, Estrecho** *strait* SE Pacific Ocean
9 W12 **Nelson House** Manitoba, C Canada
32 J4 **Nelson Lake** ◎ Wisconsin, N USA
33 T14 **Nelsonville** Ohio, N USA
29 S2 **Nelsoon River** ≈ Iowa/Missouri, C USA
85 K21 **Nelspruit** Mpumalanga, NE South Africa
78 L10 **Néma** Hodh ech Chargui, SE Mauritania
120 D13 **Neman** *Ger.* Ragnit. Kaliningradskaya Oblast', W Russian Federation
86 I9 **Neman** *Bel.* Nyoman, *Ger.* Memel, *Lith.* Nemunas, *Pol.* Niemen, *Rus.* Neman. ≈ NE Europe
Nemausus *see* Nîmes
117 F19 **Neméa** Pelopónnisos, S Greece
Německý Brod *see* Havlíčkův Brod
12 D7 **Nemegosenda** ≈ Ontario, S Canada
12 D8 **Nemegosenda Lake** ◎ Ontario, S Canada
121 H14 **Nemencinė** Vilnius, SE Lithuania
Nemetocenna *see* Arras
Nemirov *see* Nemyriv
105 O6 **Nemours** Seine-et-Marne, N France
Nemunas *see* Neman
172 R7 **Nemuro** Hokkaidō, NE Japan
172 R7 **Nemuro-hantō** *peninsula* Hokkaidō, NE Japan
172 R6 **Nemuro-kaikyō** *strait* Japan/Russian Federation
172 R7 **Nemuro-wan** *bay* N Japan
118 H5 **Nemyriv** *Rus.* Nemirov. L'vivs'ka Oblast', NW Ukraine
119 N7 **Nemyriv** *Rus.* Nemirov. Vinnyts'ka Oblast', C Ukraine
xliv G10 **Nenagh** *Ir.* An tAonach. Tipperary, C Ireland
41 R9 **Nenana** Alaska, USA
41 R9 **Nenana River** ≈ Alaska, USA
195 W8 **Nendö** *var.* Swallow Island. *island* Santa Cruz Islands, E Solomon Islands
xxxix S9 **Nene** ≈ E England, UK
129 R4 **Nenetskiy Avtonomnyy Okrug** ◐ *autonomous district* NW Russian Federation
203 W11 **Nengonengo** *atoll* Îles Tuamotu, C French Polynesia
169 U6 **Nen Jiang** *var.* Nonni. ≈ NE China
169 V6 **Nenjiang** Heilongjiang, NE China
xli O7 **Nenthead** Cumbria, NW England, UK
201 P16 **Neoch** *atoll* Caroline Islands, C Micronesia
117 D18 **Neochóri** Dytikí Ellás, C Greece
29 Q7 **Neodesha** Kansas, C USA
31 S14 **Neola** Iowa, C USA
117 M19 **Néon Karlovási** *var.* Néon Karlovásion. Sámos, Dodekánisos, Greece, Aegean Sea
Néon Karlovásion *see* Néon Karlovási
117 E16 **Néon Monastíri** Thessalía, C Greece
29 R8 **Neosho** Missouri, C USA
29 Q7 **Neosho River** ≈ Kansas/Oklahoma, C USA
127 N17 **Nepa** ≈ C Russian Federation
159 N10 **Nepal** *off.* Kingdom of Nepal. ◆ *monarchy* S Asia
158 M11 **Nepalganj** Mid Western, SW Nepal
12 L13 **Nepean** Ontario, SE Canada
38 L4 **Nephi** Utah, W USA
xliv D6 **Nephin** *Ir.* Néifinn. ▲ W Ireland
69 T9 **Nepoko** ≈ NE Zaire
20 K15 **Neptune** New Jersey, NE USA
190 G10 **Neptune Islands** *island group* South Australia
109 I14 **Nera** *anc.* Nar. ≈ C Italy
104 L14 **Nérac** Lot-et-Garonne, SW France
113 D16 **Neratovice** *Ger.* Neratowitz. Středni Čechy, C Czech Republic
Neratowitz *see* Neratovice
126 L15 **Nercha** ≈ S Russian Federation
126 L15 **Nerchinsk** Chitinskaya Oblast', S Russian Federation
126 L16 **Nerchinskiy Zavod** Chitinskaya Oblast', S Russian Federation
128 M15 **Nerekhta** Kostromskaya Oblast', NW Russian Federation
120 H10 **Nereta** Aizkraukle, S Latvia
108 K13 **Nereto** Abruzzi, C Italy
115 H15 **Neretva** ≈ Bosnia and Herzegovina/Croatia
117 C17 **Nerikós** *ruins* Lefkáda, Iónioi Nísoi, Greece, C Mediterranean Sea
120 B12 **Neringa** *Ger.* Nidden; *prev.* Nida. Neringa, SW Lithuania
85 F15 **Neriquinha** Cuando Cubango, SE Angola
120 I13 **Neris** *Bel.* Viliya, *Pol.* Wilia; *prev. Pol.* Wilja. ≈ Belorussia/Lithuania
Neris *see* Viliya
107 N15 **Nerja** Andalucía, S Spain
128 L16 **Nerl'** ≈ W Russian Federation
176 Vv13 **Nerong, Selat** *strait* Kepulauan Kai, E Indonesia
107 P12 **Nerpio** Castilla-La Mancha, C Spain
106 J13 **Nerva** Andalucía, S Spain
126 Ll13 **Neryungri** Respublika Sakha (Yakutiya), NE Russian Federation
100 L4 **Nes** Friesland, N Netherlands
96 G13 **Nesbyen** Buskerud, S Norway
94 L2 **Neskaupstadhur** Austurland, E Iceland
94 F13 **Nesna** Nordland, C Norway
28 K5 **Ness City** Kansas, C USA
xxxviii Q6 **Nesscliffe** Shropshire, W England, UK
Nesselsdorf *see* Kopřivnice
110 H7 **Nesslau** Sankt Gallen, NE Switzerland
xlii I13 **Ness, Loch** ◎ N Scotland, UK
xli V9 **Ness Point** *headland* N England, UK
Nesterov *see* Zhovkva
xl B17 **Neston** Cheshire, W England, UK
116 I12 **Néstos** *Bul.* Mesta, *Turk.* Kara Su. ≈ Bulgaria/Greece *see also* Mesta
97 C14 **Nesttun** Hordaland, S Norway
Nesvizh *see* Nyasvizh
144 F9 **Netanya** *var.* Natanya, Nathanya. Central, C Israel
xxxvii O11 **Netheravon** Wiltshire, S England, UK
100 I9 **Netherlands** *off.* Kingdom of the Netherlands, *var.* Holland, *Dut.* Koninkrijk der Nederlanden, Nederland. ◆ *monarchy* NW Europe
47 S9 **Netherlands Antilles** *prev.* Dutch West Indies. ◐ *Dutch autonomous region* S Caribbean Sea
Netherlands East Indies *see* Indonesia
Netherlands Guiana *see* Surinam
Netherlands New Guinea *see* Irian Jaya
xxxix N6 **Nether Langwith** Nottinghamshire, C England, UK
xxxvi J11 **Nether Stowey** Somerset, SW England, UK
xli P4 **Netherton** Northumberland, N England, UK
xl K10 **Nether Wasdale** Cumbria, NW England, UK
xlii K13 **Nethy Bridge** Highland, NW Scotland, UK
118 L4 **Netishyn** Khmel'nyts'ka Oblast', W Ukraine
144 E11 **Netivot** Southern, S Israel
109 O21 **Neto** ≈ S Italy
16 N2 **Nettilling Lake** ◎ Baffin Island, Northwest Territories, N Canada
31 V3 **Nett Lake** ◎ Minnesota, N USA
xxxvii Q9 **Nettlebed** Oxfordshire, C England, UK
xxxix Q5 **Nettleham** Lincolnshire, E England, UK
109 I16 **Nettuno** Lazio, C Italy
Netum *see* Noto
43 U16 **Netzahualcóyotl, Presa** ⊡ SE Mexico
Netze *see* Noteć
Neu Amerika *see* Puławy
Neubetsche *see* Novi Bečej
Neubidschow *see* Nový Bydžov
Neubistritz *see* Nová Bystřice
102 N9 **Neubrandenburg** Mecklenburg-Vorpommern, NE Germany
103 K22 **Neuburg an der Donau** Bayern, S Germany
110 C8 **Neuchâtel** *Ger.* Neuenburg. Neuchâtel, W Switzerland
110 C8 **Neuchâtel** *Ger.* Neuenburg. ◐ *canton* W Switzerland
110 C8 **Neuchâtel, Lac de** *Ger.* Neuenburger See. ◎ W Switzerland
Neudorf *see* Spišská Nová Ves
102 L10 **Neue Elde** *canal* N Germany
Neuenburg *see* Neuchâtel
Neuenburg an der Elbe *see* Nymburk
Neuenburger See *see* Neuchâtel, Lac de
110 F7 **Neuenhof** Aargau, N Switzerland
102 H11 **Neuenland** ✈ (Bremen) Bremen, NW Germany
Neuenstadt *see* La Neuveville
103 C18 **Neuerburg** Rheinland-Pfalz, W Germany
101 K24 **Neufchâteau** Luxembourg, SE Belgium
105 S6 **Neufchâteau** Vosges, NE France
104 M3 **Neufchâtel-en-Bray** Seine-Maritime, N France
111 S3 **Neufelden** Oberösterreich, N Austria
Neugradisk *see* Nova Gradiška
Neuhaus *see* Jindřichův Hradec
Neuhäusel *see* Nové Zámky
110 G6 **Neuhausen** *var.* Neuhausen am Rheinfall. Schaffhausen, N Switzerland
Neuhausen am Rheinfall *see* Neuhausen
103 I17 **Neuhof** Hessen, C Germany
Neuhof *see* Zgierz
Neukuhren *see* Pionerskiy
Neu-Langenburg *see* Tukuyu
111 W4 **Neulengbach** Niederösterreich, NE Austria
115 G15 **Neum** S Bosnia and Herzegovina
Neumark *see* Nowy Targ, Nowy Sącz, Poland
Neumark *see* Nowe Miasto Lubawskie, Toruń, Poland
Neumarkt *see* Neumarkt im Hausruckkreis, Oberösterreich, Austria
Neumarkt *see* Neumarkt Am Wallersee, Salzburg, Austria
Neumarkt *see* Środa Śląska, Wrocław, Poland
Neumarkt *see* Târgu Secuiesc, Covasna, Romania
Neumarkt *see* Târgu Mureş, Mureş, Romania
111 Q5 **Neumarkt Am Wallersee** *var.* Neumarkt. Salzburg, NW Austria
111 R4 **Neumarkt im Hausruckkreis** *var.* Neumarkt. Oberösterreich, N Austria
103 L20 **Neumarkt in der Oberpfalz** Bayern, SE Germany
Neumarktl *see* Tržič
Neumoldowa *see* Moldova Nouă
102 J8 **Neumünster** Schleswig-Holstein, N Germany
111 X5 **Neunkirchen** *var.* Neunkirchen am Steinfeld. Niederösterreich, E Austria
103 E20 **Neunkirchen** Saarland, SW Germany
Neunkirchen am Steinfeld *see* Neunkirchen
Neuoderberg *see* Bohumín
65 I15 **Neuquén** Neuquén, SE Argentina
65 H14 **Neuquén** *off.* Provincia de Neuquén. ◐ *province* W Argentina
65 H14 **Neuquén, Río** ≈ W Argentina
Neurode *see* Nowa Ruda
102 N11 **Neuruppin** Brandenburg, NE Germany
Neusalz an der Oder *see* Nowa Sól
Neu Sandec/Neusandez *see* Nowy Sącz
103 K22 **Neusäss** Bayern, S Germany
Neusatz *see* Novi Sad
Neuschliss *see* Gherla
23 N8 **Neuse River** ≈ North Carolina, SE USA
111 Z5 **Neusiedl am See** Burgenland, E Austria
113 G22 **Neusiedler See** *Hung.* Fertő. ◎ Austria/Hungary
Neusohl *see* Banská Bystrica
103 D15 **Neuss** *anc.* Novaesium, Novesium. Nordrhein-Westfalen, W Germany
Neuss *see* Nyon
Neustadt *see* Neustadt an der Aisch, Bayern, Germany
Neustadt *see* Neustadt bei Coburg, Bayern, Germany
Neustadt *see* Prudnik, Opole, Poland
Neustadt *see* Baia Mare, Maramureş, Romania
102 I12 **Neustadt am Rübenberge** Niedersachsen, N Germany
103 J19 **Neustadt an der Aisch** *var.* Neustadt. Bayern, C Germany
Neustadt an der Haardt *see* Neustadt an der Weinstrasse
103 F20 **Neustadt an der Weinstrasse** *prev.* Neustadt an der Haardt, *hist.* Niewenstat, *anc.* Nova Civitas. Rheinland-Pfalz, SW Germany
103 K18 **Neustadt bei Coburg** *var.* Neustadt. Bayern, C Germany
Neustadt bei Pinne *see* Lwówek
Neustadt in Oberschlesien *see* Prudnik
Neustadtl *see* Novo Mesto
Neustadtl in Mähren *see* Nové Město na Moravě
Neustettin *see* Szczecinek
110 M8 **Neustift im Stubaital** *var.* Stubaital. Tirol, W Austria
102 N10 **Neustrelitz** Mecklenburg-Vorpommern, NE Germany
Neutitschein *see* Nový Jičín
Neutra *see* Nitra
103 J22 **Neu-Ulm** Bayern, S Germany
Neuveville *see* La Neuveville
105 N12 **Neuvic** Corrèze, C France
Neuwarp *see* Nowe Warpno
102 G9 **Neuwerk** *island* NW Germany
103 E17 **Neuwied** Rheinland-Pfalz, W Germany
Neuzen *see* Terneuzen
128 H12 **Neva** ≈ NW Russian Federation
31 V14 **Nevada** Iowa, C USA
29 R6 **Nevada** Missouri, C USA
37 R5 **Nevada** *off.* State of Nevada; also known as Battle Born State, Sagebrush State, Silver State. ◐ *state* W USA
37 P6 **Nevada City** California, W USA
128 G16 **Nevel'** Pskovskaya Oblast', W Russian Federation
127 Oo16 **Nevel'sk** Ostrov Sakhalin, Sakhalinskaya Oblast', SE Russian Federation
126 Ll14 **Never** Amurskaya Oblast', SE Russian Federation
131 Q6 **Neverkino** Penzenskaya Oblast', W Russian Federation
105 P9 **Nevers** *anc.* Noviodunum. Nièvre, C France
20 J12 **Neversink River** ≈ New York, NE USA
191 Q6 **Nevertire** New South Wales, SE Australia
115 H15 **Nevesinje** S Bosnia and Herzegovina
120 G12 **Nevėžis** ≈ C Lithuania
130 M14 **Nevinnomyssk** Stavropol'skiy Kray, SW Russian Federation
47 W10 **Nevis** *island* Saint Kitts and Nevis
xliii F14 **Nevis, Loch** *inlet* NW Scotland, UK
Nevoso, Monte *see* Snežnik
Nevrokop *see* Gotse Delchev
142 J14 **Nevşehir** *var.* Nevshehr. Nevşehir, C Turkey
142 J14 **Nevşehir** *var.* Nevshehr. ◐ *province* C Turkey
Nevshehr *see* Nevşehir
125 Ee11 **Nev'yansk** Sverdlovskaya Oblast', C Russian Federation
xliii L24 **New Abbey** Dumfries and Galloway, SW Scotland, UK
xlii P11 **New Aberdour** Aberdeenshire, NE Scotland, UK
83 J25 **Newala** Mtwara, SE Tanzania
33 P16 **New Albany** Indiana, N USA
24 M2 **New Albany** Mississippi, S USA
31 Y11 **New Albin** Iowa, C USA
xxxvii Q12 **New Alresford** Hampshire, S England, UK
57 U8 **New Amsterdam** E Guyana
191 Q4 **New Angledool** New South Wales, SE Australia
xlii O3 **Newark** Orkney Islands, N Scotland, UK
Newark *see* Newark-on-Trent
23 Y2 **Newark** Delaware, NE USA
20 K14 **Newark** New Jersey, NE USA
20 G10 **Newark** New York, NE USA
33 T13 **Newark** Ohio, N USA
37 W5 **Newark Lake** ◎ Nevada, W USA

◆ Country ● Country Capital ◇ Dependent Territory ○ Dependent Territory Capital ◐ Administrative Region ✈ International Airport ▲ Mountain ▲▲ Mountain Range Volcano ≈ River ◎ Lake ⊡ Reservoir

Newark-on-Trent – Niš

xxxix P7 Newark-on-Trent var. Newark. Nottinghamshire, C England, UK
24 M7 New Augusta Mississippi, S USA
21 P12 New Bedford Massachusetts, NE USA
34 G11 Newberg Oregon, NW USA
23 X10 New Bern North Carolina, SE USA
22 F8 Newbern Tennessee, S USA
33 P4 Newberry Michigan, N USA
23 Q12 Newberry South Carolina, SE USA
xli Q3 New Bewick Northumberland, N England, UK
xli P8 Newbiggin Durham, N England, UK
xli R5 Newbiggin-by-the-Sea Northumberland, N England, UK
xliii L21 Newbigging South Lanarkshire, C Scotland, UK
20 F15 New Bloomfield Pennsylvania, NE USA
xxxv F5 Newborough Isle of Anglesey, NW Wales, UK
27 X5 New Boston Texas, SW USA
27 S11 New Braunfels Texas, SW USA
33 Q13 New Bremen Ohio, N USA
xliv G8 Newbridge Galway, W Ireland
xxxv K14 Newbridge Caerphilly, S Wales, UK
Newbridge see Droichead Nua
xxxv I11 Newbridge on Wye Powys, C Wales, UK
xl B15 New Brighton Wirral, NW England, UK
20 B14 New Brighton Pennsylvania, NE USA
20 M12 New Britain Connecticut, NE USA
195 N13 New Britain island E PNG
199 Hh9 New Britain Trench undersea feature W Pacific Ocean
xli P6 Newbrough Northumberland, N England, UK
20 J15 New Brunswick New Jersey, NE USA
13 V8 New Brunswick Fr. Nouveau-Brunswick. ⬖ province SE Canada
xxxvii W10 New Buckenham Norfolk, E England, UK
xliv I3 New Buildings Londonderry, NW Northern Ireland, UK
xlii P13 Newburgh Aberdeenshire, NE Scotland, UK
xliii M18 Newburgh Fife, E Scotland, UK
20 K13 Newburgh New York, NE USA
xli U2 Newburn Newcastle upon Tyne, NE England, UK
xxxvii P10 Newbury Newbury, S England, UK
xxxvii P10 Newbury ⬖ unitary authority S England, UK
xxxvi G6 Newbury Park Redbridge, SE England, UK
21 P10 Newburyport Massachusetts, NE USA
79 T14 New Bussa Niger, W Nigeria
xl M11 Newby Bridge Cumbria, NW England, UK
xlii O11 New Byth Aberdeenshire, NE Scotland, UK
197 J4 New Caledonia var. Kanaky, Fr. Nouvelle-Calédonie. ◇ French overseas territory SW Pacific Ocean
197 H5 New Caledonia island SW Pacific Ocean
183 O10 New Caledonia Basin undersea feature W Pacific Ocean
191 T8 Newcastle New South Wales, SE Australia
11 O14 Newcastle New Brunswick, SE Canada
12 I15 Newcastle Ontario, SE Canada
85 K22 Newcastle KwaZulu/Natal, E South Africa
33 P13 New Castle Indiana, N USA
22 L5 New Castle Kentucky, S USA
29 N11 Newcastle Oklahoma, C USA
20 B13 New Castle Pennsylvania, NE USA
27 R6 Newcastle Texas, SW USA
38 J7 Newcastle Utah, W USA
23 S6 New Castle Virginia, NE USA
xlv L10 Newcastle Wicklow, E Ireland
xxxviii G11 Newcastle Shropshire, W England, UK
xliv L6 Newcastle Ir. An Caisleán Nua. Down, SE Northern Ireland, UK
xli V2 Newcastle ✕ NE England, UK
Newcastle see Newcastle upon Tyne
35 Z13 Newcastle Wyoming, C USA
47 W10 Newcastle ✕ Nevis, Saint Kitts and Nevis
xxxv E12 Newcastle Emlyn Carmarthenshire, S Wales, UK
xliii N23 Newcastleton The Borders, S Scotland, UK
xxxviii J7 Newcastle-under-Lyme Staffordshire, C England, UK
xli V2 Newcastle upon Tyne var. Newcastle; hist. Monkchester, Lat. Pons Aelii. Newcastle upon Tyne, NE England, UK
xli U2 Newcastle upon Tyne ⬖ unitary authority NE England, UK
189 Q4 Newcastle Waters Northern Territory, N Australia
xliv E12 Newcastle West Ir. An Caisleán Nua. Limerick, SW Ireland
xxxv K11 Newchurch Powys, C Wales, UK
Newchwang see Yingkou
20 K13 New City New York, NE USA
33 U13 Newcomerstown Ohio, N USA
xxxvi E8 New Cross Lewisham, SE England, UK
20 G15 New Cumberland Pennsylvania, NE USA
23 R1 New Cumberland West Virginia, NE USA
xliii J22 New Cumnock East Ayrshire, W Scotland, UK
xlii P12 New Deer Aberdeenshire, NE Scotland, UK
158 I10 New Delhi ● (India) Delhi, N India
9 O17 New Denver British Columbia, SW Canada
30 J9 Newell South Dakota, N USA
23 Q13 New Ellenton South Carolina, SE USA
24 J6 Newellton Louisiana, S USA
xxxvi G9 New Eltham Greenwich, SE England, UK
30 K6 New England North Dakota, N USA
21 P8 New England cultural region NE USA
New England of the West see Minnesota
191 U5 New England Range ▲ New South Wales, SE Australia
66 G9 New England Seamounts var. Bermuda-New England Seamount Arc. undersea feature W Atlantic Ocean
40 M14 Newenham, Cape headland Alaska, USA
xxxvi L7 Newent Gloucestershire, C England, UK
144 F11 Newé Zohar Southern, E Israel
20 D9 Newfane New York, NE USA
xxxvii O13 New Forest physical region S England, UK
16 S8 Newfoundland Fr. Terre-Neuve. island Newfoundland and Labrador, SE Canada
11 R9 Newfoundland and Labrador Fr. Terre Neuve. ⬖ province E Canada
67 J8 Newfoundland Basin undersea feature NW Atlantic Ocean
66 I8 Newfoundland Ridge undersea feature NW Atlantic Ocean
66 J8 Newfoundland Seamounts undersea feature N Sargasso Sea
20 G16 New Freedom Pennsylvania, NE USA
xliii J24 New Galloway Dumfries and Galloway, SW Scotland, UK
195 U14 New Georgia island New Georgia Islands, NW Solomon Islands
195 T15 New Georgia Islands island group NW Solomon Islands
195 U14 New Georgia Sound var. The Slot. sound E Solomon Sea
32 L9 New Glarus Wisconsin, N USA
11 Q15 New Glasgow Nova Scotia, SE Canada
New Goa see Panaji
xxxvi I17 New Grimsby Isles of Scilly, SW England, UK
194 D11 New Guinea Dut. Nieuw Guinea, Ind. Irian. island Indonesia/PNG
199 H9 New Guinea Trench undersea feature SW Pacific Ocean
34 I6 Newhalem Washington, NW USA
41 P13 Newhalen Alaska, USA
31 X13 Newhall Iowa, C USA
xxxiv L16 Newham ⬖ London borough SE England, UK
12 F16 New Hamburg Ontario, S Canada
21 N9 New Hampshire off. State of New Hampshire; also known as The Granite State. ⬖ state NE USA
31 W12 New Hampton Iowa, C USA
195 N9 New Hanover island NE PNG
20 M13 New Haven Connecticut, NE USA
33 Q12 New Haven Indiana, N USA
29 W5 New Haven Missouri, C USA
xxxvii V13 Newhaven East Sussex, SE England, UK
8 K13 New Hazelton British Columbia, SW Canada
New Hebrides see Vanuatu
183 P9 New Hebrides Trench undersea feature N Coral Sea
xxxix Q2 New Holland North Lincolnshire, N England, UK
20 H15 New Holland Pennsylvania, NE USA
24 I9 New Iberia Louisiana, S USA
xxxvii U12 Newick East Sussex, SE England, UK
195 N10 New Ireland ⬖ province NE PNG
195 P10 New Ireland island NE PNG
67 A24 New Island island W Falkland Islands
20 J15 New Jersey off. State of New Jersey; also known as The Garden State. ⬖ state NE USA
20 C14 New Kensington Pennsylvania, NE USA
23 W6 New Kent Virginia, NE USA
29 O8 Newkirk Oklahoma, C USA
23 U10 Newland North Carolina, SE USA
xlii P11 New Leeds Aberdeenshire, NE Scotland, UK
30 L6 New Leipzig North Dakota, N USA
12 H9 New Liskeard Ontario, S Canada
24 G7 Newllano Louisiana, S USA
21 N13 New London Connecticut, NE USA
31 Y15 New London Iowa, C USA
31 T8 New London Minnesota, N USA
29 V3 New London Missouri, C USA
32 M7 New London Wisconsin, N USA
xliii H25 New Luce Dumfries and Galloway, SW Scotland, UK
xxxvi L16 Newlyn Cornwall, SW England, UK
xxxvi C16 Newlyn East Cornwall, SW England, UK
xlii P13 Newmachar Aberdeenshire, NE Scotland, UK
29 Y8 New Madrid Missouri, C USA
xliii K20 Newmains North Lanarkshire, C Scotland, UK
188 J8 Newman Western Australia
204 M13 Newman Island island Antarctica
12 H15 Newmarket Ontario, S Canada
21 P10 Newmarket New Hampshire, NE USA
xliv E11 Newmarket-on-Fergus Clare, W Ireland
23 U4 New Market Virginia, NE USA
xliv E13 Newmarket Cork, S Ireland
xxxix U12 Newmarket Suffolk, E England, UK
xlii D8 Newmarket Western Isles, NW Scotland, UK
23 R2 New Martinsville West Virginia, NE USA
33 U14 New Matamoras Ohio, N USA
34 M12 New Meadows Idaho, NW USA
28 R12 New Mexico off. State of New Mexico; also known as Land of Enchantment, Sunshine State. ⬖ state SW USA
xlii M11 Newmill Moray, N Scotland, UK
xliii N22 Newmill The Borders, S Scotland, UK
xxxviii K5 New Mills Derbyshire, C England, UK
xl H16 New Mills Cheshire, C England, UK
xliii J21 Newmilns East Ayrshire, W Scotland, UK
xxxvii P13 New Milton Hampshire, S England, UK
155 V6 New Mīrpur var. Mīrpur. Sind, SE Pakistan
25 S4 Newnan Georgia, SE USA
xxxvi L8 Newnham Gloucestershire, C England, UK
191 P17 New Norfolk Tasmania, SE Australia
24 K9 New Orleans Louisiana, S USA
24 K9 New Orleans ✕ Louisiana, S USA
20 K12 New Paltz New York, NE USA
33 U12 New Philadelphia Ohio, N USA
xlii P11 New Pitsligo Aberdeenshire, NE Scotland, UK
192 K10 New Plymouth Taranaki, North Island, NZ
xliv D7 Newport Mayo, NW Ireland
xliv G11 Newport Tipperary, S Ireland
xxxvii V6 Newport Essex, SE England, UK
xxxvii Q14 Newport Isle of Wight, S England, UK
xxxviii I9 Newport Shropshire, W England, UK
xxxv K14 Newport Newport, SE Wales, UK
xxxv D12 Newport Pembrokeshire, SE Wales, UK
xxxv K15 Newport ⬖ unitary authority SE Wales, UK
29 W10 Newport Arkansas, C USA
33 N13 Newport Indiana, N USA
22 M3 Newport Kentucky, S USA
31 W9 Newport Minnesota, N USA
34 F12 Newport Oregon, NW USA
21 O13 Newport Rhode Island, NE USA
23 O9 Newport Tennessee, S USA
21 N6 Newport Vermont, NE USA
34 M7 Newport Washington, NW USA
xxxv D11 Newport Bay bay SW Wales, UK
23 X7 Newport News Virginia, NE USA
xliii N17 Newport-on-Tay Fife, E Scotland, UK
xxxvii R6 Newport Pagnell Milton Keynes, SE England, UK
25 U12 New Port Richey Florida, SE USA
xliv K4 Newport Trench Cookstown, C Northern Ireland, UK
31 V9 New Prague Minnesota, N USA
46 H3 New Providence island N Bahamas
xxxv F11 New Quay Ceredigion, SW Wales, UK
xxxv K10 New Radnor Powys, C Wales, UK
xxxvi B16 Newquay Cornwall, SW England, UK
31 V10 New Richland Minnesota, N USA
13 X7 New-Richmond Québec, SE Canada
33 R16 New Richmond Ohio, N USA
32 I5 New Richmond Wisconsin, N USA
44 G1 New River ≈ N Belize
57 T12 New River ≈ SE Guyana
23 R6 New River ≈ West Virginia, NE USA
44 G1 New River Lagoon ◎ N Belize
24 J8 New Roads Louisiana, S USA
20 L14 New Rochelle New York, NE USA
31 O4 New Rockford North Dakota, N USA
xxxvii Y12 New Romney Kent, SE England, UK
xliv J12 New Ross Ir. Ros Mhic Thriúin. Wexford, SE Ireland
xli U16 New Rossington Doncaster, N England, UK
xliv K6 Newry Ir. An tIúr. Newry and Mourne, SE Northern Ireland, UK
xliv K6 Newry and Mourne ⬖ district S Northern Ireland, UK
30 M5 New Salem North Dakota, N USA
New Sarum see Salisbury
xliii L17 New Scone Perth and Kinross, C Scotland, UK
xli R5 Newsham Northumberland, N England, UK
31 W14 New Sharon Iowa, C USA
New Siberian Islands see Novosibirskiye Ostrova
25 X11 New Smyrna Beach Florida, SE USA
191 O7 New South Wales ⬖ state SE Australia
41 O13 New Stuyahok Alaska, USA
23 N8 New Tazewell Tennessee, S USA
40 M12 Newtok Alaska, USA
xli O13 Newton Lancashire, NW England, UK
xliii G19 Newton Argyll and Bute, W Scotland, UK
25 S7 Newton Georgia, SE USA
31 W14 Newton Iowa, C USA
29 N6 Newton Kansas, C USA
21 O11 Newton Massachusetts, NE USA
24 M5 Newton Mississippi, S USA
20 J14 Newton New Jersey, NE USA
23 R9 Newton North Carolina, SE USA
27 Y9 Newton Texas, SW USA
xxxvi H15 Newton Abbot Devon, SW England, UK
xl L7 Newton Arlosh Cumbria, NW England, UK
xli R9 Newton Aycliffe Durham, N England, UK
xxxvi F16 Newton Ferrers Devon, SW England, UK
xlii B11 Newtonferry Western Isles, NW Scotland, UK
xxxix X10 Newton Flotman Norfolk, E England, UK
xli N16 Newton-le-Willows St Helens, NW England, UK
xliii J20 Newton Mearns East Renfrewshire, W Scotland, UK
xliii J14 Newtonmore Highland, NW Scotland, UK
xli T12 Newton-on-Ouse North Yorkshire, N England, UK
xli R4 Newton-on-the-Moor Northumberland, N England, UK
xxxix P5 Newton on Trent Lincolnshire, E England, UK
xliii I25 Newton Stewart Dumfries and Galloway, S Scotland, UK
94 O2 Newtontoppen ▲ C Svalbard
xxxv F12 Newton Tracey Devon, SW England, UK
30 K3 New Town North Dakota, N USA
xliv F12 Newtown Cork, S Ireland
xliv J10 Newtown Laois, C Ireland
xxxv J9 Newtown Powys, E Wales, UK
xliv L4 Newtownabbey Ir. Baile na Mainistreach. Newtownabbey, E Northern Ireland, UK
xliv L4 Newtownabbey ⬖ district E Northern Ireland, UK
xliv M4 Newtownards Ir. Baile Nua na hArda. Ards, SE Northern Ireland, UK
xliv M4 Newtownards ✕ Ards, E Northern Ireland, UK
xliv I6 Newtownbutler Fermanagh, SW Northern Ireland, UK
xliv H7 Newtown Forbes Longford, C Ireland
xliv K6 Newtownhamilton Newry and Mourne, S Northern Ireland, UK
xliii N21 Newtown St Boswells The Borders, S Scotland, UK
xliv I4 Newtownstewart Strabane, W Northern Ireland, UK
xliii M16 Newtyle Angus, E Scotland, UK
31 U10 New Ulm Minnesota, N USA
30 K10 New Underwood South Dakota, N USA
27 V10 New Waverly Texas, SW USA
20 K14 New York New York, NE USA
20 G10 New York ⬖ state NE USA
37 X13 New York Mountains ▲ California, W USA
192 K12 New Zealand abbrev. NZ. ◆ commonwealth republic SW Pacific Ocean
129 O15 Neya Kostromskaya Oblast', NW Russian Federation
Neyba see Neiba
xxxv C14 Neyland Pembrokeshire, SW Wales, UK
149 Q12 Neyrīz var. Neiriz, Niriz. Fārs, S Iran
149 T4 Neyshābūr var. Nishapur. Khorāsān, NE Iran
161 J21 Neyveli Tamil Nādu, SE India
Nezhin see Nizhyn
35 N10 Nezperce Idaho, NW USA
24 H8 Nezpique, Bayou ≈ Louisiana, S USA
176 W14 Ngabordamlu, Tanjung headland Pulau Trangan, SE Indonesia
79 Y13 Ngadda ≈ NE Nigeria
N'Gage see Negage
193 G16 Ngahere West Coast, South Island, NZ
79 Z12 Ngala Borno, NE Nigeria
85 G17 Ngamiland ⬖ district N Botswana
164 K16 Ngamring Xizang Zizhiqu, W China
83 K19 Ngangerabeli Plain plain SE Kenya
164 I14 Ngangla Ringco ◎ W China
164 G13 Nganglong Kangri ▲ W China
164 K15 Ngangzê Co ◎ W China
81 F14 Ngaoundéré var. N'Gaoundéré. Adamaoua, N Cameroon
83 E20 Ngara Kagera, NW Tanzania
196 F8 Ngardmau Bay bay Babeldaob, N Palau
196 F7 Ngaregur island Palau Islands, N Palau
192 L7 Ngaruawahia Waikato, North Island, NZ
192 N11 Ngaruroro ≈ North Island, NZ
202 I16 Ngatangiia Rarotonga, S Cook Islands
192 M6 Ngatea Waikato, North Island, NZ
177 F8 Ngathainggyaung Irrawaddy, SW Burma
Ngatik see Ngetik Atoll
Ngau see Gau
174 I15 Ngawi Jawa, S Indonesia
196 C7 Ngcheangel var. Kayangel Islands. island Palau Islands, N Palau
196 E10 Ngchemiangel Babeldaob, N Palau
196 C8 Ngeaur var. Angaur. island Palau Islands, S Palau
196 E10 Ngerkeai Babeldaob, N Palau
196 F9 Ngermechau Babeldaob, N Palau
196 C8 Ngeruktabel prev. Urukthapel. island Palau Islands, S Palau
196 F8 Ngetbong Babeldaob, N Palau
201 T17 Ngetik Atoll var. Ngatik; prev. Los Jardines. atoll Caroline Islands, E Micronesia
196 E10 Ngetkip Babeldaob, N Palau
Nggamea see Qamea
195 V15 Nggatokae island New Georgia Islands, NW Solomon Islands
85 C16 N'Giva var. Ondjiva, Port. Vila Pereira de Eça. Cunene, S Angola
81 G20 Ngo Plateaux, SE Congo
178 J7 Ngoc Lac Thanh Hoa, N Vietnam
81 G17 Ngoko ≈ Cameroon/Congo
176 W14 Ngoni, Tanjung headland Maluku, Kepulauan Aru, SE Indonesia
83 H19 Ngorengore Rift Valley, SW Kenya
165 Q11 Ngoring Hu ◎ C China
Ngorolaka see Banifing
83 H20 Ngorongoro Crater crater N Tanzania
81 D19 Ngounié off. Province de la Ngounié, var. La Ngounié. ⬖ province S Gabon
81 D19 Ngounié ≈ Congo/Gabon
80 H10 Ngoura var. NGoura. Chari-Baguirmi, W Chad
80 G10 Ngouri var. NGouri; prev. Fort-Millot. Lac, W Chad
79 Y10 Ngourti Diffa, E Niger
79 Y11 Nguigmi var. N'Guigmi. Diffa, SE Niger
Nguimbo see Lumbala N'Guimbo
196 F15 Ngulu Atoll atoll Caroline Islands, W Micronesia
197 C14 Nguna island C Vanuatu
N'Gunza see Sumbe
175 N16 Ngurah Rai ✕ (Bali) Bali, S Indonesia
79 W12 Nguru Yobe, NE Nigeria
Ngwaketze see Southern
85 I16 Ngweze ≈ S Zambia
85 M17 Nhamatanda Sofala, C Mozambique
60 G12 Nhamundá, Rio var. Jamundá, Yamundá. ≈ N Brazil
62 J7 Nhandeara São Paulo, S Brazil
N'Harea see Nharêa
84 D12 Nharêa var. N'Harea, Nhareia. Bié, W Angola
Nhareia see Nharêa
178 Kk13 Nha Trang Khanh Hoa, S Vietnam
190 L11 Nhill Victoria, SE Australia
85 L22 Nhlangano prev. Goedgegun. SW Swaziland
189 S1 Nhulunbuy Northern Territory, N Australia
79 N10 Niafounké Tombouctou, W Mali
33 N5 Niagara Wisconsin, N USA
12 H16 Niagara ≈ Ontario, S Canada
12 G15 Niagara Escarpment hill range Ontario, S Canada
12 H16 Niagara Falls Ontario, S Canada
20 D9 Niagara Falls New York, NE USA
16 Pp17 Niagara Falls waterfall Canada/USA
78 K12 Niagassola var. Nyagassola. Haute-Guinée, NE Guinea
79 R12 Niamey ● (Niger) Niamey, SW Niger
79 R12 Niamey ✕ Niamey, SW Niger
79 R14 Niamtougou N Togo
81 O16 Niangara Haut-Zaïre, NE Zaire
79 O10 Niangay, Lac ◎ E Mali
79 N14 Niangoloko SW Burkina
29 U6 Niangua River ≈ Missouri, C USA
81 O17 Nia-Nia Haut-Zaïre, NE Zaire
21 N13 Niantic Connecticut, NE USA
169 U7 Nianzishan Heilongjiang, NE China
173 F7 Nias, Pulau island W Indonesia
84 O13 Niassa off. Província do Niassa. ⬖ province N Mozambique
203 U10 Niau island Îles Tuamotu, C French Polynesia
97 G20 Nibe Nordjylland, N Denmark
201 Q8 Nibok N Nauru
120 C10 Nīca Liepāja, W Latvia
Nicaea see Nice
44 J9 Nicaragua off. Republic of Nicaragua. ◆ republic Central America
44 K11 Nicaragua, Lago de var. Cocibolca, Gran Lago, Eng. Lake Nicaragua. ◎ S Nicaragua
Nicaragua, Lake see Nicaragua, Lago de
66 D11 Nicaraguan Rise undersea feature NW Caribbean Sea
Nicaria see Ikaría
109 N21 Nicastro Calabria, SW Italy
105 V15 Nice It. Nizza; anc. Nicaea. Alpes-Maritimes, SE France
Nice see Côte d'Azur
Nicephorium see Ar Raqqah
10 M9 Nichicun, Lac ◎ Québec, E Canada
170 C17 Nichinan var. Nitinan. Miyazaki, Kyūshū, SW Japan
46 E4 Nicholas Channel channel N Cuba
Nicholas II Land see Severnaya Zemlya
155 U2 Nicholas Range Pash. Selseleh-ye Kūh-e Vākhān, Taj. Qatorkŭhi Vakhon. ▲ Afghanistan/Tajikistan
22 M6 Nicholasville Kentucky, S USA
46 G2 Nicholls Town Andros Island, NW Bahamas
23 U12 Nichols South Carolina, SE USA
57 U9 Nickerie ⬖ district NW Surinam
57 V9 Nickerie River ≈ NW Surinam
157 P22 Nicobar Islands island group India, E Indian Ocean
118 L9 Nicolae Bălcescu Botoșani, NE Romania
13 P11 Nicolet Québec, SE Canada
13 Q12 Nicolet ≈ Québec, SE Canada
33 Q4 Nicolet, Lake ◎ Michigan, N USA
31 U10 Nicollet Minnesota, N USA
63 F19 Nico Pérez Florida, S Uruguay
Nicopolis see Nikopol, Bulgaria
Nicopolis see Nikópoli, Greece
124 R12 Nicosia Gk. Lefkosía, Turk. Lefkoşa. ● (Cyprus) C Cyprus
109 K24 Nicosia Sicilia, Italy, C Mediterranean Sea
109 N22 Nicotera Calabria, SW Italy
44 K13 Nicoya Guanacaste, W Costa Rica
44 L14 Nicoya, Golfo de gulf W Costa Rica
44 L14 Nicoya, Península de peninsula NW Costa Rica
Nictheroy see Niterói
113 L15 Nida ≈ S Poland
Nida see Neringa
Nidaros see Trondheim
110 D8 Nidau Bern, W Switzerland
xli Q12 Nidd ≈ N England, UK
103 H17 Nidda ≈ W Germany
Nidden see Neringa
97 F17 Nidelva ≈ S Norway
126 J10 Nidym Evenkiyskiy Avtonomnyy Okrug, N Russian Federation
112 L9 Nidzica Ger. Niedenburg. Olsztyn, N Poland
102 H6 Niebüll Schleswig-Holstein, N Germany
Niedenburg see Nidzica
101 N25 Niederanven Luxembourg, C Luxembourg
105 V4 Niederbronn-les-Bains Bas-Rhin, NE France
Niederdonau see Niederösterreich
111 S4 Niedere Tauern ▲ C Austria
103 P14 Niederlausitz Eng. Lower Lusatia. physical region E Germany
111 U5 Niederösterreich off. Land Niederösterreich, Eng. Lower Austria, Ger. Niederdonau; prev. Lower Danube. ⬖ state NE Austria
102 G12 Niedersachsen Eng. Lower Saxony, Fr. Basse-Saxe. ⬖ state NW Germany
81 D17 Niefang var. Sevilla de Niefang. NW Equatorial Guinea
85 G23 Niekerkshoop Northern Cape, W South Africa
101 G17 Niel Antwerpen, N Belgium
Niéllé see Niellé
78 M14 Niellé var. Niéllé. N Ivory Coast
81 O22 Niemba Shaba, E Zaire
113 G15 Niemcza Ger. Nimptsch. Wałbrzych, SW Poland
Niemen see Neman
94 J13 Niemisel Norrbotten, N Sweden
113 H15 Niemodlin Ger. Falkenberg. Opole, SW Poland
78 M13 Niéna Sikasso, SW Mali
102 H12 Nienburg Niedersachsen, N Germany
102 N13 Nieplitz ≈ NE Germany
113 L16 Niepołomice Kraków, S Poland
103 D14 Niers ≈ Germany/Netherlands
103 Q15 Niesky Lus. Niska. Sachsen, E Germany
Nieśwież see Nyasvizh
Nieuport see Nieuwpoort
100 O8 Nieuw-Amsterdam Drenthe, NE Netherlands
57 W9 Nieuw Amsterdam Commewijne, NE Surinam
101 M14 Nieuw-Bergen Limburg, SE Netherlands
100 O7 Nieuw-Buinen Drenthe, NE Netherlands
100 J12 Nieuwegein Utrecht, C Netherlands
100 P6 Nieuwe Pekela Groningen, NE Netherlands
100 P5 Nieuweschans Groningen, NE Netherlands
Nieuw Guinea see New Guinea
100 I11 Nieuwkoop Zuid-Holland, C Netherlands
100 M9 Nieuwleusen Overijssel, S Netherlands
100 J11 Nieuw-Loosdrecht Utrecht, C Netherlands
57 U9 Nieuw Nickerie Nickerie, NW Surinam
100 P5 Nieuwolda Groningen, NE Netherlands
101 B17 Nieuwpoort var. Nieuport. West-Vlaanderen, W Belgium
101 G14 Nieuw-Vossemeer Noord-Brabant, S Netherlands
100 P7 Nieuw-Weerdinge Drenthe, NE Netherlands
42 L10 Nieves Zacatecas, C Mexico
66 O11 Nieves, Pico de las ▲ Gran Canaria, Islas Canarias, Spain, NE Atlantic Ocean
105 P8 Nièvre ⬖ department C France
Niewenstat see Neustadt an der Weinstrasse
142 J15 Niğde Niğde, C Turkey
142 J15 Niğde ⬖ province C Turkey
85 J21 Nigel Gauteng, NE South Africa
79 V10 Niger off. Republic of Niger. ◆ republic W Africa
79 T14 Niger ⬖ state C Nigeria
69 P8 Niger ≈ W Africa
Niger Cone see Niger Fan
69 P9 Niger Delta delta S Nigeria
69 P9 Niger Fan var. Niger Cone. undersea feature E Atlantic Ocean
79 T13 Nigeria off. Federal Republic of Nigeria. ◆ federal republic W Africa
79 T17 Niger, Mouths of the delta S Nigeria
xlii K11 Nigg Highland, NW Scotland, UK
193 C24 Nightcaps Southland, South Island, NZ
12 F7 Night Hawk Lake ◎ Ontario, S Canada
67 M19 Nightingale Island island S Tristan da Cunha, S Atlantic Ocean
40 M12 Nightmute Alaska, USA
116 G13 Nigrita Kentrikí Makedonía, NE Greece
154 J15 Nihing Per. Rūd-e Nahang. ≈ Iran/Pakistan
203 V10 Nihiru atoll Îles Tuamotu, C French Polynesia
Nihommatsu see Nihonmatsu
Nihon see Japan
171 L13 Nihonmatsu var. Nihommatsu, Nihonmatu. Fukushima, Honshū, C Japan
Nihonmatu see Nihonmatsu
64 I12 Nihuil, Embalse del ⊠ W Argentina
171 K12 Niigata Niigata, Honshū, C Japan
171 K13 Niigata off. Niigata-ken. ⬖ prefecture Honshū, C Japan
170 F15 Niihama Ehime, Shikoku, SW Japan
40 A8 Niihau island Hawaii, USA, C Pacific Ocean
172 Ss13 Nii-jima island E Japan
170 Ff13 Niimi Okayama, Honshū, SW Japan
171 Kk13 Niitsu var. Niitu. Niigata, Honshū, C Japan
Niitu see Niitsu
107 P15 Níjar Andalucía, S Spain
100 K11 Nijkerk Gelderland, C Netherlands
101 H16 Nijlen Antwerpen, N Belgium
100 L13 Nijmegen Ger. Nimwegen; anc. Noviomagus. Gelderland, SE Netherlands
100 N10 Nijverdal Overijssel, E Netherlands
202 G16 Nikao Rarotonga, S Cook Islands
Nikaria see Ikaría
128 I2 Nikel' Murmanskaya Oblast', NW Russian Federation
175 Rr17 Nikiniki Timor, S Indonesia
133 Q15 Nikitin Seamount undersea feature E Indian Ocean
79 S14 Nikki E Benin
171 Kk15 Nikkō var. Nikko. Tochigi, Honshū, S Japan
Niklasmarkt see Gheorgheni
41 P10 Nikolai Alaska, USA
Nikolaiken see Mikołajki
Nikolainkaupunki see Vaasa
Nikolayev see Mykolayiv
151 U15 Nikolayevka Almaty, SE Kazakhstan
151 O6 Nikolayevka Severnyy Kazakhstan, N Kazakhstan
131 P9 Nikolayevsk Volgogradskaya Oblast', SW Russian Federation
Nikolayevskaya Oblast' see Mykolayivs'ka Oblast'
127 Nn14 Nikolayevsk-na-Amure Khabarovskiy Kray, SE Russian Federation
131 P6 Nikol'sk Penzenskaya Oblast', W Russian Federation
129 O13 Nikol'sk Vologodskaya Oblast', NW Russian Federation
Nikol'sk see Ussuriysk
40 K17 Nikolski Umnak Island, Alaska, USA
Nikol'skiy see Satpayev
131 V7 Nikol'skoye Orenburgskaya Oblast', W Russian Federation
Nikol'sk-Ussuriyskiy see Ussuriysk
116 J7 Nikopol anc. Nicopolis. Loveshka Oblast, N Bulgaria
119 S9 Nikopol' Dnipropetrovs'ka Oblast', SE Ukraine
117 C17 Nikópoli anc. Nicopolis. site of ancient city Ípeiros, W Greece
142 M12 Niksar Tokat, N Turkey
149 V14 Nīkshahr Sīstān va Balūchestān, SE Iran
115 J16 Nikšić Montenegro, SW Yugoslavia
203 R4 Nikumaroro prev. Gardner Island, Kemins Island. atoll Phoenix Islands, C Kiribati
203 P3 Nikunau var. Nukunau; prev. Byron Island. atoll Tungaru, W Kiribati
161 G21 Nilambūr Kerala, SW India
37 X16 Niland California, W USA
69 T3 Nile Ar. Nahr an Nīl. ≈ N Africa
82 G8 Nile former province NW Uganda
77 W7 Nile Delta delta N Egypt
69 T3 Nile Fan undersea feature E Mediterranean Sea
33 O11 Niles Michigan, N USA
33 V11 Niles Ohio, N USA
161 F20 Nileswaram Kerala, SW India
12 K10 Nilgaut, Lac ◎ Québec, SE Canada
164 I5 Nilka Xinjiang Uygur Zizhiqu, NW China
Nīl, Nahr an see Nile
95 N16 Nilsiä Kuopio, C Finland
160 F9 Nīmach Madhya Pradesh, C India
158 G14 Nimbāhera Rājasthān, N India
78 L15 Nimba, Monts var. Nimba Mountains. ▲ W Africa
Nimba Mountains see Nimba, Monts
Nimburg see Nymburk
105 Q15 Nîmes anc. Nemausus, Nismes. Gard, S France
158 H11 Nīm ka Thāna Rājasthān, N India
191 R11 Nimmitabel New South Wales, SE Australia
Nimptsch see Niemcza
205 R11 Nimrod Glacier glacier Antarctica
Nimroze see Nīmrūz
154 K8 Nīmrūz var. Nimroze; prev. Chakhānsūr. ⬖ province SW Afghanistan
83 F16 Nimule Eastern Equatoria, S Sudan
Nimwegen see Nijmegen
xli O7 Ninebanks Northumberland, N England, UK
161 C23 Nine Degree Channel channel India/Maldives
xliv I12 Ninemilehouse Tipperary, S Ireland
20 G9 Ninemile Point headland New York, NE USA
181 S8 Ninetyeast Ridge undersea feature E Indian Ocean
191 P13 Ninety Mile Beach beach Victoria, SE Australia
192 I2 Ninety Mile Beach beach North Island, NZ
23 P12 Ninety Six South Carolina, SE USA
xxxvii W13 Ninfield East Sussex, SE England, UK
169 Y9 Ning'an Heilongjiang, NE China
167 S9 Ningbo var. Ning-po, Yin-hsien; prev. Ninghsien. Zhejiang, SE China
167 U12 Ningde Fujian, SE China
167 P12 Ningdu Jiangxi, S China
194 E12 Ningerum Western, SW PNG
167 R9 Ningguo Anhui, E China
167 S9 Ninghai Zhejiang, SE China
Ning-hsia see Ningxia
Ninghsien see Ningbo
166 J15 Ningming Guangxi Zhuangzu Zizhiqu, S China
166 H11 Ningnan Sichuan, C China
Ning-po see Ningbo
Ningsia/Ningsia Hui/Ningsia Hui Autonomous Region see Ningxia
166 J5 Ningxia off. Ningxia Huizu Zizhiqu, var. Ning-hsia, Ningsia, Eng. Ningsia Hui, Ningsia Hui Autonomous Region. ⬖ autonomous region N China
165 X10 Ningxian Gansu, N China
178 Jj7 Ninh Binh Ninh Binh, N Vietnam
178 Kk13 Ninh Hoa Khanh Hoa, S Vietnam
194 H7 Ninigo Group island group N PNG
41 Q12 Ninilchik Alaska, USA
29 N7 Ninnescah River ≈ Kansas, C USA
205 U16 Ninnis Glacier glacier Antarctica
172 N10 Ninohe Iwate, Honshū, C Japan
101 F18 Ninove Oost-Vlaanderen, C Belgium
179 P11 Ninoy Aquino ✕ (Manila) Luzon, N Philippines
Nio see Íos
31 P12 Niobrara Nebraska, C USA
30 M12 Niobrara River ≈ Nebraska/Wyoming, C USA
81 I20 Nioki Bandundu, W Zaire
78 M11 Niono Ségou, C Mali
78 K11 Nioro var. Nioro du Sahel. Kayes, W Mali
78 G11 Nioro du Rip SW Senegal
Nioro du Sahel see Nioro
104 K10 Niort Deux-Sèvres, W France
180 H14 Nioumachoua Mohéli, S Comoros
194 G12 Nipa Southern Highlands, W PNG
9 U14 Nipawin Saskatchewan, S Canada
10 D12 Nipigon Ontario, S Canada
10 D11 Nipigon, Lake ◎ Ontario, S Canada
9 S13 Nipin ≈ Saskatchewan, C Canada
12 G11 Nipissing, Lake ◎ Ontario, S Canada
37 P13 Nipomo California, W USA
Nippon see Japan
146 K6 Niqniqīyah, Jabal an ▲ C Syria
64 I9 Niquivil San Juan, W Argentina
176 Yy10 Nirabotong Irian Jaya, E Indonesia
171 J16 Nirasaki Yamanashi, Honshū, S Japan
Niriz see Neyrīz
161 I14 Nirmal Andhra Pradesh, C India
159 Q13 Nirmāli Bihār, NE India
115 O14 Niš Eng. Nish, Ger. Nisch; anc. Naissus. Serbia, SE Yugoslavia

◆ Country ● Country Capital ◇ Dependent Territory ○ Dependent Territory Capital ⬖ Administrative Region ✕ International Airport ▲ Mountain ▲ Mountain Range Volcano ≈ River ◎ Lake ⊠ Reservoir

NISA – NORTH-WEST FRONTIER PROVINCE

106 H9 **Nisa** Portalegre, C Portugal
Nisa see Neisse
147 P4 **Nişab** Al Ḩudūd ash Shamālīyah, N Saudi Arabia
147 Q15 **Nişāb** var. Anşāb. SW Yemen
115 P14 **Nišava** Bul. Nishava. ≈ Bulgaria/Yugoslavia see also Nishava
109 K25 **Niscemi** Sicilia, Italy, C Mediterranean Sea
Nisch/Nish see Niš
172 Nn5 **Niseko** Hokkaidō, NE Japan
Nishapur see Neyshābūr
116 G9 **Nishava** var. Nišava. ≈ Bulgaria/Yugoslavia see also Nišava
120 L11 **Nishcha** Rus. Nishcha. ≈ N Belorussia
172 Qq7 **Nishibetsu-gawa** ≈ Hokkaidō, NE Japan
170 E13 **Nishi-gawa** ≈ Honshū, SW Japan
170 Ee13 **Nishi-Nōmi-jima** var. Nōmi-jima. island SW Japan
170 Bb17 **Nishinoomote** Kagoshima, Tanega-shima, SW Japan
172 Ss16 **Nishino-shima** Eng. Rosario. island Ogasawara-shotō, SE Japan
171 Hh16 **Nishio** var. Nisio. Aichi, Honshū, SW Japan
170 C13 **Nishi-Sonogi-hantō** peninsula Kyūshū, SW Japan
171 Gg14 **Nishiwaki** var. Nisiwaki. Hyōgo, Honshū, SW Japan
147 U14 **Nishtūn** SE Yemen
Nisiros see Nísyros
Nisiwaki see Nishiwaki
Niska see Niesky
115 O14 **Niška Banja** Serbia, SE Yugoslavia
10 D6 **Niskibi** ≈ Ontario, C Canada
113 O15 **Nisko** Tarnobrzeg, SE Poland
8 H7 **Nisling** ≈ Yukon Territory, W Canada
101 H22 **Nismes** Namur, S Belgium
Nismes see Nîmes
118 M10 **Nisporeni** Rus. Nisporeny. W Moldavia
Nisporeny see Nisporeni
97 K20 **Nissan** ≈ S Sweden
195 R11 **Nissan Island** island Green Islands, NE PNG
Nissan Islands see Green Islands
97 F16 **Nisser** ◎ S Norway
97 E21 **Nissum Bredning** inlet NW Denmark
31 U6 **Nisswa** Minnesota, N USA
Nistru see Dniester
117 M22 **Nísyros** var. Nisiros. island Dodekánisos, Greece, Aegean Sea
120 H8 **Nītaure** Cēsis, C Latvia
62 P10 **Niterói** prev. Nictheroy. Rio de Janeiro, SE Brazil
xliii K23 **Nith** ≈ S Scotland, UK
12 F16 **Nith** ≈ Ontario, S Canada
Nitinan see Nichinan
xxxvii P14 **Niton** Isle of Wight, S England, UK
113 I21 **Nitra** Ger. Neutra, Hung. Nyitra. Západné Slovensko, SW Slovakia
113 I20 **Nitra** Ger. Neutra, Hung. Nyitra. ≈ W Slovakia
23 Q5 **Nitro** West Virginia, NE USA
125 F11 **Nitsa** ≈ C Russian Federation
97 H14 **Nittedal** Akershus, S Norway
Niuatobutabu see Niuatoputapu
200 S11 **Niuatoputapu** var. Niuatobutabu; prev. Keppel Island. island N Tonga
200 Q15 **Niu'Aunofa** headland Tongatapu, S Tonga
Niuchwang see Yingkou
202 B16 **Niue** ◇ self-governing territory in free association with NZ S Pacific Ocean
202 F10 **Niulakita** var. Nurakita. atoll S Tuvalu
202 E6 **Niutao** atoll NW Tuvalu
95 L15 **Nivala** Oulu, C Finland
104 I15 **Nive** ≈ SW France
101 G19 **Nivelles** Walloon Brabant, C Belgium
105 P8 **Nivernais** cultural region C France
13 N8 **Niverville, Lac** ◎ Québec, SE Canada
29 T7 **Nixa** Missouri, C USA
37 R5 **Nixon** Nevada, W USA
27 S12 **Nixon** Texas, SW USA
Niya see Minfeng
152 K12 **Niyazov** Lebapskiy Velayat, NE Turkmenistan
161 H14 **Nizāmābād** Andhra Pradesh, C India
161 H15 **Nizām Sāgar** ◎ C India
129 N16 **Nizhegorodskaya Oblast'** ◈ province W Russian Federation
126 K14 **Nizhneangarsk** Respublika Buryatiya, S Russian Federation
Nizhnegorskiy see Nyzhn'ohirs'kyy
131 S4 **Nizhnekamsk** Respublika Tatarstan, W Russian Federation
131 U3 **Nizhnekamskoye Vodokhranilishche** ▣ W Russian Federation
127 O5 **Nizhnekolymsk** Respublika Sakha (Yakutiya), NE Russian Federation
127 N16 **Nizhne Leninskoye** Yevreyskaya Avtonomnaya Oblast', SE Russian Federation
126 Ii14 **Nizhneudinsk** Irkutskaya Oblast', S Russian Federation
126 Gg11 **Nizhnevartovsk** Khanty-Mansiyskiy Avtonomnyy Okrug, C Russian Federation
126 Ll6 **Nizhneyansk** Respublika Sakha (Yakutiya), NE Russian Federation
131 Q11 **Nizhniy Baskunchak** Astrakhanskaya Oblast', SW Russian Federation
126 M11 **Nizhniy Bestyakh** Respublika Sakha (Yakutiya), NE Russian Federation
131 O6 **Nizhniy Lomov** Penzenskaya Oblast', W Russian Federation
131 P3 **Nizhniy Novgorod** prev. Gor'kiy. Nizhegorodskaya Oblast', W Russian Federation
129 T8 **Nizhniy Odes** Respublika Komi, NW Russian Federation
Nizhniy Pyandzh see Panji Poyon
125 Ee11 **Nizhniy Tagil** Sverdlovskaya Oblast', C Russian Federation
129 T9 **Nizhnyaya-Omra** Respublika Komi, NW Russian Federation
129 P5 **Nizhnyaya Pesha** Nenetskiy Avtonomnyy Okrug, NW Russian Federation
125 F11 **Nizhnyaya Tavda** Tyumenskaya Oblast', C Russian Federation
126 Jj12 **Nizhnyaya Tunguska** Eng. Lower Tunguska. ≈ N Russian Federation
119 Q3 **Nizhyn** Rus. Nezhin. Chernihivs'ka Oblast', NE Ukraine
142 M17 **Nizip** Gaziantep, S Turkey
147 X8 **Nizwā** var. Nazwāh. NE Oman
Nizza see Nice
108 C9 **Nizza Monferrato** Piemonte, NE Italy
Njávdám see Näätämöjoki
Njellim see Nellim
83 H24 **Njombe** Iringa, S Tanzania
83 G23 **Njombe** ≈ C Tanzania
94 I10 **Njumis** ▲ N Norway
95 H17 **Njurunda** Västernorrland, C Sweden
96 N11 **Njutånger** Gävleborg, C Sweden
81 D14 **Nkambe** Nord-Ouest, NW Cameroon
Nkata Bay see Nkhata Bay
81 F21 **Nkayi** prev. Jacob. La Bouenza, S Congo
85 J17 **Nkayi** Matabeleland North, W Zimbabwe
84 N13 **Nkhata Bay** var. Nkata Bay. Northern, N Malawi
83 E22 **Nkonde** Kigoma, N Tanzania
81 D15 **Nkongsamba** var. N'Kongsamba. Littoral, W Cameroon
85 E16 **Nkurenkuru** Okavango, N Namibia
79 Q15 **Nkwanta** E Ghana
178 H1 **Nmai Hka** var. Me Hka. ≈ N Burma
Noardwâlde see Noordwolde
41 N7 **Noatak** Alaska, USA
41 N7 **Noatak River** ≈ Alaska, USA
xliv J7 **Nobber** Meath, E Ireland
Nobeji see Noheji
170 D15 **Nobeoka** Miyazaki, Kyūshū, SW Japan
29 N11 **Noble** Oklahoma, C USA
33 P13 **Noblesville** Indiana, N USA
172 O6 **Noboribetsu** var. Noboribetu. Hokkaidō, NE Japan
Noboribetu see Noboribetsu
61 H18 **Nobres** Mato Grosso, W Brazil
109 N21 **Nocera Terinese** Calabria, S Italy
43 Q16 **Nochixtlán** var. Asunción Nochixtlán. Oaxaca, SE Mexico
27 S5 **Nocona** Texas, SW USA
65 K21 **Nodales, Bahía de los** bay S Argentina
29 Q2 **Nodaway River** ≈ Iowa/Missouri, C USA
29 R8 **Noel** Missouri, C USA
97 C17 **Nærbø** Rogaland, S Norway
97 I24 **Næstved** Storstrøm, SE Denmark
42 H3 **Nogales** Chihuahua, NW Mexico
42 F3 **Nogales** Sonora, NW Mexico
38 M17 **Nogales** Arizona, SW USA
Nogal Valley see Dooxo Nugaaleed
104 K15 **Nogaro** Gers, S France
112 J7 **Nogat** ≈ N Poland
170 D12 **Nōgata** Fukuoka, Kyūshū, SW Japan
131 P15 **Nogayskaya Step'** steppe SW Russian Federation
104 M6 **Nogent-le-Rotrou** Eure-et-Loir, C France
105 O4 **Nogent-sur-Oise** Oise, N France
105 P6 **Nogent-sur-Seine** Aube, N France
126 I10 **Noginsk** Evenkiyskiy Avtonomnyy Okrug, N Russian Federation
130 L3 **Noginsk** Moskovskaya Oblast', W Russian Federation
127 O14 **Nogliki** Ostrov Sakhalin, Sakhalinskaya Oblast', SE Russian Federation
171 I14 **Nōgōhaku-san** ▲ Honshū, SW Japan
168 D5 **Nogoonnuur** Bayan-Ölgiy, NW Mongolia
63 C18 **Nogoyá** Entre Ríos, E Argentina
113 K21 **Nógrád** off. Nógrád Megye. ◈ county N Hungary
107 U5 **Noguera Pallaresa** ≈ NE Spain
107 U4 **Noguera Ribagorçana** ≈ NE Spain
172 N9 **Noheji** var. Nobeji. Aomori, Honshū, C Japan
103 E19 **Nohfelden** Saarland, SW Germany
40 A8 **Nohili Point** headland Kauai, Hawaii, USA, C Pacific Ocean
106 G3 **Noia** Galicia, NW Spain
105 N16 **Noire, Montagne** ⛰ S France
13 P12 **Noire, Rivière** ≈ Québec, SE Canada
12 J10 **Noire, Rivière** ≈ Québec, SE Canada
Noire, Rivière see Black River
104 G6 **Noires, Montagnes** ⛰ NW France
104 H8 **Noirmoutier-en-l'Île** Vendée, NW France
104 H8 **Noirmoutier, Île de** island NW France
171 Jj17 **Nojima-zaki** headland Honshū, S Japan
195 W8 **Noka** Nendö, E Solomon Islands
85 G17 **Nokaneng** Ngamiland, NW Botswana
95 L18 **Nokia** Häme, SW Finland
154 K11 **Nok Kundi** Baluchistān, SW Pakistan
32 L14 **Nokomis** Illinois, N USA
32 K5 **Nokomis, Lake** ▣ Wisconsin, N USA
80 G9 **Nokou** Kanem, W Chad
197 B12 **Nokuku** Espiritu Santo, W Vanuatu
97 J18 **Nol** Älvsborg, S Sweden
81 H16 **Nola** Sangha-Mbaéré, SW Central African Republic
27 P7 **Nolan** Texas, SW USA
129 R15 **Nolinsk** Kirovskaya Oblast', NW Russian Federation
xxxv C13 **Nolton** Pembrokeshire, SW Wales, UK
194 F12 **Nomad** Western, SW Papau New Guinea
170 B15 **Noma-zaki** headland Kyūshū, SW Japan
42 K10 **Nombre de Dios** Durango, C Mexico
44 I5 **Nombre de Dios, Cordillera** ⛰ N Honduras
40 M9 **Nome** Alaska, USA
31 Q6 **Nome** North Dakota, N USA
40 M9 **Nome, Cape** headland Alaska, USA
Nōmi-jima see Nishi-Nōmi-jima
12 M11 **Nominingue, Lac** ◎ Québec, SE Canada
Nomoi Islands see Mortlock Islands
170 Bb13 **Nomo-zaki** headland Kyūshū, SW Japan
200 S13 **Nomuka** island Nomuka Group, C Tonga
200 S14 **Nomuka Group** island group W Tonga
201 Q15 **Nomwin Atoll** atoll Hall Islands, C Micronesia
15 Ii8 **Nonacho Lake** ◎ Northwest Territories, NW Canada
Nondaburi see Nonthaburi
41 P12 **Nondalton** Alaska, USA
169 V10 **Nong'an** Jilin, NE China
178 I10 **Nong Bua Khok** Nakhon Ratchasima, C Thailand
178 I9 **Nong Bua Lamphu** Udon Thani, E Thailand
178 J7 **Nông Hèt** Xiangkhoang, N Laos
Nongkaya see Nong Khai
178 I8 **Nong Khai** var. Mi Chai, Nongkaya. Nong Khai, E Thailand
178 Gg15 **Nong Met** Surat Thani, SW Thailand
85 L22 **Nongoma** KwaZulu/Natal, E South Africa
178 Hh10 **Nong Phai** Phetchabun, C Thailand
159 U13 **Nongstoin** Meghālaya, NE India
85 C19 **Nonidas** Erongo, N Namibia
Nonni see Nen Jiang
42 I7 **Nonoava** Chihuahua, N Mexico
203 O3 **Nonouti** prev. Sydenham Island. atoll Tungaru, W Kiribati
178 Hh11 **Nonthaburi** var. Nondaburi, Nontha Buri. Nonthaburi, C Thailand
104 L11 **Nontron** Dordogne, SW France
189 P1 **Noonamah** Northern Territory, N Australia
30 K2 **Noonan** North Dakota, N USA
101 E14 **Noord-Beveland** var. North Beveland. island SW Netherlands
101 J14 **Noord-Brabant** Eng. North Brabant. ◈ province S Netherlands
100 H7 **Noorder Haaks** spit NW Netherlands
100 H9 **Noord-Holland** Eng. North Holland. ◈ province NW Netherlands
Noordhollandsch Kanaal see Noordhollands Kanaal
100 H8 **Noordhollands Kanaal** var. Noordhollandsch Kanaal. canal NW Netherlands
Noord-Kaap see Northern Cape
100 L8 **Noordoostpolder** island N Netherlands
47 P16 **Noordpunt** headland Curaçao, C Netherlands Antilles
100 I8 **Noord-Scharwoude** Noord-Holland, NW Netherlands
Noordwes see North-West
100 G11 **Noordwijk aan Zee** Zuid-Holland, W Netherlands
100 H11 **Noordwijkerhout** Zuid-Holland, W Netherlands
100 M7 **Noordwolde** Fris. Noardwâlde. Friesland, N Netherlands
Noordzee see North Sea
100 H10 **Noordzee-Kanaal** canal NW Netherlands
95 K18 **Noormarkku** Swe. Norrmark. Turku-Pori, SW Finland
41 N8 **Noorvik** Alaska, USA
8 J17 **Nootka Sound** inlet British Columbia, W Canada
84 A9 **Nóqui** Zaire, NW Angola
97 L15 **Nora** Örebro, C Sweden
153 Q13 **Norak** Rus. Nurek. W Tajikistan
16 P14 **Noranda** Québec, SE Canada
31 W12 **Nora Springs** Iowa, C USA
97 M14 **Norberg** Västmanland, C Sweden
12 K13 **Norcan Lake** ◎ Ontario, SE Canada
207 R12 **Nord** N Greenland
80 F13 **Nord** Eng. North. ◈ province N Cameroon
105 P2 **Nord** ◈ department N France
94 P1 **Nordaustlandet** island NE Svalbard
97 G24 **Nordborg** Ger. Nordburg. Sønderjylland, SW Denmark
Nordburg see Nordborg
97 F23 **Nordby** Ribe, W Denmark
9 P15 **Nordegg** Alberta, SW Canada
102 E9 **Norden** Niedersachsen, NW Germany
102 G10 **Nordenham** Niedersachsen, NW Germany
126 Ii4 **Nordenshel'da, Arkhipelag** island group N Russian Federation
94 O3 **Nordenskiold Land** physical region W Svalbard
102 E9 **Norderney** island NW Germany
102 J9 **Norderstedt** Schleswig-Holstein, N Germany
96 C11 **Nordfjord** physical region S Norway
96 D11 **Nordfjord** fjord S Norway
96 D11 **Nordfjordeid** Sogn og Fjordane, S Norway
94 G11 **Nordfold** Nordland, C Norway
Nordfriesische Inseln see North Frisian Islands
102 H7 **Nordfriesland** cultural region N Germany
103 K15 **Nordhausen** Thüringen, C Germany
27 T13 **Nordheim** Texas, SW USA
96 C13 **Nordhordland** physical region S Norway
102 E12 **Nordhorn** Niedersachsen, NW Germany
94 I1 **Nordhurfjördhur** Vestfirdhir, NW Iceland
94 J1 **Nordhurland Eystra** ◈ region N Iceland
94 I2 **Nordhurland Vestra** ◈ region N Iceland
180 H16 **Nord, Île du** island Inner Islands, NE Seychelles
97 F20 **Nordjylland** off. Nordjyllands Amt. ◈ county N Denmark
94 K7 **Nordkapp** Eng. North Cape. headland N Norway
94 O1 **Nordkapp** headland N Svalbard
94 L7 **Nordkinn** headland N Norway
81 N19 **Nord Kivu** off. Région du Nord Kivu. ◈ region E Zaire
94 G12 **Nordland** ◈ county C Norway
103 J21 **Nördlingen** Bayern, S Germany
95 I16 **Nordmaling** Västerbotten, N Sweden
97 K15 **Nordmark** Värmland, C Sweden
Nord, Mer du see North Sea
96 F8 **Nordmøre** physical region S Norway
102 I8 **Nord-Ostee-Kanal** canal N Germany
1 J3 **Nordostrundingen** headland NE Greenland
81 D14 **Nord-Ouest** Eng. North-West. ◈ province NW Cameroon
Nord-Ouest, Territoires du see Northwest Territories
105 N2 **Nord-Pas-de-Calais** ◈ region N France
103 F19 **Nordpfälzer Bergland** ⛰ W Germany
Nord, Pointe see Fatua, Pointe
197 H5 **Nord, Province** ◈ province C New Caledonia
94 J9 **Nordreisa** Troms, N Norway
103 D14 **Nordrhein-Westfalen** Eng. North Rhine-Westphalia, Fr. Rhénanie du Nord-Westphalie. ◈ state W Germany
Nordsee/Nordsjøen/Nordsøen see North Sea
102 H7 **Nordstrand** island N Germany
95 E15 **Nord-Trøndelag** ◈ county C Norway
xliv J12 **Nore** Ir. An Fheoir. ≈ S Ireland
xxxix V9 **Norfolk** ◈ county E England, UK
31 Q14 **Norfolk** Nebraska, C USA
23 X7 **Norfolk** Virginia, NE USA
199 Ii11 **Norfolk Island** ◇ Australian external territory SW Pacific Ocean
183 P9 **Norfolk Ridge** undersea feature W Pacific Ocean
29 U8 **Norfork Lake** ▣ Arkansas/Missouri, C USA
100 N6 **Norg** Drenthe, NE Netherlands
Norge see Norway
xli P1 **Norham** Northumberland, N England, UK
97 D14 **Norheimsund** Hordaland, S Norway
27 S16 **Norias** Texas, SW USA
171 J14 **Norikura-dake** ▲ Honshū, S Japan
126 I8 **Noril'sk** Taymyrskiy (Dolgano-Nenetskiy) Avtonomnyy Okrug, N Russian Federation
12 I13 **Norland** Ontario, SE Canada
23 V8 **Norlina** North Carolina, SE USA
32 L13 **Normal** Illinois, N USA
29 N11 **Norman** Oklahoma, C USA
Norman see Fort Norman
195 O16 **Normanby Island** island SE PNG
Normandes, Îles see Channel Islands
60 G9 **Normandia** Roraima, N Brazil
104 L5 **Normandie** Eng. Normandy. cultural region N France
104 J5 **Normandie, Collines de** hill range NW France
Normandy see Normandie
27 V9 **Normangee** Texas, SW USA
23 Q10 **Norman, Lake** ▣ North Carolina, SE USA
46 K13 **Norman Manley** ✈ (Kingston) E Jamaica
189 U5 **Norman River** ≈ Queensland, NE Australia
xxxviii M8 **Normanton** City of Derby, C England, UK
xli S14 **Normanton** Wakefield, N England, UK
189 U4 **Normanton** Queensland, NE Australia
15 Gg5 **Norman Wells** Northwest Territories, NW Canada
10 H12 **Normétal** Québec, S Canada
9 V15 **Norquay** Saskatchewan, S Canada
96 N11 **Norra Dellen** ◎ C Sweden
Norra Karelen see Pohjois-Karjala
95 G15 **Norråker** Jämtland, C Sweden
96 N12 **Norrala** Gävleborg, C Sweden
Norra Ny see Stöllet
94 G13 **Norra Storjfjället** ▲ N Sweden
94 I13 **Norrbotten** ◈ county N Sweden
Nørre Aaby see Nørre Åby
97 G23 **Nørre Åby** var. Nørre Aaby. Fyn, C Denmark
97 I24 **Nørre Alslev** Storstrøm, SE Denmark
97 E23 **Nørre Nebel** Ribe, W Denmark
97 G20 **Nørresundby** Nordjylland, N Denmark
23 N8 **Norris Lake** ▣ Tennessee, S USA
20 I15 **Norristown** Pennsylvania, NE USA
97 N17 **Norrköping** Östergötland, S Sweden
Norrmark see Noormarkku
96 N13 **Norrsundet** Gävleborg, C Sweden
97 P15 **Norrtälje** Stockholm, C Sweden
188 L12 **Norseman** Western Australia
95 I14 **Norsjö** Västerbotten, N Sweden
97 G16 **Norsjø** ◎ S Norway
126 Mm15 **Norsk** Amurskaya Oblast', SE Russian Federation
Norske Havet see Norwegian Sea
197 C13 **Norsup** Malekula, C Vanuatu
203 V15 **Norte, Cabo** headland Easter Island, Chile, E Pacific Ocean
56 F7 **Norte de Santander** off. Departamento de Norte de Santander. ◈ province N Colombia
63 E21 **Norte, Punta** headland E Argentina
23 R13 **North** South Carolina, SE USA
North see Nord
20 L10 **North Adams** Massachusetts, NE USA
115 L17 **North Albanian Alps** Alb. Bjeshkët e Namuna, SCr. Prokletije. ⛰ Albania/Yugoslavia
xli S10 **Northallerton** North Yorkshire, N England, UK
188 J12 **Northam** Western Australia
85 J20 **Northam** Northern, N South Africa
1 **North America** continent
1 N12 **North American Basin** undersea feature W Sargasso Sea
1 C5 **North American Plate** tectonic feature
20 M11 **North Amherst** Massachusetts, NE USA
xxxix O12 **Northampton** Northamptonshire, C England, UK
xxxix O11 **Northamptonshire** ◈ county C England, UK
157 P18 **North Andaman** island Andaman Islands, India, NE Indian Ocean
67 D25 **North Arm** East Falkland, Falkland Islands
23 Q13 **North Augusta** South Carolina, SE USA
181 W8 **North Australian Basin** Fr. Bassin Nord de l' Australie. undersea feature E Indian Ocean
xliii G21 **North Ayrshire** ◈ unitary authority W Scotland, UK
xliii G16 **North Ballachulish** Highland, NW Scotland, UK
33 R11 **North Baltimore** Ohio, N USA
9 T15 **North Battleford** Saskatchewan, S Canada
12 H11 **North Bay** Ontario, S Canada
10 H6 **North Belcher Islands** island group Belcher Islands, Northwest Territories, C Canada
31 R15 **North Bend** Nebraska, C USA
34 E14 **North Bend** Oregon, NW USA
xliii N19 **North Berwick** East Lothian, SE Scotland, UK
North Beveland see Noord-Beveland
North Borneo see Sabah
191 P5 **North Bourke** New South Wales, SE Australia
North Brabant see Noord-Brabant
190 F2 **North Branch Neales** seasonal river South Australia
xxxvi F14 **North Brentor** Devon, SW England, UK
46 M6 **North Caicos** island NW Turks and Caicos Islands
28 L10 **North Canadian River** ≈ Oklahoma, C USA
33 U12 **North Canton** Ohio, N USA
11 R13 **North, Cape** headland Cape Breton Island, Nova Scotia, SE Canada
192 I1 **North Cape** headland North Island, NZ
195 N9 **North Cape** headland New Ireland, NE PNG
North Cape see Nordkapp
20 J17 **North Cape May** New Jersey, NE USA
10 C9 **North Caribou Lake** ◎ Ontario, C Canada
23 U10 **North Carolina** off. State of North Carolina; also known as Old North State, Tar Heel State, Turpentine State. ◈ state SE USA
xli V14 **North Cave** East Riding of Yorkshire, N England, UK
North Celebes see Sulawesi Utara
161 J24 **North Central Province** ◈ province N Sri Lanka
99 G14 **North Channel** strait Northern Ireland/Scotland, UK
33 S4 **North Channel** lake channel Canada/USA
xxxvii S12 **Northchapel** West Sussex, SE England, UK
23 S14 **North Charleston** South Carolina, SE USA
xli R3 **North Charlton** Northumberland, N England, UK
33 N10 **North Chicago** Illinois, N USA
205 Y10 **Northcliffe Glacier** glacier Antarctica
33 Q14 **North College Hill** Ohio, N USA
27 O8 **North Concho River** ≈ Texas, SW USA
21 O8 **North Conway** New Hampshire, NE USA
xxxix V7 **North Creake** Norfolk, E England, UK
29 V14 **North Crossett** Arkansas, C USA
xxxvi J12 **North Curry** Somerset, SW England, UK
30 L4 **North Dakota** off. State of North Dakota; also known as Flickertail State, Peace Garden State, Sioux State. ◈ state N USA
xli V13 **North Dalton** East Riding of Yorkshire, N England, UK
North Devon Island see Devon Island
xliv M4 **North Down** ◈ district E Northern Ireland, UK
xxxvii U10 **North Downs** hill range SE England, UK
20 C11 **North East** Pennsylvania, NE USA
85 I18 **North East** ◈ district NE Botswana
67 G15 **North East Bay** bay Ascension Island, C Atlantic Ocean
40 L10 **Northeast Cape** headland Saint Lawrence Island, Alaska, USA
178 Mm13 **Northeast Cay** island NW Spratly Islands
83 J17 **North Eastern** ◈ province Kenya
North East Frontier Agency/North East Frontier Agency of Assam see Arunāchal Pradesh
67 E25 **North East Island** island E Falkland Islands
201 V11 **Northeast Island** island Chuuk, C Micronesia
xxxix R3 **North East Lincolnshire** ◈ unitary authority N England, UK
46 L12 **North East Point** headland E Jamaica
46 L6 **Northeast Point** headland Great Inagua, S Bahamas
46 K5 **Northeast Point** headland Acklins Island, SE Bahamas
203 Z2 **Northeast Point** headland Kiritimati, E Kiribati
46 H2 **Northeast Providence Channel** channel N Bahamas
103 J14 **Northeim** Niedersachsen, C Germany
xxxix V8 **North Elmham** Norfolk, E England, UK
31 X14 **North English** Iowa, C USA
144 G8 **Northern** ◈ district N Israel
84 M12 **Northern** ◈ region N Malawi
194 L15 **Northern** ◈ province S PNG
85 J20 **Northern** off. Northern Province; prev. Northern Transvaal. ◈ province NE South Africa
82 D7 **Northern** ◈ state N Sudan
84 K12 **Northern** ◈ province NE Zambia
82 B13 **Northern Bahr el Ghazal** ◈ state SW Sudan
Northern Border Region see Al Ḩudūd ash Shamālīyah
85 F24 **Northern Cape** off. Northern Cape Province, Afr. Noord-Kaap. ◈ province W South Africa
202 K14 **Northern Cook Islands** island group N Cook Islands
82 B8 **Northern Darfur** ◈ state NW Sudan
Northern Dvina see Severnaya Dvina
xliv I4 **Northern Ireland** var. The Six Counties. political division Northern Ireland, UK
82 D9 **Northern Kordofan** ◈ state C Sudan
197 K14 **Northern Lau Group** island group Lau Group, NE Fiji
196 K3 **Northern Mariana Islands** ◇ US commonwealth territory W Pacific Ocean
161 J23 **Northern Province** ◈ province N Sri Lanka
Northern Rhodesia see Zambia
Northern Sporades see Vóreioi Sporádes
190 D1 **Northern Territory** ◈ territory N Australia
Northern Transvaal see Northern
Northern Ural Hills see Severnyye Uvaly
xlii F10 **North Erradale** Highland, NW Scotland, UK
xliii N15 **North Esk** ≈ E Scotland, UK
86 I9 **North European Plain** plain N Europe
29 V2 **North Fabius River** ≈ Missouri, C USA
67 D24 **North Falkland Sound** sound N Falkland Islands
31 V9 **Northfield** Minnesota, N USA
21 O9 **Northfield** New Hampshire, NE USA
183 Q8 **North Fiji Basin** undersea feature N Coral Sea
xxxvii Z9 **North Foreland** headland SE England, UK
37 P6 **North Fork American River** ≈ California, W USA
41 R7 **North Fork Chandalar River** ≈ Alaska, USA
30 K7 **North Fork Grand River** ≈ North Dakota/South Dakota, N USA
23 O6 **North Fork Kentucky River** ≈ Kentucky, S USA
41 Q7 **North Fork Koyukuk River** ≈ Alaska, USA
41 Q10 **North Fork Kuskokwim River** ≈ Alaska, USA
28 K11 **North Fork Red River** ≈ Oklahoma/Texas, SW USA
28 K3 **North Fork Solomon River** ≈ Kansas, C USA
25 W14 **North Fort Myers** Florida, SE USA
33 P5 **North Fox Island** island Michigan, N USA
102 G6 **North Frisian Islands** var. Nordfriesische Inseln. island group N Germany
xli W13 **North Frodingham** East Riding of Yorkshire, N England, UK
207 N9 **North Geomagnetic Pole** pole Arctic Ocean
xli V12 **North Grimston** North Yorkshire, N England, UK
20 M13 **North Haven** Connecticut, NE USA
192 J5 **North Head** headland North Island, NZ
20 L6 **North Hero** Vermont, NE USA
37 O7 **North Highlands** California, W USA
xxxvi E15 **North Hill** Cornwall, SW England, UK
North Holland see Noord-Holland
83 I16 **North Horr** Eastern, N Kenya
157 K21 **North Huvadhu Atoll** var. Gaafu Alifu Atoll. atoll S Maldives
xxxvii W12 **Northiam** East Sussex, SE England, UK
67 A24 **North Island** island W Falkland Islands
192 N9 **North Island** island N NZ
23 U14 **North Island** island South Carolina, SE USA
33 O11 **North Judson** Indiana, N USA
North Kazakhstan see Severnyy Kazakhstan
xxxix Q4 **North Kelsey** Lincolnshire, E England, UK
xxxix O11 **North Kilworth** Leicestershire, C England, UK
33 V10 **North Kingsville** Ohio, N USA
169 Y13 **North Korea** off. Democratic People's Republic of Korea, Kor. Chosŏn-minjujuŭi-inmin-kanghwaguk. ◆ republic E Asia
xxxix R7 **North Kyme** Lincolnshire, E England, UK
159 X11 **North Lakhimpur** Assam, NE India
xliii J20 **North Lanarkshire** ◈ unitary authority C Scotland, UK
192 J3 **Northland** off. Northland Region. ◈ region North Island, NZ
199 J12 **Northland Plateau** undersea feature S Pacific Ocean
37 X11 **North Las Vegas** Nevada, W USA
xxxvii N7 **Northleach** Gloucestershire, C England, UK
xxxvi F14 **Northlew** Devon, SW England, UK
33 O11 **North Liberty** Indiana, N USA
31 X14 **North Liberty** Iowa, C USA
xxxix O3 **North Lincolnshire** ◈ unitary authority N England, UK
29 V12 **North Little Rock** Arkansas, C USA
30 M13 **North Loup River** ≈ Nebraska, C USA
xxxix P10 **North Luffenham** Rutland, C England, UK
157 K18 **North Maalhosmadulu Atoll** var. North Malosmadulu Atoll, Raa Atoll. atoll N Maldives
33 U10 **North Madison** Ohio, N USA
33 P12 **North Manchester** Indiana, N USA
33 P6 **North Manitou Island** island Michigan, N USA
31 U10 **North Mankato** Minnesota, N USA
xxxvii Q7 **North Marston** Buckinghamshire, C England, UK
25 Z15 **North Miami** Florida, SE USA
157 K18 **North Miladummadulu Atoll** atoll N Maldives
North Minch see Minch, The
xxxvi G12 **North Molton** Devon, SW England, UK
25 W15 **North Naples** Florida, SE USA
183 P8 **North New Hebrides Trench** undersea feature N Coral Sea
25 Y15 **North New River Canal** ≈ Florida, SE USA
xxxvi L8 **North Nibley** Gloucestershire, C England, UK
157 K20 **North Nilandhe Atoll** var. Faafu Atoll. atoll C Maldives
38 L2 **North Ogden** Utah, W USA
North Ossetia see Severnaya Osetiya, Respublika
37 S10 **North Palisade** ▲ California, W USA
201 U11 **North Pass** passage Chuuk Islands, C Micronesia
xxxvi J12 **North Petherton** Somerset, SW England, UK
30 M15 **North Platte** Nebraska, C USA
35 X17 **North Platte River** ≈ C USA
67 G14 **North Point** headland Ascension Island, C Atlantic Ocean
180 I16 **North Point** headland Mahé, NE Seychelles
33 S6 **North Point** headland Michigan, N USA
33 R5 **North Point** headland Michigan, N USA
41 S9 **North Pole** Alaska, USA
207 R9 **North Pole** pole Arctic Ocean
25 O4 **Northport** Alabama, S USA
25 W14 **North Port** Florida, SE USA
34 L6 **Northport** Washington, NW USA
34 L12 **North Powder** Oregon, NW USA
31 U13 **North Raccoon River** ≈ Iowa, C USA
North Rhine-Westphalia see Nordrhein-Westfalen
99 M16 **North Riding** cultural region N England, UK
98 G5 **North Rona** island NW Scotland, UK
xlii N2 **North Ronaldsay** island NE Scotland, UK
38 L2 **North Salt Lake** Utah, W USA
9 P15 **North Saskatchewan** ≈ Alberta/Saskatchewan, S Canada
xxxix P6 **North Scarle** Lincolnshire, E England, UK
37 X5 **North Schell Peak** ▲ Nevada, W USA
North Scotia Ridge see South Georgia Ridge
88 D10 **North Sea** Dan. Nordsøen, Dut. Noordzee, Fr. Mer du Nord, Ger. Nordsee, Nor. Nordsjøen; prev. German Ocean, Lat. Mare Germanicum. sea NW Europe
xli S6 **North Shields** North Tyneside, NE England, UK
37 T6 **North Shoshone Peak** ▲ Nevada, W USA
North Siberian Lowland/North Siberian Plain see Severo-Sibirskaya Nizmennost'
31 R13 **North Sioux City** South Dakota, N USA
xxxix S4 **North Somercotes** Lincolnshire, E England, UK
xliv C9 **North Sound** sound W Ireland
xlii N2 **North Sound, The** sound N Scotland, UK
xli P9 **North Stainmore** Cumbria, NW England, UK
191 T4 **North Star** New South Wales, SE Australia
North Star State see Minnesota
191 V3 **North Stradbroke Island** island Queensland, E Australia
North Sulawesi see Sulawesi Utara
North Sumatra see Sumatera Utara
xli R2 **North Sunderland** Northumberland, N England, UK
12 D17 **North Sydenham** ≈ Ontario, S Canada
20 H9 **North Syracuse** New York, NE USA
192 K9 **North Taranaki Bight** gulf North Island, NZ
202 I2 **North Tarawa** atoll Tungaru, W Kiribati
xxxvi G13 **North Tawton** Devon, SW England, UK
xxxix R4 **North Thoresby** Lincolnshire, E England, UK
xxxvii O11 **North Tidworth** Wiltshire, S England, UK
xlii E7 **North Tolsta** Western Isles, NW Scotland, UK
10 H9 **North Twin Island** island Northwest Territories, C Canada
xli O5 **North Tyne** ≈ N England, UK
xli S6 **North Tyneside** ◈ unitary authority NE England, UK
xlii A11 **North Uist** island NW Scotland, UK
xli O5 **Northumberland** ◈ county N England, UK
189 Y7 **Northumberland Isles** island group Queensland, NE Australia
11 Q14 **Northumberland Strait** strait SE Canada
34 G14 **North Umpqua River** ≈ Oregon, NW USA
47 Q13 **North Union** Saint Vincent, Saint Vincent and the Grenadines
8 L17 **North Vancouver** British Columbia, SW Canada
20 K9 **Northville** New York, NE USA
xxxix X8 **North Walsham** Norfolk, E England, UK
41 T10 **Northway** Alaska, USA
85 G21 **North-West** off. North-West Province, Afr. Noordwes. ◈ province N South Africa
North-West see Nord-Ouest
66 I6 **Northwest Atlantic Mid-Ocean Canyon** undersea feature N Atlantic Ocean
188 G8 **North West Cape** headland Western Australia
40 J9 **Northwest Cape** headland Saint Lawrence Island, Alaska, USA
84 H13 **North Western** ◈ province W Zambia
161 J24 **North Western Province** ◈ province W Sri Lanka
155 U4 **North-West Frontier Province** ◈ province NW Pakistan

◆ Country
● Country Capital
◇ Dependent Territory
○ Dependent Territory Capital
◈ Administrative Region
✈ International Airport
▲ Mountain
⛰ Mountain Range
Volcano
≈ River
◎ Lake
▣ Reservoir

◆ COUNTRY   ◇ DEPENDENT TERRITORY   ◆ ADMINISTRATIVE REGION   ▲ MOUNTAIN   ▼ VOLCANO   ⊚ LAKE
● COUNTRY CAPITAL   ○ DEPENDENT TERRITORY CAPITAL   ✕ INTERNATIONAL AIRPORT   ▲ MOUNTAIN RANGE   ✎ RIVER   ⊠ RESERVOIR

NYUYA – OLOVO

126 Kk12 **Nyuya** Respublika Sakha (Yakutiya), NE Russian Federation
126 K12 **Nyuya** ≈ NE Russian Federation
119 T10 **Nyzhni Sirohozy** Khersons'ka Oblast', S Ukraine
119 U12 **Nyzhn'ohirs'kyy** *Rus.* Nizhnegorskiy. Respublika Krym, S Ukraine
83 G21 **Nzega** Tabora, C Tanzania
78 K15 **Nzérékoré** Guinée-Forestière, SE Guinea
84 A10 **N'Zeto** *prev.* Ambrizete. Zaire, NW Angola
81 M24 **Nzilo, Lac** *prev.* Lac Delcommune. ⊡ SE Zaire

O

31 O11 **Oacoma** South Dakota, N USA
xxxix O10 **Oadby** Leicestershire, C England, UK
31 N9 **Oahe Dam** *dam* South Dakota, N USA
30 M9 **Oahe, Lake** ⊡ North Dakota/South Dakota, N USA
40 C9 **Oahu** *Haw.* O'ahu. *island* Hawaii, USA, C Pacific Ocean
172 Qq6 **O-Akan-dake** ▲ Hokkaidō, NE Japan
190 K8 **Oakbank** South Australia
21 P13 **Oak Bluffs** Martha's Vineyard, New York, NE USA
38 K4 **Oak City** Utah, W USA
39 R3 **Oak Creek** Colorado, C USA
37 P8 **Oakdale** California, W USA
24 H8 **Oakdale** Louisiana, S USA
xxxviii I9 **Oakengates** Shropshire, W England, UK
31 P7 **Oakes** North Dakota, N USA
xxxvi H12 **Oakford** Devon, SW England, UK
24 J4 **Oak Grove** Louisiana, S USA
xxxix P9 **Oakham** Rutland, C England, UK
34 H7 **Oak Harbor** Washington, NW USA
23 R5 **Oak Hill** West Virginia, NE USA
xxxix S12 **Oakington** Cambridgeshire, E England, UK
37 N8 **Oakland** California, W USA
31 T15 **Oakland** Iowa, C USA
21 Q7 **Oakland** Maine, NE USA
23 T3 **Oakland** Maryland, NE USA
31 R14 **Oakland** Nebraska, C USA
33 N11 **Oak Lawn** Illinois, N USA
xxxvii Q7 **Oakley** Buckinghamshire, C England, UK
xliii L19 **Oakley** Fife, E Scotland, UK
35 P16 **Oakley** Idaho, NW USA
28 I4 **Oakley** Kansas, C USA
33 N10 **Oak Park** Illinois, N USA
9 X16 **Oak Point** Manitoba, S Canada
34 G13 **Oakridge** Oregon, NW USA
22 M9 **Oak Ridge** Tennessee, S USA
192 K10 **Oakura** Taranaki, North Island, NZ
24 L7 **Oak Vale** Mississippi, S USA
12 G16 **Oakville** Ontario, S Canada
27 V8 **Oakwood** Texas, SW USA
193 F22 **Oamaru** Otago, South Island, NZ
xliii D21 **Oa, Mull of** *headland* W Scotland, UK
175 Q7 **Oan** Sulawesi, N Indonesia
193 J17 **Oaro** Canterbury, South Island, NZ
37 X2 **Oasis** Nevada, W USA
205 S15 **Oates Land** *physical region* Antarctica
191 P17 **Oatlands** Tasmania, SE Australia
38 I11 **Oatman** Arizona, SW USA
43 R16 **Oaxaca** *var.* Oaxaca de Juárez; *prev.* Antequera. Oaxaca, SE Mexico
43 Q16 **Oaxaca** ◐ *state* SE Mexico
Oaxaca de Juárez *see* Oaxaca
125 G8 **Ob'** ≈ C Russian Federation
12 G9 **Obabika Lake** ◎ Ontario, S Canada
Obagan *see* Ubagan
120 M12 **Obal'** *Rus.* Obol'. Vitsyebskaya Voblasts', N Belorussia
81 E16 **Obala** Centre, SW Cameroon
12 C6 **Oba Lake** ◎ Ontario, S Canada
171 H14 **Obama** Fukui, Honshū, SW Japan
xliii F17 **Oban** Argyll and Bute, W Scotland, UK
Oban *see* Halfmoon Bay
171 I(J)12 **Obanazawa** Yamagata, Honshū, C Japan
Obando *see* Puerto Inírida
106 J4 **O Barco** *var.* El Barco, El Barco de Valdeorras, O Barco de Valdeorras. Galicia, NW Spain
O Barco de Valdeorras *see* O Barco
Obbia *see* Hobyo
95 J16 **Obbola** Västerbotten, N Sweden
Obbrovazzo *see* Obrovac
Obchuga *see* Abchuha
Obdorsk *see* Salekhard
Óbecse *see* Bečej
120 I11 **Obeliai** Rokiškis, NE Lithuania
62 F13 **Oberá** Misiones, NE Argentina
110 E8 **Oberburg** Bern, W Switzerland
111 Q9 **Oberdrauburg** Salzburg, S Austria
Oberglogau *see* Głogówek
111 W4 **Ober Grafendorf** Niederösterreich, NE Austria
103 E15 **Oberhausen** Nordrhein-Westfalen, W Germany
Oberhollabrunn *see* Tulln
Oberlaibach *see* Vrhnika
103 Q15 **Oberlausitz** *physical region* E Germany
28 J2 **Oberlin** Kansas, C USA
24 H8 **Oberlin** Louisiana, S USA
33 T11 **Oberlin** Ohio, N USA
105 U5 **Obernai** Bas-Rhin, NE France
111 R4 **Obernberg am Inn** Oberösterreich, N Austria
Oberndorf *see* Oberndorf am Neckar
103 G23 **Oberndorf am Neckar** *var.* Oberndorf. Baden-Württemberg, SW Germany
111 Q5 **Oberndorf bei Salzburg** Salzburg, W Austria
Oberneustadtl *see* Kysucké Nové Mesto
191 S8 **Oberon** New South Wales, SE Australia
111 Q4 **Oberösterreich** *off.* Land Oberösterreich, *Eng.* Upper Austria. ◐ *state* NW Austria
Oberpahlen *see* Põltsamaa
103 M19 **Oberpfälzer Wald** ▲▲ SE Germany
111 Y6 **Oberpullendorf** Burgenland, E Austria
Oberradkersburg *see* Gornja Radgona
103 G18 **Oberursel** Hessen, W Germany
111 Q8 **Obervellach** Salzburg, S Austria
111 X7 **Oberwart** Burgenland, SE Austria
Oberwischau *see* Vişeu de Sus
111 T7 **Oberwölz** *var.* Oberwölz-Stadt. Steiermark, SE Austria
Oberwölz-Stadt *see* Oberwölz
33 S13 **Obetz** Ohio, N USA
Ob', Gulf of *see* Obskaya Guba
56 G8 **Obia** Santander, C Colombia
60 H12 **Óbidos** Pará, NE Brazil
106 F10 **Óbidos** Leiria, C Portugal
Obidovichi *see* Abidavichy
153 Q13 **Obigarm** W Tajikistan
172 P7 **Obihiro** Hokkaidō, NE Japan
Obi-Khingou *see* Khingov
153 P13 **Obikiik** SW Tajikistan
115 N16 **Obilić** Serbia, S Yugoslavia
131 O12 **Obil'noye** Respublika Kalmykiya, SW Russian Federation
22 F8 **Obion** Tennessee, S USA
22 F8 **Obion River** ≈ Tennessee, S USA
175 T9 **Obi, Pulau** *island* Maluku, E Indonesia
172 Oo4 **Obira** Hokkaidō, NE Japan
175 T9 **Obi, Selat** *strait* Maluku, E Indonesia
131 N11 **Oblivskaya** Rostovskaya Oblast', SW Russian Federation
127 N16 **Obluch'ye** Yevreyskaya Avtonomnaya Oblast', SE Russian Federation
130 K4 **Obninsk** Kaluzhskaya Oblast', W Russian Federation
116 J8 **Obnova** Loveshka Oblast, N Bulgaria
81 N15 **Obo** Haut-Mbomou, E Central African Republic
82 M11 **Obock** E Djibouti
Obol' *see* Obal'
Obolyanka *see* Abalyanka
176 Vv11 **Obome** Irian Jaya, E Indonesia
112 G11 **Oborniki** Poznań, W Poland
81 G19 **Obouya** Cuvette, C Congo
130 J8 **Oboyan'** Kurskaya Oblast', W Russian Federation
128 M9 **Obozerskiy** Arkhangel'skaya Oblast', NW Russian Federation
114 L11 **Obrenovac** Serbia, N Yugoslavia
114 D12 **Obrovac** *It.* Obbrovazzo. Zadar-Knin, W Croatia
Obrovo *see* Abrova
37 Q3 **Observation Peak** ▲ California, W USA
126 H7 **Obskaya Guba** *Eng.* Gulf of Ob'. *gulf* N Russian Federation
181 N13 **Ob' Tablemount** *undersea feature* S Indian Ocean
181 T10 **Ob' Trench** *undersea feature* E Indian Ocean
79 P16 **Obuasi** S Ghana
119 P5 **Obukhiv** *Rus.* Obukhov. Kyyivs'ka Oblast', N Ukraine
Obukhov *see* Obukhiv
129 U14 **Obva** ≈ NW Russian Federation
119 V10 **Obytichna Kosa** *spit* SE Ukraine
119 V10 **Obytichna Zatoka** *gulf* SE Ukraine
107 O3 **Oca** ≈ N Spain
25 W10 **Ocala** Florida, SE USA
42 M7 **Ocampo** Coahuila de Zaragoza, NE Mexico
56 G7 **Ocaña** Norte de Santander, N Colombia
107 N9 **Ocaña** Castilla-La Mancha, C Spain
39 T9 **Ocate** New Mexico, SW USA
Ocavango *see* Okavango
50 D6 **Occidental, Cordillera** ▲▲ Bolivia/Chile
50 D6 **Occidental, Cordillera** ▲▲ W Colombia
59 D14 **Occidental, Cordillera** ▲▲ W Peru
23 Q6 **Oceana** West Virginia, NE USA
23 Z4 **Ocean City** Maryland, NE USA
20 J17 **Ocean City** New Jersey, NE USA
8 K15 **Ocean Falls** British Columbia, SW Canada
Ocean Island *see* Kure Atoll
Ocean Island *see* Banaba
66 J9 **Oceanographer Fracture Zone** *tectonic feature* NW Atlantic Ocean
37 U17 **Oceanside** California, W USA
24 M9 **Ocean Springs** Mississippi, S USA
Ocean State *see* Rhode Island
27 O9 **O C Fisher Lake** ◎ Texas, SW USA
119 Q10 **Ochakiv** *Rus.* Ochakov. Mykolayivs'ka Oblast', S Ukraine
Ochakov *see* Ochakiv
Ochamchira *see* Och'amch'ire
143 Q9 **Och'amch'ire** *Rus.* Ochamchira. W Georgia
Ochansk *see* Okhansk
129 T15 **Ocher** Permskaya Oblast', NW Russian Federation
117 J19 **Óchi** ▲ Évvoia, C Greece
172 R8 **Ochiishi-misaki** *headland* Hokkaidō, NE Japan
xliii L18 **Ochil Hills** ▲ C Scotland, UK
xliii J22 **Ochiltree** East Ayrshire, W Scotland, UK
25 S9 **Ochlockonee River** ≈ Florida/Georgia, SE USA
46 K12 **Ocho Rios** C Jamaica
Ochrida *see* Ohrid
Ochrida, Lake *see* Ohrid, Lake
103 J19 **Ochsenfurt** Bayern, C Germany
25 U7 **Ocilla** Georgia, SE USA
96 N13 **Ockelbo** Gävleborg, C Sweden
Ocker *see* Oker
97 I19 **Öckerö** Göteborg och Bohus, S Sweden
25 U6 **Ocmulgee River** ≈ Georgia, SE USA
118 H11 **Ocna Mureş** *Hung.* Marosújvár; *prev.* Ocna Mureşului; prev. *Hung.* Marosújvárakna. Alba, C Romania
Ocna Mureşului *see* Ocna Mureş
118 H11 **Ocna Sibiului** *Ger.* Salzburg, *Hung.* Vizakna. Sibiu, C Romania
118 H13 **Ocnele Mari** *prev.* Vioara. Vâlcea, S Romania
118 L7 **Ocniţa** *Rus.* Oknitsa. N Moldavia
25 U4 **Oconee, Lake** ⊡ Georgia, SE USA
25 U5 **Oconee River** ≈ Georgia, SE USA
32 M9 **Oconomowoc** Wisconsin, N USA
32 M6 **Oconto** Wisconsin, N USA
32 M6 **Oconto Falls** Wisconsin, N USA
32 M6 **Oconto River** ≈ Wisconsin, N USA
106 I3 **O Corgo** Galicia, NW Spain
43 V16 **Ocosingo** Chiapas, SE Mexico
44 J8 **Ocotal** Nueva Segovia, NW Nicaragua
44 F6 **Ocotepeque** ◐ *department* W Honduras
Ocotepeque *see* Nueva Ocotepeque
42 L13 **Ocotlán** Jalisco, SW Mexico
43 R16 **Ocotlán** *var.* Ocotlán de Morelos. Oaxaca, SE Mexico
Ocotlán de Morelos *see* Ocotlán
43 U16 **Ocozocuautla** Chiapas, SE Mexico
23 Y10 **Ocracoke Island** *island* North Carolina, SE USA
104 I3 **Octeville** Manche, N France
October Revolution Island *see* Oktyabr'skoy Revolyutsii, Ostrov
45 R17 **Ocú** Herrera, S Panama
85 Q14 **Ocua** Cabo Delgado, NE Mozambique
Ocumare *see* Ocumare del Tuy
56 M5 **Ocumare del Tuy** *var.* Ocumare. Miranda, N Venezuela
79 P17 **Oda** SE Ghana
170 F12 **Ōda** *var.* Oda. Shimane, Honshū, SW Japan
94 K3 **Ódadhahraun** *lava flow* C Iceland
176 Y14 **Odammun** ≈ Irian Jaya, E Indonesia
171 Mm9 **Ōdate** Akita, Honshū, C Japan
171 J16 **Odawara** Kanagawa, Honshū, S Japan
97 D14 **Odda** Hordaland, S Norway
97 G22 **Odder** Århus, C Denmark
Oddur *see* Xuddur
31 T13 **Odebolt** Iowa, C USA
106 H14 **Odeleite** Faro, S Portugal
27 Q4 **Odell** Texas, SW USA
27 T14 **Odem** Texas, SW USA
106 F13 **Odemira** Beja, S Portugal
142 C14 **Ödemiş** İzmir, SW Turkey
Ödenburg *see* Sopron
85 I22 **Odendaalsrus** Free State, C South Africa
Odenpäh *see* Otepää
97 H23 **Odense** Fyn, C Denmark
103 H19 **Odenwald** ▲ W Germany
86 H10 **Oder** *Cz./Pol.* Odra. ≈ C Europe
Oderberg *see* Bohumín
102 P11 **Oderbruch** *wetland* Germany/Poland
Oderhaff *see* Szczeciński, Zalew
102 O11 **Oder-Havel-Kanal** *canal* NE Germany
Oderhellen *see* Odorheiu Secuiesc
102 P13 **Oder-Spree-Kanal** *canal* NE Germany
Odertal *see* Zdzieszowice
108 I7 **Oderzo** Veneto, NE Italy
124 Pp4 **Odesa** *Rus.* Odessa. Odes'ka Oblast', SW Ukraine
Odesa *see* Odes'ka Oblast'
97 L18 **Ödeshög** Östergötland, S Sweden
119 O9 **Odes'ka Oblast'** *var.* Odesa, *Rus.* Odesskaya Oblast'. ◐ *province* SW Ukraine
26 M8 **Odessa** Texas, SW USA
34 K8 **Odessa** Washington, NW USA
Odessa *see* Odesa
Odesskaya Oblast' *see* Odes'ka Oblast'
125 Ff13 **Odesskoye** Omskaya Oblast', C Russian Federation
Odessus *see* Varna
104 F6 **Odet** ≈ NW France
xlii N3 **Odie** Orkney Islands, N Scotland, UK
106 I14 **Odiel** ≈ SW Spain
78 L14 **Odienné** NW Ivory Coast
xxxvii R11 **Odiham** Hampshire, S England, UK
179 Pp12 **Odiongan** Tablas Island, C Philippines
118 L12 **Odobeşti** Vrancea, E Romania
113 H13 **Odolanów** *Ger.* Adelnau. Kalisz, SW Poland
178 J13 **Ŏdôngk** Kâmpóng Spoe, S Cambodia
27 N6 **O'donnell** Texas, SW USA
100 O7 **Odoorn** Drenthe, NE Netherlands
Odorhei *see* Odorheiu Secuiesc
118 J11 **Odorheiu Secuiesc** *Ger.* Oderhellen, *Hung.* Vámosudvarhely; *prev.* Odorhei; *Ger.* Hofmarkt. Harghita, C Romania
Odra *see* Oder
114 J9 **Odžaci** *Ger.* Hodschag, *Hung.* Hodság. Serbia, NW Yugoslavia
61 N14 **Oeiras** Piauí, E Brazil
106 F11 **Oeiras** Lisboa, C Portugal
103 G14 **Oelde** Nordrhein-Westfalen, W Germany
30 J11 **Oelrichs** South Dakota, N USA
Oels/Oels in Schlesien *see* Oleśnica
103 M17 **Oelsnitz** Sachsen, E Germany
31 X12 **Oelwein** Iowa, C USA
Oeniadae *see* Oiniádes
203 N17 **Oeno Island** *atoll* Pitcairn Islands, C Pacific Ocean
Oesel *see* Saaremaa
110 L7 **Oetz** *var.* Ötz. Tirol, W Austria
143 P11 **Of** Trabzon, NE Turkey
32 K15 **O'Fallon** Illinois, N USA
29 W4 **O'Fallon** Missouri, C USA
109 N16 **Ofanto** ≈ S Italy
xliv F9 **Offaly** *Ir.* Ua Uíbh Fhailí; *prev.* King's County. ◐ *county* C Ireland
103 H18 **Offenbach** *var.* Offenbach am Main. Hessen, W Germany
Offenbach am Main *see* Offenbach
103 F22 **Offenburg** Baden-Württemberg, SW Germany
190 C2 **Officer Creek** *seasonal river* South Australia
xxxix R12 **Offord d'Arcy** Cambridgeshire, E England, UK
xxxix W13 **Offton** Suffolk, E England, UK
Oficina María Elena *see* María Elena
Oficina Pedro de Valdivia *see* Pedro de Valdivia
117 K22 **Ofidoússa** *island* Kykládes, Greece, Aegean Sea
Ofiral *see* Sharm el Sheikh
94 H10 **Ofotfjorden** *fjord* N Norway
198 D8 **Ofu** *island* Manua Islands, E American Samoa
171 Mm12 **Ōfunato** Iwate, Honshū, C Japan
171 M10 **Oga** Akita, Honshū, C Japan
Ogaadeen *see* Ogadēn
171 M11 **Ogachi** Akita, Honshū, C Japan
171 M11 **Ogachi-tōge** *pass* Honshū, C Japan
83 N14 **Ogadēn** *Som.* Ogaadeen. *plateau* Ethiopia/Somalia
171 M10 **Oga-hantō** *peninsula* Honshū, C Japan
171 Hh14 **Ōgaki** Gifu, Honshū, SW Japan
30 L15 **Ogallala** Nebraska, C USA
174 I12 **Ogan, Air** ≈ Sumatera, W Indonesia
172 T16 **Ogasawara-shotō** *Eng.* Bonin Islands. *island group* SE Japan
12 I9 **Ogascanane, Lac** ◎ Québec, SE Canada
172 N9 **Ogawara-ko** ◎ Honshū, C Japan
79 T15 **Ogbomosho** Oyo, W Nigeria
xxxvii O9 **Ogbourne St George** Wiltshire, S England, UK
31 U13 **Ogden** Iowa, C USA
38 L2 **Ogden** Utah, W USA
20 I6 **Ogdensburg** New York, NE USA
197 L16 **Ogea Driki** *island* Lau Group, E Fiji
197 L16 **Ogea Levu** *island* Lau Group, E Fiji
25 W5 **Ogeechee River** ≈ Georgia, SE USA
Oger *see* Ogre
152 F6 **Ogiyon Shŭrkhogi** *wetland* NW Uzbekistan
171 K12 **Ogi** Niigata, Sado, C Japan
8 H5 **Ogilvie** Yukon Territory, NW Canada
8 H4 **Ogilvie** ≈ Yukon Territory, NW Canada
8 H5 **Ogilvie Mountains** ▲▲ Yukon Territory, NW Canada
Oginskiy Kanal *see* Ahinski Kanal
152 B10 **Oglanly** Balkanskiy Velayat, W Turkmenistan
25 T5 **Oglethorpe** Georgia, SE USA
25 T2 **Oglethorpe, Mount** ▲ Georgia, SE USA
108 F7 **Oglio** *anc.* Ollius. ≈ N Italy
xxxv I15 **Ogmore by Sea** Bridgend, S Wales, UK
105 T8 **Ognon** ≈ E France
175 Pp7 **Ogoamas, Pegunungan** ▲▲ Sulawesi, N Indonesia
127 N14 **Ogodzha** Amurskaya Oblast', S Russian Federation
79 W16 **Ogoja** Cross River, S Nigeria
10 C10 **Ogoki** ≈ Ontario, S Canada
10 D11 **Ogoki Lake** ◎ Ontario, C Canada
168 K10 **Ögöömör** Ömnögovĭ, S Mongolia
81 F19 **Ogooué** ≈ Congo/Gabon
81 E18 **Ogooué-Ivindo** *off.* Province de l'Ogooué-Ivindo, *var.* L'Ogooué-Ivindo. ◐ *province* N Gabon
81 E19 **Ogooué-Lolo** *off.* Province de l'Ogooué-Lolo, *var.* L'Ogooué-Lolo. ◐ *province* C Gabon
81 C19 **Ogooué-Maritime** *off.* Province de l'Ogooué-Maritime, *var.* L'Ogooué-Maritime. ◐ *province* W Gabon
170 Cc13 **Ōgori** Fukuoka, Kyūshū, SW Japan
170 Dd13 **Ōgōri** Yamaguchi, Honshū, SW Japan
116 H7 **Ogosta** ≈ NW Bulgaria
114 Q9 **Ogražden** *Bul.* Ograzhden. ▲▲ Bulgaria/FYR Macedonia *see also* Ograzhden
116 G12 **Ograzhden** *Mac.* Ogražden. ▲▲ Bulgaria/FYR Macedonia *see also* Ogražden
120 G9 **Ogre** *Ger.* Oger. Ogre, C Latvia
120 H9 **Ogre** ≈ C Latvia
114 C10 **Ogulin** Karlovac, NW Croatia
79 S16 **Ogun** ◐ *state* SW Nigeria
152 A12 **Ogurdzhaly, Ostrov** *Turkm.* Ogurjaly Adasy. *island* W Turkmenistan
Ogurjaly Adasy *see* Ogurdzhaly, Ostrov
79 U16 **Ogwashi-Uku** Delta, S Nigeria
193 B23 **Ohai** Southland, South Island, NZ
153 Q10 **Ohangaron** *Rus.* Akhangaran. Toshkent Wiloyati, E Uzbekistan
153 Q10 **Ohangaron** *Rus.* Akhangaran. ≈ E Uzbekistan
85 C16 **Ohangwena** ◐ *district* N Namibia
171 K17 **Ōhara** Chiba, Honshū, S Japan
32 M10 **O'Hare** ✈ (Chicago) Illinois, N USA
172 N8 **Ōhata** Aomori, Honshū, C Japan
192 L13 **Ohau** Manawatu-Wanganui, North Island, NZ
193 E20 **Ohau, Lake** ◎ South Island, NZ
Ohcejohka *see* Utsjoki
101 J20 **Ohey** Namur, SE Belgium
203 X15 **O'Higgins, Cabo** *headland* Easter Island, Chile, E Pacific Ocean
O'Higgins, Lago *see* San Martín, Lago
33 S12 **Ohio** *off.* State of Ohio; also known as The Buckeye State. ◐ *state* N USA
1 L10 **Ohio River** ≈ N USA
Ohlau *see* Oława
103 H16 **Ohm** ≈ C Germany
200 R16 **Ohonua** 'Eua, E Tonga
25 V5 **Ohoopee River** ≈ Georgia, SE USA
102 L12 **Ohre** *Ger.* Eger. ≈ Czech Republic/Germany
Ohri *see* Ohrid
115 M20 **Ohrid** *Turk.* Ochrida, Ohri. SW FYR Macedonia
115 M20 **Ohrid, Lake** *var.* Lake Ochrida, *Alb.* Liqeni i Ohrit, *Mac.* Ohridsko Ezero. ◎ Albania/FYR Macedonia
Ohridsko Ezero/Ohrit, Liqeni i *see* Ohrid, Lake
192 L9 **Ohura** Manawatu-Wanganui, North Island, NZ
60 J9 **Oiapoque** Amapá, E Brazil
60 J10 **Oiapoque, Rio** *var.* Fleuve l'Oyapok, Oyapock. ≈ Brazil/French Guiana *see also* Oyapok, Fleuve l'
13 O9 **Oies, Île aux** *island* Québec, SE Canada
94 L13 **Oijärvi** Oulu, C Finland
94 L12 **Oikarainen** Lappi, N Finland
196 F10 **Oikuul** Babeldaob, N Palau
20 C13 **Oil City** Pennsylvania, NE USA
20 C12 **Oil Creek** ≈ Pennsylvania, NE USA
37 R13 **Oildale** California, W USA
Oileán Ciarral *see* Castleisland
Oil Islands *see* Chagos Archipelago
117 D18 **Oiniádes** *anc.* Oeniadae. *site of ancient city* Dytikí Ellás, W Greece
117 L18 **Oinoússes** *island* E Greece
Oírr, Inis *see* Inisheer
101 J15 **Oirschot** Noord-Brabant, S Netherlands
105 N4 **Oise** ◐ *department* N France
105 P3 **Oise** ≈ N France
101 J14 **Oisterwijk** Noord-Brabant, S Netherlands
47 O14 **Oistins** S Barbados
170 D14 **Ōita** Ōita, Kyūshū, SW Japan
170 D14 **Ōita** *off.* Ōita-ken. ◐ *prefecture* Kyūshū, SW Japan
117 E17 **Oíti** ▲ C Greece
172 Oo6 **Oiwake** Hokkaidō, NE Japan
37 R14 **Ojai** California, W USA
96 K13 **Öje** Kopparberg, C Sweden
95 J14 **Öjebyn** Norrbotten, N Sweden
170 Bb12 **Ojika-jima** *island* SW Japan
42 K5 **Ojinaga** Chihuahua, N Mexico
171 K13 **Ojiya** *var.* Oziya. Niigata, Honshū, C Japan
42 M11 **Ojo Caliente** *var.* Ojocaliente. Zacatecas, C Mexico
42 D6 **Ojo de Liebre, Laguna** *var.* Laguna Scammon, Scammon Lagoon. *lagoon* W Mexico
64 I7 **Ojos del Salado, Cerro** ▲ W Argentina
107 R7 **Ojos Negros** Aragón, NE Spain
42 M12 **Ojuelos de Jalisco** Aguascalientes, C Mexico
131 N4 **Oka** ≈ W Russian Federation
85 D19 **Okahandja** Otjozondjupa, C Namibia
192 L9 **Okahukura** Manawatu-Wanganui, North Island, NZ
192 J3 **Okaihau** Northland, North Island, NZ
85 D18 **Okakarara** Otjozondjupa, N Namibia
11 P5 **Okak Islands** *island group* Newfoundland and Labrador, E Canada
8 M17 **Okanagan** ≈ British Columbia, SW Canada
9 N17 **Okanagan Lake** ◎ British Columbia, SW Canada
Okanizsa *see* Kanjiža
85 C16 **Okankolo** Otjikoto, N Namibia
34 K6 **Okanogan River** ≈ Washington, NW USA
194 I13 **Okapa** Eastern Highlands, C PNG
85 D18 **Okaputa** Otjozondjupa, N Namibia
155 V9 **Okāra** Punjab, E Pakistan
28 M10 **Okarche** Oklahoma, C USA
152 B13 **Okarem** *Turkm.* Ekerem. Balkanskiy Velayat, W Turkmenistan
201 X14 **Okat Harbor** *harbor* Kosrae, E Micronesia
24 M5 **Okatibbee Creek** ≈ Mississippi, S USA
85 C17 **Okaukuejo** Kunene, N Namibia
Okavanggo *see* Cubango/Okavango
85 E17 **Okavango** ◐ *district* NW Namibia
85 G17 **Okavango** *var.* Cubango, Kavango, Kavengo, Kubango, Okavanggo, *Port.* Ocavango. ≈ S Africa *see also* Cubango
85 G17 **Okavango Delta** *wetland* N Botswana
171 J15 **Okaya** Nagano, Honshū, S Japan
170 Ff14 **Okayama** Okayama, Honshū, SW Japan
170 F13 **Okayama** *off.* Okayama-ken. ◐ *prefecture* Honshū, SW Japan
171 I16 **Okazaki** Aichi, Honshū, C Japan
112 M12 **Okęcie** ✈ (Warszawa) Warszawa, C Poland
25 Y13 **Okeechobee** Florida, SE USA
25 Y14 **Okeechobee, Lake** ◎ Florida, SE USA
28 M9 **Okeene** Oklahoma, C USA
25 V8 **Okefenokee Swamp** *wetland* Georgia, SE USA
xxxvi G14 **Okehampton** Devon, SW England, UK
29 P10 **Okemah** Oklahoma, C USA
79 U16 **Okene** Kogi, S Nigeria
102 K13 **Oker** *var.* Ocker. ≈ NW Germany
103 J14 **Oker-Stausee** ◎ C Germany
127 O13 **Okha** Ostrov Sakhalin, Sakhalinskaya Oblast', SE Russian Federation
129 U15 **Okhansk** *var.* Ochansk. Permskaya Oblast', NW Russian Federation
127 N10 **Okhota** ≈ E Russian Federation
127 Nn11 **Okhotsk** Khabarovskiy Kray, E Russian Federation
199 I2 **Okhotsk, Sea of** *sea* NW Pacific Ocean
119 T4 **Okhtyrka** *Rus.* Akhtyrka. Sums'ka Oblast', NE Ukraine
199 Gg6 **Oki-Daitō Ridge** *undersea feature* W Pacific Ocean
85 E23 **Okiep** Northern Cape, W South Africa
Oki-guntō *see* Oki-shotō
170 Ff11 **Oki-kaikyō** *strait* SW Japan
172 P15 **Okinawa** Okinawa, SW Japan
172 Oo14 **Okinawa** *off.* Okinawa-ken. ◐ *prefecture* Okinawa, SW Japan
172 Oo14 **Okinawa** *island* SW Japan
172 Q14 **Okinoerabu-jima** *island* Nansei-shotō, SW Japan
170 D15 **Okino-shima** *island* SW Japan
170 Ff11 **Oki-shotō** *var.* Oki-guntō. *island group* SW Japan
79 T16 **Okitipupa** Ondo, SW Nigeria
177 G8 **Okkan** Pegu, SW Burma
29 N10 **Oklahoma** *off.* State of Oklahoma; also known as The Sooner State. ◐ *state* C USA
29 N11 **Oklahoma City** *state capital* Oklahoma, C USA
27 Q4 **Oklaunion** Texas, SW USA
25 W10 **Oklawaha River** ≈ Florida, SE USA
29 P10 **Okmulgee** Oklahoma, C USA
Oknitsa *see* Ocniţa
24 M3 **Okolona** Mississippi, S USA
172 Q4 **Okoppe** Hokkaidō, NE Japan
9 Q16 **Okotoks** Alberta, SW Canada
82 H6 **Oko, Wadi** ≈ NE Sudan
81 G19 **Okoyo** Cuvette, W Congo
79 S15 **Okpara** ≈ Benin/Nigeria
94 J8 **Øksfjord** Finnmark, N Norway
176 Z12 **Oksibil** Irian Jaya, E Indonesia
129 R4 **Oksino** Nenetskiy Avtonomnyy Okrug, NW Russian Federation
94 G13 **Oksskolten** ▲ C Norway
Oksu *see* Oqsu
150 M8 **Oktaybr'skiy** Kustanay, N Kazakhstan
194 E11 **Ok Tedi** Western, W PNG
Oktemberyan *see* Hoktemberyan
177 G7 **Oktwin** Pegu, C Burma
150 H10 **Oktyabr'sk** Aktyubinsk, W Kazakhstan
131 R6 **Oktyabr'sk** Samarskaya Oblast', W Russian Federation
129 N12 **Oktyabr'skiy** Arkhangel'skaya Oblast', NW Russian Federation
127 Pp12 **Oktyabr'skiy** Kamchatskaya Oblast', E Russian Federation
131 T5 **Oktyabr'skiy** Respublika Bashkortostan, W Russian Federation
131 O11 **Oktyabr'skiy** Volgogradskaya Oblast', SW Russian Federation
Oktyabr'skiy *see* Aktsyabrski
131 V7 **Oktyabr'skoye** Orenburgskaya Oblast', W Russian Federation
126 J3 **Oktyabr'skoy Revolyutsii, Ostrov** *Eng.* October Revolution Island. *island* Severnaya Zemlya, N Russian Federation
170 C15 **Ōkuchi** *var.* Ōkuti. Kagoshima, Kyūshū, SW Japan
Okulovka *see* Uglovka
171 Mm5 **Okushiri-tō** *var.* Okusiri Tô. *island* NE Japan
Okusiri Tô *see* Okushiri-tō
79 S15 **Okuta** Kwara, W Nigeria
Ōkuti *see* Ōkuchi
85 F19 **Okwa** *var.* Chapman's. ≈ Botswana/Namibia
127 O10 **Ola** Magadanskaya Oblast', E Russian Federation
29 T11 **Ola** Arkansas, C USA
Ola *see* Ala
37 T11 **Olacha Peak** ▲ California, W USA
94 J1 **Ólafsfjördhur** Nordhurland Eystra, N Iceland
94 H3 **Ólafsvík** Vesturland, W Iceland
Oláhbrettye *see* Bretea-Română
Oláhszentgyörgy *see* Sângeorz-Băi
Oláh-Toplicza *see* Toplița
37 T11 **Olancha** California, W USA
44 J5 **Olanchito** Yoro, C Honduras
44 J6 **Olancho** ◐ *department* E Honduras
97 O20 **Öland** *island* S Sweden
97 O19 **Ölands norra udde** *headland* S Sweden
97 N22 **Ölands södra udde** *headland* S Sweden
190 K7 **Olary** South Australia
29 R4 **Olathe** Kansas, C USA
63 C22 **Olavarría** Buenos Aires, E Argentina
94 O2 **Olav V Land** *physical region* C Svalbard
113 H14 **Oława** *Ger.* Ohlau. Wrocław, SW Poland
109 D17 **Olbia** *prev.* Terranova Pausania. Sardegna, Italy, C Mediterranean Sea
xlii P13 **Old Aberdeen** City of Aberdeen, NE Scotland, UK
xlii G8 **Oldany** *island* NW Scotland, UK
46 G5 **Old Bahama Channel** *channel* Bahamas/Cuba
xxxvii Q10 **Old Basing** Hampshire, S England, UK
Old Bay State/Old Colony State *see* Massachusetts
xxxix S6 **Old Bolingbroke** Lincolnshire, E England, UK
xxxviii B15 **Oldbury** Sandwell, C England, UK
xliv J7 **Oldcastle** Meath, E Ireland
8 H2 **Old Crow** Yukon Territory, NW Canada
Old Dominion *see* Virginia
xlii P11 **Old Deer** Aberdeenshire, NE Scotland, UK
Oldeberkeap *see* Oldeberkoop
100 M7 **Oldeberkoop** *Fris.* Oldeberkeap. Friesland, N Netherlands
100 L10 **Oldebroek** Gelderland, E Netherlands
100 L8 **Oldemarkt** Overijssel, N Netherlands
96 E11 **Olden** Sogn og Fjordane, C Norway
102 G10 **Oldenburg** Niedersachsen, NW Germany
102 K8 **Oldenburg** Schleswig-Holstein, N Germany
100 P10 **Oldenzaal** Overijssel, E Netherlands
94 I9 **Olderdalen** Troms, N Norway
xxxix Y13 **Old Felixstowe** Suffolk, E England, UK
xxxix R10 **Old Fletton** Cambridgeshire, E England, UK
20 J8 **Old Forge** New York, NE USA
Old Goa *see* Goa
xl H14 **Oldham** Oldham, NW England, UK
xli P15 **Oldham** ◐ *unitary authority* NW England, UK
41 Q14 **Old Harbor** Kodiak Island, Alaska, USA
46 J13 **Old Harbour** C Jamaica
xliv F15 **Old Head of Kinsale** *Ir.* An Seancheann. *headland* SW Ireland
22 J8 **Old Hickory Lake** ⊡ Tennessee, S USA
Old Line State *see* Maryland
xli O12 **Oldmeldrum** Aberdeenshire, NE Scotland, UK
Old North State *see* North Carolina
83 I17 **Ol Doinyo Lengeyo** ▲ C Kenya
9 Q16 **Olds** Alberta, SW Canada
21 O7 **Old Speck Mountain** ▲ Maine, NE USA
21 S6 **Old Town** Maine, NE USA
9 T17 **Old Wives Lake** ◎ Saskatchewan, S Canada
168 J7 **Öldziyt** Arhangay, C Mongolia
169 N10 **Öldziyt** Dornogovĭ, SE Mongolia
196 H6 **Oleai** *var.* San Jose. Saipan, S Northern Mariana Islands
20 E11 **Olean** New York, NE USA
112 O7 **Olecko** *Ger.* Treuburg. Suwałki, NE Poland
108 C7 **Oleggio** Piemonte, NE Italy
126 L13 **Olëkma** Amurskaya Oblast', SE Russian Federation
126 L13 **Olëkma** ≈ C Russian Federation
126 L12 **Olëkminsk** Respublika Sakha (Yakutiya), NE Russian Federation
119 W7 **Oleksandrivka** Donets'ka Oblast', E Ukraine
119 R7 **Oleksandrivka** *Rus.* Aleksandrovka. Kirovohrads'ka Oblast', C Ukraine
119 Q9 **Oleksandrivka** Mykolayivs'ka Oblast', S Ukraine
119 S7 **Oleksandriya** *Rus.* Aleksandriya. Kirovohrads'ka Oblast', C Ukraine
95 B20 **Ølen** Hordaland, S Norway
128 J4 **Olenegorsk** Murmanskaya Oblast', NW Russian Federation
126 K8 **Olenëk** Respublika Sakha (Yakutiya), NE Russian Federation
126 Jj9 **Olenëk** ≈ NE Russian Federation
126 Kk6 **Olenëkskiy Zaliv** *bay* N Russian Federation
128 K6 **Olenitsa** Murmanskaya Oblast', NW Russian Federation
104 I11 **Oléron, Île d'** *island* W France
113 H14 **Oleśnica** *Ger.* Oels, Oels in Schlesien. Wrocław, SW Poland
113 I15 **Olesno** *Ger.* Rosenberg. Częstochowa, S Poland
118 M3 **Olevs'k** *Rus.* Olevsk. Zhytomyrs'ka Oblast', N Ukraine
127 Nn18 **Ol'ga** Primorskiy Kray, SE Russian Federation
189 P8 **Olga, Mount** ▲ Northern Territory, C Australia
92 P2 **Olgastretet** *strait* E Svalbard
168 D5 **Ölgiy** Bayan-Ölgiy, W Mongolia
97 F23 **Ølgod** Ribe, W Denmark
106 H14 **Olhão** Faro, S Portugal
95 L14 **Olhava** Oulu, C Finland
114 B12 **Olib** *It.* Ulbo. *island* W Croatia
85 B16 **Olifa** Kunene, NW Namibia
85 E20 **Olifants** *var.* Elephant River. ≈ E Namibia
85 E25 **Olifants** *var.* Elefantes. ≈ SW South Africa
85 G22 **Olifantshoek** Northern Cape, N South Africa
196 L15 **Olimarao Atoll** *atoll* Caroline Islands, C Micronesia
Ólimbos *see* Ólympos
Olimpo *see* Fuerte Olimpo
61 Q15 **Olinda** Pernambuco, E Brazil
Olinthos *see* Ólynthos
85 I20 **Oliphants Drift** Kgatleng, SE Botswana
Olisipo *see* Lisboa
Olita *see* Alytus
107 Q4 **Olite** Navarra, N Spain
64 K10 **Oliva** Córdoba, C Argentina
107 T11 **Oliva** País Valenciano, E Spain
106 I12 **Oliva de la Frontera** Extremadura, W Spain
Olivares *see* Olivares de Júcar
64 H9 **Olivares, Cerro de** ▲ N Chile
107 P9 **Olivares de Júcar** *var.* Olivares. Castilla-La Mancha, C Spain
24 L1 **Olive Branch** Mississippi, S USA
23 O5 **Olive Hill** Kentucky, S USA
37 O6 **Olivehurst** California, W USA
106 G7 **Oliveira de Azeméis** Aveiro, N Portugal
106 I11 **Olivenza** Extremadura, W Spain
9 N17 **Oliver** British Columbia, SW Canada
105 N7 **Olivet** Loiret, C France
31 Q12 **Olivet** South Dakota, N USA
31 T9 **Olivia** Minnesota, N USA
193 C20 **Olivine Range** ▲▲ South Island, NZ
110 H10 **Olivone** Ticino, S Switzerland
Ölkeyek *see* Ul'kayak
131 O9 **Ol'khovka** Volgogradskaya Oblast', SW Russian Federation
113 K16 **Olkusz** Katowice, S Poland
24 I6 **Olla** Louisiana, S USA
xlii I2 **Ollaberry** Shetland Islands, NE Scotland, UK
64 I4 **Ollagüe, Volcán** *var.* Oyahue, Volcán Oyahue. ▲ N Chile
201 U13 **Ollan** *island* Chuuk, C Micronesia
196 F7 **Ollei** Babeldaob, N Palau
xxxix O6 **Ollerton** Nottinghamshire, C England, UK
Ollius *see* Oglio
110 C10 **Ollon** Vaud, W Switzerland
153 Q10 **Olmaliq** *Rus.* Almalyk. Toshkent Wiloyati, C Uzbekistan
106 M6 **Olmedo** Castilla-León, N Spain
58 B10 **Olmos** Lambayeque, W Peru
Olmütz *see* Olomouc
xxxvii R5 **Olney** Milton Keynes, C England, UK
32 M15 **Olney** Illinois, N USA
27 R5 **Olney** Texas, SW USA
97 L22 **Olofström** Blekinge, S Sweden
195 Y15 **Olomburi** Malaita, N Solomon Islands
113 H17 **Olomouc** *Ger.* Olmütz, *Pol.* Ołomuniec. Severní Morava, E Czech Republic
Olomuniec *see* Olomouc
125 Cc6 **Olonets** Respublika Kareliya, NW Russian Federation
179 P10 **Olongapo** *off.* Olongapo City. Luzon, N Philippines
104 J16 **Oloron-Ste-Marie** Pyrénées-Atlantiques, SW France
198 Dd8 **Olosega** *island* Manua Islands, E American Samoa
107 W4 **Olot** Cataluña, NE Spain
152 K12 **Olot** *Rus.* Alat. Bukhoro Wiloyati, C Uzbekistan
114 I12 **Olovo** E Bosnia and Herzegovina

◆ Country ● Country Capital ◇ Dependent Territory ○ Dependent Territory Capital ◐ Administrative Region ✈ International Airport ▲ Mountain ▲▲ Mountain Range ⊼ Volcano ≈ River ◎ Lake ⊡ Reservoir

OLOVYANNAYA – ÖSKEMEN

126 Kk16 **Olovyannaya** Chitinskaya Oblast', S Russian Federation
127 O06 **Oloy** ≈ NE Russian Federation
103 F16 **Olpe** Nordrhein-Westfalen, W Germany
111 N8 **Olperer** ▲ SW Austria
Olshanka *see* Vil'shanka
Ol'shany *see* Al'shany
Olsnitz *see* Murska Sobota
100 M10 **Olst** Overijssel, E Netherlands
112 L8 **Olsztyn** *Ger.* Allenstein. Olsztyn, N Poland
112 L8 **Olsztyn** *off.* Województwo Olsztyńskie. ◐ *province* N Poland
112 L8 **Olsztynek** *Ger.* Hohenstein in Ostpreussen. Olsztyn, N Poland
Olsztyńskie, Województwo *see* Olsztyn
118 I14 **Olt** ◐ *county* SW Romania
118 I14 **Olt** *var.* Oltul, *Ger.* Alt. ≈ S Romania
110 E7 **Olten** Solothurn, NW Switzerland
118 K14 **Oltenița** *prev. Eng.* Oltenitsa, *anc.* Constantiola. Călărași, SE Romania
Oltenitsa *see* Oltenița
118 H14 **Oltet** ≈ S Romania
xxxviii D15 **Olton** Solihull, C England, UK
26 M4 **Olton** Texas, SW USA
143 R12 **Oltu** Erzurum, NE Turkey
Oltul *see* Olt
152 G7 **Oltynkŭl** Qoraqalpoghiston Respublikasi, NW Uzbekistan
167 S15 **Oluan Pi** *Eng.* Cape Olwanpi. *headland* S Taiwan
Ólubló *see* Stará L'ubovňa
143 R11 **Olur** Erzurum, NE Turkey
106 L15 **Olvera** Andalucía, S Spain
Ol'viopol' *see* Pervomays'k
Olwanpi, Cape *see* Oluan Pi
17 G2 **Olympia** *state capital* Washington, NW USA
117 D20 **Olympia** Dytikí Ellás, S Greece
190 H5 **Olympic Dam** South Australia
34 F7 **Olympic Mountains** ▲▲ Washington, NW USA
124 R12 **Ólympos** *var.* Troodos, *Eng.* Mount Olympus. ▲ C Cyprus
117 F15 **Ólympos** *var.* Ólimbos, *Eng.* Mount Olympus. ▲ N Greece
117 L17 **Ólympos** ▲ Lésvos, E Greece
17 G1 **Olympus, Mount** ▲ Washington, NW USA
Olympus, Mount *see* Ólympos
117 G14 **Ólynthos** *var.* Olinthos; *anc.* Olynthus. *site of ancient city* Kentrikí Makedonía, N Greece
Olynthus *see* Ólynthos
119 Q3 **Olyshivka** Chernihivs'ka Oblast', N Ukraine
127 Q7 **Olyutorskiy, Mys** *headland* E Russian Federation
127 Pp8 **Olyutorskiy Zaliv** *bay* E Russian Federation
194 F11 **Om** ≈ W PNG
133 S6 **Om'** ≈ N Russian Federation
164 I13 **Oma** Xizang Zizhiqu, W China
172 N8 **Ōma** Aomori, Honshū, C Japan
129 P6 **Oma** ≈ NW Russian Federation
171 J14 **Ōmachi** *var.* Ōmati. Nagano, Honshū, S Japan
171 Ii17 **Omae-zaki** *headland* Honshū, S Japan
171 M11 **Ōmagari** Akita, Honshū, C Japan
xliv I4 **Omagh** *Ir.* An Ómaigh. Omagh, W Northern Ireland, UK
xliv I4 **Omagh** ◐ *district* W Northern Ireland, UK
31 S15 **Omaha** Nebraska, C USA
85 E19 **Omaheke** ◐ *district* W Namibia
147 W10 **Oman** *off.* Sultanate of Oman, *Ar.* Salṭanat 'Umān; *prev.* Muscat and Oman. ♦ *monarchy* SW Asia
133 O10 **Oman Basin** *var.* Bassin d'Oman. *undersea feature* N Indian Ocean
Oman, Bassin d' *see* Oman Basin
133 N10 **Oman, Gulf of** *Ar.* Khalīj 'Umān. *gulf* N Arabian Sea
192 J3 **Omapere** Northland, North Island, NZ
193 E20 **Omarama** Canterbury, South Island, NZ
114 F11 **Omarska** NW Bosnia and Herzegovina
85 C18 **Omaruru** Erongo, NW Namibia
85 C19 **Omaruru** ≈ W Namibia
85 E17 **Omatako** ≈ NE Namibia
Ōmati *see* Ōmachi
85 E18 **Omawewozonyanda** Omaheke, E Namibia
172 N7 **Ōma-zaki** *headland* Honshū, C Japan
Omba *see* Ambae
Ombai *see* Alor, Pulau
175 Rr16 **Ombai, Selat** *strait* Nusa Tenggara, S Indonesia
85 C16 **Ombalantu** Omusati, N Namibia
81 H15 **Ombella-Mpoko** ◐ *prefecture* S Central African Republic
xxxviii A17 **Ombersley** Worcestershire, W England, UK
Ombetsu *see* Onbetsu
85 B17 **Ombombo** Kunene, NW Namibia
81 D19 **Omboué** Ogooué-Maritime, W Gabon
108 G13 **Ombrone** ≈ C Italy
82 F9 **Omdurman** *var.* Umm Durmān. Khartoum, C Sudan
171 Jj16 **Ōme** Tōkyō, Honshū, S Japan
xliv L6 **Omeath** Louth, NE Ireland
108 C6 **Omegna** Piemonte, NE Italy
191 P12 **Omeo** Victoria, SE Australia
144 F11 **'Omer** Southern, C Israel
43 P16 **Ometepec** Guerrero, S Mexico
44 K11 **Ometepe, Isla de** *island* S Nicaragua
Om Hager *see* Om Hajer
82 I10 **Om Hajer** *var.* Om Hager. SW Eritrea
171 H14 **Ōmi-Hachiman** *var.* Ōmihachiman. Shiga, Honshū, SW Japan
8 L12 **Omineca Mountains** ▲▲ British Columbia, W Canada
115 F14 **Omiš** *It.* Almissa. Split-Dalmacija, S Croatia
114 B10 **Omišalj** Primorje-Gorski Kotar, NW Croatia
170 Dd12 **Ōmi-shima** *island* SW Japan
85 D19 **Omitara** Khomas, C Namibia
43 O16 **Omitlán, Río** ≈ S Mexico
41 X14 **Ommaney, Cape** *headland* Baranof Island, Alaska, USA
100 N9 **Ommen** Overijssel, E Netherlands
168 K11 **Ömnögovĭ** ◐ *province* S Mongolia
203 X7 **Omoa** Fatu Hira, NE French Polynesia
Omo Botego *see* Omo Wenz
Ómoldova *see* Moldova Veche
127 O6 **Omolon** Chukotskiy Avtonomnyy Okrug, NE Russian Federation
127 O7 **Omolon** ≈ NE Russian Federation
126 Ll8 **Omoloy** ≈ NE Russian Federation
171 M10 **Omono-gawa** ≈ Honshū, C Japan
83 I14 **Omo Wenz** *var.* Omo Botego. ≈ Ethiopia/Kenya
125 Ff13 **Omsk** Omskaya Oblast', C Russian Federation
125 Ff12 **Omskaya Oblast'** ◐ *province* C Russian Federation
127 O8 **Omsukchan** Magadanskaya Oblast', E Russian Federation
172 Q4 **Ōmu** Hokkaidō, NE Japan
112 M9 **Omulew** ≈ NE Poland
118 J12 **Omul, Vârful** *prev.* Vîrful Omu. ▲ C Romania
85 D16 **Omundaungilo** Ohangwena, N Namibia
170 C13 **Ōmura** Nagasaki, Kyūshū, SW Japan
85 B17 **Omusati** ◐ *district* N Namibia
170 Cc13 **Ōmuta** Fukuoka, Kyūshū, SW Japan
129 S14 **Omutninsk** Kirovskaya Oblast', NW Russian Federation
Omu, Vîrful *see* Omul, Vârful
31 V7 **Onamia** Minnesota, N USA
23 Y5 **Onancock** Virginia, NE USA
12 E10 **Onaping Lake** ◎ Ontario, S Canada
32 M12 **Onarga** Illinois, N USA
13 R6 **Onatchiway, Lac** ◎ Québec, SE Canada
31 S14 **Onawa** Iowa, C USA
172 Pp7 **Onbetsu** *var.* Ombetsu. Hokkaidō, NE Japan
xl G11 **Onchan** E Isle of Man
85 B16 **Oncócua** Cunene, SW Angola
107 S9 **Onda** País Valenciano, E Spain
113 N18 **Ondava** ≈ NE Slovakia
Ondjiva *see* N'Giva
79 T16 **Ondo** Ondo, SW Nigeria
79 T16 **Ondo** ◐ *state* SW Nigeria
169 N8 **Öndörhaan** Hentiy, E Mongolia
85 D18 **Ondundazongonda** Otjozondjupa, N Namibia
157 K21 **One and Half Degree Channel** *channel* S Maldives
197 L15 **Oneata** *island* Lau Group, E Fiji
128 L9 **Onega** Arkhangel'skaya Oblast', NW Russian Federation
125 Dd6 **Onega** ≈ NW Russian Federation
Onega Bay *see* Onezhskaya Guba
Onega, Lake *see* Onezhskoye Ozero
20 I10 **Oneida** New York, NE USA
22 M8 **Oneida** Tennessee, S USA
20 H9 **Oneida Lake** ◎ New York, NE USA
31 P13 **O'Neill** Nebraska, C USA
127 Pp13 **Onekotan, Ostrov** *island* Kuril'skiye Ostrova, SE Russian Federation
25 P3 **Oneonta** Alabama, S USA
20 J11 **Oneonta** New York, NE USA
202 I16 **Oneroa** *island* S Cook Islands
118 K11 **Onești** *Hung.* Onyest; *prev.* Gheorghe Gheorghiu-Dej. Bacău, E Romania
200 Qq15 **Onevai** *island* Tongatapu Group, S Tonga
110 A11 **Onex** Genève, SW Switzerland
128 K8 **Onezhskaya Guba** *Eng.* Onega Bay. *bay* NW Russian Federation
125 D6 **Onezhskoye Ozero** *Eng.* Lake Onega. ◎ NW Russian Federation
85 C16 **Ongandjera** Omusati, N Namibia
192 N12 **Ongaonga** Hawke's Bay, North Island, NZ
168 K9 **Ongi** Dundgovĭ, C Mongolia
168 J8 **Ongi** Övörhangay, C Mongolia
169 W14 **Ongjin** SW North Korea
161 J17 **Ongole** Andhra Pradesh, E India
168 K8 **Ongon** Övörhangay, C Mongolia
Ongtüstik Qazaqstan Oblysy *see* Yuzhnyy Kazakhstan
101 I21 **Onhaye** Namur, S Belgium
177 G8 **Onhne** Pegu, SW Burma
143 S9 **Oni** N Georgia
xliii G16 **Onich** Highland, NW Scotland, UK
31 N9 **Onida** South Dakota, N USA
170 E15 **Onigajō-yama** ▲ Shikoku, SW Japan
180 H7 **Onilahy** ≈ S Madagascar
79 U16 **Onitsha** Anambra, S Nigeria
171 Gg14 **Ono** Hyōgo, Honshū, SW Japan
197 J15 **Ono** *island* SW Fiji
171 I14 **Ōno** Fukui, Honshū, SW Japan
170 D12 **Onoda** Yamaguchi, Honshū, SW Japan
197 L17 **Ono-i-lau** *island* SE Fiji
170 Cc13 **Ōnojō** *var.* Ōnozyô. Fukuoka, Kyūshū, SW Japan
126 K16 **Onokhoy** Respublika Buryatiya, S Russian Federation
170 F14 **Onomichi** *var.* Onomiti. Hiroshima, Honshū, SW Japan
Onomiti *see* Onomichi
169 O7 **Onon Gol** ≈ N Mongolia
Ononte *see* Orontes
57 N6 **Onoto** Anzoátegui, NE Venezuela
203 O3 **Onotoa** *prev.* Clerk Island. *atoll* Tungaru, W Kiribati
Ōnozyô *see* Ōnojō
97 I19 **Onsala** Halland, S Sweden
85 E23 **Onseepkans** Northern Cape, W South Africa
106 F4 **Ons, Illa de** *island* NW Spain
188 H7 **Onslow** Western Australia
23 W11 **Onslow Bay** *bay* North Carolina, E USA
100 P6 **Onstwedde** Groningen, NE Netherlands
170 Bb16 **On-take** ▲ Kyūshū, SW Japan
171 Ii15 **Ontake-san** ▲ Honshū, S Japan
37 T15 **Ontario** California, W USA
34 M13 **Ontario** Oregon, NW USA
10 D10 **Ontario** ◐ *province* S Canada
15 Gg2 **Ontario, Lake** ◎ Canada/USA
1 L9 **Ontario Peninsula** *peninsula* Canada/USA
Onteniente *see* Ontinyent
107 S11 **Ontinyent** *var.* Onteniente. País Valenciano, E Spain
95 N15 **Ontojärvi** ◎ E Finland
32 L3 **Ontonagon** Michigan, N USA
32 L3 **Ontonagon River** ≈ Michigan, N USA
195 W11 **Ontong Java Atoll** *prev.* Lord Howe Island. *atoll* N Solomon Islands
183 N5 **Ontong Java Rise** *undersea feature* W Pacific Ocean
Onuba *see* Huelva
57 W9 **Onverwacht** Para, N Surinam
Onyest *see* Onești
190 J7 **Oodla Wirra** South Australia
190 F2 **Oodnadatta** South Australia
190 C5 **Ooldea** South Australia
29 Q8 **Oologah Lake** ⊡ Oklahoma, C USA
Oos-Kaap *see* Eastern Cape
Oos-Londen *see* East London
101 E17 **Oostakker** Oost-Vlaanderen, NW Belgium
101 D15 **Oostburg** Zeeland, SW Netherlands
100 K9 **Oostelijk-Flevoland** *polder* C Netherlands
101 B16 **Oostende** *Eng.* Ostend, *Fr.* Ostende. West-Vlaanderen, NW Belgium
101 B16 **Oostende** ✕ West-Vlaanderen, NW Belgium
100 L12 **Oosterbeek** Gelderland, SE Netherlands
101 I14 **Oosterhout** Noord-Brabant, S Netherlands
100 O6 **Oostermoers Vaart** *var.* Hunze. ≈ NE Netherlands
101 F14 **Oosterschelde** *Eng.* Eastern Scheldt. *inlet* SW Netherlands
101 E14 **Oosterscheldedam** *dam* SW Netherlands
100 M7 **Oosterwolde** *Fris.* Easterwâlde. Friesland, N Netherlands
100 I9 **Oosthuizen** Noord-Holland, NW Netherlands
101 H16 **Oostmalle** Antwerpen, N Belgium
Oos-Transvaal *see* Mpumalanga
101 E15 **Oost-Souburg** Zeeland, SW Netherlands
101 E17 **Oost-Vlaanderen** *Eng.* East Flanders. ◐ *province* NW Belgium
100 J5 **Oost-Vlieland** Friesland, N Netherlands
100 F12 **Oostvoorne** Zuid-Holland, SW Netherlands
Ootacamund *see* Udagamandalam
100 O10 **Ootmarsum** Overijssel, E Netherlands
8 K14 **Ootsa Lake** ⊡ British Columbia, SW Canada
116 L8 **Opaka** Razgradska Oblast, N Bulgaria
81 M18 **Opala** Haut-Zaïre, C Zaire
129 Q13 **Oparino** Kirovskaya Oblast', NW Russian Federation
12 H8 **Opasatica, Lac** ◎ Québec, SE Canada
114 B9 **Opatija** *It.* Abbazia. Primorje-Gorski Kotar, NW Croatia
113 N15 **Opatów** Tarnobrzeg, SE Poland
113 I17 **Opava** *Ger.* Troppau. Severní Morava, E Czech Republic
113 H16 **Opava** *Ger.* Oppa. ≈ NE Czech Republic
Ópazova *see* Stara Pazova
194 L14 **Ope** ≈ S PNG
Opécska *see* Pecica
12 E8 **Opeepeesway Lake** ◎ Ontario, S Canada
25 R5 **Opelika** Alabama, S USA
24 I8 **Opelousas** Louisiana, S USA
195 O11 **Open Bay** *bay* New Britain, E PNG
12 I12 **Opeongo Lake** ◎ Ontario, SE Canada
101 K17 **Opglabbeek** Limburg, NE Belgium
35 W6 **Opheim** Montana, NW USA
41 P10 **Ophir** Alaska, USA
Ophiusa *see* Formentera
81 N18 **Opienge** Haut-Zaïre, E Zaire
193 G20 **Opihi** ≈ South Island, NZ
10 J9 **Opinaca** ≈ Québec, C Canada
10 J10 **Opinaca, Réservoir** ⊡ Québec, E Canada
xlii F11 **Opinan** Highland, NW Scotland, UK
119 T5 **Opishnya** *Rus.* Oposhnya. Poltavs'ka Oblast', NE Ukraine
100 I8 **Opmeer** Noord-Holland, NW Netherlands
79 V17 **Opobo** Akwa Ibom, S Nigeria
128 F16 **Opochka** Pskovskaya Oblast', W Russian Federation
112 L13 **Opoczno** Piotrków, C Poland
113 I15 **Opole** *Ger.* Oppeln. Opole, SW Poland
113 H15 **Opole** *off.* Województwo Opolskie. ◐ *province* SW Poland
Opolskie, Województwo *see* Opole
150 G13 **Opornyy** Mangistau, SW Kazakhstan
Oporto *see* Porto
Oposhnya *see* Opishnya
192 P8 **Opotiki** Bay of Plenty, North Island, NZ
25 Q7 **Opp** Alabama, S USA
Oppa *see* Opava
96 G9 **Oppdal** Sør-Trøndelag, S Norway
Oppeln *see* Opole
109 N23 **Oppido Mamertina** Calabria, SW Italy
Oppidum Ubiorum *see* Köln
96 F12 **Oppland** ◐ *county* S Norway
120 J12 **Opsa** *Rus.* Opsa. Vitsyebskaya Voblasts', NW Belorussia
28 I8 **Optima Lake** ⊡ Oklahoma, C USA
192 J11 **Opunake** Taranaki, North Island, NZ
203 N6 **Opunohu, Baie d'** *bay* Moorea, W French Polynesia
85 B17 **Opuwo** Kunene, NW Namibia
152 H6 **Oqqal'a** *var.* Akkala, *Rus.* Karakala. Qoraqalpoghiston Respublikasi, NW Uzbekistan
153 V13 **Oqsu** *Rus.* Oksu. ≈ SE Tajikistan
153 P14 **Oqtogh, Qatorkŭhi** *Rus.* Khrebet Aktau. ▲▲ SW Tajikistan
152 M11 **Oqtosh** *Rus.* Aktash. Samarqand Wiloyati, C Uzbekistan
153 N11 **Oqtow Tizmasi** *Rus.* Khrebet Aktau. ▲▲ C Uzbekistan
32 J12 **Oquawka** Illinois, N USA
150 J10 **Or'** *Kaz.* Or. ≈ Kazakhstan/Russian Federation
38 M15 **Oracle** Arizona, SW USA
118 F9 **Oradea** *prev.* Oradea Mare, *Ger.* Grosswardein, *Hung.* Nagyvárad. Bihor, NW Romania
Oradea Mare *see* Oradea
115 M17 **Orahovac** *Alb.* Rahovec. Serbia, S Yugoslavia
114 H9 **Orahovica** Virovitica-Podravina, NE Croatia
158 K13 **Orai** Uttar Pradesh, N India
94 K12 **Orajärvi** Lappi, NW Finland
Oral *see* Ural'sk
76 I5 **Oran** *var.* Ouahran, Wahran. NW Algeria
191 R8 **Orange** New South Wales, SE Australia
105 R14 **Orange** *anc.* Arausio. Vaucluse, SE France
27 Y10 **Orange** Texas, SW USA
23 V5 **Orange** Virginia, NE USA
23 R13 **Orangeburg** South Carolina, SE USA
60 J9 **Orange, Cabo** *headland* NE Brazil
31 S12 **Orange City** Iowa, C USA
Orange Cone *see* Orange Fan
180 J10 **Orange Fan** *var.* Orange Cone. *undersea feature* SW Indian Ocean
Orange Free State *see* Free State
27 S14 **Orange Grove** Texas, SW USA
20 K13 **Orange Lake** New York, NE USA
25 V10 **Orange Lake** ◎ Florida, SE USA
Orange Mouth/Orangemund *see* Oranjemund
25 W9 **Orange Park** Florida, SE USA
194 M17 **Orangerie Bay** *bay* SE PNG
85 E23 **Orange River** *Afr.* Oranjerivier. ≈ S Africa
12 G15 **Orangeville** Ontario, S Canada
38 M5 **Orangeville** Utah, W USA
44 G1 **Orange Walk** Orange Walk, N Belize
44 F1 **Orange Walk** ◐ *district* NW Belize
102 N11 **Oranienburg** Brandenburg, NE Germany
100 O7 **Oranjekanaal** *canal* NE Netherlands
85 D23 **Oranjemund** *var.* Orangemund; *prev.* Orange Mouth. Karas, SW Namibia
Oranjerivier *see* Orange River
47 N16 **Oranjestad** ○ (Aruba) W Aruba
Oranje Vrystaat *see* Free State
xliv E9 **Oranmore** Galway, W Ireland
176 W9 **Oransbari** Irian Jaya, E Indonesia
Orany *see* Varėna
85 H18 **Orapa** Central, C Botswana
144 F9 **Or 'Aqiva** Haifa, W Israel
114 I10 **Orašje** N Bosnia and Herzegovina
118 G11 **Orăștie** *Ger.* Broos, *Hung.* Szászváros. Hunedoara, W Romania
Orașul Stalin *see* Brașov
113 K18 **Orava** *Hung.* Árva, *Pol.* Orawa. ≈ N Slovakia
Oravainen *see* Oravais
95 K16 **Oravais** *Fin.* Oravainen. Vaasa, W Finland
Oravicabánya *see* Oravița
118 F13 **Oravița** *Ger.* Orawitza, *Hung.* Oravicabánya. Caraș-Severin, SW Romania
Orawa *see* Orava
193 B24 **Orawia** Southland, South Island, NZ
Orawitza *see* Oravița
105 P16 **Orb** ≈ S France
108 C9 **Orba** ≈ NW Italy
164 H12 **Orba Co** ◎ W China
110 B9 **Orbe** Vaud, W Switzerland
109 G14 **Orbetello** Toscana, C Italy
106 K3 **Órbigo** ≈ NW Spain
191 Q12 **Orbost** Victoria, SE Australia
97 O14 **Örbyhus** Uppsala, C Sweden
204 I1 **Orcadas** *Argentinian research station* South Orkney Islands, Antarctica
107 P12 **Orcera** Andalucía, S Spain
35 P9 **Orchard Homes** Montana, NW USA
39 P5 **Orchard Mesa** Colorado, C USA
20 D10 **Orchard Park** New York, NE USA
Orchid Island *see* Lan Yü
117 G18 **Orchómenos** *var.* Orhomenos, Orkhómenos; *prev.* Skripón, *anc.* Orchomenus. Stereá Ellás, C Greece
Orchomenus *see* Orchómenos
108 B7 **Orco** ≈ NW Italy
105 R8 **Or, Côte d'** *physical region* C France
xlii E13 **Ord** Highland, NW Scotland, UK
31 O14 **Ord** Nebraska, C USA
Ordat' *see* Ordats'
121 O15 **Ordats'** *Rus.* Ordat'. Mahilyowskaya Voblasts', E Belorussia
38 K8 **Orderville** Utah, W USA
106 H2 **Ordes** Galicia, NW Spain
37 V14 **Ord Mountain** ▲ California, W USA
Ordos Desert *see* Mu Us Shamo
196 B16 **Ordot** C Guam
143 N11 **Ordu** *anc.* Cotyora. Ordu, N Turkey
142 M11 **Ordu** ◐ *province* N Turkey
143 V14 **Ordubad** SW Azerbaijan
107 O3 **Orduña** País Vasco, N Spain
39 U6 **Ordway** Colorado, C USA
150 L8 **Ordzhonikidze** Kustanay, N Kazakhstan
119 T9 **Ordzhonikidze** Dnipropetrovs'ka Oblast', E Ukraine
Ordzhonikidze *see* Vladikavkaz, Russian Federation
Ordzhonikidze *see* Yenakiyeve, Ukraine
Ordzhonikidzeabad *see* Kofarnihon
xxxvii M13 **Ore** East Sussex, SE England, UK
57 U9 **Orealla** E Guyana
115 G15 **Orebić** *It.* Sabbioncello. Dubrovnik-Neretva, S Croatia
97 M16 **Örebro** Örebro, C Sweden
97 L16 **Örebro** ◐ *county* C Sweden
27 W6 **Ore City** Texas, SW USA
32 L10 **Oregon** Illinois, N USA
29 Q2 **Oregon** Missouri, C USA
33 R11 **Oregon** Ohio, N USA
34 H13 **Oregon** *off.* State of Oregon; also known as Beaver State, Sunset State, Valentine State, Webfoot State. ◐ *state* NW USA
34 G11 **Oregon City** Oregon, NW USA
97 P14 **Öregrund** Uppsala, C Sweden
Orekhov *see* Orikhiv
130 L3 **Orekhovo-Zuyevo** Moskovskaya Oblast', W Russian Federation
Orekhovsk *see* Arekhawsk
Orel *see* Oril'
130 J6 **Orël** Orlovskaya Oblast', W Russian Federation
58 E11 **Orellana** Loreto, N Peru
106 L11 **Orellana, Embalse de** ⊡ W Spain
38 L3 **Orem** Utah, W USA
Ore Mountains *see* Erzgebirge/Krušné Hory
131 V7 **Orenburg** *prev.* Chkalov. Orenburgskaya Oblast', W Russian Federation
131 V7 **Orenburg** ✕ Orenburgskaya Oblast', W Russian Federation
131 T7 **Orenburgskaya Oblast'** ◐ *province* W Russian Federation
Orense *see* Ourense
196 E10 **Oreor** *var.* Koror. ● (Palau) Oreor, N Palau
196 E10 **Oreor** *var.* Koror. *island* N Palau
193 B24 **Orepuki** Southland, South Island, NZ
116 L12 **Orestiáda** *prev.* Orestiás. Anatolikí Makedonía kai Thráki, NE Greece
Orestiás *see* Orestiáda
Öresund/Øresund *see* Sound, The
193 C23 **Oreti** ≈ South Island, NZ
192 L5 **Orewa** Auckland, North Island, NZ
176 Y14 **Oreyabo** Irian Jaya, E Indonesia
xxxix Y13 **Orford** Suffolk, E England, UK
67 A25 **Orford, Cape** *headland* West Falkland, Falkland Islands
xxxix Y13 **Orford Ness** *headland* E England, UK
46 B5 **Órganos, Sierra de los** ▲▲ W Cuba
39 R15 **Organ Peak** ▲ New Mexico, SW USA
107 N9 **Orgaz** Castilla-La Mancha, C Spain
Orgeyev *see* Orhei
168 I6 **Orgil** Hövsgöl, C Mongolia
107 O15 **Orgiva** *var.* Orjiva. Andalucía, S Spain
168 I9 **Örgön** Bayanhongor, C Mongolia
119 N9 **Orhei** *var.* Orheiu, *Rus.* Orgeyev. N Moldavia
Orheiu *see* Orhei
107 R3 **Orhi** *var.* Orhy, Pico de Orhy, Pic d'Orhy. ▲ France/Spain *see also* Orhy
Orhomenos *see* Orchómenos
168 L6 **Orhon Gol** ≈ N Mongolia
104 J16 **Orhy** *var.* Orhi, Pico de Orhy, Pic d'Orhy. ▲ France/Spain *see also* Orhi
Orhy, Pic d'/Orhy, Pico de *see* Orhi/Orhy
36 L2 **Orick** California, W USA
34 L6 **Orient** Washington, NW USA
50 D6 **Oriental, Cordillera** ▲▲ Bolivia/Peru
50 D6 **Oriental, Cordillera** ▲▲ C Colombia
59 H16 **Oriental, Cordillera** ▲▲ C Peru
65 M15 **Oriente** Buenos Aires, E Argentina
107 R12 **Orihuela** País Valenciano, E Spain
119 V9 **Orikhiv** *Rus.* Orekhov. Zaporiz'ka Oblast', SE Ukraine
115 K22 **Orikum** *var.* Orikumi. Vlorë, SW Albania
Orikumi *see* Orikum
119 V6 **Oril'** *Rus.* Orel. ≈ E Ukraine
12 H14 **Orillia** Ontario, S Canada
95 M19 **Orimattila** Uusimaa, S Finland
35 Y15 **Orin** Wyoming, C USA
49 R4 **Orinoco, Río** ≈ Colombia/Venezuela
194 G15 **Oriomo** Western, SW PNG
32 K11 **Orion** Illinois, N USA
31 O5 **Oriska** North Dakota, N USA
159 P17 **Orissa** ◐ *state* NE India
Orissaar *see* Orissaare
120 E5 **Orissaare** *Ger.* Orissaar. Saaremaa, W Estonia
109 B19 **Oristano** Sardegna, Italy, C Mediterranean Sea
109 A19 **Oristano, Golfo di** *gulf* Sardegna, Italy, C Mediterranean Sea
56 D13 **Orito** Putumayo, SW Colombia
95 L18 **Orivesi** Häme, SW Finland
95 N17 **Orivesi** ◎ SE Finland
60 H12 **Oriximiná** Pará, NE Brazil
43 Q14 **Orizaba** Veracruz-Llave, E Mexico
43 Q14 **Orizaba, Volcán Pico de** *var.* Citlaltépetl. ⩚ S Mexico
97 I16 **Ørje** Østfold, S Norway
115 I16 **Orjen** ▲ Bosnia and Herzegovina/Yugoslavia
Orjiva *see* Orgiva
96 G8 **Orkanger** Sør-Trøndelag, S Norway
96 G8 **Orkdalen** *valley* S Norway
97 K22 **Örkelljunga** Kristianstad, S Sweden
Orkhaniye *see* Botevgrad
Orkhómenos *see* Orchómenos
96 H9 **Orkla** ≈ S Norway
Orkney *see* Orkney Islands
67 J22 **Orkney Deep** *undersea feature* Scotia Sea/Weddell Sea
xlii M3 **Orkney Islands** ◐ *unitary authority* N Scotland, UK
xlii N4 **Orkney Islands** *var.* Orkney, Orkneys. *island group* N Scotland, UK
Orkneys *see* Orkney Islands
26 K8 **Orla** Texas, SW USA
37 N5 **Orland** California, W USA
25 X11 **Orlando** Florida, SE USA
25 X12 **Orlando** ✕ Florida, SE USA
109 K23 **Orlando, Capo d'** *headland* Sicilia, Italy, C Mediterranean Sea
Orlau *see* Orlová
105 N6 **Orléanais** *cultural region* C France
36 L2 **Orleans** California, W USA
21 Q12 **Orleans** Massachusetts, NE USA
105 N7 **Orléans** *anc.* Aurelianum. Loiret, C France
13 R10 **Orléans, Île d'** *island* Québec, SE Canada
Orléansville *see* Chlef
xxxviii H12 **Orleton** Herefordshire, W England, UK
113 F16 **Orlice** *Ger.* Adler. ≈ NE Czech Republic
126 I15 **Orlik** Respublika Buryatiya, S Russian Federation
129 Q14 **Orlov** *prev.* Khalturin. Kirovskaya Oblast', NW Russian Federation
113 I17 **Orlová** *Ger.* Orlau, *Pol.* Orłowa. Severní Morava, SE Czech Republic
Orlov, Mys *see* Orlovskiy, Mys
130 I6 **Orlovskaya Oblast'** ◐ *province* W Russian Federation
128 M5 **Orlovskiy, Mys** *var.* Mys Orlov. *headland* NW Russian Federation
Orłowa *see* Orlová
105 O5 **Orly** ✕ (Paris) Essonne, N France
121 G16 **Orlya** *Rus.* Orlya. Hrodzyenskaya Voblasts', W Belorussia
116 M7 **Orlyak** *prev.* Makenzen, Trubchular, *Rom.* Trupcilar. Varnenska Oblast, NE Bulgaria
154 L16 **Ormāra** Baluchistān, SW Pakistan
xli Y6 **Ormesby** Redcar and Cleveland, N England, UK
xxxix Y9 **Ormesby St Margaret** Norfolk, E England, UK
179 Qq13 **Ormoc** *off.* Ormoc City, *var.* MacArthur. Leyte, C Philippines
25 X10 **Ormond Beach** Florida, SE USA
111 X10 **Ormož** *Ger.* Friedau. NE Slovenia
12 J13 **Ormsby** Ontario, SE Canada
xl C14 **Ormskirk** Lancashire, NW England, UK
Ormsö *see* Vormsi
13 N13 **Ormstown** Québec, SE Canada
Ormuz, Strait of *see* Hormuz, Strait of
105 T8 **Ornans** Doubs, E France
104 K5 **Orne** ◐ *department* N France
104 K5 **Orne** ≈ N France
94 G12 **Ørnes** Nordland, C Norway
112 L7 **Orneta** Elbląg, N Poland
97 P16 **Ornö** Stockholm, C Sweden
39 Q3 **Orno Peak** ▲ Colorado, C USA
95 I16 **Örnsköldsvik** Västernorrland, C Sweden
169 X13 **Oro** E North Korea
47 T6 **Orocovis** C Puerto Rico
56 H10 **Orocué** Casanare, E Colombia
79 N13 **Orodara** SW Burkina
107 S4 **Oroel, Peña de** ▲ N Spain
35 N10 **Orofino** Idaho, NW USA
168 I9 **Orog Nuur** ◎ S Mongolia
37 U14 **Oro Grande** California, W USA
39 S15 **Orogrande** New Mexico, SW USA
203 Q7 **Orohena, Mont** ⩚ Tahiti, W French Polynesia
Orolaunum *see* Arlon
Orol Dengizi *see* Aral Sea
201 S15 **Oroluk Atoll** *atoll* Caroline Islands, C Micronesia
11 O15 **Oromocto** New Brunswick, SE Canada
203 S4 **Orona** *prev.* Hull Island. *atoll* Phoenix Islands, C Kiribati
203 V17 **Orongo** *ancient monument* Easter Island, Chile, E Pacific Ocean
xliii D19 **Oronsay** *island* W Scotland, UK
144 I3 **Orontes** *var.* Ononte, *Ar.* Nahr el Aassi, Nahr al 'Āṣī. ≈ SW Asia
106 L9 **Oropesa** Castilla-La Mancha, C Spain
107 T8 **Oropesa** País Valenciano, E Spain
Oropeza *see* Cochabamba
169 U5 **Oroqen Zizhiqi** Nei Mongol Zizhiqu, N China
179 Qq15 **Oroquieta** *var.* Oroquieta City. Mindanao, S Philippines
42 J8 **Oro, Río del** ≈ C Mexico
61 O14 **Orós, Açude** ⊡ E Brazil
109 D18 **Orosei, Golfo di** *gulf* Tyrrhenian Sea, C Mediterranean Sea
113 M24 **Orosháza** Békés, SE Hungary
Orosirá Rodhópis *see* Rhodope Mountains
113 I22 **Oroszlány** Komárom-Esztergom, W Hungary
196 B16 **Orote Peninsula** *peninsula* W Guam
127 O9 **Orotukan** Magadanskaya Oblast', E Russian Federation
37 O5 **Oroville** California, W USA
34 K6 **Oroville** Washington, NW USA
37 O5 **Oroville, Lake** ⊡ California, W USA
0 G15 **Orozco Fracture Zone** *tectonic feature* E Pacific Ocean
66 I7 **Orphan Knoll** *undersea feature* NW Atlantic Ocean
xxxvii U10 **Orpington** Bromley, SE England, UK
31 V3 **Orr** Minnesota, N USA
97 M21 **Orrefors** Kalmar, S Sweden
xlii H12 **Orrin Reservoir** ⊡ NW Scotland, UK
190 I7 **Orroroo** South Australia
33 T12 **Orrville** Ohio, N USA
96 L12 **Orsa** Kopparberg, C Sweden
Orschowa *see* Orșova
Orschütz *see* Orzyc
121 O14 **Orsha** *Rus.* Orsha. Vitsyebskaya Voblasts', NE Belorussia
131 Q2 **Orshanka** Respublika Mariy El, W Russian Federation
110 C11 **Orsières** Valais, SW Switzerland
125 Dd13 **Orsk** Orenburgskaya Oblast', W Russian Federation
118 F13 **Orșova** *Ger.* Orschowa, *Hung.* Orsova. Mehedinți, SW Romania
96 D10 **Ørsta** Møre og Romsdal, S Norway
97 O15 **Örsundsbro** Uppsala, C Sweden
142 D16 **Ortaca** Muğla, SW Turkey
109 M16 **Orta Nova** Puglia, SE Italy
142 I17 **Orta Toroslar** ▲▲ S Turkey
56 E11 **Ortega** Tolima, W Colombia
106 H1 **Ortegal, Cabo** *headland* NW Spain
Ortelsburg *see* Szczytno
104 J15 **Orthez** Pyrénées-Atlantiques, SW France
59 K14 **Orthon, Río** ≈ N Bolivia
62 I10 **Ortigueira** Paraná, S Brazil
106 H1 **Ortigueira** Galicia, NW Spain
108 H5 **Ortisei** *Ger.* Sankt-Ulrich. Trentino-Alto Adige, N Italy
42 F6 **Ortiz** Sonora, NW Mexico
56 L5 **Ortiz** Guárico, N Venezuela
Ortler *see* Ortles
108 F5 **Ortles** *Ger.* Ortler. ▲ N Italy
xli N10 **Orton** Cumbria, NW England, UK
109 K14 **Ortona** Abruzzi, C Italy
31 R8 **Ortonville** Minnesota, N USA
153 W8 **Orto-Tokoy** Issyk-Kul'skaya Oblast', NE Kyrgyzstan
95 I15 **Örträsk** Västerbotten, N Sweden
102 J12 **Örtze** ≈ NW Germany
Oruba *see* Aruba
148 I3 **Orūmīyeh** *var.* Rizaiyeh, Urmia, Urmiyeh; *prev.* Reẓā'īyeh. Āẕarbāyjān-e Bākhtarī, NW Iran
148 J3 **Orūmīyeh, Daryācheh-ye** *var.* Matianus, Sha Hi, Urumi Yeh, *Eng.* Lake Urmia; *prev.* Daryācheh-ye Reẓā'īyeh. ◎ NW Iran
59 K19 **Oruro** Oruro, W Bolivia
59 J19 **Oruro** ◐ *department* W Bolivia
97 I18 **Orust** *island* S Sweden
Orūzgān/Orūzgān *see* Urūzgān
108 H13 **Orvieto** *anc.* Velsuna. Umbria, C Italy
204 K7 **Orville Coast** *physical region* Antarctica
xxxix S13 **Orwell** Cambridgeshire, E England, UK
xxxix X13 **Orwell** ≈ E England, UK
116 H7 **Oryakhovo** Oblast Montana, NW Bulgaria
Oryokko *see* Yalu
119 R5 **Orzhytsya** Poltavs'ka Oblast', C Ukraine
112 M9 **Orzyc** *Ger.* Orschütz. ≈ NE Poland
112 N8 **Orzysz** *Ger.* Arys. Suwałki, NE Poland
96 I10 **Os** Hedmark, S Norway
97 C14 **Os** Hordaland, S Norway
129 U15 **Osa** Permskaya Oblast', NW Russian Federation
31 W11 **Osage** Iowa, C USA
29 U5 **Osage Beach** Missouri, C USA
29 P5 **Osage City** Kansas, C USA
29 U7 **Osage Fork River** ≈ Missouri, C USA
29 U5 **Osage River** ≈ Missouri, C USA
171 Gg15 **Ōsaka** *hist.* Naniwa. Ōsaka, Honshū, SW Japan
171 Gg15 **Ōsaka** *off.* Ōsaka-fu, *var.* Ōsaka Hu. ◐ *urban prefecture* Honshū, SW Japan
Ōsaka-fu/Ōsaka Hu *see* Ōsaka
151 R10 **Osakarovka** Karaganda, C Kazakhstan
170 G15 **Ōsaka-wan** *bay* SW Japan
31 T7 **Osakis** Minnesota, N USA
45 N16 **Osa, Península de** *peninsula* S Costa Rica
62 M10 **Osasco** São Paulo, S Brazil
29 R5 **Osawatomie** Kansas, C USA
28 L3 **Osborne** Kansas, C USA
181 S8 **Osborn Plateau** *undersea feature* E Indian Ocean
xxxix Q8 **Osbournby** Lincolnshire, E England, UK
97 L21 **Osby** Kristianstad, S Sweden
Osca *see* Huesca
94 N2 **Oscar II Land** *physical region* W Svalbard
29 Y10 **Osceola** Arkansas, C USA
31 V15 **Osceola** Iowa, C USA
29 S6 **Osceola** Missouri, C USA
31 Q15 **Osceola** Nebraska, C USA
103 N15 **Oschatz** Sachsen, E Germany
102 K13 **Oschersleben** Sachsen-Anhalt, C Germany
33 R7 **Oscoda** Michigan, N USA
Ösel *see* Saaremaa
96 H6 **Osen** Sør-Trøndelag, S Norway
170 Aa12 **Ōse-zaki** *headland* Fukue-jima, SW Japan
153 T10 **Osh** Oshskaya Oblast', SW Kyrgyzstan
85 C16 **Oshakati** Oshana, N Namibia
172 Nn6 **Oshamanbe** Hokkaidō, NE Japan
85 C16 **Oshana** ◐ *district* N Namibia
126 Ii12 **Osharovo** Evenkiyskiy Avtonomnyy Okrug, N Russian Federation
12 H15 **Oshawa** Ontario, SE Canada
171 Mm13 **Oshika-hantō** *peninsula* Honshū, C Japan
85 C16 **Oshikango** Ohangwena, N Namibia
Oshikoto *see* Otjikoto
170 Cc12 **Ō-shima** *island* SW Japan
171 M7 **Ō-shima** *island* NE Japan
171 Jj17 **Ō-shima** *island* S Japan
170 G17 **Ō-shima** *island* SW Japan
172 N6 **Oshima-hantō** ▲ Hokkaidō, NE Japan
85 D17 **Oshivelo** Otjikoto, N Namibia
30 K14 **Oshkosh** Nebraska, C USA
32 M7 **Oshkosh** Wisconsin, N USA
Oshmyany *see* Ashmyany
Osh Oblasty *see* Oshskaya Oblast'
79 T16 **Oshogbo** Osun, W Nigeria
153 S11 **Oshskaya Oblast'** *Kir.* Osh Oblasty. ◐ *province* SW Kyrgyzstan
81 J20 **Oshwe** Bandundu, C Zaire
Osiek *see* Osijek
114 I9 **Osijek** *prev.* Osiek, Osjek, *Ger.* Esseg, *Hung.* Eszék. Osijek-Baranja, E Croatia
114 I9 **Osijek-Baranja** *off.* Osječko-Baranjska Županija. ◐ *province* E Croatia
108 J12 **Osimo** Marche, C Italy
126 H15 **Osinniki** Kemerovskaya Oblast', S Russian Federation
126 J14 **Osinovka** Irkutskaya Oblast', C Russian Federation
Osintorf *see* Asintorf
114 N11 **Osipaonica** Serbia, NE Yugoslavia
Osipenko *see* Berdyans'k
Osipovichi *see* Asipovichy
Osječko-Baranjska Županija *see* Osijek-Baranja
Osjek *see* Osijek
31 W15 **Oskaloosa** Iowa, C USA
29 Q4 **Oskaloosa** Kansas, C USA
xliii E17 **Oskamull** Argyll and Bute, W Scotland, UK
97 N20 **Oskarshamn** Kalmar, S Sweden
97 J21 **Oskarström** Halland, S Sweden
12 M8 **Oskélanéo** Québec, SE Canada
Öskemen *see* Ust'-Kamenogorsk

♦ Country
● Country Capital
◇ Dependent Territory
○ Dependent Territory Capital
◐ Administrative Region
✕ International Airport
▲ Mountain
▲▲ Mountain Range
⩚ Volcano
≈ River
◎ Lake
⊡ Reservoir

Oskil – Pakistan

Oskil *see* Oskol
119 W5 **Oskol** *Ukr.* Oskil. ≈ Russian Federation/Ukraine
95 D20 **Oslo** *prev.* Christiania, Kristiania. ● (Norway) Oslo, S Norway
95 D20 **Oslo** ◈ *county* S Norway
95 D21 **Oslofjorden** *fjord* S Norway
161 G15 **Osmānābād** Mahārāshtra, C India
142 J11 **Osmancık** Çorum, N Turkey
142 L16 **Osmaniye** Adana, S Turkey
xxxvi L14 **Osmington** Dorset, ~ S England, UK
97 O16 **Ösmo** Stockholm, C Sweden
xli S10 **Osmotherley** North Yorkshire, N England, UK
120 E3 **Osmussaar** *island* W Estonia
102 G13 **Osnabrück** Niedersachsen, NW Germany
112 D11 **Ośno Lubuskie** *Ger.* Drossen. Gorzów, W Poland
Osogovske Planine *see* Osogovski Planina
115 P18 **Osogovski Planina** *var.* Osogovske Planine, *Mac.* Osogovski Planini. ▲▲ Bulgaria/FYR Macedonia
Osogovski Planini *see* Osogovski Planina
172 N8 **Osore-yama** ▲ Honshū, C Japan
Oşorhei *see* Târgu Mureş
63 J16 **Osório** Rio Grande do Sul, S Brazil
65 G16 **Osorno** Los Lagos, C Chile
106 M4 **Osorno** Castilla-León, N Spain
9 N17 **Osoyoos** British Columbia, SW Canada
56 J6 **Ospino** Portuguesa, N Venezuela
100 K13 **Oss** Noord-Brabant, S Netherlands
106 H11 **Ossa** ▲ S Portugal
117 F15 **Óssa** ▲▲ C Greece
25 X6 **Ossabaw Island** *island* Georgia, SE USA
25 X6 **Ossabaw Sound** *sound* Georgia, SE USA
191 O16 **Ossa, Mount** ▲ Tasmania, SE Australia
106 H11 **Ossa, Serra d'** ▲▲ SE Portugal
79 U16 **Osse** ≈ S Nigeria
32 J6 **Osseo** Wisconsin, N USA
xli R15 **Ossett** Wakefield, N England, UK
111 S9 **Ossiacher See** ◎ S Austria
20 K13 **Ossining** New York, NE USA
96 I12 **Ossjøen** ◎ S Norway
127 P9 **Ossora** Koryakskiy Avtonomnyy Okrug, E Russian Federation
128 I15 **Ostashkov** Tverskaya Oblast', W Russian Federation
102 H9 **Oste** ≈ NW Germany
Ostee *see* Baltic Sea
Ostend/Ostende *see* Oostende
119 P3 **Oster** Chernihivs'ka Oblast', N Ukraine
97 O14 **Österbybruk** Uppsala, C Sweden
97 M19 **Österbymo** Östergotland, S Sweden
96 K12 **Österdalälven** ≈ C Sweden
96 I12 **Østerdalen** *valley* S Norway
97 L18 **Östergötland** ◈ *county* S Sweden
102 H10 **Osterholz-Scharmbeck** Niedersachsen, NW Germany
Östermark *see* Teuva
Östermyra *see* Seinäjoki
Osterode/Osterode in Ostpreussen *see* Ostróda
103 J14 **Osterode am Harz** Niedersachsen, C Germany
96 C13 **Osterøy** *island* S Norway
Österreich *see* Austria
95 G16 **Östersund** Jämtland, C Sweden
97 N14 **Östervåla** Västmanland, C Sweden
103 H22 **Ostfildern** Baden-Württemberg, SW Germany
97 H16 **Østfold** ◈ *county* S Norway
102 E9 **Ostfriesische Inseln** *Eng.* East Frisian Islands. *island group* NW Germany
102 F10 **Ostfriesland** *historical region* NW Germany
97 P14 **Östhammar** Uppsala, C Sweden
Ostia Aterni *see* Pescara
108 G8 **Ostiglia** Lombardia, N Italy
97 J14 **Östmark** Värmland, C Sweden
97 K22 **Östra Ringsjön** ◎ S Sweden
113 I17 **Ostrava** Severní Morava, E Czech Republic
112 K8 **Ostróda** *Ger.* Osterode, Osterode in Ostpreussen. Olsztyn, N Poland
Ostrog/Ostróg *see* Ostroh
130 L8 **Ostrogozhsk** Voronezhskaya Oblast', W Russian Federation
118 L4 **Ostroh** *Pol.* Ostróg, *Rus.* Ostrog. Rivnens'ka Oblast', NW Ukraine
Ostrołęckie, Województwo *see* Ostrołęka
112 N9 **Ostrołęka** *Ger.* Wiesenhof, *Rus.* Ostrolenka. Ostrołęka, NE Poland
112 M10 **Ostrołęka** *off.* Województwo Ostrołęckie, *Rus.* Ostrolenka. ◈ *province* NE Poland
Ostrolenka *see* Ostrołęka
113 A16 **Ostrov** *Ger.* Schlackenwerth. Západní Čechy, NW Czech Republic
128 F15 **Ostrov** *Latv.* Austrava. Pskovskaya Oblast', W Russian Federation
Ostrovets *see* Ostrowiec Świętokrzyski
115 M21 **Ostrovicës, Mali i** ▲ SE Albania
172 T6 **Ostrov Iturup** *island* NE Russian Federation
116 L7 **Ostrovo** *prev.* Golema Ada. Razgradska Oblast, NE Bulgaria
129 N15 **Ostrovskoye** Kostromskaya Oblast', NW Russian Federation
Ostrów *see* Ostrów Wielkopolski
Ostrowiec *see* Ostrowiec Świętokrzyski
113 M14 **Ostrowiec Świętokrzyski** *var.* Ostrowiec, *Rus.* Ostrovets. Kielce, SE Poland
112 P13 **Ostrów Lubelski** Lublin, E Poland
112 N10 **Ostrów Mazowiecka** *var.* Ostrów Mazowiecki. Ostrołęka, NE Poland
Ostrów Mazowiecki *see* Ostrów Mazowiecka
Ostrowo *see* Ostrów Wielkopolski
112 H13 **Ostrów Wielkopolski** *var.* Ostrów, *Ger.* Ostrowo. Kalisz, C Poland
Ostryna *see* Astryna
112 I13 **Ostrzeszów** Kalisz, C Poland
109 P18 **Ostuni** Puglia, SE Italy
Ostyako-Voguls'k *see* Khanty-Mansiysk
Osum *see* Osumit, Lumi i
116 I9 **Osŭm** ≈ N Bulgaria
170 Bb17 **Ōsumi-hantō** ▲▲ Kyūshū, SW Japan
170 Bb17 **Ōsumi-kaikyō** *strait* SW Japan
115 L22 **Osumit, Lumi i** *var.* Osum. ≈ SE Albania
79 T16 **Osun** ◈ *state* SW Nigeria
106 L14 **Osuna** Andalucía, S Spain
62 J8 **Osvaldo Cruz** São Paulo, S Brazil
Osveya *see* Asvyeya
xli T11 **Oswaldkirk** North Yorkshire, N England, UK
20 J7 **Oswegatchie River** ≈ New York, NE USA
29 Q7 **Oswego** Kansas, C USA
20 H9 **Oswego** New York, NE USA
xxxviii G8 **Oswestry** Shropshire, W England, UK
113 J16 **Oświęcim** *Ger.* Auschwitz. Bielsko-Biała, S Poland
171 K15 **Ōta** Gunma, Honshū, S Japan
193 E22 **Otago** *off.* Otago Region. ◈ *region* South Island, NZ
193 F23 **Otago Peninsula** *peninsula* South Island, NZ
170 E13 **Ōtake** Hiroshima, Honshū, SW Japan
192 L13 **Otaki** Wellington, North Island, NZ
171 L14 **Ōtakine-yama** ▲ Honshū, C Japan
95 M15 **Otanmäki** Oulu, C Finland
151 T15 **Otar** Zhambyl, SE Kazakhstan
172 O5 **Otaru** Hokkaidō, NE Japan
193 C24 **Otatara** Southland, South Island, NZ
193 C24 **Otautau** Southland, South Island, NZ
95 M18 **Otava** Mikkeli, SE Finland
113 B18 **Otava** *Ger.* Wottawa. ≈ SW Czech Republic
58 C6 **Otavalo** Imbabura, N Ecuador
85 D17 **Otavi** Otjozondjupa, N Namibia
171 Kk15 **Ōtawara** Tochigi, Honshū, S Japan
85 B16 **Otchinjau** Cunene, SW Angola
118 F12 **Oţelu Roşu** *Ger.* Ferdinandsberg, *Hung.* Nándorhgy. Caras-Severin, SW Romania
193 E21 **Otematata** Canterbury, South Island, NZ
120 I6 **Otepää** *Ger.* Odenpäh. Valgamaa, SE Estonia
34 K9 **Othello** Washington, NW USA
117 A15 **Othonoí** *island* Iónioi Nísoi, Greece, C Mediterranean Sea
Othris *see* Óthrys
117 F17 **Óthrys** *var.* Othris. ▲▲ C Greece
79 Q14 **Oti** ≈ N Togo
42 K10 **Otinapa** Durango, C Mexico
193 G17 **Otira** West Coast, South Island, NZ
39 V3 **Otis** Colorado, C USA
10 L10 **Otish, Monts** ▲▲ Québec, E Canada
85 C17 **Otjikondo** Kunene, N Namibia
85 C17 **Otjikoto** *var.* Oshikoto. ◈ *district* N Namibia
85 E18 **Otjinene** Omaheke, NE Namibia
85 D18 **Otjiwarongo** Otjozondjupa, N Namibia
85 D18 **Otjosondu** *var.* Otjosundu. Otjozondjupa, C Namibia
Otjosundu *see* Otjosondu
85 D18 **Otjozondjupa** ◈ *district* C Namibia
xli R13 **Otley** Leeds, N England, UK
xxxix X12 **Otley** Suffolk, E England, UK
114 C11 **Otočac** Lika-Senj, W Croatia
172 Pp6 **Otofuke-gawa** ≈ Hokkaidō, NE Japan
168 M14 **Otog Qi** Nei Mongol Zizhiqu, N China
172 Pp3 **Otoineppu** Hokkaidō, NE Japan
114 J10 **Otok** Vukovar-Srijem, E Croatia
118 K14 **Otopen** ✕ (Bucureşti) Bucureşti, S Romania
192 L8 **Otorohanga** Waikato, North Island, NZ
10 D9 **Otoskwin** ≈ Ontario, C Canada
170 F15 **Ōtoyo** Kōchi, Shikoku, SW Japan
97 E16 **Otra** ≈ S Norway
109 R19 **Otranto** Puglia, SE Italy
Otranto, Canale d' *see* Otranto, Strait of
109 Q18 **Otranto, Strait of** *It.* Canale d'Otranto. *strait* Albania/Italy
113 H18 **Otrokovice** *Ger.* Otrokowitz. Jižní Morava, SE Czech Republic
Otrokowitz *see* Otrokovice
33 P10 **Otsego** Michigan, N USA
33 Q6 **Otsego Lake** ◎ Michigan, N USA
20 I11 **Otselic River** ≈ New York, NE USA
171 H15 **Ōtsu** *var.* Ôtu. Shiga, Honshū, SW Japan
171 Jj16 **Ōtsuki** *var.* Otuki. Yamanashi, Honshū, S Japan
96 G11 **Otta** Oppland, S Norway
201 U13 **Otta** *island* Chuuk, C Micronesia
96 F11 **Otta** ≈ S Norway
201 U13 **Otta Pass** *passage* Chuuk Islands, C Micronesia
97 J22 **Ottarp** Malmöhus, S Sweden
12 L12 **Ottawa** ● (Canada) Ontario, SE Canada
32 L11 **Ottawa** Illinois, N USA
29 Q5 **Ottawa** Kansas, C USA
33 R12 **Ottawa** Ohio, N USA
12 L12 **Ottawa** *var.* Uplands. ✕ Ontario, SE Canada
12 M12 **Ottawa** *Fr.* Outaouais. ≈ Ontario/Québec, SE Canada
10 I4 **Ottawa Islands** *island group* Northwest Territories, C Canada
xxxvi I14 **Otter** ≈ SW England, UK
xli P4 **Otterburn** Northumberland, N England, UK
20 L8 **Otter Creek** ≈ Vermont, NE USA
38 L6 **Otter Creek Reservoir** ⊞ Utah, W USA
xliii G19 **Otter Ferry** Argyll and Bute, W Scotland, UK
100 L11 **Otterlo** Gelderland, E Netherlands
96 D9 **Otterøya** *island* S Norway
xlii I2 **Otterswick** Shetland Islands, NE Scotland, UK
31 S6 **Otter Tail Lake** ◎ Minnesota, N USA
31 R7 **Otter Tail River** ≈ Minnesota, C USA
xxxvi I14 **Otterton** Devon, SW England, UK
97 H23 **Otterup** Fyn, C Denmark
xxxvi I14 **Ottery St Mary** Devon, SW England, UK
101 H19 **Ottignies** Walloon Brabant, C Belgium
103 L23 **Ottobrunn** Bayern, SE Germany
194 I12 **Otto, Mount** ▲ C PNG
xli X14 **Ottringham** East Riding of Yorkshire, N England, UK
31 X15 **Ottumwa** Iowa, C USA
Ôtu *see* Ōtsu
85 B16 **Otuazuma** Kunene, NW Namibia
Otuki *see* Ōtsuki
79 V16 **Oturkpo** Benue, S Nigeria
200 Ss14 **Otu Tolu Group** *island group* SE Tonga
190 M13 **Otway, Cape** *headland* Victoria, SE Australia
65 H24 **Otway, Seno** *inlet* S Chile
Ötz *see* Oetz
110 L8 **Ötztaler Ache** ≈ W Austria
110 L9 **Ötztaler Alpen** *It.* Alpi Venoste. ▲▲ SW Austria
29 T12 **Ouachita, Lake** ⊞ Arkansas, C USA
29 R11 **Ouachita Mountains** ▲▲ Arkansas/Oklahoma, C USA
29 U13 **Ouachita River** ≈ Arkansas/Louisiana, C USA
Ouadaï *see* Ouaddaï
78 J7 **Ouadâne** *var.* Ouadane. Adrar, C Mauritania
80 K13 **Ouadda** Haute-Kotto, N Central African Republic
80 J10 **Ouaddaï** *off.* Préfecture du Ouaddaï, *var.* Ouadaï, Wadai. ◈ *prefecture* SE Chad
79 P13 **Ouagadougou** *var.* Wagadugu. ● (Burkina) C Burkina
79 P13 **Ouagadougou** ✕ C Burkina
79 O12 **Ouahigouya** NW Burkina
Ouahran *see* Oran
81 J14 **Ouaka** ◈ *prefecture* C Central African Republic
81 J15 **Ouaka** ≈ S Central African Republic
Oualam *see* Ouallam
78 M9 **Oualâta** *var.* Oualata. Hodh ech Chargui, SE Mauritania
79 R11 **Ouallam** *var.* Oualam. Tillabéri, W Niger
180 H14 **Ouanani** Mohéli, S Comoros
57 Z10 **Ouanary** E French Guiana
80 L13 **Ouanda Djallé** Vakaga, NE Central African Republic
81 N14 **Ouando** Haut-Mbomou, SE Central African Republic
81 L15 **Ouango** Mbomou, S Central African Republic
79 N14 **Ouangolodougou** *var.* Wangolodougou. N Ivory Coast
180 I13 **Ouani** Anjouan, SE Comoros
81 M15 **Ouara** ≈ E Central African Republic
78 K7 **Ouarâne** *desert* C Mauritania
13 O11 **Ouareau** ≈ Québec, SE Canada
76 K7 **Ouargla** *var.* Wargla. NE Algeria
76 F8 **Ouarzazate** S Morocco
79 Q11 **Ouatagouna** Gao, E Mali
76 G6 **Ouazzane** *var.* Ouezzane, *Ar.* Wazan, Wazzan. N Morocco
Oubangui *see* Ubangi
Oubangui-Chari *see* Central African Republic
Oubari, Edeyen d' *see* Awbāri, Idhān
100 G13 **Oud-Beijerland** Zuid-Holland, SW Netherlands
100 F13 **Ouddorp** Zuid-Holland, SW Netherlands
79 P9 **Oudeïka** *oasis* C Mali
100 G13 **Oude Maas** ≈ SW Netherlands
101 E18 **Oudenaarde** *Fr.* Audenarde. Oost-Vlaanderen, SW Belgium
101 H14 **Oudenbosch** Noord-Brabant, S Netherlands
100 P6 **Oude Pekela** Groningen, NE Netherlands
Ouderkerk *see* Ouderkerk aan den Amstel
100 I10 **Ouderkerk aan den Amstel** *var.* Ouderkerk. Noord-Holland, C Netherlands
100 I6 **Oudeschild** Noord-Holland, NW Netherlands
101 G14 **Oude-Tonge** Zuid-Holland, SW Netherlands
100 I12 **Oudewater** Utrecht, C Netherlands
Oudjda *see* Oujda
100 L5 **Oudkerk** Friesland, N Netherlands
104 J7 **Oudon** ≈ NW France
100 I9 **Oudorp** Noord-Holland, NW Netherlands
85 G25 **Oudtshoorn** Western Cape, SW South Africa
101 I16 **Oud-Turnhout** Antwerpen, N Belgium
76 F7 **Oued-Zem** C Morocco
197 H5 **Ouégoa** Province Nord, C New Caledonia
78 L13 **Ouéléssébougou** *var.* Ouolosséboougou. Koulikoro, SW Mali
79 N16 **Ouellé** E Ivory Coast
79 R16 **Ouémé** ≈ C Benin
197 J7 **Ouen, Île** *island* S New Caledonia
79 O13 **Ouessa** S Burkina
104 D5 **Ouessant, Île d'** *Eng.* Ushant. *island* NW France
81 H17 **Ouésso** La Sangha, NW Congo
81 D15 **Ouest** *Eng.* West. ◈ *province* W Cameroon
202 G11 **Ouest, Baie del'** *bay* Wallis, Wallis and Futuna
13 Y7 **Ouest, Pointe de l'** *headland* Québec, SE Canada
Ouezzane *see* Ouazzane
101 K20 **Ouffet** Liège, E Belgium
xliv D8 **Oughterard** Galway, W Ireland
xliv I6 **Oughter, Lough** ◎ N Ireland
81 H14 **Ouham** ◈ *prefecture* NW Central African Republic
80 I13 **Ouham** ≈ Central African Republic/Chad
81 G14 **Ouham-Pendé** ◈ *prefecture* W Central African Republic
79 R16 **Ouidah** *Eng.* Whydah, Wida. S Benin
76 H6 **Oujda** *Ar.* Oudjda, Ujda. NE Morocco
78 I7 **Oujeft** Adrar, C Mauritania
95 L15 **Oulainen** Oulu, C Finland
Ould Yanja *see* Ould Yenjé
78 J10 **Ould Yenjé** *var.* Ould Yanja. Guidimaka, S Mauritania
xxxix Z10 **Oulton Broad** Suffolk, E England, UK
95 L14 **Oulu** *Swe.* Uleåborg. Oulu, C Finland
95 M14 **Oulu** *Swe.* Uleåborg. ◈ *province* N Finland
95 L15 **Oulujärvi** *Swe.* Uleträsk. ◎ C Finland
95 M14 **Oulujoki** *Swe.* Uleälv. ≈ C Finland
95 L14 **Oulunsalo** Oulu, C Finland
108 A8 **Oulx** Piemonte, NE Italy
80 J9 **Oum-Chalouba** Borkou-Ennedi-Tibesti, NE Chad
78 M16 **Oumé** C Ivory Coast
76 F7 **Oum er Rbia** ≈ C Morocco
80 J10 **Oum-Hadjer** Batha, E Chad
94 K10 **Ounasjoki** ≈ N Finland
xxxix Q10 **Oundle** Northamptonshire, C England, UK
80 J7 **Ounianga Kébir** Borkou-Ennedi-Tibesti, N Chad
Ouolosséboougou *see* Ouéléssébougou
Oup *see* Auob
101 K19 **Oupeye** Liège, E Belgium
101 N21 **Our** ≈ NW Europe
39 Q7 **Ouray** Colorado, C USA
105 R7 **Ource** ≈ C France
106 G9 **Ourém** Santarém, C Portugal
106 H4 **Ourense** *Cast.* Orense; *Lat.* Aurium. Galicia, NW Spain
106 I4 **Ourense** ◈ *province* Galicia, NW Spain
61 O15 **Ouricuri** Pernambuco, E Brazil
62 J9 **Ourinhos** São Paulo, S Brazil
106 G13 **Ourique** Beja, S Portugal
61 M20 **Ouro Preto** Minas Gerais, NE Brazil
Ours, Grand Lac de l' *see* Great Bear Lake
101 K20 **Ourthe** ≈ E Belgium
171 Mm11 **Ōu-sanmyaku** ▲▲ Honshū, C Japan
xli U14 **Ouse** ≈ N England, UK
xxxvii U12 **Ouse** ≈ SE England, UK
Ouse *see* Great Ouse
104 H7 **Oust** ≈ NW France
Outaouais *see* Ottawa
13 T4 **Outardes Quatre, Réservoir** ⊞ Québec, SE Canada
13 T5 **Outardes, Rivière aux** ≈ Québec, SE Canada
xlii A10 **Outer Hebrides** *var.* Western Isles. *island group* NW Scotland, UK
32 K3 **Outer Island** *island* Apostle Islands, Wisconsin, N USA
37 S16 **Outer Santa Barbara Passage** *passage* California, SW USA
106 G3 **Outes** Galicia, NW Spain
85 C18 **Outjo** Kunene, N Namibia
9 T16 **Outlook** Saskatchewan, S Canada
95 N16 **Outokumpu** Pohjois-Karjala, SE Finland
xlii J2 **Out Skerries** *island group* NE Scotland, UK
xxxix T9 **Outwell** Norfolk, E England, UK
xxxvii U11 **Outwood** Surrey, SE England, UK
197 J5 **Ouvéa** *island* Îles Loyauté, NE New Caledonia
105 S14 **Ouvèze** ≈ SE France
190 L9 **Ouyen** Victoria, SE Australia
41 Q14 **Ouzinkie** Kodiak Island, Alaska, USA
143 O13 **Ovacık** Tunceli, E Turkey
108 C9 **Ovada** Piemonte, NE Italy
197 I14 **Ovalau** *island* C Fiji
64 G9 **Ovalle** Coquimbo, N Chile
85 C17 **Ovamboland** *physical region* N Namibia
56 L10 **Ovana, Cerro** ▲ S Venezuela
106 G7 **Ovar** Aveiro, N Portugal
116 L10 **Ovcharitsa, Yazovir** ⊞ SE Bulgaria
56 E6 **Ovejas** Sucre, NW Colombia
103 E16 **Overath** Nordrhein-Westfalen, W Germany
100 F13 **Overflakkee** *island* SW Netherlands
95 F15 **Overhalla** Nord-Trøndelag, C Norway
101 H19 **Overijse** Vlaams Brabant, C Belgium
100 N10 **Overijssel** ◈ *province* E Netherlands
100 M9 **Overijssels Kanaal** *canal* E Netherlands
94 K13 **Överkalix** Norrbotten, N Sweden
xli N12 **Over Kellet** Lancashire, NW England, UK
29 R4 **Overland Park** Kansas, C USA
101 L14 **Overloon** Noord-Brabant, SE Netherlands
101 K16 **Overpelt** Limburg, NE Belgium
xxxviii M9 **Overseal** Derbyshire, C England, UK
xxxix X7 **Overstrand** Norfolk, E England, UK
xxxvii P11 **Overton** Hampshire, S England, UK
xl M12 **Overton** Lancashire, NW England, UK
xxxv K6 **Overton** Wrexham, NE Wales, UK
37 Y10 **Overton** Nevada, W USA
27 W7 **Overton** Texas, SW USA
94 K13 **Övertorneå** Norrbotten, N Sweden
97 N18 **Överum** Kalmar, S Sweden
94 G13 **Överuman** ◎ N Sweden
168 H6 **Övgödiy** Dzavhan, C Mongolia
119 P11 **Ovidiopol'** Odes'ka Oblast', SW Ukraine
118 M14 **Ovidiu** Constanţa, SE Romania
47 N10 **Oviedo** SW Dominican Republic
106 K2 **Oviedo** *anc.* Asturias. Asturias, NW Spain
106 K2 **Oviedo** ✕ Asturias, N Spain
Ovilava *see* Wels
120 D7 **Oviši** Ventspils, W Latvia
169 P10 **Ovoot** Sühbaatar, SE Mongolia
163 O4 **Övörhangay** ◈ *province* C Mongolia
96 E12 **Øvre Årdal** Sogn og Fjordane, S Norway
97 J14 **Övre Fryken** ◎ C Sweden
94 J11 **Övre Soppero** Norrbotten, N Sweden
119 N3 **Ovruch** Zhytomyrs'ka Oblast', N Ukraine
168 J8 **Övt** Övörhangay, C Mongolia
193 E24 **Owaka** Otago, South Island, NZ
81 H18 **Owando** *prev.* Fort-Rousset. Cuvette, C Congo
171 Gg17 **Owase** Mie, Honshū, SW Japan
29 P9 **Owasso** Oklahoma, C USA
31 V10 **Owatonna** Minnesota, N USA
xliv I8 **Owel, Lough** ◎ C Ireland
181 O4 **Owen Fracture Zone** *tectonic feature* W Arabian Sea
193 H15 **Owen, Mount** ▲ South Island, NZ
193 H15 **Owen River** Tasman, South Island, NZ
22 I6 **Owensboro** Kentucky, S USA
37 T11 **Owens Lake** *salt flat* California, W USA
12 F14 **Owen Sound** Ontario, S Canada
12 F13 **Owen Sound** ◎ Ontario, S Canada
37 T10 **Owens River** ≈ California, W USA
194 K15 **Owen Stanley Range** ▲▲ S PNG
29 V5 **Owensville** Missouri, C USA
22 M4 **Owenton** Kentucky, S USA
xxxvi M14 **Owermoigne** Dorset, S England, UK
79 U17 **Owerri** Imo, S Nigeria
xliv G2 **Owey Island** *island* N Ireland
192 M10 **Owhango** Manawatu-Wanganui, North Island, NZ
23 N5 **Owingsville** Kentucky, S USA
152 K10 **Owminzatovo-Toshi** *Rus.* Gory Auminzatau. ▲▲ N Uzbekistan
79 T16 **Owo** Ondo, SW Nigeria
33 R9 **Owosso** Michigan, N USA
xxxix O4 **Owston Ferry** North Lincolnshire, N England, UK
37 V1 **Owyhee** Nevada, W USA
34 L14 **Owyhee, Lake** ◎ Oregon, NW USA
34 L15 **Owyhee River** ≈ Idaho/Oregon, NW USA
94 K1 **Öxarfjördhur** *var.* Axarfjördhur. *fjord* N Iceland
96 K12 **Oxberg** Kopparberg, C Sweden
xxxix U10 **Oxborough** Norfolk, E England, UK
9 V17 **Oxbow** Saskatchewan, S Canada
97 O17 **Oxelösund** Södermanland, S Sweden
xli N11 **Oxenholme** Cumbria, NW England, UK
xxxvii P8 **Oxford** *Lat.* Oxonia. Oxfordshire, S England, UK
193 H18 **Oxford** Canterbury, South Island, NZ
25 Q3 **Oxford** Alabama, S USA
24 L2 **Oxford** Mississippi, S USA
31 N16 **Oxford** Nebraska, C USA
20 H16 **Oxford** New York, NE USA
23 U8 **Oxford** North Carolina, SE USA
33 Q14 **Oxford** Ohio, N USA
20 I11 **Oxford** Pennsylvania, NE USA
xxxix N12 **Oxford Canal** *canal* S England, UK
9 X12 **Oxford House** Manitoba, C Canada
31 Y13 **Oxford Junction** Iowa, C USA
9 X12 **Oxford Lake** ◎ Manitoba, C Canada
xxxvii O7 **Oxfordshire** ◈ *county* S England, UK
Oxia *see* Oxyá
43 X12 **Oxkutzcab** Yucatán, SE Mexico
Ox Mountains *see* Slieve Gamph
xliii O22 **Oxnam** The Borders, S Scotland, UK
37 R15 **Oxnard** California, W USA
Oxonia *see* Oxford
xxxvii U10 **Oxted** Surrey, SE England, UK
xliii N20 **Oxton** The Borders, S Scotland, UK
12 I12 **Oxtongue** ≈ Ontario, SE Canada
Oxus *see* Amu Darya
xxxv G15 **Oxwich** Swansea, S Wales, UK
117 E15 **Oxyá** *var.* Oxia. ▲ C Greece
171 Ii13 **Oyabe** Toyama, Honshū, SW Japan
Oyahue/Oyahue, Volcán *see* Ollagüe, Volcán
171 K16 **Oyama** Tochigi, Honshū, S Japan
49 U5 **Oyapock** ≈ E French Guiana
Oyapock *see* Oiapoque, Rio
57 Z10 **Oyapok, Baie de L'** *bay* Brazil/French Guiana
57 Z11 **Oyapok, Fleuve l'** *var.* Oyapock, Rio Oiapoque. ≈ Brazil/French Guiana *see also* Oiapoque, Rio
81 E17 **Oyem** Woleu-Ntem, N Gabon
9 R16 **Oyen** Alberta, SW Canada
97 I15 **Øyeren** ◎ S Norway
168 G6 **Oygon** Dzavhan, N Mongolia
xlii H9 **Oykel** ≈ N Scotland, UK
xlii I9 **Oykel Bridge** Highland, NW Scotland, UK
127 N9 **Oymyakon** Respublika Sakha (Yakutiya), NE Russian Federation
81 H19 **Oyo** Cuvette, C Congo
79 S15 **Oyo** Oyo, W Nigeria
79 S15 **Oyo** ◈ *state* SW Nigeria
58 D13 **Oyón** Lima, C Peru
105 S10 **Oyonnax** Ain, E France
152 L10 **Oyoqighitma** *Rus.* Ayakagytma. Bukhoro Wiloyati, C Uzbekistan
152 M9 **Oyoqquduq** *Rus.* Ayakkuduk. Nawoiy Wiloyati, N Uzbekistan
34 F9 **Oysterville** Washington, NW USA
97 D14 **Øystese** Hordaland, S Norway
153 U10 **Oy-Tal** Oshskaya Oblast', SW Kyrgyzstan
153 T10 **Oy-Tal** ≈ SW Kyrgyzstan
151 S16 **Oytal** Zhambyl, S Kazakhstan
Oyyl *see* Uil
179 Qq15 **Ozamiz** Mindanao, S Philippines
Ozarichi *see* Azarychy
25 R7 **Ozark** Alabama, S USA
29 S10 **Ozark** Arkansas, C USA
29 T8 **Ozark** Missouri, C USA
29 T8 **Ozark Plateau** *plain* Arkansas/Missouri, C USA
29 T6 **Ozarks, Lake of the** ⊞ Missouri, C USA
199 Jj11 **Ozbourn Seamount** *undersea feature* W Pacific Ocean
113 L20 **Ózd** Borsod-Abaúj-Zemplén, NE Hungary
114 D11 **Ozeblin** ▲ C Croatia
127 Pp12 **Ozernovskiy** Kamchatskaya Oblast', E Russian Federation
150 M7 **Ozërnoye** *var.* Ozërnyy. Kustanay, N Kazakhstan
Ozërnyy *see* Ozërnoye
117 D18 **Ozerós, Límni** ◎ W Greece
121 D14 **Ozersk** *prev.* Darkehnen, *Ger.* Angerapp. Kaliningradskaya Oblast', W Russian Federation
130 L4 **Ozery** Moskovskaya Oblast', W Russian Federation
Özgön *see* Uzgen
109 C17 **Ozieri** Sardegna, Italy, C Mediterranean Sea
113 I15 **Ozimek** *Ger.* Malapane. Opole, SW Poland
131 R8 **Ozinki** Saratovskaya Oblast', W Russian Federation
Oziya *see* Ojiya
27 O10 **Ozona** Texas, SW USA
Ozorkov *see* Ozorków
112 J12 **Ozorków** *Rus.* Ozorkov. Łódź, C Poland
170 E14 **Ōzu** Ehime, Shikoku, SW Japan
143 R10 **Ozurget'i** *prev.* Makharadze. W Georgia

P

101 J17 **Paal** Limburg, NE Belgium
197 C13 **Paama** *island* C Vanuatu
206 M14 **Paamiut** *var.* Pâmiut, *Dan.* Frederikshåb. S Greenland
178 Gg9 **Pa-an** Karen State, S Burma
103 L22 **Paar** ≈ SE Germany
85 E26 **Paarl** Western Cape, SW South Africa
95 L15 **Paavola** Oulu, C Finland
xliii A15 **Pabbay** *island* NW Scotland, UK
xlii A10 **Pabbay** *island* NW Scotland, UK
175 P12 **Pabbiring, Kepulauan** *island group* C Indonesia
159 T15 **Pabna** Rajshahi, W Bangladesh
111 U4 **Pabneukirchen** Oberösterreich, N Austria
120 H13 **Pabradė** *Pol.* Podbrodzie. Švenčionys, SE Lithuania
58 L13 **Pacahuaras, Río** ≈ N Bolivia
Pacaraima, Sierra/Pacaraim, Serra *see* Pakaraima Mountains
58 B11 **Pacasmayo** La Libertad, W Peru
44 D6 **Pacaya, Volcán de** Ѫ S Guatemala
117 K23 **Pachía** *island* Kykládes, Greece, Aegean Sea
109 L26 **Pachino** Sicilia, Italy, C Mediterranean Sea
58 F12 **Pachitea, Río** ≈ C Peru
160 I11 **Pachmarhi** Madhya Pradesh, C India
124 N4 **Páchna** *var.* Pakhna. SW Cyprus
117 H25 **Páchnes** ▲ Kríti, Greece, E Mediterranean Sea
56 F9 **Pacho** Cundinamarca, C Colombia
160 F12 **Pāchora** Mahārāshtra, C India
43 P13 **Pachuca** *var.* Pachuca de Soto. Hidalgo, C Mexico
Pachuca de Soto *see* Pachuca
29 W5 **Pacific** Missouri, C USA
199 Jj15 **Pacific-Antarctic Ridge** *undersea feature* S Pacific Ocean
34 F8 **Pacific Beach** Washington, NW USA
37 N10 **Pacific Grove** California, W USA
31 S15 **Pacific Junction** Iowa, C USA
198-200 **Pacific Ocean** *ocean*
133 Z10 **Pacific Plate** *tectonic feature*
115 J15 **Pačir** ▲ SW Yugoslavia
190 L5 **Packsaddle** New South Wales, SE Australia
34 H9 **Packwood** Washington, NW USA
Padalung *see* Phatthalung
175 Q12 **Padamarang, Pulau** *island* C Indonesia
173 G9 **Padang** Sumatera, W Indonesia
174 Hh5 **Padang Endau** Pahang, Peninsular Malaysia
Padangpandjang *see* Padangpanjang
173 G8 **Padangpanjang** *prev.* Padangpandjang. Sumatera, W Indonesia
173 Ff7 **Padangsidempuan** *prev.* Padangsidimpoean. Sumatera, W Indonesia
Padangsidimpoean *see* Padangsidempuan
128 I9 **Padany** Respublika Kareliya, NW Russian Federation
95 M18 **Padasjoki** Häme, SW Finland
xxxvii Q6 **Padbury** Buckinghamshire, C England, UK
59 M22 **Padcaya** Tarija, S Bolivia
xxxvi C7 **Paddington** City of Westminster, SE England, UK
xxxvii V11 **Paddock Wood** Kent, SE England, UK
103 H14 **Paderborn** Nordrhein-Westfalen, NW Germany
Padeşul/Padeş, Vîrful *see* Padeş, Vârful
118 F12 **Padeş, Vârful** *var.* Padeşul; *prev.* Vîrful Padeş. ▲ W Romania
xli O14 **Padiham** Lancashire, NW England, UK
114 L10 **Padinska Skela** Serbia, N Yugoslavia
Padma *see* Brahmaputra
159 S14 **Padma** *var.* Ganges. ≈ Bangladesh/India *see also* Ganges
108 H8 **Padova** *Eng.* Padua; *anc.* Patavium. Veneto, NE Italy
84 A10 **Padrão, Ponta do** *headland* NW Angola
27 T16 **Padre Island** *island* Texas, SW USA
106 G3 **Padrón** Galicia, NW Spain
xxxvi C15 **Padstow** Cornwall, SW England, UK
120 K13 **Padsvillye** *Rus.* Podsvil'ye. Vitsyebskaya Voblasts', N Belorussia
190 K11 **Padthaway** South Australia
Padua *see* Padova
22 G7 **Paducah** Kentucky, S USA
27 P4 **Paducah** Texas, SW USA
107 N15 **Padul** Andalucía, S Spain
203 P8 **Paea** Tahiti, W French Polynesia
193 L14 **Paekakariki** Wellington, North Island, NZ
169 X11 **Paektu-san** *var.* Baitou Shan. ▲ China/North Korea
169 V15 **Paengnyŏng-do** *island* NW South Korea
192 M7 **Paeroa** Waikato, North Island, NZ
56 D12 **Páez** Cauca, SW Colombia
123 Mm4 **Páfos** *var.* Paphos. W Cyprus
123 Mm4 **Páfos** ✕ SW Cyprus
85 L19 **Pafúri** Gaza, SW Mozambique
114 C12 **Pag** *It.* Pago. Lika-Senj, W Croatia
114 B11 **Pag** *It.* Pago. *island* C Croatia
179 Qq16 **Pagadian** Mindanao, S Philippines
173 G11 **Pagai Selatan, Pulau** *island* Kepulauan Mentawai, W Indonesia
173 Ff10 **Pagai Utara, Pulau** *island* Kepulauan Mentawai, W Indonesia
196 K4 **Pagan** *island* C Northern Mariana Islands
117 G16 **Pagasitikós Kólpos** *gulf* E Greece
38 L8 **Page** Arizona, SW USA
31 Q5 **Page** North Dakota, N USA
120 D13 **Pagėgiai** *Ger.* Pogegen. Šilutė, SW Lithuania
23 S11 **Pageland** South Carolina, SE USA
83 G16 **Pager** ≈ NE Uganda
xxxvii R13 **Pagham** West Sussex, S England, UK
155 Q5 **Paghmān** Kābul, E Afghanistan
Pago *see* Pag
196 C16 **Pago Bay** *bay* E Guam, W Pacific Ocean
117 M20 **Pagóndas** *var.* Pagóndhas. Sámos, Dodekánisos, Greece, Aegean Sea
Pagóndhas *see* Pagóndas
198 C8 **Pago Pago** ○ (American Samoa) Tutuila, W American Samoa
39 R8 **Pagosa Springs** Colorado, C USA
40 H12 **Pahala** *var.* Pāhala. Hawaii, USA, C Pacific Ocean
174 H4 **Pahang** *off.* Negeri Pahang Darul Makmur. ◈ *state* Peninsular Malaysia
Pahang *see* Pahang, Sungai
174 Hh5 **Pahang, Sungai** *var.* Pahang, Sungei Pahang. ≈ Peninsular Malaysia
155 S8 **Pahārpur** North-West Frontier Province, NW Pakistan
193 B24 **Pahia Point** *headland* South Island, NZ
192 M13 **Pahiatua** Manawatu-Wanganui, North Island, NZ
40 H12 **Pahoa** *Haw.* Pāhoa. Hawaii, USA, C Pacific Ocean
25 Y14 **Pahokee** Florida, SE USA
37 X9 **Pahranagat Range** ▲▲ Nevada, W USA
37 W11 **Pahrump** Nevada, W USA
Pahsien *see* Chongqing
37 V9 **Pahute Mesa** ▲▲ Nevada, W USA
178 H7 **Pai** Mae Hong Son, NW Thailand
40 F10 **Paia** *Haw.* Pā'ia. Maui, Hawaii, USA, C Pacific Ocean
Pai-ch'eng *see* Baicheng
120 H4 **Paide** *Ger.* Weissenstein. Järvamaa, N Estonia
xxxvi H15 **Paignton** Devon, SW England, UK
192 K3 **Paihia** Northland, North Island, NZ
95 M18 **Päijänne** ◎ S Finland
116 F13 **Páïko** ▲▲ N Greece
59 M17 **Paila, Río** ≈ C Bolivia
178 I12 **Pailĭn** Bătdâmbâng, W Cambodia
56 F6 **Pailitas** Cesar, N Colombia
40 F9 **Pailolo Channel** *channel* Hawaii, USA, C Pacific Ocean
xxxix N11 **Pailton** Warwickshire, C England, UK
95 K19 **Paimio** *Swe.* Pemar. Turku-Pori, SW Finland
172 O17 **Paimi-saki** *var.* Yaeme-saki. *headland* Iriomote-jima, SW Japan
104 G5 **Paimpol** Côtes d'Armor, NW France
174 Gg9 **Painan** Sumatera, W Indonesia
65 G23 **Paine, Cerro** ▲ S Chile
33 U11 **Painesville** Ohio, N USA
xxxv J11 **Painscastle** Powys, C Wales, UK
xxxvi M8 **Painswick** Gloucestershire, C England, UK
33 S14 **Paint Creek** ≈ Ohio, N USA
38 L10 **Painted Desert** *desert* Arizona, SW USA
Paint Hills *see* Wemindji
32 M4 **Paint River** ≈ Michigan, N USA
27 P8 **Paint Rock** Texas, SW USA
23 O6 **Paintsville** Kentucky, S USA
Paisance *see* Piacenza
xliii I20 **Paisley** Renfrewshire, W Scotland, UK
34 I15 **Paisley** Oregon, NW USA
107 R10 **País Valenciano** *var.* Valencia, *Cat.* València; *anc.* Valentia. ◈ *autonomous community* NE Spain
107 O3 **País Vasco** *Basq.* Euskadi, *Eng.* The Basque Country, *Sp.* Provincias Vascongadas. ◈ *autonomous community* N Spain
58 A9 **Paita** Piura, NW Peru
197 J7 **Païta** Province Sud, S New Caledonia
175 O1 **Paitan, Teluk** *bay* Sabah, East Malaysia
106 H7 **Paiva** ≈ N Portugal
94 K12 **Pajala** Norrbotten, N Sweden
106 K3 **Pajares, Puerto de** *pass* NW Spain
56 G9 **Pajárito** Boyacá, C Colombia
56 G4 **Pajaro** La Guajira, S Colombia
Pakanbaru *see* Pekanbaru
57 Q10 **Pakaraima Mountains** *var.* Serra Pacaraim, Sierra Pacaraima. ▲▲ N South America
178 Hh11 **Pak Chong** Nakhon Ratchasima, C Thailand
127 Pp7 **Pakhachi** Koryakskiy Avtonomnyy Okrug, E Russian Federation
Pakhna *see* Páchna
153 O11 **Pakhtakor** Jizzakh Wiloyati, C Uzbekistan
201 U16 **Pakin Atoll** *atoll* Caroline Islands, E Micronesia
155 Q12 **Pakistan** *off.* Islamic Republic of Pakistan, *var.* Islami Jamhuriya e Pakistan. ◆ *republic* S Asia

◆ Country
● Country Capital
◇ Dependent Territory
○ Dependent Territory Capital
◈ Administrative Region
✕ International Airport
▲ Mountain
▲▲ Mountain Range
Ѫ Volcano
≈ River
◎ Lake
⊞ Reservoir

Pakistan, Islami Jamhuriya e – Paso de los Toros

Pakistan, Islami Jamhuriya e *see* Pakistan
178 I8 **Pak Lay** *var.* Muang Pak Lay. Xaignabouli, C Laos
Paknam *see* Samut Prakan
177 Ff5 **Pakokku** Magwe, C Burma
112 I10 **Pakość** *Ger.* Pakosch. Bydgoszcz, C Poland
Pakosch *see* Pakość
155 V10 **Pākpattan** Punjab, E Pakistan
178 H16 **Pak Phanang** *var.* Ban Pak Phanang. Nakhon Si Thammarat, SW Thailand
114 G9 **Pakrac** *Hung.* Pakrácz. Požega-Slavonija, NE Croatia
Pakrácz *see* Pakrac
120 F11 **Pakruojis** Pakruojis, N Lithuania
113 J24 **Paks** Tolna, S Hungary
Pak Sane *see* Pakxan
Paksé *see* Pakxé
178 I11 **Pak Thong Chai** Nakhon Ratchasima, C Thailand
155 R6 **Paktīā** ◐ *province* SE Afghanistan
155 Q7 **Paktīkā** ◐ *province* SE Afghanistan
175 Pp9 **Pakuli** Sulawesi, C Indonesia
83 F17 **Pakwach** NW Uganda
178 Ii8 **Pakxan** *var.* Muang Pakxan, Pak Sane. Bolikhamxai, C Laos
178 Jj10 **Pakxé** *var.* Paksé. Champasak, S Laos
80 G12 **Pala** Mayo-Kébbi, SW Chad
63 A17 **Palacios** Santa Fe, C Argentina
27 V13 **Palacios** Texas, SW USA
107 X5 **Palafrugell** Cataluña, NE Spain
109 L24 **Palagonia** Sicilia, Italy, C Mediterranean Sea
115 E17 **Palagruža** *It.* Pelagosa. *island* SW Croatia
117 G20 **Palaiá Epídavros** Pelopónnisos, S Greece
124 Nn3 **Palaichóri** *var.* Palekhori. C Cyprus
117 H25 **Palaiochóra** Kríti, Greece, E Mediterranean Sea
117 A15 **Palaiolastrítsa** *religious building* Kérkyra, Iónioi Nísoi, Greece, C Mediterranean Sea
117 J19 **Palaiópoli** Ándros, Kykládes, Greece, Aegean Sea
105 N5 **Palaiseau** Essonne, N France
Palakkad *see* Pālghāt
160 N11 **Pāla Laharha** Orissa, E India
85 G19 **Palamakoloi** Ghanzi, C Botswana
117 E16 **Palamás** Thessalía, C Greece
107 X5 **Palamós** Cataluña, NE Spain
120 J5 **Palamuse** *Ger.* Sankt-Bartholomäi. Jõgevamaa, E Estonia
191 Q14 **Palana** Tasmania, SE Australia
127 P9 **Palana** Koryakskiy Avtonomnyy Okrug, E Russian Federation
120 C11 **Palanga** *Ger.* Polangen. Palanga, NW Lithuania
149 V10 **Palangān, Kūh-e** ▲▲ E Iran
Palangkaraja *see* Palangkaraya
174 Mm10 **Palangkaraya** *prev.* Palangkaraja. Borneo, C Indonesia
161 H22 **Palani** Tamil Nādu, SE India
Palanka *see* Bačka Palanka
160 D9 **Pālanpur** Gujarāt, W India
Palantia *see* Palencia
85 I19 **Palapye** Central, SE Botswana
161 J19 **Pālār** ≈ SE India
106 H3 **Palas de Rei** Galicia, NW Spain
127 O10 **Palatka** Magadanskaya Oblast', E Russian Federation
25 W10 **Palatka** Florida, SE USA
196 B9 **Palau** *var.* Belau. ◆ *republic* W Pacific Ocean
133 Y14 **Palau Islands** *var.* Palau. *island group* N Palau
198 Aa8 **Palauli Bay** *bay* Savai'i, Western Samoa, C Pacific Ocean
178 Gg12 **Palaw** Tenasserim, S Burma
179 Oo15 **Palawan** *island* W Philippines
179 Oo15 **Palawan Passage** *passage* W Philippines
198 F7 **Palawan Trough** *undersea feature* S South China Sea
179 P10 **Palayan City** Luzon, N Philippines
161 H23 **Pālayankottai** Tamil Nādu, SE India
109 L25 **Palazzola Acreide** *anc.* Acrae. Sicilia, Italy, C Mediterranean Sea
120 G3 **Paldiski** *prev.* Baltiski, *Eng.* Baltic Port, *Ger.* Baltischport. Harjumaa, NW Estonia
114 I13 **Pale** SE Bosnia and Herzegovina
Palekhori *see* Palaichóri
175 Q7 **Paleleh, Pegunungan** ▲▲ Sulawesi, N Indonesia
175 Qq7 **Paleleh, Teluk** *bay* Sulawesi, N Indonesia
174 I11 **Palembang** Sumatera, W Indonesia
65 G18 **Palena** Los Lagos, S Chile
65 G18 **Palena, Río** ≈ S Chile
106 M5 **Palencia** *anc.* Palantia, Pallantia. Castilla-León, NW Spain
106 M3 **Palencia** ◐ *province* Castilla-León, N Spain
37 X15 **Palen Dry Lake** ◎ California, W USA
43 V15 **Palenque** Chiapas, SE Mexico
43 V15 **Palenque** *var.* Ruinas de Palenque. *ruins* Chiapas, SE Mexico
47 O9 **Palenque, Punta** *headland* S Dominican Republic
Palenque, Ruinas de *see* Palenque
Palerme *see* Palermo
109 I23 **Palermo** *Fr.* Palerme; *anc.* Panhormus, Panormus. Sicilia, Italy, C Mediterranean Sea
27 V8 **Palestine** Texas, SW USA
27 V7 **Palestine, Lake** ⊠ Texas, SW USA
109 I15 **Palestrina** Lazio, C Italy
177 F5 **Paletwa** Chin State, W Burma
161 G21 **Pālghāt** *var.* Palakkad; *prev.* Pulicat. Kerala, SW India
158 F13 **Pāli** Rājasthān, N India
178 Gg16 **Palian** Trang, SW Thailand
201 O12 **Palikir** ● (Micronesia) Pohnpei, E Micronesia
179 R17 **Palimbang** Mindanao, S Philippines
Palimé *see* Kpalimé
109 L19 **Palinuro, Capo** *headland* S Italy
117 H15 **Palioúri, Ákra** *var.* Akra Kanestron. *headland* N Greece
35 R14 **Palisades Reservoir** ⊠ Idaho, NW USA
101 J23 **Paliseul** Luxembourg, SE Belgium
160 C11 **Pālitāna** Gujarāt, W India
120 F4 **Palivere** Läänemaa, W Estonia
43 V14 **Palizada** Campeche, SE Mexico
95 L18 **Pälkäne** Häme, SW Finland
161 J22 **Palk Strait** *strait* India/Sri Lanka
161 J23 **Pallai** Northern Province, NW Sri Lanka
Pallantia *see* Palencia
108 C6 **Pallanza** Piemonte, NE Italy
xliv G11 **Pallas Grean** Limerick, SW Ireland
131 Q9 **Pallasovka** Volgogradskaya Oblast', SW Russian Federation
Pallene/Pallíni *see* Kassándra
193 L15 **Palliser Bay** *bay* North Island, NZ
193 L15 **Palliser, Cape** *headland* North Island, NZ
203 U9 **Palliser, Îles** *island group* Îles Tuamotu, C French Polynesia
107 X9 **Palma** *var.* Palma de Mallorca. Mallorca, Spain, W Mediterranean Sea
107 X9 **Palma** ✕ Mallorca, Spain, W Mediterranean Sea
84 Q12 **Palma** Cabo Delgado, N Mozambique
107 X10 **Palma, Badia de** *bay* Mallorca, Spain, W Mediterranean Sea
106 L13 **Palma del Río** Andalucía, S Spain
Palma de Mallorca *see* Palma
109 J25 **Palma di Montechiaro** Sicilia, Italy, C Mediterranean Sea
108 J7 **Palmanova** Friuli-Venezia Giulia, NE Italy
56 J7 **Palmarito** Apure, C Venezuela
45 N15 **Palmar Sur** Puntarenas, SE Costa Rica
62 I12 **Palmas** Paraná, S Brazil
61 K16 **Palmas do Tocantins** Tocantins, C Brazil
56 D11 **Palmaseca** ✕ (Cali) Valle del Cauca, SW Colombia
109 B21 **Palmas, Golfo di** *gulf* Sardegna, Italy, C Mediterranean Sea
46 I7 **Palma Soriano** Santiago de Cuba, E Cuba
25 Y12 **Palm Bay** Florida, SE USA
37 T14 **Palmdale** California, W USA
63 H14 **Palmeira das Missões** Rio Grande do Sul, S Brazil
84 A11 **Palmeirinhas, Ponta das** *headland* NW Angola
41 R11 **Palmer** Alaska, USA
21 N11 **Palmer** Massachusetts, NE USA
27 U7 **Palmer** Texas, SW USA
204 H4 **Palmer** *US research station* Antarctica
13 R11 **Palmer** ≈ Québec, SE Canada
39 T5 **Palmer Lake** Colorado, C USA
204 J6 **Palmer Land** *physical region* Antarctica
12 F15 **Palmerston** Ontario, SE Canada
193 F22 **Palmerston** Otago, South Island, NZ
202 K15 **Palmerston** *island* S Cook Islands
Palmerston *see* Darwin
192 M12 **Palmerston North** Manawatu-Wanganui, North Island, NZ
78 L18 **Palmés, Cap des** *headland* SW Ivory Coast
25 V13 **Palmetto** Florida, SE USA
Palmetto State *see* South Carolina
109 M22 **Palmi** Calabria, SW Italy
56 D11 **Palmira** Valle del Cauca, W Colombia
58 F8 **Palmira, Río** ≈ N Peru
63 D19 **Palmitas** Soriano, SW Uruguay
Palmnicken *see* Yantarnyy
37 V15 **Palm Springs** California, W USA
29 V2 **Palmyra** Missouri, C USA
20 G10 **Palmyra** New York, NE USA
20 G15 **Palmyra** Pennsylvania, NE USA
23 V5 **Palmyra** Virginia, NE USA
Palmyra *see* Tudmur
199 K7 **Palmyra Atoll** ◇ *US privately owned unincorporated territory* C Pacific Ocean
160 P12 **Palmyras Point** *headland* E India
xliii K25 **Palnackie** Dumfries and Galloway, SW Scotland, UK
xliii I25 **Palnure** Dumfries and Galloway, SW Scotland, UK
37 N9 **Palo Alto** California, W USA
27 O1 **Palo Duro Creek** ≈ Texas, SW USA
Paloe *see* Palu
Paloe *see* Denpasar, Bali, C Indonesia
174 Hh6 **Paloh** Johor, Peninsular Malaysia
82 F12 **Paloich** Upper Nile, SE Sudan
42 I3 **Palomas** Chihuahua, N Mexico
109 I15 **Palombara Sabina** Lazio, C Italy
107 S13 **Palos, Cabo de** *headland* SE Spain
106 I14 **Palos de la Frontera** Andalucía, S Spain
62 G11 **Palotina** Paraná, S Brazil
34 M9 **Palouse** Washington, NW USA
34 L9 **Palouse River** ≈ Washington, NW USA
37 Y16 **Palo Verde** California, W USA
59 E16 **Palpa** Ica, W Peru
97 M16 **Pålsboda** Örebro, C Sweden
95 M15 **Paltamo** Oulu, C Finland
175 Pp9 **Palu** *prev.* Paloe. Sulawesi, C Indonesia
143 P14 **Palu** Elâzığ, E Turkey
175 Q16 **Palu, Pulau** *island* S Indonesia
175 P8 **Palu, Teluk** *bay* Sulawesi, C Indonesia
158 I11 **Palwal** Haryāna, N India
127 Oo4 **Palyavaam** ≈ NE Russian Federation
79 Q13 **Pama** SE Burkina
180 J14 **Pamandzi** ✕ (Mamoudzou) Petite-Terre, E Mayotte
Pamangkat *see* Pemangkat
149 R11 **Pā Mazār** Kermān, C Iran
85 N19 **Pambarra** Inhambane, SE Mozambique
176 Xx10 **Pamdai** Irian Jaya, E Indonesia
176 X10 **Pami** Irian Jaya, E Indonesia
105 N16 **Pamiers** Ariège, S France
153 T14 **Pamir** *var.* Daryā-ye Pāmīr, *Taj.* Dar"yoi Pomir. ≈ Afghanistan/Tajikistan *see also* Pāmīr, Daryā-ye
Pamir/Pāmīr, Daryā-ye *see* Pamirs
155 U1 **Pāmīr, Daryā-ye** *var.* Pamir, *Taj.* Dar"yoi Pomir. ≈ Afghanistan/nTajikistan *see also* Pamir
Pāmīr-e Khord *see* Little Pamir
133 Q8 **Pamirs** *Pash.* Daryā-ye Pāmīr, *Rus.* Pamir. ▲▲ C Asia
Pâmiut *see* Paamiut
23 X10 **Pamlico River** ≈ North Carolina, SE USA
23 Y10 **Pamlico Sound** *sound* North Carolina, SE USA
27 O2 **Pampa** Texas, SW USA
Pampa Aullagas, Lago *see* Poopó, Lago
63 B21 **Pampa Húmeda** *grassland* E Argentina
58 A10 **Pampa las Salinas** *salt lake* NW Peru
59 F15 **Pampas** Huancavelica, C Peru
64 K13 **Pampas** *plain* C Argentina
57 O4 **Pampatar** Nueva Esparta, NE Venezuela
Pampeluna *see* Pamplona
106 H8 **Pampilhosa da Serra** *var.* Pampilhosa de Serra. Coimbra, N Portugal
181 Y15 **Pamplemousses** N Mauritius
56 G7 **Pamplona** Norte de Santander, N Colombia
107 Q3 **Pamplona** *Basq.* Iruñea; *prev.* Pampeluna, *anc.* Pompaelo. Navarra, N Spain
116 I11 **Pamporovo** *prev.* Vasil Kolarov. Plovdivska Oblast, S Bulgaria
142 D15 **Pamukkale** Denizli, W Turkey
23 W5 **Pamunkey River** ≈ Virginia, NE USA
158 K5 **Pamzal** Jammu and Kashmir, NW India
32 L14 **Pana** Illinois, N USA
43 Y11 **Panabá** Yucatán, SE Mexico
37 Y8 **Panaca** Nevada, W USA
117 E19 **Panachaikó** ▲▲ S Greece
12 F11 **Panache Lake** ◎ Ontario, S Canada
116 I10 **Panagyurishte** Plovdivska Oblast, W Bulgaria
174 I14 **Panaitan, Pulau** *island* S Indonesia
174 Ii14 **Panaitan, Selat** *strait* Jawa, SW Indonesia
117 D18 **Panaitolikó** ▲▲ C Greece
161 E17 **Panaji** *var.* Pangim, Panjim, New Goa. Goa, W India
45 T14 **Panama** *off.* Republic of Panama. ◆ *republic* Central America
45 T15 **Panamá** *var.* Ciudad de Panamá, *Eng.* Panama City. ● (Panama) Panamá, C Panama
45 U14 **Panamá** *off.* Provincia de Panamá. ◐ *province* E Panama
45 U15 **Panamá, Bahía de** *bay* N Gulf of Panama
200 Oo8 **Panama Basin** *undersea feature* E Pacific Ocean
45 T15 **Panama Canal** *canal* E Panama
25 R9 **Panama City** Florida, SE USA
45 T14 **Panama City** ✕ Panamá, C Panama
Panama City *see* Panamá
25 Q9 **Panama City Beach** Florida, SE USA
45 T17 **Panamá, Golfo de** *var.* Gulf of Panama. *gulf* S Panama
Panama, Gulf of *see* Panamá, Golfo de
Panama, Isthmus of *see* Panamá, Istmo de
45 T15 **Panamá, Istmo de** *Eng.* Isthmus of Panama; *prev.* Isthmus of Darien. *isthmus* E Panama
37 U11 **Panamint Range** ▲▲ California, W USA
109 L22 **Panarea, Isola** *island* Isole Eolie, S Italy
108 G9 **Panaro** ≈ N Italy
179 Q14 **Panay Gulf** *gulf* C Philippines
179 Pp13 **Panay Island** *island* C Philippines
37 W7 **Pancake Range** ▲▲ Nevada, W USA
114 M11 **Pančevo** *Ger.* Pantschowa, *Hung.* Pancsova. Serbia, N Yugoslavia
115 M15 **Pančićev Vrh** ▲ SW Yugoslavia
118 L12 **Panciu** Vrancea, E Romania
118 F10 **Pâncota** *Hung.* Pankota; *prev.* Pîncota. Arad, W Romania
Pancsova *see* Pančevo
85 N20 **Panda** Inhambane, SE Mozambique
176 X9 **Pandaidori, Kepulauan** *island group* E Indonesia
27 N11 **Pandale** Texas, SW USA
174 H7 **Pandang, Pulau** *island* W Indonesia
174 Kk9 **Pandang Tikar, Pulau** *island* N Indonesia
63 F20 **Pan de Azúcar** Maldonado, S Uruguay
120 H11 **Pandėlys** Rokiškis, NE Lithuania
161 F15 **Pandharpur** Mahārāshtra, W India
190 J1 **Pandie Pandie** South Australia
175 Pp9 **Pandiri** Sulawesi, C Indonesia
63 F20 **Pando** Canelones, S Uruguay
59 J14 **Pando** ◐ *department* N Bolivia
199 Ii10 **Pandora Bank** *undersea feature* W Pacific Ocean
97 G20 **Pandrup** Nordjylland, N Denmark
159 V12 **Pandu** Assam, NE India
81 J15 **Pandu** Equateur, NW Zaire
xxxv K13 **Pandy** Monmouthshire, SE Wales, UK
Paneas *see* Bāniyās
61 F15 **Panelas** Mato Grosso, W Brazil
120 G12 **Panevėžys** Panevėžys, C Lithuania
Panfilov *see* Zharkent
131 N9 **Panfilovo** Volgogradskaya Oblast', SW Russian Federation
81 N17 **Panga** Haut-Zaïre, N Zaire
200 Ss13 **Pangai** Lifuka, C Tonga
116 H13 **Pangaío** ▲▲ N Greece
81 G20 **Pangala** Le Pool, S Congo
83 J22 **Pangani** Tanga, E Tanzania
83 I21 **Pangani** ≈ NE Tanzania
xxxvii Q9 **Pangbourne** Newbury, S England, UK
195 U13 **Panggoe** Choiseul Island, NW Solomon Islands
81 N20 **Pangi** Maniema, E Zaire
194 H12 **Pangia** Southern Highlands, W PNG
Pangim *see* Panaji
173 F4 **Pangkalanbrandan** Sumatera, W Indonesia
Pangkalanbun *see* Pangkalanbuun
174 Ll10 **Pangkalanbuun** *var.* Pangkalanbun. Borneo, C Indonesia
174 J10 **Pangkalpinang** Pulau Bangka, W Indonesia
9 U17 **Pangman** Saskatchewan, S Canada
Pang-Nga *see* Phang-Nga
16 Nn2 **Pangnirtung** Baffin Island, Northwest Territories, NE Canada
158 K6 **Pangong Tso** *var.* Bangong Co. ◎ China/India *see also* Bangong Co
38 K7 **Panguitch** Utah, W USA
195 S12 **Panguna** Bougainville Island, NE PNG
179 Pp17 **Pangutaran Group** *island group* Sulu Archipelago, SW Philippines
27 N2 **Panhandle** Texas, SW USA
Panhormus *see* Palermo
176 X12 **Paniai, Danau** ◎ Irian Jaya, E Indonesia
81 L21 **Pania-Mutombo** Kasai Oriental, C Zaire
Panicherevo *see* Dolno Panicherevo
197 H5 **Panié, Mont** ▲ C New Caledonia
158 I10 **Pānīpat** Haryāna, N India
153 Q14 **Panj** *Rus.* Pyandzh; *prev.* Kirovabad. SW Tajikistan
153 P15 **Panj** *Rus.* Pyandzh. ≈ Afghanistan/Tajikistan
155 O5 **Panjāb** Bāmīān, C Afghanistan
153 O12 **Panjakent** *Rus.* Pendzhikent. W Tajikistan
154 L14 **Panjgūr** Baluchistān, SW Pakistan
Panjim *see* Panaji
169 U12 **Panjin** Liaoning, NE China
153 P14 **Panji Poyon** *Rus.* Nizhniy Pyandzh. SW Tajikistan
155 Q4 **Panjshīr** ≈ E Afghanistan
Pankota *see* Pâncota
79 W14 **Pankshin** Plateau, C Nigeria
169 Y10 **Pan Ling** ▲▲ N China
Panlong Jiang *see* Lô, Sông
160 J9 **Panna** Madhya Pradesh, C India
101 M16 **Panningen** Limburg, SE Netherlands
155 R13 **Pāno Āqil** Sind, SE Pakistan
124 Nn3 **Páno Léfkara** S Cyprus
124 N3 **Páno Panagiá** *var.* Pano Panayia. W Cyprus
Pano Panayia *see* Páno Panagiá
Panopolis *see* Akhmîm
31 U14 **Panora** Iowa, C USA
62 I8 **Panorama** São Paulo, S Brazil
117 I24 **Pánormos** Kríti, Greece, E Mediterranean Sea
Panormus *see* Palermo
169 W11 **Panshi** Jilin, NE China
xxxviii G9 **Pant** Shropshire, W England, UK
61 H19 **Pantanal** *var.* Pantanalmato-Grossense. *swamp* SW Brazil
Pantanalmato-Grossense *see* Pantanal
63 H16 **Pântano Grande** Rio Grande do Sul, S Brazil
175 R16 **Pantar, Pulau** *island* Kepulauan Alor, S Indonesia
23 X9 **Pantego** North Carolina, SE USA
109 G25 **Pantelleria** *anc.* Cossyra, Cosyra. Sicilia, Italy, C Mediterranean Sea
109 G25 **Pantelleria, Isola di** *island* SW Italy
Pante Macassar/Pante Makassar *see* Pante Makasar
175 Rr17 **Pante Makasar** *var.* Pante Macassar, Pante Makassar. Timor, C Indonesia
158 K10 **Pantnagar** Uttar Pradesh, N India
117 A15 **Pantokrátoras** ▲ Kérkyra, Iónioi Nísoi, Greece, C Mediterranean Sea
Pantschowa *see* Pančevo
179 Rr16 **Pantukan** Mindanao, S Philippines
43 P11 **Pánuco** Veracruz-Llave, E Mexico
43 P11 **Pánuco, Río** ≈ C Mexico
166 I12 **Panxian** Guizhou, S China
173 G7 **Panyabungan** Sumatera, N Indonesia
79 W14 **Panyam** Plateau, C Nigeria
163 N13 **Panzhihua** *prev.* Dukou, Tu-k'ou. Sichuan, C China
81 I22 **Panzi** Bandundu, SW Zaire
44 E5 **Panzós** Alta Verapaz, E Guatemala
Pao-chi/Paoki *see* Baoji
Pao-king *see* Shaoyang
109 N20 **Paola** Calabria, SW Italy
123 Jj17 **Paola** E Malta
29 R5 **Paola** Kansas, C USA
33 O15 **Paoli** Indiana, N USA
197 D14 **Paonangisu** Éfaté, C Vanuatu
175 Tt11 **Paoni** *var.* Pauni. Pulau Seram, E Indonesia
39 Q5 **Paonia** Colorado, C USA
203 O7 **Paopao** Moorea, W French Polynesia
Pao-shan *see* Baoshan
Pao-ting *see* Baoding
Pao-t'ou/Paotow *see* Baotou
81 H14 **Paoua** Ouham-Pendé, W Central African Republic
Pap *see* Pop
113 H23 **Pápa** Veszprém, W Hungary
44 J12 **Papagayo, Golfo de** *gulf* NW Costa Rica
40 H11 **Papaikou** *var.* Pāpa'ikou. Hawaii, USA, C Pacific Ocean
43 R15 **Papaloapan, Río** ≈ S Mexico
192 L6 **Papakura** Auckland, North Island, NZ
43 Q13 **Papantla** *var.* Papantla de Olarte. Veracruz-Llave, E Mexico
Papantla de Olarte *see* Papantla
203 P8 **Papara** Tahiti, W French Polynesia
192 K4 **Paparoa** Northland, North Island, NZ
193 G16 **Paparoa Range** ▲▲ South Island, NZ
117 K20 **Pápas, Ákra** *headland* Ikaría, Dodekánisos, Greece, Aegean Sea
xlii H3 **Papa Stour** *island* NE Scotland, UK
192 L6 **Papatoetoe** Auckland, North Island, NZ
193 E25 **Papatowai** Otago, South Island, NZ
xlii N2 **Papa Westray** *island* NE Scotland, UK
203 T10 **Papeete** ○ (French Polynesia) Tahiti, W French Polynesia
102 F11 **Papenburg** Niedersachsen, NW Germany
100 H13 **Papendrecht** Zuid-Holland, SW Netherlands
203 Q7 **Papenoo** Tahiti, W French Polynesia
203 Q7 **Papenoo Rivière** ≈ Tahiti, W French Polynesia
203 N7 **Papetoai** Moorea, W French Polynesia
94 L3 **Papey** *island* E Iceland
Paphos *see* Páfos
42 H5 **Papigochic, Río** ≈ NW Mexico
120 E10 **Papilė** Akmenė, NW Lithuania
31 S15 **Papillion** Nebraska, C USA
13 T5 **Papinachois** ≈ Québec, SE Canada
194 I15 **Papua, Gulf of** *gulf* S PNG
194 H13 **Papua New Guinea** *off.* Independent State of Papua New Guinea; *prev.* Territory of Papua and New Guinea, *abbrev.* PNG. ◆ *commonwealth republic* NW Melanesia
199 H10 **Papua Plateau** *undersea feature* N Coral Sea
114 G9 **Papuk** ▲▲ NE Croatia
177 G8 **Papun** Karen State, S Burma
44 L14 **Paquera** Puntarenas, W Costa Rica
57 V9 **Para** ◐ *district* N Surinam
60 I13 **Pará** *off.* Estado do Pará. ◐ *state* NE Brazil
Pará *see* Belém
126 H12 **Parabel'** Tomskaya Oblast', C Russian Federation
188 I8 **Paraburdoo** Western Australia
59 E16 **Paracas, Península de** *peninsula* W Peru
61 L19 **Paracatu** Minas Gerais, NE Brazil
198 F7 **Paracel Islands** ◇ *disputed territory* SE Asia
190 I6 **Parachilna** South Australia
155 R6 **Pārachinār** North-West Frontier Province, NW Pakistan
114 N13 **Paraćin** Serbia, C Yugoslavia
12 K8 **Paradis** Québec, SE Canada
41 N11 **Paradise** *var.* Paradise Hill. Alaska, USA
37 O5 **Paradise** California, W USA
37 X11 **Paradise** Nevada, W USA
Paradise Hill *see* Paradise
39 R11 **Paradise Hills** New Mexico, SW USA
Paradise of the Pacific *see* Hawaii
38 L13 **Paradise Valley** Arizona, SW USA
37 T2 **Paradise Valley** Nevada, W USA
117 O22 **Paradisi** ✕ (Ródos) Ródos, Dodekánisos, Greece, Aegean Sea
176 X10 **Paradoi** Irian Jaya, E Indonesia
160 P12 **Pārādwīp** Orissa, E India
Paraetonium *see* Maṭrûḥ
119 R4 **Parafiyivka** Chernihivs'ka Oblast', N Ukraine
38 K7 **Paragonah** Utah, W USA
29 X9 **Paragould** Arkansas, C USA
49 X8 **Paraguaçu** *var.* Paraguassú. ≈ E Brazil
62 J9 **Paraguaçu Paulista** São Paulo, S Brazil
56 H4 **Paraguaipoa** Zulia, NW Venezuela
64 O6 **Paraguarí** Paraguarí, S Paraguay
64 O7 **Paraguarí** *off.* Departamento de Paraguarí. ◐ *department* S Paraguay
57 O8 **Paragua, Río** ≈ SE Venezuela
59 O16 **Paraguá, Río** ≈ NE Bolivia
Paraguassú *see* Paraguaçu
64 N5 **Paraguay** ◆ *republic* C South America
49 U10 **Paraguay** *var.* Río Paraguay. ≈ C South America
Parahiba/Parahyba *see* Paraíba
61 P15 **Paraíba** *off.* Estado da Paraíba; *prev.* Parahiba, Parahyba. ◐ *state* E Brazil
Paraíba *see* João Pessoa
62 P9 **Paraíba do Sul, Rio** ≈ SE Brazil
Parainen *see* Pargas
45 N14 **Paraíso** Cartago, C Costa Rica
43 U14 **Paraíso** Tabasco, SE Mexico
59 O17 **Paraiso, Río** ≈ E Bolivia
Parajd *see* Praid
79 S14 **Parakou** C Benin
124 O3 **Paralimni** E Cyprus
117 G18 **Paralímni, Límni** ◎ C Greece
194 G15 **Parama Island** *island* SW PNG
57 W8 **Paramaribo** ● (Surinam) Paramaribo, N Surinam
57 W9 **Paramaribo** ◐ *district* N Surinam
57 W9 **Paramaribo** ✕ Paramaribo, N Surinam
Paramithiá *see* Paramythiá
58 C13 **Paramonga** Lima, W Peru
127 Pp13 **Paramushir, Ostrov** *island* SE Russian Federation
117 C16 **Paramythiá** *var.* Paramithiá. Ípeiros, W Greece
64 M10 **Paraná** Entre Ríos, E Argentina
62 H11 **Paraná** *off.* Estado do Paraná. ◐ *state* S Brazil
49 U11 **Paraná** *var.* Alto Paraná. ≈ C South America
62 K12 **Paranaguá** Paraná, S Brazil
61 J20 **Paranaíba, Rio** ≈ E Brazil
63 C19 **Paraná Ibicuy, Río** ≈ E Argentina
61 H15 **Paranaíta** Mato Grosso, W Brazil
62 H9 **Paranapanema, Rio** ≈ S Brazil
62 K11 **Paranapiacaba, Serra do** ▲▲ S Brazil
62 H9 **Paranavaí** Paraná, S Brazil
149 N5 **Parandak** Markazī, W Iran
116 I12 **Paranéstio** Anatolikí Makedonía kai Thráki, NE Greece
203 W11 **Paraoa** *atoll* Îles Tuamotu, C French Polynesia
192 L13 **Paraparaumu** Wellington, North Island, NZ
59 N20 **Parapeti, Río** ≈ SE Bolivia
56 L10 **Paraque, Cerro** ▲ W Venezuela
160 I11 **Parāsia** Madhya Pradesh, C India
117 M23 **Paraspóri, Ákra** *headland* Kárpathos, SE Greece
62 O10 **Parati** Rio de Janeiro, SE Brazil
61 K14 **Parauapebas** Pará, N Brazil
105 Q10 **Paray-le-Monial** Saône-et-Loire, C France
Parbatsar *see* Parvatsar
160 G13 **Parbhani** Mahārāshtra, C India
xli N15 **Parbold** Lancashire, NW England, UK
102 L10 **Parchim** Mecklenburg-Vorpommern, N Germany
Parchwitz *see* Prochowice
112 P13 **Parczew** Biała Podlaska, E Poland
62 L8 **Pardo, Rio** ≈ S Brazil
113 E16 **Pardubice** *Ger.* Pardubitz. Východní Čechy, C Czech Republic
Pardubitz *see* Pardubice
121 F16 **Parechcha** *Pol.* Porzecze, *Rus.* Porech'ye. Hrodzyenskaya Voblasts', W Belorussia
61 F17 **Parecis, Chapada dos** *var.* Serra dos Parecis. ▲▲ W Brazil
Parecis, Serra dos *see* Parecis, Chapada dos
106 M4 **Paredes de Nava** Castilla-León, N Spain
201 U12 **Parem** *island* Chuuk, C Micronesia
201 O12 **Parem Island** *island* E Micronesia
192 I1 **Parengarenga Harbour** *inlet* North Island, NZ
13 N8 **Parent** Québec, SE Canada
104 J14 **Parentis-en-Born** Landes, SW France
Parenzo *see* Poreč
193 G20 **Pareora** Canterbury, South Island, NZ
175 P12 **Parepare** Sulawesi, C Indonesia
117 B16 **Párga** Ípeiros, W Greece
95 K20 **Pargas** *Swe.* Parainen. Turku-Pori, SW Finland
66 O5 **Pargo, Ponta do** *headland* Madeira, Portugal, NE Atlantic Ocean
Paria, Golfo de *see* Paria, Gulf of
57 N6 **Pariaguán** Anzoátegui, NE Venezuela
47 X17 **Paria, Gulf of** *var.* Golfo de Paria. *gulf* Trinidad and Tobago/Venezuela
59 I15 **Pariamanu, Río** ≈ E Peru
38 L8 **Paria River** ≈ Utah, W USA
Parichi *see* Parychy
42 M14 **Paricutín, Volcán** Ѫ C Mexico
45 P16 **Parida, Isla** *island* SW Panama
57 T8 **Parika** NE Guyana
95 O18 **Parikkala** Kymi, SE Finland
60 E10 **Parima, Serra** *var.* Sierra Parima. ▲▲ Brazil/Venezuela *see also* Parima, Sierra
57 N11 **Parima, Sierra** *var.* Serra Parima. ▲▲ Brazil/Venezuela *see also* Parima, Serra
59 F17 **Parinacochas, Laguna** ◎ SW Peru
49 P8 **Pariñas, Punta** *headland* NW Peru
60 H12 **Parintins** Amazonas, N Brazil
105 O5 **Paris** *anc.* Lutetia, Lutetia Parisiorum, Parisii. ● (France) Paris, N France
203 Y2 **Paris** Kiritimati, E Kiribati
29 S11 **Paris** Arkansas, C USA
35 S16 **Paris** Idaho, NW USA
33 N14 **Paris** Illinois, N USA
22 M5 **Paris** Kentucky, S USA
29 V3 **Paris** Missouri, C USA
22 H8 **Paris** Tennessee, S USA
27 V5 **Paris** Texas, SW USA
Parisii *see* Paris
45 S16 **Parita** Herrera, S Panama
45 S16 **Parita, Bahía de** *bay* S Panama
Parkan/Párkány *see* Štúrovo
95 K18 **Parkano** Häme, SW Finland
29 N6 **Park City** Kansas, C USA
38 L3 **Park City** Utah, W USA
38 I12 **Parker** Arizona, SW USA
25 R9 **Parker** Florida, SE USA
31 R11 **Parker** South Dakota, N USA
37 Z14 **Parker Dam** California, W USA
31 W13 **Parkersburg** Iowa, C USA
23 Q3 **Parkersburg** West Virginia, NE USA
31 T7 **Parkers Prairie** Minnesota, N USA
179 R17 **Parker Volcano** Ѫ Mindanao, S Philippines
189 W13 **Parkes** New South Wales, SE Australia
xxxvii Y6 **Parkeston** Essex, SE England, UK
32 K4 **Park Falls** Wisconsin, N USA
xliii L23 **Parkgate** Dumfries and Galloway, SW Scotland, UK
Parkhar *see* Farkhor
12 E16 **Parkhill** Ontario, S Canada
xliv C14 **Parknasilla** Kerry, SW Ireland
31 T5 **Park Rapids** Minnesota, N USA
31 Q3 **Park River** North Dakota, N USA
31 Q11 **Parkston** South Dakota, N USA
8 L17 **Parksville** Vancouver Island, British Columbia, SW Canada
39 S3 **Parkview Mountain** ▲ Colorado, C USA
107 N8 **Parla** Madrid, C Spain
31 S8 **Parle, Lac qui** ⊠ Minnesota, N USA
117 F20 **Parlía Tyroú** Pelopónnisos, S Greece
161 G14 **Parli Vaijnāth** Mahārāshtra, C India
108 F9 **Parma** Emilia-Romagna, N Italy
33 T11 **Parma** Ohio, N USA
Parnahyba *see* Parnaíba
60 N13 **Parnaíba** *var.* Parnahyba. Piauí, E Brazil
67 J14 **Parnaíba Ridge** *undersea feature* C Atlantic Ocean
60 N13 **Parnaíba, Rio** ≈ NE Brazil
117 F18 **Parnassós** ▲▲ C Greece
193 J17 **Parnassus** Canterbury, South Island, NZ
190 H10 **Parndana** South Australia
117 H19 **Párnitha** ▲▲ C Greece
117 F21 **Párnon** ▲▲ S Greece
120 G5 **Pärnu** *Ger.* Pernau, *Latv.* Pērnava; *prev.* Rus. Pernov. Pärnumaa, SW Estonia
120 G6 **Pärnu** *var.* Parnu Jõgi, *Ger.* Pernau. ≈ SW Estonia
120 G5 **Pärnu-Jaagupi** *Ger.* Sankt-Jakobi. Pärnumaa, SW Estonia
Parnu Jõgi *see* Pärnu
120 G5 **Pärnu Laht** *Ger.* Pernauer Bucht. *bay* SW Estonia
120 F5 **Pärnumaa** *off.* Pärnu Maakond. ◐ *province* SW Estonia
159 T11 **Paro** W Bhutan
159 T11 **Paro** ✕ (Thimphu) W Bhutan
193 G17 **Paroa** West Coast, South Island, NZ
169 X14 **P'aro-ho** *var.* Hwach'ŏn-chŏsuji. ⊠ N South Korea
191 N6 **Paroo River** *seasonal river* New South Wales/Queensland, SE Australia
Paropamisus Range *see* Sefīdkūh, Selseleh-ye
117 J21 **Páros** Páros, Kykládes, Greece, Aegean Sea
117 J21 **Páros** *island* Kykládes, Greece, Aegean Sea
38 K7 **Parowan** Utah, W USA
105 U13 **Parpaillon** ▲▲ SE France
110 I9 **Parpan** Graubünden, S Switzerland
xxxvi G11 **Parracombe** Devon, SW England, UK
64 G13 **Parral** Maule, C Chile
Parral *see* Hidalgo del Parral
191 T9 **Parramatta** New South Wales, SE Australia
23 Y6 **Parramore Island** *island* Virginia, NE USA
42 M8 **Parras** *var.* Parras de la Fuente. Coahuila de Zaragoza, NE Mexico
Parras de la Fuente *see* Parras
xxxvi K12 **Parrett** ≈ SW England, UK
44 M14 **Parrita** Puntarenas, S Costa Rica
12 G13 **Parry Island** *island* Ontario, S Canada
207 O9 **Parry Islands** *island group* Northwest Territories, NW Canada
12 G12 **Parry Sound** Ontario, S Canada
112 F7 **Parsęta** *Ger.* Persante. ≈ NW Poland
30 L3 **Parshall** North Dakota, N USA
29 Q7 **Parsons** Kansas, C USA
22 H9 **Parsons** Tennessee, S USA
23 T3 **Parsons** West Virginia, NE USA
Parsonstown *see* Birr
102 P11 **Parsteiner See** ◎ NE Germany
109 I24 **Partanna** Sicilia, Italy, C Mediterranean Sea
110 J8 **Partenen** Graubünden, E Switzerland
104 K9 **Parthenay** Deux-Sèvres, W France
97 J19 **Partille** Göteborg och Bohus, S Sweden
xli O16 **Partington** Trafford, NW England, UK
109 I23 **Partinico** Sicilia, Italy, C Mediterranean Sea
113 I20 **Partizánske** *prev.* Šimonovany, *Hung.* Simony. Západné Slovensko, W Slovakia
xxxix S6 **Partney** Lincolnshire, E England, UK
xl K9 **Parton** Cumbria, NW England, UK
xliii J24 **Parton** Dumfries and Galloway, SW Scotland, UK
xliv E7 **Partry** Mayo, NW Ireland
xliv D7 **Partry Mountains** ▲▲ W Ireland
60 H11 **Paru de Oeste, Rio** ≈ N Brazil
190 K9 **Paruna** South Australia
60 I11 **Paru, Rio** ≈ N Brazil
Parvān *see* Parwān
161 M14 **Pārvatipuram** Andhra Pradesh, E India
158 G12 **Parvatsar** *prev.* Parbatsar. Rājasthān, N India
155 Q5 **Parwān** *Per.* Parvān. ◐ *province* E Afghanistan
xxxviii L7 **Parwich** Derbyshire, C England, UK
164 I15 **Paryang** Xizang Zizhiqu, W China
121 M18 **Parychy** *Rus.* Parichi. Homyel'skaya Voblasts', SE Belorussia
85 J21 **Parys** Free State, C South Africa
37 T15 **Pasadena** California, W USA
27 W11 **Pasadena** Texas, SW USA
58 B8 **Pasaje** El Oro, SW Ecuador
143 T9 **P'asanauri** N Georgia
173 G10 **Pasapuat** Pulau Pagai Utara, W Indonesia
178 Gg7 **Pasawng** Kayah State, C Burma
116 L13 **Paşayiğit** Edirne, NW Turkey
25 N9 **Pascagoula** Mississippi, S USA
24 M8 **Pascagoula River** ≈ Mississippi, S USA
118 F12 **Paşcani** *Hung.* Páskán. Iaşi, NE Romania
111 T4 **Pasching** Oberösterreich, N Austria
34 K10 **Pasco** Washington, NW USA
58 E13 **Pasco** *off.* Departamento de Pasco. ◐ *department* C Peru
203 N11 **Pascua, Isla de** *var.* Rapa Nui, *Eng.* Easter Island. *island* E Pacific Ocean
65 G21 **Pascua, Río** ≈ S Chile
105 N1 **Pas-de-Calais** ◐ *department* N France
102 P10 **Pasewalk** Mecklenburg-Vorpommern, NE Germany
9 T10 **Pasfield Lake** ◎ Saskatchewan, C Canada
Pa-shih Hai-hsia *see* Bashi Channel
Pashkeni *see* Bolyarovo
Pashmakli *see* Smolyan
179 P10 **Pasig** Luzon, N Philippines
159 X10 **Pāsighāt** Arunāchel Pradesh, NE India
143 Q12 **Pasinler** Erzurum, NE Turkey
Pasi Oloy, Qatorkŭhi *see* Zaalayskiy Khrebet
44 E3 **Pasión, Río de la** ≈ N Guatemala
174 Gg10 **Pasirganting** Sumatera, W Indonesia
Pasirpangarayan *see* Bagansiapiapi
174 H2 **Pasir Puteh** *var.* Pasir Putih. Kelantan, Peninsular Malaysia
174 L6 **Pasir, Tanjung** *headland* East Malaysia
97 N20 **Påskallavik** Kalmar, S Sweden
Páskán *see* Paşcani
112 K7 **Pasłęk** *Ger.* Preußisch Holland. Elbląg, N Poland
112 K7 **Pasłęka** *Ger.* Passarge. ≈ N Poland
154 K16 **Pasni** Baluchistān, SW Pakistan
65 I18 **Paso de Indios** Chubut, S Argentina
56 L7 **Paso del Caballo** Guárico, N Venezuela
63 E15 **Paso de los Libres** Corrientes, NE Argentina
63 E18 **Paso de los Toros** Tacuarembó, C Uruguay

◆ Country
● Country Capital
◇ Dependent Territory
○ Dependent Territory Capital
◐ Administrative Region
✕ International Airport
▲ Mountain
▲▲ Mountain Range
Ѫ Volcano
≈ River
◎ Lake
⊠ Reservoir

Paso Robles – Péronne, Lac

37 P12 **Paso Robles** California, W USA
13 Y7 **Paspébiac** Québec, SE Canada
9 U14 **Pasquia Hills** ▲▲ Saskatchewan, S Canada
155 W7 **Pasrūr** Punjab, E Pakistan
xliv J13 **Passage East** Waterford, S Ireland
32 M1 **Passage Island** *island* Michigan, N USA
67 B24 **Passage Islands** *island group* W Falkland Islands
15 I1 **Passage Point** *headland* Banks Island, Northwest Territories, NW Canada
Passarge *see* Pasłęka
117 C15 **Passarón** *ancient monument* Ípeiros, W Greece
Passarowitz *see* Požarevac
103 O22 **Passau** Bayern, SE Germany
24 M9 **Pass Christian** Mississippi, S USA
109 L26 **Passero, Capo** *headland* Sicilia, Italy, C Mediterranean Sea
179 Q13 **Passi** Panay Island, C Philippines
63 H14 **Passo Fundo** Rio Grande do Sul, S Brazil
62 H13 **Passo Fundo, Barragem de** ⊠ S Brazil
63 H15 **Passo Real, Barragem de** ⊠ S Brazil
61 L20 **Passos** Minas Gerais, NE Brazil
178 M11 **Passu Keah** *island* S Paracel Islands
120 J13 **Pastavy** *Pol.* Postawy, *Rus.* Postavy. Vitsyebskaya Voblasts', NW Belorussia
58 D7 **Pastaza** ◈ *province* E Ecuador
58 D9 **Pastaza, Río** ≈ Ecuador/Peru
63 A21 **Pasteur** Buenos Aires, E Argentina
13 V3 **Pasteur** ≈ Québec, SE Canada
153 Q12 **Pastigav** *Rus.* Pastigov. W Tajikistan
Pastigov *see* Pastigav
56 C13 **Pasto** Nariño, SW Colombia
40 M10 **Pastol Bay** *bay* Alaska, USA
39 O8 **Pastora Peak** ▲ Arizona, SW USA
107 O8 **Pastrana** Castilla-La Mancha, C Spain
174 M15 **Pasuruan** *prev.* Pasoeroean. Jawa, C Indonesia
120 F11 **Pasvalys** Pasvalys, N Lithuania
113 K21 **Pásztó** Nógrád, N Hungary
201 U12 **Pata** *var.* Patta. *atoll* Chuuk Islands, C Micronesia
38 M16 **Patagonia** Arizona, SW USA
65 H20 **Patagonia** *physical region* Argentina/Chile
Patalung *see* Phatthalung
160 D9 **Pātan** Gujarāt, W India
160 J10 **Pātan** Madhya Pradesh, C India
175 Tt8 **Patani** Pulau Halmahera, E Indonesia
Patani *see* Pattani
13 V7 **Patapédia Est** ≈ Québec, SE Canada
118 K13 **Pătâriagele** *prev.* Pătîriagele. Buzău, SE Romania
Patavium *see* Padova
190 I5 **Patawarta Hill** ▲ South Australia
190 L10 **Patchewollock** Victoria, SE Australia
xxxvi L9 **Patchway** South Gloucestershire, W England, UK
192 K11 **Patea** Taranaki, North Island, NZ
192 K11 **Patea** ≈ North Island, NZ
79 U15 **Pategi** Kwara, C Nigeria
83 K20 **Pate Island** *var.* Patta Island. *island* SE Kenya
xli R12 **Pateley Bridge** North Yorkshire, N England, UK
107 S10 **Paterna** País Valenciano, E Spain
111 R9 **Paternion** *Slvn.* Špatrjan. Kärnten, S Austria
109 L24 **Paternò** *anc.* Hybla, Hybla Major. Sicilia, Italy, C Mediterranean Sea
34 J7 **Pateros** Washington, NW USA
20 J14 **Paterson** New Jersey, NE USA
34 J10 **Paterson** Washington, NW USA
193 C25 **Paterson Inlet** *inlet* Stewart Island, NZ
100 N6 **Paterswolde** Drenthe, NE Netherlands
158 H7 **Pathānkot** Himāchal Pradesh, N India
Pathein *see* Bassein
35 W15 **Pathfinder Reservoir** ⊠ Wyoming, C USA
xliii M20 **Pathhead** Midlothian, SE Scotland, UK
178 Hh11 **Pathum Thani** *var.* Patumdhani, Prathum Thani. Pathum Thani, C Thailand
174 L14 **Pati** Jawa, C Indonesia
56 C12 **Patía** *var.* El Bordo. Cauca, SW Colombia
158 I9 **Patiāla** *var.* Puttiala. Punjab, NW India
56 B12 **Patía, Río** ≈ SW Colombia
175 T8 **Patinti, Selat** *strait* Maluku, E Indonesia
196 D15 **Pati Point** *headland* NE Guam
Pătîriagele *see* Pătâriagele
58 C13 **Pativilca** Lima, W Peru
178 Gg1 **Pātkai Bum** *var.* Patkai Range. ▲▲ Burma/India
Patkai Range *see* Pātkai Bum
117 L20 **Pátmos** Pátmos, Dodekánisos, Greece, Aegean Sea
117 L20 **Pátmos** *island* Dodekánisos, Greece, Aegean Sea
xliii I23 **Patna** East Ayrshire, W Scotland, UK
159 P13 **Patna** *var.* Azimabad. Bihār, N India
160 M12 **Patnāgarh** Orissa, E India
179 Pp13 **Patnongon** Panay Island, C Philippines
143 S13 **Patnos** Ağrı, E Turkey
62 H12 **Pato Branco** Paraná, S Brazil
33 O16 **Patoka Lake** ◎ Indiana, N USA
94 L9 **Patoniva** *Lapp.* Buoddobohki. Lappi, N Finland
115 K21 **Patos** *var.* Patosi. Fier, SW Albania
Patos *see* Patos de Minas
61 K19 **Patos de Minas** *var.* Patos. Minas Gerais, NE Brazil
Patosi *see* Patos
63 I17 **Patos, Lagoa dos** *lagoon* S Brazil
64 J9 **Patquía** La Rioja, C Argentina
117 E19 **Pátra** *Eng.* Patras; *prev.* Pátrai. Dytikí Ellás, S Greece
Pátrai/Patras *see* Pátra
117 D18 **Patraïkós Kólpos** *gulf* S Greece
94 G2 **Patreksfjördhur** Vestfirdhir, W Iceland
26 M7 **Patricia** Texas, SW USA
65 F21 **Patricio Lynch, Isla** *island* S Chile
xl F11 **Patrick** W Isle of Man
xli R10 **Patrick Brompton** North Yorkshire, N England, UK
xliv F11 **Patrickswell** Limerick, SW Ireland
xli X14 **Patrington** East Riding of Yorkshire, N England, UK
Patta *see* Pata
Patta Island *see* Pate Island
178 Hh17 **Pattani** *var.* Patani. Pattani, SW Thailand
178 Hh12 **Pattaya** Chon Buri, S Thailand
21 S4 **Patten** Maine, NE USA
37 O9 **Patterson** California, W USA
24 J10 **Patterson** Louisiana, S USA
37 R7 **Patterson, Mount** ▲ California, W USA
33 P4 **Patterson, Point** *headland* Michigan, N USA
109 L23 **Patti** Sicilia, Italy, C Mediterranean Sea
109 L23 **Patti, Golfo di** *gulf* Sicilia, Italy, C Mediterranean Sea
95 L14 **Pattijoki** Oulu, W Finland
199 Mm5 **Patton Escarpment** *undersea feature* E Pacific Ocean
29 S2 **Pattonsburg** Missouri, C USA
1 D6 **Patton Seamount** *undersea feature* NE Pacific Ocean
8 J12 **Pattullo, Mount** ▲ British Columbia, W Canada
Patuakhali *see* Patukhali
44 M5 **Patuca, Río** ≈ E Honduras
159 U16 **Patukhali** *var.* Patuakhali. Khulna, S Bangladesh
Patumdhani *see* Pathum Thani
42 M14 **Pátzcuaro** Michoacán de Ocampo, SW Mexico
44 C6 **Patzicía** Chimaltenango, S Guatemala
104 K16 **Pau** Pyrénées-Atlantiques, SW France
104 J12 **Pauillac** Gironde, SW France
177 Ff5 **Pauk** Magwe, W Burma
15 H3 **Paulatuk** Northwest Territories, NW Canada
44 K5 **Paulayá, Río** ≈ NE Honduras
24 M6 **Paulding** Mississippi, S USA
33 Q12 **Paulding** Ohio, N USA
31 S12 **Paullina** Iowa, C USA
61 P15 **Paulo Afonso** Bahia, E Brazil
40 M16 **Pauloff Harbor** *var.* Pavlor Harbour. Sanak Island, Alaska, USA
29 N12 **Pauls Valley** Oklahoma, C USA
177 Ff7 **Paungde** Pegu, C Burma
Pauni *see* Paoni
158 K9 **Pauri** Uttar Pradesh, N India
Pautalia *see* Kyustendil
176 Z11 **Pauwasi** ≈ Irian Jaya, E Indonesia
148 J5 **Pāveh** Kermānshāhān, NW Iran
130 L5 **Pavelets** Ryazanskaya Oblast', W Russian Federation
108 D8 **Pavia** *anc.* Ticinum. Lombardia, N Italy
120 C9 **Pāvilosta** Liepāja, W Latvia
129 P14 **Pavino** Kostromskaya Oblast', NW Russian Federation
116 J8 **Pavlikeni** Loveshka Oblast, N Bulgaria
151 T8 **Pavlodar** Pavlodar, NE Kazakhstan
151 S9 **Pavlodar** *off.* Pavlodarskaya Oblast', *Kaz.* Pavlodar Oblysy. ◈ *province* NE Kazakhstan
Pavlodar Oblysy/Pavlodarskaya Oblast' *see* Pavlodar
Pavlograd *see* Pavlohrad
119 U7 **Pavlohrad** *Rus.* Pavlograd. Dnipropetrovs'ka Oblast', E Ukraine
Pavlor Harbour *see* Pauloff Harbor
151 R9 **Pavlovka** Akmola, C Kazakhstan
131 V4 **Pavlovka** Respublika Bashkortostan, W Russian Federation
131 Q7 **Pavlovka** Ul'yanovskaya Oblast', W Russian Federation
131 N3 **Pavlovo** Nizhegorodskaya Oblast', W Russian Federation
130 L9 **Pavlovsk** Voronezhskaya Oblast', W Russian Federation
130 L13 **Pavlovskaya** Krasnodarskiy Kray, SW Russian Federation
119 S7 **Pavlysh** Kirovohrads'ka Oblast', C Ukraine
108 F10 **Pavullo nel Frignano** Emilia-Romagna, C Italy
29 P8 **Pawhuska** Oklahoma, C USA
xxxvi J11 **Pawlett** Somerset, SW England, UK
23 U13 **Pawleys Island** South Carolina, SE USA
178 Gg6 **Pawn** ≈ C Burma
32 K14 **Pawnee** Illinois, N USA
29 O9 **Pawnee** Oklahoma, C USA
39 U2 **Pawnee Buttes** ▲ Colorado, C USA
31 S17 **Pawnee City** Nebraska, C USA
28 K5 **Pawnee River** ≈ Kansas, C USA
33 O10 **Paw Paw** Michigan, N USA
33 O10 **Paw Paw Lake** Michigan, N USA
21 O12 **Pawtucket** Rhode Island, NE USA
Pax Augusta *see* Badajoz
117 I25 **Paximádia** *island* SE Greece
Pax Julia *see* Beja
117 B16 **Paxoí** *island* Iónioi Nísoi, Greece, C Mediterranean Sea
41 S10 **Paxson** Alaska, USA
xliii P20 **Paxton** The Borders, S Scotland, UK
32 M13 **Paxton** Illinois, N USA
128 J11 **Pay** Respublika Kareliya, NW Russian Federation
177 G8 **Payagyi** Pegu, SW Burma
110 C9 **Payerne** *Ger.* Peterlingen. Vaud, W Switzerland
34 M13 **Payette** Idaho, NW USA
34 M13 **Payette River** ≈ Idaho, NW USA
129 V2 **Pay-Khoy, Khrebet** ▲▲ NW Russian Federation
Payne *see* Kangirsuk
10 K4 **Payne, Lac** ◎ Québec, NE Canada
31 T8 **Paynesville** Minnesota, N USA
174 M4 **Payong, Tanjung** *headland* East Malaysia
Payo Obispo *see* Chetumal
63 D18 **Paysandú** Paysandú, W Uruguay
63 D17 **Paysandú** ◈ *department* W Uruguay
104 I7 **Pays de la Loire** ◈ *region* NW France
38 L12 **Payson** Arizona, SW USA
38 L4 **Payson** Utah, W USA
129 W4 **Payyer, Gora** ▲ NW Russian Federation
Payzawat *see* Jiashi
143 Q11 **Pazar** Rize, NE Turkey
142 F10 **Pazarbaşı Burnu** *headland* NW Turkey
142 M16 **Pazarcık** Kahramanmaraş, S Turkey
116 I10 **Pazardzhik** *prev.* Tatar Pazardzhik. Plovdivska Oblast, SW Bulgaria
56 H9 **Paz de Ariporo** Casanare, E Colombia
114 A10 **Pazin** *Ger.* Mitterburg, *It.* Pisino. Istra, NW Croatia
44 D7 **Paz, Río** ≈ El Salvador/Guatemala
115 O18 **Pčinja** ≈ N FYR Macedonia
200 Qq15 **Pea** Tongatapu, S Tonga
29 O6 **Peabody** Kansas, C USA
9 O12 **Peace** ≈ Alberta/British Columbia, W Canada
Peace Garden State *see* North Dakota
xxxvii U13 **Peacehaven** East Sussex, SE England, UK
9 Q10 **Peace Point** Alberta, C Canada
9 O12 **Peace River** Alberta, W Canada
25 W13 **Peace River** ≈ Florida, SE USA
9 N17 **Peachland** British Columbia, SW Canada
38 J10 **Peach Springs** Arizona, SW USA
Peach State *see* Georgia
25 S4 **Peachtree City** Georgia, SE USA
201 Y13 **Peacock Point** *point* SE Wake Island
xxxviii L5 **Peak District** *physical region* C England, UK
191 Q7 **Peak Hill** New South Wales, SE Australia
xxxix R9 **Peakirk** Cambridgeshire, E England, UK
67 G15 **Peak, The** ▲ C Ascension Island
107 O13 **Peal de Becerro** Andalucía, S Spain
201 X11 **Peale Island** *island* N Wake Island
39 O6 **Peale, Mount** ▲ Utah, W USA
41 O4 **Peard Bay** *bay* Alaska, USA
25 Q7 **Pea River** ≈ Alabama/Florida, S USA
27 W11 **Pearland** Texas, SW USA
40 D9 **Pearl City** Oahu, Hawaii, USA, C Pacific Ocean
40 D9 **Pearl Harbor** *inlet* Oahu, Hawaii, USA, C Pacific Ocean
Pearl Islands *see* Perlas, Archipiélago de las
Pearl Lagoon *see* Perlas, Laguna de
24 M5 **Pearl River** ≈ Louisiana/Mississippi, S USA
27 Q13 **Pearsall** Texas, SW USA
25 U7 **Pearson** Georgia, SE USA
xxxix Y12 **Peasenhall** Suffolk, E England, UK
27 P4 **Pease River** ≈ Texas, SW USA
xxxvii X12 **Peasmarsh** East Sussex, SE England, UK
10 F7 **Peawanuk** Ontario, C Canada
85 P16 **Pebane** Zambézia, NE Mozambique
67 C23 **Pebble Island** *island* N Falkland Islands
67 C23 **Pebble Island Settlement** Pebble Island, N Falkland Islands
115 L16 **Peć** *Alb.* Pejë, *Turk.* Ipek. Serbia, S Yugoslavia
27 R8 **Pecan Bayou** ≈ Texas, SW USA
24 H10 **Pecan Island** Louisiana, S USA
62 L12 **Peças, Ilha das** *island* S Brazil
32 L10 **Pecatonica River** ≈ Illinois/Wisconsin, N USA
110 G10 **Peccia** Ticino, S Switzerland
Pechenegi *see* Pechenihy
Pechenezhskoye Vodokhranilishche *see* Pecheniz'ke Vodoskhovyshche
128 I2 **Pechenga** *Fin.* Petsamo. Murmanskaya Oblast', NW Russian Federation
119 V5 **Pechenihy** *Rus.* Pechenegi. Kharkivs'ka Oblast', E Ukraine
119 V5 **Pecheniz'ke Vodoskhovyshche** *Rus.* Pechenezhskoye Vodokhranilishche. ⊠ E Ukraine
129 U7 **Pechora** Respublika Komi, NW Russian Federation
129 R6 **Pechora** ≈ NW Russian Federation
Pechora Bay *see* Pechorskaya Guba
Pechora Sea *see* Pechorskoye More
129 S3 **Pechorskaya Guba** *Eng.* Pechora Bay. *bay* NW Russian Federation
125 Ff6 **Pechorskoye More** *Eng.* Pechora Sea. *sea* NW Russian Federation
118 E11 **Pecica** *Ger.* Petschka, *Hung.* Ópécska. Arad, W Romania
xxxvi D8 **Peckham** Southwark, SE England, UK
26 K8 **Pecos** Texas, SW USA
27 N11 **Pecos River** ≈ New Mexico/Texas, SW USA
113 I25 **Pécs** *Ger.* Fünfkirchen; *Lat.* Sopianae. Baranya, SW Hungary
45 T17 **Pedasí** Los Santos, S Panama
Pedde *see* Pedja
191 O17 **Pedder, Lake** ◎ Tasmania, SE Australia
46 M10 **Pedernales** SW Dominican Republic
57 Q5 **Pedernales** Delta Amacuro, NE Venezuela
27 R10 **Pedernales River** ≈ Texas, SW USA
64 H6 **Pedernales, Salar de** *salt lake* N Chile
Pedhoulas *see* Pedoulás
57 X11 **Pédima** *var.* Malavate. SW French Guiana
190 F1 **Pedirka** South Australia
175 T7 **Pediwang** Pulau Halmahera, E Indonesia
120 I5 **Pedja** *var.* Pedja Jõgi, *Ger.* Pedde. ≈ E Estonia
Pedja Jõgi *see* Pedja
124 N3 **Pedoulás** *var.* Pedhoulas. W Cyprus
61 N18 **Pedra Azul** Minas Gerais, NE Brazil
106 I3 **Pedrafita, Porto de** *var.* Puerto de Piedrafita. *pass* NW Spain
78 E9 **Pedra Lume** Sal, NE Cape Verde
45 P16 **Pedregal** Chiriquí, W Panama
56 J4 **Pedregal** Falcón, N Venezuela
42 L9 **Pedriceña** Durango, C Mexico
62 L11 **Pedro Barros** São Paulo, S Brazil
41 Q13 **Pedro Bay** Alaska, USA
64 H4 **Pedro de Valdivia** *var.* Oficina Pedro de Valdivia. Antofagasta, N Chile
64 P4 **Pedro Juan Caballero** Amambay, E Paraguay
65 L15 **Pedro Luro** Buenos Aires, E Argentina
107 O10 **Pedro Muñoz** Castilla-La Mancha, C Spain
161 J22 **Pedro, Point** *headland* NW Sri Lanka
190 K9 **Peebinga** South Australia
xliii M21 **Peebles** The Borders, SE Scotland, UK
98 J12 **Peebles** *cultural region* SE Scotland, UK
33 S15 **Peebles** Ohio, N USA
20 K13 **Peekskill** New York, NE USA
xl F11 **Peel** W Isle of Man
14 Ff4 **Peel** ≈ Northwest Territories/Yukon Territory, NW Canada
15 I1 **Peel Point** *headland* Victoria Island, Northwest Territories, NW Canada
15 K1 **Peel Sound** *passage* Northwest Territories, N Canada
102 N9 **Peene** ≈ NE Germany
101 K17 **Peer** Limburg, NE Belgium
12 H14 **Pefferlaw** Ontario, S Canada
193 I18 **Pegasus Bay** *bay* South Island, NZ
123 Mm3 **Pégeia** *var.* Peyia. SW Cyprus
111 V7 **Peggau** Steiermark, SE Austria
103 L19 **Pegnitz** Bayern, SE Germany
103 L19 **Pegnitz** ≈ SE Germany
107 T11 **Pego** País Valenciano, E Spain
177 G8 **Pegu** *var.* Bago. Pegu, SW Burma
177 G7 **Pegu** ◈ *division* S Burma
176 W7 **Pegun, Pulau** *island* Kepulauan Mapia, E Indonesia
xxxvii Z10 **Pegwell Bay** *bay* SE England, UK
201 N13 **Pehleng** Pohnpei, E Micronesia
116 M12 **Pehlivanköy** Kırklareli, NW Turkey
79 R14 **Péhonko** C Benin
63 B21 **Pehuajó** Buenos Aires, E Argentina
Pei-ching *see* Beijing/Beijing Shi
xlii E13 **Peinchorran** Highland, NW Scotland, UK
102 J13 **Peine** Niedersachsen, C Germany
Pei-p'ing *see* Beijing/Beijing Shi
Peipsi Järv/Peipus-See *see* Peipus, Lake
120 J5 **Peipus, Lake** *Est.* Peipsi Järv, *Ger.* Peipus-See, *Rus.* Chudskoye Ozero. ◎ Estonia/Russian Federation
117 H19 **Peiraías** *prev.* Piraiévs, *Eng.* Piraeus. Attikí, C Greece
Peisern *see* Pyzdry
62 I8 **Peixe, Rio do** ≈ S Brazil
61 I16 **Peixoto de Azevedo** Mato Grosso, W Brazil
174 J8 **Pejantan, Pulau** *island* W Indonesia
Pejë *see* Peć
114 N11 **Pek** ≈ E Yugoslavia
178 Ii7 **Pèk** *var.* Xieng Khouang; *prev.* Xiangkhoang. Xiangkhoang, N Laos
174 Kk14 **Pekalongan** Jawa, C Indonesia
174 Gg7 **Pekanbaru** *var.* Pakanbaru. Sumatera, W Indonesia
32 L12 **Pekin** Illinois, N USA
Peking *see* Beijing/Beijing Shi
Pelabohan Kelang/Pelabuhan Kelang *see* Pelabuhan Klang
173 G5 **Pelabuhan Klang** *var.* Kuala Pelabohan Kelang, Pelabohan Kelang, Pelabuhan Kelang, Port Klang, Port Swettenham. Selangor, Peninsular Malaysia
174 J15 **Pelabuhan Ratu, Teluk** *bay* Jawa, SW Indonesia
123 L12 **Pelagie, Isole** *island group* SW Italy
Pelagosa *see* Palagruža
24 L5 **Pelahatchie** Mississippi, S USA
175 N11 **Pelaihari** *var.* Pleihari. Borneo, C Indonesia
105 U14 **Pelat, Mont** ▲ SE France
118 F12 **Peleaga, Vârful** *prev.* Vîrful Peleaga. ▲ W Romania
Peleaga, Vîrful *see* Peleaga, Vârful
126 K12 **Peleduy** Respublika Sakha (Yakutiya), NE Russian Federation
12 C18 **Pelee Island** *island* Ontario, S Canada
47 Q11 **Pelée, Montagne** ▲ N Martinique
12 D18 **Pelee, Point** *headland* Ontario, S Canada
175 R9 **Pelei** Pulau Peleng, N Indonesia
Peleliu *see* Beliliou
175 R9 **Peleng, Pulau** *island* Kepulauan Banggai, N Indonesia
175 Qq9 **Peleng, Selat** *strait* Sulawesi, C Indonesia
25 T7 **Pelham** Georgia, SE USA
113 E18 **Pelhřimov** *Ger.* Pilgram. Jižní Čechy, S Czech Republic
41 W13 **Pelican** Chichagof Island, Alaska, USA
203 Z3 **Pelican Lagoon** ◎ Kiritimati, E Kiribati
31 U6 **Pelican Lake** ◎ Minnesota, N USA
31 V3 **Pelican Lake** ◎ Minnesota, N USA
32 L5 **Pelican Lake** ◎ Wisconsin, N USA
46 G1 **Pelican Point** Grand Bahama Island, N Bahamas
85 B19 **Pelican Point** *headland* W Namibia
31 S6 **Pelican Rapids** Minnesota, N USA
Pelican State *see* Louisiana
9 U13 **Pelikan Narrows** Saskatchewan, C Canada
117 L18 **Pelinaío** ▲ Chíos, E Greece
Pelinnaeum *see* Pelinnaío
117 E16 **Pelinnaío** *anc.* Pelinnaeum. *ruins* Thessalía, C Greece
115 N20 **Pelister** ▲ SW FYR Macedonia
115 G15 **Pelješac** *peninsula* S Croatia
94 M12 **Pelkosenniemi** Lappi, NE Finland
31 W15 **Pella** Iowa, C USA
116 F13 **Pélla** *site of ancient city* Kentrikí Makedonía, N Greece
25 Q3 **Pell City** Alabama, S USA
63 A22 **Pellegrini** Buenos Aires, E Argentina
94 K12 **Pello** Lappi, NW Finland
102 G7 **Pellworm** *island* N Germany
8 H6 **Pelly** ≈ Yukon Territory, NW Canada
15 L3 **Pelly Bay** Northwest Territories, N Canada
8 I8 **Pelly Mountains** ▲▲ Yukon Territory, W Canada
Pélmonostor *see* Beli Manastir
39 P13 **Pelona Mountain** ▲ New Mexico, SW USA
Peloponnese/Peloponnesus *see* Pelopónnisos
117 E20 **Pelopónnisos** *Eng.* Peloponnese. ◈ *region* S Greece
117 E20 **Pelopónnisos** *var.* Morea, *Eng.* Peloponnese; *anc.* Peloponnesus. *peninsula* S Greece
109 L23 **Peloritani, Monti** *anc.* Pelorus and Neptunius. ▲▲ Sicilia, Italy, C Mediterranean Sea
109 M22 **Peloro, Capo** *var.* Punta del Faro. *headland* S Italy
Pelorus and Neptunius *see* Peloritani, Monti
63 H17 **Pelotas** Rio Grande do Sul, S Brazil
94 K10 **Peltovuoma** *Lapp.* Bealdovuopmi. Lappi, N Finland
125 F10 **Pelym** ≈ C Russian Federation
21 R4 **Pemadumcook Lake** ◎ Maine, NE USA
174 Kk14 **Pemalang** Jawa, C Indonesia
174 K7 **Pemangkat** *var.* Pamangkat. Borneo, C Indonesia
Pemar *see* Paimio
173 Ff5 **Pematangsiantar** Sumatera, W Indonesia
85 Q14 **Pemba** *prev.* Port Amelia, Porto Amélia. Cabo Delgado, NE Mozambique
83 K21 **Pemba** *island* E Tanzania
85 Q14 **Pemba, Baia de** *inlet* NE Mozambique
83 J21 **Pemba Channel** *channel* E Tanzania
83 J22 **Pemba North** ◈ *region* E Tanzania
83 J22 **Pemba South** ◈ *region* E Tanzania
188 J14 **Pemberton** Western Australia
8 M16 **Pemberton** British Columbia, SW Canada
31 Q2 **Pembina** North Dakota, N USA
31 Q2 **Pembina** ≈ Canada/USA
9 P15 **Pembina** ≈ Alberta, SW Canada
176 Xx15 **Pembre** Irian Jaya, E Indonesia
xxxv F14 **Pembrey** Carmarthenshire, S Wales, UK
xxxviii G12 **Pembridge** Herefordshire, W England, UK
xxxv D14 **Pembroke** Pembrokeshire, SW Wales, UK
12 K12 **Pembroke** Ontario, SE Canada
25 W6 **Pembroke** Georgia, SE USA
23 U11 **Pembroke** North Carolina, SE USA
23 R7 **Pembroke** Virginia, NE USA
xxxv C14 **Pembroke Dock** Pembrokeshire, SW Wales, UK
xxxv C13 **Pembrokeshire** ◈ *unitary authority* SW Wales, UK
Pembuang, Sungai *see* Seruyan, Sungai
xxxvii V11 **Pembury** Kent, SE England, UK
45 S15 **Peña Blanca, Cerro** ▲ C Panama
106 K8 **Peña de Francia, Sierra de la** ▲▲ W Spain
106 G6 **Penafiel** *var.* Peñafiel. Porto, N Portugal
107 N6 **Peñafiel** Castilla-León, N Spain
107 S8 **Peñagolosa** ▲ E Spain
107 N7 **Peñalara, Pico de** ▲ C Spain
xxxv D14 **Penally** Pembrokeshire, SW Wales, UK
175 Nn5 **Penambo, Banjaran** *var.* Banjaran Tama Abu, Penambo Range. ▲▲ Indonesia/Malaysia
Penambo Range *see* Penambo, Banjaran
43 O10 **Peña Nevada, Cerro** ▲ C Mexico
Penang *see* Pinang, Pulau, Peninsular Malaysia
Penang *see* Pinang
Penang *see* George Town
62 J8 **Penápolis** São Paulo, S Brazil
106 L7 **Peñaranda de Bracamonte** Castilla-León, N Spain
107 S8 **Peñarroya** ▲ E Spain
106 L12 **Peñarroya-Pueblonuevo** Andalucía, S Spain
xxxv K15 **Penarth** The Vale of Glamorgan, S Wales, UK
106 K1 **Peñas, Cabo de** *headland* N Spain
65 F20 **Penas, Golfo de** *gulf* S Chile
xxxv F12 **Pencader** Carmarthenshire, S Wales, UK
xliii N20 **Pencaitland** East Lothian, SE Scotland, UK
Pen-ch'i *see* Benxi
xxxv I15 **Pencoed** Bridgend, S Wales, UK
81 H14 **Pendé** *var.* Logone Oriental. ≈ Central African Republic/Chad
78 I14 **Pendembu** E Sierra Leone
31 R13 **Pender** Nebraska, C USA
Penderma *see* Bandırma
xxxv I13 **Penderyn** Rhondda Cynon Taff, S Wales, UK
xxxv E14 **Pendine** Carmarthenshire, S Wales, UK
xl G14 **Pendlebury** Salford, NW England, UK
34 K11 **Pendleton** Oregon, NW USA
34 M7 **Pend Oreille, Lake** ◎ Idaho, NW USA
34 M7 **Pend Oreille River** ≈ Idaho/Washington, NW USA
Pendzhikent *see* Panjakent
Peneius *see* Pineiós
106 G8 **Penela** Coimbra, N Portugal
12 G13 **Penetanguishene** Ontario, S Canada
157 H15 **Penganga** ≈ C India
167 T12 **P'engchia Yu** *island* N Taiwan
81 M21 **Penge** Kasai Oriental, C Zaire
Penghu Archipelago/P'enghu Ch'üntao/Penghu Islands *see* P'enghu Liehtao
167 R14 **P'enghu Liehtao** *var.* P'enghu Ch'üntao, Penghu Islands, *Eng.* Penghu Archipelago, Pescadores, *Jap.* Hoko-guntō, Hoko-shotō. *island group* W Taiwan
Penghu Shuidao/P'enghu Shuitao *see* Pescadores Channel
167 R4 **Penglai** *var.* Dengzhou. Shandong, E China
Peng-pu *see* Bengbu
Penhsihu *see* Benxi
Penibético, Sistema *see* Béticos, Sistemas
106 F10 **Peniche** Leiria, W Portugal
xliii M20 **Penicuik** Midlothian, SE Scotland, UK
175 Nn16 **Penida, Nusa** *island* S Indonesia
Peninsular State *see* Florida
107 T8 **Peñíscola** País Valenciano, E Spain
xli R16 **Penistone** Barnsley, N England, UK
42 M13 **Pénjamo** Guanajuato, C Mexico
Penki *see* Benxi
xxxviii B13 **Penkridge** Staffordshire, C England, UK
xxxv L6 **Penley** Wrexham, NE Wales, UK
xxxv H6 **Penmachno** Conwy, N Wales, UK
xxxv H4 **Penmaenmawr** Conwy, N Wales, UK
104 F7 **Penmarch, Pointe de** *headland* NW France
xxxv G4 **Penmon** Isle of Anglesey, NW Wales, UK
109 L15 **Penna, Ponta della** *headland* C Italy
109 K14 **Penne** Abruzzi, C Italy
Penner *see* Penneru
161 J18 **Penneru** *var.* Penner. ≈ C India
190 I10 **Penneshaw** South Australia
20 C14 **Penn Hills** Pennsylvania, NE USA
Penninae, Alpes/Pennine, Alpi *see* Pennine Alps
110 D11 **Pennine Alps** *Fr.* Alpes Pennines, *It.* Alpi Pennine; *Lat.* Alpes Penninae. ▲▲ Italy/Switzerland
Pennine Chain *see* Pennines
xli P8 **Pennines** *var.* Pennine Chain. ▲▲ N England, UK
Pennines, Alpes *see* Pennine Alps
23 O8 **Pennington Gap** Virginia, NE USA
20 I16 **Penns Grove** New Jersey, NE USA
20 I16 **Pennsville** New Jersey, NE USA
20 E14 **Pennsylvania** *off.* Commonwealth of Pennsylvania; also known as The Keystone State. ◈ *state* NE USA
20 G10 **Penn Yan** New York, NE USA
128 H16 **Peno** Tverskaya Oblast', W Russian Federation
21 R7 **Penobscot Bay** *bay* Maine, NE USA
21 S5 **Penobscot River** ≈ Maine, NE USA
190 K12 **Penola** South Australia
42 K9 **Peñón Blanco** Durango, C Mexico
190 E7 **Penong** South Australia
45 S16 **Penonomé** Coclé, C Panama
xliii K23 **Penpont** Dumfries and Galloway, SW Scotland, UK
202 L13 **Penrhyn** *atoll* N Cook Islands
199 Kk10 **Penrhyn Basin** *undersea feature* C Pacific Ocean
xxxv H4 **Penrhyn Bay** Conwy, N Wales, UK
xxxv G6 **Penrhyndeudraeth** Gwynedd, NW Wales, UK
xli N8 **Penrith** Cumbria, NW England, UK
191 S9 **Penrith** New South Wales, SE Australia
xl M8 **Penruddock** Cumbria, NW England, UK
xxxvi C17 **Penryn** Cornwall, SW England, UK
25 O9 **Pensacola** Florida, SE USA
25 O9 **Pensacola Bay** *bay* Florida, SE USA
205 N7 **Pensacola Mountains** ▲▲ Antarctica
xxxvii U11 **Penshurst** Kent, SE England, UK
190 L12 **Penshurst** Victoria, SE Australia
xxxvi E15 **Pensilva** Cornwall, SW England, UK
197 C12 **Pentecost** *Fr.* Pentecôte. *island* C Vanuatu
13 V4 **Pentecôte** ≈ Québec, SE Canada
Pentecôte *see* Pentecost
13 V4 **Pentecôte, Lac** ◎ Québec, SE Canada
15 Gg16 **Penticton** British Columbia, SW Canada
xlii M5 **Pentland Firth** *strait* N Scotland, UK
xliii L20 **Pentland Hills** *hill range* S Scotland, UK
xxxv F4 **Pentraeth** Isle of Anglesey, NW Wales, UK
xxxv H6 **Pentrefoelas** Conwy, N Wales, UK
175 Rr10 **Penu** Pulau Taliabu, E Indonesia
161 H18 **Penukonda** Andhra Pradesh, E India
177 G7 **Penwegon** Pegu, C Burma
26 M8 **Penwell** Texas, SW USA
xxxv J10 **Penybont** Powys, C Wales, UK
xxxv I13 **Pen y Fan** ▲ SE Wales, UK
xxxv H10 **Pen y Garn** ▲ W Wales, UK
xli P12 **Pen-y-ghent** ▲ N England, UK
xxxv F6 **Penygroes** Gwynedd, NW Wales, UK
175 T12 **Penyu, Kepulauan** *island group* E Indonesia
131 O6 **Penza** Penzenskaya Oblast', W Russian Federation
xxxvi L16 **Penzance** Cornwall, SW England, UK
131 N6 **Penzenskaya Oblast'** ◈ *province* W Russian Federation
127 P7 **Penzhina** ≈ E Russian Federation
127 N17 **Penzhinskaya Guba** *bay* E Russian Federation
Penzig *see* Pieńsk
38 K13 **Peoria** Arizona, SW USA
32 L12 **Peoria** Illinois, N USA
32 L12 **Peoria Heights** Illinois, N USA
33 N11 **Peotone** Illinois, N USA
20 J11 **Pepacton Reservoir** ⊠ New York, NE USA
78 I15 **Pepel** W Sierra Leone
32 I6 **Pepin, Lake** ⊠ Minnesota/Wisconsin, N USA
101 L20 **Pepinster** Liège, E Belgium
115 L20 **Peqin** *var.* Peqini. Elbasan, C Albania
Peqini *see* Peqin
42 D7 **Pequeña, Punta** *headland* W Mexico
174 I11 **Perabumulih** *var.* Prabumulih. Sumatera, W Indonesia
174 Gg4 **Perak** ◈ *state* Peninsular Malaysia
174 Gg4 **Perak, Sungai** ≈ Peninsular Malaysia
107 R7 **Perales del Alfambra** Aragón, NE Spain
117 C15 **Pérama** *var.* Perama. Ípeiros, W Greece
94 M13 **Perä-Posio** Lappi, NE Finland
13 Z6 **Percé** Québec, SE Canada
13 Z6 **Percé, Rocher** *island* Québec, S Canada
104 L5 **Perche, Collines de** ▲▲ N France
111 X4 **Perchtoldsdorf** Niederösterreich, NE Austria
188 L6 **Percival Lakes** *lakes* Western Australia
107 T3 **Perdido, Monte** ▲ NE Spain
25 O8 **Perdido River** ≈ Alabama/Florida, S USA
Perece Vela Basin *see* West Mariana Basin
118 G7 **Perechyn** Zakarpats'ka Oblast', W Ukraine
56 E10 **Pereira** Risaralda, W Colombia
62 I7 **Pereira Barreto** São Paulo, S Brazil
61 G15 **Pereirinha** Pará, N Brazil
131 N10 **Perelazovskiy** Volgogradskaya Oblast', SW Russian Federation
131 S7 **Perelyub** Saratovskaya Oblast', W Russian Federation
33 P7 **Pere Marquette River** ≈ Michigan, N USA
Peremyshl *see* Przemyśl
118 I5 **Peremyshlyany** L'vivs'ka Oblast', W Ukraine
Pereshchepino *see* Pereshchepyne
118 L9 **Pereshchepyne** *Rus.* Pereshchepino. Dnipropetrovs'ka Oblast', E Ukraine
128 L16 **Pereslavl'-Zalesskiy** Yaroslavskaya Oblast', W Russian Federation
119 Y7 **Pereval's'k** Luhans'ka Oblast', E Ukraine
131 U7 **Perevolotskiy** Orenburgskaya Oblast', W Russian Federation
127 Nn16 **Pereyaslavka** Khabarovskiy Kray, SE Russian Federation
Pereyaslav-Khmel'nitskiy *see* Pereyaslav-Khmel'nyts'kyy
119 Q5 **Pereyaslav-Khmel'nyts'kyy** *Rus.* Pereyaslav-Khmel'nitskiy. Kyyivs'ka Oblast', N Ukraine
111 U4 **Perg** Oberösterreich, N Austria
63 B19 **Pergamino** Buenos Aires, E Argentina
108 G6 **Pergine Valsugana** *Ger.* Persen. Trentino-Alto Adige, N Italy
31 S6 **Perham** Minnesota, N USA
95 L16 **Perho** Vaasa, W Finland
118 E11 **Periam** *Ger.* Perjamosch, *Hung.* Perjámos. Timiş, W Romania
13 Q6 **Péribonca** ≈ Québec, SE Canada
10 L11 **Péribonca, Lac** ◎ Québec, SE Canada
13 Q6 **Péribonca, Petite Rivière** ≈ Québec, SE Canada
13 Q7 **Péribonka** Québec, SE Canada
42 I9 **Pericos** Sinaloa, C Mexico
174 Kk7 **Perigi** Borneo, C Indonesia
104 L12 **Périgueux** *anc.* Vesuna. Dordogne, SW France
56 G5 **Perijá, Serranía de** ▲▲ Columbia/Venezuela
117 H17 **Peristéra** *island* Vóreioi Sporádes, Greece, Aegean Sea
65 H20 **Perito Moreno** Santa Cruz, S Argentina
161 G22 **Periyāl** *var.* Periyār. ≈ SW India
Periyār *see* Periyāl
161 G23 **Periyār Lake** ◎ S India
Perjámos/Perjamosch *see* Periam
29 O9 **Perkins** Oklahoma, C USA
118 L7 **Perkivtsi** Chernivets'ka Oblast', W Ukraine
45 U15 **Perlas, Archipiélago de las** *Eng.* Pearl Islands. *island group* SE Panama
45 O10 **Perlas, Cayos de** *reef* SE Nicaragua
45 N9 **Perlas, Laguna de** *Eng.* Pearl Lagoon. *lagoon* E Nicaragua
45 N10 **Perlas, Punta de** *headland* E Nicaragua
102 L11 **Perleberg** Brandenburg, N Germany
Perlepe *see* Prilep
173 G2 **Perlis** ◈ *state* Peninsular Malaysia
129 U14 **Perm'** *prev.* Molotov. Permskaya Oblast', NW Russian Federation
115 M22 **Përmet** *var.* Përmeti, Prëmet. Gjirokastër, S Albania
Përmeti *see* Përmet
129 U15 **Permskaya Oblast'** ◈ *province* NW Russian Federation
61 P15 **Pernambuco** *off.* Estado de Pernambuco. ◈ *state* E Brazil
Pernambuco *see* Recife
Pernambuco Abyssal Plain *see* Pernambuco Plain
49 Y6 **Pernambuco Plain** *var.* Pernambuco Abyssal Plain. *undersea feature* E Atlantic Ocean
67 K15 **Pernambuco Seamounts** *undersea feature* C Atlantic Ocean
190 H6 **Pernatty Lagoon** *salt lake* South Australia
Pernau *see* Pärnu
Pernauer Bucht *see* Pärnu Laht
Pērnava *see* Pärnu
116 G9 **Pernik** *prev.* Dimitrovo. Sofiyska Oblast, W Bulgaria
95 K20 **Perniö** *Swe.* Bjärnå. Turku-Pori, SW Finland
111 X5 **Pernitz** Niederösterreich, E Austria
Pernov *see* Pärnu
105 O3 **Péronne** Somme, N France
12 L8 **Péronne, Lac** ◎ Québec, SE Canada

◆ Country
● Country Capital
◇ Dependent Territory
○ Dependent Territory Capital
◈ Administrative Region
✈ International Airport
▲ Mountain
▲▲ Mountain Range
Volcano
≈ River
◎ Lake
⊠ Reservoir

PEROSA ARGENTINA – PIPLĀN

108 A8 Perosa Argentina Piemonte, NE Italy
43 Q14 Perote Veracruz-Llave, E Mexico
Pérouse see Perugia
203 W15 Pérouse, Bahía de la bay Easter Island, Chile, E Pacific Ocean
Perovsk see Kzyl-Orda
105 O17 Perpignan Pyrénées-Orientales, S France
Perran Bay see Ligger Bay
xxxvi B16 Perranporth Cornwall, SW England, UK
115 M20 Përrenjas var. Përrenjasi, Prenjas, Prenjasi. Elbasan, E Albania
Përrenjasi see Përrenjas
94 O2 Perriertoppen ▲ C Svalbard
27 S6 Perrin Texas, SW USA
25 Y16 Perrine Florida, SE USA
39 S12 Perro, Laguna del ◎ New Mexico, SW USA
104 G5 Perros-Guirec Côtes d'Armor, NW France
25 T9 Perry Florida, SE USA
25 T5 Perry Georgia, SE USA
31 U14 Perry Iowa, C USA
20 E10 Perry New York, NE USA
29 N9 Perry Oklahoma, C USA
29 Q3 Perry Lake ⊡ Kansas, C USA
33 R11 Perrysburg Ohio, N USA
27 O1 Perryton Texas, SW USA
41 O15 Perryville Alaska, USA
29 U11 Perryville Arkansas, C USA
29 Y6 Perryville Missouri, C USA
Persante see Parsęta
Persen see Pergine Valsugana
Pershay see Pyarshai
xxxviii K13 Pershore Worcestershire, W England, UK
119 V7 Pershotravens'k Dnipropetrovs'ka Oblast', E Ukraine
119 W9 Pershotravneve Donets'ka Oblast', E Ukraine
Persia see Iran
Persian Gulf see Gulf, The
Persis see Fārs
97 K22 Perstorp Kristianstad, S Sweden
143 O14 Pertek Tunceli, C Turkey
98 J10 Perth cultural region C Scotland, UK
xliii L17 Perth Perth and Kinross, C Scotland, UK
191 P16 Perth Tasmania, SE Australia
188 I13 Perth state capital Western Australia
12 L13 Perth Ontario, SE Canada
188 I12 Perth ✈ Western Australia
xliii I16 Perth and Kinross ◆ unitary authority C Scotland, UK
181 V10 Perth Basin undersea feature SE Indian Ocean
105 S15 Pertuis Vaucluse, SE France
104 E3 Pertusato, Capo headland Corse, France, C Mediterranean Sea
32 L11 Peru Illinois, N USA
33 P12 Peru Indiana, N USA
59 E13 Peru off. Republic of Peru. ◆ republic W South America
Peru see Beru
200 Oo10 Peru Basin undersea feature E Pacific Ocean
200 Oo9 Peru-Chile Trench undersea feature E Pacific Ocean
114 F13 Peručko Jezero ◎ S Croatia
108 H13 Perugia Fr. Pérouse; anc. Perusia. Umbria, C Italy
Perugia, Lake of see Trasimeno, Lago
63 D15 Perugorría Corrientes, NE Argentina
62 M11 Peruíbe São Paulo, S Brazil
161 B21 Perumalpār reef India, N Indian Ocean
Perusia see Perugia
101 D20 Péruwelz Hainaut, SW Belgium
143 R15 Pervari Siirt, SE Turkey
131 O4 Pervomaysk Nizhegorodskaya Oblast', W Russian Federation
119 X7 Pervomays'k Luhans'ka Oblast', E Ukraine
119 P8 Pervomays'k prev. Ol'viopol'. Mykolayivs'ka Oblast', S Ukraine
119 S12 Pervomays'ke Respublika Krym, S Ukraine
131 V7 Pervomayskiy Orenburgskaya Oblast', W Russian Federation
130 M6 Pervomayskiy Tambovskaya Oblast', W Russian Federation
119 V6 Pervomays'kyy Kharkivs'ka Oblast', E Ukraine
125 E10 Pervoural'sk Sverdlovskaya Oblast', C Russian Federation
127 Pp12 Pervyy Kuril'skiy Proliv strait E Russian Federation
101 F19 Perwez Walloon Brabant, C Belgium
108 I11 Pesaro anc. Pisaurum. Marche, C Italy
37 N9 Pescadero California, W USA
Pescadores see P'enghu Liehtao
167 S14 Pescadores Channel var. Penghu Shuidao, P'enghu Shuitao. channel W Taiwan
109 K14 Pescara anc. Aternum, Ostia Aterni. Abruzzi, C Italy
109 K15 Pescara ≈ C Italy
108 F11 Pescia Toscana, C Italy
110 C8 Peseux Neuchâtel, W Switzerland
129 P6 Pesha ≈ NW Russian Federation
155 T5 Peshāwar North-West Frontier Province, N Pakistan
155 T6 Peshāwar ✈ North-West Frontier Province, N Pakistan
115 M19 Peshkopi var. Peshkopia, Peshkopija. Dibër, NE Albania
Peshkopia/Peshkopija see Peshkopi
116 I11 Peshtera Plovdivska Oblast, SW Bulgaria
33 N6 Peshtigo Wisconsin, N USA
33 N6 Peshtigo River ≈ Wisconsin, N USA
Peski see Pyeski
129 S13 Peskovka Kirovskaya Oblast', NW Russian Federation
105 S8 Pesmes Haute-Saône, E France
106 H6 Peso da Régua var. Pêso da Regua. Vila Real, N Portugal
42 F5 Pesqueira Sonora, NW Mexico
104 J13 Pessac Gironde, SW France
113 J23 Pest off. Pest Megye. ◆ county C Hungary
128 J14 Pestovo Novgorodskaya Oblast', W Russian Federation
42 M15 Petacalco, Bahía bay W Mexico
Petach-Tikva/Petah Tiqva see Petah Tiqwa
144 F10 Petah Tiqwa var. Petach-Tikva, Petah Tiqva. Tel Aviv, C Israel
95 L17 Petäjävesi Keski-Suomi, C Finland
24 M7 Petal Mississippi, S USA
117 H19 Petalioí island C Greece
117 H19 Petalión, Kólpos gulf E Greece
117 J19 Pétalo ▲ Ándros, Kykládes, Greece, Aegean Sea
36 M8 Petaluma California, W USA
101 L25 Pétange Luxembourg, SW Luxembourg
56 M5 Petare Miranda, N Venezuela
43 N16 Petatlán Guerrero, S Mexico
85 L14 Petauke Eastern, E Zambia
12 J12 Petawawa Ontario, SE Canada
12 J11 Petawawa ≈ Ontario, SE Canada
Petchaburi see Phetchaburi
44 D2 Petén off. Departamento del Petén. ◆ department N Guatemala
44 D2 Petén Itzá, Lago var. Lago de Flores. ◎ N Guatemala
32 K7 Petenwell Lake ⊡ Wisconsin, N USA
12 D6 Peterbell Ontario, S Canada
xxxix R10 Peterborough prev. Medeshamstede. Cambridgeshire, E England, UK
xxxix Q10 Peterborough ◆ unitary authority E England, UK
190 I7 Peterborough South Australia
12 I14 Peterborough Ontario, SE Canada
21 N10 Peterborough New Hampshire, NE USA
xliii O14 Peterculter City of Aberdeen, NE Scotland, UK
xlii Q12 Peterhead Aberdeenshire, NE Scotland, UK
Peterhof see Luboń
199 Mm16 Peter I Island ◇ Norwegian dependency Antarctica
204 H9 Peter I Island var. Peter I øy. island Antarctica
Peter I øy see Peter I Island
xli X4 Peterlee Durham, N England, UK
Peterlingen see Payerne
207 P14 Petermann Bjerg ▲ C Greenland
9 S12 Peter Pond Lake ◎ Saskatchewan, C Canada
41 X13 Petersburg Mytkof Island, Alaska, USA
32 K13 Petersburg Illinois, N USA
33 N16 Petersburg Indiana, N USA
31 Q3 Petersburg North Dakota, N USA
27 N5 Petersburg Texas, SW USA
23 V7 Petersburg Virginia, NE USA
23 T4 Petersburg West Virginia, NE USA
xxxvii R12 Petersfield Hampshire, S England, UK
102 H12 Petershagen Nordrhein-Westfalen, NW Germany
57 S9 Peters Mine var. Peter's Mine. N Guyana
xxxviii H14 Peterstow Herefordshire, W England, UK
xxxvi Y10 Petham Kent, SE England, UK
109 O21 Petilia Policastro Calabria, SW Italy
46 M9 Pétionville S Haiti
47 X6 Petit-Bourg Basse Terre, C Guadeloupe
13 Y5 Petit-Cap Québec, SE Canada
47 Y6 Petit Cul-de-Sac Marin bay C Guadeloupe
10 K7 Petite Rivière de la Baleine ≈ Québec, NE Canada
46 M9 Petite-Rivière-de-l'Artibonite C Haiti
181 X16 Petite Rivière Noire, Piton de la ▲ C Mauritius
13 R9 Petite-Rivière-St-François Québec, SE Canada
46 L9 Petit-Goâve S Haiti
Petitjean see Sidi-Kacem
11 N10 Petit Lac Manicouagan ◎ Québec, E Canada
21 T7 Petit Manan Point headland Maine, NE USA
Petit Mécatina, Rivière du see Little Mecatina
9 N10 Petitot ≈ Alberta/British Columbia, W Canada
47 S12 Petit Piton ▲ SW Saint Lucia
Petit-Popo see Aného
Petit St-Bernard, Col du see Little Saint Bernard Pass
11 O8 Petitsikapau Lake ◎ Newfoundland and Labrador, E Canada
94 L11 Petkula Lappi, N Finland
43 X12 Peto Yucatán, SE Mexico
64 G10 Petorca Valparaíso, C Chile
33 Q5 Petoskey Michigan, N USA
144 G14 Petra archaeological site Ma'ān, W Jordan
Petra see Wādī Mūsā
117 F14 Pétras, Sténa pass N Greece
127 Nn18 Petra Velikogo, Zaliv bay SE Russian Federation
Petrel see Petrer
12 K15 Petre, Point headland Ontario, SE Canada
107 S12 Petrer var. Petrel. País Valenciano, E Spain
129 U11 Petretsovo Permskaya Oblast', NW Russian Federation
116 G12 Petrich Sofiyska Oblast, SW Bulgaria
197 H3 Petrie, Récif reef N New Caledonia
39 N11 Petrified Forest prehistoric site Arizona, SW USA
Petrikau see Piotrków Trybunalski
Petrikov see Pyetrykaw
118 H12 Petrila Hung. Petrilla. Hunedoara, W Romania
Petrilla see Petrila
114 E9 Petrinja Sisak-Moslavina, C Croatia
Petroaleksandrovsk see Türtkül
xxxvi F13 Petrockstow Devon, SW England, UK
Petrőcz see Bački Petrovac
128 G12 Petrodvorets Fin. Pietarhovi. Leningradskaya Oblast', NW Russian Federation
Petrograd see Sankt-Peterburg
Petrokov see Piotrków Trybunalski
56 G6 Petrólea Norte de Santander, NE Colombia
12 D16 Petrolia Ontario, S Canada
27 S4 Petrolia Texas, SW USA
61 O15 Petrolina Pernambuco, E Brazil
47 T6 Petrona, Punta headland C Puerto Rico
Petropavl see Petropavlovsk
119 V7 Petropavlivka Dnipropetrovs'ka Oblast', E Ukraine
151 P6 Petropavlovsk Kaz. Petropavl. Severnyy Kazakhstan, N Kazakhstan
127 Pp11 Petropavlovsk-Kamchatskiy Kamchatskaya Oblast', E Russian Federation
62 P9 Petrópolis Rio de Janeiro, SE Brazil
118 H12 Petroşani var. Petroşeni, Ger. Petroschen, Hung. Petrozsény. Hunedoara, W Romania
Petroschen/Petroşeni see Petroşani
Petroskoi see Petrozavodsk
114 N12 Petrovac Serbia, E Yugoslavia
Petrovac/Petrovácz see Bački Petrovac
115 J17 Petrovac na Moru Montenegro, SW Yugoslavia
119 S8 Petrove Kirovohrads'ka Oblast', C Ukraine
115 O18 Petrovec C FYR Macedonia
Petrovgrad see Zrenjanin
131 P7 Petrovsk Saratovskaya Oblast', W Russian Federation
128 J9 Petrovskiy Yam Respublika Kareliya, NW Russian Federation
Petrovsk-Port see Makhachkala
126 K16 Petrovsk-Zabaykal'skiy Chitinskaya Oblast', S Russian Federation
131 P9 Petrov Val Volgogradskaya Oblast', SW Russian Federation
128 J11 Petrozavodsk Fin. Petroskoi. Respublika Kareliya, NW Russian Federation
Petrozsény see Petroşani
85 D20 Petrusdal Hardap, C Namibia
119 T7 Petrykivka Dnipropetrovs'ka Oblast', E Ukraine
Petsamo see Pechenga
Petschka see Pecica
Pettau see Ptuj
111 S5 Pettenbach Oberösterreich, C Austria
xliv H4 Pettigoe Donegal, N Ireland
27 S13 Pettus Texas, SW USA
125 F13 Petukhovo Kurganskaya Oblast', C Russian Federation
Petuna see Songyuan
xxxvii S12 Petworth West Sussex, SE England, UK
111 R4 Peuerbach Oberösterreich, N Austria
64 G12 Peumo Libertador, C Chile
173 Ee3 Peusangan, Krueng ≈ Sumatera, NW Indonesia
127 O4 Pevek Chukotskiy Avtonomnyy Okrug, NE Russian Federation
29 X5 Pevely Missouri, C USA
xxxvii V13 Pevensey East Sussex, SE England, UK
xxxvii O10 Pewsey Wiltshire, S England, UK
Peyia see Pégeia
104 J15 Peyrehorade Landes, SW France
128 J14 Peza ≈ NW Russian Federation
105 P16 Pézenas Hérault, S France
113 H20 Pezinok Ger. Bösing, Hung. Bazin. Západné Slovensko, SW Slovakia
103 L22 Pfaffenhofen an der Ilm Bayern, SE Germany
110 G7 Pfäffikon Schwyz, C Switzerland
103 F20 Pfälzer Wald hill range W Germany
103 N22 Pfarrkirchen Bayern, SE Germany
103 G21 Pforzheim Baden-Württemberg, SW Germany
103 H24 Pfullendorf Baden-Württemberg, S Germany
110 K8 Pfunds Tirol, W Austria
103 G19 Pfungstadt Hessen, W Germany
85 L20 Phalaborwa Northern, NE South Africa
158 E11 Phalodi Rājasthān, NW India
158 E12 Phalsund Rājasthān, NW India
161 E15 Phaltan Mahārāshtra, W India
178 Hh7 Phan var. Muang Phan. Chiang Rai, NW Thailand
178 H14 Phangan, Ko island SW Thailand
178 Gg15 Phang-Nga var. Pang-Nga, Phangnga. Phangnga, SW Thailand
Phan Rang/Phanrang see Phan Rang-Thap Cham
178 Kk13 Phan Rang-Thap Cham var. Phanrang, Phan Rang, Phan Rang Thap Cham. Ninh Thuân, S Vietnam
178 Kk14 Phan Ri Binh Thuân, S Vietnam
178 K14 Phan Thiêt Binh Thuân, S Vietnam
Pharnacia see Giresun
27 S17 Pharr Texas, SW USA
Pharus see Hvar
178 H16 Phatthalung var. Padalung, Patalung. Phatthalung, SW Thailand
178 Hh7 Phayao var. Muang Phayao. Phayao, NW Thailand
9 U10 Phelps Lake ◎ Saskatchewan, C Canada
23 X9 Phelps Lake ◎ North Carolina, SE USA
25 R5 Phenix City Alabama, S USA
178 J8 Pheo Quang Binh, C Vietnam
Phet Buri see Phetchaburi
178 H12 Phetchaburi var. Bejraburi, Petchaburi, Phet Buri. Phetchaburi, SW Thailand
178 Hh9 Phichit var. Bichitra, Muang Phichit, Pichit. Phichit, C Thailand
24 M5 Philadelphia Mississippi, S USA
20 I7 Philadelphia New York, NE USA
20 I16 Philadelphia Pennsylvania, NE USA
20 I16 Philadelphia ✈ Pennsylvania, NE USA
Philadelphia see 'Ammān
30 L10 Philip South Dakota, N USA
101 H22 Philippeville Namur, S Belgium
Philippeville see Skikda
23 S3 Philippi West Virginia, NE USA
Philippi see Fílippoi
205 Y9 Philippi Glacier glacier Antarctica
198 G7 Philippine Basin undersea feature W Pacific Ocean
133 X12 Philippine Plate tectonic feature
179 Q13 Philippines off. Republic of the Philippines. ◆ republic SE Asia
133 X13 Philippines island group W Pacific Ocean
179 S12 Philippine Sea sea W Pacific Ocean
198 G7 Philippine Trench undersea feature W Philippine Sea
85 H23 Philippolis Free State, C South Africa
Philippopolis see Plovdiv, Bulgaria
Philippopolis see Shahbā', Syria
47 V9 Philipsburg Sint Maarten, N Netherlands Antilles
35 P10 Philipsburg Montana, NW USA
41 R6 Philip Smith Mountains ▲ Alaska, USA
158 H8 Phillaur Punjab, N India
191 N13 Phillip Island island Victoria, SE Australia
27 N2 Phillips Texas, SW USA
32 K5 Phillips Wisconsin, N USA
28 K3 Phillipsburg Kansas, C USA
20 I14 Phillipsburg New Jersey, NE USA
23 S7 Philpott Lake ⊡ Virginia, NE USA
Phintias see Licata
178 Hh9 Phitsanulok var. Bisnulok, Muang Phitsanulok, Pitsanulok. Phitsanulok, C Thailand
Phlórina see Flórina
Phnom Penh see Phnum Penh
178 J13 Phnum Penh var. Phnom Penh. ● (Cambodia) Phnum Penh, S Cambodia
178 J12 Phnum Tbêng Meanchey Preăh Vihéar, N Cambodia
38 K13 Phoenix state capital Arizona, SW USA
Phoenix Island see Rawaki
203 R3 Phoenix Islands island group C Kiribati
20 I15 Phoenixville Pennsylvania, NE USA
85 K22 Phofung var. Mont-aux-Sources. ▲ N Lesotho
178 I10 Phon Khon Kaen, E Thailand
178 I5 Phôngsali var. Phong Saly. Phôngsali, N Laos
Phong Saly see Phôngsali
178 I8 Phônhông C Laos
178 J5 Phô Rang Lao Cai, N Vietnam
Phort Láirge, Cuan see Waterford Harbour
178 Gg10 Phra Chedi Sam Ong Kanchanaburi, W Thailand
178 Hh8 Phrae var. Muang Phrae, Prae. Phrae, NW Thailand
Phra Nakhon Si Ayutthaya see Ayutthaya
177 G15 Phra Thong, Ko island SW Thailand
Phu Cưỡng see Thu Dâu Môt
177 G16 Phuket var. Bhuket, Puket, Mal. Ujung Salang; prev. Junkseylon, Salang. Phuket, SW Thailand
177 G16 Phuket ✈ Phuket, SW Thailand
177 G16 Phuket, Ko island SW Thailand
160 N12 Phulabāni prev. Phulbani. Orissa, E India
Phulbani see Phulabāni
178 K10 Phu Lôc Th,a Thiên-Huê, C Vietnam
178 J14 Phumĭ Banam Prey Vêng, S Cambodia
178 I13 Phumĭ Chŏâm Kâmpóng Spœ, SW Cambodia
178 Jj11 Phumĭ Kalêng Stœng Trêng, NE Cambodia
178 J12 Phumĭ Kâmpóng Trâbêk prev. Phum Kompong Trabek. Kâmpóng Thum, C Cambodia
178 Ii12 Phumĭ Koŭk Kduŏch Bătdâmbâng, NW Cambodia
178 K12 Phumĭ Labăng Rôtânôkiri, NE Cambodia
178 J11 Phumĭ Mlu Prey Preăh Vihéar, N Cambodia
178 I11 Phumĭ Moŭng Siĕmréab, NW Cambodia
178 I13 Phumĭ Prâmaôy Poŭthĭsăt, W Cambodia
178 I14 Phumĭ Samĭt Kaôh Kông, SW Cambodia
178 Ii11 Phumĭ Sâmraông prev. Phum Samrong. Siĕmréab, NW Cambodia
178 Jj12 Phumĭ Siĕmbok Stœng Trêng, N Cambodia
178 Jj12 Phumĭ Thalabârĭvăt Stœng Trêng, N Cambodia
178 I14 Phumĭ Veal Renh Kâmpôt, SW Cambodia
178 I13 Phumĭ Yeay Sên Kaôh Kông, SW Cambodia
Phum Kompong Trabek see Phumĭ Kâmpóng Trâbêk
Phum Samrong see Phumĭ Sâmraông
178 Kk11 Phu My Binh Đinh, C Vietnam
178 J15 Phung Hiêp Cân Thơ, S Vietnam
159 T12 Phuntsholing SW Bhutan
178 J15 Phước Long Minh Hai, S Vietnam
178 I14 Phu Quôc, Đao var. Phu Quoc Island. island S Vietnam
Phu Quoc Island see Phu Quôc, Đao
178 J6 Phu Tho Vinh Phu, N Vietnam
Phu Vinh see Tra Vinh
201 T13 Piaanu Pass passage Chuuk Islands, C Micronesia
108 E8 Piacenza Fr. Paisance; anc. Placentia. Emilia-Romagna, N Italy
109 K14 Pianella Abruzzi, C Italy
109 M15 Pianosa, Isola island Archipelago Toscano, C Italy
176 Vv11 Piar Irian Jaya, E Indonesia
47 U14 Piarco var. Port of Spain. ✈ (Port-of-Spain) Trinidad, Trinidad and Tobago
112 M12 Piaseczno Warszawa, C Poland
118 I15 Piatra Teleorman, S Romania
118 L10 Piatra-Neamţ Hung. Karácsonkő. Neamţ, NE Romania
Piauhy see Piauí
61 N15 Piauí off. Estado do Piauí; prev. Piauhy. ◆ state E Brazil
108 I7 Piave ≈ NE Italy
109 K24 Piazza Armerina var. Chiazza. Sicilia, Italy, C Mediterranean Sea
83 G14 Pibor Amh. Pībor Wenz. ≈ Ethiopia/Sudan
83 G14 Pibor Post Jonglei, SE Sudan
Pībor Wenz see Pibor
Pibrans see Příbram
38 K11 Picacho Butte ▲ Arizona, SW USA
42 D4 Picachos, Cerro ▲ NW Mexico
105 O4 Picardie Eng. Picardy. ◆ region N France
Picardy see Picardie
24 L8 Picayune Mississippi, S USA
Piccolo San Bernardo, Colle di see Little Saint Bernard Pass
64 K5 Pichanal Salta, N Argentina
153 P12 Pichandar W Tajikistan
29 R8 Picher Oklahoma, C USA
64 G12 Pichilemu Libertador, C Chile
42 F9 Pichilingue Baja California Sur, W Mexico
58 B6 Pichincha ◆ province N Ecuador
58 C6 Pichincha ▲ N Ecuador
Pichit see Phichit
43 U15 Pichucalco Chiapas, SE Mexico
24 L5 Pickens Mississippi, S USA
23 O11 Pickens South Carolina, SE USA
12 G11 Pickerel ≈ Ontario, S Canada
xli U11 Pickering North Yorkshire, N England, UK
12 H15 Pickering Ontario, S Canada
33 S13 Pickerington Ohio, N USA
10 C10 Pickle Lake Ontario, C Canada
31 P12 Pickstown South Dakota, N USA
27 V6 Pickton Texas, SW USA
25 N1 Pickwick Lake ⊡ S USA
66 N2 Pico var. Ilha do Pico. island Azores, Portugal, NE Atlantic Ocean
65 J19 Pico de Salamanca Chubut, SE Argentina
1 P9 Pico Fracture Zone tectonic feature NW Atlantic Ocean
Pico, Ilha do see Pico
61 O14 Picos Piauí, E Brazil
65 I20 Pico Truncado Santa Cruz, SE Argentina
191 S9 Picton New South Wales, SE Australia
12 K15 Picton Ontario, SE Canada
193 K14 Picton Marlborough, South Island, NZ
65 H15 Picún Leufú, Arroyo ≈ SW Argentina
Pidálion see Gkréko, Akrotíri
xxxvi M14 Piddle ≈ S England, UK
xxxvi L13 Piddletrenthide Dorset, S England, UK
161 K25 Pidurutalagala ▲ S Sri Lanka
118 K6 Pidvolochys'k Ternopil's'ka Oblast', W Ukraine
109 K16 Piedimonte Matese Campania, S Italy
29 X7 Piedmont Missouri, C USA
23 P11 Piedmont South Carolina, SE USA
19 Q12 Piedmont escarpment E USA
Piedmont see Piemonte
33 U13 Piedmont Lake ⊡ Ohio, N USA
106 M11 Piedrabuena Castilla-La Mancha, C Spain
Piedrafita, Puerto de see Pedrafita, Porto de
106 L8 Piedrahita Castilla-León, N Spain
43 N6 Piedras Negras var. Ciudad Porfirio Díaz. Coahuila de Zaragoza, NE Mexico
63 E21 Piedras, Punta headland E Argentina
59 I14 Piedras, Río de las ≈ E Peru
113 J16 Piekary Śląskie Katowice, S Poland
95 M17 Pieksämäki Mikkeli, SE Finland
111 V5 Pielach ≈ NE Austria
95 M16 Pielavesi Kuopio, C Finland
95 N16 Pielinen var. Pielisjärvi. ◎ E Finland
Pielisjärvi see Pielinen
108 A8 Piemonte Eng. Piedmont. ◆ region NW Italy
113 L18 Pieniny ▲ S Poland
113 E14 Pieńsk Ger. Penzig. Jelenia Góra, SW Poland
31 Q13 Pierce Nebraska, C USA
xli R9 Piercebridge Darlington, N England, UK
9 R14 Pierceland Saskatchewan, C Canada
117 E14 Piéria ▲ N Greece
31 N10 Pierre state capital South Dakota, N USA
104 K16 Pierrefitte-Nestalas Hautes-Pyrénées, S France
105 R14 Pierrelatte Drôme, E France
13 P11 Pierreville Québec, SE Canada
13 O7 Pierriche ≈ Québec, SE Canada
113 H20 Piešt'any Ger. Pistyan, Hung. Pöstyén. Západné Slovensko, W Slovakia
111 X5 Piesting ≈ E Austria
Pietarhovi see Petrodvorets
Pietari see Sankt-Peterburg
Pietarsaari see Jakobstad
85 K23 Pietermaritzburg var. Maritzburg. KwaZulu/Natal, E South Africa
85 K20 Pietersburg Northern, NE South Africa
109 K24 Pietraperzia Sicilia, Italy, C Mediterranean Sea
109 N22 Pietra Spada, Passo della pass SW Italy
85 K22 Piet Retief Mpumalanga, E South Africa
118 I9 Pietrosul, Vârful prev. Vîrful Pietrosu. ▲ N Romania
118 J10 Pietrosul, Vârful prev. Vîrful Pietrosu. ▲ N Romania
Pietrosu, Vîrful see Pietrosul, Vârful
108 I6 Pieve di Cadore Veneto, NE Italy
12 C18 Pigeon Bay lake bay Ontario, S Canada
29 X8 Piggott Arkansas, C USA
85 L21 Piggs Peak NW Swaziland
Pigs, Bay of see Cochinos, Bahía de
63 A23 Pigüé Buenos Aires, E Argentina
43 O12 Piguícas ▲ C Mexico
200 Qq15 Piha Passage passage S Tonga
Pihkva Järv see Pskov, Lake
95 N18 Pihlajavesi ◎ SE Finland
95 J18 Pihlava Turku-Pori, SW Finland
95 L16 Pihtipudas Keski-Suomi, C Finland
42 L14 Pihuamo Jalisco, SW Mexico
201 U11 Piis Moen var. Pis. atoll Chuuk Islands, C Micronesia
43 U17 Pijijiapán Chiapas, SE Mexico
100 G12 Pijnacker Zuid-Holland, W Netherlands
44 H5 Pijol, Pico ▲ NW Honduras
Pikaar see Bikar Atoll
128 I13 Pikalevo Leningradskaya Oblast', NW Russian Federation
196 M15 Pikelot island Caroline Islands, C Micronesia
32 M5 Pike River ≈ Wisconsin, N USA
39 T5 Pikes Peak ▲ Colorado, C USA
23 P6 Pikeville Kentucky, S USA
22 L9 Pikeville Tennessee, S USA
Pikinni see Bikini Atoll
81 H18 Pikounda La Sangha, C Congo
112 G9 Piła Ger. Schneidemühl. Piła, NW Poland
112 G10 Piła off. Województwo Pilskie, Ger. Schneidemühl. ◆ province NW Poland
64 N6 Pilagá, Riacho ≈ NE Argentina
63 D20 Pilar Buenos Aires, E Argentina
64 N7 Pilar var. Villa del Pilar. Ñeembucú, S Paraguay
64 N6 Pilcomayo, Río ≈ C South America
153 R12 Pildon Rus. Pil'don. C Tajikistan
Piles see Pylés
Pilgram see Pelhřimov
179 Q11 Pili Luzon, N Philippines
158 L10 Pīlībhīt Uttar Pradesh, N India
112 M13 Pilica ≈ C Poland
117 G16 Pílio ▲ C Greece
113 J22 Pilisvörösvár Pest, N Hungary
67 G15 Pillar Bay bay Ascension Island, C Atlantic Ocean
191 P17 Pillar, Cape headland Tasmania, SE Australia
Pillau see Baltiysk
191 R5 Pilliga New South Wales, SE Australia
xl M13 Pilling Lancashire, NW England, UK
46 H8 Pilón Granma, E Cuba
Pilos see Pýlos
9 W17 Pilot Mound Manitoba, S Canada
23 S8 Pilot Mountain North Carolina, SE USA
41 O14 Pilot Point Alaska, USA
27 T5 Pilot Point Texas, SW USA
34 K11 Pilot Rock Oregon, NW USA
40 M11 Pilot Station Alaska, USA
Pilsen see Plzeň
Pilski, Województwo see Piła
113 K18 Pilsko ▲ N Slovakia
Pilten see Piltene
120 D8 Piltene Ger. Pilten. Ventspils, W Latvia
xxxvi L11 Pilton Somerset, SW England, UK
113 M16 Pilzno Tarnów, SE Poland
Pilzno see Plzeň
39 N14 Pima Arizona, SW USA
60 H13 Pimenta Pará, N Brazil
61 F16 Pimenta Bueno Rondônia, W Brazil
58 B11 Pimentel Lambayeque, W Peru
xxxvi C8 Pimlico Westminster, SE England, UK
107 S6 Pina Aragón, NE Spain
121 I20 Pina Rus. Pina. ≈ SW Belorussia
42 E2 Pinacate, Sierra del ▲ NW Mexico
65 H22 Pináculo, Cerro ▲ S Argentina
203 X11 Pinaki atoll Îles Tuamotu, E French Polynesia
39 N15 Pinaleno Mountains ▲ Arizona, SW USA
179 Pp12 Pinamalayan Mindoro, N Philippines
174 Kk8 Pinang Borneo, C Indonesia
173 G3 Pinang var. Penang. ◆ state Peninsular Malaysia
Pinang see Pinang, Pulau, Peninsular Malaysia
Pinang see George Town
173 G3 Pinang, Pulau var. Penang, Pinang; prev. Prince of Wales Island. island Peninsular Malaysia
46 B5 Pinar del Río Pinar del Río, W Cuba
116 N11 Pınarhisar Kırklareli, NW Turkey
179 P10 Pinatubo, Mount ▲ Luzon, N Philippines
9 Y16 Pinawa Manitoba, S Canada
xxxix R8 Pinchbeck Lincolnshire, E England, UK
xxxix Q8 Pinchbeck West Lincolnshire, E England, UK
9 Q17 Pincher Creek Alberta, SW Canada
32 L16 Pinckneyville Illinois, N USA
Pincota see Pâncota
113 L15 Pińczów Kielce, S Poland
155 U7 Pind Dādan Khān Punjab, E Pakistan
Píndhos/Píndhos Óros see Píndos
155 V8 Pindi Bhattiān Punjab, E Pakistan
155 U6 Pindi Gheb Punjab, E Pakistan
117 D15 Píndos var. Píndhos Óros, Eng. Pindus Mountains; prev. Píndhos. ▲ C Greece
Pindus Mountains see Píndos
20 J16 Pine Barrens physical region New Jersey, NE USA
29 V12 Pine Bluff Arkansas, C USA
25 X11 Pine Castle Florida, SE USA
31 V7 Pine City Minnesota, N USA
189 P2 Pine Creek Northern Territory, N Australia
37 V4 Pine Creek ≈ Nevada, W USA
20 F13 Pine Creek ≈ Pennsylvania, NE USA
29 Q13 Pine Creek Lake ⊡ Oklahoma, C USA
35 T15 Pinedale Wyoming, C USA
9 X15 Pine Dock Manitoba, S Canada
9 Y16 Pine Falls Manitoba, S Canada
37 R10 Pine Flat Lake ⊡ California, W USA
129 N8 Pinega Arkhangel'skaya Oblast', NW Russian Federation
129 N8 Pinega ≈ NW Russian Federation
13 N12 Pine Hill Québec, SE Canada
9 T12 Pinehouse Lake ◎ Saskatchewan, C Canada
23 T10 Pinehurst North Carolina, SE USA
117 D19 Pineiós ≈ S Greece
117 E16 Pineiós var. Piniós; anc. Peneius. ≈ C Greece
31 W10 Pine Island Minnesota, N USA
25 V15 Pine Island island Florida, SE USA
204 K10 Pine Island Glacier glacier Antarctica
27 X9 Pineland Texas, SW USA
25 V13 Pinellas Park Florida, SE USA
8 M13 Pine Pass pass British Columbia, W Canada
15 I9 Pine Point Northwest Territories, W Canada
30 K12 Pine Ridge South Dakota, N USA
31 U6 Pine River Minnesota, N USA
33 Q8 Pine River ≈ Michigan, N USA
32 M4 Pine River ≈ Wisconsin, N USA
108 A8 Pinerolo Piemonte, NE Italy
27 W6 Pines, Lake O' the ⊡ Texas, SW USA
Pines, The Isle of the see Juventud, Isla de la
Pine Tree State see Maine
23 N7 Pineville Kentucky, S USA
24 H7 Pineville Louisiana, S USA
29 R8 Pineville Missouri, C USA
23 R10 Pineville North Carolina, SE USA
23 Q6 Pineville West Virginia, NE USA
35 V8 Piney Buttes physical region Montana, NW USA
169 W9 Ping'an Jilin, NE China
166 H14 Pingbian var. Pingbian Miaozu Zizhixian. Yunnan, SW China
163 S9 Pingdingshan Henan, C China
167 R4 Pingdu Shandong, E China
201 W16 Pingelap Atoll atoll Caroline Islands, E Micronesia
166 K14 Pingguo Guangxi Zhuangzu Zizhiqu, S China
167 Q13 Pinghe Fujian, SE China
P'ing-hsiang see Pingxiang
167 N10 Pingjiang Hunan, S China
Pingkiang see Harbin
166 L8 Pingli Shaanxi, C China
165 W10 Pingliang var. P'ing-liang. Gansu, C China
165 W8 Pingluo Ningxia, N China
Pingma see Tiandong
178 H9 Ping, Mae Nam ≈ W Thailand
167 Q1 Pingquan Hebei, E China
31 P5 Pingree North Dakota, N USA
Pingsiang see Pingxiang
167 S14 P'ingtung Jap. Heitō. S Taiwan
166 I8 Pingwu Sichuan, C China
166 J15 Pingxiang Guangxi Zhuangzu Zizhiqu, S China
167 O11 Pingxiang var. P'ing-hsiang; prev. Pingsiang. Jiangxi, S China
167 S11 Pingyang Zhejiang, SE China
167 P5 Pingyi Shandong, E China
167 P5 Pingyin Shandong, E China
62 H13 Pinhalzinho Santa Catarina, S Brazil
62 I12 Pinhão Paraná, S Brazil
63 H17 Pinheiro Machado Rio Grande do Sul, S Brazil
106 I7 Pinhel Guarda, N Portugal
xxxvi H14 Pinhoe Devon, SW England, UK
Piniós see Pineiós
195 R10 Pinipel Island island Green Islands, NE PNG
173 Ff8 Pini, Pulau island Kepulauan Batu, W Indonesia
111 Y7 Pinka ≈ SE Austria
111 X7 Pinkafeld Burgenland, SE Austria
Pinkiang see Harbin
8 M12 Pink Mountain British Columbia, W Canada
177 G3 Pinlebu Sagaing, N Burma
40 J12 Pinnacle Island island Alaska, USA
188 I12 Pinnacles, The tourist site Western Australia
190 K10 Pinnaroo South Australia
Pinne see Pniewy
102 I9 Pinneberg Schleswig-Holstein, N Germany
117 I15 Pínnes, Ákra headland N Greece
Pinos, Isla de see Juventud, Isla de la
37 R14 Pinos, Mount ▲ California, W USA
107 R12 Pinoso País Valenciano, E Spain
107 N14 Pinos-Puente Andalucía, S Spain
43 Q17 Pinotepa Nacional var. Santiago Pinotepa Nacional. Oaxaca, SE Mexico
116 F13 Pínovo ▲ N Greece
197 K7 Pins, Île des var. Kunyé. island E New Caledonia
121 I20 Pinsk Pol. Pińsk. Brestskaya Voblasts', SW Belorussia
12 D18 Pins, Pointe aux headland Ontario, S Canada
59 B16 Pinta, Isla var. Abingdon. island Galapagos Islands, Ecuador, E Pacific Ocean
129 Q12 Pinyug Kirovskaya Oblast', NW Russian Federation
59 B17 Pinzón, Isla var. Duncan Island. island Galapagos Islands, Ecuador, E Pacific Ocean
37 Y8 Pioche Nevada, W USA
108 F13 Piombino Toscana, C Italy
1 C9 Pioneer Fracture Zone tectonic feature NE Pacific Ocean
126 Ii2 Pioner, Ostrov island Severnaya Zemlya, N Russian Federation
120 A13 Pionerskiy Ger. Neukuhren. Kaliningradskaya Oblast', W Russian Federation
112 N13 Pionki Radom, C Poland
192 L9 Piopio Waikato, North Island, NZ
113 J14 Piotrków off. Województwo Piotrkowskie. ◆ province C Poland
Piotrkowskie, Województwo see Piotrków
112 K13 Piotrków Trybunalski Ger. Petrikau, Rus. Petrokov. Piotrków, C Poland
158 F12 Pīpār Road Rājasthān, N India
117 I16 Pipéri island Vóreioi Sporádes, Greece, Aegean Sea
31 S10 Pipestone Minnesota, N USA
10 C9 Pipestone ≈ Ontario, C Canada
63 E21 Pipinas Buenos Aires, E Argentina
155 T7 Piplān prev. Liaqatabad. Punjab, E Pakistan

◆ Country ● Country Capital ◇ Dependent Territory ○ Dependent Territory Capital ◆ Administrative Region ✈ International Airport ▲ Mountain ▲ Mountain Range ✱ Volcano ≈ River ◎ Lake ⊡ Reservoir

PIPMUACAN, RÉSERVOIR – PONTRHYDFENDIGAID

13 R5 **Pipmuacan, Réservoir** ⊡ Québec, SE Canada
Piqan see Shanshan
33 R13 **Piqua** Ohio, N USA
107 P5 **Piqueras, Puerto de** pass N Spain
62 H11 **Piquiri, Rio** ≈ S Brazil
62 L9 **Piracicaba** São Paulo, S Brazil
Piraeus/Piraiévs see Peiraías
62 K10 **Piraju** São Paulo, S Brazil
62 K9 **Pirajuí** São Paulo, S Brazil
65 G21 **Pirámide, Cerro** ▲ S Chile
Piramiva see Pyramíva
111 R13 **Piran** It. Pirano. SW Slovenia
64 N6 **Pirané** Formosa, N Argentina
61 J18 **Piranhas** Goiás, S Brazil
Pirano see Piran
148 I4 **Pirānshahr** Āzarbāyjān-e Bākhtarī, NW Iran
61 M19 **Pirapora** Minas Gerais, NE Brazil
62 I9 **Pirapòzinho** São Paulo, S Brazil
63 G19 **Piraraja** Lavalleja, S Uruguay
62 L9 **Pirassununga** São Paulo, S Brazil
47 V6 **Pirata, Monte** ▲ E Puerto Rico
62 I13 **Piratuba** Santa Catarina, S Brazil
xxxvii S10 **Pirbright** Surrey, SE England, UK
116 I9 **Pirdop** prev. Strednogorie. Sofiyska Oblast, W Bulgaria
203 P7 **Pirea** Tahiti, W French Polynesia
61 K18 **Pirenópolis** Goiás, S Brazil
159 S13 **Pirganj** Rajshahi, NW Bangladesh
Pirgi see Pyrgí
Pírgos see Pýrgos
63 F20 **Piriápolis** Maldonado, S Uruguay
116 G11 **Pirin** ▲▲ SW Bulgaria
Pirineos see Pyrenees
60 N13 **Piripiri** Piauí, E Brazil
120 H4 **Pirita** var. Pirita Jõgi. ≈ NW Estonia
Pirita Jõgi see Pirita
56 J6 **Píritu** Portuguesa, N Venezuela
95 L18 **Pirkkala** Häme, SW Finland
103 F20 **Pirmasens** Rheinland-Pfalz, SW Germany
103 P16 **Pirna** Sachsen, E Germany
xliii G21 **Pirnmill** North Ayrshire, W Scotland, UK
Piroe see Piru
115 Q15 **Pirot** Serbia, SE Yugoslavia
158 H6 **Pīr Panjāl Range** ▲▲ NE India
45 W16 **Pirre, Cerro** ▲ SE Panama
143 Y11 **Pirsaat** Rus. Pirsagat. ≈ E Azerbaijan
Pirsagat see Pirsaat
149 V11 **Pīr Shūrān, Selseleh-ye** ▲▲ SE Iran
94 M12 **Pirttikoski** Lappi, N Finland
Pirttikylä see Pörtom
175 T11 **Piru** prev. Piroe. Pulau Seram, E Indonesia
Piryatin see Pyryatyn
Pis see Piis Moen
108 F11 **Pisa** var. Pisae. Toscana, C Italy
Pisae see Pisa
176 Uu10 **Pisang, Kepulauan** island group E Indonesia
176 Xx11 **Pisapa** Irian Jaya, E Indonesia
201 V12 **Pisar** atoll Chuuk Islands, C Micronesia
Pisaurum see Pesaro
12 M10 **Piscatosine, Lac** ◎ Québec, SE Canada
111 W7 **Pischeldorf** Steiermark, SE Austria
Pischk see Simeria
109 L19 **Pisciotta** Campania, S Italy
59 E16 **Pisco** Ica, SW Peru
118 G9 **Pişcolt** Hung. Piskolt. Satu Mare, NW Romania
59 E16 **Pisco, Río** ≈ E Peru
113 C18 **Písek** Jižní Čechy, SW Czech Republic
33 R14 **Pisgah** Ohio, N USA
164 F9 **Pishan** var. Guma. Xinjiang Uygur Zizhiqu, NW China
119 N8 **Pishchanka** Vinnyts'ka Oblast', C Ukraine
115 K21 **Pishë** Fier, SW Albania
149 X14 **Pīshīn** Sīstān va Balūchestān, SE Iran
155 O9 **Pishin** North-West Frontier Province, NW Pakistan
155 N11 **Pishin Lora** var. Psein Lora, Pash. Pseyn Bowr. ≈ SW Pakistan
Pishma see Pizhma
Pishpek see Bishkek
175 Q13 **Pising** Pulau Kabaena, C Indonesia
Pisino see Pazin
Piski see Simeria
Piskolt see Pişcolt
153 Q9 **Piskom** Rus. Pskem. ≈ E Uzbekistan
Piskom Tizmasi see Pskemskiy Khrebet
37 P13 **Pismo Beach** California, W USA
79 P12 **Pissila** C Burkina
64 H8 **Pissis, Monte** ▲ N Argentina
43 X12 **Piste** Yucatán, E Mexico
109 O18 **Pisticci** Basilicata, S Italy
108 F11 **Pistoia** anc. Pistoria, Pistoriæ. Toscana, C Italy
34 E15 **Pistol River** Oregon, NW USA
Pistoria/Pistoriæ see Pistoia
13 U5 **Pistuacanis** ≈ Québec, SE Canada
Pistyan see Piešťany
106 M5 **Pisuerga** ≈ N Spain
112 N8 **Pisz** Ger. Johannisburg. Suwałki, NE Poland
78 I13 **Pita** Moyenne-Guinée, NW Guinea
56 D12 **Pitalito** Huila, S Colombia
62 I11 **Pitanga** Paraná, S Brazil
190 M9 **Pitarpunga Lake** salt lake New South Wales, SE Australia
199 M11 **Pitcairn Island** island S Pitcairn Islands
199 M11 **Pitcairn Islands** ◇ UK dependent territory C Pacific Ocean
xlii O13 **Pitcaple** Aberdeenshire, NE Scotland, UK
95 J14 **Piteå** Norrbotten, N Sweden
94 I13 **Piteälven** ≈ N Sweden
118 I13 **Pitești** Argeș, S Romania
Pithagorio see Pythagóreio
188 I12 **Pithara** Western Australia
105 N6 **Pithiviers** Loiret, C France
158 L9 **Pithorāgarh** Uttar Pradesh, N India
196 B16 **Piti** W Guam
108 G13 **Pitigliano** Toscana, C Italy
42 F3 **Pitiquito** Sonora, NW Mexico
Pitkäranta see Pitkyaranta
40 M11 **Pitkas Point** Alaska, USA
128 H11 **Pitkyaranta** Fin. Pitkäranta. Respublika Kareliya, NW Russian Federation
xliii K16 **Pitlochry** Perth and Kinross, C Scotland, UK
20 I16 **Pitman** New Jersey, NE USA
xlii P12 **Pitmedden** Aberdeenshire, NE Scotland, UK
114 G8 **Pitomača** Koprivnica-Križevci, N Croatia
37 O2 **Pit River** ≈ California, W USA
65 G15 **Pitrufquén** Araucanía, S Chile
Pitsanulok see Phitsanulok
Pitschen see Byczyna
xliii N18 **Pitscottie** Fife, E Scotland, UK
Pitsunda see Bichvint'a
111 X6 **Pitten** ≈ E Austria
xlii J9 **Pittentrail** Highland, NW Scotland, UK
xliii N18 **Pittenweem** Fife, E Scotland, UK
8 J14 **Pitt Island** island British Columbia, W Canada
Pitt Island see Makin
24 M3 **Pittsboro** Mississippi, S USA
23 T9 **Pittsboro** North Carolina, SE USA
29 R7 **Pittsburg** Kansas, C USA
27 W6 **Pittsburg** Texas, SW USA
20 B14 **Pittsburgh** Pennsylvania, NE USA
32 J14 **Pittsfield** Illinois, N USA
21 R6 **Pittsfield** Maine, NE USA
20 L11 **Pittsfield** Massachusetts, NE USA
191 U3 **Pittsworth** Queensland, E Australia
64 I8 **Pituil** La Rioja, NW Argentina
58 A10 **Piura** Piura, NW Peru
58 A9 **Piura** off. Departamento de Piura. ◐ department NW Peru
37 S13 **Piute Peak** ▲ California, W USA
115 J15 **Piva** ≈ SW Yugoslavia
119 V5 **Pivdenne** Kharkivs'ka Oblast', E Ukraine
119 P8 **Pivdennyy Buh** Rus. Yuzhnyy Bug. ≈ S Ukraine
56 F5 **Pivijay** Magdalena, N Colombia
111 T13 **Pivka** prev. Šent Peter, Ger. Sankt Peter, It. San Pietro del Carso. SW Slovenia
119 U13 **Pivnichno-Kryms'kyy Kanal** canal S Ukraine
115 J15 **Pivsko Jezero** ◎ SW Yugoslavia
113 M18 **Piwniczna** Nowy Sącz, S Poland
37 R12 **Pixley** California, W USA
129 Q15 **Pizhma** var. Pishma. ≈ NW Russian Federation
11 U13 **Placentia** Newfoundland, Newfoundland and Labrador, SE Canada
Placentia see Piacenza
11 U13 **Placentia Bay** inlet Newfoundland, Newfoundland and Labrador, SE Canada
179 Qq12 **Placer** Masbate, N Philippines
37 P7 **Placerville** California, W USA
46 F5 **Placetas** Villa Clara, C Cuba
115 Q18 **Plačkovica** ▲▲ E FYR Macedonia
38 L2 **Plain City** Utah, W USA
24 G4 **Plain Dealing** Louisiana, S USA
33 O14 **Plainfield** Indiana, N USA
20 K14 **Plainfield** New Jersey, NE USA
30 K8 **Plains** Montana, NW USA
26 L6 **Plains** Texas, SW USA
31 X10 **Plainview** Minnesota, N USA
31 Q13 **Plainview** Nebraska, C USA
27 N4 **Plainview** Texas, SW USA
28 K4 **Plainville** Kansas, C USA
xxxvi F7 **Plaistow** Newham, SE England, UK
117 L25 **Pláka, Ákra** headland Kríti, Greece, E Mediterranean Sea
117 J15 **Pláka, Ákra** headland Límnos, E Greece
115 N19 **Plakenska Planina** ▲▲ SW FYR Macedonia
46 K5 **Plana Cays** islets SE Bahamas
107 S12 **Plana, Isla** var. Nueva Tabarca. island E Spain
61 L18 **Planaltina** Goiás, S Brazil
85 O14 **Planalto Moçambicano** plateau N Mozambique
114 N10 **Plandište** Serbia, NE Yugoslavia
102 N13 **Plane** ≈ NE Germany
56 E6 **Planeta Rica** Córdoba, NW Colombia
31 P11 **Plankinton** South Dakota, N USA
32 M11 **Plano** Illinois, N USA
27 U6 **Plano** Texas, SW USA
25 W12 **Plant City** Florida, SE USA
24 J9 **Plaquemine** Louisiana, S USA
106 K9 **Plasencia** Extremadura, W Spain
114 C10 **Plaški** Karlovac, C Croatia
115 N19 **Plasnica** SW FYR Macedonia
125 E12 **Plast** Chelyabinskaya Oblast', C Russian Federation
11 N14 **Plaster Rock** New Brunswick, SE Canada
109 J24 **Platani** anc. Halycus. ≈ Sicilia, Italy, C Mediterranean Sea
117 G17 **Plataniá** Thessalía, C Greece
117 G24 **Plátanos** Kríti, Greece, E Mediterranean Sea
67 H18 **Plata, Río de la** var. River Plate. estuary Argentina/Uruguay
79 V15 **Plateau** ◐ state C Nigeria
81 G19 **Plateaux** var. Région des Plateaux. ◐ province C Congo
94 P1 **Platen, Kapp** headland NE Svalbard
Plate, River see Plata, Río de la
101 G22 **Plate Taille, Lac de la** var. L'Eau d'Heure. ◎ SE Belgium
Plathe see Płoty
41 N13 **Platinum** Alaska, USA
56 F5 **Plato** Magdalena, N Colombia
31 O11 **Platte** South Dakota, N USA
29 R3 **Platte City** Missouri, C USA
Plattensee see Balaton
29 R3 **Platte River** ≈ Iowa/Missouri, USA
31 Q15 **Platte River** ≈ Nebraska, C USA
39 T3 **Platteville** Colorado, C USA
32 K9 **Platteville** Wisconsin, N USA
103 N21 **Plattling** Bayern, SE Germany
29 R3 **Plattsburg** Missouri, C USA
20 L6 **Plattsburgh** New York, NE USA
31 S15 **Plattsmouth** Nebraska, C USA
103 M17 **Plauen** var. Plauen im Vogtland. Sachsen, E Germany
Plauen im Vogtland see Plauen
102 M10 **Plauer See** ◎ NE Germany
115 L16 **Plav** Montenegro, SW Yugoslavia
120 I10 **Pļaviņas** Ger. Stockmannshof. Aizkraukle, S Latvia
130 K5 **Plavsk** Tul'skaya Oblast', W Russian Federation
43 Z12 **Playa del Carmen** Quintana Roo, E Mexico
42 J12 **Playa Los Corchos** Nayarit, SW Mexico
39 P16 **Playas Lake** ◎ New Mexico, SW USA
43 S15 **Playa Vicenté** Veracruz-Llave, SE Mexico
178 K11 **Plây Cu** var. Pleiku. Gia Lai, C Vietnam
30 L3 **Plaza** North Dakota, N USA
65 I15 **Plaza Huincul** Neuquén, C Argentina
38 L3 **Pleasant Grove** Utah, W USA
31 V14 **Pleasant Hill** Iowa, C USA
29 R4 **Pleasant Hill** Missouri, C USA
Pleasant Island see Nauru
38 K13 **Pleasant, Lake** ◎ Arizona, SW USA
21 P8 **Pleasant Mountain** ▲ Maine, NE USA
29 R5 **Pleasanton** Kansas, C USA
27 R12 **Pleasanton** Texas, SW USA
193 G20 **Pleasant Point** Canterbury, South Island, NZ
21 R5 **Pleasant River** ≈ Maine, NE USA
20 J17 **Pleasantville** New Jersey, NE USA
xxxix N6 **Pleasley** Derbyshire, C England, UK
105 N12 **Pléaux** Cantal, C France
113 B19 **Plechý** Ger. Plöckenstein. ▲ Austria/Czech Republic
Plebeo see Plibo
Pleihari see Pelaihari
Pleiku see Plây Cu
103 M16 **Pleisse** ≈ E Germany
Plencia see Plentzia
192 O7 **Plenty, Bay of** bay North Island, NZ
35 Y6 **Plentywood** Montana, NW USA
107 O2 **Plentzia** var. Plencia. País Vasco, N Spain
104 H5 **Plérin** Côtes d'Armor, NW France
128 M10 **Plesetsk** Arkhangel'skaya Oblast', NW Russian Federation
Pleshchenitsy see Plyeshchanitsy
Pleskau see Pskov
Pleskauer See see Pskov, Lake
Pleskava see Pskov
114 E8 **Pleso International** ✕ (Zagreb) Grad Zagreb, NW Croatia
Pless see Pszczyna
13 Q11 **Plessisville** Québec, SE Canada
112 H12 **Pleszew** Kalisz, C Poland
10 L10 **Plétipi, Lac** ◎ Québec, SE Canada
103 F15 **Plettenberg** Nordrhein-Westfalen, W Germany
116 I8 **Pleven** prev. Plevna. Loveshka Oblast, N Bulgaria
Plevlja/Plevlje see Pljevlja
Plevna see Pleven
Plezzo see Bovec
Pliberk see Bleiburg
78 L17 **Plibo** var. Pleebo. SE Liberia
124 Oo13 **Pliny Trench** undersea feature C Mediterranean Sea
120 K13 **Plisa** Rus. Plissa. Vitsyebskaya Voblasts', N Belarus
Plissa see Plisa
114 D11 **Plitvica** Zadar-Knin, C Croatia
114 D11 **Plješevica** ▲▲ C Croatia
115 K14 **Pljevlja** prev. Plevlja, Plevlje. Montenegro, N Yugoslavia
Ploça see Ploçë
Plocce see Ploče
115 G15 **Ploče** It. Plocce; prev. Kardeljevo. Dubrovnik-Neretva, SE Croatia
115 K22 **Ploçë** var. Ploça. Vlorë, SW Albania
112 K11 **Płock** Ger. Plozk. Płock, C Poland
112 K11 **Płock** off. Województwo Płockie, Ger. Plozk. ◐ province C Poland
111 Q10 **Plöcken Pass** Ger. Plöckenpass, It. Passo di Monte Croce Carnico. pass SW Austria
Plöckenstein see Plechý
Płockie, Województwo see Płock
xlii F12 **Plockton** Highland, NW Scotland, UK
101 B19 **Ploegsteert** Hainaut, W Belgium
104 H6 **Ploërmel** Morbihan, NW France
Ploeşti see Ploieşti
118 K13 **Ploieşti** prev. Ploeşti. Prahova, SE Romania
117 L17 **Plomári** prev. Plomárion. Lésvos, E Greece
Plomárion see Plomári
105 O12 **Plomb du Cantal** ▲ C France
191 V6 **Plomer, Point** headland New South Wales, SE Australia
102 J8 **Plön** Schleswig-Holstein, N Germany
112 L11 **Płońsk** Ciechanów, C Poland
121 J20 **Plotnitsa** Rus. Plotnitsa. Brestskaya Voblasts', SW Belarus
112 E8 **Płoty** Ger. Plathe. Szczecin, NW Poland
104 G7 **Plouay** Morbihan, NW France
113 D15 **Ploučnice** Ger. Polzen. ≈ NE Czech Republic
116 I10 **Plovdiv** prev. Eumolpias, anc. Evmolpia, Philippopolis, Lat. Trimontium. Plovdivska Oblast, C Bulgaria
Plovdiv see Plovdivska Oblast
116 I11 **Plovdivska Oblast** var. Plovdiv. ◐ province C Bulgaria
32 L6 **Plover** Wisconsin, N USA
Plozk see Płock
xliv I4 **Plumbridge** Strabane, W Northern Ireland, UK
29 U11 **Plumerville** Arkansas, C USA
21 P10 **Plum Island** island Massachusetts, NE USA
34 M9 **Plummer** Idaho, NW USA
xxxvi G8 **Plumstead** Greenwich, SE England, UK
85 J18 **Plumtree** Matabeleland South, SW Zimbabwe
120 D11 **Plungė** Plungė, W Lithuania
115 J15 **Plužine** Montenegro, SW Yugoslavia
121 K14 **Plyeshchanitsy** Rus. Pleshchenitsy. Minskaya Voblasts', N Belarus
xxxvi G15 **Plym** ≈ SW England, UK
xxxvi F16 **Plymouth** Devon, SW England, UK
xxxvi F16 **Plymouth** ◐ unitary authority SW England, UK
47 V10 **Plymouth** ○ (Montserrat) SW Montserrat
33 O11 **Plymouth** Indiana, N USA
21 P12 **Plymouth** Massachusetts, NE USA
21 N8 **Plymouth** New Hampshire, NE USA
23 X9 **Plymouth** North Carolina, SE USA
32 M8 **Plymouth** Wisconsin, N USA
xxxvi F16 **Plympton** Devon, SW England, UK
xxxvi F16 **Plymstock** Devon, SW England, UK
xxxv H9 **Plynlimon** ▲ C Wales, UK
128 G14 **Plyussa** Pskovskaya Oblast', W Russian Federation
113 B17 **Plzeň** Ger. Pilsen, Pol. Pilzno. Západní Čechy, W Czech Republic
112 F11 **Pniewy** Ger. Pinne. Poznań, W Poland
108 D8 **Po** ≈ N Italy
79 P13 **Pô** S Burkina
44 M13 **Poás, Volcán** ⊼ NW Costa Rica
79 S16 **Pobè** S Benin
127 N8 **Pobeda, Gora** ▲ NE Russian Federation
Pobeda Peak see Pobedy, Pik/Tomur Feng
153 Z7 **Pobedy, Pik** var. Pobeda Peak, Chin. Tomur Feng. ▲ China/Kyrgyzstan see also Tomur Feng
112 H11 **Pobiedziska** Ger. Pudewitz. Poznań, C Poland
Po, Bocche del see Po, Foci del
29 W9 **Pocahontas** Arkansas, C USA
31 U12 **Pocahontas** Iowa, C USA
35 Q15 **Pocatello** Idaho, NW USA
178 J13 **Pochentong** ✕ (Phnum Penh) Phnum Penh, S Cambodia
130 I6 **Pochep** Bryanskaya Oblast', W Russian Federation
130 H4 **Pochinok** Smolenskaya Oblast', W Russian Federation
43 R17 **Pochutla** var. San Pedro Pochutla. Oaxaca, SE Mexico
64 I6 **Pocitos, Salar** var. Salar Quirón. salt lake NW Argentina
103 O22 **Pocking** Bayern, SE Germany
xli U13 **Pocklington** East Riding of Yorkshire, N England, UK
195 R17 **Pocklington Reef** reef SE PNG
199 Hh9 **Pocklington Trough** undersea feature W Pacific Ocean
29 R11 **Pocola** Oklahoma, C USA
23 Y5 **Pocomoke City** Maryland, NE USA
61 L21 **Poços de Caldas** Minas Gerais, NE Brazil
128 H14 **Podberez'ye** Novgorodskaya Oblast', NW Russian Federation
Podbrodzie see Pabradė
129 U8 **Podcher'ye** Respublika Komi, NW Russian Federation
113 E16 **Poděbrady** Ger. Podiebrad. Střední Čechy, C Czech Republic
176 Yy10 **Podena, Kepulauan** island group E Indonesia
130 L9 **Podgorenskiy** Voronezhskaya Oblast', W Russian Federation
115 J17 **Podgorica** prev. Titograd. Montenegro, SW Yugoslavia
115 K17 **Podgorica** ✕ Montenegro, SW Yugoslavia
111 T13 **Podgrad** SW Slovenia
Podiebrad see Poděbrady
118 M5 **Podil's'ka Vysochina** plateau W Ukraine
Podium Anicensis see le Puy
126 Ii11 **Podkamennaya Tunguska** Eng. Stony Tunguska. ≈ C Russian Federation
Pod Klošter see Arnoldstein
131 Q8 **Podlesnoye** Saratovskaya Oblast', W Russian Federation
130 K4 **Podol'sk** Moskovskaya Oblast', W Russian Federation
78 H10 **Podor** N Senegal
129 P12 **Podosinovets** Kirovskaya Oblast', NW Russian Federation
128 I12 **Podporozh'ye** Leningradskaya Oblast', NW Russian Federation
114 H9 **Podravska Slatina** Hung. Szlatina; prev. Slatina. Virovitica-Podravina, NE Croatia
114 J13 **Podromanlja** SE Bosnia and Herzegovina
Podsvil'ye see Padsvillye
118 L9 **Podu Iloaiei** prev. Podul Iloaiei. Iaşi, NE Romania
115 N15 **Podujevo** Serbia, S Yugoslavia
Podul Iloaiei see Podu Iloaiei
Podunajská Rovina see Little Alföld
128 M12 **Podyuga** Arkhangel'skaya Oblast', NW Russian Federation
58 A9 **Poechos, Embalse** ⊡ NW Peru
57 W10 **Poeketi** Sipaliwini, E Surinam
102 L8 **Poel** island N Germany
85 M20 **Poelela, Lagoa** ◎ S Mozambique
Poerwodadi see Purwodadi
Poetovio see Ptuj
85 E23 **Pofadder** Northern Cape, W South Africa
108 I9 **Po, Foci del** var. Bocche del Po. ≈ NE Italy
118 E12 **Pogăniş** ≈ W Romania
Pogegen see Pagėgiai
108 G12 **Poggibonsi** Toscana, C Italy
109 I14 **Poggio Mirteto** Lazio, C Italy
111 V4 **Pöggstall** Niederösterreich, N Austria
118 L13 **Pogoanele** Buzău, SE Romania
Pogónion see Delvinákí
115 M21 **Pogradec** var. Pogradeci. Korçë, SE Albania
Pogradeci see Pogradec
127 N18 **Pogranichnyy** Primorskiy Kray, SE Russian Federation
40 M16 **Pogromni Volcano** ▲ Unimak Island, Alaska, USA
169 Z15 **P'ohang** Jap. Hokō. E South Korea
13 T9 **Pohénégamook, Lac** ◎ Québec, SE Canada
95 L20 **Pohja** Swe. Pojo. Uusimaa, SW Finland
Pohjanlahti see Bothnia, Gulf of
95 N16 **Pohjois-Karjala** Swe. Norra Karelen. ◐ province C Finland
201 U16 **Pohnpei** ◐ state E Micronesia
201 O12 **Pohnpei** ✕ Pohnpei, E Micronesia
201 O12 **Pohnpei** prev. Ponape Ascension Island. island E Micronesia
113 F19 **Pohořelice** Ger. Pohrlitz. Jižní Morava, SE Czech Republic
111 V10 **Pohorje** Ger. Bacher. ▲▲ N Slovenia
119 N6 **Pohrebyshche** Vinnyts'ka Oblast', C Ukraine
Pohrlitz see Pohořelice
175 Qq9 **Poh, Teluk** bay Sulawesi, C Indonesia
167 P9 **Po Hu** ⊡ E China
118 G15 **Poiana Mare** Dolj, S Romania
Poictiers see Poitiers
131 N6 **Poim** Penzenskaya Oblast', W Russian Federation
197 I6 **Poindimié** Province Nord, C New Caledonia
Poindo see Lhünzhub
205 Y13 **Poinsett, Cape** headland Antarctica
31 R9 **Poinsett, Lake** ◎ South Dakota, N USA
24 I10 **Point Au Fer Island** island Louisiana, S USA
41 X14 **Point Baker** Prince of Wales Island, Alaska, USA
27 U13 **Point Comfort** Texas, SW USA
Point de Galle see Galle
46 K10 **Pointe à Gravois** headland SW Haiti
24 L10 **Pointe a la Hache** Louisiana, S USA
47 Y6 **Pointe-à-Pitre** Grande Terre, C Guadeloupe
13 U7 **Pointe-au-Pic** Québec, SE Canada
13 V5 **Pointe-aux-Anglais** Québec, SE Canada
47 T10 **Pointe Du Cap** headland N Saint Lucia
81 E21 **Pointe-Noire** Le Kouilou, S Congo
47 X6 **Pointe Noire** Basse Terre, W Guadeloupe
81 E21 **Pointe-Noire** ✕ Le Kouilou, S Congo
47 U15 **Point Fortin** Trinidad, Trinidad and Tobago
40 M6 **Point Hope** Alaska, USA
41 N5 **Point Lay** Alaska, USA
20 B16 **Point Marion** Pennsylvania, NE USA
20 K16 **Point Pleasant** New Jersey, NE USA
23 P4 **Point Pleasant** West Virginia, NE USA
47 R14 **Point Salines** ✕ (St.George's) SW Grenada
104 L9 **Poitiers** prev. Poictiers, anc. Limonum. Vienne, W France
104 K9 **Poitou** cultural region W France
104 K10 **Poitou-Charentes** ◐ region W France
105 N3 **Poix-de-Picardie** Somme, N France
Pojo see Pohja
39 S10 **Pojoaque** New Mexico, SW USA
158 E11 **Pokaran** Rājasthān, NW India
191 R4 **Pokataroo** New South Wales, SE Australia
121 P18 **Pokats'** Rus. Pokot'. ≈ SE Belarus
31 V5 **Pokegama Lake** ◎ Minnesota, N USA
192 L6 **Pokeno** Waikato, North Island, NZ
159 O11 **Pokhara** Western, C Nepal
131 T6 **Pokhvistnevo** Samarskaya Oblast', W Russian Federation
57 W10 **Pokigron** Sipaliwini, C Surinam
94 L10 **Pokka** Lapp. Bohkká. Lappi, N Finland
81 N16 **Poko** Haut-Zaïre, NE Zaire
Pokot' see Pokats'
Po-ko-to Shan see Bogda Shan
153 S7 **Pokrovka** Talasskaya Oblast', NW Kyrgyzstan
Pokrovka see Kyzyl-Suu
126 M11 **Pokrovsk** Respublika Sakha (Yakutiya), NE Russian Federation
119 V8 **Pokrovs'ke** Rus. Pokrovskoye. Dnipropetrovs'ka Oblast', E Ukraine
Pokrovskoye see Pokrovs'ke
Pola see Pula
39 N10 **Polacca** Arizona, SW USA
106 L2 **Pola de Laviana** Asturias, N Spain
106 K2 **Pola de Lena** Asturias, N Spain
106 L2 **Pola de Siero** Asturias, N Spain
203 Y3 **Poland** Kiritimati, E Kiribati
112 H12 **Poland** off. Republic of Poland, var. Polish Republic, Pol. Polska, Rzeczpospolita Polska; prev. Pol. Polska Rzeczpospolita Ludowa, Polish People's Republic. ◆ republic C Europe
Polangen see Palanga
112 G7 **Polanów** Ger. Pollnow. Koszalin, NW Poland
142 H13 **Polatlı** Ankara, C Turkey
120 L12 **Polatsk** Rus. Polotsk. Vitsyebskaya Voblasts', N Belarus
xlii G9 **Polbain** Highland, NW Scotland, UK
112 F8 **Połczyn-Zdrój** Ger. Bad Polzin. Koszalin, NW Poland
xxxvii V13 **Polegate** East Sussex, SE England, UK
152 I16 **Polekhatum** prev. Pul'-I-Khatum. Akhalskiy Velayat, S Turkmenistan
155 Q3 **Pol-e Khomrī** var. Pul-i-Khumri. Baghlān, NE Afghanistan
207 S10 **Pole Plain** undersea feature Arctic Ocean
149 P5 **Pol-e Safīd** var. Pol-e-Safid, Pul-i-Sefid. Māzandarān, N Iran
Pol-e-Safid see Pol-e Safīd
120 B13 **Polessk** Ger. Labiau. Kaliningradskaya Oblast', W Russian Federation
Polesskoye see Polis'ke
xxxviii E14 **Polesworth** Warwickshire, C England, UK
175 P11 **Polewali** Sulawesi, C Indonesia
116 G11 **Polezhan** ▲ SW Bulgaria
80 F13 **Poli** Nord, N Cameroon
Poli see Pólis
109 M19 **Policastro, Golfo di** gulf S Italy
112 D8 **Police** Ger. Politz. Szczecin, NW Poland
180 I17 **Police, Pointe** headland Mahé, NE Seychelles
117 L17 **Polichnítos** var. Polihnitos, Políkhnitos. Lésvos, E Greece
Poligiros see Polýgyros
109 P17 **Polignano a Mare** Puglia, SE Italy
105 S9 **Poligny** Jura, E France
Polihnitos see Polichnítos
Polikastro/Políkastron see Polýkastro
Políkhnitos see Polichnítos
116 K8 **Polikrayshte** Loveshka Oblast, N Bulgaria
179 Pp10 **Polillo Islands** island group N Philippines
111 Q9 **Polinik** ▲ SW Austria
123 Mm3 **Pólis** var. Poli. W Cyprus
Polish People's Republic see Poland
Polish Republic see Poland
119 O3 **Polis'ke** Rus. Polesskoye. Kyyivs'ka Oblast', N Ukraine
109 N22 **Polistena** Calabria, SW Italy
Politz see Police
Políyiros see Polýgyros
31 V14 **Polk City** Iowa, C USA
112 F13 **Polkowice** Ger. Heerwegen. Legnica, W Poland
161 G22 **Pollāchi** Tamil Nādu, SE India
111 W7 **Pöllau** Steiermark, SE Austria
201 T13 **Polle** atoll Chuuk Islands, C Micronesia
Pollensa see Pollença
Pollnow see Polanów
31 N7 **Pollock** South Dakota, N USA
94 L8 **Polmak** Finnmark, N Norway
32 L10 **Polo** Illinois, N USA
200 Qq15 **Poloa** island Tongatapu Group, N Tonga
44 E5 **Polochic, Río** ≈ C Guatemala
Pologi see Polohy
119 V9 **Polohy** Rus. Pologi. Zaporiz'ka Oblast', SE Ukraine
12 M10 **Polonais, Lac des** ◎ Québec, SE Canada
63 G20 **Polonio, Cabo** headland E Uruguay
161 K24 **Polonnaruwa** North Central Province, C Sri Lanka
118 L5 **Polonne** Rus. Polonnoye. Khmel'nyts'ka Oblast', NW Ukraine
Polonnoye see Polonne
Polotsk see Polatsk
xxxvi E16 **Polperro** Cornwall, SW England, UK
xxxvi D16 **Polruan** Cornwall, SW England, UK
111 T7 **Pöls** var. Pölsbach. ≈ E Austria
Pölsbach see Pöls
Polska/Polska, Rzeczpospolita/Polska Rzeczpospolita Ludowa see Poland
116 L10 **Polski Gradets** Burgaska Oblast, SE Bulgaria
116 K8 **Polsko Kosovo** Loveshka Oblast, N Bulgaria
35 P8 **Polson** Montana, NW USA
119 T6 **Poltava** Poltavs'ka Oblast', NE Ukraine
Poltava see Poltavs'ka Oblast'
119 R5 **Poltavs'ka Oblast'** var. Poltava, Rus. Poltavskaya Oblast'. ◐ province NE Ukraine
Poltoratsk see Asgabat
Poltavskaya Oblast' see Poltavs'ka Oblast'
120 I5 **Põltsamaa** Ger. Oberpahlen. Jõgevamaa, E Estonia
120 I4 **Põltsamaa** var. Põltsamaa Jõgi. ≈ C Estonia
Põltsamaa Jõgi see Põltsamaa
125 F10 **Polunochnoye** Sverdlovskaya Oblast', C Russian Federation
125 G8 **Poluy** ≈ N Russian Federation
120 J6 **Põlva** Ger. Põlwe. Põlvamaa, SE Estonia
95 N16 **Polvijärvi** Pohjois-Karjala, SE Finland
Pölwe see Põlva
117 I22 **Polýaigos** island Kykládes, Greece, Aegean Sea
117 I22 **Polyaígou Folégandrou, Stenó** strait Kykládes, Greece, Aegean Sea
128 J3 **Polyarnyy** Murmanskaya Oblast', NW Russian Federation
129 W5 **Polyarnyy Ural** ▲ NW Russian Federation
117 G14 **Polýgyros** var. Poligiros, Políyiros. Kentrikí Makedonía, N Greece
116 F13 **Polýkastro** var. Polikastro; prev. Políkastron. Kentrikí Makedonía, N Greece
199 Kk9 **Polynesia** island group C Pacific Ocean
117 J15 **Polýochni** site of ancient city Límnos, E Greece
43 Y13 **Polyuc** Quintana Roo, E Mexico
xxxvi C15 **Polzeath** Cornwall, SW England, UK
111 V10 **Polzela** C Slovenia
Polzen see Ploučnice
176 Ww9 **Pom** Irian Jaya, E Indonesia
58 D12 **Pomabamba** Ancash, C Peru
193 D23 **Pomahaka** ≈ South Island, NZ
108 F12 **Pomarance** Toscana, C Italy
106 G9 **Pombal** Leiria, C Portugal
78 D9 **Pombas** Santo Antão, NW Cape Verde
85 N19 **Pomene** Inhambane, SE Mozambique
112 G8 **Pomerania** cultural region Germany/Poland
112 D7 **Pomeranian Bay** Ger. Pommersche Bucht, Pol. Zatoka Pomorska. bay Germany/Poland
xliv J4 **Pomeroy** Cookstown, C Northern Ireland, UK
33 T15 **Pomeroy** Ohio, N USA
34 L10 **Pomeroy** Washington, NW USA
119 Q8 **Pomichna** Kirovohrads'ka Oblast', C Ukraine
195 O12 **Pomio** New Britain, E PNG
Pomir, Dar"yoi see Pamir/Pāmīr, Daryā-ye
29 T6 **Pomme de Terre Lake** ⊡ Missouri, C USA
31 S8 **Pomme de Terre River** ≈ Minnesota, N USA
Pommersche Bucht see Pomeranian Bay
37 T15 **Pomona** California, W USA
116 N9 **Pomorie** Burgaska Oblast, E Bulgaria
Pomorska, Zatoka see Pomeranian Bay
129 Q4 **Pomorskiy Proliv** strait NW Russian Federation
Pomorze Zachodnie see Szczecin
129 T10 **Pomozdino** Respublika Komi, NW Russian Federation
Pompaelo see Pamplona
175 Q9 **Pompangeo, Pegunungan** ▲▲ Sulawesi, C Indonesia
25 Z15 **Pompano Beach** Florida, SE USA
109 K18 **Pompei** Campania, S Italy
35 V10 **Pompeys Pillar** Montana, NW USA
Ponape Ascension Island see Pohnpei
31 R13 **Ponca** Nebraska, C USA
29 O8 **Ponca City** Oklahoma, C USA
47 T6 **Ponce** C Puerto Rico
25 X10 **Ponce de Leon Inlet** inlet Florida, SE USA
24 K8 **Ponchatoula** Louisiana, S USA
28 M8 **Pond Creek** Oklahoma, C USA
161 J20 **Pondicherry** var. Puduchcheri, Fr. Pondichéry. Pondicherry, SE India
157 I20 **Pondicherry** var. Puduchcheri, Fr. Pondichéry. ◐ union territory India
Pondichéry see Pondicherry
207 N11 **Pond Inlet** Baffin Island, Northwest Territories, NE Canada
197 I6 **Ponérihouen** Province Nord, C New Caledonia
106 J4 **Ponferrada** Castilla-León, NW Spain
192 N13 **Pongaroa** Manawatu-Wanganui, North Island, NZ
178 I12 **Pong Nam Ron** Chantaburi, S Thailand
83 C14 **Pongo** ≈ S Sudan
158 I7 **Pong Reservoir** ⊡ N India
113 N14 **Poniatowa** Lublin, E Poland
178 J13 **Pônley** Kâmpóng Chhnăng, C Cambodia
161 I20 **Ponnaiyār** ≈ SE India
9 Q15 **Ponoka** Alberta, SW Canada
131 U6 **Ponomarevka** Orenburgskaya Oblast', W Russian Federation
174 L15 **Ponorogo** Jawa, C Indonesia
128 M5 **Ponoy** Murmanskaya Oblast', NW Russian Federation
125 E5 **Ponoy** ≈ NW Russian Federation
104 K11 **Pons** Charente-Maritime, W France
Pons see Ponts
Pons Aelii see Newcastle upon Tyne
Pons Vetus see Pontevedra
xli Q6 **Pont** ≈ N England, UK
xxxv H13 **Pont Aber** Carmarthenshire, S Wales, UK
101 G20 **Pont-à-Celles** Hainaut, S Belgium
104 K16 **Pontacq** Pyrénées-Atlantiques, SW France
66 P3 **Ponta Delgada** São Miguel, Azores, Portugal, NE Atlantic Ocean
66 P3 **Ponta Delgado** ✕ São Miguel, Azores, Portugal, NE Atlantic Ocean
66 N2 **Ponta do Pico** ▲ Pico, Azores, Portugal, NE Atlantic Ocean
62 J11 **Ponta Grossa** Paraná, S Brazil
105 S5 **Pont-à-Mousson** Meurthe-et-Moselle, NE France
xxxv H14 **Pontardawe** Neath Port Talbot, S Wales, UK
xxxv G14 **Pontardulais** Swansea, S Wales, UK
xxxv G13 **Pontargothi** Carmarthenshire, S Wales, UK
105 T9 **Pontarlier** Doubs, E France
xxxv F12 **Pontarsais** Carmarthenshire, S Wales, UK
108 G11 **Pontassieve** Toscana, C Italy
104 L4 **Pont-Audemer** Eure, N France
24 K9 **Pontchartrain, Lake** ◎ Louisiana, S USA
104 I8 **Pontchâteau** Loire-Atlantique, NW France
105 R10 **Pont-de-Vaux** Ain, E France
106 G4 **Ponteareas** Galicia, NW Spain
108 J6 **Pontebba** Friuli-Venezia Giulia, NE Italy
106 G4 **Ponte Caldelas** Galicia, NW Spain
109 J16 **Pontecorvo** Lazio, C Italy
106 G5 **Ponte da Barca** Viana do Castelo, N Portugal
106 G5 **Ponte de Lima** Viana do Castelo, N Portugal
108 F11 **Pontedera** Toscana, C Italy
106 H10 **Ponte de Sor** Portalegre, C Portugal
106 H2 **Pontedeume** Galicia, NW Spain
108 F6 **Ponte di Legno** Lombardia, N Italy
xli T16 **Pontefract** Wakefield, N England, UK
9 T17 **Ponteix** Saskatchewan, S Canada
xli Q5 **Ponteland** Northumberland, N England, UK
61 N20 **Ponte Nova** Minas Gerais, NE Brazil
xxxv H9 **Ponterwyd** Ceredigion, W Wales, UK
xxxviii G10 **Pontesbury** Shropshire, W England, UK
61 G18 **Pontes e Lacerda** Mato Grosso, W Brazil
106 G4 **Pontevedra** anc. Pons Vetus. Galicia, NW Spain
106 G3 **Pontevedra** ◐ province Galicia, NW Spain
106 G4 **Pontevedra, Ría de** estuary NW Spain
32 M12 **Pontiac** Illinois, N USA
33 R9 **Pontiac** Michigan, N USA
174 Kk8 **Pontianak** Borneo, C Indonesia
109 I16 **Pontino, Agro** plain C Italy
Pontisarae see Pontoise
104 H6 **Pontivy** Morbihan, NW France
104 F6 **Pont-l'Abbé** Finistère, NW France
105 N4 **Pontoise** anc. Briva Isarae, Cergy-Pontoise, Pontisarae. Val-d'Oise, N France
9 W13 **Ponton** Manitoba, C Canada
xliv E6 **Pontoon** Mayo, NW Ireland
104 J5 **Pontorson** Manche, N France
24 M2 **Pontotoc** Mississippi, S USA
27 R9 **Pontotoc** Texas, SW USA
108 E10 **Pontremoli** Toscana, C Italy
110 J10 **Pontresina** Graubünden, S Switzerland
xxxv H10 **Pontrhydfendigaid** Ceredigion, W Wales, UK

◆ Country ● Country Capital ◇ Dependent Territory ○ Dependent Territory Capital ◐ Administrative Region ✕ International Airport ▲ Mountain ▲▲ Mountain Range ⊼ Volcano ≈ River ◎ Lake ⊡ Reservoir

PONTRILAS – PRESELI, MYNYDD

xxxviii G14 **Pontrilas** Herefordshire, W England, UK
107 U5 **Ponts** *var.* Pons. Cataluña, NE Spain
105 R14 **Pont-St-Esprit** Gard, S France
xxxv J13 **Pontsticill** Merthyr Tydfil, S Wales, UK
xxxv F13 **Pontyates** Carmarthenshire, S Wales, UK
xxxv I14 **Pontycymer** Bridgend, S Wales, UK
xxxv K14 **Pontypool** *Wel.* Pontypŵl. Torfaen, SE Wales, UK
xxxv J14 **Pontypridd** Rhondda Cynon Taff, S Wales, UK
Pontypŵl *see* Pontypool
45 R17 **Ponuga** Veraguas, SE Panama
192 L6 **Ponui Island** *island* N NZ
121 K14 **Ponya** *Rus.* Ponya. ≈ N Belorussia
109 I17 **Ponziane, Isole** *island* C Italy
190 F7 **Poochera** South Australia
xli R13 **Pool** Leeds, N England, UK
xxxvii N14 **Poole** Poole, S England, UK
xxxvii N14 **Poole** ◈ *unitary authority* S England, UK
xxxvii N14 **Poole Bay** *bay* S England, UK
xlii F10 **Poolewe** Highland, NW Scotland, UK
xl M9 **Pooley Bridge** Cumbria, NW England, UK
27 S6 **Poolville** Texas, SW USA
Poona *see* Pune
190 M8 **Pooncarie** New South Wales, SE Australia
191 N6 **Poopelloe Lake** *seasonal lake* New South Wales, SE Australia
59 K19 **Poopó** Oruro, C Bolivia
59 K19 **Poopó, Lago** *var.* Lago Pampa Aullagas. ◎ W Bolivia
192 L3 **Poor Knights Islands** *island* N NZ
41 P10 **Poorman** Alaska, USA
190 E3 **Pootnoura** South Australia
153 R10 **Pop** *Rus.* Pap. Namangan Wiloyati, E Uzbekistan
119 X7 **Popasna** *Rus.* Popasnaya. Luhans'ka Oblast', E Ukraine
Popasnaya *see* Popasna
56 D12 **Popayán** Cauca, SW Colombia
101 B18 **Poperinge** West-Vlaanderen, W Belgium
126 K7 **Popigay** Taymyrskiy (Dolgano-Nenetskiy) Avtonomnyy Okrug, N Russian Federation
126 Jj7 **Popigay** ≈ N Russian Federation
119 O5 **Popil'nya** Zhytomyrs'ka Oblast', N Ukraine
190 K8 **Popiltah Lake** *seasonal lake* New South Wales, SE Australia
xxxvi E7 **Poplar** *london borough capital* Tower Hamlets, SE England, UK
35 X7 **Poplar** Montana, NW USA
9 Y14 **Poplar** ≈ Manitoba, C Canada
29 X8 **Poplar Bluff** Missouri, C USA
35 X6 **Poplar River** ≈ Montana, NW USA
43 P14 **Popocatépetl** ⛰ S Mexico
174 Ll16 **Popoh** Jawa, S Indonesia
81 H21 **Popokabaka** Bandundu, SW Zaire
109 J15 **Popoli** Abruzzi, C Italy
195 X16 **Popomanaseu, Mount** ▲ Guadalcanal, C Solomon Islands
194 L15 **Popondetta** Northern, S PNG
114 F9 **Popovača** Sisak-Moslavina, NE Croatia
116 J10 **Popovitsa** Loveshka Oblast, C Bulgaria
116 L8 **Popovo** Razgradska Oblast, N Bulgaria
Popovo *see* Iskra
Popper *see* Poprad
32 M5 **Popple River** ≈ Wisconsin, N USA
113 L19 **Poprad** *Ger.* Deutschendorf, *Hung.* Poprád. Východné Slovensko, NE Slovakia
113 L18 **Poprad** *Ger.* Popper, *Hung.* Poprád. ≈ Poland/Slovakia
113 L19 **Poprad-Tatry** ✕ (Poprad) Východné Slovensko, N Slovakia
23 X7 **Poquoson** Virginia, NE USA
155 O15 **Porāli** ≈ SW Pakistan
192 N12 **Porangahau** Hawke's Bay, North Island, NZ
61 K17 **Porangatu** Goiás, C Brazil
121 G18 **Porazava** *Pol.* Porozow, *Rus.* Porozovo. Hrodzyenskaya Voblasts', W Belorussia
160 A11 **Porbandar** Gujarāt, W India
8 I13 **Porcher Island** *island* British Columbia, SW Canada
106 M13 **Porcuna** Andalucía, S Spain
12 F7 **Porcupine** Ontario, S Canada
66 M6 **Porcupine Bank** *undersea feature* N Atlantic Ocean
9 V15 **Porcupine Hills** ▲▲ Manitoba/Saskatchewan, S Canada
32 L3 **Porcupine Mountains** *hill range* Michigan, N USA
66 M7 **Porcupine Plain** *undersea feature* E Atlantic Ocean
14 F4 **Porcupine River** ≈ Canada/USA
108 I7 **Pordenone** *anc.* Portenau. Friuli-Venezia Giulia, NE Italy
56 H9 **Pore** Casanare, E Colombia
114 A9 **Poreč** *It.* Parenzo. Istra, NW Croatia
62 I9 **Porecatu** Paraná, S Brazil
Porech'ye *see* Parechcha
131 P4 **Poretskoye** Chuvashskaya Respublika, W Russian Federation
79 Q13 **Porga** N Benin
194 G12 **Porgera** Enga, W PNG
95 K18 **Pori** *Swe.* Björneborg. Turku-Pori, SW Finland
193 L14 **Porirua** Wellington, North Island, NZ
94 I12 **Porjus** Norrbotten, N Sweden
128 G14 **Porkhov** Pskovskaya Oblast', W Russian Federation
57 O4 **Porlamar** Nueva Esparta, NE Venezuela
xxxvi H11 **Porlock** Somerset, SW England, UK
xxxvi H11 **Porlock Bay** *bay* SW England, UK
104 I8 **Pornic** Loire-Atlantique, NW France
194 G12 **Poroma** Southern Highlands, W PNG
127 Oo15 **Poronaysk** Ostrov Sakhalin, Sakhalinskaya Oblast', SE Russian Federation
117 G20 **Póros** Póros, S Greece
117 C19 **Póros** Kefallinía, Iónioi Nísoi, Greece, C Mediterranean Sea
117 G20 **Póros** *island* S Greece
83 G24 **Poroto Mountains** ▲▲ SW Tanzania
114 B10 **Porozina** Primorje-Gorski Kotar, NW Croatia
Porozovo/Porozow *see* Porazava
205 X15 **Porpoise Bay** *bay* Antarctica
67 G15 **Porpoise Point** *headland* NE Ascension Island
67 C25 **Porpoise Point** *headland* East Falkland, Falkland Islands
110 C6 **Porrentruy** Jura, NW Switzerland
108 F10 **Porretta Terme** Emilia-Romagna, C Italy
106 G4 **Porriño** Galicia, NW Spain
94 L7 **Porsangen** *fjord* N Norway
94 K8 **Porsangerhalvøya** *peninsula* N Norway
97 G16 **Porsgrunn** Telemark, S Norway
142 E13 **Porsuk Çayı** ≈ C Turkey
Porsy *see* Boldumsaz
59 N18 **Portachuelo** Santa Cruz, C Bolivia
190 I9 **Port Adelaide** South Australia
xliv K5 **Portadown** *Ir.* Port An Dúnáin. Craigavon, S Northern Ireland, UK
xliv M5 **Portaferry** Ards, E Northern Ireland, UK
33 P10 **Portage** Michigan, N USA
20 D15 **Portage** Pennsylvania, NE USA
32 K8 **Portage** Wisconsin, N USA
32 M3 **Portage Lake** ◎ Michigan, N USA
9 X16 **Portage la Prairie** Manitoba, S Canada
33 R11 **Portage River** ≈ Ohio, N USA
29 Y8 **Portageville** Missouri, C USA
30 L2 **Portal** North Dakota, N USA
8 L17 **Port Alberni** Vancouver Island, British Columbia, SW Canada
12 E15 **Port Albert** Ontario, S Canada
106 I10 **Portalegre** *anc.* Ammaia, Amoea. Portalegre, E Portugal
106 H10 **Portalegre** ◈ *district* C Portugal
39 V12 **Portales** New Mexico, SW USA
41 X14 **Port Alexander** Baranof Island, Alaska, USA
85 I25 **Port Alfred** Eastern Cape, S South Africa
8 J16 **Port Alice** Vancouver Island, British Columbia, SW Canada
24 J8 **Port Allen** Louisiana, S USA
Port Amelia *see* Pemba
Port An Dúnáin *see* Portadown
34 G7 **Port Angeles** Washington, NW USA
46 L12 **Port Antonio** NE Jamaica
117 D16 **Pórta Panagiá** *religious building* Thessalía, C Greece
xliii G16 **Port Appin** Argyll and Bute, W Scotland, UK
27 T14 **Port Aransas** Texas, SW USA
xliv I9 **Portarlington** *Ir.* Cúil an tSúdaire. Laois/Offaly, C Ireland
191 P17 **Port Arthur** Tasmania, SE Australia
18 Mm15 **Port Arthur** Texas, SW USA
xliii E20 **Port Askaig** Argyll and Bute, W Scotland, UK
190 I7 **Port Augusta** South Australia
46 M9 **Port-au-Prince** ● (Haiti) C Haiti
46 M9 **Port-au-Prince** ✕ E Haiti
xliii G20 **Portavadie** Argyll and Bute, W Scotland, UK
xliv M5 **Portavogie** Ards, E Northern Ireland, UK
xliv K2 **Portballintrae** Coleraine, N Northern Ireland, UK
xliii H20 **Port Bannatyne** Argyll and Bute, W Scotland, UK
24 I8 **Port Barre** Louisiana, S USA
157 Q19 **Port Blair** Andaman and Nicobar Islands, SE India
27 X12 **Port Bolivar** Texas, SW USA
107 X4 **Portbou** Cataluña, NE Spain
79 N17 **Port Bouet** ✕ (Abidjan) SE Ivory Coast
190 I8 **Port Broughton** South Australia
12 F17 **Port Burwell** Ontario, S Canada
10 G17 **Port Burwell** Québec, NE Canada
190 M13 **Port Campbell** Victoria, SE Australia
13 V4 **Port-Cartier** Québec, SE Canada
193 F23 **Port Chalmers** Otago, South Island, NZ
25 W14 **Port Charlotte** Florida, SE USA
xxxvii Q13 **Portchester** Hampshire, S England, UK
40 L9 **Port Clarence** Alaska, USA
8 I13 **Port Clements** Graham Island, British Columbia, SW Canada
33 S11 **Port Clinton** Ohio, N USA
12 H17 **Port Colborne** Ontario, S Canada
13 Y7 **Port-Daniel** Québec, SE Canada
Port Darwin *see* Darwin
191 O17 **Port Davey** *headland* Tasmania, SE Australia
46 K8 **Port-de-Paix** NW Haiti
xxxv F5 **Port Dinorwic** Gwynedd, NW Wales, UK
189 W4 **Port Douglas** Queensland, NE Australia
8 J13 **Port Edward** British Columbia, SW Canada
85 K24 **Port Edward** KwaZulu/Natal, SE South Africa
60 J12 **Portel** Pará, NE Brazil
106 H12 **Portel** Évora, S Portugal
12 E14 **Port Elgin** Ontario, S Canada
47 Y14 **Port Elizabeth** Bequia, Saint Vincent and the Grenadines
85 I26 **Port Elizabeth** Eastern Cape, S South Africa
xliii D21 **Port Ellen** Argyll and Bute, W Scotland, UK
xlii N13 **Port Elphinstone** Aberdeenshire, NE Scotland, UK
Portenau *see* Pordenone
xliii H21 **Portencross** North Ayrshire, W Scotland, UK
xl F12 **Port Erin** SW Isle of Man
47 Q13 **Porter Point** *headland* Saint Vincent, Saint Vincent and the Grenadines
193 G18 **Porters Pass** *pass* South Island, NZ
85 E25 **Porterville** Western Cape, SW South Africa
37 R12 **Porterville** California, W USA
xxxvi L14 **Portesham** Dorset, S England, UK
Port-Étienne *see* Nouâdhibou
xxxv F15 **Port-Eynon** Swansea, S Wales, UK
190 L13 **Port Fairy** Victoria, SE Australia
192 M4 **Port Fitzroy** Great Barrier Island, Auckland, NE NZ
Port Florence *see* Kisumu
Port-Francqui *see* Ilebo
81 C18 **Port-Gentil** Ogooué-Maritime, W Gabon
81 C18 **Port-Gentil** ✕ Ogooué-Maritime, W Gabon
190 I7 **Port Germein** South Australia
24 J6 **Port Gibson** Mississippi, S USA
xliii H20 **Port Glasgow** Inverclyde, W Scotland, UK
xliv K3 **Portglenone** Ballymena, NE Northern Ireland, UK
xlii M11 **Portgordon** Moray, N Scotland, UK
41 Q13 **Port Graham** Alaska, USA
xxxv J14 **Porth** Rhondda Cynon Taff, S Wales, UK
xxxvi C17 **Porthallow** Cornwall, SW England, UK
79 U17 **Port Harcourt** Rivers, S Nigeria
8 J16 **Port Hardy** Vancouver Island, British Columbia, SW Canada
Port Harrison *see* Inukjuak
11 R14 **Port Hawkesbury** Cape Breton Island, Nova Scotia, SE Canada
xxxv H15 **Porthcawl** Bridgend, S Wales, UK
188 I6 **Port Hedland** Western Australia
41 O15 **Port Heiden** Alaska, USA
xlii F11 **Port Henderson** Highland, NW Scotland, UK
xxxvi B17 **Porthleven** Cornwall, SW England, UK
xxxv G6 **Porthmadog** *var.* Portmadoc. Gwynedd, NW Wales, UK
xxxvi L16 **Porthmeor** Cornwall, SW England, UK
12 I15 **Port Hope** Ontario, SE Canada
11 S9 **Port Hope Simpson** Newfoundland and Labrador, E Canada
67 C24 **Port Howard Settlement** West Falkland, Falkland Islands
xxxvi B16 **Porthtowan** Cornwall, SW England, UK
33 T9 **Port Huron** Michigan, N USA
109 K17 **Portici** Campania, S Italy
143 Y13 **Port-İliç** *Rus.* Port Il'ich. SE Azerbaijan
Port Il'ich *see* Port-İliç
106 G14 **Portimão** *var.* Vila Nova de Portimão. Faro, S Portugal
xliii G18 **Portinnisherrich** Argyll and Bute, W Scotland, UK
xxxvi D14 **Port Isaac Bay** *bay* SW England, UK
27 T17 **Port Isabel** Texas, SW USA
xxxvi J9 **Portishead** North West Somerset, SW England, UK
xxxvi D14 **Port Issac** Cornwall, SW England, UK
20 J13 **Port Jervis** New York, NE USA
57 S7 **Port Kaituma** NW Guyana
130 K12 **Port Katon** Rostovskaya Oblast', SW Russian Federation
191 S9 **Port Kembla** New South Wales, SE Australia
190 F8 **Port Kenny** South Australia
Port Klang *see* Pelabuhan Klang
xlii N11 **Portknockie** Moray, N Scotland, UK
Port Láirge *see* Waterford
xliv G10 **Portland** Tipperary, S Ireland
191 S8 **Portland** New South Wales, SE Australia
190 L13 **Portland** Victoria, SE Australia
192 K4 **Portland** Northland, North Island, NZ
33 Q13 **Portland** Indiana, N USA
21 P8 **Portland** Maine, NE USA
33 Q9 **Portland** Michigan, N USA
31 Q4 **Portland** North Dakota, N USA
34 G11 **Portland** Oregon, NW USA
22 J8 **Portland** Tennessee, S USA
27 T14 **Portland** Texas, SW USA
34 G11 **Portland** ✕ Oregon, NW USA
190 L13 **Portland Bay** *bay* Victoria, SE Australia
46 K13 **Portland Bight** *bay* S Jamaica
xxxvi L15 **Portland Bill** *var.* Bill of Portland. *headland* S England, UK
Portland, Bill of *see* Portland Bill
191 P15 **Portland, Cape** *headland* Tasmania, SE Australia
8 J12 **Portland Inlet** *inlet* British Columbia, W Canada
192 P11 **Portland Island** *island* E NZ
xxxvi L15 **Portland, Isle of** *island* SW England, UK
67 F15 **Portland Point** *headland* SW Ascension Island
46 J13 **Portland Point** *headland* C Jamaica
105 P16 **Port-la-Nouvelle** Aude, S France
Portlaoighise *see* Portlaoise
Port Laoise *see* Portlaoise
xliv I10 **Portlaoise** *var.* Port Laoise, *Ir.* Portlaoighise; *prev.* Maryborough. Laois, C Ireland
27 U13 **Port Lavaca** Texas, SW USA
xliii P14 **Portlethen** Aberdeenshire, NE Scotland, UK
190 G9 **Port Lincoln** South Australia
41 Q14 **Port Lions** Kodiak Island, Alaska, USA
xliii H26 **Port Logan** Dumfries and Galloway, SW Scotland, UK
78 I15 **Port Loko** W Sierra Leone
67 E24 **Port Louis** East Falkland, Falkland Islands
47 Y5 **Port-Louis** Grande Terre, N Guadeloupe
181 X16 **Port Louis** ● (Mauritius) NW Mauritius
Port Louis *see* Scarborough
xliv D5 **Portlurin** Mayo, NW Ireland
Port-Lyautey *see* Kénitra
190 K12 **Port MacDonnell** South Australia
191 U7 **Port Macquarie** New South Wales, SE Australia
Portmadoc *see* Porthmadog
xliv B14 **Portmagee** Kerry, SW Ireland
xlii K10 **Portmahomack** Highland, N Scotland, UK
Port Mahon *see* Mahón
46 K12 **Port Maria** C Jamaica
8 K16 **Port McNeill** Vancouver Island, British Columbia, SW Canada
11 P11 **Port-Menier** Île d'Anticosti , Québec, E Canada
41 N15 **Port Moller** Alaska, USA
xliii D15 **Port Mor** Highland, NW Scotland, UK
46 L13 **Port Morant** E Jamaica
46 K13 **Portmore** C Jamaica
194 I16 **Port Moresby** ● (PNG) Central/National Capital District, SW PNG
xliii G16 **Portnacroish** Argyll and Bute, W Scotland, UK
xlii E8 **Portnaguran** Western Isles, NW Scotland, UK
xliii C21 **Portnahaven** Argyll and Bute, W Scotland, UK
xlii I7 **Portnancon** Highland, NW Scotland, UK
Port Natal *see* Durban
27 Y11 **Port Neches** Texas, SW USA
190 G9 **Port Neill** South Australia
13 S6 **Portneuf** ≈ Québec, SE Canada
13 R6 **Portneuf, Lac** ◎ Québec, SE Canada
85 D23 **Port Nolloth** Northern Cape, W South Africa
20 J17 **Port Norris** New Jersey, NE USA
Port-Nouveau-Québec *see* Kangiqsualujjuaq
106 G6 **Porto** *Eng.* Oporto; *anc.* Portus Cale. Porto, NW Portugal
106 G6 **Porto** *var.* Pôrto. ◈ *district* N Portugal
106 G6 **Porto** ✕ Porto, W Portugal
63 I16 **Porto Alegre** *var.* Pôrto Alegre. *state capital* Rio Grande do Sul, S Brazil
Porto Alexandre *see* Tombua
84 B12 **Porto Amboim** Cuanza Sul, NW Angola
Porto Amélia *see* Pemba
Porto Bello *see* Portobelo
xliii M20 **Portobello** City of Edinburgh, SE Scotland, UK
45 T14 **Portobelo** *var.* Porto Bello, Puerto Bello. Colón, N Panama
62 G10 **Pôrto Camargo** Paraná, S Brazil
27 U13 **Port O'Connor** Texas, SW USA
Pôrto de Mós *see* Porto de Moz
60 J12 **Porto de Moz** *var.* Pôrto de Mós. Pará, NE Brazil
66 O5 **Porto do Moniz** Madeira, Portugal, NE Atlantic Ocean
61 H16 **Porto dos Gaúchos** Mato Grosso, W Brazil
Porto Edda *see* Sarandë
109 J24 **Porto Empedocle** Sicilia, Italy, C Mediterranean Sea
61 H20 **Porto Esperança** Mato Grosso do Sul, SW Brazil
108 E13 **Portoferraio** Toscana, C Italy
xliii J18 **Port of Mentieth** Stirling, C Scotland, UK
xlii E7 **Port of Ness** Western Isles, NW Scotland, UK
47 U14 **Port-of-Spain** ● (Trinidad and Tobago) Trinidad, Trinidad and Tobago
Port of Spain *see* Piarco
104 E2 **Porto, Golfe de** *gulf* Corse, France, C Mediterranean Sea
Porto Grande *see* Mindelo
108 I7 **Portogruaro** Veneto, NE Italy
37 P5 **Portola** California, W USA
197 B12 **Port-Olry** Espiritu Santo, C Vanuatu
95 J17 **Pörtom** *Fin.* Pirttikylä. Vaasa, W Finland
Port Omna *see* Portumna
61 G21 **Porto Murtinho** Mato Grosso do Sul, SW Brazil
61 K16 **Porto Nacional** Tocantins, C Brazil
79 S16 **Porto-Novo** ● (Benin) S Benin
25 X10 **Port Orange** Florida, SE USA
34 G8 **Port Orchard** Washington, NW USA
Porto Re *see* Kraljevica
34 E15 **Port Orford** Oregon, NW USA
Porto Rico *see* Puerto Rico
108 J13 **Porto San Giorgio** Marche, C Italy
109 F14 **Porto San Stefano** Toscana, C Italy
66 P5 **Porto Santo** *var.* Vila Baleira. Porto Santo, Madeira, Portugal, NE Atlantic Ocean
66 Q5 **Porto Santo** ✕ Porto Santo, Madeira, Portugal, NE Atlantic Ocean
66 P5 **Porto Santo** *var.* Ilha do Porto Santo. *island* Madeira, Portugal, NE Atlantic Ocean
62 H9 **Porto São José** Paraná, S Brazil
61 O19 **Porto Seguro** Bahia, E Brazil
109 B17 **Porto Torres** Sardegna, Italy, C Mediterranean Sea
61 J23 **Porto União** Santa Catarina, S Brazil
104 F3 **Porto-Vecchio** Corse, France, C Mediterranean Sea
61 E15 **Porto Velho** *var.* Velho. *state capital* Rondônia, W Brazil
58 A6 **Portoviejo** *var.* Puertoviejo. Manabí, W Ecuador
xliii G25 **Portpatrick** Dumfries and Galloway, SW Scotland, UK
193 B26 **Port Pegasus** *bay* Stewart Island, NZ
12 H15 **Port Perry** Ontario, SE Canada
191 N12 **Port Phillip Bay** *harbour* Victoria, SE Australia
190 I8 **Port Pirie** South Australia
xxxvi B16 **Portreath** Cornwall, SW England, UK
xlii E12 **Portree** Highland, N Scotland, UK
Port Rex *see* East London
Port Rois *see* Portrush
46 K13 **Port Royal** E Jamaica
23 R15 **Port Royal** South Carolina, SE USA
23 R15 **Port Royal Sound** *inlet* South Carolina, SE USA
xliv K2 **Portrush** *Ir.* Port Rois. Coleraine, N Northern Ireland, UK
77 W7 **Port Said** *Ar.* Būr Sa'īd. N Egypt
25 R9 **Port Saint Joe** Florida, SE USA
25 Y11 **Port Saint John** Florida, SE USA
85 K24 **Port St.Johns** Eastern Cape, SE South Africa
105 R16 **Port-St-Louis-du-Rhône** Bouches-du-Rhône, SE France
xl F12 **Port St Mary** SW Isle of Man
xliv I2 **Portsalon** Donegal, N Ireland
46 K10 **Port Salut** SW Haiti
67 E24 **Port Salvador** *inlet* East Falkland, Falkland Islands
67 D24 **Port San Carlos** East Falkland, Falkland Islands
11 S10 **Port Saunders** Newfoundland, Newfoundland and Labrador, SE Canada
85 K24 **Port Shepstone** KwaZulu/Natal, E South Africa
xlii K6 **Portskerra** Highland, N Scotland, UK
xxxvii Q13 **Portsmouth** City of Portsmouth, S England, UK
47 O11 **Portsmouth** *var.* Grand-Anse. NW Dominica
21 P10 **Portsmouth** New Hampshire, NE USA
33 S15 **Portsmouth** Ohio, N USA
23 X7 **Portsmouth** Virginia, NE USA
xxxvii Q13 **Portsmouth, City of** ◈ *unitary authority* S England, UK
xlii N11 **Portsoy** Aberdeenshire, NE Scotland, UK
12 E17 **Port Stanley** Ontario, S Canada
67 B25 **Port Stephens** *inlet* West Falkland, Falkland Islands
67 B25 **Port Stephens Settlement** West Falkland, Falkland Islands
xliv K2 **Portstewart** *Ir.* Port Stíobhaird. Coleraine, N Northern Ireland, UK
Port Stíobhaird *see* Portstewart
82 I7 **Port Sudan** Red Sea, NE Sudan
24 L10 **Port Sulphur** Louisiana, S USA
Port Swettenham *see* Klang/Pelabuhan Klang
xxxv H14 **Port Talbot** Neath Port Talbot, S Wales, UK
94 L11 **Porttipahdan Tekojärvi** ◎ N Finland
34 G7 **Port Townsend** Washington, NW USA
106 H9 **Portugal** *off.* Republic of Portugal. ◆ *republic* SW Europe
107 O2 **Portugalete** País Vasco, N Spain
56 J6 **Portuguesa** *off.* Estado Portuguesa. ◈ *state* N Venezuela
Portuguese East Africa *see* Mozambique
Portuguese Guinea *see* Guinea-Bissau
Portuguese Timor *see* Timor Timur
Portuguese West Africa *see* Angola
xliv G10 **Portumna** *Ir.* Port Omna. Galway, W Ireland
Portus Cale *see* Porto
Portus Magnus *see* Almería
Portus Magonis *see* Mahón
105 P17 **Port-Vendres** *var.* Port Vendres. Pyrénées-Orientales, S France
190 H9 **Port Victoria** South Australia
197 C14 **Port-Vila** *var.* Vila. ● (Vanuatu) Éfaté, C Vanuatu
190 I9 **Port Wakefield** South Australia
33 N8 **Port Washington** Wisconsin, N USA
xliii I26 **Port William** Dumfries and Galloway, SW Scotland, UK
59 J14 **Porvenir** Pando, NW Bolivia
65 I24 **Porvenir** Magallanes, S Chile
63 D18 **Porvenir** Paysandú, W Uruguay
95 M19 **Porvoo** *Swe.* Borgå. Uusimaa, S Finland
Porzecze *see* Parechcha
106 M10 **Porzuna** Castilla-La Mancha, C Spain
63 E14 **Posadas** Misiones, NE Argentina
106 L13 **Posadas** Andalucía, S Spain
Poschega *see* Slavonska Požega
110 J11 **Poschiavino** ≈ Italy/Switzerland
110 J10 **Poschiavo** *Ger.* Puschlav. Graubünden, S Switzerland
114 D12 **Posedarje** Zadar-Knin, W Croatia
Posen *see* Poznań
128 L14 **Poshekhon'ye** Yaroslavskaya Oblast', W Russian Federation
94 M13 **Posio** Lappi, NE Finland
Poskam *see* Zepu
Posnania *see* Poznań
175 Pp9 **Poso** Sulawesi, C Indonesia
61 P15 **Poço da Cruz, Açude** ⊡ E Brazil
175 Pp10 **Poso, Danau** ◎ Sulawesi, C Indonesia
143 R10 **Posof** Kars, NE Turkey
175 Pp9 **Poso, Sungai** ≈ Sulawesi, C Indonesia
27 R6 **Possum Kingdom Lake** ⊡ Texas, SW USA
27 N6 **Post** Texas, SW USA
Postavy/Postawy *see* Pastavy
10 I7 **Poste-de-la-Baleine** Québec, NE Canada
101 M17 **Posterholt** Limburg, SE Netherlands
85 G22 **Postmasburg** Northern Cape, N South Africa
Pôsto Diuarum *see* Campo de Diauarum
61 I16 **Pôsto Jacaré** Mato Grosso, W Brazil
111 T12 **Postojna** *Ger.* Adelsberg, *It.* Postumia. SW Slovenia
Postumia *see* Postojna
31 X12 **Postville** Iowa, C USA
Pöstyén *see* Piešťany
115 G14 **Posušje** SW Bosnia and Herzegovina
175 Pp16 **Pota** Flores, C Indonesia
117 G23 **Potamós** Antikýthira, S Greece
57 S9 **Potaru River** ≈ C Guyana
85 I21 **Potchefstroom** North-West, N South Africa
29 R11 **Poteau** Oklahoma, C USA
27 R12 **Poteet** Texas, SW USA
117 G14 **Poteídaia** *site of ancient city* Kentrikí Makedonía, N Greece
Potentia *see* Potenza
109 M18 **Potenza** *anc.* Potentia. Basilicata, S Italy
193 A24 **Poteriteri, Lake** ◎ South Island, NZ
106 M2 **Potes** Cantabria, N Spain
85 J20 **Potgietersrus** Northern, NE South Africa
27 S12 **Poth** Texas, SW USA
34 J9 **Potholes Reservoir** ⊡ Washington, NW USA
143 Q9 **P'ot'i** W Georgia
79 X13 **Potiskum** Yobe, NE Nigeria
34 M9 **Potlatch** Idaho, NW USA
35 N9 **Pot Mountain** ▲ Idaho, NW USA
115 H14 **Potoci** S Bosnia and Herzegovina
23 V3 **Potomac River** ≈ NE USA
29 W6 **Potosi** Missouri, C USA
59 L20 **Potosí** Potosí, S Bolivia
44 H9 **Potosí** Chinandega, NW Nicaragua
59 K21 **Potosí** ◈ *department* SW Bolivia
64 H7 **Potrerillos** Atacama, N Chile
44 H5 **Potrerillos** Cortés, NW Honduras
64 H8 **Potro, Cerro del** ▲ N Chile
102 N12 **Potsdam** Brandenburg, NE Germany
20 J7 **Potsdam** New York, NE USA
111 X5 **Pottendorf** Niederösterreich, E Austria
111 X5 **Pottenstein** Niederösterreich, E Austria
xxxvii T8 **Potter's Bar** Hertfordshire, SE England, UK
197 G4 **Pott, Île** *island* Îles Belep, W New Caledonia
xxxvii T5 **Potton** Bedfordshire, C England, UK
20 I15 **Pottstown** Pennsylvania, NE USA
20 H14 **Pottsville** Pennsylvania, NE USA
161 L25 **Pottuvil** Eastern Province, SE Sri Lanka
155 U6 **Potwar Plateau** *plateau* NE Pakistan
104 J7 **Pouancé** Maine-et-Loire, W France
197 H5 **Pouébo** Province Nord, C New Caledonia
197 H6 **Pouembout** Province Nord, W New Caledonia
xliv K9 **Poulaphouca Reservoir** ⊡ E Ireland
xliv D13 **Poulgorm Bridge** Kerry, SW Ireland
13 R6 **Poulin de Courval, Lac** ◎ Québec, SE Canada
20 L9 **Poultney** Vermont, NE USA
xxxvii N8 **Poulton** Gloucestershire, C England, UK
xl M14 **Poulton-le-Fylde** Lancashire, NW England, UK
197 H5 **Poum** Province Nord, W New Caledonia
xxxvi E14 **Poundstock** Cornwall, SW England, UK
61 L21 **Pouso Alegre** Minas Gerais, NE Brazil
198 Bb8 **Poutasi** Upolu, SE Western Samoa
178 Ii12 **Poŭthĭsăt** *prev.* Pursat. Poŭthĭsăt, W Cambodia
178 Ii13 **Poŭthĭsăt, Stœng** *prev.* Pursat. ≈ W Cambodia
104 J9 **Pouzauges** Vendée, NW France
Po, Valle del *see* Po Valley
108 F8 **Po Valley** *It.* Valle del Po. *valley* N Italy
113 I19 **Považská Bystrica** *Ger.* Waagbistritz, *Hung.* Vágbeszterce. Stredné Slovensko, NW Slovakia
128 J10 **Povenets** Respublika Kareliya, NW Russian Federation
192 Q9 **Poverty Bay** *inlet* North Island, NZ
114 K12 **Povlen** ▲▲ W Yugoslavia
106 G6 **Póvoa de Varzim** Porto, NW Portugal
131 N8 **Povorino** Voronezhskaya Oblast', W Russian Federation
Povungnituk *see* Puvirnituq
10 J3 **Povungnituk, Rivière de** ≈ Québec, NE Canada
12 H11 **Powassan** Ontario, S Canada
37 U17 **Poway** California, W USA
xli Q3 **Powburn** Northumberland, N England, UK
35 W14 **Powder River** Wyoming, C USA
35 Y10 **Powder River** ≈ Montana/Wyoming, NW USA
34 L12 **Powder River** ≈ Oregon, NW USA
35 W13 **Powder River Pass** *pass* Wyoming, C USA
35 U12 **Powell** Wyoming, C USA
67 I22 **Powell Basin** *undersea feature* NW Weddell Sea
38 M8 **Powell, Lake** ◎ Utah, W USA
39 R4 **Powell, Mount** ▲ Colorado, C USA
8 L17 **Powell River** British Columbia, SW Canada
33 N5 **Powers** Michigan, N USA
30 K2 **Powers Lake** North Dakota, N USA
xxxvi K14 **Powerstock** Dorset, S England, UK
23 V6 **Powhatan** Virginia, NE USA
33 V13 **Powhatan Point** Ohio, N USA
xxxviii J13 **Powick** Worcestershire, W England, UK
xxxv I10 **Powys** ◈ *unitary authority* E Wales, UK
197 I6 **Poya** Province Nord, C New Caledonia
167 P10 **Poyang Hu** ◎ S China
126 Mm16 **Poyarkovo** Amurskaya Oblast', SE Russian Federation
32 L7 **Poygan, Lake** ◎ Wisconsin, N USA
xl H16 **Poynton** Cheshire, N England, UK
111 Y2 **Poysdorf** Niederösterreich, NE Austria
114 N11 **Požarevac** *Ger.* Passarowitz. Serbia, NE Yugoslavia
43 Q13 **Poza Rica** *var.* Poza Rica de Hidalgo. Veracruz-Llave, E Mexico
Poza Rica de Hidalgo *see* Poza Rica
114 L13 **Požega** Serbia, W Yugoslavia
Požega *see* Slavonska Požega
114 H9 **Požega-Slavonija** *off.* Požeško-Slavonska Županija. ◈ *province* NE Croatia
129 U13 **Pozhva** Komi-Permyatskiy Avtonomnyy Okrug, NW Russian Federation
112 G11 **Poznań** *Ger.* Posen, Posnania. Poznań, W Poland
112 G11 **Poznań** *off.* Województwo Poznańskie, *Ger.* Posen, Posnania. ◈ *province* W Poland
Poznańskie, Województwo *see* Poznań
107 O13 **Pozo Alcón** Andalucía, S Spain
64 H3 **Pozo Almonte** Tarapacá, N Chile
106 L12 **Pozoblanco** Andalucía, S Spain
107 Q11 **Pozo Cañada** Castilla-La Mancha, C Spain
64 N5 **Pozo Colorado** Presidente Hayes, C Paraguay
65 J20 **Pozos, Punta** *headland* S Argentina
Pozsega *see* Slavonska Požega
Pozsony *see* Bratislava
57 N5 **Pozuelos** Anzoátegui, NE Venezuela
109 L26 **Pozzallo** Sicilia, Italy, C Mediterranean Sea
109 K17 **Pozzuoli** *anc.* Puteoli. Campania, S Italy
79 P17 **Pra** ≈ S Ghana
Prabumulih *see* Perabumulih
113 C19 **Prachatice** *Ger.* Prachatitz. Jižní Čechy, SW Czech Republic
Prachatitz *see* Prachatice
178 Hh11 **Prachin Buri** *var.* Prachinburi. Prachin Buri, C Thailand
Prachuab Girikhand *see* Prachuap Khiri Khan
178 H13 **Prachuap Khiri Khan** *var.* Prachuab Girikhand. Prachuap Khiri Khan, SW Thailand
113 H16 **Praděd** *Ger.* Altvater. ▲ NE Czech Republic
56 D11 **Pradera** Valle del Cauca, SW Colombia
105 O17 **Prades** Pyrénées-Orientales, S France
61 O19 **Prado** Bahia, SE Brazil
56 E11 **Prado** Tolima, C Colombia
Prae *see* Phrae
Prag/Praga/Prague *see* Praha
29 O10 **Prague** Oklahoma, C USA
113 D16 **Praha** *Eng.* Prague, *Ger.* Prag, *Pol.* Praga. ● (Czech Republic) Střední Čechy, NW Czech Republic
118 J13 **Prahova** ◈ *county* SE Romania
118 J13 **Prahova** ≈ S Romania
78 E10 **Praia** ● (Cape Verde) Santiago, S Cape Verde
85 M21 **Praia do Bilene** Gaza, S Mozambique
85 M20 **Praia do Xai-Xai** Gaza, S Mozambique
118 J10 **Praid** *Hung.* Parajd. Harghita, C Romania
28 J3 **Prairie Dog Creek** ≈ Kansas/Nebraska, C USA
32 J9 **Prairie du Chien** Wisconsin, N USA
29 S9 **Prairie Grove** Arkansas, C USA
33 P10 **Prairie River** ≈ Michigan, N USA
Prairie State *see* Illinois
27 V11 **Prairie View** Texas, SW USA
178 Ii11 **Prakhon Chai** Buri Ram, E Thailand
111 R4 **Pram** ≈ N Austria
111 S4 **Prambachkirchen** Oberösterreich, N Austria
120 H2 **Prangli** *island* N Estonia
160 J13 **Prānhita** ≈ C India
180 I15 **Praslin** *island* Inner Islands, NE Seychelles
117 O23 **Prasonísi, Ákra** *headland* Ródos, Dodekánisos, Greece, Aegean Sea
113 I14 **Praszka** Częstochowa, S Poland
121 M18 **Pratasy** *Rus.* Protasy. Homyel'skaya Voblasts', SE Belorussia
178 I10 **Prathai** Nakhon Ratchasima, E Thailand
Prathet Thai *see* Thailand
Prathum Thani *see* Pathum Thani
65 F21 **Prat, Isla** *island* S Chile
108 G11 **Prato** Toscana, C Italy
105 O17 **Prats-de-Mollo-la-Preste** Pyrénées-Orientales, S France
28 L6 **Pratt** Kansas, C USA
110 E6 **Pratteln** Basel-Land, NW Switzerland
199 L2 **Pratt Seamount** *undersea feature* N Pacific Ocean
25 P5 **Prattville** Alabama, S USA
Praust *see* Pruszcz Gdański
116 M7 **Pravda** *prev.* Dogrular. Razgradska Oblast, NE Bulgaria
121 B14 **Pravdinsk** *Ger.* Friedland. Kaliningradskaya Oblast', W Russian Federation
106 K2 **Pravia** Asturias, N Spain
xxxvi H17 **Prawle Point** *headland* SW England, UK
120 L12 **Prazaroki** *Rus.* Prozoroki. Vitsyebskaya Voblasts', N Belorussia
Prázsmár *see* Prejmer
178 J11 **Preăh Vihéar** Preăh Vihéar, N Cambodia
118 J12 **Predeal** *Hung.* Predeál. Brașov, C Romania
111 S8 **Predlitz** Steiermark, SE Austria
9 V15 **Preeceville** Saskatchewan, S Canada
Preenkuln *see* Priekule
104 K6 **Pré-en-Pail** Mayenne, NW France
xxxviii H8 **Prees** Shropshire, W England, UK
xl M13 **Preesall** Lancashire, NW England, UK
111 T4 **Pregarten** Oberösterreich, N Austria
56 H7 **Pregonero** Táchira, NW Venezuela
120 J10 **Preiļi** *Ger.* Preli. Preiļi, SE Latvia
118 J12 **Prejmer** *Ger.* Tartlau, *Hung.* Prázsmár. Brașov, S Romania
115 J16 **Prekornica** ▲▲ SW Yugoslavia
Preli *see* Preiļi
Prëmet *see* Përmet
102 M12 **Premnitz** Brandenburg, NE Germany
27 S15 **Premont** Texas, SW USA
115 H14 **Prenj** ▲▲ S Bosnia and Herzegovina
Prenjas/Prenjasi *see* Përrenjas
24 L7 **Prentiss** Mississippi, S USA
Preny *see* Prienai
102 O10 **Prenzlau** Brandenburg, NE Germany
126 Jj12 **Preobrazhenka** Irkutskaya Oblast', C Russian Federation
177 Ee9 **Preparis Island** *island* SW Burma
Prerau *see* Přerov
113 H18 **Přerov** *Ger.* Prerau. Severní Morava, E Czech Republic
Preschau *see* Prešov
12 M14 **Prescott** Ontario, SE Canada
38 K12 **Prescott** Arizona, SW USA
29 T13 **Prescott** Arkansas, C USA
34 L10 **Prescott** Washington, NW USA
32 H6 **Prescott** Wisconsin, N USA
xxxv D12 **Preseli, Mynydd** ▲▲ SW Wales, UK

◆ Country
● Country Capital
◇ Dependent Territory
○ Dependent Territory Capital
◈ Administrative Region
✕ International Airport
▲ Mountain
▲▲ Mountain Range
⛰ Volcano
≈ River
◎ Lake
⊡ Reservoir

Preservation Inlet – Putnok

193 A24 Preservation Inlet *inlet* South Island, NZ
114 O7 Preševo Serbia, SE Yugoslavia
31 N10 Presho South Dakota, N USA
60 M13 Presidente Dutra Maranhão, E Brazil
62 I8 Presidente Epitácio São Paulo, S Brazil
64 N5 Presidente Hayes *off.* Departamento de Presidente Hayes. ◐ *department* C Paraguay
62 I9 Presidente Prudente São Paulo, S Brazil
Presidente Stroessner *see* Ciudad del Este
Presidente Vargas *see* Itabira
62 I8 Presidente Venceslau São Paulo, S Brazil
199 L11 President Thiers Seamount *undersea feature* C Pacific Ocean
26 J11 Presidio Texas, SW USA
Preslav *see* Veliki Preslav
113 M19 Prešov *var.* Preschau, *Ger.* Eperies, *Hung.* Eperjes. Východné Slovensko, NE Slovakia
115 N20 Prespa, Lake *Alb.* Liqen i Prespës, *Gk.* Límni Megáli Préspa, Límni Prespa, *Mac.* Prespansko Ezero, *Serb.* Prespansko Jezero. ◎ SE Europe
Prespa, Limni/Prespansko Ezero/Prespansko Jezero/Prespës, Liqen i *see* Prespa, Lake
21 S2 Presque Isle Maine, NE USA
20 B11 Presque Isle *headland* Pennsylvania, NE USA
Pressburg *see* Bratislava
xxxv I4 Prestatyn Denbighshire, N Wales, UK
xl G17 Prestbury Cheshire, W England, UK
79 P17 Prestea SW Ghana
xxxv K10 Presteigne Powys, C Wales, UK
113 B17 Přeštice *Ger.* Pschestitz. Západní Čechy, W Czech Republic
xxxvi L14 Preston Dorset, S England, UK
xli N14 Preston Lancashire, NW England, UK
xxxix P10 Preston Rutland, C England, UK
xliii O20 Preston The Borders, S Scotland, UK
25 S6 Preston Georgia, SE USA
35 R16 Preston Idaho, NW USA
31 Z13 Preston Iowa, C USA
31 X11 Preston Minnesota, N USA
xxxvii Q11 Preston Candover Hampshire, S England, UK
23 O6 Prestonsburg Kentucky, S USA
xli P16 Prestwich Bury, NW England, UK
xliii I22 Prestwick South Ayrshire, W Scotland, UK
85 J21 Pretoria *var.* Epitoli, Tshwane. ● (South Africa-administrative capital) Gauteng, NE South Africa
Pretoria-Witwatersrand-Vereeniging *see* Gauteng
Pretusha *see* Pretushë
115 M21 Pretushë *var.* Pretusha. Korçë, SE Albania
Preussisch Eylau *see* Bagrationovsk
Preussisch-Stargard *see* Starogard Gdański
Preußisch Holland *see* Pasłęk
117 C17 Préveza Ípeiros, W Greece
39 V3 Prewitt Reservoir ⊠ Colorado, C USA
178 J13 Prey Vêng Prey Vêng, S Cambodia
150 M12 Priaral'skiye Karakumy, Peski *desert* SW Kazakhstan
126 L16 Priargunsk Chitinskaya Oblast', S Russian Federation
40 K14 Pribilof Islands *island group* Alaska, USA
115 K14 Priboj Serbia, W Yugoslavia
113 C17 Příbram *Ger.* Pibrans. Střední Čechy, W Czech Republic
38 M4 Price Utah, W USA
39 N5 Price River ≈ Utah, W USA
25 N8 Prichard Alabama, S USA
27 R8 Priddy Texas, SW USA
107 P8 Priego Castilla-La Mancha, C Spain
106 M14 Priego de Córdoba Andalucía, S Spain
120 C10 Priekule *Ger.* Preenkuln. Liepāja, SW Latvia
120 C12 Priekulė *Ger.* Prökuls. Gargždai, W Lithuania
121 F14 Prienai *Pol.* Preny. Prienai, S Lithuania
85 G23 Prieska Northern Cape, C South Africa
34 M7 Priest Lake ⊠ Idaho, NW USA
34 M7 Priest River Idaho, NW USA
106 M3 Prieta, Peña ▲ N Spain
42 J10 Prieto, Cerro ▲ C Mexico
113 J19 Prievidza *var.* Priewitz, *Ger.* Priwitz, *Hung.* Privigye. Stredné Slovensko, C Slovakia
Priewitz *see* Prievidza
114 F10 Prijedor NW Bosnia and Herzegovina
115 K14 Prijepolje Serbia, W Yugoslavia
Prikaspiyskaya Nizmennost' *see* Caspian Depression
115 O19 Prilep *Turk.* Perlepe. S FYR Macedonia
110 B9 Prilly Vaud, SW Switzerland
Priluki *see* Pryluky
64 L10 Primero, Río ≈ C Argentina
31 S12 Primghar Iowa, C USA
114 B9 Primorje-Gorski Kotar *off.* Primorsko-Goranska Županija. ◐ *province* NW Croatia
120 A13 Primorsk *Ger.* Fischhausen. Kaliningradskaya Oblast', W Russian Federation
128 G12 Primorsk *Fin.* Koivisto. Leningradskaya Oblast', NW Russian Federation
Primorsk/Primorskoye *see* Prymors'k
127 Nn17 Primorskiy Kray *prev. Eng.* Maritime Territory. ◐ *territory* SE Russian Federation
116 N10 Primorsko *prev.* Keupriya. Burgaska Oblast, SE Bulgaria
130 K13 Primorsko-Akhtarsk Krasnodarskiy Kray, SW Russian Federation
119 U13 Primors'kyy Respublika Krym, S Ukraine
115 D14 Primošten Šibenik, S Croatia
9 R13 Primrose Lake ◎ Saskatchewan, C Canada
9 T14 Prince Albert Saskatchewan, S Canada
85 G25 Prince Albert Western Cape, SW South Africa
15 I1 Prince Albert Peninsula *peninsula* Victoria Island, Northwest Territories, NW Canada
15 I3 Prince Albert Sound *inlet* Northwest Territories, N Canada
15 Mm2 Prince Charles Island *island* Northwest Territories, NE Canada
205 W6 Prince Charles Mountains ▲ Antarctica
Prince-Édouard, Île-du *see* Prince Edward Island
180 M13 Prince Edward Fracture Zone *tectonic feature* SW Indian Ocean
11 P14 Prince Edward Island *Fr.* Île-du Prince-Édouard. ◐ *province* SE Canada
11 Q14 Prince Edward Island *Fr.* Île-du Prince-Édouard. *island* SE Canada
181 M12 Prince Edward Islands *island group* S South Africa
23 X4 Prince Frederick Maryland, NE USA
8 M14 Prince George British Columbia, SW Canada
23 W6 Prince George Virginia, NE USA
207 O8 Prince Gustaf Adolf Sea *sea* Northwest Territories, N Canada
207 Q3 Prince of Wales, Cape *headland* Alaska, USA
189 V1 Prince of Wales Island *island* Queensland, E Australia
15 Jj1 Prince of Wales Island *island* Queen Elizabeth Islands, Northwest Territories, NW Canada
41 Y14 Prince of Wales Island *island* Alexander Archipelago, Alaska, USA
Prince of Wales Island *see* Pinang, Pulau
15 I1 Prince of Wales Strait *strait* Northwest Territories, N Canada
207 O8 Prince Patrick Island *island* Parry Islands, Northwest Territories, NW Canada
15 Kk1 Prince Regent Inlet *channel* Northwest Territories, N Canada
8 J13 Prince Rupert British Columbia, SW Canada
Prince's Island *see* Príncipe
xxxvii R8 Princes Risborough Buckinghamshire, C England, UK
23 Y5 Princess Anne Maryland, NE USA
205 R1 Princess Astrid Kyst *physical region* Antarctica
189 W2 Princess Charlotte Bay *bay* Queensland, NE Australia
205 W7 Princess Elizabeth Land *physical region* Antarctica
8 J14 Princess Royal Island *island* British Columbia, SW Canada
47 U15 Princes Town Trinidad, Trinidad and Tobago
xxxviii M12 Princethorpe Warwickshire, C England, UK
9 N17 Princeton British Columbia, SW Canada
32 L11 Princeton Illinois, N USA
33 N16 Princeton Indiana, N USA
31 Z14 Princeton Iowa, C USA
22 H7 Princeton Kentucky, S USA
31 V8 Princeton Minnesota, N USA
29 S1 Princeton Missouri, C USA
20 J15 Princeton New Jersey, NE USA
23 R6 Princeton West Virginia, NE USA
xxxvi G15 Princetown Devon, SW England, UK
41 S12 Prince William Sound *inlet* Alaska, USA
69 P9 Príncipe *var.* Príncipe Island, *Eng.* Prince's Island. *island* N Sao Tome and Principe
Príncipe Island *see* Príncipe
34 I13 Prineville Oregon, NW USA
30 J11 Pringle South Dakota, N USA
27 N1 Pringle Texas, SW USA
101 H14 Prinsenbeek Noord-Brabant, S Netherlands
100 L6 Prinses Margriet Kanaal *canal* N Netherlands
205 T2 Prinsesse Ragnhild Kyst *physical region* Antarctica
205 U2 Prins Harald Kyst *physical region* Antarctica
94 N2 Prins Karls Forland *island* W Svalbard
45 N8 Prinzapolka Región Autónoma Atlántico Norte, NE Nicaragua
44 L8 Prinzapolka, Río ≈ NE Nicaragua
125 Ff9 Priob'ye Khanty-Mansiyskiy Avtonomnyy Okrug, N Russian Federation
106 H1 Prior, Cabo *headland* NW Spain
31 V9 Prior Lake Minnesota, N USA
128 H11 Priozersk *Fin.* Käkisalmi. Leningradskaya Oblast', NW Russian Federation
121 J20 Pripet *Bel.* Prypyats', *Ukr.* Pryp"yat'. ≈ Belorussia/Ukraine
121 J20 Pripet Marshes *wetland* Belorussia/Ukraine
Prishtinë *see* Priština
130 J8 Pristen' Kurskaya Oblast', W Russian Federation
115 N16 Priština *Alb.* Prishtinë. Serbia, S Yugoslavia
102 M10 Pritzwalk Brandenburg, NE Germany
105 R13 Privas Ardèche, E France
109 I16 Priverno Lazio, C Italy
Privigye *see* Prievidza
114 C12 Privlaka Zadar-Knin, W Croatia
128 M15 Privolzhsk Ivanovskaya Oblast', NW Russian Federation
131 P7 Privolzhskaya Vozvyshennost' *var.* Volga Uplands. ▲ W Russian Federation
131 P8 Privolzhskoye Saratovskaya Oblast', W Russian Federation
Priwitz *see* Prievidza
131 N13 Priyutnoye Respublika Kalmykiya, SW Russian Federation
115 M17 Prizren *Alb.* Prizreni. Serbia, S Yugoslavia
Prizreni *see* Prizren
109 I24 Prizzi Sicilia, Italy, C Mediterranean Sea
115 P18 Probištip NE FYR Macedonia
174 M15 Probolinggo Jawa, C Indonesia
Probstberg *see* Wyszków
113 F14 Prochowice *Ger.* Parchwitz. Legnica, SW Poland
31 W5 Proctor Minnesota, N USA
27 R8 Proctor Texas, SW USA
27 R8 Proctor Lake ⊠ Texas, SW USA
161 I18 Proddatūr Andhra Pradesh, E India
106 H9 Proença-a-Nova Castelo Branco, C Portugal
97 I24 Præstø Storstrøm, SE Denmark
101 I20 Profondeville Namur, SE Belgium
43 W11 Progreso Yucatán, SE Mexico
126 Mm16 Progress Amurskaya Oblast', SE Russian Federation
131 O15 Prokhladnyy Kabardino-Balkarskaya Respublika, SW Russian Federation
Prokletije *see* North Albanian Alps
126 H14 Prokop'yevsk Kemerovskaya Oblast', S Russian Federation
Prökuls *see* Priekulė
115 O15 Prokuplje Serbia, SE Yugoslavia
128 H14 Proletariy Novgorodskaya Oblast', W Russian Federation
130 M12 Proletarsk Rostovskaya Oblast', SW Russian Federation
130 J8 Proletarskiy Belgorodskaya Oblast', W Russian Federation
177 Ff7 Prome *var.* Pyè. Pegu, C Burma
62 J8 Promissão São Paulo, S Brazil
62 J8 Promissão, Represa de ⊠ S Brazil
129 V4 Promyshlennyy Respublika Komi, NW Russian Federation
121 O16 Pronya *Rus.* Pronya. ≈ E Belorussia
8 M11 Prophet River British Columbia, W Canada
32 K11 Prophetstown Illinois, N USA
61 P16 Propriá Sergipe, E Brazil
104 E3 Propriano Corse, France, C Mediterranean Sea
Prościejów *see* Prostějov
Proskurov *see* Khmel 'nyts'kyy
116 H12 Prosotsáni Anatolikí Makedonía kai Thráki, NE Greece
179 Rr15 Prosperidad Mindanao, S Philippines
34 J10 Prosser Washington, NW USA
Prossnitz *see* Prostějov
113 G18 Prostějov *Ger.* Prossnitz, *Pol.* Prościejów. Jižní Morava, SE Czech Republic
119 V8 Prosyana Dnipropetrovs'ka Oblast', E Ukraine
113 L16 Proszowice Kraków, S Poland
Protasy *see* Pratasy
180 J11 Protea Seamount *undersea feature* SW Indian Ocean
117 D21 Próti *island* S Greece
116 N8 Provadiya Varnenska Oblast, NE Bulgaria
105 S15 Provence *prev.* Marseille-Marignane. ✕ (Marseille) Bouches-du-Rhône, SE France
105 T14 Provence *cultural region* SE France
105 T14 Provence-Alpes-Côte d'Azur ◐ *region* SE France
22 H6 Providence Kentucky, S USA
21 N12 Providence *state capital* Rhode Island, NE USA
38 L1 Providence Utah, W USA
Providence *see* Fort Providence
69 X10 Providence Atoll *var.* Providence. *atoll* S Seychelles
12 D12 Providence Bay Manitoulin Island, Ontario, S Canada
25 R6 Providence Canyon *valley* Alabama/Georgia, S USA
24 I5 Providence, Lake ◎ Louisiana, S USA
37 X13 Providence Mountains ▲ California, W USA
46 L6 Providenciales *island* W Turks and Caicos Islands
127 Q4 Provideniya Chukotskiy Avtonomnyy Okrug, NE Russian Federation
21 Q12 Provincetown Massachusetts, NE USA
105 P5 Provins Seine-et-Marne, N France
38 L3 Provo Utah, W USA
9 R15 Provost Alberta, SW Canada
114 G13 Prozor SW Bosnia and Herzegovina
Prozoroki *see* Prazaroki
62 I11 Prudentópolis Paraná, S Brazil
41 Q7 Prudhoe Northumberland, N England, UK
41 R5 Prudhoe Bay Alaska, USA
41 R4 Prudhoe Bay *bay* Alaska, USA
113 H16 Prudnik *Ger.* Neustadt, Neustadt in Oberschlesien. Opole, SW Poland
121 J16 Prudy *Rus.* Prudy. Minskaya Voblasts', C Belorussia
103 D18 Prüm Rheinland-Pfalz, W Germany
103 D18 Prüm ≈ W Germany
Prusa *see* Bursa
112 J7 Pruszcz Gdański *Ger.* Praust. Gdańsk, N Poland
112 M12 Pruszków *Ger.* Kaltdorf. Warszawa, C Poland
118 K8 Prut *Ger.* Pruth. ≈ E Europe
Pruth *see* Prut
110 L8 Prutz Tirol, W Austria
Pružana *see* Pruzhany
121 G19 Pruzhany *Pol.* Pružana. Brestskaya Voblasts', SW Belorussia
128 I11 Pryazha Respublika Kareliya, NW Russian Federation
119 U10 Pryazovs'ke Zaporiz'ka Oblast', SE Ukraine
Prychornomors'ka Nyzovyna *see* Black Sea Lowland
Prydniprovs'ka Nyzovyna/Prydnyaprowskaya Nizina *see* Dnieper Lowland
205 Y7 Prydz Bay *bay* Antarctica
119 R4 Pryluky *Rus.* Priluki. Chernihivs'ka Oblast', NE Ukraine
119 V10 Prymors'k *Rus.* Primorsk; *prev.* Primorskoye. Zaporiz'ka Oblast', SE Ukraine
29 Q9 Pryor Oklahoma, C USA
35 U11 Pryor Creek ≈ Montana, NW USA
Pryp"yat'/Prypyats' *see* Pripet
112 M10 Przasnysz Ostrołęka, NE Poland
113 K14 Przedbórz Piotrków, S Poland
Przemyskie, Województwo *see* Przemyśl
113 P17 Przemyśl *Rus.* Peremyshl. Przemyśl, SE Poland
113 O16 Przemyśl *off.* Województwo Przemyskie, *Rus.* Peremyshl. ◐ *province* SE Poland
113 O16 Przeworsk Przemyśl, SE Poland
Przheval'sk *see* Karakol
112 L13 Przysucha Radom, SE Poland
117 H18 Psachná *var.* Psahna, Psakhná. Évvoia, C Greece
Psahna/Psakhná *see* Psachná
117 K18 Psará *island* E Greece
117 I16 Psathoúra *island* Vóreioi Sporádes, Greece, Aegean Sea
Pschestitz *see* Přeštice
Psein Lora *see* Pishin Lora
119 S5 Psël ≈ Russian Federation/Ukraine
117 M21 Psérimos *island* Dodekánisos, Greece, Aegean Sea
Pseyn Bowr *see* Pishin Lora
Pskem *see* Piskom
153 R8 Pskemskiy Khrebet *Uzb.* Piskom Tizmasi. ▲ Kyrgyzstan/Uzbekistan
128 F14 Pskov *Ger.* Pleskau, *Latv.* Pleskava. Pskovskaya Oblast', W Russian Federation
120 K6 Pskov, Lake *Est.* Pihkva Järv, *Ger.* Pleskauer See, *Rus.* Pskovskoye Ozero. ◎ Estonia/Russian Federation
128 F15 Pskovskaya Oblast' ◐ *province* W Russian Federation
Pskovskoye Ozero *see* Pskov, Lake
114 G9 Psunj ▲ NE Croatia
113 J17 Pszczyna *Ger.* Pless. Katowice, S Poland
Ptačník/Ptacsnik *see* Vtáčnik
117 D17 Ptéri ▲ C Greece
Ptich' *see* Ptsich
117 E14 Ptolemaïda *prev.* Ptolemaïs. Dytikí Makedonía, N Greece
Ptolemaïs *see* Ptolemaïda, Greece
Ptolemaïs *see* 'Akko, Israel
123 Gg10 Ptolemy Seamounts *undersea feature* C Mediterranean Sea
121 M19 Ptsich *Rus.* Ptich'. Homyel'skaya Voblasts', SE Belorussia
121 M18 Ptsich *Rus.* Ptich'. ≈ SE Belorussia
111 X10 Ptuj *Ger.* Pettau; *anc.* Poetovio. NE Slovenia
194 E9 Pua ≈ NW PNG
63 A23 Puán Buenos Aires, E Argentina
198 B7 Pu'apu'a Savai'i, C Western Samoa
198 A7 Puava, Cape *headland* Savai'i, NW Western Samoa
58 F12 Pucallpa Ucayali, C Peru
59 J17 Pucarani La Paz, NW Bolivia
Pučarevo *see* Novi Travnik
163 U12 Pucheng Fujian, SE China
166 L6 Pucheng Shaanxi, C China
129 N16 Puchezh Ivanovskaya Oblast', W Russian Federation
113 I19 Púchov *Hung.* Puhó. Stredné Slovensko, NW Slovakia
118 J13 Pucioasa Dâmboviţa, S Romania
112 I6 Puck Gdańsk, N Poland
32 L8 Puckaway Lake ◎ Wisconsin, N USA
xxxvii U7 Puckeridge Hertfordshire, SE England, UK
65 G15 Pucón Araucanía, S Chile
95 M14 Pudasjärvi Oulu, C Finland
xxxvi M14 Puddletown Dorset, S England, UK
154 L8 Pūdeh Tal, Shelleh-ye ≈ SW Afghanistan
131 S1 Pudem Udmurtskaya Respublika, NW Russian Federation
Pudewitz *see* Pobiedziska
128 K11 Pudozh Respublika Kareliya, NW Russian Federation
xli R14 Pudsey Leeds, N England, UK
Puduchcheri *see* Pondicherry
157 H21 Pudukkottai Tamil Nādu, SE India
176 Z10 Pue Irian Jaya, E Indonesia
43 P14 Puebla *var.* Puebla de Zaragoza. Puebla, S Mexico
43 P15 Puebla ◐ *state* S Mexico
106 L11 Puebla de Alcocer Extremadura, W Spain
Puebla de Don Fabrique *see* Puebla de Don Fadrique
107 P13 Puebla de Don Fadrique *var.* Puebla de Don Fabrique. Andalucía, S Spain
106 J11 Puebla de la Calzada Extremadura, W Spain
106 J5 Puebla de Sanabria Castilla-León, N Spain
106 I4 Puebla de Trives Galicia, NW Spain
Puebla de Zaragoza *see* Puebla
39 T6 Pueblo Colorado, C USA
39 N10 Pueblo Colorado Wash *valley* Arizona, SW USA
63 C16 Pueblo Libertador Corrientes, NE Argentina
42 J10 Pueblo Nuevo Durango, C Mexico
44 J8 Pueblo Nuevo Estelí, NW Nicaragua
56 J3 Pueblo Nuevo Falcón, N Venezuela
44 B6 Pueblo Nuevo Tiquisate *var.* Tiquisate. Escuintla, SW Guatemala
43 Q11 Pueblo Viejo, Laguna de *lagoon* E Mexico
65 J14 Puelches La Pampa, C Argentina
106 L14 Puente-Genil Andalucía, S Spain
107 Q3 Puente la Reina Navarra, N Spain
106 L12 Puente Nuevo, Embalse de ⊠ S Spain
59 D14 Puente Piedra Lima, W Peru
166 F14 Pu'er Yunnan, SW China
47 V6 Puerca, Punta *headland* E Puerto Rico
39 R12 Puerco, Rio ≈ New Mexico, SW USA
59 J17 Puerto Acosta La Paz, W Bolivia
65 G19 Puerto Aisén Aisén, S Chile
43 R17 Puerto Ángel Oaxaca, SE Mexico
43 T17 Puerto Arista Chiapas, SE Mexico
45 O16 Puerto Armuelles Chiriquí, SW Panama
Puerto Arrecife *see* Arrecife
56 D14 Puerto Asís Putumayo, SW Colombia
56 L9 Puerto Ayacucho Amazonas, SW Venezuela
59 C18 Puerto Ayora Galapagos Islands, Ecuador, E Pacific Ocean
59 C18 Puerto Baquerizo Moreno *var.* Baquerizo Moreno. Galapagos Islands, Ecuador, E Pacific Ocean
44 G4 Puerto Barrios Izabal, E Guatemala
Puerto Bello *see* Portobelo
56 F8 Puerto Berrío Antioquia, C Colombia
56 F9 Puerto Boyaca Boyacá, C Colombia
56 K4 Puerto Cabello Carabobo, N Venezuela
45 N7 Puerto Cabezas *var.* Bilwi. Región Autónoma Atlántico Norte, NE Nicaragua
56 L9 Puerto Carreño Vichada, E Colombia
56 E4 Puerto Colombia Atlántico, N Colombia
44 H4 Puerto Cortés Cortés, NW Honduras
56 J4 Puerto Cumarebo Falcón, N Venezuela
Puerto de Cabras *see* Puerto del Rosario
57 Q5 Puerto de Hierro Sucre, NE Venezuela
66 O11 Puerto de la Cruz Tenerife, Islas Canarias, Spain, NE Atlantic Ocean
66 Q11 Puerto del Rosario *var.* Puerto de Cabras. Fuerteventura, Islas Canarias, Spain, NE Atlantic Ocean
65 J20 Puerto Deseado Santa Cruz, SE Argentina
42 F8 Puerto Escondido Baja California Sur, W Mexico
43 R17 Puerto Escondido Oaxaca, SE Mexico
62 G12 Puerto Esperanza Misiones, NE Argentina
58 D6 Puerto Francisco de Orellana *var.* Coca. Napo, N Ecuador
56 H10 Puerto Gaitán Meta, C Colombia
Puerto Gallegos *see* Río Gallegos
62 G12 Puerto Iguazú Misiones, NE Argentina
58 F12 Puerto Inca Huánuco, N Peru
56 L11 Puerto Inírida *var.* Obando. Guainía, E Colombia
44 K13 Puerto Jesús Guanacaste, NW Costa Rica
43 Z11 Puerto Juárez Quintana Roo, SE Mexico
57 N5 Puerto La Cruz Anzoátegui, NE Venezuela
56 E14 Puerto Leguízamo Putumayo, S Colombia
45 N5 Puerto Lempira Gracias a Dios, E Honduras
Puerto Libertad *see* La Libertad
56 I11 Puerto Limón Meta, E Colombia
56 D13 Puerto Limón Putumayo, SW Colombia
Puerto Limón *see* Limón
107 N11 Puertollano Castilla-La Mancha, C Spain
65 K17 Puerto Lobos Chubut, SE Argentina
56 I3 Puerto López La Guajira, N Colombia
107 Q14 Puerto Lumbreras Murcia, SE Spain
43 V17 Puerto Madero Chiapas, SE Mexico
65 K17 Puerto Madryn Chubut, S Argentina
Puerto Magdalena *see* Bahía Magdalena
59 J15 Puerto Maldonado Madre de Dios, E Peru
Puerto Masachapa *see* Masachapa
Puerto México *see* Coatzacoalcos
65 G17 Puerto Montt Los Lagos, C Chile
43 Z12 Puerto Morelos Quintana Roo, SE Mexico
56 L10 Puerto Nariño Vichada, E Colombia
65 H23 Puerto Natales Magallanes, S Chile
45 X15 Puerto Obaldía San Blas, NE Panama
46 H6 Puerto Padre Las Tunas, E Cuba
56 L9 Puerto Páez Apure, C Venezuela
42 E3 Puerto Peñasco Sonora, NW Mexico
57 N5 Puerto Píritu Anzoátegui, NE Venezuela
47 N8 Puerto Plata *var.* San Felipe de Puerto Plata. N Dominican Republic
47 N8 Puerto Plata ✕ N Dominican Republic
Puerto Presidente Stroessner *see* Ciudad del Este
179 Oo14 Puerto Princesa *off.* Puerto Princesa City. Palawan, W Philippines
Puerto Princesa City *see* Puerto Princesa
Puerto Príncipe *see* Camagüey
Puerto Quellón *see* Quellón
62 F13 Puerto Rico Misiones, NE Argentina
59 K14 Puerto Rico Pando, N Bolivia
56 E12 Puerto Rico Caquetá, S Colombia
47 U5 Puerto Rico *off.* Commonwealth of Puerto Rico; *prev.* Porto Rico. ◇ *US commonwealth territory* C West Indies
66 F11 Puerto Rico *island* C West Indies
66 G11 Puerto Rico Trench *undersea feature* NE Caribbean Sea
56 I8 Puerto Rondón Arauca, E Colombia
Puerto San José *see* San José
65 J21 Puerto San Julián *var.* San Julián. Santa Cruz, SE Argentina
65 I22 Puerto Santa Cruz *var.* Santa Cruz. Santa Cruz, SE Argentina
Puerto Sauce *see* Juan L.Lacaze
59 Q20 Puerto Suárez Santa Cruz, E Bolivia
56 D13 Puerto Umbría Putumayo, SW Colombia
42 J13 Puerto Vallarta Jalisco, SW Mexico
65 G16 Puerto Varas Los Lagos, C Chile
44 M13 Puerto Viejo Heredia, NE Costa Rica
Puertoviejo *see* Portoviejo
59 B18 Puerto Villamil *var.* Villamil. Galapagos Islands, Ecuador, E Pacific Ocean
56 F8 Puerto Wilches Santander, N Colombia
65 H20 Pueyrredón, Lago *var.* Lago Cochrane. ◎ S Argentina
131 R7 Pugachëv Saratovskaya Oblast', W Russian Federation
131 T3 Pugachëvo Udmurtskaya Respublika, NW Russian Federation
34 H8 Puget Sound *sound* Washington, NW USA
109 O17 Puglia *var.* Le Puglie, *Eng.* Apulia. ◐ *region* SE Italy
109 N17 Puglia, Canosa di *anc.* Canusium. Puglia, SE Italy
120 I6 Puhja *Ger.* Kawelecht. Tartumaa, SE Estonia
Puhó *see* Púchov
107 V4 Puigcerdà Cataluña, NE Spain
Puigmal *see* Puigmal d'Err
105 N17 Puigmal d'Err *var.* Puigmal. ▲ S France
78 I16 Pujehun S Sierra Leone
Puka *see* Pukë
193 E20 Pukaki, Lake ◎ South Island, NZ
40 F10 Pukalani Maui, Hawaii, USA, C Pacific Ocean
202 J13 Pukapuka *atoll* N Cook Islands
203 X9 Pukapuka *atoll* Îles Tuamotu, E French Polynesia
Pukari Neem *see* Purekkari Neem
203 X11 Pukarua *var.* Pukaruha. *atoll* Îles Tuamotu, E French Polynesia
Pukaruha *see* Pukarua
12 A7 Pukaskwa ≈ Ontario, S Canada
9 V12 Pukatawagan Manitoba, C Canada
203 X16 Pukatikei, Maunga ✱ Easter Island, Chile, E Pacific Ocean
190 C1 Pukatja *var.* Ernabella. South Australia
169 Y12 Pukch'ŏng E North Korea
115 L18 Pukë *var.* Puka. Shkodër, N Albania
192 L6 Pukekohe Auckland, North Island, NZ
192 L7 Pukemiro Waikato, North Island, NZ
202 D12 Puke, Mont ▲ Île Futuna, W Wallis and Futuna
Puket *see* Phuket
193 C20 Puketeraki Range ▲ South Island, NZ
192 N13 Puketoi Range ▲ North Island, NZ
193 F21 Pukeuri Junction Otago, South Island, NZ
121 L16 Pukhavichy *Rus.* Pukhovichi. Minskaya Voblasts', C Belorussia
Pukhovichi *see* Pukhavichy
128 M10 Puksoozero Arkhangel'skaya Oblast', NW Russian Federation
114 A10 Pula *It.* Pola; *prev.* Pulj. Istra, NW Croatia
169 U14 Pulandian *var.* Xinjin. Liaoning, NE China
169 T14 Pulandian Wan *bay* NE China
179 Rr15 Pulangi ≈ Mindanao, S Philippines
201 O15 Pulap Atoll *atoll* Caroline Islands, C Micronesia
20 H9 Pulaski New York, NE USA
22 I10 Pulaski Tennessee, S USA
23 R7 Pulaski Virginia, NE USA
176 Yy13 Pulau, Sungai ≈ Irian Jaya, E Indonesia
112 N13 Puławy *Ger.* Neu Amerika. Lublin, E Poland
xxxvii S12 Pulborough West Sussex, SE England, UK
xxxix X11 Pulham Market Norfolk, E England, UK
103 E16 Pulheim Nordrhein-Westfalen, W Germany
Pulicat *see* Pālghāt
161 J19 Pulicat Lake *lagoon* SE India
194 M12 Pulie ≈ New Britain, C PNG
Pul'-I-Khatum *see* Polekhatum
Pul-i-Khumri *see* Pol-e Khomrī
Pul-i-Sefid *see* Pol-e Safīd
Pulj *see* Pula
111 W2 Pulkau ≈ NE Austria
95 L15 Pulkkila Oulu, C Finland
125 Gg6 Pul'kovo ✕ (Sankt-Peterburg) Leningradskaya Oblast', NW Russian Federation
34 M9 Pullman Washington, NW USA
110 B10 Pully Vaud, SW Switzerland
42 F7 Púlpita, Punta *headland* W Mexico
112 M10 Pułtusk Ciechanów, C Poland
164 H10 Pulu Xinjiang Uygur Zizhiqu, W China
143 P13 Pülümür Tunceli, E Turkey
201 N16 Pulusuk *island* Caroline Islands, C Micronesia
201 N16 Puluwat Atoll *atoll* Caroline Islands, C Micronesia
27 N11 Pumpville Texas, SW USA
xxxv G12 Pumsaint Carmarthenshire, S Wales, UK
203 P7 Punaauia *var.* Hakapehi. Tahiti, W French Polynesia
58 B8 Puná, Isla *island* SW Ecuador
193 G16 Punakaiki West Coast, South Island, NZ
159 T11 Punakha C Bhutan
59 L18 Punata Cochabamba, C Bolivia
xxxv D12 Puncheston Pembrokeshire, SW Wales, UK
161 E14 Pune *prev.* Poona. Mahārāshtra, W India
85 M17 Pungoè, Rio *var.* Púnguè, Pungwe. ≈ C Mozambique
23 X10 Pungo River ≈ North Carolina, SE USA
Púnguè/Pungwe *see* Pungoè, Rio
81 N19 Punia Maniema, E Zaire
64 H8 Punilla, Sierra de la ▲ W Argentina
167 P14 Puning Guangdong, S China
64 G10 Punitaqui Coquimbo, C Chile
158 H8 Punjab ◐ *state* NW India
155 T9 Punjab *prev.* West Punjab, Western Punjab. ◐ *province* E Pakistan
133 Q9 Punjab Plains *plain* N India
95 O17 Punkaharju *var.* Punkasalmi. Mikkeli, SE Finland
Punkasalmi *see* Punkaharju
59 I17 Puno Puno, SE Peru
59 H17 Puno *off.* Departamento de Puno. ◐ *department* S Peru
63 B24 Punta Alta Buenos Aires, E Argentina
65 H24 Punta Arenas *prev.* Magallanes. Magallanes, S Chile
47 T6 Punta, Cerro de ▲ C Puerto Rico
45 T15 Punta Chame Panamá, C Panama
59 G17 Punta Colorada Arequipa, SW Peru
42 F9 Punta Coyote Baja California Sur, W Mexico
64 G8 Punta de Díaz Atacama, N Chile
63 G20 Punta del Este Maldonado, S Uruguay
65 K17 Punta Delgada Chubut, SE Argentina
57 O5 Punta de Mata Monagas, NE Venezuela
57 O4 Punta de Piedras Nueva Esparta, NE Venezuela
44 F4 Punta Gorda Toledo, SE Belize
45 N11 Punta Gorda Región Autónoma Atlántico Sur, SE Nicaragua
25 W14 Punta Gorda Florida, SE USA
44 M11 Punta Gorda, Río ≈ SE Nicaragua
64 H6 Punta Negra, Salar de *salt lake* N Chile
42 D5 Punta Prieta Baja California, NW Mexico
44 L13 Puntarenas Puntarenas, W Costa Rica
44 L13 Puntarenas *off.* Provincia de Puntarenas. ◐ *province* W Costa Rica
56 J4 Punto Fijo Falcón, N Venezuela
107 S4 Puntón de Guara ▲ N Spain
20 D14 Punxsutawney Pennsylvania, NE USA
95 M14 Puolanka Oulu, C Finland
59 J17 Pupuya, Nevado ▲ W Bolivia
167 O10 Puqi Hubei, C China
59 F16 Puquio Ayacucho, S Peru
126 H9 Pur ≈ N Russian Federation
194 I13 Purari ≈ S PNG
29 N11 Purcell Oklahoma, C USA
9 O16 Purcell Mountains ▲ British Columbia, SW Canada
107 P14 Purchena Andalucía, S Spain
29 S8 Purdy Missouri, C USA
120 I2 Purekkari Neem *prev.* Pukari Neem. *headland* N Estonia
xxxvii V9 Purfleet Essex, SE England, UK
39 U7 Purgatoire River ≈ Colorado, C USA
Purgstall *see* Purgstall an der Erlauf
111 V5 Purgstall an der Erlauf *var.* Purgstall. Niederösterreich, NE Austria
160 O13 Puri *var.* Jagannath. Orissa, E India
Puriramya *see* Buriram
xxxvi J11 Puriton Somerset, SW England, UK
111 X4 Purkersdorf Niederösterreich, NE Austria
xxxvii U10 Purley Croyden, SE England, UK
100 I9 Purmerend Noord-Holland, C Netherlands
157 G16 Pūrna ≈ C India
Purnea *see* Pūrnia
159 R13 Pūrnia *prev.* Purnea. Bihār, NE India
Pursat *see* Poŭthĭsăt, Poŭthĭsăt, W Cambodia
Pursat *see* Poŭthĭsăt, Stœng, W Cambodia
xxxvii N9 Purton Swindon, S England, UK
Purulia *see* Puruliya
156 L13 Puruliya *prev.* Purulia. West Bengal, NE India
49 G7 Purus, Rio *Sp.* Río Purús. ≈ Brazil/Peru
194 G15 Purutu Island *island* SW PNG
95 N17 Puruvesi ◎ SE Finland
24 L7 Purvis Mississippi, S USA
116 J11 Pŭrvomay *prev.* Borisovgrad. Plovdivska Oblast, C Bulgaria
174 J14 Purwakarta *prev.* Poerwakarta. Jawa, C Indonesia
174 L15 Purwodadi *prev.* Poerwodadi. Jawa, C Indonesia
174 K15 Purwokerto *prev.* Poerwokerto. Jawa, C Indonesia
174 Kk15 Purworejo *prev.* Poerworedjo. Jawa, C Indonesia
22 H8 Puryear Tennessee, S USA
160 H13 Pusad Mahārāshtra, C India
169 Z16 Pusan *off.* Pusan-gwangyŏksi, *var.* Busan, *Jap.* Fusan. SE South Korea
173 Ee4 Pusatgajo, Pegunungan ▲ Sumatera, NW Indonesia
Puschlav *see* Poschiavo
Pushkin *see* Tsarskoye Selo
131 Q8 Pushkino Saratovskaya Oblast', W Russian Federation
Pushkino *see* Biläsuvar
113 M22 Püspökladány Hajdú-Bihar, E Hungary
120 J3 Püssi *Ger.* Isenhof. Ida-Virumaa, NE Estonia
118 I5 Pustomyty L'vivs'ka Oblast', W Ukraine
128 F16 Pustoshka Pskovskaya Oblast', W Russian Federation
Pusztakalán *see* Călan
178 H1 Putao *prev.* Fort Hertz. Kachin State, N Burma
192 M8 Putaruru Waikato, North Island, NZ
Puteoli *see* Pozzuoli
167 R12 Putian Fujian, SE China
109 O17 Putignano Puglia, SE Italy
Putivl' *see* Putyvl'
43 Q16 Putla *var.* Putla de Guerrero. Oaxaca, SE Mexico
Putla de Guerrero *see* Putla
21 N12 Putnam Connecticut, NE USA
27 Q7 Putnam Texas, SW USA
xxxvi B9 Putney Wandsworth, SE England, UK
20 M10 Putney Vermont, NE USA
113 L20 Putnok Borsod-Abaúj-Zemplén, NE Hungary

◆ Country
● Country Capital
◇ Dependent Territory
○ Dependent Territory Capital
◐ Administrative Region
✕ International Airport
▲ Mountain
▲ Mountain Range
✱ Volcano
≈ River
◎ Lake
⊠ Reservoir

Putorana, Gory – Radinci

Putorana, Gory/Putorana Mountains see Putorana, Plato
126 I8 **Putorana, Plato** var. Gory Putorana, Eng. Putorana Mountains. ▲▲ N Russian Federation
64 H2 **Putre** Tarapacá, N Chile
161 J24 **Puttalam** North Western Province, W Sri Lanka
161 J24 **Puttalam Lagoon** lagoon W Sri Lanka
101 H17 **Putte** Antwerpen, C Belgium
100 K11 **Putten** Gelderland, C Netherlands
102 K7 **Puttgarden** Schleswig-Holstein, N Germany
Puttiala see Patiāla
103 D20 **Püttlingen** Saarland, SW Germany
56 D14 **Putumayo** off. Intendencia del Putumayo. ◆ province S Colombia
50 E7 **Putumayo, Río** var. Rio Içá. ≈ NW South America see also Içá, Rio
174 K8 **Putus, Tanjung** headland Borneo, N Indonesia
118 J8 **Putyla** Chernivets'ka Oblast', W Ukraine
119 S3 **Putyvl'** Rus. Putivl'. Sums'ka Oblast', NE Ukraine
95 M18 **Puula** ◎ SE Finland
95 N18 **Puumala** Mikkeli, SE Finland
120 I5 **Puurmani** Ger. Talkhof. Jõgevamaa, E Estonia
101 G17 **Puurs** Antwerpen, N Belgium
Pu'uUla'ula see Red Hill
40 A8 **Puuwai** Niihau, Hawaii, USA, C Pacific Ocean
10 J4 **Puvirnituq** prev. Povungnituk. Québec, NE Canada
34 H8 **Puyallup** Washington, NW USA
167 O5 **Puyang** Henan, C China
167 R9 **Puyang Jiang** var. Tsien Tang. ≈ SE China
105 O11 **Puy-de-Dôme** ◆ department C France
105 N15 **Puylaurens** Tarn, S France
104 M13 **Puy-l'Evêque** Lot, S France
105 N17 **Puymorens, Col de** pass S France
58 C7 **Puyo** Pastaza, C Ecuador
193 A24 **Puysegur Point** headland South Island, NZ
154 J8 **Pūzak, Hāmūn-e** Pash. Hāmūn-i-Puzak. ◎ SW Afghanistan
Puzak, Hāmūn-i- see Pūzak, Hāmūn-e
83 J23 **Pwani** Eng. Coast. ◆ region E Tanzania
81 O23 **Pweto** Shaba, SE Zaire
xxxv F7 **Pwllheli** Gwynedd, NW Wales, UK
201 O14 **Pwok** Pohnpei, E Micronesia
126 Gg10 **Pyakupur** ≈ N Russian Federation
128 M6 **Pyalitsa** Murmanskaya Oblast', NW Russian Federation
128 K10 **Pyal'ma** Respublika Kareliya, NW Russian Federation
Pyandzh see Panj
128 I6 **Pyaozero, Ozero** ◎ NW Russian Federation
177 Ff9 **Pyapon** Irrawaddy, SW Burma
121 J15 **Pyarshai** Rus. Pershay. Minskaya Voblasts', C Belorussia
126 I6 **Pyasina** ≈ N Russian Federation
116 I10 **Pyasŭchnik, Yazovir** ▣ C Bulgaria
125 B13 **Pyatigorsk** Stavropol'skiy Kray, SW Russian Federation
Pyatikhatki see P"yatykhatky
119 S7 **P"yatykhatky** Rus. Pyatikhatki. Dnipropetrovs'ka Oblast', E Ukraine
177 G6 **Pyawbwe** Mandalay, C Burma
131 T3 **Pychas** Udmurtskaya Respublika, NW Russian Federation
Pyè see Prome
177 F6 **Pyechin** Chin State, W Burma
121 G17 **Pyeski** Rus. Peski. Hrodzyenskaya Voblasts', W Belorussia
121 L19 **Pyetrykaw** Rus. Petrikov. Homyel'skaya Voblasts', SE Belorussia
95 M16 **Pyhajärvi** ◎ C Finland
95 O17 **Pyhäjärvi** ◎ SE Finland
95 L15 **Pyhäjoki** Oulu, W Finland
95 L15 **Pyhäjoki** ≈ W Finland
95 M15 **Pyhäntä** Oulu, C Finland
95 M16 **Pyhäsalmi** Oulu, C Finland
95 O17 **Pyhäselkä** ◎ SE Finland
95 M19 **Pyhtää** Swe. Pyttis. Kymi, S Finland
177 G6 **Pyinmana** Mandalay, C Burma
xxxv H15 **Pyle** Bridgend, S Wales, UK
117 N24 **Pylés** var. Piles. Kárpathos, SE Greece
117 D21 **Pýlos** var. Pilos. Pelopónnisos, S Greece
20 B12 **Pymatuning Reservoir** ▣ Ohio/Pennsylvania, NE USA
169 X15 **P'yŏngt'aek** NW South Korea
169 V14 **P'yŏngyang** var. P'yŏngyang-si, Eng. Pyongyang. ● (North Korea) SW North Korea
P'yŏngyang-si see P'yŏngyang
37 Q4 **Pyramid Lake** ◎ Nevada, W USA
39 P15 **Pyramid Mountains** ▲▲ New Mexico, SW USA
39 R5 **Pyramid Peak** ▲ Colorado, C USA
117 D17 **Pyramíva** var. Piramiva. ▲ C Greece
Pyrenaei Montes see Pyrenees
88 B12 **Pyrenees** Fr. Pyrénées, Sp. Pirineos; anc. Pyrenaei Montes. ▲▲ SW Europe
104 J16 **Pyrénées-Atlantiques** ◆ department SW France
105 N17 **Pyrénées-Orientales** ◆ department S France
117 L19 **Pyrgí** var. Pirgi. Chíos, E Greece
117 D20 **Pýrgos** var. Pírgos. Dytikí Ellás, S Greece
Pyritz see Pyrzyce
117 E19 **Pýrros** ≈ S Greece
119 R4 **Pyryatyn** Rus. Piryatin. Poltavs'ka Oblast', NE Ukraine
112 D9 **Pyrzyce** Ger. Pyritz. Szczecin, NW Poland
128 F15 **Pytalovo** Latv. Abrene; prev. Jaunlatgale. Pskovskaya Oblast', W Russian Federation
117 M20 **Pythagóreio** var. Pithagorio. Sámos, Dodekánisos, Greece, Aegean Sea
12 L11 **Pythonga, Lac** ◎ Québec, SE Canada
96 E10 **Pyttegga** ▲ S Norway
Pyttis see Pyhtää
177 G7 **Pyu** Pegu, C Burma
177 G8 **Pyuntaza** Pegu, SW Burma
159 N11 **Pyuthan** Mid Western, W Nepal
112 H12 **Pyzdry** Ger. Peisern. Konin, C Poland

Q

144 H13 **Qā' al Jafr** ◎ S Jordan
207 O11 **Qaanaaq** var. Qânâq, Dan. Thule. N Greenland
144 G7 **Qabb Eliâs** E Lebanon
Qabil see Al Qābil
Qabırrı see Iori
Qābis see Gabès
Qābis, Khalīj see Gabès, Golfe de
147 S14 **Qabr Hūd** C Yemen
Qacentina see Constantine
154 L4 **Qādes** Bādghīs, NW Afghanistan
145 T11 **Qādisīyah** S Iraq
Qadmoûs/Qadmūs see Al Qadmūs
149 O4 **Qā'emshahr** prev. 'Alīābad, Shāhī. Māzandarān, N Iran
149 U7 **Qā'en** var. Qain, Qāyen. Khorāsān, E Iran
147 U13 **Qafa** spring/well SW Oman
Qafṣah see Gafsa
169 V9 **Qagan Nur** ◎ NE China
169 Q11 **Qagan Nur** ◎ N China
Qagan Us see Dulan
164 H13 **Qagcaka** Xizang Zizhiqu, W China
Qahremānshahr see Bākhtarān
165 Q10 **Qaidam He** ≈ C China
162 L8 **Qaidam Pendi** basin C China
Qain see Qā'en
Qala Āhangarān see Chaghcharān
145 U3 **Qaḷā Diza** var. Qal 'at Dīzah. NE Iraq
Qal'ah Sālih see Qal'at Ṣāliḥ
153 R13 **Qal'aikhum** Rus. Kalaikhum. S Tajikistan
Qala Nau see Qal'eh-ye Now
147 V17 **Qalansīyah** Suquṭrā, W Yemen
Qala Panja see Qal'eh-ye Panjeh
Qala Shāhar see Qal'eh Shahr
Qalāt see Kalāt
145 W9 **Qal'at Aḥmad** E Iraq
147 N11 **Qal'at Bīshah** 'Asīr, SW Saudi Arabia
144 H4 **Qal'at Burzay** Ḥamāh, W Syria
Qal 'at Dīzah see Qaḷā Diza
145 W9 **Qal'at Ḥusayh** E Iraq
145 V10 **Qal'at Majnūnah** S Iraq
145 X11 **Qal'at Ṣāliḥ** var. Qal'ah Sālih. E Iraq
145 V10 **Qal'at Sukkar** SE Iraq
Qalba Zhotasy see Kalbinskiy Khrebet
149 Q12 **Qal'eh Bīābān** Fārs, S Iran
155 N4 **Qal'eh Shahr** Pash. Qala Shāhar. Sar-e Pol, N Afghanistan
154 L4 **Qal'eh-ye Now** var. Qala Nau. Bādghīs, NW Afghanistan
155 T2 **Qal'eh-ye Panjeh** var. Qala Panja. Badakhshān, NE Afghanistan
Qamar Bay see Qamar, Ghubbat al
147 U14 **Qamar, Ghubbat al** Eng. Qamar Bay. bay Oman/Yemen
147 V13 **Qamar, Jabal al** ▲▲ SW Oman
Qambar see Kambar
165 R14 **Qamdo** Xizang Zizhiqu, W China
197 K13 **Qamea** prev. Nggamea. island N Fiji
77 R7 **Qamīnis** NE Libya
Qamishly see Al Qāmishlī
Qânâq see Qaanaaq
Qandahār see Kandahār
82 Q11 **Qandala** Bari, NE Somalia
144 L2 **Qanṭārī** Ar Raqqah, N Syria
143 V13 **Qapiciğ Dağı** Rus. Gora Kapydzhik. ▲ SW Azerbaijan
164 H5 **Qapqal** var. Qapqal Xibe Zizhixian. Xinjiang Uygur Zizhiqu, NW China
Qapqal Xibe Zizhixian see Qapqal
Qapshagay Böyeni see Kapchagayskoye Vodokhranilishche
206 M15 **Qaqortoq** Dan. Julianehåb. S Greenland
77 U8 **Qâra** var. Qārah. NW Egypt
145 T4 **Qara Anjīr** N Iraq
Qarabāgh see Qarah Bāgh
Qaraböget see Karaboget
Qarabulaq see Karabulak
Qarabutaq see Karabutak
Qaraghandy/Qaraghandy Oblysy see Karaganda
Qaraghayly see Karagayly
145 U4 **Qara Gol** NE Iraq
Qārah see Qâra
154 J4 **Qarah Bāgh** var. Qarabāgh. Herāt, NW Afghanistan
144 G7 **Qaraoun, Lac de** var. Buḥayrat al Qir'awn. ◎ S Lebanon
Qaraoy see Karaoy
Qaraqoyyn see Karakoyyn, Ozero
Qara Qum see Garagumy
Qarasū see Karasu
Qaratal see Karatal
Qarataū see Karatau, Khrebet, Kazakhstan
Qarataū see Karatau, Zhambyl, Kazakhstan
Qaraton see Karaton
82 P13 **Qardho** var. Kardh, It. Gardo. Bari, N Somalia
148 M6 **Qareh Chāy** ≈ N Iran
148 K2 **Qareh Sū** ≈ NW Iran
Qariateïne see Al Qaryatayn
Qarkilik see Ruoqiang
153 O13 **Qarluq** Rus. Karluk. Surkhondaryo Wiloyati, S Uzbekistan
153 U12 **Qarokŭl** Rus. Karakul'. E Tajikistan
153 T12 **Qarokŭl** Rus. Ozero Karakul'. ◎ E Tajikistan
Qarqan see Qiemo
164 K9 **Qarqan He** ≈ NW China
Qarqannah, Juzur see Kerkenah, Îles de
Qarqaraly see Karkaralinsk
155 O1 **Qarqīn** Jowzjān, N Afghanistan
Qars see Kars
Qarsaqbay see Karsakpay
152 M12 **Qarshi** Rus. Karshi; prev. Bek-Budi. Qashqadaryo Wiloyati, S Uzbekistan
152 L12 **Qarshi Chŭli** Rus. Karshinskaya Step. grassland S Uzbekistan
152 M13 **Qarshi Kanali** Rus. Karshinskiy Kanal. canal Turkmenistan/Uzbekistan
Qaryatayn see Al Qaryatayn
152 M12 **Qashqadaryo Wiloyati** Rus. Kashkadar'inskaya Oblast'. ◆ province S Uzbekistan
Qasigianguit see Qasigiannguit
207 N13 **Qasigiannguit** var. Qasigianguit, Dan. Christianshåb. C Greenland
Qaşīm, Minṭaqat see Al Qaşīm
145 P8 **Qaṣr 'Amīj** C Iraq
145 R9 **Qaṣr Darwīshāh** C Iraq
148 J6 **Qaṣr-e Shīrīn** Kermānshāhān, W Iran
77 V10 **Qasr Farâfra** W Egypt
Qassim see Al Qaşīm
147 O16 **Qa'ṭabah** SW Yemen
144 H7 **Qaṭanā** var. Katana. Dimashq, S Syria
149 N15 **Qatar** off. State of Qatar, Ar. Dawlat Qaṭar. ◆ monarchy SW Asia
Qatrana see Al Qaṭrānah
149 Q12 **Qaṭrūyeh** Fārs, S Iran
Qattara Depression/Qaṭṭārah, Munkhafaḍ al see Qaṭṭâra, Monkhafad el
77 U8 **Qaṭṭâra, Monkhafad el** var. Munkhafaḍ al Qaṭṭārah, Eng. Qattara Depression. desert NW Egypt
Qaṭṭīnah, Buḥayrat see Ḥimṣ, Buḥayrat
Qaydār see Qeydār
Qāyen see Qā'en
153 Q11 **Qayroqqum** Rus. Kayrakkum. NW Tajikistan
153 Q10 **Qayroqqum, Obanbori** Rus. Kayrakkumskoye Vodokhranilishche. ▣ NW Tajikistan
145 U7 **Qazānīyah** var. Dhū Shaykh. E Iraq
Qazaqstan/Qazaqstan Respublikasy see Kazakhstan
143 T9 **Qazbegi** Rus. Kazbegi. NE Georgia
155 P15 **Qāzi Ahmad** var. Kazi Ahmad. Sind, SE Pakistan
143 Y12 **Qazimämmäd** Rus. Kazi Magomed. SE Azerbaijan
Qazris see Cáceres
148 M4 **Qazvīn** var. Kazvin. Zanjān, NW Iran
197 K12 **Qelelevu Lagoon** lagoon NE Fiji
77 X10 **Qena** var. Qinā; anc. Caene, Caenepolis. E Egypt
115 L23 **Qeparo** Vlorë, S Albania
Qeqertarssuaq see Qeqertarsuaq
207 N13 **Qeqertarsuaq** var. Qeqertarssuaq, Dan. Godhavn. S Greenland
206 M13 **Qeqertarsuaq** island W Greenland
207 N13 **Qeqertarsuup Tunua** Dan. Disko Bugt. inlet W Greenland
Qerveh see Qorveh
149 S14 **Qeshm** Hormozgān, S Iran
149 R14 **Qeshm** var. Jazīreh-ye Qeshm, Qeshm Island. island S Iran
Qeshm Island/Qeshm, Jazīreh-ye see Qeshm
148 L4 **Qeydār** var. Qaydār. Zanjān, NW Iran
148 K5 **Qezel Owzan** var. Ki Zil Uzen, Qi Zil Uzun. ≈ NW Iran
148 L5 **Qezel Owzan, Rūd-e** ≈ NW Iran
Qian see Guizhou
Qian Gorlo see Qian Gorlos
169 V9 **Qian Gorlos** var. Qian Gorlo, Qian Gorlos Mongolzu Zizhixian, Qianguozhen. Jilin, NE China
Qian Gorlos Mongolzu Zizhixian/Qianguozhen see Qian Gorlos
167 N9 **Qianjiang** Hubei, C China
166 K10 **Qianjiang** Sichuan, C China
166 L14 **Qian Jiang** ≈ S China
166 G9 **Qianning** var. Gartar. Sichuan, C China
169 U13 **Qian Shan** ▲▲ NE China
166 H10 **Qianwei** Sichuan, C China
166 J11 **Qianxi** Guizhou, S China
165 Q7 **Qiaowan** Gansu, N China
Qibilī see Kebili
164 K9 **Qiemo** var. Qarqan. Xinjiang Uygur Zizhiqu, NW China
166 J10 **Qijiang** Sichuan, C China
165 N5 **Qijiaojing** Xinjiang Uygur Zizhiqu, NW China
155 P9 **Qila Saifullāh** Baluchistān, SW Pakistan
165 S9 **Qilian** Qinghai, C China
140 Nn10 **Qilian Shan** var. Kilien Mountains. ▲▲ N China
207 O11 **Qimusseriarsuaq** Dan. Melville Bugt, Eng. Melville Bay. bay NW Greenland
Qinā see Qena
165 W11 **Qin'an** Gansu, C China
Qing see Qinghai
169 W7 **Qing'an** Heilongjiang, NE China
167 R5 **Qingdao** var. Ching-Tao, Ch'ing-tao, Tsingtao, Tsintao, Ger. Tsingtau. Shandong, E China
169 V8 **Qinggang** Heilongjiang, NE China
Qinggil see Qinghe
165 P11 **Qinghai** var. Chinghai, Koko Nor, Qing, Qinghai Sheng, Tsinghai. ◆ province C China
165 S10 **Qinghai Hu** var. Ch'ing Hai, Tsing Hai, Mong. Koko Nor. ◎ C China
Qinghai Sheng see Qinghai
164 M3 **Qinghe** var. Qinggil. Xinjiang Uygur Zizhiqu, NW China
166 L4 **Qingjian** Shaanxi, C China
166 L9 **Qing Jiang** ≈ C China
Qingjiang see Huaiyin
Qingkou see Ganyu
166 I12 **Qinglong** var. Liancheng. Guizhou, S China
167 Q2 **Qinglong** Hebei, E China
Qingshan see Dedu
165 R12 **Qingshuihe** Qinghai, C China
Qingyang see Jinjiang
169 V11 **Qingyuan** Liaoning, NE China
164 L13 **Qingzang Gaoyuan** var. Xizang Gaoyuan, Eng. Plateau of Tibet. plateau W China
167 Q4 **Qingzhou** prev. Yidu. Shandong, E China
163 R9 **Qin He** ≈ C China
167 Q2 **Qinhuangdao** Hebei, E China
166 K7 **Qin Ling** ▲▲ C China
Qin Xian see Qinxian
167 N5 **Qinxian** var. Qin Xian. Shanxi, C China
167 N6 **Qinyang** Henan, C China
166 K15 **Qinzhou** Guangxi Zhuangzu Zizhiqu, S China
Qiong see Hainan
166 L17 **Qionghai** prev. Jiaji. Hainan, S China
166 H9 **Qionglai** Sichuan, C China
166 H8 **Qionglai Shan** ▲▲ C China
166 L17 **Qiongzhou Haixia** var. Hainan Strait. strait S China
169 U7 **Qiqihar** var. Ch'i-ch'i-ha-erh, Tsitsihar; prev. Lungkiang. Heilongjiang, NE China
149 P12 **Qīr** Fārs, S Iran
164 H10 **Qira** Xinjiang Uygur Zizhiqu, NW China
Qir'awn, Buḥayrat al see Qaraoun, Lac de
144 F11 **Qiryat Gat** Southern, C Israel
144 G8 **Qiryat Shemona** Northern, N Israel
Qishlaq see Garmsār
147 U14 **Qishn** SE Yemen
144 G9 **Qishon, Naḥal** ≈ N Israel
Qita Ghazzah see Gaza Strip
162 K5 **Qitai** Xinjiang Uygur Zizhiqu, NW China
169 Y8 **Qitaihe** Heilongjiang, NE China
147 W12 **Qitbīt, Wādī** dry watercourse S Oman
167 O5 **Qixian** var. Qi Xian, Zhaoge. Henan, C China
Qīzān see Jīzān
Qizil Orda see Kzyl-Orda
Qizil Qum/Qizilqum see Kyzyl Kum
153 V14 **Qizilrabot** Rus. Kyzylrabot. SE Tajikistan
152 J10 **Qizilrawbe** Rus. Kyzylrabat. Bukhoro Wiloyati, C Uzbekistan
Qi Zil Uzun see Qezel Owzan
145 S4 **Qizil Yār** N Iraq
152 G7 **Qizqetkan** Rus. Kazanketken. Qoraqalpoghiston Respublikasi, W Uzbekistan
Qoghaly see Kugaly
Qogir Feng see K2
149 N6 **Qom** var. Kum, Qum. Markazī, N Iran
Qomisheh see Shahreẕā
Qomolangma Feng see Everest, Mount
148 M7 **Qom, Rūd-e** ≈ C Iran
Qomsheh see Shahreẕā
Qomul see Hami
Qondūz see Kunduz
Qoqek see Tacheng
Qorabowur Kirlari see Karabaur', Uval
Qoradaryo see Karadar'ya
152 G6 **Qorajar** Rus. Karadzhar. Qoraqalpoghiston Respublikasi, NW Uzbekistan
152 K12 **Qorakŭl** Rus. Karakul'. Bukhoro Wiloyati, C Uzbekistan
152 E5 **Qoraqalpoghiston** Rus. Karakalpakya. Qoraqalpoghiston Respublikasi, NW Uzbekistan
152 G7 **Qoraqalpoghiston Respublikasi** Rus. Respublika Karakalpakstan. ◆ autonomous republic NW Uzbekistan
152 H7 **Qoraŭzak** Rus. Karauzyak. Qoraqalpoghiston Respublikasi, NW Uzbekistan
Qorghazhyn see Kurgal'dzhinskiy
144 H6 **Qornet es Saouda** ▲ NE Lebanon
152 L12 **Qorowulbozor** Rus. Karaulbazar. Bukhoro Wiloyati, C Uzbekistan
148 K5 **Qorveh** var. Qerveh, Qurveh. Kordestān, W Iran
Qosshaghyl see Koschagyl
Qostanay/Qostanay Oblysy see Kustanay
149 P12 **Qoṭbābād** Fārs, S Iran
149 R13 **Qoṭbābād** Hormozgān, S Iran
144 H6 **Qoubaïyât** var. Al Qubayyāt. N Lebanon
Qoussantîna see Constantine
164 K16 **Qowowuyag** var. Cho Oyu. ▲ China/Nepal see also Cho Oyu
152 H6 **Qozoqdaryo** Rus. Kazakdar'ya. Qoraqalpoghiston Respublikasi, NW Uzbekistan
21 N11 **Quabbin Reservoir** ▣ Massachusetts, NE USA
102 F12 **Quakenbrück** Niedersachsen, NW Germany
20 I15 **Quakertown** Pennsylvania, NE USA
190 M10 **Quambatook** Victoria, SE Australia
27 Q4 **Quanah** Texas, SW USA
178 Kk11 **Quang Ngai** var. Quangngai, Quang Nghia. Quang Ngai, C Vietnam
Quang Nghia see Quang Ngai
178 K9 **Quang Tri** Quang Tri, C Vietnam
Quan Long see Ca Mau
158 L4 **Quanshuigou** China/India
xxxvi J12 **Quantock Hills** hill range SW England, UK
167 R13 **Quanzhou** var. Ch'uan-chou, Tsinkiang; prev. Chin-chiang. Fujian, SE China
166 M12 **Quanzhou** Guangxi Zhuangzu Zizhiqu, S China
9 V16 **Qu'Appelle** ≈ Saskatchewan, S Canada
10 M3 **Quaqtaq** prev. Koartac. Québec, NE Canada
63 E16 **Quaraí** Rio Grande do Sul, S Brazil
61 H24 **Quaraí, Rio** Sp. Río Cuareim. ≈ Brazil/Uruguay see also Cuareim, Río
175 P10 **Quarles, Pegunungan** ▲▲ Sulawesi, C Indonesia
xxxviii M7 **Quarndon** Derbyshire, C England, UK
Quarnero see Kvarner
109 C20 **Quartu Sant' Elena** Sardegna, Italy, C Mediterranean Sea
31 X13 **Quasqueton** Iowa, C USA
181 X16 **Quatre Bornes** W Mauritius
180 I17 **Quatre Bornes** Mahé, NE Seychelles
xxxviii J11 **Quatt** Shropshire, W England, UK
143 X10 **Quba** Rus. Kuba. N Azerbaijan
Qubba see Ba'qūbah
149 T3 **Qūchān** var. Kuchan. Khorāsān, NE Iran
191 R10 **Queanbeyan** New South Wales, SE Australia
13 Q10 **Québec** var. Quebec. Québec, SE Canada
12 K10 **Québec** var. Quebec. ◆ province SE Canada
63 D17 **Quebracho** Paysandú, W Uruguay
103 K14 **Quedlinburg** Sachsen-Anhalt, C Germany
144 H10 **Queen Alia** ✈ ('Ammān) 'Ammān, C Jordan
8 L16 **Queen Bess, Mount** ▲ British Columbia, SW Canada
8 I14 **Queen Charlotte** British Columbia, SW Canada
67 B24 **Queen Charlotte Bay** bay West Falkland, Falkland Islands
8 H14 **Queen Charlotte Islands** Fr. Îles de la Reine-Charlotte. island group British Columbia, SW Canada
8 I15 **Queen Charlotte Sound** sea area British Columbia, W Canada
8 J16 **Queen Charlotte Strait** strait British Columbia, W Canada
29 U1 **Queen City** Missouri, C USA
27 X5 **Queen City** Texas, SW USA
207 O9 **Queen Elizabeth Islands** Fr. Îles de la Reine-Élisabeth. island group Northwest Territories, N Canada
205 Y10 **Queen Mary Coast** physical region Antarctica
67 N24 **Queen Mary's Peak** ▲ C Tristan da Cunha
206 M8 **Queen Maud Gulf** gulf Arctic Ocean
205 P11 **Queen Maud Mountains** ▲▲ Antarctica
xliii L23 **Queensberry** ▲ SW Scotland, UK
xli Q14 **Queensbury** Bradford, N England, UK
Queen's County see Laois
xxxv K5 **Queensferry** Flintshire, N Wales, UK
189 U7 **Queensland** ◆ state N Australia
199 Hh10 **Queensland Plateau** undersea feature N Coral Sea
Queenstown see Cobh
191 O16 **Queenstown** Tasmania, SE Australia
193 C22 **Queenstown** Otago, South Island, NZ
85 I24 **Queenstown** Eastern Cape, S South Africa
34 F8 **Queets** Washington, NW USA
63 D18 **Queguay Grande, Río** ≈ W Uruguay
61 O16 **Queimadas** Bahia, E Brazil
84 D11 **Quela** Malanje, NW Angola
85 O16 **Quelimane** var. Kilimane, Kilmain, Quilimane. Zambézia, NE Mozambique
65 G18 **Quellón** var. Puerto Quellón. Los Lagos, S Chile
Quelpart see Cheju-do
39 P12 **Quemado** New Mexico, SW USA
27 O12 **Quemado** Texas, SW USA
46 K7 **Quemado, Punta de** headland E Cuba
Quemoy see Chinmen Tao
64 K13 **Quemú Quemú** La Pampa, E Argentina
xlii I5 **Quendale** Shetland Islands, NE Scotland, UK
xxxvii U6 **Quendon** Essex, SE England, UK
161 E17 **Quepem** Goa, W India
44 M14 **Quepos** Puntarenas, S Costa Rica
Que Que see Kwekwe
63 D23 **Quequén** Buenos Aires, E Argentina
63 D23 **Quequén Grande, Río** ≈ E Argentina
63 C23 **Quequén Salado, Río** ≈ E Argentina
Quera see Chur
43 N13 **Querétaro** Querétaro de Arteaga, C Mexico
42 F4 **Querobabi** Sonora, NW Mexico
44 M13 **Quesada** var. Ciudad Quesada, San Carlos. Alajuela, N Costa Rica
107 O13 **Quesada** Andalucía, S Spain
167 O7 **Queshan** Henan, C China
xxxvii X14 **Quesnard Point** headland Alderney, Channel Islands
8 M15 **Quesnel** British Columbia, SW Canada
39 S9 **Questa** New Mexico, SW USA
104 H7 **Questembert** Morbihan, NW France
59 K22 **Quetena, Río** ≈ SW Bolivia
155 O10 **Quetta** Baluchistān, SW Pakistan
Quetzalcoalco see Coatzacoalcos
Quetzaltenango see Quezaltenango
58 B6 **Quevedo** Los Ríos, C Ecuador
44 B6 **Quezaltenango** var. Quetzaltenango. Quezaltenango, W Guatemala
44 A2 **Quezaltenango** off. Departamento de Quezaltenango, var. Quetzaltenango. ◆ department SW Guatemala
44 E6 **Quezaltepeque** Chiquimula, SE Guatemala
179 O15 **Quezon** Palawan, W Philippines
179 P10 **Quezon City** Luzon, N Philippines
167 P5 **Qufu** Shandong, E China
84 B12 **Quibala** Cuanza Sul, NW Angola
84 B11 **Quibaxe** var. Quibaxi. Cuanza Norte, NW Angola
Quibaxi see Quibaxe
56 D9 **Quibdó** Chocó, W Colombia
104 G7 **Quiberon** Morbihan, NW France
104 G7 **Quiberon, Baie de** bay NW France
56 J5 **Quíbor** Lara, N Venezuela
44 C4 **Quiché** off. Departamento del Quiché. ◆ department W Guatemala
101 E21 **Quiévrain** Hainaut, S Belgium
42 I9 **Quila** Sinaloa, C Mexico
85 B14 **Quilengues** Huíla, SW Angola
Quilimane see Quelimane
59 G15 **Quillabamba** Cusco, C Peru
59 L18 **Quillacollo** Cochabamba, C Bolivia
64 H4 **Quillagua** Antofagasta, N Chile
105 N17 **Quillan** Aude, S France
9 U15 **Quill Lakes** ◎ Saskatchewan, S Canada
64 G11 **Quillota** Valparaíso, C Chile
161 G23 **Quilon** var. Kolam, Kollam. Kerala, SW India
189 V9 **Quilpie** Queensland, C Australia
155 O4 **Quil-Qala** Bāmīān, N Afghanistan
xliv D10 **Quilty** Clare, W Ireland
64 L7 **Quimilí** Santiago del Estero, C Argentina
59 O19 **Quimome** Santa Cruz, E Bolivia
104 F6 **Quimper** anc. Quimper Corentin. Finistère, NW France
Quimper Corentin see Quimper
104 G7 **Quimperlé** Finistère, NW France
xliv E10 **Quin** Clare, W Ireland
xlii H8 **Quinag** ▲ NW Scotland, UK
34 F8 **Quinault** Washington, NW USA
34 F8 **Quinault River** ≈ Washington, NW USA
37 P5 **Quincy** California, W USA
25 S8 **Quincy** Florida, SE USA
32 I13 **Quincy** Illinois, N USA
21 O11 **Quincy** Massachusetts, NE USA
34 J9 **Quincy** Washington, NW USA
56 E10 **Quindío** off. Departamento del Quindío. ◆ province C Colombia
56 E10 **Quindío, Nevado del** ▲ C Colombia
64 J10 **Quines** San Luis, C Argentina
41 N13 **Quinhagak** Alaska, USA
78 G13 **Quinhámel** W Guinea-Bissau
Qui Nhon/Quinhon see Quy Nhơn
Quinindé see Rosa Zárate
27 U6 **Quinlan** Texas, SW USA
63 H17 **Quinta** Rio Grande do Sul, S Brazil
107 O10 **Quintanar de la Orden** Castilla-La Mancha, C Spain
43 X13 **Quintana Roo** ◆ state SE Mexico
107 S6 **Quinto** Aragón, NE Spain
110 G10 **Quinto** Ticino, S Switzerland
29 Q11 **Quinton** Oklahoma, C USA
64 K12 **Quinto, Río** ≈ C Argentina
84 A10 **Quinzau** Zaire, NW Angola
12 H8 **Quinze, Lac des** ◎ Québec, SE Canada
85 B15 **Quipungo** Huíla, C Angola
64 G13 **Quirihue** Bío Bío, C Chile
84 D12 **Quirima** Malanje, NW Angola
191 T6 **Quirindi** New South Wales, SE Australia
57 P5 **Quiriquire** Monagas, NE Venezuela
12 D10 **Quirke Lake** ◎ Ontario, S Canada
63 B21 **Quiroga** Buenos Aires, E Argentina
106 I4 **Quiroga** Galicia, NW Spain
Quiróm, Salar see Pocitos, Salar
58 B9 **Quiroz, Río** ≈ NW Peru
84 Q13 **Quissanga** Cabo Delgado, NE Mozambique
85 M20 **Quissico** Inhambane, S Mozambique
27 O4 **Quitaque** Texas, SW USA
84 Q13 **Quiterajo** Cabo Delgado, NE Mozambique
25 T6 **Quitman** Georgia, SE USA
24 M6 **Quitman** Mississippi, S USA
27 V6 **Quitman** Texas, SW USA
58 C6 **Quito** ● (Ecuador) Pichincha, N Ecuador
Quito see Mariscal Sucre
60 P13 **Quixadá** Ceará, E Brazil
85 Q15 **Quixaxe** Nampula, NE Mozambique
166 J9 **Qu Jiang** ≈ C China
167 R10 **Qu Jiang** ≈ SE China
167 N13 **Qujiang** prev. Maba. Guangdong, S China
166 H12 **Qujing** Yunnan, SW China
152 L10 **Quljuqtov-Toghi** Rus. Gory Kul'dzhuktau. ▲▲ C Uzbekistan
Qulsary see Kul'sary
Qulyndy Zhazyghy see Kulunda Steppe
Qum see Qom
Qumälisch see Lubartów
165 P11 **Qumar He** ≈ C China
165 Q12 **Qumarlêb** Qinghai, C China
Qumisheh see Shahreẕā
153 O14 **Qumqurghon** Rus. Kumkurgan. Surkhondaryo Wiloyati, S Uzbekistan
Qunaytirah/Qunayṭirah, Muḥāfaẓat al/Qunaytra see Al Qunayṭirah
152 G7 **Qŭnghirot** Rus. Kungrad. Qoraqalpoghiston Respublikasi, NW Uzbekistan
201 V12 **Quoi** island Chuuk, C Micronesia
15 Kk6 **Quoich** ≈ Northwest Territories, NE Canada
xliii F14 **Quoich, Loch** ◎ NW Scotland, UK
85 E26 **Quoin Point** headland SW South Africa
190 I7 **Quorn** South Australia
153 R10 **Qŭqon** var. Khokand, Rus. Kokand. Farghona Wiloyati, E Uzbekistan
Qurein see Al Kuwayt
153 P14 **Qŭrghonteppa** Rus. Kurgan-Tyube. SW Tajikistan
Qurlurtuuq see Coppermine
Qurveh see Qorveh
Qusair see Quseir
143 X10 **Qusar** Rus. Kusary. NE Azerbaijan
Quşayr see Al Quşayr
77 Y10 **Quseir** var. Al Quşayr, Qusair. E Egypt
148 I2 **Qūshchī** Āzarbāyjān-e Bākhtarī, N Iran
153 N11 **Qŭshrabot** Rus. Kushrabat. Samarqand Wiloyati, C Uzbekistan
Qusmuryn see Kushmurun, Kustanay, Kazakhstan
Qusmuryn see Kushmurun, Ozero, Kazakhstan
Quṭayfah/Qutayfe/Quteife see Al Quṭayfah
Quthing see Moyeni
Quwair see Guwēr
153 S10 **Quwasoy** Rus. Kuvasay. Farghona Wiloyati, E Uzbekistan
Qu Xian see Quzhou
165 N16 **Qüxü** Xizang Zizhiqu, W China
178 Kk13 **Quy Chanh** Ninh Thuân, S Vietnam
178 Kk12 **Quy Nhơn** var. Quinhon, Qui Nhon. Binh Đinh, C Vietnam
153 O11 **Qŭytosh** Rus. Koytash. Jizzakh Wiloyati, C Uzbekistan
167 R10 **Quzhou** var. Qu Xian. Zhejiang, SE China
Qyteti Stalin see Kuçovë
Qyzylorda/Qyzylorda Oblysy see Kzyl-Orda
Qyzyltū see Kzyltu
Qyzylzhar see Kyzylzhar

R

111 R4 **Raab** Oberösterreich, N Austria
111 X8 **Raab** Hung. Rába. ≈ Austria/Hungary see also Rába
Raab see Győr
111 V2 **Raabs an der Thaya** Niederösterreich, E Austria
95 L14 **Raahe** Swe. Brahestad. Oulu, W Finland
100 M10 **Raalte** Overijssel, E Netherlands
101 I14 **Raamsdonksveer** Noord-Brabant, S Netherlands
94 L12 **Raanujärvi** Lappi, NW Finland
xlii E12 **Raasay** island NW Scotland, UK
xlii E12 **Raasay, Sound of** sound NW Scotland, UK
120 H3 **Raasiku** Ger. Rasik. Harjumaa, NW Estonia
114 B11 **Rab** It. Arbe. Primorje-Gorski Kotar, NW Croatia
114 B11 **Rab** It. Arbe. island NW Croatia
175 P16 **Raba** Sumbawa, S Indonesia
113 G22 **Rába** Ger. Raab. ≈ Austria/Hungary see also Raab
114 A10 **Rabac** Istra, NW Croatia
106 I2 **Rábade** Galicia, NW Spain
82 F10 **Rabak** White Nile, C Sudan
194 M16 **Rabaraba** Milne Bay, SE PNG
104 K16 **Rabastens-de-Bigorre** Hautes-Pyrénées, S France
123 Jj17 **Rabat** W Malta
76 F6 **Rabat** var. al Dar al Baida. ● (Morocco) NW Morocco
Rabat see Victoria
195 P10 **Rabaul** New Britain, E PNG
Rabbah Ammon/Rabbath Ammon see 'Ammān
30 K8 **Rabbit Creek** ≈ South Dakota, N USA
12 H10 **Rabbit Lake** ◎ Ontario, S Canada
197 K13 **Rabi** prev. Rambi. island N Fiji
146 K9 **Rābigh** Makkah, W Saudi Arabia
44 D5 **Rabinal** Baja Verapaz, C Guatemala
173 Ee6 **Rabi, Pulau** island NW Indonesia, East Indies
113 L17 **Rabka** Nowy Sącz, S Poland
161 F16 **Rabkavi** Karnātaka, W India
Râbniṭa see Rîbniṭa
111 Y6 **Rabnitz** ≈ E Austria
128 J7 **Rabocheostrovsk** Respublika Kareliya, NW Russian Federation
25 U1 **Rabun Bald** ▲ Georgia, SE USA
77 S11 **Rabyānah** SE Libya
77 S11 **Rabyānah, Ramlat** var. Rebiana Sand Sea, Şaḥrā' Rabyānah. desert SE Libya
Rabyānah, Şaḥrā' see Rabyānah, Ramlat
118 L11 **Răcăciuni** Bacău, E Romania
109 J24 **Racalmuto** Sicilia, Italy, C Mediterranean Sea
118 J14 **Răcari** Dâmboviţa, SE Romania
Răcari see Durankulak
118 F13 **Răcăşdia** Hung. Rakasd. Caraş-Severin, SW Romania
108 B9 **Racconigi** Piemonte, NE Italy
33 T15 **Raccoon Creek** ≈ Ohio, N USA
11 V13 **Race, Cape** headland Newfoundland, Newfoundland and Labrador, E Canada
24 K10 **Raceland** Louisiana, S USA
21 Q12 **Race Point** headland Massachusetts, NE USA
178 J15 **Rach Gia** Kiên Giang, S Vietnam
178 J14 **Rach Gia, Vinh** bay S Vietnam
78 J8 **Rachid** Tagant, C Mauritania
112 L10 **Raciąż** Ciechanów, C Poland
113 I16 **Racibórz** Ger. Ratibor. Katowice, S Poland
33 N9 **Racine** Wisconsin, N USA
12 D7 **Racine Lake** ◎ Ontario, S Canada
xxxvi H12 **Rackenford** Devon, SW England, UK
113 J23 **Ráckeve** Pest, C Hungary
xlii L5 **Rackwick** Orkney Islands, N Scotland, UK
xlii M2 **Rackwick** Orkney Islands, N Scotland, UK
Rácz-Becse see Bečej
147 O15 **Radā'** var. Ridā'. W Yemen
115 O15 **Radan** ▲ SE Yugoslavia
65 J19 **Rada Tilly** Chubut, SE Argentina
118 K8 **Rădăuţi** Ger. Radautz, Hung. Radóc. Suceava, N Romania
118 L8 **Rădăuţi-Prut** Botoşani, NE Romania
Radautz see Rădăuţi
Radbusa see Radbuza
113 A17 **Radbuza** Ger. Radbusa. ≈ SE Czech Republic
22 K6 **Radcliff** Kentucky, S USA
xl F14 **Radcliffe** Bury, NW England, UK
xxxix O8 **Radcliffe on Trent** Nottinghamshire, C England, UK
145 O2 **Radd, Wādī ar** dry watercourse N Syria
97 H16 **Råde** Østfold, S Norway
111 V11 **Radeče** Ger. Ratschach. C Slovenia
Radein see Radenci
118 J4 **Radekhiv** Pol. Radziechów, Rus. Radekhov. L'vivs'ka Oblast', W Ukraine
Radekhov see Radekhiv
111 X9 **Radenci** Ger. Radein; prev. Radinci. NE Slovenia
111 S9 **Radenthein** Kärnten, S Austria
23 R7 **Radford** Virginia, NE USA
160 C9 **Rādhanpur** Gujarāt, W India
Radinci see Radenci

◆ Country
● Country Capital
◇ Dependent Territory
○ Dependent Territory Capital
◆ Administrative Region
✈ International Airport
▲ Mountain
▲▲ Mountain Range
Volcano
≈ River
◎ Lake
▣ Reservoir

RADISHCHEVO – REGISTAN

131 Q6 **Radishchevo** Ul'yanovskaya Oblast', W Russian Federation
10 I9 **Radisson** Québec, E Canada
9 P16 **Radium Hot Springs** British Columbia, SW Canada
118 F11 **Radna** *Hung.* Máriaradna. Arad, W Romania
116 K10 **Radnevo** Khaskovska Oblast, C Bulgaria
99 J20 **Radnor** *cultural region* E Wales, UK
Radnót *see* Iernut
Rádóc *see* Rădăuţi
103 H24 **Radolfzell am Bodensee** Baden-Württemberg, S Germany
112 M13 **Radom** Radom, C Poland
112 M13 **Radom** *off.* Województwo Radomskie. ◐ *province* C Poland
118 I14 **Radomireşti** Olt, S Romania
Radomskie, Województwo *see* Radom
113 K14 **Radomsko** *Rus.* Novoradomsk. Piotrków, C Poland
119 N4 **Radomyshl'** Zhytomyrs'ka Oblast', N Ukraine
115 P19 **Radoviš** *prev.* Radovište. E FYR Macedonia
Radovište *see* Radoviš
96 B13 **Radøy** *island* S Norway
111 R7 **Radstadt** Salzburg, NW Austria
xxxvi L10 **Radstock** Bath and North East Somerset, SW England, UK
190 E8 **Radstock, Cape** *headland* South Australia
111 U10 **Raduha** ▲ N Slovenia
121 G15 **Radun'** *Rus.* Radun'. Hrodzyenskaya Voblasts', W Belorussia
126 Gg11 **Raduzhnyy** Khanty-Mansiyskiy Avtonomnyy Okrug, C Russian Federation
120 F11 **Radviliškis** Radviliškis, N Lithuania
9 U17 **Radville** Saskatchewan, S Canada
146 K7 **Raḑwá, Jabal** ▲ W Saudi Arabia
113 P16 **Radymno** Przemyśl, SE Poland
118 J5 **Radyvyliv** Rivnens'ka Oblast', NW Ukraine
Radziechów *see* Radekhiv
112 I11 **Radziejów** Włocławek, C Poland
112 O12 **Radzyń Podlaski** Biała Podlaska, E Poland
15 Hh4 **Rae** ≈ Northwest Territories, NW Canada
158 M13 **Rāe Bareli** Uttar Pradesh, N India
15 Hh7 **Rae-Edzo** Northwest Territories, NW Canada
23 T11 **Raeford** North Carolina, SE USA
101 M19 **Raeren** Liège, E Belgium
15 Kk3 **Rae Strait** *strait* Northwest Territories, N Canada
192 L11 **Raetihi** Manawatu-Wanganui, North Island, NZ
203 U13 **Raevavae** *var.* Raivavae. *island* Îles Australes, SW French Polynesia
Rafa *see* Rafah
64 M10 **Rafaela** Santa Fe, E Argentina
144 E11 **Rafah** *var.* Rafa, Rafaḩ, *Heb.* Rafiah, Raphiah. SW Gaza Strip
81 L15 **Rafaï** Mbomou, SE Central African Republic
147 O4 **Rafḩah** Al Ḩudūd ash Shamālīyah, N Saudi Arabia
Rafiah *see* Rafah
149 R10 **Rafsanjān** Kermān, C Iran
82 B13 **Raga** Western Bahr el Ghazal, SW Sudan
21 S8 **Ragged Island** *island* Maine, NE USA
46 I5 **Ragged Island Range** *island group* S Bahamas
xxxv L13 **Raglan** Monmouthshire, SE Wales, UK
192 L7 **Raglan** Waikato, North Island, NZ
24 G8 **Ragley** Louisiana, S USA
Ragnit *see* Neman
109 K25 **Ragusa** Sicilia, Italy, C Mediterranean Sea
Ragusa *see* Dubrovnik
Ragusavecchia *see* Cavtat
175 Qq12 **Raha** Pulau Muna, C Indonesia
121 N17 **Rahachow** *Rus.* Rogachëv. Homyel'skaya Voblasts', SE Belorussia
69 U6 **Rahad** *var.* Nahr ar Rahad. ≈ W Sudan
Rahad, Nahr ar *see* Rahad
Rahaeng *see* Tak
xliv J8 **Raharney** Westmeath, C Ireland
144 F11 **Rahat** Southern, C Israel
146 L8 **Rahaţ, Ḩarrat** *lavaflow* W Saudi Arabia
155 S12 **Rahīmyār Khān** Punjab, SE Pakistan
97 I14 **Råholt** Akershus, S Norway
Rahovec *see* Orahovac
203 S10 **Raiatea** *island* Îles Sous le Vent, W French Polynesia
161 H16 **Rāichūr** Karnātaka, C India
Raidestos *see* Tekirdağ
159 S13 **Rāiganj** West Bengal, NE India
160 M11 **Raigarh** Madhya Pradesh, C India
175 Q18 **Raijua, Selat** *strait* Nusa Tenggara, S Indonesia
191 O16 **Railton** Tasmania, SE Australia
xliii E19 **Rainberg Mór** *hill* W Scotland, UK
38 L8 **Rainbow Bridge** *natural arch* Utah, W USA
25 Q3 **Rainbow City** Alabama, S USA
9 N11 **Rainbow Lake** Alberta, W Canada
23 R5 **Rainelle** West Virginia, NE USA
xli N16 **Rainford** St Helens, NW England, UK
xxxvii V10 **Rainham** Havering, SE England, UK
xxxvii W9 **Rainham** The Medway Towns, SE England, UK
34 G10 **Rainier** Oregon, NW USA
34 H9 **Rainier, Mount** ⛰ Washington, NW USA
25 Q2 **Rainsville** Alabama, S USA
10 B11 **Rainy Lake** ◎ Ontario, S Canada
31 U2 **Rainy Lake** ◎ Minnesota, N USA
10 A11 **Rainy River** Ontario, C Canada
Raippaluoto *see* Replot
160 K12 **Raipur** Madhya Pradesh, C India
160 H10 **Raisen** Madhya Pradesh, C India
13 N13 **Raisin** ≈ Ontario, SE Canada
33 R11 **Raisin, River** ≈ Michigan, N USA
Raivavae *see* Raevavae
155 W9 **Rāiwind** Punjab, E Pakistan
176 U9 **Raja Ampat, Kepulauan** *island group* E Indonesia
161 L16 **Rājahmundry** Andhra Pradesh, E India
161 I18 **Rājampet** Andhra Pradesh, E India
Rajang *see* Rajang, Batang
174 Mm6 **Rajang, Batang** *var.* Rajang. ≈ East Malaysia
155 S11 **Rājanpur** Punjab, E Pakistan
161 H23 **Rājapālaiyam** Tamil Nādu, SE India
158 E12 **Rājasthān** ◐ *state* NW India
159 T15 **Rajbari** Dhaka, C Bangladesh
159 R12 **Rajbiraj** Eastern, E Nepal
160 G9 **Rājgarh** Madhya Pradesh, C India
158 H10 **Rājgarh** Rājasthān, NW India
159 P14 **Rājgīr** Bihār, N India
112 O8 **Rajgród** Łomża, NE Poland
160 L12 **Rājim** Madhya Pradesh, C India
114 C11 **Rajinac, Mali** ▲ W Croatia
160 B10 **Rājkot** Gujarāt, W India
159 R14 **Rājmahal** Bihār, NE India
159 Q14 **Rājmahāl Hills** *hill range* N India
160 K12 **Rāj Nāndgaon** Madhya Pradesh, C India
158 I8 **Rājpura** Punjab, NW India
159 S14 **Rajshahi** *prev.* Rampur Boalia. Rajshahi, W Bangladesh
159 S13 **Rajshahi** ◐ *division* NW Bangladesh
202 K13 **Rakahanga** *atoll* N Cook Islands
193 H19 **Rakaia** Canterbury, South Island, NZ
193 G19 **Rakaia** ≈ South Island, NZ
158 H3 **Rakaposhi** ▲ N India
Rakasd *see* Răcăşdia
174 Ii14 **Rakata, Pulau** *var.* Pulau Krakatau. *island* S Indonesia
164 K16 **Raka Zangbo** ≈ W China
147 U10 **Rakbah, Qalamat ar** *well* SE Saudi Arabia
xxxvii R12 **Rake** West Sussex, SE England, UK
Rakhine State *see* Arakan State
118 I8 **Rakhiv** Zakarpats'ka Oblast', W Ukraine
147 V13 **Rakhyūt** SW Oman
197 I14 **Rakiraki** Viti Levu, W Fiji
Rakka *see* Ar Raqqah
120 I4 **Rakke** Lääne-Virumaa, NE Estonia
97 I16 **Rakkestad** Østfold, S Norway
112 F12 **Rakoniewice** *Ger.* Rakwitz. Poznań, W Poland
Rakonitz *see* Rakovník
85 H18 **Rakops** Central, C Botswana
113 C16 **Rakovník** *Ger.* Rakonitz. Střední Čechy, W Czech Republic
116 J10 **Rakovski** Plovdivska Oblast, C Bulgaria
Rakutō-kō *see* Naktong-gang
120 I3 **Rakvere** *Ger.* Wesenberg. Lääne-Virumaa, N Estonia
Rakwitz *see* Rakoniewice
24 L6 **Raleigh** Mississippi, S USA
23 U9 **Raleigh** *state capital* North Carolina, SE USA
23 Y11 **Raleigh Bay** *bay* North Carolina, SE USA
23 U9 **Raleigh-Durham** ✕ North Carolina, SE USA
201 S6 **Ralik Chain** *island group* Ralik Chain, W Marshall Islands
27 N5 **Ralls** Texas, SW USA
20 G13 **Ralston** Pennsylvania, NE USA
147 O16 **Ramādah** W Yemen
Ramadi *see* Ar Ramādī
107 N2 **Ramales de la Victoria** Cantabria, N Spain
144 F10 **Ramallah** C West Bank
63 C19 **Ramallo** Buenos Aires, E Argentina
161 H20 **Rāmanagaram** Karnātaka, E India
161 I23 **Rāmanāthapuram** Tamil Nādu, SE India
160 N12 **Ramapur** Orissa, E India
144 F10 **Ramat Gan** Tel Aviv, W Israel
105 T6 **Rambervillers** Vosges, NE France
Rambi *see* Rabi
105 N5 **Rambouillet** Yvelines, N France
194 L8 **Rambutyo Island** *island* N PNG
xxxvi F16 **Rame** Cornwall, SW England, UK
159 Q12 **Ramechhap** Central, C Nepal
191 R12 **Rame Head** *headland* Victoria, SE Australia
130 L4 **Ramenskoye** Moskovskaya Oblast', W Russian Federation
128 J15 **Rameshki** Tverskaya Oblast', W Russian Federation
159 P14 **Rāmgarh** Bihār, N India
158 D11 **Rāmgarh** Rājasthān, NW India
148 M9 **Rāmhormoz** *var.* Ram Hormuz, Ramuz. Khūzestān, SW Iran
Ram Hormuz *see* Rāmhormoz
Ram, Jebel *see* Ramm, Jabal
144 F10 **Ramla** *var.* Ramle, Ramleh, *Ar.* Er Ramle. Central, C Israel
Ramle/Ramleh *see* Ramla
144 F14 **Ramm, Jabal** *var.* Jebel Ram. ▲ SW Jordan
158 K10 **Rāmnagar** Uttar Pradesh, N India
97 N15 **Ramnäs** Västmanland, C Sweden
Râmnicul-Sărat *see* Râmnicu Sărat
118 L12 **Râmnicu Sărat** *prev.* Râmnicul-Sărat, Rîmnicu-Sărat. Buzău, E Romania
118 I13 **Râmnicu Vâlcea** *prev.* Rîmnicu Vîlcea. Vâlcea, C Romania
Ramokgwebana *see* Ramokgwebane
85 J18 **Ramokgwebane** *var.* Ramokgwebana. Central, NE Botswana
130 L7 **Ramon'** Voronezhskaya Oblast', W Russian Federation
37 V17 **Ramona** California, W USA
58 A10 **Ramón, Laguna** ◎ NW Peru
12 G7 **Ramore** Ontario, S Canada
xliv J7 **Ramor, Lough** ◎ N Ireland
42 M11 **Ramos** San Luis Potosí, C Mexico
43 N8 **Ramos Arizpe** Coahuila de Zaragoza, NE Mexico
42 J9 **Ramos, Río de** ≈ C Mexico
41 R8 **Rampart** Alaska, USA
14 G5 **Ramparts** ≈ Northwest Territories, NW Canada
158 K10 **Rāmpur** Uttar Pradesh, N India
160 F9 **Rāmpura** Madhya Pradesh, C India
Rampur Boalia *see* Rajshahi
177 F6 **Ramree Island** *island* W Burma
147 W6 **Rams** *var.* Ar Rams. Ra's al Khaymah, NE UAE
149 N4 **Rāmsar** *prev.* Sakhtsar. Māzandarān, N Iran
xli O15 **Ramsbottom** Bury, NW England, UK
xxxvii O10 **Ramsbury** Wiltshire, S England, UK
95 H16 **Ramsele** Västernorrland, N Sweden
23 T9 **Ramseur** North Carolina, SE USA
xl G11 **Ramsey** NE Isle of Man
xxxix R11 **Ramsey** Cambridgeshire, E England, UK
xxxvii Y6 **Ramsey** Essex, SE England, UK
xl H10 **Ramsey Bay** *bay* NE Isle of Man
xxxv A13 **Ramsey Island** *island* SW Wales, UK
12 E9 **Ramsey Lake** ◎ Ontario, S Canada
xxxvii Z10 **Ramsgate** Kent, SE England, UK
xli Q12 **Ramsgill** North Yorkshire, N England, UK
96 M10 **Ramsjö** Gävleborg, C Sweden
160 I12 **Rāmtek** Mahārāshtra, C India
Ramtha *see* Ar Ramthā
194 H11 **Ramu** ≈ N PNG
Ramuz *see* Rāmhormoz
120 G12 **Ramygala** Panevėžys, C Lithuania
94 G12 **Rana** ≈ C Norway
158 H14 **Rāna Pratāp Sāgar** ◎ N India
175 O2 **Ranau** Sabah, East Malaysia
174 I12 **Ranau, Danau** ◎ Sumatera, W Indonesia
64 H12 **Rancagua** Libertador, C Chile
101 G22 **Rance** Hainaut, S Belgium
104 H6 **Rance** ≈ NW France
62 J9 **Rancharia** São Paulo, S Brazil
159 P15 **Rānchi** Bihār, N India
63 D21 **Ranchos** Buenos Aires, E Argentina
39 S9 **Ranchos De Taos** New Mexico, SW USA
65 G16 **Ranco, Lago** ◎ C Chile
97 C16 **Randaberg** Rogaland, S Norway
31 U7 **Randall** Minnesota, N USA
xliv K4 **Randalstown** Antrim, NE Northern Ireland, UK
109 L23 **Randazzo** Sicilia, Italy, C Mediterranean Sea
97 G21 **Randers** Århus, C Denmark
94 I12 **Randijaure** ◎ N Sweden
23 T9 **Randleman** North Carolina, SE USA
21 O11 **Randolph** Massachusetts, NE USA
31 Q13 **Randolph** Nebraska, C USA
38 M1 **Randolph** Utah, W USA
102 P9 **Randow** ≈ NE Germany
97 H14 **Randsfjorden** ◎ S Norway
94 K13 **Råneå** Norrbotten, N Sweden
78 H10 **Ranérou** C Senegal
193 E22 **Ranfurly** Otago, South Island, NZ
178 Hh17 **Rangae** Narathiwat, SW Thailand
159 V16 **Rangamati** Chittagong, SE Bangladesh
192 I2 **Rangauru Bay** *bay* North Island, NZ
21 P6 **Rangeley** Maine, NE USA
39 O4 **Rangely** Colorado, C USA
27 R7 **Ranger** Texas, SW USA
12 C9 **Ranger Lake** Ontario, S Canada
12 C9 **Ranger Lake** ◎ Ontario, S Canada
159 V12 **Rangia** Assam, NE India
193 I18 **Rangiora** Canterbury, South Island, NZ
203 T9 **Rangiroa** *atoll* Îles Tuamotu, W French Polynesia
192 N9 **Rangitaiki** ≈ North Island, NZ
193 F19 **Rangitata** ≈ South Island, NZ
192 M12 **Rangitikei** ≈ North Island, NZ
192 L6 **Rangitoto Island** *island* N NZ
Rangkasbitoeng *see* Rangkasbitung
174 Ii14 **Rangkasbitung** *prev.* Rangkasbitoeng. Jawa, SW Indonesia
178 Hh9 **Rang, Khao** ▲ C Thailand
153 V13 **Rangkŭl** *Rus.* Rangkul'. SE Tajikistan
Rangkul' *see* Rangkŭl
Rangoon *see* Yangon
159 T13 **Rangpur** Rajshahi, N Bangladesh
174 Hh7 **Rangsang, Pulau** *island* W Indonesia
161 F18 **Rānibennur** Karnātaka, W India
159 R15 **Rāniganj** West Bengal, NE India
155 Q13 **Rānīpur** Sind, SE Pakistan
Rāniyah *see* Ŗānya
27 N9 **Rankin** Texas, SW USA
15 L7 **Rankin Inlet** Northwest Territories, C Canada
191 P8 **Rankins Springs** New South Wales, SE Australia
Rankovićevo *see* Kraljevo
110 I7 **Rankweil** Vorarlberg, W Austria
Rann *see* Brežice
131 T8 **Ranneye** Orenburgskaya Oblast', W Russian Federation
xliii J16 **Rannoch, Loch** ◎ C Scotland, UK
xliii I16 **Rannoch Station** Perth and Kinross, C Scotland, UK
203 U17 **Rano Kau** *var.* Rano Kao. *crater* Easter Island, Chile, E Pacific Ocean
178 Gg14 **Ranong** Ranong, SW Thailand
195 T14 **Ranongga** *var.* Ghanongga. *island* NW Solomon Islands
203 W16 **Rano Raraku** *ancient monument* Easter Island, Chile, E Pacific Ocean
176 W9 **Ransiki** Irian Jaya, E Indonesia
94 K12 **Rantajärvi** Norrbotten, N Sweden
95 N17 **Rantasalmi** Mikkeli, SE Finland
175 N11 **Rantau** Borneo, C Indonesia
174 Hh7 **Rantau, Pulau** *var.* Pulau Tebingtinggi. *island* W Indonesia
175 Pp11 **Rantepao** Sulawesi, C Indonesia
32 M13 **Rantoul** Illinois, N USA
95 L15 **Rantsila** Oulu, C Finland
94 L13 **Ranua** Lappi, NW Finland
145 T3 **Ŗānya** *var.* Rāniyah. NE Iraq
163 X3 **Raohe** Heilongjiang, NE China
76 H9 **Raoui, Erg er** *desert* W Algeria
199 L11 **Rapa** *island* Îles Australes, S French Polynesia
203 V14 **Rapa Iti** *island* Îles Australes, SW French Polynesia
108 D10 **Rapallo** Liguria, NW Italy
Rapa Nui *see* Pascua, Isla de
Raphiah *see* Rafah
23 V5 **Rapidan River** ≈ Virginia, NE USA
30 J10 **Rapid City** South Dakota, N USA
13 P8 **Rapide-Blanc** Québec, SE Canada
12 I8 **Rapide-Deux** Québec, SE Canada
120 K6 **Räpina** *Ger.* Rappin. Põlvamaa, SE Estonia
120 G4 **Rapla** *Ger.* Rappel. Raplamaa, NW Estonia
120 G4 **Raplamaa** *off.* Rapla Maakond. ◐ *province* NW Estonia
23 X6 **Rappahonnock River** ≈ Virginia, NE USA
Rappel *see* Rapla
110 G7 **Rapperswil** Sankt Gallen, NE Switzerland
Rappin *see* Räpina
159 N12 **Rāpti** ≈ N India
59 K16 **Rapulo, Río** ≈ E Bolivia
Raqqah/Raqqah, Muḩāfaẓat al *see* Ar Raqqah
20 J8 **Raquette Lake** ◎ New York, NE USA
20 J6 **Raquette River** ≈ New York, NE USA
203 V10 **Raraka** *atoll* Îles Tuamotu, C French Polynesia
203 V10 **Raroia** *atoll* Îles Tuamotu, C French Polynesia
202 H15 **Rarotonga** ✕ Rarotonga, S Cook Islands, C Pacific Ocean
202 H16 **Rarotonga** *island* S Cook Islands, C Pacific Ocean
153 P12 **Rarz** W Tajikistan
Ras al 'Ain *see* Ra's al 'Ayn
145 N2 **Ra's al 'Ayn** *var.* Ras al 'Ain. Al Ḩasakah, N Syria
144 H3 **Ra's al Basīţ** Al Lādhiqīyah, W Syria
Ra's al-Hafgī *see* Ra's al Khafjī
147 R5 **Ra's al Khafjī** *var.* Ra's al-Hafgī. Ash Sharqīyah, NE Saudi Arabia
Ras al-Khaimah/Ras al Khaimah *see* Ra's al Khaymah
149 R15 **Ra's al Khaymah** *var.* Ras al Khaimah. Ra's al Khaymah, NE UAE
149 R15 **Ra's al Khaymah** *var.* Ras al-Khaimah. ✕ Ra's al Khaymah, NE UAE
144 G13 **Ra's an Naqb** Ma'ān, S Jordan
63 B26 **Rasa, Punta** *headland* E Argentina
176 W10 **Rasawi** Irian Jaya, E Indonesia
Râşcani *see* Rîşcani
82 J10 **Ras Dashen Terara** ▲ N Ethiopia
157 K19 **Rasdu Atoll** *atoll* C Maldives
120 E12 **Raseiniai** Raseiniai, C Lithuania
77 X8 **Râs Ghârib** E Egypt
168 D6 **Rashaant** Bayan-Ölgiy, W Mongolia
168 L10 **Rashaant** Dundgovĭ, C Mongolia
168 J6 **Rashaant** Hövsgöl, N Mongolia
xliv K3 **Rasharkin** Ballymoney, N Northern Ireland, UK
145 Y11 **Rashīd** E Iraq
77 V7 **Rashîd** *Eng.* Rosetta. N Egypt
148 M3 **Rasht** *var.* Resht. Gīlān, NW Iran
145 S2 **Rashwān** N Iraq
Rasik *see* Raasiku
115 M15 **Raška** Serbia, C Yugoslavia
121 P15 **Rasna** *Rus.* Ryasna. Mahilyowskaya Voblasts', E Belorussia
118 J12 **Râşnov** *prev.* Rîşno, Rozsnyó, *Hung.* Barcarozsnyó. Braşov, C Romania
120 L11 **Rasony** *Rus.* Rossony. Vitsyebskaya Voblasts', N Belorussia
Ra's Shamrah *see* Ugarit
131 N7 **Rasskazovo** Tambovskaya Oblast', W Russian Federation
121 O16 **Rasta** ≈ E Belorussia
Rastadt *see* Rastatt
Rastâne *see* Ar Rastān
147 S6 **Ra's Tannūrah** *Eng.* Ras Tanura. Ash Sharqīyah, NE Saudi Arabia
Ras Tanura *see* Ra's Tannūrah
103 G21 **Rastatt** *var.* Rastadt. Baden-Württemberg, SW Germany
Rastenburg *see* Kętrzyn
155 V7 **Rasūlnagar** Punjab, E Pakistan
201 U6 **Ratak Chain** *island group* Ratak Chain, E Marshall Islands
121 K15 **Ratamka** *Rus.* Ratomka. Minskaya Voblasts', C Belorussia
95 G17 **Ratan** Jämtland, C Sweden
158 G11 **Ratangarh** Rājasthān, NW India
Rat Buri *see* Ratchaburi
178 H11 **Ratchaburi** *var.* Rat Buri. Ratchaburi, W Thailand
31 W15 **Rathbun Lake** ⊠ Iowa, C USA
Ráth Caola *see* Rathkeale
xliv K9 **Rathcoole** Dublin, E Ireland
xliv G13 **Rathcormack** Cork, S Ireland
xliv H10 **Rathdowney** Laois, C Ireland
xliv L10 **Rathdrum** Wicklow, E Ireland
177 F5 **Rathedaung** Arakan State, W Burma
xlii P11 **Rathen** Aberdeenshire, NE Scotland, UK
102 M12 **Rathenow** Brandenburg, NE Germany
xliv L5 **Rathfriland** Banbridge, SE Northern Ireland, UK
xliv J9 **Rathhangan** Kildare, E Ireland
xliv E11 **Rathkeale** *Ir.* Ráth Caola. Limerick, SW Ireland
xliv K2 **Rathlin Island** *Ir.* Reachlainn. *island* N Northern Ireland, UK
xliv L2 **Rathlin Sound** *strait* NE Northern Ireland, UK
xliv F12 **Ráth Luirc** *Ir.* An Ráth. Cork, S Ireland
Ráth Maoláin *see* Rathmullan
Ráth Mealtain *see* Rathmelton
xliv I3 **Rathmelton** *Ir.* Ráth Mealtain. Donegal, N Ireland
xliv D13 **Rathmore** Kerry, SW Ireland
xliv I2 **Rathmullan** *Ir.* Ráth Maoláin. Donegal, N Ireland
xliv L10 **Rathnew** Wicklow, E Ireland
xliv K10 **Rathvilly** Carlow, SE Ireland
Ratibor *see* Racibórz
Ratisbon/Ratisbona/Ratisbonne *see* Regensburg
Rätische Alpen *see* Rhaetian Alps
40 E17 **Rat Island** *island* Aleutian Islands, Alaska, USA
40 E17 **Rat Islands** *island group* Aleutian Islands, Alaska, USA
160 F10 **Ratlām** *prev.* Rutlam. Madhya Pradesh, C India
161 D15 **Ratnāgiri** Mahārāshtra, W India
161 K26 **Ratnapura** Sabaragamuwa Province, S Sri Lanka
118 J2 **Ratne** *Rus.* Ratno. Volyns'ka Oblast', NW Ukraine
Ratno *see* Ratne
Ratomka *see* Ratamka
39 U8 **Raton** New Mexico, SW USA
145 O7 **Ratqah, Wādī ar** *dry watercourse* W Iraq
Ratschach *see* Radeče
178 H17 **Rattaphum** Songkhla, SW Thailand
xxxix V12 **Rattlesden** Suffolk, E England, UK
28 L6 **Rattlesnake Creek** ≈ Kansas, C USA
xliii L16 **Rattray** Perth and Kinross, C Scotland, UK
xlii Q11 **Rattray Head** *headland* NE Scotland, UK
96 L13 **Rättvik** Kopparberg, C Sweden
102 K9 **Ratzeburg** Mecklenburg-Vorpommern, N Germany
102 K9 **Ratzeburger See** ◎ N Germany
8 J10 **Ratz, Mount** ▲ British Columbia, SW Canada
63 D22 **Rauch** Buenos Aires, E Argentina
43 U16 **Raudales** Chiapas, SE Mexico
Raudhatain *see* Ar Rawḑatayn
Raudnitz an der Elbe *see* Roudnice nad Labem
94 K1 **Raufarhöfn** Nordhurland Eystra, NE Iceland
96 H13 **Raufoss** Oppland, S Norway
Raukawa *see* Cook Strait
192 Q8 **Raukumara** ▲ North Island, NZ
199 J12 **Raukumara Plain** *undersea feature* N Coral Sea
192 P8 **Raukumara Range** ▲▲ North Island, NZ
97 F15 **Rauland** Telemark, S Norway
95 J19 **Rauma** *Swe.* Raumo. Turku-Pori, SW Finland
96 F10 **Rauma** ≈ S Norway
Raumo *see* Rauma
120 H8 **Rauna** Cēsis, C Latvia
xxxix Q11 **Raunds** Northamptonshire, C England, UK
174 Mm16 **Raung, Gunung** ▲ Jawa, S Indonesia
160 N11 **Raurkela** *prev.* Rourkela. Orissa, E India
97 J22 **Raus** Malmöhus, S Sweden
172 R6 **Rausu** Hokkaidō, NE Japan
172 R6 **Rausu-dake** ▲ Hokkaidō, NE Japan
95 M17 **Rautalampi** Kuopio, C Finland
95 N16 **Rautavaara** Kuopio, C Finland
118 M9 **Răutel** ≈ C Moldavia
95 O18 **Rautjärvi** Kymi, SE Finland
Rautu *see* Sosnovo
203 V11 **Ravahere** *atoll* Îles Tuamotu, C French Polynesia
109 J25 **Ravanusa** Sicilia, Italy, C Mediterranean Sea
149 S9 **Rāvar** Kermān, C Iran
153 Q11 **Ravat** Oshskaya Oblast', SW Kyrgyzstan
20 K11 **Ravena** New York, NE USA
xl K10 **Ravenglass** Cumbria, NW England, UK
108 H10 **Ravenna** Emilia-Romagna, N Italy
31 O15 **Ravenna** Nebraska, C USA
33 U11 **Ravenna** Ohio, N USA
103 I24 **Ravensburg** Baden-Württemberg, S Germany
xli W10 **Ravenscar** North Yorkshire, N England, UK
189 W4 **Ravenshoe** Queensland, NE Australia
188 K13 **Ravensthorpe** Western Australia
xli O10 **Ravenstonedale** Cumbria, NW England, UK
23 Q4 **Ravenswood** West Virginia, NE USA
155 U9 **Rāvi** ≈ India/Pakistan
114 C9 **Ravna Gora** Primorje-Gorski Kotar, NW Croatia
111 U10 **Ravne na Koroškem** *Ger.* Gutenstein. N Slovenia
145 P6 **Rāwah** W Iraq
203 T4 **Rawaki** *prev.* Phoenix Island. *atoll* Phoenix Islands, C Kiribati
155 U6 **Rāwalpindi** Punjab, NE Pakistan
112 L13 **Rawa Mazowiecka** Skierniewice, C Poland
145 T2 **Ŗawāndiz** *var.* Rawandoz, Rawāndūz. N Iraq
Rawandoz/Rawāndūz *see* Ŗawāndiz
176 Vv9 **Rawarra** ≈ Irian Jaya, E Indonesia
176 V9 **Rawas** Irian Jaya, E Indonesia
145 O4 **Rawḑah** ◎ E Syria
112 G13 **Rawicz** *Ger.* Rawitsch. Leszno, W Poland
Rawitsch *see* Rawicz
188 M11 **Rawlinna** Western Australia
35 W16 **Rawlins** Wyoming, C USA
xli S16 **Rawmarsh** Rotherham, N England, UK
65 K17 **Rawson** Chubut, SE Argentina
xli P15 **Rawtenstall** Lancashire, NW England, UK
165 R16 **Rawu** Xizang Zizhiqu, W China
159 P12 **Raxaul** Bihār, N India
30 K3 **Ray** North Dakota, N USA
174 M9 **Raya, Bukit** ▲ Borneo, C Indonesia
161 I18 **Rāyachoti** Andhra Pradesh, E India
Rāyadrug *see* Rāyagarha
161 M14 **Rāyagarha** *prev.* Rāyadrug. Orissa, E India
144 H7 **Rayak** *var.* Rayaq, Riyāq. E Lebanon
Rayaq *see* Rayak
145 T2 **Ŗāyat** E Iraq
174 J10 **Raya, Tanjung** *headland* Pulau Bangka, W Indonesia
11 R13 **Ray, Cape** *headland* Newfoundland, Newfoundland and Labrador, E Canada
126 Mm16 **Raychikhinsk** Amurskaya Oblast', SE Russian Federation
131 U5 **Rayevskiy** Respublika Bashkortostan, W Russian Federation
xxxvii W8 **Rayleigh** Essex, SE England, UK
9 Q17 **Raymond** Alberta, SW Canada
24 K6 **Raymond** Mississippi, S USA
34 F9 **Raymond** Washington, NW USA
191 T8 **Raymond Terrace** New South Wales, SE Australia
27 T17 **Raymondville** Texas, SW USA
9 U16 **Raymore** Saskatchewan, S Canada
41 Q8 **Ray Mountains** ▲▲ Alaska, USA
24 H9 **Rayne** Louisiana, S USA
43 O12 **Rayón** San Luis Potosí, C Mexico
42 G4 **Rayón** Sonora, NW Mexico
178 Hh12 **Rayong** Rayong, S Thailand
27 T5 **Ray Roberts, Lake** ◎ Texas, SW USA
20 E15 **Raystown Lake** ⊠ Pennsylvania, NE USA
147 V13 **Raysūt** SW Oman
29 R4 **Raytown** Missouri, C USA
24 I5 **Rayville** Louisiana, S USA
148 L5 **Razan** Hamadān, W Iran
145 S9 **Razāzah, Buḩayrat ar** *var.* Baḩr al Milḩ. ◎ C Iraq
116 L9 **Razboyna** ▲ E Bulgaria
Razdan *see* Hrazdan
Razdolnoye *see* Rozdol'ne
Razelm, Lacul *see* Razim, Lacul
145 U2 **Ŗazga** E Iraq
116 L8 **Razgrad** Razgradska Oblast, NE Bulgaria
Razgrad *see* Razgradska Oblast
116 K7 **Razgradska Oblast** *var.* Razgrad. ◐ *province* NE Bulgaria
119 N13 **Razim, Lacul** *prev.* Lacul Razelm. *lagoon* NW Black Sea
116 G11 **Razlog** Sofiyska Oblast, SW Bulgaria
120 K10 **Rāznas Ezers** ◎ SE Latvia
104 E6 **Raz, Pointe du** *headland* NW France
Reachlainn *see* Rathlin Island
Reachrainn *see* Lambay Island
xxxvii Q9 **Reading** Reading, S England, UK
xxxvii Q9 **Reading** ◐ *unitary authority* S England, UK
20 H15 **Reading** Pennsylvania, NE USA
50 C7 **Real, Cordillera** ▲▲ C Ecuador
64 K12 **Realicó** La Pampa, C Argentina
27 R15 **Realitos** Texas, SW USA
xliv F9 **Rea, Lough** ◎ Galway, W Ireland
110 G9 **Realp** Uri, C Switzerland
178 Ii12 **Reăng Kesei** Bătdâmbâng, W Cambodia
203 Y11 **Reao** *atoll* Îles Tuamotu, French Polynesia
xxxix O9 **Rearsby** Leicestershire, C England, UK
Reate *see* Rieti
xlii K6 **Reay** Highland, N Scotland, UK
188 L11 **Rebecca, Lake** ◎ Western Australia
Rebiana Sand Sea *see* Rabyānah, Ramlat
128 H8 **Reboly** Respublika Kareliya, NW Russian Federation
172 P1 **Rebun** Rebun-tō, NE Japan
172 P1 **Rebun-suidō** *strait* E Sea of Japan
172 P1 **Rebun-tō** *island* NE Japan
108 J12 **Recanati** Marche, C Italy
xliv D8 **Recess** Galway, W Ireland
Rechitsa *see* Rechytsa
111 Y7 **Rechnitz** Burgenland, SE Austria
121 J20 **Rechytsa** *Rus.* Rechitsa. Brestskaya Voblasts', SW Belorussia
121 O19 **Rechytsa** *Rus.* Rechitsa. Homyel'skaya Voblasts', SE Belorussia
61 Q15 **Recife** *prev.* Pernambuco. *state capital* Pernambuco, E Brazil
85 I26 **Recife, Cape** *Afr.* Kaap Recife. *headland* S South Africa
Recife, Kaap *see* Recife, Cape
180 I16 **Récifs, Îles aux** *island* Inner Islands, NE Seychelles
103 E14 **Recklinghausen** Nordrhein-Westfalen, W Germany
102 M8 **Recknitz** ≈ NE Germany
101 K23 **Recogne** Luxembourg, SE Belgium
63 C15 **Reconquista** Santa Fe, C Argentina
205 O6 **Recovery Glacier** *glacier* Antarctica
61 G15 **Recreio** Mato Grosso, W Brazil
29 X9 **Rector** Arkansas, C USA
xxxvii Y10 **Reculver** Kent, SE England, UK
112 E9 **Recz** *Ger.* Reetz Neumark. Gorzów, NW Poland
101 L24 **Redange** *var.* Redange-sur-Attert. Diekirch, W Luxembourg
Redange-sur-Attert *see* Redange
20 C13 **Redbank Creek** ≈ Pennsylvania, NE USA
11 S9 **Red Bay** Québec, E Canada
25 N2 **Red Bay** Alabama, S USA
37 N4 **Red Bluff** California, W USA
26 J8 **Red Bluff Reservoir** ◎ New Mexico/Texas, SW USA
xxxiv L16 **Redbridge** ◐ *London borough* SE England, UK
32 K16 **Red Bud** Illinois, N USA
xli T8 **Redcar** Redcar and Cleveland, N England, UK
xli T8 **Redcar and Cleveland** ◐ *unitary authority* N England, UK
32 J5 **Red Cedar River** ≈ Wisconsin, N USA
9 R17 **Redcliff** Alberta, SW Canada
85 K17 **Redcliff** Midlands, C Zimbabwe
190 L9 **Red Cliffs** Victoria, SE Australia
31 P17 **Red Cloud** Nebraska, C USA
24 L8 **Red Creek** ≈ Mississippi, S USA
9 P15 **Red Deer** Alberta, SW Canada
9 Q16 **Red Deer** ≈ Alberta, SW Canada
41 O11 **Red Devil** Alaska, USA
37 N3 **Redding** California, W USA
xxxviii C17 **Redditch** Worcestershire, W England, UK
xli O4 **Rede** ≈ N England, UK
31 P9 **Redfield** South Dakota, N USA
xliii N16 **Redford** Angus, E Scotland, UK
26 J12 **Redford** Texas, SW USA
xxxix W11 **Redgrave** Suffolk, E England, UK
47 V13 **Redhead** Trinidad, Trinidad and Tobago
190 I8 **Red Hill** South Australia
40 F10 **Red Hill** *Haw.* Pu'uUla'ula. ▲ Maui, Hawaii, USA, C Pacific Ocean
xxxvii U11 **Redhill** Surrey, SE England, UK
28 K7 **Red Hills** *hill range* Kansas, C USA
11 T12 **Red Indian Lake** ◎ Newfoundland, Newfoundland and Labrador, E Canada
xxxix Y11 **Redisham** Suffolk, E England, UK
128 J16 **Redkino** Tverskaya Oblast', W Russian Federation
10 A10 **Red Lake** Ontario, C Canada
38 I10 **Red Lake** *salt flat* Arizona, SW USA
31 S4 **Red Lake Falls** Minnesota, N USA
31 R4 **Red Lake River** ≈ Minnesota, N USA
xlii M3 **Redland** Orkney Islands, N Scotland, UK
37 U15 **Redlands** California, W USA
20 G16 **Red Lion** Pennsylvania, NE USA
35 U11 **Red Lodge** Montana, NW USA
34 H13 **Redmond** Oregon, NW USA
38 L5 **Redmond** Utah, W USA
34 H8 **Redmond** Washington, NW USA
Rednitz *see* Regnitz
31 T15 **Red Oak** Iowa, C USA
20 K12 **Red Oaks Mill** New York, NE USA
104 I7 **Redon** Ille-et-Vilaine, NW France
47 W10 **Redonda** *island* SW Antigua and Barbuda
106 G4 **Redondela** Galicia, NW Spain
106 H11 **Redondo** Évora, S Portugal
41 Q12 **Redoubt Volcano** ▲ Alaska, USA
xlii F11 **Redpoint** Highland, NW Scotland, UK
9 Y16 **Red River** ≈ Canada/USA
133 U12 **Red River** *var.* Yuan, *Chin.* Yuan Jiang, *Vtn.* Sông Hông Hà. ≈ China/Vietnam
27 W4 **Red River** ≈ S USA
24 H7 **Red River** ≈ Louisiana, S USA
32 M6 **Red River** ≈ Wisconsin, N USA
Red Rock, Lake *see* Red Rock Reservoir
31 W14 **Red Rock Reservoir** *var.* Lake Red Rock. ⊠ Iowa, C USA
xxxv E13 **Red Roses** Carmarthenshire, S Wales, UK
xxxvi B17 **Redruth** Cornwall, SW England, UK
194 J15 **Redscar Bay** *bay* S PNG
82 H7 **Red Sea** ◐ *state* NE Sudan
77 Y9 **Red Sea** *anc.* Sinus Arabicus. *sea* Africa/Asia
23 T11 **Red Springs** North Carolina, SE USA
15 Gg6 **Redstone** ≈ Northwest Territories, NW Canada
9 V17 **Redvers** Saskatchewan, S Canada
79 P13 **Red Volta** *var.* Nazinon, *Fr.* Volta Rouge. ≈ Burkina/Ghana
9 Q14 **Redwater** Alberta, SW Canada
xxxv F4 **Red Wharf Bay** *bay* N Wales, UK
xxxv L15 **Redwick** Newport, SE Wales, UK
30 M16 **Red Willow Creek** ≈ Nebraska, C USA
31 W9 **Red Wing** Minnesota, N USA
37 N9 **Redwood City** California, W USA
31 T9 **Redwood Falls** Minnesota, N USA
198 Ff7 **Reed Bank** *undersea feature* C South China Sea
33 P7 **Reed City** Michigan, N USA
30 K6 **Reeder** North Dakota, N USA
xxxix Y10 **Reedham** Norfolk, E England, UK
37 R11 **Reedley** California, W USA
35 T11 **Reedpoint** Montana, NW USA
32 K8 **Reedsburg** Wisconsin, N USA
34 E13 **Reedsport** Oregon, NW USA
195 X8 **Reef Islands** *island group* Santa Cruz Islands, E Solomon Islands
193 H16 **Reefton** West Coast, South Island, NZ
22 F8 **Reelfoot Lake** ◎ Tennessee, S USA
xliv H8 **Ree, Lough** *Ir.* Loch Rí. ◎ C Ireland
Reengus *see* Ringas
xliv E12 **Reens** Limerick, SW Ireland
xxxix Q5 **Reepham** Lincolnshire, E England, UK
xxxix W8 **Reepham** Norfolk, E England, UK
37 U4 **Reese River** ≈ Nevada, W USA
100 M8 **Reest** ≈ E Netherlands
xli Q10 **Reeth** North Yorkshire, N England, UK
Reetz Neumark *see* Recz
143 N13 **Refahiye** Erzincan, C Turkey
25 N4 **Reform** Alabama, S USA
97 K20 **Reftele** Jönköping, S Sweden
27 T14 **Refugio** Texas, SW USA
112 E8 **Rega** ≈ NW Poland
Regar *see* Tursunzoda
103 O21 **Regen** Bayern, SE Germany
103 M20 **Regen** ≈ SE Germany
103 M21 **Regensburg** *Eng.* Ratisbon, *Fr.* Ratisbonne; *hist.* Ratisbona, *anc.* Castra Regina, Reginum. Bayern, SE Germany
103 M21 **Regenstauf** Bayern, SE Germany
76 I10 **Reggane** C Algeria
100 N9 **Regge** ≈ E Netherlands
Reggio *see* Reggio nell' Emilia
Reggio Calabria *see* Reggio di Calabria
109 M23 **Reggio di Calabria** *var.* Reggio Calabria, *Gk.* Rhegion; *anc.* Regium, Rhegium. Calabria, SW Italy
Reggio Emilia *see* Reggio nell' Emilia
108 F9 **Reggio nell' Emilia** *var.* Reggio Emilia, *abbrev.* Reggio; *anc.* Regium Lepidum. Emilia-Romagna, N Italy
118 I10 **Reghin** *Ger.* Sächsisch-Reen, *Hung.* Szászrégen; *prev.* Reghinul Săsesc, *Ger.* Sächsisch-Regen. Mureş, C Romania
Reghinul Săsesc *see* Reghin
9 U16 **Regina** Saskatchewan, S Canada
9 U16 **Regina** ✕ Saskatchewan, S Canada
57 Z10 **Régina** E French Guiana
9 U16 **Regina Beach** Saskatchewan, S Canada
Reginum *see* Regensburg
Registan *see* Rīgestān

◆ Country
● Country Capital
◇ Dependent Territory
○ Dependent Territory Capital
◐ Administrative Region
✕ International Airport
▲ Mountain
▲▲ Mountain Range
⛰ Volcano
≈ River
◎ Lake
⊠ Reservoir

REGISTRO – RIVIERA BEACH

62 *L11* **Registro** São Paulo, S Brazil
Regium *see* Reggio di Calabria
Regium Lepidum *see* Reggio nell' Emilia
103 *K19* **Regnitz** ***var.*** Rednitz. ≈ SE Germany
42 *K10* **Regocijo** Durango, W Mexico
106 *H12* **Reguengos de Monsaraz** Évora, S Portugal
103 *M18* **Rehau** Bayern, E Germany
85 *D19* **Rehoboth** Hardap, C Namibia
Rehoboth/Rehovoth *see* Rehovot
23 *Z4* **Rehoboth Beach** Delaware, NE USA
144 *F10* **Rehovot** ***var.*** Rehoboth, Rehovoth. Central, C Israel
83 *J20* **Rei** *spring/well* S Kenya
Reichenau *see* Rychnov nad Kněžnou, Czech Republic
Reichenau *see* Bogatynia, Poland
103 *M17* **Reichenbach** ***var.*** Reichenbach im Vogtland. Sachsen, E Germany
Reichenbach *see* Dzierżoniów
Reichenbach im Vogtland *see* Reichenbach
Reichenberg *see* Liberec
189 *O11* **Reid** Western Australia
xlii *E10* **Reidh, Rubha** *headland* NW Scotland, UK
25 *V6* **Reidsville** Georgia, SE USA
23 *T8* **Reidsville** North Carolina, SE USA
xlii *G9* **Reiff** Highland, NW Scotland, UK
Reifnitz *see* Ribnica
xxxvii *T11* **Reigate** Surrey, SE England, UK
xli *W11* **Reighton** North Yorkshire, N England, UK
Reikjavik *see* Reykjavík
104 *I10* **Ré, Île de** *island* W France
39 *N15* **Reiley Peak** ▲ Arizona, SW USA
105 *Q4* **Reims** ***Eng.*** Rheims; ***anc.*** Durocortorum, Remi. Marne, N France
65 *G23* **Reina Adelaida, Archipiélago** *island group* S Chile
47 *O16* **Reina Beatrix** ✕ (Oranjestad) C Aruba
110 *F7* **Reinach** Aargau, W Switzerland
110 *E6* **Reinach** Basel-Land, NW Switzerland
66 *O11* **Reina Sofía** ✕ (Tenerife) Tenerife, Islas Canarias, Spain, NE Atlantic Ocean
31 *W13* **Reinbeck** Iowa, C USA
102 *J10* **Reinbek** Schleswig-Holstein, N Germany
9 *U12* **Reindeer** ≈ Saskatchewan, C Canada
9 *U11* **Reindeer Lake** ◎ Manitoba/Saskatchewan, C Canada
Reine-Charlotte, Îles de la *see* Queen Charlotte Islands
Reine-Élisabeth, Îles de la *see* Queen Elizabeth Islands
96 *F13* **Reineskarvet** ▲ S Norway
192 *H1* **Reinga, Cape** *headland* North Island, NZ
107 *N3* **Reinosa** Cantabria, N Spain
xlii *M7* **Reiss** Highland, N Scotland, UK
111 *R8* **Reisseck** ▲ S Austria
23 *W3* **Reisterstown** Maryland, NE USA
Reisui *see* Yŏsu
100 *N5* **Reitdiep** ≈ NE Netherlands
203 *V10* **Reitoru** *atoll* Îles Tuamotu, C French Polynesia
97 *M17* **Rejmyre** Östergötland, S Sweden
Reka *see* Rijeka
Reka Ili *see* Ili
97 *N16* **Rekarne** Västmanland, C Sweden
15 *Ii7* **Reliance** Northwest Territories, C Canada
35 *U16* **Reliance** Wyoming, C USA
76 *I5* **Relizane** ***var.*** Ghelîzâne, Ghilizane. NW Algeria
190 *I7* **Remarkable, Mount** ▲ South Australia
56 *E8* **Remedios** Antioquia, N Colombia
45 *Q16* **Remedios** Veraguas, W Panama
44 *D8* **Remedios, Punta** *headland* SW El Salvador
Remi *see* Reims
101 *N25* **Remich** Grevenmacher, SE Luxembourg
101 *J19* **Remicourt** Liège, E Belgium
12 *H8* **Rémigny, Lac** ◎ Québec, SE Canada
57 *Z10* **Rémire** NE French Guiana
131 *N13* **Remontnoye** Rostovskaya Oblast', SW Russian Federation
176 *V13* **Remoon** Pulau Kur, E Indonesia
101 *L20* **Remouchamps** Liège, E Belgium
105 *R15* **Remoulins** Gard, S France
181 *X16* **Rempart, Mont du** ***var.*** Mount Rempart. *hill* W Mauritius
103 *E15* **Remscheid** Nordrhein-Westfalen, W Germany
31 *S12* **Remsen** Iowa, C USA
96 *I12* **Rena** Hedmark, S Norway
96 *I11* **Rena** ≈ S Norway
Renaix *see* Ronse
120 *H7* **Rencēni** Valmiera, N Latvia
120 *D9* **Renda** Kuldīga, W Latvia
109 *N20* **Rende** Calabria, SW Italy
101 *K21* **Rendeux** Luxembourg, SE Belgium
Rendina *see* Rentína
32 *L16* **Rend Lake** ⊡ Illinois, N USA
195 *U15* **Rendova** *island* New Georgia Islands, NW Solomon Islands
102 *I8* **Rendsburg** Schleswig-Holstein, N Germany
110 *B9* **Renens** Vaud, SW Switzerland
xliii *J20* **Renfrew** Renfrewshire, W Scotland, UK
12 *K12* **Renfrew** Ontario, SE Canada
xliii *H20* **Renfrewshire** ⬖ *unitary authority* W Scotland, UK
174 *H8* **Rengat** Sumatera, W Indonesia
159 *W12* **Rengma Hills** ⛰ NE India
64 *H12* **Rengo** Libertador, C Chile
118 *M12* **Reni** Odes'ka Oblast', SW Ukraine
82 *F11* **Renk** Upper Nile, E Sudan
95 *L19* **Renko** Häme, SW Finland
100 *L12* **Renkum** Gelderland, SE Netherlands
190 *K9* **Renmark** South Australia
195 *W17* **Rennell** ***var.*** Mu Nggava. *island* S Solomon Islands
189 *Q4* **Renner Springs Roadhouse** Northern Territory, N Australia
104 *I6* **Rennes** ***Bret.*** Roazon; ***anc.*** Condate. Ille-et-Vilaine, NW France
205 *S16* **Rennick Glacier** *glacier* Antarctica
9 *Y16* **Rennie** Manitoba, S Canada
xli *R3* **Rennington** Northumberland, N England, UK
37 *Q5* **Reno** Nevada, W USA
108 *H10* **Reno** ≈ N Italy
37 *Q5* **Reno-Cannon** ✕ Nevada, W USA
85 *F24* **Renoster** ≈ SW South Africa
13 *T5* **Renouard, Lac** ◎ Québec, SE Canada
20 *F13* **Renovo** Pennsylvania, NE USA
167 *O3* **Renqiu** Hebei, E China
166 *I9* **Renshou** Sichuan, C China
33 *N12* **Rensselaer** Indiana, N USA
20 *L11* **Rensselaer** New York, NE USA
107 *Q2* **Rentería** ***Basq.*** Errenteria. País Vasco, N Spain
117 *E17* **Rentína** ***var.*** Rendina. Thessalía, C Greece
xliii *I19* **Renton** West Dunbartonshire, W Scotland, UK
31 *T9* **Renville** Minnesota, N USA
xli *N7* **Renwick** Cumbria, NW England, UK
79 *O13* **Réo** W Burkina
13 *O12* **Repentigny** Québec, SE Canada
152 *K13* **Repetek** Lebapskiy Velayat, E Turkmenistan
95 *J16* **Replot** ***Fin.*** Raippaluoto. *island* W Finland
Reppen *see* Rzepin
Reps *see* Rupea
29 *T7* **Republic** Missouri, C USA
34 *K7* **Republic** Washington, NW USA
29 *N3* **Republican River** ≈ Kansas/Nebraska, C USA
15 *Ll4* **Repulse Bay** Northwest Territories, N Canada
58 *F9* **Requena** Loreto, NE Peru
107 *R10* **Requena** País Valenciano, E Spain
105 *O14* **Réquista** Aveyron, S France
142 *M12* **Reşadiye** Tokat, N Turkey
Reschenpass *see* Resia, Passo di
Reschitza *see* Reşiţa
115 *N20* **Resen** ***Turk.*** Resne. SW FYR Macedonia
62 *J11* **Reserva** Paraná, S Brazil
9 *V15* **Reserve** Saskatchewan, S Canada
39 *P13* **Reserve** New Mexico, SW USA
Reshetilovka *see* Reshetylivka
119 *S6* **Reshetylivka** ***Rus.*** Reshetilovka. Poltavs'ka Oblast', NE Ukraine
Resht *see* Rasht
108 *F5* **Resia, Passo di** ***Ger.*** Reschenpass. *pass* Austria/Italy
Resicabánya *see* Reşiţa
64 *N7* **Resistencia** Chaco, NE Argentina
118 *F12* **Reşiţa** ***Ger.*** Reschitza, ***Hung.*** Resicabánya. Caraş-Severin, W Romania
Resne *see* Resen
207 *N9* **Resolute** Cornwallis Island, Northwest Territories, N Canada
Resolution *see* Fort Resolution
16 *P4* **Resolution Island** *island* Northwest Territories, NE Canada
193 *A23* **Resolution Island** *island* SW NZ
xxxv *H14* **Resolven** Neath Port Talbot, S Wales, UK
13 *W7* **Restigouche** Québec, SE Canada
9 *W17* **Reston** Manitoba, S Canada
12 *H11* **Restoule Lake** ◎ Ontario, S Canada
56 *F10* **Restrepo** Meta, C Colombia
44 *B6* **Retalhuleu** Retalhuleu, SW Guatemala
44 *A1* **Retalhuleu** ***off.*** Departamento de Retalhuleu. ⬖ *department* SW Guatemala
xxxix *O5* **Retford** Nottinghamshire, C England, UK
105 *Q3* **Rethel** Ardennes, N France
Rethimno/Réthimnon *see* Réthymno
117 *I25* **Réthymno** ***var.*** Rethimno; ***prev.*** Réthimnon. Kríti, Greece, E Mediterranean Sea
Retiche, Alpi *see* Rhaetian Alps
101 *J16* **Retie** Antwerpen, N Belgium
113 *J21* **Rétság** Nógrád, N Hungary
xxxvii *W8* **Rettendon** Essex, SE England, UK
111 *W2* **Retz** Niederösterreich, NE Austria
181 *N15* **Réunion** ***off.*** La Réunion. ◇ *French overseas department* W Indian Ocean
132 *L17* **Réunion** *island* W Indian Ocean
107 *U6* **Reus** Cataluña, E Spain
101 *J15* **Reusel** Noord-Brabant, S Netherlands
110 *F7* **Reuss** ≈ NW Switzerland
Reuţel *see* Ciuhuru
103 *H22* **Reutlingen** Baden-Württemberg, S Germany
110 *L7* **Reutte** Tirol, W Austria
101 *M16* **Reuver** Limburg, SE Netherlands
30 *K7* **Reva** South Dakota, N USA
Reval/Revel' *see* Tallinn
128 *J4* **Revda** Murmanskaya Oblast', NW Russian Federation
125 *Ee11* **Revda** Sverdlovskaya Oblast', C Russian Federation
105 *N16* **Revel** Haute-Garonne, S France
9 *O16* **Revelstoke** British Columbia, SW Canada
45 *N13* **Reventazón, Río** ≈ E Costa Rica
108 *G9* **Revere** Lombardia, N Italy
xxxix *R6* **Revesby** Lincolnshire, E England, UK
41 *Y14* **Revillagigedo Island** *island* Alexander Archipelago, Alaska, USA
105 *R3* **Revin** Ardennes, N France
94 *O3* **Revnosa** *headland* C Svalbard
Revolyutsii, Pik *see* Revolyutsiya, Qullai
153 *T13* **Revolyutsiya, Qullai** ***Rus.*** Pik Revolyutsii. ▲ SE Tajikistan
113 *L19* **Revúca** ***Ger.*** Grossrauschenbach, ***Hung.*** Nagyrőce. Východné Slovensko, E Slovakia
160 *K9* **Rewa** Madhya Pradesh, C India
158 *I11* **Rewāri** Haryāna, N India
35 *R14* **Rexburg** Idaho, NW USA
80 *G13* **Rey Bouba** Nord, NE Cameroon
94 *L3* **Reydharfjördhur** Austurland, E Iceland
59 *K16* **Reyes** Beni, NW Bolivia
36 *L8* **Reyes, Point** *headland* California, W USA
56 *B12* **Reyes, Punta** *headland* SW Colombia
142 *L17* **Reyhanlı** Hatay, S Turkey
45 *U16* **Rey, Isla del** *island* Archipiélago de las Perlas, SE Panama
94 *H2* **Reykhólar** Vestfirdhir, W Iceland
94 *K2* **Reykjahlídh** Nordhurland Eystra, NE Iceland
94 *I4* **Reykjanes** ⬖ *region* SW Iceland
207 *O16* **Reykjanes Basin** ***var.*** Irminger Basin. *undersea feature* N Atlantic Ocean
207 *N17* **Reykjanes Ridge** *undersea feature* N Atlantic Ocean
94 *H4* **Reykjavík** ***var.*** Reikjavik. ● (Iceland) Höfudhborgarsvaedhi, W Iceland
20 *D13* **Reynoldsville** Pennsylvania, NE USA
43 *P8* **Reynosa** Tamaulipas, C Mexico
Reẓā'īyeh *see* Orūmīyeh
Reẓā'īyeh, Daryācheh-ye *see* Orūmīyeh, Daryācheh-ye
104 *I8* **Rezé** Loire-Atlantique, NW France
120 *K10* **Rēzekne** ***Ger.*** Rositten; ***prev.*** Rus. Rezhitsa. Rēzekne, SE Latvia
Rezhitsa *see* Rēzekne
119 *N9* **Rezina** NE Moldavia
116 *N11* **Rezovo** ***Turk.*** Rezve. Burgaska Oblast, SE Bulgaria
116 *N11* **Rezovska Reka** ***Turk.*** Rezve Deresi. ≈ Bulgaria/Turkey *see also* Rezve Deresi
Rezve *see* Rezovo
116 *N11* **Rezve Deresi** ***Bul.*** Rezovska Reka. ≈ Bulgaria/Turkey *see also* Rezovska Reka
Rhadames *see* Ghadāmis
Rhaedestus *see* Tekirdağ
110 *J10* **Rhaetian Alps** ***Fr.*** Alpes Rhétiques, ***Ger.*** Rätische Alpen, ***It.*** Alpi Retiche. ⛰ C Europe
xxxv *H11* **Rhandirmwyn** Carmarthenshire, S Wales, UK
110 *I8* **Rhätikon** ⛰ C Europe
xxxv *I10* **Rhayader** Powys, C Wales, UK
103 *G14* **Rheda-Wiedenbrück** Nordrhein-Westfalen, W Germany
100 *M12* **Rheden** Gelderland, E Netherlands
Rhegion/Rhegium *see* Reggio di Calabria
Rheims *see* Reims
xxxv *G10* **Rheidol** ≈ W Wales, UK
Rhein *see* Rhine
103 *E17* **Rheinbach** Nordrhein-Westfalen, W Germany
102 *F13* **Rheine** ***var.*** Rheine in Westfalen. Nordrhein-Westfalen, NW Germany
Rheine in Westfalen *see* Rheine
Rheinfeld *see* Rheinfelden
103 *F24* **Rheinfelden** Baden-Württemberg, S Germany
110 *E6* **Rheinfelden** ***var.*** Rheinfeld. Aargau, N Switzerland
103 *E17* **Rheinisches Schiefergebirge** ***var.*** Rhine State Uplands, ***Eng.*** Rhenish Slate Mountains. ⛰ W Germany
103 *D18* **Rheinland-Pfalz** ***Eng.*** Rhineland-Palatinate, ***Fr.*** Rhénanie-Palatinat. ⬖ *state* W Germany
103 *G18* **Rhein/Main** ✕ (Frankfurt am Main) Hessen, W Germany
xliii *E16* **Rhemore** Highland, NW Scotland, UK
Rhénanie du Nord-Westphalie *see* Nordrhein-Westfalen
Rhénanie-Palatinat *see* Rheinland-Pfalz
100 *K12* **Rhenen** Utrecht, C Netherlands
Rhenish Slate Mountains *see* Rheinisches Schiefergebirge
Rhétiques, Alpes *see* Rhaetian Alps
xxxv *J5* **Rhewl** Denbighshire, N Wales, UK
xlii *I8* **Rhian** Highland, NW Scotland, UK
xlii *H7* **Rhiconich** Highland, NW Scotland, UK
102 *N10* **Rhin** ≈ NE Germany
Rhin *see* Rhine
86 *F10* **Rhine** ***Dut.*** Rijn, ***Fr.*** Rhin, ***Ger.*** Rhein. ≈ W Europe
32 *L5* **Rhinelander** Wisconsin, N USA
Rhineland-Palatinate *see* Rheinland-Pfalz
Rhine State Uplands *see* Rheinisches Schiefergebirge
102 *N11* **Rhinkanal** *canal* NE Germany
83 *F17* **Rhino Camp** NW Uganda
xxxv *G7* **Rhinog Fawr** ▲ NW Wales, UK
76 *D7* **Rhir, Cap** *headland* W Morocco
xxxv *E7* **Rhiw** Gwynedd, NW Wales, UK
108 *D7* **Rho** Lombardia, N Italy
xliv *I9* **Rhode** Offaly, E Ireland
21 *N12* **Rhode Island** ***off.*** State of Rhode Island and Providence Plantations; also known as Little Rhody, Ocean State. ⬖ *state* NE USA
21 *O13* **Rhode Island** *island* Rhode Island, NE USA
21 *O13* **Rhode Island Sound** *sound* Maine/Rhode Island, NE USA
Rhodes *see* Ródos
Rhode-Saint-Genèse *see* Sint-Genesius-Rode
86 *L14* **Rhodes Basin** *undersea feature* E Mediterranean Sea
Rhodesia *see* Zimbabwe
116 *I12* **Rhodope Mountains** ***var.*** Rodhópi Óri, ***Bul.*** Rhodope Planina, Rodopi, ***Gk.*** Orosirá Rodhópis, ***Turk.*** Dospad Dagh. ⛰ Bulgaria/Greece
Rhodope Planina *see* Rhodope Mountains
Rhodos *see* Ródos
103 *I18* **Rhön** ⛰ C Germany
99 *J21* **Rhondda** S Wales, UK
xxxv *I14* **Rhondda Cynon Taff** ⬖ *unitary authority* S Wales, UK
105 *Q10* **Rhône** ⬖ *department* E France
88 *C12* **Rhône** ≈ France/Switzerland
105 *R12* **Rhône-Alpes** ⬖ *region* E France
123 *J6* **Rhône Fan** *undersea feature* W Mediterranean Sea
100 *G13* **Rhoon** Zuid-Holland, SW Netherlands
xxxv *J16* **Rhoose** The Vale of Glamorgan, S Wales, UK
xxxv *F12* **Rhos** Carmarthenshire, S Wales, UK
xxxv *E4* **Rhoscolyn** Isle of Anglesey, NW Wales, UK
xxxv *C14* **Rhoscrowther** Pembrokeshire, SW Wales, UK
xxxv *K6* **Rhosllanerchrugog** Wrexham, NE Wales, UK
xxxv *E4* **Rhosneigr** Isle of Anglesey, NW Wales, UK
xxxv *F15* **Rhossili** Swansea, S Wales, UK
xxxv *F5* **Rhostryfan** Gwynedd, NW Wales, UK
xliii *G20* **Rhubodach** Argyll and Bute, W Scotland, UK
xxxv *I4* **Rhuddlan** Denbighshire, N Wales, UK
xliii *D14* **Rhum** ***var.*** Rum. *island* W Scotland, UK
xliii *F21* **Rhunahaorine** Argyll and Bute, W Scotland, UK
Rhuthun *see* Ruthin
xxxv *J7* **Rhydycroesau** Powys, C Wales, UK
xxxv *I4* **Rhyl** Denbighshire, NE Wales, UK
xxxv *J13* **Rhymney** Caerphilly, S Wales, UK
xlii *N13* **Rhynie** Aberdeenshire, NE Scotland, UK
61 *K18* **Rialma** Goiás, S Brazil
106 *L3* **Riaño** Castilla-León, N Spain
107 *O9* **Riansáres** ≈ C Spain
158 *H6* **Riāsi** Jammu and Kashmir, NW India
174 *Gg7* **Riau** ***off.*** Propinsi Riau. ⬖ *province* W Indonesia
Riau Archipelago *see* Riau, Kepulauan
174 *I8* **Riau, Kepulauan** ***var.*** Riau Archipelago, ***Dut.*** Riouw-Archipel. *island group* W Indonesia
107 *O6* **Riaza** Castilla-León, N Spain
107 *N6* **Riaza** ≈ N Spain
83 *K17* **Riba** *spring/well* NE Kenya
106 *H4* **Ribadavia** Galicia, NW Spain
106 *J2* **Ribadeo** Galicia, NW Spain
106 *L2* **Ribadesella** Asturias, N Spain
106 *G10* **Ribatejo** *former province* C Portugal
149 *Q8* **Ribaṭ-e Rīzāb** Yazd, C Iran
85 *P15* **Ribáuè** Nampula, N Mozambique
xli *O14* **Ribble** ≈ NW England, UK
xli *O11* **Ribble Head** North Yorkshire, N England, UK
xli *O14* **Ribchester** Lancashire, NW England, UK
97 *F23* **Ribe** Ribe, W Denmark
97 *F23* **Ribe** ***off.*** Ribe Amt, ***var.*** Ripen. ⬖ *county* W Denmark
106 *G3* **Ribeira** Galicia, NW Spain
66 *O5* **Ribeira Brava** Madeira, Portugal, NE Atlantic Ocean
66 *P3* **Ribeira Grande** São Miguel, Azores, Portugal, NE Atlantic Ocean
62 *L8* **Ribeirão Preto** São Paulo, S Brazil
62 *L11* **Ribeira, Rio** ≈ S Brazil
109 *I24* **Ribera** Sicilia, Italy, C Mediterranean Sea
59 *L14* **Riberalta** Beni, N Bolivia
107 *W4* **Ribes de Freser** Cataluña, NE Spain
32 *L6* **Rib Mountain** ▲ Wisconsin, N USA
111 *U12* **Ribnica** ***Ger.*** Reifnitz. S Slovenia
119 *N9* **Rîbniţa** ***var.*** Râbniţa, ***Rus.*** Rybnitsa. NE Moldavia
102 *M8* **Ribnitz-Damgarten** Mecklenburg-Vorpommern, NE Germany
113 *D16* **Říčany** ***Ger.*** Ritschan. Střední Čechy, W Czech Republic
xli *U13* **Riccall** North Yorkshire, N England, UK
31 *U7* **Rice** Minnesota, N USA
32 *J5* **Rice Lake** Wisconsin, N USA
12 *I15* **Rice Lake** ◎ Ontario, SE Canada
12 *E8* **Rice Lake** ◎ Ontario, S Canada
25 *V3* **Richard B.Russell Lake** ⊡ Georgia, SE USA
27 *U6* **Richardson** Texas, SW USA
9 *R11* **Richardson** ≈ Alberta, C Canada
8 *I3* **Richardson Mountains** ⛰ Yukon Territory, NW Canada
193 *C21* **Richardson Mountains** ⛰ South Island, NZ
44 *F3* **Richardson Peak** ▲ SE Belize
78 *G10* **Richard Toll** N Senegal
30 *L5* **Richardton** North Dakota, N USA
12 *F13* **Rich, Cape** *headland* Ontario, S Canada
104 *L8* **Richelieu** Indre-et-Loire, C France
35 *P15* **Richfield** Idaho, NW USA
38 *K5* **Richfield** Utah, W USA
20 *J10* **Richfield Springs** New York, NE USA
20 *M6* **Richford** Vermont, NE USA
29 *R6* **Rich Hill** Missouri, C USA
xliv *K5* **Richhill** Armagh, S Northern Ireland, UK
11 *P14* **Richibucto** New Brunswick, SE Canada
110 *G8* **Richisau** Glarus, NE Switzerland
25 *S6* **Richland** Georgia, SE USA
29 *U6* **Richland** Missouri, C USA
27 *U8* **Richland** Texas, SW USA
34 *K10* **Richland** Washington, NW USA
32 *K8* **Richland Center** Wisconsin, N USA
23 *W11* **Richlands** North Carolina, SE USA
23 *Q7* **Richlands** Virginia, NE USA
27 *R9* **Richland Springs** Texas, SW USA
xli *R10* **Richmond** North Yorkshire, N England, UK
191 *S8* **Richmond** New South Wales, SE Australia
8 *L17* **Richmond** British Columbia, SW Canada
12 *L13* **Richmond** Ontario, SE Canada
13 *Q12* **Richmond** Québec, SE Canada
193 *I14* **Richmond** Tasman, South Island, NZ
37 *N8* **Richmond** California, W USA
33 *Q14* **Richmond** Indiana, N USA
22 *M6* **Richmond** Kentucky, S USA
29 *S4* **Richmond** Missouri, C USA
27 *V11* **Richmond** Texas, SW USA
38 *L1* **Richmond** Utah, W USA
23 *W6* **Richmond** *state capital* Virginia, NE USA
12 *H15* **Richmond Hill** Ontario, S Canada
193 *J15* **Richmond Range** ⛰ South Island, NZ
xxxvi *A9* **Richmond upon Thames** Richmond upon Thames, SE England, UK
xxxiv *K16* **Richmond upon Thames** ***var.*** Richmond-upon-Thames. ⬖ *London borough* SE England, UK
29 *S12* **Rich Mountain** ▲ Arkansas, C USA
33 *S13* **Richwood** Ohio, N USA
23 *R5* **Richwood** West Virginia, NE USA
xliii *O14* **Rickarton** Aberdeenshire, NE Scotland, UK
xxxvii *S8* **Rickmansworth** Hertfordshire, SE England, UK
106 *K5* **Ricobayo, Embalse de** ⊡ NW Spain
Ricomagus *see* Riom
Ridā' *see* Radā'
100 *H13* **Ridderkerk** Zuid-Holland, SW Netherlands
35 *N16* **Riddle** Idaho, NW USA
34 *F14* **Riddle** Oregon, NW USA
12 *L13* **Rideau** ≈ Ontario, SE Canada
37 *T12* **Ridgecrest** California, W USA
20 *L13* **Ridgefield** Connecticut, NE USA
24 *K5* **Ridgeland** Mississippi, S USA
23 *R15* **Ridgeland** South Carolina, SE USA
22 *F8* **Ridgely** Tennessee, S USA
12 *D17* **Ridgetown** Ontario, S Canada
Ridgeway *see* Ridgway
23 *R12* **Ridgeway** South Carolina, SE USA
xxxvii *W6* **Ridgewell** Essex, SE England, UK
xxxvii *U12* **Ridgewood** East Sussex, SE England, UK
xxxvii *S6* **Ridgmont** Bedfordshire, C England, UK
20 *D13* **Ridgway** ***var.*** Ridgeway. Pennsylvania, NE USA
xli *P6* **Riding Mill** Northumberland, N England, UK
9 *W16* **Riding Mountain** ⛰ Manitoba, S Canada
xli *P5* **Ridsdale** Northumberland, N England, UK
Ried *see* Ried im Innkreis
111 *R4* **Ried im Innkreis** ***var.*** Ried. Oberösterreich, NW Austria
111 *X8* **Riegersburg** Steiermark, SE Austria
110 *E6* **Riehen** Basel-Stadt, NW Switzerland
101 *K18* **Riemst** Limburg, NE Belgium
94 *J9* **Rieppe** ▲ N Norway
103 *O15* **Riesa** Sachsen, E Germany
65 *H24* **Riesco, Isla** *island* S Chile
109 *K25* **Riesi** Sicilia, Italy, C Mediterranean Sea
85 *F25* **Riet** ≈ SW South Africa
85 *I23* **Riet** ≈ SW South Africa
120 *D11* **Rietavas** Plungė, W Lithuania
85 *F19* **Rietfontein** Omaheke, E Namibia
109 *I14* **Rieti** ***anc.*** Reate. Lazio, C Italy
86 *D14* **Rif** ***var.*** Er Rif, Er Riff, Riff. ⛰ N Morocco
Riff *see* Rif
39 *Q4* **Rifle** Colorado, C USA
33 *R7* **Rifle River** ≈ Michigan, N USA
83 *H18* **Rift Valley** ⬖ *province* Kenya
Rift Valley *see* Great Rift Valley
120 *F9* **Rīga** ***Eng.*** Riga. ● (Latvia) Rīga, C Latvia
Rigaer Bucht *see* Riga, Gulf of
120 *F6* **Riga, Gulf of** ***Est.*** Liivi Laht, ***Ger.*** Rigaer Bucht, ***Latv.*** Rīgas Jūras Līcis, ***Rus.*** Rizhskiy Zaliv; prev. ***Est.*** Riia Laht. *gulf* Estonia/Latvia
149 *U12* **Rīgān** Kermān, SE Iran
Rīgas Jūras Līcis *see* Riga, Gulf of
13 *N12* **Rigaud** ≈ Ontario/Québec, SE Canada
35 *R14* **Rigby** Idaho, NW USA
154 *M10* **Rīgestān** ***var.*** Registan. *desert region* S Afghanistan
xliii *K20* **Riggend** North Lanarkshire, C Scotland, UK
34 *M11* **Riggins** Idaho, NW USA
11 *R8* **Rigolet** Newfoundland and Labrador, NE Canada
80 *G9* **Rig-Rig** Kanem, W Chad
120 *F4* **Riguldi** Läänemaa, W Estonia
Riia Laht *see* Riga, Gulf of
95 *L19* **Riihimäki** Häme, S Finland
205 *O2* **Riiser-Larsen Ice Shelf** *ice shelf* Antarctica
205 *U2* **Riiser-Larsen Peninsula** *peninsula* Antarctica
67 *P22* **Riiser-Larsen Sea** *sea* Antarctica
42 *D2* **Riíto** Sonora, NW Mexico
114 *B9* **Rijeka** ***Ger.*** Sankt Veit am Flaum, ***It.*** Fiume, ***Slvn.*** Reka; ***anc.*** Tarsatica. Primorje-Gorski Kotar, NW Croatia
101 *I14* **Rijen** Noord-Brabant, S Netherlands
101 *H15* **Rijkevorsel** Antwerpen, N Belgium
Rijn *see* Rhine
100 *G11* **Rijnsburg** Zuid-Holland, W Netherlands
Rijssel *see* Lille
100 *N10* **Rijssen** Overijssel, E Netherlands
100 *G12* **Rijswijk** ***Eng.*** Ryswick. Zuid-Holland, W Netherlands
94 *I10* **Riksgränsen** Norrbotten, N Sweden
172 *Q6* **Rikubetsu** Hokkaidō, NE Japan
171 *Mm12* **Rikuzen-Takata** Iwate, Honshū, C Japan
29 *O4* **Riley** Kansas, C USA
101 *I17* **Rillaar** Vlaams Brabant, C Belgium
xli *V11* **Rillington** North Yorkshire, N England, UK
Rí, Loch *see* Ree, Lough
116 *G11* **Rilska Reka** ≈ W Bulgaria
79 *T12* **Rima** ≈ N Nigeria
147 *N7* **Rimah, Wādī ar** ***var.*** Wādī ar Rummah. *dry watercourse* C Saudi Arabia
Rimaszombat *see* Rimavská Sobota
203 *R12* **Rimatara** *island* Îles Australes, SW French Polynesia
113 *L20* **Rimavská Sobota** ***Ger.*** Gross-Steffelsdorf, ***Hung.*** Rimaszombat. Stredné Slovensko, SE Slovakia
9 *Q15* **Rimbey** Alberta, SW Canada
97 *P15* **Rimbo** Stockholm, C Sweden
97 *M18* **Rimforsa** Östergötland, S Sweden
108 *I11* **Rimini** ***anc.*** Ariminum. Emilia-Romagna, N Italy
Rîmnicu-Sărat *see* Râmnicu Sărat
Rîmnicu Vîlcea *see* Râmnicu Vâlcea
155 *Y3* **Rimo Muztāgh** ⛰ India/Pakistan
13 *U7* **Rimouski** Québec, SE Canada
xlii *J8* **Rimsdale, Loch** ◎ N Scotland, UK
164 *M16* **Rinbung** Xizang Zizhiqu, W China
168 *I5* **Rinchinlhümbe** Hövsgöl, N Mongolia
64 *I5* **Rincón, Cerro** ▲ N Chile
106 *M15* **Rincón de la Victoria** Andalucía, S Spain
Rincón del Bonete, Lago Artificial de *see* Río Negro, Embalse del
107 *Q4* **Rincón de Soto** La Rioja, N Spain
96 *G8* **Rindal** Møre og Romsdal, S Norway
117 *J20* **Ríneia** *island* Kykládes, Greece, Aegean Sea
158 *H11* **Rīngas** ***prev.*** Reengus, Rīngus. Rājasthān, N India
xliv *G14* **Ringaskiddy** Cork, S Ireland
97 *H24* **Ringe** Fyn, C Denmark
96 *H11* **Ringebu** Oppland, S Norway
Ringen *see* Rõngu
xliii *J25* **Ringford** Dumfries and Galloway, SW Scotland, UK
195 *U14* **Ringgi** Kolombangara Island, NW Solomon Islands
25 *R1* **Ringgold** Georgia, SE USA
24 *G5* **Ringgold** Louisiana, S USA
27 *S5* **Ringgold** Texas, SW USA
97 *E22* **Ringkøbing** Ringkøbing, W Denmark
97 *E21* **Ringkøbing** ***off.*** Ringkøbing Amt. ⬖ *county* W Denmark
97 *E22* **Ringkøbing Fjord** *fjord* W Denmark
35 *S10* **Ringling** Montana, NW USA
29 *N13* **Ringling** Oklahoma, C USA
xxxvii *U13* **Ringmer** East Sussex, SE England, UK
96 *H13* **Ringsaker** Hedmark, S Norway
xliv *K3* **Ringsend** Coleraine, N Northern Ireland, UK
xxxix *U7* **Ringstead** Norfolk, E England, UK
97 *I23* **Ringsted** Vestsjælland, E Denmark
Rīngus *see* Rīngas
94 *I9* **Ringvassøy** *island* N Norway
xxxvii *O13* **Ringwood** Dorset, S England, UK
20 *K13* **Ringwood** New Jersey, NE USA
Rinn Duáin *see* Hook Head
xlii *M5* **Rinnigill** Orkney Islands, N Scotland, UK
102 *H13* **Rinteln** Niedersachsen, NW Germany
Rio *see* Rio de Janeiro
117 *E18* **Río** Dytikí Ellás, S Greece
58 *C7* **Riobamba** Chimborazo, C Ecuador
62 *P9* **Rio Bonito** Rio de Janeiro, SE Brazil
61 *C16* **Rio Branco** *state capital* Acre, W Brazil
63 *H18* **Río Branco** Cerro Largo, NE Uruguay
Rio Branco, Território de *see* Roraima
43 *P8* **Río Bravo** Tamaulipas, C Mexico
65 *G16* **Río Bueno** Los Lagos, C Chile
57 *P5* **Río Caribe** Sucre, NE Venezuela
56 *M5* **Río Chico** Miranda, N Venezuela
65 *H18* **Río Cisnes** Aisén, S Chile
62 *L9* **Rio Claro** São Paulo, S Brazil
47 *V14* **Rio Claro** Trinidad, Trinidad and Tobago
56 *J5* **Río Claro** Lara, N Venezuela
65 *K15* **Rio Colorado** Río Negro, E Argentina
64 *K11* **Río Cuarto** Córdoba, C Argentina
62 *P10* **Rio de Janeiro** ***var.*** Rio. *state capital* Rio de Janeiro, SE Brazil
62 *P9* **Rio de Janeiro** ***off.*** Estado do Rio de Janeiro. ⬖ *state* SE Brazil
45 *R17* **Río de Jesús** Veraguas, S Panama
36 *K3* **Rio Dell** California, W USA
62 *K13* **Rio do Sul** Santa Catarina, S Brazil
65 *I23* **Río Gallegos** ***var.*** Gallegos, Puerto Gallegos. Santa Cruz, S Argentina
63 *I18* **Rio Grande** ***var.*** São Pedro do Rio Grande do Sul. Rio Grande do Sul, S Brazil
26 *I9* **Rio Grande** ≈ Texas, SW USA
65 *J24* **Río Grande** Tierra del Fuego, S Argentina
42 *L10* **Río Grande** Zacatecas, C Mexico
44 *J9* **Río Grande** León, NW Nicaragua
47 *V5* **Río Grande** E Puerto Rico
27 *R17* **Rio Grande City** Texas, SW USA
61 *P14* **Rio Grande do Norte** ***off.*** Estado do Rio Grande do Norte. ⬖ *state* E Brazil
63 *G15* **Rio Grande do Sul** ***off.*** Estado do Rio Grande do Sul. ⬖ *state* S Brazil
67 *M17* **Rio Grande Fracture Zone** *tectonic feature* C Atlantic Ocean
67 *J18* **Rio Grande Gap** *undersea feature* S Atlantic Ocean
Rio Grande Plateau *see* Rio Grande Rise
67 *J18* **Rio Grande Rise** ***var.*** Rio Grande Plateau. *undersea feature* SW Atlantic Ocean
56 *G4* **Ríohacha** La Guajira, N Colombia
45 *S16* **Río Hato** Coclé, C Panama
27 *T17* **Rio Hondo** Texas, SW USA
58 *D10* **Rioja** San Martín, N Peru
43 *Y11* **Río Lagartos** Yucatán, SE Mexico
105 *P11* **Riom** ***anc.*** Ricomagus. Puy-de-Dôme, C France
106 *F10* **Rio Maior** Santarém, C Portugal
105 *O12* **Riom-ès-Montagnes** Cantal, C France
62 *J12* **Rio Negro** Paraná, S Brazil
65 *I15* **Río Negro** ***off.*** Provincia de Río Negro. ⬖ *province* C Argentina
63 *D18* **Río Negro** ⬖ *department* W Uruguay
49 *V12* **Río Negro, Embalse del** ***var.*** Lago Artificial de Rincón del Bonete. ⊡ C Uruguay
109 *M17* **Rionero in Vulture** Basilicata, S Italy
143 *S9* **Rioni** ≈ W Georgia
107 *P12* **Riópar** Castilla-La Mancha, C Spain
63 *H16* **Rio Pardo** Rio Grande do Sul, S Brazil
39 *R11* **Rio Rancho Estates** New Mexico, SW USA
44 *L11* **Río San Juan** ⬖ *department* S Nicaragua
56 *E9* **Ríosucio** Caldas, W Colombia
56 *C7* **Ríosucio** Chocó, NW Colombia
64 *K10* **Río Tercero** Córdoba, C Argentina
56 *J5* **Río Tocuyo** Lara, N Venezuela
Riouw-Archipel *see* Riau, Kepulauan
61 *J19* **Rio Verde** Goiás, C Brazil
43 *O12* **Río Verde** ***var.*** Rioverde. San Luis Potosí, C Mexico
37 *O8* **Rio Vista** California, W USA
114 *M11* **Ripanj** Serbia, N Yugoslavia
108 *J13* **Ripatransone** Marche, C Italy
Ripen *see* Ribe
xxxviii *M7* **Ripley** Derbyshire, C England, UK
xli *R12* **Ripley** North Yorkshire, N England, UK
xxxvii *S10* **Ripley** Surrey, SE England, UK
24 *M2* **Ripley** Mississippi, S USA
33 *R15* **Ripley** Ohio, N USA
22 *F9* **Ripley** Tennessee, S USA
23 *Q4* **Ripley** West Virginia, NE USA
107 *W4* **Ripoll** Cataluña, NE Spain
xli *R12* **Ripon** North Yorkshire, N England, UK
32 *M7* **Ripon** Wisconsin, N USA
109 *L24* **Riposto** Sicilia, Italy, C Mediterranean Sea
101 *L14* **Rips** Noord-Brabant, SE Netherlands
56 *D9* **Risaralda** ***off.*** Departamento de Risaralda. ⬖ *province* C Colombia
xxxv *K14* **Risca** Caerphilly, S Wales, UK
118 *L8* **Rîşcani** ***var.*** Râşcani, ***Rus.*** Ryshkany. NW Moldavia
158 *J9* **Rishikesh** Uttar Pradesh, N India
172 *P2* **Rishiri-suidō** *strait* E Sea of Japan
172 *Oo2* **Rishiri-tō** ***var.*** Risiri Tô. *island* NE Japan
172 *P2* **Rishiri-yama** ⩓ Rishiri-tō, NE Japan
xli *O14* **Rishton** Lancashire, NW England, UK
27 *R7* **Rising Star** Texas, SW USA
33 *Q15* **Rising Sun** Indiana, N USA
Risiri Tô *see* Rishiri-tō
104 *L4* **Risle** ≈ N France
Rîşno *see* Râşnov
29 *V13* **Rison** Arkansas, C USA
97 *G17* **Risør** Aust-Agder, S Norway
94 *H10* **Risøyhamn** Nordland, C Norway
103 *I23* **Riss** ≈ S Germany
120 *G4* **Risti** ***Ger.*** Kreuz. Läänemaa, W Estonia
13 *V8* **Ristigouche** ≈ Québec, SE Canada
95 *N18* **Ristiina** Mikkeli, SE Finland
95 *N14* **Ristijärvi** Oulu, C Finland
196 *C14* **Ritidian Point** *headland* N Guam
Ritschan *see* Říčany
37 *R9* **Ritter, Mount** ▲ California, W USA
33 *T12* **Rittman** Ohio, N USA
34 *L9* **Ritzville** Washington, NW USA
108 *F7* **Riva** ***var.*** Riva del Garda. Trentino-Alto Adige, N Italy
63 *A21* **Rivadavia** Buenos Aires, E Argentina
Riva del Garda *see* Riva
108 *B8* **Rivarolo Canavese** Piemonte, W Italy
44 *K11* **Rivas** Rivas, SW Nicaragua
44 *J11* **Rivas** ⬖ *department* SW Nicaragua
105 *R11* **Rive-de-Gier** Loire, E France
63 *A22* **Rivera** Buenos Aires, E Argentina
63 *F16* **Rivera** Rivera, NE Uruguay
63 *F17* **Rivera** ⬖ *department* NE Uruguay
37 *P9* **Riverbank** California, W USA
78 *K17* **River Cess** SW Liberia
30 *M4* **Riverdale** North Dakota, N USA
32 *I6* **River Falls** Wisconsin, N USA
9 *T16* **Riverhurst** Saskatchewan, S Canada
191 *O10* **Riverina** *physical region* New South Wales, SE Australia
82 *G8* **River Nile** ⬖ *state* NE Sudan
65 *F19* **Rivero, Isla** *island* Archipiélago de los Chonos, S Chile
9 *W16* **Rivers** Manitoba, S Canada
79 *U17* **Rivers** ⬖ *state* S Nigeria
193 *D23* **Riversdale** Southland, South Island, NZ
85 *F26* **Riversdale** Western Cape, SW South Africa
37 *U15* **Riverside** California, W USA
27 *W9* **Riverside** Texas, SW USA
39 *U3* **Riverside Reservoir** ⊡ Colorado, C USA
8 *K15* **Rivers Inlet** British Columbia, SW Canada
8 *K15* **Rivers Inlet** *inlet* British Columbia, SW Canada
xliv *F14* **Riverstown** Cork, S Ireland
9 *X15* **Riverton** Manitoba, S Canada
193 *C24* **Riverton** Southland, South Island, NZ
32 *L13* **Riverton** Illinois, N USA
38 *L3* **Riverton** Utah, W USA
35 *V15* **Riverton** Wyoming, C USA
12 *G10* **River Valley** Ontario, S Canada
11 *P14* **Riverview** New Brunswick, SE Canada
105 *O17* **Rivesaltes** Pyrénées-Orientales, S France
38 *H11* **Riviera** Arizona, SW USA
27 *S15* **Riviera** Texas, SW USA
25 *Z14* **Riviera Beach** Florida, SE USA

◆ Country
● Country Capital
◇ Dependent Territory
○ Dependent Territory Capital
⬖ Administrative Region
✕ International Airport
▲ Mountain
⛰ Mountain Range
⩓ Volcano
≈ River
◎ Lake
⊡ Reservoir

13 Q10 **Rivière-à-Pierre** Québec, SE Canada
13 T9 **Rivière-Bleue** Québec, SE Canada
13 T8 **Rivière-du-Loup** Québec, SE Canada
181 Y15 **Rivière du Rempart** NE Mauritius
47 R12 **Rivière-Pilote** S Martinique
181 O17 **Rivière St-Etienne, Point de la** *headland* SW Réunion
11 S10 **Rivière-St-Paul** Québec, E Canada
Rivière Sèche *see* Bel Air
118 K4 **Rivne** *Pol.* Równe, *Rus.* Rovno. Rivnens'ka Oblast', NW Ukraine
Rivne *see* Rivnens'ka Oblast'
118 K3 **Rivnens'ka Oblast'** *var.* Rivne, *Rus.* Rovenskaya Oblast'. ◆ *province* NW Ukraine
108 B8 **Rivoli** Piemonte, NW Italy
165 Q14 **Riwoqê** Xizang Zizhiqu, W China
101 H19 **Rixensart** Walloon Brabant, C Belgium
Riyadh/Riyāḍ, Minṭaqat ar *see* Ar Riyāḍ
Riyāq *see* Rayak
Rizaiyeh *see* Orūmīyeh
143 P11 **Rize** Rize, NE Turkey
143 P11 **Rize** *prev.* Çoruh. ◆ *province* NE Turkey
167 R5 **Rizhao** Shandong, E China
Rizhskiy Zaliv *see* Riga, Gulf of
Rizokarpaso/Rizokárpason *see* Dipkarpaz
109 O21 **Rizzuto, Capo** *headland* S Italy
97 F15 **Rjukan** Telemark, S Norway
97 D16 **Rjuven** ▲ S Norway
78 H9 **Rkiz** Trarza, W Mauritania
97 H14 **Roa** Oppland, S Norway
107 N5 **Roa** Castilla-León, N Spain
xxxix O13 **Roade** Northamptonshire, C England, UK
xxxvi F14 **Roadford Reservoir** ☒ SW England, UK
47 T9 **Road Town** ● (British Virgin Islands) Tortola, C British Virgin Islands
xlii C8 **Roag, Loch** *inlet* NW Scotland, UK
39 O5 **Roan Cliffs** *cliff* Colorado/Utah, W USA
23 P9 **Roan High Knob** *var.* Roan Mountain. ▲ North Carolina/Tennessee, SE USA
Roan Mountain *see* Roan High Knob
105 Q10 **Roanne** *anc.* Rodunma. Loire, E France
25 R4 **Roanoke** Alabama, S USA
23 S7 **Roanoke** Virginia, NE USA
23 Z9 **Roanoke Island** *island* North Carolina, SE USA
23 W8 **Roanoke Rapids** North Carolina, SE USA
23 X9 **Roanoke River** ♦ North Carolina/Virginia, SE USA
39 O4 **Roan Plateau** *plain* Utah, W USA
39 R5 **Roaring Fork River** ♦ Colorado, C USA
27 O5 **Roaring Springs** Texas, SW USA
xliv C15 **Roaringwater Bay** *bay* S Ireland
44 J4 **Roatán** *var.* Coxen Hole, Coxin Hole. Islas de la Bahía, N Honduras
44 I4 **Roatán, Isla de** *island* Islas de la Bahía, N Honduras
Roat Kampuchea *see* Cambodia
Roazon *see* Rennes
149 T7 **Robāṭ-e Chāh Gonbad** Khorāsān, E Iran
149 R7 **Robāṭ-e Khān** Khorāsān, C Iran
149 T7 **Robāṭ-e Khvosh Āb** Khorāsān, E Iran
149 R8 **Robāṭ-e Posht-e Bādām** Khorāsān, Iran
183 S8 **Robbie Ridge** *undersea feature* W Pacific Ocean
23 T10 **Robbins** North Carolina, SE USA
191 N15 **Robbins Island** *island* Tasmania, SE Australia
23 N10 **Robbinsville** North Carolina, SE USA
190 J12 **Robe** South Australia
23 W9 **Robersonville** North Carolina, SE USA
27 P8 **Robert Lee** Texas, SW USA
xliii N22 **Roberton** The Borders, S Scotland, UK
xxxvii W12 **Robertsbridge** East Sussex, SE England, UK
37 V5 **Roberts Creek Mountain** ▲ Nevada, W USA
95 J15 **Robertsfors** Västerbotten, N Sweden
29 R11 **Robert S.Kerr Reservoir** ☒ Oklahoma, C USA
40 L12 **Roberts Mountain** ▲ Nunivak Island, Alaska, USA
85 F26 **Robertson** Western Cape, SW South Africa
204 H4 **Robertson Island** *island* Antarctica
78 J16 **Robertsport** W Liberia
xliv J9 **Robertstown** Kildare, E Ireland
190 J8 **Robertstown** South Australia
Robert Williams *see* Caála
13 P7 **Roberval** Québec, SE Canada
xli V10 **Robin Hood's Bay** North Yorkshire, N England, UK
33 N15 **Robinson** Illinois, N USA
200 Oo12 **Robinson Crusoe, Isla** *island* Islas Juan Fernández, Chile, E Pacific Ocean
188 J9 **Robinson Range** ▲ Western Australia
194 L16 **Robinson River** Central, S PNG
190 M9 **Robinvale** Victoria, SE Australia
107 P11 **Robledo** Castilla-La Mancha, C Spain
56 G5 **Robles** *var.* La Paz, Robles La Paz. César, N Colombia
Robles La Paz *see* Robles
9 S17 **Roblin** Manitoba, S Canada
xxxvi F13 **Roborough** Devon, SW England, UK
195 U13 **Rob Roy** *island* NW Solomon Islands
9 S17 **Robsart** Saskatchewan, S Canada
9 N15 **Robson, Mount** ▲ British Columbia, SW Canada
27 T14 **Robstown** Texas, SW USA
27 P6 **Roby** Texas, SW USA

106 E11 **Roca, Cabo da** *headland* C Portugal
Rocadas *see* Xangongo
43 S14 **Roca Partida, Punta** *headland* C Mexico
49 X6 **Rocas, Atol das** *island* E Brazil
109 L18 **Roccadaspide** *var.* Rocca d'Aspide. Campania, S Italy
109 K15 **Roccaraso** Abruzzi, C Italy
108 H10 **Rocca San Casciano** Emilia-Romagna, C Italy
108 G13 **Roccastrada** Toscana, C Italy
xxxviii B4 **Rocester** Staffordshire, C England, UK
xxxv C13 **Roch** Pembrokeshire, SW Wales, UK
63 G20 **Rocha** Rocha, E Uruguay
63 G19 **Rocha** ◆ *department* E Uruguay
xl G13 **Rochdale** Rochdale, NW England, UK
xli P14 **Rochdale** ◆ *unitary authority* NW England, UK
104 L11 **Rochechouart** Haute-Vienne, C France
101 J22 **Rochefort** Namur, SE Belgium
104 J17 **Rochefort** *var.* Rochefort sur Mer. Charente-Maritime, W France
Rochefort sur Mer *see* Rochefort
129 N10 **Rochegda** Arkhangel'skaya Oblast', NW Russian Federation
32 L10 **Rochelle** Illinois, N USA
27 Q9 **Rochelle** Texas, SW USA
11 P13 **Rocher Percé** *island* Rocher Percé, Québec, E Canada
13 V3 **Rochers Ouest, Rivière aux** ♦ Québec, SE Canada
xxxvii V10 **Rochester** *anc.* Durobrivae. Kent, SE England, UK
xli O4 **Rochester** Northumberland, N England, UK
33 O12 **Rochester** Indiana, N USA
31 W10 **Rochester** Minnesota, N USA
19 N10 **Rochester** New Hampshire, NE USA
20 F9 **Rochester** New York, NE USA
27 P5 **Rochester** Texas, SW USA
33 S9 **Rochester Hills** Michigan, N USA
Rocheuses, Montagnes/Rockies *see* Rocky Mountains
xxxvii X8 **Rochford** Essex, SE England, UK
xliv I8 **Rochfortbridge** Westmeath, C Ireland
66 M6 **Rockall** *island* UK, N Atlantic Ocean
66 L6 **Rockall Bank** *undersea feature* N Atlantic Ocean
86 B8 **Rockall Rise** *undersea feature* N Atlantic Ocean
86 C9 **Rockall Trough** *undersea feature* N Atlantic Ocean
xxxvi I14 **Rockbeare** Devon, SW England, UK
12 E12 **Rockchapel** Cork, S Ireland
xl M6 **Rockcliffe** Cumbria, NW England, UK
xliv J6 **Rockcorry** Monaghan, NE Ireland
37 U2 **Rock Creek** ♦ Nevada, W USA
37 T10 **Rockdale** Texas, SW USA
205 N12 **Rockefeller Plateau** *plateau* Antarctica
32 K11 **Rock Falls** Illinois, N USA
25 Q5 **Rockford** Alabama, S USA
32 L10 **Rockford** Illinois, N USA
13 Q12 **Rock Forest** Québec, SE Canada
9 T17 **Rockglen** Saskatchewan, S Canada
189 Y8 **Rockhampton** Queensland, E Australia
23 R11 **Rock Hill** South Carolina, SE USA
188 I13 **Rockingham** Western Australia
23 T11 **Rockingham** North Carolina, SE USA
32 K11 **Rock Island** Illinois, N USA
27 U12 **Rock Island** Texas, SW USA
12 C10 **Rock Lake** Ontario, S Canada
31 O2 **Rock Lake** North Dakota, N USA
12 I12 **Rock Lake** ☒ Ontario, SE Canada
12 M12 **Rockland** Ontario, SE Canada
17 R7 **Rockland** Maine, NE USA
190 L11 **Rocklands Reservoir** ☒ Victoria, SE Australia
37 O7 **Rocklin** California, W USA
25 R3 **Rockmart** Georgia, SE USA
33 N16 **Rockport** Indiana, N USA
29 Q2 **Rock Port** Missouri, C USA
27 T14 **Rockport** Texas, SW USA
34 I7 **Rockport** Washington, NW USA
31 S11 **Rock Rapids** Iowa, C USA
32 K11 **Rock River** ♦ Illinois/Wisconsin, N USA
46 I3 **Rock Sound** Eleuthera Island, C Bahamas
35 U17 **Rock Springs** Wyoming, C USA
27 P11 **Rocksprings** Texas, SW USA
T9 **Rockstone** C Guyana
31 S12 **Rock Valley** Iowa, C USA
33 N14 **Rockville** Indiana, N USA
23 W3 **Rockville** Maryland, NE USA
27 U6 **Rockwall** Texas, SW USA
31 T13 **Rockwell City** Iowa, C USA
33 S10 **Rockwood** Michigan, N USA
22 M9 **Rockwood** Tennessee, S USA
27 Q8 **Rockwood** Texas, SW USA
39 U6 **Rocky Ford** Colorado, C USA
12 D9 **Rocky Island Lake** ☒ Ontario, S Canada
23 S7 **Rocky Mount** North Carolina, SE USA
23 S7 **Rocky Mount** Virginia, NE USA
35 Q8 **Rocky Mountain** ▲ Montana, NW USA
9 P15 **Rocky Mountain House** Alberta, SW Canada
39 T3 **Rocky Mountain National Park** *national park* Colorado, C USA
2 E12 **Rocky Mountains** *var.* Rockies, *Fr.* Montagnes Rocheuses. ▲ Canada/USA
44 H1 **Rocky Point** *headland* NE Belize
85 A17 **Rocky Point** *headland* NW Namibia
97 F14 **Rødberg** Buskerud, S Norway
97 I25 **Rødby** Storstrøm, SE Denmark
97 I25 **Rødbyhavn** Storstrøm, SE Denmark
11 T10 **Roddickton** Newfoundland, Newfoundland and Labrador, SE Canada

97 F23 **Rødding** Sønderjylland, SW Denmark
97 M22 **Rødeby** Blekinge, S Sweden
xlii B10 **Rodel** Western Isles, NW Scotland, UK
100 N6 **Roden** Drenthe, NE Netherlands
64 H9 **Rodeo** San Juan, W Argentina
105 O14 **Rodez** *anc.* Segodunum. Aveyron, S France
Rodholívos *see* Rodolívos
Rodhópi Óri *see* Rhodope Mountains
Ródhos/Rodi *see* Ródos
109 N15 **Rodi Gargancio** Puglia, SE Italy
xxxvii V8 **Roding** ♦ SE England, UK
103 N20 **Roding** Bayern, SE Germany
xxxviii H9 **Rodington** Shropshire, W England, UK
115 J19 **Rodiniti, Kepi i** *headland* W Albania
118 I9 **Rodnei, Munţii** ▲ N Romania
192 L4 **Rodney, Cape** *headland* North Island, NZ
40 L9 **Rodney, Cape** *headland* Alaska, USA
128 M16 **Rodniki** Ivanovskaya Oblast', W Russian Federation
121 Q16 **Rodniya** *Rus.* Rodnya. Mahilyowskaya Voblasts', E Belorussia
Rodó *see* José Enrique Rodó
116 H13 **Rodolívos** *var.* Rodholívos. Kentrikí Makedonía, NE Greece
Rodopi *see* Rhodope Mountains
117 O22 **Ródos** *var.* Ródhos, *Eng.* Rhodes, *It.* Rodi. Ródos, Dodekánisos, Greece, Aegean Sea
117 O22 **Ródos** *var.* Ródhos, *Eng.* Rhodes, *It.* Rodi; *anc.* Rhodos. *island* Dodekánisos, Greece, Aegean Sea
Rodosto *see* Tekirdağ
61 A14 **Rodrigues** Amazonas, W Brazil
181 P8 **Rodrigues** *var.* Rodriquez. *island* E Mauritius
Rodríquez *see* Rodrigues
Rodunma *see* Roanne
xliv J3 **Roe** ♦ N Northern Ireland, UK
188 I7 **Roebourne** Western Australia
85 J20 **Roedtan** Northern, NE South Africa
xxxvi B9 **Roehampton** Wandsworth, SE England, UK
100 H11 **Roelofarendsveen** Zuid-Holland, W Netherlands
Roepat *see* Rupat, Pulau
Roer *see* Rur
101 M16 **Roermond** Limburg, SE Netherlands
101 C18 **Roeselare** *Fr.* Roulers; *prev.* Rousselaere. West-Vlaanderen, W Belgium
xliii H3 **Roesound** Shetland Islands, NE Scotland, UK
15 L15 **Roes Welcome Sound** *strait* Northwest Territories, C Canada
Roeteng *see* Ruteng
Rofreit *see* Rovereto
Rogachëv *see* Rahachow
59 L15 **Rogagua, Laguna** ☒ NW Bolivia
97 C16 **Rogaland** ◆ *county* S Norway
27 T9 **Roganville** Texas, SW USA
31 P5 **Rogers** North Dakota, N USA
27 T9 **Rogers** Texas, SW USA
33 R5 **Rogers City** Michigan, N USA
Roger Simpson Island *see* Abemama
37 T14 **Rogers Lake** *salt flat* California, W USA
23 Q8 **Rogers, Mount** ▲ Virginia, NE USA
105 P5 **Rogerson** Idaho, NW USA
9 O16 **Rogers Pass** *pass* British Columbia, SW Canada
23 O8 **Rogersville** Tennessee, S USA
101 L16 **Roggel** Limburg, SE Netherlands
Roggeveen *see* Roggewein, Cabo
200 Nn12 **Roggeveen Basin** *undersea feature* E Pacific Ocean
203 X16 **Roggewein, Cabo** *var.* Roggeveen. *headland* Easter Island, Chile, E Pacific Ocean
104 F1 **Rogliano** Corse, France, C Mediterranean Sea
109 N21 **Rogliano** Calabria, SW Italy
94 G12 **Rognan** Nordland, C Norway
102 K10 **Rögnitz** ♦ N Germany
118 I6 **Rohatyn** *Rus.* Rogatin. Ivano-Frankivs'ka Oblast', W Ukraine
201 O14 **Rohi** Pohnpei, E Micronesia
Rohitsch-Sauerbrunn *see* Rogaška Slatina
155 Q13 **Rohri** Sind, SE Pakistan
158 I10 **Rohtak** Haryāna, N India
Roi Ed *see* Roi Et
201 O9 **Roi Georges, Îles du** *island group* Îles Tuamotu, C French Polynesia
159 Y10 **Roing** Arunāchal Pradesh, NE India
121 H8 **Roja** Liepāja, W Latvia
63 B20 **Rojas** Buenos Aires, E Argentina
155 R22 **Rojhān** Punjab, E Pakistan
43 Q12 **Rojo, Cabo** *headland* C Mexico
47 Q10 **Rojo, Cabo** *headland* W Puerto Rico
173 G7 **Rokan Kanan, Sungai** ♦ Sumatera, W Indonesia
173 G7 **Rokan Kiri, Sungai** ♦ Sumatera, W Indonesia
121 I11 **Rokiškis** Rokiškis, NE Lithuania
172 Nn9 **Rokkasho** Aomori, C Japan
113 B17 **Rokycany** *Ger.* Rokytzan. Západní Čechy, W Czech Republic

119 P6 **Rokytne** Kyyivs'ka Oblast', N Ukraine
118 L3 **Rokytne** Rivnens'ka Oblast', NW Ukraine
Rokytzan *see* Rokycany
164 L11 **Rola Co** ☒ W China
97 D15 **Røldal** Hordaland, S Norway
100 O7 **Rolde** Drenthe, NE Netherlands
31 O2 **Rolette** North Dakota, N USA
29 V6 **Rolla** Missouri, C USA
31 O2 **Rolla** North Dakota, N USA
110 A10 **Rolle** Vaud, SW Switzerland
189 X8 **Rolleston** Queensland, E Australia
193 H19 **Rolleston** Canterbury, South Island, NZ
193 G18 **Rolleston Range** ▲ South Island, NZ
12 H8 **Rollet** Québec, SE Canada
24 J4 **Rolling Fork** Mississippi, S USA
22 L6 **Rolling Fork** ♦ Kentucky, S USA
12 J11 **Rolphton** Ontario, SE Canada
189 N10 **Roma** Queensland, E Australia
109 I15 **Roma** *Eng.* Rome. ● (Italy) Lazio, C Italy
97 P19 **Roma** Gotland, SE Sweden
23 T14 **Romain, Cape** *headland* South Carolina, SE USA
11 P11 **Romaine** ♦ Newfoundland and Labrador/Québec, E Canada
xli Q9 **Romaldkirk** Durham, N England, UK
28 R17 **Roma Los Saenz** Texas, SW USA
116 H8 **Roman** *Hung.* Románvásár. Neamţ, NE Romania
118 L10 **Roman** *Hung.* Románvásár. Neamţ, NE Romania
xli S10 **Romanby** North Yorkshire, N England, UK
66 M13 **Romanche Fracture Zone** *tectonic feature* E Atlantic Ocean
63 C15 **Romang** Santa Fe, C Argentina
175 T15 **Romang, Pulau** *var.* Pulau Roma. *island* Kepulauan Damar, E Indonesia
xli X14 **Romang, Selat** *strait* Nusa Tenggara, S Indonesia
175 Ss15 **Romang, Selat** *strait* Nusa Tenggara, S Indonesia
113 O24 **Romania** *Bul.* Rumūniya, *Ger.* Rumänien, *Hung.* Románia, *Rom.* România, *SCr.* Rumunjska, *Ukr.* Rumuniya; *prev.* Republica Socialistă România, Roumania, Rumania, Socialist Republic of Romania, Socialist Republic of *Rom.* România. ◆ *republic* SE Europe
119 T14 **Roman-Kash** ▲ S Ukraine
xliii L21 **Romannobridge** The Borders, S Scotland, UK
25 W16 **Romano, Cape** *headland* Florida, SE USA
46 G5 **Romano, Cayo** *island* C Cuba
126 Kk15 **Romanovka** Respublika Buryatiya, S Russian Federation
131 N8 **Romanovka** Saratovskaya Oblast', W Russian Federation
110 I6 **Romanshorn** Thurgau, NE Switzerland
105 R12 **Romans-sur-Isère** Drôme, E France
201 U12 **Romanum** *island* Chuuk, C Micronesia
xliii L4 **Romanzof Mountains** ▲ Alaska, USA
105 S4 **Rombas** Moselle, NE France
176 Xx10 **Rombebai, Danau** ☒ Irian Jaya, E Indonesia
60 D7 **Romblon** ☒ N South America
176 Xx10 **Rombebai, Danau** Irian Jaya, E Indonesia
25 R2 **Rome** Georgia, SE USA
20 J9 **Rome** New York, NE USA
33 S9 **Rome** Michigan, US
Rome *see* Roma
xxxviii V9 **Romford** Havering, SE England, UK
xl H15 **Romiley** Stockport, NW England, UK
105 P5 **Romilly-sur-Seine** Aube, N France
Rominia *see* Romania
152 L11 **Romit** Bukhoro Wiloyati, C Uzbekistan
23 O3 **Romney** West Virginia, NE USA
xxxvii X12 **Romney Marsh** *physical region* SE England, UK
37 P12 **Romoland** California, W USA
23 S14 **Romond Lake** *salt flat* California, W USA
97 E24 **Rømø** *Ger.* Röm. *island* SW Denmark
119 S5 **Romodan** Poltavs'ka Oblast', NE Ukraine
131 P5 **Romodanovo** Respublika Mordoviya, W Russian Federation
Romorantin *see* Romorantin-Lanthenay
105 N8 **Romorantin-Lanthenay** *var.* Romorantin. Loir-et-Cher, C France
174 Hh5 **Rompin, Sungai** ♦ Peninsular Malaysia
96 F9 **Romsdal** *physical region* S Norway
96 F10 **Romsdalen** *valley* S Norway
96 F10 **Romsdalsfjorden** *fjord* S Norway
xxxvii O12 **Romsey** Hampshire, S England, UK
xli A11 **Rona** *island* NW Scotland, UK
35 P8 **Ronan** Montana, NW USA
23 O4 **Ronay** *island* NW Scotland, UK
Roncador Reef *see* Roncador
61 M14 **Roncador** Maranhão, E Brazil
195 W12 **Roncador Reef** *reef* N Solomon Islands
47 O6 **Roncador, Serra do** ▲ C Brazil
23 S6 **Ronceverte** West Virginia, NE USA
109 H14 **Ronciglione** Lazio, C Italy
107 N15 **Ronda** Andalucía, S Spain
96 G11 **Rondane** ▲ S Norway
61 E16 **Rondônia** *off.* Estado de Rondônia; *prev.* Território de Rondônia. ◆ *state* W Brazil
61 I10 **Rondonópolis** Mato Grosso, W Brazil

201 R4 **Rongelap Atoll** *var.* Rönlap. *atoll* Ralik Chain, NW Marshall Islands
Rongerik *see* Rongrik Atoll
164 I13 **Rong Jiang** ♦ S China
166 K12 **Rongjiang** *prev.* Guzhou. Guizhou, S China
Rong, Kas *see* Rŭng, Kaôh
178 Hh8 **Rong Kwang** Phrae, NW Thailand
201 T4 **Rongrik Atoll** *var.* Rôndik, Rongerik. *atoll* Ralik Chain, N Marshall Islands
201 X2 **Rongrong** *island* SE Marshall Islands
166 L13 **Rongshui** *var.* Rongshui Miaozu Zizhixian. Guangxi Zhuangzu Zizhiqu, S China
Rongshui Miaozu Zizhixian *see* Rongshui
120 I6 **Rõngu** *Ger.* Ringen. Tartumaa, SE Estonia
166 L15 **Rong Xian** Guangxi Zhuangzu Zizhiqu, S China
Roniu *see* Ronui, Mont
201 N13 **Ronkiti** Pohnpei, E Micronesia
Rönlap *see* Rongelap Atoll
97 L24 **Rønne** Bornholm, E Denmark
97 M22 **Ronneby** Blekinge, S Sweden
204 J7 **Ronne Entrance** *inlet* Antarctica
204 L6 **Ronne Ice Shelf** *ice shelf* Antarctica
101 E19 **Ronse** *Fr.* Renaix. Oost-Vlaanderen, SW Belgium
203 R8 **Ronui, Mont** *var.* Roniu. ▲ Tahiti, W French Polynesia
32 K14 **Roodhouse** Illinois, N USA
85 C19 **Rooibank** Erongo, W Namibia
67 N24 **Rookery Point** *headland* NE Tristan da Cunha
xli P7 **Rookhope** Durham, N England, UK
176 W10 **Roon, Pulau** *island* E Indonesia
181 V7 **Roo Rise** *undersea feature* E Indian Ocean
158 F9 **Roorkee** Uttar Pradesh, N India
101 H15 **Roosendaal** Noord-Brabant, S Netherlands
37 P10 **Roosevelt** Utah, W USA
39 N3 **Roosevelt** Utah, W USA
49 T8 **Roosevelt** W Brazil
205 O13 **Roosevelt Island** *island* Antarctica
8 L10 **Roosevelt, Mount** ▲ British Columbia, W Canada
9 P17 **Roosky** Roscommon, C Ireland
31 X10 **Root River** ♦ Minnesota, N USA
113 N16 **Ropczyce** Rzeszów, SE Poland
189 Q3 **Roper Bar** Northern Territory, N Australia
26 M5 **Ropesville** Texas, SW USA
xxxvii Q12 **Ropley** Hampshire, S England, UK
33 O12 **Ropsley** Lincolnshire, E England, UK
115 P19 **Roquefort** Landes, SW France
63 C21 **Roque Pérez** Buenos Aires, E Argentina
xliii L4 **Rora Head** *headland* N Scotland, UK
60 E10 **Roraima** *off.* Estado de Roraima; *prev.* Território do Rio Branco, Território de Roraima. ◆ *state* N Brazil
60 F9 **Roraima, Mount** ▲ N South America
176 X10 **Rori** Irian Jaya, E Indonesia
25 R2 **Ro Ro Reef** *reef* Malolo Barrier Reef
96 I9 **Røros** Sør-Trøndelag, S Norway
110 I7 **Rorschach** Sankt Gallen, NE Switzerland
95 E14 **Rørvik** Nord-Trøndelag, C Norway
121 G17 **Ros'** *Rus.* Ross'. Hrodzyenskaya Voblasts', W Belorussia
121 G17 **Ros'** *Rus.* Ross'. ♦ W Belorussia
119 O6 **Ros'** ♦ N Ukraine
46 K7 **Rosa, Lake** ☒ Great Inagua, S Bahamas
34 M9 **Rosalia** Washington, NW USA
203 W15 **Rosalia, Punta** *headland* Easter Island, Chile, E Pacific Ocean
47 T12 **Rosalie** E Dominica
37 S14 **Rosamond** California, W USA
37 S14 **Rosamond Lake** *salt flat* California, W USA
42 B4 **Rosario** Baja California, NW Mexico
42 J11 **Rosario** Sinaloa, C Mexico
42 G6 **Rosario** Sonora, C Mexico
58 G8 **Rosario** San Pedro, C Paraguay
63 E20 **Rosario** Santa Fe, C Argentina
56 H5 **Rosario** Zulia, NW Venezuela
Rosario *see* Rosario
42 K12 **Rosario, Bahía del** *bay* NW Mexico
63 C18 **Rosario del Tala** Entre Ríos, E Argentina
64 H13 **Rosario de la Frontera** Salta, N Argentina
63 F16 **Rosário do Sul** Rio Grande do Sul, S Brazil
61 H18 **Rosário Oeste** Mato Grosso, W Brazil
42 F7 **Rosarito** Baja California, NW Mexico
42 B1 **Rosarito** Baja California, NW Mexico
42 B2 **Rosarito** Baja California Sur, W Mexico
130 J6 **Rosslea** Fermanagh, N Northern Ireland, UK
12 J12 **Rosliston** ... Entre Ríos
130 M14 **Rosslau** Sachsen-Anhalt, E Germany

181 Y16 **Rose Belle** SE Mauritius
191 O16 **Rosebery** Tasmania, SE Australia
23 U11 **Roseboro** North Carolina, SE USA
27 T9 **Rosebud** Texas, SW USA
35 W10 **Rosebud Creek** ♦ Montana, NW USA
34 F13 **Roseburg** Oregon, NW USA
24 J3 **Rosedale** Mississippi, S USA
xli U10 **Rosedale Abbey** North Yorkshire, N England, UK
57 U8 **Rose Hall** E Guyana
xlii P11 **Rosehearty** Aberdeenshire, NE Scotland, UK
6 H9 **Rose Hill** W Mauritius
82 H12 **Roseires, Reservoir** *var.* Lake Rusayris. ☒ E Sudan
xxxv C14 **Rosemarket** Pembrokeshire, SW Wales, UK
xliii J11 **Rosemarkie** Highland, NW Scotland, UK
Rosenau *see* Rožnov pod Radhoštěm, Czech Republic
Rosenau *see* Rožňava, Slovakia
Rosenberg *see* Olesno, Poland
Rosenberg *see* Ružomberok, Slovakia
102 I10 **Rosengarten** Niedersachsen, N Germany
103 M24 **Rosenheim** Bayern, S Germany
Rosenhof *see* Zilupe
107 X4 **Roses** Cataluña, NE Spain
107 X4 **Roses, Golf de** *gulf* NE Spain
109 K14 **Roseto degli Abruzzi** Abruzzi, C Italy
9 S16 **Rosetown** Saskatchewan, S Canada
37 O7 **Roseville** California, W USA
31 V8 **Roseville** Minnesota, N USA
31 R7 **Rosholt** South Dakota, N USA
109 F12 **Rosignano Marittimo** Toscana, C Italy
118 I14 **Roşiori de Vede** Teleorman, S Romania
116 K8 **Rositsa** ♦ N Bulgaria
xli S14 **Rositten** *see* Rēzekne
97 I23 **Roskilde** Roskilde, E Denmark
97 I23 **Roskilde** *off.* Roskilde Amt. ◆ *county* E Denmark
Ros Láir *see* Rosslare
175 R18 **Roslavl'** Smolenskaya Oblast', W Russian Federation
xl M7 **Roskey** Cumbria, NW England, UK
9 P17 **Roosky** British Columbia, SW Canada
34 I8 **Roslyn** Washington, NW USA
101 K14 **Rosmalen** Noord-Brabant, S Netherlands
Ros Mhic Thriúin *see* New Ross
115 P19 **Rosoman** C FYR Macedonia
104 F6 **Rosporden** Finistère, NW France
xliii J25 **Rospley** Hampshire, S England, UK
xxxix Q8 **Rosrea** ... Ireland
175 Qq18 **Roti, Pulau** *island* S Indonesia
175 R18 **Roti, Pulau** *var.* Rote, Pulau. S Indonesia
191 I8 **Roto** New South Wales, SE Australia
192 N8 **Rotoiti, Lake** ☒ NZ
192 N3 **Rotoiti, Lake** ☒ North Island, NZ
34 I8 **Rotomagus** *see* Rouen
109 N19 **Rotondella** Basilicata, S Italy
104 E2 **Rotondo, Monte** ▲ Corse, France, C Mediterranean Sea
193 I15 **Rotoroa, Lake** ☒ South Island, NZ
192 N8 **Rotorua** Bay of Plenty, North Island, NZ
192 N8 **Rotorua, Lake** ☒ North Island, NZ
103 N22 **Rott** ♦ SE Germany
110 F10 **Rotten** ♦ S Switzerland
111 T6 **Rottenmann** Steiermark, E Austria
100 M12 **Rotterdam** Zuid-Holland, SW Netherlands
20 I9 **Rotterdam** New York, NE USA
xxxvii U13 **Rottingdean** Brighton and Hove, SE England, UK
97 M21 **Rottnen** ☒ S Sweden
100 N4 **Rottumeroog** *island* Waddeneilanden, NE Netherlands
100 N4 **Rottumerplaat** *island* Waddeneilanden, NE Netherlands
103 S23 **Rottweil** Baden-Württemberg, S Germany
203 O7 **Rotui, Mont** ▲ Moorea, W French Polynesia
105 P6 **Roubaix** Nord, N France
113 C15 **Roudnice nad Labem** *Ger.* Raudnitz an der Elbe. Severní Čechy, N Czech Republic
105 O4 **Rouen** *anc.* Rotomagus. Seine-Maritime, N France
176 K11 **Rouffaer Reserves** *reserve* Irian Jaya, E Indonesia
Rouffaer-Rivier *see* Tariku, Sungai
13 O10 **Rouge, Rivière** ♦ Québec, SE Canada
xxxix V8 **Rougham** Norfolk, E England, UK
22 J12 **Rough River** ♦ Kentucky, S USA
22 J12 **Rough River Lake** ☒ Kentucky, S USA
xxxix V8 **Roughton** Norfolk, E England, UK
Rouhaïbé *see* Ar Ruḥaybah
104 K11 **Rouillac** Charente, W France

xliv L6 **Rostrevor** Newry and Mourne, S Northern Ireland, UK
95 J14 **Rosvik** Norrbotten, N Sweden
25 S3 **Roswell** Georgia, SE USA
39 U14 **Roswell** New Mexico, SW USA
96 K12 **Rot** Kopparberg, C Sweden
105 J15 **Rota** Andalucía, S Spain
196 K9 **Rota** *island* S Northern Mariana Islands
27 P6 **Rotan** Texas, SW USA
Rotcher Island *see* Tamana
102 J11 **Rotenburg** Niedersachsen, NW Germany
Rotenburg *see* Rotenburg an der Fulda
103 I16 **Rotenburg an der Fulda** *var.* Rotenburg. Thüringen, C Germany
103 L18 **Roter Main** ♦ E Germany
103 J23 **Rothaargebirge** ▲ W Germany
xli Q4 **Rothbury** Northumberland, N England, UK
Rothenburg *see* Rothenburg ob der Tauber
103 J20 **Rothenburg ob der Tauber** *var.* Rothenburg. Bayern, S Germany
xxxvii S12 **Rother** ♦ S England, UK
xxxix X12 **Rother** ♦ SE England, UK
204 H6 **Rothera** UK research station Antarctica
xxxvii V12 **Rotherfield** East Sussex, SE England, UK
xli S16 **Rotherham** Rotherham, N England, UK
xli S16 **Rotherham** ◆ *unitary authority* N England, UK
193 I17 **Rotherham** Canterbury, South Island, NZ
xlii M12 **Rothes** Moray, NE Scotland, UK
xliii H20 **Rothesay** Argyll and Bute, W Scotland, UK
xli N4 **Rothiesholm** Orkney Islands, N Scotland, UK
xliii F12 **Rothienorman** Aberdeenshire, NE Scotland, UK
204 H6 **Rothschild Island** *island* Antarctica
xli S14 **Rothwell** Leeds, N England, UK
xxxix P11 **Rothwell** Northamptonshire, C England, UK
175 Qq18 **Roti, Pulau** *island* S Indonesia
175 R18 **Roti, Pulau** *var.* Rote, Pulau. S Indonesia
191 I8 **Roto** New South Wales, SE Australia
192 N8 **Rotoiti, Lake** ☒ NZ
192 N3 **Rotoiti, Lake** ☒ North Island, NZ
109 N19 **Rotondella** Basilicata, S Italy
104 E2 **Rotondo, Monte** ▲ Corse, France, C Mediterranean Sea
193 I15 **Rotoroa, Lake** ☒ South Island, NZ
192 N8 **Rotorua** Bay of Plenty, North Island, NZ
192 N8 **Rotorua, Lake** ☒ North Island, NZ
103 N22 **Rott** ♦ SE Germany
110 F10 **Rotten** ♦ S Switzerland
111 T6 **Rottenmann** Steiermark, E Austria
100 M12 **Rotterdam** Zuid-Holland, SW Netherlands
20 I9 **Rotterdam** New York, NE USA
xxxvii U13 **Rottingdean** Brighton and Hove, SE England, UK
97 M21 **Rottnen** ☒ S Sweden
100 N4 **Rottumeroog** *island* Waddeneilanden, NE Netherlands
100 N4 **Rottumerplaat** *island* Waddeneilanden, NE Netherlands
103 S23 **Rottweil** Baden-Württemberg, S Germany
203 O7 **Rotui, Mont** ▲ Moorea, W French Polynesia
105 P6 **Roubaix** Nord, N France
113 C15 **Roudnice nad Labem** *Ger.* Raudnitz an der Elbe. Severní Čechy, N Czech Republic
105 O4 **Rouen** *anc.* Rotomagus. Seine-Maritime, N France
176 K11 **Rouffaer Reserves** *reserve* Irian Jaya, E Indonesia
Rouffaer-Rivier *see* Tariku, Sungai
13 O10 **Rouge, Rivière** ♦ Québec, SE Canada
xxxix V8 **Rougham** Norfolk, E England, UK
22 J12 **Rough River** ♦ Kentucky, S USA
22 J12 **Rough River Lake** ☒ Kentucky, S USA
xxxix V8 **Roughton** Norfolk, E England, UK
Rouhaïbé *see* Ar Ruḥaybah
104 K11 **Rouillac** Charente, W France
xliv C8 **Roundstone** Galway, W Ireland
35 U9 **Roundup** Montana, NW USA
57 Y10 **Roura** NE French Guiana
Rourkela *see* Raurkela
181 Y15 **Round Island** *var.* Île Ronde. *island* NE Mauritius
12 J12 **Round Lake** ☒ Ontario, SE Canada
37 U7 **Round Mountain** Nevada, W USA
27 R10 **Round Mountain** Texas, SW USA
191 U5 **Round Mountain** ▲ New South Wales, SE Australia
27 S10 **Round Rock** Texas, SW USA
xliv C8 **Roundstone** Galway, W Ireland
35 U9 **Roundup** Montana, NW USA
xliii M3 **Rousay** *island* N Scotland, UK
105 O17 **Roussillon** *cultural region* S France
13 V? **Routhierville** Québec, SE Canada
130 Q22 **Rosa Zárate** *var.* Quinindé. Esmeraldas, NW Ecuador
142 I14 **Rosa, Hormozgān**, S Iran
119 N5 **Rostavytsya** ♦ N Ukraine
9 T15 **Rosthern** Saskatchewan, S Canada
102 M8 **Rostock** Mecklenburg-Vorpommern, NE Germany
128 L16 **Rostov** Yaroslavskaya Oblast', W Russian Federation
130 L13 **Rostov-na-Donu** *var.* Rostov, *Eng.* Rostov-on-Don. Rostovskaya Oblast', SW Russian Federation
Rostov-on-Don *see* Rostov-na-Donu
130 L12 **Rostovskaya Oblast'** ◆ *province* SW Russian Federation
101 K25 **Rouvroy** Luxembourg, SE Belgium
12 I7 **Rouyn-Noranda** Québec, SE Canada
Rouyanchengzi *see* Huachi
94 J12 **Rovaniemi** Lappi, N Finland
108 E7 **Rovato** Lombardia, N Italy
129 N11 **Rovdino** Arkhangel'skaya Oblast', NW Russian Federation
108 G8 **Rovereto** *Ger.* Rofreit. Trentino-Alto Adige, N Italy
119 P8 **Roven'ky** *var.* Roven'ki. Luhans'ka Oblast', E Ukraine
Roven'ki *see* Roven'ky
Rovenskaya Oblast' *see* Rivnens'ka Oblast'

◆ COUNTRY   ◇ DEPENDENT TERRITORY   ◎ ADMINISTRATIVE REGION   ▲ MOUNTAIN   🌋 VOLCANO   ☒ LAKE
● COUNTRY CAPITAL   ◉ DEPENDENT TERRITORY CAPITAL   ✕ INTERNATIONAL AIRPORT   ▲ MOUNTAIN RANGE   ♦ RIVER   ☒ RESERVOIR

ROVENSKAYA SLOBODA – ST-ALEXANDRE

Rovenskaya Sloboda see Rovyenskaya Slabada
108 G7 **Rovereto** Ger. Rofreit. Trentino-Alto Adige, N Italy
178 J12 **Rôviĕng Tbong** Preăh Vihéar, N Cambodia
Rovigno see Rovinj
108 H8 **Rovigo** Veneto, NE Italy
114 A10 **Rovinj** It. Rovigno. Istra, NW Croatia
56 E10 **Rovira** Tolima, C Colombia
Rovno see Rivne
131 P9 **Rovnoye** Saratovskaya Oblast', W Russian Federation
84 Q12 **Rovuma, Rio** var. Ruvuma. ≈ Mozambique/Tanzania see also Ruvuma
121 O19 **Rovyenskaya Slabada** Rus. Rovenskaya Sloboda. Homyel'skaya Voblasts', SE Belorussia
xliii N24 **Rowanburn** Dumfries and Galloway, SW Scotland, UK
191 R5 **Rowena** New South Wales, SE Australia
23 T11 **Rowland** North Carolina, SE USA
xxxvii R13 **Rowland's Castle** Hampshire, S England, UK
xli R6 **Rowlands Gill** Gateshead, NE England, UK
15 M1 **Rowley** ≈ Baffin Island, Northwest Territories, NE Canada
15 M2 **Rowley Island** island Northwest Territories, NE Canada
181 W8 **Rowley Shoals** reef NW Australia
179 Pp12 **Roxas** Mindoro, N Philippines
179 Q13 **Roxas City** Panay Island, C Philippines
23 U8 **Roxboro** North Carolina, SE USA
98 K13 **Roxburgh** cultural region SE Scotland, UK
193 D23 **Roxburgh** Otago, South Island, NZ
190 H5 **Roxby Downs** South Australia
97 M17 **Roxen** ◎ S Sweden
xxxvii T5 **Roxton** Bedfordshire, C England, UK
27 V5 **Roxton** Texas, SW USA
13 P12 **Roxton-Sud** Québec, SE Canada
xxxvii V8 **Roxwell** Essex, SE England, UK
35 U8 **Roy** Montana, NW USA
39 U10 **Roy** New Mexico, SW USA
xliv H8 **Royal Canal** Ir. An Chanáil Ríoga. canal C Ireland
32 L1 **Royale, Isle** island Michigan, N USA
39 S6 **Royal Gorge** valley Colorado, C USA
xxxviii E17 **Royal Leamington Spa** var. Leamington, Leamington Spa. Warwickshire, C England, UK
xxxvii X12 **Royal Military Canal** canal SE England, UK
xxxvii V11 **Royal Tunbridge Wells** var. Tunbridge Wells. Kent, SE England, UK
26 L9 **Royalty** Texas, SW USA
104 J11 **Royan** Charente-Maritime, W France
67 B24 **Roy Cove Settlement** West Falkland, Falkland Islands
105 O3 **Roye** Somme, N France
97 H15 **Røyken** Buskerud, S Norway
95 F14 **Røyrvik** Nord-Trøndelag, C Norway
27 U6 **Royse City** Texas, SW USA
xli S15 **Royston** Barnsley, N England, UK
xxxvii U6 **Royston** Hertfordshire, E England, UK
25 U2 **Royston** Georgia, SE USA
xli P15 **Royton** Oldham, NW England, UK
116 L10 **Roza** prev. Gyulovo. Burgaska Oblast, E Bulgaria
115 L16 **Rožaje** Montenegro, SW Yugoslavia
112 M10 **Różan** Ostrołęka, E Poland
119 O10 **Rozdil'na** Odes'ka Oblast', SW Ukraine
119 S12 **Rozdol'ne** Rus. Razdolnoye. Respublika Krym, S Ukraine
xxxvii X16 **Rozel** Jersey, Channel Islands
151 Q9 **Rozhdestvenka** Akmola, C Kazakhstan
118 I6 **Rozhnyativ** Ivano-Frankivs'ka Oblast', W Ukraine
118 J3 **Rozhyshche** Volyns'ka Oblast', NW Ukraine
Roznau am Radhost see Rožnov pod Radhoštěm
113 L19 **Rožňava** Ger. Rosenau, Hung. Rozsnyó. Východné Slovensko, E Slovakia
118 K10 **Roznov** Neamţ, NE Romania
113 I18 **Rožnov pod Radhoštěm** Ger. Rosenau, Roznau am Radhost. Severní Morava, E Czech Republic
Rózsahegy see Ružomberok
Rozsnyó see Râşnov, Romania
Rozsnyó see Rožňava, Slovakia
115 K18 **Rranxë** Shkodër, NW Albania
115 L18 **Rrëshen** var. Rresheni, Rrshen. Lezhë, C Albania
Rresheni see Rrëshen
Rrogozhina see Rrogozhinë
115 K20 **Rrogozhinë** var. Rogozhina, Rogozhinë, Rrogozhina. Tiranë, W Albania
Rrshen see Rrëshen
114 O13 **Rtanj** ▲ E Yugoslavia
131 O7 **Rtishchevo** Saratovskaya Oblast', W Russian Federation
xxxv K6 **Ruabon** Wrexham, NE Wales, UK
192 N12 **Ruahine Range** var. Ruarine. ⛰ North Island, NZ
193 L14 **Ruamahanga** ≈ North Island, NZ
Ruanda see Rwanda
xxxvi B17 **Ruan Minor** Cornwall, SW England, UK
192 M10 **Ruapehu, Mount** ▲ North Island, NZ
193 C25 **Ruapuke Island** island SW NZ
Ruarine see Ruahine Range
192 O9 **Ruatahuna** Bay of Plenty, North Island, NZ
192 Q8 **Ruatoria** Gisborne, North Island, NZ
192 K4 **Ruawai** Northland, North Island, NZ
13 N8 **Ruban** ≈ Québec, SE Canada
83 I22 **Rubeho Mountains** ⛰ C Tanzania
172 Q5 **Rubeshibe** Hokkaidō, NE Japan
Rubezhnoye see Rubizhne
115 L18 **Rubik** Lezhë, C Albania
56 H7 **Rubio** Táchira, W Venezuela
119 X6 **Rubizhne** Rus. Rubezhnoye. Luhans'ka Oblast', E Ukraine
83 F20 **Rubondo Island** island N Tanzania
126 Gg15 **Rubtsovsk** Altayskiy Kray, S Russian Federation
41 P9 **Ruby** Alaska, USA
37 W3 **Ruby Dome** ▲ Nevada, W USA
37 W4 **Ruby Lake** ◎ Nevada, W USA
37 W4 **Ruby Mountains** ⛰ Nevada, W USA
35 Q12 **Ruby Range** ⛰ Montana, NW USA
120 C10 **Rucava** Liepāja, SW Latvia
Rūdān see Dehbārez
Rudelstadt see Ciechanowiec
Rudensk see Rudzyensk
xxxvii S11 **Rudgwick** West Sussex, SE England, UK
121 G14 **Rūdiškės** Trakai, S Lithuania
97 H24 **Rudkøbing** Fyn, C Denmark
127 Nn17 **Rudnaya Pristan'** Primorskiy Kray, SE Russian Federation
151 V14 **Rudnichnyy** Kaz. Rūdnīchnyy. Taldykorgan, SE Kazakhstan
129 S13 **Rudnichnyy** Kirovskaya Oblast', NW Russian Federation
116 N9 **Rudnik** Varnenska Oblast, E Bulgaria
Rudny see Rudnyy
130 H4 **Rudnya** Smolenskaya Oblast', W Russian Federation
131 O8 **Rudnya** Volgogradskaya Oblast', SW Russian Federation
150 M7 **Rudnyy** var. Rudny. Kustanay, N Kazakhstan
126 Hh1 **Rudol'fa, Ostrov** island Zemlya Frantsa-Iosifa, NW Russian Federation
83 H16 **Rudolf, Lake** var. Lake Turkana. ◎ N Kenya
Rudolfswert see Novo Mesto
103 L17 **Rudolstadt** Thüringen, C Germany
xli W12 **Rudston** East Riding of Yorkshire, N England, UK
33 Q4 **Rudyard** Michigan, N USA
35 S7 **Rudyard** Montana, NW USA
121 K16 **Rudzyensk** Rus. Rudensk. Minskaya Voblasts', C Belorussia
106 L6 **Rueda** Castilla-León, N Spain
116 F10 **Ruen** ▲ Bulgaria/FYR Macedonia
xl G10 **Rue Point** headland N Isle of Man
82 G10 **Rufa'a** Gezira, C Sudan
104 L10 **Ruffec** Charente, W France
23 R14 **Ruffin** South Carolina, SE USA
xli N15 **Rufford** Lancashire, NW England, UK
83 J23 **Rufiji** ≈ E Tanzania
63 A20 **Rufino** Santa Fe, C Argentina
78 F11 **Rufisque** W Senegal
85 K14 **Rufunsa** Lusaka, C Zambia
120 J9 **Rugāji** Balvi, E Latvia
167 R7 **Rugao** Jiangsu, E China
xxxviii M11 **Rugby** Warwickshire, C England, UK
31 N3 **Rugby** North Dakota, N USA
xxxviii K9 **Rugeley** Staffordshire, C England, UK
102 N7 **Rügen** headland NE Germany
Ruhaybeh see Ar Ruḩaybah
167 N7 **Ru He** ≈ C China
83 E19 **Ruhengeri** NW Rwanda
Ruhja see Rūjiena
102 M10 **Ruhner Berg** hill N Germany
120 F7 **Ruhnu** var. Ruhnu Saar, Swe. Runö. island SW Estonia
Ruhnu Saar see Ruhnu
103 G15 **Ruhr** ≈ W Germany
93 V6 **Ruhr Valley** industrial region W Germany
167 S11 **Rui'an** var. Rui an. Zhejiang, SE China
167 P10 **Ruichang** Jiangxi, S China
26 J11 **Ruidosa** Texas, SW USA
39 S14 **Ruidoso** New Mexico, SW USA
167 P12 **Ruijin** Jiangxi, S China
166 D13 **Ruili** Yunnan, SW China
100 N8 **Ruinen** Drenthe, NE Netherlands
101 D17 **Ruiselede** West-Vlaanderen, W Belgium
66 P5 **Ruivo de Santana, Pico** ▲ Madeira, Portugal, NE Atlantic Ocean
42 J12 **Ruiz** Nayarit, SW Mexico
56 E10 **Ruiz, Nevado del** 🌋 W Colombia
144 J9 **Rujaylah, Ḩarrat ar** salt lake N Jordan
Rujen see Rūjiena
120 H7 **Rūjiena** Est. Ruhja, Ger. Rujen. Valmiera, N Latvia
81 I18 **Ruki** ≈ W Zaire
83 E22 **Rukwa** ◐ region SW Tanzania
83 F23 **Rukwa, Lake** ◎ SE Tanzania
27 P6 **Rule** Texas, SW USA
24 K3 **Ruleville** Mississippi, S USA
Rum see Rhum
114 K10 **Ruma** Serbia, N Yugoslavia
Rumadiya see Ar Ramādī
147 Q7 **Rumāḩ** Ar Riyāḑ, C Saudi Arabia
Rumaitha see Ar Rumaythah
Rumania/Rumänien see Romania
Rumänisch-Sankt-Georgen see Sângeorz-Băi
145 Y13 **Rumaylah** SE Iraq
145 P2 **Rumaylah, Wādī** dry watercourse NE Syria
176 V10 **Rumbati** Irian Jaya, E Indonesia
83 E14 **Rumbek** El Buhayrat, S Sudan
176 W10 **Rumberpon, Pulau** island E Indonesia
Rumburg see Rumburk
xxxix Y11 **Rumburgh** Suffolk, E England, UK
113 D14 **Rumburk** Ger. Rumburg. Severní Čechy, N Czech Republic
46 J4 **Rum Cay** island C Bahamas
101 M26 **Rumelange** Luxembourg, S Luxembourg
101 D20 **Rumes** Hainaut, SW Belgium
21 P7 **Rumford** Maine, NE USA
112 I6 **Rumia** Gdańsk, N Poland
115 J17 **Rumija** ⛰ SW Yugoslavia
105 T11 **Rumilly** Haute-Savoie, E France
145 O6 **Rūmiyah** W Iraq
Rummah, Wādī ar see Rimah, Wādī ar
Rummelsburg in Pommern see Miastko
xxxv K15 **Rumney** Cardiff, S Wales, UK
172 Oo4 **Rumoi** Hokkaidō, NE Japan
84 M12 **Rumphi** var. Rumpi. Northern, N Malawi
Rumpi see Rumphi
31 V7 **Rum River** ≈ Minnesota, N USA
xliii D15 **Rùm, Sound of** strait NW Scotland, UK
196 F16 **Rumung** island Caroline Islands, W Micronesia
Rumuniya/Rumŭniya/Rumunjska see Romania
xliv L2 **Runabay Head** headland N Northern Ireland, UK
193 G16 **Runanga** West Coast, South Island, NZ
192 P7 **Runaway, Cape** headland North Island, NZ
xl D16 **Runcorn** Cheshire, C England, UK
120 K10 **Rundāni** Ludza, E Latvia
85 L18 **Runde** var. Lundi. ≈ SE Zimbabwe
85 E16 **Rundu** var. Runtu. Okavango, NE Namibia
95 I16 **Rundvik** Västerbotten, N Sweden
83 G20 **Runere** Mwanza, N Tanzania
27 S13 **Runge** Texas, SW USA
178 I14 **Rŭng, Kaôh** prev. Kas Rong. island SW Cambodia
81 O16 **Rungu** Haut-Zaïre, NE Zaire
83 F23 **Rungwa** Rukwa, W Tanzania
83 G22 **Rungwa** Singida, C Tanzania
96 M13 **Runn** ◎ C Sweden
26 M4 **Running Water Draw** valley New Mexico/Texas, SW USA
Runö see Ruhnu
Runtu see Rundu
201 V12 **Ruo** island Caroline Islands, C Micronesia
164 L9 **Ruoqiang** var. Jo-ch'iang, Uigh. Charkhlik, Charkhliq, Qarkilik. Xinjiang Uygur Zizhiqu, NW China
165 S7 **Ruo Shui** ≈ N China
95 L18 **Ruovesi** Häme, SW Finland
114 B9 **Rupa** Primorje-Gorski Kotar, NW Croatia
190 M11 **Rupanyup** Victoria, SE Australia
174 H6 **Rupat, Pulau** prev. Roepat. island W Indonesia
174 Gg6 **Rupat, Selat** strait Sumatera, W Indonesia
118 J11 **Rupea** Ger. Reps, Hung. Kőhalom; prev. Cohalm. Braşov, C Romania
101 G17 **Rupel** ≈ N Belgium
Rupella see la Rochelle
35 P15 **Rupert** Idaho, NW USA
23 R5 **Rupert** West Virginia, NE USA
Rupert House see Fort Rupert
10 J10 **Rupert, Rivière de** ≈ Québec, C Canada
204 M13 **Ruppert Coast** physical region Antarctica
102 N11 **Ruppiner Kanal** canal NE Germany
57 S11 **Rupununi River** ≈ S Guyana
103 D16 **Rur** Dut. Roer. ≈ Germany/Netherlands
60 H13 **Rurópolis Presidente Medici** Pará, N Brazil
203 S12 **Rurutu** island Îles Australes, SW French Polynesia
Rusaddir see Melilla
85 L17 **Rusape** Manicaland, E Zimbabwe
Rusayris, Lake see Roseires, Reservoir
Ruschuk/Rusçuk see Ruse
116 K7 **Ruse** var. Ruschuk, Rustchuk, Turk. Rusçuk. Razgradska Oblast, N Bulgaria
111 W10 **Ruše** NE Slovenia
116 K7 **Rusenski Lom** ≈ N Bulgaria
xliv L8 **Rush** Ir. An Ros. Dublin, E Ireland
167 S4 **Rushan** var. Xiacun. Shandong, E China
Rushan see Rŭshon
Rushanskiy Khrebet see Rushon, Qatorkŭhi
31 V7 **Rush City** Minnesota, N USA
39 V5 **Rush Creek** ≈ Colorado, C USA
xxxix Q12 **Rushden** Northamptonshire, C England, UK
31 X10 **Rushford** Minnesota, N USA
160 N13 **Rushikulya** ≈ E India
12 D8 **Rush Lake** ◎ Ontario, S Canada
32 M7 **Rush Lake** ◎ Wisconsin, N USA
30 J10 **Rushmore, Mount** ▲ South Dakota, N USA
153 S13 **Rŭshon** Rus. Rushan. S Tajikistan
153 S14 **Rushon, Qatorkŭhi** Rus. Rushanskiy Khrebet. ⛰ SE Tajikistan
28 M12 **Rush Springs** Oklahoma, C USA
47 V15 **Rushville** Trinidad, Trinidad and Tobago
32 J13 **Rushville** Illinois, N USA
30 K12 **Rushville** Nebraska, C USA
191 O11 **Rushworth** Victoria, SE Australia
27 W8 **Rusk** Texas, SW USA
xxxix Q7 **Ruskinton** Lincolnshire, E England, UK
95 I14 **Rusksele** Västerbotten, N Sweden
120 C12 **Rusnė** Šilutė, W Lithuania
116 M10 **Rusokastrenska Reka** ≈ E Bulgaria
Russadir see Melilla
111 X3 **Russbach** ≈ NE Austria
9 V16 **Russell** Manitoba, S Canada
192 K2 **Russell** Northland, North Island, NZ
28 L4 **Russell** Kansas, C USA
23 O4 **Russell** Kentucky, S USA
195 W15 **Russell Islands** island group C Solomon Islands
22 L7 **Russell Springs** Kentucky, S USA
25 O2 **Russellville** Alabama, S USA
29 T11 **Russellville** Arkansas, C USA
22 J7 **Russellville** Kentucky, S USA
103 G18 **Rüsselsheim** Hessen, W Germany
94 K8 **Russenes** Finnmark, N Norway
Russia see Russian Federation
Russian America see Alaska
127 N17 **Russian Federation** off. Russian Federation, var. Russia, Latv. Krievija, Rus. Rossiyskaya Federatsiya. ◆ republic Asia/Europe
41 N11 **Russian Mission** Alaska, USA
36 M7 **Russian River** ≈ California, W USA
204 L13 **Russkaya** Russian research station Antarctica
126 H3 **Russkaya Gavan'** Novaya Zemlya, Arkhangel'skaya Oblast', N Russian Federation
126 J4 **Russkiy, Ostrov** island N Russian Federation
111 Y5 **Rust** Burgenland, E Austria
Rustaq see Ar Rustāq
143 U10 **Rust'avi** SE Georgia
23 T7 **Rustburg** Virginia, NE USA
Rustchuk see Ruse
94 L8 **Rustefjelbma** Finnmark, N Norway
85 I21 **Rustenburg** North-West, N South Africa
24 H5 **Ruston** Louisiana, S USA
83 E21 **Rutana** SE Burundi
64 I4 **Rutana, Volcán** ▲ N Chile
Rutanzige, Lake see Edward, Lake
Rutba see Ar Ruţbah
106 M14 **Rute** Andalucía, S Spain
175 Pp16 **Ruteng** prev. Roeteng. Flores, C Indonesia
204 L8 **Rutford Ice Stream** ice feature Antarctica
37 X6 **Ruth** Nevada, W USA
103 G15 **Rüthen** Nordrhein-Westfalen, W Germany
12 D17 **Rutherford** Ontario, S Canada
23 Q10 **Rutherfordton** North Carolina, SE USA
xliii J20 **Rutherglen** City of Glasgow, C Scotland, UK
xxxv J5 **Ruthin** Wel. Rhuthun. Denbighshire, NE Wales, UK
110 G7 **Rüti** Zürich, N Switzerland
Rutlam see Ratlām
xxxix P9 **Rutland** ◐ unitary authority C England, UK
20 M9 **Rutland** Vermont, NE USA
xxxix P9 **Rutland Water** ◎ C England, UK
23 N8 **Rutledge** Tennessee, S USA
164 G12 **Rutog** var. Rutok. Xizang Zizhiqu, W China
Rutok see Rutog
81 P19 **Rutshuru** Nord Kivu, E Zaire
100 L8 **Rutten** Flevoland, N Netherlands
131 Q17 **Rutul** Respublika Dagestan, SW Russian Federation
95 L14 **Ruukki** Oulu, C Finland
100 N11 **Ruurlo** Gelderland, E Netherlands
149 S15 **Ru'ūs al Jibāl** headland Oman/UAE
144 I7 **Ru'ūs aţ Ţiwāl, Jabal** ⛰ W Syria
83 H23 **Ruvuma** ◐ region SE Tanzania
83 I25 **Ruvuma** var. Rio Rovuma. ≈ Mozambique/Tanzania see also Rovuma, Rio
Ruwais see Ar Ruways
144 L9 **Ruwayshid, Wadi ar** dry watercourse NE Jordan
147 Z10 **Ruways, Ra's ar** headland E Oman
81 P18 **Ruwenzori** ⛰ Uganda/Zaire
147 Y8 **Ruwī** NE Oman
116 F9 **Ruy** ▲ Bulgaria/Yugoslavia
Ruya see Luia, Rio
83 E20 **Ruyigi** E Burundi
131 P5 **Ruzayevka** Respublika Mordoviya, W Russian Federation
121 G18 **Ruzhany** Rus. Ruzhany. Brestskaya Voblasts', SW Belorussia
116 I10 **Rŭzhevo Konare** var. Rŭzhevo Konare. Plovdivska Oblast, C Bulgaria
Ruzhin see Ruzhyn
116 G7 **Ruzhintsi** Oblast Montana, NW Bulgaria
119 N5 **Ruzhyn** Rus. Ruzhin. Zhytomyrs'ka Oblast', N Ukraine
113 K19 **Ružomberok** Ger. Rosenberg, Hung. Rózsahegy. Stredné Slovensko, N Slovakia
113 C16 **Ruzyně** ✕ (Praha) Praha, C Czech Republic
83 D19 **Rwanda** off. Rwandese Republic; prev. Ruanda. ◆ republic C Africa
Rwandese Republic see Rwanda
97 G22 **Ry** Århus, C Denmark
xliii G25 **Ryan, Loch** inlet SW Scotland, UK
Ryasna see Rasna
130 L5 **Ryazan'** Ryazanskaya Oblast', W Russian Federation
130 L5 **Ryazanskaya Oblast'** ◐ province W Russian Federation
130 M6 **Ryazhsk** Ryazanskaya Oblast', W Russian Federation
120 B13 **Rybachiy** Ger. Rossitten. Kaliningradskaya Oblast', W Russian Federation
128 J2 **Rybachiy, Poluostrov** peninsula NW Russian Federation
Rybach'ye see Balykchy
128 L15 **Rybinsk** prev. Andropov. Yaroslavskaya Oblast', W Russian Federation
128 K14 **Rybinskoye Vodokhranilishche** Eng. Rybinsk Reservoir, Rybinsk Sea. ▣ W Russian Federation
Rybinsk Reservoir/Rybinsk Sea see Rybinskoye Vodokhranilishche
Rybnitsa see Rîbniţa
113 I16 **Rybnik** Katowice, S Poland
113 F16 **Rychnov nad Kněžnou** Ger. Reichenau. Východní Čechy, NE Czech Republic
112 I12 **Rychwał** Konin, C Poland
9 O13 **Rycroft** Alberta, W Canada
97 L21 **Ryd** Kronoberg, S Sweden
97 L20 **Rydaholm** Jönköping, S Sweden
204 I8 **Rydberg Peninsula** peninsula Antarctica
xxxvii Q14 **Ryde** Isle of Wight, S England, UK
xxxvii X12 **Rye** East Sussex, SE England, UK
xli T11 **Rye** ≈ N England, UK
35 T10 **Ryegate** Montana, NW USA
37 S3 **Rye Patch Reservoir** ▣ Nevada, W USA
97 D15 **Ryfylke** physical region S Norway
97 H16 **Rygge** Østfold, S Norway
xli S7 **Ryhope** Sunderland, NE England, UK
112 N13 **Ryki** Lublin, E Poland
Rykovo see Yenakiyeve
130 I7 **Ryl'sk** Kurskaya Oblast', W Russian Federation
xli P12 **Rylstone** North Yorkshire, N England, UK
191 S8 **Rylstone** New South Wales, SE Australia
113 H17 **Rýmařov** Ger. Römerstadt. Severní Morava, E Czech Republic
150 E11 **Ryn-Peski** desert W Kazakhstan
171 K12 **Ryōtsu** var. Ryôtu. Niigata, Sado, C Japan
Ryôtu see Ryōtsu
112 K10 **Rypin** Włocławek, C Poland
Ryshkany see Rîşcani
Ryssel see Lille
Ryswick see Rijswijk
xli U2 **Ryton** Gateshead, NE England, UK
97 M24 **Rytterknægten** hill E Denmark
171 Kk16 **Ryūgasaki** Ibaraki, Honshū, S Japan
198 G5 **Ryukyu Trench** var. Nansei Syotō Trench. undersea feature S East China Sea
112 D11 **Rzepin** Ger. Reppen. Gorzów, W Poland
113 N16 **Rzeszów** Rzeszów, SE Poland
113 N16 **Rzeszów** off. Województwo Rzeszowskie. ◐ province SE Poland
Rzeszowskie, Województwo see Rzeszów
128 I16 **Rzhev** Tverskaya Oblast', W Russian Federation
Rzhishchev see Rzhyshchiv
119 P5 **Rzhyshchiv** Rus. Rzhishchev. Kyyivs'ka Oblast', N Ukraine

S

144 E11 **Sa'ad** Southern, W Israel
111 P7 **Saalach** ≈ W Austria
103 L14 **Saale** ≈ C Germany
103 L17 **Saalfeld** var. Saalfeld an der Saale. Thüringen, C Germany
Saalfeld see Zalewo
Saalfeld an der Saale see Saalfeld
110 C8 **Saane** ≈ W Switzerland
103 D19 **Saar** Fr. Sarre. ≈ France/Germany
103 E20 **Saarbrücken** Fr. Sarrebruck. Saarland, SW Germany
Saarburg see Sarrebourg
Saare see Saaremaa
120 D6 **Sääre** var. Sjar. Saaremaa, W Estonia
120 D5 **Saaremaa** off. Saare Maakond. ◐ province W Estonia
120 E6 **Saaremaa** Ger. Oesel, Ösel; prev. Saare. island W Estonia
94 L12 **Saarenkylä** Lappi, N Finland
Saargemund see Sarreguemines
95 L17 **Saarijärvi** Keski-Suomi, C Finland
Saar in Mähren see Žďár nad Sázavou
94 M10 **Saariselkä** Lapp. Suoločielgi. Lappi, N Finland
94 L10 **Saariselkä** hill range NE Finland
103 D20 **Saarland** Fr. Sarre. ◐ state SW Germany
Saarlautern see Saarlouis
103 D20 **Saarlouis** prev. Saarlautern. Saarland, SW Germany
110 E11 **Saaser Vispa** ≈ S Switzerland
143 X12 **Saatlı** Rus. Saatly. C Azerbaijan
Saatly see Saatlı
Saaz see Žatec
176 X9 **Saba** Irian Jaya, E Indonesia
47 V9 **Saba** island N Netherlands Antilles
144 J7 **Sab' Ābār** var. Sab'a Biyar, Sa'b Bi'ār. Ḩimş, C Syria
Sab'a Biyar see Sab' Ābār
114 K11 **Šabac** Serbia, W Yugoslavia
107 W5 **Sabadell** Cataluña, E Spain
171 Hh13 **Sabae** Fukui, Honshū, SW Japan
175 O3 **Sabah** prev. British North Borneo, North Borneo. ◐ state East Malaysia
174 Gg4 **Sabak** var. Sabak Bernam. Selangor, Peninsular Malaysia
Sabak Bernam see Sabak
40 D16 **Sabak, Cape** headland Agattu Island, Alaska, USA
83 J20 **Sabaki** ≈ S Kenya
175 P14 **Sabalana, Kepulauan** var. Kepulauan Liukang Tenggaya. island group C Indonesia
148 L2 **Sabalān, Kuhhā-ye** ▲ NW Iran
160 H7 **Sabalgarh** Madhya Pradesh, C India
46 E4 **Sabana, Archipiélago de** island group C Cuba
44 H7 **Sabanagrande** var. Sabana Grande. Francisco Morazán, S Honduras
56 E5 **Sabanalarga** Atlántico, N Colombia
43 W14 **Sabancuy** Campeche, SE Mexico
47 N8 **Sabaneta** NW Dominican Republic
56 J4 **Sabaneta** Falcón, N Venezuela
196 H4 **Sabaneta, Puntan** prev. Ushi Point. headland Saipan, S Northern Mariana Islands
176 Y12 **Sabang** Irian Jaya, E Indonesia
118 L10 **Săbăoani** Neamţ, NE Romania
161 J26 **Sabaragamuwa Province** ◐ province C Sri Lanka
Sabaria see Szombathely
160 D10 **Sābarmati** ≈ NW India
175 T6 **Sabatai** Pulau Morotai, E Indonesia
147 Q15 **Sab'atayn, Ramlat as** desert C Yemen
109 I16 **Sabaudia** Lazio, C Italy
59 J19 **Sabaya** Oruro, S Bolivia
Sa'b Bi'ār see Sab' Ābār
Sabbioncello see Orebić
154 I8 **Şāberī, Hāmūn-e** var. Daryācheh-ye Hāmūn, Daryācheh-ye Sīstān. ◎ Afghanistan/Iran see also Sīstān, Daryācheh-ye
29 P2 **Sabetha** Kansas, C USA
77 P10 **Sabhā** C Libya
69 V13 **Sabi** var. Rio Save. ≈ Mozambique/Zimbabwe see also Save, Rio
120 E8 **Sabile** Ger. Zabeln. Talsi, NW Latvia
33 R14 **Sabina** Ohio, N USA
42 I3 **Sabinal** Chihuahua, N Mexico
27 Q12 **Sabinal** Texas, SW USA
27 Q11 **Sabinal River** ≈ Texas, SW USA
107 S4 **Sabiñánigo** Aragón, NE Spain
43 N6 **Sabinas** Coahuila de Zaragoza, NE Mexico
43 O8 **Sabinas Hidalgo** Nuevo León, NE Mexico
43 N6 **Sabinas, Río** ≈ NE Mexico
24 F9 **Sabine Lake** ◎ Louisiana/Texas, S USA
94 O3 **Sabine Land** physical region C Svalbard
27 W7 **Sabine River** ≈ Louisiana/Texas, SW USA
143 X12 **Sabirabad** C Azerbaijan
Sabkha see As Sabkhah
179 P12 **Sablayan** Mindoro, N Philippines
11 P16 **Sable, Cape** headland Newfoundland and Labrador, SE Canada
25 X17 **Sable, Cape** headland Florida, SE USA
11 R16 **Sable Island** island Nova Scotia, SE Canada
12 L11 **Sables, Lac des** ◎ Québec, SE Canada
12 E10 **Sables, Rivière aux** ≈ Ontario, S Canada
104 K7 **Sable-sur-Sarthe** Sarthe, NW France
129 U7 **Sablya, Gora** ▲ NW Russian Federation
79 U14 **Sabon Birnin Gwari** Kaduna, C Nigeria
79 V11 **Sabon Kafi** Zinder, C Niger
106 I6 **Sabor, Rio** ≈ N Portugal
12 J8 **Sabourin, Lac** ◎ Québec, SE Canada
104 J14 **Sabres** Landes, SW France
205 X13 **Sabrina Coast** physical region Antarctica
146 M11 **Sabt al Ulayā** 'Asīr, SW Saudi Arabia
106 I8 **Sabugal** Guarda, N Portugal
31 Z13 **Sabula** Iowa, C USA
147 N13 **Şabyā** Jīzān, SW Saudi Arabia
Sabzawar see Sabzevār
Sabzawaran see Sabzvārān
149 S4 **Sabzevār** var. Sabzawar. Khorāsān, NE Iran
149 T12 **Sabzvārān** var. Sabzawaran; prev. Jiroft. Kermān, SE Iran
Sacajawea Peak see Matterhorn
84 C9 **Sacandica** Uíge, NW Angola
44 A2 **Sacatepéquez** off. Departamento de Sacatepéquez. ◐ department S Guatemala
106 F11 **Sacavém** Lisboa, W Portugal
31 T13 **Sac City** Iowa, C USA
107 P8 **Sacedón** Castilla-La Mancha, C Spain
118 J12 **Săcele** Ger. Vierdörfer, Hung. Négyfalu; prev. Ger. Sieben Dörfer, Hung. Hétfalu. Braşov, C Romania
10 C8 **Sachigo** Ontario, C Canada
10 C7 **Sachigo** ≈ Ontario, C Canada
10 C8 **Sachigo Lake** ◎ Ontario, C Canada
169 Y16 **Sach'ŏn** Jap. Sansenhō; prev. Samch'ŏnpŏ. S South Korea
103 O15 **Sachsen** Eng. Saxony, Fr. Saxe. ◐ state E Germany
103 K14 **Sachsen-Anhalt** Eng. Saxony-Anhalt. ◐ state C Germany
111 R9 **Sachsenburg** Salzburg, S Austria
Sachsenfeld see Žalec
15 H1 **Sachs Harbour** Banks Island, Northwest Territories, N Canada
Sächsisch-Reen/Sächsisch-Regen see Reghin
20 H8 **Sackets Harbor** New York, NE USA
11 P14 **Sackville** New Brunswick, SE Canada
21 P9 **Saco** Maine, NE USA
21 P8 **Saco River** ≈ Maine/New Hampshire, NE USA
37 O7 **Sacramento** state capital California, W USA
39 T14 **Sacramento Mountains** ⛰ New Mexico, SW USA
37 N6 **Sacramento River** ≈ California, W USA
37 N5 **Sacramento Valley** valley California, W USA
38 I10 **Sacramento Wash** valley Arizona, SW USA
107 N15 **Sacratif, Cabo** headland S Spain
xli V4 **Sacriston** Durham, N England, UK
118 F9 **Săcueni** prev. Săcuieni, Hung. Székelyhid. Bihor, W Romania
Săcuieni see Săcueni
107 R4 **Sádaba** Aragón, NE Spain
Sá da Bandeira see Lubango
144 I6 **Şadad** Ḩimş, W Syria
147 O13 **Şa'dah** NW Yemen
170 Dd14 **Sadamisaki-hinto** peninsula Shikoku, SW Japan
175 P12 **Sadang, Sungai** ≈ Sulawesi, C Indonesia
178 H17 **Sadao** Songkhla, SW Thailand
148 L8 **Sadd-e Dez, Daryācheh-ye** ◎ W Iran
xliii F22 **Saddell** Argyll and Bute, W Scotland, UK
21 S3 **Saddleback Mountain** hill Maine, NE USA
21 P6 **Saddleback Mountain** ▲ Maine, NE USA
xlii G13 **Saddle, The** ▲ NW Scotland, UK
178 J114 **Sa Đec** Đông Thap, S Vietnam
147 W13 **Sadḩ** S Oman
78 J11 **Sadiola** Kayes, W Mali
155 R12 **Sādiqābād** Punjab, E Pakistan
159 Y10 **Sadiya** Assam, NE India
145 W9 **Sa'dīyah, Hawr as** ◎ E Iraq
171 K12 **Sado** var. Sadoga-shima. island C Japan
Sadoga-shima see Sado
106 F12 **Sado, Rio** ≈ S Portugal
116 I8 **Sadovets** Loveshka Oblast, N Bulgaria
131 O11 **Sadovoye** Respublika Kalmykiya, SW Russian Federation
107 W9 **Sa Dragonera** var. Isla Dragonera. island Islas Baleares, Spain, W Mediterranean Sea
97 H20 **Sæby** Nordjylland, N Denmark
107 P9 **Saelices** Castilla-La Mancha, C Spain
Saena Julia see Siena
Saetabicula see Alzira
116 O12 **Safaalan** Tekirdağ, NW Turkey
Safad see Ẕefat
Şafāqis see Sfax
198 B8 **Safata Bay** bay Upolo, Western Samoa, C Pacific Ocean
Safed see Ẕefat
Safed, Āb-i- see Sefīd, Darya-ye
145 X11 **Şaffāf, Ḩawr aş** wetland S Iraq
97 J16 **Säffle** Värmland, C Sweden
39 N15 **Safford** Arizona, SW USA
xxxvii V6 **Saffron Walden** Essex, SE England, UK
76 E7 **Safi** W Morocco
149 V9 **Safīdābeh** Khorāsān, E Iran
148 M4 **Safīd, Rūd-e** ≈ NW Iran
130 I4 **Safonovo** Smolenskaya Oblast', W Russian Federation
142 H11 **Safranbolu** Zonguldak, N Turkey
145 Y13 **Safwān** SE Iraq
164 J16 **Saga** var. Gya'gya. Xizang Zizhiqu, W China
170 Cc13 **Saga** Saga, Kyūshū, SW Japan
170 Cc13 **Saga** off. Saga-ken. ◐ prefecture Kyūshū, SW Japan
171 Ll12 **Sagae** Yamagata, Honshū, C Japan
177 G5 **Sagaing** Sagaing, C Burma
177 G3 **Sagaing** ◐ division N Burma
171 Jj16 **Sagamihara** Kanagawa, Honshū, S Japan
171 Jj17 **Sagami-nada** inlet SW Japan
171 Jj17 **Sagami-wan** bay SW Japan
Sagan see Żagań
31 Y3 **Saganaga Lake** ◎ Minnesota, N USA
161 F18 **Sāgar** Karnātaka, W India
160 I9 **Sāgar** prev. Saugor. Madhya Pradesh, C India
13 S8 **Sagard** Québec, SE Canada
Sagarmatha see Everest, Mount
179 Qq13 **Sagay** Negros, C Philippines
Sagebrush State see Nevada
149 V11 **Sāghand** Yazd, C Iran
21 N14 **Sag Harbor** Long Island, New York, NE USA
Saghez see Saqqez
33 R8 **Saginaw** Michigan, N USA
33 R8 **Saginaw Bay** lake bay Michigan, N USA
150 H11 **Sagiz** Atyrau, W Kazakhstan
66 H6 **Saglek Bank** undersea feature W Labrador Sea
11 P5 **Saglek Bay** bay SW Labrador Sea
Saglouc/Sagluk see Salluit
104 E2 **Sagonne, Golfe de** gulf Corse, France, C Mediterranean Sea
107 P13 **Sagra** ▲ S Spain
106 F14 **Sagres** Faro, S Portugal
39 S7 **Saguache** Colorado, C USA
46 J7 **Sagua de Tánamo** Holguín, E Cuba
46 E5 **Sagua la Grande** Villa Clara, C Cuba
13 R7 **Saguenay** ≈ Québec, SE Canada
76 C9 **Saguia al Hamra** var. As Saqia al Hamra. ≈ N Western Sahara
Sagunt/Saguntum see Sagunto
107 S9 **Sagunto** var. Sagunt, Ar. Murviedro; anc. Saguntum. País Valenciano, E Spain
144 H10 **Saḩāb** 'Ammān, NW Jordan
56 E6 **Sahagún** Córdoba, NW Colombia
106 L4 **Sahagún** Castilla-León, N Spain
147 X8 **Saḩam** N Oman
70 F9 **Sahara** desert Libya/Algeria
77 U9 **Sahara el Gharbîya** var. Aş Şaḩrā' al Gharbīyah, Eng. Western Desert. desert C Egypt
77 X9 **Sahara el Sharqîya** var. Aş Şaḩrā' ash Sharqīyah, Eng. Arabian Desert, Eastern Desert. desert E Egypt
Saharan Atlas see Atlas Saharien
158 J9 **Sahāranpur** Uttar Pradesh, N India
66 L10 **Saharan Seamounts** var. Saharian Seamounts. undersea feature E Atlantic Ocean
159 Q13 **Saharsa** Bihār, NE India
69 O7 **Sahel** physical region C Africa
159 R14 **Sāhibganj** Bihār, NE India
145 Q7 **Sahīlīyah** C Iraq
144 H4 **Sāḩilīyah, Jibāl as** ⛰ NW Syria
116 M13 **Şahin** Tekirdağ, NW Turkey
155 U8 **Sāhīwāl** Punjab, E Pakistan
155 U9 **Sāhīwāl** prev. Montgomery. Punjab, E Pakistan
147 W11 **Saḩmah, Ramlat as** desert C Oman
145 T13 **Şaḩrā' al Ḩijārah** desert S Iraq
42 H5 **Sahuaripa** Sonora, NW Mexico
38 M16 **Sahuarita** Arizona, SW USA
42 L13 **Sahuayo** var. Sahuayo de José Mariá Morelos; prev. Sahuayo de Díaz, Sahuayo de Porfirio Díaz. Michoacán de Ocampo, SW Mexico
Sahuayo de Díaz/Sahuayo de José Mariá Morelos/Sahuayo de Porfirio Díaz see Sahuayo
181 W8 **Sahul Shelf** undersea feature N Timor Sea
178 Hh17 **Sai Buri** Pattani, SW Thailand
76 I6 **Saïda** NW Algeria
144 G7 **Saïda** var. Şaydā, Sayida; anc. Sidon. W Lebanon
Sa'īdābād see Sīrjān
82 B13 **Sa'id Bundas** Western Bahr el Ghazal, SW Sudan
194 J12 **Saidor** Madang, N PNG
159 S13 **Saidpur** var. Syedpur. Rajshahi, NW Bangladesh
110 C7 **Saignelégier** Jura, NW Switzerland
170 G11 **Saigō** Shimane, Dōgo, SW Japan
Saigon see Hô Chi Minh
168 I12 **Saihan Toroi** Nei Mongol Zizhiqu, N China
Saihon Tal see Sonid Youqi
Sai Hun see Syr Darya
94 M11 **Saija** Lappi, NE Finland
170 Ee14 **Saijō** Ehime, Shikoku, SW Japan
170 Dd15 **Saiki** Ōita, Kyūshū, SW Japan
176 Uu9 **Saileen** Irian Jaya, E Indonesia
95 N18 **Saimaa** ◎ SE Finland
95 N18 **Saimaa Canal** Fin. Saimaan Kanava, Rus. Saymenskiy Kanal. canal Finland/Russian Federation
Saimaan Kanava see Saimaa Canal
42 L10 **Saín Alto** Zacatecas, C Mexico
xliii P20 **St Abbs** The Borders, S Scotland, UK
xliii P20 **St Abb's Head** headland SE Scotland, UK
9 Y16 **St.Adolphe** Manitoba, S Canada
105 O15 **St-Affrique** Aveyron, S France
13 Q10 **St-Agapit** Québec, SE Canada
xxxvi B16 **St Agnes** Cornwall, SW England, UK
xxxvi I17 **St Agnes** island SW England, UK
xxxvii T8 **St Albans** anc. Verulamium. Hertfordshire, E England, UK
20 L6 **Saint Albans** Vermont, NE USA
23 Q5 **Saint Albans** West Virginia, NE USA
xxxvii N15 **St Alban's Head** var. St Aldhelm's Head. headland S England, UK
9 Q14 **St.Albert** Alberta, SW Canada
St Aldhelm's Head see St Alban's Head
13 S8 **St-Alexandre** Québec, SE Canada

◆ Country ● Country Capital ◇ Dependent Territory ○ Dependent Territory Capital ◐ Administrative Region ✕ International Airport ▲ Mountain ⛰ Mountain Range 🌋 Volcano ≈ River ◎ Lake ▣ Reservoir

St-Alexis-des-Monts -- Salhiye

13 O11 **St-Alexis-des-Monts** Québec, SE Canada
105 P2 **St-Amand-les-Eaux** Nord, N France
105 O9 **St-Amand-Montrond** *var.* St-Amand-Mont-Rond. Cher, C France
13 Q7 **St-Ambroise** Québec, SE Canada
181 P16 **St-André** NE Réunion
12 M12 **St-André-Avellin** Québec, SE Canada
104 K12 **St-André-de-Cubzac** Gironde, SW France
xliii N18 **St Andrews** Fife, E Scotland, UK
xliii N17 **St Andrews Bay** *bay* E Scotland, UK
25 Q9 **Saint Andrews Bay** *bay* Florida, SE USA
25 W7 **Saint Andrew Sound** *sound* Georgia, SE USA
Saint Anna Trough *see* Svyataya Anna Trough
xxxvii X14 **St Anne** Alderney, N Guernsey
46 J11 **St.Ann's Bay** C Jamaica
11 T10 **St.Anthony** Newfoundland, Newfoundland and Labrador, SE Canada
35 R13 **Saint Anthony** Idaho, NW USA
190 M11 **Saint Arnaud** Victoria, SE Australia
193 I15 **St.Arnaud Range** ▲▲ South Island, NZ
13 T8 **St-Arsène** Québec, SE Canada
xxxv L14 **St Arvans** Monmouthshire, SE Wales, UK
xxxv I4 **St Asaph** Denbighshire, N Wales, UK
xxxvii X17 **St Aubin** Jersey, Channel Islands
11 R10 **St-Augustin** Québec, E Canada
25 X9 **Saint Augustine** Florida, SE USA
xxxvi D16 **St Austell** Cornwall, SW England, UK
xxxvi D16 **St Austell Bay** *bay* SW England, UK
105 T4 **St-Avold** Moselle, NE France
105 N17 **St-Barthélemy** ▲ S France
104 L17 **St-Béat** Haute-Garonne, S France
xl K9 **St Bees** Cumbria, NW England, UK
xl J9 **St Bees Head** *headland* NW England, UK
181 P16 **St-Benoit** E Réunion
xxxvi D16 **St Blazey** Cornwall, SW England, UK
105 T13 **St-Bonnet** Hautes-Alpes, SE France
xliii N21 **St Boswells** The Borders, S Scotland, UK
St Botolph's Town *see* Boston
xxxvi K8 **St Briavels** Gloucestershire, C England, UK
xxxv C13 **St Brides** Pembrokeshire, SW Wales, UK
xxxv B13 **St Brides Bay** *inlet* SW Wales, UK
104 H5 **St-Brieuc** Côtes d'Armor, NW France
104 H5 **St-Brieuc, Baie de** *bay* NW France
104 L7 **St-Calais** Sarthe, NW France
13 Q10 **St-Casimir** Québec, SE Canada
12 H16 **St.Catharines** Ontario, S Canada
47 S14 **St.Catherine, Mount** ▲ N Grenada
66 C11 **St Catherine Point** *headland* E Bermuda
xliii H18 **St Catherines** Argyll and Bute, W Scotland, UK
25 X6 **Saint Catherines Island** *island* Georgia, SE USA
xxxvii P15 **St Catherine's Point** *headland* S England, UK
105 N13 **St-Céré** Lot, S France
110 A10 **St.Cergue** Vaud, W Switzerland
105 R11 **St-Chamond** Loire, E France
35 S16 **Saint Charles** Idaho, NW USA
29 X4 **Saint Charles** Missouri, C USA
105 P13 **St-Chély-d'Apcher** Lozère, S France
Saint Christopher-Nevis *see* Saint Kitts and Nevis
33 S9 **Saint Clair** Michigan, N USA
12 D17 **St.Clair** ≈ Canada/USA
191 O17 **St.Clair, Lake** ◎ Tasmania, SE Australia
12 C17 **St.Clair, Lake** *var.* Lac à L'eau Claire. ◎ Canada/USA
33 S10 **Saint Clair Shores** Michigan, N USA
105 S10 **St-Claude** *anc.* Condate. Jura, E France
47 X6 **St-Claude** Basse Terre, SW Guadeloupe
xxxv E13 **St Clears** Carmarthenshire, S Wales, UK
25 X12 **Saint Cloud** Florida, SE USA
31 U8 **Saint Cloud** Minnesota, N USA
xxxvi C15 **St Columb Major** Cornwall, SW England, UK
xlii P11 **St Combs** Aberdeenshire, NE Scotland, UK
47 T9 **Saint Croix** *island* S Virgin Islands (US)
32 J4 **Saint Croix Flowage** ⊡ Wisconsin, N USA
21 T5 **Saint Croix River** ≈ Canada/USA
31 W7 **Saint Croix River** ≈ Minnesota/Wisconsin, N USA
xliii O15 **St Cyrus** Aberdeenshire, NE Scotland, UK
xxxv B13 **St David's** Pembrokeshire, SW Wales, UK
47 S14 **St.David's** SE Grenada
xxxv A12 **St David's Head** *headland* SW Wales, UK
66 C12 **St David's Island** *island* E Bermuda
xxxvi B17 **St Day** Cornwall, SW England, UK
181 O16 **St-Denis** ○ (Réunion) NW Réunion
xxxvi C16 **St Dennis** Cornwall, SW England, UK
105 U6 **St-Dié** Vosges, NE France
105 R5 **St-Dizier** *anc.* Desiderii Fanum. Haute-Marne, N France
xxxv E11 **St Dogmaels** Ceredigion, W Wales, UK
13 N11 **St-Donat** Québec, SE Canada
xxxv I16 **St Donats** The Vale of Glamorgan, S Wales, UK
13 N11 **Ste-Adèle** Québec, SE Canada
13 N11 **Ste-Agathe-des-Monts** Québec, SE Canada
9 Y16 **Ste.Anne** Manitoba, S Canada
47 R12 **Ste-Anne** Grande Terre, E Guadeloupe
47 Y6 **Ste-Anne** SE Martinique
180 I16 **Sainte Anne** *island* Inner Islands, NE Seychelles
13 Q10 **Ste-Anne** ≈ Québec, SE Canada
13 W6 **Ste-Anne-des-Monts** Québec, SE Canada
12 M10 **Ste-Anne-du-Lac** Québec, SE Canada
13 U4 **Ste-Anne, Lac** ◎ Québec, SE Canada
13 S10 **Ste-Apolline** Québec, SE Canada
13 U7 **Ste-Blandine** Québec, SE Canada
13 R10 **Ste-Claire** Québec, SE Canada
13 Q10 **Ste-Croix** Québec, SE Canada
110 B8 **Ste.Croix** Vaud, SW Switzerland
105 P14 **Ste-Énimie** Lozère, S France
29 Y6 **Sainte Genevieve** Missouri, C USA
105 S12 **St-Egrève** Isère, E France
41 T12 **Saint Elias, Cape** *headland* Kayak Island, Alaska, USA
41 U11 **Saint Elias, Mount** ▲ Alaska, USA
8 G8 **Saint Elias Mountains** ▲▲ Canada/USA
57 Y10 **St-Élie** N French Guiana
105 O10 **St-Eloy-les-Mines** Puy-de-Dôme, C France
13 S7 **Ste-Marguerite Nord-Est** ≈ Québec, SE Canada
13 R7 **Ste-Marguerite** ≈ Québec, SE Canada
13 V4 **Ste-Marguerite, Pointe** *headland* Québec, SE Canada
13 V3 **Ste-Marguesite** ≈ Québec, SE Canada
13 R10 **Ste-Marie** Québec, SE Canada
47 Q11 **Ste-Marie** NE Martinique
181 P16 **Ste-Marie** NE Réunion
105 U6 **Ste-Marie-aux-Mines** Haut-Rhin, NE France
10 J14 **Ste-Marie, Lac** ⊡ Québec, S Canada
180 K4 **Sainte Marie, Nosy** *island* E Madagascar
104 L8 **Ste-Maure-de-Touraine** Indre-et-Loire, C France
105 R4 **Ste-Menehould** Marne, NE France
Ste-Perpétue *see* Ste-Perpétue-de-l'Islet
13 S9 **Ste-Perpétue-de-l'Islet** *var.* Ste-Perpétue. Québec, SE Canada
47 X11 **Ste-Rose** Basse Terre, N Guadeloupe
181 P16 **Ste-Rose** E Réunion
9 W15 **Ste.Rose du Lac** Manitoba, S Canada
104 J11 **Saintes** *anc.* Mediolanum. Charente-Maritime, W France
47 X7 **Saintes, Canal des** *channel* SW Guadeloupe
Saintes, Îles des *see* les Saintes
181 P16 **Ste-Suzanne** N Réunion
13 P10 **Ste-Thècle** Québec, SE Canada
105 Q12 **St-Étienne** Loire, E France
104 M4 **St-Étienne-du-Rouvray** Seine-Maritime, N France
Saint Eustatius *see* Sint Eustatius
12 M11 **Ste-Véronique** Québec, SE Canada
13 T7 **St-Fabien** Québec, SE Canada
13 P7 **St-Félicien** Québec, SE Canada
13 O11 **St-Félix-de-Valois** Québec, SE Canada
xlii P11 **St Fergus** Aberdeenshire, NE Scotland, UK
xliv M5 **Saintfield** Down, E Northern Ireland, UK
xliii J17 **St Fillans** Perth and Kinross, C Scotland, UK
104 F1 **St-Florent** Corse, France, C Mediterranean Sea
104 F1 **St-Florent, Golfe de** *gulf* Corse, France, C Mediterranean Sea
105 P6 **St-Florentin** Yonne, C France
105 N9 **St-Florent-sur-Cher** Cher, C France
105 P12 **St-Flour** Cantal, C France
28 H2 **Saint Francis** Kansas, C USA
85 H26 **St.Francis, Cape** *headland* S South Africa
29 X10 **Saint Francis River** ≈ Arkansas/Missouri, C USA
24 J8 **Saint Francisville** Louisiana, S USA
13 Q12 **St-François** ≈ Québec, SE Canada
47 Y6 **St-François** Grande Terre, E Guadeloupe
13 R11 **St-François, Lac** ◎ Québec, SE Canada
29 X7 **Saint Francois Mountains** ▲▲ Missouri, C USA
St-Gall/Saint Gall/St.Gallen *see* Sankt Gallen
104 L16 **St-Gaudens** Haute-Garonne, S France
13 R12 **St-Gédéon** Québec, SE Canada
189 X10 **Saint George** Queensland, E Australia
66 B12 **St George** N Bermuda
40 K15 **Saint George** Saint George Island, Alaska, USA
23 S14 **Saint George** South Carolina, SE USA
38 J8 **Saint George** Utah, W USA
11 R12 **St.George, Cape** *headland* Newfoundland, Newfoundland and Labrador, E Canada
195 P11 **St.George, Cape** *headland* New Ireland,
40 J15 **Saint George Island** *island* Pribilof Islands, Alaska, US
40 J15 **Saint George Island** *island* Pribilof Islands, Alaska, USA
25 S10 **Saint George Island** *island* Florida, SE USA
101 J19 **Saint-Georges** Liège, E Belgium
13 R11 **St-Georges** Québec, SE Canada
57 Z11 **St-Georges** E French Guiana
47 R14 **St.George's** ● (Grenada) SW Grenada
11 R12 **St.George's Bay** *inlet* Newfoundland, Newfoundland and Labrador, E Canada
99 G21 **Saint George's Channel** *channel* Ireland/Wales, UK
195 P10 **St.George's Channel** *channel* NE PNG
66 B11 **St George's Island** *island* E Bermuda
101 I21 **Saint-Gérard** Namur, S Belgium
St-Germain *see* St-Germain-en-Laye
13 P12 **St-Germain-de-Grantham** Québec, SE Canada
105 N5 **St-Germain-en-Laye** *var.* St-Germain. Yvelines, N France
xxxvi E16 **St Germans** Cornwall, SW England, UK
104 H8 **St-Gildas, Pointe du** *headland* NW France
105 R15 **St-Gilles** Gard, S France
104 I9 **St-Gilles-Croix-de-Vie** Vendée, NW France
181 O16 **St-Gilles-les-Bains** W Réunion
104 M16 **St-Girons** Ariège, S France
Saint Gotthard *see* Szentgotthárd
110 G9 **St.Gotthard Tunnel** *tunnel* Ticino, S Switzerland
xxxv C14 **St Govan's Head** *headland* SW Wales, UK
xxxv I10 **St Harmon** Powys, C Wales, UK
36 M7 **Saint Helena** California, W USA
67 F24 **Saint Helena** ◇ *UK dependent territory* C Atlantic Ocean
69 O12 **Saint Helena** *island* C Atlantic Ocean
85 E25 **St.Helena Bay** *bay* SW South Africa
67 M16 **Saint Helena Fracture Zone** *tectonic feature* C Atlantic Ocean
36 M7 **Saint Helena, Mount** ▲ California, W USA
23 S15 **Saint Helena Sound** *inlet* South Carolina, SE USA
33 Q7 **Saint Helen, Lake** ◎ Michigan, N USA
xl D15 **St Helens** St Helens, NW England, UK
xli N16 **St Helens** ◐ *unitary authority* NW England, UK
191 Q16 **Saint Helens** Tasmania, SE Australia
34 G10 **Saint Helens** Oregon, NW USA
34 H10 **Saint Helens, Mount** ✵ Washington, NW USA
xxxvii X17 **St Helier** ○ (Jersey) S Jersey, Channel Islands
13 S9 **St-Hilarion** Québec, SE Canada
101 K22 **Saint-Hubert** Luxembourg, SE Belgium
13 T8 **St-Hubert** Québec, SE Canada
13 P12 **St-Hyacinthe** Québec, SE Canada
St.Iago de la Vega *see* Spanish Town
33 Q4 **Saint Ignace** Michigan, N USA
13 O10 **St-Ignace-du-Lac** Québec, SE Canada
10 D12 **St.Ignace Island** *island* Ontario, S Canada
110 C7 **St.Imier** Bern, W Switzerland
xxxvi C15 **St Issey** Cornwall, SW England, UK
xxxix S11 **St Ives** Cambridgeshire, E England, UK
xxxvi L16 **St Ives** Cornwall, SW England, UK
xxxvi M16 **St Ives Bay** *bay* SW England, UK
31 U10 **Saint James** Minnesota, N USA
8 I15 **St.James, Cape** *headland* Graham Island, British Columbia, SW Canada
13 O13 **St-Jean** *var.* St-Jean-sur-Richelieu. Québec, SE Canada
57 X9 **St-Jean** NW French Guiana
13 R8 **St-Jean** ≈ Québec, SE Canada
Saint-Jean-d'Acre *see* 'Akko
104 K11 **St-Jean-d'Angély** Charente-Maritime, W France
105 N7 **St-Jean-de-Braye** Loiret, C France
104 I16 **St-Jean-de-Luz** Pyrénées-Atlantiques, SW France
105 T12 **St-Jean-de-Maurienne** Savoie, E France
104 I9 **St-Jean-de-Monts** Vendée, NW France
105 Q14 **St-Jean-du-Gard** Gard, S France
13 Q7 **St-Jean, Lac** ◎ Québec, SE Canada
104 I16 **St-Jean-Pied-de-Port** Pyrénées-Atlantiques, SW France
13 S9 **St-Jean-Port-Joli** Québec, SE Canada
St-Jean-sur-Richelieu *see* St-Jean
13 N12 **St-Jérôme** Québec, SE Canada
27 T5 **Saint Jo** Texas, SW USA
xxxvii X16 **St John** Jersey, Channel Islands
11 O15 **St.John** New Brunswick, SE Canada
28 L6 **Saint John** Kansas, C USA
78 K16 **Saint John** ≈ C Liberia
47 T9 **Saint John** *island* C Virgin Islands (US)
24 I6 **Saint John, Lake** ◎ Louisiana, S USA
21 Q2 **Saint John** *Fr.* Saint-John. ≈ Canada/USA
xl F11 **St John's** C Isle of Man
47 W10 **St John's** ● (Antigua and Barbuda) Antigua, Antigua and Barbuda
11 V12 **St.John's** Newfoundland, Newfoundland and Labrador, E Canada
39 O12 **Saint Johns** Arizona, SW USA
33 Q9 **Saint Johns** Michigan, N USA
11 V12 **St.John's** ✕ Newfoundland, Newfoundland and Labrador, E Canada
xli P8 **St John's Chapel** Durham, N England, UK
xliv F4 **St John's Point** *headland* N Ireland
xliv M6 **St John's Point** *headland* E Northern Ireland, UK
25 X11 **Saint Johns River** ≈ Florida, SE USA
xliv I3 **St Johnstown** Donegal, N Ireland
xliii J24 **St John's Town of Dalry** Dumfries and Galloway, SW Scotland, UK
xxxvi C7 **St John's Wood** Westminster, SE England, UK
47 N12 **St.Joseph** W Dominica
181 P17 **St-Joseph** S Réunion
24 J6 **Saint Joseph** Louisiana, S USA
33 O10 **Saint Joseph** Michigan, N USA
29 R3 **Saint Joseph** Missouri, C USA
22 I10 **Saint Joseph** Tennessee, S USA
24 R9 **Saint Joseph Bay** *bay* Florida, SE USA
13 R11 **St-Joseph-de-Beauce** Québec, SE Canada
10 C10 **St.Joseph, Lake** ◎ Ontario, C Canada
33 Q11 **Saint Joseph River** ≈ N USA
12 C11 **Saint Joseph's Island** *island* Ontario, S Canada
13 N11 **St-Jovite** Québec, SE Canada
123 Jj16 **St Julian's** N Malta
St-Julien *see* St-Julien-en-Genevois
105 T10 **St-Julien-en-Genevois** *var.* St-Julien. Haute-Savoie, E France
104 M11 **St-Junien** Haute-Vienne, C France
105 Q11 **St-Just-St-Rambert** Loire, E France
xxxvi L16 **St Just** Cornwall, SW England, UK
xxxvi C17 **St Keverne** Cornwall, SW England, UK
99 D8 **St Kilda** *island* NW Scotland, UK
47 V10 **Saint Kitts** *island* Saint Kitts and Nevis
47 U10 **Saint Kitts and Nevis** *off.* Federation of Saint Christopher and Nevis, *var.* Saint Christopher-Nevis. ◆ *commonwealth republic* E West Indies
9 X16 **St.Laurent** Manitoba, S Canada
St-Laurent *see* St-Laurent-du-Maroni
57 X9 **St-Laurent-du-Maroni** *var.* St-Laurent. NW French Guiana
St-Laurent, Fleuve *see* St.Lawrence
104 J12 **St-Laurent-Médoc** Gironde, SW France
11 N12 **St.Lawrence** *Fr.* Fleuve St-Laurent. ≈ Canada/USA
11 Q12 **St.Lawrence, Gulf of** *gulf* NW Atlantic Ocean
40 K10 **Saint Lawrence Island** *island* Alaska, USA
12 M14 **Saint Lawrence River** ≈ Canada/USA
101 L25 **Saint-Léger** Luxembourg, SE Belgium
11 N14 **St.Léonard** New Brunswick, SE Canada
13 P11 **St-Léonard** Québec, SE Canada
181 O17 **St-Leu** W Réunion
104 J4 **St-Lô** *anc.* Briovera, Laudus. Manche, N France
9 T15 **St.Louis** Saskatchewan, S Canada
105 V7 **St-Louis** Haut-Rhin, NE France
181 O17 **St-Louis** S Réunion
78 G10 **Saint Louis** NW Senegal
29 X4 **Saint Louis** Missouri, C USA
31 W5 **Saint Louis River** ≈ Minnesota, N USA
105 T7 **St-Loup-sur-Semouse** Haute-Saône, E France
13 O12 **St-Luc** Québec, SE Canada
47 X13 **Saint Lucia** ◆ *commonwealth republic* SE West Indies
49 S3 **Saint Lucia** *island* SE West Indies
85 L22 **St.Lucia, Cape** *headland* E South Africa
47 Y13 **Saint Lucia Channel** *channel* Martinique/Saint Lucia
85 L22 **St.Lucia Estuary** KwaZulu/Natal, E South Africa
25 Y14 **Saint Lucie Canal** *canal* Florida, SE USA
25 Z13 **Saint Lucie Inlet** *inlet* Florida, SE USA
xlii H3 **St Magnus Bay** *bay* N Scotland, UK
104 K10 **St-Maixent-l'École** Deux-Sèvres, W France
9 Y16 **St.Malo** Manitoba, S Canada
104 I5 **St-Malo** Ille-et-Vilaine, NW France
104 H4 **St-Malo, Golfe de** *gulf* NW France
46 L9 **St-Marc** C Haiti
46 L9 **St-Marc, Canal de** *channel* W Haiti
105 S12 **St-Marcellin-le-Mollard** Isère, E France
xxxvii Z11 **St Margaret's at Cliffe** Kent, SE England, UK
xlii M5 **St Margaret's Hope** Orkney Islands, NE Scotland, UK
34 M9 **Saint Maries** Idaho, NW USA
xl G12 **St Mark's** S Isle of Man
25 T9 **Saint Marks** Florida, SE USA
110 D11 **St.Martin** Valais, SW Switzerland
Saint Martin *see* Sint Maarten
33 O5 **Saint Martin Island** *island* Michigan, N USA
xxxvi I17 **St Martin's** *island* SW England, UK
xxxviii G8 **St Martin's** Shropshire, W England, UK
xxxvii V16 **St Martin's Point** *headland* Guernsey, Channel Islands
24 I9 **Saint Martinville** Louisiana, S USA
xxxvii X17 **St Mary** Jersey, Channel Islands
xlii M5 **St Mary's** Orkney Islands, N Scotland, UK
xxxvi I17 **St Mary's** *island* SW England, UK
194 K14 **St.Mary, Mount** ▲ S PNG
190 I6 **Saint Mary Peak** ▲ South Australia
191 Q16 **Saint Marys** Tasmania, SE Australia
12 E16 **St.Marys** Ontario, S Canada
40 M11 **Saint Marys** Alaska, USA
25 W8 **Saint Marys** Georgia, SE USA
29 P4 **Saint Marys** Kansas, C USA
xliii M22 **St Mary's Loch** ◎ S Scotland, UK
33 Q4 **Saint Marys** Ohio, N USA
23 R3 **Saint Marys** West Virginia, NE USA
25 W8 **Saint Marys River** ≈ Florida/Georgia, SE USA
33 Q4 **Saint Marys River** ≈ Michigan, N USA
104 D6 **St-Mathieu, Pointe** *headland* NW France
40 J12 **Saint Matthew Island** *island* Alaska, USA
23 R13 **Saint Matthews** South Carolina, SE USA
St.Matthew's Island *see* Zadetkyi Kyun
194 M8 **St.Matthias Group** *island group* NE PNG
xxxvi C17 **St Mawes** Cornwall, SW England, UK
xxxvi C15 **St Mawgan** Cornwall, SW England, UK
110 C11 **St.Maurice** Valais, SW Switzerland
xxxvi F15 **St Mellion** Cornwall, SW England, UK
xxxv K15 **St Mellons** Cardiff, S Wales, UK
13 P9 **St-Maurice** ≈ Québec, SE Canada
104 J13 **St-Médard-en-Jalles** Gironde, SW France
41 N10 **Saint Michael** Alaska, USA
St.Michel *see* Mikkeli
xxxvi C15 **St Minver** Cornwall, SW England, UK
xliii N18 **St Monans** Fife, E Scotland, UK
13 N10 **St-Michel-des-Saints** Québec, SE Canada
105 S5 **St-Mihiel** Meuse, NE France
xxxvi E15 **St Neot** Cornwall, SW England, UK
xxxix R12 **St Neots** Cambridgeshire, E England, UK
xxxv C12 **St Nicholas** Pembrokeshire, SW Wales, UK
110 J10 **St.Moritz** *Ger.* Sankt Moritz, *Rmsch.* San Murezzan. Graubünden, SE Switzerland
104 H8 **St-Nazaire** Loire-Atlantique, NW France
Saint Nicholas *see* São Nicolau
Saint-Nicolas *see* Sint-Niklaas
105 N1 **St-Omer** Pas-de-Calais, N France
104 J11 **Saintonge** *cultural region* W France
xxxvii Y7 **St Osyth** Essex, SE England, UK
13 S9 **St-Pacôme** Québec, SE Canada
13 S10 **St-Pamphile** Québec, SE Canada
13 S9 **St-Pascal** Québec, SE Canada
12 J11 **St-Patrice, Lac** ◎ Québec, SE Canada
9 R14 **St.Paul** Alberta, SW Canada
181 O16 **St-Paul** NW Réunion
40 K14 **Saint Paul** Saint Paul Island, Alaska, USA
31 V8 **Saint Paul** *state capital* Minnesota, N USA
31 P15 **Saint Paul** Nebraska, C USA
23 P7 **Saint Paul** Virginia, NE USA
79 Q17 **Saint Paul, Cape** *headland* S Ghana
105 O17 **St-Paul-de-Fenouillet** Pyrénées-Orientales, S France
67 K14 **Saint Paul Fracture Zone** *tectonic feature* E Atlantic Ocean
40 J14 **Saint Paul Island** *island* Pribilof Islands, Alaska, USA
104 J15 **St-Paul-les-Dax** Landes, SW France
23 U11 **Saint Pauls** North Carolina, SE USA
Saint Paul's Bay *see* San Pawl il-Bahar
203 R16 **St Paul's Point** *headland* Pitcairn Island, Pitcairn Islands
xxxvii X17 **St Peter** Jersey, Channel Islands
31 U10 **Saint Peter** Minnesota, N USA
xxxvii V15 **St Peter Port** ○ (Guernsey) C Guernsey, Channel Islands
25 V13 **Saint Petersburg** Florida, SE USA
Saint Petersburg *see* Sankt-Peterburg
25 V13 **Saint Petersburg Beach** Florida, SE USA
181 P17 **St-Philippe** SE Réunion
47 Q11 **St-Pierre** NW Martinique
181 O17 **St-Pierre** SW Réunion
11 S13 **St-Pierre and Miquelon** *Fr.* Îles St-Pierre et Miquelon. ◇ *French territorial collectivity* NE North America
13 P11 **St-Pierre, Lac** ◎ Québec, SE Canada
104 F5 **St-Pol-de-Léon** Finistère, NW France
105 O2 **St-Pol-sur-Ternoise** Pas-de-Calais, N France
St. Pons *see* St-Pons-de-Thomières
105 O16 **St-Pons-de-Thomières** *var.* St.Pons. Hérault, S France
105 P10 **St-Pourçain-sur-Sioule** Allier, C France
13 S11 **St-Prosper** Québec, SE Canada
105 P3 **St-Quentin** Aisne, N France
13 R10 **St-Raphaël** Québec, SE Canada
105 U15 **St-Raphaël** Var, SE France
13 Q10 **St-Raymond** Québec, SE Canada
35 O9 **Saint Regis** Montana, NW USA
20 J7 **Saint Regis River** ≈ New York, NE USA
105 R15 **St-Rémy-de-Provence** Bouches-du-Rhône, SE France
13 V6 **St-René-de-Matane** Québec, SE Canada
xxxvii W15 **St Sampson** Guernsey, Channel Islands
104 M9 **St-Savin** Vienne, W France
13 S8 **St-Siméon** Québec, SE Canada
25 X7 **Saint Simons Island** *island* Georgia, SE USA
203 Y2 **Saint Stanislas Bay** *bay* Kiritimati, E Kiribati
11 O15 **St.Stephen** New Brunswick, SE Canada
xxxvi D14 **St Teath** Cornwall, SW England, UK
41 X12 **Saint Terese** Alaska, USA
12 E17 **St.Thomas** Ontario, S Canada
31 Q2 **Saint Thomas** North Dakota, N USA
47 T9 **Saint Thomas** *island* W Virgin Islands (US)
Saint Thomas *see* São Tomé, Sao Tome and Principe
Saint Thomas *see* Charlotte Amalie, Virgin Islands (US)
13 P10 **St-Tite** Québec, SE Canada
Saint-Trond *see* Sint-Truiden
105 U16 **St-Tropez** Var, SE France
Saint Ubes *see* Setúbal
104 L3 **St-Valéry-en-Caux** Seine-Maritime, N France
105 Q9 **St-Vallier** Saône-et-Loire, C France
xliii O16 **St Vigeans** Angus, E Scotland, UK
108 B7 **St-Vincent** Valle d'Aosta, NW Italy
47 Q14 **Saint Vincent** *island* N Saint Vincent and the Grenadines
Saint Vincent *see* São Vicente
47 W14 **Saint Vincent and the Grenadines** ◆ *commonwealth republic* SE West Indies
Saint Vincent, Cape *see* São Vicente, Cabo de
104 I15 **St-Vincent-de-Tyrosse** Landes, SW France
190 I9 **Saint Vincent, Gulf** *gulf* South Australia
25 R10 **Saint Vincent Island** *island* Florida, SE USA
47 T12 **Saint Vincent Passage** *passage* Saint Lucia/Saint Vincent and the Grenadines
191 N18 **Saint Vincent, Point** *headland* Tasmania, SE Australia
Saint-Vith *see* Sankt-Vith
9 S14 **St.Walburg** Saskatchewan, S Canada
xxxvi C15 **St Wenn** Cornwall, SW England, UK
xxxviii H14 **St Weonards** Herefordshire, W England, UK
St Wolfgangsee *see* Wolfgangsee
104 M11 **St-Yrieix-la-Perche** Haute-Vienne, C France
Saint Yves *see* Setúbal
13 Y5 **St-Yvon** Québec, SE Canada
196 H5 **Saipan** *island* ● (Northern Mariana Islands) S Northern Mariana Islands
196 H6 **Saipan Channel** *channel* S Northern Mariana Islands
196 H6 **Saipan International Airport** ✕ Saipan, S Northern Mariana Islands
76 G6 **Sais** ✕ (Fès) C Morocco
Saishū *see* Cheju
Saishū *see* Cheju-do
104 J16 **Saison** ≈ SW France
174 L7 **Sai, Sungai** ≈ Borneo, N Indonesia
171 Jj16 **Saitama** *off.* Saitama-ken. ◐ *prefecture* Honshū, S Japan
170 Cc16 **Saito** Miyazaki, Kyūshū, SW Japan
Saiyid Abid *see* Sayyid 'Abid
59 J19 **Sajama, Nevado** ▲ W Bolivia
147 V13 **Sājir, Ras** *headland* S Oman
113 M20 **Sajószentpéter** Borsod-Abaúj-Zemplén, NE Hungary
85 F24 **Sak** ≈ SW South Africa
83 J18 **Saka** Coast, E Kenya
178 I11 **Sa Kaeo** Prachin Buri, C Thailand
171 Gg15 **Sakai** Ōsaka, Honshū, SW Japan
170 F14 **Sakaide** Kagawa, Shikoku, SW Japan
170 Ff12 **Sakaiminato** Tottori, Honshū, SW Japan
146 M3 **Sakākah** Al Jawf, NW Saudi Arabia
30 L4 **Sakakawea, Lake** ⊡ North Dakota, N USA
10 J9 **Sakami, Lac** ◎ Québec, C Canada
81 O26 **Sakania** Shaba, SE Zaire
152 K12 **Sakar** Lebapskiy Velayat, E Turkmenistan
180 H7 **Sakaraha** Toliara, SW Madagascar
152 I14 **Sakar-Chaga** *Turkm.* Sakarchäge. Maryyskiy Velayat, C Turkmenistan
Sakarchäge *see* Sakar-Chaga
Sak'art'velo *see* Georgia
142 F11 **Sakarya** ◐ *province* NW Turkey
142 F12 **Sakarya Nehri** ≈ NW Turkey
171 Ll11 **Sakata** Yamagata, Honshū, C Japan
126 L9 **Sakha (Yakutiya), Respublika** *var.* Respublika Yakutiya, Yakutiya, *Eng.* Yakutia. ◐ *autonomous republic* NE Russian Federation
Sakhalin *see* Sakhalin, Ostrov
127 Oo14 **Sakhalin, Ostrov** *var.* Sakhalin. *island* SE Russian Federation
127 P14 **Sakhalinskaya Oblast'** ◐ *province* SE Russian Federation
127 Nn13 **Sakhalinskiy Zaliv** *gulf* E Russian Federation
Sakhnovshchina *see* Sakhnovshchyna
119 U6 **Sakhnovshchyna** *Rus.* Sakhnovshchina. Kharkivs'ka Oblast', E Ukraine
Sakhon Nakhon *see* Sakon Nakhon
Sakhtsar *see* Rāmsar
Saki *see* Saky
143 W10 **Şäki** *Rus.* Sheki; *prev.* Nukha. NW Azerbaijan
120 E13 **Šakiai** *Ger.* Schaken. Šakiai, S Lithuania
176 Z16 **Sakiramke** Irian Jaya, E Indonesia
172 Oo16 **Sakishima-shotō** *var.* Sakisima Syotō. *island group* SW Japan
Sakiz *see* Saqqez
Sakiz-Adasi *see* Chíos
161 F19 **Sakleshpur** Karnātaka, E India
178 J9 **Sakon Nakhon** *var.* Muang Sakon Nakhon, Sakhon Nakhon. Sakon Nakhon, E Thailand
155 P15 **Sakrand** Sind, SE Pakistan
85 F24 **Sak River** *Afr.* Sakrivier. Northern Cape, W South Africa
Sakrivier *see* Sak River
Saksaul'skiy *see* Saksaul'skoye
150 K13 **Saksaul'skoye** *prev.* Saksaul'skiy, *Kaz.* Sekseüil. Kzyl-Orda, S Kazakhstan
97 I25 **Sakskøbing** Storstrøm, SE Denmark
171 Jj15 **Saku** Nagano, Honshū, S Japan
171 K16 **Sakura** Chiba, Honshū, S Japan
119 S13 **Saky** *Rus.* Saki. Respublika Krym, S Ukraine
78 E9 **Sal** *island* Ilhas de Barlavento, NE Cape Verde
131 N12 **Sal** ≈ SW Russian Federation
113 I21 **Sal'a** *Hung.* Sellye, Vágsellye. Západné Slovensko, SW Slovakia
97 N15 **Sala** Västmanland, C Sweden
175 Qq11 **Salabangka, Kepulauan** *island group* N Indonesia
13 N13 **Salaberry-de-Valleyfield** *var.* Valleyfield. Québec, SE Canada
120 G7 **Salacgrīva** *Est.* Salatsi. Limbaži, N Latvia
109 M18 **Sala Consilina** Campania, S Italy
42 C2 **Salada, Laguna** ◎ NW Mexico
63 D14 **Saladas** Corrientes, NE Argentina
63 C21 **Saladillo** Buenos Aires, E Argentina
63 B16 **Saladillo, Río** ≈ C Argentina
27 T9 **Salado** Texas, SW USA
65 J16 **Salado, Arroyo** ≈ SE Argentina
39 Q12 **Salado, Río** ≈ New Mexico, SW USA
63 D21 **Salado, Río** ≈ E Argentina
64 J12 **Salado, Río** ≈ C Argentina
43 N7 **Salado, Río** ≈ NE Mexico
149 N6 **Salafchegān** *var.* Sarafjagān. Tehrān, C Iran
79 Q15 **Salaga** C Ghana
198 Aa7 **Sala'ilua** Savai'i, W Western Samoa
118 G9 **Sălaj** ◐ *county* NW Romania
85 H20 **Salajwe** Kweneng, SE Botswana
80 H9 **Salal** Kanem, W Chad
82 I6 **Salala** Red Sea, NE Sudan
147 V13 **Şalālah** SW Oman
44 D5 **Salamá** Baja Verapaz, C Guatemala
44 J6 **Salamá** Olancho, C Honduras
64 G10 **Salamanca** Coquimbo, C Chile
43 N13 **Salamanca** Guanajuato, C Mexico
106 K7 **Salamanca** *anc.* Helmantica, Salmantica. Castilla-León, NW Spain
20 D11 **Salamanca** New York, NE USA
106 J7 **Salamanca** ◐ *province* Castilla-León, W Spain
65 J19 **Salamanca, Pampa de** *plain* S Argentina
80 J12 **Salamat** *off.* Préfecture du Salamat. ◐ *prefecture* SE Chad
80 I12 **Salamat, Bahr** ≈ S Chad
56 F5 **Salamina** Magdalena, N Colombia
117 G19 **Salamína** *var.* Salamís. Salamína, C Greece
117 G19 **Salamína** *island* C Greece
Salamís *see* Salamína
144 I5 **Salamīyah** *var.* As Salamīyah. Ḩamāh, W Syria
33 P12 **Salamonie Lake** ⊡ Indiana, N USA
33 P12 **Salamonie River** ≈ Indiana, N USA
Salang *see* Phuket
198 Bb8 **Salani** Upolu, SE Western Samoa
120 C11 **Salantai** Kretinga, NW Lithuania
106 K2 **Salas** Asturias, N Spain
107 O5 **Salas de los Infantes** Castilla-León, N Spain
104 M16 **Salat** ≈ S France
201 V13 **Salat** *island* Chuuk, C Micronesia
174 L15 **Salatiga** Jawa, C Indonesia
201 V13 **Salat Pass** *passage* W Pacific Ocean
Salatsi *see* Salacgrīva
178 Jj10 **Salavan** *var.* Saravan, Saravane. Salavan, S Laos
131 V6 **Salavat** Respublika Bashkortostan, W Russian Federation
58 C12 **Salaverry** La Libertad, N Peru
176 Uu9 **Salawati, Pulau** *island* E Indonesia
200 Nn11 **Sala y Gomez** *island* Chile, E Pacific Ocean
Sala y Gomez Fracture Zone *see* Sala y Gomez Ridge
200 O11 **Sala y Gomez Ridge** *var.* Sala y Gomez Fracture Zone. *tectonic feature* SE Pacific Ocean
63 A22 **Salazar** Buenos Aires, E Argentina
56 G7 **Salazar** Norte de Santander, N Colombia
Salazar *see* N'Dalatando
181 P16 **Salazie** C Réunion
105 N8 **Salbris** Loir-et-Cher, C France
59 G15 **Salcantay, Nevado** ▲ C Peru
47 O10 **Salcedo** N Dominican Republic
41 S9 **Salcha River** ≈ Alaska, USA
121 H15 **Šalčininkai** Šalčininkai, SE Lithuania
xxxvi G17 **Salcombe** Devon, SW England, UK
xxxvii X7 **Salcott** Essex, SE England, UK
Saldae *see* Béjaïa
56 E11 **Saldaña** Tolima, C Colombia
106 M4 **Saldaña** Castilla-León, N Spain
85 E25 **Saldanha** Western Cape, SW South Africa
Salduba *see* Zaragoza
63 B23 **Saldungaray** Buenos Aires, E Argentina
120 D9 **Saldus** *Ger.* Frauenburg. Saldus, W Latvia
xli P16 **Sale** Trafford, NW England, UK
191 P13 **Sale** Victoria, SE Australia
76 F6 **Salé** NW Morocco
76 F6 **Salé** ✕ (Rabat) W Morocco
Salehābād *see* Andīmeshk
174 Ii10 **Saleh, Air** ≈ Sumatera, W Indonesia
175 Oo16 **Saleh, Teluk** *bay* Nusa Tenggara, S Indonesia
125 G8 **Salekhard** *prev.* Obdorsk. Yamalo-Nenetskiy Avtonomnyy Okrug, N Russian Federation
198 B7 **Sālelologa** Savai'i, C Western Samoa
161 H21 **Salem** Tamil Nādu, SE India
29 V9 **Salem** Arkansas, C USA
32 L15 **Salem** Illinois, N USA
33 P15 **Salem** Indiana, N USA
21 P11 **Salem** Massachusetts, NE USA
29 V6 **Salem** Missouri, C USA
20 I16 **Salem** New Jersey, NE USA
33 U12 **Salem** Ohio, NE USA
34 G12 **Salem** *state capital* Oregon, NW USA
31 Q11 **Salem** South Dakota, N USA
38 L4 **Salem** Utah, W USA
23 S7 **Salem** Virginia, NE USA
23 R3 **Salem** West Virginia, NE USA
109 H23 **Salemi** Sicilia, Italy, C Mediterranean Sea
Salemy *see* As Salimi
xliii E17 **Salen** Argyll and Bute, W Scotland, UK
xliii F16 **Salen** Highland, NW Scotland, UK
96 K12 **Sälen** Kopparberg, C Sweden
109 Q18 **Salentina, Campi** Puglia, SE Italy
109 Q18 **Salentina, Penisola** *peninsula* SE Italy
109 L18 **Salerno** *anc.* Salernum. Campania, S Italy
109 L18 **Salerno, Golfo di** *Eng.* Gulf of Salerno. *gulf* S Italy
Salerno, Gulf of *see* Salerno, Golfo di
Salernum *see* Salerno
xl G15 **Salford** Salford, NW England, UK
xli O15 **Salford** ◐ *unitary authority* NW England, UK
Salgir *see* Salhyr
113 K21 **Salgótarján** Nógrád, N Hungary
61 O15 **Salgueiro** Pernambuco, E Brazil
Salhiye *see* Aş Şāliḩīyah

◆ Country ● Country Capital ◇ Dependent Territory ○ Dependent Territory Capital ◐ Administrative Region ✕ International Airport ▲ Mountain ▲▲ Mountain Range ✵ Volcano ≈ River ◎ Lake ⊡ Reservoir

309

SALHUS – SAN IGNACIO

96 C13 Salhus Hordaland, S Norway
119 T12 Salhyr Rus. Salgir. ≈ S Ukraine
175 S4 Salibabu, Pulau island N Indonesia
39 S6 Salida Colorado, C USA
104 J15 Salies-de-Béarn Pyrénées-Atlantiques, SW France
142 C14 Salihli Manisa, W Turkey
121 K18 Salihorsk Rus. Soligorsk. Minskaya Voblasts', S Belorussia
121 K18 Salihorskaye Vodaskhovishcha ⊠ C Belorussia
85 N14 Salima Central, C Malawi
177 Ff5 Salin Magwe, W Burma
29 N4 Salina Kansas, C USA
38 L5 Salina Utah, W USA
43 S17 Salina Cruz Oaxaca, SE Mexico
109 L22 Salina, Isola island Isole Eolie, S Italy
46 J5 Salina Point headland Acklins Island, SE Bahamas
58 A7 Salinas Guayas, W Ecuador
42 M11 Salinas var. Salinas de Hidalgo. San Luis Potosí, C Mexico
47 T6 Salinas C Puerto Rico
37 O10 Salinas California, W USA
Salinas, Cabo de see Salines, Cap de ses
Salinas de Hidalgo see Salinas
84 A13 Salinas, Ponta das headland W Angola
47 O10 Salinas, Punta headland S Dominican Republic
Salinas, Río see Chixoy, Río
37 O11 Salinas River ≈ California, W USA
xliii L19 Saline Fife, E Scotland, UK
24 H6 Saline Lake ◎ Louisiana, S USA
27 R17 Salineno Texas, SW USA
29 V14 Saline River ≈ Arkansas, C USA
32 M17 Saline River ≈ Illinois, N USA
29 N4 Saline River ≈ Kansas, C USA
107 X10 Salines, Cap de ses var. Cabo de Salinas. headland Mallorca, Spain, W Mediterranean Sea
Salisburg see Mazsalaca
xxxvii O12 Salisbury var. New Sarum. Wiltshire, S England, UK
47 O12 Salisbury var. Barouï. W Dominica
23 Y4 Salisbury Maryland, NE USA
29 T3 Salisbury Missouri, C USA
23 S9 Salisbury North Carolina, SE USA
Salisbury see Harare
16 N5 Salisbury Island island Northwest Territories, NE Canada
Salisbury, Lake see Bisina, Lake
xxxvii N11 Salisbury Plain plain S England, UK
23 R14 Salkehatchie River ≈ South Carolina, SE USA
144 I9 Şalkhad As Suwaydā', SW Syria
94 M12 Salla Lappi, NE Finland
105 U11 Sallanches Haute-Savoie, E France
107 V5 Sallent Cataluña, NE Spain
63 A22 Salliqueló Buenos Aires, E Argentina
29 R10 Sallisaw Oklahoma, C USA
82 I7 Sallom Red Sea, NE Sudan
10 J2 Salluit prev. Saglouc, Sagluk. Québec, NE Canada
Sallūm, Khalīj as see Salûm, Gulf of
11 S11 Sally's Cove Newfoundland, Newfoundland and Labrador, E Canada
145 W9 Salmān Bin 'Arāzah E Iraq
Salmantica see Salamanca
148 I2 Salmās prev. Dilman, Shāpūr. Āžarbāyjān-e Bākhtarī, NW Iran
128 I11 Salmi Respublika Kareliya, NW Russian Federation
35 P12 Salmon Idaho, NW USA
9 N16 Salmon Arm British Columbia, SW Canada
199 J5 Salmon Bank undersea feature N Pacific Ocean
Salmon Leap see Leixlip
36 L2 Salmon Mountains ▲▲ California, W USA
12 J15 Salmon Point headland Ontario, SE Canada
35 N11 Salmon River ≈ Idaho, NW USA
20 K6 Salmon River ≈ New York, NE USA
35 N12 Salmon River Mountains ▲▲ Idaho, NW USA
20 I9 Salmon River Reservoir ⊠ New York, NE USA
95 K19 Salo Turku-Pori, SW Finland
108 F7 Salò Lombardia, N Italy
Salona/Salonae see Solin
105 S15 Salon-de-Provence Bouches-du-Rhône, SE France
Salonica/Salonika see Thessaloníki
117 I14 Salonikós, Ákra headland Thásos, E Greece
118 F10 Salonta Hung. Nagyszalonta. Bihor, W Romania
106 I9 Salor ≈ W Spain
107 U6 Salou Cataluña, NE Spain
78 H11 Saloum ≈ C Senegal
44 H4 Sal, Punta headland NW Honduras
94 N3 Salpynten headland W Svalbard
144 I3 Salqīn Idlib, W Syria
95 F14 Salsbruket Nord-Trøndelag, C Norway
130 M13 Sal'sk Rostovskaya Oblast', SW Russian Federation
109 K25 Salso ≈ Sicilia, Italy, C Mediterranean Sea
109 J25 Salso ≈ Sicilia, Italy, C Mediterranean Sea
108 E9 Salsomaggiore Terme Emilia-Romagna, N Italy
Salt see As Salt
64 J6 Salta Salta, NW Argentina
64 K6 Salta off. Provincia de Salta. ◐ province N Argentina
xxxvi E16 Saltash Cornwall, SW England, UK
26 I8 Salt Basin basin Texas, SW USA
xli U9 Saltburn-by-the-Sea Redcar and Cleveland, N England, UK
xliii H21 Saltcoates North Ayrshire, W Scotland, UK
9 V16 Saltcoats Saskatchewan, S Canada
32 L13 Salt Creek ≈ Illinois, N USA
26 J9 Salt Draw ≈ Texas, SW USA
xliv K13 Saltee Islands island group SE Ireland
94 G12 Saltfjorden inlet C Norway
26 I8 Salt Flat Texas, SW USA
xxxix S4 Saltfleet Lincolnshire, E England, UK
xxxix S4 Saltfleetby St Peter Lincolnshire, E England, UK
xxxvi L10 Saltford Bath and North East Somerset, SW England, UK
27 P3 Salt Fork ≈ Texas, SW USA
29 N8 Salt Fork Arkansas River ≈ Oklahoma, C USA
33 T13 Salt Fork Lake ⊠ Ohio, N USA
28 J11 Salt Fork Red River ≈ Oklahoma, C USA
97 J23 Saltholm island E Denmark
43 N8 Saltillo Coahuila de Zaragoza, NE Mexico
190 L5 Salt Lake salt lake New South Wales, SE Australia
39 V15 Salt Lake ◎ New Mexico, SW USA
38 K2 Salt Lake City state capital Utah, W USA
xxxviii G6 Saltney Cheshire, W England, UK
63 C20 Salto Buenos Aires, E Argentina
63 D17 Salto Salto, N Uruguay
63 E17 Salto ◐ department N Uruguay
109 I14 Salto ≈ C Italy
64 Q6 Salto del Guairá Canindeyú, E Paraguay
63 D17 Salto Grande, Embalse de var. Lago de Salto Grande. ⊠ Argentina/Uruguay
Salto Grande, Lago de see Salto Grande, Embalse de
37 W16 Salton Sea ◎ California, W USA
63 I12 Salto Santiago, Represa de ⊠ S Brazil
155 U7 Salt Range ▲ E Pakistan
38 M13 Salt River ≈ Arizona, SW USA
22 L5 Salt River ≈ Kentucky, S USA
29 V3 Salt River ≈ Missouri, C USA
97 F17 Saltrød Aust-Agder, S Norway
97 P16 Saltsjöbaden Stockholm, C Sweden
23 Q7 Saltville Virginia, NE USA
Saluces/Saluciae see Saluzzo
23 Q12 Saluda South Carolina, SE USA
23 X6 Saluda Virginia, NE USA
23 Q12 Saluda River ≈ South Carolina, SE USA
175 R10 Salue Timpaus, Selat var. Selat Banggai. strait N Banda Sea
77 T7 Salûm var. As Sallūm. NW Egypt
158 F14 Salūmbar Rājasthān, N India
77 T7 Salûm, Gulf of Ar. Khalīj as Sallūm. gulf Egypt/Libya
175 Q7 Salumpaga Sulawesi, N Indonesia
161 M14 Sālūr Andhra Pradesh, E India
57 Y9 Salut, Îles du island group N French Guiana
108 A9 Saluzzo Fr. Saluces; anc. Saluciae. Piemonte, NW Italy
65 F23 Salvación, Bahía bay S Chile
61 P17 Salvador prev. São Salvador. Bahia, E Brazil
67 E24 Salvador East Falkland, Falkland Islands
24 K10 Salvador, Lake ◎ Louisiana, S USA
Salvaleón de Higüey see Higüey
106 F10 Salvaterra de Magos Santarém, C Portugal
43 N13 Salvatierra Guanajuato, C Mexico
107 P3 Salvatierra Basq. Agurain. País Vasco, N Spain
Salwa/Salwah see As Salwā
178 H5 Salween Bur. Thanlwin, Chin. Nu Chiang, Nu Jiang. ≈ SE Asia
143 Y12 Salyan Rus. Sal'yany. SE Azerbaijan
159 N11 Salyan var. Sallyana. Mid Western, W Nepal
Sal'yany see Salyan
23 O6 Salyersville Kentucky, S USA
111 V6 Salza ≈ E Austria
111 Q7 Salzach ≈ Austria/Germany
111 Q6 Salzburg anc. Juvavum. Salzburg, N Austria
111 O8 Salzburg off. Land Salzburg. ◐ state C Austria
Salzburg see Ocna Sibiului
Salzburg Alps see Salzburger Kalkalpen
111 Q7 Salzburger Kalkalpen Eng. Salzburg Alps. ▲▲ C Austria
102 J13 Salzgitter prev. Watenstedt-Salzgitter. Niedersachsen, C Germany
103 G14 Salzkotten Nordrhein-Westfalen, W Germany
102 K11 Salzwedel Sachsen-Anhalt, N Germany
158 D11 Sām Rājasthān, NW India
106 K2 Sama var. Sama de Langreo. Asturias, N Spain
56 G9 Samacá Boyacá, C Colombia
42 I7 Samachique Chihuahua, N Mexico
147 Y8 Şamad NE Oman
Sama de Langreo see Sama
Samaden see Samedan
59 M19 Samaipata Santa Cruz, C Bolivia
178 Jj11 Samakhixai var. Attapu, Attopeu. Attapu, S Laos
Samakov see Samokov
44 B6 Samalá, Río ≈ SW Guatemala
42 J3 Samalayuca Chihuahua, N Mexico
179 Q17 Samales Group island group Sulu Archipelago, SW Philippines
161 L16 Sāmalkot Andhra Pradesh, E India
47 P8 Samaná var. Santa Bárbara de Samaná. E Dominican Republic
47 P8 Samaná, Bahía de bay E Dominican Republic
46 K4 Samana Cay island SE Bahamas
142 K17 Samandağı Hatay, S Turkey
155 P3 Samangān ◐ province N Afghanistan
Samangān see Āybak
172 P8 Samani Hokkaidō, NE Japan
56 C13 Samaniego Nariño, SW Colombia
179 R12 Samar island C Philippines
131 S6 Samara prev. Kuybyshev. Samarskaya Oblast', W Russian Federation
131 S6 Samara ✕ Samarskaya Oblast', W Russian Federation
131 T7 Samara ≈ W Russian Federation
119 V7 Samara ≈ E Ukraine
195 N17 Samarai Milne Bay, SE PNG
Samarang see Semarang
144 G9 Samarian Hills hill range N Israel
56 L9 Samariapo Amazonas, C Venezuela
175 O8 Samarinda Borneo, C Indonesia
Samarkand see Samarqand
Samarkandskaya Oblast' see Samarqand Wiloyati
Samarkandski/Samarkandskoye see Temirtau
Samarobriva see Amiens
153 N11 Samarqand Rus. Samarkand. Samarqand Wiloyati, C Uzbekistan
152 M11 Samarqand Wiloyati Rus. Samarkandskaya Oblast'. ◐ province C Uzbekistan
145 S6 Sāmarrā' C Iraq
131 R7 Samarskaya Oblast' prev. Kuybyshevskaya Oblast'. ◐ province W Russian Federation
159 Q13 Samastipur Bihār, N India
78 L14 Samatiguila NW Ivory Coast
121 Q17 Samatsevichy Rus. Samotevichi. Mahilyowskaya Voblasts', E Belorussia
Samawa see As Samāwah
143 Y11 Şamaxı Rus. Shemakha. C Azerbaijan
158 H6 Samba Jammu and Kashmir, NW India
81 K18 Samba Equateur, NW Zaire
81 N21 Samba Maniema, E Zaire
175 Oo6 Sambaliung, Pegunungan ▲▲ Borneo, N Indonesia
160 M11 Sambalpur Orissa, E India
69 X12 Sambao ≈ W Madagascar
174 Kk7 Sambas, Sungai ≈ Borneo, N Indonesia
180 K2 Sambava Antsirañana, NE Madagascar
176 Ww9 Samberi Irian Jaya, E Indonesia
158 J10 Sambhal Uttar Pradesh, N India
158 H12 Sāmbhar Salt Lake ◎ N India
109 N21 Sambiase Calabria, SW Italy
118 H5 Sambir Rus. Sambor. L'vivs'ka Oblast', NW Ukraine
84 C13 Sambo Huambo, C Angola
Sambor see Sambir
63 E21 Samborombón, Bahía bay NE Argentina
101 H20 Sambre ≈ Belgium/France
45 V16 Sambú, Río ≈ SE Panama
169 Z14 Samch'ŏk Jap. Sanchoku. NE South Korea
Samch'ŏnpŏ see Sach'ŏn
83 I21 Same Kilimanjaro, NE Tanzania
110 J10 Samedan Ger. Samaden. Graubünden, S Switzerland
84 K12 Samfya Luapula, N Zambia
147 W13 Samhān, Jabal ▲ SW Oman
117 C18 Sámi Kefallinía, Iónioi Nísoi, Greece, C Mediterranean Sea
58 F10 Samiria, Río ≈ N Peru
Samirum see Semīrom
143 V11 Şämkir Rus. Shamkhor. NW Azerbaijan
178 J7 Sam, Nam Vtn. Sông Chu. ≈ Laos/Vietnam
Samnān see Semnān
Sam Neua see Xam Nua
77 P10 Samnū C Libya
198 Bb7 Samoa off. Independent State of Samoa, var. Sāmoa prev. Western Samoa ◆ monarchy W Polynesia
183 T9 Samoa Basin undersea feature W Pacific Ocean
Sāmoa-i-Sisifo see Western Samoa
114 D8 Samobor Grad Zagreb, N Croatia
116 H10 Samokov var. Samakov. Sofiyska Oblast, W Bulgaria
113 H21 Šamorín Ger. Sommerein, Hung. Somorja. Západné Slovensko, SW Czech Republic
117 M19 Sámos prev. Limín Vathéos. Sámos, Dodekánisos, Greece, Aegean Sea
117 M20 Sámos island Dodekánisos, Greece, Aegean Sea
Samosch see Szamos
173 Ff5 Samosir, Pulau island W Indonesia
Samotevichi see Samatsevichy
Samothrace see Samothráki
117 K14 Samothráki Samothráki, NE Greece
117 J14 Samothráki anc. Samothrace. island NE Greece
117 A15 Samothráki island Iónioi Nísoi, Greece, C Mediterranean Sea
Samotschin see Szamocin
xxxvi I13 Sampford Peverell Devon, SW England, UK
174 M10 Sampit Borneo, C Indonesia
174 M10 Sampit, Sungai ≈ Borneo, N Indonesia
Sampoku see Sanpoku
195 P11 Sampun New Britain, E PNG
81 N24 Sampwe Shaba, SE Zaire
27 X8 Sam Rayburn Reservoir ⊠ Texas, SW USA
178 Ii6 Sam Sao, Phou ▲▲ Laos/Thailand
97 H22 Samsø island E Denmark
97 H23 Samsø Bælt channel E Denmark
178 Jj7 Sâm Sơn Thanh Hoa, N Vietnam
142 L11 Samsun anc. Amisus. Samsun, N Turkey
142 K11 Samsun ◐ province N Turkey
143 R9 Samtredia W Georgia
61 E15 Samuel, Represa de ⊠ W Brazil
178 H15 Samui, Ko island SW Thailand
Samundari see Samundri
155 U9 Samundri var. Samundari. Punjab, E Pakistan
143 X10 Samur ≈ Azerbaijan/Russian Federation
143 Y11 Samur-Abşeron Kanalı Rus. Samur-Apsheronskiy Kanal. canal E Azerbaijan
Samur-Apsheronskiy Kanal see Samur-Abşeron Kanalı
178 Hh11 Samut Prakan var. Muang Samut Prakan, Paknam. Samut Prakan, C Thailand
178 H11 Samut Sakhon var. Maha Chai, Samut Sakorn, Tha Chin. Samut Sakhon, C Thailand
Samut Sakorn see Samut Sakhon
178 H11 Samut Songhram prev. Meklong. Samut Songkhram, SW Thailand
79 N12 San Ségou, C Mali
113 O15 San ≈ SE Poland
147 O15 Şan'ā' Eng. Sana. ● (Yemen) W Yemen
114 F11 Sana ≈ NW Bosnia and Herzegovina
82 O12 Sanaag off. Gobolka Sanaag. ◐ region N Somalia
116 J8 Sanadinovo Loveshka Oblast, N Bulgaria
205 P1 Sanae South African research station Antarctica
145 Y10 Sanāf, Hawr as ◎ S Iraq
81 E15 Sanaga ≈ C Cameroon
56 D12 San Agustín Huila, SW Colombia
179 S16 San Agustin, Cape headland Mindanao, S Philippines
39 Q13 San Agustin, Plains of plain New Mexico, SW USA
xliii D20 Sanaigmore Argyll and Bute, W Scotland, UK
40 M16 Sanak Island island Aleutian Islands, Alaska, USA
200 P11 San Ambrosio, Isla Eng. San Ambrosio Island. island W Chile
San Ambrosio Island see San Ambrosio, Isla
175 S10 Sanana Pulau Sanana, E Indonesia
175 S10 Sanana, Pulau island Maluku, E Indonesia
148 K5 Sanandaj prev. Sinneh. Kordestān, W Iran
37 P8 San Andreas California, W USA
2 C13 San Andreas Fault fault W USA
56 G8 San Andrés Santander, C Colombia
63 C20 San Andrés de Giles Buenos Aires, E Argentina
39 R14 San Andres Mountains ▲▲ New Mexico, SW USA
43 S15 San Andrés Tuxtla var. Tuxtla. Veracruz-Llave, E Mexico
27 P8 San Angelo Texas, SW USA
109 A20 San Antioco, Isola di island W Italy
44 F4 San Antonio Toledo, S Belize
64 G11 San Antonio Valparaíso, C Chile
196 H6 San Antonio Saipan, S Northern Mariana Islands
39 R13 San Antonio New Mexico, SW USA
27 R12 San Antonio Texas, SW USA
56 M11 San Antonio Amazonas, S Venezuela
56 I7 San Antonio Barinas, C Venezuela
57 O5 San Antonio Monagas, NE Venezuela
27 S12 San Antonio ✕ Texas, SW USA
San Antonio see San Antonio del Táchira
107 V11 San Antonio Abad Eivissa, Spain, W Mediterranean Sea
27 U13 San Antonio Bay inlet Texas, SW USA
63 E22 San Antonio, Cabo headland E Argentina
46 A5 San Antonio, Cabo de headland W Cuba
107 T11 San Antonio, Cabo de headland E Spain
56 H7 San Antonio de Caparo Táchira, W Venezuela
64 J5 San Antonio de los Cobres Salta, NE Argentina
56 H7 San Antonio del Táchira var. San Antonio. Táchira, W Venezuela
37 T15 San Antonio, Mount ▲ California, W USA
65 K16 San Antonio Oeste Río Negro, E Argentina
27 T13 San Antonio River ≈ Texas, SW USA
56 J5 Sanare Lara, N Venezuela
105 T16 Sanary-sur-Mer Var, SE France
27 X8 San Augustine Texas, SW USA
147 T13 Sanāw var. Sanaw. NE Yemen
43 O11 San Bartolo San Luis Potosí, C Mexico
109 L16 San Bartolomeo in Galdo Campania, S Italy
108 K13 San Benedetto del Tronto Marche, C Italy
44 E3 San Benito Petén, N Guatemala
27 T17 San Benito Texas, SW USA
56 E6 San Benito Abad Sucre, N Colombia
37 P11 San Benito Mountain ▲ California, W USA
37 O10 San Benito River ≈ California, W USA
110 H10 San Bernardino Graubünden, S Switzerland
37 U15 San Bernardino California, W USA
110 H10 San Bernardino, Passo del pass SE Switzerland
64 H11 San Bernardo Santiago, C Chile
42 J8 San Bernardo Durango, C Mexico
170 F12 Sanbe-san ▲ Kyūshū, SW Japan
42 J12 San Blas Nayarit, C Mexico
42 H8 San Blas Sinaloa, C Mexico
45 V14 San Blas off. Comarca de San Blas. ◐ special territory NE Panama
45 U14 San Blas, Archipiélago de island group NE Panama
25 Q10 San Blas, Cape headland Florida, SE USA
45 V14 San Blas, Cordillera de ▲▲ NE Panama
64 J8 San Blas de los Sauces Catamarca, NW Argentina
108 G8 San Bonifacio Veneto, NE Italy
31 S12 Sanborn Iowa, C USA
42 M7 San Buenaventura Coahuila de Zaragoza, NE Mexico
107 S5 San Caprasio ▲ N Spain
61 L21 San Carlos São Paulo, SE Brazil
64 G13 San Carlos Bío Bío, C Chile
42 E9 San Carlos Baja California Sur, W Mexico
43 N5 San Carlos Coahuila de Zaragoza, NE Mexico
43 P9 San Carlos Tamaulipas, C Mexico
44 L12 San Carlos Río San Juan, S Nicaragua
45 T16 San Carlos Panamá, C Panama
179 P9 San Carlos off. San Carlos City. Luzon, N Philippines
38 M14 San Carlos Arizona, SW USA
63 G20 San Carlos Maldonado, S Uruguay
56 K5 San Carlos Cojedes, N Venezuela
San Carlos see Quesada, Costa Rica
San Carlos see Luba, Equatorial Guinea
63 B17 San Carlos Centro Santa Fe, C Argentina
179 Q13 San Carlos City Negros, C Philippines
San Carlos de Ancud see Ancud
65 H16 San Carlos de Bariloche Río Negro, SW Argentina
63 B21 San Carlos de Bolívar Buenos Aires, E Argentina
56 H6 San Carlos del Zulia Zulia, W Venezuela
56 L12 San Carlos de Río Negro Amazonas, S Venezuela
San Carlos, Estrecho de see Falkland Sound
38 M14 San Carlos Reservoir ⊠ Arizona, SW USA
44 M12 San Carlos, Río ≈ N Costa Rica
67 D24 San Carlos Settlement East Falkland, Falkland Islands
63 C23 San Cayetano Buenos Aires, E Argentina
105 O8 Sancerre Cher, C France
164 G7 Sanchakou Xinjiang Uygur Zizhiqu, NW China
Sanchoku see Samch'ŏk
43 O12 San Ciro San Luis Potosí, C Mexico
107 P10 San Clemente Castilla-La Mancha, C Spain
37 T16 San Clemente California, W USA
63 E21 San Clemente del Tuyú Buenos Aires, E Argentina
37 S17 San Clemente Island island Channel Islands, California, W USA
105 O9 Sancoins Cher, C France
195 Z17 San Cristobal var. Makira. island SE Solomon Islands
63 B16 San Cristóbal Santa Fe, C Argentina
46 B4 San Cristóbal Pinar del Río, W Cuba
47 O9 San Cristóbal var. Benemérita de San Cristóbal. S Dominican Republic
56 H7 San Cristóbal Táchira, W Venezuela
San Cristóbal see San Cristóbal de las Casas
43 U16 San Cristóbal de Las Casas var. San Cristóbal. Chiapas, SE Mexico
200 Oo8 San Cristóbal, Isla var. Chatham Island. island Galapagos Islands, Ecuador, E Pacific Ocean
44 D5 San Cristóbal Verapaz Alta Verapaz, C Guatemala
46 F6 Sancti Spíritus Sancti Spíritus, C Cuba
105 O11 Sancy, Puy de ▲ C France
xlii I4 Sand Shetland Islands, NE Scotland, UK
97 D15 Sand Rogaland, S Norway
xliii F23 Sanda island W Scotland, UK
xliii F14 Sandaig Highland, NW Scotland, UK
175 Oo2 Sandakan Sabah, East Malaysia
190 K9 Sandalwood South Australia
Sandalwood Island see Sumba, Pulau
96 D11 Sandane Sogn og Fjordane, S Norway
116 G12 Sandanski prev. Sveti Vrach. Sofiyska Oblast, SW Bulgaria
78 J11 Sandaré Kayes, W Mali
97 J19 Sandared Älvsborg, S Sweden
96 N12 Sandarne Gävleborg, C Sweden
194 E10 Sandaun prev. West Sepik. ◐ province NW PNG
xlii C14 Sanday island NW Scotland, UK
xlii O3 Sanday island NE Scotland, UK
xxxviii I6 Sandbach Cheshire, W England, UK
xliii H19 Sandbank Argyll and Bute, W Scotland, UK
179 N14 Sand Cay island W Spratly Islands
33 P15 Sand Creek ≈ Indiana, N USA
97 H15 Sande Vestfold, S Norway
97 H16 Sandefjord Vestfold, S Norway
79 O15 Sandégué E Ivory Coast
79 P14 Sandema N Ghana
39 O11 Sanders Arizona, SW USA
26 M11 Sanderson Texas, SW USA
25 U4 Sandersville Georgia, SE USA
xxxvi K10 Sandford North West Somerset, SW England, UK
xlii N4 Sandgarth Orkney Islands, N Scotland, UK
94 H4 Sandgerdhi Sudhurland, SW Iceland
xlii P11 Sandhaven Aberdeenshire, NE Scotland, UK
xliii H25 Sandhead Dumfries and Galloway, SW Scotland, UK
30 K14 Sand Hills ▲▲ Nebraska, C USA
xxxvii R10 Sandhurst Bracknell Forest, S England, UK
xli U12 Sand Hutton North Yorkshire, N England, UK
27 S14 Sandia Texas, SW USA
37 T17 San Diego California, W USA
27 S14 San Diego Texas, SW USA
142 F14 Sandıklı Afyon, W Turkey
158 L12 Sandīla Uttar Pradesh, N India
123 J15 San Dimitri, Ras var. San Dimitri Point. headland Gozo, NW Malta
174 Gg11 Sanding, Selat strait W Indonesia
32 J3 Sand Island island Apostle Islands, Wisconsin, N USA
97 C16 Sandnes Rogaland, S Norway
94 F13 Sandnessjøen Nordland, C Norway
81 L24 Sandoa Shaba, S Zaire
113 N15 Sandomierz Rus. Sandomir. Tarnobrzeg, SE Poland
Sandomir see Sandomierz
xxxviii K8 Sandon Staffordshire, C England, UK
56 C13 Sandoná Nariño, SW Colombia
108 I7 San Donà di Piave Veneto, NE Italy
128 K14 Sandovo Tverskaya Oblast', W Russian Federation
177 Ff7 Sandoway Arakan State, W Burma
xxxvii Q14 Sandown Isle of Wight, S England, UK
xxxvi E16 Sandplace Cornwall, SW England, UK
41 N16 Sand Point Popof Island, Alaska, USA
67 N24 Sand Point headland E Tristan da Cunha
33 R7 Sand Point headland Michigan, N USA
34 M7 Sandpoint Idaho, NW USA
xlii O2 Sandquoy Orkney Islands, N Scotland, UK
xliii A15 Sandray island NW Scotland, UK
xxxix U8 Sandringham Norfolk, E England, UK
95 H14 Sandsele Västerbotten, N Sweden
8 I14 Sandspit Moresby Island, British Columbia, SW Canada
29 P9 Sand Springs Oklahoma, C USA
31 W7 Sandstone Minnesota, N USA
38 K15 Sand Tank Mountains ▲▲ Arizona, SW USA
33 S8 Sandusky Michigan, N USA
33 S11 Sandusky Ohio, N USA
33 S12 Sandusky River ≈ Ohio, N USA
85 D22 Sandverhaar Karas, S Namibia
97 L24 Sandvig Bornholm, E Denmark
97 H15 Sandvika Akershus, S Norway
96 N13 Sandviken Gävleborg, C Sweden
xxxviii B14 Sandwell ◐ unitary authority C England, UK
xxxvii Z10 Sandwich Kent, SE England, UK
32 M11 Sandwich Illinois, N USA
xxxvii Z10 Sandwich Bay bay SE England, UK
Sandwich Island see Éfaté
Sandwich Islands see Hawaiian Islands
xl M9 Sandwick Cumbria, NW England, UK
xlii I5 Sandwick Shetland Islands, NE Scotland, UK
159 V16 Sandwip Island island SE Bangladesh
xxxvii T5 Sandy Bedfordshire, C England, UK
9 U12 Sandy Bay Saskatchewan, C Canada
191 N16 Sandy Cape headland Tasmania, SE Australia
178 Mm14 Sandy Cay island NW Spratly Islands
38 L3 Sandy City Utah, W USA
33 U12 Sandy Creek ≈ Ohio, N USA
23 O5 Sandy Hook Kentucky, S USA
20 K15 Sandy Hook headland New Jersey, NE USA
152 J15 Sandykachi Turkm. Sandykgachy. Maryyskiy Velayat, S Turkmenistan
Sandykgachy see Sandykachi
152 L13 Sandykly, Peski desert E Turkmenistan
9 Q13 Sandy Lake Alberta, W Canada
10 B8 Sandy Lake Ontario, C Canada
10 B8 Sandy Lake ◎ Ontario, C Canada
25 S3 Sandy Springs Georgia, SE USA
26 H8 San Elizario Texas, SW USA
101 L25 Sanem Luxembourg, SW Luxembourg
44 K5 San Esteban Olancho, C Honduras
107 O6 San Esteban de Gormaz Castilla-León, N Spain
42 E5 San Esteban, Isla island NW Mexico
San Eugenio/San Eugenio del Cuareim see Artigas
64 H11 San Felipe var. San Felipe de Aconcagua. Valparaíso, C Chile
42 D3 San Felipe Baja California, NW Mexico
42 N12 San Felipe Guanajuato, C Mexico
56 K5 San Felipe Yaracuy, NW Venezuela
46 B5 San Felipe, Cayos de island group W Cuba
San Felipe de Aconcagua see San Felipe
San Felipe de Puerto Plata see Puerto Plata
39 R11 San Felipe Pueblo New Mexico, SW USA
San Feliú de Guixols see Sant Feliu de Guíxols
200 Oo11 San Félix, Isla Eng. San Felix Island. island W Chile
San Felix Island see San Félix, Isla
56 L11 San Fernando de Atabapo Amazonas, S Venezuela
42 C4 San Fernando var. Misión San Fernando. Baja California, NW Mexico
43 P9 San Fernando Tamaulipas, C Mexico
179 P9 San Fernando Luzon, N Philippines
179 P10 San Fernando Luzon, N Philippines
106 J16 San Fernando prev. Isla de León. Andalucía, S Spain
47 U14 San Fernando Trinidad, Trinidad and Tobago
37 S15 San Fernando California, W USA
56 L7 San Fernando var. San Fernando de Apure. Apure, C Venezuela
San Fernando de Apure see San Fernando
64 L8 San Fernando del Valle de Catamarca var. Catamarca. Catamarca, NW Argentina
San Fernando de Monte Cristi see Monte Cristi
43 P9 San Fernando, Río ≈ C Mexico
25 X11 Sanford Florida, SE USA
21 P9 Sanford Maine, NE USA
23 T10 Sanford North Carolina, SE USA
27 N2 Sanford Texas, SW USA
41 T10 Sanford, Mount ▲ Alaska, USA
44 G8 San Francisco var. Gotera, San Francisco Gotera. Morazán, E El Salvador
45 R16 San Francisco Veraguas, C Panama
179 Pp11 San Francisco var. Aurora. Luzon, N Philippines
37 L8 San Francisco California, W USA
56 H5 San Francisco Zulia, NW Venezuela
36 M8 San Francisco ✕ California, W USA
37 N9 San Francisco Bay bay California, W USA
63 C24 San Francisco de Bellocq Buenos Aires, E Argentina
42 I6 San Francisco de Borja Chihuahua, N Mexico
44 J6 San Francisco de la Paz Olancho, C Honduras
42 J7 San Francisco del Oro Chihuahua, N Mexico
42 M12 San Francisco del Rincón Jalisco, SW Mexico
47 O8 San Francisco de Macorís C Dominican Republic
San Francisco de Satipo see Satipo
San Francisco Gotera see San Francisco
San Francisco Telixtlahuaca see Telixtlahuaca
109 K23 San Fratello Sicilia, Italy, C Mediterranean Sea
San Fructuoso see Tacuarembó
84 C12 Sanga Cuanza Sul, NW Angola
58 C5 San Gabriel Carchi, N Ecuador
165 S15 Sa'ngain Xizang Zizhiqu, W China
160 E13 Sangamner Mahārāshtra, W India
158 H12 Sāngāner Rājasthān, N India
Sangan, Koh-i- see Sangān, Kūh-e
155 N6 Sangān, Kūh-e Pash. Koh-i-Sangan. ▲ C Afghanistan
126 Ll10 Sangar Respublika Sakha (Yakutiya), NE Russian Federation
175 O8 Sangasanga Borneo, C Indonesia
105 N1 Sangatte Pas-de-Calais, N France
109 B19 San Gavino Monreale Sardegna, Italy, C Mediterranean Sea
59 D16 Sangayan, Isla island W Peru
32 L14 Sangchris Lake ⊠ Illinois, N USA
175 P15 Sangeang, Pulau island S Indonesia
118 I10 Sângeorgiu de Pădure prev. Erdăt-Sângeorz, Sîngeorgiu de Pădure, Hung. Erdőszentgyörgy. Mureş, C Romania
118 I9 Sângeorz-Băi var. Singeroz Băi, Ger. Rumänisch-Sankt-Georgen, Hung. Oláhszentgyörgy; prev. Sîngeorz-Băi. Bistriţa-Năsăud, N Romania
37 R10 Sanger California, W USA
27 T5 Sanger Texas, SW USA
Sângerei see Sîngerei
103 L15 Sangerhausen Sachsen-Anhalt, C Germany
47 S6 San Germán W Puerto Rico
San Germano see Cassino
167 N2 Sanggan He ≈ E China
175 Oo16 Sanggar, Teluk bay Nusa Tenggara, S Indonesia
174 L8 Sanggau Borneo, C Indonesia
81 H16 Sangha ≈ Central African Republic/Congo
81 G16 Sangha-Mbaéré ◐ prefecture SW Central African Republic
155 Q15 Sānghar Sind, SE Pakistan
117 F22 Sangiás ▲ S Greece
Sangihe, Kepulauan see Sangir, Kepulauan
175 S4 Sangihe, Pulau var. Sangir. island N Indonesia
56 G8 San Gil Santander, C Colombia
108 F12 San Gimignano Toscana, C Italy
154 M8 Sangīn var. Sangin. Helmand, S Afghanistan
109 O21 San Giovanni in Fiore Calabria, SW Italy
109 M16 San Giovanni Rotondo Puglia, SE Italy
108 G12 San Giovanni Valdarno Toscana, C Italy
Sangir see Sangihe, Pulau
175 Rr6 Sangir, Kepulauan var. Kepulauan Sangihe. island group N Indonesia
168 K9 Sangiyn Dalay Dundgovĭ, C Mongolia
168 H9 Sangiyn Dalay Govĭ-Altay, C Mongolia
168 K11 Sangiyn Dalay Ömnögovĭ, S Mongolia
168 K8 Sangiyn Dalay Övörhangay, C Mongolia
169 Y15 Sangju Jap. Shōshū. C South Korea
178 I11 Sangkha Surin, E Thailand
175 Oo7 Sangkulirang Borneo, N Indonesia
175 Oo7 Sangkulirang, Teluk bay Borneo, N Indonesia
161 E16 Sāngli Mahārāshtra, W India
81 E16 Sangmélima Sud, S Cameroon
37 V15 San Gorgonio Mountain ▲ California, W USA
39 T8 Sangre de Cristo Mountains ▲▲ Colorado/New Mexico, C USA
63 A20 San Gregorio Santa Fe, C Argentina
63 F18 San Gregorio de Polanco Tacuarembó, C Uruguay
47 V14 Sangre Grande Trinidad, Trinidad and Tobago
165 N16 Sangri Xizang Zizhiqu, W China
158 H9 Sangrūr Punjab, NW India
46 I11 Sangster off. Sir Donald Sangster International Airport, var. Montego Bay. ✕ (Montego Bay) W Jamaica
61 G17 Sangue, Rio do ≈ W Brazil
107 R4 Sangüesa Navarra, N Spain
63 C16 San Gustavo Entre Ríos, E Argentina
Sangyuan see Wuqiao
42 C6 San Hipólito, Punta headland W Mexico
25 W15 Sanibel Sanibel Island, Florida, SE USA
25 V15 Sanibel Island island Florida, SE USA
62 F13 San Ignacio Misiones, NE Argentina

◆ Country ● Country Capital ◇ Dependent Territory ○ Dependent Territory Capital ◐ Administrative Region ✕ International Airport ▲ Mountain ▲▲ Mountain Range Volcano ≈ River ◎ Lake ⊠ Reservoir

San Ignacio – Santiago

59 L16 **San Ignacio** Beni, N Bolivia
59 O18 **San Ignacio** Santa Cruz, E Bolivia
44 M14 **San Ignacio** *var.* San Ignacio de Acosta. San José, W Costa Rica
42 E6 **San Ignacio** Baja California Sur, W Mexico
42 J10 **San Ignacio** Sinaloa, W Mexico
58 B9 **San Ignacio** Cajamarca, N Peru
San Ignacio de Acosta *see* San Ignacio
42 D7 **San Ignacio, Laguna** *lagoon* W Mexico
10 I6 **Sanikiluaq** Belcher Islands, Northwest Territories, C Canada
179 Pp9 **San Ildefonso Peninsula** *peninsula* Luzon, N Philippines
Saniquillie *see* Sanniquellie
63 D20 **San Isidro** Buenos Aires, E Argentina
45 N14 **San Isidro** *var.* San Isidro de El General. San José, SE Costa Rica
San Isidro de El General *see* San Isidro
56 E5 **San Jacinto** Bolívar, N Colombia
37 U16 **San Jacinto** California, W USA
37 V15 **San Jacinto Peak** ▲ California, W USA
63 F14 **San Javier** Misiones, NE Argentina
63 C16 **San Javier** Santa Fe, C Argentina
107 S13 **San Javier** Murcia, SE Spain
63 D18 **San Javier** Río Negro, W Uruguay
63 C16 **San Javier, Río** ⇝ C Argentina
166 L12 **Sanjiang** *var.* Guyi, Sanjiang Dongzu Zizhixian. Guangxi Zhuangzu Zizhiqu, S China
Sanjiang Dongzu Zizhixian *see* Sanjiang
171 Kk13 **Sanjō** *var.* Sanzyô. Niigata, Honshū, C Japan
59 M15 **San Joaquín** Beni, N Bolivia
57 O6 **San Joaquín** Anzoátegui, NE Venezuela
37 O9 **San Joaquin River** ⇝ California, W USA
37 P10 **San Joaquin Valley** *valley* California, W USA
63 A18 **San Jorge** Santa Fe, C Argentina
195 W15 **San Jorge** *island* N Solomon Islands
42 D3 **San Jorge, Bahía de** *bay* NW Mexico
65 J19 **San Jorge, Golfo** *var.* Gulf of San Jorge. *gulf* S Argentina
San Jorge, Gulf of *see* San Jorge, Golfo
196 K8 **San Jose** Tinian, S Northern Mariana Islands
179 Pp12 **San Jose** Mindoro, N Philippines
37 N9 **San Jose** California, W USA
63 F14 **San José** Misiones, NE Argentina
59 P19 **San José** *var.* San José de Chiquitos. Santa Cruz, E Bolivia
44 M14 **San José** ● (Costa Rica) San José, C Costa Rica
44 C7 **San José** *var.* Puerto San José. Escuintla, S Guatemala
42 G6 **San José** Sonora, NW Mexico
107 U11 **San José** Eivissa, Spain, W Mediterranean Sea
56 H5 **San José** Zulia, NW Venezuela
44 M14 **San José** *off.* Provincia de San José. ◆ *province* W Costa Rica
63 E19 **San José** ◆ *department* S Uruguay
44 M13 **San José** ✕ Alajuela, C Costa Rica
San José *see* San José del Guaviare, Colombia
San José *see* San José de Mayo, S Uruguay
179 P9 **San Jose City** Luzon, N Philippines
179 Pp13 **San Jose de Buenavista** Panay Island, C Philippines
San José de Cúcuta *see* Cúcuta
63 D16 **San José de Feliciano** Entre Ríos, E Argentina
57 O6 **San José de Guanipa** *var.* El Tigrito. Anzoátegui, NE Venezuela
64 I9 **San José de Jáchal** San Juan, W Argentina
42 G10 **San José del Cabo** Baja California Sur, W Mexico
56 G12 **San José del Guaviare** *var.* San José. Guaviare, S Colombia
63 E20 **San José de Mayo** *var.* San José. San José, S Uruguay
56 I10 **San José de Ocuné** Vichada, E Colombia
43 O9 **San José de Raíces** Nuevo León, NE Mexico
65 K17 **San José, Golfo** *gulf* E Argentina
42 F9 **San José, Isla** *island* W Mexico
45 U16 **San José, Isla** *island* SE Panama
27 U14 **San Jose Island** *island* Texas, SW USA
64 I10 **San Juan** San Juan, W Argentina
47 N9 **San Juan** *var.* San Juan de la Maguana. C Dominican Republic
59 E17 **San Juan** Ica, S Peru
47 U5 **San Juan** ○ (Puerto Rico) NE Puerto Rico
64 H10 **San Juan** *off.* Provincia de San Juan. ◆ *province* W Argentina
47 U5 **San Juan** *var.* Luis Muñoz Marin. ✕ NE Puerto Rico
San Juan *see* San Juan de los Morros
64 O7 **San Juan Bautista** Misiones, S Paraguay
37 O10 **San Juan Bautista** California, W USA
San Juan Bautista *see* Villahermosa
San Juan Bautista Cuicatlán *see* Cuicatlán
San Juan Bautista Tuxtepec *see* Tuxtepec
81 C17 **San Juan, Cabo** *headland* S Equatorial Guinea
107 S12 **San Juan de Alicante** País Valenciano, E Spain
56 H7 **San Juan de Colón** Táchira, NW Venezuela
42 L9 **San Juan de Guadalupe** Durango, C Mexico
San Juan de la Maguana *see* San Juan
56 G4 **San Juan del Cesar** La Guajira, N Colombia
42 L15 **San Juan de Lima, Punta** *headland* SW Mexico
44 I8 **San Juan de Limay** Estelí, NW Nicaragua
45 N12 **San Juan del Norte** *var.* Greytown. Río San Juan, SE Nicaragua
56 K4 **San Juan de los Cayos** Falcón, N Venezuela
42 M12 **San Juan de los Lagos** Jalisco, C Mexico
56 L5 **San Juan de los Morros** *var.* San Juan. Guárico, N Venezuela
42 K9 **San Juan del Río** Durango, C Mexico
43 O13 **San Juan del Río** Querétaro de Arteaga, C Mexico
44 J11 **San Juan del Sur** Rivas, SW Nicaragua
56 M9 **San Juan de Manapiare** Amazonas, S Venezuela
42 E7 **San Juanico** Baja California Sur, W Mexico
42 D7 **San Juanico, Punta** *headland* W Mexico
34 G6 **San Juan Islands** *island group* Washington, NW USA
42 I6 **San Juanito** Chihuahua, N Mexico
42 I12 **San Juanito, Isla** *island* C Mexico
39 R8 **San Juan Mountains** ▲▲ Colorado, C USA
56 E5 **San Juan Nepomuceno** Bolívar, NW Colombia
46 E5 **San Juan, Pico** ▲ C Cuba
203 W15 **San Juan, Punta** *headland* Easter Island, Chile, E Pacific Ocean
44 M12 **San Juan, Río** ⇝ Costa Rica/Nicaragua
43 S15 **San Juan, Río** ⇝ SE Mexico
39 O8 **San Juan River** ⇝ Colorado/Utah, W USA
San Julián *see* Puerto San Julián
63 B17 **San Justo** Santa Fe, C Argentina
111 W5 **Sankt Aegyd am Neuwalde** Niederösterreich, E Austria
111 U9 **Sankt Andrä** *Slvn.* Šent Andraž. Kärnten, S Austria
Sankt Andrä *see* Szentendre
Sankt Anna *see* Sântana
110 K8 **Sankt Anton am Arlberg** Vorarlberg, W Austria
103 E16 **Sankt Augustin** Nordrhein-Westfalen, W Germany
Sankt-Bartholomäi *see* Palamuse
103 F24 **Sankt Blasien** Baden-Württemberg, SW Germany
111 R3 **Sankt Florian am Inn** Oberösterreich, N Austria
110 I7 **Sankt Gallen** *var.* St.Gallen, *Eng.* Saint Gall, *Fr.* St-Gall. Sankt Gallen, NE Switzerland
110 H8 **Sankt Gallen** *var.* St.Gallen, Eng, Saint Gall, *Fr.* St-Gall. ◆ *canton* NE Switzerland
110 J8 **Sankt Gallenkirch** Vorarlberg, W Austria
111 Q5 **Sankt Georgen** Salzburg, N Austria
Sankt Georgen *see* Đurđevac, Croatia
Sankt-Georgen *see* Sfântu Gheorghe, Romania
111 R6 **Sankt Gilgen** Salzburg, NW Austria
Sankt Gotthard *see* Szentgotthárd
103 E20 **Sankt Ingbert** Saarland, SW Germany
Sankt-Jakobi *see* Viru-Jaagupi, Lääne-Virumaa, Estonia
Sankt-Jakobi *see* Pärnu-Jaagupi, Pärnumaa, Estonia
Sankt Johann *see* Sankt Johann in Tirol
111 T7 **Sankt Johann am Tauern** Steiermark, E Austria
111 Q7 **Sankt Johann im Pongau** Salzburg, NW Austria
111 P6 **Sankt Johann in Tirol** *var.* Sankt Johann. Tirol, W Austria
Sankt-Johannis *see* Järva-Jaani
110 L8 **Sankt Leonhard** Tirol, W Austria
Sankt Margarethen *see* Sankt Margarethen im Burgenland
111 Y5 **Sankt Margarethen im Burgenland** *var.* Sankt Margarethen. Burgenland, E Austria
Sankt Martin *see* Martin
111 X8 **Sankt Martin an der Raab** Burgenland, SE Austria
111 U7 **Sankt Michael in Obersteiermark** Steiermark, SE Austria
Sankt Michel *see* Mikkeli
Sankt Moritz *see* St.Moritz
110 E11 **Sankt Niklaus** Valais, S Switzerland
111 S7 **Sankt Nikolai** *var.* Sankt Nikolai im Sölktal. Steiermark, SE Austria
Sankt Nikolai im Sölktal *see* Sankt Nikolai
111 U9 **Sankt Paul** *var.* Sankt Paul im Lavanttal. Kärnten, S Austria
Sankt Paul im Lavanttal *see* Sankt Paul
Sankt Peter *see* Pivka
111 W9 **Sankt Peter am Ottersbach** Steiermark, SE Austria
128 J13 **Sankt-Peterburg** *prev.* Leningrad, Petrograd, *Eng.* Saint Petersburg, *Fin.* Pietari. Leningradskaya Oblast', NW Russian Federation
102 H8 **Sankt Peter-Ording** Schleswig-Holstein, N Germany
111 V4 **Sankt Pölten** Niederösterreich, N Austria
111 W7 **Sankt Ruprecht** *var.* Sankt Ruprecht an der Raab. Steiermark, SE Austria
Sankt Ruprecht an der Raab *see* Sankt Ruprecht
Sankt-Ulrich *see* Ortisei
111 T4 **Sankt Valentin** Niederösterreich, C Austria
Sankt Veit am Flaum *see* Rijeka
111 T9 **Sankt Veit an der Glan** *Slvn.* Šent Vid. Kärnten, S Austria
101 M21 **Sankt-Vith** *var.* Saint-Vith. Liège, E Belgium
103 E20 **Sankt Wendel** Saarland, SW Germany
111 R6 **Sankt Wolfgang** Salzburg, NW Austria
81 K21 **Sankuru** ⇝ C Zaire
42 D8 **San Lázaro, Cabo** *headland* W Mexico
143 O16 **Şanlıurfa** *prev.* Sanli Urfa, Urfa, *anc.* Edessa. Şanlıurfa, S Turkey
143 O16 **Şanlıurfa** *prev.* Urfa. ◆ *province* SE Turkey
143 O16 **Şanlıurfa Yaylası** *plateau* SE Turkey
63 B18 **San Lorenzo** Santa Fe, C Argentina
59 M21 **San Lorenzo** Tarija, S Bolivia
58 C5 **San Lorenzo** Esmeraldas, N Ecuador
44 H8 **San Lorenzo** Valle, S Honduras
107 N8 **San Lorenzo de El Escorial** *var.* El Escorial. Madrid, C Spain
42 E5 **San Lorenzo, Isla** *island* NW Mexico
59 C14 **San Lorenzo, Isla** *island* W Peru
65 G20 **San Lorenzo, Monte** ▲ S Argentina
42 I9 **San Lorenzo, Río** ⇝ C Mexico
106 J15 **Sanlúcar de Barrameda** Andalucía, S Spain
106 J14 **Sanlúcar la Mayor** Andalucía, S Spain
42 F11 **San Lucas** Baja California Sur, NW Mexico
42 E6 **San Lucas** *var.* Cabo San Lucas. Baja California Sur, W Mexico
42 G11 **San Lucas, Cabo** *var.* San Lucas Cape. *headland* W Mexico
San Lucas Cape *see* San Lucas, Cabo
64 J11 **San Luis** San Luis, C Argentina
44 E4 **San Luis** Petén, NE Guatemala
42 D2 **San Luis** *var.* San Luis Río Colorado. Sonora, NW Mexico
44 M7 **San Luis** Región Autónoma Atlántico Norte, NE Nicaragua
38 H15 **San Luis** Arizona, SW USA
39 T8 **San Luis** Colorado, C USA
56 J4 **San Luis** Falcón, N Venezuela
64 J11 **San Luis** *off.* Provincia de San Luis. ◆ *province* C Argentina
43 N12 **San Luis de la Paz** Guanajuato, C Mexico
42 K8 **San Luis del Cordero** Durango, C Mexico
42 D4 **San Luis, Isla** *island* NW Mexico
44 E6 **San Luis Jilotepeque** Jalapa, SE Guatemala
59 M16 **San Luis, Laguna de** ◎ NW Bolivia
37 P13 **San Luis Obispo** California, W USA
39 R7 **San Luis Peak** ▲ Colorado, C USA
43 N11 **San Luis Potosí** San Luis Potosí, C Mexico
43 N11 **San Luis Potosí** ◆ *state* C Mexico
37 O10 **San Luis Reservoir** ⊡ California, W USA
San Luis Río Colorado *see* San Luis
39 S8 **San Luis Valley** *basin* Colorado, C USA
109 C19 **Sanluri** Sardegna, Italy, C Mediterranean Sea
63 D23 **San Manuel** Buenos Aires, E Argentina
38 M15 **San Manuel** Arizona, SW USA
108 F11 **San Marcello Pistoiese** Toscana, C Italy
109 N20 **San Marco Argentano** Calabria, SW Italy
56 E6 **San Marcos** Sucre, N Colombia
44 M14 **San Marcos** San José, C Costa Rica
44 B5 **San Marcos** San Marcos, W Guatemala
44 F6 **San Marcos** Ocotepeque, SW Honduras
43 O16 **San Marcos** Guerrero, S Mexico
27 S11 **San Marcos** Texas, SW USA
44 A5 **San Marcos** *off.* Departamento de San Marcos. ◆ *department* W Guatemala
San Marcos de Arica *see* Arica
42 E6 **San Marcos, Isla** *island* W Mexico
108 H11 **San Marino** ● (San Marino) C San Marino
108 I11 **San Marino** *off.* Republic of San Marino. ◆ *republic* S Europe
64 I11 **San Martín** Mendoza, C Argentina
56 F11 **San Martín** Meta, C Colombia
58 D11 **San Martín** *off.* Departamento de San Martín. ◆ *department* C Peru
204 I5 **San Martín** *Argentinian research station* Antarctica
65 H16 **San Martín de los Andes** Neuquén, W Argentina
106 M8 **San Martín de Valdeiglesias** Madrid, C Spain
65 G21 **San Martín, Lago** *var.* Lago O'Higgins. ◎ S Argentina
108 H6 **San Martino di Castrozza** Trentino-Alto Adige, N Italy
59 N16 **San Martín, Río** ⇝ N Bolivia
San Martín Texmelucan *see* Texmelucan
37 N9 **San Mateo** California, W USA
57 O6 **San Mateo** Anzoátegui, NE Venezuela
44 B4 **San Mateo Ixtatán** Huehuetenango, W Guatemala
59 Q18 **San Matías** Santa Cruz, E Bolivia
65 K16 **San Matías, Golfo** *var.* Gulf of San Matías. *gulf* E Argentina
San Matías, Gulf of *see* San Matías
13 O8 **Sanmaur** Québec, SE Canada
167 T10 **Sanmen Wan** *bay* E China
166 M6 **Sanmenxia** *var.* Shan Xian. Henan, C China
Sânmiclăuş Mare *see* Sânnicolau Mare
63 D14 **San Miguel** Corrientes, NE Argentina
59 L16 **San Miguel** Beni, N Bolivia
44 G8 **San Miguel** San Miguel, SE El Salvador
42 L6 **San Miguel** Coahuila de Zaragoza, N Mexico
42 J9 **San Miguel** *var.* San Miguel de Cruces. Durango, C Mexico
45 U16 **San Miguel** Panamá, SE Panama
37 P12 **San Miguel** California, W USA
44 B9 **San Miguel** ◆ *department* E El Salvador
43 N13 **San Miguel de Allende** Guanajuato, C Mexico
San Miguel de Cruces *see* San Miguel
San Miguel de Ibarra *see* Ibarra
63 D21 **San Miguel del Monte** Buenos Aires, E Argentina
64 J7 **San Miguel de Tucumán** *var.* Tucumán. Tucumán, N Argentina
45 V16 **San Miguel, Golfo de** *gulf* S Panama
37 P15 **San Miguel Island** *island* California, W USA
44 L11 **San Miguelito** Río San Juan, S Nicaragua
45 T15 **San Miguelito** Panamá, C Panama
59 N18 **San Miguel, Río** ⇝ E Bolivia
58 D6 **San Miguel, Río** ⇝ Colombia/Ecuador
42 I7 **San Miguel, Río** ⇝ N Mexico
44 G8 **San Miguel, Volcán de** ⛰ SE El Salvador
167 Q12 **Sanming** Fujian, SE China
108 F11 **San Miniato** Toscana, C Italy
San Murezzan *see* St.Moritz
Sannār *see* Sennar
109 M15 **Sannicandro Garganico** Puglia, SE Italy
42 H6 **San Nicolás** Sonora, NW Mexico
63 C19 **San Nicolás de los Arroyos** Buenos Aires, E Argentina
37 R16 **San Nicolas Island** *island* Channel Islands, California, W USA
Sânnicolaul-Mare *see* Sânnicolau Mare
118 E11 **Sânnicolau Mare** *var.* Sânnicolaul-Mare, *Hung.* Nagyszentmiklós; *prev.* Sânmiclăuş Mare, Sînnicolau Mare. Timiş, W Romania
126 L15 **Sannikova, Proliv** *strait* NE Russian Federation
78 K16 **Sanniquellie** *var.* Saniquillie. NE Liberia
172 N9 **Sannohe** Aomori, Honshū, C Japan
Sanntaler Alpen *see* Savinjske Alpe
171 K15 **Sano** Tochigi, Honshū, S Japan
113 O17 **Sanok** Krosno, SE Poland
56 E5 **San Onofre** Sucre, NW Colombia
59 K21 **San Pablo** Potosí, S Bolivia
179 P11 **San Pablo** *off.* San Pablo City. Luzon, N Philippines
San Pablo Balleza *see* Balleza
37 N8 **San Pablo Bay** *bay* California, W USA
42 C6 **San Pablo, Punta** *headland* W Mexico
45 R16 **San Pablo, Río** ⇝ C Panama
179 Q11 **San Pascual** Burias Island, C Philippines
123 Jj16 **San Pawl il-Bahar** *Eng.* Saint Paul's Bay. E Malta
63 C19 **San Pedro** Buenos Aires, E Argentina
64 K5 **San Pedro** Jujuy, N Argentina
62 G13 **San Pedro** Misiones, NE Argentina
44 H1 **San Pedro** Corozal, NE Belize
42 L8 **San Pedro** *var.* San Pedro de las Colonias. Coahuila de Zaragoza, NE Mexico
64 O5 **San Pedro** San Pedro, SE Paraguay
64 O6 **San Pedro** *off.* Departamento de San Pedro. ◆ *department* C Paraguay
79 N16 **San Pedro** ✕ (Yamoussoukro) C Ivory Coast
46 G6 **San Pedro** ⇝ C Cuba
San Pedro *see* San Pedro del Pinatar
78 M17 **San-Pédro** S Ivory Coast
44 D5 **San Pedro Carchá** Alta Verapaz, C Guatemala
37 S16 **San Pedro Channel** *channel* California, W USA
64 I5 **San Pedro de Atacama** Antofagasta, N Chile
San Pedro de Durazno *see* Durazno
42 G5 **San Pedro de la Cueva** Sonora, NW Mexico
San Pedro de las Colonias *see* San Pedro
58 B11 **San Pedro de Lloc** La Libertad, NW Peru
107 S13 **San Pedro del Pinatar** *var.* San Pedro. Murcia, SE Spain
47 P9 **San Pedro de Macorís** SE Dominican Republic
42 C3 **San Pedro Mártir, Sierra** ▲▲ NW Mexico
San Pedro Pochutla *see* Pochutla
44 D2 **San Pedro, Río** ⇝ Guatemala/Mexico
42 K10 **San Pedro, Río** ⇝ C Mexico
106 J10 **San Pedro, Sierra de** ▲▲ W Spain
44 G5 **San Pedro Sula** Cortés, NW Honduras
San Pedro Tapanatepec *see* Tapanatepec
64 I4 **San Pedro, Volcán** ▲ N Chile
108 E7 **San Pellegrino Terme** Lombardia, N Italy
27 T16 **San Perlita** Texas, SW USA
San Pietro *see* Supetar
San Pietro del Carso *see* Pivka
109 A20 **San Pietro, Isola di** *island* W Italy
34 K7 **Sanpoil River** ⇝ Washington, NW USA
171 L12 **Sanpoku** *var.* Sampoku. Niigata, Honshū, C Japan
xliii K23 **Sanquhar** Dumfries and Galloway, SW Scotland, UK
42 C3 **San Quintín** Baja California, NW Mexico
42 B3 **San Quintín, Bahía de** *bay* NW Mexico
42 B3 **San Quintín, Cabo** *headland* NW Mexico
64 I12 **San Rafael** Mendoza, W Argentina
43 N9 **San Rafael** Nuevo León, NE Mexico
36 M8 **San Rafael** California, W USA
39 Q11 **San Rafael** New Mexico, SW USA
56 H4 **San Rafael** *var.* El Moján. Zulia, NW Venezuela
44 J8 **San Rafael del Norte** Jinotega, NW Nicaragua
44 J10 **San Rafael del Sur** Managua, SW Nicaragua
38 M5 **San Rafael Knob** ▲ Utah, W USA
37 Q14 **San Rafael Mountains** ▲▲ California, W USA
44 M13 **San Ramón** Alajuela, C Costa Rica
59 E14 **San Ramón** Junín, C Peru
63 F19 **San Ramón** Canelones, S Uruguay
64 K5 **San Ramón de la Nueva Orán** Salta, N Argentina
59 O16 **San Ramón, Río** ⇝ E Bolivia
108 B11 **San Remo** Liguria, NW Italy
56 J3 **San Román, Cabo** *headland* NW Venezuela
63 C15 **San Roque** Corrientes, NE Argentina
196 I4 **San Roque** Saipan, S Northern Mariana Islands
106 K16 **San Roque** Andalucía, S Spain
27 R9 **San Saba** Texas, SW USA
27 Q9 **San Saba River** ⇝ Texas, SW USA
63 D17 **San Salvador** Entre Ríos, E Argentina
44 F7 **San Salvador** ● (El Salvador) San Salvador, SW El Salvador
44 A10 **San Salvador** ◆ *department* C El Salvador
44 F8 **San Salvador** ✕ La Paz, S El Salvador
46 K4 **San Salvador** *prev.* Watlings Island. *island* E Bahamas
64 J5 **San Salvador de Jujuy** *var.* Jujuy. Jujuy, N Argentina
44 F7 **San Salvador, Volcán de** ⛰ C El Salvador
79 Q14 **Sansanné-Mango** *var.* Mango. N Togo
47 S5 **San Sebastián** W Puerto Rico
65 J24 **San Sebastián, Bahía** *bay* S Argentina
Sansenhō *see* Sach'ŏn
108 H12 **Sansepolcro** Toscana, C Italy
109 M16 **San Severo** Puglia, SE Italy
114 F11 **Sanski Most** NW Bosnia and Herzegovina
176 Ww9 **Sansundi** Irian Jaya, E Indonesia
106 K11 **Santa Amalia** Extremadura, W Spain
62 F13 **Santa Ana** Misiones, NE Argentina
59 L16 **Santa Ana** Beni, N Bolivia
44 E7 **Santa Ana** Santa Ana, NW El Salvador
42 F4 **Santa Ana** Sonora, NW Mexico
37 T16 **Santa Ana** California, W USA
57 N6 **Santa Ana** Nueva Esparta, NE Venezuela
44 A9 **Santa Ana** ◆ *department* NW El Salvador
Santa Ana de Coro *see* Coro
44 E7 **Santa Ana, Volcán de** *var.* La Matepec. ⛰ W El Salvador
42 J7 **Santa Barbara** Chihuahua, N Mexico
37 Q14 **Santa Barbara** California, W USA
44 G6 **Santa Bárbara** Santa Bárbara, W Honduras
56 L11 **Santa Bárbara** Amazonas, S Venezuela
56 I7 **Santa Bárbara** Barinas, W Venezuela
44 F5 **Santa Bárbara** ◆ *department* NW Honduras
Santa Bárbara *see* Iscuandé
37 Q15 **Santa Barbara Channel** *channel* California, W USA
Santa Bárbara de Samaná *see* Samaná
37 R16 **Santa Barbara Island** *island* Channel Islands, California, W USA
56 E5 **Santa Catalina** Bolívar, N Colombia
45 R15 **Santa Catalina** Bocas del Toro, W Panama
37 T17 **Santa Catalina, Gulf of** *gulf* California, W USA
42 F8 **Santa Catalina, Isla** *island* W Mexico
37 S16 **Santa Catalina Island** *island* Channel Islands, California, W USA
43 N8 **Santa Catarina** Nuevo León, NE Mexico
62 H13 **Santa Catarina** *off.* Estado de Santa Catarina. ◆ *state* S Brazil
Santa Catarina de Tepehuanes *see* Tepehuanes
62 L13 **Santa Catarina, Ilha de** *island* S Brazil
47 Q16 **Santa Catherina** Curaçao, C Netherlands Antilles
46 E5 **Santa Clara** Villa Clara, C Cuba
37 N9 **Santa Clara** California, W USA
38 J8 **Santa Clara** Utah, W USA
Santa Clara *see* Santa Clara de Olimar
63 F18 **Santa Clara de Olimar** *var.* Santa Clara. Cerro Largo, NE Uruguay
63 A17 **Santa Clara de Saguier** Santa Fe, C Argentina
Santa Coloma *see* Santa Coloma de Gramanet
107 X5 **Santa Coloma de Farners** *var.* Santa Coloma de Farnés. Cataluña, NE Spain
Santa Coloma de Farnés *see* Santa Coloma de Farners
107 W6 **Santa Coloma de Gramanet** *var.* Santa Coloma. Cataluña, NE Spain
106 G2 **Santa Comba** Galicia, NW Spain
Santa Comba *see* Uaco Cungo
106 H8 **Santa Comba Dão** Viseu, N Portugal
84 C10 **Santa Cruz** Uíge, NW Angola
59 N19 **Santa Cruz** *var.* Santa Cruz de la Sierra. Santa Cruz, C Bolivia
64 G12 **Santa Cruz** Libertador, C Chile
44 K13 **Santa Cruz** Guanacaste, W Costa Rica
46 I12 **Santa Cruz** W Jamaica
66 P6 **Santa Cruz** Madeira, Portugal, NE Atlantic Ocean
37 N10 **Santa Cruz** California, W USA
65 H20 **Santa Cruz** *off.* Provincia de Santa Cruz. ◆ *province* S Argentina
59 O18 **Santa Cruz** ◆ *department* E Bolivia
Santa Cruz *see* Viru-Viru
Santa Cruz *see* Puerto Santa Cruz
Santa Cruz Barillas *see* Barillas
61 O18 **Santa Cruz Cabrália** Bahia, E Brazil
Santa Cruz de El Seibo *see* El Seibo
66 N11 **Santa Cruz de la Palma** La Palma, Islas Canarias, Spain, NE Atlantic Ocean
Santa Cruz de la Sierra *see* Santa Cruz
107 O9 **Santa Cruz de la Zarza** Castilla-La Mancha, C Spain
44 C5 **Santa Cruz del Quiché** Quiché, W Guatemala
107 N8 **Santa Cruz del Retamar** Castilla-La Mancha, C Spain
Santa Cruz del Seibo *see* El Seibo
46 G7 **Santa Cruz del Sur** Camagüey, C Cuba
107 O11 **Santa Cruz de Mudela** Castilla-La Mancha, C Spain
66 Q11 **Santa Cruz de Tenerife** Tenerife, Islas Canarias, Spain, NE Atlantic Ocean
66 P11 **Santa Cruz de Tenerife** ◆ *province* Islas Canarias, Spain, NE Atlantic Ocean
62 K9 **Santa Cruz do Rio Pardo** São Paulo, S Brazil
63 H15 **Santa Cruz do Sul** Rio Grande do Sul, S Brazil
59 C17 **Santa Cruz, Isla** *var.* Indefatigable Island, Isla Chávez. *island* Galapagos Islands, Ecuador, E Pacific Ocean
42 F8 **Santa Cruz, Isla** *island* W Mexico
37 Q15 **Santa Cruz Island** *island* California, W USA
195 X8 **Santa Cruz Islands** *island group* E Solomon Islands
65 I22 **Santa Cruz, Río** ⇝ S Argentina
38 L15 **Santa Cruz River** ⇝ Arizona, SW USA
63 C17 **Santa Elena** Entre Ríos, E Argentina
44 F2 **Santa Elena** Cayo, W Belize
27 R16 **Santa Elena** Texas, SW USA
58 A7 **Santa Elena, Bahía de** *bay* W Ecuador
57 R10 **Santa Elena de Uairén** Bolívar, E Venezuela
44 K12 **Santa Elena, Península** *peninsula* NW Costa Rica
58 A7 **Santa Elena, Punta** *headland* W Ecuador
106 L11 **Santa Eufemia** Andalucía, S Spain
109 N21 **Santa Eufemia, Golfo di** *gulf* S Italy
107 S4 **Santa Eulalia de Gállego** Aragón, NE Spain
107 V11 **Santa Eulalia del Río** Eivissa, Spain, W Mediterranean Sea
63 B17 **Santa Fe** Santa Fe, C Argentina
107 N14 **Santa Fe** Andalucía, S Spain
39 S10 **Santa Fe** *state capital* New Mexico, SW USA
63 B15 **Santa Fe** *off.* Provincia de Santa Fe. ◆ *province* C Argentina
Santa Fe *see* Bogotá
46 C6 **Santa Fé** *var.* La Fe. Isla de la Juventud, W Cuba
45 R16 **Santa Fé** Veraguas, C Panama
Santa Fe de Bogotá *see* Bogotá
62 J7 **Santa Fé do Sul** São Paulo, S Brazil
59 B18 **Santa Fe, Isla** *var.* Barrington Island. *island* Galapagos Islands, Ecuador, E Pacific Ocean
25 V9 **Santa Fe River** ⇝ Florida, SE USA
61 M15 **Santa Filomena** Piauí, E Brazil
42 G10 **Santa Genoveva** ▲ W Mexico
159 S14 **Santahar** Rajshahi, NW Bangladesh
62 G11 **Santa Helena** Paraná, S Brazil
56 J5 **Santa Inés** Lara, N Venezuela
65 G24 **Santa Inés, Isla** *island* S Chile
64 J13 **Santa Isabel** La Pampa, C Argentina
45 U14 **Santa Isabel** Colón, N Panama
195 W14 **Santa Isabel** *var.* Bughotu. *island* N Solomon Islands
Santa Isabel *see* Malabo
60 D11 **Santa Isabel do Rio Negro** Amazonas, NW Brazil
63 C15 **Santa Lucia** Corrientes, NE Argentina
59 I17 **Santa Lucía** Puno, S Peru
63 F20 **Santa Lucía** *var.* Santa Lucia. Canelones, S Uruguay
44 B6 **Santa Lucía Cotzumalguapa** Escuintla, SW Guatemala
109 L23 **Santa Lucia del Mela** Sicilia, Italy, C Mediterranean Sea
37 O11 **Santa Lucia Range** ▲▲ California, W USA
42 D9 **Santa Margarita, Isla** *island* W Mexico
63 G15 **Santa Maria** Rio Grande do Sul, S Brazil
37 P13 **Santa Maria** California, W USA
66 Q4 **Santa Maria** ✕ Santa Maria, Azores, Portugal, NE Atlantic Ocean
66 P3 **Santa Maria** *island* Azores, Portugal, NE Atlantic Ocean
197 C11 **Santa Maria** *var.* Gaua. *island* Banks Islands, N Vanuatu
64 J7 **Santa María** Catamarca, N Argentina
Santa María Asunción Tlaxiaco *see* Tlaxiaco
42 G9 **Santa María, Bahía** *bay* W Mexico
85 L21 **Santa Maria, Cabo de** *headland* S Mozambique
106 G15 **Santa Maria, Cabo de** *headland* S Portugal
46 J4 **Santa Maria, Cape** *headland* Long Island, C Bahamas
109 J17 **Santa Maria Capua Vetere** Campania, S Italy
61 M17 **Santa Maria da Vitória** Bahia, E Brazil
57 N9 **Santa María de Erebato** Bolívar, SE Venezuela
106 G7 **Santa Maria de Feira** Aveiro, N Portugal
57 N6 **Santa María de Ipire** Guárico, C Venezuela
Santa María del Buen Aire *see* Buenos Aires
42 J8 **Santa María del Oro** Durango, C Mexico
43 N12 **Santa María del Río** San Luis Potosí, C Mexico
Santa Maria di Castellabate *see* Castellabate
109 Q20 **Santa Maria di Leuca, Capo** *headland* SE Italy
110 K10 **Santa Maria im Münstertal** Graubünden, SE Switzerland
59 B18 **Santa María, Isla** *var.* Isla Floreana, Charles Island. *island* Galapagos Islands, Ecuador, E Pacific Ocean
42 J3 **Santa María, Laguna de** ◎ N Mexico
63 G16 **Santa Maria, Rio** ⇝ S Brazil
45 R16 **Santa María, Río** ⇝ C Panama
38 J12 **Santa Maria River** ⇝ Arizona, SW USA
109 G15 **Santa Marinella** Lazio, C Italy
56 F4 **Santa Marta** Magdalena, N Colombia
106 J11 **Santa Marta** Extremadura, W Spain
Santa Maura *see* Lefkáda
37 S15 **Santa Monica** California, W USA
118 F10 **Sântana** *Ger.* Sankt Anna, *Hung.* Újszentanna; *prev.* Sîntana. Arad, W Romania
63 F16 **Santana, Coxilha de** *hill range* S Brazil
63 H16 **Santana da Boa Vista** Rio Grande do Sul, S Brazil
63 F16 **Santana do Livramento** *prev.* Livramento. Rio Grande do Sul, S Brazil
107 N2 **Santander** Cantabria, N Spain
56 F8 **Santander** *off.* Departamento de Santander. ◆ *province* C Colombia
Santander Jiménez *see* Jiménez
Sant'Andrea *see* Svetac
109 B20 **Sant'Antioco** Sardegna, Italy, C Mediterranean Sea
Santañy *see* Santanyí
106 J13 **Santa Olalla del Cala** Andalucía, S Spain
37 R15 **Santa Paula** California, W USA
38 L4 **Santaquin** Utah, W USA
60 I12 **Santarém** Pará, N Brazil
106 G10 **Santarém** *anc.* Scalabis. Santarém, W Portugal
106 G10 **Santarém** ◆ *district* C Portugal
46 F4 **Santaren Channel** *channel* W Bahamas
56 K10 **Santa Rita** Vichada, E Colombia
196 B16 **Santa Rita** SW Guam
44 H5 **Santa Rita** Cortés, NW Honduras
42 E9 **Santa Rita** Baja California Sur, W Mexico
56 H5 **Santa Rita** Zulia, NW Venezuela
61 I19 **Santa Rita de Araguaia** Goiás, S Brazil
Santa Rita de Cassia *see* Cássia
63 D14 **Santa Rosa** Corrientes, NE Argentina
64 K13 **Santa Rosa** La Pampa, C Argentina
63 G14 **Santa Rosa** Rio Grande do Sul, S Brazil
60 E10 **Santa Rosa** Roraima, N Brazil
58 B8 **Santa Rosa** El Oro, SW Ecuador
59 I16 **Santa Rosa** Puno, S Peru
36 M7 **Santa Rosa** California, W USA
39 U11 **Santa Rosa** New Mexico, SW USA
57 O6 **Santa Rosa** Anzoátegui, NE Venezuela
44 A3 **Santa Rosa** *off.* Departamento de Santa Rosa. ◆ *department* SE Guatemala
Santa Rosa *see* Santa Rosa de Copán
65 J15 **Santa Rosa, Bajo de** *basin* E Argentina
44 F6 **Santa Rosa de Copán** *var.* Santa Rosa. Copán, W Honduras
56 E8 **Santa Rosa de Osos** Antioquia, C Colombia
37 Q15 **Santa Rosa Island** *island* California, W USA
25 O9 **Santa Rosa Island** *island* Florida, SE USA
42 E6 **Santa Rosalía** Baja California Sur, W Mexico
56 K6 **Santa Rosalía** Portuguesa, NW Venezuela
196 C15 **Santa Rosa, Mount** ▲ NE Guam
37 V16 **Santa Rosa Mountains** ▲▲ California, W USA
37 T2 **Santa Rosa Range** ▲▲ Nevada, W USA
64 M8 **Santa Sylvina** Chaco, N Argentina
Santa Tecla *see* Nueva San Salvador
63 B19 **Santa Teresa** Santa Fe, C Argentina
61 O20 **Santa Teresa** Espírito Santo, SE Brazil
63 E21 **Santa Teresita** Buenos Aires, E Argentina
63 H19 **Santa Vitória do Palmar** Rio Grande do Sul, S Brazil
37 Q14 **Santa Ynez River** ⇝ California, W USA
Sant Carles de la Rápida *see* Sant Carles de la Ràpita
107 U7 **Sant Carles de la Ràpita** *var.* Sant Carles de la Rápida. Cataluña, NE Spain
107 W5 **Sant Celoni** Cataluña, NE Spain
37 U17 **Santee** California, W USA
23 T13 **Santee River** ⇝ South Carolina, SE USA
42 K15 **San Telmo, Punta** *headland* SW Mexico
109 O17 **Santeramo in Colle** Puglia, SE Italy
109 M23 **San Teresa di Riva** Sicilia, Italy, C Mediterranean Sea
107 X5 **Sant Feliu de Guíxols** *var.* San Feliú de Guixols. Cataluña, NE Spain
107 W6 **Sant Feliu de Llobregat** Cataluña, NE Spain
108 C7 **Santhià** Piemonte, NE Italy
63 F15 **Santiago** Rio Grande do Sul, S Brazil
64 H11 **Santiago** *var.* Gran Santiago. ● (Chile) Santiago, C Chile
47 N8 **Santiago** *var.* Santiago de los Caballeros. N Dominican Republic
42 G10 **Santiago** Baja California Sur, W Mexico
43 O8 **Santiago** Nuevo León, NE Mexico
45 R16 **Santiago** Veraguas, S Panama
59 E16 **Santiago** Ica, SW Peru

◆ Country
● Country Capital
◇ Dependent Territory
○ Dependent Territory Capital
◆ Administrative Region
✕ International Airport
▲ Mountain
▲▲ Mountain Range
⛰ Volcano
⇝ River
◎ Lake
⊡ Reservoir

SANTIAGO – SAY-UTËS

106 G3 **Santiago** *var.* Santiago de Compostela, *Eng.* Compostella; *anc.* Campus Stellae. Galicia, NW Spain
64 H11 **Santiago** *off.* Región Metropolitana de Santiago, *var.* Metropolitan. ◈ *region* C Chile
64 H11 **Santiago** ✕ Santiago, C Chile
106 G3 **Santiago** ✕ Galicia, NW Spain
78 D10 **Santiago** *var.* São Tiago. *island* Ilhas de Sotavento, S Cape Verde
Santiago *see* Santiago de Cuba, Cuba
Santiago *see* Grande de Santiago, Río, Mexico
44 B6 **Santiago Atitlán** Sololá, SW Guatemala
45 Q16 **Santiago, Cerro** ▲ W Panama
Santiago de Compostela *see* Santiago
46 I8 **Santiago de Cuba** *var.* Santiago. Santiago de Cuba, E Cuba
Santiago de Guayaquil *see* Guayaquil
64 K8 **Santiago del Estero** Santiago del Estero, C Argentina
63 A15 **Santiago del Estero** *off.* Provincia de Santiago del Estero. ◈ *province* N Argentina
42 I8 **Santiago de los Caballeros** Sinaloa, W Mexico
Santiago de los Caballeros *see* Santiago, Dominican Republic
Santiago de los Caballeros *see* Guatemala, Guatemala
44 F8 **Santiago de María** Usulután, SE El Salvador
106 F12 **Santiago do Cacém** Setúbal, S Portugal
42 J12 **Santiago Ixcuintla** Nayarit, C Mexico
Santiago Jamiltepec *see* Jamiltepec
26 L11 **Santiago Mountains** ▲ Texas, SW USA
42 J9 **Santiago Papasquiaro** Durango, C Mexico
Santiago Pinotepa Nacional *see* Pinotepa Nacional
58 C8 **Santiago, Río** ∿ N Peru
42 M10 **San Tiburcio** Zacatecas, C Mexico
107 N2 **Santillana** Cantabria, N Spain
56 I5 **San Timoteo** Zulia, NW Venezuela
Santi Quaranta *see* Sarandë
Santissima Trinidad *see* Chilung
107 O12 **Santisteban del Puerto** Andalucía, S Spain
107 U7 **Sant Jordi, Golf de** *gulf* NE Spain
107 T8 **Sant Mateu** País Valenciano, E Spain
27 S7 **Santo** Texas, SW USA
Santo *see* Espiritu Santo
62 M10 **Santo Amaro, Ilha de** *island* SE Brazil
53 W10 **Santo André** São Paulo, S Brazil
63 G14 **Santo Ângelo** Rio Grande do Sul, S Brazil
78 C9 **Santo Antão** *island* Ilhas de Barlavento, N Cape Verde
62 J10 **Santo Antônio da Platina** Paraná, S Brazil
60 C13 **Santo Antônio do Içá** Amazonas, N Brazil
59 Q18 **Santo Corazón, Río** ∿ E Bolivia
46 E5 **Santo Domingo** Villa Clara, C Cuba
47 O9 **Santo Domingo** *prev.* Ciudad Trujillo. ● (Dominican Republic) SE Dominican Republic
42 E8 **Santo Domingo** Baja California Sur, W Mexico
42 M10 **Santo Domingo** San Luis Potosí, C Mexico
44 L10 **Santo Domingo** Chontales, S Nicaragua
107 P4 **Santo Domingo de la Calzada** La Rioja, N Spain
58 B6 **Santo Domingo de los Colorados** Pichincha, NW Ecuador
Santo Domingo Tehuantepec *see* Tehuantepec
57 O6 **San Tomé** Anzoátegui, NE Venezuela
San Tomé de Guayana *see* Ciudad Guayana
107 R13 **Santomera** Murcia, SE Spain
107 O2 **Santoña** Cantabria, N Spain
Santorin/Santoríni *see* Thíra
62 M10 **Santos** São Paulo, S Brazil
67 J17 **Santos Plateau** *undersea feature* SW Atlantic Ocean
106 G6 **Santo Tirso** Porto, N Portugal
42 B2 **Santo Tomás** Baja California, NW Mexico
44 L10 **Santo Tomás** Chontales, S Nicaragua
44 G5 **Santo Tomás de Castilla** Izabal, E Guatemala
42 B2 **Santo Tomás, Punta** *headland* NW Mexico
59 H16 **Santo Tomás, Río** ∿ C Peru
59 B18 **Santo Tomás, Volcán** ⨻ Galapagos Islands, Ecuador, E Pacific Ocean
63 F14 **Santo Tomé** Corrientes, NE Argentina
Santo Tomé de Guayana *see* Ciudad Guayana
100 H10 **Santpoort** Noord-Holland, W Netherlands
Santurce *see* Santurtzi
107 O2 **Santurtzi** *var.* Santurce, Santurzi. País Vasco, N Spain
Santurzi *see* Santurtzi
65 G20 **San Valentín, Cerro** ▲ S Chile
44 F8 **San Vicente** San Vicente, C El Salvador
42 C2 **San Vicente** Baja California, NW Mexico
196 H6 **San Vicente** Saipan, S Northern Mariana Islands
44 B9 **San Vicente** ◈ *department* E El Salvador
106 I10 **San Vicente de Alcántara** Extremadura, W Spain
107 N2 **San Vicente de Barakaldo** *var.* Baracaldo. País Vasco, N Spain
59 E15 **San Vicente de Cañete** *var.* Cañete. Lima, W Peru
106 M2 **San Vicente de la Barquera** Cantabria, N Spain
56 E12 **San Vicente del Caguán** Caquetá, S Colombia
44 F8 **San Vicente, Volcán de** ⨻ C El Salvador
45 O15 **San Vito** Puntarenas, SE Costa Rica
108 I7 **San Vito al Tagliamento** Friuli-Venezia Giulia, NE Italy
109 H23 **San Vito, Capo** *headland* Sicilia, Italy, C Mediterranean Sea
109 P18 **San Vito dei Normanni** Puglia, SE Italy
166 L17 **Sanya** *var.* Ya Xian. Hainan, S China
85 J16 **Sanyati** ∿ N Zimbabwe
27 Q16 **San Ygnacio** Texas, SW USA
166 L6 **Sanyuan** Shaanxi, C China
126 L/I12 **Sanyyakhtakh** Respublika Sakha (Yakutiya), NE Russian Federation
84 C10 **Sanza Pombo** Uíge, NW Angola
Sanzyô *see* Sanjō
106 G14 **São Bartolomeu de Messines** Faro, S Portugal
62 M10 **São Bernardo do Campo** São Paulo, S Brazil
63 F15 **São Borja** Rio Grande do Sul, S Brazil
106 H14 **São Brás de Alportel** Faro, S Portugal
62 M10 **São Caetano do Sul** São Paulo, S Brazil
62 L9 **São Carlos** São Paulo, S Brazil
61 P16 **São Cristóvão** Sergipe, E Brazil
63 F15 **São Francisco de Assis** Rio Grande do Sul, S Brazil
60 K13 **São Félix** Pará, NE Brazil
São Félix *see* São Félix do Araguaia
61 J16 **São Félix do Araguaia** *var.* São Félix. Mato Grosso, W Brazil
61 J14 **São Félix do Xingu** Pará, NE Brazil
62 Q9 **São Fidélis** Rio de Janeiro, SE Brazil
78 D10 **São Filipe** Fogo, S Cape Verde
62 K12 **São Francisco do Sul** Santa Catarina, S Brazil
62 K12 **São Francisco, Ilha de** *island* S Brazil
61 P16 **São Francisco, Rio** ∿ E Brazil
63 G16 **São Gabriel** Rio Grande do Sul, S Brazil
62 P10 **São Gonçalo** Rio de Janeiro, SE Brazil
83 H23 **Sao Hill** Iringa, S Tanzania
62 R9 **São João da Barra** Rio de Janeiro, SE Brazil
106 G7 **São João da Madeira** Aveiro, N Portugal
60 M12 **São João de Cortês** Maranhão, E Brazil
61 M21 **São João del Rei** Minas Gerais, NE Brazil
61 N15 **São João do Piauí** Piauí, E Brazil
61 N14 **São João dos Patos** Maranhão, E Brazil
60 C11 **São Joaquim** Amazonas, NW Brazil
63 J14 **São Joaquim** Santa Catarina, S Brazil
62 L7 **São Joaquim da Barra** São Paulo, S Brazil
66 N2 **São Jorge** *island* Azores, Portugal, NE Atlantic Ocean
63 K14 **São José** Santa Catarina, S Brazil
62 M8 **São José do Rio Pardo** São Paulo, S Brazil
62 K8 **São José do Rio Preto** São Paulo, S Brazil
62 N10 **São Jose dos Campos** São Paulo, S Brazil
63 I17 **São Lourenço do Sul** Rio Grande do Sul, S Brazil
60 F11 **São Luís** Roraima, N Brazil
60 M12 **São Luís** *state capital* Maranhão, NE Brazil
60 M12 **São Luís, Ilha de** *island* NE Brazil
63 F14 **São Luiz Gonzaga** Rio Grande do Sul, S Brazil
106 I10 **São Mamede** ▲ C Portugal
São Mandol *see* São Manuel, Rio
49 U8 **São Manuel** ∿ C Brazil
61 H15 **São Manuel, Rio** *var.* São Mandol, Teles Pirés. ∿ C Brazil
60 C11 **São Marcelino** Amazonas, NW Brazil
60 N12 **São Marcos, Baía de** *bay* N Brazil
61 O20 **São Mateus** Espírito Santo, SE Brazil
62 J12 **São Mateus do Sul** Paraná, S Brazil
66 P3 **São Miguel** *island* Azores, Portugal, NE Atlantic Ocean
62 G13 **São Miguel d'Oeste** Santa Catarina, S Brazil
47 P9 **Saona, Isla** *island* SE Dominican Republic
180 H12 **Saondzou** ▲ Grande Comore, NW Comoros
105 R10 **Saône** ∿ E France
105 Q9 **Saône-et-Loire** ◈ *department* C France
78 D9 **São Nicolau** *Eng.* Saint Nicholas. *island* Ilhas de Barlavento, N Cape Verde
62 M10 **São Paulo** *state capital* São Paulo, S Brazil
62 K9 **São Paulo** *off.* Estado de São Paulo. ◈ *state* S Brazil
São Paulo de Loanda *see* Luanda
São Pedro do Rio Grande do Sul *see* Rio Grande
106 H7 **São Pedro do Sul** Viseu, N Portugal
66 K13 **São Pedro e São Paulo** *undersea feature* C Atlantic Ocean
61 M14 **São Raimundo das Mangabeiras** Maranhão, E Brazil
61 Q14 **São Roque, Cabo de** *headland* E Brazil
São Salvador/São Salvador do Congo *see* M'Banza Congo, Zaire, Angola
São Salvador *see* Salvador, Brazil
62 N10 **São Sebastião, Ilha de** *island* S Brazil
85 N19 **São Sebastião, Ponta** *headland* C Mozambique
106 F13 **São Teotónio** Beja, S Portugal
São Tiago *see* Santiago
81 B18 **São Tomé** ● (Sao Tome and Principe) São Tomé, S Sao Tome and Principe
81 B18 **São Tomé** ✕ São Tomé, S Sao Tome and Principe
81 B18 **São Tomé** *Eng.* Saint Thomas. *island* S Sao Tome and Principe
81 B17 **Sao Tome and Principe** *off.* Democratic Republic of Sao Tome and Principe. ◆ *republic* E Atlantic Ocean
76 H9 **Saoura, Oued** ∿ NW Algeria
62 M10 **São Vicente** *Eng.* Saint Vincent. São Paulo, S Brazil
66 O5 **São Vicente** Madeira, Portugal, NE Atlantic Ocean
78 C9 **São Vicente** *Eng.* Saint Vincent. *island* Ilhas de Barlavento, N Cape Verde
São Vicente, Cabo de *see* São Vicente, Cabo de
106 F14 **São Vicente, Cabo de** *Eng.* Cape Saint Vincent, *Port.* Cabo de São Vicente. *headland* S Portugal
Sápai *see* Sápes
Sapaleri, Cerro *see* Zapaleri, Cerro
175 Tt11 **Saparau, Pulau** *island* C Indonesia
Saparoea *see* Saparua
175 Tt11 **Saparua** *prev.* Saparoea. Pulau Saparau, C Indonesia
174 Hh8 **Sapat** Sumatera, W Indonesia
79 U17 **Sapele** Delta, S Nigeria
25 X7 **Sapelo Island** *island* Georgia, SE USA
25 X7 **Sapelo Sound** *sound* Georgia, SE USA
116 K13 **Sápes** *var.* Sápai. Anatolikí Makedonía kai Thráki, NE Greece
175 P16 **Sape, Selat** *strait* Nusa Tenggara, S Indonesia
117 D22 **Sapiéntza** *island* S Greece
63 I15 **Sapiranga** Rio Grande do Sul, S Brazil
116 K13 **Sápka** ▲ NE Greece
58 D11 **Saposoa** San Martín, N Peru
121 F16 **Sapotskino** *Pol.* Sopockinie, *Rus.* Sopotskin. Hrodzyenskaya Voblasts', W Belorussia
79 P13 **Sapoui** *var.* Sapouy. S Burkina
Sapouy *see* Sapoui
144 F12 **Sappir** Southern, S Israel
172 O5 **Sapporo** Hokkaidō, NE Japan
109 M19 **Sapri** Campania, S Italy
174 Mm15 **Sapudi, Pulau** *island* S Indonesia
29 P9 **Sapulpa** Oklahoma, C USA
148 J4 **Saqqez** *var.* Saghez, Sakiz, Saqqiz. Kordestān, NW Iran
Saqqiz *see* Saqqez
145 U8 **Sarābādī** E Iraq
178 Hh11 **Sara Buri** *var.* Saraburi. Saraburi, C Thailand
Saraburi *see* Sara Buri
26 K9 **Saragosa** Texas, SW USA
Saragossa *see* Zaragoza
Saragt *see* Serakhs
58 B8 **Saraguro** Loja, S Ecuador
130 M6 **Sarai** Ryazanskaya Oblast', W Russian Federation
Sarāi *see* Saray
160 M12 **Saraipāli** Madhya Pradesh, C India
155 T9 **Sarāi Sidhu** Punjab, E Pakistan
95 M15 **Säräisniemi** Oulu, C Finland
115 I14 **Sarajevo** ● (Bosnia and Herzegovina) SE Bosnia and Herzegovina
114 I13 **Sarajevo** ✕ C Bosnia and Herzegovina
149 V4 **Sarakhs** Khorāsān, NE Iran
117 H17 **Sarakíniko, Ákra** *headland* Évvoia, C Greece
117 I18 **Sarakinó** *island* Vóreioi Sporádes, Greece, Aegean Sea
131 V7 **Saraktash** Orenburgskaya Oblast', W Russian Federation
32 L15 **Sara, Lake** ☒ Illinois, N USA
25 N8 **Saraland** Alabama, S USA
57 V9 **Saramacca** ◈ *district* N Surinam
57 V10 **Saramacca Rivier** ∿ C Surinam
177 G2 **Saramati** ▲ N Burma
151 R10 **Saran'** *Kaz.* Saran. Karaganda, C Kazakhstan
20 K7 **Saranac Lake** New York, NE USA
20 K7 **Saranac River** ∿ New York, NE USA
Saranda *see* Sarandë
115 L23 **Sarandë** *var.* Saranda, *It.* Porto Edda; *prev.* Santi Quaranta. Vlorë, S Albania
63 H14 **Sarandi** Rio Grande do Sul, S Brazil
63 F19 **Sarandí del Yí** Durazno, C Uruguay
63 F19 **Sarandí Grande** Florida, S Uruguay
179 Rr17 **Sarangani Islands** *island group* S Philippines
131 P5 **Saransk** Respublika Mordoviya, W Russian Federation
117 C24 **Sarantáporos** ∿ N Greece
116 H9 **Sarantsi** Sofiyska Oblast, W Bulgaria
131 T3 **Sarapul** Udmurtskaya Respublika, NW Russian Federation
Sarāqeb *see* Sarāqib
144 I3 **Sarāqib** *Fr.* Saraqeb. Idlib, N Syria
56 J5 **Sarare** Lara, N Venezuela
57 O10 **Sarariña** Amazonas, S Venezuela
149 S10 **Sar Ashk** Kermān, C Iran
25 V13 **Sarasota** Florida, SE USA
119 O11 **Sarata** Odes'ka Oblast', SW Ukraine
118 I10 **Sărăţel** *Hung.* Szeretfalva. Bistriţa-Năsăud, N Romania
27 X10 **Saratoga** Texas, SW USA
20 K10 **Saratoga Springs** New York, NE USA
131 P8 **Saratov** Saratovskaya Oblast', W Russian Federation
131 P8 **Saratovskaya Oblast'** ◈ *province* W Russian Federation
131 Q7 **Saratovskoye Vodokhranilishche** ☒ W Russian Federation
Saravan/Saravane *see* Salavan
194 K12 **Sarawaget Range** *var.* Saruwaged Range. ▲ C PNG
174 M5 **Sarawak** ◈ *state* East Malaysia
Sarawak *see* Kuching
145 U6 **Saray** *var.* Sarāi. E Iraq
142 D10 **Saray** Tekirdağ, NW Turkey
78 J12 **Saraya** SE Senegal
149 W14 **Sarbāz** Sīstān va Balūchestān, SE Iran
149 U8 **Sarbīsheh** Khorāsān, E Iran
113 J24 **Sárbogárd** Fejér, C Hungary
Sârcad *see* Sarkad
xlii M7 **Sarclet** Highland, N Scotland, UK
29 S7 **Sarcoxie** Missouri, C USA
158 L11 **Sārda** *Nep.* Kali. ∿ India/Nepal
158 G10 **Sardārshahr** Rājasthān, NW India
109 C18 **Sardegna** *Eng.* Sardinia. ◈ *region* Italy, C Mediterranean Sea
109 A18 **Sardegna** *Eng.* Sardinia. *island* Italy, C Mediterranean Sea
44 K13 **Sardinal** Guanacaste, NW Costa Rica
56 G7 **Sardinata** Norte de Santander, N Colombia
Sardinia *see* Sardegna
123 K8 **Sardinia-Corsica Trough** *undersea feature* Tyrrhenian Sea, C Mediterranean Sea
24 L2 **Sardis** Mississippi, S USA
24 L2 **Sardis Lake** ☒ Mississippi, S USA
29 P12 **Sardis Lake** ☒ Oklahoma, C USA
94 H12 **Sarek** ▲ N Sweden
155 N3 **Sar-e Pol** *var.* Sar-i-Pul. Sar-e Pol, N Afghanistan
155 O3 **Sar-e Pol** ◈ *province* N Afghanistan
Sar-e Pol *see* Sar-e Pol-e Żahāb
148 J6 **Sar-e Pol-e Żahāb** *var.* Sar-e Pol, Sar-i Pul. Kermānshāhān, W Iran
176 Ww10 **Sarera, Teluk** *var.* Teluk Irian. *bay* W Pacific Ocean
153 T13 **Sarez, Kŭli** *Rus.* Sarezskoye Ozero. ◎ SE Tajikistan
Sarezskoye Ozero *see* Sarez, Kŭli
66 G10 **Sargasso Sea** *sea* W Atlantic Ocean
155 U8 **Sargodha** Punjab, NE Pakistan
80 I13 **Sarh** *prev.* Fort-Archambault. Moyen-Chari, S Chad
149 P4 **Sārī** *var.* Sari, Sāri. Māzandarān, N Iran
117 N23 **Saría** *island* SE Greece
Sariasiya *see* Sariosiyo
42 F3 **Saric** Sonora, NW Mexico
196 K6 **Sarigan** *island* C Northern Mariana Islands
142 D14 **Sarıgöl** Manisa, SW Turkey
145 T6 **Sārihah** E Iraq
143 R12 **Sarıkamış** Kars, NE Turkey
174 L6 **Sarikei** Sarawak, East Malaysia
153 U12 **Sarikol Range** *Rus.* Sarykol'skiy Khrebet. ▲ China/Tajikistan
189 Y7 **Sarina** Queensland, NE Australia
Sarine *see* La Sarine
107 S5 **Sariñena** Aragón, NE Spain
153 O13 **Sariosiyo** *Rus.* Sariasiya. Surkhondaryo Wiloyati, S Uzbekistan
Sar-i-Pul *see* Sar-e Pol, Afghanistan
Sar-i Pul *see* Sar-e Pol-e Żahāb, Iran
Sariqamish Kŭli *see* Sarykamyshkoye Ozero
155 V1 **Sarī Qŭl** *Rus.* Ozero Zurkul', *Taj.* Zŭrkŭl. ◎ Afghanistan/Tajikistan *see also* Zŭrkŭl
77 Q12 **Sarīr Tibistī** *var.* Serir Tibesti. *desert* S Libya
27 S15 **Sarita** Texas, SW USA
169 W14 **Sariwŏn** SW North Korea
116 P12 **Sarıyer** İstanbul, NW Turkey
xxxvii W15 **Sark** *Fr.* Sercq. *island* Channel Islands
113 N24 **Sarkad** *Rom.* Şărcad. Békés, SE Hungary
151 W14 **Sarkand** Taldykorgan, SW Kazakhstan
Sarkani *see* Krasnogorskoye
158 D11 **Sarkāri Tala** Rājasthān, NW India
142 G15 **Şarkikaraağaç** *var.* Şarki Karaağaç. Isparta, SW Turkey
142 L13 **Şarkışla** Sivas, C Turkey
142 C11 **Şarköy** Tekirdağ, NW Turkey
Sárköz *see* Livada
Sarlat *see* Sarlat-la-Canéda
104 M13 **Sarlat-la-Canéda** *var.* Sarlat. Dordogne, SW France
111 S3 **Sarleinsbach** Oberösterreich, N Austria
176 Y10 **Sarmi** Irian Jaya, E Indonesia
65 I19 **Sarmiento** Chubut, S Argentina
65 H25 **Sarmiento, Monte** ▲ S Chile
96 J11 **Särna** Kopparberg, C Sweden
110 F8 **Sarnen** Obwalden, C Switzerland
Sarner See ◎ C Switzerland
xxxviii G13 **Sarnesfield** Herefordshire, W England, UK
12 D16 **Sarnia** Ontario, S Canada
xxxv E7 **Sarn Meyllteyrn** Gwynedd, NW Wales, UK
118 L3 **Sarny** Rivnens'ka Oblast', NW Ukraine
175 Q10 **Saroako** Sulawesi, C Indonesia
120 L13 **Sarochyna** *Rus.* Sorochino. Vitsyebskaya Voblasts', N Belorussia
174 Hh10 **Sarolangun** Sumatera, W Indonesia
172 Q5 **Saroma** Hokkaidō, NE Japan
172 Q5 **Saroma-ko** ◎ Hokkaidō, NE Japan
Saronic Gulf *see* Saronikós Kólpos
117 H20 **Saronikós Kólpos** *Eng.* Saronic Gulf. *gulf* S Greece
108 D7 **Saronno** Lombardia, N Italy
142 B11 **Saros Körfezi** *gulf* NW Turkey
113 N20 **Sárospatak** Borsod-Abaúj-Zemplén, NE Hungary
131 P12 **Sarpa** Respublika Kalmykiya, SW Russian Federation
131 P12 **Sarpa, Ozero** ◎ SW Russian Federation
115 M18 **Šar Planina** ▲ FYR Macedonia/Yugoslavia
97 I16 **Sarpsborg** Østfold, S Norway
145 U5 **Sarqalā** N Iraq
105 U4 **Sarralbe** Moselle, NE France
xxxvii Y10 **Sarre** Kent, SE England, UK
Sarre *see* Saar, France/Germany
Sarre *see* Saarland, Germany
105 U5 **Sarrebourg** *Ger.* Saarburg. Moselle, NE France
Sarrebruck *see* Saarbrücken
105 U4 **Sarreguemines** *prev.* Saargemund. Moselle, NE France
106 I3 **Sarria** Galicia, NW Spain
107 S8 **Sarrión** Aragón, NE Spain
44 F4 **Sarstoon** *Sp.* Río Sarstún. ∿ Belize/Guatemala
Sarstún, Río *see* Sarstoon
126 M9 **Sartang** ∿ NE Russian Federation
104 E3 **Sartène** Corse, France, C Mediterranean Sea
104 K7 **Sarthe** ◈ *department* NW France
104 K7 **Sarthe** ∿ N France
117 H15 **Sárti** Kentrikí Makedonía, N Greece
172 Pp2 **Sarufutsu** Hokkaidō, NE Japan
172 Oo7 **Saru-gawa** ∿ Hokkaidō, NE Japan
Saruhan *see* Manisa
158 G9 **Sarūpsar** Rājasthān, NW India
143 U13 **Şärur** *prev.* Il'ichevsk SW Azerbaijan
Saruwaged Range *see* Sarawaget Range
Sarvani *see* Marneuli
113 G23 **Sárvár** Vas, W Hungary
149 P11 **Sarvestān** Fārs, S Iran
176 X9 **Sarwon** Irian Jaya, E Indonesia
151 P17 **Saryagach** *Kaz.* Saryaghash. Yuzhnyy Kazakhstan, S Kazakhstan
Saryaghash *see* Saryagach
Saryarqa *see* Kazakhskiy Melkosopochnik
153 W8 **Sary-Bulak** Narynskaya Oblast', C Kyrgyzstan
153 U10 **Sary-Bulak** Oshskaya Oblast', SW Kyrgyzstan
119 S14 **Sarych, Mys** *headland* S Ukraine
153 Z7 **Sary-Dzhaz** *var.* Aksu He. ∿ China/Kyrgyzstan *see also* Aksu He
151 T14 **Saryesik-Atyrau, Peski** *desert* E Kazakhstan
150 G13 **Sarykamys** *Kaz.* Saryqamys. Mangistau, SW Kazakhstan
152 F8 **Sarykamyshkoye Ozero** *Uzb.* Sariqamish Kŭli. *salt lake* Kazakhstan/Uzbekistan
Sarykol'skiy Khrebet *see* Sarikol Range
150 M10 **Sarykopa, Ozero** ◎ C Kazakhstan
151 V15 **Saryozek** *Kaz.* Saryözek. Taldykorgan, SE Kazakhstan
Saryqamys *see* Sarykamys
151 S13 **Saryshagan** *Kaz.* Saryshahan. Zhezkazgan, SE Kazakhstan
Saryshahan *see* Saryshagan
151 O13 **Sarysu** ∿ S Kazakhstan
153 T11 **Sary-Tash** Oshskaya Oblast', SW Kyrgyzstan
152 J15 **Saryyazynskoye Vodokhranilishche** ☒ S Turkmenistan
108 E10 **Sarzana** Liguria, NW Italy
42 G4 **Sásabe** *var.* Aduana del Sásabe. Sonora, NW Mexico
196 B17 **Sasalaguan, Mount** ▲ S Guam
159 O14 **Sasarām** Bihār, N India
195 W14 **Sasari, Mount** ▲ Santa Isabel, N Solomon Islands
170 C12 **Sasebo** Nagasaki, Kyūshū, SW Japan
12 I9 **Saseginaga, Lac** ◎ Québec, SE Canada
Saseno *see* Sazan
9 R13 **Saskatchewan** ◈ *province* SW Canada
9 U14 **Saskatchewan** ∿ Manitoba/Saskatchewan, C Canada
9 T15 **Saskatoon** Saskatchewan, S Canada
9 T15 **Saskatoon** ✕ Saskatchewan, S Canada
126 K7 **Saskylakh** Respublika Sakha (Yakutiya), NE Russian Federation
44 L7 **Saslaya, Cerro** ▲ N Nicaragua
40 G17 **Sasmik, Cape** *headland* Tanaga Island, Alaska, USA
121 N19 **Sasnovy Bor** *Rus.* Sosnovyy Bor. Homyel'skaya Voblasts', SE Belorussia
131 N5 **Sasovo** Ryazanskaya Oblast', W Russian Federation
27 S11 **Saspamco** Texas, SW USA
111 W9 **Sass** *var.* Sassbach. ∿ SE Austria
78 M17 **Sassandra** S Ivory Coast
78 M17 **Sassandra** *var.* Ibo, Sassandra Fleuve. ∿ S Ivory Coast
Sassandra Fleuve *see* Sassandra
109 B17 **Sassari** Sardegna, Italy, C Mediterranean Sea
Sassbach *see* Sass
100 H11 **Sassenheim** Zuid-Holland, W Netherlands
Sassmacken *see* Valdemārpils
102 O7 **Sassnitz** Mecklenburg-Vorpommern, NE Germany
101 E16 **Sas van Gent** Zeeland, SW Netherlands
151 W12 **Sasykkol', Ozero** ◎ E Kazakhstan
119 O12 **Sasyk Kunduk, Ozero** ◎ SW Ukraine
78 J12 **Satadougou** Kayes, SW Mali
107 V11 **Sa Talaiassa** ▲ Eivissa, Spain, W Mediterranean Sea
170 B17 **Sata-misaki** *headland* Kyūshū, SW Japan
28 I7 **Satanta** Kansas, C USA
161 E15 **Sātāra** Mahārāshtra, W India
198 Aa7 **Sātaua** Savai'i, NW Western Samoa
196 M16 **Satawal** *island* Caroline Islands, C Micronesia
201 R17 **Satawan Atoll** *atoll* Mortlock Islands, C Micronesia
25 Y12 **Satellite Beach** Florida, SE USA
97 M14 **Säter** Kopparberg, C Sweden
Sathmar *see* Satu Mare
25 V7 **Satilla River** ∿ Georgia, SE USA
59 F14 **Satipo** *var.* San Francisco de Satipo. Junín, C Peru
125 E11 **Satka** Chelyabinskaya Oblast', C Russian Federation
159 T16 **Satkhira** Khulna, SW Bangladesh
xli Q7 **Satley** Durham, N England, UK
160 K9 **Satna** *prev.* Sutna. Madhya Pradesh, C India
105 R11 **Satolas** ✕ (Lyon) Rhône, E France
113 N20 **Sátoraljaújhely** Borsod-Abaúj-Zemplén, NE Hungary
151 O12 **Satpayev** *prev.* Nikol'skiy. Zhezkazgan, C Kazakhstan
160 G11 **Sātpura Range** ▲ C India
170 Bb16 **Satsuma-hantō** *peninsula* Kyūshū, SW Japan
178 Hh12 **Sattahip** *var.* Ban Sattahip, Ban Sattahipp. Chon Buri, S Thailand
94 L11 **Sattanen** Lappi, NE Finland
xl M11 **Satterthwaite** Cumbria, NW England, UK
Satul *see* Satun
118 H9 **Satulung** *Hung.* Kővárhosszúfalu. Maramureş, N Romania
Satul-Vechi *see* Staro Selo
118 G8 **Satu Mare** *Ger.* Sathmar, *Hung.* Szatmárnémeti. Satu Mare, NW Romania
118 G8 **Satu Mare** ◈ *county* NW Romania
178 H17 **Satun** *var.* Satul, Setul. Satun, SW Thailand
198 Aa8 **Satupaiteau** Savai'i, W Western Samoa
Sau *see* Sava
12 F14 **Sauble** ∿ Ontario, S Canada
12 F13 **Sauble Beach** Ontario, S Canada
63 C16 **Sauce** Corrientes, NE Argentina
Sauce *see* Juan L.Lacaze
38 K15 **Sauceda Mountains** ▲ Arizona, SW USA
63 C17 **Sauce de Luna** Entre Ríos, E Argentina
65 L15 **Sauce Grande, Río** ∿ E Argentina
42 K6 **Saucillo** Chihuahua, N Mexico
97 D15 **Sauda** Rogaland, S Norway
94 J2 **Saudhárkrókur** Nordhurland Vestra, N Iceland
147 P9 **Saudi Arabia** *off.* Kingdom of Saudi Arabia, *Ar.* Al 'Arabīyah as Su'ūdīyah, Al Mamlakah al 'Arabīyah as Su'ūdīyah. ◆ *monarchy* SW Asia
103 D19 **Sauer** *var.* Sûre. ∿ NW Europe *see also* Sûre
103 F15 **Sauerland** *forest* W Germany
12 F14 **Saugeen** ∿ Ontario, S Canada
20 K12 **Saugerties** New York, NE USA
xliii N23 **Saughtree** The Borders, S Scotland, UK
Saugor *see* Sāgar
8 K15 **Saugstad, Mount** ▲ British Columbia, SW Canada
Sāūjbulāgh *see* Mahābād
104 J11 **Saujon** Charente-Maritime, W France
31 T7 **Sauk Centre** Minnesota, N USA
32 L8 **Sauk City** Wisconsin, N USA
176 Vv8 **Saukorem** Irian Jaya, E Indonesia
31 U7 **Sauk Rapids** Minnesota, N USA
57 Y11 **Saül** C French Guiana
105 O7 **Sauldre** ∿ C France
103 I23 **Saulgau** Baden-Württemberg, SW Germany
105 Q8 **Saulieu** Côte d'Or, C France
120 G8 **Saulkrasti** Rīga, C Latvia
13 S6 **Sault-aux-Cochons, Rivière du** ∿ Québec, SE Canada
33 Q4 **Sault Sainte Marie** Michigan, N USA
10 F14 **Sault Ste.Marie** Ontario, S Canada
202 E13 **Sauma, Pointe** *headland* Île Alofi, W Wallis and Futuna
176 Uu15 **Saumlaki** *var.* Saumlakki. Pulau Yamdena, E Indonesia
Saumlakki *see* Saumlaki
13 R12 **Saumon, Rivière au** ∿ Québec, SE Canada
104 K8 **Saumur** Maine-et-Loire, NW France
193 F23 **Saunders, Cape** *headland* South Island, NZ
205 N13 **Saunders Coast** *physical region* Antarctica
xxxv D14 **Saundersfoot** Pembrokeshire, SW Wales, UK
67 B23 **Saunders Island** *island* NW Falkland Islands
67 C24 **Saunders Island Settlement** Saunders Island, NW Falkland Islands
84 F11 **Saurimo** *Port.* Henrique de Carvalho, Vila Henrique de Carvalho. Lunda Sul, NE Angola
57 S11 **Sauriwaunawa** S Guyana
176 V8 **Sausapor** Irian Jaya, E Indonesia
84 D12 **Sautar** Malanje, NW Angola
78 M17 **Sauteurs** N Grenada
104 K13 **Sauveterre-de-Guyenne** Gironde, SW France
121 O14 **Sava** *Rus.* Sava. Mahilyowskaya Voblasts', E Belorussia
86 H11 **Sava** *Eng.* Save, *Ger.* Sau, *Hung.* Száva. ∿ SE Europe
44 J5 **Savá** Colón, N Honduras
35 Y8 **Savage** Montana, NW USA
191 N16 **Savage River** Tasmania, SE Australia
198 Aa7 **Savai'i** *island* NW Western Samoa
79 R15 **Savalou** S Benin
32 K10 **Savanna** Illinois, N USA
25 X6 **Savannah** Georgia, SE USA
29 R2 **Savannah** Missouri, C USA
22 H10 **Savannah** Tennessee, S USA
23 O12 **Savannah River** ∿ Georgia/South Carolina, SE USA
Savannakhét *see* Khanthabouli
46 H12 **Savanna-La-Mar** W Jamaica
10 B10 **Savant Lake** ◎ Ontario, S Canada
161 F17 **Savanūr** Karnātaka, W India
95 J16 **Sävar** Västerbotten, N Sweden
Savaria *see* Szombathely
160 C11 **Sāvarkundla** *var.* Kundla. Gujarāt, W India
118 F11 **Săvârşin** *Hung.* Soborsin; *prev.* Săvirşin. Arad, W Romania
142 C13 **Savaştepe** Balıkesir, W Turkey
Savat *see* Sawot
85 N18 **Save** Inhambane, E Mozambique
104 L16 **Save** ∿ S France
85 L17 **Save** *var.* Sabi. ∿ Mozambique/Zimbabwe *see also* Sabi
Save *see* Sava
79 R15 **Savè** SE Benin
148 M6 **Sāveh** Markazī, W Iran
118 L8 **Săveni** Botoşani, NE Romania
105 N16 **Saverdun** Ariège, S France
105 U5 **Saverne** *var.* Zabern; *anc.* Tres Tabernae. Bas-Rhin, NE France
Savichi *see* Savichy
121 O21 **Savichy** *Rus.* Savichi. Homyel'skaya Voblasts', SE Belorussia
108 B9 **Savigliano** Piemonte, NW Italy
Savigsivik *see* Savissivik
Savinichi *see* Savinichy
121 Q16 **Savinichy** *Rus.* Savinichi. Mahilyowskaya Voblasts', E Belorussia
111 T10 **Savinjske Alpe** *var.* Kamniške Alpe, Sanntaler Alpen, *Ger.* Steiner Alpen. ▲ N Slovenia
Savinski *see* Savinskiy
125 Dd6 **Savinskiy** *var.* Savinski. Arkhangel'skaya Oblast', NW Russian Federation
108 H11 **Savio** ∿ C Italy
Săvirşin *see* Săvârşin
207 O11 **Savissivik** *var.* Savigsivik. N Greenland
95 N18 **Savitaipale** Kymi, SE Finland
115 J15 **Šavnik** Montenegro, SW Yugoslavia
195 W15 **Savo** *island* C Solomon Islands
110 I9 **Savognin** Graubünden, S Switzerland
105 T12 **Savoie** ◈ *department* E France
108 C10 **Savona** Liguria, NW Italy
95 N17 **Savonlinna** *Swe.* Nyslott. Mikkeli, SE Finland
95 N17 **Savonranta** Mikkeli, SE Finland
40 K10 **Savoonga** Saint Lawrence Island, Alaska, USA
32 M13 **Savoy** Illinois, N USA
119 O8 **Savran'** Odes'ka Oblast', SW Ukraine
143 R11 **Şavşat** Artvin, NE Turkey
97 L19 **Sävsjö** Jönköping, S Sweden
Savu, Kepulauan *see* Sawu, Kepulauan
94 M11 **Savukoski** Lappi, NE Finland
Savu, Pulau *see* Sawu, Pulau
197 J13 **Savusavu** Vanua Levu, N Fiji
175 Q17 **Savu Sea** *Ind.* Laut Sawu. *sea* S Indonesia
85 H17 **Savute** Chobe, N Botswana
145 N7 **Şawāb, 'Uqlat** *well* W Iraq
144 M7 **Şawāb, Wādī aş** *dry watercourse* W Iraq
158 H13 **Sawāi Mādhopur** Rājasthān, N India
175 Tt10 **Sawai, Teluk** *bay* Pulau Seram, E Indonesia
Sawakin *see* Suakin
178 I19 **Sawang Daen Din** Sakon Nakhon, E Thailand
178 H8 **Sawankhalok** *var.* Swankalok. Sukhothai, NW Thailand
171 Kk17 **Sawara** Chiba, Honshū, S Japan
171 Jj12 **Sawasaki-bana** *headland* Sado, C Japan
39 R5 **Sawatch Range** ▲ Colorado, C USA
xxxvii U7 **Sawbridgeworth** Hertfordshire, SE England, UK
147 N12 **Sawdā', Jabal** ▲ SW Saudi Arabia
77 P9 **Sawdā', Jabal as** ▲ C Libya
Sawdirī *see* Sodiri
176 W9 **Saweba, Tanjung** *headland* Irian Jaya, E Indonesia
xliv J3 **Sawel** ▲ C Northern Ireland, UK
Sawhāj *see* Sohāg
79 O15 **Sawla** N Ghana
153 P11 **Sawot** *Rus.* Savat. Sirdaryo Wiloyati, E Uzbekistan
147 X12 **Şawqirah** *var.* Suqrah. S Oman
147 X12 **Şawqirah, Dawḩat** *var.* Ghubbat Şawqirah, Sukra Bay, Suqrah Bay. *bay* S Oman
Sawqirah, Ghubbat *see* Şawqirah, Dawḩat
xxxix T13 **Sawston** Cambridgeshire, E England, UK
191 V5 **Sawtell** New South Wales, SE Australia
xxxix R11 **Sawtry** Cambridgeshire, E England, UK
144 K7 **Şawt, Wādī aş** *dry watercourse* S Syria
175 Q18 **Sawu, Kepulauan** *var.* Kepulauan Savu. *island group* S Indonesia
Sawu, Laut *see* Savu Sea
175 Qq18 **Sawu, Pulau** *var.* Pulau Savu. *island* Kepulauan Sawu, S Indonesia
107 S12 **Sax** País Valenciano, E Spain
xxxix P9 **Saxby** Leicestershire, C England, UK
Saxe *see* Sachsen
xxxix O9 **Saxelbye** Leicestershire, C England, UK
xxxix P5 **Saxilby** Lincolnshire, E England, UK
xxxix Y12 **Saxmundham** Suffolk, E England, UK
110 C11 **Saxon** Valais, SW Switzerland
Saxony *see* Sachsen
Saxony-Anhalt *see* Sachsen-Anhalt
xxxix X12 **Saxtead** Suffolk, E England, UK
xxxix W8 **Saxthorpe** Norfolk, E England, UK
xli S14 **Saxton** North Yorkshire, N England, UK
79 R12 **Say** Niamey, SW Niger
13 V7 **Sayabec** Québec, SE Canada
Sayaboury *see* Xaignabouli
151 U12 **Sayak** *Kaz.* Sayaq. Zhezkazgan, E Kazakhstan
59 D14 **Sayán** Lima, W Peru
126 Hh15 **Sayanogorsk** Respublika Khakasiya, S Russian Federation
126 J15 **Sayansk** Irkutskaya Oblast', S Russian Federation
133 T6 **Sayanskiy Khrebet** ▲ S Russian Federation
Sayaq *see* Sayak
152 K13 **Sayat** Lebapskiy Velayat, E Turkmenistan
44 D3 **Sayaxché** Petén, N Guatemala
Şaydā/Sayida *see* Saïda
147 T15 **Sayhūt** E Yemen
31 U14 **Saylorville Lake** ☒ Iowa, C USA
Saymenskiy Kanal *see* Saimaa Canal
169 N10 **Saynshand** Dornogovĭ, SE Mongolia
168 J11 **Saynshand** Ömnögovĭ, S Mongolia
168 F7 **Sayn-Ust** Govĭ-Altay, W Mongolia
Say-Ötesh *see* Say-Utës
144 J7 **Şayqal, Bahr** ◎ S Syria
Sayrab *see* Sayrob
164 H4 **Sayram Hu** ◎ NW China
28 K11 **Sayre** Oklahoma, C USA
20 H12 **Sayre** Pennsylvania, NE USA
20 K15 **Sayreville** New Jersey, NE USA
153 N13 **Sayrob** *Rus.* Sayrab. Surkhondaryo Wiloyati, S Uzbekistan
42 L13 **Sayula** Jalisco, SW Mexico
147 R14 **Say 'ūn** *var.* Saywūn. C Yemen
150 G14 **Say-Utës** *Kaz.* Say-Ötesh. Mangistau, SW Kazakhstan

◆ Country ● Country Capital ◇ Dependent Territory ○ Dependent Territory Capital ◈ Administrative Region ✕ International Airport ▲ Mountain ▲ Mountain Range ⨻ Volcano ∿ River ◎ Lake ☒ Reservoir

SAYWARD – SERAJGONJ

8 K16 **Sayward** Vancouver Island, British Columbia, SW Canada
Saywūn *see* Say 'ūn
Sayyāl *see* As Sayyāl
145 U8 **Sayyid 'Abīd** ***var.*** Saiyid Abid. E Iraq
115 J22 **Sazan** ***var.*** Ishulli i Sazanit, ***It.*** Saseno. *island* SW Albania
Sazanit, Ishulli i *see* Sazan
Sazau/Sazawa *see* Sázava
113 E17 **Sázava** ***var.*** Sazau, ***Ger.*** Sazawa. ≈ C Czech Republic
128 J14 **Sazonovo** Vologodskaya Oblast', NW Russian Federation
104 G6 **Scaër** Finistère, NW France
xl L10 **Scafell Pike** ▲ NW England, UK
Scalabis *see* Santarém
xliii D19 **Scalasaig** Argyll and Bute, W Scotland, UK
xli W10 **Scalby** North Yorkshire, N England, UK
xl M9 **Scales** Cumbria, NW England, UK
xxxix O8 **Scalford** Leicestershire, C England, UK
xlii I4 **Scalloway** Shetland Islands, N Scotland, UK
xlii C10 **Scalpay** *island* NW Scotland, UK
xlii E13 **Scalpay** *island* NW Scotland, UK
xxxix R5 **Scamblesby** Lincolnshire, E England, UK
40 M11 **Scammon Bay** Alaska, USA
Scammon Lagoon/ Scammon, Laguna *see* Ojo de Liebre, Laguna
86 F7 **Scandinavia** *geophysical region* NW Europe
Scania *see* Skåne
xlii M5 **Scapa Flow** *sea basin* N Scotland, UK
109 K26 **Scaramia, Capo** *headland* Sicilia, Italy, C Mediterranean Sea
xlii B10 **Scarastavore** Western Isles, NW Şcotland, UK
xliii E18 **Scarba** *island* W Scotland, UK
xli W10 **Scarborough** North Yorkshire, N England, UK
12 H15 **Scarborough** Ontario, SE Canada
47 Z16 **Scarborough** ***prev.*** Port Louis. Tobago, Trinidad and Tobago
xlii H12 **Scardroy** Highland, NW Scotland, UK
193 I17 **Scargill** Canterbury, South Island, NZ
xliv A14 **Scariff Island** *island* SW Ireland
xliii C17 **Scarinish** Argyll and Bute, W Scotland, UK
xlii B9 **Scarp** *island* NW Scotland, UK
Scarpanto *see* Kárpathos
Scarpanto Strait *see* Karpathou, Stenó
xliv F10 **Scarriff** Clare, W Ireland
xli R4 **Scars, The** *headland* N England, UK
109 G25 **Scauri** Sicilia, Italy, C Mediterranean Sea
xxxix P4 **Scawby** North Lincolnshire, N England, UK
Scealg, Bá na *see* Ballinskelligs Bay
Scebeli *see* Shebeli
102 K10 **Schaale** ≈ N Germany
102 K9 **Schaalsee** ◎ N Germany
101 G18 **Schaerbeek** Brussels, C Belgium
110 G6 **Schaffhausen** ***Fr.*** Schaffhouse. Schaffhausen, N Switzerland
110 G6 **Schaffhausen** ***Fr.*** Schaffhouse. ◐ *canton* N Switzerland
Schaffhouse *see* Schaffhausen
100 I8 **Schagen** Noord-Holland, NW Netherlands
Schaken *see* Šakiai
100 M10 **Schalkhaar** Overijssel, E Netherlands
111 R3 **Schärding** Oberösterreich, N Austria
102 G9 **Scharhörn** *island* NW Germany
Schässburg *see* Sighişoara
Schaulen *see* Šiauliai
32 M10 **Schaumburg** Illinois, N USA
Schebschi Mountains *see* Shebshi Mountains
100 P6 **Scheemda** Groningen, NE Netherlands
102 I10 **Scheessel** Niedersachsen, NW Germany
11 N8 **Schefferville** Québec, E Canada
Schelde *see* Scheldt
101 D18 **Scheldt** ***Dut.*** Schelde, ***Fr.*** Escaut. ≈ W Europe
37 X5 **Schell Creek Range** ▲▲ Nevada, W USA
20 K10 **Schenectady** New York, NE USA
101 I17 **Scherpenheuvel** ***Fr.*** Montaigu. Vlaams Brabant, C Belgium
100 K11 **Scherpenzeel** Gelderland, C Netherlands
27 S12 **Schertz** Texas, SW USA
100 G11 **Scheveningen** Zuid-Holland, W Netherlands
100 G12 **Schiedam** Zuid-Holland, SW Netherlands
xliii J16 **Schiehallion** ▲ C Scotland, UK
101 M24 **Schieren** Diekirch, NE Luxembourg
100 M4 **Schiermonnikoog** ***Fris.*** Skiermûntseach. Friesland, N Netherlands
100 M4 **Schiermonnikoog** ***Fris.*** Skiermûntseach. *island* Waddeneilanden, N Netherlands
101 K14 **Schijndel** Noord-Brabant, S Netherlands
Schil *see* Jiu
101 H16 **Schilde** Antwerpen, N Belgium
Schillen *see* Zhilino
105 V5 **Schiltigheim** Bas-Rhin, NE France
108 G7 **Schio** Veneto, NE Italy
100 H10 **Schiphol** ✕ (Amsterdam) Noord-Holland, C Netherlands
Schippenbeil *see* Sępopol
Schiria *see* Şiria
Schivelbein *see* Świdwin
117 D22 **Schíza** *island* S Greece
183 U3 **Schjetman Reef** *reef* Antarctica
Schlackenwerth *see* Ostrov
111 R7 **Schladming** Steiermark, SE Austria
Schlan *see* Slaný
Schlanders *see* Silandro
102 I7 **Schlei** *inlet* N Germany
103 D17 **Schleiden** Nordrhein-Westfalen, W Germany
195 P9 **Schleinitz Range** ▲▲ New Ireland, N PNG
Schlelau *see* Szydłowiec
102 I7 **Schleswig** Schleswig-Holstein, N Germany
31 T13 **Schleswig** Iowa, C USA
102 H8 **Schleswig-Holstein** ◐ *state* N Germany
Schlettstadt *see* Sélestat
110 F7 **Schlieren** Zürich, N Switzerland
Schlochau *see* Człuchów
Schloppe *see* Człopa
103 I18 **Schlüchtern** Hessen, C Germany
103 J17 **Schmalkalden** Thüringen, C Germany
111 W2 **Schmida** ≈ NE Austria
67 P19 **Schmidt-Ott Seamount** ***var.*** Schmitt-Ott Seamount, Schmitt-Ott Tablemount. *undersea feature* SW Indian Ocean
Schmiegel *see* Śmigiel
Schmitt-Ott Seamount/ Schmitt-Ott Tablemount *see* Schmidt-Ott Seamount
13 V3 **Schmon** ≈ Québec, SE Canada
103 M18 **Schneeberg** ▲ W Germany
Schneeberg *see* Snežnik
Schnee-Eifel *see* Schneifel
Schneekoppe *see* Sněžka
Schneidemühl *see* Piła
103 D18 **Schneifel** ***var.*** Schnee-Eifel. *plateau* W Germany
Schnelle Körös/Schnelle Kreisch *see* Crişul Repede
102 I11 **Schneverdingen** ***var.*** Schneverdingen (Wümme). Niedersachsen, NW Germany
Schneverdingen (Wümme) *see* Schneverdingen
Schoden *see* Skuodas
20 K10 **Schoharie** New York, NE USA
20 K11 **Schoharie Creek** ≈ New York, NE USA
117 J21 **Schoinoússa** *island* Kykládes, Greece, Aegean Sea
102 L13 **Schönebeck** Sachsen-Anhalt, C Germany
Schöneck *see* Skarszewy
102 O12 **Schönefeld** ✕ (Berlin) Berlin, NE Germany
103 K24 **Schongau** Bayern, S Germany
102 K13 **Schöningen** Niedersachsen, C Germany
Schönlanke *see* Trzcianka
Schönsee *see* Kowalewo Pomorskie
33 P10 **Schoolcraft** Michigan, N USA
100 O8 **Schoonebeek** Drenthe, NE Netherlands
100 I12 **Schoonhoven** Zuid-Holland, C Netherlands
100 H8 **Schoorl** Noord-Holland, NW Netherlands
Schooten *see* Schoten
103 F24 **Schopfheim** Baden-Württemberg, SW Germany
103 I21 **Schorndorf** Baden-Württemberg, S Germany
102 F10 **Schortens** Niedersachsen, NW Germany
101 H16 **Schoten** ***var.*** Schooten. Antwerpen, N Belgium
191 Q17 **Schouten Island** *island* Tasmania, SE Australia
194 H9 **Schouten Islands** *island group* NW PNG
100 E13 **Schouwen** *island* SW Netherlands
47 Q12 **Schœlcher** W Martinique
Schreiberhau *see* Szklarska Poręba
111 U2 **Schrems** Niederösterreich, E Austria
103 L22 **Schrobenhausen** Bayern, SE Germany
20 L8 **Schroon Lake** ◎ New York, NE USA
110 J8 **Schruns** Vorarlberg, W Austria
Schubin *see* Szubin
27 U11 **Schulenburg** Texas, SW USA
xliv D15 **Schull** Cork, S Ireland
Schuls *see* Scuol
110 E8 **Schüpfheim** Luzern, C Switzerland
37 S6 **Schurz** Nevada, W USA
103 I24 **Schussen** ≈ S Germany
Schüttenhofen *see* Sušice
31 R15 **Schuyler** Nebraska, C USA
20 L10 **Schuylerville** New York, NE USA
103 K20 **Schwabach** Bayern, SE Germany
Schwabenalb *see* Schwäbische Alb
103 I23 **Schwäbische Alb** ***var.*** Schwabenalb, ***Eng.*** Swabian Jura. ▲▲ S Germany
103 I22 **Schwäbisch Gmünd** ***var.*** Gmünd. Baden-Württemberg, SW Germany
103 I21 **Schwäbisch Hall** ***var.*** Hall. Baden-Württemberg, SW Germany
103 H16 **Schwalm** ≈ C Germany
111 V9 **Schwanberg** Steiermark, SE Austria
110 H8 **Schwanden** Glarus, E Switzerland
103 M20 **Schwandorf** Bayern, SE Germany
111 S5 **Schwanenstadt** Oberösterreich, NW Austria
174 M9 **Schwaner, Pegunungan** ▲▲ Borneo, N Indonesia
111 W5 **Schwarza** ≈ E Austria
111 P9 **Schwarzach** ≈ S Austria
103 M20 **Schwarzach** ***Cz.*** Černice. ≈ Czech Republic/Germany
Schwarzach *see* Schwarzach im Pongau, Austria
Schwarzach *see* Svratka, Czech Republic
111 Q7 **Schwarzach im Pongau** ***var.*** Schwarzach. Salzburg, NW Austria
Schwarzawa *see* Svratka
103 N14 **Schwarze Elster** ≈ E Germany
Schwarze Körös *see* Crişul Negru
110 D9 **Schwarzenburg** Bern, W Switzerland
85 D21 **Schwarzrand** ▲▲ S Namibia
103 G23 **Schwarzwald** ***Eng.*** Black Forest. ▲▲ SW Germany
Schwarzwasser *see* Wda
41 P7 **Schwatka Mountains** ▲▲ Alaska, USA
111 N7 **Schwaz** Tirol, W Austria
111 Y4 **Schwechat** Niederösterreich, NE Austria
111 Y4 **Schwechat** ✕ (Wien) Wien, E Austria
102 P11 **Schwedt** Brandenburg, NE Germany
103 D19 **Schweich** Rheinland-Pfalz, SW Germany
Schweidnitz *see* Świdnica
103 J18 **Schweinfurt** Bayern, SE Germany
Schweiz *see* Switzerland
102 L9 **Schwerin** Mecklenburg-Vorpommern, N Germany
Schwerin *see* Skwierzyna
102 L9 **Schweriner See** ◎ N Germany
Schwertberg *see* Świecie
103 F15 **Schwerte** Nordrhein-Westfalen, W Germany
Schwiebus *see* Świebodzin
102 P13 **Schwielochsee** ◎ NE Germany
Schwihau *see* Švihov
Schwiz *see* Schwyz
110 G8 **Schwyz** ***var.*** Schwiz. Schwyz, C Switzerland
110 G8 **Schwyz** ***var.*** Schwiz. ◐ *canton* C Switzerland
12 J11 **Schyan** ≈ Québec, SE Canada
Schyl *see* Jiu
109 I24 **Sciacca** Sicilia, Italy, C Mediterranean Sea
Sciasciamana *see* Shashemenē
109 L26 **Scicli** Sicilia, Italy, C Mediterranean Sea
xxxvi I17 **Scilly, Isles of** *island group* SW England, UK
113 H17 **Ścinawa** ***Ger.*** Steinau an der Elbe. Legnica, SW Poland
Scio *see* Chíos
33 S14 **Scioto River** ≈ Ohio, N USA
38 L5 **Scipio** Utah, W USA
35 X6 **Scobey** Montana, NW USA
191 T7 **Scone** New South Wales, SE Australia
xlii E13 **Sconser** Highland, NW Scotland, UK
Scoresby Sound/ Scoresbysund *see* Ittoqqortoormiit
Scoresby Sund *see* Kangertittivaq
Scorno, Punta dello *see* Caprara, Punta
xli R10 **Scotch Corner** North Yorkshire, N England, UK
xli N12 **Scotforth** Lancashire, NW England, UK
36 K3 **Scotia** California, W USA
49 Y14 **Scotia Plate** *tectonic feature*
49 V15 **Scotia Ridge** *undersea feature* S Atlantic Ocean
204 H2 **Scotia Sea** *sea* SW Atlantic Ocean
xliii H15 **Scotland** *national region* Scotland, UK
31 Q12 **Scotland** South Dakota, N USA
27 R5 **Scotland** Texas, SW USA
23 W8 **Scotland Neck** North Carolina, SE USA
xliii F16 **Scotstown** Highland, NW Scotland, UK
205 R13 **Scott Base** *NZ research station* Antarctica
8 J16 **Scott, Cape** *headland* Vancouver Island, British Columbia, SW Canada
28 I5 **Scott City** Kansas, C USA
29 Y7 **Scott City** Missouri, C USA
205 R14 **Scott Coast** *physical region* Antarctica
20 C15 **Scottdale** Pennsylvania, NE USA
xxxix P4 **Scotter** Lincolnshire, E England, UK
205 Y11 **Scott Glacier** *glacier* Antarctica
205 Q17 **Scott Island** *island* Antarctica
28 L11 **Scott, Mount** ▲ Oklahoma, USA
34 G15 **Scott, Mount** ▲ Oregon, NW USA
36 M1 **Scott River** ≈ California, W USA
30 I13 **Scottsbluff** Nebraska, C USA
25 Q2 **Scottsboro** Alabama, S USA
33 P15 **Scottsburg** Indiana, N USA
191 P16 **Scottsdale** Tasmania, SE Australia
38 L13 **Scottsdale** Arizona, SW USA
47 O12 **Scotts Head Village** ***var.*** Cachacrou. S Dominica
199 Jj17 **Scott Shoal** *undersea feature* S Pacific Ocean
22 K7 **Scottsville** Kentucky, S USA
xlii G7 **Scourie** Highland, NW Scotland, UK
xlii I5 **Scousburgh** Shetland Islands, NE Scotland, UK
xlii L6 **Scrabster** Highland, N Scotland, UK
xliv H8 **Scramoge** Roscommon, C Ireland
31 U14 **Scranton** Iowa, C USA
20 I13 **Scranton** Pennsylvania, NE USA
xliv D8 **Screeb** Galway, W Ireland
194 G10 **Screw** ≈ NW PNG
31 R14 **Scribner** Nebraska, C USA
Scrobesbyrig' *see* Shrewsbury
12 I14 **Scugog** ≈ Ontario, SE Canada
12 I14 **Scugog, Lake** ◎ Ontario, SE Canada
xxxix P3 **Scunthorpe** North Lincolnshire, E England, UK
110 K9 **Scuol** ***Ger.*** Schuls. Graubünden, E Switzerland
Scupi *see* Skopje
Scutari *see* Shkodër
115 K17 **Scutari, Lake** ***Alb.*** Liqeni i Shkodrës, ***SCr.*** Skadarsko Jezero. ◎ Albania/Yugoslavia
Scyros *see* Skýros
Scythopolis *see* Bet She'an
27 U13 **Seadrift** Texas, SW USA
xxxvii V13 **Seaford** East Sussex, SE England, UK
23 Y4 **Seaford** ***var.*** Seaford City. Delaware, NE USA
Seaford City *see* Seaford
12 E15 **Seaforth** Ontario, S Canada
xlii C9 **Seaforth, Loch** *inlet* NW Scotland, UK
26 M6 **Seagraves** Texas, SW USA
xli S7 **Seaham** Durham, N England, UK
xli R2 **Seahouses** Northumberland, N England, UK
9 X9 **Seal** ≈ Manitoba, C Canada
190 M10 **Sea Lake** Victoria, SE Australia
85 G26 **Seal, Cape** *headland* S South Africa
67 D26 **Sea Lion Islands** *island group* SE Falkland Islands
21 S8 **Seal Island** *island* Maine, NE USA
27 V11 **Sealy** Texas, SW USA
xliii H21 **Seamill** North Ayrshire, W Scotland, UK
xxxix Y8 **Sea Palling** Norfolk, E England, UK
37 X12 **Searchlight** Nevada, W USA
29 V11 **Searcy** Arkansas, C USA
21 R7 **Searsport** Maine, NE USA
xl K10 **Seascale** Cumbria, NW England, UK
37 N10 **Seaside** California, W USA
34 F10 **Seaside** Oregon, NW USA
20 K16 **Seaside Heights** New Jersey, NE USA
xxxix T6 **Seathorne** Lincolnshire, E England, UK
xl K8 **Seaton** Cumbria, NW England, UK
xxxvi J14 **Seaton** Devon, SW England, UK
xli T8 **Seaton Carew** Hartlepool, N England, UK
xli R5 **Seaton Delaval** Northumberland, N England, UK
34 H8 **Seattle** Washington, NW USA
34 H9 **Seattle-Tacoma** ✕ Washington, NW USA
xli T10 **Seave Green** North Yorkshire, N England, UK
xxxvii Q14 **Seaview** Isle of Wight, S England, UK
193 J16 **Seaward Kaikoura Range** ▲▲ South Island, NZ
44 J9 **Sébaco** Matagalpa, W Nicaragua
21 P8 **Sebago Lake** ◎ Maine, NE USA
176 V11 **Sebakor, Teluk** *bay* Irian Jaya, E Indonesia
Sebangan, Sungai *see* Sebangau Besar, Sungai
174 M11 **Sebangan, Teluk** *bay* Borneo, C Indonesia
174 Mm11 **Sebanganu, Teluk** *bay* Borneo, C Indonesia
174 Mm11 **Sebangau Besar, Sungai** ***var.*** Sungai Sebangan. ≈ Borneo, N Indonesia
174 I8 **Sebanglea, Pulau** *island* W Indonesia
Sebaste/Sebastia *see* Sivas
25 Y12 **Sebastian** Florida, SE USA
42 C5 **Sebastían Vizcaíno, Bahía** *bay* NW Mexico
21 R6 **Sebasticook Lake** ◎ Maine, NE USA
36 M7 **Sebastopol** California, W USA
Sebastopol *see* Sevastopol'
175 Oo4 **Sebatik, Pulau** *island* N Indonesia
21 R5 **Sebec Lake** ◎ Maine, NE USA
78 K12 **Sébékoro** Kayes, W Mali
Sebenico *see* Šibenik
xl M8 **Sebergham** Cumbria, NW England, UK
42 G6 **Seberi, Cerro** ▲ NW Mexico
118 H11 **Sebeş** ***Ger.*** Mühlbach, ***Hung.*** Szászsebes; ***prev.*** Sebeşu Săsesc. Alba, W Romania
Sebes-Körös *see* Crişul Repede
Sebeşu Săsesc *see* Sebeş
33 R8 **Sebewaing** Michigan, N USA
128 F16 **Sebezh** Pskovskaya Oblast', W Russian Federation
143 N12 **Şebinkarahisar** Giresun, N Turkey
118 F11 **Sebiş** ***Hung.*** Borossebes. Arad, W Romania
Sebkra Azz el Matti *see* Azzel Matti, Sebkha
21 Q4 **Seboomook Lake** ◎ Maine, NE USA
76 G6 **Sebou** ***var.*** Sebu. ≈ N Morocco
22 I6 **Sebree** Kentucky, S USA
25 X13 **Sebring** Florida, SE USA
Sebta *see* Ceuta
Sebu *see* Sebou
175 Nn11 **Sebuku, Pulau** *island* N Indonesia
175 Oo4 **Sebuku, Teluk** *bay* Borneo, N Indonesia
176 Vv10 **Sebyar** ≈ Irian Jaya, E Indonesia
108 F10 **Secchia** ≈ N Italy
8 L17 **Sechelt** British Columbia, SW Canada
58 C12 **Sechin, Río** ≈ W Peru
58 A10 **Sechura, Bahía de** *bay* NW Peru
193 A22 **Secretary Island** *island* SW NZ
161 I15 **Secunderābād** ***var.*** Sikandarabad. Andhra Pradesh, C India
59 L17 **Sécure, Río** ≈ C Bolivia
120 D10 **Seda** Mažeikiai, NW Lithuania
29 T5 **Sedalia** Missouri, C USA
105 R3 **Sedan** Ardennes, N France
29 P7 **Sedan** Kansas, C USA
107 N3 **Sedano** Castilla-León, N Spain
106 H10 **Seda, Ribeira de** *stream* C Portugal
xli O10 **Sedbergh** Cumbria, NW England, UK
193 K15 **Seddon** Marlborough, South Island, NZ
193 H15 **Seddonville** West Coast, South Island, NZ
149 U7 **Sedeh** Khorāsān, E Iran
144 E11 **Sederot** Southern, S Israel
xxxix P8 **Sedgebrook** Lincolnshire, E England, UK
xli S8 **Sedgefield** Durham, N England, UK
xxxix U8 **Sedgeford** Norfolk, E England, UK
67 B23 **Sedge Island** *island* NW Falkland Islands
xxxviii A14 **Sedgeley** Dudley, C England, UK
xli N11 **Sedgwick** Cumbria, NW England, UK
78 G12 **Sédhiou** SW Senegal
9 U16 **Sedley** Saskatchewan, S Canada
Sedlez *see* Siedlce
125 G12 **Sednel'nikovo** Omskaya Oblast', C Russian Federation
119 Q2 **Sedniv** Chernihivs'ka Oblast', N Ukraine
38 L11 **Sedona** Arizona, SW USA
Sedunum *see* Sion
120 F12 **Šeduva** Radviliškis, N Lithuania
147 Y8 **Seeb** ***var.*** Muscat Sīb Airport. ✕ (Masqaṭ) NE Oman
Seeb *see* As Sīb
110 M7 **Seefeld in Tirol** Tirol, W Austria
85 E22 **Seeheim Noord** Karas, S Namibia
Seeland *see* Sjælland
205 N9 **Seelig, Mount** ▲ Antarctica
xxxvi M10 **Seend** Wiltshire, S England, UK
Seeonee *see* Seoni
168 E6 **Seer** Hovd, W Mongolia
104 L5 **Sées** Orne, N France
103 J14 **Seesen** Niedersachsen, C Germany
Seesker Höhe *see* Szeskie Wzgórza
102 J10 **Seevetal** Niedersachsen, N Germany
111 V6 **Seewiesen** Steiermark, E Austria
142 J13 **Şefaatli** ***var.*** Kızılkoca. Yozgat, C Turkey
155 N3 **Sefīd, Darya-ye** ***Pash.*** Āb-i-Safed. ≈ N Afghanistan
154 K5 **Sefīdkūh, Selseleh-ye** ***Eng.*** Paropamisus Range. ▲▲ W Afghanistan
76 G6 **Sefrou** N Morocco
xl L15 **Sefton** ◐ *unitary authority* NW England, UK
193 E19 **Sefton, Mount** ▲ South Island, NZ
176 U10 **Segaf, Kepulauan** *island group* E Indonesia
175 Oo3 **Segama, Sungai** ≈ East Malaysia
174 Hh6 **Segamat** Johor, Peninsular Malaysia
79 S13 **Ségbana** NE Benin
Segestica *see* Sisak
Segesvár *see* Sighişoara
176 Uu9 **Seget** Irian Jaya, E Indonesia
Segewold *see* Sigulda
128 J9 **Segezha** Respublika Kareliya, NW Russian Federation
Seghedin *see* Szeged
Segna *see* Senj
109 I16 **Segni** Lazio, C Italy
Segodunum *see* Rodez
107 S9 **Segorbe** País Valenciano, E Spain
78 M12 **Ségou** ***var.*** Segu. Ségou, C Mali
78 M12 **Ségou** ◐ *region* SW Mali
56 E8 **Segovia** Antioquia, N Colombia
107 N7 **Segovia** Castilla-León, C Spain
106 M6 **Segovia** ◐ *province* Castilla-León, N Spain
Segoviao Wangkí *see* Coco, Río
128 J9 **Segozero, Ozero** ◎ NW Russian Federation
107 U5 **Segre** ≈ NE Spain
104 J7 **Segré** Maine-et-Loire, NW France
Segu *see* Ségou
40 I17 **Seguam Island** *island* Aleutian Islands, Alaska, USA
40 I17 **Seguam Pass** *strait* Aleutian Islands, Alaska, USA
79 Y7 **Séguédine** Agadez, NE Niger
78 M15 **Séguéla** W Ivory Coast
27 S11 **Seguin** Texas, SW USA
40 E17 **Segula Island** *island* Aleutian Islands, Alaska, USA
64 K10 **Segundo, Río** ≈ C Argentina
107 Q12 **Segura** ≈ S Spain
85 G18 **Sehithwa** Ngamiland, N Botswana
160 H10 **Sehore** Madhya Pradesh, C India
195 O16 **Sehulea** Normanby Island, S PNG
155 P15 **Sehwān** Sind, SE Pakistan
111 V8 **Seiersberg** Steiermark, SE Austria
xliii F18 **Seil** *island* W Scotland, UK
28 L9 **Seiling** Oklahoma, C USA
105 S9 **Seille** ≈ E France
101 J20 **Seilles** Namur, SE Belgium
95 K17 **Seinäjoki** ***Swe.*** Östermyra. Vaasa, W Finland
10 B12 **Seine** ≈ Ontario, S Canada
104 M4 **Seine** ≈ N France
104 K4 **Seine, Baie de la** *bay* N France
Seine, Banc de la *see* Seine Seamount
105 O5 **Seine-et-Marne** ◐ *department* N France
104 L3 **Seine-Maritime** ◐ *department* N France
86 B14 **Seine Plain** *undersea feature* E Atlantic Ocean
86 B15 **Seine Seamount** ***var.*** Banc de la Seine. *undersea feature* E Atlantic Ocean
104 E6 **Sein, Île de** *island* NW France
176 Y12 **Seinma** Irian Jaya, E Indonesia
Seisbierrum *see* Sexbierum
111 U5 **Seitenstetten Markt** Niederösterreich, C Austria
Seiyu *see* Chŏnju
97 H22 **Sejerø** *island* E Denmark
112 P7 **Sejny** Suwałki, NE Poland
174 Ii13 **Sekampung, Way** ≈ Sumatera, SW Indonesia
83 G20 **Seke** Shinyanga, N Tanzania
171 I15 **Seki** Gifu, Honshū, SW Japan
167 U12 **Sekibi-sho** *island* China/Japan/Taiwan
172 Pp5 **Sekihoku-tōge** *pass* Hokkaidō, NE Japan
Sekondi *see* Sekondi-Takoradi
79 P17 **Sekondi-Takoradi** ***var.*** Sekondi. S Ghana
82 J11 **Sek'ot'a** N Ethiopia
Sekseüil *see* Saksaul'skoye
34 I9 **Selah** Washington, NW USA
174 Gg5 **Selangor** ***var.*** Negeri Selangor Darul Ehsan. ◐ *state* Peninsular Malaysia
Selânik *see* Thessaloníki
174 Hh7 **Selapanjang** Pulau Rantau, W Indonesia
178 Ii10 **Selaphum** Roi Et, E Thailand
176 Uu16 **Selaru, Pulau** *island* Kepulauan Tanimbar, E Indonesia
176 Vv11 **Selassi** Irian Jaya, E Indonesia
173 G3 **Selatan, Selat** *strait* Peninsular Malaysia
xxxviii G8 **Selattyn** Shropshire, W England, UK
41 N8 **Selawik** Alaska, USA
41 N8 **Selawik Lake** ◎ Alaska, USA
175 Pp13 **Selayar, Selat** *strait* Sulawesi, C Indonesia
97 C14 **Selbjørnsfjorden** *fjord* S Norway
xxxvii R11 **Selborne** Hampshire, S England, UK
96 H8 **Selbusjøen** ◎ S Norway
xli T14 **Selby** North Yorkshire, N England, UK
31 N8 **Selby** South Dakota, N USA
23 Z4 **Selbyville** Delaware, NE USA
142 B15 **Selçuk** ***var.*** Akıncılar. İzmir, SW Turkey
41 Q13 **Seldovia** Alaska, USA
109 M18 **Sele** ***anc.*** Silarius. ≈ S Italy
44 B5 **Selegua, Río** ≈ W Guatemala
133 X7 **Selemdzha** ≈ SE Russian Federation
133 U7 **Selenga** ***Mong.*** Selenge Mörön. ≈ Mongolia/Russian Federation
168 K6 **Selenge** Bulgan, N Mongolia
168 J6 **Selenge** Hövsgöl, N Mongolia
81 I19 **Selenge** Bandundu, W Zaire
168 L6 **Selenge** ◐ *province* N Mongolia
Selenge Mörön *see* Selenga
126 Jj16 **Selenginsk** Respublika Buryatiya, S Russian Federation
Selenica *see* Selenicë
115 K22 **Selenicë** ***var.*** Selenica. Vlorë, SW Albania
126 M7 **Selennyakh** ≈ NE Russian Federation
102 J8 **Selenter See** ◎ N Germany
Sele Sound *see* Soela Väin
105 U6 **Sélestat** ***Ger.*** Schlettstadt. Bas-Rhin, NE France
Selety *see* Sileti
Seleucia *see* Silifke
94 I4 **Selfoss** Sudhurland, SW Iceland
30 M7 **Selfridge** North Dakota, N USA
78 I15 **Seli** ≈ N Sierra Leone
78 I11 **Sélibabi** ***var.*** Sélibaby. Guidimaka, S Mauritania
Sélibaby *see* Sélibabi
Selidovka/ Selidovo *see* Selydove
128 I15 **Seliger, Ozero** ◎ W Russian Federation
38 J11 **Seligman** Arizona, SW USA
29 S8 **Seligman** Missouri, C USA
82 E6 **Selima Oasis** *oasis* N Sudan
78 L13 **Sélingué, Lac de** ⊟ S Mali
Selinoús *see* Kréstena
20 G14 **Selinsgrove** Pennsylvania, NE USA
Selishche *see* Syelishcha
128 I16 **Selizharovo** Tverskaya Oblast', W Russian Federation
96 C10 **Selje** Sogn og Fjordane, S Norway
xliii N22 **Selkirk** SE Scotland, UK
98 K13 **Selkirk** *cultural region* SE Scotland, UK
9 X16 **Selkirk** Manitoba, S Canada
9 O16 **Selkirk Mountains** ▲▲ British Columbia, SW Canada
200 Oo12 **Selkirk Rise** *undersea feature* SE Pacific Ocean
xl K10 **Sellafield Station** Cumbria, NW England, UK
xlii I1 **Sellafirth** Shetland Islands, NE Scotland, UK
117 F21 **Sellasía** Pelopónnisos, S Greece
46 M9 **Selle, Pic de la** ***var.*** La Selle. ▲ SE Haiti
104 M8 **Selles-sur-Cher** Loir-et-Cher, C France
38 K16 **Sells** Arizona, SW USA
Sellye *see* Sal'a
25 P5 **Selma** Alabama, S USA
37 Q11 **Selma** California, W USA
22 G10 **Selmer** Tennessee, S USA
181 N17 **Sel, Pointe au** *headland* W Réunion
Selseleh-ye Kūh-e Vākhān *see* Nicholas Range
xxxvii R14 **Selsey** West Sussex, SE England, UK
xxxvii R14 **Selsey Bill** *headland* S England, UK
131 S2 **Selty** Udmurtskaya Respublika, NW Russian Federation
Selukwe *see* Shurugwi
64 L9 **Selva** Santiago del Estero, N Argentina
9 T9 **Selwyn Lake** ◎ Northwest Territories/Saskatchewan, C Canada
15 Gg2 **Selwyn Mountains** ▲▲ Yukon Territory, NW Canada
189 T6 **Selwyn Range** ▲▲ Queensland, C Australia
119 W8 **Selydove** ***var.*** Selidovka, ***Rus.*** Selidovo. Donets'ka Oblast', SE Ukraine
Selzaete *see* Zelzate
Seman *see* Semanit, Lumi i
174 Ii13 **Semangka, Teluk** *bay* Sumatera, SW Indonesia
174 I13 **Semangka, Way** ≈ Sumatera, SW Indonesia
115 D22 **Semanit, Lumi i** ***var.*** Seman. ≈ W Albania
174 Kk14 **Semarang** ***var.*** Samarang. Jawa, C Indonesia
174 Kk6 **Sematan** Sarawak, East Malaysia
175 Qq17 **Semau, Pulau** *island* S Indonesia
175 Nn8 **Semayang, Danau** ◎ Borneo, N Indonesia
175 O4 **Sembakung, Sungai** ≈ Borneo, N Indonesia
81 G17 **Sembé** La Sangha, NW Congo
Semberong *see* Semberong, Sungai
174 Hh6 **Semberong, Sungai** ***var.*** Semberong. ≈ Peninsular Malaysia
174 M10 **Sembulu, Danau** ◎ Borneo, N Indonesia
Semendria *see* Smederevo
119 R1 **Semenivka** Chernihivs'ka Oblast', N Ukraine
119 S6 **Semenivka** ***Rus.*** Semenovka. Poltavs'ka Oblast', NE Ukraine
131 O3 **Semenov** Nizhegorodskaya Oblast', W Russian Federation
Semenovka *see* Semenivka
174 M16 **Semeru, Gunung** ***var.*** Mahameru. ▲ Jawa, S Indonesia
Semey/Semey Oblysy *see* Semipalatinsk
Semezhevo *see* Syemyezhava
130 L7 **Semiluki** Voronezhskaya Oblast', W Russian Federation
xxxvi M10 **Semington** Wiltshire, S England, UK
35 W16 **Seminoe Reservoir** ⊟ Wyoming, C USA
29 O11 **Seminole** Oklahoma, C USA
26 M6 **Seminole** Texas, SW USA
25 S8 **Seminole, Lake** ⊟ Florida/Georgia, SE USA
150 M8 **Semiozernoye** Kustanay, N Kazakhstan
151 V9 **Semipalatinsk** ***Kaz.*** Semey. Semipalatinsk, E Kazakhstan
151 V11 **Semipalatinsk** ***off.*** Semipalatinskaya Oblast', ***Kaz.*** Semey Oblysy. ◐ *province* E Kazakhstan
149 O9 **Semīrom** ***var.*** Samirum. Eşfahān, C Iran
40 F17 **Semisopochnoi Island** *island* Aleutian Islands, Alaska, USA
174 Ll7 **Semitau** Borneo, C Indonesia
83 E18 **Semliki** ≈ Uganda/Zaire
149 P5 **Semnān** ***var.*** Samnān. Semnān, N Iran
149 Q5 **Semnān** ***off.*** Ostān-e Semnān. ◐ *province* N Iran
101 K24 **Semois** ≈ SE Belgium
110 E8 **Sempacher See** ◎ C Switzerland
Sena *see* Vila de Sena
32 L12 **Senachwine Lake** ◎ Illinois, N USA
61 O14 **Senador Pompeu** Ceará, E Brazil
Sena Gallica *see* Senigallia
61 C15 **Sena Madureira** Acre, W Brazil
161 L25 **Senanayake Samudra** ◎ E Sri Lanka
85 G15 **Senanga** Western, SW Zambia
29 Y9 **Senath** Missouri, C USA
24 L2 **Senatobia** Mississippi, S USA
xxxvii S10 **Send** Surrey, SE England, UK
170 C15 **Sendai** Kagoshima, Kyūshū, SW Japan
171 M13 **Sendai** Miyagi, Honshū, C Japan
170 Bb15 **Sendai-gawa** ≈ Kyūshū, SW Japan
171 M14 **Sendai-wan** *bay* E Japan
103 J23 **Senden** Bayern, S Germany
160 F11 **Sendhwa** Madhya Pradesh, C India
113 H21 **Senec** ***Ger.*** Wartberg, ***Hung.*** Szenc; ***prev.*** Szempcz. Západné Slovensko, W Slovakia
29 P3 **Seneca** Kansas, C USA
29 R8 **Seneca** Missouri, C USA
34 K13 **Seneca** Oregon, NW USA
23 O11 **Seneca** South Carolina, SE USA
20 G11 **Seneca Lake** ◎ New York, NE USA
33 U13 **Senecaville Lake** ⊟ Ohio, N USA
78 G11 **Senegal** ***off.*** Republic of Senegal, ***Fr.*** Sénégal. ◆ *republic* W Africa
78 H9 **Senegal** ***Fr.*** Sénégal. ≈ W Africa
33 O4 **Seney Marsh** *wetland* Michigan, N USA
103 P14 **Senftenberg** Brandenburg, E Germany
84 L11 **Senga Hill** Northern, NE Zambia
164 G13 **Sênggê Zangbo** ≈ W China
176 Z11 **Senggi** Irian Jaya, E Indonesia
xxxv J14 **Senghenydd** Caerphilly, S Wales, UK
131 R5 **Sengiley** Ul'yanovskaya Oblast', W Russian Federation
65 I19 **Senguerr, Río** ≈ S Argentina
85 J16 **Sengwa** ≈ C Zimbabwe
Senia *see* Senj
113 H19 **Senica** ***Ger.*** Senitz, ***Hung.*** Szenice. Západné Slovensko, W Slovakia
Seniça *see* Sjenica
108 J11 **Senigallia** ***anc.*** Sena Gallica. Marche, C Italy
142 F15 **Senirkent** İsparta, SW Turkey
Senitz *see* Senica
114 C10 **Senj** ***Ger.*** Zengg, ***It.*** Segna; ***anc.*** Senia. Lika-Senj, NW Croatia
169 O10 **Senj** Dornogovĭ, SE Mongolia
94 H9 **Senja** ***prev.*** Senjen. *island* N Norway
Senjen *see* Senja
167 U12 **Senkaku-shotō** *island group* SW Japan
143 R12 **Şenkaya** Erzurum, NE Turkey
85 I16 **Senkobo** Southern, S Zambia
105 O4 **Senlis** Oise, N France
178 K13 **Senmonorom** Môndól Kiri, E Cambodia
82 G10 **Sennar** ***var.*** Sannār. Sinnar, C Sudan
xxxvi L16 **Sennen** Cornwall, SW England, UK
Senno *see* Syanno
xxxv I12 **Sennybridge** Powys, C Wales, UK
Senones *see* Sens
111 W11 **Senovo** E Slovenia
105 P6 **Sens** ***anc.*** Agendicum, Senones. Yonne, C France
Sensburg *see* Mrągowo
178 J12 **Sên, Stœng** ≈ C Cambodia
44 F7 **Sensuntepeque** Cabañas, NE El Salvador
114 L8 **Senta** ***Hung.*** Zenta. Serbia, N Yugoslavia
Šent Andraž *see* Sankt Andrä
176 Z10 **Sentani, Danau** ◎ Irian Jaya, E Indonesia
30 J5 **Sentinel Butte** ▲ North Dakota, N USA
8 M13 **Sentinel Peak** ▲ British Columbia, W Canada
61 N16 **Sento Sé** Bahia, E Brazil
Šent Peter *see* Pivka
Šent Vid *see* Sankt Veit an der Glan
194 E10 **Senu** ≈ NW PNG
Seo de Urgel *see* La See d'Urgel
160 I7 **Seondha** Madhya Pradesh, C India
160 J11 **Seoni** ***prev.*** Seeonee. Madhya Pradesh, C India
Seoul *see* Sŏul
192 I13 **Separation Point** *headland* South Island, NZ
175 O7 **Sepasu** Borneo, N Indonesia
194 F10 **Sepik** ≈ Indonesia/PNG
Sepone *see* Muang Xépôn
112 M7 **Sępopol** ***Ger.*** Schippenbeil. Olsztyn, N Poland
118 F10 **Şepreuş** ***Hung.*** Seprős. Arad, W Romania
Seprős *see* Şepreuş
Şepşi-Sângeorz/ Sepsiszentgyőrgy *see* Sfântu Gheorghe
13 W4 **Sept-Îles** Québec, SE Canada
107 N6 **Sepúlveda** Castilla-León, N Spain
174 Ii12 **Seputih, Way** ≈ Sumatera, SW Indonesia
106 K8 **Sequeros** Castilla-León, N Spain
106 L5 **Sequillo** ≈ NW Spain
34 G7 **Sequim** Washington, NW USA
37 S11 **Sequoia National Park** *national park* California, W USA
143 Q14 **Şerafettin Dağları** ▲▲ E Turkey
131 N10 **Serafimovich** Volgogradskaya Oblast', SW Russian Federation
175 Rr6 **Serai** Sulawesi, N Indonesia
101 K19 **Seraing** Liège, E Belgium
Sêraitang *see* Baima
Serajgonj *see* Shirajganj Ghat

◆ Country ● Country Capital ◇ Dependent Territory ○ Dependent Territory Capital ◐ Administrative Region ✕ International Airport ▲ Mountain ▲▲ Mountain Range Volcano ≈ River ◎ Lake ⊟ Reservoir

SERAKHS – SHEREIK

152 *I15* **Serakhs** *var.* Saragt. Akhalskiy Velayat, S Turkmenistan
176 *X10* **Serami** Irian Jaya, E Indonesia
Seram, Laut *see* Ceram Sea
Serampore/Serampur *see* Shrīrāmpur
175 *Tt11* **Seram, Pulau** *var.* Serang, *Eng.* Ceram. *island* Maluku, E Indonesia
174 *J14* **Serang** Jawa, C Indonesia
Serang *see* Seram, Pulau
174 *Kk6* **Serasan, Pulau** *island* Kepulauan Natuna, W Indonesia
174 *Kk6* **Serasan, Selat** *strait* Indonesia/Malaysia
114 *M12* **Serbia** *Ger.* Serbien, *Serb.* Srbija. ◐ *republic* Yugoslavia
Serbien *see* Serbia
Sercq *see* Sark
Serdica *see* Sofiya
131 *O7* **Serdobsk** Penzenskaya Oblast', W Russian Federation
151 *X9* **Serebryansk** Vostochnyy Kazakhstan, E Kazakhstan
126 *Ll13* **Serebryanyy Bor** Respublika Sakha (Yakutiya), NE Russian Federation
113 *H20* **Sered'** *Hung.* Szered. Západné Slovensko, SW Slovakia
119 *S1* **Seredyna-Buda** Sums'ka Oblast', NE Ukraine
120 *E13* **Seredžius** Jurbarkas, C Lithuania
142 *I14* **Şereflikoçhisar** Ankara, C Turkey
108 *D7* **Seregno** Lombardia, N Italy
105 *P7* **Serein** ≈ C France
174 *H5* **Seremban** Negeri Sembilan, Peninsular Malaysia
83 *H20* **Serengeti Plain** *plain* N Tanzania
84 *K13* **Serenje** Central, E Zambia
Seres *see* Sérres
118 *J5* **Seret** ≈ W Ukraine
Seret/Sereth *see* Siret
117 *I21* **Serfopoúla** *island* Kykládes, Greece, Aegean Sea
131 *P4* **Sergach** Nizhegorodskaya Oblast', W Russian Federation
31 *S13* **Sergeant Bluff** Iowa, C USA
169 *P7* **Sergelen** Dornod, NE Mongolia
169 *O9* **Sergelen** Sühbaatar, E Mongolia
173 *F4* **Sergeulangit, Pegunungan** ▲▲ Sumatera, NW Indonesia
126 *I4* **Sergeya Kirova, Ostrova** *island* N Russian Federation
Sergeyevichi *see* Syarhyeyevichy
151 *O7* **Sergeyevka** Severnyy Kazakhstan, N Kazakhstan
Sergiopol *see* Ayaguz
61 *P16* **Sergipe** *off.* Estado de Sergipe. ◐ *state* E Brazil
130 *L3* **Sergiyev Posad** Moskovskaya Oblast', W Russian Federation
128 *K5* **Sergozero, Ozero** ◎ NW Russian Federation
174 *L7* **Serian** Sarawak, East Malaysia
174 *J13* **Seribu, Kepulauan** *island group* S Indonesia
117 *I21* **Sérifos** *anc.* Seriphos. *island* Kykládes, Greece, Aegean Sea
117 *I21* **Sérifou, Stenó** *strait* SE Greece
142 *F16* **Serik** Antalya, SW Turkey
108 *E7* **Serio** ≈ N Italy
Seriphos *see* Sérifos
Serir Tibesti *see* Sarīr Tībistī
131 *S5* **Sernovodsk** Samarskaya Oblast', W Russian Federation
131 *R2* **Sernur** Respublika Mariy El, W Russian Federation
112 *M11* **Serock** Warszawa, C Poland
63 *B18* **Serodino** Santa Fe, C Argentina
Seroei *see* Serui
107 *P14* **Serón** Andalucía, S Spain
101 *E14* **Serooskerke** Zeeland, SW Netherlands
107 *T6* **Seròs** Cataluña, NE Spain
125 *F10* **Serov** Sverdlovskaya Oblast', C Russian Federation
85 *I19* **Serowe** Central, SE Botswana
106 *H13* **Serpa** Beja, S Portugal
Serpa Pinto *see* Menongue
190 *A4* **Serpentine Lakes** *salt lake* South Australia
47 *T15* **Serpent's Mouth, The** *Sp.* Boca de la Serpiente. *strait* Trinidad and Tobago/Venezuela
Serpiente, Boca de la *see* Serpent's Mouth, The
130 *K4* **Serpukhov** Moskovskaya Oblast', W Russian Federation
62 *K13* **Serra do Mar** ▲▲ S Brazil
Sérrai *see* Sérres
109 *N22* **Serra San Bruno** Calabria, SW Italy
105 *S14* **Serres** Hautes-Alpes, SE France
116 *H13* **Sérres** *var.* Seres; *prev.* Sérrai. Kentrikí Makedonía, NE Greece
64 *J9* **Serrezuela** Córdoba, C Argentina
61 *O16* **Serrinha** Bahia, E Brazil
61 *M19* **Serro** *var.* Sêrro. Minas Gerais, NE Brazil
Sêrro *see* Serro
Sert *see* Siirt
Sertá *see* Sertã
106 *H9* **Sertã** *var.* Sertá. Castelo Branco, C Portugal
62 *L8* **Sertãozinho** São Paulo, S Brazil
166 *F7* **Sêrtar** Sichuan, C China
176 *X10* **Serui** *prev.* Seroei. Irian Jaya, E Indonesia
85 *J19* **Serule** Central, E Botswana
174 *Ll10* **Seruyan, Sungai** *var.* Sungai Pembuang. ≈ Borneo, N Indonesia
117 *E14* **Sérvia** Dytikí Makedonía, N Greece
166 *E7* **Sêrxü** Sichuan, C China
126 *Mm15* **Seryshevo** Amurskaya Oblast', SE Russian Federation
Sé San *see* San, Tônle
Sesana *see* Sežana
175 *Nn5* **Sesayap, Sungai** ≈ Borneo, N Indonesia
Sesdlets *see* Siedlce
81 *N17* **Sese** Haut-Zaïre, N Zaire
83 *F18* **Sese Islands** *island group* S Uganda
175 *T9* **Sesepe** Pulau Obi, E Indonesia
85 *H16* **Sesheke** *var.* Sesheko. Western, SE Zambia
Sesheko *see* Sesheke
108 *C8* **Sesia** *anc.* Sessites. ≈ NW Italy
106 *F11* **Sesimbra** Setúbal, S Portugal
117 *N22* **Sesklió** *island* Dodekánisos, Greece, Aegean Sea
32 *L16* **Sesser** Illinois, N USA
Sessites *see* Sesia
108 *G11* **Sesto Fiorentino** Toscana, C Italy
108 *E7* **Sesto San Giovanni** Lombardia, N Italy
108 *A8* **Sestriere** Piemonte, NE Italy
108 *D10* **Sestri Levante** Liguria, NW Italy
109 *C20* **Sestu** Sardegna, Italy, C Mediterranean Sea
114 *E8* **Sesvete** Grad Zagreb, N Croatia
120 *G12* **Šėta** Kėdainiai, C Lithuania
Setabis *see* Xátiva
172 *N5* **Setana** Hokkaidō, NE Japan
xxxix *U9* **Setchey** Norfolk, E England, UK
105 *Q16* **Sète** *prev.* Cette. Hérault, S France
60 *J11* **Sete Ilhas** Amapá, NE Brazil
61 *L20* **Sete Lagoas** Minas Gerais, NE Brazil
62 *G10* **Sete Quedas, Ilha das** *island* S Brazil
94 *I10* **Setermoen** Troms, N Norway
97 *E17* **Setesdal** *valley* S Norway
45 *W16* **Setetule, Cerro** ▲ SE Panama
23 *Q5* **Seth** West Virginia, NE USA
Setia *see* Sezze
76 *K5* **Sétif** *var.* Stif. N Algeria
171 *I15* **Seto** Aichi, Honshū, SW Japan
170 *F14* **Seto-naikai** *Eng.* Inland Sea. *sea* S Japan
172 *Qq13* **Setouchi** *var.* Setoushi. Kagoshima, Amami-Ō-shima, SW Japan
76 *F6* **Settat** W Morocco
81 *D20* **Setté Cama** Ogooué-Maritime, SW Gabon
9 *W13* **Setting Lake** ◎ Manitoba, C Canada
xli *P12* **Settle** North Yorkshire, N England, UK
201 *Y12* **Settlement** E Wake Island
106 *F11* **Setúbal** *Eng.* Saint Ubes, Saint Yves. Setúbal, W Portugal
106 *F11* **Setúbal** ◐ *district* S Portugal
106 *F12* **Setúbal, Baía de** *bay* W Portugal
Setul *see* Satun
10 *B10* **Seul, Lac** ◎ Ontario, S Canada
105 *R8* **Seurre** Côte d'Or, C France
143 *U11* **Sevan** C Armenia
143 *V12* **Sevana Lich** *Eng.* Lake Sevan, *Rus.* Ozero Sevan. ◎ E Armenia
Sevan, Lake/Sevan, Ozero *see* Sevana Lich
79 *N11* **Sévaré** Mopti, C Mali
119 *S14* **Sevastopol'** *Eng.* Sebastopol. Respublika Krym, S Ukraine
xxxvi *G6* **Seven Kings** Redbridge, SE England, UK
xxxvii *U10* **Sevenoaks** Kent, SE England, UK
xxxv *H13* **Seven Sisters** Neath Port Talbot, S Wales, UK
27 *R14* **Seven Sisters** Texas, SW USA
8 *K13* **Seven Sisters Peaks** ▲ British Columbia, SW Canada
101 *M15* **Sevenum** Limburg, SE Netherlands
105 *P14* **Séverac-le-Château** Aveyron, S France
99 *L21* **Severn** *Wel.* Hafren. ≈ England/Wales, UK
12 *H13* **Severn** ≈ Ontario, S Canada
129 *O11* **Severnaya Dvina** *var.* Northern Dvina. ≈ NW Russian Federation
131 *N16* **Severnaya Osetiya, Respublika** *Eng.* North Ossetia; *prev.* Severo-Osetinskaya SSR. ◐ *autonomous republic* SW Russian Federation
125 *F9* **Severnaya Sos'va** ≈ N Russian Federation
127 *N17* **Severnaya Zemlya** *var.* Nicholas II Land. *island group* N Russian Federation
113 *C15* **Severní Čechy** *off.* Severočeský Kraj. ◐ *region* NW Czech Republic
113 *H17* **Severní Morava** *off.* Severomoravský Kraj. ◐ *region* E Czech Republic
xxxvi *J10* **Severn, Mouth of the** *estuary* England/Wales, UK
131 *T5* **Severnoye** Orenburgskaya Oblast', W Russian Federation
37 *S3* **Severn Troughs Range** ▲▲ Nevada, W USA
129 *W3* **Severnyy** Respublika Komi, NW Russian Federation
150 *I13* **Severnyy Chink Ustyurta** ▲▲ W Kazakhstan
129 *Q13* **Severnyye Uvaly** *var.* Northern Ural Hills. *hill range* NW Russian Federation
151 *O6* **Severnyy Kazakhstan** *off.* Severo-Kazakhstanskaya Oblast', *var.* North Kazakhstan, *Kaz.* Soltūstik Qazaqstan Oblysy. ◐ *province* N Kazakhstan
129 *V9* **Severnyy Ural** ▲▲ NW Russian Federation
Severo-Alichurskiy Khrebet *see* Alichuri Shimolí, Qatorkŭhi
126 *K14* **Severobaykal'sk** Respublika Buryatiya, S Russian Federation
Severočeský Kraj *see* Severní Čechy
Severodonetsk *see* Syeverodonets'k
128 *M8* **Severodvinsk** *prev.* Molotov, Sudostroy. Arkhangel'skaya Oblast', NW Russian Federation
Severo-Kazakhstanskaya Oblast' *see* Severnyy Kazakhstan
127 *Pp13* **Severo-Kuril'sk** Sakhalinskaya Oblast', SE Russian Federation
Severomoravský Kraj *see* Severní Morava
128 *J3* **Severomorsk** Murmanskaya Oblast', NW Russian Federation
Severo-Osetinskaya SSR *see* Severnaya Osetiya, Respublika
126 *J6* **Severo-Sibirskaya Nizmennost'** *var.* North Siberian Plain, *Eng.* North Siberian Lowland. *lowlands* N Russian Federation
125 *Ee10* **Severoural'sk** Sverdlovskaya Oblast', C Russian Federation
126 *I12* **Severo-Yeniseyskiy** Krasnoyarskiy Kray, C Russian Federation
130 *M11* **Severskiy Donets** *Ukr.* Sivers'kyy Donets'. ≈ Russian Federation/Ukraine *see also* Sivers'kyy Donets'
94 *M9* **Sevettijärvi** Lappi, N Finland
38 *M5* **Sevier Bridge Reservoir** ▣ Utah, W USA
38 *J4* **Sevier Desert** *plain* Utah, W USA
38 *J5* **Sevier Lake** ◎ Utah, W USA
23 *N9* **Sevierville** Tennessee, S USA
106 *J14* **Sevilla** *Eng.* Seville; *anc.* Hispalis. Andalucía, SW Spain
106 *J13* **Sevilla** ◐ *province* Andalucía, SW Spain
Sevilla de Niefang *see* Niefang
45 *O16* **Sevilla, Isla** *island* SW Panama
Seville *see* Sevilla
116 *J9* **Sevlievo** Loveshka Oblast, C Bulgaria
Sevluš/Sevlyush *see* Vynohradiv
111 *V11* **Sevnica** *Ger.* Lichtenwald. E Slovenia
130 *I7* **Sevsk** Bryanskaya Oblast', W Russian Federation
78 *J15* **Sewa** ≈ E Sierra Leone
41 *R12* **Seward** Alaska, USA
31 *R15* **Seward** Nebraska, C USA
8 *G8* **Seward Glacier** *glacier* Yukon Territory, W Canada
207 *Q3* **Seward Peninsula** *peninsula* Alaska, USA
Seward's Folly *see* Alaska
64 *H12* **Sewell** Libertador, C Chile
100 *K5* **Sexbierum** *Fris.* Seisbierrum. Friesland, N Netherlands
9 *O13* **Sexsmith** Alberta, W Canada
43 *W13* **Seybaplaya** Campeche, SE Mexico
181 *N6* **Seychelles** *off.* Republic of Seychelles. ◆ *republic* W Indian Ocean
69 *Z9* **Seychelles** *island group* NE Seychelles
181 *N6* **Seychelles Bank** *var.* Le Banc des Seychelles. *undersea feature* W Indian Ocean
Seychelles, Le Banc des *see* Seychelles Bank
180 *H17* **Seychellois, Morne** ▲ Mahé, NE Seychelles
94 *L2* **Seydhisfjördhur** Austurland, E Iceland
152 *J12* **Seydi** *prev.* Neftezavodsk. Lebapskiy Velayat, E Turkmenistan
142 *G16* **Seydişehir** Konya, SW Turkey
142 *J13* **Seyfe Gölü** ◎ C Turkey
Seyhan *see* Adana
142 *K16* **Seyhan Barajı** ▣ S Turkey
142 *K17* **Seyhan Nehri** ≈ S Turkey
142 *F13* **Seyitgazi** Eskişehir, W Turkey
130 *J7* **Seym** ≈ W Russian Federation
119 *S3* **Seym** ≈ N Ukraine
127 *O9* **Seymchan** Magadanskaya Oblast', E Russian Federation
116 *N12* **Seymen** Tekirdağ, NW Turkey
191 *O11* **Seymour** Victoria, SE Australia
85 *I25* **Seymour** Eastern Cape, S South Africa
31 *W16* **Seymour** Iowa, C USA
29 *U7* **Seymour** Missouri, C USA
27 *Q5* **Seymour** Texas, SW USA
116 *M12* **Şeytan Deresi** ≈ NW Turkey
111 *S12* **Sežana** *It.* Sesana. SW Slovenia
105 *P5* **Sézanne** Marne, N France
109 *I16* **Sezze** *anc.* Setia. Lazio, C Italy
117 *H25* **Sfákia** Kríti, Greece, E Mediterranean Sea
117 *D21* **Sfaktiría** *island* S Greece
118 *J11* **Sfântu Gheorghe** *Ger.* Sankt-Georgen, *Hung.* Sepsiszentgyőrgy; *prev.* Şepşi-Sângeorz, Sfîntu Gheorghe. Covasna, C Romania
119 *N13* **Sfântu Gheorghe, Braţul** *var.* Gheorghe Braţul. ≈ E Romania
77 *N6* **Sfax** *Ar.* Şafāqis. E Tunisia
77 *N6* **Sfax** ✈ E Tunisia
Sfîntu Gheorghe *see* Sfântu Gheorghe
100 *H13* **'s-Gravendeel** Zuid-Holland, SW Netherlands
100 *F11* **'s-Gravenhage** *var.* Den Haag, *Eng.* The Hague, *Fr.* La Haye. ● (Netherlands-seat of government) Zuid-Holland, W Netherlands
100 *G12* **'s-Gravenzande** Zuid-Holland, W Netherlands
xlii *D13* **Sgurr Alasdair** ▲ NW Scotland, UK
xlii *H11* **Sgurr Mor** *cliff* NW Scotland, UK
xlii *H12* **Sgurr Na Lapaich** ▲ Highland, NW Scotland, UK
Shaan/Shaanxi Sheng *see* Shaanxi
165 *X11* **Shaanxi** *var.* Shaan, Shaanxi Sheng, Shan-hsi, Shenshi, Shensi. ◐ *province* C China
Shaartuz *see* Shahrtuz
Shaba *see* Katanga
Shabani *see* Zvishavane
83 *N17* **Shabeellaha Dhexe** *off.* Gobolka Shabeellaha Dhexe. ◐ *region* E Somalia
83 *L17* **Shabeellaha Hoose** *off.* Gobolka Shabeellaha Hoose. ◐ *region* S Somalia
Shabeelle, Webi *see* Shebeli
116 *O7* **Shabla** Varnenska Oblast, NE Bulgaria
116 *O7* **Shabla, Nos** *headland* NE Bulgaria
11 *N9* **Shabogama Lake** ◎ Newfoundland and Labrador, E Canada
81 *N20* **Shabunda** Sud Kivu, E Zaire
147 *Q15* **Shabwah** C Yemen
164 *F8* **Shache** *var.* Yarkant. Xinjiang Uygur Zizhiqu, NW China
Shacheng *see* Huailai
205 *R12* **Shackleton Coast** *physical region* Antarctica
205 *Z10* **Shackleton Ice Shelf** *ice shelf* Antarctica
Shaddādī *see* Ash Shadādah
30 *K7* **Shadehill Reservoir** ▣ South Dakota, N USA
xlii *D7* **Shader** Western Isles, NW Scotland, UK
125 *Ee12* **Shadrinsk** Kurganskaya Oblast', C Russian Federation
33 *O12* **Shafer, Lake** ▣ Indiana, N USA
37 *R13* **Shafter** California, W USA
26 *J11* **Shafter** Texas, SW USA
xxxvi *M12* **Shaftesbury** Dorset, S England, UK
193 *F22* **Shag** ≈ South Island, NZ
151 *V9* **Shagan** ≈ E Kazakhstan
41 *O11* **Shageluk** Alaska, USA
126 *I16* **Shagonar** Respublika Tyva, S Russian Federation
193 *F22* **Shag Point** *headland* South Island, NZ
150 *J12* **Shagyray, Plato** *plain* SW Kazakhstan
Shāhābād *see* Eslāmābād
174 *H5* **Shah Alam** Selangor, Peninsular Malaysia
119 *O12* **Shahany, Ozero** ◎ SW Ukraine
144 *H9* **Shahbā'** *anc.* Philippopolis. As Suwaydā', S Syria
Shahbān *see* Ad Dayr
155 *P17* **Shāhbandar** Sind, SE Pakistan
155 *P13* **Shāhdādkot** Sind, SW Pakistan
149 *T10* **Shahdād, Namakzār-e** *salt pan* E Iran
155 *Q15* **Shāhdādpur** Sind, SE Pakistan
160 *K10* **Shahdol** Madhya Pradesh, C India
167 *N7* **Sha He** ≈ C China
Shahepu *see* Linze
159 *N13* **Shāhganj** Uttar Pradesh, N India
158 *C11* **Shāhgarh** Rājasthān, NW India
Sha Hi *see* Orūmīyeh, Daryācheh-ye, Iran
Shāhī *see* Qā'emshahr, Māzandarān, Iran
145 *Q6* **Shāhimah** *var.* Shahma. C Iraq
Shahjahanabad *see* Delhi
158 *L11* **Shāhjahānpur** Uttar Pradesh, N India
Shahma *see* Shāhimah
155 *U7* **Shāhpur** Punjab, E Pakistan
Shāhpur *see* Shāhpur Chākar
158 *G13* **Shāhpura** Rājasthān, N India
155 *Q15* **Shāhpur Chākar** *var.* Shāhpur. Sind, SE Pakistan
154 *M5* **Shahrak** Ghowr, C Afghanistan
149 *Q11* **Shahr-e Bābak** Kermān, C Iran
149 *N8* **Shahr-e Kord** *var.* Shahr Kord. Chahār Maḩall va Bakhtīārī, C Iran
149 *O9* **Shahreẕā** *var.* Qomisheh, Qumisheh, Shahriza; *prev.* Qomsheh. Eşfahān, C Iran
153 *S10* **Shahrikhon** *Rus.* Shakhrikhan. Andijon Wiloyati, E Uzbekistan
153 *N12* **Shahrisabz** *Rus.* Shakhrisabz. Qashqadaryo Wiloyati, S Uzbekistan
153 *P11* **Shahriston** *Rus.* Shakhristan. NW Tajikistan
Shahriza *see* Shahreẕā
Shahr-i-Zabul *see* Zābol
Shahr Kord *see* Shahr-e Kord
153 *P14* **Shahrtuz** *Rus.* Shaartuz. SW Tajikistan
149 *Q4* **Shāhrūd** *prev.* Emāmrūd, Emāmshahr. Semnān, N Iran
Shahsavār/Shahsawar *see* Tonekābon
Shaidara *see* Step' Nardara
Shaikh Ābid *see* Shaykh 'Ābid
Shaikh Fāris *see* Shaykh Fāris
Shaikh Najm *see* Shaykh Najm
144 *K5* **Shā'īr, Jabal** ▲ C Syria
160 *G10* **Shājāpur** Madhya Pradesh, C India
82 *J8* **Shakal, Ras** *headland* NE Sudan
Shakhdarinskiy Khrebet *see* Shokhdara, Qatorkŭhi
Shakhrikhan *see* Shahrikhon
Shakhrisabz *see* Shahrisabz
Shakhristan *see* Shahriston
119 *X8* **Shakhtars'k** *Rus.* Shakhtërsk. Donets'ka Oblast', SE Ukraine
127 *O15* **Shakhtersk** Ostrov Sakhalin, Sakhalinskaya Oblast', SE Russian Federation
Shakhtërsk *see* Shakhtars'k
151 *R10* **Shakhtinsk** Karaganda, C Kazakhstan
130 *L11* **Shakhty** Rostovskaya Oblast', SW Russian Federation
131 *P2* **Shakhun'ya** Nizhegorodskaya Oblast', W Russian Federation
79 *S15* **Shaki** Oyo, W Nigeria
83 *J15* **Shakīso** S Ethiopia
119 *X8* **Shakmars'k** Donets'ka Oblast', E Ukraine
31 *V9* **Shakopee** Minnesota, N USA
172 *Nn5* **Shakotan-hantō** *peninsula* Hokkaidō, NE Japan
172 *O4* **Shakotan-misaki** *headland* Hokkaidō, NE Japan
41 *N9* **Shaktoolik** Alaska, USA
83 *J14* **Shala Hāyk'** ◎ C Ethiopia
128 *M10* **Shalakusha** Arkhangel'skaya Oblast', NW Russian Federation
xxxvii *O10* **Shalbourne** Wiltshire, S England, UK
151 *U8* **Shalday** Pavlodar, NE Kazakhstan
xxxvii *P14* **Shalfleet** Isle of Wight, S England, UK
xxxvii *S11* **Shalford** Surrey, SE England, UK
131 *P16* **Shali** Chechenskaya Respublika, SW Russian Federation
147 *W12* **Shalīm** *var.* Shelim. S Oman
Shaliuhe *see* Gangca
150 *F9* **Shalkar, Ozero** *prev.* Chelkar, Ozero. ◎ W Kazakhstan
23 *V12* **Shallotte** North Carolina, SE USA
27 *N5* **Shallowater** Texas, SW USA
128 *K11* **Shal'skiy** Respublika Kareliya, NW Russian Federation
166 *F9* **Shaluli Shan** ▲▲ C China
83 *F22* **Shama** ≈ C Tanzania
9 *Z11* **Shamattawa** Manitoba, C Canada
10 *F8* **Shamattawa** ≈ Ontario, C Canada
Shām, Bādiyat ash *see* Syrian Desert
Shamiya *see* Ash Shāmīyah
147 *X8* **Shām, Jabal ash** *var.* Jebel Sham. ▲ NW Oman
Sham, Jebel *see* Shām, Jabal ash
Shamkhor *see* Şamkir
20 *G14* **Shamokin** Pennsylvania, NE USA
27 *P2* **Shamrock** Texas, SW USA
Sha'nabī, Jabal ash *see* Chambi, Jebel
145 *Y12* **Shanāwah** E Iraq
165 *T8* **Shandan** Gansu, N China
Shandī *see* Shendi
xliii *H19* **Shandon** Argyll and Bute, W Scotland, UK
167 *Q5* **Shandong** *var.* Lu, Shandong Sheng, Shantung. ◐ *province* E China
167 *R4* **Shandong Bandao** *var.* Shantung Peninsula. *peninsula* E China
Shandong Peninsula *see* Shandong Bandao
Shandong Sheng *see* Shandong
145 *U8* **Shandrūkh** E Iraq
85 *J17* **Shangani** ≈ W Zimbabwe
167 *O15* **Shangchuan Dao** *island* S China
Shangchuankou *see* Minhe
169 *P12* **Shangdu** Nei Mongol Zizhiqu, N China
167 *O11* **Shanggao** Jiangxi, S China
167 *S8* **Shanghai** *var.* Shang-hai. Shanghai Shi, E China
Shanghai *see* Shanghai Shi
167 *S8* **Shanghai Shi** *var.* Hu, Shanghai. ◐ *municipality* E China
167 *P13* **Shanghang** Fujian, SE China
166 *K14* **Shanglin** Guangxi Zhuangzu Zizhiqu, S China
85 *G15* **Shangombo** Western, W Zambia
167 *O6* **Shangqiu** *var.* Zhuji. Henan, C China
167 *Q10* **Shangrao** Jiangxi, S China
167 *S9* **Shangyu** *var.* Baiguan. Zhejiang, SE China
169 *X9* **Shangzhi** Heilongjiang, NE China
166 *L7* **Shangzhou** *var.* Shang Xian. Shaanxi, C China
169 *W9* **Shanhetun** Heilongjiang, NE China
Shan-hsi *see* Shaanxi, China
Shan-hsi *see* Shanxi, China
xxxvii *Q14* **Shanklin** Isle of Wight, S England, UK
165 *O6* **Shankou** Xinjiang Uygur Zizhiqu, W China
xliv *E14* **Shanlaragh** Cork, S Ireland
xliv *E11* **Shannon** Clare, W Ireland
xliv *G9* **Shannon** *Ir.* Ant Sionainn. ≈ W Ireland
xliv *E11* **Shannon** ✈ Clare, W Ireland
192 *M13* **Shannon** Manawatu-Wanganui, North Island, NZ
xliv *G9* **Shannonbridge** Offaly, C Ireland
xliv *H6* **Shannon Erne Waterway** *canal* N Ireland
xliv *C11* **Shannon, Mouth of the** *estuary* W Ireland
178 *H6* **Shan Plateau** *plateau* E Burma
164 *M6* **Shanshan** *var.* Piqan. Xinjiang Uygur Zizhiqu, NW China
Shansi *see* Shanxi
178 *Gg5* **Shan State** ◐ *state* E Burma
Shantar Islands *see* Shantarskiye Ostrova
127 *N13* **Shantarskiye Ostrova** *Eng.* Shantar Islands. *island group* E Russian Federation
167 *Q14* **Shantou** *var.* Shan-t'ou, Swatow. Guangdong, S China
Shantung *see* Shandong
Shantung Peninsula *see* Shandong Bandao
169 *O14* **Shanxi** *var.* Jin, Shan-hsi, Shansi, Shanxi Sheng. ◐ *province* C China
Shan Xian *see* Sanmenxia
167 *P6* **Shanxian** *var.* Shan Xian. Shandong, E China
Shanxi Sheng *see* Shanxi
166 *L7* **Shanyang** Shaanxi, C China
167 *O13* **Shaoguan** *var.* Shao-kuan, *Cant.* Kukong; *prev.* Ch'u-chiang. Guangdong, S China
Shao-kuan *see* Shaoguan
167 *Q11* **Shaowu** Fujian, SE China
167 *S9* **Shaoxing** Zhejiang, SE China
166 *M12* **Shaoyang** *prev.* Tangdukou. Hunan, S China
166 *M11* **Shaoyang** *var.* Baoqing, Shao-yang; *prev.* Pao-king. Hunan, S China
xli *N9* **Shap** Cumbria, NW England, UK
xli *N10* **Shap Fells** ▲▲ NW England, UK
xlii *N4* **Shapinsay** *island* NE Scotland, UK
129 *S4* **Shapkina** ≈ NW Russian Federation
Shāpūr *see* Salmās
164 *M4* **Shaqiuhe** Xinjiang Uygur Zizhiqu, W China
145 *T2* **Shaqlāwa** *var.* Shaqlāwah. E Iraq
Shaqlāwah *see* Shaqlāwa
144 *I8* **Shaqqā** As Suwaydā', S Syria
147 *P7* **Shaqrā'** Ar Riyāḑ, C Saudi Arabia
Shaqrā *see* Shuqrah
155 *O6* **Sharan** Urūzgān, SE Afghanistan
Sharaqpur *see* Sharqpur
Sharbaqty *see* Shcherbakty
147 *X12* **Sharbatāt** S Oman
147 *X12* **Sharbithāt, Ras** *var.* Ra's Sharbatāt. *headland* S Oman
12 *K14* **Sharbot Lake** Ontario, SE Canada
Shardara Dalasy *see* Step' Nardara
168 *H6* **Sharga** Govĭ-Altay, W Mongolia
168 *F8* **Sharga** Hövsgöl, N Mongolia
118 *M7* **Sharhorod** Vinnyts'ka Oblast', C Ukraine
168 *K10* **Sharhulsan** Ömnogŏvĭ, S Mongolia
172 *Qq6* **Shari** Hokkaidō, NE Japan
Shari *see* Chari
145 *T6* **Shārī, Buḩayrat** ◎ C Iraq
Sharjah *see* Ash Shāriqah
120 *K12* **Sharkawshchyna** *var.* Sharkowshchyna, *Pol.* Szarkowszczyzna, *Rus.* Sharkovshchina. Vitsyebskaya Voblasts', NW Belorussia
188 *G9* **Shark Bay** *bay* Western Australia
147 *Y9* **Sharkh** E Oman
Sharkovshchina/Sharkowshchyna *see* Sharkawshchyna
131 *U6* **Sharlyk** Orenburgskaya Oblast', W Russian Federation
Sharm ash Shaykh *see* Sharm el Sheikh
77 *Y9* **Sharm el Sheikh** *var.* Ofiral, Sharm ash Shaykh. E Egypt
xxxvii *S5* **Sharnbrook** Bedfordshire, C England, UK
20 *B13* **Sharon** Pennsylvania, NE USA
28 *H4* **Sharon Springs** Kansas, C USA
33 *Q14* **Sharonville** Ohio, N USA
Sharourah *see* Sharūrah
31 *O10* **Sharpe, Lake** ▣ South Dakota, N USA
xxxvi *L8* **Sharpness** Gloucestershire, C England, UK
Sharqī, Al Jabal ash/Sharqi, Jebel esh *see* Anti-Lebanon
Sharqīyah, Al Minţaqah ash *see* Ash Sharqīyah
144 *I6* **Sharqīyat an Nabk, Jabal** ▲▲ W Syria
155 *W8* **Sharqpur** *var.* Sharaqpur. Punjab, E Pakistan
147 *Q13* **Sharūrah** *var.* Sharourah. Najrān, S Saudi Arabia
129 *O14* **Shar'ya** Kostromskaya Oblast', NW Russian Federation
151 *V15* **Sharyn** *var.* Charyn. ≈ SE Kazakhstan
Sharyn *see* Charyn
85 *J18* **Shashe** Central, NE Botswana
85 *J18* **Shashe** *var.* Shashi. ≈ Botswana/Zimbabwe
83 *J14* **Shashemenē** *var.* Shashemenne, Shashhamana, *It.* Sciasciamana. S Ethiopia
Shashemenne/Shashhamana *see* Shashemenē
166 *M9* **Shashi** *var.* Sha-shih, Shasi. Hubei, C China
Shashi *see* Shashe
Sha-shih/Shasi *see* Shashi
37 *N3* **Shasta Lake** ▣ California, W USA
37 *N2* **Shasta, Mount** ▲ California, W USA
131 *O4* **Shatki** Nizhegorodskaya Oblast', W Russian Federation
152 *J13* **Shatlyk** Maryyskiy Velayat, C Turkmenistan
Shatra *see* Ash Shaţrah
121 *K17* **Shatsk** *Rus.* Shatsk. Minskaya Voblasts', C Belorussia
131 *N5* **Shatsk** Ryazanskaya Oblast', W Russian Federation
28 *J9* **Shattuck** Oklahoma, C USA
151 *P16* **Shaul'der** Yuzhnyy Kazakhstan, S Kazakhstan
9 *S17* **Shaunavon** Saskatchewan, S Canada
Shavat *see* Showot
xxxviii *I7* **Shavington** Cheshire, W England, UK
164 *K4* **Shawan** Xinjiang Uygur Zizhiqu, NW China
12 *G12* **Shawanaga** Ontario, S Canada
32 *M6* **Shawano** Wisconsin, N USA
32 *M6* **Shawano Lake** ◎ Wisconsin, N USA
xlii *C7* **Shawbost** Western Isles, NW Scotland, UK
xxxviii *H9* **Shawbury** Shropshire, W England, UK
13 *P10* **Shawinigan** *prev.* Shawinigan Falls. Québec, SE Canada
Shawinigan Falls *see* Shawinigan
13 *P10* **Shawinigan-Sud** Québec, SE Canada
144 *J5* **Shawmarīyah, Jabal ash** ▲▲ C Syria
29 *O11* **Shawnee** Oklahoma, C USA
12 *K12* **Shawville** Québec, SE Canada
Shaykh *see* Ash Shakk
145 *W9* **Shaykh 'Ābid** *var.* Shaikh Ābid. E Iraq
145 *Y10* **Shaykh Fāris** *var.* Shaikh Fāris. E Iraq
145 *T7* **Shaykh Ḩātim** E Iraq
Shaykh, Jabal ash *see* Hermon, Mount
145 *X10* **Shaykh Najm** *var.* Shaikh Najm. E Iraq
145 *W9* **Shaykh Sa'd** E Iraq
153 *T14* **Shazud** SE Tajikistan
121 *N18* **Shchadryn** *Rus.* Shchedrin. Homyel'skaya Voblasts', SE Belorussia
121 *H18* **Shchara** ≈ SW Belorussia
Shchedrin *see* Shchadryn
Shcheglovsk *see* Kemerovo
130 *K5* **Shchëkino** Tul'skaya Oblast', W Russian Federation
129 *S7* **Shchel'yayur** Respublika Komi, NW Russian Federation
151 *U8* **Shcherbakty** *Kaz.* Sharbaqty. Pavlodar, E Kazakhstan
130 *K7* **Shchigry** Kurskaya Oblast', W Russian Federation
Shchitkovichi *see* Shchytkavichy
119 *Q2* **Shchors** Chernihivs'ka Oblast', N Ukraine
119 *T8* **Shchors'k** Dnipropetrovs'ka Oblast', E Ukraine
Shchuchin *see* Shchuchyn
151 *Q7* **Shchuchinsk** *prev.* Shchuchye. Kokshetau, N Kazakhstan
Shchuchye *see* Shchuchinsk
121 *G16* **Shchuchyn** *Pol.* Szczuczyn Nowogródzki, *Rus.* Shchuchin. Hrodzyenskaya Voblasts', W Belorussia
121 *K17* **Shchytkavichy** *Rus.* Shchitkovichi. Minskaya Voblasts', C Belorussia
126 *H15* **Shebalino** Respublika Altay, S Russian Federation
xxxvi *F13* **Shebbear** Devon, SW England, UK
130 *J9* **Shebekino** Belgorodskaya Oblast', W Russian Federation
Shebelē Wenz, Wabē *see* Shebeli
83 *L14* **Shebeli** *Amh.* Wabē Shebelē Wenz, *It.* Scebeli, *Som.* Webi Shabeelle. ≈ Ethiopia/Somalia
115 *M20* **Shebenikut, Maja e** ▲ E Albania
155 *N2* **Sheberghān** *var.* Shibarghān, Shiberghan, Shiberghān. Jowzjān, N Afghanistan
150 *F14* **Shebir** Mangistau, SW Kazakhstan
33 *N8* **Sheboygan** Wisconsin, N USA
79 *X15* **Shebshi Mountains** *var.* Schebschi Mountains. ▲▲ E Nigeria
Shechem *see* Nablus
Shedadi *see* Ash Shadādah
11 *P14* **Shediac** New Brunswick, SE Canada
130 *L15* **Shedok** Krasnodarskiy Kray, SW Russian Federation
82 *N12* **Sheekh** Woqooyi Galbeed, N Somalia
xliv *I7* **Sheelin, Lough** ◎ C Ireland
40 *M11* **Sheenjek River** ≈ Alaska, USA
xliv *H2* **Sheep Haven** *Ir.* Cuan nag Caorach. *inlet* N Ireland
37 *X10* **Sheep Range** ▲▲ Nevada, W USA
xliv *B15* **Sheep's Head** *headland* S Ireland
xxxvi *F13* **Sheepwash** Devon, SW England, UK
100 *M13* **'s-Heerenberg** Gelderland, E Netherlands
xxxvii *X9* **Sheerness** Kent, SE England, UK
11 *Q15* **Sheet Harbour** Nova Scotia, SE Canada
xli *S17* **Sheffield** Sheffield, N England, UK
xli *R17* **Sheffield** ◐ *unitary authority* N England, UK
193 *H18* **Sheffield** Canterbury, South Island, NZ
25 *O2* **Sheffield** Alabama, S USA
31 *V12* **Sheffield** Iowa, C USA
27 *N10* **Sheffield** Texas, SW USA
xxxvii *T6* **Shefford** Bedfordshire, C England, UK
65 *H22* **Shehuen, Río** ≈ S Argentina
xlii *H7* **Sheigra** Highland, NW Scotland, UK
Shekhem *see* Nablus
155 *V8* **Shekhūpura** Punjab, NE Pakistan
Sheki *see* Şäki
128 *L14* **Sheksna** Vologodskaya Oblast', NW Russian Federation
127 *O4* **Shelagskiy, Mys** *headland* NE Russian Federation
29 *V3* **Shelbina** Missouri, C USA
11 *P16* **Shelburne** Nova Scotia, SE Canada
12 *G14* **Shelburne** Ontario, S Canada
35 *R7* **Shelby** Montana, NW USA
23 *Q10* **Shelby** North Carolina, SE USA
33 *S12* **Shelby** Ohio, N USA
32 *L14* **Shelbyville** Illinois, N USA
33 *P14* **Shelbyville** Indiana, N USA
22 *L5* **Shelbyville** Kentucky, S USA
29 *V2* **Shelbyville** Missouri, C USA
22 *J10* **Shelbyville** Tennessee, S USA
27 *X8* **Shelbyville** Texas, SW USA
32 *L14* **Shelbyville, Lake** ▣ Illinois, N USA
31 *S12* **Sheldon** Iowa, C USA
40 *M11* **Sheldons Point** Alaska, USA
126 *J16* **Shelekhov** Irkutskaya Oblast', C Russian Federation
Shelekhov Gulf *see* Shelikhova, Zaliv
xli *Q14* **Shelf** Bradford, N England, UK
127 *Oo9* **Shelikhova, Zaliv** *Eng.* Shelekhov Gulf. *gulf* E Russian Federation
41 *P14* **Shelikof Strait** *strait* Alaska, USA
Shelim *see* Shalīm
9 *T14* **Shellbrook** Saskatchewan, S Canada
30 *L3* **Shell Creek** ≈ North Dakota, N USA
Shellif *see* Chelif, Oued
24 *I10* **Shell Keys** *island group* Louisiana, S USA
32 *I4* **Shell Lake** Wisconsin, N USA
31 *W12* **Shell Rock** Iowa, C USA
193 *C26* **Shelter Point** *headland* Stewart Island, NZ
20 *L13* **Shelton** Connecticut, NE USA
34 *G8* **Shelton** Washington, NW USA
xxxviii *G10* **Shelve** Shropshire, W England, UK
Shemakha *see* Şamaxı
151 *W9* **Shemonaikha** Vostochnyy Kazakhstan, E Kazakhstan
131 *Q4* **Shemursha** Chuvashskaya Respublika, W Russian Federation
40 *D16* **Shemya Island** *island* Aleutian Islands, Alaska, USA
31 *T16* **Shenandoah** Iowa, C USA
23 *U4* **Shenandoah** Virginia, NE USA
23 *U4* **Shenandoah Mountains** *ridge* West Virginia, NE USA
23 *V3* **Shenandoah River** ≈ West Virginia, NE USA
79 *W15* **Shendam** Plateau, C Nigeria
82 *G8* **Shendi** *var.* Shandī. River Nile, NE Sudan
78 *I15* **Shenge** SW Sierra Leone
151 *U15* **Shengel'dy** Almaty, SE Kazakhstan
115 *K18* **Shëngjin** *var.* Shëngjini. Lezhë, NW Albania
Shëngjini *see* Shëngjin
Shengking *see* Liaoning
Sheng Xian/Shengxian *see* Shengzhou
167 *S9* **Shengzhou** *var.* Shengxian, Sheng Xian. Zhejiang, SE China
Shenking *see* Liaoning
129 *N11* **Shenkursk** Arkhangel'skaya Oblast', NW Russian Federation
166 *L3* **Shenmu** Shaanxi, C China
115 *L19* **Shën Noj i Madh** ▲ C Albania
Shenshi/Shensi *see* Shaanxi
169 *V12* **Shenyang** *Chin.* Shen-yang, *Eng.* Moukden, Mukden; *prev.* Fengtien. Liaoning, NE China
167 *O15* **Shenzhen** Guangdong, S China
160 *G8* **Sheopur** Madhya Pradesh, C India
118 *L5* **Shepetivka** *Rus.* Shepetovka. Khmel'nyts'ka Oblast', NW Ukraine
Shepetovka *see* Shepetivka
27 *W10* **Shepherd** Texas, SW USA
197 *D14* **Shepherd Islands** *island group* C Vanuatu
xxxvi *B7* **Shepherd's Bush** Hammersmith and Fulham, SE England, UK
22 *K5* **Shepherdsville** Kentucky, S USA
xxxvii *Y11* **Shepherdswell** Kent, SE England, UK
191 *O11* **Shepparton** Victoria, SE Australia
xxxvii *X9* **Sheppey, Isle of** *island* SE England, UK
xxxix *S13* **Shepreth** Cambridgeshire, E England, UK
xxxix *N9* **Shepshed** Leicestershire, C England, UK
xxxvi *L11* **Shepton Mallet** Somerset, SW England, UK
Sherabad *see* Sherobod
xxxvi *L12* **Sherborne** Dorset, S England, UK
78 *H16* **Sherbro Island** *island* SW Sierra Leone
13 *Q12* **Sherbrooke** Québec, SE Canada
xli *W4* **Sherburn** Durham, N England, UK
xli *V11* **Sherburn** North Yorkshire, N England, UK
31 *T11* **Sherburn** Minnesota, N USA
xli *T14* **Sherburn in Elmet** North Yorkshire, N England, UK
xliv *J6* **Shercock** Cavan, N Ireland
80 *H6* **Sherda** Borkou-Ennedi-Tibesti, N Chad
82 *G7* **Shereik** River Nile, N Sudan

◆ Country
● Country Capital
◇ Dependent Territory
○ Dependent Territory Capital
◐ Administrative Region
✈ International Airport
▲ Mountain
▲▲ Mountain Range
Volcano
≈ River
◎ Lake
▣ Reservoir

Sheremet'yevo – Silver State

130 K3 Sheremet'yevo ✕ (Moskva) Moskovskaya Oblast', W Russian Federation
159 P14 Shergāti Bihār, N India
29 U12 Sheridan Arkansas, C USA
35 W12 Sheridan Wyoming, C USA
xxxviii I9 Sheriffhales Shropshire, W England, UK
xli T12 Sheriff Hutton North Yorkshire, N England, UK
190 G8 Sheringa South Australia
xxxix X7 Sheringham Norfolk, E England, UK
xxxvii R6 Sherington Milton Keynes, C England, UK
xliv D15 Sherkin Island island S Ireland
126 L16 Sherlovaya Gora Chitinskaya Oblast', S Russian Federation
27 U5 Sherman Texas, SW USA
204 J10 Sherman Island island Antarctica
21 S4 Sherman Mills Maine, NE USA
31 O15 Sherman Reservoir ⊠ Nebraska, C USA
153 N14 Sherobod Rus. Sherabad. Surkhondaryo Wiloyati, S Uzbekistan
153 O13 Sherobod Rus. Sherabad. ≈ S Uzbekistan
159 T14 Sherpur Dhaka, N Bangladesh
39 T4 Sherrelwood Colorado, C USA
xxxvi M9 Sherston Wiltshire, S England, UK
101 J14 's-Hertogenbosch Fr. Bois-le-Duc, Ger. Herzogenbusch. Noord-Brabant, S Netherlands
30 M2 Sherwood North Dakota, N USA
9 Q14 Sherwood Park Alberta, SW Canada
58 F13 Sheshea, Río ≈ E Peru
149 T5 Sheshtamad Khorāsān, NE Iran
31 S10 Shetek, Lake ◎ Minnesota, N USA
xlii H3 Shetland Islands ◐ unitary authority NE Scotland, UK
xlii H1 Shetland Islands island group NE Scotland, UK
150 F14 Shetpe Mangistau, SW Kazakhstan
160 C11 Shetrunji ≈ W India
Shevchenko see Aktau
119 W5 Shevchenkove Kharkivs'ka Oblast', E Ukraine
83 H14 Shewa Gimira SW Ethiopia
167 Q9 Shexian var. Huicheng, She Xian. Anhui, E China
167 R6 Sheyang prev. Hede. Jiangsu, E China
31 O4 Sheyenne North Dakota, N USA
31 P4 Sheyenne River ≈ North Dakota, N USA
xlii D10 Shiant Islands island group NW Scotland, UK
127 Pp14 Shiashkotan, Ostrov island Kuril'skiye Ostrova, SE Russian Federation
33 R9 Shiawassee River ≈ Michigan, N USA
147 R14 Shibām C Yemen
Shibarghān see Sheberghān
171 Kk12 Shibata var. Sibata. Niigata, Honshū, C Japan
172 Qq7 Shibecha Hokkaidō, NE Japan
Shiberghan/Shiberghān see Sheberghān
172 Qq6 Shibetsu Hokkaidō, N Japan
172 Pp4 Shibetsu var. Sibetu. Hokkaidō, NE Japan
172 P5 Shibetsu var. Sibetu. Hokkaidō, NE Japan
Shibh Jazīrat Sīnā' see Sinai
Shibīn al Kawm see Shibīn el Kôm
77 W8 Shibīn el Kôm var. Shibīn al Kawm. N Egypt
149 O13 Shīb, Kūh-e ▲ S Iran
10 D8 Shibogama Lake ◎ Ontario, C Canada
Shibotsu-jima see Zelënyy, Ostrov
171 K14 Shibukawa var. Sibukawa. Gunma, Honshū, S Japan
170 Bb16 Shibushi Kagoshima, Kyūshū, SW Japan
170 C17 Shibushi-wan bay SW Japan
172 N9 Shichinohe Aomori, Honshū, C Japan
201 U13 Shichiyo Islands island group Chuuk, C Micronesia
Shickshock Mountains see Chic-Chocs, Monts
151 S9 Shiderti ≈ N Kazakhstan
151 S8 Shiderty Pavlodar, NE Kazakhstan
xlii G13 Shiel Bridge Highland, NW Scotland, UK
xlii F12 Shieldaig Highland, NW Scotland, UK
xliii F15 Shiel, Loch ◎ N Scotland, UK
xxxviii I9 Shifnal Shropshire, W England, UK
171 H15 Shiga off. Shiga-ken, var. Siga. ◐ prefecture Honshū, SW Japan
Shigatse see Xigazê
147 U13 Shiḥan oasis NE Yemen
Shih-chia-chuang see Shijiazhuang
164 K4 Shihezi Xinjiang Uygur Zizhiqu, NW China
Shihmen see Shijiazhuang
Shiichi see Shyichy
115 K19 Shijak var. Shijaku. Durrës, W Albania
Shijaku see Shijak
167 O4 Shijiazhuang var. Shih-chia-chuang; prev. Shihmen. Hebei, E China
172 Nn7 Shikabe Hokkaidō, NE Japan
155 Q13 Shikārpur Sind, S Pakistan
201 V12 Shiki Islands island group Chuuk, C Micronesia
170 Ee15 Shikoku var. Sikoku. island SW Japan
199 Gg6 Shikoku Basin var. Sikoku Basin. undersea feature N Philippine Sea
170 Ee15 Shikoku-sanchi ⛰ Shikoku, SW Japan
172 S7 Shikotan, Ostrov Jap. Shikotan-tō. island NE Russian Federation
Shikotan-tō see Shikotan, Ostrov
172 O6 Shikotsu-ko var. Sikotu Ko. ◎ Hokkaidō, NE Japan
83 N15 Shilabo SE Ethiopia
xli R3 Shilbottle Northumberland, N England, UK
131 X7 Shil'da Orenburgskaya Oblast', W Russian Federation
xli R8 Shildon Durham, N England, UK
145 V3 Shilēr, Āw-e ≈ E Iraq
159 S12 Shiliguri prev. Siliguri. West Bengal, NE India
126 Kk16 Shilka Chitinskaya Oblast', S Russian Federation
133 V7 Shilka ≈ S Russian Federation
xliv K11 Shillelagh Wicklow, E Ireland
xxxvi M13 Shillingstone Dorset, S England, UK
20 H15 Shillington Pennsylvania, NE USA
159 V13 Shillong Meghālaya, NE India
130 M5 Shilovo Ryazanskaya Oblast', W Russian Federation
170 C14 Shimabara var. Simabara. Nagasaki, Kyūshū, SW Japan
170 C14 Shimabara-wan bay SW Japan
171 Ii17 Shimada var. Simada. Shizuoka, Honshū, S Japan
170 Ee12 Shimane off. Shimane-ken, var. Simane. ◐ prefecture Honshū, SW Japan
170 F11 Shimane-hantō peninsula Honshū, SW Japan
126 M15 Shimanovsk Amurskaya Oblast', SE Russian Federation
Shimbir Berris see Shimbiris
82 O12 Shimbiris var. Shimbir Berris. ▲ N Somalia
172 P6 Shimizu Hokkaidō, NE Japan
171 Ii16 Shimizu var. Simizu. Shizuoka, Honshū, S Japan
158 I8 Shimla prev. Simla. Himāchal Pradesh, N India
Shimminato see Shinminato
171 J18 Shimoda var. Simoda. Shizuoka, Honshū, S Japan
171 Kk16 Shimodate var. Simodate. Ibaraki, Honshū, S Japan
161 F18 Shimoga Karnātaka, W India
170 Bb14 Shimo-jima island SW Japan
170 B15 Shimo-Koshiki-jima island SW Japan
83 J21 Shimoni Coast, S Kenya
170 D12 Shimonoseki var. Simonoseki; hist. Akamagaseki, Bakan. Yamaguchi, Honshū, SW Japan
171 Kk16 Shimotsuma var. Simotuma. Ibaraki, Honshū, S Japan
128 G14 Shimsk Novgorodskaya Oblast', NW Russian Federation
171 Jj14 Shinano-gawa var. Sinano Gawa. ≈ Honshū, C Japan
147 W7 Shināṣ N Oman
154 J6 Shīndand Farāh, W Afghanistan
Shinei see Hsinying
27 T12 Shiner Texas, SW USA
xli S7 Shiney Row Sunderland, NE England, UK
178 Gg1 Shingbwiyang Kachin State, N Burma
151 W11 Shingozha Semipalatinsk, E Kazakhstan
171 Gg17 Shingū var. Singû. Wakayama, Honshū, SW Japan
12 F8 Shining Tree Ontario, S Canada
170 F12 Shinji-ko var. Sinzi-ko. ◎ Honshū, SW Japan
171 Ll12 Shinjō var. Sinzyô. Yamagata, Honshū, C Japan
xlii I9 Shin, Loch ◎ N Scotland, UK
171 Ii13 Shinminato var. Shimminato, Sinminato. Toyama, Honshū, SW Japan
170 Dd12 Shinnanyō var. Shin-Nan'yō, Sinn'anyô. Yamaguchi, Honshū, SW Japan
xlii I9 Shinness Highland, NW Scotland, UK
23 S3 Shinnston West Virginia, NE USA
xliv H10 Shinrone Offaly, C Ireland
144 I6 Shinshār Fr. Chinnchâr. Ḥimṣ, W Syria
171 I16 Shinshiro var. Sinsiro. Aichi, Honshū, SW Japan
Shinshū see Chinju
172 P6 Shintoku Hokkaidō, NE Japan
83 G20 Shinyanga Shinyanga, NW Tanzania
83 G20 Shinyanga ◐ region N Tanzania
171 M13 Shiogama var. Siogama. Miyagi, Honshū, C Japan
171 J15 Shiojiri var. Sioziri. Nagano, Honshū, S Japan
170 G17 Shiono-misaki headland Honshū, SW Japan
171 Ll15 Shioya-zaki headland Honshū, C Japan
xxxvii V10 Shipbourne Kent, SE England, UK
116 J9 Shipchenski Prokhod pass C Bulgaria
xxxix V9 Shipdham Norfolk, E England, UK
166 G14 Shiping Yunnan, SW China
xli R13 Shipley Bradford, N England, UK
11 P13 Shippagan var. Shippegan. New Brunswick, SE Canada
Shippegan see Shippagan
20 F15 Shippensburg Pennsylvania, NE USA
39 O9 Ship Rock ▲ New Mexico, SW USA
39 P9 Shiprock New Mexico, SW USA
13 R6 Shipshaw ≈ Québec, SE Canada
xxxviii M13 Shipston on Stour Warwickshire, C England, UK
xli T12 Shipton North Yorkshire, N England, UK
xxxvii O7 Shipton-under-Wychwood Oxfordshire, C England, UK
127 Pp11 Shipunskiy, Mys headland E Russian Federation
166 K7 Shiquan Shaanxi, C China
126 Hh14 Shira Respublika Khakasiya, S Russian Federation
170 G16 Shirahama Wakayama, Honshū, SW Japan
159 T14 Shirajganj Ghat var. Serajgonj, Sirajganj. Rajshahi, C Bangladesh
171 Mm7 Shirakami-misaki headland Hokkaidō, NE Japan
171 L14 Shirakawa var. Sirakawa. Fukushima, Honshū, C Japan
171 Ii13 Shirakawa Gifu, Honshū, SW Japan
171 K14 Shirane-san ▲ Honshū, S Japan
171 J16 Shirane-san ▲ Honshū, S Japan
172 Pp7 Shiranuka Hokkaidō, NE Japan
172 O6 Shiraoi Hokkaidō, NE Japan
205 N12 Shirase Coast physical region Antarctica
172 Pp5 Shirataki Hokkaidō, NE Japan
149 O11 Shīrāz var. Shīrāz. Fārs, S Iran
85 N15 Shire var. Chire. ≈ Malawi/Mozambique
168 G7 Shiree Dzavhan, W Mongolia
169 O9 Shireet Sühbaatar, SE Mongolia
xxxv L14 Shirenewton Monmouthshire, SE Wales, UK
172 R6 Shiretoko-hantō headland Hokkaidō, NE Japan
172 R5 Shiretoko-misaki headland Hokkaidō, NE Japan
131 N5 Shiringushi Respublika Mordoviya, W Russian Federation
154 M3 Shīrīn Tagāb Fāryāb, N Afghanistan
155 N2 Shīrīn Tagāb ≈ N Afghanistan
172 Nn8 Shiriya-zaki headland Honshū, C Japan
150 I12 Shirkala, Gryada plain W Kazakhstan
xxxviii D16 Shirley Solihull, C England, UK
171 Ll13 Shiroishi var. Siroisi. Miyagi, Honshū, C Japan
Shirokoye see Shyroke
171 K12 Shirone var. Sirone. Niigata, Honshū, C Japan
171 I14 Shirotori Gifu, Honshū, SW Japan
171 J13 Shirouma-dake ▲ Honshū, S Japan
207 T1 Shirshov Ridge undersea feature W Bering Sea
Shirshütür see Shirshyutyur, Peski
152 K12 Shirshyutyur, Peski Turkm. Shirshütür. desert E Turkmenistan
149 T3 Shīrvān var. Shīrwān. Khorāsān, NE Iran
Shirwa, Lake see Chilwa, Lake
Shīrwān see Shīrvān
165 N5 Shisanjianfang Xinjiang Uygur Zizhiqu, W China
40 M16 Shishaldin Volcano ▲ Unimak Island, Alaska, USA
Shishchitsy see Shyshchytsy
40 M8 Shishmaref Alaska, USA
xliii G22 Shiskine North Ayrshire, W Scotland, UK
Shisur see Ash Shişar
171 I16 Shitara Aichi, Honshū, SW Japan
158 D12 Shiv Rājasthān, NW India
160 H8 Shivpuri Madhya Pradesh, C India
38 J9 Shivwits Plateau plain Arizona, SW USA
Shiwālik Range see Siwalik Range
166 M8 Shiyan Hubei, C China
166 H13 Shizong Yunnan, SW China
171 Mm13 Shizugawa Miyagi, Honshū, NE Japan
165 W8 Shizuishan var. Dawukou. Ningxia, N China
172 Oo7 Shizunai Hokkaidō, NE Japan
171 Ii16 Shizuoka var. Sizuoka. Shizuoka, Honshū, S Japan
171 Ii16 Shizuoka off. Shizuoka-ken, var. Sizuoka. ◐ prefecture Honshū, S Japan
Shklov see Shklow
121 N15 Shklow Rus. Shklov. Mahilyowskaya Voblasts', E Belorussia
115 K18 Shkodër var. Shkodra, It. Scutari, SCr. Skadar. Shkodër, NW Albania
115 K17 Shkodër ◐ district NW Albania
Shkodra see Shkodër
Shkodrës, Liqeni i see Scutari, Lake
Shkumbi/Shkumbin see Shkumbinit, Lumi i
115 L20 Shkumbinit, Lumi i var. Shkumbî, Shkumbin. ≈ C Albania
Shligigh, Cuan see Sligo Bay
126 Ii2 Shmidta, Ostrov island Severnaya Zemlya, N Russian Federation
191 S10 Shoalhaven River ≈ New South Wales, SE Australia
9 W16 Shoal Lake Manitoba, S Canada
33 O15 Shoals Indiana, N USA
170 F13 Shōbara var. Syôbara. Hiroshima, Honshū, SW Japan
170 Ff14 Shōdo-shima island SW Japan
xxxvii X9 Shoeburyness Southend-on-Sea, SE England, UK
171 Ii13 Shō-gawa ≈ Honshū, SW Japan
Shōka see Changhua
126 J3 Shokal'skogo, Proliv strait N Russian Federation
172 Oo4 Shokanbetsu-dake ▲ Hokkaidō, NE Japan
153 T14 Shokhdara, Qatorkŭhi Rus. Shakhdarinskiy Khrebet. ⛰ SE Tajikistan
151 N9 Sholaksay Kustanay, N Kazakhstan
Sholāpur see Solāpur
Sholdaneshty see Şoldăneşti
xxxvi G8 Shooters Hill Greenwich, SE England, UK
Shoqpar see Chokpar
161 G21 Shoranūr Kerala, SW India
161 G16 Shorāpur Karnātaka, C India
xxxvi E7 Shoreditch Hackney, SE England, UK
xxxvii S13 Shoreham-by-Sea West Sussex, SE England, UK
32 M11 Shorewood Illinois, N USA
Shorkazakhly, Solonchak see Kazakhlyshor, Solonchak
151 Q9 Shortandy Akmola, C Kazakhstan
Shortepa/Shor Tepe see Shūr Tappeh
195 S13 Shortland Island var. Alu. island Shortland Islands, NW Solomon Islands
195 T13 Shortland Islands island group NW Solomon Islands
Shosambetsu see Shosanbetsu
xxxvii P14 Shorwell Isle of Wight, S England, UK
172 P3 Shosanbetsu var. Shosambetsu. Hokkaidō, NE Japan
35 O15 Shoshone Idaho, NW USA
37 T6 Shoshone Mountains ⛰ Nevada, W USA
35 U12 Shoshone River ≈ Wyoming, C USA
85 I19 Shoshong Central, SE Botswana
35 V14 Shoshoni Wyoming, C USA
Shōshū see Sangju
119 S2 Shostka Sums'ka Oblast', NE Ukraine
xli Q7 Shotley Bridge Durham, N England, UK
xxxix X13 Shotley Gate Suffolk, E England, UK
193 C21 Shotover ≈ South Island, NZ
xliii K20 Shotts North Lanarkshire, C Scotland, UK
xxxix U9 Shouldham Norfolk, E England, UK
39 N12 Show Low Arizona, SW USA
Show Me State see Missouri
152 H9 Showot Rus. Shavat. Khorazm Wiloyati, W Uzbekistan
129 O4 Shoyna Nenetskiy Avtonomnyy Okrug, NW Russian Federation
128 M11 Shozhma Arkhangel'skaya Oblast', NW Russian Federation
119 Q7 Shpola Cherkas'ka Oblast', N Ukraine
Shqipëria/Shqipërisë, Republika e see Albania
24 G5 Shreveport Louisiana, S USA
xxxviii H9 Shrewsbury hist. Scrobesbyrig'. Shropshire, W England, UK
158 D11 Shri Mohangarh prev. Sri Mohangorh. Rājasthān, NW India
159 S16 Shrīrāmpur prev. Serampore, Serampur. West Bengal, NE India
xxxvii O9 Shrivenham Oxfordshire, C England, UK
xxxviii G10 Shropshire ◐ county W England, UK
xxxviii B13 Shropshire Union Canal canal W England, UK
151 S16 Shu Kaz. Shū. Zhambyl, SE Kazakhstan
Shū see Chu
166 G13 Shuangbai Yunnan, SW China
169 W9 Shuangcheng Heilongjiang, NE China
166 E14 Shuangjiang Yunnan, SW China
169 U10 Shuangliao var. Zhengjiatun. Jilin, NE China
Shuang-liao see Liaoyuan
169 Y7 Shuangyashan var. Shuang-ya-shan. Heilongjiang, NE China
Shu'aymiyah see Shu'aymīyah
147 W12 Shu'aymīyah var. Shu'aymiah. S Oman
150 I10 Shubarkuduk Kaz. Shubarqudyq. Aktyubinsk, W Kazakhstan
Shubarqudyq see Shubarkuduk
151 N12 Shubar-Tengiz, Ozero ◎ C Kazakhstan
41 S5 Shublik Mountains ⛰ Alaska, USA
Shubrā al Khaymah see Shubrâ el Kheima
124 Qq16 Shubrâ el Kheima var. Shubrā al Khaymah. N Egypt
164 E8 Shufu Xinjiang Uygur Zizhiqu, NW China
153 S14 Shughnon, Qatorkŭhi Rus. Shugnanskiy Khrebet. ⛰ SE Tajikistan
Shugnanskiy Khrebet see Shughnon, Qatorkŭhi
167 Q6 Shu He ≈ E China
Shuiding see Huocheng
Shuiji see Laixi
Shū-Ile Taūlary see Chu-Iliyskiye Gory
155 T10 Shujāābād Punjab, E Pakistan
169 W9 Shulan Jilin, NE China
164 E8 Shule Xinjiang Uygur Zizhiqu, NW China
Shuleh see Shule He
165 Q8 Shule He var. Shuleh, Sulo. ≈ C China
32 K9 Shullsburg Wisconsin, N USA
41 N16 Shumagin Islands island group Alaska, USA
152 G7 Shumanay Qoraqalpoghiston Respublikasi, W Uzbekistan
116 M8 Shumen Varnenska Oblast, NE Bulgaria
131 P4 Shumerlya Chuvashskaya Respublika, W Russian Federation
125 Ee12 Shumikha Kurganskaya Oblast', C Russian Federation
120 M12 Shumilina Rus. Shumilino. Vitsyebskaya Voblasts', NE Belorussia
Shumilino see Shumilina
127 Pp12 Shumshu, Ostrov island SE Russian Federation
118 K5 Shums'k Ternopil's'ka Oblast', W Ukraine
41 O7 Shungnak Alaska, USA
Shunsen see Ch'unch'ŏn
166 M3 Shuo Xian Shanxi, NE China
Shuo Xian/Shuoxian see Shuozhou
167 N3 Shuozhou var. Shuoxian; prev. Shuo Xian. Shanxi, C China
147 P16 Shuqrah var. Shaqrā. SW Yemen
Shurab see Shŭrob
153 O14 Shŭrchi Rus. Shurchi. Surkhondaryo Wiloyati, S Uzbekistan
153 R11 Shŭrob Rus. Shurab. NW Tajikistan
149 T10 Shūr, Rūd-e ≈ E Iran
155 O2 Shūr Tappeh var. Shortepa, Shor Tepe. Balkh, N Afghanistan
85 K17 Shurugwi prev. Selukwe. Midlands, C Zimbabwe
148 L8 Shūsh anc. Susa, Bibl. Shushan. Khūzestān, SW Iran
Shushan see Shūsh
148 L9 Shūshtar var. Shustar, Shushter. Khūzestān, SW Iran
Shushter/Shustar see Shūshtar
xxxvi J14 Shute Devon, SW England, UK
147 T9 Shuṭfah, Qalamat well E Saudi Arabia
145 V9 Shuwayjah, Hawr ash var. Hawr as Suwayqiyah. ◎ E Iraq
128 M16 Shuya Ivanovskaya Oblast', W Russian Federation
41 Q14 Shuyak Island island Alaska, USA
177 G4 Shwebo Sagaing, C Burma
177 Ff7 Shwedaung Pegu, W Burma
177 G8 Shwegyin Pegu, SW Burma
178 Gg4 Shweli Chin. Longchuan Jiang. ≈ Burma/China
177 G6 Shwemyo Mandalay, C Burma
Shyghys Qazagastan Oblysy see Vostochnyy Kazakhstan
Shyghys Qongyrat see Vostochno-Kounradskiy
121 M19 Shyichy Rus. Shiichi. Homyel'skaya Voblasts', SE Belorussia
151 Q17 Shymkent prev. Chimkent. Yuzhnyy Kazakhstan, S Kazakhstan
Shyngghyrlaū see Chingirlau
158 J5 Shyok Jammu and Kashmir, NW India
119 S9 Shyroke Rus. Shirokoye. Dnipropetrovs'ka Oblast', E Ukraine
119 O9 Shyryayeve Odes'ka Oblast', SW Ukraine
119 S5 Shyshaky Poltavs'ka Oblast', C Ukraine
121 K17 Shyshchytsy Rus. Shishchitsy. Minskaya Voblasts', C Belorussia
155 Y3 Siachen Muztāgh ⛰ NE Pakistan
Siadehan see Tākestān
154 M13 Siāhān Range ⛰ W Pakistan
148 I1 Siāh Chashmeh Āžarbāyjān-e Bākhtarī, N Iran
155 W7 Siālkot Punjab, NE Pakistan
194 K12 Sialum Morobe, C PNG
Siam see Thailand
Siam, Gulf of see Thailand, Gulf of
Sian see Xi'an
Siang see Brahmaputra
Siangtan see Xiangtan
174 J5 Siantan, Pulau island Kepulauan Anambas, W Indonesia
56 H11 Siare, Río ≈ C Colombia
179 Rr13 Siargao Island island S Philippines
194 K12 Siassi Umboi Island, C PNG
117 D14 Siátista Dytikí Makedonía, N Greece
177 Ff4 Siatlai Chin State, W Burma
179 Q15 Siaton Negros, C Philippines
179 Q15 Siaton Point headland Negros, C Philippines
120 F11 Šiauliai Ger. Schaulen. Šiauliai, N Lithuania
175 S5 Siau, Pulau island N Indonesia
85 J15 Siavonga Southern, SE Zambia
Siazan' see Siyäzän
Sibah see As Sibah
109 N20 Sibari Calabria, S Italy
Sibata see Shibata
131 X6 Sibay Respublika Bashkortostan, W Russian Federation
95 M19 Sibbo Fin. Sipoo. Uusimaa, S Finland
114 D13 Šibenik It. Sebenico. Šibenik, S Croatia
114 E13 Šibenik off. Šibenska Županija. ◐ province S Croatia
Šibenska Županija see Šibenik
Siberia see Sibir'
Siberoet see Siberut, Pulau
173 Ff9 Siberut, Pulau prev. Siberoet. island Kepulauan Mentawai, W Indonesia
173 Ff9 Siberut, Selat strait W Indonesia
Sibetu see Shibetsu
155 P11 Sibi Baluchistān, SW Pakistan
194 F15 Sibidiri Western, SW PNG
126 K10 Sibir' var. Siberia. physical region N Russian Federation
81 F20 Sibiti La Lékoumou, S Congo
83 G21 Sibiti ≈ C Tanzania
118 I12 Sibiu Ger. Hermannstadt, Hung. Nagyszeben. Sibiu, C Romania
118 I11 Sibiu ◐ county C Romania
xxxvii W6 Sible Hedingham Essex, E England, UK
31 S11 Sibley Iowa, C USA
173 Ff6 Sibolga Sumatera, W Indonesia
173 Ff6 Sibolga, Teluk var. Teluk Tapanuli. bay Sumatera, W Indonesia
xxxix S7 Sibsey Lincolnshire, E England, UK
174 Ll6 Sibu Sarawak, East Malaysia
Sibukawa see Shibukawa
44 G2 Sibun ≈ E Belize
81 I15 Sibut prev. Fort-Sibut. Kémo, S Central African Republic
179 P17 Sibutu island SW Philippines
179 P17 Sibutu Passage passage SW Philippines
179 Q12 Sibuyan Island island C Philippines
179 Q12 Sibuyan Sea sea C Philippines
201 U1 Sibylla Island island N Marshall Islands
9 N16 Sicamous British Columbia, SW Canada
Sichelburger Gerbirge see Žumberačka Gora
178 H15 Sichon var. Ban Sichon, Si Chon. Nakhon Si Thammarat, SW Thailand
166 H9 Sichuan var. Chuan, Sichuan Sheng, Ssu-ch'uan, Szechuan, Szechwan. ◐ province C China
166 I9 Sichuan Pendi basin C China
Sichuan Sheng see Sichuan
105 S16 Sicie, Cap headland SE France
109 J24 Sicilia Eng. Sicily; anc. Trinacria. ◐ region Italy, C Mediterranean Sea
109 M24 Sicilia Eng. Sicily; anc. Trinacria. island Italy, C Mediterranean Sea
Sicilian Channel see Sicily, Strait of
Sicily see Sicilia
109 H24 Sicily, Strait of var. Sicilian Channel. strait C Mediterranean Sea
44 K5 Sico Tinto, Río var. Río Negro. ≈ NE Honduras
59 H16 Sicuani Cusco, S Peru
114 I10 Šid Serbia, NW Yugoslavia
117 A15 Sidári Kérkyra, Iónioi Nísoi, Greece, C Mediterranean Sea
174 Kk8 Sidas Borneo, C Indonesia
xxxvi I14 Sidbury Devon, SW England, UK
xxxvi G9 Sidcup Bexley, SE England, UK
100 O5 Siddeburen Groningen, NE Netherlands
160 D9 Siddhapur prev. Siddhpur, Sidhpur. Gujarāt, W India
Siddhpur see Siddhapur
161 I15 Siddipet Andhra Pradesh, C India
195 O17 Sideia Island island SE PNG
175 Pp12 Sidenreng, Danau ◎ Sulawesi, C Indonesia
79 N14 Sidéradougou SW Burkina
109 N23 Siderno Calabria, SW Italy
Siders see Sierre
160 L9 Sidhi Madhya Pradesh, C India
Sidhirókastron see Sidirókastro
Sidhpur see Siddhapur
Sīdī al Hānī', Sabkhat see Sidi el Hani, Sebkhet de
77 U7 Sīdī Barrānī NW Egypt
76 I6 Sidi Bel Abbès var. Sidi bel Abbès, Sidi-Bel-Abbès. NW Algeria
76 F7 Sidi-Bennour W Morocco
76 M6 Sidi Bouzid var. Gammouda, Sīdī Bu Zayd. C Tunisia
123 K12 Sidi el Hani, Sebkhet de var. Sabkhat Sīdī al Hānī'. salt flat NE Tunisia
76 D8 Sidi-Ifni SW Morocco
76 G6 Sidi-Kacem prev. Petitjean. N Morocco
116 G12 Sidirókastro prev. Sidhirókastron. Kentrikí Makedonía, NE Greece
xliii M17 Sidlaw Hills ⛰ E Scotland, UK
204 L12 Sidley, Mount ▲ Antarctica
xxxvi J14 Sidmouth Devon, SW England, UK
31 S16 Sidney Iowa, C USA
35 Y7 Sidney Montana, NW USA
30 J15 Sidney Nebraska, C USA
20 I11 Sidney New York, NE USA
33 R13 Sidney Ohio, N USA
25 T2 Sidney Lanier, Lake ⊠ Georgia, SE USA
Sidon see Saïda
126 Hh9 Sidorovsk Yamalo-Nenetskiy Avtonomnyy Okrug, N Russian Federation
Sidra/Sidra, Gulf of see Surt, Khalīj, N Libya
Sidra see Surt, N Libya
Sīdī Bu Zayd see Sidi Bouzid
Siebenbürgen see Transylvania
Sieben Dörfer see Săcele
112 O12 Siedlce Ger. Sedlez, Rus. Sesdlets. Siedlce, E Poland
112 N11 Siedlce off. Województwo Siedleckie, var. Syedlets, Ger. Sedlez. ◐ province E Poland
Siedleckie, Województwo see Siedlce
103 E16 Sieg ≈ W Germany
103 F16 Siegen Nordrhein-Westfalen, W Germany
111 X4 Sieghartskirchen Niederösterreich, E Austria
112 O11 Siemiatycze Białystok, E Poland
178 Jj11 Siĕmpang Stœng Trĕng, NE Cambodia
178 Ii12 Siĕmréab prev. Siemreap. Siĕmréab, NW Cambodia
Siemreap see Siĕmréab
108 G12 Siena Fr. Sienne; anc. Saena Julia. Toscana, C Italy
Sienne see Siena
94 K12 Sieppijärvi Lappi, NW Finland
112 J13 Sieradz Sieradz, C Poland
112 J13 Sieradz off. Województwo Sieradzkie. ◐ province C Poland
Sieradzkie, Województwo see Sieradz
112 K10 Sierpc Płock, C Poland
26 I9 Sierra Blanca Texas, SW USA
39 S14 Sierra Blanca Peak ▲ New Mexico, SW USA
37 P5 Sierra City California, W USA
65 I16 Sierra Colorada Río Negro, S Argentina
64 I13 Sierra del Nevado ▲ W Argentina
107 P13 Sierra de Segura ⛰ S Spain
65 J16 Sierra Grande Río Negro, E Argentina
78 G15 Sierra Leone off. Republic of Sierra Leone. ◆ republic W Africa
66 M13 Sierra Leone Basin undersea feature E Atlantic Ocean
68 K8 Sierra Leone Fracture Zone tectonic feature E Atlantic Ocean
Sierra Leone Ridge see Sierra Leone Rise
66 L13 Sierra Leone Rise var. Sierra Leone Ridge, Sierra Leone Schwelle. undersea feature E Atlantic Ocean
Sierra Leone Schwelle see Sierra Leone Rise
43 U17 Sierra Madre var. Sierra de Soconusco. ⛰ Guatemala/Mexico
179 Pp9 Sierra Madre ⛰ Luzon, N Philippines
39 R2 Sierra Madre ⛰ Colorado/Wyoming, C USA
1 H15 Sierra Madre del Sur ⛰ S Mexico
1 G13 Sierra Madre Occidental var. Western Sierra Madre. ⛰ C Mexico
1 H13 Sierra Madre Oriental var. Eastern Sierra Madre. ⛰ C Mexico
46 H8 Sierra Maestra ⛰ E Cuba
42 L7 Sierra Mojada Coahuila de Zaragoza, NE Mexico
107 O14 Sierra Nevada ⛰ S Spain
37 P6 Sierra Nevada ⛰ W USA
56 F4 Sierra Nevada de Santa Marta ⛰ NE Colombia
44 K5 Sierra Río Tinto ⛰ NE Honduras
26 J10 Sierra Vieja ⛰ Texas, SW USA
39 M16 Sierra Vista Arizona, SW USA
110 D10 Sierre Ger. Siders. Valais, SW Switzerland
38 L16 Sierrita Mountains ⛰ Arizona, SW USA
Siete Moai see Ahu Akivi
78 M15 Sifié W Ivory Coast
117 I21 Sífnos anc. Siphnos. island Kykládes, Greece, Aegean Sea
117 I21 Sifnou, Stenó strait SE Greece
Siga see Shiga
197 H15 Sigatoka prev. Singatoka. Viti Levu, W Fiji
105 P16 Sigean Aude, S France
xli W13 Sigglesthorne East Riding of Yorkshire, N England, UK
Sighet see Sighetu Marmației
118 I8 Sighetu Marmației var. Sighet, Sighetul Marmației, Hung. Máramarossziget. Maramureș, N Romania
Sighetul Marmației see Sighetu Marmației
118 I11 Sighișoara Ger. Schässburg, Hung. Segesvár. Mureș, C Romania
173 E3 Sigli Sumatera, W Indonesia
94 J1 Siglufjördhur Nordhurland Vestra, N Iceland
103 H23 Sigmaringen Baden-Württemberg, S Germany
103 N20 Signalberg ▲ SE Germany
38 I13 Signal Peak ▲ Arizona, SW USA
Signan see Xi'an
204 H1 Signy UK research station South Orkney Islands, Antarctica
31 X15 Sigourney Iowa, C USA
117 K17 Sígri, Ákra headland Lésvos, E Greece
Sigsbee Deep see Mexico Basin
49 N2 Sigsbee Escarpment undersea feature N Gulf of Mexico
58 C8 Sígsig Azuay, S Ecuador
97 O15 Sigtuna Stockholm, C Sweden
44 H6 Siguatepeque Comayagua, W Honduras
107 P7 Sigüenza Castilla-La Mancha, C Spain
107 R4 Sigües Aragón, NE Spain
78 K13 Siguiri Haute-Guinée, NE Guinea
120 G8 Sigulda Ger. Segewold. Rīga, C Latvia
Sihanoukville see Kâmpóng Saôm
110 G8 Sihlsee ◎ NW Switzerland
95 K18 Siikainen Turku-Pori, SW Finland
95 M16 Siilinjärvi Kuopio, C Finland
143 R15 Siirt var. Sert; anc. Tigranocerta. Siirt, SE Turkey
143 R15 Siirt var. Sert. ◐ province SE Turkey
195 Z15 Sikaiana var. Stewart Islands. island group W Solomon Islands
Sikandarabad see Secunderābād
158 J11 Sikandra Rao Uttar Pradesh, N India
8 M11 Sikanni Chief British Columbia, W Canada
8 M11 Sikanni Chief ≈ British Columbia, W Canada
158 H11 Sīkar Rājasthān, N India
78 M13 Sikasso Sikasso, S Mali
78 L13 Sikasso ◐ region SW Mali
178 Gg3 Sikaw Kachin State, C Burma
85 H14 Sikelenge Western, W Zambia
29 Y7 Sikeston Missouri, C USA
95 J14 Sikfors Norrbotten, N Sweden
127 O16 Sikhote-Alin', Khrebet ⛰ SE Russian Federation
Siking see Xi'an
117 J22 Síkinos island Kykládes, Greece, Aegean Sea
159 S11 Sikkim Tib. Denjong. ◐ state N India
113 I26 Siklós Baranya, SW Hungary
Sikoku see Shikoku
Sikoku Basin see Shikoku Basin
85 G14 Sikongo Western, W Zambia
Sikotu Ko see Shikotsu-ko
Sikouri/Sikoúrion see Sykoúri
126 L7 Siktyakh Respublika Sakha (Yakutiya), NE Russian Federation
120 D12 Silalė Šilalė, W Lithuania
108 G5 Silandro Ger. Schlanders. Trentino-Alto Adige, N Italy
43 N12 Silao Guanajuato, C Mexico
Silarius see Sele
179 Q13 Silay off. Silay City. Negros, C Philippines
159 W14 Silchar Assam, NE India
xxxix N9 Sileby Leicestershire, C England, UK
xl K11 Silecroft Cumbria, NW England, UK
110 G9 Silenen Uri, C Switzerland
23 T9 Siler City North Carolina, SE USA
35 U11 Silesia Montana, NW USA
112 F13 Silesia physical region SW Poland
76 K12 Silet S Algeria
151 R8 Siletī var. Selety. ≈ N Kazakhstan
Siletitengiz see Siletiteniz, Ozero
151 R7 Siletiteniz, Ozero Kaz. Siletitengiz. ◎ N Kazakhstan
180 H16 Silhouette island Inner Islands, SE Seychelles
142 I17 Silifke anc. Seleucia. İçel, S Turkey
Siliguri see Shiliguri
162 J10 Siling Co ◎ W China
Silinhot see Xilinhot
198 Aa7 Silisili ▲ Savai'i, C Western Samoa
116 M6 Silistra var. Silistria; anc. Durostorum. Razgradska Oblast, NE Bulgaria
Silistria see Silistra
142 D10 Silivri İstanbul, NW Turkey
96 L13 Siljan ◎ C Sweden
97 G22 Silkeborg Århus, C Denmark
110 M8 Sill ≈ W Austria
107 S10 Silla País Valenciano, E Spain
64 H3 Sillajguay, Cordillera ▲ N Chile
120 K3 Sillamäe Ger. Sillamäggi. Ida-Virumaa, NE Estonia
Sillamäggi see Sillamäe
Sillein see Žilina
111 P9 Sillian Tirol, W Austria
xl K7 Silloth Cumbria, NW England, UK
114 B10 Šilo Primorje-Gorski Kotar, NW Croatia
29 R9 Siloam Springs Arkansas, C USA
27 X10 Silsbee Texas, SW USA
xli Q13 Silsden Bradford, N England, UK
149 W15 Sīlūp, Rūd-e ≈ SE Iran
120 C12 Šilutė Ger. Heydekrug. Šilutė, W Lithuania
143 Q15 Silvan Diyarbakır, SE Turkey
110 J10 Silvaplana Graubünden, S Switzerland
Silva Porto see Kuito
60 H12 Silva, Recife do reef E Brazil
160 D12 Silvassa Dādra and Nagar Haveli, W India
31 X4 Silver Bay Minnesota, N USA
39 P15 Silver City New Mexico, SW USA
20 D10 Silver Creek New York, NE USA
39 N12 Silver Creek ≈ Arizona, SW USA
xli N11 Silverdale Lancashire, NW England, UK
29 P4 Silver Lake Kansas, C USA
34 I14 Silver Lake Oregon, NW USA
xliv G11 Silvermine Mountains hill range Tipperary, C Ireland
37 T9 Silver Peak Range ⛰ Nevada, W USA
23 W3 Silver Spring Maryland, NE USA
Silver State see Nevada
Silver State see Colorado

◆ Country
● Country Capital
◇ Dependent Territory
○ Dependent Territory Capital
◐ Administrative Region
✕ International Airport
▲ Mountain
⛰ Mountain Range
▲ Volcano
≈ River
◎ Lake
⊠ Reservoir

SILVERSTONE – SLOV"YANOSERBS'K

xxxix O13 **Silverstone** Northamptonshire, C England, UK
xxxvi H13 **Silverton** Devon, SW England, UK
39 Q7 **Silverton** Colorado, C USA
20 K16 **Silverton** New Jersey, NE USA
34 G11 **Silverton** Oregon, NW USA
27 N4 **Silverton** Texas, SW USA
106 G14 **Silves** Faro, S Portugal
56 D12 **Silvia** Cauca, SW Colombia
110 J9 **Silvrettagruppe** ▲▲ Austria/Switzerland
xlii H4 **Silwick** Shetland Islands, NE Scotland, UK
Sily-Vajdej *see* Vulcan
110 L7 **Silz** Tirol, W Austria
180 I13 **Sima** Anjouan, SE Comoros
Simabara *see* Shimabara
Simada *see* Shimada
85 H15 **Simakando** Western, W Zambia
Simane *see* Shimane
121 L20 **Simanichy** *Rus.* Simonichi. Homyel'skaya Voblasts', SE Belorussia
166 F14 **Simao** Yunnan, SW China
159 P12 **Simara** Central, C Nepal
12 I8 **Simard, Lac** ◎ Québec, SE Canada
142 D13 **Simav** Kütahya, W Turkey
142 D13 **Simav Çayı** ≈ NW Turkey
81 L18 **Simba** Haut-Zaïre, N Zaire
194 H11 **Simbai** Madang, N PNG
195 O9 **Simberi Island** *island* Tabar Islands, N PNG
Simbirsk *see* Ul'yanovsk
12 F17 **Simcoe** Ontario, S Canada
12 H14 **Simcoe, Lake** ◎ Ontario, S Canada
82 J11 **Sīmēn** ▲▲ N Ethiopia
116 K11 **Simeonovgrad** *prev.* Maritsa. Khaskovska Oblast, S Bulgaria
118 G11 **Simeria** *Ger.* Pischk, *Hung.* Piski. Hunedoara, W Romania
109 L24 **Simeto** ≈ Sicilia, Italy, C Mediterranean Sea
173 E5 **Simeulue, Pulau** *island* NW Indonesia
119 T13 **Simferopol'** Respublika Krym, S Ukraine
119 T13 **Simferopol'** ✕ Respublika Krym, S Ukraine
Simi *see* Sými
158 M9 **Simikot** Far Western, NW Nepal
56 F7 **Simití** Bolívar, N Colombia
116 G11 **Simitli** Sofiyska Oblast, SW Bulgaria
37 S15 **Simi Valley** California, W USA
Simizu *see* Shimizu
Simla *see* Shimla
Şimlăul Silvaniei/Şimleul Silvaniei *see* Şimleu Silvaniei
118 G9 **Şimleu Silvaniei** *Hung.* Szilágysomlyó; *prev.* Şimlăul Silvaniei, Şimleul Silvaniei. Sălaj, NW Romania
Simmer *see* Simmerbach
103 E19 **Simmerbach** *var.* Simmer. ≈ W Germany
103 F18 **Simmern** Rheinland-Pfalz, W Germany
24 I7 **Simmesport** Louisiana, S USA
121 F14 **Simnas** Alytus, S Lithuania
94 L13 **Simo** Lappi, NW Finland
Simoda *see* Shimoda
Simodate *see* Shimodate
94 M13 **Simojärvi** ◎ N Finland
94 L13 **Simojoki** ≈ NW Finland
43 U15 **Simojovel** *var.* Simojovel de Allende. Chiapas, SE Mexico
Simojovel de Allende *see* Simojovel
58 B7 **Simon Bolivar** *var.* Guayaquil. ✕ (Guayaquil) Guayas, W Ecuador
56 L5 **Simón Bolívar** ✕ (Caracas) Distrito Federal, N Venezuela
Simonichi *see* Simanichy
12 M12 **Simon, Lac** ◎ Québec, SE Canada
Simonoseki *see* Shimonoseki
Šimonovany *see* Partizánske
xxxvi G11 **Simonsbath** Somerset, SW England, UK
Simonstad *see* Simon's Town
85 E26 **Simon's Town** *var.* Simonstad. Western Cape, SW South Africa
Simony *see* Partizánske
Simotuma *see* Shimotsuma
173 F6 **Simpangkaman, Sungai** ≈ Sumatera, NW Indonesia
173 F5 **Simpangkiri, Sungai** ≈ Sumatera, NW Indonesia
Simpeln *see* Simplon
101 M18 **Simpelveld** Limburg, SE Netherlands
110 E11 **Simplon** *var.* Simpeln. Valais, SW Switzerland
110 E11 **Simplon Pass** *pass* S Switzerland
108 C6 **Simplon Tunnel** *tunnel* Italy/Switzerland
Simpson *see* Fort Simpson
190 G1 **Simpson Desert** *desert* Northern Territory/South Australia
8 J9 **Simpson Peak** ▲ British Columbia, W Canada
15 L3 **Simpson Peninsula** *peninsula* Northwest Territories, NE Canada
23 P11 **Simpsonville** South Carolina, SE USA
97 L23 **Simrishamn** Kristianstad, S Sweden
127 Pp15 **Simushir, Ostrov** *island* Kuril'skiye Ostrova, SE Russian Federation
Sinā'/Sinai Peninsula *see* Sinai
173 Ee6 **Sinabang** Sumatera, W Indonesia
83 N15 **Sina Dhaqa** Galguduud, C Somalia
77 X8 **Sinai** *var.* Sinai Peninsula, *Ar.* Shibh Jazīrat Sīnā', Sīnā'. *physical region* NE Egypt
118 J12 **Sinaia** Prahova, SE Romania
196 B16 **Sinajana** C Guam
42 H8 **Sinaloa** ◐ *state* C Mexico
56 H4 **Sinamaica** Zulia, NW Venezuela
169 X14 **Sinan-ni** SE North Korea
Sinano Gawa *see* Shinano-gawa
Sināwan *see* Sīnāwin
77 N8 **Sīnāwin** *var.* Sināwan. NW Libya
85 J16 **Sinazongwe** Southern, S Zambia
177 Ff6 **Sinbaungwe** Magwe, W Burma
177 Ff5 **Sinbyugyun** Magwe, W Burma
56 E6 **Since** Sucre, NW Colombia
56 E6 **Sincelejo** Sucre, NW Colombia
177 F5 **Sinchaingbyin** *var.* Zullapara. Arakan State, W Burma
25 U4 **Sinclair, Lake** ⊡ Georgia, SE USA
8 M14 **Sinclair Mills** British Columbia, SW Canada
178 Mm15 **Sin Cowe East Island** *island* S Spratly Islands
178 Mm15 **Sin Cowe Island** *island* SW Spratly Islands
155 Q14 **Sind** *var.* Sindh. ◐ *province* SE Pakistan
160 I8 **Sind** ≈ N India
97 H19 **Sindal** Nordjylland, N Denmark
179 Q15 **Sindañgan** Mindanao, S Philippines
81 D19 **Sindara** Ngounié, W Gabon
158 E13 **Sindari** *prev.* Sindri. Rājasthān, N India
175 Q16 **Sindeh, Teluk** *bay* Nusa Tenggara, C Indonesia
116 N8 **Sindel** Varnenska Oblast, NE Bulgaria
103 H22 **Sindelfingen** Baden-Württemberg, SW Germany
161 G16 **Sindgi** Karnātaka, C India
Sindh *see* Sind
120 G5 **Sindi** *Ger.* Zintenhof. Pärnumaa, SW Estonia
142 C13 **Sındırgı** Balıkesir, W Turkey
79 N14 **Sindou** SW Burkina
Sindri *see* Sindari
155 T9 **Sind Sāgar Doāb** *desert* E Pakistan
130 M11 **Sinegorskiy** Rostovskaya Oblast', SW Russian Federation
127 O9 **Sinegor'ye** Magadanskaya Oblast', E Russian Federation
116 O12 **Sinekli** İstanbul, NW Turkey
106 F12 **Sines** Setúbal, S Portugal
106 F12 **Sines, Cabo de** *headland* S Portugal
94 L12 **Sinettä** Lappi, NW Finland
195 P11 **Sinewit, Mount** ▲ New Britain, C PNG
82 G11 **Singa** *var.* Sinja, Sinjah. Sinnar, E Sudan
80 J12 **Singako** Moyen-Chari, S Chad
Singan *see* Xi'an
174 I7 **Singapore** ● (Singapore) S Singapore
174 I7 **Singapore** *off.* Republic of Singapore. ◆ *republic* SE Asia
174 I7 **Singapore Strait** *var.* Strait of Singapore, *Mal.* Selat Singapura. *strait* Indonesia/Singapore
Singapore, Strait of/Singapura, Selat *see* Singapore Strait
175 N16 **Singaraja** Bali, C Indonesia
Singatoka *see* Sigatoka
178 H10 **Sing Buri** *var.* Singhaburi. Sing Buri, C Thailand
103 H24 **Singen** Baden-Württemberg, S Germany
Singeorgiu de Pădure *see* Sângeorgiu de Pădure
Singeorz-Băi/Singeroz Băi *see* Sângeorz-Băi
118 M9 **Singerei** *var.* Sângerei; *prev.* Lazovsk. N Moldavia
Singhaburi *see* Sing Buri
83 H21 **Singida** Singida, C Tanzania
83 G22 **Singida** ◐ *region* C Tanzania
Singidunum *see* Beograd
177 G2 **Singkaling Hkamti** Sagaing, N Burma
175 Pp12 **Singkang** Sulawesi, C Indonesia
174 Gg8 **Singkarak, Danau** ◎ Sumatera, W Indonesia
174 K7 **Singkawang** Borneo, C Indonesia
174 I8 **Singkep, Pulau** *island* Kepulauan Lingga, W Indonesia
173 F6 **Singkilbaru** Sumatera, W Indonesia
xxxvii R13 **Singleton** West Sussex, SE England, UK
191 T7 **Singleton** New South Wales, SE Australia
Singora *see* Songkhla
Singû *see* Shingū
Sining *see* Xining
109 D17 **Siniscola** Sardegna, Italy, C Mediterranean Sea
115 F14 **Sinj** Split-Dalmacija, SE Croatia
Sinja/Sinjah *see* Singa
Sinjajevina *see* Sinjavina
145 P3 **Sinjār** NW Iraq
145 P2 **Sinjār, Jabal** ▲ N Iraq
115 K15 **Sinjavina** *var.* Sinjajevina. ▲▲ SW Yugoslavia
82 I7 **Sinkat** Red Sea, NE Sudan
Sinkiang/Sinkiang Uighur Autonomous Region *see* Xinjiang Uygur Zizhiqu
Sinmartin *see* Târnăveni
169 V13 **Sinmi-do** *island* NW North Korea
Sinminato *see* Shinminato
103 I18 **Sinn** ≈ C Germany
Sinnamarie *see* Sinnamary
57 Y9 **Sinnamary** *var.* Sinnamarie. N French Guiana
Sinn'anyô *see* Shinnanyō
82 G11 **Sinnar** ◐ *state* E Sudan
Sinneh *see* Sanandaj
20 E13 **Sinnemahoning Creek** ≈ Pennsylvania, NE USA
Sînnicolau Mare *see* Sânnicolau Mare
xli U11 **Sinnington** North Yorkshire, N England, UK
Sino/Sinoe *see* Greenville
Sinoe, Lacul *see* Sinoie, Lacul
Sinoia *see* Chinhoyi
119 N14 **Sinoie, Lacul** *prev.* Lacul Sinoe. *lagoon* SE Romania
61 H16 **Sinop** Mato Grosso, W Brazil
142 K10 **Sinop** *anc.* Sinope. Sinop, N Turkey
142 J10 **Sinop** ◐ *province* N Turkey
142 K10 **Sinop Burnu** *headland* N Turkey
Sinope *see* Sinop
169 Y12 **Sinp'o** E North Korea
103 H20 **Sinsheim** Baden-Württemberg, SW Germany
Sinsiro *see* Shinshiro
Sintana *see* Sântana
174 L8 **Sintang** Borneo, C Indonesia
101 F14 **Sint Annaland** Zeeland, SW Netherlands
100 L5 **Sint Annaparochie** Friesland, N Netherlands
47 V9 **Sint Eustatius** *Eng.* Saint Eustatius. *island* N Netherlands Antilles
101 G19 **Sint-Genesius-Rode** *Fr.* Rhode-Saint-Genèse. Vlaams Brabant, C Belgium
101 F16 **Sint-Gillis-Waas** Oost-Vlaanderen, N Belgium
101 H17 **Sint-Katelijne-Waver** Antwerpen, C Belgium
101 E18 **Sint-Lievens-Houtem** Oost-Vlaanderen, NW Belgium
47 V9 **Sint Maarten** *Eng.* Saint Martin. *island* N Netherlands Antilles
101 F14 **Sint Maartensdijk** Zeeland, SW Netherlands
101 L19 **Sint-Martens-Voeren** *Fr.* Fouron-Saint-Martin. Limburg, NE Belgium
101 J14 **Sint-Michielsgestel** Noord-Brabant, S Netherlands
Sînt-Miclăuş *see* Gheorgheni
47 O16 **Sint Nicholaas** S Aruba
101 F16 **Sint-Niklaas** *Fr.* Saint-Nicolas. Oost-Vlaanderen, N Belgium
101 K14 **Sint-Oedenrode** Noord-Brabant, S Netherlands
27 T14 **Sinton** Texas, SW USA
101 G14 **Sint Philipsland** Zeeland, SW Netherlands
101 G19 **Sint-Pieters-Leeuw** Vlaams Brabant, C Belgium
106 E11 **Sintra** *prev.* Cintra. Lisboa, W Portugal
101 J18 **Sint-Truiden** *Fr.* Saint-Trond. Limburg, NE Belgium
101 H14 **Sint Willebrord** Noord-Brabant, S Netherlands
169 V13 **Sinŭiju** W North Korea
82 P13 **Sinujiif** Nugaal, NE Somalia
Sinus Aelaniticus *see* Aqaba, Gulf of
Sinus Gallicus *see* Lion, Golfe du
Sinyang *see* Xinyang
Sinyavka *see* Sinyawka
121 I18 **Sinyawka** *Rus.* Sinyavka. Minskaya Voblasts', SW Belorussia
126 Ll11 **Sinyaya** ≈ NE Russian Federation
Sinying *see* Hsinying
Sinyukha *see* Synyukha
Sinzi-ko *see* Shinji-ko
Sinzyô *see* Shinjō
113 I24 **Sió** ≈ W Hungary
179 Q16 **Siocon** Mindanao, S Philippines
Siogama *see* Shiogama
85 G15 **Sioma** Western, SW Zambia
110 D11 **Sion** *Ger.* Sitten; *anc.* Sedunum. Valais, SW Switzerland
xlii G9 **Sionascaig, Loch** ◎ NW Scotland, UK
xliv I3 **Sion Mills** Strabane, W Northern Ireland, UK
105 O11 **Sioule** ≈ C France
31 S12 **Sioux Center** Iowa, C USA
31 R13 **Sioux City** Iowa, C USA
31 R11 **Sioux Falls** South Dakota, N USA
10 B11 **Sioux Lookout** Ontario, S Canada
31 T12 **Sioux Rapids** Iowa, C USA
Sioux State *see* North Dakota
Sioziri *see* Shiojiri
179 Q14 **Sipalay** Negros, C Philippines
57 V11 **Sipaliwini** ◐ *district* S Surinam
47 U15 **Siparia** Trinidad, Trinidad and Tobago
Siphnos *see* Sífnos
169 V11 **Siping** *var.* Ssu-p'ing, Szeping; *prev.* Ssu-p'ing-chieh. Jilin, NE China
9 X12 **Sipiwesk** Manitoba, C Canada
9 W13 **Sipiwesk Lake** ◎ Manitoba, C Canada
205 O11 **Siple Coast** *physical region* Antarctica
204 K12 **Siple Island** *island* Antarctica
204 K13 **Siple, Mount** ▲ Siple Island, Antarctica
Sipoo *see* Sibbo
114 G12 **Šipovo** W Bosnia and Herzegovina
25 O4 **Sipsey River** ≈ Alabama, S USA
173 Ff10 **Sipura, Pulau** *island* W Indonesia
0 G16 **Siqueiros Fracture Zone** *tectonic feature* E Pacific Ocean
44 L10 **Siquia, Río** ≈ SE Nicaragua
179 Qq14 **Siquijor Island** *island* C Philippines
45 N13 **Siquirres** Limón, E Costa Rica
56 J5 **Siquisique** Lara, N Venezuela
161 G19 **Sira** Karnātaka, W India
97 D16 **Sira** ≈ S Norway
178 Hh12 **Si Racha** *var.* Ban Si Racha, Si Racha. Chon Buri, S Thailand
109 L25 **Siracusa** *Eng.* Syracuse. Sicilia, Italy, C Mediterranean Sea
Sirajganj *see* Shirajganj Ghat
Sirakawa *see* Shirakawa
9 N14 **Sir Alexander, Mount** ▲ British Columbia, W Canada
143 O12 **Şiran** Gümüşhane, NE Turkey
79 Q12 **Sirba** ≈ E Burkina
149 O17 **Şīr Banī Yās** *island* W UAE
97 D17 **Sirdalsvatnet** ◎ S Norway
Sir Darya/Sirdaryo *see* Syr Darya
153 O11 **Sirdaryo Wiloyati** *Rus.* Syrdar'inskaya Oblast'. ◐ *province* E Uzbekistan
Sir Donald Sangster International Airport *see* Sangster
194 H13 **Sirebi** ≈ S PNG
189 S3 **Sir Edward Pellew Group** *island group* Northern Territory, NE Australia
118 K8 **Siret** *Ger.* Sereth, *Hung.* Szeret. Suceava, N Romania
118 K8 **Siret** *var.* Siretul, *Ger.* Sereth, *Rus.* Seret, *Ukr.* Siret. ≈ Romania/Ukraine
Siretul *see* Siret
146 K3 **Sirḥān, Wādī as** *dry watercourse* Jordan/Saudi Arabia
158 I8 **Sirhind** Punjab, N India
118 F11 **Şiria** *Ger.* Schiria. Arad, W Romania
Siria *see* Syria
149 S14 **Sīrīk** Hormozgān, SE Iran
178 Hh8 **Sirikit Reservoir** ◎ N Thailand
60 K12 **Sirituba, Ilha** *island* NE Brazil
176 Ww11 **Siriwo** ≈ Irian Jaya, E Indonesia
149 R11 **Sīrjān** *prev.* Sa'īdābād. Kermān, S Iran
190 H9 **Sir Joseph Banks Group** *island group* South Australia
94 K11 **Sirkka** Lappi, N Finland
Sirna *see* Sýrna
143 R16 **Şırnak** Şırnak, SE Turkey
143 S16 **Şırnak** ◐ *province* SE Turkey
Siroisi *see* Shiroishi
161 J14 **Sironcha** Mahārāshtra, C India
Sirone *see* Shirone
Síros *see* Sýros
Sirotino *see* Sirotsina
120 M12 **Sirotsina** *Rus.* Sirotino. Vitsyebskaya Voblasts', N Belorussia
158 H9 **Sirsa** Haryāna, NW India
181 Y17 **Sir Seewoosagur Ramgoolam** ✕ (Port Louis) SE Mauritius
161 E18 **Sirsi** Karnātaka, W India
Sirte *see* Surt
190 A2 **Sir Thomas, Mount** ▲ South Australia
Sirti, Gulf of *see* Surt, Khalīj
148 J5 **Sīrvān, Rūdkhāneh-ye** *var.* Nahr Diyālá, Sirwan. ≈ Iran/Iraq *see also* Diyālá, Nahr
120 H13 **Širvintos** Širvintos, SE Lithuania
Sirwan *see* Diyālá, Nahr/Sīrvān, Rūdkhāneh-ye
9 N15 **Sir Wilfrid Laurier, Mount** ▲ British Columbia, SW Canada
12 M10 **Sir-Wilfrid, Mont** ▲ Québec, SE Canada
Sisačko-Moslavačka Županija *see* Sisak-Moslavina
114 E9 **Sisak** *var.* Siscia, *Ger.* Sissek, *Hung.* Sziszek; *anc.* Segestica. Sisak-Moslavina, C Croatia
178 J10 **Si Sa Ket** *var.* Sisaket, Sri Saket. Si Sa Ket, E Thailand
114 E9 **Sisak-Moslavina** *off.* Sisačko-Moslavačka Županija. ◐ *province* C Croatia
178 H8 **Si Satchanala** Sukhothai, NW Thailand
Siscia *see* Sisak
176 W10 **Sisember** Irian Jaya, E Indonesia
85 G22 **Sishen** Northern Cape, NW South Africa
143 V13 **Sisian** SE Armenia
207 N13 **Sisimiut** *var.* Holsteinborg, Holsteinsborg, Holstenborg, Holstensborg. S Greenland
32 M1 **Siskiwit Bay** *lake bay* Michigan, N USA
36 L1 **Siskiyou Mountains** ▲▲ California/Oregon, W USA
178 I12 **Sisŏphŏn** Bătdâmbâng, NW Cambodia
110 E7 **Sissach** Basel-Land, NW Switzerland
194 F9 **Sissano** Sandaun, NW PNG
Sissek *see* Sisak
31 R7 **Sisseton** South Dakota, N USA
149 W9 **Sīstān, Daryācheh-ye** *var.* Daryācheh-ye Hāmūn, Hāmūn-e Şāberī. ◎ Afghanistan/Iran *see also* Şāberī, Hāmūn-e
149 V12 **Sīstān va Balūchestān** *off.* Ostān-e Sīstān va Balūchestān, *var.* Balūchestān va Sīstān. ◐ *province* SE Iran
105 T14 **Sisteron** Alpes-de-Haute-Provence, SE France
34 H13 **Sisters** Oregon, NW USA
67 G15 **Sisters Peak** ▲ N Ascension Island
23 R3 **Sistersville** West Virginia, NE USA
Sistova *see* Svishtov
Sitakund *see* Sitakunda
159 V16 **Sitakunda** *var.* Sitakund. Chittagong, SE Bangladesh
159 P12 **Sītāmarhi** Bihār, N India
158 L11 **Sītāpur** Uttar Pradesh, N India
Sitaş Cristuru *see* Cristuru Secuiesc
117 L25 **Siteía** *var.* Sitía. Kríti, Greece, E Mediterranean Sea
107 V6 **Sitges** Cataluña, NE Spain
117 H15 **Sithonía** *peninsula* NE Greece
Sitía *see* Siteía
56 F4 **Sitionuevo** Magdalena, N Colombia
41 X13 **Sitka** Baranof Island, Alaska, USA
41 Q15 **Sitkinak Island** *island* Trinity Islands, Alaska, USA
177 G7 **Sittang** *var.* Sittoung. ≈ S Burma
101 L17 **Sittard** Limburg, SE Netherlands
Sitten *see* Sion
110 H7 **Sitter** ≈ NW Switzerland
111 U10 **Sittersdorf** Kärnten, S Austria
xxxvii X10 **Sittingbourne** Kent, SE England, UK
Sittoung *see* Sittang
177 F6 **Sittwe** *var.* Akyab. Arakan State, W Burma
174 Mm15 **Situbondo** *prev.* Sitoebondo. Jawa, C Indonesia
44 L8 **Siuna** Región Autónoma Atlántico Norte, NE Nicaragua
159 R15 **Siuri** West Bengal, NE India
Siut *see* Asyūt
126 M15 **Sivaki** Amurskaya Oblast', SE Russian Federation
142 M13 **Sivas** *anc.* Sebastia, Sebaste. Sivas, C Turkey
142 M13 **Sivas** ◐ *province* C Turkey
143 O15 **Siverek** Şanlıurfa, S Turkey
119 X6 **Sivers'k** Donets'ka Oblast', E Ukraine
128 G13 **Siverskiy** Leningradskaya Oblast', NW Russian Federation
119 X6 **Sivers'kyy Donets'** *Rus.* Severskiy Donets. ≈ Russian Federation/Ukraine *see also* Severskiy Donets
129 W5 **Sivomaskinskiy** Respublika Komi, NW Russian Federation
142 G13 **Sivrihisar** Eskişehir, W Turkey
101 F22 **Sivry** Hainaut, S Belgium
127 Pp9 **Sivuchiy, Mys** *headland* E Russian Federation
77 U9 **Siwa** *var.* Sīwah. NW Egypt
Sīwah *see* Siwa
158 J9 **Siwalik Range** *var.* Shiwālik Range. ▲▲ India/Nepal
159 O13 **Siwān** Bihār, N India
45 O14 **Sixaola, Río** ≈ Costa Rica/Panama
Six Counties, The *see* Northern Ireland
105 T16 **Six-Fours-les-Plages** Var, SE France
167 Q7 **Sixian** *var.* Si Xian. Anhui, E China
xliv F11 **Sixmilebridge** Clare, W Ireland
24 J9 **Six Mile Lake** ◎ Louisiana, S USA
xxxvii N12 **Sixpenny Handley** Dorset, S England, UK
145 V3 **Sīyāh Gūz** E Iraq
161 L25 **Siyambalanduwa** Uva Province, SE Sri Lanka
143 Y10 **Siyäzän** *Rus.* Siazan'. NE Azerbaijan
Sizebolu *see* Sozopol
xxxix Y12 **Sizewell** Suffolk, E England, UK
Sizuoka *see* Shizuoka
Sjar *see* Sääre
115 L15 **Sjenica** *Turk.* Seniça. Serbia, SW Yugoslavia
96 G11 **Sjoa** ≈ S Norway
97 K23 **Sjöbo** Malmöhus, S Sweden
97 I24 **Sjælland** *Eng.* Zealand, *Ger.* Seeland. *island* E Denmark
96 E9 **Sjøholt** Møre og Romsdal, S Norway
94 O1 **Sjuøyane** *island group* N Svalbard
Skadar *see* Shkodër
Skadarsko Jezero *see* Scutari, Lake
119 R11 **Skadovs'k** Khersons'ka Oblast', S Ukraine
94 I2 **Skagaströnd** *prev.* Höfdhakaupstadhur. Nordhurland Vestra, N Iceland
97 H19 **Skagen** Nordjylland, N Denmark
Skagerak *see* Skagerrak
97 L16 **Skagern** ◎ C Sweden
207 T17 **Skagerrak** *var.* Skagerak. *channel* N Europe
96 G12 **Skaget** ▲ S Norway
34 H7 **Skagit River** ≈ Washington, NW USA
41 W12 **Skagway** Alaska, USA
94 K8 **Skaidi** Finnmark, N Norway
xlii N4 **Skaill** Orkney Islands, N Scotland, UK
117 F21 **Skála** Pelopónnisos, S Greece
118 K6 **Skalat** *Pol.* Skałat. Ternopil's'ka Oblast', W Ukraine
97 J22 **Skälderviken** *inlet* Denmark/Sweden
94 I12 **Skalka** ◎ N Sweden
116 I12 **Skalotí** Anatolikí Makedonía kai Thráki, NE Greece
97 G22 **Skanderborg** Århus, C Denmark
97 K22 **Skåne** *prev. Eng.* Scania. *cultural region* S Sweden
77 N6 **Skanès** ✕ (Sousse) E Tunisia
97 C15 **Skånevik** Hordaland, S Norway
97 M18 **Skänninge** Östergötland, S Sweden
97 J23 **Skanör** Malmöhus, S Sweden
117 H17 **Skantzoúra** *island* Vóreioi Sporádes, Greece, Aegean Sea
97 K18 **Skara** Skaraborg, S Sweden
97 J18 **Skaraborg** ◐ *county* S Sweden
97 M17 **Skärblacka** Östergötland, S Sweden
xliii J22 **Skares** East Ayrshire, W Scotland, UK
97 I18 **Skärhamn** Göteborg och Bohus, S Sweden
97 I14 **Skarnes** Hedmark, S Norway
121 M21 **Skarodnaye** *Rus.* Skorodnoye. Homyel'skaya Voblasts', SE Belorussia
xli H4 **Skarpigarth** Shetland Islands, NE Scotland, UK
112 I8 **Skarszewy** *Ger.* Schöneck. Gdańsk, NW Poland
113 M14 **Skarżysko-Kamienna** Kielce, SE Poland
97 K16 **Skattkärr** Värmland, C Sweden
120 D12 **Skaudvilė** Tauragė, SW Lithuania
94 J12 **Skaulo** Norrbotten, N Sweden
113 K17 **Skawina** Kraków, S Poland
8 K12 **Skeena** ≈ British Columbia, SW Canada
8 J11 **Skeena Mountains** ▲▲ British Columbia, W Canada
xxxix T6 **Skegness** Lincolnshire, E England, UK
94 J4 **Skeidharársandur** *coast* S Iceland
95 J15 **Skellefteå** Västerbotten, N Sweden
95 I14 **Skellefteälven** ≈ N Sweden
95 J15 **Skelleftehamn** Västerbotten, N Sweden
27 O2 **Skellytown** Texas, SW USA
xli N16 **Skelmersdale** Lancashire, NW England, UK
xliii H20 **Skelmorlie** North Ayrshire, W Scotland, UK
xl M8 **Skelton** Cumbria, NW England, UK
xli U9 **Skelton** Redcar and Cleveland, N England, UK
97 J19 **Skene** Älvsborg, S Sweden
xlii J6 **Skerray** Highland, N Scotland, UK
xliv L8 **Skerries** *Ir.* Na Sceirí. Dublin, E Ireland
97 H15 **Ski** Akershus, S Norway
117 G17 **Skiáthos** Skiáthos, Vóreioi Sporádes, Greece, Aegean Sea
117 G17 **Skiáthos** *island* Vóreioi Sporádes, Greece, Aegean Sea
29 P9 **Skiatook** Oklahoma, C USA
29 P9 **Skiatook Lake** ⊡ Oklahoma, C USA
xliv D15 **Skibbereen** *Ir.* An Sciobairín. Cork, SW Ireland
94 I9 **Skibotn** Troms, N Norway
121 F16 **Skidal'** *Rus.* Skidel'. Hrodzyenskaya Voblasts', W Belorussia
xl L8 **Skiddaw** ▲ NW England, UK
Skidel' *see* Skidal'
27 T14 **Skidmore** Texas, SW USA
97 G16 **Skien** Telemark, S Norway
Skiermûntseach *see* Schiermonnikoog
112 L12 **Skierniewice** Skierniewice, C Poland
112 K12 **Skierniewice** *off.* Województwo Skierniewickie. ◐ *province* C Poland
Skierniewickie, Województwo *see* Skierniewice
76 L5 **Skikda** *prev.* Philippeville. NE Algeria
32 M16 **Skillet Fork** ≈ Illinois, N USA
97 L19 **Skillingaryd** Jönköping, S Sweden
xxxix P8 **Skillington** Lincolnshire, E England, UK
117 B19 **Skinári, Ákra** *headland* Zákynthos, Iónioi Nísoi, Greece, C Mediterranean Sea
xl K7 **Skinburness** Cumbria, NW England, UK
97 M15 **Skinnskatteberg** Västmanland, C Sweden
xliii G20 **Skipness** Argyll and Bute, W Scotland, UK
xli S12 **Skipsea** East Riding of Yorkshire, N England, UK
xli Q13 **Skipton** North Yorkshire, N England, UK
190 M12 **Skipton** Victoria, SE Australia
xli S11 **Skipton-on-Swale** North Yorkshire, N England, UK
xli T13 **Skipwith** North Yorkshire, N England, UK
xliii L21 **Skirling** The Borders, S Scotland, UK
Skiropoula *see* Skyropoúla
Skíros *see* Skýros
97 F21 **Skive** Viborg, NW Denmark
96 F11 **Skjåk** Oppland, S Norway
94 K2 **Skjálfandafljót** ≈ C Iceland
97 F22 **Skjern** Ringkøbing, W Denmark
97 F22 **Skjern Å** *var.* Skjern Aa. ≈ W Denmark
Skjern Aa *see* Skjern Å
94 G12 **Skjerstad** Nordland, C Norway
94 J8 **Skjervøy** Troms, N Norway
94 I10 **Skjold** Troms, N Norway
113 I17 **Skoczów** Bielsko-Biała, S Poland
97 I24 **Skælskør** Vestsjælland, E Denmark
111 T11 **Škofja Loka** *Ger.* Bischoflack. NW Slovenia
96 N12 **Skog** Gävleborg, C Sweden
97 K16 **Skoghall** Värmland, C Sweden
xxxv A14 **Skokholm Island** *island* SW Wales, UK
33 N10 **Skokie** Illinois, N USA
118 H6 **Skole** L'vivs'ka Oblast', W Ukraine
117 D19 **Skóllis** ▲ S Greece
xxxv A13 **Skomer Island** *island* SW Wales, UK
178 J13 **Skon** Kâmpóng Cham, C Cambodia
117 H17 **Skópelos** Skópelos, Vóreioi Sporádes, Greece, Aegean Sea
117 H17 **Skópelos** *island* Vóreioi Sporádes, Greece, Aegean Sea
130 L5 **Skopin** Ryazanskaya Oblast', W Russian Federation
115 N18 **Skopje** *var.* Üsküb, *Turk.* Üsküp; *prev.* Skoplje, *anc.* Scupi. ● (FYR Macedonia) N FYR Macedonia
115 O18 **Skopje** ✕ N FYR Macedonia
Skoplje *see* Skopje
112 I8 **Skórcz** *Ger.* Skurz. Gdańsk, N Poland
Skorodnoye *see* Skarodnaye
95 H16 **Skorped** Västernorrland, C Sweden
97 G21 **Skørping** Nordjylland, N Denmark
97 K18 **Skövde** Skaraborg, S Sweden
126 Ll14 **Skovorodino** Amurskaya Oblast', SE Russian Federation
21 Q6 **Skowhegan** Maine, NE USA
9 W15 **Skownan** Manitoba, S Canada
96 H13 **Skreia** Oppland, S Norway
Skripón *see* Orchómenos
120 H9 **Skrīveri** Aizkraukle, S Latvia
120 J11 **Skrudaliena** Daugvapils, SE Latvia
120 D9 **Skrunda** Kuldīga, W Latvia
97 C16 **Skudeneshavn** Rogaland, S Norway
85 L20 **Skukuza** Mpumalanga, NE South Africa
99 B22 **Skull** *Ir.* An Scoil. SW Ireland
24 L3 **Skuna River** ≈ Mississippi, S USA
31 X15 **Skunk River** ≈ Iowa, C USA
120 C10 **Skuodas** *Ger.* Schoden, *Pol.* Szkudy. Skuodas, NW Lithuania
97 K23 **Skurup** Malmöhus, S Sweden
Skurz *see* Skórcz
116 H8 **Skŭt** ≈ NW Bulgaria
96 O13 **Skutskär** Uppsala, C Sweden
Skvira *see* Skvyra
119 O5 **Skvyra** *Rus.* Skvira. Kyyivs'ka Oblast', N Ukraine
41 Q11 **Skwentna** Alaska, USA
112 E11 **Skwierzyna** *Ger.* Schwerin. Gorzów, W Poland
xlii D12 **Skye, Isle of** *island* NW Scotland, UK
34 I8 **Skykomish** Washington, NW USA
Skylge *see* Terschelling
65 F19 **Skyring, Peninsula** *peninsula* S Chile
65 H24 **Skyring, Seno** *inlet* S Chile
117 H17 **Skyropoúla** *var.* Skiropoula. *island* Vóreioi Sporádes, Greece, Aegean Sea
117 I17 **Skýros** *var.* Skíros. Skýros, Vóreioi Sporádes, Greece, Aegean Sea
117 I17 **Skýros** *var.* Skíros; *anc.* Scyros. *island* Vóreioi Sporádes, Greece, Aegean Sea
120 J12 **Slabodka** *Rus.* Slobodka. Vitsyebskaya Voblasts', NW Belorussia
97 I23 **Slagelse** Vestsjælland, E Denmark
95 I14 **Slagnäs** Norrbotten, N Sweden
xli O13 **Slaidburn** Lancashire, NW England, UK
xli P7 **Slaley** Northumberland, N England, UK
xliii K20 **Slamannan** Falkirk, C Scotland, UK
174 Kk15 **Slamet, Gunung** ▲ Jawa, S Indonesia
41 T10 **Slana** Alaska, USA
xliv K7 **Slane** Meath, E Ireland
xliv K11 **Slaney** *Ir.* An tSláine. ≈ SE Ireland
118 J13 **Slănic** Prahova, SE Romania
118 K11 **Slănic Moldova** Bacău, E Romania
115 H16 **Slano** Dubrovnik-Neretva, SE Croatia
128 F13 **Slantsy** Leningradskaya Oblast', NW Russian Federation
113 C16 **Slaný** *Ger.* Schlan. Střední Čechy, NW Czech Republic
xxxvi H16 **Slapton** Devon, SW England, UK
10 C10 **Slate Falls** Ontario, S Canada
29 T4 **Slater** Missouri, C USA
118 I14 **Slatina** Olt, S Romania
Slatina *see* Podravska Slatina
27 N5 **Slaton** Texas, SW USA
97 H14 **Slattum** Akershus, S Norway
9 R10 **Slave** ≈ Alberta/Northwest Territories, C Canada
70 E12 **Slave Coast** *coastal region* W Africa
9 P13 **Slave Lake** Alberta, SW Canada
125 G14 **Slavgorod** Altayskiy Kray, S Russian Federation
Slavgorod *see* Slawharad
Slavonia *see* Slavonija
114 G9 **Slavonija** *Eng.* Slavonia, *Ger.* Slawonien, *Hung.* Szlavonia, Szlavonország. *cultural region* NE Croatia
114 H9 **Slavonska Požega** *prev.* Požega, *Ger.* Poschega, *Hung.* Pozsega. Požega-Slavonija, NE Croatia
114 H10 **Slavonski Brod** *Ger.* Brod, *Hung.* Bród; *prev.* Brod, Brod na Savi. Brod-Posavina, NE Croatia
118 L4 **Slavuta** Khmel'nyts'ka Oblast', NW Ukraine
119 P2 **Slavutych** Chernihivs'ka Oblast', N Ukraine
127 N18 **Slavyanka** Primorskiy Kray, SE Russian Federation
116 J8 **Slavyanovo** Loveshka Oblast, N Bulgaria
Slavyansk *see* Slov"yans'k
130 K14 **Slavyansk-na-Kubani** Krasnodarskiy Kray, SW Russian Federation
121 N20 **Slavyechna** *Rus.* Slovechna. ≈ Belorussia/Ukraine
121 O16 **Slawharad** *Rus.* Slavgorod. Mahilyowskaya Voblasts', E Belorussia
112 G7 **Sławno** Słupsk, NW Poland
Slawonien *see* Slavonija
31 S10 **Slayton** Minnesota, N USA
xxxix Q7 **Sleaford** Lincolnshire, E England, UK
xliv B13 **Slea Head** *Ir.* Ceann Sléibhe. *headland* SW Ireland
xliii F14 **Sleat, Sound of** *strait* NW Scotland, UK
xli V12 **Sledmere** East Riding of Yorkshire, N England, UK
Sledyuki *see* Slyedzyuki
10 I5 **Sleeper Islands** *island group* Northwest Territories, C Canada
33 O6 **Sleeping Bear Point** *headland* Michigan, N USA
31 T10 **Sleepy Eye** Minnesota, N USA
41 O11 **Sleetmute** Alaska, USA
Sléibhe, Ceann *see* Slea Head
xli V10 **Sleights** North Yorkshire, N England, UK
Slēmānī *see* As Sulaymānīyah
205 O5 **Slessor Glacier** *glacier* Antarctica
xliii G22 **Sliddery** North Ayrshire, W Scotland, UK
24 L9 **Slidell** Louisiana, S USA
20 K12 **Slide Mountain** ▲ New York, NE USA
100 I13 **Sliedrecht** Zuid-Holland, C Netherlands
123 Jj16 **Sliema** N Malta
xliv F9 **Slieve Aughty Mountains** ▲▲ W Ireland
xliv H10 **Slieve Bloom Mountains** ▲▲ C Ireland
xliv D6 **Slieve Car** ▲ NW Ireland
xliv L6 **Slieve Donard** ▲ SE Northern Ireland, UK
xliv G11 **Slievefelim Mountains** ▲▲ C Ireland
xliv F6 **Slieve Gamph** *var.* Ox Mountains. ▲▲ N Ireland
xliv G11 **Slievekimalta** ▲ C Ireland
xliv C13 **Slieve Mish Mountains** ▲▲ SW Ireland
xliv H12 **Slievenamon** ▲ S Ireland
xliv I2 **Slieve Snaght** ▲ N Ireland
xlii E13 **Sligachan** Highland, NW Scotland, UK
Sligeach *see* Sligo
xliv G5 **Sligo** *Ir.* Sligeach. Sligo, NW Ireland
xliv F6 **Sligo** *Ir.* Sligeach. ◐ *county* NW Ireland
xliv F5 **Sligo Bay** *Ir.* Cuan Shligigh. *inlet* NW Ireland
xxxvii S13 **Slindon** West Sussex, SE England, UK
xli T11 **Slingsby** North Yorkshire, N England, UK
20 B13 **Slippery Rock** Pennsylvania, NE USA
97 P19 **Slite** Gotland, SE Sweden
116 L9 **Sliven** *var.* Slivno. Burgaska Oblast, E Bulgaria
116 G9 **Slivnitsa** Sofiyska Oblast, W Bulgaria
Slivno *see* Sliven
116 L7 **Slivo Pole** Razgradska Oblast, NE Bulgaria
31 S13 **Sloan** Iowa, C USA
37 X12 **Sloan** Nevada, W USA
Slobodka *see* Slabodka
129 R14 **Slobodskoy** Kirovskaya Oblast', NW Russian Federation
Slobodzeya *see* Slobozia
119 O10 **Slobozia** *Rus.* Slobodzeya. E Moldavia
118 L14 **Slobozia** Ialomiţa, SE Romania
100 O5 **Slochteren** Groningen, NE Netherlands
121 H17 **Slonim** *Pol.* Słonim, *Rus.* Slonim. Hrodzyenskaya Voblasts', W Belorussia
100 K7 **Sloter Meer** ◎ N Netherlands
Slot, The *see* New Georgia Sound
xxxvii S9 **Slough** Slough, S England, UK
xxxvii S9 **Slough** ◐ *unitary authority* S England, UK
113 J20 **Slovakia** *off.* Slovenská Republika, *Ger.* Slowakei, *Hung.* Szlovákia, *Slvk.* Slovensko. ◆ *republic* C Europe
Slovak Ore Mountains *see* Slovenské Rudohorie
Slovechna *see* Slavyechna
111 S12 **Slovenia** *off.* Republic of Slovenia, *Ger.* Slowenien, *Slvn.* Slovenija. ◆ *republic* SE Europe
Slovenija *see* Slovenia
111 V10 **Slovenj Gradec** *Ger.* Windischgraz. N Slovenia
111 W10 **Slovenska Bistrica** *Ger.* Windischfeistritz. NE Slovenia
111 W10 **Slovenska Konjice** E Slovenia
Slovenská Republika *see* Slovakia
113 K20 **Slovenské Rudohorie** *Eng.* Slovak Ore Mountains, *Ger.* Slowakisches Erzgebirge, Ungarisches Erzgebirge. ▲▲ C Slovakia
Slovensko *see* Slovakia
119 Y7 **Slov"yanoserbs'k** Luhans'ka Oblast', E Ukraine

◆ Country ● Country Capital ◇ Dependent Territory ○ Dependent Territory Capital ◐ Administrative Region ✕ International Airport ▲ Mountain ▲▲ Mountain Range ☀ Volcano ≈ River ◎ Lake ⊡ Reservoir

Slov"yans'k – South Bank

119 W6 **Slov"yans'k** Rus. Slavyansk. Donets'ka Oblast', E Ukraine
Slowakei see Slovakia
Slowakisches Erzgebirge see Slovenské Rudohorie
Slowenien see Slovenia
112 D11 **Słubice** Ger. Frankfurt. Gorzów, W Poland
121 K19 **Sluch** Rus. Sluch'. ≈ C Belorussia
118 L4 **Sluch** ≈ NW Ukraine
101 D16 **Sluis** Zeeland, SW Netherlands
114 D10 **Slunj** Hung. Szluin. Karlovac, C Croatia
112 I11 **Słupca** Konin, C Poland
112 G6 **Słupia** Ger. Stolpe. ≈ NW Poland
112 G6 **Słupsk** Ger. Stolp. Słupsk, NW Poland
112 G7 **Słupsk** off. Województwo Słupskie, Ger. Stolp. ◈ province NW Poland
Słupskie, Województwo see Słupsk
121 K18 **Slutsk** Rus. Slutsk. Minskaya Voblasts', S Belorussia
121 O16 **Slyedzyuki** Rus. Sledyuki. Mahilyowskaya Voblasts', E Belorussia
xliv B8 **Slyne Head** Ir. Ceann Léime. headland W Ireland
126 J16 **Slyudyanka** Irkutskaya Oblast', S Russian Federation
29 U14 **Smackover** Arkansas, C USA
97 L20 **Småland** cultural region S Sweden
97 K20 **Smålandsstenar** Jönköping, S Sweden
xxxix Y8 **Smallburgh** Norfolk, E England, UK
Small Malaita see Maramasike
11 O8 **Smallwood Reservoir** ◎ Newfoundland and Labrador, S Canada
121 N14 **Smalyany** Rus. Smolyany. Vitsyebskaya Voblasts', NE Belorussia
121 L15 **Smalyavichy** Rus. Smolevichi. Minskaya Voblasts', C Belorussia
76 C9 **Smara** var. Es Semara. N Western Sahara
121 I14 **Smarhon'** Pol. Smorgonie, Rus. Smorgon'. Hrodzyenskaya Voblasts', W Belorussia
114 M11 **Smederevo** Ger. Semendria. Serbia, N Yugoslavia
114 M12 **Smederevska Palanka** Serbia, C Yugoslavia
97 M14 **Smedjebacken** Kopparberg, C Sweden
118 L13 **Smeeni** Buzău, SE Romania
xxxvii Y11 **Smeeth** Kent, SE England, UK
Smela see Smila
109 D16 **Smeralda, Costa** cultural region Sardegna, Italy, C Mediterranean Sea
xxxviii B15 **Smethwick** Sandwell, C England, UK
113 J22 **Śmigiel** Ger. Schmiegel. Leszno, W Poland
119 Q6 **Smila** Rus. Smela. Cherkas'ka Oblast', C Ukraine
100 N7 **Smilde** Drenthe, NE Netherlands
9 S16 **Smiley** Saskatchewan, S Canada
27 T12 **Smiley** Texas, SW USA
Smilten see Smiltene
120 I8 **Smiltene** Ger. Smilten. Valka, N Latvia
127 O14 **Smirnykh** Ostrov Sakhalin, Sakhalinskaya Oblast', SE Russian Federation
9 Q13 **Smith** Alberta, W Canada
41 P4 **Smith Bay** bay Alaska, USA
10 I3 **Smith, Cape** headland Québec, NE Canada
28 L3 **Smith Center** Kansas, C USA
8 K13 **Smithers** British Columbia, SW Canada
xl M6 **Smithfield** Cumbria, NW England, UK
23 V10 **Smithfield** North Carolina, SE USA
38 L1 **Smithfield** Utah, W USA
23 X7 **Smithfield** Virginia, NE USA
10 I3 **Smith Island** island Northwest Territories, C Canada
Smith Island see Sumisu-jima
22 H7 **Smithland** Kentucky, S USA
23 T7 **Smith Mountain Lake** var. Leesville Lake. ⊠ Virginia, NE USA
36 L1 **Smith River** California, W USA
35 R9 **Smith River** ≈ Montana, NW USA
12 L13 **Smiths Falls** Ontario, SE Canada
35 N13 **Smiths Ferry** Idaho, NW USA
22 K7 **Smiths Grove** Kentucky, S USA
191 N15 **Smithton** Tasmania, SE Australia
20 L14 **Smithtown** Long Island, New York, NE USA
22 K9 **Smithville** Tennessee, S USA
27 T11 **Smithville** Texas, SW USA
Šmohor see Hermagor
37 Q4 **Smoke Creek Desert** desert Nevada, W USA
9 O14 **Smoky** ≈ Alberta, W Canada
190 E7 **Smoky Bay** South Australia
191 V6 **Smoky Cape** headland New South Wales, SE Australia
28 L4 **Smoky Hill River** ≈ Kansas, C USA
28 L4 **Smoky Hills** hill range Kansas, C USA
9 Q14 **Smoky Lake** Alberta, SW Canada
96 E8 **Smøla** island W Norway
130 H4 **Smolensk** Smolenskaya Oblast', W Russian Federation
130 H4 **Smolenskaya Oblast'** ◈ province W Russian Federation
Smolensk-Moscow Upland see Smolensko-Moskovskaya Vozvyshennost'
130 J3 **Smolensko-Moskovskaya Vozvyshennost'** var. Smolensk-Moscow Upland. ▲▲ W Russian Federation
Smolevichi see Smalyavichy
117 C15 **Smolikás** ▲ W Greece
116 I12 **Smolyan** prev. Pashmakli. Plovdivska Oblast, S Bulgaria
Smolyany see Smalyany
35 S15 **Smoot** Wyoming, C USA
10 G12 **Smooth Rock Falls** Ontario, S Canada
Smorgon'/Smorgonie see Smarhon'
97 K23 **Smygehamn** Malmöhus, S Sweden
204 I7 **Smyley Island** island Antarctica
23 Y3 **Smyrna** Delaware, NE USA
25 S3 **Smyrna** Georgia, SE USA
22 J9 **Smyrna** Tennessee, S USA
Smyrna see İzmır
176 W10 **Snabai** Irian Jaya, E Indonesia
xl G11 **Snaefell** ▲ C Isle of Man
94 H3 **Snaefellsjökull** ▲ W Iceland
xli T14 **Snaith** East Riding of Yorkshire, N England, UK
8 J4 **Snake** ≈ Yukon Territory, NW Canada
31 O8 **Snake Creek** ≈ South Dakota, N USA
191 P13 **Snake Island** island Victoria, SE Australia
37 Y6 **Snake Range** ▲▲ Nevada, W USA
34 K10 **Snake River** ≈ NW USA
31 V6 **Snake River** ≈ Minnesota, N USA
30 L12 **Snake River** ≈ Nebraska, C USA
35 Q14 **Snake River Plain** plain Idaho, NW USA
xli R11 **Snape** North Yorkshire, N England, UK
15 I7 **Snare** ≈ Northwest Territories, NW Canada
95 F15 **Snåsa** Nord-Trøndelag, C Norway
23 O8 **Sneedville** Tennessee, S USA
100 K6 **Sneek** Friesland, N Netherlands
xliv C14 **Sneem** Kerry, SW Ireland
Sneeuw-gebergte see Maoke, Pegunungan
97 F22 **Snejbjerg** Ringkøbing, C Denmark
xxxix Q5 **Snelland** Lincolnshire, E England, UK
xxxix U8 **Snettisham** Norfolk, E England, UK
126 I8 **Snezhnogorsk** Taymyrskiy (Dolgano-Nenetskiy) Avtonomnyy Okrug, N Russian Federation
Snezhnoye see Snizhne
113 G15 **Sněžka** Ger. Schneekoppe. ▲ N Czech Republic
111 T13 **Snežnik** Ger. Schneeberg, It. Monte Nevoso. ▲ SW Slovenia
112 N8 **Śniardwy, Jezioro** Ger. Spirdingsee. ◎ NE Poland
Sniečkus see Visaginas
119 R10 **Snihurivka** Mykolayivs'ka Oblast', S Ukraine
118 I5 **Snilow** ✕ (L'viv) L'vivs'ka Oblast', W Ukraine
113 O19 **Snina** Hung. Szinna. Východné Slovensko, E Slovakia
xxxviii L12 **Snitterfield** Warwickshire, C England, UK
119 Y8 **Snizhne** Rus. Snezhnoye. Donets'ka Oblast', SE Ukraine
xlii D11 **Snizort, Loch** inlet NW Scotland, UK
xxxvii W10 **Snodland** Kent, SE England, UK
94 J3 **Snækollur** ▲ C Iceland
96 G10 **Snøhetta** var. Snohetta. ▲ S Norway
94 G12 **Snøtinden** ▲ C Norway
xxxv G5 **Snowdon** ▲ NW Wales, UK
xxxv G5 **Snowdonia** ▲▲ NW Wales, UK
15 Ii8 **Snowdrift** ≈ Northwest Territories, NW Canada
Snowdrift see Łutselk'e
39 N12 **Snowflake** Arizona, SW USA
23 Y5 **Snow Hill** Maryland, NE USA
23 W10 **Snow Hill** North Carolina, SE USA
204 H3 **Snowhill Island** island Antarctica
9 V13 **Snow Lake** Manitoba, C Canada
39 R5 **Snowmass Mountain** ▲ Colorado, C USA
20 M10 **Snow, Mount** ▲ Vermont, NE USA
36 M5 **Snow Mountain** ▲ California, W USA
Snow Mountains see Maoke, Pegunungan
35 N7 **Snowshoe Peak** ▲ Montana, NW USA
190 I8 **Snowtown** South Australia
38 K1 **Snowville** Utah, W USA
37 X3 **Snow Water Lake** ◎ Nevada, W USA
191 Q11 **Snowy Mountains** ▲▲ New South Wales/Victoria, SE Australia
191 Q12 **Snowy River** ≈ New South Wales/Victoria, SE Australia
46 K5 **Snug Corner** Acklins Island, SE Bahamas
178 Jj13 **Snuŏl** Krâchéh, E Cambodia
118 J7 **Snyatyn** Rus. Snyatyn. Ivano-Frankivs'ka Oblast', W Ukraine
28 L12 **Snyder** Oklahoma, C USA
27 O6 **Snyder** Texas, SW USA
180 H3 **Soalala** Mahajanga, W Madagascar
180 J4 **Soanierana-Ivongo** Toamasina, E Madagascar
xxxix N8 **Soar** ≈ C England, UK
175 Ss7 **Soasiu** var. Tidore. Pulau Tidore, E Indonesia
56 G8 **Soatá** Boyacá, C Colombia
180 I5 **Soavinandriana** Antananarivo, C Madagascar
xliii D14 **Soay** island NW Scotland, UK
176 Yy12 **Soba** Irian Jaya, E Indonesia
79 V13 **Soba** Kaduna, C Nigeria
169 Y16 **Sobaek-sanmaek** ▲▲ S South Korea
82 F13 **Sobat** ≈ E Sudan
176 Z12 **Sobger, Sungai** ≈ Irian Jaya, E Indonesia
176 W10 **Sobiei** Irian Jaya, E Indonesia
130 M3 **Sobinka** Vladimirskaya Oblast', W Russian Federation
131 S7 **Sobolevo** Orenburgskaya Oblast', W Russian Federation
Soborsin see Săvârşin
170 D15 **Sobo-san** ▲ Kyūshū, SW Japan
113 G14 **Sobótka** Wrocław, SW Poland
61 O15 **Sobradinho** Bahia, E Brazil
Sobradinho, Barragem de see Sobradinho, Represa de
61 O16 **Sobradinho, Represa de** var. Barragem de Sobradinho. ⊠ E Brazil
60 O13 **Sobral** Ceará, E Brazil
107 T4 **Sobrarbe** physical region NE Spain
111 R10 **Soča** It. Isonzo. ≈ Italy/Slovenia
112 L11 **Sochaczew** Skierniewice, C Poland
130 L15 **Sochi** Krasnodarskiy Kray, SW Russian Federation
116 G13 **Sochós** var. Sohos, Sokhós. Kentrikí Makedonía, N Greece
203 R11 **Société, Archipel de la** var. Archipel de Tahiti, Îles de la Société, Eng. Society Islands. island group W French Polynesia
Société, Îles de la/ Society Islands see Société, Archipel de la
23 T11 **Society Hill** South Carolina, SE USA
183 W9 **Society Ridge** undersea feature C Pacific Ocean
64 I5 **Socompa, Volcán** ▲ N Chile
Soconusco, Sierra de see Sierra Madre
56 G8 **Socorro** Santander, C Colombia
39 R13 **Socorro** New Mexico, SW USA
Socotra see Suquţrā
178 Jj15 **Soc Trăng** var. Khanh Hung. Soc Trăng, S Vietnam
107 P10 **Socuéllamos** Castilla-La Mancha, C Spain
37 W13 **Soda Lake** salt flat California, W USA
94 L11 **Sodankylä** Lappi, N Finland
Sodari see Sodiri
35 R15 **Soda Springs** Idaho, NW USA
Soddo/Soddu see Sodo
22 L10 **Soddy Daisy** Tennessee, S USA
97 N14 **Söderfors** Uppsala, C Sweden
96 N12 **Söderhamn** Gävleborg, C Sweden
97 N17 **Söderköping** Östergötland, S Sweden
97 N17 **Södermanland** ◈ county C Sweden
97 O16 **Södertälje** Stockholm, C Sweden
82 D10 **Sodiri** var. Sawdirī, Sodari. Northern Kordofan, C Sudan
83 I14 **Sodo** var. Soddo, Soddu. SW Ethiopia
96 N11 **Södra Dellen** ◎ C Sweden
97 M19 **Södra Vi** Kalmar, S Sweden
20 G9 **Sodus Point** headland New York, NE USA
175 Rr17 **Soe** prev. Soë. Timor, C Indonesia
174 J14 **Soekarno-Hatta** ✕ (Jakarta) Jawa, S Indonesia
Soëla-Sund see Soela Väin
120 E5 **Soela Väin** prev. Eng. Sele Sound, Ger. Dagden-Sund, Soëla-Sund. strait W Estonia
Soemba see Sumba, Pulau
Soembawa see Sumbawa
Soemenep see Sumenep
Soengaipenoeh see Sungaipenuh
Soerabaja see Surabaya
103 G14 **Soest** Nordrhein-Westfalen, W Germany
100 J11 **Soest** Utrecht, C Netherlands
102 F11 **Soeste** ≈ NW Germany
100 J11 **Soesterberg** Utrecht, C Netherlands
117 E16 **Sofádes** var. Sofádhes. Thessalía, C Greece
Sofádhes see Sofádes
85 N18 **Sofala** Sofala, C Mozambique
85 N17 **Sofala** ◈ province C Mozambique
85 N18 **Sofala, Baia de** bay E Mozambique
180 J3 **Sofia** seasonal river NW Madagascar
Sofia see Sofiya
117 G19 **Sofikó** Pelopónnisos, S Greece
Sofi-Kurgan see Sopu-Korgon
116 G10 **Sofiya** var. Sophia, Eng. Sofia; Lat. Serdica. ● (Bulgaria) Grad Sofiya, W Bulgaria
116 G9 **Sofiya** ✕ Grad Sofiya, W Bulgaria
Sofiya see Sofiyska Oblast
116 G9 **Sofiya, Grad** ◈ municipality W Bulgaria
Sofiyevka see Sofiyivka
119 S8 **Sofiyivka** Rus. Sofiyevka. Dnipropetrovs'ka Oblast', E Ukraine
127 Nn14 **Sofiysk** Khabarovskiy Kray, SE Russian Federation
127 N14 **Sofiysk** Khabarovskiy Kray, SE Russian Federation
116 F10 **Sofiyska Oblast** var. Sofiya. ◈ province W Bulgaria
128 I6 **Sofporog** Respublika Kareliya, NW Russian Federation
172 Ss15 **Sōfu-gan** island Izu-shotō, SE Japan
Sog see Sog Xian
56 G9 **Sogamoso** Boyacá, C Colombia
142 I11 **Soğanlı Çayı** ≈ N Turkey
96 E12 **Sogn** physical region S Norway
96 E12 **Sogndal** var. Sogndalsfjøra. Sogn og Fjordane, S Norway
Sogndalsfjøra see Sogndal
97 E18 **Søgne** Vest-Agder, S Norway
96 D12 **Sognefjorden** fjord NE North Sea
96 C12 **Sogn Og Fjordane** ◈ county S Norway
179 R13 **Sogod** Leyte, C Philippines
168 I11 **Sogo Nur** ◎ N China
165 T12 **Sogruma** Qinghai, W China
169 X17 **Sŏgwip'o** S South Korea
162 K10 **Sog Xian** var. Sog. Xizang Zizhiqu, W China
77 X10 **Sohâg** var. Sawhāj, Suliag. C Egypt
xxxix T11 **Soham** Cambridgeshire, E England, UK
Sohar see Şuḩār
66 H9 **Sohm Plain** undersea feature NW Atlantic Ocean
102 H7 **Soholmer Au** ≈ N Germany
Sohos see Sochós
Sohrau see Żory
101 F20 **Soignies** Hainaut, SW Belgium
165 R15 **Soila** Xizang Zizhiqu, W China
105 P4 **Soissons** anc. Augusta Suessionum, Noviodunum. Aisne, N France
170 Ff14 **Sōja** Okayama, Honshū, SW Japan
158 F13 **Sojat** Rājasthān, N India
169 W13 **Sŏjosŏn-man** inlet W North Korea
118 I4 **Sokal'** Rus. Sokal. L'vivs'ka Oblast', NW Ukraine
169 Y14 **Sokch'o** N South Korea
142 B15 **Söke** Aydın, SW Turkey
201 N12 **Sokehs Island** island E Micronesia
81 M24 **Sokele** Shaba, SE Zaire
153 R11 **Sokh** Uzb. Sŭkh. ≈ Kyrgyzstan/Uzbekistan
Şokh see Sŭkh
Sokhós see Sochós
143 Q8 **Sokhumi** Rus. Sukhumi. NW Georgia
115 O14 **Sokobanja** Serbia, E Yugoslavia
79 R15 **Sokodé** C Togo
127 O10 **Sokol** Magadanskaya Oblast', E Russian Federation
128 M13 **Sokol** Vologodskaya Oblast', NW Russian Federation
112 P9 **Sokółka** Białystok, NE Poland
78 M11 **Sokolo** Ségou, W Mali
113 A16 **Sokolov** Ger. Falkenau an der Eger; prev. Falknov nad Ohří. Západní Čechy, W Czech Republic
113 O16 **Sokołów Małopolski** Rzeszów, SE Poland
112 O11 **Sokołów Podlaski** Siedlce, E Poland
78 G11 **Sokone** W Senegal
79 T12 **Sokoto** Sokoto, NW Nigeria
79 T12 **Sokoto** ◈ state NW Nigeria
79 S12 **Sokoto** ≈ NW Nigeria
Sokotra see Suquţrā
153 U7 **Sokuluk** Chuyskaya Oblast', N Kyrgyzstan
118 L7 **Sokyryany** Chernivets'ka Oblast', W Ukraine
97 C16 **Sola** Rogaland, S Norway
197 C10 **Sola** Vanua Lava, N Vanuatu
97 C17 **Sola** ✕ (Stavanger) Rogaland, S Norway
83 H18 **Solai** Rift Valley, W Kenya
176 Y15 **Solaka** Irian Jaya, E Indonesia
158 I8 **Solan** Himāchal Pradesh, N India
193 A25 **Solander Island** island SW NZ
Solano see Bahía Solano
161 F15 **Solāpur** var. Sholāpur. Mahārāshtra, W India
95 H16 **Solberg** Västernorrland, C Sweden
118 K9 **Solca** Ger. Solka. Suceava, N Romania
107 O16 **Sol, Costa del** coastal region S Spain
108 F5 **Solda** Trentino-Alto Adige, N Italy
119 N9 **Şoldăneşti** Rus. Sholdaneshty. N Moldavia
Soldau see Wkra
110 L8 **Sölden** Tirol, W Austria
29 P3 **Soldier Creek** ≈ Kansas, C USA
41 R12 **Soldotna** Alaska, USA
112 I10 **Solec Kujawski** Bydgoszcz, W Poland
63 B16 **Soledad** Santa Fe, C Argentina
57 Y11 **Soledad** Atlántico, N Colombia
37 O11 **Soledad** California, W USA
57 O7 **Soledad** Anzoátegui, NE Venezuela
Soledad see East Falkland
63 H15 **Soledade** Rio Grande do Sul, S Brazil
xxxvii P13 **Solent, The** channel S England, UK
104 F2 **Solenzara** Corse, France, C Mediterranean Sea
Soleure see Solothurn
96 C12 **Solheim** Hordaland, S Norway
129 N14 **Soligalich** Kostromskaya Oblast', NW Russian Federation
Soligorsk see Salihorsk
xxxviii D15 **Solihull** Solihull, C England, UK
xxxviii L11 **Solihull** ◈ unitary authority C England, UK
129 U13 **Solikamsk** Permskaya Oblast', NW Russian Federation
131 V8 **Sol'-Iletsk** Orenburgskaya Oblast', W Russian Federation
59 G17 **Solimana, Nevado** ▲ S Peru
60 E13 **Solimões, Rio** ≈ C Brazil
115 E14 **Solin** It. Salona; anc. Salonae. Split-Dalmacija, S Croatia
103 E15 **Solingen** Nordrhein-Westfalen, W Germany
Solka see Solca
95 H16 **Sollefteå** Västernorrland, C Sweden
97 O15 **Sollentuna** Stockholm, C Sweden
96 L13 **Sollerön** Kopparberg, C Sweden
103 I14 **Solling** hill range C Germany
97 O16 **Solna** Stockholm, C Sweden
130 K3 **Solnechnogorsk** Moskovskaya Oblast', W Russian Federation
127 Nn15 **Solnechnyy** Khabarovskiy Kray, SE Russian Federation
127 N11 **Solnechnyy** Respublika Sakha (Yakutiya), NE Russian Federation
96 H11 **Sølnkletten** ▲ S Norway
109 L17 **Solofra** Campania, S Italy
174 Gg9 **Solok** Sumatera, W Indonesia
44 C6 **Sololá** Sololá, W Guatemala
44 A2 **Sololá** off. Departamento de Sololá. ◈ department SW Guatemala
83 J16 **Sololo** Eastern, N Kenya
44 C4 **Soloma** Huehuetenango, W Guatemala
40 M9 **Solomon** Alaska, USA
29 N4 **Solomon** Kansas, C USA
195 U16 **Solomon Islands** prev. British Solomon Islands Protectorate. ◆ commonwealth republic W Pacific Ocean
195 T12 **Solomon Islands** island group PNG/Solomon Islands
28 M3 **Solomon River** ≈ Kansas, C USA
199 Hh9 **Solomon Sea** sea W Pacific Ocean
33 U11 **Solon** Ohio, N USA
119 T8 **Solone** Dnipropetrovs'ka Oblast', E Ukraine
175 R16 **Solor, Kepulauan** island group S Indonesia
130 M4 **Solotcha** Ryazanskaya Oblast', W Russian Federation
110 D7 **Solothurn** Fr. Soleure. Solothurn, NW Switzerland
110 D7 **Solothurn** Fr. Soleure. ◈ canton NW Switzerland
128 J7 **Solovetskiye Ostrova** island group NW Russian Federation
107 V5 **Solsona** Cataluña, NE Spain
115 E14 **Šolta** It. Solta. island S Croatia
Solţānābād see Kāshmar
148 L4 **Solţānīyeh** Zanjān, NW Iran
102 I11 **Soltau** Niedersachsen, NW Germany
128 G14 **Sol'tsy** Novgorodskaya Oblast', W Russian Federation
Soltūstik Qazaqstan Oblysy see Severnyy Kazakhstan
Solun see Thessaloníki
115 O19 **Solunska Glava** ▲ C FYR Macedonia
xxxv C13 **Solva** Pembrokeshire, SW Wales, UK
97 L22 **Sölvesborg** Blekinge, S Sweden
99 J15 **Solway Firth** inlet England/Scotland, UK
84 I13 **Solwezi** North Western, NW Zambia
171 Ll14 **Sōma** Fukushima, Honshū, C Japan
142 C13 **Soma** Manisa, W Turkey
83 O15 **Somalia** off. Somali Democratic Republic, Som. Jamuuriyada Demuqraadiga Soomaaliyeed, Soomaaliya; prev. Italian Somaliland, Somaliland Protectorate. ◆ republic E Africa
181 N6 **Somali Basin** undersea feature W Indian Ocean
69 Y8 **Somali Plain** undersea feature W Indian Ocean
114 J8 **Sombor** Hung. Zombor. Serbia, NW Yugoslavia
101 H20 **Sombreffe** Namur, S Belgium
42 L10 **Sombrerete** Zacatecas, C Mexico
47 V8 **Sombrero** island N Anguilla
157 Q21 **Sombrero Channel** channel Nicobar Islands, India
118 H9 **Şomcuta Mare** Hung. Nagysomkút; prev. Somcuţa Mare. Maramureş, N Romania
178 Ii9 **Somdet** Kalasin, E Thailand
101 L15 **Someren** Noord-Brabant, SE Netherlands
95 L19 **Somero** Turku-Pori, SW Finland
35 P7 **Somers** Montana, NW USA
xxxvi J12 **Somerset** ◈ county SW England, UK
66 A12 **Somerset** var. Somerset Village. W Bermuda
39 Q5 **Somerset** Colorado, C USA
22 M7 **Somerset** Kentucky, S USA
21 O12 **Somerset** Massachusetts, NE USA
Somerset East see Somerset-Oos
66 A12 **Somerset Island** island W Bermuda
207 N9 **Somerset Island** island Queen Elizabeth Islands, Northwest Territories, NW Canada
Somerset Nile see Victoria Nile
85 I25 **Somerset-Oos** Eng. Somerset East. Eastern Cape, S South Africa
85 E26 **Somerset-Wes** Eng. Somerset West. Western Cape, SW South Africa
Somerset West see Somerset-Wes
xxxix S11 **Somersham** Cambridgeshire, E England, UK
Somers Islands see Bermuda
20 J17 **Somers Point** New Jersey, NE USA
21 P9 **Somersworth** New Hampshire, NE USA
xxxvii P7 **Somerton** Oxfordshire, C England, UK
xxxvi K12 **Somerton** Somerset, SW England, UK
38 H15 **Somerton** Arizona, SW USA
20 J14 **Somerville** New Jersey, NE USA
22 F10 **Somerville** Tennessee, S USA
27 U10 **Somerville** Texas, SW USA
27 T10 **Somerville Lake** ⊠ Texas, SW USA
Someş/Somesch/ Someşul see Szamos
105 N2 **Somme** ◈ department N France
105 N2 **Somme** ≈ N France
97 L18 **Sommen** Jönköping, S Sweden
97 M18 **Sommen** ◎ S Sweden
103 K16 **Sömmerda** Thüringen, C Germany
Sommerein see Šamorín
Sommerfeld see Lubsko
57 Y11 **Sommet Tabulaire** var. Mont Itoupé. ▲▲ S French Guiana
113 H25 **Somogy** off. Somogy Megye. ◈ county SW Hungary
Somorja see Šamorín
107 N7 **Somosierra, Puerto de** pass N Spain
197 J13 **Somosomo** Taveuni, N Fiji
44 I9 **Somotillo** Chinandega, NW Nicaragua
44 I8 **Somoto** Madriz, NW Nicaragua
112 I11 **Sompolno** Konin, C Poland
107 S3 **Somport** var. Puerto de Somport, Fr. Col du Somport; anc. Summus Portus. pass France/Spain see also Somport, Col du
104 J17 **Somport, Col du** var. Puerto de Somport, Sp. Somport; anc. Summus Portus. pass France/Spain see also Somport
Somport, Puerto de see Somport/Somport, Col du
101 K15 **Son** Noord-Brabant, S Netherlands
97 H15 **Son** Buskerud, S Norway
160 L9 **Son** var. Sone. ≈ C India
45 R16 **Soná** Veraguas, W Panama
160 M12 **Sonapur** prev. Sonepur. Orissa, E India
176 Vv10 **Sonar** Irian Jaya, E Indonesia
97 G24 **Sønderborg** Ger. Sonderburg. Sønderjylland, SW Denmark
Sonderburg see Sønderborg
97 F24 **Sønderjylland** off. Sønderjyllands Amt. ◈ county SW Denmark
103 K15 **Sondershausen** Thüringen, C Germany
207 N14 **Søndre Strømfjord** ✕ W Greenland
108 E6 **Sondrio** Lombardia, N Italy
Sone see Son
Sonepur see Sonapur
59 K22 **Sonequera** ▲ S Bolivia
178 Kk12 **Sông Câu** Phu Yên, C Vietnam
178 J15 **Sông Đôc** Minh Hai, S Vietnam
83 H25 **Songea** Ruvuma, S Tanzania
176 Z11 **Songgato, Sungai** ≈ Irian Jaya, E Indonesia
169 X10 **Songhua Hu** ◎ NE China
169 Y7 **Songhua Jiang** var. Sungari. ≈ NE China
167 S8 **Songjiang** Shanghai Shi, E China
Sŏngjin see Kimch'aek
178 H17 **Songkhla** var. Songkla, Mal. Singora. Songkhla, SW Thailand
Songkla see Songkhla
169 T13 **Song Ling** ▲▲ NE China
169 W14 **Songnim** SW North Korea
84 B10 **Songo** Uíge, NW Angola
85 M15 **Songo** Tete, NW Mozambique
81 F21 **Songololo** Bas-Zaïre, SW Zaire
166 H7 **Songpan** prev. Sungpu. Sichuan, C China
169 Y17 **Sŏngsan** S South Korea
167 R11 **Songxi** Fujian, SE China
166 M6 **Songxian** var. Song Xian. Henan, C China
167 R10 **Songyin** Zhejiang, SE China
169 V9 **Songyuan** var. Fu-yü, Petuna; prev. Fuyu. Jilin, NE China
169 P11 **Sonid Youqi** var. Saihon Tal. Nei Mongol Zizhiqu, N China
169 P11 **Sonid Zuoqi** Nei Mongol Zizhiqu, N China
158 I10 **Sonīpat** Haryāna, N India
95 M15 **Sonkajärvi** Kuopio, C Finland
178 J6 **Sơn La** Sơn La, N Vietnam
155 O16 **Sonmiāni** Baluchistān, S Pakistan
155 O16 **Sonmiāni Bay** bay S Pakistan
103 K18 **Sonneberg** Thüringen, C Germany
103 N24 **Sonntagshorn** ▲ Austria/Germany
Sonoita see Sonoyta
42 E3 **Sonoita, Rio** var. Río Sonoyta. ≈ Mexico/USA
37 N7 **Sonoma** California, W USA
37 T3 **Sonoma Peak** ▲ Nevada, W USA
37 P8 **Sonora** California, W USA
27 O10 **Sonora** Texas, SW USA
42 F5 **Sonora** ◈ state NW Mexico
37 X17 **Sonoran Desert** var. Desierto de Altar. desert Mexico/USA see also Altar, Desierto de
42 G5 **Sonora, Río** ≈ NW Mexico
42 E2 **Sonoyta** var. Sonoita. Sonora, NW Mexico
Sonoyta, Río see Sonoita, Rio
148 K6 **Sonqor** var. Sunqur. Kermānshāhān, W Iran
107 N9 **Sonseca** var. Sonseca con Casalgordo. Castilla-La Mancha, C Spain
Sonseca con Casalgordo see Sonseca
56 E9 **Sonsón** Antioquia, W Colombia
44 E7 **Sonsonate** Sonsonate, W El Salvador
44 A9 **Sonsonate** ◈ department SW El Salvador
196 A10 **Sonsorol Islands** island group S Palau
114 J9 **Sonta** Hung. Szond; prev. Szonta. Serbia, NW Yugoslavia
178 Jj6 **Sơn Tây** var. Sontay. Ha Tây, N Vietnam
103 J25 **Sonthofen** Bayern, S Germany
Soochow see Suzhou
Soomaaliya/Soomaaliyeed, Jamuuriyada Demuqraadiga see Somalia
Soome Laht see Finland, Gulf of
Sooner State see Oklahoma
25 V5 **Soperton** Georgia, SE USA
178 J6 **Sop Hao** Houaphan, N Laos
Sophia see Sofiya
175 Tt5 **Sopi** Pulau Morotai, E Indonesia
Sopianae see Pécs
176 Vv11 **Sopinusa** Irian Jaya, E Indonesia
175 Tt5 **Sopi, Tanjung** headland Pulau Morotai, N Indonesia
xxxvii O13 **Sopley** Hampshire, S England, UK
83 B14 **Sopo** ≈ W Sudan
Sopockinie/Sopotskin see Sapotskino
116 I9 **Sopot** Plovdivska Oblast, C Bulgaria
112 I7 **Sopot** Ger. Zoppot. Gdańsk, N Poland
178 H8 **Sop Prap** var. Ban Sop Prap. Lampang, NW Thailand
113 G22 **Sopron** Ger. Ödenburg. Győr-Moson-Sopron, NW Hungary
153 U11 **Sopu-Korgon** var. Sofi-Kurgan. Oshskaya Oblast', SW Kyrgyzstan
158 H5 **Sopur** Jammu and Kashmir, NW India
109 J15 **Sora** Lazio, C Italy
160 N13 **Sorada** Orissa, E India
95 H17 **Söråker** Västernorrland, C Sweden
59 J17 **Sorata** La Paz, W Bolivia
Sorau/Sorau in der Niederlausitz see Żary
107 Q14 **Sorbas** Andalucía, S Spain
xliii I25 **Sorbie** Dumfries and Galloway, SW Scotland, UK
Sord/Sórd Choluim Chille see Swords
13 O11 **Sorel** Québec, SE Canada
191 P17 **Sorell** Tasmania, SE Australia
191 O17 **Sorell, Lake** ◎ Tasmania, SE Australia
108 E8 **Soresina** Lombardia, N Italy
97 D14 **Sørfjorden** fjord S Norway
96 N11 **Sörforsa** Gävleborg, C Sweden
105 R14 **Sorgues** Vaucluse, SE France
142 K13 **Sorgun** Yozgat, C Turkey
107 P5 **Soria** Castilla-León, N Spain
107 P6 **Soria** ◈ province Castilla-León, N Spain
63 D19 **Soriano** Soriano, SW Uruguay
63 D19 **Soriano** ◈ department SW Uruguay
xliii D16 **Sorisdale** Argyll and Bute, W Scotland, UK
94 O4 **Sørkapp** headland SW Svalbard
149 T5 **Sorkh, Kūh-e** ▲▲ NE Iran
xliii J22 **Sorn** East Ayrshire, W Scotland, UK
Soro see Ghazal, Bahr el
97 I23 **Sorø** Vestsjælland, E Denmark
118 M8 **Soroca** Rus. Soroki. N Moldavia
62 L10 **Sorocaba** São Paulo, S Brazil
Sorochino see Sarochyna
131 T7 **Sorochinsk** Orenburgskaya Oblast', W Russian Federation
Soroki see Soroca
196 H15 **Sorol** atoll Caroline Islands, W Micronesia
176 Uu9 **Sorong** Irian Jaya, E Indonesia
83 G17 **Soroti** C Uganda
Sørøy see Sørøya
94 J8 **Sørøya** var. Sørøy. island N Norway
106 G11 **Sorraia, Rio** ≈ C Portugal
94 I10 **Sørreisa** Troms, N Norway
109 K18 **Sorrento** anc. Surrentum. Campania, S Italy
106 H10 **Sor, Ribeira de** stream C Portugal
205 T3 **Sør Rondane Mountains** ▲▲ Antarctica
95 H14 **Sorsele** Västerbotten, N Sweden
109 B17 **Sorso** Sardegna, Italy, C Mediterranean Sea
179 Qq11 **Sorsogon** Luzon, N Philippines
107 U4 **Sort** Cataluña, NE Spain
128 H11 **Sortavala** Respublika Kareliya, NW Russian Federation
109 L25 **Sortino** Sicilia, Italy, C Mediterranean Sea
94 G10 **Sortland** Nordland, C Norway
96 G9 **Sør-Trøndelag** ◈ county S Norway
97 I15 **Sørumsand** Akershus, S Norway
120 D6 **Sõrve Säär** headland SW Estonia
97 K22 **Sösdala** Kristianstad, S Sweden
107 R4 **Sos del Rey Católico** Aragón, NE Spain
95 F15 **Sösjöfjällen** ▲ C Sweden
130 K7 **Sosna** ≈ W Russian Federation
64 H12 **Sosneado, Cerro** ▲ W Argentina
129 S9 **Sosnogorsk** Respublika Komi, NW Russian Federation
128 J8 **Sosnovets** Respublika Kareliya, NW Russian Federation
Sosnovets see Sosnowiec
131 Q3 **Sosnovka** Chuvashskaya Respublika, W Russian Federation
129 S16 **Sosnovka** Kirovskaya Oblast', NW Russian Federation
128 M6 **Sosnovka** Murmanskaya Oblast', NW Russian Federation
130 M6 **Sosnovka** Tambovskaya Oblast', W Russian Federation
128 H12 **Sosnovo** Fin. Rautu. Leningradskaya Oblast', NW Russian Federation
126 K15 **Sosnovo-Ozerskoye** Respublika Buryatiya, S Russian Federation
Sosnovyy Bor see Sasnovy Bor
113 J16 **Sosnowiec** Ger. Sosnowitz, Rus. Sosnovets. Katowice, S Poland
Sosnowitz see Sosnowiec
119 R2 **Sosnytsya** Chernihivs'ka Oblast', N Ukraine
111 V10 **Šoštanj** N Slovenia
125 F10 **Sos'va** Sverdlovskaya Oblast', C Russian Federation
56 D12 **Sotará, Volcán** ⛛ S Colombia
78 D10 **Sotavento, Ilhas de** var. Leeward Islands. island group S Cape Verde
95 N15 **Sotkamo** Oulu, C Finland
43 P10 **Soto la Marina** Tamaulipas, C Mexico
43 P10 **Soto la Marina, Río** ≈ C Mexico
43 X12 **Sotuta** Yucatán, SE Mexico
81 F17 **Souanké** La Sangha, NW Congo
78 M17 **Soubré** S Ivory Coast
117 H24 **Soúda** var. Soúdha, Eng. Suda. Kríti, Greece, E Mediterranean Sea
Soúdha see Soúda
Soueida see As Suwaydā'
116 L12 **Souflí** prev. Souflíon. Anatolikí Makedonía kai Thráki, NE Greece
Souflíon see Souflí
47 S11 **Soufrière** W Saint Lucia
47 X6 **Soufrière** ▲ Basse Terre, S Guadeloupe
104 M13 **Souillac** Lot, S France
181 Y17 **Souillac** S Mauritius
76 M5 **Souk Ahras** NE Algeria
76 E6 **Souk-el-Arba-Rharb** var. Souk el Arba du Rharb, Souk-el-Arba-du-Rharb, Souk-el-Arba-el-Rhab. NW Morocco
Soukhné see As Sukhnah
169 X14 **Sŏul** off. Sŏul-t'ŭkpyŏlsi, Eng. Seoul, Jap. Keijō; prev. Kyŏngsŏng. ● (South Korea) NW South Korea
104 J11 **Soulac-sur-Mer** Gironde, SW France
101 L19 **Soumagne** Liège, E Belgium
20 M14 **Sound Beach** Long Island, New York, NE USA
97 J22 **Sound, The** Dan. Øresund, Swe. Öresund. strait Denmark/Sweden
117 H20 **Soúnio, Ákra** headland C Greece
144 F8 **Soûr** var. Şūr; anc. Tyre. SW Lebanon
Sources, Mont-aux- see Phofung
106 G8 **Soure** Coimbra, N Portugal
9 W17 **Souris** Manitoba, S Canada
11 Q14 **Souris** Prince Edward Island, SE Canada
30 L2 **Souris River** var. Mouse River. ≈ Canada/USA
27 X10 **Sour Lake** Texas, SW USA
117 F17 **Sourpi** Thessalía, C Greece
106 H11 **Sousel** Portalegre, C Portugal
77 N6 **Sousse** var. Sūsah. NE Tunisia
12 H11 **South** ≈ Ontario, S Canada
South see Sud
85 G23 **South Africa** off. Republic of South Africa, Afr. Suid-Afrika. ◆ republic S Africa
xxxvii T9 **Southall** Ealing, SE England, UK
xxxviii M12 **Southam** Warwickshire, C England, UK
48-49 **South America** continent
2 J18 **South American Plate** tectonic feature
xxxvii P13 **Southampton** hist. Hamwih, Lat. Clausentum. City of Southampton, S England, UK
21 N14 **Southampton** Long Island, New York, NE USA
xxxvii P12 **Southampton, City of** ◈ unitary authority S England, UK
15 M5 **Southampton Island** island Northwest Territories, NE Canada
157 P20 **South Andaman** island Andaman Islands, India, NE Indian Ocean
11 Q6 **South Aulatsivik Island** island Newfoundland and Labrador, E Canada
190 E4 **South Australia** ◈ state S Australia
South Australian Abyssal Plain see South Australian Plain
199 Gg13 **South Australian Basin** undersea feature SW Indian Ocean
181 X12 **South Australian Plain** var. South Australian Abyssal Plain. undersea feature SE Indian Ocean
xliii H23 **South Ayrshire** ◈ unitary authority W Scotland, UK
39 R13 **South Baldy** ▲ New Mexico, SW USA
xli U9 **South Bank** Redcar and Cleveland, N England, UK

◆ Country
● Country Capital
◇ Dependent Territory
○ Dependent Territory Capital
◈ Administrative Region
✕ International Airport
▲ Mountain
▲▲ Mountain Range
⛛ Volcano
≈ River
◎ Lake
⊠ Reservoir

SOUTH BARRULE – STANZACH

xl F12 **South Barrule** hill S Isle of Man
25 Y14 **South Bay** Florida, SE USA
12 E12 **South Baymouth** Manitoulin Island, Ontario, S Canada
32 L10 **South Beloit** Illinois, N USA
33 O11 **South Bend** Indiana, N USA
27 R6 **South Bend** Texas, SW USA
34 F9 **South Bend** Washington, NW USA
xxxvii W9 **South Benfleet** Essex, SE England, UK
South Beveland see Zuid-Beveland
South Borneo see Kalimantan Selatan
xxxvii V11 **Southborough** Kent, SE England, UK
23 U7 **South Boston** Virginia, NE USA
190 F2 **South Branch Neales** seasonal river South Australia
23 U3 **South Branch Potomac River** ∽ West Virginia, NE USA
xxxvi G16 **South Brent** Devon, SW England, UK
193 H19 **Southbridge** Canterbury, South Island, NZ
21 N12 **Southbridge** Massachusetts, NE USA
191 P17 **South Bruny Island** island Tasmania, SE Australia
20 L7 **South Burlington** Vermont, NE USA
46 M6 **South Caicos** island S Turks and Caicos Islands
South Cape see Ka Lae
25 V3 **South Carolina** off. State of South Carolina; also known as The Palmetto State. ◈ state SE USA
South Carpathians see Carpaţii Meridionali
xli V14 **South Cave** East Riding of Yorkshire, N England, UK
South Celebes see Sulawesi Selatan
xxxvii N8 **South Cerney** Gloucestershire, C England, UK
23 Q5 **South Charleston** West Virginia, NE USA
xli R3 **South Charlton** Northumberland, N England, UK
198 F7 **South China Basin** undersea feature SE South China Sea
198 F7 **South China Sea** Chin. Nan Hai, Ind. Laut Cina Selatan, Vtn. Biên Đông. sea SE Asia
35 Z10 **South Dakota** off. State of South Dakota; also known as The Coyote State, Sunshine State. ◈ state N USA
25 X10 **South Daytona** Florida, SE USA
39 R10 **South Domingo Pueblo** New Mexico, SW USA
xxxvii R12 **South Downs** hill range SE England, UK
85 I21 **South East** ◈ district SE Botswana
67 H15 **South East Bay** bay Ascension Island, C Atlantic Ocean
191 O17 **South East Cape** headland Tasmania, SE Australia
40 K10 **Southeast Cape** headland Saint Lawrence Island, Alaska, USA
South-East Celebes see Sulawesi Tenggara
198 G14 **Southeast Indian Ridge** undersea feature Indian Ocean/Pacific Ocean
Southeast Island see Tagula Island
199 Mm16 **Southeast Pacific Basin** var. Belling Hausen Mulde. undersea feature SE Pacific Ocean
67 H15 **South East Point** headland SE Ascension Island
191 O14 **South East Point** headland Victoria, S Australia
203 Z3 **South East Point** headland Kiritimati, NE Kiribati
46 L5 **Southeast Point** headland Mayaguana, SE Bahamas
South-East Sulawesi see Sulawesi Tenggara
xliii F23 **Southend** Argyll and Bute, W Scotland, UK
9 U12 **Southend** Saskatchewan, C Canada
xxxvii X9 **Southend-on-Sea** Essex, E England, UK
xxxvii W9 **Southend-on-Sea** ◈ unitary authority SE England, UK
85 H20 **Southern** var. Bangwaketse, Ngwaketze. ◈ district SE Botswana
144 E13 **Southern** ◈ district S Israel
85 N15 **Southern** ◈ region S Malawi
85 I15 **Southern** ◈ province S Zambia
193 E19 **Southern Alps** ▲ South Island, NZ
202 K15 **Southern Cook Islands** island group S Cook Islands
188 K12 **Southern Cross** Western Australia
82 A12 **Southern Darfur** ◈ state W Sudan
194 F13 **Southern Highlands** ◈ province W PNG
9 V11 **Southern Indian Lake** ◎ Manitoba, C Canada
82 E11 **Southern Kordofan** ◈ state C Sudan
197 L15 **Southern Lau Group** island group Lau Group, SE Fiji
xii-xiii **Southern Ocean** ocean
23 T10 **Southern Pines** North Carolina, SE USA
161 J26 **Southern Province** ◈ province S Sri Lanka
xliii K23 **Southern Uplands** ▲ S Scotland, UK
Southern Urals see Yuzhnyy Ural
xxxix T10 **Southery** Norfolk, E England, UK
xliii N16 **South Esk** ∽ E Scotland, UK
191 P16 **South Esk River** ∽ Tasmania, SE Australia
9 U16 **Southey** Saskatchewan, S Canada
29 V2 **South Fabius River** ∽ Missouri, C USA
xxxix P3 **South Ferriby** North Lincolnshire, N England, UK
33 S10 **Southfield** Michigan, N USA
xxxvi R9 **Southfields** Wandsworth, SE England, UK
199 J11 **South Fiji Basin** undersea feature S Pacific Ocean
xxxvii Z11 **South Foreland** headland SE England, UK
37 P7 **South Fork American River** ∽ California, W USA
30 K7 **South Fork Grand River** ∽ South Dakota, N USA
37 T12 **South Fork Kern River** ∽ California, W USA
41 Q7 **South Fork Koyukuk River** ∽ Alaska, USA
41 Q11 **South Fork Kuskokwim River** ∽ Alaska, USA
28 H2 **South Fork Republican River** ∽ C USA
28 L3 **South Fork Solomon River** ∽ Kansas, C USA
33 P5 **South Fox Island** island Michigan, N USA
22 G8 **South Fulton** Tennessee, S USA
xxxvi D5 **Southgate** Enfield, SE England, UK
205 U10 **South Geomagnetic Pole** pole Antarctica
67 J20 **South Georgia** island South Georgia and the South Sandwich Islands, SW Atlantic Ocean
67 K21 **South Georgia and the South Sandwich Islands** ◇ UK dependent territory SW Atlantic Ocean
49 Y14 **South Georgia Ridge** var. North Scotia Ridge. undersea feature SW Atlantic Ocean
xxxvi L8 **South Gloucestershire** ◈ unitary authority W England, UK
189 Q1 **South Goulburn Island** island Northern Territory, N Australia
xxxvii R12 **South Harting** West Sussex, SE England, UK
159 U16 **South Hatia Island** island SE Bangladesh
33 O10 **South Haven** Michigan, N USA
xxxvii Q13 **South Hayling** Hampshire, S England, UK
23 V7 **South Hill** Virginia, NE USA
South Holland see Zuid-Holland
xxxvii T11 **South Holmwood** Surrey, SE England, UK
23 P8 **South Holston Lake** ⊡ Tennessee/Virginia, S USA
183 N1 **South Honshu Ridge** undersea feature W Pacific Ocean
28 M6 **South Hutchinson** Kansas, C USA
157 K21 **South Huvadhu Atoll** var. Gaafu Dhaalu Atoll. atoll S Maldives
181 U14 **South Indian Basin** undersea feature Indian Ocean/Pacific Ocean
9 W11 **South Indian Lake** Manitoba, C Canada
83 I17 **South Island** island NW Kenya
193 C20 **South Island** island S NZ
67 B23 **South Jason** island Jason Islands, NW Falkland Islands
South Kalimantan see Kalimantan Selatan
South Kazakhstan see Yuzhnyy Kazakhstan
xxxix Q4 **South Kelsey** Lincolnshire, E England, UK
xli S15 **South Kirkby** Wakefield, N England, UK
169 X15 **South Korea** off. Republic of Korea, Kor. Taehan Min'guk. ◆ republic E Asia
xxxix R7 **South Kyme** Lincolnshire, E England, UK
37 Q6 **South Lake Tahoe** California, W USA
xliii J21 **South Lanarkshire** ◈ unitary authority C Scotland, UK
27 N6 **Southland** Texas, SW USA
193 B23 **Southland** off. Southland Region. ◈ region South Island, NZ
xxxviii K13 **South Littleton** Worcestershire, C England, UK
31 N15 **South Loup River** ∽ Nebraska, C USA
157 K19 **South Maalhosmadulu Atoll** var. Baa Atoll. atoll N Maldives
12 E15 **South Maitland** ∽ Ontario, S Canada
198 Ff9 **South Makassar Basin** undersea feature E Java Sea
xxxvii U13 **South Malling** East Sussex, SE England, UK
33 O6 **South Manitou Island** island Michigan, N USA
157 K18 **South Miladummadulu Atoll** atoll N Maldives
23 X8 **South Mills** North Carolina, SE USA
xxxvii X8 **Southminster** Essex, SE England, UK
xxxvi G12 **South Molton** Devon, SW England, UK
14 G7 **South Nahanni** ∽ Northwest Territories, NW Canada
41 P13 **South Naknek** Alaska, USA
12 M13 **South Nation** ∽ Ontario, SE Canada
46 F9 **South Negril Point** headland W Jamaica
157 K20 **South Nilandhe Atoll** var. Dhaalu Atoll. atoll C Maldives
38 L2 **South Ogden** Utah, W USA
20 M14 **Southold** Long Island, New York, NE USA
204 H1 **South Orkney Islands** island group Antarctica
143 S9 **South Ossetia** former autonomous region SW Georgia
South Pacific Basin see Southwest Pacific Basin
21 P7 **South Paris** Maine, NE USA
35 U15 **South Pass** pass Wyoming, C USA
201 U13 **South Pass** passage Chuuk Islands, C Micronesia
xxxvi K12 **South Petherton** Somerset, SW England, UK
22 K10 **South Pittsburg** Tennessee, S USA
30 K15 **South Platte River** ∽ Colorado/Nebraska, C USA
33 T16 **South Point** Ohio, N USA
67 G15 **South Point** headland S Ascension Island
33 R6 **South Point** headland Michigan, N USA
South Point see Ka Lae
xl B13 **Southport** Sefton, NW England, UK
191 P17 **Southport** Tasmania, SE Australia
23 V12 **Southport** North Carolina, SE USA
21 P8 **South Portland** Maine, NE USA
xliii L19 **South Queensferry** City of Edinburgh, SE Scotland, UK
12 H12 **South River** Ontario, S Canada
23 U11 **South River** ∽ North Carolina, SE USA
xliii N5 **South Ronaldsay** island NE Scotland, UK
38 L2 **South Salt Lake** Utah, W USA
67 L21 **South Sandwich Islands** island group SE South Georgia and South Sandwich Islands
67 K21 **South Sandwich Trench** undersea feature SW Atlantic Ocean
9 S16 **South Saskatchewan** ∽ Alberta/Saskatchewan, S Canada
67 I21 **South Scotia Ridge** undersea feature S Scotia Sea
9 V10 **South Seal** ∽ Manitoba, C Canada
204 G4 **South Shetland Islands** island group Antarctica
67 H22 **South Shetland Trough** undersea feature Atlantic Ocean/Pacific Ocean
xli W2 **South Shields** South Tyneside, NE England, UK
31 R13 **South Sioux City** Nebraska, C USA
xli W13 **South Skirlaugh** East Riding of Yorkshire, N England, UK
199 I10 **South Solomon Trench** undersea feature W Pacific Ocean
xliv D10 **South Sound** sound W Ireland
191 V3 **South Stradbroke Island** island Queensland, E Australia
South Sulawesi see Sulawesi Selatan
South Sumatra see Sumatera Selatan
192 K11 **South Taranaki Bight** bight SE Tasman Sea
202 I3 **South Tarawa** atoll Tungaru, W Kiribati
South Tasmania Plateau see Tasman Plateau
xliii N5 **Southtown** Orkney Islands, N Scotland, UK
38 M15 **South Tucson** Arizona, SW USA
10 H9 **South Twin Island** island Northwest Territories, C Canada
xli O7 **South Tyne** ∽ N England, UK
xli S6 **South Tyneside** ◈ unitary authority NE England, UK
xliii A13 **South Uist** island NW Scotland, UK
xliii I4 **South View** Shetland Islands, NE Scotland, UK
xxxiv L16 **Southwark** ◈ London borough SE England, UK
xxxvi D8 **Southwark** London borough capital Southwark, SE England, UK
xxxix O7 **Southwell** Nottinghamshire, C England, UK
South-West see Sud-Ouest
South-West Africa/South West Africa see Namibia
67 F15 **South West Bay** bay Ascension Island, C Atlantic Ocean
191 N18 **South West Cape** headland Tasmania, SE Australia
193 B26 **South West Cape** headland Stewart Island, NZ
40 J10 **Southwest Cape** headland Saint Lawrence Island, Alaska, USA
178 Mm13 **Southwest Cay** island NW Spratly Islands
Southwest Indian Ocean Ridge see Southwest Indian Ridge
181 N11 **Southwest Indian Ridge** var. Southwest Indian Ocean Ridge. undersea feature SW Indian Ocean
199 Kk13 **Southwest Pacific Basin** var. South Pacific Basin. undersea feature SE Pacific Ocean
46 H2 **Southwest Point** headland Great Abaco, N Bahamas
203 X3 **South West Point** headland Kiritimati, NE Kiribati
67 G25 **South West Point** headland SW Saint Helena
27 P5 **South Wichita River** ∽ Texas, SW USA
xxxix Z11 **Southwold** Suffolk, E England, UK
xxxvii W8 **South Woodham Ferrers** Essex, E England, UK
xxxix T8 **South Wootton** Norfolk, E England, UK
21 Q12 **South Yarmouth** Massachusetts, NE USA
xxxvi G14 **South Zeal** Devon, SW England, UK
118 J10 **Sovata** Hung. Szováta. Mureş, C Romania
109 N22 **Soverato** Calabria, SW Italy
Sovetabad see Ghafurov
130 C2 **Sovetsk** Ger. Tilsit. Kaliningradskaya Oblast', W Russian Federation
129 Q15 **Sovetsk** Kirovskaya Oblast', NW Russian Federation
131 N10 **Sovetskaya** Rostovskaya Oblast', SW Russian Federation
127 O15 **Sovetskaya Gavan'** Khabarovskiy Kray, SE Russian Federation
125 F10 **Sovetskiy** Khanty-Mansiyskiy Avtonomnyy Okrug, C Russian Federation
Sovetskoye see Ketchenery
152 I15 **Sovet"yab** prev. Sovet"yap. Akhalskiy Velayat, S Turkmenistan
Sovet"yap see Sovet"yab
119 U12 **Sovyets'kyy** Respublika Krym, S Ukraine
85 I18 **Sowa** var. Sua. Central, NE Botswana
85 I18 **Sowa Pan** salt lake NE Botswana
176 Ww9 **Sowek** Irian Jaya, E Indonesia
xli S11 **Sowerby** North Yorkshire, N England, UK
85 J21 **Soweto** Gauteng, NE South Africa
Sōya-kaikyō see La Perouse Strait
172 Pp1 **Sōya-misaki** headland Hokkaidō, NE Japan
129 N7 **Soyana** ∽ NW Russian Federation
152 A8 **Soye, Mys** var. Mys Suz. headland NW Turkmenistan
84 A10 **Soyo** Zaire, NW Angola
82 J10 **Soyra** ▲ C Eritrea
Sozaq see Suzak
121 P16 **Sozh** Rus. Sozh. ∽ NE Europe
116 N10 **Sozopol** prev. Sizebolu, anc. Apollonia. Burgaska Oblast, E Bulgaria
180 J15 **Sœurs, Les** island group Inner Islands, W Seychelles
101 L20 **Spa** Liège, E Belgium
204 I7 **Spaatz Island** island Antarctica
150 M14 **Space Launching Centre** space station Kzyl-Orda, S Kazakhstan
107 O7 **Spain** off. Kingdom of Spain, Sp. España; anc. Hispania, Iberia, Lat. Hispana. ◆ monarchy SW Europe
Spalato see Split
xxxix R8 **Spalding** Lincolnshire, E England, UK
xxxix R11 **Spaldwick** Cambridgeshire, E England, UK
12 D11 **Spanish** Ontario, S Canada
38 L3 **Spanish Fork** Utah, W USA
xliv D10 **Spanish Point** headland W Ireland
66 B12 **Spanish Point** headland C Bermuda
12 E9 **Spanish River** ∽ Ontario, S Canada
46 K13 **Spanish Town** hist. St.Iago de la Vega. C Jamaica
117 H24 **Spánta, Ákra** headland Kríti, Greece, E Mediterranean Sea
xxxvi L12 **Sparkford** Somerset, SW England, UK
37 Q5 **Sparks** Nevada, W USA
Sparnacum see Épernay
97 N16 **Sparreholm** Södermanland, C Sweden
25 U4 **Sparta** Georgia, SE USA
32 J7 **Sparta** Illinois, N USA
33 P9 **Sparta** Michigan, N USA
23 R8 **Sparta** North Carolina, SE USA
22 L9 **Sparta** Tennessee, S USA
32 K16 **Sparta** Wisconsin, N USA
Sparta see Spárti
23 Q11 **Spartanburg** South Carolina, SE USA
122 F10 **Spartel, Cap** headland N Morocco
117 F21 **Spárti** Eng. Sparta. Pelopónnisos, S Greece
109 B21 **Spartivento, Capo** headland Sardegna, Italy, C Mediterranean Sea
9 P17 **Sparwood** British Columbia, SW Canada
130 I4 **Spas-Demensk** Kaluzhskaya Oblast', W Russian Federation
130 M4 **Spas-Klepiki** Ryazanskaya Oblast', W Russian Federation
127 N17 **Spassk-Dal'niy** Primorskiy Kray, SE Russian Federation
130 M5 **Spassk-Ryazanskiy** Ryazanskaya Oblast', W Russian Federation
117 H19 **Spáta** Attikí, C Greece
124 O12 **Spátha, Ákra** headland Kríti, Greece, E Mediterranean Sea
Spatrjan see Paternion
xliii H15 **Spean Bridge** Highland, NW Scotland, UK
30 I9 **Spearfish** South Dakota, N USA
27 O1 **Spearman** Texas, SW USA
67 C25 **Speedwell Island** island S Falkland Islands
67 C25 **Speedwell Island Settlement** S Falkland Islands
67 G25 **Speery Island** island S Saint Helena
47 N14 **Speightstown** NW Barbados
xl M17 **Speke** Liverpool, NW England, UK
108 I13 **Spello** Umbria, C Italy
41 R12 **Spenard** Alaska, USA
Spence Bay see Taloyoak
33 O14 **Spencer** Indiana, N USA
31 T12 **Spencer** Iowa, C USA
31 P12 **Spencer** Nebraska, C USA
23 S9 **Spencer** North Carolina, SE USA
22 L9 **Spencer** Tennessee, S USA
23 Q4 **Spencer** West Virginia, NE USA
32 K6 **Spencer** Wisconsin, N USA
190 G10 **Spencer, Cape** headland South Australia
41 V13 **Spencer, Cape** headland Alaska, USA
190 H9 **Spencer Gulf** gulf South Australia
20 F9 **Spencerport** New York, NE USA
33 Q12 **Spencerville** Ohio, N USA
xli R8 **Spennymoor** Durham, N England, UK
117 E17 **Sperchiáda** var. Sperhiada, Sperkhiás. Stereá Ellás, C Greece
117 E17 **Sperchiós** ∽ C Greece
Sperhiada see Sperchiáda
97 G14 **Sperillen** ◎ S Norway
Sperkhiás see Sperchiáda
xliv J3 **Sperrin Mountains** ▲ N Northern Ireland, UK
103 I18 **Spessart** hill range C Germany
xxxviii J13 **Spetchley** Worcestershire, W England, UK
Spétsai see Spétses
117 G21 **Spétses** prev. Spétsai. Spétses, S Greece
117 G21 **Spétses** island S Greece
xlii M11 **Spey** ∽ NE Scotland, UK
xlii M11 **Spey Bay** Moray, N Scotland, UK
103 G20 **Speyer** Eng. Spires; anc. Civitas Nemetum, Spira. Rheinland-Pfalz, SW Germany
103 G20 **Speyerbach** ∽ W Germany
109 N20 **Spezzano Albanese** Calabria, SW Italy
Spice Islands see Maluku
xliv E9 **Spiddle** Galway, W Ireland
102 F9 **Spiekeroog** island NW Germany
111 W9 **Spielfeld** Steiermark, SE Austria
67 N21 **Spiess Seamount** undersea feature S Atlantic Ocean
110 E9 **Spiez** Bern, W Switzerland
100 G13 **Spijkenisse** Zuid-Holland, SW Netherlands
41 T6 **Spike Mountain** ▲ Alaska, USA
117 I25 **Spíli** Kríti, Greece, E Mediterranean Sea
110 D10 **Spillgerten** ▲ W Switzerland
xxxix S6 **Spilsby** Lincolnshire, E England, UK
120 F9 **Spilva** ✕ (Riga) Riga, C Latvia
109 N17 **Spinazzola** Puglia, SE Italy
155 O9 **Spīn Būldak** Kandahār, S Afghanistan
xlii J10 **Spinningdale** Highland, NW Scotland, UK
Spira see Speyer
Spirdingsee see Śniardwy, Jezioro
Spires see Speyer
31 T11 **Spirit Lake** Iowa, C USA
31 T11 **Spirit Lake** ◎ Iowa, C USA
9 N13 **Spirit River** Alberta, W Canada
9 S14 **Spiritwood** Saskatchewan, S Canada
29 R11 **Spiro** Oklahoma, C USA
113 L19 **Spišská Nová Ves** Ger. Neudorf, Zipser Neudorf, Hung. Igló. Východné Slovensko, E Slovakia
143 T11 **Spitak** NW Armenia
xlii L7 **Spital** Highland, N Scotland, UK
94 O2 **Spitsbergen** island NW Svalbard
xxxv D13 **Spittal** Pembrokeshire, SW Wales, UK
Spittal see Spittal an der Drau
111 R9 **Spittal an der Drau** var. Spittal. Kärnten, S Austria
xliii L15 **Spittal of Glenshee** Perth and Kinross, C Scotland, UK
111 V3 **Spitz** Niederösterreich, NE Austria
96 D9 **Spjelkavik** Møre og Romsdal, S Norway
27 W10 **Splendora** Texas, SW USA
115 E14 **Split** It. Spalato. Split-Dalmacija, S Croatia
115 E14 **Split** ✕ Split-Dalmacija, S Croatia
115 E14 **Split-Dalmacija** off. Splitsko-Dalmatinska Županija. ◈ province S Croatia
9 X12 **Split Lake** ◎ Manitoba, C Canada
Splitsko-Dalmatinska Županija see Split-Dalmacija
110 H10 **Splügen** Graubünden, S Switzerland
Spodnji Dravograd see Dravograd
27 P12 **Spofford** Texas, SW USA
xli R13 **Spofforth** North Yorkshire, N England, UK
120 J11 **Špoģi** Daugvapils, SE Latvia
34 L8 **Spokane** Washington, NW USA
34 L8 **Spokane River** ∽ Washington, NW USA
108 I13 **Spoleto** Umbria, C Italy
32 I4 **Spooner** Wisconsin, N USA
32 K12 **Spoon River** ∽ Illinois, N USA
23 W5 **Spotsylvania** Virginia, NE USA
34 L8 **Sprague** Washington, NW USA
178 I16 **Spratly Island** island SW Spratly Islands
198 Ff7 **Spratly Islands** Chin. Nansha Qundao. ◇ disputed territory SE Asia
xxxix O12 **Spratton** Northamptonshire, C England, UK
34 J12 **Spray** Oregon, NW USA
114 I11 **Spreća** ∽ N Bosnia and Herzegovina
102 P13 **Spree** ∽ E Germany
102 P13 **Spreewald** wetland NE Germany
103 P14 **Spremberg** Brandenburg, E Germany
xxxix Q5 **Spridlington** Lincolnshire, E England, UK
27 W11 **Spring** Texas, SW USA
33 Q10 **Spring Arbor** Michigan, N USA
85 E23 **Springbok** Northern Cape, W South Africa
20 I15 **Spring City** Pennsylvania, NE USA
22 L9 **Spring City** Tennessee, S USA
38 L4 **Spring City** Utah, W USA
37 W3 **Spring Creek** Nevada, W USA
29 S9 **Springdale** Arkansas, C USA
33 Q14 **Springdale** Ohio, N USA
102 I13 **Springe** Niedersachsen, N Germany
39 U9 **Springer** New Mexico, SW USA
39 W7 **Springfield** Colorado, C USA
25 W5 **Springfield** Georgia, SE USA
32 K14 **Springfield** state capital Illinois, N USA
22 L6 **Springfield** Kentucky, S USA
20 M12 **Springfield** Massachusetts, NE USA
31 T10 **Springfield** Minnesota, N USA
29 T7 **Springfield** Missouri, C USA
33 R13 **Springfield** Ohio, N USA
34 G13 **Springfield** Oregon, NW USA
31 Q12 **Springfield** South Dakota, N USA
22 J8 **Springfield** Tennessee, S USA
20 M9 **Springfield** Vermont, NE USA
32 K14 **Springfield, Lake** ⊡ Illinois, N USA
57 T8 **Spring Garden** NE Guyana
32 K8 **Spring Green** Wisconsin, N USA
31 X11 **Spring Grove** Minnesota, N USA
11 P15 **Springhill** Nova Scotia, SE Canada
25 V12 **Spring Hill** Florida, SE USA
29 R4 **Spring Hill** Kansas, C USA
24 G4 **Springhill** Louisiana, S USA
22 I9 **Spring Hill** Tennessee, S USA
23 U10 **Spring Lake** North Carolina, SE USA
26 M4 **Springlake** Texas, SW USA
37 W11 **Spring Mountains** ▲ Nevada, W USA
67 B24 **Spring Point** West Falkland, Falkland Islands
29 W9 **Spring River** ∽ Arkansas/Missouri, C USA
29 S7 **Spring River** ∽ Missouri/Oklahoma, C USA
85 J21 **Springs** Gauteng, NE South Africa
193 H16 **Springs Junction** West Coast, South Island, NZ
189 X8 **Springsure** Queensland, E Australia
31 W11 **Spring Valley** Minnesota, N USA
20 K13 **Spring Valley** New York, NE USA
31 N12 **Springview** Nebraska, C USA
20 D11 **Springville** New York, NE USA
38 L3 **Springville** Utah, W USA
Sprottau see Szprotawa
13 V4 **Sproule, Pointe** headland Québec, SE Canada
xlii O21 **Sprouston** The Borders, S Scotland, UK
xxxix X9 **Sprowston** Norfolk, E England, UK
9 Q14 **Spruce Grove** Alberta, SW Canada
23 T4 **Spruce Knob** ▲ West Virginia, NE USA
37 X3 **Spruce Mountain** ▲ Nevada, W USA
23 P9 **Spruce Pine** North Carolina, SE USA
100 G13 **Spui** ∽ SW Netherlands
109 O19 **Spulico, Capo** headland S Italy
27 O5 **Spur** Texas, SW USA
xli Y15 **Spurn Head** headland E England, UK
101 H20 **Spy** Namur, S Belgium
97 I15 **Spydeberg** Østfold, S Norway
193 J17 **Spy Glass Point** headland South Island, NZ
8 L17 **Squamish** British Columbia, SW Canada
21 O8 **Squam Lake** ◎ New Hampshire, NE USA
21 S2 **Squa Pan Mountain** ▲ Maine, NE USA
41 N16 **Squaw Harbor** Unga Island, Alaska, USA
12 E11 **Squaw Island** island Ontario, S Canada
109 O22 **Squillace, Golfo di** gulf S Italy
109 Q18 **Squinzano** Puglia, SE Italy
174 L15 **Sragen** Jawa, C Indonesia
xliv L10 **Sraghmore** Wicklow, E Ireland
99 **Sráid na Cathrach** see Milltown Malbay
178 Jj11 **Srâlau** Stœng Trêng, N Cambodia
Srath an Urláir see Stranorlar
114 G10 **Srbac** N Bosnia and Herzegovina
Srbija see Serbia
114 K9 **Srbobran** var. Bácsszenttamás, Hung. Szenttamás. Serbia, N Yugoslavia
178 Ii14 **Srê Âmběl** Kaôh Kŏng, SW Cambodia
114 K13 **Srebrenica** E Bosnia and Herzegovina
114 I11 **Srebrenik** NE Bosnia and Herzegovina
116 M10 **Sredets** prev. Grudovo. Burgaska Oblast, SE Bulgaria
116 K10 **Sredets** prev. Syulemeshlii. Khaskovska Oblast, C Bulgaria
116 M10 **Sredetska Reka** ∽ SE Bulgaria
127 P9 **Sredinnyy Khrebet** ▲ E Russian Federation
116 N7 **Sredishte** Rom. Beibunar; prev. Knyazhevo. Varnenska Oblast, NE Bulgaria
116 I10 **Sredna Gora** ▲ C Bulgaria
127 N7 **Srednekolymsk** Respublika Sakha (Yakutiya), NE Russian Federation
130 K7 **Srednerusskaya Vozvyshennost'** Eng. Central Russian Upland. ▲ W Russian Federation
126 Ii9 **Srednesibirskoye Ploskogor'ye** var. Central Siberian Uplands, Eng. Central Siberian Plateau. ▲ N Russian Federation
129 V13 **Sredniy Ural** ▲ NW Russian Federation
178 Jj13 **Srê Khtŭm** Mŏndól Kiri, E Cambodia
113 G17 **Śrem** Poznań, W Poland
114 K10 **Sremska Mitrovica** prev. Mitrovica, Ger. Mitrowitz. Serbia, NW Yugoslavia
178 Ii11 **Srêng, Stœng** ∽ NW Cambodia
178 Ii11 **Srê Noy** Siĕmréab, NW Cambodia
Srepok, Sông see Srêpôk, Tônle
178 K12 **Srêpôk, Tônle** var. Sông Srepok. ∽ Cambodia/Vietnam
126 L15 **Sretensk** Chitinskaya Oblast', S Russian Federation
174 L17 **Sri Aman** Sarawak, East Malaysia
119 R4 **Sribne** Chernihivs'ka Oblast', N Ukraine
161 J25 **Sri Jayawardanapura** var. Sri Jayawardenepura; prev. Kotte. Western Province, W Sri Lanka
161 M14 **Srīkākulam** Andhra Pradesh, E India
161 J25 **Sri Lanka** off. Democratic Socialist Republic of Sri Lanka; prev. Ceylon. ◆ republic S Asia
139 Mm15 **Sri Lanka** island S Asia
159 V14 **Srimangal** Chittagong, E Bangladesh
Sri Mohangorh see Shri Mohangarh
158 H5 **Srīnagar** Jammu and Kashmir, N India
178 H10 **Srinagarind Reservoir** ⊡ W Thailand
161 F19 **Sringeri** Karnātaka, W India
161 K25 **Sri Pada** Eng. Adam's Peak. ▲ S Sri Lanka
Sri Saket see Si Sa Ket
113 G14 **Sroda Śląska** Ger. Neumarkt. Wrocław, SW Poland
112 H12 **Środa Wielkopolska** Poznań, W Poland
Ssu-ch'uan see Sichuan
Ssu-p'ing/Ssu-p'ing-chieh see Siping
Stablo see Stavelot
101 G15 **Stabroek** Antwerpen, N Belgium
Stackeln see Strenči
xlii J4 **Stack Skerry** island N Scotland, UK
96 C10 **Stad** peninsula S Norway
102 I9 **Stade** Niedersachsen, N Germany
xxxvii Q8 **Stadhampton** Oxfordshire, C England, UK
111 R5 **Stadl-Paura** Oberösterreich, NW Austria
121 L20 **Stadolichy** Rus. Stodolichi. Homyel'skaya Voblasts', SE Belorussia
100 P7 **Stadskanaal** Groningen, NE Netherlands
103 H16 **Stadtallendorf** Hessen, C Germany
103 K23 **Stadtbergen** Bayern, S Germany
110 G7 **Stäfa** Zürich, NE Switzerland
xliii D17 **Staffa** island W Scotland, UK
97 K23 **Staffanstorp** Malmöhus, S Sweden
103 K18 **Staffelstein** Bayern, C Germany
xli E11 **Staffin** Highland, NW Scotland, UK
xxxviii J9 **Stafford** Staffordshire, C England, UK
28 L6 **Stafford** Kansas, C USA
23 W4 **Stafford** Virginia, NE USA
xxxviii C13 **Staffordshire** ◈ county C England, UK
21 N12 **Stafford Springs** Connecticut, NE USA
117 H14 **Stágira** Kentrikí Makedonía, N Greece
120 G7 **Staicele** Limbaži, N Latvia
Ştaierdorf-Anina see Anina
xli Q9 **Staindrop** Durham, N England, UK
xxxvii S9 **Staines** Surrey, SE England, UK
xli T15 **Stainforth** Doncaster, N England, UK
xli P12 **Stainforth** North Yorkshire, N England, UK
xli W10 **Staintondale** North Yorkshire, N England, UK
111 V8 **Stainz** Steiermark, SE Austria
xli U9 **Staithes** Redcar and Cleveland, N England, UK
Stájerlakanina see Anina
119 Y7 **Stakhanov** Luhans'ka Oblast', E Ukraine
xxxvi L12 **Stalbridge** Dorset, S England, UK
110 E11 **Stalden** Valais, SW Switzerland
xxxix Y8 **Stalham** Norfolk, E England, UK
Stalin see Varna
Stalinabad see Dushanbe
Stalingrad see Volgograd
Staliniri see Ts'khinvali
Stalino see Donets'k
Stalinobod see Dushanbe
Stalinov Štít see Gerlachovský Štít
Stalinsk see Novokuznetsk
Stalinskaya Oblast' see Donets'ka Oblast'
Stalinski Zaliv see Varnenski Zaliv
Stalin, Yazovir see Iskŭr, Yazovir
xli P11 **Stalling Busk** North Yorkshire, N England, UK
113 N15 **Stalowa Wola** Tarnobrzeg, SE Poland
xli Q16 **Stalybridge** Tameside, NW England, UK
116 I11 **Stamboliyski** Plovdivska Oblast, C Bulgaria
116 J8 **Stamboliyski, Yazovir** ⊡ N Bulgaria
xxxix Q9 **Stamford** Lincolnshire, E England, UK
20 L14 **Stamford** Connecticut, NE USA
27 P6 **Stamford** Texas, SW USA
xli U12 **Stamford Bridge** East Riding of Yorkshire, N England, UK
xli Q6 **Stamfordham** Northumberland, N England, UK
xxxvi D6 **Stamford Hill** Hackney, SE England, UK
27 Q6 **Stamford, Lake** ⊡ Texas, SW USA
110 I10 **Stampa** Graubünden, SE Switzerland
Stampalia see Astypálaia
29 T14 **Stamps** Arkansas, C USA
94 G11 **Stamsund** Nordland, C Norway
29 R2 **Stanberry** Missouri, C USA
205 O3 **Stancomb-Wills Glacier** glacier Antarctica
85 K21 **Standerton** Mpumalanga, E South Africa
xli N15 **Standish** Wigan, NW England, UK
33 R7 **Standish** Michigan, N USA
xxxviii J8 **Standon** Staffordshire, C England, UK
22 M6 **Stanford** Kentucky, S USA
35 S9 **Stanford** Montana, NW USA
xxxvii W9 **Stanford-le-Hope** Essex, SE England, UK
97 P19 **Stånga** Gotland, SE Sweden
96 I13 **Stange** Hedmark, S Norway
85 L23 **Stanger** KwaZulu/Natal, E South Africa
xli Q8 **Stanhope** Durham, N England, UK
xliii L22 **Stanhope** The Borders, S Scotland, UK
Stanimaka see Asenovgrad
Stanislau see Ivano-Frankivs'k
37 P8 **Stanislaus River** ∽ California, W USA
Stanislav see Ivano-Frankivs'k
Stanislavskaya Oblast' see Ivano-Frankivs'ka Oblast'
Stanisławów see Ivano-Frankivs'k
Stanke Dimitrov see Dupnitsa
xli Q7 **Stanley** Durham, N England, UK
xliii L17 **Stanley** Perth and Kinross, C Scotland, UK
191 O15 **Stanley** Tasmania, SE Australia
67 E24 **Stanley** var. Port Stanley. ○ (Falkland Islands) East Falkland, Falkland Islands
35 O13 **Stanley** Idaho, NW USA
30 L3 **Stanley** North Dakota, N USA
23 U4 **Stanley** Virginia, NE USA
32 J6 **Stanley** Wisconsin, N USA
81 G21 **Stanley Pool** var. Pool Malebo. ◎ Congo/Zaire
161 H20 **Stanley Reservoir** ⊡ S India
Stanleyville see Kisangani
xxxvi A5 **Stanmore** Harrow, SE England, UK
44 G3 **Stann Creek** ◈ district SE Belize
Stann Creek see Dangriga
xli R5 **Stannington** Northumberland, N England, UK
127 N17 **Stanovoy Khrebet** ▲ SE Russian Federation
110 F8 **Stans** Unterwalden, C Switzerland
xxxvii V7 **Stansted** ✕ (London) Essex, E England, UK
xxxvii V7 **Stansted Mountfitchet** Hertfordshire, E England, UK
191 U4 **Stanthorpe** Queensland, E Australia
xxxix V11 **Stanton** Suffolk, E England, UK
23 N6 **Stanton** Kentucky, S USA
33 Q8 **Stanton** Michigan, N USA
31 Q14 **Stanton** Nebraska, C USA
30 L5 **Stanton** North Dakota, N USA
27 N7 **Stanton** Texas, SW USA
xxxvii Q8 **Stanton St John** Oxfordshire, C England, UK
xxxvii X7 **Stanway** Essex, SE England, UK
xxxvii N6 **Stanway** Gloucestershire, C England, UK
34 H7 **Stanwood** Washington, NW USA
119 Y7 **Stanychno-Luhans'ke** Luhans'ka Oblast', E Ukraine
110 K7 **Stanzach** Tirol, W Austria

◆ Country ● Country Capital ◇ Dependent Territory ○ Dependent Territory Capital ◈ Administrative Region ✕ International Airport ▲ Mountain ▲ Mountain Range Volcano ∽ River ◎ Lake ⊡ Reservoir

Staphorst – Sturton by Stow

100 M9 **Staphorst** Overijssel, E Netherlands
xxxvi J12 **Staple Fitzpaine** Somerset, SW England, UK
xxxix N8 **Stapleford** Nottinghamshire, C England, UK
xxxvii N11 **Stapleford** Wiltshire, S England, UK
xxxvi W11 **Staplehurst** Kent, SE England, UK
12 D18 **Staples** Ontario, S Canada
31 T6 **Staples** Minnesota, N USA
30 M14 **Stapleton** Nebraska, C USA
27 S8 **Star** Texas, SW USA
113 M14 **Starachowice** Kielce, SE Poland
Stara Kanjiža see Kanjiža
113 M18 **Stará Ľubovňa** Ger. Altlublau, Hung. Ólubló. Východné Slovensko, E Slovakia
114 L10 **Stara Pazova** Ger. Altpasua, Hung. Ópazova. Serbia, N Yugoslavia
Stara Planina see Balkan Mountains
116 L9 **Stara Reka** ≈ C Bulgaria
118 M5 **Stara Synyava** Khmel'nyts'ka Oblast', W Ukraine
118 I2 **Stara Vyzhivka** Volyns'ka Oblast', NW Ukraine
Staraya Belitsa see Staraya Byelitsa
121 M14 **Staraya Byelitsa** Rus. Staraya Belitsa. Vitsyebskaya Voblasts', NE Belarussia
131 R5 **Staraya Mayna** Ul'yanovskaya Oblast', W Russian Federation
121 O18 **Staraya Rudnya** Rus. Staraya Rudnya. Homyel'skaya Voblasts', SE Belorussia
128 H14 **Staraya Russa** Novgorodskaya Oblast', W Russian Federation
116 K10 **Stara Zagora** Lat. Augusta Trajana. Khaskovska Oblast, C Bulgaria
31 S8 **Starbuck** Minnesota, N USA
203 W4 **Starbuck Island** prev. Volunteer Island. island E Kiribati
29 V13 **Star City** Arkansas, C USA
xxxvi I14 **Starcross** Devon, SW England, UK
114 F13 **Staretina** ▲ W Bosnia and Herzegovina
Stargard in Pommern see Stargard Szczeciński
112 E9 **Stargard Szczeciński** Ger. Stargard in Pommern. Szczecin, NW Poland
195 Z17 **Star Harbour** harbour San Cristobal, SE Solomon Islands
Stari Bečej see Bečej
115 F15 **Starigrad** It. Cittavecchia. Split-Dalmacija, S Croatia
175 Qq12 **Staring, Teluk** var. Teluk Wawosungu. bay Sulawesi, C Indonesia
128 J16 **Staritsa** Tverskaya Oblast', W Russian Federation
25 V9 **Starke** Florida, SE USA
24 M4 **Starkville** Mississippi, S USA
194 E11 **Star Mountains** Ind. Pegunungan Sterren. ▲ Indonesia/PNG
103 L23 **Starnberg** Bayern, SE Germany
103 L24 **Starnberger See** ◎ SE Germany
Starobel'sk see Starobil's'k
119 X8 **Starobesheve** Donets'ka Oblast', E Ukraine
119 Y6 **Starobil's'k** Rus. Starobel'sk. Luhans'ka Oblast', E Ukraine
Starobin see Starobyn
121 K18 **Starobyn** Rus. Starobin. Minskaya Voblasts', S Belorussia
130 H6 **Starodub** Bryanskaya Oblast', W Russian Federation
112 I8 **Starogard Gdański** Ger. Preussisch-Stargard. Gdańsk, N Poland
151 P16 **Staroikan** Yuzhnyy Kazakhstan, S Kazakhstan
Starokonstantinov see Starokostyantyniv
118 L5 **Starokostyantyniv** Rus. Starokonstantinov. Khmel'nyts'ka Oblast', NW Ukraine
130 K12 **Starominskaya** Krasnodarskiy Kray, SW Russian Federation
116 L7 **Staro Selo** Rom. Satul-Vechi; prev. Star-Smil. Razgradska Oblast, NE Bulgaria
130 K12 **Staroshcherbinovskaya** Krasnodarskiy Kray, SW Russian Federation
131 V6 **Starosubkhangulovo** Respublika Bashkortostan, W Russian Federation
37 S4 **Star Peak** ▲ Nevada, W USA
Star-Smil see Staro Selo
xxxvi H16 **Start Bay** bay SW England, UK
xli Q9 **Startforth** Durham, N England, UK
xxxvi H17 **Start Point** headland SW England, UK
xlii O3 **Start Point** headland N Scotland, UK
Startsy see Kirawsk
Starum see Stavoren
121 L18 **Staryya Darohi** Rus. Staryye Dorogi. Minskaya Voblasts', S Belorussia
Staryye Dorogi see Staryya Darohi
131 T2 **Staryye Zyatsy** Udmurtskaya Respublika, NW Russian Federation
119 U13 **Staryy Krym** Respublika Krym, S Ukraine
130 K8 **Staryy Oskol** Belgorodskaya Oblast', W Russian Federation
118 H6 **Staryy Sambir** L'vivs'ka Oblast', W Ukraine
103 L14 **Stassfurt** var. Staßfurt. Sachsen-Anhalt, C Germany
113 M15 **Staszów** Tarnobrzeg, SE Poland
31 W13 **State Center** Iowa, C USA
20 E14 **State College** Pennsylvania, NE USA
20 K15 **Staten Island** island New York, NE USA
Staten Island see Estados, Isla de los
25 U8 **Statenville** Georgia, SE USA
25 W5 **Statesboro** Georgia, SE USA
States, The see United States of America
23 R9 **Statesville** North Carolina, SE USA
97 G16 **Stathelle** Telemark, S Norway
xxxvi M7 **Staunton** Gloucestershire, C England, UK
xxxvi K7 **Staunton** Gloucestershire, C England, UK
32 K15 **Staunton** Illinois, N USA
23 T5 **Staunton** Virginia, NE USA
xxxviii G13 **Staunton on Wye** Herefordshire, W England, UK
97 C16 **Stavanger** Rogaland, S Norway
xli N10 **Staveley** Cumbria, NW England, UK
xxxviii M5 **Staveley** Derbyshire, C England, UK
101 L21 **Stavelot** Dut. Stablo. Liège, E Belgium
97 G16 **Stavern** Vestfold, S Norway
Stavers Island see Vostok Island
xxxvi M7 **Staverton** Gloucestershire, C England, UK
100 J7 **Stavoren** Fris. Starum. Friesland, N Netherlands
130 M14 **Stavropol'** prev. Voroshilovsk. Stavropol'skiy Kray, SW Russian Federation
Stavropol' see Tol'yatti
130 M14 **Stavropol'skaya Vozvyshennost'** ▲ SW Russian Federation
130 M14 **Stavropol'skiy Kray** ◆ territory SW Russian Federation
117 H14 **Stavrós** Kentrikí Makedonía, N Greece
117 J24 **Stavrós, Ákra** headland Kríti, Greece, E Mediterranean Sea
117 K21 **Stavrós, Ákra** headland Náxos, Kykládes, Greece, Aegean Sea
116 I12 **Stavroúpoli** prev. Stavroúpolis. Anatolikí Makedonía kai Thráki, NE Greece
Stavroúpolis see Stavroúpoli
119 O6 **Stavyshche** Kyyivs'ka Oblast', N Ukraine
190 M11 **Stawell** Victoria, SE Australia
112 N9 **Stawiski** Łomża, NE Poland
xli W11 **Staxton** North Yorkshire, N England, UK
12 G14 **Stayner** Ontario, S Canada
39 R3 **Steamboat Springs** Colorado, C USA
22 M8 **Stearns** Kentucky, S USA
41 N10 **Stebbins** Alaska, USA
110 K7 **Steeg** Tirol, W Austria
29 Y9 **Steele** Missouri, C USA
31 N5 **Steele** North Dakota, N USA
204 J5 **Steele Island** island Antarctica
32 K16 **Steeleville** Illinois, N USA
29 W6 **Steelville** Missouri, C USA
101 G14 **Steenbergen** Noord-Brabant, S Netherlands
Steenkool see Bintuni
9 O10 **Steen River** Alberta, W Canada
100 M8 **Steenwijk** Overijssel, N Netherlands
xxxvi I10 **Steep Holm** island SW England, UK
xxxix S6 **Steeping** ≈ E England, UK
xxxvii W6 **Steeple Bumpstead** Essex, SE England, UK
xxxvii R7 **Steeple Claydon** Buckinghamshire, C England, UK
67 A23 **Steeple Jason** island Jason Islands, NW Falkland Islands
xxxix R13 **Steeple Morden** Cambridgeshire, E England, UK
182 J8 **Steep Point** headland Western Australia
118 L9 **Ştefăneşti** Botoşani, NE Romania
Stefanie, Lake see Ch'ew Bahir
15 J1 **Stefansson Island** island Northwest Territories, N Canada
119 N10 **Ştefan Vodă** Rus. Suvorovo. SE Moldavia
65 H18 **Steffen, Cerro** ▲ S Chile
110 D9 **Steffisburg** Bern, C Switzerland
97 J24 **Stege** Storstrøm, SE Denmark
118 G10 **Ştei** Hung. Vaskohsziklás. Bihor, W Romania
Steier see Steyr
Steierdorf/Steierdorf-Anina see Anina
111 T7 **Steiermark** off. Land Steiermark, Eng. Styria. ◆ state C Austria
103 J19 **Steigerwald** hill range C Germany
101 L17 **Stein** Limburg, SE Netherlands
Stein see Stein an der Donau, Austria
Stein see Kamnik, Slovenia
110 M8 **Steinach** Tirol, W Austria
Steinamanger see Szombathely
111 W3 **Stein an der Donau** var. Stein. Niederösterreich, NE Austria
Steinau an der Elbe see Ścinawa
9 Y16 **Steinbach** Manitoba, S Canada
Steiner Alpen see Savinjske Alpe
101 L24 **Steinfort** Luxembourg, W Luxembourg
102 H12 **Steinhuder Meer** ◎ NW Germany
95 E15 **Steinkjer** Nord-Trøndelag, C Norway
Stejarul see Karapelit
101 F16 **Stekene** Oost-Vlaanderen, NW Belgium
85 E26 **Stellenbosch** Western Cape, SW South Africa
100 F13 **Stellendam** Zuid-Holland, SW Netherlands
41 T12 **Steller, Mount** ▲ Alaska, USA
104 F1 **Stello, Monte** ▲ Corse, France, C Mediterranean Sea
108 F5 **Stelvio, Passo dello** pass Italy/Switzerland
105 R3 **Stenay** Meuse, NE France
102 L12 **Stendal** Sachsen-Anhalt, C Germany
120 E8 **Stende** Talsi, NW Latvia
190 H10 **Stenhouse Bay** South Australia
xliii K19 **Stenhousemuir** Falkirk, C Scotland, UK
97 J23 **Stenløse** Frederiksborg, E Denmark
xlii H2 **Stenness** Shetland Islands, NE Scotland, UK
97 L19 **Stensjön** Jönköping, S Sweden
97 K18 **Stenstorp** Skaraborg, S Sweden
xliii O19 **Stenton** East Lothian, SE Scotland, UK
97 I18 **Stenungsund** Göteborg och Bohus, S Sweden
Stepanakert see Xankändi
143 T11 **Step'anavan** N Armenia
102 K9 **Stepenitz** ≈ N Germany
31 O10 **Stephan** South Dakota, N USA
31 R3 **Stephen** Minnesota, N USA
29 T14 **Stephens** Arkansas, C USA
192 J13 **Stephens, Cape** headland D'Urville Island, Marlborough, SW NZ
23 V3 **Stephens City** Virginia, NE USA
190 L6 **Stephens Creek** New South Wales, SE Australia
192 K13 **Stephens Island** island C NZ
33 N5 **Stephenson** Michigan, N USA
11 S12 **Stephenville** Newfoundland, Newfoundland and Labrador, SE Canada
27 S7 **Stephenville** Texas, SW USA
151 P17 **Step' Nardara** Kaz. Shardara Dalasy; prev. Shaidara. grassland S Kazakhstan
xxxvi E7 **Stepney** Tower Hamlets, SE England, UK
131 O15 **Stepnoye** Stavropol'skiy Kray, SW Russian Federation
151 Q8 **Stepnyak** Kokshetau, N Kazakhstan
xliii J20 **Stepps** North Lanarkshire, C Scotland, UK
198 C9 **Steps Point** headland Tutuila, W American Samoa
117 F17 **Stereá Ellás** Eng. Greece Central. ◆ region C Greece
85 J24 **Sterkspruit** Eastern Cape, SE South Africa
131 U6 **Sterlibashevo** Respublika Bashkortostan, W Russian Federation
41 R12 **Sterling** Alaska, USA
39 V3 **Sterling** Colorado, C USA
32 K11 **Sterling** Illinois, N USA
28 M5 **Sterling** Kansas, C USA
27 O8 **Sterling City** Texas, SW USA
33 S9 **Sterling Heights** Michigan, N USA
23 W3 **Sterling Park** Virginia, NE USA
39 V2 **Sterling Reservoir** ▣ Colorado, C USA
24 I5 **Sterlington** Louisiana, S USA
131 U6 **Sterlitamak** Respublika Bashkortostan, W Russian Federation
Sternberg see Šternberk
113 H17 **Šternberk** Ger. Sternberg. Severní Morava, E Czech Republic
147 V17 **Stěroh** Suquţrā, S Yemen
112 G11 **Stęszew** Poznań, W Poland
Stettin see Szczecin
Stettiner Haff see Szczeciński, Zalew
9 Q15 **Stettler** Alberta, SW Canada
33 V13 **Steubenville** Ohio, N USA
xxxvii T7 **Stevenage** Hertfordshire, E England, UK
25 Q1 **Stevenson** Alabama, S USA
34 H11 **Stevenson** Washington, NW USA
190 E1 **Stevenson Creek** seasonal river South Australia
41 Q13 **Stevenson Entrance** strait Alaska, USA
32 L6 **Stevens Point** Wisconsin, N USA
xliii I21 **Stevenston** North Ayrshire, W Scotland, UK
41 R8 **Stevens Village** Alaska, USA
35 P10 **Stevensville** Montana, NW USA
xxxvii P8 **Steventon** Oxfordshire, C England, UK
95 E25 **Stevns Klint** headland E Denmark
8 J12 **Stewart** British Columbia, W Canada
8 J6 **Stewart** ≈ Yukon Territory, NW Canada
8 I6 **Stewart Crossing** Yukon Territory, NW Canada
65 H25 **Stewart, Isla** island S Chile
193 B25 **Stewart Island** island S NZ
189 W6 **Stewart, Mount** ▲ Queensland, E Australia
xliii I21 **Stewarton** East Ayrshire, W Scotland, UK
8 H6 **Stewart River** Yukon Territory, NW Canada
29 R3 **Stewartsville** Missouri, C USA
9 S16 **Stewart Valley** Saskatchewan, S Canada
31 W10 **Stewartville** Minnesota, N USA
Steyerlak-Anina see Anina
xxxvii T13 **Steyning** West Sussex, SE England, UK
111 T5 **Steyr** var. Steier. Oberösterreich, N Austria
111 T5 **Steyr** ≈ NW Austria
xxxvi F13 **Stibb Cross** Devon, SW England, UK
xliii O21 **Stichill** The Borders, S Scotland, UK
xxxix S6 **Stickford** Lincolnshire, E England, UK
xxxix S6 **Stickney** Lincolnshire, E England, UK
31 P11 **Stickney** South Dakota, N USA
100 L5 **Stiens** Friesland, N Netherlands
Stif see Sétif
29 Q11 **Stigler** Oklahoma, C USA
109 N18 **Stigliano** Basilicata, S Italy
97 N17 **Stigtomta** Södermanland, C Sweden
8 I11 **Stikine** ≈ British Columbia, W Canada
Stilida/Stilis see Stylida
xlii A12 **Stilligarry** Western Isles, NW Scotland, UK
97 G22 **Stilling** Århus, C Denmark
xli T13 **Stillington** North Yorkshire, N England, UK
31 W8 **Stillwater** Minnesota, N USA
29 O9 **Stillwater** Oklahoma, C USA
37 S5 **Stillwater Range** ▲ Nevada, W USA
20 I8 **Stillwater Reservoir** ▣ New York, NE USA
109 O22 **Stilo, Punta** headland S Italy
xxxix R10 **Stilton** Cambridgeshire, E England, UK
29 R10 **Stilwell** Oklahoma, C USA
115 N17 **Štimlje** Serbia, S Yugoslavia
xliii H23 **Stinchar** ≈ W Scotland, UK
27 N1 **Stinnett** Texas, SW USA
115 P18 **Štip** E FYR Macedonia
Stira see Stýra
xliii K19 **Stirling** Stirling, C Scotland, UK
xliii I19 **Stirling** ◆ unitary authority C Scotland, UK
188 J14 **Stirling Range** ▲ Western Australia
xxxvi B17 **Stithians** Cornwall, SW England, UK
95 E16 **Stjørdal** Nord-Trøndelag, C Norway
Stochód see Stokhid
xxxvii W8 **Stock** Essex, SE England, UK
103 H24 **Stockach** Baden-Württemberg, S Germany
xxxvii P11 **Stockbridge** Hampshire, S England, UK
27 S12 **Stockdale** Texas, SW USA
111 X3 **Stockerau** Niederösterreich, NE Austria
95 H20 **Stockholm** ● (Sweden) Stockholm, C Sweden
97 O15 **Stockholm** ◆ county C Sweden
xxxvi J13 **Stockland** Devon, SW England, UK
Stockmannshof see Pļaviņas
xl H16 **Stockport** Stockport, NW England, UK
xli P16 **Stockport** ◆ unitary authority NW England, UK
xli R16 **Stocksbridge** Sheffield, N England, UK
67 K15 **Stocks Seamount** undersea feature C Atlantic Ocean
37 O8 **Stockton** California, W USA
28 L3 **Stockton** Kansas, C USA
29 S6 **Stockton** Missouri, C USA
32 K3 **Stockton Island** island Apostle Islands, Wisconsin, N USA
29 S7 **Stockton Lake** ▣ Missouri, C USA
xli X6 **Stockton-on-Tees** var. Stockton on Tees. Stockton-on-Tees, N England, UK
xli S9 **Stockton-on-Tees** ◆ unitary authority NE England, UK
26 M10 **Stockton Plateau** plain Texas, SW USA
30 M16 **Stockville** Nebraska, C USA
95 H17 **Stöde** Västernorrland, C Sweden
Stodolichi see Stadolichy
178 Jj12 **Stœng Trêng** prev. Stung Treng. Stœng Trêng, NE Cambodia
115 M19 **Stogovo Karaorman** ▲ W FYR Macedonia
xxxvii W9 **Stoke** Kent, SE England, UK
Stoke see Stoke-on-Trent
xxxix P10 **Stoke Albany** Northamptonshire, C England, UK
xxxix W13 **Stoke-by-Nayland** Suffolk, E England, UK
xxxix U10 **Stoke Ferry** Norfolk, E England, UK
xxxvi H16 **Stoke Fleming** Devon, SW England, UK
xxxviii M10 **Stoke Golding** Leicestershire, C England, UK
xxxvii R7 **Stoke Hammond** Buckinghamshire, C England, UK
xxxvii R8 **Stokenchurch** Buckinghamshire, C England, UK
xxxvi D6 **Stoke Newington** Hackney, SE England, UK
xxxviii J7 **Stoke-on-Trent** var. Stoke. City of Stoke-on-Trent, C England, UK
xxxviii J7 **Stoke-on-Trent, City of** ◆ unitary authority C England, UK
xxxvii S9 **Stoke Poges** Buckinghamshire, C England, UK
xxxviii B17 **Stoke Prior** Worcestershire, W England, UK
xli T9 **Stokesley** North Yorkshire, N England, UK
190 M15 **Stokes Point** headland Tasmania, SE Australia
118 J2 **Stokhid** Pol. Stochód, Rus. Stokhod. ≈ NW Ukraine
Stokhod see Stokhid
94 I4 **Stokkseyri** Suðurland, SW Iceland
94 G10 **Stokmarknes** Nordland, C Norway
Stol see Veliki Krš
115 H15 **Stolac** S Bosnia and Herzegovina
Stolbce see Stowbtsy
103 D16 **Stolberg** var. Stolberg im Rheinland. Nordrhein-Westfalen, W Germany
Stolberg im Rheinland see Stolberg
126 L5 **Stolbovoy, Ostrov** island NE Russian Federation
Stolbtsy see Stowbtsy
121 J20 **Stolin** Rus. Stolin. Brestskaya Voblasts', SW Belorussia
97 K14 **Stöllet** var. Norra Ny. Värmland, C Sweden
Stolp see Słupsk
Stolpe see Słupia
Stolpmünde see Ustka
117 F15 **Stómio** Thessalía, C Greece
xxxvii Q10 **Stone** Buckinghamshire, C England, UK
xxxvi L8 **Stone** Gloucestershire, C England, UK
xxxviii J8 **Stone** Staffordshire, C England, UK
12 J11 **Stonecliffe** Ontario, SE Canada
xliii P14 **Stonehaven** Aberdeenshire, NE Scotland, UK
xxxvii N11 **Stonehenge** ancient monument Wiltshire, S England, UK
xliii J21 **Stonehouse** South Lanarkshire, C Scotland, UK
25 T3 **Stone Mountain** ▲ Georgia, SE USA
9 X16 **Stonewall** Manitoba, S Canada
23 S3 **Stonewood** West Virginia, NE USA
xlii A13 **Stoneybridge** Western Isles, NW Scotland, UK
xliii H25 **Stoneykirk** Dumfries and Galloway, SW Scotland, UK
12 D17 **Stoney Point** Ontario, S Canada
94 H10 **Stonglandseidet** Troms, N Norway
67 N25 **Stonybeach Bay** bay Tristan da Cunha, SE Atlantic Ocean
xlii Q1 **Stonybreck** Shetland Islands, NE Scotland, UK
37 N5 **Stony Creek** ≈ California, W USA
67 N25 **Stonyhill Point** headland S Tristan da Cunha
12 I14 **Stony Lake** ◎ Ontario, SE Canada
9 Q14 **Stony Plain** Alberta, SW Canada
23 R9 **Stony Point** North Carolina, SE USA
20 G8 **Stony Point** headland New York, NE USA
9 T10 **Stony Rapids** Saskatchewan, C Canada
41 P11 **Stony River** Alaska, USA
xxxvii R6 **Stony Stratford** Milton Keynes, C England, UK
Stony Tunguska see Podkamennaya Tunguska
10 G10 **Stooping** ≈ Ontario, C Canada
102 I9 **Stör** ≈ N Germany
97 M15 **Storå** Örebro, S Sweden
97 J16 **Stora Gla** ◎ C Sweden
97 I16 **Stora Le** Nor. Store Le. ◎ Norway/Sweden
94 I12 **Stora Lulevatten** ◎ N Sweden
94 H13 **Storavan** ◎ N Sweden
95 I20 **Storby** Åland, SW Finland
96 E10 **Stordalen** Møre og Romsdal, S Norway
Storebelt see Storebælt
97 H23 **Storebælt** var. Store Bælt, Eng. Great Belt, Storebelt. channel Baltic Sea/Kattegat
97 M19 **Storebro** Kalmar, S Sweden
97 J24 **Store Heddinge** Storstrøm, SE Denmark
Store Le see Stora Le
95 E16 **Støren** Sør-Trøndelag, S Norway
97 B14 **Store Sotra** island S Norway
94 O4 **Storfjorden** fjord S Norway
97 L15 **Storfors** Värmland, C Sweden
94 G13 **Storforshei** Nordland, C Norway
Storhammer see Hamar
102 L10 **Störkanal** canal N Germany
95 F16 **Storlien** Jämtland, C Sweden
191 P17 **Storm Bay** inlet Tasmania, SE Australia
31 T12 **Storm Lake** Iowa, C USA
31 S13 **Storm Lake** ◎ Iowa, C USA
xlii D8 **Stornoway** Western Isles, NW Scotland, UK
Storojineţ see Storozhynets'
94 P1 **Storøya** island NE Svalbard
129 S10 **Storozhevsk** Respublika Komi, NW Russian Federation
Storozhinets see Storozhynets'
118 K8 **Storozhynets'** Ger. Storozynetz, Rom. Storojineţ, Rus. Storozhinets. Chernivets'ka Oblast', W Ukraine
Storozynetz see Storozhynets'
xxxvii S12 **Storrington** West Sussex, S England, UK
94 H11 **Storriten** ▲ C Norway
21 N12 **Storrs** Connecticut, NE USA
xlii E12 **Storr, The** ▲ NW Scotland, UK
96 I11 **Storsjøen** ◎ S Norway
96 N13 **Storsjön** ◎ C Sweden
95 F16 **Storsjön** ◎ C Sweden
94 I9 **Storsteinnes** Troms, N Norway
97 I24 **Storstrøm** off. Storstrøms Amt. ◆ county SE Denmark
95 J14 **Storsund** Norrbotten, N Sweden
95 F16 **Storsylen** ▲ S Norway
94 H11 **Stortoppen** ▲ N Sweden
95 H14 **Storuman** Västerbotten, N Sweden
95 H14 **Storuman** ◎ N Sweden
96 N13 **Storvik** Gävleborg, C Sweden
97 O14 **Storvreta** Uppsala, C Sweden
31 V13 **Story City** Iowa, C USA
xxxvii T6 **Stotfold** Bedfordshire, E England, UK
9 V17 **Stoughton** Saskatchewan, S Canada
21 O11 **Stoughton** Massachusetts, NE USA
32 L9 **Stoughton** Wisconsin, N USA
xxxix W13 **Stour** ≈ E England, UK
xxxvi L12 **Stour** ≈ S England, UK
xxxvii Z10 **Stour** ≈ SE England, UK
xxxviii B15 **Stourbridge** Dudley, C England, UK
xxxviii A16 **Stourport-on-Severn** Worcestershire, W England, UK
29 T5 **Stover** Missouri, C USA
97 G21 **Støvring** Nordjylland, N Denmark
xliii N21 **Stow** The Borders, SE Scotland, UK
121 J17 **Stowbtsy** Pol. Stolbce, Rus. Stolbtsy. Minskaya Voblasts', C Belorussia
27 X11 **Stowell** Texas, SW USA
xxxix W12 **Stowmarket** Suffolk, E England, UK
xxxvii N7 **Stow-on-the-Wold** Gloucestershire, C England, UK
116 N8 **Stozher** Varnenska Oblast, NE Bulgaria
xliv I3 **Strabane** Ir. An Srath Bán. Strabane, W Northern Ireland, UK
xliv I3 **Strabane** ◆ district W Northern Ireland, UK
123 Gg10 **Strabo Trench** undersea feature C Mediterranean Sea
xliii O14 **Strachan** Aberdeenshire, NE Scotland, UK
xliii H18 **Strachur** Argyll and Bute, W Scotland, UK
xliv J10 **Stradbally** Laois, C Ireland
xxxix X11 **Stradbroke** Suffolk, E England, UK
xliv I6 **Stradone** Cavan, N Ireland
xxxix U9 **Stradsett** Norfolk, E England, UK
29 T7 **Strafford** Missouri, C USA
191 N17 **Strahan** Tasmania, SE Australia
xliii I23 **Straiton** South Ayrshire, W Scotland, UK
113 C18 **Strakonice** Ger. Strakonitz. Jižní Čechy, SW Czech Republic
Strakonitz see Strakonice
102 N8 **Stralsund** Mecklenburg-Vorpommern, NE Germany
101 L16 **Stramproy** Limburg, SE Netherlands
85 E26 **Strand** Western Cape, SW South Africa
96 E10 **Stranda** Møre og Romsdal, S Norway
xliv F5 **Strandhill** Sligo, N Ireland
xliv M5 **Strangford** Down, E Northern Ireland, UK
xliv M5 **Strangford Lough** Ir. Loch Cuan. inlet E Northern Ireland, UK
97 N16 **Strängnäs** Södermanland, C Sweden
xliv H3 **Stranorlar** Ir. Srath an Urláir. Donegal, NW Ireland
xliii H25 **Stranraer** Dumfries and Galloway, S Scotland, UK
9 U16 **Strasbourg** Saskatchewan, S Canada
105 V5 **Strasbourg** Ger. Strassburg; anc. Argentoratum. Bas-Rhin, NE France
39 U4 **Strasburg** Colorado, C USA
31 N7 **Strasburg** North Dakota, N USA
33 U12 **Strasburg** Ohio, N USA
23 U3 **Strasburg** Virginia, NE USA
119 N10 **Străşeni** var. Strasheny. C Moldavia
Strasheny see Străşeni
111 T8 **Strassburg** Kärnten, S Austria
Strassburg see Strasbourg, France
Strassburg see Aiud, Romania
101 M25 **Strassen** Luxembourg, S Luxembourg
111 R5 **Strasswalchen** Salzburg, C Austria
Stratford see Stratford-upon-Avon
xxxvi E6 **Stratford** Newham, SE England, UK
12 F16 **Stratford** Ontario, S Canada
192 K10 **Stratford** Taranaki, North Island, NZ
37 Q11 **Stratford** California, W USA
31 V13 **Stratford** Iowa, C USA
29 O12 **Stratford** Oklahoma, C USA
27 N1 **Stratford** Texas, SW USA
32 K6 **Stratford** Wisconsin, N USA
xxxix W14 **Stratford St Mary** Suffolk, E England, UK
xxxviii K13 **Stratford-upon-Avon** var. Stratford. Warwickshire, C England, UK
xxxviii D17 **Stratford upon Avon Canal** canal C England, UK
xliii J21 **Strathaven** South Lanarkshire, C Scotland, UK
xliii J19 **Strathblane** Stirling, C Scotland, UK
xlii H9 **Strathcanaird** Highland, NW Scotland, UK
xlii G12 **Strathcarron** Highland, NW Scotland, UK
xlii M13 **Strathdon** Aberdeenshire, NE Scotland, UK
191 O17 **Strathgordon** Tasmania, SE Australia
xliii M18 **Strathmiglo** Fife, E Scotland, UK
9 Q16 **Strathmore** Alberta, SW Canada
37 R11 **Strathmore** California, W USA
xlii I11 **Strathpeffer** Highland, NW Scotland, UK
12 E16 **Strathroy** Ontario, S Canada
xlii K6 **Strathy** Highland, N Scotland, UK
xlii J6 **Strathy Point** headland N Scotland, UK
xliii J18 **Strathyre** Stirling, C Scotland, UK
xxxvi E13 **Stratton** Cornwall, SW England, UK
39 W4 **Stratton** Colorado, C USA
21 P6 **Stratton** Maine, NE USA
xxxvii Q7 **Stratton Audley** Oxfordshire, C England, UK
20 M10 **Stratton Mountain** ▲ Vermont, NE USA
103 N21 **Straubing** Bayern, SE Germany
94 G12 **Straumen** Nordland, C Norway
102 O12 **Strausberg** Brandenburg, E Germany
34 K13 **Strawberry Mountain** ▲ Oregon, NW USA
31 X12 **Strawberry Point** Iowa, C USA
38 M3 **Strawberry Reservoir** ▣ Utah, W USA
38 M4 **Strawberry River** ≈ Utah, W USA
27 R7 **Strawn** Texas, SW USA
115 P17 **Straža** ▲ Bulgaria/FYR Macedonia
113 I19 **Strážov** Hung. Sztrazsó. ▲ NW Slovakia
190 F7 **Streaky Bay** South Australia
190 F7 **Streaky Bay** bay South Australia
xxxvi D9 **Streatham** Lambeth, SE England, UK
xxxvii S6 **Streatley** Bedfordshire, C England, UK
xxxvii Q9 **Streatley** Newbury, S England, UK
32 L12 **Streator** Illinois, N USA
113 J19 **Stredné Slovensko** ◆ region C Slovakia
113 C17 **Střední Čechy** off. Středočeský Kraj. ◆ region W Czech Republic
Strednogorie see Pirdop
xxxvi K11 **Street** Somerset, SW England, UK
31 O6 **Streeter** North Dakota, N USA
27 U8 **Streetman** Texas, SW USA
118 G13 **Strehaia** Mehedinţi, SW Romania
Strehlen see Strzelin
116 I10 **Strelcha** Plovdivska Oblast, C Bulgaria
126 I13 **Strelka** Krasnoyarskiy Kray, C Russian Federation
128 L6 **Strel'na** ≈ NW Russian Federation
120 H7 **Strenči** Ger. Stackeln. Valka, N Latvia
110 K8 **Strengen** Tirol, W Austria
xli T12 **Strensall** York, N England, UK
108 C6 **Stresa** Piemonte, NE Italy
Streshin see Streshyn
121 N18 **Streshyn** Rus. Streshin. Homyel'skaya Voblasts', SE Belorussia
xli P16 **Stretford** Trafford, NW England, UK
xxxix T11 **Stretham** Cambridgeshire, E England, UK
xl E16 **Stretton** Cheshire, W England, UK
xxxix Q9 **Stretton** Rutland, C England, UK
126 Gg11 **Strezhevoy** Tomskaya Oblast', C Russian Federation
97 G23 **Strib** Fyn, C Denmark
113 A17 **Stříbro** Ger. Mies. Západní Čechy, W Czech Republic
xlii P11 **Strichen** Aberdeenshire, NE Scotland, UK
194 E13 **Strickland** ≈ SW PNG
Striegau see Strzegom
Strigonium see Esztergom
100 H13 **Strijen** Zuid-Holland, SW Netherlands
65 H21 **Strobel, Lago** ◎ S Argentina
63 B25 **Stroeder** Buenos Aires, E Argentina
117 C20 **Strofádes** island Iónioi Nísoi, Greece, C Mediterranean Sea
Strofilia see Strofyliá
117 G17 **Strofyliá** var. Strofilia. Évvoia, C Greece
xliv G7 **Strokestown** Roscommon, C Ireland
102 O10 **Strom** ≈ NE Germany
xlii L6 **Stroma, Island of** island N Scotland, UK
109 L22 **Stromboli** ▲ Isola Stromboli, SW Italy
109 L22 **Stromboli, Isola** island Isole Eolie, S Italy
xlii F12 **Stromeferry** Highland, N Scotland, UK
xlii L4 **Stromness** Orkney Islands, N Scotland, UK
96 N11 **Strömsbruk** Gävleborg, C Sweden
31 Q15 **Stromsburg** Nebraska, C USA
97 K21 **Strömsnäsbruk** Kronoberg, S Sweden
97 I17 **Strömstad** Göteborg och Bohus, S Sweden
95 G16 **Strömsund** Jämtland, C Sweden
95 G15 **Ströms Vattudal** valley N Sweden
xliii I18 **Stronachlachar** Stirling, C Scotland, UK
xliii H19 **Strone** Argyll and Bute, W Scotland, UK
xlii H8 **Stronechrubie** Highland, NW Scotland, UK
29 V14 **Strong** Arkansas, C USA
Strongilí see Strongylí
109 O21 **Strongoli** Calabria, SW Italy
33 T11 **Strongsville** Ohio, N USA
117 Q23 **Strongylí** var. Strongilí. island SE Greece
xlii N3 **Stronsay** island NE Scotland, UK
xlii N3 **Stronsay Firth** inlet N Scotland, UK
xliii F16 **Strontian** Highland, NW Scotland, UK
xxxvi M8 **Stroud** Gloucestershire, C England, UK
xxxvii R12 **Stroud** Hampshire, S England, UK
29 O10 **Stroud** Oklahoma, C USA
20 I14 **Stroudsburg** Pennsylvania, NE USA
97 F21 **Struer** Ringkøbing, W Denmark
115 M20 **Struga** SW FYR Macedonia
Strugi-Kranyse see Strugi-Krasnyye
128 G14 **Strugi-Krasnyye** var. Strugi-Kranyse. Pskovskaya Oblast', W Russian Federation
116 G11 **Struma** Gk. Strymónas. ≈ Bulgaria/Greece see also Strymónas
xxxv C12 **Strumble Head** headland SW Wales, UK
115 Q19 **Strumeshnitsa** Mac. Strumica. ≈ Bulgaria/FYR Macedonia
115 Q19 **Strumica** E FYR Macedonia
Strumica see Strumeshnitsa
116 G11 **Strumyani** Sofiyska Oblast, SW Bulgaria
33 V12 **Struthers** Ohio, N USA
xlii I12 **Struy** Highland, NW Scotland, UK
116 I10 **Stryama** ≈ C Bulgaria
116 G13 **Strymónas** Bul. Struma. ≈ Bulgaria/Greece see also Struma
117 H14 **Strymonikós Kólpos** gulf N Greece
118 I6 **Stryy** L'vivs'ka Oblast', NW Ukraine
118 H6 **Stryy** ≈ W Ukraine
113 F14 **Strzegom** Ger. Striegau. Wałbrzych, SW Poland
112 E10 **Strzelce Krajeńskie** Ger. Friedeberg Neumark. Gorzów, W Poland
113 I15 **Strzelce Opolskie** Ger. Gross Strehlitz. Opole, SW Poland
190 K3 **Strzelecki Creek** seasonal river South Australia
190 J3 **Strzelecki Desert** desert South Australia
113 G15 **Strzelin** Ger. Strehlen. Wrocław, SW Poland
112 I11 **Strzelno** Bydgoszcz, C Poland
113 N17 **Strzyżów** Rzeszów, SE Poland
Stua Laighean see Leinster, Mount
25 Y13 **Stuart** Florida, SE USA
31 U14 **Stuart** Iowa, C USA
31 O13 **Stuart** Nebraska, C USA
23 S8 **Stuart** Virginia, NE USA
8 L13 **Stuart** ≈ British Columbia, SW Canada
xlii P12 **Stuartfield** Aberdeenshire, NE Scotland, UK
41 N10 **Stuart Island** island Alaska, USA
8 L13 **Stuart Lake** ◎ British Columbia, SW Canada
193 B22 **Stuart Mountains** ▲ South Island, NZ
190 F3 **Stuart Range** hill range South Australia
Stubaital see Neustift im Stubaital
97 I24 **Stubbekøbing** Storstrøm, SE Denmark
47 P14 **Stubbs** Saint Vincent, Saint Vincent and the Grenadines
111 V6 **Stübming** ≈ E Austria
116 J11 **Studen Kladenets, Yazovir** ▣ S Bulgaria
193 G21 **Studholme** Canterbury, South Island, NZ
xxxvii N14 **Studland** Dorset, S England, UK
xxxviii C17 **Studley** Warwickshire, C England, UK
Stuhlweissenberg see Székesfehérvár
Stuhm see Sztum
10 C7 **Stull Lake** ◎ Ontario, C Canada
Stung Treng see Stœng Trêng
130 L4 **Stupino** Moskovskaya Oblast', W Russian Federation
29 U4 **Sturgeon** Missouri, C USA
12 G10 **Sturgeon** ≈ Ontario, S Canada
33 N6 **Sturgeon Bay** Wisconsin, N USA
12 G11 **Sturgeon Falls** Ontario, S Canada
10 C11 **Sturgeon Lake** ◎ Ontario, S Canada
32 M3 **Sturgeon River** ≈ Michigan, N USA
22 H6 **Sturgis** Kentucky, S USA
33 P11 **Sturgis** Michigan, N USA
30 J9 **Sturgis** South Dakota, N USA
114 D10 **Šturlić** NW Bosnia and Herzegovina
xxxvi M13 **Sturminster Newton** Dorset, S England, UK
113 J22 **Štúrovo** Hung. Párkány; prev. Parkan. Západné Slovensko, S Slovakia
xxxvii Y10 **Sturry** Kent, SE England, UK
190 L4 **Sturt, Mount** hill New South Wales, SE Australia
xxxix P5 **Sturton by Stow** Lincolnshire, E England, UK

◆ Country ● Country Capital ◇ Dependent Territory ○ Dependent Territory Capital ◆ Administrative Region ✕ International Airport ▲ Mountain ▲ Mountain Range Volcano ≈ River ◎ Lake ▣ Reservoir
319

Sturt Plain – Svir', Ozero

189 P4 **Sturt Plain** *plain* Northern Territory, N Australia
189 T9 **Sturt Stony Desert** *desert* South Australia
85 J25 **Stutterheim** Eastern Cape, S South Africa
103 H21 **Stuttgart** Baden-Württemberg, SW Germany
29 W12 **Stuttgart** Arkansas, C USA
94 H2 **Stykkishólmur** Vesturland, W Iceland
117 F17 **Stylída** *var.* Stilida, Stilís. Stereá Ellás, C Greece
118 K2 **Styr** ***Rus.*** Styr'. ≈ Belorussia/Ukraine
117 I19 **Stýra** *var.* Stira. Évvoia, C Greece
Styria *see* Steiermark
Su *see* Jiangsu
Sua *see* Sowa
175 S17 **Suai** Timor, C Indonesia
56 G9 **Suaita** Santander, C Colombia
82 I7 **Suakin** *var.* Sawakin. Red Sea, NE Sudan
167 T13 **Suao** ***Jap.*** Suō. N Taiwan
Suao *see* Suau
42 G6 **Suaqui Grande** Sonora, NW Mexico
63 A16 **Suardi** Santa Fe, C Argentina
56 D11 **Suárez** Cauca, SW Colombia
195 N17 **Suau** *var.* Suao. Suaul Island, SE PNG
120 G12 **Subačius** Kupiškis, NE Lithuania
174 Jj14 **Subang** ***prev.*** Soebang. Jawa, C Indonesia
174 Gg5 **Subang** ✕ (Kuala Lumpur) Pahang, Peninsular Malaysia
133 S10 **Subansiri** ≈ NE India
120 I11 **Subate** Daugvapils, SE Latvia
145 N5 **Subaykhān** Dayr az Zawr, E Syria
165 P8 **Subei** *var.* Dangchengwan, Subei Mongolzu Zizhixian. Gansu, N China
Subei Mongolzu Zizhixian *see* Subei
174 K5 **Subi Besar, Pulau** *island* Kepulauan Natuna, W Indonesia
Subiyah *see* Aş Şubayḩīyah
28 I7 **Sublette** Kansas, C USA
114 K8 **Subotica** ***Ger.*** Maria-Theresiopel, ***Hung.*** Szabadka. Serbia, N Yugoslavia
118 K9 **Suceava** ***Ger.*** Suczawa, ***Hung.*** Szucsava. Suceava, NE Romania
118 J9 **Suceava** ◈ *county* NE Romania
118 K9 **Suceava** ***Ger.*** Suczawa. ≈ N Romania
114 E12 **Sučevići** Zadar-Knin, C Croatia
113 K17 **Sucha Beskidzka** Bielsko-Biała, S Poland
113 M14 **Suchedniów** Kielce, SE Poland
44 A2 **Suchitepéquez** ***off.*** Departamento de Suchitepéquez. ◈ *department* SW Guatemala
Su-chou *see* Suzhou
Suchow *see* Suzhou, Jiangsu, China
Suchow *see* Xuzhou, Jiangsu, China
xliv G8 **Suck** ≈ C Ireland
Sucker State *see* Illinois
194 M16 **Suckling, Mount** ▲ S PNG
59 L19 **Sucre** ***hist.*** Chuquisaca, La Plata. ● (Bolivia-legal capital) Chuquisaca, S Bolivia
56 E6 **Sucre** Santander, N Colombia
58 A7 **Sucre** Manabí, W Ecuador
56 E6 **Sucre** ***off.*** Departamento de Sucre. ◈ *province* N Colombia
57 O5 **Sucre** ***off.*** Estado Sucre. ◈ *state* NE Venezuela
58 D6 **Sucumbíos** ◈ *province* NE Ecuador
115 G15 **Sućuraj** Split-Dalmacija, S Croatia
60 K10 **Sucuriju** Amapá, NE Brazil
Suczawa *see* Suceava
81 E16 **Sud** ***Eng.*** South. ◈ *province* S Cameroon
128 K13 **Suda** ≈ NW Russian Federation
Suda *see* Soúda
119 U13 **Sudak** Respublika Krym, S Ukraine
26 M4 **Sudan** Texas, SW USA
82 C10 **Sudan** ***off.*** Republic of Sudan, ***Ar.*** Jumhuriyat as-Sudan; ***prev.*** Anglo-Egyptian Sudan. ◆ *republic* N Africa
Sudanese Republic *see* Mali
Sudan, Jumhuriyat as- *see* Sudan
xxxviii L8 **Sudbury** Derbyshire, C England, UK
xxxix V13 **Sudbury** Suffolk, E England, UK
12 F10 **Sudbury** Ontario, S Canada
Sud, Canal de *see* Gonâve, Canal de la
82 E13 **Sudd** *swamp region* S Sudan
102 K10 **Sude** ≈ N Germany
Sudest Island *see* Tagula Island
113 E15 **Sudeten** *var.* Sudetes, Sudetic Mountains, Cz./Pol. Sudety. ▲▲ Czech Republic/Poland
Sudetes/Sudetic Mountains/Sudety *see* Sudeten
94 G1 **Sudhureyri** Vestfirdhir, NW Iceland
94 J4 **Sudhurland** ◈ *region* S Iceland
176 Xx12 **Sudirman, Pegunungan** ▲▲ Irian Jaya, E Indonesia
128 M15 **Sudislavl'** Kostromskaya Oblast', NW Russian Federation
Südkarpaten *see* Carpații Meridionali
81 N20 **Sud Kivu** ***off.*** Région Sud Kivu. ◈ *region* E Zaire
Südliche Morava *see* Južna Morava
102 E12 **Süd-Nord-Kanal** *canal* NW Germany
130 M3 **Sudogda** Vladimirskaya Oblast', W Russian Federation
Sudostroy *see* Severodvinsk
81 C15 **Sud-Ouest** ***Eng.*** South-West. ◈ *province* W Cameroon
181 X17 **Sud Ouest, Pointe** *headland* SW Mauritius
197 J7 **Sud, Province** ◈ *province* S New Caledonia
130 J8 **Sudzha** Kurskaya Oblast', W Russian Federation
83 D15 **Sue** ≈ S Sudan
107 S10 **Sueca** País Valenciano, E Spain
116 I10 **Sŭedinenie** Plovdivska Oblast, C Bulgaria
Suero *see* Alzira
77 X8 **Suez** ***Ar.*** As Suways, El Suweis. NE Egypt
77 W7 **Suez Canal** ***Ar.*** Qanāt as Suways. *canal* NE Egypt
77 X8 **Suez, Gulf of** ***Ar.*** Khalīj as Suways. *gulf* NE Egypt
9 R17 **Suffield** Alberta, SW Canada
xxxix W12 **Suffolk** ◈ *county* E England, UK
23 X7 **Suffolk** Virginia, NE USA
148 J2 **Şūfīān** Āžarbāyjān-e Khāvarī, N Iran
33 N12 **Sugar Creek** ≈ Illinois, N USA
32 L13 **Sugar Creek** ≈ Illinois, N USA
33 R3 **Sugar Island** *island* Michigan, N USA
27 V11 **Sugar Land** Texas, SW USA
21 P6 **Sugarloaf Mountain** ▲ Maine, NE USA
67 G24 **Sugar Loaf Point** *headland* N Saint Helena
142 G16 **Suğla Gölü** ◎ SW Turkey
127 O8 **Sugoy** ≈ E Russian Federation
153 U11 **Sugum, Gora** ▲ SW Kyrgyzstan
164 F7 **Sugun** Xinjiang Uygur Zizhiqu, W China
175 O2 **Sugut, Sungai** ≈ East Malaysia
165 O9 **Suhai Hu** ◎ C China
168 K14 **Suhait** Nei Mongol Zizhiqu, N China
147 X7 **Şuḩār** *var.* Sohar. N Oman
168 L6 **Sühbaatar** Selenge, N Mongolia
169 P9 **Sühbaatar** ◈ *province* E Mongolia
103 K17 **Suhl** Thüringen, C Germany
110 F7 **Suhr** Aargau, N Switzerland
167 O12 **Suichuan** Jiangxi, S China
Suid-Afrika *see* South Africa
166 L4 **Suide** Shaanxi, C China
Suidwes-Afrika *see* Namibia
169 Y9 **Suifenhe** Heilongjiang, NE China
Suigen *see* Suwŏn
169 W8 **Suihua** Heilongjiang, NE China
Súilí, Loch *see* Swilly, Lough
167 Q6 **Suining** Jiangsu, E China
166 I9 **Suining** Sichuan, C China
105 Q4 **Suippes** Marne, N France
xliv H12 **Suir** ***Ir.*** An tSiúir. ≈ S Ireland
171 Gg15 **Suita** Ōsaka, Honshū, SW Japan
166 L16 **Suixi** Guangdong, S China
Sui Xian *see* Suizhou
169 T13 **Suizhong** Liaoning, NE China
167 N8 **Suizhou** ***prev.*** Sui Xian. Hubei, C China
155 P17 **Sujāwal** Sind, SE Pakistan
174 Jj14 **Sukabumi** ***prev.*** Soekaboemi. Jawa, C Indonesia
174 Kk9 **Sukadana, Teluk** *bay* Borneo, W Indonesia
171 Ll14 **Sukagawa** Fukushima, Honshū, C Japan
Sukarnapura *see* Jayapura
Sukarno, Puntjak *see* Jaya, Puncak
153 R11 **Sŭkh** ***Rus.*** Sokh. Farghona Wiloyati, E Uzbekistan
Sŭkh *see* Sokh
116 N8 **Sukha Reka** ≈ NE Bulgaria
130 J5 **Sukhinichi** Kaluzhskaya Oblast', W Russian Federation
Sukhne *see* As Sukhnah
133 Q4 **Sukhona** *var.* Tot'ma. ≈ NW Russian Federation
178 H9 **Sukhothai** *var.* Sukotai. Sukhothai, W Thailand
Sukhumi *see* Sokhumi
Sukkertoppen *see* Maniitsoq
155 Q13 **Sukkur** Sind, SE Pakistan
Sukotai *see* Sukhothai
Sukra Bay *see* Şawqirah, Dawḩat
129 V15 **Suksun** Permskaya Oblast', NW Russian Federation
170 E16 **Sukumo** Kōchi, Shikoku, SW Japan
96 B12 **Sula** *island* S Norway
129 Q5 **Sula** ≈ NW Russian Federation
119 R5 **Sula** ≈ N Ukraine
44 H6 **Sulaco, Río** ≈ NW Honduras
Sulaimaniya *see* As Sulaymānīyah
155 S10 **Sulaimān Range** ▲▲ C Pakistan
131 Q16 **Sulak** Respublika Dagestan, SW Russian Federation
131 Q16 **Sulak** ≈ SW Russian Federation
175 Rr10 **Sula, Kepulauan** *island group* C Indonesia
142 I12 **Sulakyurt** *var.* Konur. Kırıkkale, N Turkey
175 R17 **Sulamu** Timor, S Indonesia
98 F5 **Sula Sgeir** *island* NW Scotland, UK
175 Pp10 **Sulawesi** ***Eng.*** Celebes. *island* C Indonesia
Sulawesi, Laut *see* Celebes Sea
175 P11 **Sulawesi Selatan** ***off.*** Propinsi Sulawesi Selatan, ***Eng.*** South Celebes, South Sulawesi. ◈ *province* C Indonesia
175 Q9 **Sulawesi Tengah** ***off.*** Propinsi Sulawesi Tengah, ***Eng.*** Central Celebes, Central Sulawesi. ◈ *province* N Indonesia
175 Q11 **Sulawesi Tenggara** ***off.*** Propinsi Sulawesi Tenggara, ***Eng.*** South-East Celebes, South-East Sulawesi. ◈ *province* C Indonesia
175 Qq7 **Sulawesi Utara** ***off.*** Propinsi Sulawesi Utara, ***Eng.*** North Celebes, North Sulawesi. ◈ *province* N Indonesia
145 T5 **Sulaymān Beg** N Iraq
xl G11 **Sulby** N Isle of Man
97 D15 **Suldalsvatnet** ◎ S Norway
112 E12 **Sulechów** ***Ger.*** Züllichau. Zielona Góra, W Poland
112 E11 **Sulęcin** Gorzów, W Poland
79 U14 **Suleja** Niger, C Nigeria
113 K14 **Sulejów** Piotrków, S Poland
xlii J4 **Sule Skerry** *island* N Scotland, UK
Suliag *see* Sohâg
78 J16 **Sulima** S Sierra Leone
119 O13 **Sulina** Tulcea, SE Romania
119 N13 **Sulina Brațul** ≈ SE Romania
102 H12 **Sulingen** Niedersachsen, NW Germany
94 H12 **Suliskongen** ▲ C Norway
94 H12 **Sulitjelma** Nordland, C Norway
58 A9 **Sullana** Piura, NW Peru
25 N3 **Sulligent** Alabama, S USA
32 M14 **Sullivan** Illinois, N USA
33 N15 **Sullivan** Indiana, N USA
29 W5 **Sullivan** Missouri, C USA
Sullivan Island *see* Lanbi Kyun
xlii I2 **Sullom** Shetland Islands, NE Scotland, UK
98 M1 **Sullom Voe** NE Scotland, UK
105 O7 **Sully-sur-Loire** Loiret, C France
Sulmo *see* Sulmona
109 K15 **Sulmona** ***anc.*** Sulmo. Abruzzi, C Italy
Sulo *see* Shule He
116 M11 **Süloğlu** Edirne, NW Turkey
24 G9 **Sulphur** Louisiana, S USA
29 O12 **Sulphur** Oklahoma, C USA
30 K9 **Sulphur Creek** ≈ South Dakota, N USA
26 M5 **Sulphur Draw** ≈ Texas, SW USA
27 W5 **Sulphur River** ≈ Arkansas/Texas, SW USA
27 V6 **Sulphur Springs** Texas, SW USA
26 M6 **Sulphur Springs Draw** ≈ Texas, SW USA
12 D8 **Sultan** Ontario, S Canada
Sultānābād *see* Arāk
Sultan Alonto, Lake *see* Lanao, Lake
142 G15 **Sultan Dağları** ▲▲ C Turkey
116 N13 **Sultanköy** Tekirdağ, NW Turkey
179 R16 **Sultan Kudarat** *var.* Nuling. Mindanao, S Philippines
158 M13 **Sultānpur** Uttar Pradesh, N India
179 Pp17 **Sulu Archipelago** *island group* SW Philippines
198 Ff7 **Sulu Basin** *undersea feature* SE South China Sea
Sülüktü *see* Sulyukta
Sulu, Laut *see* Sulu Sea
175 Pp1 **Sulu Sea** ***Ind.*** Laut Sulu. *sea* SW Philippines
151 O15 **Sulutobe** ***Kaz.*** Sulütöbe. Kzyl-Orda, S Kazakhstan
153 Q11 **Sulyukta** ***Kir.*** Sülüktü. Oshskaya Oblast', SW Kyrgyzstan
Sulz *see* Sulz am Neckar
103 G22 **Sulz am Neckar** *var.* Sulz. Baden-Württemberg, SW Germany
103 L20 **Sulzbach-Rosenberg** Bayern, SE Germany
205 N13 **Sulzberger Bay** *bay* Antarctica
Sumail *see* Summēl
115 F15 **Sumartin** Split-Dalmacija, S Croatia
34 H6 **Sumas** Washington, NW USA
174 Gg7 **Sumatera** ***Eng.*** Sumatra. *island* W Indonesia
173 G9 **Sumatera Barat** ***off.*** Propinsi Sumatera Barat, ***Eng.*** West Sumatra. ◈ *province* W Indonesia
174 Hh11 **Sumatera Selatan** ***off.*** Propinsi Sumatera Selatan, ***Eng.*** South Sumatra. ◈ *province* W Indonesia
173 Ff6 **Sumatera Utara** ***off.*** Propinsi Sumatera Utara, ***Eng.*** North Sumatra. ◈ *province* W Indonesia
Sumatra *see* Sumatera
Šumava *see* Bohemian Forest
Sumayl *see* Summēl
145 U7 **Sumayr al Muḩammad** E Iraq
175 P17 **Sumba, Pulau** ***Eng.*** Sandalwood Island; ***prev.*** Soemba. *island* Nusa Tenggara, C Indonesia
152 D12 **Sumbar** ≈ W Turkmenistan
175 P16 **Sumba, Selat** *strait* Nusa Tenggara, S Indonesia
175 Oo16 **Sumbawa** ***prev.*** Soembawa. *island* Nusa Tenggara, C Indonesia
175 O16 **Sumbawabesar** Sumbawa, S Indonesia
83 F23 **Sumbawanga** Rukwa, W Tanzania
84 B12 **Sumbe** ***prev.*** N'Gunza, ***Port.*** Novo Redondo. Cuanza Sul, W Angola
xlii I5 **Sumburgh** Shetland Islands, NE Scotland, UK
xlii I6 **Sumburgh Head** *headland* NE Scotland, UK
113 H23 **Sümeg** Veszprém, W Hungary
82 C12 **Sumeih** Southern Darfur, S Sudan
174 Mm14 **Sumenep** ***prev.*** Soemenep. Pulau Madura, C Indonesia
Sumgait *see* Sumqayıt, Azerbaijan
Sumgait *see* Sumqayıtçay, Azerbaijan
172 Ss14 **Sumisu-jima** ***Eng.*** Smith Island. *island* SE Japan
145 Q2 **Summēl** *var.* Sumail, Sumayl. N Iraq
xli R12 **Summer Bridge** North Yorkshire, N England, UK
xxxvi C16 **Summercourt** Cornwall, SW England, UK
33 O5 **Summer Island** *island* Michigan, N USA
xlii F9 **Summer Isles** *island group* NW Scotland, UK
34 H15 **Summer Lake** ◎ Oregon, NW USA
9 N17 **Summerland** British Columbia, SW Canada
11 P14 **Summerside** Prince Edward Island, SE Canada
23 R5 **Summersville** West Virginia, NE USA
23 R5 **Summersville Lake** ⊞ West Virginia, NE USA
23 S13 **Summerton** South Carolina, SE USA
25 R2 **Summerville** Georgia, SE USA
23 S14 **Summerville** South Carolina, SE USA
41 R10 **Summit** Alaska, USA
37 V6 **Summit Mountain** ▲ Nevada, W USA
39 R8 **Summit Peak** ▲ Colorado, C USA
Summus Portus *see* Somport, Col du
31 X12 **Sumner** Iowa, C USA
24 K3 **Sumner** Mississippi, S USA
193 H17 **Sumner, Lake** ◎ South Island, NZ
39 U12 **Sumner, Lake** ⊞ New Mexico, SW USA
171 Kk13 **Sumon-dake** ▲ Honshū, C Japan
170 G15 **Sumoto** Hyōgo, Awaji-shima, SW Japan
113 G17 **Šumperk** ***Ger.*** Mährisch-Schönberg. Severní Morava, E Czech Republic
44 F7 **Sumpul, Río** ≈ El Salvador/Honduras
143 Z11 **Sumqayıt** ***Rus.*** Sumgait. E Azerbaijan
143 Y11 **Sumqayıtçay** ***Rus.*** Sumgait. ≈ E Azerbaijan
153 R9 **Sumsar** Dzhalal-Abadskaya Oblast', W Kyrgyzstan
119 S3 **Sums'ka Oblast'** *var.* Sumy, ***Rus.*** Sumskaya Oblast'. ◈ *province* NE Ukraine
Sumskaya Oblast' *see* Sums'ka Oblast'
128 J8 **Sumskiy Posad** Respublika Kareliya, NW Russian Federation
23 S12 **Sumter** South Carolina, SE USA
119 T3 **Sumy** Sums'ka Oblast', NE Ukraine
Sumy *see* Sums'ka Oblast'
165 Q15 **Sumzom** Xizang Zizhiqu, W China
129 R15 **Suna** Kirovskaya Oblast', NW Russian Federation
128 I10 **Suna** ≈ NW Russian Federation
172 Oo5 **Sunagawa** Hokkaidō, NE Japan
159 V13 **Sunamganj** Chittagong, NE Bangladesh
165 S8 **Sunan** *var.* Hongwan, Sunan Yugurzu Zizhixian. Gansu, N China
169 W14 **Sunan** ✕ (P'yŏngyang) SW North Korea
Sunan Yugurzu Zizhixian *see* Sunan
21 N9 **Sunapee Lake** ◎ New Hampshire, NE USA
xliii F16 **Sunart, Loch** *inlet* NW Scotland, UK
145 P4 **Sunaysilah** *salt marsh* N Iraq
22 M8 **Sunbright** Tennessee, S USA
35 R6 **Sunburst** Montana, NW USA
191 N12 **Sunbury** Victoria, SE Australia
23 X8 **Sunbury** North Carolina, SE USA
20 G14 **Sunbury** Pennsylvania, NE USA
63 A17 **Sunchales** Santa Fe, C Argentina
169 W13 **Sunch'ŏn** SW North Korea
169 Y16 **Sunch'ŏn** ***Jap.*** Junten. S South Korea
38 K13 **Sun City** Arizona, SW USA
21 O9 **Suncook** New Hampshire, NE USA
Sunda Islands *see* Greater Sunda Islands
35 Z12 **Sundance** Wyoming, C USA
160 M11 **Sundargarh** Orissa, E India
174 Ii14 **Sunda, Selat** *strait* Jawa/Sumatera, SW Indonesia
133 U15 **Sunda Shelf** *undersea feature* S South China Sea
Sunda Trench *see* Java Trench
133 U17 **Sunda Trough** *undersea feature* E Indian Ocean
97 O16 **Sundbyberg** Stockholm, C Sweden
xli X3 **Sunderland** *var.* Wearmouth. Sunderland, NE England, UK
xli W3 **Sunderland** ◈ *unitary authority* NE England, UK
103 F15 **Sundern** Nordrhein-Westfalen, W Germany
142 F12 **Sündiken Dağları** ▲▲ C Turkey
26 M5 **Sundown** Texas, SW USA
9 P16 **Sundre** Alberta, SW Canada
12 H12 **Sundridge** Ontario, S Canada
95 H17 **Sundsvall** Västernorrland, C Sweden
28 H4 **Sunflower, Mount** ▲ Kansas, C USA
Sunflower State *see* Kansas
174 Gg4 **Sungai Bernam** ≈ Peninsular Malaysia
174 Ii12 **Sungaibuntu** Sumatera, SW Indonesia
174 Gg9 **Sungaidareh** Sumatera, W Indonesia
178 Hh17 **Sungai Kolok** *var.* Sungai Ko-Lok. Narathiwat, SW Thailand
174 Gg10 **Sungaipenuh** ***prev.*** Soengaipenoeh. Sumatera, W Indonesia
174 Kk8 **Sungaipinyuh** Borneo, C Indonesia
Sungari *see* Songhua Jiang
Sungaria *see* Dzungaria
Sungei Pahang *see* Pahang, Sungai
178 Hh8 **Sung Men** Phrae, NW Thailand
85 M15 **Sungo** Tete, NW Mozambique
174 Ii10 **Sungsang** Sumatera, W Indonesia
116 M9 **Sungurlare** Burgaska Oblast, E Bulgaria
142 J12 **Sungurlu** Çorum, N Turkey
114 F9 **Sunja** Sisak-Moslavina, C Croatia
xli X15 **Sunk Island** East Riding of Yorkshire, N England, UK
159 Q12 **Sun Koshi** ≈ E Nepal
96 F9 **Sunndalen** *valley* S Norway
96 F9 **Sunndalsøra** Møre og Romsdal, S Norway
97 K15 **Sunne** Värmland, C Sweden
97 O15 **Sunnersta** Uppsala, C Sweden
96 C11 **Sunnfjord** *physical region* S Norway
97 C15 **Sunnhordland** *physical region* S Norway
xxxvii S10 **Sunningdale** Surrey, SE England, UK
96 D10 **Sunnmøre** *physical region* S Norway
39 N4 **Sunnyside** Utah, W USA
34 J10 **Sunnyside** Washington, NW USA
37 N9 **Sunnyvale** California, W USA
32 L8 **Sun Prairie** Wisconsin, N USA
Sunqur *see* Sonqor
27 N1 **Sunray** Texas, SW USA
24 I8 **Sunset** Louisiana, S USA
27 S5 **Sunset** Texas, SW USA
Sunset State *see* Oregon
189 Z10 **Sunshine Coast** *cultural region* Queensland, E Australia
Sunshine State *see* Florida, USA
Sunshine State *see* New Mexico, USA
Sunshine State *see* South Dakota, USA
126 Kk11 **Suntar** Respublika Sakha (Yakutiya), NE Russian Federation
41 R10 **Suntrana** Alaska, USA
154 J15 **Suntsar** Baluchistān, SW Pakistan
169 W15 **Sunwi-do** *island* SW North Korea
169 W6 **Sunwu** Heilongjiang, NE China
79 O16 **Sunyani** W Ghana
Suō *see* Suao
95 M17 **Suolahti** Keski-Suomi, C Finland
Suoločielgi *see* Saariselkä
Suomenlahti *see* Finland, Gulf of
Suomen Tasavalta/Suomi *see* Finland
95 N14 **Suomussalmi** Oulu, E Finland
170 D13 **Suō-nada** *sea* SW Japan
95 M17 **Suonenjoki** Kuopio, C Finland
178 Jj13 **Suŏng** Kâmpóng Cham, C Cambodia
128 I10 **Suoyarvi** Respublika Kareliya, NW Russian Federation
Supanburi *see* Suphan Buri
59 D14 **Supe** Lima, W Peru
13 V7 **Supérieur, Lac** ◎ Québec, SE Canada
Supérieur, Lac *see* Superior, Lake
38 M14 **Superior** Arizona, SW USA
35 O9 **Superior** Montana, NW USA
31 P17 **Superior** Nebraska, C USA
32 I3 **Superior** Wisconsin, N USA
43 S17 **Superior, Laguna** *lagoon* S Mexico
33 N2 **Superior, Lake** ***Fr.*** Lac Supérieur. ◎ Canada/USA
38 L13 **Superstition Mountains** ▲▲ Arizona, SW USA
115 F14 **Supetar** ***It.*** San Pietro. Split-Dalmacija, S Croatia
178 H11 **Suphan Buri** *var.* Supanburi. Suphan Buri, W Thailand
176 W9 **Supiori, Pulau** *island* E Indonesia
196 K2 **Supply Reef** *reef* N Northern Mariana Islands
205 O7 **Support Force Glacier** *glacier* Antarctica
143 R10 **Sup'sa** *var.* Supsa. ≈ W Georgia
Sūq 'Abs *see* 'Abs
145 W12 **Sūq ash Shuyūkh** SE Iraq
144 H4 **Şuqaylibīyah** Ḩamāh, W Syria
167 Q6 **Suqian** Jiangsu, E China
Suqrah *see* Şawqirah
Suqrah Bay *see* Şawqirah, Dawḩat
147 V16 **Suquṭrā** *var.* Sokotra, ***Eng.*** Socotra. *island* SE Yemen
147 Z8 **Şūr** NE Oman
Şūr *see* Soûr
131 P5 **Sura** Penzenskaya Oblast', W Russian Federation
131 P4 **Sura** ≈ W Russian Federation
155 N12 **Sūrāb** Baluchistān, SW Pakistan
Surabaja *see* Surabaya
174 M15 **Surabaya** ***prev.*** Soerabaja, Surabaja. Jawa, C Indonesia
97 N15 **Surahammar** Västmanland, C Sweden
174 L15 **Surakarta** ***Eng.*** Solo; ***prev.*** Soerakarta. Jawa, S Indonesia
Surakhany *see* Suraxanı
179 R17 **Surallah** Mindanao, S Philippines
143 S10 **Surami** C Georgia
149 X13 **Sūrān** Sīstān va Balūchestān, SE Iran
113 I21 **Šurany** ***Hung.*** Nagysurány. Západné Slovensko, SW Slovakia
160 D12 **Sūrat** Gujarāt, W India
Suratdhani *see* Surat Thani
158 G9 **Sūratgarh** Rājasthān, NW India
178 Gg15 **Surat Thani** *var.* Suratdhani. Surat Thani, SW Thailand
121 Q16 **Suraw** ***Rus.*** Surov. ≈ E Belorussia
143 Z11 **Suraxanı** ***Rus.*** Surakhany. E Azerbaijan
147 Y11 **Surayr** E Oman
144 K2 **Suraysāt** Ḩalab, N Syria
120 O12 **Surazh** ***Rus.*** Surazh. Vitsyebskaya Voblasts', NE Belorussia
130 H6 **Surazh** Bryanskaya Oblast', W Russian Federation
203 V17 **Sur, Cabo** *headland* Easter Island, Chile, E Pacific Ocean
114 L11 **Surčin** Serbia, N Yugoslavia
118 H9 **Surduc** ***Hung.*** Szurduk. Sălaj, NW Romania
115 P16 **Surdulica** Serbia, SE Yugoslavia
101 L24 **Sûre** *var.* Sauer. ≈ W Europe *see also* Sauer
160 C10 **Surendranagar** Gujarāt, W India
20 K16 **Surf City** New Jersey, NE USA
191 V3 **Surfers Paradise** Queensland, E Australia
23 U13 **Surfside Beach** South Carolina, SE USA
104 J10 **Surgères** Charente-Maritime, W France
125 G11 **Surgut** Khanty-Mansiyskiy Avtonomnyy Okrug, C Russian Federation
126 Hh10 **Surgutikha** Krasnoyarskiy Kray, N Russian Federation
100 M6 **Surhuisterveen** Friesland, N Netherlands
107 V5 **Súria** Cataluña, NE Spain
149 P10 **Sūrīān** Fārs, S Iran
161 J15 **Suriāpet** Andhra Pradesh, C India
179 R14 **Surigao** Mindanao, S Philippines
178 Ii11 **Surin** Surin, E Thailand
57 U11 **Surinam** ***off.*** Republic of Surinam, *var.* Suriname; ***prev.*** Dutch Guiana, Netherlands Guiana. ◆ *republic* N South America
Suriname *see* Surinam
Sūrīya/Sūrīyah, Al-Jumhūrīyah al-'Arabīyah as- *see* Syria
Surkhab, Darya-i- *see* Kahmard, Daryā-ye
Surkhandar'inskaya Oblast' *see* Surkhondaryo Wiloyati
Surkhandar'ya *see* Surkhondaryo
Surkhet *see* Birendranagar
153 R12 **Surkhob** ≈ C Tajikistan
153 P13 **Surkhondaryo** ***Rus.*** Surkhandar'ya. ≈ Tajikistan/Uzbekistan
153 N13 **Surkhondaryo Wiloyati** ***Rus.*** Surkhandar'inskaya Oblast'. ◈ *province* S Uzbekistan
143 P11 **Sürmene** Trabzon, NE Turkey
Surov *see* Suraw
131 N11 **Surovikino** Volgogradskaya Oblast', SW Russian Federation
126 Jj14 **Surovo** Irkutskaya Oblast', S Russian Federation
37 N11 **Sur, Point** *headland* California, W USA
197 F3 **Surprise, Île** *island* N New Caledonia
63 E22 **Sur, Punta** *headland* E Argentina
Surrentum *see* Sorrento
xxxvii S11 **Surrey** ◈ *county* SE England, UK
30 M3 **Surrey** North Dakota, N USA
23 X7 **Surry** Virginia, NE USA
110 F8 **Sursee** Luzern, W Switzerland
131 P6 **Sursk** Penzenskaya Oblast', W Russian Federation
131 P5 **Surskoye** Ul'yanovskaya Oblast', W Russian Federation
77 P8 **Surt** *var.* Sidra, Sirte. N Libya
97 I19 **Surte** Göteborg och Bohus, S Sweden
77 Q8 **Surt, Khalīj** ***Eng.*** Gulf of Sidra, Gulf of Sirti, Sidra. *gulf* N Libya
94 I5 **Surtsey** *island* S Iceland
143 N17 **Suruç** Şanlıurfa, S Turkey
171 Ii17 **Suruga-wan** *bay* SE Japan
174 Hh10 **Surulangun** Sumatera, W Indonesia
Süs *see* Susch
108 A8 **Susa** Piemonte, NE Italy
170 E12 **Susa** Yamaguchi, Honshū, SW Japan
Susa *see* Shūsh
115 E16 **Sušac** ***It.*** Cazza. *island* SW Croatia
Sūsah *see* Sousse
170 Ee15 **Susaki** Kōchi, Shikoku, SW Japan
170 G17 **Susami** Wakayama, Honshū, SW Japan
148 K9 **Sūsangerd** *var.* Susangird. Khūzestān, SW Iran
Susangird *see* Sūsangerd
37 P4 **Susanville** California, W USA
110 J9 **Susch** *var.* Süs. Graubünden, SE Switzerland
143 N12 **Suşehri** Sivas, N Turkey
Susiana *see* Khūzestān
113 B18 **Sušice** ***Ger.*** Schüttenhofen. Západní Čechy, SW Czech Republic
41 R11 **Susitna** Alaska, USA
41 R11 **Susitna River** ≈ Alaska, USA
131 Q3 **Suslonger** Respublika Mariy El, W Russian Federation
107 N14 **Suspiro del Moro, Puerto del** *pass* S Spain
20 H16 **Susquehanna River** ≈ New York/Pennsylvania, NE USA
99 O23 **Sussex** *cultural region* S England, UK
11 O15 **Sussex** New Brunswick, SE Canada
20 J13 **Sussex** New Jersey, NE USA
23 W7 **Sussex** Virginia, NE USA
191 S10 **Sussex Inlet** New South Wales, SE Australia
101 L17 **Susteren** Limburg, SE Netherlands
8 K12 **Sustut Peak** ▲ British Columbia, W Canada
127 Nn9 **Susuman** Magadanskaya Oblast', E Russian Federation
196 H6 **Susupe** Saipan, S Northern Mariana Islands
142 D12 **Susurluk** Balıkesir, NW Turkey
116 M13 **Susuzmüsellim** Tekirdağ, NW Turkey
142 F15 **Sütçüler** İsparta, SW Turkey
118 L13 **Şuţeşti** Brăila, SE Romania
98 I7 **Sutherland** *cultural region* N Scotland, UK
85 F25 **Sutherland** Western Cape, SW South Africa
30 L15 **Sutherland** Nebraska, C USA
193 B21 **Sutherland Falls** *waterfall* South Island, NZ
34 F14 **Sutherlin** Oregon, NW USA
155 V10 **Sutlej** ≈ India/Pakistan
Sutna *see* Satna
37 P7 **Sutter Creek** California, W USA
xxxix R8 **Sutterton** Lincolnshire, E England, UK
xxxix S11 **Sutton** Cambridgeshire, E England, UK
xxxix Y13 **Sutton** Suffolk, E England, UK
xxxvii T10 **Sutton** Sutton, SE England, UK
xxxiv K17 **Sutton** ◈ *London borough* SE England, UK
41 R11 **Sutton** Alaska, USA
31 Q16 **Sutton** Nebraska, C USA
23 R4 **Sutton** West Virginia, NE USA
10 F8 **Sutton** ≈ Ontario, C Canada
xxxvi M9 **Sutton Benger** Wiltshire, S England, UK
xxxix T8 **Sutton Bridge** Lincolnshire, E England, UK
xxxviii D14 **Sutton Coldfield** Birmingham, C England, UK
xxxix N6 **Sutton in Ashfield** Nottinghamshire, C England, UK
23 R4 **Sutton Lake** ⊞ West Virginia, NE USA
13 P13 **Sutton, Monts** *hill range* Québec, SE Canada
xxxix T5 **Sutton on Sea** Lincolnshire, E England, UK
xli T12 **Sutton-on-the-Forest** North Yorkshire, N England, UK
10 F8 **Sutton Ridges** ▲▲ Ontario, C Canada
xxxix S9 **Sutton St James** Lincolnshire, E England, UK
xxxvii P11 **Sutton Scotney** Hampshire, S England, UK
xxxvii W11 **Sutton Valence** Kent, SE England, UK
172 Nn5 **Suttsu** Hokkaidō, NE Japan
41 P15 **Sutwik Island** *island* Alaska, USA
168 K7 **Süüj** Bulgan, C Mongolia
120 H5 **Suure-Jaani** ***Ger.*** Gross-Sankt-Johannis. Viljandimaa, S Estonia
120 J7 **Suur Munamägi** *var.* Munamägi, ***Ger.*** Eier-Berg. ▲ SE Estonia
120 F5 **Suur Väin** ***Ger.*** Grosser Sund. *strait* W Estonia
153 U8 **Suusamyr** Chuyskaya Oblast', C Kyrgyzstan
197 I13 **Suva** ● (Fiji) Viti Levu, W Fiji
197 I13 **Suva** ✕ Viti Levu, C Fiji
115 N18 **Suva Gora** ▲▲ W FYR Macedonia
120 H11 **Suvainiškis** Rokiškis, NE Lithuania
Suvalkai/Suvalki *see* Suwałki
115 P15 **Suva Planina** ▲▲ SE Yugoslavia
115 M17 **Suva Reka** Serbia, S Yugoslavia
130 K5 **Suvorov** Tul'skaya Oblast', W Russian Federation
119 N12 **Suvorove** Odes'ka Oblast', SW Ukraine
Suvorovo *see* Ştefan Vodă
171 J15 **Suwa** Nagano, Honshū, S Japan
Suwaik *see* As Suwayq
Suwaira *see* Aş Şuwayrah
112 O7 **Suwałki** ***Lith.*** Suvalkai, ***Rus.*** Suvalki. Suwałki, NE Poland
112 N8 **Suwałki** ***off.*** Województwo Suwalskie, ***Lith.*** Suvalkai, ***Rus.*** Suvalki. ◈ *province* NE Poland
Suwalskie, Województwo *see* Suwałki
178 Ii10 **Suwannaphum** Roi Et, E Thailand
25 V8 **Suwannee River** ≈ Florida/Georgia, SE USA
Şuwār *see* Aş Şuwār
202 K14 **Suwarrow** *atoll* N Cook Islands
Suwaydá/Suwaydā', Muḩāfaẓat as *see* As Suwaydā'
149 R16 **Suwaydān** *var.* Sweiham. Abū Ẓaby, E UAE
Suwayqiyah, Hawr as *see* Shuwayjah, Hawr ash
Suways, Khalīj as *see* Suez, Gulf of
Suways, Qanāt as *see* Suez Canal
Suweida *see* As Suwaydā'
Suweon *see* Suwŏn
169 X15 **Suwŏn** *var.* Suweon, ***Jap.*** Suigen. NW South Korea
Su Xian *see* Suzhou
149 R14 **Sūzā** Hormozgān, S Iran
151 P15 **Suzak** ***Kaz.*** Sozaq. Yuzhnyy Kazakhstan, S Kazakhstan
Suzaka *see* Suzuka
130 M3 **Suzdal'** Vladimirskaya Oblast', W Russian Federation
167 R8 **Suzhou** *var.* Su Xian. Anhui, E China
167 P7 **Suzhou** *var.* Soochow, Su-chou, Suchow; ***prev.*** Wuhsien. Jiangsu, E China
Suz, Mys *see* Soye, Mys
171 J12 **Suzu** Ishikawa, Honshū, SW Japan
171 Hh16 **Suzuka** Mie, Honshū, SW Japan
171 Jj14 **Suzuka** *var.* Suzaka. Nagano, Honshū, S Japan
171 J12 **Suzu-misaki** *headland* Honshū, SW Japan
Svågälv *see* Svågan
96 M10 **Svågan** *var.* Svågälv. ≈ C Sweden
Svalava/Svaljava *see* Svalyava
94 O2 **Svalbard** ◇ *Norwegian dependency* Arctic Ocean
94 J2 **Svalbardhs** Nordhurland Eystra, N Iceland
97 K22 **Svalöv** Malmöhus, S Sweden
118 H7 **Svalyava** ***Cz.*** Svalava, Svaljava, ***Hung.*** Szolyva. Zakarpats'ka Oblast', W Ukraine
94 O2 **Svanbergfjellet** ▲ C Svalbard
97 M24 **Svaneke** Bornholm, E Denmark
97 L22 **Svängsta** Blekinge, S Sweden
97 J16 **Svanskog** Värmland, C Sweden
97 L16 **Svartå** Örebro, C Sweden
97 L15 **Svartälven** ≈ C Sweden
94 G12 **Svartisen** *glacier* C Norway
119 X6 **Svatove** ***Rus.*** Svatovo. Luhans'ka Oblast', E Ukraine
Svatovo *see* Svatove
Sväty Kríž nad Hronom *see* Žiar nad Hronom
178 Ii12 **Svay Chék, Stœng** ≈ Cambodia/Thailand
178 Jj14 **Svay Riĕng** Svay Riĕng, S Cambodia
94 O3 **Sveagruva** Spitsbergen, W Svalbard
97 K23 **Svedala** Malmöhus, S Sweden
120 H12 **Svėdesai** Anykščiai, NE Lithuania
95 G18 **Sveg** Jämtland, C Sweden
120 C12 **Švėkšna** Šilutė, W Lithuania
96 C11 **Svelgen** Sogn og Fjordane, S Norway
97 H15 **Svelvik** Vestfold, S Norway
120 I13 **Švenčionėliai** ***Pol.*** Nowo-Święciany. Švenčionys, SE Lithuania
120 I13 **Švenčionys** ***Pol.*** Swięciany. Švenčionys, SE Lithuania
97 H24 **Svendborg** Fyn, C Denmark
97 K19 **Svenljunga** Älvsborg, S Sweden
94 P2 **Svenskøya** *island* E Svalbard
95 G17 **Svenstavik** Jämtland, C Sweden
97 G20 **Svenstrup** Nordjylland, N Denmark
120 H12 **Šventoji** ≈ C Lithuania
119 Z8 **Sverdlovs'k** ***Rus.*** Sverdlovsk; ***prev.*** Imeni Sverdlova Rudnik. Luhans'ka Oblast', E Ukraine
Sverdlovsk *see* Yekaterinburg
131 W2 **Sverdlovskaya Oblast'** ◈ *province* C Russian Federation
126 Hh5 **Sverdrup, Ostrov** *island* N Russian Federation
Sverige *see* Sweden
115 D15 **Svetac** ***prev.*** Sveti Andrea, ***It.*** Sant'Andrea. *island* SW Croatia
Sveti Andrea *see* Svetac
Sveti Nikola *see* Sveti Nikole
115 O18 **Sveti Nikole** ***prev.*** Sveti Nikola. C FYR Macedonia
Sveti Vrach *see* Sandanski
127 O16 **Svetlaya** Primorskiy Kray, SE Russian Federation
130 B2 **Svetlogorsk** Kaliningradskaya Oblast', W Russian Federation
126 I9 **Svetlogorsk** Krasnoyarskiy Kray, N Russian Federation
Svetlogorsk *see* Svyetlahorsk
131 N14 **Svetlograd** Stavropol'skiy Kray, SW Russian Federation
Svetlovodsk *see* Svitlovods'k
121 A14 **Svetlyy** ***Ger.*** Zimmerbude. Kaliningradskaya Oblast', W Russian Federation
131 Y8 **Svetlyy** Orenburgskaya Oblast', W Russian Federation
128 G11 **Svetogorsk** ***Fin.*** Enso. Leningradskaya Oblast', NW Russian Federation
Svetozarevo *see* Jagodina
113 B18 **Švihov** ***Ger.*** Schwihau. Západní Čechy, W Czech Republic
114 E13 **Svilaja** ▲▲ SE Croatia
114 N12 **Svilajnac** Serbia, C Yugoslavia
116 L11 **Svilengrad** ***prev.*** Mustafa-Pasha. Khaskovska Oblast, SE Bulgaria
Svinecea Mare, Munte *see* Svinecea Mare, Vârful
118 F13 **Svinecea Mare, Vârful** *var.* Munte Svinecea Mare. ▲ SW Romania
153 N14 **Svintsovyy Rudnik** ***Turkm.*** Swintsowyy Rudnik. Lebapskiy Velayat, E Turkmenistan
120 I13 **Svir** ***Rus.*** Svir'. Minskaya Voblasts', NW Belorussia
128 I12 **Svir'** *canal* NW Russian Federation
Svir', Ozero *see* Svir, Vozyera

◆ Country ● Country Capital ◇ Dependent Territory ○ Dependent Territory Capital ◈ Administrative Region ✕ International Airport ▲ Mountain ▲▲ Mountain Range Volcano ≈ River ◎ Lake ⊞ Reservoir

SVIR, VOZYERA – TALLINN

121 I14 **Svir, Vozyera** *Rus.* Ozero Svir'. ◎ C Belorussia
116 J7 **Svishtov** *prev.* Sistova. Loveshka Oblast, N Bulgaria
121 F18 **Svislach** *Pol.* Świsłocz, *Rus.* Svisloch'. Hrodzyenskaya Voblasts', W Belorussia
121 M17 **Svislach** *Rus.* Svisloch'. Mahilyowskaya Voblasts', E Belorussia
121 L17 **Svislach** *Rus.* Svisloch'. ⚡ E Belorussia
Svisloch' *see* Svislach
113 F17 **Svitavy** *Ger.* Zwittau. Východní Čechy, E Czech Republic
119 S6 **Svitlovods'k** *Rus.* Svetlovodsk. Kirovohrads'ka Oblast', C Ukraine
Svizzera *see* Switzerland
126 Mm15 **Svobodnyy** Amurskaya Oblast', SE Russian Federation
116 G9 **Svoge** Sofiyska Oblast, W Bulgaria
94 G11 **Svolvær** Nordland, C Norway
113 F18 **Svratka** *Ger.* Schwarzach, Schwarzawa. ⚡ SE Czech Republic
115 P14 **Svrljig** Serbia, E Yugoslavia
207 U10 **Svyataya Anna Trough** *var.* Saint Anna Trough. *undersea feature* N Kara Sea
128 M4 **Svyatoy Nos, Mys** *headland* NW Russian Federation
126 M5 **Svyatoy Nos, Mys** *headland* NE Russian Federation
121 N18 **Svyetlahorsk** *Rus.* Svetlogorsk. Homyel'skaya Voblasts', SE Belorussia
Swabian Jura *see* Schwäbische Alb
xxxviii L9 **Swadlincote** Derbyshire, C England, UK
xxxix V9 **Swaffham** Norfolk, E England, UK
xli S10 **Swainby** North Yorkshire, N England, UK
25 V5 **Swainsboro** Georgia, SE USA
xxxvi M10 **Swainswick** Bath and North East Somerset, SW England, UK
85 C19 **Swakop** ⚡ W Namibia
85 C19 **Swakopmund** Erongo, W Namibia
xxxvi P6 **Swalcliffe** Oxfordshire, S England, UK
xli S11 **Swale** ⚡ N England, UK
xliv H6 **Swalinbar** Cavan, N Ireland
xxxix Q4 **Swallow** Lincolnshire, E England, UK
xxxvii N12 **Swallowcliffe** Wiltshire, S England, UK
xxxvii R10 **Swallowfield** Wokingham, S England, UK
Swallow Island *see* Nendö
101 M16 **Swalmen** Limburg, SE Netherlands
10 G8 **Swan** ⚡ Ontario, C Canada
xxxvii N14 **Swanage** Dorset, S England, UK
190 M10 **Swan Hill** Victoria, SE Australia
9 P13 **Swan Hills** Alberta, W Canada
67 D24 **Swan Island** *island* C Falkland Islands
Swankalok *see* Sawankhalok
31 U10 **Swan Lake** ◎ Minnesota, N USA
xxxvii V9 **Swanley** Kent, SE England, UK
23 Y10 **Swanquarter** North Carolina, SE USA
190 J9 **Swan Reach** South Australia
9 V15 **Swan River** Manitoba, S Canada
xxxv G14 **Swansea** *Wel.* Abertawe. Swansea, S Wales, UK
xxxv G14 **Swansea** ◐ *unitary authority* S Wales, UK
191 P17 **Swansea** Tasmania, SE Australia
23 R13 **Swansea** South Carolina, SE USA
xxxv G15 **Swansea Bay** *bay* S Wales, UK
21 S7 **Swans Island** *island* Maine, NE USA
30 L17 **Swanson Lake** ⊠ Nebraska, C USA
33 R11 **Swanton** Ohio, N USA
xxxix W9 **Swanton Morley** Norfolk, E England, UK
xxxix X10 **Swardeston** Norfolk, E England, UK
112 G11 **Swarzędz** Poznań, W Poland
Swatow *see* Shantou
xxxix Q8 **Swayfield** Lincolnshire, E England, UK
85 L22 **Swaziland** *off.* Kingdom of Swaziland. ◆ *monarchy* S Africa
95 G18 **Sweden** *off.* Kingdom of Sweden, *Swe.* Sverige. ◆ *monarchy* N Europe
Swedru *see* Agona Swedru
27 V12 **Sweeny** Texas, SW USA
35 R6 **Sweetgrass** Montana, NW USA
34 G12 **Sweet Home** Oregon, NW USA
27 T12 **Sweet Home** Texas, SW USA
29 T4 **Sweet Springs** Missouri, C USA
22 M10 **Sweetwater** Tennessee, S USA
27 P7 **Sweetwater** Texas, SW USA
35 V15 **Sweetwater River** ⚡ Wyoming, C USA
Sweihan *see* Suwaydān
85 F26 **Swellendam** Western Cape, SW South Africa
113 G15 **Świdnica** *Ger.* Schweidnitz. Wałbrzych, SW Poland
113 O14 **Świdnik** *Ger.* Streckenbach. Lublin, E Poland
112 F8 **Świdwin** *Ger.* Schivelbein. Koszalin, NW Poland
113 F15 **Świebodzice** *Ger.* Freiburg in Schlesien, Swiebodzice. Wałbrzych, SW Poland
112 E11 **Świebodzin** *Ger.* Schwiebus. Zielona Góra, W Poland
Święciany *see* Švenčionys
112 I9 **Świecie** *Ger.* Schwertberg. Bydgoszcz, N Poland
9 T16 **Swift Current** Saskatchewan, S Canada
100 K9 **Swifterbant** Flevoland, C Netherlands
191 Q12 **Swifts Creek** Victoria, SE Australia
xliv H3 **Swilly** ⚡ N Ireland
xliv I2 **Swilly, Lough** *Ir.* Loch Súilí. *inlet* N Ireland
xxxvi G12 **Swimbridge** Devon, SW England, UK
xxxvii O9 **Swindon** Thamesdown, S England, UK
xxxvii N9 **Swindon** ◐ *unitary authority* C England, UK
Swinemünde *see* Świnoujście
xxxvii S5 **Swineshead** Bedfordshire, C England, UK
xxxix R7 **Swineshead** Lincolnshire, E England, UK
xliv E6 **Swinford** Mayo, NW Ireland
xxxix N11 **Swinford** Leicestershire, C England, UK
xlii I3 **Swining** Shetland Islands, NE Scotland, UK
112 D8 **Świnoujście** *Ger.* Swinemünde. Szczecin, NW Poland
xli O16 **Swinton** Salford, NW England, UK
xliii P21 **Swinton** The Borders, S Scotland, UK
Swintsowyy Rudnik *see* Svintsovyy Rudnik
Świsłocz *see* Svislach
Swiss Confederation *see* Switzerland
110 E9 **Switzerland** *off.* Swiss Confederation, *Fr.* La Suisse, *Ger.* Schweiz, *It.* Svizzera; *anc.* Helvetia. ◆ *federal republic* C Europe
xliv L8 **Swords** *Ir.* Sord, Sórd Choluim Chille. Dublin, E Ireland
20 H13 **Swoyersville** Pennsylvania, NE USA
128 I10 **Syamozera, Ozero** ◎ NW Russian Federation
128 M13 **Syamzha** Vologodskaya Oblast', NW Russian Federation
120 N13 **Syanno** *Rus.* Senno. Vitsyebskaya Voblasts', NE Belorussia
121 K16 **Syarhyeyevichy** *Rus.* Sergeyevichi. Minskaya Voblasts', C Belorussia
128 I12 **Syas'stroy** Leningradskaya Oblast', NW Russian Federation
Sycaminum *see* Hefa
32 M10 **Sycamore** Illinois, N USA
130 J3 **Sychëvka** Smolenskaya Oblast', W Russian Federation
113 H14 **Syców** *Ger.* Gross Wartenberg. Kalisz, SW Poland
12 E17 **Sydenham** ⚡ Ontario, S Canada
Sydenham Island *see* Nonouti
191 T9 **Sydney** *state capital* New South Wales, SE Australia
11 R14 **Sydney** Cape Breton Island, Nova Scotia, SE Canada
Sydney Island *see* Manra
11 R14 **Sydney Mines** Cape Breton Island, Nova Scotia, SE Canada
Syedlets *see* Siedlce
Syedpur *see* Saidpur
121 K18 **Syelishcha** *Rus.* Selishche. Minskaya Voblasts', C Belorussia
121 J18 **Syemyezhava** *Rus.* Semezhevo. Minskaya Voblasts', C Belorussia
Syene *see* Aswân
119 X6 **Syeverodonets'k** *Rus.* Severodonetsk. Luhans'ka Oblast', E Ukraine
167 T6 **Syōsō Shan** *island* SE China
102 H11 **Syke** Niedersachsen, NW Germany
xli T15 **Sykehouse** Doncaster, N England, UK
96 D10 **Sykkylven** Møre og Romsdal, S Norway
117 F15 **Sykoúri** *var.* Sikouri; *prev.* Sikoúrion. Thessalía, C Greece
129 R11 **Syktyvkar** *prev.* Ust'-Sysol'sk. Respublika Komi, NW Russian Federation
25 Q4 **Sylacauga** Alabama, S USA
Sylarna *see* Sylene
96 J9 **Sylene** *Swe.* Sylarna. ▲ Norway/Sweden
159 V14 **Sylhet** Chittagong, NE Bangladesh
102 G6 **Sylt** *island* NW Germany
23 O10 **Sylva** North Carolina, SE USA
129 V15 **Sylva** ⚡ NW Russian Federation
25 W5 **Sylvania** Georgia, SE USA
33 R11 **Sylvania** Ohio, N USA
9 Q15 **Sylvan Lake** Alberta, SW Canada
35 T13 **Sylvan Pass** *pass* Wyoming, C USA
25 T7 **Sylvester** Georgia, SE USA
27 P6 **Sylvester** Texas, SW USA
8 L11 **Sylvia, Mount** ▲ British Columbia, W Canada
126 Hh12 **Sym** ⚡ C Russian Federation
xlii I3 **Symbister** Shetland Islands, NE Scotland, UK
117 N22 **Sými** *var.* Simi. *island* Dodekánisos, Greece, Aegean Sea
xxxviii H15 **Symonds Yat** Herefordshire, W England, UK
119 U8 **Synel'nykove** Dnipropetrovs'ka Oblast', E Ukraine
129 U6 **Synya** Respublika Komi, NW Russian Federation
119 P7 **Synyukha** *Rus.* Sinyukha. ⚡ S Ukraine
Syôbara *see* Shōbara
205 V2 **Syowa** *Japanese research station* Antarctica
28 H6 **Syracuse** Kansas, C USA
31 S16 **Syracuse** Nebraska, C USA
20 H10 **Syracuse** New York, NE USA
Syracuse *see* Siracusa
Syrdar'inskaya Oblast' *see* Sirdaryo Wiloyati
Syrdariya *see* Syr Darya
150 L14 **Syr Darya** *var.* Sai Hun, Sir Darya, Syrdarya, *Kaz.* Syrdariya, *Rus.* Syrdar'ya, *Uzb.* Sirdaryo; *anc.* Jaxartes. ⚡ C Asia
153 P10 **Syrdar'ya** Sirdaryo Wiloyati, E Uzbekistan
xlii J7 **Syre** Highland, N Scotland, UK
xxxix O13 **Syresham** Northamptonshire, C England, UK
144 J6 **Syria** *off.* Syrian Arab Republic, *var.* Siria, Syrie, *Ar.* Al-Jumhūrīyah al-'Arabīyah as-Sūrīyah, Sūrīya. ◆ *republic* SW Asia
144 L9 **Syrian Desert** *Ar.* Al Hamad, Bādiyat ash Shām. *desert* SW Asia
Syrie *see* Syria
117 L22 **Sýrna** *var.* Sirna. *island* Kykládes, Greece, Aegean Sea
117 I20 **Sýros** *var.* Síros. *island* Kykládes, Greece, Aegean Sea
95 M18 **Sysmä** Mikkeli, S Finland
129 R12 **Sysola** ⚡ NW Russian Federation
xxxix O9 **Syston** Leicestershire, C England, UK
Syulemeshlii *see* Sredets
131 S2 **Syumsi** Udmurtskaya Respublika, NW Russian Federation
116 K10 **Syuyutliyka** ⚡ C Bulgaria
Syvash, Zaliv *see* Syvash, Zatoka
119 U12 **Syvash, Zatoka** *Rus.* Zaliv Syvash. *inlet* S Ukraine
131 Q6 **Syzran'** Samarskaya Oblast', W Russian Federation
Szabadka *see* Subotica
113 N21 **Szabolcs-Szatmár-Bereg** *off.* Szabolcs-Szatmár-Bereg Megye. ◐ *county* E Hungary
112 G10 **Szamocin** *Ger.* Samotschin. Piła, W Poland
118 H8 **Szamos** *var.* Someş, Someşul, *Ger.* Samosch, Somesch. ⚡ Hungary/Romania
Szamosújvár *see* Gherla
112 G11 **Szamotuły** Poznań, W Poland
Szarkowszczyzna *see* Sharkawshchyna
113 M24 **Szarvas** Békés, SE Hungary
Szászmagyarós *see* Măieruş
Szászrégen *see* Reghin
Szászsebes *see* Sebeş
Szászváros *see* Orăştie
Szatmárnémeti *see* Satu Mare
Száva *see* Sava
113 P15 **Szczebrzeszyn** Zamość, SE Poland
112 D9 **Szczecin** *Eng./Ger.* Stettin. Szczecin, NW Poland
112 D9 **Szczecin** *off.* Województwo Szczecińskie; *prev.* Pomorze Zachodnie. ◐ *province* NW Poland
112 G8 **Szczecinek** *Ger.* Neustettin. Koszalin, NW Poland
Szczecińskie, Województwo *see* Szczecin
112 D8 **Szczeciński, Zalew** *var.* Stettiner Haff, *Ger.* Oderhaff. *bay* Germany/Poland
113 K15 **Szczekociny** Częstochowa, S Poland
112 N8 **Szczuczyn** Łomża, NE Poland
Szczuczyn Nowogródzki *see* Shchuchyn
112 M8 **Szczytno** *Ger.* Ortelsburg. Olsztyn, NE Poland
Szechuan/Szechwan *see* Sichuan
113 K21 **Szécsény** Nógrád, N Hungary
113 L25 **Szeged** *Ger.* Szegedin, *Rom.* Seghedin. Csongrád, SE Hungary
Szegedin *see* Szeged
113 N23 **Szeghalom** Békés, SE Hungary
Székelyhid *see* Săcueni
Székelykeresztúr *see* Cristuru Secuiesc
113 I23 **Székesfehérvár** *Ger.* Stuhlweissenberg; *anc.* Alba Regia. Fejér, W Hungary
Szeklerburg *see* Miercurea-Ciuc
Szekler Neumarkt *see* Târgu Secuiesc
113 J25 **Szekszárd** Tolna, S Hungary
Szempcz/Szenc *see* Senec
Szenice *see* Senica
Szentágota *see* Agnita
113 J22 **Szentendre** *Ger.* Sankt Andrä. Pest, N Hungary
113 L24 **Szentes** Csongrád, SE Hungary
113 F23 **Szentgotthárd** *Eng.* Saint Gotthard, *Ger.* Sankt Gotthard. Vas, W Hungary
Szentgyörgy *see* Đurđevac
Szenttamás *see* Srbobran
Szépely *see* Jebel
Szeping *see* Siping
Szered *see* Sered'
113 N21 **Szerencs** Borsod-Abaúj-Zemplén, NE Hungary
Szeret *see* Siret
Szeretfalva *see* Sărăţel
112 N7 **Szeskie Wzgórza** *Ger.* Seesker Höhe. *hill* NE Poland
113 H25 **Szigetvár** Baranya, SW Hungary
Szilágysomlyó *see* Şimleu Silvaniei
Szinna *see* Snina
Sziszek *see* Sisak
Szitás-Keresztúr *see* Cristuru Secuiesc
113 E15 **Szklarska Poręba** *Ger.* Schreiberhau. Jelenia Góra, SW Poland
Szkudy *see* Skuodas
Szlatina *see* Podravska Slatina
Szlavonia/Szlavonország *see* Slavonija
Szlovákia *see* Slovakia
Szluin *see* Slunj
113 L23 **Szolnok** Jász-Nagykun-Szolnok, C Hungary
Szolyva *see* Svalyava
113 G23 **Szombathely** *Ger.* Steinamanger; *anc.* Sabaria, Savaria. Vas, W Hungary
Szond/Szonta *see* Sonta
Szováta *see* Sovata
112 F13 **Szprotawa** *Ger.* Sprottau. Zielona Góra, W Poland
Sztálinváros *see* Dunaújváros
Sztrazsó *see* Strážov
112 J8 **Sztum** *Ger.* Stuhm. Elbląg, N Poland
112 H10 **Szubin** *Ger.* Schubin. Bydgoszcz, W Poland
Szucsava *see* Suceava
Szurduk *see* Surduc
113 M14 **Szydłowiec** *Ger.* Schlelau. Radom, C Poland

T

xlii G11 **Taagan** Highland, NW Scotland, UK
Taalintehdas *see* Dalsbruk
179 P11 **Taal, Lake** ◎ Luzon, NW Philippines
Taastrup *see* Tåstrup
113 I24 **Tab** Somogy, W Hungary
179 Q11 **Tabaco** Luzon, N Philippines
194 M7 **Tabalo** Mussau Island, NE PNG
106 K5 **Tábara** Castilla-León, N Spain
195 P9 **Tabar Island** *island* Tabar Islands, N PNG
195 P9 **Tabar Islands** *island group* NE PNG
Tabariya, Bahrat *see* Tiberias, Lake
149 S7 **Ṭabas** *var.* Golshan. Khorāsān, C Iran
45 P15 **Tabasará, Serranía de** ▲ W Panama
43 U15 **Tabasco** ◐ *state* SE Mexico
Tabasco *see* Grijalva, Río
131 Q2 **Tabashino** Respublika Mariy El, W Russian Federation
60 B13 **Tabatinga** Amazonas, N Brazil
76 G9 **Tabelbala** W Algeria
9 Q17 **Taber** Alberta, SW Canada
176 W14 **Taberfane** Pulau Trangan, E Indonesia
97 L19 **Taberg** Jönköping, S Sweden
Tabibug *see* Tabibuga
194 H12 **Tabibuga** *var.* Tabibug. Western Highlands, C PNG
203 O3 **Tabiteuea** *prev.* Drummond Island. *atoll* Tungaru, W Kiribati
179 Q12 **Tablas Island** *island* C Philippines
179 Pp12 **Tablas Strait** *strait* C Philippines
194 M16 **Table Bay** *bay* SE PNG
192 Q10 **Table Cape** *headland* North Island, NZ
11 S13 **Table Mountain** ▲ Newfoundland, Newfoundland and Labrador, E Canada
181 P17 **Table, Pointe de la** *headland* SE Réunion
29 S8 **Table Rock Lake** ⊠ Arkansas/Missouri, C USA
38 K14 **Table Top** ▲ Arizona, SW USA
194 J13 **Tabletop, Mount** ▲ C PNG
126 Mm5 **Tabor** Respublika Sakha (Yakutiya), NE Russian Federation
31 S15 **Tabor** Iowa, C USA
113 D18 **Tábor** Jižní Čechy, SW Czech Republic
83 F21 **Tabora** Tabora, W Tanzania
83 F21 **Tabora** ◐ *region* C Tanzania
23 U12 **Tabor City** North Carolina, SE USA
153 Q10 **Taboshar** NW Tajikistan
78 L18 **Tabou** *var.* Tabu. S Ivory Coast
148 J2 **Tabrīz** *var.* Tebriz; *anc.* Tauris. Āżarbāyjān-e Khāvarī, NW Iran
Tabu *see* Tabou
203 W1 **Tabuaeran** *prev.* Fanning Island. *atoll* Line Islands, E Kiribati
194 E11 **Tabubil** Western, SW PNG
179 P8 **Tabuk** Luzon, N Philippines
146 J4 **Tabūk** Tabūk, NW Saudi Arabia
146 J5 **Tabūk** *off.* Minṭaqat Tabūk. ◐ *province* NW Saudi Arabia
197 B12 **Tabwemasana, Mount** ▲ Espiritu Santo, W Vanuatu
97 O15 **Täby** Stockholm, C Sweden
43 N14 **Tacámbaro** Michoacán de Ocampo, SW Mexico
44 A5 **Tacaná, Volcán** ⚠ Guatemala/Mexico
45 X16 **Tacarcuna, Cerro** ▲ SE Panama
Tachau *see* Tachov
164 J3 **Tacheng** *var.* Qoqek. Xinjiang Uygur Zizhiqu, NW China
56 H7 **Táchira** *off.* Estado Táchira. ◐ *state* W Venezuela
167 T13 **Tachoshui** N Taiwan
113 A17 **Tachov** *Ger.* Tachau. Západní Čechy, W Czech Republic
179 R13 **Tacloban** *off.* Tacloban City. Leyte, C Philippines
59 I19 **Tacna** Tacna, SE Peru
59 H18 **Tacna** *off.* Departamento de Tacna. ◐ *department* S Peru
34 H8 **Tacoma** Washington, NW USA
20 L11 **Taconic Range** ▲ NE USA
64 L6 **Taco Pozo** Formosa, N Argentina
59 M20 **Tacsara, Cordillera de** ▲ S Bolivia
63 F17 **Tacuarembó** *prev.* San Fructuoso. Tacuarembó, C Uruguay
63 E18 **Tacuarembó** ◐ *department* C Uruguay
63 F17 **Tacuarembó, Río** ⚡ C Uruguay
85 I14 **Taculi** North Western, NW Zambia
179 R16 **Tacurong** Mindanao, S Philippines
171 Kk13 **Tadamu-gawa** ⚡ Honshū, C Japan
xli S13 **Tadcaster** North Yorkshire, N England, UK
79 V8 **Tadek** ⚡ NW Niger
76 J9 **Tademaït, Plateau du** *plateau* C Algeria
197 K6 **Tadine** Province des Îles Loyauté, E New Caledonia
82 L11 **Tadjoura** E Djibouti
82 M11 **Tadjoura, Golfe de** *Eng.* Gulf of Tajura. *inlet* E Djibouti
xxxvii Q10 **Tadley** Hampshire, S England, UK
Tadmor/Tadmur *see* Tudmur
9 W10 **Tadoule Lake** ◎ Manitoba, C Canada
13 S8 **Tadoussac** Québec, SE Canada
161 H18 **Tādpatri** Andhra Pradesh, E India
xxxvii T11 **Tadworth** Surrey, SE England, UK
Tadzhikabad *see* Tojikobod
Tadzhikistan *see* Tajikistan
169 Y14 **T'aebaek-sanmaek** ▲ E South Korea
169 V15 **Taechŏng-do** *island* NW South Korea
169 X13 **Taedong-gang** ⚡ C North Korea
169 Y16 **Taegu** *off.* Taegu-gwangyŏksi, *var.* Daegu, *Jap.* Taikyū. SE South Korea
Taehan-haehyŏp *see* Korea Strait
Taehan Min'guk *see* South Korea
169 Y15 **Taejŏn** *off.* Taejŏn-gwangyŏksi, *Jap.* Taiden. C South Korea
200 T11 **Tafahi** *island* N Tonga
107 Q4 **Tafalla** Navarra, N Spain
77 M12 **Tafassâsset, Oued** ⚡ SE Algeria
79 W7 **Tafassâsset, Ténéré du** *desert* N Niger
57 U11 **Tafelberg** ▲ S Surinam
xxxv J15 **Taff** ⚡ SE Wales, UK
Tafila/Ṭafīlah, Muḥāfaẓat aṭ *see* Aṭ Ṭafīlah
79 N15 **Tafiré** N Ivory Coast
148 M6 **Tafresh** Markazī, W Iran
149 Q9 **Taft** Yazd, C Iran
37 R13 **Taft** California, W USA
27 T14 **Taft** Texas, SW USA
149 W12 **Taftān, Kūh-e** ▲ SE Iran
37 R13 **Taft Heights** California, W USA
201 Y14 **Tafunsak** Kosrae, E Micronesia
198 Aa8 **Tāga** Savai'i, SW Western Samoa
155 O6 **Tagāb** Kāpīsā, E Afghanistan
41 O8 **Tagagawik River** ⚡ Alaska, USA
171 M13 **Tagajō** *var.* Tagazyô. Miyagi, Honshū, C Japan
130 K12 **Taganrog** Rostovskaya Oblast', SW Russian Federation
130 K12 **Taganrog, Gulf of** *Rus.* Taganrogskiy Zaliv, *Ukr.* Tahanroz'ka Zatoka. *gulf* Russian Federation/Ukraine
Taganrogskiy Zaliv *see* Taganrog, Gulf of
78 J8 **Tagant** ◐ *region* C Mauritania
154 M14 **Tagas** Baluchistān, SW Pakistan
170 D13 **Tagawa** Fukuoka, Kyūshū, SW Japan
179 P11 **Tagaytay** Luzon, N Philippines
Tagazyô *see* Tagajō
179 Qq14 **Tagbilaran** *var.* Tagbilaran City. Bohol, C Philippines
108 B10 **Taggia** Liguria, NW Italy
xliv K12 **Taghmon** Wexford, SE Ireland
79 V9 **Taghouaji, Massif de** ▲ C Niger
109 J15 **Tagliacozzo** Lazio, C Italy
108 J7 **Tagliamento** ⚡ NE Italy
179 R15 **Tagoloan** Mindanao, S Philippines
155 N3 **Tagow Bāy** *var.* Bai. Sar-e Pol, N Afghanistan
Tagtabazar *see* Takhtabazar
61 L17 **Taguatinga** Tocantins, C Brazil
195 Q17 **Tagula** Tagula Island, SE PNG
195 P17 **Tagula Island** *prev.* Southeast Island, Sudest Island. *island* SE PNG
179 Rr15 **Tagum** Mindanao, S Philippines
56 C7 **Tagún, Cerro** *elevation* Colombia/Panama
107 P7 **Tagus** *Port.* Rio Tejo, *Sp.* Río Tajo. ⚡ Portugal/Spain
66 M9 **Tagus Plain** *undersea feature* E Atlantic Ocean
203 S10 **Tahaa** *island* Îles Sous le Vent, W French Polynesia
203 U10 **Tahanea** *atoll* Îles Tuamotu, C French Polynesia
Tahanroz'ka Zatoka *see* Taganrog, Gulf of
171 I16 **Tahara** Aichi, Honshū, SW Japan
76 K12 **Tahat** ▲ SE Algeria
169 V12 **Ta He** ⚡ NE China
169 U4 **Tahe** Heilongjiang, NE China
168 G9 **Tahilt** Govĭ-Altay, W Mongolia
203 T10 **Tahiti** *island* Îles du Vent, W French Polynesia
Tahiti, Archipel de *see* Société, Archipel de la
120 E4 **Tahkuna nina** *headland* W Estonia
154 K12 **Tāhlāb** ⚡ W Pakistan
154 K12 **Tāhlāb, Dasht-i** *desert* SW Pakistan
29 R10 **Tahlequah** Oklahoma, C USA
37 Q6 **Tahoe City** California, W USA
37 P6 **Tahoe, Lake** ◎ California/Nevada, W USA
Tahoena *see* Tahuna
27 N6 **Tahoka** Texas, SW USA
34 F8 **Taholah** Washington, NW USA
79 T11 **Tahoua** Tahoua, W Niger
79 T11 **Tahoua** ◐ *department* W Niger
33 P3 **Tahquamenon Falls** *waterfall* Michigan, N USA
33 P4 **Tahquamenon River** ⚡ Michigan, N USA
145 V10 **Taḥrīr** S Iraq
8 K17 **Tahsis** Vancouver Island, British Columbia, SW Canada
Tahta *see* Takhta
77 W9 **Ṭahṭa** C Egypt
142 L15 **Tahtalı Dağları** ▲ C Turkey
59 I14 **Tahuamanu, Río** ⚡ Bolivia/Peru
58 F13 **Tahuania, Río** ⚡ E Peru
203 X7 **Tahuata** *island* Îles Marquises, NE French Polynesia
175 S6 **Tahulandang, Pulau** *island* N Indonesia
175 S5 **Tahuna** *prev.* Tahoena. Pulau Sangihe, N Indonesia
176 Yy10 **Tahun, Danau** *see* Tahun, Danau
78 L17 **Taï** SW Ivory Coast
167 P5 **Tai'an** Shandong, E China
203 R8 **Taiarapu, Presqu'île de** *peninsula* Tahiti, W French Polynesia
Taibad *see* Tāybād
166 K7 **Taibai Shan** ▲ C China
107 Q12 **Taibilla, Sierra de** ▲ S Spain
169 Q12 **Taibus Qi** *var.* Baochang. Nei Mongol Zizhiqu, N China
Taichū *see* T'aichung
167 S13 **T'aichung** *Jap.* Taichū; *prev.* Taiwan. C Taiwan
Taiden *see* Taejŏn
193 E23 **Taieri** ⚡ South Island, NZ
117 E21 **Taïgetos** ▲ S Greece
167 N4 **Taihang Shan** ▲ C China
192 M11 **Taihape** Manawatu-Wanganui, North Island, NZ
167 O7 **Taihe** Anhui, E China
167 O12 **Taihe** Jiangxi, S China
Taihoku *see* T'aipei
167 R8 **Tai Hu** ◎ E China
167 P9 **Taihu** Anhui, E China
167 O6 **Taikang** Henan, C China
172 P7 **Taiki** Hokkaidō, NE Japan
177 Fj8 **Taikkyi** Yangon, SW Burma
Taikyū *see* Taegu
169 U8 **Tailai** Heilongjiang, NE China
173 Ff10 **Tailelo** Pulau Siberut, W Indonesia
190 J10 **Tailem Bend** South Australia
xlii J10 **Tain** Highland, N Scotland, UK
167 S14 **T'ainan** *Jap.* Tainan; *prev.* Dainan. S Taiwan
117 E22 **Taínaro, Ákra** *headland* S Greece
167 Q11 **Taining** Fujian, SE China
203 W7 **Taiohae** *prev.* Madisonville. Nuku Hiva, NE French Polynesia
167 T13 **T'aipei** *Jap.* Taihoku; *prev.* Daihoku. ● (Taiwan) N Taiwan
174 Gg3 **Taiping** Perak, Peninsular Malaysia
169 S8 **Taiping Ling** ▲ NE China
172 N6 **Taisei** Hokkaidō, NE Japan
170 F12 **Taisha** Shimane, Honshū, SW Japan
111 R4 **Taiskirchen** Oberösterreich, NW Austria
65 F20 **Taitao, Peninsula de** *peninsula* S Chile
Taitō *see* T'aitung
167 T14 **T'aitung** *Jap.* Taitō. S Taiwan
94 M13 **Taivalkoski** Oulu, E Finland
95 K19 **Taivassalo** Turku-Pori, SW Finland
167 T14 **Taiwan** *off.* Republic of China, *var.* Formosa, Formo'sa. ◆ *republic* E Asia
140 Q11 **Taiwan** *var.* Formosa. *island* E Asia
Taiwan *see* T'aichung
T'aiwan Haihsia/Taiwan Haixia *see* Taiwan Strait
Taiwan Shan *see* Chungyang Shanmo
167 R13 **Taiwan Strait** *var.* Formosa Strait, *Chin.* T'aiwan Haihsia, Taiwan Haixia. *strait* China/Taiwan
167 N4 **Taiyuan** *prev.* T'ai-yuan, T'ai-yüan, Yangku. Shanxi, C China
167 R7 **Taizhou** Jiangsu, E China
Taizhou *see* Linhai
147 O16 **Ta'izz** SW Yemen
147 O16 **Ta'izz** ✕ SW Yemen
77 P12 **Tajarhī** SW Libya
153 P13 **Tajikistan** *off.* Republic of Tajikistan, *Rus.* Tadzhikistan, *Taj.* Jumhurii Tojikiston; *prev.* Tajik S.S.R. ◆ *republic* C Asia
Tajik S.S.R *see* Tajikistan
171 Kk14 **Tajima** Fukushima, Honshū, C Japan
Tajoe *see* Tayu
Tajo, Río *see* Tagus
44 B5 **Tajumulco, Volcán** ▲ W Guatemala
107 P7 **Tajuña** ⚡ C Spain
Tajura, Gulf of *see* Tadjoura, Golfe de
178 H9 **Tak** *var.* Rahaeng. Tak, W Thailand
201 U4 **Taka Atoll** *var.* Tōke. *atoll* Ratak Chain, N Marshall Islands
171 L16 **Takahagi** Ibaraki, Honshū, S Japan
170 Ff13 **Takahashi** *var.* Takahasi. Okayama, Honshū, SW Japan
170 F13 **Takahashi-gawa** ⚡ Honshū, SW Japan
Takahasi *see* Takahashi
201 P12 **Takaieu Island** *island* E Micronesia
192 I13 **Takaka** Tasman, South Island, NZ
175 P13 **Takalar** Sulawesi, C Indonesia
170 Ff14 **Takamatsu** *var.* Takamatu. Kagawa, Shikoku, SW Japan
Takamatu *see* Takamatsu
170 Cc14 **Takamori** Kumamoto, Kyūshū, SW Japan
170 Cc16 **Takanabe** Miyazaki, Kyūshū, SW Japan
175 O16 **Takan, Gunung** ▲ Pulau Sumba, S Indonesia
171 M9 **Takanosu** Akita, Honshū, C Japan
Takao *see* Kaohsiung
171 Ii13 **Takaoka** Toyama, Honshū, SW Japan
192 N12 **Takapau** Hawke's Bay, North Island, NZ
203 U9 **Takapoto** *atoll* Îles Tuamotu, C French Polynesia
192 L5 **Takapuna** Auckland, North Island, NZ
171 Gg14 **Takarazuka** Hyōgo, Honshū, SW Japan
203 U9 **Takaroa** *atoll* Îles Tuamotu, C French Polynesia
171 Jj15 **Takasaki** Gunma, Honshū, S Japan
171 Gg15 **Takatsuki** *var.* Takatuki. Ōsaka, Honshū, SW Japan
Takatuki *see* Takatsuki
171 Ii14 **Takayama** Gifu, Honshū, SW Japan
171 Hh13 **Takefu** *var.* Takehu. Fukui, Honshū, SW Japan
170 F14 **Takehara** Hiroshima, Honshū, SW Japan
Takehu *see* Takefu
xxxvii V7 **Takeley** Essex, SE England, UK
170 C13 **Takeo** Saga, Kyūshū, SW Japan
Takeo *see* Takêv
170 B17 **Take-shima** *island* Nansei-shotō, SW Japan
148 M5 **Tākestān** *var.* Takistan; *prev.* Siadehan. Zanjān, W Iran
170 D14 **Taketa** Ōita, Kyūshū, SW Japan
178 J14 **Takêv** *prev.* Takeo. Takêv, S Cambodia
178 Hh10 **Tak Fah** Nakhon Sawan, C Thailand
145 T13 **Takhādīd** *well* S Iraq
155 R3 **Takhār** ◐ *province* NE Afghanistan
Takhiatash *see* Takhiatosh
152 H8 **Takhiatosh** *Rus.* Takhiatash. Qoraqalpoghiston Respublikasi, W Uzbekistan
178 J13 **Ta Khmau** Kândal, S Cambodia
152 H9 **Takhta** *Turkm.* Tahta. Dashkhovuzskiy Velayat, N Turkmenistan
152 J16 **Takhtabazar** *var.* Tagtabazar. Maryyskiy Velayat, S Turkmenistan
151 O8 **Takhtabrod** Kokshetau, N Kazakhstan
152 H7 **Takhtakūpir** *Rus.* Takhtakupyr. Qoraqalpoghiston Respublikasi, NW Uzbekistan
Takhtakupyr *see* Takhtakūpir
148 M8 **Takht-e Shāh, Kūh-e** ▲ C Iran
79 V12 **Takiéta** Zinder, S Niger
15 I5 **Takijuq Lake** ◎ Northwest Territories, NW Canada
172 P4 **Takikawa** Hokkaidō, NE Japan
172 Pp4 **Takinoue** Hokkaidō, NE Japan
Takistan *see* Tākestān
193 B23 **Takitimu Mountains** ▲ South Island, NZ
Takkaze *see* Tekezē
172 N10 **Takko** Aomori, Honshū, C Japan
8 L13 **Takla Lake** ◎ British Columbia, SW Canada
Takla Makan Desert *see* Taklimakan Shamo
164 H9 **Taklimakan Shamo** *Eng.* Takla Makan Desert. *desert* NW China
178 Jj12 **Takôk** Môndól Kiri, E Cambodia
175 P9 **Takolekaju, Pegunungan** ▲ Sulawesi, N Indonesia
41 P10 **Takotna** Alaska, USA
Takow *see* Kaohsiung
126 Kk14 **Taksimo** Respublika Buryatiya, S Russian Federation
170 Cc13 **Taku** Saga, Kyūshū, SW Japan
8 I10 **Taku** ⚡ British Columbia, W Canada
177 G15 **Takua Pa** *var.* Ban Takua Pa. Phangnga, SW Thailand
79 W16 **Takum** Taraba, E Nigeria
203 V10 **Takume** *atoll* Îles Tuamotu, C French Polynesia
202 L16 **Takutea** *island* S Cook Islands
195 U11 **Takuu Islands** *prev.* Mortlock Group. *island group* NE PNG
121 L18 **Tal'** *Rus.* Tal'. Minskaya Voblasts', S Belorussia
42 L13 **Tala** Jalisco, C Mexico
63 F19 **Tala** Canelones, S Uruguay
Talabriga *see* Aveiro, Portugal
Talabriga *see* Talavera de la Reina, Spain
121 N14 **Talachyn** *Rus.* Tolochin. Vitsyebskaya Voblasts', NE Belorussia
155 U7 **Talagang** Punjab, E Pakistan
161 J23 **Talaimannar** Northern Province, NW Sri Lanka
119 R3 **Talalayivka** Chernihivs'ka Oblast', N Ukraine
45 O15 **Talamanca, Cordillera de** ▲ S Costa Rica
58 A9 **Talara** Piura, NW Peru
106 L11 **Talarrubias** Extremadura, W Spain
153 S8 **Talas** Talasskaya Oblast', NW Kyrgyzstan
153 S8 **Talas** ⚡ NW Kyrgyzstan
195 N11 **Talasea** New Britain, E PNG
Talas Oblasty *see* Talasskaya Oblast'
153 S8 **Talasskaya Oblast'** *Kir.* Talas Oblasty. ◐ *province* NW Kyrgyzstan
153 S8 **Talasskiy Alatau, Khrebet** ▲ Kazakhstan/Kyrgyzstan
Talat *see* Maha Sarakham
79 U12 **Talata Mafara** Sokoto, N Nigeria
175 Ss4 **Talaud, Kepulauan** *island group* E Indonesia
106 M9 **Talavera de la Reina** *anc.* Caesarobriga, Talabriga. Castilla-La Mancha, C Spain
106 J11 **Talavera la Real** Extremadura, W Spain
194 L12 **Talawe, Mount** ▲ New Britain, C PNG
25 S5 **Talbotton** Georgia, SE USA
191 R7 **Talbragar River** ⚡ New South Wales, SE Australia
64 G13 **Talca** Maule, C Chile
64 F13 **Talcahuano** Bío Bío, C Chile
160 N12 **Tālcher** Orissa, E India
27 W5 **Talco** Texas, SW USA
151 V14 **Taldykorgan** *Kaz.* Taldyqorghan; *prev.* Taldy-Kurgan. Taldykorgan, SE Kazakhstan
151 U13 **Taldykorgan** *off.* Taldykorganskaya Oblast'; *prev.* Taldy-Kurganskaya Oblast'. ◐ *province* SE Kazakhstan
Taldykorganskaya Oblast'/Taldy-Kurgan/ Taldy-Kurganskaya Oblast'/Taldyqorghan *see* Taldykorgan
153 Y7 **Taldy-Suu** Issyk-Kul'skaya Oblast', E Kyrgyzstan
153 U10 **Taldy-Suu** Oshskaya Oblast', SW Kyrgyzstan
Tal-e Khosravī *see* Yāsūj
200 Ss14 **Taleki Tonga** *island* Otu Tolu Group, C Tonga
200 Ss13 **Taleki Vavu'u** *island* Otu Tolu Group, C Tonga
104 J13 **Talence** Gironde, SW France
151 U16 **Talgar** *Kaz.* Talghar. Almaty, SE Kazakhstan
xxxv J12 **Talgarth** Powys, C Wales, UK
Talghar *see* Talgar
175 Rr10 **Taliabu, Pulau** *island* Kepulauan Sula, C Indonesia
117 L22 **Taliarós, Ákra** *headland* Astypálaia, Kykládes, Greece, Aegean Sea
Ta-lien *see* Dalian
29 Q12 **Talihina** Oklahoma, C USA
Talimardzhan *see* Tollimarjon
Talin *see* T'alin
143 T12 **T'alin** *Rus.* Talin; *prev.* Verin T'alin. W Armenia
83 E15 **Tali Post** Bahr el Gabel, S Sudan
Taliq-an *see* Tāloqān
Taliş Dağları *see* Talish Mountains
148 L2 **Talish Mountains** *Az.* Taliş Dağları, *Per.* Kūhhā-ye Ṭavālesh, *Rus.* Talyshskiye Gory. ▲ Azerbaijan/Iran
125 F11 **Talitsa** Sverdlovskaya Oblast', C Russian Federation
175 O16 **Taliwang** Sumbawa, C Indonesia
121 L17 **Tal'ka** *Rus.* Tal'ka. Minskaya Voblasts', C Belorussia
Talkang *see* Dorbod
41 R11 **Talkeetna** Alaska, USA
41 R11 **Talkeetna Mountains** ▲ Alaska, USA
Talkhof *see* Puurmani
94 H2 **Tálknafjördhur** Vestfirdhir, W Iceland
145 Q3 **Tall 'Abṭah** N Iraq
144 M2 **Tall Abyaḍ** *var.* Tell Abiad. Ar Raqqah, N Syria
xlii F11 **Talladale** Highland, NW Scotland, UK
25 Q4 **Talladega** Alabama, S USA
145 Q2 **Tall 'Afar** N Iraq
xliv L9 **Tallaght** Dublin, E Ireland
25 S8 **Tallahassee** *prev.* Muskogean. *state capital* Florida, SE USA
24 L2 **Tallahatchie River** ⚡ Mississippi, S USA
Tall al Abyaḍ *see* At Tall al Abyaḍ
145 W12 **Tall al Laḥm** S Iraq
191 P11 **Tallangatta** Victoria, SE Australia
25 R4 **Tallapoosa River** ⚡ Alabama/Georgia, S USA
105 T13 **Tallard** Hautes-Alpes, SE France
145 Q3 **Tall ash Sha'īr** N Iraq
25 Q5 **Tallassee** Alabama, S USA
145 R4 **Tall 'Azbah** NW Iraq
144 I5 **Tall Bīsah** Ḥimṣ, W Syria
xxxv G12 **Talley** Carmarthenshire, S Wales, UK
145 R3 **Tall Ḥassūnah** N Iraq
145 Q2 **Tall Ḥuqnah** *var.* Tell Huqnah. N Iraq
Tallin *see* Tallinn
120 G3 **Tallinn** *Ger.* Reval, *Rus.* Tallin; *prev.* Revel. ● (Estonia) Harjumaa, NW Estonia
120 H3 **Tallinn** ✕ Harjumaa, NW Estonia

◆ Country ● Country Capital ◇ Dependent Territory ○ Dependent Territory Capital ◐ Administrative Region ✕ International Airport ▲ Mountain ▲ Mountain Range ⚠ Volcano ⚡ River ◎ Lake ⊠ Reservoir

| ♦ COUNTRY | ◊ DEPENDENT TERRITORY | ◆ ADMINISTRATIVE REGION | ▲ MOUNTAIN | ℞ VOLCANO | ◎ LAKE |
| ● COUNTRY CAPITAL | ○ DEPENDENT TERRITORY CAPITAL | ✕ INTERNATIONAL AIRPORT | ▲ MOUNTAIN RANGE | ≈ RIVER | □ RESERVOIR |

TAWANG, TELUK – TEYATEYANENG

174 L16 Tawang, Teluk bay Jawa, S Indonesia
33 R7 Tawas Bay ◎ Michigan, N USA
33 R7 Tawas City Michigan, N USA
175 Oo4 Tawau Sabah, East Malaysia
147 U10 Ṭawīl, Qalamat at well SE Saudi Arabia
179 P17 Tawitawi island Tawitawi Group, SW Philippines
179 Pp17 Tawitawi Group island group Sulu Archipelago, SW Philippines
Ṭawkar see Tokar
xliv F7 Tawnyinah Mayo, NW Ireland
Tāwūq see Dāqūq
Tawzar see Tozeur
43 O15 Taxco var. Taxco de Alarcón. Guerrero, S Mexico
Taxco de Alarcón see Taxco
164 D9 Taxkorgan var. Taxkorgan Tajik Zizhixian. Xinjiang Uygur Zizhiqu, NW China
Taxkorgan Tajik Zizhixian see Taxkorgan
xliii L17 Tay ≈ C Scotland, UK
176 V13 Tayandu, Kepulauan island group E Indonesia
149 V6 Tāybād var. Taibad, Tāyybād, Tayyebāt. Khorāsān, NE Iran
Taybert at Turkz see Ṭayyibat at Turkī
128 J3 Taybola Murmanskaya Oblast', NW Russian Federation
83 M16 Tayeeglow Bakool, C Somalia
xliii M17 Tay, Firth of inlet E Scotland, UK
126 H13 Tayga Kemerovskaya Oblast', S Russian Federation
168 G8 Taygan Govĭ-Altay, C Mongolia
127 Oo9 Taygonos, Mys headland E Russian Federation
xliii F21 Tayinloan Argyll and Bute, W Scotland, UK
xliii J17 Tay, Loch ◎ C Scotland, UK
9 N12 Taylor British Columbia, W Canada
31 O14 Taylor Nebraska, C USA
20 I13 Taylor Pennsylvania, NE USA
27 T10 Taylor Texas, SW USA
39 Q11 Taylor, Mount ▲ New Mexico, SW USA
39 R5 Taylor Park Reservoir ⊟ Colorado, C USA
39 R6 Taylor River ≈ Colorado, C USA
23 P11 Taylors South Carolina, SE USA
22 L5 Taylorsville Kentucky, S USA
23 R6 Taylorsville North Carolina, SE USA
32 L14 Taylorville Illinois, N USA
146 K5 Taymāʾ Tabūk, NW Saudi Arabia
126 J11 Taymura ≈ C Russian Federation
126 Kk6 Taymylyr Respublika Sakha (Yakutiya), NE Russian Federation
126 J5 Taymyr, Ozero ◎ N Russian Federation
126 J5 Taymyr, Poluostrov peninsula N Russian Federation
126 Ii7 Taymyrskiy (Dolgano-Nenetskiy) Avtonomnyy Okrug var. Taymyrskiy Avtonomnyy Okrug. ◐ autonomous district N Russian Federation
178 Jj13 Tây Ninh Tây Ninh, S Vietnam
xliii G17 Taynuilt Argyll and Bute, W Scotland, UK
xliii N17 Tayport Fife, E Scotland, UK
126 Ii14 Tayshet Irkutskaya Oblast', S Russian Federation
179 Oo13 Taytay Palawan, W Philippines
174 L14 Tayu prev. Tajoe. Jawa, C Indonesia
xliii F19 Tayvallich Argyll and Bute, W Scotland, UK
Ṭāyybād/Tayyebāt see Tāybād
144 L5 Ṭayyibah var. At Taybé. Ḥimṣ, C Syria
144 J4 Ṭayyibat at Turkī var. Taybert at Turkz. Ḥamāh, W Syria
126 H9 Taz ≈ N Russian Federation
76 G6 Taza NE Morocco
145 T4 Tāza Khurmātū E Iraq
171 M10 Tazawa-ko ◎ Honshū, C Japan
Taz, Bay of see Tazovskaya Guba
23 N8 Tazewell Tennessee, S USA
23 Q7 Tazewell Virginia, NE USA
Tazimi see Tajimi
77 S11 Tāzirbū SE Libya
41 S11 Tazlina Lake ◎ Alaska, USA
126 H7 Tazovskaya Guba Eng. Bay of Taz. bay N Russian Federation
126 H8 Tazovskiy Yamalo-Nenetskiy Avtonomnyy Okrug, N Russian Federation
143 U10 T'bilisi Eng. Tiflis. ● (Georgia) SE Georgia
143 T10 T'bilisi ✕ S Georgia
81 E14 Tchabal Mbabo ▲ NW Cameroon
Tchad see Chad
Tchad, Lac see Chad, Lake
79 S15 Tchaourou E Benin
81 E20 Tchibanga Nyanga, S Gabon
Tchien see Zwedru
79 Z6 Tchigaï, Plateau du ▲ NE Niger
79 V9 Tchighozérine Agadez, C Niger
79 T10 Tchin-Tabaradene Tahoua, W Niger
80 G13 Tcholliré Nord, NE Cameroon
Tchongking see Chongqing
24 K4 Tchula Mississippi, S USA
112 I7 Tczew Ger. Dirschau. Gdańsk, N Poland
118 I10 Teaca Ger. Tekendorf, Hung. Teke; prev. Ger. Teckendorf. Bistriţa-Năsăud, N Romania
42 J11 Teacapán Sinaloa, C Mexico
202 A10 Teafuafou island Funafuti Atoll, C Tuvalu
27 U8 Teague Texas, SW USA
203 R9 Teahupoo Tahiti, W French Polynesia
202 H15 Te Aiti Point headland Rarotonga, S Cook Islands
xxxix R4 Tealby Lincolnshire, E England, UK
67 D24 Teal Inlet East Falkland, Falkland Islands
193 B22 Te Anau Southland, South Island, NZ
193 B22 Te Anau, Lake ◎ South Island, NZ
xliii E14 Teangue Highland, NW Scotland, UK
43 U15 Teapa Tabasco, SE Mexico
192 Q7 Te Araroa Gisborne, North Island, NZ
192 M7 Te Aroha Waikato, North Island, NZ
Teate see Chieti
202 A9 Te Ava Fuagea channel Funafuti Atoll, SE Tuvalu
202 B8 Te Ava I Te Lape channel Funafuti Atoll, SE Tuvalu
202 B9 Te Ava Pua Pua channel Funafuti Atoll, SE Tuvalu
192 M8 Te Awamutu Waikato, North Island, NZ
176 Xx9 Teba Irian Jaya, E Indonesia
106 L15 Teba Andalucía, S Spain
xli N10 Tebay Cumbria, NW England, UK
130 M15 Teberda Karachayevo-Cherkesskaya Respublika, SW Russian Federation
76 M6 Tébessa NE Algeria
64 O7 Tebicuary, Río ≈ S Paraguay
174 Hh11 Tebingtinggi Sumatera, W Indonesia
173 Ff5 Tebingtinggi Sumatera, N Indonesia
Tebingtinggi, Pulau see Rantau, Pulau
Tebriz see Tabrīz
143 U9 Tebulos Mt'a Rus. Gora Tebulosmta. ▲ Georgia/Russian Federation
Tebulosmta, Gora see Tebulos Mt'a
43 Q14 Tecamachalco Puebla, S Mexico
42 B1 Tecate Baja California, NW Mexico
142 M13 Tecer Dağları ▲ C Turkey
105 O17 Tech ≈ S France
79 P16 Techiman W Ghana
119 N15 Techirghiol Constanţa, SE Romania
76 A12 Techla var. Techlé. SW Western Sahara
Techlé see Techla
65 H18 Tecka, Sierra de ▲ SW Argentina
Teckendorf see Teaca
42 K13 Tecolotlán Jalisco, SW Mexico
42 K14 Tecomán Colima, SW Mexico
37 V12 Tecopa California, W USA
42 G5 Tecoripa Sonora, NW Mexico
43 N16 Tecpan var. Tecpan de Galeana. Guerrero, S Mexico
Tecpan de Galeana see Tecpan
42 J11 Tecuala Nayarit, C Mexico
118 L12 Tecuci Galaţi, E Romania
33 R10 Tecumseh Michigan, N USA
31 S16 Tecumseh Nebraska, C USA
29 O11 Tecumseh Oklahoma, C USA
xxxvi G14 Tedburn St Mary Devon, SW England, UK
194 E12 Tedi ≈ W PNG
152 H14 Tedzhen Turkm. Tejen. Akhalskiy Velayat, S Turkmenistan
152 I15 Tedzhen Per. Harīrūd, Turkm. Tejen. ≈ Afghanistan/Iran see also Harīrūd
152 H15 Tedzhenstroy Turkm. Tejenstroy. Akhalskiy Velayat, S Turkmenistan
168 I7 Teel Arhangay, C Mongolia
xli R9 Tees ≈ N England, UK
xli T8 Tees Bay bay N England, UK
12 E15 Teeswater Ontario, S Canada
202 A10 Tefala island Funafuti Atoll, C Tuvalu
60 D13 Tefé Amazonas, N Brazil
76 K11 Tefedest ▲ S Algeria
142 E16 Tefenni Burdur, SW Turkey
60 D13 Tefé, Rio ≈ NW Brazil
174 Kk14 Tegal Jawa, C Indonesia
102 O12 Tegel ✕ (Berlin) Berlin, NE Germany
101 M15 Tegelen Limburg, SE Netherlands
103 L24 Tegernsee ◎ SE Germany
109 M18 Teggiano Campania, S Italy
79 U14 Tegina Niger, C Nigeria
197 B10 Tegua island Torres Islands, N Vanuatu
44 I7 Tegucigalpa ● (Honduras) Francisco Morazán, SW Honduras
44 H7 Tegucigalpa ✕ Central District, C Honduras
Tegucigalpa see Central District, Honduras
Tegucigalpa see Francisco Morazán, Honduras
79 U9 Teguidda-n-Tessoumt Agadez, C Niger
66 Q11 Teguise Lanzarote, Islas Canarias, Spain, NE Atlantic Ocean
126 Hh13 Tegul'det Tomskaya Oblast', C Russian Federation
37 S13 Tehachapi California, W USA
37 S13 Tehachapi Mountains ▲ California, W USA
Tehama see Tihāmah
Teheran see Tehrān
79 O14 Téhini NE Ivory Coast
149 N5 Tehrān var. Teheran. ● (Iran) Tehrān, N Iran
149 N6 Tehrān off. Ostān-e Tehrān, var. Tehran. ◐ province N Iran
158 K9 Tehri Uttar Pradesh, N India
Tehri see Tikamgarh
43 Q15 Tehuacán Puebla, S Mexico
43 S17 Tehuantepec var. Santo Domingo Tehuantepec. Oaxaca, SE Mexico
43 S17 Tehuantepec, Golfo de var. Gulf of Tehuantepec. gulf S Mexico
Tehuantepec, Gulf of see Tehuantepec, Golfo de
Tehuantepec, Isthmus of see Tehuantepec, Istmo de
43 T16 Tehuantepec, Istmo de var. Isthmus of Tehuantepec. isthmus SE Mexico
1 I16 Tehuantepec Ridge undersea feature E Pacific Ocean
43 S16 Tehuantepec, Río ≈ SE Mexico
203 W10 Tehuata atoll Îles Tuamotu, C French Polynesia
66 O11 Teide, Pico de ▲ Gran Canaria, Islas Canarias, Spain, NE Atlantic Ocean
xxxv E12 Teifi var. River Teif. ≈ SW Wales, UK
Teif, River see Teifi, Afon
82 B9 Teiga Plateau plateau W Sudan
xxxvi H14 Teign ≈ SW England, UK
xxxvi H15 Teignmouth Devon, SW England, UK
Teisen see Chech'ŏn
118 H11 Teiuş Ger. Dreikirchen, Hung. Tövis. Alba, C Romania
175 N16 Tejakula Bali, C Indonesia
Tejen see Harīrūd/Tedzhen
Tejenstroy see Tedzhenstroy
37 S14 Tejon Pass pass California, W USA
Tejo, Rio see Tagus
43 O14 Tejupilco var. Tejupilco de Hidalgo. México, S Mexico
Tejupilco de Hidalgo see Tejupilco
192 P7 Te Kaha Bay of Plenty, North Island, NZ
31 S14 Tekamah Nebraska, C USA
192 I1 Te Kao Northland, North Island, NZ
193 F20 Tekapo ≈ South Island, NZ
193 F19 Tekapo, Lake ◎ South Island, NZ
192 P9 Te Karaka Gisborne, North Island, NZ
192 L7 Te Kauwhata Waikato, North Island, NZ
43 X12 Tekax var. Tekax de Álvaro Obregón. Yucatán, SE Mexico
Tekax de Álvaro Obregón see Tekax
Teke/Tekendorf see Teaca
142 A14 Teke Burnu headland W Turkey
116 M12 Teke Deresi ≈ NW Turkey
152 D10 Tekedzhik, Gory hill range NW Turkmenistan
151 V14 Tekeli Taldykorgan, SE Kazakhstan
151 R7 Teke, Ozero ◎ N Kazakhstan
164 I5 Tekes Xinjiang Uygur Zizhiqu, NW China
151 W16 Tekes Almaty, SE Kazakhstan
Tekes see Tekes He
164 H5 Tekes He Rus. Tekes. ≈ China/Kazakhstan
82 I10 Tekezē var. Takkaze. ≈ Eritrea/Ethiopia
Tekhtin see Tsyakhtsin
142 C10 Tekirdağ It. Rodosto; anc. Bisanthe, Raidestos, Rhaedestus. Tekirdağ, NW Turkey
142 C10 Tekirdağ ◐ province NW Turkey
161 N14 Tekkali Andhra Pradesh, E India
117 K15 Tekke Burnu Turk. İlyasbaba Burnu. headland NW Turkey
143 Q13 Tekman Erzurum, NE Turkey
34 M9 Tekoa Washington, NW USA
202 H16 Te Kou ▲ Rarotonga, S Cook Islands
Tekrit see Tikrīt
175 R9 Teku Sulawesi, N Indonesia
192 L9 Te Kuiti Waikato, North Island, NZ
44 H4 Tela Atlántida, NW Honduras
144 F12 Telalim Southern, S Israel
Telanaipura see Jambi
143 U10 T'elavi E Georgia
144 F10 Tel Aviv ◐ district W Israel
Tel Aviv-Jaffa see Tel Aviv-Yafo
144 F10 Tel Aviv-Yafo var. Tel Aviv-Jaffa. Tel Aviv, C Israel
144 F10 Tel Aviv-Yafo ✕ Tel Aviv, C Israel
113 E18 Telč Ger. Teltsch. Jižní Morava, S Czech Republic
194 E11 Telefomin Sandaun, NW PNG
8 J10 Telegraph Creek British Columbia, W Canada
202 B10 Telele island Funafuti Atoll, C Tuvalu
62 J11 Telêmaco Borba Paraná, S Brazil
97 E15 Telemark ◐ county S Norway
64 J13 Telén La Pampa, C Argentina
Teleneshty see Teleneşti
118 M9 Teleneşti Rus. Teleneshty. C Moldavia
106 J4 Teleno, El ▲ NW Spain
175 O8 Telen, Sungai ≈ Borneo, C Indonesia
118 I15 Teleorman ◐ county S Romania
118 I14 Teleorman ≈ S Romania
27 V5 Telephone Texas, SW USA
37 U11 Telescope Peak ▲ California, W USA
Teles Pirés see São Manuel, Rio
xxxviii I9 Telford Shropshire, W England, UK
110 L7 Telfs Tirol, W Austria
44 I9 Telica León, NW Nicaragua
44 J6 Telica, Río ≈ C Honduras
78 I13 Télimélé Guinée-Maritime, W Guinea
45 O14 Telire, Río ≈ Costa Rica/Panama
116 I8 Telish prev. Azizie. Loveshka Oblast, NW Bulgaria
43 R16 Telixtlahuaca var. San Francisco Telixtlahuaca. Oaxaca, SE Mexico
8 K13 Telkwa British Columbia, SW Canada
27 P4 Tell Texas, SW USA
Tell Abiad see Tall Abyaḍ
Tell Abiad/Tell Abyad see At Tall al Abyaḍ
Tell 'Annz see Al 'Anz
Tell Bâz see Tall Bāz
Tell Brâk see Tall Birāk
33 O16 Tell City Indiana, N USA
40 M9 Teller Alaska, USA
Tell Huqnah see Tall Ḥuqnah
161 F20 Tellicherry var. Thalassery. Kerala, SW India
22 M10 Tellico Plains Tennessee, S USA
Tell Kalakh see Tall Kalakh
Tell Mardikh see Ebla
56 E11 Tello Huila, C Colombia
Tell Shaghir Bazar see Jāghir Bāzār
Tell Shedadi see Ash Shadādah
Tell Tamr see Tall Tamir
39 Q7 Telluride Colorado, C USA
Tel'man/Tel'mansk see Gubadag
119 X9 Tel'manove Donets'ka Oblast', E Ukraine
168 H6 Telmen Nuur ◎ NW Mongolia
Teloekbetoeng see Bandarlampung
43 O15 Teloloapán Guerrero, S Mexico
Telo Martius see Toulon
129 V8 Telposiz, Gora ▲ NW Russian Federation
Telschen see Telšiai
65 J17 Telsen Chubut, S Argentina
120 D11 Telšiai Ger. Telschen. Telšiai, NW Lithuania
Teltsch see Telč
Telukbetung see Bandarlampung
173 F7 Telukdalam Pulau Nias, W Indonesia
12 H9 Temagami Ontario, S Canada
12 G9 Temagami, Lake ◎ Ontario, S Canada
202 H16 Te Manga ▲ Rarotonga, S Cook Islands
Temanggoeng see Temanggung
174 Kk15 Temanggung prev. Temanggoeng. Jawa, S Indonesia
203 W12 Tematangi atoll Îles Tuamotu, S French Polynesia
43 X11 Temax Yucatán, SE Mexico
176 X12 Tembagapura Irian Jaya, E Indonesia
133 U5 Tembenchi ≈ N Russian Federation
174 Hh10 Tembesi, Sungai ≈ Sumatera, W Indonesia
57 P6 Temblador Monagas, NE Venezuela
107 N9 Tembleque Castilla-La Mancha, C Spain
Temboni see Mitemele, Río
xxxviii J13 Teme ≈ England/Wales, UK
37 U16 Temecula California, W USA
174 Gg3 Temengor, Tasik ◎ Peninsular Malaysia
114 L9 Temerin Serbia, N Yugoslavia
Temes/Temesch see Tamiš
Temeschburg/Temeschwar see Timişoara
Temes-Kubin see Kovin
Temesmóra see Moraviţa
Temesvár/Temeswar see Timişoara
Teminaboean see Teminabuan
176 V9 Teminabuan prev. Teminaboean. Irian Jaya, E Indonesia
151 P17 Temirlanovka Yuzhnyy Kazakhstan, S Kazakhstan
151 R10 Temirtau prev. Samarkandski, Samarkandskoye. Karaganda, C Kazakhstan
12 H10 Témiscaming Québec, SE Canada
Témiscamingue, Lac see Timiskaming, Lake
13 T8 Témiscouata, Lac ◎ Québec, SE Canada
131 N5 Temnikov Respublika Mordoviya, W Russian Federation
203 Y13 Temoe island Îles Gambier, E French Polynesia
191 Q9 Temora New South Wales, SE Australia
42 H7 Témoris Chihuahua, W Mexico
42 I5 Temósachic Chihuahua, N Mexico
195 W8 Temotu off. Temotu Province. ◐ province E Solomon Islands
38 L14 Tempe Arizona, SW USA
175 P12 Tempe, Danau ◎ Sulawesi, C Indonesia
Tempelburg see Czaplinek
xliv H11 Templemore Tipperary, S Ireland
109 C17 Tempio Pausania Sardegna, Italy, C Mediterranean Sea
44 K12 Tempisque, Río ≈ NW Costa Rica
xliii L24 Templand Dumfries and Galloway, SW Scotland, UK
xxxvi D15 Temple Cornwall, SW England, UK
xliii M20 Temple Midlothian, SE Scotland, UK
27 T9 Temple Texas, SW USA
xxxvi L12 Templecombe Somerset, SW England, UK
xli T14 Temple Hirst North Yorkshire, N England, UK
102 O12 Tempelhof ✕ (Berlin) Berlin, NE Germany
xliv L4 Templepatrick Antrim, NE Northern Ireland, UK
xli N8 Temple Sowerby Cumbria, NW England, UK
xxxv D13 Templeton Pembrokeshire, SW Wales, UK
102 O11 Templin Brandenburg, NE Germany
43 P12 Tempoal var. Tempoal de Sánchez. Veracruz-Llave, E Mexico
Tempoal de Sánchez see Tempoal
43 P13 Tempoal, Río ≈ C Mexico
85 E14 Tempué Moxico, C Angola
130 J14 Temryuk Krasnodarskiy Kray, SW Russian Federation
101 G17 Temse Oost-Vlaanderen, N Belgium
65 F15 Temuco Araucanía, C Chile
193 G20 Temuka Canterbury, South Island, NZ
201 P13 Temwen Island island E Micronesia
58 C6 Tena Napo, C Ecuador
43 W13 Tenabo Campeche, E Mexico
Tenaghau see Aola
27 X7 Tenaha Texas, SW USA
41 X13 Tenake Chichagof Island, Alaska, USA
161 K16 Tenāli Andhra Pradesh, E India
Tenan see Ch'ŏnan
43 O14 Tenancingo var. Tenencingo de Degollado. México, S Mexico
203 X12 Tenararo island Groupe Actéon, SE French Polynesia
178 Gg12 Tenasserim Tenasserim, S Burma
178 H11 Tenasserim var. Taninthayi. ◐ division S Burma
100 O5 Ten Boer Groningen, NE Netherlands
xxxviii I12 Tenbury Wells Worcestershire, W England, UK
xxxv E14 Tenby Pembrokeshire, SW Wales, UK
82 K11 Tendaho NE Ethiopia
105 V14 Tende Alpes Maritimes, SE France
157 Q20 Ten Degree Channel strait Andaman and Nicobar Islands, India, E Indian Ocean
82 F11 Tendelti White Nile, E Sudan
78 G8 Te-n-Dghâmcha, Sebkhet var. Sebkha de Ndrhamcha, Sebkra de Ndaghamcha. salt lake W Mauritania
171 Ll12 Tendō Yamagata, Honshū, C Japan
76 H7 Tendrara NE Morocco
119 Q11 Tendrivs'ka Kosa spit S Ukraine
119 Q11 Tendrivs'ka Zatoka gulf S Ukraine
Tenencingo de Degollado see Tenancingo
79 N11 Ténenkou Mopti, C Mali
79 W9 Ténéré physical region C Niger
79 W9 Ténére, Erg du desert C Niger
66 O11 Tenerife island Islas Canarias, Spain, NE Atlantic Ocean
76 J5 Ténès NW Algeria
175 Oo15 Tengah, Kepulauan island group C Indonesia
175 O8 Tenggarong Borneo, C Indonesia
168 J15 Tengger Shamo desert N China
174 I4 Tenggul, Pulau island Peninsular Malaysia
Tengiz Köl see Tengiz, Ozero
151 P9 Tengiz, Ozero Kaz. Tengiz Köl. salt lake C Kazakhstan
78 M14 Tengréla var. Tingréla. N Ivory Coast
166 M14 Tengxian var. Teng Xian. Guangxi Zhuangzu Zizhiqu, S China
204 H2 Teniente Rodolfo Marsh Chilean research station South Shetland Islands, Antarctica
34 G9 Tenino Washington, NW USA
114 I9 Tenja Osijek-Baranja, E Croatia
196 B16 Tenjo, Mount ▲ W Guam
161 H23 Tenkāsi Tamil Nādu, SE India
81 N24 Tenke Shaba, SE Zaire
Tenke see Tinca
126 M7 Tenkeli Respublika Sakha (Yakutiya), NE Russian Federation
29 R10 Tenkiller Ferry Lake ⊟ Oklahoma, C USA
79 Q13 Tenkodogo S Burkina
189 Q5 Tennant Creek Northern Territory, C Australia
22 G9 Tennessee off. State of Tennessee; also known as The Volunteer State. ◐ state SE USA
39 R5 Tennessee Pass pass Colorado, C USA
22 H10 Tennessee River ≈ S USA
25 N2 Tennessee Tombigbee Waterway canal Alabama/Mississippi, S USA
101 K22 Tenneville Luxembourg, SE Belgium
94 M11 Tenniöjoki ≈ NE Finland
94 L9 Teno var. Tenojoki, Lapp. Deatnu, Nor. Tana. ≈ Finland/Norway see also Tana
Tenojoki see Tana/Teno
175 Nn3 Tenom Sabah, East Malaysia
Tenos see Tínos
43 V15 Tenosique var. Tenosique de Pino Suárez. Tabasco, SE Mexico
Tenosique de Pino Suárez see Tenosique
171 H15 Tenri Nara, Honshū, SW Japan
171 I16 Tenryū Shizuoka, Honshū, SW Japan
172 Ii15 Tenryū-gawa ≈ Honshū, C Japan
24 I6 Tensas River ≈ Louisiana, S USA
25 O8 Tensaw River ≈ Alabama, S USA
76 E7 Tensift seasonal river W Morocco
175 Pp10 Tentena var. Tenteno. Sulawesi, C Indonesia
Tenteno see Tentena
xxxvii X11 Tenterden Kent, SE England, UK
191 U4 Tenterfield New South Wales, SE Australia
25 X16 Ten Thousand Islands island group Florida, SE USA
62 H9 Teodoro Sampaio São Paulo, S Brazil
61 N19 Teófilo Otoni var. Theophilo Ottoni. Minas Gerais, NE Brazil
118 K5 Teofipol' Khmel'nyts'ka Oblast', W Ukraine
203 Q8 Teohatu Tahiti, W French Polynesia
43 P14 Teotihuacán ruins México, S Mexico
Teotilán see Teotitlán del Camino
43 Q15 Teotitlán del Camino var. Teotilán. Oaxaca, S Mexico
202 G12 Tepa Île Uvea, E Wallis and Futuna
203 P8 Tepaee, Récif reef Tahiti, W French Polynesia
42 L14 Tepalcatepec Michoacán de Ocampo, SW Mexico
202 A16 Tepa Point headland SW Niue
42 L13 Tepatitlán var. Tepatitlán de Morelos. Jalisco, SW Mexico
Tepatitlán de Morelos see Tepatitlán
42 J9 Tepehuanes var. Santa Catarina de Tepehuanes. Durango, C Mexico
Tepelena see Tepelenë
115 L22 Tepelenë var. Tepelena, It. Tepeleni. Gjirokastër, S Albania
Tepeleni see Tepelenë
42 K12 Tepic Nayarit, C Mexico
113 C15 Teplice Ger. Teplitz; prev. Teplice-Šanov, Teplitz-Schönau. Severní Čechy, NW Czech Republic
Teplice-Šanov/Teplitz/Teplitz-Schönau see Teplice
119 O7 Teplyk Vinnyts'ka Oblast', C Ukraine
126 Mm10 Teplyy Klyuch Respublika Sakha (Yakutiya), NE Russian Federation
42 E5 Tepoca, Cabo headland NW Mexico
203 W9 Tepoto island Îles du Désappointement, C French Polynesia
94 L11 Tepsa Lappi, N Finland
202 B8 Tepuka atoll Funafuti Atoll, C Tuvalu
192 N7 Te Puke Bay of Plenty, North Island, NZ
42 L13 Tequila Jalisco, SW Mexico
43 O13 Tequisquiapan Querétaro de Arteaga, C Mexico
106 J5 Tera ≈ NW Spain
79 Q12 Téra Tillabéri, W Niger
203 V1 Teraina prev. Washington Island. atoll Line Islands, E Kiribati
83 F15 Terakeka Bahr el Gabel, S Sudan
109 J14 Teramo anc. Interamna. Abruzzi, C Italy
100 P7 Ter Apel Groningen, NE Netherlands
106 H11 Tera, Ribeira de ≈ S Portugal
193 K14 Terawhiti, Cape headland North Island, NZ
100 N12 Terborg Gelderland, E Netherlands
143 P13 Tercan Erzincan, NE Turkey
66 O2 Terceira ✕ Terceira, Azores, Portugal, NE Atlantic Ocean
66 O2 Terceira var. Ilha Terceira. island Azores, Portugal, NE Atlantic Ocean
Terceira, Ilha see Terceira
118 K6 Terebovlya Ternopil's'ka Oblast', W Ukraine
131 O15 Terek ≈ SW Russian Federation
Terekhovka see Tsyerakhowka
153 R9 Terek-Say Dzhalal-Abadskaya Oblast', W Kyrgyzstan
174 Hh3 Terengganu var. Trengganu. ◐ state Peninsular Malaysia
131 X7 Terensay Orenburgskaya Oblast', W Russian Federation
60 N13 Teresina var. Therezina. state capital Piauí, NE Brazil
62 P9 Teresópolis Rio de Janeiro, SE Brazil
112 P12 Terespol Biała Podlaska, E Poland
203 V16 Terevaka, Maunga ⛰ Easter Island, Chile, E Pacific Ocean
105 P3 Tergnier Aisne, N France
45 O14 Teribe, Río ≈ NW Panama
128 K3 Teriberka Murmanskaya Oblast', NW Russian Federation
Terijoki see Zelenogorsk
Terinkot see Tarīn Kowt
Terisaqqan see Tersakkan
xxxvii W7 Terling Essex, SE England, UK
26 K12 Terlingua Texas, SW USA
26 K11 Terlingua Creek ≈ Texas, SW USA
64 K7 Termas de Río Hondo Santiago del Estero, N Argentina
142 M11 Terme Samsun, N Turkey
Termez see Termiz
Termia see Kýthnos
109 J23 Termini Imerese anc. Thermae Himerenses. Sicilia, Italy, C Mediterranean Sea
43 V14 Términos, Laguna de lagoon SE Mexico
79 X10 Termit-Kaoboul Zinder, C Niger
153 O14 Termiz Rus. Termez. Surkhondaryo Wiloyati, S Uzbekistan
109 L15 Termoli Molise, C Italy
xliv F7 Termon Donegal, N Ireland
Termonde see Dendermonde
100 P5 Termunten Groningen, NE Netherlands
175 T7 Ternate Pulau Ternate, E Indonesia
175 Ss7 Ternate, Pulau island E Indonesia
111 T5 Ternberg Oberösterreich, N Austria
101 E15 Terneuzen var. Neuzen. Zeeland, SW Netherlands
127 O17 Terney Primorskiy Kray, SE Russian Federation
109 I14 Terni anc. Interamna Nahars. Umbria, C Italy
111 X6 Ternitz Niederösterreich, E Austria
119 V7 Ternivka Dnipropetrovs'ka Oblast', E Ukraine
118 K6 Ternopil' Pol. Tarnopol, Rus. Ternopol'. Ternopil's'ka Oblast', W Ukraine
Ternopil' see Ternopil's'ka Oblast'
118 I6 Ternopil's'ka Oblast' var. Ternopil', Rus. Ternopol'skaya Oblast'. ◐ province NW Ukraine
Ternopol' see Ternopil'
Ternopol'skaya Oblast' see Ternopil's'ka Oblast'
127 Oo15 Terpeniya, Mys headland Ostrov Sakhalin, SE Russian Federation
127 Oo15 Terpeniya, Zaliv inlet Ostrov Sakhalin, SE Russian Federation
Térraba, Río see Grande de Térraba, Río
8 J13 Terrace British Columbia, W Canada
10 D12 Terrace Bay Ontario, S Canada
109 I16 Terracina Lazio, C Italy
95 F14 Terråk Troms, N Norway
28 M13 Terral Oklahoma, C USA
109 B19 Terralba Sardegna, Italy, C Mediterranean Sea
Terranova di Sicilia see Gela
Terranova Pausania see Olbia
107 W5 Terrassa Cast. Tarrasa. Cataluña, E Spain
13 O12 Terrebonne Québec, SE Canada
24 J11 Terrebonne Bay bay Louisiana, SE USA
33 N14 Terre Haute Indiana, N USA
27 U6 Terrell Texas, SW USA
Terre-Neuve see Newfoundland
Terre Neuve see Newfoundland and Labrador
35 Q14 Terreton Idaho, NW USA
xxxix T8 Terrington St Clement Norfolk, E England, UK
105 T7 Territoire-de-Belfort ◐ department E France
35 X9 Terry Montana, NW USA
30 I9 Terry Peak ▲ South Dakota, N USA
142 H14 Tersakan Gölü ◎ C Turkey
151 O10 Tersakkan Kaz. Terisaqqan. ≈ C Kazakhstan
100 J4 Terschelling Fris. Skylge. island Waddeneilanden, N Netherlands
80 H10 Tersef Chari-Baguirmi, C Chad
153 X8 Terskey Ala-Too, Khrebet ▲ Kazakhstan/Kyrgyzstan
Terter see Tärtär
107 R8 Teruel anc. Turba. Aragón, E Spain
107 R7 Teruel ◐ province Aragón, E Spain
116 M7 Tervel prev. Kurtbunar, Rom. Curtbunar. Varnenska Oblast, NE Bulgaria
95 M16 Tervo Kuopio, C Finland
94 L13 Tervola Lappi, NW Finland
Tervueren see Tervuren
101 H18 Tervuren var. Tervueren. Vlaams Brabant, C Belgium
114 H11 Tešanj N Bosnia and Herzegovina
Teschen see Cieszyn
85 M19 Tesenane Inhambane, S Mozambique
82 I9 Teseney var. Tessenei. W Eritrea
41 P5 Teshekpuk Lake ◎ Alaska, USA
168 K6 Teshig Bulgan, N Mongolia
172 Q6 Teshikaga Hokkaidō, NE Japan
172 P2 Teshio Hokkaidō, NE Japan
172 P2 Teshio-gawa var. Tesio Gawa. ≈ Hokkaidō, NE Japan
172 P3 Teshio-sanchi ▲ Hokkaidō, NE Japan
Těšín see Cieszyn
Tesio Gawa see Teshio-gawa
168 F5 Tesiyn Gol var. Tes-Khem. ≈ Mongolia/Russian Federation see also Tes-Khem
133 T7 Tes-Khem var. Tesiyn Gol. ≈ Mongolia/Russian Federation see also Tesiyn Gol
114 H11 Teslić N Bosnia and Herzegovina
8 I9 Teslin Yukon Territory, W Canada
8 I8 Teslin ≈ British Columbia/Yukon Territory, W Canada
79 Q8 Tessalit Kidal, NE Mali
79 V12 Tessaoua Maradi, S Niger
101 J17 Tessenderlo Limburg, NE Belgium
Tessenei see Teseney
12 L7 Tessier, Lac ◎ Québec, SE Canada
Tessin see Ticino
xxxvi P11 Test ≈ S England, UK
Testama see Tõstamaa
57 P4 Testigos, Islas los island group N Venezuela
39 S10 Tesuque New Mexico, SW USA
105 O17 Têt var. Tet. ≈ S France
56 G5 Tetas, Cerro de las ▲ NW Venezuela
xxxvi M8 Tetbury Gloucestershire, C England, UK
85 M15 Tete Tete, NW Mozambique
85 M15 Tete off. Província de Tete. ◐ province NW Mozambique
9 N15 Tête Jaune Cache British Columbia, SW Canada
192 O8 Te Teko Bay of Plenty, North Island, NZ
195 U15 Tetepare island New Georgia Islands, NW Solomon Islands
Teterev see Teteriv
118 M5 Teteriv Rus. Teterev. ≈ N Ukraine
102 M9 Teterow Mecklenburg-Vorpommern, NE Germany
116 I9 Teteven Loveshka Oblast, W Bulgaria
203 T10 Tetiaroa atoll Îles du Vent, W French Polynesia
107 P14 Tetica de Bacares ▲ S Spain
Tetiyev see Tetiyiv
119 O6 Tetiyiv Rus. Tetiyev. Kyyivs'ka Oblast', N Ukraine
41 T10 Tetlin Alaska, USA
xxxix S4 Tetney Lincolnshire, E England, UK
35 R8 Teton River ≈ Montana, NW USA
76 G5 Tétouan var. Tetouan, Tetuán. N Morocco
Tetova/Tetovë see Tetovo
116 L7 Tetovo Razgradska Oblast, NE Bulgaria
115 N18 Tetovo Alb. Tetova, Tetovë, Turk. Kalkandelen. NW FYR Macedonia
117 E20 Tetrázio ▲ S Greece
Tetschen see Děčín
xxxvii Q8 Tetsworth Oxfordshire, C England, UK
xxxviii A14 Tettenhall Wolverhampton, C England, UK
Tetuán see Tétouan
203 Q8 Tetufera, Mont ▲ Tahiti, W French Polynesia
131 R4 Tetyushi Respublika Tatarstan, W Russian Federation
110 I7 Teufen Sankt Gallen, NE Switzerland
42 L12 Teul var. Teul de Gonzáles Ortega. Zacatecas, C Mexico
109 B21 Teulada Sardegna, Italy, C Mediterranean Sea
Teul de Gonzáles Ortega see Teul
9 X16 Teulon Manitoba, S Canada
44 I7 Teupasenti El Paraíso, S Honduras
172 Oo3 Teuri-tō island NE Japan
102 G13 Teutoburger Wald Eng. Teutoburg Forest. hill range NW Germany
Teutoburg Forest see Teutoburger Wald
95 K17 Teuva Swe. Östermark. Vaasa, W Finland
109 H15 Tevere Eng. Tiber. ≈ C Italy
144 G9 Teverya var. Tiberias. Northern, N Israel
xliii M23 Teviot ≈ SE Scotland, UK
xliii N23 Teviothead The Borders, S Scotland, UK
Tevli see Tewli
125 Ff12 Tevriz Omskaya Oblast', C Russian Federation
193 B24 Te Waewae Bay bay South Island, NZ
xxxvi M6 Tewkesbury Gloucestershire, C England, UK
121 F19 Tewli Rus. Tevli. Brestskaya Voblasts', SW Belorussia
165 U12 Têwo var. Dêngkagoin. Gansu, C China
27 U12 Texana, Lake ◎ Texas, SW USA
29 S14 Texarkana Arkansas, C USA
27 X5 Texarkana Texas, SW USA
27 N9 Texas off. State of Texas; also known as The Lone Star State. ◐ state S USA
27 W12 Texas City Texas, SW USA
43 P14 Texcoco México, C Mexico
100 I6 Texel island Waddeneilanden, NW Netherlands
28 H8 Texhoma Oklahoma, C USA
27 N1 Texhoma Texas, SW USA
39 W12 Texico New Mexico, SW USA
26 L1 Texline Texas, SW USA
43 P14 Texmelucan var. San Martín Texmelucan. Puebla, S Mexico
29 O13 Texoma, Lake ⊟ Oklahoma/Texas, C USA
27 N9 Texon Texas, SW USA
126 I12 Teya Krasnoyarskiy Kray, C Russian Federation
85 J23 Teyateyaneng NW Lesotho

◆ Country ● Country Capital ◇ Dependent Territory ○ Dependent Territory Capital ◐ Administrative Region ✕ International Airport ▲ Mountain ▲▲ Mountain Range ⛰ Volcano ≈ River ◎ Lake ⊟ Reservoir

TEYKOVO – TÎRGU

128 M16 **Teykovo** Ivanovskaya Oblast', W Russian Federation
128 M16 **Teza** ~ W Russian Federation
43 Q13 **Teziutlán** Puebla, S Mexico
159 W12 **Tezpur** Assam, NE India
15 L8 **Tha-Anne** ~ Northwest Territories, NE Canada
85 K23 **Thabana Ntlenyana** *var.* Thabantshonyana, Mount Ntlenyana. ▲ E Lesotho
Thabantshonyana *see* Thabana Ntlenyana
85 J23 **Thaba Putsoa** ▲ C Lesotho
178 I8 **Tha Bo** Nong Khai, E Thailand
105 T12 **Thabor, Pic du** ▲ E France
Tha Chin *see* Samut Sakhon
177 G7 **Thagaya** Pegu, C Burma
Thai, Ao *see* Thailand, Gulf of
178 Jj6 **Thai Binh** Thai Binh, N Vietnam
178 Jj7 **Thai Hoa** Nghê An, N Vietnam
178 Hh10 **Thailand** *off.* Kingdom of Thailand, *Th.* Prathet Thai; *prev.* Siam. ◆ *monarchy* SE Asia
178 Hh13 **Thailand, Gulf of** *var.* Gulf of Siam, *Th.* Ao Thai, *Vtn.* Vinh Thai Lan. *gulf* SE Asia
Thai Lan, Vinh *see* Thailand, Gulf of
178 Jj6 **Thai Nguyên** Bac Thai, N Vietnam
178 J9 **Thakhèk** *prev.* Muang Khammouan. Khammouan, C Laos
159 S13 **Thakurgaon** Rajshahi, NW Bangladesh
155 S6 **Thal** North-West Frontier Province, NW Pakistan
177 G16 **Thalang** Phuket, SW Thailand
Thalassery *see* Tellicherry
178 I10 **Thalat Khae** Nakhon Ratchasima, C Thailand
111 Q5 **Thalgau** Salzburg, NW Austria
110 G7 **Thalwil** Zürich, NW Switzerland
85 I20 **Thamaga** Kweneng, SE Botswana
Thamarid *see* Thamarit
147 V13 **Thamarit** *var.* Thamarid, Thumrayt. SW Oman
147 P16 **Thamar, Jabal** ▲ SW Yemen
xxxvii Q8 **Thame** Oxfordshire, C England, UK
xxxvii T9 **Thames** ~ S England, UK
192 M6 **Thames** Waikato, North Island, NZ
12 D17 **Thames** ~ Ontario, S Canada
192 M6 **Thames, Firth of** *gulf* North Island, NZ
12 D17 **Thamesville** Ontario, S Canada
147 S13 **Thamūd** N Yemen
178 Gg9 **Thanbyuzayat** Mon State, S Burma
158 I9 **Thānesar** Haryāna, NW India
178 Jj7 **Thanh Hoa** Thanh Hoa, N Vietnam
Thanintari Taungdan *see* Bilauktaung Range
161 I21 **Thanjāvūr** *prev.* Tanjore. Tamil Nādu, SE India
Thanlwin *see* Salween
105 U7 **Thann** Haut-Rhin, NE France
178 H16 **Tha Nong Phrom** Phatthalung, SW Thailand
178 H13 **Thap Sakae** *var.* Thap Sakau. Prachuap Khiri Khan, SW Thailand
Thap Sakau *see* Thap Sakae
100 L10 **'t Harde** Gelderland, E Netherlands
158 D11 **Thar Desert** *var.* Great Indian Desert, Indian Desert. *desert* India/Pakistan
189 V10 **Thargomindah** Queensland, C Australia
156 D11 **Thar Pārkar** *desert* SE Pakistan
145 S7 **Tharthār al Furāt, Qanāt ath** *canal* C Iraq
145 R7 **Tharthār, Buḥayrat ath** ◎ C Iraq
145 R5 **Tharthār, Wādī ath** *dry watercourse* N Iraq
178 Gg14 **Tha Sae** Chumphon, SW Thailand
178 H15 **Tha Sala** Nakhon Si Thammarat, SW Thailand
116 I13 **Thásos** Thásos, E Greece
117 I14 **Thásos** *island* E Greece
xxxvii P10 **Thatcham** Newbury, S England, UK
39 N14 **Thatcher** Arizona, SW USA
178 Jj5 **Thât Khê** *var.* Tràng Dinh. Lang Sơn, N Vietnam
178 Gg9 **Thaton** Mon State, S Burma
178 J9 **That Phanom** Nakhon Phanom, E Thailand
178 I10 **Tha Tum** Surin, E Thailand
105 P16 **Thau, Bassin de** *var.* Étang de Thau. ◎ S France
Thau, Étang de *see* Thau, Bassin de
177 G3 **Thaungdut** Sagaing, N Burma
178 Gg8 **Thaungyin** *Th.* Mae Nam Moei. ~ Burma/Thailand
178 J9 **Tha Uthen** Nakhon Phanom, E Thailand
xxxvii V6 **Thaxted** Essex, SE England, UK
111 W2 **Thaya** *var.* Dyje. ~ Austria/Czech Republic *see also* Dyje
29 V8 **Thayer** Missouri, C USA
177 Ff7 **Thayetmyo** Magwe, C Burma
35 S15 **Thayne** Wyoming, C USA
177 G6 **Thazi** Mandalay, C Burma
xxxvii Q10 **Theale** Newbury, S England, UK
Thebes *see* Thíva
xliii M22 **The Borders** ◐ *unitary authority* S Scotland, UK
46 L5 **The Carlton** *var.* Abraham Bay. Mayaguana, SE Bahamas
47 O14 **The Crane** *var.* Crane. S Barbados
34 I11 **The Dalles** Oregon, NW USA
30 M14 **Thedford** Nebraska, C USA
The Hague *see* 's-Gravenhage
Theiss *see* Tisa/Tisza
15 Jj6 **Thelon** ~ Northwest Territories, N Canada
xxxvii V9 **The Medway Towns** ◐ *unitary authority* SE England, UK
xxxv G15 **The Mumbles** Swansea, S Wales, UK
9 V15 **Theodore** Saskatchewan, S Canada
25 N8 **Theodore** Alabama, S USA
38 L13 **Theodore Roosevelt Lake** ⊟ Arizona, SW USA
Theodosia *see* Feodosiya
Theophilo Ottoni *see* Teófilo Otoni
15 K13 **The Pas** Manitoba, C Canada
33 T14 **The Plains** Ohio, N USA
Thera *see* Thíra
180 H17 **Thérèse, Île** *island* Inner Islands, NE Seychelles
Therezina *see* Teresina
xxxvii U6 **Therfield** Hertfordshire, SE England, UK
117 L20 **Thérma** Ikaría, Dodekánisos, Greece, Aegean Sea
Thermae Himerenses *see* Termini Imerese
Thermae Pannonicae *see* Baden
Thermaic Gulf/Thermaicus Sinus *see* Thermaïkós Kólpos
123 Gg10 **Thermaïkós Kólpos** *Eng.* Thermaic Gulf; *anc.* Thermaicus Sinus. *gulf* N Greece
Thermiá *see* Kýthnos
117 L17 **Thermís** Lésvos, E Greece
117 E18 **Thérmo** Dytikí Ellás, C Greece
35 V14 **Thermopolis** Wyoming, C USA
191 P10 **The Rock** New South Wales, SE Australia
205 O5 **Theron Mountains** ▲ Antarctica
117 G18 **Thespiés** Stereá Ellás, C Greece
117 E16 **Thessalía** *Eng.* Thessaly. ◐ *region* C Greece
12 C10 **Thessalon** Ontario, S Canada
117 G14 **Thessaloníki** *Eng.* Salonica, Salonika, *SCr.* Solun, *Turk.* Selânik. Kentrikí Makedonía, N Greece
117 G14 **Thessaloníki** ✕ Kentrikí Makedonía, N Greece
Thessaly *see* Thessalía
86 B12 **Theta Gap** *undersea feature* E Atlantic Ocean
xxxix V11 **Thetford** Norfolk, E England, UK
13 R11 **Thetford-Mines** Québec, SE Canada
115 K17 **Theth** *var.* Thethi. Shkodër, N Albania
Thethi *see* Theth
101 L20 **Theux** Liège, E Belgium
xxxv I15 **The Vale of Glamorgan** ◐ *unitary authority* S Wales, UK
47 U9 **The Valley** ○ (Anguilla) E Anguilla
29 N10 **The Village** Oklahoma, C USA
27 W10 **The Woodlands** Texas, SW USA
xxxviii H9 **The Wrekin** ◐ *unitary authority* C England, UK
Thiamis *see* Thýamis
Thian Shan *see* Tien Shan
24 J9 **Thibodaux** Louisiana, S USA
31 S3 **Thief Lake** ◎ Minnesota, N USA
31 S3 **Thief River** ~ Minnesota, C USA
31 S3 **Thief River Falls** Minnesota, N USA
Thièle *see* La Thielle
34 G14 **Thielsen, Mount** ▲ Oregon, NW USA
Thielt *see* Tielt
108 G7 **Thiene** Veneto, NE Italy
Thienen *see* Tienen
105 P11 **Thiers** Puy-de-Dôme, C France
78 F11 **Thiès** W Senegal
83 I19 **Thika** Central, S Kenya
Thikombia *see* Cikobia
157 K18 **Thiladhunmathi Atoll** *var.* Tiladummati Atoll. *atoll* N Maldives
xxxix R6 **Thimbleby** Lincolnshire, E England, UK
Thimbu *see* Thimphu
159 T11 **Thimphu** *var.* Thimbu; *prev.* Tashi Chho Dzong. ● (Bhutan) W Bhutan
94 H2 **Thingeyri** Vestfirdhir, NW Iceland
94 I3 **Thingvellir** Sudhurland, SW Iceland
197 J6 **Thio** Province Sud, C New Caledonia
105 T4 **Thionville** *Ger.* Diedenhofen. Moselle, NE France
117 K22 **Thíra** Thíra, Kykládes, Greece, Aegean Sea
117 K22 **Thíra** *prev.* Santorin, Santoríni, *anc.* Thera. *island* Kykládes, Greece, Aegean Sea
117 J22 **Thirasía** *island* Kykládes, Greece, Aegean Sea
xli S11 **Thirsk** North Yorkshire, N England, UK
12 F12 **Thirty Thousand Islands** *island group* Ontario, S Canada
Thiruvanathapuram *see* Trivandrum
97 F20 **Thisted** Viborg, NW Denmark
Thistil Fjord *see* Thistilfjördhur
94 L1 **Thistilfjördhur** *var.* Thistil Fjord. *fjord* NE Iceland
190 G9 **Thistle Island** *island* South Australia
Thithia *see* Cicia
179 N14 **Thitu Island** *island* NW Spratly Islands
Thiukhaoluang Phrahang *see* Luang Prabang Range
117 G18 **Thíva** *Eng.* Thebes; *prev.* Thívai. Stereá Ellás, C Greece
Thívai *see* Thíva
104 M12 **Thiviers** Dordogne, SW France
94 J4 **Thjórsá** ~ C Iceland
15 L9 **Thlewiaza** ~ Northwest Territories, NE Canada
15 J9 **Thoa** ~ Northwest Territories, NW Canada
xli P5 **Thockrington** Northumberland, N England, UK
101 G14 **Tholen** Zeeland, SW Netherlands
101 F14 **Tholen** *island* SW Netherlands
28 L10 **Thomas** Oklahoma, C USA
23 T3 **Thomas** West Virginia, NE USA
29 U3 **Thomas Hill Reservoir** ⊟ Missouri, C USA
xliv G8 **Thomas Street** Roscommon, C Ireland
25 S5 **Thomaston** Georgia, SE USA
21 R7 **Thomaston** Maine, NE USA
27 T12 **Thomaston** Texas, SW USA
xliv I12 **Thomastown** Kilkenny, SE Ireland
25 O6 **Thomasville** Alabama, S USA
25 T8 **Thomasville** Georgia, SE USA
23 S9 **Thomasville** North Carolina, SE USA
37 N5 **Thomes Creek** ~ California, W USA
9 W12 **Thompson** Manitoba, C Canada
31 R4 **Thompson** North Dakota, N USA
0 F8 **Thompson** ~ Alberta/British Columbia, SW Canada
35 O8 **Thompson Falls** Montana, NW USA
31 Q10 **Thompson, Lake** ◎ South Dakota, N USA
36 M3 **Thompson Peak** ▲ California, W USA
29 S2 **Thompson River** ~ Missouri, C USA
193 A22 **Thompson Sound** *sound* South Island, NZ
15 Hh1 **Thomsen** ~ Banks Island, Northwest Territories, NW Canada
25 V4 **Thomson** Georgia, SE USA
105 T10 **Thonon-les-Bains** Haute-Savoie, E France
105 O15 **Thoré** *var.* Thore. ~ S France
39 P11 **Thoreau** New Mexico, SW USA
Thorenburg *see* Turda
xxxix R4 **Thoresway** Lincolnshire, E England, UK
94 J3 **Thórisvatn** ◎ C Iceland
94 P4 **Thor, Kapp** *headland* S Svalbard
94 I4 **Thorlákshöfn** Sudhurland, SW Iceland
Thorn *see* Toruń
xli X7 **Thornaby on Tees** Middlesborough, NE England, UK
xxxvi L9 **Thornbury** South Gloucestershire, SW England, UK
xxxix O11 **Thornby** Northamptonshire, C England, UK
xxxvi K13 **Thorncombe** Dorset, S England, UK
27 T10 **Thorndale** Texas, SW USA
xxxix W12 **Thorndon** Suffolk, E England, UK
xli U15 **Thorne** Doncaster, N England, UK
12 H10 **Thorne** Ontario, S Canada
xli S13 **Thorner** Leeds, N England, UK
xxxix R9 **Thorney** Cambridgeshire, E England, UK
xliii K23 **Thornhill** Dumfries and Galloway, S Scotland, UK
xliii J18 **Thornhill** Stirling, C Scotland, UK
xli W5 **Thornley** Durham, N England, UK
xl M13 **Thornton** Lancashire, NW England, UK
xliii M18 **Thornton** Fife, E Scotland, UK
27 U8 **Thornton** Texas, SW USA
xxxix Q3 **Thornton Curtis** North Lincolnshire, N England, UK
xli V11 **Thornton Dale** North Yorkshire, N England, UK
Thornton Island *see* Caroline Island
xli S11 **Thornton-le-Street** North Yorkshire, N England, UK
12 H16 **Thorold** Ontario, S Canada
34 I9 **Thorp** Washington, NW USA
xxxix Y12 **Thorpeness** Suffolk, E England, UK
xxxix P6 **Thorpe on the Hill** Lincolnshire, E England, UK
xxxvii Y7 **Thorrington** Essex, SE England, UK
205 S3 **Thorshavnheiane** *physical region* Antarctica
94 L1 **Thórshöfn** Nordhurland Eystra, NE Iceland
xxxvi H13 **Thorverton** Devon, SW England, UK
Thospitis *see* Van Gölü
178 Jj14 **Thôt Nốt** Cần Tho, S Vietnam
104 K8 **Thouars** Deux-Sèvres, W France
159 X14 **Thoubal** Manipur, NE India
104 K9 **Thouet** ~ W France
Thoune *see* Thun
20 H7 **Thousand Islands** *island* Canada/USA
37 S15 **Thousand Oaks** California, W USA
116 J13 **Thracian Sea** *Gk.* Thrakikó Pélagos; *anc.* Thracium Mare. *sea* Greece/Turkey
Thracium Mare/Thrakikó Pélagos *see* Thracian Sea
Thrá Lí, Bá *see* Tralee Bay
xxxix Q11 **Thrapston** Northamptonshire, C England, UK
xxxvii U11 **Three Bridges** West Sussex, S England, UK
35 R11 **Three Forks** Montana, NW USA
9 Q16 **Three Hills** Alberta, SW Canada
191 N15 **Three Hummock Island** *island* Tasmania, SE Australia
192 H1 **Three Kings Islands** *island group* N NZ
183 P10 **Three Kings Rise** *undersea feature* W Pacific Ocean
79 O18 **Three Points, Cape** *headland* S Ghana
33 P10 **Three Rivers** Michigan, N USA
27 S13 **Three Rivers** Texas, SW USA
85 G24 **Three Sisters** Northern Cape, SW South Africa
34 H13 **Three Sisters** ▲ Oregon, NW USA
195 Z16 **Three Sisters Islands** *island group* SE Solomon Islands
xli P12 **Threshfield** North Yorkshire, N England, UK
Thrissur *see* Trichūr
xli U2 **Throckley** Newcastle upon Tyne, NE England, UK
27 Q6 **Throckmorton** Texas, SW USA
xli Q4 **Thropton** Northumberland, N England, UK
188 M10 **Throssell, Lake** *salt lake* Western Australia
xlii M7 **Thrumster** Highland, N Scotland, UK
xxxvii O11 **Thruxton** Hampshire, S England, UK
117 K25 **Thrýptis** ▲ Kríti, Greece, E Mediterranean Sea
178 Jj14 **Thu Dâu Môt** *var.* Phu Cường. Sông Be, S Vietnam
178 Jj6 **Thu Do** ✕ (Ha Nôi) Ha Nôi, N Vietnam
101 G21 **Thuin** Hainaut, S Belgium
155 Q12 **Thul** Sind, SE Pakistan
Thule *see* Qaanaaq
85 J18 **Thuli** *var.* Tuli. ~ S Zimbabwe
Thumrayt *see* Thamarit
110 D9 **Thun** *Fr.* Thoune. Bern, W Switzerland
10 C12 **Thunder Bay** Ontario, S Canada
32 M1 **Thunder Bay** *lake bay* S Canada
33 R6 **Thunder Bay** *lake bay* Michigan, N USA
33 R6 **Thunder Bay River** ~ Michigan, N USA
29 N11 **Thunderbird, Lake** ⊟ Oklahoma, C USA
30 L8 **Thunder Butte Creek** ~ South Dakota, N USA
110 E9 **Thuner See** ◎ C Switzerland
178 H16 **Thung Song** *var.* Cha Mai. Nakhon Si Thammarat, SW Thailand
110 H7 **Thur** ~ N Switzerland
xli T16 **Thurcroft** Rotherham, N England, UK
110 G6 **Thurgau** *Fr.* Thurgovie. ◐ *canton* NE Switzerland
Thurgovie *see* Thurgau
Thuringe *see* Thüringen
110 J7 **Thüringen** Vorarlberg, W Austria
103 J17 **Thüringen** *Eng.* Thuringia, *Fr.* Thuringe. ◐ *state* C Germany
103 J17 **Thüringer Wald** *Eng.* Thuringian Forest. ▲ C Germany
Thuringia *see* Thüringen
Thuringian Forest *see* Thüringer Wald
xxxix Q9 **Thurlby** Lincolnshire, E England, UK
xliv H11 **Thurles** *Ir.* Durlas. Tipperary, S Ireland
xxxvi G16 **Thurlestone** Devon, SW England, UK
xxxix U13 **Thurlow** Suffolk, E England, UK
23 W2 **Thurmont** Maryland, NE USA
Thurø *see* Thurø By
97 H24 **Thurø By** *var.* Thurø. Fyn, C Denmark
xxxvii V9 **Thurrock** ◐ *unitary authority* SE England, UK
xl M7 **Thursby** Cumbria, NW England, UK
xliii L6 **Thurso** Highland, N Scotland, UK
xlii K7 **Thurso** ~ NW Scotland, UK
12 M12 **Thurso** Québec, SE Canada
xl B16 **Thurstaston** Wirral, NW England, UK
204 I10 **Thurston Island** *island* Antarctica
110 I9 **Thusis** Graubünden, S Switzerland
xli P10 **Thwaite** North Yorkshire, N England, UK
117 C15 **Thýamis** *var.* Thiamis. ~ W Greece
97 E21 **Thyborøn** *var.* Tyborøn. Ringkøbing, W Denmark
205 U3 **Thyer Glacier** *glacier* Antarctica
117 L20 **Thýmaina** *island* Dodekánisos, Greece, Aegean Sea
85 N15 **Thyolo** *var.* Cholo. Southern, S Malawi
191 U6 **Tia** New South Wales, SE Australia
65 H5 **Tía Juana** Zulia, NW Venezuela
166 J14 **Tiandong** *var.* Pingma. Guangxi Zhuangzu Zizhiqu, S China
167 O3 **Tianjin** *var.* Tientsin. Tianjin Shi, E China
Tianjin *see* Tianjin Shi
167 P3 **Tianjin Shi** *var.* Jin, Tianjin, T'ien-ching, Tientsin. ◐ *municipality* E China
165 S10 **Tianjun** *var.* Xinyuan. Qinghai, C China
166 J13 **Tianlin** *prev.* Leli. Guangxi Zhuangzu Zizhiqu, S China
Tian Shan *see* Tien Shan
165 W11 **Tianshui** Gansu, C China
156 I7 **Tianshuihai** Xinjiang Uygur Zizhiqu, W China
167 S10 **Tiantai** Zhejiang, SE China
166 J14 **Tianyang** Guangxi Zhuangzu Zizhiqu, S China
165 U9 **Tianzhu** *var.* Tianzhu Zangzu Zizhixian. Gansu, C China
Tianzhu Zangzu Zizhixian *see* Tianzhu
203 Q7 **Tiarei** Tahiti, W French Polynesia
76 J6 **Tiaret** *var.* Tihert. NW Algeria
Tiâs *see* Tiyâs
79 N17 **Tiassalé** S Ivory Coast
198 Bb8 **Ti'avea** Upolu, SE Western Samoa
Tiba *see* Chiba
62 J11 **Tibagi** *var.* Tibaji. Paraná, S Brazil
62 J10 **Tibagi, Rio** *var.* Rio Tibají. ~ S Brazil
Tibaji *see* Tibagi
Tibají, Rio *see* Tibagi, Rio
145 Q9 **Tibal, Wādī** *dry watercourse* S Iraq
56 G9 **Tibaná** Boyacá, C Colombia
81 F14 **Tibati** Adamaoua, N Cameroon
xxxvi L7 **Tibberton** Gloucestershire, C England, UK
78 K15 **Tibé, Pic de** ▲ SE Guinea
Tiber *see* Tevere, Italy
Tiber *see* Tivoli, Italy
Tiberias *see* Teverya
144 G8 **Tiberias, Lake** *var.* Chinnereth, Sea of Bahr Tabariya, Sea of Galilee, *Ar.* Bahrat Tabariya, *Heb.* Yam Kinneret. ◎ N Israel
69 Q5 **Tibesti** *var.* Tibesti Massif, *Ar.* Tibistī. ▲ N Africa
Tibesti Massif *see* Tibesti
Tibetan Autonomous Region *see* Xizang Zizhiqu
Tibet, Plateau of *see* Qingzang Gaoyuan
Tibistī *see* Tibesti
12 K7 **Tiblemont, Lac** ◎ Québec, SE Canada
145 X9 **Ţīb, Nahr aţ** ~ S Iraq
Tibnī *see* At Tibnī
190 L4 **Tibooburra** New South Wales, SE Australia
97 L18 **Tibro** Skaraborg, S Sweden
42 E5 **Tiburón, Isla** *var.* Isla del Tiburón. *island* NW Mexico
Tiburón, Isla del *see* Tiburón, Isla
25 W14 **Tice** Florida, SE USA
xxxvii W12 **Ticehurst** East Sussex, SE England, UK
Tichau *see* Tychy
116 L8 **Ticha, Yazovir** ◎ NE Bulgaria
78 K9 **Tichît** *var.* Tichitt. Tagant, C Mauritania
Tichitt *see* Tichît
110 G11 **Ticino** *Fr./Ger.* Tessin. ◐ *canton* S Switzerland
108 D8 **Ticino** ~ Italy/Switzerland
110 H11 **Ticino** *Ger.* Tessin. ~ SW Switzerland
Ticinum *see* Pavia
xli T16 **Tickhill** Doncaster, N England, UK
43 X12 **Ticul** Yucatán, SE Mexico
97 K18 **Tidaholm** Skaraborg, S Sweden
xxxvi K8 **Tidenham** Gloucestershire, C England, UK
xxxviii L5 **Tideswell** Derbyshire, C England, UK
Tidjikdja *see* Tidjikja
78 J8 **Tidjikja** *var.* Tidjikdja; *prev.* Fort-Cappolani. Tagant, C Mauritania
Tidore *see* Soasiu
175 Ss7 **Tidore, Pulau** *island* E Indonesia
Tidra, Île *see* Et Tîdra
79 N16 **Tiébissou** *var.* Tiebissou. C Ivory Coast
169 V11 **Tiefa** Liaoning, NE China
110 I9 **Tiefencastel** Graubünden, S Switzerland
Tiegenhof *see* Nowy Dwór Gdański
T'ieh-ling *see* Tieling
100 K13 **Tiel** Gelderland, C Netherlands
169 W7 **Tieli** Heilongjiang, NE China
169 V11 **Tieling** *var.* T'ieh-ling. Liaoning, NE China
158 L4 **Tielongtan** China/India
101 D17 **Tielt** *var.* Thielt. West-Vlaanderen, W Belgium
T'ien-ching *see* Tianjin Shi
101 I18 **Tienen** *var.* Thienen, *Fr.* Tirlemont. Vlaams Brabant, C Belgium
Tiên Giang, Sông *see* Mekong
153 X9 **Tien Shan** *Chin.* Thian Shan, Tian Shan, T'ien Shan, *Rus.* Tyan'-Shan'. ▲ C Asia
Tientsin *see* Tianjin
Tientsin *see* Tianjin Shi
178 K6 **Tiên Yên** Quang Ninh, N Vietnam
97 O14 **Tierp** Uppsala, C Sweden
64 H7 **Tierra Amarilla** Atacama, N Chile
39 R9 **Tierra Amarilla** New Mexico, SW USA
43 R15 **Tierra Blanca** Veracruz-Llave, E Mexico
43 O16 **Tierra Colorada** Guerrero, S Mexico
65 J17 **Tierra Colorada, Bajo de la** *basin* SE Argentina
65 I25 **Tierra del Fuego** *off.* Provincia de la Tierra del Fuego. ◐ *province* S Argentina
65 J24 **Tierra del Fuego** *island* Argentina/Chile
56 D7 **Tierralta** Córdoba, NW Colombia
106 K9 **Tiétar** ~ W Spain
62 L10 **Tietê** São Paulo, S Brazil
62 J8 **Tietê, Rio** ~ S Brazil
34 I9 **Tieton** Washington, NW USA
34 J6 **Tiffany Mountain** ▲ Washington, NW USA
33 S12 **Tiffin** Ohio, N USA
33 Q11 **Tiffin River** ~ Ohio, N USA
Tiflis *see* T'bilisi
25 U7 **Tifton** Georgia, SE USA
175 Ss11 **Tifu** Pulau Buru, E Indonesia
197 K6 **Tiga, Île** *island* Îles Loyauté, W New Caledonia
40 L17 **Tigalda Island** *island* Aleutian Islands, Alaska, USA
117 I15 **Tigáni, Ákra** *headland* Límnos, E Greece
175 O1 **Tiga Tarok** Sabah, East Malaysia
xlii A11 **Tigharry** Western Isles, NW Scotland, UK
119 O10 **Tighina** *Rus.* Bendery; *prev.* Bender. E Moldavia
xliii G20 **Tighnabruaich** Argyll and Bute, W Scotland, UK
127 P10 **Tigil'** Koryakskiy Avtonomnyy Okrug, E Russian Federation
151 X9 **Tigiretskiy Khrebet** ▲ E Kazakhstan
81 F14 **Tignère** Adamaoua, N Cameroon
11 P14 **Tignish** Prince Edward Island, SE Canada
Tigranocerta *see* Siirt
43 O11 **Tigre, Cerro del** ▲ C Mexico
58 F8 **Tigre, Río** ~ N Peru
145 X10 **Tigris** *Ar.* Dijlah, *Turk.* Dicle. ~ Iraq/Turkey
78 G9 **Tiguent** Trarza, SW Mauritania
76 M10 **Tiguentourine** E Algeria
79 V10 **Tiguidit, Falaise de** *ridge* C Niger
147 N13 **Tihāmah** *var.* Tehama. *plain* Saudi Arabia/Yemen
Tihert *see* Tiaret
T'i-hua/Tihwa *see* Ürümqi
43 Q13 **Tihuatlán** Veracruz-Llave, E Mexico
42 B1 **Tijuana** Baja California, NW Mexico
44 E2 **Tikal** Petén, N Guatemala
160 I9 **Tīkamgarh** *prev.* Tehri. Madhya Pradesh, C India
164 L7 **Tikanlik** Xinjiang Uygur Zizhiqu, NW China
79 P12 **Tikaré** N Burkina
41 O12 **Tikchik Lakes** *lakes* Alaska, USA
203 T9 **Tikehau** *atoll* Îles Tuamotu, C French Polynesia
203 V9 **Tikei** *island* Îles Tuamotu, C French Polynesia
125 B12 **Tikhoretsk** Krasnodarskiy Kray, SW Russian Federation
128 I13 **Tikhvin** Leningradskaya Oblast', NW Russian Federation
199 Ll10 **Tiki Basin** *undersea feature* S Pacific Ocean
78 K13 **Tikinsso** ~ NE Guinea
192 Q8 **Tikitiki** Gisborne, North Island, NZ
81 D16 **Tiko** Sud-Ouest, SW Cameroon
145 S6 **Tikrīt** *var.* Tekrit. N Iraq
128 I8 **Tiksha** Respublika Kareliya, NW Russian Federation
128 I6 **Tikshozero, Ozero** ◎ NW Russian Federation
126 L7 **Tiksi** Respublika Sakha (Yakutiya), NE Russian Federation
173 G8 **Tiku** Sumatera, W Indonesia
44 A6 **Tilapa** San Marcos, SW Guatemala
44 L13 **Tilarán** Guanacaste, NW Costa Rica
101 J14 **Tilburg** Noord-Brabant, S Netherlands
xxxvii V9 **Tilbury** Essex, SE England, UK
12 D17 **Tilbury** Ontario, S Canada
190 K4 **Tilcha** South Australia
Tilcha Creek *see* Callabonna Creek
31 Q14 **Tilden** Nebraska, C USA
27 R13 **Tilden** Texas, SW USA
12 H10 **Tilden Lake** Ontario, S Canada
118 G9 **Tileagd** *Hung.* Mezőtelegd. Bihor, W Romania
xxxvii Q9 **Tilehurst** Reading, S England, UK
79 Q8 **Tilemsi, Vallée de** ~ C Mali
127 Pp8 **Tilichiki** Koryakskiy Avtonomnyy Okrug, E Russian Federation
Tiligul *see* Tilihul
Tiligul'skiy Liman *see* Tilihul's'kyy Lyman
119 P9 **Tilihul** *Rus.* Tiligul. ~ SW Ukraine
119 P10 **Tilihul's'kyy Lyman** *Rus.* Tiligul'skiy Liman. ◎ S Ukraine
Tilimsen *see* Tlemcen
Tilio Martius *see* Toulon
79 R11 **Tillabéri** *var.* Tillabéry. Tillabéri, W Niger
79 R11 **Tillabéri** ◐ *department* SW Niger
Tillabéry *see* Tillabéri
34 F11 **Tillamook** Oregon, NW USA
34 E11 **Tillamook Bay** *inlet* Oregon, NW USA
157 Q22 **Tillanchāng Dwīp** *island* Nicobar Islands, India, NE Indian Ocean
97 N15 **Tillberga** Västmanland, C Sweden
Tillenberg *see* Dyleň
23 S10 **Tillery, Lake** ⊟ North Carolina, SE USA
79 T10 **Tillia** Tahoua, W Niger
xliii K19 **Tillicoultry** Clackmannan, C Scotland, UK
xxxvii X8 **Tillingham** Essex, SE England, UK
25 N8 **Tillmans Corner** Alabama, S USA
12 F17 **Tillsonburg** Ontario, S Canada
117 N22 **Tílos** *island* Dodekánisos, Greece, Aegean Sea
191 N5 **Tilpa** New South Wales, SE Australia
xxxvii N11 **Tilshead** Wiltshire, S England, UK
Tilsit *see* Sovetsk
xxxviii H8 **Tilstock** Shropshire, W England, UK
xxxviii H7 **Tilston** Cheshire, W England, UK
xliii K15 **Tilt** ~ C Scotland, UK
33 N13 **Tilton** Illinois, N USA
130 K7 **Tim** Kurskaya Oblast', W Russian Federation
56 D12 **Timaná** Huila, S Colombia
Timan Ridge *see* Timanskiy Kryazh
129 Q6 **Timanskiy Kryazh** *Eng.* Timan Ridge. *ridge* NW Russian Federation
193 G20 **Timaru** Canterbury, South Island, NZ
131 S6 **Timashevo** Samarskaya Oblast', W Russian Federation
130 K13 **Timashevsk** Krasnodarskiy Kray, SW Russian Federation
Timbaki/Timbákion *see* Tympáki
24 K10 **Timbalier Bay** *bay* Louisiana, S USA
24 K11 **Timbalier Island** *island* Louisiana, S USA
194 K12 **Timbe** ~ C Papau New Guinea
78 L10 **Timbedgha** *var.* Timbédra. Hodh ech Chargui, SE Mauritania
Timbédra *see* Timbedgha
34 G10 **Timber** Oregon, NW USA
189 O3 **Timber Creek** Northern Territory, N Australia
30 M8 **Timber Lake** South Dakota, N USA
56 D12 **Timbío** Cauca, SW Colombia
56 C12 **Timbiquí** Cauca, SW Colombia
85 O17 **Timbue, Ponta** *headland* C Mozambique
Timbuktu *see* Tombouctou
176 Vv10 **Timbuni, Sungai** ~ Irian Jaya, E Indonesia
175 Oo4 **Timbun Mata, Pulau** *island* E Malaysia
79 P8 **Timétrine** *var.* Ti-n-Kâr. *oasis* C Mali
Timfi *see* Týmfi
Timfristos *see* Tymfristós
79 V9 **Timia** Agadez, C Niger
176 X12 **Timika** Irian Jaya, E Indonesia
76 I9 **Timimoun** C Algeria
Timiris, Cap *see* Timirist, Râs
78 F8 **Timirist, Râs** *var.* Cap Timiris. *headland* NW Mauritania
151 O7 **Timiryazevo** Severnyy Kazakhstan, N Kazakhstan
118 E11 **Timiş** ◐ *county* SW Romania
12 H9 **Timiskaming, Lake** *Fr.* Lac Témiscamingue. ◎ Ontario/Québec, SE Canada
118 E11 **Timi Soara** ✕ Timiş, SW Romania
118 E11 **Timişoara** *Ger.* Temeschwar, Temeswar, *Hung.* Temesvár; *prev.* Temeschburg. Timiş, W Romania
Timkovichi *see* Tsimkavichy
79 U8 **Ti-m-Meghsoï** ~ NW Niger
102 K8 **Timmerdorfer Strand** Schleswig-Holstein, N Germany
12 F7 **Timmins** Ontario, S Canada
23 S12 **Timmonsville** South Carolina, SE USA
32 K5 **Timms Hill** ▲ Wisconsin, N USA
176 Vv9 **Timoforo** ~ Irian Jaya, E Indonesia
114 P12 **Timok** ~ E Yugoslavia
xliv E15 **Timoleague** Cork, S Ireland
60 N13 **Timon** Maranhão, E Brazil
175 Rr17 **Timor** *island* Nusa Tenggara, C Indonesia
175 S17 **Timor Sea** *sea* E Indian Ocean
175 S16 **Timor Timur** *off.* Propinsi Timor Timur, *var.* Loro Sae, *Eng.* East Timor; *prev.* Portuguese Timor. ◐ *province* S Indonesia
Timor Trench *see* Timor Trough
198 G9 **Timor Trough** *var.* Timor Trench. *undersea feature* NE Timor Sea
63 A21 **Timote** Buenos Aires, E Argentina
56 I6 **Timotes** Mérida, NW Venezuela
27 X8 **Timpson** Texas, SW USA
126 Ll13 **Timpton** ~ NE Russian Federation
95 H17 **Timrå** Västernorrland, C Sweden
22 J10 **Tims Ford Lake** ⊟ Tennessee, S USA
xlii B8 **Timsgarry** Western Isles, NW Scotland, UK
174 Hh7 **Timun** Pulau Kundur, C Indonesia
174 H3 **Timur, Banjaran** ▲ Peninsular Malaysia
179 R17 **Tinaca Point** *headland* Mindanao, S Philippines
56 K5 **Tinaco** Cojedes, N Venezuela
xliv K11 **Tinahely** Wicklow, E Ireland
66 Q11 **Tinajo** Lanzarote, Islas Canarias, Spain , NE Atlantic Ocean
195 W8 **Tinakula** *island* Santa Cruz Islands, E Solomon Islands
56 K5 **Tinaquillo** Cojedes, N Venezuela
118 F10 **Tinca** *Hung.* Tenke. Bihor, W Romania
161 J20 **Tindivanam** Tamil Nādu, SE India
76 E9 **Tindouf** W Algeria
76 E9 **Tindouf, Sebkha de** *salt lake* W Algeria
106 J2 **Tineo** Asturias, N Spain
79 R9 **Ti-n-Essako** Kidal, E Mali
xxxvii Q6 **Tingewick** Buckinghamshire, C England, UK
191 T5 **Tingha** New South Wales, SE Australia
Tingis *see* Tanger
Tinglett *see* Tinglev
97 F24 **Tinglev** *Ger.* Tinglett. Sønderjylland, SW Denmark
58 E12 **Tingo María** Huánuco, C Peru
Tingréla *see* Tengréla
164 K16 **Tingri** *var.* Xêgar. Xizang Zizhiqu, W China
97 M21 **Tingsryd** Kronoberg, S Sweden
97 P19 **Tingstäde** Gotland, SE Sweden
64 H12 **Tinguiririca, Volcán** ▲ C Chile
96 F9 **Tingvoll** Møre og Romsdal, S Norway
194 M9 **Tingwon Island** *island* N PNG
196 K8 **Tinian** *island* S Northern Mariana Islands
Ti-n-Kâr *see* Timétrine
Tinnevelly *see* Tirunelveli
97 G15 **Tinnoset** Telemark, S Norway
97 F15 **Tinnsjø** ◎ S Norway
Tino *see* Chino
117 J20 **Tínos** Tínos, Kykládes, Greece, Aegean Sea
117 J20 **Tínos** *anc.* Tenos. *island* Kykládes, Greece, Aegean Sea
159 R14 **Tinpahar** Bihār, NE India
124 O14 **Tin, Ra's al** *headland* N Libya
159 X11 **Tinsukia** Assam, NE India
xxxvi D14 **Tintagel** Cornwall, SW England, UK
78 K10 **Tîntâne** Hodh el Gharbi, S Mauritania
64 L7 **Tintina** Santiago del Estero, N Argentina
190 K10 **Tintinara** South Australia
xliii L21 **Tinto** ▲ C Scotland, UK
106 I14 **Tinto** ~ SW Spain
xliii K22 **Tinto Hills** ▲ South Lanarkshire, C Scotland, UK
79 S8 **Ti-n-Zaouâtene** Kidal, NE Mali
Tiobraid Árann *see* Tipperary
30 K3 **Tioga** North Dakota, N USA
20 G12 **Tioga** Pennsylvania, NE USA
27 T5 **Tioga** Texas, SW USA
37 Q8 **Tioga Pass** *pass* California, W USA
20 G12 **Tioga River** ~ New York/Pennsylvania, NE USA
176 Y11 **Tiom** Irian Jaya, E Indonesia
Tioman Island *see* Tioman, Pulau
174 I5 **Tioman, Pulau** *var.* Tioman Island. *island* Peninsular Malaysia
20 C12 **Tionesta** Pennsylvania, NE USA
20 D12 **Tionesta Creek** ~ Pennsylvania, NE USA
173 G11 **Tiop** Pulau Pagai Selatan, W Indonesia
175 Qq12 **Tioro, Selat** *var.* Tiworo. *strait* Sulawesi, C Indonesia
79 O12 **Tiou** NW Burkina
20 H11 **Tioughnioga River** ~ New York, NE USA
176 U10 **Tip** Irian Jaya, E Indonesia
76 J5 **Tipasa** *var.* Tipaza. N Algeria
Tipaza *see* Tipasa
44 J10 **Tipitapa** Managua, W Nicaragua
33 R13 **Tipp City** Ohio, N USA
33 O12 **Tippecanoe River** ~ Indiana, N USA
xliv G12 **Tipperary** *Ir.* Tiobraid Árann. Tipperary, S Ireland
xliv G11 **Tipperary** *Ir.* Tiobraid Árann. ◐ *county* S Ireland
xxxviii B14 **Tipton** Sandwell, C England, UK
37 R12 **Tipton** California, W USA
33 P13 **Tipton** Indiana, N USA
31 Y14 **Tipton** Iowa, C USA
29 U5 **Tipton** Missouri, C USA
38 I10 **Tipton, Mount** ▲ Arizona, SW USA
22 F8 **Tiptonville** Tennessee, S USA
10 E12 **Tip Top Mountain** ▲ Ontario, S Canada
xxxvii X7 **Tiptree** Essex, SE England, UK
161 G19 **Tiptūr** Karnātaka, W India
Tiquisate *see* Pueblo Nuevo Tiquisate
60 L13 **Tiracambu, Serra do** ▲ E Brazil
Tirana *see* Tiranë
115 K19 **Tirana Rinas** ✕ Durrës, W Albania
115 L20 **Tiranë** *var.* Tirana. ● (Albania) Tiranë, C Albania
115 K20 **Tiranë** ◐ *district* W Albania
146 I5 **Tirān, Jazīrat** *island* Egypt/Saudi Arabia
108 F6 **Tirano** Lombardia, N Italy
190 I2 **Tirari Desert** *desert* South Australia
119 O10 **Tiraspol** *Rus.* Tiraspol'. E Moldavia
192 M8 **Tirau** Waikato, North Island, NZ
142 C14 **Tire** İzmir, SW Turkey
143 O11 **Tirebolu** Giresun, N Turkey
xliii B17 **Tiree** *island* W Scotland, UK
Tîrgovişte *see* Târgovişte
Tîrgu *see* Târgu Cărbuneşti

324
◆ Country ● Country Capital ◇ Dependent Territory ○ Dependent Territory Capital ◐ Administrative Region ✕ International Airport ▲ Mountain ▲ Mountain Range Volcano ~ River ◎ Lake ⊟ Reservoir

Tîrgu Bujor – Toshkent Wiloyati

Tîrgu Bujor *see* Târgu Bujor
Tîrgu Frumos *see* Târgu Frumos
Tîrgu Jiu *see* Targu Jui
Tîrgu Lăpuş *see* Târgu Lăpuş
Tîrgu Mures *see* Târgu Mureş
Tîrgu-Neamţ *see* Târgu-Neamţ
Tîrgu Ocna *see* Târgu Ocna
Tîrgu Secuiesc *see* Târgu Secuiesc
155 *T3* **Tirich Mīr** ▲ NW Pakistan
78 *J5* **Tiris Zemmour** ◈ *region* N Mauritania
Tirlemont *see* Tienen
131 *W5* **Tirlyanskiy** Respublika Bashkortostan, W Russian Federation
Tîrnava Mare *see* Târnava Mare
Tîrnava Mică *see* Târnava Mică
Tîrnăveni *see* Târnăveni
Tírnavos *see* Týrnavos
Tirnovo *see* Veliko Tŭrnovo
160 *J11* **Tirodi** Madhya Pradesh, C India
110 *K8* **Tirol** *off.* Land Tirol, *var.* Tyrol, *It.* Tirolo. ◈ *state* W Austria
Tirolo *see* Tirol
Tirreno, Mare *see* Tyrrhenian Sea
109 *B19* **Tirso** ≈ Sardegna, Italy, C Mediterranean Sea
97 *H22* **Tirstrup** ✕ (Århus) Århus, C Denmark
161 *I21* **Tiruchchirāppalli** *prev.* Trichinopoly. Tamil Nādu, SE India
161 *H23* **Tirunelveli** *var.* Tinnevelly. Tamil Nādu, SE India
161 *J19* **Tirupati** Andhra Pradesh, E India
161 *I20* **Tiruppattūr** Tamil Nādu, SE India
161 *H21* **Tiruppur** Tamil Nādu, SW India
161 *I20* **Tiruyannāmalai** Tamil Nādu, SE India
114 *L10* **Tisa** *Ger.* Theiss, *Hung.* Tisza, *Rus.* Tissa, *Ukr.* Tysa. ≈ SE Europe *see also* Tisza
xxxvii *N12* **Tisbury** Wiltshire, S England, UK
Tischnowitz *see* Tišnov
9 *U14* **Tisdale** Saskatchewan, S Canada
29 *O13* **Tishomingo** Oklahoma, C USA
97 *M17* **Tisnaren** ◎ S Sweden
113 *F18* **Tišnov** *Ger.* Tischnowitz. Jižní Morava, SE Czech Republic
Tissa *see* Tisa/Tisza
76 *J6* **Tissemsilt** N Algeria
xxxviii *L7* **Tissington** Derbyshire, C England, UK
159 *S12* **Tista** ≈ NE India
114 *L8* **Tisza** *Ger.* Theiss, *Rom./Slvn./SCr.* Tisa, *Rus.* Tissa, *Ukr.* Tysa. ≈ SE Europe *see also* Tisa
113 *L23* **Tiszaföldvár** Jász-Nagykun-Szolnok, E Hungary
113 *M22* **Tiszafüred** Jász-Nagykun-Szolnok, E Hungary
113 *L23* **Tiszakécske** Bács-Kiskun, C Hungary
113 *M21* **Tiszaújváros** *prev.* Leninváros. Borsod-Abaúj-Zemplén, NE Hungary
113 *N21* **Tiszavasvári** Szabolcs-Szatmár-Bereg, NE Hungary
xxxvii *Q13* **Titchfield** Hampshire, S England, UK
Titibu *see* Chichibu
59 *I17* **Titicaca, Lake** ◎ Bolivia/Peru
202 *H17* **Titikaveka** Rarotonga, S Cook Islands
160 *M13* **Titilāgarh** Orissa, E India
174 *Gg4* **Titiwangsa, Banjaran** ▲▲ Peninsular Malaysia
Titograd *see* Podgorica
Titose *see* Chitose
Titova Mitrovica *see* Kosovska Mitrovica
Titovo Užice *see* Užice
115 *M18* **Titov Vrv** ▲ NW FYR Macedonia
96 *F7* **Titran** Sør-Trøndelag, S Norway
33 *Q8* **Tittabawassee River** ≈ Michigan, N USA
118 *J13* **Titu** Dâmboviţa, S Romania
81 *M16* **Titule** Haut-Zaïre, N Zaire
25 *X11* **Titusville** Florida, SE USA
20 *C12* **Titusville** Pennsylvania, NE USA
78 *G11* **Tivaouane** W Senegal
115 *I17* **Tivat** Montenegro, SW Yugoslavia
xxxvi *I13* **Tiverton** Devon, SW England, UK
12 *E14* **Tiverton** Ontario, S Canada
21 *O12* **Tiverton** Rhode Island, NE USA
109 *I15* **Tivoli** *anc.* Tiber. Lazio, C Italy
27 *U13* **Tivoli** Texas, SW USA
176 *W11* **Tiwarra** Irian Jaya, E Indonesia
147 *Z8* **Ţīwī** NE Oman
Tiworo *see* Tioro, Selat
176 *Ww12* **Tiyo, Pegunungan** ▲▲ Irian Jaya, E Indonesia
43 *Y11* **Tizimín** Yucatán, SE Mexico
76 *K5* **Tizi Ouzou** *var.* Tizi-Ouzou. N Algeria
76 *D8* **Tiznit** SW Morocco
115 *I14* **Tjentište** SE Bosnia and Herzegovina
Tjepoe/Tjepu *see* Cepu
100 *L7* **Tjeukemeer** ◎ N Netherlands
Tjiamis *see* Ciamis
Tjiandjoer *see* Cianjur
Tjilatjap *see* Cilacap
Tjiledoeg *see* Ciledug
97 *F23* **Tjæreborg** Ribe, W Denmark
97 *I18* **Tjörn** *island* S Sweden
94 *O3* **Tjuvfjorden** *fjord* S Svalbard
Tkvarcheli *see* Tqvarch'eli
42 *L8* **Tlahualillo** Durango, N Mexico
43 *P14* **Tlalnepantla** México, C Mexico
43 *Q13* **Tlapacoyán** Veracruz-Llave, E Mexico
43 *P16* **Tlapa de Comonfort** Guerrero, S Mexico
42 *L13* **Tlaquepaque** Jalisco, C Mexico
Tlascala *see* Tlaxcala
43 *P14* **Tlaxcala** *var.* Tlascala, Tlaxcala de Xicohténcatl. Tlaxcala, C Mexico
43 *P14* **Tlaxcala** ◈ *state* S Mexico
Tlaxcala de Xicohténcatl *see* Tlaxcala
43 *P14* **Tlaxco** *var.* Tlaxco de Morelos. Tlaxcala, S Mexico
Tlaxco de Morelos *see* Tlaxco
43 *Q16* **Tlaxiaco** *var.* Santa María Asunción Tlaxiaco. Oaxaca, S Mexico
76 *I6* **Tlemcen** *var.* Tilimsen, Tlemsen. NW Algeria
Tlemsen *see* Tlemcen
144 *L4* **Tlété Ouâte Rharbi, Jebel** ▲ N Syria
118 *J7* **Tlumach** Ivano-Frankivs'ka Oblast', W Ukraine
131 *P17* **Tlyarata** Respublika Dagestan, SW Russian Federation
xlii *N4* **Toab** Orkney Islands, N Scotland, UK
xlii *I5* **Toab** Shetland Islands, NE Scotland, UK
118 *K10* **Toaca, Vârful** *prev.* Vîrful Toaca. ▲ NE Romania
Toaca, Vîrful *see* Toaca, Vârful
197 *C13* **Toak** Ambrym, C Vanuatu
180 *J4* **Toamasina** *var.* Tamatave. Toamasina, E Madagascar
180 *J4* **Toamasina** ◈ *province* E Madagascar
180 *J4* **Toamasina** ✕ Toamasina, E Madagascar
23 *X6* **Toano** Virginia, NE USA
203 *U10* **Toau** *atoll* Îles Tuamotu, C French Polynesia
47 *T6* **Toa Vaca, Embalse** ⊞ C Puerto Rico
64 *K13* **Toay** La Pampa, C Argentina
165 *R14* **Toba** Xizang Zizhiqu, W China
171 *Hh16* **Toba** Mie, Honshū, SW Japan
173 *Ff5* **Toba, Danau** ◎ Sumatera, W Indonesia
47 *Y16* **Tobago** *island* NE Trinidad and Tobago
155 *Q9* **Toba Kākar Range** ▲▲ NW Pakistan
175 *T10* **Tobalai, Selat** *strait* Maluku, E Indonesia
175 *Q9* **Tobamawu** Sulawesi, N Indonesia
107 *Q12* **Tobarra** Castilla-La Mancha, C Spain
155 *U9* **Toba Tek Singh** Punjab, E Pakistan
175 *T6* **Tobelo** Pulau Halmahera, E Indonesia
xliv *F6* **Tobercurry** Sligo, N Ireland
xliii *E16* **Tobermory** Argyll and Bute, W Scotland, UK
12 *E12* **Tobermory** Ontario, S Canada
xliii *F18* **Toberonochy** Argyll and Bute, W Scotland, UK
172 *Oo5* **Tōbetsu** Hokkaidō, NE Japan
188 *M6* **Tobin Lake** ◎ Western Australia
9 *U14* **Tobin Lake** ◎ Saskatchewan, C Canada
37 *T4* **Tobin, Mount** ▲ Nevada, W USA
171 *L10* **Tobi-shima** *island* C Japan
174 *J11* **Toboali** Pulau Bangka, W Indonesia
150 *M8* **Tobol** *Kaz.* Tobyl. Kustanay, N Kazakhstan
150 *L8* **Tobol** *Kaz.* Tobyl. ≈ Kazakhstan/Russian Federation
125 *F11* **Tobol'sk** Tyumenskaya Oblast', C Russian Federation
Tobruch/Tobruk *see* Ţubruq
129 *R3* **Tobseda** Nenetskiy Avtonomnyy Okrug, NW Russian Federation
xlii *C8* **Tobson** Western Isles, NW Scotland, UK
Tobyl *see* Tobol
129 *Q6* **Tobysh** ≈ NW Russian Federation
56 *F10* **Tocaima** Cundinamarca, C Colombia
61 *K16* **Tocantins** *off.* Estado do Tocantins. ◈ *state* C Brazil
61 *K15* **Tocantins, Rio** ≈ N Brazil
25 *T2* **Toccoa** Georgia, SE USA
171 *K15* **Tochigi** *var.* Totigi. Tochigi, Honshū, S Japan
171 *Kk15* **Tochigi** *off.* Tochigi-ken, *var.* Totigi. ◈ *prefecture* Honshū, S Japan
171 *K13* **Tochio** *var.* Totio. Niigata, Honshū, C Japan
97 *I15* **Töcksfors** Värmland, C Sweden
44 *J5* **Tocoa** Colón, N Honduras
64 *H4* **Tocopilla** Antofagasta, N Chile
64 *I4* **Tocorpuri, Cerro de** ▲ Bolivia/Chile
191 *O10* **Tocumwal** New South Wales, SE Australia
56 *K4* **Tocuyo de La Costa** Falcón, NW Venezuela
158 *H13* **Toda Rāisingh** Rājasthān, N India
xxxvii *S6* **Toddington** Bedfordshire, C England, UK
108 *H13* **Todi** Umbria, C Italy
110 *G9* **Tödi** ▲ NE Switzerland
176 *Uu9* **Todlo** Irian Jaya, E Indonesia
xli *P14* **Todmorden** Calderdale, N England, UK
172 *N12* **Todoga-saki** *headland* Honshū, C Japan
61 *P17* **Todos os Santos, Baía de** *bay* E Brazil
42 *F10* **Todos Santos** Baja California Sur, W Mexico
42 *B2* **Todos Santos, Bahía de** *bay* NW Mexico
Toeal *see* Tual
Toeban *see* Tuban
xliv *D15* **Toe Head** *headland* SW Ireland
xlii *B10* **Toe Head** *headland* NW Scotland, UK
Toekang Besi Eilanden *see* Tukangbesi, Kepulauan
Tōen *see* T'aoyüan
193 *D25* **Toetoes Bay** *bay* South Island, NZ
9 *Q14* **Tofield** Alberta, SW Canada
8 *K17* **Tofino** Vancouver Island, British Columbia, SW Canada
201 *X17* **Tofol** Kosrae, E Micronesia
97 *J20* **Tofta** Halland, S Sweden
97 *H15* **Tofte** Buskerud, S Norway
97 *F24* **Toftlund** Sønderjylland, SW Denmark
200 *S13* **Tofua** *island* Ha'apai Group, C Tonga
197 *B10* **Toga** *island* Torres Islands, N Vanuatu
171 *Kk17* **Tōgane** Chiba, Honshū, S Japan
82 *N13* **Togdheer** *off.* Gobolka Togdheer. ◈ *region* NW Somalia
Toghyzaq *see* Toguzak
171 *Ii12* **Togi** Ishikawa, Honshū, SW Japan
41 *N13* **Togiak** Alaska, USA
175 *Qq8* **Togian, Kepulauan** *island group* C Indonesia
79 *Q15* **Togo** *off.* Togolese Republic; *prev.* French Togoland. ◆ *republic* W Africa
168 *F8* **Tögrög** Govĭ-Altay, SW Mongolia
168 *E7* **Tögrög** Hovd, W Mongolia
Togton-heyan *see* Tuotuoheyan
150 *L7* **Toguzak** *Kaz.* Toghyzaq. ≈ Kazakhstan/Russian Federation
39 *P10* **Tohatchi** New Mexico, SW USA
203 *O7* **Tohiea, Mont** △ Moorea, W French Polynesia
95 *O17* **Tohmajärvi** Pohjois-Karjala, SE Finland
143 *N14* **Tohma Çayı** ≈ C Turkey
95 *L16* **Toholampi** Vaasa, W Finland
168 *M10* **Töhöm** Dornogovĭ, SE Mongolia
25 *X12* **Tohopekaliga, Lake** ◎ Florida, SE USA
171 *J17* **Toi** Shizuoka, Honshū, S Japan
202 *B15* **Toi** N Niue
95 *L19* **Toijala** Häme, SW Finland
175 *Qq9* **Toima** Sulawesi, N Indonesia
170 *C17* **Toi-misaki** *headland* Kyūshū, SW Japan
175 *Rr17* **Toineke** Timor, S Indonesia
Toirc, Inis *see* Inishturk
37 *U6* **Toiyabe Range** ▲▲ Nevada, W USA
Tojikiston, Jumhurii *see* Tajikistan
153 *R12* **Tojikobod** *Rus.* Tadzhikabad. C Tajikistan
170 *F13* **Tōjō** Hiroshima, Honshū, SW Japan
41 *T10* **Tok** Alaska, USA
172 *P5* **Tokachi-dake** ▲ Hokkaidō, NE Japan
172 *Pp7* **Tokachi-gawa** *var.* Tokati Gawa. ≈ Hokkaidō, NE Japan
171 *Hh16* **Tōkai** Aichi, Honshū, SW Japan
113 *N21* **Tokaj** Borsod-Abaúj-Zemplén, NE Hungary
171 *Jj13* **Tōkamachi** Niigata, Honshū, C Japan
193 *D25* **Tokanui** Southland, South Island, NZ
82 *I7* **Tokar** *var.* Ţawkar. Red Sea, NE Sudan
142 *L12* **Tokat** Tokat, N Turkey
142 *L12* **Tokat** ◈ *province* N Turkey
Tokati Gawa *see* Tokachi-gawa
169 *X15* **Tŏkchŏk-gundo** *island group* NW South Korea
Tōke *see* Taka Atoll
202 *J9* **Tokelau** ◇ *NZ overseas territory* W Polynesia
Tőketerebes *see* Trebišov
Tokhtamyshbek *see* Tŭkhtamish
26 *M6* **Tokio** Texas, SW USA
Tokio *see* Tōkyō
201 *W11* **Toki Point** *point* NW Wake Island
Tokkuztara *see* Gongliu
153 *V7* **Tokmak** *Kir.* Tokmok. Chuyskaya Oblast', N Kyrgyzstan
119 *V9* **Tokmak** *var.* Velykyy Tokmak. Zaporiz'ka Oblast', SE Ukraine
Tokmok *see* Tokmak
192 *Q8* **Tokomaru Bay** Gisborne, North Island, NZ
171 *Hh16* **Tokoname** Aichi, Honshū, SW Japan
172 *Qq5* **Tokoro** Hokkaidō, NE Japan
192 *M8* **Tokoroa** Waikato, North Island, NZ
172 *Q6* **Tokoro-gawa** ≈ Hokkaidō, NE Japan
78 *K14* **Tokounou** Haute-Guinée, C Guinea
40 *M12* **Toksook Bay** Alaska, USA
Toksu *see* Xinhe
Toksum *see* Toksun
164 *L6* **Toksun** *var.* Toksum. Xinjiang Uygur Zizhiqu, NW China
153 *T8* **Toktogul** Talasskaya Oblast', NW Kyrgyzstan
153 *T9* **Toktogul'skoye Vodokhranilishche** ⊞ W Kyrgyzstan
Toktomush *see* Tŭkhtamish
200 *Ss12* **Toku** *island* Vava'u Group, N Tonga
172 *Qq14* **Tokunoshima** Kagoshima, Tokuno-shima, SW Japan
172 *Q14* **Tokuno-shima** *island* Nansei-shotō, SW Japan
170 *Ff15* **Tokushima** *var.* Tokusima. Tokushima, Shikoku, SW Japan
170 *F15* **Tokushima** *off.* Tokushima-ken, *var.* Tokusima. ◈ *prefecture* Shikoku, SW Japan
Tokusima *see* Tokushima
170 *E13* **Tokuyama** Yamaguchi, Honshū, SW Japan
171 *Jj16* **Tōkyō** *var.* Tokio. ● (Japan) Tōkyō, Honshū, S Japan
171 *J15* **Tōkyō** *off.* Tōkyō-to. ◈ *capital district* Honshū, S Japan
171 *K17* **Tōkyō-wan** *bay* S Japan
151 *T12* **Tokyrau** ≈ C Kazakhstan
155 *O3* **Tokzār** *Pash.* Tukzār. Sar-e Pol, N Afghanistan
201 *U12* **Tol** *atoll* Chuuk Islands, C Micronesia
192 *Q9* **Tolaga Bay** Gisborne, North Island, NZ
180 *I7* **Tôlañaro** *prev.* Faradofay, Fort-Dauphin. Toliara, SE Madagascar
168 *D6* **Tolbo** Bayan-Ölgiy, W Mongolia
Tolbukhin *see* Dobrich
62 *G11* **Toledo** Paraná, S Brazil
56 *G8* **Toledo** Norte de Santander, N Colombia
179 *Qq13* **Toledo** *off.* Toledo City. Cebu, C Philippines
107 *N9* **Toledo** *anc.* Toletum. Castilla-La Mancha, C Spain
32 *M14* **Toledo** Illinois, N USA
31 *W13* **Toledo** Iowa, C USA
33 *R11* **Toledo** Ohio, N USA
34 *F12* **Toledo** Oregon, NW USA
34 *G9* **Toledo** Washington, NW USA
44 *F3* **Toledo** ◈ *district* S Belize
106 *M9* **Toledo** ◈ *province* Castilla-La Mancha, C Spain
27 *Y7* **Toledo Bend Reservoir** ⊞ Louisiana/Texas, SW USA
106 *M10* **Toledo, Montes de** ▲▲ C Spain
108 *J12* **Tolentino** Marche, C Italy
Toletum *see* Toledo
96 *H10* **Tolga** Hedmark, S Norway
164 *J3* **Toli** Xinjiang Uygur Zizhiqu, NW China
180 *H7* **Toliara** *var.* Toliary; *prev.* Tuléar. Toliara, SW Madagascar
180 *H7* **Toliara** ◈ *province* SW Madagascar
Toliary *see* Toliara
56 *D11* **Tolima** *off.* Departamento del Tolima. ◈ *province* C Colombia
175 *Pp7* **Tolitoli** Sulawesi, C Indonesia
97 *K22* **Tollarp** Kristianstad, S Sweden
102 *N9* **Tollense** ≈ NE Germany
102 *N10* **Tollensesee** ◎ NE Germany
xli *T12* **Tollerton** North Yorkshire, N England, UK
xxxvii *X7* **Tollesbury** Essex, SE England, UK
xxxvii *X7* **Tolleshunt d'Arcy** Essex, SE England, UK
38 *K13* **Tolleson** Arizona, SW USA
152 *M13* **Tollimarjon** *Rus.* Talimardzhan. Qashqadaryo Wiloyati, S Uzbekistan
Tolmein *see* Tolmin
108 *J6* **Tolmezzo** Friuli-Venezia Giulia, NE Italy
111 *S11* **Tolmin** *Ger.* Tolmein, *It.* Tolmino. W Slovenia
Tolmino *see* Tolmin
113 *J25* **Tolna** *Ger.* Tolnau. Tolna, S Hungary
113 *I24* **Tolna** *off.* Tolna Megye. ◈ *county* SW Hungary
Tolnau *see* Tolna
81 *I20* **Tolo** Bandundu, W Zaire
Tolochin *see* Talachyn
202 *D12* **Toloke** Île Futuna, W Wallis and Futuna
32 *M13* **Tolono** Illinois, N USA
107 *Q3* **Tolosa** País Vasco, N Spain
Tolosa *see* Toulouse
175 *Qq10* **Tolo, Teluk** *bay* Sulawesi, C Indonesia
41 *R9* **Tolovana River** ≈ Alaska, USA
127 *Oo10* **Tolstoy, Mys** *headland* E Russian Federation
65 *G15* **Toltén** Araucanía, C Chile
65 *G15* **Toltén, Río** ≈ S Chile
56 *E6* **Tolú** Sucre, NW Colombia
43 *O14* **Toluca** *var.* Toluca de Lerdo. México, S Mexico
Toluca de Lerdo *see* Toluca
43 *O14* **Toluca, Nevado de** △ C Mexico
131 *R6* **Tol'yatti** *prev.* Stavropol'. Samarskaya Oblast', W Russian Federation
126 *H14* **Tom'** ≈ S Russian Federation
79 *O12* **Toma** NW Burkina
32 *K7* **Tomah** Wisconsin, N USA
32 *L5* **Tomahawk** Wisconsin, N USA
119 *T8* **Tomakivka** Dnipropetrovs'ka Oblast', E Ukraine
172 *O6* **Tomakomai** Hokkaidō, NE Japan
172 *P3* **Tomamae** Hokkaidō, NE Japan
106 *G9* **Tomar** Santarém, W Portugal
127 *O15* **Tomari** Ostrov Sakhalin, Sakhalinskaya Oblast', SE Russian Federation
117 *C16* **Tómaros** ▲ W Greece
Tomaschow *see* Tomaszów Lubelski, Poland
Tomaschow *see* Tomaszów Mazowiecki, Poland
63 *E16* **Tomás Gomensoro** Artigas, N Uruguay
119 *N7* **Tomashpil'** Vinnyts'ka Oblast', C Ukraine
Tomaszów *see* Tomaszów Mazowiecki
113 *P15* **Tomaszów Lubelski** *Ger.* Tomaschow. Zamość, SE Poland
Tomaszów Mazowiecka *see* Tomaszów Mazowiecki
112 *L13* **Tomaszów Mazowiecki** *var.* Tomaszów Mazowiecka; *prev.* Tomaszów, *Ger.* Tomaschow. Piotrków, C Poland
xlii *K13* **Tomatin** Highland, NW Scotland, UK
42 *J13* **Tomatlán** Jalisco, C Mexico
170 *F12* **Tombara** Shimane, Honshū, SW Japan
83 *F15* **Tombe** Jonglei, S Sudan
25 *N4* **Tombigbee River** ≈ Alabama/Mississippi, S USA
84 *A10* **Tomboco** Zaire, NW Angola
79 *O10* **Tombouctou** *Eng.* Timbuktu. Tombouctou, N Mali
79 *N9* **Tombouctou** ◈ *region* W Mali
xlii *J12* **Tombreck** Highland, NW Scotland, UK
39 *N16* **Tombstone** Arizona, SW USA
85 *A15* **Tombua** *Port.* Porto Alexandre. Namibe, SW Angola
85 *J19* **Tom Burke** Northern, NE South Africa
152 *L9* **Tomdibuloq** *Rus.* Tamdybulak. Nawoiy Wiloyati, N Uzbekistan
152 *L9* **Tomditow-Toghi** ▲▲ N Uzbekistan
xliii *H14* **Tomdoun** Highland, NW Scotland, UK
64 *G13* **Tomé** Bío Bío, C Chile
60 *L12* **Tomé-Açu** Pará, NE Brazil
97 *L23* **Tomelilla** Kristianstad, S Sweden
107 *O10* **Tomelloso** Castilla-La Mancha, C Spain
xliv *F10* **Tomgraney** Clare, W Ireland
xlii *H13* **Tomich** Highland, NW Scotland, UK
12 *H10* **Tomiko Lake** ◎ Ontario, S Canada
79 *N12* **Tominian** Ségou, C Mali
175 *Pp8* **Tomini, Gulf of** *var.* Teluk Tomini; *prev.* Teluk Gorontalo. *bay* Sulawesi, C Indonesia
Tomini, Teluk *see* Tomini, Gulf of
xlii *L13* **Tomintoul** Moray, N Scotland, UK
172 *Ll15* **Tomioka** Fukushima, Honshū, C Japan
172 *Jj15* **Tomioka** Gunma, Honshū, S Japan
115 *G14* **Tomislavgrad** SW Bosnia and Herzegovina
189 *O9* **Tomkinson Ranges** ▲▲ South Australia/Western Australia
126 *Ll12* **Tommot** Respublika Sakha (Yakutiya), NE Russian Federation
175 *Rr7* **Tomohon** Sulawesi, N Indonesia
56 *K9* **Tomo, Río** ≈ E Colombia
115 *L21* **Tomorrit, Mali i** ▲ S Albania
9 *S17* **Tompkins** Saskatchewan, S Canada
22 *K8* **Tompkinsville** Kentucky, S USA
175 *Pp7* **Tompo** Sulawesi, N Indonesia
188 *I8* **Tom Price** Western Australia
126 *H13* **Tomsk** Tomskaya Oblast', C Russian Federation
126 *Gg12* **Tomskaya Oblast'** ◈ *province* C Russian Federation
20 *K16* **Toms River** New Jersey, NE USA
Tom Steed Lake *see* Tom Steed Reservoir
28 *L12* **Tom Steed Reservoir** *var.* Tom Steed Lake. ⊞ Oklahoma, C USA
176 *Vv10* **Tomu** Irian Jaya, E Indonesia
194 *F13* **Tomu** ≈ W PNG
164 *H6* **Tomur Feng** *var.* Pik Pobedy, Pobeda Peak. ▲ China/Kyrgyzstan *see also* Pobedy, Pik
201 *N13* **Tomworoahlang** Pohnpei, E Micronesia
43 *U17* **Tonalá** Chiapas, SE Mexico
108 *F6* **Tonale, Passo del** *pass* N Italy
171 *Ii13* **Tonami** Toyama, Honshū, SW Japan
60 *C12* **Tonantins** Amazonas, W Brazil
34 *K6* **Tonasket** Washington, NW USA
57 *Y9* **Tonate** *var.* Macouria. N French Guiana
20 *D10* **Tonawanda** New York, NE USA
xxxvii *V11* **Tonbridge** Kent, SE England, UK
175 *Rr7* **Tondano** Sulawesi, C Indonesia
175 *Rr7* **Tondano, Danau** ◎ Sulawesi, N Indonesia
106 *H7* **Tondela** Viseu, N Portugal
97 *F24* **Tønder** *Ger.* Tondern. Sønderjylland, SW Denmark
Tondern *see* Tønder
xxxv *I15* **Tondu** Bridgend, S Wales, UK
171 *K16* **Tone-gawa** ≈ Honshū, S Japan
149 *N4* **Tonekābon** *var.* Shahsawar, Tonkābon; *prev.* Shahsavār. Māzandarān, N Iran
Tonezh *see* Tonyezh
xlii *D8* **Tong** Western Isles, NW Scotland, UK
200 *S15* **Tonga** *off.* Kingdom of Tonga, *var.* Friendly Islands. ◆ *monarchy* SW Pacific Ocean
183 *R9* **Tonga** *island group* SW Pacific Ocean
85 *K23* **Tongaat** KwaZulu/Natal, E South Africa
167 *Q13* **Tong'an** *var.* Tong an. Fujian, SE China
29 *Q4* **Tonganoxie** Kansas, C USA
41 *Y13* **Tongass National Forest** *reserve* Alaska, USA
200 *Qq16* **Tongatapu** ✕ Tongatapu, S Tonga
200 *R15* **Tongatapu** *island* Tongatapu Group, S Tonga
200 *S14* **Tongatapu Group** *island group* S Tonga
183 *S9* **Tonga Trench** *undersea feature* S Pacific Ocean
167 *N8* **Tongbai Shan** ▲▲ C China
167 *P8* **Tongcheng** Anhui, E China
166 *L6* **Tongchuan** Shaanxi, C China
166 *L12* **Tongdao** *var.* Tongdao Dongzu Zizhixian; *prev.* Shuangjiang. Hunan, S China
165 *T11* **Tongde** Qinghai, C China
101 *K19* **Tongeren** *Fr.* Tongres. Limburg, NE Belgium
Tonggou *see* Tongyu
169 *Y14* **Tonghae** NE South Korea
166 *G13* **Tonghai** Yunnan, SW China
169 *X8* **Tonghe** Heilongjiang, NE China
169 *W11* **Tonghua** Jilin, NE China
194 *L8* **Tong Island** *island* N PNG
169 *Z6* **Tongjiang** Heilongjiang, NE China
169 *Y13* **Tongjosŏn-man** *prev.* Broughton Bay. *bay* E North Korea
169 *V7* **Tongken He** ≈ NE China
178 *K7* **Tongking, Gulf of** *Chin.* Beibu Wan, *Vtn.* Vinh Băc Bô. *gulf* China/Vietnam
xliii *J25* **Tongland** Dumfries and Galloway, SW Scotland, UK
169 *U10* **Tongliao** Nei Mongol Zizhiqu, N China
167 *Q9* **Tongling** Anhui, E China
167 *R9* **Tonglu** Zhejiang, SE China
197 *D14* **Tongoa** *island* Shepherd Islands, S Vanuatu
64 *G9* **Tongoy** Coquimbo, C Chile
166 *L11* **Tongren** Guizhou, S China
165 *T11* **Tongren** Qinghai, C China
Tongres *see* Tongeren
159 *U11* **Tongsa** *var.* Tongsa Dzong. C Bhutan
Tongsa Dzong *see* Tongsa
Tongshan *see* Xuzhou
165 *P12* **Tongtian He** ≈ C China
xlii *I7* **Tongue** Highland, N Scotland, UK
46 *H3* **Tongue of the Ocean** *strait* C Bahamas
35 *X10* **Tongue River** ≈ Montana, NW USA
35 *W11* **Tongue River Resevoir** ⊞ Montana, NW USA
165 *V11* **Tongwei** Gansu, C China
165 *W9* **Tongxin** Ningxia, N China
169 *U9* **Tongyu** *var.* Tonggou. Jilin, NE China
166 *J11* **Tongzi** Guizhou, S China
42 *G5* **Tónichi** Sonora, NW Mexico
83 *D14* **Tonj** Warab, SW Sudan
158 *H13* **Tonk** Rājasthān, N India
Tonkābon *see* Tonekābon
29 *N8* **Tonkawa** Oklahoma, C USA
178 *Ii12* **Tônlé Sap** *Eng.* Great Lake. ◎ W Cambodia
104 *L14* **Tonneins** Lot-et-Garonne, SW France
105 *Q7* **Tonnerre** Yonne, C France
Tonoas *see* Dublon
37 *U8* **Tonopah** Nevada, W USA
170 *Ff14* **Tonoshō** Okayama, Shōdo-shima, SW Japan
45 *S17* **Tonosí** Los Santos, S Panama
97 *H16* **Tønsberg** Vestfold, S Norway
41 *T11* **Tonsina** Alaska, USA
97 *D17* **Tonstad** Vest-Agder, S Norway
200 *S14* **Tonumea** *island* Nomuka Group, W Tonga
143 *O11* **Tonya** Trabzon, NE Turkey
121 *K20* **Tonyezh** *Rus.* Tonezh. Homyel'skaya Voblasts', SE Belorussia
xxxv *I14* **Tonypandy** Rhondda Cynon Taff, S Wales, UK
38 *L3* **Tooele** Utah, W USA
xliv *C8* **Toombeola** Galway, W Ireland
xliv *K4* **Toome Bridge** Antrim, NE Northern Ireland, UK
xliv *G10* **Toomyvara** Tipperary, S Ireland
126 *Ii15* **Toora-Khem** Respublika Tyva, S Russian Federation
191 *O5* **Toorale East** New South Wales, SE Australia
85 *H25* **Toorberg** ▲ S South Africa
xliv *C15* **Toormore** Cork, S Ireland
xxxvi *C9* **Tooting** Wandsworth, SE England, UK
120 *G5* **Tootsi** Pärnumaa, SW Estonia
191 *U3* **Toowoomba** Queensland, E Australia
29 *Q4* **Topeka** *state capital* Kansas, C USA
113 *M18* **Topla** *Hung.* Toplya. ≈ NE Slovakia
126 *H14* **Topki** Kemerovskaya Oblast', S Russian Federation
Toplicza *see* Toplița
118 *J10* **Toplița** *Ger.* Töplitz, *Hung.* Maroshévíz; *prev.* Toplița Română, *Hung.* Oláh-Toplicza, Toplicza. Harghita, C Romania
Toplița Română/Töplitz *see* Toplița
Toplya *see* Topla
113 *I20* **Topoľčany** *Hung.* Nagytapolcsány. Západné Slovensko, W Slovakia
42 *G8* **Topolobampo** Sinaloa, C Mexico
118 *I13* **Topoloveni** Argeș, S Romania
116 *L11* **Topolovgrad** *prev.* Kavakli. Burgaska Oblast, SE Bulgaria
Topolya *see* Bačka Topola
128 *I6* **Topozero, Ozero** ◎ NW Russian Federation
34 *J10* **Toppenish** Washington, NW USA
xxxvi *I14* **Topsham** Devon, SW England, UK
189 *P4* **Top Springs Roadhouse** Northern Territory, N Australia
201 *U11* **Tora** *island* Chuuk, C Micronesia
Toraigh *see* Tory Island
201 *U11* **Tora Island Pass** *passage* Chuuk Islands, C Micronesia
149 *U5* **Torbat-e Ḩeydarīyeh** *var.* Turbat-i-Haidari. Khorāsān, NE Iran
149 *V5* **Torbat-e Jām** *var.* Turbat-i-Jam. Khorāsān, NE Iran
xxxvi *H16* **Tor Bay** *bay* SW England, UK
xxxvi *H15* **Torbay** ◈ *unitary authority* SW England, UK
xliii *G22* **Torbeg** North Ayrshire, W Scotland, UK
41 *Q11* **Torbert, Mount** ▲ Alaska, USA
33 *P6* **Torch Lake** ◎ Michigan, N USA
xxxvi *H16* **Torcross** Devon, SW England, UK
Törcsvár *see* Bran
Torda *see* Turda
106 *L6* **Tordesillas** Castilla-León, N Spain
xlii *J11* **Tore** Highland, NW Scotland, UK
94 *K13* **Töre** Norrbotten, N Sweden
97 *L17* **Töreboda** Skaraborg, S Sweden
97 *J21* **Torekov** Kristianstad, S Sweden
94 *O3* **Torell Land** *physical region* SW Svalbard
119 *Y8* **Torez** Donets'ka Oblast', SE Ukraine
xxxv *K14* **Torfaen** ◈ *unitary authority* SE Wales, UK
103 *N14* **Torgau** Sachsen, E Germany
Torgay *see* Turgay
Torgay Üstirti *see* Turgayskaya Stolovaya Strana
Torghay/Torghay Oblysy *see* Turgay
97 *N22* **Torhamn** Blekinge, S Sweden
101 *C17* **Torhout** West-Vlaanderen, W Belgium
108 *B8* **Torino** *Eng.* Turin. Piemonte, NW Italy
172 *Q13* **Tori-shima** *island* Izu-shotō, SE Japan
83 *F16* **Torit** Eastern Equatoria, S Sudan
195 *O11* **Toriu** New Britain, E PNG
154 *M4* **Torkestān, Selseleh-ye Band-e** *var.* Bandi-i Turkistan. ▲▲ NW Afghanistan
xxxvi *M9* **Tormarton** South Gloucestershire, SW England, UK
106 *L7* **Tormes** ≈ W Spain
Tornacum *see* Tournai
Torneå *see* Tornio
94 *K12* **Torneälven** *var.* Torniojoki, *Fin.* Tornionjoki. ≈ Finland/Sweden
xlii *J13* **Torness** Highland, NW Scotland, UK
94 *I11* **Torneträsk** ◎ N Sweden
11 *O4* **Torngat Mountains** ▲▲ Newfoundland and Labrador, NE Canada
26 *H8* **Tornillo** Texas, SW USA
94 *K13* **Tornio** *Swe.* Torneå. Lappi, NW Finland
Torniojoki/Tornionjoki *see* Torneälven
63 *B23* **Tornquist** Buenos Aires, E Argentina
106 *L6* **Toro** Castilla-León, N Spain
64 *H9* **Toro, Cerro del** ▲ N Chile
79 *R12* **Torodi** Tillabéri, SW Niger
Törökbecse *see* Novi Bečej
195 *S12* **Torokina** Bougainville Island, NE PNG
113 *L23* **Törökszentmiklós** Jász-Nagykun-Szolnok, E Hungary
44 *G7* **Torola, Río** ≈ El Salvador/Honduras
Toronaíos, Kólpos *see* Kassándras, Kólpos
12 *H15* **Toronto** Ontario, S Canada
33 *V12* **Toronto** Ohio, N USA
Toronto *see* Lester B.Pearson
29 *P6* **Toronto Lake** ⊞ Kansas, C USA
37 *V16* **Toro Peak** ▲ California, W USA
128 *H16* **Toropets** Tverskaya Oblast', W Russian Federation
83 *G18* **Tororo** E Uganda
142 *H16* **Toros Dağları** *Eng.* Taurus Mountains. ▲▲ S Turkey
xliii *L20* **Torphichen** West Lothian, SE Scotland, UK
xliii *N14* **Torphins** Aberdeenshire, NE Scotland, UK
xxxvi *F16* **Torpoint** Cornwall, SW England, UK
xxxvi *H15* **Torquay** Devon, SW England, UK
191 *N13* **Torquay** Victoria, SE Australia
106 *M5* **Torquemada** Castilla-León, N Spain
37 *S16* **Torrance** California, W USA
106 *G12* **Torrão** Setúbal, S Portugal
106 *H8* **Torre, Alto da** ▲ C Portugal
109 *K18* **Torre Annunziata** Campania, S Italy
107 *T8* **Torreblanca** País Valenciano, E Spain
106 *L15* **Torrecilla** ▲ S Spain
107 *P4* **Torrecilla en Cameros** La Rioja, N Spain
107 *N13* **Torredelcampo** Andalucía, S Spain
109 *K17* **Torre del Greco** Campania, S Italy
106 *I6* **Torre de Moncorvo** *var.* Moncorvo, Tôrre de Moncorvo. Bragança, N Portugal
106 *J9* **Torrejoncillo** Extremadura, W Spain
107 *O8* **Torrejón de Ardoz** Madrid, C Spain
107 *N7* **Torrelaguna** Madrid, C Spain
107 *N2* **Torrelavega** Cantabria, N Spain
109 *M16* **Torremaggiore** Puglia, SE Italy
106 *M15* **Torremolinos** Andalucía, S Spain
190 *I6* **Torrens, Lake** *salt lake* South Australia
Torrent/Torrent de l'Horta *see* Torrente
107 *S10* **Torrente** *var.* Torrent, Torrent de l'Horta. País Valenciano, E Spain
42 *L8* **Torreón** Coahuila de Zaragoza, NE Mexico
107 *R13* **Torre Pacheco** Murcia, SE Spain
108 *A8* **Torre Pellice** Piemonte, NE Italy
107 *O13* **Torreperogil** Andalucía, S Spain
63 *J15* **Torres** Rio Grande do Sul, S Brazil
Torrès, Îles *see* Torres Islands
197 *B10* **Torres Islands** *Fr.* Îles Torrès. *island group* N Vanuatu
106 *G9* **Torres Novas** Santarém, C Portugal
189 *V1* **Torres Strait** *strait* Australia/PNG
106 *F10* **Torres Vedras** Lisboa, C Portugal
107 *S13* **Torrevieja** País Valenciano, E Spain
194 *F9* **Torricelli Mountains** ▲▲ NW PNG
xxxvi *F12* **Torridge** ≈ SW England, UK
xlii *F11* **Torridon** Highland, NW Scotland, UK
xlii *F11* **Torridon, Loch** *inlet* NW Scotland, UK
108 *D9* **Torriglia** Liguria, NW Italy
106 *M9* **Torrijos** Castilla-La Mancha, C Spain
xlii *E13* **Torrin** Highland, NW Scotland, UK
20 *L12* **Torrington** Connecticut, NE USA
35 *Z15* **Torrington** Wyoming, C USA
95 *F16* **Torröjen** *var.* Torrön. ◎ C Sweden
Torrön *see* Torröjen
107 *N15* **Torrox** Andalucía, S Spain
96 *N13* **Torsåker** Gävleborg, C Sweden
97 *N21* **Torsås** Kalmar, S Sweden
97 *J14* **Torsby** Värmland, C Sweden
97 *N16* **Torshälla** Södermanland, C Sweden
Torshiz *see* Kāshmar
xxxvii *V16* **Torteval** Guernsey, Channel Islands
xliii *L24* **Torthorwald** Dumfries and Galloway, SW Scotland, UK
47 *T9* **Tortola** *island* C British Virgin Islands
108 *D9* **Tortona** *anc.* Dertona. Piemonte, NW Italy
109 *L23* **Tortorici** Sicilia, Italy, C Mediterranean Sea
107 *U7* **Tortosa** *anc.* Dertosa. Cataluña, E Spain
Tortosa *see* Ţarţūs
107 *U7* **Tortosa, Cap** *headland* E Spain
46 *L8* **Tortue, Île de la** *var.* Tortuga Island. *island* N Haiti
57 *Y10* **Tortue, Montagne** ▲▲ C French Guiana
Tortuga, Isla *see* La Tortuga, Isla
Tortuga Island *see* Tortue, Île de la
56 *C11* **Tortugas, Golfo** *gulf* W Colombia
47 *T5* **Tortuguero, Laguna** *lagoon* N Puerto Rico
143 *Q12* **Tortum** Erzurum, NE Turkey
Torugart, Pereval *see* Turugart Shankou
143 *O12* **Torul** Gümüşhane, NE Turkey
112 *J10* **Toruń** *Ger.* Thorn. Toruń, C Poland
112 *J9* **Toruń** *off.* Województwo Toruńskie, *Ger.* Thorn. ◈ *province* N Poland
Toruńskie, Województwo *see* Toruń
97 *K20* **Torup** Halland, S Sweden
120 *I6* **Tõrva** *Ger.* Törwa. Valgamaa, S Estonia
Törwa *see* Tõrva
xliv *G2* **Tory Island** *Ir.* Toraigh. *island* NW Ireland
113 *N19* **Torysa** *Hung.* Tarca. ≈ NE Slovakia
xliv *G2* **Tory Sound** *sound* N Ireland
Törzburg *see* Bran
128 *J16* **Torzhok** Tverskaya Oblast', W Russian Federation
170 *Ee15* **Tosa** Kōchi, Shikoku, SW Japan
170 *E16* **Tosa-Shimizu** *var.* Tosasimizu. Kōchi, Shikoku, SW Japan
Tosasimizu *see* Tosa-Shimizu
170 *Ee16* **Tosa-wan** *bay* SW Japan
85 *H21* **Tosca** North-West, N South Africa
108 *F12* **Toscana** *Eng.* Tuscany. ◈ *region* C Italy
109 *E14* **Toscano, Archipelago** *Eng.* Tuscan Archipelago. *island group* C Italy
108 *G10* **Tosco-Emiliano, Appennino** *Eng.* Tuscan-Emilian Mountains. ▲▲ C Italy
Tōsei *see* Tungshih
171 *J18* **To-shima** *island* Izu-shotō, SE Japan
153 *Q9* **Toshkent** *Eng./Rus.* Tashkent. ● (Uzbekistan) Toshkent Wiloyati, E Uzbekistan
153 *Q9* **Toshkent** ✕ Toshkent Wiloyati, E Uzbekistan
153 *P9* **Toshkent Wiloyati** *Rus.* Tashkentskaya Oblast'. ◈ *province* E Uzbekistan

◆ Country
● Country Capital
◇ Dependent Territory
○ Dependent Territory Capital
◈ Administrative Region
✕ International Airport
▲ Mountain
▲▲ Mountain Range
△ Volcano
≈ River
◎ Lake
⊞ Reservoir

325

Tosno – Tswaane

128 H13 **Tosno** Leningradskaya Oblast', NW Russian Federation
165 Q10 **Toson Hu** ◎ C China
168 H6 **Tosontsengel** Dzavhan, NW Mongolia
Tosquduq Qumlari *see* Goshquduq Qum
107 U4 **Tossal de l'Orri** *var.* Llorri. ▲ NE Spain
63 A15 **Tostado** Santa Fe, C Argentina
120 F6 **Tõstamaa** *Ger.* Testama. Pärnumaa, SW Estonia
102 I10 **Tostedt** Niedersachsen, NW Germany
142 J11 **Tosya** Kastamonu, N Turkey
97 F15 **Totak** ◎ S Norway
107 R13 **Totana** Murcia, SE Spain
118 H3 **Toten** *physical region* S Norway
85 G18 **Toteng** Ngamiland, C Botswana
104 M3 **Tôtes** Seine-Maritime, N France
Totigi *see* Tochigi
Totio *see* Tochio
Totis *see* Tata
201 U13 **Totiw** *island* Chuuk, C Micronesia
xxxvii P14 **Totland** Isle of Wight, S England, UK
129 N13 **Tot'ma** *var.* Totma. Vologodskaya Oblast', NW Russian Federation
Tot'ma *see* Sukhona
xxxvi H15 **Totnes** Devon, SW England, UK
57 V9 **Totness** Coronie, N Surinam
44 C5 **Totonicapán** Totonicapán, W Guatemala
44 A2 **Totonicapán** *off.* Departamento de Totonicapán. ◆ *department* W Guatemala
63 B18 **Totoras** Santa Fe, C Argentina
197 K15 **Totoya** *island* S Fiji
xxxvi D5 **Tottenham** Haringey, SE England, UK
191 Q7 **Tottenham** New South Wales, SE Australia
xli O15 **Tottington** Bury, NW England, UK
xxxvii P13 **Totton** Hampshire, S England, UK
171 Gg13 **Tottori** Tottori, Honshū, SW Japan
170 Ff13 **Tottori** *off.* Tottori-ken. ◆ *prefecture* Honshū, SW Japan
78 I6 **Touâjîl** Tiris Zemmour, N Mauritania
78 L15 **Touba** W Ivory Coast
76 G11 **Touba** W Senegal
76 E7 **Toubkal, Jbel** ▲ W Morocco
34 K10 **Touchet** Washington, NW USA
105 P7 **Toucy** Yonne, C France
79 O12 **Tougan** W Burkina
76 L7 **Touggourt** NE Algeria
79 Q12 **Tougouri** N Burkina
78 J13 **Tougué** Moyenne-Guinée, NW Guinea
78 K12 **Toukoto** Kayes, W Mali
105 S5 **Toul** Meurthe-et-Moselle, NE France
78 L16 **Toulépleu** *var.* Toulobli. W Ivory Coast
167 S14 **Touliu** C Taiwan
13 U3 **Toulnustouc** ≈ Québec, SE Canada
Toulobli *see* Toulépleu
105 T16 **Toulon** *anc.* Telo Martius, Tilio Martius. Var, SE France
32 K12 **Toulon** Illinois, N USA
104 M15 **Toulouse** *anc.* Tolosa. Haute-Garonne, S France
104 M15 **Toulouse** ✕ Haute-Garonne, S France
79 N16 **Toumodi** C Ivory Coast
76 G9 **Tounassine, Hamada** *hill range* W Algeria
177 G7 **Toungoo** Pegu, C Burma
104 L8 **Touraine** *cultural region* C France
Tourane *see* Đà Nẵng
105 P1 **Tourcoing** Nord, N France
106 F2 **Touriñán, Cabo** *headland* NW Spain
78 J6 **Tourine** Tiris Zemmour, N Mauritania
104 J3 **Tourlaville** Manche, N France
101 D19 **Tournai** *var.* Tournay, *Dut.* Doornik; *anc.* Tornacum. Hainaut, SW Belgium
104 L16 **Tournay** Hautes-Pyrénées, S France
Tournay *see* Tournai
105 R12 **Tournon** Ardèche, E France
105 R9 **Tournus** Saône-et-Loire, C France
61 Q14 **Touros** Rio Grande do Norte, E Brazil
104 L8 **Tours** *anc.* Caesarodunum, Turoni. Indre-et-Loire, C France
191 Q17 **Tourville, Cape** *headland* Tasmania, SE Australia
168 I8 **Töv** ◆ *province* C Mongolia
56 H7 **Tovar** Mérida, NW Venezuela
130 L5 **Tovarkovskiy** Tul'skaya Oblast', W Russian Federation
Tovil'-Dora *see* Tavildara
Tövis *see* Teiuş
143 V11 **Tovuz** *Rus.* Tauz. W Azerbaijan
172 N9 **Towada** Aomori, Honshū, C Japan
172 N9 **Towada-ko** *var.* Towada Ko. ◎ Honshū, C Japan
192 K3 **Towai** Northland, North Island, NZ
20 H12 **Towanda** Pennsylvania, NE USA
xxxix O13 **Towcester** Northamptonshire, C England, UK
31 W4 **Tower** Minnesota, N USA
175 Pp8 **Towera** Sulawesi, N Indonesia
xxxiv L16 **Tower Hamlets** ◆ *London borough* SE England, UK
Tower Island *see* Genovesa, Isla
188 M13 **Tower Peak** ▲ Western Australia
xli Q8 **Tow Law** Durham, N England, UK
37 U11 **Towne Pass** *pass* California, W USA
31 N3 **Towner** North Dakota, N USA
35 R10 **Townsend** Montana, NW USA
189 X6 **Townsville** Queensland, NE Australia
xliii O22 **Town Yetholm** The Borders, S Scotland, UK
Towoeti Meer *see* Towuti, Danau
175 Q10 **Towori, Teluk** *bay* Sulawesi, C Indonesia
154 K4 **Towraghoudī** Herāt, NW Afghanistan
23 X3 **Towson** Maryland, NE USA
175 Q11 **Towuti, Danau** *Dut.* Towoeti Meer. ◎ Sulawesi, C Indonesia
Toxkan He *see* Ak-say
26 K9 **Toyah** Texas, SW USA
172 Nn6 **Tōya-ko** ◎ Hokkaidō, NE Japan
171 Ii13 **Toyama** Toyama, Honshū, SW Japan
171 Ii13 **Toyama** *off.* Toyama-ken. ◆ *prefecture* Honshū, SW Japan
171 J13 **Toyama-wan** *bay* W Japan
170 F16 **Tōyo** Ehime, Shikoku, SW Japan
170 Ee14 **Tōyo** Kōchi, Shikoku, SW Japan
Toyohara *see* Yuzhno-Sakhalinsk
171 Hh16 **Toyohashi** *var.* Toyohasi. Aichi, Honshū, SW Japan
Toyohasi *see* Toyohashi
171 I16 **Toyokawa** Aichi, Honshū, SW Japan
171 Gg13 **Toyooka** Hyōgo, Honshū, SW Japan
171 Kk12 **Toyosaka** Niigata, Honshū, C Japan
171 I16 **Toyota** Aichi, Honshū, SW Japan
172 Pp2 **Toyotomi** Hokkaidō, NE Japan
170 Dd12 **Toyoura** Yamaguchi, Honshū, SW Japan
Toytepa *see* Tuytepa
76 M6 **Tozeur** *var.* Tawzar. W Tunisia
41 Q8 **Tozi, Mount** ▲ Alaska, USA
143 Q9 **Tqvarch'eli** *Rus.* Tkvarcheli. NW Georgia
Trâblous *see* Tripoli
143 O11 **Trabzon** *Eng.* Trebizond; *anc.* Trapezus. Trabzon, NE Turkey
143 O11 **Trabzon** *Eng.* Trebizond. ◆ *province* NE Turkey
11 P13 **Tracadie** New Brunswick, SE Canada
Trachenberg *see* Żmigród
13 O11 **Tracy** Québec, SE Canada
37 O8 **Tracy** California, W USA
31 S10 **Tracy** Minnesota, N USA
22 K10 **Tracy City** Tennessee, S USA
108 D7 **Tradate** Lombardia, N Italy
86 F6 **Traena Bank** *undersea feature* E Norwegian Sea
31 W13 **Traer** Iowa, C USA
106 J16 **Trafalgar, Cabo de** *headland* SW Spain
xli O17 **Trafford** ◆ *unitary authority* NW England, UK
Traiectum ad Mosam/Traiectum Tungorum *see* Maastricht
Tráigh Mhór *see* Tramore
9 O17 **Trail** British Columbia, SW Canada
60 H11 **Traíra, Serra do** ▲ NW Brazil
111 V5 **Traisen** Niederösterreich, NE Austria
111 W4 **Traisen** ≈ NE Austria
111 X4 **Traiskirchen** Niederösterreich, NE Austria
Trajani Portus *see* Civitavecchia
Trajectum ad Rhenum *see* Utrecht
121 H14 **Trakai** *Ger.* Traken, *Pol.* Troki. Trakai, SE Lithuania
Traken *see* Trakai
xliv C12 **Tralee** *Ir.* Trá Lí. Kerry, SW Ireland
xliv C12 **Tralee Bay** *Ir.* Bá Thrá Lí. *bay* SW Ireland
Trá Lí *see* Tralee
Trälleborg *see* Trelleborg
Tralles *see* Aydın
63 J16 **Tramandaí** Rio Grande do Sul, S Brazil
110 C7 **Tramelan** Bern, W Switzerland
Trá Mhór *see* Tramore
xliv J13 **Tramore** *Ir.* Tráigh Mhór, Trá Mhór. Waterford, S Ireland
97 L18 **Tranås** Jönköping, S Sweden
64 J7 **Trancas** Tucumán, N Argentina
106 I7 **Trancoso** Guarda, N Portugal
97 H22 **Tranebjerg** Århus, C Denmark
97 K19 **Tranemo** Älvsborg, S Sweden
xliii N20 **Tranent** East Lothian, SE Scotland, UK
178 Gg16 **Trang** Trang, S Thailand
176 W14 **Trangan, Pulau** *island* Kepulauan Aru, E Indonesia
Trâng Dinh *see* Thât Khê
191 Q7 **Trangie** New South Wales, SE Australia
96 K12 **Trångslet** Kopparberg, C Sweden
109 N16 **Trani** Puglia, SE Italy
63 F17 **Tranqueras** Rivera, NE Uruguay
65 G17 **Tranqui, Isla** *island* S Chile
41 V6 **Trans-Alaska pipeline** *oil pipeline* Alaska, USA
205 Q10 **Transantarctic Mountains** ▲ Antarctica
Transcarpathian Oblast *see* Zakarpats'ka Oblast'
Transilvania *see* Transylvania
Transilvaniei, Alpi *see* Carpaţii Meridionali
Transjordan *see* Jordan
180 L11 **Transkei Basin** *undersea feature* SW Indian Ocean
127 N17 **Trans-Siberian Railway** *railway* Russian Federation
Transsylvanische Alpen/Transylvanian Alps *see* Carpaţii Meridionali
96 K12 **Transtrand** Kopparberg, C Sweden
118 G10 **Transylvania** *Eng.* Ardeal, Transilvania, *Ger.* Siebenbürgen, *Hung.* Erdély. *cultural region* NW Romania
178 Jj15 **Tra Ôn** Vinh Long, S Vietnam
109 H23 **Trapani** *anc.* Drepanum. Sicilia, Italy, C Mediterranean Sea
178 J12 **Trâpeăng Vêng** Kâmpóng Thum, C Cambodia
Trapezus *see* Trabzon
116 L9 **Trapoklovo** Burgaska Oblast, E Bulgaria
xxxv G13 **Trapp** Carmarthenshire, S Wales, UK
191 P13 **Traralgon** Victoria, SE Australia
78 H9 **Trarza** ◆ *region* SW Mauritania
Trasimenischersee *see* Trasimeno, Lago
108 H12 **Trasimeno, Lago** *Eng.* Lake of Perugia, *Ger.* Trasimenischersee. ◎ C Italy
97 J20 **Träslövsläge** Halland, S Sweden
Trás-os-Montes *see* Cucumbi
106 I6 **Trás-os-Montes e Alto Douro** *former province* N Portugal
178 I13 **Trat** *var.* Bang Phra. Trat, S Thailand
Trá Tholl, Inis *see* Inishtrahull
Traù *see* Trogir
111 T4 **Traun** Oberösterreich, N Austria
111 S5 **Traun** ≈ N Austria
Traun, Lake *see* Traunsee
103 N23 **Traunreut** Bayern, SE Germany
111 S5 **Traunsee** *var.* Gmundner See, *Eng.* Lake Traun. ◎ N Austria
Trautenau *see* Trutnov
23 P11 **Travelers Rest** South Carolina, SE USA
190 L8 **Travellers Lake** *seasonal lake* New South Wales, SE Australia
33 P6 **Traverse City** Michigan, N USA
31 R7 **Traverse, Lake** ◎ Minnesota/South Dakota, N USA
193 I16 **Travers, Mount** ▲ South Island, NZ
9 P17 **Travers Reservoir** ⊠ Alberta, SW Canada
178 Jj15 **Tra Vinh** *var.* Phu Vinh. Tra Vinh, S Vietnam
27 S10 **Travis, Lake** ⊠ Texas, SW USA
114 H12 **Travnik** C Bosnia and Herzegovina
xli P14 **Trawden** Lancashire, NW England, UK
xxxv H6 **Trawsfynydd** Gwynedd, NW Wales, UK
111 V11 **Trbovlje** *Ger.* Trifail. C Slovenia
25 V13 **Treasure Island** Florida, SE USA
Treasure State *see* Montana
195 S14 **Treasury Islands** *island group* NW Solomon Islands
108 D9 **Trebbia** *anc.* Trebia. ≈ NW Italy
102 N8 **Trebel** ≈ NE Germany
105 O16 **Trèbes** Aude, S France
Trebia *see* Trebbia
113 F18 **Třebíč** *Ger.* Trebitsch. Jižní Morava, S Czech Republic
115 I16 **Trebinje** S Bosnia and Herzegovina
Trebišnica *see* Trebišnjica
115 H16 **Trebišnjica** *var.* Trebišnica. ≈ S Bosnia and Herzegovina
113 N20 **Trebišov** *Hung.* Tőketerebes. Východné Slovensko, E Slovakia
Trebitsch *see* Třebíč
Trebizond *see* Trabzon
Trebnitz *see* Trzebnica
111 V12 **Trebnje** SE Slovenia
113 D19 **Třeboň** *Ger.* Wittingau. Jižní Čechy, S Czech Republic
106 J15 **Trebujena** Andalucía, S Spain
xxxv J12 **Trecastle** Powys, C Wales, UK
xxxv J13 **Tredegar** Blaenau Gwent, SE Wales, UK
xxxvi L17 **Treen** Cornwall, SW England, UK
102 I7 **Treene** ≈ N Germany
Tree Planters State *see* Nebraska
xxxv I9 **Trefeglwys** Powys, C Wales, UK
111 S9 **Treffen** Kärnten, S Austria
xxxv C13 **Treffgarne** Pembrokeshire, SW Wales, UK
xxxv J4 **Trefnant** Denbighshire, N Wales, UK
xxxviii G8 **Trefonen** Shropshire, W England, UK
xxxv F4 **Trefor** Isle of Anglesey, NW Wales, UK
Trefynwy *see* Monmouth
xxxv H11 **Tregaron** Ceredigion, W Wales, UK
xxxvi C16 **Tregony** Cornwall, SW England, UK
104 G5 **Tréguier** Côtes d'Armor, NW France
xxxv J8 **Tregynon** Powys, C Wales, UK
xliii H15 **Treig, Loch** ◎ NW Scotland, UK
63 G18 **Treinta y Tres** Treinta y Tres, E Uruguay
63 F18 **Treinta y Tres** ◆ *department* E Uruguay
116 F9 **Treklyanska Reka** ≈ W Bulgaria
175 R10 **Treko, Kepulauan** *island group* N Indonesia
104 K8 **Trélazé** Maine-et-Loire, NW France
65 K17 **Trelew** Chubut, SE Argentina
97 K23 **Trelleborg** *var.* Trälleborg. Malmöhus, S Sweden
xxxv L14 **Trelleck** Monmouthshire, SE Wales, UK
115 P15 **Trem** ▲ SE Yugoslavia
xxxv F7 **Tremadog Bay** *bay* NW Wales, UK
13 N11 **Tremblant, Mont** ▲ Québec, SE Canada
101 H17 **Tremelo** Vlaams Brabant, C Belgium
109 M15 **Tremiti, Isole** *island group* SE Italy
32 K12 **Tremont** Illinois, N USA
38 L1 **Tremonton** Utah, W USA
107 U4 **Tremp** Cataluña, NE Spain
32 J7 **Trempealeau** Wisconsin, N USA
13 P8 **Trenche** ≈ Québec, SE Canada
13 O7 **Trenche, Lac** ◎ Québec, SE Canada
113 I19 **Trenčín** *Ger.* Trentschin, *Hung.* Trencsén. Západné Slovensko, W Slovakia
Trencsén *see* Trenčín
Trengganu *see* Terengganu
63 A21 **Trenque Lauquen** Buenos Aires, E Argentina
xxxvi L12 **Trent** Somerset, SW England, UK
xxxviii M8 **Trent** ≈ C England, UK
12 J14 **Trent** ≈ Ontario, SE Canada
Trent *see* Trento
108 F5 **Trentino-Alto Adige** *prev.* Venezia Tridentina. ◆ *region* N Italy
108 G6 **Trento** *Eng.* Trent, *Ger.* Trient; *anc.* Tridentum. Trentino-Alto Adige, N Italy
12 J15 **Trenton** Ontario, SE Canada
25 V10 **Trenton** Florida, SE USA
25 R1 **Trenton** Georgia, SE USA
33 S10 **Trenton** Michigan, N USA
29 S2 **Trenton** Missouri, C USA
30 M17 **Trenton** Nebraska, C USA
20 J15 **Trenton** *state capital* New Jersey, NE USA
23 W10 **Trenton** North Carolina, SE USA
22 G9 **Trenton** Tennessee, S USA
38 L1 **Trenton** Utah, W USA
Trentschin *see* Trenčín
xxxv I14 **Treorchy** Rhondda Cynon Taff, S Wales, UK
Treptow an der Rega *see* Trzebiatów
63 C23 **Tres Arroyos** Buenos Aires, E Argentina
63 J15 **Três Cachoeiras** Rio Grande do Sul, S Brazil
xxxvi I17 **Tresco** *island* SW England, UK
108 E7 **Trescore Balneario** Lombardia, N Italy
43 V17 **Tres Cruces, Cerro** ▲ SE Mexico
59 K18 **Tres Cruces, Cordillera** ▲ W Bolivia
xliii D17 **Treshnish Isles** *island group* W Scotland, UK
xxxvi C16 **Tresillian** Cornwall, SW England, UK
115 N18 **Treska** ≈ NW FYR Macedonia
115 I14 **Treskavica** ▲ SE Bosnia and Herzegovina
61 J20 **Três Lagoas** Mato Grosso do Sul, SW Brazil
42 H12 **Tres Marías, Islas** *island group* C Mexico
61 M19 **Três Marias, Represa** ⊠ SE Brazil
65 F20 **Tres Montes, Península** *headland* S Chile
107 O3 **Trespaderne** Castilla-León, N Spain
62 G13 **Três Passos** Rio Grande do Sul, S Brazil
63 A23 **Tres Picos, Cerro** ▲ E Argentina
65 G17 **Tres Picos, Cerro** ▲ SW Argentina
62 I12 **Três Pinheiros** Paraná, S Brazil
61 M21 **Três Pontas** Minas Gerais, SE Brazil
Tres Puntas, Cabo *see* Manabique, Punta
62 P9 **Três Rios** Rio de Janeiro, SE Brazil
xlii I4 **Tresta** Shetland Islands, NE Scotland, UK
Tres Tabernae *see* Saverne
Trestenberg/Trestendorf *see* Tăşnad
43 R15 **Tres Valles** Veracruz-Llave, SE Mexico
xxxv J13 **Tretower** Powys, C Wales, UK
96 H12 **Tretten** Oppland, S Norway
Treuburg *see* Olecko
103 K21 **Treuchtlingen** Bayern, S Germany
xxxv K5 **Treuddyn** Flintshire, N Wales, UK
102 N13 **Treuenbrietzen** Brandenburg, E Germany
97 F16 **Treungen** Telemark, S Norway
65 H17 **Trevelín** Chubut, SW Argentina
Treves/Trèves *see* Trier
108 H13 **Trevi** Umbria, C Italy
108 E7 **Treviglio** Lombardia, N Italy
106 J4 **Trevinca, Peña** ▲ NW Spain
107 P3 **Treviño** Castilla-León, N Spain
108 I7 **Treviso** *anc.* Tarvisium. Veneto, NE Italy
xxxvi B15 **Trevose Head** *headland* SW England, UK
Trg *see* Feldkirchen in Kärnten
191 P17 **Triabunna** Tasmania, SE Australia
23 W4 **Triangle** Virginia, NE USA
85 L18 **Triangle** Masvingo, SE Zimbabwe
117 L23 **Tría Nisía** *island* Kykládes, Greece, Aegean Sea
Triberg *see* Triberg im Schwarzwald
103 G23 **Triberg im Schwarzwald** *var.* Triberg. Baden-Württemberg, SW Germany
159 P11 **Tribhuvan** ✕ (Kathmandu) Central, C Nepal
56 C9 **Tribugá, Golfo de** *gulf* W Colombia
189 W4 **Tribulation, Cape** *headland* Queensland, NE Australia
110 M8 **Tribulaun** ▲ SW Austria
9 U17 **Tribune** Saskatchewan, S Canada
28 H5 **Tribune** Kansas, C USA
109 N18 **Tricarico** Basilicata, S Italy
109 Q19 **Tricase** Puglia, SE Italy
Trichinopoly *see* Tiruchchirāppalli
117 D18 **Trichonída, Límni** ◎ C Greece
161 G22 **Trichūr** *var.* Thrissur. Kerala, SW India
Tricorno *see* Triglav
191 O8 **Trida** New South Wales, SE Australia
37 S1 **Trident Peak** ▲ Nevada, W USA
Tridentum/Trient *see* Trento
111 T6 **Trieben** Steiermark, SE Austria
103 D19 **Trier** *Eng.* Treves, *Fr.* Trèves; *anc.* Augusta Treverorum. Rheinland-Pfalz, SW Germany
108 K7 **Trieste** *Slvn.* Trst. Friuli-Venezia Giulia, NE Italy
Trieste, Golfo di/Triest, Golf von *see* Trieste, Gulf of
108 J8 **Trieste, Gulf of** *Cro.* Tršćanski Zaljev, *Ger.* Golf von Triest, *It.* Golfo di Trieste, *Slvn.* Tržaški Zaliv. *gulf* S Europe
111 W4 **Triesting** ≈ W Austria
Trifail *see* Trbovlje
118 L9 **Trifeşti** Iaşi, NE Romania
111 S10 **Triglav** *It.* Tricorno. ▲ NW Slovenia
106 I14 **Trigueros** Andalucía, S Spain
117 E16 **Tríkala** *prev.* Trikkala. Thessalía, C Greece
117 E17 **Trikeriótis** ≈ C Greece
Trikkala *see* Tríkala
Trikomo/Tríkomon *see* Iskele
xliv J8 **Trim** *Ir.* Baile Átha Troim. Meath, E Ireland
110 E7 **Trimbach** Solothurn, NW Switzerland
xli S8 **Trimdon** Durham, N England, UK
xli X5 **Trimdon Colliery** Durham, N England, UK
xxxix X7 **Trimingham** Norfolk, E England, UK
111 Q5 **Trimmelkam** Oberösterreich, N Austria
31 U11 **Trimont** Minnesota, N USA
Trimontium *see* Plovdiv
Trinacria *see* Sicilia
161 K24 **Trincomalee** *var.* Trinkomali. Eastern Province, NE Sri Lanka
67 K16 **Trindade, Ilha da** *island* Brazil, W Atlantic Ocean
49 Y9 **Trindade Spur** *undersea feature* SW Atlantic Ocean
113 J17 **Třinec** *Ger.* Trzynietz. Severní Morava, E Czech Republic
xxxvii S7 **Tring** Hertfordshire, SE England, UK
59 M16 **Trinidad** Beni, N Bolivia
56 H9 **Trinidad** Casanare, E Colombia
46 E6 **Trinidad** Sancti Spíritus, C Cuba
39 U8 **Trinidad** Colorado, C USA
63 E19 **Trinidad** Flores, S Uruguay
47 Y17 **Trinidad** *island* C Trinidad and Tobago
Trinidad *see* Jose Abad Santos
47 Y16 **Trinidad and Tobago** *off.* Republic of Trinidad and Tobago. ◆ *republic* SE West Indies
65 F22 **Trinidad, Golfo** *gulf* S Chile
63 B24 **Trinidad, Isla** *island* E Argentina
109 N16 **Trinitapoli** Puglia, SE Italy
57 X10 **Trinité, Montagnes de la** ▲ C French Guiana
xxxvii X17 **Trinity** Jersey, Channel Islands
27 W9 **Trinity** Texas, SW USA
11 U12 **Trinity Bay** *inlet* Newfoundland, Newfoundland and Labrador, E Canada
41 P15 **Trinity Islands** *island group* Alaska, USA
37 N2 **Trinity Mountains** ▲ California, W USA
37 S4 **Trinity Peak** ▲ Nevada, W USA
37 S5 **Trinity Range** ▲ Nevada, W USA
37 N2 **Trinity River** ≈ California, W USA
27 V8 **Trinity River** ≈ Texas, SW USA
Trinkomali *see* Trincomalee
181 Y15 **Triolet** NW Mauritius
109 O20 **Trionto, Capo** *headland* S Italy
173 Ee4 **Tripa, Krueng** ≈ Sumatera, NW Indonesia
117 J16 **Trípiti, Ákra** *headland* Ágios Efstrátios, E Greece
144 G6 **Tripoli** *var.* Țarābulus, Țarābulus ash Shām, Trâblous; *anc.* Tripolis. N Lebanon
31 X12 **Tripoli** Iowa, C USA
Tripoli *see* Țarābulus
117 F20 **Trípoli** *prev.* Trípolis. Pelopónnisos, S Greece
Tripolis *see* Tripoli, Lebanon
Trípolis *see* Trípoli, Greece
31 Q12 **Tripp** South Dakota, N USA
159 V15 **Tripura** *var.* Hill Tippera. ◆ *state* NE India
110 K8 **Trisanna** ≈ W Austria
102 H8 **Trischen** *island* NW Germany
67 M24 **Tristan da Cunha** ◇ *dependency of Saint Helena* SE Atlantic Ocean
69 P15 **Tristan da Cunha** *island* SE Atlantic Ocean
67 L18 **Tristan da Cunha Fracture Zone** *tectonic feature* S Atlantic Ocean
178 J14 **Tri Tôn** An Giang, S Vietnam
178 U11 **Triton Island** *island* S Paracel Islands
161 G24 **Trivandrum** *var.* Thiruvanathapuram. Kerala, SW India
113 H20 **Trnava** *Ger.* Tyrnau, *Hung.* Nagyszombat. Západné Slovensko, W Slovakia
Trnovo *see* Veliko Tŭrnovo
Trobriand Island *see* Kiriwina Island
Trobriand Islands *see* Kiriwina Islands
9 Q16 **Trochu** Alberta, SW Canada
111 U7 **Trofaiach** Steiermark, SE Austria
95 F14 **Trofors** Troms, N Norway
115 E14 **Trogir** *It.* Traù. Split-Dalmacija, S Croatia
114 F13 **Troglav** ▲ Bosnia and Herzegovina/Croatia
109 M16 **Troia** Puglia, SE Italy
109 K24 **Troina** Sicilia, Italy, C Mediterranean Sea
181 O16 **Trois-Bassins** W Réunion
103 E17 **Troisdorf** Nordrhein-Westfalen, W Germany
76 H5 **Trois Fourches, Cap des** *headland* NE Morocco
13 T8 **Trois-Pistoles** Québec, SE Canada
101 L21 **Trois-Ponts** Liège, E Belgium
13 P11 **Trois-Rivières** Québec, SE Canada
57 Y12 **Trois Sauts** S French Guiana
101 M22 **Troisvierges** Diekirch, N Luxembourg
125 Ee12 **Troitsk** Chelyabinskaya Oblast', S Russian Federation
129 T9 **Troitsko-Pechorsk** Respublika Komi, NW Russian Federation
131 V7 **Troitskoye** Orenburgskaya Oblast', W Russian Federation
Troki *see* Trakai
96 F9 **Trolla** ▲ S Norway
97 J18 **Trollhättan** Älvsborg, S Sweden
96 G9 **Trollheimen** ▲ S Norway
96 E9 **Trolltindane** ▲ S Norway
60 H11 **Trombetas, Rio** ≈ NE Brazil
132 L16 **Tromelin, Île** *island* N Réunion
94 I9 **Troms** ◆ *county* N Norway
94 I9 **Tromsø** *Fin.* Tromssa. Troms, N Norway
86 F5 **Tromsøflaket** *undersea feature* W Barents Sea
Tromssa *see* Tromsø
96 H10 **Tron** ▲ S Norway
37 U12 **Trona** California, W USA
65 G16 **Tronador, Cerro** ▲ S Chile
96 H8 **Trondheim** *Ger.* Drontheim; *prev.* Nidaros, Trondhjem. Sør-Trøndelag, S Norway
96 H7 **Trondheimsfjorden** *fjord* S Norway
Trondhjem *see* Trondheim
109 J14 **Tronto** ≈ C Italy
Troodos *see* Ólympos
124 N3 **Troódos** *var.* Troodos Mountains. ▲ C Cyprus
Troodos Mountains *see* Troódos
xliii I24 **Trool, Loch** ◎ Dumfries and Galloway, SW Scotland, UK
xliii H22 **Troon** South Ayrshire, W Scotland, UK
109 M22 **Tropea** Calabria, SW Italy
38 L7 **Tropic** Utah, W USA
66 L10 **Tropic Seamount** *var.* Banc du Tropique. *undersea feature* E Atlantic Ocean
Tropique, Banc du *see* Tropic Seamount
Tropoja *see* Tropojë
115 L17 **Tropojë** *var.* Tropoja. Kukës, N Albania
Troppau *see* Opava
97 O16 **Trosa** Södermanland, C Sweden
120 H12 **Troškūnai** Anykščiai, E Lithuania
103 G23 **Trossingen** Baden-Württemberg, SW Germany
119 T4 **Trostyanets'** *Rus.* Trostyanets. Sums'ka Oblast', NE Ukraine
119 N7 **Trostyanets'** *Rus.* Trostyanets. Vinnyts'ka Oblast', C Ukraine
118 L11 **Trotuş** ≈ E Romania
46 M8 **Trou-du-Nord** N Haiti
27 W7 **Troup** Texas, SW USA
15 H8 **Trout** ≈ Northwest Territories, NW Canada
35 N8 **Trout Creek** Montana, NW USA
34 H10 **Trout Lake** Washington, NW USA
10 B9 **Trout Lake** ◎ Ontario, S Canada
35 T12 **Trout Peak** ▲ Wyoming, C USA
104 L4 **Trouville** Calvados, N France
xxxvi M10 **Trowbridge** Wiltshire, S England, UK
25 Q6 **Troy** Alabama, S USA
29 Q3 **Troy** Kansas, C USA
29 W4 **Troy** Missouri, C USA
20 L10 **Troy** New York, NE USA
23 S10 **Troy** North Carolina, SE USA
33 R13 **Troy** Ohio, N USA
27 T9 **Troy** Texas, SW USA
116 I9 **Troyan** Loveshka Oblast, C Bulgaria
116 I9 **Troyanski Prokhod** *pass* N Bulgaria
151 N6 **Troyebratskiy** Severnyy Kazakhstan, N Kazakhstan
105 Q6 **Troyes** *anc.* Augustobona Tricassium. Aube, N France
119 X5 **Troyits'ke** Luhans'ka Oblast', E Ukraine
37 W7 **Troy Peak** ▲ Nevada, W USA
115 G15 **Trpanj** Dubrovnik-Neretva, S Croatia
Tršćanski Zaljev *see* Trieste, Gulf of
Trst *see* Trieste
115 N14 **Trstenik** Serbia, C Yugoslavia
130 I6 **Trubchevsk** Bryanskaya Oblast', W Russian Federation
Trubchular *see* Orlyak
Truc Giang *see* Bên Tre
39 S10 **Truchas Peak** ▲ New Mexico, SW USA
149 P16 **Trucial Coast** *physical region* C UAE
Trucial States *see* United Arab Emirates
37 Q6 **Truckee** California, W USA
37 R5 **Truckee River** ≈ Nevada, W USA
131 Q13 **Trudfront** Astrakhanskaya Oblast', SW Russian Federation
12 J9 **Truite, Lac à la** ◎ Québec, SE Canada
44 K4 **Trujillo** Colón, NE Honduras
58 C12 **Trujillo** La Libertad, NW Peru
106 K10 **Trujillo** Extremadura, W Spain
56 I6 **Trujillo** Trujillo, NW Venezuela
56 I6 **Trujillo** *off.* Estado Trujillo. ◆ *state* W Venezuela
Truk *see* Chuuk
Truk Islands *see* Chuuk Islands
31 U10 **Truman** Minnesota, N USA
29 X10 **Trumann** Arkansas, C USA
38 J9 **Trumbull, Mount** ▲ Arizona, SW USA
xxxix T12 **Trumpington** Cambridgeshire, E England, UK
116 F10 **Trŭn** Sofiyska Oblast, W Bulgaria
xxxix X8 **Trunch** Norfolk, E England, UK
191 Q8 **Trundle** New South Wales, SE Australia
133 U13 **Trung Phân** *physical region* S Vietnam
Trupcilar *see* Orlyak
xxxvi C16 **Truro** Cornwall, SW England, UK
11 Q15 **Truro** Nova Scotia, SE Canada
27 P5 **Truscott** Texas, SW USA
118 K9 **Truşeşti** Botoşani, NE Romania
118 H6 **Truskavets'** L'vivs'ka Oblast', W Ukraine
xliv G5 **Truskmore** ▲ N Ireland
97 H22 **Trustrup** Århus, C Denmark
8 M11 **Trutch** British Columbia, W Canada
39 Q14 **Truth Or Consequences** New Mexico, SW USA
113 F15 **Trutnov** *Ger.* Trautenau. Východní Čechy, NE Czech Republic
105 P13 **Truyère** ≈ C France
xxxv E7 **Trwyn Cilan** *headland* NW Wales, UK
116 K9 **Tryavna** Loveshka Oblast, C Bulgaria
30 M14 **Tryon** Nebraska, C USA
96 J12 **Trysil** Hedmark, S Norway
96 I11 **Trysilelva** ≈ S Norway
114 D10 **Tržac** NW Bosnia and Herzegovina
Tržaški Zaliv *see* Trieste, Gulf of
112 G10 **Trzcianka** *Ger.* Schönlanke. Piła, NW Poland
112 E7 **Trzebiatów** *Ger.* Treptow an der Rega. Szczecin, NW Poland
113 G14 **Trzebnica** *Ger.* Trebnitz. Wrocław, SW Poland
111 T10 **Tržič** *Ger.* Neumarktl. NW Slovenia
Trzynietz *see* Třinec
Tsabong *see* Tshabong
168 G7 **Tsagaanchuluut** Dzavhan, C Mongolia
169 P7 **Tsagaanders** Dornod, NE Mongolia
169 S8 **Tsagaannuur** Dornod, E Mongolia
168 G8 **Tsagaan-Olom** Govĭ-Altay, C Mongolia
168 J8 **Tsagaan-Ovoo** Övörhangay, C Mongolia
168 D5 **Tsagaantüngi** Bayan-Ölgiy, NW Mongolia
131 P12 **Tsagan Aman** Respublika Kalmykiya, SW Russian Federation
25 V11 **Tsala Apopka Lake** ◎ Florida, SE USA
Tsamkong *see* Zhanjiang
Tsangpo *see* Brahmaputra
168 L9 **Tsant** Dundgovĭ, C Mongolia
85 G17 **Tsao** Ngamiland, NW Botswana
180 I4 **Tsaratanana** Mahajanga, C Madagascar
116 N10 **Tsarevo** *prev.* Michurin. Burgaska Oblast, SE Bulgaria
Tsarigrad *see* İstanbul
Tsaritsyn *see* Volgograd
128 G13 **Tsarskoye Selo** *prev.* Pushkin. Leningradskaya Oblast', NW Russian Federation
119 T7 **Tsarychanka** Dnipropetrovs'ka Oblast', E Ukraine
85 H21 **Tsatsu** Southern, S Botswana
83 J20 **Tsavo** Coast, S Kenya
85 E21 **Tsawisis** Karas, S Namibia
Tschakathurn *see* Čakovec
Tschaslau *see* Čáslav
Tschenstochau *see* Częstochowa
Tschernembl *see* Črnomelj
30 K6 **Tschida, Lake** ⊠ North Dakota, N USA
Tschorna *see* Mustvee
85 I17 **Tsebanana** Central, NE Botswana
168 G8 **Tseel** Govĭ-Altay, SW Mongolia
130 M13 **Tselina** Rostovskaya Oblast', SW Russian Federation
Tselinograd/Tselinogradskaya Oblast *see* Akmola
168 J6 **Tsengel** Hövsgöl, N Mongolia
168 E7 **Tsenher** Hovd, W Mongolia
152 E12 **Tsentral'nyye Nizmennyye Garagumy** *Turkm.* Merkezi Garagum. *desert* C Turkmenistan
85 E21 **Tses** Karas, S Namibia
Tseshevlya *see* Tsyeshawlya
168 E7 **Tsetsegnuur** Hovd, W Mongolia
168 J7 **Tsetserleg** Arhangay, C Mongolia
79 R16 **Tsévié** S Togo
85 G21 **Tshabong** *var.* Tsabong. Kgalagadi, SW Botswana
85 G20 **Tshane** Kgalagadi, SW Botswana
Tshangalele, Lac *see* Lufira, Lac de Retenue de la
85 H17 **Tshauxaba** Central, C Botswana
81 F21 **Tshela** Bas-Zaïre, W Zaire
81 K22 **Tshibala** Kasai Occidental, S Zaire
81 J22 **Tshikapa** Kasai Occidental, SW Zaire
81 L22 **Tshilenge** Kasai Oriental, S Zaire
81 L24 **Tshimbalanga** Shaba, S Zaire
81 L22 **Tshimbulu** Kasai Occidental, S Zaire
Tshiumbe *see* Chiumbe
81 M21 **Tshofa** Kasai Oriental, C Zaire
81 K18 **Tshuapa** ≈ C Zaire
Tshwane *see* Pretoria
116 G7 **Tsibritsa** ≈ NW Bulgaria
Tsien Tang *see* Puyang Jiang
116 I12 **Tsigansko Gradishte** ▲ Bulgaria/Greece
14 G3 **Tsiigehtchic** *prev.* Arctic Red River. Northwest Territories, NW Canada
129 Q7 **Tsil'ma** ≈ NW Russian Federation
121 J17 **Tsimkavichy** *Rus.* Timkovichi. Minskaya Voblasts', C Belorussia
130 M11 **Tsimlyansk** Rostovskaya Oblast', SW Russian Federation
131 N11 **Tsimlyanskoye Vodokhranilishche** *var.* Tsimlyansk Vodoskhovshche, *Eng.* Tsimlyansk Reservoir ⊠ SW Russian Federation
Tsimlyansk Reservoir *see* Tsimlyanskoye Vodokhranilishche
Tsimlyansk Vodoskhovshche *see* Tsimlyanskoye Vodokhranilishche
Tsinan *see* Jinan
Tsing Hai *see* Qinghai Hu, China
Tsinghai *see* Qinghai, China
Tsingtao/Tsingtau *see* Qingdao
Tsingyuan *see* Baoding
Tsinkiang *see* Quanzhou
Tsintao *see* Qingdao
85 D17 **Tsintsabis** Otjikoto, N Namibia
180 H8 **Tsiombe** *var.* Tsihombe. Toliara, S Madagascar
126 Kk14 **Tsipa** ≈ S Russian Federation
180 H5 **Tsiribihina** ≈ W Madagascar
180 I5 **Tsiroanomandidy** Antananarivo, C Madagascar
201 U13 **Tsis** *island* Chuuk, C Micronesia
Tsitsihar *see* Qiqihar
131 Q3 **Tsivil'sk** Chuvashskaya Respublika, W Russian Federation
143 T9 **Ts'khinvali** *prev.* Staliniri. C Georgia
121 J19 **Tsna** ≈ SW Belorussia
128 I15 **Tsna** *var.* Zna. ≈ W Russian Federation
168 K11 **Tsoohor** Ömnögovĭ, S Mongolia
171 H16 **Tsu** *var.* Tu. Mie, Honshū, SW Japan
171 K13 **Tsubame** *var.* Tubame. Niigata, Honshū, C Japan
171 Ii13 **Tsubata** Ishikawa, Honshū, SW Japan
172 Q6 **Tsubetsu** Hokkaidō, NE Japan
171 Kk16 **Tsuchiura** *var.* Tutiura. Ibaraki, Honshū, S Japan
172 N7 **Tsugaru-kaikyō** *strait* N Japan
171 Kk13 **Tsugawa** Niigata, Honshū, C Japan
172 Oo5 **Tsukigata** Hokkaidō, NE Japan
170 Dd15 **Tsukumi** *var.* Tukumi. Ōita, Kyūshū, SW Japan
168 E5 **Tsul-Ulaan** Bayan-Ölgiy, W Mongolia
85 D17 **Tsumeb** Otjikoto, N Namibia
85 F17 **Tsumkwe** Otjozondjupa, NE Namibia
170 Cc16 **Tsuno** Miyazaki, Kyūshū, SW Japan
170 D11 **Tsuno-shima** *island* SW Japan
171 H14 **Tsuruga** *var.* Turuga. Fukui, Honshū, SW Japan
170 F15 **Tsurugi-san** ▲ Shikoku, SW Japan
170 Dd15 **Tsurumi-zaki** *headland* Kyūshū, SW Japan
171 L11 **Tsuruoka** *var.* Turuoka. Yamagata, Honshū, C Japan
171 Hh15 **Tsushima** *var.* Tusima. Aichi, Honshū, SW Japan
170 C10 **Tsushima** *var.* Tsushima-tō, Tusima. *island group* SW Japan
Tsushima-tō *see* Tsushima
170 E12 **Tsuwano** Shimane, Honshū, SW Japan
170 Ff13 **Tsuyama** *var.* Tsuyama. Okayama, Honshū, SW Japan
85 G19 **Tswaane** Ghanzi, W Botswana

◆ Country ● Country Capital ◇ Dependent Territory ○ Dependent Territory Capital ◆ Administrative Region ✕ International Airport ▲ Mountain ▲ Mountain Range Volcano ≈ River ◎ Lake ⊠ Reservoir

TSYAKHTSIN – UCKFIELD

121 N16 **Tsyakhtsin** *Rus.* Tekhtin. Mahilyowskaya Voblasts', E Belorussia
121 P19 **Tsyerakhowka** *Rus.* Terekhovka. Homyel'skaya Voblasts', SE Belorussia
121 P17 **Tsyeshawlya** *Rus.* Cheshevlya, Tseshevlya. Brestskaya Voblasts', SW Belorussia
Tsyurupinsk *see* Tsyurupyns'k
119 R10 **Tsyurupyns'k** *Rus.* Tsyurupinsk. Khersons'ka Oblast', S Ukraine
Tu *see* Tsu
194 H13 **Tua** C PNG
99 **Tuaim** *see* Tuam
192 L6 **Tuakau** Waikato, North Island, NZ
xliv F8 **Tuam** *Ir.* Tuaim. Galway, W Ireland
193 K14 **Tuamarina** Marlborough, South Island, NZ
Tuamotu, Archipel des *see* Tuamotu, Îles
199 M10 **Tuamotu Fracture Zone** *tectonic feature* E Pacific Ocean
203 W9 **Tuamotu, Îles** *var.* Archipel des Tuamotu, Dangerous Archipelago, Tuamotu Islands. *island group* N French Polynesia
Tuamotu Islands *see* Tuamotu, Îles
183 X10 **Tuamotu Ridge** *undersea feature* C Pacific Ocean
178 I15 **Tuân Giao** Lai Châu, N Vietnam
179 P8 **Tuao** Luzon, N Philippines
202 B15 **Tuapa** NW Niue
45 N7 **Tuapí** Región Autónoma Atlántico Norte, NE Nicaragua
130 K15 **Tuapse** Krasnodarskiy Kray, SW Russian Federation
175 Nn2 **Tuaran** Sabah, East Malaysia
106 I6 **Tua, Rio** N Portugal
198 B7 **Tuasivi** Savai'i, C Western Samoa
193 B24 **Tuatapere** Southland, South Island, NZ
38 M9 **Tuba City** Arizona, SW USA
144 H11 **Ṭūbah, Qaṣr aṭ** *castle* Ma'ān, C Jordan
Tubame *see* Tsubame
174 Ll14 **Tuban** *prev.* Toeban. Jawa, C Indonesia
147 O16 **Tuban, Wādī** *dry watercourse* SW Yemen
63 K14 **Tubarão** Santa Catarina, S Brazil
100 O10 **Tubbergen** Overijssel, E Netherlands
Tubeke *see* Tubize
103 H22 **Tübingen** *var.* Tuebingen. Baden-Württemberg, SW Germany
131 W6 **Tubinskiy** Respublika Bashkortostan, W Russian Federation
101 G19 **Tubize** *Dut.* Tubeke. Walloon Brabant, C Belgium
78 J16 **Tubmanburg** NW Liberia
179 Qq15 **Tubod** Mindanao, S Philippines
77 T7 **Ṭubruq** *Eng.* Tobruk, *It.* Tobruch. NE Libya
203 T13 **Tubuai** *island* Îles Australes, SW French Polynesia
Tubuai, Îles/Tubuai Islands *see* Australes, Îles
42 F3 **Tubutama** Sonora, NW Mexico
56 K4 **Tucacas** Falcón, N Venezuela
61 P16 **Tucano** Bahia, E Brazil
59 P19 **Tucavaca, Río** E Bolivia
112 H8 **Tuchola** Bydgoszcz, NW Poland
113 M17 **Tuchów** Tarnów, SE Poland
25 S3 **Tucker** Georgia, SE USA
29 W10 **Tuckerman** Arkansas, C USA
66 B12 **Tucker's Town** E Bermuda
Tuckum *see* Tukums
38 M15 **Tucson** Arizona, SW USA
64 J7 **Tucumán** *off.* Provincia de Tucumán. ◆ *province* N Argentina
Tucumán *see* San Miguel de Tucumán
39 V11 **Tucumcari** New Mexico, SW USA
60 H13 **Tucunaré** Pará, N Brazil
57 Q6 **Tucupita** Delta Amacuro, NE Venezuela
60 K13 **Tucuruí, Represa de** ⊠ NE Brazil
112 F9 **Tuczno** Piła, NW Poland
xxxix X13 **Tuddenham** Suffolk, E England, UK
Tuddo *see* Tudu
107 Q5 **Tudela** *Basq.* Tutera; *anc.* Tutela. Navarra, N Spain
106 M6 **Tudela de Duero** Castilla-León, N Spain
144 K6 **Tudmur** *var.* Tadmur, Tamar, *Gk.* Palmyra; *Bibl.* Tadmor. Ḥimṣ, C Syria
120 J4 **Tudu** *Ger.* Tuddo. Lääne-Virumaa, NE Estonia
xxxv E6 **Tudweiliog** Gwynedd, NW Wales, UK
Tuebingen *see* Tübingen
126 H16 **Tuekta** Respublika Altay, S Russian Federation
106 I5 **Tuela, Rio** N Portugal
159 X12 **Tuensang** Nāgāland, NE India
142 L15 **Tufanbeyli** Adana, C Turkey
Tüffer *see* Laško
194 M15 **Tufi** Northern, S PNG
199 L3 **Tufts Plain** *undersea feature* N Pacific Ocean
Tugalan *see* Kolkhozobod
69 V14 **Tugela** SE South Africa
23 P6 **Tug Fork** S USA
41 P15 **Tugidak Island** *island* Trinity Islands, Alaska, USA
179 P8 **Tuguegarao** Luzon, N Philippines
127 N13 **Tugur** Khabarovskiy Kray, SE Russian Federation
167 P4 **Tuhai He** E China
106 G4 **Tui** Galicia, NW Spain
79 O13 **Tui** *var.* Grand Balé. W Burkina
59 J16 **Tuichi, Río** W Bolivia
66 Q11 **Tuineje** Fuerteventura, Islas Canarias, Spain, NE Atlantic Ocean
45 X16 **Tuira, Río** SE Panama
Tuisarkan *see* Tūysarkān
Tujiabu *see* Yongxiu
131 W5 **Tukan** Respublika Bashkortostan, W Russian Federation
175 R13 **Tukangbesi, Kepulauan** *Dut.* Toekang Besi Eilanden. *island group* C Indonesia
153 V13 **Tŭkhtamish** *Rus.* Toktomush, *prev.* Tokhtamyshbek. SE Tajikistan
192 O12 **Tukituki** North Island, NZ
Tu-k'ou *see* Panzhihua
124 N15 **Tūkrah** NE Libya
14 G2 **Tuktoyaktuk** Northwest Territories, NW Canada
173 Ff6 **Tuktuk** Pulau Samosir, W Indonesia
Tukumi *see* Tsukumi
120 E9 **Tukums** *Ger.* Tuckum. Tukums, W Latvia
83 G24 **Tukuyu** *prev.* Neu-Langenburg. Mbeya, S Tanzania
Tukzār *see* Tokzār
43 O13 **Tula** *var.* Tula de Allende. Hidalgo, C Mexico
43 O11 **Tula** Tamaulipas, C Mexico
130 K5 **Tula** Tul'skaya Oblast', W Russian Federation
Tulach Mhór *see* Tullamore
Tula de Allende *see* Tula
165 N10 **Tulage Ar Gol** W China
195 X15 **Tulaghi** *var.* Tulagi. Florida Islands, C Solomon Islands
Tulagi *see* Tulaghi
43 P13 **Tulancingo** Hidalgo, C Mexico
37 R11 **Tulare** California, W USA
31 P9 **Tulare** South Dakota, N USA
37 Q12 **Tulare Lake Bed** *salt flat* California, W USA
39 S14 **Tularosa** New Mexico, SW USA
39 P13 **Tularosa Mountains** ▲ New Mexico, SW USA
39 S15 **Tularosa Valley** *basin* New Mexico, SW USA
85 E25 **Tulbagh** Western Cape, SW South Africa
58 C5 **Tulcán** Carchi, N Ecuador
119 N13 **Tulcea** Tulcea, E Romania
119 N13 **Tulcea** ◆ *county* SE Romania
Tul'chin *see* Tul'chyn
119 N7 **Tul'chyn** *Rus.* Tul'chin. Vinnyts'ka Oblast', C Ukraine
Tuléar *see* Toliara
37 O1 **Tulelake** California, W USA
118 J10 **Tulgheş** *Hung.* Gyergyótölgyes. Harghita, C Romania
Tul'govichi *see* Tul'havichy
121 N20 **Tul'havichy** *Rus.* Tul'govichi. Homyel'skaya Voblasts', SE Belorussia
Tuli *see* Thuli
27 N4 **Tulia** Texas, SW USA
xliv F10 **Tulla** Clare, W Ireland
22 J10 **Tullahoma** Tennessee, S USA
xliii H16 **Tulla, Loch** W Scotland, UK
191 R12 **Tullamarine** ✕ (Melbourne) Victoria, SE Australia
xliv I9 **Tullamore** *Ir.* Tulach Mhór. Offaly, C Ireland
191 Q7 **Tullamore** New South Wales, SE Australia
105 N12 **Tulle** *anc.* Tutela. Corrèze, C France
xliii K19 **Tullibody** Clackmannan, C Scotland, UK
111 X3 **Tulln** *var.* Oberhollabrunn. Niederösterreich, NE Austria
111 W4 **Tulln** NE Austria
xlii O12 **Tulloch** Aberdeenshire, NE Scotland, UK
24 H6 **Tullos** Louisiana, S USA
xliv J11 **Tullow** *Ir.* An Tullach. Carlow, SE Ireland
xliv H5 **Tully** Fermanagh, SW Northern Ireland, UK
189 W5 **Tully** Queensland, NE Australia
128 J3 **Tuloma** NW Russian Federation
116 K10 **Tulovo** Khaskovska Oblast, C Bulgaria
29 P9 **Tulsa** Oklahoma, C USA
159 N11 **Tulsipur** Mid Western, W Nepal
xliv G7 **Tulsk** Roscommon, C Ireland
130 K6 **Tul'skaya Oblast'** ◆ *province* W Russian Federation
130 L14 **Tul'skiy** Respublika Adygeya, SW Russian Federation
194 K8 **Tulu** Manus Island, N PNG
56 D10 **Tuluá** Valle del Cauca, W Colombia
118 M12 **Tulucești** Galați, E Romania
41 N12 **Tuluksak** Alaska, USA
43 Z12 **Tulum, Ruinas de** *ruins* Quintana Roo, SE Mexico
126 Ii15 **Tulun** Irkutskaya Oblast', S Russian Federation
174 Ll15 **Tulungagung** *prev.* Toeloengagoeng. Jawa, C Indonesia
195 S11 **Tulun Islands** *var.* Kilinailau Islands; *prev.* Carteret Islands. *island group* NE PNG
130 M4 **Tuma** Ryazanskaya Oblast', W Russian Federation
56 B12 **Tumaco** Nariño, SW Colombia
56 B12 **Tumaco, Bahía de** *bay* SW Colombia
Tuman-gang *see* Tumen
44 L8 **Tuma, Río** N Nicaragua
97 O16 **Tumba** Stockholm, C Sweden
Tumba, Lac *see* Ntomba, Lac
174 M9 **Tumbangsenamang** Borneo, C Indonesia
191 Q10 **Tumbarumba** New South Wales, SE Australia
58 A8 **Tumbes** Tumbes, NW Peru
58 A9 **Tumbes** *off.* Departamento de Tumbes. ◆ *department* NW Peru
xxxv G13 **Tumble** Carmarthenshire, S Wales, UK
21 P5 **Tumbledown Mountain** ▲ Maine, NE USA
9 N13 **Tumbler Ridge** British Columbia, W Canada
178 I12 **Tumbôt, Phnum** ▲ W Cambodia
190 G9 **Tumby Bay** South Australia
169 Y10 **Tumen** Jilin, NE China
169 Y11 **Tumen** *Chin.* Tumen Jiang, *Kor.* Tuman-gang, *Rus.* Tumyn'tszyan. E Asia
Tumen Jiang *see* Tumen
57 Q8 **Tumeremo** Bolívar, E Venezuela
161 G19 **Tumkūr** Karnātaka, W India
xliii K16 **Tummel** C Scotland, UK
xliii K16 **Tummel Bridge** Perth and Kinross, C Scotland, UK
xliii K16 **Tummel, Loch** C Scotland, UK
196 B15 **Tumon Bay** *bay* W Guam
79 P14 **Tumu** NW Ghana
60 I10 **Tumuc Humac Mountains** *var.* Serra Tumucumaque. ▲ N South America
Tumucumaque, Serra *see* Tumuc Humac Mountains
191 Q10 **Tumut** New South Wales, SE Australia
Tumyn'tszyan *see* Tumen
Tün *see* Ferdows
47 U14 **Tunapuna** Trinidad, Trinidad and Tobago
62 K11 **Tunas** Paraná, S Brazil
Tunbridge Wells *see* Royal Tunbridge Wells
116 L11 **Tunca Nehri** *Bul.* Tundzha. Bulgaria/Turkey *see also* Tundzha
143 O14 **Tunceli** *var.* Kalan. Tunceli, E Turkey
143 O14 **Tunceli** ◆ *province* C Turkey
158 J12 **Tūndla** Uttar Pradesh, N India
83 I25 **Tunduru** Ruvuma, S Tanzania
116 L10 **Tundzha** *Turk.* Tunca Nehri. Bulgaria/Turkey *see also* Tunca Nehri
161 H17 **Tungabhadra** S India
161 F17 **Tungabhadra Reservoir** ◎ S India
203 P2 **Tungaru** *prev.* Gilbert Islands. *island group* W Kiribati
179 Q16 **Tungawan** Mindanao, S Philippines
174 Hh9 **Tungkal** Sumatera, W Indonesia
T'ung-shan *see* Xuzhou
167 Q16 **Tungsha Tao** *Chin.* Dongsha Qundao, *Eng.* Pratas Island. *island* S Taiwan
167 S13 **Tungshih** *Jap.* Tōsei. N Taiwan
14 G7 **Tungsten** Northwest Territories, W Canada
Tung-t'ing Hu *see* Dongting Hu
58 A13 **Tungurahua** ◆ *province* C Ecuador
97 F14 **Tunhovdfjorden** ◎ S Norway
24 K2 **Tunica** Mississippi, S USA
77 N5 **Tunis** *var.* Tūnis. ● (Tunisia) NE Tunisia
77 N5 **Tunis, Golfe de** *Ar.* Khalīj Tūnis. *gulf* NE Tunisia
77 N6 **Tunisia** *off.* Republic of Tunisia, *Ar.* Al Jumhūrīyah at Tūnisīyah, *Fr.* République Tunisienne. ◆ *republic* N Africa
Tūnisīyah, Al Jumhūrīyah at *see* Tunisia
Tūnis, Khalīj *see* Tunis, Golfe de
56 G9 **Tunja** Boyacá, C Colombia
95 F14 **Tunnsjøen** ◎ C Norway
xxxviii J7 **Tunstall** City of Stoke-on-Trent, C England, UK
xli X14 **Tunstall** East Riding of Yorkshire, N England, UK
xxxix Y12 **Tunstall** Suffolk, E England, UK
41 N12 **Tuntutuliak** Alaska, USA
153 U8 **Tunuk** Chuyskaya Oblast', C Kyrgyzstan
11 Q6 **Tunungayualok Island** *island* Newfoundland and Labrador, E Canada
64 H11 **Tunuyán** Mendoza, W Argentina
64 I11 **Tunuyán, Río** W Argentina
Tunxi *see* Huangshan
37 P9 **Tuolumne River** California, W USA
Tuong Buong *see* Tương Đương
178 J7 **Tương Đương** *var.* Tuong Buong. Nghê An, N Vietnam
166 I13 **Tuoniang Jiang** S China
165 N12 **Tuotuo He** C China
165 O12 **Tuotuoheyan** *var.* Tanggulashan, Togton-heyan. Qinghai, C China
Tüp *see* Tyup
62 J9 **Tupã** São Paulo, S Brazil
203 S10 **Tupai** *var.* Motu Iti. *atoll* Îles Sous le Vent, W French Polynesia
63 G15 **Tupanciretã** Rio Grande do Sul, S Brazil
24 M2 **Tupelo** Mississippi, S USA
126 L14 **Tupik** Chitinskaya Oblast', S Russian Federation
61 K18 **Tupiraçaba** Goiás, S Brazil
59 L21 **Tupiza** Potosí, S Bolivia
9 N13 **Tupper** British Columbia, W Canada
20 J8 **Tupper Lake** ◎ New York, NE USA
64 H11 **Tupungato, Volcán** ▲ W Argentina
169 T9 **Tuquan** Nei Mongol Zizhiqu, N China
56 C13 **Túquerres** Nariño, SW Colombia
159 U13 **Tura** Meghālaya, NE India
126 J10 **Tura** Evenkiyskiy Avtonomnyy Okrug, N Russian Federation
125 F11 **Tura** C Russian Federation
146 M10 **Turabah** Makkah, W Saudi Arabia
57 O8 **Turagua, Cerro** ▲ C Venezuela
192 L12 **Turakina** Manawatu-Wanganui, North Island, NZ
193 K15 **Turakirae Head** *headland* North Island, NZ
194 G13 **Turama** S PNG
126 I15 **Turan** Respublika Tyva, S Russian Federation
192 M10 **Turangi** Waikato, North Island, NZ
152 F11 **Turan Lowland** *var.* Turan Plain, *Kaz.* Turan Oypaty, *Rus.* Turanskaya Nizmennost', *Turk.* Turan Pesligi, *Uzb.* Turon Pasttekisligi. *plain* C Asia
Turan Oypaty/Turan Pesligi/ Turan Plain/Turanskaya Nizmennost' *see* Turan Lowland
144 K7 **Ṭurāq al 'Ilab** *hill range* S Syria
121 K20 **Turaw** *Rus.* Turov. Homyel'skaya Voblasts', SE Belorussia
146 L2 **Ṭurayf** Al Ḥudūd ash Shamālīyah, NW Saudi Arabia
Turba *see* Teruel
56 E5 **Turbaco** Bolívar, N Colombia
154 K15 **Turbat** Baluchistān, SW Pakistan
Turbat-i-Haidari *see* Torbat-e Ḥeydarīyeh
Turbat-i-Jam *see* Torbat-e Jām
56 D7 **Turbo** Antioquia, NW Colombia
Turčianský Svätý Martin *see* Martin
118 H10 **Turda** *Ger.* Thorenburg, *Hung.* Torda. Cluj, NW Romania
148 M7 **Ṭūreh** Markazī, W Iran
203 X12 **Tureia** *atoll* Îles Tuamotu, SE French Polynesia
112 I12 **Turek** Konin, C Poland
95 L19 **Turenki** Häme, SW Finland
Turfan *see* Turpan
151 R8 **Turgay** *Kaz.* Torghay. Akmola, W Kazakhstan
151 N10 **Turgay** *off.* Turgayskaya Oblast', *Kaz.* Torghay Oblysy. ◆ *province* C Kazakhstan
151 N10 **Turgay** *Kaz.* Torgay. C Kazakhstan
150 M8 **Turgayskaya Stolovaya Strana** *Kaz.* Torgay Üstirti. *plateau* Kazakhstan/Russian Federation
Turgel *see* Türi
116 L8 **Türgovishte** *prev.* Eski Dzhumaya. Razgradska Oblast, NE Bulgaria
142 C14 **Turgutlu** Manisa, W Turkey
142 L12 **Turhal** Tokat, N Turkey
120 H4 **Türi** *Ger.* Turgel. Järvamaa, N Estonia
107 S9 **Turia** E Spain
60 M12 **Turiaçu** Maranhão, E Brazil
Turin *see* Torino
118 I3 **Turiys'k** Volyns'ka Oblast', NW Ukraine
Turja *see* Tur"ya
126 K15 **Turka** Respublika Buryatiya, S Russian Federation
118 H6 **Turka** L'vivs'ka Oblast', W Ukraine
Turkana, Lake *see* Rudolf, Lake
151 P16 **Turkestan** *Kaz.* Türkistan. Yuzhnyy Kazakhstan, S Kazakhstan
153 Q12 **Turkestan Range** *Rus.* Turkestanskiy Khrebet. ▲ C Asia
Turkestanskiy Khrebet *see* Turkestan Range
113 M23 **Túrkeve** Jász-Nagykun-Szolnok, E Hungary
27 O4 **Turkey** Texas, SW USA
142 H14 **Turkey** *off.* Republic of Turkey, *Turk.* Türkiye Cumhuriyeti. ◆ *republic* SW Asia
189 N4 **Turkey Creek** Western Australia
28 M9 **Turkey Creek** Oklahoma, C USA
39 T9 **Turkey Mountains** ▲ New Mexico, SW USA
31 X11 **Turkey River** Iowa, C USA
131 N7 **Turki** Saratovskaya Oblast', W Russian Federation
Türkistan *see* Turkestan
Turkistan, Bandi-i *see* Torkestān, Selseleh-ye Band-e
Türkiye Cumhuriyeti *see* Turkey
Türkmen Aylagy *see* Turkmenskiy Zaliv
152 A10 **Turkmenbashi** *prev.* Krasnovodsk. Balkanskiy Velayat, W Turkmenistan
Türkmengala *see* Turkmen-kala
152 G13 **Turkmenistan** *off.* Turkmenistan; *prev.* Turkmenskaya Soviet Socialist Republic. ◆ *republic* C Asia
152 J14 **Turkmen-kala** *Turkm.* Türkmengala; *prev.* Turkmen-Kala. Maryyskiy Velayat, S Turkmenistan
Turkmenskaya Soviet Socialist Republic *see* Turkmenistan
152 A11 **Turkmenskiy Zaliv** *Turkm.* Türkmen Aylagy. *lake gulf* W Turkmenistan
142 L16 **Türkoğlu** Kahramanmaraş, S Turkey
46 L6 **Turks and Caicos Islands** ◇ *UK dependent territory* N West Indies
66 G10 **Turks and Caicos Islands** *island group* N West Indies
47 N6 **Turks Islands** *island group* SE Turks and Caicos Islands
95 K19 **Turku** *Swe.* Åbo. Turku-Pori, SW Finland
Turku ja Pori *see* Turku-Pori
95 K19 **Turku-Pori** *var.* Turku ja Pori, *Swe.* Åbo-Björneborg. ◆ *province* SW Finland
83 H17 **Turkwel** *seasonal river* NW Kenya
29 P9 **Turley** Oklahoma, C USA
37 P9 **Turlock** California, W USA
120 I12 **Turmantas** Zarasai, NE Lithuania
Turmberg *see* Wieżyca
192 N13 **Turnagain, Cape** *headland* North Island, NZ
Turnau *see* Turnov
xliii I13 **Turnberry** South Ayrshire, W Scotland, UK
44 H2 **Turneffe Islands** *island group* E Belize
20 M11 **Turners Falls** Massachusetts, NE USA
9 P16 **Turner Valley** Alberta, SW Canada
101 I16 **Turnhout** Antwerpen, N Belgium
111 V5 **Turnitz** Niederösterreich, E Austria
9 S12 **Turnor Lake** ◎ Saskatchewan, C Canada
113 E15 **Turnov** *Ger.* Turnau. Východní Čechy, N Czech Republic
Tŭrnovo *see* Veliko Tŭrnovo
118 I15 **Turnu Măgurele** *var.* Turnu-Măgurele. Teleorman, S Romania
Turnu Severin *see* Drobeta-Turnu Severin
Turócszentmárton *see* Martin
Turoni *see* Tours
Turon Pasttekisligi *see* Turan Lowland
Turov *see* Turaw
Turpakkla *see* Turpoqqal'a
164 M6 **Turpan** *var.* Turfan. Xinjiang Uygur Zizhiqu, NW China
Turpan Depression *see* Turpan Pendi
164 M6 **Turpan Pendi** *Eng.* Turpan Depression. *depression* NW China
164 M5 **Turpan Zhan** Xinjiang Uygur Zizhiqu, W China
Turpentine State *see* North Carolina
152 J10 **Turpoqqal'a** *Rus.* Turpakkla. Khorazm Wiloyati, W Uzbekistan
46 H8 **Turquino, Pico** ▲ E Cuba
29 Y10 **Turrell** Arkansas, C USA
45 N14 **Turrialba** Cartago, E Costa Rica
xlii O11 **Turriff** Aberdeenshire, NE Scotland, UK
145 V7 **Tursāq** E Iraq
Turshiz *see* Kāshmar
Tursunzade *see* Tursunzoda
153 P13 **Tursunzoda** *Rus.* Tursunzade; *prev.* Regar. W Tajikistan
168 J4 **Turt** Hövsgöl, N Mongolia
152 I9 **Türtkŭl** *Rus.* Turtkul'; *prev.* Petroaleksandrovsk. Qoraqalpoghiston Respublikasi, W Uzbekistan
31 O9 **Turtle Creek** South Dakota, N USA
32 K4 **Turtle Flambeau Flowage** ⊠ Wisconsin, N USA
9 S14 **Turtleford** Saskatchewan, S Canada
30 M4 **Turtle Lake** North Dakota, N USA
94 K12 **Turtola** Lappi, NW Finland
126 Jj10 **Turu** N Russian Federation
Turuga *see* Tsuruga
153 V10 **Turugart Pass** *pass* China/Kyrgyzstan
164 E7 **Turugart Shankou** *var.* Pereval Torugart. *pass* China/Kyrgyzstan
126 Hh9 **Turukhan** N Russian Federation
126 I9 **Turukhansk** Krasnoyarskiy Kray, N Russian Federation
145 N3 **Ṭurumbah** *well* NE Syria
Turuoka *see* Tsuruoka
150 H14 **Turush** Mangistau, SW Kazakhstan
62 K7 **Turvo, Rio** S Brazil
118 J2 **Tur"ya** *Pol.* Turja, *Rus.* Tur'ya. NW Ukraine
25 O4 **Tuscaloosa** Alabama, S USA
25 O4 **Tuscaloosa, Lake** ◎ Alabama, S USA
Tuscan Archipelago *see* Toscano, Archipelago
Tuscan-Emilian Mountains *see* Tosco-Emiliano, Appennino
Tuscany *see* Toscana
37 V2 **Tuscarora** Nevada, W USA
20 F15 **Tuscarora Mountain** *ridge* Pennsylvania, NE USA
32 M14 **Tuscola** Illinois, N USA
27 P7 **Tuscola** Texas, SW USA
25 O2 **Tuscumbia** Alabama, S USA
94 O4 **Tusenøyane** *island group* S Svalbard
150 K13 **Tushybas, Zaliv** *prev.* Zaliv Paskevicha. *lake gulf* SW Kazakhstan
Tusima *see* Tsushima
176 Z14 **Tusirah** Irian Jaya, E Indonesia
25 Q5 **Tuskegee** Alabama, S USA
96 E8 **Tustna** *island* S Norway
41 R12 **Tustumena Lake** ◎ Alaska, USA
112 K13 **Tuszyn** Piotrków, C Poland
143 S13 **Tutak** Ağrı, E Turkey
193 C20 **Tutamoe Range** North Island, NZ
Tutasev *see* Tutayev
128 L15 **Tutayev** *var.* Tutasev. Yaroslavskaya Oblast', W Russian Federation
xxxviii L8 **Tutbury** Staffordshire, C England, UK
Tutela *see* Tulle, France
Tutela *see* Tudela, Spain
Tutera *see* Tudela
161 H23 **Tuticorin** Tamil Nādu, SE India
115 L15 **Tutin** Serbia, S Yugoslavia
192 O10 **Tutira** Hawke's Bay, North Island, NZ
Tutiura *see* Tsuchiura
126 Ii10 **Tutonchny** Evenkiyskiy Avtonomnyy Okrug, N Russian Federation
116 L6 **Tutrakan** Razgradska Oblast, NE Bulgaria
31 N5 **Tuttle** North Dakota, N USA
28 M11 **Tuttle** Oklahoma, C USA
29 O3 **Tuttle Creek Lake** ⊠ Kansas, C USA
103 H23 **Tuttlingen** Baden-Württemberg, S Germany
175 Ss16 **Tutuala** Timor, S Indonesia
198 G9 **Tutuila** *island* W American Samoa
85 I18 **Tutume** Central, E Botswana
41 N7 **Tututalak Mountain** ▲ Alaska, USA
24 K3 **Tutwiler** Mississippi, S USA
168 L8 **Tuul Gol** N Mongolia
95 O16 **Tuupovaara** Pohjois-Karjala, SE Finland
Tuva *see* Tyva, Respublika
202 E7 **Tuvalu** *prev.* Ellice Islands. ◆ *commonwealth republic* SW Pacific Ocean
197 L17 **Tuvana-i-Colo** *prev.* Tuvana-i-Tholo. *island* Lau Group, SE Fiji
197 L18 **Tuvana-i-Ra** *island* Lau Group, SE Fiji
Tuvana-i-Tholo *see* Tuvana-i-Colo
Tuvinskaya ASSR *see* Tyva, Respublika
197 L14 **Tuvuca** *prev.* Tuvutha. *island* Lau Group, E Fiji
Tuvutha *see* Tuvuca
147 P9 **Ṭuwayq, Jabal** ▲ C Saudi Arabia
144 H13 **Ṭuwayyil ash Shihāq** *desert* S Jordan
xxxix O6 **Tuxford** Nottinghamshire, C England, UK
9 U16 **Tuxford** Saskatchewan, S Canada
178 K13 **Tu Xoay** Đắc Lắc, S Vietnam
42 L14 **Tuxpan** Jalisco, C Mexico
42 J12 **Tuxpan** Nayarit, C Mexico
43 Q12 **Tuxpán** *var.* Tuxpán de Rodríguez Cano. Veracruz-Llave, E Mexico
Tuxpán de Rodríguez Cano *see* Tuxpán
43 R15 **Tuxtepec** *var.* San Juan Bautista Tuxtepec. Oaxaca, S Mexico
43 U16 **Tuxtla** *var.* Tuxtla Gutiérrez. Chiapas, SE Mexico
Tuxtla *see* San Andrés Tuxtla
Tuxtla Gutiérrez *see* Tuxtla
Tuyama *see* Toyama
178 Jj5 **Tuyên Quang** Tuyên Quang, N Vietnam
178 K14 **Tuy Hoa** Bình Thuận, S Vietnam
178 Kk12 **Tuy Hoa** Phu Yên, S Vietnam
131 U5 **Tuymazy** Respublika Bashkortostan, W Russian Federation
148 L6 **Tūysarkān** *var.* Tuisarkan, Tuyserkān. Hamadān, W Iran
Tuyserkān *see* Tūysarkān
153 Q10 **Tuytepa** *Rus.* Toytepa. Toshkent Wiloyati, E Uzbekistan
151 W16 **Tuyuk** *Kaz.* Tuyyq. Taldykorgan, SE Kazakhstan
Tuyyq *see* Tuyuk
142 I14 **Tuz Gölü** ◎ C Turkey
129 Q15 **Tuzha** Kirovskaya Oblast', NW Russian Federation
115 K17 **Tuzi** Montenegro, SW Yugoslavia
145 T5 **Tūz Khurmātū** N Iraq
114 I11 **Tuzla** NE Bosnia and Herzegovina
119 N15 **Tuzla** Constanța, SE Romania
143 T12 **Tuzluca** Kars, NE Turkey
97 J20 **Tvååker** Halland, S Sweden
97 F17 **Tvedestrand** Aust-Agder, S Norway
128 J16 **Tver'** *prev.* Kalinin. Tverskaya Oblast', W Russian Federation
130 I15 **Tverskaya Oblast'** ◆ *province* W Russian Federation
128 I15 **Tvertsa** W Russian Federation
112 H13 **Twardogóra** *Ger.* Festenberg. Wrocław, SW Poland
xlii M4 **Twatt** Orkney Islands, N Scotland, UK
xliii P21 **Tweed** England/Scotland, UK
12 J14 **Tweed** Ontario, SE Canada
100 O7 **Tweede-Exloërmond** Drenthe, NE Netherlands
191 V3 **Tweed Heads** New South Wales, SE Australia
xli P1 **Tweedmouth** Northumberland, N England, UK
xliii L22 **Tweedsmuir** The Borders, S Scotland, UK
100 M11 **Twello** Gelderland, E Netherlands
xliv C8 **Twelve Pins, The** ▲ W Ireland
37 W15 **Twentynine Palms** California, W USA
xxxvi A9 **Twickenham** Richmond upon Thames, SE England, UK
27 P9 **Twin Buttes Reservoir** ⊠ Texas, SW USA
35 O15 **Twin Falls** Idaho, NW USA
41 N13 **Twin Hills** Alaska, USA
9 O11 **Twin Lakes** Alberta, W Canada
35 O12 **Twin Peaks** ▲ Idaho, NW USA
193 I14 **Twins, The** ▲ South Island, NZ
31 S5 **Twin Valley** Minnesota, N USA
102 G11 **Twistringen** Niedersachsen, NW Germany
193 E20 **Twizel** Canterbury, South Island, NZ
xxxvi G15 **Two Bridges** Devon, SW England, UK
31 X5 **Two Harbors** Minnesota, N USA
9 R14 **Two Hills** Alberta, SW Canada
33 N7 **Two Rivers** Wisconsin, N USA
xxxviii E13 **Twycross** Leicestershire, C England, UK
xxxvii P12 **Twyford** Hampshire, S England, UK
xxxix O9 **Twyford** Leicestershire, C England, UK
xxxvii R9 **Twyford** Wokingham, S England, UK
xliii J25 **Twynholm** Dumfries and Galloway, SW Scotland, UK
118 H8 **Tyachiv** Zakarpats'ka Oblast', W Ukraine
Tyan'-Shan' *see* Tien Shan
177 Ff3 **Tyao** Burma/India
Tyas *see* Tiyās
119 R6 **Tyas'myn** N Ukraine
25 X6 **Tybee Island** Georgia, SE USA
Tyborøn *see* Thyborøn
113 J16 **Tychy** *Ger.* Tichau. Katowice, S Poland
113 O16 **Tyczyn** Rzeszów, SE Poland
96 I8 **Tydal** Sør-Trøndelag, S Norway
xxxix S9 **Tydd St Mary** Lincolnshire, E England, UK
117 H24 **Tyflós** Kríti, Greece, E Mediterranean Sea
23 S3 **Tygart Lake** ⊠ West Virginia, NE USA
126 M15 **Tygda** Amurskaya Oblast', SE Russian Federation
23 Q11 **Tyger River** South Carolina, SE USA
34 I11 **Tygh Valley** Oregon, NW USA
xliv J5 **Tyholland** Monaghan, N Ireland
96 F12 **Tyin** ◎ S Norway
xl E14 **Tyldesley** Wigan, NW England, UK
31 S10 **Tyler** Minnesota, N USA
27 W7 **Tyler** Texas, SW USA
27 W7 **Tyler, Lake** ⊠ Texas, SW USA
24 K7 **Tylertown** Mississippi, S USA
Tylos *see* Bahrain
126 Gg12 **Tym** C Russian Federation
117 C15 **Tymfi** *var.* Timfi. ▲ W Greece
117 E17 **Tymfristós** *var.* Timfristos. ▲ C Greece
127 O14 **Tymovskoye** Ostrov Sakhalin, Sakhalinskaya Oblast', SE Russian Federation
117 J25 **Tympáki** *var.* Timbaki; *prev.* Timbákion. Kríti, Greece, E Mediterranean Sea
126 Ll14 **Tynda** Amurskaya Oblast', SE Russian Federation
31 Q12 **Tyndall** South Dakota, N USA
xliii I17 **Tyndrum** Stirling, C Scotland, UK
xli Q6 **Tyne** N England, UK
xli S6 **Tynemouth** North Tyneside, NE England, UK
99 L14 **Tyneside** *cultural region* NE England, UK
96 H10 **Tynset** Hedmark, S Norway
41 Q12 **Tyonek** Alaska, USA
Tyōsi *see* Chōshi
Tyras *see* Dniester, Moldavia/Ukraine
Tyras *see* Bilhorod-Dnistrovs'kyy, Ukraine
Tyre *see* Soûr
97 G14 **Tyrifjorden** ◎ S Norway
97 K22 **Tyringe** Kristianstad, S Sweden
127 N15 **Tyrma** Khabarovskiy Kray, SE Russian Federation
117 F15 **Týrnavos** *var.* Tírnavos. Thessalía, C Greece
131 N16 **Tyrnyauz** Kabardino-Balkarskaya Respublika, SW Russian Federation
Tyrol *see* Tirol
99 E15 **Tyrone** *cultural region* W Northern Ireland, UK
20 E14 **Tyrone** Pennsylvania, NE USA
190 M10 **Tyrrell, Lake** *salt lake* Victoria, SE Australia
86 H14 **Tyrrhenian Basin** *undersea feature* Tyrrhenian Sea, C Mediterranean Sea
123 L9 **Tyrrhenian Sea** *It.* Mare Tirreno. *sea* N Mediterranean Sea
Tysa *see* Tisa/Tisza
118 J7 **Tysmenytsya** Ivano-Frankivs'ka Oblast', W Ukraine
97 C14 **Tysnesøya** *island* S Norway
97 C14 **Tysse** Hordaland, S Norway
97 D14 **Tyssedal** Hordaland, S Norway
97 O17 **Tystberga** Södermanland, C Sweden
120 E12 **Tytuvėnai** Kelmė, C Lithuania
150 D14 **Tyub-Karagan, Mys** *headland* SW Kazakhstan
153 V8 **Tyugel'-Say** Narynskaya Oblast', C Kyrgyzstan
125 Ff13 **Tyukalinsk** Omskaya Oblast', C Russian Federation
131 V7 **Tyul'gan** Orenburgskaya Oblast', W Russian Federation
125 F11 **Tyumen'** Tyumenskaya Oblast', C Russian Federation
125 Ff10 **Tyumenskaya Oblast'** ◆ *province* C Russian Federation
126 Kk10 **Tyung** NE Russian Federation
153 Y7 **Tyup** *Kir.* Tüp. Issyk-Kul'skaya Oblast', NE Kyrgyzstan
126 I16 **Tyva, Respublika** *prev.* Tannu-Tuva, Tuva, Tuvinskaya ASSR. ◆ *autonomous republic* C Russian Federation
119 N7 **Tyvriv** Vinnyts'ka Oblast', C Ukraine
xxxv G13 **Tywi** S Wales, UK
xxxv G8 **Tywyn** Gwynedd, W Wales, UK
85 K20 **Tzaneen** Northern, NE South Africa
Tzekung *see* Zigong
43 X12 **Tzucacab** Yucatán, SE Mexico

U

84 B12 **Uaco Cungo** *var.* Waku Kungo, *Port.* Santa Comba. Cuanza Sul, C Angola
UAE *see* United Arab Emirates
203 X7 **Ua Huka** *island* Îles Marquises, NE French Polynesia
60 E10 **Uaiacás** Roraima, N Brazil
Uamba *see* Wamba
Uanle Uen *see* Wanlaweyn
203 W7 **Ua Pu** *island* Îles Marquises, NE French Polynesia
83 L17 **Uar Garas** *spring/well* SW Somalia
60 G12 **Uatumã, Rio** C Brazil
Ua Uíbh Fhailí *see* Offaly
60 C11 **Uaupés, Rio** *var.* Río Vaupés. Brazil/Colombia *see also* Vaupés, Río
151 X9 **Uba** E Kazakhstan
151 N6 **Ubagan** *Kaz.* Obagan. Kazakhstan/Russian Federation
195 N12 **Ubai** New Britain, E PNG
81 J15 **Ubangi** *Fr.* Oubangui. C Africa
Ubangi-Shari *see* Central African Republic
118 M3 **Ubarts'** *Ukr.* Ubort'. Belorussia/Ukraine *see also* Ubort'
56 F9 **Ubaté** Cundinamarca, C Colombia
62 N10 **Ubatuba** São Paulo, S Brazil
155 R12 **Ubauro** Sind, SE Pakistan
179 Qq14 **Ubay** Bohol, C Philippines
105 U14 **Ubaye** SE France
Ubayid, Wadi al *see* Ubayyiḍ, Wādī al
145 N8 **Ubaylah** W Iraq
145 O10 **Ubayyiḍ, Wādī al** *var.* Wadi al Ubayid. *dry watercourse* SW Iraq
100 L13 **Ubbergen** Gelderland, E Netherlands
170 Dd13 **Ube** Yamaguchi, Honshū, SW Japan
107 O13 **Úbeda** Andalucía, S Spain
111 V7 **Übelbach** *var.* Markt-Übelbach. Steiermark, SE Austria
61 L20 **Uberaba** Minas Gerais, SE Brazil
59 Q19 **Uberaba, Laguna** ◎ E Bolivia
61 K19 **Uberlândia** Minas Gerais, SE Brazil
103 H24 **Überlingen** Baden-Württemberg, S Germany
79 U16 **Ubiaja** Edo, S Nigeria
106 K3 **Ubiña, Peña** ▲ NW Spain
59 H17 **Ubinas, Volcán** ▲ S Peru
Ubol Rajadhani/Ubol Ratchathani *see* Ubon Ratchathani
178 I19 **Ubolratna Reservoir** ⊠ C Thailand
178 J10 **Ubon Ratchathani** *var.* Muang Ubon, Ubol Rajadhani, Ubol Ratchathani, Udon Ratchathani. E Thailand
121 L20 **Ubort'** *Bel.* Ubarts'. Belorussia/Ukraine *see also* Ubarts'
106 K15 **Ubrique** Andalucía, S Spain
Ubsu-Nur, Ozero *see* Uvs Nuur
81 M18 **Ubundu** Haut-Zaïre, C Zaire
152 K13 **Uçajy** *Rus.* Uch-Adzhi. Maryyskiy Velayat, C Turkmenistan
143 V13 **Ucar** *Rus.* Udzhary. C Azerbaijan
58 G13 **Ucayali** *off.* Departamento de Ucayali. ◆ *department* E Peru
58 F10 **Ucayali, Río** C Peru
Uccle *see* Ukkel
152 J13 **Uch-Adzhi** *Turkm.* Üçhajy. Maryyskiy Velayat, C Turkmenistan
Üchajy *see* Uch-Adzhi
131 X4 **Uchaly** Respublika Bashkortostan, W Russian Federation
151 W13 **Ucharal** *Kaz.* Üsharal. Taldykorgan, E Kazakhstan
170 C17 **Uchinoura** Kagoshima, Kyūshū, SW Japan
172 Nn6 **Uchiura-wan** *bay* NW Pacific Ocean
Uchkuduk *see* Uchquduq
Uchkurghan *see* Uchqŭrgon
152 K8 **Uchquduq** *Rus.* Uchkuduk. Nawoiy Wiloyati, N Uzbekistan
153 S9 **Uchqŭrgon** *Rus.* Uchkurghan. Namangan Wiloyati, E Uzbekistan
Uchsay *see* Uchsoy
152 G6 **Uchsoy** *Rus.* Uchsay. Qoraqalpoghiston Respublikasi, NW Uzbekistan
Uchtagan Gumy *see* Uçhtagan, Peski
152 D10 **Uchtagan, Peski** *Turkm.* Uchtagan Gumy. *desert* NW Turkmenistan
126 Mm12 **Uchur** E Russian Federation
102 O10 **Uckermark** *cultural region* E Germany
xxxvii U12 **Uckfield** East Sussex, SE England, UK

◆ Country ● Country Capital ◇ Dependent Territory ○ Dependent Territory Capital ◆ Administrative Region ✕ International Airport ▲ Mountain ▲ Mountain Range Volcano River ◎ Lake ⊠ Reservoir

Ucluelet – Ust'-Tsil'ma

8 K17 Ucluelet Vancouver Island, British Columbia, SW Canada
126 Ii14 Uda ≈ S Russian Federation
126 Mm13 Uda ≈ E Russian Federation
126 K9 Udachnyy Respublika Sakha (Yakutiya), NE Russian Federation
161 G21 Udagamandalam var. Udhagamandalam; prev. Ootacamund. Tamil Nādu, SW India
158 F14 Udaipur prev. Oodeypore. Rājasthān, N India
Udayadhani see Uthai Thani
149 N16 'Udayd, Khawr al var. Khor al Udeid. inlet Qatar/Saudi Arabia
114 D11 Udbina Zadar-Knin, C Croatia
97 I18 Uddevalla Göteborg och Bohus, S Sweden
xliii K21 Uddingston South Lanarkshire, C Scotland, UK
Uddjaur see Uddjaure
94 H13 Uddjaure var. Uddjaur. ◎ N Sweden
Udeid, Khor al see 'Udayd, Khawr al
101 K14 Uden Noord-Brabant, SE Netherlands
Uden see Udenhout
101 J14 Udenhout var. Uden. Noord-Brabant, S Netherlands
161 H14 Udgīr Mahārāshtra, C India
Udhagamandalam see Udagamandalam
158 H6 Udhampur Jammu and Kashmir, NW India
145 X14 'Udhaybah, 'Uqlat al well S Iraq
108 J7 Udine anc. Utina. Friuli-Venezia Giulia, NE Italy
183 T14 Udintsev Fracture Zone tectonic feature S Pacific Ocean
Udipi see Udupi
Udmurtia see Udmurtskaya Respublika
131 S2 Udmurtskaya Respublika Eng. Udmurtia. ◐ autonomous republic NW Russian Federation
128 J15 Udomlya Tverskaya Oblast', W Russian Federation
Udon Ratchathani see Ubon Ratchathani
178 Ii9 Udon Thani var. Ban Mak Khaeng, Udorndhani. Udon Thani, N Thailand
Udorndhani see Udon Thani
201 U12 Udot atoll Chuuk Islands, C Micronesia
127 N13 Udskaya Guba bay E Russian Federation
161 E19 Udupi var. Udipi. Karnātaka, SW India
Udzhary see Ucar
175 Q9 Uebonti, Teluk bay Sulawesi, C Indonesia
102 O9 Uecker ≈ NE Germany
102 P9 Ueckermünde Mecklenburg-Vorpommern, NE Germany
171 J14 Ueda var. Uyeda. Nagano, Honshū, S Japan
81 L16 Uele var. Welle. ≈ NE Zaire
Uele (upper course) see Uolo, Río, Equatorial Guinea/Gabon
Uele (upper course) see Kibali, Zaire
127 Q3 Uelen Chukotskiy Avtonomnyy Okrug, NE Russian Federation
102 J11 Uelzen Niedersachsen, N Germany
171 H15 Ueno Mie, Honshū, SW Japan
131 V4 Ufa Respublika Bashkortostan, W Russian Federation
131 V4 Ufa ≈ W Russian Federation
xxxvi I13 Uffculme Devon, SW England, UK
xxxvii O9 Uffington Oxfordshire, C England, UK
152 A10 Ufra Balkanskiy Velayat, NW Turkmenistan
85 C18 Ugab ≈ C Namibia
120 D8 Ugāle Ventspils, NW Latvia
83 F17 Uganda off. Republic of Uganda. ◆ republic E Africa
144 G4 Ugarit Ar. Ra's Shamrah. site of ancient city Al Lādhiqīyah, NW Syria
41 O14 Ugashik Alaska, USA
109 Q19 Ugento Puglia, SE Italy
107 O15 Ugíjar Andalucía, S Spain
105 T11 Ugine Savoie, E France
127 O15 Uglegorsk Ostrov Sakhalin, Sakhalinskaya Oblast', SE Russian Federation
129 V13 Ugleural'skiy Permskaya Oblast', NW Russian Federation
128 L15 Uglich Yaroslavskaya Oblast', W Russian Federation
128 I14 Uglovka var. Okulovka. Novgorodskaya Oblast', W Russian Federation
127 Pp5 Ugol'nyye Kopi Chukotskiy Avtonomnyy Okrug, NE Russian Federation
130 I4 Ugra ≈ W Russian Federation
xli U9 Ugthorpe North Yorkshire, N England, UK
153 V9 Ugyut Narynskaya Oblast', C Kyrgyzstan
113 H19 Uherské Hradiště Ger. Ungarisch-Hradisch. Jižní Morava, SE Czech Republic
113 H19 Uherský Brod Ger. Ungarisch-Brod. Jižní Morava, SE Czech Republic
113 B17 Úhlava Ger. Angel. ≈ W Czech Republic
Uhorshchyna see Hungary
33 T13 Uhrichsville Ohio, N USA
Uhuru Peak see Kilimanjaro
xlii D11 Uig Highland, N Scotland, UK
84 B10 Uíge Port. Carmona, Vila Marechal Carmona. Uíge, NW Angola
84 B10 Uíge ◐ province N Angola
200 Ss13 Uiha island Ha'apai Group, C Tonga
201 U13 Uijec island Chuuk, C Micronesia
169 X14 Uijŏngbu Jap. Giseifu. NW South Korea
150 H10 Uil Kaz. Oyyl. Aktyubinsk, W Kazakhstan
150 H10 Uil Kaz. Oyyl. ≈ W Kazakhstan
38 M3 Uinta Mountains ▲ Utah, W USA
85 C18 Uis Erongo, NW Namibia
85 I25 Uitenhage Eastern Cape, S South Africa
100 H9 Uitgeest Noord-Holland, W Netherlands
100 I11 Uithoorn Noord-Holland, C Netherlands
100 O4 Uithuizen Groningen, NE Netherlands
100 O4 Uithuizermeeden Groningen, NE Netherlands
201 R6 Ujae Atoll var. Wūjae. atoll Ralik Chain, W Marshall Islands
Ujain see Ujjain
113 I16 Ujazd Opole, SW Poland
Új-Becse see Novi Bečej
Ujda see Oujda
201 N5 Ujelang Atoll var. Wujlān. atoll Ralik Chain, W Marshall Islands
113 N21 Újfehértó Szabolcs-Szatmár-Bereg, E Hungary
Újgradiska see Nova Gradiška
171 H15 Uji var. Uzi. Kyōto, Honshū, SW Japan
170 Aa16 Uji-guntō island Nansei-shotō, SW Japan
83 E21 Ujiji Kigoma, W Tanzania
160 G10 Ujjain prev. Ujain. Madhya Pradesh, C India
Újlak see Ilok
'Ujmān see 'Ajmān
Újmoldova see Moldova Nouă
Újszentanna see Sântana
175 P13 Ujungpandang var. Macassar, Makassar; prev. Makasar. Sulawesi, C Indonesia
Ujung Salang see Phuket
Újvidék see Novi Sad
UK see United Kingdom
160 E11 Ukāi Reservoir ⊡ W India
83 G19 Ukara Island island N Tanzania
'Ukash, Wādī see 'Akāsh, Wādī
83 F19 Ukerewe Island island N Tanzania
145 S9 Ukhaydhir C Iraq
159 X13 Ukhrul Manipur, NE India
129 S9 Ukhta Respublika Komi, NW Russian Federation
36 L6 Ukiah California, W USA
34 K12 Ukiah Oregon, NW USA
101 G18 Ukkel Fr. Uccle. Brussels, C Belgium
120 G13 Ukmergė Pol. Wiłkomierz. Ukmergė, C Lithuania
Ukraina see Ukraine
118 L6 Ukraine off. Ukraine, Rus. Ukraina, Ukr. Ukrayina; prev. Ukrainian Soviet Socialist Republic, Ukrainskaya S.S.R. ◆ republic SE Europe
Ukrainskay S.S.R/ Ukrayina see Ukraine
84 B13 Uku Cuanza Sul, NW Angola
170 Bb12 Uku-jima island Gotō-rettō, SW Japan
85 F20 Ukwi Kgalagadi, SW Botswana
120 M13 Ula Rus. Ulla. Vitsyebskaya Voblasts', N Belorussia
142 C16 Ula Muğla, SW Turkey
120 M13 Ula Rus. Ulla. ≈ N Belorussia
168 L7 Ulaanbaatar Eng. Ulan Bator. ● (Mongolia) Töv, C Mongolia
169 N8 Ulaan-Ereg Hentiy, E Mongolia
168 E5 Ulaangom Uvs, NW Mongolia
168 E7 Ulaantolgoy Hovd, W Mongolia
168 I8 Ulaan-Uul Bayanhongor, C Mongolia
169 O10 Ulaan-Uul Dornogovĭ, SE Mongolia
165 R10 Ulan Qinghai, C China
Ulan Bator see Ulaanbaatar
168 L13 Ulan Buh Shamo desert N China
Ulanhad see Chifeng
169 T8 Ulanhot Nei Mongol Zizhiqu, N China
131 Q14 Ulan Khol Respublika Kalmykiya, SW Russian Federation
168 M13 Ulansuhai Nur ◎ N China
126 Jj16 Ulan-Ude prev. Verkhneudinsk. Respublika Buryatiya, S Russian Federation
165 N12 Ulan Ul Hu ◎ C China
195 Z16 Ulawa Island island SE Solomon Islands
144 J7 'Ulayyānīyah, Bi'r al var. Al Hilbeh. well S Syria
127 Nn13 Ul'banskiy Zaliv strait E Russian Federation
Ulbo see Olib
xxxix S15 Ulceby Lincolnshire, E England, UK
xxxix Q3 Ulceby North Lincolnshire, N England, UK
115 J18 Ulcinj Montenegro, SW Yugoslavia
xl L8 Uldale Cumbria, NW England, UK
169 O7 Uldz Hentiy, NE Mongolia
Uleåborg see Oulu
Uleälv see Oulujoki
97 G16 Ulefoss Telemark, S Norway
Uleträsk see Oulujärvi
xxxvi M8 Uley Gloucestershire, C England, UK
115 L19 Ulëz var. Ulëza. Dibër, C Albania
Ulëza see Ulëz
97 F22 Ulfborg Ringkøbing, W Denmark
100 N13 Ulft Gelderland, E Netherlands
xli R4 Ulgham Northumberland, N England, UK
168 G7 Uliastay Dzavhan, W Mongolia
196 F8 Ulimang Babeldaob, N Palau
69 T10 Ulindi ≈ W Zaire
196 H16 Ulithi Atoll atoll Caroline Islands, W Micronesia
114 N10 Uljma Serbia, NE Yugoslavia
150 L11 Ul'kayak Kaz. Ölkeyek. ≈ C Kazakhstan
151 Q7 Ul'ken-Karoy, Ozero ◎ N Kazakhstan
Ülkenözen see Bol'shoy Uzen'
Ülkenqobda see Bol'shaya Khobda
106 G3 Ulla ≈ NW Spain
Ulla see Ula
191 S10 Ulladulla New South Wales, SE Australia
159 T14 Ullapara Rajshahi, W Bangladesh
xlii G10 Ullapool Highland, N Scotland, UK
97 J20 Ullared Halland, S Sweden
107 T7 Ulldecona Cataluña, NE Spain
xli T13 Ulleskelf North Yorkshire, N England, UK
xxxix N11 Ullesthorpe Leicestershire, C England, UK
94 I9 Ullsfjorden fjord N Norway
xl M9 Ullswater ◎ NW England, UK
103 I22 Ulm Baden-Württemberg, S Germany
35 R8 Ulm Montana, NW USA
191 V5 Ulmarra New South Wales, SE Australia
118 K13 Ulmeni Buzău, C Romania
118 K14 Ulmeni Călărași, S Romania
44 L7 Ulmukhuás Región Autónoma Atlántico Norte, NE Nicaragua
196 C8 Ulong var. Aulong. island Palau Islands, N Palau
85 N14 Ulonguè var. Ulongwé. Tete, NW Mozambique
Ulongwé see Ulonguè
xl L10 Ulpha Cumbria, NW England, UK
97 K19 Ulricehamn Älvsborg, S Sweden
100 N5 Ulrum Groningen, NE Netherlands
169 Z16 Ulsan Jap. Urusan. SE South Korea
xlii I2 Ulsta Shetland Islands, NE Scotland, UK
96 D10 Ulsteinvik Møre og Romsdal, S Norway
xliv H4 Ulster province Northern Ireland, UK/Ireland
xliv J5 Ulster Canal canal Ireland/Northern Ireland, UK
175 S5 Ulu Pulau Siau, N Indonesia
126 Ll12 Ulu Respublika Sakha (Yakutiya), NE Russian Federation
44 I5 Ulúa, Río ≈ NW Honduras
142 D12 Ulubat Gölü ◎ NW Turkey
142 E12 Uludağ ▲ NW Turkey
Ulugh Muztag see Muztag Feng
164 D7 Ulugqat Xinjiang Uygur Zizhiqu, W China
142 J16 Ulukışla Niğde, S Turkey
201 O15 Ulul island Caroline Islands, C Micronesia
85 L22 Ulundi KwaZulu/Natal, E South Africa
164 M3 Ulungur He ≈ NW China
164 K2 Ulungur Hu ◎ NW China
189 P8 Uluru var. Ayers Rock. rocky outcrop Northern Territory, C Australia
xliii D17 Ulva island W Scotland, UK
197 D13 Ulveah var. Lopevi. island C Vanuatu
xl L11 Ulverston Cumbria, NW England, UK
191 O16 Ulverstone Tasmania, SE Australia
96 D13 Ulvik Hordaland, S Norway
95 J18 Ulvila Turku-Pori, SW Finland
119 O8 Ulyanivka Rus. Ul'yanovka. Kirovohrads'ka Oblast', C Ukraine
Ul'yanovka see Ulyanivka
131 Q5 Ul'yanovsk prev. Simbirsk. Ul'yanovskaya Oblast', W Russian Federation
131 Q5 Ul'yanovskaya Oblast' ◐ province W Russian Federation
151 S10 Ul'yanovskiy Karaganda, C Kazakhstan
Ul'yanovskiy Kanal see Ul'yanow Kanali
152 M13 Ul'yanow Kanali Rus. Ul'yanovskiy Kanal. canal Turkmenistan/Uzbekistan
Ulyshylanshyq see Uly-Zhylanshyk
28 H6 Ulysses Kansas, C USA
151 O12 Ulytau, Gory ▲ C Kazakhstan
126 K14 Ulyunkhan Respublika Buryatiya, S Russian Federation
151 N11 Uly-Zhylanshyk Kaz. Ulyshylanshyq. ≈ C Kazakhstan
114 A9 Umag It. Umago. Istra, NW Croatia
Umago see Umag
201 V13 Uman atoll Chuuk Islands, C Micronesia
119 O7 Uman' Rus. Uman. Cherkas'ka Oblast', C Ukraine
43 W12 Umán Yucatán, SE Mexico
Umanak/Umanaq see Uummannaq
'Umān, Khalīj see Oman, Gulf of
'Umān, Salṭanat see Oman
176 Ww12 Umari Irian Jaya, E Indonesia
160 J9 Umaria Madhya Pradesh, C India
155 R16 Umarkot Sind, SE Pakistan
196 B17 Umatac SW Guam
196 A17 Umatac Bay bay SW Guam
145 S6 Umayqah C Iraq
128 J5 Umba Murmanskaya Oblast', NW Russian Federation
144 I8 Umbāshī, Khirbat al ruins As Suwaydā', S Syria
82 A12 Umbelasha ≈ W Sudan
108 H12 Umbertide Umbria, C Italy
63 B17 Umberto var. Humberto. Santa Fe, C Argentina
194 K11 Umboi Island var. Rooke Island. island C PNG
128 J4 Umbozero, Ozero ◎ NW Russian Federation
108 H13 Umbria ◐ region C Italy
Umbrian-Machigian Mountains see Umbro-Marchigiano, Appennino
108 I12 Umbro-Marchigiano, Appennino Eng. Umbrian-Machigian Mountains. ▲ C Italy
95 J16 Umeå Västerbotten, N Sweden
95 H14 Umeälven ≈ N Sweden
41 Q5 Umiat Alaska, USA
85 K23 Umlazi KwaZulu/Natal, E South Africa
145 X10 Umm al Baqar, Hawr var. Birkat ad Dawaymah. spring S Iraq
147 U12 Umm al Ḥayt, Wādī var. Wādī Amilḥayt. seasonal river SW Oman
Umm al Qaiwain see Umm al Qaywayn
149 R15 Umm al Qaywayn var. Umm al Qaiwain. Umm al Qaywayn, NE UAE
145 Q5 Umm al Ṭūz C Iraq
144 J3 Umm 'Āmūd Ḥalab, N Syria
147 Y10 Umm ar Ruṣāṣ var. Umm Ruṣayṣ. W Oman
147 X9 Ummas Samīn salt flat C Oman
147 V9 Umm az Zumūl oasis E Saudi Arabia
82 A9 Umm Buru Western Darfur, W Sudan
82 A12 Umm Dafag Southern Darfur, W Sudan
Umm Durmān see Omdurman
144 F9 Umm el Fahm Haifa, N Israel
82 F9 Umm Inderab Northern Kordofan, C Sudan
82 C10 Umm Keddada Northern Darfur, W Sudan
146 J7 Umm Lajj Tabūk, W Saudi Arabia
144 L10 Umm Maḥfur ≈ N Jordan
145 Y13 Umm Qaṣr SE Iraq
Umm Ruṣayṣ see Umm ar Ruṣāṣ
82 F11 Umm Ruwaba var. Umm Ruwābah, Um Ruwāba. Northern Kordofan, C Sudan
Umm Ruwābah see Umm Ruwaba
149 N16 Umm Sa'īd var. Musay'īd. S Qatar
144 K10 Umm Ṭuways, Wādī dry watercourse N Jordan
40 J17 Umnak Island island Aleutian Islands, Alaska, USA
34 F13 Umpqua River ≈ Oregon, NW USA
84 D13 Umpulo Bié, C Angola
160 I12 Umred Mahārāshtra, C India
145 Y10 Umr Sawān, Hawr ◎ S Iraq
Um Ruwāba see Umm Ruwaba
Umtali see Mutare
85 J24 Umtata Eastern Cape, SE South Africa
79 V17 Umuahia Abia, SW Nigeria
62 H10 Umuarama Paraná, S Brazil
Umvuma see Mvuma
85 K18 Umzingwani ≈ S Zimbabwe
114 D11 Una ≈ Bosnia and Herzegovina/Croatia
114 E12 Unac ≈ W Bosnia and Herzegovina
25 T6 Unadilla Georgia, SE USA
20 I10 Unadilla River ≈ New York, NE USA
61 L18 Unaí Minas Gerais, SE Brazil
41 N10 Unalakleet Alaska, USA
40 K17 Unalaska Island island Aleutian Islands, Alaska, USA
193 I16 Una, Mount ▲ South Island, NZ
84 N13 Unango Niassa, N Mozambique
Unao see Unnāo
xlii H8 Unapool Highland, NW Scotland, UK
94 L12 Unari Lappi, N Finland
147 O6 'Unayzah var. Anaiza. Al Qaṣīm, C Saudi Arabia
144 L10 'Unayzah, Jabal ▲ Jordan/Saudi Arabia
Unci see Almería
59 K19 Uncía Potosí, C Bolivia
39 Q7 Uncompahgre Peak ▲ Colorado, C USA
39 P6 Uncompahgre Plateau plain Colorado, C USA
97 L17 Unden ◎ S Sweden
30 M4 Underwood North Dakota, N USA
176 Uu11 Undur Pulau Seram, E Indonesia
194 M11 Unea Island island C PNG
130 H6 Unecha Bryanskaya Oblast', W Russian Federation
41 N16 Unga Unga Island, Alaska, USA
Ungaria see Hungary
191 P8 Ungarie New South Wales, SE Australia
Ungarisch-Brod see Uherský Brod
Ungarisches Erzgebirge see Slovenské Rudohorie
Ungarisch-Hradisch see Uherské Hradiště
Ungarn see Hungary
10 M4 Ungava Bay bay Québec, E Canada
10 J2 Ungava, Péninsule d' peninsula Québec, SE Canada
Ungeny see Ungheni
118 M9 Ungheni Rus. Ungeny. W Moldavia
Unguja see Zanzibar
Üngüz Angyrsyndaky Garagum see Zaunguzskiye Garagumy
152 H11 Unguz, Solonchakovyye Vpadiny salt marsh C Turkmenistan
Ungvár see Uzhhorod
62 I12 União da Vitória Paraná, S Brazil
113 G17 Uničov Ger. Mährisch-Neustadt. Severní Morava, E Czech Republic
112 J12 Uniejów Konin, C Poland
xliii H3 Unifirth Shetland Islands, NE Scotland, UK
114 A11 Unije island W Croatia
40 L16 Unimak Island island Aleutian Islands, Alaska, USA
40 L16 Unimak Pass strait Aleutian Islands, Alaska, USA
29 W5 Union Missouri, C USA
34 L12 Union Oregon, NW USA
23 Q11 Union South Carolina, SE USA
23 R6 Union West Virginia, NE USA
64 J12 Unión San Luis, C Argentina
63 B25 Unión, Bahía bay E Argentina
33 Q13 Union City Indiana, N USA
33 Q10 Union City Michigan, N USA
20 C12 Union City Pennsylvania, NE USA
22 G8 Union City Tennessee, S USA
34 G14 Union Creek Oregon, NW USA
85 G25 Uniondale Western Cape, SW South Africa
42 K13 Unión de Tula Jalisco, SW Mexico
32 M9 Union Grove Wisconsin, N USA
47 Y15 Union Island island S Saint Vincent and the Grenadines
45 K5 Union Reefs reef SW Mexico
0 D7 Union Seamount undersea feature NE Pacific Ocean
25 Q6 Union Springs Alabama, S USA
22 H6 Uniontown Kentucky, S USA
20 C16 Uniontown Pennsylvania, NE USA
29 T1 Unionville Missouri, C USA
147 V8 United Arab Emirates Ar. Al Imārāt al 'Arabīyah al Muttaḥidah, abbrev. UAE; prev. Trucial States. ◆ federation SW Asia
United Arab Republic see Egypt
99 H14 United Kingdom off. United Kingdom of Great Britain and Northern Ireland, abbrev. UK. ◆ monarchy NW Europe
United Mexican States see Mexico
United Provinces see Uttar Pradesh
18 L9 United States of America off. United States of America, var. America, The States, abbrev. U.S., USA. ◆ federal republic
128 J10 Unitsa Respublika Kareliya, NW Russian Federation
9 S15 Unity Saskatchewan, S Canada
Unity State see Wahda
107 Q8 Universales, Montes ▲ C Spain
29 X4 University City Missouri, C USA
197 B13 Unmet Malekula, C Vanuatu
103 F15 Unna Nordrhein-Westfalen, W Germany
158 L12 Unnāo prev. Unao. Uttar Pradesh, N India
197 D15 Unpongkor Erromango, S Vanuatu
Unruhstadt see Kargowa
xlii J1 Unst island NE Scotland, UK
103 K16 Unstrut ≈ C Germany
Unterdrauburg see Dravograd
Unterlimbach see Lendava
103 L23 Unterschleissheim Bayern, SE Germany
103 H24 Untersee ◎ Germany/Switzerland
102 O10 Unterueckersee ◎ NE Germany
110 F9 Unterwalden ◐ canton C Switzerland
57 N12 Unturán, Sierra de ▲ Brazil/Venezuela
165 N11 Unuli Horog Qinghai, W China
142 M11 Ünye Ordu, W Turkey
Unza see Unzha
129 O14 Unzha var. Unza. ≈ NW Russian Federation
81 E17 Uolo, Río var. Eyo (lower course), Mbini, Uele (upper course), Woleu; prev. Benito. ≈ Equatorial Guinea/Gabon
57 Q10 Uonán Bolívar, SE Venezuela
167 T12 Uotsuri-shima island China/Japan/Taiwan
171 J13 Uozu Toyama, Honshū, SW Japan
44 L12 Upala Alajuela, NW Costa Rica
57 P7 Upata Bolívar, E Venezuela
xxxvii N10 Upavon Wiltshire, S England, UK
81 M23 Upemba, Lac ◎ SE Zaire
207 O12 Upernavik var. Upernivik. C Greenland
Upernivik see Upernavik
xl D14 Up Holland Lancashire, NW England, UK
85 F22 Upington Northern Cape, W South Africa
Uplands see Ottawa
198 Bb8 Upolu island SE Western Samoa
40 G11 'Upolu Point headland Hawaii, USA, C Pacific Ocean
xxxvi J13 Upottery Devon, SW England, UK
Upper Austria see Oberösterreich
Upper Bann see Bann
xxxix O8 Upper Broughton Nottinghamshire, C England, UK
12 M13 Upper Canada Village tourist site Ontario, SE Canada
xxxv I12 Upper Chapel Powys, C Wales, UK
20 I16 Upper Darby Pennsylvania, NE USA
30 L2 Upper Des Lacs Lake ⊡ North Dakota, N USA
193 L14 Upper Hutt Wellington, North Island, NZ
31 X11 Upper Iowa River ≈ Iowa, C USA
34 H15 Upper Klamath Lake ◎ Oregon, NW USA
36 M6 Upper Lake California, W USA
37 Q1 Upper Lake ◎ California, W USA
8 K9 Upper Liard Yukon Territory, W Canada
xliv H5 Upper Lough Erne ◎ SW Northern Ireland, UK
81 F12 Upper Nile ◐ state E Sudan
xli T13 Upper Poppleton York, N England, UK
31 T3 Upper Red Lake ◎ Minnesota, N USA
33 S12 Upper Sandusky Ohio, N USA
xxxviii K8 Upper Tean Staffordshire, C England, UK
Upper Volta see Burkina
xxxix P10 Uppingham Rutland, C England, UK
97 O15 Upplandsväsby var. Upplands Väsby. Stockholm, C Sweden
97 O15 Uppsala Uppsala, C Sweden
97 O14 Uppsala ◐ county C Sweden
40 J12 Upright Cape headland Saint Matthew Island, Alaska, USA
xxxvii Y10 Upstreet Kent, SE England, UK
xl B16 Upton Wirral, NW England, UK
22 K6 Upton Kentucky, S USA
35 Y13 Upton Wyoming, C USA
xxxviii J13 Upton upon Severn Worcestershire, W England, UK
xxxix T10 Upwell Cambridgeshire, E England, UK
147 N7 'Uqlat aṣ Ṣuqūr Al Qaṣīm, W Saudi Arabia
Uqturpan see Wushi
56 C7 Urabá, Golfo de gulf NW Colombia
Uracas see Farallon de Pajaros
Uradar'ya see Ŭradaryo
153 N13 Ŭradaryo Rus. Uradar'ya. ≈ S Uzbekistan
168 M13 Urad Qianqi var. Xishanzui. Nei Mongol Zizhiqu, N China
171 Jj17 Uraga-suidō strait S Japan
172 Pp7 Urahoro Hokkaidō, NE Japan
172 Oo8 Urakawa Hokkaidō, NE Japan
131 X6 Ural Kaz. Zayyq. ≈ Kazakhstan/Russian Federation
191 T6 Uralla New South Wales, SE Australia
Ural Mountains see Ural'skiye Gory
150 F8 Ural'sk Kaz. Oral. Zapadnyy Kazakhstan, NW Kazakhstan
Ural'skaya Oblast' see Zapadnyy Kazakhstan
131 W5 Ural'skiye Gory var. Ural'skiy Khrebet, Eng. Ural Mountains. ▲ Kazakhstan/Russian Federation
Ural'skiy Khrebet see Ural'skiye Gory
144 I3 Urām aṣ Ṣughrá Ḥalab, N Syria
191 P10 Urana New South Wales, SE Australia
191 V6 Uranga New South Wales, SE Australia
9 S10 Uranium City Saskatchewan, C Canada
60 F10 Uraricoera Roraima, N Brazil
49 S5 Uraricoera, Rio ≈ N Brazil
Ura-Tyube see Ŭroteppa
171 K16 Urawa Saitama, Honshū, S Japan
125 F10 Uray Khanty-Mansiyskiy Avtonomnyy Okrug, C Russian Federation
147 R7 'Uray'irah Ash Sharqīyah, E Saudi Arabia
32 M13 Urbana Illinois, N USA
33 R13 Urbana Ohio, N USA
31 V14 Urbandale Iowa, C USA
108 I11 Urbania Marche, C Italy
176 Uu8 Urbinasopon Irian Jaya, E Indonesia
108 I11 Urbino Marche, C Italy
xxxvii N10 Urchfont Wiltshire, S England, UK
59 H16 Urcos Cusco, S Peru
150 D10 Urda Zapadnyy Kazakhstan, W Kazakhstan
107 N10 Urda Castilla-La Mancha, C Spain
168 E7 Urdgol Hovd, W Mongolia
Urdunn see Jordan
151 X12 Urdzhar Kaz. Ürzhar. Semipalatinsk, E Kazakhstan
xli R11 Ure ≈ N England, UK
121 K18 Urechcha Rus. Urech'ye. Minskaya Voblasts', S Belorussia
Urech'ye see Urechcha
131 P2 Uren' Nizhegorodskaya Oblast', W Russian Federation
126 H9 Urengoy Yamalo-Nenetskiy Avtonomnyy Okrug, N Russian Federation
192 K10 Urenui Taranaki, North Island, NZ
197 B10 Ureparapara island Banks Islands, N Vanuatu
42 G5 Ures Sonora, NW Mexico
Urfa see Şanlıurfa
152 H9 Urganch Rus. Urgench; prev. Novo-Urgench. Khorazm Wiloyati, W Uzbekistan
Urgench see Urganch
142 J14 Ürgüp Nevşehir, C Turkey
153 O12 Urgut Samarqand Wiloyati, C Uzbekistan
164 K3 Urho Xinjiang Uygur Zizhiqu, W China
158 G5 Uri Jammu and Kashmir, NW India
110 G9 Uri ◐ canton C Switzerland
56 F11 Uribe Meta, C Colombia
56 H4 Uribia La Guajira, N Colombia
118 G12 Uricani Hung. Hobicaurikány. Hunedoara, SW Romania
59 M21 Uriondo Tarija, S Bolivia
42 I7 Urique Chihuahua, N Mexico
42 I7 Urique, Río ≈ N Mexico
58 E9 Urituyacu, Río ≈ N Peru
151 N7 Uritskiy Kustanay, N Kazakhstan
100 K8 Urk Flevoland, N Netherlands
142 B14 Urla İzmir, W Turkey
118 K13 Urlaţi Prahova, SE Romania
xliv H11 Urlingford Kilkenny, SE Ireland
131 V4 Urman Respublika Bashkortostan, W Russian Federation
153 P12 Urmetan W Tajikistan
Urmia see Orūmīyeh
Urmia, Lake see Orūmīyeh, Daryācheh-ye
Urmiyeh see Orūmīyeh
xli O16 Urmston Salford, NW England, UK
115 N17 Uroševac Alb. Ferizaj. Serbia, S Yugoslavia
153 P11 Ŭroteppa Rus. Ura-Tyube. NW Tajikistan
56 D8 Urrao Antioquia, W Colombia
Ursat'yevskaya see Khowos
168 I11 Urt Ömnögovĭ, S Mongolia
131 X7 Urtazym Orenburgskaya Oblast', W Russian Federation
61 K18 Uruaçu Goiás, C Brazil
42 M14 Uruapan var. Uruapan del Progreso. Michoacán de Ocampo, SW Mexico
Uruapan del Progreso see Uruapan
59 G15 Urubamba, Cordillera ▲ C Peru
59 G14 Urubamba, Río ≈ C Peru
60 G12 Urucará Amazonas, N Brazil
63 E16 Uruguaiana Rio Grande do Sul, S Brazil
Uruguai, Rio see Uruguay
63 E18 Uruguay off. Oriental Republic of Uruguay; prev. La Banda Oriental. ◆ republic E South America
63 E15 Uruguay var. Rio Uruguai, Río Uruguay. ≈ E South America
Uruguay, Río see Uruguay
Uruk see Erech
Urumchi see Ürümqi
164 L5 Ürümqi var. Tihwa, Urumchi, Urumqi, Urumtsi, Wu-lu-k'o-mu-shi, Wu-lu-mu-ch'i; prev. Ti-hua. autonomous region capital Xinjiang Uygur Zizhiqu, NW China
Urumtsi see Ürümqi
Urundi see Burundi
196 C15 Uruno Point headland NW Guam
127 P15 Urup, Ostrov island Kuril'skiye Ostrova, SE Russian Federation
147 P11 'Uruq al Mawārid desert S Saudi Arabia
Urusan see Ulsan
131 T5 Urussu Respublika Tatarstan, W Russian Federation
192 K10 Uruti Taranaki, North Island, NZ
59 K19 Uru Uru, Lago ◎ W Bolivia
57 P9 Uruyén Bolívar, SE Venezuela
155 O7 Ūrūzgān var. Oruzgān, Orūzgān. Ūrūzgān, C Afghanistan
155 N6 Ūrūzgān Per. Orūzgān. ◐ province C Afghanistan
172 P6 Uryū-gawa ≈ Hokkaidō, NE Japan
172 P4 Uryū-ko ◎ Hokkaidō, NE Japan
131 N8 Uryupinsk Volgogradskaya Oblast', SW Russian Federation
Ürzhar see Urdzhar
129 R16 Urzhum Kirovskaya Oblast', NW Russian Federation
118 K13 Urziceni Ialomiţa, SE Romania
U.S./USA see United States of America
170 D13 Usa Ōita, Kyūshū, SW Japan
121 L16 Usa Rus. Usa. ≈ C Belorussia
129 T6 Usa ≈ NW Russian Federation
142 E14 Uşak prev. Ushak. Uşak, W Turkey
142 D14 Uşak var. Ushak. ◐ province W Turkey
85 C19 Usakos Erongo, W Namibia
83 J21 Usambara Mountains ▲ NE Tanzania
83 G23 Usangu Flats wetland SW Tanzania
67 D24 Usborne, Mount ▲ East Falkland, Falkland Islands
102 O8 Usedom island NE Germany
101 M24 Useldange Diekirch, C Luxembourg
120 L12 Ushacha Rus. Ushacha. Vitsyebskaya Voblasts', N Belorussia
Ushachi see Ushachy
120 L13 Ushachy Rus. Ushachi. Vitsyebskaya Voblasts', N Belorussia
Ushak see Uşak
126 I2 Ushakova, Ostrov island Severnaya Zemlya, N Russian Federation
Ushant see Ouessant, Île d'
Üsharal see Ucharal
170 Bb14 Ushibuka var. Usibuka. Kumamoto, Shimo-jima, SW Japan
Ushi Point see Sabaneta, Puntan
151 V14 Ushtobe Kaz. Üshtöbe. Taldykorgan, SE Kazakhstan
65 I25 Ushuaia Tierra del Fuego, S Argentina
41 R10 Usibelli Alaska, USA
Usibuka see Ushibuka
194 I12 Usino Madang, N PNG
129 U6 Usinsk Respublika Komi, NW Russian Federation
xxxv L14 Usk Monmouthshire, SE Wales, UK
xxxv L14 Usk Wel. Wysg. ≈ SE Wales, UK
Uskočke Planine/ Uskokengebirge see Žumberačka Gora
Üsküb see Skopje
xxxv H12 Usk Reservoir ⊡ S Wales, UK
116 M11 Üsküpdere Kırklareli, NW Turkey
130 L7 Usman' Lipetskaya Oblast', W Russian Federation
120 D8 Usmas Ezers ◎ NW Latvia
129 U13 Usol'ye Permskaya Oblast', NW Russian Federation
126 J15 Usol'ye-Sibirskoye Irkutskaya Oblast', C Russian Federation
43 T16 Uspanapa, Río ≈ SE Mexico
151 R11 Uspenskiy Zhezkazgan, C Kazakhstan
105 O11 Ussel Corrèze, C France
169 Z6 Ussuri var. Usuri, Wusuri, Chin. Wusuli Jiang. ≈ China/Russian Federation
127 Nn18 Ussuriysk prev. Nikol'sk, Nikol'sk-Ussuriyskiy, Voroshilov. Primorskiy Kray, SE Russian Federation
142 J10 Usta Burnu headland N Turkey
155 P13 Usta Muhammad Baluchistān, SW Pakistan
126 K15 Ust'-Barguzin Respublika Buryatiya, S Russian Federation
127 P12 Ust'-Bol'sheretsk Kamchatskaya Oblast', E Russian Federation
131 N9 Ust'-Buzulukskaya Volgogradskaya Oblast', SW Russian Federation
110 G7 Uster Zürich, NE Switzerland
109 I22 Ustica, Isola d' island S Italy
126 J13 Ust'-Ilimsk Irkutskaya Oblast', C Russian Federation
113 C15 Ústí nad Labem Ger. Aussig. Severní Čechy, N Czech Republic
113 F17 Ústí nad Orlicí Ger. Wildenschwert. Východní Čechy, E Czech Republic
Ustinov see Izhevsk
115 J14 Ustiprača SE Bosnia and Herzegovina
125 Ff12 Ust'-Ishim Omskaya Oblast', C Russian Federation
112 G6 Ustka Ger. Stolpmünde. Słupsk, NW Poland
127 Pp10 Ust'-Kamchatsk Kamchatskaya Oblast', E Russian Federation
151 X9 Ust'-Kamenogorsk Kaz. Öskemen. Vostochnyy Kazakhstan, E Kazakhstan
127 Oo10 Ust'-Khayryuzovo Koryakskiy Avtonomnyy Okrug, E Russian Federation
126 H16 Ust'-Koksa Respublika Altay, S Russian Federation
129 S11 Ust'-Kulom Respublika Komi, NW Russian Federation
126 Jj14 Ust'-Kut Irkutskaya Oblast', C Russian Federation
126 M7 Ust'-Kuyga Respublika Sakha (Yakutiya), NE Russian Federation
130 L14 Ust'-Labinsk Krasnodarskiy Kray, SW Russian Federation
126 Mm11 Ust'-Maya Respublika Sakha (Yakutiya), NE Russian Federation
127 N9 Ust'-Nera Respublika Sakha (Yakutiya), NE Russian Federation
126 Ll13 Ust'-Nyukzha Amurskaya Oblast', S Russian Federation
126 Kk6 Ust'-Olenëk Respublika Sakha (Yakutiya), NE Russian Federation
127 O10 Ust'-Omchug Magadanskaya Oblast', E Russian Federation
126 Jj15 Ust'-Ordynskiy Ust'-Ordynskiy Buryatskiy Avtonomnyy Okrug, S Russian Federation
126 J15 Ust'-Ordynskiy Buryatskiy Avtonomnyy Okrug ◐ autonomous district S Russian Federation
129 N8 Ust'-Pinega Arkhangel'skaya Oblast', NW Russian Federation
126 Hh8 Ust'-Port Taymyrskiy (Dolgano-Nenetskiy) Avtonomnyy Okrug, N Russian Federation
116 L11 Ustrem prev. Vakav. Burgaska Oblast, SE Bulgaria
113 O18 Ustrzyki Dolne Krosno, SE Poland
Ust'-Sysol'sk see Syktyvkar
129 R7 Ust'-Tsil'ma Respublika Komi, NW Russian Federation

◆ Country ● Country Capital ◇ Dependent Territory ○ Dependent Territory Capital ◐ Administrative Region ✈ International Airport ▲ Mountain ▲ Mountain Range Volcano ≈ River ◎ Lake ⊡ Reservoir

Ust Urt – Velika Morava

Ust Urt see Ustyurt Plateau
129 O11 Ust'ya NW Russian Federation
119 R8 Ustynivka Kirovohrads'ka Oblast', C Ukraine
150 H15 Ustyurt Plateau var. Ust Urt, Uzb. Ustyurt Platosi. plateau Kazakhstan/Uzbekistan
Ustyurt Platosi see Ustyurt Plateau
128 K14 Ustyuzhna Vologodskaya Oblast', NW Russian Federation
164 J4 Usu Xinjiang Uygur Zizhiqu, NW China
175 Q10 Usu Sulawesi, C Indonesia
170 Dd14 Usuki Ōita, Kyūshū, SW Japan
44 G8 Usulután Usulután, SE El Salvador
44 B8 Usulután ◐ department SE El Salvador
43 W16 Usumacinta, Río Guatemala/Mexico
Usumbura see Bujumbura
Usuri see Ussuri
176 X12 Uta Irian Jaya, E Indonesia
38 K5 Utah off. State of Utah; also known as Beehive State, Mormon State. ◐ state W USA
38 L3 Utah Lake ◎ Utah, W USA
Utaidhani see Uthai Thani
95 M14 Utajärvi Oulu, C Finland
Utamboni see Mitemele, Río
Utaradit see Uttaradit
173 G3 Utara, Selat strait Peninsular Malaysia
172 P5 Utashinai var. Utasinai. Hokkaidō, NE Japan
Utasinai see Utashinai
176 X12 Uta, Sungai Irian Jaya, E Indonesia
200 Ss12 'Uta Vava'u island Vava'u Group, N Tonga
39 V9 Ute Creek New Mexico, SW USA
120 H12 Utena Utena, E Lithuania
39 V10 Ute Reservoir ⊠ New Mexico, SW USA
178 H10 Uthai Thani var. Muang Uthai Thani, Udayadhani, Utaidhani. Uthai Thani, W Thailand
155 O15 Uthal Baluchistān, SW Pakistan
20 I10 Utica New York, NE USA
107 R10 Utiel País Valenciano, E Spain
9 O13 Utikuma Lake ◎ Alberta, W Canada
44 I4 Utila, Isla de island Islas de la Bahía, N Honduras
Utina see Udine
61 O17 Utinga Bahia, E Brazil
Utirik see Utrik Atoll
97 M22 Utlängan island S Sweden
119 U11 Utlyuts'kyy Lyman bay S Ukraine
170 Cc14 Uto Kumamoto, Kyūshū, SW Japan
97 P16 Utö Stockholm, C Sweden
27 Q12 Utopia Texas, SW USA
100 J11 Utrecht Lat. Trajectum ad Rhenum. Utrecht, C Netherlands
85 K22 Utrecht KwaZulu/Natal, E South Africa
100 I11 Utrecht ◐ province C Netherlands
106 K14 Utrera Andalucía, S Spain
201 V4 Utrik Atoll var. Utirik, Utrōk, Utrönk. atoll Ratak Chain, N Marshall Islands
Utrōk/Utrönk see Utrik Atoll
97 B16 Utsira island SW Norway
94 L8 Utsjoki var. Ohcejohka. Lappi, N Finland
171 Kk15 Utsunomiya var. Utunomiya. Tochigi, Honshū, S Japan
131 P13 Utta Respublika Kalmykiya, SW Russian Federation
178 Hh8 Uttaradit var. Utaradit. Uttaradit, N Thailand
158 J8 Uttarkāshi Uttar Pradesh, N India
158 K11 Uttar Pradesh prev. United Provinces, United Provinces of Agra and Oudh. ◐ state N India
xxxviii K8 Uttoxeter Staffordshire, C England, UK
47 T5 Utuado C Puerto Rico
164 K3 Utubulak Xinjiang Uygur Zizhiqu, W China
41 N5 Utukok River Alaska, USA
Utunomiya see Utsunomiya
195 X9 Utupua island Santa Cruz Islands, E Solomon Islands
150 G9 Utva NW Kazakhstan
201 Y15 Utwe Kosrae, E Micronesia
201 X15 Utwe Harbor harbour Kosrae, E Micronesia
168 J7 Uubulan Arhangay, C Mongolia
120 G6 Uulu Pärnumaa, SW Estonia
207 N13 Uummannaq var. Umanak, Umanaq. C Greenland
206 L16 Uummannarsuaq var. Nunap Isua, Dan. Kap Farvel, Eng. Cape Farewell. headland S Greenland
168 E4 Üüreg Nuur ◎ NW Mongolia
Uusikaarlepyy see Nykarleby
95 J19 Uusikaupunki Swe. Nystad. Turku-Pori, SW Finland
95 L19 Uusimaa Swe. Nyland. ◐ province S Finland
131 S2 Uva Udmurtskaya Respublika, NW Russian Federation
115 L14 Uvac W Yugoslavia
27 Q12 Uvalde Texas, SW USA
161 K25 Uva Province ◐ province SE Sri Lanka
121 O18 Uvaravichy Rus. Uvarovichi. Homyel'skaya Voblasts', SE Belorussia
56 J11 Uvá, Río E Colombia
Uvarovichi see Uvaravichy
131 N7 Uvarovo Tambovskaya Oblast', W Russian Federation
125 Ff11 Uvat Tyumenskaya Oblast', C Russian Federation
202 G12 Uvea, Île island N Wallis and Futuna
83 E21 Uvinza Kigoma, W Tanzania
81 O20 Uvira Sud Kivu, E Zaire
168 E5 Uvs ◐ province NW Mongolia
168 F5 Uvs Nuur var. Ozero Ubsu-Nur. ◎ Mongolia/Russian Federation
170 E15 Uwa Ehime, Shikoku, SW Japan
170 E15 Uwajima var. Uwazima. Ehime, Shikoku, SW Japan
82 B5 'Uwaynāt, Jabal al var. Jebel Uweinat. ▲ Libya/Sudan
Uwazima see Uwajima
Uweinat, Jebel see 'Uwaynāt, Jabal al
176 Z14 Uwimmerah, Sungai Irian Jaya, E Indonesia
xxxvii S9 Uxbridge Hillingdon, SE England, UK
12 H14 Uxbridge Ontario, S Canada
Uxellodunum see Issoudun
168 M15 Uxin Qi Nei Mongol Zizhiqu, N China
43 X12 Uxmal, Ruinas ruins Yucatán, SE Mexico
133 Q5 Uy Kazakhstan/Russian Federation
150 K15 Uyaly Kzyl-Orda, S Kazakhstan
126 Mm7 Uyandina NE Russian Federation
126 I14 Uyar Krasnoyarskiy Kray, S Russian Federation
168 L10 Üydzen Ömnögovĭ, S Mongolia
Uyeda see Ueda
126 Hh3 Uyedineniya, Ostrov island N Russian Federation
79 V17 Uyo Akwa Ibom, S Nigeria
168 D8 Üyönch Hovd, W Mongolia
151 Q15 Uyuk Zhambyl, S Kazakhstan
147 V13 'Uyūn SW Oman
59 K20 Uyuni Potosí, W Bolivia
152 I9 Uzbekistan off. Republic of Uzbekistan. ◆ republic C Asia
164 D8 Uzbel Shankou Rus. Pereval Kyzyl-Dzhiik. pass China/Tajikistan
121 J17 Uzda Rus. Uzda. Minskaya Voblasts', C Belorussia
105 N12 Uzerche Corrèze, C France
105 R14 Uzès Gard, S France
153 T10 Uzgen Kir. Özgön. Oshskaya Oblast', SW Kyrgyzstan
119 O3 Uzh N Ukraine
Uzhgorod see Uzhhorod
118 G7 Uzhhorod Rus. Uzhgorod; prev. Ungvár. Zakarpats'ka Oblast', W Ukraine
126 Hh14 Uzhur Krasnoyarskiy Kray, S Russian Federation
Uzi see Uji
114 K13 Užice prev. Titovo Užice. Serbia, W Yugoslavia
Uzin see Uzyn
130 L5 Uzlovaya Tul'skaya Oblast', W Russian Federation
110 H7 Uznach Sankt Gallen, NE Switzerland
151 U16 Uzunagach Almaty, SE Kazakhstan
142 B10 Uzunköprü Edirne, NW Turkey
120 D11 Užventis Kelmė, C Lithuania
119 P5 Uzyn Rus. Uzin. Kyyivs'ka Oblast', N Ukraine

V

Vääksy see Asikkala
85 H23 Vaal C South Africa
95 M14 Vaala Oulu, C Finland
95 N19 Vaalimaa Kymi, SE Finland
101 M19 Vaals Limburg, SE Netherlands
95 J16 Vaasa Swe. Vasa; prev. Nikolainkaupunki. Vaasa, W Finland
95 K17 Vaasa Swe. Vasa. ◐ province C Finland
100 L10 Vaassen Gelderland, E Netherlands
120 G11 Vabalninkas Biržai, NE Lithuania
Vabkent see Wobkent
113 J22 Vác Ger. Waitzen. Pest, N Hungary
63 I14 Vacaria Rio Grande do Sul, S Brazil
37 N7 Vacaville California, W USA
105 R15 Vaccarès, Étang de ◎ SE France
46 L10 Vache, Île à island SW Haiti
181 Y16 Vacoas W Mauritius
34 G10 Vader Washington, NW USA
96 D12 Vadheim Sogn og Fjordane, S Norway
124 O3 Vadili Gk. Vatilí. C Cyprus
160 D11 Vadodara prev. Baroda. Gujarāt, W India
94 M8 Vadsø Fin. Vesisaari. Finnmark, N Norway
97 L17 Vadstena Östergötland, S Sweden
110 I8 Vaduz ● (Liechtenstein) W Liechtenstein
Vág see Váh
129 N12 Vaga NW Russian Federation
96 G11 Vågåmo Oppland, S Norway
114 D12 Vaganski Vrh ▲ W Croatia
Vágbeszterce see Považská Bystrica
97 L19 Vaggeryd Jönköping, S Sweden
195 U14 Vaghena var. Wagina. island NW Solomon Islands
97 O16 Vagnhärad Södermanland, C Sweden
106 G7 Vagos Aveiro, N Portugal
Vágsellye see Sal'a
94 H10 Vågsfjorden fjord N Norway
96 C10 Vågsøy island S Norway
Vágújhely see Nové Mesto nad Váhom
113 I21 Váh Ger. Waag, Hung. Vág. W Slovakia
95 K16 Vähäkyrö Vaasa, W Finland
203 X11 Vahitahi atoll Îles Tuamotu, E French Polynesia
xlii H10 Vaich, Loch ◎ NW Scotland, UK
Vaidei see Vulcan
24 L4 Vaiden Mississippi, S USA
161 I23 Vaigai SE India
203 V16 Vaihu Easter Island, Chile, E Pacific Ocean
120 I6 Väike Emajõgi S Estonia
120 I4 Väike-Maarja Ger. Klein-Marien. Lääne-Virumaa, NE Estonia
Väike-Salatsi see Mazsalaca
39 R4 Vail Colorado, C USA
200 Qq15 Vaina Tongatapu, S Tonga
120 E5 Väinameri prev. Muhu Väin, Ger. Moon-Sund. sea E Baltic Sea
95 N18 Vainikkala Kymi, SE Finland
120 D10 Vaiņode Liepāja, SW Latvia
161 H23 Vaippār SE India
203 W11 Vairaatea atoll Îles Tuamotu, C French Polynesia
203 R8 Vairao Tahiti, W French Polynesia
105 R14 Vaison-la-Romaine Vaucluse, SE France
202 G11 Vaitupu Île Uvea, E Wallis and Futuna
202 F7 Vaitupu atoll C Tuvalu
Vajdahunyad see Hunedoara
Vajdej see Vulcan
80 K12 Vakaga ◐ prefecture NE Central African Republic
116 H10 Vakarel Sofiyska Oblast, W Bulgaria
Vakav see Ustrem
143 O11 Vakfıkebir Trabzon, NE Turkey
126 H11 Vakh C Russian Federation
Vakhon, Qatorkŭhi see Nicholas Range
153 P14 Vakhsh SW Tajikistan
153 Q12 Vakhsh SW Tajikistan
131 P1 Vakhtan Nizhegorodskaya Oblast', W Russian Federation
96 C13 Vaksdal Hordaland, S Norway
129 O8 Vaksha NW Russian Federation
195 O15 Vakuta Island island Kiriwina Islands, SE PNG
Valachia see Wallachia
110 D11 Valais Ger. Wallis. ◐ canton SW Switzerland
115 M21 Valamarës, Mali i ▲ SE Albania
131 S2 Valamaz Udmurtskaya Respublika, NW Russian Federation
115 Q19 Valandovo SE FYR Macedonia
113 I18 Valašské Meziříčí Ger. Wallachisch-Meseritsch, Pol. Wałeckie Międzyrzecze. Severní Morava, E Czech Republic
117 I17 Valáxa island Vóreioi Sporádes, Greece, Aegean Sea
97 K16 Vålberg Värmland, C Sweden
118 H12 Vâlcea prev. Vîlcea. ◐ county SW Romania
65 J16 Valcheta Río Negro, E Argentina
13 P12 Valcourt Québec, SE Canada
Valdai Hills see Valdayskaya Vozvyshennost'
106 M3 Valdavia N Spain
128 I15 Valday Novgorodskaya Oblast', W Russian Federation
128 I15 Valdayskaya Vozvyshennost' var. Valdai Hills. hill range W Russian Federation
106 L9 Valdecañas, Embalse de ⊠ W Spain
120 E8 Valdemārpils Ger. Sassmacken. Talsi, NW Latvia
97 N18 Valdemarsvik Östergötland, S Sweden
107 N8 Valdemoro Madrid, C Spain
107 O11 Valdepeñas Castilla-La Mancha, C Spain
106 L5 Valderaduey NE Spain
106 L5 Valderas Castilla-León, N Spain
107 T7 Valderrobres var. Vall-de-roures. Aragón, NE Spain
65 K17 Valdés, Península peninsula SE Argentina
41 S11 Valdez Alaska, USA
58 C5 Valdéz var. Limones. Esmeraldas, NW Ecuador
Valdia see Weldiya
105 U11 Val d'Isère Savoie, E France
65 G15 Valdivia Los Lagos, C Chile
Valdivia Bank see Valdivia Seamount
67 P17 Valdivia Seamount var. Valdivia Bank. undersea feature E Atlantic Ocean
105 N4 Val-d'Oise ◐ department N France
12 J8 Val-d'Or Québec, SE Canada
25 U8 Valdosta Georgia, SE USA
96 G13 Valdres physical region S Norway
34 L13 Vale Oregon, NW USA
118 F9 Valea lui Mihai Hung. Érmihályfalva. Bihor, NW Romania
9 N15 Valemount British Columbia, SW Canada
61 O17 Valença Bahia, E Brazil
106 F4 Valença do Minho Viana do Castelo, N Portugal
61 N14 Valença do Piauí Piauí, E Brazil
105 N8 Valençay Indre, C France
105 R13 Valence anc. Valentia, Valentia Julia, Ventia. Drôme, E France
107 S10 Valencia País Valenciano, E Spain
56 K5 Valencia Carabobo, N Venezuela
107 R10 Valencia Cat. València. ◐ province País Valenciano, E Spain
107 S10 Valencia ✕ Valencia, E Spain
València/Valencia see País Valenciano
106 I10 Valencia de Alcántara Extremadura, W Spain
106 L4 Valencia de Don Juan Castilla-León, N Spain
107 U9 Valencia, Golfo de var. Gulf of Valencia. gulf E Spain
Valencia, Gulf of see Valencia, Golfo de
xliv A13 Valencia Island Ir. Dairbhre. island SW Ireland
105 P2 Valenciennes Nord, N France
118 K13 Vălenii de Munte Prahova, SE Romania
Valentia see Valence, France
Valentia see País Valenciano
Valentia Julia see Valence
105 T8 Valentigney Doubs, E France
30 M12 Valentine Nebraska, C USA
26 J10 Valentine Texas, SW USA
Valentine State see Oregon
108 C8 Valenza Piemonte, NW Italy
96 I13 Våler Hedmark, S Norway
56 I6 Valera Trujillo, NW Venezuela
199 K13 Valerie Guyot undersea feature S Pacific Ocean
Valetta see Valletta
120 I7 Valga Ger. Walk, Latv. Valka. Valgamaa, S Estonia
120 I7 Valgamaa off. Valga Maakond. ◐ province S Estonia
45 Q15 Valiente, Península peninsula NW Panama
104 E3 Valinco, Golfe de gulf Corse, France, C Mediterranean Sea
114 L12 Valjevo Serbia, W Yugoslavia
94 L9 Valjok Finnmark, N Norway
120 I7 Valka Ger. Walk. Valka, N Latvia
Valka see Valga
95 L18 Valkeakoski Häme, SW Finland
95 M19 Valkeala Kymi, S Finland
101 L18 Valkenburg Limburg, SE Netherlands
101 K15 Valkenswaard Noord-Brabant, S Netherlands
121 G15 Valkininkai Varėna, S Lithuania
119 U5 Valky Kharkivs'ka Oblast', E Ukraine
43 Y12 Valladolid Yucatán, SE Mexico
106 M5 Valladolid Castilla-León, NW Spain
106 L5 Valladolid ◐ province Castilla-León, N Spain
105 U15 Vallauris Alpes-Maritimes, SE France
xlii A11 Vallay island NW Scotland, UK
Vall-de-roures see Valderrobres
107 S9 Vall d'Uxó País Valenciano, E Spain
97 E16 Valle Aust-Agder, S Norway
107 N2 Valle Cantabria, N Spain
44 H8 Valle ◐ department S Honduras
107 N8 Vallecas Madrid, C Spain
39 Q8 Vallecito Reservoir ⊠ Colorado, C USA
108 A7 Valle d'Aosta ◐ region NW Italy
43 O14 Valle de Bravo México, S Mexico
57 N5 Valle de Guanape Anzoátegui, N Venezuela
56 M6 Valle de La Pascua Guárico, N Venezuela
56 B11 Valle del Cauca off. Departamento del Valle del Cauca. ◐ province W Colombia
43 N13 Valle de Santiago Guanajuato, C Mexico
42 J7 Valle de Zaragoza Chihuahua, N Mexico
56 G5 Valledupar Cesar, N Colombia
78 G10 Vallée de Ferlo NW Senegal
59 M19 Vallegrande Santa Cruz, C Bolivia
43 P8 Valle Hermoso Tamaulipas, C Mexico
37 N8 Vallejo California, W USA
64 G8 Vallenar Atacama, N Chile
97 O15 Vallentuna Stockholm, C Sweden
123 Ll12 Valletta prev. Valetta. ● (Malta) E Malta
29 N6 Valley Center Kansas, C USA
31 Q5 Valley City North Dakota, N USA
34 I15 Valley Falls Oregon, NW USA
Valleyfield see Salaberry-de-Valleyfield
23 S4 Valley Head West Virginia, NE USA
27 T8 Valley Mills Texas, SW USA
77 W10 Valley of the Kings ancient monument E Egypt
31 R11 Valley Springs South Dakota, N USA
22 K5 Valley Station Kentucky, S USA
9 O13 Valleyview Alberta, W Canada
27 T5 Valley View Texas, SW USA
63 C21 Vallimanca, Arroyo E Argentina
109 M19 Vallo della Lucania Campania, S Italy
110 B9 Vallorbe Vaud, W Switzerland
107 V6 Valls Cataluña, NE Spain
96 N11 Vallsta Gävleborg, C Sweden
96 N12 Vallvik Gävleborg, C Sweden
9 T17 Val Marie Saskatchewan, S Canada
120 H7 Valmiera Est. Volmari, Ger. Wolmar. Valmiera, N Latvia
107 N3 Valnera ▲ N Spain
104 J3 Valognes Manche, N France
Valona see Vlorë
Valona Bay see Vlorës, Gjiri i
106 G6 Valongo var. Valongo de Gaia. Porto, N Portugal
Valongo de Gaia see Valongo
106 M5 Valoria la Buena Castilla-León, N Spain
121 J15 Valozhyn Pol. Wołożyn, Rus. Volozhin. Minskaya Voblasts', C Belorussia
106 I5 Valpaços Vila Real, N Portugal
25 P8 Valparaiso Florida, SE USA
33 N11 Valparaiso Indiana, N USA
64 G11 Valparaíso Valparaíso, C Chile
42 L11 Valparaíso Zacatecas, C Mexico
64 G11 Valparaíso off. Región de Valparaíso. ◐ region C Chile
Valpo see Valpovo
114 I9 Valpovo Hung. Valpó. Osijek-Baranja, E Croatia
105 R14 Valréas Vaucluse, SE France
Vals see Vals-Platz
160 D12 Valsād prev. Bulsar. Gujarāt, W India
Valsbaai see False Bay
176 Uu10 Valse Pisang, Kepulauan island group E Indonesia
110 H9 Vals-Platz var. Vals. Graubünden, S Switzerland
176 Xx16 Vals, Tanjung headland Irian Jaya, SE Indonesia
95 N15 Valtimo Pohjois-Karjala, E Finland
117 D17 Váltou ▲ C Greece
131 O12 Valuyevka Rostovskaya Oblast', SW Russian Federation
130 K9 Valuyki Belgorodskaya Oblast', W Russian Federation
38 L2 Val Verda Utah, W USA
66 N12 Valverde Hierro, Islas Canarias, Spain, NE Atlantic Ocean
106 I13 Valverde del Camino Andalucía, S Spain
97 G23 Vamdrup Vejle, C Denmark
96 L12 Våmhus Kopparberg, C Sweden
95 K18 Vammala Turku-Pori, SW Finland
Vámosudvarhely see Odorheiu Secuiesc
143 S14 Van Van, E Turkey
27 V7 Van Texas, SW USA
143 T14 Van ◐ province E Turkey
143 T11 Vanadzor prev. Kirovakan. N Armenia
27 U5 Van Alstyne Texas, SW USA
35 W10 Vananda Montana, NW USA
118 I11 Vânători Hung. Héjjasfalva; prev. Vînători. Mureș, C Romania
203 W12 Vanavana atoll Îles Tuamotu, SE French Polynesia
Vana-Vändra see Vändra
126 J12 Vanavara Evenkiyskiy Avtonomnyy Okrug, C Russian Federation
13 Q8 Van Bruyssel Québec, SE Canada
29 R10 Van Buren Arkansas, C USA
21 S1 Van Buren Maine, NE USA
29 W7 Van Buren Missouri, C USA
21 T5 Vanceboro Maine, NE USA
23 W10 Vanceboro North Carolina, SE USA
23 O4 Vanceburg Kentucky, S USA
Vanch see Vanj
8 L17 Vancouver British Columbia, SW Canada
34 G11 Vancouver Washington, NW USA
8 L17 Vancouver ✕ British Columbia, SW Canada
8 K16 Vancouver Island island British Columbia, SW Canada
Vanda see Vantaa
176 Xx11 Van Daalen Irian Jaya, E Indonesia
32 L15 Vandalia Illinois, N USA
29 V3 Vandalia Missouri, C USA
33 R13 Vandalia Ohio, N USA
27 U13 Vanderbilt Texas, SW USA
33 Q10 Vandercook Lake Michigan, N USA
8 L14 Vanderhoof British Columbia, SW Canada
20 K8 Vanderwhacker Mountain ▲ New York, NE USA
189 P1 Van Diemen Gulf gulf Northern Territory, N Australia
Van Diemen's Land see Tasmania
120 H5 Vändra Ger. Fennern; prev. Vana-Vändra. Pärnumaa, SW Estonia
Vandsburg see Więcbork
36 L4 Van Duzen River California, W USA
120 F13 Vandžiogala Kaunas, C Lithuania
43 N10 Vanegas San Luis Potosí, C Mexico
Vaner, Lake see Vänern
97 K17 Vänern Eng. Lake Vaner; prev. Lake Vener. ◎ S Sweden
97 J18 Vänersborg Älvsborg, S Sweden
96 F12 Vang Oppland, S Norway
180 I7 Vangaindrano Fianarantsoa, SE Madagascar
143 S14 Van Gölü Eng. Lake Van; anc. Thospitis. salt lake E Turkey
195 V15 Vanguna island New Georgia Islands, NW Solomon Islands
26 J9 Van Horn Texas, SW USA
195 X9 Vanikolo var. Vanikoro. island Santa Cruz Islands, E Solomon Islands
Vanikoro see Vanikolo
194 E9 Vanimo Sandaun, NW PNG
127 O15 Vanino Khabarovskiy Kray, SE Russian Federation
161 G19 Vānīvilāsa Sāgara ◎ SW India
153 Q13 Vanj Rus. Vanch. S Tajikistan
118 G14 Vânju Mare prev. Vînju Mare. Mehedinți, SW Romania
127 P3 Vankarem Chukotskiy Avtonomnyy Okrug, NE Russian Federation
13 N12 Vankleek Hill Ontario, SE Canada
Van, Lake see Van Gölü
94 I8 Vanna island N Norway
95 I16 Vännäs Västerbotten, N Sweden
95 I15 Vännäsby Västerbotten, N Sweden
104 H7 Vannes anc. Dariorigum. Morbihan, NW France
105 T12 Vanoise, Massif de la ▲ E France
176 Xx10 Van Rees, Pegunungan ▲ Irian Jaya, E Indonesia
85 E24 Vanrhynsdorp Western Cape, SW South Africa
23 P7 Vansant Virginia, NE USA
96 L13 Vansbro Kopparberg, C Sweden
97 D18 Vanse Vest-Agder, S Norway
15 M4 Vansittart Island island Northwest Territories, NE Canada
95 M20 Vantaa Swe. Vanda. Uusimaa, S Finland
95 L19 Vantaa ✕ (Helsinki) Uusimaa, S Finland
34 J9 Vantage Washington, NW USA
197 K14 Vanua Balavu prev. Vanua Mbalavu. island Lau Group, E Fiji
197 C10 Vanua Lava island Banks Islands, N Vanuatu
197 J12 Vanua Levu island N Fiji
197 I12 Vanua Levu Barrier Reef reef C Fiji
Vanua Mbalavu see Vanua Balavu
197 B10 Vanuatu off. Republic of Vanuatu; prev. New Hebrides. ◆ republic SW Pacific Ocean
183 P8 Vanuatu island group, SW Pacific Ocean
197 K15 Vanua Vatu island Lau Group, E Fiji
33 Q12 Van Wert Ohio, N USA
197 K7 Vao Province Sud, S New Caledonia
Vapincum see Gap
119 N7 Vapnyarka Vinnyts'ka Oblast', C Ukraine
105 T15 Var ◐ department SE France
105 U14 Var SE France
97 J18 Vara Skaraborg, S Sweden
Varadinska Županija see Varaždin
120 J10 Varakļani Madona, C Latvia
108 C7 Varallo Piemonte, NE Italy
149 O5 Varāmīn var. Veramin. Tehrān, N Iran
159 N14 Vārānasi prev. Banaras, Benares, hist. Kasi. Uttar Pradesh, N India
129 T3 Varandey Nenetskiy Avtonomnyy Okrug, NW Russian Federation
94 M8 Varangerbotn Finnmark, N Norway
94 M8 Varangerfjorden fjord N Norway
94 M8 Varangerhalvøya peninsula N Norway
Varannó see Vranov nad Topľou
109 M15 Varano, Lago di ◎ SE Italy
120 J13 Varapayeva Rus. Voropayevo. Vitsyebskaya Voblasts', NW Belorussia
Varasd see Varaždin
114 E7 Varaždin Ger. Warasdin, Hung. Varasd. Varaždin, N Croatia
114 E7 Varaždin off. Varadinska Županija. ◐ province N Croatia
108 C10 Varazze Liguria, NW Italy
97 J20 Varberg Halland, S Sweden
Vardak see Wardag
115 Q19 Vardar Gk. Axiós. FYR Macedonia/Greece see also Axiós
97 F23 Varde Ribe, W Denmark
143 V12 Vardenis E Armenia
94 N8 Vardø Fin. Vuoreija. Finnmark, N Norway
117 E18 Vardoúsia ▲ C Greece
Vareia see Logroño
102 G10 Varel Niedersachsen, NW Germany
121 G15 Varėna Pol. Orany. Varėna, S Lithuania
13 O12 Varennes Québec, SE Canada
105 P10 Varennes-sur-Allier Allier, C France
114 I12 Vareš E Bosnia and Herzegovina
108 D7 Varese Lombardia, N Italy
118 J12 Vârful Moldoveanu var. Moldoveanul; prev. Vîrful Moldoveanu. ▲ C Romania
Varganzi see Warganza
97 J18 Vårgårda Älvsborg, S Sweden
125 F12 Vargashi Kurganskaya Oblast', C Russian Federation
97 J18 Vargön Älvsborg, S Sweden
97 C17 Varhaug Rogaland, S Norway
95 N17 Varkaus Kuopio, C Finland
94 J2 Varmahlídh Nordhurland Vestra, N Iceland
97 J15 Värmland ◐ county C Sweden
97 K16 Värmlandsnäs peninsula S Sweden
116 N8 Varna prev. Stalin, anc. Odessus. Varnenska Oblast, NE Bulgaria
116 N8 Varna ✕ Varnenska Oblast, NE Bulgaria
Varna see Varnenska Oblast
97 L20 Värnamo Jönköping, S Sweden
116 M7 Varnenska Oblast var. Varna. ◐ province NE Bulgaria
116 N8 Varnenski Zaliv prev. Stalinski Zaliv. bay E Bulgaria
116 N8 Varnensko Ezero estuary E Bulgaria
120 D11 Varniai Telšiai, W Lithuania
Varnoús see Baba
113 D14 Varnsdorf Ger. Warnsdorf. Severní Čechy, N Czech Republic
113 I23 Várpalota Veszprém, W Hungary
Varshava see Warszawa
120 K6 Värska Põlvamaa, SE Estonia
100 N12 Varsseveld Gelderland, E Netherlands
117 D19 Vartholomió prev. Vartholomión. Dytikí Ellás, S Greece
Vartholomión see Vartholomió
143 Q14 Varto Muş, E Turkey
97 K18 Vartofta Skaraborg, S Sweden
95 O17 Värtsilä Pohjois-Karjala, E Finland
Värtsilä see Vyartsilya
119 R4 Varva Chernihivs'ka Oblast', NE Ukraine
61 H18 Várzea Grande Mato Grosso, SW Brazil
108 D9 Varzi Lombardia, N Italy
Varzimanor Ayni see Ayní
128 K5 Varzuga NW Russian Federation
105 P8 Varzy Nièvre, C France
113 G23 Vas off. Vas Megye. ◐ county W Hungary
Vasa see Vaasa
202 A9 Vasafua island Funafuti Atoll, C Tuvalu
113 O21 Vásárosnamény Szabolcs-Szatmár-Bereg, E Hungary
106 H13 Vascão, Ribeira de S Portugal
118 G10 Vașcău Hung. Vaskoh. Bihor, NE Romania
Vascongadas, Provincias see País Vasco
Vashess Bay see Vaskess Bay
Vāsht see Khāsh
Vasilevichi see Vasilyevichy
117 G14 Vasilikà Kentrikí Makedonía, NE Greece
117 C18 Vasilikí Lefkáda, Iónioi Nísoi, Greece, C Mediterranean Sea
117 K25 Vasilikí Kríti, Greece, E Mediterranean Sea
121 G16 Vasilishki Pol. Wasiliszki, Rus. Vasilishki. Hrodzyenskaya Voblasts', W Belorussia
Vasil Kolarov see Pamporovo
Vasil'kov see Vasyl'kiv
121 N19 Vasilyevichy Rus. Vasilevichi. Homyel'skaya Voblasts', SE Belorussia
203 Y3 Vaskess Bay var. Vashess Bay. bay Kiritimati, E Kiribati
Vaskoh see Vașcău
Vaskohsziklás see Ştei
118 M10 Vaslui Vaslui, C Romania
118 L11 Vaslui ◐ county NE Romania
33 R8 Vassar Michigan, N USA
97 E15 Vassdalseggi ▲ S Norway
62 P9 Vassouras Rio de Janeiro, SE Brazil
94 H11 Vastenjaure ◎ N Sweden
97 N15 Västerås Västmanland, C Sweden
95 G15 Västerbotten ◐ county N Sweden
96 K12 Västerdalälven C Sweden
97 O16 Västerhaninge Stockholm, C Sweden
96 M10 Västernorrland ◐ county C Sweden
97 N19 Västervik Kalmar, S Sweden
97 M15 Västmanland ◐ county C Sweden
109 L15 Vasto anc. Histonium. Abruzzi, C Italy
97 J16 Västra Silen ◎ S Sweden
113 G23 Vasvár Ger. Eisenburg. Vas, W Hungary
119 U9 Vasylivka Zaporiz'ka Oblast', SE Ukraine
119 O5 Vasyl'kiv Rus. Vasil'kov. Kyyivs'ka Oblast', N Ukraine
126 Gg12 Vasyugan C Russian Federation
105 N8 Vatan Indre, C France
Vaté see Éfaté
xliii A14 Vatersay island NW Scotland, UK
109 G15 Vatican City off. Vatican City State. ◆ papal state S Europe
109 M22 Vaticano, Capo headland S Italy
Vatilí see Vadili
94 K3 Vatnajökull glacier SE Iceland
97 P15 Vätö Stockholm, C Sweden
197 L16 Vatoa island Lau Group, SE Fiji
180 J5 Vatomandry Toamasina, E Madagascar
118 J9 Vatra Dornei Ger. Dorna Watra. Suceava, NE Romania
118 J9 Vatra Moldoviței Suceava, NE Romania
Vatter, Lake see Vättern
97 L18 Vättern Eng. Lake Vatter; prev. Lake Vetter. ◎ S Sweden
197 H14 Vatukoula Viti Levu, W Fiji
197 H15 Vatulele island SW Fiji
119 P7 Vatutine Cherkas'ka Oblast', C Ukraine
197 J14 Vatu Vara island Lau Group, E Fiji
105 R14 Vaucluse ◐ department SE France
105 S5 Vaucouleurs Meuse, NE France
110 B9 Vaud Ger. Waadt. ◐ canton SW Switzerland
13 N12 Vaudreuil Québec, SE Canada
39 T12 Vaughn New Mexico, SW USA
56 I14 Vaupés off. Comisaría del Vaupés. ◐ province SE Colombia
56 J13 Vaupés, Río var. Rio Uaupés. Brazil/Colombia see also Uaupés, Rio
105 Q15 Vauvert Gard, S France
9 R17 Vauxhall Alberta, SW Canada
101 K23 Vaux-sur-Sûre Luxembourg, SE Belgium
180 J4 Vavatenina Toamasina, E Madagascar
200 Ss12 Vava'u Group island group N Tonga
78 M16 Vavoua W Ivory Coast
131 S2 Vavozh Udmurtskaya Respublika, NW Russian Federation
161 K23 Vavuniya Northern Province, N Sri Lanka
121 G17 Vawkavysk Pol. Wołkowysk, Rus. Volkovysk. Hrodzyenskaya Voblasts', W Belorussia
121 F17 Vawkavyskaye Wzvyshsha Rus. Volkovyskiye Vysoty. hill range W Belorussia
97 P15 Vaxholm Stockholm, C Sweden
97 L21 Växjö var. Vexiö. Kronoberg, S Sweden
129 T1 Vaygach, Ostrov island NW Russian Federation
143 V13 Vayk' prev. Azizbekov. SE Armenia
129 P8 Vazhgort prev. Chasovo. Respublika Komi, NW Russian Federation
47 V10 V.C.Bird ✕ (St John's) Antigua, Antigua and Barbuda
31 Q7 Veblen South Dakota, N USA
100 N9 Vecht Ger. Vechte. Germany/Netherlands see also Vechte
102 G12 Vechta Niedersachsen, NW Germany
102 E12 Vechte Dut. Vecht. Germany/Netherlands see also Vecht
120 I8 Vecpiebalga Cēsis, C Latvia
120 G9 Vecumnieki Bauska, C Latvia
Vedāvati see Hagari
97 J20 Veddige Halland, S Sweden
118 J15 Vedea S Romania
131 P16 Vedeno Chechenskaya Respublika, SW Russian Federation
197 H14 Ve Drala Reef reef N Fiji
97 C16 Vedvågen Rogaland, S Norway
100 O6 Veendam Groningen, NE Netherlands
100 K12 Veenendaal Utrecht, C Netherlands
101 E14 Veere Zeeland, SW Netherlands
26 M2 Vega Texas, SW USA
94 E13 Vega island C Norway
47 T5 Vega Baja C Puerto Rico
40 D17 Vega Point headland Kiska Island, Alaska, USA
97 F17 Vegår ◎ S Norway
101 K14 Veghel Noord-Brabant, S Netherlands
Veglia see Krk
116 E13 Vegorítis, Límni ◎ N Greece
9 Q14 Vegreville Alberta, SW Canada
97 K21 Veinge Halland, S Sweden
63 B21 Veinticinco de Mayo var. 25 de Mayo. Buenos Aires, E Argentina
65 I14 Veinticinco de Mayo La Pampa, C Argentina
121 F15 Veisiejai Lazdijai, S Lithuania
97 F23 Vejen Ribe, W Denmark
106 K16 Vejer de la Frontera Andalucía, S Spain
97 G23 Vejle Vejle, C Denmark
97 F23 Vejle off. Vejle Amt. ◐ county C Denmark
116 M7 Vekilski Varnenska Oblast, NE Bulgaria
56 G3 Vela, Cabo de la headland NE Colombia
Vela Goa see Goa
115 F15 Vela Luka Dubrovnik-Neretva, S Croatia
63 G19 Velázquez Rocha, E Uruguay
103 E15 Velbert Nordrhein-Westfalen, W Germany
111 S9 Velden Kärnten, S Austria
Veldes see Bled
101 K15 Veldhoven Noord-Brabant, S Netherlands
114 C11 Velebit ▲ C Croatia
116 N11 Veleka SE Bulgaria
111 V10 Velenje Ger. Wöllan. N Slovenia
202 E12 Vele, Pointe headland Île Futuna, S Wallis and Futuna
115 O18 Veles Turk. Köprülü. C FYR Macedonia
115 M20 Veleshta SW FYR Macedonia
117 F16 Velestino prev. Velestínon. Thessalía, C Greece
Velestinon see Velestino
Velevshchina see Vyelyewshchyna
56 F9 Vélez Santander, C Colombia
107 Q13 Vélez Blanco Andalucía, S Spain
106 M17 Vélez de la Gomera, Peñon de island group S Spain
107 N15 Vélez-Málaga Andalucía, S Spain
107 Q13 Vélez Rubio Andalucía, S Spain
Velha Goa see Goa
Velho see Porto Velho
114 E8 Velika Gorica Grad Zagreb, N Croatia
114 C9 Velika Kapela ▲ NW Croatia
Velika Kikinda see Kikinda
114 D10 Velika Kladuša NW Bosnia and Herzegovina
114 N11 Velika Morava var. Glavn'a Morava, Morava, Ger. Grosse Morava. C Yugoslavia

◆ Country ● Country Capital ◇ Dependent Territory ○ Dependent Territory Capital ◐ Administrative Region ✕ International Airport ▲ Mountain ▲ Mountain Range Volcano River ◎ Lake ⊠ Reservoir

Velika Plana – Villardefrades

114 N12 **Velika Plana** Serbia, C Yugoslavia
127 Pp5 **Velikaya** ∽ NE Russian Federation
128 F15 **Velikaya** ∽ W Russian Federation
Velikaya Berestovitsa *see* Vyalikaya Byerastavitsa
Velikaya Lepetikha *see* Velyka Lepetykha
Veliki Bečkerek *see* Zrenjanin
114 P12 **Veliki Krš** *var.* Stol. ▲ E Yugoslavia
116 L8 **Veliki Preslav** *prev.* Preslav. Varnenska Oblast, NE Bulgaria
114 B9 **Veliki Risnjak** ▲ NW Croatia
114 J13 **Veliki Stolac** ▲ E Bosnia and Herzegovina
Velikiy Bor *see* Vyaliki Bor
128 G16 **Velikiye Luki** Pskovskaya Oblast', W Russian Federation
129 P12 **Velikiy Ustyug** Vologodskaya Oblast', NW Russian Federation
114 N11 **Veliko Gradište** Serbia, NE Yugoslavia
161 I18 **Velikonda Range** ▲▲ SE India
116 K9 **Veliko Tŭrnovo** *prev.* Tirnovo, Trnovo, Tŭrnovo. Loveshka Oblast, N Bulgaria
Velikovec *see* Völkermarkt
129 R5 **Velikovisochnoye** Nenetskiy Avtonomnyy Okrug, NW Russian Federation
78 H12 **Vélingara** C Senegal
78 H11 **Vélingara** S Senegal
116 H11 **Velingrad** Plovdivska Oblast, SW Bulgaria
130 H3 **Velizh** Smolenskaya Oblast', W Russian Federation
113 F16 **Velká Deštná** *var.* Deštná, Grosskoppe, *Ger.* Deschnaer Koppe. ▲ NE Czech Republic
113 F18 **Velké Meziříčí** *Ger.* Grossmeseritsch. Jižní Morava, SE Czech Republic
94 N1 **Velkomstpynten** *headland* NW Svalbard
113 K21 **Vel'ký Krtíš** Stredné Slovensko, S Slovakia
195 T14 **Vella Lavella** *var.* Mbilua. *island* New Georgia Islands, NW Solomon Islands
109 I15 **Velletri** Lazio, C Italy
97 K23 **Vellinge** Malmöhus, S Sweden
161 I19 **Vellore** Tamil Nādu, SE India
Velobriga *see* Viana do Castelo
117 G21 **Velopoúla** *island* S Greece
100 M12 **Velp** Gelderland, SE Netherlands
Velsen *see* Velsen-Noord
100 H9 **Velsen-Noord** *var.* Velsen. Noord-Holland, W Netherlands
129 N12 **Vel'sk** *var.* Velsk. Arkhangel'skaya Oblast', NW Russian Federation
Velsuna *see* Orvieto
100 K10 **Veluwemeer** *lake channel* C Netherlands
30 M3 **Velva** North Dakota, N USA
117 E14 **Velvendós** *var.* Velvendos. Dytikí Makedonía, N Greece
119 S5 **Velyka Bahachka** Poltavs'ka Oblast', C Ukraine
119 S9 **Velyka Lepetykha** *Rus.* Velikaya Lepetikha. Khersons'ka Oblast', S Ukraine
119 O10 **Velyka Mykhaylivka** Odes'ka Oblast', SW Ukraine
119 W8 **Velyka Novosilka** Donets'ka Oblast', E Ukraine
119 S9 **Velyka Oleksandrivka** Khersons'ka Oblast', S Ukraine
119 T4 **Velyka Pysanivka** Sums'ka Oblast', NE Ukraine
118 G6 **Velykyy Bereznyy** Zakarpats'ka Oblast', W Ukraine
119 W4 **Velykyy Burluk** Kharkivs'ka Oblast', E Ukraine
Velykyy Tokmak *see* Tokmak
181 P7 **Vema Fracture Zone** *tectonic feature* W Indian Ocean
67 P18 **Vema Seamount** *undersea feature* SW Indian Ocean
95 F17 **Vemdalen** Jämtland, C Sweden
97 N19 **Vena** Kalmar, S Sweden
43 N11 **Venado** San Luis Potosí, C Mexico
64 L11 **Venado Tuerto** Entre Ríos, E Argentina
63 A19 **Venado Tuerto** Santa Fe, C Argentina
109 K16 **Venafro** Molise, C Italy
57 Q9 **Venamo, Cerro** ▲ E Venezuela
108 B8 **Venaria** Piemonte, NW Italy
105 U15 **Vence** Alpes-Maritimes, SE France
106 H5 **Venda Nova** Vila Real, N Portugal
106 G11 **Vendas Novas** Évora, S Portugal
104 J9 **Vendée** ◆ *department* NW France
105 Q6 **Vendeuvre-sur-Barse** Aube, NE France
104 M7 **Vendôme** Loir-et-Cher, C France
Venedig *see* Venezia
Vener, Lake *see* Vänern
108 I8 **Veneta, Laguna** *lagoon* NE Italy
Venetia *see* Venezia
41 S7 **Venetie** Alaska, USA
108 H8 **Veneto** *var.* Venezia Euganea. ◆ *region* NE Italy
116 M7 **Venets** Varnenska Oblast, NE Bulgaria
130 L5 **Venev** Tul'skaya Oblast', W Russian Federation
108 I8 **Venezia** *Eng.* Venice, *Fr.* Venise, *Ger.* Venedig; *anc.*Venetia. Veneto, NE Italy
Venezia Euganea *see* Veneto
Venezia, Golfo di *see* Venice, Gulf of
Venezia Tridentina *see* Trentino-Alto Adige
56 K8 **Venezuela** *off.* Republic of Venezuela; *prev.* Estados Unidos de Venezuela, United States of Venezuela. ♦ *republic* N South America
Venezuela, Cordillera de *see* Costa, Cordillera de la
56 I4 **Venezuela, Golfo de** *Eng.* Gulf of Maracaibo, Gulf of Venezuela. *gulf* NW Venezuela
Venezuela, Gulf of *see* Venezuela, Golfo de
66 F11 **Venezuelan Basin** *undersea feature* E Caribbean Sea
161 D15 **Vengurla** Mahārāshtra, W India
41 O15 **Veniaminof, Mount** ▲ Alaska, USA
25 V14 **Venice** Florida, SE USA
24 L10 **Venice** Louisiana, S USA
Venice *see* Venezia
108 J8 **Venice, Gulf of** *It.* Golfo di Venezia, *Slvn.* Beneški Zaliv. *gulf* N Adriatic Sea
Venise *see* Venezia
96 K13 **Venjan** Kopparberg, C Sweden
96 K13 **Venjansjön** ◎ C Sweden
161 J18 **Venkatagiri** Andhra Pradesh, E India
101 M15 **Venlo** *prev.* Venloo. Limburg, SE Netherlands
Venloo *see* Venlo
97 E18 **Vennesla** Vest-Agder, S Norway
109 M17 **Venosa** *anc.* Venusia. Basilicata, S Italy
Venoste, Alpi *see* Ötztaler Alpen
Venraij *see* Venray
101 M14 **Venray** *var.* Venraij. Limburg, SE Netherlands
120 C8 **Venta** *Ger.* Windau. ∽ Latvia/Lithuania
Venta Belgarum *see* Winchester
42 G9 **Ventana, Punta Arena de la** *var.* Punta de la Ventana. *headland* W Mexico
Ventana, Punta de la *see* Ventana, Punta Arena de la
63 B23 **Ventana, Sierra de la** *hill range* E Argentina
Ventia *see* Valence
203 S11 **Vent, Îles du** *var.* Windward Islands. *island group* Archipel de la Société, W French Polynesia
203 R10 **Vent, Îles Sous le** *var.* Leeward Islands. *island group* Archipel de la Société, W French Polynesia
108 B11 **Ventimiglia** Liguria, NW Italy
xxxvii Q14 **Ventnor** Isle of Wight, S England, UK
20 J17 **Ventnor City** New Jersey, NE USA
105 S14 **Ventoux, Mont** ▲ SE France
120 C8 **Ventspils** *Ger.* Windau. Ventspils, NW Latvia
56 M10 **Ventuari, Río** ∽ S Venezuela
37 R15 **Ventura** California, W USA
190 F8 **Venus Bay** South Australia
Venusia *see* Venosa
203 P7 **Vénus, Pointe** *var.* Pointe Tataaihoa. *headland* Tahiti, W French Polynesia
43 V16 **Venustiano Carranza** Chiapas, SE Mexico
43 N7 **Venustiano Carranza, Presa** ▣ NE Mexico
63 B15 **Vera** Santa Fe, C Argentina
107 Q14 **Vera** Andalucía, S Spain
65 K18 **Vera, Bahía** *bay* E Argentina
43 R14 **Veracruz** *var.* Veracruz Llave. Veracruz-Llave, E Mexico
43 Q13 **Veracruz-Llave** *var.* Veracruz. ◆ *state* E Mexico
45 Q16 **Veraguas** *off.* Provincia de Veraguas. ◆ *province* W Panama
Veramin *see* Varāmīn
160 B12 **Verāval** Gujarāt, W India
108 C6 **Verbania** Piemonte, NW Italy
109 N20 **Verbicaro** Calabria, SW Italy
110 D11 **Verbier** Valais, SW Switzerland
Vercellae *see* Vercelli
108 C8 **Vercelli** *anc.* Vercellae. Piemonte, NW Italy
105 S13 **Vercors** *physical region* E France
95 E16 **Verdalsøra** Nord-Trøndelag, C Norway
Verde, Cabo *see* Cape Verde
46 J5 **Verde, Cape** *headland* Long Island, C Bahamas
106 M2 **Verde, Costa** *coastal region* N Spain
Verde Grande, Río/Verde Grande y de Belem, Río *see* Verde, Río
102 H11 **Verden** Niedersachsen, NW Germany
61 J19 **Verde, Rio** ∽ SE Brazil
59 P16 **Verde, Río** ∽ Bolivia/Brazil
42 M12 **Verde, Río** *var.* Río Verde Grande, Río Verde Grande y de Belem. ∽ C Mexico
43 Q16 **Verde, Río** ∽ SE Mexico
38 L13 **Verde River** ∽ Arizona, SW USA
Verdhikoúsa/Verdhikoússa *see* Verdikoússa
29 Q8 **Verdigris River** ∽ Kansas/Oklahoma, C USA
117 E15 **Verdikoússa** *var.* Verdhikoúsa, Verdhikoússa. Thessalía, C Greece
105 S15 **Verdon** ∽ SE France
13 O12 **Verdun** Québec, SE Canada
105 S4 **Verdun** *var.* Verdun-sur-Meuse; *anc.* Verodunum. Meuse, NE France
Verdun-sur-Meuse *see* Verdun
85 J21 **Vereeniging** Gauteng, NE South Africa
Veremeyki *see* Vyeramyeyki
129 T14 **Vereshchagino** Permskaya Oblast', NW Russian Federation
78 G14 **Verga, Cap** *headland* W Guinea
63 G18 **Vergara** Treinta y Tres, E Uruguay
110 G11 **Vergeletto** Ticino, S Switzerland
20 L8 **Vergennes** Vermont, NE USA
Veria *see* Véroia
106 I5 **Verín** Galicia, NW Spain
Verin T'alin *see* T'alin
120 K6 **Veriora** Põlvamaa, SE Estonia
119 T7 **Verkhivtseve** Dnipropetrovs'ka Oblast', E Ukraine
131 W3 **Verkhiye Kigi** Respublika Bashkortostan, W Russian Federation
Verkhnedvinsk *see* Vyerkhnyadzvinsk
126 Hh11 **Verkhneimbatsk** Krasnoyarskiy Kray, N Russian Federation
128 I3 **Verkhnetulomskiy** Murmanskaya Oblast', NW Russian Federation
128 I3 **Verkhnetulomskoye Vodokhranilishche** ▣ NW Russian Federation
Verkhneudinsk *see* Ulan-Ude
126 L11 **Verkhnevilyuysk** Respublika Sakha (Yakutiya), NE Russian Federation
131 W5 **Verkhniy Avzyan** Respublika Bashkortostan, W Russian Federation
131 Q11 **Verkhniy Baskunchak** Astrakhanskaya Oblast', SW Russian Federation
119 T9 **Verkhniy Rohachyk** Khersons'ka Oblast', S Ukraine
126 Ll12 **Verkhnyaya Amga** Respublika Sakha (Yakutiya), NE Russian Federation
129 V6 **Verkhnyaya Inta** Respublika Komi, NW Russian Federation
126 Ii6 **Verkhnyaya Taymyra** ∽ N Russian Federation
129 O10 **Verkhnyaya Toyma** Arkhangel'skaya Oblast', NW Russian Federation
130 K6 **Verkhov'ye** Orlovskaya Oblast', W Russian Federation
118 I8 **Verkhovyna** Ivano-Frankivs'ka Oblast', W Ukraine
126 M8 **Verkhoyansk** Respublika Sakha (Yakutiya), NE Russian Federation
126 L8 **Verkhoyanskiy Khrebet** ▲▲ NE Russian Federation
119 T7 **Verkhn'odniprovs'k** Dnipropetrovs'ka Oblast', E Ukraine
103 G14 **Verl** Nordrhein-Westfalen, NW Germany
94 N1 **Verlegenhuken** *headland* N Svalbard
84 A9 **Vermelha, Ponta** *headland* NW Angola
105 P7 **Vermenton** Yonne, C France
9 R14 **Vermilion** Alberta, SW Canada
33 T11 **Vermilion** Ohio, N USA
24 I10 **Vermilion Bay** *bay* Louisiana, S USA
31 V4 **Vermilion Lake** ◎ Minnesota, N USA
12 F9 **Vermilion River** ∽ Ontario, S Canada
32 L12 **Vermilion River** ∽ Illinois, N USA
31 R12 **Vermillion** South Dakota, N USA
31 R12 **Vermillion River** ∽ South Dakota, N USA
13 O9 **Vermillon, Rivière** ∽ Québec, SE Canada
117 E14 **Vérmio** ▲▲ N Greece
20 L8 **Vermont** *off.* State of Vermont; also known as The Green Mountain State. ◆ *state* NE USA
115 K16 **Vermosh** *var.* Vermoshi. Shkodër, N Albania
Vermoshi *see* Vermosh
39 O3 **Vernal** Utah, W USA
12 G11 **Verner** Ontario, S Canada
104 M5 **Verneuil-sur-Avre** Eure, N France
xxxvii P10 **Vernham Dean** Hampshire, S England, UK
116 D13 **Vérno** ▲ N Greece
9 N17 **Vernon** British Columbia, SW Canada
104 M4 **Vernon** Eure, N France
25 N3 **Vernon** Alabama, S USA
33 P15 **Vernon** Indiana, N USA
27 Q4 **Vernon** Texas, SW USA
34 G10 **Vernonia** Oregon, NW USA
12 G12 **Vernon, Lake** ◎ Ontario, S Canada
24 G7 **Vernon Lake** ▣ Louisiana, S USA
25 Y13 **Vero Beach** Florida, SE USA
Verőcze *see* Virovitica
Verodunum *see* Verdun
117 E14 **Véroia** *var.* Veria, Vérroia, *Turk.* Karaferiye. Kentrikí Makedonía, N Greece
108 E8 **Verolanuova** Lombardia, N Italy
12 K14 **Verona** Ontario, SE Canada
108 G8 **Verona** Veneto, NE Italy
31 P6 **Verona** North Dakota, N USA
32 L9 **Verona** Wisconsin, N USA
63 E20 **Verónica** Buenos Aires, E Argentina
24 J9 **Verret, Lake** ◎ Louisiana, S USA
Vérroia *see* Véroia
195 P10 **Verron Range** ▲▲ New Ireland, NE PNG
105 N5 **Versailles** Yvelines, N France
33 P15 **Versailles** Indiana, N USA
22 M5 **Versailles** Kentucky, S USA
29 U5 **Versailles** Missouri, C USA
33 Q13 **Versailles** Ohio, N USA
Versecz *see* Vršac
110 A10 **Versoix** Genève, SW Switzerland
13 Z6 **Verte, Pointe** *headland* Québec, SE Canada
113 I22 **Vértes** ▲▲ NW Hungary
46 G6 **Vertientes** Camagüey, C Cuba
116 G13 **Vertískos** ▲▲ N Greece
104 I8 **Vertou** Loire-Atlantique, NW France
Verulamium *see* St Albans
101 L19 **Verviers** Liège, E Belgium
xxxvii N13 **Verwood** Dorset, S England, UK
xxxvi C17 **Veryan** Cornwall, SW England, UK
104 F1 **Vescovato** Corse, France, C Mediterranean Sea
101 L20 **Vesdre** ∽ E Belgium
119 U10 **Vesele** *Rus.* Veseloye. Zaporiz'ka Oblast', S Ukraine
113 D18 **Veselí nad Lužnicí** *var.* Weseli an der Lainsitz, *Ger.* Frohenbruck. Jižní Čechy, S Czech Republic
116 M9 **Veselinovo** Varnenska Oblast, E Bulgaria
130 L12 **Veselovskoye Vodokhranilishche** ▣ SW Russian Federation
Veseloye *see* Vesele
119 Q9 **Veselynove** Mykolayivs'ka Oblast', S Ukraine
Veseya *see* Vyasyeya
130 M10 **Veshenskaya** Rostovskaya Oblast', SW Russian Federation
131 Q5 **Veshkayma** Ul'yanovskaya Oblast', W Russian Federation
Vesisaari *see* Vadsø
Vesontio *see* Besançon
105 T7 **Vesoul** *anc.* Vesulium, Vesulum. Haute-Saône, E France
97 J20 **Vessigebro** Halland, S Sweden
97 D17 **Vest-Agder** ◆ *county* S Norway
25 P4 **Vestavia Hills** Alabama, S USA
86 F6 **Vesterålen** *island* NW Norway
94 G10 **Vesterålen** *island group* N Norway
89 W3 **Vestervig** Viborg, NW Denmark
94 H2 **Vestfirdhir** ◆ *region* NW Iceland
94 G11 **Vestfjorden** *fjord* C Norway
97 G16 **Vestfold** ◆ *county* S Norway
94 I4 **Vestmannaeyjar** Sudhurland, S Iceland
96 E9 **Vestnes** Møre og Romsdal, S Norway
97 I23 **Vestsjælland** *off.* Vestsjællands Amt. ◆ *county* E Denmark
94 H3 **Vesturland** ◆ *region* W Iceland
94 G11 **Vestvågøy** *island* C Norway
Vesulium/Vesulum *see* Vesoul
Vesuna *see* Périgueux
109 K17 **Vesuvio** *Eng.* Vesuvius. ✖ S Italy
Vesuvius *see* Vesuvio
128 K14 **Ves'yegonsk** Tverskaya Oblast', W Russian Federation
113 I23 **Veszprém** *Ger.* Veszprim. Veszprém, W Hungary
113 H23 **Veszprém** *off.* Veszprém Megye. ◆ *county* W Hungary
Veszprim *see* Veszprém
Vetka *see* Vyetka
97 M19 **Vetlanda** Jönköping, S Sweden
131 P1 **Vetluga** Nizhegorodskaya Oblast', W Russian Federation
129 P14 **Vetluga** ∽ NW Russian Federation
129 O14 **Vetluzhskiy** Kostromskaya Oblast', NW Russian Federation
131 P2 **Vetluzhskiy** Nizhegorodskaya Oblast', W Russian Federation
109 H14 **Vetralla** Lazio, C Italy
116 M9 **Vetren** *prev.* Zhitarovo. Burgaska Oblast, E Bulgaria
116 M8 **Vetrino** Varnenska Oblast, NE Bulgaria
Vetrino *see* Vyetryna
126 Ii6 **Vetrovaya, Gora** ▲ N Russian Federation
Vetter, Lake *see* Vättern
108 J13 **Vettore, Monte** ▲ C Italy
101 A17 **Veurne** *var.* Furnes. West-Vlaanderen, W Belgium
33 Q15 **Vevay** Indiana, N USA
110 C10 **Vevey** *Ger.* Vivis; *anc.* Vibiscum. Vaud, SW Switzerland
Vexiö *see* Växjö
105 S13 **Veynes** Hautes-Alpes, SE France
105 N11 **Vézère** ∽ W France
116 J9 **Vezhen** ▲ C Bulgaria
142 K11 **Vezirköprü** Samsun, N Turkey
59 J18 **Viacha** La Paz, W Bolivia
29 R10 **Vian** Oklahoma, C USA
Viana de Castelo *see* Viana do Castelo
106 H12 **Viana do Alentejo** Évora, S Portugal
106 I4 **Viana do Bolo** Galicia, NW Spain
106 G5 **Viana do Castelo** *var.* Viana de Castelo; *anc.* Velobriga. Viana do Castelo, NW Portugal
106 G5 **Viana do Castelo** *var.* Viana de Castelo. ◆ *district* N Portugal
100 J12 **Vianen** Zuid-Holland, C Netherlands
178 I8 **Viangchan** *Eng./Fr.* Vientiane. ● (Laos) C Laos
178 I6 **Viangphoukha** *var.* Vieng Pou Kha. Louang Namtha, N Laos
106 K13 **Viar** ∽ SW Spain
108 E11 **Viareggio** Toscana, C Italy
105 O14 **Viaur** ∽ S France
Vibiscum *see* Vevey
97 G21 **Viborg** Viborg, NW Denmark
31 R12 **Viborg** South Dakota, N USA
97 F21 **Viborg** *off.* Viborg Amt. ◆ *county* NW Denmark
109 N22 **Vibo Valentia** *prev.* Monteleone di Calabria; *anc.* Hipponium. Calabria, SW Italy
107 W5 **Vic** *var.* Vich; *anc.* Ausa, Vicus Ausonensis. Cataluña, NE Spain
104 K16 **Vic-en-Bigorre** Hautes-Pyrénées, S France
42 K10 **Vicente Guerrero** Durango, C Mexico
43 P10 **Vicente Guerrero, Presa** *var.* Presa de las Adjuntas. ▣ NE Mexico
Vicentia *see* Vicenza
108 G8 **Vicenza** *anc.* Vicentia. Veneto, NE Italy
Vich *see* Vic
56 J10 **Vichada** *off.* Comisaría del Vichada. ◆ *province* E Colombia
56 K10 **Vichada, Río** ∽ E Colombia
63 G17 **Vichadero** Rivera, NE Uruguay
Vichegda *see* Vychegda
128 M16 **Vichuga** Ivanovskaya Oblast', W Russian Federation
105 P10 **Vichy** Allier, C France
28 K9 **Vici** Oklahoma, C USA
xl L12 **Vickerstown** Cumbria, NW England, UK
33 P10 **Vicksburg** Michigan, N USA
24 J5 **Vicksburg** Mississippi, S USA
105 O12 **Vic-sur-Cère** Cantal, C France
31 X14 **Victor** Iowa, C USA
61 J21 **Víctor** Mato Grosso do Sul, SW Brazil
190 I10 **Victor Harbor** South Australia
63 C18 **Victoria** Entre Ríos, E Argentina
8 L17 **Victoria** Vancouver Island, British Columbia, SW Canada
47 R14 **Victoria** NW Grenada
44 H6 **Victoria** Yoro, NW Honduras
123 J16 **Victoria** *var.* Rabat. Gozo, NW Malta
118 I12 **Victoria** *Ger.* Viktoriastadt. Brașov, C Romania
180 H17 **Victoria** ● (Seychelles) Mahé, SW Seychelles
27 U13 **Victoria** Texas, SW USA
191 N12 **Victoria** ◆ *state* SE Australia
182 K7 **Victoria** ∽ Western Australia
Victoria *see* Labuan, East Malaysia
Victoria *see* Masvingo, Zimbabwe
Victoria Bank *see* Vitória Seamount
9 Y15 **Victoria Beach** Manitoba, S Canada
Victoria de Durango *see* Durango
Victoria de las Tunas *see* Las Tunas
85 I16 **Victoria Falls** Matabeleland North, W Zimbabwe
85 I16 **Victoria Falls** ✖ Matabeleland North, W Zimbabwe
85 I16 **Victoria Falls** *waterfall* Zambia/Zimbabwe
Victoria Falls *see* Iguaçu, Salto do
65 F19 **Victoria, Isla** *island* Archipiélago de los Chonos, S Chile
15 J2 **Victoria Island** *island* Northwest Territories, NW Canada
190 L8 **Victoria, Lake** ◎ New South Wales, SE Australia
70 J13 **Victoria, Lake** *var.* Victoria Nyanza. ◎ E Africa
205 S13 **Victoria Land** *physical region* Antarctica
177 F5 **Victoria, Mount** ▲ W Burma
197 I14 **Victoria, Mount** ▲ Viti Levu, W Fiji
194 K15 **Victoria, Mount** ▲ S PNG
83 F17 **Victoria Nile** *var.* Somerset Nile. ∽ C Uganda
Victoria Nyanza *see* Victoria, Lake
44 G3 **Victoria Peak** ▲ SE Belize
193 H16 **Victoria Range** ▲▲ South Island, NZ
189 O3 **Victoria River** ∽ Northern Territory, N Australia
189 P3 **Victoria River Roadhouse** Northern Territory, N Australia
13 Q11 **Victoriaville** Québec, SE Canada
Victoria-Wes *see* Victoria West
85 G24 **Victoria West** *Afr.* Victoria-Wes. Northern Cape, W South Africa
64 J13 **Victorica** La Pampa, C Argentina
205 T3 **Victor, Mount** ▲ Antarctica
37 U14 **Victorville** California, W USA
64 G9 **Vicuña** Coquimbo, N Chile
64 K11 **Vicuña Mackenna** Córdoba, C Argentina
Vicus Ausonensis *see* Vic
Vicus Elbii *see* Viterbo
35 X7 **Vida** Montana, NW USA
25 V6 **Vidalia** Georgia, SE USA
24 J7 **Vidalia** Louisiana, S USA
97 F22 **Videbæk** Ringkøbing, C Denmark
62 I13 **Videira** Santa Catarina, S Brazil
118 J14 **Videle** Teleorman, S Romania
Videm-Krško *see* Krško
Vídeň *see* Wien
106 H12 **Vidigueira** Beja, S Portugal
116 I9 **Vidima** ∽ N Bulgaria
116 G7 **Vidin** *anc.* Bononia. Oblast Montana, NW Bulgaria
160 H10 **Vidisha** Madhya Pradesh, C India
xlii I3 **Vidlin** Shetland Islands, NE Scotland, UK
27 Y10 **Vidor** Texas, SW USA
97 L20 **Vidöstern** ◎ S Sweden
94 J13 **Vidsel** Norrbotten, N Sweden
120 H9 **Vidzemes Augstiene** ▲ C Latvia
120 J12 **Vidzy** *Rus.* Vidzy. Vitsyebskaya Voblasts', NW Belorussia
65 L16 **Viedma** Río Negro, E Argentina
65 H22 **Viedma, Lago** ◎ S Argentina
47 O11 **Vieille Case** *var.* Itassi. N Dominica
106 M2 **Vieja, Peña** ▲ N Spain
42 E4 **Viejo, Cerro** ▲ NW Mexico
58 B9 **Viejo, Cerro** ▲ N Peru
120 E10 **Viekšniai** Akmenė, NW Lithuania
107 U3 **Vielha** *var.* Viella. Cataluña, NE Spain
Viella *see* Vielha
101 L21 **Vielsalm** Luxembourg, E Belgium
Vieng Pou Kha *see* Viangphoukha
25 T6 **Vienna** Georgia, SE USA
32 L17 **Vienna** Illinois, N USA
29 V5 **Vienna** Missouri, C USA
23 Q3 **Vienna** West Virginia, NE USA
Vienna *see* Wien, Austria
Vienna *see* Vienne, France
105 R11 **Vienne** *anc.* Vienna. Isère, E France
104 L10 **Vienne** ◆ *department* W France
104 L9 **Vienne** ∽ W France
Vientiane *see* Viangchan
Vientos, Paso de los *see* Windward Passage
47 V6 **Vieques** *var.* Isabel Segunda. E Puerto Rico
47 V6 **Vieques, Isla de** *island* E Puerto Rico
47 V6 **Vieques, Pasaje de** *passage* E Puerto Rico
47 V5 **Vieques, Sonda de** *sound* E Puerto Rico
Vierdörfer *see* Săcele
95 M15 **Vieremä** Kuopio, C Finland
101 M14 **Vierlingsbeek** Noord-Brabant, SE Netherlands
103 G20 **Viernheim** Hessen, W Germany
103 D15 **Viersen** Nordrhein-Westfalen, W Germany
110 G8 **Vierwaldstätter See** *Eng.* Lake of Lucerne. ◎ C Switzerland
105 N8 **Vierzon** Cher, C France
42 L8 **Viesca** Coahuila de Zaragoza, NE Mexico
120 H10 **Viesīte** *Ger.* Eckengraf. Jēkabpils, S Latvia
109 N15 **Vieste** Puglia, SE Italy
178 J9 **Vietnam** *off.* Socialist Republic of Vietnam, *Vtn.* Công Hoa Xa Hôi Chu Nghia Viêt Nam. ♦ *republic* SE Asia
178 J5 **Viêt Quang** Ha Giang, N Vietnam
Vietri *see* Viêt Tri
178 J6 **Viêt Tri** *var.* Vietri. Vinh Phu, N Vietnam
32 L4 **Vieux Desert, Lac** ◎ Michigan/Wisconsin, N USA
47 Y13 **Vieux Fort** S Saint Lucia
47 X6 **Vieux-Habitants** Basse Terre, SW Guadeloupe
121 G14 **Vievis** Kaišiadorys, S Lithuania
179 P8 **Vigan** Luzon, N Philippines
108 D8 **Vigevano** Lombardia, N Italy
109 N18 **Viggiano** Basilicata, S Italy
60 L12 **Vigia** Pará, NE Brazil
43 Y12 **Vigía Chico** Quintana Roo, SE Mexico
47 T11 **Vigie** ✈ (Castries) NE Saint Lucia
104 K17 **Vignemale** *var.* Pic de Vignemale. ▲ France/Spain
Vignemale, Pic de *see* Vignemale
108 G10 **Vignola** Emilia-Romagna, C Italy
106 G4 **Vigo** Galicia, NW Spain
106 G4 **Vigo, Ría de** *estuary* NW Spain
96 D9 **Vigra** *island* S Norway
97 C17 **Vigrestad** Rogaland, S Norway
95 L14 **Vihanti** Oulu, C Finland
155 U10 **Vihāri** Punjab, E Pakistan
104 K8 **Vihiers** Maine-et-Loire, NW France
113 O19 **Vihorlat** ▲ E Slovakia
95 L19 **Vihti** Uusimaa, S Finland
Viipuri *see* Vyborg
95 M16 **Viitasaari** Keski-Suomi, C Finland
120 K3 **Viivikonna** Ida-Virumaa, NE Estonia
161 K16 **Vijayawāda** *prev.* Bezwada. Andhra Pradesh, SE India
Vijosa/Vijosë *see* Aóos, Albania/Greece
Vijosa/Vijosë *see* Vjosës, Lumi i, Albania/Greece
Vík *see* Víkøyri
94 J4 **Vík** Sudhurland, S Iceland
96 L13 **Vika** Kopparberg, C Sweden
94 L12 **Vikajärvi** Lappi, N Finland
96 L13 **Vikarbyn** Kopparberg, C Sweden
97 J22 **Viken** Malmöhus, S Sweden
97 L17 **Viken** ◎ C Sweden
97 G15 **Vikersund** Buskerud, S Norway
126 J14 **Vikhorevka** Irkutskaya Oblast', S Russian Federation
116 G11 **Vikhren** ▲ SW Bulgaria
9 R15 **Viking** Alberta, SW Canada
86 E7 **Viking Bank** *undersea feature* N North Sea
97 M14 **Vikmanshyttan** Kopparberg, C Sweden
96 D12 **Vikøyri** *var.* Vik. Sogn og Fjordane, S Norway
95 H17 **Viksjö** Västernorrland, C Sweden
Viktoriastadt *see* Victoria
Vila *see* Port-Vila
Vila Arriaga *see* Bibala
Vila Artur de Paiva *see* Cubango
Vila Bela da Santissima Trindade *see* Mato Grosso
60 B12 **Vila Bittencourt** Amazonas, NW Brazil
Vila da Ponte *see* Cubango
66 O2 **Vila da Praia da Vitória** Terceira, Azores, Portugal, NE Atlantic Ocean
Vila de Aljustrel *see* Cangamba
Vila de Almoster *see* Chiange
Vila de João Belo *see* Xai-Xai
Vila de Macia *see* Macia
Vila de Manhiça *see* Manhiça
Vila de Manica *see* Manica
Vila de Mocímboa da Praia *see* Mocímboa da Praia
85 N16 **Vila de Sena** *var.* Sena. Sofala, C Mozambique
106 F14 **Vila do Bispo** Faro, S Portugal
106 G6 **Vila do Conde** Porto, NW Portugal
Vila do Maio *see* Maio
66 P3 **Vila do Porto** Santa Maria, Azores, Portugal, NE Atlantic Ocean
85 K15 **Vila do Zumbo** *prev.* Vila do Zumbu, Zumbo. Tete, NW Mozambique
Vila do Zumbu *see* Vila do Zumbo
106 I6 **Vila Flor** *var.* Vila Flôr. Bragança, N Portugal
107 V6 **Vilafranca del Penedès** *var.* Villafranca del Panadés. Cataluña, NE Spain
106 F10 **Vila Franca de Xira** *var.* Vilafranca de Xira. Lisboa, C Portugal
Vila Gago Coutinho *see* Lumbala N'Guimbo
106 G3 **Vilagarcía de Arousa** *var.* Villagarcía de Arosa. Galicia, NW Spain
Vila General Machado *see* Camacupa
Vila Henrique de Carvalho *see* Saurimo
104 I7 **Vilaine** ∽ NW France
Vila João de Almeida *see* Chibia
120 K8 **Viļaka** *Ger.* Marienhausen. Balvi, NE Latvia
106 I2 **Vilalba** Galicia, NW Spain
Vila Marechal Carmona *see* Uíge
Vila Mariano Machado *see* Ganda
180 G3 **Vilanandro, Tanjona** *headland* W Madagascar
Vilanculos *see* Vilankulo
120 J10 **Viļāni** Rēzekne, E Latvia
85 N19 **Vilankulo** *var.* Vilanculos. Inhambane, E Mozambique
Vila Norton de Matos *see* Balombo
106 G6 **Vila Nova de Famalicão** *var.* Vila Nova de Famalicao. Braga, N Portugal
106 I6 **Vila Nova de Foz Côa** *var.* Vila Nova de Fozcôa. Guarda, N Portugal
106 F6 **Vila Nova de Gaia** Porto, NW Portugal
Vila Nova de Portimão *see* Portimão
107 V6 **Vilanova i La Geltrú** Cataluña, NE Spain
Vila Pereira de Eça *see* N'Giva
106 H6 **Vila Pouca de Aguiar** Vila Real, N Portugal
106 H6 **Vila Real** *var.* Vila Rial. Vila Real, N Portugal
106 H6 **Vila Real** ◆ *district* N Portugal
107 T9 **Vila-real de los Infantes** *var.* Villarreal. País Valenciano, E Spain
106 H14 **Vila Real de Santo António** Faro, S Portugal
106 J7 **Vilar Formoso** Guarda, N Portugal
Vila Rial *see* Vila Real
61 J15 **Vila Rica** Mato Grosso, W Brazil
Vila Robert Williams *see* Caála
Vila Salazar *see* N'Dalatando
Vila Serpa Pinto *see* Menongue
Vila Teixeira da Silva *see* Bailundo
Vila Teixeira de Sousa *see* Luau
106 H9 **Vila Velha de Ródão** Castelo Branco, C Portugal
106 G5 **Vila Verde** Braga, N Portugal
106 H11 **Vila Viçosa** Évora, S Portugal
59 G15 **Vilcabamba, Cordillera de** ▲▲ C Peru
Vilcea *see* Vâlcea
126 Hh1 **Vil'cheka, Zemlya** *Eng.* Wilczek Land. *island* Zemlya Frantsa-Iosifa, NW Russian Federation
97 F22 **Vildbjerg** Ringkøbing, C Denmark
Vileyka *see* Vilyeyka
95 H15 **Vilhelmina** Västerbotten, N Sweden
61 F17 **Vilhena** Rondônia, W Brazil
117 G19 **Vília** Attikí, C Greece
Viliya *see* Viliya
121 I14 **Viliya** *Lith.* Neris, *Rus.* Viliya. ∽ W Belorussia
Viliya *see* Neris
120 H5 **Viljandi** *Ger.* Fellin. Viljandimaa, S Estonia
120 H5 **Viljandimaa** *off.* Viljandi Maakond. ◆ *province* SW Estonia
121 E14 **Vilkaviškis** *Pol.* Wyłkowyszki. Vilkaviškis, SW Lithuania
120 F13 **Vilkija** Kaunas, C Lithuania
207 V9 **Vil'kitskogo, Proliv** *strait* N Russian Federation
Vilkovo *see* Vylkove
59 L21 **Villa Abecia** Chuquisaca, S Bolivia
Villa Acuña *see* Ciudad Acuña
42 J4 **Villa Ahumada** Chihuahua, N Mexico
47 O9 **Villa Altagracia** C Dominican Republic
58 L13 **Villa Bella** Beni, N Bolivia
106 J3 **Villablino** Castilla-León, N Spain
56 K6 **Villa Bruzual** Portuguesa, N Venezuela
107 O9 **Villacañas** Castilla-La Mancha, C Spain
107 O12 **Villacarrillo** Andalucía, S Spain
106 M7 **Villacastín** Castilla-León, N Spain
Villa Cecilia *see* Ciudad Madero
111 S9 **Villach** *Slvn.* Beljak. Kärnten, S Austria
109 B20 **Villacidro** Sardegna, Italy, C Mediterranean Sea
Villa Concepción *see* Concepción
106 L4 **Villada** Castilla-León, N Spain
42 M10 **Villa de Cos** Zacatecas, C Mexico
56 L5 **Villa de Cura** *var.* Cura. Aragua, N Venezuela
Villa del Nevoso *see* Ilirska Bistrica
Villa del Pilar *see* Pilar
106 M13 **Villa del Río** Andalucía, S Spain
Villa de Méndez *see* Méndez
44 H6 **Villa de San Antonio** Comayagua, W Honduras
107 N4 **Villadiego** Castilla-León, N Spain
107 T8 **Villafames** País Valenciano, E Spain
43 U16 **Villa Flores** Chiapas, SE Mexico
106 J3 **Villafranca del Bierzo** Castilla-León, N Spain
107 S8 **Villafranca del Cid** País Valenciano, E Spain
106 J11 **Villafranca de los Barros** Extremadura, W Spain
107 N10 **Villafranca de los Caballeros** Castilla-La Mancha, C Spain
Villafranca del Panadés *see* Vilafranca del Penedès
108 F8 **Villafranca di Verona** Veneto, NE Italy
109 J23 **Villafrati** Sicilia, Italy, C Mediterranean Sea
Villagarcía de Arosa *see* Vilagarcía de Arousa
43 O9 **Villagrán** Tamaulipas, C Mexico
63 C17 **Villaguay** Entre Ríos, E Argentina
64 O6 **Villa Hayes** Presidente Hayes, S Paraguay
43 U15 **Villahermosa** *prev.* San Juan Bautista. Tabasco, SE Mexico
107 O11 **Villahermosa** Castilla-La Mancha, C Spain
66 O11 **Villahermoso** Gomera, Islas Canarias, Spain, NE Atlantic Ocean
Villa Hidalgo *see* Hidalgo
107 T12 **Villajoyosa** *var.* La Vila Jojosa. País Valenciano, E Spain
Villa Juárez *see* Juárez
Villalba *see* Collado Villalba
43 N8 **Villaldama** Nuevo León, NE Mexico
106 L5 **Villalón de Campos** Castilla-León, N Spain
63 A25 **Villalonga** Buenos Aires, E Argentina
106 L5 **Villalpando** Castilla-León, N Spain
42 K9 **Villa Madero** *var.* Francisco I.Madero. Durango, C Mexico
43 O9 **Villa Mainero** Tamaulipas, C Mexico
Villamaña *see* Villamañán
106 L4 **Villamañán** *var.* Villamaña. Castilla-León, N Spain
64 L10 **Villa María** Córdoba, C Argentina
63 C17 **Villa María Grande** Entre Ríos, E Argentina
59 K21 **Villa Martín** Potosí, SW Bolivia
106 K15 **Villamartín** Andalucía, S Spain
64 J8 **Villa Mazán** La Rioja, NW Argentina
Villa Mercedes *see* Mercedes
Villamil *see* Puerto Villamil
Villa Nador *see* Nador
56 G5 **Villanueva** La Guajira, N Colombia
44 H5 **Villanueva** Cortés, NW Honduras
42 L11 **Villanueva** Zacatecas, C Mexico
44 I9 **Villa Nueva** Chinandega, NW Nicaragua
39 T11 **Villanueva** New Mexico, SW USA
106 M12 **Villanueva de Córdoba** Andalucía, S Spain
107 O12 **Villanueva del Arzobispo** Andalucía, S Spain
106 K11 **Villanueva de la Serena** Extremadura, W Spain
106 L5 **Villanueva del Campo** Castilla-León, N Spain
107 O11 **Villanueva de los Infantes** Castilla-La Mancha, C Spain
63 C14 **Villa Ocampo** Santa Fe, C Argentina
42 J8 **Villa Ocampo** Durango, C Mexico
42 J7 **Villa Orestes Pereyra** Durango, C Mexico
107 N3 **Villarcayo** Castilla-León, N Spain
106 L5 **Villardefrades** Castilla-León, N Spain

♦ Country ● Country Capital ◇ Dependent Territory ○ Dependent Territory Capital ◆ Administrative Region ✈ International Airport ▲ Mountain ▲▲ Mountain Range ✖ Volcano ∽ River ◎ Lake ▣ Reservoir

Villar del Arzobispo – Vyrnwy

107 S9 Villar del Arzobispo País Valenciano, E Spain
107 Q6 Villaroya de la Sierra Aragón, NE Spain
Villarreal see Vila-real de los Infantes
64 P6 Villarrica Guairá, SE Paraguay
65 G15 Villarrica, Volcán S Chile
107 P10 Villarrobledo Castilla-La Mancha, C Spain
107 N10 Villarrubia de los Ojos Castilla-La Mancha, C Spain
20 J17 Villas New Jersey, NE USA
107 O3 Villasana de Mena Castilla-León, N Spain
109 M23 Villa San Giovanni Calabria, S Italy
63 D18 Villa San José Entre Ríos, E Argentina
Villa Sanjurjo see Al-Hoceïma
107 P6 Villasayas Castilla-León, N Spain
109 C20 Villasimius Sardegna, Italy, C Mediterranean Sea
43 N6 Villa Unión Coahuila de Zaragoza, NE Mexico
42 K10 Villa Unión Durango, C Mexico
42 J10 Villa Unión Sinaloa, C Mexico
64 K12 Villa Valeria Córdoba, C Argentina
107 N8 Villaverde Madrid, C Spain
56 F10 Villavicencio Meta, C Colombia
106 L2 Villaviciosa Asturias, N Spain
106 L12 Villaviciosa de Córdoba Andalucía, S Spain
59 L22 Villazón Potosí, S Bolivia
12 J8 Villebon, Lac ◎ Québec, SE Canada
Ville de Kinshasa see Kinshasa
104 J5 Villedieu-les-Poêles Manche, N France
Villefranche see Villefranche-sur-Saône
105 N16 Villefranche-de-Lauragais Haute-Garonne, S France
105 N14 Villefranche-de-Rouergue Aveyron, S France
105 R10 Villefranche-sur-Saône var. Villefranche. Rhône, E France
12 H9 Ville-Marie Québec, SE Canada
104 M15 Villemur-sur-Tarn Haute-Garonne, S France
107 S11 Villena País Valenciano, E Spain
Villeneuve-d'Agen see Villeneuve-sur-Lot
104 L13 Villeneuve-sur-Lot var. Villeneuve-d'Agen; hist. Gajac. Lot-et-Garonne, SW France
105 P6 Villeneuve-sur-Yonne Yonne, C France
24 H8 Ville Platte Louisiana, S USA
105 R11 Villeurbanne Rhône, E France
103 G23 Villingen-Schwenningen Baden-Württemberg, S Germany
31 T15 Villisca Iowa, C USA
Villmanstrand see Lappeenranta
Vilna see Vilnius
121 H14 Vilnius Pol. Wilno, Ger. Wilna; prev. Rus. Vilna. ● (Lithuania) Vilnius, SE Lithuania
121 H14 Vilnius ✕ Vilnius, SE Lithuania
119 S7 Vil'nohirs'k Dnipropetrovs'ka Oblast', E Ukraine
119 U8 Vil'nyans'k Zaporiz'ka Oblast', SE Ukraine
95 L17 Vilppula Häme, SW Finland
103 M20 Vils ≈ SE Germany
120 C5 Vilsandi Saar island W Estonia
119 P8 Vil'shanka Rus. Olshanka. Kirovohrads'ka Oblast', C Ukraine
103 O22 Vilshofen Bayern, SE Germany
161 J20 Viluppuram Tamil Nādu, SE India
115 I16 Vilusi Montenegro, SW Yugoslavia
101 G18 Vilvoorde Fr. Vilvorde. Vlaams Brabant, C Belgium
Vilvorde see Vilvoorde
121 J14 Vilyeyka Pol. Wilejka, Rus. Vileyka. Minskaya Voblasts', NW Belorussia
126 Kk11 Vilyuy ≈ NE Russian Federation
126 L10 Vilyuysk Respublika Sakha (Yakutiya), NE Russian Federation
126 K11 Vilyuyskoye Vodokhranilishche ⊞ NE Russian Federation
106 G2 Vimianzo Galicia, NW Spain
97 M19 Vimmerby Kalmar, S Sweden
104 L5 Vimoutiers Orne, N France
95 L16 Vimpeli Vaasa, W Finland
81 G14 Vina ≈ Cameroon/Chad
64 G11 Viña del Mar Valparaíso, C Chile
21 R8 Vinalhaven Island island Maine, NE USA
107 T8 Vinaròs País Valenciano, E Spain
Vinători see Vânători
33 N15 Vincennes Indiana, N USA
205 Y12 Vincennes Bay bay Antarctica
27 O7 Vincent Texas, SW USA
97 H24 Vindeby Fyn, C Denmark
95 I15 Vindeln Västerbotten, N Sweden
97 F21 Vinderup Ringkøbing, C Denmark
Vindhya Mountains see Vindhya Range
159 N14 Vindhya Range var. Vindhya Mountains. ▲ N India
Vindobona see Wien
22 K6 Vine Grove Kentucky, S USA
20 J17 Vineland New Jersey, NE USA
118 E11 Vinga Arad, W Romania
97 M16 Vingåker Södermanland, C Sweden
178 Jj8 Vinh Nghê An, N Vietnam
106 I5 Vinhais Bragança, N Portugal
178 K9 Vinh Linh Quang Tri, C Vietnam
Vinh Loi see Bac Liêu
178 Jj14 Vinh Long var. Vinhlong. Vinh Long, S Vietnam
115 Q18 Vinica NE FYR Macedonia
111 V13 Vinica SE Slovenia
116 G8 Vinishte Oblast Montana, NW Bulgaria
29 Q8 Vinita Oklahoma, C USA
Vinju Mare see Vânju Mare
100 I11 Vinkeveen Utrecht, C Netherlands
118 L6 Vin'kivtsi Khmel'nyts'ka Oblast', W Ukraine
114 I10 Vinkovci Ger. Winkowitz, Hung. Vinkovcze. Vukovar-Srijem, E Croatia
Vinkovcze see Vinkovci
Vinnitsa see Vinnytsya
Vinnitskaya Oblast'/Vinnytsya see Vinnyts'ka Oblast'
118 M7 Vinnyts'ka Oblast' var. Vinnytsya, Rus. Vinnitskaya Oblast'. ◆ province C Ukraine
119 N6 Vinnytsya Rus. Vinnitsa. Vinnyts'ka Oblast', C Ukraine
119 N6 Vinnytsya ✕ Vinnyts'ka Oblast', N Ukraine
Vinogradov see Vynohradiv
204 L8 Vinson Massif ▲ Antarctica
96 G11 Vinstra Oppland, S Norway
118 K12 Vintilă Vodă Buzău, SE Romania
31 X13 Vinton Iowa, C USA
24 F9 Vinton Louisiana, S USA
161 J17 Vinukonda Andhra Pradesh, E India
Vioara see Ocnele Mari
85 E23 Vioolsdrif Northern Cape, SW South Africa
84 M13 Viphya Mountains ▲ C Malawi
179 Qq11 Virac Catanduanes Island, N Philippines
128 K8 Virandozero Respublika Kareliya, NW Russian Federation
143 P16 Viranşehir Şanlıurfa, SE Turkey
160 D13 Virār Mahārāshtra, W India
9 W16 Virden Manitoba, S Canada
32 K14 Virden Illinois, N USA
Virdois see Virrat
104 J5 Vire Calvados, N France
104 J4 Vire ≈ N France
85 A15 Virei Namibe, SW Angola
Virful Moldoveanu see Vârful Moldoveanu
37 R5 Virgina Peak ▲ Nevada, W USA
47 U9 Virgin Gorda island C British Virgin Islands
xliv J7 Virginia Cavan, N Ireland
85 I22 Virginia Free State, C South Africa
32 K13 Virginia Illinois, N USA
31 W4 Virginia Minnesota, N USA
23 T6 Virginia off. Commonwealth of Virginia; also known as Mother of Presidents, Mother of States, Old Dominion. ◆ state NE USA
23 Y7 Virginia Beach Virginia, NE USA
35 R11 Virginia City Montana, NW USA
37 Q6 Virginia City Nevada, W USA
12 H8 Virginiatown Ontario, S Canada
Virgin Islands see British Virgin Islands
47 T9 Virgin Islands (US) var. Virgin Islands of the United States; prev. Danish West Indies. ◇ US unincorporated territory E West Indies
47 T9 Virgin Passage passage Puerto Rico/Virgin Islands (US)
37 Y10 Virgin River ≈ Nevada/Utah, W USA
Virihaur see Virihaure
94 H12 Virihaure var. Virihaur. ◎ N Sweden
178 Jj11 Virôchey Rôtânôkiri, NE Cambodia
95 N19 Virolahti Kymi, S Finland
32 J8 Viroqua Wisconsin, N USA
114 G8 Virovitica Ger. Virovititz, Hung. Verőcze; prev. Ger. Werowitz. Virovitica-Podravina, NE Croatia
114 G8 Virovitica-Podravina off. Virovitičko-Podravska Županija. ◆ province NE Croatia
Virovititz see Virovitica
115 J17 Virpazar Montenegro, SW Yugoslavia
95 L17 Virrat Swe. Virdois. Häme, SW Finland
97 M20 Virserum Kalmar, S Sweden
101 K25 Virton Luxembourg, SE Belgium
120 F5 Virtsu Ger. Werder. Läänemaa, W Estonia
58 C12 Virú La Libertad, C Peru
Virudhunagar see Virudunagar
161 H23 Virudunagar var. Virudhunagar. Tamil Nādu, SE India
120 I3 Viru-Jaagupi Ger. Sankt-Jakobi. Lääne-Virumaa, NE Estonia
59 N19 Viru-Viru var. Santa Cruz. ✕ (Santa Cruz) Santa Cruz, C Bolivia
115 E15 Vis It. Lissa; anc. Issa. island S Croatia
Vis see Fish
120 I12 Visaginas prev. Sniečkus. Ignalina, E Lithuania
161 M15 Visākhapatnam Andhra Pradesh, SE India
37 R11 Visalia California, W USA
Vișău see Vișeu
179 Qq12 Visayan Sea sea C Philippines
97 P19 Visby Ger. Wisby. Gotland, SE Sweden
207 N9 Viscount Melville Sound prev. Melville Sound. sound Northwest Territories, N Canada
101 L19 Visé Liège, E Belgium
114 K13 Višegrad SE Bosnia and Herzegovina
60 L12 Viseu Pará, NE Brazil
106 H7 Viseu prev. Vizeu. Viseu, N Portugal
106 H7 Viseu var. Vizeu. ◆ district N Portugal
118 I8 Vișeu Hung. Visó; prev. Vișău. ≈ NW Romania
118 I8 Vișeu de Sus var. Vișeul de Sus, Ger. Oberwischau, Hung. Felsővisó. Maramureș, N Romania
Vișeul de Sus see Vișeu de Sus
129 R10 Vishera ≈ NW Russian Federation
97 J19 Viskafors Älvsborg, S Sweden
97 J20 Viskan ≈ S Sweden
97 L21 Vislanda Kronoberg, S Sweden
Vislinskiy Zaliv see Vistula Lagoon
Visó see Vișeu
114 H13 Visoko C Bosnia and Herzegovina
108 A9 Viso, Monte ▲ NW Italy
110 E10 Visp Valais, SW Switzerland
110 E10 Vispa ≈ S Switzerland
97 M21 Vissefjärda Kalmar, S Sweden
102 I11 Visselhövede Niedersachsen, NW Germany
97 G23 Vissenbjerg Fyn, C Denmark
37 U17 Vista California, W USA
60 C11 Vista Alegre Amazonas, NW Brazil
116 J13 Vistonída, Límni ◎ NE Greece
Vistula see Wisła
121 A14 Vistula Lagoon Ger. Frisches Haff, Pol. Zalew Wiślany, Rus. Vislinskiy Zaliv. lagoon Poland/Russian Federation
116 I8 Vit ≈ NW Bulgaria
Vitebsk see Vitsyebsk
Vitebskaya Oblast' see Vitsyebskaya Voblasts'
109 H14 Viterbo anc. Vicus Elbii. Lazio, C Italy
114 H12 Vitez C Bosnia and Herzegovina
178 J15 Vi Thanh Cân Thơ, S Vietnam
Viti see Fiji
194 K12 Vitiaz Strait strait NE PNG
106 J7 Vitigudino Castilla-León, N Spain
197 H15 Viti Levu island W Fiji
126 Kk14 Vitim ≈ C Russian Federation
126 Kk13 Vitimskiy Irkutskaya Oblast', C Russian Federation
111 V2 Vitis Niederösterreich, N Austria
Vitoria see Vitoria-Gasteiz
61 O20 Vitória Espírito Santo, SE Brazil
Vitoria Bank see Vitória Seamount
61 N18 Vitória da Conquista Bahia, E Brazil
107 P3 Vitoria-Gasteiz var. Vitoria, Eng. Vittoria. País Vasco, N Spain
67 J16 Vitória Seamount var. Victoria Bank, Vitoria Bank. undersea feature C Atlantic Ocean
114 F13 Vitorog ▲ SW Bosnia and Herzegovina
104 J6 Vitré Ille-et-Vilaine, NW France
105 R5 Vitry-le-François Marne, N France
116 D13 Vítsoi ▲ N Greece
120 N13 Vitsyebsk Rus. Vitebsk. Vitsyebskaya Voblasts', NE Belorussia
120 K13 Vitsyebskaya Voblasts' prev. Rus. Vitebskaya Oblast'. ◆ province N Belorussia
94 J11 Vittangi Norrbotten, N Sweden
105 R8 Vitteaux Côte d'Or, C France
105 S6 Vittel Vosges, NE France
97 N15 Vittinge Västmanland, C Sweden
109 K25 Vittoria Sicilia, Italy, C Mediterranean Sea
Vittoria see Vitoria-Gasteiz
108 I7 Vittorio Veneto Veneto, NE Italy
183 Q9 Vitu Levu island W Fiji
199 Jj7 Vityaz Seamount undersea feature C Pacific Ocean
183 Q7 Vityaz Trench undersea feature W Pacific Ocean
110 G8 Vitznau Luzern, W Switzerland
106 I1 Viveiro Galicia, NW Spain
107 S9 Viver País Valenciano, E Spain
105 Q13 Viverais, Monts du ▲ C France
126 Ii10 Vivi ≈ N Russian Federation
24 F4 Vivian Louisiana, S USA
31 N10 Vivian South Dakota, N USA
105 R13 Viviers Ardèche, E France
Vivis see Vevey
85 K19 Vivo Northern, NE South Africa
104 L10 Vivonne Vienne, W France
197 G14 Viwa island Yasawa Group, NW Fiji
Vizakna see Ocna Sibiului
107 O2 Vizcaya Basq. Bizkaia. ◆ province País Vasco, N Spain
Vizcaya, Golfo de see Biscay, Bay of
142 C10 Vize Kırklareli, NW Turkey
126 I2 Vize, Ostrov island Severnaya Zemlya, N Russian Federation
Vizeu see Viseu
161 M15 Vizianagaram var. Vizianagram. Andhra Pradesh, E India
Vizianagram see Vizianagaram
105 S12 Vizille Isère, E France
129 R11 Vizinga Respublika Komi, NW Russian Federation
118 M13 Viziru Brăila, SE Romania
115 K21 Vjosës, Lumi i var. Vijosa, Vijosë, Gk. Aóos. ≈ Albania/Greece see also Aóos
101 H18 Vlaams Brabant ◆ province C Belgium
Vlaanderen see Flanders
100 G12 Vlaardingen Zuid-Holland, SW Netherlands
118 F10 Vlădeasa, Vârful prev. Vîrful Vlădeasa. ▲ NW Romania
Vlădeasa, Vîrful see Vlădeasa, Vârful
115 P16 Vladičin Han Serbia, SE Yugoslavia
131 O16 Vladikavkaz prev. Dzaudzhikau, Ordzhonikidze. Respublika Severnaya Osetiya, SW Russian Federation
130 M3 Vladimir Vladimirskaya Oblast', W Russian Federation
150 M7 Vladimirovka Kustanay, N Kazakhstan
Vladimirovka see Yuzhno-Sakhalinsk
130 L3 Vladimirskaya Oblast' ◆ province W Russian Federation
130 I3 Vladimirskiy Tupik Smolenskaya Oblast', W Russian Federation
Vladimir-Volynskiy see Volodymyr-Volyns'kyy
127 Nn18 Vladivostok Primorskiy Kray, SE Russian Federation
119 U13 Vladyslavivka Respublika Krym, S Ukraine
100 P6 Vlagtwedde Groningen, NE Netherlands
Vlajna see Kukavica
114 J12 Vlasenica E Bosnia and Herzegovina
114 G12 Vlašić ▲ C Bosnia and Herzegovina
113 D17 Vlašim Ger. Wlaschim. Střední Čechy, C Czech Republic
115 P15 Vlasotince Serbia, SE Yugoslavia
126 Ll7 Vlasovo Respublika Sakha (Yakutiya), NE Russian Federation
100 I11 Vleuten Utrecht, C Netherlands
100 I5 Vlieland Fris. Flylân. island Waddeneilanden, N Netherlands
100 I5 Vliestroom strait NW Netherlands
101 J14 Vlijmen Noord-Brabant, S Netherlands
101 E15 Vlissingen Eng. Flushing, Fr. Flessingue. Zeeland, SW Netherlands
Vlodava see Włodawa
Vlonë/Vlora see Vlorë
115 K22 Vlorë prev. Vlonë, It. Valona, Vlora. Vlorë, SW Albania
115 K22 Vlorë ◆ district SW Albania
115 K22 Vlorës, Gjiri i var. Valona Bay. bay SW Albania
Vlotslavsk see Włocławek
113 C16 Vltava Ger. Moldau. ≈ W Czech Republic
130 K3 Vnukovo ✕ (Moskva) Gorod Moskva, W Russian Federation
27 Q9 Voca Texas, SW USA
111 R5 Vöcklabruck Oberösterreich, NW Austria
114 D13 Vodice Šibenik, S Croatia
128 K10 Vodlozero, Ozero ◎ NW Russian Federation
114 A10 Vodnjan It. Dignano d'Istria. Istra, NW Croatia
129 S9 Vodnyy Respublika Komi, NW Russian Federation
97 G20 Vodskov Nordjylland, N Denmark
xlii I3 Voe Shetland Islands, NE Scotland, UK
xlii H2 Voe Shetland Islands, NE Scotland, UK
94 H4 Vogar Sudhurland, SW Iceland
195 N16 Vogel, Cape headland SE PNG
Vogelkop see Doberai, Jazirah
79 X15 Vogel Peak prev. Dim lang. ▲ E Nigeria
103 H17 Vogelsberg ▲ C Germany
108 D8 Voghera Lombardia, N Italy
114 I13 Vogošća SE Bosnia and Herzegovina
103 M17 Vogtland historical region E Germany
129 V12 Vogul'skiy Kamen', Gora ▲ NW Russian Federation
197 H6 Voh Province Nord, C New Caledonia
Vohémar see Iharaña
180 H8 Vohimena, Tanjona Fr. Cap Sainte Marie. headland S Madagascar
180 J6 Vohipeno Fianarantsoa, SE Madagascar
120 H5 Võhma Ger. Wöchma. Viljandimaa, S Estonia
83 J20 Voi Coast, S Kenya
78 K15 Voinjama N Liberia
105 S12 Voiron Isère, E France
111 U8 Voitsberg Steiermark, SE Austria
97 F24 Vojens Ger. Woyens. Sønderjylland, SW Denmark
114 K9 Vojvodina Ger. Wojwodina. cultural region N Yugoslavia
13 S6 Volant ≈ Québec, SE Canada
Volaterrae see Volterra
45 P15 Volcán var. Hato del Volcán. Chiriquí, W Panama
Volchansk see Vovchans'k
Volchya see Vovcha
96 D10 Volda Møre og Romsdal, S Norway
100 J9 Volendam Noord-Holland, C Netherlands
128 L15 Volga Yaroslavskaya Oblast', W Russian Federation
31 R10 Volga South Dakota, N USA
125 Gg11 Volga ≈ NW Russian Federation
Volga-Baltic Waterway see Volgo-Baltiyskiy Kanal
Volga Hills/Volga Uplands see Privolzhskaya Vozvyshennost'
128 L13 Volgo-Baltiyskiy Kanal Eng. Volga-Baltic Waterway. canal NW Russian Federation
130 M12 Volgodonsk Rostovskaya Oblast', SW Russian Federation
131 O10 Volgograd prev. Stalingrad, Tsaritsyn. Volgogradskaya Oblast', SW Russian Federation
131 N9 Volgogradskaya Oblast' ◆ province SW Russian Federation
131 P10 Volgogradskoye Vodokhranilishche ⊞ SW Russian Federation
103 J19 Volkach Bayern, C Germany
111 T9 Völkermarkt Slvn. Velikovec. Kärnten, S Austria
128 I12 Volkhov Leningradskaya Oblast', NW Russian Federation
103 D20 Völklingen Saarland, SW Germany
Volkovysk see Vawkavysk
Volkovyskiye Vysoty see Vawkavyskaye Wzvyshsha
85 K22 Volksrust Mpumalanga, E South Africa
100 L8 Vollenhove Overijssel, N Netherlands
121 L16 Vol'ma Rus. Volma. ≈ C Belorussia
Volmari see Valmiera
119 W9 Volnovakha Donets'ka Oblast', SE Ukraine
118 K6 Volochys'k Khmel'nyts'ka Oblast', W Ukraine
119 O6 Volodarka Kyyivs'ka Oblast', N Ukraine
119 W9 Volodars'ke Donets'ka Oblast', E Ukraine
131 R13 Volodarskiy Astrakhanskaya Oblast', SW Russian Federation
151 P7 Volodarskoye Kokshetau, N Kazakhstan
118 N5 Volodars'k-Volyns'kyy Zhytomyrs'ka Oblast', N Ukraine
118 K3 Volodymerets' Rivnens'ka Oblast', NW Ukraine
118 I3 Volodymyr-Volyns'kyy Pol. Włodzimierz, Rus. Vladimir-Volynskiy. Volyns'ka Oblast', NW Ukraine
128 L14 Vologda Vologodskaya Oblast', W Russian Federation
128 L12 Vologodskaya Oblast' ◆ province NW Russian Federation
130 K3 Volokolamsk Moskovskaya Oblast', W Russian Federation
130 K9 Volokonovka Belgorodskaya Oblast', W Russian Federation
117 G16 Vólos Thessalía, C Greece
128 M11 Voloshka Arkhangel'skaya Oblast', NW Russian Federation
Vološinovo see Novi Bečej
118 H7 Volovets' Zakarpats'ka Oblast', W Ukraine
116 K7 Volovo Razgradska Oblast, N Bulgaria
Volozhin see Valozhyn
131 Q7 Vol'sk Saratovskaya Oblast', W Russian Federation
79 Q17 Volta ≈ SE Ghana
Volta Blanche see White Volta
79 P16 Volta, Lake ⊞ SE Ghana
Volta Noire see Black Volta
62 O9 Volta Redonda Rio de Janeiro, SE Brazil
Volta Rouge see Red Volta
108 F12 Volterra anc. Volaterrae. Toscana, C Italy
109 K17 Volturno ≈ S Italy
115 I15 Volujak ▲ SW Yugoslavia
Volunteer Island see Starbuck Island
67 F24 Volunteer Point headland East Falkland, Falkland Islands
Volunteer State see Tennessee
116 H13 Vólvi, Límni ◎ N Greece
Volyn see Volyns'ka Oblast'
118 I3 Volyns'ka Oblast' var. Volyn, Rus. Volynskaya Oblast'. ◆ province NW Ukraine
131 Q3 Volzhsk Respublika Mariy El, W Russian Federation
Volynskaya Oblast' see Volyns'ka Oblast'
131 O10 Volzhskiy Volgogradskaya Oblast', SW Russian Federation
180 I7 Vondrozo Fianarantsoa, SE Madagascar
116 K9 Voneshta Voda Loveshka Oblast, N Bulgaria
41 P10 Von Frank Mountain ▲ Alaska, USA
117 C17 Vónitsa Dytikí Ellás, W Greece
120 J6 Võnnu Ger. Wendau. Tartumaa, SE Estonia
100 G12 Voorburg Zuid-Holland, W Netherlands
100 H11 Voorschoten Zuid-Holland, W Netherlands
100 M11 Voorst Gelderland, E Netherlands
100 K11 Voorthuizen Gelderland, C Netherlands
94 L2 Vopnafjördhur Austurland, E Iceland
94 L2 Vopnafjördhur bay E Iceland
Vora see Vorë
121 H15 Voranava Pol. Werenów, Rus. Voronovo. Hrodzyenskaya Voblasts', W Belorussia
110 I8 Vorarlberg off. Land Vorarlberg. ◆ state W Austria
111 X7 Vorau Steiermark, E Austria
100 N11 Vorden Gelderland, E Netherlands
110 H9 Vorderrhein ≈ SE Switzerland
94 J2 Vordhufell ▲ N Iceland
97 I24 Vordingborg Storstrøm, SE Denmark
115 K19 Vorë var. Vora. Tiranë, W Albania
117 H17 Vóreioi Sporádes var. Vórioi Sporádhes, Eng. Northern Sporades. island group E Greece
117 J17 Vóreion Aigaíon Eng. Aegean North. ◆ region SE Greece
117 G18 Voreíos Evvoïkós Kólpos gulf E Greece
207 S16 Voring Plateau undersea feature N Norwegian Sea
Vórioi Sporádhes see Vóreioi Sporádes
129 W4 Vorkuta Respublika Komi, NW Russian Federation
97 I14 Vorma ≈ S Norway
120 E4 Vormsi var. Vormsi Saar, Ger. Worms, Swed. Ormsö. island W Estonia
Vormsi Saar see Vormsi
126 Hh12 Vorogovo Krasnoyarskiy Kray, C Russian Federation
131 N7 Vorona ≈ W Russian Federation
130 L7 Voronezh Voronezhskaya Oblast', W Russian Federation
130 L7 Voronezh ≈ W Russian Federation
130 K8 Voronezhskaya Oblast' ◆ province W Russian Federation
Voronovitsya see Voronovytsya
Voronovo see Voranava
119 N6 Voronovytsya Rus. Voronovitsya. Vinnyts'ka Oblast', C Ukraine
126 Hh7 Vorontsovo Taymyrskiy (Dolgano-Nenetskiy) Avtonomnyy Okrug, N Russian Federation
128 K3 Voron'ya ≈ NW Russian Federation
Voropayevo see Varapayeva
Voroshilov see Ussuriysk
Voroshilovgrad see Luhans'k, Ukraine
Voroshilovgrad see Luhans'ka Oblast', Ukraine
Voroshilovgradskaya Oblast' see Luhans'ka Oblast'
Voroshilovsk see Stavropol', Russian Federation
Voroshilovsk see Alchevs'k, Ukraine
143 V13 Vorotan Az. Bärgușad. ≈ Armenia/Azerbaijan
131 P3 Vorotynets Nizhegorodskaya Oblast', W Russian Federation
119 S3 Vorozhba Sums'ka Oblast', NE Ukraine
119 T5 Vorskla ≈ Russian Federation/Ukraine
101 I17 Vorst Antwerpen, N Belgium
85 G21 Vorstershoop North-West, N South Africa
120 H6 Võrtsjärv Ger. Wirtz-See. ◎ SE Estonia
120 J7 Võru Ger. Werro. Võrumaa, SE Estonia
153 R11 Vorukh N Tajikistan
120 I7 Võrumaa off. Võru Maakond. ◆ province SE Estonia
85 G24 Vosburg Northern Cape, W South Africa
153 Q14 Vose' Rus. Vose; prev. Aral. SW Tajikistan
105 S6 Vosges ◆ department NE France
105 U6 Vosges ▲ NE France
128 K13 Voskresenkoye Vologodskaya Oblast', NW Russian Federation
130 L4 Voskresensk Moskovskaya Oblast', W Russian Federation
131 P2 Voskresenskoye Nizhegorodskaya Oblast', W Russian Federation
131 V6 Voskresenskoye Respublika Bashkortostan, W Russian Federation
96 D13 Voss Hordaland, S Norway
96 D13 Voss physical region S Norway
101 I16 Vosselaar Antwerpen, N Belgium
96 D13 Vosso ≈ S Norway
Vostochno-Kazakhstanskaya Oblast' see Vostochnyy Kazakhstan
151 T12 Vostochno-Kounradskiy Kaz. Shyghys Qongyrat. Zhezkazgan, C Kazakhstan
127 N4 Vostochno-Sibirskoye More Eng. East Siberian Sea. sea Arctic Ocean
151 X10 Vostochnyy Kazakhstan off. Vostochno-Kazakhstanskaya Oblast', var. East Kazakhstan, Kaz. Shyghys Qazagastan Oblysy. ◆ province E Kazakhstan
Vostochnyy Sayan see Eastern Sayans
Vostock Island see Vostok Island
205 U10 Vostok Russian research station Antarctica
203 X5 Vostok Island var. Vostock Island; prev. Stavers Island. island Line Islands, SE Kiribati
131 T2 Votkinsk Udmurtskaya Respublika, NW Russian Federation
129 U15 Votkinskoye Vodokhranilishche var. Votkinsk Reservoir. ⊞ NW Russian Federation
Votkinsk Reservoir see Votkinskoye Vodokhranilishche
62 J7 Votuporanga São Paulo, S Brazil
106 H7 Vouga, Rio ≈ N Portugal
117 E14 Voúrinos ▲ N Greece
117 G24 Voúxa, Ákra headland Kríti, Greece, E Mediterranean Sea
105 R4 Vouziers Ardennes, N France
119 V7 Vovcha Rus. Volchya. ≈ E Ukraine
119 V4 Vovchans'k Rus. Volchansk. Kharkivs'ka Oblast', E Ukraine
105 N6 Voves Eure-et-Loir, C France
81 M14 Vovodo ≈ S Central Africa Republic
xxxviii G14 Vowchurch Herefordshire, W England, UK
96 M12 Voxna Gävleborg, C Sweden
96 L11 Voxnan ≈ C Sweden
116 F7 Voynishka Reka ≈ NW Bulgaria
129 T9 Voyvozh Respublika Komi, NW Russian Federation
128 M12 Vozhega Vologodskaya Oblast', NW Russian Federation
128 L12 Vozhe, Ozero ◎ NW Russian Federation
119 Q9 Voznesens'k Rus. Voznesensk. Mykolayivs'ka Oblast', S Ukraine
128 J12 Voznesen'ye Leningradskaya Oblast', NW Russian Federation
150 J14 Vozrozhdeniya, Ostrov Uzb. Wozrojdeniye Oroli. island Kazakhstan/Uzbekistan
97 G20 Vrå var. Vraa. Nordjylland, N Denmark
Vraa see Vrå
116 H9 Vrachesh Sofiyska Oblast, NW Bulgaria
117 C19 Vrachíonas ▲ Zákynthos, Iónioi Nísoi, Greece, C Mediterranean Sea
119 P8 Vradiyivka Mykolayivs'ka Oblast', S Ukraine
115 G14 Vran ▲ SW Bosnia and Herzegovina
118 K12 Vrancea ◆ county E Romania
153 T14 Vrang SE Tajikistan
127 Oo2 Vrangelya, Ostrov Eng. Wrangel Island. island NE Russian Federation
114 H13 Vranica ▲ C Bosnia and Herzegovina
115 O16 Vranje Serbia, SE Yugoslavia
Vranov see Vranov nad Topľou
113 N19 Vranov nad Topľou var. Vranov, Hung. Varannó. Východné Slovensko, E Slovakia
116 H8 Vratsa Oblast Montana, NW Bulgaria
116 F10 Vrattsa prev. Mirovo. Sofiyska Oblast, W Bulgaria
114 G11 Vrbanja ≈ NW Bosnia and Herzegovina
114 K9 Vrbas Serbia, NW Yugoslavia
114 G13 Vrbas ≈ N Bosnia and Herzegovina
114 E8 Vrbovec Grad Zagreb, N Croatia
114 C9 Vrbovsko Primorje-Gorski Kotar, NW Croatia
113 E15 Vrchlabí Ger. Hohenelbe. Východní Čechy, NE Czech Republic
85 J22 Vrede Free State, E South Africa
102 E13 Vreden Nordrhein-Westfalen, NW Germany
85 E25 Vredenburg Western Cape, SW South Africa
101 I23 Vresse-sur-Semois Namur, SE Belgium
97 L16 Vretstorp Örebro, C Sweden
115 G15 Vrgorac prev. Vrhgorac. Split-Dalmacija, SE Croatia
Vrhgorac see Vrgorac
111 T12 Vrhnika Ger. Oberlaibach. W Slovenia
161 I21 Vriddhāchalam Tamil Nādu, SE India
100 N6 Vries Drenthe, NE Netherlands
100 O10 Vriezenveen Overijssel, E Netherlands
97 L20 Vrigstad Jönköping, S Sweden
110 H9 Vrin Graubünden, S Switzerland
114 E13 Vrlika Split-Dalmacija, S Croatia
115 M14 Vrnjačka Banja Serbia, C Yugoslavia
Vrondádhes/Vrondados see Vrontádos
117 L18 Vrontádos var. Vrondados; prev. Vrondádhes. Chíos, E Greece
100 N9 Vroomshoop Overijssel, E Netherlands
114 N10 Vršac Ger. Werschetz, Hung. Versecz. Serbia, NE Yugoslavia
114 M10 Vršački Kanal canal N Yugoslavia
85 H21 Vryburg North-West, N South Africa
85 K22 Vryheid KwaZulu/Natal, E South Africa
113 I18 Vsetín Ger. Wsetin. Severní Morava, E Czech Republic
113 J20 Vtáčnik Hung. Madaras, Ptacsnik; prev. Ptačnik. ▲ W Slovakia
Vuadil' see Wodil
Vuanggava see Vuaqava
197 K15 Vuaqava prev. Vuanggava. island Lau Group, SE Fiji
116 I11 Vŭcha ≈ SW Bulgaria
115 N16 Vučitrn Serbia, S Yugoslavia
101 J14 Vught Noord-Brabant, S Netherlands
119 W8 Vuhledar Donets'ka Oblast', E Ukraine
114 I9 Vuka ≈ E Croatia
115 K17 Vukël var. Vukli. Shkodër, N Albania
Vukli see Vukël
114 J9 Vukovar Hung. Vukovár. Vukovar-Srijem, E Croatia
114 I10 Vukovar-Srijem off. Vukovarsko-Srijemska Županija. ◆ province E Croatia
129 U8 Vuktyl Respublika Komi, NW Russian Federation
9 Q17 Vulcan Alberta, SW Canada
118 G12 Vulcan Ger. Wulkan, Hung. Zsilyvajdevulkán; prev. Crivadia Vulcanului, Vaidei, Hung. Sily-Vajdej, Vajdej. Hunedoara, W Romania
118 M12 Vulcănești Rus. Vulkaneshty. S Moldavia
109 L22 Vulcano, Isola island Isole Eolie, S Italy
116 G7 Vŭlchedrŭm Oblast Montana, NW Bulgaria
116 N8 Vŭlchidol prev. Kurt-Dere. Varnenska Oblast, NE Bulgaria
Vulkaneshty see Vulcănești
38 J13 Vulture Mountains ▲ Arizona, SW USA
178 K14 Vung Tau prev. Fr. Cape Saint Jacques, Cap Saint-Jacques. Ba Ria-Vung Tau, S Vietnam
197 I15 Vunisea Kadavu, SE Fiji
Vuohčču see Vuotso
95 N15 Vuokatti Oulu, C Finland
95 M15 Vuolijoki Oulu, C Finland
94 J13 Vuollerim Norrbotten, N Sweden
Vuoreija see Vardø
94 L10 Vuotso Lapp. Vuohčču. Lappi, N Finland
116 J11 Vŭrbitsa prev. Filevo. Khaskovska Oblast, S Bulgaria
116 J12 Vŭrbitsa ≈ S Bulgaria
131 Q4 Vurnary Chuvashskaya Respublika, W Russian Federation
116 G8 Vŭrshets Oblast Montana, NW Bulgaria
121 F17 Vyalikaya Byerastavitsa Pol. Brzostowica Wielka, Rus. Bol'shaya Berëstovitsa; prev. Velikaya Berestovitsa. Hrodzyenskaya Voblasts', SW Belorussia
121 N20 Vyaliki Bor Rus. Velikiy Bor. Homyel'skaya Voblasts', SE Belorussia
121 J18 Vyaliki Rozhan Rus. Bol'shoy Rozhan. Minskaya Voblasts', S Belorussia
128 H10 Vyartsilya Fin. Värtsilä. Respublika Kareliya, NW Russian Federation
121 K17 Vyasyeya Rus. Veseya. Minskaya Voblasts', C Belorussia
129 R15 Vyatka ≈ NW Russian Federation
Vyatka see Kirov
131 S16 Vyatskiye Polyany Kirovskaya Oblast', NW Russian Federation
127 Nn16 Vyazemskiy Khabarovskiy Kray, SE Russian Federation
130 I4 Vyaz'ma Smolenskaya Oblast', W Russian Federation
131 N3 Vyazniki Vladimirskaya Oblast', W Russian Federation
131 O8 Vyazovka Volgogradskaya Oblast', SW Russian Federation
121 J14 Vyazyn' Rus. Vyazyn'. Minskaya Voblasts', NW Belorussia
128 G11 Vyborg Fin. Viipuri. Leningradskaya Oblast', NW Russian Federation
129 P11 Vychegda var. Vichegda. ≈ NW Russian Federation
113 L18 Východné Slovensko ◆ region E Slovakia
113 E16 Východní Čechy off. Východočeský Kraj. ◆ region N Czech Republic
126 Jj16 Vydrino Respublika Buryatiya, S Russian Federation
121 L14 Vyelyewshchyna Rus. Velevshchina. Vitsyebskaya Voblasts', N Belorussia
121 P16 Vyeramyeyki Rus. Veremeyki. Mahilyowskaya Voblasts', E Belorussia
120 K11 Vyerkhnyadzvinsk Rus. Verkhnedvinsk. Vitsyebskaya Voblasts', N Belorussia
121 P18 Vyetka Rus. Vetka. Homyel'skaya Voblasts', SE Belorussia
120 L12 Vyetryna Rus. Vetrino. Vitsyebskaya Voblasts', N Belorussia
Vygonoskoye, Ozero see Vyhanawskaye, Vozyera
128 J9 Vygozero, Ozero ◎ NW Russian Federation
Vyhanashchanskaye Vozyera see Vyhanawskaye, Vozyera
121 I18 Vyhanawskaye, Vozyera var. Vyhanashchanskaye Vozyera, Rus. Ozero Vygonovskoye. ◎ SW Belorussia
131 N4 Vyksa Nizhegorodskaya Oblast', W Russian Federation
119 O12 Vylkove Rus. Vilkovo. Odes'ka Oblast', SW Ukraine
129 R9 Vym' ≈ NW Russian Federation
118 H8 Vynohradiv Cz. Sevluš, Hung. Nagyszőlős, Rus. Vinogradov; prev. Sevlyush. Zakarpats'ka Oblast', W Ukraine
128 G13 Vyritsa Leningradskaya Oblast', NW Russian Federation
xxxv J8 Vyrnwy Wel. Afon Efyrnwy. ≈ E Wales, UK

◆ Country ● Country Capital ◇ Dependent Territory ○ Dependent Territory Capital ◆ Administrative Region ✕ International Airport ▲ Mountain ▲ Mountain Range Volcano ≈ River ◎ Lake ⊞ Reservoir

VYSHE IVANOVSKIY BELAK, GORA – WĀṬIF

151 X9 Vyshe Ivanovskiy Belak, Gora ▲ E Kazakhstan
119 P4 Vyshhorod Kyyivs'ka Oblast', N Ukraine
128 I15 Vyshniy Volochek Tverskaya Oblast', W Russian Federation
113 G18 Vyškov Ger. Wischau. Jižní Morava, SE Czech Republic
113 F17 Vysoké Mýto Ger. Hohenmauth. Východní Čechy, E Czech Republic
119 S9 Vysokopillya Khersons'ka Oblast', S Ukraine
130 K3 Vysokovsk Moskovskaya Oblast', W Russian Federation
128 K12 Vytegra Vologodskaya Oblast', NW Russian Federation
118 J8 Vyzhnytsya Chernivets'ka Oblast', W Ukraine

W

79 O14 Wa NW Ghana
Waadt see Vaud
Waag see Váh
Waagbistritz see Považská Bystrica
Waagneustadtl see Nové Mesto nad Váhom
83 M16 Waajid Gedo, SW Somalia
100 L13 Waal ≈ S Netherlands
197 G4 Waala Province Nord, W New Caledonia
101 I14 Waalwijk Noord-Brabant, S Netherlands
101 E16 Waarschoot Oost-Vlaanderen, NW Belgium
194 G12 Wabag Enga, W PNG
13 N7 Wabano ≈ Québec, SE Canada
9 P11 Wabasca ≈ Alberta, SW Canada
33 P12 Wabash Indiana, N USA
31 X9 Wabasha Minnesota, N USA
33 N13 Wabash River ≈ N USA
12 C7 Wabatongushi Lake ◎ Ontario, S Canada
83 L15 Wabē Gestro Wenz ≈ SE Ethiopia
12 B9 Wabos Ontario, S Canada
9 W13 Wabowden Manitoba, C Canada
112 J9 Wąbrzeźno Toruń, N Poland
194 G14 Wabuda Island island SW PNG
23 U12 Waccamaw River ≈ South Carolina, SE USA
25 U11 Waccasassa Bay bay Florida, SE USA
101 F16 Wachtebeke Oost-Vlaanderen, NW Belgium
27 T8 Waco Texas, SW USA
28 M3 Waconda Lake var. Great Elder Reservoir. ⊡ Kansas, C USA
Wadai see Ouaddaï
Wad Al-Hajarah see Guadalajara
171 Gg13 Wadayama Hyōgo, Honshū, SW Japan
82 D10 Wad Banda Western Kordofan, C Sudan
77 P9 Waddān NW Libya
100 J4 Waddeneilanden Eng. West Frisian Islands. island group N Netherlands
100 J6 Waddenzee var. Wadden Zee. sea SE North Sea
xxxvii R7 Waddesdon Buckinghamshire, C England, UK
xxxix Q4 Waddingham Lincolnshire, E England, UK
xli O13 Waddington Lancashire, NW England, UK
xxxix Q6 Waddington Lincolnshire, E England, UK
8 L16 Waddington, Mount ▲ British Columbia, SW Canada
100 H12 Waddinxveen Zuid-Holland, C Netherlands
xxxvi D15 Wadebridge Cornwall, SW England, UK
9 U15 Wadena Saskatchewan, S Canada
31 T6 Wadena Minnesota, N USA
110 G7 Wädenswil Zürich, N Switzerland
23 S11 Wadesboro North Carolina, SE USA
161 G16 Wādi Karnātaka, C India
144 G10 Wādī as Sīr var. Wadi es Sir. 'Ammān, NW Jordan
Wadi es Sir see Wādī as Sīr
82 F5 Wadi Halfa var. Wādī Ḥalfā'. Northern, N Sudan
144 G13 Wādī Mūsā var. Petra. Ma'ān, S Jordan
25 V4 Wadley Georgia, SE USA
Wad Madanī see Wad Medani
82 G10 Wad Medani var. Wad Madanī. Gezira, C Sudan
82 F10 Wad Nimr White Nile, C Sudan
172 Q14 Wadomari Kagoshima, Okinoerabu-jima, SW Japan
113 K17 Wadowice Bielsko-Biała, S Poland
37 R5 Wadsworth Nevada, W USA
33 T12 Wadsworth Ohio, N USA
xli T16 Wadworth Doncaster, N England, UK
27 T11 Waelder Texas, SW USA
Waereghem see Waregem
169 U13 Wafangdian var. Fuxian, Fu Xian. Liaoning, NE China
175 S11 Waflia Pulau Buru, E Indonesia
Wagadugu see Ouagadougou
100 K12 Wageningen Gelderland, SE Netherlands
57 V9 Wageningen Nickerie, NW Surinam
15 IJ5 Wager Bay inlet Northwest Territories, N Canada
176 Y10 Wageseri Irian Jaya, E Indonesia
191 P10 Wagga Wagga New South Wales, SE Australia
188 J13 Wagin Western Australia
Wagin see Vaghena
110 H8 Wägitaler See ◎ SW Switzerland
31 P12 Wagner South Dakota, N USA
29 Q9 Wagoner Oklahoma, C USA
39 U10 Wagon Mound New Mexico, SW USA
34 J14 Wagontire Oregon, NW USA
112 H10 Wągrowiec Piła, NW Poland
155 U6 Wāh Punjab, NE Pakistan
176 U10 Wahai Pulau Seram, E Indonesia
175 O7 Wahau, Sungai ≈ Borneo, C Indonesia
Wahaybah, Ramlat Al see Wahībah, Ramlat Āl
82 D13 Wahda var. Unity State. ◐ state S Sudan
40 D9 Wahiawa Haw. Wahiawā. Oahu, Hawaii, USA, C Pacific Ocean
Wahībah, Ramlat Ahl see Wahībah, Ramlat Āl
147 Y9 Wahībah, Ramlat Āl var. Ramlat Ahl Wahībah, Ramlat Al Wahaybah, Eng. Wahibah Sands. desert N Oman
Wahibah Sands see Wahībah, Ramlat Āl
103 E16 Wahn ✕ (Köln) Nordrhein-Westfalen, W Germany
31 R15 Wahoo Nebraska, C USA
31 R6 Wahpeton North Dakota, N USA
Wahran see Oran
38 J6 Wah Wah Mountains ▲▲ Utah, W USA
40 D9 Waialua Oahu, Hawaii, USA, C Pacific Ocean
40 D9 Waianae Haw. Wai'anae. Oahu, Hawaii, USA, C Pacific Ocean
192 Q8 Waiapu ≈ North Island, NZ
193 I17 Waiau Canterbury, South Island, NZ
193 I17 Waiau ≈ South Island, NZ
193 B23 Waiau ≈ South Island, NZ
103 H21 Waiblingen Baden-Württemberg, S Germany
Waidhofen see Waidhofen an der Ybbs, Niederösterreich, Austria
Waidhofen see Waidhofen an der Thaya, Niederösterreich, Austria
111 V2 Waidhofen an der Thaya var. Waidhofen. Niederösterreich, NE Austria
111 U5 Waidhofen an der Ybbs var. Waidhofen. Niederösterreich, E Austria
176 Uu8 Waigeo, Pulau island Maluku, E Indonesia
192 L5 Waiheke Island island N NZ
192 M7 Waihi Waikato, North Island, NZ
193 C20 Waihou ≈ North Island, NZ
Waikaboebak see Waikabubak
175 P17 Waikabubak prev. Waikaboebak. Pulau Sumba, C Indonesia
193 D23 Waikaia ≈ South Island, NZ
193 D23 Waikaka Southland, South Island, NZ
192 L13 Waikanae Wellington, North Island, NZ
192 M7 Waikare, Lake ◎ North Island, NZ
192 O9 Waikaremoana, Lake ◎ North Island, NZ
193 I17 Waikari Canterbury, South Island, NZ
192 L8 Waikato off. Waikato Region. ◐ region North Island, NZ
192 M8 Waikato ≈ North Island, NZ
190 J9 Waikerie South Australia
193 F23 Waikouaiti Otago, South Island, NZ
40 H11 Wailea Hawaii, USA, C Pacific Ocean
40 F10 Wailuku Maui, Hawaii, USA, C Pacific Ocean
193 H18 Waimakariri ≈ South Island, NZ
40 D9 Waimanalo Beach Oahu, Hawaii, USA, C Pacific Ocean
193 G15 Waimangaroa West Coast, South Island, NZ
193 G21 Waimate Canterbury, South Island, NZ
40 G11 Waimea var. Kamuela. Hawaii, USA, C Pacific Ocean
40 D9 Waimea var. Maunawai. Oahu, Hawaii, USA, C Pacific Ocean
40 B8 Waimea Kauai, Hawaii, USA, C Pacific Ocean
101 M20 Waimes Liège, E Belgium
xxxix T6 Wainfleet All Saints Lincolnshire, E England, UK
160 J11 Wainganga var. Wain River. ≈ C India
Waingapoe see Waingapu
175 Pp17 Waingapu prev. Waingapoe. Pulau Sumba, C Indonesia
57 S7 Waini ≈ N Guyana
57 S7 Waini Point headland NW Guyana
Wain River see Wainganga
9 R15 Wainwright Alberta, SW Canada
41 O5 Wainwright Alaska, USA
192 K4 Waiotira Northland, North Island, NZ
192 M11 Waiouru Manawatu-Wanganui, North Island, NZ
176 X11 Waipa Irian Jaya, E Indonesia
192 L8 Waipa ≈ North Island, NZ
192 P9 Waipaoa ≈ North Island, NZ
193 D25 Waipapa Point headland South Island, NZ
193 I18 Waipara Canterbury, South Island, NZ
192 N12 Waipawa Hawke's Bay, North Island, NZ
192 K4 Waipu Northland, North Island, NZ
192 N12 Waipukurau Hawke's Bay, North Island, NZ
176 Vv13 Wair Pulau Kai Besar, E Indonesia
Wairakai see Wairakei
192 N9 Wairakei var. Wairakai. Waikato, North Island, NZ
193 M14 Wairarapa, Lake ◎ North Island, NZ
193 J15 Wairau ≈ South Island, NZ
192 P10 Wairoa Hawke's Bay, North Island, NZ
192 P10 Wairoa ≈ North Island, NZ
192 J4 Wairoa ≈ North Island, NZ
192 N9 Waitahanui Waikato, North Island, NZ
192 M6 Waitakaruru Waikato, North Island, NZ
193 F21 Waitaki ≈ South Island, NZ
192 K10 Waitara Taranaki, North Island, NZ
192 M7 Waitoa Waikato, North Island, NZ
192 L8 Waitomo Caves Waikato, North Island, NZ
192 L11 Waitotara Taranaki, North Island, NZ
192 L11 Waitotara ≈ North Island, NZ
34 L10 Waitsburg Washington, NW USA
Waitzen see Vác
192 L6 Waiuku Auckland, North Island, NZ
171 J12 Wajima var. Wazima. Ishikawa, Honshū, SW Japan
83 K17 Wajir North Eastern, NE Kenya
83 I14 Waka SW Ethiopia
81 J17 Waka Equateur, NW Zaire
12 D9 Wakami Lake ◎ Ontario, S Canada
170 G13 Wakasa Tottori, Honshū, SW Japan
171 H13 Wakasa-wan bay C Japan
193 C22 Wakatipu, Lake ◎ South Island, NZ
9 T15 Wakaw Saskatchewan, S Canada
197 I14 Wakaya island C Fiji
170 Ff15 Wakayama Wakayama, Honshū, SW Japan
170 G16 Wakayama off. Wakayama-ken. ◐ prefecture Honshū, SW Japan
28 K4 Wa Keeney Kansas, C USA
xli S15 Wakefield Wakefield, N England, UK
xli R15 Wakefield ◐ unitary authority N England, UK
193 I14 Wakefield Tasman, South Island, NZ
29 O4 Wakefield Kansas, C USA
32 L4 Wakefield Michigan, N USA
23 U9 Wake Forest North Carolina, SE USA
Wakeham Bay see Kangiqsujuaq
201 Y11 Wake Island ◇ US unincorporated territory NW Pacific Ocean
201 Y12 Wake Island ✕ NW Pacific Ocean
201 Y12 Wake Island atoll NW Pacific Ocean
201 X12 Wake Lagoon lagoon Wake Island, NW Pacific Ocean
177 F9 Wakema Irrawaddy, SW Burma
xxxvii X6 Wakes Colne Essex, SE England, UK
Wakhan see Khandūd
170 Ff15 Waki Tokushima, Shikoku, SW Japan
172 N8 Wakinosawa Aomori, Honshū, C Japan
172 Pp1 Wakkanai Hokkaidō, NE Japan
85 K22 Wakkerstroom Mpumalanga, E South Africa
12 C10 Wakomata Lake ◎ Ontario, S Canada
191 N10 Wakool New South Wales, SE Australia
Wakra see Al Wakrah
Waku Kungo see Uaco Cungo
195 S12 Wakunai Bougainville Island, NE PNG
Walachei/Walachia see Wallachia
175 Pp12 Walanae, Sungai ≈ Sulawesi, C Indonesia
161 K26 Walawe Ganga ≈ S Sri Lanka
xxxix Z11 Walberswick Suffolk, E England, UK
113 F15 Wałbrzych Ger. Waldenburg, Waldenburg in Schlesien. Wałbrzych, SW Poland
113 F15 Wałbrzych off. Województwo Wałbrzyskie, Ger. Waldenburg, Waldenburg in Schlesien. ◐ province SW Poland
Wałbrzyskie, Województwo see Wałbrzych
191 T6 Walcha New South Wales, SE Australia
103 K24 Walchensee ◎ SE Germany
101 D14 Walcheren island SW Netherlands
xxxix Q6 Walcot Lincolnshire, E England, UK
31 Z14 Walcott Iowa, C USA
35 W16 Walcott Wyoming, C USA
101 G21 Walcourt Namur, S Belgium
112 G9 Wałcz Ger. Deutsch Krone. Piła, NW Poland
110 H7 Wald Zürich, N Switzerland
111 U3 Waldaist ≈ N Austria
188 I9 Waldburg Range ▲▲ Western Australia
39 R3 Walden Colorado, C USA
20 K13 Walden New York, NE USA
Waldenburg/Waldenburg in Schlesien see Wałbrzych
9 T15 Waldheim Saskatchewan, S Canada
Waldia see Weldiya
103 M23 Waldkraiburg Bayern, SE Germany
29 T14 Waldo Arkansas, C USA
25 V9 Waldo Florida, SE USA
21 R7 Waldoboro Maine, NE USA
23 W4 Waldorf Maryland, NE USA
34 F12 Waldport Oregon, NW USA
29 S11 Waldron Arkansas, C USA
205 Y13 Waldron, Cape headland Antarctica
103 F24 Waldshut-Tiengen Baden-Württemberg, S Germany
175 Qq9 Walea, Selat strait Sulawesi, C Indonesia
Wałeckie Międzyrzecze see Valašské Meziříčí
110 H8 Walensee ◎ NW Switzerland
xxxv H9 Wales Wel. Cymru. national region Wales, UK
40 L8 Wales Alaska, USA
15 L3 Wales Island island Northwest Territories, N Canada
79 P14 Walewale N Ghana
101 M24 Walferdange Luxembourg, C Luxembourg
xxxviii G12 Walford Herefordshire, W England, UK
191 Q5 Walgett New South Wales, SE Australia
xxxviii I7 Walgherton Cheshire, W England, UK
204 K10 Walgreen Coast physical region Antarctica
31 Q2 Walhalla North Dakota, N USA
23 O11 Walhalla South Carolina, SE USA
81 O19 Walikale Nord Kivu, E Zaire
194 G9 Walis Island island NW PNG
Walk see Valga, Estonia
Walk see Valka, Latvia
31 U5 Walker Minnesota, N USA
13 V4 Walker, Lac ◎ Québec, SE Canada
37 S7 Walker Lake ◎ Nevada, W USA
xxxvii T7 Walkern Hertfordshire, SE England, UK
37 R6 Walker River ≈ Nevada, W USA
xli V14 Walkington East Riding of Yorkshire, N England, UK
xli P6 Wall Northumberland, N England, UK
30 K10 Wall South Dakota, N USA
181 U9 Wallaby Plateau undersea feature E Indian Ocean
35 N8 Wallace Idaho, NW USA
23 V11 Wallace North Carolina, SE USA
12 D17 Wallaceburg Ontario, S Canada
24 F5 Wallace Lake ⊡ Louisiana, S USA
9 P13 Wallace Mountain ▲ Alberta, W Canada
118 J14 Wallachia var. Walachia, Ger. Walachei, Rom. Valachia. cultural region S Romania
Wallachisch-Meseritsch see Valašské Meziříčí
191 U4 Wallangarra New South Wales, SE Australia
190 I8 Wallaroo South Australia
xl B15 Wallasey Wirral, NW England, UK
34 L10 Walla Walla Washington, NW USA
47 V9 Wallblake ✕ (The Valley) C Anguilla
103 H19 Walldürn Baden-Württemberg, SW Germany
102 F12 Wallenhorst Niedersachsen, NW Germany
Wallenthal see Hațeg
111 S4 Wallern Oberösterreich, N Austria
Wallern see Wallern im Burgenland
111 Z5 Wallern im Burgenland var. Wallern. Burgenland, E Austria
xxxvii Q9 Wallingford Oxfordshire, C England, UK
20 M9 Wallingford Vermont, NE USA
27 V11 Wallis Texas, SW USA
Wallis see Valais
199 Jj10 Wallis and Futuna Fr. Territoire de Wallis et Futuna. ◇ French overseas territory C Pacific Ocean
110 G7 Wallisellen Zürich, N Switzerland
202 H11 Wallis, Îles island group N Wallis and Futuna
101 H19 Walloon Brabant ◐ province C Belgium
33 Q5 Walloon Lake ◎ Michigan, N USA
xlii H4 Walls Shetland Islands, NE Scotland, UK
xli R6 Wallsend North Tyneside, NE England, UK
34 K10 Wallula Washington, NW USA
34 K10 Wallula, Lake ◎ Washington, NW USA
xxxvii Z10 Walmer Kent, SE England, UK
xl L12 Walney, Isle of island NW England, UK
23 S8 Walnut Cove North Carolina, SE USA
37 N8 Walnut Creek California, W USA
28 K5 Walnut Creek ≈ Kansas, C USA
29 W9 Walnut Ridge Arkansas, C USA
27 S7 Walnut Springs Texas, SW USA
190 L10 Walpeup Victoria, SE Australia
197 L7 Walpole, Île island SE New Caledonia
xxxix T9 Walpole St Peter Norfolk, E England, UK
41 N13 Walrus Islands island group Alaska, USA
xxxviii C14 Walsall Walsall, C England, UK
xxxviii K10 Walsall ◐ unitary authority C England, UK
xli P15 Walsden Calderdale, N England, UK
39 T7 Walsenburg Colorado, C USA
9 S17 Walsh Alberta, SW Canada
39 W7 Walsh Colorado, C USA
xxxvii W11 Walsham le Willows Suffolk, E England, UK
102 I11 Walsrode Niedersachsen, NW Germany
Waltenberg see Zalău
23 R14 Walterboro South Carolina, SE USA
Walter F. George Lake see Walter F. George Reservoir
25 R6 Walter F. George Reservoir var. Walter F. George Lake. ⊡ Alabama/Georgia, SE USA
28 M12 Walters Oklahoma, C USA
103 J16 Waltershausen Thüringen, C Germany
181 N10 Walters Shoal var. Walters Shoals. reef S Madagascar
Walters Shoals see Walters Shoal
24 M3 Walthall Mississippi, S USA
xxxix R4 Waltham North East Lincolnshire, E England, UK
xxxvii U8 Waltham Abbey Essex, SE England, UK
xxxv L16 Waltham Forest ◐ London borough SE England, UK
xxxix P8 Waltham on the Wolds Leicestershire, C England, UK
xxxvi E5 Walthamstow London borough capital Waltham Forest, SE England, UK
xli N6 Walton Cumbria, NW England, UK
xxxv K11 Walton Powys, C Wales, UK
22 M4 Walton Kentucky, S USA
20 J11 Walton New York, NE USA
xli N14 Walton-le-Dale Lancashire, NW England, UK
xxxvii Y7 Walton-on-The-Naze Essex, SE England, UK
xxxv C13 Walton West Pembrokeshire, SW Wales, UK
81 O20 Walungu Sud Kivu, E Zaire
Walvisbaai see Walvis Bay
85 C19 Walvis Bay Afr. Walvisbaai. Erongo, NW Namibia
85 B19 Walvis Bay bay NW Namibia
Walvish Ridge see Walvis Ridge
67 O17 Walvis Ridge var. Walvish Ridge. undersea feature E Atlantic Ocean
176 Yy15 Wamal Irian Jaya, E Indonesia
176 W13 Wamar, Pulau island Kepulauan Aru, E Indonesia
79 V15 Wamba Plateau, C Nigeria
81 O17 Wamba Haut-Zaïre, NE Zaire
81 H22 Wamba var. Uamba. ≈ Angola/Zaire
29 P4 Wamego Kansas, C USA
20 I10 Wampsville New York, NE USA
44 K6 Wampú, Río ≈ E Honduras
176 Xx16 Wan Irian Jaya, E Indonesia
Wan see Anhui
191 N4 Wanaaring New South Wales, SE Australia
193 D21 Wanaka Otago, South Island, NZ
193 D20 Wanaka, Lake ◎ South Island, NZ
176 Ww12 Wanapiri Irian Jaya, E Indonesia
12 F9 Wanapitei ≈ Ontario, S Canada
12 F10 Wanapitei Lake ◎ Ontario, S Canada
20 K14 Wanaque New Jersey, NE USA
176 V9 Wanau Irian Jaya, E Indonesia
193 F22 Wanbrow, Cape headland South Island, NZ
Wanchuan see Zhangjiakou
176 X11 Wandai var. Komeyo. Irian Jaya, E Indonesia
169 Z8 Wanda Shan ▲▲ NE China
207 R11 Wandel Sea sea Arctic Ocean
166 D13 Wanding var. Wandingzhen. Yunnan, SW China
Wandingzhen see Wanding
176 Z14 Wandip Irian Jaya, E Indonesia
xxxiv K16 Wandsworth ◐ London borough SE England, UK
xxxvi C8 Wandsworth London borough capital Wandsworth, SE England, UK
101 H20 Wanfercée-Baulet Hainaut, S Belgium
192 L12 Wanganui Manawatu-Wanganui, North Island, NZ
192 L11 Wanganui ≈ North Island, NZ
191 P11 Wangaratta Victoria, SE Australia
166 J8 Wangcang prev. Fengjiaba. Sichuan, C China
Wangda see Zogang
103 I24 Wangen im Allgäu Baden-Württemberg, S Germany
Wangerin see Węgorzyno
102 F9 Wangerooge island NW Germany
xxxix Y11 Wangford Suffolk, E England, UK
176 Ww11 Wanggar Irian Jaya, E Indonesia
166 J13 Wangmo var. Fuxing. Guizhou, S China
Wangolodougou see Ouangolodougou
167 S9 Wangpan Yang sea E China
169 Y10 Wangqing Jilin, NE China
178 I9 Wang Saphung Loei, C Thailand
178 H6 Wan Hsa-la Shan State, E Burma
57 W9 Wanica ◐ district N Surinam
81 M18 Wanie-Rukula Haut-Zaïre, C Zaire
Wankie see Hwange
Wanki, Río see Coco, Río
83 N17 Wanlaweyn var. Wanle Weyn, It. Uanle Uen. Shabeellaha Hoose, SW Somalia
Wanle Weyn see Wanlaweyn
xliii K22 Wanlockhead Dumfries and Galloway, SW Scotland, UK
188 I12 Wanneroo Western Australia
166 L17 Wanning Hainan, S China
178 I8 Wanon Niwat Sakon Nakhon, E Thailand
161 H16 Wanparti Andhra Pradesh, C India
Wansen see Wiązów
xxxix Q10 Wansford Cambridgeshire, E England, UK
166 L11 Wanshan Guizhou, S China
101 M14 Wanssum Limburg, SE Netherlands
xxxvi F6 Wanstead Redbridge, SE England, UK
192 N12 Wanstead Hawke's Bay, North Island, NZ
xxxvii P9 Wantage Oxfordshire, C England, UK
166 K9 Wanxian Sichuan, C China
196 F16 Wanyaan Yap, Micronesia
166 K8 Wanyuan Sichuan, C China
167 O11 Wanzai Jiangxi, S China
101 J20 Wanze Liège, E Belgium
33 R12 Wapakoneta Ohio, N USA
10 D7 Wapaseese ≈ Ontario, C Canada
34 I10 Wapato Washington, NW USA
31 Y15 Wapello Iowa, C USA
194 H12 Wapenamanda Enga, W PNG
9 N13 Wapiti ≈ Alberta/British Columbia, SW Canada
29 X7 Wappapello Lake ⊡ Missouri, C USA
20 K13 Wappingers Falls New York, NE USA
31 X13 Wapsipinicon River ≈ Iowa, C USA
194 G14 Wapumba Island island SW PNG
12 L9 Wapus ≈ Québec, SE Canada
166 H7 Waqên Sichuan, C China
23 Q7 War West Virginia, NE USA
82 D13 Warab Warab, SW Sudan
82 D14 Warab ◐ state SW Sudan
161 J15 Warangal Andhra Pradesh, C India
Warasdin see Varaždin
191 O16 Waratah Tasmania, SE Australia
191 O14 Waratah Bay bay Victoria, SE Australia
xxxix S11 Warboys Cambridgeshire, E England, UK
103 H15 Warburg Nordrhein-Westfalen, W Germany
190 I1 Warburton Creek seasonal river South Australia
188 M9 Warburton Western Australia
101 M20 Warche ≈ E Belgium
xli O9 Warcop Cumbria, NW England, UK
155 P5 Wardag var. Wardak, Per. Vardak. ◐ province E Afghanistan
Wardak see Wardag
34 K9 Warden Washington, NW USA
160 I12 Wardha Mahārāshtra, W India
xli L4 Ward Hill hill N Scotland, UK
194 L14 Ward Hunt, Cape headland S PNG
195 N16 Ward Hunt Strait strait S PNG
123 J16 Wardija, Ras il- var. Wardija Point. headland Gozo, NW Malta
145 P3 Wardīyah N Iraq
193 E19 Ward, Mount ▲ South Island, NZ
176 Ww9 Wardo Irian Jaya, E Indonesia
xxxvii U7 Ware Hertfordshire, SE England, UK
8 L11 Ware British Columbia, W Canada
101 D18 Waregem var. Waereghem. West-Vlaanderen, W Belgium
xxxvi M14 Wareham Dorset, S England, UK
101 J19 Waremme Liège, E Belgium
102 N10 Waren Mecklenburg-Vorpommern, NE Germany
176 X10 Waren Irian Jaya, E Indonesia
103 F14 Warendorf Nordrhein-Westfalen, W Germany
23 P12 Ware Shoals South Carolina, SE USA
100 N4 Warffum Groningen, NE Netherlands
83 O15 Wargalo Mudug, E Somalia
152 M12 Warganza Rus. Varganzi. Qashqadaryo Wiloyati, S Uzbekistan
Wargla see Ouargla
xxxvii R9 Wargrave Wokingham, S England, UK
194 K14 Waria ≈ S PNG
191 T4 Warialda New South Wales, SE Australia
160 F13 Wāri Godri Mahārāshtra, C India
176 W11 Warika Irian Jaya, E Indonesia
176 W13 Warilau Pulau Warilau, E Indonesia
176 Ww13 Warilau, Pulau island Kepulauan Aru, E Indonesia
178 J10 Warin Chamrap Ubon Ratchathani, E Thailand
27 R11 Waring Texas, SW USA
41 O8 Waring Mountains ▲▲ Alaska, USA
xli P5 Wark Northumberland, N England, UK
xli O2 Wark Northumberland, N England, UK
112 M12 Warka Radom, E Poland
192 L5 Warkworth Auckland, North Island, NZ
xxxvii T10 Warlingham Surrey, SE England, UK
176 V8 Warmandi Irian Jaya, E Indonesia
85 E22 Warmbad Karas, S Namibia
100 H8 Warmenhuizen Noord-Holland, NW Netherlands
xxxvi M11 Warminster Wiltshire, S England, UK
20 I15 Warminster Pennsylvania, NE USA
37 V8 Warm Springs Nevada, W USA
34 H12 Warm Springs Oregon, NW USA
23 S5 Warm Springs Virginia, NE USA
102 M8 Warnemünde Mecklenburg-Vorpommern, NE Germany
29 Q10 Warner Oklahoma, C USA
37 Q2 Warner Mountains ▲▲ California, W USA
25 T5 Warner Robins Georgia, SE USA
59 N18 Warnes Santa Cruz, C Bolivia
102 M9 Warnow ≈ NE Germany
Warnsdorf see Varnsdorf
100 M11 Warnsveld Gelderland, E Netherlands
176 Uu10 Waromge, Teluk bay Irian Jaya, E Indonesia
160 I13 Warora Mahārāshtra, C India
190 L11 Warracknabeal Victoria, SE Australia
191 O13 Warragul Victoria, SE Australia
191 O4 Warrego River seasonal river New South Wales/Queensland, E Australia
191 Q6 Warren New South Wales, SE Australia
9 X16 Warren Manitoba, S Canada
29 V14 Warren Arkansas, C USA
33 S10 Warren Michigan, N USA
31 R3 Warren Minnesota, N USA
33 U11 Warren Ohio, N USA
20 D12 Warren Pennsylvania, NE USA
27 X10 Warren Texas, SW USA
xliv L6 Warrenpoint Ir. An Pointe. Newry and Mourne, SE Northern Ireland, UK
29 S4 Warrensburg Missouri, C USA
85 H22 Warrenton Northern Cape, N South Africa
25 U4 Warrenton Georgia, SE USA
29 W4 Warrenton Missouri, C USA
23 V8 Warrenton North Carolina, SE USA
23 V4 Warrenton Virginia, NE USA
79 U17 Warri Delta, S Nigeria
xl E16 Warrington Cheshire, C England, UK
xl E16 Warrington ◐ unitary authority NW England, UK
25 O9 Warrington Florida, SE USA
25 P3 Warrior Alabama, S USA
190 L13 Warrnambool Victoria, SE Australia
31 T2 Warroad Minnesota, N USA
191 S6 Warrumbungle Range ▲▲ New South Wales, SE Australia
160 J12 Wārsa Mahārāshtra, C India
33 P11 Warsaw Indiana, N USA
22 L4 Warsaw Kentucky, S USA
29 T5 Warsaw Missouri, C USA
20 E10 Warsaw New York, NE USA
23 V10 Warsaw North Carolina, SE USA
23 X5 Warsaw Virginia, NE USA
Warsaw/Warschau see Warszawa
83 N17 Warshiikh Shabeellaha Dhexe, C Somalia
xxxix N6 Warsop Nottinghamshire, C England, UK
103 G15 Warstein Nordrhein-Westfalen, W Germany
112 M11 Warszawa Eng. Warsaw, Ger. Warschau, Rus. Varshava. ● (Poland) Warszawa, C Poland
112 L11 Warszawa off. Województwo Stołeczne Warszawskie, Eng. Greater Warsaw. ◐ province C Poland
112 J13 Warta Sieradz, C Poland
112 D11 Warta Ger. Warthe. ≈ W Poland
Wartberg see Senec
22 M9 Wartburg Tennessee, S USA
110 J7 Warth Vorarlberg, NW Austria
Warthe see Warta
175 O9 Waru Borneo, C Indonesia
176 U11 Waru Pulau Seram, E Indonesia
145 N6 Wa'r, Wādī al dry watercourse E Syria
xxxviii E17 Warwick Warwickshire, C England, UK
191 U3 Warwick Queensland, E Australia
13 Q11 Warwick Québec, SE Canada
20 K13 Warwick New York, NE USA
31 P4 Warwick North Dakota, N USA
21 O12 Warwick Rhode Island, NE USA
xxxviii E16 Warwickshire ◐ county C England, UK
12 G14 Wasaga Beach Ontario, S Canada
79 U13 Wasagu Kebbi, NW Nigeria
38 M2 Wasatch Range ▲▲ W USA
xlii M3 Wasbister Orkney Islands, N Scotland, UK
37 R12 Wasco California, W USA
31 V10 Waseca Minnesota, N USA
12 H13 Washago Ontario, S Canada
21 S2 Washburn Maine, NE USA
30 M5 Washburn North Dakota, N USA
32 K3 Washburn Wisconsin, N USA
33 S14 Washburn Hill hill Ohio, N USA
160 H13 Wāshīm Mahārāshtra, C India
xli R7 Washington Sunderland, NE England, UK
25 U3 Washington Georgia, SE USA
32 L12 Washington Illinois, N USA
33 N15 Washington Indiana, N USA
31 X15 Washington Iowa, C USA
29 O3 Washington Kansas, C USA
29 W5 Washington Missouri, C USA
23 X9 Washington North Carolina, SE USA
20 B15 Washington Pennsylvania, NE USA
27 V10 Washington Texas, SW USA
38 J8 Washington Utah, W USA
23 V4 Washington Virginia, NE USA
34 J9 Washington off. State of Washington; also known as Chinook State, Evergreen State. ◐ state NW USA
Washington see Washington Court House
33 S14 Washington Court House var. Washington. Ohio, NE USA
23 W4 Washington DC ● (USA) District of Columbia, NE USA
33 O5 Washington Island island Wisconsin, N USA
Washington Island see Teraina
21 O7 Washington, Mount ▲ New Hampshire, NE USA
28 M11 Washita River ≈ Oklahoma/Texas, C USA
xxxix T7 Wash, The bay E England, UK
34 L9 Washtucna Washington, NW USA
Wasiliszki see Vasilishki
112 P9 Wasilków Białystok, NE Poland
41 R11 Wasilla Alaska, USA
57 U9 Wasjabo Sipaliwini, NW Surinam
9 X11 Waskaiowaka Lake ◎ Manitoba, C Canada
9 T14 Waskesiu Lake Saskatchewan, C Canada
27 X7 Waskom Texas, SW USA
112 G13 Wąsosz Leszno, SW Poland
44 M6 Waspam var. Waspán. Región Autónoma Atlántico Norte, NE Nicaragua
Waspán see Waspam
172 P4 Wassamu Hokkaidō, NE Japan
110 G9 Wassen Uri, C Switzerland
100 G11 Wassenaar Zuid-Holland, W Netherlands
101 N24 Wasserbillig Grevenmacher, E Luxembourg
Wasserburg see Wasserburg am Inn
103 M23 Wasserburg am Inn var. Wasserburg. Bayern, SE Germany
103 I17 Wasserkuppe ▲ C Germany
105 R5 Wassy Haute-Marne, N France
xl L10 Wast Water ◎ NW England, UK
175 Pp12 Watampone var. Bone. Sulawesi, C Indonesia
175 Ss11 Watawa Pulau Buru, E Indonesia
xxxvi I11 Watchet Somerset, SW England, UK
Watenstedt-Salzgitter see Salzgitter
xxxix T12 Waterbeach Cambridgeshire, E England, UK
xliii M24 Waterbeck Dumfries and Galloway, SW Scotland, UK
20 M13 Waterbury Connecticut, NE USA
23 R11 Wateree Lake ⊡ South Carolina, SE USA
23 R12 Wateree River ≈ South Carolina, SE USA
xliv J13 Waterford Ir. Port Láirge. Waterford, S Ireland
xliv H13 Waterford Ir. Port Láirge. ◐ county S Ireland
xliv J13 Waterford ✕ Waterford, S Ireland
33 S9 Waterford Michigan, N USA
xliv J13 Waterford Harbour Ir. Cuan Phort Láirge. inlet S Ireland
xxxvi C15 Watergate Bay bay SW England, UK
xliv G13 Watergrasshill Cork, S Ireland
100 G12 Wateringen Zuid-Holland, W Netherlands
101 G19 Waterloo Walloon Brabant, C Belgium
12 F16 Waterloo Ontario, S Canada
13 P12 Waterloo Québec, SE Canada
32 K16 Waterloo Illinois, N USA
31 X13 Waterloo Iowa, C USA
20 G10 Waterloo New York, NE USA
xxxvii Q13 Waterlooville Hampshire, S England, UK
xliii I23 Waterside East Ayrshire, W Scotland, UK
32 L4 Watersmeet Michigan, N USA
25 V9 Watertown Florida, SE USA
20 I8 Watertown New York, NE USA
31 R9 Watertown South Dakota, N USA
32 M8 Watertown Wisconsin, N USA
24 L3 Water Valley Mississippi, S USA
xliv B14 Waterville Kerry, SW Ireland
29 O3 Waterville Kansas, C USA
19 S6 Waterville Maine, NE USA
31 V10 Waterville Minnesota, N USA
20 I10 Waterville New York, NE USA
xxxvii S8 Watford Hertfordshire, E England, UK
12 E16 Watford Ontario, S Canada
30 K4 Watford City North Dakota, N USA
147 X12 Wāṭif S Oman

◆ Country ● Country Capital ◇ Dependent Territory ○ Dependent Territory Capital ◐ Administrative Region ✕ International Airport ▲ Mountain ▲▲ Mountain Range Volcano ≈ River ◎ Lake ⊡ Reservoir

WATKINS GLEN – WHINNEYFOLD

20 G11 **Watkins Glen** New York, NE USA
Watlings Island *see* San Salvador
xxxvii Q8 **Watlington** Oxfordshire, S England, UK
176 V13 **Watnil** Pulau Kai Kecil, E Indonesia
28 M10 **Watonga** Oklahoma, C USA
9 T16 **Watrous** Saskatchewan, S Canada
39 T10 **Watrous** New Mexico, SW USA
81 P16 **Watsa** Haut-Zaïre, NE Zaire
33 N12 **Watseka** Illinois, N USA
81 J19 **Watsikengo** Equateur, C Zaire
190 C5 **Watson** South Australia
9 U15 **Watson** Saskatchewan, S Canada
205 O10 **Watson Escarpment** ▲ Antarctica
8 K9 **Watson Lake** Yukon Territory, W Canada
37 N10 **Watsonville** California, W USA
178 I8 **Wattay** ✈ (Viangchan) Viangchan, C Laos
xlii L7 **Watten** Highland, NW Scotland, UK
xlii L7 **Watten, Loch** ◎ N Scotland, UK
111 N7 **Wattens** Tirol, W Austria
xxxix V10 **Watton** Norfolk, E England, UK
22 M9 **Watts Bar Lake** ▣ Tennessee, S USA
110 H7 **Wattwil** Sankt Gallen, NE Switzerland
176 Uu12 **Watubela, Kepulauan** *island group* E Indonesia
103 N24 **Watzmann** ▲ SE Germany
194 J13 **Wau** Morobe, C PNG
83 D14 **Wau** *var.* Wâw. Western Bahr el Ghazal, S Sudan
31 Q8 **Waubay** South Dakota, N USA
31 Q8 **Waubay Lake** ◎ South Dakota, N USA
191 U7 **Wauchope** New South Wales, SE Australia
25 W13 **Wauchula** Florida, SE USA
32 M10 **Wauconda** Illinois, N USA
190 J7 **Waukaringa** South Australia
33 N10 **Waukegan** Illinois, N USA
32 M9 **Waukesha** Wisconsin, N USA
31 X11 **Waukon** Iowa, C USA
32 L8 **Waunakee** Wisconsin, N USA
32 L7 **Waupaca** Wisconsin, N USA
32 M8 **Waupun** Wisconsin, N USA
28 M13 **Waurika** Oklahoma, C USA
28 M12 **Waurika Lake** ▣ Oklahoma, C USA
32 L6 **Wausau** Wisconsin, N USA
33 R11 **Wauseon** Ohio, N USA
32 L7 **Wautoma** Wisconsin, N USA
32 M9 **Wauwatosa** Wisconsin, N USA
24 L9 **Waveland** Mississippi, S USA
xxxix Y10 **Waveney** ⁓ E England, UK
192 L11 **Waverley** Taranaki, North Island, NZ
31 W12 **Waverly** Iowa, C USA
29 T4 **Waverly** Missouri, C USA
31 R15 **Waverly** Nebraska, C USA
20 G12 **Waverly** New York, NE USA
22 H8 **Waverly** Tennessee, S USA
23 W7 **Waverly** Virginia, NE USA
101 H19 **Wavre** Walloon Brabant, C Belgium
177 G8 **Waw** Pegu, SW Burma
Wâw *see* Wau
12 B7 **Wawa** Ontario, S Canada
79 T14 **Wawa** Niger, W Nigeria
77 Q11 **Wāw al Kabīr** S Libya
45 N7 **Wawa, Río** *var.* Río Huahua. ⁓ NE Nicaragua
194 G13 **Wawoi** ⁓ SW PNG
Wawosungu, Teluk *see* Staring, Teluk
27 T7 **Waxahachie** Texas, SW USA
164 L9 **Waxxari** Xinjiang Uygur Zizhiqu, NW China
197 H14 **Waya** *island* Yasawa Group, NW Fiji
25 V7 **Waycross** Georgia, SE USA
188 K10 **Way, Lake** ◎ Western Australia
33 P9 **Wayland** Michigan, N USA
31 R13 **Wayne** Nebraska, C USA
20 K14 **Wayne** New Jersey, NE USA
23 P5 **Wayne** West Virginia, NE USA
25 V4 **Waynesboro** Georgia, SE USA
24 M7 **Waynesboro** Mississippi, S USA
22 H10 **Waynesboro** Tennessee, S USA
23 U5 **Waynesboro** Virginia, NE USA
20 B16 **Waynesburg** Pennsylvania, NE USA
29 U6 **Waynesville** Missouri, C USA
23 O10 **Waynesville** North Carolina, SE USA
28 L8 **Waynoka** Oklahoma, C USA
Wazan *see* Ouazzane
Wazima *see* Wajima
155 V7 **Wazīrābād** Punjab, NE Pakistan
Wazzan *see* Ouazzane
112 I8 **Wda** *var.* Czarna Woda, *Ger.* Schwarzwasser. ⁓ N Poland
197 K6 **Wé** Province des Îles Loyauté, E New Caledonia
xxxvi A6 **Wealdstone** Harrow, SE England, UK
xxxvii U11 **Weald, The** *lowlands* SE England, UK
194 E15 **Weam** Western, SW PNG
xli W4 **Wear** ⁓ N England, UK
Wearmouth *see* Sunderland
28 L10 **Weatherford** Oklahoma, C USA
27 S6 **Weatherford** Texas, SW USA
xl D17 **Weaver** ⁓ W England, UK
xl E17 **Weaverham** Cheshire, W England, UK
xli V12 **Weaverthorpe** North Yorkshire, N England, UK
36 M3 **Weaverville** California, W USA
29 R7 **Webb City** Missouri, C USA
198 G9 **Weber Basin** *undersea feature* S Ceram Sea
Webfoot State *see* Oregon
20 F9 **Webster** New York, NE USA
31 Q8 **Webster** South Dakota, N USA
31 V13 **Webster City** Iowa, C USA
29 X5 **Webster Groves** Missouri, C USA
23 S4 **Webster Springs** *var.* Addison. West Virginia, NE USA
175 T8 **Weda, Teluk** *bay* Pulau Halmahera, E Indonesia
67 B25 **Weddell Island** *island* W Falkland Islands
67 K22 **Weddell Plain** *undersea feature* SW Atlantic Ocean
67 K23 **Weddell Sea** *sea* SW Atlantic Ocean
67 B25 **Weddell Settlement** Weddell Island, W Falkland Islands
190 M11 **Wedderburn** Victoria, SE Australia
102 I9 **Wedel** Schleswig-Holstein, N Germany
94 N3 **Wedel Jarlsberg Land** *physical region* SW Svalbard
102 I12 **Wedemark** Niedersachsen, NW Germany
8 M17 **Wedge Mountain** ▲ British Columbia, SW Canada
xxxvi K11 **Wedmore** Somerset, SW England, UK
xxxviii B14 **Wednesbury** Sandwell, C England, UK
xxxviii B14 **Wednesfield** Wolverhampton, C England, UK
25 R4 **Wedowee** Alabama, S USA
176 Vv13 **Weduar** Pulau Kai Besar, E Indonesia
176 Vv14 **Weduar, Tanjung** *headland* Pulau Kai Besar, SE Indonesia
37 N2 **Weed** California, W USA
xxxix O12 **Weedon Bec** Northamptonshire, C England, UK
13 Q12 **Weedon Centre** Québec, SE Canada
20 E13 **Weedville** Pennsylvania, NE USA
xxxvi E14 **Week St Mary** Cornwall, SW England, UK
xxxvii Y7 **Weeley** Essex, SE England, UK
102 F10 **Weener** Niedersachsen, NW Germany
xxxviii K9 **Weeping Cross** Staffordshire, C England, UK
31 S16 **Weeping Water** Nebraska, C USA
101 L16 **Weert** Limburg, SE Netherlands
100 I10 **Weesp** Noord-Holland, C Netherlands
xli S13 **Weeton** North Yorkshire, N England, UK
191 S5 **Wee Waa** New South Wales, SE Australia
112 N7 **Węgorzewo** *Ger.* Angerburg. Suwałki, NE Poland
112 E9 **Węgorzyno** *Ger.* Wangerin. Szczecin, NW Poland
112 N11 **Węgrów** *Ger.* Bingerau. Siedlce, E Poland
100 N5 **Wehe-Den Hoorn** Groningen, NE Netherlands
100 M12 **Wehl** Gelderland, E Netherlands
Wehlau *see* Znamensk
173 E2 **Weh, Pulau** *island* NW Indonesia
Wei *see* Weifang
167 P1 **Weichang** *prev.* Zhuizishan. Hebei, E China
Weichsel *see* Wisła
103 M16 **Weida** Thüringen, C Germany
Weiden *see* Weiden in der Oberpfalz
103 M19 **Weiden in der Oberpfalz** *var.* Weiden. Bayern, SE Germany
167 Q4 **Weifang** *var.* Wei, Wei-fang; *prev.* Weihsien. Shandong, E China
167 S4 **Weihai** Shandong, E China
166 K6 **Wei He** ⁓ C China
Weihsien *see* Weifang
103 G17 **Weilburg** Hessen, W Germany
103 K24 **Weilheim** Bayern, SE Germany
191 P4 **Weilmoringle** New South Wales, SE Australia
103 L16 **Weimar** Thüringen, C Germany
27 U11 **Weimar** Texas, SW USA
166 L6 **Weinan** Shaanxi, C China
110 H6 **Weinfelden** Thurgau, NE Switzerland
103 I24 **Weingarten** Baden-Württemberg, S Germany
103 G20 **Weinheim** Baden-Württemberg, SW Germany
166 H11 **Weining** *var.* Weining Yizu Huizu Miaozu Zizhixian. Guizhou, S China
Weining Yizu Huizu Miaozu Zizhixian *see* Weining
189 V2 **Weipa** Queensland, NE Australia
9 Y11 **Weir River** Manitoba, C Canada
23 R1 **Weirton** West Virginia, NE USA
34 M13 **Weiser** Idaho, NW USA
166 F12 **Weishan** Yunnan, SW China
167 P6 **Weishan Hu** ◎ E China
103 M15 **Weisse Elster** *Eng.* White Elster. ⁓ Czech Republic/Germany
Weisse Körös/Weisse Kreisch *see* Crişul Alb
110 L7 **Weissenbach am Lech** Tirol, W Austria
103 K21 **Weissenburg** Bayern, SE Germany
Weissenburg *see* Wissembourg, France
Weissenburg *see* Alba Iulia, Romania
103 M15 **Weissenfels** *var.* Weißenfels. Sachsen-Anhalt, C Germany
111 R9 **Weissensee** ◎ S Austria
Weissenstein *see* Paide
110 E11 **Weisshorn** *var.* Flüela Wisshorn. ▲ SW Switzerland
Weisskirchen *see* Bela Crkva
25 R3 **Weiss Lake** ▣ Alabama, S USA
103 Q14 **Weisswasser** *Lus.* Běla Woda. Sachsen, E Germany
101 M22 **Weiswampach** Diekirch, N Luxembourg
111 U2 **Weitra** Niederösterreich, N Austria
167 O4 **Weixian** *var.* Wei Xian. Hebei, E China
165 V11 **Weiyuan** Gansu, C China
166 F14 **Weiyuan Jiang** ⁓ SW China
111 W7 **Weiz** Steiermark, SE Austria
166 K16 **Weizhou Dao** *island* S China
112 I6 **Wejherowo** Gdańsk, NW Poland
xxxix Q7 **Welby** Lincolnshire, E England, UK
29 Q8 **Welch** Oklahoma, C USA
26 M6 **Welch** Texas, SW USA
23 Q6 **Welch** West Virginia, NE USA
47 O14 **Welchman Hall** C Barbados
82 J11 **Weldiya** *var.* Waldia, *It.* Valdia. N Ethiopia
23 W8 **Weldon** North Carolina, SE USA
27 V9 **Weldon** Texas, SW USA
xxxix O11 **Welford** Northamptonshire, C England, UK
101 M19 **Welkenraedt** Liège, E Belgium
199 L2 **Welker Seamount** *undersea feature* N Pacific Ocean
85 I22 **Welkom** Free State, C South Africa
xli R11 **Well** North Yorkshire, N England, UK
xxxviii J13 **Welland** Worcestershire, W England, UK
xxxix R8 **Welland** ⁓ C England, UK
12 H16 **Welland** Ontario, S Canada
12 G16 **Welland** ⁓ Ontario, S Canada
12 H17 **Welland Canal** *canal* Ontario, S Canada
161 K25 **Wellawaya** Uva Province, SE Sri Lanka
xli S10 **Wellbury** North Yorkshire, N England, UK
Welle *see* Uele
xxxviii M13 **Wellesbourne** Warwickshire, C England, UK
189 T4 **Wellesley Islands** *island group* Queensland, N Australia
101 J22 **Wellin** Luxembourg, SE Belgium
xxxix P12 **Wellingborough** Northamptonshire, C England, UK
xxxviii I9 **Wellington** Shropshire, W England, UK
xxxvi I12 **Wellington** Somerset, SW England, UK
191 R7 **Wellington** New South Wales, SE Australia
12 J15 **Wellington** Ontario, SE Canada
193 L14 **Wellington** ● (NZ) Wellington, North Island, NZ
85 E26 **Wellington** Western Cape, SW South Africa
39 T2 **Wellington** Colorado, C USA
29 N7 **Wellington** Kansas, C USA
37 R7 **Wellington** Nevada, W USA
33 T11 **Wellington** Ohio, N USA
27 P3 **Wellington** Texas, SW USA
38 M4 **Wellington** Utah, W USA
193 M14 **Wellington** *off.* Wellington Region. ◆ *region* North Island, NZ
193 L14 **Wellington** ✈ Wellington, North Island, NZ
Wellington *see* Wellington, Isla
xliv J13 **Wellington Bridge** Wexford, SE Ireland
65 F22 **Wellington, Isla** *var.* Wellington. *island* S Chile
191 P12 **Wellington, Lake** ◎ Victoria, SE Australia
31 X14 **Wellman** Iowa, C USA
26 M6 **Wellman** Texas, SW USA
xxxvi L10 **Wellow** Bath and North East Somerset, SW England, UK
xxxvi K11 **Wells** Somerset, SW England, UK
31 V11 **Wells** Minnesota, N USA
37 X2 **Wells** Nevada, W USA
27 W8 **Wells** Texas, SW USA
20 F12 **Wellsboro** Pennsylvania, NE USA
23 R1 **Wellsburg** West Virginia, NE USA
192 K4 **Wellsford** Auckland, North Island, NZ
188 L9 **Wells, Lake** ◎ Western Australia
189 N4 **Wells, Mount** ▲ Western Australia
xxxix V7 **Wells-next-the-Sea** Norfolk, E England, UK
33 T15 **Wellston** Ohio, N USA
29 O10 **Wellston** Oklahoma, C USA
20 E11 **Wellsville** New York, NE USA
33 V12 **Wellsville** Ohio, N USA
38 L1 **Wellsville** Utah, W USA
38 I14 **Wellton** Arizona, SW USA
xxxix T10 **Welney** Norfolk, E England, UK
111 S4 **Wels** *anc.* Ovilava. Oberösterreich, N Austria
101 K15 **Welschap** ✈ (Eindhoven) Noord-Brabant, S Netherlands
102 P10 **Welse** ⁓ NE Germany
24 H9 **Welsh** Louisiana, S USA
xxxviii H8 **Welshampton** Shropshire, W England, UK
xxxv K8 **Welshpool** *Wel.* Y Trallwng. Powys, E Wales, UK
xli V14 **Welton** East Riding of Yorkshire, N England, UK
xxxvii T7 **Welwyn Garden City** Hertfordshire, E England, UK
xxxviii H8 **Wem** Shropshire, W England, UK
81 K18 **Wema** Equateur, NW Zaire
83 G21 **Wembere** ⁓ C Tanzania
xxxvi A6 **Wembley** Brent, SE England, UK
9 N13 **Wembley** Alberta, W Canada
10 I9 **Wemindji** *prev.* Nouveau-Comptoir, Paint Hills. Québec, C Canada
101 G18 **Wemmel** Vlaams Brabant, C Belgium
xliii H20 **Wemyss Bay** Inverclyde, W Scotland, UK
34 J8 **Wenatchee** Washington, NW USA
166 M17 **Wenchang** Hainan, S China
167 R11 **Wencheng** *prev.* Daxue. Zhejiang, SE China
79 P16 **Wenchi** W Ghana
Wen-chou/Wenchow *see* Wenzhou
166 H8 **Wenchuan** *prev.* Weizhou. Sichuan, C China
Wendau *see* Võnnu
Wenden *see* Cēsis
167 S4 **Wendeng** Shandong, E China
xxxix V9 **Wendling** Norfolk, E England, UK
83 J14 **Wendo** S Ethiopia
xxxvii V6 **Wendons Ambo** Essex, SE England, UK
xxxvii R8 **Wendover** Buckinghamshire, C England, UK
38 J2 **Wendover** Utah, W USA
12 D9 **Wenebegon** ⁓ Ontario, S Canada
12 D8 **Wenebegon Lake** ◎ Ontario, S Canada
110 E9 **Wengen** Bern, W Switzerland
167 O13 **Wengyuan** *prev.* Longxian. Guangdong, S China
xxxviii H11 **Wenlock Edge** *hill range* W England, UK
Wenmen Island *see* Wolf, Isla
201 P15 **Weno** *prev.* Moen. Chuuk, C Micronesia
201 V12 **Weno** *prev.* Moen. *atoll* Chuuk Islands, C Micronesia
164 H4 **Wenquan** Qinghai, C China
165 N13 **Wenquan** *var.* Arixang. Xinjiang Uygur Zizhiqu, NW China
166 H14 **Wenshan** Yunnan, SW China
164 H6 **Wensu** Xinjiang Uygur Zizhiqu, W China
xli T15 **Wentbridge** Wakefield, N England, UK
190 L8 **Wentworth** New South Wales, SE Australia
29 W4 **Wentzville** Missouri, C USA
xxxv J15 **Wenvoe** The Vale of Glamorgan, S Wales, UK
165 V12 **Wen Xian** Gansu, C China
167 S10 **Wenzhou** *var.* Wen-chou, Wenchow. Zhejiang, SE China
xxxviii G13 **Weobley** Herefordshire, W England, UK
36 L4 **Weott** California, W USA
101 I20 **Wépion** Namur, SE Belgium
102 O11 **Werbellinsee** ◎ NE Germany
101 L21 **Werbomont** Liège, E Belgium
85 G20 **Werda** Kgalagadi, S Botswana
Werder *see* Virtsu
83 N14 **Werdēr** SE Ethiopia
Werenów *see* Voranava
176 V11 **Weri** Irian Jaya, E Indonesia
100 I13 **Werkendam** Noord-Brabant, S Netherlands
103 M20 **Wernberg-Köblitz** Bayern, SE Germany
103 J18 **Werneck** Bayern, C Germany
103 K14 **Wernigerode** Sachsen-Anhalt, C Germany
xli O11 **Wernside** ▲ N England, UK
Werowitz *see* Virovitica
103 J16 **Werra** ⁓ C Germany
191 N12 **Werribee** Victoria, SE Australia
191 T6 **Werris Creek** New South Wales, SE Australia
Werro *see* Võru
Werschetz *see* Vršac
103 K23 **Wertach** ⁓ S Germany
103 I19 **Wertheim** Baden-Württemberg, SW Germany
100 J8 **Wervershoof** Noord-Holland, NW Netherlands
Wervicq *see* Wervik
101 C18 **Wervik** *var.* Wervicq, Werwick. West-Vlaanderen, W Belgium
Werwick *see* Wervik
103 D14 **Wesel** Nordrhein-Westfalen, W Germany
Weseli an der Lainsitz *see* Veselí nad Lužnicí
Wesenberg *see* Rakvere
102 H12 **Weser** ⁓ NW Germany
Wes-Kaap *see* Western Cape
27 S17 **Weslaco** Texas, SW USA
12 J13 **Weslemkoon Lake** ◎ Ontario, SE Canada
189 R1 **Wessel Islands** *island group* Northern Territory, N Australia
31 P9 **Wessington** South Dakota, N USA
31 P10 **Wessington Springs** South Dakota, N USA
27 T8 **West** Texas, SW USA
West *see* Ouest
32 M9 **West Allis** Wisconsin, N USA
190 E8 **Westall, Point** *headland* South Australia
West Antarctica *see* Lesser Antarctica
12 G11 **West Arm** Ontario, S Canada
xli R8 **West Auckland** Durham, N England, UK
West Azerbaijan *see* Āzarbāyjān-e Bākhtarī
144 F10 **West Bank** *disputed region* SW Asia
9 N17 **Westbank** British Columbia, SW Canada
xxxix R5 **West Barkwith** Lincolnshire, E England, UK
12 E11 **West Bay** Manitoulin Island, Ontario, S Canada
24 L11 **West Bay** *bay* Louisiana, S USA
32 M8 **West Bend** Wisconsin, N USA
159 R16 **West Bengal** ◆ *state* NE India
West Borneo *see* Kalimantan Barat
31 Y14 **West Branch** Iowa, C USA
33 R7 **West Branch** Michigan, N USA
20 F13 **West Branch Susquehanna River** ⁓ Pennsylvania, NE USA
xxxviii C15 **West Bromwich** Sandwell, C England, UK
21 P8 **Westbrook** Maine, NE USA
31 T10 **Westbrook** Minnesota, N USA
31 Y15 **West Burlington** Iowa, C USA
xli H5 **West Burra** *island* NE Scotland, UK
xxxviii G9 **Westbury** Shropshire, W England, UK
xxxvi M11 **Westbury** Wiltshire, S England, UK
xxxvi K11 **Westbury-sub-Mendip** Somerset, SW England, UK
32 J8 **Westby** Wisconsin, N USA
46 L6 **West Caicos** *island* W Turks and Caicos Islands
xliii L20 **West Calder** West Lothian, SE Scotland, UK
193 A24 **West Cape** *headland* South Island, NZ
182 L4 **West Caroline Basin** *undersea feature* SW Pacific Ocean
20 I16 **West Chester** Pennsylvania, NE USA
193 E18 **West Coast** *off.* West Coast Region. ◆ *region* South Island, NZ
27 V12 **West Columbia** Texas, SW USA
31 W10 **West Concord** Minnesota, N USA
xxxvii O12 **West Dean** Wiltshire, S England, UK
31 V14 **West Des Moines** Iowa, C USA
xxxvi F11 **West Down** Devon, SW England, UK
xxxvi D9 **West Dulwich** Lambeth, SE England, UK
xliii H19 **West Dunbartonshire** ◆ *unitary authority* W Scotland, UK
39 Q6 **West Elk Peak** ▲ Colorado, C USA
46 F1 **West End** Grand Bahama Island, N Bahamas
46 F1 **West End Point** *headland* Grand Bahama Island, N Bahamas
100 O7 **Westerbork** Drenthe, NE Netherlands
xli U10 **Westerdale** North Yorkshire, N England, UK
xlii L7 **Westerdale** Highland, N Scotland, UK
100 N3 **Westereems** *strait* Germany/Netherlands
100 O9 **Westerhaar-Vriezenveensewijk** Overijssel, E Netherlands
xxxvii V10 **Westerham** Kent, SE England, UK
102 G6 **Westerland** Schleswig-Holstein, N Germany
101 I17 **Westerlo** Antwerpen, N Belgium
21 N13 **Westerly** Rhode Island, NE USA
83 G18 **Western** ◆ *province* W Kenya
159 N11 **Western** ◆ *zone* C Nepal
194 E14 **Western** ◆ *province* SW PNG
195 T14 **Western** *off.* Western Province. ◆ *province* NW Solomon Islands
85 G15 **Western** ◆ *province* SW Zambia
188 K8 **Western Australia** ◆ *state* W Australia
82 A13 **Western Bahr el Ghazal** ◆ *state* SW Sudan
Western Bug *see* Bug
85 F25 **Western Cape** *off.* Western Cape Province, *Afr.* Wes-Kaap. ◆ *province* SW South Africa
82 A11 **Western Darfur** ◆ *state* W Sudan
Western Desert *see* Sahara el Gharbîya
120 G9 **Western Dvina** *Bel.* Dzvina, *Ger.* Düna, *Latv.* Daugava, *Rus.* Zapadnaya Dvina. ⁓ W Europe
83 D15 **Western Equatoria** ◆ *state* SW Sudan
161 E16 **Western Ghats** ▲ SW India
194 G12 **Western Highlands** ◆ *province* C PNG
xlii A10 **Western Isles** ◆ *unitary authority* NW Scotland, UK
Western Isles *see* Outer Hebrides
82 C12 **Western Kordofan** ◆ *state* C Sudan
23 T3 **Westernport** Maryland, NE USA
161 J26 **Western Province** ◆ *province* SW Sri Lanka
76 B10 **Western Sahara** ◇ *disputed territory* N Africa
Western Samoa *see* Samoa
Western Sayans *see* Zapadnyy Sayan
Western Scheldt *see* Westerschelde
Western Sierra Madre *see* Madre Occidental, Sierra
xlii I4 **Wester Quarff** Shetland Islands, NE Scotland, UK
101 E15 **Westerschelde** *Eng.* Western Scheldt; *prev.* Honte. *inlet* S North Sea
33 S13 **Westerville** Ohio, N USA
103 F17 **Westerwald** ▲ W Germany
67 C25 **West Falkland** *var.* Gran Malvina. *island* W Falkland Islands
31 R5 **West Fargo** North Dakota, N USA
196 M15 **West Fayu Atoll** *atoll* Caroline Islands, C Micronesia
xxxviii G8 **West Felton** Shropshire, W England, UK
xlii L6 **Westfield** Highland, N Scotland, UK
20 C11 **Westfield** New York, NE USA
32 L7 **Westfield** Wisconsin, N USA
West Flanders *see* West-Vlaanderen
29 S10 **West Fork** Arkansas, C USA
31 P16 **West Fork Big Blue River** ⁓ Nebraska, C USA
31 U12 **West Fork Des Moines River** ⁓ Iowa/Minnesota, C USA
27 S5 **West Fork Trinity River** ⁓ Texas, SW USA
32 L16 **West Frankfort** Illinois, N USA
100 I8 **West-Friesland** *physical region* NW Netherlands
West Frisian Islands *see* Waddeneilanden
xxxvi Z9 **Westgate on Sea** Kent, SE England, UK
xlii A12 **West Gerinish** Western Isles, NW Scotland, UK
21 T5 **West Grand Lake** ◎ Maine, NE USA
xxxix O11 **West Haddon** Northamptonshire, C England, UK
xxxvi F7 **West Ham** Newham, SE England, UK
xxxvi K10 **West Harptree** Bath and North East Somerset, SW England, UK
20 M12 **West Hartford** Connecticut, NE USA
20 M13 **West Haven** Connecticut, NE USA
29 X12 **West Helena** Arkansas, C USA
xli V11 **West Heslerton** North Yorkshire, N England, UK
xlii O13 **Westhill** Aberdeenshire, NE Scotland, UK
xxxvii U12 **West Hoathly** West Sussex, SE England, UK
30 M2 **Westhope** North Dakota, N USA
xl E14 **Westhoughton** Bolton, NW England, UK
205 Y8 **West Ice Shelf** *ice shelf* Antarctica
49 R2 **West Indies** *island group* SE North America
xlii J1 **Westing** Shetland Islands, NE Scotland, UK
West Irian *see* Irian Jaya
West Java *see* Jawa Barat
38 L3 **West Jordan** Utah, W USA
West Kalimantan *see* Kalimantan Barat
101 D14 **Westkapelle** Zeeland, SW Netherlands
xliii H21 **West Kilbride** North Ayrshire, W Scotland, UK
xl A16 **West Kirby** Wirral, NW England, UK
33 O13 **West Lafayette** Indiana, N USA
33 T13 **West Lafayette** Ohio, N USA
West Lake *see* Kagera
xxxix Y11 **Westleton** Suffolk, E England, UK
31 Y14 **West Liberty** Iowa, C USA
23 O5 **West Liberty** Kentucky, S USA
Westliche Morava *see* Zapadna Morava
xliii L21 **West Linton** The Borders, S Scotland, UK
15 I13 **Westlock** Alberta, SW Canada
xxxvi E16 **West Looe** Cornwall, SW England, UK
12 E17 **West Lorne** Ontario, S Canada
xliii K20 **West Lothian** ◆ *unitary authority* S Scotland, UK
xxxvi M14 **West Lulworth** Dorset, S England, UK
101 H16 **Westmalle** Antwerpen, N Belgium
xxxvii W10 **West Malling** Kent, SE England, UK
199 H6 **West Mariana Basin** *var.* Perece Vela Basin. *undersea feature* W Pacific Ocean
xliv H9 **Westmeath** *Ir.* An Iarmhí, Na h-Iarmhidhe. ◆ *county* C Ireland
29 Y11 **West Memphis** Arkansas, C USA
xxxvii Q12 **West Meon** Hampshire, S England, UK
xxxvii X7 **West Mersea** Essex, SE England, UK
23 W2 **Westminster** Maryland, NE USA
23 O11 **Westminster** South Carolina, SE USA
xxxiv K16 **Westminster, City of** ◆ *London borough* SE England, UK
24 I5 **West Monroe** Louisiana, S USA
20 D15 **Westmont** Pennsylvania, NE USA
29 O3 **Westmoreland** Kansas, C USA
37 W17 **Westmorland** California, W USA
xlii M3 **Westness** Orkney Islands, N Scotland, UK
194 L11 **West New Britain** ◆ *province* E PNG
West New Guinea *see* Irian Jaya
xl K7 **Westnewton** Cumbria, NW England, UK
85 K18 **West Nicholson** Matabeleland South, S Zimbabwe
31 T14 **West Nishnabotna River** ⁓ Iowa, C USA
183 P11 **West Norfolk Ridge** *undersea feature* W Pacific Ocean
xxxvi D9 **West Norwood** Lambeth, SE England, UK
27 P12 **West Nueces River** ⁓ Texas, SW USA
West Nusa Tenggara *see* Nusa Tenggara Barat
31 T11 **West Okoboji Lake** ◎ Iowa, C USA
xxxviii K8 **Weston** Staffordshire, C England, UK
35 R16 **Weston** Idaho, NW USA
23 R4 **Weston** West Virginia, NE USA
xxxvi M9 **Westonbirt** Gloucestershire, C England, UK
xxxvi J10 **Weston-super-Mare** North West Somerset, SW England, UK
xxxviii L7 **Weston Underwood** Derbyshire, C England, UK
xxxvi J12 **Westonzoyland** Somerset, SW England, UK
xxxvii N10 **West Overton** Wiltshire, S England, UK
25 Z14 **West Palm Beach** Florida, SE USA
196 E9 **West Passage** *passage* Babeldaob, N Palau
xxxvi K11 **West Pennard** Somerset, SW England, UK
25 O9 **West Pensacola** Florida, SE USA
29 V8 **West Plains** Missouri, C USA
37 P7 **West Point** California, W USA
25 R5 **West Point** Georgia, SE USA
24 M3 **West Point** Mississippi, S USA
31 R14 **West Point** Nebraska, C USA
23 X6 **West Point** Virginia, NE USA
190 G10 **West Point** *headland* South Australia
67 B24 **Westpoint Island Settlement** Westpoint Island, NW Falkland Islands
25 R4 **West Point Lake** ▣ Alabama/Georgia, SE USA
xliv D7 **Westport** *Ir.* Cathair na Mart. Mayo, W Ireland
193 G15 **Westport** West Coast, South Island, NZ
34 F10 **Westport** Oregon, NW USA
34 F9 **Westport** Washington, NW USA
33 S15 **West Portsmouth** Ohio, N USA
West Punjab *see* Punjab
xxxix Q5 **West Rasen** Lincolnshire, E England, UK
xlii M2 **Westray** *island* NE Scotland, UK
9 V14 **Westray** Manitoba, C Canada
xlii M3 **Westray Firth** *inlet* N Scotland, UK
12 F9 **Westree** Ontario, S Canada
99 L16 **West Riding** *cultural region* N England, UK
West River *see* Xi Jiang
xxxix U8 **West Rudham** Norfolk, E England, UK
xliii O21 **Westruther** The Borders, S Scotland, UK
32 J7 **West Salem** Wisconsin, N USA
xlii I2 **West Sandwick** Shetland Islands, NE Scotland, UK
67 H21 **West Scotia Ridge** *undersea feature* W Scotia Sea
West Sepik *see* Sandaun
181 N4 **West Sheba Ridge** *undersea feature* W Indian Ocean
West Siberian Plain *see* Zapadno-Sibirskaya Ravnina
33 S11 **West Sister Island** *island* Ohio, N USA
West-Skylge *see* West-Terschelling
West Sumatra *see* Sumatera Barat
xxxvii S12 **West Sussex** ◆ *county* S England, UK
xliii F20 **West Tarbert** Argyll and Bute, W Scotland, UK
100 J5 **West-Terschelling** *Fris.* West-Skylge. Friesland, N Netherlands
66 J7 **West Thulean Rise** *undersea feature* N Atlantic Ocean
31 X12 **West Union** Iowa, C USA
33 R15 **West Union** Ohio, N USA
23 R3 **West Union** West Virginia, NE USA
33 N13 **Westville** Illinois, N USA
23 R3 **West Virginia** *off.* State of West Virginia; also known as The Mountain State. ◆ *state* NE USA
101 A17 **West-Vlaanderen** *Eng.* West Flanders. ◆ *province* W Belgium
37 R7 **West Walker River** ⁓ California/Nevada, W USA
xxxvi F12 **Westward Ho** Devon, SW England, UK
xxxvii O12 **West Wellow** Hampshire, S England, UK
37 P4 **Westwood** California, W USA
xli P5 **West Woodburn** Northumberland, N England, UK
191 P9 **West Wyalong** New South Wales, SE Australia
179 N14 **West York Island** *island* N Spratly Islands
175 S15 **Wetar, Pulau** *island* Kepulauan Damar, E Indonesia
175 Ss16 **Wetar, Selat** *var.* Wetar Strait. *strait* Nusa Tenggara, S Indonesia
Wetar Strait *see* Wetar, Selat
9 Q15 **Wetaskiwin** Alberta, SW Canada
83 K21 **Wete** Pemba, E Tanzania
xl M7 **Wetheral** Cumbria, NW England, UK
xli S13 **Wetherby** Leeds, N England, UK
177 G4 **Wetlet** Sagaing, C Burma
39 T6 **Wet Mountains** ▲ Colorado, C USA
103 E15 **Wetter** Nordrhein-Westfalen, W Germany
103 H17 **Wetter** ⁓ W Germany
101 F17 **Wetteren** Oost-Vlaanderen, NW Belgium
110 F7 **Wettingen** Aargau, N Switzerland
29 P11 **Wetumka** Oklahoma, C USA
25 Q5 **Wetumpka** Alabama, S USA
xli V12 **Wetwang** East Riding of Yorkshire, N England, UK
110 G7 **Wetzikon** Zürich, N Switzerland
103 G17 **Wetzlar** Hessen, W Germany
101 C18 **Wevelgem** West-Vlaanderen, W Belgium
40 M6 **Wevok** *var.* Wevuk. Alaska, USA
25 R9 **Wewahitchka** Florida, SE USA
194 G10 **Wewak** East Sepik, NW PNG
29 O11 **Wewoka** Oklahoma, C USA
Wewuk *see* Wevok
xliv K12 **Wexford** *Ir.* Loch Garman. Wexford, SE Ireland
xliv J12 **Wexford** *Ir.* Loch Garman. ◆ *county* SE Ireland
xliv L12 **Wexford Bay** *bay* SE Ireland
xxxvi S10 **Wey** ⁓ SE England, UK
32 L7 **Weyauwega** Wisconsin, N USA
xxxix W7 **Weybourne** Norfolk, E England, UK
xxxvii S10 **Weybridge** Surrey, SE England, UK
9 U17 **Weyburn** Saskatchewan, S Canada
Weyer *see* Weyer Markt
111 U5 **Weyer Markt** *var.* Weyer. Oberösterreich, N Austria
102 H11 **Weyhe** Niedersachsen, NW Germany
xxxvii O11 **Weyhill** Hampshire, S England, UK
xxxvi L14 **Weymouth** Dorset, S England, UK
21 P11 **Weymouth** Massachusetts, NE USA
xxxvi M15 **Weymouth Bay** *bay* S England, UK
101 H18 **Wezembeek-Oppem** Vlaams Brabant, C Belgium
100 M9 **Wezep** Gelderland, E Netherlands
192 M9 **Whakamaru** Waikato, North Island, NZ
192 O8 **Whakatane** Bay of Plenty, North Island, NZ
192 O8 **Whakatane** ⁓ North Island, NZ
15 L7 **Whale Cove** Northwest Territories, C Canada
xxxviii K5 **Whaley Bridge** Derbyshire, C England, UK
xli O14 **Whalley** Lancashire, NW England, UK
xlii J3 **Whalsay** *island* NE Scotland, UK
xli Q5 **Whalton** Northumberland, N England, UK
192 L11 **Whangaehu** ⁓ North Island, NZ
192 M6 **Whangamata** Waikato, North Island, NZ
192 Q9 **Whangara** Gisborne, North Island, NZ
192 K3 **Whangarei** Northland, North Island, NZ
192 K3 **Whangaruru Harbour** *inlet* North Island, NZ
xxxix S8 **Whaplode** Lincolnshire, E England, UK
xli R12 **Wharfe** ⁓ N England, UK
27 V12 **Wharton** Texas, SW USA
181 U8 **Wharton Basin** *var.* West Australian Basin. *undersea feature* E Indian Ocean
193 E18 **Whataroa** West Coast, South Island, NZ
192 K6 **Whatipu** Auckland, North Island, NZ
xliii I25 **Whauphill** Dumfries and Galloway, SW Scotland, UK
xxxvii T7 **Wheathampstead** Hertfordshire, SE England, UK
35 Y16 **Wheatland** Wyoming, C USA
xxxix O5 **Wheatley** Nottinghamshire, C England, UK
xxxvii Q8 **Wheatley** Oxfordshire, C England, UK
12 D18 **Wheatley** Ontario, S Canada
xli S8 **Wheatley Hill** Durham, N England, UK
32 M10 **Wheaton** Illinois, N USA
31 R7 **Wheaton** Minnesota, N USA
39 T4 **Wheat Ridge** Colorado, C USA
xxxvi H11 **Wheddon Cross** Somerset, SW England, UK
27 P2 **Wheeler** Texas, SW USA
25 O2 **Wheeler Lake** ▣ Alabama, S USA
37 Y6 **Wheeler Peak** ▲ Nevada, W USA
39 T9 **Wheeler Peak** ▲ New Mexico, SW USA
33 S15 **Wheelersburg** Ohio, N USA
23 R2 **Wheeling** West Virginia, NE USA
xli U13 **Wheldrake** York, N England, UK
xl O11 **Whernside** ▲ N England, UK
xli V3 **Whickham** Gateshead, NE England, UK
190 F9 **Whidbey, Point** *headland* South Australia
xxxvi G14 **Whiddon Down** Devon, SW England, UK
xliv D14 **Whiddy Island** *island* S Ireland
188 I7 **Whim Creek** Western Australia
xl L9 **Whinlatter Pass** *pass* NW England, UK
xlii P12 **Whinneyfold** Aberdeenshire, NE Scotland, UK

◆ Country ● Country Capital ◇ Dependent Territory ○ Dependent Territory Capital ◆ Administrative Region ✈ International Airport ▲ Mountain ▲ Mountain Range ⁂ Volcano ⁓ River ◎ Lake ▣ Reservoir

WHIPSNADE – WOLEU

xxxvii S7 **Whipsnade** Bedfordshire, C England, UK
xxxix P9 **Whissendine** Rutland, C England, UK
8 L17 **Whistler** British Columbia, SW Canada
23 W8 **Whitakers** North Carolina, SE USA
xl K11 **Whitbeck** Cumbria, NW England, UK
xxxviii I13 **Whitbourne** Herefordshire, W England, UK
xli S6 **Whitburn** South Tyneside, NE England, UK
xliii K20 **Whitburn** West Lothian, SE Scotland, UK
xli V9 **Whitby** North Yorkshire, N England, UK
12 H15 **Whitby** Ontario, S Canada
xxxvii R7 **Whitchurch** Buckinghamshire, C England, UK
xxxvii P11 **Whitchurch** Hampshire, S England, UK
xxxviii H15 **Whitchurch** Herefordshire, W England, UK
xxxviii H7 **Whitchurch** Shropshire, W England, UK
8 G6 **White** ≈ Yukon Territory, W Canada
xliii O20 **Whiteadder Reservoir** ◫ S Scotland, UK
11 T11 **White Bay** *bay* Newfoundland, Newfoundland and Labrador, E Canada
22 I8 **White Bluff** Tennessee, S USA
30 J6 **White Butte** ▲ North Dakota, N USA
21 R5 **White Cap Mountain** ▲ Maine, NE USA
24 J9 **White Castle** Louisiana, S USA
190 M5 **White Cliffs** New South Wales, SE Australia
33 P8 **White Cloud** Michigan, N USA
9 P14 **Whitecourt** Alberta, SW Canada
27 O2 **White Deer** Texas, SW USA
White Elster *see* Weisse Elster
26 M5 **Whiteface** Texas, SW USA
20 K7 **Whiteface Mountain** ▲ New York, NE USA
31 W5 **Whiteface Reservoir** ◫ Minnesota, N USA
xl G14 **Whitefield** Bury, NW England, UK
35 O7 **Whitefish** Montana, NW USA
33 N9 **Whitefish Bay** Wisconsin, N USA
33 Q3 **Whitefish Bay** *lake bay* Canada/USA
12 E11 **Whitefish Falls** Ontario, S Canada
12 B7 **Whitefish Lake** ◎ Ontario, S Canada
31 U6 **Whitefish Lake** ◎ Minnesota, C USA
33 Q3 **Whitefish Point** *headland* Michigan, N USA
33 O4 **Whitefish River** ≈ Michigan, N USA
27 O4 **Whiteflat** Texas, SW USA
xliv G10 **Whitegate** Clare, W Ireland
xliv G14 **Whitegate** Cork, S Ireland
29 V12 **White Hall** Arkansas, C USA
32 K14 **White Hall** Illinois, N USA
xliv J11 **Whitehall** Kilkenny, SE Ireland
xlii N3 **Whitehall** Orkney Islands, N Scotland, UK
33 O8 **Whitehall** Michigan, N USA
20 L9 **Whitehall** New York, NE USA
33 S13 **Whitehall** Ohio, N USA
32 J7 **Whitehall** Wisconsin, N USA
xl K9 **Whitehaven** Cumbria, NW England, UK
xliv M4 **Whitehead** Carrickfergus, E Northern Ireland, UK
xlii N11 **Whitehills** Aberdeenshire, NE Scotland, UK
8 I8 **Whitehorse** *territory capital* Yukon Territory, W Canada
xxxvii P8 **White Horse, Vale of** *valley* S England, UK
xlii N13 **Whitehouse** Aberdeenshire, NE Scotland, UK
xliii F20 **Whitehouse** Argyll and Bute, W Scotland, UK
192 O7 **White Island** *island* NE NZ
xliii N19 **Whitekirk** East Lothian, SE Scotland, UK
12 K13 **White Lake** ◎ Ontario, SE Canada
24 H10 **White Lake** ◎ Louisiana, S USA
xliii H25 **White Loch** ◎ Dumfries and Galloway, SW Scotland, UK
195 N12 **Whiteman Range** ▲ New Britain, E PNG
191 Q15 **Whitemark** Tasmania, SE Australia
37 S9 **White Mountains** ▲ California/Nevada, W USA
21 N7 **White Mountains** ▲ Maine/New Hampshire, NE USA
82 F11 **White Nile** ◆ *state* C Sudan
69 U7 **White Nile** *var.* Bahr el Jebel. ≈ S Sudan
83 E14 **White Nile** *Ar.* Al Baḥr al Abyaḍ, An Nīl al Abyaḍ, Bahr el Jebel. ≈ SE Sudan
xxxvii W7 **White Notley** Essex, SE England, UK
27 W5 **White Oak Creek** ≈ Texas, SW USA
xxxvii O12 **Whiteparish** Wiltshire, S England, UK
8 H9 **White Pass** *pass* Canada/USA
34 I9 **White Pass** *pass* Washington, NW USA
23 O9 **White Pine** Tennessee, S USA
20 K14 **White Plains** New York, NE USA
30 M11 **White River** South Dakota, N USA
29 W12 **White River** ≈ Arkansas, SE USA
39 P3 **White River** ≈ Colorado/Utah, C USA
33 N15 **White River** ≈ Indiana, N USA
33 O8 **White River** ≈ Michigan, N USA
30 K11 **White River** ≈ South Dakota, N USA
27 O5 **White River** ≈ Texas, SW USA
20 M8 **White River** ≈ Vermont, NE USA
39 N13 **Whiteriver** Arizona, SW USA
27 O5 **White River Lake** ◫ Texas, SW USA
34 H11 **White Salmon** Washington, NW USA
20 I10 **Whitesboro** New York, NE USA
27 T5 **Whitesboro** Texas, SW USA
23 O7 **Whitesburg** Kentucky, S USA
White Sea *see* Beloye More
White Sea-Baltic Canal/White Sea Canal *see* Belomorsko-Baltiyskiy Kanal
65 I25 **Whiteside, Canal** *channel* S Chile
35 S10 **White Sulphur Springs** Montana, NW USA
xxxvi H14 **Whitestone** Devon, SW England, UK
xliv L7 **Whites Town** Louth, NE Ireland
23 R6 **White Sulphur Springs** West Virginia, NE USA
22 J6 **Whitesville** Kentucky, S USA
34 I10 **White Swan** Washington, NW USA
23 U12 **Whiteville** North Carolina, SE USA
22 F10 **Whiteville** Tennessee, S USA
79 Q13 **White Volta** *var.* Nakambé, *Fr.* Volta Blanche. ≈ Burkina/Ghana
32 M9 **Whitewater** Wisconsin, N USA
39 P14 **Whitewater Baldy** ▲ New Mexico, SW USA
25 X17 **Whitewater Bay** *bay* Florida, SE USA
33 Q14 **Whitewater River** ≈ Indiana/Ohio, N USA
9 V16 **Whitewood** Saskatchewan, S Canada
30 J9 **Whitewood** South Dakota, N USA
27 U5 **Whitewright** Texas, SW USA
xxxvii Z11 **Whitfield** Kent, SE England, UK
xliii I26 **Whithorn** Dumfries and Galloway, S Scotland, UK
192 M6 **Whitianga** Waikato, North Island, NZ
21 N11 **Whitinsville** Massachusetts, NE USA
xxxv E13 **Whitland** Carmarthenshire, S Wales, UK
xli S6 **Whitley Bay** North Tyneside, NE England, UK
22 M8 **Whitley City** Kentucky, S USA
23 Q11 **Whitmire** South Carolina, SE USA
xxxviii J8 **Whitmore** Staffordshire, C England, UK
33 R10 **Whitmore Lake** Michigan, N USA
205 N9 **Whitmore Mountains** ▲ Antarctica
12 I12 **Whitney** Ontario, SE Canada
27 T8 **Whitney** Texas, SW USA
27 S8 **Whitney, Lake** ◫ Texas, SW USA
37 S11 **Whitney, Mount** ▲ California, W USA
xxxvi F16 **Whitsand Bay** *bay* SW England, UK
xxxvii X9 **Whitstable** Kent, SE England, UK
189 Y6 **Whitsunday Group** *island group* Queensland, E Australia
27 S6 **Whitt** Texas, SW USA
31 U12 **Whittemore** Iowa, C USA
41 R12 **Whittier** Alaska, USA
37 T15 **Whittier** California, W USA
xli Q3 **Whittingham** Northumberland, N England, UK
xxxviii M5 **Whittington** Derbyshire, C England, UK
xli N11 **Whittington** Lancashire, NW England, UK
xxxviii G8 **Whittington** Shropshire, W England, UK
xxxviii D13 **Whittington** Staffordshire, C England, UK
xxxix O13 **Whittlebury** Northamptonshire, C England, UK
85 I25 **Whittlesea** Eastern Cape, S South Africa
xxxix R10 **Whittlesey** Cambridgeshire, E England, UK
xxxvi A9 **Whitton** Richmond upon Thames, SE England, UK
xxxv K10 **Whitton** Powys, C Wales, UK
xxxix N5 **Whitwell** Derbyshire, C England, UK
xxxvii T7 **Whitwell** Hertfordshire, SE England, UK
22 K10 **Whitwell** Tennessee, S USA
xxxviii M9 **Whitwick** Leicestershire, C England, UK
xli P15 **Whitworth** Lancashire, NW England, UK
15 I9 **Wholdaia Lake** ◎ Northwest Territories, NW Canada
190 H7 **Whyalla** South Australia
Whydah *see* Ouidah
12 F13 **Wiarton** Ontario, S Canada
175 Q11 **Wiau** Sulawesi, C Indonesia
xlii B12 **Wiay** *island* NW Scotland, UK
113 H15 **Wiązów** *Ger.* Wansen. Wrocław, SW Poland
35 Y8 **Wibaux** Montana, NW USA
29 N6 **Wichita** Kansas, C USA
27 R5 **Wichita Falls** Texas, SW USA
28 L11 **Wichita Mountains** ▲ Oklahoma, C USA
27 R5 **Wichita River** ≈ Texas, SW USA
xxxvi L10 **Wick** South Gloucestershire, SW England, UK
xlii M7 **Wick** Highland, N Scotland, UK
xxxix T11 **Wicken** Cambridgeshire, E England, UK
38 K13 **Wickenburg** Arizona, SW USA
26 L8 **Wickett** Texas, SW USA
xxxvii W8 **Wickford** Essex, SE England, UK
xxxvii Q13 **Wickham** Hampshire, S England, UK
188 I7 **Wickham** Western Australia
xxxix U12 **Wickhambrook** Suffolk, E England, UK
190 M14 **Wickham, Cape** *headland* Tasmania, SE Australia
xxxix X12 **Wickham Market** Suffolk, E England, UK
22 G7 **Wickliffe** Kentucky, S USA
xliv L10 **Wicklow** *Ir.* Cill Mhantáin. Wicklow, E Ireland
xliv K10 **Wicklow** *Ir.* Cill Mhantáin. ◆ *county* E Ireland
xliv L10 **Wicklow Head** *Ir.* Ceann Chill Mhantáin. *headland* E Ireland
xliv K10 **Wicklow Mountains** *Ir.* Sléibhte Chill Mhantáin. ▲ E Ireland
12 H10 **Wicksteed Lake** ◎ Ontario, S Canada
xxxvi L9 **Wickwar** South Gloucestershire, SW England, UK
Wida *see* Ouidah
xli R4 **Widdrington** Northumberland, N England, UK
67 G15 **Wideawake Airfield** ✕ (Georgetown) SW Ascension Island
195 P11 **Wide Bay** *bay* New Britain, PNG
xxxvi G15 **Widecombe in the Moor** Devon, SW England, UK
175 T9 **Widi, Kepulauan** *island group* E Indonesia
xl D16 **Widnes** Halton, C England, UK
112 H9 **Więcbork** *Ger.* Vandsburg. Bydgoszcz, NW Poland
103 E17 **Wied** ≈ W Germany
103 F16 **Wiehl** Nordrhein-Westfalen, W Germany
113 L17 **Wieliczka** Kraków, S Poland
113 J14 **Wieluń** Sieradz, C Poland
111 X4 **Wien** *Eng.* Vienna, *Hung.* Bécs, *Slvk.* Vídeň, *Slvn.* Dunaj; *anc.* Vindobona. ● (Austria) Wien, NE Austria
111 X4 **Wien** *off.* Land Wien, *Eng.* Vienna. ◆ *state* NE Austria
111 X5 **Wiener Neustadt** Niederösterreich, E Austria
112 G7 **Wieprza** *Ger.* Wipper. ≈ NW Poland
100 O10 **Wierden** Overijssel, E Netherlands
100 I7 **Wieringerwerf** Noord-Holland, NW Netherlands
Wieruschow *see* Wieruszów
113 I14 **Wieruszów** *Ger.* Wieruschow. Kalisz, SW Poland
111 V9 **Wies** Steiermark, SE Austria
Wiesbachhorn *see* Grosses Wiesbachhorn
103 G18 **Wiesbaden** Hessen, W Germany
Wieselburg and Ungarisch-Altenburg/Wieselburg-Ungarisch-Altenburg *see* Mosonmagyaróvár
Wiesenhof *see* Ostrołęka
103 G20 **Wiesloch** Baden-Württemberg, SW Germany
102 F10 **Wiesmoor** Niedersachsen, NW Germany
112 I7 **Wieżyca** *Ger.* Turmberg. *hill* Gdańsk, N Poland
xl E14 **Wigan** Wigan, NW England, UK
xli N16 **Wigan** ◆ *unitary authority* NW England, UK
xxxix T9 **Wiggenhall St Germans** Norfolk, E England, UK
39 U3 **Wiggins** Colorado, C USA
24 M8 **Wiggins** Mississippi, S USA
xli O13 **Wigglesworth** North Yorkshire, N England, UK
xli S13 **Wighill** North Yorkshire, N England, UK
xxxviii H12 **Wigmore** Herefordshire, W England, UK
Wigorna Ceaster *see* Worcester
xxxix O10 **Wigston** Leicestershire, C England, UK
xl L7 **Wigton** Cumbria, NW England, UK
99 H14 **Wigtown** *cultural region* SW Scotland, UK
xliii I25 **Wigtown** Dumfries and Galloway, S Scotland, UK
xliii J26 **Wigtown Bay** *bay* SW Scotland, UK
100 L13 **Wijchen** Gelderland, SE Netherlands
94 N1 **Wijdefjorden** *fjord* NW Svalbard
100 M10 **Wijhe** Overijssel, E Netherlands
100 J12 **Wijk bij Duurstede** Utrecht, C Netherlands
100 J13 **Wijk en Aalburg** Noord-Brabant, S Netherlands
101 H16 **Wijnegem** Antwerpen, N Belgium
12 E11 **Wikwemikong** Manitoulin Island, Ontario, S Canada
110 H7 **Wil** Sankt Gallen, NE Switzerland
31 R16 **Wilber** Nebraska, C USA
xli U13 **Wilberfoss** East Riding of Yorkshire, N England, UK
34 K8 **Wilbur** Washington, NW USA
29 Q11 **Wilburton** Oklahoma, C USA
190 M6 **Wilcannia** New South Wales, SE Australia
20 D12 **Wilcox** Pennsylvania, NE USA
Wilczek Land *see* Vil'cheka, Zemlya
111 U6 **Wildalpen** Steiermark, E Austria
33 O13 **Wildcat Creek** ≈ Indiana, N USA
110 L9 **Wilde Kreuzspitze** *It.* Picco di Croce. ▲ Austria/Italy
Wildenschwert *see* Ústí nad Orlicí
100 O6 **Wildervank** Groningen, NE Netherlands
102 G11 **Wildeshausen** Niedersachsen, NW Germany
110 D10 **Wildhorn** ▲ SW Switzerland
9 R17 **Wild Horse** Alberta, SW Canada
29 N12 **Wildhorse Creek** ≈ Oklahoma, C USA
30 L14 **Wild Horse Hill** ▲ Nebraska, C USA
111 W8 **Wildon** Steiermark, SE Austria
26 M2 **Wildorado** Texas, SW USA
31 R6 **Wild Rice River** ≈ Minnesota/North Dakota, N USA
Wilejka *see* Vilyeyka
205 Y9 **Wilhelm II Coast** *physical region* Antarctica
205 X9 **Wilhelm II Land** *physical region* Antarctica
57 U11 **Wilhelmina Gebergte** ▲ C Surinam
20 B13 **Wilhelm, Lake** ◫ Pennsylvania, NE USA
194 I12 **Wilhelm, Mount** ▲ C PNG
94 O2 **Wilhelmøya** *island* C Svalbard
Wilhelm-Pieck-Stadt *see* Guben
111 W4 **Wilhelmsburg** Niederösterreich, E Austria
102 G10 **Wilhelmshaven** Niedersachsen, NW Germany
Wilia/Wilja *see* Neris
20 H13 **Wilkes Barre** Pennsylvania, NE USA
23 R9 **Wilkesboro** North Carolina, SE USA
205 W15 **Wilkes Coast** *physical region* Antarctica
201 W12 **Wilkes Island** *island* N Wake Island
205 X12 **Wilkes Land** *physical region* Antarctica
xlii K10 **Wilkhaven** Highland, N Scotland, UK
9 S15 **Wilkie** Saskatchewan, S Canada
xliii L20 **Wilkieston** City of Edinburgh, SE Scotland, UK
204 I6 **Wilkins Ice Shelf** *ice shelf* Antarctica
190 D4 **Wilkinsons Lakes** *salt lake* South Australia
Wiłkomierz *see* Ukmergė
190 K11 **Willalooka** South Australia
34 G11 **Willamette River** ≈ Oregon, NW USA
xxxvi I13 **Willand** Devon, SW England, UK
191 O8 **Willandra Billabong Creek** *seasonal river* New South Wales, SE Australia
34 F9 **Willapa Bay** *inlet* Washington, NW USA
29 T7 **Willard** Missouri, C USA
39 S12 **Willard** New Mexico, SW USA
33 S12 **Willard** Ohio, N USA
38 L1 **Willard** Utah, W USA
xl B17 **Willaston** Cheshire, W England, UK
195 N11 **Willaumez Peninsula** *headland* New Britain, E PNG
39 N15 **Willcox** Arizona, SW USA
39 N16 **Willcox Playa** *salt flat* Arizona, SW USA
101 G17 **Willebroek** Antwerpen, C Belgium
47 P16 **Willemstad** ○ (Netherlands Antilles) Curaçao, Netherlands Antilles
101 G14 **Willemstad** Noord-Brabant, S Netherlands
xxxviii B14 **Willenhall** Walsall, C England, UK
xxxvi B6 **Willesden** Brent, SE England, UK
9 S11 **William** ≈ Saskatchewan, C Canada
25 O6 **William "Bill" Dannelly Reservoir** ◫ Alabama, S USA
190 G3 **William Creek** South Australia
189 T15 **William, Mount** ▲ South Australia
38 K11 **Williams** Arizona, SW USA
31 X14 **Williamsburg** Iowa, C USA
22 M8 **Williamsburg** Kentucky, S USA
33 R15 **Williamsburg** Ohio, N USA
23 X6 **Williamsburg** Virginia, NE USA
8 M15 **Williams Lake** British Columbia, SW Canada
23 P6 **Williamson** West Virginia, NE USA
33 N13 **Williamsport** Indiana, N USA
20 G13 **Williamsport** Pennsylvania, NE USA
23 W9 **Williamston** North Carolina, SE USA
23 P11 **Williamston** South Carolina, SE USA
22 M4 **Williamstown** Kentucky, S USA
20 L10 **Williamstown** Massachusetts, NE USA
20 J16 **Willingboro** New Jersey, NE USA
xxxvi V13 **Willingdon** East Sussex, SE England, UK
9 Q14 **Willingdon** Alberta, SW Canada
xxxix P5 **Willingham** Lincolnshire, E England, UK
xxxviii M8 **Willington** Derbyshire, C England, UK
xli Q8 **Willington** Durham, N England, UK
27 W10 **Willis** Texas, SW USA
110 F8 **Willisau** Luzern, W Switzerland
85 F24 **Williston** Northern Cape, W South Africa
25 V10 **Williston** Florida, SE USA
30 J3 **Williston** North Dakota, N USA
23 Q13 **Williston** South Carolina, SE USA
8 L12 **Williston Lake** ◫ British Columbia, W Canada
xxxvi I11 **Williton** Somerset, SW England, UK
36 L5 **Willits** California, W USA
31 T8 **Willmar** Minnesota, N USA
8 K11 **Will, Mount** ▲ British Columbia, W Canada
xxxix S5 **Willoughby** Lincolnshire, E England, UK
33 T11 **Willoughby** Ohio, N USA
9 U17 **Willow Bunch** Saskatchewan, S Canada
34 J11 **Willow Creek** ≈ Oregon, NW USA
41 R11 **Willow Lake** Alaska, USA
15 H7 **Willowlake** ≈ Northwest Territories, NW Canada
85 H25 **Willowmore** Eastern Cape, S South Africa
32 L5 **Willow Reservoir** ◫ Wisconsin, N USA
37 N5 **Willows** California, W USA
29 V7 **Willow Springs** Missouri, C USA
190 I7 **Wilmington** South Australia
23 Y2 **Wilmington** Delaware, NE USA
23 V12 **Wilmington** North Carolina, SE USA
33 R14 **Wilmington** Ohio, N USA
22 M6 **Wilmore** Kentucky, S USA
31 R8 **Wilmot** South Dakota, N USA
xl G17 **Wilmslow** Cheshire, W England, UK
Wilna/Wilno *see* Vilnius
103 G16 **Wilnsdorf** Nordrhein-Westfalen, W Germany
101 G16 **Wilrijk** Antwerpen, N Belgium
102 I10 **Wilseder Berg** *hill* NW Germany
69 Z12 **Wilshaw Ridge** *undersea feature* W Indian Ocean
23 V9 **Wilson** North Carolina, SE USA
27 N5 **Wilson** Texas, SW USA
190 A7 **Wilson Bluff** *headland* South Australia/Western Australia
37 Y7 **Wilson Creek Range** ▲ Nevada, W USA
25 O1 **Wilson Lake** ◫ Alabama, S USA
28 M4 **Wilson Lake** ◫ Kansas, SE USA
39 P7 **Wilson, Mount** ▲ Colorado, C USA
191 P13 **Wilsons Promontory** *peninsula* Victoria, SE Australia
xxxvii N12 **Wilton** Wiltshire, S England, UK
31 Y14 **Wilton** Iowa, C USA
21 P7 **Wilton** Maine, NE USA
30 M5 **Wilton** North Dakota, N USA
xxxvi M11 **Wiltshire** ◆ *county* S England, UK
101 M23 **Wiltz** Diekirch, NW Luxembourg
188 K9 **Wiluna** Western Australia
101 M23 **Wilwerwiltz** Diekirch, NE Luxembourg
xxxvi B10 **Wimbledon** Merton, SE England, UK
31 P5 **Wimbledon** North Dakota, N USA
xxxix S10 **Wimblington** Cambridgeshire, E England, UK
xxxvii N13 **Wimborne Minster** Dorset, S England, UK
44 K7 **Wina** *var.* Güina. Jinotega, N Nicaragua
33 O12 **Winamac** Indiana, N USA
83 G19 **Winam Gulf** *var.* Kavirondo Gulf. *gulf* SW Kenya
85 I22 **Winburg** Free State, C South Africa
xxxvi L12 **Wincanton** Somerset, SW England, UK
xxxvii N7 **Winchcombe** Gloucestershire, C England, UK
xxxvii X12 **Winchelsea** East Sussex, SE England, UK
21 N10 **Winchendon** Massachusetts, NE USA
xxxvii P12 **Winchester** *hist.* Wintanceaster, *Lat.* Venta Belgarum. Hampshire, S England, UK
12 M13 **Winchester** Ontario, SE Canada
34 M10 **Winchester** Idaho, NW USA
32 J14 **Winchester** Illinois, N USA
33 Q13 **Winchester** Indiana, N USA
22 M5 **Winchester** Kentucky, S USA
20 M10 **Winchester** New Hampshire, NE USA
22 K10 **Winchester** Tennessee, S USA
23 V3 **Winchester** Virginia, NE USA
101 L22 **Wincrange** Diekirch, NW Luxembourg
8 I5 **Wind** ≈ Yukon Territory, NW Canada
191 S8 **Windamere, Lake** ◎ New South Wales, SE Australia
Windau *see* Ventspils, Latvia
Windau *see* Venta, Latvia/Lithuania
20 D15 **Windber** Pennsylvania, NE USA
23 T3 **Winder** Georgia, SE USA
xl M10 **Windermere** Cumbria, NW England, UK
xl L10 **Windermere** ◎ NW England, UK
12 C7 **Windermere Lake** ◎ Ontario, S Canada
33 U11 **Windham** Ohio, N USA
85 D19 **Windhoek** *Ger.* Windhuk. ● (Namibia) Khomas, C Namibia
85 D20 **Windhoek** ✕ Khomas, C Namibia
Windhuk *see* Windhoek
13 O8 **Windigo** Québec, SE Canada
13 O8 **Windigo** ≈ Québec, SE Canada
Windischfeistritz *see* Slovenska Bistrica
111 T6 **Windischgarsten** Oberösterreich, W Austria
Windischgraz *see* Slovenj Gradec
39 T16 **Wind Mountain** ▲ New Mexico, SW USA
31 T10 **Windom** Minnesota, N USA
39 Q7 **Windom Peak** ▲ Colorado, C USA
189 U9 **Windorah** Queensland, C Australia
39 O10 **Window Rock** Arizona, SW USA
33 N9 **Wind Point** *headland* Wisconsin, N USA
35 U14 **Wind River** ≈ Wyoming, C USA
xxxvii S9 **Windsor** Windsor and Maidenhead, S England, UK
11 P15 **Windsor** Nova Scotia, SE Canada
12 C17 **Windsor** Ontario, S Canada
13 Q12 **Windsor** Québec, SE Canada
39 T3 **Windsor** Colorado, C USA
20 M12 **Windsor** Connecticut, NE USA
29 T5 **Windsor** Missouri, C USA
23 X9 **Windsor** North Carolina, SE USA
xxxvii R9 **Windsor and Maidenhead** ◆ *unitary authority* S England, UK
20 M12 **Windsor Locks** Connecticut, NE USA
27 R5 **Windthorst** Texas, SW USA
47 Z14 **Windward Islands** *island group* E West Indies
Windward Islands *see* Vent, Îles du, Archipel de la Société, French Polynesia
Windward Islands *see* Barlavento, Ilhas de, Cape Verde
46 K8 **Windward Passage** *Sp.* Paso de los Vientos. *channel* Cuba/Haiti
57 T9 **Wineperu** C Guyana
25 O3 **Winfield** Alabama, S USA
31 Y15 **Winfield** Iowa, C USA
29 O7 **Winfield** Kansas, C USA
27 W6 **Winfield** Texas, SW USA
23 Q4 **Winfield** West Virginia, NE USA
xxxvii R7 **Wing** Buckinghamshire, C England, UK
31 N5 **Wing** North Dakota, N USA
xli S8 **Wingate** Durham, N England, UK
xxxvii Y10 **Wingham** Kent, SE England, UK
191 U7 **Wingham** New South Wales, SE Australia
10 G16 **Wingham** Ontario, S Canada
35 T8 **Winifred** Montana, NW USA
10 F7 **Winisk** Ontario, C Canada
10 E8 **Winisk** ≈ Ontario, S Canada
10 E9 **Winisk Lake** ◎ Ontario, C Canada
26 I8 **Wink** Texas, SW USA
38 M14 **Winkelman** Arizona, SW USA
xxxvi G13 **Winkleigh** Devon, SW England, UK
9 X17 **Winkler** Manitoba, S Canada
111 Q9 **Winklern** Tirol, W Austria
Winkowitz *see* Vinkovci
xli R12 **Winksley** North Yorkshire, N England, UK
34 G9 **Winlock** Washington, NW USA
xli N13 **Winmarleigh** Lancashire, NW England, UK
79 P17 **Winneba** SE Ghana
31 U11 **Winnebago** Minnesota, N USA
31 R13 **Winnebago** Nebraska, C USA
32 M7 **Winnebago, Lake** ◎ Wisconsin, N USA
32 M7 **Winneconne** Wisconsin, N USA
37 T3 **Winnemucca** Nevada, W USA
37 R4 **Winnemucca Lake** ◎ Nevada, W USA
103 H21 **Winnenden** Baden-Württemberg, SW Germany
31 N11 **Winner** South Dakota, N USA
35 U9 **Winnett** Montana, NW USA
12 I9 **Winneway** Québec, SE Canada
24 H6 **Winnfield** Louisiana, S USA
31 U4 **Winnibigoshish, Lake** ◎ Minnesota, N USA
27 X11 **Winnie** Texas, SW USA
9 Y16 **Winnipeg** Manitoba, S Canada
9 X16 **Winnipeg** ✕ Manitoba, S Canada
1 J8 **Winnipeg** ≈ Manitoba, S Canada
9 X16 **Winnipeg Beach** Manitoba, S Canada
9 W14 **Winnipeg, Lake** ◎ Manitoba, C Canada
9 W15 **Winnipegosis** Manitoba, S Canada
9 W15 **Winnipegosis, Lake** ◎ Manitoba, C Canada
21 O8 **Winnipesaukee, Lake** ◎ New Hampshire, NE USA
24 I6 **Winnsboro** Louisiana, S USA
23 R12 **Winnsboro** South Carolina, SE USA
27 W6 **Winnsboro** Texas, SW USA
31 X10 **Winona** Minnesota, N USA
24 L4 **Winona** Mississippi, S USA
29 W7 **Winona** Missouri, C USA
27 W7 **Winona** Texas, SW USA
20 M7 **Winooski River** ≈ Vermont, NE USA
100 P6 **Winschoten** Groningen, NE Netherlands
xxxvi K10 **Winscombe** North West Somerset, SW England, UK
102 J10 **Winsen** Niedersachsen, N Germany
xxxviii H6 **Winsford** Cheshire, W England, UK
xxxvi H12 **Winsford** Somerset, SW England, UK
xxxvi K13 **Winsham** Somerset, SW England, UK
xxxviii M9 **Winshill** Staffordshire, C England, UK
xxxvii Q7 **Winslow** Buckinghamshire, C England, UK
38 M11 **Winslow** Arizona, SW USA
21 Q7 **Winslow** Maine, NE USA
20 M12 **Winsted** Connecticut, NE USA
xl M10 **Winster** Cumbria, NW England, UK
xxxviii L6 **Winster** Derbyshire, C England, UK
xli U7 **Winston** Durham, N England, UK
34 F14 **Winston** Oregon, NW USA
xxxvi M8 **Winstone** Gloucestershire, C England, UK
23 S9 **Winston Salem** North Carolina, SE USA
100 N5 **Winsum** Groningen, NE Netherlands
Wintanceaster *see* Winchester
xxxvi M13 **Winterborne Stickland** Dorset, S England, UK
xxxvi L14 **Winterbourne Abbas** Dorset, S England, UK
xxxvii O11 **Winterbourne Earls** Wiltshire, S England, UK
25 W11 **Winter Garden** Florida, SE USA
8 J16 **Winter Harbour** Vancouver Island, British Columbia, SW Canada
25 W12 **Winter Haven** Florida, SE USA
xxxix P3 **Winteringham** North Lincolnshire, N England, UK
25 X11 **Winter Park** Florida, SE USA
27 P8 **Winters** Texas, SW USA
31 U15 **Winterset** Iowa, C USA
100 O12 **Winterswijk** Gelderland, E Netherlands
110 G6 **Winterthur** Zürich, NE Switzerland
xxxix Z8 **Winterton-on-Sea** Norfolk, E England, UK
31 U9 **Winthrop** Minnesota, N USA
34 J7 **Winthrop** Washington, NW USA
xli O9 **Winton** Cumbria, NW England, UK
189 V7 **Winton** Queensland, E Australia
193 C24 **Winton** Southland, South Island, NZ
23 X8 **Winton** North Carolina, SE USA
103 K15 **Wipper** ≈ C Germany
103 K14 **Wipper** ≈ C Germany
Wipper *see* Wieprza
176 Vv9 **Wiriagar, Sungai** ≈ Irian Jaya, E Indonesia
xxxviii L7 **Wirksworth** Derbyshire, C England, UK
xl L17 **Wirral** ◆ *unitary authority* NW England, UK
190 G6 **Wirraminna** South Australia
190 F4 **Wirrida** South Australia
190 F7 **Wirrulla** South Australia
Wirsitz *see* Wyrzysk
Wirz-See *see* Võrtsjärv
xxxix S9 **Wisbech** Cambridgeshire, E England, UK
xxxvii S12 **Wisborough Green** West Sussex, SE England, UK
Wisby *see* Visby
21 Q8 **Wiscasset** Maine, NE USA
Wischau *see* Vyškov
32 J5 **Wisconsin** *off.* State of Wisconsin; also known as The Badger State. ◆ *state* N USA
32 L8 **Wisconsin Dells** Wisconsin, N USA
32 L8 **Wisconsin, Lake** ◫ Wisconsin, N USA
32 L7 **Wisconsin Rapids** Wisconsin, N USA
32 L7 **Wisconsin River** ≈ Wisconsin, N USA
35 P11 **Wisdom** Montana, NW USA
23 P7 **Wise** Virginia, NE USA
41 Q7 **Wiseman** Alaska, USA
xliii K20 **Wishaw** North Lanarkshire, W Scotland, UK
31 O6 **Wishek** North Dakota, N USA
34 I11 **Wishram** Washington, NW USA
113 P17 **Wisła** Bielsko-Biała, S Poland
112 K11 **Wisła** *Eng.* Vistula, *Ger.* Weichsel. ≈ C Poland
Wiślany, Zalew *see* Vistula Lagoon
113 M16 **Wisłoka** ≈ SE Poland
102 L9 **Wismar** Mecklenburg-Vorpommern, N Germany
31 R14 **Wisner** Nebraska, C USA
105 V4 **Wissembourg** *var.* Weissenburg. Bas-Rhin, NE France
xxxix U10 **Wissey** ≈ E England, UK
32 J6 **Wissota, Lake** ◫ Wisconsin, N USA
xxxviii H11 **Wistanstow** Shropshire, W England, UK
xliii L21 **Wiston** South Lanarkshire, C Scotland, UK
xxxv D13 **Wiston** Pembrokeshire, SW Wales, UK
xli T14 **Wistow** North Yorkshire, N England, UK
xxxix T11 **Witchford** Cambridgeshire, E England, UK
xxxvii W7 **Witham** Essex, SE England, UK
xxxix R7 **Witham** ≈ E England, UK
xxxvi L11 **Witham Friary** Somerset, SW England, UK
xxxvi H13 **Witheridge** Devon, SW England, UK
xxxix S5 **Withern** Lincolnshire, E England, UK
xli Y14 **Withernsea** East Riding of Yorkshire, E England, UK
xli X13 **Withernwick** East Riding of Yorkshire, N England, UK
xxxix U13 **Withersfield** Suffolk, E England, UK
xxxvii N7 **Withington** Gloucestershire, C England, UK
xxxviii H13 **Withington** Herefordshire, W England, UK
39 Q13 **Withington, Mount** ▲ New Mexico, SW USA
25 U9 **Withlacoochee River** ≈ Florida/Georgia, SE USA
xli O15 **Withnell** Lancashire, NW England, UK
xxxvi H12 **Withypool** Somerset, SW England, UK
112 H11 **Witkowo** Konin, C Poland
xxxvi S11 **Witley** Surrey, SE England, UK
xxxvii P8 **Witney** Oxfordshire, S England, UK
103 E15 **Witten** Nordrhein-Westfalen, W Germany
103 N14 **Wittenberg** Sachsen-Anhalt, E Germany
32 L6 **Wittenberg** Wisconsin, N USA
102 L11 **Wittenberge** Brandenburg, N Germany
105 U7 **Wittenheim** Haut-Rhin, NE France
188 I7 **Wittenoom** Western Australia
xxxvii W12 **Wittersham** Kent, SE England, UK
Wittingau *see* Třeboň
102 K12 **Wittingen** Niedersachsen, C Germany
103 E18 **Wittlich** Rheinland-Pfalz, SW Germany
102 F9 **Wittmund** Niedersachsen, NW Germany
102 M10 **Wittstock** Brandenburg, NE Germany
194 M1 **Witu Islands** *island group* E PNG
xxxvi I12 **Wiveliscombe** Somerset, SW England, UK
xxxvii X7 **Wivenhoe** Essex, SE England, UK
xxxvii Y8 **Wix** Essex, SE England, UK
112 O7 **Wiżajny** Suwałki, NE Poland
57 W10 **W.J. van Blommesteinmeer** ◫ E Surinam
112 L11 **Wkra** *Ger.* Soldau. ≈ C Poland
112 I6 **Władysławowo** Gdańsk, N Poland
Wlaschim *see* Vlašim
113 E14 **Wleń** *Ger.* Lähn. Jelenia Góra, SW Poland
112 J11 **Włocławek** *Ger./Rus.* Vlotslavsk. Włocławek, C Poland
112 I11 **Włocławek** *off.* Województwo Włocławskie, *Ger./Rus.* Vlotslavsk. ◆ *province* C Poland
Włocławskie, Województwo *see* Włocławek
112 P13 **Włodawa** *Rus.* Vlodava. Chełm, SE Poland
Włodzimierz *see* Volodymyr-Volyns'kyy
113 K15 **Włoszczowa** Kielce, S Poland
85 C19 **Wlotzkasbaken** Erongo, W Namibia
152 L11 **Wobkent** *Rus.* Vabkent. Bukhoro Wiloyati, C Uzbekistan
xxxvii S6 **Woburn** Bedfordshire, C England, UK
13 R12 **Woburn** Québec, SE Canada
21 O11 **Woburn** Massachusetts, NE USA
xxxvii S6 **Woburn Sands** Bedfordshire, C England, UK
Wocheiner Feistritz *see* Bohinjska Bistrica
Wöchma *see* Võhma
153 S11 **Wodil** *var.* Vuadil'. Farghona Wiloyati, E Uzbekistan
189 V14 **Wodonga** Victoria, SE Australia
113 I17 **Wodzisław Śląski** *Ger.* Loslau. Katowice, S Poland
100 I11 **Woerden** Zuid-Holland, C Netherlands
100 I8 **Wognum** Noord-Holland, NW Netherlands
Wohlau *see* Wołów
110 F7 **Wohlen** Aargau, NW Switzerland
205 R2 **Wohlthat Mountains** ▲ Antarctica
176 W9 **Woinui, Selat** *strait* Irian Jaya, E Indonesia
194 K15 **Woitape** Central, S PNG
Wōjjā *see* Wotje Atoll
Wojwodina *see* Vojvodina
176 W13 **Wokam, Pulau** *island* Kepulauan Aru, E Indonesia
xxxvii S10 **Woking** Surrey, SE England, UK
xxxvii R10 **Wokingham** Wokingham, S England, UK
xxxvii Q10 **Wokingham** ◆ *unitary authority* S England, UK
Woldenberg Neumark *see* Dobiegniew
xxxix R4 **Wolds, The** *hill range* E England, UK
xl V12 **Wolds, The** *hill range* N England, UK
196 K15 **Woleai Atoll** *atoll* Caroline Islands, W Micronesia
Woleu *see* Uolo, Río

◆ Country ● Country Capital ◇ Dependent Territory ○ Dependent Territory Capital ◆ Administrative Region ✕ International Airport ▲ Mountain ▲ Mountain Range ⩕ Volcano ≈ River ◎ Lake ◫ Reservoir

WOLEU-NTEM – YANAM

81 E17 **Woleu-Ntem** *off.* Province du Woleu-Ntem, *var.* Le Woleu-Ntem. ◈ *province* W Gabon
34 F15 **Wolf Creek** Oregon, NW USA
28 K9 **Wolf Creek** ≈ Oklahoma/Texas, SW USA
39 R7 **Wolf Creek Pass** *pass* Colorado, C USA
21 O9 **Wolfeboro** New Hampshire, NE USA
27 U5 **Wolfe City** Texas, SW USA
12 L15 **Wolfe Island** *island* Ontario, SE Canada
103 M14 **Wolfen** Sachsen-Anhalt, E Germany
102 J13 **Wolfenbüttel** Niedersachsen, C Germany
111 T4 **Wolfern** Oberösterreich, N Austria
xxxix U8 **Wolferton** Norfolk, E England, UK
111 Q6 **Wolfgangsee** *var.* Abersee, St Wolfgangsee. ◎ N Austria
41 P9 **Wolf Mountain** ▲ Alaska, USA
35 X7 **Wolf Point** Montana, NW USA
24 L8 **Wolf River** ≈ Mississippi, S USA
32 M7 **Wolf River** ≈ Wisconsin, N USA
111 U9 **Wolfsberg** Kärnten, SE Austria
102 K12 **Wolfsburg** Niedersachsen, N Germany
59 B17 **Wolf, Volcán** ⚠ Galapagos Islands, Ecuador, E Pacific Ocean
102 O8 **Wolgast** Mecklenburg-Vorpommern, NE Germany
110 F8 **Wolhusen** Luzern, W Switzerland
112 D8 **Wolin** *Ger.* Wollin. Szczecin, NW Poland
111 Y3 **Wolkersdorf** Niederösterreich, NE Austria
Wołkowysk *see* Vawkavysk
Wöllan *see* Velenje
xxxix P12 **Wollaston** Northamptonshire, C England, UK
15 I2 **Wollaston, Cape** *headland* Victoria Island, Northwest Territories, NW Canada
65 J25 **Wollaston, Isla** *island* S Chile
9 U11 **Wollaston Lake** Saskatchewan, C Canada
9 T10 **Wollaston Lake** ◎ Saskatchewan, C Canada
15 I3 **Wollaston Peninsula** *peninsula* Victoria Island, Northwest Territories, NW Canada
Wollin *see* Wolin
191 S9 **Wollongong** New South Wales, SE Australia
Wolmar *see* Valmiera
102 L13 **Wolmirstedt** Sachsen-Anhalt, C Germany
112 M11 **Wołomin** Warszawa, C Poland
112 G3 **Wołów** *Ger.* Wohlau. Wrocław, SW Poland
Wołożyn *see* Valozhyn
12 G11 **Wolseley Bay** Ontario, S Canada
31 P10 **Wolsey** South Dakota, N USA
xli Q8 **Wolsingham** Durham, N England, UK
112 F12 **Wolsztyn** Zielona Góra, W Poland
100 M7 **Wolvega** *Fris.* Wolvegea. Friesland, N Netherlands
Wolvegea *see* Wolvega
xxxviii B14 **Wolverhampton** Wolverhampton, C England, UK
xxxviii B13 **Wolverhampton** ◈ *unitary authority* C England, UK
Wolverine State *see* Michigan
101 G18 **Wolvertem** Vlaams Brabant, C Belgium
xxxvii R6 **Wolverton** Milton Keynes, C England, UK
xxxviii M11 **Wolvey** Warwickshire, C England, UK
xli S9 **Wolviston** Stockton-on-Tees, N England, UK
xxxviii A14 **Wombourne** Staffordshire, C England, UK
xli S16 **Wombwell** Barnsley, N England, UK
101 H16 **Wommelgem** Antwerpen, N Belgium
176 W11 **Wondiwoi, Pegunungan** ▲▲ Irian Jaya, E Indonesia
194 J13 **Wonenara** *var.* Wonerara. Eastern Highlands, C PNG
Wonerara *see* Wonenara
xxxvii S11 **Wonersh** Surrey, SE England, UK
Wongalara Lake *see* Wongalarroo Lake
191 N6 **Wongalarroo Lake** *var.* Wongalara Lake. *seasonal lake* New South Wales, SE Australia
169 Y15 **Wŏnju** *Jap.* Genshū. N South Korea
8 M12 **Wonowon** British Columbia, W Canada
169 X13 **Wŏnsan** SE North Korea
191 O13 **Wonthaggi** Victoria, SE Australia
25 N2 **Woodall Mountain** ▲ Mississippi, S USA
25 W7 **Woodbine** Georgia, SE USA
31 S14 **Woodbine** Iowa, C USA
20 J17 **Woodbine** New Jersey, NE USA
xxxix X13 **Woodbridge** Suffolk, E England, UK
23 W4 **Woodbridge** Virginia, NE USA
191 V4 **Woodburn** New South Wales, SE Australia
34 G11 **Woodburn** Oregon, NW USA
22 K9 **Woodbury** Tennessee, S USA
xxxvii X11 **Woodchurch** Kent, SE England, UK
191 V5 **Wooded Bluff** *headland* New South Wales, SE Australia
191 V3 **Woodenbong** New South Wales, SE Australia
xliv L11 **Woodenbridge** Wicklow, E Ireland
xxxvi F5 **Woodford** Redbridge, SE England, UK
xxxvi F5 **Woodford Bridge** Redbridge, SE England, UK
xxxix N13 **Woodford Halse** Northamptonshire, C England, UK
xxxvi D5 **Wood Green** Haringey, SE England, UK
xxxix R6 **Woodhall Spa** Lincolnshire, E England, UK
37 R11 **Woodlake** California, W USA
37 N7 **Woodland** California, W USA
21 T5 **Woodland** Maine, NE USA
34 G10 **Woodland** Washington, NW USA
39 T5 **Woodland Park** Colorado, C USA
195 P15 **Woodlark Island** *var.* Murua Island. *island* SE PNG
Woodle Island *see* Kuria
9 T17 **Wood Mountain** ▲▲ Saskatchewan, S Canada
32 K15 **Wood River** Illinois, N USA
31 P16 **Wood River** Nebraska, C USA
41 R9 **Wood River** ≈ Alaska, USA
41 O13 **Wood River Lakes** *lakes* Alaska, USA
190 C1 **Woodroffe, Mount** ▲ South Australia
23 P11 **Woodruff** South Carolina, SE USA
32 K4 **Woodruff** Wisconsin, N USA
27 T14 **Woodsboro** Texas, SW USA
xxxviii J8 **Woodseaves** Staffordshire, C England, UK
33 U13 **Woodsfield** Ohio, N USA
189 P4 **Woods, Lake** ◎ Northern Territory, N Australia
9 Z16 **Woods, Lake of the** *Fr.* Lac des Bois. ◎ Canada/USA
27 Q6 **Woodson** Texas, SW USA
xxxvii P7 **Woodstock** Oxfordshire, C England, UK
11 N14 **Woodstock** New Brunswick, SE Canada
12 F16 **Woodstock** Ontario, S Canada
32 M10 **Woodstock** Illinois, N USA
20 M9 **Woodstock** Vermont, NE USA
23 U4 **Woodstock**-Virginia, NE USA
21 N8 **Woodsville** New Hampshire, NE USA
192 M12 **Woodville** Manawatu-Wanganui, North Island, NZ
24 J7 **Woodville** Mississippi, S USA
27 X9 **Woodville** Texas, SW USA
28 K9 **Woodward** Oklahoma, C USA
31 O5 **Woodworth** North Dakota, N USA
xxxvi G11 **Woody Bay** *bay* SW England, UK
xxxviii H12 **Woofferton** Shropshire, W England, UK
176 Y12 **Woogi** Irian Jaya, E Indonesia
xxxvi K11 **Wookey** Somerset, SW England, UK
xxxvi M14 **Wool** Dorset, S England, UK
176 Ww9 **Wool** Irian Jaya, E Indonesia
xxxvi F11 **Woolacombe** Devon, SW England, UK
xli P2 **Wooler** Northumberland, N England, UK
xxxvi E12 **Woolfardisworthy** Devon, SW England, UK
191 V5 **Woolgoolga** New South Wales, E Australia
xxxvi G7 **Woolwich** Greenwich, SE England, UK
190 H6 **Woomera** South Australia
21 O12 **Woonsocket** Rhode Island, NE USA
31 P10 **Woonsocket** South Dakota, N USA
xxxvii I7 **Woore** Shropshire, W England, UK
33 T12 **Wooster** Ohio, N USA
xxxvii Y11 **Wootton** Kent, SE England, UK
xxxvii P7 **Wootton** Oxfordshire, C England, UK
xxxvii N9 **Wootton Bassett** Wiltshire, S England, UK
xxxviii D17 **Wootton Wawen** Warwickshire, C England, UK
82 L12 **Woqooyi Galbeed** *off.* Gobolka Woqooyi Galbeed. ◈ *region* NW Somalia
110 E8 **Worb** Bern, C Switzerland
xxxviii J13 **Worcester** *hist.* Wigorna Ceaster. Worcestershire, W England, UK
85 F26 **Worcester** Western Cape, SW South Africa
21 N11 **Worcester** Massachusetts, NE USA
xxxviii C16 **Worcester and Birmingham Canal** *canal* C England, UK
xxxviii B16 **Worcestershire** ◈ *county* C England, UK
34 H16 **Worden** Oregon, NW USA
111 O6 **Wörgl** Tirol, W Austria
xlii M4 **Work** Orkney Islands, N Scotland, UK
176 Ww14 **Workai, Pulau** *island* Kepulauan Aru, E Indonesia
xl K9 **Workington** Cumbria, NW England, UK
xxxix N5 **Worksop** Nottinghamshire, C England, UK
100 K7 **Workum** Friesland, N Netherlands
xxxix Q3 **Worlaby** North Lincolnshire, N England, UK
35 V13 **Worland** Wyoming, C USA
xxxvi G13 **Worlington** Devon, SW England, UK
Wormatia *see* Worms
101 N25 **Wormeldange** Grevenmacher, E Luxembourg
100 I9 **Wormer** Noord-Holland, C Netherlands
xliii M17 **Wormit** Fife, E Scotland, UK
103 G19 **Worms** *anc.* Augusta Vangionum, Borbetomagus, Wormatia. Rheinland-Pfalz, SW Germany
Worms *see* Vormsi
xxxvii X10 **Wormshill** Kent, SE England, UK
103 K21 **Wörnitz** ≈ S Germany
103 G21 **Wörth** Rheinland-Pfalz, SW Germany
27 U8 **Wortham** Texas, SW USA
111 S9 **Worther See** ◎ S Austria
xxxvii T13 **Worthing** West Sussex, SE England, UK
31 S11 **Worthington** Minnesota, N USA
33 S13 **Worthington** Ohio, N USA
37 W8 **Worthington Peak** ▲ Nevada, W USA
176 Y12 **Wosi** Irian Jaya, E Indonesia
176 W11 **Wosimi** Irian Jaya, E Indonesia
201 R5 **Wotho Atoll** *var.* Wōtto. *atoll* Ralik Chain, W Marshall Islands
201 V5 **Wotje Atoll** *var.* Wōjjā. *atoll* Ratak Chain, E Marshall Islands
Wotoe *see* Wotu
Wottawa *see* Otava
Wōtto *see* Wotho Atoll
xxxvi L8 **Wotton-under-Edge** Gloucestershire, C England, UK
175 Pp10 **Wotu** *prev.* Wotoe. Sulawesi, C Indonesia
100 K11 **Woudenberg** Utrecht, C Netherlands
100 I13 **Woudrichem** Noord-Brabant, S Netherlands
xxxvii V10 **Wouldham** Kent, SE England, UK
45 N8 **Wounta** *var.* Huaunta. Región Autónoma Atlántico Norte, NE Nicaragua
175 R12 **Wowoni, Pulau** *island* C Indonesia
175 Qq12 **Wowoni, Selat** *strait* Sulawesi, C Indonesia
83 J17 **Woyamdero Plain** *plain* E Kenya
Woyens *see* Vojens
Wozrojdeniye Oroli *see* Vozrozhdeniya, Ostrov
xxxix Q5 **Wragby** Lincolnshire, E England, UK
Wrangel Island *see* Vrangelya, Ostrov
41 Y13 **Wrangell** Wrangell Island, Alaska, USA
40 C15 **Wrangell, Cape** *headland* Attu Island, Alaska, USA
41 S11 **Wrangell, Mount** ▲ Alaska, USA
41 T11 **Wrangell Mountains** ▲▲ Alaska, USA
207 S7 **Wrangel Plain** *undersea feature* Arctic Ocean
xxxix S7 **Wrangle** Lincolnshire, E England, UK
xlii G6 **Wrath, Cape** *headland* N Scotland, UK
39 W3 **Wray** Colorado, C USA
xl M14 **Wrea Green** Lancashire, NW England, UK
46 K13 **Wreck Point** *headland* C Jamaica
85 C23 **Wreck Point** *headland* W South Africa
25 V4 **Wrens** Georgia, SE USA
xxxix Z11 **Wrentham** Suffolk, E England, UK
xli U14 **Wressle** East Riding of Yorkshire, N England, UK
xxxix V10 **Wretham** Norfolk, E England, UK
xxxv K6 **Wrexham** Wrexham, NE Wales, UK
xxxv K6 **Wrexham** ◈ *unitary authority* NE Wales, UK
29 R13 **Wright City** Oklahoma, C USA
204 J12 **Wright Island** *island* Antarctica
11 N9 **Wright, Mont** ▲ Québec, E Canada
27 X5 **Wright Patman Lake** ⊡ Texas, SW USA
38 M16 **Wrightson, Mount** ▲ Arizona, SW USA
25 U5 **Wrightsville** Georgia, SE USA
23 W12 **Wrightsville Beach** North Carolina, SE USA
37 T15 **Wrightwood** California, W USA
15 Gg7 **Wrigley** Northwest Territories, W Canada
xxxvi K10 **Wrington** North West Somerset, SW England, UK
113 G14 **Wrocław** *Eng./Ger.* Breslau. Wrocław, SW Poland
113 G14 **Wrocław** *off.* Województwo Wrocławskie. ◈ *province* SW Poland
Wrocławskie, Województwo *see* Wrocław
112 F10 **Wronki** *Ger.* Fronicken. Piła, NW Poland
xxxvii V10 **Wrotham** Kent, SE England, UK
xxxvii O9 **Wroughton** Swindon, S England, UK
xxxviii H10 **Wroxeter** Shropshire, W England, UK
xxxix X9 **Wroxham** Norfolk, E England, UK
xxxvii P6 **Wroxton** Oxfordshire, C England, UK
112 H11 **Września** Poznań, C Poland
112 F12 **Wschowa** Leszno, W Poland
Wsetin *see* Vsetín
188 I12 **Wubin** Western Australia
169 W9 **Wuchang** Heilongjiang, NE China
Wuchang *see* Wuhan
Wu-chou/Wuchow *see* Wuzhou
166 M16 **Wuchuan** *var.* Meilu. Guangdong, S China
166 K10 **Wuchuan** *prev.* Duru. Guizhou, S China
169 O13 **Wuchuan** Nei Mongol Zizhiqu, N China
169 V6 **Wudalianchi** Heilongjiang, NE China
165 O11 **Wudaoliang** Qinghai, C China
147 Q13 **Wuday'ah** *spring/well* S Saudi Arabia
79 V13 **Wudil** Kano, N Nigeria
166 G12 **Wuding** Yunnan, SW China
166 L4 **Wuding He** ≈ C China
190 G8 **Wudinna** South Australia
163 P10 **Wudu** Gansu, C China
166 L9 **Wufeng** Hubei, C China
167 O11 **Wugong Shan** ▲▲ S China
163 P7 **Wuhai** Nei Mongol Zizhiqu, N China
167 O9 **Wuhan** *var.* Han-kou, Han-k'ou, Hanyang, Wuchang, Wu-han; *prev.* Hankow. Hubei, C China
167 Q7 **Wuhe** Anhui, E China
Wuhsi/Wu-hsi *see* Wuxi
Wuhsien *see* Suzhou
167 Q8 **Wuhu** *var.* Wu-na-mu. Anhui, E China
Wūjae *see* Ujae Atoll
166 K11 **Wu Jiang** ≈ C China
Wujlān *see* Ujelang Atoll
79 W15 **Wukari** Taraba, E Nigeria
166 H11 **Wulian Feng** ▲▲ SW China
166 G13 **Wuliang Shan** ▲▲ SW China
176 U15 **Wuliaru, Pulau** *island* Kepulauan Tanimbar, E Indonesia
166 K11 **Wuling Shan** ▲▲ S China
111 Y5 **Wulka** ≈ E Austria
Wulkan *see* Vulcan
111 T3 **Wullowitz** Oberösterreich, N Austria
Wu-lu-k'o-mu-shi/Wu-lu-mu-ch'i *see* Ürümqi
81 D14 **Wum** Nord-Ouest, NE Cameroon
166 H12 **Wumeng Shan** ▲▲ SW China
166 K14 **Wuming** Guangxi Zhuangzu Zizhiqu, S China
102 I10 **Wümme** ≈ NW Germany
Wu-na-mu *see* Wuhu
176 Y11 **Wunen** Irian Jaya, E Indonesia
10 D9 **Wunnummin Lake** ◎ Ontario, C Canada
82 D13 **Wun Rog** Warab, S Sudan
103 M18 **Wunsiedel** Bayern, E Germany
102 I12 **Wunstorf** Niedersachsen, NW Germany
177 G3 **Wuntho** Sagaing, N Burma
103 F15 **Wupper** ≈ W Germany
103 E15 **Wuppertal** *prev.* Barmen-Elberfeld. Nordrhein-Westfalen, W Germany
166 K5 **Wuqi** Shaanxi, C China
167 P4 **Wuqiao** *var.* Sangyuan. Hebei, E China
103 L23 **Würm** ≈ SE Germany
79 T12 **Wurno** Sokoto, NW Nigeria
103 I19 **Würzburg** Bayern, SW Germany
103 N15 **Wurzen** Sachsen, E Germany
166 L9 **Wu Shan** ▲▲ C China
164 G7 **Wushi** *var.* Uqturpan. Xinjiang Uygur Zizhiqu, NW China
Wusih *see* Wuxi
67 N18 **Wüst Seamount** *undersea feature* S Atlantic Ocean
Wusuli Jiang/Wusuri *see* Ussuri
167 N3 **Wutai Shan** ▲ C China
166 H10 **Wutongqiao** Sichuan, C China
165 P6 **Wutongwozi Quan** *spring* NW China
194 E9 **Wutung** Sandaun, NW PNG
101 H15 **Wuustwezel** Antwerpen, N Belgium
194 G8 **Wuvulu Island** *island* NW PNG
165 U9 **Wuwei** *var.* Liangzhou. Gansu, C China
167 R8 **Wuxi** *var.* Wuhsi, Wu-hsi, Wusih. Jiangsu, E China
Wuxing *see* Huzhou
166 L14 **Wuxuan** Guangxi Zhuangzu Zizhiqu, S China
166 K11 **Wuyang He** ≈ S China
169 X6 **Wuyiling** Heilongjiang, NE China
163 T12 **Wuyi Shan** ▲▲ SE China
167 Q11 **Wuyishan** *prev.* Chong'an. Fujian, SE China
168 M13 **Wuyuan** Nei Mongol Zizhiqu, N China
166 L17 **Wuzhi Shan** ▲ S China
165 W8 **Wuzhong** Ningxia, N China
166 M14 **Wuzhou** *var.* Wu-chou, Wuchow. Guangxi Zhuangzu Zizhiqu, S China
20 H12 **Wyalusing** Pennsylvania, NE USA
190 M10 **Wycheproof** Victoria, SE Australia
99 K21 **Wye** *Wel.* Gwy. ≈ England/Wales, UK
xxxvii X11 **Wye** Kent, SE England, UK
Wyłkowyszki *see* Vilkaviškis
xxxix N8 **Wymeswold** Leicestershire, C England, UK
xxxix O9 **Wymondham** Leicestershire, C England, UK
xxxix W10 **Wymondham** Norfolk, E England, UK
31 R17 **Wymore** Nebraska, C USA
190 E5 **Wynbring** South Australia
189 N3 **Wyndham** Western Australia
31 R6 **Wyndmere** North Dakota, N USA
29 X11 **Wynne** Arkansas, C USA
29 N12 **Wynnewood** Oklahoma, C USA
191 O15 **Wynyard** Tasmania, SE Australia
9 U15 **Wynyard** Saskatchewan, S Canada
35 V11 **Wyola** Montana, NW USA
190 A4 **Wyola Lake** *salt lake* South Australia
33 P9 **Wyoming** Michigan, N USA
35 V14 **Wyoming** *off.* State of Wyoming; also known as The Equality State. ◈ *state* C USA
35 S15 **Wyoming Range** ▲▲ Wyoming, C USA
191 T8 **Wyong** New South Wales, SE Australia
xl M13 **Wyre** ≈ NW England, UK
112 G9 **Wyrzysk** *Ger.* Wirsitz. Piła, W Poland
Wysg *see* Usk
112 O10 **Wysokie Mazowieckie** Łomża, E Poland
112 M11 **Wyszków** *Ger.* Probstberg. Ostrołęka, NE Poland
112 L11 **Wyszogród** Płock, C Poland
23 R7 **Wytheville** Virginia, NE USA

X

82 Q12 **Xaafuun** *It.* Hafun. Bari, NE Somalia
82 Q12 **Xaafuun, Raas** *var.* Ras Hafun. *headland* NE Somalia
Xábia *see* Jávea
44 C4 **Xaclbal, Río** *var.* Xalbal. ≈ Guatemala/Mexico
143 Y10 **Xaçmaz** *Rus.* Khachmas. N Azerbaijan
82 O12 **Xadeed** *var.* Haded. *physical region* N Somalia
165 O14 **Xagquka** Xizang Zizhiqu, W China
178 I6 **Xai** *var.* Muang Xay, Muong Sai. Oudômxai, N Laos
164 F10 **Xaidulla** Xinjiang Uygur Zizhiqu, W China
178 I7 **Xaignabouli** *prev.* Muang Xaignabouri, *Fr.* Sayaboury. Xaignabouli, N Laos
178 J7 **Xai Lai Leng, Phou** ▲ Laos/Vietnam
164 L15 **Xainza** Xizang Zizhiqu, W China
164 L16 **Xaitongmoin** Xizang Zizhiqu, W China
85 M20 **Xai-Xai** *prev.* João Belo, Vila de João Bel. Gaza, S Mozambique
Xalbal *see* Xaclbal, Río
82 P13 **Xalin** Nugaal, N Somalia
178 I6 **Xam Nua** *var.* Sam Neua. Houaphan, N Laos
84 D11 **Xá-Muteba** *Port.* Cinco de Outubro. Lunda Norte, NE Angola
85 C16 **Xangongo** *Port.* Rocadas. Cunene, SW Angola
143 W12 **Xankändi** *Rus.* Khankendi; *prev.* Stepanakert. SW Azerbaijan
143 V11 **Xanlar** *Rus.* Khanlar. NW Azerbaijan
116 J13 **Xánthi** Anatolikí Makedonía kai Thráki, NE Greece
60 H13 **Xanxerê** Santa Catarina, S Brazil
83 O15 **Xarardheere** Mudug, E Somalia
133 W8 **Xar Moron** ≈ NE China
Xarra *see* Xarrë
115 L23 **Xarrë** *var.* Xarra. Vlorë, S Albania
84 D12 **Xassengue** Lunda Sul, NW Angola
107 S11 **Xàtiva** *var.* Jativa; *anc.* Setabis. País Valenciano, E Spain
Xauen *see* Chefchaouen
62 K10 **Xavantes, Represa de** *var.* Represa de Chavantes. ⊡ S Brazil
164 I7 **Xayar** Xinjiang Uygur Zizhiqu, W China
Xäzär Dänizi *see* Caspian Sea
178 Jj9 **Xé Bangfai** ≈ C Laos
178 Jj10 **Xé Banghiang** *var.* Bang Hieng. ≈ S Laos
Xégar *see* Tingri
33 R14 **Xenia** Ohio, N USA
Xeres *see* Jeréz de la Frontera
117 E15 **Xeriás** ≈ C Greece
117 G17 **Xeró** ▲ Évvoia, C Greece
85 H18 **Xhumo** Central, C Botswana
167 N15 **Xiachuan Dao** *island* S China
Xiacun *see* Rushan
Xiaguan *see* Dali
165 U11 **Xiahe** *var.* Labrang. Gansu, C China
167 Q13 **Xiamen** *var.* Hsia-men; *prev.* Amoy. Fujian, SE China
166 L6 **Xi'an** *var.* Changan, Sian, Signan, Siking, Singan, Xian. Shaanxi, C China
166 L10 **Xianfeng** Hubei, C China
Xiang *see* Hunan
167 N7 **Xiangcheng** Henan, C China
166 F10 **Xiangcheng** *prev.* Qagchêng. Sichuan, C China
166 M8 **Xiangfan** *var.* Xiangyang. Hubei, C China
Xianggang *see* Hong Kong
167 N10 **Xiang Jiang** ≈ S China
Xiangkhoang *see* Pèk
178 Ii7 **Xiangkhoang, Plateau de** *var.* Plain of Jars. *plateau* N Laos
167 N11 **Xiangtan** *var.* Hsiang-t'an, Siangtan. Hunan, S China
167 N11 **Xiangxiang** Hunan, S China
Xiangyang *see* Xiangfan
167 S10 **Xianju** Zhejiang, SE China
166 F8 **Xianshui He** ≈ C China
167 N9 **Xiantao** *var.* Mianyang. Hubei, C China
167 R10 **Xianxia Ling** ▲▲ SE China
166 K6 **Xianyang** Shaanxi, C China
164 L5 **Xiaocaohu** Xinjiang Uygur Zizhiqu, W China
169 W6 **Xiao Hinggan Ling** *Eng.* Lesser Khingan Range. ▲▲ NE China
166 M6 **Xiao Shan** ▲▲ C China
166 M12 **Xiao Shui** ≈ S China
167 P6 **Xiaoxian** *var.* Xiao Xian. Anhui, E China
166 G11 **Xichang** Sichuan, C China
43 P11 **Xicoténcatl** Tamaulipas, C Mexico
Xieng Khouang *see* Pèk
Xieng Ngeun *see* Muong Xiang Ngeun
165 X10 **Xifeng** Gansu, C China
166 J11 **Xifeng** Guizhou, S China
Xigang *see* Helan
164 L16 **Xigazê** *var.* Jih-k'a-tse, Shigatse, Xigaze. Xizang Zizhiqu, W China
166 I8 **Xi He** ≈ C China
165 W11 **Xihe** Gansu, C China
Xihuachi *see* Heshui
165 Q7 **Xijian Quan** *spring* NW China
165 W10 **Xiji** Ningxia, N China
166 M14 **Xi Jiang** *var.* Hsi Chiang, *Eng.* West River. ≈ S China
166 K15 **Xijin Shuiku** ⊡ S China
Xilagani *see* Xylaganí
166 I13 **Xilin** *prev.* Bada. Guangxi Zhuangzu Zizhiqu, S China
169 Q10 **Xilinhot** *var.* Silinhot. Nei Mongol Zizhiqu, N China
Xilokastro *see* Xylókastro
Xin *see* Xinjiang Uygur Zizhiqu
167 R10 **Xin'anjiang Shuiku** ⊡ SE China
Xin'anzhen *see* Xinyi
169 Q7 **Xin Barag Youqi** *var.* Altan Emel. Nei Mongol Zizhiqu, N China
169 R7 **Xin Barag Zuoqi** *var.* Amgalang. Nei Mongol Zizhiqu, N China
169 W12 **Xinbin** Liaoning, NE China
167 O7 **Xincai** Henan, C China
165 V8 **Xincheng** *var.* Yinchuanzhan. Ningxia, N China
167 O13 **Xinfeng** Jiangxi, S China
167 O14 **Xinfengjiang Shuiku** ⊡ S China
169 T13 **Xingcheng** Liaoning, NE China
84 E11 **Xinge** Lunda Norte, NE Angola
167 P12 **Xingguo** Jiangxi, S China
165 S11 **Xinghai** Qinghai, C China
167 R7 **Xinghua** Jiangsu, E China
Xingkai Hu *see* Khanka, Lake
167 P13 **Xingning** Guangdong, S China
166 I13 **Xingren** Guizhou, S China
167 O4 **Xingtai** Hebei, E China
61 J14 **Xingu, Rio** ≈ C Brazil
165 P6 **Xingxingxia** Xinjiang Uygur Zizhiqu, NW China
166 I13 **Xingyi** Guizhou, S China
164 I6 **Xinhe** *var.* Toksu. Xinjiang Uygur Zizhiqu, NW China
Xin Hot *see* Abag Qi
165 T10 **Xining** *var.* Hsining, Hsi-ning, Sining. *province capital* Qinghai, C China
167 O4 **Xinji** *prev.* Shulu. Hebei, E China
167 P10 **Xinjian** Jiangxi, S China
Xinjiang *see* Xinjiang Uygur Zizhiqu
168 D8 **Xinjiang Uygur Zizhiqu** *var.* Sinkiang, Sinkiang Uighur Autonomous Region, Xin, Xinjiang. ◈ *autonomous region* NW China
166 H9 **Xinjin** Sichuan, C China
Xinjin *see* Pulandian
169 U12 **Xinmin** Liaoning, NE China
166 M12 **Xinning** Hunan, S China
Xinpu *see* Lianyungang
167 P5 **Xinwen** *prev.* Suncun. Shandong, E China
Xin Xian *see* Xinzhou
167 N6 **Xinxiang** Henan, C China
167 O8 **Xinyang** *var.* Hsin-yang, Sinyang. Henan, C China
167 Q6 **Xinyi** *var.* Xin'anzhen. Jiangsu, E China
167 Q6 **Xinyi He** ≈ E China
167 O11 **Xinyu** Jiangxi, S China
164 I5 **Xinyuan** *var.* Künes. Xinjiang Uygur Zizhiqu, NW China
Xinyuan *see* Tianjun
168 M14 **Xinzhao Shan** ▲ N China
167 N3 **Xinzhou** *var.* Xin Xian. Shanxi, C China
106 H4 **Xinzo de Limia** Galicia, NW Spain
Xions *see* Książ Wielkopolski
167 O7 **Xiping** Henan, C China
165 T11 **Xiqing Shan** ▲▲ C China
61 N16 **Xique-Xique** Bahia, E Brazil
117 E14 **Xirovoúni** ▲ N Greece
Xishanzui *see* Urad Qianqi
166 J11 **Xishui** Guizhou, S China
167 O9 **Xishui** Hubei, C China
169 R10 **Xi Ujimqin Qi** *var.* Bayan Ul Hot. Nei Mongol Zizhiqu, N China
166 K11 **Xiushan** Sichuan, C China
167 O10 **Xiu Shui** ≈ S China
164 J16 **Xixabangma Feng** ▲ W China
166 M7 **Xixia** Henan, C China
Xixona *see* Jijona
Xizang *see* Xizang Zizhiqu
Xizang Gaoyuan *see* Qingzang Gaoyuan
166 E9 **Xizang Zizhiqu** *var.* Thibet, Tibetan Autonomous Region, Xizang, *Eng.* Tibet. ◈ *autonomous region* W China
169 U14 **Xizhong Dao** *island* N China
Xolotlán *see* Managua, Lago de
165 N9 **Xorkol** Xinjiang Uygur Zizhiqu, NW China
43 X14 **Xpujil** Quintana Roo, E Mexico
Xuancheng *see* Xuanzhou
178 Jj9 **Xuân Đuc** Quang Binh, C Vietnam
166 L9 **Xuan'en** Hubei, C China
166 K8 **Xuanhan** Sichuan, C China
167 O2 **Xuanhua** Hebei, E China
167 P4 **Xuanhui He** ≈ E China
167 Q8 **Xuanzhou** *var.* Xuancheng. Anhui, E China
167 N7 **Xuchang** Henan, C China
143 X10 **Xudat** *Rus.* Khudat. NE Azerbaijan
83 M16 **Xuddur** *var.* Hudur, *It.* Oddur. Bakool, SW Somalia
82 O13 **Xudun** Nugaal, N Somalia
166 L11 **Xuefeng Shan** ▲▲ S China
44 F2 **Xunantunich** *ruins* Cayo, W Belize
169 W6 **Xun He** ≈ NE China
166 L7 **Xun He** ≈ C China
166 L14 **Xun Jiang** ≈ S China
169 W5 **Xunke** Heilongjiang, NE China
167 P13 **Xunwu** Jiangxi, S China
167 O3 **Xushui** Hebei, E China
166 L16 **Xuwen** Guangdong, S China
166 I11 **Xuyong** *var.* Yongning. Sichuan, C China
167 P6 **Xuzhou** *var.* Hsu-chou, Suchow, Tongshan; *prev.* T'ung-shan. Jiangsu, E China
116 K13 **Xylaganí** *var.* Xilagani. Anatolikí Makedonía kai Thráki, NE Greece
117 F19 **Xylókastro** *var.* Xilokastro. Pelopónnisos, S Greece

Y

166 H9 **Ya'an** *var.* Yaan. Sichuan, C China
190 L10 **Yaapeet** Victoria, SE Australia
81 D15 **Yabassi** Littoral, W Cameroon
83 J15 **Yabēlo** S Ethiopia
172 Pp5 **Yabetsu-gawa** *var.* Yūbetsu-gawa. ≈ Hokkaidō, NE Japan
116 H9 **Yablanitsa** Loveshka Oblast, W Bulgaria
45 N7 **Yablis** Región Autónoma Atlántico Norte, NE Nicaragua
126 Kk16 **Yablonovyy Khrebet** ▲▲ S Russian Federation
168 J14 **Yabrai Shan** ▲▲ NE China
47 U6 **Yabucoa** E Puerto Rico
197 K14 **Yacata** *island* Lau Group, E Fiji
166 J11 **Yachi He** ≈ S China
34 H10 **Yacolt** Washington, NW USA
56 M10 **Yacuaray** Amazonas, S Venezuela
59 M22 **Yacuiba** Tarija, S Bolivia
59 K16 **Yacuma, Río** ≈ C Bolivia
161 H16 **Yādgīr** Karnātaka, C India
23 R8 **Yadkin River** ≈ North Carolina, SE USA
23 R9 **Yadkinville** North Carolina, SE USA
131 P3 **Yadrin** Chuvashskaya Respublika, W Russian Federation
197 I13 **Yadua** *prev.* Yandua. *island* NW Fiji
172 Oo17 **Yaeyama-shotō** *var.* Yaegama-shotō. *island group* SW Japan
77 O8 **Yafran** NW Libya
197 L15 **Yagasa Cluster** *island group* Lau Group, E Fiji
172 Oo3 **Yagashiri-tō** *island* NE Japan
67 H21 **Yaghan Basin** *undersea feature* SE Pacific Ocean
127 Nn9 **Yagodnoye** Magadanskaya Oblast', E Russian Federation
Yagotin *see* Yahotyn
80 G12 **Yagoua** Extrême-Nord, NE Cameroon
165 Q11 **Yagradagzê Shan** ▲ C China
Yaguachi *see* Yaguachi Nuevo
58 B7 **Yaguachi Nuevo** *var.* Yaguachi. Guayas, W Ecuador
Yaguarón, Río *see* Jaguarão, Rio
171 I16 **Yahagi-gawa** ≈ Honshū, SW Japan
119 Q11 **Yahorlyts'kyy Lyman** *bay* S Ukraine
119 Q5 **Yahotyn** *Rus.* Yagotin. Kyyivs'ka Oblast', N Ukraine
42 L12 **Yahualica** Jalisco, SW Mexico
81 L17 **Yahuma** Haut-Zaïre, N Zaire
142 K15 **Yahyalı** Kayseri, C Turkey
178 Gg15 **Yai, Khao** ▲ SW Thailand
171 Kk15 **Yaita** Tochigi, Honshū, S Japan
171 Ii17 **Yaizu** Shizuoka, Honshū, S Japan
166 G9 **Yajiang** Sichuan, C China
121 O14 **Yakawlyevichi** *Rus.* Yakovlevichi. Vitsyebskaya Voblasts', NE Belarus
169 S6 **Yakeshi** Nei Mongol Zizhiqu, N China
34 I9 **Yakima** Washington, NW USA
34 J10 **Yakima River** ≈ Washington, NW USA
116 G7 **Yakimovo** Oblast Montana, NW Bulgaria
Yakkabag *see* Yakkabogh
153 N12 **Yakkabogh** *Rus.* Yakkabag. Qashqadaryo Wiloyati, S Uzbekistan
154 L12 **Yakmach** Baluchistān, SW Pakistan
79 O12 **Yako** W Burkina
41 W13 **Yakobi Island** *island* Alexander Archipelago, Alaska, USA
81 K16 **Yakoma** Equateur, N Zaire
116 H11 **Yakoruda** Sofiyska Oblast, SW Bulgaria
Yakovlevichi *see* Yakawlyevichi
131 T2 **Yakshur-Bod'ya** Udmurtskaya Respublika, NW Russian Federation
172 N6 **Yakumo** Hokkaidō, NE Japan
170 B17 **Yaku-shima** *island* Nansei-shotō, SW Japan
41 V12 **Yakutat** Alaska, USA
41 U12 **Yakutat Bay** *inlet* Alaska, USA
Yakutia/Yakutiya/Yakutiya, Respublika *see* Sakha (Yakutiya), Respublika
126 Mm11 **Yakutsk** Respublika Sakha (Yakutiya), NE Russian Federation
178 Hh17 **Yala** Yala, SW Thailand
190 D6 **Yalata** South Australia
xxxvi W11 **Yalding** Kent, SE England, UK
33 S9 **Yale** Michigan, N USA
188 I11 **Yalgoo** Western Australia
116 O12 **Yalıköy** İstanbul, NW Turkey
81 L14 **Yalinga** Haute-Kotto, C Central African Republic
121 M17 **Yalizava** *Rus.* Yelizovo. Mahilyowskaya Voblasts', E Belarus
46 L13 **Yallahs Hill** ▲ E Jamaica
24 L3 **Yalobusha River** ≈ Mississippi, S USA
81 H15 **Yaloké** Ombella-Mpoko, W Central African Republic
166 E7 **Yalong Jiang** ≈ C China
142 E11 **Yalova** İstanbul, NW Turkey
Yaloveny *see* Ialoveni
Yalpug *see* Ialpug
Yalpug, Ozero *see* Yalpuh, Ozero
119 N12 **Yalpuh, Ozero** *Rus.* Ozero Yalpug. ◎ SW Ukraine
119 T14 **Yalta** Respublika Krym, S Ukraine
169 W12 **Yalu** *Chin.* Yalu Jiang, *Jap.* Oryokko, *Kor.* Amnok-kang. ≈ China/North Korea
Yalu Jiang *see* Yalu
125 F12 **Yalutorovsk** Tyumenskaya Oblast', C Russian Federation
142 F14 **Yalvaç** Isparta, SW Turkey
172 N12 **Yamada** Iwate, Honshū, C Japan
170 Cc14 **Yamaga** Kumamoto, Kyūshū, SW Japan
171 L12 **Yamagata** Yamagata, Honshū, C Japan
171 Ll12 **Yamagata** *off.* Yamagata-ken. ◈ *prefecture* Honshū, C Japan
170 Bb16 **Yamagawa** Kagoshima, Kyūshū, SW Japan
170 Dd12 **Yamaguchi** *var.* Yamaguti. Yamaguchi, Honshū, SW Japan
170 Dd12 **Yamaguchi** *off.* Yamaguchi-ken, *var.* Yamaguti. ◈ *prefecture* Honshū, SW Japan
Yamaguti *see* Yamaguchi
129 X5 **Yamalo-Nenetskiy Avtonomnyy Okrug** ◈ *autonomous district* N Russian Federation
126 Gg6 **Yamal, Poluostrov** *peninsula* N Russian Federation
171 J16 **Yamanashi** *off.* Yamanashi-ken, *var.* Yamanasi. ◈ *prefecture* Honshū, S Japan
Yamanasi *see* Yamanashi
Yamanīyah, Al Jumhūrīyah al *see* Yemen
131 W5 **Yamantau** ▲ W Russian Federation
126 K16 **Yamarovka** Chitinskaya Oblast', S Russian Federation
Yamasaki *see* Yamazaki
13 P12 **Yamaska** ≈ Québec, SE Canada
171 Jj17 **Yamato** Kanagawa, Honshū, S Japan
199 Gg4 **Yamato Ridge** *undersea feature* S Sea of Japan
170 G14 **Yamazaki** *var.* Yamasaki. Hyōgo, Honshū, SW Japan
191 V5 **Yamba** New South Wales, SE Australia
83 D16 **Yambio** *var.* Yambiyo. Western Equatoria, S Sudan
Yambiyo *see* Yambio
116 L10 **Yambol** *Turk.* Yanboli. Burgaska Oblast, E Bulgaria
81 M17 **Yambuya** Haut-Zaïre, N Zaire
176 Uu15 **Yamdena, Pulau** *prev.* Jamdena. *island* Kepulauan Tanimbar, E Indonesia
170 Cc13 **Yame** Fukuoka, Kyūshū, SW Japan
177 G6 **Yamethin** Mandalay, C Burma
194 G11 **Yaminbot** East Sepik, NW PNG
171 L15 **Yamizo-san** ▲ Honshū, C Japan
189 U9 **Yamma Yamma, Lake** ◎ Queensland, C Australia
78 M16 **Yamoussoukro** ● (Ivory Coast) C Ivory Coast
39 P3 **Yampa River** ≈ Colorado, C USA
119 S2 **Yampil'** Sums'ka Oblast', NE Ukraine
118 M8 **Yampil'** Vinnyts'ka Oblast', C Ukraine
127 Oo10 **Yamsk** Magadanskaya Oblast', E Russian Federation
158 J8 **Yamuna** *prev.* Jumna. ≈ N India
158 I9 **Yamunanagar** Haryāna, N India
Yamundá *see* Nhamundá, Rio
151 U8 **Yamyshevo** Pavlodar, NE Kazakhstan
165 N16 **Yamzho Yumco** ◎ W China
126 Ll6 **Yana** ≈ NE Russian Federation
195 P15 **Yanaba Island** *island* SE PNG
170 C13 **Yanagawa** Fukuoka, Kyūshū, SW Japan
170 E13 **Yanai** Yamaguchi, Honshū, SW Japan
161 L16 **Yanam** *var.* Yanaon. Pondicherry, E India

◆ Country ● Country Capital ◇ Dependent Territory ○ Dependent Territory Capital ◈ Administrative Region ✕ International Airport ▲ Mountain ▲▲ Mountain Range ⚠ Volcano ≈ River ◎ Lake ⊡ Reservoir

YAN'AN – YUN SHUI

166 L5 **Yan'an** *var.* Yanan. Shaanxi, C China
Yanaon *see* Yanam
131 U3 **Yanaul** Respublika Bashkortostan, W Russian Federation
120 O12 **Yanavichy** *Rus.* Yanovichi. Vitsyebskaya Voblasts', NE Belorussia
Yanboli *see* Yambol
146 K8 **Yanbu' al Baḩr** Al Madīnah, W Saudi Arabia
23 T8 **Yanceyville** North Carolina, SE USA
167 R7 **Yancheng** Jiangsu, E China
165 W8 **Yanchi** Ningxia, N China
166 L5 **Yanchuan** Shaanxi, C China
191 O10 **Yanco Creek** *seasonal river* New South Wales, SE Australia
191 O6 **Yanda Creek** *seasonal river* New South Wales, SE Australia
190 K4 **Yandama Creek** *seasonal river* New South Wales/South Australia
167 S11 **Yandang Shan** ⛰ SE China
197 G5 **Yandé, Île** *island* Îles Belep, W New Caledonia
Yandua *see* Yadua
165 O6 **Yandun** Xinjiang Uygur Zizhiqu, W China
78 L13 **Yanfolila** Sikasso, SW Mali
81 M18 **Yangambi** Haut-Zaïre, N Zaire
164 M15 **Yangbajain** Xizang Zizhiqu, W China
Yangchow *see* Yangzhou
166 M15 **Yangchun** Guangdong, S China
167 N2 **Yanggao** Shanxi, C China
Yanggeta *see* Yaqeta
Yangiabad *see* Yangiobod
Yangibazar *see* Dzhany-Bazar, Kyrgyzstan
Yangi-Bazar *see* Kofarnihon, Tajikistan
Yangiklshak *see* Yangiqishloq
152 M13 **Yangi-Nishon** *Rus.* Yang-Nishan. Qashqadaryo Wiloyati, S Uzbekistan
153 Q9 **Yangiobod** *Rus.* Yangiabad. Toshkent Wiloyati, E Uzbekistan
153 O10 **Yangiqishloq** *Rus.* Yangiklshak. Jizzakh Wiloyati, C Uzbekistan
153 P11 **Yangiyer** Sirdaryo Wiloyati, E Uzbekistan
153 P9 **Yangiyŭl** *Rus.* Yangiyul'. Toshkent Wiloyati, E Uzbekistan
166 M15 **Yangjiang** Guangdong, S China
Yangku *see* Taiyuan
Yang-Nishan *see* Yangi-Nishon
177 G9 **Yangon** *Eng.* Rangoon. ● (Burma) Yangon, S Burma
177 G8 **Yangon** *Eng.* Rangoon. ◈ *division* SW Burma
166 K17 **Yangpu Gang** *harbour* Hainan, S China
167 N4 **Yangquan** Shanxi, C China
167 N13 **Yangshan** Guangdong, S China
178 Kk13 **Yang Sin, Chu** ▲ S Vietnam
Yangtze *see* Chang Jiang, C China
Yangtze Kiang *see* Chang Jiang
166 G11 **Yangyuan** Sichuan, C China
167 R7 **Yangzhou** *var.* Yangchow. Jiangsu, E China
166 L5 **Yan He** ≈ C China
169 Y10 **Yanji** Jilin, NE China
Yanji *see* Longjing
31 Q12 **Yankton** South Dakota, N USA
Yannina *see* Ioánnina
126 M6 **Yano-Indigirskaya Nizmennost'** *plain* NE Russian Federation
Yanovichi *see* Yanavichy
161 K24 **Yan Oya** ≈ N Sri Lanka
164 K6 **Yanqi** *var.* Yanqi Huizu Zizhixian. Xinjiang Uygur Zizhiqu, NW China
Yanqi Huizu Zizhixian *see* Yanqi
167 P2 **Yan Shan** ⛰ E China
167 Q10 **Yanshan** Jiangxi, S China
166 H14 **Yanshan** *prev.* Hekou. Yunnan, SW China
169 X8 **Yanshou** Heilongjiang, NE China
126 Ll6 **Yanskiy Zaliv** *bay* N Russian Federation
191 O4 **Yantabulla** New South Wales, SE Australia
167 R4 **Yantai** *var.* Yan-t'ai; *prev.* Chefoo, Chih-fu. Shandong, E China
120 A13 **Yantarnyy** *Ger.* Palmnicken. Kaliningradskaya Oblast', W Russian Federation
116 J9 **Yantra** Loveshka Oblast, N Bulgaria
116 K9 **Yantra** ≈ N Bulgaria
167 P5 **Yanzhou** Shandong, E China
81 E16 **Yaoundé** *var.* Yaunde. ● (Cameroon) Centre, S Cameroon
196 I14 **Yap** ◈ *state* W Micronesia
196 F16 **Yap** *island* Caroline Islands, W Micronesia
59 M18 **Yapacani, Rio** ≈ C Bolivia
176 Ww12 **Yapa Kopra** Irian Jaya, E Indonesia
Yapan *see* Yapen, Selat
Yapanskoye More *see* Japan, Sea of
79 P15 **Yapei** N Ghana
10 M10 **Yapeitso, Mont** ▲ Québec, E Canada
176 X10 **Yapen, Pulau** *prev.* Japen. *island* E Indonesia
176 X9 **Yapen, Selat** *var.* Yapan. *strait* Irian Jaya, E Indonesia
63 E15 **Yapeyú** Corrientes, NE Argentina
142 I11 **Yapraklı** Çankın, N Turkey
182 M3 **Yap Trench** *var.* Yap Trough. *undersea feature* SE Philippine Sea
Yap Trough *see* Yap Trench
Yapurá *see* Caquetá, Río, Brazil/Colombia
Yapurá *see* Japurá, Rio, Brazil/Colombia
176 U11 **Yaputih** Pulau Seram, E Indonesia
197 I13 **Yaqaga** *island* N Fiji
197 H13 **Yaqeta** *prev.* Yanggeta. *island* Yasawa Group, NW Fiji
42 G6 **Yaqui** Sonora, NW Mexico
34 E12 **Yaquina Bay** *bay* Oregon, NW USA
42 G6 **Yaqui, Río** ≈ NW Mexico
176 Y14 **Yar** *channel* Irian Jaya, E Indonesia
56 K5 **Yaracuy** *off.* Estado Yaracuy. ◈ *state* NW Venezuela
152 E13 **Yaradzhi** *Turkm.* Yarajy. Akhalskiy Velayat, C Turkmenistan
Yarajy *see* Yaradzhi
129 Q15 **Yaransk** Kirovskaya Oblast', NW Russian Federation
xxxvi J13 **Yarcombe** Devon, SW England, UK
142 F17 **Yardımcı Burnu** *headland* SW Turkey
xxxix P12 **Yardley Hastings** Northamptonshire, C England, UK
xxxix X9 **Yare** ≈ E England, UK
129 S9 **Yarega** Respublika Komi, NW Russian Federation
118 I7 **Yaremcha** Ivano-Frankivs'ka Oblast', W Ukraine
201 Q9 **Yaren** SW Nauru
129 Q10 **Yarensk** Arkhangel'skaya Oblast', NW Russian Federation
161 F16 **Yargatti** Karnātaka, W India
171 Ii14 **Yariga-take** ▲ Honshū, S Japan
147 O15 **Yarīm** W Yemen
56 F14 **Yarí, Río** ≈ SW Colombia
56 K5 **Yaritagua** Yaracuy, N Venezuela
Yarkand *see* Yarkant He
Yarkant *see* Shache
164 E9 **Yarkant He** *var.* Yarkand. ≈ NW China
155 U3 **Yarkhūn** ≈ NW Pakistan
xxxvi L12 **Yarlington** Somerset, SW England, UK
Yarlung Zangbo Jiang *see* Brahmaputra
118 L6 **Yarmolyntsi** Khmel'nyts'ka Oblast', W Ukraine
169 T11 **Yar Moron** ≈ N China
xxxvii P14 **Yarmouth** Isle of Wight, S England, UK
Yarmouth *see* Great Yarmouth
11 O16 **Yarmouth** Nova Scotia, SE Canada
xxxvi M10 **Yarnbrook** Wiltshire, S England, UK
Yaroslav *see* Jarosław
128 L15 **Yaroslavl'** Yaroslavskaya Oblast', W Russian Federation
128 K14 **Yaroslavskaya Oblast'** ◈ *province* W Russian Federation
126 Kk12 **Yaroslavskiy** Respublika Sakha (Yakutiya), NE Russian Federation
191 P13 **Yarram** Victoria, SE Australia
191 O11 **Yarrawonga** Victoria, SE Australia
190 L4 **Yarriarraburra Swamp** *wetland* New South Wales, SE Australia
xliii M22 **Yarrow** The Borders, S Scotland, UK
xliii M22 **Yarrow Feus** The Borders, S Scotland, UK
126 Gg8 **Yar-Sale** Yamalo-Nenetskiy Avtonomnyy Okrug, N Russian Federation
126 I12 **Yartsevo** Krasnoyarskiy Kray, C Russian Federation
130 I4 **Yartsevo** Smolenskaya Oblast', W Russian Federation
56 E8 **Yarumal** Antioquia, NW Colombia
197 H13 **Yasawa** *island* Yasawa Group, NW Fiji
197 G13 **Yasawa Group** *island group* NW Fiji
79 V12 **Yashi** Katsina, N Nigeria
79 S14 **Yashikera** Kwara, W Nigeria
153 T14 **Yashilkŭl** *Rus.* Ozero Yashil'kul'. ◎ SE Tajikistan
Yashil'kul', Ozero *see* Yashilkŭl
171 Ll11 **Yashima** Akita, Honshū, C Japan
170 Dd14 **Ya-shima** *island* SW Japan
170 E14 **Yashiro-jima** *island* SW Japan
131 P13 **Yashkul'** Respublika Kalmykiya, SW Russian Federation
152 F13 **Yashlyk** Akhalskiy Velayat, C Turkmenistan
Yasinovataya *see* Yasynuvata
116 N10 **Yasna Polyana** Burgaska Oblast, SE Bulgaria
126 M14 **Yasnyy** Amurskaya Oblast', SE Russian Federation
178 J10 **Yasothon** Yasothon, E Thailand
191 R10 **Yass** New South Wales, SE Australia
Yassy *see* Iaşi
170 Ff12 **Yasugi** Shimane, Honshū, SW Japan
149 N10 **Yāsūj** *var.* Yesuj; *prev.* Tal-e Khosravī. Kohkīlūyeh va Būyer Aḩmadī, C Iran
142 M11 **Yasun Burnu** *headland* N Turkey
119 X8 **Yasynuvata** *Rus.* Yasinovataya. Donets'ka Oblast', SE Ukraine
142 C15 **Yatağan** Muğla, SW Turkey
171 M9 **Yatate-tōge** *pass* Honshū, C Japan
xxxvi L9 **Yate** South Gloucestershire, SW England, UK
197 J7 **Yaté** Province Sud, S New Caledonia
29 P6 **Yates Center** Kansas, C USA
193 B21 **Yates Point** *headland* South Island, NZ
15 Kk7 **Yathkyed Lake** ◎ Northwest Territories, NE Canada
176 U15 **Yatoke** Pulau Babar, E Indonesia
81 M18 **Yatolema** Haut-Zaïre, N Zaire
171 J15 **Yatsuga-take** ▲ Honshū, S Japan
170 C14 **Yatsushiro** *var.* Yatusiro. Kumamoto, Kyūshū, SW Japan
170 C15 **Yatsushiro-kai** *bay* SW Japan
144 F11 **Yatta** *var.* Yuta. S West Bank
83 J20 **Yatta Plateau** *plateau* SE Kenya
xxxvii Q9 **Yattendon** Newbury, S England, UK
xxxvi K10 **Yatton** North West Somerset, SW England, UK
Yatusiro *see* Yatsushiro
59 F17 **Yauca, Río** ≈ SW Peru
47 S6 **Yauco** W Puerto Rico
176 Xx9 **Yauke** Irian Jaya, E Indonesia
Yaunde *see* Yaoundé
Yavan *see* Yovon
Yavarí *see* Javari, Rio
58 G9 **Yavari Mirim, Río** ≈ NE Peru
42 G7 **Yavaros** Sonora, NW Mexico
160 I13 **Yavatmāl** Mahārāshtra, C India
56 M9 **Yaví, Cerro** ▲ C Venezuela
45 W16 **Yaviza** Darién, SE Panama
144 F10 **Yavne** Central, W Israel
118 H5 **Yavoriv** *Pol.* Jaworów, *Rus.* Yavorov. L'vivs'ka Oblast', NW Ukraine
Yavorov *see* Yavoriv
170 E15 **Yawatahama** Ehime, Shikoku, SW Japan
Ya Xian *see* Sanya
xxxix R10 **Yaxley** Cambridgeshire, E England, UK
142 L17 **Yayladaği** Hatay, S Turkey
129 V13 **Yayva** Permskaya Oblast', NW Russian Federation
129 V12 **Yayva** ≈ NW Russian Federation
149 Q9 **Yazd** *var.* Yezd. Yazd, C Iran
149 Q8 **Yazd** *off.* Ostān-e Yazd, *var.* Yezd. ◈ *province* C Iran
Yazgulemskiy Khrebet *see* Yazgulom, Qatorkŭhi
153 S13 **Yazgulom, Qatorkŭhi** *Rus.* Yazgulemskiy Khrebet. ⛰ S Tajikistan
24 K5 **Yazoo City** Mississippi, S USA
24 K5 **Yazoo River** ≈ Mississippi, S USA
131 Q5 **Yazykovo** Ul'yanovskaya Oblast', W Russian Federation
111 U4 **Ybbs** Niederösterreich, NE Austria
111 U4 **Ybbs** ≈ C Austria
97 G22 **Yding Skovhøj** *hill* C Denmark
117 G20 **Ýdra** *var.* Ídhra, Idra. Ýdra, S Greece
117 G21 **Ýdra** *var.* Ídhra. *island* S Greece
117 G20 **Ýdras, Kólpos** *strait* S Greece
178 Gg10 **Ye** Mon State, S Burma
191 O12 **Yea** Victoria, SE Australia
xli R13 **Yeadon** Leeds, N England, UK
xxxvi G16 **Yealm** ≈ SW England, UK
xxxvi G16 **Yealmpton** Devon, SW England, UK
80 I5 **Yebbi-Bou** Borkou-Ennedi-Tibesti, N Chad
164 F9 **Yecheng** *var.* Kargilik. Xinjiang Uygur Zizhiqu, NW China
107 R11 **Yecla** Murcia, SE Spain
42 H6 **Yécora** Sonora, NW Mexico
xli V11 **Yedingham** North Yorkshire, N England, UK
Yedintsy *see* Edineţ
128 J13 **Yefimovskiy** Leningradskaya Oblast', NW Russian Federation
176 Uu9 **Yeflio** Irian Jaya, E Indonesia
130 K6 **Yefremov** Tul'skaya Oblast', W Russian Federation
Yêgainnyin *see* Henan
143 U12 **Yeghegis** *Rus.* Yekhegis. ≈ C Armenia
151 T10 **Yegindybulak** *Kaz.* Egindibulaq. Karaganda, C Kazakhstan
130 L4 **Yegor'yevsk** Moskovskaya Oblast', W Russian Federation
Yehuda, Haré *see* Judaean Hills
83 E15 **Yei** ≈ S Sudan
167 P8 **Yeji** *var.* Yejiaji. Anhui, E China
Yejiaji *see* Yeji
125 Ee11 **Yekaterinburg** *prev.* Sverdlovsk. Sverdlovskaya Oblast', C Russian Federation
Yekaterinodar *see* Krasnodar
Yekaterinoslav *see* Dnipropetrovs'k
126 Mm15 **Yekaterinoslavka** Amurskaya Oblast', SE Russian Federation
131 O7 **Yekaterinovka** Saratovskaya Oblast', W Russian Federation
78 K16 **Yekepa** NE Liberia
131 T3 **Yelabuga** Respublika Tatarstan, W Russian Federation
Yela Island *see* Rossel Island
131 O8 **Yelan'** Volgogradskaya Oblast', SW Russian Federation
119 Q9 **Yelanets'** *Rus.* Yelanets. Mykolayivs'ka Oblast', S Ukraine
125 G13 **Yelanka** Novosibirskaya Oblast', C Russian Federation
127 Nn15 **Yel'ban'** Khabarovskiy Kray, E Russian Federation
130 L7 **Yelets** Lipetskaya Oblast', W Russian Federation
129 W4 **Yeletskiy** Respublika Komi, NW Russian Federation
78 J11 **Yélimané** Kayes, W Mali
Yelisavetpol *see* Gäncä
Yelizavetgrad *see* Kirovohrad
127 O13 **Yelizavety, Mys** *headland* SE Russian Federation
127 Pp11 **Yelizovo** Kamchatskaya Oblast', E Russian Federation
Yelizovo *see* Yalizava
131 S5 **Yelkhovka** Samarskaya Oblast', W Russian Federation
xlii I2 **Yell** *island* NE Scotland, UK
161 E17 **Yellāpur** Karnātaka, W India
9 U17 **Yellow Grass** Saskatchewan, S Canada
Yellowhammer State *see* Alabama
9 O15 **Yellowhead Pass** *pass* Alberta/British Columbia, SW Canada
15 Hh8 **Yellowknife** *territory capital* Northwest Territories, W Canada
15 I7 **Yellowknife** ≈ Northwest Territories, NW Canada
194 F10 **Yellow River** ≈ NW PNG
25 P8 **Yellow River** ≈ Alabama/Florida, S USA
32 I4 **Yellow River** ≈ Wisconsin, N USA
32 J6 **Yellow River** ≈ Wisconsin, N USA
32 K7 **Yellow River** ≈ Wisconsin, N USA
Yellow River *see* Huang He
163 V8 **Yellow Sea** *Chin.* Huang Hai, *Kor.* Hwang-Hae. *sea* E Asia
35 S13 **Yellowstone Lake** ◎ Wyoming, C USA
35 T13 **Yellowstone National Park** *national park* Wyoming, NW USA
35 Y8 **Yellowstone River** ≈ Montana/Wyoming, NW USA
xlii I2 **Yell Sound** *strait* N Scotland, UK
29 U9 **Yellville** Arkansas, C USA
126 Hh11 **Yeloguy** ≈ C Russian Federation
152 J14 **Yëloten** *prev.* Iolotan', *Turkm.* Yolöten. Maryyskiy Velayat, S Turkmenistan
121 M20 **Yel'sk** *Rus.* Yel'sk. Homyel'skaya Voblasts', SE Belorussia
xxxix N11 **Yelvertoft** Northamptonshire, C England, UK
xxxvi F15 **Yelverton** Devon, SW England, UK
79 T13 **Yelwa** Kebbi, W Nigeria
125 Ee12 **Yemanzhelinsk** Chelyabinskaya Oblast', C Russian Federation
23 R15 **Yemassee** South Carolina, SE USA
147 O15 **Yemen** *off.* Republic of Yemen, *Ar.* Al Jumhūrīyah al Yamanīyah, Al Yaman. ◆ *republic* SW Asia
118 M4 **Yemil'chyne** Zhytomyrs'ka Oblast', N Ukraine
128 M10 **Yemtsa** Arkhangel'skaya Oblast', NW Russian Federation
128 M10 **Yemtsa** ≈ NW Russian Federation
129 R10 **Yemva** *prev.* Zheleznodorozhnyy. Respublika Komi, NW Russian Federation
119 X7 **Yenakiyeve** *Rus.* Yenakiyevo; *prev.* Ordzhonikidze, Rykovo. Donets'ka Oblast', E Ukraine
Yenakiyevo *see* Yenakiyeve
177 Ff6 **Yenangyaung** Magwe, W Burma
178 Jj5 **Yên Bai** Yên Bai, N Vietnam
191 P9 **Yenda** New South Wales, SE Australia
176 W10 **Yende** Irian Jaya, E Indonesia
79 Q14 **Yendi** NE Ghana
164 E8 **Yengisar** Xinjiang Uygur Zizhiqu, NW China
124 O3 **Yeniboğaziçi** *var.* Ayios Seryios, *Gk.* Ágios Sérgios. E Cyprus
124 Oo2 **Yenierenköy** *var.* Yialousa, *Gk.* Agialoúsa. NE Cyprus
Yenipazar *see* Novi Pazar
142 E12 **Yenişehir** Bursa, NW Turkey
Yenisei Bay *see* Yeniseyskiy Zaliv
126 Hh8 **Yenisey** ≈ Mongolia/Russian Federation
126 I13 **Yeniseysk** Krasnoyarskiy Kray, C Russian Federation
207 W10 **Yeniseyskiy Zaliv** *var.* Yenisei Bay. *bay* N Russian Federation
131 Q12 **Yenotayevka** Astrakhanskaya Oblast', SW Russian Federation
128 L4 **Yenozero, Ozero** ◎ NW Russian Federation
Yenping *see* Nanping
41 Q11 **Yentna River** ≈ Alaska, USA
xxxvi H13 **Yeoford** Devon, SW England, UK
188 M10 **Yeo, Lake** *salt lake* Western Australia
191 R7 **Yeoval** New South Wales, SE Australia
xxxvi L12 **Yeovil** Somerset, SW England, UK
42 H6 **Yepachic** Chihuahua, N Mexico
189 Y8 **Yeppoon** Queensland, E Australia
130 M5 **Yeraktur** Ryazanskaya Oblast', W Russian Federation
Yeraliyev *see* Kuryk
152 F12 **Yerbent** Akhalskiy Velayat, C Turkmenistan
126 Jj12 **Yerbogachen** Irkutskaya Oblast', C Russian Federation
143 T12 **Yerevan** *var.* Erevan, *Eng.* Erivan. ● (Armenia) C Armenia
143 U12 **Yerevan** ✈ C Armenia
131 O12 **Yergeni** *hill range* SW Russian Federation
Yeriho *see* Jericho
37 R6 **Yerington** Nevada, W USA
142 J13 **Yerköy** Yozgat, C Turkey
116 L13 **Yerlisu** Edirne, NW Turkey
Yermak *see* Aksu
151 R9 **Yermentau** *Kaz.* Ereymentaū, Jermentau. Akmola, C Kazakhstan
151 R9 **Yermentau, Gory** ⛰ C Kazakhstan
129 R5 **Yermitsa** Respublika Komi, NW Russian Federation
37 V14 **Yermo** California, W USA
126 Ll14 **Yerofey Pavlovich** Amurskaya Oblast', SE Russian Federation
101 F15 **Yerseke** Zeeland, SW Netherlands
131 Q8 **Yershov** Saratovskaya Oblast', W Russian Federation
129 P9 **Yërtom** Respublika Komi, NW Russian Federation
58 D13 **Yerupaja, Nevado** ▲ C Peru
Yerushalayim *see* Jerusalem
107 R4 **Yesa, Embalse de** ⊞ NE Spain
151 V15 **Yesik** *Kaz.* Esik; *prev.* Issyk. Almaty, SE Kazakhstan
151 O8 **Yesil'** *Kaz.* Esil. Turgay, N Kazakhstan
142 K15 **Yeşilhisar** Kayseri, C Turkey
142 L11 **Yeşilırmak** *anc.* Iris. ≈ N Turkey
xlii L4 **Yesnaby** Orkney Islands, N Scotland, UK
39 U12 **Yeso** New Mexico, SW USA
Yeso *see* Hokkaidō
131 N15 **Yessentuki** Stavropol'skiy Kray, SW Russian Federation
126 J9 **Yessey** Evenkiyskiy Avtonomnyy Okrug, N Russian Federation
107 P12 **Yeste** Castilla-La Mancha, C Spain
Yesuj *see* Yāsūj
191 T4 **Yetman** New South Wales, SE Australia
xxxvi L13 **Yetminster** Dorset, S England, UK
78 L4 **Yetti** *physical region* N Mauritania
xliii L18 **Yetts o'Muckhart** Clackmannan, C Scotland, UK
177 G4 **Ye-u** Sagaing, C Burma
104 H9 **Yeu, Île d'** *island* NW France
Yevlakh *see* Yevlax
143 W11 **Yevlax** *Rus.* Yevlakh. C Azerbaijan
119 S13 **Yevpatoriya** Respublika Krym, S Ukraine
125 B17 **Yevreyskaya Avtonomnaya Oblast'** *Eng.* Jewish Autonomous Oblast. ◈ *autonomous province* SE Russian Federation
130 K12 **Yeya** ≈ SW Russian Federation
164 I10 **Yeyik** Xinjiang Uygur Zizhiqu, W China
130 K12 **Yeysk** Krasnodarskiy Kray, SW Russian Federation
Yezd *see* Yazd
Yezerishche *see* Yezyaryshcha
Yezo *see* Hokkaidō
120 N11 **Yezyaryshcha** *Rus.* Yezerishche. Vitsyebskaya Voblasts', NE Belorussia
Yialí *see* Gyalí
Yialousa *see* Yenierenköy
169 V7 **Yi'an** Heilongjiang, NE China
Yiannitsá *see* Giannitsá
166 I10 **Yibin** Sichuan, C China
164 K13 **Yibug Caka** ◎ W China
166 M9 **Yichang** Hubei, C China
166 L5 **Yichuan** Shaanxi, C China
163 W3 **Yichun** Heilongjiang, NE China
169 X6 **Yichun** *var.* I-ch'un. Heilongjiang, NE China
167 O11 **Yichun** Jiangxi, S China
Yidu *see* Qingzhou
196 C15 **Yigo** NE Guam
167 Q5 **Yi He** ≈ E China
169 X8 **Yilan** Heilongjiang, NE China
142 C9 **Yıldız Dağları** ⛰ NW Turkey
142 L13 **Yıldızeli** Sivas, N Turkey
169 U4 **Yilehuli Shan** ⛰ NE China
169 S7 **Yimin He** ≈ NE China
165 W8 **Yinchuan** *var.* Yinch'uan, Yin-ch'uan, Yinchwan. Ningxia, N China
Yinchuanzhan *see* Xincheng
Yinchwan *see* Yinchuan
Yindu He *see* Indus
167 N14 **Yingde** Guangdong, S China
167 O7 **Ying He** ≈ C China
169 U13 **Yingkou** *var.* Ying-k'ou, Yingkow; *prev.* Newchwang, Niuchwang. Liaoning, NE China
Yingkow *see* Yingkou
167 N8 **Yingshan** Hubei, C China
167 P9 **Yingshan** Hubei, C China
167 Q10 **Yingtan** Jiangxi, S China
Yin-hsien *see* Ningbo
164 H5 **Yining** *var.* I-ning, *Uigh.* Gulja, Kuldja. Xinjiang Uygur Zizhiqu, NW China
166 K11 **Yinjiang** Guizhou, S China
177 Ff4 **Yinmabin** Sagaing, C Burma
169 N13 **Yin Shan** ⛰ N China
Yin-tu Ho *see* Indus
165 P15 **Yi'ong Zangbo** ≈ W China
Yioúra *see* Gyáros
83 J14 **Yirga 'Alem** *It.* Irgalem. S Ethiopia
63 E19 **Yi, Río** ≈ C Uruguay
83 E14 **Yirol** El Buhayrat, S Sudan
Yirshi *see* Yirxie
169 S8 **Yirxie** *prev.* Yirshi. Nei Mongol Zizhiqu, N China
167 Q5 **Yishui** Shandong, E China
Yisrael/Yisra'el *see* Israel
Yíthion *see* Gýtheio
Yitiaoshan *see* Jingtai
169 W10 **Yitong** Jilin, NE China
165 P5 **Yiwu** *var.* Aratürük. Xinjiang Uygur Zizhiqu, NW China
169 U12 **Yiwulü Shan** ⛰ N China
169 T12 **Yi Xian** Liaoning, NE China
167 N10 **Yiyang** Hunan, S China
167 Q10 **Yiyang** Jiangxi, S China
167 N13 **Yizhang** Hunan, S China
95 K19 **Yläne** Turku-Pori, SW Finland
95 L14 **Yli-Ii** Oulu, C Finland
95 L14 **Ylikiiminki** Oulu, C Finland
94 N13 **Yli-Kitka** ◎ NE Finland
95 K17 **Ylistaro** Vaasa, W Finland
94 K13 **Ylitornio** Lappi, NW Finland
95 L15 **Ylivieska** Oulu, W Finland
xxxv G7 **Y Llethr** ▲ NW Wales, UK
95 L18 **Ylöjärvi** Häme, SW Finland
97 N17 **Yngaren** ◎ C Sweden
xxxv J14 **Ynysybwl** Rhondda Cynon Taff, S Wales, UK
27 T12 **Yoakum** Texas, SW USA
79 X13 **Yobe** ◈ *state* NE Nigeria
172 Nn4 **Yobetsu-dake** △ Hokkaidō, NE Japan
176 Xx10 **Yobi** Irian Jaya, E Indonesia
82 L11 **Yoboki** C Djibouti
170 C12 **Yobuko** Saga, Kyūshū, SW Japan
24 M4 **Yockanookany River** ≈ Mississippi, S USA
24 L2 **Yocona River** ≈ Mississippi, S USA
176 Yy15 **Yodom** Irian Jaya, E Indonesia
174 Kk15 **Yogyakarta** *prev.* Djokjakarta, Jogjakarta, Jokyakarta. Jawa, C Indonesia
174 Kk16 **Yogyakarta** *off.* Daerah Istimewa Yogyakarta, *var.* Djokjakarta, Jogjakarta, Jokyakarta. ◈ *autonomous district* S Indonesia
172 O5 **Yoichi** Hokkaidō, NE Japan
44 G6 **Yojoa, Lago de** ◎ NW Honduras
81 G16 **Yokadouma** Est, SE Cameroon
171 H15 **Yōkaichi** *var.* Yôkaiti. Shiga, Honshū, SW Japan
Yôkaiti *see* Yōkaichi
171 H15 **Yokkaichi** *var.* Yokkaiti. Mie, Honshū, SW Japan
Yokkaiti *see* Yokkaichi
81 E15 **Yoko** Centre, C Cameroon
172 Qq12 **Yokoate-jima** *island* Nansei-shotō, SW Japan
172 N9 **Yokohama** Aomori, Honshū, C Japan
171 Jj16 **Yokohama** Kanagawa, Honshū, S Japan
171 Jj17 **Yokosuka** Kanagawa, Honshū, S Japan
170 F12 **Yokota** Shimane, Honshū, SW Japan
171 M11 **Yokote** Akita, Honshū, C Japan
172 Nn7 **Yokotsu-dake** ▲ Hokkaidō, NE Japan
79 Y14 **Yola** Adamawa, E Nigeria
81 L19 **Yolombo** Equateur, C Zaire
Yolöten *see* Yëloten
176 W10 **Yomber** Irian Jaya, E Indonesia
172 T16 **Yome-jima** *island* Ogasawara-shotō, SE Japan
78 K16 **Yomou** Guinée-Forestière, SE Guinea
176 Y15 **Yomuka** Irian Jaya, E Indonesia
196 C16 **Yona** E Guam
170 Ff12 **Yonago** Tottori, Honshū, SW Japan
172 O17 **Yonaguni** Okinawa, SW Japan
172 Nn16 **Yonaguni-jima** *island* Nansei-shotō, SW Japan
172 Pp14 **Yonaha-dake** ▲ Okinawa, SW Japan
169 X14 **Yonan** SW North Korea
171 L13 **Yonezawa** Yamagata, Honshū, C Japan
167 Q12 **Yong'an** *var.* Yongan. Fujian, SE China
165 T9 **Yongchang** Gansu, N China
167 P7 **Yongcheng** Henan, C China
169 Z15 **Yŏngch'ŏn** *Jap.* Eisen. SE South Korea
166 J10 **Yongchuan** Sichuan, C China
165 U10 **Yongdeng** Gansu, C China
133 W9 **Yongding He** ≈ E China
167 P11 **Yongfeng** Jiangxi, S China
164 L5 **Yongfengqu** Xinjiang Uygur Zizhiqu, W China
169 X13 **Yŏnghŭng** E North Korea
165 U10 **Yongjing** Gansu, C China
169 Y15 **Yŏngju** *Jap.* Eishū. C South Korea
Yongning *see* Xuyong
166 E12 **Yongping** Yunnan, SW China
166 G12 **Yongren** Yunnan, SW China
166 L10 **Yongshun** *var.* Lingxi. Hunan, S China
167 P10 **Yongxiu** *var.* Tujiabu. Jiangxi, S China
166 M12 **Yongzhou** Hunan, S China
20 K14 **Yonkers** New York, NE USA
105 Q7 **Yonne** ◈ *department* C France
105 P6 **Yonne** ≈ C France
56 H9 **Yopal** *var.* El Yopal. Casanare, C Colombia
164 E8 **Yopurga** *var.* Yukuriawat. Xinjiang Uygur Zizhiqu, NW China
xli T13 **York** *anc.* Eboracum, Eburacum. York, N England, UK
xli T13 **York** ◈ *unitary authority* N England, UK
188 J12 **York** Western Australia
25 N5 **York** Alabama, S USA
31 Q15 **York** Nebraska, C USA
20 G16 **York** Pennsylvania, NE USA
23 R11 **York** South Carolina, SE USA
12 J13 **York** ≈ Ontario, SE Canada
13 X6 **York** ≈ Québec, SE Canada
189 V1 **York, Cape** *headland* Queensland, NE Australia
190 I9 **Yorke Peninsula** *peninsula* South Australia
190 I9 **Yorketown** South Australia
21 P9 **York Harbor** Maine, NE USA
23 X6 **York River** ≈ Virginia, NE USA
99 M16 **Yorkshire** *cultural region* N England, UK
xli P10 **Yorkshire Dales** *physical region* N England, UK
9 V16 **Yorkton** Saskatchewan, S Canada
27 T12 **Yorktown** Texas, SW USA
23 X6 **Yorktown** Virginia, NE USA
32 M11 **Yorkville** Illinois, N USA
44 I5 **Yoro** Yoro, C Honduras
44 H5 **Yoro** ◈ *department* N Honduras
172 Pp14 **Yoron-jima** *island* Nansei-shotō, SW Japan
79 N13 **Yorosso** Sikasso, S Mali
37 R8 **Yosemite National Park** *national park* California, W USA
170 Ff14 **Yoshii-gawa** ≈ Honshū, SW Japan
170 Ff15 **Yoshino-gawa** *var.* Yosino Gawa. ≈ Shikoku, SW Japan
131 Q3 **Yoshkar-Ola** Respublika Mariy El, W Russian Federation
Yosino Gawa *see* Yoshino-gawa
176 Y15 **Yos Sudarso, Pulau** *var.* Pulau Dolak, Pulau Kolepom; *prev.* Jos Sudarso. *island* E Indonesia
176 Z10 **Yos Sudarso, Teluk** *bay* Irian Jaya, E Indonesia
169 Y17 **Yŏsu** *Jap.* Reisui. S South Korea
172 Nn5 **Yotei-zan** ▲ Hokkaidō, NE Japan
xliv H14 **Youghal** *Ir.* Eochaill. Cork, S Ireland
xliv H14 **Youghal Bay** *Ir.* Cuan Eochaille. *inlet* S Ireland
20 C15 **Youghiogheny River** ≈ Pennsylvania, NE USA
166 K14 **You Jiang** ≈ S China
xxxviii L6 **Youlgreave** Derbyshire, C England, UK
191 Q9 **Young** New South Wales, SE Australia
9 T15 **Young** Saskatchewan, S Canada
63 E18 **Young** Río Negro, W Uruguay
190 G5 **Younghusband, Lake** *salt lake* South Australia
190 J10 **Younghusband Peninsula** *peninsula* South Australia
192 Q10 **Young Nicks Head** *headland* North Island, NZ
193 D20 **Young Range** ⛰ South Island, NZ
203 Q15 **Young's Rock** *island* Pitcairn Island, Pitcairn Islands
9 R16 **Youngstown** Alberta, SW Canada
33 V12 **Youngstown** Ohio, N USA
165 N9 **Youshashan** Qinghai, C China
Youth, Isle of *see* Juventud, Isla de la
79 N11 **Youvarou** Mopti, C Mali
166 K10 **Youyang** Sichuan, C China
169 Y7 **Youyi** Heilongjiang, NE China
153 P13 **Yovon** *Rus.* Yavan. SW Tajikistan
xxxviii L9 **Yoxall** Staffordshire, C England, UK
xxxix Y11 **Yoxford** Suffolk, E England, UK
142 J13 **Yozgat** Yozgat, C Turkey
142 K13 **Yozgat** ◈ *province* C Turkey
64 O6 **Ypacaraí** *var.* Ypacaray. Central, S Paraguay
Ypacaray *see* Ypacaraí
64 P5 **Ypané, Río** ≈ C Paraguay
Ypres *see* Ieper
116 I13 **Ypsário** *var.* Ipsario. ▲ Thásos, E Greece
33 R10 **Ypsilanti** Michigan, N USA
36 M1 **Yreka** California, W USA
Yrendagüé *see* General Eugenio A. Garay
195 N8 **Ysabel Channel** *channel* N PNG
xxxv H6 **Ysbyty Ifan** Conwy, N Wales, UK
xxxv H10 **Ysbyty Ystwyth** Ceredigion, W Wales, UK
12 K8 **Yser, Lac** ◎ Québec, SE Canada
153 Y8 **Yshtyk** Issyk-Kul'skaya Oblast', E Kyrgyzstan
Yssel *see* IJssel
105 Q12 **Yssingeaux** Haute-Loire, C France
97 K23 **Ystad** Malmöhus, S Sweden
xxxv H13 **Ystalyfera** Neath Port Talbot, S Wales, UK
xxxv G11 **Ystrad Aeron** Ceredigion, W Wales, UK
xxxv I13 **Ystradfellte** Powys, C Wales, UK
xxxv H13 **Ystradgynlais** Powys, C Wales, UK
xxxv J14 **Ystrad Mynach** *var.* Ystrad-mynach. Caerphilly, SE Wales, UK
Ysyk-Köl *see* Balykchy, Kyrgyzstan
Ysyk-Köl *see* Issyk-Kul', Ozero, Kyrgyzstan
Ysyk-Köl Oblasty *see* Issyk-Kul'skaya Oblast'
xlii P12 **Ythan** ≈ NE Scotland, UK
Y Trallwng *see* Welshpool
96 C13 **Ytre Arna** Hordaland, S Norway
96 B12 **Ytre Sula** *island* S Norway
95 G17 **Ytterhogdal** Jämtland, C Sweden
126 M10 **Ytyk-Kyuyel'** Respublika Sakha (Yakutiya), NE Russian Federation
Yu *see* Henan
Yuan Jiang *see* Red River
167 S13 **Yüanlin** *Jap.* Inrin. C Taiwan
167 N3 **Yuanping** Shanxi, C China
167 O11 **Yuan Shui** ≈ S China
170 G16 **Yuasa** Wakayama, Honshū, SW Japan
194 H10 **Yuat** ≈ N PNG
37 O6 **Yuba City** California, W USA
172 Oo6 **Yūbari** Hokkaidō, NE Japan
172 P6 **Yūbari-sanchi** ⛰ Hokkaidō, NE Japan
37 O6 **Yuba River** ≈ California, W USA
82 H13 **Yubdo** W Ethiopia
172 Q5 **Yūbetsu** Hokkaidō, NE Japan
Yūbetsu-gawa *see* Yabetsu-gawa
43 X12 **Yucatán** ◈ *state* SE Mexico
49 O3 **Yucatan Basin** *var.* Yucatan Deep. *undersea feature* N Caribbean Sea
Yucatán, Canal de *see* Yucatan Channel
43 Y10 **Yucatan Channel** *Sp.* Canal de Yucatán. *channel* Cuba/Mexico
Yucatan Deep *see* Yucatan Basin
Yucatan Peninsula *see* Yucatán, Península de
43 X13 **Yucatán, Península de** *Eng.* Yucatan Peninsula. *peninsula* Guatemala/Mexico
38 I11 **Yucca** Arizona, SW USA
37 V15 **Yucca Valley** California, W USA
167 P4 **Yucheng** Shandong, E China
167 N4 **Yuci** Shanxi, C China
133 X5 **Yudoma** ≈ E Russian Federation
167 P12 **Yudu** Jiangxi, C China
Yue *see* Guangdong
166 M12 **Yuecheng Ling** ⛰ S China
189 P7 **Yuendumu** Northern Territory, N Australia
166 H10 **Yuexi** Sichuan, C China
167 N10 **Yueyang** Hunan, S China
129 U14 **Yug** Permskaya Oblast', NW Russian Federation
129 P13 **Yug** ≈ NW Russian Federation
127 N11 **Yugorenok** Respublika Sakha (Yakutiya), NE Russian Federation
125 F10 **Yugorsk** Khanty-Mansiyskiy Avtonomnyy Okrug, C Russian Federation
125 G6 **Yugorskiy Poluostrov** *peninsula* NW Russian Federation
114 M13 **Yugoslavia** *off.* Federal Republic of Yugoslavia, *SCr.* Jugoslavija, Savezna Republika Jugoslavija. ◆ *federal republic* SE Europe
152 K14 **Yugo-Vostochnyye Garagumy** *prev.* Yugo-Vostochnyye Karakumy. *desert* E Turkmenistan
Yugo-Vostochnyye Karakumy *see* Yugo-Vostochnyye Garagumy
167 S10 **Yuhuan Dao** *island* SE China
166 L14 **Yu Jiang** ≈ S China
127 Nn7 **Yukagirskoye Ploskogor'ye** *plateau* NE Russian Federation
120 L11 **Yukhavichy** *Rus.* Yukhovichi. Vitsyebskaya Voblasts', N Belorussia
130 J4 **Yukhnov** Kaluzhskaya Oblast', W Russian Federation
Yukhovichi *see* Yukhavichy
81 J20 **Yuki** *var.* Yuki Kengunda. Bandundu, W Zaire
Yuki Kengunda *see* Yuki
28 M10 **Yukon** Oklahoma, C USA
1 F4 **Yukon** ≈ Canada/USA
Yukon *see* Yukon Territory
41 S7 **Yukon Flats** *salt flat* Alaska, USA
14 F5 **Yukon Territory** *var.* Yukon, *Fr.* Territoire du Yukon. ◈ *territory* NW Canada
143 T16 **Yüksekova** Hakkâri, SE Turkey
126 Jj11 **Yukta** Evenkiyskiy Avtonomnyy Okrug, C Russian Federation
170 Dd13 **Yukuhashi** *var.* Yukuhasi. Fukuoka, Kyūshū, SW Japan
Yukuhasi *see* Yukuhashi
Yukuriawat *see* Yopurga
129 O9 **Yula** ≈ NW Russian Federation
189 P8 **Yulara** Northern Territory, N Australia
131 W6 **Yuldybayevo** Respublika Bashkortostan, W Russian Federation
25 W8 **Yulee** Florida, SE USA
164 K7 **Yuli** *var.* Lopnur. Xinjiang Uygur Zizhiqu, NW China
167 T14 **Yüli** C Taiwan
166 L15 **Yulin** Guangxi Zhuangzu Zizhiqu, S China
166 L4 **Yulin** Shaanxi, C China
167 T14 **Yüli Shan** ▲ E Taiwan
166 F11 **Yulongxue Shan** ▲ SW China
38 H14 **Yuma** Arizona, SW USA
39 W3 **Yuma** Colorado, C USA
56 K5 **Yumare** Yaracuy, N Venezuela
65 G14 **Yumbel** Bío Bío, C Chile
81 N19 **Yumbi** Maniema, E Zaire
165 R8 **Yumen** *var.* Laojunmiao, Yümen. Gansu, N China
165 Q7 **Yumenzhen** Gansu, N China
164 J3 **Yumin** Xinjiang Uygur Zizhiqu, NW China
Yun *see* Yunnan
142 G14 **Yunak** Konya, W Turkey
47 O8 **Yuna, Río** ≈ E Dominican Republic
40 I17 **Yunaska Island** *island* Aleutian Islands, Alaska, USA
166 M6 **Yuncheng** Shanxi, C China
59 L18 **Yungas** *physical region* E Bolivia
Yungki *see* Jilin
Yung-ning *see* Nanning
166 I12 **Yun Gui Gaoyuan** *plateau* SW China
Yunjinghong *see* Jinghong
166 M15 **Yunkai Dashan** ⛰ S China
Yunki *see* Jilin
166 E11 **Yun Ling** ⛰ SW China
167 N9 **Yunmeng** Hubei, C China
163 N14 **Yunnan** *var.* Yun, Yunnan Sheng, Yünnan, Yun-nan. ◈ *province* SW China
Yunnan *see* Kunming
Yunnan Sheng *see* Yunnan
170 Cc15 **Yunomae** Kumamoto, Kyūshū, SW Japan
167 N8 **Yun Shui** ≈ C China

◆ Country
● Country Capital
◇ Dependent Territory
○ Dependent Territory Capital
◈ Administrative Region
✈ International Airport
▲ Mountain
⛰ Mountain Range
△ Volcano
≈ River
◎ Lake
⊞ Reservoir

YUNTA – ZHUOZHOU

190 J7 **Yunta** South Australia
167 Q14 **Yunxiao** Fujian, SE China
166 K9 **Yunyang** Sichuan, C China
200 Nn10 **Yupanqui Basin** *undersea feature* E Pacific Ocean
Yuratishki *see* Yuratsishki
121 I15 **Yuratsishki** *Pol.* Juraciszki, *Rus.* Yuratishki. Hrodzyenskaya Voblasts', W Belorussia
Yurev *see* Tartu
126 H14 **Yurga** Kemerovskaya Oblast', S Russian Federation
58 E10 **Yurimaguas** Loreto, N Peru
131 P3 **Yurino** Respublika Mariy El, W Russian Federation
43 N13 **Yuriria** Guanajuato, C Mexico
129 T13 **Yurla** Komi-Permyatskiy Avtonomnyy Okrug, NW Russian Federation
Yuruá, Río *see* Juruá, Rio
116 M13 **Yürük** Tekirdağ, NW Turkey
164 G10 **Yurungkax He** ≈ W China
129 Q14 **Yur'ya** *var.* Jarja. Kirovskaya Oblast', NW Russian Federation
Yur'yev *see* Tartu
129 N16 **Yur'yevets** Ivanovskaya Oblast', W Russian Federation
130 M3 **Yur'yev-Pol'skiy** Vladimirskaya Oblast', W Russian Federation
119 V7 **Yur"yivka** Dnipropetrovs'ka Oblast', E Ukraine
126 K6 **Yuryung-Khaya** Respublika Sakha (Yakutiya), NE Russian Federation
44 I7 **Yuscarán** El Paraíso, S Honduras
167 P12 **Yu Shan** ▲ S China
128 I7 **Yushkozero** Respublika Kareliya, NW Russian Federation
165 R13 **Yushu** Qinghai, C China
131 P12 **Yusta** Respublika Kalmykiya, SW Russian Federation
128 I10 **Yustozero** Respublika Kareliya, NW Russian Federation
143 Q11 **Yusufeli** Artvin, NE Turkey
170 E15 **Yusuhara** Kōchi, Shikoku, SW Japan
129 T14 **Yus'va** Permskaya Oblast', NW Russian Federation
Yuta *see* Yatta
167 P2 **Yutian** Hebei, E China
164 H10 **Yutian** *var.* Keriya. Xinjiang Uygur Zizhiqu, NW China
64 K5 **Yuto** Jujuy, NW Argentina
64 P7 **Yuty** Caazapá, S Paraguay
166 G13 **Yuxi** Yunnan, SW China
167 O2 **Yuxian** *prev.* Yu Xian. Hebei, E China
171 M11 **Yuzawa** Akita, Honshū, C Japan
129 N16 **Yuzha** Ivanovskaya Oblast', W Russian Federation
Yuzhno-Alichurskiy Khrebet *see* Alichuri Janubí, Qatorkŭhi
Yuzhno-Kazakhstanskaya Oblast' *see* Yuzhnyy Kazakhstan
127 Oo15 **Yuzhno-Sakhalinsk** *Jap.* Toyohara; *prev.* Vladimirovka. Ostrov Sakhalin, Sakhalinskaya Oblast', SE Russian Federation
131 P14 **Yuzhno-Sukhokumsk** Respublika Dagestan, SW Russian Federation
125 Ee12 **Yuzhnoural'sk** Chelyabinskaya Oblast', C Russian Federation
126 I13 **Yuzhno-Yeniseyskiy** Krasnoyarskiy Kray, C Russian Federation
151 Z10 **Yuzhnyy Altay, Khrebet** ▲ E Kazakhstan
Yuzhnyy Bug *see* Pivdennyy Buh
151 O15 **Yuzhnyy Kazakhstan** *off.* Yuzhno-Kazakhstanskaya Oblast', *Eng.* South Kazakhstan, *Kaz.* Ongtüstik Qazaqstan Oblysy; *prev.* Chimkentskaya Oblast'. ◈ *province* S Kazakhstan
127 Oo10 **Yuzhnyy, Mys** *headland* E Russian Federation
131 W6 **Yuzhnyy Ural** *var.* Southern Urals. ▲ W Russian Federation
165 V10 **Yuzhong** Gansu, C China
Yuzhou *see* Chongqing
105 N5 **Yvelines** ◈ *department* N France
110 B9 **Yverdon** *var.* Yverdon-les-Bains, *Ger.* Iferten; *anc.* Eborodunum. Vaud, W Switzerland
Yverdon-les-Bains *see* Yverdon
104 M3 **Yvetot** Seine-Maritime, N France
Yylanly *see* Il'yaly

Z

153 T12 **Zaalayskiy Khrebet** *Taj.* Qatorkŭhi Pasi Oloy. ▲ Kyrgyzstan/Tajikistan
Zaamin *see* Zomin
Zaandam *see* Zaanstad
100 I10 **Zaanstad** *prev.* Zaandam. Noord-Holland, C Netherlands
Zabadani *see* Az Zabdānī
121 L18 **Zabalatstsye** *Rus.* Zabolot'ye. Homyel'skaya Voblasts', SE Belorussia
114 L9 **Žabalj** *Ger.* Josefsdorf, *Hung.* Zsablya; *prev.* Józseffalva;. Serbia, N Yugoslavia
Zāb aş Şaghīr, Nahraz *see* Little Zab
126 L16 **Zabaykal'sk** Chitinskaya Oblast', S Russian Federation
Zāb-e Kūchek, Rūdkhāneh-ye *see* Little Zab
Zabeln *see* Sabile
Zabéré *see* Zabré
Zabern *see* Saverne
147 N16 **Zabīd** W Yemen
147 O16 **Zabīd, Wādī** *dry watercourse* SW Yemen
Żabinka *see* Zhabinka
Ząbkowice *see* Ząbkowice Śląskie
113 G15 **Ząbkowice Śląskie** *var.* Ząbkowice, *Ger.* Frankenstein, Frankenstein in Schlesien. Wałbrzych, SW Poland
112 O10 **Zabłudów** Białystok, NE Poland
114 D8 **Zabok** Krapina-Zagorje, N Croatia
149 W9 **Zābol** *var.* Shahr-i-Zabul, Zabul; *prev.* Nasratabad. Sīstān va Balūchestān, E Iran
Zābol *see* Zābul
149 W13 **Zāboli** Sīstān va Balūchestān, SE Iran
Zabolot'ye *see* Zabalatstsye
79 Q13 **Zabré** *var.* Zabéré. S Burkina
113 G17 **Zábřeh** *Ger.* Hohenstadt. Severní Morava, E Czech Republic
113 J16 **Zabrze** *Ger.* Hindenburg, Hindenburg in Oberschlesien. Katowice, S Poland
155 O7 **Zābul** *Per.* Zābol. ◈ *province* SE Afghanistan
Zabul *see* Zābol
44 E6 **Zacapa** Zacapa, E Guatemala
44 A3 **Zacapa** *off.* Departamento de Zacapa. ◈ *department* E Guatemala
42 M14 **Zacapú** Michoacán de Ocampo, SW Mexico
43 V14 **Zacatal** Campeche, SE Mexico
42 M11 **Zacatecas** Zacatecas, C Mexico
42 L10 **Zacatecas** ◈ *state* C Mexico
44 F8 **Zacatecoluca** La Paz, S El Salvador
43 P15 **Zacatepec** Morelos, S Mexico
43 Q13 **Zacatlán** Puebla, S Mexico
150 F8 **Zachagansk** Zapadnyy Kazakhstan, NW Kazakhstan
117 D20 **Zacháro** *var.* Zaharo, Zakháro. Dytikí Ellás, S Greece
24 J8 **Zachary** Louisiana, S USA
119 U6 **Zachepylivka** Kharkivs'ka Oblast', E Ukraine
Zachist'ye *see* Zachystsye
121 L14 **Zachystsye** *Rus.* Zachist'ye. Minskaya Voblasts', NW Belorussia
42 L13 **Zacoalco** *var.* Zacoalco de Torres. Jalisco, SW Mexico
Zacoalco de Torres *see* Zacoalco
43 P13 **Zacualtipán** Hidalgo, C Mexico
114 C12 **Zadar** *It.* Zara; *anc.* Iader. Zadar-Knin, W Croatia
114 C12 **Zadar-Knin** *off.* Zadarsko-Kninska Županija. ◈ *province* SW Croatia
177 G14 **Zadetkyi Kyun** *var.* St. Matthew's Island. *island* Mergui Archipelago, S Burma
69 Q9 **Zadié** *var.* Djadié. ≈ NE Gabon
165 Q13 **Zadoi** Qinghai, C China
130 L7 **Zadonsk** Lipetskaya Oblast', W Russian Federation
77 X8 **Za'farâna** E Egypt
155 W7 **Zafarwāl** Punjab, E Pakistan
124 P1 **Zafer Burnu** *var.* Cape Andreas, Cape Apostolas Andreas, *Gk.* Akrotíri Apostólou Andréa. *headland* NE Cyprus
109 J23 **Zafferano, Capo** *headland* Sicilia, Italy, C Mediterranean Sea
116 M7 **Zafirovo** Razgradska Oblast, NE Bulgaria
117 L23 **Zaforá** *island* Kykládes, Greece, Aegean Sea
106 J12 **Zafra** Extremadura, W Spain
112 E13 **Żagań** *var.* Zagań, Żegań, *Ger.* Sagan. Zielona Góra, W Poland
120 F10 **Žagarė** *Pol.* Zagory. Joniškis, N Lithuania
77 W7 **Zagazig** *var.* Az Zaqāziq. N Egypt
76 M5 **Zaghouan** *var.* Zaghwān. NE Tunisia
Zaghwān *see* Zaghouan
117 G16 **Zagorá** Thessalía, C Greece
Zagorod'ye *see* Zaharoddzye
Żagory *see* Žagarė
Zágráb *see* Zagreb
114 E8 **Zagreb** *Ger.* Agram, *Hung.* Zágráb. ● (Croatia) Grad Zagreb, N Croatia
148 L7 **Zāgros, Kūhhā-ye** *Eng.* Zagros Mountains. ▲ W Iran
Zagros Mountains *see* Zāgros, Kūhhā-ye
114 O12 **Žagubica** Serbia, E Yugoslavia
113 L22 **Zagyva** ≈ N Hungary
Zaharo *see* Zacháro
121 G19 **Zaharoddzye** *Rus.* Zagorod'ye. *physical region* SW Belorussia
149 W11 **Zāhedān** *var.* Zahidan; *prev.* Duzdab. Sīstān va Balūchestān, SE Iran
Zahidan *see* Zāhedān
Zahlah *see* Zahlé
144 H7 **Zahlé** *var.* Zaḩlah. C Lebanon
Zāhmet *see* Zakhmet
113 O20 **Záhony** Szabolcs-Szatmár-Bereg, NE Hungary
147 N13 **Zahrān** 'Asīr, S Saudi Arabia
145 R12 **Zahrat al Baṭn** *hill range* S Iraq
123 I12 **Zahrez Chergui** *var.* Zahrez Chergúi. *marsh* N Algeria
131 S4 **Zainsk** Respublika Tatarstan, W Russian Federation
84 A10 **Zaire** *prev.* Congo. ◈ *province* NW Angola
Zaire *see* Congo
114 P13 **Zaječar** Serbia, E Yugoslavia
85 L18 **Zaka** Masvingo, E Zimbabwe
126 J16 **Zakamensk** Respublika Buryatiya, S Russian Federation
118 G7 **Zakarpats'ka Oblast'** *Eng.* Transcarpathian Oblast, *Rus.* Zakarpatskaya Oblast'. ◈ *province* W Ukraine
Zakarpatskaya Oblast' *see* Zakarpats'ka Oblast'
Zakataly *see* Zaqatala
Zakháro *see* Zacháro
Zakhidnyy Buh/Zakhodni Buh *see* Bug
152 J14 **Zakhmet** *Turkm.* Zähmet. Maryyskiy Velayat, C Turkmenistan
145 Q1 **Zākhō** *var.* Zākhū. N Iraq
Zākhū *see* Zākhō
Zákinthos *see* Zákynthos
113 L18 **Zakopane** Nowy Sącz, S Poland
80 J12 **Zakouma** Salamat, S Chad
117 L25 **Zákros** Kríti, Greece, E Mediterranean Sea
117 C19 **Zákynthos** *var.* Zákinthos. Zákynthos, W Greece
117 C20 **Zákynthos** *var.* Zákinthos, *It.* Zante. *island* Iónioi Nisoi, Greece, C Mediterranean Sea
117 C19 **Zakynthou, Porthmós** *strait* SW Greece
113 G24 **Zala** *off.* Zala Megye. ◈ *county* W Hungary
113 G24 **Zala** ≈ W Hungary
144 M4 **Zalābiyah** Dayr az Zawr, C Syria
113 G24 **Zalaegerszeg** Zala, W Hungary
106 K11 **Zalamea de la Serena** Extremadura, W Spain
106 J13 **Zalamea la Real** Andalucía, S Spain
169 U7 **Zalantun** *var.* Butha Qi. Nei Mongol Zizhiqu, N China
126 J15 **Zalari** Irkutskaya Oblast', S Russian Federation
113 G23 **Zalaszentgrót** Zala, SW Hungary
Zalatna *see* Zlatna
118 G9 **Zalău** *Ger.* Waltenberg, *Hung.* Zilah; *prev. Ger.* Zillenmarkt. Sălaj, NW Romania
111 V10 **Žalec** *Ger.* Sachsenfeld. C Slovenia
119 S9 **Zalenodol's'k** Dnipropetrovs'ka Oblast', E Ukraine
112 K8 **Zalewo** *Ger.* Saalfeld. Olsztyn, N Poland
147 N9 **Ẓalim** Makkah, W Saudi Arabia
82 A11 **Zalingei** *var.* Zalinje. Western Darfur, W Sudan
Zalinje *see* Zalingei
118 K7 **Zalishchyky** Ternopil's'ka Oblast', W Ukraine
Zallah *see* Zillah
100 J13 **Zaltbommel** Gelderland, C Netherlands
128 H15 **Zaluch'ye** Novgorodskaya Oblast', NW Russian Federation
Zamak *see* Zamakh
147 Q14 **Zamakh** *var.* Zamak. N Yemen
142 K15 **Zamantı Irmağı** ≈ C Turkey
Zambesi/Zambeze *see* Zambezi
85 G14 **Zambezi** North Western, W Zambia
85 K15 **Zambezi** *var.* Zambesi, *Port.* Zambeze. ≈ S Africa
85 O15 **Zambézia** *off.* Província da Zambézia. ◈ *province* C Mozambique
85 I14 **Zambia** *off.* Republic of Zambia; *prev.* Northern Rhodesia. ◆ *republic* S Africa
179 Q16 **Zamboanga** *off.* Zamboanga City. Mindanao, S Philippines
56 E5 **Zambrano** Bolívar, N Colombia
112 N10 **Zambrów** Łomża, E Poland
85 L14 **Zambué** Tete, NW Mozambique
79 T13 **Zamfara** ≈ NW Nigeria
Zamojskie, Województwo *see* Zamość
58 C9 **Zamora** Zamora Chinchipe, S Ecuador
106 K6 **Zamora** Castilla-León, NW Spain
106 K5 **Zamora** ◈ *province* Castilla-León, NW Spain
Zamora *see* Barinas
58 A13 **Zamora Chinchipe** ◈ *province* S Ecuador
42 M13 **Zamora de Hidalgo** Michoacán de Ocampo, SW Mexico
113 P15 **Zamość** *Rus.* Zamoste. Zamość, SE Poland
113 P15 **Zamość** *off.* Województwo Zamojskie, *Rus.* Zamoste. ◈ *province* SE Poland
Zamoste *see* Zamość
166 G7 **Zamtang** *prev.* Gamda. Sichuan, C China
77 O8 **Zamzam, Wādī** *dry watercourse* NW Libya
81 F20 **Zanaga** La Lékoumou, S Congo
43 T16 **Zanatepec** Oaxaca, SE Mexico
107 S9 **Záncara** ≈ C Spain
Zancle *see* Messina
164 G14 **Zanda** Xizang Zizhiqu, W China
100 H10 **Zandvoort** Noord-Holland, W Netherlands
41 P8 **Zane Hills** *hill range* Alaska, USA
33 T13 **Zanesville** Ohio, N USA
148 L4 **Zanjān** *var.* Zenjan, Zinjan. Zanjān, NW Iran
148 L4 **Zanjān** *off.* Ostān-e Zanjān, *var.* Zenjan, Zinjan. ◈ *province* NW Iran
Zante *see* Zákynthos
83 J22 **Zanzibar** Zanzibar, E Tanzania
83 J22 **Zanzibar** *Swa.* Unguja. *island* E Tanzania
83 J22 **Zanzibar Channel** *channel* E Tanzania
83 J22 **Zanzibar North** ◈ *region* E Tanzania
83 J22 **Zanzibar South** ◈ *region* E Tanzania
83 J22 **Zanzibar West** ◈ *region* E Tanzania
171 L13 **Zaō-san** ▲ Honshū, C Japan
167 N8 **Zaoyang** Hubei, C China
126 I14 **Zaozernyy** Krasnoyarskiy Kray, S Russian Federation
167 Q6 **Zaozhuang** Shandong, E China
30 L4 **Zap** North Dakota, N USA
114 L13 **Zapadna Morava** *Ger.* Westliche Morava. ≈ C Yugoslavia
128 H16 **Zapadnaya Dvina** Tverskaya Oblast', W Russian Federation
Zapadnaya Dvina *see* Western Dvina
113 H20 **Západné Slovensko** ◈ *region* W Slovakia
113 A17 **Západní Čechy** *off.* Západočeský Kraj. ◈ *region* W Czech Republic
126 H10 **Zapadno-Sibirskaya Ravnina** *Eng.* West Siberian Plain. *plain* C Russian Federation
Zapadnyy Bug *see* Bug
150 E9 **Zapadnyy Kazakhstan** *off.* Zapadno-Kazakhstanskaya Oblast', *Eng.* West Kazakhstan, *Kaz.* Batys Qazaqstan Oblysy; *prev.* Ural'skaya Oblast'. ◈ *province* NW Kazakhstan
126 Hh15 **Zapadnyy Sayan** *Eng.* Western Sayans. ▲ S Russian Federation
65 H15 **Zapala** Neuquén, W Argentina
64 I4 **Zapaleri, Cerro** *var.* Cerro Sapaleri. ▲ N Chile
27 Q16 **Zapata** Texas, SW USA
46 D5 **Zapata, Península de** *peninsula* W Cuba
63 G19 **Zapicán** Lavalleja, S Uruguay
67 J19 **Zapiola Ridge** *undersea feature* SW Atlantic Ocean
67 L19 **Zapiola Seamount** *undersea feature* S Atlantic Ocean
128 I2 **Zapolyarnyy** Murmanskaya Oblast', NW Russian Federation
119 U8 **Zaporizhzhya** *Rus.* Zaporozh'ye; *prev.* Aleksandrovsk. Zaporiz'ka Oblast', SE Ukraine
Zaporizhzhya *see* Zaporiz'ka Oblast'
119 U9 **Zaporiz'ka Oblast'** *var.* Zaporizhzhya, *Rus.* Zaporozhskaya Oblast'. ◈ *province* SE Ukraine
Zaporozhskaya Oblast' *see* Zaporiz'ka Oblast'
Zaporozh'ye *see* Zaporizhzhya
42 L14 **Zapotiltic** Jalisco, SW Mexico
164 G13 **Zapug** Xizang Zizhiqu, W China
143 V10 **Zaqatala** *Rus.* Zakataly. NW Azerbaijan
165 P13 **Zaqên** Qinghai, W China
165 Q13 **Za Qu** ≈ C China
142 M13 **Zara** Sivas, C Turkey
Zara *see* Zadar
Zarafshan *see* Zarafshon
153 P12 **Zarafshon** *Rus.* Zeravshan. W Tajikistan
152 L9 **Zarafshon** *Rus.* Zarafshan. Nawoiy Wiloyati, N Uzbekistan
Zarafshon *see* Zeravshan
153 O12 **Zarafshon, Qatorkŭhi** *Rus.* Zeravshanskiy Khrebet, *Uzb.* Zarafshon Tizmasi. ▲ Tajikistan/Uzbekistan
Zarafshon Tizmasi *see* Zarafshon, Qatorkŭhi
56 E7 **Zaragoza** Antioquia, N Colombia
42 I5 **Zaragoza** Chihuahua, N Mexico
43 N6 **Zaragoza** Coahuila de Zaragoza, NE Mexico
43 O10 **Zaragoza** Nuevo León, NE Mexico
107 R5 **Zaragoza** *Eng.* Saragossa; *anc.* Caesaraugusta, Salduba. Aragón, NE Spain
107 R6 **Zaragoza** ◈ *province* Aragón, NE Spain
107 R5 **Zaragoza** ✈ Aragón, NE Spain
149 S10 **Zarand** Kermān, C Iran
154 J9 **Zaranj** Nīmrūz, SW Afghanistan
120 I11 **Zarasai** Zarasai, E Lithuania
64 N12 **Zárate** *prev.* General José F.Uriburu. Buenos Aires, E Argentina
107 Q2 **Zarautz** *var.* Zarauz. País Vasco, N Spain
Zarauz *see* Zarautz
Zaravecchia *see* Biograd na Moru
Zarāyīn *see* Zarēn
130 L4 **Zaraysk** Moskovskaya Oblast', W Russian Federation
57 N6 **Zaraza** Guárico, N Venezuela
Zarbdar *see* Zarbdor
153 P11 **Zarbdor** *Rus.* Zarbdar. Jizzakh Wiloyati, C Uzbekistan
148 M8 **Zard Kūh** ▲ SW Iran
128 I5 **Zarechensk** Murmanskaya Oblast', NW Russian Federation
155 Q7 **Zareh Sharan** Paktīkā, E Afghanistan
41 Y14 **Zarembo Island** *island* Alexander Archipelago, Alaska, USA
145 V4 **Zarēn** *var.* Zarāyīn. E Iraq
155 Q7 **Zarghūn Shahr** *var.* Katawaz. Paktīkā, SE Afghanistan
79 V13 **Zaria** Kaduna, C Nigeria
118 K2 **Zarichne** Rivnens'ka Oblast', NW Ukraine
126 H14 **Zarinsk** Altayskiy Kray, S Russian Federation
118 J12 **Zărneşti** *Hung.* Zernest. Braşov, C Romania
117 J25 **Zarós** Kríti, Greece, E Mediterranean Sea
102 O9 **Zarow** ≈ NE Germany
Zarqa/Zarqā', Muḩāfaẓat az *see* Az Zarqā'
113 G20 **Záruby** ▲ W Slovakia
58 B8 **Zaruma** El Oro, SW Ecuador
112 E13 **Żary** *Ger.* Sorau, Sorau in der Niederlausitz. Zielona Góra, W Poland
56 D10 **Zarzal** Valle del Cauca, W Colombia
44 I7 **Zarzalar, Cerro** ▲ S Honduras
158 I5 **Zāskār** ≈ NE India
158 I5 **Zāskār Range** ▲ NE India
121 K15 **Zaslawye** Minskaya Voblasts', C Belorussia
118 K7 **Zastavna** Chernivets'ka Oblast', W Ukraine
113 B16 **Žatec** *Ger.* Saaz. Severní Čechy, NW Czech Republic
Zaumgarten *see* Chrzanów
152 G10 **Zaunguzskiye Garagumy** *Turkm.* Üngüz Angyrsyndaky Garagum. *desert* N Turkmenistan
27 X9 **Zavalla** Texas, SW USA
101 H18 **Zaventem** Vlaams Brabant, C Belgium
101 H18 **Zaventem** ✈ (Brussel/Bruxelles) Vlaams Brabant, C Belgium
Zavertse *see* Zawiercie
116 L7 **Zavet** Razgradska Oblast, NE Bulgaria
131 O12 **Zavetnoye** Rostovskaya Oblast', SW Russian Federation
162 M3 **Zavhan Gol** ≈ W Mongolia
114 H12 **Zavidovići** N Bosnia and Herzegovina
126 Mm16 **Zavitinsk** Amurskaya Oblast', SE Russian Federation
125 F12 **Zavodoukovsk** Tyumenskaya Oblast', C Russian Federation
Zawia *see* Az Zāwiyah
113 K15 **Zawiercie** *Rus.* Zavertse. Katowice, S Poland
77 P11 **Zawīlah** *var.* Zuwaylah, *It.* Zueila. C Libya
144 I4 **Zāwiyah, Jabal az** ▲ NW Syria
111 Y3 **Zaya** ≈ NE Austria
177 G8 **Zayatkyi** Pegu, C Burma
151 Y11 **Zaysan** Vostochnyy Kazakhstan, E Kazakhstan
Zaysan Köl *see* Zaysan, Ozero
151 Y11 **Zaysan, Ozero** *Kaz.* Zaysan Köl. ◎ E Kazakhstan
165 R16 **Zayü** *var.* Gyigang. Xizang Zizhiqu, W China
Zayyq *see* Ural
46 F6 **Zaza** ≈ C Cuba
118 K5 **Zbarazh** Ternopil's'ka Oblast', W Ukraine
118 J5 **Zboriv** Ternopil's'ka Oblast', W Ukraine
113 F18 **Zbraslav** Jižní Morava, SE Czech Republic
118 K6 **Zbruch** ≈ W Ukraine
Žďár *see* Žďár nad Sázavou
113 F17 **Žďár nad Sázavou** *Ger.* Saar in Mähren; *prev.* Žďár. Jižní Morava, C Czech Republic
118 K4 **Zdolbuniv** *Pol.* Zdolbunów, *Rus.* Zdolbunov. Rivnens'ka Oblast', NW Ukraine
Zdolbunov/Zdolbunów *see* Zdolbuniv
112 J13 **Zduńska Wola** Sieradz, C Poland
119 O4 **Zdvizh** ≈ N Ukraine
Zdzięciół *see* Dzyatlava
113 I16 **Zdzieszowice** *Ger.* Odertal. Opole, SW Poland
Zealand *see* Sjælland
196 K6 **Zealandia Bank** *undersea feature* C Pacific Ocean
65 H20 **Zeballos, Monte** ▲ S Argentina
85 K20 **Zebediela** Northern, NE South Africa
115 L18 **Zebë, Mal** *var.* Mali i Zebës. ▲ NE Albania
Zebës, Mali i *see* Zebë, Mal
23 V9 **Zebulon** North Carolina, SE USA
114 K8 **Žednik** *Hung.* Bácsjózseffalva. Serbia, N Yugoslavia
101 C15 **Zeebrugge** West-Vlaanderen, NW Belgium
191 N16 **Zeehan** Tasmania, SE Australia
101 L14 **Zeeland** Noord-Brabant, SE Netherlands
31 N7 **Zeeland** North Dakota, N USA
101 E14 **Zeeland** ◈ *province* SW Netherlands
85 I21 **Zeerust** North-West, N South Africa
100 K10 **Zeewolde** Flevoland, C Netherlands
144 G8 **Ẕefat** *var.* Safed, *Ar.* Safad. Northern, N Israel
Żegań *see* Żagań
Zehden *see* Cedynia
102 O11 **Zehdenick** Brandenburg, NE Germany
Zē-i Bādīnān *see* Great Zab
Zeiden *see* Codlea
152 M14 **Zeidskoye Vodokhranilishche** ⊠ E Turkmenistan
Zē-i Kōya *see* Little Zab
189 P7 **Zeil, Mount** ▲ Northern Territory, C Australia
100 J12 **Zeist** Utrecht, C Netherlands
103 M16 **Zeitz** Sachsen-Anhalt, E Germany
165 T11 **Zêkog** Qinghai, C China
Zelaya Norte *see* Atlántico Norte, Región Autónoma
Zelaya Sur *see* Atlántico Sur, Región Autónoma
101 F17 **Zele** Oost-Vlaanderen, NW Belgium
112 N12 **Żelechów** Siedlce, E Poland
115 H14 **Zelena Glava** ▲ SE Bosnia and Herzegovina
115 I14 **Zelengora** ▲ S Bosnia and Herzegovina
128 I5 **Zelenoborskiy** Murmanskaya Oblast', NW Russian Federation
131 R3 **Zelenodol'sk** Respublika Tatarstan, W Russian Federation
128 G12 **Zelenogorsk** *Fin.* Terijoki. Leningradskaya Oblast', NW Russian Federation
130 K3 **Zelenograd** Moskovskaya Oblast', W Russian Federation
120 B13 **Zelenogradsk** *Ger.* Cranz, Kranz. Kaliningradskaya Oblast', W Russian Federation
131 O15 **Zelenokumsk** Stavropol'skiy Kray, SW Russian Federation
172 Rr7 **Zelënyy, Ostrov** *var.* Shibotsu-jima. *island* NE Russian Federation
Železna Kapela *see* Eisenkappel
Železna Vrata *see* Demir Kapija
114 L11 **Železniki** Serbia, N Yugoslavia
100 N12 **Zelhem** Gelderland, E Netherlands
115 N18 **Želino** NW FYR Macedonia
115 M14 **Željin** ▲ C Yugoslavia
103 K17 **Zella-Mehlis** Thüringen, C Germany
111 P7 **Zell am See** *var.* Zell-am-See. Salzburg, S Austria
111 N7 **Zell am Ziller** Tirol, W Austria
Zelle *see* Celle
111 W2 **Zellerndorf** Niederösterreich, NE Austria
111 U7 **Zeltweg** Steiermark, S Austria
121 G17 **Zel'va** *Pol.* Zelwa. Hrodzyenskaya Voblasts', W Belorussia
120 H13 **Želva** Ukmergė, C Lithuania
Zelwa *see* Zel'va
101 E16 **Zelzate** *var.* Selzaete. Oost-Vlaanderen, NW Belgium
120 E11 **Žemaičių Aukštumas** *physical region* W Lithuania
120 C12 **Žemaičių Naumiestis** Šilutė, SW Lithuania
Zembin *see* Zyembin
131 N6 **Zemetchino** Penzenskaya Oblast', W Russian Federation
81 M15 **Zémio** Haut-Mbomou, E Central African Republic
43 R16 **Zempoaltepec, Cerro** ▲ SE Mexico
101 G17 **Zemst** Vlaams Brabant, C Belgium
114 L11 **Zemun** Serbia, N Yugoslavia
Zendajan *see* Zendeh Jan
154 J5 **Zendeh Jan** *var.* Zendajan, Zindajān. Herāt, NW Afghanistan
Zengg *see* Senj
114 H12 **Zenica** C Bosnia and Herzegovina
Zenjan *see* Zanjān
Zen'kov *see* Zin'kiv
Zenshū *see* Chŏnju
Zenta *see* Senta
170 Ff14 **Zentsūji** *var.* Zentûzi. Kagawa, Shikoku, SW Japan
Zentûzi *see* Zentsūji
84 B11 **Zenza do Itombe** Cuanza Norte, NW Angola
114 H12 **Žepče** N Bosnia and Herzegovina
25 W12 **Zephyrhills** Florida, SE USA
199 J10 **Zephyr Reef** *reef* Antarctica
164 F9 **Zepu** *var.* Poskam. Xinjiang Uygur Zizhiqu, NW China
153 Q12 **Zeravshan** *Taj./Uzb.* Zarafshon. ≈ Tajikistan/Uzbekistan
Zeravshan *see* Zarafshon
Zeravshanskiy Khrebet *see* Zarafshon, Qatorkŭhi
103 M14 **Zerbst** Sachsen-Anhalt, E Germany
151 P8 **Zerenda** Kokshetau, N Kazakhstan
112 H12 **Żerków** Kalisz, C Poland
110 E11 **Zermatt** Valais, SW Switzerland
Zernest *see* Zărneşti
110 J9 **Zernez** Graubünden, SE Switzerland
130 L12 **Zernograd** Rostovskaya Oblast', SW Russian Federation
Zestafoni *see* Zestap'oni
143 S9 **Zestap'oni** *Rus.* Zestafoni. C Georgia
100 H12 **Zestienhoven** ✈ (Rotterdam) Zuid-Holland, SW Netherlands
115 J16 **Zeta** ≈ SW Yugoslavia
15 J2 **Zeta Lake** ◎ Victoria Island, Northwest Territories, N Canada
100 L12 **Zetten** Gelderland, SE Netherlands
103 M17 **Zeulenroda** Thüringen, C Germany
102 H10 **Zeven** Niedersachsen, NW Germany
100 M12 **Zevenaar** Gelderland, SE Netherlands
101 H14 **Zevenbergen** Noord-Brabant, S Netherlands
126 M14 **Zeya** Amurskaya Oblast', SE Russian Federation
133 X6 **Zeya** ≈ SE Russian Federation
Zeya Reservoir *see* Zeyskoye Vodokhranilishche
149 T11 **Zeynalābād** Kermān, C Iran
126 M14 **Zeyskoye Vodokhranilishche** *Eng.* Zeya Reservoir. ⊠ SE Russian Federation
106 H8 **Zêzere** ≈ C Portugal
Zgerzh *see* Zgierz
144 H6 **Zgharta** N Lebanon
112 K12 **Zgierz** *Ger.* Neuhof, *Rus.* Zgerzh. Łódź, C Poland
113 E14 **Zgorzelec** *Ger.* Görlitz. Jelenia Góra, SW Poland
Zhabdün *see* Zhongba
121 F19 **Zhabinka** *Pol.* Żabinka, *Rus.* Zhabinka. Brestskaya Voblasts', SW Belorussia
Zhaggo *see* Luhuo
165 R15 **Zhag'yab** Xizang Zizhiqu, W China
150 L9 **Zhailma** *Kaz.* Zhayylma. Kustanay, N Kazakhstan
151 V16 **Zhalanash** Almaty, SE Kazakhstan
Zhalashash *see* Dzhalagash
151 S7 **Zhalauly, Ozero** ◎ NE Kazakhstan
121 G16 **Zhaludok** *Rus.* Zheludok. Hrodzyenskaya Voblasts', W Belorussia
Zhaman-Akkol', Ozero *see* Akkol', Ozero
151 R16 **Zhambyl** *prev.* Aulie Ata, Auliye-Ata, Dzhambul. Zhambyl, S Kazakhstan
151 Q14 **Zhambyl** *off.* Zhambylskaya Oblast', *Kaz.* Zhambyl Oblysy; *prev.* Dzhambulskaya Oblast'. ◈ *province* S Kazakhstan
Zhambyl Oblysy/Zhambylskaya Oblast' *see* Zhambyl
Zhamo *see* Bomi
151 S12 **Zhamshy** ≈ C Kazakhstan
150 M15 **Zhanadar'ya** Kzyl-Orda, S Kazakhstan
151 O15 **Zhanakorgan** *Kaz.* Zhangaqorghan. Kzyl-Orda, S Kazakhstan
165 N16 **Zhanang** Xizang Zizhiqu, W China
151 T12 **Zhanaortalyk** Zhezkazgan, C Kazakhstan
151 Q16 **Zhanatas** Zhambyl, S Kazakhstan
Zhangaözen *see* Novyy Uzen'
Zhangaqazaly *see* Novokazalinsk
Zhangaqorghan *see* Zhanakorgan
167 O2 **Zhangbei** Hebei, E China
Zhangdian *see* Zibo
169 X9 **Zhangguangcai Ling** ▲ NE China
151 W10 **Zhangiztobe** Semipalatinsk, E Kazakhstan
165 W11 **Zhangjiachuan** Gansu, N China
166 L10 **Zhangjiajie** *var.* Dayong. Hunan, S China
167 O2 **Zhangjiakou** *var.* Changkiakow, Zhang-chia-k'ou, *Eng.* Kalgan; *prev.* Wanchuan. Hebei, E China
167 Q13 **Zhangping** Fujian, SE China
167 Q13 **Zhangpu** Fujian, SE China
169 U11 **Zhangwu** Liaoning, NE China
165 S8 **Zhangye** Gansu, N China
167 Q13 **Zhangzhou** Fujian, SE China
169 W6 **Zhan He** ≈ NE China
Zhänibek *see* Dzhanibek
166 L16 **Zhanjiang** *var.* Chanchiang, Chan-chiang, *Cant.* Tsamkong, *Fr.* Fort-Bayard. Guangdong, S China
Zhansügirov *see* Dzhansugurov
169 V8 **Zhaodong** Heilongjiang, NE China
Zhaoge *see* Qixian
166 H11 **Zhaojue** Sichuan, C China
167 N14 **Zhaoqing** Guangdong, S China
164 H5 **Zhaosu** *var.* Mongolküre. Xinjiang Uygur Zizhiqu, NW China
166 H11 **Zhaotong** Yunnan, SW China
169 V9 **Zhaoyuan** Heilongjiang, NE China
169 V9 **Zhaozhou** Heilongjiang, NE China
151 X13 **Zharbulak** Semipalatinsk, E Kazakhstan
164 J15 **Zhari Namco** ◎ W China
150 I12 **Zharkamys** *Kaz.* Zharqamys. Aktyubinsk, W Kazakhstan
151 W15 **Zharkent** *prev.* Panfilov. Taldykorgan, SE Kazakhstan
128 H17 **Zharkovskiy** Tverskaya Oblast', W Russian Federation
151 W11 **Zharma** Semipalatinsk, E Kazakhstan
150 F14 **Zharmysh** Mangistau, SW Kazakhstan
Zharqamys *see* Zharkamys
121 N14 **Zhary** *Rus.* Zhary. Vitsyebskaya Voblasts', N Belorussia
Zhaslyk *see* Jasliq
126 Ll11 **Zhatay** Respublika Sakha (Yakutiya), NE Russian Federation
164 J14 **Zhaxi Co** ◎ W China
Zhayylma *see* Zhailma
Zhdanov *see* Beyläqan, Azerbaijan
Zhdanov *see* Mariupol', Ukraine
Zhe *see* Zhejiang
167 R10 **Zhejiang** *var.* Che-chiang, Chekiang, Zhe, Zhejiang Sheng. ◈ *province* SE China
Zhejiang Sheng *see* Zhejiang
151 S7 **Zhelezinka** Pavlodar, N Kazakhstan
121 C14 **Zheleznodorozhnyy** *Ger.* Gerdauen. Kaliningradskaya Oblast', W Russian Federation
126 J13 **Zheleznodorozhnyy** Irkutskaya Oblast', C Russian Federation
Zheleznodorozhnyy *see* Yemva
130 J7 **Zheleznogorsk** Kurskaya Oblast', W Russian Federation
126 Jj14 **Zheleznogorsk-Ilimskiy** Irkutskaya Oblast', C Russian Federation
131 N15 **Zheleznovodsk** Stavropol'skiy Kray, SW Russian Federation
Zhëltyye Vody *see* Zhovti Vody
Zheludok *see* Zhaludok
Zhem *see* Emba
166 K7 **Zhenba** Shaanxi, C China
166 I13 **Zhenfeng** Guizhou, S China
Zhengjiatun *see* Shuangliao
165 X10 **Zhengning** Gansu, N China
169 Q12 **Zhengxiangbai Qi** Nei Mongol Zizhiqu, N China
167 N6 **Zhengzhou** *var.* Ch'eng-chou, Chengchow; *prev.* Chenghsien. Henan, C China
167 R8 **Zhenjiang** *var.* Chenkiang. Jiangsu, E China
169 U9 **Zhenlai** Jilin, NE China
166 I11 **Zhenxiong** Yunnan, SW China
166 K11 **Zhenyuan** *prev.* Wuyang. Guizhou, S China
167 R11 **Zherong** Fujian, SE China
Zhetiqara *see* Dzhetygara
150 F15 **Zhetybay** Mangistau, SW Kazakhstan
166 M11 **Zhexi Shuiku** ⊠ C China
151 O12 **Zhezdy** Zhezkazgan, C Kazakhstan
151 O12 **Zhezkazgan** *Kaz.* Zhezqazghan; *prev.* Dzhezkazgan. Zhezkazgan, C Kazakhstan
151 O13 **Zhezkazgan** *off.* Zhezkazganskaya Oblast', *Kaz.* Zhezqazghan Oblysy; *prev.* Dzhezkazganskaya Oblast'. ◈ *province* C Kazakhstan
Zhezkazganskaya Oblast'/Zhezqazghan/Zhezqazghan Oblysy *see* Zhezkazgan
166 M9 **Zhicheng** Hubei, C China
Zhidachov *see* Zhydachiv
165 Q12 **Zhidoi** Qinghai, C China
126 Jj15 **Zhigalovo** Irkutskaya Oblast', S Russian Federation
126 L9 **Zhigansk** Respublika Sakha (Yakutiya), NE Russian Federation
131 R6 **Zhigulevsk** Samarskaya Oblast', W Russian Federation
120 D13 **Zhilino** *Ger.* Schillen. Kaliningradskaya Oblast', W Russian Federation
131 O8 **Zhirnovsk** Volgogradskaya Oblast', SW Russian Federation
Zhitarovo *see* Vetren
Zhitkovichi *see* Zhytkavichy
131 P10 **Zhitkur** Volgogradskaya Oblast', SW Russian Federation
Zhitomir *see* Zhytomyr
Zhitomirskaya Oblast' *see* Zhytomyrs'ka Oblast'
130 J5 **Zhizdra** Kaluzhskaya Oblast', W Russian Federation
121 N18 **Zhlobin** Homyel'skaya Voblasts', SE Belorussia
Zhmerinka *see* Zhmerynka
118 M7 **Zhmerynka** *Rus.* Zhmerinka. Vinnyts'ka Oblast', C Ukraine
155 R9 **Zhob** *var.* Fort Sandeman. Baluchistān, SW Pakistan
155 R8 **Zhob** ≈ C Pakistan
Zhodino *see* Zhodzina
121 L15 **Zhodzina** *Rus.* Zhodino. Minskaya Voblasts', C Belorussia
126 Mm3 **Zhokhova, Ostrov** *island* Novosibirskiye Ostrova, NE Russian Federation
Zholkev/Zholkva *see* Zhovkva
Zholsaly *see* Dzhusaly
Zhondor *see* Jondor
164 I15 **Zhongba** *var.* Zhabdün. Xizang Zizhiqu, W China
166 F11 **Zhongdian** Yunnan, SW China
Zhonghua Renmin Gongheguo *see* China
165 V9 **Zhongning** Ningxia, N China
167 N15 **Zhongshan** Guangdong, S China
205 X7 **Zhongshan** *Chinese research station* Antarctica
166 M6 **Zhongtiao Shan** ▲ C China
165 V9 **Zhongwei** Ningxia, N China
166 K9 **Zhongxian** *var.* Zhong Xian. Sichuan, C China
167 N9 **Zhongxiang** Hubei, C China
167 O7 **Zhoukou** *var.* Zhoukouzhen. Henan, C China
Zhoukouzhen *see* Zhoukou
167 S9 **Zhoushan** Zhejiang, S China
167 S9 **Zhoushan Qundao** *Eng.* Zhoushan Islands. *island group* SE China
118 I5 **Zhovkva** *Pol.* Żółkiew, *Rus.* Zholkev, Zholkva; *prev.* Nesterov. L'vivs'ka Oblast', NW Ukraine
119 S7 **Zhovti Vody** *Rus.* Zhëltyye Vody. Dnipropetrovs'ka Oblast', E Ukraine
119 Q10 **Zhovtneve** *Rus.* Zhovtnevoye. Mykolayivs'ka Oblast', S Ukraine
Zhovtnevoye *see* Zhovtneve
116 K9 **Zhrebchevo, Yazovir** ⊠ C Bulgaria
169 V13 **Zhuanghe** Liaoning, NE China
165 W11 **Zhuanglang** Gansu, C China
151 P15 **Zhuantobe** *Kaz.* Zhūantöbe. Yuzhnyy Kazakhstan, S Kazakhstan
167 Q5 **Zhucheng** Shandong, E China
165 V12 **Zhugqu** Gansu, C China
167 N15 **Zhuhai** Guangdong, S China
Zhuizishan *see* Weichang
Zhuji *see* Shangqiu
130 I5 **Zhukovka** Bryanskaya Oblast', W Russian Federation
167 O3 **Zhuozhou** *prev.* Zhuo Xian. Hebei, E China

◆ Country ● Country Capital ◇ Dependent Territory ○ Dependent Territory Capital ◈ Administrative Region ✈ International Airport ▲ Mountain ▲ Mountain Range ▲ Volcano ≈ River ◎ Lake ⊠ Reservoir

Key

◆ COUNTRY   ◇ DEPENDENT TERRITORY   ᴧ ADMINISTRATIVE REGION   ▲ MOUNTAIN   ᴧ VOLCANO   ◎ LAKE

● COUNTRY CAPITAL   ○ DEPENDENT TERRITORY CAPITAL   × INTERNATIONAL AIRPORT   ᴧ MOUNTAIN RANGE   ≈ RIVER   ⊞ RESERVOIR

PICTURE CREDITS

DORLING KINDERSLEY *would like to express their thanks to the following individuals, companies and institutions for their help in preparing this atlas.*

Earth Resource Mapping Ltd., *Egham, Surrey*

Brian Groombridge, World Conservation Monitoring Centre, *Cambridge*

The British Library, *London*

British Library of Political and Economic Science, *London*

The British Museum, *London*

The City Business Library, *London*

King's College, *London*

National Meteorological Library and Archive, *Bracknell*

The Printed Word, *London*

The Royal Geographical Society, *London*

University of London Library

Paul Beardmore
Philip Boyes
Hayley Crockford
Alistair Dougal
Reg Grant
Louise Keane
Zoe Livesley
Laura Porter
Andy Summers

Every effort has been made to trace the copyright holders and we apologize in advance for any unintentional omissions. We would be pleased to insert the appropriate acknowledgement in any subsequent edition of this publication.

Adams Picture Library: 88CLA. **G. Andrews:** 194CR. **Ardea, London Ltd:** K. Ghana 156C; M. Iijima 140TC; R. Waller 154TCR. **Aspect Picture Library:** P. Carmichael 137CRB, 166TR; G. Tompkinson 202CRA. **Axiom Photographic Agency:** C. Bradley 154CA, 165CA; J. Holmes xiv CRA, xxxvii CRB, xxiv BCR, 156TCR, 172TL, 172BR; J. Morris 77TL, 77CRB; J. Spaull 134BL. **Bridgeman Art Library:** Collection of the Earl of Pembroke, Wilton House xx BC. **J. Allan Cash Ltd:** 8BC, 62CL, 71CL, 73CL, 74CRB, 78BC, 89BL, 111BR, 144BCL, 147TL, 160CR, 186BR, 189TR. **Bruce Coleman Ltd:** 100CLB; S. Alden 199BR; atlantide xxxvi TCR, 144BR; E. Bjurstrom 147BR; T. Buchholz xv CL, 33CA; J. Burton xxiii CRi; J. Cancalosi 189AR; B. J. Coates 199BC; B. Coleman 65TL; B. & C. Colhoun 38CR; A. Compost xxiii CBRi; Dr S. Coyne 47TL; G. Cubitt xvi TL, 173BCL, 186TR, 192TR; P. Davey xxxvii CLB, 123CBL; N. Devore 197CBL; S.J. Doylee xxii CRii; H. Flygare xvii CA; M.P. & L. Fogden 17C; J. Foott Productions xxiii CBRii, 9 CRA; M. Freeman 93CRB; G. Gualco 146C; B. Henderson 201CR; Dr.C. Henneghien 71C; C. Hughes 71BCL; J. Johnson 41CR, 207TR; J. Jurka 93CLA; S. J. Krasemann 35TR; H. Lange 8CRA, 70CA; L. Lee Rue III 157BCL; C. Lockwood 34BC; M. McCoy 195TR; L.C. Marigo xxii BC, xxxvii CLA, 88CB; J. Murray xv C, 187BR; Orion Press 172TR; Orion Service & Trading Co. 171tr; C. Ott 18BL; Dr. E. Pott 42CLA, 89CB, 95BL, 204 CLB; F. Prenzel 197C, 201CB; M. Read 44BR, 45CRB; H. Reinhard xxii CRi, xxxvii TCR, 204BR; J. Shaw xix TL; K.N. Swenson 204BC; P. Terry 117TL; N.Tomalin 56BCL; H. Van Den Berg 71CR; P. Van Gaalen 88TR; 102CL U. Walz; P. Ward 80CLA; S. Widstrand 59TR; K. Wothe 93 CLB, 181TCL; J.T. Wright 131BR. **Colorific!:** Black Star/ M. Koene 57TR; J. Prupp 167BCR; R. Rogers 59BR; M. Yamashita 179CA; Bill Wisneski 126TC, 205BR. **Comstock:** 110CRB. **D. Cousens:** 153CRA. **Sue Cunningham Photography:** 53CR. **James Davis Travel Photography:** 11C, 21BC, 58CRB, 59CLA, 63BCL, 122CB, 166CA, 187CRA, 203BR. **George Dunnet:** 128CA. **Environmental Picture Library:** C. Westwood 130CL. **Eye Ubiquitous:** L. Fordyce 10CLA; L. Johnstone 6CRA, 32C; S. Miller xxi CA; M. Southern 75BLA. **FFOTOGRAFF:** C. Aithie 137CL; N. Tapsell 164CL. **G.S.F. Picture Library:** xvi BR, xxiv CRA, 110BR, 126BR; Solarfilma 99TC. **Robert Harding Picture Library:** xvii TC, xxv CRA, xxx CLA, 13CRA, 39CB, 41CLA, 52BL, 101TC, 116TC, 125BR, 138CLA, 148CB, 149TL, 153TR, 173CA, 173CB, 177BR; P.G. Adam 111CLA; D. Atchison-Jones 72CLB; J. Bayne 74CB; Bildagentur Schuster 82CRA; Bowman 52BR; 55CA, 64CL, 72CRA; C. Campbell xxi BC;

R. Cundy 71BR; F. Frerck 53BL; G. Corrigan 165CRB, 167CRB; Delu 81CRB; Financial Times 148BR; T. Gervis 7CR; I. Griffiths xxx CL, 79TL; T. Hall 177CRA; D. Harney 148CA; G. Hellier xv CR, 135BL; F. Jackson 143BCR; P. Koch 145TR; S. Massif xv CB; A. Mills 90CLB; L. Murray 116TL; G. Renner 76CB, 204C; R. Richardson 120CB; E. Rooney 128TR; Sassoon xxiv CL, 154CBL; P. Scholey 184TR; M. Short 143TL; E. Simanor XXXVII CR; V. Southwell 145CR; J. Strachan 44TR, 136BCR; C. Tokeley 140CLA; A.C. Waltham xvii CLB, xxii CLiii, 144CR, 167C; Westlight 39CR; N. Wheeler 145CBL. **Paul Harris:** 126TL, 174TC. **The Hutchison Library:** 6BL, 140BCL; P .Collomb 143CE; C. Dodwell 137TR; N. Durrell McKenna xxxvi BCR; S. Errington 72CB; P. Hellyer 148BC; J. Horner xxxvi TCL; R.I. Lloyd 134CRA; J. Nowell 135CLB, 149TCR; A. Zvoznikov xxii CLii. **The Image Bank:** 89BR; A. Becker xxiv BL; J. Banagan 202CB; K. Forest 169TR; P. Hendrie 174BCL; M. Isy-Schwart 201C, 203CL; M. Khansa 124BR; T. Madison 177CCR; C. Molyneux 143CRiii; K. Mori 201TC; C. Navajas xviii TR; Ocean Inc.199CBL; S. Proehl 6CLB; T. Rakke xix TR; M. Reitz 206CA; M. Romarelli 177BL; G.A. Rossi 157BCR; 184CLB; B. Roussel 111TL; S. Satushek xvii BC; J. Van Os xvii TC; Bullaty/Lomeo xxiv TCL; M.J. Spielman xxiv TCR; Stockphotos/ J. M. Spielman xxiv TCL; J. Holmes xxiv BL; Silvestris 181TCR; D. Smith xxii BCL; A. Wharton xxiii BL; Van Wiseswli 126TC, 205BR. **Mountain Camera:** J. Cleare 159TC; C. Monteath 159CR. **Nature Photographers Ltd:** E.A. Janes 114CB. **Network Photographers Ltd:** Rapho/C. Sappa 121BR. **Natural History Photographic Agency:** N.J. Dennis xxiii CLii; D. Heuchlin xxiii CLA; J. Jeffrey 138BL; 27BR, 40TR; R. Tidman 166CLB; D. Tomlinson 151CR. **Nottingham Trent University:** V. Waltham xiv CA, 159CRB. **OSF:** Dr. Allan xxii TR; H.R. Bardarson xviii CB; D. Bown xxiii CBLii; M. Brown 146BL; M. Colbeck 153CAR; L. Gould xxiii CRA; D. Guravich xxiii TR; M. Hill 59TL, 205TR; C. Menteath 140 CLA; S. Osolinski 84CA; R. Packwood 74CA; M. Pitts 187CC; N. Rosing xxiii CBLi, 199CA; J. Cornish 108BL; T. Craddock xxiv TR; P. Degginger 38C; Demetrio 5BR; N. DeVore xxiv BCL; A. Diesendruck 62BR; S. Egan 89CRA; R. Elliott xxii BCR; S. Elmore 21C; R. Frerck 122TCi; J. Garrett 75CR; S. Grandadam

N. Cooper 84CB, 159TC; J.L. Dugast 177CB, 178BCR; J. Hartley 92C, 75CRA; J. Holmes 155BCR; J. Morris 78CRB; M. Rose 152TR; D. Sansoni 161C; L.C. Stowers 169TL. **Pictor International Ltd:** xiv BR, xv CRB, xix TC, xx 18B, 22TR, 22CRB, 24CL, 25CB, 28C, 29CB, 32CRA, 36BR, 36CR, 36CB, 40C, 40CRB, 100TC, 101TR, 108CLB, 177TCR, 178BR, 179CR, 188BL, 193TL. **Pictures Colour Library:** xxi BCL, xxii BR, xxxvi BCL, 6BR, 13TR, 17TR, 21TL, 22BL, 26C, 26CLA, 29TR, 34TR, 38CB, 43CA, 45CRA, 70BL, 92CRA, 101BR, 108CRB, 108CA, 108TR, 109CLA, 170BC, 171BR, 199CL. **Planet Earth Pictures:** D. Barrett 154CBL, 192CA; R. Coomber 17BL; G. Douwma 201BL; E. Edmonds 181BR; H.C. Heap 124TR; J. Lythgoe 206BL; A. Mounter 137BCR, 180CR; M. Potts 6CA; P. Scoones xxx TR; D. Tackitt 180BR; J. Waters 55BCL. **Popperfoto/Reuters:** J. Drake xxxii CL. **Rex Features Ltd:** 170CR; Antelope xxxiii CLB; M. Friedel xxx CR; I. McIlgorm xxx CBR; J. Shelley xxx CR; Sipa Press: xxx CRA; Sipa Press/Ali xxxx CBL; Chamussy 184BL. **Russia & Republics Picture Library:** M. Wadlow 120CA, 121CB, 128TL,128C, 128CB, 128BR,130TR. **SCR Library:** J. King 151BR. **Science Photo Library:** CNES, 1990 Distribution Spot Images xi BC; Earth Satellite Corporation xix CRA, XXXI CR; F. Gohier xi CR; J. Heseltine xvi TC; K. Kent xv CLB; P. Menzel xv BL; NASA x BC; D. Parker xiv CB; Peter Arnold Inc./ R.J. Wainscoat xi BC; University Of Cambridge Collection Air Pix 89CLB; D. Weintraub xi BA. **South American Pictures:** 59BL, 64TR; Guyana Space Centre 52TR; R. Francis 54BL; T. Morrison 52CR, 54TR, 56TR, 62BL, 63C. **Southampton Oceanography:** xviii BL. **Sovfoto/ Eastfoto:** xxxii CRB. **Spectrum Colour Library:** 52BC, 166BC. **Still Pictures:** C. Caldicott 79TR; A. Crump 197CL; M. & C. Denis-Huot xxii BL, 80TC, 83BL; M. Edwards xxi AR, 55BL, 71CLB, 99CR, 161BR; J. Frebet 55LCB; M. Gunther 123BR; E. Parker 54CL; R. Seitre 137CA,138TL 138BL. **Frank Lane Picture Agency:** xxi TC, 95TL; J. Holmes xxi BL; Silvestris 181TCR; D. Smith xxii BCL; A. Wharton xxiii BL; Van Wiseswli 126TC, 205BR.

12BR; C. Harvey 71TL; G. Hellier 172CR; D. Hughes xxxi CBR; A. Husmo 93TC; G. Irvine 33BL; G. Johnson xvii TR, 138CLB; A. Kehr 115CA; R. Koskas xvi TR; J. Lawrence 77CRA; L. Lefkowitz 7CA; M. Lewis 47CLA; S. Mayman 57BR; Murray & Assoc. 47CR; N. Parfitt xxxvii CL, 70TCR, 83TL; R. Passmore 123TR; N. Press xvi CB; E. Pritchard 90CA, 92C; T. Raymond 23BL; L. Resnick 76BR; M. Rogers 82CRB; C. Saule 92CRA; 7CLA; S. Schulhoff xxvi TL; D. Smith 7CLA; P. Seaward 36C; M. Segal 34BL; V. Shenai 158CL; R. Sherman 28CLA; H. Sitton 142CR; R. Smith 58CA; S. Studd; 110CLAH. Strand 65TR; P. Tweedie 185CR; L. Ulrich 19BL; M. Vines 19TL; A.B. Wadham 62CR; J. Warden 65BCL; R. Wells 25CR, 200BL; G. Yeowell 36BL. **Telegraph Colour Library:** 63TCR, 63BR; J. Sims 28BR. **Topham Picturepoint Ltd:** 54BR, 137BCL, 139CR, 168BR, 174TR, 176BC. **Travel Ink:** Andrew Cowin 90TR. **Trip:** 146BR, 150CA, 161CR; B. Ashe 167CRA; D. Cole 202CR, 202BCL; D. Davis 91BL; I. Deineko xxxi TR; J. Dennis 24BL; Dinodia 160CL; A. Gasson 155CR; W. Jacobs 45TL, 56BL, 185BC, 186CLA, 193CBR, 197BL; P. Kingsbury 114C; T. Knight 185BR; V. Kolpakov 151BR; T. Noorits 89TL, 121TR, 152CL; R. Power 43TR; N. Ray 176C; E. Smith 191TL, 191TC; V. Sidoropolev 151TR. **Woodfin Camp Associates Inc.:** 94CRB. **World Pictures:** xv CA, xvii CRA, 25CB, 25BR, 26BL, 37BL, 42TR, 53T, 73BL, 82TCR, 84TR, 85BL, 88BR, 100BR, 102TC, 103TC, 123CB, 124BL, 167BCL, 168CLB, 180CBL, 180BC, 187BL, 190CB, 191C, 192CL, 193CR. **ZEFA:** xvi BR, xxvi CB, xviii CL, 11BL, 12TC, 17CA, 23TL, 24BR, 27BL, 34TC, 38BR, 71CLA, 81BL, 83BR, 89CRB, 94C, 100C, 100CLA, 101BL, 102BR, 108TL, 120CRA, 122BL, 126CRB, 128CLA, 170CA, 191CRA. **Additional Photography:** G. Dann; H. Taylor; J. Young

Additional British Isles Pictures
Bruce Coleman Ltd.: C. James xxxix TC. **J. Allan Cash Ltd.:** xl BR, xli CL, xiv CL. **Colorific!:** G. Satterley xli C. **James Davis Travel Photography:** xxxvi CL, xxxvi TR, xxxix CRA. **Eye Ubiquitous:** xl C. **Chris Fairclough Colour Library:** xli BR. **Robert Harding Picture Library:** xxxv TC; Craven xxxv BL; S. Harris xli BCL; Jacobs xxxvii TL; R. Rainford xliv BL; A. Williams xl TR, xxxviii BR. **Images Colour Library:** xl BL, xlii BL, xxxix TR. **Leeds Castle Foundation:** xxxix CL. **Pictor International Ltd.:** xlii BR. **Telegraph Colour Library:** R. Antrobus xxxix BR. **Additional Photography:** Rob Reichenfeld xxxix BC, xxxix BL.

NORTH AMERICA

 CANADA
PAGES 8–16

 UNITED STATES OF AMERICA
PAGES 17–41

 MEXICO
PAGES 42–43

 BELIZE
PAGES 44–45

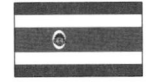 COSTA RICA
PAGES 44–45

 EL SALVADOR
PAGES 44–45

 GUATEMALA
PAGES 44–45

 HONDURAS
PAGES 44–45

SOUTH AMERICA

 GRENADA
PAGES 46–47

 HAITI
PAGES 46–47

 JAMAICA
PAGES 46–47

 ST KITTS & NEVIS
PAGES 46–47

 ST LUCIA
PAGES 46–47

 ST VINCENT & THE GRENADINES
PAGES 46–47

 TRINIDAD & TOBAGO
PAGES 46–47

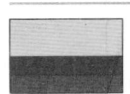 COLOMBIA
PAGES 56–57

AFRICA

 URUGUAY
PAGES 62–63

 CHILE
PAGES 64–65

 PARAGUAY
PAGES 64–65

 ALGERIA
PAGES 76–77

 EGYPT
PAGES 76–77

 LIBYA
PAGES 76–77

 MOROCCO
PAGES 76–77

 TUNISIA
PAGES 76–77

 LIBERIA
PAGES 78–79

 MALI
PAGES 78–79

 MAURITANIA
PAGES 78–79

 NIGER
PAGES 78–79

 NIGERIA
PAGES 78–79

 SENEGAL
PAGES 78–79

 SIERRA LEONE
PAGES 78–79

 TOGO
PAGES 78–79

 BURUNDI
PAGES 82–83

 DJIBOUTI
PAGES 82–83

 ERITREA
PAGES 82–83

 ETHIOPIA
PAGES 82–83

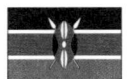 KENYA
PAGES 82–83

 RWANDA
PAGES 82–83

 SOMALIA
PAGES 82–83

 SUDAN
PAGES 82–83

EUROPE

 SOUTH AFRICA
PAGES 84–85

 SWAZILAND
PAGES 84–85

 ZAMBIA
PAGES 84–85

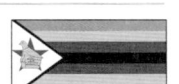 ZIMBABWE
PAGES 84–85

 DENMARK
PAGES 94–97

 FINLAND
PAGES 94–95

 ICELAND
PAGES 94–95

 NORWAY
PAGES 94–97

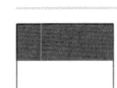 MONACO
PAGES 104–105

 ANDORRA
PAGES 106–107

 PORTUGAL
PAGES 106–107

 SPAIN
PAGES 106–107

 ITALY
PAGES 108–109

 SAN MARINO
PAGES 108–109

 VATICAN CITY
PAGES 108–109

 AUSTRIA
PAGES 110–111

 BOSNIA & HERZEGOVINA
PAGES 114–115

 CROATIA
PAGES 114–115

 MACEDONIA
PAGES 114–115

 YUGOSLAVIA
PAGES 114–115

 BULGARIA
PAGES 116–117

 GREECE
PAGES 116–117

 MOLDAVIA
PAGES 118–119

 ROMANIA
PAGES 118–119

ASIA

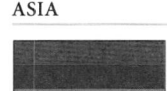 ARMENIA
PAGES 142–143

 AZERBAIJAN
PAGES 142–143

 GEORGIA
PAGES 142–143

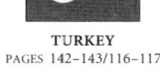 TURKEY
PAGES 142–143/116–117

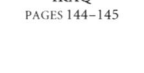 IRAQ
PAGES 144–145

 ISRAEL
PAGES 144–145

 JORDAN
PAGES 144–145

 LEBANON
PAGES 144–145

 IRAN
PAGES 148–149

 KAZAKHSTAN
PAGES 150–151

 KYRGYZSTAN
PAGES 152–153

 TAJIKISTAN
PAGES 152–153

 TURKMENISTAN
PAGES 152–153

 UZBEKISTAN
PAGES 152–153

 AFGHANISTAN
PAGES 154–155

 PAKISTAN
PAGES 154–157

SOUTH KOREA
PAGES 162–163/168–169

TAIWAN
PAGES 166–167

JAPAN
PAGES 170–172

BRUNEI
PAGES 173–176

INDONESIA
PAGES 173–176

MALAYSIA
PAGES 173–176

SINGAPORE
PAGES 173–176

BURMA
PAGES 177–179

AUSTRALASIA & OCEANIA

 MAURITIUS
PAGES 180–181

 SEYCHELLES
PAGES 180–181

 AUSTRALIA
PAGES 188–191

 NEW ZEALAND
PAGES 192–193

 PAPUA NEW GUINEA
PAGES 194–195

 SOLOMON ISLANDS
PAGES 194–195

 MARSHALL ISLANDS
PAGES 196/201

MICRONESIA
PAGES 196/201